# SPORTS PAGES

OF THE

Los Angeles Times

HARRY N. ABRAMS, INC.,
PUBLISHERS, NEW YORK

# SPO
# PA

O F

Los Ang

ENLARGED AND
UPDATED EDITION

RTS

GES

T H E

eles Times

WITH A NEW CHAPTER
BY EARL GUSTKEY

EDITED AND WITH TEXT BY BILL SHIRLEY
INTRODUCTION BY JIM MURRAY

Enlarged and Updated Edition

Designer: Kenneth R. Windsor

ISBN 0-8109-3554-6



Published in 1991 by Harry N. Abrams, Incorporated, New York
A Times Mirror Company


Printed and bound in the United States of America

# CONTENTS

# INTRODUCTION

BEFORE THERE WAS O. J. SIMPSON, THERE WAS COTTON WARBURTON. BEFORE THE Dodgers, there were the Hollywood Stars. Before Steve Garvey, there was Jigger Statz. Before the L.A. Rams, there were the L.A. Wolves. Jackie Robinson played for them.

The first black big-league baseball player came from here. So did most of the white ones.

The Olympic Games were held here, not Philadelphia, not New York, not Boston. The first Olympic Village was erected here. We showed the world how to conduct an Olympiad. A community that could bring its water from three hundred miles away, draw oil from its sea, and man-make a harbor, a community that manufactured the world's dreams, could put on an Olympics in its spare time in the middle of a depression.

The sun shone 350 days a year, a city was carved where only mesquite and mustard and scrub oak were put by nature; its trees, people, architecture, and manufacture were imported. But its lifestyle was its own. And sports were an integral part of that lifestyle, maybe *the* integral part.

A case could be made that Los Angeles *made* pro football. It saved pro baseball. It popularized pro basketball. For generations the Olympic team was peopled with Southern Californians. There wasn't an empty lot that didn't have a cast of shot-putters, javelin-throwers, high-jumpers, pole-vaulters, and just plain runners on it. You imagined Athens looked like this in the glory that was Greece.

The attitude of Southern California was always "Why not?" Its people found a new phrase to describe it at the end of the twentieth century; "laid back" was a purely California invention.

Bowl games started here. The first $100,000 horse race was run here. For decades, every Indianapolis race car, or almost every one, was built here. Half the field came from here.

The Olympic team was 60 to 80 percent Southern Californian. It's where the Charlie Paddocks, Rafer Johnsons, Bob Mathiases, and Parry O'Briens first made their marks. And toed their marks.

Sports is a legacy in Los Angeles. It was all waiting there for Marcus Allen, O. J., Mike Garrett, Lynn Swann, and before them the Musicks, the Mohlers, the Landsdells, Saunders, Pinckerts. John Wayne played football at USC. It was all there. The tradition, the encouragement, the zest. It was as much a part of the life as the oranges, the oil, the sound stages.

The East never understood. The people there thought Los Angeles was just that funny little place where movies were made because the light was so good and the air clear (a melancholy recollection today indeed!). L.A. was just Charlie Chaplin and Mae Busch. The East thought the Dodgers brought sports culture here. It seriously miscalculated the sports quotient of L.A.

Los Angeles regularly drew a million people to its baseball parks. Or thereabouts. The minor league Angels had season attendances of up to 700,000. The "Hollywood" Stars drew 300,000 to 400,000. Even in the big leagues only the Yankees were drawing a million at the time. To give you an idea, the St. Louis Browns drew only 80,000 fans *the whole year*. The East didn't realize Hollywood was just a part of L.A. It was only a real estate subdivision. The million attendance was furnished by one city. And it was paying for an inferior product of the grand old game. Baseball never dreamt of annual attendances in the three millions—a commonplace when the Dodgers moved West. L.A. didn't need the Dodgers half so much as the Dodgers needed L.A. As *baseball* needed L.A.

No one ever heard of 104,000 people for a football game till USC began to play Notre Dame. No one ever heard of 100,000 at a pro game till the Rams began to play the San Francisco 49ers, the Green Bay Packers, the Unitas Colts.

The citizenry is sports daffy. Check your broker on his lunch hour. Try the squash court. The tennis court. If your lawyer is in court, find out which one. It may not be the law court.

The people here don't just go to the beach. They play volleyball on it. Muscle Beach is a part of Americana, a happy-hunting-ground of adagio dancers, gymnasts, weightlifters, and muscle builders. Narcissism-by-the-sea. You don't just take a box lunch to the ocean. You take a surfboard, a wind-sailer, an outrigger.

Back East they told Walter O'Malley when he was contemplating his Dodger move, "You'll never get the Los Angeles native away from the beach, his swimming pool, or the tennis court on the weekend. You'll bomb out there." O'Malley played his games at night. But still they came on weekends. There is no finite perimeter to L.A.'s love of sports.

The movie moguls, wherever they came from—Hungary or Canarsie—developed a California love of sports or the outdoors. The old ones bet on them. The younger ones played them. They chose, of all things, polo. Which gave rise to the studio-lot joke "From Poland to polo in one generation."

Golf soon followed. The movie crowd, vibrant, self-confident, disrespectful of old taboos, refused to accept the stricture that golf was just for people who came over on the *Mayflower*. It was for people who came over in steerage, too. Barred from the select, snooty, Old Los Angeles and Pasadena courses, they built their own. More lavish, more fun, and more picturesque in many cases.

The movie crowd loved the USC Trojans. And they loved prizefighters. Charlie Chaplin always surrounded himself with young girls—and young prizefighters. Al Jolson bought his own fighter—Henry Armstrong, no less. Friday-night fights at the Hollywood Legion were social soirees. Here Jolson punched Walter Winchell. Here Lady Astor had her own fighter, Enzo Fiermonte. He couldn't fight much, but he was beautiful to look at.

The movie crowd began to buy racehorses. A case could be made that L. B. Mayer lost his preeminent position in town because he dabbled so heavily in racehorses that the parent company, Loew's, Inc., lost confidence in him. His horses, like his pictures, were good but not great. He could never win the Kentucky Derby. But when he had his dispersal sale, he sold many of the studs and broodmares who would sire winners. When he died of leukemia it was said he lamented the loss of his racing stable far more than his acting stable.

The movies made USC into a football power. They subsidized athletes, gave them summer jobs, winter jobs, and even year-round jobs. John Wayne came over to John Ford simply because he was a football player. So did Ward Bond and Grant Withers. Producers like Aaron Rosenberg and Ben Hibbs were All-American football players at USC. Cotton Warburton became a cutter. Movie stars frequently entertained the entire USC football team. One flaming redhead of the jazz era was said to have entertained them personally, and intimately. They were celebrities to the celebrities.

A Coliseum football game was always a gaudy show, a Hollywood premiere. The Rockne mystique at Notre Dame didn't start here, but it reached full flower here. Everyone knows how a future president of the United States played a Notre Dame halfback, George Gipp, here, but few remember he also played Grover Cleveland Alexander, the pitcher, too. Sports movies never made money, but that never stopped Hollywood from making them.

Love of sports became endemic. Robert Benchley once described L.A. as "two million people going to their tennis courts." He complained there was "no one to drink with on the weekends when the sun was out."

L.A. is the only American community to host two Summer Olympic Games. L.A. showed the world how it was done in 1932. Because housing was a major problem for countries impoverished by the Great Depression, the organizing committee built the first Olympic Village—low-cost housing for the athletes of the world—which was sold at a profit at the Games' end. Many standards of show business and merchandising were applied to dramatize the Games and give them the aspect of something more than an athletic festival. The Olympics went Hollywood.

Tennis became a religion. The house that didn't have a swimming pool had a tennis court. The incomparable May Sutton,who learned her game on the backyard courts of Pasadena,electrified the tennis world when, at the age of sixteen, she won the U.S. women's championship and the following year won Wimbledon. She headed a long line of awesome women players to come out of California—Hazel Hotchkiss, Molla Mallory, Helen Wills, Alice Marble, Maureen Connolly, Billie Jean King.

The men fared no less well. "Little" Bill Johnston, Maurice McLoughlin ("The Comet"), Ellsworth Vines, Donald Budge, Jack Kramer, Pancho Gonzales, all came off the public courts of California. The Los Angeles Tennis Club, run with iron autocracy by the late Perry T. Jones, became a spawning ground of Davis Cup teams, Wimbledon and Forest Hills champions, and, when players became good anywhere in the world, they gravitated to Jones and L.A. to hone their skills. A Tony Trabert came from Cincinnati but Alex Olmedo hitchhiked all the way from Peru.

The movie-star players spanned the generations from Charlie Chaplin to Charlton Heston to Johnny Carson. It was in Los Angeles that the custom of wearing shorts even in championship play came into vogue. The Californians typically hated the inhibitions of long skirts and long trousers. It was a Los Angeles girl, Gussie Moran, who popularized the fashion of showing panties on a court. She scandalized the royal family with her lace frillies, but today her costume would be suitable for a game in a nunnery.

The notion that Californians are great, empty-headed, or sawdust-brained globs too concerned with their muscles and not enough with their minds owes its beginnings to the area's fondness for athletics. How could someone be a serious human being if he was out playing the ad court in doubles on a day the national budget was being debated? Who could go surfing instead of going to gloomy old museums? What manner of people didn't care about the Middle East so long as the surf was up, the

Dodgers at home, all lifts open at Mammoth, there was a drag race at Orange County, a foursome was forming up at Riviera, or they needed a partner for doubles at Chuck Heston's? What kind of people preferred working on their tans to poring over Shakespeare folios at the Huntington Library on a Sunday afternoon? What kind of a pagan culture was this? Was the sun a god, the sea a religion, a game a rite?

No, it was just a people with a great zest for life and joy, released from the gloom and cloudy climes and past tradition and musty old customs like a Victorian living room where someone suddenly throws the windows open and pulls down the camphor-smelling drapes. California was volleyball at the beach, a diving board in the backyard, a tennis racket in the convertible, a golf bag in the garage, skis in the trunk of the car. It was a tailgate picnic at the Rose Bowl, "Fight On For USC!" Gershwin writing a fight song for UCLA, it was Saturday-night-at-Dodger-Stadium but go home in the seventh inning no matter what because you had a (choose one) golf, tennis, volleyball, water polo game in the morning—or maybe you were going to crew down to Ensenada.

So, sports is a way of life in Los Angeles and Southern California? No. Life is a way of life.

JIM MURRAY

# 1883
# 1892

THE YEAR WAS 1883. JOHN L. SULLIVAN WAS THE HEAVYWEIGHT BOXING CHAMPION OF THE WORLD. IN the first baseball game played under lights, Fort Wayne, Indiana, defeated Quincy, Illinois, 19–11, in seven innings, at Fort Wayne. Pitcher Charles "Hoss" Radbourn won forty-four games for the Providence Nationals, and umpires in the National League got salaries for the first time. The American record for the 100-meter dash was 10¼ seconds, and the best time for the mile was 4:30 4/5. Jumpers were going as high as five feet, eight inches and as far as twenty-one feet, seven inches. A new game, football, was becoming popular among such colleges as Yale, Princeton, Rutgers, Harvard, and Columbia, and a horse named Leonatus won the Kentucky Derby in two minutes, forty-three seconds.

Americans were playing tennis, golf, baseball, and football; they were punching each other out in prizefights and they were racing horses. But the nation was not yet hooked on sports, and there was little evidence that games would become a national obsession. Newspapers, including the *Los Angeles Daily Times*, didn't give them much attention. In fact in the early 1880s *The Times* did not have a sports section. It carried short items on games and races on the first page under such headings as "Day Dispatches" and "Times Telegrams" and often buried them among reports of floods, fires, murders, lynchings, and outbreaks of cholera and yellow fever. There were more ads than news, even on the first page.

But before the decade was out, a YMCA instructor in Springfield, Massachusetts, named James Naismith, had fastened two peach baskets to a gymnasium balcony and invented basketball; Richard Sears had won the first United States tennis championship; two professional baseball leagues, the National and the American Association, were in business; football rivalries between Yale and Harvard and Army and Navy had begun; and the bare-knuckle era of boxing had ended and James J. Corbett was the new heavyweight champion.

John L. Sullivan, the last of the bare-knuckle champions, won the title by knocking out Paddy Ryan in nine rounds in 1882, and in the last championship match fought with bare fists, he stopped Jake Kilrain in seventy-five rounds in 1889. *The Times* carried a long report of that famous fight as its top story on Page One.

On September 7, 1892, Corbett and Sullivan met in New Orleans and, probably for the first time, boxers used gloves in a championship fight and fought three-minute rounds under Marquis of Queensberry Rules. Corbett knocked Sullivan out in the twenty-first round and won a purse of twenty-five thousand dollars as well as a ten-thousand-dollar side bet from Sullivan.

Buchanan, the winner of the 1884 Kentucky Derby, was ridden by the famed black jockey Isaac Murphy, who also won aboard Riley in 1890 and Kingman in 1891. The crowd was so large at the 1891 Derby, it was reported, "that locomotion was almost impossible. The inner field presented one mass of humanity." But while the famous race drew large crowds, it did not attract many horses. Only four raced in 1891 and three in 1892. Fields of at least twenty are common today.

In fact today sports are bigger in every way. Television brings sports events into living rooms, often magnifying them beyond their importance. Newspapers have bigger and better sports sections, and the reporting is deeper, more literate.

On these *Los Angeles Times* pages are headlines and portions of reports that will remind you of some of the events and some of the athletes who have made history, one way or another. There are stories of achievements and records; man's ability to run faster, jump higher and farther, and play better apparently has no bounds. But there are also headlines that deal with deaths, defeats, politics, and cheating.

The best was yet to come in 1892. Baseball would have its World Series, professional football its Super Bowl, auto racing its Indianapolis 500, college football its Rose Bowl, and the world its modern Olympic Games. Brighter stars would replace Murphy, Sullivan, and Corbett.

Obviously all the great events could not be included in a hundred-year history. After all, there were 36,525 sports-page candidates, and most of them qualified.

# LOS ANGELES DAILY TIMES.

VOL. III. LOS ANGELES CALIFORNIA, TUESDAY MORNING, JUNE 5, 1883.—WITH SUPPLEMENT. 155.

## Day Dispatches.

[By the Western Associated Press.]

### PACIFIC COAST NEWS.

**Beer, Illustrated Newspaper and Palace Cars in San Francisco.**

SAN FRANCISCO, June 4.—The combination of lager-beer brewers formed in this city a year ago, was broken by the smaller brewers refusing to enter into the compact and by their underselling the combination. When it was formed the price of hops rose in two weeks from 35 cents to $1.10 a pound.

A new weekly, illustrated paper will be started in this city shortly. It will have new presses, its artists and writers will be imported.

Geo. M. Pullman, proprietor of the Pullman Palace cars, is in this city for the purpose of coming to an agreement with the managers of the Central Pacific Railroad for running his cars though from Ogden to San Francisco, and by the Southern route. While the prospects of the project are good, the Central Pacific still hold out that no definite settlement has yet been made, though it is conceded to be necessary to adopt a plan.

**The Wheat Crop and Ocean Freights.**

SAN FRANCISCO, June 4. It is pointed out that in the absence of an Isthmus canal or ship railway a large wheat yield on this coast means an important advance in ocean freights all over the world. This fact was illustrated in 1866-67, in 1872 73, 1876 77 and still more forcibly in 1880 81. The United States coasting law increases the difficulties by sharply limiting the supply of bondage available for the business of this coast. And that in view of these difficulties it is not surprising that it took California nearly two years to market the 1880 crop entailing an estimated loss to California farmers of fully ten million dollars. With a large crop this year this loss is duplicated.

**The A. & P. on Piles at the Needles.**

SAN FRANCISCO, June 5. A special to the Call from Mojave, Colorado, states that regular trains on the Atlantic & Pacific are now running to the Needles on the Colorado river. Passengers at present are transferred over the river by ferry. The Atlantic & Pacific Company are having considerable trouble driving piles at the crossing of the Colorado, owing to high water and the bed of the river being quicksand. The piling washes out nearly as fast as driven. If the river continues to rise they will have to abandon the building of the bridge until the water falls.

**Seattle Settlings.**

SEATTLE, W. T., June 4. Work on the new wharf and warehouse of the Improvement Company will commence shortly. A capacity of 5,000 tons will be thus added to the dock room of the company. This improvement must be completed before the fall crops are due.

Of the Third street school property, four lots will be sold to-morrow for the purpose of raising funds for a $65,000 school building in Seattle.

It is stated that the railroad company will try the experiment of making its cars at this place with a view to establishing a manufactory at Seattle.

Coal shipments from Seattle for the month just closed amount to a total of 11,814 tons. The output for the present month will undoubtedly be largely in excess of the above figures.

### BLAINE, LOGAN AND GRANT.

**What the Latter Thinks About the Former as Candidates.**

LOUISVILLE, June 4.—General and Mrs. Grant arrived in this city last night, remaining until this afternoon, when they left for Lexington. A Courier Journal reporter interviewed Grant on the political situation, the latter expressing the opinion that Blaine and Logan were each very strong men for the Republican nomination in 1884.

### GENERAL DISPATCHES.

**The Oar—The Coming Single and Double Scull Race.**

CHICAGO, June 4.—Among the entries for the single and double scull races at Pullman, June 22d and 23d, to date, are: Single scull, Hanlan, Ross, George Hosmer, Charles E. Courtney, Plaisted and Elliot. Double scull: Geo. Hosmer and John McKay, Hanlan and Lee, Weisberger and Selwing. The course is on Lake Calumet, at the suburban village of Pullman, just south of the city, where the most elaborate and complete arrangements for seating and otherwise accommodating from fifteen to twenty thousand people have been made. Both races will be three miles with turn.

**Sunday Trains Stopped.**

NEW HAVEN, June 3. The Sunday trains on the Housatonic railroad were stopped to-day by the Massachusetts authorities. The clergymen of Berkshire Co., Mass., presented a petition against running trains on Sunday, but the railroad disregarded them.

**A Steel Mill Resumes.**

CHICAGO, June 4.—The Calumet Iron and Steel Company, at South Chicago, which has been closed for several days, debating whether it would accept the Pittsburg schedule, started again this morning with half of its usual force.

### IN FOREIGN LANDS.

**A Royal Shoulder-Hitter Vanquishes Mace and Slade.**

LONDON, June 4.—On the arrival of Jem Mace and the Maori, Slade, Lord Charles Beresford challenged both to a set-to without gloves. Mace accepted the challenge. The Prince of Wales was present, as were also a large crowd of aristocratic sports and private gentlemen. After several rounds Mace failed to come to time and acknowledged defeat. Lord Beresford, after finishing Mace, invited Slade to enter the ring. Warned by Mace's treatment, the Maori refused.

**Warned to Leave Ireland.**

DUBLIN, June 4.—James Carey and the other informers who testified at the Phoenix Park murderers have been notified that they must indicate places out of the country to which they would be sent. Carey protested that he would remain in Dublin. The authorities pointed out that they would receive no police protection and that on no condition would be allowed in Ireland.

**Agitators Released.**

DUBLIN, June 4.—Davitt, Healy a[nd] Quinn were released from Kilmain[ham] jail this afternoon.

**How the San Buenav[entura] ... Amuse Th[emselves].**

From the Ventura Signal ...

R. William For[d] ... the name of " ... a part of ... Little Ba... his tail ... [illegible]

## Times Telegrams

[Western Associated Press Night Report.]

### A SECOND SUEZ CANAL.

**Confidence of De Lesseps and his Associates in the Enterprise.**

PARIS, June 4.—At a meeting of the Suez Canal Company to-day it was proposed by De Lesseps to examine into the project for the construction of a second canal across the Isthmus. Adopted unanimously. De Lesseps assured the meeting that the English directors were given local assistance, and prophesied that another canal would be built

DeLesseps stated that improvements now being made, at a cost of 30,000,000 francs, would suffice for a traffic of ten million tons a year. The company had, a year ago, decided on building a second route. They could accomplish this within the limits of their own lands, but could do the work much more rapidly and conveniently if the Egyptian Government would grant fresh concessions. He said the notification for obtaining aid from England on this object were proceeding favorably.

### A CROWNER'S 'QUEST.

**The Brooklyn Bridge Inquiry—The Testimony Adduced.**

NEW YORK, June 4.—The inquest began to-day in the case of twelve victims of the recent panic on the Brooklyn bridge. McMartin, superintendent, testified to the facts of the occurrence as learned by him. He stated that at the time of the disaster there were twenty-two special police officers on the bridge. A railing had been put up at the stairway since the accident, but the witness said this precaution would not remedy matters in case of another panic.

Jas. T. Stranahan, trustee, said, on days when there was an unusual pressure of travel the wagon road would be thrown open to the public, as a temporary way. If it should seem best additional walks for foot passengers could be constructed on each side of the carriage-way.

### SPORTS.

**The Great Rowing Match for $5,000 a Side.**

ROCHESTER, N. Y., June 4.—Courtney accepts the offer of the manufacturing company and will give bonds in $10,000 to row his best in a race with Hanlan for a purse of $5000. Probably the race will be rowed at Cincinnati, St. Louis or Chicago. The Pittsburg, Fort Wayne and Chicago road to-day brought to the city an excursion train of eleven carloads of employees in its shops at Fort Wayne to visit the Exposition of railway appliances. The company furnished transportation free.

**Wrestling Match.**

SAN FRANCISCO, June 4.—The wrestling match this evening between Muldoon, champion of America, who beat the Scotch champion, Donald Dinnie, and Jules Rigal, champion of France, terminated in another victory for Muldoon. The wrestling was in Græco-Roman style, two throws out of three. The first tussle lasted twenty-one minutes, fifty-eight and a half seconds. The second, thirty-two minutes, thirty-six and a half seconds. It was evident from the beginning that the Frenchman was overmatched, his short height, five feet four inches, telling against him. The match was held in Union Hall and was witnessed by about 2700 people. The match was for $500 a side and gate money of $2700 was taken. It is reported that Donald Linnie has challenged Muldoon to wrestle again.

### IN PARLIAMENT.

**The Duke of Albany and the Governor-Generalship of Canada.**

LONDON, June 4.—Gladstone declined to answer as to whether the services of the Duke of Albany as Governor-General of Canada had been refused. The Government, he said, were aware of the willingness of the Duke to render services to his crown and country. He added that this feeling did the Duke the highest honor.

Kennard asked whether the Government would represent that registration of a new set of claims at Washington by the Alabama Claims Commissioner was in violation of the intentions of the Geneva Conference.

Lord Edmund Fitzmaurice replied that it was not the intention of the Government to interfere in the matter in any way.

### IN OTHER LANDS.

**Nihilism in the Russian Army.**

LONDON, June 4.—The Pall Mall Gazette publishes another portion of a letter from a Russian Nihilist, Stepniak, in which he declares that a widespread society exists in the Russian army composed exclusively of officers, including many colonels of regiments. In regard to the present quiescence of the Nihilists he says they would be foolish to attempt a revolt when the enemy is alert. An attempt to assassinate the Czar might still form the beginning of a revolt or *coupe d'etat*, but such an attempt of itself, he says, is no longer of importance.

**Nihilists at the Bottom of it.**

ST. PETERSBURG, June 4.—A secret inquiry into the riot which occurred on the streets of St. Petersburg last Monday evening, shows that it was instigated by Nihilists.

**Garibaldi's Statue.**

ROME, June 4.—The statue of Garibaldi was unveiled at Caprera yesterday.

### GENERAL DISPATCHES.

**The Regular Suicide—a Nickel Fraud.**

SAN FRANCISCO, June 4.—John Thompson, a native of Pennsylvania, forty-one years of age, committed suicide this morning at 1206½ Howard street, by cutting his throat. A deep gash about an inch in length was found in the left side of the neck, severing the carotid artery. A gash was also found in the right arm, severing an artery. The deceased left a wife and two children.

Paul Ruegg was arrested by United States Detective Henry Finnegass this afternoon, charged with passing a five-cent nickle for a five-dollar piece.

**Dynamite vs. Petroleum.**

NEW YORK, June 4.—The customs authorities of Rio de Janeiro recently seized and confiscated as dynamite a large shipment of petrolatum or petroleum jelly. The agent was compelled to pay a heavy fine, although he protested the goods were not explosive. He appealed to the Custom House Inspector and offered to prove the articles were purely medical preparations. The Inspector declined to return the goods. The agent cabled the owner here to appeal to the Emperor for redress.

**Fresno Murder.**

FRESNO, Cal., June 4.—Joe Foster shot A. J. Beckwith in a feud near Millerton to-day. He fired two shots, inflicting mortal wounds. Cause, Beckwith had caused Foster's arrest for stealing.

**The Prison Inquiry**

SACRAMENTO, June 4. The hearing of the matter of the prison directors ... up before the ... and J. Wallace this morning. After ... upon a plan of ... an adjournment was ... morrow morning. [illegible]

### WASHINGTON.

**The New Revenue Commissioner.**

WASHINGTON, June 5.—Walter Evans, Commissioner of Internal Revenue, called at the White House to-day and paid his respects to the President. He was presented by Postmaster General Gresham. The President referred in a general way to the proposed consolidation of the Internal Revenue districts, and informed the Commissioner that he would dispose of the question as soon as possible.

**The Issue of Silver Dollars.**

WASHINGTON, June 4.—The issue of standard silver dollars during the week ending June 2d was 166,000. During the corresponding period last year, 117,000.

**Postal News.**

WASHINGTON, June 4.—Owing to the order issued by Postmaster-General Gresham, requiring first and second-class postmasters to attend personally to the duties of their offices, a number of applications for leaves of absence have already been received at the department.

The Mexican mail service from New Orleans and Galveston has been resumed.

**A Texas Tornado.**

GALVESTON, Texas, June 4.—A Greenville special says: A tornado struck here last evening in a northwesterly direction with terrific force and torrents of rain for twenty minutes, and the total destruction of the town seemed imminent. A survey of the city shows a hundred and fifty houses blown down, and a large number of old buildings more or less injured. There was only one life lost, although several persons were seriously injured.

### WASHINGTON TERRITORY.

**Observations of a Gentleman lately from Tacoma—Not a Paradise.**

A reporter of the TIMES met Dr. H. Bell lately from New Tacoma, Washington Territory, where for some time he has charge of the medical department of the Northern Pacific Railroad Company, and had an excellent opportunity to judge of the commercial, agricultural and mineral resources of the Territory. Dr. Bell states that business of all kinds throughout is very much overdone and there are many idle men. While of course there are great opportunities for enterprise, there are also many drawbacks. The climate is one of the most serious of these. A rainfall of from ninety to one hundred and two inches per annum is by no means uncommon in Western Washington, and there is much cold, damp, foggy and disagreeable weather at all seasons. When it starts to rain there it rains for all it is worth, sometimes for two weeks at a stretch.

The doctor does not consider Washington a healthy country. Typhoid, malarial fevers and diphtheria have been very prevalent during the past three years, and with the breaking up of large tracts of new land these diseases are continually on the increase. While the country is growing rapidly and has good schools, very fair society and many commercial advantages, it hardly proves satisfactory to a majority of the immigrants who have located there. The agricultural districts are covered with a very heavy growth of timber, which can only be cleared off at great expense, and the land, when cleared, is fit for nothing but grain, potatoes and vegetables. Fruit of almost every description is a failure.

Eastern Washington has a very cold climate, the thermometer in the Spokan valley ranging from 30 to 65 degrees below zero last winter. It is not a desirable country for immigrants accustomed to a mild climate. The Territory will undoubtedly grow, despite the drawbacks above alluded to, and become in time a flourishing State, but it will be well for all those who are thinking of leaving comfortable homes to take up a residence there to know that they will find many difficulties to contend with.

### JOHN CHINAMAN'S DEVICE.

**Why One of our County Officials Thinks the Chinese Must Go.**

The ways of the Mongolian are past finding out, and our efficient District Attorney probably realizes that fact at present more fully than ever before. Rumor has it that Mr. White is about to take a helpmeet to himself, and, be this true or otherwise, it is certain that a few days ago he hired a suit of apartments in the Baker block and commenced preparations that look suspiciously like housekeeping. The rooms, while spacious and pleasant in every respect, looked to Mr. White as if the use of a scrubbing brush and soap on the floors would be a decided improvement, and he decided to make the experiment. Accordingly Chinatown was notified and from a variety of candidates, which Mr. White with his usual ability questioned regarding their experience and credentials, one was selected, and after a few parting words of caution as to the necessity of doing a thorough job he was left to make the best of the situation. John took a careful survey of the surroundings and perfected a plan of operations which, while it temporarily proved perfectly satisfactory to him, rather startled the occupants of the rooms below. His idea was a simple one and consisted in procuring a piece of hose, attaching it to the faucet and turning the water on so that it would flow over the floor. This performance continued for some time, when suddenly the occupants of the rooms of the Board of Trade below discovered a fine head of water coming through the ceiling and deluging the carpets and furniture lately purchased at heavy expense. It is needless to add that John's little labor-saving scheme of house-cleaning was summarily ... and Mr. White feels that he has another strong point to make against Chinese immigration during the next campaign.

**Santa Ana News.**

Standard, June 2.]

Eastern orders have been received during the week for seven car-loads of Santa Ana valley oranges. Prices are stiffening.

The Los Angeles papers report that a man was seriously hurt at Santa Ana by being hit over the head with a shovel. We have heard of no such an affair here, but a man was seriously hurt at Spadra a few days ago by this means.

John Stine, formerly Superintendent of the Santa Ana Valley Irrigation Company, has taken a contract to build about a mile and a half of ditch for the Carpenter Water Company. N. W. Stowell has a mile of cement pipe ready to put down for the same company.

Two gentlemen from Riverside are here visiting Laguna, Ocean View and other points, with a view of selecting a place at which they and others from Riverside propose erecting cottages as summer resorts.

Mr. Sherman Page, formerly a leading lawyer of Minnesota, will shortly remove from Orange to Los Angeles.

W. H. H. Clayton, who has just completed the school census of the district, informs us that there are 205 children in the Orange school district between the ages of five and seventeen years. There are also 97 in the district under five years of age.

The late rains have greatly improved the barley crop. Many places were sown quite late, and where it was possible to irrigate it has been done. ... the water supply has ... and the result will be a ... increase in the quantity ...

It is probable that ... sheep will be shipped from this ... Eastern ... the freights from ... [illegible]

# LOS ANGELES DAILY TIMES.

VOL. V...NO. 292. LOS ANGELES, CALIFORNIA, WEDNESDAY MORNING, NOVEMBER 12, 1884. FIVE CENTS.



## NEW YORK.

### The Eyes of the World Centered There.

#### THE OFFICIAL COUNT PROGRESSING.

**A List of the Counties in Which the Canvass Has Been Completed Likelihood of Settlement To-day.**

The canvass of the returns by the County Supervisors in New York has so far developed no errors of a serious nature. Thirty-three out of the sixty counties which compose the State have been heard from officially, and their returns do not differ materially from the figures furnished directly after the election. Twenty-seven counties still remain to be heard from. New York and Kings being among the number. It is quite probable that in these two counties the Republican National Committee base their hopes of overcoming Cleveland's alleged plurality. The result may not be known for several days yet.

#### IN NEW YORK CITY.

**How the Count is Progressing—Adjournment.**

*Associated Press Dispatches to The Times.*

NEW YORK, Nov. 11. To-day at noon the Board of Aldermen were sworn in as a Board of County Canvassers. Charles B White (Rep.) was elected Chairman of the Board. The room was filled with lawyers, interested in the count, and spectators. Among the lawyers present representing the Republican National and State Committees were Wm. M. Evarts, Col. Geo. Bliss, Robert Sewell, Clarence A. Seward and Wm Allen Butler. The Democratic National and State Committees were represented by General Francis C. Barlow, Franklin Bartlett, Aaron J. Vanderpool, Charles P. Miller, Francis M. Scott, Francis L. Stetson, Edward B Bacon, and James C. Carter. A resolution was offered that none but those having business with the Board should be allowed to remain in the room during its sessions. This was laid on the table. The required committees were appointed on protests supervising of returns, etc. William P. Kirk (Tammany) read a protest against any votes being counted that were cast for William R. Grace for Mayor, on the ground that it has been publicly and semi-officially asserted and vouched for by many people that Grace was not a naturalized citizen. This matter was referred to the Committee on Protests. The Board then adjourned until to-morrow. The Committees witness the count, which was only interrupted by the offering of four affidavits of men who declared they had voted for Butler in Smithfield, but believed their votes were credited to Cleveland. The Board of canvassers took no notice of the affidavits.

#### CANVASSING THE VOTES.

**How the Situation Stood at Midnight.**

NEW YORK—Midnight Nov. 11.—Up to this hour the result of the ballot for Presidential Electors has been declared in 33 of the 60 counties of this State. The list of previous reports of County Clerks showed a Democratic plurality of 1,280. To-day's canvass shows a net loss to Blaine of 4 votes. The remaining 27 counties, with two exceptions, have reported progress, and will, for the most part, report the result of their canvass to-morrow. No mention is made of any serious discrepancy in the count of the several counties which did not to-day complete their official canvass. They reported that there was no reason to believe that when completed the figures would show any change from those already given. The canvassed returns received by the Democratic State Committee from 24 counties indicated a change of 6 votes in favor of Blaine against 60 in Livingston in favor of Cleveland. No returns have been received by the Republican National Committee at the Victoria Hotel, and Chairman Draper, of the Republican State Executive Committee, could not be found. General John Knapp, a stalwart Republican from Auburn, said he believed the official canvass would make no material change in the published returns. "If there is any hitch," said he, "it will be in New York and Kings counties. Up in the country the people knew twenty-four hours after the closing of the polls what the result is. I think it is a sure thing." The official canvass of the Kings county Board of Supervisors returns in six wards examined to-day, beginning with the first, showed Cleveland to have 14,219 votes, and Blaine 8,216.

#### THE COUNT IN THE STATE.

**Reports of Progress in Different Counties.**

NEW YORK, Nov. 11. Several counties have reported to the Secretary the official canvass up to 2 p. m., but in none of them have any notable changes taken place. One county found irregularities that compelled an adjournment until to-morrow. The irregularities were, however, purely technical. Machinery in New York and Kings counties will move slowly, and no statement of final results will be made for some days.

SARATOGA.

SARATOGA, Nov. 11. The Saratoga county official canvass gives Blaine 8,190; Cleveland, 5,846, Butler, 92, St. John, 425.

NIAGARA COUNTY.

The Board of County Canvassers of Niagara county met this morning and adjourned until to-morrow evening.

SCHOHARIE.

SCHOHARIE, N. Y., Nov. 11. The official canvass of the vote in Schoharie county give the following figures: Blaine, 3,172, Cleveland 5,529, Butler, 37; St. John 173.

QUEENS COUNTY.

In Queens county the Supervisors sent back the returns of nine districts to the Inspectors. In each case the Inspectors failed to give the total number of the votes cast. When the returns from the first district of the first ward of Long Island City, were presented the counsel representing the Republican State Committee questioned their validity, claiming they were not signed by properly qualified inspectors. He said he had been told that Heany, chairman of the Board of Inspectors left the polling place and had received no ballots and had not been present when they were cast and counted and that another person had taken his place and signed the returns without being duly qualified. Supervisor McLaughlin suggested that the objections of the counsel were interfering with the work of the Board and moved that the canvass proceed. This course was adopted and no further notice was taken of the counsel's objection. The counsel also claimed that the vote of Newtown is in excess of the registry, but upon inspection of the registry book it was discovered it was several hundred less. It is now almost certain that there will be no change in the figures already published showing Cleveland's majority to be 1922. The Board convenes at 9 a. m. to-morrow and expects to complete the canvass of the electoral vote before noon.

RICHMOND.

The official vote of Richmond county is declared as follows: Blaine 3,164, Cleveland 5,135, Butler 75, St. John 90.

FULTON.

Fulton county: Blaine 4,617, Cleveland 3,521, Butler 38, St. John 227.

HAMILTON.

Hamilton county: Blaine 521, Cleveland 567, Butler 1, St. John 21.

OTSEGO.

The Board of Canvassers of Otsego county assembled to-day, but finding errors in the returns adjourned until to-morrow afternoon.

LIVINGSTON.

The Board of Canvassers of Livingston county met to-day, but finding errors in some of the returns sent them back for correction, and adjourned until to-morrow. The Chairman of the Board authorizes the statement that Blaine's plurality in the county is 1,152.

CLINTON.

The Clinton county official vote is: Blaine, 5,973, Cleveland, 5,151; Butler, 19; St. John, 35.

RENSSELAER.

The Rensselaer county official vote is: Blaine, 13,759; Cleveland, 13,414, Butler, 686; St. John, 416.

KINGS.

The Kings County Board of Canvassers met to-day. A number of citizens were present, as also counsel representing the Republican and Democratic National and State Committees. John G. McKane was elected chairman, and the usual committees appointed, after which the Board went to work on the canvass.

The Queens County Board of Canvassers also organized to-day, and will probably complete its electoral votes this afternoon.

The Board of Canvassers of Suffolk county also got to work to-day on the vote within their jurisdiction. Lawyers are present representing both the Republican and Democratic parties in Queens and Suffolk counties, to see a fair canvass.

SENECA.

The Seneca county official vote is: Blaine, 3,309; Cleveland, 3,627; Butler, 59; St. John, 119.

WARREN.

The Warren county official vote is: Blaine, 3,577; Cleveland, 2,793; Butler, 179, St. John, 123.

ULSTER.

In Ulster county some returns were sent back to the inspectors, owing to irregularities which do not affect the Presidency. Democrats and Republicans are represented by counsel.

OTSEGO.

The Otsego county vote is: Cleveland, 7,307; Blaine, 6,871; Butler, 84; St. John, 432.

NIAGARA.

The Niagara county vote is: Blaine, 5,875; Cleveland, 6,193.

ONTARIO.

The official vote of Ontario county cannot be ascertained until to-morrow, the Board of Canvassers having adjourned until 11 o'clock.

MONROE.

In Monroe county the Board of Supervisors met to-day as a Board of Canvassers. A motion to canvass electoral votes first was lost. The point was raised and sustained by the chairman, that only towns whose Supervisors have original certificates of the returns signed by the Inspector of Election, could be legally canvassed. Only 7 out of 35 Supervisors had such certificates with them. Three of these towns were canvassed and found all right. The Board then adjourned until to-morrow afternoon.

COLUMBIA.

The Supervisors of Columbia county adjourned until to-morrow for corrected returns from the first districts of Chatham and Copake.

CHAUTAUQUA.

Chautauqua county gives Blaine 10,670, Cleveland 5,861, Butler 431, St. John 540.

CAYUGA.

The Cayuga county vote is: Blaine, 9,206; Cleveland, 6,041; Butler, 421; St. John, 591.

LIVINGSTON.

Livingston county stands: Blaine, 5,191; Cleveland, 4,039; Butler, 118; St. John, 375.

SCHENECTADY.

Schenectady county: Blaine, 3,260; Cleveland, 2,977; Butler, 41; St. John, 106. Electoral returns from nine election districts were without tickets attached, and were sent back for correction. The Board meets again to-morrow to canvass.

DUCHESS.

Duchess county is half completed. Returns from several towns were sent back to have clerical errors corrected.

WYOMING.

Wyoming county stands: Blaine, 4,441; Cleveland, 3,189; Butler, 53; St. John, 488.

ORANGE.

Orange county: Returns of several towns and districts were sent back for correction on account of clerical errors. None were material.

TOMPKINS.

N. Y., 11.—The Ithaca Board of Canvassers of Tompkins county adjourned until to-morrow noon.

BROOME AND CHENANGO.

BINGHAMTON, N. Y., 11.—The canvass of votes for the Presidential electors in Broome and Chenango counties is not yet completed, owing to clerical errors.

ONEIDA.

UTICA, N. Y., 11. The Board of Canvassers of Oneida county adjourned until to-morrow on account of defective returns from the First and Fourth wards.

AT ROME.

ROME, 11.—Errors are simply clerical. The County Clerk's returns show Blaine 13,780, Cleveland 13,820, Butler 189, St. John 894, blanks 3.

ALBANY COUNTY.

ALBANY, Nov. 11 - The sub-Committee of the Board of County Canvassers met this evening. The Twelfth Ward matter was considered. The Democratic candidate, in whose favor the change of vote was made, refused to profit by it. The effect will be to elect the Republican candidates for County Treasurer and Coroner. The vote on Presidential electors will be officially canvassed to-morrow. There will be no change as far as known. The plurality for Cleveland is 650.

GENESEE COUNTY.

BUFFALO, N. Y., Nov. 11—The Courier's special from Batavia says the Board of Canvassers of Genesee county found several technical errors, and sent the returns back for correction. They adjourned till to-morrow. It is not thought the errors mentioned will make any difference in the majority first given for Blaine.

ERIE AND CATTARAUGUS.

BUFFALO, N. Y., Nov. 11.- The County Canvassers began work on the Erie county vote and to-night finished the Presidential vote without making any change from Blaine's majority of 1,490. Dispatches to the Courier confirm the old figures in Cattaraugus county, 1,398 majority for Blaine.

NIAGARA COUNTY.

LOCKPORT, N. Y., Nov. 11. — The Niagara county official vote will be Blaine electors each 5875, Cleveland each 6193. Owing to a clerical error in the returns the Board adjourned until to-morrow.

YATES.

Yates county: Blaine, 3,191; Cleveland, 1,918; Butler, 130; St. John, 200.

ORLEANS.

Orleans county: Blaine, 36 electors, 3,997; Cleveland, 2,908; Butler, 68; St. John, 669.

PUTNAM.

Putnam county: Blaine, 2,103; Cleveland, 1,526; Butler, 4; St. John, 99.

TIOGA.

Tioga county: Blaine 4367, Cleveland 3379, Butler 204, St. John 401.

OSWEGO.

Oswego county: Blaine 9976, Cleveland 7434, Butler 265, St. John 560.

CATTARAUGUS.

Cattaraugus county: Blaine 7463, Cleveland 6065, Butler 372, St. John 939.

WESTCHESTER.

Westchester county: Blaine 11,286, Cleveland 12,524, Butler 255, St. John 137. Returns of all the towns, except Ossinning and Newcastle, canvassed. There will not be any change in the result.

ROCKLAND.

Rockland county: Blaine 2,592, Cleveland 3,697, Butler 28, St. John 123.

LEWIS.

Lewis county: Blaine 3,854, Cleveland 3,778, Butler 14, St. John 114.

WAYNE.

Wayne county: Blaine 6,843, Cleveland 4,740, Butler 168, St. John 133.

HERKIMER.

Herkimer county: Blaine 6,138, Cleveland 5,328, Butler 56, St. John 327.

ONONDAGA.

Onondaga county: Blaine 16,892, Cleveland 13,165, Butler 99, St. John 601.

ALLEGHANY.

Alleghany county: Blaine 6,668, Cleveland 3,886, Butler 736, St. John 488.

WASHINGTON.

Washington county gives Blaine 7,337; Cleveland, 4,222; Butler, 115; St. John, 225.

ESSEX.

Essex county: Blaine 4,551; Cleveland, 2,776, Butler, 61; St. John, 65.

MADISON.

Madison county: Blaine 6,608; Cleveland, 4,864; Butler, 86; St. John, 529.

MONTGOMERY.

Montgomery county: Blaine 5,505, Cleveland 5,413, Butler 48, St. John 134.

STEUBEN.

Steuben county: Blaine 10,047, Cleveland 9,060, Butler, 48; St. John 901.

FULTON AND HAMILTON.

Fulton and Hamilton counties: Blaine's plurality 1,047, showing no change from former figures. The Board of Canvassers of Wayne county sent out committees to the several towns to reconvene the inspectors to correct clerical errors in the returns. No change is expected in the figures already published. Chautauqua county gives 4,809 majority for Blaine, and Wyoming county 1,252 majority for Blaine.

DUCHESS.

POUGHKEEPSIE, Nov. 11. The canvass for Duchess county will probably be finished to-morrow. The Supervisors from several towns have sent back to have clerical errors only corrected.

JEFFERSON.

WATERTOWN, N. Y., Nov. 11. The Board of Canvassers of Jefferson county adjourned until 12 o'clock to-morrow.

LIST OF MISSING COUNTIES.

NEW YORK, Nov. 11. The following counties have yet to report officially on the vote for Presidential Electors at the recent election: Albany, Broome, Chemung, Chenango, Columbia, Cortland, Delaware, Duchess, Erie, Franklin, Genesee, Greene, Jefferson, Kings, Livingston, Monroe, New York, Oneida, Orange, Oswego, Queens, St. Lawrence, Schuyler, Suffolk, Sullivan, Tompkins, and Ulster.

## CALIFORNIA.

**Beaten by One Vote—Carothers Beaten for Congress.**

SAN FRANCISCO, Nov. 11.—In the official canvass of the vote of Alameda county by the Board of Supervisors, it was ascertained that in the Fifty-second Assembly District, T. C. Morris (Dem.) was elected, instead of N. B. Tyler (Rep.), as previously announced. The vote was, Morris 924, Tyler 923.

No later returns have been received this morning of the vote in the First Congressional District, but returns received and published in the morning papers confirm last night's dispatch and agree in showing that Henley (Dem.) will have a majority which, when full returns are in from Del Norte county, will probably bring it up to forty.

SAN FRANCISCO, Nov. 11. W. D. English, Chairman of the Democratic State Central Committee, has just sent the following to the Associated Press: "Herewith I hand you an estimate for Congress in the First District. Del Norte, Trinity, Shasta, and Plumas, one estimated, gives the Republicans all they claim in those four counties.' Del Norte, Carothers, 30; Humboldt, 275; Trinity, 257; Siskiyou, Henley, 145; Shasta, Carothers, 68; Modoc, Carothers, 130; Lassen, 40; Plumas, Henley, 160; Sierra, 486; Tehama, Henley, 75; Colusa, 756; Mendocino, 222; Lake, 207; Sonoma, Carothers, 111; Napa, 349. Total, Henley 1,575, Carothers 1,504.

**The Democrats Call for Funds.**

NEW YORK, Nov. 11.—Republican National Committee have moved to Victoria Hotel, and Chairman Jones, Senator Hobart, and Messrs. Elkins, Chaffee and Converse are to-day awaiting the reports of the official count in the State. Hon. Emory A. Storrs, in an interview this afternoon said: "It is the duty of Blaine to insist on a fair count, for he has not been running for fun, but as a representative of some millions of people." The Democratic National Committee to-day issued a call to those interested in Cleveland and Hendricks for money with which to defray extraordinary expenses occasioned by the threatened dispute of the electoral vote of the State of New York.

**Neither Party Yields.**

NEW YORK, Nov. 11.—The Mail and Express says: "The official count of the ballot in every county of the State is now in progress. The work will be very thorough. Neither party yields an inch. Every figure will be closely scrutinized in the counties of the State. A week is usually consumed at the work. In this city and in Kings county less time is required. Four years ago the official canvass of the State was not completed until November 20th, over a week distant. Prominent lawyers on both sides will watch the count."

**John Kelly Talks.**

NEW YORK, Nov. 11.—John Kelly of Tammany Hall said to-night: "There is no political significance in the election of Alderman Waite (Rep.) as President of the Board of Supervisors by the votes of Tammany Aldermen." Mr. Kelly adds: "Waite has often voted with the Tammany Democrats in the Board, and the latter have only corresponded with the retiring Alderman's desire for the courtesy of election." Kelly declares the Tammany Aldermen will watch the count of the electoral vote as a cat watches a mouse.

**Kings County Republicans.**

NEW YORK, Nov. 11.—At a meeting of the Republican General Committee of Kings county, to-night, State Senator Albert Daggett moved to drop from the rolls the names of all those members who voted for Cleveland. Alexander Forman and Edwin Packard, the latter a delegate to the Republican Chicago Convention, admitted they did not support Blaine. The motion was not acted on. The resignation of W. C. Beecher, a son of Rev. Henry Ward Beecher, was accepted.

**The Plenary Council.**

BALTIMORE, Nov. 11. – The Plenary Council reassembled at the seminary of St. Sulpice to-day, and the work of the first chapter of proposed action was taken up. This afternoon a conference was held at the archiepiscopal residence, composed principally of priests. Archbishops Alemany of San Francisco and Kenrick of St. Louis, are the only Archbishops present who attended as such the first Plenary Council of 1852. Of the Bishops who attended the second Plenary Council, Archbishops Elder, Lamy and Fechand and Bishops Hennessey, Degoesbriand, Loughlin and O'Connell are the only survivors. At vespers in the Cathedral Bishop Becker of Wilmington preached on "The Church and Science."

**The Next Congress.**

WASHINGTON, Nov 11. - Mr. McPherson, Secretary Republican Congressional Committee, says that from the most authentic information he has been able to secure the next House of Representatives will consist of 182 Democrats, 141 Republicans, 1 Greenbacker (Brumm of Pennsylvania), and 1 Fusionist (Weaver of Iowa)—a Democratic majority over all of 39. As compared with the membership of the various parties in the present House, this estimate shows a loss of 19 votes to the Democrats and 4 to the Independents, and a gain of 22 Republican and 1 Fusionist vote.

**Disorderly Sailors Punished.**

ANNAPOLIS, Md., Nov. 11.—Sentences were passed on the United States sailors who on August 31st seized articles of freight, confectionery and stores, and acted in a manner so disorderly on the steamer Carolina, from Baltimore to Norfolk, that the lady passengers were greatly alarmed. John Cunningham was given three years in prison on Cob dock, New York, and a loss of $864 pay. Judah Lind and Joseph Oliver were given one year each in prison and a loss of $117 pay.

**Steel Men in Conference.**

PHILADELPHIA, Pa., Nov. 11.—A conference begun to-day with closed doors at the office of the American Iron and Steel Association. On one side are the members of the Gun Foundry Board of the United States Government appointed to inquire into the best means for the manufacture of heavy guns adopted to modern warfare. On the other are representatives of the leading steel manufacturers of the country.

**Democratic Jollification in Indianapolis.**

INDIANAPOLIS, Nov. 11.—The Democratic State jollification here to-day was largely attended, but there was not a great number of visitors from outside the city. Between 3 and 4 o'clock this afternoon a meeting was organized at Circle Park, where Governor Hendricks and ex-Senator McDonald spoke. At night there was a torchlight parade, which Mr. Hendricks reviewed from a stand on Washington street. There was a great crowd on the streets and much enthusiasm. Everything passed off in good order.

**No Parades in Philadelphia.**

PHILADELPHIA, Pa., Nov. 11.—The Press says: "It seems to be settled that there will will be no Democratic parade here on Thursday, no matter how the official count of New York's vote goes. It is the disposition of the leaders of the Democracy that in the present state of public feeling parades and other demonstrations of rejoicing should be avoided."

**Michigan's Vote.**

DETROIT, Nov. 11.—Twenty out of eighty counties have reported on the vote for electors. Blaine pluralities 6,954. Fusion pluralities 2,254; Blaine's net plurality in twenty counties 4,700. Six other counties report the work of the canvassers as not completed. The counties not heard from will not materially change the figures sent heretofore. Full figures will not be in for a few days. In many counties the canvass has been postponed.

**Liberated Suspects.**

DUBLIN, Nov. 11. Patrick N. Fitzgerald, Fenian suspect, was arrested in London last April on a charge of treason, a felony, and was acquitted. Owing to his acquittal the crown abandoned the Fubbercurry cases, and all prisoners were released. They were received by friends with great rejoicing.

**Nevada Legislature.**

SAN FRANCISCO, Nov. 11.—With three counties to hear from, the Nevada Legislature will stand: Senate Fifteen Republicans, five Democrats; Assembly Thirty-one Republicans, nine Democrats. Republican majority on joint ballot, thirty-two.

**Mr. Blaine at Home**

AUGUSTA, Me., Nov. 11. Mr. Blaine remains quietly at home. He appears to be waiting like everybody else, and occupies himself about his ordinary affairs and entertaining friends who call.

**Blaine's Plurality in Oregon.**

PORTLAND, Ogn., Nov. 11. Unofficial returns from every county in the State gives Blaine a plurality at 2,100.

## MAUD S.

### The Great Mare Again Lowers Her Record.

#### A HALF-SECOND MORE KNOCKED OFF.

**In Spite of Weather and Prognostications, the Mare Makes a Mile in 2:09¾—Particulars of the Event.**

*Associated Press Dispatches to The Times.*

LEXINGTON, Ky., Nov. 11. Maud S. has proved herself a greater mare than ever her old owner, Vanderbilt, or her present owner, Robert Bonner, expected that she was. Hiram Woodruff, an old-time trainer of trotting horses, laid it down as an iron-clad law that you could never have a fast mile after the frost had struck the ground. Last week ice formed repeatedly and took the elasticity from the soil and sober-headed men like Dr. Herr said it was too late for Maud S. to attempt to do what no horse except herself had ever done. Enthusiasts, however, predicted that the record would be broken. The day was bright for November, but the expert does no look for muscles to be flexible when Indian summer comes. There was a large gathering of the very best people of the Blue Grass region at the fair grounds track. A placard, conspicuously posted on the grand stand, said: "No betting allowed." At half-past 11 Bair came out behind the Queen and gave her a warming-up mile in 2:26¾. The judges and timers were Major H. C. McDowell, Colonel B. West and W. H. Wilson. In the opposite stand Mr. Bonner held his watch, flanked on both sides by General G. F. Robinson, Mr L. F. Brodhead, Mr. Richard Anderson and Hamilton Busby. The conditions under which the performance was made were written in the record-book: "Maud S. will start to beat her own record of 2:09¾, and should she beat the record Woodburn Farm, where she was bred, will commemorate the achievement by awarding to her through the Kentucky Trotting-horse Breeders' Association a cup with the time made by her engraved thereon." Bair jogged around the track, went to the head of the stretch, came down and nodded for the word. The great mare did not make a single misstep. The time of the first quarter was 32¾, half mile 1:04, three-quarter pole 1:37, and here Mr. Bowerman joined her with a runner hitched to a sulky. The finish was strong, as the judges stopped their watches at 2:09¾. A majority of the outside watches made it 2:09. The scene, when the queen returned to the stand for Bair to weigh, was indescribable. It was the greatest performance of the kind ever witnessed in the world, and the Kentuckians shouted as only Kentuckians can. Mr. Bonner's first congratulatory dispatch was to Vanderbilt. The mare will now be turned out for the winter.

**The Coming Meeting of the Pacific Blood Horse Association.**

CHICAGO, Nov. 11.—Binnette, the sensational three-year-old daughter of Billet, whose wonderful performances at Louisville and Latonia in the fall caused her to be regarded as the Miss Woodford of the western turf, has been leased, so it is stated, to California parties by her owners, Bowman & Co., and will run in a four-mile dash at San Francisco week after next at the meeting of the Pacific Coast Blood Horse Association, in which Baldwin's, Haggin's, and other well-known stables will take part. At the close of this meeting part of the Rancho Del Paso stable will journey to Mobile in charge of Captain T. G. Moore, where they will be wintered and prepared for the coming engagements in the Southwest and East next Spring. It is more than probable that some of the other California stables which have engagements this side of the Rockies next spring will also be wintered there, as Captain Cottrell has demonstrated that horses can be trained there to good advantage during the winter months and the Magnolia track affords every facility for that purpose.

#### THE CHOLERA.

**An Alarming Increase of the Disease in Paris.**

PARIS, Nov. 11.—Between noon and 11 o'clock last night, 27 fresh cases of cholera and eleven deaths were reported in this city. These numbers do not include additional cases and deaths which occurred at the hospitals. In numerous instances the victims were seized by the dread disease in the most sudden manner. With hardly a premonition, they were stricken in the streets, in omnibuses, and other public places, or when pursuing their ordinary vocations. The hospitals set apart for the use of cholera patients are already full to overflowing, and others are being placed in readiness as rapidly as circumstances will permit. Many cases occurred among the troops in garrison. In nearly all the barracks some of the soldiers have been attacked. If the epidemic continues, an order will be issued closing the public schools. The eastern and central sections of the city are the ones most affected. The residences occupied principally by English and American people, are in most excellent condition.

MADRID, Nov. 11.—On account of the continued existence of cholera in France, the Spanish government has directed that all persons arriving overland from that country shall submit to a quarantine of ten days at the Spanish frontier.

BERLIN, Nov. 11.—Imperial Boards of Health of Germany and Austria-Hungary, acting in concert, are endeavoring to adopt measures to prevent cholera securing an entrance into either country.

PARIS, Nov. 11.—Up to noon to-day there were 36 deaths from cholera, including those in the hospitals. Victor Guichard, senior, a member of the Chamber of Deputies, died to-day, while conversing with a colleague at Pollis, Bourbon. His age was 81. Brisson, in Chambers, announced his death, and the Chambers adjourned.

**Civil Service Examinations.**

WASHINGTON, Nov. 11.—A series of examinations for the examination of applicants for the departmental service at Washington has been arranged for December for the west and south: Friday, December 5, Denver; Friday, 12, San Francisco; Wednesday, 17, Los Angeles, Cala.; Monday, 22, Fort Worth; Wednesday, 24, San Antonio; and Saturday, 27, Houston. These examinations will be two grades "limited" and "general." The limited is for copyists at a salary of $720 to $900 a year and the general is for clerkships at a salary of $1000 and upward. Persons desiring to make application and be examined at these examinations can obtain application blanks and a copy of the civil service law rules and regulations of the postmaster at either of the places named or of the Civil Service Commission at Washington, and as in most cases there will not be time to admit of application being forwarded to the Commissioner and notice of application returned to applicants, the application duly executed may be brought to examination and delivered to the Chief Examiner.

**Piutes Going on the War-Path.**

SAN FRANCISCO, Nov. 11. A Winnemucca, Nev., dispatch says the Piutes are going on the war-path against the Washoe Indians. A large number of the first named tribe left here to-day for the Pyramid reservation, where they hold a council to-day to decide what action to take. Lieut. Connell, of McDermott, left here yesterday for Wadsworth to endeavor to restore amicable relations between the two tribes. The cause of the trouble was the killing of one or two Piutes by the Washoes.

**Connecticut's Returns.**

HARTFORD, Conn., Nov. 11. Official returns at the Secretary of State's office show the Republican candidates for State Secretary, Treasurer and Comptroller, voted for a week ago to have pluralities over the Democratic candidates of about 125 each. Waller (D) for Governor was the only one on the ticket getting a plurality. The Legislature will have the choosing of the entire State ticket. The Legislature is Republican.

**The Wine Yield.**

ST. HELENA, Nov. 12. The grape picking season is nearly finished and the quantity of wine manufactured will be fully 50 per cent. in excess of last season throughout Napa valley.

**Hinton's Appointment Invalid.**

SAN FRANCISCO, Nov. 11. Superior Judge Finn has decided that the appointment of W. M. Hinton by Governor Stoneman as Police Commissioner in place of R. P. Hammond is invalid.

**Passed Its Third Reading.**

LONDON, Nov. 11. In the Commons to-day the Franchise bill passed its third reading without division.

## GENERAL SCHOFIELD'S REPORT.

**Operations in the Department of Missouri During the Past Year.**

CHICAGO, Nov. 11. The annual report of Major-General Schofield, commanding the Division of the Missouri, published to-day, treats of the operations in that Division during the past year. The roster of troops in the Division shows seven regiments and two companies of cavalry, nineteen regiments and one company of infantry, four batteries of field artillery. The report urges the necessity for liberal appropriations to provide permanent shelter and barracks for troops in the Division. It refers to the destitute condition of certain Indian tribes in the Department of the Platte, and urges means for their relief. It urges the necessity for a practical school for field artillery, fashioned after schools of application for infantry and cavalry at Fort Leavenworth. It mentions the encampments of the Illinois National Guard during the months of June and August, when an inspection of troops occurred by Lieutenant-Colonel Sweitzer, Eighth Cavalry. General Schofield, in this connection, invites attention to the importance of schools for the practical instruction of the militia of the several States. The urgent need is for the education of both officers and men in the use of the modern rifle, in field manœuvres necessary to make the fire of the rifle effective, and in the detail of army life, both in camp and in garrison. One year of such instruction to young men between 17 and 20 years of age would make, he argues, excellent soldiers, far more valuable than many times their number of untrained militia. The national government might well give reasonable aid to these schools in money, military materials and experienced instructors, such as would make the system inexpensive to the States.

## COMING EXCURSIONISTS.

**List of Names of Those Who Will Arrive Wednesday.**

*Special Dispatch to The Times.*

NEEDLES, Cal., Nov. 11.—The following is the list of passengers to arrive Wednesday afternoon with the R. M. Baker & Co. excursion in charge of S. J. Mathes:

*For Los Angeles*—Mrs. Juda A. Sabine, Edward D. Sabine, Colorado Springs, Col.; H. C. Wallby, Lincoln, Ill.; Mrs. W McPherrin, Arthur McPherrin, Royal McPherrin, Paul McPherrin, Nellie McPherrin, Clarinda, Iowa; George J. Fackler, Mrs. George J. Fackler, Miss Lizzie Fackler, Kansas City; Miss Nannie Gregory, Longwood, Mo.; C. Clemons, Kansas City, Mo.; Miss Clara Weaver, Miss Minnie Pollock St. Louis, Mo.; Miss Labreds, Carren, Ill.; O. P. Hayes, San Jose; J. E. Hayes, Mrs. J. E. Hayes, May Hayes, Archie Hayes, Ambrose Hayes, Harper, Conn.; Theo. Twining, Washington, Kas.; H. C. Witmer, Miss Victoria Witmer, Jeda, Wis.; W. J. Lavarco, Chicago; J. C. Cook, St. Paul, Minn.; Mrs. E. C. Cook, Mooresville, Ind.; Mrs. A. V. Pocoobhoff, Los Angeles; W. C. Hayes, Mrs. W. C. Hayes, Petersburg, O.; L. P. Suley, Mrs. L. P. Suley, Lula Suley, Juan Suley, Pauline Suley, Erbert Suley, Reynoldsville, Pennsylvania; W. S. Jones, Mrs. W. S. Jones, Kansas City; Miss Mattie Knight, Sycamore, Ills.; A. C. Tubbs, Aurora, Ills.; Ann Nye, Northwood, Ia.; R. M. Watson, Clayton, N. J.; Mrs. R. M. Watson, Miss Edith Watson, Clayton, N. J.; John Peaslee, Mrs. John Peaslee, Bertha Peaslee, Addie Peaslee, Miss E. Large, Linn e Peaslee, Dewitt, Ia.; D. A. Bentley, Mrs. Dabandi, Greely Bentley, Dollie Bentley, Los Angeles; S. Cheesbrough, Glenn Falls, N. Y.; Miss L. Broomhall, Mrs. G. E. Nye, George Nye, Muscatine, Ia.; Mrs. J. M. Stowell, Ray Stowell, Fred. Stowell, Des Moines; Dr. A. C. Orr, Rochester, Ind.; L. H. Gibbs, Mrs. L. H. Gibbs, Louis Gibbs, Earl Gibbs, Des Moines; A. G. Brown, Mrs. A. G. Brown, Brockway Centre, Mich.; G. W. Murdell, Mrs. G. W. Murdell, Casmobia, Ill.; Mrs. Fannie Lybarger, Miss Fannie Lybarger, Chas. Lybarger, Casmobia, Ill.; A. Durant, Mrs. A. Durant, L. Auren, J. H. Hearn, Lillie Hearn, Marshalltown, Ia.; J. Chambers, Mrs. J. Chambers, Mitchell, Iowa; Miss Ruham Wright, Elk Lick, Pa.; Miss Ida Rouday, C. P. Dunham, Mrs. Dr. Adams, Marshalltown, Ia.; K. W. Macomber, Mrs. Macomber, Miss Laura Macomber, Louis, Ia.; L. Grant, Atlantic, Ia.; F. M. Johnson, Lawrenceburg, Ind.; L. C. Mason, Norwalk, Conn.; R. Bigelow, L. White, Northwood, Ia.; Mrs. E. White, Chas. White, Edward White, Holton, Ia.

*For San Francisco*—Miss J. Black, San Francisco; H. T. Arthur, Mrs. H. T. Arthur, DeWitt, Ia.; J. W. Ross, Kansas City; Miss M. Cox, B. Alf Sturitt, Miss Alden, Oneida, Ill.; J. H. Long, Mrs. J. P. Losigh, Miss Eva Albe, St. Johns, Mich.; Mrs. E. F. Rice, Barre; Miss J. K. Whitehead, Mrs. J. K. Whitehead, Miss Edith Whitehead, Edward Whitehead, Mrs. S. A. Tregs, Mt. Rose, Mo.; P. S. Eastman, Mrs. Eastman, Nora Eastman, Bert Eastman, Osage, Ia.; J. Beck, Port Huron, Mich.; J. H. Cummings, Milwaukee; J. M. S. Potter, Indianapolis.

*For Pomona.*—Mrs. L. P. Crawford, Helen Crawford, Pomona.

*For Riverside.*—Jas. Lee, Mrs. Jas. Lee, Miss May Morris, Elmwood, Ill., Mrs. E. A. Corins, Altoona, Ill.; Julia Goddard, Edwin Goddard, Galesburg, Ill.

## YESTERDAY'S FIRE.

**Three Thousand Dollars' Worth of Property Burned.**

The alarm of fire at six p. m. yesterday was caused by the burning of three houses opposite the Alameda Hotel, near the junction of Alameda and Upper Main streets. The fire started in a blacksmith shop and was soon communicated to the wagon and carpenter shops near by. The house occupied by Peter Miller was also partially burned. The railroad company's yard locomotive was promptly on the ground, and played a good stream on the fire from the zanja. The fire department were slow about getting on water on account of an insufficient supply. When, however, water was obtained good work was done. The blacksmith and wagon shops were totally destroyed. The carpenter shop and residence were only partially burned. The blacksmith shop belonged to Fred Simon, and was insured for $600. Its value, including the wagon shop, was $1,200. The carpenter shop belongs to W. A. Spaulding, formerly of the Express, and cost $1,000. It was not learned if it was insured. The residence occupied by Mr. Miller belonged to John O'Neill, and was valued at about $800. Mr. Miller had $500 insurance on his furniture. Everything in the house was saved, although it was considerably damaged in its removal. The fire started from the forge in the blacksmith shop, which Mr. Simon left burning while he went to his supper, intending to return and work late into the night. When first seen the flames were spreading rapidly inside the shop, with the above results.

**Excursion to Temecula, San Diego County.**

Messrs. Charnock, Morrill & Robinson will run an excursion train from Los Angeles to the new colony of Temecula on Saturday, the 15th instant, leaving Los Angeles at 6:15 a. m., passing through Pomona, Colton, Riverside, and Elsinore, and arriving on the ground at 10 a. m.

Teams will be at hand to convey parties over the lots and lands the company are offering for sale at extremely low prices and very easy terms. This is the best opportunity now presented in California to secure cheap and first-class lands. Cheapness of wood, purity and abundance of water, and ample transportation facilities make this one of the most desirable localities in Southern California. For particulars, maps, etc., inquire of Charnock, Morrill & Robinson, rooms 11 and 12, Widney Block, on First street, between Main and Spring streets.

Round trip tickets sold for only $[illegible].

**Annual Report of Zanjero.**

The Zanjero has prepared his report showing the following sales of water during the year ending November [illegible]

[illegible]

# LOS ANGELES DAILY TIMES.

VOL. VII.—NO. 133. LOS ANGELES, CALIFORNIA, FRIDAY MORNING, MAY 15, 1885. FIVE CENTS.



## The Times.

Office—Temple, Main and New High.

An interesting government statement relative to farm-labor wages is telegraphed to-day.

"Sheridan at Stone River," a stirring poem dedicated to the Army of the Cumberland, is printed on the second page.

Yesterday, sad to say, was another bad day for General Grant. He is far from being out of danger, and the disease may take a fatal turn when least expected. But let us hope that the result will be otherwise.

England's latest scheme for disposing of the troublesome Soudan is for the Porte to take possession and run the Mahdi's machine for him. Turkey is thinking of it, and the Mahdi remains to be heard from.

A most extraordinary and impolitic nomination would be that of Zach Montgomery, of California, for Assistant Attorney General for the Interior Department, which has been suggested by Attorney-General Garland. Montgomery is a bitter political and religious bigot, and a sworn enemy of our public school system. He is n. g.

The Russian idea of the frontier question is to extend the line upon the first exhibition of "disorder" on the part of the Afghans. This is neat but not gaudy, and does infinite credit to the long diplomatic head of De Giers. The Afghans will doubtless be found a very disorderly people whenever the Northern Bear concludes to make a descent upon Herat.

Boston Traveller: No conversion since the days of St. Paul has been more remarkable than that of George William Curtis. Only last summer he described the Democratic party as "very hungry and very thirsty," but last week he alluded to Mr. Pendleton as leader of "a party that holds the spoils system is a crime."

An article from the Montreal Gazette, entitled "Four Great Generals," which is reprinted on the second page of to day's Times, contains and interesting and intelligent, though brief, estimate of the respective military abilities o Generals Grant, McPherson, Sherman and Sheridan, with a warm and high encomium upon Grant by Sherman.

Labouchere had an idea that the Queen should have provided the Princess Beatrice's £6000 annuity. That was not the Queen's idea, however, and Parliament seems to have agreed with her. No matter what becomes of Ireland, Afghanistan or Egypt, it is of the first importance that the royal family be not permitted to come to want.

An extra session of the Legislature, for the purpose of taking a "whack" at the subject of irrigation, is possible. If held, it will afford an excellent opportunity for certain ambitious statesmen to work the gubernatorial racket. The question of irrigation, unless it be of the sort that is practiced at the bars of the capital, will probably be secondary to the other.

The friends of Sunset Cox cannot persuade the President to withdraw his name for the Turkish mission. Mr. Cox himself desires to go to Constantinople. He will make a worthy successor to General Lew Wallace, and perhaps bring out as notable a book, during his official stay at the court of the "unspeakable Turk," as "Ben Hur."

Nearly all old Californians who go East to live find that the "hankering" for California returns upon them so strong that they are not contented until they have once more set foot on the Golden Shore. L. P. Sellers, of Bangor, Maine, is one of these. He writes to the Times-Mirror Company: "I am an old Californian, and would like one of your papers, because I must go back there as soon as ever I can."

In consequence of his recent injuries, General Seridan has been compelled to decline giving a reception to his comrades in Los Angeles. The fact is sincerely regretted by the veterans, who would all be rejoiced to take the commander by the hand and give him the mystic grasp of loving comradeship. It is expected that the General will be well enough to leave Santa Monica and come up to Los Angeles to-day. He may push on at once, without stopping here. May health and safety attend him and his!

The New York Commercial's Washington special says: "That the Administration, in seeking men on whom to confer office, should seem to show a preference to Southerners, particularly Confederates, has given rise to some comment in military circles. All over the North are many brave men and good Democrats who fought in the Union army, yet not one who was conspicuous in that army has received an office." General Rosecrans, since appointed Register of the Treasury—a sort of chief clerkship—is an exception. He has had Presidential aspirations, but is put off with a bureau office, while Confederates are sent to represent the country abroad. By all means give the Confederates a chance.

The President has done a good thing, for which we gladly give him credit. He has revoked the appointment of James Blackburn as Internal Revenue Collector for the Lexington, Kentucky, district, an appointment procured by his brother, ex-Governor Blackburn, present United States Senator from that State, with the co-operation of other Democratic politicians of like extreme views. The writing of the following letter in 1861, by James Blackburn, is what "cooked his goose":

Abingdon, Va., October 2, 1861.

*My Dear Wife*: I have left you and our children in the land of the despot, but God grant that I may soon be able to make the Union men of Kentucky feel the edge of my knife. From this day I hold every Union traitor as my enemy, and from him I scorn to receive quarter, and to him I will never grant my soul in death, for they are cowards and villains enough. Brother Henry and I arrived here without hindrance. I have had chills all the way, but I hope to live to kill forty Yankees for every chill that I ever had. I learn that Hardee is still in Arkansas. Lee is reported inactive, and if this prove true, I will tender my resignation, to go immediately to Kentucky. I hope that I will do my duty as a rebel and free man. Since I know the Union men of Kentucky, I intend to begin the work of murder in earnest, and if ever I spare one then may hell be my portion. I want to see Union blood run deep enough for my horse to swim in. Your husband,

James Blackburn.

Mr. Blackburn, being relieved from the necessity of looking after Uncle Sam's internal revenue, will now have more time to contemplate the past. Mr. Blackburn appears to be a fool—or was one in 1861.

The Salvation Army at Stockton defies the Chief of Police, who has notified them [illegible]

## WASHINGTON.

### A Californian's Chances for an Office.

SUNSET COX MUST GO TO TURKEY.

A Delegation of His Constituents Visit the President, but Cleveland Declines to Withdraw His Name.

*Associated Press Dispatches to The Times.*

New York, May 14.—The Tribune's Washington special says: It is understood that Attorney-General Garland has recommended the appointment as Assistant Attorney-General for the Interior Department of Zachary Montgomery, of San Francisco. It is said Montgomery is an old and intimate personal friend of the Attorney-General, who places a high estimate upon his legal abilities. The World's Washington special says: It is said the wife of Judge Field will be appointed Vice Regent of the Ladies' Mount Vernon Society of California at a meeting of the Grand Council of ladies at the home of Washington on Wednesday next.

THE ADMINISTRATION'S PLANS.

New York, May 14.—Secretary Bayard, in a letter to the Minister Roberts Banquet Committee, says: "This government has no plan inconsistent with the integrity, prosperity and development of every state in the entire hemisphere. Our policies, commercial or political, are such as cannot fail to strengthen the cause of law, order and morality, and of such I am sure Mr. Roberts will prove himself an able and worthy representative."

REDUCING THE FORCE.

Washington, May 14.—Six clerks and one messenger in the office of the Supervising Architect of the Treasury were dismissed to-day, and the salaries of three of the principal clerks were reduced in order to bring the expenditures of the office within the limit of the appropriations for the current fiscal year ending June 30. The changes will lessen the current expenses of the office about $1200.

LEAVES OF ABSENCE.

Hereafter leaves of absence will be granted to clerks and employes of the Treasury Department for not more than thirty days for each year of service, and for proportionate periods for shorter terms of service, reckoning back to the last leave of absence granted for the full time then due, but not more than one year. All absences for any cause whatever during the time within the right to which leave has accrued will be deducted.

WANT HER RETAINED.

An army delegation, consisting of Surgeon General Murray, Inspector General Baird, Assistant Adjutant General O. D. Greene, General H. J. Hunt, General Ayres and Lieutenant Colonel Hudson, called upon the President and urged the retention of Miss Sumner, daughter of General Sumner, as Postmistress at Charlottesville.

### SUNSET COX.

The President Refuses to Withdraw His Name as Minister to Turkey.

Washington, May 14.—A delegation of the constituency of Congressman Cox of New Yord called on President Cleveland to-day. After the ceremony of introduction Judge McCarthy addressed the President on behalf of the delegation, stating the purpose of their visit to Washington. They had seen Mr. Cox, and urged him in behalf of all classes of people in his district to decline the appointment as Minister to Turkey and represent them in Congress. They had not prevailed, and now came to ask the President to advise Mr. Cox to decline. With this Judge McCarthy handed the President an engrossed copy of the resolutions. The President said the proposition was a singular one to make to him. He had found a good man, such a one as he wanted to help run the administration, and here came his friends to say he was a good man and yet to ask him (the President) to let him go. He was afraid the proposition would be a sort of boomerang for those who made it.

Judge McCarthy—"We feel, Mr. President, knowing him as we do——"

The President—"It won't do. I must have the lion's share of the good things for the Administration, and the more resolutions you pass calling Mr. Cox a good man the more I shall hold on to him."

Something was said by the delegates about the difficulty of filling Mr. Cox's place. "You have," said the President, "a district full of good men. Send us along a good man. I won't interfere in your district, but I want him, and you won't get me to back out. Your mission is unsuccessful."

Mr. Cox felt he had a word to say. He had served sixteen years and had formed a host of warm attachments. All these gentlemen know that this request came from no suggestion of his.

The President—"It is very complimentary to you and me, too. I feel that I have been building perhaps better than I know."

A delegate said it would be very gratifying to his constituents to have Mr. Cox remain. It would be very hard to fill his place.

Mr. Cox said he used to be in a great hurry to get up to the House promptly, but some one had told him the government could run without him, and he had found it so. The President had made this appointment with so much kindness, he felt himself bound to go where sent. They could always find a good Democrat in the district, and could always elect him. After some further talking and a round of hand-shaking, the delegation withdrew.

### Loss of a Steamer in the Willamette.

Portland, Org. May 14.—The steamer City of Salem struck on a rock at Rock Island rapids in the Willamette, twenty miles above this city this afternoon and sank to her hurricane deck. She broke her shaft the day before and was coming down in tow of the steamer Isabel. Her cargo consisted of eighty tons of flour, half of which was saved in a damaged condition. No lives were lost. As the steamer's hull was not bulk-headed and the water is very swift and the banks rocky, it will hardly be possible to save anything but the machinery. The steamer was owned jointly by the Capitol Mills Company of Salem and Wm. Reid of Portland, and was valued at $18,000. Not insured.

### Minister McLean Presents His Credentials.

Paris, May 14.—Mr. Morton, retiring United States Minister, to-day presented his letters of recall to President Grevy. They then lunched together. Afterwards Mr. McLean presented his credentials to the President and delivered an address, to which M. Grevy replied, welcoming the new Minister and thanking him for the sentiment expressed in his address. M. Grevy assured Mr. McLean he would always find in France a most sympathetic co-operation in everything calculated to promote the welfare of the American Republic.

### Rumors of an Extra Session of the Legislature.

San Francisco, May 14.—Rumors of an extra session of the Legislature to pass an irrigation law are again in circulation. It is asserted that meetings of irrigationists have been held in this city, and that they have secured the signatures of a majority of members of each House to a petition for the session, coupled with a pledge not to prolong its duration over fifteen days. Several prominent Senators and politicians express the belief that the call will be made within thirty days.

### Grand Lodge I. O. O. F.

San Francisco, May 14.—Election of officers, Grand Lodge, I. O. O. F., terminated at 12:45 this afternoon as follows: Grand Master, Nath. Cook, of Santa Clara; Deputy Grand Master, C. T. McEachran, of St. Helena; Grand Warden, Elwood Bruner, of Sacramento; Grand Secretary, W. B. Lyon, of San Francisco; Grand Treasurer, Geo. B. Lemont, of San Francisco; and Grand Representative, J. W. E. Wilson, of San Francisco.

### The Illinois Senatorship.

Springfield, Ill., May 14.—After ten unsuccessful ballots to-day for United States Senator, at 10:05 the joint assembly took a recess till 8:30 a. m. to-morrow. This is done to prevent Weaver being sworn in.

Springfield, May 14.—About 10:30, after the Democrats had adjourned, Weaver, the new member from the Thirty-Fourth District, was taken into the house and sworn in by Judge Grose. The fight now will be to have him recognized by the chair. This will come in the morning.

### On a Tour of Inspection.

Chicago, May 14.—Secretary Endicott arrived here to-day on a tour of inspection. He left to-night for Fort Leavenworth, and will also visit Fort Snelling and the arsenal at Rock Island, Ill. Regarding the mooted transfer of the Indians to the War Department he said he was not prepared to speak definitely, but that he believed it might prove advantageous on the score of economy.

[illegible]

### REVOLVER AND BOWIE-KNIFE.

In the Hands of Two Desperate Men—They Do Some Damage.

New York, May 14.—About 8:30 to-night an altercation occurred between Larry O'Brien, a well-known broker and politician, and George Trueman, a sporting character, belonging to Chicago. The former was probably fatally stabbed, and the latter was shot twice. The affray was the outcome of a quarrel to-night. O'Brien met Trueman on the corner of Broadway and Twenty-seventh streets and accused him of attempted blackmail. The remark enraged Trueman, who gave utterance to some strong language. His remarks so exasperated O'Brien that he lifted his cane and struck the other man a heavy blow on the head. Without warning Trueman drew a murderous-looking bowie-knife and plunged it into his opponent's abdomen, inflicting a gash eight inches long. A policeman immediately arrested Trueman, and while in the custody of the officer a pistol shot was heard and a bullet from O'Brien's revolver lodged in the prisoner's back. He broke away from the officer and a second bullet from the same source lodged in Trueman's left shoulder. Both men were taken to the Twenty-Ninth Precinct Police Station, and thence removed to the New York hospital. The excitement in the locality was intense. The cause of the quarrel is said to be an attempt on the part of Trueman to blackmail a Wall street friend of O'Brien's. The friend is supposed to be Mr. Kelly of the firm of Kelly & Bliss, bookmakers. A charge of felonious assault was made against both men at the station house. The knife used has a blade a foot long and an inch and a quarter wide. O'Brien declined to take an anesthetic while his wound was being sewed up, and both men indulged in recriminations while their wounds were being dressed in the same ward in the hospital. To-night both men were resting quietly, but the result of the injuries is likely to be fatal in each case.

### WINNIPEG AFFAIRS.

Riel Will Be Hanged if Caught—The Northcote Safe.

Chicago, May 14.—The Daily News has Winnipeg intelligence of an authentic nature that the train with provisions which left Swift Current a week ago was attacked by Poundman and his Indians and captured after a fight, in which several were wounded and two killed. Thirty-one teams and twenty-one teamsters were captured. Ten teamsters escaped. The train was within thirteen miles of Battleford.

Winnipeg, May 14.—The latest news from the front is contained in the following dispatch, received this afternoon by Commissioner Wrigley: "The Northcote is safe, but ran through a terrible fire at Batouche from both banks of the river, and the rebels tried to capture her by lowering the ferry cable, but they were not quick enough. They carried away the smokestack and whistle, however. Three were wounded but slightly, the boat being barricaded with beef boxes and hay and oats. Plenty of provisions and fodder at the front; also ammunition, and things look brighter. We expect this defeat will wind up the business. The rebels are delivering themselves up. Will insist upon Riel being hanged." The report that Riel has gone down the river is not much credited in Winnipeg, as all good judges say he would thereby place himself in the way of being captured. As for the rebels who are surrendering, it is not likely anything further will be done with them. Many of them were no doubt misled by Riel and Dumont, and others were coerced into joining the rebels.

### THE SHARON CASE.

A Batch of Affidavits to be Filed by Sarah Althea.

San Francisco, May 14.—The Chronicle to-morrow will publish the following: On Monday next about sixty affidavits will be filed in Judge Sullivan's court by counsel for plaintiff in the Sharon divorce case. They are intended to refute the Kowalsky depositions, which brought in question and reflected upon the plaintiff's virtue while living at the Baldwin and Grand hotels prior to 1880, when her connection with William Sharon began. "I have not found it necessary," said Sarah Althea, "to get affidavits from the bell boys and servants. Those which I have are all from respectable and well-known people. If you will not publish their names I will let you see the affidavits." She did so. Nearly all of them are brief, and most of them are made by persons who resided at the hotels mentioned when she did. They cover thirteen years of her life previous to 1880. The affiants testify that they never heard a word against her virtue and chastity until the Sharon affair; that her companions were respectable ladies, and in several cases wives of deponents, and that no men visited her rooms at suspicious hours.

### FARM LABOR.

Statistics of Wages Paid in Different Sections of the Country.

Washington, May 14.—The monthly statistical publication of the Agricultural Department for May, which will be issued within two or three days, contains a comprehensive statement of the wages paid farm laborers in all parts of the country, based upon what Mr. Dodge, statistician of the department, believes to be entirely trustworthy data: Eastern States, $25.30; Middle States, $23.19; Southern States, $14.27; Western States, $22.26; California, $28.75. The amount of labor seeking employment in agricultural districts at the present time is unusually large, yet there are many localities in almost every section of the country in which there is more or less complaint of a scarcity of labor. The report closes with a practical suggestion that in manufacturing towns and cities offices be opened, either by the labor unions or by benevolent citizens, through which communications may be opened between unemployed city workmen and farmers needing help, so that the reputable and worthy city laborer may have means of making known his true character, instead of starting on foot at a venture, subject to the risk of being mistaken for a professional tramp.

### A Bad Day for General Grant.

New York, May 14.—Yesterday was acknowledged to be a bad day for General Grant. He suffered with his throat and could only speak with difficulty. The afternoon brought him no relief, even though it brought Dr. Douglas, and it was not until early this morning that he fell into a slumber, superinduced by an extra quantity of morphine. This morning he awoke feeling a little easier, but not at all improved in his general condition. Dr. Douglas's statements imply that the General is not improving in the same ratio as hitherto. The weather has a very depressing influence.

New York, May 14.—General Grant was a little easier this evening. Fred Grant and Dr. Douglas state he is really a very sick man.

### The London Exhibition of 1886.

London, May 14.—The Executive Council of the American exhibition to be held here in 1886 have, after examining the merits of the various sites for the exhibition, to-day given preference to that at Earl's Court, Kensington, in close proximity to the site of the South Kensington Animal Exhibition and of equal area, about twenty-two acres. The American exhibition will have its own railway station and its own grounds, and be in direct communication with all railroad systems of the United Kingdom. Visitors will be enabled by this arrangement to see both the British, Colonial and American exhibitions without going from under cover.

### Earnings of the Southern Pacific.

New York, May 14.—The following is the statement for February of the railroads mentioned: Southern Pacific of New Mexico—Gross earnings, $56,711; operating expenses, $24,680; net earnings, $32,030. Southern Pacific of Arizona—Gross earnings, $137,516; operating expenses, $60,155; net earnings, $77,362. Southern Pacific of California—Gross earnings, $247,359; operating expenses, $131,397; net earnings, $115,961. Southern Pacific of California, Northern Division—Gross earnings, $82,300; operating expenses, $54,029; net earnings, $28,270.

### Fire at Santa Barbara.

Santa Barbara, May 14.—A dwelling house belonging to George Parker was entirely destroyed by fire this afternoon. Mrs. Parker was baking bread and had a big fire in the stove, and the roof where the stove pipe passed through caught, taking the house, furniture and wearing apparel. But little was saved. Loss about $1000. No insurance.

### Death of Benjamin H. Coit.

San Francisco, May 14.—Benjamin Howard Coit, well known in this city, where he acted as caller of the San Francisco Stock Board, died suddenly at his residence this morning of heart disease. Death occurred during sleep.

[illegible]

## RUSSIA'S PLANS.

### She Will Extend the Boundary at Pleasure.

PROGRESS OF THE NEGOTIATIONS.

The New Frontier Line Described—Colonel Alikhanoff Still at Merv with Russian Troops.

*Associated Press Dispatches to The Times.*

London, May 14.—A dispatch from Tirpul to the Daily Telegraph says that the people of Afghanistan expect that England will avenge the defeat of the Afghans by the Russians, or indemnify the Ameer for his losses.

London, May 14.—Lord Granville is communicating with Russia in regard to keeping order on the new Russo-Afghan frontier. It is reported that De Giers has asked whether England will accept the responsibility for acts of frontier tribes nominally under the control of the Ameer. It is the intention of De Giers to leave Russia free to extend the frontier on the first excuse of tribal disorders.

London, May 14.—The Standard says: It is rumored that the Russian reply raises a difficulty in regard to the basis of delimitation. It is expected that a commission of officers will be appointed to examine the northwest frontier of India with a view to taking into consideration measures for the defense of Afghanistan. Merchants residing at Merv have petitioned Russia to allow an Afghan agency there.

Vienna, May 14.—A dispatch from St. Petersburg to the Political Correspondence says the basis of the Anglo-Russian agreement appears to consist in the abolition of the neutral zone in favor of a direct boundary between Russia and Afghanistan. Russian government circles think this will secure a lasting peace, the neutral zone having been a constant cause of discussion.

Hongkong, May 14.—The Russian Minister at Pekin is much concerned over English occupation of Queipaart. Vladivostok is closed to foreign vessels, unless brought in by a Russian pilot.

London, May 14.—Negotiations which have been resumed in London between Russia and England respecting the Afghan question are making satisfactory progress. Some further explanations are still necessary from both sides before satisfaction with the general agreement already reached can be secured, but it is not believed this will delay the final adjustment. M. Lessar, chief of the Russian commission on the Afghanistan frontier question, expects at every moment to be instructed to proceed forthwith to Asia for the work of delimitating the frontier.

AN ANNUITY FOR THE PRINCESS BEATRICE.

London, May 14.—In the House of Commons this afternoon Gladstone stated he did not know whether Russia's answer concerning the Afghan frontier agreement reached by Lord Granville, Earl of Kimberly, Baron De Staal and M. Lessar, and submitted to the Czar for approval, had yet arrived in London. Negotiations between the two governments continue, Gladstone said, and the government were unaware of any further Russian advance. The latest telegrams received make no mention of any advance. Gladstone then moved, and Sir Stafford Northcote seconded, the granting of an annuity of £6000 to Princess Beatrice on the occasion of her forthcoming marriage. Labouchere opposed the motion. He thought the Queen should provide the annuity. The annuity was voted by 335 against 38.

THE NEW AFGHAN FRONTIER.

Simla, India, May 14.—The new Afghan frontier line starts at a point north of Zulfikar, and runs thence eastward to Chamara Bhid. From the latter place the line extends northward down the Kushk river to Gauzit Khan, and proceeds thence eastward and south to Penjdeh, to Katioja Sahl.

Teheran, May 14.—Colonel Alikhanoff, who commanded the Russians in their attack on Penjdeh, remains at Merv with 2000 troops. The Russians have two batallions of infantry and 800 cavalry, with two batteries at Sarakhs. They have strong outposts at Pul-i-Khatum and Zulfikar.

### THE TURF.

A Great Day at Louisville—Races at Other Places.

Louisville, May 14.—Never in the history of the Louisville Jockey Club has a better opening day been known than met this afternoon for Derby day. Visitors from all over the land swelled the crowd that witnessed the races to nearly thirty thousand. Weather beautiful. Track never in better condition. First race, ladies' stakes, two-year-old fillies, five furlongs—Bonita won, Pure Rye second, Vice third; time 1:04. Second race, one and a quarter miles—Woodman won, Boatman second, Leman third; time 2:10. The event of the day was the Kentucky Derby. The starters were Joe Cotton (favorite), Biersan, Favor, Irish Pat and Tenbooker, Thistle, Clay Pate, Keokuk, Playfair and Lord Coleridge. Pooling was unusually heavy before the race, and the interest and excitement intense. A good start was made out of the chute. Favor, who was not at all lame, took the lead and cut out the pace, closely followed by Keokuk and Biersan, Cotton bringing up the rear. The horses were all well bunched when they passed the grand stand, and the mile finish from that on was one of the prettiest races ever seen here. Favor ran out at the three-quarter pole, and Morris's other entry (Biersan) went into win, but could not. Joe Cotton ran easily till near the finish, and passed Biersan without much urging, and won the race by half a length, Biersan second, Tenbooker third, Favor fourth and the others bunched close in behind. The time was 2:37¼. Such pushing, rushing and shouting was never heard nor seen. It was a great race, the time being second only to that of Pat Malloy in the Derby of 1879, when it was made in 2:37. The closing race was mile heats for maidens three-year-olds and upwards—Monocrat won in two straight heats. Compensation ran second in the first, but Slocum won in the second heat, Compensation third; time 1:44, 1:44¼.

Washington, May 14.—Attendance large and track in good condition. Seven furlongs, three-year-olds and upwards—King Lion won, Eva K. second, Queen Esther third; time, 1:31¼. Mile, for mares, all ages—Farewell won, Pink Cottage second, Hatef third; time, 1:45¼. Mile and one-eighth, three-year-olds—Tecumseh won, Jennie Doe second, Wickham third; time 1:58¾. Mile, three-year-olds and upwards—Greenfield won, Winston second, Mintmore third; time, 1:45¾. Mile and a quarter, three-year-olds and upwards—Lyda Stanhope won, Hilarity second, Bald Hornet third; time, 2:11¾.

Memphis, May 14.—Class 2:45, trotting—Katie Isler won, Edgers second, Charles M third, Belle Isle fourth; time, 2:38¼, 2:39¼, 2:37½, 2:37¼, 2:38, 2:38¼. Second race, free for all—Phyllis won, Executor second, Texas Bill third, Sleepy Joe fourth; time, 2:27¼, 2:26¼, 2:26¼, 2:25.

Philadelphia, May 14.—Suffolk Park trotting races. Frank Ellis won the 2:40 class. Best time, 2:30¼. The 2:30 class race was taken by Mayflower. Best time, 2:30¼. The 2:24 class was won in straight heats by Mambrino Sparkle. Best time, 2:24¼. The 2:24 class for pacers was unfinished.

### The Murderer Maxwell.

New York, May 14.—A special from Philadelphia says: "In New York Walter Lennox Maxwell, who was arrested in New Zealand for the murder of Preller in St. Louis, made a statement that he was a brother of Lord Herries, and several times spoke of his aristocratic connections. In February last Bernard C. Maxwell, second brother of Lord Herries, was in Philadelphia on business and sailed for Europe in March, and has since been heard from in London. It is a queer coincidence that he has a brother Walter Lennox Maxwell, who came here from Australia and settled for awhile on a ranch in Colorado, though nothing has been heard of him for some time. Some points of resemblance and these coincidences have given rise to a belief that the companion of the murdered man, who is now under arrest, either knew Lord Herries's brother or assumed his name purposely to mislead."

### Roller-Skating Contest.

New York, May 14.—Roller-skating contest, 1 o'clock—Snowden, 883; W. Boyst, 865; Maddocks, 844; Shoes, 815; Francis, 673; Harriman, 600; Omelia, 485; Walton, 476.

### Picnickers Poisoned.

Atlanta, May 14.—About a hundred persons were to-day poisoned at a picnic at Tallulah Falls, through a chemical change made in the ice-cream freezer. All are recovering.

### A Distinguished Arrival at the Pico House.

A few days ago Baron and Baroness Haignet, of France, arrived in the city and took rooms at the Pico House. Baron Haignet is one of the wealthiest land owners of France, and was an intimate friend of the late Emperor Louis Napoleon. [illegible]

### TWO SUICIDES.

One Near Redwood City and the Other in Shasta Valley.

Redwood City, May 14.—This morning Andrew Larson, gardener at N. J. Britton's place, about one and one half miles from town, was found in the gardener's house lying back across the bed with the top of his head blown off, and a single-barreled shot-gun with an empty cartridge was lying across his feet, which were resting on the floor. It was at first thought to be an accident, but an unsigned note was found in his trunk written in English, directing all his effects to be sent to a cousin in Iowa.

Yreka, May 14.—Warren Winchester, an old resident of this county, of late years engaged in stock raising in Shasta Valley, suicided by shooting himself with a rifle on Wednesday afternoon. The coroner was notified to-day and went to his place and took possession of his effects. He was a native of North Carolina, aged 71 years. His sister resides in Louisville, Ky. The following note was found near him: "My mind is gone; my health is gone, and I am willing to die, so God bless my sister and all. No blame on any one for this act. I do it myself. God have mercy on my soul." His name was signed to the note.

### THE SOUDAN.

Negotiations for Turning it Over to the Porte.

London, May 14.—Negotiations [illegible] proceeding with Turkey for the [illegible] occupation of Suakim and the Soudan [illegible] the following basis. The Porte [illegible] to assist in suppressing the slave [illegible] and in developing external [illegible] relations. Besides the formal [illegible] made through Fehmi Pasha, if the [illegible] accepts, an English company will [illegible] the option of securing a concession to construct the railway to Berber and will receive other trading rights. Granville is also negotiating with the Italian government concerning an alternative scheme for the occupation of the Red Sea littoral in the event of failure to come to an agreement with the Porte. Reforma [illegible] Rossegna of Rome and other Liberal Italian papers are opposed to Italian occupancy of Egypt unless England promise armed support in the event of Italy being involved in a European quarrel. The Italian military journal Esercito approves of the occupation of Egypt by Italy.

### A BIG ENTERPRISE.

A Los Angeles Colonization Scheme On the Mojave.

San Bernardino Index, May 13.]

Deeds have been filed and placed on record for the purchase of 30,386 acres of land, lying in townships 2 and 3 north and range 5 west. It was purchased of Julius Fink, of San Francisco, by H. L. Macneil, of Los Angeles, for himself and his associates. The price paid was $75,000.

This land lies to the northward of the mountain range that shuts in this valley. It comprises both bottom land along the Mojave river and high mesa land. This latter is mostly a red loam, very similar to that of Riverside, Lugonia and other successful and flourishing settlements in this valley. The line of the California Southern extension, which will be the main line of the great Atlantic and Pacific [illegible]

[illegible]

### A Thin Case.

J. J. Flanigan, ex-waiter at the Santa Barbara ... had J. ... Scott ... Hotel ... charge of embezzlement ... [illegible]

### Official Arithmetic.

[illegible]

### Bentley—Wiester.

Mr. E. H. Bentley, of the firm of Wicks, Lucas and Bentley ... [illegible]

### Down a Trap.

John Scott, who is totally blind in one eye ... [illegible]

### STATE AND COAST.

The fruit shipments from Vacaville now average from twelve to fifteen tons daily.

[illegible]

# LOS ANGELES SUNDAY TIMES.

VOL. X.---NO. 89. LOS ANGELES, CALIFORNIA, SUNDAY MORNING, SEPTEMBER 12, 1886.—SIX-PAGE EDITION. FIVE CENTS.

## The Times.

Office—Temple, Main and New High

HE fell down.

THE bosses must go.

TRAMPS are not trumps

IT is the handwriting upon the wall.

COLONIZATION doesn't always do the work.

THE Burlingame Brigade needed a few more convicts.

LET's see—did the Express say anything about "six delegates?"

EX-GOV. MANSFIELD has been talked of for State Senator. We do not know his own intentions in the matter.

THE bosses begin to believe that it would be money in their pockets if the Burlingame Brigade had never been born.

THE Express's able test, designed to "disfranchise the mugwumps" died a bornin.' It was not found convenient to apply to anyone, yesterday.

THE bosses concentrated their whole power, their machinery, their patronage and their money, on the Third Ward. And they were downed.

THE returns from all the county primaries, received up to last night, are printed elsewhere in the TIMES. The full list of delegates-elect will be published in the next issue.

THE TIMES has no desire to be unduly hard on its 'steemed evening contrumpery in this, the hour of affliction, but still would like the s. e. c. to understand that there is "punishment after dea..."

THE splendid service done by citizens of the Third Ward yesterday, in rescuing it from the clutch of the bosses, will stand as a convincing proof of the invaluable advantage of organization, union and work. Shoulder to shoulder and back to back is the thing.

THE Republican State Central Committee has decided to open the campaign on the 18th inst. at the Wigwam, in San Francisco, when addresses will be delivered by John F. Swift and other able speakers. There will be opened a fire all along the line on the same date.

AMONG the powers and duties of the next County Convention of the Republican party will be the election of a new County Central Committee. It will be important that that body, when elected, appoint an efficient executive committee to manage the impending local campaign.

THE TIMES in the primary contest just closed, has been fighting for the people's right to manage their own political affairs in their own way, as against the impertinent interference of bosses. The TIMES is gratified and encouraged by the result of yesterday's contest at the primary polls. The people themselves won the fight. The people are always right when they can be aroused, and when once aroused they are simply terrible in their power.

GENERAL VANDEVER, who was expected to arrive in Los Angeles from San Buenaventura yesterday, has been detained, and will not be here until the middle of this week. He is called elsewhere first, but will be here in time for the big meeting of the 18th inst., which has been appointed by the State Executive Committee. The General is ready for the fray, and exceedingly anxious to begin the work of the campaign. He will endeavor to carry it on to the satisfaction of his frends and the Republican party, and the TIMES does not doubt that he will succeed fully. He believes that victory awaits us, and we share his confidence.

### BRIEFS.

A marriage license was issued yesterday to S. Sindlinger and Rosina Vogel.

J. W. Batcheller, of Fruitland, adds his name to the list of candidates for County Assessor.

Filed in the Recorder's office: 62 deeds, 21 mortgages, 15 satisfactions, 1 marriage license and 9 miscellaneous papers.

Miss C. B. Meeker, lecturer of the Grand Lodge of Good Templars, will speak at Trinity M. E. church, Fort street, at 7:30 o'clock this evening.

The entire $2500 of stock of the Grape Growers' and Wine Makers' Association, has been disposed of. There is talk of watering the same—that is, the stock, not the brandy.

### PERSONAL NEWS.

Rev. W. J. Chichester and his two sons arrived safely on Friday from their eastern trip.

Alexander Badlam, of San Francisco, arrived in Los Angeles yesterday by the express from the north.

Judge Alex. Campbell was summoned by telegraph yesterday to Tucson on law business, and left on the east-bound express at 2:30.

Dr. S. D. Bowker, of Kansas City, has been in our city the past two weeks, and says that no place in all our country has better prospects for the future than Los Angeles.

#### A Critical Trial.

J. W. Davis, Jr., the Colton banker, came into the city the past week to buy the best piano he could buy in Los Angeles. His wife, who is a fine singer and thorough musician, lately from Pittsburg, accompanied him. They spent a whole day and evening in critically comparing the leading makes of pianos sold here by the different houses, and finally selected the Decker Bro's. baby-grand as being the best piano to be found.

There is a growing demand for the baby-grand style of piano, as the country fills up with wealthy people, and the Decker Bro's. baby (or pony) grand is undoubtedly the nearest perfection that the art of pianoforte-making has yet reached.

Among the recent purchasers of this magnificent instrument, we have heard of Baron Rognist, Dr. Burbank, the Ellis Villa College and Rev. Williel Thomson, of Pasadena, and the trade in grands seems to be confined chiefly to the Decker Bro's.

#### The Best of All.

Adams street is considered the most desirable location for a home. It is now to be gravelled, and there is to be a stone sidewalk all the way from Figueroa and Washington to Adams and Severance. Remember this when you attend the auction sale of lots in the Severance tract, to be held Wednesday, September 15th. Only one-quarter cash required, balance in one, two and three years.

#### Beaumont.

Beautiful maps of this new town and colony lands in San Gorgonio Valley, Southern California's great sanitarium, may now be had by calling on the Southern California Investment Company, 114 ... street, Nadeau block.

#### ...parisons are odious.

... doubt that the auction ... Severance tract will ... the lots are all large ... to buy them. ... and the adver-

## PACIFIC COAST.

### The State Legislature Finally Adjourns.

A THEATRICAL SENSATION AT 'FRISCO.

The Democracy Utters its Preliminary Howl—A Steamer Ashore—A Young Robber's Severe Sentence.

*Associated Press Dispatches to The Times.*

SACRAMENTO, Sept. 11.—The Senate met at 10:30.

The report of the Committee on Attachés, recommending payment of mileage to Senators and the statutory officers of the Senate, came up as the special order.

A message was here received from the Assembly notifying the Senate of its concurrence in the Senate resolution to adjourn *sine die* at 12:30 p. m. to-day.

The report of the committee was then adopted by a *viva voce* vote.

The Cross resolution providing half pay for all attachés during five days of the recess, except the president, secretary, postmistress, sergeant-at-arms, clerk and mail carrier, was adopted.

President Daggett, at 12:30, declared the Senate adjourned *sine die*. In so doing, he stated that while the extra session had not accomplished the objects of those who caused its call, it had still been productive of a vast amount of benefit to the people of the State, by reason of the discussion that had been held.

#### Assembly.

SACRAMENTO, Sept. 11.—The Assembly met at 10 a. m.

The Committee on Expenses, to which had been referred the resolution to grant to officers, clerks and attachés pay during recess, submitted a majority and minority report. The majority report proposed to give all officers, clerks and attachés pay during recess, while the minority report allowed pay only to the sergeant-at-arms, postmistress, assistant clerk, mail carrier, porter, watchman and rear porter. The aggregate amounted to $646. The minority report was adopted.

The Senate resolution to adjourn *sine die* to-day, at 12:30, was taken up. The vote stood 27 in favor and 11 opposed—38 in all; three less than a quorum.

Mr. Walrath moved a call of the House.

In half an hour a quorum was obtained, and the concurrent resolution to adjourn *sine die*, at 12:30 p. m., was then adopted by a vote of 38 to 9.

At 12:30 p. m. the Speaker declared the Assembly adjourned *sine die*.

#### SAN FRANCISCO.

A Theatrical Divorce Suit—Heavy Sentence—Notes.

SAN FRANCISCO, Sept. 11.—A suit for divorce was filed to-day by Jennie Gedge against her husband, George Gedge, better known as George Osbourne, the well-known actor of this city. She alleges cruelty as the ground for divorce, saying that, on the 6th of this month he assaulted her with a pistol.

Steve Clay, aged 19, was brought up for sentence before Judge Murphy this morning, having been convicted of snatching a purse containing $500, on June 28th, from an old lady, named Mrs. Sharfer, after dazing her by striking her in the face. The crime was committed in broad daylight. The judge, after reviewing the case, said that the crime was, in his judgment, a most atrocious one, and concluded by sentencing the prisoner to fifteen years in Folsom.

Maurice Connell, one of the survivors of the Greely expedition, re-enlisted in the Signal Corps of the army to-day. He will be stationed in this city.

#### STATE POLITICS.

The Democratic Campaign Opened at San Francisco.

SAN FRANCISCO, Sept. 11.—Odd Fellow's Hall, the scene of the recent Democratic convention, was the place where the Democracy of California opened the campaign to-night by a ratification meeting. Over 2000 people crowded the hall, which is still decorated with the same banners and hangings that were noticed during the proceedings of the convention. Hon. George A. Johnson, of Sonoma, presided over the meeting, and started the ball of the campaign rolling with a warm speech of welcome. The Democratic standard-bearer, Washington Bartlett, was introduced, and was received with tumultuous cheering. His speech was not a lengthy one, but at the conclusion the applause was deafening. Patrick Reddy, of Mono, Stephen M. White, of Los Angeles, and J. P. Irish, of this city, followed in turn and made eloquent addresses. A number of stands were erected in front of the building, from which Hon. T. F. Barry, Charles Gildea, Senator J. D. Spencer, Hon. J. W. Sinom and several others addressed large audiences.

REPUBLICAN NOMINATIONS.

JACKSON, Cal., Sept. 11.—The Republican County Convention met to-day and nominated J. C. Brusie for Assemblyman. E. C. Voorhies was indorsed for Joint Senator of Amador and Calaveras counties.

#### MARINE MISHAPS.

The Steamer Sardonyx Ashore—A Schooner in Trouble.

VICTORIA, B. C., Sept. 11.—The steamship Sardonx is ashore on Gabrista reef, near Nanaimo. She went on at high tide, and, being light, it is thought she will be floated again without sustaining serious damage.

SAN FRANCISCO, Sept. 11.—A dispatch was received at the Merchants' Exchange this morning stating that the schooner Eliza Miller, loaded with grain from Hueneme for San Francisco, had gone ashore one and one-half miles north of the lighthouse at Hueneme, and was leaking slightly. It is believed that she will get off at the rise of the tide.

#### Morosini's Missing Daughter.

NEW YORK, Sept. 11.—Randolph Aronson, manager of the Casino, received the following telegram last night:

"DAYTON, N. J., Sept. 11.—Will report on Monday morning sure.

"MRS. SCHILLING."

Aronson thought the dispatch genuine, and said he had never doubted that Mrs. Schilling would appear at the appointed time. Her ten days leave of absence will be up on Monday.

The World insists that Victoria Morosini-Schilling is at her father's house, and that a reconciliation was brought about by George D. McClellan, the young man who is accused by Victoria's husband of having run away with her.

#### Turf Topics.

SAN FRANCISCO, Sept. 11.—The Flatbush stakes, seven-eighth of a mile, for two year-olds, were won by Haggin's King Fox. Time, 1:27¾—the best time on record for two-year-olds, and within a quarter of a second of breaking the record for all ages.

SAN FRANCISCO, Sept. 11.—A private dispatch received here states that Dwyer Bros.' celebrated filly Dewdrop, for which they paid $29,000 a short time ago, died at noon to-day. The cause is unknown.

#### The Quebec Elections.

OTTAWA, Ont., Sept. 11.—It is officially announced that the elections for the Province of Quebec will take place on October 12th. Nominations will be made five days earlier.

## FIENDISH WORK.

Attempt to Wreck Trains at Chicago—Dynamite Used.

CHICAGO, Sept 11—At ten minutes before 12 o'clock last night James Calvin, a night operator, sitting in the signal tower of the Lake Shore company at the intersection of the main and stockyards tracks, was blinded by an explosion. The tower is thirty feet high. Calvin had noticed nothing unusual, when he was suddenly startled by seeing a column of smoke arise at one side of the structure followed by a deafening explosion. A twenty-inch piece of gas-pipe was found, showing that it was dynamite which caused this explosion. The theory of the police is that the wreckers hoped to blow up the tower, and when a passenger train came along to turn the switch, and thus they would have plunged the train into the mass of freight cars lining the tracks. Another attempt to wreck a train took place last night about eight o'clock, when the Lake Shore road was receiving from the Illinois Central a train of twenty-eight cars. The switch was turned and fifteen cars derailed. Several arrests have been made, but nothing definite has been learned from the men arrested.

#### A TRUNK TRAGEDY.

A Medical Student Implicated in a Ghastly Affair.

TOLEDO, O., Sept. 11.—This forenoon a trunk arrived by the Wheeling and Lake Erie road from Bellevue, which exhaled so horrible an odor as to drive the baggageman from his post. It was placed on the platform and the police authorities notified. Soon after their arrival, E. Wilson, who had come from Bellevue on the Lake Shore railroad, arrived with a dray and presented a check for the trunk. He was immediately arrested and the trunk opened, when it was found to contain the body of a woman packed in hay. Wilson and the trunk were then taken to the police station where the Coroner examined the body. It was that of a woman about twenty, much emaciated and partly dressed in underclothing of the finest quality. Wilson is a school teacher of Ithaca, O., and last winter was a student of the Toledo Medical College. He is held on a charge of grave-robbery. He refuses to talk.

#### The Washouts.

SAN FRANCISCO, Sept. 11.—In reference to the repairs of washouts near Albuquerque, the Atlantic and Pacific have received the following telegram from their General Manager, D. B. Robinson:

"We have had one or two small washouts on the First Division, but nothing serious. The track has been laid again, and everything is all right. The Santa Fé has had one or two bad ones, but they have also repaired all damages. Traffic was resumed yesterday."

#### The Los Angeles Towel Co.

A new enterprise which is being developed in our city, by a couple of gentlemen who have just arrived from the East, promises to be a great convenience to the live business men of our city. In the course of a few days they will call upon the professional and business men, soliciting their subscription. We bespeak for them a liberal patronage.

#### Eastern Visitors

Wishing to post themselves on the value of select residential property should attend the auction sale of lots in Severance's orange grove, on Adams street, Wednesday, September 15th. This is well known as the best location in Los Angeles, and such an opportunity will not occur again.

#### For Constable.

J. B. Sanchez, President of the Spanish Republican Club, announces himself as a candidate for Constable of Los Angeles Township, subject to the action of the Republican convention.

#### Adams Street Lots.

Remember to attend the Severance auction of lots, on Adams street, Wednesday, September 15th. Only 10 per cent. down, 15 per cent. in thirty days, balance in one, two and three years. Property will double in value before twelve months are over.

#### Now Be Careful

Or you will want Electric Railway Homestead Association lots at $290 when you can't get them.

#### The Effect

Of the Pico Electric Railway on value of property near it, is truly wonderful. Yesterday evening a gentleman was offered a piece of property for $750, and this morning it was sold for $1500. The railway will have the same effect in the Electric Railway Homestead lots.

#### Go and See

The Severance orange trees on Adams street. They are the finest in the land. Lots in this tract will be sold at auction Wednesday, September 15th. Read the advertisement.

#### Only a Little More

Than ½ of the Electric Railway Homestead Association lots remain to be sold. Buy quick or you wont get the $290.

#### Nearly Every Mail

Brings orders for lots from distant parties. The Electric Railway Homestead Association lots wont last but a few days at $290.

#### No Other Tract

Compares with that of the Electric Railway Homestead Association. Secure your lots now. Price only $290.

#### Counters and Fixtures For Sale.

Dillon & Kenealy having retired from the dry good business in Los Angeles, will sell their counters and fixtures, in their store corner Main and Requena, on Wednesday and Thursday the 15th, and 16th inst. Dillon & Kenealy.

#### The Trees and Flowers

On the Electric Railway Homestead Association tract are beautiful; water splendid, and the "title is perfect."

#### No Trouble at All

To sell lots in the Electric Railway Homestead Association tract. All we ask is to see the property.

#### At a Premium.

The Electric Railway Homestead Association lots will undoubtedly sell at a premium equal to all the money invested before the distribution. Speculators, think of it!

#### The Best Investment.

You can possibly make is to buy in the Alcantara Grove Tract at the great auction sale, Saturday, September 19th.

#### Monte Vista.

Most beautifully situated, charming scenery, delightful climate, unsurpassed soil, abundance of pure mountain water, no fogs, no frost, 1500 feet above sea level. It is nature's sanitarium. Don't fail to see this magnificent colony. Maps and full particulars at 30 South Spring street.

#### Free Carriage all this Week

To the Alcantara Grove Tract, on Main street, Seville street and Grand avenue, from 30 South Spring street.

#### Long Beach Township.

The Township of Los Nietos was yesterday divided on the north line of township range 4 south, and the Township of Long Beach created in the south division.

#### Found Guilty.

Robert Collins, the man arrested at the instance of the Humane Society for atrocious abuse of his overloaded horse, came up before Justice Austin yesterday forenoon. Judge Alex. Campbell represented the Society. Collins was convicted, and will be sentenced to-morrow.

#### Methodist Conference.

The annual conference of the Methodist Episcopal church will meet in San Diego next week, and a number of ministers are already in Los Angeles en route to the scene of their labors.

## THE CUP CONTEST.

### A Second Big Victory for the Mayflower.

THE GALATEA AGAIN BADLY BEATEN.

The Race Easily Won—The Queen's Cup to Stay in This Country for Another Year.

*Associated Press Dispatches to The Times.*

NEW YORK, Sept. 11.—To-day's race has decided upon which side of the Atlantic the America's cup shall stay, at least for another year. It resulted in a glorious victory for the sloop Mayflower When she finished this evening, at 6:15:40, the Galatea was nearly two miles astern. The course was twenty miles to leeward and return from Scotland lightship. The race was sailed in a breeze that blew fresh from the northwest for three hours, then canting two points to the westward, it grew light, the last hours of the contest being little better than a drift. The Mayflower only had eight minutes and twenty seconds to spare when she crossed the finish line, as the time limit of the race was seven hours. The Galatea was defeated on every point of sailing. In the run out to the outer mark with spinnakers set, the Galatea was beaten 13:45, and in the windward work over half an hour. There is great rejoicing among yachtmen here to-night, while the Bostonians are fairly wild with delight.

LIEUT. HENN UNDER THE WEATHER.

Off Whistle buoy at 10:15 A. M., the Galatea was cast off. Her crew soon made sail, while the Mayflower's crew did the same, both setting their club topsails. When the judges' boat ran along side the Galatea, Lloyd Phœnix, representing the New York Yacht Club, told the Regatta Committee that Lieut. Henn was very sick in the cabin, and that he wished the course to be made fifteen miles instead of twenty, so as to be sure to finish within a reasonable time. In case it should fall calm he wished the Luckenbach to tow the cutter back, if the race was not completed, so that he could see a doctor early. Secretary Robinson said that he would consult with Gen. Paine as to the length of the course. That gentleman, when seen, said that he would leave the matter entirely in the hands of the committee. They decided that the course should be southeast twenty miles, and streaming back to the Galatea that course was given to them. Capt. Bradford was sailing the cutter. Beaver Webb looked after the sails, while Mrs. Henn peeped out of the companion-way with an anxious look in her eyes, for her husband's condition alarmed her considerably.

A fleet of steam and sailing craft, nearly as large as that of Thursday, had assembled near the starting point, Scotland lightship. Mammoth flags bedecked the steamers Grand Republic and Columbia, and the iron steamers Siren, Orpheus and Taurus were black with their human freight of yachting enthusiasts. The breeze was freshening every moment, and as it was the first time the yachts had come together where the first half of the contest was to be sailed to leeward, there was much discussion as to the probable result.

A MAGNIFICENT START.

When the starting signal was given at 11:20 a. m. the Mayflower was in an excellent position, square to the northwest of the imaginary line drawn between Scotland light-ship and the Luckenbach, lying a cable's length to the northward of it. Her spinnaker boom was down to port and thirty seconds after the signal her great sails blossomed out amid wild cheers from the thousands on the Grand Republic. With her main boom broad off to starboard her pyramid of snowy sails gleaming in the sunlight, and a shower of foam at her sides the Boston beauty dashed across the line well in the lead.

The cutter was a quarter of a mile to the westward. When the whistle blew she came along with the wind abeam till she crossed the bow of the lightship close aboard. Then quartering away her spinnaker was sheeted out exactly on tide and the third day's battle was begun.

The official time of the start was: Mayflower, 11:22:40 a. m.; Galatea, 11:24:10 a. m.

THE TWENTY-MILE RUN.

With a twenty-mile run before them there was an excellent opportunity to test their speed in a steady breeze and with very little sea to impede their progress. That a "stern chase" is a long one was never better illustrated than in that twenty-mile run. For about twenty minutes the Galatea held her own with the sloop, but after that she was practically out of the race, for the Mayflower was leading her nearly a mile when half the distance to the outer mark was covered. The steamboat captains regarded past warnings, and kept well away from the contestants.

AT THE OUTER MARK.

At 12:50 p. m. the outer mark hove in sight, and in half an hour the fleet of steamers, numbering thirty-one in all, had gathered around it to await the coming of the yachts. The wind had fallen and had canted a point to westward.

The iron sloop-yacht Priscilla accompanying the yachts over the course. She had all her light sails set, and led the Mayflower at noon by a quarter of a mile and seemed to be out sailing the racers.

Down came the trio like white-winged birds before the wind. The Mayflower's balloon jib-topsail came in at 1:41:30 p. m., and four minutes later in came her spinnaker, and at 1:53 she gybed to port and came for the mark close hauled on the starboard tack. Luffing grandly round it a few moments later amid the serenade of the steam whistles, the pride of Boston began her windward work with a lead of nearly a mile. The Galatea gybed at 1:52:30, having "doused" her spinnaker three minutes before.

The time of rounding the outer mark was: Mayflower, 1:55:05 p. m.; Galatea, 2:10:20.

The Priscilla luffed the mark only three minutes after the Mayflower.

THE CHASE TO WINDWARD.

The Galatea made a very pretty picture as she lay down to her scuppers and began her chase to windward after the sloop. Both had about all the wind they wanted to carry club topsails in. Capt. Stone put the Mayflower about at 1:55 and stood to the northward. Beaver Webb was sailing the Galatea. He refused to tack. At 2:20 Capt. Stone brought the Boston sloop around again. She was then over a mile on the cutter's beam. Two minutes before going about, the Mayflower took in her club topsail. She carried her working topsail for an hour, when the wind having lightened considerably she set the club topsail again. The Galatea having set hers shortly before. Both yachts went about at 4:20 and stood to the northward. They were off Deal Beach at this time, and the wind was growing lighter every moment. The Mayflower was lucky enough to hold the light air under the land, while the Galatea lay almost becalmed for twenty minutes. The cutter tacked at 4:37 and made a short cut in shore going about again at 4:45. From here the sail up the New Jersey beach was little better than a drift.

THE MAYFLOWER WINS.

As the Mayflower slowly approached the finish, the excitement became intense among the passengers on board the steamers. There was no longer any fear that the Mayflower would be defeated, but the time, seven hours, had almost expired, and there was great fear that after being so near the goal, the Boston sloop might not be able to finish. Just as all hope was dying out, the breeze freshened, and with only 8 minutes and 20 seconds to spare, the Mayflower shot across the finish line close hauled on the port tack, just as the sun sank to rest in a crimson halo behind Sandy Hook. The cheering and whistling and the waving of thousands of handkerchiefs lasted fully ten minutes, the crew of the victorious sloop waving and cheering themselves till the yacht was long past the finish. The Galatea finished 31 minutes 18 seconds after the Mayflower. As she came to an anchor the Mayflower's crew gave her three rousing cheers, which the Englishmen answered.

The following shows the records of the race: Mayflower—start, 11:12:40 a. m.; finish, 6:11:40 p. m.; elapsed time, 6 hours 49 minutes; corrected time, 6 hours 49 minutes. Galatea—start, 11:24:10 a. m.; finish, 6:42:58; elapsed time, 7 hours, 18 minutes, 4 seconds; corrected time, 7 hours, 18 minutes, 9 seconds.

## LOS ANGELES LAND BUREAU.

An Important Move of the Largest Real Estate House on the Pacific Coast.

During the past week important improvements have been going on in the Wilson Block, No. 20 West First street, in this city. The interior of the store is fitted with the most modern conveniences for a land business, comprising private offices, counters, safes, and complete appointments. In the city of San Francisco the firm of Easton & Eldridge is a household word. The same people transact their business in the interior of the State under the corporate name of the Pacific Coast Land Bureau, with their principal place of business in San Francisco, with sub-agencies in the several counties of California. An agency of the Land Bureau had been maintained in this city for several years; but now the business in their line has assumed such proportions that they have concluded to open a separate house in this city.

The Los Angeles Land Bureau has been incorporated with a paid-up capital of $100,000, and the first Board of Directors is composed of Geo. W. Frink, President; Wendell Easton, Vice-President; Jas. B. Lankershim, Treasurer; F. B. Wilde, Secretary; W. B. Matthews, Salesman.

The house will do a general real estate business, buying and selling of property at auction or private sale, collect rents, hold power of attorney for absentees. The subdivision of city and suburban properties will be a specialty. The entire fittings for the office, including safes and office furniture, were purchased in this city, it being the policy of the company to identify their business with our community. The city of Los Angeles is to be congratulated and should feel proud of this new departure in real estate circles, which will have an immediate and permanent effect in legitimatizing the growing business of buying and selling lands.

#### A Card from Justice Ranney.

*To the Editor of the Times*—SIR: On general principles the public has such a thorough distrust of the truthfulness of any charge made by Horace Bell in his Porcupine, against any public official, that it is simply ridiculous to go into print to give him or his charges any denial. I have for such reason hitherto ignored all the false accusations he has made against me as the Justice of the Peace of this township.

"In the Porcupine of this date, however, is a specific charge intended to place me before the Republican delegates, to be elected to-day, as a corrupt official. The bills I have presented to the county for each of the six months, ending June 30th last, are stated, and it is further charged that the bill for June has been refused by the Board of Supervisors, and that I will sue the county for the same. This is wilfully false. The Board has never refused either to audit that bill or any other bill that I have presented to the county, and for the simple reason that every bill that I have presented has been authorized by law. Bell says: "Are the bills honest, legal and just?" and he answers his question by saying, "No, they are not." Now this allegation is simply and willfully false. Every bill was expressly authorized by law. The law prescribes and fixes the fees of justices of the peace. I am, therefore, authorized to make out my bills in conformity with the fee bill of the statute. I have done this, and have in no instance exceeded it. The Board of Supervisors called Deputy District Attorney Knox before it, to counsel upon every bill for May last. He carefully inspected the bill and the docket of my court, and in a written report and also a verbal statement to the Board, he informed the Board my bill was in no respect violative of law. The only charge that has been made against my bills is, that I made out several complaints where several were arrested for the same offense, instead of giving the parties all in one complaint. There is no provision of law that compels or requires me to do this, hence I violated no law in drawing separate complaints. The Porcupine says I violated law. The Porcupine pretends to be a lawyer. I therefore challenge it to produce any law of the State, that directs me to do otherwise than I have done. The Porcupine cannot show that I have violated any fee bill or statute of this State, or that I have in any particular robbed the county. In a late issue that paper stated I had taken illegally $50,000 during my term of office, and that both the District Attorney and Deputy District Attorney Knox had been oftentimes asked to prosecute me for taking fees illegally. I deny the charge in toto. The Porcupine cannot point to a single case wherein I have charged this county one dollar unlawfully. I challenge it to name the case and point out the law violated. Bell knows his statement is wholly and absolutely false. I have asked the District Attorney and Deputy District Attorney Knox if they knew of any case wherein I have violated the law, and they both deny that they have any such knowledge; further Deputy District Attorney Knox informs me that neither the editor of the Porcupine or anyone else has ever pointed out to him any violation by me of the law in such case, or has asked him to prosecute me therefor. The utter falsity of the charges against me as made by Bell in his paper, and reiterated for the last year, are known to every lawyer in the city who has chosen to ascertain the facts, and it is equally well known to himself. Bell has undertaken to dictate to the Republicans of this county that they shall not again recommend me or re-elect me, and to accomplish his purpose he has simply followed his usual course of wilfull misrepresentation, and deliberate falsification. Respectfully,

R. RANNEY,

Justice of the Peace, Los Angeles Township.
September 11, 1886.

#### Further Denial.

The Rev. P. W. Dorsey has returned from San Bernardino. He called at the TIMES editorial room yesterday and again protested his innocence in the Brown-Brown marital imbroglio. When all the facts in the case develope themselves, or are developed, the TIMES will publish them.

#### Subscriptions

To the Electric Railway Homestead Association tract are coming from every direction. You must buy quick if you want any at $290.

#### Still They Go.

No tract ever put on the Los Angeles market met with such rapid sales as the Electric Railway Homestead Association Tract.

#### Triumphantly Acquitted.

Conductor J. U. Henry, of the C. S. R. R., was tried at Colton yesterday, on the charge of being implicated in the recent ticket swindle. He was triumphantly acquitted, and his excellent reputation fully vindicated.

#### Nothing Like Them Ever Sold

In this city. Those beautiful Alcantara Grove lots, 50x150, covered with beautiful trees.

#### Save Your Dollars

And make the best investment you ever made in your life at the Alcantara Grove sale on Saturday, September 19th.

#### Some Property Titles

Are not good. Those of the Electric Railway Homestead Association are good, and are open to investigation, at our expense, if found imperfect.

#### The Electric Railway Homestead Association

Don't put any property on the market till they are sure of the "title." Think of this before investing elsewhere.

## BLAINE.

### His Closing Speech in the Maine Campaign.

DEMOCRATIC DUPLICITY DENOUNCED.

The Weakness of the Prohibition Party Illustrated—The Third Party the Democrats' Only Hope.

*Associated Press Dispatches to The Times.*

GARDINER, Me., Sept. 11.—The last rally of the Republican campaign in the State was held in the spacious coliseum in this city to-night. In the course of his remarks Blaine said: "It is worth while in this last hour for discussion, standing as we are on the eve of election, to recall the peculiarities of this campaign, for certainly the general arguments submitted to the people have been, on the side of the opposition, filled with contradictions, not to say absurdities. The Democrats have apparently been unable to define their position on any question. In the leading national issue of protection, they have been timid and irresolute to the last degree, occasionally putting forward rank free trade arguments through some one of their speakers and recalling or qualifying them in one of their leading organs on the succeeding day. Their organ argues in Maine for Morrison's tariff bill as a whole, and yet is afraid to touch any one of the many features of that bill, in which the commercial agricultural and manufacturing interests of Maine are injured or destroyed. [Applause.] The most learned doctor of Salamanca would be unable to find any thread of consistency, any line of logic, any dash of common sense in the mode in which the Democratic party has conducted its campaign on that great issue. They seem, indeed, to have kept up a mere show of a fight on behalf of their own party, while depending in reality for any possible chance of victory upon the diversion and distraction caused by a third party, and the third party in turn has exhibited as striking peculiarities as the Democrats themselves in their mode of conducting their campaign. General Neal Dow, who has for the last quarter of a century stood for the two continents as the great witness of the value and effectiveness of prohibition, now declares that for thirty years it has not done a bit of good in the suppression of the liquor traffic in Maine. [Laughter.] Gen. Dow has thus apparently been willing to set at naught his own testimony throughout this longer period in order to achieve a victory against the Republicans. If there be consistency in political action, if there be honor and fair dealing among men, the Republican party and its candidates exhibit both in their campaign, which, so far as I have had a word to say, is now closed. I bid you a cordial good-night." [Tremendous applause.]

#### The Soledad Extension.

MISSION SAN MIGUEL, Sept. 11.—Ground is being broken on the west side of the river, four miles from San Miguel, on the Soledad extension of the Southern Pacific railroad.

#### French Conversational Soiree

Prof. J. P. Garneau gave a French conversational *soirée* last night at the Conservatory of Music, corner of South Main and Fifth streets. Recitations in French were given by the Misses Brousseau and Valentine and Prof. Garneau. Piano selections were rendered by Misses Tingley and Valentine and vocal music by Misses Calhoun, Bennett, and Anna Wiseman. The evening concluded with organ selections by Mrs. Valentine. The affair was a success and well attended and was very creditable to Prof. Garneau.

#### Stationery and Confectionery.

The establishment of Messrs. Off & Greer, No 45 N. Main street, is growing very popular with our citizens. They have everything in the fancy and staple stationery line. Eastern papers, periodicals and magazines. Subscriptions are taken for leading periodicals at publishers' rates. The California department is complete in every respect.

The finest confectionery can be found here. Meister's celebrated ice-cream always on hand—the neatest ice-cream parlors for ladies in the city. French candies of every variety. Fresh caramels of the choicest selection. They are doing a very large business, in consequence of their excellent quality.

#### The "White Goods" Day,

But a few weeks more and our Grand Annual Clearance Sale will be at an end. We have labored assiduously, not only to reduce our stock, but also to show purchasers our sincerity in every proposition offered. Importations of fall and winter goods are daily arriving. Dress goods in latest styles, foreign notions in unique designs, and, to give proper attention to fall stock, we are compelled to make short work of our entire line of ladies' muslin wear, which we propose to place on our counters next Wednesday, September 15. The appended list will contain the finest assortment of chemises, dressing sacques, night dresses, drawers, aprons, skirts and children's long and short dresses that can be found on the Pacific coast.

J. M. Hale & Co.'s Grand Clearance Sale, Wednesday, September 15.

The unparalleled presentation for the day will be 800 ladies' chemises, on extra finished muslin, 25c each.

Each chemise has three rows of Alicienne puffing and finished on bands and top with good quality of Irish lace. Each garment is worth fully 60c and is displayed for public inspection in south show window. In assorted sizes and extra length. In connection with this line will be offered 500 pairs ladies' drawers, superfine muslin, 25c each.

This garment has three rows of Alicienne puffing, with Irish lace trimming, and, like the chemise, is worth 60c. No exaggeration at all is given with this description, and everything guaranteed exactly as represented. This line of drawers is also displayed in south show window, and we invite general inquiry concerning the values offered.

J. M. Hale & Co.'s Grand Clearance Sale, Wednesday, September 15.

175 ladies' night dresses at 50c each. This garment is worth its regular price, $1, and is only sold at 50c because we do not care to carry over such an immense quantity of one kind. Trimmed with cambric embroidery and beautifully tucked, it presents an appearance not excelled by any $1 garment. Displayed in north show window.

89 ladies' chemises at 50c each. Heavy muslin bands, tucked and stitched, tucked yoke, edged with ruffles; worth 85c. Five dozen pairs ladies' drawers at 50c each. Wide hem and two groups of fine tucks, eight tucks in a group; worth 80c.

39 pairs ladies' drawers at 75c each. Embroidery ruffle, on fine muslin, with two groups of fine tucks; worth $1.25. 24 ladies' night dresses at 75c each, with fine embroidery and tucking, and at one-half price; worth $1.50.

92 ladies' "Mother Hubbard" chemises at $1 each. 40 ladies' chemises, Pompadour style, at $1 each; embroidery edged; worth $1.75. 20 pairs ladies' drawers at $1 per pair; worth $1.75. 73 dressing sacques at $1; worth $1.75. 90 night dresses at $1; worth $1.75.

100 ladies' white skirts at 50c each. Cambric flounce and group tucks, two groups in each flounce; worth 75c. 75 ladies' white and ecru aprons at 50c each; "Mother Hubbard" style, with lace inserting; worth 75c. 90 children's dresses at 50c each; cambric tucking and beautifully flounced; worth 75c.

12 dozen ladies' chemises at 75c each. Yoke of fine solid tucks with center edged with inserting; neck and sleeves with embroidery; in "Mother Hubbard" style also. 75 children's dresses at 75c each; fine cambric muslin; embroidery on sleeves and neck; pleated back and yoke front; worth $1.25.

6 dozen fancy aprons at 75c each. 5 dozen infants' slips at 75c each. The chemises, drawers, night dresses, children's dresses and infants' slips, together with the aprons, are about one-half value.

We will also offer our entire line of chemises, dressing sacques, drawers, night dresses, in higher grades, at one-half value. Everything must go regardless of price. The first and last opportunity of this kind for this season.

J. M. Hale & Co.'s Grand Annual Clearance Sale, Wednesday, September 15

7 and 9 N. Spring street, opposite Postoffice

## Church Notices.

CHURCH OF THE UNITY, OPERA House.—At 11 a. m., subject of Dr Fay's sermon: "Religious Sense Conditional,"—a word with the materialist and agnostic.

FIRST CONGREGATIONAL CHURCH, corner Hill and Third streets.—A. J. Wells, pastor. Preaching by the pastor at 11 a. m. and 7:30 p. m. Morning subject, "Grecian Culture and the Signs of the Times."

REORGANIZED CHURCH OF JESUS Christ of Latter Day Saints, Knights of Pythias Hall, 24 S. Spring street, upstairs Preaching every Sunday at 11 a. m. Subject, September 12th, 19th, 26th: "The Stick of Ephraim; or, Book of Mormon." All are invited to attend.

FIRST PRESBYTERIAN CHURCH, Fort and Second sts.—Rev. W. J. Chichester, pastor, will preach this morning at 11 o'clock. All cordially invited. No evening service.

MASONIC HALL, BRYSON BLOCK, 29 S. Spring street. Religious services conducted by Dr. Charles McLean every Sunday, at 3 p. m.

FORT HILL MISSION—ON PHILADELphia st., just west of cemetery. Opening services at 11 a. m., to-day.

## ANNOUNCEMENTS FOR OFFICE.

#### For County Auditor.

A. A. MONTANO is a candidate for COUNTY AUDITOR, subject to the action of the Republican Convention.

#### For County Treasurer.

W. N. MUNROE announces himself as a candidate for COUNTY TREASURER, subject to the action of the Republican Convention.

E. N. McDONALD, of Wilmington, is a candidate before the Republican Convention for the office of COUNTY TREASURER.

J. T. HADDOX of El Monte, announces himself as a candidate for COUNTY TREASURER, subject to the decision of the Republican Convention.

L. M. LA FETRA, of Azusa, will be a candidate for the office of COUNTY TREASURER subject to the action of the Republican County Convention.

#### For Supervisor.

THOMAS BANBURY, of Pasadena, is a candidate for SUPERVISOR, from the First district, subject to the action of the Republican Convention.

JAMES FOORD, of San Gabriel, is a candidate for SUPERVISOR, subject to the action of the Republican Convention.

#### For County Surveyor.

JOHN GOLDSWORTHY announces himself as a candidate for COUNTY SURVEYOR, subject to the decision of the Republican Convention.

#### For County Assessor.

J. W. BATCHELLER, of Fruitland is a candidate for COUNTY ASSESSOR, subject to the decision of the Republican Convention.

J. W. MYERS, of Newhall, announces himself as a candidate for COUNTY ASSESSOR, subject to the action of the Republican Convention.

C. C. MASON, of Fulton Wells, announces himself as a candidate for COUNTY ASSESSOR, subject to the decision of the Republican Convention.

#### County Superintendent of Schools.

J. C. OLIVER is a candidate for COUNTY SUPERINTENDENT OF SCHOOLS, subject to the decision of the Republican Convention.

## Special Notices.

Dissolution—This 10th day of September, 1886, the co-partnership in real estate and commission business heretofore existing between J. J. Southworth and H. B. Pinney is dissolved by mutual consent, said H. B. Pinney retiring, J. J. Southworth continuing the business, who will collect and pay all bills of the firm. J. J. SOUTHWORTH, H. B. PINNEY.

Moorhouse & Reichert, 146 S. Spring st., carpenter jobbing; stepladders a specialty; plaster paris ornaments for sale. Telephone 341.

G. A. R.—Frank Bartlett Post No. 6 meets every TUESDAY EVENING in Good Templar's Hall, N. Main st. A cordial invitation extended to all visiting Comrades. HORACE BELL, P. B., SAM KUTZ, Adjutant.

## TERMS OF THE TIMES.

PUBLISHED EVERY DAY, MONDAYS INCLUDED.

SERVED BY CARRIERS:

| | |
|---|---|
| DAILY and SUNDAY, per week | $ .20 |
| DAILY and SUNDAY, per month | .85 |

BY MAIL, POST PAID:

| | |
|---|---|
| DAILY and SUNDAY, per month | .85 |
| DAILY and SUNDAY, per quarter | 2.25 |
| DAILY and SUNDAY, per year | 9.00 |
| SUNDAY, per year | 2.00 |
| WEEKLY MIRROR, per year | 2.00 |

THE TIMES *is the only morning Republican newspaper printed in Los Angeles that owns the exclusive right to publish here the telegraphic "night report" of the Associated Press, the greatest news-gathering organization in the world. Our franchise has recently been renewed for a long term of years.*

SUBSCRIBERS, when writing to have the address of their paper changed, should also state the former address.

CORRESPONDENCE solicited from all quarters. Timely local topics and news given the preference. Use one side of the sheet only, write plainly, and send real name for the private information of the Editor.

TELEPHONES—Business Office........No. 29
Editorial (3 bells)......No. 29

**Address THE TIMES-MIRROR COMPANY,**
TIMES BUILDING,
N.E. cor. First and Fort sts., Los Angeles, Cal.

ENTERED AT POSTOFFICE AS 2D-CLASS MATTER.

# The Times.

**BY THE TIMES-MIRROR COMPANY.**

H. G. OTIS,
President and General Manager.
ALBERT McFARLAND,
Vice-Prest., Treas. and Business Manager.
WM. A. SPALDING, Secretary.


### *REMOVED.*

*The office of the Times-Mirror Company is removed to the new Times Building, northeast corner of First and Fort streets (first floor)—entrance, for the present on the Fort-street side. Open day and night.*

### POINTS OF THE MORNING'S NEWS.

An American citizen locked up in a Mexican jail for refusing to vote at the late election....Montrose wins the Kentucky Derby....Rumors of the death of Parnell....California wines cornered by San Francisco dealers....Great damage to the grape crop by frosts....The San Bernardino and Bear Valley Railroad locating its line....The Burlington road's project for reaching San Francisco....Fire at Suisun....Mutiny on the ship Occidental....Strike of Northern Pacific laborers...The schooner Wing and Wing ashore at Crescent City....Germany and Russia quarreling over grain duties....Races at Baltimore....B'nai B'rith Convention at Memphis....Kentucky State Republican Convention....Reunion of the Society of the Army of the Cumberland at Washington....Fire at Flagstaff....Smuggled opium seized at San Francisco....British vessels seized in Alaskan waters to be sold. ....Powderly denies the reported dissensions among the Knights of Labor....Higher wages for Pacific coast sailors...Wool-growers in convention at St. Louis....Gold found in Monterey county....Editor O'Brien speaks at Montreal......Fatalities at El Paso......Street railway franchise granted in San Luis Obispo.....An old man arrested at Monterey for the murder of Hansen....Justice Wood, of the Supreme Court, dangerously ill......The Maxwell land case......Treasurer Jordan's successor appointed....Loss of a steamer in the Straits of Malacca. ......Conflicting reports regarding the fate of the Mexican officers sentenced to death for the Nogales outrage.

THE Sacramento Record-Union prints a picture of the Los Angeles Normal School as the proposed Normal building to be built in Chico. It will do.

THE important industry of concentrating the wine-must of Southern California has been founded by Hon. J. de Barth Shorb, and will be in operation at San Gabriel this season.

IN another column will be found some sewer suggestions by a prominent Omaha engineer. He thinks Col. Waring too much interested in royalties on the patents he represents to be able to give purely disinterested advice. Mr. Rosewater's remarks are worth consideration.

THE monarchical governments of Europe are declining to take part in the Paris Exposition of 1889, because that exposition is designed to celebrate the hundredth anniversary of the period when France shook off monarchial rule and began a career which made her a Republic.

THE proposed universal language called Volapük will come in for discussion by Richmond Walker in the forthcoming (June) number of The American Magazine. It is said that the grammar of this speech can be learned in an hour, and it has already been adopted by 10,000 people. Volapük may be a good language, but we opine that it will not become popular until it adopts a title that will stay on people's stomachs.

IN his address at the recent organization of the Anti-Poverty Society, in New York, Dr. McGlynn said: "Religion will never be right until we shall have a democratic pope walking down Broadway with a stove-pipe hat on his head and carrying an umbrella under his arm. In my opinion that man will be the greatest of popes. Instead of having men carry him on their shoulders, he will have the laugh on them, for he will carry them in his heart."

IN the forthcoming entertainments of the National Opera Company the ladies of Los Angeles will have an opportunity to display their graciousness and good sense by doffing their high hats, as they did on the occasion of the Patti Concert. These entertainments are also to be given in a large hall with flat floor, and the occasion for continuing the reform so auspiciously begun remains the same. Ladies, shall we chalk down another white mark for you?

### IMPORTANT BUSINESS ANNOUNCEMENT.

**The Times-Mirror Printing and Binding House.**

Last evening a contract was signed consolidating the important and successful job-printing establishment of Kingsley & Barnes, No. 20 North Spring street, with the Times-Mirror printing and binding house, which have within the past twelve months been materially enlarged and improved.

The consolidation is to take effect on the 1st day of June next, and, as soon as practicable, the first-named printing-office will be removed to the new Times Building, where the combined concerns will occupy parts of three floors, and will constitute, by all odds, the largest, best-equipped, most complete printing and binding establishment on the southern coast. It will be under the immediate management of Messrs. John A. Kingsley and Thomas F. Barnes, gentlemen long and well known in the printing art in this city. This fact is a guarantee of the successful conduct of the united concerns and an earnest of increased efficiency. The reputation of both establishments for fine work will be maintained and strengthened under the consolidation.

The offices now brought together have, in the past twelve months, done a business combined of more than $40,000, and, being strengthened by this union, will, in the coming year, without doubt, do a still larger business.

The corporate name to be taken by the consolidated concern is THE TIMES-MIRROR PRINTING AND BINDING HOUSE. It will be equipped with ten steam presses, large and small, together with other necessary machinery, and a great quantity and variety of new and fashionable type, etc., thus fitting it for the rapid execution of all classes of book, mercantile, legal and general printing and binding in a superior manner.

Still further improvements are in contemplation, especially in the book-bindery; and our friends, the public, may rest assured that all orders committed to the Times-Mirror Printing and Binding House for execution will be taken care of with more promptness and efficiency than ever before, and that printing will be done at prices that will meet eastern and San Francisco tariffs for first-class work.

This more complete separation of their book and job-printing and book-binding business from their newspaper duties will enable the proprietors of THE DAILY TIMES and WEEKLY MIRROR to give closer attention to these favorite journals, and thus increase their efficiency.

We anticipate the best results from the new arrangement.

### A Glance at Los Angeles.

Society, like individuals, has its infancy and its manhood—eras of development and change that mark its progressive history. For a decade or two the city of Los Angeles has been in a transition state. Fifteen years ago it was not particularly noted for its æsthetic culture. It was largely a business community, giving its attention to trade, busy with agricultural and horticultural experiments, without much aggressiveness of spirit, or very large expectations for its future. There was, of course, somewhat of Yankee enterprise here, and a good deal of faith in future possibilities. Yet there was no very extensive outreaching for trade, and no thought of any business rivalry with San Francisco. The home markets did not offer very much that was attractive. Supplies came largely from abroad. Land was cheap but other things were high, and luxuries were none too plenty. Even building, ten years ago, did not speak much, generally, either, for the taste or the wealth of the community. There were but few modern houses. There was little demand for finished and elegant architecture. There was small variety in our homes. There were few churches and places of amusement, and the latter were, by no means, of the best. But now all of this is changed. Our growth has been so rapid that even San Francisco has come to regard us as a dangerous rival. Her jealousy vents itself in many uncalled-for attacks upon us. She is not slow to resort to misrepresentation, if so she may hinder our progress. She sees business that she has controlled slipping from her and passing into our hands. She sees us becoming a great railroad center, with a network of transcontinental lines not only feeding our business and making transportation cheap for us, but bringing to us the largest tide of immigration and capital that is coming to the State. Our caravansaries are continually being multiplied, yet they remain full to overflowing. Building is active, yet she observes that we cannot build fast enough to supply the demand for homes. The building that is now being done is for the future. It is solid and substantial. It is also attractive. The best architects are in demand here. Our homes and our public buildings are not behind those of any city of our size. There is not a street where the signs of improvements are not visible. It is impossible to go beyond the sound of the hammer. With all of our rapid advancement building has never, perhaps, been more active than it is today. Public as well as private improvements are progressing rapidly. Los Angeles is one of the widest awake cities on the continent. She is not going to rest much longer without well-paved streets and extensive and handsomely-improved public parks. She has also decided to give a generous patronage to none but the best in the way of amusements. She wanted to hear Patti, and was ready to subscribe liberally for the pleasure. She wants the great American Opera Company, and she will give it as large and appreciative an audience as it could secure in San Francisco. She lacks nothing in the way of accommodation for the best talent, and her people have a right to demand now as much consideration from artists and professionals as have the people of San Francisco and the majority of eastern cities. Her right is based upon the ability to pay for, and a culture sufficient to appreciate, the best talent. When this fact is generally known, it goes without saying that professionals of genuine excellence will not pass us by. We shall soon be able to command as much professional ability as New York or Boston, and artists will feel that it is as well worth their while to come to us here.

In addition to all this, we have climatic attractions that will lure them, and a season in Southern California will have charms such as neither New York nor Boston can never offer.

A significant feature for the future of this section is this, that whereas a few years ago travel in this direction was largely of the tourist class, who came for the sake of pleasure, or as the means of temporary escape from inclement season; it now embraces in a large degree persons coming here for permanent settlement, and it is not now, as some years ago, confined to any particular season, but is active all the year round. This rapid and steady influx of population and of capital will work out the most desirable results. No spirit of jealousy can stay this incoming tide; no amount of misrepresentation can hold it back. Los Angeles is destined to grow and to witness such development as has never before been shown in the history of any section of the Union. This city has but just begun the work of advancement, and she will go on without let or hindrance, developing her resources, building up her manufacturing interests, increasing her agricultural and horticultural wealth to the end of her history.

### Railroad Speculations.

The San Diego Union of the 10th inst. contains the following surmises as to certain phases of the railroad situation in Southern California, which will be read with interest here:

"The Southern Pacific suit to condemn the old Texas Pacific right-of-way into San Diego has been dismissed. This probably means that the Southern Pacific is not going to build into San Diego at present. The dismissal of the suit, if that is its meaning, gives color to the report that the Atchison, Topeka and Santa Fé and the Southern Pacific have divided the State of California between them, the Santa Fé agreeing not to invade that portion lying north of a line drawn from Mojave to the coast, and the Southern Pacific not to build additional lines south of this line. This compact is terminable only after three years' notice by either company. Of course, either company may break it with impunity, and, to guard against surprises of this sort, each company will complete surveys now in progress, and be ready to build new lines in self-defense on short notice. It may be better, from one point of view, for San Diego just now, and for some time in the future, to have one railroad than two. If the Santa Fé had a line to San Francisco the large traffic to contend for there would concentrate the attention of both roads on that point to the neglect of San Diego; whereas, in the present state of things, San Diego is the Santa Fé's only ocean terminus, and it must perforce make the most of it.

"On the other hand, there are those who see in the railroad project from Yuma to San Diego and Ensenada a possible Southern Pacific scheme for reaching San Diego with a direct line and also the trade of the rapidly developing section below the line. Developments in the direction of this enterprise will be watched with interest, at any rate."

SENSATIONS have been crowding upon Los Angeles of late, but we have escaped the vitriol-thrower until now. A quiet house on College street was the scene yesterday evening of one of those horrors—a woman throwing upon a man's face the living fire of sulphuric acid. The matter is a shocking one; though, if the woman's story is true, it is entirely improbable that she will be brought to book. It may be suggested, however, that even to repel a ravisher, the revolver is rather more American than the vitriol vial.

THE San Diego Union is a well-meaning paper generally, but when it drops into a grave mistake like the following, it should be corrected with a club. The Union says:

"An important measure has been passed by the Congress of Chili, providing for a new trunk-line across the South American continent, which, it is said, 'will ruin the English coal trade.' Won't it be too—too Chili—without coal?"

THE Alta thinks it is time the fool and his pistol should be parted.

### AMUSEMENTS.

GRAND OPERA-HOUSE.—*Rudolph, Baron von Hollenstein*, is the production of a somewhat noted playwright, Bronson Howard. In the shape presented by George S. Knight it is announced as "re-arranged" by A. R. Cazauran. It is not a matter of much importance which of the literary lights is to be credited with the best of the work, as the piece itself is simply a stringing together of familiar melodramatic incidents. It is written up, of course, for Mr. Knight, who represents again the German gentleman, with a tendency to over-indulgence in strong potations. But on this occasion he has an opportunity for some very effective acting, and he makes every point tell by his incisive delivery, while his touches of quiet pathos were natural enough.

For its successful representation, the piece requires a different class of support. Mr. Knight's company is entirely out of its element in such a piece. Foy is a good specialty actor, but as "Whitworth Lawrence, a man of iron," the villain of the play, he is ludicrously miscast. Much of the weight of the piece falls on Miss Therese Newcombe, who was altogether inadequate for the part of the loving and suffering wife. Mrs. Knight has little to do, but sings as nicely and dresses as tastefully as usual. The rest of the company call for no special mention.

It is some time since we have had a combination of such light caliber on the boards of the Grand Opera-house. The attendance last night was quite good, though not nearly up to the standard of the opening night.

This evening *Over the Garden Wall* will be repeated.

# PACIFIC COAST.

## California Wine Cornered by Dealers.

### Immense Loss to the Grape Crop Through Recent Frosts.

### Big Gold Find in the Southern Part of Monterey County.

**Alleged Outrage on an American Citizen in Mexico -Imprisoned for Refusing to Take Part in the Late Election in Sonora—Coast Notes.**

*By Telegraph to The Times.*

SAN FRANCISCO, May 11.—[Special.] A rise in California wine and brandy is among the probabilities of the next few days. Recently the wine merchants of this city have been buying all the wine they could get at reasonably low figures, and it is said that they have control of nine-tenths of the marketable wine in the cellars of the State as well as a good hold on that which will be in a condition to sell within the next two years. Their operations have been conducted very quietly, and it was not until they had the larger part of all the wine secured that producers began to suspect that something unusual was being done. Persons familiar with the situation are of the opinion that the prices of retailers to consumers will advance from 25 to 50 cents per gallon and perhaps more. The wine merchants themselves laugh knowingly when questioned about the matter, and neither deny nor confirm the rumor that they have cornered the market. Out of four interrogated this morning not one would answer definitely, beyond saying that such a thing might be possible, as the supply of wine in the State is not large and may be placed at from 20,000,000 to 25,000,000 gallons. The frosts in the wine districts of Sonoma and Napa which have continued during the past few days, it is believed, will largely conduce to the success of such a movement if it is really in progress.

### JACK FROST.

**His Icy Fingers Play Havoc with the Grape Crop.**

SAN FRANCISCO, May 11.—[By the Associated Press.] Dispatches received here today state that there were severe frosts yesterday morning and this morning in the Sonoma, Napa, Livermore, and Santa Clara valleys, and severe injury was done to most of the vineyards in those districts. A gentleman who arrived from the Napa valley last evening, said that the vineyards were black from frost. In consequence of reports of the damage, there was a marked advance in the price of wine by those dealers and producers who have large stocks on hand. Tomorrow, John L. Beard and Juan Galleges, of Mission San José, will start on a tour of inspection through the Napa and Sonoma valleys. They will report the results there observed to the Viticultural Commission. The frost at Mission San José, last night, was so severe as to kill all bean plants in the gardens. The latest frosts ever known in the vineyard districts of upper California in previous seasons was on the 5th of May.

NAPA, May 11.—There has been frost for three mornings. The young vines are injured somewhat. In some localities there is great injury. Generally, the damage is not considered great.

LOOMIS, May 11.—The largest crop of grapes in Placer county for many years is almost a total loss. The rain of Monday, followed by a norther, brought frost for the past two nights, and many fruits and vegetables were also injured. The loss is enormous.

### THE NANAIMO HORROR.

**Some of the Victims Members of the A. O. U. W.**

SEATTLE (Wash.), May 11.—By the Associated Press.] Since the explosion at Nanaimo there has been much speculation among members of the Ancient Order of United Workmen in this city as to the number of members of that order who had fallen victims to the disaster. As this was a matter which, in a financial sense, nearly concerned members of the order, Past Master T. H. Cann yesterday telegraphed to Master William Bone, of Nanaimo, inquiring for information. Master Bone was among those killed in the disaster, and the telegram fell into the hands of Foreman B. S. Smith, who answered as follows:

NANAIMO (B. C.), May 10.—*To T. H. Cann, Past Master, etc.:* Eight Workmen killed, one badly injured.

(Signed) B. S. SMITH, Foreman.

VICTORIA (B. C.), May 11.—The Coroner's inquest in the case of the mine disaster has been postponed until Wednesday, the 25th of May. The postponement was taken to allow a thorough examination of the mine by experts, with a view to giving some information as to the cause of the explosion.

SAN FRANCISCO, May 11.—The subscription fund for the relief of the widows and orphans of the victims of the Nanaimo mine disaster now amounts to over $6000. Charles Crocker has donated $1000.

### A RICH FIND.

**Gold in the Anthracite Coal Fields of Monterey County.**

SAN LUIS OBISPO, May 11.—[By the Asssociated Press.] A report was brought to this city today of the discovery of gold in the mountains bordering on the coast of Monterey county, just north of the San Luis Obispo line, the immediate location being the San Carbojoro rancho. The find is a short distance east of what is known as the anthracite coal-fields of Monterey county. The discovery was made by an old-timer named Cruikshank, who, while working in the hills, struck a lead of quartz, and following it up found the quartz to be rich with the precious metal and containing considerable free gold. The ore is the richest the miners have ever seen and a company has already been formed. Last Saturday the reports reached San Simon, and Sunday morning saw an exodus of men and boys, all eagerly traveling toward the gold fields on foot and by saddle-horses.

### IN A SONORA JAIL.

**Alleged Outrage on an American Citizen in Mexico.**

TUCSON (Ariz.), May 11.—[By the Associated Press.] The Citizen today published a letter dated Saharipa (Sonora, Mexico), April 20th, and signed J. D. Garcia. The writer says he is an American-born citizen, and that last Sunday he was accosted by the Prefect of the district to vote for him at the election then being held. Garcia refused, on the ground of being an American, and the Prefect sent him to jail, where he has been ever since, with scarcely any sustenance.

### A STEAMER SUNK.

**Many Lives Lost in the Straits of Malacca.**

SAN FRANCISCO, May 11.—[By the Associated Press.] The steamer City of Rio Janeiro has arrived today from China and Japan. She brings news of a terrible marine disaster in the Straits of Malacca. The steamer Benton, plying between Singapore, Penang and Malacca, was run into about midnight March 29th by the steamer Fair Penang, shortly after leaving Malacca, and sunk within half an hour. Of 200 persons aboard only fifty thus far are known to have been saved. Most of those lost are natives. After the collision the Fair Penang continued on her way. The loss to vessel and cargo was $60,000.

**A Tragic Chapter from El Paso.**

EL PASO (Tex.), May 11.—The suicide of John Martin, a brakeman, and the killing of Martinez by a Southern Pacific train yesterday is followed today by the finding of the dead body of Jesus Gunonez near the street railroad corral. The latter was a carpenter by trade and came here from Chihuahua. He had been gambling for several nights, in company with several friends, and won considerable money. He was literally disemboweled, and had a wound in the left side, over the heart. It is believed that he was murdered for his money.

# THE RAILWAYS.

**Burlington's Scheme for a Line to San Francisco—A Baltimore and Ohio Rumor—New Line Projected.**

*By Telegraph to The Times.*

SAN FRANCISCO, May 11.—[By the Associated Press.] It is currently reported that the Burlington Company intend to reach San Francisco with an extension of their system just as soon as possible. The proposed route begins at Denver, thence along Grand River past Glenwood Springs and Grand Junction, in Colorado, thence through Utah and Nevada by the most direct route westward to San Francisco. It is stated that the Burlington route has entered into agreements with the Union Pacific Company whereby but one track is to be built. Whichever road builds this track will use it for a time, and as soon as the other desires the use of it an opportunity will be given; provided that one-half of the expense of maintenance is paid by each. This new agreement has healed all differences which formerly existed between the roads. It has not been decided as yet when work will be commenced.

A BALTIMORE AND OHIO RUMOR.

NEW YORK, May 11.—A rumor was circulated in Wall street today that the following arrangement had been made to take Baltimore and Ohio stock under the Garrett option. The Ives-Stayner party to take $3,000,000, Jay Gould $6,000,000, Pullman and Adams Express party $6,000,000, other parties smaller amounts. No confirmation could be obtained, but the statement caused a sharp dump in the market.

TO OPEN UP BEAR VALLEY.

SAN BERNARDINO, May 11.—The San Bernardino and Bear Valley Narrow-gauge Railroad Company commenced the location of their line up along the mountain sides north of this city this morning. The road will be about twenty-five miles in length, passing through thousands of acres of fine timber and opening up Bear Valley, the great water-shed of Southern California. It will be owned and operated by local capital.

RESISTING HIGH FREIGHT RATES.

NEW YORK, May 11.—Individual operators and shippers of anthracite coal have organized to resist the enforcing of advanced tariffs by the coal-carrying railroads, and purpose to make up a case and take it to the Interstate Commerce Commission with a demand that the rate on anthracite coal be reduced to a comparative level with the rates on other articles.

**The Ball Field.**

CINCINNATI, May 11.—Rain stopped the game.

ST. LOUIS, May 11.—Game called on account of rain.

CLEVELAND (O.), May 11.—Cleveland, 7; Brooklyn, 12.

LOUISVILLE, May 11.—Game called on account of rain.

NEW YORK, May 11.—New York, 9; Washington, 8.

DETROIT, May 11.—Detroit, 18; Pittsburgh, 2.

CHICAGO, May 11.—Chicago, 11; Indianapolis, 6.

BOSTON, May 11.—Boston, 4; Philadelphia, 9.

**Arrested for the Hansen Murder.**

MONTEREY, May 11.—A man 60 years old, named Hall, was arrested today charged with the shooting of Hansen down the coast. Hall was interviewed and protests his innocence, and says that he has never seen Hansen in his life. Hall lives sixteen miles from where the shooting occurred. He was taken to Hansen's cabin, but the latter was so weak that he failed to recognize him. Hansen has one bullet in his head and one under the left eye, and death is only a matter of a few days. Hall will have an examination before Judge Westfall this week.

**Rescued from the Desert.**

SACRAMENTO, May 11.—J. E. Dixon, formerly proprietor of the Crescent City Hotel, of this city, and subsequently of the Russ House, at Tucson, was reported by a dispatch last night as having wandered and been lost in the desert. Mrs. Dixon and daughter are visiting Sacramento and received a dispatch this morning saying that he had been found, but was merely alive from hunger and thirst. The wife and daughter left for Tucson this afternoon.

**Kentucky Republicans.**

LOUISVILLE, May 11.—At midnight the State Republican Convention is still in session at Masonic Temple, in this city. Hon. W. O. Bradley, of Lancaster, has been nominated for Governor; Mat O'Doherty, of Louisville, for Lieutenant-Governor; Hon. F. Lane, of Hopkinsville, for Attorney-General, and R. D. Davis, of Carter, for Auditor. There were about 1000 delegates present.

**Forced to Be a Soldier.**

SAN FRANCISCO, May 11.—The Bulletin's Murphy (Cal.) special says: "News has just reached here that J. B. Fruchier, an American citizen who left here last October to visit France, was seized on his arrival there, imprisoned, denied counsel and forced to serve in the French army. He is now in the Seventh Regiment of the line, in the garrison of Capors."

**Want Their Wages Raised.**

PORTLAND (Or.), May 11.—The machinists employed in the foundries here have asked their employers to raise their wages from $3 to $3.25 per day, to take effect Monday, May 16th.

**A Dwelling Burned.**

LAKEPORT, May 11.—William McElroy's house, one mile north of town, caught fire on the roof this afternoon and burned down, together with contents. Loss, $2000; no insurance.

# FAVORITES BEATEN

## The Kentucky Derby Won by Montrose.

### Baldwin's Horse Throws Up His Tail and Peters Out.

### A Bad Day for the Knowing Backers of Sure Steeds.

**Other Turf Matters—Maryland Jockey Club Races—Secretary Vail Ends the Long Row in the National Trotting Association by Resigning His Place.**

*By Telegraph to The Times.*

LOUISVILLE (Ky.), May 11.—[By the Associated Press.] The bay colt Montrose, son of Duke of Montrose, dam Patti, wins the great Kentucky Derby. It was not a great race, but it was a pretty one. The time, 2:39¼, makes a poor comparison with Ben Ali's last year, when the latter lowered the Derby record to 2:36½ after a magnificent contest, but it is not bad. The weather in the morning looked a little threatening, and at 2 o'clock a slight shower fell. It lasted only a few minutes, though, and did not affect the track in the least. Long before the first drop fell streams of vehicles and street cars, packed and crammed, had filled Churchill Downs with immense throngs, second in numbers only to the memorable gathering at the Ten Broeck-Mollie McCarthy race. The field was open to the public, and it looked as if about one-half of the big commonwealth of Kentucky had been dumped down there. In the grand stand the gay costumes of ladies at the north end and the fluttering of their fans afforded a pleasant contrast to the mass of humanity packed together like sardines over all the other space available. There must have been 20,000 people present. Gen. Robinson, of Lexington; Col. Green, of St. Louis, and Col. M. Lewis Clark were the judges.

The horses got off in the first race without much trouble. It was for maiden 2-year-olds, and there were seven starters. Cast-steel won in the fast time of 1:03¼; distance, five-eighths of a mile.

The second race, a mile and a quarter, was won handily by Montana Regent in 2:11½.

The crowd grew nervous waiting for the big event of the day, and there was a murmur of applause when Col. Clark rang the bell for the Derby. Jim Gore was first out of his paddock. He galloped by the stand slowly, and was greeted with cheers. His fore-feet were wrapped in red flannel, and he appeared stiff. Pendennis came next. The dark-brown Californian looked well and attracted much attention. When Banburg appeared, however, he was greeted with loud cheers, showing where most of the money was. He looked fit, and his backers were confident. The friends of Pendennis were also quite enthusiastic. Lucky Baldwin had said before the race that he was a better horse than Goliath, and that was conclusive enough to many who got within range of the circulation of the statement. Out of the original 119 entries there were only seven started. Those were: Banburg (who was ridden by Blaylock), Jacobin (Stoval), Clarion (Arnold), Montrose (Lewis), Pendennis (Murphy), Jim Gore (Fitzpatrick) and Banyan (Godfrey).

The post odds were: Seven to 5 against Banburg, 4 to 1 against Jacobin, 15 to 1 against Clarion, 15 to 1 against Montrose, 8 to 1 against Pendennis, 3 to 1 against Jim Gore, 7 to 1 against Banyan. The distance was a mile and a half. They started out. Billy Cheatham, of Nashville, who sent them off, had only to drop his flag once in vain. The second time, after a breathless silence, "They're off!" went up simultaneously from thousands of throats in the grand stand. Jacobin led off, followed closely by Banyan and Montrose, with the rest in a bunch. As they swerved into the stretch Banyan leaped to the front. Montrose maintained a good second, and Jacobin third place. Down the stretch the whole lot of them closed up beautifully, Montrose keeping well to the front all the time. As they came down past the grand-stand a great shout arose as they flew by in the order named: Jacobin, Banburg, Banyan, Jim Gore, Pendennis and Clarion. Jim Gore seemed to be taking things easy, maintaining his position past the quarter. Montrose still led; Banyan, another son of King Ban, third; Pendennis sixth, and Jacobin had dropped back to the last place. At the end of the mile the positions were not materially changed. Jim Gore seemed to falter, but gathered himself up and moved up to the third place at the three-quarter pole. There Montrose still led, Banyan alongside, Gore and Banburg second. They whirled into the stretch, and Fitzpatrick was seen to be urging the popular son of Hindoo. As they came around the turn Pendennis threw up his tail and gave up. He ran a miserable race from beginning to end. Montrose still led, to the surprise of al Fitzpatrick had been instructed to win with Jim Gore if he had to kill the colt, and as he laid on the lash in the stretch, the horse was plainly seen to be limping. Lewis gave Montrose the rein, as it was nip and tuck between the two for a moment, but Montrose held on nobly, and passed under the string the winner by two lengths, Jim Gore second. He had led with apparent ease from the grand-stand, without a touch of the whip, and looked able to go another quarter. Jacobin was third; Banburg, the favorite, fourth; Clarion fifth; Banyan sixth; Pendennis last. Jim Gore was limping terribly at the finish. It is thought that he will never be able to start again. Montrose is owned by Labold Bros., of Cincinnati, and was bred by Milton Young. Time was 2:39¼. The timers were W. S. Barnes, Ed Corrigan and B. C. Thomas.

MARYLAND JOCKEY CLUB RACES.

BALTIMORE, May 11.—The weather today was beautiful, the attendance large and track heavy.

Three-quarters of a mile, for 3-year-olds and upwards—Anarchy won; McLaughlin, second; Barnum, third. Time, 1:21½.

For 3-year-olds, one mile—Queen Elizabeth won; Matawan, second; Lizzie Baker, third. Time, 1:50.

For 2-year-olds, half-mile—Satisfaction won; Tonique, second; Belle Dor, third. Time, 53½.

Mile and half a furlong—Enigma won; Panama, second. Time, 1:53.

Mile—Paymaster and Mahoney ran a dead heat; Maia, third. Time, 1:50. In the run off Mahoney won. Time, 1:51.

SECRETARY VAIL RESIGNS.

CHICAGO, May 11.—Tonight a long and stubborn fight against Vail, secretary of the National Trotting Association, was brought to a close by the resignation of Secretary Vail. His resignation was accepted with but one dissenting vote, that of a Mr. Buckley, a friend of Vail.

**A Liberal Franchise.**

SAN LUIS OBISPO, May 11.—At a meeting last night of the City Council a street-railway franchise was granted to Edwin Goodall and associates for a term of thirty years. The streets granted comprise so many in all directions that there is no room for any other company. The franchise stipulates that Goodall commence work in thirty days, and to have two miles completed in six months, and that fare shall not exceed 5 cents per mile.

# DERBY DAY.

## The Great Racing Event at Louisville.

### A Chicago Horse Carries Off the Honors in Grand Style.

### The Favorite Beaten by the Almost Unknown Macbeth.

**Exciting Scenes During the Great Race—How the Winner's Jockey Handled His Horse—Previous Record of Macbeth—A Bonanza to His Owner.**

*By Telegraph to The Times.*

LOUISVILLE (Ky.), May 14.—[By the Associated Press.] Another Kentucky Derby has been run, another favorite beaten, and another great thoroughbred crowned with the laurel wreath of victory and excellence, bestowed where superiority in horse flesh is best understood, leaps into fame and brings his owner a fortune. Macbeth, the great dark son of Macduff, dam Agnes, belonging to the well-known Chicago stable of Hankins, is the equine hero in Kentucky tonight, and though the choice of the sons of the blue grass turfmen was the fine-looking chestnut son of Falsetto, Gallifet, they tip their glasses to the Chicago winner with the plaudit that it was well and nobly done. The first day of the Louisville spring meeting was cold, threatening and disagreeable, but the chilling western wind did not prevent the attendance of an immense throng at Churchill's downs. If anything, the crowd was larger than that of last year, and when the sun shone our shortly after the first race, its beams fell on a mass of humanity which filled the grand-stand, lawn, betting-booths, field and every spot from which a sight of the track was obtainable. Vehicles of every description, the tops covered with black forms, filled the Derby field, and the fence along the track for a quarter of a mile on either side of the timer's stand was surged against by a pushing mob. The track was about as fast as it ever is, being considered by the trainers a second or two slow. The judges were the regular ones, Col. C. F. Gray and Col. Lew Clark. The starter was James Caldwell.

THE GREAT EVENT.

The Derby was the great one of the day and of the meeting. Gallifet and Alexandria, composing the Melbourne stable entry, sold good favorites and lots of good Kentucky shekels went on odds of 4 to 5. The Chevalier was next in favor at 3 to 1, the odds against the others being about 12 to 1, White 6 to 1, Macbeth 8 to 1, Zeb Ward 10 to 1, Long Roll, the Sharper entry, being scratched half an hour before the race.

Gallifet and Alexandria were first to show on the track, and they were greeted with cheers as they swung by the stand in a half-mile spin together. The Chevelier, a magnificent black colt, received an ovation as he went past the stand, indicating what was known to be a fact, that his backers were numerous and enthusiastic. White received some recognition, but Macbeth comparatively little. Zeb Ward and Autocrat were quietly admired by those who are fond of toying with short ones. After one false start, Caldwell got them off the chute in great style and the fun began.

Cheveller led away with Autocrat and Gallifet close up, White third and the others not far off. Into the stretch they swerved, out of the unpopular chute, Col. Zeb Ward holding in front for what was to be only short-lived glory, Alexandria second, White third, Chevelier fourth, Gallifet fifth, Autocrat sixth and Mebeth last.

Covington, on the winner of Gayoso Hotel stakes at Memphis, and other leading southern events, was playing an admirable waiting game, which he kept up, and which, if McCarty on Gallifet had better adhered to, might have led to a more interesting finish. Passing the grand stand, Alexandria moved to the fore to the music of thousands of throats. There his stable companion was second, Chevalier third, White, Macbeth, Ward and Autocrat back in a bunch. Rounding the turn into the back stretch, Gallifet's jockey seemed to become impatient, and let the chestnut have his head, running first by a length almost the entire length to the next turn, the Chevalier second and Macbeth third. Ward had dropped away back, and Alexandria and Autocrat had also appeared to weary of the rapid pace set by the fleet son of Falsetto.

MACBETH WINS.

As they approached the turn, Covington was seen to give Macbeth more head, and the colt answered like the staying one he proved himself to be. By the time the head of the long run home was reached, he had collared Gallifet and was running easy. McCarty began to use the lash on the favorite, but at the eighth pole it was evident to all that it was no use. Macbeth was running easy with head up and without the least urging. Gallifet was working hard, and as Macbeth passed under the wire a length in front of him he looked severely punished and ready to quit. White was third, two lengths behind, Alexandria, a bad fourth, Chevalier fifth, Autocrat sixth, Ward seventh and last. The time was 2:38¼, and compares favorably with that made in former Derbies. Macbeth won in a gallop, and seemed ready to go another quarter.

It was stated after the race that the Chicago stable had certainly won $70,000 on Macbeth, if not more. They closed the winter books on him in New Orleans, this city and probably at other places. That the strapping big dark colt will be heard from again is assured by this performance, as indeed was indicated by his first-class running in the South. Many now think that he was not allowed to win at Nashville and Lexington, as he might have, in order to secure the big odds that were to be had today—8 to 1.

MACBETH'S RECORD.

It is rather astonishing that odds of 8 to 1 were obtainable against Macbeth, looking at his first-class performances in the South. Macbeth started frequently as a 2-year old, doing most of his running at Louisville and Latonia. At the latter place, in the fall, he won the Kimball stakes, three-quarters of a mile. Beyond this, his performances attracted but little attention until this year, when his winning the one and an eighth miles handicap at Memphis in 1:55½, with White Nose second and Panama third, and subsequently the Gayoso-hotel stakes from Long Chance and Frederick, brought him into prominence as a Derby candidate. He ran second in the Merchants' Stakes at Memphis, Little Minch winning in 2:10. He was beaten at Nashville in the Troubadour Stakes by Cruiser, Emperor of Norfolk and Volante, and also by Leo in another race at the same place. Poteen beat him at Lexington in the Distillers' Stakes, he running second and the time being 2:08. He ran second in Chevalier Phœnix Hotel stakes. White started six or eight times as a 2-year-old, running second a number of times in only ordinary field and not winning or doing anything worthy of note. He ran second to Emperor of Norfolk at Nashville in the Lawyers' stakes, the first part of this month, Cruiser being third. The distance was one and three-fourths miles, and the time 2:09½.

SUMMARY OF THE DAY.

First race—Owing to a mistake, this race had to be run over after it had been won by Liberty, the favorite, Madstone second, Santa Cruz third. After they got off a second time, Madstone won, Santa Cruz second, Liberty third. Time, 1:02¾.

Club purse, one and one-sixteenth miles—Terra Cotta won, Barrister second, Jacobin third. Time, 1:50.

Kentucky derby, $2500 added, $500 to second, $200 to third. Starters—Alexandria 118 (Jones), Autocrat 118 (Hamilton), Col. Zeb Ward 118 (Blaylock), Gallifet 118 (McCarthy), Macbeth 115 (Covington), The Chevalier 118 (Lewis), White 118 (Withers). Auction pools—Melbourne Stable $50, Chevalier $27, Macbeth $11, White $8, field $11. Books—Melbourne stable 4 to 5, The Cavalier 3 to 1, Autocrat 12 to 1, White 6 to 1, Macbeth 9 to 1, Zeb Ward 10 to 1. Macbeth won handily by a length, Gallifet second, two lengths in front of White, third; the other horses strung out. Time, 2:38¼.

Selling, three-quarter-mile heats—Persimmons won the first heat, Lela May second, Lida L. third. Time, 1:15¾. In the second heat Persimmons won again, Lela May second, Lida L. third. Time, 1:16.

## CONSOLIDATION.

### Southern Pacific and Its Many Branches Amalgamated.

SACRAMENTO, May 14.—[By the Associated Press.] Articles were filed in the Secretary of State's office today of association, incorporation, amalgamation and consolidation of the Southern Pacific Railroad Company, the San José and Alameda Railroad Company, the Pajaro and Santa Cruz Railroad, the Southern Pacific Branch Railroad Company, the San Pablo and Tulare Railroad Company, the San Pablo and Tulare Extension Railroad Company, the San Ramo Valley Railroad Company, the Stockton and Copperopolis Railroad, the Stockton and Tulare Railroad Company, the San Joaquin Valley and Yosemite Railroad Company, the Los Angeles and San Diego Railroad Company, the Los Angeles and Independence Railroad Company, the Long Beach, Whittier and Los Angeles County Railroad Company, the Long Beach Railroad Company, the Southern Pacific Railroad Extension Railroad Company, and the Pomona and San Bernardino Railroad Company. The articles set forth that the Southern Pacific is the owner of railroads and franchises, the aggregate of which is 1454.32 miles in length.

The lengths of the other roads are given, and it is stated that an amalgamation and consolidation of their capital stocks, debts, properties, assets and franchises will be mutually advantageous. The directors of the respective roads agree to the amalgamation, and that it shall go into effect at once. The name of the consolidated corporation is the Southern Pacific Company. The object of the corporation is to operate and construct double-track steam railroads, the railroad and its branches to be 2538.80 miles in length. The directors are Charles F. Crocker, Timothy Hopkins, Charles Mayne, W. V. Huntington, N. T. Smith, J. L. Willcut and A. N. Towne.

The capital stock is $142,900,000, divided into 1,429,000 shares of a par value of $100 each.

## BASE-BALL.

### The Weather Unfavorable for Games in the East.

CHICAGO, May 14.—[By the Associated Press.] Anson's colts won today's game by superior playing all around. Krock's pitching was a mystery to the New Yorkers, except when Roger Conner, in the first inning, made a home-run drive over the wall. Score: Chicago, 5; New York, 1.

PITTSBURGH, May 14.—The weather was miserably cold today, and good playing was difficult. Henderson's wild pitching and some villainous fielding lost the game for the home team. Score: Pittsburgh, 5 Boston, 6.

INDIANAPOLIS, May 14.—Five hundred people attended the game today. The weather was very cold and damp. Healy's pitching was an important feature, and won the game, together with some good hitting. Score: Indianapolis, 7; Washington, 1.

DETROIT, May 14.—No game—rain.

PHILADELPHIA, May 14.—The Athletics-Baltimore game was called at the commencement of the fifth inning, on account of rain. Score: 4 to 1, in favor of Baltimore.

CLEVELAND, May 14.—Cleveland, 3; Brooklyn, 7. Five innings—snow and darkness.

ST. LOUIS, May 14.—St. Louis, 6; Kansas City, 4.

## THE TRAIN ROBBERS.

### Mexican Justice to Be Meted Out to Them.

NOGALES (Ariz.), May 14.—[By the Associated Press.] Conrad Rolling has been arrested at Huachuca, and is believed to be the leader of the band of train-robbers who attacked the train on the Sonora Railroad on Friday night.

It was the intention to give Rolling and Taylor, the supposed Agua Zarca train-robbers, a hearing this afternoon, but the District Attorney telegraphed that the magistrate has no jurisdiction, as the crime was committed in Mexico. It was expected that there would be pretty strong evidence against both parties in the examination, as evidence of a circumstantial nature is strong against both Taylor and Rolling. The Mexican authorities last night arrested two men, who, they are pretty certain, were the robbers. A large detachment of Mexican troops arrived this morning from Guaymas. The troops will be used to execute the death sentence should any of the prisoners now in jail prove to have been in the robbery.

### The English Grain Trade.

LONDON, May 14.—The Mark Lane Express says: "The English wheat trade is slow, and previous rates are difficult to sustain. Foreign wheat is quiet. In London prices have been maintained, but in Liverpool they are a fraction cheaper. Flour is firm. Corn at Liverpool is 1d per cental dearer. Oats are in demand at an advance of 3d. Linseed is weak and prices declined 6d. Today there was a better demand for wheat, and both English and foreign rose 6d. Flour was 6d higher. Oats 6d to 1s dearer."

### To Work a Copper Mine.

SANTA FE (N. M.), May 14.—Articles of association of the Santa Fé Copper Company were filed today by Jay A. Hubbell of Michigan, Stephen W. Dorsey of New York and others of New Mexico. The capital stock is $5,000,000. The object is the working of an extensive blanket vein of copper ore at San Pedro, in this county. The mine is well known as the Cañon del Agua Grant mine, so long in litigation.

### Left Their Plunder Behind.

ELKO (Nev.), May 14.—The store of Hull, Wells Fargo's agent and County Treasurer, was broken into last night, and a box containing $3000 in silver and $1000 in gold coin was removed and carried on a wheelbarrow to the foot of a hill a quarter of a mile distant, where it was found intact this morning.

### Changed Its Manager.

PHILADELPHIA, May 14.—The Journal of United Labor, the official organ of the Knights of Labor, has been placed in charge of A. M. Deway, publisher of the Labor Journal at Detroit. The paper has never been a financial success, although it has a large circulation.

### Suing His Daughter's Abductors.

PITTSBURGH (Pa.), May 14.—The father of Minnie Rosa Parsons, the young lady alleged to have been abducted, recently, today began a suit for damages against Ensign Ryan, U. S. N., and J. H. Mead. Process was granted for their arrest.

### Burned at Sea.

SAN FRANCISCO, May 14.—It is announced by cable from London that the German bark Marie Rierbeck, from Genoa to this city, was burned at sea. The crew is safe. The vessel was valued at $14,000, and the cargo at $100,000.

### Sketchley's New Ostrich Farm

RED BLUFF, May 14.—Mr. Sketchley moved his ostriches this morning on drays to the farm on the Sacramento River.

A grand reception was tendered to Dr. Sketchley this evening.

### A Hog-thief's Escape.

RED BLUFF, May 14.—Bob Henderson, arrested a few days on the charge of stealing hogs, escaped from the County Jail last night by sawing off a bar in the window of his cell.

### The Queen of the Pacific.

SAN FRANCISCO, May 14.—The Queen of the Pacific was taken to the Union Iron Works today. She will there be given a thorough overhauling.

# EASTERN TOPICS.

## The Mystery of Beem's Death Grows Deeper.

### Farmers Driven from Their Homes Along the Mississippi.

### Frightful Accident on the Santa Fe Road in Colorado.

**The First Carrier Pigeon Arrives from the Great Buffalo Hunt in Texas—The Great Sugar Trust to Be Taken to Task.**

*By Telegraph to The Times.*

CHICAGO, May 14.—The mystery of Gen. Martin Beem's death was tonight made more peculiar than ever by the action of the Veteran Union League, the organization which undertook to investigate the matter. The report from the committee charged with the task was submitted to a meeting of the league this evening. The gist of the report was that Gen. Beem had been murdered, but that no blame attached to his wife. No explanation was vouchsafed for such a state of affairs. The committee asked for additional time to probe deeper into the subject. By vote of the league this was granted, but later a reconsideration was moved and the committee discharged, thus apparently shelving the whole business, so far as Gen. Beem's old comrades are concerned. A feature of the meeting was the reading of a strong letter from Mrs. Beem demanding virtually a vindication or prosecution.

## TERRIBLE ACCIDENT.

### A Railway Collision Causes a Fearful Explosion.

FOUNTAIN (Colo.), May 14.—A horrible railway casualty occurred here at 2:45 this morning. At 2:41, the north-bound "Thunderbolt" stopped at the station for orders. She had hardly come to a stand-still when a caboose with four loaded freight cars, which had broken away from the through freight at Colorado Springs, 13 miles away, came dashing down the long grade at lightning speed, crashing into the express and piling the caboose and first car into ruins on top of the engine and baggage car. The car next to the caboose was a huge tank of naptha, which being wrecked scattered the oil over the depot, cars and adjoining buildings. It caught fire, and in an instant everything was in a sheet of flames. The engineer and fireman escaped somewhat injured. The Pullman and two day coaches of passengers were hastily detached from the burning baggage car and run down the track to a safe distance from the fire, which had now enveloped the depot, and was rapidly approaching a car of the runaway freight, when an alarm was given that this car was loaded with powder and for every one to

RUN FOR THEIR LIVES.

All who heard the warning attempted to obey, but had gone but a short distance when 17,000 pounds of giant powder with which the car was loaded exploded, shaking the earth as though by an earthquake. Twenty houses in the city were almost totally destroyed, together with the new Baptist Church, which was blown from its foundation and scattered over acres of ground. Men and women were knocked senseless, and pieces of broken rails, car-wheels and timbers were carried with terrific force for half a mile. A number of freight cars standing on the side track were blown to atoms. The passengers in the "Thunderbolt" were severely shaken up, and a number cut by pieces of glass from the windows, but none were seriously injured. The yard of the Newton Lumber Company took fire, and was completely destroyed. People standing a quarter of a mile from the explosion were hit by flying fragments and badly wounded.

THE DEAD ARE

C. F. Smith, manager of the Newton Lumber Company. He was trying to extinguish the flames of the depot when the explosion occurred, and was badly wounded, dying in an hour. A piece of iron was blown through his body, the hole being two inches in diameter.

The remains of an unknown man were found underneath the engine after the fire was extinguished.

Lawrence Weichart, a German carpenter, while assisting to put out the fire in the lumber-yard, was struck on the head by a flying bolt, and died in two hours.

H. Hutchins, a merchant 60 years old, standing at a door some distance away, was struck by an iron bar and died this afternoon. The wounded number about 30. None of them will die, although all are painfully injured.

The loss to the town, which was completely ruined, is estimated at $60,000, while the amount of the railroad's loss is variously estimated at from $75,000 to $100,000. All the wounded are residents of this place except W. Knight of St. Louis and J. C. Munn of Tombstone, who had their faces badly cut.

## THE METHODISTS.

### Proposed Limitation of the Bishops' Term of Office.

NEW YORK, May 14.—[By the Associated Press.] Bishop Merrill presided at today's session of the Methodist Conference. The Committee on Episcopacy was asked to report Tuesday upon a resolution to elect bishops for a term of eight years. At present the bishops hold office for life, as a matter of usage.

A resolution was offered to the effect that the conference express the opinion that the Blair Educational Bill is a good measure. The resolution was referred to the Committee on State of the Church. Rev. John Miley of Drew Theological Seminary read his report as fraternal delegate to the Methodist Church South, and Rev. Isaac W. Joyce of Cincinnati read his report as fraternal delegate to the General Conference of the Methodist Church in Canada.

A resolution was introduced, asking the Committee on Episcopacy to provide for balloting for bishops so that one candidate shall be balloted for at a time.

The Rev. Dr. J. M. Buckley offered a substitute to the effect that the vote will be taken by orders; that lay delegates and ministerial delegates vote separately. This caused a general and rather excited discussion. It was said that there was lobbying going on for candidates, but the members denied it. Finally, in order to end the discussion ex-Gov. Cumback of Indiana moved the previous question. A number of amendments were offered. When the vote was taken everything was voted down and the discussion closed.

The Southern California Conference offered a resolution that German missions on the Pacific be organized into an annual conference. Referred to the Committee on boundaries. Adjourned.

## FLEEING FROM FLOODS.

### Dwellers by the Mississippi Driven from Their Homes.

ST. LOUIS, May 14.—[By the Associated Press.] The river is steadily rising here, and the inhabitants on the American bottoms are moving portable property back to the bluffs. Reports from the north are alarming, and if any levee or the Madison dike breaks the loss will be millions. A regular exodus has taken place from the river bottoms. The entire town of Alexandria, Mo., is inundated with five feet of water, and the damage is very heavy. People are being taken as fast as possible to the high lands several miles back of the town. The levee is now being patrolled for miles by sentinels whose duty is to summon assistance when any break is observed.

MORE TALES OF DISASTER.

CHICAGO, May 14.—Dispatches to the Associated Press from several points along the upper Mississippi River give accounts of great losses to property owners and vast inundations. The levee that protects the Say bottoms gave away at an early hour this morning and the men engaged in strengthening it had to run for their lives. An opening 100 yards wide was made and the water rushed through and into the bottoms with a roar. Couriers hastened through the bottoms warning farmers of the break and there was a wild chase, driving the stock to the highlands. The bottoms are in Illinois and embrace about 100,000 acres of land, and reach from a point opposite Lordsiana, Mo., to a point opposite Hannibal. At the broadest place they are nearly five miles and the overflows make a great turbulent sea.

At 6 a.m. the Indian Grave levee gave way and submerged 14,900 acres of low lands, 5000 acres of which was planted in wheat.

The levee broke about six miles above Quincy, Ill., on the Missouri side.

The break at Alexandria has covered a great area—800,000 acres of land—in the midst of which is a modern Venice with impromptu crafts of all kinds and sizes. Water floods the town of Alexandria from 2 to 6 feet deep. The people were in a manner prepared for the flood, and the suffering is not great. The bottom was planted in wheat and corn, and the farming community reckon their loss at figures aggregating $300,000. Most of the live stock had been driven to the bluffs.

The situation at Keokuk is becoming very serious, the railroad yards being entirely submerged and many mills compelled to shut down. At the Government works at Keokuk the stage was 19 feet 1 inch, five inches above the high-water mark of 1881 and within 25 inches of the highest mark on record, that of 1851.

At Burlington, Davenport and other points the water at 10 o'clock tonight is within a few inches of the highest mark known, and is steadily rising. Many establishments near the river are being flooded, and goods are being hurriedly removed. Hopes are expressed that the rise will cease soon.

## THE POLITICAL FIELD.

### Woodburn to Be Shelved by His Nevada Constituents.

WINNEMUCCA (Nev.), May 14.—Many delegates and candidates are here to attend the Republican State Convention tomorrow. Senator Stewart will be elected delegate to the National Convention if not indorsed for President tonight. Bartine of Carson, who came here a candidate for Supreme Judge, is said to have the best show for Congress. The fight for Judge is narrowed down to Leonard, the present incumbent, and Murphy, formerly Attorney-General. The delegates say that Woodburn telegraphed that he would accept a renomination, but they are not disposed to humor him.

THE CAMPAIGN IN NEW YORK.

BUFFALO, May 14.—The Republican State Convention assembles here Wednesday, and it is accepted as a foregone conclusion that Senator Frank Hiscock, ex-Senator Warner Miller, ex-Senator Thomas C. Platt and Chauncey M. Depew will be chosen delegates to the Chicago convention.

NEW YORK, May 14.—The Democratic State Convention meets here tomorrow. The delegates-at-large to the St. Louis convention will probably be Senator Raines, Roswell P. Flower, Hugh McLaughlin and Smith Weed or ex-Mayor Cooper.

THE LABOR PARTIES.

CINCINNATI, May 14.—Delegates to the two national conventions of the Union Labor and United Labor parties are coming in rapidly. The Union Labor Convention will meet at noon tomorrow, at the Odeon. The United Labor will meet at the same time at the Grand Opera-house. Jerse Harper, the most prominent man in the United Labor party, is here. Dr. McGlynn, among the foremost of the Union Labor party, is on the ground.

STILL BALLOTING.

NASHVILLE, May 14.—The Democratic State Convention met at noon and proceeded to ballot for Governor. The thirty-first ballot resulted as follows: Taylor, 727; Trousdeale, 489; McConnell, 111. Necessary to a choice, 886.

## THE SUGAR TRUST.

### A Legal Assault on the Great Combination

NEW YORK, May 14.—[By the Associated Press.] The Attorney-General today made an investigation of the sugar trust on a petition signed by Hugh J. Grant, Richard Crocker and Thomas F. Gilroy, whose complaint against the sugar trust has already been made public. They claim that it is illegal for a number of reason. The defendant's counsel declared that the complainants were well-known politicians, who had introduced a bill in the State Legislature making it a crime to combine for the purpose of fixing the prices of commodities; that this bill said nothing about a combination to fix the price of labor, and that this movement appeared to be for the purpose of arraying labor against capital. It was wholly for political effect. It was unfair and unjust to subject sugar refiners to these annoyances to serve some one's political ends. The Attorney-General will make known his decision as to whether or not he will proceed against the trust in about two weeks.

## BLAZING OIL.

### A Night of Terror in a Pennsylvania Town.

OIL CITY (Pa.), May 14.—[By the Associated Press.] The fire has burned itself out and all danger has passed. The first reports are greatly exaggerated, and the loss will not exceed $100,000.

The great overflow, watched with so much terror, occurred shortly before 2 o'clock this morning. The tank emptied its flames and contents, and huge islands of burning oil, some of them a hundred feet in diameter, flowed down the creek. Booms proved useless, and the fierce fire swept on, burning several dwellings, the Western New York and Pennsylvania Railroad bridge and a large barrel factory. There was very little sleep in the city last night, as it was feared the town would be destroyed.

## A TRUSTY BIRD.

### A Pigeon Brings News of the Great Bison Hunt.

GARDEN CITY (Kan.), May 14.—A carrier pigeon bringing the first news from the buffalo-hunting expedition of the Chicago Times, has arrived here from headquarters. At the Upper Canadian River in Northwestern Texas, 185 miles distant, two small groups of bisons had been sighted, and it was evident that the hunters were close upon the trail of the main herd. Considerable sport was had in lassoing three buffalo calves.

### Street Duel at Sutter City.

MARYSVILLE, May 14.—P. D. Gardemeyer, a real-estate speculator of Sutter City, and a man named McNabb fired seven shots at each other, at that place, this morning, at 25 feet range, without any bullets taking effect. McNabb threatened Gardemeyer because he believed that the latter was instrumental in having his son arrested for selling liquor without a license. No arrests were made.

### A Prominent San Diegan Dead.

SAN DIEGO, May 14.—A. B. Lowrie of the wholesale house of McIntyre & Lowrie of Boston, Mass., and one of the heaviest stockholders in the Atchison, Topeka and Santa Fé Railroad, also president of the San Diego Land and Town Company, died at National City today. The remains were taken to Boston tonight.

### The Transcontinentals.

SAN FRANCISCO, May 14.—There are gathered here from the general offices of all the transcontinental railway lines officials in the operating service of their roads who have come to attend the meeting of their association, which will be called tomorrow. From talks with members already on the ground it is gathered that this meeting will be not altogether a quiet one.

### Pacific Methodist College.

SANTA ROSA, May 14.—People from various sections of the State are in attendance at the commencement exercises of the Pacific Methodist College in this city. Contests for the Anderson medal for the best recitation by a young lady and the Hardin medal for the best oration took place this evening at the Athenæum.

### Snow in Michigan.

MARQUETTE (Mich.), May 14.—A snow and sleet storm has prevailed for the last 24 hours and snow is still falling rapidly.

## IN ASHES.

### A Washington Territory Town Almost Destroyed.

PORTLAND (Or.), May 14.—News is just received from Goldendale, Wash., that the town was nearly destroyed by fire yesterday. All the business portion of the town is laid in ashes. The fire department consisted only of a hook and ladder company, which was practically helpless to stay the course of the flames. The total loss will reach $175,000; total insurance, $50,000.

PORTLAND (Or.), May 14.—Later reports from Goldendale show that the losses by fire are much heavier than at first reported. Eight blocks were laid in ashes and over 79 houses destroyed. No lives were lost. The fire lasted four hours. The hook and ladder-house was burned early during the fire and left the citizens powerless. The total loss will reach over $200,000, with only about $50,000 insurance. The following is a list of the principal losses: Sig Sichel, general merchandise, $35,000; Cummings & Cram, $25,000; Sentinel Publishing Company, $4000; J. M. Keers & Co., drugs, $6000; C. R. Van Alstyne, groceries, $15,000; Mrs. C. R. Van Alstyne, millinery, $1000; Childings, $3500; A. P. Hotaling & Co., building, $12,000; hook and ladder apparatus, $3500; William Dickson, livery stable, $4000; Hiram Wing, groceries, $3000; courthouse and county jail, $10,000; Sloper Downer, sash and door factory, $3000; William Melligen, general merchandise, $5000; D. D. McFall, building and hardware store, $9000; Victor Gobat, jeweler, $3000; D. W. Pierce, dwelling and lumberyard, $5000; Bold & Fenton, agricultural implements, $4000; B. W. Snoover, furniture, $4000; W. H. Ward, building and saddlery stock, $6000; H. D. Young, furniture factory, store and dwelling, $6000; M. E. Church and parsonage, $3000; John Hess, dwelling, $3000; W. H. Chappel, hotel, $4000; Simpson, drug store, $5000.

A light breeze was blowing when the fire broke out, but as the flames gained headway the wind naturally increased. In less than an hour it seemed to be a gale blowing from every point of the compass. Farmers in the neighborhood seeing the flames, hurried to render assistance, and did good service with teams. A number of men and women fainted from overwork, exhaustion and excitement. There were several physicians on hand, but they could do little good, as the drug stores, with their contents, were destroyed. Considerable want and destitution is said to prevail.

## IN NO HURRY.

### The Southern Pacific Will Not Go to San Diego Just Yet.

SAN FRANCISCO, May 14.—[By the Associated Press.] A local paper will tomorrow contain this bit of speculation as to certain railroad probabilities: "The Southern Pacific Company is evidently in no great hurry to reach San Diego. It may extend its line down there in the course of the next two years, or it may not. Mr. Huntington's idea of the scheme is said to have been that the road would be a very profitable one, and ought to be built, but he would not recommend the payment of fancy sums for rights of way. The report has gained ground that the Southern Pacific Company was negotiating for the purchase of the San Diego and Elsinore Railroad. Asked as to the truth of the report today, Charles F. Crocker said that there was little in it. There was no doubt that the San Diego and Elsinore Company was willing to sell. It had, in fact, drawn up an agreement for purchase, which had been submitted to the Southern Pacific Company's directors for their approval and signatures, but as yet it had received neither. The route was one not favored by the Southern Pacific people. 'When we go to San Diego,' said the Colonel, 'it will not be that way.' On the other hand, there are those sage prophets in the railroad world who predict that the Southern Pacific Company will be fighting the Santa Fé on its own ground in San Diego within a year."

### Fatally Injured

VISALIA, May 14.—Frank O'Neal, aged 80, was run over this morning by a wagon near Visalia. He was brought here and died this afternoon.

### The Weather.

SIGNAL OFFICE, LOS ANGELES, May 14.—At 4:07 a.m. today the thermometer registered 53; at 12:07 p.m., 74; 7:07 p.m., 60. Barometer for corresponding periods, 29.95, 29.95, 29.92. Maximum temperature, 78; minimum temperature, 51. Weather clear.

INDICATIONS.

SAN FRANCISCO, May 14—Indications for the 24 hours commencing at 4 a.m., May 15th, for California: Local rains, followed by fair weather, in northern portion; generally fair weather in southern portion; nearly stationary temperature.

# The  Times.

EIGHTH YEAR. LOS ANGELES, TUESDAY, JULY 9, 1889. PRICE: Single Copies 5 Cents. By the Week, 8 Cents.





For Additional Classified Advertisements, See Second Page.


# ORANGE COUNTY.

## Its First Convention Held Yesterday.

### Non-partisan, but Somewhat Sultry All the Same.

### A Lively Breeze in the Outset, Followed by a Big Bolt.

### Delegate Head Heads a Bolt—The Seceders Retire and Lift Up Their Voices in Protestation—The Nominations.

ORANGE, July 8.—[Special.]—The Orange non-Partisan Citizens' Convention for the nomination of candidates to fill the offices of the new county of Orange, met here today at 10 a.m., at the Rochester Hotel, with a full delegation present. A. Cauldwell, chairman of the Executive Committee making the call, took the platform at 10 sharp and called the convention to order. He then read the call, including an address to the people of the county. The address is as follows:

*To the Citizens of Orange County*: In issuing the above call for a Citizens' Convention for Orange County, we have felt that party politics, in the national sense, have no proper place in our own local public business; that it is of great importance that the affairs of the new county shall be started aright in the direction of an economical, honest and energetic conduct of public business, freed from the exigencies of partisan politics, and that these objects can best be accomplished by a movement of this character. The delegates to this convention will come direct from the people, and we feel sure that a body of men so selected will nominate candidates whose high character and standing in private life will be their certificate of fitness and ability for public station. Beyond the issuance of the call the matter is left where it properly should be, in the hands of the voters in each precinct.

This call had been signed by about 100 voters, representing 16 precincts of the county. After completing the reading, Mr. Cauldwell announced that W. P. Northcross would act as temporary chairman, and S. M. Craddick as temporary secretary. Mr. Northcross spoke of the business of the hour, and that business, he thought, was to nominate good and true men to fill the various offices in the new county.

C. C. Wright of the Orange delegation, moved that the chairman appoint three committees as follows: A committee on permanent organization and order of business; a committee on credentials; and a committee on resolutions.

The motion, being seconded, was announced by the chair.

A delegate from Santa Ana got the floor, and opposed the proceedings as high-handed and exceptional, and wanted to know if a few individuals proposed to run the convention.

Chairman Northcross replied that the proceedings were not without precedent, but were regular and orderly, because there was no convention until an organization was effected.

A delegate from Tustin sailed into the chairman in rough order, saying if two or three men were to transact all the business the rest of the convention might as well retire for good.

The chairman took issue with the delegate, and a half-dozen men were on their feet, talking and shouting at the top of their voices. Chairman Northcross came down from the platform, after placing Mr. Cauldwell in the chair, and defended his course and that of the chairman of the Executive Committee in a cool and deliberate manner, which soothed the excited delegates to some extent.

The Tustin member, however, was not satisfied, and insisted on talking and finally moved to proceed to the election of a new chairman, and was promptly ruled out of order. He appealed to the convention, but his appeal was ignored. He was finally got to his seat, when the chairman announced the following committeemen:

*On Credentials*—George Irvine, Richard Eagan, A. Cauldwell, J. A. McFadden, A. F. Gardner.

*Organization and Order of Business*—J. A. Pfeiffer, John W. Irons, John Cadman, George A. Whidden and S. J. Findley.

*On Resolutions*—A. McDermott, Joshua Parker, B. M. Litton, H. Goff, W. H. Watts.

At 10:30 the convention took a recess until 1 o'clock p.m., awaiting reports of the several committees.

#### AFTERNOON SESSION.

##### Two-thirds of the Convention Secede—Nominations Made.

ORANGE, July 8.—[Special.] The afternoon session of the convention was called to order at 1:15 o'clock. When order was restored, J. W. Ballard from Tustin arose and offered the following resolution:

"Resolved, that it is the sense of the delegates assembled that, up to this time, this convention is not an organized body, inasmuch as the delegates present have had no voice in the selection of its presiding officers, and that now we proceed to the organization of the convention and the election of a temporary chairman and secretary, and that said election be had by vote of precincts here represented."

The resolution was promptly ruled out of order and Mr. Ballard took his seat.

DELEGATE HEAD PROTESTS.

H. W. Head of Garden Grove arose to his feet, and, speaking to the delegates, said: "Every delegate present can certainly see by this time that it is the determination of a few men to run this convention. The great majority of this convention seems powerless. Now, I, for one, do not propose to sacrifice my independence and manhood by submitting to such an outrage, and I therefore declare my intention of withdrawing from this meeting, and ask all who feel as I do to go out with me. Let us go to some place where we can transact the business for which we were elected."

He added that he was sorry to take such a step, for he loved Orange very much, but he thought it was the only course left open to him. Then, waving aloft his hat, he called upon the delegates to follow, and started across to the door, and, amid hisses, left the room, followed by all of the Garden Grove delegation, all from Santa Ana, and most of those from Newport, Westminster, Tustin, Anaheim and Newhope, comprising about two-thirds of the convention.

The Committee on Credentials and Organization reported and the report was adopted. The temporary organization was made permanent.

The Committee on Resolutions reported and the report was adopted.

NOMINATIONS MADE.

A motion here prevailed to nominate candidates, and A. Cauldwell proposed to place in nomination Col. I. E. Messmore of Orange for Superior Judge, which was made by acclamation.

E. E. Edwards of Santa Ana was nominated for District Attorney.

J. A. Peiffer of St. James was nominated for Clerk.

George J. Mosbaum of Santa Ana was nominated for Auditor.

T. A. West of St. James was nominated for Sheriff.

T. J. Lockhart of Orange was nominated for Treasurer.

Fred Smythe of Anaheim was nominated for Assessor.

J. P. Greely of Fullerton was nominated for Superintendent of Schools.

S. J. Findley of Santa Ana was nominated for Surveyor.

Dr. I. D. Mills of El Modena was nominated for Coroner.

Candidates for Supervisor were nominated as follows: No. 2, Jacob Ross; No. 4, S. Armor; No. 5, S. B. Lewis. No. 3 was held over.

This completing the nominations, the convention at 3:30 p.m. adjourned sine die.

THE SECEDERS.

The seceding delegates got together on the outside of the building and appointed an indignation committee to prepare an address to the people of the county, setting forth the cause for their action on the occasion. The fifth and sixth clauses of the resolutions are as follows:

"We appeal to the voters of Orange county not to permit a sectional issue, separate in all respects from the election of officers, to be a means whereby unsuitable men may be elected to office in payment for influence exercised in behalf of the county seat. In the interest of a clean election and sound government, we urge that the issue of the county seat and the election of officers be settled by the voters as separate and independent questions, each upon its own merits." HORATIO.

# THE BURNED TOWN.

### MORE ABOUT THE BAKERSFIELD FIRE.

#### List of the Principal Losses and Insurance—Aid Tendered from Los Angeles—The Hungry Are Fed.

*By Telegraph to The Times.*

BAKERSFIELD, July 8.—[By the Associated Press.] One life was lost in yesterday's fire. Patrick O'Donnell, aged 45 years, was burned to death in the St. James Hotel.

The following are the heavier approximate losses and insurance:

Southern Hotel $142,000, insurance $55,000; the boarders $5000, no insurance.

Dinkelspiel Bros. $75,000, insurance $55,000.

Kern Valley Bank $25,000, no insurance.
L. McKelvey $8000, insurance $4000.
Masonic Temple $20,000, insurance $14,000.
A. C. Maude $15,000, insurance $3000.
Kern Californian $10,000
Mrs. Denver $6000, insurance $5000.
A. Kratzmer $8000, insurance $3500.
P. Galtes $35,000, insurance $17,500.
H. M. F. Levison $8000, insurance $5000.
Chinatown $35,000.
A. P. Eyreud $40,000.
A. J. McLeod $22,000, insurance $2500.
Mrs. F. A. Tracey $8000, insurance $3000.
J. Wallers $9000, insurance $5100.
S. W. Wible $20,000, insurance $4200.
H. Hirschfield $30,000, insurance $15,000.
Haggin's Land Department $2000.
A. Weill $60,000, insurance $25,000.
J. Neiderauer $12,000, insurance $5000.
Goldburg & Gumpertz $17,000, insurance $6000.
O. O. Matson $25,000, insurance $10,000.
O. D. Fish $15,000, insurance $6,000.
Arlington Hotel $9800, insurance $5000.
W. H. Scribner $25,000, insurance $7,000.
G. H. Wheeler $20,000, insurance $8000.
J. S. Drury $10,000, insurance $4500.
O'Boyle Bros. $30,000, insurance $16,000.
W. H. Harron $10,000, insurance, $5000.

The small losses are not here enumerated nor is all the insurance yet known, but the losses known aggregate $899,500, insurance $340,150.

Early this morning from Carr & Haggin's ranches came three teams, the first loaded with meat, the second with vegetables, and the third with groceries, under orders to go to every house and hand over every thing that was asked for, free of charge. Los Angeles, through its Mayor this morning tendered anything that Bakersfield should ask for. A meeting of citizens was called to return thanks for the sympathy manifested.

## BASE-BALL.

### The Giants Open Their New Grounds Auspiciously.

NEW YORK, July 8.—[By the Associated Press.] The Giants' new grounds, at One Hundred and Fifty-fifth street and Eighth avenue, were formally opened this afternoon. The various entrances had to be closed long before the game started, as at that time every foot of ground from where the game could be seen was occupied. Several trainloads arrived, but the would-be spectators went sorrowfully back to the city, after offering the gate-keepers sums ranging from $1 to $10 to allow them to enter the grounds. The Giants won, Pittsburgh's errors making the result:

| | | | | | | | | | | |
|---|---|---|---|---|---|---|---|---|---|---|
| New York | 0 | 0 | 4 | 0 | 1 | 0 | 0 | 2 | 0 | —7 |
| Pittsburgh | 0 | 0 | 2 | 0 | 0 | 0 | 0 | 3 | 0 | —5 |

Base hits: New York, 14; Pittsburgh, 7. Errors: New York, 1; Pittsburgh, 9. Batteries: Crane and Ewing, Galvin and Miller. Umpire, Powers.

PHILADELPHIA, July 8.—The Phillies had it all their own way in the opening game with Indianapolis this afternoon.

| | | | | | | | | | | |
|---|---|---|---|---|---|---|---|---|---|---|
| Philadelphia | 1 | 1 | 3 | 0 | 2 | 3 | 1 | 0 | 0 | —11 |
| Indianapolis | 1 | 0 | 0 | 0 | 0 | 0 | 0 | 0 | 0 | —1 |

Base hits: Philadelphia, 14; Indianapolis, 5. Errors: Philadelphia, 1; Indianapolis, 7. Batteries: Shriver and Sanders, Daily and Getzein and Rusie. Umpire, McQuaid.

WASHINGTON, July 8.—The Senators broke their long list of defeats today by outplaying Chicago in a well-contested and interesting game.

| | | | | | | | | | | |
|---|---|---|---|---|---|---|---|---|---|---|
| Washington | 0 | 1 | 0 | 0 | 0 | 3 | 0 | 0 | 0 | —4 |
| Chicago | 0 | 0 | 1 | 1 | 0 | 0 | 1 | 0 | 0 | —3 |

Base hits: Washington, 4; Chicago, 7. Errors: Washington, 3; Chicago, 2; Batteries: Mack and Ferson, Hutchinson and Farrell. Umpire, Lynch.

BOSTON, July 8.—The home team won this afternoon through their excellent playing.

| | | | | | | | | | | |
|---|---|---|---|---|---|---|---|---|---|---|
| Boston | 0 | 6 | 0 | 0 | 0 | 0 | 0 | 0 | 0 | —6 |
| Cleveland | 0 | 0 | 0 | 0 | 0 | 0 | 1 | 0 | 0 | —1 |

Base hits: Boston, 9; Cleveland, 6. Errors: Boston, 2; Cleveland, 4. Batteries: Clarkson and Bennett; Bakely and Zimmer. Umpire, Curry.

CINCINNATI, July 8.—Athletics, 3; Cincinnati, 11.

ST. LOUIS, July 8.—St. Louis, 14; Columbus, 0.

KANSAS CITY, July 8.—Brooklyn, 8; Kansas City, 4.

LOUISVILLE, July 8.—Baltimore, 2; Louisville, 5.

### Ex-Premier Norquay's Obsequies.

WINNIPEG, July 8.—The late John Norquay, ex-Premier of Manitoba, was given a state burial this afternoon. The militia, police, fire brigade, judges, members of the Legislature, Board of Trade, City Council and other civic bodies took part in the parade. The funeral was the largest ever seen in the Canadian Northwest.

# SULLIVAN WINS.

## Kilrain Defeated in the Great Fight.

### The Baltimore Man Faces the Bostonian for Seventy-five Rounds,

### But Is Practically Beaten from the Beginning.

#### Kilrain Weeps and Hints that He Was Drugged—Thirty Thousand People Witness the Big Fight.

*By Telegraph to The Times.*

NEW ORLEANS, July 8.—[By the Associated Press.] The big fight is over. Kilrain has been fairly, squarely, honestly and honorably whipped in a contest in which the beaten man has no cause to be ashamed of his defeat. There is no manner of doubt that Jake Kilrain is a game man and a good fighter, and the men who saw him fight today will put up their money on him the next time he enters the ring against any living man except Sullivan. No account of this much-talked-of contest will be complete unless the thread of narratives is taken up at the time of the departure of the first train from New Orleans on Monday. At 1:30 o'clock the rush for admission to the $15 coaches was something indescribable. Thousands of men surrounded the depot for hours before the announced time of departure, and madly jostled each other for a favorable position. When the doors were fairly opened the crush was frightful, and 200-pound men were lifted off their feet and suspended in the air by mere force of the forward and backward pressure. It took nearly two hours to seat the $15-ticket holders, and some had to occupy camp stools in the aisles. Just before the $15 train started from New Orleans it was discovered that scores of men and boys had concealed themselves on the cross-beams connecting the wheels, while others hung on to the long iron rods connecting the trucks. The greater number, however, were perched on the roofs of the cars, in some cases as many as 25 on a coach. The interlopers were discovered and driven off by the police before starting, but, once the train was in motion, they swarmed back like so many flies, and remained to the end of the journey. Ninety per cent. of the foolhardy actors were beardless boys, ranging from 13 to 19. The most reckless deed of all was that of three young rascals, who concealed themselves on the inner side of the cowcatcher, and were never disclosed.

THE RING AT RICHBURG.

The ring was pitched at Richburg, Miss., in a clearing on the edge of a pine forest near the little village. The ring was on a patch of green turf, and surrounding it on three sides were tiers of seats ten feet high, put up by an enterprising local speculator, who charged $2 for the privilege of a seat. Unfortunately, however, he occupied the space set aside for the inner-ring seat-holders, and those who had paid $15 for accommodation there claimed the right to sit in the improvised amphitheater without extra charge. The local man, who had taken the risk of receiving $2 for the occupancy of the seats, appealed to the crowd to pay him, and made the point that the gentlemen who were occupying them were in honor bound to accept his terms. The crowd jeered the suggestion.

The alleged reporter's stand was composed of three rows of seats on a level with the ring and provided with a rough wooden board in front of them to be used as rests for writing pads. There was room for 20 in each row, but the occupants of the second row could see nothing, their view being obstructed by those who sat on the same level in the first row. Outside of the ring the villagers sat on wood and wagons piled with lumber, while others enjoyed the sight from rudely constructed platforms, six or seven feet high. Small boys as usual had the best view from elevated perches in surrounding pine trees. Enterprising photographers had three cameras in position on ladders and took views of the crowd and surroundings.

It was 8 o'clock when the first train reached Richburg, but even at that early hour the three upper rows of seats were found occupied by Richburgers who had sat on their elevated perches since daylight waiting for the show to begin. The assembled multitude sat broiling under the blaze of the hot sun. Those who had umbrellas were allowed to open them, but the intimation was plain and general that when the fight began umbrellas would have to go. After paying $15, and after coming a hundred miles to see the fight, the crowd was in no temper to tolerate any obstructions to the view. The general aspect of the crowd was anything but tough. The hoodlum element was largely outnumbered by an eminently respectable crowd. Professional men, merchants and bankers, some from New Orleans and others from neighboring States, were present to a preponderating degree. Many of the spectators came from points as far distant as San Francisco in the West and New York and Boston in the East, but these were mostly of the sporting variety, bookmakers, gamblers and professional pugilists.

PASSING THE MILITIA.

While the holders of gilt-edge tickets at $15 each were disembarking and scrambling for places of vantage at the ring side, the $10 people on the second train were having experiences between New Orleans and the battle-ground. At 2:40 o'clock the train, which was booked to leave at 2 o'clock, started, and then those who had secured seats settled themselves comfortably, many going to sleep. At every station crowds of people shouted at the train as it rushed by, but no stop was made. About a mile beyond East Pearl River a company of Mississippi militia who had been sent down to the State line yesterday afternoon to prevent the fight, was found. The speed of the train had been increased, and it ran by them at the rate of 40 miles an hour, the crowds hooting and yelling at them in derision. In the last coach were a number of prominent sports from the East. Principal among them were Joe Coburn, Dominick McCaffrey, Birt Foley and Billy Madden. It was a noteworthy fact that although the passengers on train No. 2 had among them some of the roughest characters in New Orleans, they were very quiet and orderly. Few of them were drunk.

At 9 o'clock the second train reached the battle ground, after several vexatious and long delays. The locomotive did not have power enough to draw the train up the grade of a round curve. The coaches were also in poor running order, hot boxes being frequent and causing much delay. Within 13 miles of the battle ground half of the train was detached to wait the return of the locomotive. When the train arrived at its destination a rush was made to the ring, which was pitched half a mile from the depot.

A BROILING MULTITUDE.

It was 9 o'clock and ten minutes before the train of the $10 men made its appearance, and in five minutes after its arrival the amphitheater was packed with a mass of eager and perspiring humanity, something like 30,000 in number. By this time a friendly cloud spread over the face of the sun and tempered its burning rays. The crowd waited patiently and in good humor. Many were hungry, all thirsty and tired, but there was no relief except at the hands of a colored man who peddled cheese sandwiches of doubtful age at 15 cents apiece, while another colored man peddled


[Continued on Fourth Page.]

THE POLICE BOSSES Were treated to a real sensation at their meeting yesterday. ARMY HEADQUARTERS Are to be moved from Los Angeles to the city of San Francisco.

# The Los Angeles Times.

THE KENTUCKY DERBY Was won by Riley in 2:45, the slowest time on record. FURTHER ACCOUNTS Of the high-handed doings of the Democratic Mayor of Cedar Keys.

NINTH YEAR. LOS ANGELES, THURSDAY, MAY 15, 1890. PRICE: Single Copies 5 Cents. By the Week, 5 Cents.



# A TERRORIZED TOWN.

## A Reign of Terror at Cedar Keys, Fla.

Further Accounts of the Antics of the Democratic Mayor.

Carlisle Gaining in the Contest for the United States Senate.

Tammany Succeeds in Staving Off Inquiry Into Recently Exposed Scandals—Triple Murder in Pennsylvania.

*By Telegraph to The Times.*

CEDAR KEYS (Fla.), May 14.—[By the Associated Press.] A United States marshal and four deputies arrived here last night for the purpose of arresting Mayor Cottrell and the City Marshal on the charge of interfering with Government business. The City Marshal has been arrested, but Cottrell is hiding. A perfect reign of terror has been created by the actions of these two men for several weeks past. Some of their deeds were related in yesterday's dispatches. Full details of what they have been doing will not be known until Cottrell is locked up, for people do not dare to speak against him as long as he is at liberty.

He has had men whipped, and has insulted women. He has paraded the streets with a loaded shotgun threatening to kill people. He shot at the lighthouse-keeper, cut a man with a knife, and forced his own reëlection, because it was worth a man's life to vote against him.

He made his mistake, however, when he assaulted Collector of Customs Pinkerton, and has now drawn upon himself the Federal force.

Cottrell was formerly an inspector of customs under the Democratic Collector, but was removed by the present Administration, and has been very bitter toward the Republican Collector, finally assaulting and threatening to kill him.

### TAMMANY RELIEVED.

The Inquiry Into Its Methods Staved Off for a Time.

CHICAGO, May 14.—[By the Associated Press.] A special from New York says: It is believed there will be no more meetings of the legislative investigation committee for some time. It is rumored that a deal has been fixed up to stop the inquiry into the affairs of the city, much to the relief of the Tammany leaders. Ivins of the committee is going to Europe, and will remain abroad all summer. Whether Boardman will continue the investigation or not during the summer will be decided at a secret caucus which meets this afternoon.

Senator Fassett is in the city, and will attend the caucus.

"You may depend upon it that there will be no investigation until just before election," said an independent politician.

The wife of Senator Fassett is one of the heirs of the late Charles Crocker. The Crocker estate in California will be divided on June 5th, and Senator Fassett will go to California to protect his wife's interest.

### A GHASTLY CRIME.

A Family of Three Persons Butchered at Their Home.

WASHINGTON (Pa.), May 14.—[By the Associated Press.] News reached here today of a triple murder, committed at Bentleysville, near here, last night. John Crouch, an aged and wealthy farmer, his wife and grown-up son, were found this morning with their throats cut from ear to ear. The door of the house was standing open, and the bed clothing, furniture and walls were bespattered with blood. The scene was horrible and the news spread rapidly about the village. The murdered persons were the wealthiest in that section of the country, and the theory is that the murder was committed to get money, which it was generally supposed they kept about the house. Searching parties started out in all directions, but no clew was found of the perpetrators. There being no telegraph or telephone facilities nothing more can be learned tonight.

### CARLISLE GAINING

In the Race for Beck's Seat in the Senate.

FRANKFORT (Ky.), May 14.—[By the Associated Press.] The Democratic caucus tonight took four ballots, only six names being voted upon: Carlisle, McCreary, Lindsay, Knott, Moore and Settle. Messrs. Buckner, McKinsey and Reeves were left out entirely.

The fourth ballot stood: Carlisle, 39, a gain of 5 over the first ballot; McCreary, 12, a gain of 2 over the first ballot; Lindsay, 28; Knott, 16; Moore, 12; Settle, 7.

Carlisle is undoubtedly stronger tonight, and his men are in a mood to push the contest to a close tomorrow.

### A Pair of Bond Thieves.

NEW YORK, May 14.—Regarding the robbery of John H. Wallace, editor of Wallace's Monthly, Inspector Byrnes says the party who stole the $40,000 worth of bonds from Wallace was Leslie McLeod, assistant editor of the magazine. It was at first supposed that young Robert Wallace stole them. McLeod has been identified by officials of the Safe Deposit Company as the man who went to the vaults on Wednesday and on Thursday morning the bonds were missing. It is known that young Wallace on Thursday afternoon negotiated $10,000 worth of bonds. On the same day he took a steamer for Havana. Great surprise is expressed at the action of young Wallace.

### Two Hungarians Killed.

CLEARFIELD (Pa.), May 14.—A work train on the Beach Creek road was run into by a local freight today 25 miles from here. Two Hungarians were killed and several seriously hurt.

### DEMANDS CONCEDED.

A Railroad Grants the Requests of its Employes.

TERRE HAUTE (Ind.), May 14.—[By the Associated Press.] For several days there have been rumors of trouble on the Ohio and Mississippi road. Grand Chief Sargent of the Brotherhood of Firemen was asked about it tonight, and said that 30 days ago a grievance committee of engineers and firemen asked President Barnard for a change in wages and certain rules. He offered some concessions to the engineers, who declined them unless the firemen were recognized. On May 6th Chief Arthur of the engineers and Chief Sargent of the firemen called but Barnard refused to treat with them as official representatives of their brotherhoods.

The Supreme Council of the Confederation of Railway Employés, consisting of officers of the firemen, brakemen, conductors and switchmen, was notified and had an interview yesterday with President Barnard. After considerable discussion an agreement was reached by which the labor organizations were recognized for the first time on this road. An increase in wages was obtained and changes in rules for the benefit of the men also. One interesting feature of the agreement is that the council which the engineers have so far kept out of secured the benefits for the engineers.

## A GRAND WEDDING.

YOUNG SENATOR WOLCOTT THE HAPPY MAN.

His Bride a Well-known Society Lady of Buffalo, N. Y.—The Ceremony Performed in That City.

*By Telegraph to The Times.*

BUFFALO, May 14.—[By the Associated Press.] At high noon today St. Paul's Cathedral was the scene of a beautiful wedding, when Rt. Rev. Arthur Cleveland Cox, Bishop of the diocese of western New York, united in marriage Hon. Edward Oliver Wolcott, United States Senator from Colorado, and Mrs. Frances Metcalfe Bass, daughter of the late James H. Metcalfe. As the choir boys were chanting, the procession turned into the center aisle. They were followed by the ushers, George Porter, Thomas Carr, Carleton Smith and George Carey; the bride coming last with her son, Lyman Metcalfe Bass. The best man was Henry R. Wolcott and among the group of friends who stood near were Hon. Sherman S. Rogers, Robert Cameron Rogers and Mr. and Mrs. Edwin T. Evans.

The bridal robe, a Worth creation, was of white satin. It was brocaded in roses, forming a train which opened over a petticoat of plain white satin, banded with fringes of crystal and silver. It had a slightly pointed bodice with collar of point lace and full front of silk mull, finished with a cincture of white and silver, below which fell a mull sash softly turned into a truelover's knot, while at the throat sparkled the groom's gift, a superb pendant of diamonds, formed of immense stones surrounded by smaller ones. The flowers carried were a cluster of La France roses.

After the ceremony breakfast was served at the residence of Mrs. James H. Metcalfe, on North street. At 4 o'clock Senator and Mrs. Wolcott left for New York in a special car, the interior of which was filled with flowers.

The groom is a descendant of Oliver Wolcott, who was in Washington's Cabinet, and for over a quarter of a century his ancestors were governors of Connecticut. He has the honor of being the youngest United States Senator. The cards announced that Mr. and Mrs. Wolcott will be at home on Thursday, June 5th and 12th, from 4 until 6 o'clock, at 1221 Connecticut avenue, the beautiful residence built in Washington by Senator Cameron for his daughter.

### SOUTHERN METHODISTS.

Strong Prohibition Resolutions Reported—Action Deferred.

ST. LOUIS, May 14.—[By the Associated Press.] In the general conference of the Methodist Church, South, the committee on revivals recommended various changes in the discipline for the benefit of Methodists in Mexico. The publishing committee recommended the offering of a premium for a series of catechisms. A lively debate followed.

The committee on temperance reported in favor of unfermented wine for the sacraments whenever practicable, and approved the resolutions introduced last week opposing all laws licensing or permitting the manufacture or sale of intoxicating liquors as a beverage, "because," says the report, "such laws provide for a continuance of the traffic, and furnish no protection against its ravages. The proper attitude of Christians toward the drink traffic should be uncompromising opposition, and voluntary total abstinence is the sole and true ground of personal temperance, and complete legal prohibition of the traffic is the duty of the Government."

The report went to the calendar, and will, no doubt, cause much debate when it comes up for consideration.

### Snow in the East.

NECHE (N. D.), May 14.—Eight inches of snow fell last night, and it is still snowing.

ST. PAUL, May 14.—Snow and rain fell in Northern Minnesota and North Dakota today and farmers welcome it for their crops. In most places the snow was quite heavy.

### Fell Down a Shaft.

SAN ANDREAS, May 14. — Robert Benson, aged 22 years, fell into an unused shaft 45 feet deep at Central Hill and was almost instantly killed.

### San Franciscans at Baltimore.

BALTIMORE, May 14.—Mr. and Mrs. Spear arrived today from San Francisco to attend the national conference of Charities and Corrections.

### A Floral Festival.

SANTA CRUZ, May 14.—The floral festival, under the patronage of the Woman's Aid Society, opened this morning at the Fair Pavilion to continue through the week.

# RILEY THE WINNER.

## The Slowest Kentucky Derby on Record.

The Race Run Over the Muddiest of Tracks—Time, 2:45.

Letcher Comes in Second and Robespierre Takes Third Place.

Other Events of the Opening Day at the Louisville Course—The Linden Park Racing Record—Other Sporting News.

*By Telegraph to The Times.*

LOUISVILLE (Ky.), May 14.—[By the Associated Press.] The features of the opening day of the spring meeting of the Louisville Jockey Club were great crowds, some very lively, though not heavy betting, and mud; and then the Kentucky Derby, which was run in the slowest time on record. It rained heavily all night and until 10 o'clock this morning. At 2 o'clock the heavens were clear, and when the bell called for the first race, fully twenty thousand people were present. While the bets placed by individuals were not heavy, except in a few instances, the aggregate of money that changed hands was very great. A good many were unable to place their money, as the jam was so great. The track was slush at the opening. The slightest canter scattered the mud for several feet on either side, and with every great bound in running, mud and water dashed yards away in every direction. As the racing progressed, the mud dried a little, and became more sticky.

The opening events were as follows: Five furlongs, 2-year-olds—Grandpa won, Liberty Bell second, Gen. Caldwell third. Time, 1:07½.

Mile, all ages—Uncle Bob won, Glockner second, Warpeak third. Time, 1:46½.

THE DERBY.

Next came the Derby, and Riley won it. None of the other five could touch him on that muddy track, and it is doubtful if Bill Letcher, who alone proved to be in the same class, could have pushed the great son of Longfellow even over a dry track. Isaac Murphy's riding was superb. The occasion required a jockey who could keep his horse in hand and prevent him from killing himself by running away. Murphy did this admirably. He had his horse under complete control throughout, held him back to let the others set the pace through the mud, kept the way open before him to take advantage of every favor the dreadful track offered, and win the race.

There were six starters: Riley (Murphy), Prince Fonso (Overton), Palisade (Britton), Bill Letcher (Allen), Robespierre (Francis), Outlook (Breckinridge).

They were off with the first tap of the drum, with Letcher in the lead, Palisade second, Outlook third, the others bunched. At the quarter Robespierre led, Outlook was second, Palisade third, and the others were scattered. At the half Riley was first by a head in front of Robespierre. At the three-quarters Riley began his race, and the rest began whipping for life. Riley went to the front, Bill Letcher being second, Robespierre third, and the rest straggling.

In the stretch Riley was two lengths in front of Letcher and coming easily, and Robespierre was third. Letcher then began to come under a heavy whip, and for a moment it looked like his race, but Murphy loosened the reins and Riley responded nobly, coming under the wire a winner by a length and three quarters. Robespierre was a length behind Letcher; Palisade was back two lengths more, and Fonso nearly neck and neck with him, while Outlook was 10 lengths in the rear. Time, 2:45.

CLOSING EVENT.

Three-quarters of a mile, heats, all ages—First heat: White Nose won, Loveland second, Friendless third; time, 1:19½. Second heat: White Nose won, Loveland second, Banner Bearer third; time, 1:20.

### Linden Park Races.

LINDEN PARK, May 14.—This was the closing day of the meeting.

Six and a half furlongs—Stockton won, Gloster second, Lady Pulsifer third. Time, 1:22½.

Five furlongs—[illegible]saquena filly won, Mandolin colt second, Trestle third. Time, 1:02½.

Mile—Supervisor won, Black Thorn second, Puzzle third. Time, 1:43½.

Seven-eighths of a mile—Prince Howard won, Brian Boru second, Stonemason third. Time, 1:30½.

Five-eighths of a mile—Coapman won, Osceola second, Little Barefoot third. Time, 1:03.

Six and a half furlongs—Bill Barnes won, Louis E. second, Bohemian third. Time, 1:22.

Five furlongs—Buckstone won, King Arthur second, John Atwood third. Time, 1:03.

### The Congregationalists.

SANTA BARBARA, May 14. — The fourth annual convention of the general Congregational Association of Southern California assembled here today. About one hundred delegates are in attendance.

The convention of the Woman's Home Missionary Society of the Congregational Church of Southern California is also in session.

### A School-book Combine.

INDIANAPOLIS, May 14.—A St. Louis special to the Sentinel announces that the new American School-book Company recently organized, has acquired a controlling interest in the Standard School-book Company of St. Louis. The Standard is the most extensive school-book concern outside of the combination.

### The Odd Fellows.

SAN FRANCISCO, May 14.—At the session of the Odd Fellows' Grand Lodge this morning, a series of amendments to the constitution were adopted.

# THE BLUE TRIUMPHANT.

## Yale Defeats Harvard in the Great Football Match.

### Twenty Thousand Spectators Witness the Exciting Contest.

### The New Haven Lads Finally Victors by a Score of 10 to 0.

**The Cambridge Team Outplayed from the Start—Their Line Fatally Weak—Scenes and Incidents of the Struggle.**

*By Telegraph to The Times.*

SPRINGFIELD (Mass.,) Nov. 21.—[By the Associated Press.] The great football game is over, and Yale has won—10 to 0. Fully 20,000 people saw the blue wave victorious on Hampden Park today, and when the great contest was over it was the unanimous conviction that the best team had won. All the morning the clouds hung heavily, but later the sun came out and the last requisite was added to make the day perfect. The story of the game is simply one of the supremacy of Yale over Harvard. The Cambridge eleven was simply outplayed and the best team won. The Harvard rush line was fatally weak and of little assistance to her half-backs, while Yale's line was almost perfect. The great Heffelinger fairly eclipsed his reputation and easily proved himself to be the greatest guard in the country. Mackie was no match for him. For general all-round work behind the line Bliss carried off the honors of the day. His tackling and rushing were phenomenal. In punting he was a match for the Harvard captain. Behind the line no word of criticism can be charged to the Harvard team, but without any support they were helpless against Yale's fine tacklers. The blocking off was wretched and the Yale rushers were down on the backs before they could start. Hallowell, Newell, Lake and Corbett did some brilliant individual work, but the lack of team work neutralized it. Trafford's great punting did much to keep down the score. Much disappointment was felt with the work of the Yale captain. He managed his men finely, but when the ball went to him he repeatedly lost ground. It was a kicking game throughout. After Yale scored the first touch down in four minutes Harvard began to punt, and continued these tactics during the rest of the game. In the first half the ball was in the Harvard's territory most of the time. In the second half Harvard forced the playing much of the time and Trafford twice had a chance to try for a goal from the field but failed both times.

This city was owned today by wearers of the blue and crimson. Hotels and streets were crowded since morning, and the early and late trains added thousands to the throngs. The betting last evening was nearly even, but today odds were given on the Yales. Most of the Harvard men arrived last night and at 11:45 a.m. The Yale delegation came at noon by two special trains. Most of the city stores were decorated impartially. All the smaller New England colleges were represented, Amherst and Williams sending the largest delegations on special trains. At 11 a.m. the Yale men were offering $100 to $60, which Harvard's backers accepted readily. At 10:30 several hundred persons were waiting for the gates of Hampden Park to open, and at 11, when the gates swung back, a steady stream set in from way down Main street. This line of would-be spectators was two miles long, though the game was not to begin for three hours. Fourteen separate entrances were provided to prevent a rush, and the work of placing the vast throng and seating those entitled to seats went on with little friction. One hundred and sixty uniformed officers were on hand to preserve order.

When play began the field was in as perfect condition as could be desired. Experts pronounced it without question the best football field in the country. Not a breath of air was stirring and the weather conditions were most favorable for any game. The grand stands which encircle the entire field were packed with a gay and happy throng half an hour before the game was scheduled to begin. The long wait was enlivened by college yells and cheers, so that it did not seem long.

Harvard was first in the field. Yale followed shortly after. Harvard won the toss and took the north end. Yale had the ball. Yale gained ten yards on a wedge and McClung gained thirty yards in a run around the end. The ball was within a yard of Harvard's goal line in three minutes and a touch down was made by McClung. Yale missed a goal. Score 4 to 0 in favor of Yale. Yale then returned to center, and on a put by Trafford the ball was carried into Yale's territory, but the New Haven men were playing a powerful game and yard by yard forced the ball back until it was at Harvard's thirty-yard line. Trafford then again got the ball and again punted it back to the Yale thirty-yard line, where Yale gained possession of the ball. McCormick then punted for Yale, but little was gained and Harvard got the ball. Her men then formed a wedge and gained five yards more.

At the end of the first half the ball was near center field in Yale's territory, the score stand Yale 4, Harvard 0. The second half began at ten minutes past 3, with the ball in Harvard's keeping. After vainly trying to break through Yale's line Tafford punted for thirty yards, but Yale got the ball and began to slowly force it back to the center. Harvard finally secured the ball and it was snapped to Tafford, who, by a lucky punt, sent it to Yale's twenty-five yard line, but this availed nothing, as McCormick on a strong punt drove the ball to center, and on a fumble by Harvard got the ball. Harvard seemed to be playing a stronger game than during the first half. Bliss then started on a run around the end and gained Harvard's twenty-five yard line, but here he was downed and Trafford got in another of his punts and the ball once more went back to center, but here Bliss again got it, and by another run carried it to Harvard's twenty-five yard line. The ball was slowly worked back to the center, where it again fell into Yale's hands, but she lost it on four downs. Yale got the ball after Harvard gained ten yards, but McClung failed to get around and McCormick sent the ball to the twenty-five yard line, when Harvard got it. By a fumble Bliss got the ball and carried it across the line and McClung reached the goal; score, Yale 10, Harvard 0.

The teams were again lined up at the center and Harvard gained ten yards, but Yale soon forced the ball back to center but lost it, and Trafford tried for a goal from the field, but failed. The Harvard men began to play with desporation and soon had forced the ball to Yale's twenty-five-yard line, where Trafford again tried to kick a goal, but again failed, and Yale getting the ball, made a gain of twenty yards, but here time was called and Yale won by a score of 10 to 0.

# BURIED ALIVE.

**Several Laborers Entombed in Brooklyn—Efforts to Rescue Them.**

BROOOLYN (N. Y.,) Nov. 21.—[By the Associated Press.] This afternoon a new conduit extension under course of construction burst and submerged a number of laborers. To add to the horror a large gas pipe running parallel with the conduit broke, filling the place with gas.

Four laborers, and possibly seven, were buried alive. Hugh Murray, and two Italians, known only by numbers, were completely entombed. Another Italian was partially buried and before he could be rescued another load of sand caved in, carrying him out of sight. Ernest Pallis was rescued unconscious.

While the rescuers were at work another cavein occurred and Frank Bezine, an Italian, was buried. The work of rescue is being pushed as rapidly as possible, but it is impossible to reach the bodies before tomorrow.

# ALL WANT THE PLUM.

## Delegations at Work to Secure the Republican Convention.

**Omaha Men Try to Work the President, but in Vain—De Young Says San Francisco will Win the Prize.**

*By Telegraph to The Times.*

WASHINGTON, Nov. 21.—[By the Associated Press.] Representatives of Omaha, Minneapolis, San Francisco and Detroit have opened headquarters at the Arlington Hotel for their campaign to secure the vote of the National Republican Committee for the next national convention. Omaha, Minneapolis and San Francisco have full delegations here. Cincinnati and Detroit have their advance guards on hand, which will be reinforced tonight by the arrival of large delegations of workers. New York also had an advance guard at work here this morning and their regular headquarters were opened this afternoon, when a large delegation arrived. No delegation is expected from Chicago, as it is generally understood that the World's Fair city is satisfied with the honors already accorded her by Congress in giving her the fair.

Members of the Nebraska delegation called in a body this morning and paid their respects to the President. The visitors were cordially received, but were unable to pursuade the President to express preference for their city. Members of the delegation for Minneapolis called later in the day, but were equally unsuccessful in causing the President to commit himself.

Col. Biethen of Minneapolis, reviewing the situation tonight, said: "The West objects to New York, believing that no political aid could come from holding the convention in New York. The Mest believes that if the convention was held in the Mississippi or Missouri Valleys it would give the Republican cause great aid, insure absolute control of the Western and Northwestern States, even to the reclamation of Iowa. But the West just as radically believes that to hold the convention in New York is to surrender to Wall street. While this is puerility so far as actual effects are concerned every man here from Minneapolis, Omaha and California, would swear that it would cost the Republicans of the Mississippi and Missouri valleys from one-quarter to one-third of the granger vote, which simply means defeat in Iowa, Minnesota, Kansas and doubtful results in Wisconsin and Montana." Blethen thinks these arguments are having their effect with the committee.

"Minneapolis, Omaha and California are emphatic for an open ballot, there having been," said Blethen, "a rumor that the committee was discussing the propriety of a secret ballot. This, the West construes to be in favor of New York."

All contestants tonight aver with much confidence that they have every reason to believe that their affairs are progressing smoothly and each one thinks their city will capture the convention.

The New York city delegation reached here this afternoon, upward of 100 men, representing the Republical clubs of the city of New York, the Hotel Men's Association, General Citizens' Committee and others. Thoy have headquarters at the Arlington and are working hard tonight. Minneapolis is making a grand push for the convention. California is making a splendid show under the guidance of Editor de Young, of the San Francisco Chronicle, and Omaha's demand is being vigorously pushed by Editor Rosewater, of the Bee.

M. H. de Young, member of the National Committee from California, is gratified at the progress San Francisco is making in her fight for the convention. "There is going to be a long-drawn-out contest," he said tonight, "but San Francisco will get the prize. The prospects for it never looked brighter than they do tonight."

**An Aristocratic London Wedding.**

LONDON, Nov. 21.—Lady Sarah Isabel Augusta Spencer Churchill, youngest sister of the Duke of Marlborough and Lord Randolph Churchill, was married today to Lieut. Gordon C. Wilson, son of Sir Samuel Wilson. The ceremony took place in St. George's Church, Hanover square, the Archbishop of Canterbury officiating. The building was crowded to the doors with the wealth and fashion of England. The Prince of Wales and Duke of Cambridge were conspicuous guests.

**Snow in the East.**

ST. PAUL (Minn.,) Nov. 21.—Over half a foot of snow fell in this city and vicinity this morning.

DENVER (Colo.,) Nov. 21.—A hurricane prevailed this forenoon, which changed to a heavy snow, which continued till this evening. Telegraphic communication with the East was cut off for several hours. The weather is very cold. The storm is general throughout the State.

**Cornell Scores a Victory.**

DETROIT, Nov. 21.—The Cornell-Ann Harbor football match resulted in favor of the Ithaca boys, 58 to 12. Hard rain fell all the morning and during most of the game and made playing rather difficult.

# GRANGERS COMBINE.

## The Farmers' Alliance Gathering in Everything in Sight.

### Consolidation with the F. M. B. A. Men Practically Effected.

### The Charges Against McCune Promptly Laid on the Table.

**No Recognition Hereafter to be Paid to the Faction of the Alliance Which Opposes the Sub-treasury Scheme.**

*By Telegraph to The Times.*

INDIANAPOLIS, Nov. 21.—[By the Associated Press.] The Alliance and Farmers' Mutual Benefit Association have practically amalgamated, though each refused to adopt resolutions looking to a consolidation. But the two organizations are as firmly united as if formal resolutions had been adopted. The arrangements look to the disappearance of the Farmers' Mutual Benefit Association before its next national meeting. Last night and today the Alliance has been initiating into its membership many of the most prominent members of the Farmers' Mutual Benefit Association. They go back to their homes to proselyte among the sub-lodges. The Alliance agreed to admit sub-lodges of the Farmers' Mutual Benefit Association into the Alliance upon payment of $1 for blanks. It is reported that before the time for the next annual meeting of the Farmers' Mutual Benefit Association nearly all the lodges will have joined the Alliance.

The Supreme Council of the Alliance adopted a resolution instructing Alliance Congressmen not to enter caucuses of the old political parties. This was amended by instructing them not to vote for any man for Speaker who does not support the Ocala platform.

The committee which had the protest of the anti-sub-treasury people in hand reported that the antis refused to present their case and the matter had therefore been dropped.

U. P. Duncan of South Carolina was indorsed for appointment to the Interstate Commerce Commission vice Bragg, deceased.

Several changes were made in the constitution. One disqualifies business agents from membership, the reason being that it may become necessary for the council to sit in judgment on the agents. Other changes permit females to pay the per capita tax, thus becoming a basis for representation; repeal the clause allowing persons of mixed occupations to become members; restrict membership to farmers and farm laborers; abolish the provision by which presidents of all State Alliances are made a national legislation committee, and providing for a special committee to act as an advisory board to the president.

The council today listened to General Lecturer Wright, of the Knights of Labor, who set forth the troubles of the Clothing Union with the Rochester Labor Exchange. It will be remembered that Master Workman James Hughes was arrested and convicted on a charge of conspiracy in this lock-out case. The Council adopted resolutions condemning the exchange, expressing the belief that the jury was packed, and calling "upon all fair-minded people to let the goods of these Rochester manufacturers alone."

The charges made by McAllister of the Anti-sub-treasury Committee against McCune were laid on the table. The Committee on Federation reported, recommending confederation with the Knights of Labor, Farmers' Mutual Benefit Association and a dozen other orders. The report was accepted and delegates from each State were chosen to represent the council at the February assembly of these confederated orders.

A resolution was passed favoring the granting of pensions by the issuing of full legal tender paper money to all honorably discharged Union soldiers who were disabled or in needy circumstances.

The report of the committee appointed to confer with the anti-sub-treasury people, and which is briefly referred to above, takes occasion in closing to deny that the Supreme Council shut the door in the faces of Dr. Yeaman and friends. The report asserts that two or more of them were Alliance men, with the pass word, and could have taken seats with the council and presented their complaint. This would been an orderly and brotherly way of settlement, "but," says the report, "the refusal of Dr. Yeaman to join in public discussion involving his protest and the Ocala platform settles one fact: That it was not the desire of the anti-sub-treasuryites to inform or convince this council of error. Your committee recommends to the brotherhood that for the future no attention be given or recognition granted to any one claiming to be an Alliance man, while at the same time affiliating with the band known as the McAllister and Yeaman anti-sub-treasuryites."

**Bullion Blockade Broken.**

NEW ORLEANS, Nov. 21.—A Tampico, Mex., special says: "The bullion blockade, which has been in effect here for the past month, is broken and 22,400 bars of silver, accumulated here, are being exported as rapidly as transportation facilities will permit. This delay in bullion shipments was caused by the Monterey smelters refusing to pay the government charges of $3, made for assaying every bar exported. The assay charges have now been reduced to $2 for every 135 marks. This result is not entirely satisfactory to smelters, but they must accept it for the present."

**Texas Drought Broken.**

DENNISON (Tex.,) Nov. 21.—A drought which prevailed here since the early summer months, and caused great suffering and inconvenience, is broken. There has been a steady rain for twenty-four hours and indications point to continued rain. Thousands of tons of hay and miles of fencing were destroyed by fires caused by the excessive dry spell.

**Death of Rev. Thomas Hill.**

BOSTON, Nov. 21.—Rev. Thomas Hill, ex-president of Harvard College, died at Waltham this morning, aged 73.



# REVOLT IN PERSIA.

**The Shah's Soldiers Kill 200 Rebels and Capture Their Leaders.**

LONDON, Nov. 21.—[By Cable and Associated Press.] A dispatch from Teheran, the capital of Persia, states that the Mujtahid, or High Priest of the Shiah sect, which is the predominant religious sect of the country, its followers numbering nearly 7,000,000, recently fomented a revolt in Mazanderan, a province in Northern Persia. The government took prompt measures, but the rebels made determined resistance against the Shah's soldiers. They were not defeated until 200 of their number had been lost. The loss of the troops was twenty killed. A large number of rebels, including the leader, the priest, were taken prisoners and summary justice will be meted out to them.

# The Los Angeles Times

THE COUNTY CONVENTION CONTINUED ITS LABORS YESTERDAY. — CORBETT DEFEATED SULLIVAN IN THE TWENTY-FIRST ROUND.

ELEVENTH YEAR. TWELVE PAGES. THURSDAY MORNING, SEPTEMBER 8, 1892. 5:00 O'CLOCK A. M. PRICE: SINGLE COPIES, 5 CENTS; BY THE WEEK, 5 CENTS




# CORBETT WINS

## John L. Sullivan no Longer Champion.

### The Californian Knocks Him Out in Twenty-one Rounds.

### The Huge Bruiser Pounded to Jelly and Streaming With Blood.

**Corbett Finishes Fresh and Without a Mark—Sullivan Says He Has Fought Once too Often in the Ring.**

*By Telegraph to The Times.*

NEW ORLEANS, Sept. 7.—[By the Associated Press.] The laurels have shifted and John L. Sullivan has had some new sensations. So has James J. Corbett. One has been knocked off the pedestal of the pugilistic championship and the other has climbed into his place. The California heavyweight, Corbett, has knocked out the champion, John L. Sullivan, and won besides some $85,000. Furthermore, it appeared to spectators, if the truth be told, as though Corbett won easily.

The impression left by the rapid spectacle is that Sullivan was at no moment in the path of success, and the physical evidences of this were apparent at the finish. Corbett, the winner, at the moment of his victory, was keen, quick and alert in every round. Although marked by bruises and blood, his face was aglow with a steady interest. His face wore a half smile, and he was ready to attack his foe with a ferocious force, so that had that foe been able to rise there were conditions of victory.

Sullivan was reeking with blood, smashed, bruised, jellied and nearly, if not quite, insensible. These were the evidences of defeat and it was when these had been established that the laurels shifted and a new man had been born in the championship.

Why was Sullivan dethroned? He, himself, had contributed to the causes of his own downfall. If his life had known no excess Sullivan would have been able to fight and struggle more effectively to retain his prestige. He is not relatively so good a man at 34 as hundreds of other men at that age. His face is furrowed, not alone by years, but by his methods of living. His ponderous body also bore traces, not alone of time, but of easy living. His condition was not comparable with that of his foe. It could not be. There was a cumulation of age and wide freedom which could not be trained away without impairing the man. Sullivan, too, has been overconfident. He had been contemptuous of the needful measures for his perfect condition. He was Sullivan, and Sullivan could not lose in battle. Corbett has taught him otherwise, and now he is starting with eight years less of life's inevitable wear. Had he conserved his powers and perfected the methods of their use, charging his heart meanwhile with confidence, he would have become king of his kind. His was the

The victor and vanquished.

capital of brawn and muscle upon which to build up the fortune of victory and reputation.

It may not be carelessly said that Corbett at 26 years of age is a better man than Sullivan was at that age, but assuming that they were equally good men at equal ages, the analysis of this victory comes back to the fact that, while some men of 34 may whip some men of 26 the elder man, to be the victor, must not have added his own methods of depletion to those which the silent years so surely employ.

Sullivan came forward tonight into the glare of twenty electric lights, his senses fed by the shouts of those who will flout him now. If the majority believed in him, why should not the champion believe in himself? So while they yelled with worshiping plaudits he sat down in his corner, and with easy interest scanned the powerful fellow opposite.

Somehow there is a homage in the eager attention the trainers bestow upon their champion, and tonight, while Sullivan enjoyed this, his heavy form sunk down. As he sat awaiting for the preliminaries those who scanned him

JAMES J. CORBETT.

closely saw welts of flesh on his abdomen rolling far over the edge of his firmly drawn belt. It should not have been the obesity of age, for the man tonight should be in the prime of his years. It was the distention surely following wine suppers and hot dinners of rich food. While sitting thus under the eyes of hundreds whose scrutiny was sharpened by their money being on the result, Sullivan was in turn studying his foe. In the opposite corner, out of which all victors in the Olympic Club have gone to victory, sat a beautiful specimen of human flesh and bone. Sullivan saw a smiling and confident face; he saw a neck that had poise and strength; he saw a chest deep enough to hold a bellows; he saw a pair of browned shoulders where piles of muscles crept and glided beneath the skin. He beheld, outstretched upon the ropes, while the trainers did their service, a pair of arms as long as those of a windmill, bunched with lithe driving muscles with the blood and nerve of youth. The champion beholds a foe whose figure was clean cut and rounded in its lines. There was no adipose to clog his lungs or burden the freedom of his actions. Like a racer was Corbett, trim, solid, balanced physically at every point, unless, indeed his long legs seemed a trifle light for the muscular shoulders and body. But those who doubted the power of lithe underlimbs could not know how like steel they had been tempered to bend without breaking under stress and tension. Doubles Sullivan learned later what iron thews lay along the slender columns that held up the man.

When the fight began Corbett came up prancing, verily prancing. He teetered about Sullivan like a carpet amateur, and while the crowd laughed, Sullivan smiled as though amused. So did Corbett. But one of them grew terribly serious before the night had grown much older, while the other continued with a smile on his face, and is smiling yet. As they came up to the second round the crowd was treated to what has gone down into history as "the Sullivan rush." His awful right flew out, but finding lodgment only for an instant, a glancing shot on the back of the catlike fellow, who wheeled suddenly and slammed his left on the big man's stomach. The crowd yelled. The cheers for his foe's cleverness nettled the champion, though he smiled in a derisive way while Corbett laughed in his face. The spectacle was new to oldtimers. Never before had they seen any man laugh in Sullivan's face.

So it went on. There was an onslaught by the champion, but there was no teetering then. Straight and swift as lightning Corbett's left shot forth and landed with a shock on Sullivan's jaw. Sullivan would brook no such liberties. To be sure he had not yet landed a blow of any moment on Corbett, but after such an affront he would kill his presumptuous foe. The big fellow's jaw closed, his lower lip became pushed up against its fellow, and the crowd cried, "See Sullivan's mug now!" Corbett heeded the injunction. Again his right shot away and returned and—could it be?—blood stained Sullivan's nose and trickled over his lips.

Surely now he would grind Corbett to atoms, and he tried, but away flew Corbett's left and right, landing squarely on the damaged nose again and again. The blows splashed the blood over Sullivan's face until it was dripping with fluid. Could this be? Sullivan receiving such indignities and permitting his assailant to live? Yet so it was.

Another time the men lined up and Sullivan's face bore the prophecy of defeat. His eyes were anxious; his face was pale; it had a surprised and troubled expression, and the conviction was being forced on the crowd that there was a possibility that Sullivan was to go down. Corbett continued to land on Sullivan's stomach, jaw and three times on his bleeding nose, that was growing pulpy. Again and again Sullivan led but failed and lurched forward with the force of his unlanded blows. Could it be that he was becoming weak while Corbett was unruffled? And so it was, and so it continued from round to round until, in the fifteenth, the bleeding champion betrayed clearly the outcome of it all. It was only a matter of time.

When for the twentieth time the men stood up, hope had gone from Sullivan's face. Defeat was putting its iron in his heart. He knew it and showed it. There came a clinch and a break, and as Sullivan heavily backed away Corbett rained his face with blows until it was a mass of blood and bruises. His body was smeared with blood, he seemed heavy, and led no more, but waited only for the end. And all the time Corbett was smiling in his face.

The end was in the next, the twenty-first round. Sullivan hugged Corbett's neck, but it cost him dearly, for the fresh, agile fellow again spattered blood from Sullivan's nose. The big fellow responded as best he could, and tried to clinch. Corbett shoved the champion off. He staggered back and then began the final strokes. Corbett felt victory in his reach, and followed his man, slamming right and left on his nose, jaw, neck, eyes and mouth. Finally with a terrible swing, he knocked Sullivan clear off his feet, and a moment later the champion that was lay flat on his back, still more or less covered with blood, and as he lay there his great frame was a dire picture of the fall of the great. The count of the referee began and Sullivan moved, rolled over, got on one knee and both hands, and essayed to rise, while Corbett advanced to punch him more should he succeed. But it was useless. The great bulk of what had been the champion reeled and again went down, and the "Ten and out!" of the referee told the battle was over.

A more pitiable sight than was the champion has seldom been seen in a prize ring. Corbett leaped up then and helped to lift Sullivan to his chair. Sullivan could not recognize him. His head rolled helplessly. Corbett shook his hand and he did not know it. His star had set; a new one had risen.

### BEFORE THE FIGHT.

**Intense Excitement Everywhere—The Men at the Ringside.**

NEW ORLEANS, Sept. 7.—[By the Associated Press.] The excitement which has prevailed in this city has had no parallel since the Italian assassins were lynched eighteen months ago. There has been no subject of conversation discussed in any quarter save the fistic event of the evening, in which every portion of the country is more or less deeply interested. It apparently effected the outside world as deeply as it did the participants in the battle. Both Sullivan and Corbett were known to be in prime condition, and the greatest fight of the series was looked forward to by all with keenness. There was a universal move in the direction of the Olympic Club even before the evening began to fall. Business men, lawyers and journalists took their dinners down town and had their vehicles ordered early. They were willing to wait at the club, but they were unwilling to waste time in going down. At 6 o'clock carriages were already heading down Canal street, which was crowded with people, and vehicles were passing down the intersecting streets, the carriages reaching the scene of battle. Down in the neighborhood of the club for blocks and blocks carriages were strung along the curbstones and every street corner had a crowd.

The Sullivan poople came to the club first. They took a carriage at the hotel before 7 o'clock and drove leisurely down with a string of hacks. Sullivan looked strong and determined. He walked with a jaunty air and came in so easy with a line of people entering at the time that few noticed him.

Big Jim Corbett followed in the wake of the champion, coming in fifteen minutes later. When his party pulled up in front of the door the street was cleared and an avenue opened into the building. Corbett came in first with a light step and his face wreathed in smiles. The first sign of the contest for the championship of America came in the person of Police Captain Barrett, who went into the ring at five minutes before 9 o'clock. The scales upon which the gloves were weighed were laid beside the center of the post. Ex-Mayor Guillotte, who acted as master of ceremonies, entered the arena a few minutes later and made a speech, warning the spectators not to violate any of the rules of the club.

Sullivan entered the ring first. He was dressed in green trunks and black shoes and socks. He looked in perfect condition. Corbett followed a moment later, looking pale and finely drawn beside his bulky antagonist. He wore an air of confidence, however. He smiled and nodded to his acquaintances around the ring, though he was said by some people to be a little nervous.

Police Captain Barrett stepped to the center of the ring and presented Prof. John Duffy with a beautiful silver ice bowl and ladel. John Donaldson and Billy Delaney were announced as Corbett's seconds with Bat Masterson as timekeeper. Charles Johnson and Jack McAuliffe were the seconds for John L. Sullivan. Frank Moran was his timekeeper. In the toss for corners Corbett won and chose the lucky one that Dixon and McAuliffe fought in.

Gloves were weighed and found to be according to law and they were given to the fighters. In the parley which was held in the center of the ring, Corbett looked entirely out-classed in point of build, though his friends relied upon his cleverness to win the battle. The pivot blow and back heeling were barred by mutual consent, and the men after agreeing to fight fair went to their corners to get ready for the fray.

### THE BATTLE BY ROUNDS.

**How the Californian Outfought and Conquered the Champion.**

NEW ORLEANS, Sept. 7.—[By the Associated Press.] It was 9:10 o'clock when the men stepped to the center of the ring. They shook hands and time was called.

First round—Both men stopped, lightly countering, and Sullivan immediately became the aggressor. He made a left lead, but was stopped. Corbett danced all about his opponent, eyeing him closely. Sullivan made a rush, but Jim backed away. Sullivan also attempted a left-hander, but Jim cleverly avoided it. Sullivan looked vicious as he played for an opening. He next attempted a right-hand stomach punch, but the blow fell short. Sullivan tried to corner Jim, but the latter slipped away. The gong sounded and not a blow had been landed by either man.

Second round—Sully was still the aggressor. He upper cut Jim and touched him again with his left hand a little later. Jim eyed his man closely, and when Sullivan rushed the Californian would slip away. Sullivan landed a heavp right on the shoulder, but received a stomach punch in return.

Third round—Corbett ducked away from a heavy lunge. Sully followed him about the ring trying for his stomach. Jim's head missed a heavy left hander, and Sully looked vicious. Jim landed two heavy stomach punches and Sully missed a vicious right. Each hit the other on the head. Corbett then stepped out of harm's way, but came back quickly and landed his left on the stomack. He also planted a heavy blow on the champion's ear, sending his head back. Both men were fighting hard when the gong sounded. Sullivan was ringing wet with perspiration.

Fourth round—Sullivan missed with his left, but he chased Jim around the ring, and finally landed a light left. Corbett stepped up close, attempting to punch the stomach, but John was guarding with the right. The champion followed up his man all over the ring, but received a heavy left-hand swing for his pains. Jim landed with both hands on Sullivan's head as the round ended, and the champion went to his corner with a sneering smile.

Fifth round—Sullivan stepped to the center with a smile, and Corbett touched his nose with his left. The champion tried to land his left on the stomach and the men clinched, Sullivan landing his first heavy right. Sullivan missed a fearful left-hander and staggered forward from the force of the blow. Tha men boxed cautiously for an opening, and the champion seemed eager for hot work. He followed his antagonist all around the ring. The first blood came from Sullivan's nose. The fighting was fast and furious, and Sullivan nearly fell on the ropes from left-hand jabs on the head. As the round ended Corbett landed a heavy right on the champion's head.

Sixth round—Both men landed light lefts and Sullivan's nose was bleeding again. The champion war beginning to look tired, for he missed with his right as he aimed for the jaw. Corbett took plenty of time and used the entire ring to maneuver in. He landed a light stomach punch and hit the champion in the face. A little later there was a heavy exchange of lefts on the head, and Sullivan seemed angry. He slapped his opponent with his left hand, but Corbett landed with blows on the head and ran away. The men walked to the center of the ring and it began to look as if some of the fight was out of Sully. Jim landed a heavy left on Sullivan's head and the champion went to his corner, looking tired.

Seventh round—Corbett walked right up to Sullivan and barely avoided a left-hand punch. The champion kept trying his hardest for a right on the jaw, but the foxy Corbett was not there. The champion landed two light blows on the head, and Corbett sent in hot shot from his left. He jabbed Sullivan continually on the nose in this round and blood flowed freely. Jim was cheered to the echo for his skillful fighting. Sullivan was forced on the ropes by a heavy right on the jaw, and, as the gong sounded, received a heavy left on the jaw.

Eighth round—Sullivan landed a light left on the stomach and received a left on the mouth. Jim was now the aggressor. Sullivan hit Corbett in a clinch and the audience yelled "foul." Both exchanged heavy lefts, but Jim cleverly ducked a mighty right. Jim, after a narrow escape from another right, sent his left in the champion's stomach, forcing him to the ropes. Jim landed a heavy left on the mouth, which brought blood and a smile from the champion, who looked fatigued.

Ninth round—Sullivan was puffing when he came up this time. Both exchanged good lefts. Sullivan received a light one on the ear and got another on the nose, but evened up matters a little with his right. Jim landed a heavy left on the nose and both men hugged each other in a clinch. Sullivan was missing many of his blows now, although when he did land his blows were twice as heavy as those of his antagonist. Jim had much the best of Sullivan.

Tenth round—Sullivan attempted to land a left, but the blow fell short. He followed his opponent, however, and

### POINTS OF THE MORNING'S NEWS.

BY TELEGRAPH.

No cases of cholera have occurred in New York city and the scare is subsiding, but reports from Hamburg show no abatement of the disease....The poet Whittier is dead....Sensational testimony was brought out in the McWhirter inquest at Fresno....Vermont has gone overwhelmingly Republican....The American Bankers' Association is in session in San Francisco....More Christians have been massacred in China....Nancy Hanks trotted a mile in 2:07 on a regulation track at St. Paul....Senator Cullom made a great speech at Joliet, Ill.

IN AND ABOUT THE CITY.

A day of surprises in the Republican County Convention....The Colonels won the opening game of the Oakland-Los Angeles series....Native Sons to leave for Santa Barbara today....Meeting of the Southern California World's Fair Association....The city flooded with "green goods" circulars.

# 1893
# 1902

THE WORLD MADE LITTLE NOTE OF A MEETING ORGANIZED IN PARIS IN 1894 BY PIERRE DE COUBERTIN, a young French baron with the quixotic notion that sports could help bring peace to a troubled world. Seventy-nine delegates from nine nations, including the United States, responded to Baron de Coubertin's invitation and agreed to revive the Olympic Games, selecting Athens, Greece, for the First Olympiad of modern times.

For two years Baron de Coubertin pursued his noble ideal, telling everyone who would listen that the day competition "among oarsmen, runners, and fencers took its place among the customs of Europe, the cause of peace [would] have received a new and powerful support."

Sports, he reasoned, would produce better humans; better humans would produce a better world; and a better world would produce peace. On April 5, 1896, fifteen centuries after Emperor Theodosius I of Rome had banned the ancient Games because they had disintegrated into pagan festivals, the Olympics were born again when King George I of Greece declared open the Games of the First Olympiad.

Only a handful of Americans competed in what was largely a European show that got little publicity in this country. The first Games got off to a shaky start, mired in political controversy, setting a tone that marred almost every Olympics that followed.

While Greek sports fans accepted the Games with enthusiasm, historians noted that politicians didn't think much of the idea. There was no official support from a country in political turmoil. Suggestions were made that the Games be delayed until 1900 to celebrate the start of a new century and be moved to Paris. The baron's estimate of expenses was challenged and a threat made that the Greek government would not authorize a lottery to raise money for the Games. Baron de Coubertin, in fact, made plans to move the competition to Budapest if Greece rejected it.

But with the help of Greece's Crown Prince, Baron de Coubertin won the fight, and the Games remained in Athens. Americans won nine of the twelve track and field events and three gold medals in pistol shooting. The competition also included weightlifting, Greco–Roman wrestling, swimming, cycling, lawn tennis, fencing, and gymnastics.

Ironically, following the success of the first Games, the Greeks said the festival belonged to them permanently, an idea supported by American athletes but opposed by Baron de Coubertin. An argument for making Athens the permanent home of the Olympics was to be heard again in the 1970s and 1980s after the murders in Munich, the scandalous costs of Montreal, and the boycott of Moscow.

But the 1900 Olympics were held instead in Paris as scheduled. Again, there was almost as much controversy as competition. The games were so poorly organized and so spoiled by "athletic politics . . . it was indeed a wonder that the Olympic movement survived," wrote former *Times* Sports Editor Bill Henry in his history of the Games.

There was little evidence after the first two revivals of this ancient competition that it would become the world's biggest and most important sports event. And only three more Olympics would be held before war would cancel one.

The United States continued its domination of track and field events at Paris, winning seventeen of the twenty-three, but won only one other competition, the tug of war. Other new events included rowing, yachting, archery, and water polo.

Americans were more interested in professional baseball than they were in a tug of war, archery, and gymnastics among amateurs in foreign countries. Boston, Baltimore, Brooklyn, and Pittsburgh dominated the National League, and in an era when a home-run champion might hit fewer than ten a season, Bobby Lowe of Boston and Ed Delahanty of Philadelphia became the first two batters to hit four in one game.

Bob Fitzsimmons, a boxer from England who never weighed more than 170 pounds, won the heavyweight championship in 1897 by knocking out Jim Corbett in fourteen rounds. Undefeated as middleweight champion, Fitzsimmons lost his heavyweight championship the first time he defended it when Jim Jeffries stopped him in eleven rounds in 1899.

The purse for the Kentucky Derby, which was more than $500,000 in 1982, had grown to $6,000 by 1896, an increase of $5,000 over the first Derby in 1875. A horse named The Winner finished seventh in 1896, thus establishing one of the best bar arguments in history. Who wouldn't bet that The Winner couldn't finish seventh in the Derby?

# The Los Angeles Times

THE EAST-BOUND SOUTHERN PACIFIC OVERLAND WAS DERAILED NEAR BEAUMONT. — THE BILL FOR THE CREATION OF SAN ANTONIO COUNTY DEFEATED IN THE SENATE.

TWELFTH YEAR. TWELVE PAGES. THURSDAY MORNING, MARCH 9, 1893. 4:00 O'CLOCK A.M. PRICE: SINGLE COPIES, 5 CENTS; BY THE WEEK, 5 CENTS




## TODAY'S BULLETIN —OF— The Times.

MARCH 9, 1893.

(BY TELEGRAPH): Defeat of San Antonio County Bill in the Senate....Fitzsimmons scores an easy victory over Hall....Honolulu celebrated Washington's birthday and the proposed treaty....No extra session of Congress probable....Wreck on the Southern Pacific near Beaumont....De Lesseps on the witness stand.

IN AND ABOUT THE CITY.

Washout on the California Southern near Lamanda Park....Trial of the Holmes forgery case commenced....Four Supreme Court opinions received for filing....Anniversary missionery meeting at Immanuel Church....Proceedings of the Supervisors....Business transacted by the Fire Commissioners....News from neighboring counties.

WEATHER INDICATIONS.

For Southern California: Clearing; warmer along the southwestern coast; variable winds.



# FITZ WINS.

## An Easy Victory for the Champion.

### A Terrific Blow on the Chin Knocks Jim Hall Out.

### Only Four Rounds Required to Settle the Great Contest.

**Both Men in Fine Form—The Knock-out Blow One of the Hardest Ever Delivered in the Prize Ring.**

*By Telegraph to The Times.*

NEW ORLEANS, March 8.—[By the Associated Press.] The battle of middleweights is over. The March carnival of pugilism has become prize-ring history, and Bob Fitzsimmons stands before the country as Hall's conqueror and the winner of the largest purse ever fought for. A magnificent crowd in point of size and personnel saw the great battle tonight. Clubs and managers have tried for several months to bring the Australians together, and it was only successfully accomplished after numerous disappointments and failures in the negotiations. Each principal was regarded as a wonder in his class. The men are somewhat similar in build. Both are giants, strong, healthy, big-boned, long-armed, and stubborn, formidable fighters, adepts in science, experienced in the ring, hard punchers, and each with a distinctive style. So close was the match considered for a long time that even money was wagered. Today Hall was strongly a favorite, but the influx of Fitzsimmons men and money beat down Hall, and made Fitzsimmons for a time the favorite. Neither man worked hard on the last day. Each remained quiet, except when Fitzsimmons went to take out naturalization papers and Hall to dine with Charley Mitchell.

The men fought at catch-weights for superiority only, and a purse of $40,000, and $2500 went to the loser and the remainder to the winner. The audience, which filled the immense auditorium, was variously estimated at between four thousand and forty-five hundred. The financial result of the fight is not yet known, but the general opinion is that the club lost several thousand dollars by the entertainment.

PERFECT ARRANGEMENTS.

Arrangements at the ringside were perfect. The crowd was representative in character and thoroughly cosmopolitan. The two principals reached the arena in ample time to prepare themselves for the battle. Both men were trained to a fine point, but neither had taken off much flesh. The men entered the ring at 9 o'clock promptly, Hall leading the procession. He was loudly cheered, as was Fitzsimmons, who came in waving the American flag. The men chosen to look after Hall's interests were Lightweight Champion McAuliffe, Charley Mitchell, Squire Abbingdon, Baird and John Kline holding the watch. Fitzsimmons had men with less reputation, but not less faithful, than Hall's attendants—Billy Fitzsimmons, his brother; Martin Julian and Frank Bosworth, and D. G. O'Malley keeping time. Referee Duffy made a neat speech, counselling the usual good order and cautioned the men about fouls and the usual club rules. Capt. Barrett weighed the gloves, finding them of lawful weight, and handed them to Martin Julian, who took them over to Hall for his choice, and Mitchell selected his principal's gloves. Referee Duffy announced the pivot blow barred, and the men stripped.

THE FIGHT BY ROUNDS.

Round 1—Usual handshaking, and both men stepped nimbly to the center and feinted for an opening. Fitz attempted a left upper-cut, but Hall backed away. He failed a second time, and the men clinched. Hall then led for Fitz's stomach and received a tap on the shoulder. Fitz scored a heavy left on Hall's mouth and right on his heart without a return. Hall made a wild left swing, and Fitz smilingly dodged. Fitz landed a heavy left and dodged a return. Hall landed a heavy right on the ear, and Fitz clinched. Hall hit Fitz on the head as the round closed.

Round 2—Fitz missed a left on the stomach, and immediately after a right on the body, because Hall clinched. The men were extremely cautious. Hall received a heavy left on his stomach, responding with a left on Fitz's head. Hall landed a heavy left, and received a good return on the head. Fitz forced Hall into a corner, but the latter clinched to avoid punishment. Fitz tried to land a left, but was neatly stopped. Both men, in a hot rally, scored hits on the head.

Round 3—Fitz was the aggressor, landing on the stomach, and later on the body and head. Then Hall landed two heavy lefts on the face and a heavy right upper cut. Fitz clinched to save himself, and Duffy had difficulty in parting them. Fitz continued clinching to avoid punishment.

Round 4—Hall came up the aggressor. Fitz landed a heavy right on the jaw, knocking Hall into the middle of the ring. The blow was a tremendous right-hand swing, and landed full on the point of the jaw. Hall was a long time coming to, and was finally helped to his corner by Fitzsimmons.

The referee awarded the contest to Fitzsimmons, who waved the United States flag over his head, walked to his opponent's corner and shook hands, and as he was leaving the ring, received a tremendous ovation.

AN EASY VICTORY.

The fight was the easiest that Fitzsimmons has had in America, and the blow that knocked Hall out is universally said to be the hardest any prize ring habitue ever witnessed. The audience rose to their feet and a tremendous shout went up. Hall lay unconscious on the carpet, a look of agony on his face. It was feared he had suffered serious injury, but his seconds, with the club officials and doctors, ran quickly to the prostrated pugilist, and, applying restoratives, gradually brought him back to consciousness. Fitzsimmons ran around the ring hastily, pulling off his gloves, and helped to resuscitate his conquered foe. When Hall was brought to he was carried limp to a chair, where he remained until able to go to his dressing-room. Fitz was frenzied with delight over his comparative easy victory.

AFTER THE FIGHT.

After Hall had been brought back to consciousness Fitzsimmons skipped nimbly to his room, and, without putting on his clothes, drew on a heavy overcoat and jumped into a carriage with his wife and drove to his quarters. A great crowd congregated in front of the winner on Canal street, giving him a rousing welcome as he drove up. After he had gone up stairs Fitzsimmons came out on the balcony and made a modest speech. Afterward, in his room, he said to an Associated Press representative: "Hall is the cleverest man I ever met. He clearly out-pointed me in the third round. But he thought, because some of my blows fell short, I could not reach him, and I fooled him. I can only say I am very lucky to win as soon as I did."

The Hall people were dejected. Hall was the picture of tribulation in his corner before he was led to his room, and his seconds looked like men who had lost their best friends. Hall blamed himself, and his seconds blamed him by innuendo for carelessness. He lost a superb opportunity, and a princely purse and reputation, and all in a moment of over confidence, and they had reason to lament the swing chance that brought a splendid form to the carpet a whipped man. For three rounds it was a superb exhibition of clean hitting, deft maneuvers and skill, dodging and audacious swinging. There was more fighting in those three rounds, according to the rules, than in the entire battle between Sullivan and Corbett last September, and memory does not supply in ring history a match of men so difficult to pick a superior. Hall felt he could win when three rounds were gone. He meant to force matters in the fourth, but for a moment he was unguarded and lost a fortune. Hall remained in his room an hour after the fight was over. For a long time he was dazed and uncommunicative. What he said was little, but it meant volumes. "I got it on my jaw, that was all." It is all he could or would say.

## WRECK ON THE S. P.

### Accident to the Eastbound Express Near Beaumont.

**A Lone Tramp Stealing a Ride Has a Few Ribs Broken—Passengers and Crew Escape Without Injury.**

*By Telegraph to The Times.*

COLTON, March 8.—[By the Associated Press.] The eastbound Southern Pacific train was wrecked this side of Beaumont today. The culvert over a dry arroyo was weakened by the heavy rain. Two engines crossed safely. The mail and baggage and express cars and one day coach jumped the track. The mail car rolled down an embankment fifteen feet. A tramp was crushed between the baggage and express cars and had three ribs broken and his head cut. The passengers raised $50 and sent the tramp to Beaumont for treatment. The westbound train was sidetracked near Beaumont. The wreck will be cleared tonight.

[The above dispatch is considerably exaggerated, according to the statements of local Southern Pacific officials, who give the following version of the wreck: No. 19, overland passenger train eastbound, due at Beaumont at 10:12 yesterday afternoon, when about a mile and a half west of that place, struck a small culvert, which had given way owing to the heavy rains. The train was going up a steep grade, and was drawn by two engines, one of which, with the baggage car, slipped off the rails. A tramp, who was stealing a ride between, was pinched. The accident was so slight that no wrecking train was sent out, and it was expected to have everything straight within a few hours. No. 19 was hauled back to Colton, where the passengers were made comfortable, while No. 20, westbound, was taken back to Beamont, where a heavy snowstorm was prevailing. Owing to the heavy grade, the train was making slow progress, or the accident might have been more serious.

## WASHINGTON'S SENATOR.

**Allen Likely to Be Appointed by the Governor**

OLYMPIA (Wash.,) March 8.—[By the Associated Press.] The Legislature will, in all probability, adjourn tomorrow night without electing a United States Senator. The opposition of the Republican factions has stood firm through the daily balloting for nearly two months, and John B. Allen, who sought reëlection, has held fifty-two votes, within six of the coveted reëlection. Turner, Allen's Republican opponent, has held the key to the situation with twenty-four votes, who have withstood the appeals and influence of Allen's supporters and friends. The Democrats, with twenty-seven votes, have, from time to time, complimented the leaders of the party, but never a break outside the ranks, and the nine Populists whose votes have been valued so highly, refused to yield. Two ballots will be taken at noon tomorrow as usual, and both houses, it is expected, will meet at 7 p.m. and ballot until midnight, when the session closes. It is confidently asserted that in case of no election Gov. McGraw will appoint Allen. The talk of an extra session is subsiding.

**Death of an Aged Mason.**

PORTLAND (Or.,) March 8.—William Gardner, said to have been the oldest Mason in the United States, died here today, aged 97. He joined the Masons in Scotland in 1816. His home, previous to coming here, was in Kansas City, Mo.

**A Whittier Boy Pardoned.**

SACRAMENTO, March 8.—Gov. Markham today pardoned Henry N. Laskey from the Whittier Reform School. Laskey was sentenced in the Superior Court of San Diego county for eight years for burglary.

# KNOCKED OUT.

## The San Antonio County Bill Defeated.

### The Senate Rejects the Measure by a Vote of 24 to 11.

### Pomona Advocates Confident of Victory Up to the Last Moment.

**Mathews and Carpenter Recipients of Congratulations—San Diego Harbor Appropriation Passes the House.**

*By Telegraph to The Times.*

SACRAMENTO, March 8.—[Special.] The Senate today refused to pass the San Antonio Bill by a vote of 24 to 11. Up to the last moment, the Pomona delegates claimed that at the most they would only lack about two votes to carry the measure. The vote was a complete surprise, and the size of the majority against county division is considered the result of the personal efforts of Senators Mathews and Carpenter. Both have been indefatigable since the fight began, and since the result was announced, have been the recipients of many congratulations.

The $150,000 San Diego Harbor Appropriation Bill was passed in the House tonight by a large vote. The same bill is also on the third-reading file in the Senate.

LEGISLATIVE PROCEEDINGS.

**The San Antonio Bill Defeated in the Senate.**

SACRAMENTO, March 8.—[By the Associated Press.] *Senate.*—The bill creating the county of San Antonio came up for third reading. Mr. Mathews opposed its passage. [The result is given in the special above.]

The Senate refused to reconsider the Bretz Mutual Insurance Bill.

Mr. Leeds's amendment, placing the regulation of railroad rates and fares in the hands of the Legislature, was taken up and discussed.

Recess.

The bill to provide for the transfer of money from one county treasury to another, when a new county has been formed, was passed.

The Assembly bill to pay the Dougherty claim for work on the bay of San Francisco, which amounts to about $500,000, was finally killed.

The urgency file was taken up.

The Assembly joint resolution relating to the free and unlimited coinage of silver was adopted.

The bill to retire the teachers of the public schools of the State upon partial pay was finally passed. Notice of reconsideration was given.

The bill to prohibit the employment of persons who are related by affinity or consanguinity to chief or other officers of any department of government of the State was defeated by a vote of 27 to 8.

In the Senate tonight the bill exempting State property from assessment by municipal and county governments was finally passed.

Adjourned.

*Assembly.*—The Judiciary Committee reported back the substitute Reassessment Bill, with amendment. As amended the substitute provides that railroads shall be reassessed at the tax rate levied for the years in which the taxes remain unpaid, instead of at the 1893 rate. This is the same as the original Shanahan bill.

A number of appropriation bills were passed.

Recess.

The Senate constitutional amendment, providing that cities shall have only one board of supervisors, was passed by a vote of 35 to 8.

A large number of bills were given a second reading, among which was the bill providing that health and market inspectors shall consist of practical plumbers.

Mr. McGowan's bill, making it unlawful to refuse admission to places of amusement, came up.

Mr. Larue moved to strike out the enacting clause, which motion was carried and the bill killed.

Opposition to the Kings County Bill was renewed by a motion to reconsider, which was lost, and the bill ordered immediately transmitted to the Senate.

Mr. Ragsdale's Mutual Insurance Bill, which was defeated yesterday, was brought up for reconsideration, and finally passed by a vote of 42 to 33.

Mr. Shanahan got two of his bills up as cases of urgency, which were read first, second and third times, and finally passed. Both provide for the serving of summons without the State by means of publication.

Mr. Conway's bill providing that water corporations shall not charge more than the actual cost of material and labor for water connections was also passed. Recess.

In the Assembly tonight the bill for an appropriation of $200,000 for seawall thoroughfares and piers in the harbor of San Diego, was passed and immediately transmitted to the Senate.

Mr. Emeric's bill for the protection of fish was taken up, and a motion was made to strike out the enacting clause, and the remarkable discovery was made that the bill contained no enacting clause. An amendment was offered supplying one, but it was lost, and the bill defeated.

At a caucus of the leading Democrats of the Senate and Assembly tonight, it was determined to substitute the Seawall Reassessment Bill for the Carpenter substitute, when the latter comes up in the House tomorrow.

**Call for a New Party.**

PITTSBURGH (Pa.,) March 8.—A call has been issued for a conference in this city on the 16th inst. of the Prohibitionists, woman suffragists and others interested in a general reform of the Government, to organize a new national party. It is signed by 1800 Western Pennsylvania people, including many ministers and several public characters. The tariff and silver are among the topics for discussion.

## CANADIAN RECIPROCITY.

**Canada's Version of the Conference with Blaine.**

OTTAWA (Ont.,) March 8.—[By the Associated Press.] The Governor-General has transmitted to Parliament the record of the conference at Washington on February 15, 1892, between the Canadian delegates and Blaine. The following portion, which relates to reciprocity, is the Canadian version:

Blaine said he could understand why Canada was reluctant to enter into a treaty of unlimited reciprocity, but no other arrangement would suit the United States, and it must be accompanied by discrimination in favor of the United States, especially against Great Britain, which was America's great competitor, and it must be likewise accompanied by the adoption of a uniform tariff for the United States and Canada, equal to that of the United States. Unless such points were guarded there could be no security, on the one hand, from smuggling along the border line of over three thousand miles, or, on the other, of maintaining the present protective policy of the United States. Blaine added: "We would expect to have the Canadians to compete with in manufacturing, but no one else, and that a treaty for natural products alone could not be discussed."

## A PIRATICAL CREW.

### Mutiny on Board the American Bark Hesper.

**A Miscarried Plot to Murder the Captain and Officers and Sail the Seas Under the Black Flag.**

*By Telegraph to The Times.*

HONOLULU, March 1.—[By the Associated Press.] The American bark Hesper, Capt. Sodergren, arrived here February 21, with an account of a mutiny on January 13, which resulted in the death of Second Mate M. Fitzgerald. The Hesper left Newcastle, N. S. W., December 22 with a cargo of coal for San Francisco. The plot was hatched by Thomas Leclair, Herman Sparf, Hans Hansen, Thomas Green and Edward Larsen to murder the captain, first and second mates, cook and a Greek sailor, and then run the vessel either to China or the Chilean coast and sell the cargo and fit the bark out for a piratical cruise. On the night of January 13, Leclair hid himself amidships, and as Mate Fitzgerald passed him sprang upon him, striking him a blow on the back of his head with a hatchet. The mate fell, but Leclair struck at him until his victim ceased to struggle. Sparf and Hansen joined him and proposed to throw the mate's body overboard. Leclair wanted first to call the captain and dispatch him, and on the other two refusing, he went aft alone. Sparf and Hansen then threw the mate's body overboard. Leclair told the man on watch at the wheel to call the captain, but the latter refused to do so. Shortly after midnight First Mate Lucas went to Capt. Sodergren's cabin and told him that the second mate was not to be found. The two went on deck, where they were joined by the carpenter. Search resulted in their finding the deck covered with blood. Capt. Sodergren learned from Seaman Thomas Green that the latter had been asked by Leclair and others to assist in throwing the captain overboard. The latter thereupon ordered the men's arrest. The bark was headed for Tahiti. While on the way there Green and Larsen attempted to release the other men, without success. When the Hesper reached Tahiti the five men were taken before United States Consul Doty. Sparf and Hansen confessed, which Leclair also did finally. The five men were sent to jail to remain until the arrival of the bark Tropic Bird, bound for San Francisco, February 15, when they were taken there for trial.

## MASSACHUSETTS CRIMINALS.

**A Concerted Plan of Escape Frustrated.**

BOSTON, March 8.—[By the Associated Press.] A concerted plan of convicts to break from the State Prison in a body has been frustrated. The prisoners have been supplied by secret means with nearly one hundred revolvers. The plan was to kill any one who opposed them. Information reached the officials in season to balk the scheme. Discipline is said to have been utterly lax, convicts dominating the officers. Pistols had been furnished them at $20 each by some one. Gov. Russell is acting warden at the State Prison today. He will personally oversee the search of the prison for weapons. Convicts will be locked in cells, and dealt with individually. It is stated a new warden will be appointed at a special meeting of the Governor and Council this afternoon.

## CORRUPT LEGISLATORS.

**Idaho's Lawmakers Accept Bribes from Lobbyists.**

BOISE (Idaho,) March 8.—[By the Associated Press.] Gov. McConnell today addressed a letter to the District Attorney, in which he charged that various members of the late Legislature had accepted money bribes from lobbyists for different college and other schemes. The legislators thus corrupted, he says, belong to all three parties. "State officers will furnish you such information," says the Governor, "which will probably place you in a position where you can obtain such evidence as will lead to the arrest and punishment of offenders, both inside and outside the Legislature."

**Bill Dalton Gets a Life Sentence.**

INDEPENDENCE (Kan.,) March 8.—Bill Dalton has been sentenced to imprisonment for life on a plea of guilty of murder in the second decree, for his part in the Coffeyville battle last fall.

**The Western Union's New President.**

NEW YORK, March 8.—Gen. Thomas T. Eckert has been chosen president and general manager of the Western Union.

**A Mississippi Hanging.**

MAGNOLIA (Miss.,) March 8.—L. K. Ford was hanged today for the murder of Marshal R. A. Clay a year ago.

# JOY IN HAWAII.

## The Proposed Treaty Causes Rejoicing.

### The Stars and Stripes Displayed More Than Ever Before.

### Washington's Birthday Generally Observed as a Holiday.

**Reception on Board the Mohican—Minister Stevens's Opinion of the Treaty—A Bit of History.**

*By Telegraph to The Times.*

HONOLULU, March 1.—[By the Associated Press.] The early part of the present week witnessed scenes of much enthusiasm in Honolulu, and the Stars and Stripes were probably more generally displayed than at any time in Hawaiian history. The arrival of the steamship China from San Francisco Monday, February 20, followed by that of the Australia on February 22, brought intelligence that caused great satisfaction to the provisional government and the American party on the islands. On the first named date, when it became known that President Harrison and his Cabinet had decided upon a favorable course in regard to the disposition of the islands, excited throngs gathered about the mail dock, postoffice and news stands, and discussed the information received with much ardor. The prompt action of the administration in the matter was warmly commended by Americans, irrespective of party affiliations, as well as by many of the German residents and of the more intelligent natives.

WASHINGTON'S BIRTHDAY.

The scene, however, was nothing like that of February 22, when the Australia brought the news that the message from President Harrison, providing for a treaty of annexation of the islands, had gone to the Senate, and that as far as the American Government was concerned the islands were probably a part of the United States when the Australia arrived. The day was the anniversary of the birth of Washington, and was being observed as a general holiday. The streets were filled with natives and others in their best attire. Flags were floating from many buildings and from the vessels in the harbor, the whole forming, in the bright sunlight, a pretty setting for the introduction of the startling effects furnished by the steamer from San Francisco.

Col. Soper, commanding the provisional government forces, was applauded when he expressed himself in favor of a salute of 100 guns in honor of the occasion, providing he were given authority therefor. On board the United States flagship Mohican Admiral Skerrett and staff were holding a reception, and hither came all of the prominent personages of Honolulu, exclusive of the more pronounced royalists.

The Associated Press dispatch from Washington, announcing the receipt of the annexation message by the Senate was shown to the Admiral and Captain Wiltz and President Dole, Minister of Finance Jones, and others of the provisional government. It proved to be the latest intelligence received, and the dispatch was handed about and read with many expressions of satisfaction.

NEWS OF THE TREATY.

United States Minister Stevens, owing to the recent loss of his daughter, did not attend the anniversary exercises, but the dispatch was shown to him subsequently, and he also stated that, so far as he knew, it was the latest information received. The Minister declined to speak officially, but expressed his individual opinion by saying: "I expected there would be some opposition in the House, and am surprised somewhat to find, by the columns of the newspapers received, that there is about the same unanimity there as appears to prevail in the Senate. I think the matter is settled except as to minor details."

As to whether the Queen should receive an annual pension or a certain sum in full, Mr. Stevens thought that if $250,000 were appropriated in a lump sum it would be divided between the deposed Queen and the Princess. As to the government of the islands under annexation, he though, as does President Dole, that the manner in which Louisiana was governed after its acquisition was best, but that the District of Columbia mode, with a board of commissioners, one of whom to be nominally governor, would solve many local problems. The United States, he considered, was disposed to be liberal in the matter of treating with native Hawaiians, and the white residents here were willing to concede many points, so that they secured annexation. Government lands would be turned into homesteads for the benefit of Hawaiians under such restrictions that they would not be able to dispose of them in a trifling manner, and poll taxes would probably be reduced to a nominal sum; other taxes would be made reasonable and the natives would doubtless be recognized in the distribution and patronage of minor offices and appointments.

CLEGHORN TRANQUIL.

A. S. Cleghorn, Collector of Customs, and father of the Princess Kaiulani, was not surprised at the news from Washington. "I had hoped, though," he said, "to see the Princess placed on the throne, backed by an American protectorate." Mr. Cleghorn said his daughter is at the finishing school of Mrs. Rook, at Brighton, England. It had been arranged that she should shortly make a tour of the United States, but the revolution had somewhat upset these plans.

At the close of last week a rumor was current on the streets of Honolulu that the Senate would not ratify the treaty of annexation, and it is stated several wagers were made that the Queen would come again to the throne. Several members of the Advisory Council, discussing the rumor, said that if the United States should refuse to take action it would drive the provisional gov-

# THE FOOTBALL CRAZE

## The Whole Country is Crazy on the Subject.

### What Harvard, Princeton, Yale and the Other Big Teams are Going to Do.

### How the Game Commenced in the United States—Plans as Mapped Out for the Current Season.

NEW YORK, Nov. 1.—(Special Correspondence.) The old order of four seasons per year has been changed. There are really only two—the Bob Cook and the Walter Camp seasons. The Bob Cook season begins with December 1 and lasts until the 'varsity race is rowed at New London. The Walter Camp season begins when the 'varsity eight-oared supremacy is settled, and lasts until the Thanksgiving games are played. The intervening time between Thanksgiving and December 1 is occupied by the surgeon, who mends the shattered and touseled creatures, who leave the field half-crazed in victory, or gloomy in defeat.

The lay world is just beginning to hear about football matters of this year. But the collegians have been talking football for the last three months. Until the Harvard-Yale supremacy is settled they may go to classes and may recite well, but their thoughts will be on football. Even the gray-haired professors will forget their duties so much as to stop in the middle of a recitation and mutter in a whisper: "Can we win? Is Hinkey really the right man? Will he bring the boys into proper shape?"

There is only one man in New Haven who is more prominent than Walter Camp. I forget his name, but I think he is president of the university. Camp will go up to New Haven to remain until the Harvard-Yale game is settled, early in November. He now makes flying visits to the boys, and gives them the advantage of his erudition and experience. The "boys" gather around him in the rubbing-down room, their chins cupped in their hands, and listen to all that Mr. Camp says, while Capt. Hinkey strikes Napoleonic attitudes and strolls back and forth and thinks—and thinks, and thinks—like some general planning a battle. Taciturn Capt. Hinkey has been caught making useless speeches on three occasions since he entered college. The first was: "We were beaten fairly," uttered after the Princeton victory of last Thanksgiving. The second was: "We must work this year, boys," uttered on the occasion of his meeting "the boys" to begin the fall practice at Traver's Island in August. The third was a little swear word, uttered after Williams scored against Yale. "The boys" have all the confidence in the world in Capt. Hinkey, even if he is as dumb as an oyster, and he lost the Thanksgiving-day game, to the everlasting chagrin of old Eli.

AT OLD HARVARD.

At Cambridge Capt. Emmons and his men are on their mettle. They have hopes just as they have had hopes for a great many years, only to have them shattered in the great game at Sprinfield. What Camp is to Yale, Arthur Cumnock is to Harvard. Cumnock captained the victorious crimson team of '91 and the Yale men say sarcastically that the only reason that Harvard makes so much of him is because his was the only team from Cambridge which beat Eli's sons for fifteen years. Cumnock was the handsomest football captain on record, and some Wellesley girls could not resist the impulse to kiss him after his great victory. Just now he is connected with a large wholesale dry goods house on Leonard street, and instead of studying the problems of the field, he is studying the patterns of dress goods. He runs up to Cambridge as often as he can get the time, and helps the boys out with suggestions.

PRINCETON'S THREE GREAT MEN.

Princeton had three great men, any one of whom might be called the Camp of old Nassau. Savage was her most famous captain. They called him "lemons" because he was so sour. He swore like a trooper on the field, and was never known to praise a man. But he won games, and that is what counts. He is now a prosperous business man in the West. "Snake" Ames, who played on the Princeton team four years, 1886-89, got his name because he could work his way through a rush line as a snake goes through a woodpile. He once made two touchdowns in a game with Harvard, the only points made, something never done before or since. Like Savage,

Capt. Emmons of Harvard.

he is in business and exceedingly prosperous. Then there was their great Hector Cowan who could run with two men on his back, the ball against breast, and whistle at the same time. He was a raw-boned country boy when he came to college, and they called him "The Haypitcher" until he went down to the running track one day, and clad in an $8 suit of clothes, beat all the other fellows at sprinting. That settled it. He immediately became a hero. But he never overcame his awkwardness or his unfortunate manner of blushing, stuttering and stammering in the presence of admiring college girls. He always steadfastly avoided everything in petticoats. He was as gentle as a lamb off the field; but upon it he was as rough—well, we are simply taking the words out of a professor's mouth—as the devil. They said he prayed before he played. Anyway, he said he wouldn't serve in a team captained by swearing "Lemons" Savage, whereupon Savage resigned, as he preferred the freedom of his tongue to any college honor. Whether it was "Lemons'" swearing or the "Haypitcher's" praying which won the victories while the two were on the team is still a matter of great doubt. Cowan is now a sedate Presbyterian preacher. Not one of Nassau's three giants has taken active interest in Princeton's teams after graduation. If any one had he could have been to his alma mater what Camp is to Yale.

Although Camp was a great captain it is the interest he has taken in the game which has given him his prominent position more than a recognized superiority over all other footballists. Frank W. Peters, who captained Yale in '85, and made a victorious crew out of green men, is generally considered by football experts to have been Camp's superior. But Peters left football when he left college. Camp was the captain of Yale's first successful team and has never lost his interest in the game. He is of a nature which makes him popular with collegians. The boys will mind him when they will mind no one else. Consequently, one plan of action is settled upon and followed out, which is always best, while the other teams having three or four heads never present so strong a team play as the New Haven men.

"DOGGIE" TRENCHARD.

And since Princeton has no Camp she trusts implicitly in Capt. "Doggie" Trenchard. In doing this, she does well. "Doggie" is a wonderful little fellow. Because he is so nicknamed is no sign that he is not respected, even revered. If George Washington was captain of the Princeton team he would be called "peanuts," because he came from Virginia, or something else equally absurd. That is the Princeton way. His dogged ways have given funny little Trenchard his funny name. He is a great man. He can raise a cheer when Dr. Patten would be regarded with cold indifference. Most of these names I have mentioned are history now, and forgotten by the public. But at their colleges they are everything, and will be held in loving remembrance as long as football lasts.

And football seems to have come to stay.

AMERICA IS FOOTBALL MAD.

Boys of six years and wearing long hair are talking knowingly about "punts," "flying wedges" and the like. They look forward to the time when they shall play upon the high school team, then upon the grammar school or preparatory school team, then upon the college team and make a touchdown, which saves the day, and be carried off the field on the muscular arms of a score of football lunatics. There are half a dozen preparatory schools which act as feeders to the various college teams. At Andover and Philips Exeter, the enthusiasts even go so far as to carry on regular proselyting campaigns among the grammar schools in order to secure the promising young athletes for their schools, and, of course, Harvard and Yale men know for months beforehand what footballists are coming from Andover and Exeter. You must not forget that there is just as great rivalry between the freshmen teams of the different colleges as there is between the picked college teams.

But not all of the great football players of today began playing when they were ten years of age. The grammar-school-trained and academy-trained boy often finds himself supplanted by a novice. A big, hulking freshman from the country will walk down to the field to watch the men play. He remarks that he believes he can play the game himself—such is the story of Heffelfinger. He makes a try in the practice, and the captain finds that he has encountered a genius—for a man may have a genius for football as well as for anything else—which sets the whole college into a spasm of joy.

FOOTBALL IN THE WEST.

Football has now become as popular in the West as in the East. Every college has its team and belongs to some college league, and, as many of the Western institutions are coeducational, the victorious young athletes do not have to go as far as their Eastern brothers for feminine praise of their prowess. The same rules apply in the West as in the East, but the game is not played so roughly; or at least, fewer accidents have resulted. In the smaller colleges where the men cannot afford to train so finely as they do in the East the players wear thick wool toboggan caps and keep their hair cut down to the length of that of an ordinary individual. Because there is no such rivalry between any of the Western colleges as between Harvard, Yale and Princeton: the sport does not become the all-engrossing mania that it is in the Eastern universities. The larger Western colleges have graduates of Harvard, Yale and Princeton to coach them and not infrequently when a strong man is developed in a Western college he is induced to come East, and, knowing the warm reception he will receive, the opportunity is seldom missed.

THE FOOTBALL PLAYER.

The football player is a broad-shouldered, smooth-faced, bright-eyed, long-haired young man, is a good fellow to know (if he has not grown egotistical through his victories,) and is really our modern knight-errant who fights for the honor of his alma mater, instead of his family name, and to win the praise from my lady in laces as he stands before her in his ripped, mud-bespattered, and sometimes blood-bespattered, suit, bruised, but triumphant. And now he wears an armor the same as the old knight. He has a mask for his nose and mouth, pads for ears, caps for his shoulders, pads for his stomach, shin protectors and bandages for his legs and arms to prevent him from being mauled and bruised and killed. Yet, with all of these to protect him, he sometimes loses his life. But more American college men die of causes traceable to lack of exercise than in playing football. The world is bound to have its knights, anyway, and our footballist is of a better sort than a blustering, threatening swashbuckler or the insipid creature sometimes met at afternoon teas.

HOW THE GAME STARTED HERE.

Speaking of the footballist's armor, it is interesting to note how rapidly football has developed in this country. It is only twenty years since the Rugby game was introduced. Then the players wore long trousers, the shirt of the track-athlete, with handkerchiefs tied around their heads. Of course, both Harvard and Yale claim to have introduced football. It would never do for one of the universities to allow an honor completely to the other. Rev. R. S. Shaff, a pastor at Jacksonville, Ill., declares that Yale and Columbia played a game according to Rugby rules in 1872, Columbia winning. In 1870 he was studying in Germany. His chum was an Oxford man, who explained and glorified the Rugby game. Young Shaff brought an oval leather ball across the water with him. He exhibited it to some of his college mates in his room. They guyed him about it unmercifully and said it might do for the nursery, but not for men. But he finally persuaded them to try a game. They liked it so well that Yale has been wedded to football ever since.

Harvard has another version of the introduction of the pigskin ball. "The Crimson" played two games of football in Cambridge against McGill University of Montreal in the spring of '74. The first game, according to old-fashioned rules, was won by the Harvard men. In the second game, in which they claim the Rugby rules for the first time prevailed, both sides failed to score.

Capt. Hinkey of Yale.

In the fall of '74 the Harvards played against an all-Canada team at Montreal. They were, peculiarly enough, for the most part undersized men. They found their opponents were giants. Montreal society turned out with a great flutter of feathers to see the little Yankees humiliated. They poked fun at the little Yankees, and said to the little Yankees: "What do you think your little fellows can do against our big fellows, anyway?" But that's the way the big Gauls used to scoff at the little Romans in Caesar's legions—before a battle.

The little Yankees used their heads, which is the way of Yankees—big and little. The big Canadians started with a solid phalanx (which was the germ of the famous up-to-date flying wedge) to carry the ball irresistibly down the field. But the little Yankees got them tangled up before they had gone a rod. Then there was a shout down at the Canadian end of the field. Little Billee Seaman, the smallest Yankee of them all, had just slid in between the big fellow's legs, and,

Capt. Trenchard of Princeton.

while they were squabbling, he had kicked a goal, and stood with his hands in his pockets, an enfant terrible smile upon his chubby face. Before the game was over little Billee Seaman had demonstrated that he could get through almost any sort of a hole. With British persistence the Canadians tried their phalanx again, and again, and every time little Billee Seaman, or some other little Yankee, would slip away with the ball and kick a goal. And after he had kicked a goal little Billee Seaman couldn't resist a little smile, which was full of suggestion. Finally the giant Canadians were completely demoralized, and the big captain, who stood head and shoulders above little Billee Seaman, went up to little Billee Seaman and said menacingly:

"You don't play fair. You slide right between our legs, and get away from us. You don't play the way we do."

"We just play to win," said little Billee Seaman, smiling some more. His playing, it is needless to say, was strictly within the rules.

Dr. William Seaman is now medical examiner for the Equitable Life Assurance Society for a large salary, but he is still known up at the Harvard Club as "Little Billee Seaman, who didn't play according to custom, but just slipped between their legs and kicked a goal."

In '75 Harvard vanquished Yale at Rugby. In '76 Yale turned the tables under the captainship of Eugene V. Baker. Walter Camp played in this team and was captain in '77, '78 and '79. And Yale has won continuously ever since with the one exception when Arthur Cumnock led Harvard to a glorious victory.

IT TAKES BRAINS AS WELL AS LONG HAIR.

Football is an intellectual as well as a muscular game, as the public may be surprised to know. To play it sucessfully a man must have a cool head. The signalling which most of the uninitiated do not understand, is always done by means of numbers. Each man has his number; and the spaces between them are numbered. The quarter back gives the orders.

Suppose the right end is numbered 12 and the left half back is numbered 1 and the quarter back wants the left half back to go around the right end, the quarter back will say: 7—12—13 or 5—12—13, or 50—12—13, the first number being known as a bluff and counts for nothing—so the enemy will not be able to nearn the signals. It takes considerable training you will readily understand, to respond immediately to these signals which are rattled with lightning rapidity from the quarter back's lips. Naturally, the quarter back must have the best head of any many on the team. He is the field officer of the team.

There are a number of technical changes in the rules of football this year, with which all football experts are by this time familiar.

For interfering with a player in attempt to make a fair catch, the penalty has been increased from five to fifteen yards, thus preventing interfering as a matter of advantage, which formerly, was often done. This will also stop a great deal of unnecessary rough play. The time of the game has been reduced to thirty-five minutes for each half, and ten minutes intermission, which, it is calculated, will lead to faster play all around. Rule No. 20 is doubtless the most apparent and important to the ordinary spectator. It reads:

"The ball shall be kicked off at the beginning of each half; and whenever a goal has been obtained the side which has lost the goal shall kick off. If the ball go into touch before it has been touched by an opponent, it shall be brought back and kicked off again. If it be kicked into touch a second time it shall go as a kick-off to the opponents."

This does away with our old familiar friend, the wedge. It renders the playing more open, and when we get to the big games we shall doubtless see some very clever team work as a second good result. Mass and momentum plays are also prohibited.

In the case of a touchback, resulting from a drop kick at the goal on the first down, the line of kick out shall be the ten-yard line instead of the twenty-five-yard line. This change was made to encourage drop kicking. When a man has been tackled and thrown, the ball shall be considered down at that spot and the umpire will stop further piling upon him—another blow at unnecessary roughness. Ten yards for fouls is another penalty which has been increased, and has already shown a tendency to make their occurrence less frequent.

Still the new rules do not seem to have been of any use in preventing the men from being bruised and battered as much as of old. There's scarcely a man on any one of the teams who has not already been laid up for a day or two by some injury. Harvard has been particularly unfortunate. Most of her men have been on crutches two or three times. Dr. Eliot, who is quaintly humorous, often asks one of the professors who calls upon him, with an inimitable inflection on the last word of the question:

"Football again today—how many were killed and wounded?"

THE BIG TEAMS.

Sherman, Butterworth, Adee, Hinkey, Hickock and Greenway are the old men who will play with Yale this year, and Brewer, Lewis, Newell, Waters and Emmons are the veterans from crimson who will face the blue at Springfield.

The personnel of the two teams on the great day, will probably be as follows:

| | | |
|---|---|---|
| Hinkey | Left end | Moulton |
| Chadwick | Left tackle | Hallowell |
| McCrea | Left guard | Murchio |
| Stillman | Center | Frank Shaw |
| O. Hickcok | Right guard | J. N. Shaw |
| Murray | Right tackle | Gould |
| Greenway | Right end | Arthur Brewer |
| Adee | Quarter back | Beall |
| Thorne | Left half back | Hayes |
| Miles | Right half back | Dunlap |
| Butterworth | Full back | Brewer |

The determination of the independent young undergraduates of Yale and Princeton not to play on Thanksgiving day, breaking a tradition so dear to the alumni of both institutions, and robbing New York of her great Thanksgiving-day diversion, has brought an avalanche of censure down upon their heads. What New York has lost Philadelphia has won in the great Harvard-University of Pennsylvania game. Capt. Knipe is a wonderful man, and the game between his men and Capt. Emmon's athletes will be quite as interesting as that between Harvard and Yale at Springfield. With this year's Springfield contest the five-year Yale-Harvard agreement is completed. This will result doubtless in a great four-cornered league, in which Pennsylvania will have the place which her prowess during the last three years has won for her. Regretfully, but surely, Harvard and Yale have been forced to see clearly that Old Nassau and the U. of P. are foemen worthy of their steel.

IT MAKES MONEY, TOO.

Patti, Barnum and Bernhardt may boast about boxoffice receipts, but they have never taken in so much at any performance as the $35,000 which the Princeton-Yale game in New York yielded last year, and that was only $5000 more than the amount paid by the enthusiasts who saw Harvard beaten at Springfield. This money is divided between the colleges and it is all swallowed up by the numerous expenses of training and caring for these very precious young men who fight the battles on the gridiron field.

But money is of little object to the athletic organizations of big colleges. The devoted alumni will supply deficiencies. Therefore, from a pecuniary standpoint Thanksgiving day's game holds no attraction compared to preservation of the honor of dear old Yale and dear old Princeton. There is another reason besides that that five days is not sufficient for the Yalesians to recover from the effects of their game with Harvard with which the general public is not familiar and which in part accounts for Yale's refusal to play on Thanksgiving day. Nearly everybody who attends these games wears the Yale or Princeton colors. To see his college colors adorning the lapel of a saloon-keeper's or a racing tout's coat makes a graduate or an undergraduate fairly shiver with horror. Shrewd observers also say, but for the popularity of the Yale-Princeton game in New York, among a class other than collegiate, the professional football league would never have been inaugurated and college men had always hoped that the American game of football might be kept free of professionalism—purely a gentlemanly sport. Therefore, Yale and Princeton will not allow what one Yale senior called "New York's unwashed" to spend their holiday shouting for the blue, and the orange and black.

### Little Boy Blue.

The little toy dog is covered with dust,
But sturdy and stanch he stands,
And the little tin soldier is wet with rust,
And his musket molds in his hands.

Time was when the little dog was new
And the soldier was passing fair,
And that was the time when our Little Boy Blue
Kissed them and put them there.

"Now, don't you go till I come," he said,
"And don't you make any noise!"
So toddling off to his trundle-bed
He dreamt of his pretty toys.

And as he was dreaming, an angel song
Awakened our Little Boy Blue—
Oh! the years are many, the years are long,
But the little toy friends are true.

Aye! faithful to Little Boy Blue they stand,
Each in the same old place,
Awaiting the touch of a little hand,
The smile of a little face.

And they wonder, as, waiting these years through
In the dust of that little chair,
What has become of our Little Boy Blue
Since he kissed them and put them there.

EUGENE FIELD.

### Vote it Strong.

Vote your vote, and vote it strong!
Everything is going wrong;
Winter coming—cold and snow,
Laboring man, what will he do?
To the soup-house he must go,
Democrats have made it so.

Vote your vote, and vote it strong!
Everything is going wrong;
Prices down on what you grow,
Money coming very slow;
If you want these things to stay,
Go and vote the same old way.

Vote your vote, and vote it strong!
Everything is going wrong;
Free-trade good times all pretense,
Cotton down to just five cents;
Wheat is forty cents or less;
Prospects dark, we must confess.

Vote your vote, and vote it strong!
Everything is going wrong;
Debts increasing every day,
Less ability to pay;
Knock out Grove, the heavy-weight,
Vote the grand old ticket straight!

# REHEARING BEGUN

## Tax Cases Argued Before a Full Court.

### The Government Will Not Touch on the Municipal Bond Feature.

### Attorney Guthrie of the Opposing Counsel Says That the Income Act Should be Sent Back to Congress.

*Associated Press Leased-wire Service.*

WASHINGTON, May 6.—The Supreme Court, with its full membership of nine justices on the bench for the first time in many months, began the hearing today of the income-tax suits. Justice Jackson of Tennessee, who has been absent from Washington the greater part of the past year seeking restoration to health, took his seat with extraordinary interest attached to his presence, since he assumes practically the position of umpire upon the vital question of the principle upon which the law is based, and which divides the other justices into equal factions. Justice Jackson did not appear to be feeble, but it was plainly evident that he was far from being a well man, and that only by a strong effort did he sit throughout the hearing.

Most conspicuous among the spectators in court was Postmaster-General Wilson, the chairman of the Ways and Means Committee that framed the tariff act; Representative McMillan of Tennessee, chairman of the sub-committee which drafted the income-tax provisions, and ex-Speaker Crisp of the House. The attendance of lawyers and others having an unofficial interest in the matter was noticeably smaller than at the first argument of the law, and after the usual contingent of casual tourists had satisfied their curiosity to obtain a sight of the prominent men, the courtroom was not crowded. But two arguments are to be made for each side—one by Atty.-Gen. Olney and Assistant Attorney-General Whitney for the government, and by W. G. Guthrie and Joseph Choate for the appellants, who are Messrs. Hyde and Pollock. Today Guthrie delivered his speech and Whitney began his, which he will finish tomorrow. As the time assigned is five hours to each side, the arguments will be closed Wednesday afternoon.

Before Guthrie began, the Chief Justice, after calling the case, stated that in response to the suggestion of the Attorney-General, which the court interpreted as virtually a motion for a rehearing, the court had decided to permit counsel to go into all questions involved.

Guthrie began by saying that counsel for the appellants in the cases had been subjected to considerable criticism for their motions for a rehearing, but they had felt justified in the realization of the fact that there were many points still undecided in the definite and final adjudication of which the entire country was vitally interested, and he assured all concerned that the counsel for the appellants in the prsent case would approach it in a spirit of the highest patriotism and with no desire for mere self-aggrandizement. He said that the question involved was a constitutional one and added:

"The Constitution is the political creed and conscience of the nation, which must control and rule our destiny in so far as this court shall preserve it intact, according to its letter and its spirit, or permit the darkness of error to affront its light, so will our future see progress or decline, happiness or misery, glory or shame. There can be no law inconsitent with the fundamental law and a century of error cannot overrule the Constitution. The question is not to be determined by considerations of present expediency or practicability or hardship, but according to the lights, the purposes, the intention of the framers, and as they intended the Constitution to operate, so must we enforce it today. The people are not to be deprived of inherited rights, such as are ibedded in our Constitution, by mere precedent or technical application of the rule of stare decisis."

The point of contention, he said, was that the authorities establish the principle that taxation upon the income of one class of property is as objectionable as upon another. He charged the Hilton case with being the sole cause of all the error in this matter. It was, he said, a political case, in which the administration of Washington was pitted against the anti-Federalists, and a case in which local prejudice cut an important figure. He controverted the opinion that the decision in the Hilton case had been accepted as deciding that only the capitation tax and the land tax were direct taxes, and asked, if this was so, why it was Congress, in 1796, less than thirty days after the decision was rendered, had instructed the Secretary of the Treasury, by resolution, to report a plan for laying direct taxes by apportionment.

Guthrie then presented at some length the contention that, as it was clearly the intention of Congress to have the law act as a whole upon the incomes, the provisions which are unquestionably void, invalidate the whole act. The law, he said, expressly included rents and other incomes from land and personal property, and the language covers also the income from municipal bonds. The government has insisted that it was not only the intention, but within the power of Congress to tax the income from municipal bonds. The object of the act is single and entire, that is to say, the taxation of income from all sources. In order to preserve the provisions now remaining, the court must strike out words actually used, such as rents, income and product of land.

He declared that the act should be sent back to Congress, because it is arbitrary and unjust, and in violation of the express provisions of the Constitution. He then took up the question of exemptions and limitations, repeating much of the argument advanced at the first hearing, and asked the court to declare the whole act unconstitutional because of the exemptions. Replying to the suggestion of Atty.-Gen. Olney that, in the light of the recent decision, the government should refund the money collected under former income-tax laws, Guthrie said:

"The people of the United States gladly paid the income tax to defray the expenses of the war, and would make similar sacrifices today if it were necessary. Congress has not returned the cotton tax, although it was clearly sectional, partial and unfair. Has it ever been advanced as a principle of justice and morality that if you decide a certain interpretation of the customs laws has been erroneous, every man who had paid without protest, is entitled to have his duties refunded?"

Guthrie concluded at 3 o'clock and was followed by Assistant Attorney-General Whitney on behalf of the government. Whitney complained of the brief time given for preparing for the rehearing. He said that the government would not again present any argument on the question of municipal bonds. He did not suppose any tax law had ever been enacted which made express mention of all possible exemptions. If such a requirement were to be applied there would be very few valid laws.

As to the question of exemptions of rentals from real estate, that was different. The government had hopes this question would be so presented as to obtain a reversal of the former opinion. He contended that the bills in the case asked for no special relief in case of rentals. He announced the historical and definitive argument would be handed to the court in the shape of a brief. Whitney said the appellants relied principally upon the system of economics of John Stuart Mill, which had not come into existence at the time the Constitution was adopted, and he contended that the distinctions between direct and indirect taxes were so abstruse that it was not possible to incorporate it in a written constitution.

Whitney, in criticising the opposition for going so far back into history for precedents, said he had not intended to go back further than 1689, but as the appellants had gone to 1189, he would himself give some precedents of that date.

"Can't you," asked the Chief Justice, in a tone which appeared to contain a spirit of banter, "go back further than that?"

"I might," replied Whitney, "but I should not tax the patience of the court to that extent; but for the precedent of my much-learned friends on the other side." He said he would agree to stop short of 1189 if Choate would, whereupon Choate assured Whitney and the court that he would stop several centuries short of that date.

Whitney referred at some length to the distinctions between the words tax and duty in English legislation. He said this distinction had been very sharp and the word tax had been applied and where the word duty could not be made to cover the case. "If," he said, "the framers of the Constitution were acquainted with Blackstone, they were familiar with the English classification."

A peculiarity of the English system since 1689 was that everything called a tax was laid by the rule of apportionment, whereas, everything called a duty was laid by the rule of uniformity. The thorough understanding of this principle by the Democrats of the convention explained the apparent lack of interest in the discussion of the distinction in these matters. The important question with them appeared to be that of the proper distribution of taxes to be made according to the apportionment. He contended that the direct taxes were traceable to the English land tax, and it was impossible to levy such a tax except by apportionment. The system of apportionment among countries was the same in this country in the early days as in England. At this point Whitney was interrupted by the adjournment of the court for the day.

# ROUSING THE PEOPLE.

## CUBAN AGITATORS AT WORK IN CAMAGUAY.

### The Flower of the Spanish Forces Sent to That District—Mayor Garcia of Santa Spiritu Resigns—A Surrender.

*Associated Press Leased-wire Service.*

NEW YORK, May 6.—A special to the World from Havana says that agitators of the revolution are said to be working hard in the Camaguay regions. Spain's best-disciplined soldiers are being sent to that section as an uprising there would be fatal to Spanish rule. During the last war some 80,000 men revolted in that district, and a large column once came very near Havana.

Marcus Garcia, the Mayor of Santa Spiritu, has sent in his resignation, and is in Santa Clara. No little importance is attached to this step. A native of Cuba, and a desperate and brave leader in the first revolution, he is extremely popular in the whole province of Puerto Principe, where he has lived all his life. As Mayor of Santa Spiritu he has been devoted to the welfare of the people, personally conducting all forces in pursuing the many bandits that operated in that neighborhood, which he contrived to exterminate.

The whole district of Camaguay would blindly follow him should he once more desire it. He has been summoned to Havana to account to Gen. Campos for his strange resignation. In Rio Grande, in the neighborhood of Sancti Spiritu, men have revolted, and are trying to induce Justo Sanchez, a leader of the past war, to take command of them. At present the leaders are a Cuban named Castillo and a Spaniard named Quintero.

There is a rumor that an expedition 2000 strong is liable to land in Vuelto Abajo, at the extreme western end of the island of Cuba. Nothing definite can be ascertained in regard to it. The story appears to have been purposely set afloat by stock exchange speculators.

INSURGENTS AT MANZANILLO.

KEY WEST (Fla.) May 6.—Reports have been repeatedly circulated in Cuba and Florida that Callazo, an insurgent leader, has landed in Spain. After a long investigation Callaza has been discovered at Tampa

The Spanish government finds great difficulty in getting provisions, etc., to troops at Bayamo. The American tug Pedro Pablo has been converted into a transport. All the fortifications under Manzanillo have been destroyed by the insurgents. The province is virtually in their hands.

REBELS SURRENDER.

HAVANA, May 6.—Twenty members of a band of rebels at Villas, commanded by Quintin Bravo, have surrendered.

THE NEW SPANISH MINISTER.

WASHINGTON, May 6.—Senor Enrique Dupuy de Lome, the new Spanish Minister, was presented to the President today by Acting Secretary of State Uhl. The Minister presented his letters accrediting him in the name of King Don Alfonso XIII, and referred to the fact that he had come for the third time to serve his sovereign at Washington. He referred to "the bonds, already a century old, which join Spain and the United States," and spoke felicitously of his late meeting with President Cleveland during the World's Fair at Chicago. He assured the President of the affection of the Queen Regent and her government for himself and the American people.

President Cleveland replied in an equally pleasant strain, assuring the Minister of his pleasure to welcome him again to Washington. "It augurs well, Mr. Minister," said the President, "for the sake of your mission, that you come among us not only inspired by the amicable desires of your government, but as a personal friend."

A CORRESPONDENT TO BE INVESTIGATED.

WASHINGTON, May 6.—The State Department has been asked to investigate the case of Manuel Fuentes, the correspondent of the New York World, who was arrested near Santiago de Cuba on a charge of aiding the revolutionists, it being charged that he endeavored to sell arms to them. This charge is denied.

## CALIFORNIA ATHLETES.

### The University Team Arrives at Princeton Today.

*Associated Press Leased-wire Service.*

PRINCETON (N. J.) May 6.—The University of California athletic team will arrive in Princeton tomorrow direct from California. A. W. North, the manager of the team, is already in Princeton, having come on a few days in advance of the team. On his way here from California, North stopped over at Denver, Chicago and Ann Arbor, where he succeeded in arranging for meets for his team on their return trip. Immediately after the California-Princeton meet on next Saturday the men will go to Philadelphia, where they will remain during the California-Pennsylvania meeting on May 18 and until the Mott Haven games of May 24 and 25.

The following meets have been arranged for the team while on its tour: Princeton, May 11; Pennsylvania, May 18; Mott Haven, games, May 24 and 25; Ann Arbor, June 5 or 8; Chicago Athletic Club, June 15; Denver Athletic Club at Chicago, June 15; Denver Athletic Club and combined Colorado colleges at Denver, on June 22. In addition to these an exhibition meet may be arranged with Syracuse University at Syracuse on May 29 and a joint meet will be held on June 10 with either the University of Wisconsin at Madison or the University of Illinois at Champaign. Several entries will also be made in the Western intercollegiate games in Chicago June 1.

[SPORTING RECORD.]

# A BATTLE OF GIANTS

## Steve O'Donnell Defeats Jake Kilrain.

### The American Was Winded in the Thirteenth Round but Lasted Twelve More.

### Halma Wins the Kentucky Derby in Splendid Style—The California Athletic Team—Baseball in the East and Races.

*Associated Press Leased-wire Service.*

CONEY ISLAND (N. Y.) May 6.—Since Goddard and Maher fought here in December, 1892, there has not been a heavyweight contest brought off in the vicinity of New York.

The fact that Jake Kilrain of Baltimore and Steve O'Donnell of Australia were to meet here tonight at catch-weights in a 25-round go attracted a large crowd of sports, as every person who had an opportunity was anxious to see these two heavyweight pugilists prove who was the better man, after the very unsatisfactory ten-round draw which they fought a short time ago in Boston.

After a minor bout between locals, George F. Green, better known as "Young Corbett" of San Francisco, was given an opportunity of showing his prowess. His antagonist was Jim Holmes of New York. They met at 135 pounds for eight rounds. The Californian had as seconds Young Griffo, Billy Delaney of San Francisco, John McVey of Philadelphia and Jim McCabe of Fordham. The men behind Holmes were William Holmes, Charley O'Brien and Pete Dunn of New York.

"Young Corbett" showed himself clever, but his blows lacked steam. He was knocked down in the third round. "Young Corbett" led in the fifth and sixth and in the latter he smashed Holmes right and left on the body and face at will. Holmes was very groggy. He stopped after Green had smashed him twice in the face in the next round, and Green was declared the winner.

The event of the evening was then ordered. There were about six thousand people in the house when the announcer gave out the names of the seconds. Billy Delaney, John McVey, Mike Dunn and Benny Murphy were to look after O'Donnell, and Ernest Gebhardt, L. A. Duke and Al Halford of Baltimore were to take care of Kilrain. Champion Corbett was not in the house, but his manager, Billy Brady, sat close by the ringside. "Parson" Davies of Chicago was also an interested spectator. O'Donnell climbed through the ropes at 9:50 o'clock and Young Griffo was then among the seconds, who by this time numbered half a dozen. Kilrain arrived a minute later, and, in comparison with his tall opponent, he looked as big as an elephant. O'Donnell's weight was said to be 185 pounds and Kilrain's 30 pounds more. The latter looked very beefy. The men shook hands at 10 o'clock.

First round—Both men sparred very carefully for a minute. Kilrain led left on neck and O'Donnell went to his knees. O'Donnell jabbed his left on the chest. Kilrain punched his left into O'Donnell's chin and got away from a swing. He repeated this a moment later.

Second round—O'Donnell led left, but failed and Jake sent his left in once more on the chin. Steve put his left on the wind lightly and then the same hand visited Kilrain's eye and nose three times. Kilrain landed the left on the neck and chin. Steve led the left, but Jake threw it off. As the gong sounded Kilrain landed on the chest with a straight left.

Third round—Kilrain led the left for the head, but fell short and his arms stopped a lead of Steve's for the stomach. Kilrain gave a right and left-hand smash in the face. After a clinch he jabbed again in the face, and both punched on the body. Jake got in lightly with the left on the neck and then landed on Steve's face. O'Donnell tried twice for the face and head, but fell short.

Fourth round—After a few passes O'Donnell got in on the stomach with his left, and Jake countered on the neck. Jake smashed his right in the face and the men clinched. Jake landed on the face with the left and once more on the neck with his right. Then he jabbed his left on the face and got a left on the face and a left-hander on the nose in return.

Fifth round—Again Jake's left reached Steve's face and the latter countered. He put in a very hard left on Kilrain's stomach and then jabbed the same hand on Jake's jaw. Kilrain returned with his left on the face. Both countered on the head with their lefts and then Steve put a left on the stomach. Jake went full on the face with his left.

Sixth round—O'Donnell led the left on the face and Jake got in his left again. O'Donnell landed the left on the neck and they clinched. Kilrain stopped a hard one meant for his wind. After a clinch Steve landed on the body and Jake swung his right on the head.

Seventh round—Steve tapped Jake's face lightly with his left and then sent in three lefts. Jake jabbed his left and then failed on three leads. Steve jabbed his lift twice on Jake's cheek and once more on the face. Exchanges on the body followed and then Kilrain put his left on the face. He stopped two hard leads for the head very cleverly.

Eighth round—Jake came up smiling. He landed a left on the face and led for the head, but O'Donnell ducked and Jake immediately landed his right on the face. O'Donnell put back his left on the nose. Rapid right and left-hand exchanges followed and the Baltimore man's nose began to bleed.

Ninth round—Kilrain's nose was bleeding. Both landed on the face and body. O'Donnell put his left twice in quick succession on Jake's cheek. Jake got in a left on the chin and O'Donnell placed a hot one on Jake's damaged nose. They clinched and afterwards they exchanged right and left-hand blows on the face and body.

Tenth round—O'Donnell led off with a left on the jaw. Jake landed a left on the cheek and swung lightly on the face. Steve put in his left twice on the face and Kilrain sent in a left on the body. O'Donnell sent his left three times in the face and Jake sent back only one in return. Both landed lightly with the left on the face.

Eleventh round—Light taps opened this round and then Steve landed twice heavily on the stomach, Steve's left went to the ribs and then twice more to the face. He went in again and hit Kilrain four times on the face and body without a return.

Twelfth round—Kilrain led off with a left jab in the face and put Steve's head back with a left on the neck. Steve put in two lefts on the face and Kilrain landed left on the chest. Steve smashed Jake on the body. Jake led on the face. Both jabbed with their lefts on the face. Jake got in a good one on Steve's jaw and the latter did the same trick.

Thirteenth round—O'Donnell swung his right, but fell short and then got in twice on the face. Jake hit back with a hard right swing on the neck. Then they smashed right and left on the body and face at close quarters and Jake was very weak. He was nearly gone when the gong rang.

Fourteenth round—O'Donnell led and landed twice on the face and placed a vicious right in the wind. Jake put his right on the face. Steve's right went hard on the ribs and it made Jake grunt. O'Donnell jabbed his right on the wind three times, and then went twice to the face with the left and once with his right. Kilrain was clearly winded.

Fifteenth round—O'Donnell landed a heavy right on the body. Both countered on the neck. Steve then smashed right and left on face and body. He jabbed his right and left on the face and body. Jake countered lightly on the neck. This was O'Donnell's round.

Sixteenth round—Steve slapped Jake's face, and, after a light interchange, he put his right heavily on Jake's jaw. Kilrain tapped him on the neck, and, while Steve kept up a tattoo on the face with his left, he placed his right frequently on the ribs and stomach.

Seventeenth round—Steve led off with a hard right on the body and again on the mouth. He kept up jabbing his right on the body. Jake landed lightly on the face, but was heavily countered on the neck. Jake put in a good right-hand body-blow, but O'Donnell finally reached his face, damaging his left eye badly.

Eighteenth round—Steve landed on the chin and again on the neck. He put his right hand over the heart and then countered on the face and neck. Jake put his left on the body and received a crack on the jaw in return. Steve put a right smash on the body, and Jake countered on the head. O'Donnell hit Jake on the badly-damaged eye and nearly closed it.

Nineteenth round—Both jabbed with the left on the face. Steve landed a left on Jake's face four times. Jake put his left back on the neck. O'Donnell sailed in and punched hard, without a return until the end of the round.

Twentieth round—Jake sent his left twice for the face, but was easily stopped, and O'Brien planted a right swing on the ribs. He kept jabbing Kilrain, who attempted to get back, but without effect. Kilrain was very groggy when the gong sounded.

Twenty-first round—Jake's face showed evident signs of his punishment, but he was still very game. He led off with a left on the neck. O'Donnell fought him around the ring. When at close quarters he put his right on the body and sent his left over on the jaw. Kilrain fell like a log to the floor, and, although he managed to get up within the required ten seconds, the referee, Tim Hurst, stopped the bout at the request of the police. Jake would have been put out with one more punch. Time of the last round, 1 min., 19 sec.; time of the fight, 1 hr., 20 min., 10 sec.

Although Kilrain rose within the stipulated ten seconds, O'Donnell was awarded the decision, the bout practically ending in a knock-out.

## NO MORE FIGHTS.

### The Louisiana Supreme Court Rules Against Boxing Exhibitions.

*Associated Press Leased-wire Service.*

NEW ORLEANS (La.) May 6.—The State Supreme Court today handed down a decision reversing the decision of the District Court, in which the lower court ruled that prize-fighting as recently conducted here might be continued.

The decision was rendered in the appealed case of the State of Louisiana vs. the Olympic Club. The Supreme Court rules that the recent alleged boxing exhibitions were nothing more or less than prize-fights and that as such they are prohibited by the State law. The injunction originally prayed for is granted and prize-fighting in New Orleans will hereafter be prohibited. Associate Justice Watkins filed a dissenting opinion.

WHERE WILL CORBETT GO NOW?

TALLAHASSEE (Fla.) May 6.—The Senate today passed the bill prohibiting prize-fighting and glove contests in Florida, giving sheriffs power to arrest offenders without warrants, making all participants alike liable, the offense being deemed a felony and punishable by a fine of $2500 to $5000 and imprisonment of not more than five years, or both fine and imprisonment, at the discretion of the court.

## THE KENTUCKY DERBY.

### Halma Wins the Great Race—Twenty-five Thousand Spectators.

*Associated Press Leased-wire Service.*

LOUISVILLE (Ky.) May 6.—Fair ladies waved their handkerchiefs and sturdy men joined in the lusty cheer that greeted the son of the great sire, when Halma passed under the wire a winner of the twenty-first Kentucky Derby, this afternoon. Such rejuvenated activity and enthusiasm was never before witnessed on a racecourse, for the historic Churchill Downs presented a scene that will go down to posterity. The Kentucky Derby is an event to which all Kentuckians look forward with a just pride, and this afternoon the New Louisville Jockey Club established a new era in the history of racing in Kentucky, the home of the thoroughbred.

It was a grand victory, too, for Byron McClelland's entry. That Kentuckians have not lost their enthusiasm for the horse was evidenced by the crowd that throged the superb stand, betting-ring and every other available place to see th classic event. It will nver b known just how many pairs of yes centered upon little "Soup" Perkins as he guided Halma under the wire an easy winner, but the most conservative place the number at 25,000.

Before the arrival of the noon hour, the journey of the thousands to Churchill Downs began. The boulevard leading to the course was crowded with vehicles of every description from the antiquated two-wheel conveyance to the more modern English cart. All the city buildings and many of the larger establishments gave a half-holiday to their clerks and all went to see the Kentucky Derby. At the Downs there was a scene never before witnessed in the history of that grand old course. The magnificent new stand, which has a seating capacity of nearly 10,000, was inadequate to hold the vast throng. Every place of vantage about the stands, the paddock and the stables was occupied, while in and about the betting-stand it was one solid mass of humanity. The betting-stand, from the time the first odds were chalked on the board until the flag fell in the closing event, was almost one immovable mass. Men jostled against each other and essayed to elbow their way through the throng in their efforts to place their money, but the fifteen bookies who were there to accommodate the public could not handle more than one-half the money.

Halma won the Derby as he pleased, and not once did Perkins find it necessary to use the rawhide, for the colt assumed the lead from the very fall of the flag and set the pace to the finish. He was not urged a foot of the route, and when he passed the stand for the last time there were four good lengths of daylight between the son of Hanover and the hard-ridden Basso, who was second.

There was enthusiasm when the first two events were run, but when the winners were posted in the second race, there was augmented activity, for the Kentucky Derby would soon be a thing of the past. The sound of the saddling bell had hardly died away, before Curator, with Overton up, came out of the paddock and cantered around in front of the stand. The Bashford Manor colt was applauded, but, with the appearance of Laureate, it increased, and when Halma, with Perkins up, and Basso, with Martin astride, paraded in front of the vast crowd, it gave vent to its approval with one long-continued cheer that lasted almost until the candidates had reached the half-mile pole, where Starter Pettingill, flag in hand, awaited them.

While the thousands were eagerly watching the horses that were to contest for the event, all was activity in the betting ring. If 10,000 people endeavored to place a bet on the first two races, everybody wanted to back their choice in the Derby, and bookies found it an arduous task to handle half of the bills that were shoved at them. Halma, on performance, was entitled to be the favorite, and he was, in the judgment of both the spectators and bookmakers, for the first odds posted were 2 to 5. Even at those prohibitive odds, there was a rush to place money on him, and when the flag went down the best obtainable was 1 to 3, while several books had rubbed him off the board. Basso was not without friends, and loads of money went on him at 4 to 1 to win and 3 to 5 for the place, and not once did the odds change after they had once been posted. Laureate, too, had a big following at 9 to 2, and 4 to 5 for the place, while Curator, at 15 to 1, was not altogether friendless.

At 3:55 o'clock all eyes were turned toward the half-mile pole, for there the Derby candidates awaited the order to start on the journey which was to make one of their number famous. They lined up, and at the first attempt were sent away well bunched, with Halma, the favorite, showing in front by a neck. There was not a length's difference between the four horses.

Martin wanted to save Basso for the final struggle, and as they rounded the first turn he drew the colt up and at the quarter was last, but he took good care that the distance which separated him from Halma did not become too great. Halma had the lead by a head from Curator, who had moved up to second, while Laureate was third and half a length back. A mighty shout went up as Halma passed under the wire for the first time with Perkins pulling at the reins. Laureate was second and Curator third. Halma and Laureate went neck and neck around the lower turn and when they reached the three-quarter pole Perkins's mount was leading by a head, with Laureate still after him and Curator a head in front of Basso.

"Basso has quit!" was the cry that passed, and the Falsetto colt was indeed showing signs of fatigue, but when they had passed the mile Martin began riding, and when they showed in the stretch for the final run Basso was second.

"Basso wins!" was shouted almost simultaneously from a thousand or more throats as Martin, riding furiously, went after Halma who, apparently, was running with the same ease as when he went by the stand for the first time. The bay colt, however, had run his race, and although Martin rode him to the very wire, the best he could do was to finish four good lengths behind Halma with Laureate third, the same distance from Basso, and Curator last by five lengths from Laureate. It was a hollow victory for Halma and the great son of Hanover landed the prize without a struggle.

There were no sensational finishes, and but two favorites won. Potentate, in the first event, broke the track record for six furlongs, which was 1:18.

Six furlongs, maiden three-year-olds: Potentate won, Sister Mary second, Insomnia third; time 1:13¾.

Four furlongs, maiden two-year-olds: Reprieve won, Realm second, Forget third; time 0:49.

The Kentucky Derby, for three-year-olds, one mile and a half, worth $3300: Byron McClelland's black colt Halma, by Hanover—Julia L., 122, (Perkins,) 1 to 3, won; C. H. Smith's b. c. Basso, by Falsetto, 122, (Martin,) 4 to 1, second; Laureate third; time 2:37½. Curator also ran. The fractional time was: Quarter, 0:26; half, 0:51½; three-quarters, 1:17¾; mile, 1:44; mile and a half, 2:37½.

One mile, selling: Cattaraugus won, La Creole second, Fred Gardiner third; time 1:42¼.

Five furlongs, maiden two-year colts and geldings: Hernani won, Rondo second, Otho third; time 1:03¼.

## EASTERN BASEBALL.

### Pittsburgh, Boston, Chicago and Cincinnati Winners.

*Associated Press Leased-wire Service.*

PITTSBURGH, May 6.—Pittsburgh 12, base hits 12, errors 1.

Brooklyn 1, base hits 4, errors 5.

Batteries—Colclough and Kinslow; Gumbert, Daily and Grim.

BOSTON-ST. LOUIS.

ST. LOUIS, May 6.—St. Louis 6, base hits 8, errors 4.

Boston 8, base hits 11, errors 3.

Batteries—Clarkson and Peitz; Nichols and Ganzel.

CHICAGO-WASHINGTON.

CHICAGO, May 6.—Chicago 4, base hits 8, errors 1.

Washington 0, base hits 5, errors 1.

Batteries—Hutchinson and Kittredge; Mack and McGuire.

CINCINNATI-NEW YORK.

CINCINNATI, May 6.—Cincinnati 4, base hits 11, errors 2.

New York 3, base hits 10, errors 1.

Batteries—Parrott and Vaughn; Rusie and Schriever.

NO GAME.

CLEVELAND, May 6.—No game; rain.

LOUISVILLE, May 6.—The Louisville-Philadelphia game was postponed on account of the Derby.

## AGAINST SUNDAY GAMES.

### Mass-meeting at Chicago to Protest Against Sunday Baseball.

*Associated Press Leased-wire Service.*

CHICAGO, May 6.—Three hundred persons attended a mass-meeting held at the People's Institute to protest against Sunday saloons and Sunday baseball games. The meeting was held under the auspices of the Internation Sunday Observance League. The Rev. M. M. Parkhurst gave scriptural reasons why Sunday traffic and Sunday amusements should be forbidden. The Rev. W. S. Leach said that it was a degradation of the American flag that it should wave over a baseball field with a Sunday game in progress.

Bishop Fallows said that he had been told by a person who had canvassed the subject that all professional players except one were opposed to Sunday games. The Rev. Thomas E. Cox called on all Roman Catholics to discontinue the Sunday traffic in liquor and to stay away from the ball games.

T. B. Gault said that to arrest the managers and players would cause too much annoyance in return. He thought the only way to stop the game was by injunction. It is intended to take this course.

## BAY DISTRICT.

### Starter Merrill Makes His First Appearance and is Cheered.

*Associated Press Leased-wire Service.*

SAN FRANCISCO, May 6.—Four favorites won today and the talent fared well in consequence. Staretr Merrill, who relieved Starter Ferguson, made his first appearance and his work was so satisfactory that the crowd gave him a round of cheers.

Six furlongs: Red Glen won, Nelson second, Linville third; time 1:15¼.

About six furlongs: Mamie Scott won, Raindrop second; Gold Dust third; time 1:14.

One mile: Midas won, Arundel second, Fortuna third; time 1:41.

About six furlongs: Hueneme won, San Luis Rey second; Alaric third; time 1:14½.

Five and a half furlongs: Arnette won, Rico second, Rel Alta third; time 1:04¼.

Seven furlongs, inside course: Tar and Tartar won, May Day second, Hy Dy third; time 1:34¼.

## REFUSED TO SELL ALIX.

### Salisbury Offered Thirty Thousand for the Little Trotter.

*Associated Press Leased-wire Service.*

NEW YORK, May 6.—It is said that Monroe Salisbury and Morris J. Jones declined an offer of $30,000 for Alix a few days ago. One report has it that the proposition came by cable from France, while according to another story Ed Decernea, the well-know broker in trotters, made the bid. If there is any truth in either rumor it is likely that the prospective buyer is James Gorden Bennett.

### Chicago Races.

CHICAGO, May 6.—Five furlongs: Belle Foster won, Blue Bell second, Libertine tird; time 1:05.

One mile, selling: Lester won, Pepper second, George W. third time 1:47½.

Six furlongs, selling: Willie L. won, Via second, James V. Carter third; time 1:08.

Four and a half furlongs: Sallie Clicquot won, Harmony second, Carrie C. third; time 0:58¾.

One mile and a furlong, hurdle: Walter A. won, Roeder second, Uncertainty third; time 2:06.

### Roby Must Close.

VALPARAISO (Ind.) May 6.—The fight to close the gates at the Roby racetrack will begin in earnest tomorrow. Prosecuting Attorney Heard of this city said tonight that warrants would be issued tomorrow for every one connected with the racetrack. Sheriff Hayes will go to Roby with warrants to arrest the whole crowd. The plan is to make arrests every day until the gambling is stopped. If necessary Gov. Matthews will send 500 militia.

### Blackburn Wins.

LONDON, May 6.—Count von Bordeleben was beaten today by John Blackburn in the match of the British Chess Club after sixty-four moves. Score: Blackburn, 3; Von Bordeleben, 1; drawn, 2.

### A Foreign Book.

CINCINNATI, May 6.—It is stated that there will be a foreign book at the Latonia track this year. The work of constructing a big poolroom at the track was begun today.

## FLASHES FROM THE WIRES.

Rear-Admiral Amy, U. S. A., retired, is very ill.

Prof. Karl Vogt, M. D., the well-known philosopher and author, died at Geneva, Switzerland, yesterday.

Secretary Gresham is reported to have had a satisfactory day today and the crisis is said to have passed.

It is reported that a compromise of the Manitoba school question may be expected before the meeting of the Legislature.

It is announced that the Whiteway party in New Foundland is planning to abandon the negotiations for a confederation with Canada.

Col. William Berry, department commander of the Army of the Cumberland, died suddenly of apoplexy at Quincy, Ill., aged 58 years.

A Boise, Idaho, dispatch says that John Gehrig and Alexander Strutchen were drowned Saturday near Shoshone, while attempting to ford Wood River.

At Brockton, Mass., the shoe manufacturers have advanced the prices of shoes 15 to 20 cents a pair. The increased cost of leather is given as the cause.

Charles H. and Henry Delaney arrested in connection with the blind pool expose at Pittsburgh, a few months ago, have been found guilty of conspiracy to defraud.

The superintendent of the Carson (Nev.) mint has relieved J. T. Jones, the assistant melter and refiner, and has asked for Secretary Carlisle's approval of the action. The removal will be approved.

The tank steamer Lumen is ashore off Long Branch in a dangerous position. At low-tide the water where the Lumen lies is but eighteen feet deep. The draft of the steamer is eighteen feet. She is surrounded by rocks.

A special to the Chicago Record from Bay City, Mich., says that Greenwood, Ogewamo county, is believed to have been destroyed by forest fires today. No information has come from there since 7 o'clock last night.

A dispatch to the London Times from Odessa says advices from the cholera-infected districts show that the epidemic is seriously increasing. Unless measures are immediately taken the disease is likely to spread throughout Russia and reach the rest of Europe.

Acting Commissioner Smith has received the following dispatch from Ralph Hall, Indian agent at Turtle Mountain Reservation: "I think the trouble is settled. The prisoners surrendered and the mob has been dispersed without bloodshed."

William E. Gladstone, in a letter to Franch Seymour Stevenson, chairman of the Anglo-Armenian Association, says that the conduct of the Sultan and Turkish government on the Armenian question has been worse than their conduct regarding Bulgaria in 1876.

Fire early yesterday destroyed M. Strausse & Co.'s tannery, Postal Station A, Groben's coal-yard, barns, several freight cars, two dwellings, a number of horses, and a large amount of stock in East Buffalo. The loss is estimated at $250,000 with $125,000 insurance.

A terrible hailstorm did much damage in Omaha yesterday. Hailstones as large a hen's eggs fell and filled the streets. Much property was destroyed, mostly glass and young trees. The damage will amount to thousands of dollars. But little glass remains in windows fronting south.

The forest fires which began Sunday in the vicinity of Glen Hazel are still burning fiercely. It is estimated the damage caused by yesterday's fire at Glen Hazel, including the sawmill, lumber-yard, railroad property and the consequent loss of revenue to the railroad companies on account of the interruption of traffic, will foot up near $1,000,000.

A dispatch to the London Standard from Rome says the papal nuncio has received orders to inform the nations to which they are credited that any message of congratulations or any participation in the September fetes in honor of the two hundred and fiftieth anniversary of the Italian entry into Rome will be considered injurious and insulting to the Pope and the Holy See.

A farewell dinner was given last night at the Savoy Hotel, London, to George W. Smalley, the well-known newspaper correspondent, who will soon start for New York, where he will represent the London Times. Many journalists were present. Among the guests were the Hon. Thomas F. Bayard, American Ambassador; Lord Russell Kilowen, Lord Chief Justice of England; Sir Henry James, Poultney Bigelow and Moberly Bell of the Times.

A few weeks ago the wife of Albert Zerkles, a poor farmer living three miles north of Decatur, Ind., gave birth to triplets, all girls. Acting on the suggestion of a friend, they were named Frances, Ruth and Esther, and the father wrote to President Cleveland, telling him of the event and the christening of his daughters, and asking him to buy them each a new dress. Zerkles has now been greatly surprised and gratified at receiving a check for $500 signed by Grover Cleveland.

Additional advices to Paris from Mejunga regarding the victory of the French on Betaiboka River on Friday show that the Hovas lost 300 men, including several important chiefs. The French losses were only one killed and four wounded.

The Parliamentary secretary to the Colonial office, Sydney Burton, in the House of Commons yesterday afternoon, replying to a question, said that no request had been received from Canada to call a conference of British colonies to discuss the details of laying the proposed Pacific cable.

In the case of the Corporation of Catholic Bishops of Nesqually, Washington Territory, versus John T. Gibon, R. T. Yeatman and the United States, the decision of the United States Court for the District of Washington has been affirmed by the Supreme Court. The Supreme Court has rendered a decision in the case of David B. Sayre, involving the constitutionality of the court-martial law, appealed from the Circuit Court of Virginia, which released Sayre on a writ of habeas corpus. It reversed the judgment of the court below.

Secretary Smith has decided that the State of South Dakota is not entitled to the 50,000 acres of valuable land in the Yankton-Sioux reservation which the State recently took steps to secure for its own use. The entire reservation comprises about 168,000 acres and the 50,000 claimed by the State included some of the most valuable lands in South Dakota. The reserve was to have been opened for settlement within a few days, but final action was deferred pending the decision of the disputed question. It is now presumable that the President will promulgate the proclamation within a few days and that the opening will take place thirty days thereafter.

The action of the Pension Bureau in construing the legal meaning of dependence under the act of June 27, 1890, has been reversed by Assistant Secretary of the Interior Reynolds in a decision on a dependent mother's case. The ruling provides where the property possessed by a mother having no other means of support is so small that it will not yield an income sufficient to support her during her life, it should not deprive her of the right to a pension. By "adequate means of support" the law is interpreted to mean not merely enough to supply the necessaries of life for a limited period of years, but a comfortable maintenance of the pensioner during the remainder of her life.

# SECESH IN HAWAII.

## A Movement to Separate the Group.

### Evidence Showing That the British Are Fomenting Another Native Rebellion.

### If Successful Kaiulani is to be the Queen—Gresham Refuses to Protect Naturalized Hawaiians—Thurston.

*Associated Press Leased-wire Service.*

SAN FRANCISCO, May 6.—The following advices per steamer Gaelic were received today:

HONOLULU, April 29.—Minister Hatch has received a communication from Secretary Gresham, through United States Minister Willis, in regard to naturalized Hawaiians applying for the protection of the United States. The communication deals entirely with the case of J. F. Bowler, who called upon the United States to interfere in his behalf. Bowler was convicted of a charge of misprision of treason in connection with the recent rebellion. Secretary Gresham states that the United States government cannot interfere, and in giving reasons calls attention to the fact that Bowler has taken the oath of allegiance required for becoming a naturalized citizen of Hawaii. No reference is made to the other prisoners coming under possible American jurisdiction. Secretary Gresham's letter will be made public at a meeting of the councils to be held this week.

Evidence is at hand that shows that British influence is at work in Honolulu. The natives are in a state of expectancy and word has been passed quietly among them that within a short space of time restoration would be a fact. In that event Kaiulani is to be made Queen. Bishop Willis, the head of the English church in this country, is said to be the man who is going among the natives with the information. British Consul Hawes is also mentioned in this connection. This renewed hope on the part of the natives has given the annexation movement a severe set-back.

Rumors of a impending revolution are still rife and the stories are of such a nature that no little alarm is felt in government circles. Information comes from the island of Hawaii to the effect that the residents are contemplating secession from the group, claiming as a reason for the step that they do not receive their share of money for public improvements.

The Hawaiian government is now putting into effect measures to equalize and perhaps change altogether the immigration stream. A limited number of Chinese field-laborers are to be brought in under restrictions, by authority of the act of 1892. For the present the Board of Immigration will refuse all applications for further importations of Japanese contract-laborers.

It is the intention of the government and the planters to encourage by every means immigration from Europe. Negotiations are now under way for more Portuguese. In this regard matters may shape themselves in a manner that may detain Minister Thurston in this country. It is understood that a new immigration bureau is to be created, and if so he will be offered the chairmanship. The government has received no word from Secretary Gresham regarding Minister Thurston's alleged recall.

President Dole celebrated his fifty-first birthday anniversary on April 23. During the day a petition was circulated praying that amnesty be granted the political prisoners. By 5 o'clock in the afternoon about five hundred names had been affixed to the petition. An hour later the document was presented to the President, who replied that he would submit it to the councils for action.

The Sugar Trust's new arrangement, that of shipping No. 2 sugar around the Horn to Atlantic ports, is creating havoc with vessels that ply between San Francisco and Honolulu. Vessels that formerly had no trouble securing cargoes are now compelled to leave port in ballast. The last two that left in this manner are the brig W. G. Irwin and the bark Albert. The latter vessel departed for the Sound on the 27th inst. Capt. Griffith has not been up north since 1889.

The German bark Triton from Liverpool, now in port at Honolulu, passed a burning vessel in the south seas. Capt. Schon reports that on March 4, in lat. 10 deg. 40 min. S., long. 111 deg. 40 min. W., a burning four-masted iron ship was sighted. On approaching within speaking distance it was discovered to be an English vessel, evidently coal-laden, but on account of darkness her identity could not be learned. Her four masts were standing, but her decks appeared to be burned out. The derelict was of about twenty-five hundred tons register; her top sides were black with painted ports, the bottom being painted dark red. A current of about two and a half miles an hour was running to the westward, gradually setting the burning ship toward the Marquesas Islands, where Capt. Schon thought she would land in about six weeks' time.

## NEW COMMISSIONERS.

### Gotham's Police Board Takes Office—Some Tart Letters.

*Associated Press Leased-wire Service.*

NEW YORK, May 6.—Theodore Roosevelt, Col. Fred Grant and A. Parker were sworn in as Police Commissioners to succeed Martin, Kerin and Murray, when the board, which consists of four members met, Roosevelt was elected president and Parker treasurer.

Before relinquishing his office Commissioner Murray sent a letter to Mayor Strong refusing to comply with the request for his resignation. In concluding the letter, Murray said:

"The party of which I am a member, and which, prior to your election as Mayor, you were identified with, through its representatives in the Legislature, with mistaken confidence in your discretion, fairness and Republicanism, conferred upon you an arbitrary power of removal. This power shall not be used with vindictiveness, nor, exercised for the purpose of building up factional dissentions. The spirit of this act you have violated. The exercise of the power by you, however narrow, capricious or unjust, I cannot prevent. If you think you can afford to employ this power, do so. I can afford to be made its innocent victim."

Kerwin today gave out a second letter to the Mayor, in which he went into more details in regard to the alleged violation of ante-election pledges by Strong than he did in his letter of last Saturday. Both Kerwin and Murray are Platt Republicans. In his letter Kerwin says:

"The record proves that you are false to every promise you made, and, in the face of overwhelming evidence, you have not dared to deny your wanton treachery. The patient people of this city, my dear sir, will not forget that you are silent in the face of charges of the most damaging character directly crediting you with being untruthful in your statements and false to the pledges subscribed by you. They will not soon forget the explanation you made when you startled the community with the false declartion that the city's finances had been tampered with. Least of all, will any self-respecting citizen forget your conduct in going outside of this city for persons to conduct the affairs of the municipality. In doing this you gratuitously insulted every man who cast a vote at the last election."

### Drowned i a Bathtub.

YERINGTON (Nev.) May 6.—James O'Hara, a mining man of this place, was found dead in a bathtub at Hind's Springs today. It is supposed he was overcome, as he was sick at the time.

Two Sheets—14 Pages.

# The Times

LOS ANGELES

XVth YEAR. [75 CENTS PER MONTH, OR 2½ CENTS A COPY.] TUESDAY MORNING, APRIL 7, 1896. PRICE 3 CENTS. [ON RAILWAY TRAINS THE SUNDAY TIMES] 5c



## A SUDDEN RISE

### From Typewriter to the Inheritor of Several Millions.

(BY ASSOCIATED PRESS WIRE.)

CLEVELAND (O.,) April 6.—Miss Gertrude Hopkins, one of the official stenographers in the Common Pleas Court, who has a surplus of personal beauty, will shortly have a typewriter for sale cheap, unless she wants to keep it as a memento of "former days." Miss Hopkins has discovered that she is an heiress to $7,000,000.

Her mother, formerly a Miss Barker, was born in New York in 1836. Miss Josephine Barker was the daughter of James Barker, who was born in England. The latter was a fourth son, and as the English law at the time gave all the property to the eldest son, he came to America. Later the eldest son, who inherited the property, becoming dissolute, sold away his life interests.

A change in the English laws turned the attention of the American Barkers to the property, and they began suit to recover the life interests. Solicitors have been retained to look after Miss Hopkins's interests. It is stated that there are very good prospects of her winning the case. There are not many claimants, and if the suit is won, Miss Hopkins will be very wealthy.

### Order of Pente "Busted."

PHILADELPHIA, April 6.—The Order of Pente, a beneficial organization, which agreed to pay the members large profits after seven years, assigned today. The assets and liabilities amount to many thousands of dollars.

## A GEORGIA TRAGEDY.

### Miss Sallie Owen Killed by Dentist Ryder at Talboton.

ATLANTA, (Ga.,) April 6.—A special to the Journal from Talboton, Ga., says that Miss Sallie Emma Owen was shot and instantly killed last night in the parlor of J. H. McCoy's residence by Dr. W. L. Ryder, a dentist. A. Persons, a candidate for Congress, was standing beside Miss Owen. He was also shot at, but received only a flesh wound. It is presumed that Miss Owen refused to marry Ryder.

Miss Owen was a graduate of the Wesleyan Female College and belonged to one of the wealthiest and most aristocratic families of Georgia. Ryder was captured a few miles from town. He had made an unsuccessful attempt to commit suicide by cutting his throat.

### Hanged for Murder.

HELENA (Mont.,) April 6.—William Biggerstaff, colored, was hanged here this morning for the murder of Richard Johnson, the champion fighter of Montana. He exhibted an unlooked-for coolness. The execution was most successful and his neck was broken. He was pronounced dead in eight and a half minutes after jerking up the body.

### Methodists Ask No Appropriation.

NEW YORK, April 6.—At today's session of the Methodist Episcopal Conference, New York district, a resolution was adopted without opposition approving the action of the House of Representatives refusing to vote appropriations to sectarian schools.

## THE MORNING'S NEWS —IN— The Times

### IN BRIEF.

**The City—Pages 5, 6, 7, 8, 9, 10, 11, 14.**

Shameful betrayal of trust by City Councilmen....T. A. Lewis discusses charges of cruelty in the Huse case....Broadway tunnel plans adopted....Possessory interests adjudged to be subject to taxation....Judge Smith publicly justifies Le Compte Davis....A female bicyclist's experience with a mule....Work of the Oil Inspector criticised....Quarrel over the transfer of a saloon....Agricultural District Park directors object to Williams, the lessee....Statistics showing working of police department for March....Crude oil takes another jump....Transfer of Boys and Girls' Society Home.

**Southern California—Page 13.**

Culpable faith-cure people of Pomona will escape punishment....Broom-corn crop at Whittier....Evidence in the Southern murder trial at Santa Ana all in....San Pedro citizens will attend the free harbor mass-meeting....Water rates advanced at Covina....Fish and gold nuggets from the San Gabriel river....Col. A. G. Gassen assaults a newspaper man at San Diego....Southern Pacific circulating harbor petitions in outside towns....Horse brutally beaten at San Bernardino....Contest between Banning Water Company stockholders gets into court....Temperance lodge organized on the warship Thetis....Discussions at the Ontario Farmers' Institute....Overland expedition to Durango, Mexico....Sugar-beet culture attracting attention at Hueneme.

**Pacific Coast—Page 3.**

The Ukiah stage upset and burned with its contents—The driver killed....New York and Boston mine-owners making a tour of inspection...."White Hat" McCarthy raises the money to prevent the sale of his horses....David E. Morgan meets a horrible death at Stanton, Ariz....Mayor Carlson of San Diego announces himself as an independent candidate for Congress....Rich gold discoveries in the southeastern part of Kern County....A pottery firm insolvent....The indictment against Attorney Coffin of Heney trial notoriety, is quashed....The Vanderbilt party return to Sacramento from Oregon and go East today....Linton sentenced to ten years for manslaughter.

**General Eastern—Pages 1, 2, 3.**

The River and Harbor Bill passes the House—Representative McLachlan [illegible] the measure with a view to increased appropriations, but is cut off....The Cuban resolutions adopted by an overwhelming majority—The funding bill and its status—Snappy debate over the Postoffice Appropriation Bill in the Senate—Senator Allen discusses the spoils system, and says Cleveland is a disgrace....Gen. Harrison married to Mrs. Dimmick....The Supreme Court adjourns for a week, without passing upon the Wright law....Panic caused by fire in a Chicago church....Dentist Ryder kills the girl who rejected him, and shoots at a Congressional candidate....Conference of Ballington Booth and his sister....Annual gathering of Latter-day Saints....President Cleveland sends secret agents to Cuba.

**By Cable—Pages 1, 2.**

American contestants win in the preliminary Hellenic games at Athens....The Ailsa wins the cruising race from Nice to Monaco....Arabs rout the dervishes at Hoyet—Anxiety felt at Cairo for the safety of the Egyptian advance guard....Result of the vote on the Cuban resolutions anxiously awaited at Madrid—The fighting in the island.

**At Large—Pages 1, 2, 3.**

Dispatches were also received from Helena, Mont.; New York, Salt Lake, Philadelphia, Silver City, N. M.; Washington, Buluwayo, Africa; Butte, Chicago, London, Paris and other places.

**Financial and Commercial—Page 12.**

Visible supply of grain at New York....Active demand for sheep at Chicago....Stock market active at New York....Money on call easier....Good trade in grain at Chicago, Liverpool and San Francisco....Gold shipments....Stocks and bonds....Coast markets.

**Weather Forecast.**

SAN FRANCISCO, April 6.—For Southern California: Generally fair on Tuesday; fresh to brisk westerly winds.

## THE BOOTHS.

### Ballington's Sister Entreats Him to Return—A Cablegram.

NEW YORK, April 6.—Ballington Booth and his sister, Mrs. Booth-Tucker, had a protracted conference, lasting from 10 o'clock last night until 4:30 o'clock this morning, in Ballington Booth's residence, Montclair, N. J. There was no lack of cordiality, but it is understood that the entreaties of Mrs. Booth-Tucker were addressed to Ballington to return. At the Salvation Army headquarters in this city today, there being present the Booth-Tuckers, Commissioner Carleton, Maj. Matan and Secretary Lewis, a cablegram to Gen. William Booth was prepared, but its contents were not divulged.

The following statement was made by Commander and Mrs. Ballington Booth in the headquarters of the Volunteers: "We have met and had an interview with our sister, Mrs. Booth-Tucker, and wish it distinctly understood that our attitude is absolutely unchanged and that our future plans for the Volunteers will go forward as heretofore stated."

### Minister Terrell Reports.

WASHINGTON, April 6.—Mr. Terrell, Minister to Constantinople, arrived at Washington last night. Today he had a long interview with Assistant Secretary Adee, describing to him at length the conditions existing in Turkey. He saw Secretary Olney only a short time, to pay his respects. The Minister expects to remain in Washington for a few days. Asked how long he would be in the United States, Minister Terrell referred vaguely to the departmental regulations permitting a leave of absence for sixty days from his post. He declined to say whether he intended to return to Turkey, or when.

[SPORTING RECORD.]

# NEW AND OLD.

## American Boys Leading At Athens.

## Modern Brawn in the Ancient Athletic Games.

### Eighty Thousand People Witness the Contests.

**The Lawrence Prizefighting Outfit Bound Over for Manslaughter and Slugging—Showalter is a Champion—Races.**

(BY ASSOCIATED PRESS WIRE.)

ATHENS, April 6.—(By Atlantic Cable.) The athletic contests, which are intended by the projectors as a revival of the ancient Hellenic contests, opened today, and the preliminary exercises were accompanied by an impressive ceremonial. Great enthusiasm was manifested by the people, and the occasion is being observed as a national festival, the city being gaily and brilliantly decorated, and thousands of sightseers being abroad. Many visitors are here, attracted by the athletic events.

The day opened with a religious ceremony, the singing of a Te Deum in the cathedral. This was attended by the royal family and a great throng of spectators and auditors. Although the sky was overcast and threatened rain, this did not detract in any degree from the enthusiastic interest in the sports. The number of spectators who looked on at the contests is estimated at 80,000. The royal family entered the inclosure at 3 o'clock, except the Crown Prince Constantine, the Duke of Sparta, who has been an active factor in the making of the arrangements for the contests, and who today accompanied the Organization Committee.

The Crown Prince and the committee met King George as he advanced in the midst of the arena. There he was welcomed by his son on behalf of the committee, the Crown Prince begging him to take over the Stadion, which had been restored as nearly as possible to its pristine condition through the generosity of M. Averoff, whose statue was unveiled yesterday. King George, in reply, praised the incomparable beauty of the restored structure, and cordially welcomed the athletic young men who have come from all parts of the world to lend additional brilliancy to the festival. The King then took formal possession of the Stadion in the name of Greece.

The united military bands, playing as one, then rendered a hymn, while the King, the members of the royal family and their attendants, took the place which had been allotted to them, all overlooking the arena from an advantageous point of view and at the same time in sight of those who had gathered to witness the games.

The vast concourse of people, eager with interest, yet silent and attentive under the open sky, listened to the ceremony, the religious touch which was given to the exercises, the historic associations of the place and the almost reverent purpose manifested to revive in some sort and preserve the memory of the cherished glories of antiquity, all appealed strongly to the mind of each of the 80,000 persons who were ranged about the arena.

All this was a stimulus to the young athletes gathered to test their prowess and all were eager in the competition although the utmost courtesy was manifested in the intercourse of the contestants.

The members of the American teams of Princeton and the Boston Athletic Association came into the arena in excellent condition and full of confidence, and the Greeks were plainly in fear of their American competitors. The result proved that the confidence of the Americans and the fears of the Greeks were both fully warranted, the Americans carrying off first honors in each event in which they entered. Today's contests were preliminary trials, and so decided nothing definitely as to the final awards of victory. The trials were running races at 100 metres, 400 metres and 500 metres and throwing the discus, a sport as old as Greece itself and to which the putting the shot of modern athletics is most nearly allied. The hop, skip and jump was also contested and won by an American.

In the 100 metres dash, the first heat was won by F. A. Lane of the Princeton team; Zokoloy, a Hungarian, second; time 12 2-5s.

In the second heat, at 100 meters, Thomas P. Curtis of the Boston Athletic Association won; Chaalkokondghis, a Greek, coming in second; time 12 4-5s.

In the third heat of the 100 meters, Thomas E. Burke of the Boston Athletic Association won; Osman, a German, second, time 11 4-5s. The fourth heat in the 100meter dash is fixed for Friday.

In the running race for 800 meters none of the Americans competed.

In throwing the discus Capt. Robert Garrett of Princeton won against the Greeks, Paras, Revolpulo and Verie.

In the 400 meters, running dash first heat: H. B. Jameson of Princeton won, Osman, the German, being second. In the second heat Thomas F. Burke won, Gimely, an Englishman, being second.

Of the above-mentional Americans, F. A. Lane is from Franklin, O. He prepared for Princeton at the Wittenborg College, Springfield, O.

Thomas H. Curtis was born in San Francisco and is 24 years old. He has been a football player and is considered the most promising hurdler in America. He is of medium height and weighs 145 pounds trained.

Thomas E. Burke is not yet 21. He weighs 144 pounds. He was born in Boston, and won his spurs at the international games between the New York Athletic Club and the London Athletic Club in New York, when he ran the 440 yards in 49s.

Robert Garrett of Baltimore is 20 years of age, weighs 178 pounds and stands 6 feet 2 inches in height.

Jameson is from Peoria, Ill. He is 22 years of age, weighs 152 and is 5 feet 8 inches in height.

### Showalter the Champion.

PHILADELPHIA, April 6.—J. W. Showalter tonight won the chess championship of the United States, and a purse of $750 by defeating Emil Kemeny of this city in the fifteenth game of the match. Score, Showalter, 7; Kemeny, 4; drawn, 4

### CHARGED WITH MANSLAUGHTER.

**Arthur Bradley Arraigned for Killing His Adversary.**

(BY ASSOCIATED PRESS WIRE.)

LAWRENCE (Mass.,) April 6.—Arthur Bradley of Haverhill, one of the principals in the fatal prizefight here Saturday night, was arraigned today, charged with manslaughter and prizefighting and ten others were charged with being present and aiding and abetting the fight. Bradley was bound over to the grand jury in $2500 on the charge of manslaughter, and $2000 on the charge of prizefighting. The other defendants were bound over in $1000 each.

### San Francisco Races.

SAN FRANCISCO, April 6.—The weather was fine and the track slow. Three favorites, two second choices and an outsider won.

Half a mile: Sister Adelle won, Modestia second, Parthamax third; time 0:52.

Five and a half furlongs: Mobalasca won, Pat Murphy second, Irma third; time 1:10¼.

One mile: Imp. Miss Brummel won, Maj. Cook second, Yankee Doodle third; time 1:44¾.

One and one-sixteenth miles: Sister Mary won, Sam Leake second, Peter II third; time 1:51½.

Seven furlongs: Walter J. won, All Smoke second, Perseus third; time 1:31½.

Seven furlongs: Nelson won, Nephew second, Pollock third; time 1:31¼.

### The Ailsa Won.

NICE, April 6.—In the cruising race from here to Monaco and return today the Ailsa won, Satanita second and Britannia third.

### Murderer Linton Sentenced.

JACKSON, April 6.—Henry Linton, convicted of manslaughter in the killing of Henry Vogel, was sentenced today to ten years in San Quentin, the extreme penalty.

## PANIC IN A CHURCH.

### WHAT THREATENED TO BE A HOLOCAUST.

**Mad Crush of the Members of the Second Baptist Congregation to Escape Peril—The Minister and the Organ Kept On—A Brave Sexton.**

(BY ASSOCIATED PRESS WIRE.)

CHICAGO, April 6.—Eighteen hundred people were in the seats and aisles of the Second Baptist Church last night and Rev. Dr. W. M. Lawrence, pastor of the venerable and historic place of worship, was in the midst of an eloquent sermon, when it was noticed by a few in the congregation that the ceiling was on fire. Before a word could be said, however, a blazing brand fell among the flowers which surrounded the pulpit. Instantly there was a rush for the door. Over the roar of the stampeded worshippers came the reassuring voice of pastor Lawrence: "There is no danger."

But the worshippers, distracted beyond control, did not pause. Again did the pastor cry out: "If you will resume your seats, I will finish my sermon," but as he uttered the last word another blazing brand fell and then the chandelier, with its 105 lights, tottered to one side and a sheet of flame rolled over the pastor's head. The terrified worshippers waited for no further counsel. They stormed through the aisles, over the pews and were wedged in a struggling mass at the doors. Organist Howard Wells now attempted to quell the panic. The voice of the pastor was lost in the tumult, but the great roar of the organ could be heard. Its melody, however, had no effect. A woman who lay upon the threshold was being trampled on when a patrolman dragged her upon the steps. She was taken away bleeding and in a swoon by friends who were summoned. Using force in some instances and calling upon the people to take their time, the policeman fought his way into the auditorium, where he picked up three old women who had fainted.

When the tumult was at the height Capt. George Cressy marched the boys' brigade down the aisles and ordered them to save the flowers and pulpit chairs. Then the beautiful Easter decorations were torn from the altar, and, following them came the pulpit itself, leaving the pale but calm-faced pastor still standing in a downfall of burning embers and Organist Wells running his fingers over the keyboard in a thundering rendition of the hymn, "Onward, Christian Soldiers."

Sexton Allison had not been unmindful of his charge during all the panic. When the worshippers arose and stormed the doors he ran to the balcony, climbed a ladder which led to the attic and, fighting his way through the heavy smoke, reached the big burner and the flames that were rapidly making their way through the roof. He was accompanied by David Murry. Without waiting for the firemen whom Usher Toates was making haste to summon, the aged sexton stripped himself of his coat and sought to smother the flames with the garment, but the fire had gained such headway that it not only destroyed the coat, but severely burned the hands of the courageous fighter.

The sexton's vest was then used to whip the flames, but this, too, proved of no avail and it was not until water was brought in pails from the auditorium that the fire was extinguished. When the firemen dashed up before the hundreds of frightened people who still filled the streets and dragged their leads of hose through Easter lilies, palms and hyacinths to the gallery, one man, blackened, stripped of coat and vest and so badly burned that he could scarcely clutch the rounds of the ladder, came down from aloft. It was the sexton.

"The fire is out, boys," he gasped out, for he was all but suffocated by smoke.

But the firemen hammered away in the lath and plaster to make sure their services were not needed and when they left the place a great, ragged hole in the ceiling, which completely encircled the chandelier, told of the narrow escape of the venerable structure. Sexton Allison said that the fire was undoubtedly caused by a leak in the big gaspipes which supplied the chandeliers. The injuries of those hurt in the stampede are not serious.

THE FLOOR SANK.

OMAHA (Neb.,) April 6.—A panic was narrowly averted at the South Tenth-street Episcopal Church last night. The services had scarcely begun when a portion of the auditorium floor sank from two to four feet, jostling the worshippers and frightening the women. Everybody was able to get out without injury.

# GOBS OF PORK.

## The River and Harbor Bill Passes.

## Big Sums for Many Sections Except San Pedro.

### Southern California's Hope Now in the Senate.

**Representative McLachlan Makes an Effort to Secure Discussion but Fails—Senator Allen Roasts Cleveland.**

(BY TELEGRAPH TO THE TIMES.)

WASHINGTON (D. C.,) April 6.—(Special Dispatch.) The Rivers and Harbors Bill, making an appropriation of $60,000,000, including the continuing contracts, passed under suspension of rules, not allowing debate or amendment. Mr. McLachlan proposed a suspension of the rules in order to endeavor to get a larger appropriation for San Pedro. He made the following speech:

"I am opposed to the motion of the gentleman from New York to suspend the rules and pass this bill, for the reason that if this course is pursued, it will give no opportunity to any one to offer any amendments to this important measure, making appropriations aggregating over $60,000,000 of the people's money, including the continuous contracts provided therein. I assume that the Committee on Rivers and Harbors have faith in the justice and merits of the bill that it has presented here today, and if I am right in this assumption that committee can surely have no valid objection to submitting its labors and conclusions to the deliberate judgment of this house, and give us a reasonable opportunity to investigate them ourselves. The members of this committee will not claim to be infallible, or assume that their judgment upon many features of this bill is superior to that of the whole House.

"This bill is far from being satisfactory to me or the people whom I represent. San Pedro harbor, the point in my district where two great transcontinental railroads touch tidewater on the Pacific Coast, has received most miserly consideration at the hands of this committee, notwithstanding the most reasonable demands that we made of it, and I urge you to defeat this resolution to suspend the rules and pass this bill so that I may have an opportunity to present to this house the merits of our claims for San Pedro and Southern California. Having had an opportunity to do that, I must be satisfied with the result, but if this resolution prevails, I will have no opportunity to present our case to the House, and must submit to the wrong perpetrated by the committee against an improvement that deserves far better consideration than it has received at the hands of the committee.

"There are other localities that have similar grievances against the provisions of this bill, and we simply demand an opportunity to be heard. This is reasonable; that is just."

As he wanted an increase his motion was voted down. Increases are never allowed, opening up, as they do, endless debates. W.

WILL FIGHT IN THE SENATE.

WASHINGTON, April 6.—(Special Dispatch.) The River and Harbor Bill as it passed the House this afternoon carried all California appropriations with it. There is no doubt, however, that a strong fight will be made in the Senate to change some of the California items. One of the amendments proposed is to place Oakland harbor under the continuing-contract system, as originally intended by the House committee, then an effort will be renewed to have the amount of the San Pedro appropriation increased to $392,000 and have that work also placed under the continuing-contract system. The friends of Santa Monica will not be asleep either. They want an appropriation of $2,800,000 authorized, the work to be done under the contract system.

The Oakland and San Pedro projects have the indorsement and will be pushed by Senators White and Perkins, while Santa Monica will be left in the hands of railroad men who are now fighting the California Mineral-land Classification Bill.

SENATE AND HOUSE.

WASHINGTON, April 6.—The Senate spent the entire day on the Postoffice Appropriation Bill, but did not complete it. The bill served to bring out some sharp criticisms by Senator Gorman on the administration of the Postoffice Department and by Senator Allen on alleged iregularities resulting from the civil service system. Senator Allen repeated the sensational charges as to the large money contributions said to have been made in the interest of Mr. Cleveland and Gen. Harrison. The charge that Mr. Wanamaker contributed a large sum toward Gen. Harrison's election led to an emphatic denial from Senator Hawley. Senator Allen alluded to the President as "His Majesty" and as the chief mugwump of the country. The vote on the Postoffice Bill will be taken tomorrow.

The House today adopted the conference report on the Cuban resolutions by a vote of 224 to 27 and passed the River and Harbor Appropriation Bill under suspension of the rules, after a lively debate of forty minutes, by a vote of 216 to 40. The report on the Cuban resolutions had been debated Friday and Saturday and the vote today was taken directly after the reading of the journal. Eighteen Republicans and nine Democrats voted against the report. After the most determined opposition of those opposed to the recognition of the insurgents in the Senate and House there were but ten more votes against the report than against the original resolutions. The former vote was 262 to 17. By its action today the House agreed to the Senate resolutions and disposed of the Cuban question for the present. Those resolutions were as follows:

"Resolved, That, in the opinion of Congress, a condition of public war exists between the government of Spain and government proclaimed and for some time maintained by force of arms by the people of Cuba, and that the United States of America should maintain a strict neutrality between the contending powers, according to each all the rights of belligerents in the ports and territory of the United States.

"Resolved, further, that the friendly offices of the United States should be offered by the President to the Spanish government for the recognition of the independence of Cuba."

The River and Harbor Bill passed today carries an actual appropriation of $10,330,560 and authorizes contracts for thirty-two new projects, with a limit of cost of $51,251,210. Only forty minutes' debate was allowed. Mr. Hooker, chairman of the River and Harbor Committee, attempted to secure an extension of this time, but first Mr. Maguire of California and then Mr. Grosvenor of Ohio objected.

The debate was very spirited. Mr. Dockery of Missouri attacked the recklessness with which it was proposed to extend the "continuing contract" system on the bill, a natural result, he claimed, of the policy of giving the government's promise to pay instead of paying cash. He admitted, however, the great economy of the contract system, which Mr. Burton of Ohio had stated from official reports to be 30 per cent.

Mr. Hepburn of Iowa also made a vigorous assault on the bill, which he said had enough "pork" in it to insure its passage. He devoted himself particularly to the Mississippi River Commission, the work of which he denounced. This brought forth a reply from Mr. Catchings, the former chairman of the River and Harbors Committee, and a defense of the measure from Mr. Hooker of New York, the present chairman. When the vote was finally taken the majority in favor of it was so overwhelming that its opponents were unable to secure the ayes and nays.

Before the House adjourned the New Mexican Bond Bill was defeated and the bill to open the Assinaboine Military Reservation was passed.

### FIFTY-FOURTH CONGRESS.

REGULAR SESSION.

(BY ASSOCIATED PRESS WIRE.)

WASHINGTON, April 6.—SENATE: Many Senators were absent of late in their seats. Messrs. Chandler of New Hampshire, Harris of Tennessee, Lindsay of Texas, Patmo of Ilinois, and Thurston of Nebraska. Among the bills favorably reported was one to prevent wholesale divorces in the territories by requiring a year's residence before application.

Senator Frye of Maine introduced a bill to pension the widow of the late Gen. Thomas L. Casey at $100 a month.

Senator Call of Florida made an ineffectual effort to take up the Cuban resolution offered by him some days ago, proposing the immediate use of the United States Navy to protect American citizens in Cuba and to prevent barbarities.

Senator Allison insisted that the appropriation bills must be kept to the front.

Senator Call gave notice that he would move to take up the Cuban resolutions tomorrow.

The Postoffice Appropriation Bill was taken up, the pending question being that of the consolidating of the country and suburban postoffices as adjuncts to the city or the metropolitan districts.

Senator Wolcott advocated the reform as essential to the vast postal service of the country, small postoffices being created at the rate of over two thousand a year, and the aggregate army of 70,000 postmasters maintaining separate accounts with Washington. He believed the change would do away with the system of giving postoffices as rewards for political services, the Democratic grocery store-keeper running the postoffice of one administration and the Republican grocery store-keeper running it the next administration.

Senator Wolcott said he was by no means friendly with the present administration, yet he desired to commend the able and intelligent conduct of the Postoffice Department under Postmaster-General Wilson. The Senator added that this was a move toward throwing off the domination of the spoils system from the postal service. "Civil service is," he said, "largely an acquired taste, but any public man who has remained here through an opposing administration and has seen men appointed to office as a reward for political dirty work, unworthy men, not fit to hold office, many of them unintelligent and unprincipled men—then one can appreciate the virtues of civil service."

Senators Wolcott and Gorman joined issue over some references of the former to the Elliott City, Md., absorption of the Baltimore postoffice, the latter saying he knew all about the matter and did not, like Senator Wolcott, get his information at second-hand.

Senator Wolcott said that any differences that might exist between the Postmaster-General and one or two Senators ought to give way before the needs of public service

Senator Gorman argued that Senator Wolcott sought to place the subject on a low plane. He sought to intimate that this was a mere personal and political question.

"If it is a political question," exclaimed Senator Gorman with intense sarcasm, "then I congratulate the Postoffice Department that a distinguished Senator on the other side of the chamber can be its defender on this occasion. There has been a suspicion among many Democrats that many acts of this administration could consistently be defended by some Republicans.

Senator Gorman rejected the idea that the postoffices were a huge spoils system. He served under Democratic administrations and under Republican administrations, and the mere appointment of postmasters was not anything to him. He said he knew, from recent events, that any resolution by him would be rejected. Senator Gorman said that his observation of civil service reformers was that they were the first to get their friends into office, and then to keep them there. Referring to the Postmaster General, Senator Gorman said it would be well for that official to listen to the people and serve them rather than to be delivering lectures on tariff and gold and silver. It would be well, said Senator Gorman, to return to the old rule that when we found a man constantly proclaiming his virtue there was a rascal near at hand.

The Senator said he hoped to see a Postmaster General, no matter what his politics might be, who would really re-

Part I—News Sheet—Pages 1 to 8.

# The Los Angeles Times

XVIth YEAR. [At the Counter....3 Cents.] [By the Month.....75 Cents.] THURSDAY MORNING, MARCH 18, 1897.—TWO PARTS: 14 PAGES. PRICE {On Streets and Trains / At All News Agencies} 5c



# THE NEW WORLD'S CHAMPION.

## Fitzsimmons Won the Big Fight in Fourteen Furious Rounds.

### Corbett Was Caught Off His Guard at the Moment When Victory Seemed Assured.

### IT WAS A BATTLE ROYAL FROM START TO FINISH.

**Jim Had the Best of the Contest Till a Terrible Blow Under the Heart Put Him Out—He Recovered Almost Immediately and Begged for Another Chance to Prove His Right to the Championship Belt—The New Champion Says He Has Honors Enough and Will Retire from the Ring—The Arena Was Spattered with Gore Drawn from Fitzsimmons's Face Under the Rain of Corbett's Blows—Scenes and Incidents at the Ring Side Graphically Told.**

[BY THE TIMES' SPECIAL WIRE.]

CARSON (Nev.,) March 17.—[Special Dispatch.] Like the evening sun which drops slowly behind the hills and fills with a burst of evanescent glory the hushed sky, James J. Corbett, the cleverest, cleanest fighter the world has ever produced, sank slowly upon his right knee beside the ropes of the arena wherein stood his only rival, and ten seconds later the air was rent with the yells of the frenzied multitude which almost breathless had waited for this instant.

There was something awful in the impulse which prompted this fearful outcry from the vast assemblage, and almost instinctively the thought flashed upon the mind that here again was the Roman amphitheater of old, its wolfish masses thirsting for human blood, ready at any instant with thumbs turned downward to cry, "Habet, habet!"

Human nature was at its worst. Probably not a man of the 5000 but sat the fight out, nerved to eagerness for but one thing—the blow which should lay his gladiator's foeman prostrate and senseless in the dust. Some may have expected otherwise, and have wagered on a draw or may have believed in their hearts that the contest was to be false, but when this splendid pair of human battering rams entered the ring and faced each other for the fray, which for the time being bore in its possibilities the proportions of life and death, not a man of them all but had a desire tugging at his heart, whispering fiercely, "Sick him, Corbett," or "Knock him out, Fitz," and when the end came, as I have said, the yells of the frenzied multitude rent the air.

Men hugged each other, cast canes, hats, hankerchiefs and newspapers into the air, and with the clamor of tongues of Babel told each other and everybody who chose to listen what they thought of it and how it happened.

It was a great fight. I have seen some big batles in the course of the three years that the California Athletic Club was at the height of its fame, and pugilistic talent was imported from abroad much as we import blooded horses or rare wines, and I have read with interest descriptions of famous contests which I have not seen, but this, the latest, stands pre-eminent above them all. Corbett, the invincible; Corbitt who licked the popular idol Sullivan while but a stripling; "Gentleman Jim," the hope of the lovers of clean sport defeated; Why, at first thought is seems impossible, but those who saw that fight saw otherwise.

It is too stale a saying to be repeated, that Corbett is not a puncher. He depends on jabs and swings to win his battles, and his vivacity and cleverness at ducking to save him from defeat. But as Waterloo was lost to Napoleon through an error of judgement, so Corbett defeated himself today by a trifling mistake which instinct should have told him to have shunned.

About the middle of the fourteenth round, after each had rained varied blows on his antagonist's head, Fitzsimmons countered Corbett's right hand lead. Corbett should have stepped back. Instead of this, in his eagerness to get both hands home on Fitzsimmons, he merely threw his head back. This naturally impelled his body forward. Quick as a flash, Fitzsimmons shot his left into Corbett'e jaw and delivered a hook blow with his right slightly under Corbett's heart. That finished him so far as this fight is concerned. Like a tree at whose base the ax had been laid he came down slowly, his head erect and his features set. Then as the reaction of the awful blow came home to him, he lifted his left hand to his heart and horror and pain distorted his mouth and filled his eyes with such a look of suffering I never wish to behold again. He was near the ropes, just to the right of that side of the ring which was nearest to the main entrance gate.

Slowly, while the referee was counting the precious seconds, he brought himself up a little more erect, then he essayed to rise, but rolled over with an exclamation of pain, and some of those present thought his leg was broken. With fixed eyes, apparently knowing nothing, but one thing, and that he must rise, he again tried. He grasped the lower rope with his right hand and sought to pull himself up, but collapsed and while being lefted in the strong arms of his seconds, who had now crowded around him, amid a tumult indescribable, the fatal "Ten—out" was pronounced by Referee Siler and the battle had been lost and won.

Scarcely had Corbett been stood on his fefet and the words broken upon his ear that he was defeated, than he frantically essayed to make toward Fitzsimmons, who stood bewildered, surrounded by a yelling mob, scarcely knowing what was done or what he had to do. But when his seconds announced that the referee had given him the fight, and the mob piled into the ring to shake hands with him, his mouth opened above the ropes and he shot at his wife, who stood below, flushed and trembling, one of those grins of his which once seen will ever be remembered.

It was a long time before Corbett could be pacified, and Brady added fuel to the flame of the crowd's torment by making an offer to back Corbett against Fitzsimmons for another fight for $20,000 or $25,000 a side. The crowd lingered upon the scene, loath to leave, but finally filed slowly out, those who had backed Fitzsimmons being exultingly joyous, while those who had pinned their faith on Corbett, were insisting that he was the better man, pointing to the fact that he had Fitzsimmons all but out in the sixth round.

ROBERT FITZSIMMONS, CHAMPION OF THE WORLD.

The defeated champion went almost tearfully to his dressing-room, which was guarded by the faithful Jeffries. "I was not licked," he moaned. With him entered his trainers and seconds and a few chosen friends, and then the door was locked.

Corbett complained that Fitzsimmons had struck him in the stomach and many spectators carried away that impression.

John L. Sullivan, Billy Jordan, John Brink and other shining lights described it to me as a blow under the heart, and that is the way the newspapermen saw it also. Jordan said, to be exact, the blow might have been said to have landed over the spleen. He declared that no doubt Corbett was the better man, but did not know what to say about another fight.

"Parson" Davies was asked what he thought of the outcome. "Well," he said, and then shrugged his shoulders, "there you are. It was a splendid fight and on doubt another will come of it."

The Los Angeles delegates, Assemblymen Dennery, Bettman and Lacy, ex-Speaker Lynch and Secretary Steppacher, all agreed that it was worth coming miles to see, though they were not all satisfied with the outcome.

The interior of the arena presented a striking picture during the progress of the contest. In the center of the great twelve-sided amphitheater was the ring on a raised platform. To the right of it was a huge square box, which contained the kinetoscope, whose work today will picture this event to all posterity. "Boxes," or spaces divided off by a low railing of rough pine lumber, surrounded the ring to the extent of a couple of acres, and from those rose tiers of seats divided by barbed wire into two classes, those to which the price of admission charged was $20, and others to which a $10 entrance fee was charged. Common varnished pine chairs were placed in the boxes, and all else was pine boards glistening in warm sunlight and their newness. No roof but the vaulting, cloud-flecked blue sky covered the arena. The $10 and $20 seats were fairly well filled in spots, and the "boxes" nearest the stage were crowded with well-to-do citizens of this great country, or gentlemen atached to the ring as a means of acquiring wealth.

Many complaints were made by the spectators about the niggardly management which would not allow one to go to the entrance even for a look outside, without charging him therefor. One disgruntled individual figured that Stuart was charging $240 for sixteen square feet of space, and I heard several of those who occupied "boxes," for which they paid $40 a seat, six chairs to a "box," complain of being crowded and wish they had paid $20 for a reserved seat, or $10 for a chance to shuffle around on the upper tiers. As a matter of fact, those in these two classes of seats had a more unobstructed view than those who occupied "boxes" on the floor. For my double eagle, and because of my being a newspaper man, I secured a good seat in a $40 box, twenty feet from the ringside, and was fortunate in having a box to myself, with the exception of a young man from Los Angeles named Norton, who was fortunate enough to win $40 of Capt. Merry's money with his $27 by backing Fitzsimmons.

Across the aisle on my right, and one box back, sat the terrible John L. Sullivan, in a dark suit of mixed goods, black overcoat with velvet collar, clean shaven, a cigar between his teeth, and a plug hat with a broad black band. I asked Sullivan who was in his party. "Frank Dunn, the Kelliher brothers, Lewis and Tom Jones," he said. "I will go from here to St. Louis, where my show opens on Sunday." The big fellow looks pasty about the face, but appeared to be in fairly good health. He is still the idol of lovers of fistic sport, and every once in a while the shout went up, "Sullivan, Sullivan," whereat the ex-champion would endeavor to suppress a gratified smile.

At 10:38 o'clock, Billy Jordan, the old-time master of ceremonies of the California Athletic Club of San Francisco, climbed through the ropes into the ring. "Frank P. Dunn of Boston," he said, "on behalf of John L. Sullivan, challenges the winner of the contest for $5000 and will put up $1000 now with the New York World as a forfeit."

Sullivan was called for and mounted the platform. He said: "Gentlemen, there is no necessity for me saying any more than what Mr. Jordan has told you. I mean what I say—I am going one more battle. I think there's one more fight in me."

This speech he repeated to those on the opposite side of the arena, and took his seat amid cheers and applause.

Shortly afterward, Billy Madden appeared to announce that he had $2500 in Tom Lewis's hands to back Joe Goddard against the winner, the fight to take plice inside of a year, and also had $2500 of Sharkey money placed with the New York Journal's representatives for the same purpose. This brought the yell of "Sharkey, Sharkey!" in response to which the tough-mugged adversary of Lanky Bob who won his way to prominence by making a hard fight against Corbett and winning from the kangaroo fighter by what a majority of the sporting writers call a bogus foul, mounted to the stage, and with a roll as if aboard ship, advanced to the ropes when he oraculated in husky tones: "I have met both of these men, and I would like the first chance. I don't think they've got anything on me."

This beautiful sample of English was the signal for a yell of delight from his admirers, while spectators who were not impressed by his appearance sarcastically remarked that there would be something on him if Fitz or Corbett ever struck him again.

Sharkey occupied a seat with the Examiner staff much of the time. He did not look the athlete in his dark suit, black overcoat and square-topped dicer, but his scarred features were ugly enough to make him conspicuous among the short-haired fraternity.

Before the fight began, I found ex-Senator John J. Ingalls seated by Max W. Newberry of the Examiner's staff of artists in the front row of boxes. "Yes, I have come a long way to see this gathering," he said to me, "and from the financial view of this showing, I'm afraid my mission is a failure."

The brainy ex-Senator looked brown and well. He wore a brown suit, a snuff-colored overcoat and a black soft hat. He had reference to Dan Stuart's enterprise and not to his own, for I understand the Examiner pays him a very fancy figure for "doing" the picturesque features of the fight, which he afterward told me with a smile, "was very interesting."

Wyatt Earp, he of Fitzsimmons-Sharkey notoriety, sat in a box several rows back of Sullivan, and, in fact, there were notables "too numerous to mention." The first row of seats next to the ring was set aside for newspaper men from the big cities, and here could be found such noted men in their profession as Bowden of the New Yorw Press; Jim Whitfield of the Kansas City Times; Lou Houseman of the Chicago Inter Ocean; George Siler of the Chicago Tribune who refereed the fight; Rocap of the Philadelphia Record; Harry Wilford of the Cincinnati Enquirer; Ennis of the Boston Herald; Jack Taylor of the Boston Globe; Charles Seymour of the Chicago Chronicle; Carl Smith of the Chicago Record; Joe Eakins, Billy Inglis, Howard Hackett and Ed Bowen of the New York World and others. Langdon Smith of the New York Herald said to me that the attendance was not what he had expected, nor what it deserved. He thought some of these papers, he probably had in mind "Long Green's" Examiner, were responsible for this, as they had "tied it up" too close. The Examiner sent here eighteen people, under the guise of special writers, to take up space and crowd out actual working newspapermen. T. T. Williams and big Bill Naughton were the high cock-a-lorums of this gang, while ex-Senator Ingalls, pugilist Sharkey and William Muldoon, the wrestler, lent dignity thereto. Mrs. Mary Davison also helped out on pictures, though Newberry denied she was in the arena. Swinnerton and Erson and Edgren were others of the artistic talent of that sheet.

A number of women were scattered throughout the audience, and at 11:30 o'clock, Mrs. Fitzsimmons, in a black dress and hat and a long sealskin sacque, was ushered down the aisle from the northeast entrance to the corner selected for her husband.

Fifteen minutes later "One-eyed" Connolly, an old-time scrapper from Chicago, in response to yells from the crowd, entered the ring to make a speech. The most noticeable thing about Mr. Connolly was his bad eye and his jag. He got as far as, "Gentlemen, this is no time for speeches," when an attendant rushed into the ring and grappled with him, ordering him out. The one-eyed, nothing daunted, kicked out behind at his captor, and continued his talk, saying: "Fighters are ready." Here the management interfered, and Mr. Connolly was summarily called down.

These incidents helped to fill up the two hours' delay while awaiting the arrival of a special train.

At 11:55 o'clock, Bat Masterson hurried down the main aisle and called to those on the stage: "Both are ready."

About the same time thunders of applause announced the arrival of Fitzsimmons. He came down the northeastern aisle in the wake of a big policeman, followed by Roeber, Julian, Stelzner and Hickey. Fitzsimmons was clad in a long dressing gown of light blue, with red circles and half-circles figured therein.

Corbett came down the aisle to my right about the same time, also being hailed with loud acclamation. He circled around to the aisle whence Fitzsimmons came in and took a seat in that corner, while the sandy-haired apparition from Australia sat in the corner of the stage to my left. Corbett was followed by Delaney, White, McVey, Billy Woods and John Donaldson, all of whom were behind him as he fought.

Corbett was clad in a brown-striped bathing robe. Fitzsimmons eyed him curiously, and then arising from his seat, paced up and down the ring, sizing up his opponent from time to time, and evidently thinking hard. Corbett seeing him, also took to pacing on his own side.

At 12:02 o'clock Madden introduced Fitzsimmons, Corbett and Siler, all of whom were greeted with demonstrations of delight. Fitzsimmons stripped, looking brown and ruddy. He wore a blue and white breechcloth, with a belt of tiny American flags in silk. Corbett looked white beside his opponent, and appeared more finely drawn. He wore a red breechcloth. Both men had regulation fighting shoes.

After Fitzsimmons had "sized up" his rival, he called over the ropes to his wife: "I will lick him or he will lick me—that's all." Mrs. Fitzsimmons sat below her husband's chair all during the fight and was greatly concerned for his safety at several times, especially during the famous sixth round, when Corbett was hammering Fitzsimmons to the floor with what seemed irresistible blows. One of the most grotesque features of this whole exhibition was Fitzsimmons leering at his wife from over Corbett's shoulder, and winking at her with his right eye, while his mouth and nose were streaming with thick gore. In fact, so often did he repeat this winking process that some of his adherents declared he paid too much attention to his wife and not enough to Corbett.

The men smiled continually in clinches, but it was in a stereotyped way which did not disguise the fact that both were anxious. When the men met in the ring, and Corbett offered the usual hand-shake, Fitzsimmons did not respond, and Julian called out "No shake no shake." "No shake" returned Corbett. "All right" and with the air of a man who would say "That settles it" he returned to his corner.

Time was called at seven minutes past noon, and for nearly an hour these two men faced each other, though it had been said that Corbett would whip Fitzsimmons in six rounds. The latter disappointed his friends in that he did not make so many drives for which he is noted, but on the other hand he showed up harder, tougher, more wiry and more vicious. Corbett was light on his feet, more active and more clever but his blows often lacked steam and it was painfully apparant throughout the fight that he was not husbanding his wind and strength. He should not have "mixed up" with Fitzsimmons, for at in-fighting, with permission to hit during clinches, Fitzsimmons, who strikes a powerful blow showed up to better advantage than at out-fighting. His swings were nearly always wild and more than once he nearly sprawled over the ring as Corbett cleverly ducked. Fitzsimmons lost his temper once or twice and drove Corbett about the ring regardless of danger to himself. He was a horrible sight with the lower part of his face streaming with blood and his right ear tinged with life fluid from a cut, while Corbett bore not a mark, though his skin was tinged in places with his opponents gore. Outside of a front tooth which was knocked out in the thirteenth, and a red spot made by the final blow, he appeared after the battle to be in as good condition as ever, but if they ever meet again, my judgement will go with Fitzsimmons as physically the stronger. C. E. WASHBURN.

## FITZ IS STRICTLY IN IT.

## PRELIMINARY GOSSIP.

**A Cinch Game Worked by Metropolitan Newspapers.**

[BY THE TIMES' SPECIAL WIRE.]

CARSON (Nev.,) March 17.—[Special Dispatch.] It is a beautiful morning. The snow on the hillsides is glistening in the bright sunlight and the frost is rapidly disappearing from the sidewalks under the grateful warmth. There are

## GOLDEN DAYS RETURNED

### A RENAISSANCE OF MINING IN ARIZONA.

**Ledges Near Gleason Getting Richer as Depth is Attained—New Strikes Made in Sight of the Old Town of Yuma.**

[BY THE TIMES' SPECIAL WIRE.]

YUMA (Ariz.,) March 17.—[Special Dispatch.] Late arrivals from Gleason, the scene of the new strike in the Short Horn Mountains, give out sensational reports of developments there. The King of Arizona ledge, the original discovery, which was four feet wide on top and was estimated to be worth $2000 per ton, has now widened to twelve feet, at a depth of twenty feet, and the ore is continually growing richer.

Reports from Gleason and from other portions of the county where the rich strikes are being made, are fanning the flames of excitement, and Yuma county is now being prospected as never before; in fact, as no portion of Arizona ever was. On the streets, which are filled with strangers, no talk is heard but of mining, and every one has his pockets and hands full of rock.

Yesterday an old miner discovered a ledge of gold-bearing rock which those who have tested it claim to be very rich, directly across the river from Yuma, on the Indian Reservation. The ledge runs underneath the Catholic Church connected with the Indian mission. He will probably not be allowed by the authorities to work the mine, be it ever so rich.

Work is progressing on the strike made in South Yuma by Cooke of Los Angeles. As depth is attained the ledge grows wider and better-looking. A contract has been let for one hundred feet of development work, and the work will be pushed. It seems a return to the days of "forty-nine," and mortars, gold pans and horn spoons are in demand.

### THE BORREGO GANG.

**Their Only Hope is Now in President McKinley.**

[BY ASSOCIATED PRESS WIRE.]

SANTA FE (N. M.,) March 17.—The four Borrego assassins will be executed one week from this date unless ex-Delegate Catron, who is still hard at work in Washington, induces President McKinley to reopen the case and reverse Cleveland's decision denying a commutation of sentence.

It is too late to have Gov. Thornton relieved, and his successor appointed and qualified before the day of the execution. From this source the accused men have given up all idea of securing relief, but they are still hopeful that McKinley will act.

Dist.-Atty. J. H. Crist, who prosecuted these criminals, has arrived in Washington and was expected to have a conference with the Attorney-General today urging that the law take its course.

### AN HEIRESS KIDNAPED.

**Stolen in Returning from School and Held for Ransom.**

[BY ASSOCIATED PRESS WIRE.]

ST. LOUIS, March 17.—Ella Burden, 11 years old, who is an heiress to $100,000, has been inexplicably missing from her home since Monday. She lived with her grandmother, Mrs. Burden, at No. 5032 Minerva street, and left home Monday for the Dozier School, where she was regarded as one of the brightest and prettiest of several hundred pupils. At 3:30 o'clock in the afternoon, the usual hour, she left school for home and went a part of the way with several other girls, to a point where she usually took a car for home. Nothing has been heard of her since.

The only theory for her disappearance is that she has been kidnaped and is being held by her captors until a sufficient ransom is offered. A large reward has been offered for her return.

### LOST CATTLE.

**Hard Winter Played Havoc with Herds on the Ranges.**

[BY ASSOCIATED PRESS WIRE.]

MINNEAPOLIS (Minn.,) March 17.—A special from Mandan and Dickinson states that it is generally believed that 75 per cent. of the range animals have already succumbed to the winter, the chinook yesterday coming too late to save them. It is impossible to travel over the range, and no exact figures can be had. Bad Lands ranges, which have been crowded the past years, will have but few cattle this season. It is stated that Pierre Wibaux puts his loss at a million dollars, as 250,000 young Utah cattle he put on the range last fall are all dead.

### A FRANTIC FATHER.

**Kills His Two Little Children and Himself.**

[BY ASSOCIATED PRESS WIRE.]

PHILADELPHIA, March 17.—Frederick Franks, in a fit of insanity, shot and killed his son William, aged 9, shot and badly wounded his daughter Amelia, aged 5, and then sent a bullet into his breast near the heart, at his home in this city this morning. Franks made elaborate preparations for the terrible work. He arose earlier than usual, and told his wife to go to a grocery store for something for breakfast, while he made coffee. While she was gone the tragedy occurred.

# INCOME TAX DEBATE.

## SUBJECT UNEXPECTEDLY BOBS UP IN THE SENATE.

**Senator Mills Offers a Direct Tax Clause as an Amendment to the Constitution.**

## THE PROPOSITION DEFEATED.

### LAID ON THE TABLE BY A STRICT PARTY VOTE.

**Fortifications Appropriation Bill Agreed To—Railway Debt Adjustment and Other Topics Under Consideration.**

[ASSOCIATED PRESS NIGHT REPORT.]

WASHINGTON, May 4.—Quite unexpectedly a brief but sharp debate was precipitated in the Senate today in the income-tax proposition. A resolution proposing an amendment to the Constitution of the United States in relation to the succession to the Presidency was under discussion. Mr. Mills of Texas proposed an amendment in the form of a new section intended to authorize Congress to lay a tax on incomes in such form as to meet the requirements of the decision of the Supreme Court. He was sharply criticised for endeavoring to place such a rider on a resolution which practically all Senators favored, but stood his ground and insisted upon a vote on his amendment.

The amendment was defeated, 32 to 29, all the Republicans voting against the amendment and all the Democrats, except Mr. Caffery of Louisiana, together with the Populists and Silver Republicans, voting in favor of it.

The joint resolution which was adopted reads as follows:

"In all cases not provided for by article 2, clause 5, of the Constitution, where there is no person entitled to discharge the duties of the office of President, the same shall devolve upon the Vice-President.

"The Congress may by law provide for the case where there is no person entitled to hold the office of President or Vice-President, declaring what officer shall act as President and such officer shall act accordingly until the disability shall be removed or a President shall be elected."

The conference report on the Fortifications Appropriation Bill was agreed to.

### FIFTY-FIFTH CONGRESS.

REGULAR SESSION.

[ASSOCIATED PRESS DAY REPORT.]

WASHINGTON, May 4.—SENATE.—When the Senate convened today the chaplain delivered an invocation relating to the war, praying that our course be maintained as the cause of justice, equity and humanity. "Crown our arms with success and bring the war to a speedy and triumphant close, so that we may honor God, help the oppressed and deliver them from their bondage, and return to our own accustomed labors and trains of thought and of light."

On presenting an amendment to the war revenue measure providing for issuance of treasury notes instead of bonds, Mr. Stewart of Nevada said it was well understood that bonds as provided for in the bill were a favorite investment of the capitalists, while the treasury notes provided for by this amendment were the favorite method of the people in meeting emergency obligations.

Mr. Stewart's amendment was a substitute for the loan and bond section of the bill, and provided for the issuance of $500,000,000 of treasury notes which would be ample probably for the conduct of the existing war. The amendment was referred to the Finance Committee.

The conference report on the Fortification Bill was agreed to.

A House bill authorizing the Supreme Lodge of the Knights of Pythias to erect and maintain a sanitarium on the government reservation at Hot Springs, Ark., was passed.

Further conference was ordered on the bill extending the homestead laws to Alaska.

### RAILWAY ADJUSTMENT.

[ASSOCIATED PRESS NIGHT REPORT.]

WASHINGTON, May 4.—Mr. Gear of Iowa, chairman of the Pacific Railroads Committee, called up and obtained consideration for a bill authorizing a commission consisting of the Secretary of the Treasury, the Secretary of the Interior, and the Attorney-General to effect an adjustment between America and the Sioux City and Pacific Railroad Company in relation to certain bonds issued by the government, in aid of the construction of the railroad.

An amendment to the bill, offered by Mr. Harris of Kansas, provides that the commission may not accept less in settlement of the government's claim than the principal of the bonds issued in aid of the construction of the road.

Mr. Morgan of Alabama, delivered an extended speech upon the measure, in the course of which he indicated the great importance of the measure as a precedent.

At the conclusion of Mr. Morgan's speech, Mr. Cockrell of Missouri secured the passage of the following bill:

"That the Secretary of the Treasury is hereby directed to make a report showing therein the value of the silver bullion in the treasury, and the amount of the seigniorage and the amount of the existing treasury notes issued in its purchase, and the amount of standard silver dollars coined under the act of July 14, 1870, and the amount of the seigniorage and the amount of treasury notes redeemed in such dollars and retired."

Mr. Harris continuing the debate upon the pending Railroad Bill, urged the adoption of his amendment, as the very least that Congress could do in protecting the interests of the country.

Mr. Pettigrew of South Dakota said that the Sioux City Railroad was a link so important to the Northwestern system, that, if the government should insist upon the payment of its principal claim in full, about $1,600,000, the Northwestern, would pay it. He declared that the Northwestern officials had for years falsified the returns from the Sioux City Railroad, with the plan in view of securing the road at a nominal price. He said he proposed to offer an amendment to the amendment providing that not less than $3,000,000 should be accepted by the commission in settlement of the government's claims.

The proposed amendment to the Constitution in relation to the succession to the Presidency was favorably reported from the Judiciary Committee.

Mr. Mills of Texas offered the following amendment, in the form of a new section:

"Sec. 2—Direct taxes shall not be apportioned among the several States which may be included within this Union, according to their respective numbers, but Congress shall have power to lay and collect direct taxes as other taxes, duties, imposts and excises are levied and collected."

Mr. Mills explained that his amendment was offered in order that the points raised by the Supreme Court against the income-tax proposition might be met.

Mr. Hoar made an appeal to Mr. Mills to withhold his amendment, promising at any time in the future he would assist him in getting consideration for his income-tax amendment.

Mr. Mills insisted upon his amendment and Mr. Hoar then moved to lay it on the table.

Upon this the ayes and nays were demanded.

Pending the voting, Mr. Mills, when pressed by Mr. Hoar for a reason for insisting upon his amendment at this time, said: "I want to tie on the pending resolution so that it may reach the American people, who are in favor of it."

Discussing the amendment, Mr. Mills declared the war might set aflame the whole of Europe, and this country might be involved for years, yet the Congress had no power to raise money except by taxing what is now taxed and by the issuance of bonds. It had no power to make the great incomes pay their proportion of the taxes.

Mr Foraker of Ohio announced that he was both in favor of the resolution and the pending amendment. He was in favor, he said, of an income tax. It was, however, under the circumstances, better to lay the amendment on the table.

In the course of other remarks on the amendment by Mr. Mills and Mr. Stewart, Mr. Chandler pressed them hard to know why they were not willing to separate propositions which had not the slightest relation to one another. Not receiving a satisfactory reply, he commented sarcastically on the order of statesmanship that induced them to employ such tactics.

Mr. Hoar declared that the income tax proposition was as big a piece of demagogueism as was ever conceived.

He inquired of Mr. Stewart how much the millionaire mine-owners of Nevada contribute to the State through the State income tax?

Evading the question, Mr. Stewart replied that there were no millionaire mine-owners in Nevada, as they had been ruined by Republican legislation.

The ayes and nays were called on the motion to lay the proposed amendment on the table, and it was carried, 32

After some further debate upon the resolution, in the course of which both Mr. Hoar and Mr. Bacon said that it was not intended to cover, and did not cover cases of contested Presidential elections, the resolution was agreed to, the necessary two-thirds voting for it.

At 3:35 p.m., the Senate went into executive session and when the doors were reopened, Mr. Hawley presented the report of the conference of the bill suspending the law relating to the purchase of supplies by the quartermaster's department of the army.

Mr. Hawley, after the reading of the report, moved that it be agreed to.

Mr. Morgan thought the proposed law was unwise and imprudent. He said that it was most extraordinary that bureau officers should be authorized to go into the open market and purchase unlimited supplies.

After a brief debate on the report, it was laid over until tomorrow. Then, at 5 o'clock, the Senate adjourned.

### IN THE HOUSE.

WASHINGTON, May 4.—The House today adopted the conference report upon the Fortifications Bill. The remainder of the session was consumed with the consideration of the Alaskan Land Bill, and a resolution for the repeal of an act prohibiting the passage of importations in bond through the territory of the United into the "free zone." The latter was passed, but the Alaskan measure went over.

### HOUSE PROCEEDINGS.

[ASSOCIATED PRESS DAY REPORT.]

WASHINGTON, May 4.—HOUSE.—In the House today, Mr. Grosvenor (Rep.) of Ohio called up as a privileged report from the Committee on Ways and Means a resolution to repeal a joint resolution prohibiting the passage of goods in bond through this country into the free zone of Mexico, affecting importation along the northern border of Mexico. The effect of the resolution, Mr. Grosvenor said, would tend to reduce smuggling.

Mr. Lanham of Texas raised a point of order against the bill, claiming that it did not raise revenues. The Speaker overruled the point of order and in doing so, construed "raising revenue" as contemplated, as being equivalent to "affecting revenue."

The House went into committee of the whole to consider the resolution.

The resolution passed after a discussion by Messrs. Grosvenor, Slayden and Cooper for, and Mr. Stephens against it.

Mr. Hemenway presented the conference report upon the Fortifications Appropriation Bill, and it was adopted.

### SUDDEN ADJOURNMENT.

[ASSOCIATED PRESS DAY REPORT.]

WASHINGTON, May 4.—The conference report upon the act extending the homestead laws and providing for the right-of-way for railroads in Alaska was called up by Mr. Lacey of Iowa.

The conference eliminated the features from the bill providing for the appointment of a commission to consider the North Atlantic fishing and other trade relations controversies with Canada, upon which the House on Monday rejected the report upon a point of order.

Mr. Lacey explained the bill as reported from conference. He then moved the previous question, but Mr. Pitney, who had opposed the passage of the bill, raised the point of no quorum.

Mr. Lacey immediately moved to adjourn, and an adjournment was taken at 4:20 o'clock.

## WAR REVENUE BILL.

**Bond Issue Depends Upon the Vote of Senator J. P. Jones.**

[ASSOCIATED PRESS NIGHT REPORT.]

WASHINGTON, May 4.—The Senate Committee on Finance, which was in session the greater part of the day, devoted itself principally to a discussion of the bond provision of the War Revenue Bill. The Democrats contended that the feature could and should be dispensed with, while the Republicans held that a bond issue was necessary to carry on the war. The Democrats will formally suggest some substitute proposition within a day or two. Whether their plan will meet success in committee will depend upon the vote of Senator Jones of Nevada, who holds the balance of power.

## CHASKA IS GOOD NOW.

**Noted Sioux Indian Commits Suicide in Jail.**

[ASSOCIATED PRESS NIGHT REPORT.]

NIOBRARA (Neb.,) May 4.—Samuel Campbell Chaska has committed suicide. Chaska was a full-blooded Sioux Indian. Ten years ago he graduated with high honors from Carlisle, and shortly afterward became famous by marrying Cora Belle Fellows of Washington.

Neither the wealth of his fashionable society wife, nor his learning acquired by years of study at Carlisle, could eradicate the Sioux traits that generations had left in his blood.

In a few years he drifted back to the reservation and sunk to the level of a common blanket Indian again. His wife left him years ago. Chaska was in jail at the time of his death, charged with stealing horses.

[SPORTING RECORD.]

# HE MET HIS MASTER.

## LIEBER KARL COMPELLED TO LOWER HIS COLORS.

**He Led at the Start of the Kentucky Derby, but Plaudit Thundered in Ahead.**

## SIX THOUSAND DOLLAR STAKE.

### FIFTEEN THOUSAND PEOPLE SAW SIMMS RIDE TO VICTORY.

**Up Guards Captures the Chester Cup Stakes in England—Lively Games of Ball—Racing Summaries.**

[ASSOCIATED PRESS NIGHT REPORT.]

LOUISVILLE, May 4.—Lieber Karl met his master today. He lowered his colors to a grander, better horse, for Plaudit, like the aristocrat of the turf that he is, won the honors of the class by nobly responding to a call for speed in a way that will long be remembered by the 15,000 people who saw it.

Derby day dawned dark and gloomy, and by 10 o'clock the rain came and continued at intervals until 2 o'clock. The sandy soil of the track absorbed it however, and the going was not over a second or a half slow when the bell sounded.

The field was sent away in the first breakaway, with Lieber Karl in front, Isabey second, Plaudit third, and Han D'Or last. These positions were maintained as they went around the lower turn, and when they were straightened out in the back stretch Lieber Karl was a length and a half in front, while Simms had brought Plaudit up to second.

Down the home stretch they went, and as the horses passed for the final turn, Simms went to work on Plaudit, and no thoroughbred ever responded better. Each stride enabled him to cut down the distance, and when they faced the wire in the stretch Lieber Karl had but a half a length the advantage, with Plaudit still lessening the distance.

They were on even terms at the eighth pole, and then amid the lusty shouts of the throng and the stands the son of Himyar thundered down the track and to the wire, winner of the twenty-fourth Kentucky Derby. Isabey was third, a half length away, and Han D'Or last by two lengths. Results:

Five and one-half furlongs: J. H. C. won, Bangle second, Johnny Williams third; time 1:09½.

One mile: Kris Kringle won, Past Kauvar second, Mill Stream third; time 1:45.

Half mile: Glad Hand won, Preliminary second, Bridal Tour third; time —.

Kentucky Derby, one mile and a quarter, three-year-olds, stake $6000: Plaudit, 117 (Simms,) 3 to 1, won; Lieber Karl, 122 (T. Burns) 2 to 5, second; Isabey, 117 (Knapp,) 20 to 1, third; time 2:09.

Four and a half furlongs: Parker Bruce won, Duke of Baden second, Laurenton third; time 0:57¾.

Six furlongs: Rey Salazar won, Lady Irene second, Sarah third; time 1:18.

### AQUEDUCT RESULTS.

[ASSOCIATED PRESS NIGHT REPORT.]

NEW YORK, May 4.—Results at Aqueduct:

Five furlongs: Judge Wardell won, Queen of Beauty second, Continental third; time 1:02.

Five furlongs: Ninety Cents won, Problem second, Canteloupe third; time 1:03.

About seven furlongs: Warrenton won, Mazarine second, Storm King third; time 1:26¾.

The Jamaica stakes, five furlongs: Vertigo won, Autumn second, Roysterer third; time 1:02.

About seven furlongs: Nearest won, Pink Chambray second, Ella Daly third; time 1:27.

Mile and forty yards: Wordsworth won, Filament second, Festa third; time 1:46 4-5.

### OAKLAND EVENTS.

[ASSOCIATED PRESS NIGHT REPORT.]

SAN FRANCISCO, May 4.—The weather at Oakland was fine and the track fast. Results:

Five furlongs: Emma Rey, 97 (Clawson,) 2 to 1, won; Lona Marie, 97 (McNichols,) 6 to 1, second; Brown Prince, 99 (Wainwright,) 12 to 1, third; time 1:03. Cyaro, Rebecca Wells, Kitty Blake, Stangelo, Charline Lemon and Quirte also ran.

Four furlongs: Excursion, 104 (Thorpe,) 1 to 2, won; Rey Hooker, 101 (McNichols,) 25 to 1, second; Mallakwa, 108 (Piggott,) 12 to 1, third; time 0:49. Faversham, The Miller, Britomartis, Simi, Uhler, Racebud, Zaccatoso also ran.

Four and a half furlongs, selling: E. Come, 107 (Piggott,) 4 to 1, won; Melay, 106 (Gouin,) 10 to 1, second; Ojai, 101 (Ruiz,) 2 to 1, third; time 0:56¼. Also Ran II, Leo, Vertner, Obdaidian, Distance, La Parasseuse also ran.

Mile an an eighth: Judge Denny, 111 (Clawson,) 5 to 1, won; Satsuma, 116 (Shields,) 3 to 5, second; Ostler Joe, 116 (Thorpe,) 5 to 2, third; time 1:55. No other starters.

Seven furlongs, selling: San Antonio, 110 (Clawson,) 7 to 5, won; Watomba, 108 (Thorpe,) 3 to 1, second; Imp. Missioner, 108 (Piggott) 7 to 2, third; time 1:28½. Elsemore, Duke of York II, El Moro, Lady Ashley, P. A. Finnegan, Sadie Schwarts, On Gua Nita also ran.

Six furlongs, selling: San Mateo, 114 (Piggott,) even, won; Sport McAllister, 108 (Gouin,) 25 to 1, second; Mamie Scott, 97 (McNichols,) 4 to 1, third; time 1:14¾. Lucky Star, Charles A., Widow Jones, Zarro, Walter J., Pat Murphy, William O'B., Howard, Miss Ruth, Ricardo, Alma also ran.

### UP GUARDS WINS.

[ASSOCIATED PRESS NIGHT REPORT.]

LONDON, May 4.—At the second day's racing of the 1898 meeting today, Maj. Westenra's four-year-old bay colt Up Guards won the Chester cup, a handicap of 2550 sovereigns, nearly two miles and a quarter. Sixteen horses ran.

### PIRATES LOSE TO THE COLTS.

[ASSOCIATED PRESS NIGHT REPORT.]

PITTSBURGH, May 4.—The game was slow and uninteresting. Attendance, 1200. Score:

Pittsburgh, 3; base hits, 10; errors, 4.
Chicago, 7; base hits, 8; errors, 4.
Batteries—Tannehill and Schriver; Griffith and Donahue.
Umpires—Swartwood and Wood.

### TROLLEY-DODGERS WIN.

[ASSOCIATED PRESS NIGHT REPORT.]

NEW YORK, May 4.—The Brooklyns won today without an effort. Score:

Brooklyn, 11; base hits, 8; error, 1.
Washington, 2; base hits, 7; errors, 7.
Batteries—Yeager and Grimes; Mercer and Farrell.
Umpires—Connolly and Lynch.

### SPIDERS' BUNCHED HITS WON.

[ASSOCIATED PRESS NIGHT REPORT.]

CLEVELAND, May 4.—Cleveland bunched its hits in the fourth and made four runs, winning the game. Score:

Cleveland, 8; base hits, 13; error, 1.
Louisville, 3; base hits, 12; errors, 3.
Batteries—Wilson and Seimmer; Downing and Wilson.
Umpires—McDonald and O'Day.

### ORIOLES WIN AT HOME.

[ASSOCIATED PRESS NIGHT REPORT.]

BALTIMORE, May 4.—Errors by Cross gave the Orioles two runs and the game. Attendance, 1200. Score:

Baltimore, 4; base hits, 8; errors, 0.
Philadelphia, 2; base hits, 6; errors, 2.
Batteries—McJames and Clark; Wheeler and McFarland.
Umpires—Curry and Snyder.

### GIANTS DEFEAT BOSTONS.

[ASSOCIATED PRESS NIGHT REPORT.]

NEW YORK, May 4.—In the seventh inning, with three men on bases, Davis rapped a good single to center field, which was fumbled by Hamilton. Three men came over the rubber, and New York was never headed. Attendance, 3000. Score:

New York, 8; base hits, 11; error, 1.
Boston, 3; base hits, 6; errors, 3.
Batteries—Rusie and Warner; Stivetts and Bergen.
Umpires—Andrews and Emslie.

### NO GAME AT CINCINNATI.

[ASSOCIATED PRESS NIGHT REPORT.]

CINCINNATI, May 4.—Cincinnati-St. Louis game postponed; rain.

## G.A.R. RESOLUTIONS.

**Any One Who Served Under the Flag to Be Eligible.**

[ASSOCIATED PRESS NIGHT REPORT.]

AMSTERDAM (N. Y.,) May 4.—A. H. Perry Post, No. 400, has adopted unanimously a resolution to amend the constitution of the Grand Army of the Republic so as to make eligible to membership all who have served under the flag of the United States in any war.

Confederate veterans who have since served the United States in war, may also become members. The present constitution provides that only veterans of the rebellion on the Union side may become members.

J. A. Maxwell, of the council of adminstration of the State Department, introduced the resolution and will bring it before the coming State and national encampments.

**At New York Hotels.**

NEW YORK, May 4.—[Exclusive Dispatch.] E. C. Mueller of Los Angels is at the Marlboro.

## FEDERATION OF LABOR.

**Colorado Forces Claim They Can Carry the Next Legislature.**

[ASSOCIATED PRESS NIGHT REPORT.]

COLORADO SPRINGS (Colo.,) May 4.—A call was made for a State Constitutional Convention by the third annual convention of the Federation of Labor of Colorado meeting in this city. The labor forces claim that they will be able to carry the next Legislature, which convenes in January, and through that body the Constitutional convention will be called.

Radical legislation in the interests of organized labor will be demanded. The convention declares for an eight-hour law; against child labor, and in favor of the federation entering politics to secure needed legislation. The convention is by far the most important held in behalf of labor in Colorado.

## THE UNIVERSITY CLUB.

**Permanent Organization Effected. An Address by James B. Scott.**

The first regular meeting and banquet of the newly-organized University Club were held last evening at the Maison Dorée. A permanent organization was effected W. A. Spalding being elected president, C. C. Wright, vice-president, and Russ Avery, secretary and treasurer. Standing committees were appointed as follows: Membership, James B. Scott, Leslie R. Hewitt and J. D. Gish; Social Entertainment, E. W. Camp, W. T. Craig and D. W. Edelman; Finance, T. D. Mott, Jr., Warren E. Lloyd and W. H. Workman, Jr.

After the conclusion of the banquet an excellent addres wa delivered by James B. Scott upon "The Cuban War from the Standpoint of International Law." A general discussion followed, Percy R. Wilson, T. D. Mott, Jr., Prof. E. T. Pierce, Russ Avery, E. W. Camp and Dr R. W. Bell participating, the latter reading an original poem.

Those present were:

| | |
|---|---|
| H. C. Head, | C. C. Wright, |
| W. H. Workman, Jr., | James B. Scott, |
| Richard J. Dillon, | Percy R. Wilson, |
| H. A. Kiefer, | Arthur G. Van Gorder, |
| Edward W. Holmes, | C. C. Van Liew, |
| J. G. Warren, | B. M. Davis, |
| Warren E. Lloyd, | Willis Booth, |
| R. D. Emery, | D. J. Frick, |
| H. Z. Osborne, Jr., | S. M. Haskins, |
| R. M. Bell, | L. S. Thorpe, |
| W. T. Craig, | A. Davidson, |
| D. W. Edelman, | C. W. Hodgson, |
| Edward North, | S. B. Osborne, |
| W. F. Burbank, | E. T. Pierce, |
| J. W. Hart, | B. L. Mills, |
| E. W. Camp, | L. K. Chase, |
| T. D. Mott, Jr., | H. C. Brown, |
| W. A. Spalding, | Russ Avery. |

## ARSON OR ACCIDENT.

**Cobbler Rehwald's Shop Set on Fire.**

About 12:30 o'clock this morning a small blaze was discovered in the cobler's shop of L. Rehwald at No. 205 Fifth street.

Rehwald is the man who came near being a victim of mob violence yesterday afternoon because of his alleged unpatriotic utterances.

The parties who discovered the fire in the shop forced an entrance, and, once inside, found a box filled with sawdust, upon which some liquid had been poured. The box was covered with a sheet of leather, and this prevented the sawdust from breaking into a blaze, the confined smoke smothering the flames.

The only damage done was to burn a portion of the leather thrown over the box.

The origin of the fire will be a matter of police investigation. A number of people who were on the street near the shop all evening say that the old shoemaker visited his place about an hour before the fire was discovered, and that absolutely no other parties had been around the place, owing to the warning of the police earlier in the evening.

The doors of the shop were found locked and the windows tightly fastened when the men who discovered the incipient blaze sought to effect an entrance. For this reason, and because persons claim to have seen Rehwald in and around his shop, the rumor that he set fire to his own place gained currency last night, and, as stated, the matter will be fully investigated. Other than a few broken window panes, no damage was done to the place.

# RECRUITING THE ARMY.

## IT IS TO BEGIN AT ONCE THROUGHOUT THE COUNTRY.

**All Regiments Will Be Brought Up to Their Full Strength—As Fast as Enlisted the Men Will Be Sent to the Front.**

[SPECIAL CORRESPONDENCE OF THE TIMES.]

WASHINGTON, April 29.—Recruiting for the regular army under the Reorganization Bill will begin at once.

No additional machinery is necessary for inaugurating this work, as all of it can readily be done through the recruiting officers and board now scattered around the country. A circular letter of instructions has been prepared, giving directions for the work, which will be prosecuted as rapidly as possible.

The recruiting will be done at all the army posts throughout the country, and at the places where the regiments are now located. there being no limit on enlistments for the regular army on acco unty of locality, as there is in the volunteer service. Nor will any limit be placed on the total number enlisted through fear of exceeding the force authorized by law. Under the present army requirements, only about one out of every eleven applicants is accepted, and even with the relaxation probable on account of the war necessity, there is no reason to expect that the 30,000 and odd additional men needed will be procured with any undue speed.

Few people understand the constitution of the reorganized army, nor how the present force of 25,000 is to be increased to 61,000.

Briefly, this will be done by recruiting up the present companies to about twice their present strength, and by the constitution of two additional companies, and the filling out of two skeleton companies, now existing in each regiment.

The infantry regiments today consist of ten companies of about sixty men each, and two skeleton companies with no men, but with a full complement of officers. Under the new bill, these eight companies will be filled out to 106 men; two new companies of 106 each will be constituted, and the two skeleton companies will also be filled out. By this means a regiment of infantry will be increased from 480 men to 1272. The changes in the cavalry and artillery will be similar, though not so large, as this branch of the service is already organized on the twelve-company formation.

Our peace-time army is so small that it has been possible for us to be wonderfully select in its members, and it is unmatched by any on earth. Every man in it, at the time of his enlistment, is required to be between 21 and 30 years of age, of good habits and character, unmarried, and to conform to certain arbitrary regulations in regard to height and weight. In spite of the talk of certain newspapers about the dog's life that a soldier is supposed to lead, the fact remains that admission to the regular army is highly prized at all times, in most parts of the country, and there has never been the least scarcity of would-be recruits.

During the present excitement there will be little difficulty about applicants. As fast as they are enlisted, the men will be sent directly to the front to join their regiments. This is in order to give them the advantages that arise from association with trained comrades and trained officers, and enable them to learn the difficult lessons of discipline as quickly as possible. Army officers calculate that a soldier can be made under these circumstances in one-eighth of the time that would be required if his associations were entirely with other recruits.

It is said some of the State organizations wish to be advised in advance of where they are to be sent and are opposed to any separation of their commands. It is provided in the act of the organization of the volunteer army that State commands enlisting in a body shall be preserved intact. The War Department will respect this, of course, but it is extremely doubtful whether the department would undertake to guarantee that the entire quota of a State should always be kept together. In fact, this would seem to be an impossibility.

No one can tell in advance what the exigencies of war may at any time require, and troops once mustered in the service of the government have no recourse but to march where they are ordered. It might be that the two regiments of infantry and the four batteries from California would be kept together during the period of hostilities. On the other hand, the regiment might be in one place and each of the four batteries in another. In war and in the movements of armed forces the law of necessity rises superior to all others.

The War Department has issued its instructions to the officers sent out to muster in the volunteer troops of the country into the United States service. They differ in some degree from those in use in the regular army, chiefly in the greater liberality they show toward the physical qualifications of the volunteers.

The instructions provide that all volunteers are to be minutely examined by a medical officer of the United States detailed for that purpose, or by physicians engaged by the mustering officer and the regimental commander for the purpose. The physical qualifications of the volunteers as to height, weight and health are the same as those for the regulars, but the other qualifications of age and being unmarried, are not held binding. In fact, it is expressly provided that volunteers may be between 18 and 45 years of age, instead of between 21 and 30, as with the regulars.

In cavalry commands, the horses will also be examined carefully. They are required to be between five and nine years old. The United States regulation equipments only will be acceptable. consisting of a saddle, blanket, bridle, with curb and a halter of the regulation pattern. Every officer and man must be the owner of his own horse.

MARRIOTT.

**Plague in Hongkong.**

TACOMA (Wash.,) May 4.—The steamship Columbia, from the Orient, brings Hongkong advices to April 6. During the week previous to that date cases of bubonic plague in Hongkong had increased rapidly and the colonial government was considering various measures for preventing a spread of the malady.

[SPORTING RECORD.]

# JEFFRIES A KINGPIN.

## KNOCKS OUT FITZSIMMONS IN THE ELEVENTH ROUND.

**The Los Angeles Pugilist Proved to Be a Wonder and Kept Up an Invincible Jabbing at the Former Champion.**

**Lanky Bob Knocked Flat Upon His Back in the Second Round and Loses Blood in the Third.**

**Cambridge University Plays Cricket, Cook County Cyclers and the L.A.W.—Horse Races.**

[BY DIRECT WIRE TO THE TIMES.]

CONEY ISLAND SPORTING CLUB (N. Y.,) June 9.—[Exclusive Dispatch.] Big Jim Jeffries of Los Angeles is the champion pugilist of the world. At the Coney Island Athletic Club tonight he defeated Robert Fitzsimmons in a fast and vicious contest that went eleven rounds. He fought with the coolness and precision of a veteran, and at no time was he in danger of meeting with defeat. It was a fair and square contest, marked by a brilliant display of science on both sides, and was fairly and squarely won. The young Californian showed himself a master at every point in the game, and won as he pleased after he had taken the measure of his opponent.

To those who had seen him before he offered the greatest surprise. He was no longer a clumsy, awkward boxer, hesitating to lead or to follow an advantage, but a finished fighter, keen and alert for an opening, and swift to take and follow an advantage when it came to him. He came to the ring in superb condition, and the first round that he fought had no apparent effect upon him. As he stood over the prostrate form of his bleeding and unconscious opponent he looked fit to go on for another hour. He was punished throughout the fight, for no man can engage the wonderful Australian, who never before met reverse, without being hit hard and often; but he stood up to it with a lion-like courage, and never faltered.

He showed an entirely different method of boxing. He crouched very low, with his left arm extended, and Fitzsimmons seemed lost as to the best method of finding him. His defense was nearly perfect. He also showed wonderful improvement in footwork and hitting power. He was as lively as a lightweight on his feet, and repeatedly ducked the undercutting swings of his opponent. He has stopped cuffing and chopping. He punches and hooks and swings with the precision of a finished boxer.

It was a great battle, and the young victor will probably remain the champion for years to come. He has size, weight and speed, and the comparative ease with which he defeated Fitz, whom they all feared, will give him wonderful confidence.

Jeffries won a fortune by his wonderful victory, and furnished one of the greatest upsets in the history of pugilistic betting. Hundreds of thousands of dollars were placed on him at the ruling odds of 2 to 1. Fitz was regarded as a sure winner, and was liberally backed. It was admitted that he was at a disadvantage, as far as youth, weight and reach were concerned, but his backers relied upon his speed and cleverness to pull him through. It was thought that he would simply stand away from his man, and jab and chop him to a finish. In reality, he found himself pitted against a man just as fast as himself and equally clever as a boxer. He went in with every confidence, only to be fooled by the young giant whom he faced, and then beaten to a knockout by superior strength.

The credit for Jeffries's notable victory belongs to the men who prepared him. Billy Delaney, who developed the Corbett that whipped John L. Sullivan, was his guide. With the eye of an expert, he studied and guarded Jeffries's physical development and care, and Tommy Ryan and Jim Daly taught him the science of the ring. In six weeks they accomplished, with the excellent material in their hands, what ordinarily takes years of actual experience to do. They had raw material, and they whipped it into shape.

As is usually the case, the man on the short end of the betting had the crowd behind him, and the young Californian was cheered on to victory. When it became apparent that he was standing his opponent off and taking the lead, he jumped into marvelous popularity, and New York will tomorrow hail him as King. He will retain his popularity, for he is as modest as a girl. He prepared for the battle without a word of disrespectful nature for his opponent, and was calm in victory. He had said in calm, but determined way, that he was going to win. He believed it, and realization was but proof of his words. Again, he is the first American in this half of the century to win the championship, and among the thousands of patrons of the ring he will be hailed for that respect.

It was California's night in pugilism, for principal, manager and trainer claim the Golden State as home. In the house, too, there was a hopeful little band of Californians, who cheered their favorite from the handshake to the count-out. It was one of the few heavyweight championship events ever pulled off in New York, and it was Gotham's first chance of seeing Fitzsimmons in a real contest, and the fight provoked tremendous interest.

It was 9 o'clock before the auditorium of the clubhouse began to fill up. The crowd was a most remarkable one. There were delegations from almost every city of importance in the United States and Canada, and in the number were all the sporting men of note. Professional New York, however, contributed the largest portion of the great audience that numbered nearly ten thousand and paid about $100,000 for its sport.

Both men entered the ring in splendid shape, and the fight proved that they were so. There was but little time lost in the ring. Nobody paid any attention to the announcements, and drowned the voice of Frank Burns, who made them. The impatient, eager crowd had not come for speeches, but to see the fight. Jeffries quietly slid off a red sweater and a pair of black trousers, and showed the most remarkable physique that those present had ever seen. Great masses of muscle lay on his back, chest and shoulders, but it played lightly and swiftly when he moved.

Fitzsimmons was finely drawn and lithe, and looked like a greyhound when he tossed off his blue bathrobe. They were both under twoscore of great

JAMES J. JEFFRIES, WHO BY HIS DEFEAT OF FITZSIMMONS HAS BECOME THE CHAMPION OF THE WORLD.

electric lights that burned on the gallery over their heads, to furnish light for the vitascope pictures, and seemed like actors under a huge calcium.

When the gong sent them away, they both began to size one another up, and nothing effective was done in the opening round. Fitz was aggressive in the second and until the eighth round, but Jeffries stood up to him and fought him back to a standstill. The Cornishman went down before a straight left in the second round, and Jeffries kept putting his head back. Fitz persistently pressed the Californian, but he had met his match, and was powerless to land an effective blow. He put his left on the young Californian's eye in the fifth round and cut it, but Jeffries came back gamely and fought on.

The Californian used his left effectively on the face and body, and also brought his right into play on the body repeatedly. Fitzsimmons tried all his tricks and devices, but was either blocked or countered harder than he led. After the seventh round the young Californian had things all his own way. The eighth round was all his. He sent the Australian staggering against the ropes with a left-hander and again landed his left. Fitz went to his corner dazed.

Fitz came back fairly strong in the ninth round, only to be beaten back. It was all Jeffries's way, and there was consternation in the Fitzsimmons corner. The crowd saw the inevitable result, and there were hoarse yells for the Californian to go in.

In the tenth round Fitz was beaten to a standstill, and it was only the call of time that saved him. He was down twice, and was done for when he staggered to his corner.

The end came after a minute and a half of fighting in the eleventh round. It was left and right from Jeffries, and the Australian, who had always never known defeat, dropped down unconscious. His seconds frantically called to him, but their words fell upon deaf ears. Referee Siler and the timers called off the ominous count of ten, and there was a roar of applaus that shook the building up. A new champion was heralded.

Jeffries's seconds swarmed around and embraced him, and in an instant hundreds of spectators broke for the ring. The police stopped the advance, and while Jeffries slipped through the ropes and ran for his dressing-room, Fitzsimmons, still limp and unconscious, was carried to his corner. He was some time in reviving, and then did not know he was beaten or that he had been in a fight.

### FIGHT BY ROUNDS.

[BY DIRECT WIRE TO THE TIMES.]

CONEY ISLAND SPORTING CLUB (Ringside,) June 9.—When time was called for the first round Bob dances as Jeffries feints. They break instantly, and Jeffries is short of a left jab for the head. Jeffries is short with a left again, but touches the wind and puts a left on the neck.

Second round—Jeffries misses a left for the head, and Bob rushes and puts a left on the neck and a right over the heart. Jeffries closes into a light clinch, then, crouching, pushes a left to the stomach, but his right swing only grazes Bob's shoulder. Jeffries rushes two lefts to the wind and chest, then jabs the face twice with the left. Fitz swings a right to the shoulder. Jeffries shoots a straight left to the jaw and Bob goes down squarely. He is soon up and starts to rush, but his left and right drives for the head are neatly blocked.

Third round—A clinch to open. Fitzsimmons missed a left, and Jeffries comes back with a left on the nose, and the claret shows on Fitzsimmons's face. Bob plants a good right over the heart, and after an exchange of left-handers, Fitzsimmons pokes the left to the neck, and Jeffries comes back hard on Fitzsimmons's ribs with a left, and a right to the stomach. Jeffries jabs the left twice to the face. Jeffries puts a stiff one on the stomach with the left and repeats it a little later. Fitzsimmons hooks a left to the ear, and his right goes over Jeffries's head, and an instant later Jeffries ducks another one. Now Jeffries ducks into a stiff left, catching it on the mouth. The men were sparring at the bell.

Fourth round—Jeffries misses a left, but ducks Fitzsimmons's right swing. Fitzsimmons misses a left for the stomach, and Jeffries puts a good right over the heart. His left for the wind is stopped, but he shoots a hard left to the neck. Fitzsimmons smiles and hooks a right to the ear; Jeffries planting a sledge-hammer right over the heart. Another miss of Fitzsimmons's right draws Jeffries's right to his ribs. Fitzsimmons puts a light left to the mouth and brings his right to the ear, and Jeffries ducks into a stiff left swing. He rushes Bob to the ropes, good footwork carrying Fitzsimmons out of danger.

Fifth round—Bob puts a left straight on the mouth and Jeffries misses a left for the head. Fitz cuts the eye with his right. Both miss lefts. Bob shoots a left to the bad eye and swings to the ear with the same glove. Bob puts a left straight on the mouth, and Jeffries misses a left for the head. Fitz cuts Jeffries's eye with his right. Both miss lefts. Bob shoots a left to the bad eye and swings to the ear with the same glove. Jeffries sends a left to the wind and a right to the ribs. Fitz rushes and puts a left on the neck, and Jeffries misses a savage left swing. Jeffries shoots a straight left to Fitz's mouth, and Fitz tries a left for the solar plexus. Jeffries plants a left on the chin, then jabs the face with a short-arm left. Fitzsimmons misses two lefts, and Jeffries hooks the right, sending Bob to his knees. He is up in a jiffy, and Jeffries pushes a right on the ribs and a left on the nose, Bob replying with a light left on the head. At the close Jeffries jabs. Fitzsimmons gets a left on the stomach. Jeffries's work has pleased his friends, but Bob's friends feel as confident as ever.

Sixth round—Fitz was up and ready ten seconds before the gong. He swings a right to the back of Jeffries's ear, then jabs the latter's face with the left, Jeffries countering with his left on the mouth. Bob jabs a left to the chin, but misses a right, and Jeffries swings a left to the forehead. Jeffries ducks, with a right hook on the ear. They swap left-facers and Bob misses a right swing, Jeffries smashing the wind with the right. Bob puts Jeffries across the ring.

Seventh round—Fitzsimmons runs Jeffries across the ring, but is short with the left, and Jeffries sends a hot left to the face. They come together, Jeffries's right slapping Bob's side, sounding like a drum. Jeffries barely touches the chin, Bob stopping handsomely. Jeffries clinches against the next two leads, but Bob puts a right on the ear. Jeffries answering with a right on the ribs. Fitzsimmons lands a light left on the neck, then a straight left to the mouth. Both miss lefts, then swap rights on the head. Fitzsimmons stops Jeffries's swing, and puts two lefts on the mouth and neck, cutting the mouth severely. Jeffries's left goes over the shoulder and Bob digs a right wickedly under the heart. The gong then sounds.

Eighth round—Jeffries's legs are worked upon vigorously by his attendant. Bob puts a left to the neck, but misses a right swing. Jeffries sends a left to the ribs. He missed a right swing. Jeffries put a left to the ribs, Bob putting a straight one on the mouth. Bob put a left to the neck, but misses a right swing. Bob misses a right, and Fitz jolts Jeffries with the left; then shoots to the mouth and follows again to the jaw. There are two clinches, and Jeffries shoves a right to the ribs, Fitz reaching the chin with his left. Fitz sent a straight left to the eye, Jeffries touching the stomach with his left. Bob sent a left over Jeffries's shoulder, and Jeffries swings his left a foot over Bob's head. A straight left on the jaw sends Fitz reeling to the ropes. Out in the center he clinches, then swings a hard left to Jeffries's head. The bell rings.

Ninth round—Jeffries jabs a left on the mouth. Another left from Jeffries to the mouth, and then he hits to the neck. The men swap rights. Jeffries's left draws more blood from Bob's nose. Bob misses a right, and Jeffries puts a right on the ribs. Jeffries's left finds the chin and Jeffries pokes a left to the face. Bob comes back with a straight left on the mouth. Jeffries swings twice with the left on the head. Fitz hooks a left to the neck. They swap lefts on the head. Bob plants a left on the neck.

Tenth round—Jeff springs in and hugs Bob. After the break he pokes a left to Bob's chest, then a left to the jaw, Bob replying with a left on the eye. Fitz misses a left hook, ducking nicely Jeff's right, and is stopped by Bob's elbow. Bob puts a left on the cheek,, Jeffries missing his answer, Fitz misses a left and a right swing, and Jeffries jabs a left to the mouth. Fitz crowds him to the corner. Jeffries shoots a straight to the jaw. Bob falls flat on his back and takes eight seconds to arise. When he gets up Jeffries swung a right to the neck, and again Bob is down. He gets up, but is sent to his knees by a left, when he arises he clinches, and the bell is heard. Just as the bell sounds Fitz swings a wild left. Fitz is very groggy.

Eleventh round—Fitz was up briskly for this round. He misses a left for the head. Jeffries clinches. Fitz misses a right jab, Jeffries jolting the neck with a left. Fitz uses a left on the stomach and a right on the chest. Fitz misses a right, and Jeffries plants a right over the heart. Jeffries sent a straight left to the mouth, sending Bob's head back, but Bob is still there. He puts a left on the shoulder. Jeffries puts a right on the wind and a left to the eye. Two more lefts from Jeffries on Bob's head, then Jeffries jabs the left twice like lightning. Now two left swings go to the neck and jaw, and a right swing is sent to the point of the jaw and the Cornishman falls prone.

He falls on his side and rolls over on his back. The referee counts 1, 2, 3, 4, 5, 6, Bob rolls over. Then 7, 8, 9, 10. Fitzsimmons is out, and Jeffries is champion of the world. The referee waves his hands to the seconds to carry Fitzsimmons to his corner. They lift him, still unconscious, and sit him in his chair. He revives rapidly.

Meanwhile a shouting, cheering crowd surrounds Jeffries in his corner. Fitz sits disconsolate in his chair, and the Californian crosses the ring and shakes hands. Jeffries leaves the ring in the center of a shouting, howling mob.

It was a great fight, and was fought on its merits. It is another illustration that youth and strength are too big handicaps for age to encounter. Fitz left the platform a few moments after the battle.

ROBERT FITZSIMMONS.

### OUT OF THE WEST.

**Sturdy Young Giant Comes to Uphold California Prowess.**

[ASSOCIATED PRESS NIGHT REPORT.]

NEW YORK, June 9.—James J. Jeffries, another sturdy young giant, has come out of the West to whip champion pugilists. At the arena of the Coney Island Athletic Club tonight he defeated Robert Fitzsimmons, world's champion in two classes—middleweight and heavyweight—in eleven rounds of whirlwind fighting. He came to the ring a rank outsider, and left it the acknowledged master of the man he defeated. He was never at any time in serious danger, and after the size-up in the early rounds of the contest, took the lead. He had the Australian whipped from the ninth round.

It was acknowledged that Jeffries would have an immense advantage in weight, height and age, but the thousands who tipped and backed his opponent to win, were sure that he was slow, and that he would, in that respect, be at the mercy of the pastmaster at the science of fighting, whom he was to meet. He proved, on the contrary, that he was just as fast as the man he met, and beat him down to unconscious defeat in a fair fight.

Jeffries is a veritable giant in stature, and marvelously speedy for his immense size. Less than a year ago he appeared in New York a great, awkward, ungainly boy. Today he is the lithe, active, alert trained athlete. The men who prepared him for his fight worked wonders with him. They taught him a nearly-perfect defense, improved his foot movement and instructed him in the methods of receiving punishment. If he cares for himself he will probably be able to successfully defend the title for many years.

The defeated pugilist was as good as on the crispy morning when, on the plains of far-away Nevada, he lowered the colors of the then peerless Corbett. He was just as active, just as clever, just as tricky and just as fearless of punishment. He went unfalteringly to his defeat. He was the aggressor even at the moment when he was bleeding and unsteady, and when he was stunned by the blows he received, he reeled instinctively toward his opponent. He was fighting all the time, and punished his opponent, but found him a different opponent than any he had met, and in a difficult attitude to fight.

Jeffries fought from a crouching attitude that was hard to get at. He held his head low, his back was bent down, and his left arm was extended. He kept jabbing away with the left, and found no trouble in landing it. It was there that his superior reach told. That giant arm served as a sort of a human fender to ward off danger. He showed an excellent defense, and the ability to use both hands with skill. He is game, too, for he never shrank from his punishment. It was a great fight to watch, and it commenced and ended amid scenes of intense excitement. It was all very dramatic.

The men fought before a crowd of 9000 persons, and stood up in a great beam of blinding white light. It was like a thousand calciums, and it showed their great white bodies in strange relief. When the blood came it was of more intense red than usual.

There was no suggestion of interference from the police. Chief Devery occupied a seat by the ringside, but he never entered the ring. When it was over he sent Capt. Kenney to clear the ring. The contest was pulled off without wrangle, and was devoid of the brutal elements that Chief Devery alleged that he feared.

Never was a crowd handled with greater order and less friction. It was all perfectly orderly. There was absolutely no confusion attendant upon the assemblage and housing of the big crowd. Several thousand of those who were provided with tickets came to the beach late in the afternoon, and their action relieved the pressure during the early hours of the evening. The lateness of the hour at which the contestants were announced to appear kept the crowd from seeking the Coney Island Club house very early, and Coney Island, with its merry-go-rounds, Ferris wheels, gilded cafés, jugglers and bespangled dancers, furnished ample amusement and entertainment during the wait.

It all made a strange scene. Crowds thronged the streets, and surged around among the stands and stalls of the ready-tongued fakirs. The lights of the curious town were never brighter and the strange devices that made apologetic music were never worked harder. The many places where liquids were sold were packed to overflowing, and everywhere the buz of conversation was freighted with fight talk. It was on everybody's lips. Enthusiasts touted their favorites. Here Fitzsimmons would win in a walk; there Jeffries was a sure victor. The newsboys shouted late extras that told all about it, and fakirs offered the latest pictures of the two giants who were to fight.

There was plenty of money ready on both sides, but nobody liked the odds. The Jeffries men wanted 2 to 1 for their money, and the Fitzsimmons men were slow to give it. The great house filled very slowly, and it was after 9 o'clock before the police had to bestir themselves and clear the aisles. Time seemed to drag, and the absence of any preliminary contest gave the crowd a fight appetite. They began calling for the performance at 9:30, and at 9:45 o'clock were demonstrative.

Jeffries was the first of the principals to appear. He came through the main entrance and walked the length of the hall at 9:20 o'clock to an accompaniment of cheers, while Fitzsimmons, who was accompanied by his Spartan-like wife, gained the building and dressing-room by a rear door. The disagreement as to the conditions of clinches and breaks was discussed and settled outside of the ring, and there was but little delay when the terms were agreed upon.

Fitzsimmons entered the ring at 10:05 o'clock, and was made the occasion of a rather theatrical demonstration. Julian was first, and then came the fighter. The seconds were next in line, and then followed two men bearing a great floral piece that was almost funeral in its appearance. It was inscribed "Good uck to the Champion," but the flowers were wilted. Fitzsimmons bowed ceremoniously to it.

Jeffries was next in the arena, and, like his opponent, got a demonstration. Fitzsimmons looked lanky and thin, but his skin was clear, his eye bright and his step elastic. He made a great display of American flags at his waist. Jeffries looked sturdy and massive, and seemed a little nervous. He got the worst of the assignment of corners, for the electric lights shown into his face, and he blinked at them in a nervous sort of way. Siler, too, looked colorless and ill at ease.

There was no trying delay in the

[THE PHILIPPINES.]

# AGGIE A DEAD ONE.

## Belief Grows That He Was Slain.

## He Fell Among the Savages Beyond Bintoc.

### American Garrison Attacked and Twenty Soldiers Killed.

[A. P. NIGHT REPORT.]

MANILA, May 2, 7:05 p.m.—[By Manila Cable.] Gen. Funston has discovered a rebel warehouse near Cabanatuan, province of New Ejija, containing all the archives of the Malolos government, Aguinaldo's correspondence up to the time of his flight, and much valuable historical matter. The belief is growing that Aguinaldo was killed by the Igorottes. There is no proof that he has been alive since Maj. Peyton C. March of the Thirty-third Regiment abandoned the chase after the Filipino leader in the Benquet Mountains. An insurgent officer who recently surrendered to Gen. Young says that the insurgent general Tinio holds this belief. Tinio held regular communication with Aguinaldo until December 18, since when he has heard nothing from him, and thinks Aguinaldo would find means to communicate with him if alive.

Maj. March's information was that there were only half a dozen soldiers with Aguinaldo when he fled beyond the Bintoc wilderness where the savages are hostile to all strangers. Friends of Aguinaldo's wife assert that she has heard nothing from him since they parted. She is in a delicate condition, and nearly prostrated with worry. Therefore she has not been informed of the death of her child, and thinks it has been with friends at Bacoor.

The Sultan of Sulu, with a retinue including several of his wives, has sailed for Singapore, ostensibly on a religious mission. A Hongkong dispatch to a Manila paper says the Sultan has gone to Singapore in order to protest to the British against the Americans establishing a tariff against imports, claiming that it is a violation of the treaty of 1877 between Spain, Great Britain and Germany, Germany guaranteeing the Sulu Islands free trade, whereas the Americans have established a tariff nearly doubling the prices of tobacco, rice and the Sulu staples of life, most of which are imported from Singapore.

The Filipino crew on the steamship Escano recently mutinied in the channel between Cebu and Leyte and killed the captain, the mate and the owners, Señor Escano and his son, with knives after a desperate struggle. The mutineers then scuttled the ship, and escaped to the Leyte Mountains with some $28,000.

#### ATTACK ON A GARRISON.

TWENTY AMERICANS KILLED.

[A. P. DAY REPORT.]

MANILA, May 2.—[By Manila Cable.] The American garrison at Catubig, island of Samar, consisting of thirty men of the Forty-third Regiment, has been attacked by rebels. Twenty of the Americans were killed. The remainder were rescued.

The Americans were quartered in the Catubig Church, which the enemy, numbering several hundred men, surrounded and fiercely attacked. The Americans fought for two days, and then the rebels managed to ignite the roof of the church, and it burned away and finally fell upon those inside the edifice. The walls remained intact, however, and were used as a shelter by the besieged Americans for three days longer, the enemy attacking the building on all sides at once.

The Americans continued firing from the windows and doors of the church and did good execution among the Filipinos. It is estimated that over two hundred of the latter were killed, many dead bodies being removed from the scene of the fighting. After five days' resistance by the Americans, a lieutenant and eight men arrived from Laoag and engaged the besiegers, who, thereupon, retired.

The fortunate arrival of these reinforcements prevented the annihilation of the main force entrenched in the church, who had repeatedly declined to surrender when ordered. The ten survivors were without food; had little ammunition, and were exhausted when relieved.

This fight has encouraged the Filipinos, who are now acting in an aggressive manner, and threatening that section of the coast, particularly the town of Cataram, whence the garrison will probably be withdrawn to Laoag.

#### GEN. OTIS ON CONDITIONS.

TALKS BEFORE STARTING HOME.

[BY DIRECT WIRE TO THE TIMES.]

MANILA, May 2.—[Exclusive Dispatch.] Gen. Otis will probably start for home at the end of this week. The transport Meade is here awaiting his orders. In view of his near departure, Gen. Otis consented last night to talk for publication. The military situation was naturally the first topic with which he dealt. He regarded the effectual stamping out of the insurrection as perhaps the most substantial object he has accomplished here. He said:

"You know I am rather pessimistic. I am not inclined to take the sanguine view prevailing in certain quarters; yet I have held the opinion for some time that the thing is entirely over. I cannot see where it is possible for guerrillas to effect any reorganization, concentrate in any force, or accomplish anything serious. We have 116 posts north of Manila, and 94 south of the city.

"Everywhere people are giving valuable information, and are almost daily disclosing hidden arms and other insurgent property. Filipinos who want peace are beginning to appreciate the power of the Americans to protect them, and are giving effective coöperation. The remnants of guerrilla bands are thoroughly scattered, and they are unable to remain for any time in any place. Even the insurgent leaders recognize the necessity of the Americans staying here. They admit that a strong government is essential to the peace and prosperity of the islands. I asked Señor Mabini, Aguinaldo's minister of foreign affairs, only the other day, if he did not know that the United States were necessary to the Philippines. He replied that he did. I then asked him what the insurgents were fighting for, and he answered that their object was to get the best terms. Even the best of them have thus been deluded into believing that they could wrest conditions from us."

To the question: "Do you think the insurrection could have been avoided by any change in our attitude early in 1898?" Gen. Otis replied: "No, it was inevitable from the start. When Aguinaldo left Hongkong and came to Cavite it was with the intention of fighting the Americans. Independence was the junta's scheme even then. Recently we have come into possession of proof that when Aguinaldo went to Hongkong from Singapore the whole subject was discussed at a big meeting of the junta. They planned that Aguinaldo should come to Manila with American assistance, make a show of coöperation until the Spaniards were expelled and then drive the Americans out."

Gen. Otis thinks Aguinaldo is hiding in Isabella province, with 400 men. He does not believe the reports that he is dead. He declares that conditions are unfavorable just yet for civil government, and that it must come slowly. The recently-appointed native officers are treacherous and plots are constantly being exposed. The general believes new civil government and a new penal code will be long steps toward reconstruction and will settle the friar question. He advocates the exclusion of Chinese, who monopolize business. He called attention to the fact that the revenues of the islands already practically equal Spain's collections. Spain's largest receipts in any one year were $18,000,000. American receipts last month were $1,400,000, largely through the customs. There is a general demand for schools, the supply of school books being exhausted. Three hundred thousand dollars is being expended on roads. In conclusion, Gen. Otis said:

"When once the Filipinos recognize the beneficence of our institutions they will quickly adopt them, adapting themselves to the changed conditions. Thereafter trouble will be out of the question, but Americans need good men here; men who are strong, clean, honest and intelligent; men who will realize the work to be done and sympathize with the people, and men who are anxious to do the best for the United States and the islands."

To secure such men Gen. Otis favors a good-salaried civil service.

## ALASKAN FOX FARMS.

### A LITTLE-KNOWN INDUSTRY OF THE NORTHWEST.

[Chicago Journal:] Uncle Sam has a considerable reputation as a landlord, but few persons know that part of his rent roll income is derived from leasing islands for the culture of foxes. This is the case, however, on the coast of Alaska, where such an island commands an annual rental of $100. For this the government gives the tenant a written contract securing him in the exclusive occupancy of his island and for this particular purpose.

To the farmer who has found it necessary to exercise all his ingenuity in order to get rid of the foxes as a pest, the idea of deliberately breeding them, and even maintaining a farm for their comfort, seems almost preposterous. The fox, in those places where his presence is most deplored, seems to have no difficulty in making a living without human aid. But the experience of breeders in Alaska has shown that the fur foxes must be handled with the utmost care in order not to wreck the fortunes of the investor, for it takes not a little capital to go into the business on a large scale.

On the finest fox farms in Alaska every pair of breeding animals used at the start cost $150 to $200. The work has been in progress for fifteen years or more, yet practically the first dollar of profit has yet to show itself. Good money has been poured after bad, running well up into the thousands, and this expenditure is still going on, for the shareholders believe they have a money-making idea if they can only wait long enough.

#### EXPERIMENTS IN BREEDING.

It is on the Atu and Pribilof islands that the blue fox was first found, but the supply is now nearly exhausted. As the Pribilofs are a government reservation, no live animals can be taken away without a special permit, and all the skins which the natives obtain there they are obliged to sell to the North American Commercial Company. The price paid is $5 a pelt.

The first systematic experiment in blue fox breeding was made with twenty-two foxes taken from the Pribilof Islands and landed on North Semidi Island, a barren and unknown waste. Although no one knew the habits of the foxes and everything had to be done tentatively, including the finding of artificial means of feeding them, still, from the progeny of these pioneer foxes, nearly twenty other islands have been stocked. Some of the barren islands of Alaska, indeed, show no sign of doing good for any other use.

The method of caring for the foxes is substantially the same everywhere. Each island has a keeper and one or two native assistants. They put up the food for the animals during the summer, consisting of unmarketable fish, blubber and oil, and cornmeal. The foxes come at a regular hour every day to be fed, like ordinary domestic animals, and soon learn to know their caretakers, but continue suspicious and wild in the presence of strangers.

#### MAY START BEAR FARMS.

One of the first problems which had to be mastered was how to catch the foxes without harming their skins, as it would not do to shoot them or use any kind of sharp instruments in their capture. Another consideration is the necessity of leaving those animals uninjured which are to be continued in use for breeding.

Fox traps are, therefore, used. But the chief virtue of these had its drawbacks; for all the foxes come into the traps, attracted by the bait, and when those which are to be kept for breeding purposes find that no harm comes to them, they become not only fearless but greedy, and hurry to run in and spring the traps as soon as set to the great annoyance of the breeder and the hindrance of the proper business. The foxes set apart for breeding are marked by clipping the hair at the tips of the tails so as to prevent confusion with the others or recounting.

It is considered probable that the domestication of the fox will set a vogue for the domestication of other fur-bearing animals and thus build up a very valuable and permanent industry. The Russian sable is one of the animals talked of in connection with this idea. One enthusiast has already evolved the notion that an island set apart for raising bears would be a good thing. He has launched his experiment and has already a dozen or more bears, but the market seems still too well stocked to make much of a demand for his special product.

#### Fatal Engine Explosion.

ROSEBURG (Or.,) May 2.—One of the engines of the Booth-Kelly Lumber Company, five miles east of Saginaw, exploded this morning, killing Engineer O. Fredrickson of Cottage Grove and seriously injuring H. Rudolph and Otto Anlauf of Comstock, Or.

## EXPLOSION.

(CONTINUED FROM FIRST PAGE.)

rescuing party. He was the first one in the mine and the last to leave it. His brother, Foreman William Parmely, perished in No. 4.

One of the miners sent over from Castle Gate to aid in the rescue work talked interestingly when he came out of the tunnel. "The explosion is the most disastrous, so far as loss of life is concerned, that has ever occurred in America," said he. "There will be two hundred dead when we are through work. In the great explosion at Almy, Wyo., a few years ago, sixty-seven men were killed. We had some hard experiences today going through the mine. Several times members of our party were overcome by the damp, but we got them out in time. We found the bodies of the men in every conceivable shape, but generally they were lying on their stomachs with their arms about their faces. The men died almost instantly when struck by the damp, and did not suffer. They just became unconscious, and were asphyxiated. Their faces were all calm and peaceful, as though they had just fallen asleep.

"The men in No. 1 might possibly have escaped had they started to run as soon as the explosion in No. 4, which is connected with it, occurred. Evidently, they did not appreciate this fact until too late, as they put on their coats and arranged their tools before starting. They started, however, just in time to meet the damp half way. The bodies found near the entrance are badly crushed and bruised, as they got the full force of the explosion. They are few in number, however. Mine No. 1 is damaged comparatively little, but No. 4 is badly damaged."

Dan Davis, well known to Utah Welshmen, is among the dead, and David T. Evans, a favorite amateur actor here, perished in the mine. The three Gatherum brothers of Provo have been taken out dead.

Superintendent W. G. Sharp resumed work with a will at 8 o'clock, when a rescue party of sixteen, directed by State Mine Inspector Gomer Thomas, and including Messrs. Sharp, Frank Cameron, superintendent at Castle Gate, and James Harrison, entered the tunnel of No. 1. It was not long before the bodies commenced to come out.

All efforts are now being concentrated to bring out a large number of bodies known to be in No. 4, where eighty-five men perished. Here the force of the explosion broke down the timbers, and the bodies can only be got at through No. 1. Up to noon 149 bodies had been brought out.

A sad picture was presented about the mouth of No. 4 tunnel, where, with drawn features and haggard face, sat young John Miller, a helper, waiting for the bodies of his three brothers, Harry, Rance and Isaac, to be brought out. E. J. Roe, a young man who was working in the bottom of No. 6 shaft, bears on his person the evidence of his frightful experience. His face is a mass of lacerations from the flying slack, while his head is cut and his body bruised, but he is alive and thankful. When the damp struck him, he was literally knocked out of immediate danger, and some instinct guided the blinded and almost senseless man to the pure air.

Sam Wicherly, the well-known volunteer, who served in Battery M, has an even more thrilling experience. The force of the explosion from the No. 6 raise carried him clear beyond the damp zone, and today he is pluckily serving with a rescue party.

The theory of Bishop Parmely is that some of the Fins, recently imported, secretly took giant powder down into the mine to assist them in their work. They were exceedingly anxious to make a good showing, and as much money as possible, and it is thought that this form of explosive was used in order that great bodies of coal could be more easily dislodged. It is thought that when the giant powder was touched off, it ignited some of the dust, of which every coal mine in the country has more or less.

Inquiry among the miners disclosed the fact that they entertained various opinions regarding the terrible affair, some being exceedingly bitter in their denunciation of the company. Others took a more conservative view of the matter, and said it was one of those things over which no man has control, and for which no man or men should be held responsible.

A curious fact connected with the affair is that five men, Thomas Seller, Alexander C. Wilson, John Wilson, Harry Taylor and John Reddoes, who were working outside of the mine, were very severely hurt.

John Wilson was blown with his horse a distance of over two hundred yards across the bottom of the cañon. The back of his skull was crushed and something had been driven into his abdomen. He is in a terrible plight. Thomas Sellers was fifty yards away from the mouth of the tunnel, but he had his right foot crushed; shoulder knocked out of place and his back badly hurt. Harry Taylor was severely bruised.

Three hundred and ninety-eight men entered the mines for work yesterday morning, and a great majority of these have perished. The Mayor of Salt Lake has issued a proclamation, appointing a committee to receive subscriptions for the relief of the destitute.

#### TWO HUNDRED CORPSES.

[A. P. DAY REPORT.]

SALT LAKE, May 2.—A special to the Deseret News from Scofield at 10:30 o'clock this morning, says:

"At this hour 201 bodies have been recovered. It is now known that between three and four hundred men entered the mines, and it is also known that a great majority of them have been killed.

"The appalling nature of the disaster had not fully dawned upon the people of this place last night, as the company kept the grief-stricken wives and children away from the scene of operations. All night long lights were kept burning in every home in Scofield and Winter Quarters, and the moans of mothers and piteous cries of the many orphans are heartrending. The two camps have always been conspicuous for the large number of married men employed. This fact makes the disaster more appalling and far-reaching in its results. Several families have been robbed of all their male representatives. Among the dead are about twenty young boys, who acted as couplers and trap boys.

Just how the catastrophe occurred is not known, and probably will never be definitely known, as various reasons are being attributed. At Provo a mass meeting has been held for the relief of the families of the victims and $3000 was subscribed.

#### FIGURES VARY.

[A. P. NIGHT REPORT.]

SALT LAKE, May 2.—A special to the Herald from Scofield, Utah, says:

"It seems that at least 250 men have been killed in the mine accident. The accurate figures will not be known for some days. The mine managers say it will be impossible to secure a list of names until the dead bodies have been brought out and identified.

"Superintendent Sharp says that there were 300 men in the mine at the time of the explosion. Of these it is impossible to account for more than sixty. In the turmoil and confusion, those who escaped cannot be seen. There is great variance between the figures given by Superintendent Sharp and those given by Mine Superintendent Parmley."

[SPORTING RECORD.]

# ON THE YALE TRACK.

## Berkeley Athletes Fit for Contests.

## Plaw Startles the Easterners the First Thing.

### Prince of Wales's Nag a Winner. Baseball and Races.

[A. P. NIGHT REPORT.]

NEW HAVEN (Ct.,) May 2.—[Exclusive Dispatch.] Nine lithe track athletes, representing the University of California, arrived here this afternoon. They went at once to the clubhouse at the Yale field, where they deposited their luggage and took on light practice on the track. Plaw, the Pacific Coast champion hammer-thrower, gave the Yale spectators at practice a shock by hurling the hammer 150 feet despite the fact that he was just off a sleeping car, after a four days' ride. Capt. Drum said tonight:

"Our nine athletes are tired by their long ride, but not a man is out of condition. We shall practice tomorrow on the Yale field, and are confident of making a showing comparing well with our home records. We have decided to remain in New Haven till next Monday, when we shall go to Princeton to train for our dual games with the Tigers."

Capt. Drum tonight announced the following official entries for the games with Yale on Saturday: W. P. Drum, 100, 220 and 400-yard dashes; J. D. Hoffman, jumps and pole vault; A. Plaw, hammer and shot; C. R. Broughton, broad jump, 100-yard dash; Roy Woolsey, shot put, 120-yard hurdles; Roy Service, mile run, hurdles; Charles Moser, half-mile run; Anthony Cadogan, sprints; Tyrell Hamlen, hurdles.

#### CORBETT GETTING TIRED.

WANTS ACTION AND NO TALK.

[BY DIRECT WIRE TO THE TIMES.]

NEW YORK, May 2.—[Exclusive Dispatch.] As the date of the encounter between Jim Jeffries and Jim Corbett draws nigh and the chances of the Seaside Sporting Club receiving a license from police commissioners grows dimmer, Corbett tires of uncertainty and wants the question of the battle ground settled without further parley. As there are available places aside from this club to pull off the combat, Corbett is now willing to go elsewhere, and for the first time since the match was made he is perfectly satisfied to let the affair take place at Westchester.

Tom O'Rourke, when told that Corbett was willing to fight at Westchester said: "I have nothing to say. The club will get the license, and we will be able to pull off the fight May 11."

#### EASTERN BASEBALL.

EXCITEMENT AT PITTSBURGH.

[A. P. NIGHT REPORT.]

PITTSBURGH, May 2.—The game today was of the hair-raising sort. Both tied the score in the ninth, amid great excitement. In the tenth, Beaumont scored the winning run on a single by McCreery. The attendance was 5500. Score:

Pittsburgh, 6; hits, 9; errors, 3.
St. Louis, 5; hits, 10; errors, 1.
Batteries — Leaver and Zimmer; Young and O'Connor.
Umpire—Hurst.

BOSTON-BROOKLYN.

[A. P. NIGHT REPORT.]

BROOKLYN, May 2.—Boston outplayed Brooklyn at all points today, and won in a canter. Dineen went up in the air in the third, but after that steadied himself. Kitson was knocked out of the box in the fourth round, Howell taking his place. The attendance was 2100. Score:

Boston, 10; hits, 14; errors, 1.
Brooklyn, 5; hits, 7; errors, 5.
Batteries—Dineen and Sullivan; Kitson, Howell and McGuire.
Umpire—Emslie.

PHILADELPHIA-NEW YORK.

[A. P. NIGHT REPORT.]

NEW YORK, May 2.—Grady's indifferent playing at third base and timely batting aided the Philadelphias in scoring another victory over the New Yorks this afternoon. The New Yorks drove Piatt to the bench in the third, and Donohue, who relieved him, stayed the New Yorks' batting. The attendance was 3000. Score:

Philadelphia, 7; hits, 16; errors, 2.
New York, 5; hits, 9; errors, 3.
Batteries—Piatt, Donohue and McFarland; Hawley and Bowerman.
Umpire—Connolly.

KANSAS CITY-MILWAUKEE.

[A. P. NIGHT REPORT.]

MILWAUKEE, May 2.—Milwaukee, 5; Kansas City, 9.

MINNEAPOLIS-CHICAGO.

[A. P. NIGHT REPORT.]

MINNEAPOLIS, May 2.—Minneapolis, 2; Chicago, 12.

DETROIT-CLEVELAND.

[A. P. NIGHT REPORT.]

CLEVELAND, May 2.—Cleveland, 5; Detroit, 6.

BUFFALO-INDIANAPOLIS.

[A. P. NIGHT REPORT.]

BUFFALO, May 2.—Buffalo, 10; Indianapolis, 4.

POSTPONED GAME.

[A. P. NIGHT REPORT.]

CHICAGO, May 2.—Cincinnati-Chicago game postponed on account of rain.

#### PRINCE OF WALES'S NAG.

WINS EASILY AT NEWMARKET.

[A. P. DAY REPORT.]

LONDON, May 2.—[By Atlantic Cable.] The Two Thousand Guineas Stakes, run at Newmarket today, was won by the Prince of Wales's Diamond Jubilee. Bonarosa and Sidus finished second and third, respectively, in a field of ten.

Great crowds saw the race. The Prince of Wales watched his colors carried to victory, and the subsequent reception accorded him, showed how popular was Diamond Jubilee's success.

Sir R. Waldie Griffith's View Holl, ridden by Martin, led to the furlong post, when Diamond Jubilee drew clear, followed by Sidus, and, making the remainder of the running, won easily by four lengths. A length separated second and third horses. The betting was 11 to 4 against Diamond Jubilee; 5 to 1 against Bonarosa, and 100 to 1 against Sidus. L. Reiff rode Bonarosa. Tod Sloan rode, but was unplaced.

#### ONE CLOSE FINISH.

HEADWATER WINS THE RACE.

[A. P. NIGHT REPORT.]

SAN FRANCISCO, May 2.—While the racing at Oakland today was of a very good quality, it was rather devoid of incident. There was only one close finish—in the handicap—that caused a good deal of interest. Headwater, Pat Morrissey and Sly finished close together. Headwater won, although Sly might have received the verdict with a little more luck. Mortgage showed what a clever filly she is with light weight up by beating True Blue rather handily at a mile in 1:39¾.

OAKLAND SUMMARIES.

[A. P. NIGHT REPORT.]

SAN FRANCISCO, May 2.—The weather at Oakland was fine, and the track fast. Results:

Four furlongs: Loneliness, 97 (Logue,) 4 to 1, won; Loyal S., 103 (Bassinger,) 8 to 1, second; Illusion, 106 (Bozeman,) 5 to 2, third; time 0:49. Tiolita, Aphrodis, Wardman, Cliorente, Too Hot, Impotente, Ada Fox and Mafeking also ran.

One mile and a quarter: Mamie G., 90 (Logue,) 5 to 1, won; Col. Root, 10 (Bozeman,) 10 to 1, second; Ramlet, 92 (Holmes,) 12 to 1, third; time 2:07½. Poorlands, Twinkle Twinkle, Croker, Rapido, Meadow Lark, Avero, Lion d'Or and P. A. Finnegan also ran.

One mile: Mortgage, 94 (Ranch,) 4 to 5, won; True Blue, 111 (H. Stewart,) 3 to 1, second; Captive, 114 (Bozeman,) 13 to 2, third; time 1:39¾. Olinthus and Anita B. also ran.

Six furlongs: Headwater, 116 (Buchanan,) 2 to 7, won; Pat Morrissey, 98 (Ranch,) 7 to 2, second; Sly, 115 Powell,) 3 to 1, third; time 1:14. Rio Chico, Gusto, Pompilo, Ramboula, Moscow Boy, Leipzig, Alas and Bonibell also ran.

One and one-eighth miles: Gauntlet, 101 (Bassinger,) 9 to 1, won; Lena, 106 (I. Powell,) 12 to 1, second; Twinkler, 106 (Shaw,) 14 to 5, third; time 1:56. Snipes, Storm King, Grand Sachem, Terrene, Morinel, Casdale and Moringa also ran.

One and one-quarter miles: Coda, 100 (Mounce,) 3 to 1, won; Glen Ann, 106 (I. Powell,) 8 to 1, second; Grady, 95 (Fauntleroy,) 8 to 1, third; time 2:07½. Faunette, Mary Kinsella, Whaleback, Fashion Plate, Dr. Marks, Ace, Duke of York and Dare III also ran.

#### Long Shots at Aqueduct.

NEW YORK, May 2.—In the fifth race at Aqueduct today two horses, McGrathiana Prince and Laudeman, ran first and second, with 100 to 1 quoted against each of them in places. The odds-on favorite was third. Results:

Seven furlongs: Sparrow Wings won, Wax Taper second, Dutch Comedian third; time, 1:26.

Six furlongs: El Fin Conig won, Elex second, Insurrection third; time, 1:14 3-5.

About seven furlongs: Ragged Sailor won, Mercer second, George Lebar third; time, 1:26.

Six furlongs: Boney Boy won, Robert Metcalf second, Lady Linsey third; time, 1:14 3-5.

About seven furlongs: McGrathiana Prince won, Laudeman second, Kimmage third; time, 1.27.

#### On Nashville's Fast Track.

NASHVILLE, May 2.—The weather was clear, and track fast. Results:

Six furlongs: Shrove Tuesday won, Wedding Guest second, Clipsetta third; time, 1:15¼.

Seven furlongs: The Pride won, Eitholin second, Bohul third; time, 1:27½.

Mile and one-sixteenth: Windward won, Behuath second, Lennep third; time, 1:48¾.

Nine-sixteenths mile: Clorita won, Denman Thompson second, Yobel third; time, 0:55¾.

Thirteen-sixteenths mile: Sir Eldon won, Koscio second, Two Annies third; time, 1:22.

Thirteen-sixteenths mile: Crystalline

# The World of Sports Throughout the Land---Baseball, Racing, Fistiana, Coursing.

## LOOLOOS RETURN HOME ONCE MORE.

### RAIN PREVENTS A GAME BUT 'FRISCO LOSES.

**Work of the Local Team on the Trip—Seven Games Won and Six Lost—Batting and Fielding Averages—Games Local and Elsewhere.**

Jupiter Pluvius took a hand in the baseball arena yesterday and knocked out all sorts of homers, triples, doubles, while the single swats were something awful. He outplayed his opponents at every point of the game and they were simply "not in it." They'd have got good and wet if they had been. It rained. No game for Los Angeles. 'Frisco and Oakland managed to scratch out seven innings and the metropolis was downed. 'Twas a good deed, and Pete Lohman has a vote of thanks from several and sundry baseball fans who inhabit the City of the Angels. We are a good second and Manager Morley is wearing a smile that has no limit.

The exiled gladiators are e'en now speeding on their way toward their own stamping grounds. They will be with us tomorrow for a month's stay. A warm welcome will be extended to them when they insert their spikes into local dirt once more. Nobly have they fought and conquered and the town is theirs. They have invaded the lines of the enemy and have taken many scalps. While they have not escaped unscathed, and there are a few wounded in the lists, and Big Chief Hutch is hobbling about on one piece of underpinning, they will be nursed and cared for and put in fine fighting trim to welcome those swatters from San Francisco who open in this city next Thursday.

The Looloos have surpassed the fondest expectations by the work on the trip. They have played in all thirteen games, and of these have won seven. They have fought their way into the lead and are almost there now. They left with a record of three games won and two lost, and come back with ten won and eight lost. A reputation has been established on the trip which makes them the drawing card of the league. They have played a consistent game throughout and have fought hard against a hard game. They now repose in a secure notch thirty points ahead of the next team.

A look at the individual work of the team will show that there are some weak spots, which should be strengthened. There is but one man on the slab who can be depended upon. His name is Oscar Jones. Hale lacks experience and steadiness. Hartwell is an unknown quantity as yet. Johnson has not made good. All of the last three may develop into bright particular stars, but they do not at the present time scintillates with bright, effulgent rays. The comedian will, perhaps, do better when the hot weather comes. A series at home may help Hale and Hartwell. But from appearances it would seem that to get one other good erliable man, who can be relied upon to pitch steady ball, would be the proper move. With two men to pitch even average ball, the sticking ability of the team ought to make it a big winner.

Hank Spies at the plate is the best man in the league. Hutchinson at first cannot possibly be improved upon. Charlie Reilly at third is the proper man, and King Kelly at short is all right. Brockhoff should be taken from the second sack and put into center. He is one of the finest outfielders in the business. Slugger Householder should be moved over to right. A new man should be found on second, one who is a good fielder, fast on the bases and a sure sacrifice hitter, even if he don't knock the cover off the ball. Neither Swindells nor Bowman is hiting at all. Outfielders who don't rank over .200 with the stick are of no use, no matter what their fielding abilities may be. Yet both of these men are hard workers and might improve with the weather. Swindells should be retained if possible, in case anything should happen to Spies.

Then reconstruct that batting order once more. Let Brockhoff lead off as now. Put the new infielder in the second notch for sacrifice and fast going to first. Capt. Hutchinson is hitting that ball too hard to waste his ability in that line. Move him down to third and just keep hands off Slugger Householder. He is where he belongs in the fourth place. Spies, Reilly, Kelly are good, and there you have it. Then there would be a little more hitting toward the lower end of the order where it is badly needed. There was a game or two that might have been pulled out of the fire with a little—just a little—hitting down at the bottom of the list.

### DOWN TO DEFEAT.

OAKLAND WINS AT 'FRISCO.

[BY THE NEW ASSOCIATED PRESS—P.M.]

SAN FRANCISCO, April 28.—The wet weather prevented the playing of baseball at Recreation Park this afternoon.

The morning game at Oakland was called at the end of the seventh inning, with the score standing seven to six, in favor of the Oakland nine, which made the winning run in the last inning. Score:

SAN FRANCISCO.

| | A.B. | R. | B.H. | P.O. | A. | E. |
|---|---|---|---|---|---|---|
| Hildebrand, cf. | 3 | 0 | 0 | 3 | 0 | 0 |
| Croll, rf. | 4 | 0 | 1 | 2 | 0 | 0 |
| Krug, ss. | 3 | 0 | 0 | 2 | 1 | 0 |
| Holland, lf. | 3 | 1 | 1 | 2 | 0 | 0 |
| Pabst, 1b. | 2 | 2 | 1 | 3 | 0 | 0 |
| Graham, c. | 1 | 1 | 0 | 5 | 1 | 1 |
| Nordyke, 2b. | 3 | 1 | 2 | 1 | 4 | 3 |
| J. Reilly, 3b. | 2 | 1 | 1 | 1 | 2 | 0 |
| Shea, p. | 2 | 0 | 1 | 0 | 1 | 1 |
| Totals | 23 | 6 | 7 | *19 | 9 | 5 |

OAKLAND.

| | A.B. | R. | B.H. | P.O. | A. | E. |
|---|---|---|---|---|---|---|
| Drennan, cf. | 3 | 1 | 1 | 2 | 1 | 1 |
| Francks, ss. | 3 | 0 | 1 | 3 | 2 | 0 |
| Arellanes, 2b. | 4 | 1 | 1 | 1 | 2 | 0 |
| Streib, 1b. | 3 | 1 | 0 | 6 | 0 | 0 |
| Dunleavy, lf. | 3 | 2 | 2 | 3 | 0 | 0 |
| Moore, 3b. | 4 | 0 | 1 | 1 | 1 | 0 |
| Moskiman, rf. | 4 | 1 | 1 | 1 | 2 | 0 |
| Lohman, c. | 1 | 1 | 0 | 4 | 2 | 0 |
| Russell, p. | 1 | 0 | 0 | 0 | 0 | 0 |
| Babbitt, p. | 1 | 0 | 0 | 0 | 1 | 1 |
| Totals | 27 | 7 | 7 | 21 | 11 | 2 |

*One man out when the game was called in the seventh inning.

SCORE BY INNINGS.

| | 1 | 2 | 3 | 4 | 5 | 6 | 7 | |
|---|---|---|---|---|---|---|---|---|
| San Francisco | 0 | 1 | 0 | 5 | 0 | 0 | 0 | —6 |
| Oakland | 1 | 1 | 4 | 1 | 0 | 0 | 0 | —7 |

SUMMARY.

Runs responsible for—Shea, 3; Russell, 3.
Three-base hit—Nordyke.
Two-base hits—Dunleavy, Moskiman, Holland, Pabst.
Sacrifice hit—Russell.
First base on errors—Oakland, 2;
First base on balls—San Francisco, 6; Oakland, 7.
Left on bases—San Francisco, 4; Oakland, 8.
Struck out—By Shea, 3; by Russell, 1; by Babbitt, 1.
Hit by pitcher—J. Reilly and Holland.
Double plays—Lohman to Francks, Drennan to Babbitt to Francks.
Passed ball—Graham.
Wild pitches—Shea, Babbitt, 2.
Time, 2h.
Umpire—J. O'Connell.

BATTING AVERAGES.

The hitting of the Looloos dropped off some the past week, that one game in which Stricklett had them guessing and held them down to two hits playing havoc with their averages. Eddie Householder lost 12 points; while Spies dropped 45; Hutchinson gained 3 and Charley Reilly dropped 5; Brockhoff fell from .383 to .238, and there was a corresponding slump all along the line. The team batting average is .222; not high enough to win that pennant. The full table of averages up to date is as follows:

| Name— | A.B. | Hits. | Total Bases. | Runs. | Pr. ct. |
|---|---|---|---|---|---|
| Brockhoff | 58 | 19 | 23 | 15 | .328 |
| Hutchinson | 66 | 20 | 27 | 14 | .303 |
| Householder | 62 | 26 | 39 | 12 | .419 |
| Spies | 54 | 16 | 17 | 9 | .296 |
| Reilly | 47 | 15 | 18 | 8 | .319 |
| Kelly | 67 | 15 | 24 | 10 | .224 |
| Swindells | 54 | 10 | 12 | 5 | .185 |
| Bowman | 67 | 12 | 14 | 2 | .179 |
| Jones | 24 | 3 | 3 | 0 | .125 |
| Johnson | 20 | 3 | 4 | 3 | .150 |
| Hale | 18 | 1 | 1 | 0 | .055 |
| Hartwell | 12 | 1 | 1 | 1 | .083 |

Team total, .222.

FIELDING.

There has been quite a marked improvement in fielding, and the hard-hitting center fielder in particular has made a big jump. Every man on the team has bettered himself some in the records, with the exception of Brockhoff, who lost just one little point. The team fielding average is .925. The full table is as follows:

| Name— | Total chances. | Chances accepted. | Errors. | Per cent. |
|---|---|---|---|---|
| Brockhoff | 94 | 83 | 11 | .883 |
| Hutchinson | 153 | 150 | 3 | .980 |
| Householder | 49 | 42 | 7 | .857 |
| Spies | 126 | 122 | 4 | .968 |
| Reilly | 70 | 65 | 5 | .929 |
| Kelly | 119 | 110 | 9 | .915 |
| Swindells | 30 | 29 | 1 | .967 |
| Bowman | 49 | 48 | 1 | .979 |
| Jones | 21 | 19 | 2 | .905 |
| Johnson | 38 | 36 | 2 | .947 |
| Hale | 10 | 9 | 1 | .900 |
| Hartwell | 16 | 14 | 2 | .875 |

Team total, .925.

BATTERY WORK.

Oscar Jones continues to be the star twirler of the Looloos, not only in point of effectiveness, but also in percentage of games lost and won. He has won six games out of nine pitched, and his great effectiveness is apparent from the figure, .836. Johnson and Hartwell have each won and lost a game, while Hale has won two and lost three. The latter, however, has pitched the best ball of the two, with .785 as the degree of effectiveness. The full table is as follows:

| | A.B. | Hits. | Runs. | Per ct. | Games. | Won. | Lost. | Per ct. |
|---|---|---|---|---|---|---|---|---|
| Jones | 256 | 42 | 22 | .836 | 9 | 6 | 3 | .667 |
| Johnson | 84 | 26 | 14 | .692 | 2 | 1 | 1 | .500 |
| Hale | 153 | 33 | 26 | .785 | 5 | 2 | 3 | .400 |
| Hartwell | 95 | 23 | 8 | .758 | 2 | 1 | 1 | .500 |

LEAGUE STANDING.

| | Won. | Lost. | Per cent. |
|---|---|---|---|
| San Francisco | 11 | 8 | .579 |
| Los Angeles | 10 | 8 | .556 |
| Oakland | 10 | 8 | .556 |
| Sacramento | 6 | 11 | .353 |

LONG BEACH WINS.

LONG BEACH, April 28.—[Regular Correspondence.] A large and enthusiastic audience witnessed the best-played game of ball ever seen on a Long Beach diamond on the High School campus Saturday, between Pasadena High School and Long Beach High School. The features of the game were the strong battery work of Darby and Cook of the home team, and the home run of L. Rafferty for the visitors. The drive was the second ball pitched in the game, and was clearly earned, going far beyond the right fielder. It was the only run made by the visitors.

Following is the score:

Pasadena ............1 0 0 0 0 0 0 0 0—1
Long Beach ..........1 2 0 0 3 0 0 0 x—6

LOCAL AMATEUR GAMES.

The second Horse Shoes defeated the Tribunes Saturday, on the grounds at Seventh and Crocker streets, by a score of 20 to 13. Hutchinson and Gambel were in the points for the winners. A return game will be played next Saturday.

The Tigers fell victims to the Cahuenga team Saturday, by a score of 8 to 5.

OTHER BALL GAMES.

[BY THE NEW ASSOCIATED PRESS—P.M.]

CHICAGO, April 28.—In the presence of 16,500 spectators, the American League champions gave Cleveland a thorough drubbing this afternoon, pounding Baker all over the lot. Score:

Chicago, 13; hits, 23; errors, 2.
Cleveland, 1; hits, 7; errors, 2.
Batteries—Griffith and Sullivan; Baker and Wood.

DETROIT, April 28.—(American League.) For the third time in the opening series with Milwaukee, the home team won this afternoon with a great batting rally in the ninth inning. Score:

Detroit, 12; hits, 15; errors, 4.
Milwaukee, 11; hits, 16; errors, 4.
Batteries—Sevier, Frisk, Cronin and Buelow and McAllister; Dowling and Leahy.

CHICAGO, April 28.—Two singles, a double and a triple, followed by Green's muff gave the Cincinnati National League team four runs in the sixth inning, two more in the eighth, and the game. Attendance 8500. Score:

Chicago, 4; hits, 10; errors, 1.
Cincinnati, 6; hits, 11; errors, 1.
Batteries—Cunningham and Chance; Phillips and Peitz.
Umpire—Emslie.

## NEW ATHLETIC CLUB HAS COME TO STAY.

### ORGANIZATION ADDED TO LOCAL FIELD.

**Alpha Club Will Continue in the Field—Griffin and Kennedy, Smith and Bernstein in Training for Coming Fights—News of the Ring.**

The mix-up in the pugilistic affairs of the city has gradually worked itself out until it has at last assumed some semblance of definite form. The much-talked-of new athletic club is a certainty. It has the backing of men of money, whose reputations are beyond impeachment. It will have for its manager T. J. McCarey, a man who is well known to the local sporting

SOLLY SMITH.

fraternity. The entrance of the new club in the field will hardly have any effect upon the Alpha people. They have been doing exceptionally well in their efforts to provide good sport in the city, and they have a large following. The entrance of the Republican Athletic Club into the game again gives the city three organizations of this character, and there should certainly be some good fights during the summer.

On Friday night next Billy Walsh and Kid Long meet at Turner Hall in a twenty-round go. Both of the lads are well known, and should put up a clever fight. There will be a fast preliminary of ten rounds. The next fight scheduled is that between Joe Kennedy and Hank Griffin, which is booked to take place in Hazard's Pavilion on the 7th. Griffin is in hard training at San Pedro, where he has Billy Woods for a running mate. He is reported as hard as nails. Kennedy has been working his weight down in San Francisco, but will arrive in this city today, finishing his training at the quarters of the Alpha Athletic Club. On the Friday night following, Solly Smith and Joe Bernstein will try conclusions for twenty rounds at the same place. Both

JOE BERNSTEIN.

of these men have reputations of a national character, and are two of the cleverest men who ever donned the gloves. Both of them are in the city and in hard training for the fight.

The Smith-Bernstein fight will be the magnet which will bring to this city for the first time Terry McGovern, the pugilistic wonder of the country today. Terry is so fast that he has been giving away weight to men and beating them out in a walk. The Brooklyn boy will challenge the winner of the fight at Hazard's Pavilion at the ringside. He is matched at this writing to meet Aurelio Herrera, the Bakersfield favorite, to go twenty rounds before the club which offers the largest purse. There is a side bet of $5000 to $3500 that McGovern will win. The new athletic club of this city is after the fight, and has good prospects of getting it.

On Wednesday night next Jim Tremble goes up against Al Neill at Bakersfield. Tremble lost to Billy Woods in this city a few weeks ago, but has been training hard for this fight. On paper it looks as if Neill should have a walkover. Tremble is clever, but he hasn't a knockout punch in his repertoire. Neill is as good in every way, and has two good hands with plenty of steam behind them.

BOWLING.

EVENTS ON LOCAL ALLEYS.

The event of the week in bowling circles was the overwhelming defeat administered to the Chutes by the Brunswick-Balke-Collender team on Friday night. The surprise was the greater in that it was so totally unlooked for. Individually with but a single exception the members of the Chutes team are considered stronger than the men who won from them. They have rolled up large scores in practice and have come to look upon themselves as practically invulnerable.

The defeat cannot be laid to bad form, that is, in the sense athletic. It was due to some very bad habits which a number of the boys possess. One of these is that of losing their heads in trying situations, and another one that should be sedulously guarded against in a bowler, that of playing to the grand stand. The scores made were not even good. A man who will bowl 185-180-175 is a much better man to have on the team than one who will double the century mark in one of his games and fall off woefully in the others. Inconsistent work, bowling that was far below what they really can do, was the cause of the Chutes defeat.

Nearly all of the new alleys which are to be placed in the various bowling resorts of the city have arrived and are being put in position as fast as possible. Before the week is over the facilities will be increased threefold. The interest in the game has caused all the proprietors to spend large amounts in equipments which will make the Los Angeles alleys second to none in the country.

The only game of the week is at nines on Friday night in Dysinger's alleys. It will be between the Oaks and the Imperials, with the following line-up:

| Oaks. | Imperials. |
|---|---|
| Yaeger | Austin |
| Durand | Meyer |
| Fitzmyer | E. Dutzler |
| Farquhar | Putzman |
| Thompson | C. Dutzler |

KENTUCKY DERBY.

ALARD SCHECK THE FAVORITE.

[BY THE NEW ASSOCIATED PRESS—P.M.]

LOUISVILLE (Ky.,) April 29.—In the Kentucky Derby tomorrow it is thought to be certain that Alard Scheck will be first choice in the betting, and His Eminence second choice, and many turf followers tonight say that the chances that the finish will find these two horses in the same position as the betting. The Tennessee crowd will back Scheck heavily, especially the Memphis part of it, and Lexington and the bluegrass contingent are said to be ready to bet a fortune on Sanazaro, who by some is thought to have quite a chance.

The track is lightning fast, and as the weather promises to be perfect, a new record may be made. The crowd bids fair to be the largest ever seen at Churchill Downs. Cincinnati has arranged to send two trainloads, and Indianapolis, St. Louis and Chicago will be well represented. The entries and jockeys follow: Alard Scheck (Henry,) Sanazaro (O'Connor,) His Eminence (Winkfield,) Amur (Boland,) Driscoll (Cochran.)

AFTER TWENEY YEARS.

ENGLISH FOOTBALL ENTHUSIASM

[BY THE NEW ASSOCIATED PRESS—P.M.]

LONDON, April 29.—The Tottenham Hotspur football team, which replayed Saturday at Bolton with the Sheffield United team the final game for the association cup, and won back the trophy lost twenty years ago, arrived home at 1 o'clock this morning.

Thousands were still waiting the arrival of the players, with bands, flags and lanterns, and the team was uproariously welcomed. The crowds paraded the suburbs with the heroes of the occasion, and there was a torchlight procession, in which the trophy was displayed.

## SHARPSHOOTERS END THEIR TOURNAMENT.

### FULL SCORE OF TWO DAYS' EVENTS AT ROUND HILL.

**Belknap Does Some Consistent Work—Frick Makes Phenomenal Score in Championship Event—Westcott Wins the Re-entry at 500 Yards.**

The second day of the fifth semi-annual tournament of the Los Angeles Sharpshooters came to an end yesterday with the big event on Round Hill range. A light, changeable wind prevailed throughout, making good tickets hard to get. Although the riflemen did not turn out in the force which the event justified, yet the shoot was one of the most successful ever held in Southern California.

Belknap did the most consistent shooting of the two days. It was unfortunate that Frick was the first man up in the championship event, for he did such phenomenal shooting that he scared out a number of possible entries. His score was 215, and he won by a large margin. The best centers in connection with the ring reëntry will be measured and be ready for distribution Monday evening at Joe Singer's.

The full scores for the two days are as follows:

Championship event—Frick, 215; Belknap, 203; Leighton, 200; Hauerwaas, 195; Averill, 192; Variel, 181; Barrett, 176.

Ring reëntry; possible 75; three tickets to win—

| | | | | | Total. |
|---|---|---|---|---|---|
| 1 | Belknap | 74 | 70 | 68 | 212 |
| 2 | Frick | 71 | 70 | 70 | 210 |
| 3 | Hauerwaas | 72 | 66 | 65 | 203 |
| 4 | Singer | 68 | 68 | 66 | 202 |
| 5 | Leighton | 68 | 68 | 66 | 202 |
| 6 | Wescott | 64 | 63 | 63 | 190 |
| 7 | Harper | 65 | 62 | 63 | 190 |
| 8 | Variel | 64 | 61 | 60 | 185 |

Merceandise event; possible 75; three tickets to win—

| | | | | | Total. |
|---|---|---|---|---|---|
| 1 | Belknap | 69 | 68 | 68 | 205 |
| 2 | Leighton | 70 | 65 | 65 | 200 |
| 3 | Hauerwaas | 68 | 67 | 65 | 200 |
| 4 | Rishel | 66 | 65 | 60 | 191 |
| 5 | Wescott | 67 | 62 | 61 | 190 |
| 6 | Singer | 62 | 62 | 62 | 186 |
| 7 | Harper | 62 | 62 | 60 | 184 |
| 8 | Casey | 61 | 60 | 57 | 178 |
| 9 | Barrett | 61 | 59 | 53 | 173 |
| 10 | Taylor | 61 | 56 | 52 | 168 |
| 11 | J. Mason | 6 | 54 | 52 | 166 |
| 12 | Freytag | 56 | 52 | 51 | 159 |
| 13 | Freeman | 54 | 48 | 47 | 149 |
| 14 | Wolff | 60 | 45 | 44 | 149 |
| 15 | Marquis | 55 | 44 | 43 | 142 |
| 16 | Dan Kohler | 45 | 44 | 40 | 129 |

Five hundred yards, reëntry; possible 60—Wescott, 55; Lee, 52; Mehl, 52; Freeman, 50.

Five hundred yards, reëntry; possible 60—Wescott, 55; Lee, 52; Mehl, 52; Freeman, 50.

COURSING.

CRAWFORD LASS IN THE FINALS.

Crawford Lass won the final from Hotfoot at Coursing Park yesterday after a hard and gruelling course. Hotfott had been racing hard all day, and although he led, the Lass outstayed him. Frosty Morn gave Crawford Lass a hard rub, as they ran two ties before the judge could pick the winner.

Young Fleetfoot showed sudden improvement and beat Storm King on the short end of 1 to 6. Mollie H, the clever little hound from Compton, ran into third money by hard coursing and was withdrawn on account of hard races. Dick Adams's St. Gertrude ran in fine form.

WON BY WEDGEWOOD.

[BY THE NEW ASSOCIATED PRESS—P.M.]

SAN FRANCISCO, April 28.—The deciding course in the 112-dog open stake at Union Coursing Park today was won by Wedgewood, who defeated Little Sister by a score of 4 to 1.

**The Tonnesen Art Pictures**

That accompany the Sunday Times every Sunday are fine enough to hang in any parlor. Bring or send them back to The Times office and they will be mounted, passe-partout style, for 25 cents each. Where there is postage or express charges to pay, of course, that expense must be borne by the owners of the pictures.

## Normal School Track Team That Went to Santa Barbara.

The track team of the Los Angeles Normal School journeyed to Santa Barbara Saturday to attend the interscholastic meet and went down to defeat. While they were beaten out by both Santa Barbara and Throop, yet it was a hard-fought field, and the honors were won only after a closely-contested day.

The track was not in the best of condition and a strong wind prevented better records being made. In the 100-yard sprint, Thomas of Santa Barbara beat the gun and the race had to be run over because of protest. Gallup of Los Angeles then went in and won as he pleased in the good time of 10 2-5s. Gallup also romped in an easy winner in the 220-yard dash. Stanley Howland made a game fight for the mile run, but was beaten out by Enos of San Luis Obispo. Gallup should have won out in the fifty-yard sprint, but the hard work told on him, and he tailed in to Gould of Throop.

Butler did some good work at pole vaulting, carrying the second honor to the San Luis man. Gallup landed second in the 440-yard event, and Chandler was the second man in the running broad jump. The boys were somewhat disappointed as to the results, as they confidently expected to carry the day.

Athletics at the Normal School are pushed as never before. Tennis courts are being made and a grand stand is being erected on the field. Now that the field day is over, the members of the basket-ball team will go into training once more, and games will be played weekly.



## HIDALGO'S GOSSIP.

The midwinter racing season, the longest continuous season in the world (and altogether too long for the good of the sport, here or anywhere else,) is in its sere and yellow leaf. Tanforan closed its gates on Saturday night, not to reopen them until next October; and if it could be deferred until ten days before Christmas, so much the better. It is evident to the most inexperienced eye that cheating with horses has ceased to be a crime in the opinion of most owners; and more especially of those whose horses come out here to race during the winter months. There is hardly a horse at any of the tracks whose true form is not known within thirty days after the opening of these midwinter meetings. Of course, there are exceptions, like Waring, for instance, whom everybody thought to be "all out" at seven furlongs, but who turned out to be such a top sawyer at a mile and a quarter, with 127 pounds up, that there were people in California ready and willing to match him against any horse in America to go two miles with 120 on each; and to let the acceptor stipulate the amount of the wager for which the proposition was accepted. When Waring won the San Francisco Handicap with 117 pounds in the saddle, beating such cracks as The Lady, Vesuvian, Star Chamber, and horses of that class, people said to me, "How did you come to overlook Waring in such a race as that, with this horse in at seven to ten pounds less than he had won with at the East?" My answer was that he had never won at distances above a mile, and had been frequently beaten at a mile there. So far as ordinary races go, one might have played him at those odds (9 to 2,) but not in a field of eighteen horses, with at least six contestants that were put in only for pacemakers to kill off just such horses as Waring had previously shown himelf to be. On previous performances, there were at least six of those horses that figured to beat him. This, however, was an exceptional case and against the general rule.

In a general way, at San Francisco, during the past six months they have had six races each day—two purses, at from seven to ten pounds below the scale, and four selling races, in which $1200 horses, and, in some cases, even more valuable, have been entered at $200 or $300, so as to get a light weight. Once in a great while, somebody would "get his back up" and run up the winning horse to about his true value, when the owner would bid the usual $5 and retain him for future depredations. Whenever a horse got as well known as Scotch Plaid (who has won his last eight outings,) then the game was to have him beaten. Now, there are many ways to get a horse beaten. You will hear a great many men say, "Oh, that horse was pulled. He has won at that distance before and beaten better horses than these." Very true, but pulling did not do it. All a boy has to do to lose a race is to disobey the instructions of the trainer. If the horse is "a front runner," as they say in this country, all he has to do is to take him back and make a waiting race of it. His horse will have fretted himself to death long before the rider calls on him for a final effort on the home stretch. Suppose that the trainer gets his horse in good shape and thinks he can win at a mile if he can get through the first half of his journey without any material effort. He instructs the boy to that effect, and then comes somebody to bribe the jockey. No sooner is the flag down than out goes the boy and makes all the running. At the quarter he leads by four lengths and at the half by eight. He comes into the stretch, four lengths to the good, but all pumped out. He finishes "outside of the money," and his owner is given a start down the toboggan toward bankruptcy. The boy generally excuses himself on the ground that he had to sweat out so much in order to ride at 103 pounds that it took all his strength away, and he could not control the horse's action.

They used to have selling races in Australia, at all the tracks, until the decency of the people rose up against them. In 1893-4 the four leading tracks of that country—the Randwick and Rosehill at Sydney, and the Felmington and Caulfield at Melbourne—abolished them at once and for all time. Don't you suppose that this style of racing would be revived if there was any merit in it? But it never has been, and most of the men who practice it, at the backwoods meetings, are treated on the metropolitan track as if they were pariahs and outcasts. It is regarded by the most intelligent men on the antipodean turf as detrimental to the interests of true sport, and, therefore, worthy only of condemnation. The Englishman (or the Australian, who is merely a transplanted Englishman) is a very conservative individual. He is slow to condemn any proposition, but once he does so, it stays "down and out" for an indefinite period.

Do you suppose that you could have any such legislation on the American turf as that inaugurated by the antipodean clubs, seven years ago, in the interest of decent racing? If you do, you don't know your own country. Just attempt to bring about such a reform as was started by the Victoria Racing Club, in 1893, and then see whom you will be obliged to fight. First would come James B. Haggin, who owns about four hundred mares and fifty-odd stallions; and you would hear him say, in tones of almost freezing politeness: "Why, gentlemen, if you abolish selling races, you will do my business a great injury. I am selling over three hundred head of yearlings annually at auction, and you certainly cannot hope for all of them to show stake-form. Then you will also be doing injustice to poor owners who cannot afford to pay entrance fees to the races for which their horses contend." After his "smile that was childlike and bland," would come Gen. W. H. Jackson of Nashville, who owns ten sires and about two hundred mares. He would give the same song and dance as the Sphinx of Del Paso, save in a little more virulent language, for he is an ex-Confederate brigadier and a fighter "from away back" at almost any kind of a game. Abolish the selling races, as they have done at the antipodes, and those two breeders, between them, would be obliged to sell two hundred colts and fillies, annually, for prices ranging from $75 to $125, that now average over $400 at auction. So you see whom you would antagonize in these United States of ours. Over in Australia there is no breeder who ever sends over thirty or forty yearlings to the auction block, and it was this condition that made the abolishment of selling races possible in that country.

Here, on the other hand, you find millionaires and owners of rich mines entering their horses in selling races at one-tenth of their value, in order to get light weights on them, while in Australia, the pillars of the turf—like the late James White, Donald Wallace and William R. Wilson—were content to nominate their horses in stake events and rich handicaps, leaving the selling races to poor owners who had only two or three horses. And even at that, these races grew to be so prolific of fraud and jobbery that the two leading clubs abolished them altogether, for the reasons above stated. But so long as our track betting is carried on exclusively by bookmakers, we shall have selling races; and the public will go home, cursing and kicking splinters off the railroad ties at every step of the way.

I am willing and ready today to make one of 100 men to put up $1000 each to build a track on which no bookmaking shall be allowed; and where no selling races shall be run under an ypretense whatever; but I never expect to see the day when such a reform in racing will be inaugurated in this country. The matter has already gone too far to admit of anything in the shape of reconstruction; and so the thing will go on, from year to year, until we have legislation that will close up all the tracks indefinitely, as was done in New Jersey in 1895. All the trades people are against so much racing, because it tends to impoverish not merely the rich, but the wage-worker as well. The butcher and the baker are against it, and the candlestick maker will not be long in following suit.

There will be some good sport at Riverside during the coming week, with horses carrying heavy weights, and ridden to win. The British colonists of that section are men who love good sport, and will spare no pains to bring about a fair field and no favor. There will be no bookmaking on the ground—nothing but Paris mutuals, in which the odds regulate themselves. Such sport does, and always will, commend itself to the lovers of fair play, one of whom is HIDALGO.

## THIRTY THOUSAND VISITORS.

**Sunday Attendance at the Pan-American Exposition—"Sandpaper Finish" Not Obtainable by the First of May.**

[BY THE NEW ASSOCIATED PRESS—P.M.]

BUFFALO (N. Y.,) April 28.—Today's attendance at the Pan-American Exposition was very large. Fully 30,000 persons passed through the gates, about 75 per cent. of them paying for admission. Although the exposition is still far from complete, every one seemed satisfied with what there was to see.

The managers of the exposition had been working for a unique distinction—that of having all things in readiness for the opening day, and had it not been for the storm their hopes would have no doubt been fulfilled. As it is, the "sand-paper finish" which the management has striven for cannot be accomplished by May 1.

An event on the opening day, next Wednesday, will be the flight of 5000 carrier pigeons, carrying the news of the opening of the exposition.

## PYTHIAN UNIFORM RANK.

**Commander-in-Chief Carnahan Says There Will Be No Secession from the Supreme Lodge.**

[BY THE NEW ASSOCIATED PRESS—P.M.]

INDIANAPOLIS, April 28.—Commander-in-Chief James H. Carnahan of the Uniform Rank, Knights of Pythias, said tonight that a secession from the Supreme Lodge by the Uniformed Rank is utterly impossible. He stated that the rumor had its origin in a report of a district meeting held in Cleveland, O., last February.

Early in May Gen. Carnahan will go on a tour of inspection of the various uniform ranks of the country, and late in the year will arrive in San Francisco, to make arrangements with a number of other supreme officers for the national convention and encampment of the Uniform Rank, the latter numbering nearly sixty thousand men.

CRIPPLE CREEK GOLD.

COLORADO SPRINGS (Colo.,) April 28.—Carefully-compiled statistics by the Gazette show that the gold production of the Cripple Creek district up to the close of the present month makes a grand total of over $100,000,000. Gold was first discovered in this camp in 1889.

# Stanford Players Unable to Score Against the Bully Buckers from Michigan

## THE FIRST HALF THE REAL THING.

### *Enormous Crowd Sees the Michigan Back-breakers Make Monkeys of the Stanford Footballists.*

ELEVEN staunch Wolverines from far-off Michigan yesterday downed the California Bear on the football gridiron at Pasadena. When the game was called near the end of the second half, on account of the gathering darkness, the famed escutcheon of the University of Michigan bore forty-nine additional points. Stanford had failed to score.

For the visitors the game concluded a remarkable series of victories. In eleven games played this season the Michigan team made 550 points, an average of 50 points to the game. None of the teams were able to make a single score against them.

At the outset yesterday's game was a furious struggle. The Stanford boys had set their hearts upon making at least one touchdown. The hearts of the Cardinals were in every play, and for a time it seemed that Stanford would hold its own against the fierce rushes of the eastern giants. It was anybody's game for the first twenty minutes, although Michigan from the beginning showed superior form.

Then the boys from Ann Arbor tried a trick play near the west-side line. All the team made a rush around the right end, leaving Heston, the left half-back, with the ball. This play deceived Stanford, and with a clear field the fast Michigander sprinted down the side lines for 25 yards. With the ball on the 5-yard line, Michigan twice tried unsuccessfully to get the spheroid across the goal mark. On the third trial Snow wriggled through the center for the coveted distance, just twenty-three minutes after play began.

CARDINALS LOSE HEART.

This touchdown seemed to mark the end of the equal struggle. Stanford lost heart. The Cardinals' play lacked vim and snap. Occasionally there were rallies, when exceptionally fine football was played, but after the first touchdown it was easy to see that Michigan must win.

But no one believed that the score would be as large as the ... proved. It was not until Stanford went to pieces in the second half that it was possible for the Michigan players to pile up the score almost at will.

From the start it was college football. The game was an exhibition of good, clean sport, and of the kind which lovers of athletic prowess wish to see. The Michigan team played hard and fast, and Stanford, although overwhelmed, played with grit until the last moment.

There was plenty of excitement, for in a sense California was pitted against Michigan. It was a struggle between prominent college teams from the two States. Few people thought the Stanford team had much chance against a team that has been rated with Harvard, and every good gain was the more vigorously applauded because unexpected.

It was billed as Tournament of Roses Day in the Crown of the Valley, but the football game was the subject on every tongue. While the parade was passing the Hotel Green in the morning, the crowd took turns in gazing at the pageant and debating the respective merits of the football players. When the teams passed in their tallyhos they were cheered to the echo.

COLOR COINCIDENCE.

Because of a coincidence the entire town seemed to be in sympathy with Michigan. Blue and gold were the Michigan colors, and also the colors of the Tournament of Roses. Every house along the principal streets was decked with the colors, but it was impossible to tell whether in honor of the flowers or the visiting football players.

When the colors first began to appear the Stanford players at the Hotel Green were very much mystified at the strong following of the easterners. They surreptitiously tore down all the blue and gold banners they could find near the hotel. After they had removed a particularly fine silken banner from one of the balconies of the hotel the mistake was discovered and the manager was implored to restore the missing emblem to the lady whose patriotic spirit had led her to hang it from her balcony.

No sooner had the flower-bedecked traps and tallyhos and the dashing caballeros passed up Colorado street than the pilgrimage to the football park began. The new Tournament Park, which was utilized for the first time yesterday, is located at the corner of California and Wilson streets, over a mile from the center of Pasadena, and thither the throng of humanity pressed. Forgetful of the noon-day meal, thousands of people went to the park almost as soon as the parade was over. Every means of locomotion was used. Hundreds walked rather than try to get aboard the street cars. One long line of humanity strung out Colorado street to Wilson, and thence south to the park. The street was crowded with vehicles of every kind. The automobile, the Victoria, and the heavy farm wagon vied for possession of the road. Men came on bicycles and on horseback. Every street car was loaded until no more could possibly hold on.

CRUSH AT THE GATE.

But a barrier to further progress was set at the gates of the park. A tremendous crowd gathered there, but could get no farther. It seemed to be the design of the management to have everybody that was going to attend the game banked in the crowd on the outside before any were allowed admission. For hours the crowd stood good-naturedly in the hot sun waiting for a chance to get inside.

On the other side of the fence was H. L. Van Schaick and one policeman. They were afraid to start the crowd, for fear of what finally happened, anyway. About 2 o'clock, another minion of the law arrived, and thus reinforced Van Schaick got on top of the fence and admonished everybody to get in line for the one small door that led into the park. As there were 3000 people on the outside, jammed against the fence, about twenty independent lines were at once formed and all headed for the entrance. Each line claimed to be the original and only line by which entrance to the park could be gained. Soon there was a commotion at the gate, and to further admonish the people to get in line the gate was closed.

This gave the cue to one small boy, who knows a thing or two about getting on a football field, whether the management wills or no. The youngster got a man to boost him up where he could get a look over the fence. With his hands on the top of the 9-foot boards Young America surveyed the prospect. It seemed to please him. In about a minute there was a convulsive twitch of the youngster's knee joints, which developed soon into a writhing motion that landed him on the top. A moment he sat there unconcerned, and then dropped over. As he didn't come back on the toe of the management's boot, another boy tried it. He paused a moment before disappearing to tell the rest of the small boys that all was clear.

STAMPEDE OVER FENCE.

Then came the stampede. Small boys first and then grown men. Quicker than it takes to tell, the fence clear around the field was a kaleidoscopic scene of heads that suddenly appeared above the top from the outside and disappeared below on the inside. Van Schaick and his lone policeman were battling fiercely on the inside with two of the offenders, and meanwhile hundreds were scaling the fence. It is estimated that 2000 people took advantage of the opportunity.

While many hundred people got inside of the field by the way of the top of the fence, the number by no means represented a loss to the management. Most of the men and many of the boys had tickets, but despaired of ever getting through the one small entrance way. There was one reporter among the fence climbers who had "bucked" the entrance gate for about an hour, and concluded that there are times where patience ceases to be a virtue.

Aside from this unfortunate occurrence, there were many other ways in which the management was not prepared to handle the crowd. Not enough ushers were provided, and the spectators had to play a little football to get to their reserved seats. A crowd from the side lines took advantage of the lack of organization to appropriate over 300 seats on the bleachers. The special policemen were entirely at sea. Pasadena is such a peaceful town that when a big crowd gathers the policemen seem to be lost in wonder at the antics of the rough element.

GRAND STAND INSPIRATION.

After the crowd was seated, the grand stand presented an inspiring sight. Tiers on tiers of expectant faces, quickened by the excitement of the moment, made a pretty picture from the gridiron. Ladies with Stanford leanings wore bright red waists that shone vividly in the warm sun. There were cardinal pennants and blue and gold pennants. For the moment the heat was forgotten. Rich dresses were dragged through the deep dust with utter disregard. Everybody was out to see the game.

Across from the grand stand a space was reserved for the turnouts. The tallyhos of the Winsor grammar and Pasadena High Schools and that of Throop Polytechnic Institute were ranged along the side lines, the occupants wearing the same costumes as in the parade. The fence on three sides of the field was crowned with a row of human "rail birds," which made the field look as though inclosed by a black line.

Hundreds found lodgment in the branches of the like oak trees that grow just outside the grounds. During the game the like oaks bore such a heavy crop of live boys and men that they presented a most amusing spectacle.

By many the crowd was estimated at 10,000, but the managment gave the more conservative estimate of 8000. Owing to the large number that jumped the fence no accurate figures could be obtained. It is certain that the game netted a handsome profit after paying all the expenses of the two teams. The amount was placed at about $6000 at the close of the game.

WARRIORS COME.

Stanford's team was the first to arrive. The Cardinal players came in two tallyhos wearing big red sweaters. Michigan's players did not arrive on the field until 2:50 o'clock, fully thirty minutes after their rivals. The appearance of both teams was the signal for enthusiastic cheering.

After a short preliminary practice, which gave Sweeley a chance to exhibit his ability to kick the "spiral" punt, the game was on. How the hearts of the girls in the red waists must have pounded when Stanford put on so bold a front. One little lady just above the press box could not restrain her enthusiasm. Every time the Stanford boys made a good play she jumped to her feet in perfect ecstacy and waved a long red flag.

Not far from where she sat was another firm admirer of Stanford, although from his language it is probable that he never spent much time at the university.

"Wal, I guess youse fellers hain't found Stanford sech an easy thing as they might be. Are they, Michigan? Hey!" said the youth who wore a flaming-red necktie and a torrid band of red around his hat, on which he had stuck a big California poppy. "They hain't so easy as some of those eastern fellers you met, is they?"

And all through the game this fervid "rooter" shouted for Stanford every time there was the slightest provocation. His comments on the players delivered in a megaphone voice kept the grand stand in a roar.

But despite cheers and encouragement, Stanford steadily lost ground after the first touchdown. Once a splendid rally was made and the ball was taken from Michigan on the one-yard line. Then the Stanford sympathizers "gave 'em the ax."

CRUTCHES ON THE FIELD.

Toward the end of the game, when Michigan was fast running up the score, Lewis P. Bansbach, the Stanford quarter-back, who was prevented from playing because of two sprained ankles received in practice, got wildly excited. He came on the grounds limping with the aid of crutches, but when he saw the Michigan eleven forcing his team down the field he demanded to be put in the game. Before any one knew it he had thrown away the crutches and was out on the field. Phil Wilson and a Stanford player picked him up and put him back in a chair on the side lines, much to his disgust.

"Let me play," he demanded. "I can play, and they need me. Why do I have to sit here and watch that team running all over us. Let me get in the game."

But Bansbach was forced back into the chair while the unbidden tears coursed freely down his face. Such is the spirit that makes good college football.

SPECTACULAR GAME.

The score tells the story of the struggle. Michigan played a much faster game than Stanford, and had more lasting ability. Sweeley's punts were about ten yards better than those of Fisher or Traeger. From a spectacular point of view there have been few games in this section to equal that of yesterday, because of the great amount of kicking. Stanford was forced to kick almost constantly, and Michigan profited by doing so. Sweeley kicks a spiral punt that goes high in the air. Yesterday he frequently punted fifty and sixty yards.

Stanford frequently fumbled the ball. Both teams were penalized for off side plays. Stanford's captain showed poor judgment in trying to place kick goals from the forty and forty-five-yard lines, but the Stanford players saw that it was their only chance to score. Stanford was never able to carry the ball into Michigan territory more than ten or fifteen yards, and almost the entire game was played in Stanford territory.

Sweeley place kicked a goal from the field near the end of the first half, which is the only goal from the field that Michigan has kicked in a match game this year.

Considering his lack of experience Tarpey did good work at quarter. The end players on both teams did fine work. They were down the field on every kick, and no long runs were made around the end by either team. Cooper, Traeger, Slaker and McGilvray did good work for Stanford. Fisher did not play up to his usual form.

Sweeley, Redden, Shorts, Herrnstein and Heston were most in evidence for Michigan, although the team work was so perfect that no particular credit obtains to any one man, except Sweeley for his punts and Shorts for his defensive work.

Technically speaking, Michigan lost no prestige through yesterday's game. The team successfully kept Stanford out of Michigan territory. Stanford was unable to break the record of fifteen yards as the longest gain made against Michigan during the year. None of the Michigan players were compelled to leave the field.

Neither team was in the best football form, as was evidenced by the fact that thirty-two minutes was taken out in the first half for delays. One hour and seven minutes was the elapsed time of the first half, and fifty minutes that of the second half, with ten minutes left to play.

STANFORD GETS THE BALL ON THE ONE-YARD LINE.

ROOSEVELT OF STANFORD HAS TO LEAVE THE GAME.

## STORY OF THE FRAY FOR COVETED HONORS.

### HOW TEAMS AND MEN FOUGHT FOR THEIR COLORS.

**Details of the Memorable Struggle in Which Stanford Was Overwhelmingly Defeated and Michigan Cut a Wide Swath in the West.**

Game was called at 2:57 o'clock, with Michigan on the south side of the field and Stanford on the north, the latter team in possession of the ball. The line-up was as follows:

| Michigan. | | Stanford. |
|---|---|---|
| Gregory | center | Lee |
| Wilson | right guard | Thompson |
| McGugin | left guard | Roosevelt |
| Shorts | right tackle | McFadden |
| White (capt.) | left tackle | Traeger |
| Sweeley | right end | Cooper |
| Redden | left end | Preston |
| Weeks | quarter-back | Tarpey |
| Herrustein | right half | Fisher (capt.) |
| Heston | left half | Slaker |
| Snow | full-back | McGilvray |

Sweeley kicked 40 yards to McGilvray, who returned the ball 10 yards by some clever dodging of outstretched arms. The ball was put in play, but went to Michigan on a fumble. Herrustein, Snow and McGugin each did a line buck for a total gain of 11 yards, and followed this with two ineffectual plays against the line. Snow made two telling straight bucks for 10 yards, but on the next play the ball went to Stanford on a foul. McGilvray sent the spheroid down the field on a punt for 25 yards and Sweeley received it, but was tackled without making any ground.

The teams remained stationary for a few plays and Stanford gained the pigskin on a fumble. Treager kicked for 10 yards, but Sweeley returned the punt 30 yards to Tarpey. Stanford threw its backs against the Michigan line, but made no headway, and Fisher kicked 50 yards to the easterners' 10-yard line. Sweeley, with his mighty kicking legs, returned the ball 35 yards to Slaker, who was tackled without and Shorts took the pigskin down the field in three plays against the line for a gain of 7 yards, and White fumbled on a criss-cross, but recovered. Weeks kicked 10 yards and Snow was there to get the ball. Shorts, by a straight buck, gained 4 yards, and after Sweeley's unsuccessful end run, repeated the dose for 3 yards more. Snow advanced 5 yards on a buck to Stanford's 5-yard line, but the Michiganders found, once more, an invincible wall to hurl themselves against, and the cardinals took the ball on downs. Fisher removed the scene of battle 25 yards down the field by a gaining. McFadden bucked right tackle for 7 yards, one of the best gains made by Stanford during the game.

The same tactics proved ineffectual for two more plays, and Treager tried a place kick for goal from Michigan's 40-yard line. The ball fell short 10 yards and Sweeley returned on a 40-yard punt. The ball was caught by Fisher, who made no perceptible gain. Michigan gained the ball on a fumble and advanced Heston 30 yards, but Stanford recovered the pigskin and terminated a series of small gains with another place kick from the Michigan's 45-yard line.

This netted Stanford 20 yards, but Sweeley diminished this one-third by a grand-stand run without interference. The ball was carried through Stanford's line for a series of small gains, and then Heston went down the west side line for a brilliant 25-yard dash. This was one of the best of the game and was executed by means of a fake kick. This brought the ball to Stanford's 5-yard line, but the mighty Michiganders hurled themselves in vain against the Stanford's invincible line for three downs, but Snow was finally sent through center for a touchdown, and Shorts kicked a goal.

Score: Michigan, 6; Stanford, 0.

It took the undefeated champions of the Middle West twenty-three minutes, including elapsed time, to make their first touch down, but thereafter the tale was different.

Traeger kicked 40 yards to Sweeley, who returned a spiral 50 yards to Tarpey, but the latter failed to gain. Slaker was sent through the left tackle for 4 yards, and McFadden increased this another yard by the same play. Treager circled right tackle for 2 yards and McGilvray took 5 more through center. Slaker won 2 yards more around left tackle, and McGilvray made a vain rush against center and fumbled the ball. Sweeley punted for 35 yards, and on Tarpey's fumble Weeks cabbaged the pigskin, but was brought down by Cooper in a brilliant tackle. Sweeley made an exhibition punt of 60 yards clear, and the ball rolled back of Stanford's goal. McFadden kicked from the 25-yard line, and Sweeley came dodging back for an advance of 25 yards, but Cooper, in another grand-stand tackle brought him down. Shorts made a cross buck through left tackle for 4 yards, and in the melée that followed Roosevelt was injured, and Van Sickle was substituted. Heston advanced 5 yards on a straight buck, and Redden encompassed right end for 2 yards more.

Here followed a series of line bucks which netted the easterners only small gains, but advanced the ball irresistibly toward their opponents' goal. The ball was carried by this means to Stanford's 5-yard line, and then ensued a mighty struggle of muscle and weight. Stanford's line held like a rock, though, and Michigan could not advance past her 1-yard line. Stanford received the ball on downs at this point, when her goal was in such danger, and the situation was relieved by Fisher's 25-yard kick. Sweeley received the ball, but made no appreciable gain on his run. A double pass from Heston to Redden advanced the ball 2 yards, and Shorts duplicated the gain with a straight buck. Sweeley gained 3 yards with a left-end run and Shorts 4 yards on a cross buck. Snow and Heston each made a try against the line, but with no results, and Weeks executed the quarter-back kick for 15 yards to Fisher, who returned the ball on a punt 20 yards. Heston kick to Sweeley, and Treager was there to tackle him before he coud advance. Shorts, Snow and Herrustein made 14 yards in a series of straight bucks, and then Sweeley tried for goal on a place kick at Stanford's 20-yard line, and sent the ball beautifully between the poles for an additional 5 points.

Score: Michigan, 11; Stanford, 0.

The ball went back to the center of the field, and Traeger kicked off for 50 yards, but Sweeley returned it the 50 and added 15, the longest punt of the game. Tarpey managed to fumble the long punt, and Gregory was there to pick the pigskin up, but made no advance. A place kick, executed by Sweeley, sent the ball back of Stanford's line for 30 yards, but Tarpey received the spheroid and punted back 15 yards to the Stanford's 25-yard line. Redden got the ball and by a sensational run, which the California boys vainly tried to stop, scored a touchdown. Shorts kicked a goal.

Score: Michigan, 17; Stanford, 0.

SECOND HALF.

On the kick off, Traeger sent a 50-yard punt to Sweeley, who returned the ball a similar distance to Tarpey; the latter fumbled and enabled Michigan to secure the pigskin. Time was called with the ball in Stanford territory.

Time of first half, including elapsed time, 1h. 7m.

Score, first half, Michigan, 17; Stanford, 0.

The blue stockings arranged themselves on the north side of the gridiron and those of the cardinal hosiery on the south when the time was called for the beginning of the second half. Traeger started the game with a low punt for 20 yards, and Shorts made a dodging run for 12 yards. Sweeley advanced the pigskin on a punt for 45 yards, but Tarpey did the fumble act again and allowed Heston to secure it. Heston made a dive and run through the left tackle for 12 yards, and after two unsuccessful line bucks, Hernnstein secured another dozen around left end. Before the dust had cleared he duplicated the play with a gain of 5 yards more, and advanced the ball to Stanford's 2-yard line. Snow found a hole and carried the pigskin over for a touchdown. Shorts failed to kick goal.

Score: Michigan, 22; Stanford, 0.

Traeger punted on the kick off over the Michiganders' goal line, and Sweeley came back with a 50-yard effort, which McGilvray caught and returned 20 yards on a run. He followed this with a 3-yard buck through left tackle, and Traeger hit right tackle for 2 yards more. Fisher sent a 40-yard spiral to Sweeley, who returned for the same distance, and the ball was captured by McGilvray, who failed to advance. Fisher tried a left-end run, but was forced back with a 5-yard loss, and McFadden kicked for 30 yards. Sweeley recovered 10 yards of this on a spectacular dash, and Traeger brought him down by a brilliant tackle. Sweeley sent a diagonal punt for 15 yards and Slaker fumbled to Weeks. Sweeley resorted to the punt and sent the ball over Stanford's line for 40 yards. Tarpey fumbled and Redden secured the ball and by a 25-yard run made a touchdown. Shorts kicked a goal. Score: Michigan, 28; Stanford, 0.

Traeger kicked over the Michigan line and Sweeley punted in return 50 yards to Slaker, who made a good run without interference for 15 yards.

At this point in the game McGilvray was obliged to retire and Allen was substituted. Slaker went to fullback.

Slaker kicked 30 yards and Sweeley returned the ball on a 16-yard punt to Allen, who advanced 5 yards. Stanford lost the ball on downs, and Sweeley executed an end run for 5 yards, followed by line bucks of Snow and Short, which netted 5 yards more. Two fake kicks were tried unsuccessfully, and Heston made a buck for 3 yards, following it up with an end run which gained 7 yards. This play brought the ball to Stanford's 5-yard line, and Snow made the necessary distance and a touchdown by a line buck. Shorts failed to kick goal. Score: Michigan, 33; Stanford, 0.

Fisher kicked off for 40 yards and Sweeley returned for 30 yards to Slaker, who was pushed back 5 yards. McFadden kicked 30 yards to Sweeley, who returned the ball to McFadden on a 60-yard drive. The latter was downed on Stanford's 5-yard line. McFadden punted 20 yards out of bounds and Michigan secured the ball. Herrnstein gained 6 yards on a double pass and 2 yards more on a straight buck. Snow made a great buck through center for 15 yards and landed the ball behind Stanford's goal. No goal. Score: Michigan, 38; Stanford, 0.

Fisher kicked off 25 yards, and Herrnstein took 5 yards from this by a run without interference. On a fake kick, Heston advanced 5 yards, and Sweeley kicked 55 yards to Allen, who failed to cover any ground. McFadden kicked 30 yards to Sweeley, who made a dash back for 20 yards. A double pass sent Herrnstein around left end for 13 yards. Sefton was at this point in the game substituted at right end for Cooper, who was unable to proceed. By a series of line bucks and a right-end play by Heston for 5 yards, the ball was advanced to Stanford's 10-yard line.

Hauvemen was substituted for Traeger, who was the fourth man to retire from the game on Stanford's side. The Michiganders played no substitutes throughout the whole game.

Another series of line bucks followed, and Snow was finally sent through center for 3 yards and a touchdown. Shorts kicked a goal. Score, Michigan, 44; Stanford, 0.

Stanford was nearly fagged out when the beginning of the end approached, but played with fine grit, while the Michigan men were still fresh and strong.

McFadden kicked off for 45 yards and Sweeley returned the ball on a punt the same distance. McFadden secured the ball and sent it back out of bounds 20 yards. By a fake kick Heston made a magnificent 45-yard run down the west-side line, but was tackled very cleverly by Preston. Snow and Herrnstein advanced the ball 9 yards by two plays against the line, and Herrnstein secured a touchdown by a 22-yard dash through right tackle. Shorts failed to kick goal.

A MICHIGAN BUCK THROUGH TACKLE.

FORMING UP FOR ONE OF MICHIGAN'S ATTACKS.

# 1903
# 1912

AS A NEW CENTURY BEGAN, BASEBALL HAD A NEW LEAGUE—AND A NEW CONTROVERSY. THE OLD Western League had become the American League, and the new kid on the block immediately demanded major status. But it was not until 1903 that the established National League, which already had such stars as Honus Wagner and Christy Mathewson, recognized its rival as an equal.

When Boston won the American League championship that season it played the National League winner, Pittsburgh, in an unofficial World Series that went virtually unnoticed, even in the cities where it was played. Boston won the best five-of-nine series in eight games, which drew only about a hundred thousand spectators.

Boston also won the American League championship the following year, but John McGraw, manager of the National League champion New York Giants, refused to meet the American League team in another series. The American League, in McGraw's view, was still an upstart minor league. But the Series resumed in 1905, with McGraw's Giants beating Connie Mack's Philadelphia Athletics, four games to one, and it has continued every year, even through two world wars.

Baseball already had its first .400 hitter, Napoleon Lajoie (.422 in 1901), and a great batting champion in Honus Wagner, but overshadowing the achievements of the stars of this era was a colossal mistake, the infamous "Merkle Boner."

On September 23, 1908, Fred Merkle of the New York Giants failed to touch second base, thus preventing the winning run from scoring against the Chicago Cubs. As a result of the 1–1 tie, the teams finished even for the season and Chicago won a playoff game to determine the championship. What is not usually remembered about Merkle's "boner" is that twenty thousand spectators rioted after the play and chased the umpires off the field.

The fascination of Americans with automobiles probably started with the building of this country's first one in the 1890s, and the first race, it has been suggested, probably was held as soon as the second one appeared. The earliest races among Duryeas, Wintons, and Stanleys were mostly on roads between cities. But by 1903 Barney Oldfield and others were winning races on one-mile circular dirt tracks at speeds up to 65 miles per hour. On straight tracks, racers were driving almost 100 miles per hour. Oldfield drove a "Winton Bullet" to victory on a dirt track in Los Angeles in 1903 and averaged 65.6 miles per hour.

In 1910 Ralph DePalma averaged 75 miles per hour in a Fiat while winning a fifty-mile race at the Playa del Rey Motordrome. On the same day on the same track a driver named Ray Harroun won a hundred-mile race. The next year at Indianapolis, Harroun won the first five-hundred-mile race at an average speed of 74.5 miles per hour.

The Olympic Games of 1904, staged in St. Louis as part of its Louisiana Purchase Exposition, was a strange affair that had little to do with Olympic ideals or international competition. Few foreign contestants competed, and athletes from the United States won all but thirteen of the more than ninety events that were staged from May to November.

Some of the events bearing the "Olympic" name featured thirteen-year-old schoolboys. And long before Rosie Ruiz made headlines by running only part of the Boston Marathon, a fellow identified as Fred Lorz was driven half the distance of the 1904 Olympic marathon in a wagon and got his picture taken with Alice Roosevelt, the president's daughter, as she presented him a laurel wreath as the champion. The real winner arrived a few minutes later.

There was a marked improvement in the organization of the 1908 Games, and the London festival went so smoothly that historian Bill Henry said, "The Olympic Games had arrived!" The United States, with 160 entries, won twenty-two events, but the United Kingdom, with 839 athletes, won fifty-seven.

The successful Games staged in Stockholm, Sweden, in 1912 featured the victories of the American Indian Jim Thorpe in the decathlon and pentathlon, a remarkable feat that made him famous as the "world's greatest living athlete." Thorpe was later stripped of his medals when it was learned that he had accepted money for playing baseball, and it was not until the winter of 1983 that his family got them back.

Finishing fifth in the pentathlon in Stockholm was a young American lieutenant named George Patton. His worst score was in shooting; he used an army revolver instead of a target pistol.

Home-News Sheet.
CITY AND COUNTRY.

# Los Angeles Daily Times

Part II.—8 Pages.
FINANCE AND TRADE.

XXII[D] YEAR. SATURDAY, AUGUST 15, 1903. PRICE 3 CENTS.

# JIM JEFFRIES AN EASY WINNER.

## Champion Manifests Decided Superiority Over James J. Corbett and Knocks Him Out in the Tenth Round.

### Mammoth Crowd at the Ringside—Men in Splendid Condition and Good Humor.

[BY DIRECT WIRE TO THE TIMES.]

**SAN FRANCISCO, Aug. 14.—[Exclusive Dispatch.] Jeffries knocked out Corbett in the tenth round.**

**First preliminary—Frank Smith of Los Angeles and Harry Sheridan of San Rafael fought a draw.**

**Second preliminary—Jack Evans won from James Fairbanks of San Francisco in the second round.**

SAN FRANCISCO, Aug. 14.—[Exclusive Dispatch.] The battle for the heavyweight championship of the world tonight at the Mechanics Pavilion between Champion James J. Jeffries and James J. Corbett ended in the tenth round, with a clean knockout for Jeffries. The blow with which he settled this battle was the exact duplicate of the blow he administered to Fitzsimmons last year in the eighth round of that historic fight.

The fight tonight was a revelation in regard to the improvement of Jeffries in speed and skill, and the first six rounds were a great disappointment to Corbett's admirers, who looked to see him make a much better showing. It was not until after the sixth round that Corbett developed any skill in evading Jeff's rushes and getting inside to deliver any effective blows. Even in the last returns of the fight, when he hit Jeffries repeately in the mouth, he seemed to have no punishing power. Jeff outclassed him completely in punishing power, and even in the quickness of his blows. Had the fight lasted the limit, the decision must have gone to Jeffries as he forced the pace right from the start, and had he not been checked by Corbett's repeated clinching, he would have fought uninterruptedly throughout each round.

In contrast with his work in the Ruhlin and Fitzsimmons fights, Jeffries put up a far cleverer fight, and showed that the claims made for his superior speed and shiftiness were well founded; in fact, Corbett, the acknowledged superior of all heavyweights in the boxing art, did not make so good a showing against Jeffries as Fitzsimmons did. He did not draw any blood from the champion, nor did he manifestly distress him with any of the blows that he landed on the mouth and nose.

In the first four rounds Corbett made a very poor showing, as he clinched repeatedly, and seemed unable to keep off Jeff's rushes. He lost much strength in these rounds because of Jeff's rough tactics. Jeff followed his man around the ring, his long left held ready for a punch. He only adopted about half his usual crouch, and in this way he was able to land with punishing power repeatedly on Corbett's wind, despite Corbett's cleverness in blocking swings and in ducking to escape right and left swings to the head.

In the fifth round Corbett began to show signs of the severe punishment he had received. He was too slow after one clinch to escape a terrible blow directly over the belt, which dropped him to the carpet, all doubled up, and his face writhing from the force of the savage punch. Rising on one knee, he looked anxiously at Timekeeper Harting, and at the count of nine seconds he rose and resumed fighting, Jeffries tried to end the battle, but Corbett skillfully staved him off and saved himself from further punishment until the gong sounded.

Again the sixth round Corbett went down with a blow on the mouth, and took the count of nine seconds. Again the gong saved him. In the seventh round Corbett had evidently received some pointers from Tommy Ryan, for he adopted entirely new tactics, using very cleverly his left shoulder to block Jeff's rushes and getting in stiff uppercuts and punches in the face in the clinches.

The eighth was Corbett's best round, as he showed extraordinary cleverness in evading punches, and his swiftness in delivering blows on Jeff's face aroused the hopes of his admirers that he might go the limit. The ninth, however, showed that these hopes were false. Corbett repeatedly landed with right and left on Jeff's moutt, but though the champion spit blood, he was not distressed for a moment, and he landed both left and right just over Corbett's belt, so that the latter went to his corner very tired and groggy.

In the tenth it was evident that Jeffries meant to settle matters, for he rushed his man once around the ring, and when near Corbett's own corner landed a left-hand punch that brought Corbett to his knees. It was the heaviest blow, as well as the cleanest, that Jeffries had delivered, and from the expression on Corbett's face it was evident that he could not last many seconds. He made a game effort to prolong the fight by clinching, but Jeffries threw him off as though he were a child, and then landed with his left again on Corbett's wind, bringing him down in a heap. It was so evident that Corbett could make no showing, even though he should rise, that Tommy Ryan, after the timekeeper had counted five, threw up the sponge, and the referee gave the fight to Jeffries.

For several minutes after he fell, Corbett lay on the carpet. Then his seconds lifted him into a chair, and he vomited from the effects of the blow. This relieved him a trifle. He was helped to his feet, and Jeffries shook hands with him, and congratulated him on the good showing he had made.

As Corbett staggered across the ring, and went down the stairs, supported by his brother on one side and Yank Kenny on the other, he said with a smile to several of his friends, who crowded about him: "He is too damned big and strong for me; that's all there is to it."

Referee Graney said the fight was square throughout and that both men showed every inclination to obey orders. It was one of the cleanest and best of fights between big men ever seen in San Francisco, and the verdict of all who saw it was that there is no man in the ring today who can face Champion Jeffries with the slightest chance of success.

#### FIGHT BY ROUNDS.

SENT FROM THE RINGSIDE.

[BY DIRECT WIRE TO THE TIMES.]

SAN FRANCISCO, Aug. 14.—[Exclusive Dispatch.] Nine p.m.—Flashlight photographers have just entered the ring with their apparatus, and the pugilists will be photographed as soon as they enter. It was learned that Corbett has received many messages from theatrical promoters from all parts of the world, offering him extravagant inducements to appear in monologue stunts, win or lose. Every seat in the vast building now has its occupant. Corbett and Jeffries will soon file out of their dressing-rooms.

#### JEFF FIRST TO ENTER.

9:12 p.m.—Jeffries was the first to enter the ring. As he tripped through the ropes he was accorded a tremendous ovation. He was followed quickly by Corbett, who received the greater amount of applause. Jeffries looked in splendid condition, and said as he entered the ring that he was fit to fight for a king's ransom. Corbett was clad in a long white robe, which made his face look pale. Physically, however, he could not have looked better. Corbett is seconded by Yank Kenny, Sam Berger, Pop Dare and Thomas Regan. Jeffries is looked after by his brother Jack, Billy Delaney, Bob Fitzsimmons and Joe Kennedy.

Jeffries was introduced by Announcer Jordan as the champion of the world. He was vigorously applauded. Corbett was introduced as James J. Corbett of San Francisco, and was enthusiastically cheered.

Challenges were read from Jack Monroe and Jack Johnson, the colored champion. Eddie Graney, the referee, was then introduced as the "Native Son of the Golden West."

Jeff had on black trunks, entwined with the American flag. Corbett looked confident as he pulled the bandages off his hands and greeted his friends with encouraging smiles. The men are now in Corbett's corner, arguing about the contest. Jeffries went to his corner and calmly surveyed the audience, while waiting for Corbett to finish removing the bandages and don the gloves.

#### FIRST ROUND.

First round—They came to the center instantly, and Jeffries chased Corbett around and missed a left swing for the jaw. They then came together and parted carefully. Jeffries tried left for the body and head, but was blocked. Jim tried left swing and then got a right to body. Jeffries followed it with a left high on the body, and they mixed it, Corbett getting light rights to the body, and Jeffries then put a light over the heart and a hard left to the body. Jeffries seemed inclined to force matters. Corbett shot right to the body, and they came to a clinch. Jeffries hooked left to jaw and Corbett bored in with right to the wind. As the bell rang, Jeffries went to his corner smiling. Jeffries had a little the better of the round. Both fought very carefully throughout. Jeffries astonished his backers by his agility.

Second round—They went to a clinch, and Jeffries got left to Corbett's neck. As they came out of a clinch Jeffries landed left hard on Jim's nose. Jeff swung hard with left. Corbett rushed inside it. They came together again, and Jeffries got left to chest. Jeffries also got in a right to body. Corbett caught Jeffries a vicious left swing on the head, and the champion then put a light right to the jaw. Jim ducked a left for the head and landed a right on the neck in return. In return he received a heavy right jolt to the ribs. Bell rang. Jeffries seemed to have plenty of steam behind his blows and showed much cleverness.

#### CORBETT CLAIMS A FOUL.

Third round—The men came together, and were separated without any blows. Jeff landed a left swing on Jim's neck, and followed him around, landing another left to the wind. Corbett was chased around the ring, and Jeff put a straight left hard to the body. Jeff caught Jim on the jaw with a vicious right, and they clinched. Corbett claimed a foul, and Jeff swung left and right to jaw. Corbett protested to the referee that Jeff was holding on, and landed a savage right to jaw. Jeff sent in left swing to the jaw. They went into a clinch. Jeff broke it up with stiff right and left to the body, and the gong rang. The round was Jeff's, although Corbett succeeded in landing some telling blows.

#### CORBETT ON HIS KNEES.

Fourth round—They went into a clinch, and Jeffries forced Corbett's head back with left hook to the jaw, and followed it with two lefts to the head. Jeffries jarred Corbett with a raking left to the jaw, followed it with a left cross to the head. Corbett put his left twice to the head and they came together in a hard clinch. Jeffries uppercut Corbett with a powerful left to the body, and Jim jabbed Jeffries with left to the face. Corbett clinched constantly, and Jeffries landed a hard left to the body. Another left and right to the body by Jeffries sent Jim to his knees. He took a count of nine on one knee, and waded into Jeffries, but the latter rushed at him and landed a hard right to the heart. Jim looked anxious at the sound of the bell. It was a welcome sound to him.

Fifth round—They did not get to the center on time, owing to Jeff's glove being examined by the police captain. The examination was satisfactory. Jeff rushed in with a left to the wind, and Corbett got in a left swing to the wind twice. Corbett feinted with left and swung a right to the head. Jeffries landed a hard left swing to the head and followed it quickly with a similar blow. Again Jeffries swung, and landed right and left to the neck. Jeffries met Jim at all points, and outfought him at what was supposed to be Corbett's forte. Corbett rallied, and delivered some good rights and lefts to the face. Jeffries swung with left twice and landed on the face, and Jim clinched to avoid punishment. The bell rang, and Jeffries again went to his corner smiling.

Sixth round—Both missed left leads, and they went to a clinch. Jeff crouching. Jim blocked two hard rights, and the champion sent Jim to the floor with a stiff left to the jaw. Jim took the count, and came into a clinch. Jeffries was unrelenting, and landed left and right, while Jim hung on to avoid punishment. Corbett put right and left hard to the jaw, and Jeff rushed Corbett into his corner, but did not land. Just as the bell sounded Corbett uppercut Jeff on the jaw with a hard right, but did not feaze the champion. Corbett went to his corner smiling, but looked very fatigued.

#### CORBETT GETS GAY.

Seventh round—Jeff rushed Jim about the ring, and went to a clinch. Jeff stopped Jim with a left on the face, but it was not hard. Jeff drove a hard left to the body that was blocked, and followed it with a left to the jaw and with two more to the same place. Corbett yelled out, "He can't knock me out." This angered Jeff. Jim then put a right to the head and a hard left to the wind. Jeff got in a light left to the body, followed with a left swing to the jaw. Jim came back with three stiff lefts and rights on the face and the bell found them in a clinch. Corbett smiled, and went to his corner. At this stage, Jeff has a long lead.

Eighth round—Corbett led with left for head, and Jeffries bored in effectually. Jeffries got right to body, and Jim put in three light lefts and rights to the face, but Jeffries smiled. Jim got a left to the face, and in return received a heavy right swing on the neck. A clinch followed. Jeffries caught Jim with a right to the jaw and a left to the body. Corbett came back with a stiff jolt to the face, and followed with two more to the same place. Jeff received a smart left on the face, and Jim cleverly ducked two lefts and uppercut Jeff on

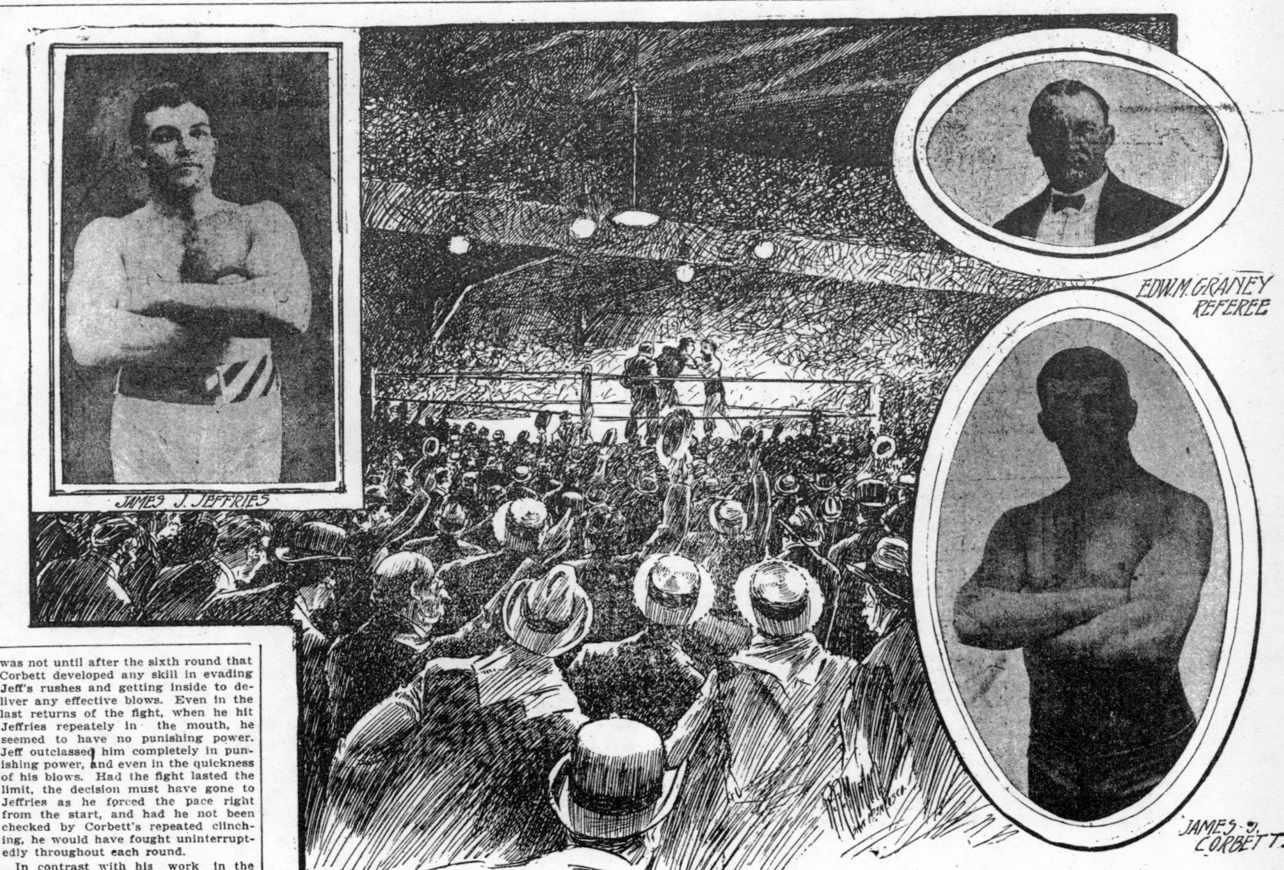


EIGHTH ROUND—THE EXCITED THRONG ATT HE GREAT FIGHT.

SPORTING SECTION.

The Field of Sports. FAR AND NEAR.

# Los Angeles Sunday Times

Part III.-4 Pages. COMPLETE REPORTS.

XXIIIrd YEAR. SUNDAY MORNING, JULY 10, 1904. PRICE 5 CENTS



## BROOMSTICK WINS RACE.

*Takes Twenty-five Thousand Dollar Prize by Head.*

*Brighton Handicap the Waterloo of Irish Lad.*

*Fall Meeting of the Coney Island Jockey Club.*

[BY DIRECT WIRE TO THE TIMES.]

BRIGHTON BEACH, July 9.—The fourth race today, the Brighton Handicap, value $25,000, one mile and a quarter: Broomstick, 6 to 1, won; Irish Lad, 7 to 5, second; High Ball, third; time 2:02 4-5.

The time announced, 2:02 4-5, beats the best previous record for the distance, which was 2:03 1-5, made by Waterberry with 124 pounds, July 8, 1903. Broomstick carried 104 pounds.

The start was prompt, and as the field passed for the first time, Irish Lad was leading, with Broomstick second and High Ball third. These positions remained unchanged around the paddock turn and into the back stretch.

Passing the three-quarters pole, Broomstick moved up to Irish Lad and they ran head and head until well into the stretch, when both boys, Burns on Broomstick and Hildebrand on Irish Lad, sat down to drive hard, and in a furious finish Broomstick won by a head. Irish Lad was five lengths in front of High Ball. Waterboy was never dangerous and finished fifth. Hermis was scratched.

Irish Lad pulled up very lame and will probably never race again.

### IRISH LAD'S OVATION.

[BY DIRECT WIRE TO THE TIMES.]

NEW YORK, July 9.—[Exclusive Dispatch.] Irish Lad, beaten, but still king of thoroughbreds, got an ovation after the finish of the Brighton Handicap this afternoon as remarkable as justified by his truly wonderful performance. When S. S. Brown's new champion, Broomstick, trotted back to the judges' stand with the world's record of 2:02 1-5 for a mile and a quarter, 30,000 turf lovers gave him splendid greetings. But when Irish Lad came limping back, barely able to stand on his right leg, the crowd rose to a man and cheered long and loud. It was a grand testimonial to the speed and gameness of this truly greatest of American thoroughbreds.

Twenty feet from the wire, Irish Lad, after leading the entire distance, faltered, tossed his head and laid back his ears as if in great pain. Broomstick, with nose at Irish Lad's neck, felt the lash of ever-vigilant Tommy Burns's whip, and with one mighty leap, had taken the greatest turf contest in history by a bare nose.

Four lengths back came Highball, winner of the American Derby, then Eugenia Burch, a head in front of the deposed California champion, Waterboy, who got a miserable ride from Jockey Lyne. Even at his best, it is doubtful if Waterboy could have beaten either Broomstick or Irish Lad. The hero of the race was Irish Lad, for he conceded nine pounds to the winner, carried him the first mile in 1:37 4-5, and then was beaten only by breaking down almost under the wire.

Irish Lad, the greatest of American thoroughbred,s will probably never race again. Before the race, it was given out by his owners, Duryea & Whitney, that the colt was afflicted with ringbone, and, win or lose, he would never enter a race again. He will be retired at once to the Whitney breeding farm in Kentucky.

Waterboy was the favorite in the great race, and probably a quarter of a million was bet on the Californian by the rank and file of the holiday crowd present. He was plainly short and got a very bad ride in the bargain.

### BROOMSTICK RAN UNBACKED.

Broomstick ran practically unbacked and bookmakers made the biggest kind of killing ever recorded in a single race. Ort Wells, who was second choice, was outrun from the beginning. His owner, John W. Drake, wagered $30,000 on his colt and told the clubhouse contingent he did not think the colt could lose with weights. Bookmakers got every cent of this rich picking, as Ort Wells did not run in the money.

Californians got back part of their losses by backing the gelding Et Tu Brute, bred near San José, to win the fifth race, at six furlongs. Backed from sevens to three at the post, Et Tu Brute got off well and won in a fierce drive by a neck from Divination.

Duryea and Whitney, on the showing of two-year-olds thus far, seem to have the rich futurity to be run at the fall meeting of the Coney Island Jockey Club at their mercy. Their stable uncovered two this week that promise to be world beaters. Bumble Bee is surely of stake caliber, and Iota, Sandringham-Clemintina, the filly which won a maiden start Friday, developed a genuine turf sensation. The filly refused to break and the field of eleven were twenty lengths away before she left the barrier. Iota had caught the bunch leading into the stretch and when a sixteenth from the wire had beaten all but Salt and Pepper; thirty yards from the wire the two were nose and nose, and Iota won cleverly by a neck. It was a remarkable exhibition of speed and gameness in the youngster, and those who witnessed it pronounced Iota a better filly than unbeaten Tanya, in the same barn. Tanya ran unbeaten at Morris Park and Gravesend, setting a new mark for five furlongs.

### FAIR-GROUNDS SUMMARY.

[BY THE ASSOCIATED PRESS—P.M.]

ST. LOUIS, July 9.—Five furlongs: Benson Hurst won, The Hebrew second, Blumenthal third; time 1:01.

Mile and a sixteenth: First One won, Second Mate second, Sister Lillian third; time 1:57¾.

The Union Championship stakes, six furlongs: Dishabil won, Broomhandle second, Miss Inez third; time 1:20.

Six furlongs: Lansdowne won, Our Lillie second, Orient third; time 1:21¼.

Mile and three-sixteenths: Bessie McCarthy won, Thane second, Hymettus third; time 2:01¾.

Mile and a sixteenth: Decoration won, Poor Quoi second, Miss Betty third; time 2:00.

### ASCOT AUTO BRUSHES.

GARBUTT AND RYUS TIED.

Fine sport was anticipated by the members of the Automobile Club of Southern California at Ascot Park yesterday in the five-mile race arranged between J. W. Sefton, Jr., of San Diego, in a Pope-Toledo, and Turner in his Peerless. There has been much contention over the respective speed values of these two kinds of machines, and keen interest was shown when the race was called. Disappointment was strong when, near the end of the third mile, Sefton had to withdraw on account of a minor trouble with his machine, which is new and not entirely smooth running yet. Each car carried four persons. Next Saturday a Peerless and a Pope-Toledo will be matched again.

In the brush between the two fast drivers, Garbutt and Ryus, consisting of two five-mile heats, Garbutt won the first heat, in 6 min. 32 2-5 secs., and Ryus the second heat, in 6 mins. 37 secs.

H. A. Bingham, in an Olds touring car, won a three-mile race against Eager in a one-cylinder Rambler, in 7 mins. 21 1-5 secs.

## "FARMING OUT" OVERLOOKED.

NATIONAL ASSOCIATION BLINKS AT COMMON PRACTICE.

**Doc Reisling's Case Discussed, but Only With View to its Eastern Bearing—Los Angeles Case Left in the Cold—Association is Tried Out.**

Garry Herrmann and his associates on the National Baseball Association took what is regarded as a most important step when they decided that the disposal of Moriarity to Fall River by the Chicago National League Club, with the understanding that he should be returned, is perfectly legal and within the laws of the national agreement regarding "farming." The commission in President Johnson's office decided not to change the wording of the peace agreement on the subject of farming, as the ruling, to quote Secretary Bruce, "is already as clear as it can be made." But it ruled that each case should be brought before them.

Moriarity was "sold" to Fall River with the understanding that President Hart should have the privilege of buying him back should he desire to do so. As the arrangement was as clear a piece of farming as any this year, the decision of the commission to sidestep the real issue is held to open the door to similar acts by other clubs and to legalize other cases which are already matters of history.

It was ruled that Toledo should lose the services of Reisling and O'Hara unless the claims due Pittsburg and Cleveland respectively for the players shall be paid. The same ruling was made in regard to Bonner, for whom Kansas City now owes money to Cleveland.

Nothing was said about Los Angeles' claim on Reisling. He is still pitching for Toledo, and probably will finish the season there. The National Association thus far has done the Coast no good.

### Target Shooting.

TACOMA (Wash.) July 9.—Washington won in the three days' competition target shooting at American Lake by 26 points; the army was second and Oregon third.

There will be a team bluerock shoot this morning at the grounds of the Los Angeles Gun Club near Sherman, to which all shooters are invited.

## GREAT IS JOY OF OUTDOORS.

*Bloom for Milady's Cheeks in the Open Air.*

*From Heights to the Sea the Place to be.*

*New Cure for Many Ills is Free to All.*

The glory of a day out of doors!

There is nothing like it in the world for bringing bloom to the cheek, brightness to the eye, elasticity to the step and a general restoration of lost health.

Great is the joy of spending the entire time in the open air, among the trees and birds, where all is harmonious; at the seashore, lake or mountain, where are found renewed vigor and health, after indulging in exercise of fishing, rowing, driving, riding, walking, hill or mountain climbing. It is sure to drive away "the blues" and makes the heart light and gay.

The open air treatment is a simple and most efficacious method of bringing about a permanent cure of persons whose systems are "run down" by worry, overwork and nervous affections.

The great success attending the open-air treatment is just now attracting the attention of thoughtful people everywhere. Women especially, whose lungs are weak, and who are suffering and unhappy by reason of a "rundown" condition, are taking the cure.

The proper thing to do is to remain out of doors every day as much as possible, and to indulge in some form of exercise, whether it be walking hill or mountain climbing, rowing, fishing, riding or sitting out of doors, inhaling the health-giving ozone. The entire day should be spent out of doors; the object being to gain all the possible advantages accruing from the outdoor life, which has been demonstrated to be so beneficial to people who seek juvenation of their bodily system.

Those who pursue this outdoor life are greatly astonished and overjoyed in a brief period of time, to observe that the cheeks upon which have blazed the death badge, are gradually developing the rich, even glow of vigorous life. It is the sleep of the desert wanderer who has found water and life in an oasis, after following mirages till body and brain and soul had sickened almost unto death.

The chief point not to be lost sight of is to be sure and remain in the open air as much as possible. Do not be afraid if the weather is a little cool. Warm wraps will keep out the cold. Some enthusiasts of the new cure, who have been blessed with a generous quantity of hair, have accustomed themselves to go hatless in all kind of changeable weather, whether in the mountains, seashore or country, and have received no evil results from such exposure.

Of course proper food taken in correct quantities is also a feature of the new cure. Some persons have been known to progress rapidly on a diet of raw eggs and plenty of milk, consumed at regular intervals.

It is well to retire to bed early and endeavor to sleep at least eight hours, also to avoid eating when bodily or mentally tired or in a state or nervous excitement. Do not smoke or drink liquor, wine or beer, except by special permission, but drink plenty of good milk and water between meals. Never take any kind of walking, breathing, or other exercises when you are tired, nor take them to the extent of getting tired.

Many of the men and women who are at present pursuing the open-air treatment, and who are making the fight for life, are expected to be exposed to the free, unwarmed air of nature the greater portion of the day. They must take exercise and rest, until health and strength come back in swelling tide.

Particularly at this time of the year nature affords ample opportunity for persons with worn-out systems, whose physical conditions have been run down, to seek the outdoor treatment.

The languid and tired feeling experienced by the man or woman suffering possibly from some disease that is sapping life away, vanishes like smoke in a short time, if such persons have recourse to boating, sailing or fishing for continuous days at mountain, lake or seashore. The eye brightens, the ruddy complexion returns to the pallid cheek, the step becomes more elastic, strength and merry laughter are again visible in the form that was previously more or less emaciated, all the result of the open-air treatment.

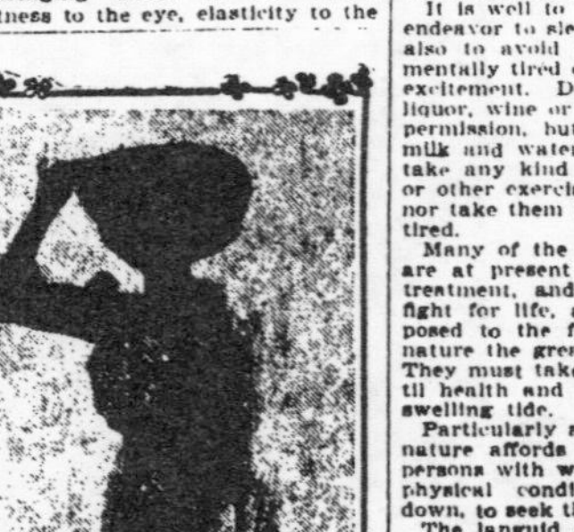

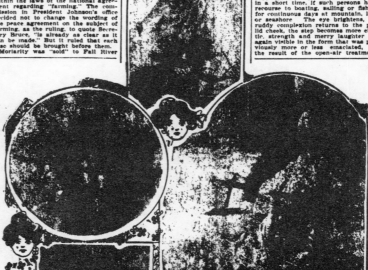

How Milady Reaps the Benefits of Southern California Atmosphere

The latter has not only changed and improved the physical condition of the devotees of the new cure, but the eagerly sought change is likely to be permanent.

Let milady take a row over the placid stream in a boat that is to her liking, remaining out some hours, and she will discover on her return to shore that the bracing air and exercise undergone, if continued for several days, will make a "new woman" of her, her health being restored.

Another good means of regaining lost health by the open air treatment is by daily practice of hill or mountain climbing, which invigorates the system, and while seemingly tiresome, really is productive of much good, which is experienced after a reasonable night's rest.

Don't be afraid to ascend the hilltops or high embankments, while the wind sometimes is blowing furiously, but take up a position on the lofty eminence and inhale the pure, fresh air, that means so much to your worn-out system. It will do you an immense amount of good and you will be well repaid for your visits, especially if they are repeated a number of times.

One does not necessarily have to take any or all of the mentioned forms of exercise to be assured of good results from the open air treatment.

Take to the seashore, mountain, lake or country and live the entire time out of doors, if you wish to regain lost health. Conform to the simple regulations laid down and discipline yourself to the agreeable task required in the matter of partaking of various kinds of exercise. To some people this new form of outdoor treatment may not appeal very strongly, and they may balk against the plan laid down.

Many, however, realizing the wisdom of the regulations and their physical helplessness in many instances, set themselves for the struggle like soldiers going into battle with the odds somewhat against them.

But, later on, to their great satisfaction, they find their condition improving for the better, and they happily discover that they are on the road to recovery. Then they watch the quavering needle of the weighing scale as closely as a mariner watches his compass and with far more eagerness. They discover that they are gaining flesh and that their health is improving. The open air treatment is responsible for it.

## TITLE STILL ANDERSON'S.

*National Open Golf Champion for This Year.*

*Competition at Chicago Has Sensational Finish.*

*Amateur Oarsmen's Regatta an Olympian Affair.*

[BY DIRECT WIRE TO THE TIMES.]

CHICAGO, July 9, 1904.—[Exclusive Dispatch.] Willie Anderson of the Apawamis Country Club of Rye retains the title of the national open golf champion this year, as he won the twenty-two hole competition for the honor at the Glenview Club, which came to a conclusion this afternoon, with a score of 303.

This is the third year that he has won the championship, being successful last year and in 1901. In addition to the title of national champion, he is also western open champion, having won the title at Grand Rapids last week.

Anderson receives in addition to $200 in cash, a gold medal emblematic of the championship and will retain the custody of the championship cup. Gilbert Nicholls of the St. Louis Country Club took second money, with a score of 308, while Fred McKenzie of Onwentsia, once amateur champion of Scotland, was third with 309.

In accomplishing a feat which has never before been equaled in the history of the national championship—winning it three times—Anderson made a sensational finish, his score for the last eighteen holes being 72, which was only equaled by one contestant during a tournament—Alexander Campbell of Boston.

Anderson originally came from North Berwick, Scotland, where he learned to play the game as a boy. He has been in the United States for five years and at one time was connected with the Oconomowoc, Wis., Golf Club. He is the son of "Old Tom" Anderson, the green keeper of Braid's Rod Public Links, Edinburgh, Scotland. Willie is 24 years old.

Chandler Egan of Exmoor, the western amateur champion of 1902, won the gold medal for amateurs, returning a score of 329, twenty-six strokes behind Anderson. Egan had 163 at the conclusion of yesterday's play, and this morning made 83 and this afternoon also 83.

The tournament has been remarkable for the reversals of form, as exhibited by some of the professionals in succeeding rounds. Some of the contestants played phenomenal golf for one round and then would take a decided slump.

### MAYOR WEAVER'S STAND.

HARD BLOW TO BRUISERS.

[BY DIRECT WIRE TO THE TIMES.]

NEW YORK, July 9.—[Exclusive Dispatch.] Followers of the pugilistic game got a hard knock Friday, when Mayor Weaver of Philadelphia shut the doors in the face of Fitzsimmons and O'Brien. There was no mistaking Weavers's sincerity, so there was no trifling. Philadelphia has had a surfeit of the plug-ugly business of late, and Weaver, personally, is in sympathy with the decent element of the city.

It looks as though the ministers of Quakertown were inspired at the last moment to make the strong protest they did, and that inspiration was probably Mayor Weavers himself. It looks as though Philadelphia is about ready to join New York in shutting out bruisers, and giving California a tighter monopoly on the fighting business.

### AMATEUR OARSMEN'S REGATTA.

OLYMPIC EVENT THIS YEAR.

[BY DIRECT WIRE TO THE TIMES.]

NEW YORK, July 9.—[Exclusive Dispatch.] The thirty-second annual championship regatta of the National Association of Amateur Oarsmen will this year be an Olympian affair open to all amateur clubs in the world. The regatta will be held at Crevecoeur Lake, St. Louis, July 29 and 30.

In addition to challenge cups and plate of the national association, each winning oarsmen or sculler will receive a "national die," gold medals, to each of which will be attached a gold bar with the word "Olympic," emblematical of the world's championship.

Oarsmen will receive very low special rates from all railways. Lou Scholes, the young Irish-Canadian who won the English diamond sculls and smashed the record in doing so, will meet Frank Greer of Boston, who won the championship last year.

### NEW RIFLE.

SAN BERDOO MAN'S DESIGN.

A. E. Perris, chief clerk of the Santa Fé oil department at San Bernardino, has received the first sample of the "Perris Special," a rifle which he recently designed for a prominent eastern arms manufacturing company, to meet the demand for a lighter and shorter gun than is now made by that company.

The new gun is fitted with a 20-inch round barrel with Sheard copper bead front sight and flat-top Rocky Mountain rear. The rear sight is brought back so that it rests just in front of the receiver, which gives a much greater distance between the front and rear sights than is now used on rifles, and increases the accuracy of the arm. The stock is shorter than on the regular arm, and fitted with a handsome hard rubber shotgun butt plate, which enables the user to operate the gun without taking it from the shoulder. The gun weighs six and one-half pounds, and is pronounced by experts who have examined it the finest field and saddle gun on the market. The new gun is credited with all the advantages of the light weight of the carbine, but without the disadvantages of the cumbersome stock and ring at the side of the receiver, which is now put on all the light carbines.

### HELENE IS GONE.

The auxiliary sloop Helene, a popular fishing boat around Ocean Park, carried away her mooring Friday night while her owners were uptown attending some social function, and the boat drifted helplessly in on the beach. All night she bumped, and this afternoon when the breeze came up she began going to pieces. Her engine and fittings were mostly recovered; the rest of her is now too wet even for good firewood.

SPORTING SECTION.

The Pink Sheet.
THE FIELD OF SPORTS.

# Los Angeles Sunday Times

Part III—4 Pages
SPORTS AND SPORTSMEN.

XXIVTH YEAR. SUNDAY MORNING, OCTOBER 15, 1905. ON ALL NEWS STANDS. TRAINS AND STREETS. | 5 CENTS





## HEMERY WINS AUTO RACE.

*Heath Finishes Second and Tracy Third.*

*Winner Scorched at Seventy Miles an Hour.*

*Foxhall Keene Crashes Into Telephone Pole.*

[BY DIRECT WIRE TO THE TIMES.]

NEW YORK, Oct. 14.—[Exclusive Dispatch.] While the Frenchmen shouted and cried, and the Americans bit their lips with disappointment, August Hemery, driver of the eighty-horse-power Darracq car, won the race for the W. K. Vanderbilt, Jr., cup over the Long Island course today, after one of the most sensational speed contests ever held.

Hemery, who had climbed up from fourth place in the race to the leadership at the finish, made the remarkable time of four hours, thirty-six minutes and eight seconds for the total of 283 miles of the course. At times he went at the terrific speed of seventy miles an hour and narrowly escaped several smashes on the route, that was fraught with danger at every turn. He defeated Heath, the other representative of France, who was striving for first place over Lancia, the Italian, and when the latter was practically put out of the race by a bad accident near the finish, Heath swept past him and seemed sure of winning the great contest.

It was then that Hemery, the French driver, pressed so hard that the American had to take second place at the close of the contest, and then Tracy, the other American contestant, took third place over Lancia, who finished fourth.

KEENE HAS ACCIDENT.

While going at the terrific speed of eighty miles an hour, Foxhall Keene, in his 120-horse power Mercedes, crashed into a telephone pole in Willis avenue, between Albertsons and Lakeville, smashing his machine, but he himself and his mechanic escaped all injury. Mr. Keene, who was second in the race at that point, was put out of the race permanently by the accident. At this point of the road a clump of trees form, with the telephone and telegraph poles, the most dangerous obstruction to the racing cars. The road is narrow at this point, and the slightest swerve means to crash into the poles and trees on either side of the road.

Lancia, who set a hot pace

Hemery, the winner

**Two foreigners who made great showing in Vanderbilt cup chase yesterday.**

### INDIANS' VICTORY.

CO. F BADLY BEATEN.

[BY DIRECT WIRE TO THE TIMES.]

RIVERSIDE, Oct. 14.—[Exclusive Dispatch.] By a score of 88 to 0 the Sherman Indians swept Co. F football team off the field today. Notwithstanding the terrible drubbing, Co. F is unanimous in saying that the Indians play the whitest football of any team on the Coast. The Indians were like a whirlwind. They started in with a touchdown on Co. F's kickoff and the game wound up with the three goals from touchdowns and another from the field in the last five minutes. Tortes kicked the goal from the field.

Co. F played bravely, but they were simply not in it with Hempel's speedy braves. The Indians bucked the line for 10 yards at a time; went round the ends for 60 yards and played with the city team as though they were babies. It was all speed. If any team expects to shut the Indians out this year, they will have to hobble the braves. The game was of two halves of twenty and fifteen minutes. The Indians averaged a goal every three minutes of the play. The line-up was as follows:

| Sherman Indians | | Co. F. |
|---|---|---|
| Kennedy | left end | Patton |
| Lugo | left tackle | Poole |
| H. Coleman | left guard | Emmons |
| C. Coleman | center | Lichtwerk |
| Blacktooth | right guard | Schurer<br>Schneider |
| Lubo | right tackle | McMahon |
| Scholder (C.) | right end | Bailey |
| Chas. Coleman | quarterback | Wilson<br>Croft |
| Neafus | left halfback | Locke |
| McGee | fullback | Rose (C.)<br>Willett |
| Tortes | right half | Ferguson<br>Anderson |

The Indians played as subs Fulwilder, tackle; Whipple, guard; Bullock, quarter; Lupe Lugo, fullback, and Baldy, end. The soldier boy subs were Schneider, Brown and Fisher.

### SHOT PUTTER COMES.

WANTS HIGHEST HONORS.

[BY DIRECT WIRE TO THE TIMES.]

NEW YORK, Oct. 14.—[Exclusive Dispatch.] Dennis Horgan, the champion shot-putter of the British Isles, who formerly held the world's record with the 16-pound shot, has arrived in New York, and will stay in this country indefinitely. When seen at the Pastime Athletic Club he stated that the object of his visit was to win back the world's record, which Ralph Rose and Wesley Coe have wrested from him during the last year. Horgan's record of 48 feet 2 inches stood a number of years, and was considered unbeatable until Rose, the California boy, sent the iron ball an unheard of distance of 48 feet 7½ inches. The Irishman's pride was further humbled last August, when W. W. Coe of Somerville, Mass., set the mark up to 49 feet 6 inches. When Horgan read of this he made arrangements to come to America and stay until he had retrieved his lost laurels. Horgan's last visit to this country was in 1900, when he easily won the American shot-putting championship.

### HARVARD WINS.

HARD FOUGHT GAME.

Harvard 8, Pasadena High School 0.

One of the grittiest football games of the season was played yesterday afternoon on the Harvard School campus between the Harvard Military School eleven and the Pasadena High School team.

Harvard won by hard line bucking, but every inch of ground was stubbornly contested by the lads from Pasadena, who had evidently come to town to win.

The first half resulted 6 to 0, in favor of Harvard, who in order to cross their opponent's goal, were forced to adopt a close formation.

There were no sensational runs during the game, but in the second half the play opened up with a good exhibition of punting.

Pasadena was weak on offensive play, and failed to gain any great advantage when given the ball. The boys were strong in defensive work and allowed few openings.

Both teams were penalized for off side playing, the home team losing the most ground for this offense.

Near the end of the second half, the crowd was given a pretty exhibition of football when the pigskin was punted in a corkscrew curve far down the field by Ball of Harvard. Little of Pasadena missed the catch and the ball went bouncing over the goal line. Gibbs of Pasadena grabbed the ball and tried to repair the damage with a quick run. He was downed behind his own goal line by a neat tackle and two points were added to Harvard's score by the safety thus gained.

The line up:

| Harvard | | Pasadena |
|---|---|---|
| Darling | right guard | Lee |
| Coulter | right tackle | Ross |
| Okey | rear end | Wheeler |
| Zuill | center | Patterson |
| Lee | left guard | Reynolds |
| Cross | left tackle | Underwood |
| Duff | left end | Hotaling |
| W. Cline | quarterback | Little |
| Keating | right half | Crawford |
| H. Cline | left half | Patton |
| Ball | fullback | Blick |

The officials were: Frank Boren, referee; W. A. Ellis, umpire. The halves were twenty minutes each.

### COURSING RACES.

THREE STAKES ON CARD.

[BY DIRECT WIRE TO THE TIMES.]

SAN FRANCISCO, Oct. 14.—[Exclusive Dispatch.] A champion stake of twelve entries, a reserve of thirty-two and an open of forty-four, make up the card for tomorrow. One round of the open stake was run today, leaving twenty-two dogs in this stake for tomorrow. The champion and reserve stakes are made up of the best dogs in their respective classes, and it is needless to say the many spectators will be furnished with an excellent days' sport. The management has succeeded in matching the two notable performers, Sacramento Boy and Homer Boy. They will meet next Sunday, October 22, for a purse of $250. The winner will have to raise the flag in three trials out of five. No two dogs are better known to followers of the leash than these two grand greyhounds.

A large delegation will be on hand from Sacramento to witness this trial for supremacy.

## GIANTS WIN BALL HONORS.

*Shut Out Philadelphia in the Final Game.*

*Christy Mathewson Was the Cause of It.*

*Large and Enthusiastic Crowd Sees Contest.*

[BY DIRECT WIRE TO THE TIMES.]

POLO GROUND, NEW YORK, Oct. 14.—[Exclusive Dispatch.] All hail to the conquerors, the Giants. They won the game 2 to 0. Who won? Mathewson won.

The Giants took the fifth game of the world's series from the Athletics and the fifth game carried with it the baseball championship of the world. Mathewson's pitching did it. Bender was great. The mighty chief had on his war paint, but he gave two bases on balls at the wrong time and that hurt his team. His team played an errorless game. Mathewson allowed six hits and Bender five, but Bender was wild at the wrong time. It was the fourth shut-out for the Athletics, who in thirty-six innings failed to score. Great are the Giants, but greater is "Christy."

About thirty thousand fans saw the game. At 1:30 o'clock both bleacher stands were packed and jammed to suffocation and the crowd was beginning to stand around the center of the field boundary ropes. There was not a seat to be had in the lower section of the big pavilion and in the upper section most of the reserved seats had been taken. A band helped enliven the preliminary practice, which was as brisk and snappy as any one could wish to see.

### BRITT AMBITIOUS.

WANTS NELSON AGAIN.

[BY DIRECT WIRE TO THE TIMES.]

SAN FRANCISCO, Oct. 14.—[Exclusive Dispatch.] Jimmy Britt appears to be drawing bigger houses than Battling Nelson did in Denver. Britt writes as follows to a friend in this city: "I have been drawing bigger houses than Nelson since leaving Frisco, and seem to be more popular in defeat than I ever was in victory. I played a week in Salt Lake and was treated fine by both press and public. My boxing partner failed to show up one night, and instead of boxing I did my monologue. It was a great success, and now I am compelled to do it wherever I show. I arrived in Denver Sunday morning, and was met at the depot by Otto Floto and Battling Nelson. That afternoon I opened the biggest house in the history of the theater. Had I beaten Jeffries in a punch it could not have been better. Had a talk with Nelson in which I told him I thought I was his master, and that I wanted the first chance at him. He said he would fight me again as soon as he finished his engagement. I still think I can beat him."

### HYLAS FIRST.

WINS RICH STAKE.

[BY THE ASSOCIATED PRESS—P.M.]

NEW YORK, Oct. 14—Thomas Hitchcock, Jr.'s, Hylas, the 8 to 5 favorite, won the champion steeplechase in the presence of 25,000 persons at Belmont Park today. T. P. Phelan's Ben Crockett, paying 2 to 1 for the place, was second and Mr. Cotton's Jimmy Lane third. The Champion steeplechase is one of the richest events of its kind in the East, the winner receiving a little over $10,000 in adition to a $500 plate. A splendid field of timber-toppers faced the starter for this event, which is over the trying journey of three and a half miles. Results:

Six furlongs: Penrhyn won, Arklirta second, Lancastrian third; time 1:12 3-5.

The champion steeplechase, about three miles and a half: Hylas won, Ben Crockett second, Jimmy Lane third; time 6:57.

Handicap, six furlongs: Tiptoe won, Snow second, Bridgeman third; time 1:13 1-5.

Seven furlongs: Townes won, Holloway second, Gentian third; time 1:27 3-5.

Two and one-quarter miles: St. Bellant won, Ostrich second, Bedouin third; time 3:57 2-5.

One mile and three-sixteenths: Monsieur Baucaire won, Red Knight second, Israelite third; time 1:59.

### GOLF HONORS.

PAULINE MACKAY WINS.

[BY THE ASSOCIATED PRESS—P.M.]

NEW YORK, Oct. 14.—The final contest for the women's national golf championship began today between Miss Margaret Curtis and Miss Pauline Mackay at the Norris country links at Covent Station, N. J. Miss Curtis represents the Essex Country Club of Manchester-by-the-Sea, Mass., and Miss Mackay the Oakley Country Club of Watertown, Mass.

Weather conditions were excellent. Miss Curtis was the favorite because of the low scores which she has been making over the course in the preliminary rounds.

Miss Pauline Mackay won the woman's national golf championship, defeating Miss Margaret Curtis by 1 up in 18 holes.

## BETTER LUCK ALONG BEACHES.

**FISHERMEN FINDING SPORT AT ALL THE RESORTS.**

**Halibut, Croakers, Surf Fish, Sea Trout, Bass, Yellowtail and Yellowfins Taking Hold at the Various Vantage Points—Jack Smelts Quit Biting for a Time.**

Fishermen have been having all kinds of sport during the week which closed yesterday.

Croakers, halibut, yellowfins, yellowtail and bass were the piscatorial programme. At most of the beaches some kind of fish was running well enough to afford good sport.

San Pedro Bay produced a number of croakers and a few yellowfins during the rising tides. Halibut are beginning to bite better as the colder weather comes on, and their flesh is becoming more palatable.

The bass fishing outside is first class, and seems to be growing better all the time. Big yellow-bellies are to be had at the breakwater and at Port Los Angeles.

At the southern resorts some surf fish of fair size are feeding in considerable numbers. West Newport and Huntington Beach, are both good points for fishermen's research.

The yellowtail at Newport are biting with considerable regularity, and one can almost depend on going out on the wharf and getting at least one "strike" of a good-sized one. Some weighing thirty-five pounds have been seen—and lost through broken gear.

At Redondo mackerel, yellowtail and halibut are the prevailing game with occasional sea trout thrown in for variety.

Manhattan fishing is quiet, and there is little doing at Hermosa, though some anglers report good sport casting off the beach for yellowfins.

Hyperion, ill-smelling place of the sewer wharf, is little frequented nowadays, the difficulties of fishing there being such as to deter most anglers. Halibut bite there at times, and occasionally yellowtail run past the pier head.

Jack smelts are plentiful, but they are not biting very well at present.

### BUSH LEAGUE.

NEW ONE TALKED.

[SPECIAL CORRESPONDENCE OF THE TIMES.]

SANTA BARBARA, Oct. 14.—Again the formation of a bush baseball league has sprung up, and is being agitated in several of the cities of the southern part of the State. Manager Van Dervort of this city has been receiving communications from influential baseball men of Los Angeles and other cities in regard to joining the league with his Channel City team, and he has expressed a willingness to be one of them.

A similar league, which embraced the larger and smaller cities of the southern part of the State was started two years ago, but it died after a series of winter games and squabbles. The whole organization was one big fight from start to finish, but while it lasted it was interesting to ball players and fans alike. It is said that the plans now being made on the quiet are more stable and far-reaching than those launched two years ago, and if carried into action, will put a number of minor ball teams into a series of games that will interest the residents of every town and hamlet in Southern California. Santa Barbara now has a strong team in constant practice, and will be out after the pennant when it is unfurled to the breeze.

### RACERS FOR COAST.

LYMAN BUYS TWO.

[BY DIRECT WIRE TO THE TIMES.]

NEW YORK, Oct. 14.—[Exclusive Dispatch.] It was reported at Belmont Park yesterday that J. G. Lyman has purchased for California racing the mare Geranium and the gelding Roycroft. The sum of $1000 has been mentioned as the amount paid to C. M. Dowell.

### CROSS-COUNTRY MEET.

WILL COME IN NOVEMBER.

[BY DIRECT WIRE TO THE TIMES.]

NEW YORK, Oct. 14.—[Exclusive Dispatch.] The National Cross Country Championships of the Amateur Athletic Institution of the United States will be held under the auspices of the New York Athletic Club at Travers Island, N. Y., on November 30.

### CRICKET.

CRICKET MATCH TODAY.

An interesting cricket game is scheduled for this afternoon at Agricultural Park between the Los Angeles eleven and the St. George Cricket team. The game will be called at 3 o'clock.

There is much interest being taken in the sport and there is a prospect of several lively games in the near future. On next Sunday the winning team in the game of this afternoon will play a picked eleven from Santa Monica.

The fielding positions of the players in today's game:

| LOS ANGELES. | | ST. GEORGE. |
|---|---|---|
| H. Justice | bowler | Barwell |
| F. Justice | shortslip | Price |
| Higgins | mid-on | Johnson |
| Moles | cover-point | F. Brown |
| Calderbank | longstop | Sweet |
| Eyer | longslip | Packman |
| Pierce | leg | Barwell |
| Wood | point | T. Brown |
| Hughes | long-on | Gadsden |
| Cooper | long-off | Trowbridge |
| Montague | wicket-keeper | Meggett |

### Latonia Card.

CINCINNATI (O.) Oct. 14.—Latonia results:

Five and a half furlongs: Calabash won, Miltiades second, Granada third; time 1:07 3-5.

One mile: Varieties won, John Lyle second, Thespian third; time 1:40 3-5.

Six furlongs: Santon won, Covina second, Chief Milliken third; time 1:14 1-5.

One mile and fifty yards: Shawana won, Brancas second, Devout third; time 1:43 2-5.

Six and a half furlongs: Hogan won, Lady Esther second, Nifo third; time 1:21.

One mile and three-sixteenths: Marshall Ney won, Mae Hanlon second, Brand New third; time 1:59 1-5.

## COLUMBIA MEN DISQUALIFIED.

*Three Crack Men Declared Not Eligible.*

*Harvard Wins Poor Contest from Springfield.*

*Yale Takes Easy Game from Holy Cross.*

[BY DIRECT WIRE TO THE TIMES.]

**FOOTBALL RESULTS.**

| | | | |
|---|---|---|---|
| Sherman Ind. | 88 | Co. F. | 0 |
| Harvard | 12 | Springfield | 0 |
| Yale | 18 | Holy Cross | 0 |
| Virginia Techs | 32 | West Point | 6 |
| Pennsylvania | 5 | N. Carolina | 0 |
| Princeton | 48 | Bicknell Col. | 0 |
| Columbia | 11 | Williams | 5 |
| Chicago | 16 | Indiana | 5 |
| Michigan | 18 | Vanderbilt | 0 |
| Perdue | 12 | Wabash | 0 |
| Cincinnati | 12 | Earlham | 0 |
| Wisconsin | 21 | Notre Dame | 0 |
| Illinois | 12 | St. Louis | 6 |

NEW YORK, Oct. 14.—[Exclusive Dispatch.] Columbia football men were thrown into a panic when it was learned this week that Capt. Thomas J. Thorpe, Douglass Carter and W. M. Starbuck were declared out of football for the season. With these men out of the game, Columbia fears greatly the outcome of not only the game with the members of the "big four," but also those with the smaller elevens. Thorpe has been dropped from college, while Carter has been declared ineligible for an indefinite period, and Starbuck during the present academic year. The men under the ban were all matriculated in the school of mines, where a specially high standard of scholarship must be preserved, and it was owing to their failure to keep up to it that they got into trouble with Dean Sever. It was rumored for some time that Thorpe was in difficulty on account of his scholarship, but it was not thought such drastic action would be taken. He entered college three years ago, and in his first two years stood very well, having only one condition. Last year he was injured playing football so that his eyes were affected, and consequently he had to refrain from study. Carter understood he could become eligible by working off one condition, and took the examination for it yesterday, only to learn later that he was debarred from athletics because he had failed to advance with his class.

The greatest surprise, however, was the case of Starbuck, which had been passed on earlier in the season, so that he was allowed to play in the earlier games, having been declared eligible by the regular committee. One of the professors in the school of mines stated that there were eight more ball players who were under consideration for the same treatment that was accorded to the three disqualified, and that absolutely no favor would be shown to a man merely because he was an athlete.

Thorpe would probably have been the greatest tackle playing the game this fall, and it will be practically impossible to fill his place. Carter and Starbuck were among the best candidates for the position of fullback, the former being an especially good punter. In the almost impossible schedule that the blue and white is attempting this year, the chance for anything like success is unlooked for by the students with these men out of the game.

HARVARD WINS.

[BY DIRECT WIRE TO THE TIMES.]

CAMBRIDGE (Mass.) Oct. 14.—[Exclusive Dispatch.] By the score of 12 to 0, Harvard this afternoon defeated the eleven from the Springfield training school. The showing made by Harvard disgusted the coaches. Springfield's strength was a surprise to everyone.

YALE'S EASY VICTORY.

[BY DIRECT WIRE TO THE TIMES.]

NEW HAVEN, Oct. 14.—[Exclusive Dispatch.] Yale skunked Holy Cross on the Yale field this afternoon, scoring herself a safe eighteen points. The visitors, however, outplayed the home team a few minutes during the first half.

PENN'S GAME.

[BY DIRECT WIRE TO THE TIMES.]

PHILADELPHIA (Pa.), Oct. 14.—[Exclusive Dispatch.] Pennsylvania scored only 5 points against North Carolina on Franklin field this afternoon. The Southern team's tackling bothered the home players considerably. The final score was Pennsylvania 5, North Carolina 0.

SOLDIERS BEATEN.

[BY DIRECT WIRE TO THE TIMES.]

WEST POINT, Oct. 14.—[Exclusive Dispatch.] The West Point eleven lost to the Virginia Techs by the embarrassing score of 32 to 6. The Army was weakened by the loss of three of its best players. From the start the Virginia boys had little trouble with the army lines.

PRINCETON'S BIG SCORE.

[BY DIRECT WIRE TO THE TIMES.]

PRINCETON, Oct. 14.—[Exclusive Dispatch.] The Tigers rolled up a score of 48 to 0 against Bucknell College eleven here today. The game was a succession of plunges for gain. Bucknell was too light and mobile to hold the striped players at any point.

COLUMBIA VICTORIOUS.

[BY DIRECT WIRE TO THE TIMES.]

NEW YORK, Oct. 14.—[Exclusive Dispatch.] After a hard-fought battle with the pigskin warriors of Williams' College, their old-time enemies on the checkerboard, Columbia this afternoon came off victorious with a score of 11 to 5. Williams' five points came in the second half when Brown, the left half, carried the ball over.

### TOURISTS ARRIVE.

LULL'S PARTY ON ROAD.

[BY DIRECT WIRE TO THE TIMES.]

RIVERSIDE, Oct. 14.—[Exclusive Dispatch.] An eight-car automobile party of forty-five Angelenos, guests of Mr. and Mrs. L. C. Lull, arrived here between 6 and 7 o'clock. Mr. and Mrs. Lull came in on the last car at 7 o'clock. They are being entertained at the Glenwood Tavern. The trip from Los Angeles was devoid of notable incident. The best time made was three hours and fifty minutes. Tomorrow Mr. and Mrs. Lull have invited Frank A. Miller and sixteen of his friends to join the Angelenos on a tour of the valley.

# Nelson's Rowdy Tactics Bring Hisses From Thousands.

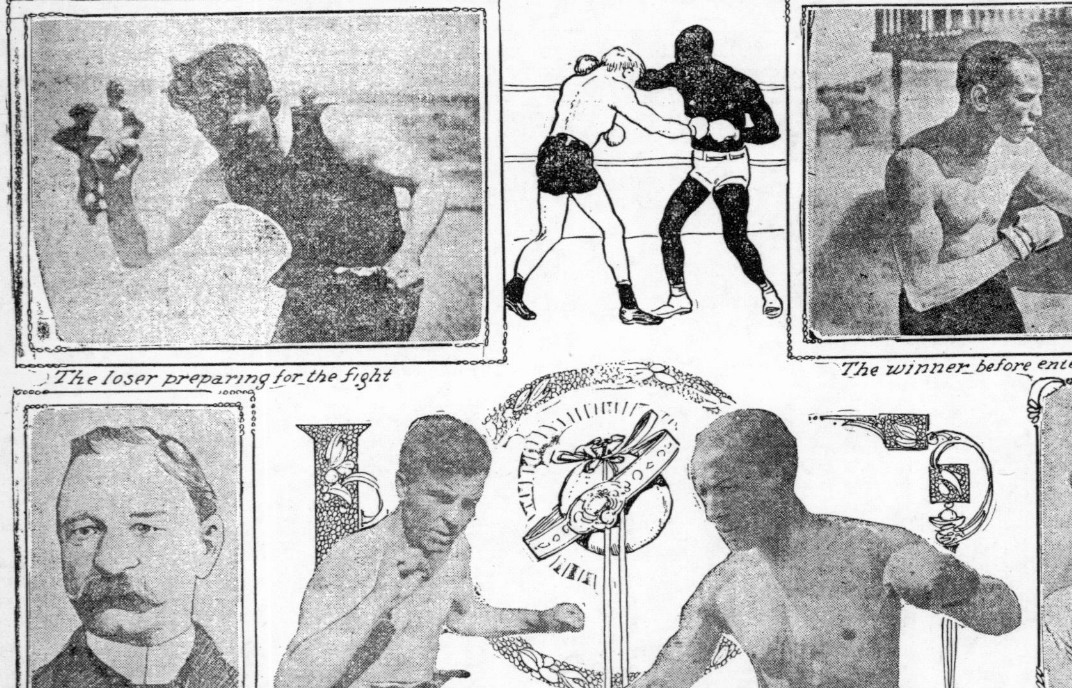

The loser preparing for the fight

The winner before entering the ring

George Siler Referee

Ole Elliott Sec'y Goldfield A.C.

A Corner in the Goldfield Athletic Club-Rooms

Gans and Nelson in fighting

The foul that ended the fight.

The Exciting Goldfield Event—Principals and Episodes of the Day.

at the ground. He was dressed in a sloppy old gray suit of clothes. Tim McGrath squatted in front of him and talked in a low voice, giving remarks to which Bat did not listen.

Gans crossed to the timekeeper's side and leaned over the ropes, saying anxiously, "Now, I don't want no sponge throwing from no seconds butting in the ring, and I don't want no fouls."

"Same here," said Bat. As the timekeepers took their places, Tex Rickard brought four husky deputy sheriffs to the ring.

"The first man who speaks to any timekeeper I want you to knock down," Tex said. Nobody spoke to the timekeepers.

SHOUTS FOR ROOSEVELT, JR.

Gans went to his corner under a big umbrella, while Larry Sullivan of Goldfield announced that 100 deputy sheriffs would keep order and that Teddy Roosevelt's son was in the audience. The crowd began to yell, "Roosevelt, Roosevelt," but Sullivan said, "Oh, shut up." And they shut up. Larry's speech was a wonder of English grammar.

Just before the fight began, Gans crossed the ring and dared Nelson to bet $1200 against $2000. Bat shook his head. Then the gong, with the two fighters crouching and tense. Siler, the referee, wandered around like some placid old gentleman out for a morning walk.

Bat bored in hard at first, oblivious of the storm of blows. It was not a pretty fight. They clung and struggled and punched. Bat was no match for the darky as a boxer. But Bat's old pounded head came back into it like bull dog.

DANE BLEEDS FREELY.

By the third round Bat was bleeding from the nose, and his cauliflower ear and mouth, but he was as strong as a tiger. At the end of the fifth round Gans, stopped and looked with silent sarcasm at Bat's bloody face as the Dane went to his corner. Joe kept keeping away and punching Bat's bloody face at long distance.

"Close to him, Bat," called Nolan soothingly. "He likes those," shouted Nolan as Bat swung to Gans's stomach. Bat's face was streaming and his body was spotted with blood as he went to his corner. The claret spattered onto Gans. As the seventh round ended, a big nigger wench in blue jumped up in a chair and yelled "foul," but Siler did not allow it.

Bat came back like a young bull in the next round and the crowd went frantic. Through round after round, the gladiators stood shoulder to shoulder, butting, shoving and roughing it. It was a wearing down match. Blood was dripping in gobs from both men. Gans's chalky eyes were rolling. As the thirteenth round began, Nolan leaned far over the ropes and yelled: "Stay right with him, Bat, its a hundred to one on you."

NELSON BECOMES ROWDY.

Gans's answer was to rush Bat against the ropes as a policeman forces back a crowd, and he held him there, struggling to bend him back. Bat made a dirty, little rowdy of himself in the fourteenth round. Gans knocked him through the ropes, and reached over to help him up. As he did so Bat struck him in the stomach. At the end of the round both fighters stood still in the center of the ring, glaring at each other.

Then one of them struck out. Nelson cursed and tried to kick Gans. Joe's lean brown leg kicked back. Neither kick landed, and the crowd yelled in derision. Bat Nelson will never live down the memory of that dirty kick.

Bat was knocked down in his own corner in the fifteenth. Joe helped him up and dealt him a stinging blow as he got to his feet. Gans gave a wonderful exhibition of boxing in that round. Bat lunged out viciously for his woolly head and it was not there. Swinging, the brown body flitted, and both men fell through the ropes, Nelson underneath.

SPECTATORS IN FIGHT.

Nelson's scalp was cut, but he came back in a few seconds. Two men in a box started to rival with the fight and the crowd was in agony which contest to watch. Gans was bleeding from the mouth and his gloves were soaked with blood.

As the two pugilists came close over the press correspondents' table it was a horrible sight, two straining, dripping bodies and bloody agonized faces. Bat was pounded enough to have killed twenty Jimmy Britts. Bat went groggy and was holding his hands before his face, helpless to stave off the storm of blows. The twentieth gong saved him, but he came up strong and full of fight for the twenty-first round.

As the twenty-third round began, some one yelled "Skiddoo" for somebody, and it looked like Gans to skiddoo, too. Bat butted his shoulder against the coon's body, and drove fearful piston-rod blows into Gans's stomach until the coon looked weak and faint, staring with dreadful chalky eyes. The Dane's left eye was now almost shut, but his blows were strong and fresh.

BOTH FIGHTERS WEARY.

Bat came up quick and strong for the twenty-fifth round, but Gans looked tired and worn. Laying his head on Gans's shoulder Bat pounded him furiously in the stomach until Gans rallied in a whirlwind of sheer desperation. Gans began dodging again and Bat lost strength beating empty air.

Bat was going after Gans like a tiger, when Gans suddenly hit him a blow on the jaw that sent him staggering backward half dazed. Gans leaped after him and slung in punches until Bat was tottering, head down, about the ring. The gong saved him.

Hisses and boos for Nelson closed the thirtieth round. After the gong Bat stood still, sticking out his bloody chin in defiance and glaring as savagely as was possible with one eye bunged shut. Suddenly he reached out and gave Gans a savage shove. The referee jumped between them before they could mix it.

SAYS GANS TO NOLAN.

As they came together for the thirty-first, Gans leaned over Bat's shoulder and said tauntingly to Nolan over in Bat's corner: "I feel sorry for you."

Bat suddenly walked into a right-hand punch full in the face in the thirty-second. He looked up in stunned surprise and his knees quaked as he stumbled backward, but again the gong saved him.

Bat looked like a boy with mumps when he went to his corner at the end of the thirty-third. One eye was swollen shut. He was cut and beaten until he was a hideous, maimed thing. Gans dragged himself wearily to his corner.

A man in a white undershirt leaned over and said: "Uppercut him, Joe." Nolan replied from his corner: "Put him out in his own corner, Bat."

## BONE IN GANS'S HAND BROKEN.

### FIGHTS BRAVELY ON DESPITE THE SERIOUS HANDICAP.

**Negro's Sportsmanlike Work Wins Praise on All Sides, Being in Sharp Contrast to Rowdy Actions of Fast-Firing Opponent—Nelson Hissed as Milling Ends.**

ARENA (Goldfield, Nev.) Sept. 3.—Battling Nelson deliberately fouled Joe Gans in the forty-second round of the best and longest fight seen anywhere in many years. Both men were tired when the fight ended, but Gans was apparently the stronger. He was away ahead on points, and had smashed and cut Nelson all through the fight without being badly hurt himself.

Shortly after the forty-second round commenced the men were in their usual clinch. Nelson had his head on Gans's shoulder and his arm down. Several times he hit Gans below the belt, apparently feeling for a vital spot. At last he drew back his right arm and hit Gans a vicious blow square in the groin. The colored boy sank to his knees and rolled over on his back. Referee Siler, without hesitation, ordered Nelson to his corner, and awarded the fight to Gans on a foul.

Siler's decision received almost unanimous approval. The foul was so obvious that not even men who had bet on Nelson could say that it had not been committed. All through the long contest Nelson had employed rough tactics. He repeatedly butted Gans and had to have his head hauled away by the referee.

SILER TALKS OF FOUL.

Referee Siler stated to the Associated Press that while he would not say that the foul was intentional, there was no doubt but that it had been committed. Nelson, he said, had used his usual tactics all through the fight, and while he knew that Nelson was butting whenever he had an opportunity, he did not disqualify him for that, because he saw that it was not hurting Gans, and as no other referee had disqualified Nelson for doing the same thing, he did not feel like doing it. Besides, the people were there to see the fight, and he did not want to disappoint them.

Siler was loudly cheered as he left the ring, as was Gans, who was carried to his dressing-room. Nelson and his seconds were hissed as they departed. Billy Nolan, Nelson's manager, made a disconnected statement, in which he said that Gans had promised not to claim the decision on a foul, and yet he jumped at the very first opportu-

(Continued on Fourth Page.)

## PITH OF NEWS FROM THE MIDDLE WEST.

[BY DIRECT WIRE TO THE TIMES.]

CHICAGO, Sept. 3.—[Exclusive Dispatch.] Repenting of the rain and clouds in which he wrapped Chicago yesterday, Prof. Frankenfield today announced that the city would enjoy two days of the finest weather he had in stock. If tomorrow equals today's sample, the forecaster will be as popular here as Bryan. Maximum temperature was 70 deg., minimum, 66 deg. The wind was in the north, and reached 24 miles an hour. Middle West temperatures:

Alpena, 56; Bismarck, 82; Cairo 76; Cheyenne, 64; Cincinnati, 78; Cleveland, 70; Davenport, 70; Denver, 70; Des Moines, 72; Detroit, 70; Devil's Lake, 80; Dodge City, 66; Dubuque, 70; Duluth, 62; Escanaba, 58; Grand Rapids, 64; Green Bay, 64; Helena, 76; Huron, 72; Indianapolis, 72; Kansas City, 74; Marquette, 54; Memphis, 78; Milwaukee, 66; North Platte, 68; Omaha, 70; Rapid City, 76; St. Louis, 76; St. Paul, 74; Sault Sainte Marie, 52; Springfield, Ill., 72; Springfield, Mo., 74; Wichita, 72.

LEAGUE CLUBS' STANDING.

National League—Chicago, .748; Pittsburgh, .650; New York, .642; Philadelphia, .447; Cincinnati, .413; Brooklyn, .412; St. Louis, .368; Boston, .320.

American League—New York, .597; Chicago, .595; Philadelphia, .555; Cleveland, .551; St. Louis, .525; Detroit, .475; Washington, .388; Boston, .320.

MUELLER CERTIFICATES FIGHT.

The first point in the legal battle to determine the legality of the Mueller municipal street-railway certificates was decided by Judge Windes, today, against the city, in allowing two intervening petitioners to file their appearances and objections along with the original bill of complaint. Although containing many of the points raised in the first bill, the new objections to the Mueller certificates are such as to increase the intricacy of the forthcoming legal battle. Walter L. Fisher, Mayor Dunne's $1000-a-year expert, argued against the permitting of the additional petitioners to come into court, but after several hours arguing, Judge Windes ordered their petition filed.

NORTH SIDE CRUSADE.

The crusade against disreputable hotels was extended to the North Side tonight. Six hotels north of the river were raided by the police, and nearly one hundred persons were arrested. Ira B. Cook, the Evanston millionaire and owner of the Hotel Cecil, which was raided last week, appeared in police court today charged with being the owner of a building rented for immoral purposes. He gave bonds for appearance later.

SHOT AT AND DROWNED.

[BY DIRECT WIRE TO THE TIMES.]

JANESVILLE (Wis.) Sept. 3.—[Exclusive Dispatch.] Frank McLaughlin, aged 15 years, was drowned in Rock River this afternoon. McLaughlin and a companion were returning from a picnic, and playfully took a rowboat from the shore for a short ride. When the boat was in midstream the owner missed it, and is alleged to have taken a shot at the boys, which so frightened them that the McLaughlin boy jumped and disappeared beneath the water's surface.

# BURNS GETS DECISION IN VERY POOR FIGHT.

## *All Bets Declared Off by Order of McCarey—Box Office Disagreement Alleged to Be Cause—Promoters Lose Money on Advertised Purse.*

### HINTS THAT IT WAS CROOKED.

Manager Tom McCarey on whose orders the bets were declared off when asked this morning to state some reason for his action said:

"There were enough suspicious circumstances for me to believe that something might be wrong, and to cause my action. I do not consider that any one was hurt by having the bets declared off, while they might have been wronged if they had been allowed to stand. That is all the reason I will give tonight. I do not care to implicate any one at this time."

TOMMY BURNS and Jack O'Brien put up the cheapest fight for the highest priced admission in the history of Los Angeles pugilism, in their bout at Naud Junction, last night.

Burns received the decision at the end of twenty rounds, but it was through no good work of his, for O'Brien would not fight except in spurts measured by seconds of time, and during the remainder of the three minutes of each round he sped about the ring with Burns alternately chasing him and standing in the center of the ring looking on in disgust; and when O'Brien did make a stand, Burns refused to lead.

All bets were declared off by Referee Charles Eyton before the men stepped into the middle of the ring. Manager McCarey ordered this action, and Eyton refused to give a reason at the ringside, but referred all questions to McCarey.

The house was away below expectations and the promoters have lost money on the venture. The battle was delayed by Billy Nolan demanding his share of the purse or a binding guarantee, and the crowd waited a full hour before the men reached a settlement.

The majority of the spectators seemed of the opinion that the fight should have been declared no contest, but as a deciseion was in order, Burns was given the verdict, O'Brien not even protesting or evincing any interest in the action of the referee.

Had the price of admission been ordinary, the crowd would have felt no more than disgust, but as the patrons paid fancy prices to witness the battle, they expected the participants to put up a fast exhibition throughout. Instead, the fighters loafed on their job and a feeling of discontent with the whole affair is prevalent among visitors and local fight fans who have witnessed good battles.

O'Brien did very little fighting, and Burns did less than in their first contest. Burns was willing enough to mix it up, but when he might have gone in and taken a chance he became cautious and danced about until the opportunity to really mix it was lost.

Very little punishment was dealt by either man. A real good blow was not struck. Burns inflicted the more punishment, but nearly every blow delivered by him was struck at close range when the men were coming together or glanced off at long range. O'Brien had nothing but a left jab with an occasional right which he failed to deliver often because he was afraid to get in close.

O'Brien at times ran for dear life never minding the storm of hisses which arose. Then when Burns got in close and mixed it with him he held on desperately, as he did in the first battle. Referee Eyton refused to allow the men to stay together unless they got busy in the infighting, and promptly broke them. Nevertheless, they were locked in each other's embrace for many minutes of the fight for which the spectators were paying $500 a minute. While the men were dancing in the ring or chasing about the same rate of money was being paid.

Burns cut O'Brien above the nose and on the left eyelid. He also battered his mouth so that O'Brien was spitting blood throughout most of the fight. O'Brien raised a roof on Burns's right eyelid and puffed his eyes, nose, and mouth with his left jabs. Burns's nose bled considerably, and he also spat blood at times. Otherwise the men were not injured and came out of the battle apparently fresh, considering they had indulged in twenty rounds of work.

Bettors who wagered large sums of money demand a specific reason why the bets were declared off. Commissioners received much money from Easterners visiting Los Angeles, to bet on one man or the other. Those who bet on Burns want to know why the bets were declared off, as they are unable to cash on Burns, who won.

#### CROWD IMPATIENT.
#### HAD LONG WAIT.

The big pavilion looked like an empty barn at 7:30 o'clock, for the electric parade kept many people away, and the festivities of the Shriners kept the nobles up town. There were not over 400 people in the house when the parade started, but each car brought the sports and at 7:45 o'clock the house began to fill rapidly, and by 8 o'clock was over half full. Every minute brought more people, and at 8:30, when the preliminary boys came on, there were close to 4000 in their seats.

There were many new faces around around the ring, there being probably 1000 Shriners present, and at least fifty wore their fezes. A list of the best-known men present might read like a page from the directories of a hundred cities. There were fezes there that had Medina, Al Malaikah, Islam, Moslem, India and El Riad embroidered on them—and there were others.

Coffroth of San Francisco's ex-fight trust, Squires manager, Kennedy, and dozens of others equally well known in the sporting world were at the ringside.

At 8:45 o'clock when the preliminary came on, there were few vacant seats in the house with the exception of a number of $30 chairs and the seats in the corners up under the roof. It was a good-natured crowd that guyed every one, smoked, cheered, yelled, hooted, laughed and even sang, a big bunch in the east side of the building singing about forty verses of that good old song, "We're here because we're here." This kept the crowd lively for there was a long wait, as is always the case after the curtain-raiser was through with. Hundreds smoked after Megaphone Cook had made a real speech asking the crowd to stop it. As the time slipped on without either Burns, O'Brien or Manager McCarey coming forth, the singing and yelling increased in volume, but there was a few minutes' break in the din at 9:45 o'clock when one of Burns' handlers came into the ring with a bucket. A few minutes later O'Brien appeared and was greeted with cheers and after he was seated the noise died away a trifle, but every minute of the time crowds talked, yelled, whistled, until Burns entered the ring at 9:50 o'clock.

Burns looked White as he sat in his corner while O'Brien appeared a trifle red in the face. After Burns had been seated a few minutes, O'Brien arose and walked to Burns's corner and shook hands with him. Tommy extended his hand and not only did not arise, but looked at O'Brien's feet.

It was stated at this time that the long wait was due to the fact that both Burns and O'Brien wanted the other to go into the ring first and finally O'Brien went in first, after the physicians had examined both men.

#### SLUGGING MATCH.
#### MURRAY AND ERVIN DRAW.

Dick Murray and Jimmy Erwin had one grand slugging match in the preliminary. They boxed (or fought) to a draw and the six rounds was all either man cared for, as they could scarcely more than stand when the gong rang down the act. The decision of Referee Tommy Walsh was received with cheers, as both boys had worked hard to win and the honors were about as even as could be expected in any fight.

Both boys are built on the battleship lines and they opened their heavy batteries from the tap of the gong. Most of the heavy shots were spent because of poor calculation of distance, but enough blows landed on each to have sunk the cruiser type of fighter. Murray carried the heavier armor, for in the earlier rounds Ervin landed the most blows, but Murray came back for more and gradually wore Ervin down until in the last round he had him on more than even terms and earned a draw.

Ervin landed repeatedly on the jaw and wind with terrific rights but the red-headed Irishman only smiled and came back for more. Ervin's best blow was a heavy uppercut, which he landed on face and stomach with telling effect.

Ervin was the better boxer and skipped out of harm's way many times, but he never lost an opportunity to mix it when the right chance came. The bout gave good satisfaction.

#### SULLIVAN AND KELLY.
#### READY FOR FRIDAY BATTLE.

Jack (Twin) Sullivan and Hugo Kelly saw the Burns-O'Brien fight last night, and each expressed the belief that he could defeat either man. Neither put great emphasis on his statement, however, for they have all they can attend to to take care of one another, Friday night, when they meet for the middleweight championship.

Betting on the Sullivan-Kelly fight is even money and take your choice. Never were two men more evenly matched, in the eyes of Los Angeles fans. Sullivan is a master of ring generalship and craft, while Kelly is rugged and has a good head. Sullivan is great on defense and has a way of hiding the fact that he is hurt and thus tiding over many a crisis safely. Kelly can hit hard and also absorb much punishment. He is the proverbial "tough nut."

Sullivan has a large following in Los Angeles through the good work done in his nine battles in this city. Since he cut out the dirty work after his first fight with Jim Flynn, Sullivan seems to be a different man, and his boxing is pleasing to Los Angeles fans. Kelly also is well known here, having boxed Sullivan a draw about a year ago, and fought Burns a draw nearly two years ago.

Both men are in good condition and their fight ought to be interesting during every minute of every round.

#### Flynn Challenges.

Jim Flynn is caught between the devil and the deep blue. He is too heavy for a middleweight and too light to fight in the legitimate heavyweight class. He challenged the winner of last night's battle, but really is lighter than either O'Brien or Burns. He is ready to fight Kelly or Jack Sullivan but will not agree to make the weight of 158 pounds, as he says he would weaken too much to do himself justice. Flynn is willing to fight any man in the world, but his weight, either way, is against him, except in the little used light heavyweight class.

While rowing on the lake near the Eastside Athletic Club, yesterday, Flynn fell out of the boat into deep water and was compelled to swim ashore with his heavy clothes on.

Flynn attempted to show off before a crowd of friends on land by standing up in the bow—hence the "accident."

### SPORTING EVENTS

**TODAY.**

Baseball, 3 o'clock, Chutes Park; cars going south on Main street and Grand avenue. San Francisco and Los Angeles teams of Pacific Coast League.

**FRIDAY.**

Boxing bout between Hugo Kelly and Jack (Twin) Sullivan for the middleweight championship, 8 o'clock, at Naud Junction. Downey-avenue cars on Broadway, or Eastlake Park cars on Spring street.

Baseball, 3 o'clock, Chutes Park.

Carnival of equestrian sports and barbecue, Fiesta Park; Grand-avenue and Pico cars on Broadway.

**SATURDAY.**

Baseball, 3 o'clock, Chutes Park.

**SUNDAY.**

Auto races, 1:30 o'clock, at Agricultural Park; Jefferson-street cars on Main, or University cars on Spring street.

Baseball, 2:30 o'clock, Chutes Park.

#### Abe Attell's Offer.

Abe Attell received an offer to fight in Ogden, Utah, last night, and agreed to meet any man his weight, provided the money is in sight. Abe is "yours truly for business" every time.

"I will fight any one up to Jeffries, and anywhere from the desert to New York, if they can show me the coin," says the featherweight champion.

# WILLIS PROVES TO BE BIG JOKE.

### LOOLOOS SLAP HIS CURVES ALL OVER THE LOT.

**Fourteen Swats and Three Bungles Result in Many Useless Scores. Dillon Hits Home Run Under the Right Field Fence—Fireman Esola Plays Nasty Trick.**

Los Angeles 9, San Francisco 4.

After the Looloos got through with Willis at the ball game yesterday, he looked as if he had walked 247 miles across the hot sands and then had the camel step on his head. If he had been the fall guy for the entire conclave he would not have been any worse off.

Dillon was back in the game for the first time in a week and he put Hosp in to pitch. Of course they call this one a busher, but he showed he is about as good as any of them, yesterday, for he held the Grafters to six scattered hits. He was wild, however, and gave no less than eight bases on balls, but he had perfect support and was never in danger.

The Looloos seemed to straighten out everything that poor Willis had, the last inning being the only one in which they did not make a hit. The total was fourteen swats, and eight of these came in the first three innings, and, mixed in with two soaks in the legs, two passes, two errors and a sacrifice, brought in eight runs. It was all very easy and the score was so much one-sided that no one thought of trying to make any spectacular plays.

The only two features of the game was Dillon's home run through a hole in the right field fence and Fireman Esola's strong arm play in the first of the seventh inning when he deliberately grabbed Delmas' arm and prevented him from making a double play at first base. Of course Derrick didn't see this and Willis, on whom the double would have been made, scored later on. It made no difference, however, for the locals were too far ahead to lose, but this man Esola will have to be watched hereafter.

The visitors began with a run, from two passes, a sacrifice and a single, and their final three came from four passes, an out and two singles.

In the fisrt scoring for the Looloos, three singles, two sacrifices, two errors and a hit by pitcher made three runs. Three more came in the next inning from two passes, a sacrifice, a single and a two-bagger; and in the third, two runs were made off three singles, a hit by pitcher and a useless fielder's choice. The last run was Dillon's homer through a hole in the fence.

The score:

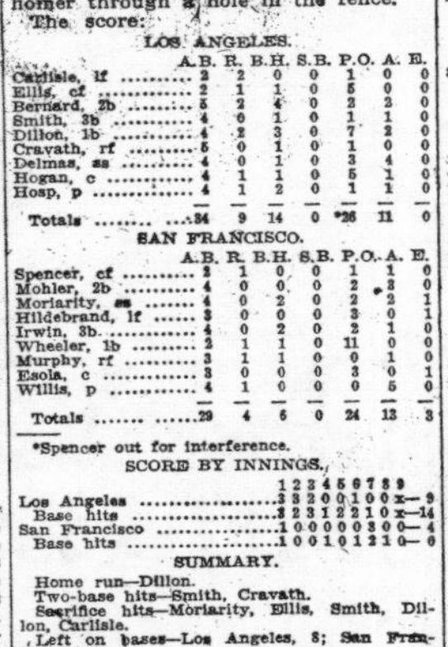

LOS ANGELES.

| | A.B. | R. | B.H. | S.B. | P.O. | A. | E. |
|---|---|---|---|---|---|---|---|
| Carlisle, lf | 2 | 2 | 0 | 0 | 1 | 0 | 0 |
| Ellis, cf | 2 | 1 | 1 | 0 | 5 | 0 | 0 |
| Bernard, 2b | 5 | 2 | 4 | 0 | 2 | 2 | 0 |
| Smith, 3b | 4 | 0 | 1 | 0 | 1 | 1 | 0 |
| Dillon, 1b | 4 | 2 | 3 | 0 | 7 | 2 | 0 |
| Cravath, rf | 5 | 0 | 1 | 0 | 1 | 0 | 0 |
| Delmas, ss | 4 | 0 | 1 | 0 | 3 | 4 | 0 |
| Hogan, c | 4 | 1 | 1 | 0 | 5 | 1 | 0 |
| Hosp, p | 4 | 1 | 2 | 0 | 1 | 1 | 0 |
| Totals | 34 | 9 | 14 | 0 | *26 | 11 | 0 |

SAN FRANCISCO.

| | A.B. | R. | B.H. | S.B. | P.O. | A. | E. |
|---|---|---|---|---|---|---|---|
| Spencer, cf | 2 | 1 | 0 | 0 | 1 | 1 | 0 |
| Mohler, 2b | 4 | 0 | 0 | 0 | 2 | 3 | 0 |
| Moriarity, ss | 4 | 0 | 2 | 0 | 2 | 2 | 1 |
| Hildebrand, lf | 3 | 0 | 0 | 0 | 3 | 0 | 1 |
| Irwin, 3b | 4 | 0 | 2 | 0 | 2 | 1 | 0 |
| Wheeler, 1b | 2 | 1 | 1 | 0 | 11 | 0 | 0 |
| Murphy, rf | 3 | 1 | 1 | 0 | 0 | 1 | 0 |
| Esola, c | 3 | 0 | 0 | 0 | 3 | 0 | 1 |
| Willis, p | 4 | 1 | 0 | 0 | 0 | 5 | 0 |
| Totals | 29 | 4 | 6 | 0 | 24 | 13 | 3 |

*Spencer out for interference.

SCORE BY INNINGS.

| | 1 | 2 | 3 | 4 | 5 | 6 | 7 | 8 | 9 | |
|---|---|---|---|---|---|---|---|---|---|---|
| Los Angeles | 3 | 3 | 2 | 0 | 0 | 1 | 0 | 0 | x | 9 |
| Base hits | 3 | 2 | 3 | 1 | 2 | 2 | 1 | 0 | x | 14 |
| San Francisco | 1 | 0 | 0 | 0 | 0 | 0 | 3 | 0 | 0 | 4 |
| Base hits | 1 | 0 | 0 | 1 | 0 | 1 | 2 | 1 | 0 | 6 |

SUMMARY.

Home run—Dillon.
Two-base hits—Smith, Cravath.
Sacrifice hits—Moriarity, Ellis, Smith, Dillon, Carlisle.
Left on bases—Los Angeles, 8; San Francisco, 8.
First base on called balls—Off Hosp, 8; off Willis, 2.
Struck out—By Hosp, 4; by Willis, 2.
Double play—Hosp to Hogan to Dillon.
First base on errors—Los Angeles, 1.
Hit by pitched ball—Wheeler, Carlisle, Ellis.
Time of game—2h. 5m.
Umpire—Derrick.

#### PORTLAND WINS.
#### BAT AT CRITICAL TIME.

[BY THE ASSOCIATED PRESS—P.M.]

SAN FRANCISCO, May 8.—Portland captured today's game from Oakland by being able to connect safely with the pitching of Wright when men were on bases. Wright's failure to cut the plate at critical times also figured in the run-getting. Oakland landed on Kinsella for five hits and three runs in the fourth inning, but with the exception of that period he was effective. Score:

PORTLAND.

| | A.B. | R. | B.H. | S.B. | P.O. | A. | E. |
|---|---|---|---|---|---|---|---|
| Shinn, ss | 5 | 0 | 0 | 0 | 1 | 0 | 1 |
| Lovett, cf | 4 | 1 | 1 | 1 | 4 | 0 | 0 |
| Casey, 2b | 1 | 1 | 1 | 0 | 3 | 4 | 0 |
| McCreedie, rf | 4 | 0 | 1 | 1 | 3 | 0 | 0 |
| Dunleavy, 3b | 3 | 1 | 1 | 1 | 2 | 0 | 2 |
| Donahue, c | 4 | 1 | 0 | 0 | 3 | 2 | 0 |
| Croll, lf | 2 | 0 | 0 | 0 | 1 | 0 | 0 |
| Carson, 1b | 4 | 0 | 2 | 1 | 10 | 0 | 0 |
| Kinsella, p | 4 | 0 | 0 | 0 | 0 | 3 | 0 |
| Totals | 31 | 4 | 6 | 4 | 27 | 9 | 3 |

OAKLAND.

| | A.B. | R. | B.H. | S.B. | P.O. | A. | E. |
|---|---|---|---|---|---|---|---|
| Smith, lf | 4 | 0 | 0 | 0 | 1 | 0 | 0 |
| Van Haltren, cf | 4 | 1 | 2 | 0 | 1 | 0 | 0 |
| Heitmuller, rf | 4 | 1 | 2 | 0 | 0 | 0 | 0 |
| Eagan, ss | 3 | 0 | 0 | 0 | 2 | 3 | 0 |
| Hackett, c | 4 | 1 | 1 | 0 | 5 | 0 | 2 |
| Haley, 2b | 4 | 0 | 2 | 0 | 1 | 6 | 1 |
| Bigbie, 1b | 4 | 0 | 3 | 0 | 17 | 0 | 0 |
| Devereaux, 3b | 4 | 0 | 0 | 0 | 0 | 2 | 0 |
| Wright, p | 3 | 0 | 1 | 0 | 0 | 6 | 0 |
| Totals | 34 | 3 | 11 | 0 | 27 | 17 | 3 |

SCORE BY INNINGS.

| | 1 | 2 | 3 | 4 | 5 | 6 | 7 | 8 | 9 | |
|---|---|---|---|---|---|---|---|---|---|---|
| Portland | 0 | 1 | 0 | 1 | 2 | 0 | 0 | 0 | 0 | 4 |
| Base hits | 0 | 2 | 0 | 1 | 1 | 0 | 1 | 0 | 1 | 6 |
| Oakland | 0 | 0 | 0 | 3 | 0 | 0 | 0 | 0 | 0 | 3 |
| Base hits | 1 | 2 | 0 | 5 | 1 | 1 | 1 | 0 | 0 | 11 |

SUMMARY.

Sacrifice hit—Croll.
Hits—Off Wright, 4.
Struck out—By Kinsella, 3; by Wright, 4.
Balk—Kinsella.
Double plays—Carson (unassisted,) Casey to Shinn.
Passed ball—Hackett.
Wild pitch—Kinsella.
Time of game—1h. 47m.
Umpire—Perrine.

#### WINS EASILY.
#### ST. VINCENT'S BEATS POMONA.

CLAREMONT, May 8.—St. Vincent's College defeated the Pomona College in the first intercollegiate game of the season to be played on the Pomona diamond this afternoon, by a score of 3 to 1. Pomona lost the game on fielding errors.

The feature of the game was the fine work of both batteries. Phillips, of St. Vincent's, struck out 16 men and allowed 7 hits, while Gally struck out 7, and allowed the hard hitting Catholics but 4 swats. In a number of innings the superb pitching of Gally was all that saved Pomona from a worse defeat. St. Vincent's had men on third a number of times with only one man down but Gally would pitch himself out of the box and shut them out.

The Saints first score came in the first of the third, when Philips hit for one base, took second on Spurgeon's error in center, third on Flick's hot drive to short, and scored on Walden's muff of Mahoney's throw. Their other two runs came in the second, when on errors by Canterbury and Graf and Flick's single, both McCann and Flick crossed the plate.

Pomona scored their tally in the sixth, when Bob Spurgeon singled, went to third on Ammon's muff of Flick's throw, and scored on McCann's muff of Ammon's throw.

The score:

POMONA.

| | A.B. | R. | B.H. | S.B. | P.O. | A. | E. |
|---|---|---|---|---|---|---|---|
| R. Spurgeon, c | 4 | 1 | 2 | 0 | 7 | 2 | 0 |
| Walden, 1b | 4 | 0 | 0 | 0 | 16 | 0 | 3 |
| Mahoney, ss | 4 | 0 | 1 | 0 | 2 | 4 | 1 |
| W. Spurgeon, cf | 4 | 0 | 1 | 0 | 0 | 0 | 1 |
| Metcalf, rf | 4 | 0 | 0 | 0 | 0 | 0 | 0 |
| Graf, lf | 4 | 0 | 0 | 1 | 0 | 0 | 0 |
| Canterbury, 3b | 3 | 0 | 0 | 0 | 0 | 3 | 2 |
| Birdsall, 2b | 4 | 0 | 2 | 0 | 1 | 8 | 0 |
| Gally, p | 3 | 0 | 1 | 0 | 1 | 1 | 1 |
| Totals | 34 | 1 | 7 | 2 | 27 | 18 | 8 |

ST. VINCENT'S.

| | A.B. | R. | B.H. | S.B. | P.O. | A. | E. |
|---|---|---|---|---|---|---|---|
| Lamar, ss | 5 | 0 | 1 | 0 | 0 | 1 | 0 |
| McCann, 3b | 5 | 1 | 0 | 0 | 1 | 1 | 1 |
| Flick, 2b | 5 | 1 | 1 | 1 | 0 | 3 | 0 |
| Cunningham, cf | 4 | 0 | 0 | 0 | 0 | 0 | 0 |
| Lane, c | 4 | 0 | 0 | 0 | 14 | 4 | 1 |
| Olahassa, rf | 3 | 0 | 0 | 0 | 0 | 0 | 0 |
| Winne, lf | 3 | 0 | 0 | 0 | 0 | 0 | 0 |
| Phillips, p | 4 | 1 | 1 | 0 | 0 | 2 | 0 |
| De Ybarrando, rf | 1 | 0 | 0 | 0 | 0 | 0 | 0 |
| Brannen, lf | 1 | 0 | 1 | 0 | 0 | 0 | 0 |
| Totals | 35 | 3 | 4 | 1 | 15 | 11 | 4 |

SUMMARY.

Two-base hit—Gally.
First base on called balls—Off Gally, 3; off Phillips, 1.
Struck out—By Phillips, 16; by Gally, 7.
Hit by pitched ball—Cunningham.
Time of game—1h. 40m.
Umpire—Moorman.

#### NATIONAL LEAGUE.
#### POOR OLD BROOKLYN.

[BY THE ASSOCIATED PRESS—P.M.]

BROOKLYN, May 8.—Chicago outplayed Brooklyn today, winning by a big margin. Score:

Chicago, 12; hits, 16; errors, 1.
Brooklyn, 4; hits, 8; errors, 7.
Batteries—Brown and Kling; Strickett and Bergen, Butler.

#### HEAVY BATTING GAME.

[BY THE ASSOCIATED PRESS—P.M.]

PHILADELPHIA, May 8.—St. Louis hit Sparks and Moran hard and Buckley clinched the game by a great stop of Titus's hit. Score:

St. Louis, 6; hits, 13; errors, 1.
Philadelphia, 4; hits, 11; errors, 2.
Batteries—McGlynn and Noonan; Sparks, Moran, McQuillin and Jacklitsch.

#### AMERICAN GAMES.
#### FIENE'S WILDNESS LOSES.

[BY THE ASSOCIATED PRESS—P.M.]

CHICAGO, May 8.—Because of Fiene's wildness in the sixth inning followed by Flick's three-base hit Chicago lost to Cleveland today. Score:

Chicago, 5; hits, 9; errors, 0.
Cleveland, 7; hits, 7; errors, 3.
Batteries—Altrock, Fiene and McFarland; Moore, Joss and Wakefield.

#### POSTPONED GAME.

St. Louis-Detroit game called off, rain.

#### NATIONAL LEAGUE.
#### PFEFFER'S NO HIT GAME.

[BY THE ASSOCIATED PRESS—P.M.]

BOSTON, May 8.—Pfeffer shut out Cincinnati without a hit or run today and Boston won easily. Score:

Boston, 6; hits, 8; errors, 1.
Cincinnati, 0; hits, 0; errors, 4.
Batteries—Pfeffer and Brown; Mason and Schlei.

#### SHUT-OUT GAME.

[BY THE ASSOCIATED PRESS—P.M.]

NEW YORK, May 8.—In a fast and well-played game New York shut out Pittsburgh today. Score:

Pittsburgh, 0; hits, 4; errors, 1.
New York, 4; hits, 9; errors, 1.
Batteries—Leifield and Phelps; Mathewson and Bresnahan.

#### CLUBS' STANDING.

PACIFIC COAST LEAGUE.

| | Played. | Won. | Lost. | P.c. |
|---|---|---|---|---|
| Los Angeles | 28 | 20 | 8 | .714 |
| San Francisco | 31 | 16 | 15 | .516 |
| Oakland | 30 | 15 | 15 | .500 |
| Portland | 31 | 9 | 22 | .310 |

NATIONAL LEAGUE.

| | Played. | Won. | Lost. | P.c. |
|---|---|---|---|---|
| New York | 20 | 17 | 3 | .850 |
| Chicago | 19 | 16 | 3 | .842 |
| Pittsburgh | 15 | 9 | 6 | .600 |
| Philadelphia | 17 | 10 | 7 | .588 |
| Boston | 18 | 8 | 10 | .444 |
| Cincinnati | 18 | 7 | 11 | .389 |
| St. Louis | 20 | 4 | 16 | .200 |
| Brooklyn | 17 | 1 | 16 | .059 |

AMERICAN LEAGUE.

| | Played. | Won. | Lost. | P.c. |
|---|---|---|---|---|
| Chicago | 23 | 18 | 5 | .783 |
| New York | 17 | 11 | 6 | .647 |
| Philadelphia | 17 | 10 | 7 | .583 |
| Cleveland | 20 | 9 | 11 | .450 |
| Boston | 17 | 8 | 10 | .444 |
| Washington | 16 | 5 | 11 | .313 |
| St. Louis | 19 | 5 | 14 | .263 |

#### SCANDAL AT OAKLAND.

**Stewards Investigating Suspicious Races—Logistilla Runs Last Though Favorite.**

[BY THE ASSOCIATED PRESS—P.M.]

SAN FRANCISCO, May 8.—Logistilla proved a great disappointment when she failed to get any of the money in the Zig Zag Handicap at Oakland, today. The good mare, despite her heavy impost, was a strong favorite, but was outrun all the way. J. C. Clem won in a drive from Bedford, the pacemaker. Cembury and Misty's Pride were two outsiders to land.

The stewards at Oakland are making a thorough investigation into several races run during the past two days. In connection with the case of Jockey J. H. Hunter, who was suspended yesterday, the officials feel that they have some corroboration of their belief that the boy pulled Meringue and Ethel Day. It is said that two agents, some bookmakers and several trainers may be involved. The sudden improvement of Woolma and Tonic are also under investigation.

Six furlongs, selling: Cembury, 106 (Mentry,) 13 to 1, won; Rose Cherry, 105 (Borel,) 20 to 1, second; Calla, 104 (Fischer,) 7 to 2, third; time, 1:14 3-5. Poinsettia, Curriculum, Lassen, Menden, Bazzini, Salable, Paladini, Remember and Nancy W. finished as named.

Six furlongs: Bemay, 109 (Keogh,) 13 to 10, won; Tawasentha, 104 (Fischer,) 8 to 1, second; Elmdale, 109 (W. Kelley,) 10 to 1, third; time, 1:15 1-5. Hilo de Oro, Azusa, Bon Vivant, Blanche, Pescadora, Golden Sentiment, Ray Bennet and John H. Sheehan finished as named.

One mile and 50 yards, selling: Royal Maxim, 110 (A. Williams,) 5 to 2, won; Tonic, 105 (A. Walsh,) 8 to 1, second; Seven Bells, 110 (R. Davis,) 7 to 1, third; time, 1:45 3-5. Mohawk, Tetanus, Talentosa, Eulalie B., Arcourt, Carmania, George Kilborn and Elota finished as named.

One mile and a furlong, Zig Zag Handicap, purse $1000: J. C. Clem, 100 (C. Ross,) 3 to 1, won; Bedford, 106 (W. Kelley,) 23 to 5, second; Eduardo, 96 (McRae,) 9 to 1, third; time, 1:52 2-5. Logistilla also ran.

Six furlongs, selling: Misty's Pride, 102 (Kirschbaum,) 20 to 1, won; Dorado, 104 (Fischer,) 40 to 1, second; Banposal, 107 (T. Sullivan,) 17 to 1, third; time, 1:13 4-5. Royal Rogue, Gossiper, The Borgian, Boloman, Bribery, Silverskin and E. M. Brattain finished as named.

Five and a half furlongs, purse: Blagg, 95 (W. Kelley,) 11 to 5, won; Oceanshore, 90 (C. Ross,) 3 to 1, second; St. Francis, 100 (Keogh,) 9 to 1, third; time, 1:07. Native Son, Fireball, Grasscutter, Lotta Gladstone and Van Ness finished as named.

#### Querido Wins Chester.

LONDON, May 8.—The Chester Cup, a handicap of 2500 sovereigns for two-year-olds and upward at two miles and a quarter, was run at Chester, today, and won by Querido. Bibani was second and Torpoint was third. Twelve horses started. Querido, which is a French horse, was ridden by Johnny Reiff, the American jockey, and won by a length and a half. Bridge of Caney, ridden by Danny Maher, the American jockey, was fourth.

#### Director of Athletics.

NEW YORK, May 8.—Francis S. Banks has tendered his resignation as chairman of the Columbia University Committee on Athletics and also as graduate director of the Columbia University Rowing Club. President Butler has tendered the appointment as chairman of the committee on athletics to Albert W. Putnam, '97, an old Columbia football man, and the latter has accepted. He will assume his duties on July 1.

# FREIGHT TIED UP BY STRIKE.

### TRANS-ATLANTIC LINERS GO WITH SMALL CARGOES.

**Longshoremen's Fight for More Pay Is Continued in New York and May Cause Postponement of Annual Police Parade, Owing to Need for Armed Protection.**

[BY DIRECT WIRE TO THE TIMES.]

NEW YORK, May 8.—[Exclusive Dispatch.] At a loss of hundreds of thousands of dollars daily to the steamship companies and men involved and to the importers and exporters of the country, the strike of the longshoremen here today was continued, with no end now in sight.

On the one side the heads of every one of the transatlantic lines and a majority of the coastwise companies declare they cannot grant the men the advance in wages demanded. On the side of the strikers it is contended that there had not been a break in the ranks of the 10,000 men who first went out and that they have practically paralyzed the water freight traffic of the port.

They appeared sanguine and their agents are at work on the leaders of the truck drivers' unions to have that great army of men go out in sympathy. This attempt, it is acknowledged, has not yet made any headway.

Every ship that steamed for a foreign port today went out with much less than a full cargo, although the passenger traffic was not impaired.

There was a growing feeling of resentment on the part of the strikers and their friends, noticeable in Manhattan and Brooklyn. This culminated in many cases of violence in which severe injuries were received and about seventeen arrests made.

The most serious case was in Williamsburg, where strikers or their friends attacked in the early evening about 200 strike-breakers returning to their homes. Many were cut and bruised and it took police reserves with their clubs and revolvers to subdue the riot. There were thirteen arrests.

Police Commissioner Bingham early in the afternoon, fearing more violence, ordered every policeman of his department on reserve and may postpone the annual parade on Saturday so that his force may keep ready for any emergency.

Efforts were still being made by Civic Federation officials to get strikers and employers together, but this was without any result.

Piers from the Battery to Thirty-fourth street were guarded by the police and private detectives; outside of these points only a few trucks were moving freight, which lay piled in heaps along the water front.

In various halls there were hourly meetings and there was speaking on the rights and wrongs of the strikers and their confidence in ultimate victory. In the offices of the big steamship companies there were frequent conferences and meetings which brought the declaration that there could be no concessions.

# QUEER BRITISH TRADITIONS.

### ODD THINGS SOME MAYORS HAVE TO ENDURE.

**In One Town the Election Is Held in Church Belfry, in Another the Mayor Is Ducked, in Another His Weight Is Recorded and in Another He Gets a Perquisite of Coal.**

American college fraternities and other secret orders require of their initiates few more curious or exacting "stunts" than the citizens of many towns in the British Isles still exact from successful candidates for the office of Mayor.

The Englishman is known to stick to old ways about as tenaciously as the Old Man of the Sea stuck to Sinbad the Sailor, but some of the Mayoral ceremonies still observed in the ancient towns may be described in American slang as "the limit."

Moreover, in places where these old customs have been allowed to die a natural death an attempt is being made to resurrect them. This is the result of many noblemen and men of wealth having defeated business men in the run for office, the former having more time and regard for the preservation of the ancient ceremonies, many of which date back to the middle ages.

The strangest of these ceremonies and customs, as described by the Washington Times, are now observed in the so-called cinque ports, of which Lord Curzon was once lord warden, and where, at Walmar Castle, the late Lady Curzon was taken with her serious illness.

ELECTIONS IN CHURCH BELFRY.

The oldest of the towns, a tributary of and belonging to the cinque ports, is Brightlingsea, a little place famous for its oysters, and for having furnished skippers for several American cup challengers, the last of these having been Capt. Sycamore.

Although it has a town hall, Brightlingsea's municipal election is held in the belfry of the parish church on the first Monday in January. The church bell summons the voters, and they gather in procession at the church yard gate. Headed by the deputy, for such is the chief magistarte called, and other officials with ancient names, they proceed to the belfry.

A ship's captain carries the deputy's regalia, consisting of a truncheon and a handsome chain formed of gold models of oysters and silver models of fish. The keeper of the records asks the freemen to elect a "deputy for the cinque ports liberty." Several nominations being made, the nominees have to retire while the balloting is done. None can refuse to accept any office to which he is elected on penalty of confiscation of his property.

At the recent election W. B. Penlock was elected by a majority of one vote. He assumed the office after journeying to Sandwich, the ancient royal town, where he was installed. He then returned in full regalia to his own city hall, where he was proclaimed deputy. A fish dinner, to which all freemen of any cinque were invited, wound up the day in a blaze of glory.

Among the other ceremonies which attend the election of mayors in England is a queer one at Tiverton, a famous old country town in Devonshire. There the "ducking" of the Mayor is an invariable part of the programme.

A stream of water was presented to the town by Isabella, Countess of Devon, some six centuries ago. Annually since then, according to the conditions of the inheritance, the town's chief magistrate and the high bailiff have been thrown bodily into the water to remind the officials and citizens that the stream is a gift of the kind Countess.

As may be imagined this method of perpetuating the noble lady's memory is uncommonly effective and, however futile it may seem, it cannot be said to be as "dry" as some of the inauguration ceremonies the newer towns put up with.

WEIGHED IN THE BALANCE.

The mayors of High Wycombe in Buckinghamshire are literally weighed in the balance and apparently never found wanting. This is for some reason unknown in High Wycombe. It may be that in the Middle Ages—for the custom has been continued for centuries—ponderosity was considered a qualification for office holding. As the ceremony only is performed publicly at both the beginning and end of the Mayor's term of office and the figures are carefully recorded, the purpose may be to ascertain whether the magistrate has grown "fat" in public office—anyhow, the custom would show some interesting figures if carried out in American cities.

The origin of municipal "graft" may perhaps be traced back to the Middle Ages in the Irish town of Limerick, where for centuries past the Mayor has got his coal free. He has, in fact, the strange privilege of levying a toll of a quarter of a ton of coal on every cargo brought into the city, and as 500 or 600 coal-laden ships enter the port every year he gets plenty of fuel, the greater portion of which he is said to give to the poor. The coal dealers of Limerick have made repeated attempts to down this custom of "legitimate graft" through the courts, but the judge has insisted that tradition must not be sacrificed to justice.

THROWING THE DART IN CORK.

The Lord Mayor of Cork annually claims harbor jurisdiction by throwing a dart. Escorted by all the city officials and invited guests, he steams in a launch to a certain spot in the bay and from the bow of the boat he throws a dart as far seaward as possible. This point defines the boundaries belonging to the city so far as claiming proper duties and harbor rights is concerned. As it is naturally to Cork's advantage that the dart should go as far as possible, the respective mayors do considerable practicing before election, each trying to outdo his predecessor.

In Chard, Somersetshire, the municipal council nominates church officers. The Mayor must attend in state the services at the parish church on Easter Sunday. During the worship a loud knock at the doors interrupts the services and a verger invites the knocker to enter. The chief of police, armed with a strange sort of immense mace, marches up the aisle to the minister and presents a document containing the nominations. These are officially read and the worship continues.

MUST PREACH ON MARRIAGE.

The Mayor of Cardiff, in Wales, be he married or single, must annually deliver a little sermon on the privileges and duties of marriage. This is done when he hands over to the most virtuous servant girl of the city a dowry of $150 at the time of her marriage. This dowry was provided for by the late Marquis of Bute for the purpose of enabling deserving couples to marry and it is always presented publicly.

# LATEST SPORTING NEWS, LOCAL AND TELEGRAPHIC.

RAILROADS REFUSE.

## GANS-NELSON FIGHT IS OFF.

*Nothing Doing for Lightweights on the Desert.*

*Promoter Rickard Cannot Get Low Railroad Rates.*

*New Champ Will Go to Chicago to Attend Banquet.*

[BY DIRECT WIRE TO THE TIMES.]

SALT LAKE, July 22.—[Exclusive Dispatch.] The Battling Nelson-Joe Gans fight, scheduled for Labor Day at Ely, Nev., was called off by Tex. Rickard this afternoon after the Nevada promoter had failed to get cheap rates over the railroads for the fight. A rate of $14.65 for the round trip was the best Rickard could get from Salt Lake City, so he called off the match. Nelson was at the conference with the railroad officials and was disappointed because he could not get another chance at the black man.

The Battler will get two-thirds of the $1000 posted with J. T. Clark of San Francisco by Tex. Rickard as a guarantee that he would pull off the fight. Gans will get the other third.

Nelson will go from here to Denver and then to Chicago, where the Danish Rifle Club will entertain him August 31 at a banquet, the date having been changed from July 25.

Rickard was to have put up his $10,000 forfeit last Saturday, but the time was extended to give him a chance to negotiate terms with the railroads. If Rickard had secured rates he could have pulled off the fight with small loss, but without these he would have lost heavily. As it is he is only out $1000.

This ends the much-discussed return match between Gans and Nelson in Nevada, but it is probable that some San Francisco promoter will make a good offer for the lightweights to settle the question as to which is real champion. Selig says he will keep Gans in San Francisco for some time in hope of getting a fight.

### BLACK JOE CHESTY.

PACKY MAY GO NORTH.

[BY DIRECT WIRE TO THE TIMES.]

SAN FRANCISCO, July 22.—[Exclusive Dispatch.] Selig said tonight that if Nelson has other plans and refuses a return match here, Gans will fight any lightweight in the world, winner take all, and bet $5000 on the side.

Frank Goings, connected with the Jeffries Athletic Club of Los Angeles, was in conference tonight with Freddie Welsh, trying to secure his signature to a contract to fight Young Otto before the Jeffries club on August 14. As Welsh thinks he stands a chance of getting on with either Nelson or Gans for the September date in San Francisco, he would not give Goings a definite answer. He figures that Willis Britt will be in the city inside of forty-eight hours, and prefers to wait his coming.

The news from Rickard is likely to send McFarland and Gilmore back to San Francisco as quickly as possible. McFarland still itches for a chance at Nelson, and thinks he could wrest from him the lightweight title. Here is his chance, for Nelson is foot loose and might be persuaded into signing up, as Willis wants to keep him busy.

### KELLY SHOWS WELL.

PLEASES NORTHERN BUGS.

[BY DIRECT WIRE TO THE TIMES.]

SAN FRANCISCO, July 22.—[Exclusive Dispatch.] Hugo Kelly, of Chicago has made a hit with local fight fans by his boxing. Though he did not extend himself, Kelly showed such speed and hitting power in a short bout with Joe Reilly, a local fighter, that he impressed every one who saw him in action as the best thing that has reached here from Chicago since Packey McFarland blew in and took the wind out of Jimmy Britt.

Another thing in his favor is his magnificent condition. Kelly slipped one over on O'Connor. He held out for 158 at 6 o'clock, though it is easy to see he could have made 154 at 3 o'clock, as originally planned. Ferretti is tickled over the way he fooled O'Connor, Ketchel's manager.

It looks as though Jack Welsh would agree to referee the Ketchel-Kelly fight. Welsh is official referee of Marisch's club, but he became very grouchy on the public after the Gans-Nelson battle and declared he would retire. If Welsh refuses to serve, the choice will lie between Eddie Smith and Billy Roche. Eddie Hanlon is in fine form for his fight Saturday night with Johnny Murphy, but the public has made Murphy a 10 to 7 favorite, as it is believed Hanlon has gone back so far he can't recover. If Murphy wins he will be in a position to challenge some of the top-notch lightweights.

### Tennis Players Chosen.

LONDON, July 22.—M. J. Richie, J. C. Hart, the Irish champion, and K. Powell of Cambridge University, have been selected to represent the United Kingdom in an effort to bring back the Dwight F. Davis lawn-tennis challenge cup from Australia. The men will start from London in October.

### Warren After Fish.

Smith Warren has gone to Catalina for a two weeks' fishing trip, and will probably do something to make the other nimrods sit up and look around, for he is said to be the best "outside" or deep-water fisherman in this end of the State. No one seems to know just why he is, but the fact that he catches all kinds of big fish without great effort when other men have but indifferent success, proves he is something out of the ordinary.

### Three Deer Slain.

Edward Allen and Vernon Carr of South Pasadena returned late Tuesday afternoon from a three days' deer-hunting trip to the Simi section in Ventura county. Allen got a four-point buck, and Carr shot one that had six points, while a friend who was in the party also secured a fine buck.

### Two Have Hopes.

Charley Finch and John Wiedenbach left yesterday for Ravenna, near Lang station, where they will remain all week trying to get some deer that Finch is said to have staked out in the Gleason Mountains.

### Fight to Draw.

SAN DIEGO, July 22.—Billy Snailham of San Francisco and Kid Texas of Pueblo fought twenty fast rounds here tonight. At the end of the bout both men were very tired, but neither had the advantage, and the referee declared the contest a draw.

TWO MORE RECORDS SECURED.

## AMERICANS DO WELL IN STADIUM EVENTS.

[ASSOCIATED PRESS NIGHT REPORT.]

LONDON, July 22.—Comparative gloom pervaded the American camp tonight. The athletes from over the seas had strongly cherished hopes of repeating yesterday's grand record in making clean sweeps in the track events, but a dark horse in the person of the South African youth, R. E. Walker, upset the calculations. Walker broke the tape in what is considered the most important event in the Olympic games, the 100-meters dash, a short two feet in front of J. A. Rector, the University of Virginia crack, thereby putting an end to the astonishing succession of American triumphs which had begun to sadden the Britons.

Shoulder and shoulder, Walker, Rector and the Canadian star, Kerr, ran down the straight course with Cartmell, the Pennsylvania sprinter, close behind. At the half-way mark, Walker forged slightly ahead, but at the tape less than a yard separated the first three men, with the Canadian only a few inches behind the Virginian in third place.

The American team did remarkably well at the stadium today, but success had elated them to the point where they were satisfied with nothing less than everything in sight. A world's record by C. J. Bacon, of the Irish-American A.C., in the 400-meters hurdles, which he won in 55s.; an Olympic record of 24 feet, 6½ inches by F. C. Irons, of Chicago A.A., in the running broad jump, and the victory of G. S. Dole, of Yale, in the featherweight wrestling, out of seven finals should be a satisfactory day's performance.

Great Britain, as usual, came second among the countries, with S. V. Bacon winning the middleweight wrestling, and the English team defeating the Belgians in the water polo. The African colonial flag was raised to the masthead to signalize Walker's great sprint, and Finland, whose representative, Saarla, conquered all comers in the Graeco-Roman wrestling bouts, having no flag, brought forth the standard bearing the word "Finland," which the Finns carried in the opening parade, and it was elevated on the flagpole.

WALKER HONORED.

Walker received an ovation seen only once in a lifetime on an athletic field, when 40,000 people rose with a great cheer and filled the air with hats, while the boy, this morning unknown but whose name fills London tonight, was lifted on the shoulders of enthusiastic friends. The only demonstration approaching this during the meeting was the tumult after Sheppard's sensational win in the 800 meters yesterday, but that was feeble by comparison, because Walker is a Britisher, and the English public is not partial toward American successes.

This is due partly to the fact that it is a bitter pill to the keenest sporting nation on earth to take second place in any contest, and it is also true that the Americans incurred some unpopularity by their protests, which the London newspapers and the Olympic officials interpret as a reflection upon the honesty of the English judges, and resented accordingly.

The American contingent had feared that Kerr, the Canadian, would rob them of the 100-meters dash, but they had not considered Walker dangerous. No one accepted the national misfortune more gracefully than Rector. When spoken to regarding Walker's victory, the Virginian said:

"Walker is a faster runner than I, and that is all there is to say."

LONDON EXCITED.

The Olympic games are developing into a huge success. While the meeting started discouragingly with the weather and other conditions against it, London is fast becoming athletic mad. People everywhere talk of nothing but the Olympian runners and jumpers, and the women seem as much interested as the men. Great crowds gather around the ticket offices to secure the best seats for the final days, and a big attendance is certain from this on.

It would be hard to imagine a finer spectacle than the stadium presented today. From athletic, social and spectacular standpoints, it quite equaled the expectations of the promoters. Queen Alexandra and other members of the royal family were present, and congratulated the African runner on his victory. The stands contained 40,000 persons, of whom at least one-half were women, whose multi-colored costumes presented a fascinating picture. The American section was truly American, with waving flags and noise-making instruments. There was organized cheering by a large band of collegians under the leadership of a frantic youth, brandishing a huge club and shouting "rah, rah, rah. Bacon." which was heartily taken up by the others, when the first American victory of the day was proclaimed. This caught the fancy of the crowd immensely, as did the Americans cheering for Walker, who, although he defeated their favorite, was as cordially greeted as their own countrymen.

The picture in the arena was worthy of applause. When the Queen entered the royal box, the runners were striving with every muscle set in the 400-meters race around the track, divers were throwing double somersaults from the tower, and brawny wrestlers were struggling in the Graeco-Roman contests. On the platform at either end of the oval a band of Danish lady gymnasts, who were the most attractive novelty of the meeting, arrayed in white uniforms and yellow stockings, were engaged in a graceful exercise. The jumping events were conducted on the green turf in the center of the stadium and, altogether, today's meeting furnished a series of thrilling pictures and quite as much excitement and close finishes as yesterday.

AMERICANS WIN HURDLES.

In addition to Walker's sprint, the 400-meter hurdle and the semi-final heats of the 400 and 200-meter flat races were memorable events. The Americans had the hurdles to themselves.

C. J. Bacon, the Irish-American Athletic Club, and Harry L. Hillman, New York Athletic Club, between whom there was as warm a rivalry as between the men of different nationalities, ran clear away from their English rivals, Burton and Tremer. The Americans rounded the turn yards ahead of the Englishmen and found it out for first place in the stretch, Bacon reaching the tape slightly in the lead.

On Hillman's previous record, he was expected to win, for at the Olympic games in St. Louis in 1904, he ran the distance in 53s., but as he had knocked down two hurdles, a world's record was not made. When he was defeated today, Hillman's bride, who was sitting in the stand, burst into tears.

J. B. Taylor of the Irish-American Athletic Club, the colored University of Pennsylvania runner; J. C. Carpenter of Cornell University, and D. R. Robinson of Yale, won their heats in the semi-finals of the 400 meters, with the English champion Halswell, their only opponent, for the final. Halswell's feat in lowering the Olympic record was easily one of the most brilliant performances of the day. He covered the distance in 48 2-5s.; breaking Harry Hillman's record of 49 1-5s., made at St. Louis in 1904. Taylor's time was 49 4-5s. Halswell is picked as the winner of the final which will be tomorrow, but Taylor if he is in his best form, Americans at least believe, may succeed in reaching the tape first.

R. Cloughen, Irish-American Athletic Club, and N. J. Cartmell, Pennsylvania, won two of the four semi-finals of the 200 meters and will oppose Kerr of Canada and Hawkins of the United Kingdom in the final. The public is backing the Canadian to win. All of the heats in this event resulted in close finishes.

W. F. Hamilton, Chicago A. A., gave Kerr so close a race that a majority of the spectators thought that he had won until they heard the official announcement. Cloughen beat George, who was England's chief hope, while Hawkins, in a heat in which no Americans were entered, shut out Roche, another British favorite.

ACCIDENT TO DIVER.

A sensation occurred during the high diving. Cane, England's representative, struck the water heavily and failed to come to the surface. A bystander plunged into the tank and brought Cane ashore. The Englishman, however, suffered no more serious injury than temporary loss of wind.

The Olympic managers tendered their official thanks to the rescuer, whose name is Johaansen, and who is the holder of King Edward's cup for life-saving.

Soon after this the German, Nicolia, finished a double somersault from the high tower by striking the water at full length like a sand bag. An American, N. C. Grote, of the Missouri A. C., promptly dived after him, but the German, who came up almost immediately, rejected the offer of rescue and swam ashore unaided.

Counting all the events held within and outside of the stadium including many games in which the United Kingdom alone competed, the score up to date stands:

United Kingdom, 32; America, 17; Sweden, 5; Norway, and France, 2 each; Canada, Germany, Belgium, Italy, Finland, South Africa, 1 each.

The score in the field and track events, in which the American team came over to participate in, is as follows:

America, 75; United Kingdom, 56 1-3; Sweden, 12; Greece, 6; South Africa, 5; Canada, Norway, Italy, 3 each; France, and Hungary, 1 1-3 each; Australia, Germany, Finland, 1 each.

SUMMARIES.

In the first section of the running broad jump, Cook, American, was first with a jump of 22 ft. 10½ in.; Bellah, American, second, 21 ft. 9½ in.; Haleyes, Hungary, third, 21 ft. 5½ in.; Bleaen, United Kingdom, fourth, 21 ft. 1½ in.

In the second section Kelly, American, covered 23 ft. 3¼ in., beating Ahearne and Bellerby, the United Kingdom's best men. John J. Brennan, Marquette University, was second, with 22 ft. 6½ in.; Weinstein, Germany, third, 22 ft. 2¾ in.; Ahearne, fourth, 22 ft. ¾ in., and Bellerby, fifth, with 21 ft. 1¾ in.

In the third section, Irons, America, Jumped 24 ft. 5 in., beating the Olympic record. Mount Pleasant, the Carlisle School Indian athlete, was second to Irons, with a jump of 22 ft. 4½ in. Williams, United Kingdom, was third, 21 ft. 10 in.

In the fourth section, Murray, United Kingdom, was first with 22 ft. ¼ in.; Lukeman, Canada, second, with 21 ft. 7 in., and Watt, United Kingdom, third, 21 ft. ¾ in. There were no Americans in this section.

In the fifth section, Bricker, Canada, was first with 23 ft. 3 in. There were no Americans competing.

The final of the running broad jump was won by F. C. Irons, Chicago A.A., with 24 ft. 6½ in., which is a new Olympic record. Daniel J. Kelly, Irish-American A.C., was second with 23 ft. 3¼ in., and Bricker, Canada, was third, with 23 ft. 3 in. E. T. Cooke, Cornell University, and John J. Brennan, Marquette University, got certificates of merit for their jumps, 22 ft. 10 in., and 22 ft. 6¼ in., respectively.

The final in the 400-meter hurdle race was won by J. C. Bacon, Irish-American A. C. Harry L. Hillman, N. Y.A.C., was second, and Tremer, United Kingdom, third. The time of the winner was 55s.

Bacon and Hillman had it all their own way in this event. It was only a question which one of them would come in first. They rounded the turn yards ahead of Burton and Tremer and fought it out for first place in the stretch. Bacon succeeded in beating his team-mate and his time, 55s, establishes a new Olympic record.

The first heat in the final of the 400-meter flat race was won by J. C. Carpenter, Cornell. Davis, United Kingdom, was second, and N. A. Merriam, University of Chicago, was third. Time, 49 2-5s.

The second heat in this event was won by Halswelle, United Kingdom. Time, 48 4-5s. Montague, United Kingdom, was second; Nichols, United Kingdom, third, and William C. Prout, Boston, A.A., fourth.

Third heat—Taylor, Irish-American A.C., won in 49 4-5s.; H. P. Ramey, Chicago A.A., second; Ryle, United Kingdom, third.

Fourth heat—D. R. Robbins, Yale University, won in 49s; Sebert, Canada, second; J. C. Atlee, Princeton University, did not finish when he saw that Robbins had won.

The judges made a correction in Halswelle's time in the second heat. He covered the 400 meters in 48 2-5s., a record for this distance. He then ran on to the quarter-mile mark and his time for this distance was 48 4-5s.

In the first heat of the semi-finals 200-meters flat race, Kerr, Canada, beat Hamilton, America, by the barest margin, only a foot; time 22 2-5s.

Cartmell, America, won the second heat with Sherman and Huff, America, second and third; time, 22 3-5s.

The third heat went to Cloughen, America, in 22 3-5s.

Hawkins, United Kingdom, defeated his team-mate Roche, in the fourth heat by a yard in 22 2-5s. No Americans were drawn in this heat.

The final in the middleweight to 160-pound catch-as-catch-can wrestling, was won on points by S. V. Bacon, United Kingdom, Relwyskow, United Kingdom, was second.

Saarela, Finland, won the Graeco-Roman light heavy to 205 pounds wrestling competition.

In the first bout in the wrestling match for featherweights, up to 133 pounds, Dole, America, defeated Cockings, United Kingdom, on points.

In the second bout, catch-as-catch-can, Dolan, America, beat Webster, United Kingdom.

In the semi-final of the catch-as-catch-can, Dole threw McKie, United Kingdom.

G. S. Dole, Yale University, won the final in the catch-as-catch-can wrestling match, defeating Slim, England.

In the fourth heat of the high diving, Stanberg, Sweden, was first with 79.2 points and Arbin, Sweden, second with 76.8 points.

The fifth heat was won by Anderson, Sweden, with 73.5 points, Aro, Finland, was second, with 69.3 points, and H. C. Grote, Missouri Athletic Club, third, with 62.8.

WHITE WINGS STRETCHING.

## "TIMES" CUP RACE ON SATURADY.

FOUR YACHTS HAVE ENTERED FOR VALUABLE TROPHY.

**Three Boats of South Coast Club and One from San Diego the Contestants—Entry of Junior Club of Griefer City Is Barred Owing to Conditions of Deed of Gift.**

The Aeolus of the San Diego club, and the Venus, Wasp and Michief II of the South Coast Yacht Club, completed the entry list for the annual race for The Times perpetual trophy, to be sailed Saturday afternoon off San Pedro. The Trilby, the boat entered last week by the Junior Club of San Diego, has been withdrawn, owing to the stipulations of the deed of gift, which requires clubs which enter yachts to have been organized at least one year, and the Junior Club has been organized but six months. The Mischief I has also declined to compete, which makes the event a four-cornered race, with boats entered of a very even class.

The San Diego yacht arrived at the harbor port yesterday afternoon, and will be put on the ways today to undergo a few finishing touches, and be measured in order that she may be classified according to the conditions of the race.

The South Coast club boats are also being treated in final preparation for the crucial contest, and the committee will arrange the time allowances tomorrow, according to the respective measurements of each craft.

The course, as adopted by the Racing Committee, starts between the end of the San Pedro breakwater and a flag buoy set in a southerly direction therefrom, thence to the whistling buoy off Point Vincente, leaving said buoy to port; thence return to the point of beginning, passing between the end of the breakwater and the flag buoy. The preparatory gun will be fired at 12:55 and the starting gun at 1 o'clock p.m. A time allowance will be given for a course of seventeen miles.

The judges' boat will leave the clubhouse anchorage at 12 o'clock, and will follow the contestants in close proximity throughout the course.

The members of the South Coast club are planning to make a gala day of Saturday, and will give an elaborate "smoker" at the clubhouse in the evening following the race in honor of the visiting San Diego yachtsmen.

TRUE FISH TALES.

## GOOD FISHING OFF CATALINA.

VISITING NIMRODS LAND VERY LARGE SPECIMENS.

**Immense Yellowtail Hooked by St. Louis Angler Still Excites Island Experts—C. G. Conn Catches Almost One Ton of Fish During First Three Days of Visit.**

[SPECIAL CORRESPONDENCE OF THE TIMES.]

AVALON, July 22.—The sixty and one-fourth-pound yellowtail caught by L. W. Weinheimer, the St. Louis angler, is the talk of sporting men here assembled. That Simpson's world record catch should be so soon and so narrowly matched is a matter of amazement even to experienced anglers hereabouts who are just beginning to realize that such denizens of the yellowtail variety swim these waters. Weinheimer's misfortune in not being able to bring his fish promptly to the official scales has without doubt, cost him both the world record and the handsome signet ring put up by Simpson as a prize to the first angler who surpassed his record.

At 11 o'clock Monday night A. W. Hooper left for Clemente again intent on winning further honors, and looking for big game. Mr. Simpson, the English angler still lingers here, loth to tear himself away from what he pronounces to be the finest sport he has found anywhere in his travels round the globe. He has asserted from the beginning that his record is bound to be eclipsed and is firm in the belief that more than one twin to his big catch swims Clemente waters. Mr. Weinheimer is having his big yellowtail mounted for preservation.

He has fished extensively in Florida waters and in the Wisconsin lakes for the famous muscallonge, but declares that the angling here beats anything he has seen before. "During five hours' fishing at Clemente, day before yesterday," he says, "I took six yellowtail, four weighing in excess of twenty pounds, one weighing thirty-seven pounds, and my last—and greatest—which I am confident weighed fully sixty-two pounds, when I took it out of the water. Will I try again before leaving Avalon? Yes, I guess so. I'm going from here to Aransas Pass to take a whack at the tarpon down there that Murphy and Hooper are telling me about."

Shortly after Weinheimer's return last night and before the excitement had died down, incident to his phenomenal fish, the McCausland party arrived from Clemente and a crowd gathered on the fisherman's wharf to welcome them. George McCausland brought back a forty-two and a half pound yellowtail, which entitles him to a gold button and his father registered a thirty-two and a half pound fish, for which he wins a silver button. P. Mooney, who went with them, reports that he played a 250-pound jewfish on light tackle for three hours and then lost him. Had Mooney been successful in landing his prize, he would have made a world record for light tackle catches.

C. G. Conn, "the gentleman from Indiana," caught three more jewfish and an immense 360-pound shark which runs his total since reaching Avalon three days ago, up to almost a ton of fish, the weight of his eight big black sea bass and the shark totaling over 1700 pounds. The shark was fully fifteen feet long and was the largest of its kind taken here for years, although not of the "man-eating" variety.

FISHING IMPROVES.

Fishing has picked up wonderfully within the last few days, and today the waters were alive with rock bass, yellowtail, white sea bass and other varieties, affording great sport. Never have so many white sea bass been seen here. W. /. Simpson and C. F. Holder report having passed hundreds of them between Sugar Loaf and Long Point yesterday and Mr. Simpson caught several of them.

One of the interesting features of the recent government official trip to San Clemente was that, while Messrs. Pinchot, Flint, Holder, Woodruff and Houghton fished for two weeks, they all used tackle so light that they could not take a fish in less than half an hour, and often an hour and a half, and every fish not needed for a specimen or for the table was released. This is the doctrine the Tuna Club was organized to teach.

A school of tuna was seen jumping off Pebbly Beach yesterday and created much excitement, but up to date none have been taken, but an unknown fish towed an angler about White's Landing for two hours on Sunday. The first yellowfin tuna of the season was taken Monday. This is the greatest sport of which Santa Catalina boasts.

Anglers are finding the conveniences of the Tuna Club a great addition to their pleasure. There is a private landing for boats, and in the long tackle room are thirty or more lockers devised for anglers, so that rods can be hung properly. Line driers are so arranged that they can be used at any time, and many other conveniences are there which makes the Tuna Club headquarters the best equipped organization in the country. In the rush Saturday nights a number of Tuna Club members find the sleeping rooms of great service when the hotels are not equal to the demand.

The club library has received a set of books from Casper Whitney, the well-known editor of Outing, and E H. Brewster, president of the Light Tackle Club, has presented the library with a set of Forest and Stream. The directors purpose making this library one of the best in California on the subject of fish and angling. H. Gray Griswold, the famous New York Angler, and an old member of the club, has presented it a set of pictures showing some of his remarkable catches in Florida, and Mr. Caldwell has given the club a fine photograph of his famous swordfish catch.

### BOTH MEN READY.

PUGS FINISH TRAINING.

Both Battling Johnson and Al Kaufman finished their hard work yesterday for their fight tomorrow night at McCarey's pavilion that will settle the heavyweight championship of the Coast. Kaufman presumably holds the title now and many of the local sports look to see a new cnampion after tomorrow.

Kaufman is said to have weighed 196 pounds yesterday, while Johnson tipped the scales at 185 pounds. They will enter the ring at about these figures and Johnson expects to be able to give away ten pounds on account of his great gameness and his strength. There have been rumors flying around that Kaufman was not in the best of condition to meet such a tough one as Johnson, but as Billy Delaney seems to be satisfied with the condition of his man, no one else need complain, since Kaufman is risking his reputation on the result of the fight.

Both men put in a hard day yesterday and while Kaufman was still without a sparring partner he made up for it with shadow boxing and all-around gymnastic work. Each man will do a little road work this morning.

### Seattle Card.

SEATTLE, July 22.—Results:

Five furlongs: Anna May won, Belle Griffon second, Nuns Veiling third; time, 1:01 1-5.

Five furlongs: Nasmerito won, Miss Worth second, Larry Mulligan third; time, 1:01.

Five furlongs: Belle Kinney won, Abbey second; Miss Fairbanks third; time, 1:00 1-5.

NEAR THE FINISH.

## THREE HAVE PERFECT SCORE.

*No Change in Conditions in Hower Trophy Contest.*

*Official Pacing Car Runs Off Bank Into Ditch.*

*Final Run of Schedule Ends Today at Saratoga..*

[BY DIRECT WIRE TO THE TIMES.]

BETHLEHEM (N. H.) July 22.—[Exclusive Dispatch.] Again the Chicago Motor Club team in the Glidden tour came through the day with a perfect score, and still this team and the Pierce-Buffalo and Peerless-Columbus teams are at the top with clean records. No change took place today in the Hower trophy contest—the Premier, two Pierces and two Stoddard-Daytons still retaining clean scores.

Two penalizations occurred today in the Glidden contest, Marmon No. 22 breaking a wheel and withdrawing tonight. Oakland No. 28 was penalized nine points for being late. Both cars were previously penalized.

R. M. Owen, who has driven the Reo car with a perfect score to date, is anxious that the Olds Motor Works insist that the Olds car in the Chicago club continue in the contest in the event of a tie at Saratoga. Superintendent Ralph Owen of the Olds factory is a brother of R. M. Owen, and there is much hope tonight that family influence will keep the Olds car in the tour to the finish.

Frank Yeagers, in a Studebaker, threw a front tire crossing a bridge today, and dashed against the rail. His car arrived two minutes ahead of its schedule, with a fender broken. There was no penalization. All the other Studebakers arrived an hour ahead of time.

The official pacing car, containing Charles J. Glidden and Chairman F. B. Hower, ran off a steep bank today, throwing its passengers twenty feet. Nobody was injured severely, and Ralph Estips, in the Packard press car, dragged the big Pierce from the ditch.

Chairman Hower made the first on-coming car, another Pierce, the temporary pacemaker, and thereby caused much dissatisfaction among contestants who recalled last year's similar incident when Hower refused to substitute a Royal Tourist for the official cars.

Tomorrow's run is to Saratoga, finishing the scheduled trip. Owing to the distance of nearly 200 miles, the start from here will be at 6 o'clock in the morning.

### Strike-breakers in Mines.

BIRMINGHAM (Ala.) July 22.—Two trainloads of imported labor, strike-breakers, were placed in the mines today in the Birmingham district with military escort and there was not the least interference on the part of the strikers or sympathizers.

THE MOB!

# GIANTS LEAD WILD RIOTING.

*Twenty Thousand Fans Chase Umpires from Field.*

*Crowd Assaults Players and Latter Retaliate.*

*National League in Chaotic Condition as Result.*

[BY DIRECT WIRE TO THE TIMES.]

NEW YORK, Sept. 23.—[Exclusive Dispatch.] The third game of the sensational series between the on-rushing Cubs and the blown Giants, ended in a riot at the Polo Grounds this afternoon, when an angry mob of 20,000 fans chased Umpires Emslie and O'Day from the field and interrupted one of the most sensational contests ever seen in this part of the country.

The trouble cropped up in the ninth inning. With McCormick on third and Merkle at first, Bridwell rapped a beauty over second base. Instead of running to second Merkle waited till Bridwell overhauled him and the two immediately beat it for the clubhouse. In the meantime Johnny Evers grasped the situation and called to Hofman for the ball. By this time McCormick had crossed the plate and the crowd had swarmed onto the field.

A couple of "rummies" jostled Evers as he went to make the catch at second and the ball bounced off his back to Pfiester. The pitcher promptly returned it to the bag, but McGinnity, who saw what was being pulled off by the Cubs, intercepted the throw and tried to make off with the spheroid. He was tackled by the entire Chicago infield, and after being jostled about a great deal, ptiched the ball into the crowd. Emslie here called Merkle out, and when Evers carried the intelligence to O'Dea, Hank ordered the field cleared for action.

By this time fully 5000 of the bleacher rabble were around the veteran official, but amid cat calls and hisses and threats of violence he stood his ground. The police finally broke through to his rescue and hustled O'Day into the little pen under the grand stand. O'Day declared as he was unwillingly closeted that the game would have to proceed, and ordered the police to clear the grounds.

Frank Chance tried to get to O'Day, but was jostled back by the crowd. After he was closeted with Emslie for half an hour both umpires declared they had made no decision and that the game would stand 2 to 1 in favor of the Giants, under protest. No official ruling has yet been made.

McGraw, without a pitcher left in condition to work except his minor-league recruits, declares angrily that he will not play two games tomorrow, and that he claims the game.

PULLIAM DENIES RUMOR.

While the game has been protested by the Chicago Club, President Pulliam denied tonight that he had taken any action in the matter, as he cannot tell and will not do so until the case has been presented to him in the regular announcement. Following is Pulliam's statement:,

"The New York stock ticker tonight, having carried this statement: 'Harry Pulliam, president of the National League, decides today's game between Chicago and New York a tie, and announces that it must be played over,' say such statement is unauthorized. I have made no decision, and I will not until the matter is presented to me in regular form."

The score:

Chicago, 1; hits, 5; errors, 3.

New York, 2; hits, 7; errors, 0.

Batteries—Pfeister and Kling; Mathewson and Bresnahan.

Umpires—O'Day and Emslie.

BEGINNING WORK.

# GIANT TACKLE IS TO RETURN.

HIGH SCHOOL IN LUCK TO GET VETERAN TACKLE.

**Prep School Eleven Schedules Games With Colleges and Holds Open Dates for Interscholastic Championships With Northern Schools—Santa Ana Has Nerve.**

The first football practice of the season for the Los Angeles High School squad will be held this afternoon at Fiesta Park, when many candidates are expected to turn out in answer to the call of Coach Noble. After the flurry of registration, the Blue and White rooters are anxious to get a line on the new material available to fill the vacancies by graduation of last season's stars, and a large crowd of enthusiasts will attend the initial appearance of the men today.

The season's schedule of games has been arranged by Coach Noble as follows:

October 10—U.S.C. and L. A. High at Fiesta Park.

October 17—St. Vincents and L. A. High at Fiesta Park.

October 24.—Pomona and L. A. High at Fiesta Park.

November 7—Santa Ana High and L. A. High at Fiesta Park.

November 14—Occidental and L. A. High at Fiesta Park.

November 21 and Thanksgiving Day are reserved for possible games with the northern interscholastic champions, and as several teams have already written for contests, the games seem certain.

Adamson, last year's star tackle, who was not expected to return this year, has been heard from, and says he will be back before the season is very far advanced.

Francis Gates a 170-pound half back, has registered from Boone Academy, Berkeley, and seems a likely candidate to fill Mitchell's berth in case Stan is unable to play a part or whole of the season.

PLAY CLASS GAMES.

U.S.C. TEAMS IN STRUGGLE..

In a hard fought contest the sophomore eleven defeated the freshman team in the annual class game at the University of Southern California, yesterday afternoon, the score being 5 to 0. The single touchdown was made in the last part of the first period, Right Half Skinner of the upper classmen crossing the goal after three desperate line bucks.

The game was played on Bovard Field before a noisy crowd of class partisans.

The fourth and third academy teams played a close game, neither team being able to score. The line-up displayed many fast, clever players who will doubtless do yeoman's service on the second eleven. The teams will play off the tie this afternoon, and tomorrow the winner of today's game will meet the sophomores in the deciding contest for the championship of the campus teams.

The contest showed the underclass elevens possessed of some excellent material for the 'varsity. Reed and Ickes, the opposing quarters, gave a heady, clever exhibition, Reed making the longest run of the game on a fake kick, and Ickes appeared to advantage in open field work.

Geller and Thompson of the "baby" backfield, also played well, and Gower and Goodnow at end were very effective in guarding the wing. Hall and Skinner were the strong players on the sophs, and Paulin hit the line for good gains.

The line-up of the teams was as follows:

| Sophomores. | | Freshman. |
|---|---|---|
| Wallace | right end | Goodnow (c) |
| Williames | right tackle | Murray |
| Murray | right tackle | Williams |
| Bruce | right guard | Hatch |
| Traynor | center | Davidson |
| Richardson | left guard | Malcolm |
| Grace | left tackle | Allen |
| Henderson | left end | Geller |
| Reed | quarter | Ickes |
| Hall | left half | Hogan |
| Skinner | right half | Gower |
| Paulin | fullback | Thompson |
| Fourth Preps. | | Third Preps. |
| Huston | right end | Hall |
| Longshore | right tackle | Law |
| McQuigg | right guard | Powell |
| Rocho | center | Bunker |
| Sargeant | left guard | Mann |
| Ward | left tackle | Henderson |
| Hummel | left end | Martin |
| Reiche | quarter | Halloway |
| D. Wallace | left half | Bartholomew |
| Hunter | right half | Fiersman |
| P. Lorentzen | fullback | Murdock |

Umpire—Cromwell.

Pomona Practice.

CLAREMONT, Sept. 23.—Twenty-two men reported for football practice yesterday afternoon on Alumni field. Considering that college does not open until today, yesterday and Monday having been given up to registration, the number out is very promising. Of the twenty-two nearly all are new men, comparatively few of the old 'varsity men having as yet returned. Today's practice will probably draw out veterans, as in addition to Capt. Taylor, Mahoney, half; Birdsall, half; Vail, quarter, and Benner, end; with perhaps several more, are all ready to get into their suits.

The afternoon's work was light, Coach Stanton giving the men only practice with kicks and handling punts, falling on the ball, and starting for the linemen. Most of the material appears to be pretty green, and the recruits will have to pass some time mastering the rudiments of the game.

One or two of the new men showed up exceedingly well; Carver, the half-miler from Occidental, while new to the game, gives promise of developing into an aggressive player. At present he seems rather clumsy, but with practice ought to turn out a strong plunging back. Shutt from Santa Monica High handles himself well, and shows good football instinct for a freshman. He weighs about 160 pounds, and should make the old 'varsity halves hustle to hold their positions before the season is out. It is possible that he may be tried at quarter.

Much satisfaction is felt here at U. S.C.'s decision to enter the conference. While opinions are expressed in some quarters regretting that the university seems to come in with feelings of being unjustly treated, the general attitude is that of gratification at the prospect of renewed friendly relations, and confidence that time and intimacy will show how sincerely Pomona has desired to get the Southern California institutions together in an agreement that would secure to all a wise and fair basis of competition.

LONG BEACH TENNIS.

**Eastern Experts Win Majority of the Games in Round Robin Tourney at Long Beach.**

The eastern tennis players who arrived here yesterday showed their class by finishing close to the top in the round-robin tourney played yesterday afternoon on the courts of the Hotel Virginia at Long Beach. It was an opportunity afforded local tennis enthusiasts to see the visitors in action on cement courts, and the men showed they were at home on these.

Niles and Brown won 30 games; Wright and Johnson, 24; Bell and Bundy, 23; Duncan and Variel, 17, and Rogers and Sinsabaugh, 16. Today the teams will be Wright and Johnson, Bundy and Bell, Rogers brothers, Duncan and Variel, and Sinsabaugh and Brown. Mr. Niles is compelled to leave for the East today, as he must reach Harvard by next Wednesday. He is captain of the tennis team in the big college, and unless he is there to register he will be disqualified.

The visitors were taken for a ride around this city yesterday morning, and will be shown Pasadena and environs this morning by auto, if the weather is pleasant.

FUSE HURTS MOTORMAN.

Philip Reis, 30 years of age, a motorman living at No. 634 Towne avenue, was painfully burned on the face and hands last night, by the explosion of the fuse on his car. Reis, with his conductor and an inspector, crawled beneath the car on the dead track in Agricultural Park. The headlight of the car would not work, and the men were searching for the trouble when the fuse blew out. Reis was thrown from beneath the car. He was hurried to the Receiving Hospital, where his injuries were dressed. Later he was sent to his home. His eyesight may be impaired.

CIRCUS WAGON WINS.

While a Main-street car was going north near Eighteenth street late last night, the brake refused to hold the wheels on the slippery track and it collided with a circus wagon. The wagon was only slightly injured, but the front part of the car was completely wrecked. No one was hurt, although there was a general shaking up.

IMPERIAL NEXT.

Imperial Valley delegates to the National Irrigation Congress, to be held in Albuquerque next week, have asked the Los Angeles representatives to join them in an effort to secure the 1910 convention for the valley. W. C. Mendenhall of this city, will act as chairman of the Chamber of Commerce delegation to the Albuquerque meeting.

UNDELIVERED TELEGRAMS.

At the office of the Postal Telegraph Company there are telegrams for Una Melrose, Seelda Theobald, Mrs. J. H. Watrous, Mrs. C. M. Lee and H. C. Goldrick.

*TRANSFER PATTERNS.*

*The Times, on Sunday, October 4, and each Sunday thereafter, will distribute to each subscriber and purchaser of the paper a four-page TRANSFER PATTERN-SECTION. It is a unique, exclusive, attractive feature of particular interest and value to women. It will not injure the most delicate fabrics, and so simple that a child can successfully manipulate the process.*







SMASHED.

# NEW RECORD TO SAN DIEGO.

*Rambler Roadster Cuts Time Over One Hour.*

*Lower Mark Could Have Been Easily Made.*

*Road in Horrible Shape for Fast Driving.*

[BY DIRECT WIRE TO THE TIMES.]

SAN DIEGO, Sept. 23.—[Exclusive Dispatch.] In an attempt to break a record for the Chanslor and Lyons cup for the best round-trip time between this city and Los Angeles, L. B. Harvey, with a Rambler four-cylinder roadster, was successful, completing the circuit in eleven hours, twenty-one and one-half minutes.

The trip to Los Angeles by way of Escondido, Elsinore, Corona and Pomona was covered in six hours, two minutes, while the return trip was made over the coast route in five hours, nineteen and one-half minutes. The previous record held by the Great Smith roadster was beaten by one hour, six and one-half minutes.

Harvey, accompanied by Fred Roberts, a local machinist, and Lonis Miller, a local newspaper man, left the Union building at 6:10 o'clock yesterday morning. They made Escondido in one hour and three minutes, and rolled up in front of The Times building in Los Angeles at 12:12 o'clock. After stopping eight minutes for gasoline and water the start on the return trip was made at 12:22 o'clock.

Harvey, knowing that he had the former record broken by a good margin, made no effort to break the coast record, but, taking his time so as to not be behind the Great Smith record, reached the Union office at 5:41½ p.m.

Harvey had no mishap on the way, either going or coming. He reports the roads in horrible shape for a record run, and in many places he can hardly account for the manner in which they got along at the record-breaking clip they were driving.

SPORTING SECTION.

The Pink Sheet. IN THE FIELD OF SPORTS

# Los Angeles Sunday Times

Part VI— Pages. ROUND-UP, OF THE WEEK.

XXVIII[TH] YEAR. SUNDAY MORNING, JULY 11, 1909. On All News Stands, Trains and Streets. | 5 CENTS.



FERRIS AND SHETTLER TROPHIES THE PRIZES.

# APPERSON BEATS THE VANDERBILT CUP RACE TIME AND CHALMERS-DETROIT WINS SMALL CAR EVENT.

## POINTS OF THE SANTA MONICA ROAD RACE.

Big car race won by Apperson, driven by Harris Hanshue, in 3h., 8m. 3s.

Small car rac won by Chalmers-Detroit, driven by Bert Dingley, in 3h. 38m. 35s.

Average time of Apperson was 64.44 miles, which breaks the Vanderbilt cup record.

Average time of the Chalmers-Detroit was 55.5 miles.

Fifty thousand persons saw the races from various vantage points.

The Dick Ferris trophy goes to Leon T. Shettler, agent for the Apperson.

The Leon T. Shettler trophy goes to the Western Motor Car Co., agents for the Chalmers-Detroit.

Not an injury worthy the name was reported and the accidents to cars were but trivial.

The management of the big event was excellent, and no time was lost in getting the cars off.

There was no serious trouble between the management or the city and private parties over the handling of seats and concessions.

Chadwick, Second

## FAST AS THE WIND.

Averaging 64.44 miles per hour over the entire course, Harris Hanshue, in the Apperson "Jackrabbit," won the great automobile road race for the Ferris Trophy on the Santa Monica course yesterday morning, in one of the most thrilling auto contests ever held on this continent.

The time was 3h. 8m. 3s. for the 202.417 miles. The average time was better than that made in the Vanderbilt race last year, and the performance will live long in the annals of the sport.

The Apperson jumped into the lead in the eleventh lap and maintained its advantage until the end. Bruno Seibel, in the Chadwick, was second, having made a wonderful run, after a rather tame start. His time was 3h. 15m. 30s.

The Stearns, with Frank Free driving, was third. The fast car led the field for several laps, and was a close second during the greater part of the contest. The Stearns's time was 3h. 19m. 52s.

The Locomobile was fourth, Murray Page finishing the race in 3h. 21m. 15s.

The Stoddard-Dayton crossed the line fifth, in 3h. 24m.

GREAT CROWDS.

Fifty thousand persons witnessed the race. Every vantage point about the 8.417-mile course was occupied. Automobiles were driven across grain fields and cabbage patches in order to get a position along the course. On Nevada avenue and the Palisades, the people were packed along the roadside, ten deep. The stands were but half-full, but the roofs of the buildings were crowded, and there was not a window that overlooked the course that did not half a half-dozen spectators.

The race was not marred by bad accidents. Several drivers had narrow escapes. The Haynes went into the ditch on its fourteenth lap, and had to quit, but Driver Shannon and Machinist La Casse were not seriously hurt. The course was well patroled and the management could not have been better, except that the timing system was not as efficient as it might have been.

Dick Ferris, donor of the cup, occupied a box at the finish, and was given an ovation when he arose after repeated calls for a speech. Ferris came across the continent to witness the struggle. He says the course is the fastest in the world and predicts that all road records will eventually be lowered on the Santa Monica course.

The Apperson will receive the $1000 Ferris Trophy, one of the handsomest silver cups ever offered for any race. Cup and base is 3½ feet high and weighs thirty-three and a half pounds. It contains 400 ounces of pure silver and is lined with gold.

The fastest lap was made by the Lozier, which Tettzlaff drove in 6m. 50 3-5s., in the first round. The car held the lead at the beginning of the race.

SECOND EVENT.

Nearly everybody remained for the light car race. The thousands who had witnessed the thrilling struggle of the morning had no desire to leave. Another such contest was promised with cars lighter, but, for their weight, equally as fast as the speed-devouring demons which had thrilled the spectators during the morning session.

For an hour lunches were enjoyed. Every automobile party spread a picnic lunch, and during the interval awaited the start of the second race. Lined along the course, the thousands of automobiles were left standing, while those in them awaited expectantly the popping of the exhausts which would tell that the second race was on.

Along Nevada avenue the spectators were massed in a solid body. On every vantage point the crowd swarmed like flies. There was not a foot of frontage which had not been preëmpted at 12 o'clock. Many went without lunch rather than give up the position which they had gained when the crowd moved at the finish of the big event.

At the Soldiers' Home, where the veterans had gathered to watch the race, the throng was packed in solid lines. It was impossible to get standing room near the course at the turn where the road sweeps past the grand stand erected for the old soldiers.

Along the Palisades the automobiles took the best vantage points. On one little knoll at least 200 machines had been parked, the occupants craning their necks to watch the cars as they whizzed past.

ON THE SNAKE TURN.

Again, down at the "S" turn there were thousands of people who wanted to watch the cars come through the zigzag at sixty miles an hour. Every house along the course had its race party. Porches were lined and in several instances small grand stands had been erected where the races could be watched to better advantage.

Clarence Smith, in the Maxwell, almost drove into the money in the little race. He finished fourth, close to the Buick. It was Smith's first race, and he kept his car on the course for lap after lap, making fast time for the entire race.

Bob Greer, in the Mitchell, drove a consistent race. Again the Mitchell remained on the course through the entire contest. The Cadillac was forced to go into the peddock after Christopherson had been obliged to give his lead to the Mitchell.

The Regal, driven by C. H. Bigelow, finished consistently. Though it was never in the running, the little car made a good showing and finished with a burst of speed that did credit

(Continued on Second Page.)

Stearns, Third, rounding the Nevada turn.

Apperson Car, with Harris Hanshue at the Wheel,
winning the great road race and the Dick Ferris trophy at Santa Monica yesterday. The Chadwick was second and the Stearns third.

HAD CORRECT DOPE.

# MAJORITY OF GUESSERS NAMED RIGHT CARS.

*Apperson's and Chalmers' Backers' Faith Justified by the Result. Ten Best Estimaters Within Three to Ten Seconds of Time Figured.*

It appears from the result of the great classic Santa Monica road race that the majority of the guessers on the outcome had the straight "dope" as to the cars destined to win.

Out of a total of 25,132 guesses submitted in The Times guessing contest, 6552, or a little more than one-fourth of the total number of guesses, named the Apperson as the winner in the race for the Ferris cup. Out of a total of 22,204 guesses as to the winner of the Shettler cup, 7994 favored the Chalmers-Detroit. The fact that these two cars carried off the honors is very good proof that the majority of the persons who figured on the race made a close study of the cars and drivers, and exercised sound judgment in picking the winners and estimating the speed that would be attained.

Hundreds of persons participating in the contest came within a few minutes of estimating the time correctly, and quite a number came within less than 60 seconds of forecasting the correct figures.

The coupons were all numbered in the order in which they were received at The Times office and in the case of tie guesses, the one bearing the lowest number will be awarded the prize.

HOW THEY GUESSED.

Following is the score list showing the number of guesses recorded in favor of each car.

BIG CAR RACE.

| | |
|---|---|
| Apperson | 6552 |
| Locomobile | 3909 |
| Thomas | 3132 |
| Stearns | 1969 |

(Continued on Fifth Page.)

SAILING.

# WASP IS VICTOR OF "TIMES" CUP.

SAILS CLOSE RACE WITH SAN DIEGO YACHT GRETCHEN.

**Mah Pe Sailed Fast Race, But Her Measurements Set Her Back Though She May Yet Be Given Trophy—Skipper Wood Hangs by Broken Bowstay and is Drenched.**

The Times Challenge Cup was won by the Wasp of the South Coast Yacht Club yesterday afternoon at San Pedro, with a minute and a half to spare. The little craft crossed the line at the end of the San Pedro breakwater at 4:42:55, beating the Gretchen by a scratch.

The contest was one of the best ever held in the South. The victory was so close that when the steamer Cabrillo, following in the wake, nearly threw the Wasp out of her course, she had only a fraction over a minute in which to finish the lead.

It is barely possible that the trophy may be snatched by the Mah Pe, which entered the race with the understanding that her measurements would be taken later. It is not believed that the Mah Pe is eligible, although her great displacement compared with her small sail area brings her well down to the thirty-five-foot class.

The real race was between the Wasp and Gretchen and the Mischief II. The start was one of the best ever seen on the Coast. They were off in a bunch after circling around and around the starting flag waiting for the second gun at 1:10 o'clock.

The Mah Pe, with a great area of canvas, was so close to the other nine craft that they could hardly be noticed.

The real sport of the race was furnished by Skipper Warren Wood of the Mischief I. The yacht broke its bowstay just as it crossed the line. For fifteen minutes the skipper hung in a sling under the bow of the yacht with the swells breaking over him. Finally the line was fastened and he was hauled out of his precarious position.

MAH PE RACES.

As the yachts rounded the Pt. Firmin whistling buoy, the Mah Pe raced up the coast to Point Vincent, far in advance of the other contestants. She took one long tack two miles out to sea against the westward wind. All the other boats kept close to shore, with short tacks, ranging from one-quarter to three-quarters of a mile in length.

The Aeolus passed the Mischief II two miles above the lighthouse, not far behind the Mah Pe. Back and forth the Gretchen, Mischief II and the Wasp tacked. They did not change their relative positions for some time. The Gretchen was in the lead, followed by

(Continued on Ninth Page.)

# SPORTING NEWS, LOCAL AND TELEGRAPHIC.

SPACE EATERS.

## OLDFIELD DRIVES HUNDRED MILES AN HOUR ON PIEPAN.

*Crowd Sees Kerscher Beat De Palma in Sensational Ten-Mile Race, But Italian Driver Wins Honors in Fifty-Mile World Record-Breaking Contest on the Motordrome.*

BARNEY OLDFIELD smashed the half mile and kilometer automobile records at the Motordrome yesterday afternoon, and did what he said he would do when the meet opened—drove the Benz faster than 100 miles an hour on the board course. With Benny Kerscher as mechanician, Oldfield went away from the wire at a terrific clip and made the half in 17.97s.

Had Oldfield finished the mile he must certainly have lowered his own record of 36.22s. He was making 105.56 miles an hour as he flew past the half-mile mark. Then he shut off, knowing he had clipped the half-mile mark. He should have made the last half mile faster than the first had he kept on driving.

In a second record-breaking attempt Oldfield smashed the kilometer mark, making the five-eighths of a mile in 22.88s. The Benz did not quite reach the 100-mile-an-hour mark on this trial, but Barney clipped more than two seconds from the former kilometer mark.

Four thousand persons saw the speed trials yesterday. The day was ideal Motordrome weather. It was warm enough to be comfortable on the bleachers. It was the first time that so large a crowd had witnessed a race meet on a mid-week day on any track near Los Angeles. The crowd looked small, howhowever, on the large track and compared with the Sunday throng the parking space for automobiles looked almost empty.

Benny Kerscher, with the Darracq, was the sensation in the ten-mile race. Under the coaching of Oldfield, Benny went out to defeat De Palma if possible. De Palma drove the Fiat Cyclone, a sixty-horse-power car, wonderfully fast, which has helped De Palma to make world records. Kerscher drove the Darracq, the 100-horse-power car which won the Vanderbilt cup race in the days when that affair was the biggest event in motordom.

THEY'RE OFF.

Starter Fred Wagner sent the men off in a splendid start, but Benny shot to the pole and hit a terrific clip. De Palma went after the "Flying Dutchman," but Kerscher came into the stretch at the end of the first mile nearly fifty yards to the good. Oldfield slowed his wild Dutchman down another notch, and De Palma shot up to even terms. Then Benny threw the Darracq's throttle open again and sailed away, only to be cautioned again by Oldfield.

For mile after mile this was repeated with Kerscher keeping the lead. De Palma gave some wonderful exhibitions of jockeying with his smaller car, but try as he would the Italian boy could not get the pole. Benny wriggled all over the track but he kept the lead always, looking at Oldfield for advice as he swung around into the stretch.

On the eighth mile, while Benny was still in the lead, Barney gave him the signal and he was away for his first big victory. He grinned in great glee as he raced past the grand stand. He was winning and could not conceal his joy.

De Palma gave Kerscher a race for every foot of the journey. He sent the little "Cyclone" to the limit of its power and speed, but Benny was too fast. He had been given the word by his chief and he drove with the throttle wide open and the Darracq dancing all over the course.

STEADY GAIT WINS.

Kerscher won, with De Palm aclose behind. His time of 7m. 1.92s. was not sensational, though it was fast. It is doubtful if Kerscher would have won but for the generalship of Barney Oldfield who managed the race for the plucky driver who always had a tendency to "drive his head off" if left alone.

The five-mile handicap was won by the Stoddard-Dayton starting 15s. ahead of Oldfield on scratch. The Marmon starting with the Stoddard was a close second and the Isotta, also starting with the Stoddard, was third. This was one of the prettiest races of the day as Alvan McMurtrie gauged the speed of the three cars to a nicety.

The Cole "Thirty" started more than a minute to the good. The Palmer Singer was second in length of handicap and the Stoddard, Marmon and Isotta were away together just 15s. ahead of the Knox. It was a race for every minute of the journey with the Stoddard winning by a length.

Some one called Al Livingston a "quitter," when the Stoddard-Dayton man desired to keep his car out of the fifty-mile race. The Stoddard's radiator was leaking and Livingston was afraid of injuring the engine.

Nettled at the remark, Livingston said:

"Well, I'll drive anyhow, and show you I'm no quitter."

He started and took second place in a race in which the world record for fifty miles was broken by the Fiat "Cyclone," driven by Ralph De Palma. The latter's time, 37m. 55.53s. clips nearly two minutes from the former world record for the fifty miles held by the Isotta.

HARD FIGHT.

This race developed into a duel between the Darracq and the Fiat, with De Palma in the lead and Kerscher showing all kinds of speed. Once Kerscher shot into the lead, remained there for half a lap and then was slowed down by Oldfield. Kerscher trailed De Palma for thirty-nine miles. Kerscher went out in his fortieth mile with a flat tire.

Once, when Kerscher was pressing the Fiat closely, De Palma waved defiance at Oldfield as he noticed the champion signalling to Kerscher. It seemed almost foolhardy for De Palma to appear so confident. The result showed, however, that he always had the race well in hand. He won easily.

The Fiat 'Ninety," driven by Bragg, turned a mile in 37.89s. during a three-mile trial against time. Bragg shut off his motor at the end of the second mile. His time for the two miles was 1:15.96s.; beating Kerscher's best time for the two-mile mark.

Kerscher in the Darracq went three miles for a world record and turned the trick. His time was 1m. 57.71s., a new world record. The old mark, held by himself, was 1m. 58.96s.

The Buick "Forty," driven by Nikrent, broke a world record for ten miles against time, in the 301-450 cu. in. class. The Buick's time was 7m. 35.87s.

De Palma drove the Fiat "Ninety" a mile in an effort to break Barney Oldfield's track record of 36.22. His time was 37.67s.

Interest in the closing three days' races centers in the Oldfield-Robertson match which has taken the place of the Oldfield-De Palma race. Robertson was sick yesterday and did not appear. It is promised that he will be on hand Friday. Robertson is to drive his Simplex "Ninety," one of the fastest cars on the course, and Oldfield his Blitzen Benz, the fastest car on the Motordrome.

### TIME TRIALS.

ONE-HALF MILE.

| | |
|---|---|
| Oldfield in Benz | :17.91 |

ONE KILOMETER.

| | |
|---|---|
| Oldfield in Benz | :22.88 |

ONE MILE.

| | |
|---|---|
| Oldfield in Benz | :37.38 |
| De Palma in Fiat 90 | :37.67 |

TWO MILES.

Bragg in Fiat 90:

| Miles. | By Laps. | Total. |
|---|---|---|
| 1 | :37.89 | :37.89 |
| 2 | :38.07 | 1:15.96 |

THREE MILES.

Kerscher in Darracq:

| Miles. | By Laps. | Total. |
|---|---|---|
| 1 | :39.28 | :39.28 |
| 2 | :39.24 | 1:18.52 |
| 3 | :39.19 | 1:57.71 |

TEN MILES.

Nikrent in Buick:

| Miles. | By Laps. | Total. |
|---|---|---|
| 1 | :47.52 | :47.52 |
| 2 | :46.45 | 1:33.97 |
| 3 | :44.95 | 2:18.92 |
| 4 | :45.00 | 3:03.92 |
| 5 | :44.99 | 3:48.91 |
| 6 | :45.33 | 4:34.24 |
| 7 | :45.48 | 5:19.72 |
| 8 | :46.41 | 6:05.13 |
| 9 | :45.32 | 6:50.37 |
| 10 | :45.42 | 7:35.87 |

### TIME OF RACES.

Fifty miles, free-for-all:

| Miles. | By 5-laps. | Total. |
|---|---|---|
| 5 | 3:36.16 | 3:36.16 |
| 10 | 3:41.92 | 7:18.08 |
| 15 | 3:58.43 | 11:06.51 |
| 20 | 3:38.03 | 14:44.54 |
| 25 | 3:49.67 | 18:34.21 |
| 30 | 4:08.74 | 22:42.95 |
| 35 | 3:49.58 | 26:32.53 |
| 40 | 3:47.65 | 30:20.18 |
| 45 | 3:54.02 | 34:14.20 |
| 50 | 3:41.33 | 37:55.53 |

Ten miles, free-for-all:

| Miles. | By Laps. | Total. |
|---|---|---|
| 1 | :41.39 | :41.39 |
| 2 | :41.86 | 1:23.25 |
| 3 | :41.98 | 2:05.23 |
| 4 | :41.39 | 2:46.62 |
| 5 | :42.99 | 3:29.61 |
| 6 | :40.73 | 4:10.34 |
| 7 | :42.98 | 4:53.32 |
| 8 | :41.83 | 5:35.25 |
| 9 | :41.80 | 6:17.05 |
| 10 | :44.87 | 7:01.92 |

Five miles, free-for-all handicap:

| Order of Finish. | Handicap. | Total. |
|---|---|---|
| Stoddard-Dayton | :12 | 3:50.55 |
| Marmon | :10 | 3:50.82 |
| Isotta | :11 | 3:51.45 |

## THE TIMES AUTOMOBILE RACING FORM CHART.

LOS ANGELES, April 13, 1910.—Fourth day Motordrome races. Weather, clear and windy. Starter, F. J. Wagner; referee, S. B. Stevens; timer, C. H. Warner; judges, Charles Burman, Robert Marsh, Ralph W. Smith, Ed R. Maier; handicapper, A. A. McMurtry.

FIRST RACE—Ten miles, free-for-all, class E. Prizes: First, $200; second, $100.

| Index. | 16 Auto and Owner— | H.P. | B. | S. | P. Dis. | Driver. | 1 | 2 | 3 | 4 | 5 | 6 | 7 | 8 | 9 | 10 |
|---|---|---|---|---|---|---|---|---|---|---|---|---|---|---|---|---|
| 13 | Darracq | 4-100 | 6¾ | 5½ | 787.2 | Kerscher | 1 | 1 | 1 | 1 | 1 | 1 | 1 | 1 | 1 | 1 |
| 6 | Fiat Cyclone | 4-60 | 5½ | 5⅛ | 487.0 | De Palma | 2 | 2 | 2 | 2 | 2 | 2 | 2 | 2 | 2 | 2 |

Time—7m. 1 92-100s. Off—3:12.

Start, rolling, good. Darracq took the pole and lead in first mile and was never headed, winning by four lengths over the Fiat. Kerscher drove just fast enough to win in order to save tires for the fifty-mile race. De Palma tried three times to pass Darracq, closing up to within one and one-half lengths in the fifth mile.

SECOND RACE—Five miles, handicap, free-for-all, class D. Prizes: First, $100; second, $50.

| Index. | 17 Auto and Owner— | H.P. | B. | S. | P. Dis. | Driver. | Handicap. | 5 |
|---|---|---|---|---|---|---|---|---|
| 15 | Stoddard-Dayton (Fessenden) | 4-50 | 5¼ | 5¾ | 486.1 | Livingstone | :12 | 1 |
| 15 | Marmon (Nordyke & M. Co.) | 4-30 | 4½ | 4½ | 286.3 | Harroun | :10 | 2 |
| 15 | Isotta (Motor Import Co.) | 4-45 | 5⅛ | 6 | 495.1 | Marquis | :11 | 3 |
| 14 | Knox (B. Oldfield) | 6-60 | 5 | 4¾ | 559.5 | Oldfield | Scratch | .. |
| 15 | Palmer-Singer (P.-S. M. Co.) | 6-60 | 4⅞ | 5½ | 616.9 | Lescault | :43 | .. |
| 11 | Cole (H. O. Vogel) | 4-30 | 4 | 4 | 201.1 | Endecott | :50 | .. |

Time—3m. 50 55-100s. Off—3:26.

Start, standing, good. Stoddard-Dayton won on fractional margin of 32-100 seconds from the Marmon, which was 73-100 seconds ahead of the Isotta, making the calculations of Handicapper McMurtry nearly perfect. Knox gained slowly during entire race, but did not have the speed to overcome the handicap, which was based on the mark of 43s. for the Knox.

THIRD RACE—Fifty miles, free-for-all, class D. Prizes: First, $200; second, $100; third, $50.

| Index. | 18 Auto and Owner— | H.P. | B. | S. | P. Dis. | Driver. | 5 | 10 | 15 | 20 | 25 | 35 | 40 | 45 | 50 |
|---|---|---|---|---|---|---|---|---|---|---|---|---|---|---|---|
| 16 | Fiat Cyclone | 4-60 | 5½ | 5⅛ | 487.0 | De Palma | 1 | 1 | 1 | 1 | 1 | 1 | 1 | 1 | 1 |
| 17 | Stoddard-Dayton (Fessenden) | 4-50 | 5¼ | 5¾ | 486.1 | Livingstone | 4 | 4 | 4 | 4 | 4 | 4 | 2 | 2 | 2 |
| 17 | Marmon (Nordyke & M. Co.) | 4-30 | 4½ | 4½ | 286.3 | Harroun | 3 | 3 | 3 | 3 | 3 | 3 | 3 | 3 | 3 |
| 16 | Darracq (B. Oldfield) | 4-100 | 6¾ | 5½ | 787.2 | Kerscher | 2 | 2 | 2 | 2 | 2 | 2 | .. | .. | .. |
| 17 | Isotta (Motor Import Co.) | 4-45 | 5⅛ | 6 | 495.1 | Marquis | 5 | .. | .. | .. | .. | .. | .. | .. | .. |

Time—37m. 55 53-100s. Off—4:08.

Start, rolling, good. Fiat Cyclone took the lead and pole from Darracq in second mile, keeping to the front in every mile except the twenty-first, when the Darracq, which had followed about twenty-five yards behind, jumped ahead for a half-mile, but the Cyclone spurted and passed it. Fiat won without stopping by time margin of 2m. 37 44-100s. over Stoddard-Dayton. Darracq was close second to Fiat until thirty-seventh mile, when right rear tire was thrown and Kerscher retired with car to pits. Marmon lapped Stoddard-Dayton in eighteenth mile and held third position easily one-half lap behind leaders until thirty-eighth mile, when rear tire blew out. Harroun changed tire at pits and finished third, 15.59s. behind the Stoddard. Stoddard faltered in the fifth and was passed by the Marmon. Livingston claimed he had radiator trouble. Stoddard was then lapped by Fiat and Darracq in fourteenth mile, and by Fiat again in the thirty-sixth mile, but finished race without stop, second to the Fiat. Isotta drove close to Marmon and Stoddard until seventh mile, when Isotta broke bearing between third cylinder piston rod and crank shaft and

Ralph De Palma (Below) After Winning Fifty-Mile Race, at the Motordrome yesterday. Above on the right is Harris Hanshue, the driver who was injured Sunday; beside him at the wheel is Leon T. Shettler, the Apperson agent.

NECK AND NECK.

## BINOCULAR WINS FEATURE RACE.

THISTLE BELLE OUTGAMED IN THE CLOSING STRIDES.

**Modesworth Rides First Winner When He Lands Oceanshore in Front in Mile Drive—Goldfinn Exonerated on Showing in the Early Stages of Race by Judges.**

[ASSOCIATED PRESS NIGHT REPORT.]

OAKLAND, April 13.—Thistle Belle in the feature event was beaten a head by Binocular, which closed with a rush. Molesworth rode his first winner here when he landed Oceanshore in front. Owing to the fact that Goldfinn did not run any better in the early stages of her race today, Gross was exonerated by the stewards.

Five furlongs, selling: Sainest, 105 (Selden,) won; Mollie Montrose, 108 (Shale,) second; Amethyst, 113 (Thomas,) third; time, 1:07 3-5. Arthur Hyman, Burning Bush, Swagerlator, Sir Barry, Bonnie Reg, Banrose, Father Downey, Angelface and Salomy Jane finished as named.

Five and one-half furlongs, selling: Argonaut, 115 (Mentry,) won; Tramotor, 115 (Coburn,) second; Emma G, 108 (Gargan,) third; time, 1:08. Creston, E. M. Fry, Cotytto, Bill Kinney, and Paul Clifford finished as named.

Mile, selling: Dixie Dixon, 87 (Thomas,) won; French Cook, 109 (Mentry,) second; Hush Money, 109 (Taylor,) third; time, 1:41 4-5. Tremargo, Rubric, Morling, J. C. Clem, Cobleskill and Mr. Bishop finished as named.

Futurity course, selling: Binocular, 96 (Selden,) won; Thistle Belle, 104 (Williams,) second; Goldfinn, 109 (Mentry,) third; time, 1:10. Sewell, Balronia and Banorella finished as named.

Mile, selling: Oceanshore, 101 (Molesworth,) won; Cocksure, 103 (Williams,) second; Hampass, 100 (Koris,) third; time, 1:41 4-5. Colbert, Gene Russell, Silver Line, Dorothy Ledgett, Birth, Lady Rensselaer and Eudora finished as named.

Futurity course, selling: Ilex, 103 (Selden,) won; Gelico, 93 (Callaghan,) second; Lord Clinton, 104 (Williams,) third; time, 1:11 1-5. Silk Calopes, Clara Sal, Eddie Graney, Estelle M., Roberta and Alder Gulch also ran.

THURSDAY'S ENTRIES.

Futurity course, selling: Rey el Tovar, Siscus, 108; Passenger, 107; Juan, Pride of Lismore, Gramercy, 105; Camera, 103; W. V. Brumby, 100; Glare, 99; Galene Gale, 98.

Four furlongs, selling: Ban Ann, 107; Bessie C., 106; Lacamargue, 105; Emory K., 104; Ard Lake, 103; Abella, West Point, 100; Joe Wells, Lady M. M., 99; Othalo, 95; Kiefer, 92.

Mile and twenty yards, selling: Aftermath, Goldway, Don Enrique, Wolfville, 112; French Cook, 111; Orilene, Livius, 110; Giles, Mike Jordan, 107; Spring Ban, 105; Nasmerito, 103; Contra Costa, 90.

Five furlongs, handicap: Cloudlight, 112; Likely Dieudonne, 107; Nagazam, Meddling Hannah, 100; Napa Nick, 98; Fern L., 92; Kid North, 86.

Mile and twenty yards, selling: Pickaway, Cataline, Kaiserhoff, 112; Mattie Mack, 110; Tiflis, Right Sort, 108; Theo Case, My Pal, 107; Melton Cloth, 103; Lanita, 101; Silver Grain, 95; Tom O'Malley, 87.

lerd, 112; Ampedo, St. Francis, 110; Marse Abe, 109; Father Stafford, Faneuil Hall, 108; Banonica, Airs, 107; Balnade, 105; Anne McGee, Gretchen G., 104.

JAMESTOWN STRUGGLES.

KING WINS HANDICAP.

[ASSOCIATED PRESS NIGHT REPORT.]

JAMESTOWN (Va.) April 13.—Five furlongs: Laughing Eyes won, Demetros second, Fire Brand third; time 1:04 3-5.

Four furlongs: Maromara won, May Weed second, Jack Ryan third; time 0:51 3-5.

Handicap, five and one-half furlongs: King of Yolo won, Plantland second, Howlet third; time 1:11 2-5.

Five furlongs: Grenade won, Racing Belle second, Amorel third; time 1:01 4-5.

Mile: Lois Cavanaugh won, Dander second, Smug third; time 1:44 2-5.

For hunters, under auspices of Norfolk Hunt Club, six furlongs: Jim won, Garret second, Monsoon third; time 1:23.

JACKSONVILLE CARD.

HOFFMAN DEFEATED.

[ASSOCIATED PRESS NIGHT REPORT.]

JACKSONVILLE, April 13.—The feature of today's races was the defeat of Hoffman in the main event by Ethon.

Five and one-half furlongs: Lista won, Inferno Queen second, Hurlock third; time 1:08.

Four furlongs: Renovator won, Chess second, Grand Peggy third; time 0:49 1-5.

Six furlongs: M. J. Whelon won, Herksman second, Fay O. third; time 1:14 2-5.

Six furlongs: Ethon won, Hoffman second, Eye White third; time 1:11 4-5.

Six furlongs: Elizabethan won, Morpeth second, McLeod F. third; time 1:14 3-5.

Six furlongs: Chilla won, Begone second, Bonnie Bard third; time 1:13 3-5.

Mile and one-sixteenth: Mystifier won, Jack Right second, El Oro third; time, 1:47 2-5.

ANGELENO IS FREE.

LAWTON (Okla.) April 13.—Indictments against Carroll W. Gates, a Los Angeles millionaire, on a charge of conspiracy to defraud the government out of thirteen sections of land in Northwest Oklahoma, and civil suits to recover the land, were dismissed here today by Assistant United States Attorney Zimmerman.

Flying: Racing: Shooting: Fishing: Ball.

Part III—In the Field of Outdoor Sports.

# The Los Angeles Times

The Pink Sheet—4 Pages—Illustrated.

XXXth YEAR. FRIDAY MORNING, OCTOBER 27, 1911. PRICE: [illegible]



# MACK'S ATHLETICS WIN WORLD'S CHAMPIONSHIP

**Dick Wayne,**

A featherweight of brilliant promise, who will box Chester Moss tomorrow in the preliminaries.

No Fights.

## EXHIBITIONS IN MILWAUKEE.

### FIGHTING BARRED BUT GORE SHOW IS O.K.

*Gus Christie and Maurice Sayers Go Six Rounds to Draw—Preliminaries Sprinkle Gore Freely. Four Four-Round and One Six-Round Contest Make Up Bill.*

[BY DIRECT WIRE TO THE TIMES.]

MILWAUKEE, Oct. 26.—[Exclusive Dispatch.] Although the Wolgast-McFarland fight was forbidden by the Sheriff a few weeks ago the Cathedral Athletic Club, an organization of young men in the gymnasium attached to St. John's Catholic Cathedral, tonight staged an exhibition boxing match between Gus Christie and Maurice Sayers, who went a six-round draw. Some of the preliminaries were bloody affairs.

The announcers were careful to announce the different bouts as exhibition glove contests, but some of the preliminaries were real fights, if it takes a nose bleed induced by a poke to the nose, to constitute a boxing exhibition a fight.

Mark Connedy was roughly handled by "Yub" Rice, another youngster, the boys drawing blood plentifully from each other and applause equally plentiful from the spectators.

Battling Dempsey and Bill Driscoll boxed a draw in the semi-windup. There were four four-round bouts and one of six rounds.

TO USE NEW GRIDIRON

LONG BEACH, Oct. 26.—The first game of football to be played on the new gridiron at the Polytechnic School here will take place Saturday afternoon of this week, when the local High School eleven will go up against the school team from Ontario. Great interest in this first game is shown among the students here.

Get 'Em Guessing.

## KIRKWOOD PUZZLE TO LOCAL BOXING FANS.

*On Eve of Big Fight With Rivers at Vernon, Question of Who Will Win Is Paramount—Rivers Has Everything to Gain by Winning and Will Make the Try of His Career.*

BY GREY OLIVER.

GEORGE KIRKWOOD, who is to battle with Young Rivers tomorrow afternoon at the Vernon Arena is a puzzle.

He is a department store clerk, a driver of a sprinkling wagon, a common laborer, prize-fighter, pool player and cashier for a bookmaker on a race track. His father and twin brothers worked for years on the boats of the Mississippi River.

Could you guess what this kind of a boy would be?

He might be a divinity student, a clerk in a candy store or an undertaker's assistant, but what is he?

A boxer who won the amateur championship of the South and the Pacific Coast; a boy who has fought twenty-five fights and lost but one decision and this was when he substituted for another fighter who could not toe the mark.

This is a very good record for any boy in the boxing game and yet the local fight bugs are willing to bet two to one that he will be beaten if the weather permits him to meet Joe Rivers in the Vernon Arena tomorrow aftrnoon.

"Of course this betting proposition does not effect me in the least," declared Kirkwood yesterday in his room at the St. Ignatius Club at Aliso and Anderson streets where he is training. "I wouldn't care if he was a million to one. That doesn't make him win."

And Kirkwood laughed. Now whenever you see a boxer laugh without being afraid that someone is watching him it is generally a foregone conclusion that he is not much afraid of what may happen.

"Of course I'm a fighter for that's my business and I like it. I expect to stay in the business too, even if I lose. I'm from Missouri and have got to be shown why I should not stick at it. I was born in St. Louis twenty-three years ago and have been fighting only three years.

HOW HE STARTED.

"When I was a kid I used to work in a department store in St. Louis and my father and my two twin brothers worked on the boats on the Mississippi River. Father had a pair of boxing gloves on his boat and used to bring 'em home at night and tried to get my brothers to box. They wouldn't do it because they did not care for it.

"When he found this out he tried to get me into it. I was only 8 years old then and he used to put the gloves on and get down on his hands and knees and putting the other pair on my hands he would have me box with him. I did that night after night just to please him and then I got to liking it.

"However, I didn't think much of it at that but I used to go to the amateur shows frequently. I was about 16 years old then. One night some fellow was not on hand to box and some fellow who knew I had boxed a little told the manager about me and he asked me to go on. I did and beat the boy easily. He never laid a glove on me.

"After that I went on frequently and won six fights right off the reel. Later on I went to Louisville and knocked two fellows out in a series of bouts for the championship of the South and won the title. In 1909 I went to the Seattle Exposition and won the Coast title for amateurs, knocking out one fellow and getting the decision over another. Then I went back to St. Louis and beat Oliver Kirk who won the championship at the St. Louis Fair. After that I went to San Francisco."

Kirkwood does not hand out this dope with any apparent desire to boost himself, but gives it merely as a bunch of facts, which he says can easily be verified. He is far from being a typical fighter. He is more of the Freddie Welsh gentleman style. He has a rather soft voice and none of the Jim Flynn or Bat Nelson swagger.

Whether or not he can fight is another thing. He knocked the life out of Rivers in the first round of their four-round bout in San Francisco, but Rivers stalled out the four rounds and got a draw. He is not a boxer and is not hard to hit, but he has a right counter that is said to be a wonder. He is weak on the defense. So was Bat Nelson, but he generally won if anyone would fight instead of box.

FINE LARGE RECORD.

Kirk has lost but one in twenty-five, so he says, and this entitles him to more than passing notice, although he has never fought more than ten rounds. Preliminary boys around San Francisco do not get a longer chance than that. He has beaten Johnny Roach, Jimmy Carroll, Charles Rodgers, Roy Moore, Billy Canole, Ray Baughman, Marty Kane, Jimmy Melville and Eddie Weber and some of the sports from San Francisco declare that he was fighting stronger in the tenth round of some of his bouts than in the first. This proves that any fighter can generally go the distance he trains for.

Whether or not Kirkwood has the class remains to be seen. Like Nelson, he is a slow beginner and does not carry the fight to his man. He wants it carried to him, but they do say he is some infighter and can hit a hard blow. Any boy who has driven a sprinkling wagon, worked in a department store and paid off tickets at the rear door of a bookmaker's box should be strong in both his head and his hands.

The dope favors Rivers tomorrow, for he is both a good boxer and a hard hitter, but he may be treated to another Kilbane surprise and he may have the easiest picking in the world. Kirkwood is down to weight, while it is reported that Rivers will be kept busy making 123 pounds, which is the weight agreed upon. If Kirkwood is nervous, he did not show it yesterday, when I saw him working at the St. Ignatius Club.

He is not favored by the sports, because he is unknown here, but everyone will want to see him in action just to find out if he is a bear. He is hairy enough to be one. Withal he is a pleasant fellow to meet and his sister, Mrs. Carter, in this city, and his mother back in old St. Louis will be the most anxious women in the country until they hear what may happen tomorrow afternoon.

### KIRKWOOD READY FOR JOE RIVERS.

Joe Rivers and George Kirkwood did practically nothing of any consequence yesterday in the training line for their scheduled bout tomorrow afternoon at the Vernon Arena.

Rivers was the busy one of the two for he boxed with two of his sparring partners in the afternoon at Doyle's Vernon camp and seemed to be in fine shape. He looks to be as good as ever and his many friends maintain that he will win in jig time tomorrow. He says he will be down to the stipulated weight of 123 pounds and if

(Continued on Fourth Page.)

**"Chief" Bender,**

Phenomenal pitcher of the Athletics whose wonderful work was a feature of the world series games.

Score 13 to 2.

## ATHLETICS WIN SERIES WITH INDIAN TWIRLER.

*Philadelphian Victory Makes Mack's Men Twice the World's Champions—Games Set New Record for Attendance and Gate Receipts—Quaker Players Get Over Three Thousand Apiece for Their Share.*

[BY A. P. NIGHT WIRE TO THE TIMES.]

ALL RECORDS for attendance and receipts for a world's championship series were broken. The National Baseball Commission tonight gave out the following figures:

Attendance 179,851.

Total receipts $342,364.30.

Of this amount the players received $127,910.61.

Each club received $90,108.72, and the National Commission's share was $34,236.25.

PHILADELPHIA, Oct. 26.—Hail! Philadelphia Athletics champions of the world for the second successive year.

In an exhibition of batting seldom seen in a premier baseball series the American League team defeated New York today in the sixth game of the series by the overwhelming score of 13 to 2, thus giving them the four necessary games out of the six played to carry off baseball's greatest honor.

It was more than a mere defeat for the Giants. It was a rout.

With the victory goes 60 per cent. of $127,910.61, or $76,746.37, of which each athletic player will receive $3654.59.

The losers will receive the remainder, $51,164.24, or $2436.39 for each New York player.

Coming from behind after New York had scored one run in the first inning, the Athletics tied the score in the third, won the game in the fourth by making four runs, made it a little safer in the sixth when they added another run, and crushed the Giants in the seventh under an avalanche of seven hits, which with a couple of misplays, added seven more runs to the total.

SENSATIONAL HITTING.

The sensational hitting of all the pitchers the New Yorkers sent into the box aroused the excited crowds to the greatest enthusiasm. With victory in their grasp, the Athletics appeared to let down, and when the seventh inning was over, the cheering thousands started to leave the grounds.

The struggling National League champions sent in three pitchers to stem the tide, but all were hit almost alike, Wiltse getting the worst whaling. The two others were Ames, who started the game, and Marquard, who followed Wiltse into the box.

Thirteen hits for a total of seventeen bases was the record shown by the hit column when the game was over. Every member of the team got a bingle with the exception of Collins and Bender, but the former made a timely sacrifice that helped to score a run.

When the game began, Catcher Thomas was the only member of the White Elephant team that had not made a hit in the series. He got into the honor column in the seventh inning and the Athletic players themselves cheered Thomas.

Murray of the New York team is the only one of its regulars who failed to connect with any Athletic pitcher in the series for a hit.

To "Chief" Bender, the wonderful Chippewa Indian twirler, goes the credit of pitching the final victory. His work in the box surpassed the exhibition he gave in the first game on the polo grounds in New York. Three singles and a double were all the New Yorks could garner off his delivery.

The two base hit was made by Doyle in the first inning, and he scored later when Murphy muffed an easy fly. From this time, the Indian was never in trouble. New York got a single in the third and one in the fifth. In the ninth Bender appeared to let down and let Herzog hit him, and subsequently scored. It was the third game Bender pitched, and his second [illegible] in the three days.

PLENTY OF ERRORS.

Despite the terrific hitting by the Athletics and the fact that a total of eight errors were made by the two teams, the game was brilliantly played. Numerous spectacular [illegible] brought the cheering crowd to its feet.

Devore, left fielder for New York, robbed Lord of a three-base hit by a great sprint, catching his long fly in center field. Baker and Davis made sensational running catches of [illegible] flies and Collins electrified the spectators by a stop and throw of a terrific grounder back of second base that no one thought he could reach.

The Philadelphia team was charged with five errors and all of them were made on the easiest kind of chances. Two of New York's three errors were wild throws, which virtually started its downfall.

The crowd that saw the Athletics win the championship was the smallest of the series, numbering 20,[illegible], but what it lacked in numbers was made up in enthusiasm. There was little noise until the third inning, when the Athletics tied the score, and when the home team cut loose in the fourth and subsequent rounds, there was never a let-up in the cheering.

Every player was given a rousing hand-clapping as he stepped to the plate, rank errors were overlooked, and finally the Athletics so far outclassed the Giants in the hitting department that the crowd began to cheer in derision every time an Athletic player was thrown out by a New York man.

The fourth inning was noisy, but it was nothing compared to the seventh, when ten Athletics stepped to the plate to take a crack at the pitching.

CHEERS FOR WINNERS.

A bit of sentiment on the part of Capt. Harry Davis was cheered when he sent the injured McInnes [illegible] the game in the ninth. "Stuffy" took the last put-out and officially figured in the series.

"Chief" Meyers retired near the end of the game in favor of Wilson, probably for the same reason.

Before the game began it looked as though Plank would be the pitcher and there was some surprise among the enthusiasts when Connie Mack sent Bender into the box. The "chief" proved he could pitch more than twice a week.

Philadelphia made nine hits and eleven runs in the two feature innings of the game.

In the fourth, with the score a tie, Baker opened the inning with a slashing single to center field. The crowd called on Murphy to bring him around and he almost did it by landing Baker on third with a single to center field. The veteran Davis then came up and hit a grounder to Doyle, who threw to the plate, but Baker was in with the run by a beautiful slide under Meyers.

This run gave the home team the lead.

With none out, Barry laid down a bunt and, in fielding the ball to first, Ames hit Barry on the head and the ball rolled out to right field. [illegible] play and Davis rounded the bases to the plate. Barry put on steam and started to sprint to second. [illegible] made a poor throw to catch the [illegible]

(Continued on Second Page.)

## WORLD'S SERIES IN SEASONS PAST; SCORE: NATIONAL 4, AMERICAN 4.

**1903.**

The first series ever played between the respective champions of the American and National leagues started at Boston, October 1, 1903. Pittsburgh, the National champs, and the Boston Americans being the contenders. Boston won five of the eight games played as follows:

| Clubs—Where played. | Score. | Attend. |
|---|---|---|
| Pitts.-Boston, at Boston | 7-3 | 16,242 |
| Boston-Pitts., at Boston | 3-0 | 9,415 |
| Pitts.-Boston, at Boston | 4-2 | 18,801 |
| Pitts.-Boston, at Pittsburgh | 5-4 | 7,600 |
| Boston-Pitts., at Pittsburgh | 11-2 | 12,322 |
| Boston-Pitts., at Pittsburgh | 6-3 | 11,556 |
| Boston-Pitts., at Pittsburgh | 7-3 | 17,038 |
| Boston-Pitts., at Boston | 3-0 | 7,455 |
| Total receipts over $50,000. | | 100,429 |

The members of the Boston team at that time were Dineen, Hughes, Young, Gibson and Winters, pitchers; Criger and Farrell, catchers; Lachance, first base; Ferris, second base; Parent, shortstop; Collins, third base; Dougherty, left field; Stahl, center field; Freeman, right field.

The Pittsburgh players were Leever, Phillippi, and Kennedy, pitchers; Phelps and Smith, catchers; Bransfield, first base; Ritchey, second base; Wagner, shortstop; Leach, third base; Clarke, left field; Beaumont, center field; Sebring, right field.

**1905.**

In 1904, there were no post-season games, but the year following, the Philadelphia Athletics and the New York Giants came together with the following results:

| Clubs—Where played. | Scr. | Attend. | Rcts. |
|---|---|---|---|
| N. Y.-Ath., at Phil. | 3-0 | 17,955 | $12,[illegible] |
| Ath.-N. Y., at N. Y. | 3-0 | 24,992 | 18,[illegible] |
| N. Y.-Ath., at Phil. | 9-0 | 10,991 | [illegible] |
| N. Y.-Ath., at N. Y. | 1-0 | 13,598 | [illegible] |
| N. Y.-Ath., at N. Y. | 2-0 | 24,187 | 17,[illegible] |
| Totals | | 91,723 | [illegible] |

The winners' roster read Mathewson and McGinnity, pitchers; Bresnahan and Bowerman, catchers; McGann, first base; Gilbert, second base; Dahlen, shortstop; Devlin, third base; Mertes, left field; Donlin, center field; Strang and Browne, right field.

The Athletic players were Bender, Plank and Coakley, pitchers; Powers, catcher; Davis, first base; Murphy, second base; M. Cross, shortstop; L. Cross, third base; Hartsel, left field; Hoffman, center field; Seybold, right field.

**1906.**

In 1906, the Cubs, under Chance, won their first pennant, but were defeated by the White Sox in the series.

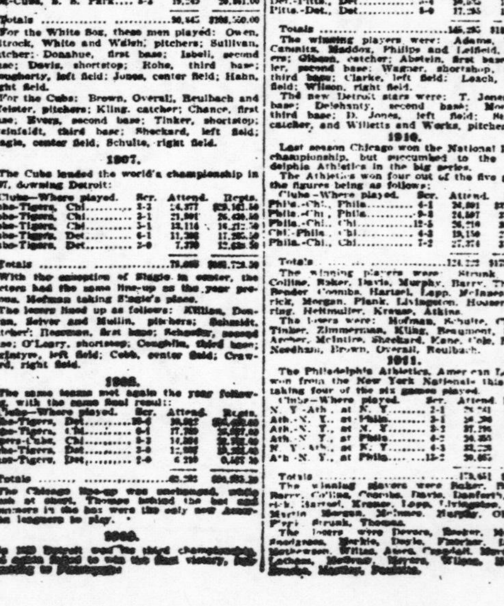

| Clubs—Where played. | Scr. | Attend. | Repts. |
|---|---|---|---|
| Sox-Cubs, W. S. Park | 2-1 | 12,693 | $13,919.00 |
| Cubs-Sox, S. S. Park | 7-1 | 12,595 | 13,[illegible].00 |
| Sox-Cubs, W. S. Park | 3-0 | 13,667 | 14,066.50 |
| Cubs-Sox, S. S. Park | 1-0 | 18,384 | 19,249.50 |
| Sox-Cubs, W. S. Park | 8-6 | 23,257 | 22,[illegible].00 |
| Sox-Cubs, S. S. Park | 8-3 | 19,249 | 20,[illegible].00 |
| Totals | | 99,845 | $106,550.00 |

For the White Sox, these men played: Owen, Altrock, White and Walsh, pitchers; Sullivan, catcher; Donahue, first base; Isbell, second base; Davis, shortstop; Rohe, third base; Dougherty, left field; Jones, center field; Hahn, right field.

For the Cubs: Brown, Overall, Reulbach and Pfeister, pitchers; Kling, catcher; Chance, first base; Evers, second base; Tinker, shortstop; Steinfeldt, third base; Sheckard, left field; Slagle, center field, Schulte, right field.

**1907.**

The Cubs landed the world's championship in 1907, downing Detroit:

| Clubs—Where played. | Scr. | Attend. | Repts. |
|---|---|---|---|
| Cubs-Tigers, Chi | 3-3 | 24,377 | $23,161.50 |
| Cubs-Tigers, Chi | 3-1 | 21,901 | 26,420.50 |
| Cubs-Tigers, Chi | 5-1 | 13,114 | 16,[illegible].50 |
| Cubs-Tigers, Det | 6-1 | 11,306 | 17,[illegible].50 |
| Cubs-Tigers, Det | 2-0 | 7,370 | 12,[illegible].50 |
| Totals | | 78,[illegible] | $[illegible].50 |

With the exception of Slagle in center, the victors had the same line-up as the year previous, Hofman taking Slagle's place.

The losers lined up as follows: Killian, Donovan, Seiver and Mullin, pitchers; Schmidt, catcher; Rossman, first base; Schaefer, second base; O'Leary, shortstop; Coughlin, third base; McIntyre, left field; Cobb, center field; Crawford, right field.

**1908.**

The same teams met again the year following, with the same final result:

| Clubs—Where played. | Scr. | Attend. | Repts. |
|---|---|---|---|
| Cubs-Tigers, Det | 10-6 | [illegible] | [illegible] |
| Cubs-Tigers, Chi | 6-1 | 17,760 | [illegible] |
| Tigers-Cubs, Chi | 8-3 | 14,[illegible] | [illegible] |
| Cubs-Tigers, Det | 3-0 | 12,[illegible] | [illegible] |
| Cubs-Tigers, Det | 2-0 | 6,210 | [illegible] |
| Totals | | 62,[illegible] | $[illegible] |

The Chicago line-up was unchanged, while Bush at short, Thomas behind the bat and Summers in the box were the only new American leaguers to play.

**1909.**

In 1909 Detroit won its third championship and again failed to win the final victory, succumbing to Pittsburgh.

| Clubs—Where played. | Scr. | Attend. | Repts. |
|---|---|---|---|
| Pitts.-Det., Pitts | 4-1 | 29,264 | $40,271.50 |
| Det.-Pitts., Pitts | 7-2 | 30,915 | 41,[illegible] |
| Pitts-Det., Det | 8-6 | 18,277 | 20,476.00 |
| Det.-Pitts., Det | 5-0 | 17,036 | 21,[illegible].00 |
| Pitts.-Det., Pitts | 8-4 | 21,706 | [illegible] |
| Det.-Pitts., Det | 5-4 | 10,535 | 12,517.50 |
| Pitts.-Det., Det | 8-0 | 17,[illegible] | 19,677.00 |
| Totals | | 145,[illegible] | $188,302.50 |

The winning players were: Adams, Willis, Camnitz, Maddox, Philips and Leifield, pitchers; Gibson, catcher; Abstein, first base; Miller, second base; Wagner, shortstop, Byrne, third base; Clarke, left field; Leach, center field; Wilson, right field.

The new Detroit stars were: T. Jones, first base; Delehanty, second base; Moriarity, third base; D. Jones, left field; Stanage, catcher, and Willetts and Works, pitchers.

**1910.**

Last season Chicago won the National League championship, but succumbed to the Philadelphia Athletics in the big series.

The Athletics won four out of the five games, the figures being as follows:

| Clubs—Where played. | Scr. | Attend. | Repts. |
|---|---|---|---|
| Phila.-Chi., Phila | 4-1 | 26,891 | $37,[illegible] |
| Phila.-Chi., Phila | 9-3 | 24,597 | 35,137.00 |
| Phila.-Chi., Chi | 12-5 | 26,210 | 36,751.50 |
| Chi.-Phila., Chi | 4-3 | 19,150 | 27,[illegible].50 |
| Phila.-Chi., Chi | 7-2 | 27,374 | 37,116.50 |
| Totals | | 124,222 | $173,980.00 |

The winning players were: Strunk, Lord, Collins, Baker, Davis, Murphy, Barry, Thomas, Bender, Coombs, Hartsel, Lapp, McInnes, Derrick, Morgan, Plank, Livingston, Houser, Oldring, Heitmuller, Krause, Atkins.

The losers were: Hofman, Schulte, Chance, Tinker, Zimmerman, Kling, Beaumont, Evers, Archer, McIntire, Sheckard, Kane, Cole, Richie, Needham, Brown, Overall, Reulbach.

**1911.**

The Philadelphia Athletics, American League, won from the New York Nationals this year, taking four of the six games played.

| Clubs—Where played. | Scr. | Attend. | Repts. |
|---|---|---|---|
| N. Y.-Ath., at N. Y. | 2-1 | 38,[illegible] | $77,[illegible] |
| Ath.-N. Y., at Phila | 3-1 | 26,286 | 42,[illegible] |
| Ath.-N. Y., at N. Y. | 3-2 | 37,216 | 75,[illegible] |
| Ath.-N. Y., at Phila | 4-2 | 24,355 | 40,[illegible] |
| N. Y.-Ath., at N. Y. | 4-3 | 33,228 | [illegible] |
| Ath.-N. Y., at Phila | 13-2 | 20,485 | 30,[illegible] |
| Totals | | 179,851 | $342,364 |

The winning players were Baker, Bender, Barry, Collins, Coombs, Davis, Danforth, Derrick, Hartsel, Krause, Lapp, Livingston, Lord, Martin, Morgan, McInnes, Murphy, Oldring, Plank, Strunk, Thomas.

The losers were Devore, Becker, Murray, Snodgrass, Merkle, Doyle, Fletcher, Devlin, Mathewson, Wiltse, Ames, Crandall, Marquard, Latham, McGraw, Meyers, Wilson, Herzog, Drucke, [illegible]

The Los Angeles Times

*The Pink Sheet—4 Pages—Illustrated.*

XXXI[ST] YEAR. MONDAY MORNING, JULY 8, 1912. PRICE: Single Copies, on Streets and Trains, 5 Cents. Per Month, Per Copy, Delivered, 2½ Cents.

World Beaters.

# AMERICAN TEAM HAS BIG DAY.

*Sprinters Make Clean Sweeps in Century Dash.*

*Thorpe Wins Pentathlon; Donahue Third.*

*Jumpers and Long-Distance Runners in Front.*

[By Atlantic Cable and by Wireless from Chicago to The Times.]

BY JAMES H. RANDALL.

STOCKHOLM, July 7.—Realizing their determination to astonish the natives of the Olympic stadium, the American team signalized the second day's athletic tournament by a clean sweep of the 100-meters race and a bumper crop of other notable victories.

Ralph H. Craig won the century in 10 4-5s, Alvin T. Meyer was second, and Donald F. Lippincott, the record-breaker of Saturday, was third.

This wholesale triumph of the Americans created the wildest enthusiasm and not a little heart-burning among the vanquished.

"Yankee Doodle," played not indifferently by one of the bands, was given in compliment to the prides of the sprinting track, who left the rest of the world's athletes bunched among the "also rans."

Duke Kahanamoku came home first in the second heat of the 100 meters swimming race, free style, doing the acquatic sprint in 1m., 3 4-5s. James Thorpe won the Pentathlon, having only nine points recorded against him in the running broad jump, throwing the javeline and the discuses and the 200 and 1500-meters race. Third honors in this event were captured by a lad from Los Angeles, James J. Donohue, with twenty-nine points. George L. Horine and five other Americans were among the eleven who qualified for the finals in the running high jump.

Right down the card the Americans covered themselves with honors and their superiority, team for team, is now placed beyond dispute. The boys were keyed up to the last note of tension, each encouraged the other. Tonight they are jubilant and they are heroes among the people of this city.

MARVEL AT HORINE.

Horine's jumping style took the breath of the onlookers away from them. He is in magnificent form and when he crossed the lathe at a clear horizontal by a simultaneous impulse, the silent Swedes burst out with a "whew," which sounded like a scream of a thousand sirens.

While the day was perfect for the field and track sports in the stadium, the bicycle racers, sent away at 2 o'clock in the morning, found everything against them. The roads were in bad shape and the hills were numerous and steep. One hundred and twenty cyclists, representing almost every nationality, started on the long 200-mile race round Lake Maelar. Among them were six Americans, John Becht, Empire City Wheelmen; Alvin Loftus, Providence, R. I., attached to the New York Athletic Club; Carl O. Shutte, Kansas City, attached to the St. Louis Cycling Club; W. C. Martin, St. Louis Cycling Club; Jerome Steinert, Atlas Bicycle Club, and Jesse Pike, Century Road Club of America.

With the race two-thirds over, about half of the starters were still riding. Lewis, the representative of South Africa, held the lead, while John Becht, Alvin Loftus and Carl Shutte were among the first twenty-five.

No prettier sprinting race has been run at any Olympic contest than was the 100-meter dash. Four Americans, Meyer, Craig, Belote and Lippincott, went to the tape.

Only one competitor, G. H. Patching, the South African crack, was there from another country to make the Americans extend themselves.

At the first start, Patching and Belote beat the pistol and were called back. Five times the five men in their tense nervousness were off before the pistol crack. Then they started with the crack of the pistol as one man. On an absolutely level line they flashed down the cinder path.

CRAIG FORGES AHEAD.

Not one man forged a hairsbreadth ahead of the other until Ralph Craig, calling upon his best strength, burst ahead and fell across the line, the winner by a foot. How the others finished only the officials could say exactly, from the stands they seemed to be running a perfectly dead heat. The American flag flashed to the top of the mast, showing that the United States had carried off another prize.

Great interest centered in the running high jump trials. The American team was confident of qualifying most of their men and they did. Six of the eleven who qualified by clearing

(Continued on Fourth Page.)

## OFFER AD $32,500 TO FIGHT PACKY.

Ad Wolgast received a telegram from William O'Day yesterday offering him $32,500 to fight Packy McFarland in San Francisco on Labor Day.

He also received two different offers—each of $20,000—to fight Rivers in Sacramento.

He says he will not return a definite answer until he hears from Joe Rivers relative to a fight on Labor Day.

"I can fight Packy any time," he says, "but this Mexican won't last long. If I don't get a fight with him this summer some one else will put him out of business."

## *Yankees Invincible in Olympiad.*

American Athletes Who Shone Yesterday at Stockholm.

"Duke" Kahanamoku, the Hawaiian swimmer, broke a world's record in the 100-meter swim. Jim Thorpe, the Carlisle Indian, won the pentathlon, the five-event competition, and James Donahue of this city, "our Jim," took second. Melvin Sheppard, the veteran middle-distance runner, was slightly off color, but he did the work.

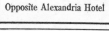

## WHIFFS FROM THE OLD SPORT PIPE

A pleasant custom was inaugurated yesterday at the Los Angeles Athletic Club. Hereafter ladies will be admitted to the main dining-room every Sunday night between 6 and 8 o'clock.

Although yesterday was the first time, the dining-room was filled with handsomely gowned women and their escorts. Several members entertained supper parties.

The House Committee announces that the "Sunday suppers" are frankly an experiment, to be discontinued if unpopular. The indications are that they will become a charming feature of club life.

**Ad Saw Fight.**

Ad Wolgast had a chance to take in the Rivers-Wolgast fight yesterday. The finished moving pictures were put on at the studio at Edendale.

The champ was immensely pleased with them.

"You can see clearly the whole fracas at the end," he said. "Jack Welsh not only counted Rivers out, but took about twelve seconds to count ten. The pictures show that I didn't commit a foul. I took three or four cracks at the Mexican's stomach; then missed with my right and fell over on top of him with my legs spread wide apart. Instead of the referee picking me up, the pictures show that I grabbed hold of him to keep from falling."

**Not Edifying.**

The employment of Larry Sullivan as announcer at Vernon on the Fourth was a somewhat amusing diversion, but Larry as a fixture will do the fight game no good here. His record in connection with fights and other things is not one that will adorn the fight game in this or any other town.

**Undulating Bill.**

Bill Tozer, the pitcher, always makes me think of Maude Allen, the classical dancer. When he runs bases Bill's arms wave and undulate as he floats along. If the orchestra should strike "The Spring Song," I always feel perfectly certain that Bill would waft, with witching grace, clear around the bases for a home run.

After More Honors.

# TETZLAFF TO RACE AT PORTLAND TOMORROW.

[BY DIRECT WIRE TO THE TIMES.]

PORTLAND (Or.) July 7.—[Exclusive Dispatch.] A two days' automobile racing meet will open here Tuesday with Teddy Tetzlaff and Barney Oldfield as star performers. The Country Club dirt track will be the scene of the races and coming with Oldfield are Heinmann, with a Benz, and Bill Fritch, Cino factory pilot. The Fiat team includes, in addition to Tetzlaff, Hewlett, Verbeck, Hill and Maggio.

Eight events will be on the programme each day. The races will be from five to 151 miles in length. Among the local drivers who will compete are Frank Tauscher, H. J. Groat and Dundee. Tauscher will drive his special Cole racer. Groat will pilot a Stearns, and Dundee will drive the famous "Whistling Billie," a White creation.

The advance guard of the racing contingent has arrived in the person of Jimmy Rogers, aviator and auto pilot.

Rogers immediately set to work campaigning for a series of free-for-all races in an effort to secure the presence of Ralph Mulford, Hughie Hughes, and other international drivers, in addition to the Tetzlaff-Oldfield squads contracted for by the officials of the speed carnival.

Golf Honors.

# FRANK WADE IS THE NEW CHAMPION AT BEVERLY.

BY ALMA WHITAKER.

FRANK WADE defeated H. N. H. Woodcock in the finals for the San Gabriel Country Club championship yesterday by three up and two to play.

It must be confessed that the new champion has sprung a surprise upon us, for there were very few who believed that he could defeat Woodcock in such a close match. That Woodcock might conceivably have been off his usually brilliant game and thus fallen an easy prey to the steady golfer, was expected; but that a really close game in which Woodcock could in no wise be described as "off" should still see Wade the winner was a surprise indeed, and his success calls for heartiest congratulations.

In the morning round it was a ding-dong game all the way, neither player showing his best form, but with shining spots at intervals. The drive-off was not very prepossessing and they both missed short putts on the first green, halving the hole for five. Then Woodcock showed off with one of his fine drives, which Wade's skilful second shot counterbalanced and made them level for two. This, too, they subsequently halved for five par figures, Wade holing a very long putt.

Number 3 went to Woodcock for three, who made up for an indifferent drive with a good putt. From the fourth Woodcock's second shot was a gem and landed him dead for the hole, but alas, for human weakness, it took him two putts to get in. Wade on the other hand laid his third shot dead and holed it comfortably, thereby halving a hole in par 4, which had seemed practically in Woodcock's pocket.

The fifth, too, was halved for four, a par three, and both players took the sixth in six, par figures, playing neck and neck most of the way. The seventh went to Woodstock for three to Wade's five, leaving Woodcock two up, to which lead he added No. 8 in par figures. But Wade was in no wise abashed and he played imputurbally on with that consistent calm for which he is noted, with the result that his patience was rewarded at the next hole.

From the ninth Woodcock made a really dashing drive. Too dashed dashing, as he afterwards observed, for it bounded into the road with every intention of staying there, so that its owner picked up and conceded the hole, which Wade did in six. The champion followed this up with a neat three at the tenth, for which he holed a very long putt, leaving Woodcock's lead reduced to one up.

The eleventh trembled in the balance while Woodcock carefully—oh,

(Continued on Fourth Page.)

Even Break.

# NAGLE WINS ANOTHER GAME.

*Beats Oaks Because Angels Hit Ball Hard.*

*Tozer Loses Battle in First Three Innings.*

*Patterson and Moore Shine in Fielding.*

BY GREY OLIVER.

Los Angeles, 6; Oakland, 5. Morning game.

Oakland, 5; Los Angeles, 3. Afternoon game.

Couldn't be any hard feelings yesterday, for each team won a game.

Angels won in the morning because they hit Durbin for no less than eighteen swats and yet they had to have a ninth inning rally before they could do this. For this reason it was one of the most remarkable ball games ever seen in this section.

Just imagine a team getting eighteen hits and making but six runs. Do you get that? And if Dillon had not put in two extra batsmen the chances are that there would have been a tie game.

In the afternoon the Oaks got theirs early off Tozer and after he had lost the game Dillon stuck in Leverenz. Just why no one knows.

As a baseball proposition the morning game was the best, as it always is on Sunday. The Angels made more than twice as many hits as the Oaks and then had a hard time winning. At that they had to lug in two extra batsmen in the ninth inning and had not these made good hits the game would have ended in a tie.

Smith was thrown out of the morning game for kicking on a decision and Howard and Mitze made home runs. Aside from these the big thing of the game was Patterson's great left-handed catch of Smith's foul to the Christmas trees back of third in the seventh inning.

Durbin was the flinger Sharpe stuck in and although he was hit all over the lot he only failed to get by because the locals hit him in the ninth.

Nagle showed some of his old-time form for the locals by pitching an eight-hit game and he would have won with his mouth open had not Core dropped an easy fly in the eighth inning. This muff came with two out and allowed three runs to come in and as these tied the score the Angels had to play the ninth inning.

The Angels started off in the second with their first run on Metzer's pass and singles by Driscoll and Smith and the second one came in the fourth on three singles and a sacrifice.

Howard made the third run with his homer over the left fence in the sixth with two out and the fourth one came in the seventh from a single and steal by Core and hits by Moore and Metzger.

ANGELS ARE WEAK.

The Oaks could do nothing with Nagle after Mitze's homer in the second, until the eighth, when all kinds of runs poured in. Mitze and Durbin singled. Patterson lifted a fly to right field and Leard struck out. Then with two out and two men on Zacher beat out an infield hit, filling the bases. Coy slapped out a fly to Core in center and it was such an easy catch that Core muffed it and the three runners scored. Right after this Hetling whanged out a double to left center and Coy raced across the plate.

The situation looked very bad for the locals until they managed to tie the score in the last of the eighth on Nagle's single, Howard's infield out and a double by Core.

The Oaks could do nothing in their half of the ninth for the first three men up were easy outs. In the locals' half Metzger was an easy out at first and then Driscoll lined a single to center. Dillon got scared about this time and put in Brooks to bat for Smith. This bird responded by cracking out a double to left that put Driscoll on third. Then Page was put in to hit for Nagle and he lined a single over third that scored Driscoll with the winning run, there being but one out.

FAST MATINEE GAME.

The matinee contest was a fairly good one in the way of hitting for both Tozer and Killilay were touched for nine swats. Five off Tozer were made in the first three innings and

(Continued on Second Page.)

## PLAYERS WHO "JAW" TO BE "PINCHED."

[BY DIRECT WIRE TO THE TIMES.]

WALLA WALLA (Wash.) July 6.—[Exclusive Dispatch.] Umpires in the Western Tri-State League who officiate in games in this city in the future will have a sinecure hereafter as the result of an order issued yesterday.

Mayor A. J. Gillis instructed Chief of Police "Mike" Davis to arrest all players disputing an umpire's decision and charge them with disorderly conduct. The order is the result of a recent visit of the Mayor to a game, in which there was considerable "beefing."

During the contest, the Mayor's wife, who accompanied him, was struck by a bag of peanuts thrown by a bibulous fan. This act is expected to cause the issuing of "rules for rooting" by his honor in the near future.

*Flying: Racing: Shooting: Fishing: Ball.*

*Part III—In the Field of Outdoor Sports.*

The Los Angeles Times

*The Pink Sheet—4 Pages—Illustrated.*

XXXIst YEAR. TUESDAY MORNING, JULY 16, 1912. PRICE: Single Copies, on Streets and Trains, 5 Cents. Per Month, Per Copy, Delivered, 2½ Cents.

# OLYMPIC GAMES END WITH CHEERS FOR AMERICA.

C.D.Reidpath. E.R.Mercer.

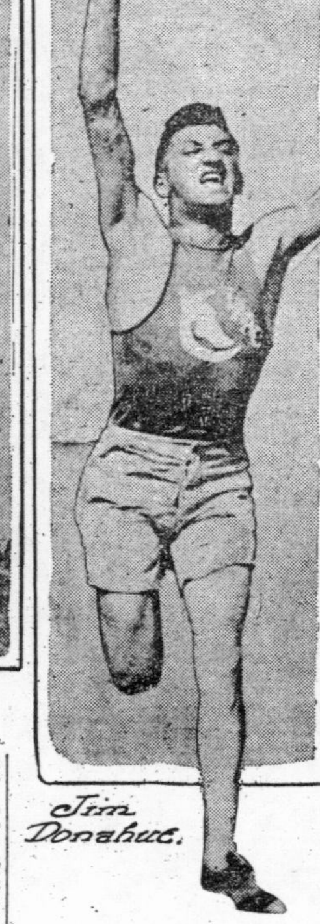

Jim Donahue.

Koehlemainen. James Thorpe.



Angels—Senators.

## P. O'ROURKE SPITS FIRE.

*Says Hap Hogan Will Get Busted on Jaw.*

*Angels Expect to Fatten on the Senators.*

*But Deacon Van Buren Says Nothing Doing.*

BY OWEN R. BIRD.

The Sacramento baseball team came rolling into our city last night in its usual good spirits, and when asked if it was feeling right the team responded that all was well and the same old stuff went this time as before and would until baseball was dead.

Manager Van Buren, the new leader of the Solons, was wearing that preoccupied air that all truly great men have when about to enter the field of battle.

"These Seraphs are going like wild fire," said Van Buren, "and to lick them we will have to hit out a good streak of speed." Van is like Jimmie Johnson, Owen Moran's manager, who always boosts the other fellow, so if anything happens on the unlooked-for slate there will be a good alibi in the ice box.

Patsy O'Rourke, the former manager of the Senators, and who now is just playing second base to while the time away until he settles in his own mind which offer he will take from the other clubs that are after his number, said the team was in fair shape, but was having a slight slump, only he did not say "slight."

The heavers that are going the best with the up-State men are Spider Baum, Arrelanes and Schwenck. Baum is the steady one of the bunch, while the others named seem to have a lot on the ball. The team as a whole is not hitting up to par now, but they say that they always find the batting eye while here, so have no fear of Cap Dillon's pets. All this will be proven during the next six days.

PATSY SPEAKS.

After leaving the hotel the bunch scattered, and O'Rourke went to Hap Hogan's, where he began to demonstrate how to play fifty-ball straight pool. After breaking and making a ten-ball run, and then, sluffing off with some really rotten shots, he leaned on his cue and, with the light streaming over his flaming red necktie, said: "I always get a bum jinx in this Hogan place, 'cause I always come up here with red in me glim. That Irishman gets on my nerves and there is nothing I like better than to mix with him on the field."

"Yes, some day you will get the hook for about five weeks from the president," said one of the players, looking on. "Who, me?" said Pat. "No, you got me mixed with some of the other guys. Say, any time that Hogan gets fresh I get right after him and you don't see him tearing my can off, do you? No, and he never will.

GOES TOO FER.

"This Hogan goes too fer wid that kid thing," said Patsy, "and some day a guy who don't know him and treats him like you would your father will step up and bust him on the jaw. I only hope fer his own sake and his face that he don't start it with some of these quiet guys he don't know, 'cause I look to see him eating grass some of these days."

After getting this out of his system he went on with the pool game and made up the lead that he had lost during the heated discussion of the "Peerless Leader."

BASEBALL TAME.

O'Rourke says that there is too much of the nice social element in the Coast League and it will never be a real, up-to-date league until the players get busy on the field and hate each other. Now, this may be the right dope, but to the present writing it only seems to bring on fines and other less-pleasant things; but every man has a right to his own opinions.

The Angels have just finished a hard series with the Tigers and expect to fatten up in every line on the Sacramento delegates. The team as a whole is playing better ball than they did during the first part of the season and seem to have more of that old "Crossing-the-Delaware Pep" than before. It must be remembered that Hogan won several of his games during the past series by terrible ninth-inning finishes after the Dillon crew had had all the best of it for eight and a half innings.

When men get up and make singles with two outs and two strikes, what are you going to do? Why, lose the game with the best grace possible. But the point of this argument goes to show that the Angels are really fighting now and are willing to come from the rear, whereas during the first part of the season, when the enemy got two runs in front, the whole gang was inclined to dog it.

The local heavers are right for this series unless several corks were drawn in the two Sunday battles, but we will not be able to find out about the corks until the series is really under way.

Play ball.

## WOLGAST-RIVERS FIGHT FORBIDDEN.

[A. P. NIGHT WIRE TO THE TIMES.]

STOCKTON (Cal.) July 15.—All hope of holding the Wolgast-Rivers fight in this city on Admission Day was abandoned this afternoon, when, during a meeting of business men with Dist.-Atty. E. P. Foltz, that official announced that under the law the bout, as it would be undoubtedly conducted, would be illegal, and would not be permitted by him.

Mr. Foltz stated to the committee that the law at best straddled the prize-fight question so that its interpretation is doubtful, and, in view of the widespread sentiment against it, he would not permit the fight to be held in the county.

## WILL PUT HORN IN PLACE OF KAUFMAN

[BY A. P. NIGHT WIRE TO THE TIMES.]

SAN FRANCISCO, July 15.—The unexpected illness of Al Kaufman, who was to have fought Charley Miller before the Tuxedo Club at Dreamland Rink on the night of July 31, has brought a serious halt in the white hope elimination process that is being conducted by the fight promoters all over the country. Kaufman was training faithfully for his second "come-back" trial, when he was stricken and forced to take to his bed.

Eddie Graney, promoter and matchmaker, said today that the date he holds will not be cancelled. He is negotiating with Charley Horn, another local heavyweight, to meet Miller. Horn disposed of Al Williams, a sparring partner of Jim Flynn, in easy fashion, a few nights ago. Tim McGrath, manager for Horn, says that he and his charge have been looking for the opportunity now before them.

"Horn will win from Miller," said McGrath, "and then they will not be able to stop him until he is in a position to make his bid for a try at the championship."

## ENGLAND WINS GAME IN CRICKET SERIES.

The fourth of the triangular test matches, for the cricket championship of the world, was won by England at Leeds yesterday. The scores were as follows: England, 242 and 238 to the 147 and 159 by South Africa. England won by 174 runs.

The fifth of these world series games starts today, when Australia crosses bats with South Africa at Lords.

## Winners of World-Fame.

Thorpe won first in the decathlon. James Donahue of Los Angeles yesterday took second in the pole vault in the decathlon. Mercer, the University of Pennsylvania all-around athlete, won first in the pole vault, in the decathlon. Koehlemainen, the Finnish runner, yesterday won the 8000-meter cross-country run. The King of Sweden personally congratulated him. Reidpath of Syracuse University was a member of the American relay team that won the 1600-yard event yesterday.

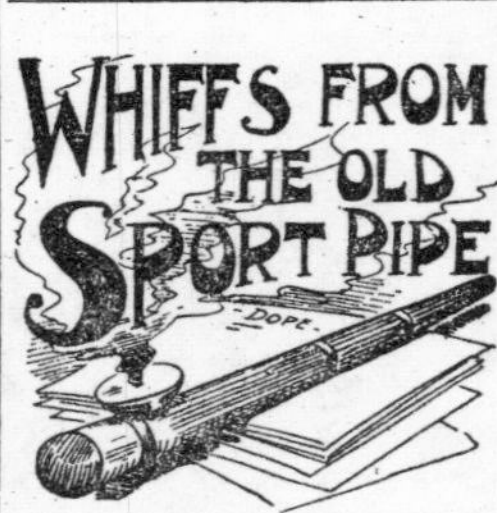



J. J. Canavan was the last of the local automobile men to see Bert Smith. It was in the hotel at Las Vegas. The Ocean-to-Ocean Highway-builder and Col. Del M. Potter, the organizer, were housed in that hotel near the depot, and Canavan, who was on his way East, ran over to the hotel on a stop-over, for the sole purpose of getting cooled off. He heard that Bert was in the house and he went up to his room with a greeting from Los Angeles. Bert was in the little tin bathtub, and in getting out to greet him, he splashed water all over Canavan's new suit.

Winnie Cutter, one time slab performer for San Francisco and Sacramento, and later known as a coach of college teams from U.S.C. to the University of Oregon, is now in Santa Barbara. He seemingly has settled down and retired from active sporting circles, to take up the strenuous duties of a telephone lineman.

Arthur Lang, a former St. Vincent's boy, has joined the fire department of Fresno. The lad also pitches on the Fresno team and is attracting more than his share of attention in the twilight town.

Among the college athletes who are vacationing in these parts are Tom Coleman of Stanford, Tom Ybarando of Santa Clara, Louis Cass of Stanford, Hill Hatch of Santa Clara and Bill Mahoney of Michigan.

Harry Price, the old U.S.C. and Poly High boy, who was with Sacramento during the first part of the season, and later went into the brush of the San Joaquin Valley, has been signed for the catcher's role on the Austin (Tex.) team. He had expected to leave for his new berth today, but the illness of his mother prevented his departure, and it will very probably be the last of the week before he gets away.

W. K. Merrill, manager of the Santa Barbara baseball team, has come through with the information that Walter Johnson will winter in Southern California again.

One of the best-known members of Denver sporting circles, John Bramer, is in Los Angeles. The man from the Mile High City will remain here for a short time only, as he is on a honeymoon and business calls him on his merry way; but it is rumored that he will return to Southern California to make his home, as soon as matters can be closed up in Denver. Bramer has been looking over some of South-

(Continued on Fourth Page.)

Honors the Winners.

## KING PUTS WREATHS ON YANKEE HEROES' BROWS.

*Dramatic Scene in Olympic Stadium When Prizes Are Awarded—South Africa Wins Marathon—Portuguese Runner Dies—Thorp, Carlisle Indian, Greatest All-Round Athlete in World.*

[BY A. P. NIGHT WIRE TO THE TIMES.]

## AMERICA SCORES MORE THAN ALL REST PUT TOGETHER.

| | United States | Finland | Sweden | England | Canada | Greece | Germany | Norway | France | Hungary | Italy | South Africa |
|---|---|---|---|---|---|---|---|---|---|---|---|---|
| 100 meter | 6 | 0 | 0 | 0 | 0 | 0 | 0 | 0 | 0 | 0 | 0 | 0 |
| Pentathlon | 4 | 0 | 0 | 0 | 0 | 0 | 0 | 2 | 0 | 0 | 0 | 0 |
| Throw Jav. B. H. | 0 | 2 | 3 | 0 | 0 | 0 | 0 | 0 | 0 | 1 | 0 | 0 |
| Standing Broad Jump | 3 | 0 | 0 | 0 | 0 | 3 | 0 | 0 | 0 | 0 | 0 | 0 |
| 1000 meter | 2 | 4 | 0 | 0 | 0 | 0 | 0 | 0 | 0 | 0 | 0 | 0 |
| Running High Jump | 4 | 0 | 0 | 0 | 0 | 0 | 2 | 0 | 0 | 0 | 0 | 0 |
| 800 meter | 6 | 0 | 0 | 0 | 0 | 0 | 0 | 0 | 0 | 0 | 0 | 0 |
| Throw Jav. E. H. | 0 | 6 | 0 | 0 | 0 | 0 | 0 | 0 | 0 | 0 | 0 | 0 |
| 400 meter relay | 0 | 0 | 2 | 3 | 0 | 0 | x | 0 | 0 | 0 | 0 | 0 |
| Putting shot | 6 | 0 | 0 | 0 | 0 | 0 | 0 | 0 | 0 | 0 | 0 | 0 |
| 5000 meter | 0 | 3 | 0 | 1 | 0 | 0 | 0 | 0 | 2 | 0 | 0 | 0 |
| 1500 meter | 3 | 0 | 0 | 3 | 0 | 0 | 0 | 0 | 0 | 0 | 0 | 0 |
| 200 meter | 5 | 0 | 1 | 0 | 0 | 0 | 0 | 0 | 0 | 0 | 0 | 0 |
| Shot put, either hand | 5 | 1 | 0 | 0 | 0 | 0 | 0 | 0 | 0 | 0 | 0 | 0 |
| Pole vault | 6 | 0 | 0 | 0 | 0 | 0 | 0 | 0 | 0 | 0 | 0 | 0 |
| 1000 meter walk | 0 | 0 | 0 | 2 | 3 | 0 | 0 | 0 | 0 | 0 | 1 | 0 |
| Discus, Best H. | 3 | 3 | 0 | 0 | 0 | 0 | 0 | 0 | 0 | 0 | 0 | 0 |
| Running Broad Jump | 3 | 0 | 1 | 0 | 2 | 0 | 0 | 0 | 0 | 0 | 0 | 0 |
| 110 meter hurdle | 6 | 0 | 0 | 0 | 0 | 0 | 0 | 0 | 0 | 0 | 0 | 0 |
| 400 meter | 4 | 0 | 0 | 0 | 0 | 2 | 0 | 0 | 0 | 0 | 0 | 0 |
| 3000 meter team race | 3 | 0 | 2 | 1 | 0 | 0 | 0 | 0 | 0 | 0 | 0 | 0 |
| Discus, right and left H. | 0 | 5 | 1 | 0 | 0 | 0 | 0 | 0 | 0 | 0 | 0 | 0 |
| Standing high jump | 5 | 0 | 0 | 0 | 0 | 1 | 0 | 0 | 0 | 0 | 0 | 0 |
| Marathon | 1 | 0 | 0 | 0 | 0 | 0 | 0 | 0 | 0 | 0 | 0 | 5 |
| Throwing hammer | 4 | 0 | 0 | 0 | 2 | 0 | 0 | 0 | 0 | 0 | 0 | 0 |
| 1600 meter team race | 3 | 0 | 0 | 1 | 0 | 0 | 0 | 0 | 2 | 0 | 0 | 0 |
| Hop, Step and Jump | 0 | 0 | 6 | 0 | 0 | 0 | 0 | 0 | 0 | 0 | 0 | 0 |
| Decathlon | 3 | 0 | 3 | 0 | 0 | 0 | 0 | 0 | 0 | 0 | 0 | 0 |
| 6000 meter cross country | 3 | 0 | 3 | 0 | 0 | 0 | 0 | 0 | 0 | 0 | 0 | 0 |
| Totals | 88 | 24 | 22 | 11 | 7 | 6 | 2 | 2 | 4 | 1 | 1 | 5 |

x—Finished second but was disqualified.

STOCKHOLM, July 15.—The last day of the track and field sports in the stadium brought no sensation. The games reached their culmination in the Marathon. The curtain falls on the Olympic with the United States well in front in the total points in all sports to date, and with a sweeping victory in the field and track events which for years have constituted the programme at meetings in America and Great Britain and to which athletics of these nations devote their energies.

The awarding of all prizes by the King, who placed laurel wreaths on the heads of the victors and shook hands with all the winners, took place in the stadium this afternoon. The American team led the march of triumphant athletes who, arrayed before the King, formed an assemblage of picked men and women of the world of sports never seen in one body before.

The triumphs of the day were divided for the most part between the United States and the northern nations. The latter, particularly Sweden, scored a number of points in wrestling and aquatic sports in which the Americans did not figure.

DONOHUE PROMINENT.

James Thorp, the Carlisle Indian School student, proved himself the greatest all-round athlete of the world in the decathlon, which provided a variety of tests of speed, strength and quickness, while Eugene L. Mercer, University of Pennsylvania; George W. Philbrook, Notre Dame, and James L. Donohue, Los Angeles A. C., were prominent in the second class.

The American quarter-milers ran away with the 1600-meters relay, as predicted, Sheppard, Lindberg, Meredith and Reidpath showing their heels to rivals. England probably would have taken second place instead of France, but her first man, Nicol, developed lameness.

The hop, step and jump proved wholly a Swedish event. The northern country took the three leading places and divided the cross-country race of 8000 meters, which really was a test of cliff climbing and ability to penetrate underbrush, with the husky Finn second, while the English team was third. The Americans for the first time in this class of work were absolute outsiders.

Two events have cast a shadow on the Olympic games. The Portuguese runner, F. Lazaro, who ran in the Marathon, died today from sunstroke, and Lieut. Lawrence, an officer of the Eighteenth Hussars, was thrown into a ditch during the military competition, suffering concussion of the brain and other serious injuries.

DRAMATIC SPECTACLE.

It seemed marvelous that any capacity to shout was left in Stockholm after the last nine days, but the victors got all that was due them when they received their laurels.

The presentation of the prizes at 3

(Continued on Third Page.)

1913
1922

THE OLYMPIC GAMES SCHEDULED FOR 1916 WERE CANCELED DUE TO WORLD WAR I, BUT THE FIGHTING in Europe did not have much effect on sports in America. Major events such as baseball's World Series and the Kentucky Derby were not interrupted, but the Indianapolis 500 was canceled in 1917 and 1918. For the most part, however, the U.S. sports show went on.

In fact before the decade ended, the era in America known as the "Golden Age of Sports" had begun. Such great personalities as Babe Ruth, Rogers Hornsby, Ty Cobb, Bobby Jones, Bill Tilden, Red Grange, and Jack Dempsey began to be noticed.

Ruth had the lowest earned-run-average, 1.75, in the American League in 1916 while pitching for the Boston Red Sox, and five years later he set a record by hitting fifty-nine home runs as an outfielder for the New York Yankees. Hornsby and Cobb hit more than .400 several times while winning batting championships, and Cobb, in 1915, won his ninth batting title in a row.

Walter Camp's All-America football teams contained some familiar names: Paul Robeson of Rutgers, George Gipp of Notre Dame, and Bo McMillen of little Centre College. Tilden won two men's singles championships at Wimbledon and three U.S. Opens in the early twenties. The dominant woman at Wimbledon in that era was France's Suzanne Lenglen.

Another filly made a name for herself at Louisville in the 1915 Kentucky Derby when Regret became the first of her sex to win the nation's number one horse race. How great an achievement was it? It would be sixty-five years before another filly won the Derby. Twenty-nine others have failed. The great gelding Exterminator, who was to finish out of the money only sixteen times in eight years and a hundred races, won the 1918 Derby.

Eight years had passed since the last Games at Stockholm when the VII Olympics opened in Antwerp, Belgium, in 1920. The war-torn Belgian capital had been awarded the Games only a few months after the last shot of World War I had been fired, and there was little time to get ready. The hastily built stadium seated only thirty thousand, and the Games, Baron Pierre de Coubertin later noted, did not possess the "scope and sumptuousness that had been previously planned."

But three names that would be long remembered by sports fans played prominent roles at Antwerp. Charlie Paddock of the University of Southern California won the 100-meter dash, Finland's Paavo Nurmi won the 10,000-meter run, and the United States' Duke Kahanamoku swam to victory in the 100 meters just as he did at Stockholm in 1912.

College football had become so dangerous earlier in the century—18 players killed and 159 seriously injured in one year—that President Roosevelt ordered the game cleaned up. By this time the sport had become a major attraction in America, spreading from the East to the Midwest, where such schools as Notre Dame and Illinois were powers.

In 1913 Notre Dame upset Army 35–13, with a startling new offensive weapon, a forward pass brilliantly executed by Gus Dorais and Knute Rockne. In 1919 the Praying Colonels of Centre College, led by Bo McMillen, upset Harvard, 6–0. That same year Rockne, who was now the Notre Dame coach, had the first of five undefeated teams. Pop Warner was making a name for himself at Pittsburgh. What Amos Alonzo Stagg didn't invent for football, it has been said, Warner did.

Meanwhile on the West Coast a new power was coming of age, the USC Trojans under Coach Gus Henderson. In four years, 1919–22, the Trojans won thirty of thirty-three games. And at Pasadena, the Rose Bowl, first played in 1902 with Michigan beating Stanford, 49–0, resumed in 1916 with Washington State defeating Brown, 14–0.

Collegians had the game to themselves for a long time; there was no competition from professionals. But in 1920, at a Hupmobile agency in Canton, Ohio, George Halas and others formed the American Professional Football Association, which later became the National Football League. Twelve teams, including Halas's Staleys of Decatur, Illinois, paid a membership fee of a hundred dollars and elected Jim Thorpe president.

Jack Johnson, who had won the heavyweight boxing championship by beating Jim Jeffries in 1910, lost the title on April 5, 1915, when he was knocked out by Jess Willard in the twenty-sixth round at Havana, Cuba. Willard was a big fellow, standing 6′7″ and weighing about 265 pounds. But on July 4, 1919, in Toledo, Ohio, William Harrison (Jack) Dempsey, weighing only about 190, knocked Willard down seven times in the first round and won the championship when his opponent had to quit before the fourth round began.

A major scandal rocked baseball in 1920 when it was disclosed that eight Chicago White Sox players had conspired to throw the 1919 World Series that was won by Cincinnati, five games to three. The eight players, including Shoeless Joe Jackson, were banned from baseball and a new commissioner, Judge Kenesaw Mountain Landis, was elected to keep the game pure.

IN THE FIELD OF SPORTS

The Los Angeles Times

XXXIInd YEAR. WEDNESDAY, SEPTEMBER 10, 1913.—8 PAGE PART III.





# COOPER DEFEATS WORLD-FAMOUS AUTO DRIVERS.

Whiz-z-z.

## FLIGHT OF A WHITE STREAK.

*With Red Demon Motors in Pursuit.*

*That's What the Big Corona Race Was Like.*

*A Thrilling Description of the Stutz's Victory.*

BY R. A. WYNNE.

In the minds of over 100,000 Southern Californians there remains this morning the picture of a ghostly white thing fleeing screamingly around and around pursued by three giant red monsters which seemed to be bursting their mighty hearts in their titanic efforts to overtake the elusive white shape.

It was the vivid memory of those last twenty laps in the wonderful free-for-all race at Corona yesterday, when Earl Cooper and his white Stutz won both the heavy car and the free-for-all events from the greatest field of competitors ever gathered at a road race in the West.

Barney Oldfield had turned turtle in his giant Mercer when he had a nice lead of two laps and Cooper had leaped into the lead like a white flash of light. The speed had become terrific. The 100,000 spectators who lined the three miles of the speedway a hundred and more deep on both sides were dizzy in counting the flashing cars as they leaped into view for a second and seemed to drop from sight like a flash of light. The pace increased until the very air was odorous of burning rubber from the mistreated tires. Wishart, in his Mercer, went out with engine trouble. De Palma, fighting valiantly in the last Mercer, also gave up the ghost. There remained only the three Fiats with Tetzlaff, Verbeck and Hill driving and the elusive and fleet Stutz to fight it out in the free-for-all.

AFTER THE STUTZ.

The Fiats started out to get the Stutz. They were said to have the speed and it seemed a foregone conclusion that one of them would finally reach the Stutz and pass her.

Here began one of the most brilliant and stubborn fights ever seen on a race track. Tetzlaff in his mighty 120 Fiat crept up to within striking distance of the Stutz, but to the astonishment of the spectators, there he hung. The Stutz seemed to become a thing of life. It leaped into view from under the drooping pepper trees one instant and the next instant it was disappearing under the bending trees at the distant curve in the track. The Fiats plunged, roaring defiance, after the Stutz, but the margin of separation remained the same. The spectators arose in a mass as they realized that Cooper had suddenly displayed speed that was marvelous and was actually holding the mighty 120 Fiats at arm's length.

In the train of Tetzlaff and his Fiat roared Verbeck and then Hill. The three foreign cars seemed to be imbued with the drivers' fierce longing to overhaul that fleeing white shape in front. A dozen laps were covered in what seemed to be a deadlock. Something must give, as that awful pace could not continue.

In the pits the Stutz helpers stood spellbound at the marvelous showing of their own car. In the Fiat pits the helpers stood with tires waiting and implements in hand to rush through the expected tire change.

SIGNALS FOR TIRES.

Suddenly the mechanician with Cooper was seen to throw up one hand as they shot into the lower turn and a deep groan went up from the spectators. Cooper was coming in for a change of tire. As his car slowed and jerked to a standstill and while the feverish and almost hysterical mechanics "yanked" the car up on a jack

(Continued on Third Page.)

## WINNERS AND PRIZES IN CORONA SPEED BATTLE.

LIGHT car event. Distance 102.45 miles, for cars of 230 cubic inches and under. Purse $1750. Buick, Ed Waterman driver, won; time, 1h. 37m. 26s.; Reo, Earle Jackson driver, second, time, 1h. 41m. 6 2-5s.; Studebaker, Frank B. Goode driver, third; time, 1h. 46m. A new world record for the Buick. Average 63 miles an hour.

Heavy car race. Distance 251.97 miles. Purse $3000. Cars of 231 to 450 cubic inches: Stutz, Earl Cooper driver, won; time, 3h. 21m 29 1-5s.; Marmon, C. H. Taylor driver, second; time, 4h. 9m. 33s.; National, Tony Jeanette driver, third. New world record for the Stutz; average 75 miles an hour.

Free-for-all, 300 miles. Purse $5250: Stutz, Earle Cooper, won; time, 4h. 2m. 38s. Fiat, Frank Verbeck, second; time 4h. 10m. 20s; Fiat, George Hill, third; time not given. Average of 74½ miles an hour.

Battle Royal.

## COOPER WINS GRAND PRIZE CORONA MOTOR ROAD RACE.

*Barney Oldfield Wrecks His Mercer to Avoid Killing a Boy—Teddy Tetzlaff Loses to Stutz Racer in Thrilling Fight for World Championship — Studebaker Turns Turtle in Light Event—Many Thrills.*

BY BERT C. SMITH.

ONE HUNDRED THOUSAND spectators saw Earl Cooper, in the Stutz, win the Corona road race yesterday. A new world champion was born in the race that was tense with excitement. That white, ghostly Stutz, with two men crouched low behind the cowl, kept bouncing over the wire for lap after lap with speed unslackened save when a tire was changed.

Barney Oldfield led that great race for fifty-nine laps. The crowd was wild. Woman danced and cheered, then cheered again. The man who had won so many track victories was to be victor in the greatest road race ever held. Barney sent that Mercer out to a wonderful lead, and when two laps ahead, and while leading the entire field of sixteen cars, the world champion's finish came in a sensational wreck.

With Cooper close behind him, Barney went into the first curve beyond the grand stands at ninety miles an hour. Even Teddy Tetzlaff failed to pass the flying Mercer, which Barney was handling so well. It looked like Oldfield's race. Eager to see the leader, the crowd surged close to the curb. That finish was tragic, and in that wreck Oldfield showed himself to be every inch a man.

BARNEY SAVED BOY.

Overcome by excitement, a 9-year-old lad raced out on that course directly in front of Oldfield's winning Mercer. Frank Sandhoffer, the mechanician, saw the boy, but so did Barney. Quick as a flash, Oldfield whirled his steering wheel to avoid the boy. He turned so quickly that the front wheel of the Mercer crumpled, the car lurched to the curb and Mechanician Sandhoffer was thrown out and crushed under the car.

The boy was saved. The little fellow, frightened almost to death, went screaming to his mother's side. The mangled mechanician was picked up tenderly and hurried to the field hospital. How Barney escaped no one will ever be able to say. The car did not turn turtle, but Oldfield, trembling like a leaf, climbed out of the wreckage and walked back to the pits followed by a crowd. Barney had saved the boy, but at a fearful cost.

It will never be known just how Barney would have figured in that race. His car was running perfectly. The engine was in splendid shape. The accident settled things for Oldfield, and Cooper took the lead, never to lose it again until he had won both the heavy event and the free-for-all in a wonderful dash.

COOPER'S TRIUMPH.

Earl Cooper defeated the world's best drivers. He was matched with Ralph de Palma, Teddy Tetzlaff, Spencer Wishart and Barney Oldfield, and he won. The trophies and prize money are his and he is the new world motor champion and his Stutz is one of the greatest little cars that ever was sent into a motor battle.

Ed Waterman, on the Buick, won that light event. It was a race with many thrills. Two cars shot out into a strong lead. Waterman's Buick and Frank B. Goode's Studebaker changed places lap after lap, first one having the lead, only to see the other take the pace.

Came another fast car into the squabble of that race. The Buick took a long lead over Goode's Studebaker. Then Rev. Earl Schnack sent his Ford into second place. The pace was too hot for the little car to maintain. The preacher could not catch the flying Buick. From the rear ranks came a flying meteor, the Studebaker, driven by William Rhodes, an Alhambra man, whose mechanic was Billy Warren, also of Alhambra.

These two boys began to send that Studebaker from ninth place to seventh, then to fifth, then right up until the car was second and making a strong bid for first. With only two more laps to go, Rhodes came across the tape a hundred yards behind the Buick. Waterman, in his excitement, shot over the line and then tried to back to the wire. His mistake might have been fatal to a man following close behind.

Quick to see his advantage, Rhodes

(Continued on Fifth Page.)

## WORLD RECORDS IN CORONA RACE.

Teddy Tetzlaff in the Fiat drove the fastest lap in 1m. 52s.

Barney Oldfield led the field for fifty-nine laps at an average of seventy-eight miles an hour.

World records were broken in the light event and in the heavy car race.

Oldfield's wreck cut down the speed of the cars in the big race and prevented a world record.

Five persons were injured, but no one was killed in the Corona road race.

Bill Warren, mechanician on the Studebaker, was the most seriously hurt. He may have sustained a fractured skull. He is still unconscious.

The attendance at Corona is estimated at more than 100,000 spectators.

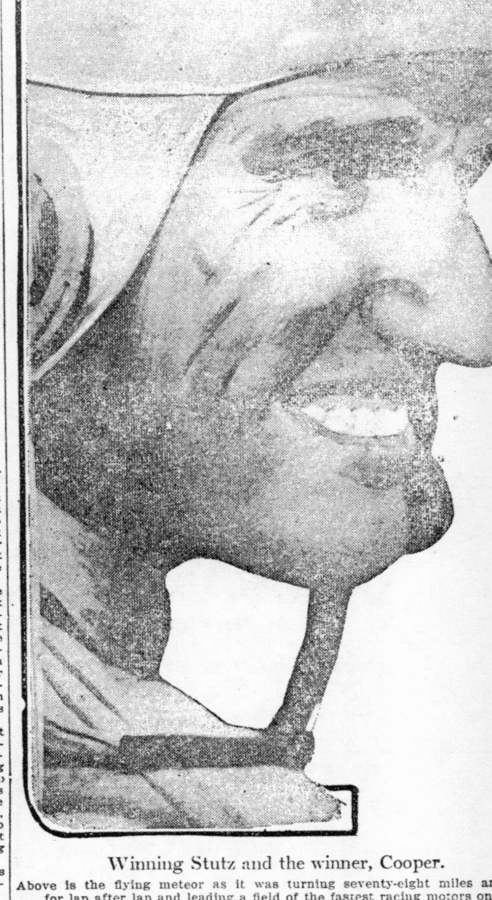

Winning Stutz and the winner, Cooper.

Above is the flying meteor as it was turning seventy-eight miles an hour for lap after lap and leading a field of the fastest racing motors on earth. Below the face of the man who drove that white car into two remarkable victories in the same day.

With the Mechanics.

## HOW A WASHER MISPLACED IN THE PITS LOST A RACE.

BY BONNIE GLESSNER.

FUNNY old Father Time, the shifting sands of whose hour-glass are said to check off each passing second or fraction thereof, must have been a very busy man if he gave a personal supervision to the repair pits at the Corona road race yesterday, for there, more than at any other section of the polished race course that rims the Crown City, was time vitally valuable.

Across from the grand stand were the repair pits—boarded enclosures that are pits in name only—and here men struggled throughout the long, hot day, fighting, fighting desperately for every second of the precious time that relentlessly slipped away, carrying with it, as the case might be, fame, money, or the plaudits of friends.

Like the vortex of a giant whirlpool, the pits caught the passing cars, one after another, and held them captive while time-mad men bent brain and muscle to the task of releasing them quickly. Like bits of flotsam they circled the vortex. Now whirling up for a brief space of time, only to roar madly away when released or, slowly eddying in, to cling to the edge of the pits for many heart-breaking seconds, then careen wildly away in the wake of the more fortunate cars.

BURNED-UP SECONDS.

Life's great happenings seem to always hang on trivial things. Thus the misplacing of the washer of the valve spring cost the National car second place in the heavy car race.

(Continued on Eighth Page.)

Photo by G. B. Keyes.

When Eddie Pullen crashed into the fence.

A wonderful photograph taken at the exact moment when Pullen, who was leading the field at an average of eighty-two miles an hour, burst his right front tire on the Nevada-avenue turn and tore head-on into the fence, breaking the spindle of his front axle and being eliminated from the running.

But Busy.

## RALPH'S PIT WAS UNUSED.

*Vanderbilt Winner Never Went Near It.*

*But Much Happened There, Nevertheless.*

*Helpers Aided Materially His Victory.*

BY AD G. WADDELL.

When Fred J. Wagner dipped the checkered flag in honor of Ralph De Palma, winner of the great Vanderbilt cup race, yesterday, the Mercedes pit crew indulged in a stag tango party.

"Get a black cigar for Tommy," begged George Shillo, one of the pit men.

George Townsend, the New Yorker who helped Ralph with his car, left the pit on the run and came back with a roll of something which he claimed to be a cigar.

"Tommy must have a cigar," he explained; "if I don't have one for him he will be sore."

"Tommy" was Tommy Alley, the mechanician of De Palma's car.

Moving picture men had their cameras rigged around the three sides of the pit and on the tracks to the rear. Professional and amateur photographers were wedged in on all sides.

That was the end of the long session in the Mercedes pit.

HOW THEY FIGURED.

It was figured in the pit that Barney would cross the tape first, but take second place by less than thirty seconds, as he had started 75 seconds ahead of De Palma. In the final stages, the Mercer began to creep ahead and the picture men began to forsake the Mercedes pit for that of the famous old speed king, who was gaining ground.

Then it was that some of the hard luck that had been showing up at intervals all day, hit Barney. He drew up at his pit at the end of the thirty-first lap with a bad tire.

"It's all over now," said Townsend; "if his tires will hold out, Ralph has it. A stop will kill his chances."

Louis Sorrell sat in the disabled Mason's pit on one side and Frank Goode, who had been forced to retire from the race with his Apperson, sat in the pit on the other side.

The unfortunate Mason mechanic

(Continued on Fourth Page.)

The Vanderbilt.

## BARNEY CHASED ELUSIVE RALPH BUT RAN SECOND.

*Italian Driver Sat Back in His Machine and Simply Drove Into First Place, Letting Everybody Else Get Excited—Mercer Driver Nearly Won, but Not Quite. Carlson in Mason Good Third.*

BY HARRY A. WILLIAMS.

THE Vanderbilt cup, most highly-prized trophy in American motordom, remains in the De Palma family.

The great Italian pilot, stuffed with spaghetti and seated serenely in his Mercedes, proved his right to retain this valuable piece of junk, when he sent the white torpedo-like car home a winner at Santa Monica yesterday, reeling off 294 miles at the dizzy average of 75.5 an hour for a new record in this event.

This is his second victory in the Vanderbilt classic in as many years, and equals the achievement of Harry Grant in winning two straight.

De Palma drove a great race, a wonderful race and he had good luck. His generalship was perfect, and plunging around the course at a death-defying speed, he showed no more excitement than a farmer winding an eight-day clock.

De Palma won without batting an eye, taking a chew or wiping his nose.

Rah for Ralph!

BARNEY CLOSE UP.

Barney Oldfield, fighting with his Mercer down to the last 200 yards of the race, after having been goaded into driving the tires almost off his machine, sped past the tape a good second and 1m. and 20s. behind the fleeing Mercedes.

By the nineteenth lap the race had developed into a speed slaughtering duel between these two, and from then on they battled round and round the course, always in sight of each other, except when one disappeared momentarily around a turn.

Two things beat Oldfield. One was the superb generalship of De Palma. The other was costly delays in the pit. Three times, Oldfield was forced to stop for tires, gas and oil.

Never did the Mercedes falter. It swung over the entire distance as steadily as though harnessed to the solar system. As the great machine reeled off lap after lap, even the mechanics in the Mercedes pit leaned over the rail and gazed wonderingly at the performance.

Of fuel and oil De Palma had enough. His tires did not fail him, and his machine clicked off the miles with clocklike regularity from the instant that it bounded forward in

(Continued on Second Page.)

## WHAT HAPPENED TO THE CARS THAT DIDN'T PLACE.

THE Isotta, driven by Harry Grant, went out in the first lap. Grant had worked until 3 o'clock yesterday morning, welding the piston broken in practice Wednesday and when the repaired piston went wrong, other complications set in and he said last night that there was but one chance in a thousand that he would start Saturday in the Grand Prize, as he also had cracked a cylinder.

The Mason, driven by Dave Lewis, came into the pits with a broken piston at the end of the first lap. It was reported that a piece of piston metal had broken off and worked under the exhaust valve. A new valve was put in, but this did not remedy the trouble and the car never started on the second lap.

Spencer Wishart drove the Mercer No. 2 into the pits at the end of the second lap with a cracked cylinder which put him out of the competition.

The Fiat Ninety, driven by Frank Verbeck, went out on the tenth lap with a broken valve, but limped to the pits and retired from the race.

The English Sunbeam went out on the tenth lap with a broken axle.

The Apperson, driven by Frank Goode, broke an oil line and was out of the race after eleven laps.

The Mercer, driven by Edwin Pullen, was wrecked on the Wilshire boulevard turn when in the lead at the end of thirteen laps.

Guy Ball's Marmon broke a feed pipe near the Soldiers' Home and was forced to retire on the sixteenth lap.

Stutz, car No. 3, driven by Gil Anderson, went out on the eighteenth lap with a broken drive shaft.

Tony Janette in the Alco, went out in the twenty-second lap, when near the bridge over the course on Ocean avenue. Janette's retirement was charged to a cracked cylinder.

Joerimann in the Touraine, was running in fifth place, with five laps to go when Cooper finished fourth. Fifth place was given to the youngster in the Touraine and he was flagged down.

Congratulating the winner.

Ralph De Palma surrounded by a swarm of enthusiastic friends after the race and trying to shake hands with them all at once. On the extreme right is Tom Alley, his mechanician.

The Los Angeles Times

XXXIVth YEAR. TUESDAY MORNING, APRIL 6, 1915.—4 PAGES. PART III.



# JESS WILLARD WORLD'S HEAVYWEIGHT CHAMPION

### NEW CHAMP'S RING CAREER.

| | | |
|---|---|---|
| **1911—** | | |
| K. | Ed Burke | 3 rds. |
| K. | Louis Fink | 3 rds. |
| K. | Al Mandino | 4 rds. |
| K. | Joe Kavanaugh | 11 rds. |
| K. | Bill Schiller | 4 rds. |
| W. | Frank Lyon | 10 rds. |
| W. | Mike Comiskey | 10 rds. |
| **1912—** | | |
| K. | John Young | 6 rds. |
| K. | Frank Bowers | 3 rds. |
| K. | John Young | 5 rds. |
| W. | Arthur Pelky | 10 rds. |
| W. | Luther McCarty | 10 rds. |
| K. | Sailor White | 1 rd. |
| K. | Soldier Kearns | 8 rds. |
| **1913—** | | |
| K. | Frank Bauer | 5 rds. |
| K. | Jack Leon | 4 rds. |
| L. | Gunboat Smith | 20 rds. |
| D. | Charley Miller | 4 rds. |
| K. | Al Williams | 8 rds. |
| K. | Bull Young | 11 rds. |
| **1914—** | | |
| K. | George Rodel | 9 rds. |
| K. | One-round Davis | 2 rds. |
| W. | Carl Morris | 10 rds. |
| K. | George Rodel | 5 rds. |
| K. | Dan Daly | 9 rds. |
| **1915—** | | |
| K. | Jack Johnson | 26 rds. |

New Champion of World.

## ASSOCIATED PRESS HINTS THAT JOHNSON QUIT.

### *Ex-champion Sends White Wife From Arena and Jumps Up After Count.*

*Negro Pugilist Sees He Cannot Win so When Knocked Down Takes Count Rather than Further Punishment—End Dazes Spectators, Who Rush into Ring — Willard Escorted to City.*

[BY ATLANTIC CABLE AND A. P.]

HAVANA, April 5.—Jack Johnson, exiled from his own country, today lost his claim to fistic fame as the heavyweight champion of the world, the title being wrested from him by Jess Willard, the Kansas cowboy, the biggest man who ever entered the prize ring.

Today's fight probably has no parallel in the history of ring battles. For twenty rounds Johnson punched and pounded Willard at will, but his blows grew perceptibly less powerful as the fight progressed, until at last he seemed unable or unwilling to go on.

Johnson stopped leading and for three or four rounds the battle between the two huge men was little more than a series of plastic poses of white or black gladiators.

So it was until the twenty-fifth round, when Willard got one of his widely-swinging, windmill right-hand smashes to Johnson's heart. This was the beginning of the end.

JOHNSON SENDS WIFE HOME.

When the round closed Johnson sent word to his wife that he was all in and told her to start for home. She was on the way out and was passing the ring in the twenty-sixth round, when a stinging left to the body and a cyclonic right to the jaw caused Johnson to crumple on the floor of the ring, where he lay partly outside the ropes until the referee counted ten, and held up Willard's hand in token of his newly-won laurels.

There is much discussion tonight and probably will be for a long time, among the followers of the fighting game, as to whether Johnson was really knocked out. In the sense of being smashed into unconsciousness, he certainly was not put out.

The consensus of opinion is that Johnson expected and knew that there was no possibility of his winning, so when knocked down he chose to take the count rather than rise and stand further punishment.

Johnson has often stated that fighting is a business and he would not foolishly submit to repeated knockdowns when he found he had met his master. A second or two after Jack Welch, the referee, had counted ten, Johnson quickly got up. It was well that he did so, for a moment later a rush of spectators to the fighting platform all but smothered the pugilists.

For an instant it seemed as if trouble was threatened, but some fifty or more of the several hundred soldiers stationed about the fight arena jumped into the ring and formed circles around the vanquished and victor.

Under escort of the soldiers, Willard and Johnson left the ring and went to their dressing rooms, while the crowd cheered and broke into wild discussion.

WILLARD LEAVES.

Willard was out of his dressing-room in a few moments, and in an automobile on his way back to Havana. He was escorted half way to the city from the Marianao race track, where the fight was held, by a troop of Cuban cavalry.

Crowds lined the streets and narrow roadways and the new white champion was loudly cheered. He was decidedly the favorite of the crowd all through the fight, and tonight is the hero of the island.

Automobiles returning to the city from the fight flew white flags and thus the news spread far and wide that the white challenger had defeated the negro champion. As Willard came along, the crowds in the streets waved flags and handkerchiefs tied to sticks. At one point a group of negro children, who had evidently heard that Johnson was the victor, waved black flags at the white champion, who was much amused.

MODEST CHAMPION.

Willard probably is the most modest champion who ever stepped out of a prize ring, taking his victory as philosophically as he had looked forward to the fight. Neither he nor Johnson showed much evidence of having been engaged in a heavyweight championship battle. The new champion's lip, right ear and left cheek showed slight cuts, but at no time was there more than a drop or two of blood in evidence.

In this respect the fight was in great contrast to the Johnson-Jeffries fight at Reno, five years ago, when Jeffries was cut to pieces and blood splashed over the spectators at the ringside. Evidently thinking that this condition might prevail again today, Johnson objected to the presence of a white woman in the newspaper seats just outside the ropes, and she was relegated to a place farther back.

CLEAN FIGHT.

On the contrary, no fight between heavyweights that has gone to a finish was cleaner or less brutal. Johnson's left eye was partly closed in the early rounds, but not sufficiently to interfere with his fighting. His lip also was cut inside and his famous golden smile flashed from a very red setting.

The end of the fight came with a suddenness that dazed the spectators. It followed two or three rounds of almost complete idleness on the part of the contestants, and the crowd settled down to a long drawn out struggle, believing that it would go the full limit of the forty-five rounds without either being able to register a knockout.

EARLY ROUNDS.

The early rounds were filled with flashes of Johnson's former wonderful speed when he would rain rights and lefts to Willard's body and face, delivering ten blows to one of the big white challenger's. Through all this time, Willard was strictly on the defensive, and on one occasion Johnson

(Continued on Second Page.)

### FITZ BEATEN AT SAME AGE.

James J. Jeffries defeated Bob Fitzsimmons and won the world's heavyweight championship on the day that he was 37 years and 5 days old. Jess Willard won the title from Jack Johnson on the day that the black champion was 37 years and 5 days of age.

Tickled to Death.

## JIM JEFFRIES COACHED WILLARD FOR TITLE BOUT.

*Man Whom Johnson Beat Tells Cowboy to Stay Away and Make Negro Lead—Fight is not Fake and Jess Won Because He had the Goods is How the One-time Champion Describes Outcome.*

BY AD G. WADDELL.

NO MAN in Los Angeles was more delighted with the result of the Willard-Johnson fight than James J. Jeffries. Probably no man in this country was more interested in the outcome of the Havana match than the man who lost the heavyweight title to the burly negro at Reno in 1910.

"I figured Willard to win, and am sure glad that he did win," said the former world's heavyweight champion last night. "I always did figure Willard a better man than the black, and when Harry Monohan went down to Havana and saw that Jess was in better condition than Johnson, I was sure that we would have a white champion if Willard would only fight as he was told.

"Before Willard went away from Los Angeles I spent hours with him, and pounded one thing into his head—that was to stay away and let Johnson bring the fight to him. He did that, didn't he?

"All the rounds that were reported

(Continued on Second Page.)

Jess Willard,

The cowboy pugilist, who yesterday knocked out Jack Johnson and restored the championship to the white race.

All After Jess.

## HEAVYWEIGHTS GET BUSY WITH MANY CHALLENGES.

[BY A. P. NIGHT WIRE.]

NEW YORK, April 5.—Willard's victory over Johnson and the fact that the world's heavyweight title has passed into the custody of a white pugilist was welcome news to those identified with pugilism and to other sport followers in Greater New York. Tonight virtually nothing but the big fight was talked about in the hotels and cafes where sporting men gathered.

Everywhere the prevailing impression was that Johnson's defeat by the big Kansan would give a stimulus to boxing and make the sport more popular all over the United States. Now that the title is held by an American, who will be ready to defend it without hindrance on his native soil, the promoters of fistic contests here see a big future for Willard and look forward to some good bouts being arranged for him when he is ready to entertain a challenge for the championship.

"Gunboat" Smith, Jim Coffey, and Al Reich, all of whom have their homes in this city, have issued challenges to the "cowboy" champion. In all probability this trio, as well as many others in the heavyweight division, will have to wait some time before Willard will consent to a match for the title. His managers and backers have mapped out an itinerary of exhibitions and theatrical engagements for Willard in preference to having him defend his laurels in the ring in the near future.

Willard, as challenger for the title, had a host of friends here who wished him well and hoped for him to win, but only a handful of them placed any wagers on his chance of success. Very little money changed hands at the odds exceeding 2 to 1 against Willard, while some of the bettors accepted as low as 6 to 5 for fairly large amounts.

### CHECH BUYS OREGON LAND.

[BY DIRECT WIRE—EXCLUSIVE DISPATCH]

ALBANY (Or.) April 5.—Charles Chech, pitcher of the Los Angeles team, and W. H. Page, who played second base for the Angels last year, have become, not "bloated bondholders," but Oregon orchard-land buyers, and have taken tracts at Linn Haven, one of the most fertile in the Willamette Valley. Their neighbor is Marty O'Toole, the famous pitcher who was sold two years ago by St. Paul to Pittsburgh for $22,000, the then record price.

## HOW BIG JESS WILLARD KNOCKED OUT JOHNSON.

[BY A. P. NIGHT WIRE.]

HAVANA, April 5.—Round 26—Johnson rose slowly from his chair and Willard met him more than two-thirds of the way across the ring. Willard stabbed a long left into the negro's face, sending his head bobbing back. Before the champion could recover his position, Willard swung a smashing right which landed full on Johnson's stomach. Johnson was flung against the ropes by the force of the blow and he clinched on the rebound.

The cowboy tried to tear loose, but the black man held grimly with eyes closed and legs shaking. Just before the referee broke them Johnson looked over Willard's shoulder toward the box where his wife had been, his eyes showing a dazed, tired, puzzled expression.

As soon as Welch had broken the clinch, Jess rushed again, forcing the negro into Willard's corner, where the finish came. Johnson was slow in guarding, and his strong, youthful opponent hooked a swinging left to the body. The fading champion's legs quivered and again the towering giant feinted for the body. Johnson dropped his guard and Willard won the title with a quick, hard swing to the exact point of the jaw.

The negro's knees folded up under him, and he sank slowly to the floor and rolled over on his back, partly under the ropes.

Welch waved Willard back and began to count. Up and down swung the referee's hand, but Johnson never moved. His eyes were glassy, only the whites being visible. At the count of "ten" Welch turned and held up Willard's hand and a new champion replaced Johnson, who was still stretched on the floor of the ring. Time of round, 1 minute 26 seconds.

Davis Cup Winners.

## TENNIS POPULAR IN ANTIPODES.

EIGHTY-FIVE PER CENT. OF POPULACE PLAYS.

**Australian Says His Countrymen Conduct Tennis on Scientific Basis. Lays Blame on Excessive Cost of American Courts for Lack of Interest in Game in this Country.**

They take their tennis seriously over in Australia. It is the belief of Alfred S. Baker, tennis player and business man of Sydney, that fully 85 per cent. of the men, women and children of the country play the game, many of them with marked skill.

"We are a country of tennis players," Mr. Baker said yesterday at the Angelus. "You can count twelve private tennis courts in one block in Sydney and the other large cities of the country. It has seemed to me that nearly everybody who had room for a tennis court improved the opportunity to build one.

"The tennis clubs are affiliated. Tennis playing is conducted on a scientific basis. The great interest in tennis began to develop in Australia about ten years ago when we began to think about taking the Davis cup. We won it, held it three years, lost it and now have it again."

The visitor believes that less than 1 per cent. of Americans play tennis. The number he regards as ridiculously low. It appears to him, however, that interest in the game is growing.

"The habit of building expensive courts is one of the things that discourages tennis in America," Mr. Baker continued. "I learn that it is not uncommon for as much as $500 to be spent on a court. The average cost of a court in our country is about $50. The less expensive courts really are the most satisfactory. Courts with a covering of sod or of the natural earth, or 'chipped' courts, as we call them, are the most satisfactory. I regard the cement covered courts, popular here, as an abomination. They are terribly hard on the feet and they give too much bounce to the ball."

*The Pink Pages—Sporting News—The Foremost Recent Events Graphically Told.*

The Los Angeles Times

PART III—4 PAGES. | FRIDAY MORNING, OCTOBER 13, 1916. —TWO-PAGE BUDGET. | IN THE VAN | First in Sporting News First in all Automobiling

# RED SOX CINCH WORLD'S CHAMPIONSHIP IN FIFTH GAME OF BIG SERIES.

Fair Enough.

## TRIPLE PLAY FOR TWO BITS.

*Showing Coast Ball is Better than that of Majors.*

*Angels Continue to Swat the Poor Oaklets.*

*Bradley Hogg is Surprised in the Seventh.*

BY HARRY A. WILLIAMS.

World series may come and world series may go, but the Coast League season wags on until October 29.

With Boston bloated with its own greatness, and Brooklyn gone the way of Babylon, we pursue the even tenor of our virtuous way, and for more than two weeks yet the fans will be able to go out to Washington Park and get a run for their money.

QUITE INTERESTING.

They were given one of these runs yesterday, many of them, in fact—eleven all told—the final score being 8 to 3 in favor of Los Angeles, and were permitted to witness something for two-bits which was denied the big league boobs who pungled up at the minimum rate of three bucks per boob per game, to wit: a triple play.

In the course of beating Oakland, which is a greatly reinforced aggregation, it became necessary for the Angeles to execute one of these three-ply stunts, and they did so without hesitation.

This necessity arose in the seventh inning after Del Howard executed a Del Gainer and scored two with a pinch hit. The Angels pulled out of this inning breathing hard and with their heads barely above the surface. By a sudden assault on the unsuspecting Bradley W. Hogg, Oakland scored three and came within one tally of wiping out a four-run lead which Los Angeles had compiled with painstaking care in the first and fourth. As the poets say, more about this inning and the triple play anon.

ALL SETTLED.

The game continued close until the eighth, when the Angels penetrated Speed Martin and his support for four runs so as to sew the thing up and have nothing to worry about in the ninth.

Hitting was free on our side at all times, while the Oaks displayed considerable freedom with the bat from the seventh to the ninth, inclusive. The pressure was so great that Del Howard was compelled to use three pitchers and an equal number of pinch-hitters. This amply refutes the rumor that the war had caused a shortage of pinch-hitters. Two of Oakland's pinch-hitters delivered, which is more than can be said of his pitchers. With two out of his pinch-hitters hitting, they had a percentage of .666 for the day as against .000 for the pitchers. If composed entirely of pinch-hitters the Oaks would be a very dangerous ball team.

TOUGH GUYS.

At that, the tailenders shou'l not be sneezed at, even if this is ideal weather for sneezing. It should be recalled that with a weaker line-up than they now have they did as well against Portland last week as Vernon did the week before.

Howard handled his pitchers diplomatically. Instead of yanking them openly, he slid them gently aside to let somebody bat for them. This is a good system because it does not jar the pitcher's confidence in himself. The pitchers were eased out of the game as follows: Gardner batted for Prough in the fifth, Howard for Beer in the seventh, and Harwood for Martin in the ninth. No runs were scored off Sammy, but he was wilder than some of those guys who bet on Brooklyn, and was threatened with serious consequences at all times.

The fielding was as tight as the hitting was free. It had to be. Otherwise neither side might never have been retired. Both clubs played errorless ball until the ninth, when the Oaks took an inning off and booted a couple. The work of Bobby Davis

(Continued on Second Page.)

*The Dangers of the Dodgers. . . . . . . No. 6.*

THAT "SHORE" WAS AN AWFUL WALLOP!

THE DODGERS

0

HIT 'EM FOUR TIMES AND WIN A WORLD CHAMPIONSHIP

I THANK YOU!

CHAMP

RED SOX

BOSTON

JINGLE JINGLE

THE LONG END

GALE

Hoss Racing.

## LEE AXWORTHY LOWERS RECORD.

TROTS MILE WITH WAGON IN TWO-TWO-THREE.

**Volga Fails to Lower Her Own Time—Deputy Sheriff Spills in Two-ten Pace — Official Programme Ended—Horses to go After Records Today.**

[BY A. P. NIGHT WIRE.]

LEXINGTON (Ky.) Oct. 12.—Lee Axworthy, champion trotting stallion of the world, driven to a wagon by one of his owners, Harry K. Devereaux of Cleveland, lowered the wagon record of 2:05 1-4 for trotting stallions to 2:02 3-4 on the final day of the forty-fourth annual meeting of the Kentucky Trotting Horse Breeders' Association here today.

Volga, champion three-year-old mare, started to beat her mark of 2:04 1-2, but tired in the stretch after trotting the third quarter in 30 1-4 and completed the mile in 2:05 1-4.

These two exhibitions featured the final programme, the three races on the card being won in straight heats. Locust Bug took the 2:20 trot, Little Frank D the 2:10 pace, and Binville the 2:12 trot. Valentine held the reins on Little Frank D and Locust Bug, putting him up among the leading drivers of the meeting. Cox leads the list with eight victories and Murphy is second with six.

In the first heat of the 2:10 pace, The Deputy Sheriff fell going up the back stretch. Crossman, driving Major A, pulled up and barely missed the spill, and Whitehead, driving Hal Leaf, was thrown into the infield, but was not injured. Hal Leaf finished the mile without a driver. All the horses were placed by the judges, Hal Leaf getting third place in the first heat and winning second money in the race.

Though the official programme was completed today the meeting will be continued tomorrow to permit horsemen to start their horses for records. Cox, Murphy, Geers, Edman and Pastime are among the stables that will be shipped to Atlantic, while others will go to Rock-

(Continued on Second Page.)

What do They Care.

## RECORD DUCK OPENING SURE, DESPITE WEATHER.

OPENING of the general game seasons at 5.28 next Sunday morning finds gunners faced by a combination of conditions almost without precedent in Southern California sporting annals.

LOOKED GOOD.

Two weeks ago a record-breaking opening day seemed certain. Sprigs fairly "elbowed" each other off the artesian-overflows of the duck clubs. Those with water were in luck. Quail were in evidence everywhere throughout the brushlands of hill and washes, while wheat and Kaffir corn stubbles looked like conventions with all-day sessions. Ducks were pouring into the drowned lands by day and by night.

Then came the rains, to the discomfiture of beet growers and bean harvesters. Welcomed at first by shooters, repeated showers shifted the scenes from as sunny as summer to the gloom of the clouds themselves as the ducks sailed for the south—squadrons of 'em—and few coming down from San Joaquin and Owens Valley to take their places.

THE RESULT.

A quiet storm with little precipitation and early in the season had produced the expected result. Natural feed in the south is sprouted already. The quail have moved back to the hills, where green grass is springing up everywhere, and water is even more abundant than the deer and dove hunters reported it last month.

The prospect is not bad enough to discourage a single shooter, but from the most brilliant in years it has shrunk to merely better than average, with the biggest stock of native-bred birds in years awaiting those who are willing to walk, and can hit the artful dodgers of the hillsides after a hard day's "hike" mostly up and down.

COME LATER.

The ducks will be coming along later in a record-breaking November flight as records go the last ten years; and enough birds are now in the country to give general limits the opening morning in the "first flight" before the sun clears the summit of Santiago—which is quite as it should be.

But, good as the shooting will be for everybody, it will fall far short of the bee-like buzzing of myriad shots that would have offered the relatively few favored clubs that had water independent of the rainfall. As many ducks will be killed in the aggregate and perhaps even more, but they will be wider distributed.

GOOD HUNTING.

Clubmen, road hunters, and those of the "unattached," who prey not upon the bounty of others, but go far afield to where ducks are doing damage and the rancher's welcome goes forth to the visiting gunner—all will get ducks Sunday.

Reports covering all of Southern California have been compiled by the Fish and Game Commission's experts following investigations of deputies and experts, checked by reports of sportsmen during the deer and dove seasons just closed. With scarcely an exception, they agree that the quail crop is appreciably better than last year, and young birds still can be distinguished, showing a late brood.

Most of the birds seen are well-grown and strong, but not wild, and the law seems to have been observed more generally about Los Angeles than ever before. Quail are plentiful right in the city throughout the San Fernando Valley washes, and many limits will be shot there Sunday as the local authorities are avoiding making the extension of the city obnoxious by enforcing provisions based upon congested population.

Throughout the Calabasas, "posting" of ranches is general, but in the open territory birds are plentiful. Throughout the Simi, the large holdings are also closed, such as the 26,000-acre Strathearn Rancho, but north and west of Moorpark quail are very plentiful. Ventura county in general has raised more quail than in several years; the same is, however, true of every county in Southern California.

LOTS OF 'EM.

The northern hill section of Los Angeles, from Saugus north, east and west, is literally alive with quail, and the men who know how to hunt the birds, and can hit them on the hills, will need tog o no farther. Antelope Valley ranchers claim damage by quail to Kaffir corn and other crops, particularly such vegetables as peas, raised for domestic use, and more or less shooting of a sporadic nature has been done, an offender being arrested and fined $50 for "soonering" last week.

The San Gabriel and other river washes east of town are full of quail and rabbias, and limits will be killed quite generally the first day, after which the canny birds locate the thick brush and willow tangles, where ten men and a whole kennel of dogs cannot dislodge them.

IN TOWN.

A surprising number of quail will be shot the first day right in town, as dove hunters, slipping out for an evening shoot have found some fine bands that will be good for fifteen birds in a Sunday morning round-up.

Lower Orange and all of San Diego county from San Onofre to

(Continued on Third Page.)

And Now It's All Over.

## ERNIE SHORE HEAVES THREE-HIT GAME, DESPITE CHILLY WEATHER.

*New Record for Attendance and Receipts is Set in Final Game—Superior Ability of the Winners is Apparent Throughout Pastime.*

[BY A. P. NIGHT WIRE.]

BOSTON, Oct. 12.—The Boston Americans won the championship of the baseball universe here this afternoon when they defeated the Brooklyn Nationals, 4 to 1, in the fifth and final game of the world's series of 1916. The greatest gathering in the history of the American national sport witnessed the victory, 42,620 fans departing after the contest, convinced that the Bostons were the baseball machine par excellence of recent years.

UNDEFEATED.

As a result of the four games-to-one conquest over Brooklyn, Boston is tonight celebrating its fifth victory in world's series since 1903, and there is added joy in the fact that never in its history has a Boston team been forced to bow to the superior prowess of a rival in such a combat.

The victory over Brooklyn today was so clean-cut and decisive that there was left no ground for argument. That the better team won the championship was obvious. Before the speed and curves of Ernest Shore, the Brooklyns were well-nigh helpless, while Jeff Pfeffer, the last hope of Brooklyn, proved unequal to the task of holding Boston in check.

DODGERS LEAD.

Although the Nationals were first to score, their advantage was short-lived, and once the Bostons unlimbered their heavy batting artillery any doubt regarding the outcome of the game was dissipated, so closely did Shore hold the Brooklyn clan in the mystery of his deceptive delivery.

The invaders from Greater New York were able to score only three hits for a similar total of bases, and the solitary run scored was unearned. It was the result of a pass, a sacrifice, and an out and a passed ball. Boston, on the other hand, got ten bases on seven hits, and two of its four runs were earned.

TOO CHILLY.

Although the contest was played before a record throng of fans, there was only a moderate amount of enthusiasm, the chilling weather and the ease with which Boston disposed of its opponents dulling the edge of such outbursts which sprang from grand stands and bleachers at the more thrilling points of the game.

The day was bitter cold, with a piercing wind from the east. The spectators, who paid $83,873 to witness the triumph of the American League champions, came prepared for the November-like weather. Overcoats, fur wraps and heavy gloves were much in evidence.

NEW FEATURES.

Aside from Shore's clever cold-weather hurling and a sensational running shoe-top catch by Wheat off Shore in the fifth, and its mate by Lewis in the eighth, when he robbed Merkle, batting for Pfeffer, of an apparently sure double, the game was devoid of feature plays.

Immediately after Scott had clinched the championship by gobbling Mowrey's short fly for the final out of the game the spectators rushed upon the field and fell in behind the Royal Rooters and their band for a parade. On the first circuit of the diamond they captured President J. J. Lannin of the Boston club and then crossed the field after President C. H. Ebbets of Brooklyn. Amid the cheers of the fans the rival club executives joined arms and led the march, while thousands in the stands stayed to watch the celebration.

PLAYERS RUN.

The players, however, did not wait to take part in the impromptu ceremonies. Both teams rushed for their dressing-rooms and there were few if any congratulations. Manager Robinson did not meet Manager Carrigan in his dash across the field and there was no public greeting or hand clasp between the pair. Many of the fans, however, shook hands with the Boston players and with Manager Carrigan, who said again that he had retired from professional baseball with today's game.

As was the case in yesterday's game, Brooklyn was the first to score. Its only and unearned tally came in the second session, when Shore issued his only pass of the day, Cutshaw to first. Mowrey sacrificed him to second, from which point he moved to third on Olson's infield out and scored when Shore uncovered the plate with a passed ball.

ALL TIED UP.

Boston immediately tied the score in their half of the same inning when Lewis tripled to left and came home as Wheat threw the ball, recovered from Gardner's high fly, wide of the plate in an effort to get Lewis at the plate.

The Red Sox added two more in the next turn at bat. Cady hit a bounder over Daubert's head. Hooper walked. Cady scored when Olson threw Janvrin's grounder into center field in an attempted double play. Hooper romped home from third on Shorten's hot one over second. The fourth and final run was manufactured in the fifth on Hooper's single and Janvrin's double. After that the Red Sox, aided by Shore's air-tight pitching, played defensive ball and Brooklyn never threatened.

NEW RECORD.

The attendance and receipts for today's game established a new record in this department of world's series history, supplanting the figures made in the same park October 11 a year ago, when the amounts were a few hundred less. Neither the total attendance or money taken in at the box office surpassed the banner records made in 1911 and 1912.

(Continued on Second Page.)

## COMPOSITE BOX SCORE OF THE WORLD'S SERIES.

BROOKLYN.

| | Ab | R | H | 2b | 3b | Hr | So | Bb | Sb | Sh | Po | A | E | Batg | Fldg |
|---|---|---|---|---|---|---|---|---|---|---|---|---|---|---|---|
| Myers, cf | 22 | 2 | 4 | 0 | 1 | 1 | 3 | 1 | 0 | 0 | 10 | 1 | 0 | .182 | 1.000 |
| Daubert, 1b | 17 | 1 | 3 | 0 | 1 | 0 | 3 | 2 | 0 | 0 | 42 | 3 | 0 | .176 | 1.000 |
| Merkle, 1b | 3 | 0 | 1 | 0 | 0 | 0 | 0 | 2 | 0 | 0 | 9 | 0 | 1 | .333 | .900 |
| Stengel, rf | 11 | 2 | 4 | 0 | 0 | 0 | 0 | 0 | 0 | 1 | 3 | 1 | 1 | .364 | .800 |
| Johnston, rf | 10 | 1 | 3 | 0 | 1 | 0 | 0 | 1 | 0 | 0 | 1 | 0 | 1 | .300 | .500 |
| Wheat, lf | 19 | 2 | 4 | 0 | 1 | 0 | 0 | 2 | 1 | 0 | 13 | 0 | 1 | .211 | .857 |
| Cutshaw, 2b | 19 | 2 | 2 | 1 | 0 | 0 | 1 | 1 | 0 | 0 | 17 | 12 | 2 | .106 | .935 |
| Mowrey, 3b | 17 | 2 | 3 | 0 | 0 | 0 | 1 | 3 | 0 | 1 | 8 | 15 | 1 | .176 | .958 |
| Olson, ss | 17 | 1 | 4 | 0 | 1 | 0 | 2 | 2 | 0 | 2 | 9 | 12 | 4 | .235 | .840 |
| Meyers, c | 10 | 0 | 2 | 0 | 1 | 0 | 0 | 0 | 0 | 0 | 21 | 8 | 0 | .200 | 1.000 |
| Miller, c | 8 | 0 | 1 | 0 | 0 | 0 | 1 | 0 | 0 | 1 | 8 | 2 | 0 | .250 | 1.000 |
| Marquard, p | 3 | 0 | 0 | 0 | 0 | 0 | 1 | 0 | 0 | 0 | 0 | 3 | 0 | .000 | 1.000 |
| Pfeffer, p | 4 | 0 | 1 | 0 | 0 | 0 | 2 | 0 | 0 | 0 | 0 | 2 | 0 | .250 | 1.000 |
| Smith, p | 5 | 0 | 1 | 1 | 0 | 0 | 0 | 0 | 0 | 0 | 1 | 8 | 0 | .200 | 1.000 |
| Coombs, p | 3 | 0 | 1 | 0 | 0 | 0 | 0 | 0 | 0 | 0 | 0 | 2 | 0 | .333 | 1.000 |
| Cheney, p | 0 | 0 | 0 | 0 | 0 | 0 | 0 | 0 | 0 | 0 | 0 | 0 | 1 | .000 | .000 |
| Rucker, p | 0 | 0 | 0 | 0 | 0 | 0 | 0 | 0 | 0 | 0 | 0 | 0 | 0 | .000 | .000 |
| Dell, p | 0 | 0 | 0 | 0 | 0 | 0 | 0 | 0 | 0 | 0 | 0 | 0 | 0 | .000 | .000 |
| O'Mara, pinch | 1 | 0 | 0 | 0 | 0 | 0 | 1 | 0 | 0 | 0 | 0 | 0 | 0 | .000 | .000 |
| Totals | 170 | 13 | 34 | 2 | 6 | 1 | 15 | 14 | 1 | 5 | 142 | 69 | 12 | .200 | .946 |

BOSTON.

| | Ab | R | H | 2b | 3b | Hr | So | Bb | Sb | Sh | Po | A | E | Batg | Fldg |
|---|---|---|---|---|---|---|---|---|---|---|---|---|---|---|---|
| Hooper, rf | 21 | 6 | 7 | 1 | 1 | 0 | 0 | 2 | 1 | 0 | 8 | 2 | 0 | .333 | 1.000 |
| Janvrin, 2b | 23 | 2 | 5 | 3 | 0 | 0 | 6 | 0 | 0 | 1 | 7 | 14 | 2 | .217 | .913 |
| Walker, cf | 11 | 1 | 3 | 0 | 1 | 0 | 2 | 1 | 0 | 0 | 4 | 0 | 0 | .273 | 1.000 |
| Shorten, cf | 7 | 0 | 4 | 0 | 0 | 0 | 1 | 0 | 0 | 1 | 3 | 0 | 0 | .571 | 1.000 |
| Walsh, cf | 3 | 0 | 0 | 0 | 0 | 0 | 0 | 0 | 0 | 0 | 1 | 0 | 0 | .000 | 1.000 |
| Hoblitzel, 1b | 17 | 3 | 4 | 1 | 1 | 0 | 1 | 6 | 0 | 0 | 64 | 3 | 0 | .235 | 1.000 |
| Lewis, lf | 16 | 3 | 6 | 2 | 1 | 0 | 1 | 1 | 0 | 5 | 9 | 1 | 0 | .375 | 1.000 |
| Gardner, 3b | 16 | 2 | 3 | 0 | 0 | 2 | 1 | 0 | 0 | 2 | 7 | 20 | 2 | .187 | .931 |
| Scott, ss | 16 | 1 | 2 | 0 | 1 | 0 | 1 | 1 | 0 | 2 | 6 | 22 | 2 | .125 | .933 |
| Cady, c | 4 | 1 | 1 | 0 | 0 | 0 | 0 | 3 | 0 | 0 | 11 | 1 | 0 | .200 | 1.000 |
| Thomas, c | 7 | 0 | 1 | 1 | 0 | 0 | 1 | 0 | 0 | 1 | 11 | 4 | 0 | .143 | 1.000 |
| Carrigan, c | 3 | 0 | 2 | 0 | 0 | 0 | 1 | 0 | 0 | 1 | 3 | 1 | 0 | .667 | 1.000 |
| Shore, p | 6 | 0 | 0 | 0 | 0 | 0 | 5 | 1 | 0 | 0 | 1 | 5 | 0 | .000 | 1.000 |
| Mays, p | 1 | 0 | 0 | 0 | 0 | 0 | 1 | 0 | 0 | 0 | 0 | 4 | 0 | .000 | 1.000 |
| Ruth, p | 5 | 0 | 0 | 0 | 0 | 0 | 1 | 0 | 0 | 0 | 1 | 5 | 0 | .000 | 1.000 |
| Foster, p | 1 | 0 | 0 | 0 | 0 | 0 | 1 | 0 | 0 | 0 | 1 | 1 | 0 | .000 | 1.000 |
| Leonard, p | 3 | 0 | 0 | 0 | 0 | 0 | 1 | 1 | 0 | 0 | 0 | 0 | 0 | .000 | .000 |
| Gainer, pinch | 1 | 0 | 1 | 0 | 0 | 0 | 0 | 0 | 0 | 0 | 0 | 0 | 0 | 1.000 | .000 |
| McNally, pinch | 0 | 1 | 0 | 0 | 0 | 0 | 0 | 0 | 0 | 0 | 0 | 0 | 0 | .000 | .000 |
| H'k'n, pinch | 0 | 1 | 0 | 0 | 0 | 0 | 0 | 1 | 0 | 0 | 0 | 0 | 0 | .000 | .000 |
| Totals | 161 | 21 | 39 | 8 | 5 | 2 | 24 | 17 | 1 | 13 | 147 | 83 | 6 | .242 | .974 |

SUMMARY.

Two-base hits—Lewis (2,) Hooper, Janvrin (3,) Smith, Cutshaw, Thomas, Hoblitzel. Three-base hits—Walker, Hoblitzel, Wheat, Meyers, Scott, Olson, Daubert, Hooper, Johnston, Myers, Lewis. Home runs—Myers, Gardner (2.) Stolen bases—Wheat, Hooper. Sacrifice hits—Janvrin, Scott (2,) Lewis (5,) Thomas, Stengel, Olson (2,) Miller, Carrigan, Gardner (2,) Shorten. Double plays—Janvrin to Scott to Hoblitzel; Hooper to Cady; Gardner to Janvrin to Hoblitzel; Scott to Janvrin to Hoblitzel (2;) Mowrey to Cutshaw to Daubert. Myers to Miller. Left on bases—Brooklyn, 32; Boston, 31. First base on errors—Brooklyn, 5; Boston, 6. Bases on balls—Off Marquard, 6; off Pfeffer 4, off Shore, 3; off Smith, 6; off Ruth, 3; off Mays, 3; off Coombs, 1; off Leonard, 4, off Cheney, 1. Hits—Off Marquard, 12 in 11 innings; off Shore, 12 in 17 2-3 innings; off Pfeffer, 7 in 10 2-3 innings; off Smith, 7 in 13 1-3 innings, off Ruth, 6 in 14 innings, off Mays, 7 in 5 innings, off Foster, 3 in 3 innings; off Leonard, 5 in 9 innings; off Cheney, 4 in 3 innings off Rucker, 1 in 2 innings; off Dell, 1 in 1 inning. Struck out—By Marquard, 9, by Shore, 9; by Pfeffer, 5; by Smith, 2; by Ruth, 4; by Mays, 2; by Foster, 1; by Leonard, 3; by Cheney, 5; by Rucker, 3. Wild pitches—Pfeffer (2.) Passed ball—Cady. Umpires—Connolly, Dineen, O'Day and Quigley.

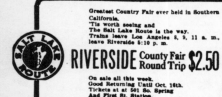

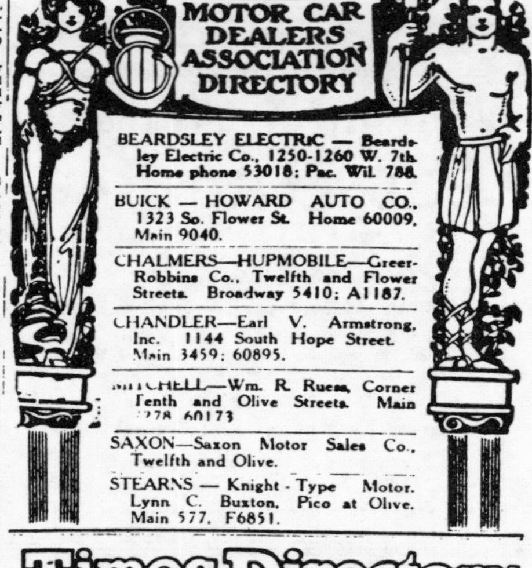

*The Pink Pages—World's Series—The Foremost Events Graphically Told.*

The Los Angeles Times

Pages 3 and 4
FINANCIAL MARKETS

TUESDAY MORNING, OCTOBER 16, 1917.—PART III: 4 PAGES.

# WHITE SOX DOWN GIANTS AND GRAB 1917 WORLD BASEBALL CHAMPIONSHIP.

All Over.

## NEW YORKERS FALTER IN FATAL FOURTH AND LOSE.

### *Windy City Gets the Title for First Time Since Cub 1908 Victory.*

[BY A. P. NIGHT WIRE.]

NEW YORK, Oct. 15.—Coming out of the West like Lochinvar of old, the Chicago Americans won the world series baseball championship this afternoon, defeating the New York Nationals, 4 to 2, in the sixth and deciding game of the 1917 diamond classic.

For the first time in almost a decade the titular banner will flutter over the fans in the Middle West metropolis next spring when the series pennant is raised at Comiskey Park as evidence of the superiority of the White Sox in the great national game.

After winning the first two games on their home field and losing the next two at the Polo Grounds, the Chicago clan clinched the gonfalon with two straight victories, one at Comiskey Park and the other at the lair of the Giants.

The New York club did not go down to defeat today without desperate resistance. The battle was surcharged with sensational situations and thrilling plays, but the invading combination with the edge of a one-game lead was not to be denied. It was the Giants who eventually broke under the strain of the conflict.

With "Rube" Benton, the towering southpaw from Clinton, N. C., waging a pitching duel for the locals against the curves of Urban Faber, the Cascade (Iowa) hurler of the White Sox, the battle was fought through three full innings without either team giving the slightest margin either offensively or defensively. In the "fatal fourth," however, the Giants faltered for just a moment and seizing their advantage, the players of Chicago rushed the breach and captured the first world series championship emblem won by the city on the shores of Lake Michigan since Frank Chance's Cubs defeated the Detroit Americans in the struggle of 1908.

SOX BEST.

While the Nationals made a game rally in the fifth, and the Sox added another run in the ninth, the three runs scored by the Chicago team in the fourth session were the deciding factor. The play in this inning convinced the thirty-odd thousand spectators present that for this season, at least, the pennant-winning club of the American League is better than that which won the six months' race in the senior organizaion.

That the championship should be decided in the fourth inning was in keeping with the feature and factor play throughout the series. The Chicago club scored its winning run in this inning during the first game and collected five in the second contest in the same period. In the third and fourth contests, won by the Giants, the winning team scored the only runs of the battle in the fourth inning of the third and the first of the five runs in the fourth game, which was a 5-to-0 shutout in favor of New York. The scoring of Saturday proved an exception, but today the Sox reverted to their original system and, aided by misplays by the Giants, closed the series with a decisive victory.

The largest assemblage of spectators to witness any game of the present interleague combat was on hand when the rival clubs grappled. According to the official figures, 33,969 persons paid admission to the Polo Grounds, their contributions totaling $73,348. Of this sum, the stockholders of the two clubs each will receive $33,006.06 and the National Commission $7334.80. The players ceased to participate in the gate receipts after the fourth game, but they will receive $152,888.58 as their share, this amount being divided 60 per cent. to the Chicago team and 40 per cent. to the New York players. The total receipts for the six games amounted to $425,878 and, after subtracting the money paid to the players, the two clubs each are richer by $115,200.81 and the National Commission $42,587.80.

THE CLIMAX.

As was befitting the climax of the baseball year, the day was the best of the ten through which the battle raged. Under these favorable conditions the thousands of fans entered into the spirit of the play with more

(Continued on Second Page.)

*The Battle of Ball Run—Finished. . . By HATLO.*

American on Top.

## SOX VICTORY POPULAR IN BIGGEST PART OF COUNTRY

### *Middle West, Coast and South Solidly Behind Chicago Team.*

BY HARRY A. WILLIAMS.

NOW that the traditions of the American League have been upheld, there is little more to be said.

Fans here will revert to the Coast League race, while those elsewhere will go into winter quarters.

It remained for the White Sox to uphold these traditions, Cleveland having failed to do so against Cincinnati, and the Browns falling down on the job to the Cardinals. For a time it seemed that the balance might be restored by the National entries defeating the American League clubs in every post-season series, but with something really worth while at stake—the championship of the world—the American rose superior, and overcame all obstacles, including Slim Sallee, Ferdinand Schupp and Rube Benton.

Chicago's victory was a popular one except in New York and other parts of the extreme and self-sufficient East, where the opinion prevails that spring bottom pants and hair oil are still worn by everybody living south of Atlantic City and west of Buffalo. In no other world series has sectional feeling been so marked. The West and South were solidly for the Sox.

ATTITUDE HERE.

This attitude here was due to a number of things. One was the presence of six former Coast League boys on the Chicago club. Then Charles A. Comiskey, the biggest figure in baseball, is one of our prime boosters. When not actually training in Southern California, he is singing its praises. And Commy can sing. I heard him once with two quarts of champagne under his belt. Then there was a touch of human nature, known as egotism. In New York, Chicago is known as "the West." Los Angeles is more so. People here who would not know the difference between baseball and quoits, were pulling for Chicago to win. Their somewhat indefinable yearning was due to a vague desire to see the championship move farther West.

Persons who had never before shown any interest in baseball inquired feverishly for the results. One lady called up after the fourth game in New York. From her questions it was easy to see that she didn't know whether they were playing baseball or football. When told that New York had won, she spilled a couple of juicy sobs into the phone. In war we have attained that broad nationalism that recognizes only one country and one flag, but when it comes to baseball sectionalism is still rampant.

The genuine fans were guided in their choice, if they made any, partly by their sympathies and to a degree by their judgment. There was still another class—the bettors—who relied on cold blooded calculations.

Comiskey by his thoroughgoing Americanism also compiled a big following here and elsewhere. He was one of the founders of the younger league, for which the name "American" was happily chosen. Also it was he who conceived the idea of making this a "Star Spangled" world series, prior to which he pledged a part of his income to the Red Cross. Doubtless the National league and its champions are fully as patriotic. But Commy's patriotism was more outspoken. He is typically western.

The series itself was a combination of good and bad baseball. Although the result was always in doubt, the White Sox must be given the edge by virtue of winning four out of six games. Furthermore, they were the only club to win a victory away from home. They outplayed their rivals on the whole, and in the last analysis appeared to outgame them. Some will claim that they were more ably managed, but that is largely a matter of personal opinion, and brings up too many involved problems of baseball to form a rapid-fire opinion. From this distance failure to pull Sallee earlier in Saturday's game looked like faulty generalship, and yet he has been criticised by few baseball men.

It seems that McGraw felt forced to rely on his left-handers—the men who had won for him in the regular season. Plainly, he did not have a particle of faith in his right-handers. The inevitable result of this was that the Sox would get wise to his southpaws, and they began getting wise about the seventh inning last Saturday. Had the Giants won that game it would be necessary now to play a seventh. This disposes of the claim made in some quarters that McGraw was trying to prolong the series.

Rowland made his only false move when he failed to start Russell in the third game, instead of waiting until the fifth, after the series had been tied. When his team was two games to the good was the proper time to do his experimenting. Of course, failure to start Russell in the third game had no effect on the series, as the Sox couldn't score on Benton, but it nevertheless was the logical time, and would have given

(Continued on Second Page.)



## ANGEL-TIGER BATTLE TODAY.

Interest in Coast League baseball, which has been lagging during the world series, will take a fresh start this afternoon, when the Angels hook up with the Tigers in what may prove to be the deciding series of the season.

The season has two weeks to run. In order to nose out San Francisco it will be necessary for the Angels to gain two games on the Seals during that time. They are now a game and a half behind. San Francisco plays Salt Lake in the latter city, starting today.

## BOXING PROGRAMME TONIGHT AT VERNON.

Phil Salvadore, Sacramento lightweight, and Billy Cappelli of San Pedro, will clash in the four-round main event at the Vernon Athletic Club tonight. Salvadore got off to a flying start last week when he defeated Young Ketchell, terror of the 133 pounders. Cappelli is an aggressive battler and is expected to put up his usual whirlwind fight.

Johnny Rees, of the Naval Reserves, and Louie Rees, local lightweight, are slated for the semi-windup. The boys claim no relationship and will get their first introduction when they get in the ring.

The preliminary programme follows: Billy Moore vs. Mikey O'Brien, 135 pounds; Eddie Huse vs. Dick McManus, 145 pounds; Frank O'Campo vs. Al Anderson, 130 pounds; Sidney White vs. Charlie Grove, 116 pounds.

## YALE MAN HEADS ATHLETIC LEAGUE.

[BY A. P. NIGHT WIRE.]

NEW YORK, Oct. 15.—Robert Fleming Blair of Yale University, has been elected president of the Intercollegiate Association of Amateur Athletes of America at the annual meeting here. Other officers chosen were Joseph A. Esquirol, treasurer, and Hubert G. Larsen, acting secretary.

## COMMISSION BARS ALL BARNSTORMING.

[BY A. P. NIGHT WIRE.]

NEW YORK, Oct. 15.—Players participating in the world's series will be forbidden to engage in post-series games, it was announced here today by the National Commission. From each player's share in the world series money the sum of $1000 will be retained until January 1 as a means of enforcing the new rule.

## FLATLANDERS HOOK UP WITH PASADENA.

A gridiron argument between Los Angeles and Pasadena High schools has been arranged for Friday afternoon on the Pasadena High gridiron. The L. A. High Flatlanders were an unknown quantity until they fought Long Beach to a 6-6 tie last Saturday, thereby surprising many of the prep school dopesters.

Coach Glen Whittle of L. A. has three teams on the field every evening. He has secured the services of "Handsome Fred" Featherstone, former head coach, for the training of the second team.

## THE GAME PLAY BY PLAY.

[BY A. P. DAY WIRE.]

FIRST HALF—The umpires conferred with the managers at the plate before the game to discuss rules for field discipline. Judge Hylan, Democratic candidate for Mayor, threw out the ball. John Collins up. Strike one. Foul, strike two. Fletcher came in behind Benton and took Collins's hopper and threw him out. McMullin up. Ball one. McMullin sent up a weak foul to Rariden. Eddie Collins up. The stands booed Eddie Collins to the echo. Strike one. Collins singled sharply over second. Jackson up. Strike one. Herzog took Jackson's slow roller and tossed him out. No runs, one hit, no errors.

Second half—Burns up. Eddie Collins threw out Burns at first, Burns hitting at the first ball pitched. Herzog up. Strike one. Ball one. Herzog shot a single over McMullin's head, the stands breaking into a cheer. Kauff up. Foul, strike one. Strike two. Ball one. Kauff struck out, Faber's wide curves being too much for him. Zimmerman up. Ball one. Zimmerman sent a long drive right into Jackson's hands. No runs, one hit, no errors.

SECOND INNING.

First half—Felsch up. Strike one. Ball one. Ball two. Strike two. Ball three. Felsch struck out, failing to offer at the third strike. Gandil up. Gandil punched a single over the middle bag. Weaver up. Herzog threw out Weaver, Gandil moving to second. Schalk up. Strike one. Zimmerman threw out Schalk, making a nice play on the Chicago catcher's grounder. No runs, one hit, no errors.

Second half—Fletcher up. Strike one. Schalk ran down the line and took Fletcher's roller and threw him out. Robertson up. Foul, strike one. Eddie Collins took Robertson's smash and got his man at first. Holke up. Ball one. Holke got a double against the left-field fence. A little higher, it would have gone into the stands for a home run. Rariden up. Eddie Collins threw out Rariden, who hit the first ball pitched. No runs, one hit, no errors.

THIRD INNING.

First half—Faber up. Ball one. Ball two. Strike one. Foul, strike two. Foul. Faber struck out. John Collins up. Foul, strike one. John Collins popped to Herzog. McMullin up. Benton was employing a quick drop ball which he kept around the batters' knees. Strike one. Ball one. Strike two. Foul. McMullin fanned. It was Benton's third strike out and the crowd cheered him. No runs, no hits, no errors.

Second half—Benton up. Ball one. Strike one. Foul, strike two. Ball two. Faber burned an out curve over for a third strike and Benton sat down. Burns up. Ball one. Burns sent a hot liner to Felsch. Herzog up. Foul, strike one. Ball one. Ball two. Herzog sent a high fly out to Felsch. No runs, no hits, no errors.

FOURTH INNING.

First half—Eddie Collins up. Foul, strike one. Foul, strike two. Ball one. Zimmerman took Collins's grounder and threw wildly to the stands, Collins going to second. Jackson up. Foul, strike one. Foul, strike two. Ball one. Ball two. Jackson sent up a high fly to Robertson, who dropped the ball. Eddie Collins dashed to third, Jackson holding first when Robertson threw to third. Felsch up. Foul, strike one. The New York infield came in on the grass. Benton took Felsch's grounder and ran over to tag Collins. Benton tossed to Zimmerman, who ran after Collins and chased the Sox second baseman across the plate for a run. Gandil up. Jackson and Felsch scored on Gandil's single to right. Gandil was thrown out stretching his hit, Robertson to Herzog. Weaver up. Weaver sent a long fly to Burns. Schalk up. Ball one. Strike one. Ball two. Ball three. Schalk shot a hot single into left. Faber up. Ball one. Strike one. Ball two. Ball three. Strike two. Red Faber walked. John Collins up. Strike one. Fletcher threw out John Collins. Three runs, two hits, two errors.

Second half—Kauff up. Foul, strike one. Eddie Collins took Kauff's roller and threw him out. Zimmerman up. Strike one. Ball one. Strike two. Ball two. Zimmerman sent a high fly to John Collins. Fletcher up. Fletcher bounced a hit off McMullin's glove. The ball bounced to Weaver, who nearly threw the New York shortstop out by a line-shot throw. Robertson up. Robertson flied to Felsch. No runs, one hit, no errors.

FIFTH INNING.

First half—McMullin up. Ball one. Ball two. Strike one. Ball three. Strike two. Benny Kauff robbed McMullin of a hit, coming in fast and getting his line drive. Eddie Collins up. Ball one. Strike one. Ball two. Burns took Collins's easy fly. Jackson up. Strike one. Jackson struck at the ball so hard that he fell down and the crowd jeered. Ball one. Foul, strike two. Herzog threw out Jackson. No runs, no hits, no errors.

Second half—Holke up. Foul, strike one. Strike two. Holke struck out on three pitched balls. Rariden up. Ball one. Foul, strike one. Ball two. Ball three. Strike two. Rariden walked, making Faber pitch to him. Wilhoit batted for Benton. Wilhoit up. Ball one. Ball two. Strike one. Strike two. Foul. Ball three. Wilhoit also walked, Faber becoming unsteady. Burns up. Burns forced Wilhoit, Weaver to Eddie Collins, Rariden going to third. Herzog up. Ball one. Rariden and Burns scored on Herzog's three-base hit off the right-field wall. The stands were in a frenzy. Kauff up. Kauff fouled out to Gandil. Two runs, one hit, no errors.

SIXTH INNING.

First half—Perritt went into the box for New York. Felsch up. Ball one. Ball two. Strike one. Ball three. Felsch walked. Perritt lost his man trying to work the corners of the plate. Gandil up. Strike one. Felsch went out stealing, Rariden to Fletcher. Strike two. Gandil struck out on three pitched balls. Weaver up. [illegible]

[illegible]

Ball one. Strike one. Leibold popped to Herzog, who dropped the ball and then ran over to first, touching both Schalk, who was standing on the bag, and the bag as well. Leibold was declared out and Schalk was ruled as being safe. McMullin up. Ball one. Strike one. Foul, strike two. McMullin struck out. No runs, no hits, no errors.

Second half—The official scorer scores the play on Leibold as an assist for Herzog and a putout for Holke in the seventh inning. Rariden up. Strike one. Strike two. Foul. Leibold went into right field in place of John Collins. Ball one. Foul. Foul. Ball two. Rariden went out to Gandil, unassisted. Perritt up. Ball one. Perritt got a line single over second. Burns up. Strike one. Foul, strike two. Ball one. Foul. Foul. Ball two. Ball three. Burns lofted to Weaver. Herzog up. Ball one. Foul, strike one. On a short passed ball Perritt dashed to second and then ran to third when Schalk's wild throw got away from Collins. Ball two. Herzog popped to Weaver. No runs, one hit, one error.

EIGHTH INNING.

First half—It was announced that the official attendance was 33,006. Eddie Collins up. Strike one. Collins went out to Holke unassisted. Jackson up. Foul, strike one. Ball one. Jackson sent a hit into right field, for a base. Felsch up. Ball one. Ball two. Felsch fouled out to Holke. Gandil up. Strike one. Strike two. Foul. Foul. Foul. Kauff made a corking catch of Gandil's long fly. No runs, one hit, no errors.

Second half—Kauff up. Ball one. Kauff flied out to Leibold. Zimmerman up. Strike one. Ball one. Weaver threw out Zimmerman, robbing him of a hit. Fletcher up. Ball one. Ball two. Foul, strike one. Strike two. McMullin threw out Fletcher. No runs, no hits, no errors.

NINTH INNING.

First half—Weaver up. Foul, strike one. Ball one. Weaver got a single to left field. Schalk up. Ball one. Ball two. Strike one. Schalk fouled to Zimmerman. Faber up. On the hit-and-run play, Faber bunted, Weaver going to second. Faber's bunt was a sacrifice and he was thrown out, Perritt to Holke. Leibold up. Strike one. Weaver scored when Kauff dropped Leibold's line drive close to the ground. The official scorer gives Leibold a hit. McMullin up. Ball one. Ball two. Strike one. Leibold went to second on Kauff's throw to the plate. Zimmerman threw out McMullin. One run, two hits, one error, the official scorer giving Kauff an error on his throw to the plate.

Second half—Robertson up. Foul, strike one. Foul, strike two. Robertson claimed the ball struck his hand and Umpire Klem allowed it. Holke up. Collins threw out Holke at first, Robertson going to second. Rariden up. Strike one. Ball one. Ball two. Foul, strike two. Ball three. Foul. Rariden fanned. McCarty batted for Perritt. Strike one. Collins tossed out McCarty. No runs, no hits, no errors.

## AX OF FACULAY FALLS ON BROOKS.

The faculty ax will keep Ed Brooks out of an Occidental football jersey this season. The mighty Tiger full-back of last year registered at the Eagle Rock school last Saturday, and the "profs" have decided that he cannot imbibe enough learning by next Thursday to make him eligible for the game with the California Bears at Berkeley on Saturday afternoon. Consequently, Brooks has decided to repair to the fastnesses of Arizona, where he is big chief over a bunch of Mexicans in a copper mine.

While down-hearted over the loss of Brooks yesterday, the Tigers were cheered somewhat when it became known that Don Odell, who received a twisted ankle in last Saturday's game, will be in the best of shape for the Bear argument, and that "Tiny" Smith, who was rudely knocked on the bean by some budding Polyite in a practice game last week, will also be in the line-up.

The Tigers will leave for the north at 5 o'clock p.m. Thursday, over the Santa Fe. To put the Bengals on edge, Manager Brandstetner is trying to arrange a practice contest with Pasadena High Wednesday afternoon. The Occidental freshmen are slated to meet Polytechnic on the same date, and a double-header is being planned.

Brandstetner has received a communication from the Denver School of Mines offering the Tigers a two-year contract, one game to be played here and the next year's argument at Denver. "Brandy" wishes to sleep over this document before rendering a decision.

COAST LEAGUE STANDING.

| | Won. | Lost. | Pct. |
|---|---|---|---|
| San Francisco | 111 | 88 | .558 |
| Los Angeles | 108 | 88 | .551 |
| Portland | 103 | 94 | .523 |
| Salt Lake | 95 | 92 | .508 |
| Oakland | 94 | 103 | .477 |
| Vernon | 79 | 120 | .397 |

GAMES THIS WEEK.

Los Angeles and Vernon here.
San Francisco in Salt Lake.
Portland in Oakland.

## STATISTICS OF WORLD'S SERIES.

WHITE SOX.

| | Batting average. | Fielding average. |
|---|---|---|
| Leibold, rf | .400 | 1.000 |
| J. Collins, rf | .286 | .622 |
| McMullin, 3b | .125 | 1.000 |
| E. Collins 2b | .409 | 1.000 |
| Jackson, lf | .305 | 1.000 |
| Felsch, cf | .273 | 1.000 |
| Gandil, 1b | .261 | .986 |
| Weaver, ss | .333 | .866 |
| Schalk, c | .263 | .950 |
| Faber, p | .143 | 1.000 |
| Cicotte, p | .143 | .857 |
| Russell, p | .000 | .000 |
| Danforth, p | .000 | 1.000 |
| Williams, p | .000 | .000 |
| Risberg | .500 | .000 |
| Lynn | .000 | .000 |
| Totals | .274 | .955 |

GIANTS.

| | Batting average. | Fielding average. |
|---|---|---|
| Burns, lf | .277 | 1.000 |
| Herzog, 2b | .316 | .923 |
| Kauff, cf | .160 | .875 |
| Zimmerman, 3b | .120 | .920 |
| Fletcher, ss | .200 | .896 |
| Robertson, rf | .636 | .888 |
| Holke, 1b | .286 | .985 |
| McCarty, c | .400 | .888 |
| Rariden, c | .384 | 1.000 |
| Sallee, p | .166 | 1.000 |
| Perritt, p | 1.000 | 1.000 |
| Schupp, p | .250 | 1.000 |
| Anderson, p | .000 | 1.000 |
| Tesreau, p | .000 | .000 |
| Benton, p | .000 | 1.000 |
| Wilhoit | .000 | .000 |
| Totals | .263 | .957 |

## GOTCH IMPROVING; HAS GOOD CHANCE.

[BY A. P. NIGHT WIRE.]

CHICAGO, Oct. 15.—The condition of Frank Gotch, former world's champion wrestler, has improved so rapidly that his physicians said today he would be able to leave the hospital tomorrow. Gotch, suffering from acute congestion of the kidneys, was taken to the hospital last Wednesday. The former champion will regain his health, his physicians said, if he takes a long rest.

## LIGHTWEIGHTS WILL HAVE GAME TODAY.

The Polytechnic High lightweight squad and Whittier State are scheduled for a gridiron argument in the Quaker town this afternoon. The Mechanic lightweights went down to defeat before St. Vincent's last week, but claim they were greatly outweighed by the Saints. Whittier State, as yet, is an unknown quantity.

GUN CLUB SHOOT.

The Los Angeles Gun Club held a turkey shoot and practice shoot Sunday. The scores:

E. K. Mobler, 20 yards, 186x200; W. A. Cornelius, 19 yards, 186x200; Owen Council, 19 yards, 182; William Kennedy, 18 yards, 181; C. E. Groat, 17 yards, 118x125; Seth Hart, 17 yards, 117x125; C. W. Fish, 19 yards, 112x125; S. H. Wilson, 18 yards, 95x100; Mrs. Groat, 17 yards, 94x100; W. R. Shepherd, 16 yards, 92x100; F. Free, 19 yards, 86x100; A. L. Hunt, 16 yards, 88x100; H. A. Hunt, 18 yards, 8x100; P. L. Fallis, 16 yards, 80x100; J. C. Rendler, 16 yards, 70x100; L. L. Sheldon, 16 yards, 66x75; E. J. Brown, 16 yards, 59x75; F. Schiffman, 16 yards, 47x50; M. D. Towne, 16 yards, 40x50; H. Wilson, 16 yards, 39x50; Frank Chance, 16 yards, 37x50; L. A. Wisler, 16 yards, 37x60; E. S. Brown, 16 yards, 37x50; C. D. Wagner, 16 yards, 33x50; M. D. Roberts, 16 yards, 34x50; H. B. Fuerst, 16 yards, 32x50; H. H. Durgee, 16 yards, 31x50; A. H. Honey, 16 yards, 31x50; E. A. Ulman, 16 yards, 27x50; W. King, 16 yards, 25x50; W. W. Sweeney, 16 yards, 12x50; George Cline, 16 yards, 21x25; W. Kays, 16 yards, 21x25; J. L. Brown, 16 yards, 21x25; L. Calder, 16 yards, 19x25; J. D. Neuls, 16 yards, 13x25; F. H. Teeple, 16 yards, 16x25; R. A. Rucker, 16 yards, 13x25; F. L. Rucker, 16 yards, 13x25; W. A. Earnshow, 16 yards, 12x25; L. R. Merritt, 16 yards, 12x25; A. L. Tunison, 16 yards, 9x20; N. Reeves, 16 yards, 7x15; Mrs. Tunison, 16 yards, 5x10; Mrs. Sheldon, 16 yards, 3x5.

Turkey Winners—W. A. Cornelius, two turkeys; S. H. Wilson, two turkeys; Seth Hart, one turkey; William Kennedy, one turkey; Frank Free, one turkey; Owen Council, one turkey.

A number of the shooters tied for the turkeys in the different events, but in the shoot-off lost out.

## SAM M'VEY, NEGRO HEAVYWEIGHT, WINS.

[BY A. P. NIGHT WIRE.]

COLON, Oct. 15.—Sam McVey and Jim Johnson, negro heavyweight pugilists, fought twenty-five rounds here yesterday. McVey won the decision.



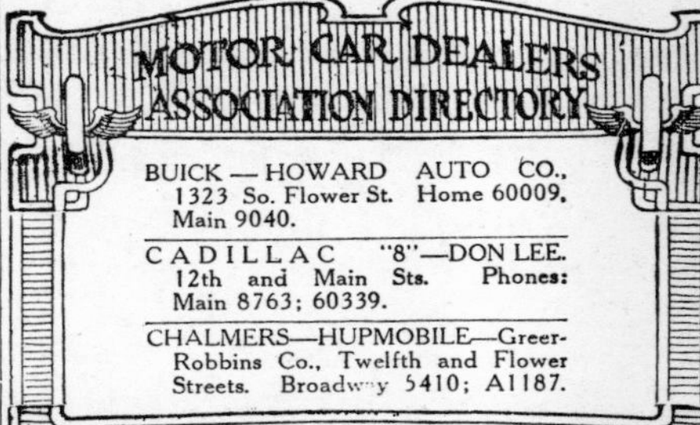

# Classified Liners.

## HORSES, MULES, CATTLE, ETC.
For Sale, Exchange, Wanted.

### For Sale.

FOR SALE—AUCTION. AUCTION. Horses, mares, mules, wagons, Buggies and harness, Tuesday, May 14, 10 a.m. 609 East 7th st. If in need of anything in the above line, do not fail to attend our Tuesday sale, as we will have all classes to offer. All stock sold must be as represented or money refunded. Stock at private sale. Horses and mules for hire. W. N. SNOWDEN, Prop. Phone Pico 417. Sam Watkins, Auctioneer.

FOR SALE—90 HEAD OF EXTRA FINE DAIRY COWS. ABOUT 20 OF THESE COWS WILL BE fresh in the next two weeks. The rest are all milking. Holstein, Durham, Guernsey and Jersey. 5 or 6 head of nice gentle family cows, 2 purebred Holstein bulls. Will take cows in exchange and will sell on time to responsible parties. Cows delivered any place in the city free of charge. COR. NADEAU AND ALAMEDA. South 1967.

FOR SALE—TEAM HORSES, BROWN AND BAY, weigh 2200, sound, good workers, $165. Team gray mares, closely mated, weigh 2400. Good workers, $125. One bay horse, weight 1200; 7 years, $100. One black horse, weight 1400, $135. Stock for hire. SNOWDEN'S, 609 E. 7th. Phone Pico 417.

FOR SALE—GOOD BRED, YOUNG BROOD BOAR, Berkshire and Poland-China, about 250 lbs. Also 6 White Leghorn roosters, choice. R. F. D. 14, BOX 465, Los Angeles. 3rd house west of Cudahy ave., on Anna st., Cudahy.

FOR SALE—TEAM HORSES, HARNESS AND wagon, suitable for fruit wagon; horses 8 years old. Owner leaving town. Corner MAIN AND HOMEWARD AVE. Take Moneta car.

FOR SALE—2 FINE WORK HORSES, 2900 pounds, age 9 and 11, cheap. MIDWICK COUNTRY CLUB, Ramona Acres, L. A. Co. Alhambra 99.

FOR SALE — BLACK JERSEY-GUERNSEY COW, fresh, giving 4 gallons of the richest milk. 916 BEATRICE AVE., near Sisters' Hospital.

FOR SALE—FRESH JERSEY COW, 3 YEARS OLD, tuberculin tested; easy milker, giving 4 gal. Will sell cheap. 1046 E. JEFFERSON.

FOR SALE — HOGS. 100 CHOICE FEEDERS, weighing 100 to 150 lbs., all good. DENNISON BROS., Ojai, Cal.

FOR SALE—OR RENT, FARM MULES. SEE W. A. GILLETTE, 1307 Fair Oaks ave., South Pasadena.

FOR SALE—OR RENT, 4 GOOD WORK MULES, 1 heavy team of horses, 3 small cheap horses, 2 farm wagons, buggy and harness. Call 707 E. SEVENTH ST.

FOR SALE—FRESH 5-YEAR-OLD JERSEY COW and calf, giving 5 gals. daily; can't be beat for butter. 4500 HUNTINGTON DRIVE, East 3454.

FOR SALE—2 YOUNG HORSES, STUDEBAKER 3½-ton wagon, smooth flat rack (nearly new,) harness, plows, and Jersey cow. MOOR, 746 E. Colorado blvd., Eagle Rock.

FOR SALE—LITTLE PIGS, BROOD SOWS, MIGHT trade for good cow. SHOEMAKER, Route 4, box 835, L. A.

FOR SALE—FRESH COW, JERSEY-DURHAM, 4½ gallons, would trade for dry cows or heifers. 404 S. MARENGO, West Alhambra.

FOR SALE—FOUR LARGE FINE BREWERY horses. WIELAND BREWERY, 112 S. Central ave. Home phone 10579, Sunset, Pico 468.

FOR SALE—POLAND CHINA PIGS, LITTLE and big; also sows and boar. VAUGHAN RANCH, 8th and Maclay, San Fernando.

FOR SALE—TUBERCULIN TESTED YOUNG JERSEY cow, $85. DELAGARRIGNE, Ocean Park Heights. R. 1, Box 263, Palms.

FOR SALE—2 JERSEY COWS, NEARLY FRESH. Apply 204 SUNOL DRIVE. Take E. First st. car to Rowan, walk 5 blocks east to Sunol.

FOR SALE—THOROUGHBRED HORSE. PRACTIcally new harness and wagon. A bargain. Call 35526.

FOR SALE—2 JERSEY COWS, 2 YEARS OLD, just fresh, very choice cows. Call today. 4445 SANTA FE AVE.

FOR SALE—ONE GOOD HORSE FOR RANCH, 1000 lbs., rubber tired buggy, harness, saddle, bridle, in first class condition. 1121 W. 36TH PL.

FOR SALE—GRAY HORSE, SEVERAL WAGONS and harness; give long trial to responsible parties. 639 SAN PEDRO.

FOR SALE— $45 buys good mare, wagon, surry and harness. 762 IVY ST., Watts. Watts car to Latin.

FOR SALE—OR EXCHANGE — 14-MONTHS-OLD registered Holstein bull, ¾ white, for piano. 1672 FISKE AVE., Pasadena, Colorado 4805.

FOR SALE—TEAM OF HORSES, 6 AND 8 years, weight 2500, just from work, cheap for cash. Call 775 S. SAN PEDRO ST.

FOR SALE—GOOD SPAN OF RANCH MARES. Apply 546 S. CLARENCE ST.

FOR SALE — RIDING AND DRIVING PONY, cheap. 148 W. 89TH ST. Vermont 6145.

FOR SALE—ONE TEAM OF MULES AND HARness, cheap. 1156 MAPLE AVE.

FOR SALE—FINE JERSEY COW, GOOD MILKer. Call Monday, 1224 W. 54TH ST.

FOR SALE—GOOD SOUND HORSE, MUST SELL. Ver. 3224. 626 N. KINGSLEY.

FOR SALE—WHITE MARE, 1000 POUNDS, 903 W. WASHINGTON.

FOR SALE—11 COWS, A1 MILKERS, ONE HOLstein bull. ARTESIA, 7122, F. C. PAYTON.

FOR SALE—2 FRESH COWS. SOUTH 2878W.

### For Exchange.

FOR EXCHANGE—GOOD WORK HORSE, FOR goats or chickens. HOME 59366.

### Wanted.

WANTED — HOGS. WISH TO MEET A PARTY who has 25 to 100 head of hogs (brood sows and stockers) and who is short of the right kind of feed; we have a going ranch in San Diego Co., between Fallbrook and Escondido, gravity flow of the very best mountain water in cement pipes for irrigation; 3-room house, good barn, water piped to faucets to both; water is free; fine patch of alfalfa; 35 acres wheat and barley; 5 tons milo maize in barn, 25 acres plowed and ready to plant; will exchange half interest in team, wagons, feed and farm implements for half interest in hogs and will give competent, thorough going farmer full charge. For further particulars, see N. BLACKSTOCK, room 704, Title Guarantee Bldg., Los Angeles.

WANTED—I OWN SUMMER RESORT AND 700 acres on Big Bear Lake—120-acre meadow. Big demand for riding animals. Will give party furnishing same feed for stock and all the money he makes first year. Apply at once. C. E. MILLER. 910 Van Nuys Bldg.

WANTED—COWS, COWS, HIGHEST CASH PRICES paid, thin or fat bulls and calves. Call for everywhere. H. FROELICH, 1343 Girard st. Broadway 3818.

WANTED—WE PAY CASH FOR HOGS, ANY NUMber and kind considered. DURBIN & FORBES, Broadway 4170. 722 San Fernando Bldg. Stock yards, South 2712-J.

WANTED — TEAM OF BLOCKY HORSES OR mules, weight about 2600 lbs.; young and sound; must be cheap for cash. Hollywood 1240.

WANTED—BUTCHER WANTS COWS, CALVES, bulls. I buy old horses. Phones: SOUTH 3602J1, VERMONT 6015.

## POULTRY—PET STOCK—
Supplies—For Sale, Exchange, Wanted.

### Poultry and Poultry Supplies.

FOR SALE—BABY CHICKS EVERY DAY, THOUSands of them, all popular varieties, supplied by experienced hatchers and reliable breeders. Better chicks cannot be had from any source. Intending purchasers will do well to inspect our supply. Our round, metal, fireless brooder is economical and safe. Chicks properly cared for will prove profitable this season. Baby ducks. Baby turkeys. Hatching eggs by the setting or incubator lots. Used incubators at bargain prices. Good breeding stock a specialty. Foods, appliances, books and supplies. We buy, sell and exchange everything in hair, fur and feathers. FANCIERS' EXCHANGE, 640 S. Main st.

FOR SALE — SIX PENS, HAMBURGS SEAbrights, White Wyandottes, Partridge Rocks, Partridge Wyandottes and Anconas. Blue ribbon stock, cheap. Two stands bees, wire and coop. Southeast corner 35th and Maple. W. E. KERN. Call Sunday.

FOR SALE—A PEN OF 9 BARRED ROCK HENS and rooster, also one pen of 6 light Brahmas, good laying strain. Through breeding for this season. Light Brahma and Barred chicks at reduced prices. Call or write T. M'NAMARA, 3421 Beswick st.

WANTED—WHO HAS 100 WHITE LEGHORN PULlets, 8 weeks old or older, they will exchange for my 23 young does, a buck and 35 young, 5 weeks old? Address M. E. DOOLITTLE, Burbank, Cal.

WANTED—ABOUT 75 YOUNG TURKEYS, ABOUT 7 or 8 weeks old; also 150 young Rhode Island Red pullets, of good strain; apply, giving price and full particulars. J. WILLIAMS, Supt. of Bolsa Chica Gun Club, Huntington Beach, Cal.

FOR SALE—ONE DOZEN OR MORE FINE LAYing hens, White Leghorns, McFarlane, heavy laying strain. 7611 SANTA MONICA BLVD., Hollywood.

FOR SALE — BABY CHICKS, HATCHING EGGS, poultry, etc. PIONEER HATCHERY, 320 S. Spring st. F1635; Main 3653. Sales yard, 815 S. LOS ANGELES ST. F1637.

FOR SALE—OR TRADE—1 NEW 200-EGG JUBIlee incubator, cost $30; will sell cheap. Call SOUTHERN CALIFORNIA MUSIC CO., 332 S. Broadway. Ask for Mr. Butler.

FOR SALE — 500 BABY CHICKS, McFARLAND strain Leghorns, 23c each, or $20 per hundred. Inquire Monday after 12 o'clock, 2440 S. MAIN. Park Poultry Co., South 1435W.

FOR SALE — FINE LOT WHITE AND BROWN Leghorns, few Rhode Islands, the bunch at $12 dozen. Call at 232 S. PARK VIEW ST. Temple or W. First car.

FOR SALE—FIRST AND SECOND-PRIZE SILVER Wyandotte, 2 doz. or part; beautiful strain; $2.25 each. Also pheasant and pigeons. SOUTH 5800-M.

FOR SALE—BABY CHICKS, BARRED ROCKS, Rhode Island Reds, White Leghorns. REDWING HATCHERY, 2030 E. Florence. South 5035-W. Delivered.

FOR SALE—SETTING EGGS AT REDUCED PRICE. Anconas, White Leghorns, Reds, heavy laying strain, $1 per setting. 126 E. AVE. 37. East 333.

WANTED — TWO TO FOUR HUNDRED GOOD stock White Leghorn pullet chicks, eight to ten weeks old. State stock and price. HENRY MERZ, Burbank.

FOR SALE—140 WHITE LEGHORN HENS AND pullets, laying. 12 mated Carneaux pigeons. 621 S. 6TH ST., Alhambra. Phone Alhambra 370W.

FOR SALE—FINE 10 BLUE ANDALUSIAN chickens, 9 hens and rooster, $20; also 10 Plymouth Rocks. 5632 HAROLD WAY.

FOR SALE—5 HENS AND ROOSTER, THORoughbred White Brahmas, will sell cheap. Call at 3606 DENKER AVE. Vermont 1403.

## POULTRY—PET STOCK—
Supplies—For Sale, Exchange, Wanted

### Poultry and Poultry Supplies.

FOR SALE— PRE-REMOVAL SALE. GERMAIN'S POULTRY DEPARTMENT. On July 1 we move to Sixth and Main sts., and are now offering attractive bargains in every department of our large store. A few of our Poultry Supply specials follow: West Coast Egg More (35c value,) 20c. C.E.F. Fountain, special 50c. Otas & Moe line galvanized feeders and fountains.

INCUBATOR SPECIALS. Cyphers Superior (hot water,) 130-egg size, $16.95. Cyphers Columbia (hot air,) 140-egg size, $16.95. Cyphers Columbia (hot air,) 250-egg size, $23.65.

BUCKEYE INCUBATORS AND BROODERS. We are California agents for the celebrated Buckeye Incubators and brooders, the most scientific hatchers and brooders on the market.

POULTRY FOODS. Coulson's No. 1 Condition Powder keeps baby chicks in a strong, vigorous condition. We have a full line of Coulson's foods and remedies for all ages of fowls. Coulson's Laying Mash is an excellent egg producer, and should be kept before laying hens all the time. Contains all the necessary ingredients for egg making.

DARLING'S MEAT CRISPS contain the highest per cent. of protein of any food on the market. Protein is absolutely necessary to the health of a fowl, and Darling's Meat Crisps offer the most economical means of feeding it.

DISINFECT NOW. Don't let those lice, mites and other germs get a foothold in your flock. They breed rapidly during hot weather, and are big profit reducers. Paint your coops inside and out with Carbola—it paints and disinfects with one operation.

For general disinfecting in large poultry yards, etc., use Crude Carbolic Acid.

EGGS FOR HATCHING. Get your eggs for hatching from Germain's. We carry eggs from reliable breeders only—in all standard varieties, including turkey, geese and duck eggs.

EGG CARRIERS. Egg carriers, egg boxes, egg scales, egg testers.

E-Z EGG PRESERVER. Preserve those eggs the easy way; keeps eggs just like fresh for ten months. Easy to use; economical.

GERMAIN SEED AND PLANT CO., 10996. 326-328-330 S. Main st. Main 996.

FOR SALE— BABY CHICKS! BABY CHICKS! Thousands of chicks on hand Monday, many varieties, and every day also.

FREE HATCHERY EXHIBIT. 15,000 eggs incubating here every day. 3000 chicks hatching Monday, visitors welcome, thousands of chicks on hand Monday of many varieties.

FIRELESS BROODERS—No worry, no danger of fires; will raise very healthy chicks; 50-chick size, $1.25; 100-chick size, $2.50; 150-chick size, $3.50. Outdoor hot water brooder, rainproof, 18 square feet floor space, only $17.50; 150-chick hot water indoor brooder, 12 square feet floor space, only $8.

HATCHING EGGS THAT HATCH—Mammoth Bronze turkey eggs, $2.50 per dozen; Buff Orpington eggs, $1.50 for 15; Barred Rocks, Reds, Anconas, $1.25 for 15. We can supply eggs in large lots of several varieties.

USED INCUBATORS. One 540 Pioneer, good as new, $35, cash or easy terms; one Success 130-egg, good as new, $7; two used 200-chick hot water brooders, $11 each, delivered to you.

200-CHICK HOT WATER BROODERS. The best and lowest priced brooder on the market, contains 18 square feet of floor space, and sold at a low price and on easy terms. Investigate this.

BREEDING STOCK. Rhode Island Reds, Barred Rocks, Minorcas, Wild Mallard Ducks, Pekin Ducks, White Leghorn hens and pullets. Ancona year-old hens, one fine pen of Partridge Rocks. Visit our sales yard anyway.

PIGEONS—RABBITS. All kinds of rabbits and pigeons for breeding stock. 815 South Los Angeles street.

VISITORS ALWAYS WELCOME. THE PIONEER HATCHERY, Main 3653. 320 S. Spring st. F1635.

FOR SALE—BLUE ANDALUSIAN, BLACK MInorca, Rhode Island Red and White Leghorn baby chicks and setting eggs, from our prizewinning beautiful pens; our blue Andalusians are unsurpassed and from heavy laying strain. Black Minorcas and McConnell's strain, from large typo, heavy-laying hens. Visitors invited to inspect our unsurpassed mating pens, setting eggs $1 to $2.50. BLACK AND BLUE HATCHERY, 5307 Meridian st. Phone 39458. Take Garvanza car marked York blvd., off York, cor. Avenue 58.

FOR SALE—BLACK MINORCA HATCHING EGGS, $2 per setting, for remainder of season. Your opportunity to secure extra fine eggs from our high-record, prize-winning strain of birds that have both SIZE AND QUALITY and lay those FAMOUS LARGE, WHITE EGGS. BLACK MINORCA GARDENS, 2111 S. Wilson ave., Monterey Park, Alhambra. Phone 167-R. El Monte car, Convent Sta.

FOR SALE—2000 BABY CHICKS, MONDAY AND Tuesday, R. I. Reds, Barred Rocks, Anconas, Brown Leghorns, White Minorcas, Black Minorcas, White Wyandottes. Monday, MacFarlane White Leghorns, $12 per 100. Special price on Anconas. 100 LYTTLE'S White Rocks, SHEPPARD Anconas, DU BOIS White Orpingtons. Brooder free with each 100 Anconas, Monday. Rabbits and pigeons. D. E. DOKE, 743 S. Los Angeles st.

FOR SALE—P. COOK EXTRA SELECT WHITE Leghorn baby chicks, 200-egg strain, 12½ cents; Anconas, Rocks and Reds, 15 cents each; 75 Ancona pullets, our own raising, 75 cents each; 25 extra fine young White Leghorn hens, $1.25 each; 200 milk-fed broilers, 35 cents lb.; small broilers, 30 cents each. P. COOK CHICK RANCH, 3017 S. Main st. Tel. South 1302.

FOR SALE—INSURE YOUR CHICKS BY FEEDing Pratts Baby Chick Food for the critical first three weeks; then add Pratts Poultry Regulator to a good developing ration and watch 'em grow. Satisfaction guaranteed or money refunded. Seed, feed and poultry supply dealers everywhere.

REID'S POULTRY PASTE— For body lice, scaly leg, head lice. One application guaranteed to keep birds free from lice for six months, or money refunded. Costs ½c a bird. At your dealer's, 25c and 50c, or mailed prepaid upon receipt of price. D. R. REID, 201 S. Middleton st. Huntington Park, Cal.

FOR SALE—4-DAYS-OLD THOROUGHBRED R. I. Red chicks, 20c each, from large dark red hens, excellent early layers; mated to cockerels from prize-winning stock, each over standard weight, and wonderful color; also eggs $1.50 setting. Every egg fertile or money back; will sell a few hens from my breeding yards at reduced prices. WEST 3915. 2531 W. JEFFERSON.

FOR SALE—VALENTINE'S CHOICE CORN FATtened table poultry, Plymouth Rock pullets, Rhode Island Red baby chicks, with mother hen. 22 well-bred Brown Leghorn laying hens, $1 each. H. M. VALENTINE, 1005 Verdugo road, Los Angeles city limits, Phone Green 216, Glendale.

FOR SALE—HATCHING THIS WEEK. R. I. Reds, Buff Orpingtons, White Minorcas and Black Langshans. Finest stock. Lowest prices. Will also sell 500 fancy White Leghorn laying hens. QUALITY EGG RANCH, Bingham Station, Santa Ana line or phone Monday, F3087, Broadway 1335. L. A. office.

FOR SALE—PEKING DUCKLINGS, 28C. PEKIN hatching eggs, special for Sunday, Monday, 75c setting. Rocks, Reds, Black Minorcas, $1 for 15. Call POULTRY RANCH, Vermont 555.

FOR SALE—9 GOSLINGS, 75C EACH. 4206 NASSAU ST. Take E. First st. car, Rowan ave., 3 block south.

FOR SALE—8 LAYING PULLETS, R. I. REDS, 2 pullets with 30 chickens, 1 rooster. Call Monday, 1711 MAPLE AVE.

FOR SALE—RHODE ISLAND REDS, 200 McFARlin chicks, 1 week to 8 weeks. 1040 W. 43RD ST.

FOR SALE—GENTLE 2-QT. MILCH GOAT, $20; year-old hornless Nubian doe, $30. 4555 GLEN ALBYN DRIVE. Garvanza car to Avenue 45½.

FOR SALE—HATCHING EGGS, RHODE ISLAND Reds, $1 for 15; $6 for 100. 3800 BROOKLYN AVE. Boyle 1755.

FOR SALE—THOROUGHBRED ANCONA YEARling hens, heavy layers. Not in Glendale. GLENDALE 1046-J.

FOR SALE—PHEASANT EGGS FOR HATCHING from beautiful large birds. HALE BROWN, 745 Whittier st. Phone 51926.

FOR SALE—A THOROUGHBRED RHODE ISLAND Red rooster, Weaver strain. 633 E. 50TH ST. San Pedro st. car.

FOR SALE — CHICKENS, 10 WHITE LEGHORNS for $6; must do your own carting. Call in rear house of 833 E. ADAMS ST.

FOR SALE—WHITE LEGHORN EGGS, 15 FOR 65 cents. Martin and McFarlane strain. Duck eggs, 12 for 75 cents. 5024 SECOND AVE. 79589.

FOR SALE — FINE LARGE PAIR BOURBON (red) turkeys, eggs; also pheasant eggs, young later. EAST 3935 or SOUTH 518W.

FOR SALE—HATCHING EGGS, RHODE ISLAND Reds, $1 for 15; $6 for 100. 3800 BROOKLYN AVE. Boyle 1755.

FOR SALE—15 FERTILE EGGS, $1. THORoughbred Rhode Island Reds. Fine deep red stock. 20344. 127 WEST 17TH ST.

FOR SALE—SETTING HENS, ALSO SETTING eggs, fancy Rhode Island Red eggs, 15 for $1. 644 N. HOBART. 568094.

FOR SALE—BIG RHODE ISLAND RED ROOSter, 12 months old, bantams and canaries. 522 CONCORD. Boyle 1691.

FOR SALE—DUCKS, ALL BREEDS, YOUNG AND old. VAUGHAN RANCH, 8th and Maclay, San Fernando.

FOR SALE—ONE DOZEN NICE, CLEAN RHODE Island Red hens, price $1.35 each. 550 E. COLORADO, Eagle Rock City. Phone Garvanza 259.

FOR SALE—WHITE MINORCA HATCHING EGGS and baby chicks, choice stock. LEECH POULTRY YARDS, 1170 W. 37th place. 77780.

FOR SALE—36 YOUNG McFARLAND WHITE Leghorn hens, $12 dozen. Call Sunday, 314 S. SOTO ST. East 4th st. car.

FOR SALE—PEN PARTRIDGE ROCKS, PRIZE birds L. A. Show. Sell cheap. Address H, box 142, TIMES OFFICE.

FOR SALE—FULL BLOOD PARTRIDGE ROCKS, 8 hens, 1 rooster, year old. 1221 S. MARIPOSA, Sunday or evenings.

FOR SALE—BROILERS, MILK AND CORN FED, fat and juicy, at Valley Grove farm, First st., Lankershim, near Universal City.

FOR SALE—YOUNG ORPINGTON ROOSTER, $5. Also 2 broody hens. BDWY. 2086.

FOR SALE—BROWN LEGHORN HENS, $1.10 each. 1892 W. JEFFERSON ST.

FOR SALE—NINE ANCONA LAYING PULLETS, $1.25 each. 3673 S. VAN NESS AVE.

FOR SALE—THOROUGHBRED WHITE LEGHORN laying pullets. Make your own selection. 28275.

TO LET—CARLOAD GOOD WORK MULES WITH harness. D. H. GOODIN, 790 Lyon st.

FOR SALE—400 6-WEEKS-OLD CHICKS, 18c each. Phone 29270. 5931 S. FLOWER.

FOR SALE—7 YOUNG BARRED ROCK HENS, $1.50 each. 153 W. 61ST.

FOR SALE—WHITE ORPINGTON EGGS FOR hatching. 15 for $1. 330 E. JEFFERSON.

FOR SALE—150 WHITE LEGHORN CHICKS, 5 days old, 12½c each. BOYLE 2054.

FOR SALE—SINGLE COMB WHITE LEGHORN pullets, laying. 1658 W. 38TH PLACE.

FOR SALE—1 DOZEN BROWN LEGHORNS, $16. Apply 1600 W. 50TH ST.

FOR SALE—BARRED ROCK EGGS, $1 PER setting of 15. 261 N. JOHNSON ST. 31110.

FOR SALE—HEN, 8 FINE STRAIN RED CHICKS. 1834 W. ADAMS. Reasonable.

## POULTRY—PET STOCK—
Supplies—For Sale, Exchange, Wanted

### Poultry and Poultry Supplies.

FOR SALE—32 HENS, LEGHORNS AND RHODE Island Reds. VERMONT 125.

FOR SALE—FINE LAYING HENS, 1122 SANTEE. MAIN 6091.

FOR SALE—BARRED ROCK EGGS, $1 PER SETting of 15. 261 N. JOHNSTON ST. 31110.

FOR SALE—PURE HENTAIL CAMPINE COCKERels. 338 NEWLAND ST. Gar. 1135.

FOR SALE—SETTING HENS. PHONE 20444.

### Pigeons, Birds, etc.

FOR SALE— FEATHERED PETS At Pre-Removal Prices. About July 1 we move to Sixth and Main sts. We want to reduce our stocks and are therefore offering high-class decorative and singing birds at special low prices. You've always wanted a bird for your home, and now's the time to gratify your desire at small cost. We offer trim little Paroquettes (miniature parrots) at $5.50 a pair. They make wonderful pets, and their bright coloring makes them highly attractive. White Java Sparrows, with bright red bills, at $4; blue with red bills at $3.50 pair; Zebra Finches, with their stripes, checks and spotted wings and red bills, make an attractive ornament for any home —$3 pair. Society Finches, demure little birds dressed in brown and white, at $2.50 pair.

CAGES—FOODS—ACCESSORIES. Few firms in the West carry a larger or more diversified stock of cages than we—you have almost every type of cage to select from. We also have a complete assortment of perches, swings, chains, brackets, springs, bird baths, seed and water cups, wire cage cloth, bird nesting, bird nests, and special foods, color foods, singing foods, and dependable remedies.

GERMAIN SEED AND PLANT CO., 10996. 326-328-330 S. Main st. Main 996.

FOR SALE— BIRDLAND. The long-expected birds from Australia have arrived in fine shape. In this shipment we received the wonderful Lady Goulds, Diamond, Gold and other pretty finches. We can right now show the best selection of song and aviary birds of all kinds; also ornamental land and water fowl, monkeys, etc. Chameleons, small turtles are also here, and we have some good gold and fancy fish, globes, cages, food, remedies and all other accessories.

TALKING PARROTS. Some of all kinds and of the best grades to select from, every bird guaranteed.

DOGS. Our Dog Department at NO. 216 MERCANTILE PLACE, offers a nice lot of puppies of different breeds; also a full line of kennel supplies and all the standard foods and remedies. Illustrated catalogue free to those interested. L. M. GRIDER, 1301 Central ave., and 216 Mercantile Place, Los Angeles, Cal.

FOR SALE—CHEAP, ABOUT 50 THOROUGHbred blue barred Homer or carrier pigeons, big squab kind. I paid $1 each, but will sell at 25c each if you take all. The squabs retail at 50c each. A. S. VANDEGRIFT, Burr ave., La Canada, or 302 S. Broadway, Los Angeles, Cal. A2236, Pico 635.

FOR SALE— PHEASANTS. CHEAP. Three BEST varieties left. SELLING OUT. Take 'em away, "your own price." Baby pheasants 15c. Eggs $1 per dozen. Milo maize feed, $3.25 per hundred. Bantam setting hens, everything goes. MORGAN'S PHEASANT FARM, 244 East 61st st. OPEN SUNDAY.

FOR SALE—I'M LEAVING TO JOIN THE COLors, must dispose of my squab plant, 75 pairs Red Carneaux, Splash and Buff pigeons, highgrade stock and steady workers. Full equipment. Cor. McPherrin and Garslon ave., Ramona Park. Address K, box 369, TIMES SPRING ST. BRANCH.

FOR SALE—CANARIES— Some good Hertzmountain males. Beautiful singers, bred from Imported stock. Also a few females. Salesroom at the ELITE HAT CLEANERS, 514 W. 6th.

FOR SALE—BEAUTIFUL SINGING ROLLER with female now mating. One large double dome and perch mating cage. Two Hendryx brass cages with wall derricks and springs. Two glass bath cabinets. Reasonable. Phone MR. BARRETT, 10250; Main 7215. Sunday excepted.

FOR SALE—PHEASANTS AND EGGS; ALSO BABY pheasants. Golden, Silver, Reeves, Amherst, Berci color, Ring-neck eggs, 10 cents each. The RUTH PHEASANTRY, 340 Crosby st., R.F.D., No. 2, box 251, Pasadena, 3 blocks beyond end of Lincoln ave. car line, 1 block east. Phone Colorado 886.

FOR SALE—55 PAIR OF THE FINEST RED Carneaux pigeons, banded, mated and working. $1 per pair. Address W. W. WOLCOTT, 10th and Alameda st., Burbank, Cal.

FOR SALE—REASONABLE, NIGHTINGALES, Goldfinches, Nonpareil, Zebras, Cuban, Spice, many other finches. Pheasants' eggs, 75c per doz. Quail eggs free. 121 W. 47TH PLACE.

FOR SALE — PHEASANT EGGS, GOLDEN AMherst and Reeves, fresh and reasonable price; also laying pheasants, cheap. PHONE 51225.

FOR SALE—BEAUTIFUL WARBLERS, $2.50. Mated pairs, some with young. 1808 ALLESANDRO.

FOR EXCHANGE—HAVE TWO FEMALE SILver pheasants, one year old. Will exchange one for male. Ad. J. box 15, TIMES OFFICE.

FOR SALE—LADY GOULD FINCHES, MATED pairs of red-headed and black-headed beauties. BIRD EMPORIUM, 820 Summit ave.

FOR SALE—CRIMSON, SHAFTAIL, OWL, MASKed and Diamond Finches. Best assortment of aviary birds. BIRD EMPORIUM, 820 Summit ave.

FOR SALE—CANARY BIRDS AND A BEAUTIful cage. Call Sunday and evenings, 1222 W. 27TH ST.

WANTED — GOOD SINGING CANARIES AND aviary birds. LYNWOOD PET STOCK SHOW, 439½ S. Hill st.

FOR SALE—BEAUTIFUL YELLOW GERMAN roller and cage. 1827 N. ALEXANDRIA AVE. 599617.

FOR SALE—YELLOW CANARY WARBLERS, DAY and night singers, $3.50. Vermont 5460—26321. 1101 W. VERNON AVE.

FOR SALE—12 PAIRS CARNEAUX PIGEONS FOR $10. 1818 ACACIA.

FOR SALE—RINGNECK PHEASANT EGGS, $1.50 doz. 215 E. 45TH ST.

FOR SALE—WHITE QUACKLESS DUCK HATCHing eggs. PHONE HOLLYWOOD 1422.

FOR SALE—PEACOCK, RING-NECKED PHEASants, trio, $10. 2310 E. FIRST. Boyle 2114.

FOR SALE—AVIARY CANARY BIRDS, MALES, $3.50. Phone 559138, mornings or evenings.

FOR SALE—GOLDEN PHEASANT EGGS, 15C each. 1920 RODNEY DR. Hollywood 3883.

FOR SALE—SIX NICE FEMALE CANARIES, ALso singers. 747 E. 21ST ST.

FOR SALE—30 CARNEAUX PIGEONS, $12. 731 WEST 11TH ST.

FOR SALE—GERMAN ROLLER CANARIES, male and female. 156 E. 45TH ST.

### Ducks, Geese, Turkeys.

FOR SALE—WHITE MUSCOVY DUCKLINGS, PANama Exposition strain, 30c each. CALDWELL RABBIT FARM, 2520 San Fernando blvd.

FOR SALE—FORTY 11 WEEKS PEKIN DUCKS, about 3½ to 4 lbs. WILSHIRE 3358.

FOR SALE—BABY TURKEYS AND TURKEY EGGS, Barred Rock, White Minorca hens. 938 W. 63RD PLACE. Vermont 327.

WANTED—INDIAN RUNNER LAYING DUCKS. Call SOUTH 2567W.

FOR SALE—MUSCOVY DUCKLINGS AND EGGS. 52921. 930 GRATTAN ST.

### Bees and Honey.

FOR SALE—PURE ITALIAN BEES. WORK DONE and lessons given in bee-keeping. Rt. 2, box 296, INGLEWOOD.

WANTED—I BUY HONEY IN ANY QUANTITY. Drop me a line. W. B. BOWIE, 2934 Francis ave., Los Angeles.

### Goats, Milch, etc.

FOR SALE—SOME VERY FINE TOGGENBURG Saanan, Nubian milch goats, fresh, giving two to four quarts each. Large uders and easy milkers. If your goat has disappointed you we will take it in exchange on a real milker, registered and pure breed billy goats for service, fee $2 to $5. Goats called for, delivered and boarded. Call Sunday if you like. Bring your goat with you if you wish to exchange. 5735 CENTRAL AVE. South 1323W.

FOR SALE — 60 MILCH GOATS, FRESH AND coming fresh, young, gentle, large teats, udders, heavy milkers; pure bred; unequaled Toggenburg bucks for service; hornless bucks rented; dry goats taken in exchange; called for, delivered anywhere. Visitors welcome. Information cheerfully given. Postage for reply. No Sunday business. SHEDDAN BROS., 6124 Central. Route 12, box 7. South 6915.

FOR SALE—FORTY-FIVE HEAD PURE BRED Angora goats, also fifty to seventy-five head of grade milk goats. A bargain if taken soon at NADEAU RANCH, 6 miles east of Saugus. R. Nadeau, Saugus, Cal.

FOR SALE—TWO YOUNG PURE BRED TOGG. bucks and 35 head of young grade does. Information, 85 N. HOLLISTON, Pasadena. Colo. 8101.

FOR SALE—TWO ¾ TOGGENBURG GOAT KIDS, male and female, age 3 months, bargain if taken at once. Address box 63, R.F.D., SAN GABRIEL, Cal., 2 blocks east San Gabriel car line.

FOR SALE — NATURALLY HORNLESS TOGGENburg goats, fresh and coming fresh, beautifully marked doe kids, no scrubs. 142 N. EASTLAKE.

FOR SALE—MILCH GOAT, BEEN FRESH TWO months, gives one quart milk, cheap. Sunday only. Take West Sixth st. car to end of line. 612 EL CENTRO AVE.

FOR SALE—OR EXCHANGE—TWO TOGGENburg buck kids, after a 4-quart milker, 2½ months old, for milch goat or nanny kid. 1206 E. 41ST ST.

WANTED—MILCH GOATS OR KIDS, ALSO TOGgenburg billy kid, good stock. Exchange for fine Wilton rug, 13x14, rockers, buggy, medical battery. 1314 W. AVE. 63.

FOR SALE—FRESH NUBIAN GRADE DOE, $35, or will take part cash and Indian Runner ducks. Call SOUTH 2567W.

FOR SALE—THREE-QUART MILCH GOAT AND two (2) month-old doe kids, part Toggenburg. 11617 GALE ST., Hawthorne, Cal.

WANTED—PURE BLOOD GOATS. WHAT HAVE you? Highest cash price paid. Give description. Address E, box 282, TIMES OFFICE.

FOR SALE—TWO NICE LOOKING TOGGENBURG grade does, just fresh, both are hornless and have hornless kids. VERMONT 2791.

WANTED—GOATS. PURE BLOOD. WHAT HAVE you? Highest price paid. Give description. Address E, box 282, TIMES OFFICE.

FOR SALE—4-QUART MILCH GOAT, WITH KID, $50. 1401 MILFORD ST., Glendale. Phone Red 160. Call Sunday morning.

FOR SALE—A GOOD MILCH GOAT, $25; ALSO Nubian doe, $20; these are bargains. H. S. SEELY, 3545 Mission road. East 970.

FOR SALE—2 FRESH GOATS, 2 YOUNG NANnies, 4 months old, all hornless. 6210 S. MAIN. South 788.

FOR SALE—GOOD GOAT, AND 2 KID GOATS, is milking 4 quarts a day. Price $65, or will trade for cows. 644 W. AVENUE 50.

FOR SALE—FRESH SAANAN GOAT, GIVING 3 quarts daily. 7816 MONETA AVE.

## POULTRY—PET STOCK—
Supplies—For Sale, For Exchange.

### Goats, Milch, etc.

WANTED—LATE MODEL ROADSTER. CALL 26112 or 23280.

FOR SALE—GOOD FRESH GOAT, $15, INCLUDing kid. Call evenings. 4320 MOSHER.

FOR SALE—FRESH MILCH GOATS AND KIDS, $20 up. 139 E. 62ND ST.

FOR SALE—MILK GOAT, $20. 5538 DUARTE. Watts car to 55th st.

FOR SALE—TWO-QUART, FRESH, HORNLESS, gentle family goat, young, with kid. 790154.

FOR SALE—FRESH MILK GOAT, CHEAP, GIVing 3 quarts. 1019 E. 57TH ST.

FOR SALE—FRESH YOUNG GOAT AND KID, $25. Maple ave. car. 5025 SAN PEDRO.

FOR SALE—FRESH GOAT, GIVING 2½ PINTS A day, $15. 153 GIFFORD ST., Bell Station.

### Rabbits, Hares, etc.

FOR SALE—YOU ARE CORDIALLY INVITED TO attend the regular meeting of the Southern California Pet Stock Association, to be held Monday evening, May 14, 1918. Second floor, Times Building, at 8 p.m., subject: "The Fancy Rabbit"—Angoras, English Lops, Japanese, French silvers, etc. Bring your specimen, for judging. Lots of interesting and valuable information for the novice and any one interested in this fast-growing industry. SOUTHERN CALIFORNIA PET STOCK ASSOCIATION, C. E. Chittick, Secy.

FOR SALE—NEW ZEALAND, BELGIAN, FLEMish Giant, and fur bearers, we buy breeding rabbits of all kinds. FANCIERS' EXCHANGE, 640 S. Main st.

FOR SALE—6 DOES, 1 YEAR OLD, WITH YOUNG 5 weeks old, $3.50 each; 6 does, 1 year old, bred, $2.50 and $3 each; 11 does, 4½ months old, nearly ready to breed, $1.50 each. 342 ANGELENO AVE., Burbank.

FOR SALE—UTILITY NEW ZEALAND RED RABbits and young, 7 to 8 pounds, $3; 8 to 9 pounds, $3.50; others, 30c. G. W. CLEMSON, Shoup and Oxnard blvd., near Owensmouth.

FOR SALE — NEW ZEALAND AND BELGIAN Bucks, also Flemish, New Zealand and Belgian does, fryers. Wilshire 704. 4002 SUNSET BLVD., corner of Sanborn. Hollywood car.

FOR SALE—FLEMISH GIANTS, EXTRA FINE stock bucks and does. 1714 W. 38TH PLACE. Call before 2:30 Sunday. Week-days after 5:30 p.m.

FOR SALE—THOROUGHBRED FLEMISH GIANTS and New Zealands. Bucks and does. Beautiful stock, reasonable. PALM RABBITRY, 1110 W. 17TH.

FOR SALE—50 FINE NEW ZEALAND DOES, 10 with litters. Bucks, young stock. After Sunday. 415 E. COLORADO BLVD., Glendale.

FOR EXCHANGE—BELGIAN BUCK FOR BELgian or New Zealand buck, young. 533 W. QUEEN ST., Inglewood.

FOR SALE—FLEMISH GIANT DOES AND BUCKS. Also hutches. No reasonable offer refused. 828 W. 56TH ST.

FOR SALE—WE SPECIALIZE IN PHOTOGRAPHing rabbits and chickens. GRAHAM PHOTO CO. 110½ S. Broadway.

FOR SALE—RAISE RABBITS FOR US, PAY $3 each. Send 10c booket and particulars. H. E. GIBSON CO., Arcadia, Cal.

WANTED—WILL PAY HIGHEST MARKET PRICE for rabbits and poultry. H. C. PELPHREY, Inglewood. Sunset 207-W.

FOR SALE—1 FLEMISH DOE AND BUCK, 1 Belgian doe with 9 young, 1 New Zealand doe and 4 young bucks, also hutches. 1034 WALL ST.

FOR SALE — 200 RABBITS, FLEMISH AND New Zealand does, some with litters also some fine bucks, the large kind. 1106 W. 70TH ST.

FOR SALE — THOROUGHBRED NEW ZEALAND from registered stock, reasonable prices. Utility bucks and does, $2. 130 E. AVENUE 43.

FOR SALE—SEVERAL YOUNG FLEMISH BUCKS, exchange for good does; will buy does. Watts car, Florencita Park. WILSON, 1714 Santa Marie.

FOR SALE—NEW ZEALAND AND GIANT RABbits, 75 cents and up. Bred does, $2.50. 7880 SANTA MONICA BLVD. Holly 2495.

FOR SALE—NEW ZEALAND RED AND BLACK and white fur rabbits. 616 N. BENTON WAY, city. West Temple car.

FOR SALE—1 PAIR BLACK KAIGAIS, 1 GOLDen Kaigai buck; 8 young Flemish Giants. 1207 N. Virgil. Hollywood 2870.

WANTED — RABBITS, FROM TWO TO THREE pounds, 15c pound. Phone 22GJ. J. C. SPENSER, Inglewood.

FOR SALE—BRED DOES, SOME YOUNG DOES, also some sanitary hutches. 545 N. CORONA, Laguna Bell Acres. Rennington.

FOR SALE—SOME BEAUTIFUL YOUNG BREEDing stock, from prize-winners. 4560 HUNTINGTON DRIVE. East 3454.

FOR SALE—MY NEW ZEALAND-NILROY DOES, some with young, all must go, cheap. 1639 TALMADGE ST., East Hollywood.

FOR SALE—$2 UP. FEW FLEMISH GIANTS, does and bucks, also service of good buck, $1. 710 W. VERNON.

FOR SALE—STOCK RABBITS, BRED, $1.50 each. 718 WATERLOO, Wil. 2584.

FOR SALE—FINAL CLEAN-UP, BIG STOCK OF rabbits and hutches. 1453 W. 49TH ST.

WANTED—RABBITS, 2 TO 4 LBS., WILL CALL. A. H. HUNT, R. R. 4, Box 585, City. Vt. 5343.

FOR SALE—BUCK AND BRED DOE, CHEAP. 4338 BURNS AVE.

FOR SALE—BUCK, DOE AND YOUNG. 239 W. 50TH ST. Phone South 7090R.

FOR SALE—RABBITS AND MARINE GRAY. 750005.

FOR SALE—30 BELGIANS, LARGE AND SMALL. 1116 CASTALIA ST., Bairdstown.

FOR SALE—BELGIAN, FLEMISH AND ANGORA, also hutches. 648 W. 16TH ST.

FOR SALE—YOUNG BRED DOES. GLENDALE 865-W.

FOR SALE—THOROUGHBRED FLEMISH GIANT and rich red New Zealand. 911 WEST 20TH.

FOR SALE—FLEMISH AND NEW ZEALANDS. Choice stock. Phone WEST 5430.

FOR SALE—RABBIT ALFALFA, $23. ROBBINSON & COTA, 910 S. Los Angeles. Main 7517.

### Dogs and Dogs at Stud.

AT STUD—SCOTCH COLLIE FROM CHAMPION stock, stud fee $10, from same sire puppies for sale, males $10, females $5. MRS. SPITTERS, Orpington ave., North Inglewood.

FOR SALE—MALE AND FEMALE PEDIGREED Collies, brother and sister, ten months old. Have papers. Male $40; female, $25. Address K, box 344, TIMES SPRING ST. BRANCH.

FOR SALE—ACCOUNT OF MOVING WILL SELL my two male thoroughbred Scotch Collie pups at half price, four months old and beautifully marked. WEST 2962.

FOR SALE—PEDIGREED TOY BLACK AND TAN puppies, beauties, also very fine male at stud. Call after Sunday, 1233 W. 5TH ST.

FOR SALE—1-YEAR-OLD SPITZ, $2; GOOD LOOKer; fine watchdog. Playfellow. GARVANZA 1663.

FOR SALE—BEAUTIFUL FRENCH BULLDOG puppies, $25. Bostons, $10. Telephone BOYLE 3431.

FOR SALE—BEAUTIFUL HELL HOUND PUPpies. LYNWOOD PET STOCK SHOW, 439½ S. Hill st.

FOR SALE—ENGLISH TOY FOX TERRIER PUPpies, beauties, pedigreed. Cheap. 2708 S. MAIN. 23780.

AT STUD—DANDY JIM AND TINY TAD, CURLY coated, typical toy poodles. 5310 TEMPLETON ST. East 1737; 35488.

WANTED—SMALL DOG FOR PET; ONE USED TO auto preferred; will take puppy to train; state breed and price. 1906 LOS FELIZ BLVD.

FOR SALE—YOUNG AIREDALE DOG, MALE, fine stock, pedigreed, very reasonable. Call any morning. 2018 MAGNOLIA AVE. 25185.

AT STUD—PRINCE WAKAKAI, FINEST YOUNG English bull on the Coast; massive head, heavy bone; six champions in pedigree. Fee $15. 160 W. 63RD ST.

FOR SALE—$10 BUYS BOSTON BULL WATCH dog, full grown male, house and auto broke. Dandy watch dog and playmate. Phone BROADWAY 2320.

FOR SALE—COLLIE PUPS, 7 MONTHS OLD, eligible to registration. Males, $10 and $15. 823 HICKORY ST. Watts local to Latin station, walk east.

FOR SALE—FINE TOY FOX TERRIER PUPpies, can be seen any day before 1 p.m. at 8125 HAMILTON WAY. Off Sunset blvd. and Elza ave.

FOR EXCHANGE—HALF COYOTE, HALF BULLdog. Want thoroughbred bloodhound pup or other unusual. Address J, box 124, TIMES OFFICE.

FOR SALE — CHIHUAHUA FEMALE, BUCKSKIN color, bred, price $15. 1436 VALENCIA. West 3382.

FOR SALE — SPITZ-POMERANIAN PUPPIES, males, $5; females, $3. Phone Glendale 1102J. Or call 1553 OAK ST., Glendale.

FOR SALE—PEDIGREED BOSTON TERRIER pups, beautifully marked. HOLLYWOOD 2326. 1911 N. Van Ness.

FOR SALE—FOUR THOROUGHBRED SCOTTISH terrier pups, finest in the State, 2 males and 2 females. 1230 AVENUE 56.

FOR SALE—TWO BOSTON BULL TERRIERS, highly pedigreed, cheap. Must sell, leaving city. Phone 71279. 2006 W. 29TH PLACE.

FOR SALE—7 YOUNG COYOTES, $2 FOR ONE OR $7 for all. LOWELL MERRILL, Phone 124-J-3, Ontario.

FOR SALE—PEDIGREED BOSTON TERRIER puppies, for least money. 1260 EAST SEAUSON. South 5716-R.

FOR SALE—ENGLISH BULL MALE PUP, MAhogany brindle, thoroughbred. 6925 MIRAMONTE BLVD., near Compton ave.

FOR SALE—THOROUGHBRED AIREDALE PUP, black and tan, only $10. 9001 MENLO AVE.

FOR SALE—IRISH TERRIER PUPPY, 6 MONTHS old, pedigreed stock. 830 WEST 73RD ST.

FOR SALE—COLLIE PUPPIES, $5 EACH, BEAUties. HUNT, 1219 W. 110th st. Ver. 5343.

FOR SALE—POINTER AND SETTER PUPS, FROM fine hunting stock. 851 S. ST. ANDREWS PL. 568313.

WANTED — GENUINE SCOTCH COLLIE PUP from 2 to 6 months old. Phone Main 8874 or call 1018 VAN NUYS BLDG. Mornings only.

FOR SALE—PEDIGREE, TOY, BOSTON TERRIER, female, puppy. Cheap. 219 E. 28TH ST. 21535.

FOR EXCHANGE—BROWN MALE WATCH DOG, part bull, very bright. SOUTH 1615-W.

FOR SALE — POMERANIAN PUPPIES, CHEAP. Can be seen at 908 S. HOPE ST. Monday.

FOR SALE—PEDIGREED ENGLISH BULLDOG, 2 brood bitches, 1 male. 674 W. 63RD ST.

FOR SALE—MALE AIREDALE, REASONABLE. 2411 W. 27TH. 75735.

FOR SALE—3 BULL PUPS, 1 MONTH OLD. 568059.

FOR SALE—$2 EACH BUYS PUPPIES, PLAYFUL, good watchdogs. 626 MAPLE AVE.

FOR SALE—BOSTON TERRIER PUP, SIRE BONnie Boo. WILSHIRE 1180. Stud dogs.

FOR SALE—2 PEDIGREED PEKINESE DOGS. Color tan. Beauties. HOLLYWOOD 693.

FOR SALE—AIREDALE, THOROUGHBRED, AUTO trained. E. 636. 649 AMETHYST.

## POULTRY—PET STOCK—
Supplies—For Sale, Exchange, Wanted

### Dogs and Dogs at Stud.

THE EXCLUSIVE DOGGERY— Classy dogs, and guaranteed health. The cleanest and most sanitary dog shop on the Pacific Coast. Breeds of all kinds generally on hand. If you want the best, we have them. Also a full line of remedies, collars, leashes, harness, etc. Veterinary in attendance. At stud—Boston terrier, Radio A.K.C. 217090. The best son of Ch. Little Tony Wagner, weight 14 lbs. Fee $10. THE DOG SHOP, 302 W. Ninth st. Bdwy. 7665.

FOR SALE—OPENING. THE LYNWOOD PET STOCK SHOW, 439½ S. Hill st. opens Monday, May 13, 1918. Visitors will be welcome. You will find a clean stock of pets, gold fish, supplies and cages. Bring in your pets, we will buy or handle on commission. Veterinarian in attendance. Phones Pico 3256, East 970; A4443. Branch at 3545 Mission Road.

FOR SALE—PUPPIES AND GROWN DOGS OF all kinds. We specialize in good dogs. One litter of police puppies from registered stock, $100 each. Ranch dogs and crossbreeds at nominal prices. Harness, collars, leads, chains, remedies, foods. We buy good puppies of all breeds. FANCIERS' EXCHANGE, 640 S. Main st.

FOR SALE—PEDIGREED ENGLISH BULL pups. Beautifully marked. Very reasonable. 525½ S. OLIVE ST.

AT STUD—THAT SENSATIONAL BULLDOG, HEYwood Marco, imported. An international winner and sire of large litters of promising puppies in England. Only a youngster, but he tops the lot. For particulars apply DR. MOXLEY'S KENNELS, 1410 E. Washington.

FOR SALE—AND AT STUD, COCKER SPANIELS, thoroughbred puppies and grown dogs from registered blue ribbon parents at very reasonable prices. THE SAN MARINO COCKER KENNELS, Porterville, Cal. Box 181, R.R. No. 2.

AT STUD—ENGLISH BULLDOG, THE INTERNAtional champion, Toll Bar Jack, fee $25; eight highest quality pups sired by him can be seen at DAVID'S BULLDOG KENNELS, 1110 S. Rowan ave., Los Angeles, Cal. Boyle 791.

FOR SALE—ENGLISH BULL, FEMALE, BRED to Sir Roxmodel, cheap if taken at once. Also puppies for sale, sired by Sir Roxmodel and Princess Roxine, 3 months old. 1195 W. 38TH PLACE. 77785.

FOR SALE—AIREDALE PUPPIES, 2 MONTHS old; one male, 10 months old; one female, 14 months old. Bargain. 1310 W. 25TH ST. West 561.

THE DOG SHOP— CLASSY, GUARANTEED, HEALTHY DOGS. THE EXCLUSIVE DOGGERY. 302 W. 9TH ST. BDWY. 7665.

FOR SALE—6 MONTHS OLD FEMALE BULL terrier, beautiful marked, fine watch dog and house broke; sell cheap. Call from 8 a.m. to 2 p.m. to 3803 SAN PEDRO ST., City.

FOR SALE—BEAUTIFUL MALE SCOTCH COLLIE pups, some almost white, $5 up. Also Silver Persian kittens. 436 W. 87TH ST., between Figueroa and Moneta.

FOR SALE—TWO BEAUTIFUL WHITE ALASkan puppies, males. Five weeks old. $7 each. T. T. McCARTY, 345 S. Rugby ave. Phone South 5760-M.

FOR SALE—BEAUTIFUL BOSTON PUPPIES, highly pedigreed, ideal markings, screw tails, sired by Riddell's Little Model. None better in city. Price $25, $35 and $50. 1344 S. HOPE.

AT STUD—OR FOR SALE—BLENHEIM, 2½-LB. black and tan, chocolate or seal brown, 3-lb. Chihuahua, very small black Pekinese. 1436 VALENCIA. West 3382.

FOR SALE—SEAL BRINDLE AND WHITE BULL terrier, male, five months old. Perfect markings, good stock. Sunday only $5. Well worth $10. 4219 LA SALLE AVE.

FOR SALE—TWO GOOD ENGLISH BULL BROOD matrons, or would exchange for pupies, or other pet stock. H. S. SEELY, 3545 Mission road. East 970.

FOR SALE—FRENCH BULL, MALE, 1 YEAR old, $15. PHONE 560163.

FOR SALE—YOUNG BOSTON BULLDOG, VERY cheap. 3251 E. 2ND ST.

FOR SALE—THOROUGHBRED AIREDALE PUPpy, Male, 4 months old. Phone 35095.

### Cats.

STATEMENT— Have moved back to my old home, 1436 VALENCIA ST., and will continue my cat business at war time prices. Apache Redruff, deep orange; Shamrock, light silver; Bonnie Rex, white, blue eyed; are the largest studs in this city; all are line bred. Service $2. Phone WEST 3382.

WANTED—GOOD HOME FOR LITTLE BLACK kitten; for sale, beautiful Persian kitten, exchange orange or smoke male, breeding for white. Phone WEST 6325. 22510.

FOR SALE—2 PEDIGREED SILVER MALE KITtens. Sire Marmaduke. GLENDALE, 1553.

AT STUD—PRINCE INTO, MASSIVE CREAM PERsian, fee reasonable. Cats and kittens for sale. COZEE KENNELS, 1774 E. Jefferson st. So. 4845J.

FOR SALE — WHITE ANGORA KITTENS; 6 weeks old; very fine stock; price reasonable. 1707 W. 55TH ST.

FOR SALE—THOROUGHBRED PEDIGREED Persian cats. SOUTH 2813-R.

CATS AT STUD—BLUE, SILVER AND ORANGE. Kittens for sale, all colors. 640 S. MAIN ST.

FOR SALE—THOROUGHBRED ANGORA KITTEN. Phone West 3572. 1663 W. 25TH.

### Wanted.

WANTED—CATTLE, HAVE PASTURE FOR CARE of cattle all summer. Will take them on shares. F. H. HARTH, 431½ W. 4th st., Santa Ana.

WANTED—SETTING OF SILVER SPANGLED Hamburgs, also White Crested Black Polish eggs. Address L, HUNT, 356 S. Westmoreland ave.

WANTED—POULTRY, ALL KINDS, HIGHEST prices paid; call for them anywhere. L. A. POULTRY EX., 2212 Central ave. South 5548.

## TOO LATE—
To Classify.

[The hour for closing many of the columns of The Times "Liner" Section Saturday night is 8 o'clock. Subsequent to this hour, developments often occur in commercial and domestic affairs which make it necessary to seek quick and effective publicity. Therefore, this "Too Late to Classify" column often offers greater bargains and more money-making opportunities than any other section of The Times.]

MUST SELL AT ONCE AT HALF THE PRICE to produce, five-room furnished cottage in Hollywood, large lot, 20 bearing fruit trees, all kinds, 30 Rhode Island Red laying pullets, four fine cockerels, two milch goats, rabbits, fine Jersey and Hereford bull calf, plently free pasture, lot all fenced, small cottage on rear, sheds, chicken corrals, hutches, fine young cedar hedge, splendid rose garden, very artistic little home, just the place for a studio. Have position in East and must go at once. Inquire on premises from owner. Price $1800, half cash, balance mortgage to suit. 1118 CITRUS AVE., Hollywood, one block west of Highland avenue, ½ block north of Santa Monica blvd. No city taxes; no sickness ever been in this house.

POTTERY MANUFACTURER WANTS ADDITIONal capital for the manufacture of vitrified hotel ware and other clay products. Have large orders on file. Also want 10 acres on R.R. trackage. Must have natural gas and water. Samples at laboratory. AMERICAN CHINA CO., 200 Lankershim Bldg., 3rd and Spring sts., city.

FOR SALE—OR EXCHANGE—3 TRUST DEEDS, one for $1150, $1200, at 7 per cent., on modern bungalows, one $3500, at 8 per cent., on income property. Just like cash. Want good automobile for one, clear country for balance. Address PJ, box 412, TIMES SPRING ST. BRANCH.

FOR SALE—IMPORTED AFRICAN DATE PALM OFFSHOOTS, PRICE UPON APPLICATION. ADDRESS J, BOX 16, TIMES OFFICE.

FOR SALE—SOUTH HOLLYWOOD BUNGALOW, bargain. Lexington ave., near Western ave. 6 rooms, very attractive, large lot. Price $3250. KWIS & CRAM, 704 Union Oil Bldg. F2334.

FOR SALE—NICE BUILDING LOT, 15TH ST., in San Pedro, 1½ blocks from Pacific ave. Particulars. 1325 W. 23RD.

SPECIAL SALE PRICE—EVERY PERSON GETS half soles put on for this week only. Will put on high-grade rubber heels for 25c. Regular price 50c. SILENT SHOE HOSPITAL, 760 W. 6th St. BUSY BEE SHOE HOSPITAL, 830 W. 7th St.

FOR EXCHANGE—4-ROOM BUNGALOW, SANTA Monica, furnished, 5 blocks from the water. Want small ranch or city. Address K, box 383, TIMES SPRING ST. BRANCH.

WANTED—PARTNER IN ESTABLISHED NURSery, experience not necessary. Good proposition for reliable man. Phone South 2996-M, 8 a.m. to 7 p.m. After sunday address K, box 521, TIMES SPRING ST. BRANCH.

FINANCE WANTED— FINANCIAL BACKING OF $1000 WANTED by chemist to handle new rubber tire preservative; capable of big things; profitable deal offered. CHEMIST, 607 S. Figueroa st.

GROCERY STOCK WANTED FOR ALL OR PART exchange for 10 acres, well located, clear, $3500. EVANS, 641 Lebanon. Pico 1343.

WANTED—TO BUY GOOD FIVE-ROOM HOUSE to be moved off lot. Address K, box 393, TIMES SPRING ST. BRANCH.

FOR SALE—CORNER LOT, CENTER WATTS, $150, terms. Sacrifice. WILSHIRE 2032.

FOR EXCHANGE—FORT WORTH, TEXAS, property, for Los Angeles property. BDWY. 3469.

FOR SALE—OR EXCHANGE—MAKE ME AN OFfer for equity in 8-room bungalow, suburban; also acre and half foothills, $3000; mortgage. Address J, box 294, TIMES OFFICE.

HELLO, BEAUMONT, CAL., WHERE THE RED apples grow! 160 acres, 2 miles from Beaumont, 40 acres under cultivation; can be had for $3000, terms to suit. Address J, box 108, TIMES OFFICE.

FOR SALE—NEAR BEAUMONT, CAL., FAMOUS for its red apples! 5-room cottage and 2 acres apples; 50 big red cherry trees. Also berries and mixed fruit trees; fine place for chickens; all for $1000; this is a real bargain. Address J, box 98, TIMES OFFICE.

FOR EXCHANGE—IN HOLLYWOOD, 50 ACRES, fruit land, fine soil, 3 acres in red mountain cherries and almonds. 2 miles from Beaumont, Cal. Exchange for cottage or clear lot in Hollywood. Address H, box 175, TIMES OFFICE.

FOR SALE — SEVEN-ROOM BUNGALOW, CORner, thoroughly good, at a price which probably gives more value than any other offering in this paper. Call 1476 W. FIRST ST., Glendale.

# Latest Sporting News—Baseball.

The Turf.

## EXTERMINATOR TRUE TO NAME.

*Kilmer's Acquisition is Kentucky Derby Winner.*

*Victor in Racing Classic by Length Over Escoba.*

*Result of Event on Sloppy Track Big Surprise.*

[BY A. P. NIGHT WIRE.]

LOUISVILLE (Ky.) May 10.—One of the greatest crowds that ever witnessed the Kentucky Derby, today saw W. S. Kilmer's recent acquisition, Exterminator, ridden by Jockey W. Knapp, win the forty-fourth renewal of that classic handily by one length from K. D. Alexander's Escoba. Eight lengths back came Viva America, who had set the early pace, while the public choice, A. K. Macomber's War Cloud, was fourth.

The race was run over a sloppy track and under the circumstances, the time, 2m. 10 4-5s., was good.

Exterminator's victory came as a great surprise to most of the spectators, as few had conceded the gelding a chance.

The start was good, Exterminator getting off in fifth place, which he still held by a length at the quarter. At the half the gelding had moved up to fourth place, which he held by half a length and at the three-quarters he was first by a head. At the mile he had dropped back a little and was second by four lengths. Coming into the stretch, he moved up on Escoba and in the final drive he moved away, finishing with a generous length to spare.

Escoba was second at the start and ran a good race throughout, never dropping further back than third place. The colt made a determined effort in the last furlong but tired rapidly in the last sixteenth and was going back at the wire.

War Cloud went to the post a heavy favorite at odds of $1.45 to $1, and his showing proved a great disappointment.

The gross value of the race was $18,475, of which $14,700 went to the winner. Of the remainder, $2500 went to Escoba, $1000 to Viva America, while War Cloud saved his entry and starting fees.

## BAPTISTS FALL BEFORE THROOP.

### CROWN CITY COLLEGIANS GET STRANGLE HOLD ON THE TITLE.

[LOCAL CORRESPONDENCE.]

REDLANDS, May 11.—Throop took a strangle hold on the college conference championship in baseball here this afternoon by beating the University of Redlands 5 to 1. Lukens had the Indian sign on the Baptists and three hits in remote frames tell the story.

Throop got off in the second frame. Otis knocked a high one to Holt in left field, who misjudged it and dropped the ball. Then up came Lukens and lammed one out against the left field fence. While Holt got his hands on the ball he could not hold it. Otis scored on Potts's fly to Campbell and Taylor brought in Lukens with a two-base hit into center field. Throop connected again in the fifth when Krause walked and Twitcham got a hit. Krause scored on Cummings's error and Twitcham on a hit by Emler. In the sixth Potts got a base on Cummings's error and was scored by Twitcham's single. Redlands scored in the ninth when Kilby walked, stole second and third and came home when Lukens threw the ball away. The score:

| THROOP. | AB | R | H | O | A |
|---|---|---|---|---|---|
| Krause,cf | 3 | 1 | 0 | 0 | 0 |
| T'cham,rf | 5 | 1 | 4 | 1 | 0 |
| Sil'thorn,c | 5 | 0 | 0 | 11 | 1 |
| Emler,ss | 4 | 0 | 1 | 1 | 2 |
| Otis,lf | 5 | 1 | 0 | 1 | 0 |
| Lukens,p | 5 | 1 | 0 | 1 | 2 |
| Potts,2b | 5 | 1 | 1 | 2 | 3 |
| Davis,1b | 4 | 0 | 0 | 10 | 0 |
| Taylor,3b | 4 | 0 | 1 | 0 | 0 |
| Totals | 40 | 5 | 7 | 27 | 8 |

| REDLANDS. | AB | R | H | O | A |
|---|---|---|---|---|---|
| C'mings,ss | 3 | 0 | 0 | 0 | 3 |
| Lackey,ss | 1 | 0 | 0 | 0 | 3 |
| Trine,1b | 3 | 0 | 0 | 12 | 0 |
| Kilby,rf | 4 | 1 | 0 | 2 | 0 |
| Rhodes,cf | 4 | 0 | 1 | 1 | 0 |
| Smith,c | 4 | 0 | 0 | 7 | 0 |
| Al'tara,2b | 3 | 0 | 0 | 2 | 0 |
| Holt,lf | 3 | 0 | 1 | 0 | 0 |
| C'pbell,3b | 3 | 0 | 0 | 2 | 5 |
| Dye,p | 1 | 0 | 1 | 0 | 1 |
| Wiese,p | 2 | 0 | 0 | 1 | 0 |
| Totals | 31 | 1 | 3 | 27 | 12 |

SCORE BY INNINGS.

| | 1 | 2 | 3 | 4 | 5 | 6 | 7 | 8 | 9 | |
|---|---|---|---|---|---|---|---|---|---|---|
| Throop | 0 | 2 | 0 | 0 | 2 | 1 | 0 | 0 | 0 | 5 |
| Base hits | 1 | 1 | 1 | 0 | 2 | 1 | 1 | 0 | 0 | 7 |
| Redlands | 0 | 0 | 0 | 0 | 0 | 0 | 0 | 0 | 1 | 1 |
| Base hits | 0 | 0 | 1 | 0 | 0 | 0 | 1 | 1 | 0 | 3 |

SUMMARY.

Earned run—Throop, 1. Two-base hit—Taylor. Bases on balls—Off Dye, 2; off Wiese, 2; off Lukens, 1. Struck out—By Dye, 3; by Wiese, 2; by Lukens, 11. Umpire—Johnson. Errors—Cummings, 2; Holt, 2; Trine, Lukens, Potts.

## GRAND RAPIDS MAN COMING TO TIGERS.

Infielder Alcock, who was with Grand Rapids last year and who is regarded as a cracking good infielder or outfielder, is expected to join Bill Essick's Tigers either today or tomorrow. He left Grand Rapids some days ago and is due now in Los Angeles. It is more than likely that the newcomer will be used in right field as soon as he reports.

## CRAWFORD HURT; OUT OF GAME.

Sam Crawford, one of the greatest baseball favorites that ever played in Los Angeles, may be lost to the fans for some time. In the seventh inning of yesterday's game between Vernon and the Angels, Sam turned his ankle as he reached second base on a long single to right field. Several minutes elapsed before he was able to regain his feet. He then had to be helped off the field.

Doc Finlay examined the injured member and quickly recommended an X-ray examination and the ankle was put under the rays. No bones were found to be broken, but is was discovered that several ligaments had been severely strained. Under the best conditions it is hardly likely that Crawford will be able to get back into the line-up for a fortnight.

As utility players are difficult to obtain just now it is more than likely that Killefer will play center field this afternoon. Cooper may be sent to right, in which case Caldwell, the new utility man, will play at second. Crawford will remain in Los Angeles until the Angels return for their series with the Seals the week of May 21-26.

## BASEBALL STANDINGS.

### COAST LEAGUE.

| | W. | L. | P.c. | | W. | L. | P.c. |
|---|---|---|---|---|---|---|---|
| Salt Lake | 21 | 15 | .583 | Oakland | 18 | 20 | .474 |
| Vernon | 20 | 18 | .526 | Sacramento | 17 | 18 | .486 |
| Los Angeles | 20 | 19 | .513 | S. Francisco | 16 | 22 | .421 |

YESTERDAY'S RESULTS.

Los Angeles, 4; Vernon, 0.
Sacramento, 4; Oakland, 3 (11 innings.)
Salt Lake, 3; San Francisco, 2.

### NATIONAL LEAGUE.

| | W. | L. | P.c. | | W. | L. | P.c. |
|---|---|---|---|---|---|---|---|
| New York | 18 | 3 | .857 | Philadelphia | 8 | 11 | .421 |
| Chicago | 13 | 6 | .674 | Brooklyn | 7 | 12 | .368 |
| Pittsburgh | 11 | 9 | .550 | St. Louis | 7 | 14 | .333 |
| Cincinnati | 11 | 12 | .478 | Boston | 6 | 14 | .300 |

YESTERDAY'S RESULTS.

Pittsburgh, 2; New York, 0.
Boston, 6; Chicago, 4.
St. Louis-Philadelphia, wet grounds.
Brooklyn-Cincinnati, rain.

### AMERICAN LEAGUE.

| | W. | L. | P.c. | | W. | L. | P.c. |
|---|---|---|---|---|---|---|---|
| Cleveland | 12 | 9 | .571 | Washington | 10 | 11 | .476 |
| Boston | 13 | 10 | .565 | St. Louis | 9 | 10 | .474 |
| New York | 12 | 10 | .545 | Detroit | 7 | 10 | .412 |
| Chicago | 9 | 8 | .529 | Philadelphia | 8 | 12 | .400 |

YESTERDAY'S RESULTS.

New York, 6; Detroit, 5.
Philadelphia, 1; Chicago, 0.
Washington, 1; Cleveland, 0.
St. Louis, 4; Boston, 2.

### WESTERN LEAGUE.

| | W. | L. | P.c. | | W. | L. | P.c. |
|---|---|---|---|---|---|---|---|
| Des Moines | 9 | 2 | .818 | Wichita | 5 | 5 | .500 |
| Omaha | 7 | 4 | .636 | Hutchinson | 4 | 7 | .364 |
| Topeka | 7 | 4 | .636 | Sioux City | 3 | 8 | .273 |
| Joplin | 5 | 5 | .500 | St. Joseph | 3 | 8 | .273 |

YESTERDAY'S RESULTS.

St. Joseph, 6; Sioux City, 2.
Joplin-Wichita, rain.
Hutchinson, 3; Topeka, 4.
Omaha, 10; Des Moines, 3.

### AMERICAN ASSOCIATION.

| | W. | L. | P.c. | | W. | L. | P.c. |
|---|---|---|---|---|---|---|---|
| Louisville | 8 | 1 | .889 | Columbus | 4 | 5 | .444 |
| Milwaukee | 7 | 2 | .778 | St. Paul | 3 | 6 | .333 |
| Kansas City | 6 | 3 | .667 | Minneapolis | 2 | 7 | .222 |
| Indianapolis | 5 | 5 | .500 | Toledo | 2 | 8 | .200 |

YESTERDAY'S RESULTS.

Minneapolis, 0; Milwaukee, 6.
St. Paul, 2; Kansas City, 11.

### PACIFIC COAST INTERNATIONAL.

Spokane, 2; Seattle, 4.
Aberdeen, 2; Portland, 4.
Tacoma, 2; Vancouver, 5.

### SOUTHERN ASSOCIATION.

Birmingham, 4; Chattanooga, 1.
Atlanta, 10; Nashville, 0.
New Orleans, 4; Little Rock, 0.
Mobile, 0; Memphis, 1.

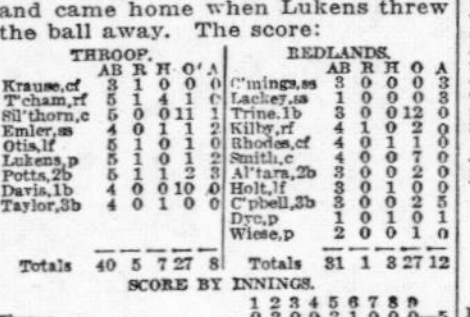

## ANGELENOS CONTEST IN BICYCLE MEET.

[LOCAL CORRESPONDENCE.]

RIVERSIDE, May 11.—The twelve-mile road race arranged by local dealers for bicycle day was participated in by a bunch of the fastest bicycle riders of the present day. The winners were Ralph Kingsley of Los Angeles (scratch,) who finished in 31m. 1s., and Desmond Fletcher of this city (handicap,) who finished first in 33m. 3s. net time. There were twenty-five entrants. Robert Gerwing of Santa Ana finished one-fifth second behind Fletcher, while George Gerwing, a brother, finished third, just one-fifth second later. Charles Fuller Gates was master of ceremonies.

## BEES BUNCH HITS; GET LEAD AND GAME.

[BY A. P. NIGHT WIRE.]

SAN FRANCISCO, May 11.—Salt Lake and San Francisco fought on fairly even terms until the sixth inning, when the Bees bunched three hits off Smith for a one-run lead, which the Seals were unable to overcome. Hunter, Seal outfielder, was banished from the game for disputing a decision at the plate. The series now stands three and two, with San Francisco on the short end. The score:

| SALT LAKE. | AB | R | H | O | A |
|---|---|---|---|---|---|
| Farmer,cf | 4 | 1 | 2 | 3 | 0 |
| Siglin,2b | 5 | 0 | 1 | 2 | 6 |
| Ryan,lf | 4 | 0 | 3 | 4 | 1 |
| Orr,ss | 3 | 1 | 1 | 1 | 3 |
| Chapelle,rf | 4 | 0 | 0 | 2 | 0 |
| Sheeley,1b | 2 | 0 | 1 | 13 | 0 |
| Sands,2b | 3 | 0 | 1 | 1 | 2 |
| Konnick,c | 4 | 1 | 1 | 1 | 1 |
| Leverenz,p | 3 | 0 | 0 | 0 | 0 |
| Totals | 32 | 3 | 10 | 27 | 13 |

| SAN FRANCISCO. | AB | R | H | O | A |
|---|---|---|---|---|---|
| Maggert,cf | 3 | 1 | 0 | 0 | 0 |
| Pick,3b | 3 | 0 | 1 | 2 | 3 |
| Hunter,lf | 3 | 0 | 1 | 2 | 0 |
| Koerner,1b | 4 | 1 | 0 | 11 | 2 |
| Downs,2b | 4 | 0 | 1 | 6 | 2 |
| Goldie,lf,rf | 3 | 0 | 0 | 0 | 0 |
| Brooks,c | 4 | 0 | 2 | 1 | 3 |
| Corhan,ss | 4 | 0 | 1 | 2 | 5 |
| Smith,p | 4 | 0 | 1 | 1 | 1 |
| Hummel,rf | 1 | 0 | 0 | 2 | 0 |
| Totals | 33 | 2 | 7 | 27 | 16 |

SCORE BY INNINGS.

| | 1 | 2 | 3 | 4 | 5 | 6 | 7 | 8 | 9 | |
|---|---|---|---|---|---|---|---|---|---|---|
| Salt Lake | 0 | 0 | 2 | 0 | 0 | 1 | 0 | 0 | 0 | 3 |
| San Francisco | 0 | 1 | 1 | 0 | 0 | 0 | 0 | 0 | 0 | 2 |

SUMMARY.

Error—Farmer. Stolen bases—Orr, Sands, Hunter. Three-base hit—Farmer. Sacrifice hit—Leverenz. Bases on balls—Off Smith, 3; off Leverenz, 3. Struck out—By Smith, 1. Double plays—Corhan to Koerner to Pick; Sands to Sheeley; Pick to Koerner. Runs responsible for—Smith, 3; Leverenz, 1.

At Washington Park.

## PERTICA GOOD IN PINCHES.

*Killefer's Men Defeat Vernon Four to Nothing.*

*Roy Mitchell Touched up Hard in Third.*

*Five Hits Quickly Blossom into Four Runs.*

BY EDWIN F. O'MALLEY.

Pertica, the Angelic juvenile, wrought havoc with Bill Essick yesterday, carrying him down the line for nine circles while the Killefers corralled four runs. The kid pitched a good game in the pinches, but was wobbly in his control, so wobbly that when the dust of hostilities had lifted six f.o.b.'s were chalked up against him. Roy Mitchell heaved well except in one inning when he was touched up for five bingles which blossomed into four runs. Roy had been out of the game for a long time on account of an injured rib. He was desirous in the extreme to make good yesterday—a desire that led him to give an attentive ear to the machinations of Baal.

This old offender enticed Roy to resort to a lady's beauty parlor to make good and Roy responded with a big R. It is a well known fact that a compost of talcum powder and soap when furtively applied to a rotundity of horsehide will make the said rotundity play the village cut-up in flirting over the plate. Ah—but where to locate his base of operations—that was the rub! Mitch is nothing if not original. Using his girth as a sort of Mason and Dixon's line he decided to go below it for his parlors. Just below a garter of cerulean blue, on his right leg, Roy planted a goodly mixture of his magic compost.

### RUBS HIS CALF.

It was noticed a number of time that when the Vernon hurler stooped to put dirt on the ball he covertly rubbed his right calf. Red Killefer, who has an eye like the famous Lecocq, complained to Casey at the beginning of the seventh that Roy was drugging the ball.

"Step right this way," motioned Pearl to Mitchell, who sheepishly approached the plate. It was at this juncture that Fournier, who has a keen eye for the Hogarthian line of beauty, pranced to the rubber, dropped enthusiastically to his knees, ran a trembling finger over the cerulean blue garter and then gave Roy's right leg a resounding smack. It was the same thing as if one hit a bag of lime. "Stop tickling me, Jacques," blushed Roy. "Mitch you have a perfect right," returned Jacques, "to your opinion and——

Casey, of course, had to butt in at this point. He came up with a handful of talcum powder. "I'm detected," purred Roy, as a vanity glass and powder puff were pried from beneath that blue garter by the nervous and sedulous Fournier, "but I'll promise to be good hereafter." Casey took him at his word and the game proceeded.

### HERE IS THE WAY.

Here is the way the Angels smothered the ball in the third canto: Bolesy singled to left and scurried to second on Little Bo-Peepy's scorcher in the same place. Pertica produced air vacuums. Killefer banged a beauty to right for two bags scoring Boles and Pepe. Terry put Red on third by a single to left and filched the keystone. Fournier ambled. Crawford singled to right putting Red and Terry over the rubber. Fournier went to third on the throw-in and Sam second. As he reached the bag, Crawford twisted his ankle and limped off the field, Caldwell taking his place. Ellis fouled to De Vormer and Cooper ended the scrimmage by the Mitchell-Borton route. Four runs, five hits.

Vernon had its best opportunity to score in the sixth, but Johnny Powers had his fingers crossed and messed up the whole thing. R. Mitchell and Daley walked. J. Mitchell grounded out to Fournier and Chadbourne walked. Borton and Hosp, however, disseminated the barley, the former flying to Ellis and Farnz ingloriously whiffing. En passant might gurgle—an excellent Saturday attendance, the size of which made the cockles of Johnny Powers's heart and that of Pete Cunningham dance like an Easter day sun. Bill Essick's troubles follow:

| LOS ANGELES. | AB | R | H | O | A |
|---|---|---|---|---|---|
| Killefer,2b | 3 | 1 | 1 | 2 | 2 |
| Terry,ss | 2 | 1 | 1 | 2 | 2 |
| Fournier,1b | 3 | 0 | 0 | 9 | 2 |
| Crawford,rf | 2 | 0 | 1 | 0 | 0 |
| Ellis,lf | 2 | 0 | 0 | 1 | 0 |
| Cooper,cf | 4 | 0 | 0 | 1 | 1 |
| Boles,c | 4 | 1 | 2 | 4 | 0 |
| Pepe,3b | 3 | 1 | 1 | 3 | 1 |
| Pertica,p | 4 | 0 | 1 | 0 | 1 |
| Caldwell,rf | 2 | 0 | 0 | 4 | 1 |
| Totals | 29 | 4 | 7 | 27 | 9 |

| VERNON. | AB | R | H | O | A |
|---|---|---|---|---|---|
| Daley,lf | 1 | 0 | 0 | 2 | 0 |
| J.M'chell,ss | 3 | 0 | 0 | 3 | 2 |
| C'bourne,cf | 3 | 0 | 0 | 2 | 0 |
| Borton,1b | 4 | 0 | 2 | 7 | 0 |
| Hosp,2b | 4 | 0 | 1 | 3 | 1 |
| Snyder,lf | 3 | 0 | 0 | 2 | 0 |
| Wist'zil,3b | 3 | 0 | 0 | 1 | 1 |
| DeVormer,c | 3 | 0 | 1 | 5 | 1 |
| R.M'chell,p | 3 | 0 | 1 | 2 | 5 |
| Mathes,x | 1 | 0 | 0 | 0 | 0 |
| Totals | 28 | 0 | 5 | 27 | 10 |

x—Batted for Snyder in ninth.

SCORE BY INNINGS.

| | 1 | 2 | 3 | 4 | 5 | 6 | 7 | 8 | 9 | |
|---|---|---|---|---|---|---|---|---|---|---|
| Los Angeles | 0 | 0 | 4 | 0 | 0 | 0 | 0 | 0 | 0 | 4 |
| Base hits | 0 | 0 | 5 | 1 | 0 | 0 | 0 | 0 | 1 | 7 |
| Vernon | 0 | 0 | 0 | 0 | 0 | 0 | 0 | 0 | 0 | 0 |
| Base hits | 1 | 0 | 1 | 1 | 0 | 0 | 0 | 0 | 2 | 5 |

SUMMARY.

Stolen base—Terry. Two-base hits—Killefer, Boles. Sacrifice hits—Terry, 2; Boles. Struck out—By R. Mitchell, 4; by Pertica, 4. Bases on balls—Off R. Mitchell, 4; off Pertica, 6. Runs responsible for—R. Mitchell, 4. Double plays—R. Mitchell to Wisterzil; Pepe to Killefer; Caldwell to Fournier. Hit by pitched ball—Killefer, Wisterzil. Passed ball—De Vormer. Time of game—1h. 55m. Umpire—Casey.

## SENATORS CAPTURE GAME IN ELEVENTH.

[BY A. P. NIGHT WIRE.]

SACRAMENTO, May 11.—Forsythe's single, a sacrifice hit and an error scored the winning run for Sacramento in the eleventh inning, after Oakland had tied the score in the ninth. The score:

| OAKLAND. | AB | R | H | O | A |
|---|---|---|---|---|---|
| Hawks,rf | 4 | 0 | 0 | 0 | 0 |
| Wares,2b | 5 | 1 | 1 | 3 | 5 |
| Mid'ton,lf | 5 | 0 | 1 | 1 | 1 |
| Miller,cf | 5 | 2 | 2 | 2 | 0 |
| Gardner,1b | 3 | 0 | 0 | 16 | 0 |
| C'ensen,3b | 4 | 0 | 1 | 3 | 2 |
| Croll,ss | 4 | 0 | 1 | 3 | 5 |
| Murray,c | 4 | 0 | 0 | 2 | 1 |
| Krause,p | 4 | 0 | 2 | 0 | 2 |
| Totals | 38 | 3 | 8 | 30 | 16 |

| SACRAMENTO. | AB | R | H | O | A |
|---|---|---|---|---|---|
| Eldred,rf | 5 | 0 | 3 | 2 | 0 |
| Wolter,cf | 5 | 0 | 0 | 6 | 0 |
| Wilie,lf | 5 | 0 | 1 | 1 | 0 |
| F'sythe,1b | 5 | 1 | 2 | 19 | 0 |
| Fisher,c | 4 | 0 | 2 | 1 | 4 |
| Rodgers,2b | 4 | 1 | 1 | 1 | 6 |
| Pinelli,3b | 4 | 1 | 1 | 0 | 1 |
| Downey,ss | 4 | 0 | 1 | 2 | 6 |
| Leake,p | 4 | 1 | 0 | 1 | 1 |
| Totals | 40 | 4 | 11 | 33 | 18 |

One out when winning run was scored.
Eldred called out in eighth for not touching first.

SCORE BY INNINGS.

| | | | | | | | | | | | | |
|---|---|---|---|---|---|---|---|---|---|---|---|---|
| Oakland | 0 | 0 | 0 | 1 | 0 | 0 | 0 | 0 | 2 | 0 | 0 | 3 |
| Sacramento | 0 | 0 | 0 | 0 | 2 | 0 | 1 | 0 | 0 | 0 | 1 | 4 |

SUMMARY.

Errors—Hawks, Wares, Miller, 2; Downey, Leake. Stolen bases—Wolter, Wilie, Pinelli. Home runs—Miller, 2. Three-base hits—Eldred, Rodgers. Two-base hits—Fisher, Eldred, Wares. Sacrifice hits—Hawks, Gardner, Rodgers. Bases on balls—Off Krause, 1. Struck out—By Krause, 1; by Leake, 1. Double plays—Croll to Gardner; Croll to Christensen. Runs responsible for—Krause, 3; Leake, 3.

The Los Angeles Times

SATURDAY MORNING, JULY 5, 1919.

SPORTS MOTORING FILMLAND DRAMA

# MORMONS BIFF TIGERS TWICE.

*Bees Upset Dope by Copping Both Games.*

*Sailor Stroud has Better of Lefty Mitchell.*

*Leverenz Too Good for Bengals in a.m. Contest.*

BY HARRY A. WILLIAMS.

Salt Lake was all swelled up last night, and had just cause to be, having won two ball games and one world's championship in one day. That is enough honor for one Fourth, and outside of the ball games we rejoice heartily with Jack Cook and other denizens of the Utah metropolis in the gaining of their new-found laurel. True, Salt Lake is not the birth place of Jack Dempsey, but that city claims to be his home, and backed up said claim by betting 3 to 1 on the challenger, with few takers, which merely proves there are more than three wise men residing there.

TAKE A PAIR.

It is not believed that they would have offered the same odds on their ball team, but the Bees upset the dope by copping both pastimes. Such is baseball. Salt Lake won, 2 to 1 and 3 to 2, scores which are eloquent of high-class stuff on both sides. The second battle went eleven rounds, which was more than the Toledo folks got for their money. After what the Bees have done to the Tigers in the last two days, and the Beavers accomplished in the ninth against the Angels yesterday afternoon, a good many people are inclined to revise their opinions about it being a two-club race.

Both managers being averse to losing on the Fourth, which is a day dedicated to the commemorating of great victories, trotted out some of their best pitching bets. Leverenz and Dell hooked up in the morning pastime, while Stroud was pitted against Fromme and Mitchell in the afternoon fracas.

HEAVY THINKING.

Not realizing what was to happen later, but suspecting what might happen, Salt Lake scored enough runs in the first round to keep the score tied until the eleventh. Between the first and the eleventh the Tigers counted two, thereby confirming their suspicions that the score might be tied.

When Maggert and Krug opened the first inning with singles, things looked dark for Fromme, and the appearances were not misleading. Art immediately soaked Mulvey, filling the sacks. Rumbler resorted to a force-out of Mulvey as the surest way of getting Maggert over the pan. Sheeley although he had trained faithfully, seemed to be out of form, and popped a fly to Chadbourne, which was too short for anybody to score. Some of the experts opined that Johnson was trained too fine, but he upset them with a single that counted Krug.

Mulligan rammed the ball against the sod so hard that it bounced into the air for an infield single. This left the bases full, and Byler left them the same way by allowing a third strike to be called on him. Byler did this again in the third round, although he had seen it demonstrated, but a short time before that the only way to win is by swinging.

When Stroud opened the second with a single, Essick motioned for Willie Mitchell, who was warming up in the place set aside for that purpose. Willie, however, was not fully heated up, and Maggert was allowed to sacrifice until he was called to the center of the arena. He soon disposed of the visitors, and with the aid of some superlative fielding by High, held them back until the eleventh.

Vernon started scoring in the second, acing one Edington's single. High's walk, a force-out and Krug's overthrow of first in trying to complete a double. Hits by De Vormer and Chadbourne knotted the score in the third.

A NEAR RALLY.

Salt Lake showed signs of copping in the ninth. Mulligan walked and Mitchell potted Byler with a fast one, putting two on with nobody out. Stroud sacrificed. This put runners on second and third. Every time Mitchell pitched to Maggert, Mulligan would run down the line and give a life-like imitation of starting to steal home. He did this once too often, or rather the last time he forgot to go back to third. De Vormer pegged to Me sel, and Mulligan found himself cut off from his base. His only alternative was to beat it home. Meusel, having longer legs, pursued and overtook him.

Johnson provided the eleventh inning crisis by leading off with a single. He sprang the unexpected by stealing second, and Mulligan sacrificed him to third. Byler, having learned the value of swinging, slammed one toward left until Mitchell went up and hawked the ball as it took a high hop. Johnson already was so far on his way home with the winning run that Johnny had to content himself with throwing Butch out at first. Stroud grounded to Mitchell.

ZOWIE—A TRIPLE.

Meusel lammed out a beautiful triple to left center in the home half of the eleventh. Borton followed with a fly to Maggert which would

(Continued on Second Page.)

# JOE STECHER TRIMS LEWIS.

[BY A. P. NIGHT WIRE.]

OMAHA (Neb.) July 4. — Joe Stecher of Dodge, Neb., defeated Ed (Strangler) Lewis of San Jose, Cal., in two straight falls in a wrestling match staged here today. Stecher won the first fall in one hour and forty-seven minutes and the second fall in fourteen minutes. He took each fall with a body scissors and wrist lock.

Lewis was on the defensive throughout and was given little opportunity to employ his specialty, the headlock. The match was fairly fast and interesting throughout. Earl Caddock, world's champion, refereed.

# SOUTHERNERS WIN ROW.

[BY A. P. NIGHT WIRE.]

SAN FRANCISCO, July 4.—The San Diego Rowing Club crew won the main event in the championship regatta of the Pacific Coast Association of Oarsmen held here today when, after a gruelling contest, it took the senior four-oared race by approximately one-quarter of a length.

The race was over a one and one-half mile course. It was a close and spirited event which was not decided definitely until the visitors, when near the finish, by a burst of speed outdistanced a team representing the South End Rowing Club of this city. The Ariel Rowing Club crew finished a close third.

Among other races and the order in which the different clubs finished were:

Junior four-oared race, Dolphins, San Francisco; South End, San Francisco; San Diego, San Diego; Ariels, San Francisco.

United States Navy cutter race: Training ship Boston, crew from the United States Shipping Board training station at Mare Island.

Senior single sculls: Bill Wilson, South End; Bill Ringen, Dolphins.

Canoe race, San Diego, Dolphins; South End.

Junior singles sculls: G. Arnholdt Smith, San Diego; E. Brown, Ariels; Ruddy Illing, South End; "Bud" Sterling, Dolphins.

Intermediate four-oared race: South Ends; San Diego; Ariels.

The races were held in China Basin in San Francisco Bay and attracted a large crowd.

# LOUIS CHEVROLET FIRST.

[BY A. P. NIGHT WIRE.]

TACOMA (Wash.) July 4.—Piloting his machine at an average speed of ninety-seven miles an hour, Louis Chevrolet, this afternoon won first prize in the eighty-mile race at the Tacoma Speedway after having captured first honors in the sixty-mile event and third in the forty-mile contest.

Eddie Hearne was second in the main event and Cliff Durant, third.

Ralph K. Mulford was second in the sixty-mile event and Hearne, third. The forty-mile race was won by Mulford with Durant second and Chevrolet third.

More than 35,000 persons witnessed the three events for the Pacific Coast championship, which goes to Chevrolet.

Mulford, who was doubtful about starting in the second race, of sixty miles, on account of spark plug trouble, was second at the end of the tenth lap.

He started from the pits from a standing start after the other four drivers had crossed the tape with a flying start. He caught all the drivers except Chevrolet before the first twenty miles had been reeled off.

Hearne, third, followed by Resta and Durant. The first twenty miles of the second race were made at a trifle over 101 miles an hour by Chevrolet.

Mulford led at the end of the tenth lap of the first race. His speed for the twenty miles was at the rate of 110 miles an hour, the fastest time yet made on the speedway. He was followed by Durant, Hearne, Resta and Chevrolet. Chevrolet had been in third place until the beginning of the tenth lap, when he was forced into the pits by tire trouble.

Mulford, driving at the rate of almost exactly 100 miles an hour, won the forty-mile race on the Tacoma speedway this afternoon. He finished the forty miles in 24m. 2 2-5s. The race was a contest between Mulford and Durant. Chevrolet finished third, with Hearne and Resta following.

The second race of sixty miles was won by Louis Chevrolet. He led the field all the way. Mulford, Hearne, Durant and Resta finished in the order named. The time of Chevrolet was 36m. 47 1-5s. at the rate of ninety-eight and one-half miles an hour.

With Mulford and Chevrolet each having won a race, interest was keen in the third and last event, the eighty-mile grind. At the end of the first ten laps, Chevrolet led, closely pressed by Mulford, with Hearne, Resta and Durant following.

The $15,000 in prize money is distributed on points, the position of the drivers in each race counting in their final standing.

# VETERANS LAND ON YOUNGSTERS.

*Maury and Mack Play Way to the Tennis Finals.*

*Browne and Wayne to be Their Opponents.*

*Northern Team Eliminated in Semi-finals.*

BY HOWARD ANGUS.

Old age may have been butchered in Toledo's sweltering sun yesterday and served raw with spinach, but he certainly cavorted all over the tennis courts at Long Beach, playfully slapping youngsters on the wrists.

Those two weather-stained veteran teams of McLoughlin and Bundy and Browne and Wayne eliminated all comers in the Pacific Coast doubles tennis championships and will battle today for the right to represent the West in the national event. The match will be held this afternoon and promises to produce the most kittenish and classy tennis of the year in spite of the alleged creaking joints and shaking legs of the veterans.

BROWN AND WAYNE.

The dapper Mr. Browne and the serious-looking Mr. Wayne defeated two teams that fairly radiate youth. In the morning Godshall and Berry went down, 6-0, 6-2, 6-0, and in the afternoon San Francisco's two tea drinkers, Bates and Parker, bit the dust, 6-2, 6-3, 5-7, 6-1.

McLoughlin and Bundy spent the day defeating other members of their sporting store. In the dawning hours they eliminated partner Sinsabaugh and young Davies of Hollywood, 8-6, 6-0, 6-1, and in the twilight of evening their chief clerk, Harvy Snodgrass, and his playing mate with the poetical hair, Ketchum, 6-4, 6-2, 6-1.

STANDING ROOM.

The tournament drew a large attendance and forced the management to hang up the "standing room" only sign. The crowd was notable for the fine silk suits worn by the ladies and the variety of flannel trousers and flashy hosiery displayed by the men. It was strictly a holiday crowd. Again it demonstrated that past fame is alluring. When Bundy and McLoughlin appeared, trailing their aged glory behind them, Sinsabaugh hurried to take down the standing-room sign and came out of the crush looking like Jess Willard on round three.

Bates and Parker in their match showed to much better advantage than yesterday. They forced Browne and Wayne to play tennis. The northerners took the third set, 5-7, after the southerners had them 4-1 and later 5-2. Their demonstration of the fighting spirit elated the crowd and resulted in Browne and Wayne dragging themselves listlessly from the court. Nat Browne's famous mustached smile was only seen at odd fleeting moments.

Because of the wind the southerners could not work their already overworked lob and won on straight drives and cuts and such like.

TEA DRINKING.

The northerners tried to make the vets fall for the tea drinking with the score two wins and one defeat for them just as was the case with the Barker brothers. But Browne and Wayne drank cup for cup and came back the lightest on their feet.

The tea drinking evidently gave the daper old-young man with the mustache a bright idea, for he was heard to invite some of his dry looking friends in a low voice well covered with his hand to accompany him to his room after the match. They stole out with the tread of leopards on the march and came back looking slick.

Snodgrass and Ketchum did more than open the pores of McLoughlin and Bundy's skin. When the match was over Bundy looked as if somebody had been ducking him in the ocean. He was probably the wettest man in Long Beach yesterday. His opponents specialized on him and Bundy sent them back as much as they gave. He looked very fast on his feet and is playing better tennis than he has since the Davis cup matches. His shots were not of the blinding kind, but they certainly made the unsophisticated youngsters blush at times. Once when Bundy dropped the ball just over the net, leaving them flat footed back near the wire they looked like a couple of kids whose mother had caught them in her rouge box.

GOOD ENOUGH.

The work of McLoughlin and Bundy gave one the impression that they were playing just good enough to win. When it was necessary to take a point they did. When it was a matter of small consequence they dashed into long practice rallies. McLoughlin's service was probably the slowest of the four. He was accused yesterday of trying to copy Nat Brown's famous lolly pop serve. He modestly denied the allegation.

Sea-dog Cliff Herd and his aviator friend, Kenny Hawks, played an exhibition match with Winnie and Mace and son. The well-known operatic star, who claims to be the only singing athlete proved conclusively that he had his land legs with him. He played ferociously. His lesson with Hawks was excellent, he having taught the aviator the blinker system last night.

In addition to the championship match today, Simpson Sinsabaugh promises to arrange some special features. So there will be enough tennis and none to spare.

Jack Dempsey, the New Heavyweight Champion of the World.

This photograph, taken and copyrighted by the Keystone view service during a training bout, shows new champion just as he might have looked to Willard after landing one of those terrific clips to the chin.

# CROWD ROASTS DURING PRELIMINARIES

[BY A. P. DAY WIRE.]

TOLEDO (O.) July 4. — Everybody had a bed last night, it was said, largely for the reason that every Toledoan who could went into the lodging-house business for the occasion. Early today they were astir, turning out of Pullmans, hotels, vacant stores given over to cots, seeking breakfast and turning their steps toward the great arena at Bayview Park.

ON JOB EARLY.

The road to the park was alive and bustling with the dawn, nor was it entirely asleep during the night, for now and then a truck loaded with supplies for the vendors moved out in the darkness. With the daylight traffic increased, policemen and soldiers were early at their stations.

In the arena carpenters were still busy putting on the final touches to the vast amphitheater with its 80,000 seats. Thousands of these were still on sale this morning. Every road leading into the city saw automobiles bringing their loads of fight enthusiasts from near-by cities and some from a distance.

Detectives from all the principal cities of the land were mingling in the crowds, while 500 Toledo citizens were sworn in to aid the regular city police force in maintaining order. How the vast throng was to get back into the city was a problem concerning which there was more hope than confidence.

SERVICE POOR.

It was admitted that the street cars were totally inadequate to the task of bringing the crowd back to town. Two main thoroughfares were available for automobiles and pedestrians, but great congestion was anticipated and it was thought certain that thousands would have to make their way back on foot.

Parking space for 21,000 automobiles at $2 each was available outside the arena. The money goes to the city.

Willard remained favorite in the betting. One man paraded the streets with a sign on his automobile reading: "I will bet this machine against $1000 on Dempsey."

Emergency ambulance and all police patrol wagons were at police headquarters for instant use in event of trouble of any sort.

All physicians in Toledo were registered with the police and were available for emergency.

PRELIMINARIES.

The first preliminary was called at 11 o'clock, a six-round go between Tommy O'Boyle of Toledo, 116 pounds, and Solly Epstein of Indianapolis, 114 pounds. Tom Bodkin of Pittsburgh, referee, decided the contest a draw.

The crowd continued to gather but slowly, only a few thousand spectators being present when the first preliminary started.

The second preliminary, just before noon, scheduled to go six rounds, between "Wop" English and Battling Wendt, both of Toledo, ended in the first round, English winning by a knockout.

At noon the crowd was rapidly gathering, the arena being about one-third filled.

Among the thousands of coatless and collarless spectators was a good sprinkling of women.

The third preliminary, a scheduled six-round contest between Tommy Long of Detroit and Johnny Lewis of Toledo, ended in the third round, with a knockout victory for Lewis.

BLISTERING.

By noon the vertical sun was serving up the attendance en casserole. The breeze continued, but confined its efforts to fluttering the flags on the arena. It did not dip into the bowl of the amphitheater.

The seats were filling steadily with a crowd which to a man had discarded coats, and largely collars. A Bedouin effect was produced by the numerous spectators who covered their heads with handkerchiefs surmounted by their hats.

The temperature in the press seats was 112 deg. in the sun under which everybody sat. There was no shade in which to take a more conservative reading.

A small blaze was started at the ringside by a cigarette stump. It was extinguished with a pail of drinking water, which happened to be at hand.

CHAMPION FAN.

A member of a big party from Toronto, whose train was parked near another special from California, reported meeting the last word in fight enthusiasts in the Coast party. This man was totally blind, but paid $60 for a seat under a 112-deg. sun for a show which he could only imagine from what his friends told him and from memories of fights of earlier days before he was imprisoned in darkness.

A brass band made spasmodic efforts to play jazz, but made a sorry work of it. The brass instruments were so hot they almost burnt the hands of their players and all the pep had sweated from the snare drum. The envy of all was the aviator who looped, swirled and gyrated above. He looked cool, in any event.

ON THE ALTAR.

Up in the squared circle, as if on a sacrificial altar, the performers in the preliminaries slugged and slipped, panted and bled, exposed to the full fury of the sun. The sweat poured off them in rivulets as they sought to engage the attention of an almost oblivious crowd. Few even heard their names as they were announced.

Only their seconds seemed really interested. At the interval the latter crawled through the ropes and sprayed them with water and cooled their spines and pulses with ice. At 1:15 o'clock p.m., the band had apparently given up efforts to entertain.

The only thermometer in the press stand rose straight up to 12[illegible] deg. which was at the top of the [illegible]. A place was found for it [illegible] flooring away from the sun. [illegible] it dropped back to 10[illegible]. Again placed by the side of telegraph instruments, its fever returned and in ten minutes it was again at 120, leaving to conjecture where it might

(Continued on Third Page.)

# LEFT HOOK LICKS JESS.

*Blow that Dempsey had Rehearsed Wins Jack the Title.*

BY BENNY LEONARD,

Lightweight Champion of the World.

[EXCLUSIVE DISPATCH.]

TOLEDO (O.) July 4. — A left hook, perfectly timed, accurately placed and powerfully delivered won the heavyweight championship of the world for Jack Dempsey here this afternoon. Shortly after Dempsey and Jess Willard squared off in the first round Jack shot this punch, the one that he had rehearsed so thoroughly throughout his training, to Willard's jaw. It landed squarely on what is known as the "button." Willard's knees sagged, his arms dropped to his side, a faraway look came into his eyes.

Dempsey took in the situation at a glance. He knew that he had stung Jess. The crown loomed big and glittering before his vision, and, without losing one precious second, the man who a few minutes later was to be the new heavyweight champion turned loose the whirlwind attack that has carried him to the top of the ladder in record time.

END IN THIRD.

This hurricane assault of Dempsey's has brought him from oblivion into the rose-tinted glare of the calcium. The end did not come until after the third round had passed and Willard was unable to come up for the fourth round when his chief adviser Walter Monaghan, threw in the towel signalizing defeat, but it was that first left hook that won for him.

Undoubtedly the shortest space of time on record. From a nobody to a champion in little more than a year is going some. Of course, Dempsey has been fighting more than a year but until twelve months ago there were few who had heard of the Utah cyclone.

Before diving into the technical points of the battle which culminated with the dethroning of Willard and the crowning of a new king, I wish to go on record as saying that Dempsey is a real champion. He has all the attributes that go to make him a champion. He has youth, he has speed, he has stamina.

He has strength and he is willing. He should be champion for some time to come.

JESS TANNED.

As the two men entered the ring, Willard wearing a broad smile of confidence, they appeared to be in the best of condition. The thousands who had not seen Willard in his training and were getting their first glimpse of the champion, openly voiced their surprise at the way Jess looked. He was tanned from training in the open and he seemed to feel his great strength. Glancing across the ring to where Dempsey was seated beneath a broad sunshade held by Big Bill Tate, a smile flitted across Willard's face.

If he entertained a thought of what was in store for him he certainly covered it masterfully. There was no outward sign to indicate that the champion was in the least fearful of his smaller opponent. As they stood together receiving their final instructions from Ollie Pecord, the referee, the disparity in their sizes was apparent. Dempsey seemed like a lightweight alongside of the giant Willard. A murmur of astonishment at the difference in their statures rippled through the vast crowd. Many of those who had picked Dempsey to win were not so sure their judgment had been justified. They were inclined to feel they might have underrated the superman.

JACK CALM.

In great contrast to the smiling confidence of Willard was Dempsey. He was not nervous but appeared to be extremely serious. Not the semblance of a smile adorned his face. In his eyes was a look of seriousness. He was all business. He listened intently to Pecord's instructions and then asked a few questions regarding the kidney punch, the rabbit punch and the manner of breaking from the clinches. He acted his part as challenger like a great showman. There was nothing affected about him. He was almost retiring in his efforts to avoid anything that might be mistaken for egotism. And then came the fight.

As the two men advanced from their corners at the sound of the opening gong neither made any pretense of shaking hands. Willard moved forward a few paces toward a neutral corner. Dempsey shuffled forward cautiously. It was apparent that Jack had fully made up his mind to adhere to the programme of battle he had outlined to me before the fight. He was not in the ring to take any chances. To those who watched his movements closely it was apparent he was supremely confident.

DROPS SMILE.

Willard must have noticed this as they approached each other for the smile which had draped his face disappeared and in its place came a look of concern. It was the first indication on Willard's part that he realized a youth, brimful of determination and supported by great strength, was about to attack him in an effort to strip him of his title.

Before a blow had been struck they fell into a clinch and Willard tried to rest his great weight on Dempsey. Jack soon wiggled clear just as the referee called "break." Thereupon Jack started stepping quickly around the ring. He moved in and out and around. He was drawing Willard out. He was making Willard tax what little strength he had in his legs. Willard led with a left jab but Dempsey easily

(Continued on Third Page.)

# EXACTLY WHAT HAPPENED.

[BY A. P. NIGHT WIRE.]

TOLEDO (O.) July 4.—Following is the Willard-Dempsey fight by rounds:

ROUND ONE.

Willard loomed up like a Goliath against his five-inch shorter David and opened the engagement by pumping his long left twice into Dempsey's face with force enough to make the latter blink. The challenger missed a swing and, slipping into a clinch, landed three body blows with his left hand, carrying but little force. Willard held him easily in a clinch and partly turning him around used his rapier-like left again, once to the head and once to the body after the break. Then Dempsey, as he had got the range, opened his heavy artillery and swung a jarring left to the jaw, followed by a right and left to the body. The almost superhuman power of the punches was immediately apparent. A partly silly, partly stupid expression overspread the champion's face and as he rocked on his heels his whole body quivered. He pulled himself together and as Dempsey crowded in again, shot a left to the mouth and repeated to the eye. The blows did not even cause his youthful Nemesis to hesitate, and dodging past the outstretched left as it snapped for the third time, he whipped over a right and a left almost simultaneously, the blows landing flush on Willard's jaw and for the first time in his championship career Willard was dropped to the floor. He was up again at the count of six only to be sent to the canvas with another right as he rose slowly to his feet, the blood beginning to pour from his mouth. He turned away from his opponent, who struck again twice with his right, Willard falling on his hands and knees. When he arose Dempsey crowded him into a corner and with a right and left to the face sent him to the floor again. As he arose a fusillade of body blows dropped him in a corner where he sat when the bell terminated the round and led Dempsey to believe that Willard had been counted out.

ROUND TWO.

Dempsey started where he left off, and Willard with a big cut under his eye appeared to be in a bad way. He managed to snap a left to Dempsey's face and a puny right uppercut to the chin. Dempsey replied with several body drives and Willard fell partly through the ropes. When he regained his feet he stumbled into a clinch, but Dempsey easily tore loose and proceeded to batter him almost at will, the champion retaliating with but three feeble stabs to the face during the melee. When Willard went to his corner he fell heavily into his chair and it was seen that his right eye was completely closed and that side of his face was swollen entirely out of shape while Dempsey was unmarked.

ROUND THREE.

The final session was simply a series of rapid-fire swings which fell on Willard's face and body with pile-driver power, which left Willard completely helpless as he staggered about the ring and wobbled along the ropes utterly unable to defend himself. Blood bubbled from his mouth with every gasp for breath while the crowd about the ringside began to yell to Referee Pecord to stop it. Just as the bell rang and Willard collapsed in his chair he spat out a tooth and it was seen that he was in bad condition. As he sat lolling from side to side his chief second, Walter Monahan, talked earnestly to him and when Willard nodded his head Monahan walked over and spoke to Pecord. The referee threw up his hands and hurried to Dempsey's corner. He gesticulated to the [illegible] and finally pulled Dempsey toward the center of the ring before the new champion realized that Willard's seconds had thrown up the sponge. As soon as he grasped the situation he started for Willard's corner and the late titleholder arose and stepped weakly to meet him. They shook hands and Willard muttered something in reply to Dempsey's remarks and the fight had passed into history.

# REDS ANNEX ANOTHER GAME AND BASEBALL CHAMPIONSHIP OF WORLD.

## CINCY CAPTURES WORLD'S SERIES.

*Eller Proves Too Much for the Sox Sluggers.*

*Williams Knocked Out of Box in First Canto.*

*Jackson Makes Longest Hit of Game for Homer.*

[BY A. P. NIGHT WIRE.]

CHICAGO, Oct. 9.—The world's baseball championship pennant for 1919 will fly from Redland Field, Cincinnati, next season.

Pat Moran's athletes invaded hostile territory today and cornered the eighth and deciding game against the White Sox by a score of 10 to 5.

As expert baseball it was as funny as a sack race. Nearly everything possible happened, including a comic four-run rally by the athletes in the pale hosiery. It never would have happened just as it did if the sun had not entered the lists and blinded the visiting fielders. It was all the funnier for the reason that the Sox were nine runs behind at the time.

The Reds, after dropping two games on their own grounds on the banks of the Ohio, permitting the Sox to get back in the running for the big emblem, started after the deciding game at the onset. They descended on Claude Williams's left-handed offerings with a determination which sent him into seclusion before the third man was out, and Bill James, who hurls from the other side, was trotted out.

Three runs were scored off Williams and one off James. It was the latter's first appearance in the series and he led a terrible life until the sixth, when with two men on the sacks he was given the beckoning finger by Manager Gleason, and Roy Wilkinson, also a right-hander, came forth, to remain through the balance of the game. The Reds continued their onslaught and sent three runs across the rubber.

ROY IS WILD.

In the seventh the rangy hurler was somewhat wild and walked two men, but no runs were scored by the champions-to-be. In the eighth, they annexed another and let it go at that. Their position was so sure that they appeared indifferent, even bored, at he Sox rally, which had the effect, largely, of merely stretching out the contest into the longest of the series, namely 2h. 27m.

The remarkably good weather of the series was again in evidence

(Continued on Second Page.)

## HOUCK MAY USE SPITTER TODAY.

This will be "spit-ball day" in the series between Vernon and St. Paul, and Bill Essick is figuring on using Byron Houck, providing the latter's arm is right. In case Houck turns up wrong, Essick will send in Dell with his dry delivery.

Mike Kelley will use Niehaus, one of his left-handers, against the Tigers. Neihaus, on the records, is Kelley's second best bet with a season mark of twenty-three wins and thirteen defeats for a percentage of .639.

## FINISHING TOUCHES ADDED BY THE REDS.

WIN BALL GAME AND WORLD'S CHAMPIONSHIP FROM THEIR AMERICAN BRETHREN.

Play-by-play summary of the final ball game in the world's series won in a handy manner by the Cincinnati Reds:

FIRST INNING.

CINCINNATI—Rath up. Strike one. Foul, strike two. Rath opened the contest with a pop fly that Risberg got in short left. Daubert up. Strike one. Daubert singled to center. It was a line drive that Liebold made a great effort for but could not quite reach before it touched the ground. Groh up. Strike one. Groh fouled the first one off. Ball one. Foul, strike two. Groh fouled the third ball into the left-field pavilion. Groh singled to right. It was a short hit that cleared over first base and Daubert held second. Roush up. Ball one, strike one. Roush doubled past first base to the right-field pavilion fence, scoring Daubert, and putting Groh on third. Duncan up. James is warming up for Chicago. Foul, strike one. Ball one. Duncan doubled to left field, scoring Groh and Roush. It was a line drive that went over Weaver's head and Jackson fielded in the extreme left-field corner. This was enough for Williams, and "Big Bill" James went into the box for Gleason's team. Kopf up. Ball one. Ball two. Strike one. Ball three. James could not locate the plate properly and walked Kopf. Duncan retained second. Neale up. Strike one. Strike two. Neale took a terrific swipe at the second strike but missed. Ball one. Neale fanned, the third strike being called on him. Rariden up. Ball one. James almost made a wild pitch but Schalk recovered the ball before any damage could be done. Rariden lofted a Texas leaguer hit over first base, scoring Duncan and putting Kopf on third. Eller up. The crowd gave Eller a hand clap ovation when he went into the batter's box. Foul, strike one. Ball one. Rariden stole second. Ball two. Eller ended the inning by flying out to Felsch. The Reds displayed the most consecutive hitting of the series in this inning. Their wallops off Williams were all clean hits. FOUR RUNS, FIVE HITS, NO ERRORS.

CHICAGO—Liebold up. Strike one. Eller's first pitch was over the pan. Liebold started for the Sox with a clean single to left that Duncan fielded fast and prevented him from stretching it into a double. Ed Collins up. Strike one. Ball one. Ed Collins doubled to left, Duncan fumbling the hit and Ed Collins reached second while Liebold went to third. Weaver up. Ball one. Strike one.

(Continued on Second Page.)

## THEY'RE OFF AT ASCOT TODAY.

*Lovers of Horse Racing to See Sport's Renewal.*

*Big Stampede to be One of the Day's Features.*

*Movie Ladies' Derby Comprises Many Entrants.*

BY ED O'MALLEY.

All lovers of horse racing will have a chance to enjoy themselves to the top of their bent this afternoon at Ascot Park, when the first of a three days' meeting will be given. Some of the best horses that were campaigned at the recent Reno meeting will compete in the various stakes and excellent sport can be reasonably looked forward to. At least fifteen good jockies will be on hand, to accept mounts and this will insure adequate riding ability.

One of the best stables that is now at the course is that of Al Monroe, the well-known local tire man. Al has three fine thoroughbreds in Little Jake, Emelda and Snowy Morn. Joe McBride will do all his riding and Joe is regarded as one of the best pilots in the West. Jim Sharkey is doing Monroe's training and Al declares he will have a good thing to uncork before the meeting is over.

HORSES GALORE.

Over 200 bangtails are now stabled at the course and this should cause big entry lists in the various events. Among the stables ready for the three races today are those of the Millerick brothers, Bob Anderson, Charles Bustillos, George Faulkner, Wade and Buchanan, H. W. Barnes, W. Singleton, J. D. Stadler, C. H. James, Frank Rheinhart and H. W. Crawford. The best of the jockies at Reno, headed by Powers, the star rider, are here.

The largest event of its kind ever attempted, the Stampede in reality ushers in the fall and winter festival season and marks the return—if for only three days—of the sport of kings. In addition to the twelve running races, which carry rich purses, there will be a score of daily wild west contests, which will decide the all-American championship. To the winner of this coveted cowboy honor will go the beautiful trophy given by Mayor M. P. Snyder who will make the presentation in person.

CALL FOR POLICE.

Yesterday a call had to be made for police to separate two rival camps. The cowboys were going at it in a manner which threatened to determine many of the contests before the opening of the show. Some of the cowboys who will participate are Art Acord, Hoot Gibson, Bob Anderson, Yakima Cannuck, Cliff Burrell, Skeeter Bill Robinson, Arizona Brady, Cheyene Bill Adams, Shorty Valdez, Walla Walla Tony, Calgary Marsten and Long Jim Brinker.

When one event is over the second, under the direction of "Buck" Buchanan, will be put on immediately. Special chutes have been built to take care of the stock, some of which is very wild, judging from injuries to men who have attempted to handle the sagebrush horses and the longhorn steers.

PARADE TODAY.

There will be a parade downtown this morning in which all of the contestants will appear. This will include the women performers among whom are Dorothy Morell, Dolly Mullins, Hazel Paget and others. The women riders will have a special event, the "Movieland's Ladies' Derby" for the It trophy.

The big aerial thrill will be provided by Elsie de Villiers who will leap from a speeding airplane at an elevation of 3000 feet. This is the first time that this hazardous feat ever has been attempted by a woman. It was announced, last night, that the gates would be opened to the public at noon and that the show would begin promptly at 2:30 o'clock.

The following are the entries for today's races:

First race, five furlongs, "The Come Back," claiming, purse $275:

| | |
|---|---|
| Borel | 110 |
| Belmaduthy | 110 |
| Forum | 115 |
| Ki. | 115 |
| Miss Brush | 110 |
| Prospero's Son | 110 |
| Santiago White | 115 |
| Von Dillion | 115 |
| Walter Whitaker | 110 |

Second race, five furlongs, "Thomas H. Ince" cup, claiming, purse $275:

| | |
|---|---|
| Dot H. | 110 |
| Duly Fashion | 115 |
| Hugh Angleton | 110 |
| Lantern | 110 |
| McLleland | 110 |
| Master Franklin | 115 |
| Muriel's pet | 110 |
| Orien Kripp | 118 |
| Ring | 115 |

Third race, six furlongs, "The Santa Anita Stakes," purse $415:

| | |
|---|---|
| Col. Boyle | 108 |
| Dickie W. | 117 |
| Delaney | 113 |
| Fireplace | 108 |
| Hyndia | 108 |
| Judge Ellsworth | 113 |
| Marguerita W. | 113 |
| Sam Hill | 113 |
| Toy Miss | 118 |
| Wall Street | 113 |
| Yorkest | 113 |

TO OPEN WINTER BALL.

SANTA BARBARA, Oct. 9.—The Winter League baseball season will be opened here on next Sunday with a big parade, which will include the City Council, a twenty-piece band and both ball clubs. City Manager Craig will pitch the first ball and award the prize for the best name for the new ball park. The Universal Club of Los Angeles will play here. Batteries—Universal: Ford Tally, pitcher, Price, catcher; Santa Barbara: Hensling, pitcher, Lewis, catcher.

*The Base-Ballsheviki—No. 8 - - - - - - - By GALE.*

## AH, HA! ST. PAUL JARS BENGALS.

*Master Griner Uncovers Deceptive Delivery.*

*Fromme Mussed up Considerably in the Seventh.*

*Visitors Show Abundance of Speed and Pep.*

BY HARRY A. WILLIAMS.

The complacency of the Coast League was considerably jarred yesterday, when St. Paul put over a 5 to 0 win on the Vernon Tigers in the second game of the western world series.

However, without a desire to detract from the achievement of the distinguished visitors, it may be said that they made up for all the "breaks" that they didn't get on the opening day, and concerning which Mr. Mike Kelley, the camp chair manager, made some bitter complaints. Had there been a cloudburst of rubies and diamonds yesterday Mr. Kelley's athletes would have been standing right under it with a dishpan. That's how lucky they looked.

CHUCKING DUEL.

For six rounds the affair was a flinging duel between Art Fromme and big Dan Griner, with both men pitching airtight ball, although frequently in the hole. In the seventh, however, Mr. Kelley, who from his camp chair had been studiously observing the general build and speed of Fromme, changed his mode of attack and directed his players to surround Art with bunts.

And between bunts and bad hops Fromme was busier than a new cat in a strange alley. Art never did look like a world's champion on bunt since his bum knee, a[illegible]ed the habit of popping out of [illegible]ace about three years ago, and yesterday he lived up to his reputation. Kelley reserved this form of attack

(Continued on Second Page.)

## REDS BURN UP THE SOX.

BY I. E. SANBORN.

[EXCLUSIVE DISPATCH.]

CHICAGO, Oct. 9.—After half a century of rooting, Cincinnati baseball fans came into their own today, when their Reds cinched the world's championship in the eighth game of the world's greatest world's series, and it was significant that they burned up the White Sox by a score of 10 to 5, on the anniversary of the day Mrs. O'Leary's cow burned up nine-tenths of Chicago, forty-eight years ago.

In spite of their defeat, which was written in the books many eons ago, the White Sox lost no friends today, and all Chicago took off its hat to Patrick Moran and his Reds with the same feeling which the gamest fist fighter of all time crystallized into language when he said he was glad the championship remained in America.

Chicago can lose a world's championship to Cincinnati with better grace and with less bitterness than to any other city in either circuit, because Pat Moran, who won it, has a warm spot in the hearts of all Chicago fans. They were rooting every round for Kid Gleason, but if the gray-haired leader of the White Sox had to lose there was no one in baseball to whom the fans would rather lose than to the pilot of the Reds.

GET BIG LEAD.

The world's series was over five minutes after today's game started, and uncovered the guy at whom Dame Rumor has been shooting for a week. The Reds were given a lead of four runs in one-third of an inning, and raised it to five in the next round. Still the Gleasons preserved their unbeaten spirit, and before the game was over rapped Hod Eller so hard that it looked doubtful if he could finish the scrap. Lest you forget, Eller was the shine ball boy who struck out six White Sox in succession in the fifth game of the series, and held the Gleasons to three widely-scattered swats.

Today under a handicap that would have made the average team quit the White Sox hammered Eller's shiner for ten hits and if Ed Roush had not come to the rescue of his moundsman with a miraculous catch in the ninth inning we might be hurrying to catch a train for Cincinnati to play the ninth game of the series

The Reds batted one of Boss Gleason's two aces out of the American League forever with only one out in the first inning. Three runs scored before Big Bill James could be rushed to the rescue. There was some criticism of Gleason's choice because he did not use Dick Kerr, but who the h—l would he have had for the cinch game if he had wasted wee Richard on a battle that was lost almost before the big crowd found its seats.

The Reds found big Bill's slants for frequent hits but scored only three runs off him, until he gave unmistakable signs of losing contro' with nobody out in the sixth after two Reds got on. Wilkinson then was sent to James's relief merely to prepare him for next year, when Gleason expects to win a world's championship, and the youngster finished well after a poor showing in the sorry sixth.

JOE'S GREAT SWAT.

The Sox were beaten 10 to 1 up to the eighth inning and their only tally had been scored on a home run by Joe Jackson into the right-field bleachers in an attempt to beat the blow that Babe Ruth put over that spot a few weeks previous. In the eighth they whaled away at Eller's delivery so hard that they scored four runs and compelled Moran to send Jim Ring out to warm up. Then in the ninth with Eddie Murphy walking in place of Wilkinson the Gleasons would have closed some more of the gap between themselves and their conquerors if Roush had not made a sensational diving and somersault catch of a line drive by Leibold, which would have been good for at least two tallies if it had gone through.

The crowd, which nearly filled the plant, was in marked contrast to the meager attendance at Wednesday's game in Cincinnati and was a token of Chicago's appreciation of the gameness of its White Sox in coming from nowhere in the home stretch of the world's series and making themselves almost an even bet for the big pennant.

Murphy opened the ninth with a walk. Leibold whaled a liner to right center and Roush copped it by a diving catch, skidding on his right ear for a couple of yards afterward. Collins made his third hit of the day, but Weaver flied and Rath intercepted a hot one from Jackson, closing the world's series of 1919.

## HICKEY LIKES WESTERN SERIES.

Los Angeles, in the estimation of President Hickey of the American Association, has qualified as a city which will support post-season championship series.

"On what I have seen in the first two games, I stand ready on behalf of the American Association to sign an agreement at once to make these series a permanent thing," declared Mr. Hickey last night. "With this in view the association next season will play 164 games instead of 152, so that there will be only about four days' difference in the closing of the two seasons. This means there will be no long lay-off for the association champions, and they will come to the Coast on edge."

## TIGERS AND QUAKERS TO CLASH TOMORROW.

FIRST BIG GRID STRUGGLE OF YEAR TO COME OFF AT HADLEY FIELD.

What should be the most successful intercollegiate football season that the south has ever known will be officially opened tomorrow afternoon when the rival varsity elevens of Occidental and Whittier colleges meet on Hadley Field, Whittier, for their first tanbark encounter since America's entrance into the world war.

As a result of war-time conditions, every college and university in the south suffered a great depletion in the ranks of the male portion of its student body, with the result that the athletic teams representing them were of a distinctly inferior grade. In the case of Whittier College, so few men were left in school that the Quakers were unable to put a football team on the field last season. With the return of peace conditions the enrollment of men in the southern colleges is the largest that has ever been known, and Whittier, like the rest, is putting a team on the field that will fight it out for the Southern California championship.

TAKES NO CHANCES.

Coach Van Cleve of the Whittier aggregation has allowed only very meager news to reach this city as to the strength of the Quaker team, or as to the style of play which the up-country lads will use. But "Fox" Stanton is not taking any chances, and is working his Tiger proteges overtime in the attempt to have them in the best possible condition for the coming struggle. During the past week the Bengals have improved 50 per cent. in the quality of their game. Hard scrimmage and lots of it has been the order of the day on the Oxy campus, and the results are manifest in every department of the game, as played by Stanton's men.

Special interest attaches to Armond Powers, husky center for the Tigers, in the coming game; for Powers was once a student of the school against whom he will be playing, having attended Whittier in his freshman year. Powers has been playing a whale of a game all season, and can be expected to give a good account of himself on Saturday. Capt. Bruce Kirkpatrick, who until this season has always played on the line, will be seen in the backfield in the coming struggle, Stanton having switched the Tiger leader to the position of full-back.

HALF-BACK SMITH.

"Speed" Smith, the man who has been playing the most spectacular ball of any member of the Tiger team, will probably hold down one half-back position, with Fred Curtis at the other half, and "Bob" Madden, a three-year letter man, at quarter. Just who will start the game for the Bengals in the line is still very much of an uncertain quantity.

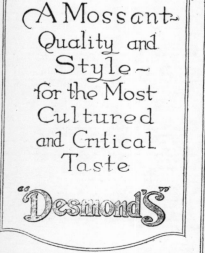

# THE TIMES PAGE of BASEBALL and LATE SPORTING NEWS

## WALTER MAILS BLANKS ANGELS.

*Eccentric Portsider Heaves Excellent Game.*

*Killefer's Pets Make Strong Rally in Ninth.*

*Brown Pitches Well, but Plays in Tough Luck.*

BY ED O'MALLEY.

A number of commodities went up yesterday including the Los Angeles baseball club, but our gentle Angels' flight was an aerial soar under the magic wand of Walter Mails, who defeated them something like 4 to 0. Walter came rightly by his laurels for he was at his best and to make matters doubly sure his team-mates played faultlessly behind him. Not a ripple of any kind bobbed up to ruffle his keenly sensitive disposition.

So effectively did he heave 'em over that in most instances the pill was poked into the air for little lazy fouls or easy flies to the outfield. His hop ball worked to a nicety and so thoroughly did he hold the Angels in his mitt that only five assists were credited to the Senators in the nine innings. Mails is purely a child of temperament. Just flutter him for a moment by a jazz remark or an error by his team-mates and he becomes confusion's masterpiece.

PLAYED PERFECTLY.

Well, to make a long story short—the Angels yesterday had no jazz to hurl at him and the Yippers seemed as if they couldn't make an error even though they tried. In the light of yesterday's work we doubt whether there was a team west of the Mississippi River that could have defeated Mails.

His one big and only scare came in the last of the ninth inning. Crawford flied to Schang and just then when everybody was trekking toward the exit, Johnny Bassler rifled a hot one to center for a single. Rube Ellis, who is usually true blue in a pinch, darted one to left for another single. Niehoff then sent a groan through the grand stand by elevating to Schang. Pete Lapan after making several vicious lunges into the air staved matters off for a moment by drawing a pass. It was now up to Chief Killefer. The bags were filled and a timely swat might still save the day. Red had two strikes called on him.

SHOT IN A GROOVE.

Then like a shot out of a cannon, Mails grooved the next one for the prettiest strike imaginable. Killefer had evidently closed his eyes and trusted to the fates, for the umpire called it a "ball" amid a storm of protest. Red finally grasped at a straw and tilted the next one over to McGaffigan in the form of a dwarf fly and the rally died a most natural death.

If Mails pitched superbly the fact must not be overlooked that Curly Brown was also there. Brown would have won nine games out of ten on his work of yesterday. He is surely getting to be the unlucky kid and had it not been for a questionable decision of Byron's in the ninth inning when it looked as if Bassler had nabbed Grover off second on his throw to McAuley, the game might have been projected into extra innings and a different result registered.

GRAB IN NINTH.

The visitors grabbed the persimmon in the first part of the ninth inning as follows: Grover shot a hot one to McAuley, who made a dandy stop, but threw high to Zeider, the ball going into the grand stand and Grover toddling to second. Mails made a perfect bunt down the third-base line and beat the throw to first. McGaffigan got Brown in a hole and shot a groover to right for a single, scoring Grover and sending Mails to second. Schang hit to Brown, who threw to Niehoff, forcing Mails at third.

Cady biffed a single to center, which Killefer allowed to get through his legs and the hit went for a double, McGaffigan and Schang scoring. Orr went out, McAuley to Zeider. Sheehan walked and pulled off a double steal with Cady, the latter tallying. Compton was an easy out, Crandall to Zeider. The score:

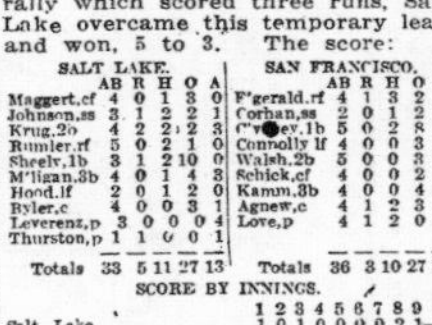

| SACRAMENTO. | AB | R | H | O | A |
|---|---|---|---|---|---|
| M'G'an,2b | 4 | 1 | 1 | 3 | 1 |
| Schang,rf | 3 | 1 | 0 | 5 | 0 |
| Cady,c | 4 | 1 | 2 | 4 | 0 |
| Orr,ss | 4 | 0 | 0 | 2 | 0 |
| Sh'han,1b | 3 | 0 | 0 | 5 | 1 |
| Comtron,cf | 4 | 0 | 0 | 1 | 1 |
| Kopp,lf | 3 | 0 | 1 | 2 | 0 |
| Grover,3b | 3 | 1 | 0 | 3 | 1 |
| Mails,p | 2 | 0 | 1 | 1 | 1 |
| Totals | 30 | 4 | 5 | 26 | 5 |

| LOS ANGELES. | AB | R | H | O | A |
|---|---|---|---|---|---|
| Killefer,cf | 4 | 0 | 1 | 1 | 0 |
| McAuley,ss | 3 | 0 | 0 | 1 | 4 |
| K.C'all,2b | 1 | 0 | 0 | 2 | 5 |
| Zeider,1b | 3 | 0 | 0 | 11 | 2 |
| C'wford,rf | 4 | 0 | 0 | 5 | 1 |
| Bassler,c | 4 | 0 | 2 | 2 | 2 |
| Ellis,lf | 4 | 0 | 2 | 1 | 0 |
| Niehoff,3b | 4 | 0 | 0 | 3 | 3 |
| Brown,p | 2 | 0 | 1 | 1 | 1 |
| Lapan,x | 0 | 0 | 0 | 0 | 0 |
| Totals | 29 | 0 | 6 | 27 | 18 |

Zeider out in eighth for interference.

x—Batted for Brown in ninth.

SCORE BY INNINGS.

| | 1 | 2 | 3 | 4 | 5 | 6 | 7 | 8 | 9 | |
|---|---|---|---|---|---|---|---|---|---|---|
| Sacramento | 0 | 0 | 0 | 0 | 0 | 0 | 0 | 0 | 4 | —4 |
| Base hits | 0 | 0 | 0 | 0 | 1 | 0 | 1 | 0 | 3 | —5 |
| Los Angeles | 0 | 0 | 0 | 0 | 0 | 0 | 0 | 0 | 0 | —0 |
| Base hits | 1 | 1 | 0 | 0 | 1 | 0 | 1 | 0 | 2 | —6 |

SUMMARY.

Errors—McAuley, 3. Two-base hit—Cady. Stolen bases—Killefer, Bassler, Cady, Sheehan. Sacrifice hits—Schang, Killefer, Zeider, K. Crandall. Struck out—By Mails, 3; by Brown, 1. Bases on balls—Off Mails, 4; off Brown, 2. Runs responsible for—Brown, 2. Double plays—Niehoff to Zeider to Niehoff; Compton to McGaffigan; K. Crandall to McAuley to Zeider; Crawford to Zeider. Time of game—1h. 40m. Umpires—Anderson and Byron.

## TILDEN SPEARS BRITISH TITLE.

*Defeats Patterson in Tennis Championships.*

*American Doubles Team Wins With Dispatch.*

*Miss Ryan of California Has Edge on Crown.*

[BY CABLE AND ASSOCIATED PRESS.]

WIMBLEDON, July 3.—William T. Tilden of Philadelphia won the British lawn tennis championship in singles on the courts here today. Tilden defeated Gerald L. Patterson of Australia, the title holder, in the challenge round, 2-6, 6-3, 6-2, 6-4.

Tilden's victory was the climax of the long series of games against the world's greatest experts through which he had come during the past week. Throughout his play has been consistent and brilliant, and today he took the measure of the Australian by a combination of brilliant plays and clever strategy. He found his opponent's weakest points and, after the first set, which Patterson won, directed his play against the Australian's weakness, capturing the next three sets and the match.

C. S. Garland of Pittsburg and N. Norris Williams II of Boston won the finals in the British tennis doubles championship today by defeating A. R. F. Kingscote and J. C. Parke, of the British cup team. The Americans took three of the four sets played. The score was 4-6, 6-4, 7-5, 6-2.

It was red-letter day for Williams. He was the directing brain and outstanding personality of the match. His opponents served up on his backhand until they found he always made brilliant returns down the center line. They then attacked his forehand, only to find that the pace of his return of ten put the ball away. Williams's play generally was brilliant.

In fast-volleyed exchanges at the net he smashed finely and frequently sent over winning services which the Englishman could not touch.

Garland did not start so well, but in the fourth set he played brilliantly. The features of his game were general all-around steadiness, forehand driving and extraordinary quickness at the net. Sometimes he thus returned balls which it appeared impossible for him to get and scored on them.

Gerald L. Patterson of Australia and Mlle. Suzanne Lenglen of France defeated Randolph Lycett of Australia and Miss Elizabeth Ryan of California in the finals of the mixed doubles in the British lawn-tennis championship tournament here today. The winners took the match in straight sets, 7-5, 6-3.

The finals in the ladies' doubles championship was won by Mlle. Lenglen and Miss Ryan of California. They beat Mrs. Lambert Chambers and Mrs. Larcombe in straight sets, 6-4, 6-0.

## MAGDALEN COLLEGE WINS CREW BATTLE.

DEFEATS LEANDER FOR EIGHT-OARED CHAMPIONSHIP—THAMES SHOWS SPEED.

[BY CABLE AND ASSOCIATED PRESS.]

HENLEY ON THAMES, July 3.—Magdalen College, Oxford, defeated the Leander eight-oared crew in the final race for the grand challenge cup here this morning. Magdalen won by two lengths, the crew making the distance in 7 minutes and 24 seconds.

The final in the diamond sculls, was won by J. Beresford, Jr., who defeated D. H. L. Gollan. Beresford took the lead by half a length at the quarter-mile and gradually extended the margin to the finish, winning by three lengths. The time was 8 minutes, 57 seconds.

The Thames challenge cup was won by the crew of the Thames Rowing Club, which defeated the eight of Caius College by a length. The time was 7 minutes, 43 seconds.

## SALT LAKE RALLIES AND WALLOPS SEALS.

[BY A. P. NIGHT WIRE.]

SAN FRANCISCO, July 3.—Despite a sixth-inning San Francisco rally which scored three runs, Salt Lake overcame this temporary lead and won, 5 to 3. The score:

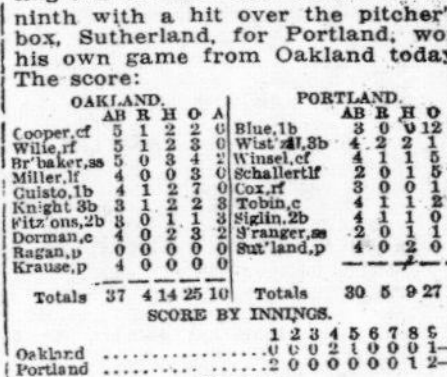

| SALT LAKE. | AB | R | H | O | A |
|---|---|---|---|---|---|
| Maggert,cf | 4 | 0 | 1 | 3 | 0 |
| Johnson,ss | 3 | 1 | 2 | 2 | 1 |
| Krug,2b | 4 | 2 | 2 | 2 | 3 |
| Rumler,rf | 5 | 0 | 2 | 1 | 0 |
| Sheely,1b | 3 | 1 | 2 | 10 | 0 |
| M'ligan,3b | 4 | 0 | 1 | 4 | 3 |
| Hood,lf | 2 | 0 | 1 | 2 | 0 |
| Byler,c | 4 | 0 | 0 | 3 | 1 |
| Leverenz,p | 3 | 0 | 0 | 0 | 4 |
| Thurston,p | 1 | 1 | 0 | 0 | 1 |
| Totals | 33 | 5 | 11 | 27 | 13 |

| SAN FRANCISCO. | AB | R | H | O | A |
|---|---|---|---|---|---|
| F'gerald,rf | 4 | 1 | 3 | 2 | 0 |
| Corhan,ss | 2 | 0 | 1 | 2 | 3 |
| C'v[illegible]ey,1b | 5 | 0 | 2 | 8 | 1 |
| Connolly,lf | 4 | 0 | 0 | 3 | 0 |
| Walsh,2b | 5 | 0 | 0 | 3 | 3 |
| Schick,cf | 4 | 0 | 0 | 2 | 0 |
| Kamm,3b | 4 | 0 | 0 | 4 | 3 |
| Agnew,c | 4 | 1 | 2 | 3 | 3 |
| Love,p | 4 | 1 | 2 | 0 | 2 |
| Totals | 36 | 3 | 10 | 27 | 15 |

SCORE BY INNINGS.

| | 1 | 2 | 3 | 4 | 5 | 6 | 7 | 8 | 9 | |
|---|---|---|---|---|---|---|---|---|---|---|
| Salt Lake | 1 | 0 | 1 | 0 | 0 | 0 | 0 | 2 | 1 | —5 |
| San Francisco | 0 | 0 | 0 | 0 | 0 | 3 | 0 | 0 | 0 | —3 |

SUMMARY.

Errors—Corhan, Walsh, 2. Two-base hits—Johnson, Agnew, 2; Sheely, Fitzgerald, Krug, Caveney. Bases on balls—Off Leverenz, 5; off Love, 5. Struck out—By Leverenz, 1; by Love 3; by Thurston, 1. Winning pitcher—Leverenz.

## LEONARD AND WHITE SET.

[BY A. P. NIGHT WIRE.]

BENTON HARBOR (Mich.) July 3.—Benny Leonard, lightweight champion of the world, and Charley White of Chicago, challenger for the title, wound up their training today for their ten-round championship battle here Monday afternoon.

White practically finished his boxing work yesterday and today did only enough work to keep his muscles loosened. The challenger is in remarkably fine condition.

Leonard, however, may pull on the gloves for the benefit of his admirers tomorrow when he will continue to do his road work to sharpen his wind. He declares he is as fast as ever after his long layoff and asserts he will defend his title in true championship form.

Officials of the State Boxing Commission made the prediction today that the receipts of the contest will likely reach $65,000.

Leonard worked hard today, boxing two rounds with Teddy Murphy and finishing with a three-round bout with Joe Benjamin, Pacific Coast lightweight. He also did considerable shadow boxing and wrestling and covered five miles on the road. He expects to box two or three rounds tomorrow and also do some road work.

Although a referee's decision is permitted in Michigan, none will be rendered Monday. White must either knock out Leonard or be the victim of a foul blow to win the title.

Benton Harbor and St. Joseph began filling up rapidly tonight with thousands of visitors. The advance sale of seats has reached $32,000. With three preliminaries, the first to start at 3 o'clock central standard time, White nad Leonard probably will not enter the ring until 5 o'clock.

## BUDDY RYAN TO JOIN SENATORS.

Buddy Ryan, who played left field a number of years for the Salt Lake baseball team and who has been playing in the Idaho League, will join Bill Rodgers's Sacramento team here today and will probably be seen in left field. Ryan was always regarded as one of the Coast League's best batters and unless he has gone back considerably, should be of big help to the Senators.

## STANDING OF THE CLUBS

PACIFIC COAST LEAGUE.

| | W. | L. | P.c. | | W. | L. | P.c. |
|---|---|---|---|---|---|---|---|
| Salt Lake | 50 | 35 | .588 | Portland | 40 | 40 | .500 |
| Vernon | 52 | 38 | .578 | Oakland | 38 | 51 | .427 |
| Los Angeles | 48 | 38 | .558 | Sacramento | 36 | 49 | .424 |
| S. Francisco | 44 | 41 | .518 | Seattle | 34 | 50 | .405 |

Yesterday's Results.

Sacramento, 4; Los Angeles, 0.
Salt Lake, 5; San Francisco, 3.
Portland, 5; Oakland, 4.
Seattle, 12-7; Vernon, 7-4.

NATIONAL LEAGUE.

| | W. | L. | P.c. | | W. | L. | P.c. |
|---|---|---|---|---|---|---|---|
| Cincinnati | 37 | 27 | .578 | Boston | 29 | 29 | .500 |
| Brooklyn | 35 | 31 | .530 | Pittsburg | 30 | 31 | .492 |
| Chicago | 35 | 33 | .515 | New York | 31 | 37 | .456 |
| St. Louis | 35 | 33 | .515 | Philadelphia | 26 | 38 | .406 |

Yesterday's Results.

Cincinnati, 5; Chicago, 3.
Pittsburg, 3; St. Louis, 1.
Philadelphia, 5; Brooklyn, 2.
New York-Boston game postponed, wet grounds.

AMERICAN LEAGUE.

| | W. | L. | P.c. | | W. | L. | P.c. |
|---|---|---|---|---|---|---|---|
| New York | 48 | 23 | .676 | Boston | 31 | 32 | .492 |
| Cleveland | 45 | 22 | .672 | St. Louis | 33 | 36 | .478 |
| Chicago | 40 | 28 | .588 | Detroit | 21 | 45 | .318 |
| Washington | 33 | 29 | .532 | Philadelphia | 17 | 52 | .246 |

Yesterday's Results.

Chicago, 11; St. Louis, 3.
Cleveland, 6; Detroit, 3.
New York, 4-5; Philadelphia, 2-0.
Boston-Washington game postponed rain.

AMERICAN ASSOCIATION.

Columbus, 3; Toledo, 4.
Milwaukee, 4; Kansas City, 2.
St. Paul 9; Minneapolis, 4.
Indianapolis, 4; Louisville, 4 (called ninth, wet grounds.)

SOUTHERN ASSOCIATION.

Little Rock, 10; New Orleans, 3.
Birmingham, 12; Nashville, 7.
Memphis, 3; Mobile, 7.
Atlanta, 4; Chattanooga, 1.

WESTERN LEAGUE.

Tulsa, 9; Oklahoma City, 5.
St. Joseph, 6; Omaha, 3.
Joplin, 0; Wichita, 1.
Des Moines, 3; Sioux City, 4.

## SEATTLE KNOCKS OUT TWO TIGER PITCHERS.

[BY A. P. NIGHT WIRE.]

SATTLE, July 3.—Seattle knocked two Vernon pitchers, Shellenback and Piercey, out of the box today and won both ends of a double-header. The scores:

First game.

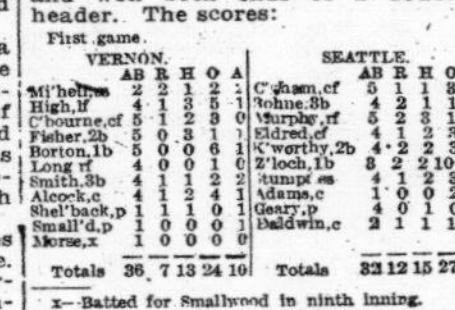

| VERNON. | AB | R | H | O | A |
|---|---|---|---|---|---|
| Mi'hell,ss | 2 | 2 | 1 | 2 | 1 |
| High,lf | 4 | 1 | 3 | 5 | 1 |
| C'bourne,cf | 5 | 1 | 2 | 3 | 0 |
| Fisher,2b | 5 | 0 | 3 | 1 | 1 |
| Borton,1b | 5 | 0 | 0 | 6 | 1 |
| Long,rf | 4 | 0 | 0 | 1 | 0 |
| Smith,3b | 4 | 1 | 1 | 2 | 2 |
| Alcock,c | 4 | 1 | 2 | 4 | 1 |
| Shel'back,p | 1 | 1 | 1 | 0 | 1 |
| Small'd,p | 1 | 0 | 0 | 0 | 1 |
| Morse,x | 1 | 0 | 0 | 0 | 0 |
| Totals | 36 | 7 | 13 | 24 | 10 |

| SEATTLE. | AB | R | H | O | A |
|---|---|---|---|---|---|
| C'gham,cf | 5 | 1 | 1 | 3 | 0 |
| Bohne,3b | 4 | 2 | 1 | 1 | 4 |
| Murphy,rf | 5 | 2 | 3 | 1 | 0 |
| Eldred,cf | 4 | 1 | 2 | 3 | 0 |
| K'worthy,2b | 4 | 2 | 2 | 3 | 3 |
| Z'loch,1b | 3 | 2 | 2 | 10 | 0 |
| Stumpf,ss | 4 | 1 | 2 | 3 | 4 |
| Adams,c | 1 | 0 | 0 | 2 | 0 |
| Geary,p | 4 | 0 | 1 | 0 | 1 |
| Baldwin,c | 2 | 1 | 1 | 1 | 0 |
| Totals | 32 | 12 | 15 | 27 | 12 |

x—Batted for Smallwood in ninth inning.

SCORE BY INNINGS.

| | 1 | 2 | 3 | 4 | 5 | 6 | 7 | 8 | 9 | |
|---|---|---|---|---|---|---|---|---|---|---|
| Vernon | 1 | 0 | 2 | 0 | 0 | 0 | 0 | 0 | 4 | — 7 |
| Seattle | 0 | 0 | 0 | 3 | 3 | 0 | 0 | 0 | 6 | —12 |

SUMMARY.

Three-base hits—Mitchell, Murphy, High. Two-base hits—Chadbourne, Fisher, Alcock, Cunningham. Bases on balls—Off Shellenback, 1; off Smallwood, 2. Innings pitched—By Shellenback, 4 1-3. Runs responsible for—Geary, 7; Shellenback, 6; Smallwood, 5. Losing pitcher—Shellenback. Errors—Smith, Mitchell.

Second game.

| VERNON. | AB | R | H | O | A |
|---|---|---|---|---|---|
| Mi'hell,ss | 4 | 2 | 3 | 6 | 3 |
| High,lf | 4 | 0 | 0 | 1 | 0 |
| C'bourne,cf | 4 | 1 | 2 | 1 | 0 |
| Fisher,2b | 4 | 1 | 1 | 3 | 3 |
| Borton,1b | 4 | 0 | 2 | 6 | 1 |
| Morse,rf | 4 | 0 | 0 | 3 | 2 |
| Smith,3b | 4 | 0 | 0 | 1 | 3 |
| D'vorm'r,c | 3 | 0 | 0 | 3 | 2 |
| Piercy,p | 2 | 0 | 0 | 0 | 1 |
| Alcock,x | 1 | 0 | 1 | 0 | 0 |
| Small'd,p | 0 | 0 | 0 | 0 | 0 |
| Totals | 34 | 4 | 9 | 24 | 15 |

| SEATTLE. | AB | R | H | O | A |
|---|---|---|---|---|---|
| Cun'ham,lf | 5 | 3 | 3 | 1 | 0 |
| Bohne,3b | 3 | 1 | 2 | 1 | 0 |
| Murphy,rf | 3 | 0 | 1 | 4 | 0 |
| Eldred,cf | 2 | 2 | 2 | 3 | 1 |
| Ken'hy,2b | 3 | 1 | 2 | 2 | 2 |
| Z'loch,1b | 4 | 0 | 1 | 10 | 0 |
| Stumpf,ss | 3 | 0 | 1 | 2 | 4 |
| Baldwin,c | 4 | 0 | 1 | 4 | 1 |
| Gardner,p | 4 | 0 | 1 | 0 | 0 |
| Totals | 31 | 7 | 15 | 27 | 8 |

x—Batted for Piercy in ninth inning.

SCORE BY INNINGS.

| | 1 | 2 | 3 | 4 | 5 | 6 | 7 | 8 | 9 | |
|---|---|---|---|---|---|---|---|---|---|---|
| Vernon | 1 | 0 | 0 | 0 | 0 | 3 | 0 | 0 | 0 | —4 |
| Seattle | 1 | 0 | 1 | 1 | 0 | 2 | 2 | 0 | x | —7 |

SUMMARY.

Errors—Morse, Smith (2,) De Vormer, Baldwin. Two-base hits—Mitchell, Cunningham (2,) Eldred, Borton, Kenworthy, Zamloch. Bases on balls—Off Piercy, 2. Struck out—By Gardiner, 4; by Piercy, 1. Innings pitched—By Piercy, 6. Runs, responsible for—Piercy, 4. Losing pitcher—Piercy.

## PITCHER SUTHERLAND WINS OWN CONTEST

[BY A. P. NIGHT WIRE.]

PORTLAND (Or.) July 3.—Putting two runners over the pan in the ninth with a hit over the pitcher's box, Sutherland, for Portland, won his own game from Oakland today. The score:

| OAKLAND. | AB | R | H | O | A |
|---|---|---|---|---|---|
| Cooper,cf | 5 | 1 | 2 | 2 | 0 |
| Wilie,rf | 5 | 1 | 2 | 3 | 0 |
| Br'baker,ss | 5 | 0 | 3 | 4 | 2 |
| Miller,lf | 4 | 0 | 0 | 3 | 0 |
| Guisto,1b | 4 | 1 | 2 | 7 | 0 |
| Knight,3b | 3 | 1 | 2 | 2 | 3 |
| Fitz'ons,2b | 3 | 0 | 1 | 1 | 3 |
| Dorman,c | 4 | 0 | 2 | 3 | 2 |
| Ragan,p | 0 | 0 | 0 | 0 | 0 |
| Krause,p | 4 | 0 | 0 | 0 | 0 |
| Totals | 37 | 4 | 14 | 25 | 10 |

| PORTLAND. | AB | R | H | O | A |
|---|---|---|---|---|---|
| Blue,1b | 3 | 0 | 0 | 12 | 0 |
| Wist'zil,3b | 4 | 2 | 2 | 1 | 1 |
| Winsel,cf | 4 | 1 | 1 | 5 | 0 |
| Schaller,lf | 2 | 0 | 1 | 5 | 0 |
| Cox,rf | 3 | 0 | 0 | 1 | 0 |
| Tobin,c | 4 | 1 | 1 | 2 | 0 |
| Siglin,2b | 4 | 1 | 1 | 0 | 4 |
| S'ranger,ss | 2 | 0 | 1 | 1 | 4 |
| Sut'land,p | 4 | 0 | 2 | 0 | 3 |
| Totals | 30 | 5 | 9 | 27 | 12 |

SCORE BY INNINGS.

| | 1 | 2 | 3 | 4 | 5 | 6 | 7 | 8 | 9 | |
|---|---|---|---|---|---|---|---|---|---|---|
| Oakland | 0 | 0 | 0 | 2 | 1 | 0 | 0 | 0 | 1 | —4 |
| Portland | 2 | 0 | 0 | 0 | 0 | 0 | 0 | 1 | 2 | —5 |

SUMMARY.

Errors—Wilie, Brubaker. Struck out—By Ragan, 1; by Krause, 1. Bases on balls—Off Ragan, 2; off Krause, 3. Two-base hits—Spranger, Guisto, Brubaker. Three-base hit—Wisterzil. Innings pitched—By Ragan 1 1-3. Losing pitcher—Krause. Runs responsible for—Ragan, 2; Sutherland, 4; Krause, 3.

## TAKES QUALIFYING HONORS.

[BY A. P. NIGHT WIRE.]

DEL MONTE, July 3.—R. D. Skelly of Riverside won the qualifying honors in the Independence Day golf tournament, which started here today. His gross was 79.

## AUTO THIEVES COP FOUR CARS.

The following automobiles were stolen from the streets of Los Angeles yesterday: Buick '17, touring, dark green, 261331; Ford '14, roadster, 240726; Ford '19, touring, 221297, and Hudson speedster, 46349. Any one seeing any of these cars will please notify the auto theft bureau of the Auto Club of Southern California, or police headquarters.

## MAJOR LEAGUE RESULTS.

### CHAMPIONS DEFEAT CUBS IN THE RAIN.

[BY A. P. NIGHT WIRE.]

CINCINNATI, July 3.—In a game that was held up by rain for half an hour at the end of the fifth inning, the champions defeated the Cubs. The Reds won off Martin in the sixth and seventh. The fielding of See in center was a leading feature. Catcher Killefer of the Cubs, who had been out of the game for a month with a broken finger, was badly cut about the face in the fifth, when a foul tip broke his mask. He was forced to retire. The score:

| CHICAGO. | AB | R | H | O | A |
|---|---|---|---|---|---|
| Flack,rf | 2 | 0 | 0 | 2 | 0 |
| Hendrix,x | 1 | 0 | 0 | 0 | 0 |
| Barber,rf | 1 | 0 | 0 | 1 | 0 |
| H'locher,ss | 4 | 1 | 1 | 3 | 3 |
| Terry,2b | 4 | 0 | 3 | 3 | 3 |
| R'ertson,lf | 4 | 0 | 0 | 2 | 0 |
| Merkle,1b | 4 | 1 | 1 | 7 | 1 |
| Paskert,cf | 3 | 1 | 1 | 2 | 0 |
| Herzog,3b | 4 | 0 | 1 | 1 | 1 |
| Killefer,c | 2 | 0 | 0 | 2 | 2 |
| Daly,c | 1 | 0 | 1 | 0 | 1 |
| Tyler,p | 1 | 0 | 0 | 1 | 2 |
| O'F'rell,xx | 1 | 0 | 0 | 0 | 0 |
| Martin,p | 0 | 0 | 0 | 0 | 1 |
| Vaughn,p | 0 | 0 | 0 | 0 | 0 |
| Totals | 32 | 3 | 8 | 24 | 14 |

| CINCINNATI. | AB | R | H | O | A |
|---|---|---|---|---|---|
| Rath,2b | 4 | 2 | 2 | 1 | 5 |
| Groh,3b | 3 | 0 | 1 | 0 | 2 |
| Roush,1b | 4 | 0 | 2 | 12 | 0 |
| Duncan,lf | 2 | 2 | 1 | 0 | 0 |
| Kopf,ss | 4 | 1 | 1 | 1 | 1 |
| Neale,rf | 2 | 0 | 0 | 3 | 0 |
| See,cf | 3 | 0 | 0 | 6 | 1 |
| Allen,c | 2 | 0 | 0 | 3 | 0 |
| Wingo,c | 1 | 0 | 0 | 1 | 0 |
| Sallee,p | 3 | 0 | 0 | 0 | 2 |
| Totals | 28 | 5 | 7 | 27 | 11 |

x—Batted for Flack in fifth.
xx—Batted for Tyler in fifth.

SCORE BY INNINGS.

| | 1 | 2 | 3 | 4 | 5 | 6 | 7 | 8 | 9 | |
|---|---|---|---|---|---|---|---|---|---|---|
| Chicago | 0 | 0 | 0 | 2 | 1 | 0 | 0 | 0 | 0 | —3 |
| Cincinnati | 0 | 0 | 1 | 2 | 0 | 1 | 1 | 0 | x | —5 |

SUMMARY.

Errors—Terry, Tyler, Allen. Two-base hits—Rath, Groh, Terry. Three-base hits—Terry, Paskert. Stolen base—Roush. Sacrifice hits—Groh, Duncan, Neale, See, Martin. Double plays—See to Rath; Rath to Kopf to Roush. Left on bases—Chicago, 4; Cincinnati, 6. Bases on balls—Off Sallee, 1; off Tyler, 1; off Martin, 2. Hits—Off Tyler, 4 in 4 innings; off Martin, 2 in 2 1-3; off Vaughn, 1 in 1 2-3. Struck out—By Sallee, 2; by Tyler, 1; by Martin, 1. Wild pitch—Tyler. Losing pitcher—Martin. Umpires—Klem and Emslie. Time of game—2h. 5m.

### COOPER TOO NIFTY FOR THE CARDINALS.

[BY A. P. NIGHT WIRE.]

ST. LOUIS, July 3.—St. Louis could do nothing with Cooper in the pinches today and Pittsburg won, 3 to 1. Caton's triple drove in the winning runs. The score:

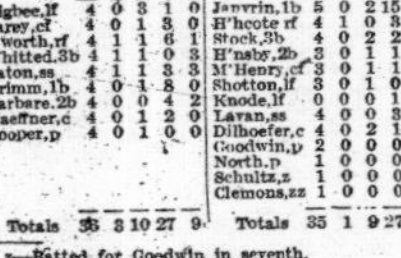

| PITTSBURG. | AB | R | H | O | A |
|---|---|---|---|---|---|
| Bigbee,lf | 4 | 0 | 3 | 1 | 0 |
| Carey,cf | 4 | 0 | 1 | 3 | 0 |
| S'worth,rf | 4 | 1 | 1 | 6 | 1 |
| Whitted,3b | 4 | 1 | 1 | 0 | 3 |
| Caton,ss | 4 | 1 | 1 | 3 | 3 |
| Grimm,1b | 4 | 0 | 1 | 8 | 0 |
| Barbare,2b | 4 | 0 | 0 | 4 | 2 |
| Haeffner,c | 4 | 0 | 1 | 2 | 0 |
| Cooper,p | 4 | 0 | 1 | 0 | 0 |
| Totals | 36 | 3 | 10 | 27 | 9 |

| ST. LOUIS. | AB | R | H | O | A |
|---|---|---|---|---|---|
| Janvrin,1b | 5 | 0 | 2 | 15 | 0 |
| H'hcote,rf | 4 | 1 | 0 | 3 | 0 |
| Stock,3b | 4 | 0 | 2 | 2 | 4 |
| H'nsby,2b | 3 | 0 | 1 | 1 | 4 |
| M'Henry,cf | 3 | 0 | 1 | 1 | 0 |
| Shotton,lf | 3 | 0 | 1 | 0 | 0 |
| Knode,lf | 0 | 0 | 0 | 1 | 0 |
| Lavan,ss | 4 | 0 | 0 | 3 | 2 |
| Dilhoefer,c | 4 | 0 | 2 | 1 | 2 |
| Goodwin,p | 2 | 0 | 0 | 0 | 1 |
| North,p | 1 | 0 | 0 | 0 | 1 |
| Schultz,z | 1 | 0 | 0 | 0 | 0 |
| Clemons,zz | 1 | 0 | 0 | 0 | 0 |
| Totals | 35 | 1 | 9 | 27 | 14 |

z—Batted for Goodwin in seventh.
zz—Batted for Shotton in eighth.

SCORE BY INNINGS.

| | 1 | 2 | 3 | 4 | 5 | 6 | 7 | 8 | 9 | |
|---|---|---|---|---|---|---|---|---|---|---|
| Pittsburg | 0 | 0 | 0 | 0 | 0 | 3 | 0 | 0 | 0 | —3 |
| St. Louis | 1 | 0 | 0 | 0 | 0 | 0 | 0 | 0 | 0 | —1 |

SUMMARY.

Error—Carey. Three-base hit—Caton. Stolen bases—Stock, McHenry. Sacrifice hit—Hornsby. Left on bases—Pittsburg, 6; St. Louis, 9. Bases on balls—Off Cooper, 1. Hits—Off Goodwin, 10 in 7 innings; off North, none in 2. Struck out—By Cooper, 1. Wild pitch—Goodwin. Losing pitcher—Goodwin. Umpires—Moran and Rigler. Time of game—1h. 50m.

### PHILLIES BUNCH HITS AND DOWN BROOKLYN.

[BY A. P. NIGHT WIRE.]

BROOKLYN, July 3.—The Phillies bunched three hits off Mamaux for two runs in the second inning and two more hits with a pass and two errors in the sixth today, stopping Brooklyn's winning streak. The clubs will play a double-header tomorrow. The score:

| PHILADELPHIA. | AB | R | H | O | A |
|---|---|---|---|---|---|
| R'lings,2b | 4 | 0 | 1 | 0 | 4 |
| W'liams,cf | 4 | 1 | 1 | 6 | 0 |
| Stengel,rf | 4 | 1 | 0 | 1 | 0 |
| Meusel,lf | 4 | 0 | 0 | 2 | 0 |
| Fletcher,ss | 3 | 2 | 2 | 5 | 3 |
| P'lette,1b | 4 | 1 | 2 | 13 | 0 |
| R.M'er,3b | 3 | 0 | 2 | 0 | 6 |
| M.Wheat,c | 3 | 0 | 0 | 0 | 0 |
| G.Smith,p | 3 | 0 | 0 | 0 | 2 |
| Totals | 32 | 5 | 8 | 27 | 15 |

| BROOKLYN. | AB | R | H | O | A |
|---|---|---|---|---|---|
| Olson,ss | 4 | 0 | 0 | 1 | 4 |
| J'nston,3b | 4 | 0 | 0 | 2 | 5 |
| Kilduff,2b | 4 | 0 | 0 | 2 | 0 |
| Z.Wheat,lf | 3 | 1 | 1 | 1 | 0 |
| Myers,cf | 4 | 1 | 1 | 5 | 1 |
| K'etchy,1b | 4 | 0 | 3 | 8 | 1 |
| Neis,rf | 2 | 0 | 0 | 0 | 1 |
| Griffith,rf | 2 | 0 | 2 | 1 | 0 |
| C.Miller,c | 4 | 0 | 0 | 7 | 0 |
| Mamaux,p | 1 | 0 | 0 | 0 | 0 |
| S.Smith,p | 0 | 0 | 0 | 0 | 0 |
| Mohart,p | 0 | 0 | 0 | 0 | 0 |
| Mitchell,x | 1 | 0 | 0 | 0 | 0 |
| Elliott,xx | 1 | 0 | 0 | 0 | 0 |
| Totals | 34 | 2 | 7 | 27 | 12 |

x—Batted for Mamaux in sixth.
xx—Batted for S. Smith in eighth.

SCORE BY INNINGS.

| | 1 | 2 | 3 | 4 | 5 | 6 | 7 | 8 | 9 | |
|---|---|---|---|---|---|---|---|---|---|---|
| Philadelphia | 0 | 2 | 0 | 0 | 0 | 3 | 0 | 0 | 0 | —5 |
| Brooklyn | 0 | 0 | 0 | 0 | 0 | 0 | 1 | 0 | 1 | —2 |

SUMMARY.

Errors—Rawlings, R. Miller, Konetchy, Neis. Two-base hits—Fletcher, 2; Paulette, 2; Z. Wheat, Griffith. Stolen base—Neis. Sacrifice hits—R. Miller, G. Smith. Left on bases—Philadelphia, 4; Brooklyn, 6. Bases on balls—Off Mamaux, 2; off G. Smith, 1. Hits—Off Mamaux, 7 in 6 innings; off S. Smith, 1 in 2; off Mohart, none in 1. Struck out—By Mamaux, 2. Losing pitcher—Mamaux. Umpires—Harrison and Hart.

DEAF BALL STARS ARRIVE.

An aggregation of deaf baseball players arrived from San Francisco yesterday for a game with the Los Angeles Silents at Exposition Park. The battle will start promptly at 10:30 this morning. The local Silents are prepared for a close and interesting game. Batteries for the Northerners, Lard and Lee; for Los Angeles, Allen and Burson.

### YANKEES GRAB SIX FROM CONNIE MACK.

[BY A. P. NIGHT WIRE.]

PHILADELPHIA, July 3.—New York made a clean sweep of the six-game series by winning both games of today's double-header from Philadelphia. Errors gave New York a commanding lead in the first inning of the first game, but the second was a battle between Naylor and Collins until the ninth, when errors by Myatt and Perkins decided it. The scores:

First game:

| NEW YORK. | AB | R | H | O | A |
|---|---|---|---|---|---|
| Gleich,lf | 4 | 1 | 1 | 2 | 0 |
| Ward,ss | 5 | 1 | 2 | 5 | 5 |
| Pipp,1b | 5 | 0 | 1 | 14 | 0 |
| Ruth,rf | 4 | 1 | 3 | 0 | 0 |
| Meusel,3b | 5 | 0 | 1 | 1 | 4 |
| Bodie,cf | 4 | 0 | 1 | 2 | 0 |
| Pratt,2b | 4 | 1 | 2 | 2 | 5 |
| Ruel,c | 2 | 1 | 2 | 1 | 0 |
| Mays,p | 2 | 0 | 0 | 0 | 5 |
| Totals | 35 | 5 | 13 | 27 | 19 |

| PHILADELPHIA. | AB | R | H | O | A |
|---|---|---|---|---|---|
| Witt,2b | 3 | 0 | 2 | 4 | 4 |
| Thomas,3b | 4 | 0 | 0 | 0 | 4 |
| Walker,lf | 4 | 0 | 0 | 1 | 0 |
| Dugan,ss | 4 | 0 | 0 | 2 | 3 |
| Strunk,cf | 3 | 0 | 3 | 1 | 0 |
| Perkins,c | 2 | 0 | 0 | 5 | 0 |
| Myatt,rf | 3 | 0 | 0 | 1 | 0 |
| Griffin,1b | 3 | 0 | 0 | 13 | 1 |
| Perry,p | 3 | 0 | 0 | 0 | 5 |
| Totals | 29 | 0 | 5 | 27 | 17 |

SCORE BY INNINGS.

| | 1 | 2 | 3 | 4 | 5 | 6 | 7 | 8 | 9 | |
|---|---|---|---|---|---|---|---|---|---|---|
| New York | 3 | 0 | 0 | 1 | 0 | 0 | 0 | 1 | 0 | —5 |
| Philadelphia | 0 | 0 | 0 | 0 | 0 | 0 | 0 | 0 | 0 | —0 |

SUMMARY.

Errors—Pipp, Bodie, Witt, Thomas. Two-base hits—Meusel, Reul, Ward, Pratt, 2. Sacrifice hits—Mays, 2; Ruel, 2. Double plays—Pipp, unassisted; Pratt to Ward to Pipp; Mays to Ward to Pipp; Dugan to Griffin; Thomas to Dugan to Griffin. Left on bases—New York, 9; Philadelphia 4. Bases on balls—Off Mays, 2; off Perry, 2. Struck out—By Mays, 1; by Perry, 2. Umpires—Friel and Dineen. Time of game—1h. 23m.

Second game:

| NEW YORK. | AB | R | H | O | A |
|---|---|---|---|---|---|
| Gleich,lf | 4 | 0 | 0 | 5 | 0 |
| Ward,ss | 4 | 0 | 0 | 0 | 2 |
| Pipp,1b | 3 | 1 | 1 | 10 | 1 |
| Ruth,rf | 3 | 0 | 1 | 2 | 0 |
| Meusel,3b | 4 | 0 | 0 | 1 | 2 |
| Bodie,cf | 4 | 1 | 1 | 3 | 0 |
| Pratt,2b | 4 | 1 | 2 | 2 | 3 |
| Hannah,c | 3 | 1 | 0 | 3 | 1 |
| Collins,p | 4 | 0 | 2 | 1 | 2 |
| Totals | 33 | 4 | 7 | 27 | 11 |

| PHILADELPHIA. | AB | R | H | O | A |
|---|---|---|---|---|---|
| Witt,2b | 4 | 0 | 0 | 5 | 1 |
| Thomas,3b | 4 | 1 | 2 | 1 | 1 |
| Walker,lf | 3 | 0 | 0 | 1 | 0 |
| Dugan,ss | 3 | 0 | 0 | 3 | 2 |
| Strunk,cf | 2 | 0 | 0 | 3 | 0 |
| Burrus,1b | 3 | 0 | 0 | 8 | 0 |
| Perkins,c | 3 | 0 | 0 | 4 | 1 |
| Myatt,rf | 3 | 0 | 0 | 2 | 0 |
| Naylor,p | 2 | 0 | 1 | 0 | 4 |
| Bigbee,x | 1 | 1 | 1 | 0 | 0 |
| Totals | 28 | 2 | 4 | 27 | 9 |

x—Batted for Naylor in ninth.

SCORE BY INNINGS.

| | 1 | 2 | 3 | 4 | 5 | 6 | 7 | 8 | 9 | |
|---|---|---|---|---|---|---|---|---|---|---|
| New York | 0 | 0 | 0 | 1 | 0 | 0 | 0 | 0 | 3 | —4 |
| Philadelphia | 0 | 0 | 0 | 0 | 0 | 0 | 1 | 0 | 1 | —2 |

SUMMARY.

Errors—Perkins, Myatt. Two-base hits—Collins, Thomas. Sacrifice hits—Walker, Dugan. Double play—Collins to Ward to Pipp. Left on bases—New York, 6; Philadelphia, 2. Bases on balls—Off Collins, 1; off Naylor, 4. Struck out—By Collins, 2; by Naylor, 3. Umpires—Dineen and Friel. Time of game—1h. 49m.

### CLEVELAND EASILY PUTS IT ON DETROIT.

[BY A. P. NIGHT WIRE.]

DETROIT, July 3.—By bunching hits in four innings Cleveland netted six runs and easily won the second game of the series from Detroit. Aside from the hitting of the visitors the game was featureless. The score:

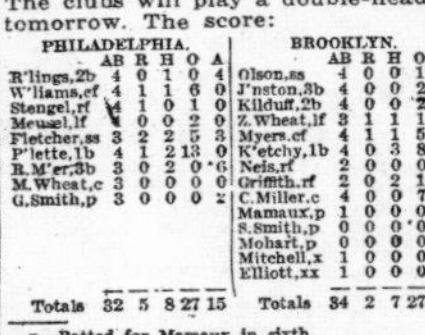

| CLEVELAND. | AB | R | H | O | A |
|---|---|---|---|---|---|
| Evans,lf | 5 | 3 | 3 | 2 | 0 |
| C'pman,ss | 2 | 1 | 1 | 2 | 6 |
| Speaker,cf | 2 | 1 | 0 | 3 | 0 |
| Wood,rf | 3 | 0 | 2 | 3 | 0 |
| G'rdner,3b | 4 | 1 | 1 | 1 | 2 |
| W'ganss,2b | 4 | 2 | 0 | 0 | 1 | 5 |
| J'nston,1b | 4 | 0 | 1 | 13 | 0 |
| O'Neill,c | 3 | 0 | 1 | 2 | 0 |
| Bagby,p | 4 | 0 | 0 | 0 | 1 |
| Totals | 29 | 6 | 9 | 27 | 14 |

| DETROIT. | AB | R | H | O | A |
|---|---|---|---|---|---|
| Young,2b | 4 | 2 | 1 | 2 | 3 |
| Bush,ss | 2 | 0 | 1 | 1 | 3 |
| Shorten,cf | 3 | 0 | 0 | 2 | 1 |
| Veach,lf | 4 | 0 | 0 | 1 | 0 |
| F'gstead,rf | 4 | 0 | 0 | 4 | 0 |
| Ellison,1b | 4 | 0 | 1 | 14 | 0 |
| Pinelli,3b | 4 | 0 | 2 | 0 | 4 |
| Stanage,c | 2 | 0 | 0 | 3 | 1 |
| Manion,c | 1 | 0 | 0 | 0 | 1 |
| Oldham,p | 3 | 1 | 1 | 0 | 2 |
| Hale,z | 1 | 0 | 0 | 0 | 0 |
| H'man,zz | 0 | 0 | 0 | 0 | 0 |
| Totals | 32 | 3 | 6 | 27 | 15 |

z—Batted for Stanage in seventh.
zz—Batted for Oldham in ninth.

SCORE BY INNINGS.

| | 1 | 2 | 3 | 4 | 5 | 6 | 7 | 8 | 9 | |
|---|---|---|---|---|---|---|---|---|---|---|
| Cleveland | 2 | 0 | 2 | 0 | 0 | 1 | 1 | 0 | 0 | —6 |
| Detroit | 1 | 0 | 2 | 0 | 0 | 0 | 0 | 0 | 0 | —3 |

SUMMARY.

Errors—Young, Stanage. Three-base hits—Chapman, Evans. Stolen bases—Chapman, Evans. Sacrifice hits—Wood, Shorten, Chapman, Wambsganss 2. Double play—Pinelli to Young to Ellison. Left on bases—Cleveland, 4; Detroit, 7. Bases on balls—Off Bagby, 4; off Oldham, 4. Struck out—By Oldham, 3; by Bagby, 1. Wild pitch—Oldham. Umpires—Nallin and Connolly. Time of game—1h. 39m.

### WHITE SOX SMEAR IT ON THE BROWNS.

[BY A. P. NIGHT WIRE.]

CHICAGO, July 3.—Chicago found Weilman and Leifield for sixteen hits, totaling twenty-four bases, and easily defeated St. Louis. The score:

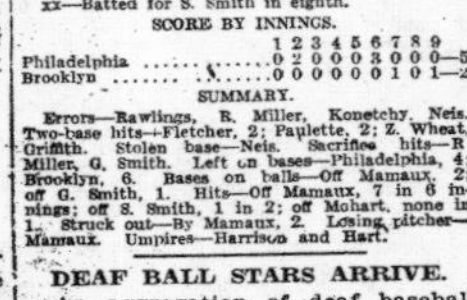

| ST. LOUIS. | AB | R | H | O | A |
|---|---|---|---|---|---|
| Tobin,rf | 4 | 0 | 2 | 2 | 0 |
| Gedeon,2b | 4 | 0 | 0 | 2 | 1 |
| Sisler,1b | 4 | 0 | 1 | 8 | 0 |
| J'ohson,cf | 4 | 1 | 1 | 1 | 0 |
| K.W'ms,lf | 3 | 2 | 2 | 2 | 0 |
| Gerber,ss | 3 | 0 | 1 | 3 | 3 |
| Billings,c | 4 | 0 | 1 | 5 | 3 |
| T'pson,3b | 4 | 0 | 1 | 1 | 1 |
| Weilman,p | 1 | 0 | 0 | 0 | 4 |
| Leifield,p | 0 | 0 | 0 | 0 | 0 |
| E.Smith,x | 1 | 0 | 0 | 0 | 0 |
| Severeid,xx | 1 | 0 | 0 | 0 | 0 |
| Totals | 33 | 3 | 9 | 24 | 12 |

| CHICAGO. | AB | R | H | O | A |
|---|---|---|---|---|---|
| Leibold,rf | 3 | 0 | 0 | 1 | 0 |
| E.C'lins,2b | 4 | 2 | 3 | 4 | 3 |
| Weaver,3b | 4 | 2 | 3 | 2 | 4 |
| Jackson,lf | 5 | 1 | 2 | 1 | 0 |
| Felsch,cf | 5 | 1 | 2 | 2 | 0 |
| J.C'lins,1b | 5 | 3 | 3 | 13 | 0 |
| Risberg,ss | 5 | 1 | 2 | 1 | 7 |
| Schalk,c | 3 | 0 | 1 | 3 | 1 |
| Faber,p | 2 | 1 | 0 | 0 | 1 |
| Totals | 36 | 11 | 16 | 27 | 13 |

x—Batted for Weilman in seventh.
xx—Batted for Leifield in ninth.

SCORE BY INNINGS.

| | 1 | 2 | 3 | 4 | 5 | 6 | 7 | 8 | 9 | |
|---|---|---|---|---|---|---|---|---|---|---|
| St. Louis | 0 | 0 | 0 | 1 | 0 | 0 | 1 | 0 | 1 | —3 |
| Chicago | 0 | 1 | 0 | 2 | 8 | 1 | 0 | 4 | x | —11 |

SUMMARY.

Error—Weilman. Two-base hits—Weaver, J. Collins, Tobin, Billings. Three-base hits—J. Collins, Jackson, 2. Stolen base—E. Collins. Sacrifice hits—Weaver, Leibold. Double plays—Faber to Weaver to J. Collins; Billings to Gerber; E. Collins to J. Collins. Left on bases—St. Louis, 6; Chicago, 8. Bases on balls—Off Weilman 4; off Faber, 3; off Leifield, 1. Innings pitched—By Weilman, 6; by Leifield, 2. Struck out—By Weilman, 4; by Faber, 2. Wild pitches—Weilman, Leifield. Losing pitcher—Weilman. Umpires—Evans and Hildebrand.

## JIUJITSU BATTLE A DRAW.

Ed ("Strangler") Lewis and Gero Mayaki, exponents of jiujitsu, the Japanese art of strangling one another to a fall, wrestled to a draw at the Los Angeles Athletic Club last night. The bout was staged in three sessions of thirty minutes each with ten-minute intermissions.

Lewis had the better of the third period, and was the aggressor for the last fifteen minutes. He secured several dangerous head locks and head scissors, and it looked bad for the Jap, but he always managed to wriggle out in time to escape disastrous punishment.

After appraising the show in a rough sort of way the bugs that packed the club gymnasium voted it a tremendous success. Not being experts in the strangle-as-strangle stuff some of the holds went over their head, but they howled themselves hoarse as first Lewis and then Miyaki squirmed out of each other's clutches.

BULL WAS THERE.

The men came into the ring promptly at 9 o'clock. The Strangler was seconded by Bull Montana, the handsome kamerad of Spike Robinson. A sawed-off son of the Mikado was in Miyaki's corner. Little Tokio rose up and screeched a welcome to Miyaki when he crawled through the ropes.

When Referee Pat Higgins called the men to the center of the ring for their instructions the great disparity in height and weight made it look like a crime to send the Jap against the towering Lewis. It was said the Jap weighed 170 pounds and Lewis 250 pounds.

But once the wild action started the ringsiders wasted no sympathy on the Jap. Mayaki scrambled out of Lewis's pet holds with the greatest impunity. Head locks, arm locks and bar locks all looked alike to the Jap. Lewis ripped the Jap's jacket to pieces in the first session and time was called for repairs.

A PET STUNT.

One of the Strangler's pet stunts was to obtain a good grip on Mayaki's jacket, hoist him in midair, whirl him around a few times and bang him on the floor with much gusto. Nothing gentle about this jiujitsu stuff.

The brown-skinned wrestler had the science of jiujitsu, but Lewis had the brute strength. The Strangler has been studying the stuff for some time, but he has a lot to learn. It was no trouble for him to get on top of the Jap, but it was another thing for him to make Miyaki cry quits, which signifies a fall in jiujitsu.

The Nipponese pulled one good trick when Lewis had a dangerous head lock on him. He inserted his fingers between the Strangler's ribs and tickled him. Lewis jumped up immediately.

The first two sessions were about even, though it appeared that Lewis had a bit the better of it at the end of the second. The Jap went to his corner breathing hard.

## VETERANS LOSE DOUBLES MATCH

*McLoughlin, Bundy Beaten by Wayne and Browne.*

*Former National Champs Display Little Class.*

*Northern Teams Sail Through Matches Easily.*

BY PAUL LOWRY.

The thirty-third annual tennis tourney for the doubles championship of the Pacific Coast will go into history as marking the passing of what was a few years ago one of America's foremost doubles team. Upon the championship court of the Los Angeles Country Club yesterday afternoon McLoughlin and Bundy, former and three-time national champions, went down to defeat at the hands of Nat Browne and Claude Wayne in a four-set match. The scores were 6-3, 3-6, 6-4, 7-5.

An indication of just how far McLoughlin and Bundy have slipped in the short period of one year may be gained by a perusal of the score between the same teams in the tourney of 1919. Then McLoughlin and Bundy won in three straight sets, 6-2, 6-2, 6-2.

Yesterday's battle was just as bitterly fought, just as keenly contested at that of 1919. But there was something lacking. Wayne and Browne played just as good a game as they are capable of, and their court tactics were impeccable. But McLoughlin and Bundy, and particularly McLoughlin were but shells of their former selves.

Simpson Sinsabaugh, grand old veteran of the game, whispered a whole mouthful at the conclusion of the match, when he said, "Slow, wasn't it?"

SLOW IT WAS.

Slow it was. Browne and Wayne knew their opponents' weakness, and they played to them. Lobs, short ones, deep ones and puzzling ones kept McLoughlin and Bundy charging hither and thither, the inevitable result being a smash into the net or a slam outside. The irony of fate. Any man who a few years ago would have called a match slow in which McLoughlin appeared would have been labeled a candidate for Norwalk.

The furious, unbridled energy of the dashing Maury was known throughout the length and breadth of the land. His hurricane service had been heralded far and wide. In the fourth set yesterday with McLoughlin and Bundy leading in games 5 to 4 Bundy beseeched his auburn haired team-mate for a few of the 1910 services. The point score of that game tells a whole story. Mac lost a love game.

TOOK THE NEXT.

Wayne took the next game on his service, making the score 6-5. With Bundy serving on the twelfth game, an out and a net by McLoughlin and the same by Bundy ended the match. Bundy, if anything, was the steadier of the two throughout the argument. The lack of a confident overhead game, due to a short period of practice, was what really lost the match for McLoughlin and Bundy.

The two northern teams—Davis and Griffin and Kinsey and Kinsey—romped through their third-round matches and are now in the semi-finals. Davis and Griffin defeated Reynolds and Reed, 6-2, 6-4, 6-4, in a match featured only by the fun which the northerners obtained by running their opponents all over the court after impossible shots.

In the lower bracket of the draw Kinsey and Kinsey overwhelmed Allen and Ferrandini, 6-0, 6-1, 6-0. The Southern Californians never had a chance with the team from the Bay City.

Snodgrass and Reinke trampled on Gene Warren and Fred Adams, 6-3, 6-4, 10-8.

NORTH VS. SOUTH.

The narrowing of the field finds two northern teams and an equal number from the south in the running. It will be north against the south this afternoon. The Kinseys take on Snodgrass and Reinke of the south at 2 p.m. Griffin and Davis tackle the other southern hopes, Wayne and Browne, Monday morning. Both northern teams are favorites, but either or both of the southern combinations may upset the dope. An exhibition mixed doubles match will be played at 3 p.m. today between May Sutton Bundy and Tom Bundy on one side of the net and Mary Browne and Willis Davis on the other side.

The summaries:

SECOND ROUND.

Reynolds and Reed defeated Marsh and Morgan, 12-10, 6-0, 7-5; Allen and Ferrandini defeated Hopkins and Darhanian, 6-3, 4-6, 7-5, 7-5; Warren and Adams defeated Davies and Johns, 6-3, 6-8, 7-5, 1-6, 7-5.

THIRD ROUND.

Davis and Griffin defeated Reynolds and Reed, 6-2, 6-2, 6-4; Wayne and Browne defeated McLoughlin and Bundy, 6-3, 3-6, 6-4 7-5; Kinsey and Kinsey defeated Allen and Ferrandini, 6-0, 6-1, 6-0; Snodgrass and Reinke defeated Warren and Adams, 6-3, 6-4, 10-8.

GOODYEAR BASEBALL.

The Goodyear Regulars will play the Ventura nine this afternoon at Ventura. The Goodyears under Manager R. G. Norris have lost only four games out of eighteen played since the team was organized.

## BANKS OF YALE BEATS 'EM ALL.

*Takes Intercollegiate Tennis Crown at Haverford.*

*Plays Consistently Throughout the Tournament.*

*Robinson, Harvard, Slaughtered at the Net.*

[EXCLUSIVE DISPATCH.]

PHILADELPHIA, July 3.—L. Maxwell Banks of Yale won the intercollegiate tennis championship this afternoon, defeating Dwight Parker Robinson, Jr., Harvard, in the finals, 6-3, 6-3, 6-4. The match was played before a big gathering of tennis fans on Court No. 1 of the Mercer Cricket Club, Haverford.

EXCELLENT FORM.

Banks, who is the New England champion, played in excellent form, at no time allowing his oppenent to get a commanding lead. Throughout the tournament Banks has displayed a remarkable ability for diagnosing his opponents' game and then proceeding to play the shots that he judges will put his antagonist at his worst. So it was today. Banks, on many occasions, put the ball just over the net, forcing Robinson to go to the barrier, and then would pass him. Often Robinson went to the net of his own accord and on those occasions his trips were just as disastrous as though he had been drawn there by Banks's clever short shots. At no time during the first set, when Robinson was at the net, did he make a point consistently. Banks drove the ball with disconcerting accuracy down the side lines, many of these passing Robinson, far out of his reach and as he was outgenerald into taking a place position.

Robinson's service takes were more severe than Banks's but the little Yale man handled his opponent's delivery without apparent effort, driving it into either corner with equal facility whether he had to take it on the back or the forehand.

A REAL FEATURE.

Banks's play throughout the tournament has been one of the features. He has displayed nothing except a back court game. This is due to the fact that he is very short and has little reach, which almost excludes him from the net before he thinks of it. But Banks well deserved to win the title, for his game was by far the most consistent of any of the players, who competed for the title of 1920. The point score of today's match follows:

First set:

| | | | | | | | | | | |
|---|---|---|---|---|---|---|---|---|---|---|
| Banks | 7 | 5 | 4 | 4 | 2 | 4 | 9 | 4 | 4 | —47—6 |
| Robinson | 9 | 3 | 6 | 2 | 4 | 0 | 7 | 2 | 1 | —35—3 |

Second set:

| | | | | | | | | | | |
|---|---|---|---|---|---|---|---|---|---|---|
| Banks | 4 | 5 | 4 | 3 | 4 | 4 | 7 | 4 | 4 | —37—6 |
| Robinson | 0 | 7 | 1 | 5 | 2 | 2 | 7 | 2 | 0 | —26—3 |

Third set:

| | | | | | | | | | | | |
|---|---|---|---|---|---|---|---|---|---|---|---|
| Banks | 1 | 4 | 5 | 2 | 3 | 4 | 8 | 4 | 1 | 4 | —36—6 |
| Robinson | 4 | 0 | 3 | 4 | 5 | 1 | 6 | 2 | 4 | 2 | —31—4 |

Banks—120 points, 18 games.
Robinson—92 points, 10 games.

## SPEED DEMONS TO RACE AT TACOMA.

ELEVEN OF THE WORLD'S BEST DRIVERS TO CONTEND FOR RICH PRIZES.

The eyes of the automobile racing world will be on the Pacific Coast tomorrow, when the famous racing drivers who took part in the recent Indianapolis and Uniontown (Pa.) speedway classics will renew their unending battle for supremacy on the big oval at Tacoma's ninth annual motor sweepstakes.

This year one race of 115 laps, or approximately 223 miles, will be run, instead of three shorter events as last July 4, when races of 40, 60 and 80 miles were held. Louis Chevrolet made the highest score at last year's meet, his victory in the 60 and 80-mile events giving him the lion's share of the points and the $7300 prize money. Eddie Hearne, Cliff Durant, Ralph Mulford and Dario Resta, the only other contenders, shared in this sum in the order named.

This year eleven riders will contend for seven prizes aggregating $22,500, this year's first prize of $10,000 greatly overtopping the entire purse offered a year ago.

The rest of the prize money will be divided as follows: Second, $5000; third, $2500; fourth, $1700; fifth, $1200; sixth, $1100; seventh, $1000.

Three Duesenbergs are entered, with Jimmy Murphy, Tommy Milton and Eddie O'Donnell at the wheel. Gaston Chevrolet, who just a year ago set up a new 100-mile record on the Sheepshead Bay speedway, his time of 54m. 17.8s. being three seconds better than the best previous mark, will drive a Monroe, as will Roscoe Sarles, last year's Ascot victor.

The two Joes, Boyer and Thomas, will pilot Frontenacs at Tacoma, the remaining entries being Eddie Hearne in the Revere, Cliff Durant in his Chevrolet, Ralph Mulford in the Mulford Special and Ralph De Palma in the Ballot.

## HORNSBY HITS CENTURY MARK.

*First Ball Player in National League to Do It.*

*Babe Ruth Continues to Hit in Very Fair Form.*

*George Sisler Remains Up in the Four Hundred.*

[BY A. P. NIGHT WIRE.]

CHICAGO, July 3.—Roger Hornsby, the St. Louis star, banged out his one hundredth hit of the season in Wednesday's game against Cincinnati, the first player in the National League to touch the century mark. Hornsby slipped slightly in his batting, but continued to hold a comfortable lead among the regulars who have participated in thirty-five or more games, according to averages released and which include games of Wednesday. The St. Louis crack is topping the hitters with an average of .380.

Cy Williams, Philadelphia outfielder, slammed out another homer, which gave him eight, and Robertson, Chicago, who was sharing honors with Hornsby last week as runner-up, also belted a circuit drive, breaking the tie with the St. Louisan, and placing himself one behind Williams.

"Babe" Ruth, the home-run king of the New York club, bagged a brace of homers in the doubleheader with Philadelphia Wednesday, which gave him a total of twenty-four, only five behind the world's record, which he made last year. Ruth is steadily climbing to the top among the batters of the American League who have participated in thirty-five games or more. He is hitting .374, just twenty points behind Tris Speaker of Cleveland and Joe Jackson of Chicago, who are sharing the honor of runners-up to George Sisler, the St. Louis star, who is batting .413. Speaker and Jackson are hitting .394.

## SPEED DEMON BADLY HURT IN AUTO RACE.

[EXCLUSIVE DISPATCH.]

EL CENTRO, July 3.—Jim Mealey, driving a Dodge car, in a fifty-lap race on the local half-mile track for the championship of Imperial Valley, today turned turtle in the thirtieth lap, rolled over an embankment and suffered injuries which may cause his death. Both legs were broken and it is feared he is internally injured.

At the time of the accident Mealey was leading the field by a lap and a half and appeared to be a certain winner as he had not yet been forced to stop. Several cars were closely bunched and some said that it looked as if Mealey had been edged off the big bowl, but there was no direct evidence to prove this. Fred Hacket, driving an Overland, won the race in slow time.

## L.A.A.C. WRESTLERS WIN AT PORTLAND.

Calvin Patten and Allan Ferguson of the Los Angeles Athletic Club both won their matches in the Pacific Coast Olympic wrestling tryouts at Portland, according to a wire received last night by Walter Miller.

Patten won in the 135-pound class and Ferguson in the 145-pound class. They return here Monday, and go on to Boston for the final tryouts this month.

## SMASHES WORLD'S SWIMMING MARK.

[BY A. P. NIGHT WIRE.]

NEW YORK, July 3.—The World's outdoor swimming record for women for 500 yards, with four turns, was broken here today by Miss Ethelda Bleibtrey of Brooklyn, a probable contestant in the Olympic games. Miss Bleibtrey also broke the American outdoor record for women for 300 yards. Her time for the 500-yard race was 7 minutes, 22 2-5 seconds, and for the 300-yard race, 4 minutes, 18 2-5 seconds.

The former world's record for women for 500 yards with four turns was made by Clair Galligan of New Rochelle, N. Y., in Los Angeles, in 1918.

## CLAY COURT TENNIS TILT.

[BY A. P. NIGHT WIRE.]

CHICAGO, July 3.—With entries closing Thursday to the tenth annual national clay court tennis championship to begin here next Saturday, the caliber of stars already entered indicated an exceptionally well matched field for both men's singles and doubles, which are the two championships to be decided. Prominent among the entries so far are: W. E. Davis and Roland Roberts of San Francisco; Vincent Richards of New York; Walter Hayes and Ralph Burdick of Chicago; Joe Armstrong of Minneapolis and Fred Josties and Theodore Drewes of St. Louis.

Last year William M. Johnston of San Francisco won the singles clay court honors. He is at present in England.

## JOHNSON FIGHT PROHIBITED

[BY A. P. NIGHT WIRE.]

SAN DIEGO, July 5.—Gov. Estaban Cantu of Lower California, in a telegram received today at Tia Juana from Mexicali, prohibits the scheduled twenty-round fight of Monday between Jack Johnson, formerly heavyweight champion, and Al Norton, a Pacific Coast heavyweight.

A petition from Tia Juana merchants protesting against the contest was sent to Gov. Cantu a few days ago and is said to have resulted in his prohibiting the match. In the petition the merchants set forth that such a contest would give Tia Juana undesirable notoriety. The telegram received from the Governor by a committee of Tia Juana merchants reads:

"Regarding the petition for not permitting the boxing match of the negro, Johnson, will say that this government, in view of your argument, will not permit such match."

# ARIZONA G.O.P. GIVES PLATFORM

*Council Indorses Republican National Ticket.*

*Commends Gov. Campbell and His Administration.*

*Labor Plank Asks Square Deal for All Workers.*

[EXCLUSIVE DISPATCH.]

PHOENIX, Sept. 28.—All day the party councils have been working on platforms and party organization, in accordance with the terms of the primary laws. There was unusual secrecy concerning the platforms, both sides fearing that thunder might be stolen by the opposition.

The Republicans released their platform this evening.

DISTINGUISHED LIST.

The Bourbons' subcommittee on platform has an especially distinguished list, including Chairman Joseph Morgan, head of the State organization of the Knights of Columbus; Senator Marcus A. Smith, Secretary of State Mit Simms, their candidate for Governor; Atty.-Gen. Wiley A. Jones and L. D. Clark, editor of the Tucson Star.

INDORSE CAMPBELL.

The Republicans indorse the national ticket and platform, hailing the approach of restoration of constitutional government and the end of autocratic rule. There is strong indorsement of Gov. Campbell and his administration, especially commending the Governor for his stand against the policy of the State Land Department in leasing and disposing of the vast land heritage of Arizona for a song and calling for a clean-up of the land department and an ending of the policy of tieing up these lands in the hands of a chosen few.

Indorsement is also given Ralph H. Cameron and James R. Dunseath for Congress.

There is a call for return to the sound reclamation policy, inaugurated under the administration of President Roosevelt, with recommendation that Congress appropriate for completion of the work or reclamation of arid lands, with preference rights secured to service men and women.

FAITH IN HIGHWAYS.

Faith is declared in the continued construction of highways in Arizona with special reference to roads for national reservations.

Indorsement is given the civil service bill, now before the voters, giving preference to soldiers and sailors, as something that will prevent creation in the future of political machines.

LABOR PLANK.

The labor plank states: "We believe in the application of the square deal to all citizens and to all classes of citizens, and to that end advocate the adoption of all measures tending to bring labor and capital into closer relationship and harmony. We believe in the just rights of labor.

"We believe that the wage-earner is entitled to a commensurate wage, reasonable hours of service, healthful working conditions and a share in determining the conditions under which his personal co-operation shall be given in all productive enterprises."

**Fever Takes Consular Clerk.**

[BY A. P. NIGHT WIRE.]

VERA CRUZ, Sept. 28.—Dr. Albert Hedrick, a clerk in the United States Consular Service, died last night from yellow fever.

## MAHARG'S STORY OF FIXED GAMES.

[BY A. P. NIGHT WIRE.]

PHILADELPHIA, Sept. 28.—The first, second and final games of last year's world's series were "thrown" to Cincinnati by eight members of the Chicago Americans, according to revelations said to have been made by Billy Maharg, former boxer and well known in local sporting circles.

Maharg's story, as printed today in the Philadelphia North American, says that he and Bill Burns, former American League pitcher, were the first to be approached in the conspiracy.

"I received a wire from Burns from New York the middle of last September, inviting me to take a hunting trip with him down on his ranch in New Mexico," said Maharg. "We were to take Bill James, one of the White Sox pitchers, with us. James had nothing to do with the subsequent events, but, while we were there in a room talking, Cicotte came in and started to talk in a low voice to Burns.

"I heard enough to know that he said that a group of prominent players of the White Sox would be willing to 'throw' the coming world's series if a syndicate of gamblers would give them $100,000 on the morning of the first game.

SAW GAMBLERS.

"When Cicotte left, Burns turned to me and repeated Cicotte's conversation, part of which I had heard. Burns said: 'Do you know any gamblers who would be interested in this proposition?' I said I would go to Philadelphia and see what I could do. Burns said he would have to go to Montreal to close an oil deal and that he would wire me about the progress of the deal.

"I then went to Philadelphia and saw some gamblers. They told me it was too big a proposition for them to handle, and they recommended me to Arnold Rothstein, a well-known and wealthy New York gambler.

"In the meantime Burns and I had returned to New York and I went over again and joined him. We met Rothstein by appointment and put the proposition up to him. He declined to get into it. He said he did not think that such a frame-up could be possible.

"We left Rothstein and hung around New York for awhile. I returned to Philadelphia, thinking that everything was off until I received the following telegram from Bill Burns:

" 'Arnold R. has gone through with everything. Got eight in. Leaving for Cincinnati at 4:30.' I went the next day and joined Burns. He said that after I had left New York he ran into Abe Attell, the fighter, who had gone to Rothstein and fixed things up. Burns said he had seen Cicotte and that eight members of the team were in the deal.

"Attell was in Cincinnati and had a gang of about twenty-five New York gamblers with him. He said they were working for Rothstein.

ATTELL REFUSED TO PAY.

"I had my first suspicion on the morning of the first game, when Burns and I visited Attell. We asked for the $100,000 to turn over to the White Sox players to carry out our part of the deal.

"Attell refused to turn over the $100,000, saying that they needed the money to make bets. He made a counter-proposal that $20,000 would be handed the players at the end of each losing game. Burns went to the Sox players and they seemed satisfied with the new arrangement.

"Burns told me that he saw the players were restless and wanted the full amount, and he was afraid they would not keep up the agreement.

"The players, however, told Burns that, if they lost behind Cicotte and Williams, they wouldn't win for Kerr. So we went to Chicago and bet all of our personal winnings of the first two days on Cincinnati to win the third game. As a matter of fact, the Sox got even with us by winning this game.

"Burns and I lost every cent we had in our clothes. The upshot was that Attell and his gang cleaned up a fortune and the Sox players were double-crossed out of $90,000 that was coming to them."

## ABE ATTELL DENIES PART IN SCANDAL.

[BY A. P. NIGHT WIRE.]

NEW YORK, Sept. 28.—Abe Attell, former featherweight pugilist, who has been named as a ringleader in the baseball gambling scandal, said here tonight that he had retained a lawyer to take care of his interests, and that in a day or two he would make a statement that would "shoot the lid sky-high."

"You can say," he said, "that the story placing the responsibility upon me for passing the $100,000 to the White Sox is a lie. It looks to me that Arnold Rothstein is behind the stories. I am surprised at this because I have been a good friend of Rothstein.

"He is simply trying to pass the buck to me. It won't go.

"You can see that some one is trying to make it appear that I was responsible for the deal at the Astor. Well, I can tell you that I was not responsible for it. Maharg's story of the fake telegrams and all the rest, as far as I am concerned, is all bunk."

## JAP "SMOKE SCREEN" ALLEGED BY BARROWS.

POSSESSION OF CALIFORNIA LANDS BY ORIENTALS MEANS END, HE SAYS.

[BY A. P. NIGHT WIRE.]

BERKELEY, Sept. 28.—Possession of land in California by Japanese means the doom of the United States, President David P. Barrows of the University of California said in a statement today setting forth his stand on the Japanese question. Japan is raising a "smoke screen" in California to divert attention from what he termed "a bold move" in Asia. His statement follows, in part:

"California is intensely interested in keeping the American citizen on the land. No nation can hold together unless it controls the soil. Therefore, we cannot allow our agricultural lands to pass into the hands of aliens. We are trying to hold a large frontier in California, much larger than people in other sections of the country realize, unless they have visited the Pacific Coast.

"Under the 'smoke screen' which Japan is raising in pretense of domestic agitation in California, she is undoubtedly planning a bold move in either Siberia, Manchuria or Mongolia. She is trespassing upon the sacred rights of China, to all of which we are indifferent.

"We Californians are accused in the East of being sensationalists. We have little sympathy from others, except those who have been here and understand how fast California is falling into the hands of the Japanese. However, California sees the menace and is united to oppose it.

"In this connection the University of California is trying to do its part in making life on the farm not only tolerable, but inviting. We believe we can do this if we are attentive in instructing our students toward its merits. The University of California acts as an agent for the rest of the State in an attempt to raise its own standards to that of a great protectorate for its own labor."

# WHITE SOX CONFESS FAKE.

*Greatest Scandal in Baseball History Shakes American League.*

(Continued from First Page.)

the others would be sent them at once. With his voice trembling, Mr. Comiskey, who has owned the White Sox since the inception of the American League, said this was the first time scandal had ever touched his "family" and that it distressed him too much to talk about it.

RUSH OF PLAYERS.

The rush of players to bare their part in the affair started today when Cicotte appeared and asked permission to testify. Cicotte wept, court attaches said, and exclaimed in anguish his sorrow for his two small children as he told how he did his utmost to lose rather than win the 1919 world series, after he had "found" $10,000 beneath his bedroom pillow where it had been placed by professional gamblers.

He said he lobbed the ball to the plate so slowly "you could read the trademark on it," in the first game at Cincinnati, when he was taken out of the box after three and two-thirds innings had been played.

THE CONFESSION.

A court official who was present when Cicotte went on the stand described the scene when the star pitcher broke down and cried as he told the jury of his part in the series "fixing."

"My God, think of my children," he cried. Cicotte has two small children.

"I've lived a thousand years in the last year," the court official quoted him as saying.

"I never did anything I regretted so much in my life," the witness added, according to the State official. "I would give anything in the world if I could undo my acts in the last world series. I've played a crooked game and I have lost, and I am here to tell the whole truth."

The story Cicotte is said to have told the jury follows in every essential particular that told in Philadelphia by Maharg last night.

CICOTTE'S STORY.

"In the first game at Cincinnati I was knocked out of the box," Cicotte told the jury, according to the court official. "I wasn't putting a thing on the ball. You could have read the trade-mark on it when I lobbed the ball up to the plate.

"In the fourth game, played at Chicago, which I also lost, I deliberately intercepted a throw from the outfield to the plate which might have cut off a run. I muffed the ball on one occasion. At another time in the same game I purposely made a wild throw. All the runs scored against me were due to my own deliberate errors. I did not try to win."

Jackson said that throughout the series he either struck out or else hit easy balls when hits would have meant runs.

When Jackson finished his testimony before the grand jury he was taken into custody by a deputy sheriff. A court official said that Jackson testified that he received his money in a Cincinnati hotel and that Risberg and McMullin were the principal "pay-off" men.

JACKSON'S STORY.

Jackson stated that he received his money from Claude Williams.

According to the court official, Jackson testified that, while each player implicated was approached individually, each knew about the others. He said that Cicotte also had testified to this effect.

Jackson also testified that Gandil, Risberg and McMullin were the only clique that existed and that Gandil was the leader of this.

He said that the players thought Gandil had double-crossed them, but afterwards found out it was Abe Attell, who had failed to pay the money he promised.

Last year's world's series records show that in the first inning of the first game he started by hitting Rath, first Cincinnati batter. Daubert followed with a single over second base that sent Rath to third, and he scored when Groh flied to Jackson, Rath beating Jackson's throw to the plate.

CHICAGO TIES.

Chicago tied in the next inning, Kopf putting Jackson on second with a wild throw. Felsch sacrificed him to third and Gandil hit safely in center, scoring Jackson.

The end of Cicotte's pitching and the runs that ultimately won the game were scored by Cincinnati in the fourth inning. All the damage was done with two out. With Kopf on first, Neale and Wingo singled; Reuther, the hard-hitting Cincinnati pitcher, drove a three-base hit to the center-field bleachers. Rath doubled and Daubert singled, the combination resulting in five runs. Wilkinson took Cicotte's place after Daubert's single and Groh flied to Felsch. The final score was 9 to 1.

## GAME AT CHICAGO DELIBERATELY THROWN.

The fourth game played at Chicago was also deliberately thrown away, according to the court officials, who heard Cicotte's statement to the grand jury. The Reds won, 2 to 0, Ring, pitching for Cincinnati, holding the American League champions to three hits. Both Cincinnati runs were made in the fifth inning when two of Cincinnati's hits were bunched with a wild throw to first by Cicotte and a bad throw to the plate by Jackson, which the pitcher intercepted and muffed. The play of this inning was sent over the Associated Press wires as follows:

"Roush was out, Schalk to Gandil, the ball rolling half way to the pitcher's box. Duncan was safe when Cicotte threw his drive wide to first, the ball going to the stand and Duncan reaching second. Kopf singled to left and Duncan stopped at third, but scored when Jackson threw wild to the plate. Kopf reached second.

"The official scorer gives Cicotte the error for muffing Jackson's throw. Neale sent one over Jackson's head and Kopf scored. Neale reached second. It was a two-base hit. Wingo out, Ed Collins to Gandil, Neale going to third. Ring drove a vicious grounder that Ed Collins got and threw him out at first. Two runs, two hits, two errors."

The rest of the game was played sharply and so far as the records show, cleanly. Cicotte pitched the nine innigs.

## CICOTTE A WINNER IN THE SIXTH GAME.

Cicotte's next appearance in the series was in the sixth game when Cincinnati had four victories against one defeat, Richard Kerr, the diminutive left-handed pitcher having shut out the champions in the third game. The veteran twirler, who today confessed the big gambling deal, went through nine innings and held his opponents to seven hits. Chicago won, 4 to 1, hitting Sallee hard in the first five innings. Jackson and Felsch each got two hits and drove in all of Chicago's runs.

Billy Maharg, Philadelphia prizefighter, who last night in Philadelphia, issued a statement connecting Cicotte with the gambling deal and charging that Abe Attell, former fighter, headed the gambling clique, asserted that the Sox were double-crossed by Attell and never received $100,000 which had been promised them. It was late in the series before they found this out, Maharg asserted, as Attell kept postponing the day of settlement, saying he needed the money to bet.

## WILLIAMS DEFEATED IN FINAL CONFLICT.

Besides the two defeats registered against Cicotte in the series, three others were chalked up against Claude Williams. The latter, a "side arm" left-hander, was wild in the second and fifth games, which went to the Reds, 4 to 2 and 5 to 0. In the eighth and last game of the series he was found for four solid hits in the first inning and that game and the title of world's champions went to Cincinnati, 10 to 5. Williams's lack of control was generally recorded as the cause of his defeats, the record of the second contest saying:

"While Cincinnati obtained only four hits, these came at opportune times when they had been preceded by bases on balls off Williams."

The fifth game was a shutout triumph for Hod Eller, the big "shine ball" expert of Cincinnati's pitching staff. Only three hits were made off him and he established a world series record by striking out the side in two successive innings.

Four of Cincinnati's five runs were grouped in the sixth inning. Eller doubled, Rath scored him with a single and moved to second on Daubert's "bunt, perfectly laid," as the report of the game said. Williams walked Groh. Roush drove a three-base hit to Felsch's territory, scoring two runners, and tallied himself after Duncan flied to Jackson.

Both Cicotte and Jackson were closeted with the grand jury for a considerable time today. Court officials reported that they told their stories in substantial detail. As they left the room they were taken in custody by detectives and taken away. Their detention was not in the nature of an arrest and it was announced that they would be released later.

Cicotte, who earlier in the day had vehemently denied any part in the alleged plot as described by Maharg at Philadelphia, admitted on the stand, officials of the court said, that the Philadelphian's story was substantially correct.

## GANDIL IS ACCUSED BY OTHER PLAYERS.

The court officials also quoted Cicotte as saying that the players had believed that "Chick" Gandil, who, he said, was interested in the dealings with the gamblers, had "doubled-crossed" them and that Maharg's story was the first intimation they had that Attell had "held out" on the $100,000 which had been promised them.

The eight players named in the true bills had been with the White Sox for periods ranging from four to nine years. Cicotte was purchased from Boston in 1912 for the waiver price. Joe Jackson was bought from Cleveland in 1915 for a large sum in cash and some players. Felsch was purchased from Milwaukee of the American Association in 1914; McMullin from Los Angeles in 1916; Risberg from Vernon of the Pacific Coast League in 1916; Williams from Salt Lake City in 1916, and Weaver from York, Pa., in 1911. The purchase price of the eight, paid by Comiskey, represents a tidy fortune.

The investigation by the grand jury will continue until all phases of baseball gambling have been bared, it was said by officials. The investigation started two weeks ago following reports that a game played here August 31 by the Cubs and Philadelphia Nationals was "fixed" and the inquiry into last year's world series came up only as an incident to the other inquiry.

## SEVERAL COUNTS ARE PROBABLE IN RETURN.

Assistant State's Attorney Hartley Replogle, in charge of the case, said tonight that indictments to be drawn up tomorrow on today's true bills may contain several counts. The true bills specified but one alleged offense, "conspiracy to commit an illegal act." The penalty upon conviction is one to five years in the penitentiary and a fine of not more than $10,000.

"This is just the beginning," Mr. Replogle said. "We will have more indictments within a few days and before we get through we will have purged organized baseball of everything crooked and dishonest.

"We are going after the gamblers now. There will be indictments within a few days against men in Philadelphia, Indianapolis, St. Louis, Des Moines, Pittsburg, Cincinnati and other cities. More baseball players also will be indicted. We've got the goods on these men and we are going the limit."

Harry Grabiner, secretary of the White Sox, announced that the club would play out the schedule to the end though it had to "employ Chinamen" to fill the vacancies in the team.

## COMISKEY MAKES PUBLIC STATEMENT.

Mr. Comiskey tonight made this statement to the Associated Press:

"The consideration which the grand jury gave to this case should be greatly appreciated by the general public. Charles A. McDonald, chief justice and the foreman of the grand jury, Harry Brigham and his associates, who so diligently strived to save and make America's great game the clean sport which it is, are to be commended in no uncertain terms by all sport followers, in spite of what happened today. And, thank God, it did happen. Forty-four years of baseball endeavor have convinced me more than ever that it is a wonderful game and a game worth keeping clean.

"I would rather close my ball park than send nine men on the field with one of the men holding a dishonest thought toward clean baseball—the game which John McGraw and I went around the world with to show the people on the other side.

"We are far from through yet. We have the nucleus of another championship team with the remainder of the old world's championship team."

He named the veterans, Eddie and John Collins, Ray Schalk, Urban Faber, Dick Kerr, Eddie Murphy, "Nemo" Leibold and Amos Strunk, and declared that with addition of Hodge, Falk, Jourdan and McClellan "I guess we can go along and win the championship yet."

## OWNER OF YANKEES WOULD DONATE CLUB.

[BY A. P. NIGHT WIRE.]

NEW YORK, Sept. 28.—A telegram offering to place the entire New York American baseball team at the disposal of Charles A. Comiskey, who today suspended seven of his players indicted in connection with alleged fixing of games, was sent tonight to the White Sox club owner by Jacob Ruppert and T. L. Huston, owners of the Yankee club.

The message follows:

"Your action in suspending players under suspicion, although it wrecks your entire organization and perhaps your cherished life work, not only challenges our admiration but excites our sympathy and demands our practical assistance. You are making a terrible sacrifice to preserve the integrity of the game. So grave and unforeseen an emergency requires unusual remedies.

"Therefore, in order that you may play out your schedule, and if necessary, the world series, our entire club is placed at your disposal. We are confident that Cleveland sportsmanship will not permit you to lose by default and will welcome the arrangement. We are equally certain that any technicalities in carrying it out can be readily overcome by action of the National Commission."

## OFFER IMPOSSIBLE; COMISKEY PLEASED.

[BY A. P. NIGHT WIRE.]

CHICAGO, Sept. 28.—When told of the offer of the New York Americans to Comiskey to turn their club over to the Chicago White Sox, Harry Grabiner, secretary of the Sox, said:

"Of course, it is impossible, but the offer will bring tears to the old man's eyes."

"It's a splendid offer and one I appreciate from the bottom of my heart, but I'm afraid there is no way I can accept it," said Charles A. Comiskey when informed that Jacob Ruppert and T. L. Huston, owners of the New York Yankees, had offered to place their entire team at the disposal of the Chicago team to replace the men he suspended.

"The league rules definitely say that no trades or transfers can be made after August 31," he explained, "so I know that such an act would not be sanctioned by the league, but it was a wonderful thing for them to do."

President Ban Johnson of the American League could not be reached. When Ray Chapman, Cleveland shortstop, was killed Owen Bush of Detroit offered to transfer to Cleveland. Mr. Johnson said then it could not be done because of the league rule cited by Mr. Comiskey.

## WHAT THE WHITE SOX PLAYERS RECEIVED.

According to reports of the testimony of Eddie Cicotte before the grand jury, the White Sox players received the following amounts for their part in "throwing" the series:

Eddie Cicotte, pitcher, $10,000.

Claude Williams, pitcher, $10,000.

Joe Jackson, outfielder, $5000.

"Buck" Weaver, third baseman, $5000.

"Happy" Felsch, outfielder, $1000.

Oscar Risberg, shortstop, $2000.

"Chick" Gandil, first baseman, $20,000.

Fred McMullin, utility, $15,000.

William Sullivan, an investigator for the State's Attorney's office, to-

EVERY MORNING IN THE YEAR. Los Angeles Times DAILY FOUNDED DECEMBER 4, 1881.
The Times Building, First and Broadway.
$1.05 per Month { DELIVERED BY CARRIER } Single Copies: Daily, 3 Cents; Sunday, 10 Cents, Everywhere.
By Mail, in Postal Zones 1 to 4, including California, Arizona, Nevada, Utah, Yearly, $12.00; Monthly, $1.05. In Zone 5, including Colorado, Idaho, Montana, New Mexico, Oregon, Washington, Yearly, $16.00; Monthly, $1.50. In Zones 6, 7 and 8, balance of States, Canada and Mexico, Yearly, $18.00; Monthly $1.50. POSTAGE PREPAID.
Entered as second class matter, December 4, 1881, at the Postoffice at Los Angeles, Cal., under the Act of March 3, 1879.
WEDNESDAY MORNING, SEPTEMBER 29, 1920. Vol. XXXIX. No. 302.

night told how Eddie Cicotte happened to confess the plot to "throw" the series, which uncovered all the details of the scheme. Sullivan accompanied the club south on this spring's training trip, at Comiskey's invitation, trying to confirm Comiskey's suspicions that the series had been "thrown."

He failed to learn anything definite then, but last Monday night Cicotte came to him, saying:

"I've got a load on my chest."

Sullivan sent him to Comiskey and today the club owner heard his star twirler's confession. Comiskey directed Cicotte to the club's attorney for advice and the latter, Alfred Austria, took the pitcher before the grand jury, where he unloosed the "load on his chest," with tears of remorse streaming down his cheeks.

Eddie Cicotte and Joe Jackson were not promised immunity from prosecution or extra consideration in return for their confessions today that they had "thrown" world series games, Austrian said tonight.

"Cicotte and Jackson made signed confessions," he said. "Cicotte first signed an immunity waiver which made it possible to indict him on his own evidence. They are liable to prosecution and will be given the same treatment as the other players."

Hartley Replogle, prosecutor of the case, said that "full legal prosecution would follow."

## GLEASON CONFIDENT DESPITE SCANDAL.

"We're going to win the pennant and then the world's series in spite of this," Manager Gleason of the White Sox said tonight.

"The thing has come to a head and I'm glad of it," he said. "I've been working on this affair with Mr. Comiskey for a long time and it has kept me under a tremendous strain. I'm mighty happy that it's all cleared up.

"The men on my team now are real men and real ball players and we're going to win the pennant and then the world's series, in spite of this scandal."

## GANDIL SOLD HOME HERE A WEEK AGO.

"Chick" Gandil, indicted today in Chicago in connection with the White Sox gambling charges, came here last winter with his wife and bought a home. Early in the spring he left for St. Anthony, Idaho, to manage a ball club, but returned soon, saying his health was better in California. He participated in five games with the Bakersfield team of the San Joaquin Valley Baseball League after returning from Idaho. About a week ago he sold his home and announced he was leaving for New Orleans. Nothing has been heard of him since.

## MAHARG WOULD TELL ALL FOR $10,000.

[BY A. P. NIGHT WIRE.]

PHILADELPHIA, Sept. 28.—Billy Maharg, the former boxer, who last night made sensational disclosures regarding the "fixing" of world series games in 1919, tonight accepted the invitation of Charles Comiskey, president of the Chicago White Sox, to testify at Chicago. In a telegram to Comiskey, Maharg says:

"I accept your offer to tell what I know about the crooked world's series of 1919 and will go to Chicago and testify provided you leave a certified check for $10,000 with Harvey Woodruff, sports editor of the Chicago Tribune, to be turned over to me after I testify. Please answer."

## PLAN OF FRAZEE TO AID COMISKEY.

[BY A. P. NIGHT WIRE.]

BOSTON, Sept. 28.—H. H. Frazee, president of the American League club, said tonight he believed it to be the duty of each club in the league to give one of its players to the Chicago club in order to assist in its rehabilitation, in case the Chicago players indicted by the grand jury are found guilty. He announced that he would make such an offer on behalf of his own club immediately.









# WHITE SOX INDICTED.

*Eight Took Part in Bribe Plan.*

*Cicotte and Jackson Tell How They Intentionally Let Cincinnati Win.*

*Implicate Other Players and Tell of the Amounts of Money Taken.*

[BY A. P. NIGHT WIRE.]

CHICAGO, Sept. 28.—Indictments were voted against eight baseball stars today and confessions obtained from two of them, when Charles A. Comiskey, owner of the oft-time champion Chicago White Sox, smashed his pennant-chasing machine to clean up baseball. The confessions told how the Sox threw last year's world's championship to Cincinnati for money paid by gamblers.

Seven Sox regulars and one former player had true bills voted against them by the Cook county grand jury. The seven were immediately suspended by Mr. Comiskey. With his team only half a game behind the league-leading Cleveland Indians, the White Sox owner served notice on his seven stars that if they were found guilty he would drive them out of organized baseball for the rest of their lives.

MONEY UNDER PILLOWS.

Officials of the court, desirous of giving the national game the benefit of publicity in its purging, lifted the curtain on the grand jury proceedings sufficiently to show a great hitter, Joe Jackson, declaring that he deliberately just tapped the ball; a picture of one of the world's most famous pitchers, Cicotte, in tears, and glimpses of alleged bribes of $5000 or $10,000 discovered under pillows, or on beds, by famous athletes about to retire.

Around the courtroom at one time or another were some of baseball's greatest leaders, among them John J. McGraw, manager of the New York Giants, awaiting a call to testify tomorrow; and John Heydler, president of the National League, who testified today.

THE MEN INVOLVED.

The exact nature of the information Mr. Comiskey put before the grand jury was not disclosed. The men whom the jury involved as a result of testimony uncovered by their owner were:

Eddie Cicotte, star pitcher who waived immunity and confessed, according to court attaches, that he took a $10,000 bribe.

Arnold "Chick" Gandil, former first baseman.

"Shoeless Joe" Jackson, heavy-hitting left fielder.

Oscar "Happy" Felsch, center-fielder.

Charles "Swede" Risberg, shortstop.

Claude Williams, pitcher.

George "Buck" Weaver, third baseman.

Fred McMullin, utility player.

STORY OF CICOTTE.

Cicotte, according to court attaches, told the grand jury he received $10,000 from the gamblers, finding the money under the pillow when he returned to his hotel room on the night before the first game at Cincinnati.

"I refused to pitch a ball until I got it," they quoted him as saying.

Jackson, it was said, testified he was promised $20,000 by Chick Gandil, but received only $5000. Claude Williams, according to the witnesses, got $10,000.

"Buck" Weaver, after learning of his indictment and suspension, denied that he had agreed to help throw any world's series games and that he had received any of the money.

"I batted .333 and made four errors out of thirty chances in the world's series," he said. "That should be a good-enough alibi."

While the grand jurors voted their true bills Comiskey, the "old Roman" seated in the midst of his crumbling empire out at White Sox park, issued the telegram suspending those involved, paid off Weaver, Cicotte and Jackson on the spot, and announced that checks for pay due

(Continued on Second Page.)

# SIXTEEN YEARS OF STRIVING AGAIN BRINGS McGRAW A CHAMPIONSHIP.

## GIANTS WIN THE BLUE RIBBON OF BASEBALL.

### *Capture World Series Championship in as Thrilling Nip and Tuck Combat as Has Ever Been Fought.*

[BY A. P. NIGHT WIRE.]

NEW YORK, Oct. 13.—World's champions, 1921, the New York National League baseball club.

The Giants won by defeating the Yankees in the eighth game of the world's series at the Polo Grounds today. The American League champions died fighting hard in a classic twirling duel between their pitching ace—Waite Hoyt, and Art Nehf, the Giants' star left-hander. However, they lacked the necessary punch, the National League team taking the game by 1 to 0 and the series, five games to three.

The Giants' victory gives Manager John J. McGraw his second world's champion team. The New York Nationals, seven-time pennant winners under McGraw, captured the world's title against the Athletics of the American League in 1905, but although winning the bunting five times since they have been baffled every time until this year, twice bowing to the Athletics, once to the Red Sox and once to the White Sox.

A DIFFERENT STORY.

This year, with a National League entrant that had shown its high class by coming from behind late and beating the Pittsburg Pirates to the flag, the world's series told a different story. Off to a poor start through loss of the first two games, the Giants gamely came back, spedily evened up the series and then, with but a slight let-up while getting their second wind, rounded into the stretch with a rush and pushed through with three straight victories to their final triumph. In every victory except today's they came from behind. Thus, one of the best and most hotly contested series in the history of the sport was won cleanly and in the final analysis, decisively, by a club, whose gameness and all-around ability will be generally conceded.

As for the underlying reason for the success of the McGraw men reports may differ, but there seems little cause to doubt that the most widely propounded opinion will be that it was because of a preponderance of high-class pitching. The series showed but two of Manager Miller Huggins's twirlers capable of pitching winning ball—Mays and Hoyt—while the Giants put forward a trio of masters in Douglas, Barnes and Nehf.

WITH FLAG FLYING.

Out-hit by the Giants in nearly every game and by many points in the series, the Yankees none the less made a hard fight by their smartness in manufacturing runs out of scant material and the superb work done by Mays and Hoyt in six of the eight battles. Their championship craft went down with flag flying and tonight their loyal supporters were

(Continued on Third Page.)

## RECEIPTS RECORDS BROKEN.

### *Present World's Series Was Greatest Financially in the History of Game.*

[BY A. P. NIGHT WIRE.]

NEW YORK, Oct. 13.—The 1921 world series, ended today, set new financial and attendance records. Total receipts for the eight games were $900,233, contributed by 269,976 spectators.

This was $177,819 more than the best previous gate collected in the 1919 series between Cincinnati and Chicago, when the total was $722,414 for the eight games of that year. The attendance in the series just closed was also 18,075 greater than the eight games of the Giants-Boston American play in 1912, when the total count registered 251,901, which has stood as a record for nine years.

As a result of the former gate receipts, all those who participate in the sharing of the funds will receive more than any of their predecessors in similar positions. The Giants as winners collect 60 per cent of 75 per cent of the players' share of the receipts for the first five games, amounting to $131,635, which, divided among some twenty-five eligible men, gives approximately $5265 to each. Under the plan of distributing 25 per cent among club players finishing second and third in both major leagues, the Cleveland Americans and the Pittsburg Nationals will divide $43,878.34 equally, while the two St. Louis teams, as third place clubs, share $29,252.22.

The magnates also come in for a record division of the money. The advisory board, which succeeded the National Commission, will take as its 15 per cent share $135,034.95. The club owners' share will amount to $472,675.82.



*The Knickerbocker Kids—No. 10 - - - - By GALE*

## WORLD'S SERIES CLEAN FROM START TO FINISH.

### *Humorist Lauds Sportsmanlike Play of Both Yanks and Giants; Hoyt Praised to Skies.*

BY IRVIN S. COBB.

[EXCLUSIVE DISPATCH.]

POLO GROUNDS (New York) Oct. 13.—Let others sing, as doubtless they will, of a finish to a world's series rag hunt so loaded with thrill and suspense that literally it out-drammers drama itself. Let others sing, with a hey-niddy-noddy or a fol-de-rol-day or whatever is proper to sing with under such circumstances, of a winning team which coming twice from behind with a rush and a roar, finally with its all-lengths of hickory raps out taps for its rivals.

Let yet others sing of an outfit who meet defeat with heads bloodied but unbowed, their records as a club and as individuals unstained by any sullying taint of saffron. Finally, let all hands sing of a sapling of a kid from Brooklyn, name of Hoyt, who in twenty-seven innings of pitching is scored on but twice, and one of those scores bred of an error. For surely this youngster deserves his meed of words and music. It is the first time in a communal history when anybody from Brooklyn has lasted out the full of a week in Manhattan without requiring the attention either of the police or the medical profession.

CLEAN SPORT.

As I was saying, let others sing of those things. If anyone would sing of the world's series of which I have had personal cognizance—and I believe the only world's series that ever was—which is played out to its ultimate conclusion without signs of breaking or faltering from their side, a world's series that is marked, so far as a bystander can figure, by clean sportsmanship from the start to finish; a world's series in which there are no quitters, none who flinches from the gaff, none who soldiers or sulks or weakens, none who, whether winning or losing, failing or sceuceeding, refuses to give of the best that is in him to the role he has essayed in the crowning seasonal classic of the national game. There was a lot of gore spilling in these eight days but not so much yellow displayed as

(Continued on Second Page.)

## LANDIS IS FOR SEVEN GAME TILT.

### *Supreme Commissioner to Recommend Shorter Baseball Series Next Year.*

[BY A. P. NIGHT WIRE.]

NEW YORK, Oct. 13.—Federal Judge K. M. Landis, commissioner of baseball, in a statement tonight said he would recommend that a seven-game series, instead of nine, be played next season. He also declared that owing to the high class of baseball played, there would be small chance of reducing admission fees next year.

## KIENHOLTZ REFEREE OF OXY-U.S.C. GAME.

At the regular weekly meeting of the Southern California Football Officials Association last night at Hotel Angelus, W. S. Kienholtz was named as referee of the Occidental-U.S.C. fracas at Patterson Field tomorrow. Foley will assist Kienholtz as umpire, while Call and Brennan will officiate as head linesman and field judge, respectively.

## *Dudley's Mare Victor in the Trotting Race.*

[BY A. P. NIGHT WIRE.]

LEXINGTON (Ky.) Oct. 13.—Jeanette Rankin, owned by George E. Dudley of Youngstown, O., made it a double in the Lexington Grand Circuit meeting today when she accounted for the Ashland 2:11 trot in straight heats. E. Colorado was her closest contender. The winner trotted the two heats in 2:05 and 2:05 1-4.

Klio, bay mare, by Peter the Great-Axward Belle, driven by Pittman, also made it a double on the meeting when she captured the 2:17 trot, a split heat affair, after losing the first heat to Alma Todd. Alma Todd got second money.

The 2-year-old trot and the 2:09 pace were easy for Peter Earl and Roger C., both taking first money in straight heats.

The judges declared off all bets on the 2:17 trot, following the finish in the last heat during which Palin handling the reins on Alma Todd did not appear to put up a very strong finish. This action, however, did not affect the division of the purse, Klio being given first money.

Summary:

Two-year-old trotters, two in three, purse $1000:

| | | |
|---|---|---|
| Peter Earl, b.c., by Peter the Great (Cox) | 1 | 1 |
| Collateral, br.c. | 2 | 2 |
| Eleanor Worthy, b.f. | 3 | 3 |
| Dewey the Great, b.c. | 4 | 4 |
| Dot Belwin | Dis. | |

Time—2:12½, 2:10½.

The 2:09 pace, two in three, purse $1000:

| | | |
|---|---|---|
| Roger C, ch.g., by Major C (Palin) | 1 | 1 |
| Wanda May, gr.m. | 6 | 2 |
| The Jack, b.g. | 2 | 7 |
| Charley Sweet, b.g. | 3 | 4 |
| Loleta, b.m. | 9 | 3 |
| Captain Shirley, ch.g. | 4 | 6 |

Flo Patch, Uriko, Direct Light and Osage Girl also started.

Time—2:07¼, 2:03¾.

The Ashland, 2:11 trot, two in three, purse $2000:

| | | |
|---|---|---|
| Jeanette Rankin, ch.m. by San Francisco (McDonald) | 1 | 1 |
| E. Colorado, b.h. | 2 | 2 |
| Emma Harvester, b.m. | 3 | 3 |
| Voltage, br.c. | 5 | 4 |
| Bilston, br.h. | 4 | 5 |
| Miss Emma Todd, b.f. | 6 | 6 |

Time—2:05, 2:05¼.

The 2:17 trot, two in three, purse $1000:

| | | | |
|---|---|---|---|
| Klio, b.m. by Peter the Great (Pittman) | 2 | 1 | 1 |
| Alma Todd, br.m. | 1 | 2 | 2 |
| Bessie Worthy, b.m. | 3 | 6 | 3 |
| Peter Alation, ch.g. | 4 | 4 | 4 |
| Alice G. Forbes, br.m. | 6 | 3 | 5 |
| Noble Argot, blk.g | 5 | 5 | Dis. |

Time—2:07¼, 2:09½, 2:07¼.

## *Tickets for the Bear-U.S.C. Tilt Reach H. Bruce.*

Graduate Manager Henry Bruce of U.S.C. yesterday received his allotment of tickets for the U.S.C.-California football game at Berkeley on November 5. The quota is 3013. and Bruce says the sale will be limited to students, alumni and friends of the university. Those who come under this head may mail their checks to Bruce and receive their pasteboards from him.

## MISSION BOY BEST OF RACING HOUNDS.

[BY A. P. NIGHT WIRE.]

EAST ST. LOUIS (Ill.) Oct. 13.—About 150 entries were in the kennels of the St. Clair race track for racing greyhounds at the close of the first day's races. The majority of entries are from Oklahoma and California.

Mission Boy, a brindle, known as the Man O'War of dogdom, won the feature event, the fourth, or inaugural stakes races, purse $25, over a three-eighths of a mile course, in 39 4-5 seconds. Cannibal King, the brindle, finished second and Esybara, brindle, third.

## GIANTS IN NAME AND DEEDS; RAWLING A STAR AT SECOND; PERFECT BALANCE COPS BUN.

BY GEORGE KELLY,
First Baseman of the Giants.

[EXCLUSIVE DISPATCH.]

POLO GROUNDS (New York) Oct. 13.—Giants in name, in deeds the same.

Having waited since 1905, John J. McGraw again guided his team to the championship of the baseball world. He failed in 1911, 1912, 1913 and 1917, but the club of 1921 came through and there was a greater thrill in this victory, for we downed the Yankees, rivals for popularity in this city.

"The greatest game for the biggest prize, with the most sensational finish." These were the words of hundreds of fans after the game was over.

Well, we will let it go at that, but before anyone says any more about championship of 1921 let them shake hands with Johnny Rawlings. Rawlings started the play that saved the game and prevented us from going extra innings or possibly nine games with the Yankees.

HUGS EARTH.

When Baker hit that ball down toward right field every ounce of power in the strong body of the Maryland farmer was behind it. The ball hugged the earth and Rawlings dove for it. He got it rolling over and over, but came up and threw Baker out to me. Ward was racing for second and kept right on. I saw the play in the making and cut loose a throw to Frank Frisch. The peg had to be perfect,

(Continued on Second Page.)

## ANGEL RALLY CLAMPS IT.

### *Hornsby's Lads Batter Pill in Seventh Canto and Mission Nine Drops Two in a Row.*

BY HARRY A. WILLIAMS.

America's baseball championship having passed over to the National League by virtue of Giant prowess, it was opportune that Rogers Hornsby, batting boss of that circuit, should lead Los Angeles to a 3 to 2 win over the San Francisco Missions on the same day.

It was in the seventh inning that the Angels scored their three runs and put the frosted kibosh on the Northerners with a rally that had the bugs standing up on their stiff legs. Prior to that time the game was strictly Mission style, with the bell ringing once in the second and again in the fifth, which was not enough to make a real chime. But from that moment on El Camino Real was closed to Harry Heilman's militant missionaries, who are carrying the gospel of big league hitting to the benighted cash customers of California.

HAS A SHADE.

Prior to the spiffy seventh Tony Faeth had a shade on Jay Gould, but that round with three singles and a double put the edge on the other side.

Hornsby didn't play a hand in the winning sortie, but his fielding, especially in the sixth, unquestionably turned the Missions back from what would otherwise have been an easy victory. His stop of Siglin's grounder back of second in that frame, snuffed out two runs, and in the second his toss to Baldwin cut off a score at the plate. But for these two plays the Heilman horde would have piled up such a lead that the Angel efforts of the seventh would have been far from adequate, meaning insufficient or not enough thereof.

Heilman continued to hit 'em where they ain't, lining a single and a double in four trips, and hammering across the second Mission run. On another occasion he was out at first on a hard smash to Gould, and fourthly he grounded to Brown.

Lefty O'Doul, with two singles and a double, was really the game's shining light as a swatter.

One out in the second when Pete

(Continued on Second Page.)

## *Orioles Down Louisville and Grab the Lead.*

[BY A. P. NIGHT WIRE.]

BALTIMORE (Md.) Oct. 13.—The Baltimore Internationals went to the front today in its series with Louisville of the American Association by winning the fifth game, 10 to 5. The series now stands three to two in favor of the Orioles. The score:

| | R. | H. | E. |
|---|---|---|---|
| Louisville | 5 | 10 | 2 |
| Baltimore | 10 | 14 | 0 |

Batteries—Kobb, Wright, Cullop, Sanders and Meyers; Ogden and Egan.

## OLD TIGERS AGAIN MAUL THE SEALS.

[BY A. P. NIGHT WIRE.]

SAN FRANCISCO, Oct. 13.—The Vernon Winter League team defeated San Francisco again today, 10 to 7. George Sisler, leader of the Vernon club, got two singles and a double in four times up and made one stolen base. Ty Cobb got two singles and a double in four trips to the plate and stole two bases. Couch, San Francisco pitcher, made two erriors in the sixth inning and these helped to beat him.

VERNON.

| | AB | R | H | O | A |
|---|---|---|---|---|---|
| Cooper,cf | 5 | 1 | 2 | 4 | 0 |
| Wolfer,lf | 6 | 1 | 2 | 3 | 4 |
| Sisler,1b | 4 | 1 | 3 | 11 | 0 |
| Smith,3b | 4 | 0 | 1 | 0 | 4 |
| Knight,2b | 5 | 1 | 2 | 2 | 5 |
| Sneider,rf | 5 | 2 | 2 | 4 | 0 |
| Mitze,c | 3 | 2 | 1 | 1 | 0 |
| Kingdon,ss | 4 | 1 | 1 | 2 | 0 |
| Jones,p | 4 | 1 | 2 | 0 | 3 |
| Totals | 40 | 10 | 16 | 27 | 18 |

SAN FRANCISCO.

| | AB | R | H | O | A |
|---|---|---|---|---|---|
| Pinelli,3b | 5 | 2 | 2 | 0 | 6 |
| Willie,rf | 3 | 1 | 1 | 1 | 6 |
| Cobb cf | 4 | 0 | 3 | 2 | 0 |
| O'C'nell,1b | 4 | 1 | 1 | 11 | 2 |
| C'ourne,lf | 4 | 1 | 1 | 1 | 0 |
| Ellison,2b | 4 | 0 | 1 | 5 | 0 |
| Rhyne,ss | 5 | 1 | 3 | 4 | 4 |
| Yelle,c | 4 | 0 | 0 | 2 | 0 |
| Couch,p | 3 | 1 | 1 | 1 | 1 |
| Kremer,p | 1 | 0 | 0 | 1 | 1 |
| Jenkins,x | 1 | 0 | 1 | 0 | 0 |
| Totals | 38 | 7 | 14 | 28 | 17 |

x—Batted for Kremer in ninth.

SCORE BY INNINGS.

| | 1 | 2 | 3 | 4 | 5 | 6 | 7 | 8 | 9 | |
|---|---|---|---|---|---|---|---|---|---|---|
| Vernon | 0 | 1 | 1 | 0 | 1 | 3 | 4 | 0 | 0 | 10 |
| Base hits | 2 | 1 | 2 | 1 | 2 | 2 | 5 | 1 | 0 | 16 |
| San Francisco | 1 | 0 | 2 | 0 | 1 | 0 | 1 | 0 | 2 | 7 |
| Base hits | 2 | 0 | 3 | 1 | 1 | 1 | 3 | 0 | 2 | 14 |

SUMMARY.

Errors—Kingdon, Couch, 2; Pinelli, Yelle. Six runs 10 hits, off Couch, 27 at bat, in 6 innings. Stolen bases—Cobb, 2; Chadbourne, Sisler, Jones, Cooper. Home run—Schneider. Two-base hits—Cobb, Rhyne, 2; Sisler, Pinelli, Knight, Schneider, Mitze. Sacrifice hits—Smith, Cobb, O'Connell, Jones, Kingdon. Bases on balls—Off Couch, 2; off Jones, 6; off Kremer, 2. Struck out—By Kremer, 2. Double play—Knight to Kingdon to Sisler. Runs responsible for—Couch, 3; Jones, 7; Kremer, 4. Left on bases—Vernon, 9; San Francisco, 10. Charge defeat to Couch. Time of game—2h. Umpires—Reardon and Toman.

## ARGENTINA WINS.

[BY CABLE AND ASSOCIATED PRESS.]

BUENOS AIRES, Oct. 13.—Argentina is the winner of the first international tennis tournament for the championship of South America, which ended yesterday.

## OFFICIAL BOX SCORE OF THE DECIDING GAME.

NATIONALS.

| | A.B. | R. | B.H. | P.O. | A. | E. |
|---|---|---|---|---|---|---|
| Burns, cf | 4 | 0 | 1 | 3 | 0 | 0 |
| Bancroft, ss | 3 | 1 | 0 | 0 | 4 | 0 |
| Frisch, 3b | 4 | 0 | 0 | 2 | 3 | 0 |
| Young, rf | 2 | 0 | 1 | 0 | 0 | 0 |
| Kelly, 1b | 4 | 0 | 0 | 13 | 1 | 0 |
| E. Meusel, lf | 4 | 0 | 1 | 1 | 0 | 0 |
| Rawlings, 2b | 4 | 0 | 3 | 4 | 4 | 0 |
| Snyder, c | 2 | 0 | 0 | 4 | 0 | 0 |
| Nehf, p | 4 | 0 | 0 | 0 | 0 | 0 |
| Totals | 31 | 1 | 6 | 27 | 12 | 0 |

AMERICANS.

| | A.B. | R. | B.H. | P.O. | A. | E. |
|---|---|---|---|---|---|---|
| Fewster, lf | 3 | 0 | 0 | 2 | 0 | 0 |
| Peckinpaugh, ss | 2 | 0 | 0 | 2 | 2 | 1 |
| Miller, cf | 4 | 0 | 1 | 1 | 0 | 0 |
| R. Meusel, rf | 4 | 0 | 0 | 2 | 0 | 0 |
| Pipp, 1b | 3 | 0 | 1 | 11 | 0 | 0 |
| Ruth, z | 1 | 0 | 0 | 0 | 0 | 0 |
| Ward, 2b | 3 | 0 | 1 | 0 | 2 | 0 |
| Baker, 3b | 3 | 0 | 0 | 1 | 3 | 0 |
| Schang, c | 3 | 0 | 0 | 8 | 1 | 0 |
| Hoyt, p | 3 | 0 | 1 | 0 | 3 | 0 |
| Totals | 29 | 0 | 4 | 27 | 11 | 1 |

z—Batted for Pipp in ninth.

SCORE BY INNINGS.

| | | | | | | | | | | |
|---|---|---|---|---|---|---|---|---|---|---|
| Giants | 1 | 0 | 0 | 0 | 0 | 0 | 0 | 0 | 0 | 1 |
| Yankees | 0 | 0 | 0 | 0 | 0 | 0 | 0 | 0 | 0 | 0 |

SUMMARY.

Two-base hits—Rawlings, 2. Stolen bases—Young. Sacrifice—Snyder, 2. Double plays—Bancroft, Rawlings and Kelly; Rawlings, Kelly and Frisch. Left on bases—Nationals, 9; Americans, 7. Bases on balls—Off Nehf, 5; off Hoyt, 4. Struck out—Nehf, 3; Hoyt, 7. Wild pitch—Nehf. Umpires—At plate—Chill; first base, Rigler; second base, Moriarty; third base, Quigley. Time, 1h. 58m.

The Los Angeles Times

TUESDAY MORNING, JANUARY 3, 1922.

SPORTS MOTORING FILMLAND DRAMA

# WASHINGTON-JEFFERSON FOOTBALL ELEVEN OUTSMARTS CALIFORNIA.

## *Erickson Was a Thorn in the Side of California All Day.*

Red and Black Halfback Skirting Brick Muller's End for a Big Gain.

In the third quarter, Erickson, aided by Capt. Stein's marvelous interference, scooted around Muller's flank for a 25-yard run, but stepped outside the field of play and fifteen yards of the dash was disallowed. Nisbet of California (with his back to the runner) has been spilled and Erb has been hit just as he is about to leap at the runner. The blocker that got Erb did a nose dive into a gooey puddle and came up with eyes and mouth full of mud and gumbo. Cranmer is running up at the extreme left. W. and J.'s strong interference was one of the big features of the day. Photo by F. M. Litchfield, Times staff photographer.

## NISBET'S TOE STAVES OFF EASTERN TRIUMPH.

### *Booting of Big Blonde Fullback All That Stands Between W. and J. and a Muddy Victory.*

BY PAUL LOWRY.

If Washington and Jefferson's football team isn't the best in the East it is at least the best eastern team that ever played before a Tournament of Roses crowd at Pasadena. Outclassed in every single department of play with the exception of kicking, California was lucky to come out on the even end of a 0-to-0 score in the annual continental classic.

W. and J. offered the smartest exhibition of football ever uncorked in the West, surpassing anything shown here by Pennsylvania, Harvard or Ohio State. Nothing but masterful punting on the part of Archie Nisbet, California fullback, kept the Bear goal line unsullied. That and the fact that Stein, captain and right end, of the Washington and Jefferson team, was outside when Brenkert, by a magnificent effort, reversed his field on a run from a fake punt formation and sped 40 yards over the goal line just before the end of the first quarter.

This was one of the high spots of a tremendously thrilling game, played on a football links covered with wet grass and slippery mud. It was a run that called into play all the elements of early interference, straight arm and change of pace and particularly difficult of execution because of the uncertain footing.

**SIX FIRST DOWNS.**

W. and J.'s line charged low and hard and fast, blocked perfectly and made it possible for Coach Neale's backs to pierce the California line or skirt the ends. Six first downs were rolled up by the Presidents to California's two.

California's big moment came in the final quarter, when big Brick Muller, rumbling in from his position at right end, hurried Brenkert and the Red and Black kicker's boot sliced only 13 yards up the field and outside. This was the big break California had been waiting for, and Andy Smith rushed the reserves into the fray. Dunn replaced Nichols at halfback and Morrison went in for Nisbet. From the W. and J. 23-yard line the Bears made 7 yards in three trials, but the following play nearly brought grief to California.

It was a forward pass to Morrison with three men going out and while Morrison completed the toss he couldn't hold on to the ball, dropping it when tackled. Erickson, the scintillating star of the contest, scooped it up and dashed down the sidelines. He had practically a clear field for a touchdown, but slipped and was pounced upon and shoved out of bounds

The wet field defeated Califor-

(Continued on Third Page.)

## REFUSED TO TAKE BEARS SERIOUSLY.

### *Presidents Not at All Awed by California's Fame; Enjoyed the Contest Hugely.*

BY KAYO.

The whole trouble seemed to be that Washington and Jefferson's football players wouldn't take the California "wonder-team" seriously.

Forty-thousand football fans from all parts of California crowded into the stands at Tournament Park, Pasadena, yesterday and spent most of the time wondering why the heavens didn't open and strike the Presidents dead for giggling at critical points and daring to kid the Bears.

Usually when the California team gets down to the opposition's 20-yard line, the opposition slaps each other on the collective back, gets a desperate look on its face and gallops back and forth along the line of scrimmage yelling "fight." Opposition ought to tremble when California gets on its 20-yard line, and that's all there is to it.

**WOULDN'T TREMBLE.**

But Washington and Jefferson positively refused to tremble. When the Bears rushed down to within striking distance the Presidents appeared just as cheerful and appeared to be having just as good a time as when California was at the other end of the field. Perhps their tackling was a little more deadly, perhaps they tightened up a bit but they never gave any signs of fearing that the mighty California machine was going to run over 'em and flatten 'em.

Apparently Washington and Jefferson came on the field with the intention of having a real, all-around good time and they had it. They rushed up and wiped the mud from their hands on the referee's neat white shirt. When a

(Continued on Second Page.)

## NAVY REFUSES ALLIANCE.

BOSTON, Jan. 2.—The Navy Department will not enter an alliance with the Amateur Athletic Union. This was the answer today of Capt. C. R. Train, U.S.N., to the A.A.U's. proposal that the Army and Navy join with it in the conduct of amateur athletics.

"I still think as does Admiral Washington, chief of personnel, that it is not wise for a department of the Federal government to ally itself with the A.A.U.," Capt. Train wrote in the letter which was made public here by President William C. Prout of the A.A.U. We both feel that the existing rules of the A.A.U. amply cover contact between the Navy Department and that organization. The sound activities of your organization for the advancement of amateur sports has our hearty admiration."

President Prout explained that the alliance was proposed to the Army and Navy as a result of an amendment to the A.A.U. rules providing that if they adopted registration systems which provide for investigation and the certificate of amateur registrants service athletes with such credentials could compete in A.A.U. events.

## EDDIE O'DOWD WINS POPULAR DECISION.

[BY A. P. NIGHT WIRE.]

COLUMBUS (O.) Jan. 2.—Eddie O'Dowd of Columbus, won the judges' decision over Patsy Flanagan of St. Louis in twelve rounds today. Each weighed 117 pounds.



## *W. and J. Coach Says Breaks Were Missing*

BY EARLE NEALE,
Washington and Jefferson Head Coach.

I am entirely satisfied with the showing my men made against California, and if they had had a few more breaks of the game they would have won. The Washington and Jefferson team outplayed California throughout, and only needed a little luck to prove it in the score.

The slippery condition of the playing field was quite a handicap to my team, in spite of the general opinion, especially in the kicking department. The work of some of the officials was far from satisfactory to me.

## SALISBURY WINS DEL MONTE GOLF TOURNEY.

[BY A. P. NIGHT WIRE.]

DEL MONTE, Jan. 2. — R. Walker Salisbury of Burlingame, Cal., and Salt Lake City won the New Year's tournament here today by defeating E. I. Neustader of Portland, Or., one up in the finals. H. F. Elliott of Porterville, Cal. and L. V. Bentley lost in the semifinals. Blair Foster of San Francisco, won the second flight, Phil Bekeart, Jr., of San Francisco, the third flight, and Dr. J. F. McMath the fourth. Mrs. W. J. Matson of San Mateo won the women's finals.

## SAYS PRESIDENTS ARE GOOD SPORTS.

BY GEORGE LATHAM,
Captain of California Eleven.

The outcome of the game was what could be expected on such a field. It is hard for the spectators to realize the difficulty of playing on a sloppy gridiron, and I would certainly like to have another chance at Washington and Jefferson on a dry field. I am confident that California could win under better playing conditions.

Washington and Jefferson certainly has a fine team and every man on it is a good sportsman.

## ERICKSON IS THE INDIVIDUAL STAR OF ANNUAL CLASSIC; IS OF ALL-AMERICAN CALIBER

BY GLOOMY GUS HENDERSON,
U.S.C. Football Coach.

**Everyone who saw the big intersectional football game at Tournament Park yesterday is convinced that it was the greatest East-vs.-West affair that has ever been staged at Pasadena. The Washington and Jefferson eleven may not be the greatest team in the East, but it played the best brand of football of any of the eastern teams that have been seen in action in the annual New Year's Day tussle.**

Using a formation which was a variation of the old punt formation, the W. and J. team got the Bears on the run with the opening kickoff, and had Andy Smith's men backed up to dangerous territory before they knew what it was all about. California had a busy time of it trying to diagnose this attack, but the Presidents worked it throughout the game with wonderful success.

W. and J.'s interference was beautiful during the march down the field at the start of the game. Toomey interrupted things by intercepting a forward pass when the Washington and Jefferson machine was all fixed for a touchdown, and would undoubtedly have broken loose for a score if the field had not been sloppy. This incident shows how quickly the tide of battle can change in modern football.

One minute we thought W. and J. had scored a touchdown, and the next it looked as if Toomey was off for a touchdown in California's favor.

The rest of the game was featured by Nisbet's kicking and Erickson's open field running. Nisbet's headwork in his booting was the best I have ever seen. He averaged 42 yards from the line of scrimmage, which means that his punts went 52 yards. This is considerable of a record when it is

(Continued on Second Page.)

## COAST IS NOT SUPERIOR.

### *Game Demonstrates East Does Not Have to Take a Back Seat to Football as Played in West.*

BY WALTER H. ECKERSALL,
Field Judge of Washington and Jefferson-California Game and Former Chicago Gridiron Star.

**In a great battle featured by hard, vicious tackling and clever blocking by the eastern eleven, football teams representing California and Washington and Jefferson struggled to a scoreless tie at Tournament Park before a gathering of 45,000 fans.**

**It was a great struggle played under adverse conditions. The heavy rain of Sunday and Sunday night left the field in poor shape. This condition hampered the open play of both teams, although W. and J. successfully executed one forward pass for a good gain.**

On the other hand the Bears attempted a few forward tosses, but the passes failed to gain, as only two were completed and both behind the line of scrimmage.

**DECIDED ADVANTAGE.**

On straight football, W. & J. had a decided advantage which was offset by the brilliant punting of Archie Nisbet. In fact, it was this player's clever toe work which kept California in the game and at times compelled W. & J. to fight with its back in the shadow of its own goal posts.

Despite the breaks, which were in favor of California, the invaders fought with dogged determination and staved off defeat when things looked darkest. The men played with an aggressiveness, which brought rounds of applause from the large crowd, most of which was partial to the Native Son eleven.

California can be justly criticized for poor work at the end of the first half. An exchange of punts, combined with a few line plunges placed the oval on the W. & J. 15-yard line. At this stage, time was called for an injured player. Captains of both teams were told there was only two seconds left to play. The ball rested directly in front of the goal posts. Instead of calling upon Irving Toomey, a fairly re-

(Continued on Third Page.)

## *Bears Played Their Best, Says Smith.*

BY ANDY SMITH,
Head Coach of the University of California.

My men put everything they had into the game with Washington and Jefferson, but could not penetrate the Easterners' strong defense on the muddy field. I am sorry the conditions prevented California from using their usual spectacular plays, and am convinced that if the game had been played on a dry field California would have won.

I have nothing but praise for the Washington and Jefferson squad. It is a real team and gave us a real battle.

## *Club Meets Santa Clara Five Tonight.*

The third and deciding basketball game between the L.A.A.C. and Santa Clara College will be staged tonight in the club gym. In their first encounter the Catholics took the Mercury men down the line, but lost in the second engagement. Tonight the rival teams will settle matters once and for all, and a rough and thrilling exhibition is expected. The game will be open to the public. It will start at 8:30 p.m.

## WANTS TO PLAY BEARS AGAIN.

BY RUSSELL STEIN,
Captain of W. and J. Eleven.

If California and Washington and Jefferson could each go halfway across the continent to meet in a football game I am sure my team would win. The long trip, coupled with the slippery field, handicapped my men to a great extent, and I am sorry we can't take another crack at California's wonder team under more favorable conditions.

The fact that we used only eleven men during the entire game is an indication, I think, of our superiority.

# 1923
# 1932

THE OLYMPIC GAMES, PLAGUED BY POLITICAL AND FINANCIAL PROBLEMS EVER SINCE THEY WERE REVIVED in 1896, finally became at Los Angeles in 1932 the international celebration of peace and goodwill Baron Pierre de Coubertin had hoped they would be.

With nine years to prepare for the X Olympics, Los Angeles had the resources and enthusiasm to stage them in ideal conditions: fine facilities and splendid weather. For the first time, a city had built a special village to house Olympic athletes. And despite a worldwide depression, the Games, for the most part, went off smoothly. On July 30 more than a hundred thousand spectators filled the Coliseum for the Opening Ceremonies. Athletes from forty nations marched in a dazzling parade.

The competition that followed was dazzling, too. Records fell in bundles. The women, led by the United States star Mildred (Babe) Didrikson, broke every track-and-field standard. Attendance records also were set.

The Los Angeles Games were not without problems, however. A political flap with Japan caused China to enter at the last minute, and Cheng Chun-liu, described as "a handsome but none too swift sprinter," became the sole representative of four hundred million Chinese. The splendid runner from Finland, Paavo Nurmi, was ruled a professional and barred from competing in the marathon.

In the 3,000-meter steeplechase, an official who was to hold the lap numbers became ill, his substitute got confused, and the runners took an extra lap. Babe Didrikson, who had already won the 80-meter hurdles and the javelin, lost a tie for a third gold medal when it was ruled that she was "diving" over the bar in the high jump, which at that time was illegal.

The Olympics of 1924 returned to Paris and were featured by the remarkable endurance running of Nurmi, "The Flying Finn," who won four races from 1,500 to 10,000 meters. And movie fans will remember the success of British stars H. M. Abrahams, who won the 100 meters, and E. H. Liddell, the 400-meter champion. They were featured in the film *Chariots of Fire*. In the same year the first Winter Olympics were held in Chamonix, France.

Women competed in track and field for the first time in the 1928 Games at Amsterdam. Forty-six nations, a record, competed. At age thirty-two, Nurmi set a record in the 10,000-meter run but finished second in the 5,000 meters and 3,000-meter steeplechase. In the Winter Games at St. Moritz, Switzerland, the same year, a fifteen-year-old schoolgirl from Norway, Sonja Henie, won a gold medal in figure skating and a place in history. She won the event again at Lake Placid, New York, in 1932, adding the glamour that is part of the sport today by skating in satin costumes.

Professional sports in these years were dominated by boxers, notably Jack Dempsey and Gene Tunney, and the New York Yankees' Babe Ruth. In 1926 Ruth hit three home runs in a World Series game, a record. And on September 30, 1927, he hit his sixtieth home run of the regular season for another record.

Dempsey, who had won the world heavyweight championship by beating Jess Willard in 1919, did not lose it until September 23, 1926, when Tunney won a ten-round decision. Tunney gave him a return match the following year, and in their famous "long count" fight in Chicago he retained the championship on another ten-round decision.

The "long count" came when Dempsey knocked Tunney down in the seventh round. The referee did not start counting immediately because Dempsey hovered over his opponent. Under an Illinois rule, he should have retreated to the corner farthest from Tunney. By the time Dempsey did this and the referee began his count, Tunney had recovered. At the count of nine, he got up and went on to win the fight.

While champion, Dempsey fought an unforgettable match with Luis Firpo of Argentina, "the Wild Bull of the Pampas." In three minutes, fifty-seven seconds of fighting at New York's Polo Grounds on September 14, 1923, Dempsey knocked Firpo down seven times and the Argentine got up and smashed the champion through the ropes into the press section. Sportswriters shoved Dempsey back into the ring, and he knocked out Firpo in the second round.

In 1930 a twenty-eight-year-old amateur golfer, Bobby Jones, won four major events—the U.S. and British Opens and the U.S. and British amateur tournaments—and retired. Such a "Grand Slam" had never been achieved, and no golfer has done it since.

The nation was shocked on March 31, 1931, when Knute Rockne, the Notre Dame football coach, died in a plane crash in Kansas. His team had won 105 games, lost 12, and tied 5. On November 21 of that year, USC won a memorable game from the Irish, 16–14, in Chicago's Soldier Field.

But among all the victories and achievements of this era, a "bone-head" play stands out. In the 1929 Rose Bowl game, the California center, Roy Riegels, picked up a Georgia Tech fumble on the 35-yard line, headed for the Tech goal line, spun around to avoid a tackle, got confused, and raced toward his own end zone. A teammate caught him on the one-yard line and headed him in the right direction, but it was too late; he was tackled. When California punted from its own end zone, Georgia Tech blocked the kick for a safety and won the game, 8–7.

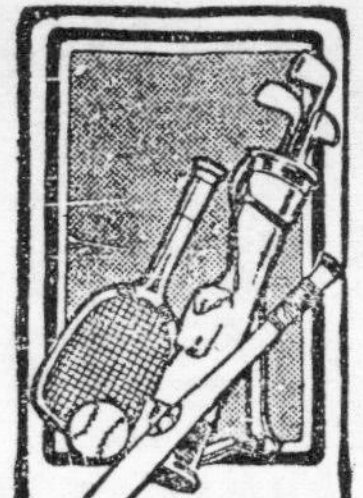

# SPORT NEWS
## The Los Angeles Times

SATURDAY MORNING, SEPTEMBER 15, 1923.

# FIRPO JUST MISSES VICTORY

## ARGENTINE'S RIGHT HAS CHAMPION ALMOST OUT

### *Lack of Ring Knowledge on Part of Firpo Saves Dempsey From Being Knocked Cuckoo in First*

BY SID SUTHERLAND
[EXCLUSIVE DISPATCH]

POLO GROUNDS (New York) Sept. 14.—The American style of fighting, when exemplified by a Jack Dempsey, is still the best. He showed it in two rounds here tonight. The Argentine method of deciding pugilistic supremacy is good, but not quite as good. He proved it in the first round. But it was good, none can deny it.

How good it was you can hear from 85,000 persons who sat paralyzed with astonishment as Firpo knocked the heavyweight champion of the world through the ropes, entirely out of the ring and on to the heads and shoulders of stunned newspaper men in the first row.

Can the Argentino hit with that right hand? Can he assimilate punishment? To both questions the answer is a thunderous YES whose genuiness ever the king of fighters will acknowledge.

**COULDN'T FINISH JACK**

Can the Argentino take advantage of a victory lying in the hollow of his hand? No. Nor does he know what to do when he has a heavyweight title holder leaning against the ropes, hands hanging at his sides, face a smear of blood, eyes blank with the onrushing unconsciousness that was following one of the worst beatings ever handed to a champion.

Never has such a first round been fought within the memory of the oldest and most ardent boxing fan. Never have four-score thousand spectators been jerked to their feet by so amazing an exhibition of pure gameness as that displayed by the visitor to our shores. Never have hard-boiled sporting scribes dropped their pencils, opened their mouths in incredulity and held their breaths at the fight of a man, knocked down six times within a minute, arise to his feet and slash and beat the champion into submission for the balance of the round.

Two things beat Firpo. Handicapped by his lack of knowledge of the referee's orders in the first clinch, he turned his head a second to glance at the arbiter, Johnny Gallagher. At that instant the alert Dempsey dropped his left on the foreigner's jaw and Firpo collapsed on his face.

The second thing that helped Dempsey retain his title by the narrowest margin in history was the complete absence of boxing intelligence on the part of a man who had the crown on his brow.

And it was the latter fault that earned for Firpo his Omaha moniker—gorgonzola cheese. Had he been capable of exercising an ounce, a feather's weight of ring generalship, the record books would have contained this entry:

Firpo stopped Dempsey in one round.

But why dwell on what does not exist?

When the gong rang, Dempsey shot from his corner. He catapulted across the canvas and met Firpo in his own corner. There was no weaving of his body, no strategy. He shifted his right and whipped a left hook to the cheek bone. Firpo backed along the ropes, and sidled to the middle of the ring.

**TIGER-LIKE**

Jack was on him like a tiger. He feinted with his left and when Firpo raised his arms sank a terrific right into the stomach. Firpo bent down and rushed into a clinch. The referee shouted at both men, knocked their arms loose and said something to Firpo.

The Argentine foolishly turned his head and Jack let fly. The bigger man went down, took a count of seven on his knee (Dempsey standing far too close for compliance with the rules) and arose. He drove three hard- side-swiping rights to Jack's left kidney and took a right to the chin that sent him down for a toll of five.

When Firpo arose Jack dropped him with a right uppercut that brought a stream of blood from his nose and mouth. This time the referee counted nine and it appeared to be over.

The ability to "take it" on which was made one unwise forecast that I can attest to, and the magnificent courage, heretofore doubted by the 'fight experts" whose wisdom in ring affairs surpasses this scribe's, brought the stupified Buenos Aires giant to his tottering legs.

Dempsey crowded his apparently hopelessly beaten opponent and hooked a right uppercut that overthrew the taller man for the fourth time. He arose at six, Dempsey for the first time and the only at the command of the judges, retiring across the ring until the fallen man arose.

Once more there was a flurry of gloves, a clinch, a bit of Jack's famous in-fighting and down the Argentin went again. After arising at seven he was once more floored with a right cross.

How fortunate for Jack that he had duplicated the Toledo feat by knocking his foe to the canvas six times in the first round.

For at this moment Firpo, battered, bloody, stunned, went into action, a rally that has never been

(Continued on Twelfth Page)

## FIRPO STOPPED BY CHAMP

### *Challenger Counted Out After Flooring Dempsey Twice and Being Dropped Seven Times*

(Continued from First Page)

they leaped at each other once more. Dempsey again was the quicker on the attack and Firpo went down under the crushing blows of the champion. He arose only to go down once more. Now there was no doubt of the outcome. The challenger, bleeding and tottering, forced himself to his feet, carrying on largely by instinct. Dempsey stepped in, whipped his left to the body and then a short right to the chin that sent Firpo sprawling on his back, staring vacantly at the glare of lights overhead.

The Argentine tried feebly to turn over, to gather strength to rise. His fighting heart called him back to the fray, but the body that had withstood one of the most terrific assaults the ring has ever known, could not respond.

He lay flat at the count of ten, after fifty-seven seconds of the round had elapsed and was helped to his corner by the victorious champion.

Then that vast throng, whipped to a fever pitch of excitement by the sensational struggle of these two slugging gladiators, gave vent to an ovation that echoed and reechoed from Coogan's Bluff as Dempsey's hand was raised in victory.

Ringside spectators rushed for the ring, some hurdling three rows of press benches to get at the champion and lift him to their shoulders. For a moment it seemed that the frenzy might assume the proportions of a riot, but the police, after a struggle, gained control.

And, while the American had fulfilled popular expectations and the most venturesome predictions of critics by his short and spectacular triumph, the challenger received an ovation in defeat for the fight that marked him among the most courageous battlers who ever sought the world's title.

Dempsey won because he was the "Dempsey of Toledo," the smashing, mauling, relentless assailant, who battered Jess Willard into submission four years ago and ascended the heavyweight throne. Firpo proved himself a dangerous challenger, despite the briefness of his stand against the champion, but his inexperience, the lack of an all-around fighting equipment to reinforce his powerful right, caused his downfall in the face of Dempsey's superior speed and generalship.

The outcome proved that sheer strength and hitting power alone, plus a courageous heart, could not survive against experienced skill, swiftness of foot and equally as formidable punching prowess.

Dempsey had to call on his all to survive that withering comeback of Firpo's in the first round after the Argentine had been floored five times. But the fact that he had the reserve, the stamina and courage to weather that sudden and terrific storm and emerge triumphant demonstrated conclusively that he is the present-day "Champion of Champions," and in the belief of those who saw him tonight, one of the greatest of all time.

Dempsey's victory answered the riddle of his battle with Tommy Gibbons at Shelby, Mont., last July. It proved that the champion had not lost his punch, that Gibbons lasted the limit simply because he waged a defensive fight, intent upon staying the limit, and that against a foe ready to struggle toe to toe, Dempsey can give and take the mightiest punches and in the end win.

## BANDIT ROBS FILLING STATION MAN OF CASH

E. Murrin, employee of an oil station at Sixth and Alameda streets was robbed of approximately $70 last night by an unmasked bandit who walked into Murrin's station, covered him with a gun and ordered him to put all the money he had into a canvas sack he handed to Murrin. The bandit walked across the street and drove away in a light automobile, accompanied by two other

# JOHNSTON AFTER TILDEN'S TITLE

[P. & A. Photo]

**Little Bill Tries It Again**

California's favorite son, as far as tennis goes, gets another chance to crown Big Bill Tilden of Philadelphia today in the finals for the national tennis title. Little Bill has a hundred rooters, where Big Bill has one, but if Johnston doesn't succeed in winning this time the folks are going to think that is can't be done.

## DOCTORS FAVORED DEMPSEY

### *Examining Physicians Predicted Firpo's Knockout at Hands of Jack Within Four Rounds*

[EXCLUSIVE DISPATCH]

NEW YORK, Sept. 14.—That Luis Angel Firpo would not last more than two or three rounds against Jack Dempsey was the verdict of four reputable physicians who examined the Argentine at the office of the boxing commission this afternoon several hours before the battle. Although the physicians did not come out in the open with their declaration, they individually voiced an opinion when asked to do so by the reporters. Close examination of Luis revealed to the students of physical culture that Firpo was far from being in the same physical condition as his opponent, who was pronounced by Dr. Walker, head of the board of physicians, and William Muldoon, chairman of the boxing commission, as being the finest specimen they ever had seen.

"How does he look?" several reporters asked Dr. Walker as soon as he and his colleagues had completed their tests with the Argentinian.

"Well," replied the brother of State Senator Jimmy Walker, "I don't like to make any statement. You boys should know from the figures I've just given you how he compares with Dempsey."

"Does that mean that Firpo is not in proper condition?" was fired back at the doctor.

"I wouldn't say that. But if you insist I'll say that he lacks the essentials which make for a perfect or even a near perfect

(Continued on Twelfth Page)

## FACES CHAMP IN FINAL ROUND OF PLAY TODAY

### *National Singles Championship to be Prize When Two Bills Meet for Thirteenth Time*

BY WILLIAM T. TILDEN II
World's Tennis Champion, 1920-21
[EXCLUSIVE DISPATCH]

PHILADELPHIA, Sept. 14.—The battle of Bills, big and little, will continue tomorrow in the final round of the lawn tennis championship of the United States, for little Bill Johnston defeated Francis T. Hunter, 6-4, 6-2, 7-5, and I eliminated B. I. C. Norton of England, 6-3, 7-5, 6-2, in the semifinals at Germantown Cricket Club today

Johnston was too sound and too severe for Hunter. The New Rochelle star fought gamely and gallantly against the all-around strength of the Californian's game, but he could not quite match the little world champion in speed and steadiness. Johnston centered his attack on Hunter's backhand, pounding his terrific drive down into the left corner and following into the net behind it. Hunter was forced to defend the ball, seldom having a chance to use his own booming forehand wallop. Johnston held the advantage from the opening, although Hunter missed a great chance when he was 15-40 and 5-4 on Johnston's service with two chances to bring the score to 5-all. Johnston, however, pulled out of the hole and won the set, 6-4.

**HUNTER FALTERS**

The second set was all Johnston. He broke Hunter's defense completely and routed the New Yorker, winning decisively. The third set, found Hunter waging a desperate fight, with his backhand weakening under the terrible pounding of the Californian. Johnston ran to 5-3, but Hunter, with his back to the wall, bravely lifted his game to tie the score at 5-all. He was rushing the net with the same daring which had won for him against Richards. However, Johnston had the ground game which Richards lacked to hold Hunter and in a burst of glorious driving the world's champion broke through and took the next two games and the match, 6-4, 6-2, 7-5.

Brian I. C. Norton played a heady and aggressive game against me in the other semifinal match, but his wildness in the pinches gave me an edge in every set that allowed me to run out the match three in a row. The glaring weakness of Norton's deep backhand was very apparent under the torrent of deep drives which I directed on his left corner.

The little English star made many marvelous shots, sensational recoveries and brilliant rallies but he could not meet the pace and was forced to bow in three sets, 6-3, 7-5, 6-2.

**OLD RIVALS**

Tomorrow will be the thirteenth sanctioned meeting of Little Bill Johnson and me. At the moment we stand even at six matches each. Not only are we tied in matches but even in sets, each of us have won twenty-four. It is hard to find any pair of players so evenly matched over a period of years and anyone who dares to prophecy the result of tomorrow's meeting is indeed a person of discernment. It seems fitting that either one or the other of us should have the honor of placing his name on the new championship cup which comes into competition this year, for it is almost beyond the realm of possibility that either of us could win it outright, yet the ultimate victor may value that name as I do those of William A. Larned and Maurice E. McLoughlin which adorn the trophy I won last year. Surely time must lay Little Bill and me in the discard soon, maybe this year, and I know who ever wins tomorrow will be proud to have his name handed down on the new trophy. Little Bill looked very good at times today and I know his wonderful ability to rise to his best when the great test is at hand. I look to see a long and bitter battle tomorrow. I have never been in better condition mentally and physically and if he beats me, as he may well do, it is because he is a better player. I know should victory be mine no one will be heartier in his congratulations or more sincere than Little Bill. That is why I face the match with pleasure no matter what the outcome.

"Linesman ready?

"Players ready?"

"Final round national singles championship of the United States William M. Johnston vs. W. T. Tilden, II. play!"

## BLIND BARITONE IS SEEN IN NEW ROLE

Earl Houk, the blind Elk and well-known baritone, said to be the only sightless man in the world who can follow a baseball game by sound, has blossomed into the field of canned music.

Yesterday he for the first time sat spellbound under the sound of his own voice, and it is even said that he applauded himself. Earl recently sang a couple of records for the phonograph, and they came out yesterday. They are "Here's to Our Absent Brother" and "Vacant Chair," both Elk melodies, as may be guessed from the title.

## *HACKLEY IS VICTOR AT HOLLY*

### *Easily Disposes of Kid Koster in the Main Event; Eddie Roberts Wins*

Jimmy Hackley easily won the main event from Kid Koster last night at the Hollywood Stadium. The clash was rather disappointing as Koster would not fight and took every opportunity that offered itself to close in and hang on. Hackley was willing enough, but it requires two to make a fight. Hackley had every round.

The semi-windup went to Eddie Roberts, who easily disposed of Terry Adams. In the first round Roberts shot a straight left to the jaw, toppling Adams over for the count of nine. In the fourth round Adams was knocked down again, taking the count of seven. The third round was even. In the special event Jack Lewis and Joe Medina put up a fast draw.

Dan Tobey through his own solicitation was the recipient of an avalanche of straw cadies which were hurled into the ring from all sides. It required but a short time for several of the ring attendants to reduce this mess to a crumpled bunch by the stamping route.

Al Jennings made an eloquent appeal for the victims of the Japanese earthquake which the crowd responded to with a nice donation.

Sailor Foster and Rolly Edwards put up a fast draw. Billy Harold received a very unpopular decision over Kid Louie. The crowd voiced its disapproval by giving Louie a great hand as he left the ring. Paul Wilkins proved a set-up for Sammy Santos. Santos won by a technical knockout in the first round. Frankie Dolan was too clever for Art Springer, giving him a good lesson in boxing.

## *Middleweights Box at Lyceum Club Tonight*

Jack Powell, a new middleweight sensation will trade blows tonight with Red Williams of Oakland in the main event at the Lyceum A.C. Williams has been having things his own way the past few months with the boys in his division but tonight he will take on an opponent that will stand toe-toe with him. The semi-wind-up will bring together Sailor Tommy Reyes, U.S.S. Nevada, and Benny Diaz, hero of last week's show. It is expected that this battle will loom up with the main event for both are of the slashing type, and love to mix from the start of the gong. A classy special event will have Ted Frenchie swapping punches with Sailor Young Bruno, U.S.S. Nevada, considered to be one of the best in his division in the Pacific Fleet. Other bouts follow: Harley Hite vs. Sailor Lane, 145 pounds; Roy Hillard vs. Young Manila, 114 pounds, and Kid Payo vs. Young Siki in the curtain raiser.

## MUSHY CALLAGHAN IS AFTER MORE SCALPS

Mushy Callaghan, newsboy featherweight champ, wants action at Vernon or Hollywood. Callaghan has been going great and in his last bout scored a knockout over Frankie Herman at Vernon. Manager Carlo Curtis of the newsboys' gym is trying to land Mushy a bout.

**BOXERS IN A DRAW**

[BY A. P. NIGHT WIRE.]

OKLAHOMA CITY, Sept. 14.—Tommy Loughran, Philadelphia light-heavyweight, and Jimmy Delaney of St. Paul, were awarded a draw by the referee at the end of twelve rounds of slow boxing here tonight.

Art instruction is practically unknown in schools of Turkey, but it is expected that water-color painting will be taken up in the near future.

*Still Bosses the World*

Jack Dempsey, Heavyweight Champion

## JACK DEMPSEY SAYS

[BY A. P. NIGHT WIRE]

RINGSIDE, POLO GROUNDS (New York) Sept. 14.—Jack Dempsey admitted tonight after his victory with Luis Angel Firpo that he never had received such a socking in his life.

"I won as I thought I would," said Jack, "but I can truthfully say that I never had such a fight in all my life. When he socked me on the chin in the first round, knocking me through the ropes after I had knocked him down, I thought my finish had come.

"Those who told me that Firpo would be a soft mark certainly were talking through their hats. After he slammed me with that first right, I knew that I had a fight on my hands. Firpo is dangerous every second. I hit him with everything I had and certainly was surprised when he continued to crawl off the floor.

"He is game and the hardest puncher I ever faced. It was the first time I was knocked down since I became champion, and I'll never forget it. I saw 8,000,000 stars when I got that punch on the chin that knocked me out of the ring."

## LUIS ANGEL FIRPO SAYS

[EXCLUSIVE DISPATCH]

NEW YORK, Sept. 14.—Luis Firpo: "Dempsey is a real champion and deserved his victory. I had him dizzy in the first round and if he is a gentleman he will admit it. I would have preferred to wait a year before meeting him and took the bout against my better judgment. Had I waited a year, I believe there would have been a different result. The referee told us in his instructions in case of a knockdown to go to a neutral corner and remain there until the other man regained his feet. Dempsey did not do this, but stood over me on several occasions. For this I blame only the referee. I am not hurt and I do not know what I shall do in the immediate future."

## JACK KEARNS SAYS

[EXCLUSIVE DISPATCH]

NEW YORK, Sept. 14.—Jack Kearns made the following statement: "The bout ended just as I thought, but Firpo also was stronger than I had expected. When Dempsey came to his corner at the end of the first round, he said, 'Gee, Jack, he hit me a couple of pipps,' but he said it with a smile and then I knew he was all right. Jack was dazed in the first round, but what fighter wouldn't be dazed after he was knocked backward through the ropes? Dempsey came through all right and he's still the best heavyweight in the world."

## HORATIO LAVELLE SAYS

[EXCLUSIVE DISPATCH]

NEW YORK, Sept. 14.—Horatio Lavelle said: "We are disappointed, of course, for those of us who were close to him felt that Firpo would knock Dempsey out, but we think that Firpo showed himself a brave man and also a great fighter. After the first round all of us who were with Firpo in his corner thought that he would win, but Dempsey showed wonderful courage and his showing in the second round was wonderful."

## ARGENTINA GROANS AT FIRPO'S DEFEAT

[BY CABLE AND ASSOCIATED PRESS.]

BUENOS AIRES, Sept. 14.—The defeat of Luis Angel Firpo by Jack Dempsey was a stunning disappointment to the tens of thousands of people who thronged the streets of Buenos Aires tonight hopeful of receiving the news that the Argentine fighter had won for his country the championship of the world.

When it became known that Firpo had lost, groans were to be heard among the crowds in front of the bulletin boards and some of the people wept.

Public schools were established in Egypt by the government thirty years ago.

## TAYLOR AND BOWEN COP BOWLERS' TITLE

Following the tenth round of the bowling doubles championship tournament for the B. H. Dyas Company gold medals, held this week at the Angelus Academy alleys, Cy Taylor and Johnny Bowen practically cinched the title. Ernie Shay and Turner came from nowhere and are in second place. Blume and Bennett are third, Phelps and Mitchell fourth and Lustig and Groshong fifth.

An opening doubles sweepstakes tournament will be held at the Anbelus Academy tomorrow night, while on Monday evening a special doubles match between Mrs. Meador and Mrs. Scott and Mrs. Taylor and Mrs. Cruthers will be held.

## RETURN BOUT PROBABLE

[BY A. P. NIGHT WIRE]

RINGSIDE, POLO GROUNDS (New York) Sept. 14.—Tex Rickard, who promoted the Dempsey-Firpo bout tonight, announced at the close of the drama that he was ready to stage another bout between the champion and his Argentine challenger next summer, and a bout between Firpo and Harry Wills, American negro.

# Red Grange Scores Victory for Illinois Over Michigan, 39 to 14, Almost Single-Handed

## RUNS WILD IN BIG TEN GAME

### *Scores Five Touchdowns With Sensational Runs*

### *Yost's Proteges Demoralized in Opening Quarter*

### *But Play Real Football in Remaining Periods*

[EXCLUSIVE DISPATCH]

URBANA (Ill.) Oct. 18.—Michigan never knew Harold "Red" Grange, the Illini wild cat until today. They don't know him yet, for they could not find him. But the Ann Arbor boys know of him—from the score board. The great halfback of Bob Zupke's football team simply ran all over the Michigan players in the first quarter of their grid battle here today at the new Illinois stadium and crushed the proteges of "Hurry Up" Yost before they even realized they were in a contest. The final score was 39 to 14 in favor of Illinois, but it was 27 to 0 at the end of the first period when Grange raced down the field four times for touchdowns.

Grange had torn Michigan to pieces before the game had gone more than fifteen seconds because he received the first kick off from Capt. Steger of the Wolverines and from his own 5-yard line, ran and dodged and tore his way ninety-five yards for a touchdown. Right then and there Michigan knew it was up against something it hadn't seen in football before.

WHEATON LAD LOOSE

Three more times in that first quarter Grange got loose for long runs for touchdowns. His second one came after about five minutes of play and was sixty-seven yards in length. The joyful Illini rooters were hardly through cheering that thrilling play before the red-headed Wheaton lad got loose again for another, 56 yards in length, and before the quarter was ended he took the ball on the Michigan 44-yard line and dashed through the whole team for a fourth touchdown.

In that first period he made four as sensational open-field runs as have been seen in years.

It is doubtful if anything near its equal has been seen in the West since the days of Walter Eckersall. Going into the game Michigan was figured to have an equal chance to win. The four startling runs in the first quarter by young Grange made Illinois a 100-to-1 shot. He carried the ball for a total of 262 yards on those four plays and Michigan was a crushed and beaten foe.

The second quarter had hardly begun when Coach Zupke called his star from the game to save him for other foes to come later in the season though he was back in the fray for the entire second half but content to make one touchdown, the final run for it being only eleven yards. He did a lot of plunging and passing in the second half but never again got loose for a long and thrilling dash.

GAME WARRIORS

Michigan must be given credit for gameness. After the horrible experience of the first quarter, the Yost men recovered their senses and their famous Michigan spirit and fought as no Michigan team ever has fought in the past. They were fighting a hopeless battle but they fought with admirable spirit and gameness and for the last three quarters of the game more than played Illinois to a standstill, Illinois making only twelve points after the first quarter while Michigan gathered fourteen.

## GRANGE SETS A FEW RECORDS

[BY A. P. NIGHT WIRE]

ILLINOIS STADIUM, URBANA (Ill.) Oct. 18.—This is the record of Harold (Red) Grange sensational 22-year-old Illinois halfback, perhaps the outstanding gridiron star of America last season, in today's Michigan-Illinois game:

Scored five touchdowns—four in less than twelve minutes of play.

Broke away for successive runs of 90, 65, 55 and 45 yards for touchdowns.

Scooped up the ball on the very first kick-off and raced 90 yards, dodging through Michigan's tacklers for a touchdown.

Carried the ball in twenty-one plays and gained the astonishing distance of 402 yards.

## BRONCHOS WIN FROM TIGERS

(Continued from First Page)

and Mishkin had been taken out exhausted, and Johnson, playing left end for Oxy, let Babcock get around him, Smith missed a tackle, and the fleet Santa Clara back oozed over the line for a score wrapped in the enthusiastic embrace of Bud Teachout, who had overtaken Babcock just in time to convince him that making touchdowns on the Occidental team isn't the most pleasant job in the world. An attempt to convert via the drop-kick roue was gummed up.

The game ended ten seconds after the succeeding kick-off.

Although the entire Occidental team looked like a million dollars until the final quarter, Renius at center and Godett at end were the outstanding individuals, their vicious tackling stopping the Bronchos' attempts to make years with excellent results. McHann, Stevens Capt. Ridderhoff, Wheeler and Ebers also sparkled in behalf of Oxy, while Mishkin showed excellent judgment in selecting his plays, and ran back Casanova's punts for sizable gains on several occasions.

ENDS TOUGH

McKee, who played safety for Santa Clara most of the time, seldom had an opportunity to run back any of Ridderhoff's tall punts, as the Oxy ends smeared him in his tracks time after time. Although Ridderhoff outbooted Casanova as far as bona fide kicking is concerned, the latter got off several low-bounding boots which gained a lot of valuable distance for the Bronchos.

Oxy made eight first downs to seven for Santa Clara, the visiting team moving the sticks six times in the last quarter.

The line-ups:

| Santa Clara (12.) | | Occidental (0.) |
|---|---|---|
| Malley | L.E.R. | Hazeltine |
| Leonard | L.T.R. | Conde |
| Nolan | L.G.R. | McHann |
| Boeckstadt | C. | Renius |
| Duff | R.G.L. | Westgate |
| Gallagher | R.T.L. | Stevens |
| Toso | R.E.L. | Godett |
| McKee | Q. | Mishkin |
| Casanova | L.H.R. | Wheeler |
| Bundy | R.H.L. | Ebers |
| Fawke (C.) | F.B. | Ridderhoff (C.) |

Substitutions—For Santa Clara, Nock for Nolan, Rianda for Casanova, Babcock for Bundy, Bedolla for McKee, Sumner for Leonard, Barrelout for Malley, Schultz for Fawke, Hulsman for Schultz; for Occidental Porter for Ebers, McDonald for Westgate, Teachout for Hazeltine, Gregory for Mishkin, Hitch for Stevens, Betts for McDonald, Buxton for Ridderhoff, Johnson for Godett, Mishkin for Gregory, Smith for Mishkin.

Touchdowns, Bundy, Babcock.

SCORE BY QUARTERS

| | | | | |
|---|---|---|---|---|
| Santa Clara | 0 | 0 | 0 | 12—12 |
| Occidental | 0 | 0 | 0 | 0—0 |

Officials—Dick Rutherford, referee; Gillette, umpire; Wells, head linesman; Ritchie, field judge.

## LENGTHY PASS DECIDES GAME

### *U.S.S. California Wins Over Mississippi, 13 to 9*

### *Ballinger's 45-Yard Heave to Nidds Wins Scrap*

### *Mississippi Lead is Wiped But by Great Play*

[EXCLUSIVE DISPATCH]

TRONA FIELD, LOS ANGELES HARBOR, Oct. 18.—With two minutes to play and his team in a bad hole, Ensign Herb Ballinger, substitute quarter of the U.S.S. California eleven, took a short pass from Tiny Walker and then shot the ball forty-five yards over the entire U.S.S. Mississippi team to Joe Nidds, who was waiting on the goal line. Ballinger kicked goal a moment later and gave the California a 13-to-9 victory.

Today's affair was the first game of United States battle fleet championship series for both squads and in the first two quarters this fact was very noticeable. Neither ship was able to get the ball within striking distance of the goal despite plentiful fumbles and badly executed passing attempts. The California during the game attempted sixteen passes of which thirteen fell short. The Mississippi attempted six and completed five.

BOTH SCORE

In the third quarter, however, the boys all started off in mid-season form, the first spectacular score being a field goal from the 30-yard line by Dooley, the Mississippi's fullback. A few minutes later, though, California kicked out of danger, the Mississippi's safety man-fumbled and Taylor, left end, recovered and carried the ball thirty yards down the field for a touchdown.

But the Mississippi immediately uncorked a rapid series of passes interspersed with a thirty-five-yard run through a broken field by Lawrence. A short pass put the ball under the shadow of the goal posts and Dooley went over.

The Mississippi 9-to-6 lead looked good as the game drew to a close with the ball in the middle of the field. Ballinger dropped back on the next formation to receive a short job from Walker and then heaved the ball forty-five yards in a perfect pass to Nidds, who put the ball over the line without leaving his tracks. Ballinger kicked goal. In the remaining minute of play California had the ball on the one-foot line at the final whistle.

FORMER NAVY STAR

Herb Ballinger, by the way, is the Los Angeles Harbor boy who went in as substitute half in last year's Navy-Princeton game, which he won for the Navy with a goal from midfield.

Duforth, who started at full for the California, showed plenty of ability and Dooley and Brown vied for the honors on the Mississippi eleven. The Mississippi has an extraordinary line and with their offense polished up should give the Idaho a hard fight for fleet title.

Today on the same field the U.S.S. Colorado and Maryland teams will scramble in their first meeting of the year. The line-ups:

| U.S.S. Mississippi (9) | | U.S.S. California (13) |
|---|---|---|
| Lawrence | L.E.R. | Nidds |
| Ma. Eachran | L.T.R. | Dunn |
| Norton | L.G.R. | Youngblood |
| Ellis | C. | Ward |
| Lee | R.G.L. | Hanson |
| Ragsdale | R.T.L. | Linnett |
| Van Rel | R.E.L. | Sybersky, Taylor |
| Armstrong | Q. | Matthews, Ballinger |
| Brown | L.H.R. | Bliss |
| Dooley | R.H.L. | Walker |
| Furlough | F. | Duforth, Newhall |

SCORE BY QUARTERS

| | | | | |
|---|---|---|---|---|
| U.S.S. California | 0 | 0 | 7 | 6—13 |
| U.S.S. Mississippi | 0 | 0 | 9 | 0—9 |

SUMMARY

Touchdowns—Taylor, Dooley Nidds. Goal from touchdown—Ballinger. Field goal—Dooley. Completed passes—U.S.S. California, 3; U.S.S. Mississippi, 5. Officials Referee, Ensign Hughes, U.S.S. Pennsylvania; umpire, Lieut. Fitz, U.S.S. Pennsylvania; head linesman, Ensign Hoffman, U.S.S. Pennsylvania; field judge, Ensign Cameron, U.S.S. Pennsylvania.

Emergency transportation needs following the earthquake in Japan caused a boom in motorcycle sales, 2060 being imported in six months this year.

## OBSERVATIONS
### By the INNOCENT BYSTANDER, BILL HENRY

Football is certainly a grand old pastime, not only to gaze upon and argue about and play but likewise as a contributor to the health and wealth of the community by giving the contractors something to do in the matter of building stadiums. Of course there's our own Coliseum, the biggest in the world, with its seating capacity of nearly 90,000. Through the fact that U.S.C. largely monopolizes its use, and properly do, because the Trojans are our leading institution in an athletic way, a lot of people believe that it is the property of the local university.

Such is not the case, however. The Coliseum is public property and belongs jointly to the city and county, which makes it quite different from the averaged stadium in itself. Our Coliseum, therefore, was not designed solely for football but as a sort of outdoor civic auditorium with athletic events only to form a part of its usefulness. Band concerts, great public speeches and other community activities are to take place inside its massive concrete walls.

• • •

The University of Illinois yesterday celebrated the opening and dedication of its massive new stadium, the occasion being the Michigan-Illinois football game. This stadium is the newest and certainly one of the most magnificent of its kind in the world. It cost $2,000,000 and seats 65,000 people. All are seated at the side of the field, there being a huge double-decked stand on either side. A third similar stand, to be erected at one end of the field, will raise the capacity to about 85,000.

All visible portions of the stands are decorated in faced brick and carved limestone and along the upper level of both sides are great collonades of stone columns dedicated to the Illinois dead in the World War. The space underneath the seats is divided into rooms for athletic purposes, including two rooms forty feet high, sixty feet wide and 200 feet long, each large enough to accommodate five simultaneous basketball games.

• • •

Excitement over intercollegiate football, which has manifested itself chiefly in the building of stadiums, is even more manifest out here in connection with traveling over long distances to see games. We think nothing out here of traveling 500 miles to see our football teams play, and if we don't go by train, we go by boat or use the family flivver as a means of transportation.

Paul Davis of Stanford was down here a few days ago with the news that Stanford will have six special trains coming south for the game with U.S.C. at the Coliseum on November 8. In addition there will be a mob on the Harvard and dozens of automobiles. Stanford students and alumni have just about completed arrangements to charter the entire Biltmore Hotel, or as much of it as they can get for the day of the game.

• • •

U.S.C.'s preparations for invading the lair of the Golden Bear at Berkeley on November 1 are equally stupendous. Out at Trojandom they fully expect to have 3000 rooters at Berkeley, all of whom will make the trip in the hope and expectation that the Bears will meet their first defeat in four years at the hands of the local eleven.

The Southern Pacific will run a flock of special trains to Berkeley and it is also expected that the Yale or Harvard will be chartered. Most of Pomona College walked out a week ago to make the trip to Berkeley and thereby caused terrific mental anguish among the faculty members. There is nobody who will go to the limit for something he likes, like the college student who likes football.

## LOYOLA IS BEATEN BY LA VERNE

### *Brethren Take Lions Into Camp by Walking Off With 15-to-0 Game*

Uncorking a host of trick plays, combined with the brilliant passing combination of the Brook Brothers, the classy La Verne College grid warriors took the Loyola College down a peg by registering a 15-to-0 victory over the Lions on the Loyola turf, yesterday afternoon.

In the first quarter the Brethren worked their way down deep into the bewildered Lion's territory, losing the ball on Loyolas' 3-yard line. Hoffman fumbled and recovered the ball behind the line where he was downed for a safety.

Lowry was injected at quarter and the Lions regained their pep. Lowry and "Big Chief" Brown, Loyola half, by their stellar line plunging placed the ball on La Verne's 10-yard line, but lacked the punch to put it over. At this period of the game Loyola suffered its worst jolt, by the injury of Brown, who was the Lion's most consistent yard gainer.

During the second quarter Loyola continually threatened the visitors' goal line, at one time taking the ball to their 1-yard line, but for some reason or other couldn't score.

At the beginning of the last period, Betts of La Verne recovered a fumble and took it over for the first touchdown of the game. Brooks booted it over for the extra point, making the score 9 to 0.

Early in the last quarter La Verne completed its final touchdown by a thirty-yard pass from Brook to Glick. After this Loyola made a desperate rally tossing a flock of completed passes, but to no avail.

La Verne received what breaks there were, completing only seven first downs to Loyola's ten.

| Loyola College. | | La Verne College. |
|---|---|---|
| Brown | L.E.R. | Lehmer |
| Krack | L.T.R. | Root |
| Deasy & Sherwood | L.G.R. | Brubaker |
| | C. | Dickey |
| Donohue | R.G.L. | Martens |
| Furlong | R.T.L. | Marshburn |
| O'Hara | R.E.L. | Betts |
| Hoffman | Q. | O. Brooks |
| Tunney | L.H.R. | Welch |
| N. Brown | R.H.L. | Glick |
| Hoeffer | F. | J. Brooks |

Substitutions—Loyola, Haddock, Lowry, Duffey, McIsaacs, Murrin, Mannion; La Verne, Hoff, Hartman, Boets.

Touchdowns—Betts, Glick.

Goals after touchdown—Brooks.

SCORE BY QUARTERS

| Team— | 1 | 2 | 3 | 4 | Ttl. |
|---|---|---|---|---|---|
| La Verne | 2 | 0 | 6 | 7 | 15 |
| Loyola | 0 | 0 | 0 | 0 | 0 |

Referee, Brennan; umpire, Evans; head linesman, Mahoney.

## MISSOURI BARELY NOSES OUT AMES

[BY A. P. NIGHT WIRE]

AMES (Iowa) Oct. 18.—After fighting evenly without scoring for three and one-half quarters, the University of Missouri football team defeated Iowa State College here today, 7 to 0, when a forward pass, Whiteman to O'Sullivan, was good for eighteen yards and a touchdown. Walsh added the extra point by kicking goal.

New York City will have two players in the national pocket billiard race.

## QUAKERS BEAT GRIZZLY TEAM

### *Score of Fiercely Fought Game is 6 to 0*

### *Jimmy Cline's Men Give Poets Terrific Battle*

### *Stratton Scores Lone Marker for Perry's Club*

[EXCLUSIVE DISPATCH]

WHITTIER, Oct. 18.—Whittier College barely nosed out a win here today over Jimmy Cline's fighting eleven from the Southern Branch by a 6-0 margin. The Poets were forced to fight with their backs to the wall for three quarters, defending their goal line from the vicious smashes of Peake and Timmons and three times the Grizzlies advanced the ball to kicking distance but Turney failed to convert the attempt.

The break that beat the Bruins occurred in the last quarter when Parisi allowed a bounding punt to roll out of his hands and cross the goal line where Stratton, Quaker tackle, curled around it. Hastings blocked the kick on the Poets' try for the extra point. The Whittier team had failed to make a first down up to this point but forthwith proceeded to rip the Grizzly line to shreds, Pendleton and Ferguson leading the attack. Pendleton furnished the fans a thrill by dashing through tackle for 50 yards to the Bear goal line but was called back on an offside play. Ray Johns also performed brilliantly for the Quakers.

Peake, Bishop, Hastings, Timmons and Cashon did the heavy work for the losers but the pace was too hot and the entire Cub team crumbled in the last ten minutes, the whistle saving them from another score. The Branch made five first downs to four for Whittier and completed three passes out of eleven attempts while the Poets were unsuccessful in four attempts at the aerial route.

The line-ups:

| Whittier College (6.) | | Southern Branch (0.) |
|---|---|---|
| Johns | R.E.L. | Cashon |
| Rothsearmel | R.T.L. | Bishop |
| Morris | R.G.L. | Jarvis |
| Word | C. | Hastings |
| A. Behnke | L.G.R. | Hollingsworth |
| H. Behnke | L.T.R. | Gardner |
| A. Clark | L.E.R. | Breese |
| Weightman | Q. | Timmons |
| Denny | R.H.L. | Jackson |
| Ferguson | L.H.R. | Turney |
| Red Clark | F. | Peake |

Substitutions—For Whittier, Ashton for A. Clark, Pendleton for Denny, Latson for A. Behnke, A. Clark for Weightman, Stratton for H. Behnke, A. Behnke for Latson, Compton for A. Clark, Robinson for Morris, M. Johnson for A. Behnke; for Southern Branch, Parisi for Timmons, Williams for Jarvis.

Touchdown—Stratton.

Officials—Peterson, referee; Jessen, umpire; Call, head linesman; Mallette, field judge.

SCORE BY QUARTERS

| Team— | 1 | 2 | 3 | 4 | Ttl. |
|---|---|---|---|---|---|
| Whittier College | 0 | 0 | 0 | 6 | 6 |
| Southern Branch U. C. | 0 | 0 | 0 | 0 | 0 |

## POMONA ELEVEN WINS OVER CALTECH TEAM

Smashing over for the only touchdown of the game in the third quarter, the Pomona College team defeated Caltech, 7 to 0, at Claremont yesterday afternoon. McCully made the score and Capt. Clarke added the extra point. Caltech came back strong and made five first downs to Pomona's one in the fourth period, but was unable to count.

## OXY FROSH-TOILERS TIE

The Occidental Freshman football team and Manual Arts High's tanbark artists played two quarters of peppy football and ended in a 13-to-13 tie at the Coliseum yesterday. Both teams showed strong offensives, but were weak on the defense. Plenty of first downs were made on both sides. Long runs and many completed passes made the game interesting but not particularly hard fought.

The frosh scored first when a long pass to Ross made nearly thirty yards to Manual's 20-yard line. The frosh took the ball around the ends, threw a few passes, scoring on four downs. Manual practically duplicated the performance three minutes later, and taking advantage of a fumbled punt, took the ball on the frosh 20-yard line and made yards once for the touchdown. The quarter ended with the ball in the Tiger babes' possession of their own 45-yard line.

In the second period, Manual held for downs and the frosh punted. After the run-back, Manual took the ball to the 40 yard mark, and there fumbled. Ross recovered for Occidental. A long pass gained twenty yards. Two end runs put the ball on the 5-yard line, and two bucks put it over. The Artisans staged a parade when they got the ball. The Occidental kick-off went to Howe on the 10-yard line. The Toiler half went twenty yards before being downed. Then, Manual made five first downs, around the ends and over the tackles and went right down the field for seventy yards, never losing the ball, to a touchdown. The half ended a moment later.

## *San Diego Wins Over Fullerton With Much Ease*

[EXCLUSIVE DISPATCH]

SAN DIEGO, Oct. 18.—Fullerton High led the San Diego High School at the end of the first quarter in a game played here today, 7 to 6, but that was only the signal for the San Diegans to start working and at the end of the game the score read San Diego, 33; Fullerton, 7. Four of the touchdowns made by the locals were by fine bucks and the other was made when L. Peterson intercepted a pass and ran sixty yards for a touchdown.

Yesterday's game was the first for San Diego in the Coast prep league. It was an auspicious start for the locals and the outlook for the future is more heartening than previously figured. Ritchey made three of the San Diego touchdowns on line bucks and Reed crashed the line for another. Peterson's tally was the final of the game.

## SOLONS WAKE UP AND ANNEX COUPLE

[BY A. P. NIGHT WIRE]

SACRAMENTO, Oct. 18.—The Senators shoved a pair of rookies on the hill today and managed to come through with a twin win over the Bees 7 to 3, and 7 to 6. The second game was called at the end of the eighth inning because of darkness. The scores:

First game

SALT LAKE AB R H O A — SACRAMENTO AB R H O A

[illegible]

SCORE BY INNINGS

[illegible]

SUMMARY

[illegible]

Second game

SALT LAKE AB R H O A — SACRAMENTO AB R H O A

[illegible]

SCORE BY INNINGS

[illegible]

(Called end 8th inning darkness.)

SUMMARY

[illegible]

Cyril J. H. Tolley, British amateur golf champion of 1920, and captain of this year's British Walker Cup team, has decided to remain in America. He may make his headquarters in New York and is expected to play in late season exhibition matches. Tolley is the second British amateur golf champion to settle in the United States. [illegible] preceded him and is a figure in California circles.

## POMONA ELEVEN BEATS CALTECH

(Continued from First Page)

Caltech, and Bob Heilbron at tackle played bang-up football, while Neher at half, and McCully at full shone brightly for the Sagehens.

| Pomona (7) | | Caltech (0) |
|---|---|---|
| Worden | L.E.R. | Holme |
| Vernon | L.T.R. | Heilbron |
| Lang | L.G.R. | Larabee |
| Robles | C. | Nickell |
| Burger | R.G.L. | Moore |
| Barnham | R.T.L. | Seymour |
| Draper | R.E.L. | Brunner |
| Clark | Q. | Foster |
| Smith | L.H.R. | Stanton |
| Neher | R.H.L. | Johnson |
| McCully | F. | Alderman |

Substitutions—For Pomona—Leavitt for Lang, Tart for Burger, Merritt for Smith. For Caltech Jones for Holme, Kinsey for Larabee, Hill for Nickell.

Touchdown—McCully.

Goal after touchdown—Clark.

SCORE BY QUARTERS

| | 1 | 2 | 3 | 4 | Total |
|---|---|---|---|---|---|
| Pomona | 0 | 0 | 7 | 0 | 7 |
| Caltech | 0 | 0 | 0 | 0 | 0 |

Officials—Referee, Foley; umpire, Solomon; head linesman, Griffith; field judge, Kirkpatrick.

## Standings

PACIFIC COAST LEAGUE

| | W | L | Pct. | | W | L | Pct. |
|---|---|---|---|---|---|---|---|
| Seattle | 108 | 90 | .545 | Salt Lake | 101 | 96 | .508 |
| Los Angeles | 106 | 91 | .5380 | Vernon | 96 | 103 | .482 |
| S. Franc's | 107 | 92 | .5376 | Portland | 89 | 107 | .454 |
| Oakland | 102 | 98 | .510 | Sacramento | 88 | 112 | .431 |

Yesterday's Results

Los Angeles, 2-3; Vernon, 1-0.
Seattle, 6; Portland, 2.
San Francisco, 10-15; Oakland, 6-4.
Sacramento, 7-7; Salt Lake, 6-3.

How the Series Stand

Los Angeles, 4; Vernon, 1.
Seattle, 5; Portland, 0.
San Francisco, 4; Oakland, 1.
Sacramento, 3; Salt Lake, 2.

Games Today

Vernon at Los Angeles.
Oakland at San Francisco.
Seattle at Portland.
Salt Lake at Sacramento.

## EL CENTRO ELEVEN BEATS ACADEMY TEAM

[EXCLUSIVE DISPATCH]

SAN DIEGO, Oct. 18.—El Centro defeated the Army and Navy Academy 6 to 0 in a hard-fought game today. Allen of the El Centro eleven made two field goals in the fourth quarter, scoring the only points made during the game. Long runs by Hein and Sawyer featured for the El Centro team.

## UTAH TRAMPLES OVER ARIZONA

[BY A. P. NIGHT WIRE]

SALT LAKE CITY, Oct. 18.—University of Utah football eleven won from the University of Arizona here today 32 to 7. The weather was crisp and the field fast. The game was witnessed by a crowd of about 4000 football fans.

## DIXON DEFEATS WARREN

### *Only One Upset Marks Play in Opening Round of County Tennis Championship Tournament*

Only one notable upset marked the opening round of play in the annual Los Angeles county championship tennis tournament at the Los Angeles Tennis Club yesterday. It came when Victor Dixon outsteadied Eugene Warren, 7-5, 6-4. Harvey Snodgrass and Walter Wesbrook, who are expected to face each other in the finals of the men's singles, both drew defaults yesterday.

Play will continue today. Yesterday's results:

Dick Skeen defeated Joe Bixler, default.
J. De Lara defeated Walker, 6-0, 6-1.
J. Stepp Jr. defeated Ward Johnson, default.
Ted Easton defeated J. Barron, 6-1, 6-2.
John Thomas defeated D. Miller, 6-2, 6-2.
T. Barron defeated R. Malone, 6-2, 6-4.
L. A. White Jr. defeated Ben James, default.
A. Bennett defeated George Bergstrom, 6-2, 6-3.
Joe Phillips defeated D. Smith, 6-3, 6-4.
Issenhuth defeated Dodge D. Jenner, 6-4, 3-6, 6-3.
S. Katow defeated R. Laird, default.
Charles Wessner defeated Charles Bennett, default.
Sheldon defeated Stevens, 6-3, 6-2, 6-4.
Wesbrook defeated Francis Dean, default.
Mrs. Mullineaux defeated Mrs. Phillips, 6-8, 6-3, 6-4.
Mrs. Henry defeated Mrs. Robson, 6-1, 6-0.
Thomas and Bennett defeated Bergstrom and Barron, default.
Miller and Malone defeated Ted Easton and partner, default.
Walker and D. Jenner defeated White and partner, default.
Mrs. Sullivan defeated Miss D. Robinson, 6-1, 6-2.
Wessner defeated Marsh, 6-2, 5-7, 6-4.
Paul Greene defeated Bixler, default.
Miss Muriel James defeated Mrs. Mullineaux, 6-3, 6-1.
C. A. Barker defeated Sturdevant, 6-0, 6-1.
Master defeated Phillips, 7-5, 6-1.
V. Dixon defeated E. A. Warren, 7-5, 6-4.
Stindorf defeated Quisenberry, 6-1, 7-5.
Meyer defeated White, 3-6, 6-0, 6-2.
Snodgrass defeated Reynolds, default.
Wabraushek defeated Langdon, 6-2, 6-4.
R. H. F. Variel defeated B. Ingham, 6-0, 6-0.
Perry Jones defeated Ben Anderson, 6-1, 6-1.
Quisenberry and Nelson defeated Meyer and Marsh, 6-2, 6-4.
Robinson and White defeated Anderson and partner, default.
Master and W. Jones defeated Variel and Dr. Harvey, 6-3, 6-4.
C. A. Barker defeated Meyer, 6-4, 7-5.

Today's schedule of play:

9 A.M.

Court 1—Norval Craig vs. L. White.
Court 2—Ted Easton vs. Alan Evans.
Court 3—Dewitt Miller vs. James Barron.
Court 4—Tree Stephens vs. Joe Bixler.
Court 5—Alley vs. Rievorro.
Court 6—Charles Barrington vs. A. Bennett.
Court 7—Sue E. Dunlap vs. Helen Brooks.
Court 8—Bryant and Dirkmann vs. Gibson and Dohilia.
Court 9—Muriel James vs. Elizabeth Corr.
Court 10—Dudley Smith vs. George Bergstrom.

10 A.M.

Court 1—Ted Van Kits vs. Ray Nelson.
Court 2—Dorothy Robinson vs. Anne Feitt.
Court 3—Dick Skeen vs. Ted Easton.
Court 4—M. Cohen vs. J. Doeg.
Court 5—E. Bennett vs. Bill Palmer.
Court 6—Bill Doeg vs. R. Roberts.
Court 7—Phillips vs. Katow.
Court 8—Wilma Hays vs. Florence Marshall.

11 A.M.

Court 1—Ralph Stindorf vs. Bob Variel.
Court 2—Mrs. William Henry vs. Miss Muriel James.
Court 3—Winner Bryant and Dixon vs. Gibson and Dohilia vs. Barker and Stansbaugh.
Court 4—Miller and Malone vs. Walker and D. Jenner.
Court 5—Maryline Conroy vs. Louise Jones.
Court 7—John Stepp Jr. vs. J. De Lara.
Court 8—Frances Lee vs. O'Hara Parret.

12 NOON

Court 1—Mitchell vs. Jack Reed.
Court 2—Winner Van Kits vs. Nelson vs. Master.
Court 4—Easton and Doeg vs. Bennett and Bixler.
Court 5—Hastings and Harwood vs. Malone and Baumgarten.
Court 6—Stephens and Healy vs. Palmer and D. Smith.
Court 7—Bergstrom and Barron vs. Evans and Barrington.
Court 8—Evelyn Pettit vs. Katherine Wilson.

1 P.M.

Court 1—V. Green vs. Perry Jones.
Court 2—Mrs. Henry and Snodgrass vs. Mr. and Mrs. Phillips.
Court 3—Conrad Bryant vs. Wilson.
Court 4—Warren and Stindorf vs. Stepp and Stepp.
Court 6—Thomas vs. Ransom.
Court 7—Wessner and De Lara vs. Joe Bixler and partner.
Court 8—Doris Doeg vs. Anne Fenton.

2 P.M.

Court 1—Snodgrass vs. winner Alley vs. Rievorro.
Court 2—Wesbrook vs. Wabraushek.
Court 3—Winner Cohen vs. J. Doeg vs. R. Brady.
Court 4—Issenhuth vs. A. Bennett.

3 P.M.

Court 1—Snodgrass and Wesbrook vs. Rievorro and partner.
Court 2—Winner Warren and Stindorf vs. Stepp and Stepp vs. Robinson and White.
Court 3—P. Jones and Reed vs. Wilson and Mitchell.
Court 4—Wabraushek and partner vs. Curtis and Curtis.
Court 5—Issenhuth and Skeen vs. Thomas and Ransom.

4 P.M.

Court 1—Dixon and Greene vs. Master and W. Jones.
Court 2—Winner Snodgrass and Wesbrook vs. Rievorro and partner vs. Nelson and Quisenberry.
Court 3—Mrs. Sullivan and Perry Jones vs. Mr. and Mrs. Mullineaux.
Court 4—Craig and J. Doeg vs. E. Ransom and Phillips.

# McTigue Loses World Title to Berlenbach

SUNDAY MORNING, MAY 31, 1925.

# U.S.C. WINS PHILADELPHIA TRACKFEST

## PETER DE PAOLO COPS INDIANAPOLIS MOTOR CLASSIC

### LOCAL YOUTH SETS RECORD

*Bennett Hill Close Second in Hoosier Classic*

*Speedway Race Replete With Minor Spills*

*Racing Feature Witnessed by 145,000 Fans*

BY J. L. JENKINS
[EXCLUSIVE DISPATCH]

INDIANAPOLIS, May 30. Peter De Paolo, the youth who brought a pair of tiny shoes worn by his year-old baby and hooked them to the front springs of his cyclonic Duesenberg racing car, won the greatest speed contest in the annals of the sport today, and carried home a snug fortune estimated at $25,000 for his four hours and fifty-six minutes of supreme struggle.

Roaring into the lead from the starting tape, he set a pace above

Peter De Paolo.

104 miles an hour for the twenty-two cars entered in the race, and held it for lap after lap in the fastest 100 miles ever seen on the Hoosier oval. He was relieved but once during the long grind and drove consistently and hard for his victory.

Something of the speed attained may be imagined from the fact that all of the first four cars in the race exceed the average time made a year ago by the Joe Boyer-Corum winning combination.

**ALL RECORDS FELL**

Practically all of the speedway records fell in the alleged unlucky thirteenth revival. In the first place, De Paolo and Duray spattered all former speed records by qualifying their cars at 113 miles an hour earlier in the week. Then Uncle Sam turned loose the flood of race fans and hung up an estimated 145,000 attendance record for the big day before all of the twelve pilots that finished set new marks in each division of the race proper.

Next to De Paolo's drive, the performance of Harry Miller's new idea of automobile constructin—the front wheel drive—proved the most interesting feature. The new car, practically untried until today, not only stood up under the terrific strain for the whole distance, but also outran a score of the finest standard race cars ever produced. The new job made itself felt early in the race when Dave Lewis went out after the leaders and stayed in the front ranks until forced into the pits for fuel. He stayed at the wheel until he had reeled off 425 miles and then turned the car over to Bennie Hill, whose mount had broken up early in the game. Hill, always a hard driver, put scores of thrills into the last few laps by outfooting the leader in a desperate attempt to close up the two-and-one-half-mile handicap he was laboring under, and bringing the car in, but one minute behind the flying Italian.

**REPLETE WITH THRILLS**

The race this year was replete with minor spills and with wonderful repair and pit work. For the first time, tire manufacturers had refused to build the old standard, high-pressure race tire, and had equipped practically all of the cars entered with balloon type, or low air pressure doughnuts. When the first 100 miles had been covered the drivers found that they had misjudged some of the riding qualities of their equipment and many of them were forced in to readjust shock absorbers and change the air pressure. Contrary to the general

(Continued on Page 7, Column 4)

### HOW THEY FINISHED

| Place | Driver | Car | Time | M.P.H. |
|---|---|---|---|---|
| 1 | Peter De Paolo | Duesenberg | 4:56:39.47 | 101.13 |
| 2 | Bennie Hill | Junior 8 | 4:57:33.15 | 100.82 |
| 3 | Phil Shafer | Duesenberg | 5:59:26.79 | 100.18 |
| 4 | Harry Hartz | Miller | 5:03:21.59 | 98.89 |
| 5 | Tommy Milton | Miller | 5:08:25.71 | 97.21 |
| 6 | L. L. Corum | Miller | 5:09:31.11 | 96.91 |
| 7 | Ralph De Palma | Miller | 5:09:46.06 | 96.85 |
| 8 | Peter Kreis | Duesenberg | 5:11:26:86 | 96.32 |
| 9 | W. E. Shattuc | Miller | 5:13:20.48 | 95.74 |
| 10 | Pietro Bordino | Fiat | 5:16:37.97 | 94.75 |
| 11 | Fred Comer | Miller | 5:16:48.71 | 94.70 |
| 12 | Frank Elliot | Miller | 5:25:15.71 | 92.23 |

### SOME OF THE TROJAN TRACK HEROES

Here are five of the seven U.S.C. performers who gathered the points which brought the I.C.A.A.A.A. championship to Los Angeles for the first time in history. At the upper left is Leighton Dye, who won the high hurdles; at the upper right Alden Ross, who tied for fourth in the high jump. Kenneth Grumbles, who cinched victory for the Trojans by his win in the low hurdles, is in the center. Bottom, from left to right, are the great U.S.C. weight men—Norman Anderson, who placed third in both shot and discus, and Bud Houser, who captured the discus and grabbed second in the shotput.

### Stanford Wins Pacific Coast Track Honors

[BY A. P. NIGHT WIRE]

STADIUM, SEATTLE, May 30. The sunny southern State of the Pacific Coast triumphed East and West today. While the University of Southern California was taking the American intercollegiate track championship at Philadelphia, Leland Stanford University handily won the Pacific Coast Conference intercollegiate meet here with 63 1-2 points.

The other contenders placed as follows in distribution of the 165 points for the fifteen events.

University of Washington, 46 1-2; University of Montana, 15 1-2; Oregon Agricultural College, 15; University of Oregon, 13; Washington State College, 8.5; University of Idaho.

Eight conference records were broken and two of the new marks also broke records for all the colleges on the Pacific Coast.

Glenn Hartranft, Cardinal, who was on the American Olympic team last year, was accorded the premier honor of the day, breaking two of the records, one of which he had just set himself yesterday in the qualifications. In the discus and the shotput Hartranft took from Gus Pope, of Washington, crowns worn for four years. The figures of the meet left Washington Pacific Northwest Intercollegiate Conference champoint. Contestants pronounced natgiven above. Stanford does not belong to this conference. Whitman sent five men to compete for Northwest glory, but none took a point. Contestants pronounced natural conditions perfect. Rain threatened the preliminaries yesterday but today turned clear and moderately warm, with a breeze so light that it was counted of no effect.

Pacific all-college records broken were:

Broad jump—Proc Flannigan, Oregon, held it 23ft. 4½in., May 15, 1925, Seattle. Flannigan broke it 23ft. 5 8-10in.

Mile relay—Montana held it, 3:24, Missoula, May 23, 1925. Stanford broke it, 3:23.4.

Pacific Intercollegiate Coast Conference records broken were:

Shotput—Glenn Hartranft held it, 48ft. 7 3-8in., May 29, 1925, Seattle. Hartranft broke it, 50ft. 1 3-10in.

Mile run—Walkley, Oregon, held it, 4:28, 1921. Drummond Wilde, Washington, broke it, 4:24.5.

High hurdles—Wells, Stanford,

(Continued on Page 7, Column 2)

### WESTBROOK IN TENNIS TITLE PLAY

*Harold Godshall Also is Survivor to Enter the Finals Today*

SACRAMENTO, May 30.—California's leading tennis players will meet in the finals of the Central California championship tournament at the Sutter Lawn Tennis Club tomorrow, the stars having survived the semifinal rounds today. In the men's singles William M. Johnston of San Francisco, former world's champion, will meet Walter Westbrook of Los Angeles in the upper half and Harold Godshall, ranking player of Los Angeles, Elmer Griffin and Bud Chandler of the University of California will contest in the lower bracket.

Helen Wills, national women's champion, worked her way into the finals by defeating Eleanor Tennant of San Francisco without much trouble.

The feature match of the day was between Bill Johnston and Gervais Hillis of the University of California. Hillis won the second set from Johnston and forced him to a

(Continued on Page 2, Column 5)

### ASTORIA BATTLER TAKES DECISION IN TAME BOUT

*New Light-heavyweight Champ Forces Issue Throughout Tilt at Yankee Ball Park*

BY HARRY NEWMAN
[EXCLUSIVE DISPATCH]

YANKEE STADIUM, NEW YORK, May 30.—Paul Berlenbach defeated Mike McTigue in a fifteen-round bout here tonight in the main event of the Milk Fund show. As the result he is now the new light-heavyweight champion of the world, but it was a miserable exhibition of boxing all the way.

Berlenbach forced the issue from the opening bell, but there was too much senseless clinching and mauling to please the fans. Had it not been for Berlenbach there would not have been any fight at all. The Astoria kid had to step out and make the issue, but he did not have his knockout sock with him, and they just shuffled through the fifteen rounds.

Once McTigue threatened to get Paul with a knockout and that was in the sixth round when McTigue nailed Paul with a succession of rights to the chin and just for a brief period it looked as if Paul was going to leave the contest. But after that mishap Paul shook everything McTigue had to deal out over his shoulder.

From the eighth round on it was all Berlenbach and while it was not much of an exhibition to look at, Berlenbach was clearly en-

(Continued on Page 7, Column 2)

### VOTE ON EAST-WEST GRID GAME

*Pacific Coast Conference Takes Control of Classic of Rose Tournament*

[BY A. P. NIGHT WIRE]

SEATTLE, May 30.—Control of the annual New Year's football game at Pasadena was given to the Pacific Coast Managers' Association in an agreement between that body and the Pasadena Tournament of Roses Committee, which was ratified by the Managers' Association last night and announced here today.

The University of California delegate did not vote on the question.

Schedules for basketball, tennis, crew, wrestling and track for 1926 were drawn up. The Washington-California crew race was scheduled for April 10 at Seattle. The Pacific Coast Conference track and field meet was awarded to Stanford University May 26, being moved up one week on the sport calender so that the southern institutions could enter teams and still compete in the annual intercollegiate meet in the East.

The University of Washington relay carnival was set for May 1.

The question of baseball schedules was left until the December meeting of the conference, which is to decide whether the diamond sport will be continued in its present form by the conference schools, cut down to a sectional sport or dropped.

Cross-country runs were raised to a standard of minor sport in the conference and the championship meet for 1925 was awarded Moscow, Idaho, May 7.

### Tilden Bows to Richards in Tourney

[EXCLUSIVE DISPATCH]

MOUNTAIN STATION (N. J.) May 30.—Vincent Richards kicked over the traces today. Before 1200 spectators the young New York star defeated William T. Tilden, II., in the final round of the invitation tournament at the Orange Lawn Tennis Club, 4-6, 6-1, 7-5, 6-4.

### FUENTE-MORE SCRAP POSTPONED A WEEK

Sandy More, who was to have met Tony Fuente in the Mexicali arena this afternoon, will be unable to fulfill his engagement, according to "Pop" Nealis of the Newsboys' Club. More was fouled by Capt. Bob Roper at Wilmington last Wednesday and is still in bed. According to Nealis, who was in communication with Promoter Joe Flores of Mexicali, yesterday, the bout will be held next Sunday.

**NAVY DEFEATS ARMY.**

[BY A. P. NIGHT WIRE]

WEST POINT (N. Y.) May 30.—Navy's track team defeated Army here today, 72 1-2 points to 62 1-2.

### TROJANS CAPTURE MEET BY AMASSING 33 POINTS

*Princeton Athletes Finish Second in I.C.4A. Annual Carnival on Philadelphia Field*

[EXCLUSIVE DISPATCH]

PHILADELPHIA, May 30.—The intercollegiate track-and-field championship went west this afternoon when the brawny sons of the University of Southern California scored 33 points to win from the cream of athletes who came here from all over the country to participate in the forty-ninth annual college classic on Franklin Field.

**TROJAN COUNTERS**

Discus throw—Houser, 5 points; Anderson, 3 points.

Shot put—Houser, 4 points; Anderson, 3 points.

High hurdles—Dye, 5 points; Stever, 3 points.

Low hurdles—Grumbles, 5 points.

100-yard dash—Lloyd, 2 points; Taylor, 1 point.

High jump—Ross, 1½ point.

Pole vault—White, ½ points.

High point men—Houser, 9; Anderson, 6.

Although the Trojans won easily it was not until the semifinal event, the 220-yard low hurdles, was run, that the Californians were assured of victory. When K. L. Grumbles dashed ahead of a classy field to win this event, he clinched the title for his team.

**YALE THIRD**

Yale, former title-holder, had a mighty tussle with Princeton for second honors, with the latter beating its ancient rival 28½ points to 26½ for Yale. University of Pennsylvania and Georgetown were tied for fourth place with 22 points each, Cornell won sixth place with 16½ points, while California University barely nosed out Harvard for seventh position with 12½ points to the Crimson's 12.

Southern California led in first place with three 5-point markers. Bud Houser, with a mighty heave of 150ft. 2 1-4in. broke the I.C.A.A.A.A. discus record. His heave was 10ft. 2 1-8in. better than the former record made by Glenn Hartranft of Stanford in 1924. Houser's team-mate, Anderson, added three points to the total scored by California in this event by taking third place.

**THREE VICTORIES**

The other three first places captured by Southern California were in the 120-yard high hurdles, won by L. W. Dye and in the 220-yard low hurdles in which Grumbles nosed out Scattergood of Princeton to win at the tape.

The individual scoring honors of the Southern California team go to Bud Houser. The husky Californian totaled nine points for his team. He took second place to Hills of Princeton in the shotput when the Orange and Black champion made a record-breaking heave of 49ft. 9 5-8in., which bettered his mark of yesterday.

Next to Houser's performance the outstanding feature for Southern California was the work of L. W. Dye in the high hurdles. Dye opened up from the start, setting a terrific pace and came in an easy winner over Wolff of Pennsylvania in the fast time of

(Continued on Page 8, Column 3)

### O'BRIEN MOVES TO DEMPSEY GYMNASIUM

Tommy O'Brien yesterday transferred his training quarters from Pirrone's baseball park to Jack Dempsey's gymnasium and soon had the gallery sitting up noticing his marvelous footwork at shadow boxing and skipping the rope. He went through a siege of sparring with Eddie Cole, Jack Clark and Eddie Cochrane, letting loose his terrific right several times with telling effect. Tommy will continue the hard grind until next Wednesday and will then taper off.

### BUD TAYLOR DUE FROM EAST THIS AFTERNOON

Bud Taylor, who fights Jimmy McLarnin at Doyle's Tuesday night, will arrive on the Golden State Limited from Chicago this afternoon. He will train at the Newsboys' Club at 3 o'clock, Gig Rooney having been instructed to provide him with three good sparring partners. Gig picked out Joe Oakes, August Gotto and Babe Picato for the purpose.

## LEWIS AND STECHER ANNEX MAT BATTLES

### Wayne Munn is Vanquished by Strangler

BY WALTER ECKERSALL
[EXCLUSIVE DISPATCH]

MICHIGAN CITY (Ind.) May 30.—Endurance combined with a superior knowledge of the game gave Ed (Strangler) Lewis a victory over Wayne (Big) Munn, two out of three falls here this afternoon.

Munn won the first fall in 24m. 55s. with his favorite crotch and half-Nelson hold. In this fall the former Nebraska football player outwrestled Lewis, who only secured an offensive position once. On several occasions he attempted headlocks only to be shook off with apparent ease.

Lewis, however, came back with kindled determination in the second fall and finally whittled the big fellow down to his size. He bided his time and at the end of three successive headlocks, pinned Munn's shoulders to the mat after 32m. 12s. of grappling.

Strangler came back with renewed confidence for the third and deciding fall. He pulled and tugged his opponent about the ring, tiring him as he pushed him about. He finally secured the opportunity. Wayne had broken a headlock after a great effort. Lewis clamped on another and brought Wayne's shoulders to the mat after 7m. 15s. of wrestling.

Lewis's victory was due to his wonderful condition and staying powers. He entered the ring weighing 219 pounds, the lightest he has been for any match in five years. He relied mostly on his headlock, although on a few occasions he secured underneath wristlocks mainly to weaken Munn's arms. He did not even attempt a toe hold, but sent Munn to the canvas several times by leg holds. On other occasions he tripped Wayne to secure the offensive positions.

Munn worked well during the

(Continued on Page 2, Column 2)

### Zbyszko Loses Grappling Duel in Two Falls

[BY A. P. NIGHT WIRE]

ST. LOUIS (Mo.) May 30.—Joe Stecher, Nebraska scissors marvel, who lost the heavyweight wrestling championship to Ed "Strangler" Lewis four years ago, again reached the pinnacle of the wrestling world by defeating Stanislaus Zbyszko, title-claimant, in straight falls here tonight.

Stecher won both falls with his favorite hold, the first in one hour and twenty-three minutes and the second in five minutes.

Zbyszko, veteran of thirty years on the mat, fought gamely, but after the first fifteen minutes was largely on the defensive and finally was forced to give up to full body scissor holds. Stecher was declared the winner just as the sun was setting.

Time after time, Stecher was on top, but Zbyszko pulled his arms and legs underneath so effectively that Stecher was unable to complete the scissors.

Zbyszko used the flying mare as his chief offensive weapon, but it was not effective. The match was staged in St. Louis University athletic field before a crowd estimated at 13,500. The purse was $50,000, of which $10,000 was posted by Joe Stecher and his brother and manager, Anton Stecher. Zbyszko was to get the purse, win or lose.

The Stechers announced yesterday that in event Joe won today he would meet any legitimate challenger except Ed Lewis, whom, they asserted, had refused, while champion, to give Joe a chance to regain the title.

ST. LOUIS (Mo.) May 30.—Stanislaus Zbyszko, veteran Pole, who was taken to a hospital here this afternoon after his championship match with Joe Stecher, of Nebraska, was found to be suffering from internal injuries, several broken ribs and injuries to his back, it was learned tonight.

# GENE TUNNEY DETHRONES DEMPSEY AS RING KING

# *Champ Only Shadow of Dempsey of Old*

## POWER IS LOST BY "IRON MIKE"

*Willard's Master Fails to Show Former Condition*

*Fighting Instinct Sole Asset Possessed by ex-King*

*Jack Sorry Spectacle at End of One-Sided Ring Bout*

BY HARVEY WOODRUFF

PHILADELPHIA, Sept. 23. (Exclusive)—Jack Dempsey, shorn tonight of the title he has worn for seven years, was but a shadow of the bronzed panther-like young chap who pounded Jess Willard into quick submission at Toledo, in 1919.

JACK DEMPSEY.

Dempsey's judgment of distance was poor, the power behind his blows which upset Gunboat Smith, Willard, Bill Brennan, Carpentier, Miske, and Firpo was lacking.

To those who have seen his great battles of the past, Dempsey was a sorry specimen at the end of the ten rounds of milling, which elevated Tunney to the pugilistic pinnacle.

In one respect, and one respect only, Dempsey was the Dempsey of old; that was his fighting instinct. But fighting instinct without the other qualities which made Dempsey terrifying and formidable was valueless.

The fighting instinct was evident from the time the champion, Jack, now no longer Champion Jack, sprang from his corner in the first round and started to carry the battle to Tunney with the same tactics which we have observed in every battle we have seen him fight. It was evident

(Continued on Page 12, Column 6)

## TUNNEY WINS; BOHEMIA DINS

**Greenwich Village Stages Celebration as Native Son Trips Dempsey**

NEW YORK, Sept. 23. (AP)—Abington Square, a part of Greenwich village and the home of Gene Tunney, new heavyweight champion of the world, tonight celebrated the victory of a favorite son.

Crowds with bells, horns and other noise-making instruments, thronged the streets as news of the victory over Jack Dempsey reached them. Some invaded neighboring churches and soon church bells added their peals to the clamor.

Bonfires were lighted in the center of the square.

## *Gene Sure He Could Master Jack Dempsey*

RINGSIDE, SESQUICENTENNIAL STADIUM, PHILADELPHIA, Sept. 23. (AP)—Gene Tunney's smile, laid aside for a thin-lipped look of determination during his victorious fight, returned as he left the ring, mobbed by a wildly enthusiastic group of friends and handlers.

"I am naturally gratified," was the first comment of the studious ex-marine. "I knew soon after the start that I was the champion's master. I fought a carefully planned battle and it succeeded to the fondest of my expectations. Dempsey was game. He gave me trouble but I was never doubtful of the outcome."

### NET STAR HURT

The Pomona College tennis team has been hit again by injuries. Lee Mills, frosh captain last year, is laid up with an infected foot and will be unable to play for some time.

## DEMPSEY ONLY SECOND-RATER

*Man Killer of Old Becomes Tottering Has-Been*

*Tunney Unmarked Keeps Smile Throughout Battle*

*Record-Breaking Crowd Dazed at Champ's Defeat*

BY WESBROOK PEGLER

RINGSIDE, SESQUICENTENNIAL STADIUM, PHILADELPHIA (Pa.) Sept. 23.—With his face beaten into a bloody mask, Jack Dempsey passed the heavyweight championship of the world along to Gene Tunney tonight at the end of ten rounds of fighting that began in a trickle of rain and wound up in a downpour. More than 130,000 frantic citizens stood in the rain, open-mouthed and only able to utter weird squawks as Dempsey tottered to his corner at the last bell, with his left eye sealed shut and the entire left side of his face bulging like some horrible growth to plunge into the arms of his handlers in collapse. Tunney, unmarked and with the same rather pained smile on his face that he wore when he entered the ring, turned to his people in his corner, dazed almost as badly as Dempsey by the unexpected ease with which he had beaten the fellow who held the championship since the summer of 1919, under the awesome title of the man-killer.

### SECOND-RATER

It wasn't a man-killer that Gene Tunney fought, but a timid, pawing second-rater who might have lost to a Bartley Madden or a Charlie Weinert. The Dempsey who used to tear out of his corner at the clang of the first bell as though some one had set fire to his trunks, came out with his guard up and, to the amazement of the greatest throng that ever saw a prizefight, leaped into a clinch with his arms at Tunney's waist.

Tunney, the instinctive counter fighter, shrunk back into the angle of his corner as Dempsey walked at him, not the headlong Dempsey who flung himself at Luis Firpo, but a mincing Dempsey, who crossed the ring with something of William T. Tilden's gait in his stride and didn't even offer a punch when he got there. Inasmuch as Dempsey hadn't hit him on the way in, Tunney grabbed his arms in the clinch and discovered that he could handle this dark-browed fellow with the gauzy little patches of bandage glued to his eyebrows like horns. So Tunney parted Dempsey's arms and, as they stepped away, he flipped in a right for the jaw that went

Continued on Page 12, Column 4)

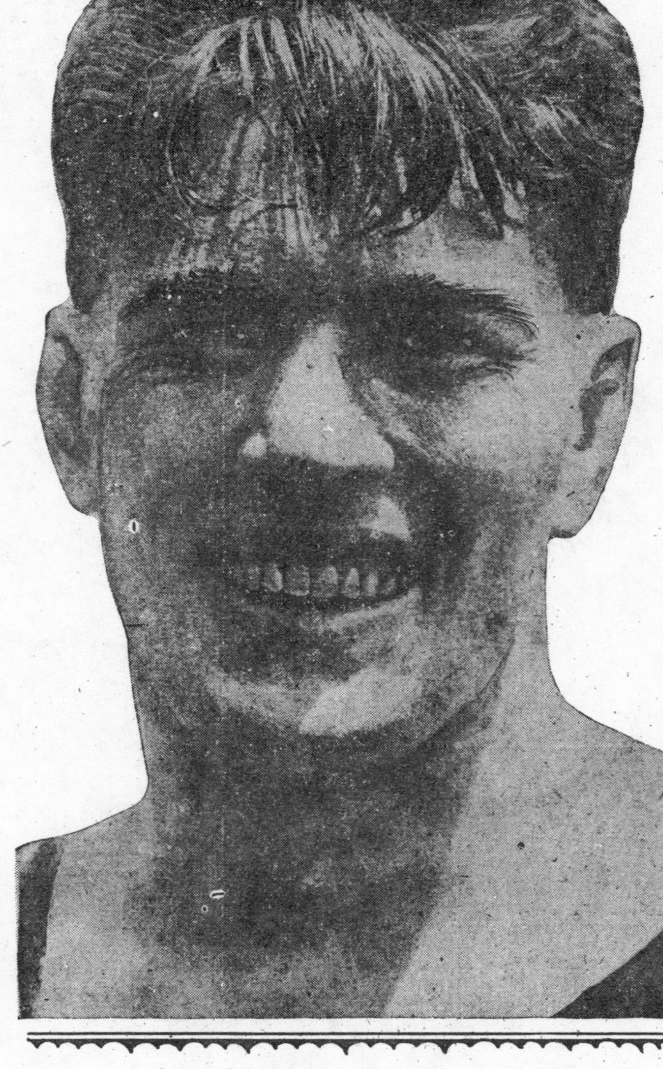

Gene Tunney, the Newest Heavyweight Champion

A seven-year quest that would have rivaled Jason's search for the Golden Fleece ended in Philadelphia yesterday when James Joseph Tunney won the heavyweight championship of the world fro mJack Dempsey. Gene Tunney, bor nin New York, May 25, 1898, of Irish-American nationality, won the boxing championship of the A. E. F. in 1919, after developing his fistic ability with the marines. He began his professional career in 1919, won the light heavyweight championship of America from Battling Levinski, then losing and regaining this title in bouts with Harry Greb withing a year. He forsook 175-pound ranks after knocking out gaging in 14 no-decision bouts, losing one verdict an bouts, winning 30 by knockouts, 14 on decisions, en-Georges Carpentier in 1924. He has engaged in 60 d figuring in one "no-contest."

## MARINE EASILY POUNDS WAY TO DECISIVE WIN

*Record Crowd of 132,000 Fans Sees Champion Deposed in Ten-Round Bout Via Verdict Route*

### JACK PATHETIC FIGURE AFTER LOSING TITLE

PHILADELPHIA, Sept. 23. (Exclusive)—Jack Dempsey, ex-heavyweight champion of the world, lay in a state of collapse in his dressing-room after the bout. Around him were gathered only a few friends and several marine and police officers. All Dempsey's friends had words of consolation to offer, however. Speaking from a rubbing table and swathed to his chin in blankets, he said:

"I have no alibis to offer. I lost to a good man, an American—a man who speaks the English language—I have no alibi."

As Dempsey lay back and closed his eyes, Gene Normile, his manager, again inclosed the ex-champion's head with his arms. Philadelphia Jack O'Brien stood on his right side soothing and petting him. A doctor in uniform stood on the other side of the table.

The doctor worked over the long gash in Dempsey's left eye. Each time he touched it Dempsey's face twitched and he pulled away. Soon another doctor arrived and both worked on Dempsey together.

Big Bill Tate stood at Dempsey's feet. He looked glum and said nothing. Normile said nothing. Dempsey lay silent.

Only the soothing words of O'Brien and the cautions of the doctors' voices filled the room under the stand.

Dempsey finally grew still under the handling and looked like he was asleep. O'Brien or Normile spoke to him and he didn't answer. They shook him slightly, but he did not respond.

Finally the doctor said: "Let him alone, he's tired."

(Continued from First Page)

clear it so that the announcer could make known the formal decision.

Tunney won eight of the ten rounds by so decisive a margin that no doubt was left of his supremacy the Associated Press score sheets showed. None of the rounds was scored for the champion and only in the sixth and seventh was he conceded better than an even break. In both of these, it was more a case of Tunney's cautiousness than Dempsey's own attacking success that affected the scoring.

### CHALLENGER CAUTIOUS

But for his hesitancy to open up and put all his guns into action, Tunney might have won by a knockout or scored an even more decisive victory. The challenger was cautious at first because he feared Dempsey was holding back, purposely shifting his customary rushing tactics to upset the Marine's plan of battle. But Tunney found a ready mark for his blows and as he discovered himself outpunching Dempsey consistently at close and long range, he became more aggressive and more confident.

This confidence grew as the battle progressed through the drenching downpour, but Tunney always was a bit wary. Now and then, in such rounds as the fourth, sixth and seventh, Dempsey connected with solid smashes to the head, driving in with a flash of his old ferocity. But the spark soon faded from these outbursts.

The champion's downfall and the disappointment in his showing was reminiscent of the defeat of James J. Jeffries by Jack Johnson in the first heavyweight battle Tex Rickard ever promoted, in 1910. Dempsey, like Jeffries, went into the ring a big favorite, only to exhibit little championship fighting qualities.

Chiefly because of Dempsey's lethargy and Tunney's intermittent cautiousness, the bout had few thrills, few spectacular moments of the sort that have punctuated most of Dempsey's battles since he dethroned Willard on July 4, 1919.

## TITLE GO LACKS CLASS

*Heavyweight Crown Changes Hands by Decision Route for First Time in Four Decades.*

RINGSIDE, SESQUICENTENNIAL STADIUM, PHILADELPHIA, Sept. 23. (AP)—The heavyweight title passed tonight from Jack Dempsey, to Gene Tunney on a judges' decision for the first time in nearly four decades of glove fighting.

Every previous champion, from the days of John L. Sullivan's reign, has passed from the throne by way of a knockout. Down through an illustrious line—Sullivan, Corbett, Fitzsimmons, Jeffries, Burns, Johnson and Willard—the count of ten has been tolled to effect every shift of the scepter.

Dempsey's downfall ended a seven-year reign that shared the distinction of being the longest on record. Johnson was the only other title-holder to rule for as long a period.

There were no knockdowns nor the semblance of any, except for one or two occasions when the fighters each slipped on the soaked and slippery surface of the ring.

Tunney was in command from the start. Before the bell had ended the first round, with the crowd amazed at Dempsey's slowness, the challenger had begun to seize his opportunities. As the champion swung wildly, the former Marine worked in his left jabs and crossed with solid rights that shook Dempsey up.

From then on, with monotonous regularity, Tunney beat off Dempsey's rushes with jolting blows to the head and body. The challenger gave ground more often than Dempsey, but it was for strategic purposes, not because he was suffering much punishment. Tunney's right eye was cut in one exchange, in the seventh round, and blood flowed from the reopening of cuts on his lips, but these did not bother him to any extent. He took Dempsey's stiffest punches without flinching and ducked or blocked most of the others.

Tex Rickard's weather luck finally failed for the first time since he began promoting boxing's biggest spectacles, but the soaked tens of thousands, including many women, refused to leave their seats. Many had come prepared, but the big majority took their drenching smilingly and stuck to the finish to cheer the advent of a new reign in pugilism.

The rain started lightly at first, shortly after Dempsey and Tunney entered the ring. During an unusually long delay caused by the taping of their hands, it increased in intensity. By the time the final bell sounded, the two gladiators were spattered by solid sheets of water. Tunney's gloves, soaked and crimson with Dempsey's blood, literally splashed their way to victory.

## TUNNEY'S GLOVES FIND EASY TARGET IN DEMPSEY'S FACE

BY GRANTLAND RICE

PHILADELPHIA, Sept. 23. (Exclusive)—Gene Tunney, the fighting marine, is the new heavyweight champion of the world.

In the presence of 130,000 people, who sat through a driving rainstorm in Philadelphia's big Sesquicentennial Stadium, Gene Tunney gave Dempsey one of the worst beatings any champion ever took. He not only outpointed Dempsey in every one of the ten rounds, but the challenger hammered the champion's face all out of shape.

It was like nothing human when the tenth round ended, Dempsey's left eye was entirely closed. There was a deep opening under Dempsey's right eye.

It poured a steady stream of blood, he was bleeding at both the mouth and nose as a faucet might run a crimson stream; in addition to all this his face was knocked almost out of shape. By a queer turn of fate he was almost exactly the same ghastly sight at Philadelphia as was Jess Willard seven years ago at Toledo. He was beaten every bit as badly, although he was never knocked from his feet. Gene Tunney fought one of the most surprising fights of his career. With a pouring rain beating down on the ring which left the footing slippery and treacherous, Tunney met Dempsey's wild, savage rushes with stiff lefts and rights to the face. These jabs and punches, delivered from short range, carried terrific power. They cut Dempsey's face into a flutter of crimson ribbons, they threw him off his balance and left him dazed and bewildered.

Tunney appeared extremely confident from the start and he fought with the same confidence to the end of the battle.

## ROUND-BY-ROUND STORY OF HEAVYWEIGHT TITLE BATTLE

BY CHARLES W. DUNKLEY
(BY ASSOCIATED PRESS.)

### ROUND ONE

Tunney was short with a left and they clinched in the corner. After the breakaway they traded punches to the body. Dempsey missed a left and Tunney drove a right to the head Dempsey drove both fists to the body at close quarters. Dempsey hooked a left to the head and they clinched. Tunney landed a right to the jaw and missed another right to the same spot. They clinched. Dempsey backed away from a right. Dempsey ducked a right to the head. Dempsey crowded into Tunney and got two light lefts to the head. Tunney ducked a right and Dempsey fell into the ropes. They traded rights to the head. Tunney rocked Dempsey with a right to the jaw and was pounding him furiously to the body at the bell.

### ROUND TWO

Tunney ran away with Dempsey after him. They clinched without damage. Dempsey hooked a left to the head and two rights to the body as Tunney retreated. Dempsey chased Gene to a corner punishing him around the ring.

Tunney was bleeding from the mouth. Tunney landed a light left to the head. Dempsey drove Tunney to a corner with a left and right to the head. Tunney landed a light right to the head. They clinched in a corner without damage. Tunney landed a left to the head and they clinched. Dempsey missed a left hook but sunk two rights to the body. Tunney backed away and landed a half dozen punches to the head. They were engaged in a furious body attack as the bell ended the round.

### ROUND THREE

The rain was starting to fall heavily. They boxed cautiously and Dempsey missed a left and right to the head, with Tunney backing away. Jack ducked three light lefts but was nailed with a right to the jaw Tunney drove a right to the body as Jack came in. Tunney nailed Dempsey with a right to the jaw as they clinched. The blow staggered Dempsey. They exchanged blows to the head and clinched. Tunney planted a right to the body, backing Dempsey to the ropes. They clinched at the edge of the ring. Tunney ripped a right to the head and Jack chased him into a corner without damage. Jack sunk a right to the body and got a right to the head.

### ROUND FOUR

Dempsey sent a left to the jaw, knocking Tunney into the ropes. Tunney hung on as Dempsey drove his fist to the body. Jack chased the challenger into a corner, driving his left to the body. Dempsey was bleeding from a cut on the left eye. Dempsey missed a left hook to the head. Dempsey was short with a left to the head and they clinched. Gene stepped away from a left to the body. Tunney nailed Dempsey with a right as the champion came in. Tunney backed away from a right and landed three punches to the head. Tunney nailed Dempsey with a right, as

(Continued on Page 14, Column 4)

MONDAY MORNING, OCTOBER 11, 1926.

# CARDS BEAT YANKS AND CAPTURE WORLD SERIES

## ALEXANDER IS HERO OF THRILLING 3-TO-2 WIN

### *Pitching Ace Rescues Haines in Seventh and Whiffs Lazzeri With the Bases Filled*

(Continued from First Page)

as effective as ever to cap the climax of his heroic role.

Not since the famous right arm of Walter Johnson pulled the Senators to their first world's championship in 1924 has there been anything so colorful as this finish of Alexander's. Two years ago, however, the big train came back vigorously after being twice defeated, while this time the stalwart Nebraskan stepped into the breach with two victories already behind him.

**CREDIT TO HAINES**

Alexander did not get official crtdit today for the victory that would have put him among the honor-roll men who have won three world's series games. The verdict goes down on the books in Haines's name, but the glory belongs to Alexander, the 39-year-old warrior, who was sold "down the river" a short time ago as a Chicago Cub discard.

Thwarted as they were by Alexander's great stand, it was, nevertheless a heartbreaking defeat for the Yankees, who battled desperately to overcome a margin they had yielded in the fourth inning when the Cardinals, aided by two errors by Koenig and Meusel, scored all their three runs. It was heart-breaking for Waite Hoyt, young right-hander, who had twirled brilliantly even when his support sagged, and it was heart-breaking for Babe Ruth, whose fourth home run of the series, again shattering all world's championship records, had put the Yankees in the lead and upset the confidence of Haines, hero of a shutout victory over the American League champions in St. Louis.

But it was thrilling just the same for the Cardinals, themselfs victims of unfortunate "breaks" in previous games, yet possessed of the fighting spirit and pluck to come back when their cause seen lost and capture, on foreign soil, the final two games that carried them to the world's championship.

Forty years is a long time between titles but this conquering clan, the first National League pennant winner St. Louis has ever had, came through under fire to establish its right to the peak. Back in 1886, when St. Louis, then in the old American Association, was in the throes of its first and last pennant-winning streak, its representatives triumphed over the Detroit Nationals

(Continued on Page 12, Column 3)

### CARDS CHAMPS

**ST. LOUIS**

| | AB | R | H | PO | A | E |
|---|---|---|---|---|---|---|
| Holm, cf | 5 | 0 | 0 | 2 | 0 | 0 |
| Southworth, rf | 4 | 0 | 0 | 0 | 0 | 0 |
| Hornsby, 2b | 4 | 0 | 2 | 4 | 1 | 0 |
| Bottomley, 1b | 3 | 1 | 1 | 14 | 0 | 0 |
| Bell, 3b | 4 | 1 | 0 | 0 | 4 | 0 |
| Hafey, lf | 4 | 1 | 2 | 3 | 0 | 0 |
| O'Farrell, c | 3 | 0 | 0 | 3 | 2 | 0 |
| Thevenow, ss | 4 | 0 | 2 | 1 | 3 | 0 |
| Haines, p | 2 | 0 | 1 | 0 | 4 | 0 |
| Alexander, p | 1 | 0 | 0 | 0 | 0 | 0 |
| Totals | 34 | 3 | 8 | 27 | 14 | 0 |

**NEW YORK**

| | AB | R | H | PO | A | E |
|---|---|---|---|---|---|---|
| Combs, cf | 5 | 0 | 2 | 2 | 0 | 0 |
| Koenig, ss | 4 | 0 | 0 | 2 | 3 | 1 |
| Ruth, rf | 1 | 1 | 1 | 2 | 0 | 0 |
| Meusel, lf | 4 | 0 | 1 | 3 | 0 | 1 |
| Gehrig, 1b | 2 | 0 | 0 | 11 | 0 | 0 |
| Lazzeri, 2b | 4 | 0 | 0 | 2 | 1 | 0 |
| Dugan, 3b | 4 | 1 | 2 | 2 | 3 | 1 |
| Severeid, c | 3 | 0 | 2 | 3 | 1 | 0 |
| Hoyt, p | 2 | 0 | 0 | 0 | 1 | 0 |
| Paschal, x | 1 | 0 | 0 | 0 | 0 | 0 |
| Adams, xx | 0 | 0 | 0 | 0 | 0 | 0 |
| Collins, c | 1 | 0 | 0 | 0 | 0 | 0 |
| Pennock, p | 1 | 0 | 0 | 0 | 1 | 0 |
| Totals | 32 | 2 | 8 | 27 | 10 | 3 |

x—Paschal batted for Hoyt in sixth.

xx—Adams ran for Severeid in sixth.

**SCORE BY INNINGS**

| | |
|---|---|
| St. Louis | 000300000—3 |
| Hits | 101300120—8 |
| New York | 001001000—2 |
| Hits | 121012100—8 |

**SUMMARY**

Two-base hit—Severeid. Home run—Ruth. Sacrifices — Haines, O'Farrell, Koenig, Bottomley. Left on bases—St. Louis, 7; New York, 10. Bases on balls—Off Haines, 5 (Ruth 3, Gehrig 2;) off Alexander, 1 (Ruth.) Struck out—By Haines, 2 (Lazzeri 2;) by Alexander, 1 (Lazzeri;) by Hoyt, 2 (Hafey, Haines.) Hits off Hoyt, 5 in six innings; off Pennock, 3 in three; off Haines, 8 in six and two-thirds; off Alexander, 0 in two and one-third. Winning pitcher—Haines. Losing pitcher—Hoyt. Umpires—Hildebrand (at plate,) Klem (at first base,) Dineen (second base,) O'Day (third base.) Time of game 2:15.

## STATISTICS ON WORLD SERIES

NEW YORK, Oct. 10. —Standing of the clubs:

| Team | W | L | Pct. |
|---|---|---|---|
| Cardinals | 4 | 3 | .571 |
| Yankees | 3 | 4 | .429 |

**RESULTS OF GAMES:**

First game—Yankees 2; Cardinals 1.

Second game—Cardinals 6; Yankees 2.

Third game—Cardinals 4; Yankees 0.

Fourth game—Yankees 10; Cardinals 5.

Fifth game—Yankees 3; Cardinals 2; (ten innings.)

Sixth game—Cardinals 10; Yankees 2.

Seventh game—Cardinals 3; Yankees 2.

**SUNDAY'S TOTAL:**

Attendance 38,093.
Receipts $140,091.00.
Advisory Council's share $21,013.65.
Each club's share $24,769.34.
Each league's share $24,769.34.

**TOTALS FOR THE SERIES:**

Attendance 328,051.
Total receipts $1,207,864.
Player's share (first four games only) $372,300.51.
Advisory Council's share $181,179.60.
Each club's share $158,595.97.
Each league's share $158,595.97.



*The "Babe" In the Woods, No. 9* . . . . . . . . By BOB DAY

## SUZANNE SUBDUES OUR MARY

### *French Tennis Star Wins Pro Tilt; Illness Forces Snodgrass to Default*

NEW YORK, Oct. 10. (AP)—Suzanne Lenglen easily triumphed over her American professional rival, Mary K. Browne of Santa Monica, Cal., 6-2, 6-1, at Madison Square Garden tonight in the second series of exhibition tennis matches.

Mary Browne

Miss Browne put up a plucky battle but she was decisively outplayed. A crowd estimated at 3500, as compared with an opening - night attendance fixed at 13,000, saw the match.

In a men's singles match, Vincent Richards, former Davis Cup star, was leading Harvey Snodgrass of Los Angeles, 6-4, 4-1, when Snodgrass had to default because of illness.

Howard Kinsey and Harvey Snodgrass teamed against Vincent Richards and Paul Feret to win the single set of a men's doubles match, 6-2.

In the mixed doubles, with Richards as her partner, Mlle. Lenglen again opened up her barrage of spectacular drives to aid in sweeping Miss Browne and Snodgrass to a single set defeat by a 6-2 count.

## LAUBERDER VICTOR IN HOLLYWOOD PLAY

W. G. Lauberder finished all even in a match-play-against-par tournament staged at the Hollywood Country Club yesterday and won the event. G. A. Druin placed second, 1 down, with E. M. Phillips 2 down. J. C. Beggs, M. G. Dedall and L. Wrese were all 3 down against par. Mrs. A. G. Shagrue defeated Mrs. W. E. Amor in the play-off for the tie in the putting contest. A number of women players are expected out to the course this week to start practice for the match-play event which is to begin the 18th inst.

## FOUR GOLFERS TIE FOR FIRST HONORS

The professional handicap tournament at the California Country Club yesterday ended with four golfers tied for first. M. Morse, Roy Compton, E. S. Estes and T. R. Theney each scored a net 70. S. T. Stonerod and Graham Bakel were next in line with 71's, while D. P. O'Keefe, Earl Crenshaw, Walter Hambley and A. Seablom tallied 72's. A silver golf bag cocktail shaker was the prize.

### PROFESSIONAL GRID RESULTS

**NATIONAL LEAGUE**

Detroit, 10; Kansas City, 0.
Bears, 7; New York Giants, 0.
Milwaukee, 13; Racine, 2.
Chicago Cardinals, 13; Green Bay, 7.
Pottsville, 24; Dayton, 6.
Providence, 19; Columbus, 0.
Akron, 0; Canton, 0. (Tie.)

**AMERICAN LEAGUE**

Wilson's Wildcats, 23; Brooklyn, 0.
New York, 19; New Britain, 6.

## POETS TACKLE GRIZZLIES

### *Undefeated Southern Conference Squads in Big Game at Whittier Saturday Afternoon*

BY BRAVEN DYER

The big football game of this week for Southern California Conference fans takes place at Whittier, where Leo Calland's rejuvenated Poets entertain Coach Bill Spaulding's up-and-coming Southern Branch aggregation. Last year the Quakers trotted onto Moore Field, scored a touchdown early in the game and then battled their heads off to hold the lead and eventually did. Grizzly supporters have never forgiven the Poets for this and anybody who even hails from Whittier is regarded with distrust by all those who have the welfare of Spaulding and his boys at heart.

That 7-to-0 defeat wrecked Southern Branch's title hopes, no other conference squad being able to flatten the Grizzlies during the 1925 season. Saturday's clash at Whittier will have much the same championship flavor for the losing team will be out of the conference race for keeps, particularly if the Poets happen to be on the short end of the score for the Quakers have already been tied.

Bill Spaulding

There is virtually no way of comparing the teams by scores of this year, as the two squads have not met a common foe. Such procedure went out of style long ago, anyway. We looked over both squads earlier in the season and there was little to choose between them.

**POETS HAVE VETERANS**

The Quakers are a veteran outfit with the exception of Earl Clevenger at one guard berth, while the Grizzlies, sporting less letter men, have given rather concrete evidence of possessing more potential power than their rivals. Such was the case last year, however, and the Quakers refused to be bothered, scoring their touchdown in a businesslike manner and then outfighting the Grizzlies to hold their slim margin.

Calland's charges have seemingly recovered from the bruising they received at the hands of U.S.C. His team's 13-to-6 victory over Caltech is indicative of defensive as well as offensive strength. Conference followers are aware that in Denny, Pendleton, Clark and Phelan the Poets have plenty of offensive power, but after what happened to the Whittier line in the U.S.C. game there was some doubt as to the quality of Leo's forward wall, despite the presence of a lot of bulky veterans. The Trojans, however, wore their rivals out by sheer force of numbers on that date and Whittier's showing against Caltech removes virtually all doubt as to the defensive ability of the Poets.

At that we doubt if the Caltech backfield can compare in strength with Fleming, Fields, LaBucherie and Birlenbach. This Grizzly combination carries weight plus speed and the Whittier line will be sorely tried when the first two chaps start pounding the line and LaBucherie begins skirting the ends.

The Grizzly backfield tore San Diego's line wide open Saturday and that score of 42 to 7 ought to afford Calland and company plenty of food for thought. It is the largest count ever run up by a Southern Branch team. The Southerners were battered about somewhat by Pomona the week before and this didn't help 'em any.

It should be a great game with plenty of drama and Whittier's new

(Continued on Page 12, Column 5)

### FOOTBALL STANDINGS

**COAST CONFERENCE**

| | W. | L. | Pct. |
|---|---|---|---|
| So. California | 1 | 0 | 1.000 |
| Oregon Aggies | 1 | 0 | 1.000 |
| Washington | 1 | 0 | 1.000 |
| Idaho | 1 | 0 | .000 |
| California | 0 | 0 | .000 |
| Stanford | 0 | 0 | .000 |
| Washington State | 0 | 1 | .000 |
| Oregon | 0 | 1 | .000 |
| Montana | 0 | 2 | .000 |

**Games Saturday**

U.S.C. vs. Occidental at Coliseum (nonconference.)
Oregon Aggies at California.
Idaho at Washington.
Montana at Washington State.
Nevada at Stanford (nonconference.)

**Southern California**

| | | | |
|---|---|---|---|
| So. California | 74 | Whittier | 0 |
| So. California | 42 | Santa Clara | 0 |
| So. California | 16 | Wash. State | 7 |

**California**

| | | | |
|---|---|---|---|
| California | 13 | Santa Clara | 6 |
| California | 32 | Olympic Club | 0 |
| California | 7 | St. Mary's | 26 |

**Stanford**

| | | | |
|---|---|---|---|
| Stanford | 13 | Caltech | 6 |
| Stanford | 44 | Fresno | 7 |
| Stanford | 19 | Occidental | 0 |
| Stanford | 7 | Olympic Club | 3 |

**Oregon Aggies**

| | | | |
|---|---|---|---|
| Oregon Aggies | 67 | Multnomah | 0 |
| Oregon Aggies | 49 | Montana | 0 |
| Oregon Aggies | 23 | Gonzaga | 6 |

**Washington**

| | | | |
|---|---|---|---|
| Washington | 20 | U.S.S. N. M. | 0 |
| Washington | 33 | Col. Puget Snd. | 0 |
| Washington | 28 | Willamette | 0 |
| Washington | 23 | Oregon | 9 |

**Washington State**

| | | | |
|---|---|---|---|
| Wash. State | 35 | College of Idaho | 0 |
| Wash. State | 7 | So. Cal. | 16 |

**Oregon U.**

| | | | |
|---|---|---|---|
| Oregon | 44 | Willamette | 0 |
| Oregon | 0 | Pacific | 0 |
| Oregon | 9 | Washington | 23 |

**Idaho**

| | | | |
|---|---|---|---|
| Idaho | 0 | Montana State | 0 |
| Idaho | 27 | Montana | 12 |

**Montana**

| | | | |
|---|---|---|---|
| Montana | 0 | Oregon Aggies | 49 |
| Montana | 12 | Idaho | 27 |

**Southern Conference**

| | W. | L. | T. | Pct. |
|---|---|---|---|---|
| Pomona | 2 | 0 | 0 | 1.000 |
| Occidental | 1 | 0 | 0 | 1.000 |
| So. Branch | 1 | 0 | 0 | 1.000 |
| Whittier | 1 | 0 | 1 | 1.000 |
| Caltech | 0 | 1 | 0 | .000 |
| Redlands | 0 | 1 | 0 | .000 |
| La Verne | 0 | 1 | 1 | .000 |
| San Diego | 0 | 2 | 0 | .000 |

**Games Saturday**

So. Branch at Whittier.
Caltech at Pomona.
Redlands at San Diego.

**Pomona**

| | | | |
|---|---|---|---|
| Pomona | 20 | San Diego | 6 |
| Pomona | 27 | La Verne | 6 |

**Southern Branch**

| | | | |
|---|---|---|---|
| So. Branch | 25 | Santa Barbara | 0 |
| So. Branch | 42 | San Diego | 7 |

(Continued on Page 12, Column 6)

## BAMBINO OUTHITS HORNSBY

### *Ruth Takes All Hitting Honors in Contest With Cardinal Leader*

While the Cards and Yanks were battling for honors, a lot of attention was centering on the duel between Babe Ruth and Rogers Hornsby, respective sluggers of the St. Louis and New York championship teams. Babe carted off all honors.

BABE RUTH

The big Bambino played in all seven games, appeared at the plate on twenty official occasions, got six hits and scored six runs. His average was .300. Four of the Babe's six bingles were homers, the other two being mere singles. Babe's four circuits established uncountable records, incidentally.

On eleven of his appearances the Babe was walked, and only twice did he fan. In addition, he rang up the greatest number of total bases—eighteen; and tied Bill Southworth of the Cards for the number of runs scored—six.

In the field Ruth handled ten chances without an error, two of his catches being of the spectacular variety. He had no sacrifices, and stole a base—the only one which the Yankees gathered.

The great Rajah, pilot of the new champs, had a hitting average of .250. He was at the platter twenty-eight times, got seven hits and scored two runs. One of Hornsby's bingles was for two bases, the rest being singles. He walked twice, fanned the same number of times and stole one base.

Hornsby was great in the field. He handled the ball thirty-six times, including four double plays, and did not make an error.

## *Wilson Stars in Victory Over Brooklyn*

NEW YORK, Oct. 10.—George Wilson brought his Pacific Coast Wild Cats to Commercial Field this afternoon and before a big crowd almost single-handedly clawed his way to a 23-0 victory over Brooklyn's "two-horse" eleven. Wilson, in his Brooklyn debut, lived up to all expectations. This sandy-haired, stocky-built crashing halfback, in real wildcat fashion, scored one touchdown, was at one end of a forward pass, which resulted in another score, and otherwise performed in brilliant style.

| Wild Cats. | | Brooklyn. |
|---|---|---|
| Flaherty | L.E. | Hunsinger |
| Johnston | L.T. | Prendergast |
| Busch | L.G. | Howard |
| Walters | C. | Pollock |
| A. Wilson | R.G. | Taylor |
| Erickson | R.T. | Kozlek |
| Vesser | R.E. | Harrison |
| Bross | Q. | Stuhldreher |
| G. Wilson | L.H. | Bolger |
| R. Morrison | R.H. | Britton |
| D. Morrison | F. | Layden |

**SCORE BY QUARTERS**

| | | | | |
|---|---|---|---|---|
| Wild Cats | 0 | 13 | 3 | 7—23 |
| Brooklyn | 0 | 0 | 0 | 0—0 |

Touchdowns—D. Morrison, Wilson, Illman. Points after touchdown—Lawson, 2 (placements.)

Goal from field—Lawson (placement from 25-yard line.)

## ST. LOUIS GOES WILD WITH JOY

**Terrific Din As Missouri City Hears of Team's Win Over Yankees**

ST. LOUIS, Oct. 10. (AP)—St. Louis went wild with joy late today when news was flashed that the St. Louis Cardinals had won the world's series. Whistles, bells and automobile horns joined in a terrific din.

Downtown streets, usually almost deserted on Sunday, were filled with fans in front of radio loudspeakers and scoreboards.

Jubilant fans danced, threw their hats in the air and hugged each other.

If office buildings had not been closed, the streets undoubtedly would soon have been covered with paper thrown from windows as they were when news was received that the Cardinals had won the city's first pennant in thirty-eight years and when the victorious team came home.

The name of Alexander the Great was on everyone's lips. A great cheer went up from the crowds when in the seventh inning with the bases filled, the veteran pitcher relieved Haines and struck out Lazzeri for the third out.

## *Place Ducats on Sale for U.S.C.-Card Tilt*

Twenty-two thousand seats to the U. S. C.-Stanford grid tilt in the Coliseum on the 30th inst. have already been reserved, according to Arnold Eddy, ducat dispenser of the local institution, but something like 50,000 are still available.

The 22,000 disposed of were sold to students of the university, alumni, and fans who applied for season ducats some time ago, while a number were sent to Stanford for disposal.

The remaining 50,000 for the most part, are available to the general public at $2.00, and are on sale at the B. H. Dyas Company.

## HOFF REITERATES SUIT INTENTION

MINNEAPOLIS (Minn.) Oct. 10. (AP) Charles Hoff, world's champion pole vaulter, has begun his fight to remain in the United States, he announced here tonight.

Denied extension of his stay in America by immigration authorities, Hoff will file a second appeal Monday. He will confer with Charles W Seaman, Minneapolis immigration inspcetor, tomorrow regarding the disputed points in the controversy. Should his appeal be denied, he will be forced to return to Norway on the 15th inst.

Hoff is appearing at a local theater.

## STARS DIVIDE WITH BEAVERS

### *Ducks Rout Hulvey and Cop First Game, 8 to 3*

### *Singleton Bests Lingrel in 1-to-0 Final Duel*

### *Portland Captures Series by 4-to-3 Margin*

BY BOB RAY

While some 5000 fans looked on and at times actually rooted despite the fact that the Coast League clubs are playing out the rest of the schedule for no reason at all, Portland and Hollywood split even in yesterday's twin bill at Wrigley Field. The Beavers won the opener, 8 to 3, but went down to defeat in the finale when "Sheriff" Singleton bested Ray Lingrel in a 1-to-0 hurling duel. It might be added that it was the latter contest that caused the fans to actually root.

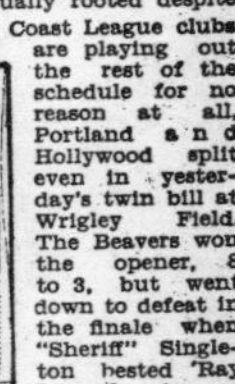

"SHERIFF" SINGLETON.

Portland's Beavers annexed the series, four games to three, but failed to pass the Sacramento Senators in their attempt to land a first-division berth. The Beavers are still a half-game behind the Solons, which they will try to make up this week in their series with the champion Angels.

Getting back to the contests, Lingrel and Singleton put on a midseason duel in the nightcap and the players even got into the spirit of the thing and backed up both twirlers with good support.

The game was originally slated to go seven innings, but neither Singleton nor Lingrel allowed a run in these frames, so an extra round was necessary.

**SHERIFF WON GAME**

The Sheriff won his own ball game in the eighth because he had to. Singleton was first up in the extra frame and he reached first when Lingrel hit him on the elbow of his pitching arm. The Sheriff knew that he wouldn't be able to pitch any more, so he completed the circuit when Gooch sacrificed and Dudley Lee slapped a double down the left-field line. Singleton made certain of the victory by sprinting in from second a la Charley Paddock, crossing the plate before "Red" Smith, who wound up the game in left for the Beavers, even got to the ball.

Portland passed up its best chance to score in the first inning, which Metz opened with a single to Coumbe. However, Metz's stay on the sacks was very short, for when Coumbe threw the ball past Singleton, who covered the bag, the Portland infielder started out for second. However, Les Cook was on the job and picked up the wild heave and tossed to Singleton in plenty of time to get Metz, who by that time had started back to first. Singleton let Cook's throw squirt through his hands, but Johnny Kerr was backing up the Sheriff this time to throw back to Singleton

(Continued on Page 12, Column 4)

# Strategy and Endurance Save Fight Crown

FRIDAY MORNING, SEPTEMBER 23, 1927.

# TUNNEY FLASHES STRONG FINISH TO WIN VERDICT

## DEMPSEY LOSES TO BETTER MAN

*Ring Craft Carries Champ Through Seventh*

*Fistic King Criticised for "Bicycle Act"*

*Tunney Ranks With Famous Old-time Battlers*

BY WALTER ECKERSALL

CHICAGO, Sept. 22.—Superior ring generalship and endurance, two of the most important qualifications of a fighter, enabled Gene Tunney to retain his heavyweight championship in the battle with Jack Dempsey on Soldier Field tonight.

It was Tunney's ring craft which enabled him to weather the seventh round when he was sent to the canvas by two left hooks followed by a right cross and it was his endurance which enabled him to outfinish the challenger in the closing rounds.

It would have been suicide for Tunney to have traded punches with Dempsey after that unexpected knockdown in the seventh. He did what any smart fighter would have done. He hung on and kept the challenger at long range by stabbing Jack with left leads. In this manner he permitted his head to clear and when he answered the bell for the eighth round he was himself once again.

The champion may be criticised for mounting the bicycle and making Dempsey chase him after he had taken the nine-count. There was nothing else for him to have done. In fact it was his own carelessness that permitted Dempsey to reach him with that first wicked left hook, which was the starter of the knockdown.

**In the eighth round, Tunney sent the challenger to the floor for a one-count with sort of an overhand right cross. Dempsey was up as Paul Beeler, the timekeeper, tolled off the count of one. These were the only two knockdowns of the fight, but the one scored by Dempsey was by far the most damaging. Tunney, however, was smart enough to take the full count and made no effort to get up until the count of eight. He was clearly on his feet before the count of ten.**

That Tunney was entitled to the decision was shown by the verdict of the two judges, Sheldon Clark, chairman of the athletic committee of the Chicago Athletic Association, and George Lytton, local business man and Dave Barry, the referee, which gave Dempsey the sixth and seventh rounds and all the rest to Tunney.

It simply was the case of the boxer against the fighter and in a short fight the former is the victor in the great majority of cases. The champion was too smart. He feinted Dempsey into position so that he could be nailed with straight left leads which generally were followed by right crosses right on the jaw. The champion made few attempts to start his punches for the body. The attack which Jack followed early in the fight was shifted to the head as the battle wore on.

It was a clean fight, contrary to the expectations of many who thought

(Continued on Page 10, Column 4)

## STILL THE CHAMP!

Gene Tunney, the scholar of Speculator, came close to losing his heavyweight crown to Jack Dempsey, the former title-holder, in the seventh round when he went down for a nine-count before the Manassa Mauler's attack, but he came back strong to win anyway and prove his claim as a real champion. Here's a pen and ink sketch of Tunney by Gordon L'Allamand of "The Times" art staff.

## DEMPSEY DEFEATED BY SINGLE SECOND

*Slashing Finish Won Decision for Champion After Great Two-Fisted Battle; Tunney Wobbly After Being Dropped in Seventh*

BY ALAN J. GOULD
Associated Press Sports Editor

SOLDIER FIELD, CHICAGO, Sept. 22. (AP)—Gene Tunney, the man of destiny, is still heavyweight champion of the world but his crown was perilously close to being toppled from his head tonight by the gallant thrust of the old warrior, Jack Dempsey, in the greatest boxing spectacle of all time.

Tunney's hand was raised in victory at the end of a slashing, smashing battle but only because he had the courage and fighting power for a sensational finish after being knocked down for a count of nine in the seventh round by Dempsey's vicious two-handed attack.

**Only one second, in this seventh round, separated Dempsey from the greatest victory of his career, and an achievement no other ex-champion had ever recorded, but Tunney back on his feet, slipped from range, cleared his head and weathered as stormy a session as he has ever experienced.**

Safely past that crisis, Tunney finished the last three rounds like a champion, regained confidence, taking the aggressive and beating Dempsey into defeat with a two-handed, well-timed attack to the head. With his title in danger, Tunney had the stuff to put on a victorious rally. At the close of the final round, both eyes cut and badly bleeding, Dempsey was groggy and reeling, "out on his feet." So battered was the old champion, his last charge expended, that he did not seem to know the battle was over and had to be led to his corner.

**Tunney's victory was not without dispute, however, for there were scores in the ringside section who thought the champion was saved from losing his crown in the seventh round by a count that was actually several seconds longer than the toll of nine.**

It was unquestionably a "long count"—from twelve to fourteen

(Continued on Page 13, Column 4)

## GENE SMARTER, SAYS LEONARD

*Outboxed and Outpunched Jack, Declares Benny*

*Tunney Got a Bit Careless in Seventh Round*

*Dempsey Better Than in His Philadelphia Bout*

BY BENNY LEONARD
(Undefeated Lightweight Champion.)

CHICAGO, Sept. 22.—Gene Tunney proved too smart for Jack Dempsey in the ring here tonight. He outboxed and outpunched his challenger in all but the seventh round of their fight. In that round Tunney became careless and tried to swap punches with Dempsey with the idea of knocking him out. In the anxiety of his effort he let go a few overhand rights that missed Dempsey. Then over near Dempsey's corner when Tunney was just getting ready to throw a right, Dempsey loosed one of those old-time attacks of his, shot a short left hook which caught Tunney flush on the jaw. Tunney went back on his heels and was starting to go down from the punch when Jack hooked him with a right and another left to the jaw which plopped him down much more quickly.

BENNY LEONARD

### TUNNEY DAZED

Tunney was down and dazed. Dempsey did not go to a neutral corner but stood there and the referee, Dave Barry, motioned him to a neutral corner, and took up the count. At the count of four, Tunney was in a sitting position on the ropes, taking the full advantage of the count like a good ring general. He got up and then kept backing away from Dempsey.

**The next round Dempsey went down from a little punch, a right, but it was more because Dempsey was a bit wobbly on his legs than because the punch was hard that Dempsey sort of slipped to the floor. He was up in a jiffy, however, and the blow did not hurt him.**

Gene Tunney and Jack Dempsey fought exactly as I predicted they would. Tunney, the boxer, stayed away and waited for Dempsey to lead, most of the time, but in the second round he showed a stiff attack. Tunney thought he might have a chance to knock out Dempsey and he fought hard and fast in spots.

The only thing was that Gene got careless in that seventh round and Dempsey got lucky with his punches.

### BENNY WAS RIGHT

I told you that he would be lucky with his punches but that I did not think he would be lucky enough to enable him to score a knockout. That's just what happened.

As soon as Tunney got up after that knockdown and was circling around retreating from Dempsey, Jack, finally slowing down to a walk in his chase of Tunney, got tired and motioned to him to stop, making a sort of "come hither" gesture with his gloved hand.

**Just imagine Jack Dempsey not being able to catch a fellow who is backing up, especially after a knockdown, when everyone knows that a man coming forward ought to be able to go faster that way than his opponent can go backward, ordinarily. That proved to me that Dempsey's legs were weak.**

Dempsey kept hitting for the body, just as I predicted he would. Jack

(Continued on Page 10, Column 5)

## Estelle Breaks Down as She Hears News

CHICAGO, Sept. 22. (AP)—Estelle Taylor, wife of Jack Dempsey, collapsed in her suite at a fashionable North Shore hotel tonight, a Chicago newspaper says, after she heard over the radio that her husband had been defeated in his comeback attempt against Gene Tunney.

## RING RULE EXPLAINED BY PREHN

*Count Over Boxer Given Knockdown Elucidated by Illinois Commissioner*

SOLDIER FIELD, CHICAGO, Sept. 22. (AP)—Under interpretation of the rules of the Illinois State Athletic Commission a count over a boxer who has been knocked down cannot begin until his opponent has gone to the "farthest corner," Paul Prehn, commissioner, explained tonight when asked whether Gene Tunney had not had the benefit of a long count in the seventh round.

JACK DEMPSEY

Jimmy De

Jimmy Forest, former trainer of Dempsey, sat in the challenger's corner with a stop watch and said Gene got a twelve-second count. Others said thirteen or fourteen, while Dempsey's handlers claimed it was fifteen seconds.

Dave Barry, the referee, warned Dempsey to go to a corner and when the ex-champion hesitated, withheld his count, together with the official knockdown timekeeper. When Dempsey moved off, the toll was taken up.

The rule of the commission, on which varying ringside interpretations were put, reads:

"When a knockdown occurs, the timekeeper shall immediately arise and announce the seconds audibly as they elapse. The referee shall first see that the opponent retires to the farthest corner and then, turning to the timekeeper, shall pick up the count in unison with the timekeeper, announcing the seconds to the boxer on the floor. Should the boxer on

(Continued on Page 10, Column 6)

## DEMPSEY COMEBACK HOPES FADE IN CLOSING ROUNDS

*Manassa Mauler Risks All in One Big Splurge, But Champ Stages Rally to Retain His Crown*

(Continued from First Page)

in the lead. Each was behind. Each came back.

Tunney fought like a champion, and richly deserves the title he retains. Dempsey fought like the splendid, courageous man he is. "God, what a man," said Gene Normile, who was in Dempsey's corner last year, as the challenger survived the fourth and all but scored a knockout in the seventh.

**As the rounds went, Tunney won six and Dempsey four, but the general consensus of ringside opinion is that Dempsey really knocked Tunney out, and failed to profit by it when he did not get into a neutral corner fast enough.**

The preliminaries got under way at 8:05 with Big Boy Peterson and Johnny Russell as the dish. The flood of light which greeted the boxers when the big arcs were turned on made the ring as bright as day and brought a roar of approval from the big crowd.

Just as Peterson was awarded the nod over Russell a few spattering raindrops began to fall at 8:30. Customers of the Dempsey-Tunney fight at Philadelphia last year had visions of another horrible experience, but the spattering ceased almost as soon as it started.

Two boys who have battled on the Coast met in the second preliminary, Chuck Wiggins winning in six rounds over Sailor Jimmy Byrne.

Davy Miller refereed the third fight between George Manley and Yale Okum, thereby destroying the hopes of his supporters that he would be the third man in the ring for Dempsey and Tunney.

Manley won and the decks were cleared for the big event of the evening, which Rickard had promised would go on sharply at 9:30. A courier passed along press row and announced that Gus Wilson had gone to Tunney's dressing-room to supervise the bandaging.

However, something went wrong, because at 9:30 Jack McCann and Billy Vidabeck, who was one of Tunney's sparring partners, climbed in the ring and were introduced.

### GATE $2,800,000

Another message to the press row from one of Rickard's henchmen brought the information that the promoter in law estimated the gate at $2,800,000 and the attendance at 150,000.

Virabeck was announced as the winner of the fourth six-rounder, which was a horrible example of biffing and with the hour at 9:55 everybody began craning their necks for the expected coming of the champion and the challenger.

A big shout arose as Dempsey was observed coming down the aisle. He climbed into the ring preceded by Leo Flynn, his manager, and Jerry the Greek, his trainer, and Gus Wilson. Jack was outfitted in a big white sweater and white bath robe with flowing sleeves. Jack had big black initials, J. D. on his bath robe.

Dempsey spotted Gene Normile sit-

(Continued on Page 12, Column 3)

## HOI POLLOI MINGLE WITH BEST PEOPLE AT CHICAGO

BY WESTBROOK PEGLER

CHICAGO, Sept. 22.—The best people of the nation, of whom Mr. Tex Rickard is so exceedingly fond, and some other people, presumably not so good, gathered tonight in a mass of 150,000 in Chicago's memorial built to honor the soldier dead and watched another prize fight costing nigh onto $3,000,000 which ended after the fashion of multi-million-dollar prize fights, in a wrangle.

**Gene Tunney came back after being knocked down in the seventh round to hit Dempsey a bat behind the left ear in the eighth and floor him, face downward and well spread out. At the end of the tenth round he won the decision of the two amateur or gentlemen judges and the referee, but while the 140,000 people were still jammed in the aisles inching their way out of the huge concrete cup on the margin of Lake Michigan, the voice of Mr. Leo Percentage Flynn, manager for Mr. Dempsey was heard rising in strident sounds of complaint, known in the language of the trade as the squawk.**

Mr. Flynn claimed that his gentleman had knocked Tunney down twice and should have had the decision therefor and he also insisted that Mr. Tunney, when he was knocked to the heel of his white silk trouserettes, was allowed to rest not for nine seconds, but thirteen. The fact was that Tunney did go down twice, the second time in the tenth round, but this time it was for only

(Continued on Page 10, Column 5)

## BATTLING AT CLOSE QUARTERS

Here are Jack Dempsey, defeated challenger, (in dark trunks) and Gene Tunney, champion, boring in during the first round at the Soldiers' Field, Chicago, last night. The P. & A. picture was transmitted over Pacific Telephone and Telegraph lines from the scene of the conflict.

## BLOW BY BLOW STORY OF DEMPSEY-TUNNEY BATTLE

### ROUND ONE

Dempsey missed a left lunge falling into a clinch. Jack punched again with two left hooks to the ribs. In the clinch that followed he clipped Gene four times with a right on the back of the head. They sparred cautiously, Dempsey preferring to feint for openings while Tunney laid back. Gene snapped a left to Dempsey's chin and followed with a solid right smash to the chin. Jack fell into a clinch taking another right to the head as he came in. Jack dropped a left on Tunney's body. Jack backed away while the champion followed him across the ring with a volley of lefts and rights to the head close to the ropes. Gene missed an overhand right as the bell sounded.

### ROUND TWO

Dempsey was fighting cautiously, apparently seeking to evade a disastrous first-round spasm like that at Philadelphia last fall. They came out boxing again and Gene shot a left and right to chin. They were dancing, boxing high. Gene dropped an overhand right on Dempsey's chin after chasing him to a corner. Another right missed. Dempsey smashed a left to the body and three lefts to the chin before Tunney could tie him up. Hands high, Jack dodged away from a right. There was little action as they sparred carefully in the center. Tunney's left was short, but Dempsey merely fell into a clinch. Gene missed two more lefts while Jack clipped two short left hooks to the body. As Dempsey lunged low Tunney missed again but managed to catch himself and fleck two soft lefts to Jack's face as the round ended.

### ROUND THREE

Again they boxed carefully, slowly in the center of the ring. Dempsey apparently was trying to tantalize Tunney into leading and making an open fight of it. Tunney sneaked over a pretty left jab but took a half-dozen raps on the back of the neck. Gene took the offensive, driving Dempsey into the ropes, where Jack tied him tight. As they bobbed in the center Tunney led and fell into Dempsey's straight right smash to the body. Gene held while Jack clouted both hands to the midsection. A right smash to the heart drove Tunney back. As they fiddled about Dempsey wove in close again to cuff the back of Tunney's head with his right and dig his left twice to the champion's ribs.

### ROUND FOUR

Dempsey took the offensive but Tunney's right cracked on his chin. Gene's left found the same mark. While Dempsey rapped two lefts to the body Gene complained that the blows were foul and fought Jack des-

(Continued on Page 11, Column 3)

## LOOKS LIKE JACK MISSED THAT ONE

From the picture below it appears that Tunney dodged a hard wallop during the second round of last night's ten-round title bout at Chicago. Dave Barry, who refereed the affair, is watching the big fellows. The P. & A. picture was transmitted over Pacific Telephone and Telegraph lines.

# Ruth Crashes Sixtieth Homer for New Record

SATURDAY MORNING, OCTOBER 1, 1927.

# TROJANS FACE REAL TEST IN SANTA CLARA TODAY

## BRONCOS DOPED TO GIVE LOCALS GREAT BATTLE

### *Passing Attack of Visitors and Punting of Simoni Sure to Extend Jones's Eleven*

BY BRAVEN DYER

Some years ago, so history tells us, a gang of Greeks stowed away in a horse and invaded the sacred walls of Troy, startling the doughty Trojans well out of their wits. Ever since then, so the bedtime story runs, the Trojans have had little use for horsies, colts or other animals of similar lineage.

It is therefore with no little fear and trembling that the Trojans of U.S.C. go against the Broncos of Santa Clara at the Coliseum this afternoon. Word has come down from the north that the Broncos are very, very tough and inclined to be skittish. Holding California to a 14-to-6 count is indicative of something. Probably punch and power, and the Trojans will be very much on their guard when the bucking Broncos bust onto the greensward this afternoon around 2:45 o'clock.

BUD CUMMINGS

Adam Walsh, the big Broncho buster, drove his charges into town yesterday and during the afternoon gave them a short workout at the Coliseum. Even our unpracticed eye told us that Mr. Walsh had gathered together a group of exceedingly determined athletes, all of whom are bent on doing something valiant to wipe out the memory of last year's 42-to-0 defeat at the hands of the Trojans.

TWO BIG TACKLES

In the first place Santa Clara has two big, powerful, experienced tackles and any smart coach will tell you that's half the battle in forming a football team. The gentlemen answer to the names of Red Chisholm and Tiny Leonard. Each weighs 200 pounds and each looks tougher than a cafeteria steak. In fact, Leonard is so hard that Walsh won't let him run signals with the varsity for fear he'll forget himself and mangle somebody. Ahart, another 200-pounder, took his place yesterday, while Leonard performed on the second-stringers, where damage done is less likely to be fatal to the team's success.

Secondly the Broncos also have a high-class, meaty center in Mr. Guido Granucci. Nearly all the Broncos are called Guido. For instance there's Simoni, the sensational sophomore kicker, who was also christened with this front handle. And Guido Barsi,

(Continued on Page 10, Column 4)

## BRUINS AND FRESNO TO MIX TODAY

### *Northern Team Doped to Give Locals Real Grid Battle*

BY EDWARD LAWRENCE

There being some doubt as to the exact status of Fresno State, footballically speaking, the U.C.L.A. Bruin will be no better than an even bet in this afternoon's contest on Moore Field.

JOE FLEMING.

That the northern athletes were tumbled, 33 to 0, by Stanford last Saturday is nothing against them, but rather says plenty in their favor. It is rumored that Pop Warner's eleven can punch holes in any team this side of the Rockies, which adds luster to the Teachers' feat of holding the score down to five touchdowns.

Fresno State can match the Bruin veterans man for man with a few left over among the twenty-seven members making up the squad. The Bruins will have a slight edge in weight, which may prove the deciding factor in the game, but there the advantage ceases.

USE AERIAL ATTACK

Meager reports from the north would indicate that the Teachers use an effective overhead game, interspersing forward passes with laterals. Santa Barbara State's few gains against the Bruins last week were made through the air, a point of weakness in the Bruin defense.

Not that Coach Bill Spaulding

(Continued on Page 10, Column 2)

## RARIN' TO GO! - - - By Bruce Russell

## TODAY'S GRID MENU

LOCAL

U.S.C. vs. Santa Clara at Coliseum.

U.S.C. frosh vs. Burbank High at Coliseum (preliminary.)

U.C.L.A. vs. Fresno State College at Moore Field.

U.C.L.A. frosh vs. Visalia J. C. at Moore Field (preliminary.)

Southwestern at Loyola.

Caltek vs. Redlands at Rose Bowl.

La Verne at Whittier.

California Christian College at San Diego State.

PACIFIC COAST

Stanford vs. St. Mary's at Palo Alto.

California vs. Nevada at Berkeley.

Arizona vs. Occidental at Tucson.

Olympic Club vs. St. Ignatius at San Francisco.

Washington vs. Willamette at Seattle.

Washington State vs. Idaho College at Pullman.

Oregon vs. Pacific University at Eugene.

Oregon Aggies vs. California Aggies at Corvallis.

Idaho vs. Montana State at Moscow.

Montana vs. Mt. St. Charles at Missoula.

Gonzaga vs. Cheney at Spokane.

GENERAL EASTERN

Army vs. Detroit at West Point.

Brown vs. Albright at Providence.

Bucknell vs. Geneva at Lewisburg.

Butler vs. Louisville at Indianapolis.

(Continued on Page 11, Column 2)

## GOLDSTEIN IS BEATEN BY HUGHES

### *Cleveland Boxer Carries Away Verdict Over Boston Boy at Hollywood*

Tommy Hughes, who hails from Cleveland, where he learned the rudiments of the manly art from Johnny Kilbane, former featherweight champion, walked off with an easy verdict over Harry Goldstein, Boston 112-pounder, in last night's flyweight tournament match at the Hollywood Legion Stadium.

Hughes captured eight out of the ten rounds and out-pointed the Boston battler all the way. Goldstein earned an even break in two rounds but that was the best he could do against the more - clever, harder - hitting Hughes.

There were three knockdowns, with Goldstein the victim each time, and all three came in the sixth round. Hughes put Harry on the canvas for a two count the first time with a left hook to the jaw. Goldstein bounced up and was promptly knocked down again by a right to the chin. Harry only stayed down for one this time and was soon dropped for another one count by a left hook. Goldstein weathered the series of knockdowns nicely and was getting in some good raps before the round ended.

Goldstein showed that he is as thrifty as his name would imply; in the eighth, after Hughes had knocked one of his gold teeth out, Harry looked around

(Continued on Page 11, Column 6)

## HOW TROJANS AND BRONCOS LINE UP AT COLISEUM TODAY

| U.S.C. No. | Player | Weight | Position | Weight | Player | SANTA CLARA No. |
|---|---|---|---|---|---|---|
| 30 | Boren | 178 | LER | 177 | Chisholm | 37 |
| 10 | Hibbs | 195 | LTR | 202 | Caresse | 7 |
| 35 | Anthony | 200 | LGR | 170 | Granucci | 15 |
| 39 | Fox | 197 | C | 198 | Schenone | 14 |
| 27 | Heiser | 194 | RGL | 168 | Leonard | 35 |
| 8 | Scheving | 185 | RTL | 200 | Falk | 30 |
| 12 | Steponovich | 170 | REL | 164 | Barsi | 19 |
| 2 | Capt. Drury | 185 | Q | 184 | B. Cummings | 2 |
| 15 | Saunders | 178 | LHR | 145 | McCormick | 11 |
| 21 | L. Thomas | 185 | RHL | 155 | Simoni | 21 |
| 24 | Edelson | 170 | F | 180 | Koller | 10 |

U.S.C.—Kemp (1,) Ryan (3,) Chambers (4,) Lejane (5,) Moses (6,) Gowder (7,) Wilcox (9,) Tappaan (11,) Dihel (13,) La Velle (14,) Templeton (16,) Williams (17,) M. Thomas (18,) Hoff (19,) Elliott (20,) Bonham (22,) Moser (23,) Barragar (25,) McCaslan (26,) Beattie (29,) Porter (31,) Coyle (32,) Ward (33,) McCabe (34,) Anthony (35,) Aleksi (36,) Kreiger (37,) Schaub (38.)

Santa Clara—E. Cummings (1,) Haakinson (4,) Morey (12,) Miller (28,) McCormick (11,) Fawley (9,) Hassler (26,) Breen (32,) Valine (33,) Kerckhoff (6,) Clatk (20,) Ahart (36,) O'Daniels (22,) McGovern (18,) Phelan (34,) Regan (31,) Loughery (8,) Sidener (16,) Sherman (3,) Terremere (25.)

## Football Results

LOCAL

L. A. High, 18; Venice, 0.
Polytechnic, 19; Santa Monica, 0.
Franklin, 0; Glendale, 0.
Hollywood, 12; Pasadena, 0.
Long Beach, 7; Manual Arts, 0.
Woodrow Wilson, 6; Anaheim, 6.

SOUTHERN CALIFORNIA

Orange, 25; Tustin, 0.
Pomona, 5; Covina, 0.
Monrovia, 27; South Pasadena, 0.

EASTERN

Still College, 7; Midland, 0.
Buena Vista, 7; Doana College, 0.
Furman, 20; North Carolina, 0.
Alabama, 31; Southwestern of Memphis, 0.
Pennsylvania, 19; Central, 6.
Baylor U., 20; Trinity U., 12.
Daniel Baker, 3; West Texas Teachers' College, 0.
University of Chattanooga, 44; Western Kentucky Teachers, 6.
Little Rock College, 10; Hendrix College, 27.
Central Normal, 66; Vincennes U., 0.
St. Olaf, 14; Augsburg, 7.
Moorehead Teachers, 0; St. Cloud Teachers, 7.

## TIGER FLOWERS COPS DECISION OVER LATZO

WILKESBARRE (Pa.) Sept. 30. (AP) Tiger Flowers, former middleweight champion, tonight battled his way to a judges' decision over Pete Latzo of Scranton, former welterweight title-holder, in ten rounds.

VINCENT MEETS MEYERS

OAKLAND, Sept. 30. (AP)—Billy Vincent of Los Angeles and Pete Meyers of San Francisco, middleweights, meet in the ten-round main bout of the opening program of the Acorn Athletic Club here tomorrow night.

# *Reds Prevent Bucs From Cinching Flag*

## BAMBINO'S HIT BEATS SOLONS

### *Veteran Zachary Victim of Record-Breaking Poke*

### *Circuit Hit Scores Koenig and Gives Yanks Win*

### *Babe Has One More Game in Which to Boost Mark*

NEW YORK, Sept. 30. (AP)—Babe Ruth's sixtieth homer of the season, creating a new major league record, carried the New York Yankees to a 4-to-2 win over the Washington Senators today.

With the score tied at 2-2 in the eighth, Koenig tripled with one out and came home as Ruth shattered his old mark of fifty-nine homers with a bull mashie shot into the sun seats of the right-field stand. Ruth also hit two singles and scored three of New York's runs.

BABE RUTH

Tuning his pitchers for the world series, Manager Miller Huggins worked Pipgras and Pennock in relay today and the pair held Washington to five hits.

The Senators took an early lead in the fourth inning, scoring two runs on three hits. Goslin singled and after two were out, a single and steal by Ruel and Bluege's one-baser counted the tallies. The Yankees got to Tom Zachary for single runs in the fourth and sixth innings to set the stage for Ruth's record-smashing climax. Score:

| WASHINGTON | AB | R | H | O | A | NEW YORK | AB | R | H | O | A |
|---|---|---|---|---|---|---|---|---|---|---|---|
| Rice,rf | 3 | 0 | 1 | 2 | 0 | Combs,cf | 4 | 0 | 0 | 3 | 0 |
| Harris,2b | 3 | 0 | 0 | 3 | 4 | Koenig,ss | 4 | 1 | 1 | 3 | 5 |
| Vanzel,cf | 4 | 0 | 1 | 1 | 0 | Ruth,rf | 3 | 3 | 3 | 4 | 0 |
| Goslin,lf | 4 | 1 | 1 | 5 | 0 | Gehrig,1b | 4 | 0 | 2 | 10 | 0 |
| Judge,1b | 4 | 0 | 0 | 8 | 0 | Meusel,lf | 3 | 0 | 1 | 3 | 0 |
| Ruel,c | 3 | 1 | 1 | 2 | 0 | Lazzeri,2b | 3 | 0 | 0 | 2 | 2 |
| Bluege,3b | 3 | 0 | 1 | 1 | 4 | Dugan,3b | 3 | 0 | 1 | 1 | 1 |
| Gillis,ss | 4 | 0 | 0 | 2 | 1 | Bengough,c | 3 | 0 | 1 | 1 | 2 |
| Zachary,p | 2 | 0 | 0 | 0 | 1 | Pipgras,p | 3 | 0 | 0 | 0 | 2 |
| Johnson,x | 1 | 0 | 0 | 0 | 0 | Pennock,p | 1 | 0 | 0 | 0 | 1 |
| Totals | 31 | 2 | 5 | 24 | 10 | Totals | 31 | 4 | 9 | 27 | 13 |

x—Batted for Zachary in 9th.

SCORE BY INNINGS

Washington ............... 0 0 0 2 0 0 0 0 0—2
New York ............... 0 0 0 1 0 1 0 2 x—4

SUMMARY

Error—Gehrig. Two-base hit—Rice. Three-base hit—Koenig. Home run—Ruth. Stolen bases—Ruel, Bluege, Rice. Sacrifice—Meusel. Double plays—Harris to Bluege; Gillis to Harris to Judge. Left on base—New York, 4; Washington, 7. Base on balls—Pipgras, 4; Pennock, 1; Zachary, 1. Struck out—Zachary, 1. Hits—off Pipgras, 4 in 6 innings; off Pennock, 1 in 3. Hit by pitcher—Rice by Pipgras. Winning pitcher—Pennock. Umpires—Dineen, Connolly and Owens. Time—1h. 38m.

## *Hagenlacher Boosts Lead*

CHICAGO, Sept. 30. (AP)—Eric Hagenlacher of Germany tonight strengthened his grip on Welker Cochrane's world 18.2 balkline billiard crown, by winning the second block of their titular 1500-point match to gain a lead of 1000 to 708.

Hagenlacher won the second 500-point block 500 to 376. He also won the first, played last night, 500 to 332.

The point score of tonight's block: Hagenlacher: 4 (left over from last night's unfinished run,) 3, 135, 10, 84, 2, 113, 17, 39, 20, 11, 2, 1, 59—total 500—average, 35 10-14—high run, 135

Cochrane—54, 6, 4, 0, 45, 26, 22, 38, 85, 94, 2, 0, 0—total, 376—average, 28 12-13—high run, 94.

Grand match inning average:
Hagenlacher—33 10-30.
Cochrane—23 18-30.
High-match run—Hagenlacher, 154; Cochrane, 94.

NELSON STOPS LEABO

SAN BERNARDINO, Sept. 30. (AP)—Al Nelson of Los Angeles knocked out Skip Leabo, San Bernardino lightweight, in the sixth round here last night.

## HOLLYWOOD STARS DEFEAT SEATTLE IN NINTH, 8 TO 7

Bud Lowell's long sacrifice fly to Callaghan, with one out and men on second and third, allowed Red Bouton to romp over the plate in the ninth inning and give the Hollywood Stars an 8-to-7 victory over Red Killefer's Seattle Indians. The win made it three straight for the Sheiks and gave them a 3-to-1 lead in the series.

The contest, although featured by loose play on both sides, was exciting enough, as far as the score was concerned, with both clubs coming from behind a couple of times.

Seattle, after trailing from the first inning, when the Stars made four runs, took the lead in the eighth inning, when Kimmick tripled against the center-field bricks, came in with the tying run when Twombly dropped Borreani's fly for a two-base error, and Guilland, who replaced Nance in the seventh, followed with a single to right that scored Borreani. Borreani's run gave the Tribe a 6-to-5 lead.

Hollywood came back with two runs in its half of the eighth to again go out in front. Sherlock dropped Lowell's pop fly for a starter and Frederick followed with a single. Kerr sacrificed. Heath, batting for Cook, hit to Hudgens and Lowell was trapped between third and home.

(Continued on Page 10, Column 3)

## *Donald Signs Berlenbach-Walker Go*

NEW YORK, Sept. 30.—Mickey Walker, world's middleweight champion, and Paul Berlenbach, former world's light-heavyweight champion, were signed today by Dick Donald, Pacific Coast promoter, to fight ten rounds to a decision at Los Angeles. No exact date has been set for the meeting, but the battlers agreed to fight on one of three dates to be designated by the promoter, November 21, 22 or 23. According to Jack Kearns, Walker's manager, the boys will fight for the "world's light-heavy middleweight title," which sounds nice and may look well on bill posters.

## RABBIT PUNCHES

BY PAUL LOWRY

THE same colleges, the same field, and the same day of the year—the first Saturday in October. That applies to the little pigskin tussle between U.S.C. and Santa Clara which is scheduled for public consumption at the Coliseum this afternoon. But the same score? you ask. Hardly, unless the day of miracles is here and Howard Jones has made seasoned linesmen out of raw material.

The score was 42 to 0 in U.S.C.'s favor last year, but Santa Clara this year is fresh from a close game with California in which the Bears nosed out a 14-to-6 victory and Santa Clara has the vets, so the struggle this afternoon should be close. Gone are Badgro, Schaub, Cravath, Gorrell and Cox from the Trojan

(Continued on Page 11, Column 5)

## LUCAS UPSETS PIRATE CRAFT

### *Cincinnati Bunches Hits to Capture 2-to-1 Game*

### *Pittsburgh Rally in Eighth Falls Short of Tie*

### *Paul Waner Fails in Pinch to End Corsair Flash*

HOW THEY STAND

| | W. | L. | Pc. |
|---|---|---|---|
| Pittsburgh ........ | 93 | 59 | .612 |
| St. Louis .......... | 91 | 61 | .599 |
| New York .......... | 90 | 62 | .592 |
| Chicago ............ | 85 | 67 | .559 |
| Cincinnati ......... | 74 | 77 | .490 |
| Brooklyn .......... | 64 | 87 | .424 |
| Boston ............. | 57 | 94 | .377 |
| Philadelphia ....... | 62 | 99 | .385 |

Yesterday's Results
Cincinnati, 2; Pittsburgh, 1.
Philadelphia, 12; Boston, 2.
Brooklyn, 10; New York, 5.

Games Today
Pittsburgh at Cincinnati.
Chicago at St. Louis.
New York at Brooklyn.
Philadelphia at Boston.

CINCINNATI, Sept. 30. (AP)—Checked in all but one inning by the brilliant twirling of Red Lucas and the sensational defensive work of Hughie Critz around second base, the league-leading Pittsburgh Pirates lost to Cincinnati 2 to 1 today, thereby prolonging the settlement of the superheated National League pennant race with only two days to go.

PAUL WANER

Lucas, ace of the Reds' twirling staff, held the Buccaneers to six hits, two of which were bunched in an eighth-inning rally that fell one run short of knotting the score after the Cincinnati clan had fallen on Vic Aldridge in the sixth and seventh frames for the tallies that turned out to be the deciding margin.

The setback left the Bucs

(Continued on Page 10, Column 3)

# Gene Tunney Announces Retirement From Ring

WEDNESDAY MORNING, AUGUST 1, 1928. C

# PADDOCK QUALIFIES FOR 200-METERS; BORAH OUT

## CHAMP DESERTS BOXING THRONE

*Ten Years in Game is Long Enough for Tunney*

*Present Contenders Unable to Attract Public*

*Rickard to Conduct Tourney to Find New King*

BY EDWARD J. NEIL
Associated Press Sports Writer

NEW YORK, July 31. (AP)—As dramatically as he entered the boxing game ten years ago, Gene Tunney, heavyweight champion, stepped from his throne today and back into private life — finished with the ring forever.

TEX RICKARD

Amid surroundings that lent every aid to his desire to retire "as gracefully as possible" from the game that has made him an international figure, grown to a giant in strength and size, and a millionaire, since that desperate day ten years ago when he sought a fight in order to eat, the big marine, with a husky note in his voice, told fifty newspaper men and friends he was through.

**For days rumors had circulated that Tunney's final ring engagement took place in the Yankee Stadium last Thursday night when Tom Heeney, best of the present crop of challengers, succumbed to the champion's merciless power and ring mastery in eleven rounds. But Gene refused to confirm these stories until he stood today at the side of William Muldoon, the 82-year-old New York State boxing commissioner and "Grand old man of sport," to talk to those who had gathered in the ancient's honor.**

Then, standing before the lunch-

(Continued on Page 2, Column 2)

## Trojan-Irish Grid Game to Get $5 Top

## CHOICE SEATS TO COST MORE

*Advance Marks Raise of $2 Over 1926 Game*

*Howard Jones Returns Home from Wisconsin*

*Trojans May Tackle Huskies in Track Meet*

BY BRAVEN DYER

Best seats to the Notre Dame University of Southern California football game in the Los Angeles Coliseum December 1 will cost purchasers $5 each, according to an announcement from the Trojan graduate manager's office yesterday. This marks an advance of $2 over price of tickets to the same contest here two years ago, and also is the first time in history that any Coliseum game has commanded a $5 top. The price applies to the majority of seats.

HOWARD JONES

Other interesting developments at the Trojan institution were the return of Head Football Coach Howard Jones from the East, and the announcement that Southern California and the University of Washington will probably enter into a home-and-home agreement on track meets. Negotiations with the Huskies will be carried on in San Francisco within two weeks, when Gwynn Wilson, Trojan manager, goes north to confer with Ed Campbell of Washington and Alfred Masters of Stanford.

This meeting is primarily to discuss resumption of football hostili-

(Continued on Page 3, Column I)

## NO MORE OF THIS SORDID STUFF FOR GENE TUNNEY

In announcing his retirement as heavyweight champion yesterday Tunney indicated, although he did not make it a flat-footed threat, that he would indulge in no more one-sided orgies as the one pictured here with—the tenth-round episode in the fight with Heeney at New York recently, when the challenger was chopped to the floor and only saved by the bell for another spasm.

[P. & A. photos]

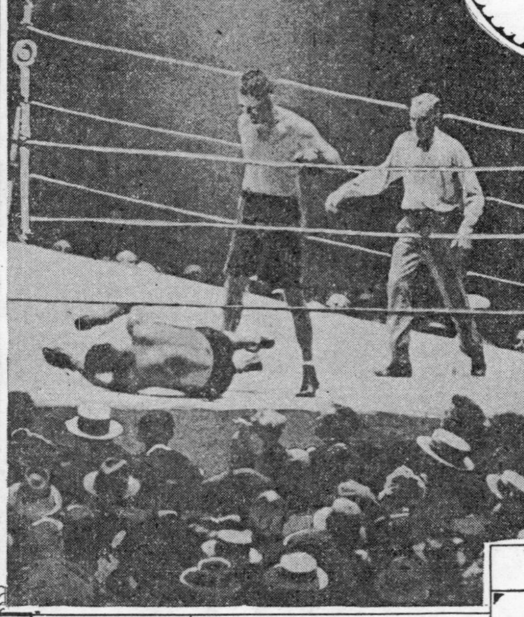

## DYE AND ANDERSON IN HURDLE FINALS TODAY

### Miss Copeland Cops Second in Discus

BY BILL HENRY
"Times" Staff Correspondent

AMSTERDAM, July 31.—Miss Lillian Copeland of the Pasadena Athletic and Country Club brought the American flag to the top of the pole here today by taking second place in the women's discus event after a terrific battle against entries from Poland, Sweden and Germany.

LILLIAN COPELAND

The Pasadena girl made two splendid tosses near the finish of the competition and won over all but Halina Konopacka of Poland, a tall, powerfully built maiden, who broke the world's record with a toss of 129ft. 11in., not to mention a few infinitesimal fractions of an inch in addition.

Maybelle Reichardt, another Pasadena girl, was just outside the money in seventh place.

DYE BEST BET

Pacific Coast male athletes qualified well in the 110-meter hurdles and 200-meter sprint. Leighton Dye of the Los Angeles Athletic Club and long-legged Steve Anderson of the University of Washington both ran 14 4-5s., equalling the world's record. Both will have to hurry, however, to defeat Weightman-

(Continued on Page 4, Column 1)

### Hahn Defeated by Lowe in 800 Meters

(Continued from Page 1, Part 1)

Leighton Dye and Stephen Anderson, each equalling the former world's record of 14 4-5 seconds made by Earl Thomson in 1920.

American sprinters suffered a fresh setback in the 200-meter trials when Charley Borah was nosed out for the second qualifying place by Percy Williams, the Canadian youth,

**HOW COAST MEN FARED**

CHARLES PADDOCK, L.A. A.C.: Qualified for semifinals of 200 meters today; finals also to be run.

CHARLES BORAH, L.A.A.C.: Shut out in second trial of 200 meters.

LEIGHTON DYE, L.A.A.C.: Qualified for finals of 110-meter hurdles today.

STEVE ANDERSON, Washington: Qualified for finals of 110-meter hurdles today.

EARL FULLER, Olympic Club: Failed to place in finals of 800 meters, finishing ninth.

on top of his 100-meter triumph yesterday. Helmut Koernig, German ace, captured the heat, equaling the Olympic record of 21 3-5s, but it was a real battle between Williams and Borah. The American appeared to have the place cinched, but lacked the stamina to meet Williams's closing rush. The Canadian just got the width of his chest across the line first.

The other three Americans each

(Continued on Page 4, Column 1)

## YANKEES LEAD BY 42 POINTS

AMSTERDAM, July 31. (AP)—Although Americans have captured only three of the eight Olympic championships decided thus far, the United States tonight still held a commanding lead in points on the field at Amsterdam. Scoring 16 points today under the unofficial scoring system the United States has rolled up 71 points to 29 for her nearest rival of the moment, Great Britain, who tallied only 10 points today. Unable to place in either of the two men's finals today, Finland saw herself passed in the standing by both Sweden and Germany.

Scoring 10 points for first place, 5 for second, 4 for third, 3 for fourth, 2 for fifth and 1 for sixth,, the standings tonight were:

| | Previous total | 800 meters | Broad jump | Grand total |
|---|---|---|---|---|
| United States | 55 | 2 | 14 | 71 |
| Great Britain | 19 | 10 | .. | 29 |
| Sweden | 16 | 5 | .. | 21 |
| Germany | 9 | 4 | 5 | 18 |
| Finland | 17 | .. | .. | 17 |
| Canada | 10 | 3 | .. | 13 |
| Ireland | 10 | .. | .. | 10 |
| France | 4 | 1 | .. | 5 |
| Haiti | 0 | .. | 5 | 5 |
| Italy | 4 | .. | .. | 4 |
| Philippines | 3 | .. | .. | 3 |
| South Africa | 2 | .. | .. | 2 |
| Japan | 1 | .. | .. | 1 |
| Holland | 0 | .. | 1 | 1 |

## HEATH'S WALLOP IN TENTH WINS THRILLER FOR STARS

BY BOB RAY

If you like thrills you should have been out at Wrigley Field yesterday and seen Oscar Vitt's scrappy Stars come from behind to nose out the Mission Bells, 4 to 3, in the tenth inning of the series opener. The victory put the Stars in the league lead, Sacramento losing.

Just when the Bells apparently had the contest stowed away, 3 to 1, and two were out in the last half of the ninth, Dud Lee and Johnny Kerr singled to revive hopes of victory on the Hollywood bench. Whereupon, Skipper Vitt called Frank Shellenback, the slugging slabster, in to pinch hit for Twombly and all that Shelly did was to lambast one of Herman Pillette's offerings off the concrete base of the center-field bleachers for a double, Lee and Kerr legging it home to knot the count and send the fans back to their seats.

**And then in the home half of the tenth, after Carlyle had been disposed of, Mickey Heath connected solidly with one of Pillette's pitches and the ball soared off his bat in the general direction of the center-field fence. The ball came down on top of the brick wall and then bounced jauntily out into Thirty-ninth street for a home run**

(Continued on Page 2, Column 5)

MICKEY HEATH

## RUETHER HANGS UP NINETEENTH WIN AS SEALS DEFEAT ANGELS

SAN FRANCISCO, July 31.—Dutch Ruether of the Seals turned in his nineteenth win of the year today at the expense of the Angels, breezing through to an easy 7-to-2 victory.

The Angels got a run in the first inning. With one man out Burkett singled and after Tolson was out on a fly to center, Berger singled. Schulmerich popped a weak fly to center field that Averill and Jolly allowed to drop between them and Burkett scored.

The Seals came back savagely at the expense of Barfoot. Johnson opened with a triple. He scored while Crosetti was being thrown out by Barfoot. Then followed singles by Averill, Suhr and Jolley; a sacrifice fly by Mishkin and a double by Rhyne. Four runs scored.

A double by Suhr, an infield out and a sacrifice fly by Jolley put over another run in the third. A single by Crosetti and a home run by Averill accounted for the two runs in the fifth. Barfoot left the game after the fifth and Weathersby finished. He was not scored on but the Seals had runs enough and to spare by that time.

The Angels were helpless before

(Continued on Page 3, Column I)

## STANDINGS AND RESULTS IN MAJOR AND MINOR LEAGUES

**PACIFIC COAST LEAGUE**

| | W. | L. | Pct. |
|---|---|---|---|
| HOLLYWOOD | 21 | 9 | .700 |
| Sacramento | 20 | 10 | .667 |
| San Francisco | 18 | 12 | .600 |
| Oakland | 16 | 14 | .533 |
| Missions | 15 | 15 | .500 |
| LOS ANGELES | 13 | 17 | .433 |
| Portland | 10 | 20 | .333 |
| Seattle | 7 | 23 | .233 |

Yesterday's Results

HOLLYWOOD, 4; Missions, 3 (10 innings.)
San Francisco, 7; LOS ANGELES, 2.
Portland, 8; Seattle, 1.
Oakland, 7; Sacramento, 6.

Games Today

Missions vs. HOLLYWOOD at Wrigley Field.
LOS ANGELES at San Francisco.
Oakland at Sacramento.
Seattle at Portland.

**AMERICAN LEAGUE**

| | W. | L. | Pct. |
|---|---|---|---|
| New York | 70 | 31 | .693 |
| Philadelphia | 64 | 36 | .640 |
| St. Louis | 52 | 52 | .500 |
| Cleveland | 47 | 55 | .461 |
| Washington | 46 | 57 | .447 |
| Chicago | 45 | 56 | .446 |
| Detroit | 42 | 57 | .424 |
| Boston | 38 | 60 | .388 |

Yesterday's Results

Chicago, 7; Washington, 5.
Detroit, 7; Boston, 2.

(Continued on Page .3, Column 3)

## LOS ANGELES OFFICIALLY AWARDED 1932 OLYMPICS

Despite the agitation to take the Olympic Games away from Los Angeles, California will have the world classic of 1932, and as much of the world as can get here will come to see them, was the report of William May Garland, president of the California Tenth Olympiad Association, in a message received here yesterday from Amsterdam. Garland is in the Dutch city observing the progress of the games there and getting suggestions to aid in their staging in Los Angeles in 1932. He is accompanied by Zack J. Farmer, secretary of the association.

## COOPER WHIPS LA SALLE IN OLYMPIC MAIN EVENT

BY PAUL LOWRY

Farmer Joe Cooper plastered Bobby La Salle at will in the main event at the Olympic last night and won every round with the exception of the fifth and sixth. A low punch caused Referee Wright to stop the fight momentarily in the fifth and send Cooper to his corner for a breathing spell.

When the boys resumed their biffing Cooper appeared to have a charley horse in his left leg and was barely able to stand. For two rounds the leg bothered him, but from the seventh on he ripped home left and right-hand uppercuts to La Salle's face until that young man's mouth looked like a badly mutilated tomato. It was puffed and bruised and red with gore at the finish.

BOBBY LASALLE

**About the only place La Salle hit Cooper was back of the left ear and on the left side. Most of the time his wild swings whistled through the air or wrapped themselves around Cooper's neck.**

In the semi-wind-up there was a mild upset when Charley Pinto defeated Johnny Vacca in ten fast rounds. It was a far better fight than the main event and saw Pinto winning with a neat left-hand attack to Vacca's body.

Pinto is from Buffalo and once fought Fidel LaBarba's conqueror a draw, but was hardly rated strong

(Continued on Page 4, Column 7)

## ALAN HERRINGTON WINS IN SEABRIGHT NET TOURNEY

SEABRIGHT (N. J.) July 31. (AP)—The East met the West and the South met the East in the two chief matches of the Seabright invitation tennis tournament today, adding a sectional flavor to the interest in the play.

**The East was victorious in one match, Julius Seligson of New York and Lehigh University, the intercollegiate singles champion, defeating Berkeley Bell of Austin, Tex., in three sets, 3-6, 7-5, 6-4. Seligson's victory repeated his triumph over the Texan in the finals of the Metropolitan turf court championship on Sunday.**

In the second match the West triumphed. Alan Herrington of San Francisco, who holds the intercollegiate title in the doubles, won after a long tussle from Sidney B. Wood of Forest Hills, N. Y. The scores were 6-3, 12-10.

Ricardo Tapia of Mexico and Gordon Lum, captain of the Chinese Davis Cup team, staged the longest and most bitterly contested match of the day with the Mexican finally winning, 7-5, 5-7, 6-4.

Like the Seligson-Bell match, the encounter between Watson Washburn, former Davis Cup player, and William Aydelotte, national indoor champion, also was their second meeting within a few days. The two New Yorkers also met in the Metropolitan championship. Wash-

(Continued on Page .3, Column 4)

## BERT RITCHIE, TROJAN GRID STAR, NOT ELIGIBLE IN FALL

Bert Ritchie, former San Diego High School athletic star, will not be eligible for football this fall at the University of Southern California, according to word at the Trojan institution yesterday. Ritchie showed up in good style as a fullback in spring practice and was counted on as sure point winner in the hurdles on the track team. Bert was a freshman last fall but did not play football.

SPORTS
Los Angeles Times

PATHETIC FIGURES
GENT WHO HAD TICKET ON 50 YD. LINE BUT WHO WAS CAUGHT IN A ROSE PARADE MOB YESTERDAY AND ARRIVED AT THE ROSE BOWL FIFTEEN MINUTES AFTER THE GAME WAS OVER

BRUCE RUSSELL

WEDNESDAY MORNING, JANUARY 2, 1929. C

# GOLDEN BEARS LOSE TO ENGINEERS

## HOW ENGINEERS MEASURED BEARS FOR 8-TO-7 TRIMMING

Here are two remarkable action photos showing Georgia Tech scoring eight points at the Rose Bowl yesterday afternoon. Top photo is of "Stumpy" Thomason crossing the California goal line in the third period. Eisan has missed the tackle and is stretched out on the ground. Lumpkin is next to him, with Umpire Art Badenoch in the middle of the picture. Below, Vance Maree is shown knocking down Lom's punt with his arms. Note the ball right off his hands. These two plays were the highlights of the game. [Photos by Paul Strite and C. E. Thompson, Times staff photographers]

## GEORGIA TECH TEAM WINS NATIONAL GRID HONORS

### Riegels's Error Gives Tornado Chance to Win

**HEART BROKEN!**

Roy Riegels, captain-elect of the California varsity, was heartbroken last night over his now famous play in the Georgia Tech game. He declared he had no excuses to make, that he was merely mixed up in his directions and that the first he knew that anything was wrong was when Lom grabbed him by the arm on the goal line. Riegels said he was not groggy or goofy from a pounding in the line. His splendid play during the second half rather bears out this statement. No man, battered as some of the southern writers insinuate Riegels was, could come back and play the football Riegels did. Lom declared he sensed that Riegels was out of step the minute he turned around. Benny said he chased him, hollering for him to stop, but that because of the din by the crowd Riegels could not hear him. That's the inside of one of football's queerest plays.

(Continued from Page 1, Part 1)

yards in surpassing numbers to Tech, had missed three other opportunities to score.

**Once Eisan was in the clear on a regular Brick Muller heave from Capt. Phillips, but slipped and fell only five yards from the goal line. Again, Barr was standing on the Georgia Tech goal line, but a rifle shot from Benny Lom went right through his arms. And in the first quarter, after Lom had slipped around a Tech end for thirty-six-yard run from fake punt formation, the Bears missed fire by delaying their forward passing attack until the fourth down.**

When they did try a pass it was obvious—a fake place kick on which Barr was smeared for a twelve-yard loss.

Georgia Tech proved to be as good a football team as the experts said it was. It had a fast-charging, hard-hitting line—one of the most consistent forward walls that ever performed in a Rose Bowl classic.

**ALL STARRED**

There wasn't a single outstanding individual on it with the possible exception of Capt. Pund, but there never was a moment of the game when one of those linesmen wasn't rising to the heights to achieve some bit of distinction when it was most needed.

Sometimes it was Jones and Waddey, the ends, who until they tired in the last period, never gave the California safety men half a chance to run back punts. They were down on Breakenridge and Eisan with every boot.

Then there was Maree, who blocked the kick that resulted in the safety and 2 points. And Thrash and Watkins. Drennon bobbed up ever and anon to knife through and spoil California's sequence of plays. And Westbrook, the other guard. And there was Capt. Pund to intercept forward passes, play a roving center on the

(Continued on Page 2, Column 6)

### Breaks Decide Annual Battle in Rose Bowl

BY BRAVEN DYER

The breaks of the game! Wowie! Had there been many more the entire assemblage of 65,000 fans would have been seeking the bughouse last night.

ROY RIEGELS

Picture yourself a football game in which one team fumbled the ball into the hands of its foe, only to have it fumbled back to the original possessors on the very next play. Not once, but many times. Picture, if you can, a game in which a seasoned performer ran 64 yards to the wrong goal line and was prevented from scoring 2 points for the opposition only by the determination of one of his team-mates.

**WIN HONORS**

Picture this and much more, including blocked kicks, intercepted passes, numerous penalties and frequent yelps for time out, and you have some conception of the struggle that took place in the Pasadena Rose Bowl yesterday when Georgia Tech gained a stranglehold on national grid honors by beating California, 8 to 7.

But if you were not present you can go on picturing until you're blue in the face and you'll never know half the thrills that went with a game of football that was a nightmare for coaches and players, but a treat filled with pulse-quickening surprises for the spectators.

It was bad football, from a fundamental standpoint, but it was so darned thrilling that you could forgive practically every error that occurred.

**The scores all came suddenly and unexpectedly. Georgia Tech tallied on a safety in the second quarter and followed up with a touchdown by Stumpy Thomason in the third period. California went scoreless until the final minutes of play when Capt. Phillips took a pass over the goal line and Barr added the extra point.**

But the play that will live forever in the minds of those who attended the battle was that 64-yard gallop by Roy Riegels, captain-elect of the Bears. The play has been written about in books for many, many years. Coaches with a penchant for telling yarns like to spill it at all banquets. It has been the basis of many a magazine thriller. But to see it pulled on the field of play, right before your eyes, is something else again.

When Columbus started out to explore the world he took a compass with him. But Roy Riegels of the Bears, having played on football fields for many years, never dreamed he would need such an instrument

(Continued on Page 3, Column 4)

## HERE ARE STATISTICS ON GEORGIA TECH-BEAR TILT

BY AL PARMENTER

| | Tech | Bears |
|---|---|---|
| Yardage gained on running plays | 157 | 167 |
| Yardage gained on forward passes | 23 | 109 |
| Total yardage gained from scrimmage | 180 | 276 |
| Forward passes attempted | 2 | 17 |
| Forward passes completed | 1 | 9 |
| Forward passes intercepted by | 1 | 0 |
| Number of punts | 10 | 10 |
| Average length of punts | 38 | 43 |
| Touchdowns | 1 | 1 |
| Tries for point after touchdown made | 0 | 1 |
| Safety | 1 | 0 |
| Number of penalties against | 5 | 3 |
| Yardage lost through penalties | 35 | 10 |
| First downs from scrimmage | 4 | 6 |
| First downs on passes | 1 | 5 |
| Total first downs | 5 | 11 |
| Fumbles by | 4 | 2 |
| Fumbles recovered by | 3 | 4 |

Yardage gained from scrimmage by Tech backs:

| | |
|---|---|
| Mizell | 77 |
| Thomason | 40 |
| Lumpkin | 32 |
| Dunlap | 8 |

Yardage gained from scrimmage by California backs:

| | |
|---|---|
| Lom | 113 |
| Barr | 24 |
| Schmidt | 20 |
| Cockburn | 7 |
| Rice | 5 |
| Breakenridge | 1 |

**THE LINE-UPS**

| California | | Georgia Tech. |
|---|---|---|
| Avery | L.E.R. | Waddey |
| Fitz | L.T.R. | Maree |
| H. Gill | L.G.R. | Drennon |
| Riegels | C. | Pund |
| Schwarz | R.G.L. | Westbrook |
| Bancroft | R.T.L. | Thrash |
| Phillips | R.E.L. | Jones |
| Breakenridge | Q. | Schulman |
| Lom | L.H.R. | Thomason |
| Barr | R.H.L. | Mizell |
| Schmidt | F. | Lumpkin |

**SCORE BY PERIODS**

| | | | | |
|---|---|---|---|---|
| California | 0 | 0 | 0 | 7—7 |
| Georgia Tech | 0 | 2 | 6 | 0—8 |

**SUBSTITUTES**

California: Miller for Riegels, Schichtling for Barr, C. Handy for Schwarz, Cockburn for Schmidt, Rice for Schichtling, Norton for Avery, Riegels for Miller; Breakenridge for Eisan, Schmidt for Cockburn, Beckett for Gill.

Georgia Tech: Durant for Schulman, Dunlap for Mizell, Watkins for Maree, Holland for Jones.

Scoring: Touchdowns—Thomason, Phillips. Conversions—Barr. Safety—Breakenridge for California.

## BREAKS DECIDE GEORGIA WIN OVER GOLDEN BEARS

BY "CHICK" MEEHAN
Coach, New York University
[Copyright, 1929, by Bell Syndicate.]

In a hard football battle, between two great lines, Georgia Tech defeated California 8 to 7 yesterday.

COACH MEEHAN.

The Yellow Jackets blocked two punts, and those two feats won the game for them.

If breaks ever decided a football game, they did yesterday. There were plenty of breaks throughout the entire game, and Tech was quick to take advantage of every opportunity to score. The first one came after one of the most exciting and spectacular plays ever seen on a football field. In the second period, with four minutes to play of the first half, and the ball on Tech's 24-yard line, Thomason whirled around California's right end for a gain of eleven yards, and was tackled so ferociously by Lom, that he fumbled the ball, and it went spinning toward the boundary line, when Riegels, the California center, who played a brilliant game throughout, scooped up the ball and started for a touchdown for California that eventually turned out to be a safety for Georgia Tech.

**As he passed, Thomason tried to push him out of bounds, but missed him. Riegels then reversed his field, and ran toward the center, and to everyone's surprise, turned, and ran the other way. The California team immediately started taking out men, clearing his pathway, despite the fact that he was running toward his own goal. He finally got into the clear, and Lom, who was chasing after him, yelled frantically in his ear to turn around. At this point it became a most exciting race, until they reached the one-foot line, when Lom caught him by the wrist, and wheeled him around, to start him in the other direction. As he did this, Pund, Georgia Tech center, brought him to earth with a vicious thud.**

On the next play, and before the

(Continued on Page 2, Column 8)

## PLAY-BY-PLAY STORY OF GEORGIA TECH'S TRIUMPH OVER CALIFORNIA ELEVEN

BY BRAVEN DYER

At 2 o'clock the bowl was practically filled, indicating a capacity crowd when the whistle blew. Georgia Tech came on the field for limbering up exercises shortly before 2 o'clock, indulging in light punting practice, which was featured by the mighty boots of Bob Parham. After the Golden Tornado left the field, California came on the scene of action and took up six minutes of punting and passing practice.

**Charles Wesley Keppen, the demon announcer, broadcast the line-ups. Schulman was announced as the starting quarterback for Georgia Tech, and Breakenridge took up the same duties for the Bears. Coach Alexander of the Engineers planned on letting his regular signal-barker, Bob Durant, sit on the bench for awhile to observe the type of Bear attack. It was considerably more of a surprise than was Price's feat in starting Breakenridge in place of Eisan, for the Bear sub had been working with the regulars almost every practice since the team arrived.**

**FIRST QUARTER**

Captains Phillips and Pund met in the middle of the field and shook hands with each other and the officials. Phillips won the toss and elected to receive in the south end of the field. Waddey, right end for the visitors, kicked off to Schmidt, who received on his 15-yard line, and fumbled, but recovered and returned the ball to the 34-yard line. Barr hit right tackle for a yard. Lom dropped back to pass, but instead of passing, raced around right end, reversed his field, and galloped to Georgia Tech's 28-yard line, where he was stopped by Thomason. Barr went through right tackle for 2½ yards. Barr hit right guard for 2 yards, being stopped by Lumpkin. Tech was playing a six-man line against the Bears, with Lumpkin and Pund backing up the line. Lom went through right tackle for 1 yard. With Breakenridge in position to hold the ball, Barr went back for a place kick, but instead of kicking attempted to pass, but was downed in his tracks by Waddey before he could get rid of the ball. Tech took the ball on its own 34-yard line.

**Thomason hit right tackle for a yard. Running from punt formation, Mizell skirted right end and dashed down the sidelines until he was run out of bounds on the 50-yard line. However, the ball was brought back and Tech penalized 5 yards for having a backfield man in motion, placing the ball on the 30-yard line. Mizell's run was a pretty piece of work. Mizell punted to Breakenridge, who was downed on the 41-yard line.**

On a reverse, Barr went through right tackle for 4 yards. Schmidt hit left guard for 2 yards. Barr hit right guard for 3½ yards, but the ball was brought back and Tech penalized 5 yards for offside, giving California a first down on Tech's 48-yard line. On a reverse, Lom broke through left tackle for 7 yards, being brought down by Mizell. Tech returned to a seven-man line in an effort to stop California's running attack. Thrash stopped Lom for no gain. Schmidt hit the middle of the line for a yard. He fumbled, but recovered. Lom punted out of bounds on Tech's 16-yard line.

Thomason made 2 yards at right tackle. Mizell punted to Breakenridge, who was downed in his tracks on California's 49-yard line by Jones and Waddey.

**On a reverse, Lom failed to gain, Drennon made the tackle. Lom went back to pass, and attempted a repitition of the play on which he made so much yardage earlier in the game,**

(Continued on Page 2, Column 4)

## "FRAGILE" TECH FORWARDS WIN GLORY FOR GEORGIA

BY DICK HAWKINS
Sports Editor Atlanta Constitution

ROSE BOWL, PASADENA, Jan. 1. National champions. All Dixie is rolling those words around its mouth like a Pickaninny rolls a stalk of sugar cane. Georgia Tech's Golden Tornado, called "fragile and smaller than their opponents," fought the Golden Bears of California like they have never been fought before and won a football game, 8 - 7. That is the story without any of its thrills.

"STUMPY" THOMASON

To tell all those thrills would take a Webster, a Dickens and a Service all rolled into one. Some people would call that game sloppy. There were fumbles and there were queer plays till hades wouldn't have it, but after all the score is the thing that counts. Tomorrow the score will be the only part of the game left to memory.

**Roy Riegels, captain-elect for next year, is a sad boy tonight. He did what you read about in books and seldom see when he recovered a fumble and raced 64 yards toward his own goal before he discovered his mistake. Just after that big Vance Maree, one of Tech's "fragile" linemen, smashed through and blocked a punt which was covered by Barr for a safety. This furnished the deciding score of the game and some will call it luck for Tech. Luck, dear readers, is that which happens outside the agency of man. The fact that Mr. Riegels was beaten to the point where he didn't know where his own goal was is not a matter of luck, it's a matter of football fight. By the same token the numerous fumbles by Tech ball carriers were not luck for California. They were the result of savage tackling by California's fighting Bears. Let's hear no more talk of luck and what might have been.**

The Tornado of Tech was victo-

(Continued on Page 2, Column 2)

SPORTS
Los Angeles Times

THURSDAY MORNING, JANUARY 2, 1930.

# PANTHERS SUNK BY TROJANS, 47 TO 14

## A SHINING TROJAN HERO---OFFENSIVELY AND DEFENSIVELY

The top photo shows Erny Pinckert (No. 17) taking a forward pass from Russ Saunders for the second Trojan touchdown in the first period. Pinckert catching the ball on the 15-yard line, and although he was tackled on the 10-yard line he squirmed out of Parkinson's grasp. Big George Dye is the lumpy gentleman seen running toward Pinckert, the Trojan center hurrying along to form interference for Pinckert. At the bottom Pinckert is seen in a different role—that of a protecting back who has batted down a pass intended for All-American Joe Donchess, following Uansa's 68-yard run on the first scrimmage play of the game. Pinckert scored on his pass, and saved a score on the Pitt toss.
[Photos by Paul Strite, Times staff photographer]

## TROJANS STUN GRIDIRON FANS

*Easy Victory Astonishes Tremendous Crowd*

*Polished Passing Attack Smashes Panthers*

*"Formation B" Functions With Usual Fumbles*

BY BRAVEN DYER

Flashing the greatest offensive maneuver ever revealed in a major gridiron combat on the western slope, the Trojans of Southern California yesterday passed and slashed their way to an astounding 47-to-14 triumph over the hitherto undefeated Panthers of Pittsburgh.

GARRETT ARBELBIDE

Seventy-one thousand fans looked on in amazement as the proteges of Howard Jones raced up and down the Rose Bowl turf for one touchdown after another, putting to complete rout the team which had been rated in the same class with Notre Dame by eastern critics.

It was the most crushing defeat ever suffered by a Rose Bowl contestant since the annual East vs. West games were inaugurated, back in 1916.

SET RECORD

Southern California's smashing victory gives that institution two wins in as many Rose Bowl games. The Trojans are the only eleven, East, West, Midwest or South with such a record. The other triumph was scored over Penn State in 1923.

The ease with which the Trojans amassed 26 points in the first half left the capacity crowd stunned with astonishment. Most of us had looked for a tough first quarter, and not a few expected that the Panthers would be leading at the end of the second period.

Therefore, the astounding spectacle of Pitt, an undefeated team, boasting no less than four bona-fide all-Americans, trailing by four touchdowns at the half-way mark left practically everybody speechless.

**This writer said yesterday morning that the Trojans had the stuff to win if they played as they could play. It was also stated that if Jones's men did their stuff properly, Pitt would not be able to stop them.**

Well, the Trojans were right and that settled Pitt in no uncertain fashion. It is doubtful if any team ever exhibited a more polished passing attack in a major football game than that which Russ Saunders and Marshall Duffield unleashed yesterday afternoon.

Ride the Panthers for their poor defense if you want to, and they deserve it, but at the same time give Jones and his boys credit for knowing how and where to throw the ball and what was more important, how to catch it. Pitt had pass chances too, but the Panther receivers were not in the same class with Troy's ends and halfbacks, none of whom fell down when called upon in a pinch.

The Trojans massacred their foes with such apparent ease that a lot of people are wondering today how it all came about. It looked like some kind of a game instead of a battle.

In brief, the scoring came about in this manner:

PITT HALTED

After Toby Uansa had paralyzed Trojan rooters with that pulse-quickening 68-yard run of his around Troy's left end in the first minute of play, Jones's boys gave a perfect imitation of that great stand of theirs on the 2-yard line at Stanford. Only this time the ball was out a bit farther, Toby having been overhauled from behind by

(Continued on Page 13, Column 3)

## JONES LOUD IN PRAISE OF TROJANS

*Panthers' Pass Defense Weakened by Trying to Stop Line Plays*

BY BOB RAY

Pittsburgh laid itself open to Southern California's passing attack by building its defense to stop the Trojans' running plays.

HOWARD JONES.

That, in a nutshell, was the way Coach Howard Jones, his usually serious countenance illuminated by a wide smile of victory, summed up the Trojans' 47-to-14 triumph over the hitherto unbeaten Pittsburgh Panthers in yesterday's annual Rose Bowl football battle.

"Of course," said Jones, "my boys played a great game of football, and I don't think anyone will deny that, while the Panthers unquestionably were not at the top of their game. I was more than

(Continued on Page 13, Column 2)

## TROJANS PRAISED BY PITT

*Sutherland and His Men Laud U.S.C. After Game at Rose Bowl*

BY FRANK ROCHE

"U.S.C. has come ahead, we have gone back since Thanksgiving Day The Trojans played beautiful football, we fell down." The above statement was gleaned from Coach Jock Sutherland of the Pittsburgh football team as he was leaving the field with his players following the game yesterday at the Rose Bowl. Sutherland, who is usually a tight-lipped individual, was high in his praise of the Trojan football team.

"JOCK" SUTHERLAND

"The Trojans are the equal of any team in the country. I have seen few teams function better than U.S.C. did against us." he commented as he walked to the dressing-rooms at the Bowl. "My team's defense against Howard Jones's passing attack simply went to pieces," he said rather dryly. When pressed for an explanation on that question, Sutherland simply said he had none to give.

**"You might quote me on one thing," he said turning to the**

(Continued on Page 13, Column 4)

## DAZZLING AERIAL ATTACK BLASTS PITT'S RECORD

*Crowd of 70,000 Spectators Views Overwhelming Defeat of East's Best Bet in Rose Bowl*

### HOW THEY SCORED

First quarter—Saunders passed to Edelson for 25 yards. Shaver kicked goal. Troy recovers Walinchus's fumble on Pitt 30. Saunders passed to Pinckert. Shaver missed.

Second quarter—Troy recovers fumble on Pitt 28. Duffield goes over. Baker missed goal. Duffield pass to Mortensen to the Pitt 2-yard line. Duffield scored. Baker converted.

Third quarter—Saunders scored on 50-yard drive. Shaver converted. Uansa passed to Walinchus for 28 yards. Parkinson converted. Saunders passed to Edelson for 42 yards. Baker converted.

Four quarter—Williams passed to Collins for 25 yards. Parkinson converted. Duffield passed to Wilcox for 61 yards. Duffield converted.

(Continued from Page 1, Part I)

it was in stark and staring figures on the score board:

Southern California, 26; Pittsburgh, 0.

Shades of William Penn! It was a catastrophe.

And it was worse after the third quarter got under way. Saunders scored another touchdown, and the tally read 33 to 0 against Pittsburgh with its redoubtable all-American quartet composed of Uansa, Montgomery, Parkinson and Donchess.

SKILL WASTED

But all the skill and the craft and the football brains and fight possessed by these good players proved unavailing against Southern California's uncrowned all-Americans.

And all the predictions made by Pop Warner, Knute Rockne and other master minds of football that Pitt would beat the Trojans were buried along with the Panthers under the avalanche of Southern California touchdowns.

It was a grand and glorious day for the Trojans—a day in which they rose to heights supreme and delivered a real knockout punch to the pride of the East.

**The victory was the Trojans' second in the annual East-West games at Pasadena, the S.C. boys having defeated Penn State, 14 to 3, in 1923.**

That team was coached by Elmer (Gloomy Gus) Henderson, and today's eleven was the first that has seen New Year's action under the direction of Howard Harding Jones.

It was a sweet afternoon for Jones, who sat on the bench and watched his players parade up and down the field for one score after another—parade in form that saw them a better team than when they beat Washington State and still later crush Carnegie Tech in early December.

Even Toby Uansa's dazzling run for 68 yards on the first scrimmage play of the game was lost sight of in the sparkling array of plays that followed.

Pitt was unable to crown Uansa's run with a touchdown, the fleet Pitt left halfback having been hauled down from the rear by Russ Saunders on the Trojans' 14-yard line. Parkinson and Walinchus made 7 yards in three plays, but Pinckert knocked down Walinchus's intended pass to Donchess over the goal line.

PINCKERT HERO

And right now is a good time to say something about this young Pinckert person. He was one of the real stars of the game. His blocking and interference running were well-nigh perfect, and his defensive play, backing up the line on Pitt smashes and smearing forward passes. was unusual.

Pitt made its only scores in the same manner by which the Trojans scored so often—through the air—but Pinckert was responsible for neither.

The Panthers had a splendid line and hard-running backs, and they amassed 223 yards to the Trojans' 141 by rushing, but the story of their downfall is revealed in the air figures.

**The Trojans gained 297 yards with their passes, to 80 made by Pitt. The Panthers were caught flat footed time after time. They were unable to solve the deception of the Trojan air attack. Sometimes the ball went sailing over the heads of the secondary defense or wide to the right or left.**

Once Edelson took the ball right out of the hands of the astonished Uansa's grasp and continued merrily on his way to a touchdown.

Here's the toll in brief:.

First period: From the Trojans' 46-yard line Saunders passed to Edelson on the 30-yard line, and Edelson raced over the goal line. He caught the ball over Walinchus's head, and was tackled in the end zone by Uansa. Shaver kicked goal. Score, 7 to 0. From the Pitt 25-yard line Saunders passed to Pinckert, and Parkinson missed the tackle on the 10-yard line. Shaver missed goal. Score, 13 to 0.

Second period: Duffield, who had entered the game for Saunders, sent a quick kick over the heads of the Pitt secondary defense men. Wilcox and Arbelbide recovered Clark's fumble on the Pitt 19-yard line and in six plays Duffield went over. The play on fourth down started from near the right side lines, and Duffield, racing in and out, scampered wide to the left. He outguessed the last Pitt man who had a chance to get him—Donchess, who had moved over from the other side—and went over for the score. Baker's kick hit the uprights, and the score was 19 to 0. Duffield a few plays later passed to Mortenson for a gain of 50 yards, and the ball was on the Pitt 3-yard line. On a spin play Duffield smashed through center. Baker kicked the goal and the score was 26 to 0 at half time.

PANTHERS TALLY

Third period: Pinckert intercepted a Pitt pass and ran it back 5 yards to the middle of the field. In eight plays, on five of which Saunders carried the ball, the Trojans were over the goal line again. Saun-

(Continued on Page 12, Column 7)

## TROJAN SUPREMACY IS SHOWN

*Thundering Herd Had Great Advantage in Everything Except Yardage From Scrimmage; Uansa Well Bottled With Exception of Opening Dash; S. C. Passes Score*

BY RALPH HUSTON

The Thundering Herd of the University of Southern California was forced to bow to Pittsburgh in one thing, yesterday—yards from scrimmage. The Panthers chalked up 223 yards in 49 attempts, against 141 for the Trojans in 47 tries, but it was that stubborn work in the front wall that enabled the Trojans to pass their way to the most crushing victory in the history of the Rose Bowl game.

GAIUS SHAVER

The Trojans completed eight out of fifteen passes for a total of 297 yards, against the 80 yards which the Panthers gained in four successful passes out of twenty attempts. Both teams intercepted three overhead tosses.

The Trojans made ten first downs, against eight for the enemy, both teams making six from scrimmage. Touchdowns are not counted as first downs.

**Toby Uansa, Pitt's all-American halfback, rang up 84 yards from scrimmage, but some 68 of that was on one play. In the other ten times he carried th ball, he was held to 16 yards, an average of 1.6 per try.**

Russ Saunders was the hardest-working back on the field, carrying the ball twenty-one times for a tot-l gain of 64 yards, an average of just about 3 yards per play.

Gaius Shaver and Marshall Duffield outpunted "Pug" Parkinson, the other Panther all-American back, an average of 15 yards per punt. Shaver booted three times, varying from 61 to 36 yards, for an average of 48 yards per boot, while Duffield added a quick kick of 53 yards. Parkinson kicked seven times, averaging 34.5 yards.

Both teams fumbled twice, and on each occasion the opposing eleven recovered.

The Trojan combined total of yardage gained from scrimmage and passes was 438 yards, against 303 for Pittsburgh. The S. C. backs lost just 13 yards in scrimmage plays, while Pitt lost 41. Rooney sufferde most of this when Tappaan downed him for a 20-yard loss when he dropped back to pass.

The complete details:

| | S.C. | P. |
|---|---|---|
| Total yardage gained from scrimmage | 141 | 223 |
| Number of yards lost from scrimmage | 13 | 41 |
| Forward passes attempted | 15 | 20 |
| Forward passes comp'eted | 8 | 4 |
| Forward passes incomplete | 4 | 13 |
| Forward passes intercepted | 3 | 3 |
| Total yardage gained from forward passes | 297 | 89 |
| Total yardage. scrimmage and passes | 438 | 303 |
| First downs from scrimmage | 6 | 6 |
| First downs from passes | 3 | 2 |
| First downs on penalties | 1 | 0 |
| Total first downs | 10 | 8 |
| Total number of scrimmage plays | 47 | 49 |

(Continued on Page 13, Column 7).

## MODERNISM ROSE BOWL KEYNOTE

*Pony Blimp Adds Roar to Clicking Sound Cameras, and Cheers of 70,000 Fans as Trojans Crush Panthers; Dramatic Moments Thrill Vast Throng*

BY JEAN PLANNETTE

Another New Year football classic is finish-'

The end of the gridiron season, which used to be marked by a tangle of horse-drawn vehicles around Tournament Park reached new heights yesterday with a capacity crowd of 70,000 in the Rose Bowl. Thousands of automobiles threaded their way over the boulevards and through the foothills. Sound cameras clicked, and the roar of the Goodyear pony blimp added the final note of modern progress to the scene.

HARRY EDELSON

The long-rumored storm failed to materialize and the weather was perfect—unless you were rooting for Pittsburgh. Proceedings began with the Trojan band massed with the Pasadena Elks' band as a courteous representation for Pittsburgh. The Trojan pony cannons fired a salute as the flag was borne aloft by a huge cluster of balloons in the national colors. Patriot-- may be a sentimental illusion, but the sight of 70,000 people rising to the strains of the "Star Spangled Banner" was enough to thrill the most hardened cynic.

**The Trojans yesterday returned a large portion of football prestige to the West and at the same time cinched the national championship for Notre Dame. Even the most rabid S.C. fan was amazed at the ease with which the warriors of Troy humbled the Panthers. Troy resembled what the mythical all-American team should be in action. There are seemingly no mistakes to be pointed out to any individual. Best of all, it was a seniors' field day and every one of the de-**

(Continued on Page 13, Column 7)

## OVERWHELMING ATTACK, NOT HEAT, BEAT PITT

BY RUSSELL J. NEWLAND
Associated Press Sports Writer

ROSE BOWL (Pasadena) Jan. 1. (AP)—Crashing, swirling giants who asked no quarter and yielded none, Southern California's Trojans ripped and tore a Pittsburgh Panther defense to shreds here today to rout the previously undefeated mythical champions of the East, 47-14—the most decisive beating taken by a losing team since this classic was established, fourteen years ago.

The great intersectional struggle that annually heralds the New Year in this far-off corner of the nation saw a Pittsburgh eleven that placed four men on all-American teams this past season completely outclassed from opening kick-off to closing gun.

All the vaunted power of the Panther team that brought it nine straight victories during the year of 1929 went for naught against a Trojan offensive that brushed everything before it.

The game had barely gotten under way when Southern California cleats had dug their first message in turf behind the Pittsburgh goal line. Six times again, in the ensuing fifty-four minutes of play, Trojan toters of the ball explored the ground where points are found.

**By land and air the young gridiron warriors who fight for the Cardinal and Gold of South-**

(Continued on Page 13, Column 7)

## EASTERNERS SHOCKED BY TROJAN GRID TRIUMPH

BY WALTER ECKERSALL

PASADENA, Jan. 1. (Exclusive)—Outclassed in practically every department of the game, Southern California defeated Pittsburgh, the undefeated eastern eleven, here today in the Rose Bowl, 47 to 14.

WALTER ECKERSALL

The Trojans, who played one of the best games of the year, had a much stronger attack than the Panthers, and they made ground when yards meant scores. Their defense was almost as strong, although they permitted Pittsburgh to score by the use of two forward passes. Pitt was unable to penetrate the stiff Southern California defense and it was not until they started to forward-pass that the easterners made any ground.

Pitt had absolutely no forward-pass defense, and three of the Trojans' touchdowns were the results of forward passes thrown over the back men of the box defense. In the second half, Pitt resorted to the diamond defense and the Trojans' passes were not so successful.

**The result of this game and the defeat of Carnegie Tech by the Trojans, and the victory of Stanford over the Army is a wonderful boost for the caliber of football played in this section. The eastern elevens were defeated decisively, and to-**

(Continued on Page 13, Column 1),

# Gallant Fox Wins Kentucky Derby Laurels

SPORTS
Los Angeles Times

SUNDAY MORNING, MAY 18, 1930. C

# ERIC KRENZ BREAKS OWN WORLD'S DISCUS RECORD

## JOCKEY SANDE PILOTS VICTOR

*Triumphant Steed Wins by Three Lengths*

*Gallant Knight Second at Churchill Downs*

*Throng of 70,000 Fans Sees Turf Classic*

**(Continued from Page 1, Part I)**

denly became an oriflamme of victory, a sure beacon of success. As Sande and Gallant Fox breezed into the lead at the half-mile post 70,000 spectators suddenly understood that the race was over. For they know what form means down this way, form and class, and here was the horse that had all the form and class of this race. There was no one else even close. There was no one else as close as the outposts of a Siberian frontier. Sande set his pace and opened up as much gray daylight as he needed and from that point on it was merely a question as to who might finish second or third.

There was all the tradition in the world back of his race. There was double-dyed tradition. In the first place, Gallant Fox was bred at the oldest nursery of the American thoroughbred. He was bred at the Belair stables between Baltimore and Washington, which dates back before George Washington's time, back around 1750. This stable raced horses against Gen. Washington before he was ever known as a general and statesman. The breeding spot that sent Gallant Fox into action goes back beyond the time of Washington. Lighthorse Harry Lee, Mad Anthony Wayne, Lord Cornwallis and the revolutionary knights of forgotten years. Ned O, who finished third, came from the same breeding center.

**ECHO OF TRADITION**

Now there is another echo of tradition. Back in 1919, a matter of eleven years ago, Earl Sande had his chance to ride the winner of the Preakless and the Kentucky Derby. But he was sure that Billy Kelly could beat Sir Barton in the Derby, so he picked the former and Sir Barton doubled up for a victory in two of the May classics. Sande could not put Billy Kelly in front of the Canadian horse. Eleven years is a long time to wait. In this stretch or span of time Sande has been in and out of the racing game. He was thought to be all through and washed up some years ago. Few thought he would ever come back to racing greatness. Balked in his main ambition when he was in his prime, just after the war, he finally had his chance this year. Gallant Fox was the vehicle waiting for a rider who could reclaim some of the past glory that belonged to Sir Barton and Man o'

**(Continued on Page 3, Column 3)**

# Stars Win Thriller From Seattle

## GREEN'S HOMER DECIDES ISSUE

*Hollywood Captures 8-to-7 Game from Indians*

*Ninth-Inning Circuit Clout Nets Two Tallies*

*Sheiks Cinch Weekly Series With Ball Victory*

**BY BRAVEN DYER**

Frank Merriwell, famous athletic hero of fiction, had nothing on Harry Green, fence-busting outfielder of the Hollywood Stars!

HARRY GREEN

Coming to bat in the last of the ninth yesterday, his team one run behind and Mike Gazella perched on second base with two out, Hard-hitting Harry hammered his second homer of the day over the left-field fence and Hollywood made it four straight over Seattle.

The count was 8 to 7, and Green's powerful clubbing in the closing stanza was all that saved Hollywood from defeat.

**In the seventh inning, with two out and Otis Brannon on first base, Green caught one of Rudy Kallio's slants and wafted it over the left-field wall. This cut Seattle's lead down, the count being 7 to 6, after Harry's initial circuit clout.**

**BIG SURPRISE**

More than half of the assembled multitude had started for the exits when Green came through with his second swat in the ninth frame. Harry was a utility player last year, but his heavy hitting caused Manager Oscar Vitt to make a place for him in left field this season and as a result Green is the leading slugger on the Hollywood club. You can't ask for any more than he did yesterday!

Unless Seattle gets better pitching today the Stars seem destined to walk off with the twin bill. Vitt's boys are slapping the apple soundly right now and being half a dozen runs behind, as they were yesterday, apparently means nothing in their young lives. Dutch Ruether, who won Seattle's lone game this week, will probably be on the mound in one of today's games, with House hurling the other. Hulvey, Wetzel

**(Continued on Page 6, Column 2)**

## TURNING THE TABLES ON STANFORD'S STAR

Telephoto by P. & A. shows Frank Wykoff of the University of Southern California winning the 100-yard dash in 9.7s, at Stanford yesterday, thereby gaining revenge for his defeat last month at the hands of Hec Dyer. From left to right the sprinters are Dyer, Gilberson (Stanford), Maurer (S.C.) Wykoff (S.C.) and Howell (S.) Maurer was thir.. behind Dyer, with Howell fourth. Dyer did his stuff in the 220, when he trimmed Wykoff in 21.5s.

## A WINNING COMBINATION

Here is shown Gallant Fox and Jockey Earl Sande—the popular combination taken just after winning the fifty-sixth Kentucky Derby at Churchill Downs yesterday afternoon in a drizzling rain before 70,000 spectators. Below the finish of the classic is shown with Gallant Fox three lengths ahead of Gallant Knight. Nedo appears in third-money position. [Upper photo by A. P. telephoto. Lower picture by P. & A. telephoto.]

## FOUR SOUTHLAND NET CHAMPIONSHIPS TO BE SETTLED HERE TODAY

**Today's Schedule**

**12:30—Women's singles final, Midge Gladman vs. Gladys Patz.**

**1:30—Men's singles final, Keith Gledhill vs. Ellsworth Vines.**

**3:00—Women's doubles final, Midge Gladman and Josephine Cruickshank vs. May Sutton Bundy and Violet Doeg.**

**4:00—Men's doubles final, Keith Gledhill and Ellsworth Vines vs. Dr. Gerald Bartosh and Jack Tidball.**

**YESTERDAY'S FINAL**

**Helen Marlowe and Ellsworth Vines retained their Southern California mixed doubles championship by beating Dorothy Workman and Jack Tidball, 7-5, 6-4.**

Helen Marlowe and Ellsworth Vines, defending champions from 1929, became the first 1930 Southern California title holders, when they defeated the challenging pair of Dorothy Workman and Jack Tidball, 7-5, 6-4, in the final round of mixed doubles. Some idea of what California is developing for the future may be gained from the fact that none of the four finalists is yet 20 years of age.

KEITH GLEDHILL

Four championships will be settled today. Marjorie Gladman, 1929 champion, meets Gladys Patz in the women's singles, and with Josephine Cruickshank will debate the women's doubles title against Mrs. May Sutton Bundy and Violet Doeg. The men's events feature Keith Gledhill meeting Ellsworth Vines in the singles final, and then the two will team up to face Gerald Bartosh and Jack Tidball for the doubles championship. The first match takes place at 12:30.

**Gladys Patz and Mrs. Esther Bartosh, 1929 women's doubles champions, bit the dust in a bitterly fought semifinal match in which they were unable to down the battling Santa Monica team of Mrs. Bundy and her neice, Violet Doeg. After Miss Patz and Mrs. Bartosh had captured the first set 8-6, Mrs. Bundy with her youthful partner settled down to take the next two at 6-4 and 6-2. They will give Miss Gladman and Miss Cruickshank a real run for the championship today.**

The two women's semifinals were in strange contrast. Miss Patz, facing the formidable Miss Deike who has the scalps of the two "first ten" players already this season, wore her opponent down by varying the length of her shots to win at 6-3, 7-5. Miss Gladman won rather easily over Helen Marlowe who was extremely unsteady and erred repeatedly to lose 6-2, 6-2. Miss Patz defeated Miss Gladman twice last year and this battle will be warm.

In the men's division, Keith Gledhill, just off the train from Stanford, had just a little too much variety and steadiness to his game for his fellow Santa Barbaran, Henry Culley, and won 7-5, 6-2. Gerald Bartosh put up a terrific battle against Ellsworth Vines before going down by the stupendous score of 12-10, 8-6. Vines and Gledhill had quite a battle in subduing Lester Stoefen and Henry Culley, 6-4, 3-6, 6-3, in a semifinal.

## Bruins, Cards Split Honors in Net Event

EUGENE (Or.) May 17. (AP)—The University of California at Los Angeles and Stanford University divided the honors today in the concluding rounds of the Coast Conference tennis play.

Albert Lewis of U.C.L.A., won the conference singles title by taking the measure of Stanley Almquist of Oregon in the finals, in a hard-fought three-set match, 5-7, 6-2, 7-5.

**The Stanford doubles team, Ted Easton and Bob Hall, won from the Washington combination composed of Lloyd Nordstrom and Bill Newkirk, 6-4, 6-0.**

The Lewis-Almquist match was in doubt until the final point was scored. The match went to deuce five times.

At the beginning of the deciding set the Oregon player won the first two games, but Lewis rallied and took his own service in the third game. From then on until the end Lewis was the aggressor. Although Almquist's drives were harder and more deadly, he was not so steady as the U.C.L.A. star.

## OAKS DRUB ANGELS TWICE

*Acorns Cop Both Ends of Double-Header from Los Angeles, 5 to 2; 8 to 0*

OAKLAND, May 17. (Exclusive)—Playing before an overflow crowd at Emeryville today, Carl Zamloch's Oaks cinched their series with the Angels by winning both games of a double-header, 5 to 2 in the first contest and 8 to 0 in the nightcap, which was called at the end of the seventh by agreement.

"Poison Ivy" Andrews, former New York Yankee, who was batted from the box in his first four starts for the Oaks, came through with a six-hit exhibition to beat the Angels in the first contest. Four of the hits were bunched into the sixth inning by Statz, Schulmerich Jacobs and Harper for the only Angel scores.

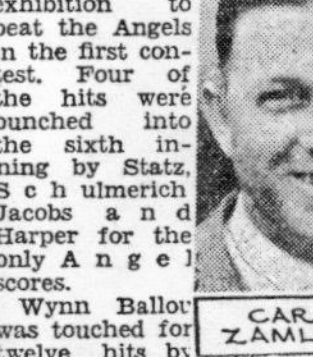

CARL ZAMLOCH

Wynn Ballou was touched for twelve hits by the Oaks and few of them were wasted. The timely hitting was done by Martin, Arlett, De Viveiros and Ernie Lombardi. The last named went to bat for De Viveiros in the seventh and delivered a single that scored two runs to cinch the first game.

Jim Edwards was Zamloch's selection for the second game and he blanked the Angels with only three hits.

First game:

| | AB | H | O | A |
|---|---|---|---|---|
| Haney,3b | 3 | 0 | 1 | 1 |
| Statz,cf | 4 | 1 | 5 | 0 |
| Sigafoos,2b | 3 | 0 | 0 | 2 |
| S'merich,lf | 4 | 1 | 1 | 0 |
| Jacobs,1b | 4 | 1 | 11 | 0 |
| Harper,rf | 5 | 1 | 2 | 0 |
| Dittmar,ss | 4 | 1 | 2 | 3 |
| Hannah,c | 2 | 1 | 2 | 0 |
| Ballou,p | 3 | 0 | 0 | 3 |
| Horne,x | 0 | 0 | 0 | 0 |
| P'ker,xx,2b | 0 | 0 | 0 | 0 |
| Skiff,c | 0 | 0 | 0 | 0 |
| Warren,z | 1 | 0 | 0 | 0 |
| Moore,zz | 1 | 0 | 0 | 0 |
| Totals | 34 | 6 | 24 | 9 |

| OAKLAND | AB | H | O | A |
|---|---|---|---|---|
| Uhalt,lf | 5 | 3 | 1 | 0 |
| B'baker,2b | 4 | 1 | 2 | 3 |
| Martin,cf | 4 | 2 | 4 | 0 |
| Arlett,rf | 3 | 1 | 1 | 0 |
| Vergez,3b | 2 | 0 | 1 | 0 |
| Fenton,1b | 3 | 2 | 6 | 2 |
| D'veros,ss | 2 | 1 | 1 | 0 |
| Read,c | 4 | 1 | 7 | 1 |
| Andrews,p | 3 | 0 | 2 | 0 |
| Lombardi,y | 1 | 1 | 0 | 0 |
| Dean,ss | 0 | 0 | 2 | 1 |
| Anton,yy | 0 | 0 | 0 | 0 |
| Totals | 37 | 12 | 27 | 7 |

x—Ran for Hannah in seventh.
xx—Batted for Sigafoos in eighth.
z—Batted for Ballou in ninth.
zz—Batted for Haney in ninth.
y—Batted for Deviveros in seventh.
yy—Ran for Lombardi in eighth.

**(Continued on Page 2, Column 2)**

## DIEGEL BEATS ABE MITCHELL

*Local Pro Scores Victory Over Britisher*

LONDON, May 17. (AP)—Leo Diegel, with steady but not spectacular golf, today scored the first American professional victory in Britain this season when he defeated Abe Mitchell in a thirty-six-hole match at Moor Park, 1 up.

LEO DIEGEL

The American professional champion sent home a long putt for a birdie 2 to win at the home hole after the British pro had staged a rally which brought him from the rear. Mitchell at one time was 4 down.

Meanwhile the other American golf forces are moving to new fields. The Walker Cup players, after taking possession of the international trophy at Sandwich last night, motored to London today to spend the week-end sightseeing.

Bobby Jones may play another match with the Prince of Wales and Monday the full Walker Cup squad will turn out at Sunningdale for a golf magazine's thirty-six-hole medal competition.

**COLLEGE TRACK**

Army, 87½; Colgate, 43½.
Harvard, 89 2-3; Dartmouth, 45 1-3.

# Standings and Results

**PACIFIC COAST LEAGUE**

| | W. | L. | Pct. |
|---|---|---|---|
| Sacramento | 24 | 15 | .615 |
| Oakland | 24 | 16 | .600 |
| LOS ANGELES | 21 | 17 | .553 |
| San Francisco | 21 | 19 | .525 |
| Missions | 18 | 20 | .474 |
| Seattle | 18 | 21 | .462 |
| HOLLYWOOD | 17 | 21 | .447 |
| Portland | 12 | 26 | .316 |

**Yesterday's Results**

HOLLYWOOD, 8; Seattle, 7.
Oakland, 5-8; LOS ANGELES, 2-0.
Sacramento, 12; San Francisco, 9.
Missions, 7; Portland, 2.

**How the Series Stand**

HOLLYWOOD, 4; Seattle, 1.
Oakland, 5; LOS ANGELES, 1.
Sacramento, 3; San Francisco, 2.
Missions, 3; Portland, 2.

**Games Today**

(All double-headers)

Seattle vs. HOLLYWOOD at Wrigley Field.
LOS ANGELES at Oakland.
San Francisco at Sacramento.
Portland at Missions.

**NATIONAL LEAGUE**

| | W. | L. | P.c. |
|---|---|---|---|
| New York | 14 | 11 | .560 |
| St. Louis | 15 | 12 | .556 |
| Chicago | 16 | 13 | .552 |
| Brooklyn | 14 | 12 | .538 |
| Pittsburgh | 13 | 12 | .520 |
| Cincinnati | 12 | 14 | .462 |
| Boston | 11 | 14 | .440 |
| Philadelphia | 8 | 15 | .348 |

**Yesterday's Results**

Boston, 4-4; New York, 3-3 (first game ten innings.)
Philadelphia, 14; Brooklyn, 6.
Pittsburgh, 7; Cincinnati, 5.
Chicago-St. Louis, rain.

**Games Today**

Boston at New York.
Brooklyn at Philadelphia.
Cincinnati at Pittsburgh.
Chicago at St. Louis.

**AMERICAN LEAGUE**

| | W. | L. | P.c. |
|---|---|---|---|
| Washington | 20 | 9 | .690 |
| Philadelphia | 17 | 10 | .630 |
| Cleveland | 14 | 12 | .538 |
| New York | 12 | 12 | .500 |
| Chicago | 11 | 13 | .458 |
| Boston | 12 | 15 | .444 |
| St. Louis | 10 | 16 | .385 |
| Detroit | 10 | 19 | .345 |

**Yesterday's Results**

Chicago, 4-6; Cleveland, 1-2.
Detroit, 12; St. Louis, 7.
Washington, 16; Philadelphia, 5.
New York, 3; Boston, 2.

**Games Today**

St. Louis at Detroit.
Cleveland at Chicago.

**(Continued on Page 6, Column 2)**

## CARD CAPTAIN BETTERS MARK BY FOUR FEET

*Trojans Win Intercollegiate Track Championship With Stanford in Second Place*

**BY PAUL LOWRY**
**Sports Editor of "The Times"**

STANFORD STADIUM, May 17.—A mighty heave from the brawny right arm of Eric Krenz, Stanford captain, and a new world's record in the discus went into the record books here today.

The new mark is 167ft. 5⅜in.

The marvelous throw shattered Krenz's own record of 163ft. 8 3-4in., and eventually will displace the approved world's mark which now stands to the credit of Bud Houser.

ERIC KRENZ

The international federation approve these new feats every two years, and Krenz's record will not come up for scrutiny until 1932.

It was in the Stanford Stadium that Houser threw the platter for a world's record four years ago.

**And it was therefore, quite fitting that Krenz, in rare form, should reclaim the mark for Stanford in its own stadium.**

**NO FLUKE**

It was by no fluke that Krenz today laid claim to an undisputed record.

Three times he bettered his own existing records. His throws in order were: 163ft. 10 1-2in.; 164ft. 8in.; 167ft. 5 3-8in.

**The 164-foot toss was disqualified, the officials ruling that his foot was outside the circle when he started the throw.**

**Krenz thereupon unleashed his 163ft. 10 1-2in. toss and soon followed it up with the new world's record.**

Krenz's feat was the bright and shining feature of the annual California intercollegiate track-and-field championships.

**TROJANS WIN**

The University of Southern California lived up to the dope sheets and won the meet with a total of 78 13-15 points, but as the result of several upsets Stanford made the meet much closer than expected.

The Cardinals were second with 62 1-15 points, followed by California with 17 1-30 and U.C.L.A., 7 1-30.

**Second only to Krenz's remarkable performance, was the sprint duels between Frank Wykoff of S.C. and Hec Dyer of Stanford in the 100 and 220.**

**And the question as to who is the best sprinter in the State is still unsettled.**

Wykoff won the 100 by five feet in 9 7-10s. And Dyer had the same edge in the 220 in 21 5-10s. A breeze strong enough to hamper the

**(Continued on Page 2, Column 5)**

## MEXICANS NEXT FOR CUP SQUAD

*Doeg and Allison Both Win Matches from Canadians to Sweep Series*

PHILADELPHIA, May 17. (AP)—The United States Davis Cup tennis team goes forth to meet the Mexican racket wielders at Washington, D. C., next week with a clean record of five victories and no defeats in its elimination contest with the Canadian tennis players here this week.

JOHNNY DOEG

After the United States team had won two singles matches and one doubles contest yesterday to earn the right to meet Mexico in the remaining American zone tie, John Doeg of Santa Monica, and Wilmer Allison, Austin, Tex., today added two more victories to the count.

**Doeg defeated Dr. Jack Wright of Canada, 6-2, 6-3, 6-2, and Allison followed this up by winning from Marcel Rainville, Canada, 6-2, 6-2, 7-5.**

The two victories today were not needed to give the Americans the right to meet Mexico, but they put all they had into their game and played as if the result of the meet depended on their performance. There seems to be no doubt about the outcome of either match, although for a moment it appeared that Rainville would defeat Allison's ambition to win in straight sets.

**In the three matches yesterday, John Van Ryn defeated Wright, and George M. Lott, Jr., won from Rainville, and then Van Ryn and Allison won the doubles contest from Wright and Willard Crocker.**

The winner of the engagement at Washington next week will meet the winning team in the European zone play and, if again victorious, will go to France to meet the French team

**(Continued on Page 5, Column 2)**

## NAVY CREW WINS FOUR CORNERED BOAT CLASH

CAMBRIDGE (Mass.) May 17. (AP) The Navy crew won a four-cornered regatta here today on the Charles River. Massachusetts Tech finished a half a length behind the Middies, Harvard a length behind Tech and Pennsylvania trailed the Crimson by four lengths. The water was rough and the race rowed in the twilight, it being delayed several hours because of water conditions.

**Harvard won the 150-pound rowing event on the Charles today, defeating Massachusetts Tech's oarsmen by a half-length over the mile and five-sixteenths Henley distance. Pennsylvania was a poor third, two lengths behind Tech. Harvard's time was 7m. 3 2-5s.**

The M. I. T. junior varsity crew repeated its win of two weeks ago by beating Harvard and Pennsylvania in 9m. 26s. Harvard finished eight seconds after Tech and Pennsylvania trailed the Crimson.

The water was so rough that while the Harvard crew was waiting to get onto a float after the race their shell filled with water and broke in the middle. The oarsmen were dumped in the river.

The Harvard freshman crew ran away with the one-mile and three-quarters race with the yearlings of Tech and Pennsylvania. The Crimson boat led Tech by six lenths to the finish and the Pennsylvanians

**(Continued on Page 2, Column 2)**

## FRANCE BEATS BRITISH; TILDEN AIDS ENGLISH

PARIS, May 17. (AP)—Despite the whole-hearted and formidable assistance of Big Bill Tilden, England was able to gain only the short end of a 5-to-4 score in nine matches of an intercountry tennis tournament with France today.

**The excellent form displayed by the seven-time American champion, competing for England as an honorary member of the British Lawn Tennis Club, was the brightest feature of the day's play to American spectators who vowed that Tilden's long winter campaign on the Riviera had enabled him to appear on the Paris courts in the best form he has shown in years.**

Big Bill paired with Bunny Austin, young British star, in the featured doubles match of the series and was the strongest player on the courts in beating Henri Cochet and Jacques Brugnon, who will team in the Davis Cup doubles final round, 2-6, 6-4, 6-4. Tilden never lost his service and played as brilliantly as in the heyday of his career. Cochet also was superb.

Aside from the doubles conquest of Tilden and Austin, England's victories were scored by the second-string doubles combination of I. G. Collins and J. C. Gregory, who beat Jean Borotra and Rene De Buzzy, 6-2, 7-5, and in two singles, Austin defeated Brugnon, 8-6, 6-2, and Nigel Sharpe beat Pierre Landry, 6-4, 6-3.

For the French, Borotra turned in a singles victory over H. G. N. Lee, 3-6, 6-1, 6-4, and De Buzzlet defeated Gregory, 6-3, 8-6. Antione Gentien beat Collins, 8-6, 6-3. Two French veterans outscored their British rivals, Roger Guillemaut nosing out M. J. G. Ritchie, 12-10, 6-4, while Francois Blanchy, champion of France in olden days, won the contest for veterans over 40 years of age, from A. L. Kingscote, 6-3, 4-6, 6-1.

# Bobby Jones Wins National Amateur Title

SPORTS
Los Angeles Times

SUNDAY MORNING, SEPTEMBER 28, 1930. C

# TROJANS ROLL UP 52-TO-0 SCORE AGAINST BRUINS

## FOURTH IN ROW FOR ATLANTAN

*Crushes Homans in Finals by 8 and 7 Margin*

*No New Worlds to Conquer as Georgian Wins*

*Amateur Event Just a Breeze for Golf's Greatest*

(Continued from Page 1, Part I)

ticipated, largely because "Calamity Jane," the Jones putter, was far from her usually consistent self.

**DRAMATIC CLIMAX**

Jones became 9 up at the twenty-second, with only fourteen to go, and the crowd became frienziedly eager to be in on the "kill," but it went seven more holes. At the twenty-seventh, Homans cut away a hole with a fine birdie 2. At the twenty-eighth, it looked to be all over until Bobby took two shots to get out of a trap and barely saved a half in "buzzard" 6's. It was now dormie 8 and the throng broke all bounds in its wild gallop to the eleventh hole, down into the woods and along the creek—the twenty-ninth hole of the match.

**Gallery marshals were ruthlessly brushed aside or knocked down in the wild charge to catch a glimpse of the last putt. Jones and Homans were nearly engulfed after they played their second shots well to the green. Surrounded by marines, the contestants and officials pushed their way to the green.**

Jones was twenty-five feet away from the cup and putted dead for his four. A hush fell over the tremendous crowd, covering the hills and knolls, the woods and fairway. Homans putted from twenty feet, the ball rolled close, but missed and a wild shout went up from the crowd. Almost instantly there was a wild rush for the green and Jones. For a few seconds, it looked as

(Continued on Page 5, Column 7)

# *Vines Conquers Mangin in Title Court Battle*

## PASADENA STAR TAKES LAURELS

*Lanky Youngster Scores in Three-Set Match*

*Mrs. Harper, Miss Morrill Take Doubles Crown*

*Two Upsets Registered in Women's Singles*

BY RALPH HUSTON

Ellsworth Vines, the youthful Pasadena "giant-killer," yesterday added another victim to his long list of conquests when he blasted his way to a straight-set victory over Gregory Mangin of Georgetown University in the finals of the men's singles in the fourth annual Pacific Southwest tournament at the Los Angeles Tennis Club. The scores were 14-12, 6-3, 6-4.

ELLSWORTH VINES.

In winning, Vines joined the list of tournament winners that includes Bill Tilden, Henri Cochet and Johnny Doeg, present national champion. It also was Vines's fourth straight victory over a seeded player in the tournament.

Vines defeated Carl Busch, local player, in the first round, and Leonard Dworkin, U.C.L.A. star, in the second. In the third he conquered G. Lyttleton Rodgers, Irish Davis Cup captain, who had beaten him in the men's nationals. Rodgers was seeded No. 8. The quar-

(Continued on Page 5, Column 2)

## UP AND OVER WITH MUSICK AND MOHLER

Top photo shows Jim "Sweet" Musick stepping through the Bruin line for a bit of yardage at the Coliseum yesterday. Jim did some hefty line smacking and this was one of the few times he wasn't bent horizontal as he plowed into the Bruins. Arbelbide, Trojan end, is No. 44 in the play. At the bottom Orv Mohler is seen being tackled by McMillan of the Bruins after knocking off some yards through right tackle. Mohler was the ground-gaining star of the game, the Bruins experiencing considerable difficulty in putting their hands on him.

(Photos by Tommy Burns, Associated Press Photographer.)

## S.C. RESERVES LACK STRENGTH

*First String Very Good but Others Only Fair*

*Orv Mohler Slated to Play Plenty of Ball*

*Spaulding's Seconds Show Some Promise*

BY BILL HENRY

Query—How good are the Trojans?

Answer—Good enough to beat the Bruins, 52 to 0.

And that's about all you could find out from yesterday's frolic at the Coliseum. The first-string Trojans are very good. They ought to be. Several of the first eleven played last year and the year before for Jones against such opposition as Stanford, California, Notre Dame, Carnegie Tech and Pittsburgh.

HOWARD JONES.

The second string looked passable and without any doubt Orv Mohler is going to see a lot of varsity action. He looks and acts very much like Don Williams, and will make a great alternate for Duffield. He had a terrible case of butterfingers trying to hold the ball on attempts to add the extra point, but that was his worst apparent failing.

**Getting down into the third string, Mr. Jones's players began to look very ordinary. Spark-plug Maloney is going to be popular with the crowd, but probably not with Mr. Jones. He likes to reach his destination by means of all the way stations and Jones doesn't like his ball carriers to make side trips en route to the goal line.**

Bill Spauding's Bruins looked like a fair country ball club with lots of big powerful candidates anxious to do something for the dear old school but not quite sure just what they ought to do. Bill's boys need a lot of polishing, but by the end of the season will annoy a lot of their opponents. Bill's second string

(Continued on Page 5, Column 5)

## JONES'S TEAM IMPRESSIVE

*Musick and Mohler Display Marked Ability*

*Bruins Fail to Show Offense Worth Mentioning*

*Spaulding's Boys Play Fair Ball on Defense*

BY PAUL LOWRY

The Trojans tamed the Bruins just as had been expected, and in so doing gave approximately 40,000 customers their first taste of Pacific Coast Conference football at the revamped Coliseum yesterday.

MARSHALL DUFFIELD

When the score-keeper got through chalking up the digits the board at the peristyle end of the big bowl read:

Southern California, 52; U.C.L.A., 0.

It wasn't as bad as last year—not by 24 points—and Bruin supporters are thankful for small favors these days.

In years to come the worm will turn, and as one Bruin rooter said to his best girl as they walked through the tunnel: "Some of these days we'll be coming out here to see a U.C.L.A. victory."

While Howard Jones's 1930 edition of the Thundering Herd failed to roll up as many points as last year they looked just about as impressive.

That is, the varsity did. The second and third-stringers aren't quite as hot as in 1929, and therein lies the main difference.

On the other hand, the 1930 Bruins were stronger defensively than last year, although they were just as weak on offense.

**EIGHT OF 'EM**

The Trojans scored eight touchdowns against their Westwood rivals yesterday, the scores being fairly evenly distributed throughout the contest.

**Two touchdowns arrived in the first period, two more in the second, three in the third, and in the final quarter—when the third varsity was in operation—one was pushed over the last stripe.**

Sharing honors in this touchdown parade were Marshall Duffield with three scores, Musick with two; Orv Mohler, the sophomore signal

(Continued on Page 2, Column 6)

## CUBS THUMP REDS AGAIN

*Chicago Makes it Three in Row Over Cincinnati Ball Club; Wilson Raises Record*

CHICAGO, Sept. 27. (AP)—The Cubs made it three in a row from the Cincinnati Reds today when they slugged Kolp and Rixey for a 13-to-8 win. Pat Malone went the route for his twentieth victory of the year.

Hack Wilson raised the National League home run record by knocking out his fifty-fifth and fifty-sixth home runs of the year and batted in four runs to raise his mark to 188. Gabby Hartnett hit homers in the second and third to raise his total to thirty-seven. Malone also hit one out of the park.

| CINCINNATI | AB | H | O | A | CHICAGO | AB | H | O | A |
|---|---|---|---|---|---|---|---|---|---|
| Swans'n.cf | 5 | 3 | 4 | 0 | Blair.2b | 6 | 4 | 2 | 6 |
| Call'han.lf | 3 | 2 | 1 | 0 | English.ss | 2 | 0 | 3 | 4 |
| Crawf'd.2b | 4 | 1 | 4 | 4 | Cuyler.rf | 4 | 2 | 0 | 0 |
| C'inello.3b | 5 | 1 | 1 | 1 | Wilson.cf | 4 | 2 | 2 | 0 |
| Heilm'n.rf | 5 | 1 | 1 | 0 | D.Taylor.lf | 5 | 1 | 3 | 0 |
| Stripp.1b | 3 | 2 | 10 | 0 | Hartnett.c | 5 | 3 | 6 | 0 |
| Gooch.c | 4 | 0 | 2 | 1 | Kelley.1b | 5 | 1 | 10 | 1 |
| Duroc'r.ss | 3 | 1 | 1 | 3 | Bell.3b | 4 | 2 | 1 | 2 |
| Kolp.p | 2 | 0 | 0 | 0 | Malone.p | 5 | 2 | 0 | 1 |
| Rixey.p | 1 | 0 | 0 | 2 | | | | | |
| Walker.x | 1 | 0 | 0 | 0 | | | | | |
| Totals | 36 | 11 | 24 | 11 | Totals | 40 | 17 | 27 | 14 |

x—Batted for Rixey in ninth.

SCORE BY INNINGS

Cincinnati ........4 0 1 0 0 0 0 0 3— 8
Chicago ..........0 2 1 4 0 2 2 2 x—13

SUMMARY

Errors—Crawford, Blair. Runs batted in—Crawford, 2; Cuccinello, Stripp, 3; Hartnett, 3; Malone, 2; Cuyler, 3; Wilson, 4; Blair, Callaghan, 2. Two-base hits—Callaghan, 2; Stripp, Bell, Heilmann, Blair, Hartnett, Crawford. Three-base hits—Blair, Bell. Home runs—Hartnett, 2; Wilson, 2; Malone. Stolen base—D. Taylor. Sacrifice hits—Crawford, Cuyler. Double plays—Blair to English to Kelley; Durocher to Crawford to Stripp; English to Blair to Kelley. Left on base—Cincinnati, 6; Chicago, 12. Bases on balls—Off Kolp, 4; Rixey, 4; Malone, 4. Struck out—By Kolp, 2; Malone, 6. Hits batted—Off Kolp, 8 in 3 2-3 innings; Rixey, 9 in 4 1-3. Losing pitcher—Kolp. Umpires—Magerkurth, Rigler and Pfirman. Time of game—2h.

## STANFORD FRESHMAN TIE JAYSEE ELEVEN

STANFORD UNIVERSITY, Sept. 27. (AP)—The Sacramento Junior College eleven and the Stanford University freshmen battled to a 13-13 tie here today. The flashy work of Tony Danadio enabled the visitors to tie the score in the last four minutes of play.



## FOOTBALL RESULTS

LOCAL

Southern California, 52; U.C.L.A., 0.
S.C. Frosh, 7; Santa Ana J.C., 0.
Compton J.C., 32; Santa Monica J.C., 0.
Riverside J.C., 12; San Bernardino J.C., 0.
Chaffey J.C., 6; Fullerton J.C., 0.
Loyola High, 40; Ventura, 0.
Monrovia High, 25; El Monte, 13.
Black Fox, 13, S.C. Military, 0.
Santa Barbara High, 7; Hoover, 0.

PACIFIC COAST

California, 19; Santa Clara, 7.
Stanford, 18; Olympic Club, 0.
Washington, 48; Whitman, 0.
Washington State, 47; College of Idaho, 12.
Montana State, 7; Idaho, 6.
Stanford Frosh, 13; Sacramento J.C., 13.
California Frosh, 0; San Mateo J.C., 0.
Arizona, 57; Arizona Frosh, 0.
Montana, 52; Mt. St. Charles, 0.

EAST

Yale, 38; Maine, 0.

(Continued on Page 6, Column 2)

## OLD-TIMERS' NIGHT! NEXT THURSDAY OVER KHJ

Tune in and hear Dean B. Cromwell, coach of the Southern California national intercollegiate track-and-field champions, tell you about some of the heroes of yesteryear—the has-beens with athletic pasts who have settled in Southern California. Listen to Bill Henry of The Times tell you about the days when Los Angeles High School was the little red school on top of the hill, and of his classmates who became famous college athletes. Paul Lowry, sports editor of The Times, will interview these old-timers, and if you want any questions answered send them to The Times Sports Edition of the Air. Next Thursday night from 9:30 to 10 you will have them answered over KHJ.

## *HUSKIES IN EASY WIN OVER WHITMAN ELEVEN*

BY FRANK G. GORRIE
Associated Press Sports Writer

SEATTLE (Wash.) Sept. 27. (AP)—Notre Dame football as coached by Jimmy Phelan, new University of Washington mentor, was exhibited here today for the first time with great success as the Huskies conquered Whitman College, 48 to 0.

It was the opening game of the season for both schools, and a non-conference tilt.

A hard rain up until game time held the attendance down to 10,000 but the small band of spectators were dished up a flashy brand of ball.

Fight as they did, the Missionaries were unable to stop the shifting offensive of the Huskies and the Purple and Gold squad romped up and down the new turf field virtually at will to pile up touchdowns.

Washington scored two touchdowns in the first period, one safety in the second, one touchdown in the third and four in the last quarter.

**Two sensational runs, one an 88-yard dash by Clarence Bled-**

(Continued on Page 3, Column 3)

## STANFORD TRIUMPHS, 18-0

*Cardinal Regulars Do Scoring Against Olympic Club in Second and Fourth Quarters*

STANFORD UNIVERSITY, Sept. 27. (AP)—Forced to call on their first-string men in scoring moments, Stanford University's football team defeated the Olympic Club of San Francisco, 18 to 0, here today.

The Stanford second-string eleven battled the clubmen on even terms until late in the second period, when the Cardinal regulars were inserted and proceeded to score in a hurry.

A forward-lateral pass from Simkins to Neill to Moffatt, another short pass from Simkins to Moffatt and a reverse over left tackle by Moffatt netted 57 yards and a touchdown.

A try for point failed.

**The Cardinals scored twice in the final period. Early in the quarter an Olympic Club punt was blocked by Ehrhorn, Stanford tackle, and was recovered by Bogue on the Olympic Club 4-yard line. Hillman went over left guard for the touch down. A moment later an intercepted pass, a 25-yard jaunt around left end by Moffatt, and two smashes at center by Simkins took the ball over for the third touchdown.**

The Olympic Club showed little in the matter of offense, a 33-yard dash by Left Half Schlichting in the second period being their longest gain. Schimmel, center, and Ford, end, stood out in defensive play.

Line-up and summary:

| Stanford (18) | | Olympic Club (0) |
|---|---|---|
| Colvin | L.E. | Ford |
| Bogue | L.T. | Kuhn |
| Hand | L.G. | Barnard |
| Taylor | C. | Schimmel |
| Dawson | R.G. | Greger |
| Ehrhorn | R.T. | Spiedel |
| Doub | R.E. | Davison |
| Allen | Q. | Boberg |
| Hardy | L.H. | Melbourne |
| Clark | R.H. | Fredericks |
| Caddel | F.B. | Pomeroy |

SCORE BY QUARTERS

Stanford ............ 0 6 0 12—18
Olympic ............ 0 0 0 0— 0

Touchdowns—Moffatt (sub. for Hardy;) Simkins (sub. for Caddel;) Hillman (sub. for Allen.

Referee, Herb Dana; umpire, Sam Dolan; field judge, R. B. Leland; head linesman, Bill Kelley.

## HOW TROY RUINED BRUINS

| U.C.L.A. | Pos. | U.S.C. |
|---|---|---|
| Haight | L.E.R. | Arbelbide |
| Norfleet | L.T.R. | R. Brown. |
| Jones | L.G.R. | Shaw |
| Oliver | C. | Williamson |
| Hampton | R.G.L. | Baker |
| McMillan | R.T.L. | Hall |
| Wellendorf | R.E.L. | Wilcox |
| Solomon (C.) | Q. | Duffield (C.) |
| Decker | L.H.R. | Pinckert |
| Roberts | R.H.L. | Apsit |
| N. Duncan | F. | Musick |

SCORE BY QUARTERS

U.S.C. .................................. 13 13 20 6—52
U.C.L.A. ................................ 0 0 0 0— 0

Scoring: Touchdowns—Duffield 3, Musick 2, Mohler (sub for Duffield) 2, Ritchey (sub for Musick) 1. Points after touchdowns: Placekicks—Baker 1, Kirkwood (sub for Apsit) 1, Musick, 2.

SUBSTITUTIONS

U.C.L.A.—J. Duncan for Hampton, Bailie for Norfleet, Bergdahl for Solomon, Stoeffen for Haight, Willoughby for McMillan, Goodstein for Oliver, Carter for Jones, Forster for Roberts, Dennis for Decker, Thoe for N. Duncan, Mulhaupt for Wellendorf, Bradbury for J. Duncan, Grossman for Thoe, Zimmerman for Bradbury, Waldron for Stoeffen, Sorrenson for Mulhaupt, Reinhard for Zimmerman, Milum for Goodstein.

U.S.C.—Mohler for Duffield, Ritchey for Musick, Tipton for Pinckert, Kirkwood for Apsit, Plaehn for Hall, Gentry for Shaw, Hawkins for Williamson, Armistead for R. Brown, Clark for Arbelbide, Sparling for Wilcox, Jensen for Baker, Maloney for Mohler, Thompson for Hall, Deranian for Jensen, Beatty for Maloney, Biggs for Arbelbide, Winfield for Shaw.

Officials: Sid Foster, referee; Bruce Kirkpatrick, umpire; Verne Landreth, head linesman; Horace Gillette, field judge.

# Pittsburgh Trounces Cubs, 9-5, to Even Series

SPORTS
Los Angeles Times

WEDNESDAY MORNING, APRIL 1, 1931. C

# ROCKNE'S TRAGIC DEATH STUNS SPORTING WORLD

## PIRATES RALLY TO CINCH TILT

*Malone Is Rapped for Five Runs in Eighth Round*

*Phillips Gets Two Homers; Gus Suhr Wallops One*

*Kremer and Wood Pitch Win for Smoky City Squad*

BY BOB RAY

Rajah Hornsby's clouting Clubs from Chicago were given a dose of their own medicine in the form of a 9-to-5 capsule of defeat from the Pittsburgh Pirates yesterday at Wrigley Field. The Buc triumph, achieved off the offerings of Perce Lay Malone, evened up the series at one all, so today's contest will settle the argument between the National League rivals until they open the season in a couple of weeks.

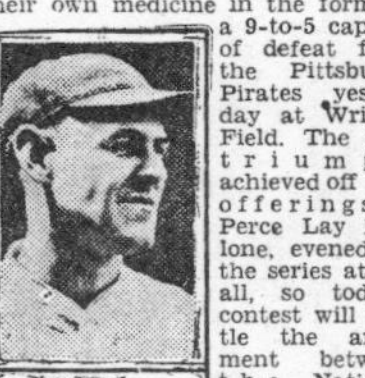
RAY KREMER

Remy Kremer and young Charley Wood hurled for the Pirates, the latter taking the mound in the seventh with the score tied, so gets credit for the victory. The Cubs got only eight hits off the two twirlers, while Malone was rapped for twelve, including two homers by Ed Phillips and another by Gus Suhr, not to mention numerous triples, doubles and singles.

**The Cubs, aided by Pittsburgh errors in the second and third innings, took a four-run lead off Kremer's hurling. In the second round two were out when Bell singled to left and Grimm followed with a one-base shot to center. Malone aided his own cause with another single to center that scored Bell. Grimm also came in when Traynor let L. Waner's throw roll through**

(Continued on Page 15, Column 6)

## GLICK BEATEN BY TOWNSEND

*Canadian Wins Decision Over Brooklyn Scrapper*

*Veteran Boxer Outclassed in Rough Ring Battle*

*Hamas Finishes Erickson in First Round of Go*

BY KAY OWE

Billy Townsend, Vancouver blond, beat Joe Glick, veteran of nearly 300 fights, in the ten-round main event at the Olympic last night.

BILLY TOWNSEND.

It was a rough, tough battle all the way, both boys winding up with cuts over each eye. Townsend won because he had youth and stamina, and inflicted the severer punishment.

In the early rounds Glick's greater experience stood him in good stead, but he could not stave off the bull-like rushes of his younger opponent forever and in the fifth round he receipted for a bad beating.

**From then on Glick fought bravely but Townsend piled up an appreciable margin in each round with a relentless attack to head and body.**

There were no knockdowns, although on two or three occasions unusually hard wallops to the face slowed Glick enough to make him teeter and cover.

The semi-wind-up saw Steve Hamas, the former Penn State boy, score his ninth straight local knockout. This one was at the expense of Man Mountain Erickson, who outweighed the 188½-pound Hamas by twenty-five pounds.

**Erickson went out in the first**

(Continued on Page 15, Column 3)

## INTIMATE GLIMPSES OF KNUTE ROCKNE AT NOTRE DAME

At the top (left,) we have Rockne and his room-mate, Gus Dorais. Dorais was captain of the Notre Dame eleven in 1912, Rockne in 1913—their final season. Dorais played quarter, Rockne left end. The Dorais-Rockne passing combination is famous in football lore. At the right is Rockne as a track athlete in 1912. He held a record of 12ft. 10in. in the pole vault and also was a good broad jumper. The 1924 Four Horsemen team was generally hailed as Rockne's best. The Horsemen are shown in the middle photo—Miller, Layden, Crowley and Stuhldreher reading from left to right. Below is the last photo taken of Rockne on the Coast. It shows him with Jimmy Phelan (left,) at the time of a visit to Seattle, where Phelan coaches the University of Washington. Phelan is being mentioned as a possible successor to Rockne The photo of Rockne and Dorais, and of Rocke in track costume were loaned by Bill Cook of this city, who was on the football squad with Rockne in 1912 and 1913.

## MUCH SPECULATION AS TO SUCCESSOR OF WIZARD

*Many Prominent Coaches on List of Probable Candidates to Take Notre Dame Position*

BY RALPH HUSTON

While the sports world stood stunned by the tragic death yesterday of Knute K. Rockne, speculation as to his possible successor as head coach at Notre Dame was rife.

Many colleges and universities all over the country are now coached by men who played football under Rockne at Notre Dame. Four of these are now on the Pacific Coast — "Slip" Madigan at St. Mary's, "Clipper" Smith at Santa Clara, Tom Lieb at Loyola and Jimmy Phelan at Washington.

EDWARD "SLIP" MADIGAN

Others include Gus Dorais, now at Detroit U; Harry Stuhldreher of Four Horsemen fame, at Villanova; Charley Bachman of Florida and Jim Crowley, also of the Four Horsemen, who is coaching at Michigan State.

**All of these coaches were prominently mentioned as possible successors to Rockne at Notre Dame. Dorais, whose Detroit team has lost only one game in the last three years, was quarterback of the Irish at the same time that Rockne played end. Dorais was captain of the 1912 team, and Rockne captained the 1913 machine.**

Lieb coached the unbeaten Notre Dame team of 1929, when Rockne was too ill to take charge, and came to Loyola last year. It was generally believed that it would be impossible for Notre Dame to sign a new coach this year, as most of the mentors are under long-term contracts. "Hunk" Anderson, Rockne's assistant coach, probably will be left in charge this season, it was said.

HOST OF FRIENDS

Rockne made a host of friends in Southern California during the four times he brought his teams to Los Angeles. In 1925 the great Four Horsemen trampled Stanford in the annual Tournament of Roses game in Pasadena.

**In 1926 the Irish opened a series of games with the Trojans of the University of Southern California. They won that game, 13-12, and returned in 1928 to lose, 27-14. The Irish returned last year under the leadership of Frank Carideo to**

(Continued on Page 14, Column 4)

## RICE PAYS TRIBUTE TO HIS FRIEND

*"There Are Few People Who Can't Be Replaced—Rockne Is One of Them"*

BY GRANTLAND RICE
(Copyright, 1931, by North American Newspaper Alliance)

The sudden, tragic death of Knute Rockne, Notre Dame's great football coach, comes as one of the greatest shocks the world of sport has ever known. Here was not only a rare genius on the football field, but a personality that for years had caught and held the attention of millions, one of the most attractive personalities this generation has developed along any line.

**Knute Rockne could have been an outstanding figure in any career or profession he might have adopted. He had brains, ability, character and the vital qualities of leadership. He stuck to football because that was the game he loved and because it belonged to the type of younger men who were his kind. Football is a game that demands spirit and action, and Knute Rockne had these elements to a rare degree. He knew football and he knew how to teach football, having shown this teaching ability as a chemistry professor at Notre Dame before he took up football coaching. Beyond this he had the knack of appealing to the student in the right way, the knack of holding interest and attention. And more than all, he had the imagination that belongs to genius. And he had the ability to transfer a lot of his imagination to his team.**

PATH TO SUCCESS

I spent most of the afternoon and evening with Knute on one of his last trips east. We were discussing

(Continued on Page 14, Column 2)

## ROCKNE DEATH SHOCKS COACHES

*Coast Mentors Send Expressions of Grief Over Passing of Famous South Bend Football Wizard; Howard Jones Overwhelmed by Tragedy; Warner, Ingram Stunned*

*(Lack of space makes it impossible to print even a small percentage of the expressions of grief over Knute Rockne's passing. Those that follow are from prominent coaches on the Coast.—Ed. note.)*

**HOWARD JONES**, head football coach at the University of Southern California, said:

"I have just learned of the tragedy, and I am too overwhelmed to say much. I can hardly realize that he has gone. I can feel the great grief of the sports world in losing Rockne, one of its outstanding figures, but then, too, I feel a personal loss, for he was my friend. We have had many bitter battles on the football field, but Rockne has always been to me the greatest of all coaches, and I am glad to have had the opportunity of playing his teams. He instilled in his men the same fine qualities that made him the great man he was; courage, hard playing, strict adherence to the rules, but above all, sportsmanship

(Continued on Page 15, Column 5)

## PHELAN'S FEAR FOR OLD COACH BECOMES REALITY

SEATTLE, March 31. (AP)—Informed of the death of Knute Rockne, Jimmy Phelan, University of Washington football coach and Rockne's first captain at Notre Dame, said:

"I am stunned, and still, this terrible loss is the answer to a presentiment that has followed me for months. A presentiment that Knute Rockne, my great friend and adviser, was in some kind of danger.

**"When he went to the hospital in Rochester, Minn., I had a secret fear of the outcome, and I cannot tell why. But that fear has stayed with me and I have been unable to leave it behind.**

**"The greatest man who ever held the helm in football, coaching work, the greatest man outside of football and one of the greatest minds in the United States was Knute Rockne and his loss through death is irreparable.**

"There is no one who can fill Rockne's place, either in football or as a man. He was pre-eminent in his line and one of our greatest men of the day. **We are all losers by his passing."**

## IRISH LOST BUT THIRTEEN TILTS IN FOURTEEN YEARS

**In fourteen years as head football coach at the University of Notre Dame Knute Rockne led only thirteen defeated teams from the field. He coached five undefeated teams, those of 1919, 1920, 1924, 1929 and 1930. The complete record follows:**

| Year Captain | Won | Lost | Tied | Pct. |
|---|---|---|---|---|
| 1917—Jimmy Phelan | 7 | 1 | 0 | .875 |
| 1918—Peter Bahan | 6 | 1 | 0 | .857 |
| 1919—Peter Bahan | 9 | 0 | 0 | 1.000 |
| 1920—Frank Coughlin | 10 | 0 | 0 | 1.000 |
| 1921—Eddie Anderson | 10 | 1 | 0 | .909 |
| 1922—Glen Carberry | 8 | 1 | 1 | .888 |
| 1923—Harvey Brown | 8 | 1 | 0 | .889 |
| 1924—Adam Walsh | 10 | 0 | 0 | 1.000 |
| 1925—Clem Crowe | 7 | 2 | 1 | .777 |
| 1926—Hearndon-Edwards | 8 | 1 | 0 | .889 |
| 1927—John Smith | 7 | 1 | 1 | .875 |
| 1928—Fred Miller | 5 | 4 | 0 | .556 |
| 1929—John Law | 9 | 0 | 0 | 1.000 |
| 1930—Tom Conley | 9 | 0 | 0 | 1.000 |
| Totals | 113 | 13 | 3 | .896 |

## ROCKNE DID MUCH TO POPULARIZE FOOTBALL

BY ALAN GOULD
Associated Press Sports Editor

NEW YORK, March 31. (AP)—All his life was speed. Do it right, but do it quickly, he taught his quarterbacks. The best way to win is to pull the unexpected.

And so, with the swiftness characteristic of his whole life, Knute Rockne's death today closed the career of the most spectacular figure in American football, leaving it dazed and shaken from the loss of a personality woven into the very fabric of the sport.

**To those who have known and appreciated Rockne's genius as a creative mind and leader, those who have gone out on the gridirons to fight their young hearts out for the coach they worshipped, to those who have sat at the fountain of his football knowledge and set forth to make their own careers as disciples of his famous "system" — Rockne's passing seems almost too shocking to believe.**

It takes from football the most

(Continued on Page 15, Column 4)

# Twenty Grand Captures Derby by Four Lengths

SPORTS
Los Angeles Times

SUNDAY MORNING, MAY 17, 1931. C

# EASTMAN TIES WORLD'S MARK AS TROY WINS

## SWEEP ALL IS SECOND HORSE

*Mate Finishes Third; Winner Sets New Record*

*Old Rosebud's Mark Broken by Mrs. Whitney's Colt*

*Sixty Thousand Watch Turf Classic in Kentucky*

(Continued from Page 1, Part I)

spectators responded to the thrill of Twenty Grand's great feat with an ovation rivaling that accorded the popular conquest of Earle Sande and Gallant Fox a year ago. The West was prepared for this third successive triumph for the East and responded with a spontaneous outburst of enthusiasm as the rose wreath was draped over Twenty Grand's arched neck and the gold Derby trophy was presented to Mrs. Whitney by Charles Curtis, Vice-President of the United States.

### SEVENTEEN-YEAR RECORD SMASHED

LOUISVILLE (Ky.) May 16.—In winning the fifty-seventh Kentucky Derby before 50,000 spectators this afternoon, Twenty Grand broke a Derby record that had stood since 1914. Mrs. Helen Hay Whitney's victorious horse ran the distance in 2:01 4-5, displacing the 2:03 2-5, which Old Rosebud reeled off seventeen years ago. Twenty Grand finished four lengths in front of Sweep All and seven lengths ahead of Mate. The triumph netted the Greentree Stable $48,725.

**TAKES COMMAND**

It was a horse race for at least a mile of the route, until Twenty Grand took complete command, and there was plenty of consolation for the West in the ability of one of its hopes, Sweep All, to split the highly favored eastern pair. Boys Howdy and Pittsburgher, two of the well-liked long shots among Kentuckians, faded from contention, but Spanish Play came strong to finish fourth and in the money.

The race carried a gross value of $58,725 and was worth $48,725 to Twenty Grand. Sweep All won $6000 for his owner, while Mate took the third price, $3000, and Spanish Play fourth money of $1000.

For the climax event of a bright, sunshiny day, that contrasted sharply with the drab, rainy derbies of the past three years, the field of twelve crack 3-year-olds went to the post for the race that annually focuses national and even world-wide interest.

As the pulses of the thousands of onlookers quickened and as radio broadcasters and telegraph wires flashed their words afar, the bluebloods of the turf swayed nervously in the starting stalls, then bounded forward to the rereberberating cry, "They're off."

It was not a perfect start and as the field dashed for positions down the stretch, and past the crowded stands for the first time, Twenty Grand appeared caught in the jumble of flashing color and galloping horseflesh. The favorite was tenth as they swept past the first-quarter pole, with the Mongol, rank outsider and 100-to-1 shot, nosed in front of the well-bunched pack.

Down the first turn, the field began to spread out. Prince D'Amour, another long shot, and the only gelding in the field, moved to the front, but was quickly replaced by Walter J. Salmon's Ladder, which finished third in the Preakness.

Down the stretch the battle for positions continued and for the first time, the favorites made the moves that caused their backers to breathe more easily. Sweep All, on the outside, rushed to the front at three-quarters followed by Twenty Grand, Mate, Ladder and Boys Howdy in that order.

For a moment Mate, under Jockey George Ellis's urging, seemed about to take the lead. Instead, Twenty Grand, responded with a rush that carried the big colt quickly past his conqueror of a week ago, and past Sweep All into the van. Coming around the turn into the home stretch, Twenty Grand had the race in hand.

**MATE OUTCLASSED**

There was not doubt of the outcome at any stage of the last quarter, for Mate was thoroughly beaten and Sweep All had too much ground to make up in a game finish.

Twenty Grand ran that smashing last quarter in :24 2-5 seconds, adding three lengths to his margin of four lengths over Sweep All and turning the tables on Mate by the decisive margin of seven lengths.

The fractional times were: :23 1-5 for the quarter, :47 2-5 for the half, 1:12 for the three quarters, 1:37 2-5

(Continued on Page 4, Column 2)

## TWO WORLD RECORD RACES THAT GENERATED THRILLS

The 100-yard dash in 9 5-10s., equaling the recognized world's record, and the 440 in 47 4-10s., equaling Ted Meredith's world record made in 1916. Those were the remarkable races reeled before a big crowd at the Olympic stadium yesterday. The striking photo at the top shows Frank Wykoff of the University of Southern California leading Hec Dyer of Stanford to the tape in the 100. Wykoff's own world's record of 9 4-10s., which he made twice last year, has not yet been accepted by the International Federation, which meets once every two years, and will not meet again until 1932. The photo below shows Ben Eastman of Stanford winning the "quarter of the century" from Vic Williams of S.C. Hables of Stanford was third in the 100 although Maurer of S.C. at the far side of the track appears to have the edge.

[Photo of 100-yard dash by Joe Mingo of Wide World. Photo of 440 race by Fred Coffey, Times Staff photographer]

## STANFORD STAR EQUALS TED MEREDITH'S RECORD

*Blond Ben Captures Quarter Mile in 47 2-5s.; Cromwell's Team Wins by Lopsided Score*

BY BRAVEN DYER

Blond Ben Eastman, Stanford's big bertha of the track, fired his opening blast at the world's 440-yard record yesterday at the Olympic Stadium and scaled the throne previously occupied only by Ted Meredith of Pennsylvania.

Combining the speed of a frightened gazelle with the smooth-striding form of a champion, Blond Ben tied Meredith's mark of 47 2-5s. in the greatest quarter-mile race ever staged on the Pacific Coast.

Vic Williams of Southern California, national A.A.U. champion, pushed Blond Ben to his sensational feat, trailing his northern foe by slightly more than a yard in a spectacular finish which saw the great Trojan runner expending every ounce of energy in a futile effort to nip Eastman at the tape.

ERNEST PAYNE

The best way of describing the race is to say that it was all that it was advertised to be. Talked about, raved about, written about and dreamed about for lo these many months, the battle provided 20,000 frenzied fans with their greatest kick of the day.

### WHAT S.C. DID

It was a field day for Troy at the Olympic Stadium yesterday. Dean Cromwell's team broke six of the ten meet records, smashed and tied one other. The Trojans won nine first places and placed second in all but three, taking second in every event they did not win. Every Trojan performed as well, or better than expected in his special event. Yesterday's victory climaxed two years of undefeated competition on the Coast for Cromwell's charges.

**BLOND BEN STEALS SHOW**

Eastman's feat was the outstanding feature of the California intercollegiates which sparkled with so many brilliant performances that a separate story could well be devoted

(Continued on Page 2, Column 5)

## ANGELS DEFEAT PORTLAND, 8-1

*Malcom Moss in Great Form to Vanquish Ducks*

*Mails Chased in Fourth as Cherubs Score Five Runs*

*Summa Tallies Four Safeties Against Former Mates*

BY BOB RAY

With Malcolm Moss in sensational form, Jack Lelivelt' Angeles breezed to an easy 8-to-1 triumph over Portland last night at Wrigley Field to take a three-to-two edge in the series.

MALCOLM MOSS

The Ducks might have been impersonating rolling stones for they were able to gather but one run off Moss, whose dazzling fast ones and sharp-breaking downers accounted for seven strikeouts and that run would not have scored had not Barton misplayed Bowman's double that scored Woodall from first after two were out in the seventh.

**The Great Mails started against Moss, but was chased in the fourth when the Cherubs rammed across five runs to sew up the struggle. Joe Bowman replaced the Portland southpaw and also receipted for his share of the lacing doled out by Seraph bats.**

Homer Summa had a big eve-

(Continued on Page 3, Column 2)

## OLYMPIC SHIFT SUGGESTED

*Transfer of Final Tryouts for Track Team From Chicago to Los Angeles Urged by Committee*

CHICAGO, May 16. (AP)—The track-and-field committee of the American Olympic Association tonight recommended the final tryouts for the 1932 American track team be transferred from Chicago to Los Angeles. July 15 and 16 were decided on as dates for the tryouts. The recommendation must be approved by the association's directorate.

Decision to shift the site of the tryouts, originally awarded to Chicago, came when plans were revealed to hold the 1932 Intercollegiate Association of Amateur Athletes of America championships on the Pacific Coast. It would be unfair, the committee decided, to require Coast athletes to travel to Chicago for final trials, and then return so far west for the international games at Los Angeles on July 30-August 14.

The committee also decided that four semifinal meets will be held, one of them to be an I.C.A.A.A.A. event. The National Collegiate Association meet at Chicago and two other open meets will b- recognized as semifinal meets.

One of the open events will be held at Chicago and the other at San Francisco, probably during the week of July 4-9, 1932.

**OLYMPIC SHIFT**

**Winners of the first three places in each event of the four semifinal trials will be eligible to compete in the finals at Los Angeles, although a committee, yet to be appointed, will prune the list on the basis of performances.**

To offset any additional expense to eastern and midwestern athletes by the shift to Los Angeles the Pacific Coast committee representatives said their section would guarantee transportation and expenses from Chicago to the Coast and return. Eastern and midwestern athletes or their organizations will be responsible for their own fare and expenses to Chicago.

The Olympic committee was expected to approve the shift from Chicago to Los Angeles.

## HOLLYWOOD STARS MOP UP ACORN OUTFIT TWICE

OAKLAND, May 16. (Exclusive) The Hollywood Stars made it five straight wins over the Oaks tonight by defeating them in the afternoon game, 6 to 0, when Frank Shellenback pitched a six-hit game and coming back in the night game for a 6-to-3 victory when Charley Wetzel kept nine hits well scattered.

**Monte Pearson, who had been giving Sam Gibson of the Seals a tough race for pitching honors, was named as Manager Carl Zamlock's selection to try and stop the Stars in the night ball game but he was nicked for three runs on four hits in the fourth inning and when the Stars started to pound him again in the sixth Frank Tubbs went in but before he could get the side retired three more runs scored.**

**The Vittmen took the lead in the first inning of the afternoon contest when Lee walked, took second on Brannan's bunt, stole third and counted on Hill's long fly. Sherlock scored in the third on a walk, Severeid's single and an infield out.**

In the seventh Carlyle singled, Sherlock sacrificed and Gazella doubled to right to bring Cleo home.

**Brannan's single and Dave Barbee's homer over the left-field fence added to more off Ortman in the eighth. The final Star score was made off Ludolph in the ninth on singles by Severeid and Gazella and Shellenback's long fly.**

Shellenback was accorded brilliant support by Dud Lee and Ortie Brannan, who made four double Bplays and handled nineteen

(Continued on Page 2, Column 4)

## YALE CONQUERS HARVARD

PRINCETON (N. J.) May 16. (AP) Yale's wide margin of superiority in the field events enabled the Eli trackmen to overcome a 30-point lead which the Tigers gained in the track events and the Bulldogs

(Continued on Page 2, Column 4)

## ENGINEERS, BEARS SIGN

BERKELEY, May 16. (AP)—Georgia Tech and the University of California will play two football games, one next fall and the other in 1932, Graduate Manager W. W. Monahan announced here today.

## HUSKIES VANQUISH OREGON

WASHINGTON STADIUM (Seattle) May 16. (AP)—Battling a cold blustering wind and intermittent downpours of rain, the University of Washington Huskies swamped the University of Oregon Webfoot-

(Continued on Page 2, Column 4)

# DESPERATE TROJAN RALLY VANQUISHES IRISH

SPORTS
Los Angeles Times
Vol. L. SUNDAY MORNING, NOVEMBER 22, 1931. [PART VI-a.]

[Wide World telephoto]

They Should Have Had Him, But They Didn't

And Gaius Shaver, Troy's star quarterback, got away for an 8-yard gain on this line play in the first quarter of yesterday's thriller at South Bend. It looks like, in this telephoto at least, that Shaver should have been stopped at the line of scrimmage by the Notre Dame man awaiting him, but Shaver wiggled his hips, and slid away for an 8-yard gain. This was during the Trojans' first-period drive that almost netted them a touchdown.

## NOTRE DAME GRID REIGN ENDED BY BAKER'S GOAL

### *Hunk Praises Trojan Squad for Comeback*

BY HEARTLY (HUNK) ANDERSON
Coach of the Notre Dame Football Team

NOTRE DAME (Ind.) Nov. 21.—I have nothing but the highest praise for Coach Howard Jones and his Southern California football team which today defeated Notre Dame, 16 to 14, for the first defeat suffered by the Irish in three years.

A team that is losing 14 to 0 as the fourth quarter begins and comes back to win deserves all the credit that I or anybody else can give it. And because of their victory I take o.. my hat to them.

The strong finish, which netted the small margin of victory was due, I think, to the excellent generalship of Orv Mohler as well as his line plunging. He seemed able to detect holes in the line and run through them with much success.

**Gus Shaver comes in for much praise for his work. The big quarterback accounted for considerable yardage through our line, particularly on spinners and reverse plays. He accounted for the second Trojan touchdown on a lateral pass much similar to the one Notre Dame used in scoring its second marker.**

For the Notre Dame team the work of Marchie Schwartz at left halfback and Charlie Jaskwhich at quarterback was outstanding. In the line, Nordie Hoffman, Joe Kurth, Capt. Yarr and Ed Krause played commendable football.

IRISH LET DOWN

The real cause for the defeat, I think, was a letdown after the 14 points had been rolled up.

As a coincidence, the same thing happened in the game with Southern California in 1929 at Soldier Field, when Russ Saunders ran through the entire Notre Dame team with the kick-off after a Notre Dame score. Notre Dame had let down

(Continued on Page 4, Column 1)

### *Battling Troy Gridders Pull Win From Fire*

(Continued from Page 1, Part I)

riod and then followed this up with another devastating drive which brought about the field goal by Baker.

ADJECTIVES NEEDED

Noah Webster's diction book does not contain enough adjectives to describe the way in which the Trojans refused to be licked. Perhaps they themselves do not know how they did it, but do it they did in the face of disheartening setbacks and against what appeared to be impossible odds.

Here was the situation one minute before the end of the third quarter: Notre Dame had 14 points. The Irish had scored in the first half and then, as if to prove their superiority beyond all peradventure of a doubt, came smashing back with another touchdown almost as soon as the third period opened. Jackwhich had place-kicked both points and the score of 14 to 0 looked as big as the population of China. In fact it looked a darn sight larger than that, if possible, because of the consummate ease with which the Irish scored those two touchdowns.

**In other words the Irish were in command of the situation and everybody, apparently, but the Trojans knew it. Schwartz had been whizzing around his own right end repeatedly for long gains. Banas, on that twisting 32-yard run which ended up on Troy's 3-yard line, had made the Trojans look positively silly. And the ease with which Schwartz went over for the touchdown presaged others to come.**

But instead of disheartening the Trojans this second tally made them mad. Made them so mad that they finally did the impossible. Fighting fiercely for first downs which on several occasions were gained only by a matter of inches, the Southern California players literally swept the redoubtable South Benders off their feet with the savageness of their attack. No team in modern football history ever faced a more hopeless situation and worked out of it the way the Trojans did this afternoon.

Here is the story of that gallant rush which enabled Southern Cali-

(Continued on Page 5, Column 8)

## SCHALDACH HERO AS BEARS DEFEAT STANFORD, 6-0

### *California Gains "Promised Land" With First Victory Over Foes Since 1923 Grid Triumph*

BY PAUL LOWRY
Sports Editor of "The Times"

PALO ALTO, Nov. 21.—The ghost of Andy Smith came back to Stanford Stadium this afternoon. On the same field where one of his "wonder teams" dedicated the opening of Stanford's big bowl with a smashing 42-to-7 victory ten years ago the battling Bears of California entered the promised land again today.

California beat Stanford, 6 to 0, with a slashing, hard-running attack led by Hank Schaldach, who struck down the Indians with the trident in the way of a brilliant triple thrust. He ran, he passed and he kicked Stanford into submission before a crowd of 87,500 fans.

RALSTON GILL

He scored the only touchdown of the day early in the second quarter, and he got away for a 45-yard run in the last period that looked like a touchdown. Jack Hillman, brother of the Stanford captain, had to haul down the flying Schaldach from behind to save the day on the Stanford 15-yard line.

SWEET SWEET

The victory was the sweetest music in years to sons of California. They hadn't won from Stanford since Don Nichols led the next to the last of the so-called "wonder teams" to victory by a 9-to-0 score in 1923.

California has waited eight long years for a chance to tear up the Stanford goal posts. Today, when the last gun popped, there was a wild rush for both posts. Eager hands grasped the uprights. Human bodies were hoisted to the crossbars. In a trice both goal posts were reduced to kindling wood.

**Around the field went the serpentine of victory. It was a great day for California and the California boys and girls made the most of it. Eight years is a long time to wait.**

California's victory was deserved. The Bears fought hard for what they got, and while Stanford battled just as hard not to let them

(Continued on Page 2, Column 6)

### *OLD BEAR FINDS ITS LOST GROWL*

*Long Despised Berkeley Grid Animal Finally Scalps Warner*

BY HARRY CARR
"Times" Staff Representative

STANFORD UNIVERSITY, Nov. 21.—In the second quarter, that old sea dog, Navy Bill Ingram, sitting with his elbows on his knees, squinted, his eyes balefully at Pop Warner across the field. It was like John Paul Jones sailing up to challenge the trim Serapis with an old patched-up leaking Yankee frigate.

BILL INGRAM

The long despised, battered old Berkeley Bear was about to growl.

Suddenly Pop Warner hitched around in his seat with a startled jerk as the ball shot like a bullet from Schaldach's big paw straight into the arms of Smith for a 10-yard gain.

Navy Bill smiled a grim slow smile.

Like an indignant old she-elephant starting to trumpet, Pop threw away his cigarettes and scrambled to his feet, his overcoat streaming in the wind as he glared down the field. Shaldach had plunged through the slim white-

(Continued on Page 4, Column 5)

## TROJAN GRID MEN BARE HEADS AT ROCKNE'S GRAVE

SOUTH BEND (Ind.) Nov. 21. (Exclusive)—In the excitement and joy of their triumph over Notre Dame, the Trojans of Southern California did a thing this evening which should further cement the friendly relations between the two institutions. As the fleet of automobiles brought the victorious party back to the railroad station. Coach Howard Jones ordered the return routed via the cemetery where Knute Rockne is buried. Arriving at the great leader's grave the entire Trojan squad, cripples and all, got out of the cars and stood with bared heads while Jones placed a wreath of flowers on the stone. The Trojan mentor spoke feleingly of Notre Dame's immortal coach and then requested a minute of silence. No word was spoken as the players observed this ritual and returned to their cars for the drive to the station.

## YALE DEFEATS HARVARD, 3-0

*Albie Booth's Drop Kick Wins Thrilling Game*

*Crimson Domination Over Eli Finally Ended*

*Wood Overshadowed by Play of Diminutive Rival*

BY GRANTLAND RICE
(Copyright, 1931, by North American Newspaper Alliance, Inc.)

BOSTON, Nov. 21. (Exclusive)—Fate, the strange, bewildering will-o'-the-wisp that directs so many destinies, has a way of evening up. In the gray twilight of the Harvard stadium this afternoon Albie Booth finished his football assault on Harvard amid the roaring acclaim that belongs to victory as Barry Wood lay on his own 1-yard line, covered by two Blue tacklers at the final whistle.

ALBIE BOOTH.

Harvard's unbeaten season and Harvard's three-year domination over Yale and Albie Booth came to a dramatic and abrupt end as Booth's winning drop kick from the 13-yard line sent Yale spinning out in front by the score of 3 to 0 with less than three minutes to play. It so happened that a smashing, slashing defensive war between two evenly matched teams suddenly turned into a Blue storm and an Eli tumult as big John Wilbur, Yale's star left tackle, blocked Barry Wood's attempted punt on Harvard's 45-yard line and then dived across the ball.

**Here, with only about three minutes to go, was the last big chance for Yale and Booth after spending three years hooked to a Crimson leash. And Booth leaped to this last chance with everything he had.**

On the second play, Albie fired a forward pass to Barres, Yale's alert right end, and the pass car-

(Continued on Page 4, Column 2)

## OREGON TRIMS BRUINS, 13-6

*Webfooters Defeat U.C.L.A. at Olympic Stadium*

*Temple and Mikulak Smash Westwooders' Hopes*

*Bergdahl's Absence Felt by Spaulding Team*

BY EDWARD LAWRENCE

U.C.L.A. couldn't fill Lenny Bergdahl's shoes in the Olympic Stadium yesterday afternoon. This fact, plus the presence of two green-clad power trucks in the Oregon backfield, Mark Temple and Mike Mikulak, gave the Webfeet a 13-to-6 victory before some 15,000 shivering fans.

NORM DUNCAN.

Without Bergdahl, the Bruins lost the spark that carried them to victory over St. Mary's two weeks ago, and bogged down at the crucial moments, taking advantage of but one of three scoring opportunities.

TIED AT HALF

Blocked punts, fumbles, and penalties paved the way for Oregon and Bruin touchdowns in the first half, the teams leaving the field tied, 6 to 6, at half time. The Webfeet came back in the third quarter to make the only sustained drive of the day, a 74-yard march that ended in the winning touchdown.

**Temple, Mikula and company, and the Oregon sophomore back is all that has been said of him, registered first on the score board in the initial period. Bob Decker put his team in the hole right off the bat when Heyden, Webfoot center, came in fast to block his punt on the Bruin 6-yard line. The sturdy U.C.L.A. line held, Capt. Norman Duncan catching Temple behind the line of scrimmage on the final thrust. But the Bruins were not so fortunate a few mo-**

(Continued on Page 3, Column 2)

## YEP, TROY'S HORSE CAN KICK

| NOTRE DAME (14) | | U.S.C. (16) |
|---|---|---|
| Kosky | L.E. | Sparling |
| Culver | L.T. | Brown |
| Harriss | L.G. | Rosenberg |
| Yarr | C. | Williamson |
| Hoffman | R.G. | Stevens |
| Kurth | R.T. | Smith |
| Devore | R.E. | Arbelbide |
| Jaskwhich | Q.B. | Shaver |
| Schwartz | L.H. | Mallory |
| Sheeketski | R.H. | Pinckert |
| Banas | F.B. | Musick |

SCORE BY QUARTERS

| | | | | |
|---|---|---|---|---|
| Notre Dame | 0 | 7 | 7 | 0—14 |
| Southern California | 0 | 0 | 0 | 16—16 |

Touchdowns—Notre Dame: Banas, Schwartz. Southern California: Shaver, 2.

Points after touchdown—Notre Dame: Jaskwhich, 2. Southern California: Baker.

Field goal—Baker (Southern California.)

SUBSTITUTES

Notre Dame—Krause for Culver, Brancheau for Sheeketski, Host for Kosky, Kozak for Kurth, Mahoney for Devore, Wunsch for Hoffman, Leahy for Banas, Leonard for Leahy, Murphy for Jaskwhich, Milheam for Sheeketski.

Southern California—Mohler for Shaver, Erskine for Smith, Clark for Mallory, Baker for Rosenberg, Hall for Brown, Palmer for Arbelbide, Griffith for Mohler.

Officials—Birch (Earlham,) referee; Gillette (Oregon,) umpire; Barker (Chicago,) field judge; Wyatt (Missouri,) head linesman.

## FOOTBALL RESULTS

LOCAL

Oregon, 13; U.C.L.A., 6.
Pomona, 6; Occidental, 0.
Loyola, 13; Olympic Club, 0.
Whittier, 19; Redlands, 7.
U.S.S. Maryland, 41; U.S.S. Tennessee, 0.
U.S.S. Texas, 6; U.S.S. Pennsylvania, 6.

JUNIOR COLLEGES

Chaffey, 6; Pomona, 6.
San Bernardino, 8; Citrus, 6.
Compton, 7; Loyola frosh, 0.

HIGH SCHOOLS

Fullerton, 0; Long Beach, 0.
Santa Ana, 14; Alhambra, 6.
San Diego, 40; Glendale, 0.
Taft High School, 14; Bakersfield, 7.
Ventura High, 38; Lompoc, 7.
San Diego A. & M., 13; Caltech frosh, 0.
San Luis Obispo, 19; Santa Barbara, 13.

PACIFIC COAST

California, 6; Stanford, 0.
Washington State, 13; Gonzaga, 6.
San Francisco U., 40; Nevada, 7.
Arizona, 14; De Paul, 13.
Flagstaff State, 13; Tempe State, 7.
Puget Sound, 25; Pacific U., 6.

EAST

Yale, 3; Harvard, 0.
Syracuse, 0; Columbia, 0.
Southern Methodist, 13; Navy, 6.
West Virginia, 19; Penn State, 0.
Army, 54; Ursinus, 6.
Georgetown, 13; Villanova, 6.
Bucknell, 14; Fordham, 13.
Holy Cross, 16; Loyola (Md.,) 14.
Brown, 19; New Hampshire, 13.
Lafayette, 13; Lehigh, 7.
Allegheny, 7; W. Va. Wesleyan, 3.
Hobart, 13; Rochester, 7.
Duquesne, 13; North Dakota, 7.
Delaware, 31; Haverford, 0.
Juniata, 25; Waynesburg, 6.
Tufts, 7; Massachusetts, 7.
Grove City, 20; Thiel, 0.
Penn Military, 12; Susquehanna, 0.
Springfield, 78; Vermont, 0.
St. Vincent, 13; New River, 6.
Dickinson, 14; Muhlenberg, 6.
Boston College, 18; Boston U., 6.
St. Josephs, 20; Washington College, 0.
Union, 7; Rensselaer, 2.
Geneva, 18; Westminster, 0.

MIDWEST

Southern California, 16; Notre Dame, 14.
Northwestern, 19; Iowa, 0.
Purdue, 19; Indiana, 0.
Kansas, 14; Missouri, 0.
Nebraska, 23; Iowa State, 0.
Wisconsin, 12; Chicago, 7.
Michigan, 6; Minnesota, 0.
Ohio State, 40; Illinois, 0.
DePauw, 13; Wabash, 7.

(Continued on Page 5, Column 8)

## GEORGIA BEATS AUBURN

### *Bulldogs Forced to Give Utmost to Capture Grid Battle by 12-to-6 Score*

MEMORIAL STADIUM (Columbus, Ga.) Nov. 21. (Exclusive)—Geared to the highest pitch in fighting intensity, a good game Auburn team took everything the highly favored Bulldogs from Athens, Ga., could throw at them here this afternoon, yielding a meager 12-to-6 conquest to the celebrated conquerors of Yale and New York University.

It was Georgia's markedly superior physical resources that told the tale in the end, an advantage in power and mechanical precision overcoming in the second half the sheer inspirational battle being waged by the visitors from the loveliest village across the river.

**The Bulldogs' first touchdown came early in the third period, and resulted from a march of 62 yards in which four straight first downs were rung up. Little Homer Key, playing before his home folks, started things with a 25-yard sweep around end to the Tigers' 33. After three plays netted only 4 yards, the Georgians gambled and got away with it, Whire catapaulting through tackle for 7 yards and a first down.**

Two plunges by Mott brought 11 yards and another first down. Key and Mott picked up 5 between them and Big Jodie Whire took the ball for those last 5½ yards and a touchdown.

The second Georgia counter came early in the last period, after getting organized late in the third. The boys traveled 52 yards to make this one, Whire and Mott teaming up with short but consistent gains through the wilting Tiger line. A 15-yard dash by Buster put the ball on the 1-yard stripe and the final quarter opened and on the next play he took it over.

Rallying their flagging forces, Auburn came back gamely to score themselves a few minutes later. The Tigers traveled 78 yards to do it, too. Hitchy-Coo Hitchcock, Auburn's star

(Continued on Page 2, Column 8)

[Chicago Tribune telephoto]

Once Marchy Didn't March

Marchmont Schwartz, Notre Dame's great all-American halfback, was the leading ground-gainer of the South Bend game yesterday, but he didn't get away every time. This telephoto shows Ray Sparling, Trojan wingman, stopping the husky Irish star on a jaunt around end, without gain. The chubby young man with the pleased expression on his face on the ground, is Ernie Smith, mammoth Trojan tackle.

OLYMPIC GAMES SECTION
Los Angeles Times
EQUAL RIGHTS
LIBERTY UNDER THE LAW — TRUE INDUSTRIAL FREEDOM
VOL. LI. SUNDAY MORNING, JULY 31, 1932. [PART VI-a.]


# MULTITUDE ACCLAIMS OPENING OF OLYMPICS

Great March of Athletes in Olympic Stadium Showing Vast Crowd Assembled for Opening

(Carroll photo)

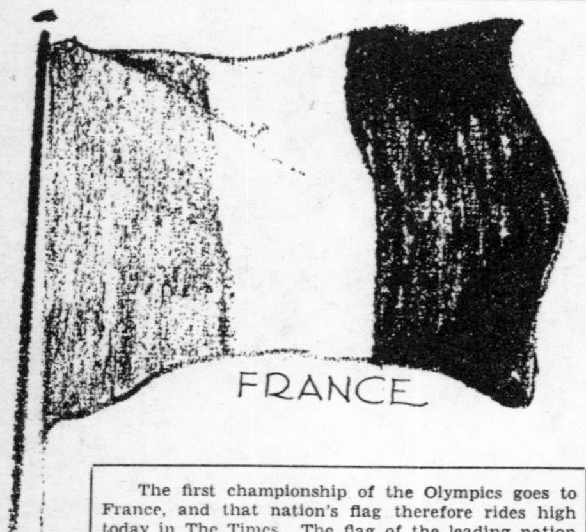


The first championship of the Olympics goes to France, and that nation's flag therefore rides high today in The Times. The flag of the leading nation will occupy this space daily.

## CITIUS, FORTIUS, ALTIUS CALL IT A "FAIR MOB"

### *Three Musketeers of Olympia Agree Curtis and Count Wear Nifty Toppers*

BY RALPH HUSTON

Those three venerable Musketeers of Olympia—Citius, Altius and Fortius—stood on the peristyle at the Olympic Stadium, yesterday, leaned on their spears, and talked the situation over.

"Quite a gathering," observed Citius, scraping a muddy boot on the base of the Olympic torch.

"Yeah, fair mob. Feels good, at that, to be back at the old stand."

"Nice stadium. They didn't have anything like this back in Elis. Looks like there are more people outside than in. They're all lined up out in back waiting to watch the athletes march in and out, and Zeuz only knows how many are here in front, without tickets."

**"PIPE THE TOPPERS"**

"Hope they keep those speeches short. I'll never forget one time Demosthenes got started in one of the old Games, and they'd been forced to postpone the athletic events three times before he finally got through."

"Well, we're getting under way. Here comes Vice-President Curtis, and Count de Baillet-Latour. Pipe the toppers! Is that a nifty, or isn't it? William May Garland looks distinguished in that outfit. Wonder if Zack Farmer will wear his iron hat? Nope. There he is, and he hasn't even changed his shirt. Guess there's been so much work he couldn't get away from the office."

**"Did you hear that? Some Beverly Hills humorist, who used to be a cowboy until he took up polo, pulls the nifty of the year. 'They look like a bunch of undertakers out here to bury Nurmi!' That's a classic!"**

"Greece leads again, eh? That's a nice honor. Say, did you ever hear "The Star-Spangled Banner"

(Continued on Page 4, Column 1)

### *Today's Events*

ATHLETICS

2:30 p.m.—400-meter hurdles—men (trials)—Stadium.
2:30—High jump—men—Stadium.
2:30—Shot put—men—Stadium.
3:00—100 meters—men (trials 1)—Stadium.
4:00—800 meters—men (trials)—Stadium.
4:30—100 meters—men (trials 2)—Stadium.
5:00—400-meter hurdles—men (trials 2)—Stadium.
5:30—Javelin—ladies—Stadium.
5:30—10,000 meters—men (final)—Stadium.

3:00—Weight lifting—Olympic Auditorium.
7:30—Weight lifting—Olympic Auditorium.
1:00—Fencing (foils)—Armory.

## FIRST CHAMPION HAILED

The first victory in the Olympic Games of 1932 at Los Angeles goes to Rene Duverger, French weight lifter, competing in the lightweight division.

Rene Duverger of France became the first Olympic champion when he captured the lightweight weight-lifting championship last night with a total of 715 points, breaking the old Olympic record of 711 points. He raised 214½ pounds in the two-hand military tress, 225½ pounds in the two-hand snatch and 275

(Continued on Page 2, Column 5)

## STIRRING MARCH OF ATHLETES AROUSES CHEERS OF CROWD

### *Swelling Strains of National Anthem From Giant Band and Chorus as Pride of Nations Open Olympics Holds Throng Tense*

BY BRAVEN DYER

It may be a physical impossibility for goose pimples actually to sprout through a person's shirt but as 105,000 pulse-quickened souls stood bareheaded in the Olympic Stadium yesterday afternoon this phenomenon was experienced by even the most calloused observer.

Lieut. Harold William Roberts was leading his magnificent mixed chorus of 2000 voices in a marvelous rendition of the national anthem and so inspiring was the presentation that you could almost feel the epidermis rising on your next door neighbor.

Spectacles may come and go but it is doubtful if there ever will be another such as yesterday's—certainly never in the lifetime of most of those who witnessed the mammoth pageant of color and music. And uppermost in the minds of those who helped to jam the huge stadium to capacity will be the memory of that stirring anthem, a choral achievement that will never be forgotten.

As to the athletes themselves, the greatest gathering of brawn and sinew the world has ever known, they filed slowly past in military procession, more than 1500 from all corners of the world. The dramatic entry of Greece, birthplace of both the ancient and modern Olympic Games, was the signal for

(Continued on Page 2, Column 3)

## *JIM THORPE DENIED ONE LITTLE TICKET; WEEPS AS HUGE PARADE PASSES*

BY PAUL LOWRY

Jim Thorpe, the Indian, cried when the big parade went by. He was the saddest man in the huge throng of 105,000 persons at the Olympic Stadium.

Jim was in the press box, recipient of a last-minute gift after getting the cold shoulder at ticket headquarters.

They forgot that Jim was a great hero for the United States twenty years ago.

But Jim remembered.

He sobbed softly to himself when the United States flag dipped in salute before the Vice-President's box.

Big Jim had cause for his sorrow.

At Stockholm in 1912 he won the all-around championship for America by a margin so large that the second-place man was in another league.

Then they took Jim's medals away. They said he had played a wee bit of semi-professional baseball. They erased Jim's name from the

(Continued on Page 4, Column 7)

**TRIO SWELLS AVERAGES**

Three of the ten leading hitters of the American League in 1931 increased their averages over that of 1930. These three players were the three topnotch sluggers last season, Simmons, Ruth and Morgan.

**FINNEY'S HITTING HELPS**

The powerful hitting of Louis Finney has helped Portland a lot this year. Finney places fourth among the hitters of the Coast League with an average better than .370.

OLYMPIC GAMES SECTION
Los Angeles Times
EQUAL RIGHTS — LIBERTY UNDER THE LAW — TRUE INDUSTRIAL FREEDOM

VOL. LI. C — MONDAY MORNING, AUGUST 1, 1932.

# FIVE MARKS BROKEN IN OLYMPICS

The United States having triumphed yesterday in Olympic events, its flag rides today as the victor's symbol on The Times' flagpole.

## FIRST DAY MARKED BY MANY SENSATIONS

### *Spectators Kept on Toes as Records Fall; Excellent Bills Slated for Today*

BY PAUL LOWRY

Climaxed by a new world's mark and record-shattering performances all along the line, the Games of the Tenth Olympiad were well under way yesterday.

Track and field, opening at the Olympic Stadium, saw Mildred (Babe) Didrikson break the world's javelin standard for women by more than eleven feet, while new Olympic records were set in 100 meters, shot put, 10,000 meters and 400-meter hurdles.

Fencing opened at the Armory with a surprisingly large crowd in attendance while weight liftin: wound up at the Olympic Auditorium last night.

Two other sports—wrestling and cycling—start today with track and field and fencing continuing at their respective stadiums. Track runs for eight days, winding up with the Marathon next Sunday. Fencing lasts fourteen days.

In brief these were the high lights of yesterday's competition:

**TRACK**

Javelin throw for women—"Babe" Didrikson of the United States established a new Olympic and world's record with a throw of 143ft. 4in.

100 meters—Eddie Tolan of the United States set a new Olympic record of 10.4s. Jonath of Germany also bettered the old mark with 10.5s. Both races were semifinal heats.

400-meter hurdles—Hardin of the United States and Tisdall of Ireland tied for new Olympic mark honors with semifinal heats of 52.8s.

Shot put—Leo Sexton, giant New Yorker, slashed the former Olympic record with a toss of 52ft. 6 13-16in.

10,000-meter run—J. Kusocinski, the Pole, broke the great Paavo Nurmi's Olympic standard by running the distance in 30m. 11.4s.

**WEIGHT LIFTING**

Jsmayr of Germany captured the middleweight division honors with Galimberti of Italy second and Hipfinger of Austria third.

France assured itself of the weight lifting team trophy when Raymond Suvigny won the featherweight division last night. Wolpert of Germany was second and Anthony Terlazzo of the United States third.

In the heavyweight class, the concluding event, Jaroslav Skobia was the winner with Psenicka of Czecho-Slovakia second and Strassberger of Germany third.

**FENCING**

**In the foils elimination team tourney the United States defeated Argentina, 10 to 6; Denmark won from Mexico, 11 to 5; France downed Argentina, 12 to 4, and Italy whitewashed Mexico, 16 to 0.**

**Four teams thus qualified for the finals—the United States, Denmark, Italy and France.**

**Lieut. Calnan of the United States, who took the Olympic oath for all the competing athletes at the opening ceremonies Sunday, was the first to win a fencing bout. He defeated Saucedo of Argentina, five touches to four.**

**VICTORY CEREMONY**

The first victory flag run up on the center pole at the Olympic Stadium was in honor of Rene Duverger, the French dancing master, who won the lightweight class in the weight-lifting finals Saturday night. This preceded the start of the track events.

The second victory flag was also the tricolor of France. It was for Louis Hostin, the croupier, who won the light-heavyweight honors in weight lifting.

Not until the good right arm of Leo Sexton beat back the challenge of the giants of Europe in the shot put did the United States put a flag on the victory pole. A small flag went up for Henry Duey's third place in the light-heavyweight division of weight lifting, but it was Sexton who propelled the big standard up the main mast.

Before the day was out Canada and Poland each scored first-place triumphs, and flung their banners to the breeze—McNaughton in the high jump and Kusocinski in the 10,000 meters.

**HIGH LIGHTS**

One of the biggest features of the day was Duncan McNaughton's win in the high jump. A University of Southern California boy, he has never at any time this year been considered the kingpin of Dean Cromwell's leapers. He tied for third at 6ft. 2in. with Stewart of S.C. in the I.-C.-4-A. meet while Van Osdel, a team-mate, was tying O'Connor of Columbia for first at 6ft. 4in.

McNaughton was born in Canada, but the Canadian team was not sure about giving him a place on the squad until after he tried out after its arrival here. He leaped 6ft. 3in. and was permitted to wear the Maple Leaf. He responded by winning the jump-off of a four-way tie with Van Osdel and Johnson of the United States and Toribio of the Philippines.

McNaughton did it by the **simple** process of wearing al lhis rivals **out.** This event was considered **almost** an American cinch. Van Osdel, **Spitz** and Johnson had all tied at 6ft. 6 5-8in. in the American trials at Palo Alto, but they didn't have it yesterday. Spitz went out at 6ft. 4in. and Johnson couldn't stand the strain of the extra jumps.

**METCALFE FAVORED**

While Tolan broke the Olympic record Ralph Metcalfe, the Marquette Negro, still looks like America's best bet in the 100 meters. Jonath of Germany runs powerfully, and Yoshioka of Japan is a fast little fellow. Percy Williams, the defending champion, barely escaped defeat in the semifinals of the 100. He just nipped Berger of Holland at the tape.

Although he doesn't look it Kusocinski is just as great a distance runner as the marvelous Paavo Nurmi. He probably could have smashed Nurmi's world mark in the 10,000 meters, but loafed in after he ran Iso-Hollo of Finland into the ground on the last curve.

Today's program sees the competition wax even hotter than yesterday with the following events listed:

Track (Olympic Stadium)—Semifinals, 100 meters for men; hammer throw, finals 100 meters for men; finals, 400-meter hurdles for men, trials, **100 meters for ladies; semi-**

(Continued on Page 10, Column 3)

Taking the Maple Leaf for a High Ride

Although he was considered only the fourth-best jumper on the University of Southern California track team, Duncan McNaughton carried the **colors of Canada to victory in the Olympic Games high jump yesterday, soaring 6ft. 5⅝in. His college team-mate, Bob Van Osdel, representing the United States, was second and Simeon Toribio of the Phillipine Islands third. McNaughton and Van Osdel actually tied for first place, but the young Canadian won the jump-off.**

## SEXTON HURLS SHOT FOR NEW OLYMPIC RECORD

### *Mighty Irishman Tosses Pellet 52ft. 6 3-16in. to Set American Flag Fluttering on Victory Pole*

BY RALPH HUSTON

A great broth of a bhoy—one that would warm the heart of Dr. Patrick O'Callaghan himself, begorry—sent the Stars and Stripes to the victory pole in the Olympic Stadium for the first time yesterday, but it also set the harps tinkling in Tara's ancient halls.

Leo Sexton, gigantic, massive colossus with the face of Erin, the shield of America on his chest, hurled the 16-pound shot farther than it ever had been hurled before in the Olympic Games. Fifty-two feet, 6 and 3-16th inches he hurled it to smash to smithereens the Olympic record.

"I'm sick, and I'm tired of these Brixes, these Rotherts and these Hirschfelds," said Irish Leo Sexton in New York these few short weeks ago. "I have nothing against the Germans. They're fine fellows all, but it's time a good Irishman won a shot put, and I think I'll do it."

He threw the shot all over the place in the eastern indoor **meets. He threw it farther when he moved outdoors. He won the American tryouts.** He moved to Bovard Field to work out, and when Franisek Douda, the giant Czecho-Slovakian tossed it 53ft. 6in. in practice, Irish Leo Sexton muttered to himself and threw one 53ft. 10½in.

Irish Leo didn't have to throw that far yesterday. They made him go 52ft. plus, and that's where he threw that sixteen-pound ball, with a mighty effort on his last throw **that brought frenzied cheers from the 60,000 spectators who had turned**

(Continued on Page 13, Column 1)

*Mighty "Babe" Does It Again*

World Record in Javelin Shattered

Here's Babe Didrikson, the Texas flash, showing how she threw weapon ten feet farther than any other girl in history.

## NEW OLYMPIC CHAMPIONS

**Shot put—Leo Sexton (United States,) 52ft. 6 3-16in. (New Olympic record.)**

**High jump—Duncan McNaughton (Canada,) 6ft. 5⅝in.**

**10,000-meter run—Janusz Kosocinski (Poland,) 30m. 11.4s. (New Olympic record.)**

**Javelin throw (women) — Mildred (Babe) Didrikson (United States,) 143ft. 4in. (New world's record.)**

**WEIGHT LIFTING**

**Featherweight — Raymond Suvigny (France,) 632½ pounds.**

**Lightweight—Rene Duverger (France,) 715 pounds. (New Olympic record.)**

**Middleweight—Rudolf Jsmayr (Germany,) 759 pounds.**

**Light-heavyweight—Louis Hostin (France,) 803 pounds.**

**Heavyweight—Jardslav Skobia (Czecho-Slovakia,) 836 pounds.**

## *"GEE, MY HAND SLIPPED," WAILS BABE IN SMASHING RECORD BY ELEVEN FEET*

BY MURIEL BABCOCK

**If the mighty "Babe's" hand hadn't slipped, she might have thrown that javelin clean through the grand stand.**

Captured in the midst of an informal running broad jump up the stairs en route to a bath and some clean clothes in her room at the Chapman Park Hotel, "Babe" Mildred Didrikson, who yesterday broke the world's woman javelin record by eleven good feet, admitted her feat was kind of a mistake.

"No, I haven't got a new technique," she said grinning, "my hand slipped when I picked up the pole. It slid along about six inches and then I got a good grip again. And then I threw and it just went."

**And it would have gone 155 or 160 feet, interposed Coach Fred L. Steers at this point, if the Babe's hand hadn't done the shimmy.**

"Do I feel good about it? Sure," said Babe. "I just felt like throwing. I'm awful glad I did what I did."

And she disappeared into her room.

The mighty Babe's return to the hotel from Olympic Stadium yesterday afternoon assumed the proportions of triumphal entrance.

Clambering out of a bus, (not a private limousine or even a taxi) along with a lot of other woman athletes, the Babe ducked into the hotel to find all the girls lined up to clap and cheer for her.

**Somebody yelled, "What a woman!" Babe grinned appreciatively and headed for the elevator, about fifty fans in pursuit. Three autograph hunters leaped upon her. Babe stopped and signed the proffered books. Somebody tapped her upon the left shoulder, with "Congratulations, Babe!"**

Somebody tapped her on the right shoulder, with "Swell work, Babe."

Then, "Say, where's the report on the event?" and she headed for the ticker in the hotel lobby whence all news stories of the events are tapped out as they occur. She found her name and the records, which seemed all right and then scuttled for her room and change of clothes.

## *Kozeluh Wins Tennis Crown*

CHICAGO, July 31. (AP)—Karl Kozeluh of Czecho-Slovakia today won the professional tennis championship of the United States by defeating Hans Nusslein, youthful German, 6-2, 6-2, 7-5. Kozeluh, who is 36 years of age and holder of the world professional championship for seven years, eliminated Big Bill Tilden in a hard-fought semifinal match Saturday.

## *TODAY'S EVENTS*

2:30 p.m.—ATHLETICS, Olympic Stadium.
2:30 p.m.—100 meter, men (semifinal.)
2:30 p.m.—Throwing hammer, men.
3:00 p.m.—100 meter, men (finals.)
3:30 p.m.—400-meter hurdles, men (final.)
3:45 p.m.—100 meter, ladies (trials I.)
5:00 p.m.—100 meter, ladies (semifinals.)
5:15 p.m.—3000-meter steeplechase, men (trials.)
9:00 a.m.—FENCING (foil teams,) Armory.
1:00 p.m.—FENCING (foil teams,) Armory.
11:00 a.m.—WRESTLING (free style,) Olympic Auidtorium.
6:00 p.m.—WRESTLING (free style,) Olympic Auditorium.
7:30 p.m.—TRACK CYCLING, Rose Bowl.
1000-meter scratch (trials.)
2000-meter tandems (trials.)
1000-meter scratch (reclassification.)
1000-meter by time (trials.)

## BABE DIDRIKSON CRACKS WORLD JAVELIN RECORD

### *Flat and Hurdle Races Thrill as Athletic History Written in Afternoon Trials*

BY BRAVEN DYER

While the greatest collection of bulky-muscled behemoths and iron-limbed luminaries the world has ever known struggled all afternoon in their futile efforts to crack world's records, it remained for a mere slip of a girl from Texas to prove that the female of the species is not only more deadly than the male but also more reliable when it comes to shattering official standards.

Mildred (Babe) Didrikson, 128 pounds of feminine dynamite, came through yesterday when all competitors of the so-called stronger sex failed in their world record-wrecking attempts.

Kusocinski's victory was the first ever scored by Poland in an Olympic Games track and field program. It was the first time Finland had ever lost the 10,000-meter race.

Yesterday was the second time in Olympic history that the United States failed to win the high jump. Con Leahy winning for Ireland in 1906. Leahy was trained in this country, as was McNaughton, yesterday's winner.

Not since 1912 has Great Britain failed to place a man in the finals of the 100 meters.

More than 50,000 spectators joined in a wild cheer as the doughty Dedrikson dame rifled the javelin 143ft. 4in. on her very first effort a mighty heave which erased the former world mark of 132ft.

**GERMAN'S TRY FUTILE**

This magnificent throw, uncorked before most of the spectators, realized the event was under way, closed the javelin competition right then and there. Fraulein Ellen Braumuller of Germany, holder of the record before "Babe" broke into the picture, put everything she had into her work, but couldn't quite match the skill and strength of this confident kid from the wilds of the Lone Star State.

**The amazing feature of "Babe's" toss was that it might just as well have traveled ten feet more, but for the fact that she threw the wand much after the manner of a catcher pegging to second base. The heave had absolutely no elevation and sailed practically in a straight line from the time it left Miss Didrikson's mighty right arm until it dug its way into the green turf of the Olympic Stadium.**

With "Babe" it was just a case of doing what she had boasted of ever since her arrival in Los Angeles. She has no compunctions about admitting that she's good and her great sorrow at this time is that they will let her compete in only three events. Several weeks ago she won the national A.A.U. championship all by herself, scoring 30 points.

**GAMES' MARKS FALL**

Although all the males, straining with might and main throughout four hours of red-hot competition, were unable to match the record-smashing feats of the "Babe," they did manage to shatter a half-dozen Olympic Games' standards, which was a pretty fair average for the opening day's festivities.

In fact, in every event but the high jump and 800-meter run the men contenders lowered Olmypic records and if this becomes a habit with them, as seems likely, the official statisticians are going to have a lot of work on their hands.

Second only to Miss Didrikson was gigantic Leo Sexton of the New York Athletic Club who smashed the Olympic shot-putting standard with a tremondous toss of 52ft. 6 3-16in. Leo missed tying Emil Hirschfeld's official world mark by a little more than an inch, but made good his boast to annex the event for the United States.

**Nobody deserved a place of honor yesterday more than Harlow Rothert, the former Stanford boy, who exceeded the fondest expectations of his admirers by placing second to Sexton.**

It was less than two weeks ago that Harlow's younger brother Lowry was killed in an automobile accident. The kid was just beginning to show promise of taking his brother's place as an athletic star at Stanford and the blow was a terrific one to Harlow. I have an idea that Rothert's greatest inspiration yesterday was the memory of his younger brother and the thought that he (Harlow) must do something to perpetuate the family name in international competition now that it is impossible for his brother to carry on in his footsteps.

**Olympic records fell in other events as follows:**

**100-meter run—10.4s. by Ed-**

(Continued on Page 12, Column 1)

## FRENCH ANNEX WEIGHT-LIFTING

### *Tri-Color Athletes Capture Three of Five Titles*

### *Skobia, Czecho-Slovakian, Cops Heavyweight Honors*

### *Jsmayr, Germany, Suvigny of France Also Victors*

BY BOB RAY

When the last of the five Xth Olympiad weight-lifting champions was crowned at the Olympic Auditorium last night, the chanticleer of France let out a lusty crow to tell the world that the mighty sons of La Belle France had captured three of the crowns. The other two titles were won by Germany and Czecho-Slovakia.

The weight-lifting ended none too soon for Announcer Charley Keppen, who is reported to be bordering on a complete breakdown as a result of trying to pronounce the trick names of the invaders, as well as some of the more fancy American cognomens. Keppen's tonsils are scattered all over the Olympic Auditorium, backfiring right out of his throat on good old Czecho-Slovakian, Argentine, German, French and Italian names.

**The feature of last night's final program was the dethroning of Joe Strassberger, the 287-pound German champion of the 1928 Olympics, by two mighty Czechs — Jaroslav Skobia, who won with a record-breaking total of 836 pounds, and Vaclav Psenicka, a pudgy little 220-pound Prague mechanic.**

Strassberger and Psenicka really tied with totals of 830½, but the Olympiad ruling gives the preference to the smaller man in case of a tie. So Strassberger, despite the fact that he also bettered his 1928 Olympiad total of 819½, was forced to be satisfied with third place.

In the other event staged last night Raymond Suvigny of France won the featherweight title with a total of 632½ pounds to tie the Olympiad record. Second was Hans Wolpert, chunky little German, while third, and making the best showing of any of the Americans, was Anthony Terlazzo, a Hoboken office worker, who had to quit his job to make the United States team.

**THE CHAMPIONS**

**The five Xth Olympiad weight-lifting champions are: Heavyweight, Skobia, an electrician in Prague, Czecho-Slovakia. Light-heavyweight, Louis Hostin, a croupier in a French gambling casino. Middleweight, Rudolf Jsmayr, a young Munich lawyer. Lightweight, Rene Duverger, a Parisian dance professor. Featherweight, Suvigny, a French accountant.**

Interest last night centered chiefly in the heavyweight division where Strassberger, who runs a Munich cafe and possesses a bay window that speaks well of the food he serves, was a favorite. Jovial Joe got off to a good start with a heave of 275 pounds in the military press, but he was unable to keep pace with the two younger Czechs in the two-hand snatch and two-hand clean and jerk and, like all champions must sometimes do, had to meet defeat.

**YANKS TOO LIGHT**

Marcel Dumoulin, who works in a French auto factory, took fourth in the heavyweight lifting, while the two Americans, Albert Manger and Howard Turbyfill, wound up the procession. Manger, who is a Baltimore lithographer, and Turbyfill, a Corona blacksmith, looked like pygmies alongside the beefy Europeans. By training off a few pounds they could have made the light-heavyweight division, where they would have made a good showing. Turbyfill has been lifting weights but one year. He'll be a threat in 1936.

**Final heavyweight results, with the best lifts in the military press, two-hand snatch and two-hand clean and jerk, respectively, and the totals follow: Skobia, Czecho-Slovakia, 247½, 253, 335—836. Psenicka, Czecho-Slovakia, 247½, 258½, 324½ — 830½. Strassberger, Germany, 275, 242, 313½—830½. Dumoulin, France, 209, 236½, 308 — 753½. Manger, United**

(Continued on Page 14, Column 7)

## *Gin Chow Sees Jus' Litty Rain*

Gin Chow consulted his magic books and predicts rain on the 7th inst.

"Not so hard rain—jus' litty rain. But rain anyhow."

Gin says there will be no very hot days during the period of the Games.

OLYMPIC GAMES SECTION
Los Angeles Times
EQUAL RIGHTS
LIBERTY UNDER THE LAW — TRUE INDUSTRIAL FREEDOM
VOL. LI. C. TUESDAY MORNING, AUGUST 2, 1932.

# TOLAN WINS DISPUTED 100 METERS

IRELAND

The flag of Ireland floats at the mast-head today as the result of first places won in the 400-meter hurdles and hammer throw.

## SECOND DAY A THRILLER, NATIONS DIVIDE HONORS

### *Michigan Negro and Irish Doctor Outstanding Heroes of Colorful Spectacle*

### TODAY'S TRACK STANDINGS

The United States added to its lead in the track and field standings, men's division, with the following results yesterday, points being scored 10-5-4-3-2-1 for the first six places:

| | Previous total | Hammer throw | 100 meters | 400-meter hurdle | Grand total points |
|---|---|---|---|---|---|
| United States | 25 | 6 | 18 | 9 | 58 |
| Ireland | .. | 10 | .. | 10 | 20 |
| Finland | 11 | 5 | .. | .. | 16 |
| Poland | 10 | .. | .. | .. | 10 |
| Canada | 10 | .. | .. | .. | 10 |
| Germany | 6 | .. | 4 | .. | 10 |
| Czecho-Slovakia | | .. | .. | .. | 4 |
| Philippine Islands | | .. | .. | .. | 4 |
| New Zealand | 3 | .. | .. | .. | 3 |
| Sweden | 1 | 3 | .. | 1 | 5 |
| Japan | 1 | .. | 1 | .. | 2 |
| South Africa | .. | .. | 2 | .. | 2 |
| Italy | .. | .. | .. | 2 | 2 |
| Great Britain | .. | .. | .. | 3 | 3 |
| Argentine | .. | 1 | .. | .. | 1 |

BY PAUL LOWRY

A Michigan Negro, an Irish doctor from County Cork and an Irish forester from Tipperary combined forces to steal Olympic honors yesterday.

Tolan, O'Callaghan and Tisdell. Those were the names.

They were the heroes on an afternoon of amazing and spectacular performances—an afternoon which saw four Olympic records broken and the flag of Ireland flown from the victory pole twice.

By nations this is what happened:

**IRELAND**

Tisdell, a forester from Tipperary, won the 400-meter hurdles in new world's record time of 51.8s., but his mark was disallowed because he knocked over the last hurdle. He is virtually a rank beginner, having run only five 400-meter races in his life. Dr. Pat O'Callaghan, the mental specialist of County Cork, was trailing Porhola, the Finn, until his last throw, but he showed the typical fighting Irish spirit and beat Porhola by over five feet in the hammer throw.

**IRISH NOW SECOND**

Dr. O'Callaghan is 6ft. 2in. in height and weighs 245 pounds. He was the defending champion, having won at Amsterdam four years ago. His mark yesterday was 176ft. 11½in. Ireland's 20 points in the hammer and hurdles moved the Irish up to second place in the track-and-field standings.

**UNITED STATES**

**Eddie Tolan, the "Midnight Express," won the 100 meters from Ralph Metcalfe in new Olympic record time of 10.3s. This ties the world's mark held by Percy Williams of Canada, who was eliminated in one of the semifinal heats.**

Williams was the defending champion. Tolan's victory over Metcalfe was disputed. Those on the finish line thought Metcalfe had a tie at least, and the majority of the press sleuths favored Metcalfe. Lawson Robertson, head coach of the American team, collected bets on Metcalfe's "win." Hardin was second in the 400-meter hurdles and F. Morgan Taylor, third. Hardin was given credit for a new Olympic record of 52s. flat when Tisdall's mark was rejected because of the spilled hurdle. Zaremba and McDougall took third and fifth, respectively, in the hammer throw. Conner, another entry, fouled on all three qualifying throws. America scored 33 points to lead track and field with a total of 58.

**POLAND**

**Stella Walsh, the little lady who had trouble in deciding whether to run for the land of her birth or the land of her adoption, set a new women's world record in the 100-meter of 11.9s. The former mark was 12s. flat. This happened in one of the early heats.**

**GREAT BRITAIN**

Lord Burghley, the defending champion in the 400-meter hurdles, was able to get no better than a fourth after a valiant battle.

Tom Ebenson bettered the 3000-meter steeplechase mark by three seconds. His time in a trial heat was 9m. 18.8s.

**FINLAND**

Iso-Hollo made Ebenson's glory short lived when he lowered the Olympic record in the 3000-meter steeplechase to 9m. 14.6s. in another heat.

**SOUTH AFRICA**

Joubert placed fifth in a 100-meter field where the greatest sprinters in Olympic Games history went to their marks.

**ITALY**

Facelli, toast of Mussolini in the 400-meter hurdles, placed fifth in a world-record shattering race. But in another sport of the day—fencing—Italy emerged in a three-way tie with the United States and France. The United States made its best showing of Olympic Games

(Continued on Page 12, Column 2)

### TODAY'S EVENTS

2:30 p.m.—ATHLETICS, Olympic Stadium.
2:30 p.m.—110-meter hurdles, men (trials 1.)
2:30 p.m.—Broad jump, men.
2:30 p.m.—Discus, women.
3 p.m.—200 meters, men (trials 1.)
3:45 p.m.—800 meters, men (final.)
4 p.m.—100 meters, women (final.)
4:15 p.m.—110-meter hurdles, men (semifinals.)
4:45 p.m.—5000 meter, men (trials.)
5:30 p.m.—200 meters, men (trials 2.)
1 p.m.—FENCING (foil, men and women.) Armory.
11 a.m.—WRESTLING (free style.) Olympic Auditorium.
6 p.m.—WRESTLING (free style.) Olympic Auditorium.
7:30 p.m.—TRACK CYCLING, Rose Bowl (Pasadena.)
1000-meter scratch (quarterfinals.)
1000-meter scratch (reclassification.)
4000-meter pursuit race (trials.)
4000-meter pursuit race (quarterfinals)
9 a.m.—PENTATHLON (equestrian) secret course. Starts Riviera Country Club.

METCALFE
YOSHIOKA
JOUBERT
SIMPSON
JONATH
TOLAN

[Upper photo by Fred Coffey, Times photographer]
[Lower photo by Wide World]

The Race They'll Always Argue Over

Who do you think won this race? These two pictures taken from different angles show the finals of the 100-meter dash, yesterday's Olympic Games feature race. Movies of the finish show Eddie Tolan winning to accord with the selection of the officials. However, the majority of the fans and practically all the "experts" in the press box believed Ralph Metcalfe to be the winner. But as both represented Uncle Sam it really didn't make much difference. Jonath, of Germany, nosed out George Simpson, another Yankee, for third, with Joubert, of South Africa, fifth. Yoshioka, of Japan, was sixth.

## *SURE AND YOU CAN'T BEAT THOSE SONS OF OULD ERIN; VICTORY FLAG UP AGAIN*

BY RALPH HUSTON

You can have your Flying Finns. You can have your ambling Americans. You can have your powerful Poles. I'll take the wild Irish for mine!

Twice Ould Ireland sent its sons against the world yesterday. And twice those stalwart, brawny lads sent the green, white and gold of Erin to the top of the Victory Mast.

Dr. Patrick O'Callaghan! Was there ever a more fighting man?

Robert Morton Newburgh Tisdall! Was there ever a faster?

"Never!" shouts Tipperary.

"Never!" yells Cork.

"Never!" echoes Dublin, as all Ireland joins in.

Brave Brian Boru, and great Cuchulain sat on a cloud, hung their feet over the side, and rent high heaven with their shouts. Ould Erin has done it again.

And how that little brave band of patriots, sent here to show the world what Ireland could do, shouted.

"Come on, Bob! Beat the Eyetalian! Beat Burghley!"

(Continued on Page 12, Column 1)

## CAMERA SHOWS TOLAN WINNER BY TWO INCHES

### *Electro-Photographic "Camera-Clock" Reveals Scant Margin Between Victor and Ralph Metcalfe*

Eddie Tolan won over Ralph Metcalfe by two inches in the 100-meter final at the Olympic Stadium yesterday afternoon. This was the verdict last night of the electro-photographic "camera-clock," according to Gustavus Kirby, American member of the board of judges. All the judges said their official decision, giving Tolan the victory, was sustained by the motion pictures.

Tolan's time, by the "camera-clock," was 10.28s., as compared with the official hand time of 10.3s., equaling the world record.

**Kirby stated that the pictures show Tolan got his chest into the tape first, while still camera shots indicated that Metcalfe, who starts slowly, was going away from Tolan after they hit the tape.**

**In the women's 100-meter semifinal, first heat, the order of finish as announced at the conclusion of the race was changed last night by official action of the I.A.A.F. Council when they reversed the order of the second and third place winners.**

The amended results give second place to Wilde, U.S.A., and third place to Dollinger of Germany. The results of this heat remain unchanged.

This action was taken after studying the pictures taken at the finish line by the electrical timer.

## *AMERICANS DEFEATED IN FENCING*

### *France Beats United States as Competitions Go on After Tie*

**France defeated the United States in the first round last evening by a score of 11 to 5. The United States then faced Italy and the latter took a lead of five bouts to none.**

BY EDITH DURBIN

After almost seven hours of careful, tense, exhaustive fighting yesterday at the State Armory, the first place honors in foil team competition were divided between Italy, France and United States in a three-way tie for first in Olympic battle. Each of these countries defeated the other two and the fourth entry, Denmark. Competition was started later in the evening to decide the winner.

**There was more than one surprise and upset! The first was the defeat of France by United States, the only time America has ever beaten France at her own game. Not for one minute during the contest between these two nations was either of them sure to win.**

Calnan and Levis, the first two men to fight for America, defeated Gardere and Bondoux. This gave United States an initial lead of 2 points. The next three bouts were won by France. From that time until the 8 to 8 score was recorded, necks were strained and hands were gripped by American and French alike.

At the end of the competition

(Continued on Page 12, Column 3)

## ITALY GRABS CYCLING LEAD

### *Nine Countries Represented in 1000-Meter Race*

### *British and French Also Put Up Contest*

### *Total of 8000 Fans Witness Events at Pasadena*

BY BOB RAY

ROSE BOWL (Pasadena) Aug. 1. Pedal-pushing prides of France, Holland, Denmark, Italy, Great Britain, Canada, Australia, Mexico and the United States unlimbered their legs on the Rose Bowl saucer tonight as the cycling program of the Tenth Olympiad got under way for a three-night stand.

Honors, if any, in the trials of the 1000-meter scratch and 4000-meter pursuit races were captured by Italy, France, Holland, Great Britain and Australia, with the Italians achieving the distinction of breaking their Olympiad record in the 4000-meter pursuit race by more than fifteen seconds. British and French riders also bettered this same mark but they didn't do so by such an emphatic margin as did the sons of Mussolini. Some 8000 fans turned out for the opening night's program, which, according to the writer's opinion, was almost totally lacking in thrills. However, they say that the excitement doesn't begin until all the lesser lights are weeded out so here's hoping they show something tomorrow and Wednesday nights.

**CONTINUE TODAY**

Tomorrow night's program will see the quarter-finals and reclassifications in both the 1000-meter scratch and 4000 pursuit races as well as the trials and reclassification of the 2000-meter tandem scramble.

**The evening started off with the heats of the 1000-meter scratch race being run off. There is probably nothing more boring than heats of a 1000-meter scratch race, but evidently they are a part of the Olympics and must be suffered through just like measles, smallpox, mumps and various other children's diseases.**

It seems that during the first 800 meters of these scratch races the contenders try to see how slow they can go; it's no end of good clean fun watching three boys on bicycles dilly-dally along, jockeying for the pole position as they hit the 200-meter mark, where the sprint begins. They only take the time of the last 200-meter sprint. In these

(Continued on Page 12, Column 5)

### *Attendance Record Also Endangered*

Although official figures have not yet been announced, estimates by officials indicate that the attendance for the first two days of track and field at the present Olympic Games has approximately equaled the total attendance for the entire program for the Games at Amsterdam in 1928. Olympic officials estimate 120,000 people saw the programs Sunday and yesterday. The official total at Amsterdam for the entire schedule of track and field was slightly in excess of 130,000.

## METCALFE CLOSE SECOND AS JONATH TAKES THIRD

### *Simpson Captures Fourth Place; Most Observers Say Marquette Flash Struck Tape First*

BY BRAVEN DYER

An ebony streak with horn-rimmed spectacles pinned back to his ears by adhesive tape yesterday brought back to the United States the sprinting championship of the world. Twelve long years since Charles W. Paddock last won an Olympic Games 100-meter dash for Uncle Sam but in the brief space of 10.3 seconds yesterday afternoon Eddie Tolan of Detroit recaptured the laurels which other American sprinters were unable to gain at Paris and Amterdam. It was the first running triumph ever scored by a Negro athlete during modern Olympic competition.

Where all our white hopes failed in the past, Tolan delivered. And backing him up to make Uncle Sam's victory the more conclusive was Ralph Metcalfe, another nimble-footed Negro from the Midwest. There was no question as to the superiority of these two black boys who make the ace of spades look like the queen of hearts by comparison.

**ARGUMENT OVER FIRST**

**But there was a wide difference of opinion among scribes and laymen when it came to deciding which of the two colored flyers had hit the tape first. The finish was one of those dead-heat affairs which produce never-ending arguments.**

Tolan, earlier in the afternoon, won the first semifinal heat, or so it was announced, when most of us in the press box figured Yoshioka of Japan had led the former University of Michigan ace to the ribbon. The time was 10.7s.

Metcalfe's powerful, space-eating strides carried him to victory in the second heat, the muscular Marquette man coming with his usual last-minute rush at the finish to lead his team-mate, George Simpson, and Arthur Jonath of Germany across the line. Ralph's time was 10.6s.

**METCALFE FAVORED**

**So the final lacked the international rivalry which would have flared up had Jonath won one of the heats. It was Tolan vs. Metcalfe in a rematch following their spectacular duels during the American trials, when diminutive Eddie trailed his more muscular team mate to the tape in both the 100 and 200 meters.**

And there weren't many in the vast crowd of 50,000 fans who believed that sawed-off Eddie could turn the trick.

The six finalists were Tolan, Metcalfe, Jonath, Yoshioka, Simpson

(Continued on Page 10, Column 1)

## STELLA GETS BIG SURPRISE

### *Miss Walsh Couldn't Believe Record Shattered*

### *Says She Was Running With Not Much Effort*

### *Heavy Schedule Today for Polish Sensation*

BY MURIEL BABCOCK

There wasn't anybody in the whole Olympic Stadium yesterday afternoon who was any more surprised than the big piece of Polack muscle and beef that is Stella Kalsh—greatest woman runner—when she learned that she had broken a world's record in the first heat.

**"I thought I had done about 12 at the most," she told me, a broad grin illuminating a face smeared heavily with cold cream, as she emerged from her shower at Chapman Park Hotel yesterday.**

"I didn't think I was working hard at all. I wasn't gritting my teeth and working at all. I was just taking it easy. It was one of the easiest races I ever ran.

**TWO WAYS**

"You know there are two ways of running. That's for me, anyway. One is when I grit my teeth and pull hard. The other is when I relax. My trainer has been after me to relax more and take it easy and that's what I did yesterday. It certainly helps."

Does she think if she works a little harder in the finals she can run around a man's time?

**"Oh, of course not," she said firmly, flustered at the idea, but**

(Continued on Page 12, Column 8)

### NEW OLYMPIC CHAMPIONS

**TRACK AND FIELD**

**Hammer throw—Dr. Patrick O'Callaghan (Ireland,) 176ft. 11½in. (Retained championship.)**

**100-meter dash—Eddie Tolan (United States,) 10.3s. (New Olympic record.)**

**400-meter hurdles—Robert Tisdall (Ireland,) 51.8s. (Record not allowed because last hurdle knocked down.)**

**FENCING**

**Team foils—France, Italy and the United States finished in triple tie.**

OLYMPIC GAMES SECTION
Los Angeles Times
EQUAL RIGHTS
LIBERTY UNDER THE LAW — TRUE INDUSTRIAL FREEDOM
VOL. LI. C — WEDNESDAY MORNING, AUGUST 3, 1932.

# DISASTERS MAR HOT PENTATHLON

UNITED STATES

Stars and Stripes goes on top today with two first places. Poland and Great Britain each won a first place.

## FIRST PLACE WINNERS

Number of first places won yesterday:

| | | |
|---|---|---|
| United States | 2 | (Track and field) |
| Poland | 1 | (Track and field) |
| Great Britain | 1 | (Track and field) |

Total number of first places won to date (all sports):

| | | | |
|---|---|---|---|
| United States | 5 | France | 4 |
| Poland | 2 | Ireland | 2 |
| Great Britain | 1 | Canada | 1 |
| Germany | 1 | Czecho-Slovakia | 1 |

## AMERICA LEADS, IRELAND SECOND, CANADA THIRD

### *Sensations Continue as World and Olympic Records Fall Fast and Furious*

## BOX SCORE OF OLYMPICS

The box score shows the number of places and points scored yesterday, with total number of points scored by Olympic athletes:

**TRACK AND FIELD—MEN**

(Points scored 10-5-4-3-2-1 for six places)

| | 1st | 2nd | 3rd | 4th | 5th | 6th | Prev. pts. scored | Grand ttl. to date |
|---|---|---|---|---|---|---|---|---|
| United States | 1 | 1 | 0 | 1 | 2 | 1 | 58 | 81 |
| Ireland | 0 | 0 | 0 | 0 | 0 | 0 | 20 | 20 |
| Canada | 0 | 1 | 1 | 0 | 0 | 0 | 10 | 19 |
| Finland | 0 | 0 | 0 | 0 | 0 | 0 | 16 | 16 |
| Great Britain | 1 | 0 | 0 | 0 | 0 | 0 | 3 | 13 |
| Poland | 0 | 0 | 0 | 0 | 0 | 0 | 10 | 10 |
| Germany | 0 | 0 | 0 | 0 | 0 | 0 | 10 | 10 |
| Sweden | 0 | 0 | 0 | 1 | 0 | 0 | 5 | 8 |
| Philippines | 0 | 0 | 0 | 0 | 0 | 0 | 4 | 4 |
| Czecho-Slovakia | 0 | 0 | 0 | 0 | 0 | 0 | 4 | 4 |
| New Zealand | 0 | 0 | 0 | 0 | 0 | 0 | 3 | 3 |
| South Africa | 0 | 0 | 0 | 0 | 0 | 0 | 2 | 2 |
| Italy | 0 | 0 | 0 | 0 | 0 | 0 | 2 | 2 |
| Japan | 0 | 0 | 1 | 0 | 0 | 1 | 2 | 7 |
| Argentine | 0 | 0 | 0 | 0 | 0 | 0 | 1 | 1 |

**TRACK AND FIELD—WOMEN**

| | 1st | 2nd | 3rd | 4th | 5th | 6th | Prev. pts. scored | Grand ttl. to date |
|---|---|---|---|---|---|---|---|---|
| United States | 1 | 1 | 1 | 0 | 1* | 0 | 13 | 33½ |
| Germany | 0 | 0 | 0 | 0 | 2* | 0 | 9 | 15½ |
| Poland | 1 | 0 | 1 | 0 | 0 | 1 | 0. | 15 |
| Japan | 0 | 0 | 0 | 0 | 0 | 0 | 3 | 3 |
| Canada | 0 | 1 | 0 | 0 | 0 | 0 | 0 | 5 |
| Great Britain | 0 | 0 | 0 | 1 | 0 | 0 | 0 | 3 |

*—Indicates tie for fifth in 100 meters.

**FENCING**

| | 1st | 2nd | 3rd | 4th | 5th | 6th | Total Points |
|---|---|---|---|---|---|---|---|
| France | 1 | 0 | 0 | 0 | 0 | 0 | 10 |
| Italy | 0 | 1 | 0 | 0 | 0 | 0 | 5 |
| United States | 0 | 0 | 1 | 0 | 0 | 0 | 4 |
| Denmark | 0 | 0 | 0 | 1 | 0 | 0 | 3 |

BY PAUL LOWRY

Victory in the classic 800 meters, long an Olympic legacy of John Bull's, is still his cherished possession.

Tom Hampson, bespectacled son of Great Britain, came from behind to win with a smashing finish and maintain the standard of British supremacy set by the immortal G. A. Hill and Douglass Lowe in the last three Olympiads.

On the road to his spectacular triumph Hampson set a new world's record of 1m. 49.8s. to beat back two cousins—Alex Wilson and Phil Edwards of Canada.

Olympic records being a drug on the market, the athletes set three new world standards yesterday and equaled still another.

Two American flags went up on the victory pole as against one by Poland and another by Great Britain.

By nations this is what happened:

UNITED STATES

Ruth Osburn, a corn-fed girl from Missouri, set the first world's record of the day when she tossed the discus 131ft. 8in. This beat the old mark made by Halinaa Konopacka of Poland at Amsterdam in 1928 by approximately two feet. But Miss Osburn's glory was short-lived. Lilian Copleland of the University of Southern California flicked the platter out to the 133ft. 2in. mark, and this was the winning throw. The two American girls with their first and second places added 15 points to the women's total, which is now 33½ as against Germany's 15½ and Poland's 15. Miss von Bremen scored 4 in the 100 meters and Miss Wilde 1½.

**George Saling, long - legged collegian from Iowa, was the winner of one of the semifinal**

(Continued on Page 10, Column 4)

## TOWERING SWEDE WINS FIRST WRESTLING CROWN

BY HARRY A. WILLIAMS

John Ritchthoff, a towering titian-skinned Nordic, was last night crowned the first Olympic wrestling champion of the present tournament, when he successfully defended his 1928 championship against N. Hirschl, a bulky Austrian, the only grappler of that country entered.

Richthoff won by the decision route as he did the night before from Jack Riley. He snagged the title at Amsterdam four years ago, but was forced to renew it.

HEADS STUDY CLUB

Richthoff wrestled under the colors of Sweden, his home being in Limhamn in the southern part of that country. He is a cement worker and originally built up his magnificent physique shouldering this weighty material. During the past ten years he has been president of the Men's Study Club of Limhamn, and also chairman of the Swedish Chess Club of that city. Whenever traveling his first act in reaching a city is to look up the museums. He is also a good singer, but not a soprano.

**Richthoff weighs 235 pounds, and once held the wrestling championship of Europe in both free style and Greco-Roman, and for ten years has been the champion of Sweden in both styles.**

Richthoff did not prove aggressive in his two matches here, but explained this by the fact that he had to meet only two men and the 1 point charged against him in each decision victory could not cause his overthrow, while if he had taken chances there would have been the danger of sustaining falls himself, which would have eliminated him.

Melvin Clodfelter, only hope of

(Continued on Page 12, Column 2)

Spectacular Fall Fails to Hurt Either Rider or Horse

Lieut. Petnehazy of Hungary on Aeronauta made one of the most sensational spills of the opening day of the Pentathlon. This remarkable photograph was made by Tommy Burns of the Associated Press at the last jump of the Fox Hills course. Neither horse nor rider was seriously hurt. (Photo copyrighted)

## RIDERS, HORSES HURT IN SPILLS

*Bo Lindman of Sweden Held Winner of Event*

*Mexican Contestant Badly Injured by Fall*

*Swedish Champion Well Up at Finish of Ride*

BY FRANK ROCHE

The pentathlon opened with a day of thrills and disasters.

**Baron de Freitas Branco de Heredia's horse "Dan Anthony" ran away with him and all but killed himself and his rider. Baron de Haredia is from Portugal.**

**Anguiano De la Fuente of Mexico spilled with "Brown Arrow" with the result that the rider had to be removed to Inglewood Hospital with serious injuries. The horse may be saved.**

**Lieut. Petnehazy of Hungary took a header with Aeronauta at the last hurdle. It looked like sure death for both. By some miracle they managed to get up and finish.**

**Lieut. S. A. Thofelt of Sweden took three falls with "Noria," any one of which looked as though both rider and horse would be killed. Horse and rider managed to survive and finish. Thofelt, winner of the 1928 pentathlon, came to the finish line covered with mud and dirt from head to feet.**

Those were only some of the high lights of a morning which bristled with hectic action.

Lieut. Bo Lindman of Sweden won first place; Lieut. Mayo, United States, second.

The other riders finished in the following order: Vernon Barlow, Great Britain; Count Oxenstierna, Sweden; Charles Legard, Great Britain; Ivan Duranthon, France; Simonetti, Italy; Eugenio Pagnini, Italy; Conrad Miersch, Germany; Tibor Benko, Hungary; Willi Remer, Germany; Clayton Mansfield, United States; Frencesco Pacini, Italy; Sven Thofelt, Sweden; Imre Petnehazy, Hungary; Morales Mendoza, Mexico; Helmuth Naude; Willem Van Rhijn, Holland; Elmer Somfai, Hungary; Rafael De Sousa, Portu; gal Sebastiao De Heredia, Portugal; Ortega Casanova, Mexico; Augiano De La Fuente, Mexico; Jeffrey McDougal, Great Britain. The last three men were disqualified for getting off course.

Winner's time, 8m. 7 3-5s. First nine had no faults called against them.

The pentathlon started at Fox Hills at 8 a.m. in the presence of about 5000 spectators.

The finish was in the hills at Manchester near Inglewood Boulevard.

TWENTY-FIVE IN SADDLES

Twenty-five officers from various cavalry regiments of Europe and America took part.

The course was 4888 meters (about three and a half miles.) There were sixteen obstacles that had to be jumped.

**The horses were supplied by the United States Cavalry. Under the rules, none of the contestants had ever ridden over the course. The route was a secret; the rider found his way by following flags.**

No rider had ever seen the horse he was to ride until he mounted.

Hardly had the event gotten under way before Dan Anthony, one of America's crack cavalry mounts reared up and hrew Baron de Heredia high and dry. Dan Anthony ran five miles before he was captured.

RUNS AWAY AGAIN

They came back and went through the start after Lieut. Brady of the United States had gotten

(Continued on Page 13, Column 1)

## TOM HAMPSON OF GREAT BRITAIN SETS NEW 800-METER RECORD

### *English Pedagogue Runs Race in 1m. 49.8s. and Beats Wilson of Canada by One Yard; Negro Wins Broad Jump for United States*

BY BRAVEN DYER

Thomas Hampson, the powerful, bespectacled professor from St. Albans in Hertfordshire, England, yesterday sent the Union Jack to the top of the victory flag pole for the first time in the 1932 Olympic Games.

He won the greatest 800-meter race in history and beat a field of the finest half-milers that ever faced a starter's gun. It was the scholarly gentleman's final Olympic Games. He will never run again after he goes home to a hero's welcome.

Running with all the ease and confidence that has characterized Great Britain's famous middle-distance aces for the last twenty years, the picturesque pedagogue blazed his way to a new world's record of 1m. 49.8s. This time was so sensational that had it not been for the orgy of record breaking going

(Continued on Page 10, Column 1)

## BLONDE VALKYRIE OF FOILS SWEEPS ALL BEFORE HER

BY EDITH DURBIN

Helene Mayer, the beautiful blonde Valkyrie of the swords, swept evertyhing before her at the fencing bouts yesterday.

She is the woman champion of the world in foil fencing, championship winner of the 1928 Olympics and champion of Germany.

**Now she goes to the semifinals in this Olympic.**

Four men and Miss Mayer defeated their eight opponents.

From each of the four pools for men six fencers will enter the semifinals with these champions. Bougnal, France; Palacios, Argentina; Bloch, Denmark; Every, United States; Cattiau, France; Mund, Belgium; Levis, United States; Graffenried, Switzerland; Gardère, France; Larraz, Argentina; DeBour-

(Continued on Page 14, Column 1)

## NEW OLYMPIC CHAMPIONS

**TRACK AND FIELD**

**Men**

800 meters—Tom Hampson, Great Britain, 1m. 40.8s. (New world's record.)

Broad jump—Ed Gordon, United States, 25ft. ¾in.

**Women**

100 meters—Stella Walsh, Poland, 11.9s. (New world's record.)

Discus throw—Lillian Copeland, United States, 133ft. 2in. (New world's record.)

**WRESTLING**

Heavyweight—J. C. Richthoff, Sweden, retained championship.

## *WORLD'S CHAMPION FOR HALF-HOUR, EXPERIENCE OF TALL MISSOURI GAL*

BY RALPH HUSTON

For a half-hour yesterday a big, gawky country girl from Shelbyville, Mo., was champion of the world.

Four months after she had first picked up a discus, to see how heavy it was, she had broken the world's record in the Olympic competition for the world's championship. A half-hour later one of her own team-mates had beaten her best throw and she had to be content with second place.

**Ruth Osburn, 18 years of age, almost 6 feet tall and weighing about 150 pounds, decided to be a discus thrower four months ago. The football coach at Shelbyville (Mo.) High School had encouraged her. Less than three weeks ago she won the American final tryouts with a record-breaking toss of 133ft. 3-4in.**

Yesterday in the Olympic Stadium she sent her first throw 131ft. 8in., approximately two feet past the flag indicating the world's rec-

(Continued on Page 12, Column 1)

## *Today's Events*

At Olympic Stadium:

2:30 p.m. — Semifinals, 200 meters, men.

2:30 p.m.—FINALS, pole vault, men.

2:30 p.m. — FINALS, discus throw, men.

3 p.m.—80-meter hurdles, women (trials.)

3:45 p.m.—FINALS, 110-meter hurdles, men.

5 p.m.—FINALS, 200 meters, men.

5:15 p.m.—1500 meters, men (trials.)

1:30 p.m.—50,000 meter walk, men, starts at clubhouse on Riverside Drive near Griffith Park.

6:30 p.m.—50,000 meter walk, finish, same place.

**PENTATHLON**

8 a.m.—Fencing, Armory Olympic Park.

1 p.m.—Fencing, Armory, Olympic Park.

**WRESTLING**

11 a.m.—Free style, Olympic Auditorium, 1801 South Grand avenue.

7:30 p.m.—FINALS, free style, Olympic Auditorium, 1801 South Grand avenue.

**TRACK CYCLING**

7:30 p.m.—FINALS, Rose Bowl, Pasadena.

OLYMPIC GAMES SECTION

Los Angeles Times

EQUAL RIGHTS

LIBERTY UNDER THE LAW — TRUE INDUSTRIAL FREEDOM

VOL. LI. C — THURSDAY MORNING, AUGUST 4, 1932.

# TOLAN FLASHES TO NEW RECORD

UNITED STATES

Again the Stars and Stripes goes on top today with four first places. Great Britain, Italy and Sweden each won a first place.

## FIRST-PLACE WINNERS

Number of first places won yesterday:

| | | |
|---|---|---|
| United States | 4 | (Track and field) |
| United States | 3 | (Wrestling) |
| Sweden | 2 | (Wrestling) |
| France | 1 | (Wrestling) |
| Finland | 1 | (Wrestling) |
| Great Britain | 1 | (Track and field) |
| Italy | 1 | (Cycling) |
| France | 1 | (Cycling) |
| Australia | 1 | (Cycling) |
| Holland | 1 | (Cycling) |

Total number of first places won to date (all sports):

| | | | |
|---|---|---|---|
| United States | 12 | France | 6 |
| Ireland | 2 | Poland | 2 |
| Great Britain | 2 | Sweden | 2 |
| Italy | 1 | Germany | 1 |
| Canada | 1 | Czecho-Slovakia | 1 |
| Finland | 1 | Australia | 1 |
| Holland | 1 | | |

## AMERICA RUNS RAMPANT, CHALKS UP FOUR FIRSTS

### *Scores 70 Points for Total of 151; Great Britain Second With 28; Ireland Third*

### BOX SCORE OF OLYMPICS

The box score shows the number of places and points scored yesterday with total number of points scored by Olympic athletes.

**TRACK AND FIELD—MEN**

(Points scored 10-5-4-3-2-1 for six places)

| | 1st | 2nd | 3rd | 4th | 5th | 6th | Previous points | Grand total |
|---|---|---|---|---|---|---|---|---|
| United States | 4 | 3 | 3 | 1 | 0 | 0 | 81 | 151 |
| Great Britain | 1 | 0 | 0 | 1 | 1 | 0 | 13 | 28 |
| Ireland | 0 | 0 | 0 | 0 | 0 | 0 | 20 | 20 |
| Canada | 0 | 0 | 0 | 0 | 0 | 0 | 19 | 19 |
| Germany | 0 | 0 | 0 | 2 | 0 | 1 | 10 | 17 |
| Finland | 0 | 0 | 0 | 0 | 0 | 0 | 16 | 16 |
| Japan | 0 | 1 | 0 | 0 | 1 | 0 | 7 | 14 |
| Poland | 0 | 0 | 0 | 0 | 0 | 0 | 10 | 10 |
| Sweden | 0 | 0 | 0 | 0 | 0 | 0 | 8 | 8 |
| Italy | 0 | 0 | 1 | 0 | 1 | 0 | 2 | 8 |
| France | 0 | 0 | 1 | 1 | 0 | 0 | 0 | 7 |
| Latvia | 0 | 1 | 0 | 0 | 0 | 0 | 0 | 5 |
| Philippines | 0 | 0 | 0 | 0 | 0 | 0 | 4 | 4 |
| Czecho-Slovakia | 0 | 0 | 0 | 0 | 0 | 0 | 4 | 4 |
| Hungary | 0 | 0 | 0 | 0 | 1 | 1 | 0 | 3 |
| New Zealand | 0 | 0 | 0 | 0 | 0 | 0 | 3 | 3 |
| South Africa | 0 | 0 | 0 | 0 | 0 | 1 | 2 | 3 |
| Argentina | 0 | 0 | 0 | 0 | 1 | 0 | 1 | 3 |
| Brazil | 0 | 0 | 0 | 0 | 0 | 1 | 0 | 1 |

**TRACK AND FIELD—WOMEN**

No changes because no finals.

| | | | |
|---|---|---|---|
| United States | 33½ | Canada | 5 |
| Germany | 15½ | Japan | 3 |
| Poland | 15 | Great Britain | 3 |

**CYCLING**

| | 1st | 2nd | 3rd | 4th | 5th | 6th | Total Points |
|---|---|---|---|---|---|---|---|
| France | 1 | 2 | 1 | 0 | 0 | 0 | 24 |
| Holland | 1 | 1 | 0 | 1 | 0 | 0 | 18 |
| Italy | 1 | 0 | 1 | 1* | 0 | 0 | 17 |
| Great Britain | 0 | 1 | 1 | 1* | 0 | 0 | 12 |
| Australia | 1 | 0 | 0 | 0 | 0 | 0 | 10 |
| Canada | 0 | 0 | 0 | 1 | 0 | 1 | 4 |
| Denmark | 0 | 0 | 1 | 0 | 0 | 0 | 4 |
| United States | 0 | 0 | 0 | 0 | 1 | 0 | 2 |

*Tie for fourth.

**WRESTLING (Free Style)**

| | 1st | 2nd | 3rd | 4th | Total Points |
|---|---|---|---|---|---|
| United States | 3 | 2 | 0 | 1 | 43 |
| Sweden | 2 | 1 | 2 | 0 | 33 |
| Finland | 1 | 1 | 2 | 0 | 23 |
| Hungary | 0 | 2 | 1 | 0 | 14 |
| France | 1 | 0 | 0 | 0 | 10 |
| Austria | 0 | 0 | 2 | 0 | 8 |
| Canada | 0 | 1 | 0 | 0 | 5 |

BY PAUL LOWRY

America's biggest day in all Olympic history.

This epitomizes the brilliant showing of the athletes wearing the Stars and Stripes on the fourth day of the track and field championships.

First, second and third in the 200 meters.

First, second and third in the 110-meter hurdles.

First, third and fourth in the pole vault.

First and second in the discus throw.

Four new Olympic records, including a new world standard in the eighty-meter hurdles for women. Yes—and for Mildred (Babe)

(Continued on Page 15, Column 1)

## EVENTS TODAY

**TRACK, FIELD AND GAMES**
Olympic Stadium

10 a.m.—Field hockey, Japan vs. India.
2:30 p.m.—400 meters, men, first trials.
2:30 p.m.—FINALS, javelin throw, men.
2:30 p.m.—FINALS, hop, step and jump, men.
3:45 p.m.—FINALS, 1500 meters, men.
4 p.m.—400 meters, men, second trials.
4:30 p.m.—FINALS, 80-meter hurdles, women.

**WRESTLING**
Olympic Auditorium

11 a.m.—Greco-Roman.
7:30 p.m.—Greco-Roman.

**FENCING**
Armory, Olympic Park

1 p.m.—Foils, women's finals. Men's semifinals.

**CYCLING, ROAD RACE**

8 a.m.—Starts Moorpark via. Oxnard. Finish at Castellammare, north of Santa Monica.

**PENTATHLON**
Elysian Park

9 a.m.—Shooting.

[Wide World photo]

Bill Miller Going in Search of a Couple of Clouds

The doughty American pole vaulter who won first yesterday is shown here during competition, which resulted in his triumph at 14ft. 1⅞in.

## ROGERS WANTS TO LET JUDGES IN ON SECRET

### *Will Says Tell 'Em Who Won So They Won't Have to Go to Movies to Find Out*

BY WILL ROGERS

BEVERLY HILLS, Aug. 3.—Arise and face the victory flag. Ceremonie old—antique, proto—colair.

I have been a patron of these games now all summer, and there is something that I think should be rectified. They are run fine, marvelous attendance, keen appreciation, splendid performances, but there is just one little hitch, I think that the judges should be notified in some way who wins the various events, so they will know it on the day it happens. As things are now they have to go to the movies at night and see the pictures to see who won. now I think that they should know who these winners are as soon as the audience does.

In fact, I don't think it should be kept a secret by the audience from the judges, the judges are evidently nice fellows and come a long way and shouldn't be kept in the dark as long as they are on every event.

**ALL IN THE DARK**

**What I think the trouble is there is so many of 'em out there, that part of 'em do see enough of each race or event to get an idea who won, but the rest of 'em can't see because the first couple of hundred are in their way, well by the time the ones in the front rows can relay the information to the other thousands**

(Continued on Page 18, Column 1)

## GREEN ANNEXES LENGTHY WALK

### *Pink-Cheeked Briton Wins 50,000-Meter Event*

BY IRVING ECKHOFF

Pink-cheeked son of old England, Thomas William Green had too much grit and energy for the rest of the field in the gruelling 50,000-meter walk held yesterday afternoon over the paved roads of Griffith Park.

Green won the long grind in 4h.

(Continued on Page 17, Column 5)

## UNITED STATES MATMEN CARRY OFF THREE TITLES

OLYMPIC WRESTLING CHAMPIONS 1932

Bantamweight, R. Pearce, United States.

Featherweight, H. Pihlajamaki, Finland.

Lightweight, C. Pacome, France.

Welterweight, J. Van Bebber, United States.

Middleweight, Ivar Johansson, Sweden.

Light-heavyweight, P. Mehringer, United States.

Heavyweight, J. Richjthoff, Sweden.

BY HARRY A. WILLIAMS

These United States may not be known especially as a "rasslin" country, but three of its athletes specialized in that sport sufficiently to bring home three titles in the finals of the Olympiad free-style wrestling tournament at Olympic Auditorium last night and thereby give this country the Olympic team title in this respect.

These winners were Bob Pearce, bantamweight, Stillwater, Okla.; Jack Van Bebber, lightweight, Los Angeles, and Pete Mehringer, light-heavyweight, sophomore and Big Six conference all-star tackle at the University of Kansas. Pearce and Van Bebber are graduates of the A. & M. University at Stillwater, Okla., and both coached by Ed Gallagher. Pearce plans a teacher's career, and Van Bebber is employed by a local chain grocery store.

H. Pihlajamaki, the new featherweight champion, lives at Vassa and is a policeman. Pacome, the freshly fledged lightweight champion, recently graduated from the University of Lille, and will take up the practice of law.

Sweden, a nation much given to fishing, yesterday was the early seagull that grabbed the grunion, winning the only daylight wrestling championship of the Tenth Olympiad. Ivar Johansson reached the goal of his ambitions, the middleweight title, several hours ahead of time by throwing Bob Hess, of Iowa State College, in the short time of 2m. 10s., thereby becoming the daylight limited of the tournament.

Mr. Johansson, if he won at all, was not supposed to have done so until last night.

This match, the second of the morning session, was listed as a semifinal, but on checking up it was found that by tossing young Mr. Hess violently on his ear he had won the championship on the spot. This gave Sweden the first pair of titles, Johan Richthoff, hav-

(Continued on Page 14, Column 8)

## NEW OLYMPIC CHAMPIONS

**TRACK AND FIELD**

200-meter dash—Eddie Tolan, U.S., 21.2s. (New Olympic record.)

Pole vault—Bill Miller, U.S., 14ft. 1⅞in. (New Olympic record.)

Discus throw—John Anderson, U.S., 162ft. 4⅞in. (New Olympic record.)

110-meter hurdles—George Saling, U.S., 14.6s. (Equals Olympic record.)

50,000-meter walk—Thomas William Green, G.B., 4h. 50m. 10s.

**WRESTLING**

Middleweight—Ivar Johansson, Sweden.

## BABE BREAKS RECORDS EASIER THAN DISHES

BY GRANTLAND RICE

[Copyright, 1932, by the North American Newspaper Alliance, Inc.]

World's records to Mildred Babe Tex Didrikson, the Texas thunderbolt, are merely playthings in a toy shop. She takes them in her stride, whether it calls for a brawny arm or a pair of flying feet or the co-ordination of a lean, lithe body.

The Babe never fails or flutters. In the first Olympic javelin throw she ever made a few days ago the bounding Babe set a new world's record.

In the first Olympic eighty-meter hurdle she had ever run, the same Dallas entry set another world's record, reducing the old mark from 12.2s. to 11.8s.

This was only the first trial heat where the Babe was under no pressure, winning out alone.

**This is the first time in**

(Continued on Page 17, Column 4)

## SIMPSON AND METCALFE DECISIVELY DEFEATED

### *Negro Whizzes Over 200-Meter Route in 21.2s. for Mark; American Wins Vault*

BY BRAVEN DYER

Eddie Tolan, Detroit Negro, is the new "world's fastest human." He proved it yesterday afternoon to the satisfaction of more than 75,000 spectators. Running through the twilight shadows of a perfect August afternoon, the stubby colored boy decisively defeated his team-mates, George Simpson and Ralph Metcalfe, in the fastest 200-meter race ever run in the Olympic Games.

On Monday Tolan won the 100 meters from Metcalfe. Most of the assembled spectators thought sawed-off Eddie got the best of this decision. The race was closer than the skin on a wrinkled prune.

**But yesterday Tolan's superiority was unquestioned. He had a margin of four feet and the result stunned the huge crowd which had been led to believe that Metcalfe was unbeatable over this distance.**

**RECORD SMASHED**

Tolan's time was 21.2s. This smashed the Olympic record of 21.6s., which has stood since 1904. For almost thirty years the best sprinters in the world have been shooting at this mark. Until yesterday they did not even come close.

The race was really decided as soon as Starter Franz Miller of Germany fired his gun. Sounds funny, doesn't it? But Tolan got by far the best start of the six finalists. He was on the pole with the rest ahead of him in staggered lanes. Unconsciously he must have felt that the others had an advantage. Actually they did not for the official surveyors have this staggered-lane business all figured out to decimals.

**THERE THEY GO**

**At any rate Eddie was rolling when Miller's gun banged. This slight advantage sent him away flying while the others were just beginning to dig up the track with their finely-tuned legs. Around the curve they blazed. Tolan was in lane one, Metcalfe next to him and then Simpson. Arthur Jonath of Germany, chief foreign threat, ran clear on the outside.**

Seventy-five thousand pairs of eyes centered on the chunky Detroit Negro and the white-skinned Teuton. They swept up the straightaway, 100 yards to the tape.

Simpson and Metcalfe began to creep up slowly on Tolan. Jonath must have felt his advantage slipping. He dug in furiously, arms flying a la Charley Paddock. But the steady strides of Simpson and Metcalfe carried them smoothly onward.

**TOLAN STUMBLES**

**Twenty yards from the finish Tolan actually began to widen the margin between himself and Simpson. Three yards to go. Tolan stumbled slightly, righted himself and carried on courageously. Simpson and Metcalfe smashed the tape almost shoulder to shoulder. But they were more than a yard behind Eddie, who is as elusive as an eel over these short sprint routes.**

By his victory Tolan becomes the

(Continued on Page 12, Column 1)

## KNEE SPRAINED, SECOND IN RACE

### *Game Monrovia Girl on Tail of Famed "Babe"*

### *And She Lost Only by a Hair's Breadth*

### *Might Have Won—Well, She Doesn't Mind*

BY MURIEL BABCOCK

The tall, thin girl who finished second to the mighty "Babe" Didrikson in the hurdles yesterday, ran with a bandaged left knee which she literally had to drag over the white fences.

"Babe" tied the world and Olympic record of 11.8s.

The girl with the bandaged knee—Simone Shaller of Monrovia—in her first six months of big competitive running, was probably a tenth of a second slower.

**MISSED HER SUGAR**

"If I'd had my lump of sugar before I started maybe I could have done better," she said with a twinkle in her black eyes after the race. "Nope, I'm not a bit tired, my knee doesn't hurt and I can run again tomorrow.

**"Lump of sugar? Oh, I just like to chew one about an hour before a race. It gives me energy, I think. But I forgot it today in the excitement. I was awfully excited about 1 o'clock. But I forgot it when I got out on the track—I didn't mind the crowd a bit like I thought I would."**

The bandaged knee? Simone banged it against a hurdle in practice two weeks ago. For a time it looked as if she were out of the Olympics for good. But last Thursday, less than a week ago, she went gingerly on the field again. The knee worked. It worked again yesterday.

It is so tightly tied that she cannot bend it more than half its usual distance. It is so tightly tied that instead of being its usual limber self, and giving her added momentum as she takes the hurdle, it drags.

There is nothing really the matter with the knee, she tells you. It just isn't up to snuff. (Tough, isn't it, when a knee won't work properly and will let you run only second place to a girl like "Babe" Didrikson?)

With black curly hair, a narrow

(Continued on Page 14, Column 7)

## *Off on Another Record-Smashing Tour*

[A. P. photo]

"Babe" Didrikson Lowers Olympic Mark in 80-Meter Hurdles

That "iron girl" from Dallas came through again at the Olympic Stadium yesterday with a victory. Not satisfied with winning the javelin throw in the Games, the Texas miss negotiated the hurdles in 11.8s., thereby bettering the 80-meter time of 12.2s. Simone Schaller of Pasadena was second in the event, while Marjorie Clark of South Africa finished third. Betty Taylor of Canada took fourth place. The above photo shows "Babe" going over the hurdles ahead of the field. Michi Nakanishi appears about to crash the "gate."

OLYMPIC GAMES SECTION

Los Angeles Times

EQUAL RIGHTS

LIBERTY UNDER THE LAW — TRUE INDUSTRIAL FREEDOM

VOL. LI. C — FRIDAY MORNING, AUGUST 5, 1932.

# MAYO LEADS PENTATHLON

## *Mark in 1500-Meter Race Smashed*

ITALY

Italy's flag goes on top today with three first places. Finland, Japan, Austria and the United States each won a first place.

### FIRST-PLACE WINNERS

Number of first places won yesterday:

| | | | |
|---|---|---|---|
| Italy | 3 | Japan | 1 |
| United States | 1 | Austria | 1 |
| Finland | 1 | | |

Total number of first places won to date (all sports:)

| | | | |
|---|---|---|---|
| United States | 13 | France | 6 |
| Italy | 4 | Ireland | 2 |
| Poland | 2 | Great Britain | 2 |
| Sweden | 2 | Finland | 2 |
| Japan | 2 | Austria | 1 |
| Germany | 1 | Canada | 1 |
| Czecho-Slovakia | 1 | Australia | 1 |
| Holland | 1 | | |

## ITALY AND FINLAND SHINE AS RECORDS FALL AGAIN

### *America Has Poorest Day, but Still Far in Lead; England Drops to Third Place*

### BOX SCORE OF OLYMPICS

The box score shows the number of places and points scored yesterday with total number of points scored by Olympic athletes.

TRACK AND FIELD—MEN

(Points scored 10-5-4-3-2-1 for six places)

| | 1st | 2nd | 3rd | 4th | 5th | 6th | Previous points | Grand total |
|---|---|---|---|---|---|---|---|---|
| United States | 0 | 0 | 0 | 1 | 1 | 3 | 150 | 158 |
| Finland | 1 | 1 | 1 | 0 | 0 | 0 | 16 | 35 |
| Great Britain | 0 | 1 | 0 | 0 | 0 | 0 | 29 | 34 |
| Japan | 1 | 0 | 1 | 0 | 0 | 0 | 14 | 28 |
| Ireland | 0 | 0 | 0 | 1 | 0 | 0 | 20 | 23 |
| Canada | 0 | 0 | 1 | 0 | 0 | 0 | 19 | 23 |
| Germany | 0 | 0 | 0 | 1 | 0 | 0 | 17 | 20 |
| Italy | 1 | 0 | 0 | 0 | 0 | 0 | 8 | 18 |
| Sweden | 0 | 1 | 0 | 0 | 1 | 0 | 8 | 15 |
| Poland | 0 | 0 | 0 | 0 | 0 | 0 | 10 | 10 |
| France | 0 | 0 | 0 | 0 | 0 | 0 | 7 | 7 |
| Latvia | 0 | 1 | 0 | 0 | 0 | 0 | 0 | 5 |
| Philippines | 0 | 0 | 0 | 0 | 0 | 0 | 4 | 4 |
| Czecho-Slovakia | 0 | 0 | 0 | 0 | 0 | 0 | 4 | 4 |
| Hungary | 0 | 0 | 0 | 0 | 0 | 0 | 3 | 3 |
| New Zealand | 0 | 0 | 0 | 0 | 0 | 0 | 3 | 3 |
| South Africa | 0 | 0 | 0 | 0 | 0 | 0 | 3 | 3 |
| Argentina | 0 | 0 | 0 | 0 | 0 | 0 | 3 | 3 |
| Holland | 0 | 0 | 0 | 0 | 1 | 0 | 0 | 2 |
| Brazil | 0 | 0 | 0 | 0 | 0 | 0 | 1 | 1 |

TRACK AND FIELD—WOMEN

| | 1st | 2nd | 3rd | 4th | 5th | 6th | Previous points | Grand total |
|---|---|---|---|---|---|---|---|---|
| United States | 1 | 1 | 0 | 1 | 0 | 0 | 33½ | 51½ |
| Germany | 0 | 0 | 0 | 0 | 0 | 0 | 15½ | 15½ |
| Poland | 0 | 0 | 0 | 0 | 0 | 0 | 15 | 15 |
| Canada | 0 | 0 | 0 | 0 | 0 | 1 | 5 | 6 |
| Great Britain | 0 | 0 | 0 | 0 | 1 | 0 | 3 | 5 |
| South Africa | 0 | 0 | 1 | 0 | 0 | 0 | 0 | 4 |
| Japan | 0 | 0 | 0 | 0 | 0 | 0 | 3 | 3 |

CYCLING

| | 1st | 2nd | 3rd | 4th | 5th | 5th | Previous points | Grand total |
|---|---|---|---|---|---|---|---|---|
| Italy | 2 | 1 | 0 | 1 | 0 | 0 | 17 | 45 |
| France | 0 | 0 | 0 | 0 | 1 | 0 | 24 | 26 |
| Holland | 0 | 0 | 0 | 0 | 0 | 0 | 18 | 18 |
| Great Britain | 0 | 0 | 0 | 1 | 0 | 1 | 12 | 16 |
| Denmark | 0 | 1 | 0 | 0 | 1 | 0 | 4 | 11 |
| Australia | 0 | 0 | 0 | 0 | 0 | 0 | 10 | 13 |
| Sweden | 0 | 0 | 2 | 0 | 0 | 0 | 0 | 8 |
| Canada | 0 | 0 | 0 | 0 | 0 | 0 | 4 | 4 |
| United States | 0 | 0 | 0 | 0 | 0 | 0 | 3 | 3 |

FENCING

| | 1st | 2nd | 3rd | 4th | 5th | 6th | Previous points | Grand total |
|---|---|---|---|---|---|---|---|---|
| France | 0 | 0 | 0 | 0 | 0 | 0 | 10 | 10 |
| Austria | 1 | 0 | 0 | 0 | 0 | 0 | 0 | 10 |
| Italy | 0 | 0 | 0 | 0 | 0 | 0 | 5 | 5 |
| Great Britain | 0 | 1 | 0 | 0 | 0 | 0 | 0 | 5 |
| United States | 0 | 0 | 0 | 0 | 0 | 0 | 4 | 4 |
| Hungary | 0 | 0 | 1 | 0 | 0 | 0 | 0 | 4 |
| Denmark | 0 | 0 | 0 | 0 | 0 | 0 | 3 | 3 |
| Belgium | 0 | 0 | 0 | 1 | 0 | 0 | 0 | 3 |
| Germany | 0 | 0 | 0 | 0 | 1 | 0 | 0 | 2 |
| Holland | 0 | 0 | 0 | 0 | 0 | 1 | 0 | 1 |

BY PAUL LOWRY

The light blue of Finland and the dark blue of Italy predominated on the fifth day of the track and field championships of the Tenth Olympiad.

Men in the light blue won the first three places in the javelin throw—Jarvinen, Sippala and Penttila.

A fiery, dashing young man in dark blue ran Finland's famed distance men into the ground—Luigi Beccali.

But to make it a real day for Italy, her cyclers won the 100-kilometer race in both individual and team divisions.

And in order not to startle the cash customers, who have become accustomed to it, four new Olympic marks and two world records were set

It was America's poorest day, the boys wearing the Stars and Stripes scoring only 9 points. However, there is little danger of the United States being overtaken. Her total is 158, as against Finland's 35 and Great Britain's 33.

By nations:

**ITALY**

Luigi Beccali is the new Olympic champion in the 1500 meters. He ran a heady race after letting Glenn Cunningham of the United States and Phil Edwards of Canada pile up a fifteen-yard lead in the first three laps. Beccali came with a rush in the last seventy yards, and won going away. His new Olympic time of 3m. 51.2s. betters the time made by Larva of Finl-nd at the last Olympics by two full seconds. Larva was last yesterday.

This was the first running victory Italy has ever scored in any of the modern Olympic Games, which is reason enough for Mussolini to give Beccali a distinguished service medal.

In the 100-kilometer cycling race Attilio Pavesi was first with Segato second and Olmo fourth. Thus, by running almost one-two-three, Italy also won the team championship, which is decided by the placing of the individuals.

**FINLAND**

But for Italy's splurge, Finland would have walked off with scoring honors for the day despite the Finns' disappointment in not placing men in one of their favorite distances—the 1500 meters.

Matti Jarvinen, the world's champion, had no trouble in winning the

(Continued on Page 14, Column 6)

[A. P. photos]

The Victor and the Vanquished
Ellen Preis of Austria, new fencing queen (left,) and Helene Mayer of Germany, the deposed champion.

## ITALIANS TAKE BIKE CLASSIC

### *Both Individual and Team First Places Won*

BY BOB RAY

"Viva L'Italia!"

That's about all you can say after yesterday's Olympiad cycling feature, the grueling 100-kilometer road race, which saw the blue-jerseyed sons of Italy, led by Attilio Pavesi, sweep team honors as well as first, second and fourth places in the pedal-pumping scramble for individual glory.

The winner, Pavesi, a young fellow so good looking that he might easily get a job in the movies were it not for the fact that he is tied up with a contract in Mussolini's military, churned over the pavement from Moorpark to Castellammare, just north of Santa Monica, in the record time of 2h. 28m. 5 3-5s. The youthful Italian soldier outraced his nearest rival, Guglielmo Segato, also of Italy, by 1 minute and 15 4-5 seconds.

HE GOES RIGHT ON

**Segato, however, might have won but for a spill, suffered when he took the Saticoy curve too fast. Bicycle and rider skidded almost thirty feet after striking the pavement, Segato leaving no little epidermis on the highway. But the plucky Italian refused aid from either traffic officers or the Red Cross first-aid truck, righted his cycle amid the cheers of the fans and pedaled off to a second place for Italy.**

Segato knew that he would have been disqualified had he accepted any outside aid. It would have taken nothing short of a broken

(Continued on Page 14, Column 4)

## *Sproul Hits U.S.C. Bowl Lease Plan*

Dr. Robert Gordon Sproul, president of the University of California, yesterday entered into the controversy between the University of Southern California and the University of California at Los Angeles over the former's request for a blanket ten-year lease on the Olympic Stadium.

Dr. Sproul asked the City Council, which, with the Board of Supervisors, has control of the structure, not to create a situation which may be prejudicial to the growth of the University of California.

## *BOXERS PUT INTO SHAPE FOR GAMES*

### *Much Speculation as to Outcome of Bouts, but Argentina Strong*

Argentina's wild bull in the amateur fistic ring, Santiago Alberto Lovell, admits there is one fighter who will take part in the Olympic Games competition next week of whom he is afraid. In fact, Lovell, the man ring experts tabbed as the favorite to win the heavyweight honors, comes right out and says he will not fight this lad. Lovell said he is frightened.

"Who is the feared man?" George Hussey, dean of boxing followers,

(Continued on Page 17, Column 2)

## EVENTS TODAY

Swimming Stadium, Olympic Park

9 a.m.—Pentathlon, swimming.

Olympic Stadium

10 a.m.—Decathlon, 100 meters.
11 a.m.—Decathlon, broad jump.

Olympic Stadium

2:30 p.m.—400 meters, men, semifinals.
2:30 p.m.—Decathlon, shot put.
3:15 p.m.—FINALS, 5000 meters men.
3:30 p.m.—Decathlon, high jump.
4:30 p.m.—FINALS, 400 meters, men.
5:30 p.m.—Decathlon, 400 meters, men.

Olympic Auditorium

11 a.m.—Wrestling, Greco-Roman.
7:30 p.m.—Wrestling, Greco-Roman.

Armory, Olympic Park

8 a.m. and 1 p.m.—Fencing, sword teams.

Los Angeles Harbor

12 noon, yatching.

## GIRL UNCROWNS FENCING QUEEN

### *Ellen Preis Triumphs as Helene Mayer Fails*

BY EDITH DURBIN

Flashing steel uncrowned the blond Valkyrie of the swords yesterday. Sparks flew and swords glittered. But Helene Mayer could not hold her first-place honors against the expert foilswomen she met.

Ellen Preis of Austria fought her way through a tie with Heather Guinness of Great Britain to the championship of the women's individual foil for the 1932 Olympics. As loser by one touch in the fight for first place, Miss Guinness became the second-place winner. Until the fence-off each of these girls had won eight bouts and lost one.

**Erna Bogen of Hungary, who placed second at Amsterdam, won third place in this event yesterday. And fourth-place winner was Mary Addams of Belgium, who was the first to beat Helene Mayer and set the spark of defeat which brought to the last champion only fifth place.**

MEN WINNERS

Men who, because of their places in the semifinals yesterday, will enter the finals of the individual foil competition for men are: Levis of United States, Casmir of Germany, Cattiau of France, Larraz of Argentina, Gaudini of Italy, Marzi of Italy, Guaragna of Italy, Palacios of Argentina, Bougnol of France and Lloyd of England.

These represent the five highest men from each of the two pools fenced yesterday.

SHE EATS ORANGE

**After her first bout, which she lost to Miss Addams, Helene Mayer sat very still for some time, chin on hand and elbow on knee, thinking it over. After all, what was one bout lost? She still had all the chance in the world to come through on top. So she calmly ate an orange, throwing the peel on the floor under her chair.**

Then came her bout with Erna Bogen, the Hungarian champion, who ran Helene a close race at the 1928 Games, and then -on second place. This was a very long bout, both of the girls being exhausted before it finished. On the surface each maintained absolute control and poise. But the tenseness could be felt in the atmosphere. Miss Mayer faced another defeat, 5 to 4.

MORE DISCOMFORT

**This time the German girl showed more signs of discomfort. As she came to her chair, she shrugged her shoulders, seeming to say that she had not been able to do what she wanted. There was no criticism of the decisions detectable on her face.**

She had fenced three bouts and

(Contnued on Page 22, Column 4

## ITALIAN GIVES BLOW TO FINNS

### *Beccali Speeds Over Route in 3m. 51.2s.*

### *Two Seconds Clipped Off Old Olympic Record*

### *Great Britain and Canada Second and Third*

BY BRAVEN DYER

Finland's domination of the distances is definitely ended.

Luigi Beccali, swarthy son of sunny Italy, gave the Finns their second mortal thrust of the week yesterday. Rushing up from the rear with all the fury these fiery Italians can generate when aroused, Mussolini's messenger made short work of the supposedly invincible Purje and Larva.

His coal-black hair flashing in the brilliant sunlight, Beccali reeled off the fastest 1500 meters ever recorded in the Olympic Games. He ran the distance, 120 yards less than a mile, in 3m. 51.2s. Larva set the old record, 3m. 53.2s. during the 1928 Games.

HE'S HERO NOW

By his spectacular victory, Beccali steps to the front rank of Italy's heroes. He becomes the first Italian to win a running race in the Olympics. Not only this, but only one other Latin ever won an Olympic event. This was Ugo Frigerio, king of the walkers for many years. So Beccali will go home to the greatest welcome ever accorded an Italian athlete.

**Finland's downfall was complete. No Finn finished among the first six. Larva, the defending champion, was last in the field of twelve starters. It was the first time Finland had lost this race since 1920, her first Olympic Games.**

Janusz Kusocinski, the pudgy Pole, gave the Finns their first rude shock on Sunday. He won the 10-000-meter classic from Iso-Hollo. This was the first time Finland had ever lost this race. Nurmi's countrymen swept four distance races at Amsterdam. They have now lost two of their titles, which is a terrible blow for the proud Finns.

CAME UNHERALDED

Beccali's triumph was as convincing as it was surprising. He came here unheralded and unsung. All we knew was that he had made the best time registered in Europe during the 1931 season. But it was not considered nearly good enough to beat the highly touted Finns. Larva had won in 1928 and Purje was

(Continued on Page 14, Column 1)

## AMERICAN SETS GREAT MARK IN SHOOTING TEST

### *He Scores 197 of Possible 200; Italian Second, Swede Third; Contestants Swim Today*

**AND THE SOLDIERS WAIT——**

In lonely little garrisons on the Afghan frontier . . . in gray old barracks in Berlin and Vienna . . . at the quadrangle of the Horse Guards in Whitehall . . . under the white desert sun at Fort Riley . . . in the cold gray halls of the War College . . .

Everywhere that there are soldiers the bulletins of the pentathlon are eagerly scanned.

Wednesday morning, the waiting garrisons read that a Swedish officer had been the finest rider; Thursday that another Swede led the world as a swordsman; this morning they will learn that a young lieutenant of our galloping field artillery out-shot the world's finest marksmen.

BY FRANK ROCHE

"Ready on the left; ready on the right; ready on the firing line." Bang—and an American shot forward to take the lead in the modern pentathlon. That was the picture yesterday morning at the Elysian Park rifle range where the third day's test of man in the pentathlon took place.

It was a young American field artillery officer from Fort Sill, Okla., named Richard Mayo, who stole the show from competitors of ten nations. Mayo, a lieutenant in rank, stepped forward to take the honors in the pistol shooting from some of the finest shots of the world's leading armies.

CHANCE TO WIN

**He bombarded the Swedish dynasty in the pentathlon so heavily that this morning it appears for the first time in the history of this event the Swedes will be forced to abdicate—and the United States, thanks to Lieut. Mayo, has a chance to succeed them.**

Mayo registered the highest score in the shooting. He had had twenty hits for a total of 197 points.

That victory along with his second place in the equestrian event on the opening day and a tie for fourth place in the fencing on Wednesday gives Lieut. Mayo the best score to date.

HOW THEY RANK

**Mayo now has 7½ points for three days' competition. His nearest competitor is an Italian army officer named Carlo Simonetti, who has a total of 17 points. Simonetti took third yesterday in the shooting.**

Sweden got a second place in the shooting when Count Oxenstierna, a naval officer, came through with a score of 194 for twenty shots. Oxenstierna took fourth in the

(Continued on Page 18, Column 7)

## SISTER A-JITTER AS BABE WINS

### *For First Time, Mrs. Cole Sees Athlete in Action*

### *Excited Dash Made to Hug Victor Following Race*

### *Another Blood Relative of Texan in Stands*

BY MURIEL BABCOCK

Babe Didrikson's sister, a usually placid sewing and cooking housewife head of a Santa Monica bungalow, Mrs. C. F. Cole, sat in Olympic stands yesterday and for the first time in her life had the thrill of watching the younger Didrikson girl run. More than run, break a world's record, become a two-time Olympic champion.

Mrs. Cole was all a-jitter.

When the gun cracked, she was on her feet with a yell. As the Babe vaulted neatly over the final hurdle, a bare winner, she sank into her seat exhausted.

Then, "Mamma must know this just the same as we do. She's listen-

(Continued on Page 18, Column 2)

Lieut. Richard Mayo
Here's the winner of the shooting event in the pentathlon yesterday, the victory placing him out in front in the five-day competition.

# OLYMPIC GAMES SECTION
# Los Angeles Times

LIBERTY UNDER THE LAW — EQUAL RIGHTS — TRUE INDUSTRIAL FREEDOM

VOL. LI. C SATURDAY MORNING, AUGUST 6, 1932.


# CARR BEATS EASTMAN, SETS MARK

Finland, Italy and the United States each won a championship yesterday. Three flags share equally the honor.

## FIRST-PLACE WINNERS

Number of first places won yesterday:

| | | |
|---|---|---|
| United States | 1 | (Track and field) |
| Finland | 1 | (Track and field) |
| Italy | 1 | (Fencing) |

Total number of first places won to date (all sports:)

| | | | |
|---|---|---|---|
| United States | 14 | France | 6 |
| Italy | 5 | Finland | 3 |
| Ireland | 2 | Great Britain | 2 |
| Poland | 2 | Sweden | 2 |
| Japan | 1 | :stria | 1 |
| Germany | 1 | Canada | 1 |
| Czecho-Slovakia | 1 | Australia | 1 |
| Holland | 1 | | |

Wee Willie Shows Heels to Blazin' Ben Again in Amazing Race

Here's the finish of the 400-meter duel yesterday in which Carr beat Eastman in the world record time of 46.2s.

[Times photo by Bill Snyder]

## AMERICA BOOSTS OLYMPIC LEAD, FINLAND SECOND

### *United States Total Points Now 180; Great Britain Holds Third With 34*

BY PAUL LOWRY

Olympic boxing starts next Tuesday, but the preliminaries were staged at the Olympic Stadium yesterday. A photographer punched an usher in the nose, and Lauri Lehtinen of Finland put on the swellest exhibition of blocking ever seen anywhere.

Lehtinen's feat even overshadows the third straight victory for Bill Carr over Ben Eastman in the 400 meters with a marvelous world's record tag to it of 46.2s.

The Finn's stunt came in the finals of the 5000 meters. Twice Hill of the United States tried to pass Lehtinen in the final ninety meters. Twice the Finn moved over in front of Hill. The next time Hill tried the inside lane. Lehtinen swung over there.

**And that was the way they finished with a fine old boxing hiss rending the air. It should have been a cheer. You will see no finer blocking when the boys start throwing leather at the Olympic Auditorium next week.**

(Continued on Page 11, Column 3)

## BODY FAILS BUT HE CARRIES ON

### Ovation Given Nippon Lad Lap Behind

[A. P. photo]

Schoichiro Takenaka Sticks to It

BY IRVING ECKHOFF

Stubby little legs fighting on and on. Sweat running down his forehead . . . blinding his eyes. The body weakened but the mind ruling supreme. One thought carrying through. Must finish; don't give up.

A lion-hearted little Japanese schoolboy named Schoichiro Tak-

(Continued on Page 11, Column 6)

## WEE WILLIE BREAKS ALL MARKS FOR 400 METERS

### *Time of 46.2s. Amazes Throng; Blazin' Ben in Game Finish; Wilson Takes Third*

BY BRAVEN DYER

All hail the greatest quarter miler of all time. Wee Willie Carr of Pine Bluff, Ark.

For the third time in five weeks the pint-sized Pennsylvania student showed his twinkling heels to Blazin' Ben Eastman of Stanford. More than 50,000 spectators fell back into their seats yesterday limp with exhaustion after watching wee Willie win the greatest 400-meter race ever run on this planet.

Running the best race of his spectacular career, Eastman was still unable to beat his diminutive Nemesis. Blazin' Ben was back in his early-season form all right, but it wasn't enough. Not by five feet.

AMAZING FEAT

But Ben's magnificent effort forced Wee Willie to a new world's record. The time, 46.2s., was almost unbelievable. No one but Wee Willie could crash the gates of the hall of fame at such blinding speed.

They started in lanes, six of them, Walters of South Africa, Eastman of Stanford, Wilson of Canada, Carr of Pennsylvania, Gordon of Los Angeles and Golding of Australia in that order from the pole. Six in the race but all eyes on Wee Willie and Blazin' Ben. It might just as well have been a two-man match for all the crowd cared.

"Eastman's in the right spot," said Ben's supporters as the runners went to their lanes. "He's behind Carr on the staggered start and thus knows how fast he has to run."

**But they reckoned wrong. They forgot that Wee Willie could run 400 meters just a little faster than any mortal who ever lived. They forgot that Wee Willie had been improving with every start and that he himself did not know the full limit of his running ability.**

OFF THEY GO

"Auf de Plaetze," said Franz Miller, the starter, in his most perfect German. "Fertig," continued the eminent Herr Miller. And then the sound of the gun, fired from midfield. Slowly at first, but furiously after the first three strides, the six speedsters sped on their way, Carr way out in the middle of the

(Continued on Page 11, Column 1)

## AQUATIC STARS IN BIG SPLASH

### *Two Water Polo Clashes on Opening Program Today*

### *Hungarian, German Teams to Meet in Grudge Battle*

### *World's Speediest Paddlers in Preliminary Trials*

BY BOB RAY

Swimming makes its big splash in the Tenth Olympiad today when the world's greatest human fish gather at the Olympic Park Stadium for a full days' program that will feature 100-meter free-style trials for both men and women, trials in the women's 200-meter breast-stroke and, probably most exciting of all, two water polo games.

HELENE MADISON

The aquatic-minded mermaids and mermen began their day's labors at 9 o'clock this morning, and take up their splashing again after lunch at 3 o'clock, so the fans are in for plenty of thrills.

**Although the swimming trials will bring world's cham-**

(Continued on Page 10, Column 2)

## AMERICAN YACHTS SWEEP TO VICTORY IN TWO EVENTS

BY WALDO DRAKE

LOS ANGELES HARBOR, Aug. 5. American racing sailors broke even with the rest of the sea-going world on San Pedro Bay today as the Olympic seven-day yachting program got under way to the accompaniment of a lusty westerly breeze, a stiff chop and sunlit skies. Victory went to the Americans in the star-class and eight-meter events and the Yankee sailors also finished in the money in the other two divisions, the six-meter class and the tiny twelve-foot monotype sloops.

SWEDES FURNISH SURPRISE

The one big surprise of the day was the sound drubbing meted out to the American six-meter Gallant by the beautiful Swedish sloop Bissbi, to win in her class by the wide margin of three minutes and fifteen seconds. Bissbi, reported good only in medium weather, met Gallant in the heavy weather that the Los Angeles yacht is supposed to revel in and badly outpointed and outfooted her in an eighteen-mile breeze Bissbi's elapsed time for the twelve miles, twice around the Point Fermin triangle, was 2h. 12m. 2s. The Canadian entry, Caprice, was third in 2h. 17m.

**Tore Holm, sailing Bissbi, got her away to a perfect windward start and rounded the Point Fermin whistler after the first short beat of a mere mile, with a lead of one minute. Thereafter she was never threatened by Gallant on any leg of the course. Caprice, sailed by Harold Jones, found the weather to her liking but was indifferently handled on the windward legs.**

In the eight-meter class, Owen Churchill, sailing his husky double-ended Angelita, won by more than four minutes—as expected—over Santa Maria, raced by Ron Maitland for Canada, his only competitor. Angelita, unless she suffers a serious casualty, is almost a certainty to take eight-meter honors throughout the week.

GRAY WINS STAR CLASS

Victory in the star class went to the soft-spoken Gilbert Gray of New Orleans, sailing his white witch, Jupiter, for the United States, Skipper Gray, disdaining to reef, though most of the foreigners did, put Jupiter over the course in the excellent star-boat time of 2h. 38m. 42s., beating Colin Ratsey, the English entry, Joy, by an even five minutes—which is an exceeding wide margin of victory in a star-class race. Gunnar Asther, in the Swedish star, for Sweden, was third, six minutes astern of Joy. These three boats are quite obviously the "class" of the Olympic star class entries and should stage an inter-

(Continued on Page 11, Column 7)

*Finnish Finish*

[A. P. photo]

Lehtinen Winning 5000-Meter Final

Ralph Hill, American star (right,) is shown being nosed out by less than a stride in his race with Lauri Lehtinen of Finland, at the Stadium yesterday. The European runner thrice crossed his rival in their duel on the stretch. Hill recovered his lane too late to snag the glory for America. Some 60,000 spectators lustily booed the result.

## MAYO HOLDS PENTATHLON LEAD FOR CLIMAX TODAY

### *Young American With Sore Heel Must Run Race of His Life to Beat Swedes for Title*

PENTATHLON STANDING

| Name, Nation— | Riding | Fencing | Shooting | Swimming | Total |
|---|---|---|---|---|---|
| Mayo (America) | 2 | 4½ | 1 | 14 | 21½ |
| Oxenstierna (Sweden) | 4 | 14 | 2 | 5 | 25 |
| Thofelt (Sweden) | 15 | 1 | 9 | 1 | 26 |
| Lindman (Sweden) | 1 | 2½ | 19 | 9 | 31½ |
| Simonetti (Italy) | 8 | 6 | 3 | 15 | 32 |

BY FRANK ROCHE

On the slim legs of a young field artillery officer out of Ft. Sill, Okla., Lieut Richard Mayo by name, depend the chances of America to win the modern pentathlon for the first time in history.

Mayo just did cling to his lead in this gruelling test of man yesterday in taking fourteenth place in the swimming, which was the fourth event of the competition. The Swedes, past masters at the pentathlon, closed in on the young American like a pack of bloodhounds with the scent of victory in their nostrils.

**A Swedish naval officer, Count Oxenstierna, thrashed his way to fifth place in the swimming event over a 300-meter course at the Olympic Swimming Stadium. Another Swede, Lieut. Thofelt, of Stockholm's crack regiment, the First, finished first in the swimming.**

The navy man, who left his tor-

(Continued on Page 11, Column 2)

## FINN WINS 5000-METER RACE AS CROWD BOOES

### *Lane Blocking Charge as Plucky American Strives to Pass Lehtinen in Finale*

BY BRAVEN DYER

Finland finally won a running race, her first of the Olympic Games. But in achieving this triumph she lost her reputation for clean sportmanship.

The vast majority of 50,000 spectators raised their voices in a chorus of booes at the Olympic Stadium yesterday afternoon. This unsual outburst, never condoned in polite circles, was aimed at Lauri Lehtinen, greatest of all Finnish distance runners. It continued until the announcer's voice, over the loud speaker, pleaded: "Remember, these people are our guests."

Lehtinen and Ralph Hill of Klamath Falls, Or., came around the final turn of the gruelling 5000-meter race in a two-man struggle that had the huge crowd on its feet. Hill, probably the best distance runner America ever had, prepared to make his closing sprint. Earlier in the week he defeated Lehtinen by a marvelous burst of speed during the final 150 yards of their trial heat. The Finn, no doubt recalled this.

CROWD AMAZED

Ralph challenged, and swung wide to pass his foe on the outside. To the astonishment of all the spectators on the south side of the stadium Lehtinen cut out and blocked Hill's progress. Halted in his bid for victory by these tactics, Hill broke his stride. There was nothing else for him to do. The Oregon boy then swung back and attempted to pass the Finn on the inside.

**Remembering Hill's terrific sprint earlier in the week, Lehtinen cut back with his rival and to the amazement and indignation of spectators prepared to block the Oregonian's path again. But Lehtinen didn't quite achieve his objective. Hill slipped through and came racing up the track with everything he had. Despite the fact that he was virtually starting**

(Continued on Page 10, Column 4)

## AMERICANS SAY RACE NOT FAIR

### *Kirby Avers He Would Have Disqualified Finn*

BY ALAN GOULD

Sports Editor, Associated Press

American track and field officials last night expressed regret that the tactics of Lauri Lehtinen, young Finnish runner, prevented a "fairly run" race and deprived Ralph Hill, American star, of the chance to make his best effort in the stretch of the 5000-meter Olympic final.

So far as the Amateur Athletic Union was concerned, through its president, Avery Brundage, the case rested with the statement they did not consider the race "fairly run" but would make no protest.

Others, including Gustavus T. Kirby, the American chief finish judge, who was a close observer of the disputed tactics by which Lehtinen interfered with Hill in the last 100 meters, were more outspoken. Mr. Kirby, although not officially having any part in the final decision of the referee, Arthur Holz of Germany, to accept Lehti-

(Continued on Page 8, Column 2)

## WHAT THE EXPERTS SAY—

Joe Binks, English writer and former mile-run champion of Great Britain. It was a foul. We would not tolerate such tactics in England. I don't know whether Hill could have beaten Lehtinen or not but the finish was so close that the American might have done so had it not been for the foul.

Georges Root, Paris newspaper man: It was a very evident foul.

Dr. Willy Miesl, German writer: Were I an official I could do nothing but disqualify Lehtinen. It was a very evident foul. I think Lehtinen was the better man, but it is not right to win that way.

Ted Collingwood, Australian sports writer: Lehtinen crossed over in front of Hill twice. I would call it a foul both times. If the man in front handicapped the man behind by interference the man in front should be disqualified.

Jules Ladoumegue, holder of the world's 1500-meter record, a Frenchman: I would rather not give my opinion for publication.

Charles Paddock, former sprint champion: It was a very palpable foul. A champion is supposed to win cleanly and fairly, particularly in the Olympic Games.

Will Rogers: It looked as if Lehtinen, or whatever his name is, made the mistake of zigging when he should have zagged.

## EVENTS TODAY

SWIMMING, Swim Stadium, Olympic Park

9 a.m.—100 meters, free style, men. Trials.
9:30 a.m.—200-meter breast stroke, women. Trials.
10:10 a.m.—Water polo, United States vs. Brazil.

OLYMPIC SCTADIUM

10 a.m.—DECATHLON, 110-meter hurdle.
11 a.m.—DECATHLON, discus throw.

ARMORY, Olympic Park

9 a.m.—Fencing, sword teams.

OLYMPIC AUDITORIUM, 1801 South Grand avenue

11 a.m.—Wrestling, Greco-Roman.

SUNSET GOLF CLUB, 4201 Crenshaw Boulevard

9 a.m.—PENTATHLON, cross-country run. Start.

LOS ANGELES HARBOR

12 noon—Yachting.

OLYMPIC STADIUM

2:30 p.m.—100-meter relay, four to team. Men. Trials.
2:30 p.m.—DECATHLON, pole vault.
3:15 p.m.—100-meter relay, four to team. Women. Trials.
4 p.m.—FINAL, 3000-meter steeplechase. Men.
4:30 p.m.—DECATHLON, javelin throw.
4:30 p.m.—400-meter relay, four to team. Men. Trials.
5:30 p.m.—DECATHLON, 1500 meters.

SWIMMING, Swim Stadium, Olympic Park

3 p.m.—100-meter free style, women. Trials.
3:30 p.m.—100-meter free style, men. Semifinals.
3:40 p.m.—Water polo, Germany vs. Hungary.

# OLYMPIC GAMES SECTION

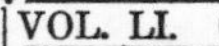

**Los Angeles Times**

EQUAL RIGHTS

LIBERTY UNDER THE LAW — TRUE INDUSTRIAL FREEDOM

VOL. LI. C — SUNDAY MORNING, AUGUST 7, 1932.




# RECORDS FALL IN AMAZING ARRAY

FINLAND

SWEDEN

UNITED STATES

Finland, Sweden and the United States each won a championship yesterday. Three flags share equally the honor.

## HOW NATIONS STAND

The unofficial point totals for the Olympic Games follow:

| | | | |
|---|---|---|---|
| United States | 321½ | Holland | 21 |
| Finland | 91 | Hungary | 21 |
| Germany | 89½ | Czecho-Slovakia | 19 |
| France | 89 | Denmark | 19 |
| Italy | 81½ | Australia | 18 |
| Great Britain | 66½ | South Africa | 9 |
| Sweden | 57 | New Zealand | 6 |
| Canada | 42 | Latvia | 5 |
| Japan | 31 | Belgium | 3 |
| Poland | 25 | Philippines | 4 |
| Austria | 23 | Argentina | 1 |
| Ireland | 23 | Brazil | 1 |

## DECATHLON SENSATION MARKS EXCITING DAY

### *Bausch's Feat Amazes Thousands; Daily Blunder Chalked Up by Officials in Stadium*

## FIRST-PLACE WINNERS

Number of first places won yesterday:

| | | |
|---|---|---|
| Sweden | 1 | (Modern pentathlon.) |
| Finland | 1 | (300-meter steeplechase.) |
| United States | 1 | (Decathlon.) |

Total number of first places won to date (all sports:)

| | | | |
|---|---|---|---|
| United States | 15 | France | 6 |
| Italy | 5 | Finland | 4 |
| Sweden | 3 | Ireland | 2 |
| Great Britain | 2 | Poland | 2 |
| Japan | 1 | Austria | 1 |
| Germany | 1 | Canada | 1 |
| Czecho-Slovakia | 1 | Australia | 1 |
| Holland | 1 | | |

BY PAUL LOWRY

Jim Bausch's new and marvelous world's record in the gruelling decathlon and the daily blunder of the I.A.A.F. officials were the big features of the seventh day of the Olympiad.

Count no day perfect when the officials don't make at least one bobble at the stadium.

The score is at least one per day, as follows:

**(1.) Placed Yoshioka third when he won a semifinal heat of the 100 meters.**

**(2.) Gave first to Tolan when he was third in a 100-meter heat.**

**(3.) Looking at the pole vault when Noel of France, made a long throw in the discus.**

**(4.) Balled up the staggered start in the 200 meters and made Metcalfe run farther than the man on the pole.**

**(6.) Permitted a palpable foul by Edwards in the 800 meters.**

**(7.) Passed up a foul by Lehtinen in the 5000 meters with no other decision than to let the matter rest.**

**(8.) Forced the runners in the 3000-meter steeplechase to run an extra lap.**

America added to its point total yesterday with a first and fourth in the decathlon, a third and sixth in the 3000-meter steeplechase and a third in the modern pentathlon.

The score in track and field now stands at 202 for the United States as against 68 for Finland and 41 for Great Britain.

### UNITED STATES

Jim Bausch, America's dark horse in the decathlon, smashed the former Olympic record to smithereens with a grand total of 8462.23 points, and in so doing hung up a world's standard that will take a lot of beating. The big Kansan virtually cinched the event when he scored better than 1000 points in two of the last three events on the program—pole vault and javelin. Buster Charles couldn't keep the big lead he piled up on Friday, but managed to come in fourth for the best showing America has made in this event since the days of Jim Thorpe.

Although Lieut. Richard Mayo held the lead at the end of four events in the modern pentathlon he couldn't keep up with the Swedes on the fifth day. He tried gamely in the 4000-meter cross-country race, but he finished far back and his final standing was third. However, he did beat Thofelt, champion of the Games four years ago.

In the 3000-meter steeplechase Joe McCluskey wound up third after a long stretch sprint with Evenson of Great Britain. McCluskey was a stride back. Dawson took the sixth place in this event.

**Swimming opened with an assault on the women's 100 free style Olympic record. It was smashed three** times, the final mark going to Eleanor Garatti Saville at 1m. 8.5s., four-tenths second better than Helene Madison.

### SWEDEN

Yesterday Swedish athletes placed one-two-four in the event. Count Oxenstierna was first, Bo Lindman second and S. Thofelt, the 1928 champion, fourth.

### GERMANY

Both Eberle and Sievert proved to be consistent performers in the decathlon, and placed third and fifth, respectively, with point totals of 8030.80 and 7941.07, respectively. Remer an Miersch took fifth and sixth places in the modern pentathlon.

### FINLAND

Iso-Hollo simply played with the field in the 3000-meter steeplechase. In spite of the extra lap he ran tirelessly and was over 100 yards ahead at the finish. It was announced that the time over the prescribed distance would have been a new Olympic record. Including the extra lap the time was 10m.

(Continued on Page 6, Column 2)

## JAPANESE TAKE HONORS IN SWIMMING EVENTS

### *Aquatic World Bows to Nipponese Paddlers; Girls Break Marks With Reckless Abandon*

BY BOB RAY

It's the Japanese crawl now!

First it was the Australian crawl, then they changed its nationality to American, but after yesterday's sensational Olympiad performances by the rising sons of Nippon, the aquatic world must now acknowledge that the Japanese variation of the famous swimming stroke is better than its predecessors.

Featuring the opening of the Olympic Games aquatic program was the establishment of a new Olympiad record by Yasuji Miyazaki, a lithe, brown-skinned son of Japan. He outdistanced the world's best in the semifinals of the men's 100-meters free style swim yesterday afternoon to thrill 5000 fans, besting the previous Olympic record set in 1928 by the great Johnny Weissmuller and giving every indication that he will go further in his triumphs by breaking the Weissmuller's world's mark tomorrow in the finals.

Qualifying along with Miyazaki for the finals were two Japanese team rates, Tatsugo Kawaishi and Zenjiro Takahashi, and a valiant trio of Americans—Al Schwartz, Ray Thompson and Manuella Kalili. These six fight it out for the Olympiad championship tomorrow, but there are none who will predict anything but a Japanese triumph.

The performance of Miyazaki outshone the efforts of the world's greatest mermaids, even though they did manage to shatter Olympic records with the customary abandon that has infested the athletes in all sports of the magnificent Xth Olympiad.

Record smashing by the female of the paddling species began bright and early—in the first race held during the morning program to be exact.

DENNIS FIRST

The honor went to a 16-year-old Australian schoolgirl, Clare Dennis, who lunged her way through the waters of the Los Angeles Swimming Stadium to set a new standard in the 200-meters breast stroke event.

Little Miss Dennis, when informed that her time of 3m. 8.2s. had bettered the previous Olympic record for the event, literally jumped with joy and a broad smile, which she just couldn't control, blossomed out.

**"When do the papers come out?" she asked, and you just couldn't help being glad with her over her record-breaking feat.**

Shortly after in the third heat of the event Hideko Maehata, stockiest of the girls on the Japanese women's swim squad but still appearing quite small beside her rivals, plowed her way to a victory in time that also beat the Olympic mark of 3m. 11.4s., set by Hilda Schrader of Germany during the 1928 Games at Amsterdam. Miss Maehata's time was 3m. 10.7s. The Nipponese maiden, unlike Miss Dennis, smiled and appeared a bit embarrassed when congratulated for her victory.

The third Olympic record to sink below the waves before the onslaught of the great field of women swimmers was Albina Osipowich's 100-meter free-style mark of 1m. 11s., set in 1928.

FIVE TIMES

Five times was this standard bettered during the heats staged yesterday afternoon and, punctured with holes, it settled slowly into oblivion.

**Eleanor Garatti Saville, a San Francisco matron, turned in the best time for the event, 1m. 8.5s., in winning the final of four heats. Previously the great Helene Madison had pruned the standard down to 1m. 8.9s., right after Joyce Cooper, stately English miss, had lowered the mark to 1m. 9s. The other mermaids who bettered the Olympiad record were Josephine McKim, dainty American miss, and Willy den Ouden, a cute little 14-year-old paddler from Holland.**

It was a day of superlative performances, but it was the great swimming of the Nipponese, Miyazaki, that stood out like the torch on the peristyle of the Olympic Stadium.

The Japanese youngster found himself arrayed against Dr. Stephen Barany, a great Hungarian swimmer who took second to Weissmuller in the Amsterdam Olympics, Szekely, another Hungarian, and the two Americans, Kalili and Thompson, in the semifinals. And what a race it was.

Barany, swimming with that stiff-arm stroke so popular with the European mermen, started off at a

(Continued on Page 3, Column 1)

*"Jolly Well Done"—as One Mermaid to Another*

[A. P. photos by Tommy Burns]

British Miss Congratulates Japanese Victor

After Hideko Maehata defeated Margery Hinton in the trials of the women's 200-meter breast stroke yesterday at the Olympic Swimming Stadium, the English girl promptly rushed up and praised the little Japanese paddler. Quite a difference in size between the sturdy daughter of Great Britain and the little Nipponese maid. And Miss Maehata is the largest member of the Japanese women's swimming squad. Lower photo shows the finish of the race, Miss Maehata just reaching the end of the tank and Miss Hinton submerged as she was about to go through her final strokes.

## STEEPLECHASE CROWN TO FINN

*Extra Lap Run Off Through Judge's Mistake*

*Distance of 3450 Meters Made in 10m. 33.4s.*

*American Relay Team Sets New World Mark*

BY BRAVEN DYER

Volmari Iso-Hollo, a young typesetter from Finland, won the picturesque 3000-meter steeplechase yesterday afternoon, but had to go an extra lap to be crowned Olympic Games champion.

This wierd happenstance, unheard of in Olympic Games competition, came about because officials went sound asleep and neglected to flag the field of ten runners at the conclusion of their seventh and final lap.

Nobody was able to discover what the officials were actually doing when this faux pas occurred, but loud snores from the field indicated that somebody was fast in the arms of Morpheus.

RACE NOT CLOSE

Fortunately the race was not close. Iso-Hollo took the lead after the second lap and never lost it. You can picture the pickle in which officials would have found themselves but for the Finn's rapidity. Mr. Iso-Hollo's time was 10m. 33.4s. for 3450 meters. It was estimated that he turned the regulation distance of 3000 meters in 9m. 18.4s. Iso-Hollo set a new Olympic record of 9m. 14.6s. during trial heats early in the week.

**Although the program was the least attractive yet presented to Olympic spectators, those 40,000 souls who found their way to the stadium saw three world records fall. The American sprint relay team of Kiesel, Toppino, Dyer and Wykoff started it in their trial heat by running 400 meters in 40.6s. The old mark was 40.8s. Shortly after this the Yankee 1600-meter relay squad of Fuqua, Ablowich, Warner and Carr shattered the second mark. With each man touring 400 meters they turned the distance in 3m. 11.8s. The old mark of 3m. 12.6s. was made by Stanford last year. Jim Bausch closed the afternoon's entertainment by smashing the decathlon standard in a blazing finish.**

Joe McCluskey of the United States was the only runner affected by the faux pas of officials in the steeplechase. The Fordham boy was actually second at the conclusion of the regulation distance, but faded on the final lap and was passed by Tom Evenson of Great Britain.

DECISION AGAIN LATE

The Englishman, although beating McCluskey over the longer route, finished approximately eighty yards behind Iso-Hollo. Maitilainen of Finland, was fourth, followed by Bailey of Great Britain, and Glenn Dawson of Oklahoma. Dawson ran well during the early stages of the race, as did the two Britishers, but none of the trio was able to match Iso-Hollo's withering pace over the last four laps.

It was almost two hours after the race ended before any official announcement came over the loudspeaker. But denizens of the press box knew something had been amiss, because unofficial timers caught the men in 10m. 33.8s., and also saw the runners clear the water jump once more than required.

Officials had been talking to the entries during the meantime. They had the privilege of demanding that the race be rerun. None of them seemed to care much about this, and you couldn't blame them, for this grind is a torturing one. It's bad enough to run two miles on the flat without having a flock of hurdles bobbing up in front of you. McCluskey did the sporting thing by waiving his right to second place, so the awards were apportioned on the basis of the 3450-meter excursion.

WIND-UP TODAY

Today winds up the greatest track-and-field program the world has ever known. If you doubt this

(Continued on Page 5, Column 1)

## EVENTS TODAY

**SWIM STADIUM, Olympic Park**

9:30 a.m.—Diving exhibition.
10 a.m.—International race, 200 meters, free style. Men.
10:15 a.m.—Water polo, Germany and Hungary reserves vs. United States.

**OLYMPIC AUDITORIUM, 1801 South Grand avenue**

11 a.m.—Wrestling, Greco-Roman.

**LOS ANGELES HARBOR**

12 noon—Yachting.

**OLYMPIC STADIUM**

2:30 p.m.—High jump, women.
2:30 p.m.—100-meter relay, men, semifinals.
3 p.m.—FINALS, 100-meter relay, women.
3:30 p.m.—MARATHON, start.
3:30 p.m.—FINALS, 100-meter relay, men.
3:45 p.m.—LACROSSE, United States vs. Canada.
4:30 p.m.—FINALS, 400-meter relay, men.
6:05 p.m.—Time approximate, Marathon finish.

**SWIM STADIUM, Olympic Park**

3 p.m.—100-meter, free style, women, semifinals.
3:20 p.m.—FINALS, 100-meter, free style, men.
3:35 p.m.—Springboard diving, men and women.
4:05 p.m.—Water polo, Germany and Hungary vs. Hollywood Athletic Club.
4:50 p.m.—Water polo, Japan vs. United States.

**ARMORY, Olympic Park**

2 p.m.—Fencing, sword teams.

**OLYMPIC AUDITORIUM, 1801 South Grand avenue**

7:30 p.m.—Wrestling, FINALS, Greco-Roman.

Tickets for today and tomorrow on sale at each stadium.

## MAYO BEATEN IN PENTATHLON

*American Finally Bows in Defeat to Oxenstierna*

*Strong Finish Wins Honor for Swede Navy Officer*

*Yankee Collapses at End of Cross-country Run*

BY FRANK ROCHE

To the victors belong the spoils. To the Swedes belong the modern pentathlon. An American almost wrested it from them this time, but failed by a tiny margin. History repeated itself in this gruelling test of men, which terminated yesterday after five terrific days of competition.

The Swedes, led by a handsome young naval officer, a nobleman in his own right, Lieut. Johan Gabriel

(Continued on Page 4, Column 1)

## HERE ARE NEW RECORDS

400-meter relay—New world's record of 40.6s., by American team composed of Bob Kiesel, Emmett Toppino, Hector Dyer and Frank Wykoff. Old records 40.8s. flat held by German team and 1931 U.S.C. squad.

1600-meter relay—New world's record of 3m. 11.8s. by the United States team composed of Ivan Fuqua, Edgar Ablowich, Karl Warner and William Carr. Old record 3m. 12.6s., held by 1931 Stanford team.

100-meter men's free style—New Olympic record of 58s. flat by Yasuji Miyazaki, Japan. Old record 58 3-5s. set by Johnny Weissmuller, United States, 1928.

100-meter women's free style—New Olympic record of 1m. 8.5s., by Eleanor Garratti Saville, United States. Old recordfl 1m. 11s., set by Albina Osipowich, United States, 1928.

200-meter women's breast stroke—New Olympic record of 3m. 8.2s., by Claire Dennis, Australia. Old record, 3m. 11.4s., set by Hilda Schrader, Germany, 1928.

Decathlon—New world record of 8462.23 points by Jim Bausch of Kansas. Old world record of 8053.29 by Paavo Yrjola of Finland. Jarvinen of Finland did 8255.27 in 1930.

## DOCTOR'S ABSENCE EXPLAINED

**Ask any good Irishman at Olympic Village about Dr. Patrick O'Callaghan's sore thumb.**

**"Oh! Why, the doctor's thumb is all right."**

**But it isn't, and that sore right thumb kept the good doctor out of the decathlon.**

**For the doctor loves to fight and fight he will, say his comrades.**

## BAUSCH WINS IN DECATHLON

*Yes, He's Nephew of Your Old Uncle Sam*

*They Crown Him Greatest Athlete of All*

*Second Honors Awarded to Jarvinen, Finland*

BY RALPH HUSTON

The greatest gosh-durned athlete this old globe of ours has ever seen is a nephew of your Uncle Sam.

He is Jarring Jim Bausch, the Kansas Colossus, who can run faster, jump higher and throw things farther than any man, woman or child in the world.

He's old Citius, Altius and Fortius rolled into one, is Jarry Jim, who smashed every existing record and every record anybody ever thought would exist yesterday, when he won

(Continued on Page 4, Column 4)

## *Jim Bausch's Iron-Man Feat Greatest Ever*

When Jim Bausch, American all-around star from Kansas, captured the Olympic decathlon championship, smashing the world and Olympic records to smithereens, he scored the greatest all-around performance of all time. Bausch amassed a total of 8462.23 points in the ten-event two-day iron-man test. Paavo Yrojolo of Finland made the former Olympic record in 1928. It stood at 8053.29 points.

OLYMPIC GAMES SECTION

Los Angeles Times

EQUAL RIGHTS — LIBERTY UNDER THE LAW — TRUE INDUSTRIAL FREEDOM

VOL. LI. C MONDAY MORNING, AUGUST 8, 1932.

# ZABALA BREAKS MARATHON MARK

Flags of Sweden and the United States today share honors alike at the top of The Times, each having won four championships. Argentina, Japan, France, Italy, Germany and Finland each won a first place.

## FIRST-PLACE WINNERS

Number of places won yesterday:

| | | |
|---|---|---|
| United States | 3 | (Track and Field) |
| Japan | 1 | (Swimming) |
| Argentina | 1 | (Marathon) |
| Finland | 1 | (Wrestling) |
| Sweden | 4 | (Wrestling) |
| Italy | 1 | (Wrestling) |
| Germany | 1 | (Wrestling) |

Total number of first places won to date (all sports:)

| | | | |
|---|---|---|---|
| United States | 18 | France | 6 |
| Italy | 6 | Finland | 5 |
| Sweden | 7 | Ireland | 2 |
| Great Britain | 2 | Poland | 2 |
| Japan | 2 | Austria | 1 |
| Germany | 2 | Canada | 1 |
| Czecho-Slovakia | 1 | Australia | 1 |
| Holland | 1 | Argentina | 1 |

That Great Moment When Finish Line Was Reached

[Wide World Photos]

Juan Zabala finishing Marathon is shown at left. The dramatic moment after the finish when he is supported by admirers while the crowd cheered is pictured at right.

## TRACK AND FIELD EVENTS CLOSE, HISTORY WRITTEN

### *Thirteen World Records Broken; America Leads; Finns Second, Britons Third*

## HOW NATIONS STAND

The unofficial point totals for the Olympic Games (all sports) follow:

| | | | |
|---|---|---|---|
| United States | 381½ | Czecho-Slvakia | 24 |
| Italy | 130½ | Ireland | 23 |
| Finland | 129 | Hungary | 21 |
| Sweden | 124 | Denmark | 19 |
| Germany | 105½ | Australia | 18 |
| France | 104 | Argentina | 14 |
| Great Britain | 88½ | South Africa | 12 |
| Canada | 58 | Belgium | 6 |
| Japan | 57 | New Zealand | 6 |
| Holland | 27 | Latvia | 5 |
| Austria | 27 | Philippines | 4 |
| Poland | 25 | Brazil | 1 |

BY PAUL LOWRY

The world's greatest track and field competition ever held has come to a close. In eight days of super-brilliant performances the Tenth Olympiad produced the following:

(1.) Twenty new Olympic and seven world records for men in twenty-three events.

(2.) Six new Olympic and world records for women in six events.

(3.) The astounding point total of 218 for the United States as against 72 for Finland and 55 for Great Britain.

(4.) An all-time record attendance that approached the 500,000 mark for the duration of the track-and-field contests.

Juan Zabala's victory in the classic Marathon closed the track division of the Tenth Olympiad, but not until United States teams had set new world standards of 40s. flat and 3m. 8.2s. in the 400 and 1600-meter relays, respectively.

This was the crowning touch to the greatest orgy of record shattering the world has ever known. Only marks in the high jump, hammer throw and broad jump escaped annihilation.

UNITED STATES

Flying around the track with the speed of bullets Kiesel, Toppino, Dyer and Wykoff bit a huge chunk off their own record made the day

(Continued on Page 12, Column 7)

## JAPANESE BOY CROWNED FIRST SWIMMING KING

### *Miyazaki Wins 100-Meters Finals; Willy den Ouden Smashes Mark in Women's Semifinals*

BY BOB RAY

A churning, yellow-capped figure that cut through the waters like a torpedo bent on destruction. That was Yasuji Miyazaki, 15-year-old Japanese school-boy, yesterday as he proved himself the fastest swimmer in the world and won for himself, and Japan, the title as 100-meter men's free style champion of the Tenth Olympiad.

Like a torpedo swishing through the waves—legs kicking so rapidly that they looked like blades of an electric fan and arms plunging into and rising out of the water faster and faster — Miyazaki glided to the finish line to explode for the second time the previous Olympic record for the distance that was set by the great Johnny Weissmuller in the 1928 Games.

HELENE MADISON

Miyazaki's time of 58.2s., however, did not equal his 58s. flat made in Saturday's semifinals. But it did crack Weissmuller's winning time of 58.6s., made at Amsterdam.

**After it was over and the record time had been announced to the stands, Miyazaki was appropriately put up on a pedestal to pose for photographs. A happy Japanese boy was Miyazaki as he stood there—the new champion of the world.**

"Banzai" upon "Banzai" were roared down upon him from frenzied Japanese rooters and Miyazaki, standing there grinning, had to acknowledge the shouts by waving a towel over his head at the cheering stands.

EARNS RIGHT TO TITLE

Miyazaki proved beyond a doubt his right to the title of Olympic

(Continued on Page 13, Column 1)

## NURMI-ZABALA RACES HINTED

Paavo Nurmi, who had hoped to win the Olympic Marathon as the crowning achievement of his great athletic career, said yesterday that the course for the 1932 race was the easiest in the history of the Games, and that he was confident he could have done 2h. 20m. if he had been permitted to run. An unverified report said that Nurmi and Juan Carlos Zabala, the winner, will tour the country in a series of match races, presumably professional.

## TRACK RECORDS TOPPLED IN SENSATIONAL TIME

### *Men's and Women's Relay Marks Fall and Girl Wins High Jump Title From Babe Didrikson*

BY BRAVEN DYER

After what happened at the Olympic Stadium yesterday afternoon more than 75,000 fans are prepared to testify that there is no known limit to human ability. After smashing two relay records to smithereens during the trial heats Saturday, the United States baton-passing athletes went out yesterday and lowered the first marks by such sensational running that it left the huge crowd gasping for breath.

Perhaps it was the inspiration of the girls that started yesterday's brilliant performances. At any rate, four American girls cracked the first mark and from that time until Juan Carlos Zabala won the classic Marathon the spectators were treated to one sensation after another.

RECORDS FALL

**Five events and five new Olympic records. Four new world records. It's time somebody called a halt, just to give us a rest and give the next generation time to catch up.**

**The record-breaking, which gives no indication of ceasing, started early. Four fleet maidens representing the United States, carried the baton 400 meters in world-record time.**

They smashed the official standard by more than a second, running the distance in 47s. flat. The old mark was 48.4s., set by Canada in the 1928 Olympics.

It was by far the most closely contested relay of the Games and the United States won only because Miss Wilhelmina von Bremen had too much sprint for Hilda Strike of Canada over the final 100 meters.

SIX TEAMS START

Six teams started, Holland, Germany, Great Britain and Japan entering in addition to the Yankees and Canadians. It was a two-team race from the opening gun between Canada and the United States. Mary L. Crew sent the Yankee gals ahead in the first 100 meters, running against Mildred Frizzell. And fleet-footed Evelyn Furtsch of Tustin, Cal., put the United States a little farther out in front on the next stretch.

**There wasn't a great deal of difference between the teams as they swung around the curve on the third section, Mary Frizzell of Canada regaining the yard lead from Annette Rogers of the United States. Canada, however, was unfortunate when Miss Frizzell got only a fair pass to Hilda Strike, while Miss Rogers gave the baton to Wilhelmina von Bremen perfectly.**

FOOT TO SPARE

With a yard lead Miss von Bremen sped for the tape, followed closely by Miss Strike. The tall, blonde American girl was just a wee bit stronger physically than her rival and although Miss Strike cut down the margin at the finish, Miss Von Bremen carried the ribbon away with about a foot to spare.

**Miss Rogers, who was also entered in the high jump going on at the same time as the relay, returned to her leaping as soon as the baton-passing event had been concluded.**

Great Britain was third. Miss Ethel Johnson, Gwendoline Alice

(Continued on Page 10, Column 5)

## ARGENTINE RUNNER CLIPS MINUTE OFF OLD MARK

### *Finish Dramatic as 75,000 Cheer; England Second, Finland Third, America Seventh*

BY BRAVEN DYER

Six weeks ago Juan Carlos Zabala "collapsed" and failed to finish "The Times" Marathon.

Toward twilight last evening the sound of trumpets from atop the Olympic Stadium signified his approach at the head of the greatest distance runners from all over the world.

The last note of the trumpeters had hardly died away before the swarthy son of South America came pounding through the tunnel to the accompaniment of the greatest ovation ever accord-finish The Times Marathon.

More than 75,000 spectators stood on their toes and cheered the midget Argentine youth all the way around the oval. They knew the torture of this twenty-six-mile grind and they were acknowledging the gameness of the 20-year-old schoolboy from Buenos Aires.

THREE MORE FOLLOW

While the plaudits of the multitude grew into a deafening roar, three other runners appeared as if by magic. They were Samuel Ferris of Great Britain, Armas Toivonen of Finland and Duncan McLeod Wright, another Englishman.

**No more spectacular finish has ever been recorded in the Olympic Games. After traveling more than twenty-six miles four runners were on the track at the same time and they had only three-quarters of a lap to run inside the stadium.**

Zabala was just about to cross the line as the fourth member of this quartet appeared through the tunnel. Ferris was 200 yards behind. Toivonen was less than half this distance to the rear of Ferris. Wright followed within forty yards of the Finn.

The crowd was quick to catch the drama of the occasion and each man, as he came to the end of the

(Continued on Page 10, Column 1)

## FRANCE, ITALY FENCING CHIEFS

### *Two Countries to Fight It Out; America Next*

The balance of power has been maintained!

France and Italy are taking turn about as victors in fencing. For France won the epee team championship Sunday afternoon.

The Olympic foil team competition was won last week by France, but Italy returned and gave tit for tat by winning the foil individual championship. The score between France and Italy in the Sunday contest was 9 to 7.

UNITED STATES THIRD

United States beat Belgium, 8 to 2, and thereby places third. This carries out to date Lieut. Calnan's prediction that the United States would take a place in each event. But only half of the fencing events are over!

France and Italy succeeded in beating the United States yester-

(Continued on Page 12, Column 1)

## 'ALL HAIL—SHE BEAT MIGHTY BABE!'

### Dramatic Story Behind Winner of High Jump Contest

[A. P. Photo]

Jean Shiley

BY MURIEL BABCOCK

The mighty Babe Didrikson goes home to Texas tomorrow minus one Olympic championship she thought to acquire, but minus not one atom of that self-confidence that has been with her from the start.

"I jumped as high as she did, or higher," she told me when I asked her what she thought of the judges' decision giving Jean Shiley, American girl, the Olympic win.

And again in the lobby, to some visitors who asked her what happened, she made the same remark.

"Did you know you were diving instead of jumping the correct way?"

"Nope."

"Did you ever have any trouble

(Continued on Page 14, Column 6)

## YESTERDAY'S RECORDS

Yesterday's Olympic performers ran true to form and continued the epidemic of record breaking. Here they are:

4x100-meter relay (women) new world record of 47s. by United States team (Carew, Furtsch, Rogers, Von Bremen.)

4x100-meter relay (men) new world record of 40s. by U.S. team (Kiesel, Toppino, Dyer, Wykoff.)

4x400-meter relay—new world record of 3m. 8.2s. by U.S. team (Fuqua, Ablowich, Warner, Carr.)

High jump (women)—new world record by **JEAN SHILEY, U.S.A.**, 5ft. 5¼in.

**Marathon—New Olympic record of 2h. 31m. 36s. by Juan Zabala (Argentina.)**

## EVENTS TODAY

**SWIMMING, Olympic Park**

**Morning**

8:30 a.m.—Springboard diving, men, finals.

**Afternoon**

3:00 p.m.—Finals, 100-meter free style, women.
3:10 p.m.—400-meter free style, men, trials.
4:10 p.m.—Water polo, Brazil vs. Germany.
4:45 p.m.—Water polo, Hungary vs. Japan.

**OLYMPIC STADIUM**

8:00 a.m.—Assignment of jurors calisthenics.
2:30 p.m.—Field hockey, United States vs. Japan.
8:00 p.m.—Football, Princeton, Yale, Harvard graduates vs. Stanford, U.S.C. and U.C. graduates.

**FENCING, Armory, Olympic Park**

9:00 a.m.—Swords.
1:00 p.m.—Swords.

**LOS ANGELES HARBOR**

12:00 Noon—Yachting.

Tickets for today and tomorrow are on sale at each stadium.

OLYMPIC GAMES SECTION
Los Angeles Times
EQUAL RIGHTS
LIBERTY UNDER THE LAW · TRUE INDUSTRIAL FREEDOM
VOL. LI. TUESDAY MORNING, AUGUST 9, 1932.

# WEST BEATS EAST GRIDDERS, 7 TO 6

UNITED STATES

Uncle Sam's banner goes to top of The Times today with three championships won. Hungary took one first place.

## HOW NATIONS STAND

| | | | |
|---|---|---|---|
| United States | 419½ | Czecho-Slovakia | 24 |
| Italy | 137½ | Ireland | 23 |
| Finland | 130 | Denmark | 19 |
| Sweden | 124 | Australia | 20 |
| Germany | 107½ | Argentina | 14 |
| France | 104 | South Africa | 13 |
| Great Britain | 88½ | Belgium | 6 |
| Canada | 61 | New Zealand | 6 |
| Japan | 58 | Switzerland | 5 |
| Holland | 32 | Latvia | 5 |
| Hungary | 31 | Philippines | 4 |
| Austria | 27 | Brazil | 1 |
| Poland | 25 | | |

Water Flashes Churn to Speed Marks

Little Willy den Ouden of Holland (left) and Helene Madison of the United States as They Appeared on Eve of Great Race Yesterday, which Helene Won

[Wide World photo of Miss Den Ouden, A. P. of Miss Madison]

## TRIUMPHS IN SWIMMING RAISE AMERICAN SCORE

### *Victories of Helene and Mickey in Race and Diving Bolster Up Hopes of Beating Japan*

#### FIRST-PLACE WINNERS

Number of first places won yesterday:

| | | |
|---|---|---|
| United States | 2 | (Swimming) |
| Hungary | 1 | (Gymnastics) |

Total number of first places won to date (all sports:)

| | | | |
|---|---|---|---|
| United States | 21 | Sweden | 7 |
| France | 6 | Italy | 6 |
| Finland | 5 | Great Britain | 2 |
| Japan | 2 | Germany | 2 |
| Ireland | 2 | Poland | 2 |
| Czecho-Slovakia | 1 | Holland | 1 |
| Austria | 1 | Canada | 1 |
| Australia | 1 | Argentina | 1 |
| Hungary | 1 | | |

BY PAUL LOWRY

A dark-brown man with a thinning thatch and a close-cropped mustache pulled Micky Riley down on a bench and embraced him with a bear-like hug. A girl with wavy blonde locks dropped on her knees and looked up adoringly into the boy's eyes.

The man with the tanned skin was Fred Cady, Mickey's coach. The girl with the curly hair was Georgia Coleman, Mickey's sweetheart.

Mickey Riley had just won the springboard diving championship of the world for the United States.

**A few minutes later there was another touching scene. Three boys in a circle had thrown their arms around one another-er's shoulders. They patted each other on the back. They looked happy enough to cry. They were Riley, Harold (Dutch) Smith and Dick Degener. The announcer had just broadcast the information that they placed one-two-three for the United States.**

Thus was America's counter-challenge to Japan's opening thrust in the water events of the Tenth Olympiad touched off. Where Japan scored 17 points with a first, second and fifth in the 100-meter free style for men American came back with 19 in the springboard diving.

This happened in the morning.

HELENE TRIUMPHS

In the afternoon America's greatest mermaid, Helene Madison, swam to her first Olympic championship. Where Holland's Willemjntje Den Ouden had churned the water to a new Olympic record in the semifinal heats of the 100-meter free style for women Helene saved her speed and her strength for the finals. She was rewarded by a new Olympic record of 1m. 6.8s.

**American cleaned up here again with first, third and fourth places and 17 points.**

**But the Japanese threat is still in the air**

Y. Yokoyama set a new Olympic

(Continued on Page 12, Column 7)

## FISTS FLY AT OLYMPICS, OFFICERS QUELL RIOT

### *Mob Action Starts When Brazilian Polo Players Rush Hungarian Official After Decision*

BY BOB RAY

Fists flew and a general riot ensued out at the Los Angeles Swimming Stadium as an enraged Brazilian water polo team charged a Hungarian referee yesterday to provide the most exciting incident of the Xth Olympiad.

Bela Komjadi was the water polo official who was the center of the attack, which resulted in Brazil's septet being disqualified from further participation in the championships. Three Brazilian players, L. Da Silva, goalie; A. Serpa, left back, and C. Branco, a reserve, also were barred from further participation in the swimming events of the Games.

**And to add a bit more excitement to the melee that occurred on the edge of the pool Los Angeles police manhandled Dr. Leo Donath of Hungary, who is the secretary of the International Swimming Association. Dr. Donath tried to get to the center of the fracas and police, thinking he wasgoing to join in the fisticuffs, slammed him back against the concrete wall in front of the press box. The officers then were told who the bespectacled Hungarian official was.**

The riot was the aftermath of the water polo game between Germany and Brazil, which the Germans won, 7 to 3.

Komjadi, who denies he is coach of the Hungarian water-polo team, although other squars declare that he is, inflicted a total of forty fouls against the Brazilians to only four called on Germany and was repeatedly booed by the spectators for his methods of officiating. He

(Continued on Page 12, Column 1)

## HELENE, MICKEY CAPTURE TITLES

### *Miss Madison Flashes to Victory in Pool*

BY BOB RAY

"Queen" Helene Madison still is queen of the aquatic waves, and Mickey Riley, a Los Angeles boy from Boyle Heights, is the new Olympic Games springboard diving champion.

This was decided at yesterday's swimming and diving program at the Los Angeles Stadium when the tall American girl from Seattle beat back the challenge of 14-year-old Willy den Ouden of Holland to win the 100-meter free style finals and Riley, whose real name is Galitzen, outshone the best amateur spring-

(Continued on Page 14, Column 2)

## HELENE ALMOST LATE FOR RACE

Helene Madison was almost late to her own race yesterday.

Helene, who always changes into her swimming suit in the apartment of a friend, came sauntering through the center tunnel leading to the starting board just as the clock ticked 3.

"I didn't know I was late until somebody grabbed me and told me to hurry," she said afterward. "I looked and the announcer was already calling off the event. I ran and jumped into the pool to get wet and get a quick workout—I had to do that—then we were swimming.

"After it was all over I cried. I was terribly happy about winning because I have been pointing for this race for two years."

She didn't fight her hardest during the first lap.

"I took a lead of the field and instead of trying to gain on that, I just tried to keep it. It was much easier for me in the finish. I wasn't exhausted. I'm not tired now."

## *QUEEN HELENE THROUGH RACING---IT COSTS TOO MUCH TO BE CHAMPION*

BY MURIEL BABCOCK

Helene Madison is swimming her last races this week.

She will retire from big competition swimming with the end of the Olympic Games.

This announcement from her father, Charles Madison of Seattle, came yesterday morning a good four hours before the big, tall girl went into her 100-meter battle.

**"Whether she wins or loses, and, of course, we're hoping she makes her last race her best and comes out Olympic champion, she is through," Father Madison said.**

"She's had an awful lot of swimming in the last few years. And I think she's had about enough. It has gotten so it is nothing but one race after another.

ALL FED UP

"She's fed up herself with all of it. I don't think she has the same zest for racing that she used to have. She's hit her peak. She's won her records, got them all practically, and now it's time she did something else."

**I saw Father Madison, a big, well-built, genial man, and Mother Madison, vigorous, snapping-eyed, tall, like Helene, in the Pasadena home of Mrs. Madison's sister about 10:30 o'clock of a morning. They had driven down from Seattle for the Games.**

Father Madison, in golf knickers, lounging in an easy chair, smoking one cigarette after another, talked of Helene's early exploits, of the first time they realized she had championship caliber, of her days as a little girl when she collected all the stray cats and dogs of the neighborhood and brought them home to be fed and cared for.

MOTHER ON JOB

Mother Madison, in fresh, bright pajamas, alternated her attention between the sewing machine and the conversation. She was busy taking a tuck in Helene's official red jacket. "It has to be done for this afternoon," she explained. "It was one of the things they gave her and it was too big—needed some alterations."

**They seemed like nice, sensible people. Like your father and mother, like mine. Pretty proud of all that Helene has done, but not overly impressed with what it means to her as far as her life is concerned. Anxious that she shouldn't go "too champion," anxious that she should be like the rest of the girls and boys she knows.**

"I suppose it has been a tremendous thing, having a great champion in the family," I remarked.

"Well," said Father Madison, with a twinkle in his eye, "it hasn't been what you might think. The house has sort of revolved about this

(Continued on Page 13, Column 5)

## TOUCHDOWN NEAR CLOSE OF GAME NETS VICTORY

### *Shaver Goes Over for Score and Kirwan Adds Extra Point; Early Tussle Close*

BY BRAVEN DYER

What started out to be a very ordinary football game became a thrilling battle in the closing quarter at the Olympic Stadium last night and 60,000 fans cheered twenty-two husky gridiron warriors to the echo as the Western All Stars defeated the Eastern eleven, 7 to 6. The struggle was witnessed by the largest crowd that ever saw a major game at night.

Trailing, 6 to 0, with but eight minutes of play remaining, the Pacific Coast athletes drove 65 yards down the field in fifteen plays to score their touchdown. Lugging the ball on practically every play was Gaius (Gus) Shaver, former All-American back of the University of Southern California. And it was the ex-Trojan thunderbolt who finally tallied the touchdown with but three minutes of action left.

SHAVER BREAKS LOOSE

Arrived at the 23-yard mark, Shaver suddenly broke loose and scampered to the 4-yard line before White was able to bounce him out of bounds. The eastern gridders, remindful of their heroic work in other tight spots -- they repulsed their foes three times on the 5-yard line—stood with their backs to the wall and fought their heads off to the last ditch.

Shaver made two at center. On second down the ball was still nine inches from the goal. Another smash by Shaver and the pigskin was two inches from a touchdown. On his fourth and final crack Gus drove over right tackle, leaping high into the air and got the tally amid thunderous cheers. Ed Kirwan, former California quarterback, kicked goal and that was the victory.

SCORE BY QUARTERS

| | | | | |
|---|---|---|---|---|
| East | 0 | 0 | 0 | 6—6 |
| West | 0 | 0 | 0 | 7—7 |

SCORING

Touchdowns—Strange (Yale,) for East; Shaver (U.S.C.,) for West.

Conversions—Kirwan (California,) for West.

SUBSTITUTIONS

East—Crickard for Mays, Gahagan for Bouscaren, Strange for Myerson, Yeckley for Hall, Lead for Barres, Wister for Hamley, Zundel

(Continued on Page 13, Column 1)

## ROWING STARS ALL SET TO GO

### *Seven Championships at Stake This Week*

### *Three Classes Ready for Opening Heats Today*

### *Finals Saturday Expected to Draw Over 100,000*

**The rowing races start at 3 p.m. today instead of 1 p.m. as formerly announced in the official program.**

BY RALPH HUSTON

**The navies and the armies of the world swing into action this week in peace-time competition that tops the second half of the Olympic Games program.**

**While cavalry mounts and officers contest in the gruelling and thrilling equestrian events the Olympic Marine Stadium at Long Beach will be the scene of bitter battles for seven rowing championships.**

The oarsmen get into action today, with three of the seven classes meeting in the opening heats. Singles scullers, pairs without coxswains and fours with coxswains will struggle over the 2000-meter course with winners advancing to the finals, which are scheduled for Saturday.

Tomorrow the popular eight-oared flotillas, the double sculls, and fours

(Continued on Page 15, Column 1)

## WHEN BRAZILIAN SPIRIT BOILED OVER

**Here** is a remarkable action photo of yesterday's riot at the Swimming Stadium. Brazilian water polo players became aroused at the asserted unfair decisions of the referee and charged him to provoke a riot that police were forced to quell. The referee, Bela Komjadi of Hungary, is cringing in a dugout between the milling police and angry Brazilian players. The player glowering down at Komjadi is Da Cilva, 200-pound Brazil goalie, while the one whose arm is upraised is Jacobina, a forward. [A. P. photo by E. F. Tinsley]

## AMERICA ANNEXES FIRST YACHTING CHAMPIONSHIP

BY WALDO DRAKE

All four favorite skippers continued their consistent march toward Olympic yachting titles off Point Fermin yesterday, as the fourth round of the seven-day sailing program was run off before a ten-mile westerly.

**Commodore Owen Churchill captured for the United States the first yachting title of the Tenth Olympiad by sailing his eight-meter sloop Angelita to her fourth straight victory over Santa Maria, the Canadian entry. Sir Ronald Maitland, the Canadian skipper, informed the judges last night that since the Angelita had defeated him so decisively and because there is no chance for the Santa Maria, even if she wins all three remaining races, he and his crew acknowledged the Angelita as the Olympic champion.**

Bissbi, the Swedish whirlwind, won her fourth successive start in the six-meter division, beating the American boat Gallant by the enormous margin of five minutes and twenty seconds.

Caprice, sailing for Canada, was again third. A remarkable thing about Bissbi's performance today is that she sailed the twelve-mile windward and leeward course in the fresh breeze in 2h. 24m. 20s., a minute and six seconds better than the much heavier eight-meter Angelita's time over the same route. She now has 12 points in the series against 8 for Gallant, so that she may finish second in all of the remaining races and still win the title. Numerous bets have been placed among the Southland racing sailors, however, that Bissbi will win all seven races without a break. That is an astonishing performance to expect of any racing yacht, but both Bissbi, her skipper, Tore Holm, and her faultless crew have proved an astonishing combination practically unbeatable as far as Gallant and Caprice are concerned in any weather or on any point of sailing.

**In the star-class, Skipper Gilbert Gray of New Orleans continued his no less remarkable performance by winning again with the American sloop Jupi-**

(Continued on Page 13, Column 6)

## EVENTS TODAY

ROWING

Long Beach

3 p.m.—Four oar with coxswain, two heats.
3:40 p.m.—Two oar without coxswain, two heats.
4:20 p.m.—Single sculls, two heats.

SWIMMING

Olympic Park

Morning

10 a.m.—400-meter free style, men (semifinals.)
10:30 a.m.—100-meter back stroke, women (trials.)
10:50 a.m.—Exhibition high diving, men.
11:05 a.m.—Exhibition high diving, women.

Afternoon

3 p.m.—Springboard diving, women.
3:15 p.m.—FINALS, 400-meter free style, men.
3:30 p.m.—Water polo, Germany and Hungary reserves vs. United States reserves.
4:15 p.m.—Water polo, Brazil vs. Japan.

OLYMPIC STADIUM

8 a.m.—Gymnastics, parallel bars, horizontal bar, Indian clubs.
2:30 p.m.—Lacrosse, Canada vs. United States.

OLYMPIC AUDITORIUM, 1801 South Grand avenue

2 p.m.—Boxing.
8 p.m.—Boxing.

FENCING

Armory, Olympic Park

1 p.m.—Swords.

LOS ANGELES HARBOR

12 noon—Yachting.

Tickets for today and tomorrow at each stadium.

# OLYMPIC GAMES SECTION

# Los Angeles Times

EQUAL RIGHTS

LIBERTY UNDER THE LAW — TRUE INDUSTRIAL FREEDOM

VOL. LI. C WEDNESDAY MORNING, AUGUST 10, 1932.


# MORE OLYMPIC RECORDS CLIPPED

UNITED STATES

Again the United States flag goes to the top of The Times with three championships won yesterday. Australia, Japan, Hungary, Sweden and Italy each won a first place.

## HOW NATIONS STAND

The unofficial point totals for the Olympic Games (all sports) follow:

| | | | |
|---|---|---|---|
| United States | 489½ | Poland | 25 |
| Italy | 154½ | Czecho-Slovakia | 24 |
| Finland | 141 | Ireland | 23 |
| Sweden | 134 | Denmark | 23 |
| Germany | 107½ | Argentina | 15 |
| France | 104 | South Africa | 13 |
| Great Britain | 93½ | Belgium | 6 |
| Japan | 75 | New Zealand | 6 |
| Canada | 69 | Switzerland | 5 |
| Hungary | 50 | Latvia | 5 |
| Holland | 32 | Philippines | 4 |
| Australia | 31 | Brazil | 1 |
| Austria | 26 | | |

When the United States Got Its Worst Drubbing in Rowing Classic

Poland's two-man boat is shown sweeping to victory in heat of race at Long Beach yesterday, with the oarsmen of France close behind and the Americans a poor third.

[Times photo by Bill Snyder]

## NIPPONESE HAVE GREAT DAY ANNEXING POINTS

### *Sons of Japan Add Fifteen Tallies to Their Total; Americans Star in Gymnastics*

## FIRST-PLACE WINNERS

Number of first places won yesterday:

| | | |
|---|---|---|
| United States | 3 | (Gymnastics) |
| Australia | 1 | (Swimming) |
| Japan | 1 | (Swimming) |
| Hungary | 1 | (Gymnastics) |
| Sweden | 1 | (Yachting) |

Total number of first places won to date (all Sports:)

| | | | |
|---|---|---|---|
| United States | 25 | Sweden | 8 |
| France | 6 | Italy | 6 |
| Finland | 5 | Japan | 3 |
| Great Britain | 2 | Germany | 2 |
| Australia | 2 | Hungary | 2 |
| Ireland | 2 | Poland | 2 |
| Czecho-Slovakia | 1 | Holland | 1 |
| Austria | 1 | Canada | 1 |
| Argentina | 1 | | |

BY PAUL LOWRY

Japan carried its threat to the peace and security of American minds still farther in the swimming contests of the Tenth Olympiad yesterday.

Winning one race and outdistancing the field in the semi-final heat of another race, the slim sons of Nippon carried on the amazing story of record breaking that has made this Olympic Games the most sensational in history.

Japan added fifteen points to its total to America's eight in the water sports.

Only in minor sport, where Japan offered no challenge, was the United States able to pile up the points.

YANKS ADD TEN MORE

This was in gymnastics, where three first places, carrying with them ten points apiece, fattened the American total.

**No day in the Olympics is complete without new records, and yesterday was no exception. Four swimming marks were hung up—Jauan's 8m. 58.4s. in the 800-meter relay race for men, Claire Dennis's 3m. 6.3s. in the 200-meter breast stroke for women, Eleanor Holm's 1m. 18.3s. in the 100-meter back stroke and Takashi Yokoyama's 4m. 51.4s. in the 400-meter semifinals for men.**

Today Japan sends Tokoyama out to beat America's Buster Crabbe and S. Taris of France, the world's champion, in the 400-meter free-style swim.

However, not all the glory of the day went to Japan and America.

Bissbi, the Swedish six-meter boat, won the championship by beating America's Gallant for the fifth straight time.

Hungary also got on the map with a victory in gymnastics, Stephen

(Continued on Page 18, Column 1)

## OLYMPIC FIGHTS OPENED BY JEERING OF REFEREE

### *Al Romero Loses to British Welter on Foul in Sensational Fight; Mexicans Protest Verdict*

BY PAUL LOWRY

Fouling David McCleave of Great Britain in the last thirty seconds of the third round, Al Romero of Mexico lost a sensational battle at the Olympic last night. It was the featured wind-up of the first day of boxing in the Olympic Games.

Romero, local Mexican welterweight, was out in front by a couple of blocks when he hit McCleave low. The Englishman had been on the canvas twice in the first two rounds. He came back to make a hot fight of it in the last round.

Following an examination by three doctors it was announced that no evidence of a foul had been discovered. However, the decision stood despite a heated protest by the Mexican delegation. The In-

(Continued on Page 16, Column 1)

## HORSES, RIDERS IN ACTION TODAY

### *Dressage Event First to Show Mount's Ability*

Horses come triumphantly into the Olympic Games today.

The first event will be the Dressage.

This will last two days.

It will be held at the Raviera Country Club.

Teams are entered from Sweden, Mexico, France and the United States . . . each country entering three horses and riders.

The nearest approach to "dressage," in the language of the lay-

(Continued on Page 14, Column 1)

## *New Records*

Subjects of King Neptune assaulted world and Olympic recors yesterday. Here they are:

800-meter relay—Japan (Miyazaki, Yusa, Toyoda, Yokoyama) 8m. 58s., a new Olympic record and likely to be accepted as world record.

200-meter breast-stroke (women) new world record of 3m. 6.3s. by Clare Dennis of Australia.

100-meter back-stroke (women) new world record of 1m. 18.3s. by Eleanor Holm of the United States.

## *Yankee Water Poloists Tie German Squad*

Never once in the lead but refusing to quit their gallant, albeit somewhat rough, battling against a favored European team, a hard-fighting band of Los Angeles Ath-

(Continued on Page 16, Column 2)

## *PARADE OF GYMNASTS TO OPEN FETE TONIGHT*

**Full details of the international gymnastic carnival in which 1000 athletes will participate as a feature of the Olympic gymnastic competition at Olympic Stadium at 8 p.m. tonight, have been announced by officials.**

**Starting with a grand parade of athletes, rivaled only by the parade of nations at the opening ceremonies, the show will be presented in acts.**

**After the parade the athletes will march to a reserved section of seats in the east end of the stadium, leaving the entrants representing the Turnverein-Germania, 250 men and women, on the field for the first**

(Continued on Page 16, Column 4)

## PEARCE THRILLS THRONG IN SINGLE SCULL VICTORY

### *Bobby Easy Winner Over Yank; Poland Flag Waves as Two Rowing Trials Annexed*

BY RALPH HUSTON

OLYMPIC MARINE STADIUM (Long Beach) Aug. 9.—Bobby Pearce, Australia's mighty man of maritime maneuvers, sculled his way to an easy victory today in the first heat of the 1932 Olympic singles sculls championship, and definitely demonstrated that all the experts who had picked him to retain the crown he won at Amsterdam in 1928 were somewhat more than Wright.

Forced to row only against Bill Miller, the American champion, because of the withdrawal of Herbert Buhtz, German entrant, Pearce rowed his way, easily and lazily,

(Continued on Page 12, Column 1)

## ITALIAN WINNER IN SWORD TEST

### *Cornaggia-Medici Carries Off Individual Epee Title*

BY EDITH DURBIN

The Italians are at the top of the see-saw again. Giancarlo Carnaggia-Medici, known to the European fencing aristocracy as "The Gentleman of Milan," was winner of the individual epee competition yesterday afternoon.

Battling his way up from the bottom at the beginning of the event, the descendant of the ancient

(Continued on Page 17, Column 2)

## FIELD DAY HELD BY SWIM STARS

### *Two World's Marks Fall in in Exciting Events*

### *Eleanor Holm Hangs Up New Back-stroke Standard*

### *Mermaids Shine as Races in Full Swing*

BY BOB RAY

A dainty American beauty who once spurned an offer to enter the Follies, a 16-year-old Australian schoolgirl, and four of those super-swimmers that Japan is rearing to astonish the aquatic world, shared honors in yesterday's program as another page of record-shattering

(Continued on Page 15, Column 1)

## BISSBI WINS SIX-METER YACHT TITLE FOR SWEDEN

BY WALDO DRAKE

Bissbi, the Swedish whirlwind masquerading as a six-meter sloop, yesterday trounced Gallant, erstwhile American Olympic hope, for the fifth successive time, off Point Fermin, thereby sewing up Sweden's second Olympic six-meter sailing championship. She spotted Gallant, excellently sailed by Ted Conant, a nice lead and the windward berth at the start of the race and then slipped out of the so-called "impossible position" to win by the wide gap of 3m. 18s.

Caprice, which has been contend-

(Continued on Page 14, Column 1)

[Large picture by Carroll, inset by Wide World]

What Happens When World's Greatest Sculler Starts Sculling

Here is Bobby Pearce of Australia, setting too fast a pace for William Miller of the United States in heat of individual sculls race at Long Beach course yesterday. Inset is Bobby Pearce himself.

[Wide World photo]

Strain Too Great—Italian Faints

Here is Ricardo Divora of the Italian crew, who collapsed after a hot race in which he and his fellow countrymen swept to victory over Germany, New Zealand and Brazil in the four oar with coxswain contest.

# GOLDEN BEAR CREW OUTCLASSES CANADA

[Times photo by Bill Snyder]

California Crew Sweeps to Stirring Triumph Over Canadian Oarsmen

Berkeley's Golden Bears, America's representatives in the eight-oared event, came through in fine fashion yesterday at the Olympic rowing course to beat the highly touted Leander crew of Canada. The Yanks won by a scant length. The Bears represented the United States at Amsterdam in 1928 and brought home the championship.

OLYMPIC GAMES SECTION
Los Angeles Times
EQUAL RIGHTS
LIBERTY UNDER THE LAW — TRUE INDUSTRIAL FREEDOM
VOL. LI. C — THURSDAY MORNING, AUGUST 11, 1932.

UNITED STATES

Four championships captured yesterday by the United States sends the Stars and Stripes to the top of The Times today. France won one first place.

## SONS OF UNCLE SAM AGAIN WIN CRUSHING VICTORIES

### *Americans Snag Four Firsts and Make Sensational Sweep of Women's Diving Events*

BY BRAVEN DYER

Smashing victories scored by Uncle Sam's sons and daughters sent the United States point total soaring again yesterday. It was as big a day as this country has had during the Olympic Games. Four firsts, with a sensational clean sweep in the women's diving, gave followers of the red, white and blue something to shout about for a long time to come.

No more spectacular triumph has been recorded during the international classic than that of Clarence (Buster) Crabbe in the 400-meter swim. This husky son of the Hawaiian Islands defeated Jean Taris of France by inches in the most thrilling finish recorded at the Swimming Stadium.

Crabbe had to come from behind in the last fifty meters to accomplish his feat and as it was the two great swimmers were only one-tenth of a second apart at the finish.

**RECORD LOWERED**

Keeping pace with the breakers of track and field records, all six finalists in the 400-meter swim lowered the Olympic record. Crabbe's time was 4m. 48.4s., with that of Boy Charlton, Australian, who was sixth, 4m. 58.6s. The old Olympic mark was 5m. 1.6s., made by Alberto Zorrilla of the Argentine in 1928.

**Second only to Crabbe's tri-**

(Continued on Page 15, Column 4)

## HOW NATIONS STAND

**The unofficial point totals for the Olympic Games (all sports) follow:**

| | | | |
|---|---|---|---|
| United States | 557½ | Poland | 25 |
| Italy | 181½ | Czecho-Slovakia | 24 |
| Finland | 150½ | Ireland | 23 |
| Sweden | 141 | Denmark | 23 |
| France | 130½ | Argentina | 15 |
| Germany | 110½ | South Africa | 13 |
| Great Britain | 98 | Belgium | 6 |
| Japan | 84 | New Zealand | 6 |
| Canada | 73 | Switzerland | 5 |
| Hungary | 61½ | Latvia | 5 |
| Holland | 33 | Philippines | 4 |
| Australia | 32 | Brazil | 1 |
| Austria | 27 | | |

## CRABBE ANNEXES SWIM THRILLER BY INCHES

### *Yank Noses Out Taris of France to Set 400-Meter Mark; American Girls Sweep Diving Event*

BY BOB RAY

The spell of Japan's domination in the men's Olympic swimming events was broken yesterday, broken by two giants of men—Buster Crabbe of America and Jean Taris of France—and the American proved himself supreme in a finish that gave 10,000 cheering fans a thrill of a lifetime. He won by inches in the finals of the 400-meter free style to give the United States its first Olympic championship in the men's events.

It was a battle of champions, for Taris holds the world's record for the distance, and it took a champion to beat a champion. Both annihilated the previous Olympic mark as they splashed their way up and down the pool eight times in a battle that took all that was in them and left onlookers limp with excitement.

**FRENCHMAN LEADS**

Taris, the Frenchman, led all the way until the last few meters, when Crabbe, fighting with a determination that would not be thwarted, caught up with his rival and then grasped the finish rail just one-tenth of a second before the sturdy son of France.

**It was the first men's swimming final yet decided that had not been won by Japan's water-wonders, and Buster, his heart set on winning, after his victory, could no more hold back the rush of enthusiasm that enveloped him than could the throng of American aquatic rooters in the stands.**

Before Buster could get out of the water his dad leaned down over the edge of the pool to give his son—his champion—a kiss that probably will mean more to both of them, in years to come, than the gold medal that goes to a "Champion Olympique."

**EAR-TO-EAR SMILE**

In answer to the ringing congratulatory shouts from the fans, Buster simply bounced up and down in the water, a smile that went from ear to ear and back again overspreading his face. Buster was glad, and he wanted the world to know it.

Crabbe's triumph, coming on top of Georgia Coleman's victory in the women's springboard diving finals, made it a great day for the United States. Two championships out of two finals held, and both won by America.

It was an emphatic victory for the American women in the diving event, little Katherine Rawls of Miami, and Jane Fauntz of Chicago capturing second and third places for a clean sweep.

**Returning to that thrilling 400-meter finals, Taris started**

(Continued on Page 14, Column 1)

## UNITED STATES HAS BIG DAY

Yesterday was one of the biggest days ever enjoyed by the United States in Olympic competition. Triumphs by Buster Crabbe in the 400-meter swim, Georgia Coleman, Kathryn Rawls and Jane Fauntz in the ten-foot diving and the victory of the California crew over Canada at Long Beach kept the American flag waving in the breeze. The star boat, Jupiter, although finishing third in yesterday's heat, won this competition with thirty-eight points and cannot be defeated for the title. Americans finished one-two-three in the tumbling and our boxers are still among the best in the program of fisticuffs. For the first time the U.S.A. scored in the dressage, taking third at Riviera with the famous French horse Taine, the winner.

## MAGNIFICENT TAINE WINS COVETED DRESSAGE TITLE

### *Commandant Lesage Rides French Gelding in Intricate Tests; America's Olympic Third*

BY FRANK ROCHE

The most highly educated horse on earth today is Taine, black gelding son of France.

This thoroughbred, mounted by Commandant Xavier Lesage, senior instructor of Samur, won his right to this coveted honor yesterday morning at Riviera Country Club Olympiad arena when he gave a lesson in dressage to nine other mounts representing the nations of the world.

**France's system of horsemanship boomed again when Commandant Marion took second honors with the fine horse Linon. The United States registered as Capt. Tuttle and his noble animal Olympic, a former thoroughbred race horse, took third place. This marked the first time in history that the Americans have placed so high in Olympic Games dressage competition.**

Nature provided the perfect setting in California's Riviera for the crowning of Centaur.

Flashing against the crowded tiers of appreciative humanity were the scarlets, blues, gold, silver, greys and kahki of the world's military leaders in the field of equestrian sport.

**It was the horse's day and no**

(Continued on Page 12, Column 1)

[Carroll photo]

The End of the Trail

Canada's four-oared crew gave its all but failed to beat the blue-shirted Italian quartet yesterday at Long Beach. This remarkable photo shows the Canadian boat immediately after it crossed the finish line. Only one of the four is still erect. Two others are slumped down with their heads bowed. The other boy can be seen lying on his back completely exhausted.

## CALIFORNIA OARSMEN PUT ON WHIRLWIND FINISH

### *Leander Eight in Valiant Effort, but Loses by Three-Quarters Length; Crowd Thrilled*

BY RALPH HUSTON

MARINE STADIUM (Long Beach) Aug. 10.—By three-quarters of a length, California's amphibious Golden Bears defeated the great Leander crew of Canada today, in the "crucial" heat of the Olympic eight-oared rowing championships.

By three-quarters of a length, gained largely in the last 200 meters of the gruelling 2000-meter grind, "California's crew in California's Olympics" surged over the finish line in this man-made lagoon, to qualify for the finals of the blue-ribbon classic, which will be held here Saturday.

Just three-quarters of a length, but a margin of victory gained in so convincing a fashion that already the experts are convinced that it will be Italy, not Canada, which California will have to beat in those same finals. Italy already has qualified.

**STILL HAS CHANCE**

The blazing, blue-shirted Romans won the first heat of the eight-oared event today, smashing the favored Great Britain boat down under a torrent of power and fast stroking. Canada, and the rest of the defeated boats, have another chance to qualify tomorrow, in the repachage races, which will select the two other crews to go into the finals against the United States and Italy.

**Slow to start, but fast to finish, California's valiant eight shot across the finish line with tremendous force, generated by a sudden high-stroking rush in the last 200 meters that forced the Canadians, determined as they were, to acknowledge defeat.**

The four boats — United States, Canada, Germany and New Zealand were off to a perfect start. Canada immediately opened up with a furious forty-beat stroke to take the early lead, followed by Germany in second position, New Zealand third, and the Californians last.

They were well bunched, with Canada having a slight lead for the next few hundred meters. At 500 meters, Canada led by eight feet over the Americans, with Germany third and New Zealand fourth. Coming to the 1000-meter mark, Canada was hitting about thirty-six strokes to the minute, and the Californians had picked up to the same spot, and were threatening.

**The breeze had died down, but Lane No. 1, where the Bears were stroking, was a bit rough. Passing the 1000-meter mark, Norrie Graham, midget coxswain, called upon his men to overhaul the flying Leander crew. Increasing the beat only slightly, the Bears appeared to find new power to send into their oars. Stroke by stroke they overhauled the battling men from Hamilton.**

Stroke by stroke they gradually forged to the front.

**"DOWN THEY COME"**

At 1500 meters, the Californians were in front by a quarter of a length. Forty strokes to the minute they hammered out. Steady as clockwork. Smoothly. The game Canadians raised the beat to forty-two and above, but they could not match California's surging, amazing power. It was still a great boat race. The Bears led by three-quarters of a length. Canada had the same margin over Germany, and New Zealand was hot on the trail of the oarsmen from the Fatherland.

At 1750 meters Graham gathered

(Continued on Page 16, Column 1)

## JUPITER MAKES IT TWO FOR YANKEE YACHTSMEN

BY WALDO DRAKE

Gilbert Gray, master helmsman from New Orleans, yesterday won the Olympic star-class yachting title for the United States by bringing his sloop Jupiter home third in the last, but one of the seven Olympic races off Point Fermin. Jean Herbulot, canny Frenchman from Cannes, won the race in Tramontane, when he beat Ernest Ratsey, sailing the British boat Joy, by 59s., but Jupiter's third-place finish gives her a total of 38 points, so that she is Olympic champion without sailing today's final race.

Tramontane and Joy, however, are tied for second honors with 29 points and it is a certainty that the scrap today between these two excellent skippers, with two good boats, is going to be by all odds the most torrid affair of the entire race week. Except for losing all his points in the first race when his

(Continued on Page 16, Column 6)

OLYMPIC GAMES SECTION
Los Angeles Times
EQUAL RIGHTS
LIBERTY UNDER THE LAW — TRUE INDUSTRIAL FREEDOM

VOL. LI. FRIDAY MORNING, AUGUST 12, 1932.

# ELEANOR HOLM WINS SWIM CROWN

ITALY

Italy's flag goes to the top of The Times today with three championships won. The United States won two first places while India, Holland and Hungary captured one each.

## HOW NATIONS STAND

The unofficial point totals for the Olympic Games (all sports) follow:

| | | | |
|---|---|---|---|
| United States | 613½ | Poland | 29 |
| Italy | 228 | Czecho-Slovakia | 24 |
| Finland | 158½ | Ireland | 23 |
| Sweden | 141 | Argentina | 15 |
| France | 135½ | South Africa | 13 |
| Germany | 113½ | India | 10 |
| Great Britain | 107 | Belgium | 6 |
| Japan | 94 | New Zealand | 6 |
| Hungary | 76½ | Switzerland | 5 |
| Canada | 75 | Latvia | 5 |
| Holland | 43 | Philippines | 4 |
| Australia | 37 | Spain | 4 |
| Austria | 27 | Brazil | 1 |
| Denmark | 27 | | |

## RECORDS STILL TOPPLE AS OLYMPICS NEAR END

### *India's Crack Field Hockey Team Drubs America, 24 to 1; Boxing Finals Tomorrow*

## FIRST-PLACE WINNERS

Number of first places won yesterday:

| | | |
|---|---|---|
| Italy | 4 | (Gymnastics, fencing) |
| United States | 2 | (Swimming, gymnastics) |
| India | 1 | (Field hockey) |
| Holland | 1 | (Yachting) |

Total number of first places won to date (all sports:)

| | | | |
|---|---|---|---|
| United States | 31 | Great Britain | 2 |
| Italy | 11 | Australia | 2 |
| Sweden | 8 | Poland | 2 |
| France | 8 | Holland | 2 |
| Finland | 5½ | Czecho-Slovakia | 1 |
| Japan | 3 | Austria | 1 |
| Hungary | 2½ | Argentine | 1 |
| Germany | 2 | India | 1 |
| Ireland | 2 | Canada | 1 |

India's famous field hockey team, unbeaten in two Olympic Games, came more than 12,000 miles for the easiest competition of this gigantic international program. Yesterday the colorful athletes slaughtered the United States under a deluge of goals. The score was 24 to 1 and might have been worse, but the visitors gradually ran themselves to death peppering the net with one spectacular shot after another.

In 1928 the turbaned thunderbolts swept through the Amsterdam Olympics without a single score registered against them.

India's opponents improved this time. They got two goals. One was scored by Japan and the other by the United States. If there is any fun in moral victories the Japanese and Yankees have it coming—but it is doubtful if they are doing any shouting.

**SWIM CROWN WON**

Miss Eleanor Holm, who passed up the Follies for a berth on the American swimming team, came through for the United States yesterday. She won the 100 meters backstroke for women before 10,000 spectators at the swimming stadium. Bonnie Mealing of Australia finished second, four yards behind the American beauty.

**Japan's youthful stars dominated the situation in the men's events. Y. Tsuruta and R. Koike broke the Olympic record in the 200 meters breast stroke trials. S. Makino splashed his way to a new Olympic mark in one of the 1500-meter heats. His time was 19m. 53.3s. for the grind.**

Buster Crabbe, winner of the 400 meters final the day before, put up a strong battle in his heat of the 1500 meters yesterday, but had to bow to the superior speed of Kitamura, 14-year-old Japanese sensation. The young Japanese negotiated the distance in 19m. 55.2s.

**RIDERS TAKE GLORY**

Two American horsemen, Maj. Harry Chamberlain, ace of the Yankee riders, and Capt. E. Y. Argo, topped a brilliant field in the first day of the three-day test at Riviera.

**Continuation of the rowing heats at Long Beach sent Canada and Great Britain into the finals of the eight-oared event, slated for tomorrow. By winning their heats these two crews stamped themselves as worthy foes for California and Italy in the classic eight-oared race.**

Although neither the Englishmen nor Canucks were able to equal the fast time registered by Italy on the preceding day, this was due

(Continued on Page 12, Column 3)

## HOLLAND LANDS FOURTH OLYMPIC YACHT TROPHY

BY WALDO DRAKE

Young Bob Maas yesterday rang down the curtain on the Olympic yacht racing program at Los Angeles Harbor by winning for Holland the twelve-foot dinghy championship. The Dutch boy's victory was due in no sense of the word to spectacular work—for he won but two races out of eleven—but simply because he sailed consistently in every event.

**LYON TAKES OPENER**

In the two final races sailed off Cabrillo Beach yesterday by the tiny twelve-footers, Bill Lyon of the United States won his first race in the morning event, sailed in only a ghost of a breeze—while victory in the afternoon affair went to long and lanky Silo Treleani of Italy. The final event of the "round robin" series was sailed in a twenty-mile westerly that afforded the European skippers plenty of the breeze for which they have been asking all week.

**Bob Maas finished seventh and ninth out of ten starters in yesterday's races, but his point total is 85 markers, against 79 for LeBrun, of France, who takes second honors. Third is Amat Cansino of Spain, with 77 points; fourth, Edgar Behr of Germany with 74 points; while Reginald Dixon of Canada is fifth with 72 and Ernest Ratsey of Great Britain, sixth, with 70 points. For the United States, Bill Lyon took 67 points and seventh place.**

The sympathy of all yachtsmen who witnessed the Olympic regatta goes out to the two French skippers, Jean Herbulot of the good star-class sloop Tramontane, and Jacques LeBrun, sailing in the twelve-foot class. LeBrun, probably the best of all the monotype skippers, would now be the champion but for having been disqualified yesterday in the morning race on protest of the Italain Treleani. LeBrun finished fourth in the event and the 8 points he lost cost him the championship.

Herbulot, who handles the tiller

(Continued on Page 10, Column 3)

## AMERICA LEADS IN HORSE EVENT

*Chamberlin First in One of Three-Day Tests*

*Second Honors Also Taken by United States*

*Holland, Winner for 1928, Given Third Place*

BY FRANK ROCHE

For the first time in the history of the Olympic Games equestrian competition the Stars and Stripes of the United States were raised to the top of the masthead. Maj. Harry Chamberlin, ace of American horsemen, and his mount, Pleasant Smiles, saw to this yesterday at the Riviera Club as the first chapter in the three-day event, the most gruelling test of a horse known, was run off.

Not only did the United States win first prize in the high schooling competition, but they topped it off by taking second honors when Capt. E. Y. Argo and Honolulu Tomboy were judged next best.

**HOLLAND THIRD**

Holland, the winner of the 1928 Olympic Games prize in the three-day event, took third honors. Lieut. Pahud De Mortanges and Marcroix accounted for that position.

**They put the horse's memory to test yesterday.**
**Today they test his heart.**

Starting at 8:45 o'clock this morning, this crack field of horses and men will participate in the second phase of the three-day event known as the endurance test.

Only one horse and rider missed his routine yesterday. Capt. Barrigueete, the Mexican who was riding Monza, went halfway through the forty-one movements when it was discovered that he had overlooked something. The judges rushed from the pavilion and the performance was held up.

However, the judges sent the Mexican back over the route again and he went through it without a miss.

**HORSE TAKES JUMP**

Mexico had another bad break when El Trero, a fiery looking animal, jumped out of the arena. His rider, Capt. Perez Allendo, regained his poise quickly.

The first horse in the arena was Japan's gelding, Kyu Gun, ridden by the popular Lieut.-Col. Kido. Kyu Gun is Japanese bred of Australian parents. He differed in appearance as did the others in the three-day competition from the horses that performed Wednesday in Dressage.

**Kido and Kyu Gun went along in cool fashion. The little Japanese got a big hand when he came to a halt with a snappy salute at the end of the ride.**

Next in the ring was Duiveltje, one of Holland's great horses, with Lieut. Schummelketel up. This animal has four prettily marked white feet. Duiveltje is a mahogany bay. He appeared to have plenty of fire and should give a good account of himself in the terrific test today.

The little Mexican Monza was next.

**AMERICAN APPLAUDED**

The first American horse and rider in the arena yesterday was Lieut. Earl Thomson and Jenney Camp. They made a fine impression on the spectators, who gave them a tremendous hand as they completed their performance.

Sweden sent Marokan and Capt. Hallberg of the Royal Hussars into the arena next. They went through the motions without much ado and got a hand for their coolness as they trotted off.

**Capt. Nara of Japan's crack field artillery strutted in on Sonshin. This rangy-looking**

(Continued on Page 10, Column 1)

Kusuo Kitamura Found This Worse Than the Race

He was terrified to the point of panic when a horde of newspaper photographers closed in on him at the conclusion of his sensational victory over Buster Crabbe at the Swimming Stadium.

[Times photo]

## TWO FAST ENGLISH CREWS WIN PLACES FOR FINALS

### *American Supremacy Challenged as Great Britain and Canada Come Back Strong*

BY RALPH HUSTON

MARINE STADIUM (Long Beach) Aug. 11.—Britannia, majestic ruler of the seas, will send forth two boats Saturday to challenge the supremacy of the United States in the Olympic eight-oared rowing championship.

Great Britain and Canada today won the two reclassification heats in the blue-ribbon event, gaining the right to meet the United States' representative, California, and Italy, in the final struggle over the 2000-meter route.

The Cambridge crew, representing Great Britain, showed to much better effect than it did in losing to Italy to triumph over New Zealand in the first heat today, while Canada, beaten by California yesterday, flashed to victory over Germany and Japan. Rowing straight into a stiff breeze, neither victor was able to equal the time made by either California or Italy yesterday, the 6m. 28.2s. figure made by the blue-shirted Italians being four-fifths of a second faster than that turned in by California. Canada rowed 7m. 3 1-5s. today, and Great Britain 6m. 49s.

The entire program today was made up of these reclassification events, crews beaten in earlier races being given a second chance to qualify for the final races scheduled tomorrow and Saturday.

**The United States leads all nations with finalists in five of the seven events. Great Britain**

(Continued on Page 13, Column 1)

## CAN YOU BEAT IT! WHAT'S USE HAVING YOUR NAME IN TYPE?

You can be a world champion and the hottest headline name of the day, and still folks won't know you.

The mighty Babe—Didrikson is the last name—sat in a parked automobile in downtown Los Angeles late yesterday afternoon. She was waiting, with a couple of Texas friends, to start for the airport to take off for home—Dallas is the town.

A friendly Los Angeles policeman, noticing the Texas license, stopped to talk.

Yep, she was in town for the Olympics, Babe told him. Had he seen any of the games?

He had, he admitted, "but, say, I never did get to the stadium when that girl from Texas was performing. I'd sure like to have seen her. They say she was a wow."

"You're lookin' at her right now, pardner," Babe told him.

The copper almost fell over backward. Babe had to produce a couple of letters and show him her wrist watch with her name engraved thereon to convince him.

They left him—for Dallas—standing on the sidewalk and shaking his head in bewilderment.

## *HUNGARY SABER TEAM WINS AND ITALY SECOND*

BY EDITH DURBIN

If ever you need a second in a saber duel, pick a Hungarian!

Victorious against United States, Italy and Poland by large margins, the Hungarians won highest honors in the Olympic saber team competition fenced yesterday afternoon at the State Armory.

Italy placed second through her

(Continued on Page 10, Column 7)

## AMERICAN GIRL IN CLOSE RACE

*Bonnie Mealing, Australia, Comes in Second*

*Holland Threat Withdraws Due to Insect Bite*

*Contest Seen by 12,000 as Many Turned Away*

BY BOB RAY

Eleanor Holm, one of your Uncle Sam's niftiest nieces, brought another Olympic swimming championship to America yesterday when she backstroked her way to a decisive triumph over the world's best in the only final race at the stadium.

A capacity crowd of 12,000 fans—many persons were turned away from the gates — saw the fair Eleanor, the girl who turned down a contract from Ziegfeld in order to keep on with her aquatic career, splash her way to the Olympic title that placed her on top of the swimming world in her chosen event.

**FOUR YARDS AHEAD**

**Arms flailing backward and red-tinted fingernails flashing in the sunlight and shadows, Miss Holm reached the finish of the 100 meters four yards ahead of Bonnie Mealing, Sydney girl who carried Australia's hopes. Next came Valerie Davies, good-looking British brunette fro mWales; Phyllis Harding, Great Britain's former record-holder for the event: Joan McSheehy, tall, striking New York blande, and finally, Joyce Cooper, veteran English paddler of the 1928 Olympiad.**

Although she failed to equal her world and Olympic record of 1m. 18.3s., established in the semifinals, Miss Holm won decisively from a great field that lacked only, Marie Braun-Philipsen, husky Dutch swimmer who was unfortunately unable to race because of a sudden attack of blood poisoning. The Holland girl, who won the event at Amsterdam in 1928, was bitten by an insect in the pool during the morning trials of the women's 400 meters and had to withdraw when complications set in.

Another American miss, Lenore Kight, of Pennsylvania, established a new Olympic record in the morning's 400-meter free-style trials when she negotiated the distance in 5m. 40.9s. to better Martha Norelius's mark of 4m. 42.8s. set at Amsterdam in the 1928 Games.

Miss Kight's two American mates, Helene Madison and Norene Forbes, also qualified for the semifinals of the 400 meters.

**JAPAN TRIUMPHS**

In the men's trials of 1500 meters and 200 meters breast stroke events, and in the semifinals of the men's 100 meters backstroke, the brown sons of Japan swept to triumph, qualifying their three entrants in each of the events.

Two Japanese swimmers, Y. Tsuruta and R. Koike, broke the Olympic record for the 200 meters breast stroke, turning in identical times of 2m. 46.2s., while in the 1500 meters S. Makino, another Nipponese flash, set the fastest time of 19m. 53.3s. fo rthe lengthy grind.

**Kitamura, the 14-year-old Japanese phenom, won the feature heat of the 1500-meter trials, leading both Buster Crabbe, America's 400-meter champion, and Jean Taris of France in the fine time of 19m. 55.2s. Crabbe and Taris put on**

(Continued on Page 12, Column 1)

## EVENTS TODAY

**LACROSSE**
**Will Rogers announcing, at Olympic Stadium**
2:30 p.m.—Canada vs. United States.

**SWIMMING**
**Olympic Park**
Morning
9 a.m.—FINALS. High diving, women.
9:45 a.m.—400-meter free style, women, semifinals, two heats.
Afternoon
3 p.m.—200-meter breast stroke, men, semifinals, two heats.
3:20 p.m.—1500-meter free style, men, semifinals, two heats.
4:20 p.m.—FINALS, 100-meter back stroke, men.
4:35 p.m.—FINALS, 100-meter relay, women.
4:55 p.m.—WATER POLO, Germany vs. Japan.

**ROWING**
**Long Beach Marine Stadium**
3 p.m.—Four oar with coxswain.
3:40 p.m.—Two oar without coxswain.
4:20 p.m.—Single sculls.
5 p.m.—Two oar with coxswain.

**EQUESTRIAN SPORTS**
**Riviera Country Club**
8:15 a.m.—Three Day Event, Steeple and Cross Country.

**BOXING**
**Olympic Auditorium, 1801 South Grand avenue**
2 p.m. and 8 p.m.

**FENCING**
**Armory, Olympic Park**
8 a.m. and 1 p.m.

**GYMNASTICS**
**Olympic Stadium**
8 a.m.—Parallel Bars and Flying Rings.

**SHOOTING**
**Elysian Park**
9 a.m. and 2 p.m.—Pistols.

**YACHTING**
**Los Angeles Harbor**
12 noon.
Tickets for today and tomorrow at all stadiums.

## HERE'S LOOKING AT YOU, ELEANOR

Pretty Miss Eleanor Holm, who yesterday scored another triumph for United States by beating a brilliant field for the Olympic championship in the 100-meter back stroke for women. Miss Holm set the world's and Olympic record for the event in the semifinals but did not equal it yesterday.

[Times photo]

OLYMPIC GAMES SECTION

Los Angeles Times

EQUAL RIGHTS — LIBERTY UNDER THE LAW — TRUE INDUSTRIAL FREEDOM

VOL. LI. C SATURDAY MORNING, AUGUST 13, 1932.

# JAPANESE SMASH SWIM RECORDS

UNITED STATES

Four championships won yesterday keeps the Stars and Stripes at the top of The Times. Italy, won two first places while Japan, Germany, Great Britain and Australia each took one.

## HOW NATIONS STAND

The unofficial point totals for the Olympic Games (all sports) follow:

| Nation | Points | Nation | Points |
|---|---|---|---|
| United States | 680½ | Austria | 27 |
| Italy | 264 | Czecho-Slovakia | 24 |
| Finland | 165½ | Ireland | 23 |
| France | 144½ | Argentina | 15 |
| Sweden | 144 | New Zealand | 14 |
| Germany | 130½ | South Africa | 13 |
| Great Britain | 124 | India | 10 |
| Japan | 116 | Belgium | 6 |
| Hungary | 86½ | Switzerland | 5 |
| Canada | 78 | Latvia | 5 |
| Australia | 47 | Philippines | 4 |
| Holland | 46 | Spain | 4 |
| Poland | 42 | Brazil | 4 |
| Denmark | 29 | Uruguay | 4 |

## JAPANESE MERMEN TAKE STRANGLE-HOLD ON TITLE

### *Nipponese Swimmers Pass Yankees in Point Column; American Girls Uphold Their End*

BY BRAVEN DYER

When Wallace Irwin began his "Letters of a Japanese Schoolboy" little did he realize the sturdy sons of Nippon would one day be the toast of the world in the Olympic Games. That day has now arrived. Thanks to the sensational swimming of her brown-skinned paddlers Japan passed the United States in the race for point honors yesterday and now appears certain to capture the Olympic Games championship in this branch of competition.

Japan's total is now 56 to 46, for the United States, with additional first places due today. This is only for men's events, the American girls having upheld their end magnificently.

**Fourteen-year-old Kusuo Kitamura, 15-year-old Shozo Makino, 16-year-old Reizo Koike and Masaji Kiyokawa, who is an old man compared to the others, showed the rest of the world how to go places in the water. When these kids get their full growth they'll probably have to carry anchors to give their foes a chance.**

Kiyokawa won the 100-meter backstroke title and two of his countrymen, Irie and Kawatsu made it a clean sweep by taking second and third.

Makino shattered the Olympic record in his semifinal heat of the grueling 1500 meters, swimming the distance in 19m. 38.7s., as compared to the old mark of 19m. 51.8s. In this heat the nimble Nippon, who gained terrific speed by powerful leg action, defeated Buster Crabbe of the United States, who, however, qualified for the final today.

Little Kitamura won the other heat in 19m. 51.6s., also breaking the Olympic record. Jean Taris, famous French swimmer, piled up an early lead in this race but the smooth-swimming son of Nippon cut loose with a terrific sprint in the closing laps and Taris could do nothing about it.

**To add to Japan's day of days, all her swimmers qualified for the 200-meter breast-stroke final this afternoon. Reizo Koike won his heat, followed by Yoshiyuki Tsuruta, while Shigeo Nakagawa was third in the other test.**

Had it not been for the feminine

(Continued on Page 10, Column 6)

## THEY DIDN'T WAIT FOR TIME OR TIDE

It used to be noised about that "time and tide wait for no man," but these four stellar women sprinters put a little reserve English on the axiom when they paddled to a new world's record in the 4x400 meters relay yesterday. They are Josephine McKim, Helen Johns, Eleanor Geratti Saville and Helene Madison, and they turned the 400 meters in 4m. 38s. [A. P. photo]

[Carroll photo]

They See Olympic Glory in the Distance

Jenny Camp, ace of the world's courageous horses, skimming over one of the rigid high jumps on the cross-country run. Lieut. E. F. Thomson is the rider.

## NIPPONESE BOYS HAVE GREAT DAY

### *First Three Places Nabbed in Backstroke Final*

### *Olympic Mark Lowered for 1500-Meter Race*

### *Two Capacity Crowds See Thrilling Events*

BY BOB RAY

With Japan's sensational aquatic wonders sweeping the boards in the men's events and America's marvelous mermaids upholding the Stars and Stripes in the women's competion, two capacity crowds were treated to a day of thrills and record breaking in yesterday's morning and afternoon Olympic programs at the swimming stadium.

After Dorothy Poynton, Georgia Coleman and Marion Dale Roper had finished one-two-three for the United States in the women's high diving to open the morning performance, a great American quartet, composed of Josephine McKim, Helen Johns, Eleanor Garatti Saville and Helene Madison, wound up the day in a blaze of glory by breaking through the water to a new world's record of 4m. 38s. in the women's 4x100 meters relay.

RECORDS SMASHED

But in between these two magnificent efforts by the fair Yankee divers and paddlers it was all Japan. Nipponese performers carried off the first three places in the 100 meters backstroke, the only men's final to take place, and the Rising Sun of Japan also waved supreme in semifinals of the 1500 meters free style and the 200 meters breast stroke. Olympic records were cracked to smithereens in both of the latter two events by the Japanese wonders of the waves.

**The outstanding exhibition of the day was provided by Shozo Makino, 16-year-old Japanese schoolboy, who doffed his horn-rimmed glasses in the second heat of the 1500-meters, dived in and then negotiated the gruelling distance in the spectacular time of 19m. 51.8s. to hang up a new Olympic record. Just previously, in the first semifinal, Makino's 14-year-old team-mate, Kuzuo Kitamura had reeled off the distance in 19m. 51.6s. to lower Arne Borg's Olympic mark of 1928 by .02s.**

Japanese enthusiasts are predicting that Makino and Kitamura will finish one-two in the finals today, but they will be given plenty of competition by America's Buster Crabbe, 400-meter champion, and Jean Taris, the favorite aquatic son of France. It should be a whale of a race, but it seems almost inconceivable that the winner will be able to get under the record set by Shozo.

In the breast-stroke semifinals all three Japanese entries qualified for today's finals when Reizo Koike, another 16-year-old wonder, spread-eagled his way to victory in the first heat in the record time of 2m. 44.5s. Yoshiyaki Tsuruta, the Japanese who set the previous Olympic mark of 2m. 48.8s. at Amsterdam, finished second to Koike and succeeded in bettering his old mark, also. Tsuruta was timed in 2m. 45.4s.

Erwin Sietas, husky German, and Teofilo Yldefonzo, spectacular Filipino, also got under the 1928 record in the second heat of the semifinals.

Summary:

**In the diving Miss Poynton, 16-year-old Fairfax High School girl, outclassed the field despite injuries to her back and ribs suffered in practice Thursday. She took the lead from the start and wound up with almost a 5-point lead over Georgia Coleman, the springboard champion. Marion Dale Roper, another local girl, was a close third to Miss Coleman.**

Pretty Ingeborg Sjoquist of Sweden led the invading feminine forces, while the other two places went to Ingrid Larsen of Denmark and Etsuko Kamakura of Japan.

The men's backstroke finals saw Masaji Kiyokawa score an easy vic-

(Continued on Page 11, Column 6)

## AMERICAN HORSES DASH TO NEW GLORY IN TEST

### *Lieut. Thomson With Jenny Camp Rides to First-Place Honors; Dutch Champion Well Up*

BY FRANK ROCHE

An American horse and rider won!

An American team won!

Jenny Camp, bay mare, with Lieut. E. F. Thomson, United States Army, up, is the most courageous horse in the world today.

Maj. H. D. Chamberlin, with Pleasant Smiles; Capt. E. Y. Argo, on Honolulu Tomboy, and Lieut. E. F. Thomson comprising America's team in the three-day equestrian event, defeated the international field when every one of the Yankee riders finished the gruelling twenty-two and one-half-mile test yesterday with commendable scores. The race was the second day's event in the three-day horse competition.

It must be the dream of every thoroughbred horse at sometime or other to win this grueling Olympic event, conducted yesterday over Southern California's picturesque country just outside the city limits of Los Angeles. For some it was a nightmare.

A huge amphitheater provided by nature herself was the setting for the endurance test that started at Beverly Boulevard and then moved on to the Riviera field, where the horses and mounts performed on a very tricky steeplechase course which all but took the life's blood of two of the contestants.

More than 100,000 persons lined the twenty-two-and-a-half-mile course watching the cross-country, obstacle jumps and the mile-and-one-third gallop to the finish. Spectators stood on hilltops, alongside the highway and on top of automobiles at vantage points from the Riviera to Baldwin Hills. Thousands of automobiles were parked adjacent to the course and the occupants stood in the heat of the noonday sun eagerly scanning the

(Continued on Page 8, Column 1)

## SCORES OF HORSES

Here are the standings in the three-day equestrian event:

| Rider | Horse | Nation | 1st day | 2nd day | Totals |
|---|---|---|---|---|---|
| Lt. Thomson | Jenny Camp | U.S. | 300 | 1271 | 1571 |
| Lt. de Mortanges | Marcroix | Holland | 311.8 | 1242 | 1553.8 |
| Lt. von Rosen | Sunnyside Maid | Sweden | 310.6 | 1241.5 | 1552.1 |
| Maj. Chamberlin | Pleasant Smiles | U.S. | 340.3 | 1107.5 | 1447.8 |
| Capt. Hallberg | Marokan | Sweden | 290 | 1129 | 1419 |
| Lt. Schummeketel | Duivelte | Holland | 267.5 | 1105 | 1372.5 |
| Capt. Yamamoto | Kingo | Japan | 257.3 | 1092.5 | 1349.8 |
| Capt. Argo | Honolulu Tomboy | U.S. | 333 | 907.5 | 1240.5 |
| Lt. van Lennep | Henk | Holland | 277.5 | 797.5 | 1075 |

Team totals for two days:

United States .................... 4259.33

Holland .................... 4001.33

Note: Holland and the United States are the only nations that remain in team competition.

## HOPES OF AMERICANS DIMMED AS SALICA AND FEARY LOSE RING TIFFS

### NATIONS' BOXING SCORE

| Nation | Won | Lost | Nation | Won | Lost |
|---|---|---|---|---|---|
| United States | 12 | 6 | Denmark | 3 | 2 |
| Germany | 10 | 5 | Great Britain | 3 | 3 |
| Italy | 8 | 7 | Mexico | 2 | 5 |
| South Africa | 7 | 3 | Finland | 2 | 2 |
| Argentina | 7 | 5 | Philippines | 1 | 3 |
| Sweden | 4 | 2 | Ireland | 1 | 5 |
| Canada | 4 | 6 | Greece | 0 | 1 |
| France | 3 | 6 | New Zealand | 0 | 3 |
| Hungary | 3 | 1 | Japan | 0 | 5 |

BY PAUL LOWRY

Uncle Sam's chances of winning the boxing championships of the Tenth Olympiad suffered a rude setback last night. Two of his representatives—Louis Salica, flyweight, and Fred Feary, heavyweight from Stockton—passed out of the picture.

As a result only two Americans are left in the finals—Eddie Flynn, welterweight, and Carman Barth, middleweight.

Three other countries have the United States topped. Germany, Argentina and South Africa will each send three men into the last round, and between them they offer little solace or comfort to Yankee Battlers. Then there is Italy with two men in the running.

The American finalists have to face two of the toughest fighters in the tournament. Flynn meets Erich Campe of Germany and the Barth tangles with a young bull from the Argentine pampas named Amado Azar.

Only in total matches won and lost does the United States lead—12 and 6, as against 10 and 5, by Germany.

The most atrocious decision of the week kept Louis Salica, United States flyweight, from reaching the finals. He defeated Stephen Enekes easily, but the Hungarian was given

(Continued on Page 10, Column 1)

## BOBBY PEARCE ROWS TO TITLE

### *Australian Wins Olympic Crown Second Time*

### *Crack Boatsman Announces Scull Career at End*

### *Bill Miller Given Second Place for America*

MARINE STADIUM, LONG BEACH, Aug. 12.—Bobby Pearce, one of the greatest oarsmen ever to scull through the briny, closed his spectacular career here today by capturing, for the second time, the Olympic singles scull crown, a feat never before accomplished in Olympic history.

His long arms giving him a tremendous reach, his huge shoulders generating tremendous power, the Australian drove to victory over three rivals, in the most important of the four Olympic rowing championships decided today.

Pearce said, when he arrived here several weeks ago, that the present Olympics would mark the close of his rowing career.

NEW CHAMPIONS

The newly crowned champions are:

Singles sculls—Bobby Pearce, Australia.

Pairs without coxswain—Lewis Clive and Hugh R. A. Edwards, Great Britain.

**Pairs with coxswain—Joseph A. Schauers, stroke; Charles M. Kieffer, bow, and Edward F.**

(Continued on Page 11, Column 1)

## EVENTS TODAY

ROWING

Long Beach Marine Stadium

3 p.m.—FINALS. Four oar without coxswain.
3:40 p.m.—FINALS. Double sculls.
4:20 p.m.—FINALS. Eight-oar shells.

EQUESTRIAN SPORTS

Olympic Stadium

2:30 p.m.—Three-day event. Jumps.

SWIMMING

Olympic Park

Morning

9 a.m.—FINALS. High diving. Men.
11 a.m.—Trials for international relay race.

Afternoon

3 p.m.—Exhibition high diving. Men.
3:15 p.m.—FINALS. 200-meter breast stroke. Men.
3:30 p.m.—FINALS. 400-meter free style. Women.
3:45 p.m.—FINALS. 1500-meter free style. Men.
4:15 p.m.—Exhibition high diving. Women.
4:30 p.m.—Water polo. Japan vs. Hungary.

FENCING

Armory, Olympic Park

1 p.m.—Sabers.

BOXING

Olympic Auditorium, 1801 South Grand avenue
2 p.m. and 8 p.m.

SHOOTING

Elysian Park

9 a.m. and 2 p.m.—Carbines.

Tickets will be on sale at each stadium.

## *THEY CAME QUIETLY—LEAVE IN GLORY*

BY MURIEL BABCOCK

Their glory now belongs to the past.

Girl athletes of the Tenth Olympiad, moderns of moderns, who flashed their twentieth-century prowess for brief moments on Olympic field and in Olympic pool, are getting their bags packed ready to go home. Back home to jobs, to school, to sewing and cooking and the more prosaic duties of everyday life.

SOME HAVE GONE

Some of the girls have already gone. Stella Walsh and the Polish contingent. Babe Didrikson, the British and Canadian track and field teams, the Austrians. The little Brazil girl has gone back to the coffee ship in the harbor.

The Germans go on Monday. The Dutch girls depart Wednesday. Little Miss Ingeborg Sjoquist, the Swedish diver—despite all the conversation about her potential motion-picture qualities—is going quietly back to Sweden. She leaves tonight.

Yvonne Godard goes Monday with the French boys. The Danish girls are supposed to leave Monday; also the lone South African who is left in the hotel.

SIDE TRIP PLANNED

The Japanese swimming team is taking a little side trip en route home. Mrs. Shirayama, chaperon and coach, has made arrangements for them to see Yosemite National Park, but the track and field girls are sailing the first of the week.

The four Australian girls, who were the first to arrive in Los Angeles, will be among the last to leave. They will be at Chapman Park Hotel all next week. They have seen the girls from other countries come into Los Angeles country by country, and now they will see them depart. Thelma Kench, the New Zealand sprinter, will be the very last to go. There is no boat for New Zealand for another two weeks.

VOL. LI. C SUNDAY MORNING, AUGUST 14, 1932. 

# GOLDEN BEARS NOSE OUT CLOSE CREW VICTORY

[Carroll photo]

On Their Way to Second Successive Olympic Crew Championship

California's Golden Bears are shown leading the sturdy sons of Italy in the pulsating eight-oared boat race at Long Beach yesterday. Canada is third, followed by Great Britain. The picture shows the position just before the finish.

Once more the Stars and Stripes goes to the top of The Times with seven championships won. Hungary won three first places, Japan, South Africa and Argentina each won two, while Great Britain, Canada and Holland won one each.

## AMERICA SPLITS DAY'S THRILLS WITH JAPAN

### HOW NATIONS STAND

The unofficial point totals for the Olympic Games (all sports) follow:

| | | | |
|---|---|---|---|
| United States | 799½ | Argentina | 40 |
| Italy | 300 | Denmark | 34 |
| Sweden | 170 | Austria | 30 |
| Finland | 169½ | Ireland | 26 |
| Germany | 166½ | Czecho-Slovakia | 24 |
| France | 150½ | New Zealand | 14 |
| Japan | 150 | Philippines | 14 |
| Great Britain | 146 | Mexico | 13 |
| Hungary | 126½ | India | 10 |
| Canada | 99 | Belgium | 6 |
| Holland | 61 | Switzerland | 5 |
| Australia | 50 | Latvia | 5 |
| Poland | 42 | Spain | 4 |
| South Africa | 41 | Brazil | 4 |
| | | Uruguay | 4 |

Closing their competition in a glory, athletes representing Japan and the United States, hogged the limelight in yesterday's final day of Olympic Games competition.

Swimmers from the Land of the Rising Sun captured the 1500-meter

(Continued on Page 2, Column 1)

## QUEEN HELENE SETS NEW WORLD'S SWIM RECORD

### *Mark Smashed for 400 Meters; Buster Crabbe Badly Beaten by Two Japanese Boys*

BY BOB RAY

Two American girls broke the world's record in the 400-meters, a pair of Japan's famous schoolboys smashed to smithereens the Olympic Games 1500-meters mark, and they rang down the curtain on the greatest swimming meet in history as the Xth Olympiad's aquatic program ended yesterday before 12,000 fans who crowded to capacity the Los Angeles Stadium.

"Queen" Helene Madison lowered her own world's record by 2.5s. to win the women's thrilling 400-meters finals, but she had to do it to barely beat out pretty Lenore Kight, Yankee miss from Pittsburgh, by less than a foot.

Kusuo Kitamura, 14-year-old Japanese phenom, lowered the old 1500-meter mark by 39.4s., swimming the distance in the second fastest time ever made, but still had a battle on his hands right to the finish from his 16-year-old Nipponese mate, Shozo Makino.

**YANKS WIN DIVING**

In one of the other two finals decided yesterday America continued to maintain its world superiority in the diving with Harold (Dutch) Smith, Mickey Riley and Frank Kurtz taking the first three places in the high-platform event. This effort gave the sons and daughters of United States first, second and third places in all four diving events—a feat never before accomplished by one country in Olympic Games competition.

**The fourth final of the day ended with Yoshiyuki Tsuruta, defending Japanese champion, beating out his 14-year-old rival—Reizo Koike—for the title in the 200-meter breast stroke. Koike set a new Olympic record in the event in Friday's semifinals so he has that to console him even though Tsuruta did win the championship.**

Japan's great paddlers won every men's swimming event but the 400 meters, which went to Buster Crabbe of America, to capture the aquatic title, but the sensational mermaids of United States made a run-away of the women's Olympic competition to even up the score.

**The most exciting race of the final day was staged by Miss Madison and Miss Kight in the 400-meter classic. Almost shoulder to shoulder they swam—Queen Helene and Princess Lenore—as eight times up and down the pool they gave their all in a magnificent race that will never be forgotten by those who saw it.**

**BUT LENORE DID**

Who was this mite of a miss from Pennsylvania who was daring to end the reign of Queen Helene, the greatest woman swimmer of all time? Surely she couldn't keep up this killing pace, which left all the others trailing in their wake, down that last fifty meters. But Lenore Kight did. By ever so slight a margin Miss Madison was leading as they began a final sprint. Twenty-five meters to go and the crowd screaming and yelling for these two courageous Amazons.

Legs pumping faster and faster, arms flailing the waves in a flurry of foam, they battled side by side in their lanes marked off by red strips of wood that stood out in bold relief against the green-blue water.

**Every last ounce of effort they put into their last few strokes and grasped for the finishing rail—Queen Helene the winner by inches, still the ruler of the waves, but Lenore even greater**

(Continued on Page 2, Column 1)

## GREAT EQUESTRIAN JUMPERS WILL VIE TODAY AT STADIUM

Prix des Nations, one of the most thrilling events in horse competition, is on the Olympic equestrian bill this afternoon at the stadium as the grand finale of the Games. Horsemen representing five of the world's leading nations send the pick of their jumpers into this competition today. The nations entered are the United States, Japan, Sweden, Holland and Mexico. The horsemen will compete over a course on which will be from sixteen to twenty jumps that will average from four-feet three to five-feet three in height.

## *YANKEE HORSEMEN WIN FIRST TEAM VICTORY IN OLYMPICS HISTORY*

BY FRANK ROCHE

Strike up the band! Play "Yankee Doodle!" The American equestrian team rode to town with an Olympic feather in its hat yesterday as the three-day event, themostgruelling test of a horse known to man was concluded.

**Led by its ace horseman, Maj. Harry Chamberlin, the Americans took the team championship in Olympic equestrian sports for the first time in history. Chamberlin and his team buddies, Lieut. Earl Thomson and Capt. E. Y. (Eddie) Argo cinched the title yesterday at the stadium, defeating Holland's crack trio, Lieut. de Mortanges, Lieut. Schummelketel and Lieut. von Lennep, in the last phase of the three-day test over twelve hazardous jumps.**

Holland took the individual championship, thanks to its massive horse Marcroix, ridden by Lieut Pahud de Mortanges of the Dutch cavalry service. The victory of Marcroix and Lieut. de Mortanges was the second Olympic Games honor—Marcroix having placed second in Amsterdam in 1928.

**JENNY CAMP STAR**

But Marcroix had to have everything that has been said about him to defeat America's fine little bay mare Jenny Camp, and young Lieut. Earl Thomson of our Fort Riley cavalry school. There were less than 3 points difference in the ratings between Marcroix and Jenny Camp on the judges' cards following yesterday's performance. Morcroix had 186.1, and Jenny Camp 189.

**For sometime to come there will be discussion in horse circles about the judging of the two performances of Lieut. Thomson and Lieut. de Mortanges if the aftermath that followed the announcement of the decision is any criterion.**

Thomson had 60 points in penalties called against him after covering the jumping course. Jenny Camp, his mare, did not hesitate once and had only one knockdown. She flicked two feet in the water on that jump for just an instant. The horse before Jenny Camp, Duiveltje, a Dutch horse ridden by Lieut. Schummelketel, had one refusal. Also Duiveltje knocked down a jump and touched the water with two feet. For that the judges gave the pair 58 in penalties. Thomson's performance, which was within a hair breadth of being clean, netted him 60 in penalties.

**THOMSON ON SPOT**

Thomson went into the competition in the lead, having won the toughest part of the three-day event—the endurance phase.

**Marcroix had 40 in penalties called against him which sent the title back to Holland for another four years. The big Dutch horse turned in a great performance but at that he had a knockdown and tipped his feet in the water jump.**

The Americans had the satisfaction of having the cleanest performance of the day, in addition to winning the team championship. Little Capt. Eddie Argo on Honolulu Tomboy, a fine mare, rode like a will-of-the-wisp. They barely touched a leaf on any of the jumps as they skipped around the course. The judges had a hard time giving Capt. Eddie any penalties, but they did decide to give him one for 3-4 of a point. That must have been for coming early to the training field one day last week.

Argo's performance brought the

(Continued on Page 4, Column 1)

## ITALY SECOND, CANADA THIRD IN EXCITING RACE

### *Oarsmen in Neck to Neck Finish in Most Spectacular Battle of Olympic Program*

BY RALPH HUSTON

MARINE STADIUM (Long Beach) Aug. 13.—Eight tall, husky boys from California's Inland Empire, and a small, hawk-nosed young man from Pendleton, Or., heart of the great Northwest, are the best oarsmen of the world.

Born and raised in agricultural communities, these stalwarts, from the University of California, representing the United States, today, won the most sensational crew race in Olympic history. Many of them had never seen an oar until they went to college, but today they are monarchs of all they survey.

But only by one foot are the Golden Bears the rowing champions of the world. One foot, gained through the last five meters of this gruelling classic, was the margin of victory these fighting Golden Bears had over the blue-shirted huskies from Italy. About three-quarters of a length back of these stout-hearted Italians came the feared Canadian crew, which had two feet on the Cambridge eight, representing Great Britain.

**HUGE CROWD SEE RACE**

More than 50,000 people saw this great race, which will go down in rowing history as one of the classics of all time. The valiant Bears, second in the early stages of the race, took the lead at the half-way post. Two hundred meters from home they saw that margin swirled away as the high-stroking Italians surged past with a mighty sweep and power.

**Maddened, the Bears swept up their stroke. Inch by inch the prow of the shell crept up to even terms. Inch by inch it forged in front. Twenty-five meters from home it was a dead heat. Five meters to go, and Italy seemed to have gone on top again. From somewhere those maddened Bears found new power. From somewhere they discovered new-found strength. From somewhere they brought forth a frenzied burst of speed. And somehow they shot home a winner by a margin so narrow that no one knew who had won until the judges made their decision.**

"California's crew in California's Olympics" had kept the faith. They had no great Pete Donlan at stroke, as had the California crew in 1928. They had no shirt-waving Don Blessing at coxswain. They had no color. But they did have eight smooth-working oarsmen. They did have power. They did have speed. They did have heart, and courage, and the will to win. They needed all of that to win today.

**GLORIOUS IN DEFEAT**

They needed it to beat those blue-shirted Italians. Italy is great, but California is one-foot greater. Too much praise cannot be given the Italians for their majestic, mighty efforts. And they were glorious in defeat.

"How much?" they asked the judges, after the decision had been rendered. "Only that. Too bad. Well, okeh," and they warmly grasped the hands of the men who had beaten them.

**There was a slight delay at the start. A fairly strong cross-breeze was blowing, and the Canadians fouled the bow-line, which holds the shells in position at the start of the race. Finally they got away, and the Italians, hitting a high forty-two, immediately jumped into the lead, closely followed by the Bears, Canada and Great Britain in that order.**

At 350 meters the Americans and Italy were almost even. Italy was maintaining its high stroke, so typical of all Italian crews. The Americans were rowing about thirty-six. The 500-meter mark found the Bears finally in front, a spurt having carried them to a quarter-length advantage over Italy. Canada and Great Britain, neck and neck, were a half-length behind.

**BREEZE INTERFERES**

Passing the opening which leads to Alamitos Bay, Norrie Graham ran into trouble. The breeze, always strongest in lane No. 1, pushed

(Continued on Page 2, Column 2)

## FLYNN, BARTH WIN GAMES RING TITLES

### *Two Americans Annex Olympic Boxing Championships to Give Yankees Team Honors; Lovell Wins Heavyweight Crown*

BY PAUL LOWRY

The United States won the final spoils of the Tenth Olympiad—the boxing championships.

Aided by a gift decision to Carmen Barth, Cleveland, O., American boxers captured titles in the welterweight and middleweight classes, and finished with a slight margin over Argentina and South Africa.

Both these countries won a pair of crowns, but the United States had two first and three third places as against two firsts and a second for Argentine and two firsts for South Africa.

**As a crowning touch to the championships the winners were herded into the ring after the fights, introduced and then left to the mercy of the photographers and the autograph hounds.**

The fluky decision to Barth in the middleweight class gave the United States the team title.

He was outpointed decisively by Amado Azar, young bull of the Argentine, but the nod went to the American, and was in keeping with the one that eliminated Louis Salica, United States flyweight, from the tournament in the semi-finals.

**POLICEMAN BEATEN**

Eddie Flynn of New Orleans cinched his crown by scoring a knockdown in the last round. He beat Erich Campe, a German policeman.

Three Germans fought in the finals. None of them won, but each was presented with a bouquet of red roses tied with streamers in Germany's national colors.

One unofficial total gave the United States 9 points for the team championship, Argentine 8, South Africa 7, and Germany 6.

Hungary crowned the first Olympic Games boxing champion when Stephen Enekes of Budapest defeated Francisco Cabanas, Mexico's lone representative in the flyweight finals.

It was a close, hard-fought battle

(Continued on Page 4, Column 1)

### BOXING CHAMPS

**Flyweight — Stephen Enekes (Hungary.)**

**Bantamweight — Horace Gwynne (Canada.)**

**Featherweight—Carmelo Robledo (Argentina.)**

**Lightweight — Lawrence Stevens (South Africa.)**

**Welterweight — EDWARD FLYNN (UNITED STATES.)**

**Middleweight — CARMEN BARTH (UNITED STATES.)**

**Light-heavyweight — David Carstens (South Africa.)**

**Heavyweight—Santiago Lovell (Argentina.)**

(Carroll photo)

Olympic Champions—But What a Finish!

By the scant margin of one-fifth of a second the Golden Bears of California defeated Italy in the eight-oared final at Long Beach yesterday afternoon. Canada is shown coming up for third honors.

1933
1942

MANY AMERICANS NEEDED A LIFT AS THE GREAT DEPRESSION CONTINUED INTO THE 1930s, AND MANY got it from sports. Splendid achievements in virtually all sports marked the era, events so remarkable they not only helped to take people's minds off the economy but they continue to stir memories today.

Baseball's first All-Star game was played as part of the Chicago World's Fair in 1933, and the following year in the second game, Carl Hubbell of the New York Giants struck out five American League batters in a row with his baffling screwball. The batters were Babe Ruth, Lou Gehrig, Jimmie Foxx, Al Simmons, and Joe Cronin—five of the best.

On June 15, 1938, a Cincinnati pitcher, Johnny Vander Meer, pitched his second consecutive no-hit game, beating Brooklyn, 6–0. No other pitcher has been able to duplicate that remarkable feat.

Two streaks that are still major league records were set by Lou Gehrig and Joe DiMaggio. Gehrig, the New York Yankees' first baseman, played a record 2,130 consecutive games before illness forced him from the lineup on April 30, 1939. Gehrig died two years later, on June 2, 1941.

The other record—a record that has resisted assaults from the game's greatest stars for more than forty years—was Joe DiMaggio's fifty-six-game hitting streak. Starting on May 15, 1941, the Yankee star hit safely ninety-one times and batted .408 until two Cleveland pitchers, Jim Bagby and Al Smith, stopped him without a hit on July 17.

In 1936 the nation's baseball writers voted the first five players into the Hall of Fame, selecting Ty Cobb, Babe Ruth, Christy Mathewson, Honus Wagner, and Walter Johnson.

In 1933 boxing got a new heavyweight champion when a giant Italian named Primo Carnera knocked out Jack Sharkey in the sixth round with a right uppercut. But Carnera's reign lasted less than a year. On June 14, 1934, Max Baer knocked the Italian down twelve times in eleven rounds to win the title. The championship changed hands again the next summer when James J. Braddock beat Baer on a fifteen-round decision.

Meanwhile a young black boxer from Detroit named Joe Louis—and known as the "Brown Bomber" —was making news. After being knocked out in the twelfth round by the German Max Schmeling, in a 1936 fight, Louis got a shot at Braddock's championship on June 22, 1937, and won it by a knockout in the eighth round. At age twenty-three Louis became the youngest boxer to hold the heavyweight title and only the second black man, the first being Jack Johnson.

Horse racing had been a popular sport in New York for many years, and the Kentucky Derby was fifty-nine years old before Southern California got its first major track. On December 26, 1934, the Santa Anita Turf Club held the first races on its spacious Arcadia grounds. The next year Azucar won the first Santa Anita Handicap.

Gene Sarazen produced one of golf's most dramatic moments in the 1935 Masters tournament. Seemingly out of contention, he sank a 220-yard 4-wood shot on the fifteenth hole in the final round to record the most famous double-eagle in history. He eventually won the championship in a playoff.

May 25, 1935, was a day track-and-field fans will long remember. Here is what a slender black Ohio State sophomore named Jesse Owens did that day in the Big Ten outdoor championships at the University of Michigan:

3:15 P.M.—Won 100-yard dash, equaling Frank Wykoff's world record of 9.4 seconds.

3:25 P.M.—Long jumped 26 feet, 8¼ inches to break the world record. Pressed for time, Owens took only one jump.

3:34 P.M.—Broke the world record in the 220-yard dash by three-tenths of a second, winning in 20.3 seconds.

4:00 P.M.—Broke an eleven-year-old world record by winning the 220-yard low hurdles in 22.6 seconds.

Owens gained even more fame in the 1936 Olympic Games at Berlin, winning four gold medals. He won the 100-meter dash in 10.3 seconds, a time that broke the Olympic and world record but was not recognized because of the wind. However his record of 20.7 seconds for the 200-meter dash was allowed. He also broke the Olympic record in the long jump, sailing 26 feet, 5⁵⁄₁₆ inches, and ran a lap on the winning 400-meter relay team, which set a world record of 39.8 seconds.

The Berlin Olympics were knee deep in controversy before they began. While the Los Angeles Games were still in progress in 1932, one Nazi newspaper denounced the Olympics as an "infamous festival dominated by Jews." Hitler came to power after Germany was awarded the Games, and there were attempts by some countries, including the United States, to take them away from Berlin.

But in Berlin the Games remained, and about five thousand athletes from fifty-two nations competed in what was technically and artistically a splendid competition. However, Hitler caused a flap by congratulating German winners and snubbing champions from other countries.

It has been widely reported that Owens was one of the athletes snubbed. But Owens did not win his first medal until later in the competition and by then, by most accounts, Hitler had stopped congratulating the winners. One black American athlete ignored by Hitler was the high-jump winner Cornelius Johnson. But saying it was Owens makes a better story, of course, because no athlete had so dominated the Olympic Games.

# CARNERA FLATTENS SHARKEY IN SIXTH

SPORTS
Los Angeles Times
FRIDAY MORNING, JUNE 30, 1933.

## Bill Henry Says—

NEW YORK, June 29. (Exclusive)—Just a few of the things I'd like to see happen at the A.A.U. national track and field championships at Chicago tomorrow night:

Ben Eastman really spring a comeback and confound all hands by winning the 800 meters in 1m. 50s. or better—he'd have to run that fast probably to beat Glenn Cunningham and Hornbostel.

Glenn Cunningham take the world's 1500-meter and mile run records away from Jules Ladoumegue of France in one race—they'll let him run on to the mile if he wants to.

Walter Marty of Fresno State flabbergast the East by beating George Spitz and breaking the world's record to boot.

**WHAT PROBABLY WILL TAKE PLACE**

And here are a few things I rather expect will happen when the boys get together on Soldier Field:

Ralph Metcalfe to win both sprints and beat Jesse Owens—who is likely to become a bit agitated in such fast company.

The saddle-colored Cleveland high-school wonder to out-leap all the big college and athletic club stars in the broad jump.

Louisiana State's sensational team to suffer a reaction from the N.C.A.A. victory and not do quite so well this time.

Somebody in the discus and shot to get those weapons out far enough to leave the folks gaping and gasping.

**U. S. DAVIS CUP TEAM IS SERIOUS**

Saw John Van Ryn, Wilmer Allison and George Lott—three-quarters of the United States Davis Cup squad, off for Europe the other night.

A midnight sailing is quite an event, too.

"They're pulling that same old bunk about Cochet and Borotra—but those birds will be in there playing the same championship tennis," the boys said.

The public interested in the return of the Davis Cup need not fear that the American team doesn't know what it's up against.

The boys are really in earnest. They're not worrying about the French until they get by the winners in the final round.

**DOUBLES TEAM IS VITAL FACTOR**

No matter whom they meet a great deal is going to depend on the two boys of whom the least is said—Lott and Van Ryn, the doubles team.

The singles matches frequently are divided.

And the team with the winning doubles combination is the one that comes home with the bacon.

If Australia beats England—as is certainly possible, Crawford is likely to win two singles matches.

Yes, he might beat the great Vines.

And France will always be dangerous as long as Cochet is playing—no matter how bad he looked in the French championships.

**TENNIS POLITICS IN THE OFFING**

The American scheme of letting Lott and Van Ryn, an experienced combination, worry about the doubles and leaving Vines and Allison free to concentrate on singles is a good move.

I hope that politics doesn't interfere.

There are a lot of volunteers trying to run the Davis Cup squad and the best they're likely to do is to ruin our chances of winning.

## SERAPHS SLUG SEAL HURLERS FOR 11-7 WIN

### *Cherubs Capture Third in Row*

BY BOB RAY

Unleashing their best shots in the second inning to chase across seven runs, Mons. Jacques Lelivelt's ascending Angels clinched yesterday's contest early and then coasted to an 11-to-7 triumph over Skipper Ike Caveney's trained Seals, who enacted the role of victims.

The victory gave the Seraph sluggers their third straight over San Francisco, and, as an added attraction, enabled Leroy Herrmann, the side-winding ace of the Cherub chucking corps, to chalk up his fourteenth triumph of the current campaign. Mr. Herrmann, however, was pounded for thirteen hits by the losers and did nothing to distinguish himself.

**Bill Henderson, who used to be known as a speed-ball pitcher, but didn't look like one yesterday, started on the mound for the San Franciscans and escaped to the showers uninjured during that second-inning Angel bombardment. Ed Stutz replaced Henderson in time to get on the throwing end of Jim Oglesby's mighty home-run wallop into the bleachers, which ended the scoring for the big round.**

Caveney told young Dick Freitas, youthful southpaw, to go in and see what he could do about the very embarrassing situation and what he did was to yield four more Seraph runs during the remainder of the struggle.

The contest was punctuated by five home runs, which brought the total of circuit clouts to thirteen for the week. Jack Fenton and Jerry Donovan hit the bulb out of the lot for the Seals, while Oglesby, Jigger Statz and Hughie McMullen blasted four-baggers for the home guards. Mr. McMullen, by the way, completely circled the bases after hitting the bulb into the center-field stands, thus dispelling all talk that he didn't have enough energy to do so. Hughie, you know, hit the ball over the right-field screen in the tenth inning to win Wednesday's game, but stopped at first base. Thus, he didn't get credit for his homer and the Angels won by a score of 6 to 5, instead of 8 to 5, which really doesn't seem very important anyway, although some people thought it was.

Inasmuch as the Angels sewed up the game in the second inning, your correspondent deems this a very appropriate time to let you in on the details of this seven-run scoring orgy.

**Lillard opened the round with a fly on Donovan, but Dittmar walked and Orv Mohler, who filled in at second base for the injured Jimmy Reese, followed with a single. Herrmann also walked and the bases were bulging with prospective Angel tallies. Statz beat out a high bouncer to Henderson and Dittmar scored. McMullen, batting second in the revamped line-up, poked a hit to right and in came Mohler and Herrmann. Henderson retreated under fire and Stutz toured in to the mound from the bull pen. Steinback bounced a torrid smash over Garibaldi's head and Statz scored, McMullen pulling up at third. The Angel catched crossed the plate while Gudat was forcing Stainback, and then Oglesby cleaned up with his line smash into the bleachers. Lillard then fanned to end the round.**

**HERRMANN ON ROPES**

The Seals got to Herrmann for a run in the third, two more in the fifth and had Leroy hanging on the ropes in the eighth and ninth when they added their final four. But in the meantime the Angels were occasionally doing things to Mr. Frei-

(Continued on Page 12, Column 3)

## When the Leaning Tower of Pisa Fell on Sharkey

The Gabby Gob must have experienced some such sensation, if any, when Primo Carnera hit the heavyweight champion with his ponderous right hand in the sixth round of last night's fight. Photo shows Jack stretched full length on the canvas, with Primo standing to one side admiring his handiwork. Referee Donovan is about to rush over and raise Carnera's ham-like duke in token of victory.
[Associated Press telephoto]

## UPPERCUT TO CHIN PUTS JACK DOWN FOR COUNT

### *Italian Giant Lands Terrific Wallop to End Title Bout Before Crowd of 12,000*

(Continued from Page 1, Part I)

his rubber guard for his teeth hanging drunkenly half in and half out.

Primo pranced to his corner and the referee started to count.

It was just a formality.

At ten the huge Italian leaped into the air, waving his arms like a crazy man. He rushed about the ring taking bows and accepting imaginary applause.

His seconds charged in and he grabbed them and in each arm swung them in the air like a kid with a pair of dolls.

But the eyes of the crowd were not for the new champion.

For once Jack Sharkey—the lippy Lithuanian—the hated smart aleck—the fresh guy who had been booed for seven years—had the sympathy of the crowd.

**COULDN'T GET UP**

There was no question of his rising to his feet. He was way past that. His seconds rushed out and dragged him to his corner, swabbing his temples with wet towels, showering smelling salts into his nostrils, slapping his cheeks while his soaking head wobbled uncertainly on his neck.

It took two minutes of hard work to bring him around.

He stared unbelievingly at his seconds.

He blinked.

He understood—his head dropped—he looked up questioningly again at Johnny Buckley, his manager and his friend.

He staggered to his feet and started across the ring to congratulate his opponent who pranced wildly two-thirds of the way across to meet him.

The crowd roared.

The king was dead—make way for King Kong Carnera.

Mr. Sharkey, like Jackie Fields, Young Corbett and Tony Canzoneri before him, had learned that it's bad luck to defend a championship this year.

It's open season on title-holders.

**BOTH TRIED**

And for the benefit of the suspicious the only thing about the battle that looked as though it might be framed was the pictures they took of the ex-champion face down on the canvas.

Both fighters tried—and the astounding feature of Carnera's fight was not his strength—everybody knew about that—but his ferocity.

He was the savage killer rather than the good-natured side show freak—and 260 pounds of maddened Italian was more than Sharkey could handle.

Sharkey was first in the ring and after the customary introductions, which included Jack Dempsey and Gene Tunney, the fight was on.

Carnera surprised Sharkey by his aggressiveness in the first round and staggered the champion in addition to nearly throwing him through the ropes coming out of a clinch. Sharkey landed a terrific right to Carnera's jaw, but the giant fought back fiercely instead of going down. Carnera's edge in the first was evened up by Sharkey's more careful boxing and hard rights to the body in the second stanza, and Sharkey had a narrow margin in the third as a result of similar methods. The fourth was devoid of decisive action, but in the fifth the champion stung the gigantic Italian with a hard left and the bull-like rush of the enraged challenger brought a warning from the referee for backhand hitting. The champion had all the best of it.

**JACK HELPLESS**

Carnera caught Sharkey against the ropes at the start of the sixth round and beat him unmercifully. The champion was partly wrestled to the floor in his own corner, but came back swinging wildly. A hard right stung Primo and as Sharkey was bent over near the ropes the mammoth challenger brought up a right uppercut that landed squarely on the champion's jaw and stretched him helpless on the floor.

The first giggle of the evening took place a few minutes before

(Continued on Page 10, Column 7)

## *Blow-by-Blow of Fight for Heavy Crown*

ROUND ONE

The huge Carnera moved majestically out of his corner like an ancient broad-beamed whaler under full sail. Sharkey dove for him, but Primo caught his left hook on his big right paw. As they came together, Carnera bounced his ponderous right fist twice off Sharkey's side, but took a hard left hook to the head. Sharkey ripped back in with both hands to the body, but as he pulled away, Carnera's left hook caught him off balance, hurled him across the ring, and nearly drove him through the ropes. Incensed, the blazing champion flailed back in again with both hands, landing a left and right to Carner's head, but again the tremendous Italian heaved him across the ring as though he were a child and into the far ropes. Sharkey took Carnera's right to the body and banged a beautiful right off the Italian's long chin, the best punch of the round as the bell sounded.

ROUND TWO

Boxing carefully, Carnera led with his long left and smothered Sharkey as the champion drove to close quarters. Sharkey bounced his right off Primo's broad chest and grunted so he could be heard all over the ringside as he flung a long right that missed. Another terrific right to the jaw didn't miss and Carnera bounced back into the ropes as Sharkey followed him with a hard left hook to the head. Lunging in after feinting like a fox darting in on its prey, Sharkey lunged again and his right cracked on Carnera's chin. Primo enveloped the champion in his huge arms as Sharkey tried to get a punch at his body. Sharkey was sneering at the tremendous Italian as he feinted, searching for an opening, with Carnera pinned against the ropes as the gong sounded.

ROUND THREE

Sharkey was fighting a very careful, very heady fight, moving constantly around, feinting for openings. He got Carnera set, but his right bounced from the Italian's defending left arm as though it had hit a lamp post. Again Sharkey flung himself in, and as Carnera's arms flailed about, missing him with a dozen punches. The champion drove a furious right to the head and a left hook to the body. Carnera was falling back more and more on the defensive as Sharkey looped over a left to the head feinting to bring Carnera's arms up, and smashed his left into the huge Italian's side. Sharkey wove in with a hard right to the body, but Carnera roughed him with both hands about the head as he pushed him along the ropes. The bell caught Sharkey tearing back for more.

ROUND FOUR

Carnera stuck out his long left hand, but Sharkey slipped under it, pulled away from three more stabs and shot inside for a quick volley into the Italian's body. The champion was away again before Carnera could swing his huge hands into action. Standing back now with his left poised, waiting constantly for Sharkey to come to him and missing often, Carnera took two hard lefts to the head and a right to the body before he managed to rough in close and drawing a warning from Referee Donovan. They paced around the ring making left jabs and Carnera suddenly swung a hard right to the head. Carnera grabbed Sharkey's left hand, pulled him in and flailed his head with both hands, drawing a warning for holding and hitting, then another for backhanding. Primo threw Sharkey into the ropes again as though he were slinging a volley ball as the bell rang.

ROUND FIVE

Sharkey poked at Carnera's body with a left and threw the giant's fists down, but Primo put his hands up in time to block a shot to the chin. As Sharkey banged a left to the body, Carnera grabbed him, held him and banged him with his free hand, drawing another warning from the referee, but Sharkey merely sneered and smashed his left to the Italian's ribs again. Carnera hooked two lefts to Sharkey's jaw, but the champion followed him around the ring, feinted his hands down and smashed a terrific right to the giant's temple. Carnera wobbled like a brick chimney that is starting to come down, but he held and recovered quickly as Sharkey failed to fight clear of his tremendous arm, but Sharkey was right back on him, swinging left hooks to the head, with his right cocked for a finisher. He chased Carnera to a corner, but the bell rang before he could do more than fire a long left to the jaw.

ROUND SIX

Keeping close to Carnera's waist, Sharkey stabbed up into the Italian's face, then hooked two lefts to the body. Carnera drove in with both hands, catching Sharkey off balance, and as he thumped the champion around the ring, Sharkey slipped to the floor. He was caught off balance and came up without a count to weave in on the Italian. Carnera held the champion off with his left and ripped four ponderous rights to Sharkey's body. A right uppercut floored Sharkey and he was counted out.

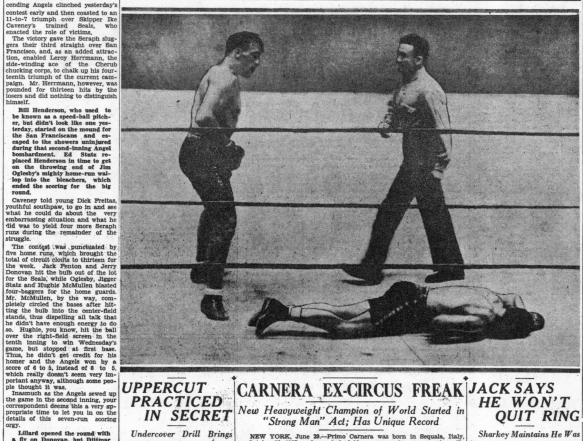

## *UPPERCUT PRACTICED IN SECRET*

### *Undercover Drill Brings Championship to Carnera, Who Was in Great Shape*

MADISON SQUARE GARDEN BOWL (New York) June 29. (AP)—**A secret right uppercut, practiced in utmost privacy—the punch everybody said he didn't have—was the blow that tonight brought the heavyweight championship of the world to Primo Carnera.**

**"Every day I practice it for months," the man mountain crowed in his gutteral broken English as he sat in his dressing room after his sensational victory over Jack Sharkey.**

**"Nobody thought Primo had uppercut. I show 'em, hah?**

**"I felt better every round"—he illustrated with a flourish of his huge fists. "I just feeling good when he went down. He never hurt me once," and the great fellow pounded his chest and grinned with an expanse**

(Continued on Page 10, Column 8)

## CARNERA EX-CIRCUS FREAK

### *New Heavyweight Champion of World Started in "Strong Man" Act; Has Unique Record*

NEW YORK, June 29.—Primo Carnera was born in Sequala, Italy, on October 25, 1907, and as a lad of 12 was engaged as a carpenter. He paid little attention to school, preferring to spend his spare time in wandering about the countryside.

When he was 14 he made his way to France, trying his hand at many occupations, but finding none that proved fascinating enough to keep him stationary.

During one of his periods of unemployment, then 16 years of age, he chanced to stop in front of a street circus in a French Province, and this action was the turning point of his career. For his great size made him conspicuous, and the circus manager, on the lookout for a new attraction, picked him out of the crowd and offered him a job as a strong man, with bed, board and an opportunity to see the country as his reward. The youth took the job.

**He traveled throughout France for several years. One of his appearances carried him near Paris, where Leon See, a sports promoter, saw him. See promptly asked the young giant if he would consider a boxing career. Carnera hestiated but after much persuasion consented.**

Carnera's official record, tactfully edited by his various proprietors, listed seventy-four fights, claimed fifty-six knockouts and thirteen decisions and acknowledged five defeats, including one administered by Sharkey. Of all his fights, however, the professional opinion of the prize-fight industry was inclined to regard only half a dozen as sincere contests or shooting matches.

Carnera had come to the business as a human monstrosity, a circus freak, and much of his career had been devoted to mere sham battles with decrepit hulks or notorious rabbits, selected by managers who had no confidence in him and did not wish to take any unnecessary risks.

**Carnera's record was a census of all the noted horizontalists of the last twenty years, including such picturesque and pathetic failures as Jim Sigman, diving Dan O'Dowd and the cour-**

(Continued on Page 10, Column 2)

## *JACK SAYS HE WON'T QUIT RING*

### *Sharkey Maintains He Was Too Rusty, Doesn't Want to Hang Up Gloves*

**MADISON SQUARE GARDEN BOWL (New York) June 29. (AP)—Slowly and painfully, Jack Sharkey made his way tonight from the pit that was both the scene of his coronation and downfall, and, after shaking off the effects of Primo Carnera's paralyzing right uppercut, he declared he would fight again.**

**"Will I hang up my gloves?" he asked as soon as his fuddled head cleared. "No," he said, "I won't hang them up. I'm going to fight again, maybe in a couple of weeks, when I am not so rusty. That's what is wrong with me now."**

**His statement that he intended to remain active in the ring, however, was far from being a ringing declaration of purpose.**

**It may be that Sharkey was still dazed when he denied that**

(Continued on Page 10, Column 7)

## Wild Scenes as Vast Venetian Is Crowned New King of Heavies

Photo on the left shows Jack Sharkey being dragged to his corner following sixth round knockout at the hands of Primo Carnera. On the right, Sharkey, after being revived, is walking unsteadily to his corner after having congratulated his conqueror. Note the smile of contentment on the handsome features of the Ambling Alp and the fond tenderness of his many handlers. [Associated Press telephotos]

## AZTECA, CASANOVA HERE

### *Mexicans Take Limbering Up Exercises at Gym With Serious Work to Begin Today*

BY BILL POTTS

Kid Azteca, bearing but few ring scars and a marked resemblance to Bert Colima, and Baby Casanova, who showed great promise as a push-cart vendor of ice cream until he entered the ring, were unveiled before a critical handful of experts yesterday at the Ringside Gym.

The pair, who arrived here Wednesday by plane from Mexico, did no boxing, but went through light calisthenics and limbering-up exercises. They plan to don the leather mittens for the first time today.

**Azteca, 19-year-old welterweight champion of the republic, is training for his pending engagement with Ceferino Garcia on the same card which features Casanova against Young Tommy at the Olympic July 11.**

Although it was difficult to get an accurate gauge on Azteca's ability, his bag-punching maneuvers proved he is of the combination slugger-boxer type. His best stock in trade seems to be a vicious left hook and jab.

He is rather tall—five feet nine inches—for a welterweight, and tipped the scales at 143 pounds after yesterday's workout. In twenty-three fights, the wiry Mexican has been defeated only by Tommy White and Eddie Frisco. Azteca, whose real name is Luis Villanueva, later reversed the White verdict and had previously whipped Frisco.

Neither Azteca nor Casanova speaks English, but willingly divulged the following information through an interpreter: Azteca's home is in Juarez and Mexico lost a pretty fair tailor and chauffeur when he turned fighter. So far neither has noticed any effect from the change of climate. Their manager, Jimmy Fitten, is building an arena in Mexico and probably will not be here for the fight. They were practically abducted by Al Lang, who met them at the airport and whisked them to the Ringside Gym before rival owners could get to them.

## *Seattle Horse Racing Season Due to Start*

SEATTLE (Wash.) June 29. (Exclusive)—Legalized horse racing returns here Saturday when the Silver Lake track lifts the barrier and sends the frisky "nags" on their merry way. The Silver Lake season will continue until July 22, according to data released by the State Racing Commission. Another plant, the Washington Jockey Club, will tentatively open on August 2.

# RAMAGE RALLIES TO WHIP ROSENBLOOM

## Jewels That Gleamed on Diamond in All-Star Baseball Battle

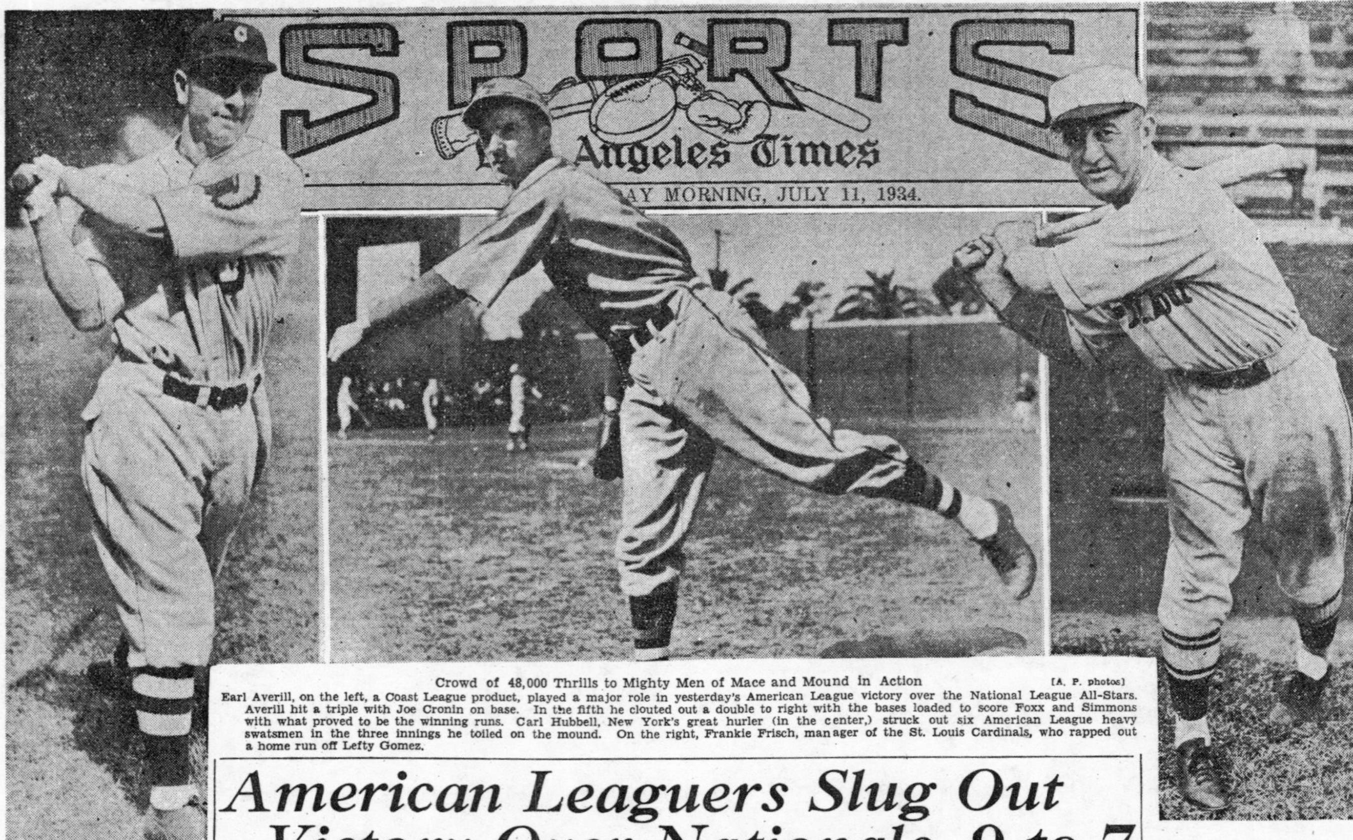


Crowd of 48,000 Thrills to Mighty Men of Mace and Mound in Action [A. P. photos]

Earl Averill, on the left, a Coast League product, played a major role in yesterday's American League victory over the National League All-Stars. Averill hit a triple with Joe Cronin on base. In the fifth he clouted out a double to right with the bases loaded to score Foxx and Simmons with what proved to be the winning runs. Carl Hubbell, New York's great hurler (in the center,) struck out six American League heavy swatsmen in the three innings he toiled on the mound. On the right, Frankie Frisch, manager of the St. Louis Cardinals, who rapped out a home run off Lefty Gomez.

## Bill Henry Says—

"WHEN I don't know where I'm goin', I figure it's time to quit," said the husky young man in his shirt sleeves.

Not a bad idea, either.

And particularly so when your profession happens to be the hazardous one of driving racing automobiles.

They don't all do it.

In fact, a little less foolishness and a little more thinking would probably have saved a whole lot of drivers' lives.

**STUBBLEFIELD LOOKS FOR THRILLS**

Stubby Stubblefield, whose thick arms have steered him to fame on many tracks, likes the thrill of driving.

But he's no sap.

He quit Ascot because he found the cars did strange things; he's coming back to Ascot because it's been changed.

And for the better.

Stubby has an idea that the dirt turns and shorter course will be a whole lot more thrilling.

**DIRT TURNS TAKE REAL DRIVING**

"It takes more real driving to get somewhere on a dirt track—you have to battle the steering wheel all the time.

"And that's fun.

"The drivers get more kick out of it and so do the spectators—the best drivers really ought to win.

"It'll be popular.

"I'm inclined to think that automobile racing will come back strong if they stick to half-mile dirt tracks," he said.

**SOME TRACKS DON'T MEAN ANYTHING**

Stubby, to be frank about it, doesn't think much of the board or paved speedways for automobile races.

They don't mean anything.

He likes the kind of tracks where the best driver has a chance to win even if a lot of the cars are faster than his.

Driving skill counts.

On some speedways the worst drivers may win, thanks to fast cars, and the best drivers be accidentally killed.

**THINKS INDIANAPOLIS IS HOT STUFF**

"If you ask me," said Stubby, "I think that Indianapolis is the finest speedway in the whole world.

"It takes driving.

"You have to know how to drive, you have to have a good car and you have to be in shape to last the race out.

"Condition counts.

"When I race at Indianapolis I work out with pulleys and weights like a fighter to get in top-notch condition."

**CAUSE OF SCIENCE IS ADVANCED**

Stubby insists that the scientific laboratory label attached to Indianapolis isn't any joke.

He's serious about it.

He drove one of the Diesel-engined cars this year and thinks the race taught the engineers a lot of lessons.

Particularly about fuel.

This year, hoping to slow the race down, a fuel limit was placed on the cars—they had to go the 500 miles on forty-five gallons of gas.

**PRIVATE CARS SURE TO BENEFIT**

Frankly, most of 'em thought they couldn't average better than eleven miles on a gallon at 100 miles an hour—but they did, and easily.

They learned something.

Without any doubt at all the economy feature that they picked up will be passed along, in time, to your car and mine.

Thanks, for that!

But Stubby thinks Ascot's new dirt turns will provide plenty of thrills whether they produce any scientific data or not.

## Santa Monica Road Classic Has Birthday

"Ca-a-a-r coming!"

Twenty-five years ago yesterday that announcement split the balmy atmosphere at Santa Monica for the first time. The occasion was the first Santa Monica road race and it was won by a muscular young man who has played end on the point-a-minute Michigan team. He drove an Apperson Jackrabbit at the hair-raising average of about sixty miles an hour. His name was Harris M. Hanshue and he's one of the head men of General Aviation, which flies the air mail hither and yon about the United States of America.

## Londos Must Defend Title Against Lewis

CHICAGO, July 10. (AP)—Jim Londos, wrestling champion, was ordered by the Illinois Athletic Commission to meet Ed (Strangler) Lewis in a title match within ninety days, an encounter which would net him a $40,000 guarantee or a privilege of 40 per cent of the net gate receipts.

The order was made yesterday when Ed White, manager of Londos, asked two weeks of grace to consider the offer of Joe Foley, general manager of the Chicago Stadium operating company, at those terms.

## Tennis Stars Sail for Home

LONDON, July 10. (AP)—Still in possession of the Wightman trophy, women's international tennis prize, Carolin Babcock, Sarah Palfrey and Josephine Cruickshank today left London for Southampton to board the Leviathan, en route home.

Helen Hull Jacobs, captain of the team which successfully defended the cup against England at Wimbledon last month, is suffering from a sore throat, of which there was an epidemic during the Wimbledon championships, and will take a later boat.

## Mack Signs to Battle Jackson

Ritchie Mack, recently voted the best boxer Texas has produced under the new boxing law, was signed yesterday to meet Young Peter Jackson, California's lightweight contender, at the Olympic next Tuesday night.

The credentials of Mack consist of a win and a draw with Kid Azteca of Mexico City, and decisions over Tracey Cox, Manuel Quintero, Billy Hogan, Manuel Villa and others.

## Cavalcade in Speedy Tune-up

CHICAGO, July 10. (AP)—Cavalcade, favorite for the $35,000 classic at Arlington Park Saturday, turned in a sensational workout today over a sloppy track, running the classic distance of a mile and a quarter in 2:08 3-5.

## American Leaguers Slug Out Victory Over Nationals, 9 to 7

## ANGELS RETURN FOR CIVIL WAR GO WITH STARS

### Double-header on Tap Tonight

BY BOB RAY
"Times" Staff Representative

SOMEWHERE ON THE ESPEE, July 10.—Mr. J. Lelivelt's Angels return home tomorrow night sadder, wiser, and, most important of all, richer, if that adjective may still be used in connection with baseball. Their record of consecutive winning series has been stopped at twenty-nine, "Scow" Thomas, after winning fifteen straight games this year and a total of twenty-two in a row without a defeat, has finally met his Waterloo, and the Angels are in third place instead of the customary first, but the Los Angeles boys return from the great Northwest with plenty of financial balm to sooth their wounded pride.

Mr. Lelivelt's lads lost all their records at Seattle, but they set one in doing so when they drew down the fattest check that has been handed to a visiting Coast League club this season. And they drew it in only five days of play, for the Fourth of July was pool day, with the league taking all of the receipts.

**SEATTLE ON MAP**

Bill Klepper and his assistants certainly have put baseball back on the map at Seattle and if the Indians can keep up in the race this year the rotund boss of the Tribe will get back a lot of the money he's lost in the pastime.

But while the national pastime is booming at Seattle it is dying a slow death in Portland, where the visiting clubs' share is just about enough to pay for the hungry athletes' coffee and cake. Tom Turner has made rather a mess of things. He tore down instead of built up the Ducks, put himself in as manager when Walter McCredie was forced to bed with arthritis, and he's more or less in bad with the Portland baseball writers. And the Portland fans, who will turn out in flocks when given a winner, are staying away in large numbers. About the best thing that could happen for for baseball at Portland would be

(Continued on Page 11, Column 2)

## CARL HUBBELL'S MOUND WIZARDRY THRILLS FANS

### Lon Warneke, Van Mungo Victims of Savage Batting Assault in Fifth; Averill Stars

BY EDWARD J. NEIL
Associated Press Sports Writer

NEW YORK, July 10. (AP)—For three magnificent innings the National League today showed the American League and 48,363 howling faithful the finest pitcher in baseball—Carl Owen Hubbell. Then everyone relaxed, and the second annual battle of the all-stars turned into nothing so much as the major league equivalent of the married men vs. single men at the annual Sunday-school picnic.

The American Leaguers finally won, 9 to 7, with a typical blasting display that blew long Lon Warneke of the Cubs right out of the box and scattered the offerings of his successor, Van Mungo of the Dodgers, all over the premises in a six-run outburst in the fifth inning. The Americans then proceeded to clinch the contest, marking their second straight victory in the two-year all-star series, thanks to the brilliant relief pitching of young Mel Harder of the Cleveland Indians. Rarely, however, in a match of such magnitude has the play ever degenerated so quickly and so completely from the sublime to the ridiculous as it did after Hubbell's magnificent display.

**GOMEZ BESTED**

For three innings, the greatest southpaws in the game, Hubbel of the world's champions and Lefty Vernon Gomez of the Yanks, locked in the pitching duel the baseball world has long been awaiting, and the honors rested entirely with the lanky, screwball twister from Oklahoma.

Facing the greatest hitting array ever assembled, the master fanned six men in the first two innings—five of them in a row—and all they happened to be were Babe Ruth, Lou Gehrig, Jimmy Foxx, Al Simmons and Joe Cronin, manager of the rival array. Bill Dickey, Yankee catcher, cracked him for a single to break up the succession with two out in the second, but he got his hurling rival, Gomez, which was like shooting birds on the ground after what he had just done.

**SETTLES DOWN**

A trifle unsteady at the start—when he allowed Charley Gehringer of the Tigers, to open the game with a single to center that Wally Berger of the Braves, fumbled into two bases—Hubbell settled down after passing Heinie Manush of the Senators and started on his mag-

(Continued on Page 12, Column 1)

## MIDWESTERN FANS SUPPORT OWN ATHLETES

### Local Tabulation to Be Given

BY BRAVEN DYER

First official returns from headquarters indicate that far western football players are going to have a tough time landing on the all-star squad which is to oppose the Chicago Bears at the World's Fair on August 31.

Compliation of votes last night by the Chicago Tribune showed only one Pacific Coast player on the first eleven. The chap enjoying this distinction is Aaron "Rosy" Rosenberg, the rough-and-ready running guard of the 1933 Trojans who is now working in a local motion-picture studio. Our "Rosy" leads all the guards by a margin of more than 100 votes, but the names of other Coast athletes are conspicuous by their absence.

Of course, Rosenberg has quite an advantage on many of the Pacific Coast players. He appeared twice in South Bend, once when the Trojans won that 16-to-14 game from Notre Dame, and again last season. Fans who saw him in those battles won't soon forget his playing,

(Continued on Page 11, Column 2)

## Maxie Only Wanted to Sit This One Out

Rosenbloom Down in the Tenth But 'Twas Only a Slip [A. P. photo]

Above is shown the light-heavyweight champion weary and worn out as a result of the rally waged by Lee Ramage in the latter rounds of their non-title bout at the Olympic last night. The San Diego boy was not in the immediate vicinity of Maxie's presence when the latter slipped. George Blake is the referee who awarded Ramage the decision.

## YANKEE BOAT REPULSES CHALLENGE OF RAINBOW

### Foremost Candidate to Represent America in Cup Defense Remains Undefeated

BY LEONARD M. FOWLE, JR.

[Copyright, 1934, by North American Newspaper Alliance, Inc.]

NEWPORT (R. I.) July 10.—The sloop Yankee remains undefeated by an eligible contender for America's Cup defense honors. She again demonstrated her all-around ability by trouncing Rainbow in a 28½-mile triangular race by a margin of 5m. 27s.

Vanitie seems to be the jinx of the Boston syndicate's craft, but the Lambert boat is not a candidate, only a trial horse. If Yankee can continue to shellack Rainbow and Weetamoe, her after-guard need not worry greatly when she lowers her colors to Vanitie.

Yankee outdistanced the newest of American Class J sloops on all points of sailing under wind conditions between eight and fourteen knots. There no longer can be any doubt that Yankee has established herself as a very strong contender for the defender's role.

Luck may have played a part in her victory, as she received a lift

(Continued on Page 11, Column 1)

## Pacho Loses Bout Verdict, LaSalle Wins

NEW YORK, July 10. (U.P.)—Tony Falco, Philadelphia lightweight, won a close decision over Bobby Pacho of Los Angeles at Coney Island tonight. A butt on the head in the third round cut Pacho's forehead and hampered him during the rest of the fight. Pacho shaded him with sharper punching. Falco weighed 141½; Pacho 137 1-4.

Kenny La Salle, Los Angeles welterweight, outpointed Young Firpo, Pennsgrove, N. J., in ten rounds.

## Pasek Recalled by White Sox

OAKLAND, July 10. (AP)—Gloomy faces worn by Oakland baseball club owners today were explained by a telegram from the Chicago White Sox recalling Catcher Johnny Pasek immediately. Pasek had been bludgeoning the ball for the Oaks. He had been farmed out here on a forty-eight-hour recall notice. The Sox intend to send him to another minor league club as the result of a new deal.

Before the Pasek developments cropped up, the Oaks leaders were cheered by the return yesterday of Bernard Uhalt, outfielder. Uhalt was turned back by the White Sox after a trial.

## Iowa Promotes Football Coach

AMES (Iowa) July 10. (AP)—Ossie Solem, head football coach at the University of Iowa, today was appointed director of athletics and head of the department of physical education at the university to succeed Dr. E. H. Lauer, resigned. The appointment was made by the State Board of Education. Solem, who came to Iowa in 1932 from Drake University, will continue as football coach. Dr. Lauer accepted the deanship of the college of liberal arts at the University of Washington.

**GIBBS DEFEATS BLACK**

CHICAGO, July 10. (U.P.)—Jack Gibbs, 162 pounds, Orange, Texas, won an eight round fight tonight from George Black, 157, Milwaukee. Gibbs knocked Black down six times. Lou Terry, 140, St. Louis and Lou Taylor, 139, Chicago, fought five rounds to a draw.

## SAN DIEGO BOY EARNS VERDICT AS RIVAL TIRES

### Champ Totters at Finish

BY BILL POTTS

The three R's of boxing, Ramage, Rosenbloom and Referees, still had the fistic fraternity puzzled last night after exactly two weeks of wrestling with the problem.

The only intelligible solution advanced was that at last two wrongs do seem to make a right!

More than half of the crowd of 5000 spectators at the Olympic last night were responsible for such a theory when they vociferously cheered Referee George Blake's decision that Lee Ramage had proven to be a better man than Slapsie-Maxie Rosenbloom after ten rounds of enthusiastic mauling which was almost a repetition of their draw two weeks ago.

**THRONG APPLAUDS LEE**

In the first fight Rosenbloom appeared to have won easily, but got only an even break from Referee Harry Lee for his efforts. Last night the Harlem harlequin was not nearly as impressive, but he did have a slight edge and should have received no worse than a draw.

Most of the partisan crowd broke out into a wild burst of applause as Lee's tired arm was raised. The downstairs "experts," however, viewing the proceedings with less favoritism, were united in the belief that Rosenbloom had received the worst of it for the second time in two weeks. Our score sheet showed five rounds for Slapsie-Maxie, four for the San Diego stripling and one even.

Duplicating his do-or-die attack of their first encounter, Ramage battled his way to victory in the final two rounds when he put his head down and followed Rosenbloom, desperately tired, relentlessly all over the ring, shooting punches into every available opening without let-up. The crowd was on its feet cheering like mad at the spectacle of the clean-cut young schoolboy, driving the slightly bald and elderly looking champion before him. He had Maxie in a bad way at the finish.

**STIRRING SPECTACLE**

It was a stirring spectacle and as sparkling rally as ever a beaten man has put on in the Olympic ring.

Rosenbloom was far ahead as they went into the ninth round and it seemed that the only way Ramage could win was by a knockout, and Lee needs something more than his busy fists with which to administer a Mickey Finn.

His daring, last-minute assault must have won over the heart of every red-blooded man and woman in the place regardless of whom they thought should have won the fight.

There were no knockdowns although Rosenbloom fell flat on his haunches in the tenth round when he stepped in a slippery spot on the canvas.

**COASTS AT INTERVALS**

Maxie usually started each round with a wild flurry of slaps and jabs that built up a clean margin and allowed him to coast at intervals. This proved a most wise procedure as he was dead tired and reeling around the ring in distress at the finish. If it had gone another minute he probably would have gone down from exhaustion. Ramage was equally weary.

In the semi-wind-up Tony Cancela, good-looking Mexican heavyweight, got over in impressive fashion when he stopped Tony Sousa in the fourth round. Cancela, obviously not in the best of shape, dropped the first two rounds, but found the range with a biting left to drop Sousa in the fourth for an eight count and flatten him with a right that traveled about six inches.

**ONE-PUNCH VICTORY**

Leo Kelly, knocked down for a short count, climbed off the floor and kayoed Bill Thomas with one punch in the first round. Manuel Victoria won all the way from Ray Kaiser and Cannonball Green and Angus Morgan went to a slow draw in the opener.

Weights on the main event were 186 for Ramage and 184½ for Rosenbloom.

**MARIANNE HUNT WINS**

PROVIDENCE (R. I.) July 10. (AP) Among upsets marking play in the Rhode Island singles championships on the turf courts at Agawam Hunt here today, Miss Marianne Hunt of Los Angeles, defeated Mae Ceurvorst of Wichita, Kan., fourth seeded woman entrant, 6-2, 3-6, 6-4.

## ILLINOIS REFUSES TO ENFORCE LEVINSKY BAN

### Rift Reported in Agreements Between Athletic Bodies; Chicago May Stage Lasky Go

A rift in the supposedly air-tight and puncture-proof agreement between the "Big Three"—the athletic commissions of the States of California, New York and Illinois—was indicated late last night in a wire received here.

The telegram, sent by Joseph Triner, chairman of the Illinois State Athletic Commission, emphatically stated that that group would not recognize California's suspension of King Levinsky, Chicago's peddler of fish and fists. The wire read:

**REJECTS BAN**

"California State Athletic Commission:

"At meeting today our commission decided that it could not concur in your suspension of King Levinsky because suspension was based on nonpayment of civil debts.

[Signed] "Illinois State Athletic Commission, Joseph Triner, chairman."

Inasmuch as the "Big Three" had mutually agreed to recognize and abide by each other's decisions, the action taken by the Illinois body automatically makes the pact invalid.

**FIGHT PLANNED**

Rumors have been circulated about rather freely that a Levinsky-Art Lasky fight is planned in Chicago for a September date and the action of the Illinois commission in refusing to bar the Kingfish, is construed as a means to opening the way for the battle.

# DIZ DEAN HURLS CARDS TO WORLD TITLE

C WEDNESDAY MORNING, OCTOBER 10, 1934.

## Bill Henry Says—

EVERY year there are a flock of form reversals on the gridiron on the first couple of Saturdays. This year they were more frequent and a lot more startling. And we, therefore, have an unusually interesting season coming up. Here are just a few impressions after a study of the scoring statistics of last week:

**FIVE TOUGH TEAMS**

What city in the United States has five college teams within spitting distance of the City Hall that could win a majority of games from California, Stanford, St. Mary's, Santa Clara and S.F.U.? Looks like San Francisco is the grid capital this year.

**PIGSKIN HOUNDS**

Clipper Smith and Slip Madigan must teach the same bloodbound system of football. Kellogg of St. Mary's fumbled on the California goal line and Team-mate Schreiber of Moraga flopped on it for a touchdown. The next day Falaschi of Santa Clara fumbled on the S.F.U. goal line and Team-mate McGee chased it across and fell on it.

**YEP, THE SAME GUY**

The guy who ran wild for Minnesota against Nebraska was the same Stan Kostka who came out to Oregon with Doc Spears and Mike Mikulak. When Doc went back to Wisconsin, Kostka went back with him but ran afoul of a Big Ten rule prohibiting players from transferring with a coach. Doc shipped him to Minnesota. He weighs 210 pounds and can outsprint pretty nearly anybody you want to name.

**BUT, CAN HE CROON?**

Just mention anybody you've seen in recent years who could do as many things as well as Ed Goddard of Washington State. He will punt or quick kick with Alustiza of Stanford. He can pass with the best of 'em. He runs hard interference. And when have you seen a tougher safety man to drag down? Quite a find!

**TROUBLE AHEAD?**

When somebody predicted that the Trojans "might" lose two games this year somebody pointed out that a very good football team "might" lose to Washington State, Pittsburgh, Stanford, California, Washington and Notre Dame and not be disgraced. Those are six pretty tough customers this year.

**WHAT DO YOU THINK?**

Wonder if Purdue was saving Purvis to beat Notre Dame this week? He didn't play against Rice last Saturday. Two bits to a plugged nickle both Purdue and Notre Dame are a lot better than they looked last Saturday. Another two bits says that anybody who fools around with any of those Texas football teams is looking for trouble.

**IN THE BIG TEN**

Iowa and Minnesota are living up to advance notices in the Big Ten and likewise Ohio State. Chicago is the dark-horse outfit. Can't tell for sure about the Maroons until they tangle with an aroused Michigan team this week. Boy, will those Wolverines be mad after thinking over their Michigan State beating for a week!

**THEODORATOS AMIBITOUS**

One of the interested spectators last Saturday at the Coliseum was Jim Londos, the wrestling champ. He's a buddy of his fellow-Greek, George Theodoratos. He has an idea that George would make a swell wrestler but the burly Cougar wants to make the All-American football team this year, win the intercollegiate shot this summer and then win the world's heavyweight boxing championship.

**OUR ONLY HOPE!**

The only football team of any prominence in our neighborhood that hasn't enjoyed a seat on the mourner's bench this year is Loyola. The Lions have looked pretty good in spots so far. In fact, better than that. They've also looked not so good. All hands are anticipating a full house when they play Santa Clara next Sunday.

**PASS IT AROUND**

The local pro footballers have been standing the crowds on their heads with their Rugby passing. Not having any high-priced coaches who are scared of their jobs the boys toss the ball around, sometimes four of five of them handling it on impromptu passing plays. What college coach is going to get smart and do it?

**PICKED UP ON THE RUN**

In a practice game against the freshmen Notre Dame didn't miss a goal after touchdown in four tries . . . but they missed the one that would have tied the game with Texas . . . Somebody in

(Continued on Page 12, Column 1)

## DEAN FACES LONDOS IN TITLE MAT BOUT TONIGHT

### *Behemoth Hill-Billy Squirms With Champ as Colossal Collection of Pachyderms Risk Life and Limb*

BY BILL HENRY

Bellowing, trumpeting and pawing the earth like peevish hippopotami squabbling over the rights to an African water hole, eighteen head of assorted behemoths will clash tonight at Wrigley Field in the greatest program of assault and battery ever perpetrated locally under a wrestling license. Some 30,000 customers are expected at the giant squirm.

The high spot on the card of nine encounters will bring together World's Wrestling Champion Jim Londos, a Grecian statue of Hercules come to life, and Frank (Man Mountain) Dean, a bearded Georgia hill-billy weighing 317 pounds, whose string of sensational victories on the local mat have brought him a crack at the title.

**WEIRD COLLECTION**

The eight other bouts will feature a cross-section of the strange conglomeration of pugnacious pachyderms roughly grouped together under the general head of "wrestlers." They include college football players, acrobats, life guards, longshoremen, a bearded Hindu and even a couple of regular old-time wrestlers who are on the card to justify the issuance of a wrestling permit for the brawl.

It ought to be a large evening.

**HE CAN WRESTLE**

Champion Jim Londos was a star when the boys really used to wrestle and is one of the few who have been able to hold up their end in the modern free-for-all style which features butting, kicking, choking and other parlor tricks. Not only is Jim a fine wrestler and an accomplished showman but he can talk a college professor deaf, dumb and blind on such topics as archeology and the classics and can do it in any one of nine or ten languages.

Man Mountain Dean, the bearded Samson, has squashed some eight or nine opponents in succession and has attracted a huge following of enthusiastic rooters who hope to see him pluck the champion's arm off and beat him over the head with it or do something equally cute. The skeptics, on the other hand, claim that he's a big false alarm who can't wrestle a lick. Mr. Dean himself dodges the issue and points out that he can pack the joint with cash customers and it doesn't make any difference whether he knows the difference between a half nelson and an oyster on the half shell or not.

**WEAPONS SPIKED**

Some mysterious authority, presumably the State Athletic Commission, has deprived the two main eventers of their most formidable offensive weapons, according to an announcement by Prof. Lou Daro, the well known scientist and collector of rare objects, who imported tonight's performers.

Londos will not be permitted to use his pet "unconscious hold," by means of which he puts pressure on a nerve in the neck of his opponent and lulls him gently into dreamland. Londos squawked violently at the ruling but was finally calmed by his manager, Ed White of Chicago, who told him that the hold was no good against the Man Mountain for the reason that you couldn't tell whether he was unconscious or not anyway.

**DAISY SIDETRACKED**

Dean's chances were materially crippled when the commission refused to permit Daisy Dean, his husky wife, to act as his chief second. Daisy has a quaint way of picking up a stool or typewriter or other suitable missile and cracking her 317 pound darling's opponent over the head with same. The commission ruled that she could demonstrate her wifely affection and loyalty any place except at the ringside.

The Man Mountain's chief offensive weapon in his local bouts has been what has been referred to as a running broad jump. The Georgia Goliath hurls his opponent to the mat then takes a running leap into the air and lands, rumble seat first, on his prostrate opponent. It seems to have a very quieting effect on the boys.

Rumors have been circulated to the effect that the Man Mountain not only isn't a hill-billy from Georgia but that his name isn't even Dean. Dean counters with the statement that Jim Londos's real

(Continued on Page 11, Column 2)

## STATE GOLF CARD FIXED

### *Open Schedule Again Revised*

After a session lasting until almost midnight Junior Chamber of Comermce officials and delegates representing Southern California communities last night drew up a new schedule for the next California open golf season. It followed acrimonious debate, climaxed by censure of the National Professional Golfers' Association by Olin Dutra, national open champion.

Olin Dutra

**P.G.A. AT FAULT**

This body sanctioned a trip to Honolula and Australia by six eastern stars—Paul Runyan, Craig Wood, Leo Diegel, Ky Laffoon, Denny Shute and Harry Cooper—interfering with the start of the California season. None of the communities with these drawing stars absent cared to open the schedule.

The new program, subject to replacements by the P.G.A. for the touring players, who won't be back until December 29, calls for Lakewood to open the tournament season December 13. Pasadena follows, provided the P.-G.A. can supply such drawing cards as Willie McFarlane, Joe Kirkwood, Gene Sarazen, Johnny Golden, Tommy Armour and Ed Dudley.

San Jose, which previously had a week-end date, will be asked to accept dates for its $1500 affair that will allow other and richer tourneys to come in on a tight schedule.

The new program follows:

December 13, 14, 15, 16, California open, $1500.

December 20, 21, 22, 23, Pasadena open, $4000.

December 28, 29, 30, Riverside amateur-pro, $2000.

January 4, 5, 6, Santa Monica open, $2500.

January 12, 13, 14, L.A. open, $5000.

January 18, 19, 20, Sacramento, $2500.

January 26, 27, San Jose (?) $1500.

February 1, 2 3, 4, Oakmont open, $6500.

February 7, 8, 9, 10, Agua Caliente open, $5000.

## STANFORD IN STIFF DRILL

STANFORD UNIVERSITY, Oct. 9. (AP)—In fighting trim, Stanford's football warriors drilled here today for their intersectional battle with invaders from Northwestern University Saturday.

Except for Bobby Grayson, slashing fullback, all members of the Stanford squad participated in stiff workouts today and yesterday. Grayson is nursing a hip injury.

Coach "Tiny" Thornhill said he would not know until tomorrow whether he will use Grayson in the game. He declared another scrimmage will be held tomorrow and light workouts Thursday and Friday devoted to defensive practice.

The Stanford coach said he was encouraged with his team's 17-to-0 win over Oregon last week and was particularly pleased with the showing made by the reserves.

## ART LASKY IN LINE FOR HAMAS OR SCHMELING GO

### *Commission "Suggests" Steve Give Jewish Boy Another Chance or Lose Future Bouts*

NEW YORK, Oct. 9. (Exclusive)—Steve Hamas was put on the spot and Art Lasky was given a Mexican stand-off by the New York State Boxing Commissioners today.

Lasky's plea for a reversal of Referee Billy Cavanaugh's decision in favor of Hamas at the Garden last Friday night was denied by the solons—Gen. John J. Phelan, Bill Brown and Chick Goodman.

Art Lasky

While Cavanaugh's action may have been drastic, he was entirely justified in calling the fourth frame of their ten-round fracas against Lasky because of a back-hand slap Art flipped at Steve's chin, Gen. Phelan declared.

As solace to Lasky, the commissioners "suggested," since they cannot arbitrarily command, that Hamas give his victim an early return match over the fifteen-round route.

They indicated that if Hamas avoids Lasky's demands that Art, and not Hamas, will get first consideration when it comes to deciding the logical challenger of Max Baer in a heavyweight championship bout here next summer.

If Hamas ducks Lasky's demand for a return fight—and both Steve and Charley Harvey, his manager, have indicated they'll have no more of the hard-hitting westerner—Art will seek a match with Max Schmeling. Hamas, who holds a decision over the German, must then content himself with Primo Carnera, so far as available opponents are concerned. Lasky has already held Da Preem to a ten-round draw, but Hamas hasn't met the Italian.

"I'm trying to match Lasky and Hamas for fifteen rounds," Jimmy Johnston, promoter of Madison Square Garden, announced tonight. "If Steve doesn't want to fight, we'll get Schmeling. If Lasky beats the German he will be the logical opponent for Max Baer."

# *Clemens Back at Half, Powers at Guard as S.C. Party Leaves*

### *The Greek Has a Name for Him*

You can hire Man-Mountain Dean to haunt a house any night but tonight as the Man-Mountain will be busy grappling with Jeemy Londos, Grecian wonder, who claims the world's wrestling championship. The bout is scheduled for Wrigley Field and tops a card of nine bouts.

## RED BIRDS COP TITLE

### *Columbus Defeats Toronto in Ninth and Deciding Game to Triumph*

COLUMBUS (O.) Oct. 9. (AP)—The Columbus Red Birds, champions of the American Association, tonight added the 1934 minor league championship to their collection, defeating the Toronto Leafs, International League titleholders, 13 to 8, in the ninth and deciding game of the little World Series.

This afternoon Toronto defeated Columbus, 5 to 1, knotting the series at four games each.

| First game: | R. | H. | E. |
|---|---|---|---|
| Toronto | 5 | 11 | 2 |
| Columbus | 1 | 7 | 2 |

Schott and Heving; Klinger, Teachout and O'Dea.

| Second game: | R. | H. | E. |
|---|---|---|---|
| Toronto | 8 | 13 | 1 |
| Columbus | 13 | 16 | 2 |

Hollingsworth, Blake, Hilcher and Heving; Greer, Heusser and O'Dea.

## *Frisch to Boss Cards Again in 1935 Campaign*

ST. LOUIS, Oct. 9. (AP)—Frankie Frisch, as everyone who gave it a thought suspected all along, will manage the St. Louis Cardinals, new world champions, again 1935.

While the job always has been regarded as safe for the old Fordham flash, official word from the head man of the front office was not forthcoming until today.

"I think Frisch is a great manager," President Sam Breadon said in Detroit. "I think he has a great deal of courage and that he is the kind of man I want to handle my ball club. I have not talked terms, but he will handle the club next season."

## *Here's Data on Tonight's Huge Grappling Card*

Bouts tonight and order in which they will be run off:

Pat O'Shocker vs. Jack Ganson, one fall, fifteen-minute time limit.

Matros Kirilenko vs. Abie Goldberg, one fall, fifteen-minute time limit.

Dick Daviscourt vs. Jagat Singh, one fall, twenty-minute time limit.

Sammy Stein vs. Cosey Colombo, one fall, twenty minutes.

Paul Boesch vs. Ernie Dusek, one fall, twenty minutes (emergency bout.)

George Zaharias vs. Joe Savoldi, one fall, thirty minutes.

Champion Jim Londos vs. Man Mountain Dean, best two out of three falls to a finish.

Ray Steele vs. Joe Malcewicz, one fall, twenty minutes.

Nick Lutze vs. Howard Cantonwine, one fall to a finish.

**MORE FACTS**

Place—Wrigley Field, Forty-first street and Avalon Boulevard.

Starting time — Preliminaries, 8:30 p.m.; main event, 10 o'clock.

Referee—To be appointed today by athletic commission.

Capacity—40,000.

Expected attendance—Between 35,000 and 40,000. Take street cars marked 'S," "V" and "H."

**HOW THEY TAPE**

| Champion Jim Londos | | Man Mountain Dean |
|---|---|---|
| Argos, Greece | | Tucker, Ga. |
| 38 | Age | 35 |
| 202 | Weight | 317 |
| 5 ft. 8¼ | Height | 5 ft. 11¼ |
| 74¼ in. | Reach | 74 in. |
| 46—51 | Chest | 56—61 |
| 18½ in. | Neck | 23 in. |
| 18½ in. | Biceps | 20¾ in. |
| 15 in. | Forearm | 17 in. |
| 9 in. | Wrist | 10½ in. |
| 33 in. | Waist | 48 in. |
| 25 in. | Thigh | 26 in. |
| 18 in. | Calf | 18 in. |
| 11 in. | Ankle | 11 in. |

## *Pacific Points for California*

STOCKTON (Cal.) Oct. 9. (U.P.)—Coach Amos Alonzo Stagg and his College of Pacific squad who held the Trojans of Southern California to a slim 6 points two weeks ago today were pointing toward their game this Saturday with the Bears of California. Stagg claims that his team is in much better shape than when it met the southerners, and will give the Bears a tough battle.

## CARD FANS CUT LOOSE

### *St. Louis Goes Wild After Home Team Carries Off World Series Title*

ST. LOUIS, Oct. 9. (AP)—A St. Louis celebration over the Cardinal baseball team, new world champions, started slowly today, but tonight the town had gone wild.

Noise began shortly after "Dizzy" Dean racked up the last goose egg against the Detroit Tigers in the ninth inning. The delirium gradually mounted to a frenzied uproar.

After a dinner-hour lull, celebrating fans poured into the downtown district in automobiles of all descriptions, jamming the streets and creating a din that threatened to split the eardrums.

Motors backfired, horns blared, and sirens screamed. And those old stand-bys, the family wash boiler and the rim from the family car's extra tire, trailed behind automobiles at the end of ropes, contributed their clanking cacophony to the tumult.

## WINSTON GUEST LEADS TEAM TO POLO VICTORY

WESTBURY (N. Y.) Oct. 9. (AP)—Winston Guest's Templeton team today rode back to the polo heights it occupied two years ago, defeating Seymour Knox's defending Aurora four in the final match for the national open championship. The score was 10 to 7.

Continuing the brilliant play he showed in the East-West matches, Guest dominated the game with his hard riding and long drives to Mike Phipps at No. 1. Guest, riding No. 2 position, scored three goals, while Phipps counted four times, Raymond Guest twice and Stewart Iglehart once.

## TEAM HOLDS HARD DRILL

### *Offense Clicks in Practice*

*Troy Boasts Record of Not Losing Two Consecutive Games in Ten Years*

BY BRAVEN DYER
"Times" Staff Representative

ON BOARD THE TROJAN SPECIAL, Oct. 9.—Whizzing across the desert early this evening, Southern California's party of pigskinners was cheered by the knowledge that during the past ten years no Trojan team has ever lost two consecutive games in the same season.

Headed for Pittsburgh, and what 90 per cent of the fans think is a sound thumping, the forty-three youngsters who must carry Troy's colors into battle are resolved that this record shall not be shattered.

**TEAM CLICKS**

Had you seen them in their final workout at Bovard Field this afternoon you would have sensed their grim determination to make immediate amends for their sorry showing thus far this year. Howard Jones drilled them for more than two hours, driving first this man and then that, with the result that Troy's offense showed signs of actually clicking for the first time this season.

A surprising change in tactics was noted. Jones had Russell Powers, 185 pound scrub player, operating at the running guard slot. Cal Clemens was sent back to his right half spot. The Head Man was so impressed with Powers' grid prowess that he may start the new comer in the Pitt game.

As a result of today's strenuous workout at Bovard Field Jones added three players to the party an hour before the train pulled out. They were Gar Matthews, quarterback; Pete Kovac, guard, and Jim Sutherland, left halfback.

**NEW PICTURES**

Immediately following a sumptous repast served by Chief Steward Bill Rutledge, the athletes retired to the lounge car and sat through a two-hour motion-picture show.

Minus the services(?) of Cliff Herd and Gordon Campbell, who generally take turns acting as his bridge partner, Mr. Jones was reluctantly forced to call upon Mark Kelly and Sid Ziff to help him out.

(Continued on Page 11, Column 2)

## *BALL FANS APPROVED BY LANDIS*

### *"Can't Blame the Crowd," Says Baseball's Arbiter After Demonstration*

DETROIT, Oct. 9. (AP)—Kenesaw Mountain Landis, commissioner of baseball, said tonight that he "couldn't blame the crowd" for its violent demonstration toward Joe Medwick, St. Louis Cardinal left fielder, which halted today's World Series game for seventeen minutes in the sixth inning.

The 17,000 occupants of the left-field bleachers were expressing their resentment for what they apparently believed was an attempt by Medwick to spike Marvin Owen, Tiger infielder, as he slid into third after tripling. Others considered the in-

(Continued on Page 10, Column 4)

## TROTTER GOES TO CENTER IN BRUIN GRID WORKOUT

### *Duke to Play Pivot Position Against Montana Grizzlies in Coliseum Saturday*

BY IRVING ECKHOFF

Back to his first love went Duke Trotter, gigantic Bruin lineman, when Bill Spaulding counted noses yesterday before the U.C.L.A. workout for the Montana game Saturday in the Coliseum.

The schnozzle of Larry McConnel, second-string center, was practically missing so the Bruin masterminds switched Trotter from guard to center, at which position he will probably play against the Grizzlies.

Duke Trotter

Duke will alternate with Sherman Chavoor, soph pivot man who has been the number one man to date. McConnell is bruised up considerably and won't see much action Saturday. The injuries were incurred during scrimmages since the Oregon mess two weeks back.

Trotter was highly pleased with the change and said that center was his favorite position, anyway.

**OTHER CHANGES**

Replacing Duke at guard was Wendle Womble, husky blond boy from Sacramento Jaysee. He will share a good portion of the work with Bob Barr, sophomore.

The other guard position is being handled by Verdi Boyer single-handed.

Ray Allington and Chuck Pike, a couple of first-year men, are functioning at right end, subbing for Sinclair Lott and Bob Schroeder, both on the side lines with injuries.

Julian Smith is aiding Bob McChesney at left end, which should be bad news for Montana fans.

(Continued on Page 12, Column 1)

## TIGER FANS STAGE RIOT

### *Medwick Chased From Field*

*Sixth-Inning Demonstration Holds Up Game Seventeen Minutes as Cards Win*

BY ALAN GOULD
Associated Press Sports Editor

DETROIT, Oct. 9. (AP)—Completing the spectacular saga of the Deans with a history-making climax, the great Jerome Herman (Dizzy) Dean pitched St. Louis to the baseball championship of the world today with a record shutout triumph, 11 to 0, as the Cardinal clouting crew slaughtered the pitching staff of the Detroit Tigers in as wild and riotous a finish as any World Series has ever witnessed.

Judge Landis

**SMASHING RALLY**

The National League champions blasted the last defense of Mickey Cochrane's battered Bengals with a smashing seven run attack in the third. They bombarded six pitchers all told for a total of 17 hits while Dizzy Dean, turning in the fourth victory for his team and family, emerged from the seventh and final game with the most lopsided series shutout margin since Christy Mathewson blanked the Athletics, 9 to 0, in 1905.

Before the clouting Cardinals dashed off the field with the final decision, four games to three, and their third world championship in the nine years, they survived a riotous outburst by the left field bleacher fans who let loose a barrage of missiles, aimed at Joe (Ducky) Medwick, interrupted the game for seventeen minutes and subsided only after the St. Louis leftfielder and cleanup clouter was removed from the game, mainly for safety's sake, by Baseball Commissioner Kenesaw Mountain Landis.

**WILD DEMONSTRATION**

The demonstration, one of the worst in series history, was prompted by a run-in at third base in the Cardinal half of the sixth inning, when Medwick slid into the bag after a booming triple to right and exchanged kicks with Marvin Owen, Tiger infielder. The two players almost came to blows before they were separated by players and umpires, but Medwick's return to his position at the end of the inning was the signal for a wild outbreak by the thousands packed in the temporary open stands of left field.

Medwick was the target for fruit, hot dogs and a few dozen pop bottles, all of which he dodged before beating a retreat to the infield, where his team-mates clustered around him. Yelling and hooting, the crowd quickly littered up most of deep left field with food or anything else they could get their hands on.

**ANOTHER VOLLEY**

Players, umpires, and finally Manager Cochrane went out to plead for order, but on each of three times that Medwick tentatively

(Continued on Page 10, Column 8)

## *BOX SCORE*

ST. LOUIS (N. L.)

| | A.B. | R. | H. | O. | A. | E. |
|---|---|---|---|---|---|---|
| Martin, 3b | 5 | 3 | 2 | 0 | 1 | 0 |
| Rothrock, rf | 5 | 1 | 2 | 4 | 0 | 0 |
| Frisch, 2b | 5 | 1 | 1 | 3 | 5 | 0 |
| Medwick, lf | 4 | 1 | 1 | 1 | 0 | 0 |
| Fullis, lf | 1 | 0 | 1 | 1 | 0 | 0 |
| Collins, 1b | 5 | 1 | 4 | 7 | 2 | 1 |
| Delancey, c | 5 | 1 | 1 | 5 | 0 | 0 |
| Orsatti, cf | 3 | 1 | 1 | 2 | 0 | 0 |
| Durocher, ss | 5 | 1 | 2 | 3 | 4 | 0 |
| J. Dean, p | 5 | 1 | 2 | 1 | 0 | 0 |
| Totals | 43 | 11 | 17 | 27 | 12 | 1 |

DETROIT (A. L.)

| | A.B. | R. | H. | O. | A. | E. |
|---|---|---|---|---|---|---|
| White, cf | 4 | 0 | 0 | 3 | 0 | 1 |
| Cochrane c | 4 | 0 | 0 | 3 | 2 | 0 |
| Gehringer, 2b | 4 | 0 | 2 | 3 | 5 | 1 |
| Goslin, lf | 4 | 0 | 0 | 4 | 0 | 1 |
| Rogell, ss | 4 | 0 | 1 | 3 | 2 | 0 |
| Greenberg, 1b | 4 | 0 | 1 | 7 | 0 | 0 |
| Owen, 3b | 4 | 0 | 0 | 1 | 2 | 0 |
| Fox, rf | 3 | 0 | 2 | 3 | 0 | 0 |
| Auker, p | 0 | 0 | 0 | 0 | 0 | 0 |
| Rowe, p | 0 | 0 | 0 | 0 | 0 | 0 |
| Hogsett, p | 0 | 0 | 0 | 0 | 0 | 0 |
| Bridges, p | 2 | 0 | 0 | 0 | 0 | 0 |
| Marberry, p | 0 | 0 | 0 | 0 | 0 | 0 |
| xG. Walker | 1 | 0 | 0 | 0 | 0 | 0 |
| Crowder, p | 0 | 0 | 0 | 0 | 0 | 0 |
| Totals | 34 | 0 | 6 | 27 | 11 | [illegible] |

x—Batted for Marberry in 8th.

| | | | | | | | | | | |
|---|---|---|---|---|---|---|---|---|---|---|
| St. Louis | 0 | 0 | 7 | 0 | 0 | 2 | 2 | 0 | 0 | —11 |
| Detroit | 0 | 0 | 0 | 0 | 0 | 0 | 0 | 0 | 0 | — 0 |

Runs batted in—Frisch, 3; Collins, 2; Delancey, 1; J. Dean, 1; Medwick, 1; Martin, 1; Rothrock, 1.

Earned runs—St. Louis, 10.

Two-base hits — Rothrock, 2; J. Dean, 1; Frisch, 1; Delancey, 1; Fox, 2.

Three-base hits—Medwick, 1; Durocher, 1.

Stolen bases—Martin, 2;

Double plays—Owen to Gehringer to Greenberg.

Left on bases—St. Louis, 9; Detroit, 7.

Bases on balls — Off Auker, 1 (Rothrock;) Hogsett, 2 (Orsatti, Martin;) Marberry, 1 (Orsatti.)

Struck out—By J. Dean, 5 (Greenberg, 3; Bridges, White;) by Crowder, 1 (Rothrock;) by Auker, 1 (Martin;) by Bridges, 2 (J. Dean, Delancey.)

Hits—Off Auker, 6 in 2⅓ innings; off Rowe, 2 in ⅓ innings; off Hogsett, 2 in 0 innings (pitched to four batters in third;) off Bridges 6 in 4⅓ innings; off Marberry 1 in 1 inning; off Crowder, 0 in 1 inning.

Losing pitcher—Auker.

Umpires — Geisel (A.L.) plate; Reardon (N.L.) first base; Owen (A.L.) second base; Klem (N.L.) third base.

Time of game—2h. 19m.

# Hawaiians Rally to Beat Bear Eleven, 26-13

Los Angeles Times Sports

C WEDNESDAY MORNING, DECEMBER 26, 1934.

# HIGH GLEE WINS $5000 CHRISTMAS RACE

### *When High Glee Brought His Ticket Holders a Real Christmas Present at Santa Anita*

High Glee, a rank outsider, shown galloping to a thrilling victory in the $5000 Christmas Stakes, feature race of the inaugural program at Santa Anita Park. Chictoney (No. 10) was second, more than a length behind the victor. Riskulus, owned by Norman Church, was third. Top Row (No. 4) was fourth and Time Supply, the favorite, fifth. High Glee paid $14.60. Silvio Coucci jockeyed High Glee to victory. Fans who had tickets on Chictoney received a surprise when prices of $39.00 to place and $13.40 to show were posted.

## *Bill Henry* Says—

THOUGHTS of a guy trying to recover from neckties, turkey, stick candy, Christmas cards and all the other things that go with the celebration of the happy Yule season.

**FOR CHRISTMAS?**

Some college is going to pick up a prize package in this boy Harry Smith of Chaffey. He is built on bungalow lines, strong as a bull, aggressive and fast. He annoyed Long Beach no end the other afternoon in the prep finals and would make a fine Christmas present for some haggard coach, who is wondering where he's going to get a really good guard.

**TENNIS PREVIEW**

The indoor tennis tournament that starts at the Ambassador tonight is likely to be unusually interesting with three red-hot Davis Cup prospects in Donald Budge of San Francisco, Frank Shields of New York and Gene Mako of Los Angeles battling. Last year Jane Sharp started the sensational play that put her in this year's first ten at this tournament. Incidentally it was packed every night. Better hurry.

**ME-FIRST-ERS FOILED**

It is being rumored around that when the pro golfers sent by the association to Australia departed on their journey, that all got together and agreed to whack up the prizes regardless of who won 'em. They didn't declare Jimmy Thomson in on the divvy because he was paying his own way. Then Jimmy up and won the big prize of the whole trip. I wonder who's laffing now?

**SOME NEW STARS**

In the 1936 Olympic Games you can look to the swimmers to provide the new names and new records. They do it every time. Holland has Willy Den Ouden, a 15-year-old girl, to bust all of Helene Madison's records wide open.

**DIDN'T GO SO FAST**

The two-man racing cars out at Mines Field averaged only fifteen miles an hour faster than the litstock cars did last February over an infinitely more difficult course. The condition of the track, however, had a great deal to do with it. For quite a time the boys were averaging almost ninety miles an hour. If they put the lads on again a few weeks hence and the track is in shape they might keep the average up close to the 100-mile-an-hour mark.

**THIS IS SOMETHING NEW**

Has it occurred to you that the Rose Bowl situation is unique? This is the first time the new Bowl has ever been filled to its capacity of 84,400. It is the first time it has ever been sold out before Christmas. The day the Trojans nearly filled it they sold 30,000 tickets the day of the game. It is probably the largest football crowd of the year in the United States also.

**UP AGAINST CLASS**

This may be a little out of season, but you can begin feeling sorry for Dink Templeton and his Stanford track prospects for this year. He won't be right up there as usual. The Tropans will have a sensational team of veterans and some great newcomers. The dark horse bunch to watch out for are Brutus Hamilton's Californians. They've been getting tougher every year and they're about due.

**STARS MISSING**

Where are all the outstanding fighters that usually crop up during the course of every new year? This has been a pretty punk twelve months, fistically speaking. Madison Square Garden can't find anybody who'd draw flies at an outdoor fight in Florida. And who looks like an opponent for the mighty Maxie Baer?

**A BREAK FOR NAGS**

Santa Anita is going to do several unusual things. You'll see more than the usual atention paid to the horses. There are a number of good races planned for the 2-year-olds and the races leading up to the four-mile "Marathon" for the older horsse will be the first of such length in this country in years.

## *What's Doing in Sports at Local Arenas*

WRESTLING—"Man Mountain" Dean vs. Jim Londos at Olympic, 8:30 p.m.

FOOTBALL—Alabama team works out at Occidental College, 2 p.m.

BASKETBALL—Two games. Glendale J.C. vs. Baxter Club, Fresno State vs. Universal Studio, 7:15 p.m., at Glendale High.

## BEARS DROP GRID GAME

### *Townies Capture Tilt, 26-13*

*California Warriors Routed in Last Half to Drop Hawaii Struggle*

HONOLULU, Dec. 25. (AP)—Fifteen thousand football fans of Hawaii sat amazed and watched the Honolulu town team, led by a pair of local firemen, trounce the University of California, 26 to 13, here today.

The Townies, after a disastrous local season, played far over their heads, while the California varsity functioned slowly and uncertainly. Among the spectators were many doleful experts who had figured the mainland team to be at least twenty-one points better than the local aggregation.

**RAINBOWS NEXT**

California will play the Roaring Rainbows of the University of Hawaii here New Year's Day.

Trailing 13 to 12 at half time, the Townies drove brilliantly for another touchdown and the extra point in each of the last two quarters. Dashing through the California line and around the ends, and occasionally varying their attack by taking to the air, the locals outplayed the visitors throughout after the first quarter.

**WILLIAMS SCORES**

The first California score climaxed a 46-yard drive, featured by a 28-yard pass from Halfback Arleigh Williams to Bob Brittingham, end, which placed the ball on the Townies' 13-yard line. A 15-yard penalty gave the Golden Bears the ball on the Townies 1-yard line, from which point Williams crashed through the line for the touchdown. The versatile halfback added the extra point with a placement kick.

The town team came back with a 77-yard drive, with Hiram Kaakua, a lanky Hawaiian, and Tim Blaisdell, both firemen, sweeping the ends and advancing the ball to California's 10-yard line, where the ball was lost on downs.

**BEARS SCORE AGAIN**

As the second period opened an 18-yard pass from California's Eddie Vallejo to Halfback Ken Moeller put the ball on the Townies' 9-yard marker. Frank Walker, fullback, stabbed the line for a touchdown. Vallejo failed to convert when his place kick was wide. This was California's last sally into scoring territory.

Then the Townies got under way. A 16-yard pass from Fernandez to Howell began a 43-yard drive. Kaakua swept around end for 6 yards and then tossed a 21-yard forward

(Continued on Page 10, Column 4)

High Glee, C. V. Whitney's brown filly, is shown basking in the victor's limelight. Jockey Silvio Coucci is up. Mayor George H. Williams of Arcadia and Mrs. Hal Roach bestowed the traditional floral wreath on High Glee.

## ALABAMA IN HARD DRILL

*Coach Thomas Sends Tide Through Stiff Practice Behind Locked Gates*

BY BRAVEN DYER

While most of the sportively inclined citizenry of Southern California attended the opening of the Santa Anita race track, Coach Frank Thomas sent his University of Alabama gridders through a stiff workout at the Rose Bowl yesterday afternoon.

The practice session was a secret one and the southern mentor barred the gates to everybody while he drilled his charges for the better part of two hours. Absence of suitable weather during their late practice periods while at home handicapped the Dixie lads and Thomas lost no time yesterday giv-

(Continued on Page 6, Column 6)

## *Flower of Cinemaland Flocks to Santa Anita*

### Al Jolson, Mary Brian, Gable and Scores of Other Celebrities Rub Elbows at New Track

BY READ KENDALL

Filmdom entirely forgot its world of make-believe to migrate to the Santa Anita track yesterday for the renewal of horse racing in Los Angeles . . . They rubbed elbows with Angelenos and society folk, jostled through the crowd of 39,000 spectators to get a hot dog or place a bet and joined in the cheer that swept over the giant racing plant as the horses left the barrier for the first race.

Al Jolson, with his wife, Ruby Keeler on his arm seen heading for the ticket window to place his bet. Jolson knows every horse there is to know and is a devout follower of the tracks. You couldn't have kept him home even with a broken leg . . . Mary Brian the cynosure of all eyes in about the slickest outfit noticed in the clubhouse. It was a tow-toned chartreuse woolen ensemble. Her mother was with her but Dick Powell was noticeably missing . . .

Over in a corner of the dining-room in the clubhouse sat Gene

(Continued on Page 10, Column 2)

## GROOMS IN RACE STRIKE

*Stable Hands, Enraged Over "Louse Ring," Almost Spoil Program*

Santa Anita's big opening-day crowd came closer to disappointment yesterday than any one of the 39,000 even remotely suspected.

For several hours the entire program of eight races was completely scrapped. The grooms—over 700 strong—struck. They refused to lead a horse to the receiving barn. They were finally appeased by Christopher FitzGerald, the presiding steward, and today they have a session with Carleton Burke, head of the Racing Commission, for a final showdown.

It all happened over the so-called "louse ring." The Santa Anita management wired off a section at the west end of the terrace, near the barns, where the grooms can view

(Continued on Page 10, Column 1)

## STRENUOUS SCRIMMAGES AT END FOR STANFORD

STANFORD UNIVERSITY, Dec. 25. (AP)—His squad back in shape after a series of illness and injuries which had given him some nerve-racking days, Coach C. E. (Tiny) Thornhill today announced the end of heavy scrimmaging for his Stanford football players, who are preparing for the Pasadena Rose Bowl game.

Only Bobby Grayson, the All-America back and Stanford's best signal caller, remained on the slightly doubtful list today as the Cards drew a day of rest in celebration of Christmas—and Grayson confidently expects to be ready to meet Alabama's great Crimson Tide one week hence.

Except for Jim (Monk) Moscrip, stellar left end, and Robert (Horse) Reynolds, All-America tackle, the practice field was empty here today. The pair couldn't stay away from the enclosed turf, and they spent over an hour exercising.

Thornhill will collect his squad—that is, those who haven't left for the south already—for a final workout here tomorrow afternoon. It will be an informal practice. The team leaves at 9 p.m. for Pasadena and will have two workouts at Brookside Park there Thursday.

## *Few Long Shots; Many "Big Shots" of Sports World at Santa Anita*

BY BOB RAY

There may have been a scarcity of long shots at Santa Anita yesterday, but there were plenty of "big shots" of the athletic world on hand to help welcome legalized horse racing back to Southern California for the first time since the days when hour-glass figures, William Jennings Bryan and croquet were current topics of conversation and amusement.

Leading the parade was none other than Will Rogers, who talks a fine game of polo when he isn't twitting the lawmaking bodies of this great commonwealth. Will apparently has degenerated into a tout, but not of the common garden variety because he told everybody to bet on Vanita, who only breezed home to pay $30.40 in the third race.

Also among those present was Lou Daro, the rassling impresario, wearing a white carnation in his lapel and a look of amazement on his face. Lou wouldn't state whether he was trying to get a job as jockey for Man Mountain Dean or whether he was just attempting to sign up a race horse for a finish match with one of his rasslers.

The hoss-racing profession was represented by Lou Anger, Joe Schenk's right-hand man at Agua Caliente, and Bill Kyne, Bay Meadows track owner, who brought down a party of sportmen.

Gene Normile, who managed Jack Dempsey in the post-Kearns era, who also on hand. Gene at one time operated a book at Tijuana

(Continued on Page 8, Column 8)

## WHITNEY'S STILL LEAD

### *Filly Captures Rich Classic*

*High Glee's Victory Brings More Glory to Famous Racing Stables*

BY OSCAR OTIS

You'll read a lot about Santa Anita's opening yesterday. You'll read, those of you who weren't out there, about a 39,000 turnout, a near-record pari-mutuel handle for California, the spectacle, the pomp, and the show that marked Santa Anita's inaugurual of a fifty-three-day meeting.

You'll hear a lot today about the beauty of the plant, the color of the throng, the bets won and lost, the drama of racing itself.

**THE STORY**

But right now you'll read about a bit of a filly named High Glee racing in the sky-blue silks and Eton brown cap of a young New York sportsman named Whitney.

High Glee won the Christmas Stakes from a California horse named Chictoney and a Los Angeles-owned horse called Riskulus. She won fairly and squarely as a good horse should. Her victory was really a triumph for California racing, as the presence of the Whitney silks at any race track is the final hallmark of quality.

**RICH GENT**

Three generations ago in New York there lived an enormously wealthy fellow named Whitney. He was an astute business man, and built up one of the largest fortunes in the history of American finance.

He not only loved business but sport as well. He turned to the turf for recreation. He went first class. He was a power in the Jockey Club, that august body which controls racing in America., He bought a farm and some fine thoroughbreds. To this day his stock has dominated American racing.

The venerable Whitney served his country as well as the turf. He distinguished himself as a member of the Cabinet and in other lines of

(Continued on Page 7, Column 1)

## CHICTONEY IN SECOND

### *Riskulus Third in Classic*

*Crowd of 39,000 Witnesses Surprising Victory of Whitney Horse*

The scared little horse in the stabling paddock was the winner of the big $5000 Christmas stakes. High Glee they registered her as a yearling. She's the daughter of an exotic-named father, Pharamond II.

Time Supply, the big favorite, and Head Play, the beauty king, didn't have the punch.

In the lee of the majestic Sierra Madre Mountains and with a crowd of 39,000 persons looking on they gave horse racing back to Southern California with a smashing surprise in the first big feature spin at Santa Anita.

**BROWN FILLY**

High Glee, a little brown 3-year-old filly belonging to one of the blue bloods of the East, C. V. Whitney, walked off with the $5000 Christmas stakes by over a length. Chictoney, a California horse, was second, and Riskulus, a Los Angeles-owned horse, was third by the same distance. The time was 1:37 for the mile.

Second at the start and first at the finish. That was the sensational performance of the norse little Silvio Coucci, the Bronx Express, wearing the Eton blue and brown colors of the Whitney stables, rode yesterday.

**COUCCI UP**

It was Coucci's second victory of the day and it pulled him up to within striking distance of Maurice Peters for the year's jockey leadership. Peters has ridden 213 winners and Coucci 211.

Gauging his pace perfectly little Coucci didn't make his bid for victory until the head of the stretch was reached. Chictoney had set the pace and High Glee had followed it. Together they fought off all challenges. They were a friendly team.

But when they rounded the turn and hit the straightaway the friendship ceased. Coucci used his bat for the first time and High Glee responded with a wild leap that carried her past Chictoney like the wind.

**ALL OVER**

It was all over by the time they hit the eighth pole. They might just as well have stopped the race right there. There was not catching High Glee and Riskulus, who had something in reserve, finished a length and a half ahead of the tiring Top Row, world record holder.

Time Supply and Head Play, the big favorites, were never in the running. Winner of the last two big handicaps of the year—$25,000 races at Narragansett and Bay Meadows—Time Supply finished fifth. He was an 8-to-5 favorite but he left his race in the Bay Meadows mud a week ago last Sunday.

**HEAD PLAY LAST**

Head Play, living up to an old reputation and fractious at the start, wound up last after being sent outside the stall gate at the start. Lee Humphries, "Little Red," riding "Big Red" couldn't get his mount into the competition at any stage of the game.

The vivid burnt orange colors of the Mrs. Silas B. Mason stables loomed up brightly, but the gorgeous horse Tommy Taylor trained so hard for the race couldn't get back to the wars after over a year's lay-off.

He looked a champion in the stabling paddock. He pricked up his ears and gazed about majestically, but when it came to matching strides with other great stars in a field of twelve "Big Red" was sunk.

**THREE HORSE RACE**

The tingling duel of horse flesh and hard riding that saw High Glee

(Continued on Page 10, Column 5)

## TWENTY GRAND MAY GO TO POST ON SATURDAY

*Greentree Stable's Mighty Champion Nominated for $2500 Santa Maria Handicap*

Although Head Play failed in his first comeback trial this is not going to deter Twenty Grand from making a noble effort in the Santa Maria $2500 stake race on Saturday. Trainer Bill Brennan yesterday entered the 1931 Kentucky Derby winner under the nom de course of Mrs. Payne Whitney, the Greentree Stables. Gillie, a filly, and Peradventure, a 2-year-old, will be running mates.

And from the C. V. Whitney barns will come Trumpery, stablemate of High Glee, yesterday's winner of the $5000 Christmas stakes.

Marooned, a crack sprinter from the LeMar stables, will make his first start at the track, and Clyde Phillips, who scratched Semaphore in the big Christmas Day feature, will send him to the post.

Bill Brennan

Blessed Event is a world record holder who will make his initial start. He is owned by Al Tarn, who sent Polish Beau home in front in the seventh race yesterday.

Horse and owner—

Twenty Grand, Greentree Stable.
Gillie, Greentree Stable.
Peradventure, Greentree Stable.
Marooned, Le Mar Stock Farm.
Frisky Matron, Mrs. Alberta E. Ryan.
Trumpery, C. V. Whitney.
Sweeping Light, Eskay Stable.
Wise Daughter, Milky Way Stable.
Teralice, Percy M. Pike.
Red Wagon, A. C. Compton.
Ima Count, Northway Stable.
Chance Line, Mrs. Ray Pollard.
Wacoche, A. G. Tarn.
Blessed Event, A. G. Tarn.
Pitter Pat, Belair Stud.
Rock X., Tranquility Farm.
Royal Blunder, Thomas Donley.
Laughing Queen, William R. Coe.
Semaphore, Mrs. Clyde Phillips.
Leros, J. C. Ellis.
Sarada, F. A. Griffith.
Cutie Face, F. A. Griffith.

# AZUCAR'S VICTORY NETS HIS OWNER $108,400

*When Azucar (Sugar in Any Kind of Language) Bought Himself $108,400 Worth of Oats*

Azucar (Spanish for sugar) made good his name yesterday when he won the classic Santa Anita Handicap, world's richest turf race. Azucar is shown crossing the finish line two lengths ahead of Ladysman (No. 5.) Time Supply (No. 6) was third. Ted Clark, who set the pace, can be seen running at the rail. He is just about to be passed by Top Row, fourth place winner. Azucar netted his owner, F. M. Aiger, the staggering sum of $108,400. The victor is a reformed steeplechase jumper. [A. P. photo]

## WINNER STORMS IN FROM BEHIND TO ANNEX STAKE

### *Alger's Steed Defeats Challenges of Time Supply and Ladysman in Battle on Stretch*

BY OSCAR OTIS

Now that the $100,000 Santa Anita Handicap has been written into the record books, now that Azucar has been crowned the winner, let us glance into the actual running of the race and profit by the lessons it has shown.

The Santa Anita, considering the size of the field with twenty starters, was an amazingly true-run race. Not a single starter but did not have a chance to run at some stage of the journey and, although the traffic was intense in spots, as Bill Henry so aptly puts it, each and every horse was clear at one time or another and had a free dash for it. Even so, very few horses were badly shut off at any stage.

Azucar was clearly the best horse. Victory netted his owner, Fred M. Alger, Jr., $108,400. Azucar came from behind, and in the stretch maintained his position easily in front when challenged by Time Supply and Ladysman. The latter found a clear opening at the head of the stretch after having been hemmed in on the rail at the far turn, but even so was running easily most of the way.

**FORWARDLY PLACED**

Time Supply was forwardly placed at all times. The horse had not a valid excuse, just not having enough on the ball as against Azucar and Ladysman. Even so, Time Supply turned in a smashing effort and one that will make him dangerous in future handicap races wherever he may choose to campaign on the American turf.

Top Row got through on the rail as usual to finish fourth. He dearly loves to run on the rail and saved ground while many of the others were taking the overland route on the outside.

**"EKKY" LACKS SPEED**

Equipoise was on the outside most of the way, and while he got none the best of it, he was not badly banged around. Equipoise just simply did not have enough speed to catch those horses, and failed to come on when called upon in the stretch.

High Glee could never catch Ted Clark, the early pacemaker. Ted tired and stopped to a walk just as he figured to do after hitting up the fast clip he did for the first mile. Faireno had a run for it, but faltered when the real racing began. Mate was forwardly placed early and wilted after a half mile.

**START DELAYED**

Head Play acted badly and delayed the start, was finally started from the outside, and failed to show much actual running ability once the field got under way. Gusto and Good Goods were never prominent. Riskulus had early speed but stopped badly, apparently not being in very good frame of mind with his spread hoof aching. Sarada, Sweeping

(Continued on Page 27, Column 5)

## OWENS RUINS JUMP MARK

### *Negro Boy Does 25ft. 9in.*

*Other Records Wrecked in Weight Toss, Dash and 1500-Meter Run*

NEW YORK, Feb. 23. (AP)—Five world record performances, including two by Ohio State's brilliant Negro athlete, Jesse Owens, and another by the all-conquering Glenn Cunningham marked an exciting battle for the national senior A.A.U. indoor track and field championships tonight before a near capacity crowd of 15,000 in Madison Square Garden.

**TWO EQUALED**

Two other world indoor marks were equaled, with new championship meet records set up in seven events, all told, as the New York Athletic Club easily retained the team championship. Wearers of the winged foot compiled 36 points.

Cunningham, again demonstrating his complete mastery over all rivals, raced to a forty-yard triumph over Bill Bonthron and lowered his own indoor 1500-meter record to 3m. 50.5s. The only surprise was Bonthron's comeback to beat his Pennsylvania rival, Gene Venzke, for second place by a two-yard margin.

**RECORD LEAP**

Owens, the all-around star of the meet, successfully defended his broad-jump title with a new record leap of 25ft. 9in., and then lost out by inches to another Negro, Ben Johnson of Columbia, in a record-breaking battle for honors in the 60-meter dash. Owens lowered the world record to 6.6s. in the semi-finals, which saw the elimination of the defending champion, Ralph Metcalfe of Marquette, but Johnson flashed to the tape first in similar record time to beat Owens in the final by six inches.

**OFF FORM**

Metcalfe, who had shared the former record of 6.7s., was off form and among the principal upset victims of the night. The outstanding surprise, however, came in the 1000-meter run in which the great Charles Hornbostel of Indiana, previously undefeated indoors this winter, apparently pulled a muscle, pulled up and finished next to last. Hornbostel thus lost his title to Glen Dawson of Tulsa, Okla., and withdrew from the 600 meters.

Other world records were set in the 1500-meter walk by Hank Cieman of Toronto in 6m. 7.3s. and in the thirty-five-pound weight throw by Henry Dreyer, Rhode Island State, with 55ft. 3¾in.

**BEARD WINS**

Percy Beard of the N.Y.A.C. equaled his own world mark of 8.6s. in capturing the sixty-five-meter high hurdles.

Only six champions emerged in

(Continued on Page 29, Column 6)

# Los Angeles Times Sports

CC SUNDAY MORNING, FEBRUARY 24, 1935.

## *Bill Henry Says—*

SOMEWHERE over the hill, where they take care of such things, the old man with the scythe is saying to his helpers that it's about time to prepare a headstone which will have engraved upon it:

"Here Lies Horse Racing."

And when his helpers ask him what other words ought to be carved on the monument he'll tell 'em to prepare the same old inscriptions:

"Killed by Its Friends."

That's the history of horse racing and it looks very much as though it would be as true this time as it has been in the past.

**ENOUGH HORSE RACING IS SUFFICIENT**

Yesterday the original fifty-three-day meeting of the Santa Anita track came to an end, though it has been extended for a couple of weeks longer by an indulgent racing board.

It's been quite a show, too.

In a setting unequaled for grandeur, amid beautiful surroundings, devoid of any breath of scandal, managed in a style that is certainly in strange contrast to the haphazard muddle of most racing plants, the finest horses in the world have performed in a race meet whose success has far surpassed the most rosy dreams of its sponsors.

**"HORSEMEN" PREDICTED GIGANTIC FLOP**

And, let we forget, let's remember that the "horsemen" who talk out of the corners of their mouths and to whom horse racing is a matter of form charts, whispers, odds and such things, made the following predictions:

(1.) Santa Anita would never be built.

(2.) If it was built, it would be a flop.

(3.) None of the "big-name" horses would be here.

(4.) If they came, none of the "big-name" horses would go to the post because they were all broken-down cripples.

These weren't the assertions of the enemies of horse racing. That's what the so-called "horsemen" themselves all had to say about the track.

**TOO MUCH RACING SURE TO KILL SPORT**

The demand of the horsey gentry who like to call themselves

(Continued on Page 29, Column 2)

## JANE SHARP WINS TITLE

*Helen Pedersen Beaten in National Indoor Final, 11-9, 6-1*

NEW YORK, Feb. 23. (AP)—Overcoming a three game deficit in the first set when she shifted to a forecourt position after vainly trying to match her opponent from the baseline, Eleanor Jane Sharp of Pasadena, Cal., today became women's national indoor tennis champion.

She defeated Helen Pedersen of Stamford, Conn., national girl's grass court titlist, who for the second consecutive year was denied the championship, 11-9, 6-1. A year ago Miss Pedersen was beaten in the final in straight sets by Norma Taubele. A gallery of close to 1000 watched the contest.

After a 10 minute rest Miss Sharp came back for her third final of the tournament, pairing with Gregory Mangin of Newark, former men's indoor titleholder, to defeat

(Continued on Page 29, Column 7)

## *Bronc Baseball Team Defeats Stanford, 5-3*

STANFORD UNIVERSITY (Cal.) Feb. 23. (AP)—Four runs in the first three innings and another in the ninth gave the Santa Clara University baseball team a 5-to-3 victory over the Stanford Indians here today.

The Santa Clarans' attack in the early frames drove Johnny Campbell, Stanford hurler, from the mound. He was relieved by Stan Anderson.

"Schoolhouse" Banks, Santa Clara hurler, allowed but two hits.

The score:

| | | R. | H. | E. |
|---|---|---|---|---|
| Santa Clara | 031 000 001— | 5 | 7 | 5 |
| Stanford | 000 003 000— | 3 | 2 | 6 |

Banks and Bassi; Campbell, Anderson, Heringer and Ferro, Morgan.

## *Trojan Cagers Defeat California Five, 36-26*

### Bears Ahead at Half-Time, but S.C. Squad Comes From Behind With Guttero Leading Attack

BY BOB RAY

California's Golden Bears, swamped 60-32 by Southern California Friday evening, gave the fast-traveling Trojans a real basketball battle at the Olympic last night, but in the end the Berkeley boys once more bowed to Sam Barry's basket-bombers by a score of 36-26.

The victory gave the Trojans, who have already clinched the southern division championship and are just waiting to see whether they're going to play Oregon State or Washington for the Pacific Coast Conference title, a clean sweep over their arch-rivals from California in the four-game series.

**BEAR DEFENSE TIGHT**

Nibs Price's quintet, showing a complete reversal of the terrible form they exhibited Friday, even went so far as to grab the lead at the end of a nip-and-tuck first half, 14-12. The Bears presented a tight defense that had the Trojans worried until they finally got under way in the second period.

Lee Guttero, Troy's candidate for All-American center honors, led the S.C. scorers by registering five field goals and four free throws for 14 points. This brought Guttero's season point total to 173, a new southern division scoring record.

**JACK HUPP INJURED**

Jack Hupp, lanky Trojan forward, scored 9 points, the same number made by big Dave Meek, the California center. Hupp injured his ankle in a spill midway in the second half, but Jerry Gracin filled in nicely for him to register 6 points.

After Troy had jumped off to a 7-0 lead, the Bears, with Meek and Kopke doing most of the scoring, rallied to finally move ahead, 13-8.

(Continued on Page 29, Column 8)

## *STANFORD WINS OVER BRUIN FIVE*

*Westwooders Beaten by Indians in Long-Range Basket Duel, 35-16*

STANFORD UNIVERSITY, Feb. 23. (AP) — In a long-range sharp-shooting duel, Stanford's basketball Indians defeated the University of California at Los Angeles Bruins, 35 to 16, here tonight.

It was the second straight win for the Indians, who downed U.C.L.A., 33 to 28 last night, and their fourth victory in eleven starts in the Pacific Coast Conference's southern-division race.

The Indians bottled up the Bruins with a tight defensive tonight and then banged away with wild shots from the middle of the floor to hit the mark often enough for their overwhelming victory.

John Ball, U.C.L.A. high-scoring center, was closely guarded but managed to lead his team with six points. Rod Bost, right forward, led the Stanford scoring with 9 points.

The Indians took the lead early

(Continued on Page 29, Column 1)

## NITTINGER COPS TITLE

*Don Defeats Van, 6 and 5, to Bring College Golf Crown to Southern California*

DEL MONTE, Feb. 23. (AP)—Defeating Bill Van, 6 and 5, Don Nittinger carried off the Pacific Coast intercollegiate golf championship for the University of Southern California today at Pebble Beach.

Van, also of U.S.C., was trailing at the end of the first round today, carding 82 for the first eighteen to Nittinger's 78. This afternoon he showed signs of overcoming the lead, but on the second hole he failed by a poor putt to make an eagle and from then on it was easy going for the winner. They finished at the thirteenth when Nittinger sank a beautiful ten-foot putt.

U.S.C. carried the title south from Stanford, holder for the last two years through Lawson Little, who was unable to compete in this tournament.

Stanford suffered from the beginning of play this year, when Nittinger created an upset by defeating Don Edwards, runner-up on the State amateur finals last year.

## *Denver Bettors Win $300,000*

DENVER, Feb. 23. (AP)—A Denver betting syndicate won $300,000 on Azucar when he finished first in the Santa Anita $100,000 Handicap race today, the News says.

The Denverites wagered $20,000 on Azucar at odds of 15 to 1, the paper says.

An additional $35,000 was wagered on the race by Denverites, the paper estimated. Most of this was bet on the favorites.

## *Azucar Breezes in as Wind Comes Up*

BY BILL HENRY

The day was made to order for Azucar. Game old Ted Clark, bless his courageous soul, skittish little High Glee and gorgeous Big Red Head Play battered their hearts out bucking a thirty-mile gale as they led the way down the backstretch. Azucar, beautifully held on the rail, let the others kill themselves bucking the wind and then breezed home in front of the gale like a yacht with all sails sets.

**Depression Notes**

Well, well, well! So this is the Depression! You should have seen the folks battling like steers in a stampede to lay the family bankroll on the line. More than $150,000 had been wagered on the handicap before the horses got on the track and they wagered almost as much

(Continued on Page 27, Column 6)

## *Racing Form Chart for Santa Anita Handicap*

**3898**—SIXTH RACE—One mile and one-quarter. For 3-year-olds and up. The Santa Anita Handicap.— Purse $100,000 added, plus all entrance and starting fees to the winner. Net value to winner, $108,400; second, $10,000; third, $5000; fourth, $2500.

| Index No. | Horse. | Wt. | P.P. | St. | ¼ | ½ | ¾ | Str. | Fin. | Jockey. | Odds to $1 |
|---|---|---|---|---|---|---|---|---|---|---|---|
| 3790 | Azucar | 117 | 3 | 2 | 14hd | $11^{3}$ | $4^{2}$ | $1^{2}$ | $1^{2}$ | Woolf | 12.40 |
| 3807 | Ladysman | 117 | 4 | 6 | 7hd | 8½ | $3^{3}$ | 2hd | $2^{1}$ | Richards | 5.20 |
| 3737 | Time Supply | 118 | 2 | 1 | $3^{3}$ | $3^{1\frac{1}{2}}$ | $2^{1\frac{1}{2}}$ | 3hd | $3^{2}$ | Luther | 12.10 |
| 3737 | Top Row | 109 | 18 | 15 | $11^{1\frac{1}{2}}$ | $16^{1}$ | $8^{1\frac{1}{2}}$ | 4½ | 4½ | Peters | 26.70 |
| 3822 | Ted Clark | 103 | 12 | 5 | $1^{4}$ | $1^{6}$ | $1^{2}$ | $5^{1}$ | 5[illegible] | Meade | 6.30 |
| 3737 | Mate | 120 | 6 | 4 | 4hd | 5hd | 9½ | 6½ | 6hd | Albrecht | 35.10 |
| 3861 | Equipoise | 130 | 19 | 12 | 12hd | $12^{1\frac{1}{2}}$ | $12^{2}$ | $7^{1}$ | $7^{1\frac{1}{2}}$ | Workman | 1.70 |
| 3861 | Gusto | 117 | 5 | 17 | $18^{6}$ | $14^{1}$ | 7hd | $8^{1}$ | 8½ | Arcaro | 28.30 |
| 3845 | Frank Ormont | 108 | 11 | 19 | 20 | 20 | 15½ | 9hd | 9hd | Maiben | 6.30 |
| 3861 | Twenty Grand | 126 | 7 | 1 | $9^{1}$ | 13hd | $14^{3}$ | $13^{1}$ | 10hd | Coucci | 10.30 |
| 3861 | Sweeping Light | 108 | 1 | 3 | 10hd | 10hd | $11^{1}$ | $10^{1}$ | $11^{1\frac{1}{2}}$ | Haas | 6.30 |
| 3737 | Riskulus | 111 | 9 | 7 | $8^{1}$ | 6hd | 6½ | $11^{3}$ | $12^{5}$ | Westrope | 6.30 |
| 3790 | Fleam | 104 | 10 | 13 | $15^{1\frac{1}{2}}$ | 17hd | 13hd | 12½ | $13^{1}$ | Saunders | 33.40 |
| 3861 | Sarada | 106 | 15 | 20 | $19^{5}$ | $19^{3}$ | $19^{1}$ | $16^{1}$ | $14^{2}$ | McCown | 6.30 |
| 3845 | Mad Frump | 102 | 20 | 18 | 17hd | $18^{1\frac{1}{2}}$ | 16½ | $14^{3}$ | $15^{6}$ | Turk | 6.30 |
| 3845 | Precursor | 103 | 14 | 10 | $8^{2}$ | $7^{2}$ | $10^{1\frac{1}{2}}$ | $15^{3}$ | $16^{4}$ | Mauro | 6.30 |
| 3676 | High Glee | 107 | 16 | 8 | 2hd | 2½ | $17^{1}$ | $17^{2}$ | $17^{2}$ | Robertson | 1.70 |
| 3790 | Good Goods | 107 | 8 | 16 | 16hd | 15½ | 18½ | $18^{1}$ | $18^{1\frac{1}{2}}$ | Jones | 32.80 |
| 3790 | Head Play | 117 | 13 | 9 | $5^{1}$ | $4^{2}$ | 5hd | $19^{3}$ | $19^{6}$ | Kurtsinger | 10.50 |
| 3737 | Faireno | 120 | 17 | 14 | 13½ | 9hd | 20 | 20 | 20 | Malley | 33.40 |

Time, :22 2-5, :45 1-10, 1:36, 2:02 1-5. Two-dollar mutuels paid: Azucar, $26.80, $9.00, $6.60; Ladysman, $5.20, $4.60; Time Supply, $8.40. Winner ch. g. 7, T. Milesius-Clarice. Trained by J. Ruston. Went to post 4:33½, off 4:38. Start good, won easily, others driving.

Azucar, splendidly ridden, lacked the necessary early speed to keep up but gained gradually and coming strongly after entering the stretch got to the front in the final furlong and although bearing out a trifle near the end, won easily. Ladysman, also well handled, ran a smashing race and saved all possible ground in the late stages. Time Supply had his speed, and, remaining close to the pace in the early part, held on well in the final drive. Top Row ran a courageous race and was going gamely at the finish. Ted Clark opened up a long lead while making the pace but tired in the stretch. Equipoise was off rather slowly, was in close quarters on backstretch and was never a dangerous contender. High Glee had some early speed but never threatened Ted Clark, the pacemaker. Twenty Grand was never a dangerous contender at any stage. Faireno was close enough up in early stages but stopped badly. Mate could not keep up. Head Play acted badly at the post and started from outside the stalls, lacked his usual early speed. The others were outpaced. Scratched—Gillie. Overweights—High Glee, 2 pounds; Ted Clark, 3; Precursor, 3.

## *When There Was Nothing Backward About Ted Clark Except His Companions*

Four lengths to the good as the field headed into the stretch and running like he was being chased by a pack of hungry wolves. That was Ted Clark yesterday as he came dangerously close to scoring a stunning upset in the $100,000 Handicap at Santa Anita. The ex-selling plater's blinding speed left him in the long stretch run to the tape and he struggled home fifth as Azucar, Ladysman, Time Flight and Top Row whizzed by. Azucar, the victor, can be seen in second place, having fought his way through the field on the rail position. Time Supply on the outside of Azucar, finished third. [Times photo by George Strock]

## *WOOLF NETS $10,000 BY GREAT RIDE*

*Azucar's Jockey Enriched Ten Per Cent of Purse for Turf Triumph*

"If you want a statement from me," said F. M. Alger, Jr., owner of Azucar, the horse that won the $100,000 added Santa Anita Handicap yesterday, "just say that Jockey Georgie Woolf rode a wonderful race and is deserving of all the credit possible.

"What are our future plans for Azucar? Well, right now we're all so elated over the great victory that I'm not sure just when we'll leave Santa Anita. However, I plan to race Azucar in Detroit, and then we expect to take him to England. No, we're not sure whether we'll try him in the steeplechase running again. We'll just wait a while and see how things develop."

Alger, who is stopping at the Huntington Hotel in Pasadena, stated that Woolf would be given a bonus of about 10 per cent, which means that the young jockey will be some $10,000 richer because of his sensational winning ride.

## *Betting "Take" at Santa Anita Shaved*

SANTA ANITA PARK (Arcadia, Cal.) Feb. 23. (UP)—The Los Angeles Turf Club announced at the conclusion of the Santa Anita Handicap today that for the remainder of the racing meet it would take only a 6 per cent "cut" of the amount of money to pass through the betting booths.

For the fifty days of the meet, to today, the club received 8 per cent and the State 4 per cent. The meet here runs daily except Sunday until March 9.

## *What's Doing in Sports at Local Arenas*

**SUNDAY**

SOCCER—Two games at Loyola Stadium, 1 p.m.

POLO — Finals of Pacific Coast championship at Midwick, 2:15 p.m.; Sharpshooters vs. Santa Barbara at Riviera, 2 p.m.

RUGBY—Three games at Gilmore Stadium, 1 p.m.

YACHTING—Finals of Mid-winter regatta at Los Angeles Harbor, 12 a.m.

MOTORBOATING — Regatta at Newport Harbor, 2 p.m.

# Shellenback to Hurl Against Ducks Tomorrow

MONDAY MORNING, APRIL 8, 1935.

# SARAZEN TIES WOOD FOR AUGUSTA TITLE

## Bill Henry Says—

THE scantily attired boys from the University of Michigan who arrive in Los Angeles today for a three-day stay en route to meet the California Bear track team would appear to have undertaken a pretty large task if their best performances are correct as sent in by Robert P. Dockeray. Incidentally there's a big Michigan dinner at the Roosevelt tonight.

Willis Ward, the great Negro athlete, has marks of 9.6s. in the 100, 14.5s. in the high hurdles, 6ft. 7⅛in. in the high jump and 24ft. 2in. in the broad jump. Brother Ward is good enough for anybody's league. Sam Stoller, 9.7s. for the 100 yards, Capt. Harvey Smith with 1m. 54.8s. for the half and 4m. 23.5s. for the mile, and David Hunn with 13ft. 6in. for the pole vault are other outstanding performers.

Five seniors, eight juniors and nine sophomores make up the team and in view of the fact that the team has had no outdoor competition, they'll have a doubly difficult task trying to trim those pesky Bears. They're tough! Ask the Trojans!

**TRACK RECORDS THREATENED**

Good-by two Southern California Conference track records in one fell swoop, says Johnny Whitehead, who writes in to predict that John Baker of Whittier College will crack the two-mile conference meet record of 9m. 48.7s. made by Scovell of Occidental and the best time mark of 9m. 47.2s. made by Nick Carter of Occidental.

Baker, who was a good runner a couple of years ago and then stayed out of college a couple of seasons, has been running the mile and two-mile races this year and has a best mark in the mile of 4m. 33.6s. Whitehead thinks he'll do 9m. 40s. for the two miles at Occidental on Saturday in the conference meet.

**SIX-DAY SURVIVOR HEARD FROM**

Frank Drury, who assisted in keeping score on the six-day bike riders at the Olympic a few weeks ago, comes to life again after sleeping off the effects of his six-day activity at the score sheets to say that San Francisco's "New Century Wheelmen" have moved into their old quarters at 1001 Oak street, San Francisco, and, if desired, we can drop in and visit the six-day bike riders who are sitting up nights training for the next six-day race in May up at the Dreamland Rink. Wonder if they serve raw hamburger for breakfast, like the six-day bike riders do?

**WHO'S WHO ON TROY GRIDIRON**

Somebody signing himself "Home Town Booster" wrote in and wanted to know who was playing on the Trojan gridiron varsity these bright spring days. Some of the veterans aren't out this spring but here's a rough idea of how the first and second strings are lining up:

| First | | Second |
|---|---|---|
| Gaisford | L.E. | Williams |
| Hull | L.T. | Lund |
| Brosseau | L.G. | Roberts |
| Kuhn | C. | Hughes |
| Sanders | R.G. | Shuey |
| McNeish | R.T. | Rose |
| Bettinger | R.E. | Rodeen |
| Howard | Q. | Davis |
| Kidder | L.H. | Sutherland |
| Propst | R.H. | Langley |
| Clark | F. | Lynch |

They change these line-ups every night but the boys named on the two teams give a pretty fair indication of being varsity prospects.

**GEORGE ANDERSON OR DUBBY HOLT?**

The question of sprint supremacy between George Anderson, the California flyer, and Dubby Holt of Fresno State seems to be filling the air these days and folks are harking back to prep school duels between these two boys.

Coach A. W. Walton, who had Anderson at Muir Tech and who, by the way, has had plenty of other wonderful boys over at the Pasadena school, has sent me the dope. They met in two 100-yard dashes, two 220s and a relay race while in high school. Holt won the 100 both times and Anderson won both furlongs. Here's what Coach Walton says about the relay.

In the relay Holt got away to a six-yard lead, but Anderson nipped him near the tape, they bumped slightly and somebody dropped a baton. The race was very close and the judges, in debating their decision, thought that Holt had

(Continued on Page 11, Column 2)

## What's Doing in Sports at Local Arenas

**MONDAY**

WRESTLING — Lansdowne vs. McCann at Hollywood, 8:30 p.m.

BOXING — Amateur fights at Ocean Park arena, 8:30 p.m.

## SHEIK BOSS MAKES BOW

### Shellenback in First Start

*Portland Club Opens Three Game Series Tomorrow Against Hollywood*

BY BOB RAY

Frank Shellenback, popular pilot of the Hollywood Sheiks, will doff his managerial toga and don his pitching paraphernalia in a quick-change act out at Wrigley Field tomorrow when he makes his first start of the season on the mound against the Portland Ducks.

"Shelly" was scheduled to pitch one of yesterday's games, but rain caused postponement of the Sheiks' double bill with the Angels. So now he will serve up his assortment of spitballs against Manager Buddy Ryan's Ducks as he makes his 1935 mound debut.

Frank wavered for a while trying to decide whether he should pitch or give the assignment to Grant Bowler, the speedballer from Detroit, but finally picked himself.

**TO PITCH AGAINST VITTMEN**

"Now I can pitch Tuesday," says Shellenback, "and then get enough rest to come back in next Sunday's double-header against Oscar Vitt's Oaks at Oakland. I imagine we ought to be able to cook up a little excitement with me pitching against my former boss for the first time."

Portland comes here with a team that appears to have everything but capable pitching. Buddy Ryan says his infield, composed of Harry Davis at first, Bill Cissell at second, "Wimpy" Wilburn at short and Gil English at third, is the best in the league—both defensively and offensively.

In the outfield are Blackerby, Bongiovanni, Clabaugh and Metzler. Ryan predicts that Bongiovanni will be sold to the majors this year. And behind the plate Bill Cronin, former Angel, and Hal Doerr will share the catching duties.

**A'S PROMISE PITCHERS**

Ed Bryan, one of the best control pitchers in the circuit, is slated to be Shellenback's opponent in the series opener. Dutch Ulrich, Hal Turpin, Hobo Carson and Pudgy Gould are the only other experienced slabsters on the Portland squad. However, Jake Wade, a southpaw turned over to the club by Detroit, is expected to join the Portlanders here. And Connie Mack has promised to send two hurlers as soon as the major legaue race opens.

Skipper Jack Lelivelt's Angels, seeking their third straight pennant, leave tonight for Sacramento for three games against a highly improved gang of Senators. The Seraphs will have twenty players on their first road trip.

**ANGELS SIGN GABLER**

Glenn Gabler, who started his baseball career with the Angels, but has since performed for about four other clubs, was signed by the Los Angeles club yesterday and will be taken on the trip. Gabler will be used for relief work.

"Tarzan" Meola will be the starting hurler against Sacramento, with "Ramrod" Nelson and "Swifty" Garland slated to start the other two games in Sacramento.

The following Angels will make the trip: Pitchers Meola, Nelson, Campbell, Garland, Kimball, Buxton, Harris and Gabler; Catchers Veltman, Goebel and Gibson; Infielders Oglesby, Reese, Dittmar, Lillard, Mattick and Mesner, and Outfielders Gudat, Carlyle and Statz.

## Bengal Nine to Invade Arizona

Occidental College's championship baseball team, with a secure grip on first place in the Southern California Conference race, will take a week off from its title defense campaign and invade Arizona this Thursday, according to Coach Bill Anderson.

The Bengals meet the University of Arizona at Tucson on Thursday, Friday and Saturday afternoons and for the first time this season will be the underdogs, as the Wildcats have one of the strongest college nines in the Southwest.

## MICHIGAN TRACK SQUAD TO ARRIVE TODAY FOR VISIT

Fielding (Hurry Up) Yost, Michigan athletic director; Track Coach Charles B. Hoyt, their wives and twenty-five University of Michigan track athletes in addition to Willis Ward, the Wolverines' colored one-man track team, will stop over here three days to prepare for Saturday's invasion of Berkeley to face University of California in a dual meet.

The party arrives at Alhambra at 7:50 this morning and will go directly by bus to their headquarters at the Hollywood Roosevelt Hotel.

According to the schedule arranged for them by A. J. Sturzenegger, Bill Spaulding's right-hand man at U.C.L.A. and former assistant to Yost, the Wolverines will work out today, tomorrow and Wednesday at Hollywood High School each morning and at Westwood in the afternoon.

Michigan is undefeated this season, having won the Midwestern Conference and A.A.U. sectional indoor titles with more points than the total amassed by second and third-place teams combined in each meet.

**The team and coaches will be guests of the Michigan Alumni Association during their stay here.**

## Touch All the Bases, Babe, It's Out of the Lot

Babe Ruth was the Sultan of Swat again yesterday at Newark where he pounded out two home runs to enable the Boston Braves to defeat the International League Bears, 10 to 8. This Wirephoto shows the Bambino clouting his second homer, which was described as the longest ever made at Newark Park. The Babe hit his homers in the first and second innings. The catcher is Willard Hershberger, ex-Hollywood Sheik.

(AP) Wirephoto

## United States Menaces Japan Swim Supremacy

### Dazzling Performances in A.A.U. Championships Buoys Hopes of Yankees in Olympic Games

NEW YORK, April 7. (AP)—On the basis of developments in the National Collegiate A.A. and National Senior A.A.U. swimming championships the last ten days the United States can look forward to the 1936 Olympics with new hope of checking Japan's natators, surprise conquerors of the world three years ago at Los Angeles.

After watching the pick of the country's mermen in the two major indoor championships, the swimming committee of the Amateur Athletic Union, headed by Bob Kiphuth, veteran Yale coach, today selected a group of forty-five swimmers to point for the final tryouts for an All-American team which will invade Japan this summer for a three-day international meet.

The team, which will be selected at the national outdoor championships to be held some time in July at a place yet to be designated, will include fourteen swimmers, one diver—probably Dick Degener, Marshall Wayne or Elbert Root—and Kiphuth as manager, although no definite selections have been officially made, there is no disputing the fact that the No. 1 will be 20-year-old Jack Medica, the Pacific powerhouse, who hung up a world's record of 5m. 16.3s. for 500 yards, decimating his old mark of 5m. 26.6s., and turned in a 2m. 10.8s. "220" to capture the national championship for that distance in the fastest time ever made in titular competition.

The swimmers designed as candidates for the All-American team to invade Japan are:

Backstroke—Kiefer, Zehr, Al Vande Weghe, Paterson, N. J.; Taylor Drysdale, University of Michigan; Sandy Sinkiewicz, Detroit A.C.; Gordon Chalmers, Newark A.C.; C. Salie, Ohio State; R. Westerfield, Iowa University, and Johnny Kaye, Southern California.

Breast stroke—John Higgins, Providence; Jack Kasley, University of Michigan; John Schmieler and Ray Kayne, Detroit A.C.; Max Brydenthal, Lake Shore A.C., and Paul Friesel, Brooklyn.

100-yard free style—Peter Fick, New

(Continued on Page 10, Column 8)

## BET PARLAY NETS $58,181 TO PLUNGER

LYONS (France) April 7. (UP)—An unnamed plunger broke the provincial pari-mutuel record for winnings today when he pyramided a 50-franc win and 50-franc place four-way parlay into 481,542 francs ($58,181.77.)

His bets were on Perseis, Hanoi, Rentenmark and Folle Passion at Longchamps, and all finished first.

**SANTA MONICA RUGGERS TIE**

Although they were held to a 3-to-3 tie by the Pasadena A.C. fifteen in a muddy battle staged yesterday, the Santa Monica ruggers won the league championship and the Prosser Cup.

## HIXON LOSES GOLF MATCH

*Capt. A. Bullock-Webster Wins Lakeside Tourney*

Capt. A. Bullock-Webster, former State amateur champion, won the Lakeside invitation golf tournament yesterday by defeating his team-mate from the Midwick Country Club, youthful Frank Hixon, 1 up.

The All-Midwick final produced splendid golf, considering that most of the round was played in a steady drizzle of rain. Bullock-Webster, 43, and preparing for a shot at the British amateur this summer, carded a 76 to a 78 for Hixon.

**QUALIFIED TOGETHER**

Oddly enough, the two players had qualified together on Tuesday, Hixon winning medal honors with the only subpar round, a brilliant 69. Bullock-Webster had a 78. It was also something of a coincidence that Frank was beaten yesterday on the eighteenth green, which happened to be the only hole he didn't par during his sensational qualifying round.

**HIXON LEADS**

The eighteenth, a par three hole of 240 yards, found both on in two shots yesterday. Hixon, putting first, failed to get up, his putt stopping inches short. Bullock-Webster then sank his putt to win the tournament.

Hixon was 1 up at the end of

(Continued on Page 11, Column 2)

## They Carried Off Lakeside Silverware

Capt. A. Bullock Webster (second from left) is shown being congratulated by Frank Hixon, whom he beat 1 up on the eighteenth hole yesterday in the golf final at Lakeside. Left to right: Brandon Hurst, tournament chairman; Bullock-Webster, Hixon, and James B. Irsfeld, president of Lakesid-

## Ruth Hits Two Homers as Boston Braves Win

### Bambino's Second Circuit Wallop Longest Ever Made at Newark; Bears Outslugged, 10-8

NEWARK (N. J.) April 7. (AP)—Two home runs by Babe Ruth enabled the Boston Braves of the National League to defeat the Newark Bears, champions of the International League, 10 to 8, today.

Ruth's first home run came in his first appearance at the plate. It was a hard line drive into the right-field bleachers. The second in the sixth inning started the Braves on a hitting spree which netted seven runs. This second homer was the longest ever made at the local park, an attendant said.

| | | R. | H. | E. |
|---|---|---|---|---|
| Boston (N.) | .......100 007 110— | 10 | 13 | 1 |
| Newark (I.L.) | .....403 001 000— | 8 | 11 | 0 |

Prim, Benton, Frankhouse and Hogan, Lewis; Makosky, Miller, Spittler, Kleinhans and Hershberger, Baker.

**RED SOX NOSE OUT BIRMINGHAM**

BIRMINGHAM (Ala.) April 7. (AP) The Boston Red Sox today lent Catcher Bob Smith to Birmingham and beat the Barons, 7 to 6, their second victory over the southerners in two days.

Manager Joe Cronin of the Sox, nursing an injured wrist, watched his team from the bench.

| | | R. | H. | E. |
|---|---|---|---|---|
| Boston (A.) | .......300 210 001— | 7 | 12 | 1 |
| Birmingham | .......100 120 002— | 6 | 13 | 2 |

**COSTLY CINCY ROOKIE OUT WITH LEG INJURY**

COLUMBIA (S. C.) April 7. (AP)—Serious doubt that Johnny Mize—$55,000 rookie first baseman—will start the season with the Cincinnati Reds, developed today as the team was rained out at Charlotte, and came on here for a resumption of the series with Detroit tomorrow.

In yesterday's game, Mize pulled a tendon in his leg, injured last year while playing with Rochester.

(Continued on Page 11, Column 3)

## BLACKPOOL IN BID FOR MAX BAER

LONDON, April 7. (AP)—Blackpool, Great Britain's "Coney Island," has entered the free-for-all competition for a heavyweight championship match between Max Baer and Max Schmeling.

Harry Wilkinson, representing a Blackpool syndicate, cabled an offer of £60,000 (about $291,600) to Baer on Saturday, says the Herald.

**JAPANESE IN TWIN WIN**

SAN DIEGO, April 7. (AP)—The barnstorming Tokio Giants, Japan's star baseball team, split a double-header here today in the rain, losing to the Texas Liquor House, 13 to 3, and winning from the Whippets, 4 to 1, in a six-inning affair. Both the Liquor House and Whippets are sandlot aggregations.

## TWO STARS IN PLAY-OFF

### "Double Eagle" Made by Gene

*Stocky Italian Gets Two On Par Five Hole to Tie at Augusta*

BY GRANTLAND RICE



AUGUSTA (Ga.) April 7.—Millions of stars and duffers have played billions of golf shots in the 500-year history of the ancient green. But Gene Sarazen played one in the final round of the masters' tournament at Augusta that holds all records for all time.

Standing in the middle of the fifteenth fairway, 230 yards from the cup after a 255-yard drive, the stocky, swarthy Italian was three strokes back of Craig Wood, the leader, with only four holes left to play. A mere miracle would be of no help. The big New Jersey blond had posted his 282 with a brilliant finish and this lead looked safer than a dozen Gibraltars.

**SHIFTS TO SPOON**

A gallery of more than 2000 was banked back of Sarazen and packed back of the green. Sarazen took out an iron and then shifted to a spoon. The white ball was lying closely on soft, wet turf. Gene had a pond to carry in front of the green.

And then, as he swung, the double miracle happened. The ball left the face of his spoon like a rifle shot. It never wavered from a direct line to the pin. As it struck the green, a loud shout went up. This suddenly turned into a deafening, reverberating roar as the ball spun along its way and finally disappeared into the cup for a double eagle 2—a 2 on a 485-yard hole where even an eagle 3 wouldn't have helped.

**WOOD OVERTAKEN**

As a result of this incredible happening against odds of a million to one, Gene Sarazen and Craig Wood meet tomorrow at thirty-six holes to play off the tie at 282. Sarazen, three strokes back, picked up these strokes on one hole and the vocal cataclysm that sent its thunder over the red hills of Georgia must have lasted five minutes.

With Olin Dutra, open champion, in third place at 284, Henry Picard fourth at 286 and Denny Shute fifth at 287, Lawson Little finished sixth with 288, one of the finest rounds of the day.

**JONES THRILLED**

It remained for Bobby Jones, in a triple tie for twenty-fifth place, to get his thrill from Sarazen's amazing performance on the fifteenth hole — one shot in golf that will never be forgotten by those lucky enough to see it played.

"That was one golf shot," Bob said to me, "that was beyond all imagining, and golf is largely imagination. From duffer to star we all dream of impossible shots that might come off. This one was beyond the limit of all dreams, when you consider all the surrounding circumstances. I still don't believe what I saw."

**LEADERS FALTER**

The fourth round of the masters' tournament found Craig Wood leading, with Olin Dutra, Henry Picard and Gene Sarazen in close pursuit. The day was chilly and dark, with a roistering wind whipping the course. One by one the leaders be-

(Continued on Page 11, Column 6)

## HERE'S HOW GOLF PRIZE WAS SPLIT

AUGUSTA (Ga.) April 7. (AP)—Craig Wood of Deal, N. J., and Gene Sarazen of Brookfield Center, Ct., who ran a dead heat with totals of 282 in the Augusta national tournament, will battle through thirty-six holes tomorrow for the big prize of $1500 with $800 going to the loser.

Distribution of prize money for other finishers and their seventy-two-hole totals follows:

|  |  |  |
|---|---|---|
| $600 | Olin Dutra | 284 |
| $500 | Henry Picard | 286 |
| $400 | Denny Shute | 287 |
| $300 | Paul Runyan | 289 |
| $250 | Victor Ghezzi | 290 |
| $137.50 | Joe Turnesa | 291 |
| $137.50 | Bobby Cruickshank | 291 |
| $137.50 | Byron Nelson | 291 |
| $50 | Johnny Revolta | 292 |
| $50 | Ray Mangrum | 292 |

## GORMAN MAY ESTABLISH UNIQUE ICE HOCKEY RECORD

TORONTO, April 7. (AP)—Thomas Patrick Gorman, the garruluous Ottawa Irishman, surveyed the hockey world from a perch on the top today as his Montreal Maroons and the Toronto Maple Leafs moved on to Montreal to continue the 1935 struggle for the Stanley Cup and the world's professional hockey championship.

With the Maroons leading two games to none, Gorman had in his grasp a unique record in the annals of the ice sport. A year ago he coached the Chicago Blackhawks and won the Stanley Cup in a furiously contested final series against Detroit. This season he shifted to Montreal and built up the Maroons into a team that today stood as an odds-on favorite to capture the trophy in three straight games.

The Maroons won the opener of the three-out-of-five series, 3 to 2, in an overtime clash here Thursday. Last night they made it two straight by the even more decisive margain of 3 to 1. The next two games, if the series goes that far, are scheduled for Montreal Tuesday and Thursday.

# Lawson Little Defeats Tweddell, One Up

Los Angeles Times Sports

SUNDAY MORNING, MAY 26, 1935.

# OWENS BREAKS THREE WORLD RECORDS

## Bill Henry Says—

THE office was pretty dark as I walked in anxious to take advantage of the early-morning quiet to write some pretty deep observations. The editor on the graveyard shift didn't raise his eyes or his voice in recognition as I strolled between the deserted desks over to the sports department. In the dim light I discerned, on the main copy desk where the night editor does his nightly stint with sound effects in the form of complaints and unprintable remarks, a good-sized paper bag with card attached on which was printed, "To Bill Henry, Sports Editor."

**THE EDITOR GETS A PRESENT**

My heart beat just a little faster. A present, perhaps, from the staff or possibly a little token from a reader or a feminine admirer—after all, you know, there's something about graying temples that gets the more appreciative of the fair sex. A moment of happy speculation as to the contents—and then I opened it.

It contained an assortment of walnuts, peanuts, hickory nuts, chestnuts and a card on which was scribbled, "Nuts—to you, my pal." I didn't have to look on the other side. Such a vulgar thought could come from only one source—

The Office Cynic!

**THE OFFICE CYNIC IS IN AGAIN**

My face must have registered my feelings for I heard a snicker from behind the filing cabinet and I knew he was there. I didn't have to look. I could picture him as I had on dozens of occasions, sprawled out in my favorite swivel chair with those big clumsy feet up on my desk.

Disgusting fellow!

There was no use trying to ignore him. Or insult him. "Well," I said, "this is a surprise! It seems to me that the last time you were up here you were heading east to go to work—as you called it with that rare sense of humor of yours—sitting behind the judges at the McLarnin-Ross fight and making so much noise they wouldn't dare give the fight to anybody but your pal, McLarnin."

**HE WISHES TO MAKE A COMPLAINT**

"Well," he growled, "Mebbe I'm goin' yet. Been kind busy with social engagements." He was fumbling around with shaky fingers trying to put a crease in a tattered pair of obviously slept-in pants. "I can't get outta this dump too soon for me."

"Nor me, either," I interrupted.

He paid no attention to the sarcasm. "The town is a flop anyhow," he continued. "You farmhands don't even go for a good thing like a rassin' tournament. Say, I had a job all lined up to act as doorkeeper and interpreter for them two Khan boys, the Abyssinian Assassins, but the people in this burg didn't appreciate a rassin' tournament enough to make it worth while to bring 'em here from Harlem—I mean Abyssinia."

**HE THINKS WE ARE UNAPPRECIATIVE**

"Well," I countered, "I'm deeply interested in science myself." As a matter of fact, I have been intending to drop down and write a treatise on the scientific use of leverages and highly technical holds by the wrestlers but apparently they weren't feeling particularly scientific the night I saw them. In fact, they seemed a trifle primitive in the operation of their art, kicking, biting, slugging and giving vent to their emotions in a series of grimaces such as I never discerned on the faces of such fellow-delvers into the realm of science as Prof. Einstein or Dr. Miliken."

I suddenly realized that the fellow wasn't listening, in fact, was sidling toward the door.

**HE TAKES A VERY DIRTY DIG**

"Wait a minute," I said, feeling sort of sorry for him. "Where are you going? How are you going to eat?"

He gave me a nasty look.

"Don't worry," he said. "I got me a job with the Relief. Sumpin' soft. It don't require a strong back like pick and shovel work, or a judgment of time and distance like street cleanin'. I'm on the newspaper they're gettin' out. No brains required. I'm Sportin' Editor!"

## What's Doing in Sports at Local Arenas

**SUNDAY**

BASEBALL—Hollywood vs. Los Angeles at Wrigley Field, 1:30 p.m.

SOCCER—Two games at Loyola Stadium, 1 p.m.

EQUESTRIAN CARNIVAL—Program at Riviera, 1:30 p.m.

TENNIS — Southern California junior championship at Midwick, all day.

## LITTLE IN LINKS WIN

### Britisher Bows to Champion

*California Star Retains Amateur Title After Strenuous Match*

ST. ANNE'S-ON-THE-SEA (Eng.) May 25. (AP)—William Lawson Little, Jr., the colossus from California, fixed the mantle of golfing greatness more firmly on his shoulders today when he defeated Dr. William Tweddell, a 38-year-old British physician, 1 up, in thirty-six holes and won the British Amateur golf championship for the second straight time.

Thus the 24-year-old San Francisco shotmaker became the first player in history to win three consecutive national amateur golf crowns and the third man ever to register a "double" in the fifty years of this championship.

During a sensational struggle which saw the husky holder of the British and American Simon-pure titles 3 up at the end of the morning round, only to be brought back on even terms with six holes to go in the home stretch, Little played some of the grandest gold in his career. He withstood paralyzing pressure over the final, windswept passage to subdue Tweddell, the winner of the 1927 championship, who made a bold bid to restore the crown to England on the last nine holes.

**WHEN IT COUNTED**

Desperately needing a 4 on the final hole to assure victory, the American skillfully got off one of the most testing shots of the tournament, hemmed in on three sides by a gallery of almost 10,000, which had verged on riotous conduct over the prospect of witnessing Little's downfall.

Standing on the thirty-sixth tee, Little was dormie one. Tweddell, having the honor by virtue of winning the previous hole, divided the fairway with a 250-yard drive. Earlier Little had been belting the ball from the tees fairly consistently about 300 yards.

Down the stretch, he was hard pressed and sacrificed accuracy for distance. He sliced his drive into a swarm of spectators standing in the rough and the ball settled on a bare spot.

**PROTECTS PELLET**

His fore-caddy, with a stick flying an American flag, rushed to the spot and fell on all fours, animal-like, to prevent the rampaging spectators from tampling on the ball. Little slowly ambled up to the ball and with characteristic impassiveness viewed the situation without a sign of emotion. One hundred yards distant was the green, with two yawning traps in between. It took the marshals fully five minutes to move the crowd back to permit Little to get a free swipe at the ball. He chose a spade mashie lobbed the pellet beautifully to clear the traps and it came to rest on the green twenty-eight feet from the hole. Tweddell planted his approach three feet inside of Little's.

That recovery had a revitalizing effect on the champion. For the first time during the final match he smiled. He took less time than usual in lining up the putt and then rolled

(Continued on Page 21, Column 7)

**BANK TEAM TRIUMPHS**

The Bank of America baseball team swamped the Goddard Jackson Pump Co. nine, 16 to 3, yesterday at Fairfax High.

| | R. | H. | E. |
|---|---|---|---|
| Bank of America | 16 | 13 | 2 |
| Goddard Pump Co. | 3 | 9 | 3 |

Gresham and Mueller; Gray and Castro.

**NEW KINDA LOVE**

VALLEY FORGE (Pa.) May 25. (AP)—Cadets at Valley Forge Military Academy here have contrived a new "spring salad" of sports which has made a big hit. It's a sort of field hockey played on roller skates on a big paved court, with discarded brooms for mallets and a volleyball or basketball as the "puck."

### Here's Greatest Leap Ever Made by Civilized Man

The alert eye of Wirephoto brings you Jesse Owens at the top of his amazing jump yesterday of 26ft. 8¼in. in the Big Ten meet at Ann Arbor, Mich. Owens's leap surpassed Chuhei Nambu's world record by more than six inches. Note the great heighth the Ohio State Negro has attained. Owens also broke the world's records for the 220 and low hurdles and tied the 100-yard dash mark. (AP) Wirephoto

## Wells Pitches Sheiks to Win Over Seraphs

### Reese's Bobbles and Umpire Kelly's Error Factors in Triumph of Hollywood Outfit

**BY BOB RAY**

"Jes lak shootin' possum down in Alabam'," remarked Big Ed Wells. Hollywood's leading southpaw and Alabama5s leading possum hunter, after he'd hurled Shelly's Sheiks to a 4-2 victory over the Angeles yesterday at Wrigley Field.

And Wells was right, for in only one inning did the Leliveltians cause him any trouble. In the other eight frames the Hollywood portsider with the No. 13 shoes, went about his business, with never a worry or a care. Wells yielded but seven hits, and three of them came in the fifth

**BAD INNING**

But despite Wells's steady slabbing, the Sheiks needed a little outside assistance from Jimmy Reese and Umpire Joe Kelly to put across what proved to be their winning runs. Reese and Kelly had a bad inning in the fifth, the Angel-second-sacker being charged with two errors and the umpire one as Hollywood scored a run to break a 2-2 tie. The final Hollywood tally came across in the eighth as the usually steady Reese, with a double play in front of him that would have retired the side, heaved the ball wide to first.

It was a tough game for Ralph Buxton, young Angel right-hander, to lose despite the fact that he was touched for eleven hits, but Wells really deserved the victory.

**SERIES TIED**

Hollywood's triumph not only tied up the civil war series at 1-all, but also kept Los Angeles from going into first place. However, Oscar Vitt's Oaks look like they're choking up and it'll just be a few days before the Angels oust them from first place.

Although the Angels lost the ball game they swept the argumentative field with their forensic efforts, all

(Continued on Page 20, Column 3)

## BERGERE IN RACE GRIND

*Hollywood Pilot Qualifies as Complications and Crack-up Develop*

INDIANAPOLIS, May 25. (AP)—Skids marked the resumption today of qualifying trials for the 500-mile race to be run May 30 at the Indianapolis Motor Speedway. Cliff Bergere of Hollywood was the first to join qualifiers when he made the dash at an average of 114.162 miles per hour.

A pilot tuning up for the trials wrecked his car on one of the treacherous turns and a householder living just across the road from the big track threatened through court action to ditch the entire race, contending that it is a public nuisance and a dangerous event.

**WILLIAMS CRASHES**

The mishap occurred to the car driven by Merrill (Doc) Williams of Anderson, Ind. He was speeding at 100 miles per hour when his car suddenly scooted toward the outside retaining wall, gammed it and caromed to the inside wall. Williams escaped the fate of two drivers and a mechanic who died in similar accidents last Tuesday. Thrown clear of the machine as it skidded,

(Continued on Page 20, Column 3)

## ROOKIES IN LIMELIGHT

*Blanton, Whitehead Astound Baseball World With Winning Ways*

NEW YORK, May 25. (AP)—Two freshman twenty-game-winning pitchers in one season—one in each league? That seems, indeed, to be the bright prospect that has turned the attention of both big leagues squarely on two rookie pitchers this season—Darrell Elijah (Cy) Blanton of the Pittsburgh Pirates and John Whitehead of the rampant Chicago White Sox.

**FIVE WINS**

Before the season was a full month old each of these sensations had produced five victories to top their respective leagues in games won and had satisfied all who came to see them pitch that they had the stuff to justify their low-hit performances.

Now twenty-game-winning pitchers are rare enough in this day and agé of large mound staffs and liberal use of relief hurlers, and fellows who can come up with twenty victories in their first season under the big top are naturally still scarcer. That's why talk of Blanton and Whitehead dominates all the baseball gabfests nowadays.

**ALL-TIME HIGH**

Speculation as to just how far these newcomers will carry their first-season spurts more or less automatically puts them into some very fast company indeed, for if they crash the twenty-games lists they can rank, in that respect at least, with such as Grover Cleveland Alexander, Wesley Cheek Ferrell and Vernon (Lefty) Gomez.

Alex, of course, with his twenty-eight victories and thirteen defeats for the Phillies when he broke in 'way back in 1911, has the all-time record for first-year victories. He turned out to be quite a pitcher, as his National League record of 696 games hurled in the twenty years from 1911 through 1930—several of them thirty-games-won years—and his five years' leadership in earned run averages would indicate.

## Rosemont Winner Over Omaha in Withers Mile

### Famous Stretch Drive of Kentucky Derby and Preakness Victories Fails to Bring Results

NEW YORK, May 25. (AP)—The famous stretch drive that carried William Woodward's Omaha to easy victories in the Kentucky Derby and the Preakness failed to get results today as the chestnut son of Gallant Fox bowed to William Du Pont's Rosemont in the sixtieth running of the Withers Mile at Belmont Park.

Meeting Rosemont for the first time, Omaha found his stretch drive matched stride for stride as he dropped the decision and the purse of $11,250 by one and one-half lengths for his first major defeat of the year. Mrs. Payne Whitney's Plat Eye wa s another one and one-half lengths to the rear, while stretched out behind the three leaders were six other top-notch 3-year-olds.

**WINGING ALONG**

The crowd of 20,000 made Omaha the 1-to-2 choice and as the chestnut flyer swung around the sweeping bend leading into the home stretch it appeared as if their confidence would be justified. The Derby and Preakness winner, running in full stride, had moved up from sixth to third place and was rapidly cutting in on the advantage held by the pace-setting Plat Eye.

He was still third at the turn for home, a quarter of a mile from the judges, but Rosemont, with Wayne Wright riding one of his famous finishes, was now winging along in front with one and one-half lengths to spare. Another sixteenth of a mile and Omaha had passed Plat Eye, but there was no catching Rosemont.

**VAST IMPROVEMENT**

Showing vast improvement over

(Continued on Page 19, Column 6)

## HOMER ORGY BY BAMBINO

*Ruth Clears Bases Trio of Times but Braves Bow to Bucs, 11-7*

PITTSBURGH, May 25. (AP)—Rising to the glorious heights of his heyday, Babe Ruth, the Sultan of swat, crashed out three home runs against Pittsburgh today but they were not enough and Boston took an 11-to-7 defeat before a crowd of 10,000.

Babe Ruth

The stands rocked with cheers for the Mighty Babe as he enjoyed a field day at the expense of Pitchers Red Lucas and Guy Bush, getting a single besides the three circuit blows in four times at bat and driving in altogether six runs.

Ruth left the game amid an ovation at the end of the Braves' half of the seventh inning and after his third home run—a prodigious clout that carried clear over the right-field grandstand, bounded into the street and rolled into Schenley Park. Baseball men said it was

(Continued on Page 19, Column 1)

## JESSE SETS NEW MARKS

### Startling Times Registered

*Low Hurdles, Furlong, Broad Jump Standards Ruined by Negro Sensation*

ANN ARBOR (Mich.) May 25. (AP) Jesse Owens, spectacular Ohio State Negro, gave one of the ostm amazing demonstrations of versatility in track and field history here today as he shattered three world's records and equalled a fourth to dominate completely the thirty-fifth annual Western Conference meet.

Michigan won its fourteenth team championship, but instead of a runaway as had been expected, had to battle Owens and Ohio State down to the last event for the decision. The Wolverines amassed 48 points, to 43½ for the Buckeyes.

**CLIMAX OF DAY**

Owens climaxed his great afternoon's performance with a leap of 26ft. 8½in. in the broad jump, a new world mark.

Even without the astonishing leap which set him off in a class by himself as the all-time greatest broad jumper, the nicomparable 21-year-old sophomore still would have turned in an almost matchless day.

Before surpassing the accepted world record of 26ft. 2⅛in. for the jump, set by Chuhei Nambu of Japan in 1931, Owens tied Frank Wykoff's world 100-yard dash standard of 9.4s.

**ADDED RECORDS**

After his jump he raced to spectacular world record-smashing triumphs in the 220-yard dash and the 220-yard low hurdles. Running by himself after the first few strides, he finished the furlong in 20.3s. The performance was three-tenths of a second under Roland Locke's world record, shaded Locke's American mark of 20.5s., and beat Ralph Metcalfe's collegiate mark of 20.4s.

Apparently just as fresh as when he started his day of days, Owens completed his conquest of records by winning the low hurdles in 22.6s., four-tenths of a second under the listed world standard held jointly by Charles Brookins of Iowa, and Norman Paul, Southern California ace.

**PERFECT LEAP**

That jump, about which track fans are likely to be talking for a long time—unless Owens gives them something else to talk about soon—was just about a perfect effort.

He blazed down the turf runway on his first attempt with every ounce of his amazing speed, struck the takeoff squarely and rocketed off into space. Before he landed it was apparent that he had achieved the record at which he had been shooting all season. The judges of the event withheld announcement as they checked and re-checked the leap, but the 10,000 spectators knew, when Owens started jumping up and down, that it was a record effort.

**GREAT PERFORMANCE**

These four almost matchless victories more than equalled the splen-

(Continued on Page 22, Column 8)

## Buc Fans Like Babe Herman

PITTSBURGH, May 25. (Exclusive)—Despite his trials and tribulations in the early games of the season, Babe Herman is in the good graces of Pirate fans. Herman had to leave the line-up more than two weeks ago with a bad foot, but he went in at first base this week in place of the injured Gus Suhr and is playing a good game at the gateway position.

Pittsburgh fans know all about the more or less hapless Herman. They like him personally and are willing to overlook his fielding shortcoming if he is able to hit even close to his stride. His fielding weakness is an open secret among the thousands who sit in the left field stands, yet these same fans cheer Babe whenever he gets hold of one at the plate.

### Rosemont Shows Heels to Omaha in Withers Mile

William Woodward's Omaha, Derby and Preakness winner, is shown being bested by William Dupont's Rosemont in the Withers mile yesterday at Belmont Park. Rosemont won by one and one-half lengths. The time was 1m. 36 3-5s. Plat Eye was third. (AP) Wirephoto

## Here's Detailed List of Owens's Day's Work

ANN ARBOR (Mich.) May 25. (AP)—Here is what Jesse Owens did today:

(1.) Bettered all existing records for the running broad jump with a leap of 26ft. 8¼in. The best previous jump was 26ft. 2⅛in. by Chuhei Nambu of Japan in 1931.

(2.) Ran 220 yards in 20.3s., outdoing the best that the world's fastest humans had been able to do to date for the furlong. The recognized world record in 20.6s. by Roland Locke of Nebraska, set in 1926.

(3.) Stepped over the 220-yard low hurdles in 22.6s., putting in the shade the performances of such great hurdlers as Charlie Brookins, Norman Paul, Jack Keller and Dick Rockaway. Owens bettered the world record of 23s. flat set by Brookins in 1924.

(4.) Equalled the world's record for the 100-yard dash by sprinting the century in 9.4s. All the timers' watches caught Owens on the fast side of 9.4s.

Owens's records will be offered for adoption as world marks. He did not use starting blocks and the wind, brisk at first, died down as Owens set his marks.

# SCHMELING KNOCKS OUT LOUIS IN TWELFTH

Los Angeles Times Sports

SATURDAY MORNING, JUNE 20, 1936. • C

## WORLD MARK FOR 400 SET BY WILLIAMS

### *Negro Runs 46.1 at N.C.A.A.*

*Towns Does 14.1 in Hurdles as Owens Stars and Troy Qualifies Eighteen*

CHICAGO, June 19. (AP)—America's premier collegiate athletes, striving for berths on Uncle Sam's Olympic team, smashed two world records and tied another in the preliminaries of the national collegiate track and field championships today.

The slim crowd of less than 2000 sitting in sun-drenched Stagg Field, saw Ohio State's black streak of lightning, Jesse Owens, holder of four world's records, easily qualify in the four events in which he competed.

Archie Williams of California, America's newest quarter-mile sensation, started the record breaking by running the 400 meters faster than any human has done before. Running with long, beautiful strides, the Pacific Coast champion reeled off the distance in 46.1s., knocking a tenth of a second off the mark hung up by Bill Carr of Pennsylvania in the 1932 Olympic Games. Williams, a Negro, coasted to the tape, indicating he had enough reserve to have improved his performance if pressed at the finish.

**NEW RECORD**

The second world mark to fall was in the 110 meters high hurdles, with Forest Towns, Georgia's timber-topping ace, clearing the sticks in 14.1s. This eclipsed the recognized world's mark of 14.2s. made by Percy Beard of Auburn in 1934.

Owens, in his dazzling performances today, bettered the Olympic record in the broad jump, sailing through space 25ft. 10 7-8in. on his second qualifying leap. While the listed Olympic record is 25ft. 4 3-4in. by Edward B. Hamm of Georgia Tech, Owens a year ago leaped 26ft. 8 1-4in. in the Western Conference championship meet, an applied-for world's mark.

**LONGER RACE**

Owens also qualified in the 100 meters run, the 200 meters run and the 220 yards low hurdles. Through a mistake at the start, Owens was forced to travel 110 meters in the 100 meters event because officials started the runners from the high hurdles mark instead of the proper starting line. Owens galloped to victory in 11.2s., breaking the tape six feet ahead of George Boone of Southern California. He won his heat in the 200 meters run in 21.4 without extending himself and in the 220-yard hurdles, second within thirty yards of the finish, turned on the steam to take first place in 23.7s.

On the basis of today's performances, Southern California, the defending champions, rates as the big threat to repeat. The Trojans qualified eighteen men for the finals tomorrow, with California next with eight and Wisconsin and Ohio State third with six each. Michigan and Stanford were fourth with five each.

**JUMPERS IN TIE**

The Buckeyes, with Owens as their ace, may prove dangerous in the team championship fight, for they bagged 18 points today in the two finals held. Their two dusky jumpers, David Albritton and Melvin Walker, tieing for the championship in the high jump final with leaps of 6ft. 6 1-8in. Walker attempted to clear 6ft. 9 3-8in., two-eighths of an inch above the world mark, and came within a hair's breadth of making it. He cleared the bar and after his body hit the ground the bar jiggled for an instant and then toppled off, ruining his effort.

Besides the world marks, two national collegiate records were shattered after the 276 young men from eighty universities and colleges finished their day's assault. Kenneth Carpenter of Southern California established a new meet mark in the discus with a toss of 167ft. 1½in. to erase the record of 163ft. 3 3-4in.

(Continued on Page 18, Column 3)

## *'GATE' FOR BOUT ONLY $547,531*

NEW YORK, June 20. (AP)—Despite indications that the Yankee Stadium was fully two-thirds full, it was officially announced the paid attendance was only 39,878 for the Louis-Schmeling fight. The gross receipts were set at $547,531, with a net "gate" of $464,945. This meant each of the principals, splitting 60 per cent of the net proceeds, would collect approximately $125,000.

## Schmeling Fight With Braddock This Fall

NEW YORK, June 19. (AP)—Mike Jacobs, who staged the Max Schmeling-Joe Louis heavyweight bout tonight, said he plans to match Schmeling with James J. Braddock for the world's heavyweight title this fall.

"I've got Schmeling signed and I can get Braddock," he said. "I'll probably put the show on here although I do not think New York did right by tonight's show by any means."

Jacobs, who has Louis under contract until 1940, hasn't lost faith in the Brown Bomber.

"Maybe that licking will do him good," he said. "Anyway, he'll be back before long, bowling them over right and left just as he used to."

### *When "Condemned Man" Turned Executioner and Slaughtered Joe Louis*

**Blasted by the heavy right fist of Max Schmeling in a terrific twelfth-round barrage, Joe Louis slumps to the canvas as Referee Donovan motions the German to his corner.**

**As early as the fourth round the erstwhile Brown Bomber, felt the sting of Max's right hand. Here's Joe resting on hands in fourth round as Max starts to walk away.**

Associated Press Wirephotos

## SUPER-MAN BELTED OUT BY GERMAN

### *Stunning Upset Thrills Crowd*

*Detroit Negro Destroyed by Vicious Right-Hands of Teuton Schlager*

(Continued from First Page)

punches that brought the tears to his eyes and the crowd to its feet.

He swung that sucker punch until his bigger, younger opponent—the master boxer of the age, the man who could have beaten Dempsey—collapsed under a battering barrage no human mechanism could absorb.

It was one man against the world, a man who had lived cleanly, a man who believed in himself, a sucker with a sucker punch—and courage.

After the fight Louis said that it was Schmeling's first solid right-hand punch near the start of the fourth round that made strings of the sinews of his legs. He said he bruised the knuckles on both his hands.

And Schmeling?

**BRADDOCK NEXT**

"I told you that I wasn't afraid," he said. "I told you that I had studied Louis and believed that he was made to order for me. I waited until I had my chance and the first time I hit him with my right I knew I had him. My great ambition is to fight Jim Braddock and be the first man to win the world's heavyweight championship back after losing it."

Oh, yes—regarding my fearless prediction that Joe could end this fight early or late, depending on whether Marva, his wife, wanted to go to the second feature or the midnight show—I'm now convinced that Marva didn't want to go to any show at all.

**CHAMPIONS APPEAR**

First to enter the ring was Max Schmeling closely followed by Louis and while the gloves were being put on, a string of ex-champions were introduced and then the announcer set a new all-time record by requesting the audience to "cast aside all prejudism" three Boston sports writers were carried out unconscious after this one.

The referee was Arthur Donovan. The judges were Charley Lynch and George Lecron.

They sparred cautiously at the bell and Schmeling surprised Louis with a vicious right which barely missed the black boy's chin. They sparred very carefully for the rest of the round with each waiting for the other to lead. Schmeling was making Joe lead and Joe didn't want to.

**STRANGE INCIDENT**

A strange incident occurred in the second round when in the midst of a clinch Schmeling motioned to his corner and both fighters started to sit down. Apparently Schmeling thought he heard the bell, but they came back and sparred fruitlessly with no damage being done.

Max caught Louis with a hard right to the jaw in the third that shook the colored boy out of his lethargy and brought the crowd up with a yell, but Louis came back with a series of stiff lefts that started the German's eyes to puffing. Schmeling was a more baffling problem to hit than Louis's more recent opponents.

Schmeling backed cautiously away and showed a good deal respect for Louis in the fourth, still avoiding anything that looked like a damaging punch. Suddenly Schmeling swung a terrific right that caught Louis flush on the chin and the dark boy's legs wobbled. Louis sank to the floor, but bobbed up without electing to take a count. The Uhlan swarmed over him like a flash, swinging punch after punch, and the excitement was so intense that they swapped punches for several seconds after the bell.

**WEATHERS STORM**

Schmeling spun Louis again with another right at the start of the fifth, but Louis weathered the storm successfully. He had no defense for the German's lightning right and only the fact that it was landing high on his head kept the punches from flooring the Negro, who came back gamely and showed remarkable recuperative ability. Louis was out at the bell and staggered to his corner barely able to keep his feet.

The Bomber's seconds worked over him frantically at the corner between rounds, while Max eagerly awaited the gong.

Schmeling landed a terrific right as they came to the center of the ring for the sixth and Louis had lost his aggressiveness and was pawing Schmeling with a long left that had no sting. The whole left side of his face was badly swollen from the German's punches and he was again wobbly at the bell. It was the third round in succession on which Louis was practically saved by the bell.

Louis came out with a new style

(Continued on Page 18, Column 6)

## *FOUL BLOWS FORCE MAX TO DEAL OUT KNOCKOUT*

YANKEE STADIUM, NEW YORK, June 19. (U.P.)—"Hah! Hah!"

Those were the first sounds made by Max Schmeling when he returned to his dressing-room tonight—a "victim" who turned the tables on his would-be "executioner."

A dozen or more sports writers—"experts" who had done most of their worrying over what round Joe Louis would belt the German out—were assembled in the Yankee dressing-room when Max arrived. They swarmed about the former heavyweight champion to congratulate him.

But all Max could say was: "Hah! Hah! I guess I fooled you guys, no?" And his words were echoed—or rather, magnified—by Joe Jacobs, Max's "human sounding-board" manager.

A wide grin split Schmeling's face from ear to ear as Jacobs picked up the conversation for the "Schmeling-Jacobs" troupe.

"Where's all dem guys?" Joe said with a blast that rattled the dressing-room windows. "—Dem name-the-round guys; dem name-de-punch duys; dem name-the-minute guys?"

Max finally got his chance to say something.

"I had him in the fourth round," he said, "but my eye bothered me.

(Continued on Page 18, Column 8)

## BLOW-BY-BLOW DESCRIPTION OF FIGHT

**FIRST ROUND**

They advanced to the center of the ring slowly. Max missed with a hard right to the jaw. They sparred and Louis came in with two punches to the body. Max feinted and Louis was short with a left jab. Schmeling scored with a left to the face. Louis was short with a right to the body. Louis shot a right uppercut to the chest and landed a right and left to the jaw.

Joe rocked Max's head with a left hook to the jaw. Schmeling weaved and came in covering his head with his elbows. Joe stabbed stiffly with a long left to the face. They exchanged long lefts to the face. They clinched along the ropes and after the break Schmeling rushed and missed with an overhand right. Louis pinned Max against the ropes but his punches landed on the German's shoulders.

**SECOND ROUND**

Schmeling weaved and jabbed lightly with his left. Louis shot a left and right to the neck and the German retreated. Louis missed with a short left to the jaw. Joe jabbed and Max backed away slowly. Max took a left and a right to the chin. Louis hooked his left to the side of the head. Max landed a right to the head. The German backed away from a right uppercut. In a half clinch Max left-hooked to the side of the head.

Schmeling retreated to his corner and weaved out of the path of a long left hook. Louis jabbed five times without a return. Both men started for their corners thinking the bell had rung and the referee called them back. Louis hooked a solid left to the pit of the stomach. Max weaved back cautiously out of the way of Louis's left.

**THIRD ROUND**

They sparred waiting for an opening. Max's left eye was cut. Schmeling landed a hard right to Joe's head, the hardest blow so far. Louis rushed in with two left hooks to the head, driving Max to a neutral corner while Joe left jabbed repeatedly without a return. Max continued to retreat and he bobbed under Louis's left and right. Joe stabbed

(Continued on Page 18, Column 4)

## *'HE WAS BEAT; BEAT BAD,' SAYS JOE'S RING PILOT*

YANKEE STADIUM, NEW YORK, June 19. (U.P.)—Joe Louis, the so-called "merciless mutilator," stalked into the ring to fight Maxie Schmeling like a conquering Roman gladiator, but was carried out by a procession remindful of a funeral.

For twenty minutes after the fight he lay on his dressing-room table not even trying to talk, but mumbling responses to questions of his managers and trainer, Jack Blackburn, who seemed the most hurt by the crushing defeat of "Chappie."

His jaws so swollen he could not get them open, Joe lay there more like a corpse than a man who forty-five minutes before was joking with Blackburn and yawning in anticipation of another good night's sleep.

Both of the Brown Bomber's thumbs were badly sprained. Blackburn said Joe told him he hurt the left one in the fourth round, the session when "Der Mox" first floored him. No excuses were offered by his managers, Julian Black or John Roxborough.

"He was beat all right; beat bad," Black said. "I don't know what was the matter with him. He was a sucker for that short right."

While Blackburn cut gloves and tape from his hands, Joe lay there motionless. His trainer had to lift

(Continued on Page 18, Column 6)

# OWENS WINS 100-METERS; WYKOFF FOURTH

*Remarkable Radio Wirephotos Score Triumph of Speed With American Winners in Olympics*

Glenn Hardin, chief hope of the United States in the 400-meter hurdles, is shown here taking the last barrier to win his heat at Berlin yesterday in 53.9s. The picture was radioed from Berlin to New York and sent via Wirephoto to The Times. (AP) Wirephoto

Jesse Owens wasn't the only American who dominated the Olympic sprints yesterday; here's a radiophoto sent from Berlin to New York and Wirephotoed to Los Angeles showing Helen Stephens, Missouri farm girl, setting a new world's record of 11.4s. for the women's 100-meter dash in her trial heat at Berlin yesterday. Miss Fulton clipped 4-10ths of a second off the old mark held by Stella Walsh of Poland. Finals of this race will be held tomorrow. (AP) Wirephoto

## RACE MARK THROWN OUT

### *Helen Stephens Sets Record*

*Negro's 10.2 Effort in 100 Meters Disallowed by Committeemen*

BY ALAN GOULD
Associated Press Sports Editor

BERLIN, Aug. 3. (AP)—American speed ruled the Olympic straightaway today with a succession of smashing triumphs down a rain-drenched stretch before the third straight capacity crowd of 100,000 spectators.

Officials of the International Amateur Athletic Federation ruled out Jesse Owens's world record-breaking performance of 10.2s. made yesterday, deciding there was too much of a favoring wind, but they couldn't keep the brown Buckeye bullet from capturing the 100-meter crown.

**WYKOFF FOURTH**

Owens achieved the first objective in his bid for three Olympic titles—he resumes work in the 200-meter run and the broad jump tomorrow—by beating Ralph Metcalfe, Chicago Negro, by a meter (39.37 inches) in world and Olympic standard equaling time of 10.3s. Frank Wykoff, Carpinteria (Cal.) three-time Olympian, was fourth among the six finalists.

The Negro pair, keen rivals for the last two years on American cinderpaths, shared speed honors with the 19-year-old Fulton (Mo.) flyer, Helen Stephens, who twice shattered the listed world 100-meter record of 11.8s.

**JUST LIKE OWENS**

She stepped the distance over a heavy track in 11.4s. in her first trial and then captured her semifinal test in 11.5s., thus decisively breaking Stella Walsh's world standard and spread-eagling her opponents just as decisively as Owens.

Miss Stephens's record, made with a medium following wind, will stand overnight pending a possible recount as in the case of Owens by the ruling solons of the I.A.A.F. in their regular morning post-mortem session.

**HAMMER TO GERMANY**

The United States increased her point-scoring margin despite the German challenge in the weight events. Teutons won the first two places in record-shattering hammer throw competition.

Completion of five men's events—high jump, shot put, hammer throw, 10,000 meters and 100 meters—in the first two days found the Americans amassing 46 points, 30 of which were gained by Negroes. The Germans showed 31¼ points, shading Finland by a point.

Meanwhile the United States was fortified strongly for tomorrow's features, not only by Miss Stephen's dominance among the women sprinters, but by qualifying all three entries in both the 400-meter low hurdles and the 800-meter flat race.

**HURDLERS QUALIFY**

Glenn Hardin of Greenwood, Miss., defending champion and holder of the Olympic and world marks, and Joe Patterson of the United States Naval Academy and Oklahoma City, captured two of the three hurdle trials, qualifying for the semifinal, while Dale Schofield of Provo, Utah, ran second in his heat but also made the grade.

John Woodruff, University of Pittsburgh Negro freshman, Harry Williamson of High Point, N. C., and bespectacled Charles F. (Chuck) Hornbostel of Evansville, Ind., swept through the second 800-meter tests in which nine qualified for the final. Woodruff, following orders to the letter, raced an amazingly fast first quarter in 52s. flat and registered the fastest trial, 1m. 52.7s.

**VIRTUAL CLOUDBURST**

The final of the 100 meters was the focal point of a day marred by a virtual cloudburst as well as a fight during a soccer match lost by the Americans to Italy, 1 to 0.

The huge crowd, including Reichsfuehrer Adolf Hitler, tensely watched every move as the American trio in the sprint toed the marks and broke perfectly. A roar swelled from the vast concrete stadium as Owens took command quickly, led Wykoff by a yard half way down the straightaway and

(Continued on Page 12, Column 5)

Los Angeles Times Sports

R TUESDAY MORNING, AUGUST 4, 1936.

## Bill Henry Says—

BERLIN, Aug. 3.—Tomorrow's program is, in many ways, one of the very best in the Games. It's pretty hard to beat the 400-meter hurdles and the 800-meter flat race for thrills and the finals in both events will be run off at about the time you're reading this. There are also finals in the broad jump and the ladies's discus — which look like push-overs for Owens of the U.S.A. and Fraulein Mauermeier of Germany—and heats in the 200 meters and 5000 meters flat races. The gal fencers get under way, too, and in the morning the exhibition of gliding at the aerdrome ought to be worth going miles to see. Things are getting hotter every day—you hardly know what show to watch.

**ANCIENT MARK WAS HARD TO BEAT**

The boys at Los Angeles took a terrible revenge on the 200-meter record which had stood longer than any other on the track and field books. Archie Hahn, the University of Michigan sprinter, won the event in 1904 at St. Louis in 21.6s.—on a straightaway—and ever since that time the race has been run around a curve in the Olympic Games and until 1932 it was never beaten although it had been equaled.

But in 1932 Metcalfe and Tolan put it at 21.5s., then Luti of Argentina and Jonath of Germany shoved it down to 21.4 and finally Tolan, winning the final, did 21.2s. which was going some. Now, with Owens boasting a mark of

(Continued on Page 12, Column 1)

## Here's Olympic Games at a Glance

BY THE ASSOCIATED PRESS

**TRACK AND FIELD**

Jesse Owens captured 100-meter championship with Ralph Metcalfe second and Frank Wykoff fourth; Helen Stephens twice bettered world record in women's 100-meter trials as Annette Rogers also qualified for finals; Karl Hein of Germany won the hammer throw title with toss of 56.49 meters (185ft. 4 1-16in.,) breaking Olympic record; John Woodruff, Charley Hornbostel and Harry Williamson qualified for 800-meter finals; Harold Manning, Joe McCluskey and Glen Dawson for the 3000-meter steeplechase finals, and Glenn Hardin, Joe Patterson and Dale Schofield for the 400-meter hurdles semifinals; Bill Rowe and Don Favor finished fifth and sixth in hammer throw; Harriet Bland, St. Louis girl, was eliminated in first heat of women's 100-meter trials.

Team point standings (on unofficial 10-5-4-3-2-1 basis:)

Men's track and field—United States, 46; Germany, 31¼; Finland, 30¼; Japan, 5½; Sweden, 5; Holland, 4; Great Britain, 2; Argentina, 1.

Women's track and field—Germany, 16; Poland, 4; Austria, 3; Japan, 2.

Polo round-robin—Great Britain defeated Mexico, 13-11.

Soccer—Italy defeated United States, 1-0; Norway defeated Turkey, 4-0.

Wrestling—Ross Flood, bantamweight; Francis Millard, featherweight, and Harley Strong, lightweight, gained third round as Frank Lewis, welterweight; Richard Voliva, middleweight, and Kay Clemons, light-heavyweight, won their first-round matches. Roy Dunn, heavyweight, was thrown by Nils Akerlind of Sweden but remained in the competition.

Weight lifting—A York (Pa.) weight lifter, Tony Terlazzo, figured in his first Olympic championship ceremony of the day as a result of his victory in the featherweight class.

Werner Houstin of France successfully defended his Olympic light-heavyweight weight-lifting title with a lift of 782.20 pounds, as the two Americans in the competition, William Good, Reamstown, Pa., and John Miller, Salunga, Pa., finished seventh and ninth, respectively.

## YANK SOCCER TEAM UPSET

### *Row Marks Tilt at Berlin*

*Two Americans Injured as Italians Score 1 to 0 Victory*

BERLIN, Aug. 3. (AP)—America's Olympic soccer team literally went down fighting today in losing a 1-0 decision before a crowd of 7000 including the Italian Crown Prince, Umberto.

Two Americans, George Nemchik, Trenton, N. J., and Bill Fiedler, Philadelphia, were injured during a bruising game in which the German referee, Weingaertner, frequently was forced to warn the Italians for rough tactics.

**KICKED IN TUMMY**

The climax of the bitter struggle was reached early in the second half when Nemchik was kicked in the stomach by one of the Italians. A few minutes later, after the Italians had scored the lone goal of the game, Fiedler suffered torn ligaments in his knee when pushed roughly by Piccini of the rival team.

Weingaertner "put the thumb" on the Italian, ordering him from the game. Three times he tried to get Piccini to leave but finally gave up. A half dozen Italian players swarmed over the referee, pinning his hands to his sides and clamping hands over his mouth. The game was formally finished with Piccini still in the line-up.

**ITALIANS JEERED**

The crowd jeered the Italians and cheered the Americans most of the way. The American team manager, Elmer Schroeder, Philadelphia, said after the game that Fiedler

(Continued on Page 13, Column 5)

# *Baby Arizmendi Favored Over Armstrong in Battle Tonight*

## HITLER CAN'T GREET STARS

### *Der Fuehrer at Games Again*

*Receptions Barred Because Leader Can't Spend All His Time at Stadium*

BERLIN, Aug. 3. (U.P.)—Adolf Hitler again attended the Games today, arriving to the accompaniment of vociferous "Heils" which echoed and re-echoed across the vast stadium. Der Fuehrer remained at the stadium for two hours and a half, applauding and saluting the various winners regardless of their nationality. However, he did not receive either the German hammer-throw winners or the United States Negroes who ran one-two in the 100 meters.

Hitler officially announced today he would forego receiving any more winners because it was impossible for him to remain constantly at the stadium, and failure to honor all champions might arouse feeling among some of the foreigners. Hitler's decision apparently was made as a result of the interpretations placed on his departure yesterday just in time to prevent him from receiving the two Negroes, Cornelius Johnson and Dave Albritton, who finished first and second in the high jump.

## *Happiest Day of His Life for Jesse Owens*

Negro Sprinter Gets Thrill of a Lifetime by Victory in 100-Meters Dash

BY EDWARD BEATTIE
United Press Staff Correspondent

BERLIN, Aug. 3. (U.P.)—To say that Jesse Owens got the "thrill of a lifetime" from his smashing victory in the Olympics 100-meter dash today would be putting it mildly.

Bedecked with the laurel wreath and clasping the gold medal symbolic of his triumph, the Buckeye Bullet said he never expected to experience so much joy again—not even if he completes his hoped-for "triple" by winning the running broad jump final tomorrow and the 200-meter final on Wednesday.

"This is the happiest day in my life—I guess it's the happiest I will ever have," Jesse said.

**HOUNDED FOR AUTOGRAPH**

A pack of Germans, young and old, followed Owens from the track to the showers and before he could discuss his experiences at any length he had to give his autograph. For each of the hero-worshipers Owens signed his familiar, "Yours Sincerely, Jesse Owens."

Fully ten minutes after the crowd left the Negro star, still in track togs and still wearing the laurel wreath around his neck, did nothing but contemplate his gold medal. Over and over again he said, "This is the prettiest thing I ever got."

"I just didn't know what to do when I stood on that stand before

(Continued on Page 12, Column 8)

## Complete Results of Olympic Events

BERLIN, Aug. 3. (AP)—Summaries in Olympic track and field competition today:

100-meter final—Won by **JESSE OWENS, UNITED STATES,** 10.3s. (ties listed world and Olympic records;) second, **RALPH METCALFE, UNITED STATES,** 10.4s; third, Martin Osendarp, Holland, 10.5s.; fourth, **FRANK WYKOFF, UNITED STATES**; fifth, Erich Borchmeyer, Germany; sixth, Hans Strandberg, Sweden.

Hammer-throw final—Won by Karl Hein, Germany, 56.49 meters (185ft. 4 1-16in.) (new Olympic record; betters old record of 179ft.

(Continued on Page 12, Column 4)

## TITLE BOUT TO BE HELD

### *Mexican Picked Over Negro*

*Crowd of 20,000 Expected to See Wrigley Field Ring Attraction*

BY JACK SINGER

Nineteen, no, it was twenty years ago, two men in uniform—a sailor and a soldier—sat in a Manila cafe.

The sailor was talking as he gazed abstractedly over the broad, blue expanse of water to the point where the sea and the sky blended into one. "Some day," he said, "I'm going to promote a world's championship fight."

The soldier looked into his glass of bubble water and replied: "Yes, and some day I'm going to manage a world's champion."

The sailor was Joe Waterman. The soldier was Wirt Ross. And tonight the dreams of one, perhaps both, come true at Wrigley Field where Baby Arizmendi of Mexico squares off against Henry Armstrong, St. Louis Negro managed by the ex-soldier, Wirt Ross, for the featherweight championship of the world as recognized by the California Athletic Commission and nine sister States.

The strange gate magic of a

(Continued on Page 13, Column 4)

## *LELIVELT, KILLEFER REINSTATED*

Jack Lelivelt, manager of the Los Angeles ball club, and Bill Killefer, boss of the Sacramento team, will not sit on the side lines when their teams oppose each other at Wrigley Field tomorrow night.

W. C. Tuttle, president of the Pacific Coast League, last night lifted the fifteen-day suspensions on both pilots.

Lelivelt was suspended last Wednesday following a run-in with Umpire Hollis Leake in Tuesday's game against San Diego in the border city.

Killefer was suspended Friday after an argument with Umpire Snyder during Wednesday night's game with Portland in the north.

Prexy Tuttle said he was not yet prepared to lift his thirty-day suspension of Jimmy Reese, Angel second-sacker, who was banished following last Tuesday's row in San Diego. Tuttle intimated, however, that Jimmy might not be required to serve "full time."

Arnold Statz, third of the Angels suspended last week, joins his club tomorrow night, his five-day term having now elapsed.

## What's Doing in Sports Today

BOXING—Baby Arizmendi vs. Henry Armstrong at Wrigley Field for featherweight championship of world, 8 30 p.m.

SOFTBALL—Games at Fiedler Field Loyola Stadium, McLaglen Stadium, Belvedere, all 7 30 p.m.

MIDGET AUTO RACING—Speed program at Atlantic Stadium, 8:15 p.m.

## *American Sprinters Who Ran One-Two in 100-Meter Dash*

Jesse Owens, left, and Ralph Metcalfe talk it over during a recent track meet. They were right together again yesterday in the 100-meter finals of the Olympic Games, Owens winning in 10.3s. to tie the Games record and Metcalfe finishing second, just as he did four years ago at the Coliseum. Owens competes again today in the broad jump. (AP) photo

## TODAY'S OLYMPIC BILL

BERLIN, Aug. 3. (AP)—The schedule for the third day of the XIth Olympics tomorrow:

**OLYMPIC STADIUM**

10.30 a.m.—Broad jump trials; women's discus trials; men's 200-meter trials. (Subtract nine hours for Pacific Coast time.)
3 p.m.—400-meter hurdles semifinals.
3:15 p.m.—Women's discus trials and finals.
3.30 p.m.—200-meter semifinals.
4 p.m.—Women's 100-meter finals.
4:30 p.m.—Broad jump semifinals and finals.
5:30 p.m.—400-meter hurdles finals.
5:45 p.m.—800-meter finals.
6 p.m.—5000-meter trials.
6:10 p.m.—Norwegian gymnastics.

**FIELD HOCKEY STADIUM**

4:30 p.m.—Field hockey eliminations, Holland vs. Belgium; France vs. Switzerland.

**MAYFIELD**

2 p.m.—Polo, Germany vs. Hungary.

**GYMNASIUM**

9 a.m.—Women's fencing, foils, first round; men's fencing; team foils, semifinals.
1 p.m.—Women's foils, second round.
3 p.m.—Men's team foils, finals.

**RUHLEBEN SHOOTING STANDS**

9 a.m.—Modern pentathlon, pistol shooting.

**HERTHA SPORTS CLUB**

5 30 p.m.—Soccer football eliminations, Sweden vs. Japan.

**POST STADIUM**

5 30 p.m.—Soccer football eliminations, Germany vs. Luxemburg.

**DEUTSCHLAND HALL**

10 a.m.—Catch-as-catch-can wrestling eliminations.
7 p.m. Catch-as-catch-can wrestling finals.

**STAAKEN AIRDROME**

11 a.m. Glider plane exhibition.

# OWENS WINS BROAD JUMP AND CRACKS RECORD

*Radiophoto Brings First Pictures of American Olympic Victories by Jesse Owens and Helen Stephens*

Whether it's on the ground or in the air Jessie Owens, sensational Ohio State Negro, flies through the air, as this remarkable picture, transmitted from Berlin to New York by radio and then sent to Los Angeles by Wirephoto, aptly shows. Owens, who won the Olympic 100-meter championship Monday, yesterday captured the broad jump crown with this great jump of 26ft. 5 21-64in., a new Olympic record.

Radio and (AP) Wirephoto

This photo, radioed from Berlin to New York and thence transmitted to Los Angeles by the magic of Wirephoto, shows Helen Stephens, American female flier from Fulton, Mo., receiving her laurel wreath after winning the 100-meters dash yesterday. Kaethe Krause, Germany, third place, and Stella Walsh, second place, of Poland, flank Miss Stephens on the victory stand.

Radio and (AP) Wirephoto

## HARDIN COPS HURDLE RACE

### *Helen Stephens Wins Sprint*

*Woodruff Scores Triumph in 800-Meter Run for United States*

BY ALAN GOULD
Associated Press Sports Editor

BERLIN, Aug. 4. (AP)—Scaling the heights to Olympic track and field conquest unknown since pre-war days, the United States today ended all doubt about team supremacy, capturing first places in all three men's events, dividing honors in the two women's contests with Germany and producing the first double winner of the Eleventh Olympiad in an amazingly unbeatable Jesse Owens.

Ohio State's redoubtable Negro shattered Olympic records most every time he made a move in the day-long competition in two events. He twice bettered the 200-meter mark, coasting to 21.1s. victories in the qualifying trails, and then climaxed the day by bettering the broad jump mark five times, winding up with a final leap of 8.06 meters, 26ft. 5 21-64in.

SEEKS TRIPLE TODAY

This jumping feat, which buried the previous mark of 7.73 meters, 25ft. 4 11-16in., made by Edward Hamm in the 1928 Games, gave a second gold medal and oak tree to the tan thunderbolt who is poised to complete a triple triumph in the decisive 200-meter tests tomorrow.

The decisive but non-record-breaking victories of Glenn Hardin, Greenwood, Miss., in the 400-meter hurdles and John Hughey Woodruff, Connellsville (Pa.) Negro, in the 800-meter run, combined with Owens's latest contribution ended any idea that the point battle for the team title will be close.

YANKEES WELL AHEAD

Completion of three of eight days of Olympic blue ribbon competition found the United States totaling 83 points in eight events—more than double Germany's 38¾ points. The Teutons had the satisfaction of pushing Owens to record-jumping flights, but picked up only 7½ points while Finland went scoreless and remained in third place with 30¼ points.

Helen Stephens of Fulton, Mo., sharing the feminine spotlight with Germany's record-breaking discus thrower, Gisela Mauermayer, continued the United States' sprinting sweep. The Missourian beat five rivals decisively, including Poland's defending champion, Stella Walsh, in the women's 100-meter clash, bettering the listed world record for the third time. She won the title in 11.5s., one-tenth of a second short of her own best mark in yesterday's trials.

ROBINSON QUALIFIES

Meanwhile, two mates, dusky Matthew (Mack) Robinson of Pasadena, Cal., and Bobby Packard of Rockford, Ill., University of Georgia freshman, accompanied Owens through the 200-meter trials into the semi-finals.

Don Lash of Auburn, Ind., and Louis Zamperini of Torrance, Cal., emerged unimpressively among fifteen qualifiers in the 5000-meter trials in which the finals will be held Friday. Tom Deckard of Bloomington, Ind., the third American 5000-meter entry, was eliminated.

The weather turned blustery with the day's usual shower, but Reichsfuehrer Adolf Hitler and another capacity crowd of 100,000 jammed the big concrete stadium most of the day with Owens the main magnet.

Der Fuehrer joined in terrific ap-

(Continued on Page 14, Column 3)

Los Angeles Times Sports

CC WEDNESDAY MORNING, AUGUST 5, 1936.

# *ARMSTRONG WINS TITLE*

## OWENS GETS NEEDED REST

### *Negro Kept Off Relay Team*

*Buckeye Bullet Will Make Final Appearance in Olympics Today*

BERLIN, Aug. 4. (AP)—Jesse Owens will be all through with the Olympics after he has run in the 200-meter semifinals and, assuming he qualifies, in the finals tomorrow.

Jesse, who hates to stand around, had hoped to run one leg of the 400-meter sprint relay, but Lawson Robertson, track coach, feels the Ohio Negro has done just about enough for one Olympics.

Robertson has not yet decided who will make up the 400-meter relay team, but Marty Glickman, Sam Stoller and Foy Draper are considered certainties on the basis of trials the last two days. Frank Wykoff probably will be the fourth man.

Eddie O'Brien, Al Fitch, Harold Cagle and Robert Young definitely are slated for the 1600-meter relay team.

## *Jarrett and Brundage May Smoke Peace Pipe*

### Eleanor's Hubby Plans Conference With Olympic Nabob; Miss Holm Anxious to Rejoin Team

BERLIN, Aug. 4. (AP)—Art Jarrett, actor-husband of Eleanor Holm Jarrett, disbarred American swimming star, arrived today and announced plans to arrange a conference with Avery Brundage, president of the American Olympic Committee, for the purpose of gaining his wife's reinstatement to the Olympic team if that still is possible.

If he discovers Mrs. Jarrett definitely is off the squad, Jarrett said he wanted to be given full information as to the events leading up to the committee's disbarment of the backstroke champion.

Mrs. Jarrett was removed from the team on the day the squad reached Hamburg for violating training rules forbidding drinking and late hours.

Jarrett emphasized that he was making no threats nor deciding on any course of action until he has had an opportunity of conferring with Brundage and other officials.

He hoped to contact the A.O.C. president tonight. He has been advised, unofficially, that all chance of his wife's reinstatement has vanished but Eleanor, still hoping for a chance, said:

"I still have a week in which I could get into condition if permitted to compete and I believe I could win."

## *Famed Swimmer Traffic Victim*

PARIS, Aug. 4. (AP)—Cartonnet Jacques, former world-record breaststroke swimmer, was seriously injured in an automobile accident today.

Jacques lowered the world records in the 200-meter breast-stroke to 2:39.6 and the 200-yard breaststroke to 2:25.2 last year.

## ARIZMENDI LOSES BOUT

### *Decision Earned by Negro*

*Mexican Feather Bows to Foe Before 16,000 at Wrigley Field*

BY JACK SINGER

Petey Sarron, N.B.A. featherweight champion of the world, his face an ashen white, an empty ache in the pit of his stomach, squirmed in his seat and choked as he watched Henry Armstrong, the chocolate lancer, hammer Baby Arizmendi into the most brutal, ruthless defeat of his brilliant eleven-year stretch of ring warfare last night at Wrigley Field.

Paling perceptibly as he blinked with frightened eyes that saw Armstrong, the infernal machine, smoke the idol of Mexico out of the ring with burning, searing leather to take every one of ten rounds and with it recognition in California as world's featherweight champion,

(Continued on Page 17, Column 2)

## *Bill Henry Says—*

BERLIN, Aug. 4.—Discus tossers may come and discus tossers may go but Bud Houser, only two-time winner in this event in Olympic history, will stick for a long time in the minds of athletes as a great competitor. He won his first title in 1924 as a schoolboy at Paris. He repeated in 1928 at Amsterdam after muffing his early throws so badly that when he stepped into the circle for his final toss he wasn't in the first five.

BUD HOUSER'S WIN HAD DRAMA

Houser wound up and let one go for the championship and a new Olympic record of slightly better than 155 feet, and that's what you call coming through when you're up against it. Incidentally in the same event another American, Corson, made all his throws without removing his sweat pants. It developed later that he'd forgotten to bring his track pants to the stadium and there wasn't anybody big enough to loan him any. At Los Angeles in 1932 the winner John Anderson had the distinction of setting a new Olympic record on four successive throws, 157ft., 160ft., 162ft. ¾in. and 162ft. 4⅞in. The winner this year'll probably go 10 feet better than that!

SWIVEL-HIPPED BOYS DO THEIR STUFF

The modern pentathlon boys, being soldiers, probably don't mind getting up early but they're first again with their shooting competition starting at 9 in the morning. The fencers start at the same time and keep at it afternoon and evening as well. After some heats during the morning the big event at the Stadium is the departure at 1 p.m. of the pedestrians on their 50,000-kilometer stroll from which they're due to return about 5 p.m. Meantime we'll see heats in the 80-meter hurdles for ladies, 110-meter hurdles for men and the 1500 meters too. Also finals in the 200 meters, discuss, and pole vault. Lacrosse, polo, weight-lifting, soc-

(Continued on Page 14, Column 1)

## *American Crew Oozes Power in Trial Spin*

### Don Hume Again at Stroke as Husky Boatload Impressive; Italy Feared by Yankees

BERLIN, Aug. 4. (AP)—American Olympic oarsmen settled into the second week of training today with the University of Washington crew showing consistent improvement.

Don Hume, stroke of the crew, apparently was completely recovered from his cold and is stroking so well that Coach Al Ulbrickson considers the crew now is equal to its form when it won in the trials at Princeton.

The Huskies' best time trial to date is 6m. 36s. made under adverse water and wind conditions.

The British, Hungarian and Italian eights now are regarded as the principal threats in preference to the Swiss crew which won the Henley Grand Challenge Cup.

The Australian all-police crew is considered powerful but, like the Japanese, erratic.

Cecil Pearce, Australian sculler, has impressed the American sweep-swingers and they predict he will keep the singles title in the family. His cousin Bobby won the last two Olympic sculls titles.

## *What's Doing in Sports Today*

BASEBALL—Sacramento vs. Los Angeles at Wrigley Field, double-header, first game 7:30 p.m.

WRESTLING—Dave Levin vs. Chief Little Wolf at Olympic Auditorium, 8:30 p.m.

SOFTBALL—Games at Fiedler Field, Loyola Stadium, Belvedere, all at 7:45 p.m.

LOUIS STARTS TRAINING

POMPTON LAKES (N. J.) Aug. 4. (UP)—Joe Louis returned to his lucky training spot today to prepare for his coming fight with ex-Heavyweight Champion Jack Sharkey. It was here that the Detroit Negro trained for Carnera, Baer and Uzcudun.

## OLYMPICS AT A GLANCE

BY THE ASSOCIATED PRESS

TRACK AND FIELD

United States makes clean sweep of three men's finals as Jesse Owens captured the broad jump at new Olympic record distance of 8.06 meters, 26ft.5 21/64in., Glenn Hardin takes the 400-meter low hurdles crown, and Johnny Woodruff romps off with 800-meter championship; Helen Stephens eclipses listed Olympic record in taking women's 100-meter title in 11.5s.; Owens, clocked twice in 21.1s., one-tenth of a second under the Olympic standard, qualifies for 200-meter semifinals along with Bobby Packard and Mack Robinson; Don Lash and Louis Zamperini qualify for 5000 meters final but Tom Deckard is eliminated; Gisela Mauermayer of Germany takes women's discus championship with new Olympic record toss of 47.63 meters, 156ft. 3⅜in., as Miss Stephens and Mrs. Gertrude Wilhelmsen, Americans sail even to qualify for the finals; Chuck Hornbostel and Harry Williamson finish fifth and sixth in 800-meter final, Joe Patterson takes fourth place in 400-meter hurdles final, and Annette Rogers places fifth in women's 100-meter final.

TEAM STANDINGS

(On unofficial 10-5-4-3-2-1 basis)

Men's track and field: United States, 83; Germany, 38¾; Finland, 30¼; Japan, 9½; Canada, 9; Italy, 7½; Sweden, 5; Holland, 4; Philippines, 4; Poland, 3; Great Britain, 2; Brazil, 2; Argentina, 1; Greece, 1.

Women's track and field: Germany, 38; Poland, 14; United States, 12; Japan, 7; Austria, 3; Sweden, 1.

Wrestling: Ross Flood, bantamweight; Francis Millard, featherweight, and Harley Strong, lightweight, reach fourth round; Frank Lewis, welterweight; Dick Voliva, middleweight, and Roy Clemons, light-heavyweight, win and gain third round. Roy Dunn, heavyweigh, is eliminated.

Soccer: Japan upset Sweden, 3 to 2.

Polo: Germany, 8; Hungary, 8; tie.

Yachting: American boats fare badly as competition opens in four classes, finishing third in star class, seventh in the six-meter and eight-meter divisions and seventeenth in the monotype class.

Field hockey eliminations: Afghanistan, 6; Denmark, 6, tie. Holland, 2; Belgium, 2, tie. France, 2; Switzerland, 1.

## *Complete Results of Olympic Events*

BERLIN, Aug. 4. (AP)—Following are the complete results of today's competitions in the Olympic track and field events:

Broad jump final—Won by **JESSE OWENS, UNITED STATES,** 8.06 meters, 26ft. 5 21-64in. (new Olympic record;) second, Lutz Long, Germany, 7.87 meters, 25ft. 9 27-32in.; third, Naoto Tajima, Japan, 7.74 meters, 25ft. 4 47-64in.; tied for fourth, Arturo Maffei, Italy, and Wilhelm Leichum, Germany, 7.73 meters, 25ft. 4 21-64in.; sixth, **ROBERT CLARK, UNITED STATES,** 7.67 meters, 25ft. 1 31-32in.

400-meter hurdles finals—Won by **GLENN HARDIN, UNITED STATES,** 52.4s.; second, Johnny Loaring, Canada, 52.7s.; third, Miguel White, Philippines, 52.8s.; fourth, **JOSEPH PATTERSON, UNITED STATES,** 53.0s.; fifth, Magalhaes Padilha, Brazil, 54.0s.; sixth, Christos Mantikas, Greece, 54.2s.

800-meter final—Won by **JOHN WOODRUFF, UNITED STATES,** 1m. 52.9s.; second, Mario Lanzi, Italy, 1m. 53.3s.; third, Phil Edwards, Canada, 1m. 53.6s.; fourth, Kazimierz Kucharski, Poland, 1m. 53.8s.; fifth, **CHARLES HORNBOSTEL, UNITED STATES,** 1m. 54.6s.; sixth, **HARRY WILLIAMSON, UNITED STATES,** 1m. 55.8s.; seventh, Gerald Backhouse, Australia; eighth, Brian MacCabe, Great Britain; ninth, Juan Anderson, Argentina.

Women's 100-meter final—Won by **HELEN STEPHENS, UNITED STATES,** 11.5s. (betters Olympic record;) second, Stella Walasiewicz, Poland, 11.7s.; third, Kathe Krauss, Germany, 11.9s.; fourth, Marie Dollinger, Germany; fifth, Annette Rogers, United States; sixth, Emmy Albus, Germany.

Women's discus throw final—Won by Bygisela Mauermayer, Germany, 47.63 meters, 156ft. 3 3-8in. (betters

(Continued on Page 14, Column 7)

## *No Place for the Baby Even if He Was Armed*

Baby Arizmendi, Mexican featherweight, is shown trying to cover up and avoid the barrage of blows aimed in his direction by Henry Armstrong in last night's fight at Wrigley Field. Armstrong's easy victory won him recognition from the California Boxing Commission as world's champion.

Times photo by George Strock

# OWENS, CARPENTER, MEADOWS BREAK RECORDS

## *Bill Henry* *Says—*

BERLIN, Aug. 5.—There'll be a ›llow in the grandstands here ›morrow, so I'm told, whom I'm ›axious to meet. He's sort of in a ›ass by himself. In fact, there ›asn't been anyone like him since ›everal hundred years B. C.—if ›ou get what I mean. His name Mr. Jarvinen and the folks get ›eal lyrical when they refer to ›im as the Diagoras of Finland.

**INLAND'S JARVINEN UITE A CHAP**

In case you haven't brushed up ›n your history recently, the late ›Ir. Diagoras not only was an ›lympic champion himself, but ›ved to see his three sons all ›owned Olympic champions, too. ›his led a contemporary to re›ark, "Die, Diagoras, for thou hast ›othing short of divinity to de›re," which, if it was said by a ›alous rival, was the ancient ›reek version of "I'll be glad when ›u're dead, you rascal you." The ›ntemporaneous Mr. Jarvinen ›asn't done quite that well, but ›e won the discus throw, Greek ›yle, at the Greek Olympics of ›06 and placed in the discus in ›ndon in 1908. Back in 1932 he ›d three sons all on the Olympic ›am, Kalle a shot putter, Akilles, ›cathlon star, and Matti, javelin ›ampion. He hopes to see at ›ast Matti repeat here and, for ›e, I hope he does. He's some ›an!

**'HAT'S DOING AT THE AMES TODAY**

They start the day off by weigh›g the Greco-Roman wrestlers at a.m. at the Olympic Village ›d the boys start grappling right ›terward. Modern pentathlon ›ntestants have their swimming ›st. Track and field starts off ›th trials in the javelin, 400 me›rs and hop, step and jump in ›e morning and in the afternoon ›'ll see finals in the javelin, hop, ›ep and pump, eighty-meter hur›es for women and 110-meter ›rdles for men and the classic ›00-meter final. Late in the aft›noon polo, handball, hockey and ›ccer matches are scheduled, ›ncing and wrestling go on both ›ternoon and evening and the ›clists have heats in the 1000 ›eters ad 4000-meter pursuit race. ›p at Kiel the yachtsmen have at all day.

**URDLERS DON'T WIN RECORD TIME**

The 110-meter hurdle event ›ever seems to be won in record ›me in the Olympic Games. Earl ›homson of Canada did it in 1920 ›hen he set the mark at 14.8s. ›y the time they'd finished racing Paris four years later nobody ›d even equaled the mark and Amsterdam in 1928 the final ›as won in 14.8s. by Atkinson of ›uth Africa while trailing him, fifth place, was team-mate ›eightman-Smith who had set a ›w mark of 14.6s. in a semifinal ›at. About the same thing hap›ned in Los Angeles in 1932 when ›aling won the final in 14.6s. after ›ck Keller had run 14.5s. in one ›mifinal and he himself had done ›.4s. in the other. So watch for ›e boys to break records, if they ›, in the heats rather than in the ›als.

**ARSMEN BOAST UPERSTITIONS**

I wonder how the oarsmen and on the subject of supersti›on this year? They're so far ›vay that it's pretty hard to catch ›with them. The California ›ew which represented the U.S.A. 1932 had a superstition that ›roke Ed Salisbury had to break ›n oar before every big race. ›very time he did it, they won. ›hey were badly worried before ›e Olympic finals because there ›adn't been any signs of a frac›re—but just four years ago to›ay, on the eve of the finals, big ›d reported a break. At first they

Continued on Page 13, Column 1)

## *American Woman Athletes Shown at Work and at Play in Olympic Games*

Kathlyn Kelly preparing for her specialty, the high jump.

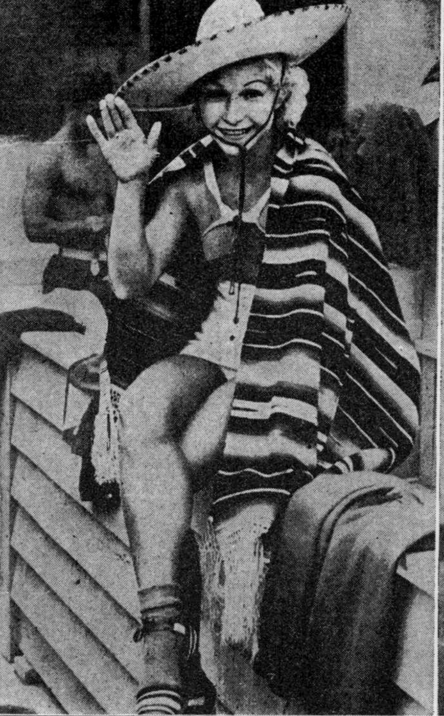

Dorothy Poynton Hill, Los Angeles diver, goes Latin.

Helen Stephens, fastest woman, also hurls the discus.

(AP) Wirephotos

## LEVIN WINS OVER CHIEF

### *Redskin Rammed by Easterner*

*Savage Slammed by Steinke in Semifinal Match at Olympic*

BY JACK SINGER

Prof. L. Daro, as president of the College of Hard Shocks the foremost exponent of the "Boo Deal," presented another of his weekly series of pachyderm productions last night at his Olympic torture chamber which was designed with great civic pride to establish Los Angeles as the center of art and culture.

Entitled "When Knighthood Was In Cauliflower" and co-starring that eminent mat-inee idol, Dapper Dave Levin, and the man made famous by the Three Little Pigs, Chief Little Wolf, Prof. Daro's latest "expose-ition" of nature in the raw was enthusiastically received by 7500 patrons, who came to see what Chief of Police Davis listed as justifiable homicide.

**DAVE QUALIFIES**

Although it required half the evening to accomplish his purpose, Dapper Dave, getting into the swim of things after the ring was soaked with sweat, decided to deliver a "mash" note in person and eliminated Little Wolf in two straight falls.

Dapper Dave, who addresses himself as "world champion" every time he sits down and writes himself a letter, thus qualified to represent the cause of law and order against Senor Vincent Lopez, who is Prof. Daro's favorite champion at the present hour, at Wrigley Field August 19.

Late last night Prof. Daro was found mumbling deliriously with a box of headache tablets in his hand "The greatest show in the whole world and all I get is 7500 people here tonight," moaned the professor as he swallowed three aspirins

**THAT OLYMPIAD**

"No doubt the Olympic Games had something to do with it," helpfully advanced Mr. Sid Marks. "You know that Citius, Altius, Fortius stuff and things."

"The Olympic Games?" replied Prof. Daro. "What is that Olympic Games? I give the public games at the Olympic every week. Who

(Continued on Page 12, Column 3)

Los Angeles Times Sports

C THURSDAY MORNING, AUGUST 6, 1936.

## *Radiophoto Faster Than Owens in Flashing Photo of Victory*

That loud noise you heard yesterday morning was Jesse Owens cracking his third record of the 1936 Olympic Games. This picture, radioed to New York from Berlin and flashed to Los Angeles via Wirephoto, shows the Buckeye Bullet annexing his third Olympic title—the 200-meter dash crown in the new Olympic record time of 20.7s. At the right is Mack Robinson of Pasadena Jaysee, who won second place while Martin Osendarp of Holland, center, nabbed third place.

(AP) Radio and Wirephoto

## SACS STOP SALVESON

### *Seraphs Divide Twin Bill*

*Angel Hurler Fails in Try for Thirteenth in Row as Solons Cop, 4-0*

BY BOB RAY

Sacramento's Solons, formerly known as Two-Gun Tuttle's Bushers, stopped Jack Salveson's string of twelve straight victories last night as they humbled our drooping Angels, 4-0, in the opener of a nocturnal double bill.

But the Angels got revenge in the nightcap when they bunched bingles with five Sacramento errors to get an even break by triumphing, 5-2, as Scow Thomas held the Sacs to four safeties. Johnny Chambers was the victim of the Seraph hitting and the Solon fielding.

Salveson, seeking to hurdle the sinister No. 13 in his string of triumphs, allowed only five hits, but two were bunched with a walk and a pair of errors as the Sacs scored three runs in the first inning. That was the ball game.

**PIPPEN BLANKS ANGELS**

Harold (Cotton) Pippen proved Salveson's Nemesis. The lanky, towheaded Sacramento right-hander kept seven Seraph hits well spaced and never allowed an Angel to advance past second base.

All of the Angels except Steve Mesner, who banged out a double and two singles, and Red Russell, who collected a pair of hits, found Cotton decidedly tough pitching.

The Angels, on orders from Prexy Dave Fleming, presented a rearranged line-up, shoving in their youthful recruits in an effort to stop a losing streak that was extended to five in a row. The bargain-bill lured a crowd of 6000 fans.

**MATTICK'S ERRORS HURT**

The Sacs, who believe in making hay instead of hitting it when the sun goes down, got to Salveson for three runs in the first frame of the opener. A couple of errors by Mattick played a prominent part in the uprising.

Morehouse hit the first pitch against the left field fence for two bases. Adams rapped Salveson's second offering to Mattick, who threw wildly to first. Adams went

(Continued on Page 12, Column 3)

## TRIPLE FOR NEGRO STAR

### *Jesse Captures 200 Meters*

*Southern California Aces Annex Pole Vault and Discus Laurels*

BY ALAN GOULD
Associated Press Sports Writer

BERLIN, Aug. 5. (AP)—Incomparable Jesse Owens, whose blazing bursts of speed and jumping ability have thrilled nearly half a million spectators on four successive days, completed his classic Olympic triple title conquest in record-smashing style in the rain today.

Approximately 75,000 spectators, the smallest crowd yet occupying the huge stadium any afternoon, made up in cheers what it lacked in numbers as the dynamic American Negro added the 200-meter title to his previous triumphs in the 100-meter sprint and the broad jump.

Pursued by his dusky Pasadena (Cal.) team-mate, Matthew (Mack) Robinson, who finished second, the Ohio State all-around star ended an unbeaten campaign by lowering the world as well as the Olympic mark around one turn to 20.7s.

**BIG DAY**

Owens, in contributing the fifth American Negro triumph in these Games, featured another big day in which the United States team soared well over the 100 mark in the team point standing, leaving all rivals far behind.

In addition to the 200-meter final, Americans finished one-two in the discus throw with big Ken Carpenter of Compton, Cal., beating his California rival, Gordon (Slinger) Dunn, by hurling the platter 50.48 meters, 165ft. 7 29-64in. for a new Olympic record.

Another gold medal was added to the steadily growing American collection by Earle Meadows of Fort Worth, Tex. The Southern California Trojan soared to the Olympic mark-smashing height of 4.35 meters, 14ft. 2 15-16in., eclipsing the old record of 14ft. 1 7-8in. made by Bill Miller at Los Angeles four years ago.

**RETAIN TITLE**

The day's competition saw Great Britain retain the 50-kilometer walk championship as Harold Whitlock clipped nearly twenty minutes from the record, winning in 4h. 30m. 41.4s., and Uncle Sam's 110-meter hurdling trio and 1500-meter triumvirate qualify in stirring trials marks by the elimination of Stanley Wooderson, Great Britain's "metric mile hope."

Reichsfuehrer Adolf Hitler was driven from his official box by a heavy downpour of rain just after Owens flashed across the finish line for his third triumph and wasn't among the thousands who remained and thundered acclaim when the Negro stepped up for the third time to be crowned with a laurel wreath and given his third gold medal and oak tree that will be planted on Ohio State's campus.

Surmounting dismal weather conditions throughout his four-day stretch, Owens set two new Olympic records, equaled a third besides adding his name twice to the world record list by equaling the 100-meter mark of 10.3s. in addition to his 200-meter mark this afternoon.

**ACHIEVES TRIPLE**

Owens thus became the fourth American to capture three or more championships in one Olympiad and the first athlete to achieve a triple since peerless Paavo Nurmi ran them all dizzy in 1924 at Paris.

The Negro joined the company of Arthur Kraenzlein, who won four events in 1900, Ray Ewry, who swept three standing jumps twice in 1900 and 1904, and Archie Hahn, triple sprint winner in 1904.

The day's only reversals for the Americans, not unexpected, came in the women's 110-meter hurdles and the Marathon walk in which new Olympic marks were set in both events.

The trio of American girls reached the semifinals in the timber-topping feature but Anne Vrana O'Brien of Huntington Beach, Cal., was shut out in the first heat by Italy's Trebisonda Valla in 11.6s., equaling the world mark as well as clipping one-tenth of a second from the Olympic standard.

Tidye Pickett, Chicago Negro girl, fell at the second hurdle and hurt her foot severely, while Simone Schaller of Monrovia, Cal., was eliminated on a photographic recount, the judges reversing themselves and yielding the third qualifying place to Claudia Testoni of Italy.

European walkers, led by Britain's

(Continued on Page 10, Column 7)

## *Red Tape Cut; Records Submitted*

BERLIN, Aug. 5. (AP)—Reversing the customary procedure whereby world records achieved by Americans must await approval at the convention of the Amateur Athletic Union, Avery Brundage, president of the A.A.U., today cut the red tape and arranged approval of this year's outstanding marks by the International Amateur Athletic Federation forthwith.

**MARKS LISTED**

These included Forrest Towns's 14.1s. mark in the high hurdles, George Varoff's pole vault of 14ft. 6½in., Cornelius Johnson's and Dave Albritton's high jumps of 6ft. 9¾in. and Glenn Morris's decathlon mark of 7800 points.

Jesse Owens's mark of 10.2s. for the 100 meters, made in Chicago at the N.C.A.A. meet, June 20, was rejected by the I.A.A.F. records committee, because, said Brundage, "the track was found to be a few inches short." Thus, Owens, who won his third Olympic title today, lost his second attempt to gain undisputed possession of this mark. In the Olympic trials Sunday it was thrown out because of a slight favoring wind.

**FURLONG RECORD UP**

Owens's record in the 220-yard dash of 20.3s., made in the 1935 Big Ten championships, also was offered, as the new 200-meter mark and given committee approval.

The 220-yard low hurdles and the 100-yard marks set by Owens were not submitted, according to Brundage.

The entire batch of records, including the ten the committee found in order last week, are due for final consideration at the I.A.A.F. congress October 8.

## JARRETT TO FILE SUIT

### *Eleanor's Husband Plans Legal Action Against Olympic Committee*

BERLIN, Aug. 5. (AP)—Arthur Jarrett announced late tonight his intention of taking legal action against the American Olympic Committee upon returning to New York with his wife, Eleanor Holm Jarrett, who was dismissed from the Olympic team on its arrival in Germany.

After being refused a conference by Avery Brundage, president of the American Olympic Committee, Jarrett in a statement asserted he would take "the proper steps, first to obtain the facts about the case, which the American Olympic Committee apparently tried to conceal, and secondly, to get redress for damages to my wife's reputation."

**FAIL TO MEET**

Jarrett and Brundage failed to get together for a conference, despite the former's efforts during the past two days. They conferred lengthily by telephone, however, apparently getting nowhere.

Brundage told Jarrett, as well as newspapermen, that "the case is closed and there is nothing I can say, nor any information I can add, that hasn't already been given out. All I can do is refer you to the

(Continued on Page 10, Column 2)

## YESTERDAY'S OLYMPICS AT A GLANCE

BY THE ASSOCIATED PRESS

**TRACK AND FIELD**

Jesse Owens completed his Olym›ic "triple," winning 200-meter title ›n new world record time of 20.7s.; ›lack Robinson, Pasadena, Cal., runs ›econd.

Earle Meadows captures pole vault, ›oosting Olympic record to 4.35 me›ers (14ft. 2 15-16in.;) Bill Sefton ›nishes fourth and Bill Graber ›fth.

Discus championship goes to Ken ›arpenter with new Olympic rec›rd toss of 50.48 meters, as Gor›on Dunn places second; Walter ›Vood fails to qualify for finals.

Harold Whitlock, Great Britain, ›lips nearly twenty minutes off ›lympic standard in winning 50,›00-meter walk in 4h. 30m. 41.4s.; ›mericans, Albert Mangan, Ernest ›oehler and George Crosbie finish ›wenty-first, twenty-third and twen›y-sixth, respectively.

Gene Venzke, Glenn Cunningham ›nd Archie San Romani all qualify ›r finals of 1500-meter run, as Stan›ey Wooderson, British hope, is ›liminated.

Forrest Towns, Fritz Pollard and ›oy Staley all win their heats in qualifying for semifinals of 110-meter high hurdles.

All three American girls in women's 80-meter hurdles, Simone Schaller, Anne Vrana O'Brien and Tidye Pickett, are eliminated as Trebisonda Valla, Italy, equals world record of 11.6s., and clips one-tenth second off Olympic standard.

Unofficial team point standings (on 10-5-4-3-2-1 basis:)

Men's track and field—United States, 128; Germany 41¾; Finland, 30¼; Japan, 18 13-22; Great Britain 12 1-11; Italy, 11 13-22; Canada, 11 1-11 Holland, 9; Switzerland, 8; Sweden, 5 1-11; Norway, 5; Philippines, 4; Latvia, 4; Czechoslovakia, 3 1-11; Poland, 3 1-11; Brazil, 2; Greece, 2; Argentina, 1; Austria, 2-11; Hungary, 2-11.

Women's track and field: Germany, 38; Poland, 14; United States, 12; Japan, 7; Austria, 3; Sweden, 1.

Modern Pentathlon — Gotthardt Handrick, Germany; Sven Thofelt, Sweden, and Charles Leonard, St. Petersburg, hold first three places after four events of five-event test have been completed. Alfred Starbird and Fred Weber, other American entries, rank ninth and tenth, respectively.

Field hockey—Japan, 5; United States 1. India, 4; Hungary, 0.

Polo—Argentina, 15; Mexico, 5.

Fencing—Schacherer Elek, Hungary, wins women's foils championship with Helene Mayer, Germany, second. American entrants eliminated in semifinals. Hugh Alessandroni and William Pecora, Americans, eliminated in second round of men's foils competition.

Soccer—Poland, 3; Hungary, 0. Austria, 2; Egypt, 0.

Yachts—Great Britain leads with 49 points after first day's actual competition in four divisions. United States far back with 19 points.

Weight lifting—Joseph Menger. Germany, wins heavyweight and Khadr El Touni of Egypt takes middleweight weight-lifting titles. American middleweights, Stan Kratkowsky, Detroit, and Walter Good, York, Pa., finish fifth and fourteenth, respectively. In the heavyweight class, Americans John Grimek and David Mayor finish ninth and twelfth, respectively.

Hitler draws crowd to final matches.

## *Games Track Summary*

BERLIN, Aug. 5. (AP)—Summaries in today's Olympic track and field competition:

200-meter semifinals (first three qualify for finals:)

First semifinal—Won by **MATTHEW ROBINSON, UNITED STATES**, 21.1. (betters listed Olympic record of 21.2, set by Eddie Tolon, United States, 1932, and equals new Olympic record set by Jesse Owens yesterday;) second, Orr, Canada, 21.3; third, Van Beveren, Holland, 21.5; **FOURTH, BOBBY PACKARD, UNITED STATES**; fifth, Neckermann, Germany; sixth, Grimbeek, South Africa.

Second semifinal — **WON BY JESSE OWENS, UNITED STAETS, 21.3**; second, Osendarp, Holland, 21.5; third, Haenni, Switzerland, 21.6; fourth, Theunissen, South Africa; fifth, Humber, Canada; sixth, McPhee, Canada.

Women's 80-meter hurdle quarter finals (first three qualify for semifinals:)

First heat—Won by Testoni, Italy, 12.0; second, Tiffen, England, 12.2; third, Lanitis, Greece, 12.6; fourth, Puschberger, Austria; fifth, Mabille, France.

Second heat—Won by Webb, England, 11.8; second, Eckert, Germany, 12.0; **THIRD, TIDYE PICKETT, UNITED STATES**, 21.4; fourth, Mitsui, Japan; fifth, Kolbach, Austria.

Third heat—Won by Taylor, Can-

(Continued on Page 10, Column 3)

## *Polish Writer Calls Helen Stephens 'Man'*

WARSAW, Aug. 5. (Exclusive)—An accusation that Helen Stephens, American sprinter who broke the world's record for the women's 100-meter Olympic dash at Berlin, is in reality a man was made today by the special correspondent of the Polish newspaper Kurier Poranny.

His report was tinged with indignation against the United States for having assertedly permitted a man to run in the women's race. Miss Stephens yesterday defeated the Polish star, Stanislawa Walasiewicz, known in the United States as Stella Walsh, in the 100-meter dash.

**SOMETHING "SCANDALOUS"**

"It is scandalous that the Americans entered a man in a women's competition," the correspondent stated. "Miss Walasiewicz would have gained first place if she had competed only against women. It was not her fault if she was defeated by Stephens who should have been running with Owens and the other American male stars."

American Olympic authorities last week recommended that women athletes entered in the international events be subjected to a sex examination. The move was referred to various individual sports federations for a decision.

**BRUNDAGE'S IDEA**

The motion, advanced by Avery Brundage, president of the American Olympic Committee, was intended to make certain that entrants were correctly qualified for women's competitions.

This recommendation led observers to recall in May of this year Mary Edith Weston, noted English girl athlete, was formally proclaimed a man after undergoing two

(Continued on Page 14, Column 3)

# LOUIS KNOCKS OUT BRADDOCK IN EIGHTH ROUND

Los Angeles Times Sports

R WEDNESDAY MORNING, JUNE 23, 1937.

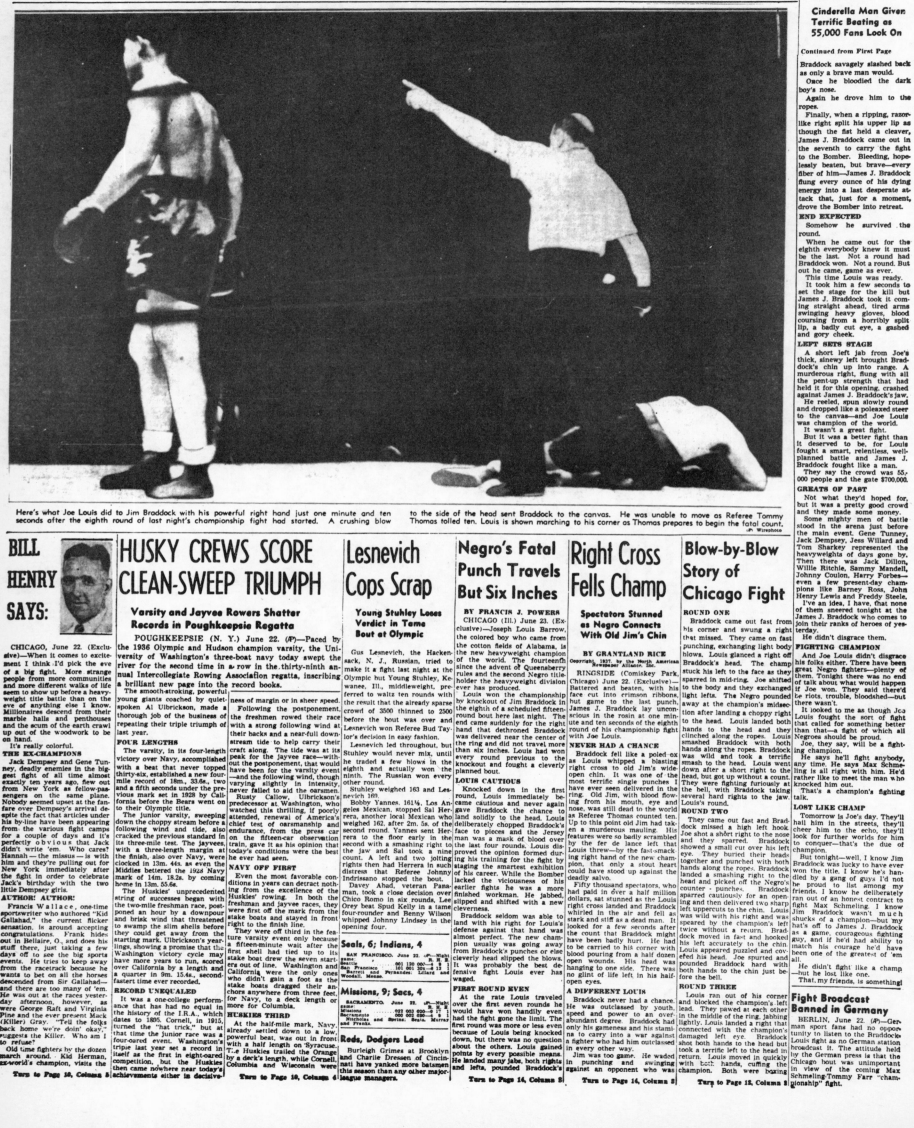

Here's what Joe Louis did to Jim Braddock with his powerful right hand just one minute and ten seconds after the eighth round of last night's championship fight had started. A crushing blow to the side of the head sent Braddock to the canvas. He was unable to move as Referee Tommy Thomas tolled ten. Louis is shown marching to his corner as Thomas prepares to begin the fatal count. (AP) Wirephoto

## Negro Wins Ring Title

### Cinderella Man Given Terrific Beating as 55,000 Fans Look On

Continued from First Page

Braddock savagely slashed back as only a brave man would.

Once he bloodied the dark boy's nose.

Again he drove him to the ropes.

Finally, when a ripping, razor-like right split his upper lip as though the fist held a cleaver, James J. Braddock came out in the seventh to carry the fight to the Bomber. Bleeding, hopelessly beaten, but brave—every fiber of him—James J. Braddock flung every ounce of his dying energy into a last desperate attack that, just for a moment, drove the Bomber into retreat.

**END EXPECTED**

Somehow he survived the round.

When he came out for the eighth everybody knew it must be the last. Not a round had Braddock won. Not a round. But out he came, game as ever.

This time Louis was ready.

It took him a few seconds to set the stage for the kill but James J. Braddock took it coming straight ahead, tired arms swinging heavy gloves, blood coursing from a horribly split lip, a badly cut eye, a gashed and gory cheek.

**LEFT SETS STAGE**

A short left jab from Joe's thick, sinewy left brought Braddock's chin up into range. A murderous right, flung with all the pent-up strength that had held it for this opening, crashed against James J. Braddock's jaw.

He reeled, spun slowly round and dropped like a poleaxed steer to the canvas—and Joe Louis was champion of the world.

It wasn't a great fight.

But it was a better fight than it deserved to be, for Louis fought a smart, relentless, well-planned battle and James J. Braddock fought like a man.

They say the crowd was 55,000 people and the gate $700,000.

**GREATS OF PAST**

Not what they'd hoped for, but it was a pretty good crowd and they made some money.

Some mighty men of battle stood in the arena just before the main event. Gene Tunney, Jack Dempsey, Jess Willard and Tom Sharkey represented the heavyweights of days gone by. Then there was Jack Dillon, Willie Ritchie, Sammy Mandell, Johnny Coulon, Harry Forbes—even a few present-day champions like Barney Ross, John Henry Lewis and Freddy Steele.

I've an idea, I have, that none of them sneered tonight at the James J. Braddock who comes to join their ranks of heroes of yesterday.

He didn't disgrace them.

**FIGHTING CHAMPION**

And Joe Louis didn't disgrace his folks either. There have been great Negro fighters—plenty of them. Tonight there was no end of talk about what would happen if Joe won. They said there'd be riots, trouble, bloodshed—but there wasn't.

It looked to me as though Joe Louis fought the sort of fight that called for something better than that—a fight of which all Negroes should be proud.

Joe, they say, will be a fighting champion.

He says he'll fight anybody, any time. He says Max Schmeling is all right with him. He'd rather like to meet the man who knocked him out.

That's a champion's fighting talk.

**LOST LIKE CHAMP**

Tomorrow is Joe's day. They'll hail him in the streets, they'll cheer him to the echo, they'll look for further worlds for him to conquer—that's the due of champion.

But tonight—well, I know Jim Braddock was lucky to have ever won the title. I know he's handled by a gang of guys I'd not be proud to list among my friends. I know he deliberately ran out of an honest contract to fight Max Schmeling. I know Jim Braddock wasn't much shucks of a champion—but my hat's off to James J. Braddock as a game, courageous fighting guy, and if he'd had ability to match his courage he'd have been one of the greatest of 'em all.

He didn't fight like a champ—but he lost like one.

That, my friends, is something!

## BILL HENRY SAYS:

CHICAGO, June 22. (Exclusive)—When it comes to excitement I think I'd pick the eve of a big fight. More strange people from more communities and more different walks of life seem to show up before a heavyweight title battle than on the eve of anything else I know. Millionaires descend from their marble halls and penthouses and the scum of the earth crawl up out of the woodwork to be on hand.

It's really colorful.

**THE EX-CHAMPIONS**

Jack Dempsey and Gene Tunney, deadly enemies in the biggest fight of all time almost exactly ten years ago, flew out from New York as fellow-passengers on the same plane. Nobody seemed upset at the fanfare over Dempsey's arrival despite the fact that articles under his by-line have been appearing from the various fight camps for a couple of days and it's perfectly obvious that Jack didn't write 'em. Who cares? Hannah — the missus — is with him and they're pulling out for New York immediately after the fight in order to celebrate Jack's birthday with the two little Dempsey girls.

**AUTHOR! AUTHOR!**

Francis Wallace, one-time sportswriter who authored "Kid Gallahad," the current flicker sensation, is around accepting congratulations. Frank hides out in Bellaire, O., and does his stuff there, just taking a few days off to see the big sports events. He tries to keep away from the racetrack because he wants to bet on all the horses descended from Sir Gallahad—and there are too many of 'em. He was out at the races yesterday afternoon, however, as were George Raft and Virginia Pine and the ever present Mack (Killer) Gray. "Tell the folks back home we're doin' okay," suggests the Killer. Who am I to refuse?

Old time fighters by the dozen march around. Kid Herman, ex-world's champion, visits the

Turn to Page 10, Column 5

## HUSKY CREWS SCORE CLEAN-SWEEP TRIUMPH

### Varsity and Jayvee Rowers Shatter Records in Poughkeepsie Regatta

POUGHKEEPSIE (N. Y.) June 22. (AP)—Paced by the 1936 Olympic and Hudson champion varsity, the University of Washington's three-boat navy today swept the river for the second time in a row in the thirty-ninth annual Intercollegiate Rowing Association regatta, inscribing a brilliant new page into the record books.

The smooth-stroking, powerful young giants coached by quiet-spoken Al Ulbrickson, made a thorough job of the business of repeating their triple triumph of last year.

**FOUR LENGTHS**

The varsity, in its four-length victory over Navy, accomplished with a beat that never topped thirty-six, established a new four-mile record of 18m., 33.6s., two and a fifth seconds under the previous mark set in 1928 by California before the Bears went on to their Olympic title.

The junior varsity, sweeping down the choppy stream before a following wind and tide, also cracked the previous standard in its three-mile test. The jayvees, with a three-length margin at the finish, also over Navy, were clocked in 13m. 44s. as even the Middies bettered the 1928 Navy mark of 14m. 18.2s. by coming home in 13m. 55.6s.

The Huskies' unprecedented string of successes began with the two-mile freshman race, postponed an hour by a downpour and brisk wind that threatened to swamp the slim shells before they could get away from the starting mark. Ulbrickson's yearlings, showing a promise that the Washington victory cycle may have more years to run, scored over California by a length and a quarter in 9m. 15.4s., second-fastert time ever recorded.

**RECORD UNEQUALED**

It was a one-college performance that has had no equal in the history of the I.R.A., which dates to 1895. Cornell, in 1915, turned the "hat trick," but at that time the junior race was a four-oared event. Washington's triple last year set a record in itself as the first in eight-oared competition, but the Huskies then came nowhere near today's achievements either in decisiveness of margin or in sheer speed.

Following the postponement, the freshmen rowed their race with a strong following wind at their backs and a near-full down-stream tide to help carry their craft along. The tide was at its peak for the jayvee race—without the postponement, that would have been for the varsity event—and the following wind, though varying slightly in intensity, never failed to aid the oarsmen.

Rusty Callow, Ulbrickson's predecessor at Washington, who watched this thrilling, if poorly attended, renewal of America's chief test of oarsmanship and endurance, from the press car on the fifteen-car observation train, gave it as his opinion that today's conditions were the best he ever had seen.

**NAVY OFF FIRST**

Even the most favorable conditions in years can detract nothing from the excellence of the Huskies' rowing. In both the freshman and jayvee races, they were first off the mark from the stake boats and stayed in front right to the finish line.

They were off third in the feature varsity event only because a fifteen-minute wait after the first shell had tied up to its stake boat drew the seven starters out of line. Washington and California were the only ones who didn't gain a foot as the stake boats dragged their anchors anywhere from three feet, for Navy, to a deck length or more for Columbia.

**HUSKIES THIRD**

At the half-mile mark, Navy, already settled down to a low, powerful beat, was out in front with a half length on Syracuse. The Huskies trailed the Orange by a deck's length, while Cornell, Columbia and Wisconsin were

Turn to Page 10, Column 4

## Lesnevich Cops Scrap

### Young Stuhley Loses Verdict in Tame Bout at Olympic

Gus Lesnevich, the Hackensack, N. J., Russian, tried to make it a fight last night at the Olympic but Young Stuhley, Kewanee, Ill., middleweight, preferred to waltz ten rounds with the result that the already sparse crowd of 3500 thinned to 2500 before the bout was over and Lesnevich won Referee Bud Taylor's decision in easy fashion.

Lesnevich led throughout, but Stuhley would never mix, until he traded a few blows in the eighth and actually won the ninth. The Russian won every other round.

Stuhley weighed 163 and Lesnevich 169.

Bobby Yannes, 161½, Los Angeles Mexican, stopped Sal Herrera, another local Mexican who weighed 162, after 2m. 5s. of the second round. Yannes sent Herrera to the floor early in the second with a smashing right to the jaw and Sal took a nine count. A left and two jolting rights then had Herrera in such distress that Referee Johnny Indrissano stopped the bout.

Davey Abad, veteran Panaman, took a close decision over Chico Romo in six rounds, Lee Orey beat Spud Kelly in a tame four-rounder and Benny Wilson whipped Johnny Lindsey in the opening four.

## Seals, 6; Indians, 4

SAN FRANCISCO, June 22. (AP)—Night game:

| | | R. | H. | E. |
|---|---|---|---|---|
| Seattle | 001 120 000 | 4 | 9 | 1 |
| San Francisco | 101 001 30x | 6 | 12 | 1 |

Barrett and Fernandes; Lillard and Woodall, Monzo.

## Missions, 9; Sacs, 4

SACRAMENTO, June 22. (AP)—Night game:

| | | R. | H. | E. |
|---|---|---|---|---|
| Missions | 022 003 020 | 9 | 17 | 1 |
| Sacramento | 000 002 020 | 4 | 9 | 1 |

Nitcholas and Sprinz; Seats, Murray and Franks.

## Reds, Dodgers Lead

Burleigh Grimes at Brooklyn and Charlie Dressen of Cincinnati have yanked more batsmen this season than any other major-league managers.

## Negro's Fatal Punch Travels But Six Inches

BY FRANCIS J. POWERS

CHICAGO (Ill.) June 23. (Exclusive)—Joseph Louis Barrow, the colored boy who came from the cotton fields of Alabama, is the new heavyweight champion of the world. The fourteenth since the advent of Queensberry rules and the second Negro title-holder the heavyweight division ever has produced.

Louis won the championship by knockout of Jim Braddock in the eighth of a scheduled fifteen-round bout here last night. The end came suddenly for the right hand that dethroned Braddock was delivered near the center of the ring and did not travel more than six inches. Louis had won every round previous to the knockout and fought a cleverly planned bout.

**LOUIS CAUTIOUS**

Knocked down in the first round, Louis immediately became cautious and never again gave Braddock the chance to land solidly to the head. Louis deliberately chopped Braddock's face to pieces and the Jersey man was a mask of blood over the last four rounds. Louis disproved the opinion formed during his training for the fight by staging the smartest exhibition of his career. While the Bomber lacked the viciousness of his earlier fights he was a more finished workman. He jabbed, slipped and shifted with a new cleverness.

Braddock seldom was able to land with his right for Louis's defense against that hand was almost perfect. The new champion usually was going away from Braddock's punches or else cleverly head slipped the blows. It was probably the best defensive fight Louis ever has waged.

**FIRST ROUND EVEN**

At the rate Louis traveled over the first seven rounds he would have won handily even had the fight gone the limit. The first round was more or less even because of Louis being knocked down, but there was no question about the others. Louis gained points by every possible means. He landed many jabs, both rights and lefts, pounded Braddock's

Turn to Page 14, Column 8

## Right Cross Fells Champ

### Spectators Stunned as Negro Connects With Old Jim's Chin

BY GRANTLAND RICE



RINGSIDE (Comiskey Park, Chicago) June 22. (Exclusive)—Battered and beaten, with his face cut into crimson ribbons, but game to the last punch, James J. Braddock lay unconscious in the rosin at one minute and ten seconds of the eighth round of his championship fight with Joe Louis.

**NEVER HAD A CHANCE**

Braddock fell like a poled ox as Louis whipped a blasting right cross to old Jim's wide-open chin. It was one of the most terrific single punches I have ever seen delivered in the ring. Old Jim, with blood flowing from his mouth, eye and nose, was still dead to the world as Referee Thomas counted ten. Up to this point old Jim had taken a murderous mauling. His features were so badly scrambled by the fer de lance left that Louis threw—by the fast-smacking right hand of the new champion, that only a stout heart could have stood up against the deadly salvo.

Fifty thousand spectators, who had paid in over a half million dollars, sat stunned as the Louis right cross landed and Braddock whirled in the air and fell as stark and stiff as a dead man. It looked for a few seconds after the count that Braddock might have been badly hurt. He had to be carried to his corner with blood pouring from a half dozen open wounds. His head was hanging to one side. There was no glint of life left in his half-open eyes.

**A DIFFERENT LOUIS**

Braddock never had a chance. He was outclassed by youth, speed and power to an over-abundant degree. Braddock had only his gameness and his stamina to carry into a war against a fighter who had him outclassed in every other way.

Jim was too game. He waded in punching and swinging against an opponent who was

Turn to Page 14, Column 8

## Blow-by-Blow Story of Chicago Fight

**ROUND ONE**

Braddock came out fast from his corner and swung a right that missed. They came on fast punching, exchanging light body blows. Louis glanced a right off Braddock's head. The champ stuck his left to the face as they sparred in mid-ring. Joe shifted to the body and they exchanged light lefts. The Negro pounded away at the champion's midsection after landing a choppy right to the head. Louis landed both hands to the head and they clinched along the ropes. Louis smashed Braddock with both hands along the ropes. Braddock was wild and took a terrific smash to the head. Louis went down after a short right to the head, but got up without a count. They were fighting furiously at the bell, with Braddock taking several hard rights to the jaw. Louis's round.

**ROUND TWO**

They came out fast and Braddock missed a high left hook. Joe shot a short right to the nose and they sparred. Braddock showed a small cut over his left eye. They buried their heads together and punched with both hands along the ropes. Braddock landed a smashing right to the head and picked off the Negro's counter - punches. Braddock sparred cautiously for an opening and then delivered two sharp left uppercuts to the chin. Louis was wild with his right and was speared by the champion's left twice without a return. Braddock moved in fast and hooked his left accurately to the chin. Louis appeared puzzled and covered his head. Joe spurted and pounded Braddock hard with both hands to the chin just before the bell.

**ROUND THREE**

Louis ran out of his corner and blocked the champion's left lead. They pawed at each other in the middle of the ring, jabbing lightly. Louis landed a right that connected with the champion's damaged left eye. Braddock shot both hands to the head but took a terrific left to the head in return. Louis moved in quickly with both hands, cuffing the champion. Both were boxing

Turn to Page 12, Column 8

## Fight Broadcast Banned in Germany

BERLIN, June 22. (AP)—German sport fans had no opportunity to listen to the Braddock-Louis fight as no German station broadcast it. The attitude held by the German press is that the Chicago bout was unimportant in view of the coming Max Schmeling-Tommy Farr "championship" fight.

# Vander Meer Hurls Second No-Hit, No-Run Game

Los Angeles Times Sports

CC THURSDAY MORNING, JUNE 16, 1938.

## BITTER RING ENEMIES---CHAMPION ARMSTRONG AND CHAMPION AMBERS---MEET HERE

"Don't fight here, boys," warns Manager Al Weill, center. "Wait till you get paid for it." Henry Armstrong, left, and Lou Ambers, right, meet July 26 with the welter and lightweight titles at stake.

Ambers, left, shakes hands with Armstrong. The next time they meet they will touch gloves in the ring in New York and attempt to maim each other.

The welter-featherweight champion and the lightweight king compare biceps and fore-arms. Armstrong will rest here before leaving for the East. Ambers boxes Jimmy Vaughn at the Olympic next Tuesday in a tune-up.

Times photos by J. H. McCrory

## BILL HENRY SAYS:

When a veteran—or, in deference to the ladies—an ex-champion reasserts supremacy over the field as Ralph Guldahl, the golfer, and Helen Wills Moody, the tennis player, have done quite recently it makes fine copy for the scribblers but it furrows the foreheads of the thinkers.

**VETERAN'S INNINGS**

It's a fine thing to see the old-timers refuse to bow their heads before the onrush of bubbling youth. It gives the authors a chance to dwell upon the sterling physical and mental characteristics of the old-timers, point the finger impolitely at the shortcomings of the younger generation and in general to depart on a highly sentimental literary debauch over the high qualities and noble traits of the veterans as compared with the tendency of the newcomers to fold up and die when the going gets really tough.

**GULDAHL AND MOODY**

Speaking in behalf of the scribblers, my heartfelt thanks to Ralph Guldahl for winning the Open golf championship quite unexpectedly for the second time, and to Dame Moody for proving to be the solid rock as of yore in the Wightman Cup—but after Guldahl, after Moody—what? Or, perhaps I should ask, whom? Or should it be who? Anyhow—my point is that the deep thinkers in the world of sport always bob up and inquire, under such circumstances, what we're going to do for real champions when such as Moody and Guldahl do begin to crack and come apart at the seams.

**YOUTH IS MISSING**

Our Wightman Cup team, of course, scored a glorious victory over the British gals—but look who did it. La Moody is certainly no spring chicken. Alice Marble is a veteran of quite a few years of tournament play and is always uncertain even though she has moments when her game is positively inspired. Helen Jacobs has gone to pieces physically and is always bobbing up with a sprain, strain or other infirmity. Sarah Palfrey Fabyan, our one great doubles player, has been in the top flight for a decade. The only youngster on the team, Dorothy Bundy, lacks soundness in her game.

**YATES IS PROMISING**

Charley Yates, of course, looks like a coming "great" in the golf world but there's a lot of difference between doing your stuff in the amateurs and repeating in the ranks of the icy-veined professionals — just ask Lawson Little. The youngsters really have quite a job on their hands breaking through the upper-crust of golf and tennis greats. You can go a long distance with experience

Turn to Page 13, Column 4

## JOE E. BROWN'S HORSES COP TWO TURF RACES

BY PAUL LOWRY

The movies hogged the limelight at Hollywood Park yesterday with Joe E. Brown, Robert Riskin and Bing Crosby sharing the thunder.

Senor Brown of the wide orifice was tops with a double—Kay Em Bee in the second race and that good old stretch runner, Barnsley, in the sixth.

Bing Crosby's High Strike, a California bred that he acquired at the Marchbank dispersal sale over a year ago, captured the Balboa, one of the features, by five open lengths.

As a matter of fact, all the features of the day went to the esteemed gentlemen mentioned in the opening paragraph. Barnsley grabbed off the Hawthorne, and Dogaway, owned by Riskin, who goes in for writing rather than crooning or funmaking, gathered in the Pasadena Handicap in a photo-finish with Bill Farnsworth.

**CORKING RACES**

All three races were corkers. A crowd estimated at 15,000 persons saw the day's program of eight races, wagering a total of $313,629.

A non-starter since last December, when he failed in the $10,000 California breeders' champion stakes at Santa Anita, High Strike won as his rider pleased yesterday—by five lengths—from Count Pan and Sky Grenade, running the distance in 1:12 3/5 over a fast track.

**EASY VICTORY**

The Crosby win was decisive long before the finish line was reached where the Dogaway conquest was not settled until the closing strides. Barnsley had to drop back around the far turn, but when he turned on the heat in the stretch there was no denying the gold and brown color bearer.

Both the Brown standard bearers rewarded their backers handsomely—Kay Em Bee $30 and

Turn to Page 13, Column 3

## Nagurski Winner Over Joe Savoldi

BY MATT PHAN

"Jumping Joe" Savoldi, the Fullback of Notre Dame, no relation to the Hunchback, led with his shin last night at the Olympic and that is why Bronko Nagurski, Minnesota's triple-sweat man, is still the world's heavyweight rassling champion today.

Missing a flying drop kick, Signor Savoldi fell on his head, thus injuring his pride, among other things, and giving the Minnesota powerhouse a one-fall victory after 29m. 12s. of gripping grappling and football tactics.

**JOE CARRIED OUT**

As the result of the accident. "Jumping Joe" was pronounced unable to continue by the team physician, Dr. Lloyd Mace, who ordered the injured man carried to the dressing room for further observation.

Signor Savoldi has nobody but himself to blame for the catastrophe inasmuch as he attempted a quick kick on fourth down with the ball, or fall, in his own territory, poor strategy to say the least.

**BRONKO PENALIZED**

Prior to the disastrous finale Nagurski had been penalized half the distance to his own goal line for illegal use of the hands,

Turn to Page 11, Column 1

## Mrs. Moody, Budge Seeded First in Wimbledon Tennis

LONDON, June 15. (AP)—Falling into the easier hal' of the draw, Helen Wills Moody tonight became a 5-to-2 favorite to win the greatest women's Wimbledon tennis tournament of a decade.

In sharp contrast to the men's division where America's Don Budge was favored at the unprecedented odds of 1 to 5, Mrs. Moody was rated a bare point ahead of Alice Marble of San Francisco, who was listed at 3 to 1 in the betting odds.

Seedings, made today for the tournament, which opens Monday, found Mrs. Moody and Miss Marble occupying the first two positions, followed by Jadwiga Jedrzejowska of Poland, Mrs. Hilda Krahwinkel Sperling of Germany, Mme. Rene Mathieu of France, Kay Stammers of England, Mrs. Sarah Palfrey Fabyan of Brookline, Mass., and Margaret (Peggy) Scriven of England.

Much to the surprise of most experts, Helen Jacobs, former British and American champion, and Anita Lizana of Chile, current American titleholder, were left out of the seeded list. It still is doubtful whether Miss Jacobs will be able to play. She was forced to withdraw from last week's Wightman Cup matches because of an injured nerve in her right arm.

Miss Marble was placed at the top of the draw with Mrs. Moody at the bottom. Thus, potentially, the greatest women's tennis battle of the year was set up for the finals July 2.

The only seeded player in Mrs. Moody's quarter will be Miss Stammers, but Mrs. Bobby Heine Miller of South Africa, Mrs. Har-

Turn to Page 13, Column 6

## Guldahl and Mangrum Tie

### Pair Deadlock With 144's at Halfway Mark in Western Open

ST. LOUIS, June 15. (AP)—It was a case of thirty-six holes behind him, thirty-six holes ahead of him and Ray Mangrum beside him as Ralph Guldahl reached the halfway mark in his quest for a third consecutive Western Open golf championship today with the gangling Dayton (O.) pro sharing the lead.

Mangrum, stroking a smooth course over the treacherous Westwood terrain, brought in his second straight 72 for a 144 total as Guldahl, alone in the lead with a par 71 yesterday, came in with a 73 for his second round.

**STARS TRAIL**

As par was the only winner throughout the day, other sharpshooters who were on Guldahl's heels yesterday still were stalking him and still others slowly faded into the background.

Little Paul Runyan of White Plains, N. Y., added a 36-37—73 today to his 72 to be deadlocked with Sam Snead of White Sulphur Springs, W. Va., at 145, one stroke behind the leaders. Snead also added a 73 today to reach his total.

**STROKE BEHIND**

Jimmy Hines, the New York redhead, and Bob Hamilton, a dark horse from Evansville, Ind., were a stroke behind Snead and Runyan. Hines was out in even par 35 today but went two over on the in nine for a 73. Hamilton, in the 74 bracket at the end of yesterday's play, was one of the

Turn to Page 11, Column 2

## Armstrong, Lou Ambers Meet Here

BY JACK SINGER

Far, far away from the turbulent, seething scene of training camps, official weigh-ins, betting odds, $200,000 gates, ballyhoo and all the giddy, maddening whirl of a championship fight Henry Armstrong and Lou Ambers shook hands here yesterday.

The next time they meet they will touch gloves in the ring under the searching incandescents at Madison Square Garden Bowl, New York, on the night of July 26.

**DRAMATIC MEETING**

The room was charged with tense electricity as Armstrong, welter and featherweight champion of the world, and Ambers, king of the lightweights, dramatically faced each other. Al Weill, Ambers's manager, obviously nervous, shuffled his feet and swabbed his clammy brow with a handkerchief. The others stood in strained, awkward silence.

Suddenly Ambers's chiseled Italian features brightened into a broad smile, revealing a row of white teeth. Armstrong, the kinky killer of the ring, grinned sheepishly. And, like a rubber band that had been stretched too far, the tenseness snapped and broke and was, in turn, supplanted by a comforting, radiant warmth.

**JUST LUCKY**

Ambers feinted with a chuckle and led with: "Congratulations, Henry. Glad you won."

Armstrong countered with a left and right grin, replying: "Thanks, Lou. I was pretty lucky to beat Ross."

Lou led with a left, pushing his hair off his forehead, and

Turn to Page 10, Column 3

## Seals Take Gift Game

### Hollywood's Errors Enable San Francisco to Claim 14-4 Victory

BY BOB RAY

Red Killefer's Hollywood Stars have only one thing to be thankful for this morning. There weren't many fans out at Wrigley Field last night to see them put on their worst exhibition of the season as they lost their second straight to the San Francisco Seals by a 14-to-4 score that doesn't tell the half of it.

The Stars practically gave the game to Lefty O'Doul's lads, being guilty of a half-dozen errors, four of which were bunched in the second inning when the Seals made eight runs on only two hits.

**SHORES COASTS**

Presented with this generous lead, which grew to 10-0 in the third inning, Big Bill Shores coasted to an easy victory although touched for thirteen hits by the Hollywooders.

Stu Bolen, who started for Hollywood, was as wild as his support was wobbly and gave way to Jim Prendergast, rookie southpaw secured from Kansas City by way of Seattle, in the terrible second.

The Seals never scored an earned run until the ninth when they added their final cluster of four—three of which came on Ted Norbert's homer. Tommy Carey hit a homer, as well as two singles, for the Stars.

**CUT LOOSE**

All went well for one inning, but in the second round the Seals broke loose to score eight runs—all unearned—on two hits,

Turn to Page 11, Column 3

## VANDER MEER BREAKS ALL RECORDS IN MAJORS

### Youthful Cincinnati Southpaw Repeats Saturday's Feat Against Dodgers

BROOKLYN, June 15. (AP)—Johnny Vander Meer, 23-year-old Cincinnati Reds' southpaw, broke all major league pitching records tonight by hurling his second straight no-hit, no-run game, blanking the Dodgers, 6 to 0.

The fast-balling youngster, in his first full year in the major leagues, pitched a no-hitter against the Boston Bees only last Saturday.

**BASES LOADED**

Eight Dodgers reached base, all by walks, but the 190-pounder from Midland Park, N. J., pitched his way out of the pinches on each occasion. In the ninth inning, he loaded the bases with one out on passes, but forced one runner at the plate and then got Leo Durocher on a fly ball to end the threat.

Never before in the history of the major leagues, ancient or modern, has any pitcher hurled two no hitters in a single season, let alone in two consecutive games. In fact, only eight have pitched two no-hitters over their entire career.

**SEVENTH VICTORY**

The victory was Vander Meer's seventh of the season against two defeats.

In hurling his second no-hitter, Vander Meer also broke Dazzy Vance's National League record for consecutive hitless innings. His nine tonight, coupled with his nine against Boston Saturday, and the final one-third of an inning against the New York Giants in his previous start, June 5, gave him a record of 18⅓ innings, one full inning better than the listed mark of 17⅓ set by Dazzy Vance in 1925.

The major league record in this respect is held by Cy Young, for a twenty-three-inning stretch in 1904, but Young's mark was accomplished by pitching assignments of two, six, nine and six innings.

**ELEVEN-HIT ATTACK**

The Reds backed up Vander Meer with an eleven-hit attack off three Brooklyn pitchers, featuring Buck McCormick's second homer of the season, with

Turn to Page 11, Column 2

## Angel Winning Streak Ended

### Lowly Acorns Rally to Defeat Seraphs by 9-7 Score

OAKLAND, June 15. — The lowly Oaks rose up in all their outraged might tonight to snap the Los Angeles winning streak. Scoring five runs of Dutch Lieber and Jittery Joe Berry in the eighth inning, they scored a 9-to-7 victory. A single by Jolley and doubles by Abreu and Kelleher sent Lieber to the showers.

Raimondi, first man to face Berry, singled infield to fill the bases. Gibson doubled, scoring Kelleher with the tying run, and Conroy, batting for Lindell, was given a free pass.

**GIBSON SCORES**

Hill walked, forcing in Raimondi. Luby and Bolyard popped out, and Jolley lifted a dinky fly to the pitcher's box. The ball bounced out of Berry's glove and Gibson scored.

With the series tied at one all, Truck Hannah announced Lillard as his starting pitcher tomorrow night.

Seeking their ninth consecutive victory, Los Angeles held a 5-to-3 lead over Oakland in the fourth inning tonight.

**LIEBER TRIPLES**

Doubles by Gudat, Rothrock and Mayo and singles by Russell and Cihocki accounted for four runs in the first inning.

Pitcher Dutch Lieber tripled in the second and scored on a wild pitch by Jack Lindell, the

Turn to Page 10, Column 5

**BABE RUTH PROVES LUCKY FOR VANDER MEER**

Just before Johnny Vander Meer pitched his second consecutive no-hit, no-run game Babe Ruth wished him good luck. The result proved that the Babe is a lucky guy to have around.

(AP) Wirephoto

## Schmeling-Louis Fight Gate May Pass Million-Dollar Mark

NEW YORK, June 15. (AP)—With the fistic fireworks just a week away, Promoter Mike Jacobs today put a definite tag of $470,000 on the advance sale for the Joe Louis-Max Schmeling world heavyweight championship fight.

He predicted a good "break" from the weather would mean gross receipts in excess of $1,000,000 for the title show at the Yankee Stadium, June 22.

"Today, with the half-million mark in sight, we are only $14,000 behind the advance sale for the Louis-Baer fight ten days before that bout," said Jacobs.

The Louis-Baer fight, in 1935, grossed $948,252 from the ticket sales. Receipts from the sale of radio and picture rights put it over the million dollar mark.

"We banked $48,000 Monday, $47,000 yesterday and around $50,000 today," Jacobs continued. "We need only $67,000 to match the total Baer-Louis advance sale and we will do that much business tomorrow at the rate things are going."

The heaviest demand, Jacobs added, has been for the $30 ringside seats, of which there are thirty-eight rows. He said 75 per cent of the advance orders have come from out-of-town fans.

# Los Angeles Times Sports

CC TUESDAY MORNING, JANUARY 3, 1939.


# TROJANS BEAT DUKE, 7-3, ON LAST MINUTE PASS

## WHEN IRON DUKES' GOAL LINE WAS DENTED FOR FIRST TIME

Duke hearts sank, Trojan throats roared and 93,000 spectators went berserk when Al Krueger (No. 62) snagged Doyle Nave's last-minute pass in the end zone for the touchdown that beat Duke, 7 to 3, yesterday in the Rose Bowl. On the scene, too late, are Eric Tipton (20,) halfback, and Bailey (47,) end. Carroll photo

## Nave-Krueger Toss Scores

### Aerial Bomb Wipes Out Blue Devils' 3-Point Lead in Final Minute of Play; Ruffa Boots Field Goal for Losers

BY BRAVEN DYER

Stymied by the rock-ribbed defense of Duke's durable Devils, Southern California called on Doyle Nave in the last two minutes of play at the Rose Bowl yesterday afternoon.

With the ball 34 yards from the promised land and Duke leading, 3-0, Doyle threw four consecutive strikes to Al Krueger and the last was a perfect pitch in the end zone for the winning touchdown.

**WASN'T THERE**

And I wasn't there to see the "Frank Merriwell" finish!

I had left with four minutes of the game remaining because somebody has to get out the paper. Gus Henderson, Steve Hannigan, Hal Chanslor and I were just pulling out in my chariot when over the radio came this announcement:

"Nave is back—he's going to pass—he's throwing the ball—it's in the end zone and it's complete to Krueger for a TOUCHDOWN!"

**RARE RESTRAINT**

There is no truth in the dastardly report that I promptly fainted at the wheel. The three gentlemen with me will testify that I kept right on driving in to town just as if nothing had happened. The hell I did—I let out a yell which all but shattered the windshield and promptly began jabbering like an idiot.

The gridirony of it all practically slays me!

I have suffered vicariously for two years while watching Doyle Nave squirming on well-worn benches from Los Angeles to Seattle and all the way back to Ohio State and Notre Dame. And then I'm not even present when he pulls the most spectacular triumph in all Trojan history! And still there are some people who say a sports writer leads an ideal existence. From now until my boy Doyle graduates I'm going to stick to the end of every game even if the paper never comes out.

**HOWARD CAN COACH**

There is no truth in the report that I have now joined the wolves who habitually demand the resignation of Howard Jones. After due deliberation I have decided to let Howard coach next fall—but only with the implicit

Turn to Page 14, Column 3

## Doyle Nave Thankful

### Hero Grateful to Jones for Affording Him Golden Chance

BY BOB RAY

"Thanks for the opportunity of getting into the game, coach."

It was Doyle Nave, Troy's "forgotten man," who pitched that touchdown pass, talking to Howard Jones in the S.C. dressing rooms.

"Don't thank me," said Jones with a startled look on his weather-beaten face. "Let me thank you!"

Nave, who pitched four successive "strikes" into the ham-like hands of "Antelope Al" Krueger during those frantic final four minutes, entered the game with a bandage over a cut on his forehead—a scrimmage memento. As he was being patched up by Doc Thurber after the game, Doyle, who hadn't played long enough this season to get a letter, asked the doc: "I wonder if I'll get a letter, anyway?"

"Sure," answered the Trojan medico, "and I'm in favor of giving you a whole alphabet."

Krueger, who seems to have formed a habit of catching crucial touchdown passes in the waning seconds of halves or the end of games, was for giving all the credit to Nave.

"Nave is without a peer as a passer," said Krueger, "and all you have to do is break loose from the defenders and look for the ball. It's a cinch to be there because Doyle waits until he sees you are free before he shoots a bullet pass right to you. A pass-receiver can't keep free for long and Nave's ability to

Turn to Page 14, Column 2

## BILL HENRY SAYS:

"The Rose Bowl game?" said Mr. George Preston Marshall as he eyed the Duke-Trojan fracas from a nifty vantage spot on the 50-yard line, "why it's the best game of its kind that there is—but one of these days the pro-bowl game is going to be both bigger and better."

**THE "PRO-BOWL"**

Now, Mr. Marshall gets around quite a lot and he's something of an authority on such matters and before you get in an argument with him you'd better be sure you know what you're talking about. Mr. Marshall's Washington Redskin football team, which won the world's title a year ago, has an advance sale of season tickets that will compare favorably with that of any college in the country. He has taken as many as 15,000 fans from Washington to New York to see his team play the team that recently took the title away from him, the New York Giants. George knows his pigskins—and a lot of other things, too.

**THE COMING GAME**

"Professional football is the best football played anywhere," said Mr. Marshall, continuing his oration. "Our coaches don't have any alumni gunning for their scalps, but they have a vociferous and wildly enthusiastic lot of followers who stick with the teams for the very good reason that they like 'em. The job of a professional coach is not only to play winning football, but particularly to play interesting football. Fans will stick with a losing team if it plays interesting football. Only the most rabid alumni will stick with a team that plays uninteresting football. Professional

Turn to Page 17, Column 4

## MAIN MAN SURPRISE WINNER IN NEW YEAR HANDICAP

BY PAUL LOWRY

"Happy New Year," thundered Main Man to Movie Man Louis B. Mayer at Santa Anita yesterday.

"Same to you," responded Movie Man Mayer as he led Main Man into the winner's circle at the end of the $10,000 New Year Handicap, accepted a check for $8350, a huge silver trophy from the Monrovia Chamber of Commerce and gayly waved one free hand to friends in the Turf Club.

Mayer had just seen his Main Man capture the New Year Handicap by two and one-quarter lengths from the highly favored Ligaroti and Sweepalot, with the 8-5 first choice, Specify, still farther back. Heelfly, third choice, finished fifth.

**MAYER HAPPY**

The movie man had a right to be happy. He has spent lavishly in acquiring a topnotch racing stable in the past few months, and it was the second time in as many days of racing that his blue and pink silks had come down in front. Flying Bonny won for him on opening day.

Main Man's victory was the big surprise of the afternoon. He had finished far back to Specify and Ligaroti in the San Francisco Handicap at Tanforan, but yesterday he dropped five pounds and got out in front at the break and was never headed. He ran a brilliant race, and those who waited for him to come back to his field were rudely disappointed. He was in front from start to finish.

**JOCKEY WOOLF UP**

Trained to the pink by T. D. (Pinky) Grimes and ridden by the Old Ice Man himself, Georgie Woolf, Main Man never left the issue in doubt. He went postward a bad fourth choice in the

Turn to Page 17, Column 1

## GRID SCORES

Trojans, 7; Duke, 3.
U.C.L.A., 32; Hawaii, 7.
T.C.U., 15; Carnegie Tech, 7.
Tennessee, 17; Oklahoma, 0.
St. Mary's, 20; Texas Tech, 13.
North, 7; South, 0.
Utah, 26; New Mexico, 0.
West, 14; East, 0.

## Davey O'Brien Leads T.C.U. to 15-7 Victory Over Tartans

NEW ORLEANS, Jan. 2. (AP)—That little giant of the gridiron, David O'Brien of All-America fame, uncorked his famous right arm today to pass the Horned Frogs of Texas Christian into a 15-to-7 triumph over Carnegie Tech's Tartans in the Sugar Bowl classic.

With the exception of one brief spell in the wildest game of the Sugar Bowl history, the Southwest Conference champions monopolized the fifth annual struggle as O'Brien, a 152-pound quarterbacking dynamo, directed the nation's No. 1 eleven to a well-earned victory.

Ably supporting O'Brien's devastating aerial attack was a powerful display of ball carrying by Fullback Connie Sparks and Halfback Johnny Hall behind what was probably the biggest and best line the Southwest had produced.

O'Brien's support on the catching end by Don Looney, Earl Clark and Durward Horner stood out in the attack that saw the Frogs, trailing at the half, 6-7, and on the short end of a score for the first time in 11 consecu-

Turn to Page 18, Column 1

## Trojans Fail to Impress Wallace Wade

BY FRANK FINCH

This may have been Wallace Wade's last trip to the Rose Bowl.

He admitted as much yesterday afternoon as he emerged from the Duke dressing room, bitterly disappointed by the sudden, spectacular surge of the Trojans that punctured Duke's perfect defensive record and enabled Southern California to keep its Rose Bowl slate untarnished.

Asked if he would like to bring another Duke team west to avenge yesterday's "—and sud-

Turn to Page 14, Column 8

## WARBURTON THINKS TROJANS PILFERED MOVIE SCRIPT

BY COTTON WARBURTON
Trojan All-American for Season of 1933

Southern California stole the final page of a Hollywood movie script to snatch that Duke game out of the fire over in the Rose Bowl yesterday afternoon, 7 to 3.

That dramatic finish — with Doyle Nave and Al Krueger co-starring would be a standard fadeout out around our studio—but "reel" life and real happenings don't always conform.

Get this picture:

A fourth-string quarterback—sometimes lucky to get in for a single play—pitches four perfect strikes to the same fellow for half the distance of the field and the winning touchdown with only 40 seconds remaining!

Studio bosses might have said—and they go for most anything—that was laying it on a bit too thick. But 93,000 humans can attest it actually happened over in Pasadena. Doyle Nave "out-Frank Merriwelled" the famous hero of college fiction.

It must have been a mighty sweet moment to that plucky substitute who refused to get the jitters under fire. In my playing days I often dreamt of scoring touchdowns like that one, but it never came to pass—at least, not that dramatic.

Maybe I had best retire from

Turn to Page 18, Column 6

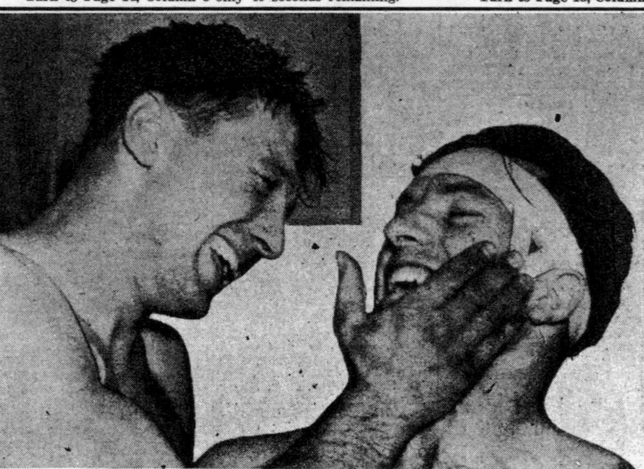

**BOYS WHO GAVE BLUE DEVILS THE DEVIL**

Al Krueger gives Doyle Nave an affectionate pat on the cheek in the Trojan showers last night. Krueger caught Nave's aerial shot that gave Troy a 7-3 win. (AP) photo

## Statistical Story of Troy's Win

| TROJANS | | BLUE DEVILS |
|---|---|---|
| 165 | Yards gained from scrimmage | 122 |
| 30 | Yards lost from scrimmage | 36 |
| 135 | Net yards gained from scrimmage | 86 |
| 84 | Yards gained from forward passes | 53 |
| 8 | Yards lost from passes | 1 |
| 211 | Total yards gained, pass and scrimmage | 139 |
| 9 | First downs from running plays | 4 |
| 4 | First downs from forward passes | 2 |
| 0 | First downs from penalties | 2 |
| 13 | Total number of first downs | 8 |
| 31 | Forward passes attempted | 13 |
| 13 | Forward passes completed | 6 |
| 2 | Forward passes had intercepted | 1 |
| 16 | Forward passes incomplete | 6 |
| 16 | Number of punts | 15 |
| 652 | Total yardage of punts | 608 |
| 40.8 | Average length of punts | 40.5 |
| 2 | Punts had blocked | 1 |
| 64 | Total yards from punt runbacks | 66 |
| 4.4 | Average yards of punt runbacks | 4.1 |
| 5 | Number of penalties | 3 |
| 35 | Yards lost from penalties | 25 |
| 0 | Fumbles made | 2 |
| 0 | Own fumbles recovered | 0 |
| 2 | Opponent's fumbles recovered | 0 |
| 1 | Field goals attempted | 1 |

**BALL CARRIERS**

| SOUTHERN CALIF. | T.C.B. | Y.G. | Y.L. | N.Y.G. | Ave. | Pts. |
|---|---|---|---|---|---|---|
| Lansdell | 12 | 105 | 9 | 96 | 8 | |
| Morgan | 2 | 0 | 6 | 0 | -3 | |
| Sangster | 2 | 0 | 1 | 0 | - ½ | |
| Anderson | 6 | 30 | 3 | 27 | 4½ | |
| Banta | 4 | 12 | 0 | 12 | 3 | |
| Jones | 4 | 15 | 4 | 11 | 3¾ | |
| Day | 4 | 4 | 5 | -1 | - ¼ | |
| Krueger | 1 | 2 | 0 | 2 | 2 | 6 |
| Gaspar | | | | | | 1 |
| **DUKE** | | | | | | |
| Spangler | 1 | 0 | 7 | 0 | -7 | |
| Tipton | 16 | 98 | 23 | 65 | 5 | |
| O'Mara | 8 | 19 | 0 | 19 | 2⅓ | |
| G. McAfee | 3 | 20 | 5 | 15 | 5 | |
| W. McAfee | 1 | 0 | 1 | 0 | -1 | |
| Robinson | 1 | 5 | 0 | 5 | 5 | |
| Ruffa | | | | | | 3 |

Legend—T.C.B., times carried ball; Y.G., yards gained; Y.L., yards lost; N.Y.G., net yards gained; Ave., average; Pts., points.

# Bears Annihilate Redskins, 73-0, Capture Pro Bowl Bid

**TOUCHDOWN, ALMOST**—Charlie Malone caught this 42-yard pass from Sammy Baugh close to the Bears' goal, but the Redskins couldn't get it over in yesterday's championship game. Bears in the photo are Raymond McLean, No. 57, and Robert Snyder, No. 47. (AP) Wirephoto

**HOW IT STARTED**—On the second play of yesterday's pro championship game, Bill Osmanski, Bear fullback, took the ball and raced 68 yards for the first touchdown. Osmanski is shown here evading hopeful Redskin tacklers. After the massacre was over the Redskins found themselves thoroughly scalped, 73-0. (AP) Wirephoto

## Chicago Team Runs Wild

### All Scoring Records Fall as Washington Crumbles Before Foe

BY SID FEDER

WASHINGTON, Dec. 8. (AP)—Chicago's bruising Bears took candy from a baby today in winning professional football's "World Series."

The big fellows from the Windy City had no trouble smashing all kinds of scoring and ground-gaining records to crush a completely outclassed tribe of Washington Redskins, 73 to 0, and take the championship of the National Professional Football League. It was the worst beating ever handed out in league history.

**CONSOLATION**

About the only thing the Redskins had to smile about, if there was anything at all, was the crowd of 36,034 contributed to the biggest play-off melon the players ever have sliced. The net gate was $102,280, of which the players' pool amounted to $54,562.80, with the Bears taking $873.99 each. The Redskins received $606.25 each for their cuffing.

Victory qualified the Bears to play in the Pro Bowl game at Los Angeles.

The Bears, beaten in Griffith Stadium, 7-3, last month by the Redskins, wasted no time today showing that this one, with the chips down, was a different game. They scored on their second play from scrimmage, about one minute after the kickoff. They scored the next two times they had their hands on the ball, and from there on it was simply a slaughter.

**RECORDS FALL**

Before they finished they easily eclipsed the old play-off record of 30 points which the New York Giants piled up against the Bears of '34. From there they went on to shatter the league's all-time high scoring mark of 64 points which Philadelphia rolled up against Cincinnati six years ago.

Before the first half had ended these big bruisers from the West had shattered the play-off record for most yards gained rushing—173 by the '34 Giants. Their total yardage was 'way in front of the 441 record the 1937 Redskins piled up against the Bears.

There was no particular standout among the Bears. They were all good.

**M'CHESNEY SHINES**

Sid Luckman, the old Columbia quarterback, directed the team from the difficult "T" formation in smart style; Clyde Turner, the rugged center from Hardin-Simmons playing his first year in pro ball, spearheaded a line that never stopped. The ball-carrying backs—George McAfee, ex-Duke; Ray Nolting, from Cincinnati; Bill Osmanski, from Holy Cross, and Joe Maniaci, late of Fordham—made the Redskins look like papooses.

For Washington the most heroic figure was Bob McChesney, big end from U.C.L.A. who played a good portion of the game although his right hand wore a cast. By all odds the standout Washington performer was "Wee Willie" Wilkin, who learned his football at St. Mary's of California and played a whale of a game at tackle all afternoon.

**ONE GESTURE**

As far as the scoring was concerned—well, it had the "experts" in the press box writing with both hands trying to keep up. The Bears scored three touchdowns in each of two periods, four in the third and took it easy only in the second quarter when they counted but once.

They rolled up only 17 first downs while the Redskins counted 18, but that was because the Bears scored in almost every way possible—passing, running, intercepting passes and what have you. They even scored a point after touchdown by a for-

Turn to Page 11, Column 4

PAGE 9 MONDAY, DECEMBER 9, 1940 PART II

**GIVE UP, JIMMY?**—Jimmy Johnston gained only one yard for the Redskins in this play yesterday before being swarmed by Bears. Sid Luckman is putting on a clutch; the others are Bill Osmanski, No. 9; Danny Fortmann, No. 21, and George McAfee, No. 5. (AP) Wirephoto

## SPORT POST-SCRIPTS

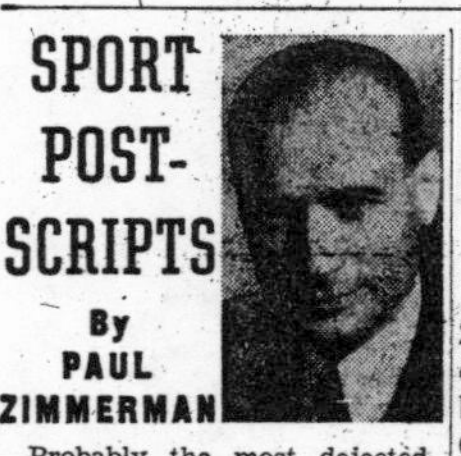

By PAUL ZIMMERMAN

Probably the most dejected Trojan after the final game with Notre Dame Saturday was a chunky fellow named Floyd Phillips.

After playing second fiddle last year to Harry Smith and doing a great job, Phillips had hoped to blossom out as a star running guard for Southern California this season.

**TOUGH LUCK**

But it was not to be. Floyd suffered a broken bone in his left foot in the second game of the season and he never got into a game after that although Troy could have used him; and how.

"I was ready to go," said Phillips after the game. "The doctors said I could play against the Irish. I wanted to the worst way."

Coach Howard Jones, however, realized that however willing Floyd might be, that it would not be wise to send him in there. Because no gridster can be out of a key spot all season and still play his better game the first time he gets back.

So Phillips bowed out, without getting a chance to do his stuff again and that's one of the toughest things about this game of football—having to trudge off the field without getting a chance at a final fling and the resultant plaudits of the multitude.

**KRUEGER TOO**

The same dejection shrouded Al Krueger, who left the contest early with a shoulder injury.

Maybe Antelope Al could not have caught some of those dying-gasp passes pitched at the other ends. But maybe he could have, too. He did, of course, get enthusiastic recognition from the fans as he departed early—slowly sauntering into the tunnel and football oblivion after being the pass-catching hero in Troy's great Rose Bowl victories over Duke and Tennessee.

And while we are being a bit sentimental, we can't overlook Big Ben Sohn, who played All-America football in his last three games against Washington, U.C.L.A. and Notre Dame. How Sohn could be left off all the Coast All-Star teams this fall is more than I can see. It is true that he started slow but by the same measure, some of those selected finished that way.

**WATCH BOBBY**

And when you discuss All-Star teams, where were the

Turn to Page 10, Column 7

## Bulldogs Top Bombers in League Tilt, 28-7

BY BOB SMYSER

Los Angeles' Bulldogs whipped the San Diego Bombers, 28 to 7, yesterday at Gilmore Stadium, and main result of the afternoon's activities was further proof that the border town brigade still has the weakest offense in Pacific Coast Professional League circles.

It was a savage tilt, highlighted by a lot of rough stuff in the third quarter that delighted the 9000 fans, but the Bombers never were really in the ball game as far as the scoring went.

**ONE PERFECT PLAY**

Except for a perfectly executed pass play in the fourth quarter, and a couple of razzle-dazzle lateral pass thrillers in the final minutes, the Bombers showed little aptitude for advancing the ball against the rugged proteges of Ike Frankian.

Meanwhile, the Bulldogs pushed across a touchdown in the second period, roughed it up a bit in the third, and then went on a scoring spree in the fourth.

Big shot in the last quarter was Red Elder, a veteran performer in local pro circles, who ripped apart the stiff Bomber defense with a savage assault that carried the Bulldogs 76 yards in 11 plays and ended with their second score.

The Bombers—tired lads by then—never recovered from that attack.

**ROUGH STUFF**

The rough-house activity began right when the third period opened, Izzy Cantor flaring up when a couple of Bombers hit him extra hard on a tackle. Izzy was benched for the rest of the game by the officials. Later on, Bulldog Norm Lehnert had a couple of scrapes with his foes but managed to remain in the hostilities. The Bulldogs twice drew roughing penalties during the hot going.

Speed Burner Howard Cleveland engineered Los Angeles to

Turn to Page 10, Column 3

## Santa Anita 'Cap Weights Due Today

BY PAUL LOWRY

Another period of "watchful waiting" will end this afternoon with the release by Racing Secretary Webb Everett of weights for the seventh running of the Santa Anita Handicap.

It is quite naturally assumed that W. L. Brann's Challedon, "horse of the year" in both 1939 and 1940, will be awarded top impost.

**NO WEIGHT LIMIT**

But it is assumed, with equal conviction, that Challedon will not be given more than 130 pounds although there is no limit such as existed during the early years of Santa Anita racing.

It is not the purpose of this department to guess Everett's mind on the weights he will dish out for 92 eligibles, but as far as Challedon is concerned the lines are pretty well drawn.

A year ago Everett gave Challedon 128 pounds as against 129 for Kayak II and 130 for Seabiscuit. The Santa Anita racing secretary said he didn't believe Challedon was any Cavalcade, which he had weighted at 129 as against Equipoise's 130 six years ago.

**TOO MANY EXCUSES**

And more recently he has put himself on record to the effect one must make too many excuses for Challedon to place him in the list of "greats"—to wise and to wit, defeat by Eight Thirty in the Massachusetts Handicap and Hash in the Narragansett Special. Both times Challedon carried 130 pounds.

It is true that Challedon won the Hollywood Gold Cup with 133 pounds up, but his chief rival—Kayak II—was far from being in tip-top condition that day.

It will be interesting to see just what Everett does with Kayak II, winner of the Handicap in 1939 and second to Seabiscuit last spring—a race that many thought Kayak II could have won if he had not been

Turn to Page 12, Column 1

## AL WRIGHT SOLD TO PORTLAND

SAN FRANCISCO, Dec. 8. (AP)—Al (A-1) Wright, second baseman of the San Francisco Seals of the Pacific Coast Baseball League, was sold today to the Portland club.

The sale, for an undisclosed cash sum, was announced by Manager Frank O'Doul in a telegram to Walter Mails, the Seals' public relations director. O'Doul is en route home from the minor league baseball meeting in Atlanta.

## Open Golf Play Ends in Tie

### Mangrum, McCormick Card Totals of 288 at Los Serranos Links

BY CHARLES CURTIS

Lloyd Mangrum, Texan who migrated to California before taking a professional's job in Chicago, pocketed first-prize money in the Southern California Open golf championship yesterday at Los Serranos Country Club in Chino but he had to share scoring honors with Bruce McCormick, long-hitting Flintridge amateur.

Mangrum and McCormick finished with 288 totals, eight over par for the 72-hole grind, as the early round pace-setters collapsed under the strain of the last day firing on the difficult rolling fairways and hard-packed greens.

**PLAY-OFF SUNDAY**

The lads who finished in the dead heat will play off for the Southland Open crown next Sunday morning in an 18-hole match. The tournament was staged for the benefit of the Casa Colina Home for Crippled Children in Chino.

The first and second-round leader, Don Erickson of Baldwin Fairways, blew himself out of the title when he took a 78 yesterday morning. And at the end of that morning round Fay Coleman, popular Cheviot Hills (California) club pro, had climbed into first position with a 215 aggregate. But he eliminated himself when he took a total of 80 strokes in the afternoon.

That left a wide-open race for the title and until the last three-

Turn to Page 10, Column 2

## Big Ten Irks Coast Moguls

DEL MONTE, Dec. 8. (AP)—Action of Big Ten representatives in reaffirming their stand against postseason football games, including the Rose Bowl, reacted on Pacific Coast Conference delegates like a punch on the nose, it was learned here tonight on the eve of the annual meeting of the big western circuit.

One of the Coast bigwigs, who asked his name not be used, said sentiment among his associates indicated they intended to drop negotiations looking toward a tie-up with the Middle Western conference in which the champions of the two federations would meet annually in the Rose Bowl.

## Challenge Cup Soccer

Detroit Chrysler, 2; Cleveland Delarda, 0.

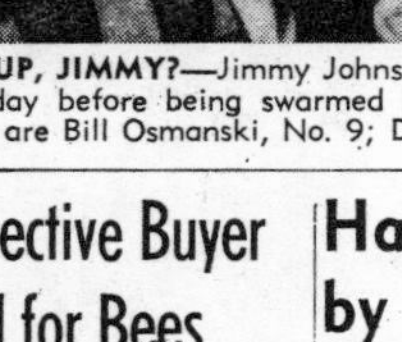

## Prospective Buyer Found for Bees

NEW HAVEN (Ct.) Dec. 8. (AP)—Albert H. Powell, wealthy retired New Haven coal dealer, said tonight he expected to complete "before long" negotiations for his purchase of the Boston Bees of the National Baseball League.

Powell said completion of the deal, disclosed in Boston today by C. F. Adams, the Bees' chief owner, would be delayed until the return of Bob Quinn, general manager of the club, from Chicago where he is to attend a baseball meeting this week. He declined to indicate how much money was involved.

"Of course, Mr. Quinn will stay with the club, if I can persuade him," said Powell, "and I think I can."

Quinn stopped off at New Haven this morning while en route to Chicago for a discussion of the transaction, Powell said.

## Hank Luisetti Reinstated by Amateur Athletic Union

DENVER, Dec. 8. (AP) — A strong effort to place the national A.A.U. outdoor track and field championships on a yardage basis was beaten after heated debate at the national Amateur Athletic Union convention today.

The board of governors voted, 71 to 18, to retain the metric system used for the last 10 years. Yards were substituted for meters at the national indoor meet in 1939.

The union also voted to reinstate Angelo (Hank) Luisetti, former Stanford basketball star, to his amateur status. He had been barred from A.A.U. play for turning movie actor.

Dr. L. W. Olds of Ypsilanti, Mich., track and field committee chairman, told the convention that a return to the yardage system "would help sell track and field to the American public."

"The sport is not as active as it should be," Olds said. "This is shown by the fact we do not yet have a single concrete bid for the 1941 outdoor championships."

Avery Brundage, president of the American Olympic Committee, and J. Lyman Bingham of Chicago, assistant to the A.A.U. president, led the battle against dropping the metric measurements.

"The metric system has nothing to do with any lack of interest in track sports," Brundage said. He argued that "the A.A.U. would stultify itself by making this change and would cause endless confusion."

Officers elected today at the convention were: president, Laurence di Benedetto, New Orleans; first vice-president, Fred L. Steers, Chicago; second vice-president, James M. Roche, New Haven, Ct.; third vice-president, Lewis H. Mahony, Denver; fourth vice-president, William L. Bailey, High Point, N. C.; secretary-treasurer, Daniel J. Ferris, New York; assistant to the president, L. Lyman Bingham, Chicago.

## BOWL TICKETS ALL SOLD OUT

PASADENA, Dec. 8.—All tickets for the Nebraska-Stanford Rose Bowl game save the 15,000 which will be put up for public sale Wednesday morning, have been sold, game headquarters here revealed tonight.

The public sale begins Wednesday morning at 8:30. Each purchaser will be limited to four tickets and only cash will be accepted. The ducats will be sold at the five outside ticket booths on the east side of the Rose Bowl. There will be 15 windows open, to keep the lines moving as fast as possible. The tickets are $4.40 each.

# Joe Louis Stops Conn in 13th to Retain Championship

## SPORT POST-SCRIPTS

By PAUL ZIMMERMAN

If you are one of those who has craned your neck to the breaking point at a preview and got jostled by the throng to get a glimpse of a movie star;

If you are one of several hundred thousand Southland bowlers who never got anything but personal satisfaction out of the dough you have spent at a bowling alley;

Well, the millennium arrives for you tomorrow night.

**EVERYTHING FREE**

Because the Greek Theater at Griffith Park will be thrown open to you "free for nothing" tomorrow night.

There you will get to see a swell program by stars of the radio and screen and, in addition, there will be 2000 door prizes thrown in for good measure.

"Sounds screwy," you say?

Sure, but it is a fact, nevertheless.

The "how come" is that this is the opening gun of the Los Angeles Bowling Association, the Bowling Proprietors' Association and the Junior Chamber of Commerce in their drive to bring the American Bowling Congress to Los Angeles in 1944.

**GREAT SHOW**

Charlie Vance, field representative of the A.B.C., will be on hand as a decidedly interested observer. If the bowling fans pack the place, it is a cinch he will go east to give a glowing report on the spirit in the City of the Angels.

All the Bowling Congress means to us is something like 25,000 guests from across the nation who will spend about 3,000,000 bucks in good, old long green to entertain themselves while here. And you can't beat that.

Vance gets the honor of crowning Carole Landis, 20th Century-Fox glamour gal, as the "300 Girl," an honor several thousand swains at the bowl would fight for—or haven't you seen Carole? Other outstanding entertainers include Red Skelton, Eddy Foy Jr., Cee Pee Johnson, the demon drummer, and those famous song writers, Hoagie Carmichael and Johnny Mercer.

**BAY CITY WANTS IT**

Incidentally, we have a potent rival for the 1944 congress in a little burg named San Francisco.

Since the West Coast can have the national bowling tourney only once in seven years, Los Angeles is going to have to put up its dukes and fight off the Bay City's bid right now or forget the whole thing.

The 1944 site will be named at the next A.B.C., which takes place at Columbus in 1942, and it is up to Los Angeles to crack its heels and get going on a drive that will make the bowling world sit up and take notice.

**WAR TAKES STAR**

Death of Janusz Kusocinski, great Polish distance runner, at the hands of the Gestapo stirs deep memories of almost a decade ago.

Kusocinski was the first runner to break the monopoly that had been Finland's in the distance events of the Olympics. His triumph in the 10,000 meters came early in the games—on a Sunday—and the 50,000 in the stadium came up with a great applause when he left Volmari Iso-Hollo, the Finn, far behind and then almost walked through the tape in Olympic record time.

To the Polish people here Janusz immediately became a popular idol—even more so than Stella Walsh.

**HE CELEBRATED**

It was my privilege to sit at Janusz's left at a sumptuous dinner at the Polish dining hall in the Olympic Village that night. There was a great deal of celebration and much boisterous conversation by everyone but Kusocinski.

Janusz was busy catching up on desserts after his training grind. He started out with pineapple pie, had two bowls of strawberries and cream and topped this off with a couple of helpings of ice cream.

Kusocinski wasn't much on English and John Roman, Polish attache, helped me get an interview across.

**MORE SPEED**

The thing I'll never forget about our talk was his answer to the question of whether or not he could have run the race faster. Janusz's blue eyes lighted up as he said:

"Of course I could have but why should I? There was none to beat me."

Kusocinski at that time voiced a besetting ambition. He hoped someday to accumulate enough money to purchase a racing car and make a name for himself on the speedways of Europe.

P.S.: Anyone who saw Janusz walk in ahead of Iso-Hollo that August day in 1932 would know he wouldn't be the kind of a guy to bow to an oppressor.

BATTLE'S END—Billy Conn is shown here making a futile attempt to get up as Referee Eddie Josephs is about to count "ten." Champion Joe Louis stands in a neutral corner after delivering the blow which brought him victory in this his 18th defense of his ring title.

GOING DOWN—After making a game stand for over 12 rounds, Billy Conn starts for the canvas, a victim of one of Joe Louis' crushing punches. Conn is shown here heading for the floor in the fatal 13th round. Louis stands over him. (AP) Wirephoto

Los Angeles Times Sports

THURSDAY, JUNE 19, 1941

## Challenger Ahead Until Fatal Knockout Punch

### Pittsburgh Boxer Amazes Brown Bomber With Clever Exhibition of Ringcraft

BY SID FEDER

POLO GROUNDS (New York,) June 18. (AP)—Joe Louis held onto his world heavyweight championship tonight—but he never came closer to losing it.

For 12 full rounds Billy Conn, the "fresh kid" from Pittsburgh who wasn't supposed to have a "prayer," the good little man who was laughed at as a challenger gave the Brown Bomber more than he sent. Then Joe found the range and with a fearful bombardment that lasted less than a minute and a half he chopped Conn down in the 13th.

**CONN HELPLESS**

The curly-haired Irish kid was literally beaten to the floor, and helpless, remained there as Referee Eddie Josephs counted him out. He made an effort to get up at "10," but he couldn't make it.

The greatest crowd to see a fight since 72,000 turned out for the second Louis-Schmeling tussle three years ago was on its feet and howling at the finish. A total of 54,487 cash customers contributed to an approximate gross gate of $450,000.

Thus, Louis stretched his all-time record run as "king of the ring" to 18 straight defenses, but as the fight ended, a roaring crowd that jammed this big National League park wondered if two seconds might not have meant the difference between the old boss or a cry for "the King is dead, long live the King."

**ROUSING BATTLE**

For Billy was counted out at 2:58 of the 13th after the most rousing heavyweight title fight since Tony Galento and the Bomber put on their old-fashioned slugfest two years ago. And, had he been able to make those two seconds to the 14th, he might have stayed out of harm's way for two more rounds, to win on a decision. For the 12 completed rounds, he was master. On the Associated Press' score card he led eight rounds to four at that point, making it an absolute "must" for Joe to put the crusher on to keep his crown.

**IRISH COMES OUT**

But win or lose for C[illegible] brother, this was a scrap [illegible] started out just as he had in[illegible]cated in his training camp. He had Billy Boy hanging on by the end of the second. Then something happened. Mostly, it was Billy's "Irish" coming out. Through the third and fourth he started to tag Joe, with no more concern for the destroyer's dynamite than if Louis' hands were feather dusters.

Starting with the sixth and going right on through the 12th, with the possible exception of the 10th, when Joe opened up, Billy banged away at the headman as though he held a lease on him. He waded in, particularly in the eighth and ninth.

Two swinging left hooks right on the whiskers in the 12th round staggered Joe, and for a few moments the crowd, which packed the upper and lower grandstands and filled every one of the 14,000 infield seats, went absolutely wild.

But came the 13th, and with the unlucky number all the black cats in the world must have trotted out in front of Billy. He was grinning now, and as confident as if he were taking on a

Turn to Page 22, Column 3

## Padres Slug Stars, 15-12

### Pitchers Parade as Rival Batters Fatten Averages

BY AL WOLF

At a late hour last night, a portly party who was foaming at the mouth and screaming incoherently was led out of Gilmore Field. He was the official scorer of the evening's alleged baseball game between San Diego and Hollywood.

An examination of his book full of hen scratches revealed that the Padres had outlasted the Stars to gain a 15-12 decision after three hours of this and that.

**SECOND STRAIGHT**

The outcome gave the visitors their second triumph of the series and extended Hollywood's string of losses to exactly 10 in a row, thereby dropping the cinema city fraternity to seventh place in the standings.

In the aforementioned scorekeeper's ledger were listed six Hollywood flingers and a mere five Padre moundsmen. Also listed were a total of 34 base hits, half a dozen errors, home runs by Bill Brenzel of the locals and Johnny Jensen of the visitors and even a long list of umpires. Seems that Arbiter Henry Fanning was smacked by a batted ball and had to go home, whereupon various players of both teams took turns robbing each other.

**ROSENBERG INJURED**

One other casualty was incurred, the Stars' Harry Rosenberg spraining his ankle and having to be carried from the scene.

Despite what happened last night, the clubs will collide again tonight as advertised. At a late hour last night Manager Bill Sweeney and Ced Durst were scouring the highways and by-

Turn to Page 20, Column 6

## GIANTS, BUCS IN 11-INNING TIE

### Fight Broadcast Halts Game for 56 Minutes

PITTSBURGH, June 18. (AP)—In a game interrupted for a 56 minute broadcast of the Billy Conn-Joe Louis fight, the New York Giants and Pittsburgh Pirates tonight battled 11 innings to a 2-2 tie before 24,000 fans. Mel Ott got his 17th home run of the year for the visitors and Bob Elliott drove in both Pirate runs in the first inning with a triple.

| NEW YORK | AB | H | O | A | PITTSBURGH | AB | H | O | A |
|---|---|---|---|---|---|---|---|---|---|
| Bartell.ss | 5 | 2 | 2 | 5 | Gustine.2b | 4 | 1 | 7 | 5 |
| Rucker.cf | 5 | 2 | 3 | 1 | Handley.3b | 5 | 3 | 0 | 3 |
| Danning.c | 5 | 0 | 8 | 0 | V'ghan.ss | 4 | 0 | 2 | 2 |
| Ott.rf | 4 | 1 | 0 | 1 | Elliott.rf | 5 | 2 | 1 | 0 |
| Young.1b | 5 | 0 | 15 | 0 | V.R'bays.lf | 4 | 1 | 4 | 0 |
| Moore.lf | 3 | 1 | 0 | 0 | F'tcher.1b | 5 | 0 | 14 | 1 |
| Orengo.3b | 5 | 1 | 0 | 3 | D'M'gio.cf | 5 | 2 | 2 | 0 |
| W'head.2b | 4 | 0 | 5 | 4 | Lopez.c | 3 | 0 | 1 | 1 |
| Wittig.p | 1 | 0 | 0 | 0 | An'son.z | 0 | 0 | 0 | 0 |
| O'Dea.x | 1 | 0 | 0 | 0 | Davis.c | 1 | 0 | 1 | 0 |
| Melton.p | 2 | 1 | 0 | 5 | Butcher.p | 4 | 1 | 1 | 5 |
| Totals | 40 | 8 | 33 | 19 | Totals | 40 | 10 | 33 | 17 |

x Batted for Wittig in 4th.
z—Ran for Lopez in 9th.

SCORE BY INNINGS

New York ..... 0 1 0 1 0 0 0 0 0 0 0—2
Pittsburgh ..... 2 0 0 0 0 0 0 0 0 0 0—2

SUMMARY

Runs scored—Ott, 2; Gustine, Handley. Runs batted in—Elliott, 2; Ott, Orengo. Two-base hit—Handley. Three-base hit—Elliott. Home run—Ott. Stolen base—Handley. Sacrifice—Vaughan. Double play—Rucker to Young. Left on bases—New York, 8; Pittsburgh, 9. Bases on balls—Off Wittig, 1; Butcher, 3; Melton, 2. Struck out — By Wittig, 1; Melton, 5; Butcher, 2. Hits—Off Wittig, 4 in 3 innings; Melton, 6 in 8. Wild pitch—Butcher. Umpires — Conlan, Goetz and Reardon. Time of game—2h. 43m. Attendance—24,738.

## Scribes Have Conn Ahead Before 13th

NEW YORK, June 18.—Up to the time that Billy Conn ran into a ring full of Joe Louis' fists in the 13th round tonight, the Pittsburgh challenger, despite the margin of weight against him, had scored more blows and won more rounds in the scheduled 15-round encounter.

Count of the Associated Press boxing experts gave Conn eight rounds and Louis four, ending the 12th. The United Press gave Conn six rounds, five to the champion, and one—the 10th—even.

## Round-by-Round Story of Conn's Great Stand

NEW YORK, June 18. (AP)—The blow-by-blow account of Joe Louis' successful 13-round defense of his world's championship against Billy Conn tonight here follows:

**ROUND ONE**

Louis rushed across the ring, trying to back Conn into a corner. Joe jabbed to the forehead as Billy backed away. Conn jabbed lightly to the face. After tossing a short straight left, Billy slipped to the seat of his pants but was up with no count. In a half clinch, Joe hooked hard to the head. Conn fired a left to the body but took left and right to the head against the ropes. Conn hooked twice to the head but took two hard rights and a left to the ear in return. He was dancing all around Louis. Billy's left poked Joe's nose. Louis jabbed a hard left to the eye at the bell. Louis' round.

**ROUND TWO**

Billy continued to dance around Joe as the champion stalked him. Conn jabbed to the nose as Louis was wild with a right. Twice more Billy jabbed and backed off. Billy poked a left to the eye and received the same treatment. Conn jabbed to the nose, then Louis backed him into a corner and fired left, right, left and right to the head. For a moment Conn appeared hurt. Then he lashed out with a hook of his own. Joe fired both hands to head and body. Conn fought back, throwing both hands to the head and hooking hard to the body. Joe dug two hard lefts and one right to the ribs. Conn hooked a left to the eye at the bell, and the crowd roared. Conn was beating Louis to the punch. Louis' round.

**ROUND THREE**

Louis continued trying to corner the challenger. Conn's hook to the ear brought a hard hook to the head. Joe dug a right to the stomach and threw another to the head. Billy bounced a left off the chin. Louis swung a left hook to the forehead. Conn twice threw lefts to the head. Joe tossed two lefts into the body. Billy bounced a left off the jaw. They traded stiff lefts, then Conn fired both hands to Louis' head. A "mouse" appeared under Louis' left eye. Louis threw a left at the bell that skinned Conn's right eye. Conn's round.

**ROUND FOUR**

Louis still stalked Billy. Conn landed a straight left to the stomach and a right to the ear. Billy hooked to the body and nailed Joe with a hard right cross to the head. Conn moved in fast and tagged Louis with two straight lefts and a right to the eye. Billy stuck two straight lefts into Joe's face and then in a half clinch flailed away with his right. Joe held on momentarily. As Conn bore in again he caught a hook to the jaw. Louis fired a left to the ear. Billy bounced a right off the chin but took a left to the head. Conn shot a right to the eye as Joe hooked hard to the head. The crowd was in a continuous uproar. Conn fired two more rights to Joe's eye. Louis nailed a smashing left hook to the nose at the bell. He was beating Louis to the punch. Conn's round.

**ROUND FIVE**

Joe caught Billy with a straight left, then crossed a right. After Billy hooked two lefts to the ear, they traded jabs. Billy hooked to the head but took a hard left in the pit of the stomach. Billy's right chipped Joe's jaw, but Conn received four punches to the body in a half clinch. They traded left uppercuts in midring. Billy threw a hard left to the body and a smashing right as they came out of a half clinch. Conn poked two lefts to the head. As Billy fired a left to the body, Joe connected with a smashing right. Joe pummeled Conn's body and then nailed him with a vicious right. Joe landed half a dozen more punches and Conn was hurt. Louis was all out now. Conn was trying to hold at the bell. A short hook just before the bell cut Billy over the right eye. Louis' round.

**ROUND SIX**

They traded left hooks as Billy danced away fast. Conn socked two lefts to the head but took a left, right and left to the body. In a half clinch Billy tossed a right to the ear as Joe continued to bang his midsection. Billy came out of a half clinch throwing left, right and left to the head. Conn hooked to the eye. Billy threw a left to the jaw as Louis tossed both hands to the body. Billy bounced a hard left off Joe's eye, added two more lefts. Then Louis threw a left to the head and a right to the body. Conn was dancing away at the bell. Conn's round.

**ROUND SEVEN**

Billy looked stronger as he jabbed Joe's nose. Louis jabbed twice to the head. Joe dug a left to the body. Joe tried to pin Billy and the challenger danced off. They traded hooks to the head. Joe caught Conn against the ropes with a hard hook to the body but Billy bounced out with a left to the eye. Conn caught Joe with two hooks to the head and left and right to the body. Louis pumped his left to the ribs. Billy hooked to the ear and, in close, bounced a right off the other ear. Billy tagged Joe with a short right to the chin as Louis smashed at his body. Conn's round.

**ROUND EIGHT**

Louis bounced left and right off Billy's head, adding two fists to the body. Billy fired his right three times in close. Louis threw a right to the jaw. Conn bounced his right off Joe's eye. They struck straight lefts at long range. Billy threw two rights to the head in close. Conn caught Louis at close

Turn to Page 22, Column 1

## Fight Fan Dies From Heart Attack

REDDING, June 18. (AP)—Jack Rester died of a heart attack tonight while listening to the Billy Conn-Joe Louis fight over the radio with his twin brother, Bill. In the middle of the 10th round, Rester fell out of his chair.

## McCarthy Hits Racing Rule

### Attorney Horse Owner Attacks California's Responsibility Law

Neil S. McCarthy, attorney and an owner of a string of thoroughbreds racing at Hollywood Park, issued a statement yesterday in which he decried the interpretation of California racing laws which makes the owner the absolute insurer and responsible for the condition of horses when they go to the post.

**LONE DEVELOPMENT**

McCarthy has been retained as counsel for several of the nine owners ordered to appear before the California Horse Racing Board Monday to show cause why their licenses should not be revoked because of urinalysis tests which chemists said showed nine thoroughbreds racing at the Inglewood oval had been stimulated with caffeine.

His statement was the lone development in the case, which reached a white heat Saturday when Chairman Jerry Giesler issued his "show cause" orders.

"The issue with Chairman Giesler of the Horse Racing Board," read the statement in part, "is not and at no time has been whether anyone guilty of tampering with any animals should be apprehended and punished. Such ac-

Turn to Page 20, Column 4

## MACKS HELD TO FOUR HITS AS FELLER WINS 14TH GAME

PHILADELPHIA, June 18. (AP) Rapid Robert Feller won his 14th game of the season today as the Cleveland Indians defeated the Athletics 14 to 2 and increased their American League lead to three games.

Feller gave the A's just four hits—the same number as last week when he shut out the Mackmen, 2-0, for his 13th victory—while his Tribal mates slammed out 17 safeties, including five home runs and four doubles.

**HOME RUNS GALORE**

Eight of their hits and seven of their runs, including Lou Boudreau's two-run homer, came in the second inning and drove Les McCrabb out of the box to be replaced by Chubby Dean. First Baseman Hal Trosky connected for home runs on successive times at bat and Ken Keltner and Ray Mack each clouted one four-bagger.

Everyone in the Cleveland line-up made at least one blow except Feller, who fanned twice.

**FANS EIGHT BATTERS**

In winning his 14th against three defeats, the young right-hander gave only two walks and struck out eight Mackmen to boost his strikeout total to 119 for the campaign.

The Athletics' two runs came singly, the first in the second when Bob Johnson and Eddie Collins walked and Pete Suder singled, and the other in the fourth when Johnson tripled and came home on Frankie Hayes' long fly.

The largest week-day crowd of the season, 10,507, watched the slugfest.

| CLEVELAND | AB | H | O | A | PHILADELPHIA | AB | H | O | A |
|---|---|---|---|---|---|---|---|---|---|
| Boudr'u.ss | 4 | 3 | 2 | 2 | Branc'o.ss | 4 | 0 | 4 | 5 |
| Peters.ss | 0 | 0 | 0 | 1 | Moses.rf | 4 | 1 | 2 | 0 |
| Keltner.3b | 6 | 3 | 1 | 1 | Miles.lf | 4 | 0 | 1 | 0 |
| Walker.lf | 6 | 1 | 0 | 0 | Johns'n.1b | 3 | 1 | 9 | 1 |
| Heath.rf | 6 | 2 | 1 | 0 | Hayes.c | 4 | 0 | 4 | 0 |
| Campb'l.cf | 4 | 1 | 4 | 0 | Collins.cf | 3 | 1 | 3 | 0 |
| Trosky.1b | 5 | 3 | 9 | 0 | Suder.3b | 3 | 1 | 1 | 0 |
| Mack.2b | 5 | 2 | 1 | 4 | Davis.2b | 3 | 0 | 3 | 4 |
| Hemsley.c | 4 | 2 | 8 | 0 | McCrabb.p | 0 | 0 | 0 | 1 |
| Feller.p | 4 | 0 | 1 | 1 | Dean.p | 3 | 0 | 0 | 1 |
| Totals | 44 | 17 | 27 | 9 | Totals | 31 | 4 | 27 | 12 |

SCORE BY INNINGS

Cleveland .......... 0 7 2 1 0 1 2 1 0—14
Philadelphia ........ 0 1 0 1 0 0 0 0 0— 2

SUMMARY

Runs scored—Boudreau, 3; Keltner, 2; Walker, Heath, Trosky, 3; Mack, 2; Hemsley, Feller, Johnson, 2. Errors—Johnson, Brancato. Runs batted in—Boudreau, 3; Keltner, 3; Heath, Campbell, 2; Mack, Hemsley, Feller, Trosky, 2; Hayes, Suder. Two-base hits—Mack, Campbell, Boudreau, Hemsley. Three-base hit—Johnson. Home runs—Boudreau, Mack, Trosky, 2; Keltner. Stolen base—Heath. Sacrifice — Feller. Double play—Brancato to Johnson. Left on bases—Philadelphia, 4; Cleveland, 8. Bases on balls—Off McCrabb, 1; Dean, 3; Feller, 2. Struck out—By Feller, 8; McCrabb, 1; Dean, 2. Hits—Off McCrabb, 7 in 1 1-3 innings; Dean, 10 in 7 2-3. Balk—Feller. Losing pitcher—McCrabb. Umpires—Ormsby, Rommel and Pipgras. Time of game—1h. 54m. Attendance—10,507.

## Bout Date Changed

WATERBURY (Ct.) June 18. (AP)—Promoter George Mulligan announced tonight the Irwin (Kay) Kaplan of Los Angeles-Wicky Harkins of Philadelphia boxing bout slated here Thursday would take place June 26 instead.

## Urge Me Surprise Winner Over Favored Jubal Junior

BY PAUL LOWRY

U. H. Plavan, the man who put over the Kay-Diane coup at Hollywood this summer, is still living right. Having lost Kay-Diane in a claiming race for twice her purchase price—after she had won over $4000 in purses for him—Plavan sent Urge Me to the post yesterday to knock over Jubal Junior, the shortest-priced favorite of the meeting.

It all happened in the fifth race, a six-furlong dash for sprinters with a $6000 claiming tag on their noses.

Urge Me took command soon after the break, piled up a nice lead and saved enough for Jubal Junior's challenge in the stretch to win by half a length from the public choice in 1:11. Journey On was third.

Jubal Junior went to the post at 1 to 2 and might have been closer, or even victorious, if he had not been forced to break from the rail position.

In the featured Beaufremont at seven furlongs Vain Grove was an easy two length winner

Turn to Page 20, Column 7

# Two Cleveland Hurlers End DiMaggio's Hitting Streak

## SPORT POST-SCRIPTS

By PAUL ZIMMERMAN

If a year's suspension is a just and reasonable penalty to be imposed on Eddie Mayo for a run-in with an umpire the other day, then President William G. Bramham of the National Association of Professional Baseball Leagues, who so ruled, had best give the game back to Abner Doubleday, who originated it.

We do not propose to argue, this fine day, over what the Los Angeles third baseman did or did not do in that squabble nor his ethics in this specific case.

**FAILED OF DUTY**

But we insist that President W. C. Tuttle of the Pacific Coast League failed of his responsibility to the player when he did not give President Bramham all the facts of the case in requesting a ruling.

Tuttle, whom we prefer to dispose of by calling him the "complacent" type, admits that Bramham was informed only of the fact that his report indicated Umpire Ray Snyder had been spat upon.

Any baseball fan who has followed Mayo since he came to the Angels will attest to the fact that Eddie never before has been guilty of misconduct of even a moderate degree; that he is the spirited, conscientious, hard-working type of which the Angels, the entire league and all organized baseball for that matter need in much greater quantities.

**DEBT TO PUBLIC**

As president of the league, Author Tuttle owes it to the fans to foster and protect the Mayo species instead of breaking his spirit by permitting an excessive and costly suspension that deprives the star infielder of his livelihood for 12 solid months.

As for Bramham, I am in no position to say what sort of a despotic ruler he thinks he is to hand down such a suspension without first giving Mayo a defense.

But certainly it is impossible for him to rule wisely from several thousand miles away on a fragmentary report. It is an actual fact that Mayo could have gone out on the street and whapped the first policeman he met, with intent to do bodily harm, and received a lighter fine through the bar of justice.

**LEFT UNSAID**

Anyone who knows Eddie Mayo at all—and President Tuttle should—realizes that the infielder was entirely out of character if he did expectorate upon Snyder.

Mr. Tuttle admits that the penalty was much more severe than he had expected, but in the same breath he says he intends to do nothing further in the matter except to forward Mayo's appeal if Eddie chooses to make one.

It isn't what the league president told Bramham so much as what he left unsaid, and Mr. Tuttle might just as well face the music, since he now is washing his hands of the whole thing after neatly passing the buck.

**BAD UMPIRING**

To present the case properly, President Tuttle might honestly have told Bramham that his umpires had booted so many decisions in this hot city series that any finely trained athlete easily might have lost his head over just one more close play whether this one happened to be called right or not.

He might have gone even farther and admitted that the officiating of ball games in the Coast League this season, as displayed in these parts at least, has been little short of comic absurdity in striking instances.

Yes, Mr. Tuttle might have said a lot of things to temper a rather casual incident that flared up and died out almost without notice that Sunday afternoon.

**KNITTING BEE**

Of course, if Mr. Tuttle and Mr. Bramham want the meek to inherit baseball, that's a different thing.

If they want "milktoast" players, why, maybe they had best issue an official statement so that what few baseball fans remain can take themselves to the roque courts for an exhilarating afternoon or evening instead.

Me, I've never been much on siding with umpires anyway. And I admit jealousy is the reason. It always makes me sore when hard-working ball players get fined for beefing at guys who draw a day's salary for a couple of hours of blind man's buff.

**P.S.:** Come to think of it, maybe Tuttle and Bramham shouldn't try to give the game back to Doubleday when they get through. Abner probably would rise up from the grave and say, "No, thanks. You keep the corpse."

**SWIMMING TRIO**—These three misses, all Los Angeles Athletic Club swimming stars, take part in all-star aquatic exhibition Sunday at Santa Monica Deauville Club. They are Lorraine Ogg, Corinne Smith and Natalie Rogers.

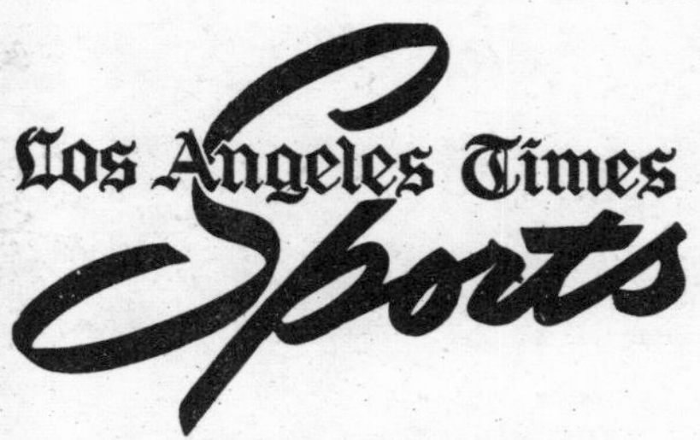

Los Angeles Times Sports

FRIDAY, JULY 18, 1941

## Mioland Likely Victor in Hollywood Gold Cup

### For Fourth Time in as Many Years Howard's Entry to Go Postward as Classic Favorite

BY PAUL LOWRY

For the fourth time in as many years C. S. (Lucky Charlie) Howard tomorrow will send the favorite to the post in the $75,000 Hollywood Gold Cup.

Mioland, the Oregon-bred son of Mio D'Arezzo, yesterday sizzled five-eighths in :59 2-5 to cinch public choice honors and sent erstwhile lukewarm supporters tumbling over one another to climb aboard the Howard bandwagon for the big race.

Twice in the past three years the Howard horses have made good—Seabiscuit in 1938, Kayak II in 1939. Only in the 1940 running when Kayak II and Advocator tumbled before the powerful charge of Challedon have the red and white silks of the San Francisco automobile magnate gone under.

**HOWARD'S NEMESIS**

But lurking in the background for this year's running of the great summer classic is little Nick Wall, the nemesis of the Howard silks in so many important races—Stagehand over Seabiscuit in the 1938 Santa Anita Handicap, Jacola over Seabiscuit in the Laurel Mile, Today over Seabiscuit in the Santa Anita race when the Biscuit broke down and Bay View over Mioland in the last Santa Anita Handicap.

Wall is to ride the paperweight Paperboy (98,) the English-bred colt which finished a powerful fourth in the Derby to Staretor. The tiny veteran was billed to pilot Cinesar in yesterday's third race, but his plans were changed and he took a plane from New York for the Coast last night.

**PAPERBOY WORKS**

Paperboy was given a seven-furlong tightener yesterday morning, returning to Trainer Darrell Cannon after stepping the first half in :47 4-5, three quarters in

Turn to Page 25, Column 3

## Riddle Cops 11th Straight

### Sensational Cincy Hurler Keeps Record Clean as Giants Lose, 5-4

NEW YORK, July 17. (AP) Elmer Riddle, the year's pitching sensation, achieved his 11th victory without a defeat tonight as the Cincinnati Reds squeezed past the New York Giants, 5 to 4. Riddle gave up 10 hits and made a faltering start, but did not allow a run after the fourth inning.

The Reds clustered seven of their nine hits for three runs in the first inning and two more in the third before Bill Lohrman gave up the Giants' hurling chore. Fiddler Bill McGee held them helpless the rest of the way

Turn to Page 23, Column 3

## Smith, Bagby Shackle Joe

### Record String Snapped at 56, but Yanks Triumph Before 67,468 by 4-3

CLEVELAND, July 17. (AP) The fast-stepping New York Yankees strengthened their hold on first place tonight with their second consecutive victory over the Cleveland Indians, 4 to 3, in a tight battle before 67,468, to go seven games ahead. Joe DiMaggio's hitting streak was snapped at 56 straight games as Al Smith and Jim Bagby retired him three times and walked him a fourth.

Lefty Gomez stopped the Indians with four hits and one run for eight innings, but the slim southpaw was routed by the determined Redskins in a ninth-inning rally. Fireman Johnny Murphy pitched a triple to Larry Rosenthal, batting for Ray Mack, to allow two runs but bore down to retire Pinch Hitters Clarence Campbell and Hal Trosky and Roy Weatherly to end the game.

**KELTNER STOPS JOE**

DiMaggio's streak, started May 15 against Chicago, might have been extended but for some sharp

### DiMaggio's Record

His batting record for the season now is:

| G. | A.B. | R. | H. | H.R. | Pct. |
|---|---|---|---|---|---|
| 85 | 334 | 80 | 124 | 20 | .371 |

For the 56-game hitting streak which ended last night:

| G. | A.B. | H. | 2B | 3B | H.R. | Pct. |
|---|---|---|---|---|---|---|
| 56 | 223 | 90 | 16 | 4 | 15 | .403 |

fielding by Ken Keltner, Cleveland third baseman. In the first and seventh innings he made sensational stops of hot smashes and threw out the rangy Yankee outfielder. The other time Smith pitched to DiMaggio he walked him on a 3-and-2 pitch.

Joe had his last chance in the eighth, coming to bat against Bagby with the bases filled and one out. However, he bounded to Lou Boudreau for a fast double play.

After the game DiMaggio said: "I can't say that I'm glad it's over. Of course I wanted to go on as long as I could.

"Now that the streak is over, I just want to get out there and keep helping to win ball games."

**EXPERT OPINES**

Bagby, who threw the double-play pitch to DiMaggio, said it was simply a "straight fast ball."

"That's the kind of a pitch you either hit or don't hit," he smiled. "There's no sense in throwing a slow curve to a guy like DiMaggio. Fortunately, he hit right for our side."

Smith had nothing to say about helping break DiMaggio's record. He appeared downcast because of losing the game, but did remark that he received "great help from Keltner with getting DiMaggio out."

The largest crowd in night baseball history saw two home runs, Gerry Walker getting his fourth of the season for Cleveland's first run in the fourth and Joe Gordon putting the Yanks

Turn to Page 22, Column 1

## Missing Figures Enter Stimulation Hearing

BY PAUL ZIMMERMAN

A fantastic story of an elusive individual, tentatively identified as "Speedy," who dropped a small sack of cube sugar and caffeine pills as he fled from Hollywood Park on the morning of June 25, was told at the stimulation hearing before the California Horse Racing Board at the State Building yesterday.

C. Jerry Jones, an investigator for the Hollywood Turf Club, said the man, who has not been seen since, had created suspicion by his actions around the cafeteria kitchen in the stable area.

**OTHERS MISSING**

The investigator disclosed that two other men seen with Speedy at the cafeteria kitchen also are missing. They are James McDonald, a groom who had been employed in the Bob White stable which races Brown China—one of the nine horses implicated in the caffeine investigation—and Austin (Tex) Russell, another groom.

It was Russell, according to Jones' testimony, who identified Speedy in the presence of Jack Mackenzie, general manager of Hollywood Park. At that time, the investigator said, he quizzed Russell as to what disposition he intended to make of the contents of the small sack.

**MAN VANISHES**

"What was Speedy going to do with the sugar?" Jones said he asked Russell.

"You mean that stuff he was going to scatter around?" the investigator said Russell replied.

Jones said Russell disappeared the day after he talked to him. McDonald, whom the investi-

Turn to Page 25, Column 2

## Stars Win Out in Ninth, 4-3

### Pippen's Masterpiece Ruined as Gudat 'Loses' Schulte's Timely Blow

BY BOB SMYSER

They staged another one of those ninth-inning spine-tinglers out at Gilmore field last night with Bill Sweeney's Hollywood Stars cracking out four runs in a wild last frame that gave them a 4-3 victory over Oakland and just about broke the heart of a gent named Henry Pippen.

Pippen, who goes under the nickname of Cotton, went into the ninth as the evening's hero. On the mound for Oakland, he had given up two scratch hits and appeared to be on his way to a shutout.

**STARS FIND RANGE**

But — in keeping with the series tradition of thrilling last innings—the Twinks suddenly found their range on the Acorn right-hander and plastered him for two runs, loaded the bases and still had none away.

At this point Pippen bore down to get two men out without any further scoring. But it only paved the way for Ham Schulte to dump a double into left field — a blow that Marv Gudat appeared to lose in the lights—and send two runs across the plate to make it 4-3 as the local rooters went haywire.

**DASSO'S NINTH**

Thus did Frankie Dasso squeeze through with his ninth victory of the season. He pitched a creditable game, giving up only eight hits and fanning seven men. It was Pippen's 10th defeat and made his season's average .500.

The triumph also gave Holly-

Turn to Page 22, Column 3

## Eddie Mayo Begins Battle

### Angel Veteran Opens Campaign Against Stiff Suspension

Eddie Mayo's fight against the one-year suspension slapped on him by President W. C. Tuttle of the Pacific Coast League got under way yesterday when the veteran third baseman of the Los Angeles ball club went into conference with David P. Fleming, Angel prexy.

Mayo's heavy penalty was inflicted Wednesday by Tuttle, coming as a result of the player's bitter argument with Umpire Ray Snyder at Gilmore Field last Sunday — an argument which Snyder alleges was climaxed by Mayo spitting in the arbiter's face.

**MEET AGAIN TODAY**

Fleming, who returned from Catalina Island yesterday, wasn't able to give much time to Mayo because of pressing business affairs and he has scheduled another conference with the player today.

"I want to see how much information I can gather before taking any definite action in Mayo's behalf," declared Fleming. "We are certainly going to wage a fight against this suspension, but I can't as yet declare our course."

**EDDIE DENIES CHARGE**

Mayo vehemently denies that he spat in Snyder's face. The Angel ball player, one of the most valuable men in the Pacific Coast League and "sparkplug" of the Seraphs, is confident that the suspension can and will be lifted.

## Jimmy Clark Upset in Quarter-final Round

INDIAN CANYON (Spokane, Wash.) July 17. (AP)—Defeat of the tournament medalist and red-hot favorite, Jimmy Clark, provided a thundering climax today to third-round and quarter-finals matches of the 1941 national public links golf championship.

The handful of fans who braved hot, muggy weather to gallery the main attraction of the quarter-finals could hardly believe it, but there was 20-year-old Clark sent to the sidelines by an opponent who wasn't conceded the ghost of a chance to beat the tournament favorite.

Clark had sailed through three matches without trouble until he hooked up with Jack Kerns, an insurance underwriter in Denver and a corking good golfer on the side.

When the 18-hole match ended on the 17th green the applause was for the boy from the Rocky Mountain metropolis. He played winning golf all the way. Sensational in spots for the first four holes he was four under par—

Turn to Page 25, Column 4

## JOCKEY PEARSON UNDER KNIFE

Jockey Billy Pearson, injured last Tuesday in a three-horse spill at Hollywood Park, will be operated on by Dr. T. J. Bluechel tomorrow morning at Hollywood Hospital.

Surgery is required on the sensational rider's left shoulder. He suffered a badly shattered collarbone in the mishap.

## ANGELS NAB THIRD IN ROW

SAN FRANCISCO, July 17.—For the third straight night the Seals looked at sharp pitching this evening to lose to the Angels. The score was 4 to 2 and the winner was Frankie Totaro, former San Francisco prep star.

Totaro allowed but four hits but had to be lifted in the eighth to cut off a possible Seal rally. With the score 4-2, Totaro walked Fain and Carroll to open the eighth and Manager Arnold (Jigger) Statz came loping in from center field to find out why.

He evidently learned enough, because he sent Totaro to the baths and recalled Jittery Joe Berry from the bench. Berry struck out Fernandez, forced White to roll out and Lazzeri to pop-foul out.

San Francisco struck first in the fifth when, with two away, Ogrodowski walked and came around on a sacrifice and Fain's single.

The visitors made a pair of runs in the sixth on Schuster's double, singles by Warstler and

Turn to Page 22, Column 1

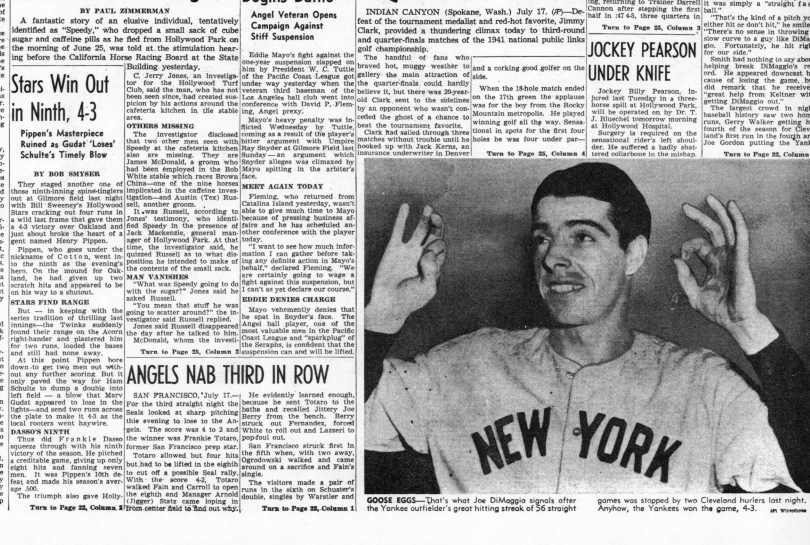

**GOOSE EGGS**—That's what Joe DiMaggio signals after the Yankee outfielder's great hitting streak of 56 straight games was stopped by two Cleveland hurlers last night. Anyhow, the Yankees won the game, 4-3. (AP) Wirephoto

# Warmerdam Vaults 15 ft. 7 1-4 in. for Record

## Sport Postscripts

By PAUL ZIMMERMAN

Dr. F. C. Allen, the basketball physician from Kansas, is off his feed again.

It should be explained at the outset that Dr. Allen, sometimes called Phog for reasons never adequately explained, hasn't been well since our Justin McCarthy Barry of Southern California sold the National Collegiate Association on the idea that the center jump had given the game to the string beans and had taken the spectator appeal out of the sport.

**SLIGHT TOUCHES**

Dr. Allen had slight touches of illness years ago when Kansas University took him out of the athletic directorship. Phog had pursued a custom of giving the Jayhawker school's choice athletic jobs to cage players to the detriment of the football team. It might be added that football hasn't recovered there yet.

And he had similar gnawing pains in the pit of his stomach when he suddenly wasn't named to take the Olympic basketball team to Berlin in 1936, just at a time when he had visions of a swell free trip—and publicity.

So, you see, his is something of a chronic case and it may be far beyond a cure.

**RACE TRACK**

The result is that whenever his Jayhawkers get a basketball setback—which isn't frequent—Dr. Allen starts squawking about eliminating the center jump.

Last year he said the fast game was burning out athletes—giving them bad hearts. Someone came along to refute the charge and Phog retired to the sidelines.

Now he says "race track" basketball has made it impossible for the officials to keep up with the play and the result is bad whistle tooting.

"Basketball," says he, "is a pell-mell, slam-bang scramble" because the center jump is gone and "good officials can't get the job done because they aren't allowed to ride motorcycles on the floor."

**HARD TO FOLLOW**

It is difficult to follow the good doctor's reasoning because good officials and bad were missing a lot of fouls back in the days when two Jack-the-beanstalks leaped ceilingward to get the tip-off after each score.

Never was it the business of the referee to keep on the heels of the man with the ball. It always has been the official's business to keep out of the way so plays and players are free to do what they can about getting that bloated bulb through the basket.

And if the referee can't do just a little running so he can see what goes, then he's too old for the business anyway.

**IT'S TERRIBLE**

Just in case his argument didn't get across, Dr. Allen added:

"The game is a terrible affair from the players' viewpoint. It's just a race, a collision and a shot."

That's his 1941 tune with new words.

All of which indicates that the good doctor has been sitting too close to the court or too far from the stands, as the case may be. He should try a spectator's pew some time just to get the point of view of the cash customer. After all, the fellow who shells out his dough to see the game is the guy who has kept Dr. Allen in business more years than he cares to admit.

The cash customer happens to be the guy who likes "race track" basketball and the doctor might just as well cease butting his head against the stone wall.

**CAGES TRIED**

Getting back to the officials this business of putting them in cages above the baskets is novel but hardly exciting. How would you like to have your baseball umpires rolled out in lion cages? Or your football arbiters on a traveling crane that rolls along the sidelines?

Of course not. You want 'em out where you can see 'em and where they can get full benefit of your impressions of them. They're part of the show, whether anyone likes it or not.

It's like that gag of having the fight referee officiate from outside the ropes. A noble experiment, no doubt, but it just never worked.

Some wise guy came up with the idea of putting the basketball official in the stands instead of in the cages. Strictly a theorist's notion, we calls it, unless he planned to put the spectators on the court with the players.

**P.S.:** Otherwise it might become a slight case for the coroner and good cage officials already are too scarce.

## Mayo Asked to Take Cut

### Angel Third Sacker Very Unhappy About It and Refuses to Sign Up

BY AL WOLF

Contract dissatisfaction among members of the local baseball colony continued to grow yesterday. Joining the five Hollywood pastimers (Bob Kahle, Roy Joiner, Johnny Dickshot, Bill Atwood and Del Young) who Friday were revealed to have fired back unsigned 1942 tickets was Outfielder Harry Rosenberg.

And across town at Wrigley Field, President Clarence Rowland of the Los Angeles Angels was visited by Third Baseman Eddie Mayo, who was very unhappy upon discovering that he is in line for a salary slash. Rowland also admitted that he is in the midst of a mail-order argument with First Baseman Phil Weintraub, who recently returned his unsigned contract from Milwaukee.

**ANY CUT HURTS**

Mayo insisted that he wasn't a holdout, that yesterday's discussion was "very palsy-walsy" and that he believed everything would work out all right. He declined to state how much pay reduction he was asked to take but said, "Any pay cut at all is bad enough, I think." Eddie has been taking a course in plastics engineering this winter but said yesterday he had no idea of giving up baseball.

Mayo, it will be remembered, was the party of the first part in last summer's alleged spitting episode with Umps Ray Snyder, a happening which caused his suspension by Pacific Coast League Prexy W. C. Tuttle from July 13 to Sept. 4, when the national executive committee, to which Mayo had appealed after Minor League Czar William Bramham had upheld Tuttle's action, ordered his reinstatement.

**GOT NO PAY**

Mayo received no salary for his eight weeks of enforced idleness and a claim for the wages which he subsequently filed with Tuttle was turned down.

The popular infielder was hitting over .300 when suspended and was rated perhaps the best defensive hot-corner man in the circuit. The benching dulled his batting eye to the extent that he wound up with .286 for the 109 games he got into. He had been considered amost a cinch to go up to the majors prior to difficulties, which were attended by a veritable storm of fan support.

**FAIR OFFER**

Rowland believed the terms offered Mayo to be a private matter but added that "I think we made him a very fair offer." Rowland also refused to state whether Weintraub was getting a cut in pay. The Angels were none too excited over the large Jewish infielder's play last season, his first with the club. He batted .302 and hit 18 homers, but was slow afield and on the paths.

Rosenberg wrote Business Manager Oscar Reichow from San Francisco that he would quit baseball rather than accept a reduction in salary, which Reichow admitted was the situation. Rosenberg was peeved last season because of being relegated to the

Turn to Page 10, Column 7

## Nevada Takes Lead in Ski Tourney

RENO (Nev.) Feb. 14. (AP)—Taking the first three places in the jumps and third place in the down mountain race, University of Nevada led on points today at the end of the first day's competition in the sixth annual Nevada intercollegiate ski tournament.

Nevada's combined points in both events totaled 197. University of California, with 185, was second; Oregon State, 161, third; Stanford, 147, fourth; California Polytechnic, 85, fifth, and U.C.L.A., 57, sixth.

Stanford's ski artist, Bobby Blatt, won the down mountain in 1.032 minutes. Bill Nelson, Nevada, leaped 102 feet to win the jumps.

The slalom and cross-country races will be held tomorrow.

Summaries:

Down mountain race—Individual winners: First, Bobby Blatt, Stanford, 1.032m.; second, Harry Morgan, California, 1.069; third, Bill Bechdolt, Nevada, 1.073. Team winners: First, Stanford, 100 points; second, Nevada, 97.04; third, California, 94.21; fourth, Oregon State, 92.38.

Jumping—Individual winners: First, Bill Nelson, Nevada, 102ft.; second, Bill Bechdolt, Nevada, 100.5ft.; third, Ashley Van Slyck, Nevada, 96ft. Team winners in jump: First, Nevada, 100 points; second, California, 91.6 points; third, Oregon State, 68.7 points.

GETTING THE BIRD—Evelyn Boldrick, former national women's badminton champion reached the semifnals yesterday in the Southern California championships on the courts of the Pasadena Badminton Club.

Times photo by Jack Herod

## Pepper Martin Due Here Soon

### Sacramento Manager Opens Rookie School in Fullerton Feb. 23

Pepper Martin, manager of the Sacramento Solons, is due in Fullerton one week from tomorrow to start training his squad for the 1942 Pacific Coast League season.

Although the main Solon outfit is not due to report until March 2, Coach Ken Penner is already on hand and he and Martin will conduct a rookie school beginning one week from tomorrow and running for 10 days.

Off to a flying start last year, Sacramento went out in front by a dozen or more games in the Coast League race but faltered in the stretch and finally tied San Diego for second behind the pennant-winning Seattle club.

Martin's gang met the Rainiers in the Shaughnessy play-off finals, after trimming San Diego four straight, but were defeated by Seattle.

## Detroit Lions Name Latshaw to Staff

DETROIT, Feb. 14. (AP)—The Detroit Lions, professional football club, announced today the appointment of Robert Latshaw, former Detroit newspaperman, as business manager, succeeding Charles Chaplin, resigned.

## Alsab Finishes Fourth in Hialeah Feature

HIALEAH (Fla.) Feb. 14. (U.P.)—Alsab, 1941 2-year-old champ and future-book favorite for the Kentucky Derby, finished out of the money for the second straight time at Hialeah Park today when he ran fourth behind the victorious Bright Willie in the Biscayne Purse.

Bright Willie, a three-year-old colt owned by Mrs. Ralph McIlvain, streaked home in new track record time of 1:36 3-5 for a mile at the lavish Florida plant while Sir War finished second and Incoming third. Alsab was several lengths off the pace and never entered the contention.

**EARLY LEAD**

The winner moved into the lead in the early stages and held Sir War easily at the end. He was ridden by the veteran Alf Robertson and carried 118 pounds, eight less than the top-weighted Alsab, to a mutuel return of $8.40, $3.70 and $2.80 across the board. Alsab defeated only two horses in the small field—Wood Robin and Eternal Peace.

Sir War paid $5.70 and $3.20 and Incoming $4.70 to show.

**SECOND DEFEAT**

The defeat was the second suffered by Alsab within eight days and removed much of the luster from his brilliant 1941 record. Last week he finished sixth behind American Wolf in the Bahamas Handicap but Owner Al Sabath blamed Jockey Conn McCreary for the defeat. Today Alsab was ridden by Eddie Arcaro—but did no better under the circumstances.

Bright Willie won by three lengths after holding the pace from the quarter pole. Sir War was a steady second and had a length and three-quarters over Incoming, who was another length and a half ahead of Alsab. The latter, an odds-on favorite, broke last and moved up to fourth at the head of the stretch but was unable to improve his position and was six lengths away from the leader at the end.

**TRANSIENT WINS**

In the $5000 added Evening Handicap which was overshadowed by the second straight defeat of Alsab, Mrs. Vera S. Bragg's Transient continued the downfall of favorites by wearing down Sweet Willow in the stretch to win going away.

Transient, handled by Eddie Arcaro, was kept close to the pace for a half mile and took the lead in the stretch to finish five lengths before Sweet Willow, who was three lengths ahead of The Swallow. The time for the seven furlongs was 1:23 3/5.

## Freeman Wins Birdie Match

### Pomona College Star Nears Men's Singles Title at Pasadena

Dave Freeman, the Pomona College athlete who holds a couple of national titles in the sport, advanced a step nearer the 1942 Southern California badminton men's singles crown last night at the Pasadena Badminton Club.

**SANDERSON VICTIM**

San Diego's Neil Sanderson bowed to the blond, young veteran by counts of 15-6, 18-14 in a quarterfinals match.

Skeeter Erikson of Pasadena advanced to the semifinals when he smashed Al Blatz of Santa Monica, 15-10, 15-7.

**BIGGEST UPSET**

Biggest upset of the day was the victory of Sally Williams over Elizabeth Anselm of San Francisco in the women's singles. Scores were 11-5, 11-8. Miss Williams is from Spokane and attends school in Claremont.

U.C.L.A.'s Evelyn Boldrick, defending champ, easily got to the semifinals by defeating Miss

Turn to Page 10, Column 7

## Flying Dutchman Cracks Every Existing Mark

### Amazing Californian Starts at 14ft. 4in., Then Makes History on Seventh Leap

BOSTON, Feb. 14. (AP)—Corny Warmerdam, the 28-year-old San Francisco schoolmaster who holds all the world pole-vaulting records, made the highest one in history, 15ft. 7¼in., on his third and final try at that height before 14,281 fans at the 53rd Boston A.A. track games.

After a half-hour rest, Warmerdam resumed his battle against the stratosphere and tried to clear a height only two inches less than 16 feet. He made three rapid tries and appeared over on his final one, but while descending his body grazed the bar just enough to knock it off its pins.

The amazing Californian did not start competing on the Boston Garden's runway, lengthened to 131 feet for the occasion, until the bar was raised to 14ft. 4in. He negotiated that and 14ft. 8⅝in. and, on a second try, cleared 15ft. 2in., a performance that improved his week-old indoor record by 1⅝ inches.

**RICE VICTOR**

Chunky Greg Rice, the Notre Dame product now competing for the New York A.C., turned in the fastest two miles in Boston's history, 8m. 53.4s., and ran the legs off his supposedly outstanding rival, Gilbert Dodds of the Boston A.A., in the Billings feature.

Rice, a winner at Philadelphia last night, laid well back until Dodds took the lead away from the veteran Joe McCluskey at the mile mark and did not get really interested until the fourth last lap. Then he forged ahead with ease, started really digging and went on to beat Dodds, a transplanted Nebraskan, by a good 50 yards.

**MAC MITCHELL WINS**

Les MacMitchell, New York University's sensational miler, captured the blue-ribbon Hunter event with a yard to spare on Earl Mitchell of Indiana, with a 4m. 11.8s. performance. MacMitchell set the pace for the first eight laps, permitted Mitchell and Jim Rafferty of the New York A.C., who finished third, to lead for single turns, and then uncorked his finishing drive.

Returning to his favorite distance, John Borican of Asbury Park, N.J., the indoor world record holder, led every inch of the way while defeating the veteran Gene Venzke of the New York A.C. by two yards in the Lapham "1000."

Borican, beaten in the Penn A.C. mile in Philadelphia last night by Campbell Kane of Indiana, never was seriously challenged as he romped to the tape in 2m. 12.3s. Kane, off last in the five-man field, managed to move up to third, only to be overhauled by Les Eisenhart of Port Clinton, O., inches from the finish line. Bowdoin's Alan Hillman was the trailer.

**DUGGER EQUALS MARK**

Ed Dugger, Tufts' I.C.4-A. high hurdles champion, now of Dayton, O., equaled the world indoor record of 5.6s. set here last year by Fred Wolcott, while leading that Texan by two feet in the final of the 45-yard timber topping. George Gilson of Holy Cross placed third and Walter Hall of Tufts was fourth.

Penn State's Norwood Ewell equaled the meet's record of 5.3s. in capturing the Briggs 50-yard special from Howard Caldwell of Amherst by inches. Sergt. Tom Carter of Ft. Devens, recent Pittsburgh star, gained the sprint's third honors.

Chuck Beetham of Columbus, O., cut a fifth of a second off his own Boston record by uncorking a terrific gun-lap sprint that carried him to the finish line a good 10 yards ahead of Roy Cochran

Turn to Page 12, Column 6

## Harbert in Texas Lead

### Youngster Has Total of 137 for 36 Holes; Byron Nelson Fires 67

SAN ANTONIO, Feb. 14. (AP)—Professional golf's doughty sophomore, Melvin (Chick) Harbert of Battle Creek, Mich., led the Texas open golf tournament at the end of 36 holes today — and well deserved it—but there's another guy and another story.

It doesn't concern Harbert, who carved a 69 out of Willow Springs under trying conditions for his halfway total of 137 that outdid the field by three strokes. It is the story of Lord Byron Nelson, the Texas boy now of Toledo, who was National Open titlist two years ago.

**WHAT A ROUND!**

The freckled Texan had a 67. He didn't have a putt of more than 15 feet for a birdie. He missed a 14-inch putt and he three-putted one green from a mere 10 feet.

"Today's round goes up there with the 66 I had at Augusta, Ga., in 1937 as the finest round I ever played," said Nelson as he walked off the home green, "and in that 66 I had 34 putts."

The 67 today gave Nelson a 141 total—good for a share of third place with Herman Keiser of Akron, O., who tacked a 70 to his opening 71.

**SNEAD SECOND**

Second to Harbert was Slammin' Samuel Jackson Snead — who had a 69 despite a spectator's ill-timed shout on the 16th green which made him miss a 3-foot putt—and Sam Byrd of Ardmore, Pa., both with 140. Snead was working on a first-round 70, while Byrd had a great 68 today.

Nelson played in company with Bing Crosby and Jimmy Demaret.

Crooner Crosby's game suffered and he had 83 for a 160, but Demaret, another Texan now of Detroit, was sharp for his 71 and 145 total.

**HARBERT UNDER PAR**

Harbert, 27 next week, fashioned a 3-under-par 33 on the outgoing nine and then drew the gallery by grabbing birdies at the 10th and 11th to go 5 under.

But over on the long 14th, par 4 hole, he faded his tee shot out of bounds and wound up with 6. On the 18th, still 3 under, he pushed his tee shot to an island in the middle of a creek, played beautifully out 180 yards to the left of the green but failed to get close enough for his par putt. He was just missing greens all the way around but laying them dead on chip shots.

Leading scorers:

| | |
|---|---|
| Melvin Harbert, Battle Creek, Mich. | 68-69—137 |
| Sam Snead, Hot Springs, Va. | 71-69—140 |
| Sam Byrd, Ardmore, Pa. | 72-68—140 |
| Herman Keiser, Akron, O. | 71-70—141 |
| Byron Nelson, Toledo, O. | 74-67—141 |
| Ben Hogan, Hershey, Pa. | 70-71—141 |
| Jimmy Thomson, Del Monte, Cal. | 72-70—142 |
| E. J. Harrison, Chicago | 67-75—142 |
| Lloyd Mangrum, Chicago | 69-73—142 |
| x-Johnny Dawson, Hollywood | 71-71—142 |
| Henry Ransom, Philadelphia | 71-71—142 |
| Jim Milward, Madison, Wis. | 73-70—143 |
| Lawson Little, San Francisco | 72-71—143 |
| Joe Brown, Des Moines | 70-74—144 |
| Jimmy Gauntt, Longview, Tex. | 72-72—144 |
| Jack Grout, West Pittson, Pa. | 68-77—145 |
| Jimmy Demaret, Detroit | 74-71—145 |
| Willie Goggin, New York | 71-74—145 |
| Leland Gibson, Kansas City | 70-75—145 |
| Chandler Harper, Portsmouth, Va. | 73-72—145 |

x—Amateur

## Sabin, Skeen Reach Finals of Net Play

WEST PALM BEACH (Fla.) Feb. 14. (U.P.)—Little Wayne Sabin of Reno, Nev., entered his bid for a third Florida championship today by defeating Bruce Barnes of Houston, Tex., 6-3, 6-4, 6-4, in the semifinal round of the $1000 Gulf Stream professional tennis tournament.

Dick Skeen, third-seeded player from Beverly Hills, Cal., ranked second nationally, hit his stride for the first time in the Florida professional circuit to defeat Bob Harmon of Oakland, Cal., and advance to the finals. Skeen took the sets, 9-7, 6-3, 6-2.

In the doubles semifinals Welby Van Horn and Sabin defeated Walter Senior, West Palm Beach, and Jan Zozeluh, Ft. Lauderdale, 8-6, 8-6, 6-4. They will play Barnes and Harmon tomorrow.

BEATEN AGAIN—Here's Alsab, 1941 juvenile champion, running fourth in yesterday's feature at Hialeah. In his second race as a 3-year-old, Alsab finished seven lengths behind Bright Willie (2,) Sir War (1) and Incoming (3.) Alsab also was out of the money last time.

(AP) Wirephoto

1943
1952

WORLD WAR II VIRTUALLY SHUT DOWN SPORTS IN AMERICA. THE HEAVYWEIGHT BOXING CHAMPIONSHIP was frozen for the duration while Joe Louis served in the armed forces. All major auto racing was suspended from 1942 through 1945. Baseball continued, but with most good players in military service, the quality of the sport suffered drastically.

All major golf championships were canceled, as was Wimbledon, the most important tennis tournament in the world. Not even the Olympic Games, a sports festival dedicated to peace and goodwill, could survive the fighting. The Games of 1940 and 1944 were canceled.

However the Kentucky Derby went on as scheduled during the war years, and in 1943 Count Fleet became the sixth horse to win the triple crown (Derby, Preakness, and Belmont Stakes). John Longden and Eddie Arcaro were the leading jockeys of the era.

When the war ended, sports rebounded bigger, better, and more popular than ever. Ringside spectators paid a record hundred dollars for a seat to see Louis knock out Billy Conn in the eighth round of his first postwar fight on June 19, 1946, at Yankee Stadium.

Ted Williams, who like many athletes missed three seasons due to the war, hit two home runs to lead the American League to a 12–0 victory in the 1946 All-Star baseball game. In the same year Cleveland star Bob Feller pitched a no-hit game against the Yankees and set a season record by striking out 348 batters. The Cleveland Rams of the National Football League moved to Los Angeles in 1946 and in 1951 brought the city its first professional championship by beating the Cleveland Browns.

A former UCLA athlete, Jackie Robinson, played second base for Brooklyn in 1947 and became the first black player in major league history. And before the season ended, black players were used in the American League for the first time.

The 1947 World Series between the Yankees and Dodgers featured one of the most exciting games in the history of the event. Floyd (Bill) Bevens of the Yankees pitched a no-hit game for eight and two-thirds innings but lost it, 3–2, on a double by Cookie Lavagetto, the Dodgers' only hit.

The Olympic Games, held for the first time in twelve years, returned to London in 1948 while the city was still rationing food and war damage was visible. The Olympic Village was a former Royal Air Force base; the athletes slept in barracks.

Mel Patton, the United States' best sprinter from the University of Southern California, finished fifth in the 100-meter dash but won the 200 meters. The most memorable moment of the 1948 Games came when Bob Mathias, a seventeen-year-old schoolboy from Tulare, California, won the decathlon. Competition on the second day of the event started at 10:00 A.M. and continued until 10:30 P.M. Flashlights were used so Mathias and other contestants could see to throw the javelin and pole vault.

In one of the finest performances in any Olympic Games, Fanny Blankers-Koen of Holland won four gold medals in track and field, winning the 100- and 200-meter dashes, the 80-meter hurdles, and leading her 400-meter relay team to victory.

The Soviet Union, isolated from the capitalist sports world for forty years, entered an Olympic team at Helsinki, Finland, in 1952, for the first time since it competed at Stockholm in 1912, and immediately the United States' domination of the Olympics was threatened. The USSR, in fact, won sixty-eight medals and claimed, by a point system based on all medals in all events, a "team victory" in what was designed as an individual competition. The use of sports as political propaganda began. Germany and Japan, barred from the 1948 Games, were allowed to compete in 1952.

The United States dominated track and field events at Helsinki, winning fourteen of twenty-four events and setting ten records. Bob Mathias again won the decathlon, but the star of the show was Emil Zatopek of Czechoslovakia, who won the 5,000 and 10,000 meters and the marathon.

In 1949, and for the first time since 1937, the world had a new heavyweight boxing champion. Joe Louis retired and Ezzard Charles won the title by beating Jersey Joe Walcott on a fifteen-round decision. Louis came out of retirement the following year, but Charles beat him in fifteen rounds to keep the championship. By 1952 the title had changed hands twice, Walcott winning it from Charles and Rocky Marciano taking it away from Walcott.

Two more great thoroughbreds, Assault in 1946 and Citation in 1948, won horse racing's triple crown.

All the news of this newsy era was not good news, however. Jockey George Woolf was killed in an accident at Santa Anita in 1946, and race driver Rex Mays died in a crash at Del Mar in 1949. Babe Ruth said goodbye to New York baseball fans at Yankee Stadium in June of 1948 and died two months later. A major fire gutted the Hollywood Park racetrack in 1949.

| EAST-WEST | | SUGAR BOWL | | COTTON BOWL | | ORANGE BOWL | | SUN BOWL | |
|---|---|---|---|---|---|---|---|---|---|
| East | 13 | Tennessee | 14 | Texas | 14 | Alabama | 37 | 2nd Air Force | 13 |
| West | 12 | Tulsa | 7 | Georgia Tech | 7 | Boston Col. | 21 | Hardin-Simmons | 7 |

# Georgia Team Called Great in Action Packed Tilt

## Sport Postscripts

By PAUL ZIMMERMAN

If you think directing a visiting Rose Bowl team is all beer and skittles, you should have worn the shoes of Coach Wallace Butts, the Georgia grid master, and made his rounds here for the 10 days prior to the classic that took place yesterday.

Personally, if it were our assignment, we would ask the university authorities for a staff composed of a lawyer, social secretary, ticket agent, public relations council, bodyguard, chauffeur, private detective, valet and the customary assistant coaches and team trainer.

**SOME GUY**

Taking it on his own, as this good-natured Georgian has done, a fellow should be a combination of Chamber of Commerce delegate, orator, movie and radio actor, politician, opera singer, psychologist and gourmand. Also a football coach.

Of course, a guy can turn his back on everyone, shut his ears to all pleas, don a pair of smoked glasses, cut the telephone line and lock the world out entirely. We've had a Rose Bowl coach or two wh› did that. But Coach Butts wouldn't be that kind of a guy.

When he stepped off the train in Pasadena a week ago Monday afternoon he announced his platform.

**COUNTRY BOY**

"First of all," said Wally, "I have a football coaching job to be done.

"But I also want youall to be my friends. I don't want to make anyone mad at me. I'm just a country boy in the big town for the first time and I want to do the right thing—just so I get a chance to coach my football team."

Now, you can't hate a coach like that. And he lived up to his word to the limit. If you think not, follow Wally through the 10 days prior to yesterday's game.

**BLUE MONDAY**

Monday, Dec. 21 — Train arrives four hours late. Greeted by swarm of photographers and reporters at train. Pursued by reporters and photographers to hotel. Finally gets to his hotel rooms. Sends his clothes out to be pressed. Answers continuous stream of telephone calls from people seeking tickets, proposing publicity stunts, suggesting promotion gags, offering scout reports, suggesting scoring plays. Meets with Rose Tournament Committee after dinner. Blue Monday for sure.

Tuesday, Dec. 22—Two practice sessions. Second given over to photographers and newsreel men. Poses every way imaginable.

Wednesday, Dec. 23—Actually gets to coach team. Gets evening off, too. Worries over Sinkwich's injuries.

Thursday, Dec. 24—Two practice sessions. Poses for Christmas Eve pictures. Makes banquet speech. Interviewed on radio program.

**LOVE FEAST**

Friday, Dec. 25.—Practice. Christmas dinner and team party. More pictures. More radio.

Saturday, Dec. 26—Practice. Studio trip. Breaks bread with rival U.C.L.A. coaches at dinner.

Sunday, Dec. 27—No rest. Practice. Attends Pro All-Star-March Field grid game.

Monday, Dec. 28—Practice. Does raft of recordings for broadcast by short wave to armed forces.

Tuesday, Dec. 29—More recordings for service programs. U.C.L.A. alumni luncheon speech. Practice. Rose Bowl open house in evening.

Wednesday Dec. 30—Speech at Breakfast Club. Speech at Kickoff luncheon. Personal appearance on Kay Kyser's radio program. Oh, yes, and grid practice in the afternoon. Wonders what ails his stomach.

Thursday, Dec. 31—Lull before storm. Gets acquainted with team again. Worries about game. Treats strained vocal chords. Fasts to recover from gastronomical disturbances resulting from enforced "rubber

Turn to Page 13, Column 6

KICK BLOCKED—Here is Willard (Red) Boyd, Georgia tackle, blocking Bob Waterfield's punt on the first play of the fourth quarter. The ball bounded out of the end zone for an automatic safety and two points. Riddle is No. 22. Behind Waterfield is Poschner, Georgia end, who helped to rush the Bruin kicker.

Times photo by Charley Strite

## Game Thrills 90,000 Fans

### U.C.L.A. Considered Lucky to Hold Score Down to 9 Points

BY BRAVEN DYER

The chap who wrote "Georgia on My Mind" must have been thinking about the great Dixie football team which defeated U.C.L.A., 9 to 0, yesterday in the famed Rose Bowl.

Certain it is that none of the 90,000 exhausted spectators who sat in on yesterday's superthriller ever will forget the smashing sons of the South.

For sustained action there never has been a Rose Bowl contest to equal this one. Nine points ordinarily would not indicate much offensive football but the slashing Bulldogs came so close to scoring on at least five the slashing Bulldogs came close to scoring on at least five other occasions.

**BRUINS LUCKY**

Seldom has a Rose Bowl team rolled up such a commanding margin in first downs (24 to 5) and yardage (373 to 159) and emerged with so few points on the scoreboard.

The Bruins can thank their lucky stars they got off as fortunately as they did.

Only their fighting hearts kept them in the ball game for three full quarters. In defeat, the U.C.L.A. fans can well be proud of the gallant stand which Babe Horrell's boys made yesterday afternoon. Nothing short of such dogged determination could have kept the score from mounting into the 20's or 30's.

The Bruins were mighty fortunate, for instance, that those sprained ankles prevented Coach Wally Butts from employing Frankie Sinkwich in the same backfield with Charley Trippi except for brief moments during the terrific battle.

**GREATEST COMBINATION**

It was difficult to imagine what might have happened to the Westwood lads had Fireball Frankie been physically sound. I'll venture the opinion that Sinkwich and Trippi together, when both are right, constitute one of the greatest two-man backfield combinations ever to trod the Rose Bowl turf.

Trippi was the spearhead of Georgia's brilliant attack. He ran the ball for 115 yards, or 18 more than the entire Bruin backfield could gain. His deadly passes punctured U.C.L.A.'s secondary defense with telling effect.

It was due largely to this sensational sophomore that Georgia had the ball most of the game, running off more than twice as many plays as the Bruins, 96 to 47. You can't win without the football and most of the time the Bulldogs wouldn't give it up until they were deep in Bruin territory.

**FRANKIE SCORED**

Sinkwich could hardly be called an important cog in Georgia's attack yesterday, but on several occasions he revealed the brand of football which brought him the nation's highest athletic honors. And it was Frankie who scored the clinching touchdown in the final quarter, driving over his own right tackle from the 5-foot mark.

Obviously in great pain because of his injured ankles, Sinkwich nevertheless displayed terrific drive on at least three occasions, once smashing through for eight yards and later for 13.

When he left the game at the end of the first half he limped so badly few expected him to return. But come back he did, determined to make up for the costly first-half fumble which prevented a Georgia score. When the supreme test came, Frankie showed the stuff of which champions are made by crashing over for the only touchdown of the game.

**ALMOST STOPPED**

Even then the battling Bruins almost stopped him, knocking Frankie back onto the playing field, but not until his forward progress had carried him into the end zone. Referee Landreth looked to the head linesman, Ralph Coleman, who signaled the touchdown.

Lamar Davis was almost as brilliant as Trippi. He came within one player (Waterfield) of returning the opening kickoff for a touchdown. Only Bob's deadly tackle stopped the Georgia flyer

Turn to Page 13, Column 3

## Tennessee Overpowers Tulsa Grid Team, 14-7

NEW ORLEANS, Jan. 1. (AP)—Tennessee overpowered Tulsa, 14-7, here today before an estimated Sugar Bowl crowd of 70,000 but the Oklahomans got off to a fast start and staged a blazing finish that might have tied the ball game except for a last-minute pass interception by Tennessee's end, Jim Powell.

In the dying seconds of the game, trailing by seven points, Tulsa's N. A. Keithley hit his ends with a pair of 17-yard passes to open a drive that carried from his own 40 to Tennessee's 29 and kept pitching them until he reached the 12 where Powell stopped the circus.

**TENNESSEE DRIVES**

Today's game was a case of too much Tennessee drive as the Vols came from behind to score a touchdown in the second and a safety in the third and came again for six points in the final period.

Big Bobby Cifers, tailback and Walter Slater, his alternate, were the Tennessee standouts, Cifers taking the fire out of Tulsa's punting with his own brilliant kicking and battering runbacks of Tulsa's kicks. He averaged about 15 yards on his returns.

The statistics gave Tulsa minus 39 yards running to Tennessee's 208. On the other hand the Tulsa Hurricane netted 168 yards in the air to Tennessee's 88.

**PASS TO SCORE**

This startling aerial strength exploded against Tennessee for the game's opening touchdown.

All-America Glenn Dobbs whipped five consecutive passes, four of them to Saxon, his end, without a miss. The barrage gained 57 yards and Clyde Leforce, Dobbs' substitute at tailback, hit Wingman Cal Purdin for the score. Leforce kicked point.

The thrust started late in the first period and ended early in the second.

Tennessee lashed back in the same period, carrying from its own 40 to a touchdown without giving up the ball.

**SLATER HURLS**

Slater's passing and running, coupled with the line-plunging of Bernard Gold, substitute fullback, plowed to the Tulsa 3 and Gold hurdled center for the touchdown. Charles Mitchell's attempted conversion was wide.

Slater led a second drive two minutes later, getting off two long passes for a total of 30 yards, then laying one in End Al Hust's hands in the end zone. But the officials had signaled the

Turn to Page 13, Column 7

## Tide Smashes Eagles, 37-21

### Alabama Rallies After Slow Start to Win Orange Bowl Thriller

MIAMI (Fla.) Jan. 1. (AP)—Sarasota is winter quarters of Ringling Bros.' Circus—but the greatest show on earth was right here in the Orange Bowl today as Alabama's Crimson Tide rolled back from apparent defeat to overwhelm Boston College, 37-21, before 30,000 football fans.

'Bama's crimson-shirted powerhouse, playing for the first time in this tropical bowl classic, spotted Boston 14 points in the first quarter before it got rolling. But when it did — when Russ Craft, Dave Brown, Johnny August and little Russ Mosley started digging up the turf—the best that Boston College could throw in its way wasn't enough to stop the Tide.

**TIDE GAMBLES**

'Bama scored thrice in the second quarter to once for the Eagles and with three minutes to play in the half, B.C. was leading, 21-19. But now the Tide was gambling.

Craft, on the ancient Statue of Liberty play, scooted 11 yards around left end for first down on B.C.'s 15. Russ Mosley pegged two short passes to Ends Samp Sharp and Babs Roberts to reach the 8, then missed an attempted pitch to Roberts for the touchdown.

**EAGLES STOPPED**

With 30 seconds left to play, and one shot left in the locker, 'Bama dropped back to the 15 for a field goal. George Hecht, guard, sent the ball spinning from placement directly through the uprights, and 'Bama led 22-21 as the half ended.

Eagle adherents hoped for a reversal in the last half, with All-America Mickey Holovak break-

Turn to Page 14, Column 2

Los Angeles Times Sports

SATURDAY, JANUARY 2, 1943

## Texas Line Powers Over Georgia Tech by 14-7

DALLAS, Jan. 1. (AP)—Texas' massive line beat Georgia Tech into the Cotton Bowl turf for three quarters today and the Yellow Jackets' rally in the final minutes paid off with only one touchdown as the Southeastern Conference team lost to the Longhorns, 14-7.

It was a thrilling battle of long runs and many passes but the real story was in the play of Texas' forward wall that battered the Techs from goal line to goal line while the Longhorns' halfbacks ripped and tore their way to touchdowns in the first and third periods.

A crowd of 36,000—much larger than expected—watched Texas, Southwest Conference champion, play one of its best games.

**CASTLEBERRY STOPPED**

Texas stopped Clint Castleberry, Tech freshman star, practically cold and the speedy Longhorn backs rolled up 201 yards from scrimmage.

Texas scored on a 52-yard drive in the first period. Joe Schwarting, brilliant Longhorn wingman, recovered Pat McHugh's fumble to set up the score. McKay pitched two passes to Wally Scott to send the ball to the Tech 29.

Jackie Field, Roy McKay and Max Minor alternated in smashing the line down to the Georgians' 4. McKay tried guard for 1, then passed over the goal line where Castleberry bunted the ball into Minor's hands for a touchdown. Field kicked the point.

The next Texas touchdown was the most sensational play of the game—a dodging, twisting 60-yard run by the fleet Field.

Jackie took a punt on the Texas 40 and ran straight down the field with only one Georgia Tech hand being laid on him. He crossed the goal line with five Longhorns running interference.

**67-YARD DRIVE**

The Tech score was the climax of a 67-yard surge. From the Georgia 33 Castleberry and Bobby Sheldon took cracks at the line to advance 10 yards. Sheldon then uncorked a pass to Jack Marshall who ripped his way to the Texas 24. Castleberry picked up 2 at the line.

Then he slanted one of his left-handed passes to Jack Helms who took it for 16 yards. Three plunges made only 3 yards but Dave Eldredge resurrected the statue-of-liberty play to whip around left end for a touchdown. Bob Jordan converted.

Tech came pounding back to drive to the Texas 3 with only

Turn to Page 13, Column 4

## Bowl Gives Red Cross $50,000

Following the Rose Bowl game, officials of U.C.L.A., Georgia, the Pacific Coast Conference and the Tournament of Roses joined in announcing a gift of $50,000 to the Red Cross. The gift was announced in a telegram sent to Norman H. Davis, Red Cross chairman, at Washington, D.C. It said:

"We wish to give the National Red Cross $50,000 from the proceeds of the New Year's Rose Bowl football game."

Chairman Davis' acceptance on behalf of the Red Cross was received two hours later.

## Eastern All-Stars Nip Western Eleven, 13-12

SAN FRANCISCO, Jan. 1. (AP)—A smooth-operating band of college all-stars brought the East its first football triumph over the West in five years today, edging out the Westerners, 13 to 12, in a spine-tingling charity game before a near-capacity crowd of 58,000 in Kezar Stadium.

The two teams, evenly matched, played a brand of football as wide open as a church door, and it was anybody's ball game until the final gun. The West had power aplenty on the hoof and the East had the edge in fleetness afoot, but both outfits took to the air early in this 18th annual Shrine classic and yardage was reeled off in spectacular fashion.

**PASSERS SPARKLE**

Two great opposing passers, Columbia's Paul Governali for the East and Washington State's Bob Kennedy for the West, turned in handsome jobs. Governali tossed one touchdown pass and paved the way for the East's second score on another aerial thrust. Kennedy, passing fiercely all afternoon, scored on a lateral and passed a long one later to set up his team's second tally.

It was a matter of failures at the try for point after touchdown that gave the East its first win over the West since 1937 when Princeton's Ken Sandback kicked a field goal for a 3-0 victory.

**WESTERNERS TRICKY**

Speed and aerial trickery were supposedly the East's main stock in trade, as against the West's bulk, but the way the not-so-famous Westerners tossed the ball around and cut fancy capers from their strategic T formation had the Easterners back on their heels much of the game and forced them to fight to the last minute to preserve their narrow edge.

This is the way the touchdown-a-period scoring went:

First quarter—Midway in the period Steve Filipowicz, Fordham's Mr. Five By Five fullback, cut through the line for 14 yards to the West 34. Governali then unleashed a beautiful long pass to End Dave Schreiner of Wisconsin, who pulled the ball out of the sky over the goal line with Westerners swarming about him. Al Klug, substitute tackle from Marquette, booted the important place kick to make it 7-0.

**JURKOVICH PASSES**

Second quarter—The West, finding the Eastern line a little tough, began to shoot passes, California's Jim Jurkovich and Kennedy doing the tossing. This

Turn to Page 14, Column 4

## Bombers Down Hardin-Simmons

### 2nd Air Force Rallies in Final Period to Take Sun Bowl Game, 13-7

EL PASO (Tex.) Jan. 1. (AP) Outplayed during the first half and trailing for more than three quarters of the game, the red-white-and-blue-clad Bombers of the 2nd Air Force came from behind in the Sun Bowl today to score a battering 13-7 victory over the wily Border Conference champions of Hardin-Simmons University.

**MOBLEY INTERCEPTS**

An overflow crowd of nearly 16,000 contributed the proceeds of the game to service relief funds.

The Cowboys from the plains of West Texas, sparked by a freshman fullback named Camp Wilson and little Doc Mobley at half, swarmed over the burly Bombers in the second quarter and went into a 7-0 lead with Wilson scoring over his left tackle.

Mobley, the nation's leading ground gainer this season, set up the Cowboy tally when he intercepted a pass by Billy Sewell, Washington State's passing star last season, and romped 66 yards to the Air Force 9-yard line. Hardin-Simmons failed to score then, but after the Bombers punted out to their 29, big Camp Wilson rammed over the goal line on the next play on a 29-yard ride.

**PENALTIES HELP**

In the third, however, the Bombers came back after a 52-yard punt by Sewell set the Cowhands back on their heels. Big Vic Spadaccini, now a lieutenant in the Air Forces but for three years fullback at Minnesota and later with the Cleveland Rams, steamed over from the 1-yard stripe. Capt. Al Bodney, a Tulane product, missed the conversion and the Cowboys still led.

The Bomber offensive went into gear in the fourth, aided by

Turn to Page 12, Column 1

# COUNT FLEET CAPTURES KENTUCKY DERBY

## The Sports Parade

By BRAVEN DYER

There are so many outstanding performers in the latest version of the Ice-Capades that each is worth almost a complete column. As skilled athletic entertainers they are tops in their profession. Only after years of constant practice have they attained such proficiency and only by keeping in shape are they able to maintain their perfection and popularity.

Take the cute little Ice-Capets, for instance. They skate in at least eight shows per week and also rehearse two or three times. Skating makes 'em hungry and eating adds weight. They jump on the scales twice each week and if there's a bulge on the wrong side of the indicator that's bad news for the cuties. No more dessert, girlies.

The Ice-Capets buy their own skates, costing around $23 per pair and also buy their own made-to-order skating boots which cost $35. Generally the girls wear out two pairs of skates per season.

**SKATING ONE YEAR**

Martha (Trixie) Firschie, the amazingly cute and efficient little juggler, started her career at the age of 10 in Vienna. She has toured 27 countries and came to the United States in 1938. It was just one year ago that she began doing her act on skates. To watch her you'd think she had been born with 'em on.

Pert Donna Atwood may become more popular than Sonja Henie, Belita or any of the others who have had top billing for years. The 18-year-old redhead has everything in her favor. She's cute, doesn't mind hard work, has youth on her side and already has displayed enough ability to presage a brilliant career.

**IMAGINE THAT**

On opening night at the Pan-Pacific Donna took one spill. She did it gracefully, once she found it was inevitable. Only it happened right in front of John Harris, Mr. Big of the show. Donna wrinkled her nose, smiled and said: "Imagine seeing you here, Mr. Harris."

Red McCarthy's popularity is a tribute to long years of practice. He started his skating career carrying a sign which advertised chocolate nut candy bars. Red skated so fast nobody could read what was on his shirt, so they fired him and Red became a speed champion. He's cracked up so many times and broken so many bones he long ago lost count.

**LITTLE SHAVER**

The kids, of course, will chuckle at Chuckie Stein, the midget who has such a difficult time carrying my lady's lengthy train, after first appearing in the role of a mouse. Chuckie is just under four feet tall, weighs 62 pounds and is 22 years of age. This season marks his pro debut.

Eighteen men with the show last season are now in the service. Phil Taylor was in the last war. His stilt skating tops anything ever tried in this field. Megan Taylor, his daughter, won the world's figure skating title in 1939.

Life begins at well past 40 for those "Old Smoothies," who glide their way into your hearts with their graceful act. Orrin Markhus and Irma Thomas, they are, and the ease with which they cover the rink is a lesson to those who make hard work of everything they try to do.

Eleanor O'Meara is a charming Canadian girl who is making her professional debut right here in Los Angeles. Those of us who have seen her skate can vision a brilliant future for the young lady.

**ALL THE ANSWERS**

If there's something special you want to know about figure skating, ballroom skating or anything tricky on ice just get in touch with Bob Dench and his wife, Rosemarie. They've written a book on ice skating and it has all the answers. British born, they came to America in 1938 and they've been here ever since. Bob expects to join the British Air Force soon, although he's too old for combat duty.

That blond ballerina, Vera Hruba, was five times figure skating champion of Czechoslovakia. Vera gets better every time she appears here. The chic Czech cuts a cute caper.

**STAR BOWLER**

Bernie Lynam, who does that hilariously funny stunt on skis, is one of the best athletes in the huge cast. He tops 'em all at bowling, seldom dropping below the 250 mark. He lost his partner, Larry Jackson, to Uncle Sam and may go himself before long.

Among the cuddly (I was only told) Ice-Capets is Mercedes Wheeler from Wichita. Most versatile of all the "line" girls, Mercedes is a fancy diver, played basketball and tennis in high school and high-jumped. Right now Mercedes wants to try her hand at golf.

One fine feature of the show is Tom Barry, the commentator. And you don't need grandma's ear trumpet to know what he's talking about.

AT THE FINISH—Here's the overhead finish of the 69th running of the Kentucky Derby with Count Fleet winning by three lengths from Blue Swords and Slide Rule another six lengths back. Mrs. John Hertz's son of Reigh Count ran the mile and a quarter in 2:04, paid $2.80 to-win and picked up $60,725. (AP) Wirephoto

Los Angeles Times Sports

SUNDAY MORNING, MAY 2, 1943

## ANGELS SLAP STARS, 11-8, COP SERIES

### Eight Pitchers Yield 35 Hits as Seraphs Overcome Five-Run Deficit in 10 Innings

BY AL WOLF

There's nothing dead about the balls Los Angeles and Hollywood are using in their current series at Gilmore Field—but we're not so sure about the pitchers.

Thirty-five hits rattled off the bats yesterday as the Seraphs won, 11-8, in 10 innings, the second overtime tussle in as many days.

Eight flingers flung, four on each side, as the Angels banged 18 safeties, including a homer by Johnny Ostrowski, and the Twinks bagged 17, including a round-tripper by Roy Younkers. That made it an aggregate of 134 base blows in the five games between the cross-town rivals.

**Padres Win, Too**

Yesterday's triumph assured the Cherubs of their second straight triumphant series of the season and kept them abreast of San Diego, which downed Portland in another extra-inning fray.

The engagement closes this afternoon with the customary Sabbath double-header. Play starts earlier, at 1 o'clock, because the Seraphs have to catch an early train for the Northwest. Manager Charley Root and Bill Thomas will toss for the home forces against Ken Raffensberger and Paul Gehrman.

Hollywood got off to a 5-0 lead in the first two frames yesterday, knocking Don Osborn out of the box early in the initial inning, and still held a comfortable 7-3 lead after five panels by socking Oren Baker freely, too.

**Erautt Blows Up**

But in the sixth Eddie Erautt blew up and the count was tied before Pappy Joiner could get the side out.

Ostrowski's limit larrup put the Angels ahead in the top of the eighth, but the Stars evened it again in the last half when Johnny Dickshot's "sure out" bounder with two away suddenly bounced over Roy Hughes' head and brought in Art Lilly from third.

In the tenth, though, the Seraphs pounded the tar out of Pat McLaughlin, who pitched like he was throwing the 16-pound shot. Four hits off McLaughlin and one off Ronnie Smith provided three tallies and gave the Sweeneys their fourth win in five games with the Roots.

McLaughlin was charged with the defeat, while Pete Mallory, No. 3 in the Angel

Turn to Page 16, Column 4

## Padres Humble Beavers, 4-3

SAN DIEGO, May 1. (AP)—San Diego combined two hits in the 11th inning to defeat Portland, 4 to 3, today and remain in a tie with Los Angeles for the Coast League lead. It was the third 11-inning victory for the Padres over the Beavers this week.

Jensen led off the 11th by walking. Walter Lowe doubled, and Jensen was called out at the plate in trying to score on the double. Lowe moved to third after Jack Calvey and Morry Abbott were intentionally passed, Jack Whipple, batting for Al Olsen, singled to bring Lowe home with the deciding marker.

Forrest Orrell, losing pitcher, held the Padres hitless until the fifth inning, when they scored two runs.

The Beavers scored a run in the seventh to tie up the game. They went ahead in the eighth when Jack O'Neill singled and scored on Ted Gullic's one-bagger.

The Padres tied the score in their half of the eighth on two singles, a sacrifice, a walk and a fly by Swede Jensen.

| PORTLAND | AB | H | O | A |
|---|---|---|---|---|
| O'Neill,ss | 5 | 1 | 5 | 5 |
| Th'pson,rf | 5 | 1 | 0 | 0 |
| Rogers,2b | 4 | 1 | 2 | 2 |
| Gullic,cf | 5 | 1 | 3 | 1 |
| Barton,1b | 5 | 1 | 11 | 0 |
| Owen,3b | 4 | 1 | 0 | 3 |
| Gill,lf | 4 | 0 | 6 | 0 |
| East'w'd,c | 4 | 2 | 4 | 2 |
| Orrell,p | 4 | 0 | 0 | 2 |
| Totals | 40 | 8 | b31 | 15 |

| SAN DIEGO | AB | H | O | A |
|---|---|---|---|---|
| Whe'ler,2b | 2 | 0 | 1 | 2 |
| McD'ld,1b | 4 | 0 | 12 | 1 |
| Pat'ett,cf | 4 | 1 | 4 | 0 |
| Salkeld,c | 4 | 1 | 2 | 0 |
| Jensen,lf | 4 | 0 | 4 | 0 |
| Lowe,3b | 4 | 1 | 2 | 1 |
| Calvey,ss | 4 | 1 | 6 | 4 |
| Abbott,rf | 3 | 1 | 1 | 0 |
| Olsen,p | 3 | 0 | 1 | 2 |
| Ball'ger,a | 1 | 0 | 0 | 0 |
| C'teaux,2b | 2 | 1 | 0 | 3 |
| Morgan,z | 0 | 0 | 0 | 0 |
| Whi'ple,aa | 1 | 1 | 0 | 0 |
| Totals | 46 | 7 | 33 | 13 |

b—One out when winning run scored.
a—Batted for Wheeler in 5th.
aa—Batted for Olsen in 11th.
z—Ran for Ballinger in 5th.

SCORE BY INNINGS

Portland ..... 0 1 0 0 0 0 0 1 1 0 0 0—3
San Diego .... 0 0 0 0 2 0 0 1 0 0 1—4

SUMMARY

Error—O'Neill. Runs responsible for—Olsen, 3; Orrell, 4. Bases on balls—Off Olsen, 3; Orrell, 8. Struck out—By Olsen, 2; Orrell, 4. Left on bases—Portland, 7; San Diego, 11. Two-base hits—Barton, Easterwood, Abbott, Rogers, Lowe. Sacrifice—McDonald. Stolen base—Patchett. Runs batted in—Gill, Ballinger, McDonald, Easterwood, Gullic, Jensen, Whipple. Double plays—Caillteaux to Calvey to McDonald; O'Neill to Barton. Time of game—2h. 20m. Umpires—Hood and Widner.

## RACING FANS BET $5,803,120

NEW YORK, May 1. (AP)—Although many turf followers had difficulty in getting to their favorite betting booths today, an estimated 124,279 did find their way to the tracks and wagered $5,803,120 at six ovals.

| Track | Betting | Attendance |
|---|---|---|
| Churchill Downs | $1,081,899 | *60,000 |
| Jamaica ........ | 1,934,863 | 27,608 |
| Pimlico ........ | 862,571 | 17,171 |
| Narragansett ... | 735,780 | *18,000 |
| Bay Meadows ... | 412,000 | * 8,000 |
| Beulah Park .... | 56,007 | * 3,500 |
| Totals ........ | $5,803,120 | 124,279 |

*—Estimated.

## Arsenal Gunners Win Before 75,000

LONDON, May 1. (AP) — The Arsenal Gunners today won the League South football cup and set up a scoring record for Wembley Stadium by whipping Charlton Athletic, 7-1, before a crowd of 75,000 including members of the War Cabinet.

## Tigers Score in 15th to Nip Tribe, 3 to 2

DETROIT, May 1. (AP)—Rookie Dick Wakefield lined a single to left field in the 15th inning today to score Roger Cramer from third base and give the Detroit Tigers a 3-to-2 victory over the Cleveland Indians.

Cramer, who had doubled off 38-year-old Joe Heving to open the sixth extra frame, moved up on a sacrifice by Ned Harris. Manager Lou Boudreau rushed in Lefty Al Smith to pitch to Wakefield, $52,000 beauty, but the rookie hammered a three-two pitch to break up the game.

The victory, fourth straight for Detroit, dropped the Indians out of joint possession of the American League lead with the New York Yankees, who beat Washington. The Tigers and Indians now are tied for second, just a notch ahead of the Senators.

The Tigers gathered 12 hits off three of four Cleveland pitchers while Hal White and Paul (Dizzy) Trout limited the Indians to eight. But Cleveland outfielders twice threw Pinky Higgins out at the plate before the end came in the 15th.

| CLEVELAND | AB | H | O | A |
|---|---|---|---|---|
| Hock't,cf | 7 | 2 | 3 | 1 |
| B'dreau,ss | 6 | 1 | 7 | 4 |
| Keltn'r,3b | 5 | 1 | 0 | 6 |
| Heath,lf | 6 | 0 | 0 | 0 |
| Cul'bine,rf | 5 | 2 | 0 | 1 |
| Den'ng,1b | 6 | 1 | 15 | 2 |
| Mack,2b | 6 | 0 | 5 | 7 |
| Des'tels,c | 1 | 0 | 2 | 3 |
| Edwards,x | 1 | 0 | 0 | 0 |
| Rosar,c | 4 | 0 | 9 | 1 |
| Ken'dy,p | 1 | 0 | 1 | 0 |
| Naynick,p | 0 | 0 | 0 | 1 |
| Dean,xx | 0 | 0 | 0 | 0 |
| Heving,p | 3 | 1 | 1 | 2 |
| Smith,p | 0 | 0 | 0 | 0 |
| Totals | 51 | 8 | y43 | 28 |

| DETROIT | AB | H | O | A |
|---|---|---|---|---|
| Cram'r,cf | 6 | 1 | 5 | 0 |
| Harris,rf | 5 | 0 | 5 | 0 |
| Wakef'd,lf | 7 | 2 | 1 | 0 |
| York,1b | 6 | 2 | 17 | 3 |
| Higgins,3b | 4 | 2 | 1 | 3 |
| Bl'dw'h,2b | 2 | 1 | 3 | 5 |
| Hoover,ss | 5 | 1 | 5 | 4 |
| Rich'ds,c | 5 | 1 | 3 | 2 |
| White,p | 4 | 1 | 2 | 3 |
| Radcliff,z | 1 | 1 | 0 | 0 |
| Parsons,c | 0 | 0 | 1 | 0 |
| Trout,p | 2 | 0 | 2 | 1 |
| Totals | 47 | 12 | 45 | 21 |

y—One out when winning run scored.
x—Batted for Desautels in 5th.
xx—Batted for Naymick in 5th.
z—Batted for Richards in 14th.

SCORE BY INNINGS

Cleveland ...... 000 020 000 000 000—2
Detroit ........ 020 000 000 000 001—3

SUMMARY

Error—Mack. Runs batted in—Hoover, White, Wakefield, Hockett, 2. Two-base hits—Bloodworth, Boudreau, Cramer. Stolen base—Bloodworth. Sacrifices—Bloodworth, 2; Higgins, Harris. Double plays—Boudreau to Mack to Denning; Mack to Boudreau to Denning. Left on bases—Cleveland, 7; Detroit, 11. Bases on balls—Off Kennedy, 1; Naymick, 1; Heving, 4; White, 1; Trout, 2. Struck out—By Naymick, 1; Heving, 5; White, 2; Heving, 2. Hits—Off Kennedy, 6 in 2 innings (none out in 3rd;) Naymick, 0 in 2; Heving, 5 in 10 1-3; Smith, 1 in 0 (pitched to one batter in 15th;) White, 5 in 10; Trout, 3 in 5. Wild pitch—Trout. Winning pitcher—Trout. Losing pitcher—Heving. Umpires—Weaver, Rue and Pipgras. Time of game—2h. 48m. Attendance (paid,) 3425.

## TROY SPIKEMEN TOP U.C.L.A. TEAM, 71-60

### S.C. Hands Bruins Tenth Straight Loss but Weak Spots Indicate Loss to Bears Saturday

BY JOHN DE LA VEGA

A University of Southern California track squad that is only a shadow of the usual Trojan juggernauts edged out U.C.L.A., 71-60, in their annual meet at the Coliseum yesterday, but in triumph S.C. displayed such glaring weaknesses that it will be a minor miracle if they can get over California next Saturday.

True, S.C. chalked up its 10th straight win over the Westwoods without the services of two certain first-place winners, Shot-putter Ron Thomas and Half-miler Paul Iacono. Thomas has a sprained finger and Iacono has a cold.

**Off Form**

But the startling facts of the day were that even the supposed topnotchers on the S.C. squad are still a long way from top form, as indicated by the winning times and distances.

Best marks of the afternoon were turned in by Trojans Edsel Curry and Doug Miller, in the broad jump and javelin. Curry hopped 23ft. 8in., while Miller tossed the javelin 188ft. 1in. Both efforts are their best of the season.

Cliff Bourland, who was ailing with an aggravated sinus most of the week, was allowed to enter the 100 and he came through with an eyelash victory over Teammate Jim Jenkins. The time was only 10.1s., however.

**Weak Spots**

S.C. did even worse than expected in the distances; U.C.L.A. took 25 of the possible 27 digits in the 880, mile and two-mile. Craig Tyler and Mode Perry ran one, two in the half; Densmore and Perry outstepped Trojan Field Berry in the mile and S.C. didn't even have an entry in the two-mile.

Other Trojan soft spots were the high jump and pole vault, in which Harley Tinkham was S.C.'s lone representative. He cleared only 5ft. 11in. in the jump which was good enough for a tie for first, and vaulted but 11ft. 6in.

The mile relay proved the best competitive event, with Anchorman Bruce Miller making up 10 yards on Bruin Ken Boyd in the stretch to win going away. Had

Turn to Page 17, Column 2

## Bear Trackmen Wallop Fresno

BERKELEY, May 1. (AP)—The University of California track team defeated Fresno State, 111 to 20, today in a dual meet. Carlson, leaping 13ft. 6in. in the pole vault, gave Fresno its only first place. A crowd of 2000 saw the events.

Ralph Dewey, California distance man, won both the mile and the two-mile.

Hal Davis, California, beat Peyton Jordan of St. Mary's Pre-flight in the 100-yard dash, running it in 9.6s.

Jordan, who ran by special invitation and did not figure in the scoring, defeated Davis last week.

The summary:

Mile run—Dewey (C.,) Ring (C.,) McCarthy (C.) Time, 4m. 20.4s.

440-yard dash—Dunn (C.,) Prader (C.,) Baker (F.) Time, 49.6s.

100-yard dash—Davis (C.,) Jurkovich (C.,) Hunt F.) Time, 9.6s.

120-yard high hurdles—Angelich (C.,) Smith (C.,) Waldron (C.) Time, 14.9s.

880-yard run—Klemmer (C.,) Shropshire (F.,) Stone (C.) Time, 1m. 53.9s.

220-yard dash—Davis (C.,) Hunt (F.,) Ribisi (C.) Time, 21.2s.

Two-mile run—Dewey (C.,) Kisling (F.,) Tom E. Gay (C.) Time, 9m. 33.2s.

220-yard low hurdles—Angelich (C.,) Smith (C.,) Waldron (C.) Time, 24.1s.

Mile relay—California (Davis, Stone, Prader, Dunn.) Time, 3m. 26.4s.

Pole vault—Carlson (F.,) 13ft. 6in.; Croswird (C.,) 13ft.; Harris (C.,) 12ft. 6in.

Shot-put—Bernhard (C.,) 46ft. 6in.; Lamoure (F.,) 45ft. 6¾in.; Hill (C.,) 44ft. 7¼in.

High jump—Tie between De Pries (C.) and Ennis (C.,) 5ft. 11in.; Friedman (C.) 5ft. 9in.

Javelin—Carson (C.,) 182ft.; Tuttle (C.,) 175ft.; Laitinen (C.,) 174ft.

Broad jump—Knecht (C.,) 22ft. 11¾in.; Weisend (C.,) 21ft. 11¼in.; Tom A. Gay (C.,) 21ft. 10in.

Discus—Jurkovich (C.,) 144ft. 8¾in.; Bernhard (C.,) 140ft. 11½in.; Hunter (F.,) 139ft. 1in.

## Colorado Trackmen Win

SALT LAKE CITY, May 1. (AP) — Don Cieber's powerful spring in the mile relay carried the University of Colorado track squad to a 72-66 victory over University of Utah today.

## HOT DOG, IT'S STILL DERBY

LOUISVILLE (Ky.) May 1. (AP)—Despite an Office of Price Administration freeze of food and drink prices at early April levels the annual Derby gouge was on today.

Kentucky Derby visitors found prices hiked way up and O.P.A. officials here said they were besieged with complaints.

The local O.P.A. staff was short-handed because most of the investigators are in Harlan County checking cost of living prices.

## Riverland Sets Track Record in Winning Dixie Handicap

BALTIMORE, May 1. (AP)—Turning on his familiar blazing finish, Riverland carried the colors of Harold A. Clark's Louisiana farm to victory in the 39th running of the tradition-steeped Dixie Handicap before a crowd of more than 17,000 persons today.

Running the mile and three-sixteenths of Maryland's oldest stake race in 1:56 2/5, the big Coldstream gelding shaved two-fifths of a second off the former track record, held since 1938 by Pompoon and Seabiscuit.

Just back of the former plater as he hit the wire were Max Hirsch's Attention and Hal Price Headley's Anticlimax. Attention also finished second in the 1942 renewal of the Dixie won by Whirlaway.

Despite his smashing victory in the Excelsior Handicap at Jamaica last Saturday, Riverland was held at second choice in the wagering, the Hirsch-trained entry of Attention and A. J. Saccett's Tola Rose being favored.

Riverland returned $5.70, $2.60 and $2.20 across the board.

At the finish the winner had a half-length lead over Attention, which was a head in front of Anticlimax. Tola Rose finished fourth in the field of seven.

The victory was worth $17,775 and boosted Riverland's all-time winning to $96,295.

## Longden Says Count Fleet the Greatest

CHURCHILL DOWNS, LOUISVILLE (Ky.) May 1. (AP) The toughest part of piloting Count Fleet to victory in the 69th running of the Kentucky Derby today was waiting for the race to start, Jockey Johnny Longden announced after the big race.

It was a relief to get off from the post, he declared.

"I never had a bit of trouble after we got away from the gate. We went to the top somewhere around the half to the three-quarters and I didn't have to work keeping him there.

"Blue Swords? Sure, I saw him coming. I just gave the Count a little nudge and he gave out some more. That's all."

**Son Sees Victory**

Johnny's triumph was shared by his son, Vance, 12-year-old cadet at the San Rafael Military Academy, San Rafael, Cal.

Mrs. Longden is in a New York hospital, awaiting the arrival of another member of the family.

Vance, who comes within a hair's breadth of being as tall as his father, watched the race with Mr. and Mrs. John D. Hertz, and accompanied them to the presentation stand where Mrs. Hertz, Count Fleet's owner, received the gold trophy from Governor Keen Johnson.

"Did you get to see the race good?" was the first question Longden put to his son.

"Sure, just wonderful," the boy shouted above the tumult raised by autograph seekers.

**First Derby Win**

Longden, 35 years old and a native of Wakefield, Eng., has been around the big tracks and had some of the better mounts for quite a few years, but the Count was his first Derby winner.

From the moment he knew he was going to ride the Hertz pride in the Derby, Longden said, he was confident of a win.

The news in midafternoon that owner Warren Wright had

Turn to Page 18, Column 1

## Blue Swords Runs Second

### Slide Rule Third as Longden Coasts in With Favorite

BY SID FEDER

CHURCHILL DOWNS, LOUISVILLE (Ky.) May 1. (AP) — The Fleet sailed into port with the 69th Kentucky Derby today without even getting up a full head of steam.

Just as was predicted almost unanimously for this wartime renewal of the ancient turf classic, Mrs. John Hertz's Count Fleet—he has been tagged "The Fleet" or "The Count" ever since he skyrocketed to turf prominence a year ago—made a parade of his renewal of this ancient run for the roses.

**As Expected**

A comparatively slim crowd estimated as 60,000 by Col. Matt Win, the Downs' impresario, compared to the 90,000's of other years, roared him home as he did just what he was supposed to, in the way he was supposed to do.

But he didn't need their roars, because he took the lead when he wanted to in this mile-and-a-quarter "heartbreaker" and there wasn't another galloper in the race with enough get-up-and-go in his hoofs even to challenge him.

**Ocean Wave Out**

The only hopeful who might have made him speed up from a waltz to a two-step was Warren Wright's Ocean Wave and the Wave wasn't even on the track. Three hours before the plaintive notes of "My Old Kentucky Home" drifted over this picturesque race course, Ocean Wave, was withdrawn because of an injured leg—and whatever horse race this Derby might have been stayed right in his barn with him.

As a result, the Fleet broke out in full battle array after bouncing along with some of the others in the field of 10 for half a mile and from there on it was just a gallop. At the wire he was three lengths in front of Blue Swords, the pride and joy of Allen T. Simmons, Akron (O.) radio station owner, and nine in front of Slide Rule, from the barn of W. E. Boeing, the Seattle airplane manufacturer.

**Burnt Cork Last**

And all the way back, they were stretched out just like that, all the way back to Burnt Cork, the entry of Eddie Anderson—Rochester of the radio—who was just as unanimously the prerace prediction to finish last as the Count was to be first to the pay-off line for the pile of bank notes amounting to $60,725 which was waiting for the winner.

The victory of the Hertz hurricane, freely forecast after he was backed down to 1 to 2 in the "future books"—shortest price in Derby history —,and knocked down to 2 to 5 in the mutuel machines today, was about the only thing in this Derby that didn't fit into the pattern which made this the strangest of all of Col. Matt Winn's annual affairs at the picturesque Downs.

**The Pay-off**

Count Fleet paid his backers $2.80 to win, $2.40 to place and $2.20 to show for a $2 ticket. Blue Swords paid $3.40 and $3.00. Slide Rule paid $3.20.

The folks saw quite a horse in the Fleet, a colt which already is being tabbed as "the greatest since Man o' War" and considerably more than "just a chip off the old block" of his daddy, Reigh Count, which slopped through the mud to victory in the 1928 derby.

**Goes Away**

He broke up with the leaders today, played with them until they rounded the clubhouse turn, then said, "So long, pals," and went away. Only once in

Turn to Page 18, Column 1

## Kentucky Derby Chart



CHART OF THE KENTUCKY DERBY, CHURCHILL DOWNS—SEVENTH RACE—$75,000 added, mile and one-quarter, for 3-year-olds, weight for age. Net value to winner, $60,725; second, $8000; third, $3000; fourth, $1000. Winner, br.c. 3, by Reigh Count—Quickly (Haste.) Trained by G. D. Cameron. Bred by Mrs. John D. Hertz. Time: :12 1-5, :23 1-5, :34 2-5, :46 3-5, :59 2-5, 1:12 3-5, 1:25, 1:37 3-5, 1:50 2-5, 2:04.

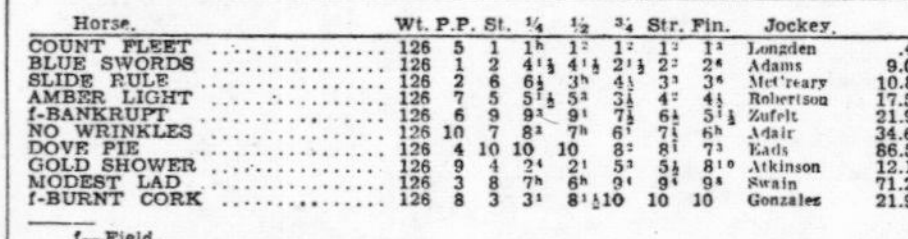

| Horse. | Wt. | P.P. | St. | ¼ | ½ | ¾ | Str. | Fin. | Jockey. | |
|---|---|---|---|---|---|---|---|---|---|---|
| COUNT FLEET | 126 | 5 | 1 | $1^{h}$ | $1^{2}$ | $1^{2}$ | $1^{3}$ | $1^{3}$ | Longden | .40 |
| BLUE SWORDS | 126 | 1 | 2 | $4^{1\frac{1}{2}}$ | $4^{1\frac{1}{2}}$ | $2^{1\frac{1}{2}}$ | $2^{2}$ | $2^{6}$ | Adams | 9.00 |
| SLIDE RULE | 126 | 2 | 6 | $6\frac{1}{2}$ | $3^{h}$ | $4\frac{1}{2}$ | $3^{3}$ | $3^{6}$ | McCreary | 10.80 |
| AMBER LIGHT | 126 | 7 | 5 | $5^{1\frac{1}{2}}$ | $5^{3}$ | $3\frac{1}{2}$ | $4^{2}$ | $4\frac{1}{2}$ | Robertson | 17.50 |
| f-BANKRUPT | 126 | 6 | 9 | $9^{3}$ | $9^{1}$ | $7\frac{1}{2}$ | $6\frac{1}{2}$ | $5^{1\frac{1}{2}}$ | Zufelt | 21.90 |
| NO WRINKLES | 126 | 10 | 7 | $8^{2}$ | $7^{h}$ | $6^{1}$ | $7\frac{1}{2}$ | $6^{h}$ | Adair | 34.60 |
| DOVE PIE | 126 | 4 | 10 | 10 | 10 | $8^{2}$ | $8^{1}$ | $7^{3}$ | Eads | 86.50 |
| GOLD SHOWER | 126 | 9 | 4 | $2^{4}$ | $2^{1}$ | $5^{3}$ | $5\frac{1}{2}$ | $8^{10}$ | Atkinson | 12.10 |
| MODEST LAD | 126 | 3 | 8 | $7^{h}$ | $6^{h}$ | $9^{4}$ | $9^{4}$ | $9^{8}$ | Swain | 71.20 |
| f-BURNT CORK | 126 | 8 | 3 | $3^{1}$ | $8^{1\frac{1}{2}}$ | 10 | 10 | 10 | Gonzalez | 21.90 |

f—Field.

TWO-DOLLAR MUTUELS PAID

| | | | |
|---|---|---|---|
| COUNT FLEET ...... | 2.80 | 2.40 | 2.20 |
| BLUE SWORDS ...... | | 3.40 | 3.00 |
| SLIDE RULE ........ | | | 3.20 |

EQUIVALENT ODDS TO $1

| | | | |
|---|---|---|---|
| COUNT FLEET ...... | .40 | .20 | .10 |
| BLUE SWORDS ...... | | .70 | .50 |
| SLIDE RULE ........ | | | .60 |

COUNT FLEET began fast, was hustled along until reaching the stretch, shook off the bid of GOLD SHOWER and, responding to a shaking up, won handily. BLUE SWORDS, away well, was in hand until reaching the last half mile, came determinedly when subjected to punishment but was not good enough for the winner, though easily best of the others. SLIDE RULE saved fround while outrun to the half-mile pole, was blocked when moving up approaching the stretch and, taken out for the drive, could not reach the leaders when subjected to punishment. AMBER LIGHT raced evenly under restraint until reaching the mile, made a game bid entering the stretch but tired near the finish. BANKRUPT, outrun until the final quarter, failed to respond when called upon in the stretch. NO WRINKLES, on the outside throughout, could not better his position and had no excuse. DOVE PIE swerved to the inside after the start and was never a serious contender. GOLD SHOWER, much used engaging COUNT FLEET in the first three-quarters, gave way badly thereafter. MODEST LAD, bothered slightly after the start by DOVE PIE, was always far back. BURNT CORK began fast, displayed good speed in the first half mile and then quit.

# TROJANS CLUB HUSKIES IN ROSE BOWL

Los Angeles Times Sports
SUNDAY MORNING, JANUARY 2, 1944

## Bowl Football Scores

ROSE BOWL—S.C., 29; Washington, 0.
KEZAR STADIUM—West, 13; East, 13.
SUGAR BOWL—Georgia Tech, 20; Tulsa, 18.
COTTON BOWL—Texas, 7; Randolph Field, 7.
ORANGE BOWL—Louisiana State, 19; Texas A. & M., 14.
SUN BOWL—Southwestern of Texas, 7; New Mexico, 0.
OIL BOWL—Southwestern Louisiana Institute, 24; Arkansas A. & M., 7.
ARAB BOWL—Army, 10; Navy, 7.

## HUSKIES RUN AFOUL OF BOWL TRADITION

### Inspired Trojans Make Most of Foes' Inability to Throw or Bat Down Forward Passes

BY AL WOLF

You can put this in your meerschaum and puff it:

Southern Cal never again will be a Rose Bowl underdog, even if the entire squad's in the town lockup at kickoff time.

The boys who made Washington a 1-3 favorite, a 12½-point favorite, took the cure yesterday. They'll never, never forget the little fact that putting a Trojan team in the Pasadena platter is just like waving a red flag at an ill-tempered bull—only worse.

Troy yesterday was perhaps the most inspired football team I ever saw. Washington was one of the biggest flops I can remember.

**David and Goliath**

On a fast field those 29 points would have been small change.

It was David and Goliath all over again, with Jim Hardy playing the slingshot role.

Washington was ponderous and powerful, but Washington also was slow and inept. Washington was a gridiron Carnera, lunging clumsily, pawing thin air and bellowing with rage, while Southern Cal, a Corbett or a Louis, combined fast footwork with punishing jabs and heavy punches that almost made you shudder in sympathy for the big fella.

Washington's pass defense was pitiful to behold—and Washington's own passing was worse yet. As soon as Troy opened up midway in the second period it was apparent that the Huskies were dead ducks. And when the Huskies tried to fight fire with fire their own tosses were so bad that they really were good—most of 'em fell to the ground so far short of their targets that S.C.'s alert defenders couldn't intercept.

**Robinson Overrated**

Sam Robinson—"greatest Washington back since George Wilson"—was vastly overrated. He was a defensive standout, but didn't exactly set the world on fire as a ball packer. Jack Tracy, rated as one of the Coast's top ends, twice was suckered badly by Troy's aerials.

Of course, there's another way of looking at the whole thing.

S.C. would have made an awful lot of football teams look bad yesterday.

That Trojan line was simply terrific. The return of Norm Verry was just what the doctor ordered for S.C.'s forwards. They all went wild.

Washington obviously had a crusher offense, but Verry and Bill Gray and John Ferraro and the others blunted and hog-tied and piled it up by playing the greatest game of their careers. Gray and Verry at a peak together were much too much. They simply couldn't be handled.

**What a Catch!**

Jim Hardy's passing, of course, was superb. Eddie Saenz was a constant gadfly. Georgie Callanan was a ball of fire. And when did you see a better running catch than Gordon Gray made for the game's third touchdown?

But most amazing of all was Troy's lack of fumbling. The Cravathmen had been undisputed world's champs in this department, but yesterday they held on tight and gleefully pounced on Husky bobbles for a change.

## Trojan Players Not Surprised Over Victory

BY STUART BELL

"The boys proved what I knew they were all season—a fine football team."

That is what Coach Jeff Cravath of the Trojans said yesterday after S.C. defeated Washington, 29 to 0, in one of the Rose Bowl's greatest upsets.

Cravath and the players said it wasn't much of an upset for them because they thought all along they had an even chance to win.

"It was marvelous," Jeff said, and there were traces of tears in his eyes.

"I thought of Howard Jones as I sat on the bench," said Cravath, "and actually prayed that the Trojans might win for him. I did not tell the boys that. There was no sentimental appeal to any of the players."

**No Pep Talk**

"He didn't even make a pep talk before the game," said George Callanan, who caught touchdown passes all over the field and was one of Troy's brightest stars. "All he said was, 'Boys, it's your ball game,' and it was."

Callanan said that Washington played a very clean game.

"Those fellows patted us on the back, helped us off the ground and more than once complimented us on some good piece of work."

Cravath refused to single out any one Trojan for praise.

"The entire team was magnificent," he declared. "Sure, Bill Gray played a great game. Who didn't? What about Ainslie Bell, for instance? He had not played 30 minutes for us all year, yet he played the entire first quarter, ran the team to perfection and turned over a confident aggregation to Jim Hardy.

**Turning Point**

"As for Hardy, I kept him on the bench the first period. I felt he would do better if I could talk to him as the game progressed. You saw what he did, throwing those passes and kicking. He was steady as could be."

Cravath thought the turning point of the game came with the first touchdown. After that one, he felt sure the Huskies could be passed against and beaten decisively.

Jeff declared that the presence of Norm Verry was a very important factor in the victory.

"He not only played a great game," said Cravath, "but he proved a fine leader. He was inspiration at all times. They believed in him and the kind of ball he can play. His leg stood up in great shape, too."

**Praise for Saksa**

Verry thought Frank Saksa, the Huskies' right guard, did the best line job for the visitors.

Cravath said Pest Welch had plenty of sympathy coming for not having sufficient competition to keep his team on playing edge for a big game.

"He might have done better on a wet field. Our passing game would have been handicapped and their backfield power behind a big line would have been harder to stop."

## Braddock, Ex-World Champ, Now Captain

NEW YORK, Jan. 1. (AP)—James J. Braddock, former heavyweight boxing champion, began the new year today by being promoted from a first lieutenant to a captain.

Braddock, attached to the Brooklyn Army base, was commissioned in the Army Oct. 3, 1942.

NO. 1—Jim Hardy passes to George Callanan for 11 yards and the game's first touchdown as S.C. upset Washington, 29-0, in the Rose Bowl yesterday. The play took place 40 seconds before the first half ended.
Times Miracle Eye Photos by J. H. McCrory

## Washington Grids Laud Play of Trojan Line

BY PAUL LOWRY

In other columns you will read that touchdown pitches from Jim Hardy and Ainslee Bell to George Callanan and Gordon Gray won an astonishing New Year's football game for Southern California from Washington, 29 to 0.

But if you had come with me into the Husky dressing room after the ball game you would have learned that it was the unsung Trojan linemen who turned the Washington machine inside out and balked its thunder.

In particular it was Norm Verry, John Ferraro and Bill Gray, guard, tackle and center, respectively, who were the sore thumbs in the Husky side all day long.

**Too Much Verry**

From Coach Ralph (Pest) Welch on down it was the same story.

"That guy Verry," said Welch, "oh, what a headache he was to us."

"I couldn't handle that man Ferraro," said Right End Jack Tracy, best of the Washington wingmen.

"No wonder we couldn't get going," said Fullback Gail Bruce. "That trio haunted us all day long. Every time we started something they bobbed up like ghosts."

"Verry was the toughest guard I faced all season," declared Bill Ward, big, black-haired 220-pounder who is the star of the Husky forward wall. "He was the big cog in the Trojan team."

**No Moaning**

The dressing room under the big cement bowl was a sober, quiet place as the Huskies filed in after the final whistle.

There was no moaning and gnashing of teeth where a celebration had been anticipated. The Huskies had been outplayed, they knew it and they praised their rivals accordingly.

Coach Welch didn't attempt to explain the size of the score except to say that the Trojans got every break and the Huskies none at all.

Welch attributed the Huskies' lack of sharpness to the fact they hadn't played a game in two months.

"But," he added quickly, "the Trojans were hot today, they outplayed us and they deserved to win."

## Tuskegee Tops Clark, 12-7, in Vulcan Bowl

BIRMINGHAM (Ala.) Jan. 1. (AP)—With breaks figuring in most of the scoring, the Tuskegee Institute Tigers defeated the Clark College Panthers, 12 to 7, today in the third annual Vulcan Bowl.

| | | | | |
|---|---|---|---|---|
| Tuskegee | 0 | 6 | 6 | 0—12 |
| Clark | 7 | 0 | 0 | 0— 7 |

Scoring: Tuskegee—Touchdowns, Griggs, Tabor; Clark—Touchdown, Harper; Extra Point, Haynes (pass.)

## S.C. Registers Biggest Upset of Grid Season

BY ARCH WARD
Chicago Tribune Sports Editor

PASADENA, Jan. 1.—Southern California, which never has lost a Rose Bowl game, today defeated Washington, which never has won the event, 29 to 0, in one of the most surprising developments of a football season replete with upsets.

Undefeated in its abbreviated schedule, Washington was a top-heavy favorite. The Huskies, conquerors of March Field, which in turn overwhelmed the Trojans, were supposed to have the better line and speedier backs.

The crowd of 70,000 saw the S.C. line out-charge Washington's from start to finish. The Huskies' famed backs, Sam Robinson and Al Akins, never had a chance to break loose. They were fenced in behind their own line most of the afternoon. Trojan ends and tackles were forever seeping through Washington defenses to harry the forward passer, most of whose tosses were wide of their target.

Play was fairly even as long as it stayed on the ground, but S.C., with a sharpshooter named Jim Hardy doing most of the passing, had a marked advantage in aerial attack. All four Trojan touchdowns were made on passes.

Individual honors for the victorious Trojans were widely distributed. Dick Jamison, left guard who did the punting, repeatedly kicked out of bounds inside Washington's 10-yard line. The middle of the S.C. line—Jamison and Norm Verry at guards and Bill Gray at center—throttled every assault. George Callanan and Gordon Gray each caught two touchdown passes. Milford Dreblow, who only a year ago was a substitute back at Santa Ana High School, averaged 6 yards per try in his four trips as a ball carrier.

Above all, the team had poise, spirit and the will to win. Washington sagged noticeably after S.C. got its second touchdown.

## Skyhawks Edge Panthers, 4-3

Al and Eddo Papike were a little too hot on the ice last night at the Pan-Pacific for the Pasadena Panthers, and the San Diego Skyhawks nosed out the local hockey club, 4 to 3.

Al scored two of the Skyhawk goals and Eddo tallied the final one to break a 3-3 deadlock and down Charlie Sands and his game squad which came from behind twice to tie the score.

| Panthers | | Skyhawks |
|---|---|---|
| Wolf | G. | LePrenci |
| Sands | W. | Maracle |
| MacDonnell | W. | Markovich |
| McLean | D. | A. Papike |
| Page | D. | E. Papike |
| Dowell | C. | Bots |

Panther spares: Beauchamp, Smith, LeBouf, Droulliard, LeDuc.
Skyhawk spares: Palkovich, Swan, Strutz, Blatnick.
Referees: Jack Abel and Chuck Pilsbury.

FIRST PERIOD
Scoring: 1—Skyhawks—A. Papike, unassisted, 11m. 30s.; 2—Panthers—Dowell (MacDonnell, Sands) 14m. 48s.; 3—Skyhawks—A. Papike (Bots) 16m. 42s.

SECOND PERIOD
Scoring: 4—Panthers—Droulliard (Le Duc, Le Bouef.) 16m. 45s.; 5—Skyhawks—Palkovich (Blatnick), 19m. 24s.
Penalties—Palkovich, Page (2,) E. Papike, Swan, A. Papike.

THIRD PERIOD
Scoring: 6—Panthers—Sands, unassisted, 45s.; 7—Skyhawks—E. Papike (Maracle Markovich) 12m. 34s.
Penalty—Maracle.
Saves—Wolf, 30; LePrinci, 26.

## STATISTICAL STORY OF TROJAN WIN

| | Huskies | Trojans |
|---|---|---|
| Total yards gained running | 132 | 141 |
| Yards lost running | 9 | 20 |
| Net yards gained, running | 123 | 121 |
| Forward passes attempted | 23 | 16 |
| Forward passes completed | 4 | 9 |
| Forward passes intercepted | 0 | 3 |
| Forward passes incomplete | 16 | 7 |
| Total yards gained, passing | 51 | 112 |
| Total yards intercepted passes returned | 0 | 38 |
| Total net yards gained passes, running | 174 | 233 |
| First downs, running plays | 5 | 3 |
| First downs, forward passes | 2 | 4 |
| First downs, penalties | 0 | 1 |
| Total first downs | 7 | 8 |
| Total number scrimmage plays | 62 | 65 |
| Number kickoffs | 1 | 5 |
| Average length kickoffs | 58 | 47.80 |
| Average length kickoff returns | 27.50 | 12.00 |
| Number punts | 8 | 10 |
| Total yardage punts | 255 | 383 |
| Average length punts | 31.37 | 38.30 |
| Total yardage punt returns | 48 | 35 |
| Average length punt returns | 9.60 | 5.83 |
| Number penalties | 2 | 3 |
| Yards lost, penalties | 10 | 25 |
| Ball lost on downs | 2 | 2 |
| Total number fumbles | 2 | 2 |
| Own fumbles recovered | 0 | 2 |
| Ball lost on fumbles | 2 | 0 |

YARDAGE GAINED BY BACKS

| Huskies— | TCB | TYA | YL | Net | Avg. |
|---|---|---|---|---|---|
| Robinson | 13 | 49 | 3 | 46 | 3.54 |
| Kramer | 9 | 39 | 3 | 36 | 4.00 |
| Akins | 9 | 54 | 3 | 51 | 5.67 |
| Totals | 31 | 132 | 9 | 123 | 3.98 |

| Trojans— | TCB | TYA | YL | Net | Avg. |
|---|---|---|---|---|---|
| Saenz | 10 | 43 | 7 | 36 | 3.60 |
| G. Callanan | 5 | 18 | 0 | 18 | 3.60 |
| Evans | 5 | 37 | 0 | 37 | 7.40 |
| Parsons | 2 | 1 | 0 | 1 | 0.50 |
| Whitehead | 6 | 10 | 0 | 10 | 1.66 |
| Hardy | 1 | 0 | 9 | −9 | −9.00 |
| Dreblow | 4 | 24 | 0 | 24 | 6.00 |
| Shipkey | 1 | 3 | 0 | 3 | 3.00 |
| Curry | 3 | 4 | 2 | 2 | 0.66 |
| McFadden | 2 | 1 | 2 | −1 | −0.50 |
| Totals | 39 | 141 | 20 | 121 | 3.11 |

## Vikings Play Hispano Eleven

Second pairings in the all-important City Cup tournament, soccer football classic, will be held at Loyola Stadium this afternoon, with the colorful Hollywood-Hispano eleven facing Northrop Vikings in the featured tussle at 3 p.m.

Victoria A.C. will stack up against the fighting Shipbuilders in the early game, slated for 1 p.m. Last week Victoria got off to a 3-to-0 edge over the Shipbuilders, only to have the Boatmen tally three in the second period and wind up in a tie.

## National Hockey Loop

Toronto, 5; Boston, 2.
Montreal, 4; Chicago, 0.

## S.C. Romps to Upset Win, 29-0

Continued from Page 1, Part 1

enough to throw one more pass in the fourth stanza. This was a perfect strike to his brother Don, but the youthful end failed to hold the ball.

**Eight of Fifteen**

All told Jim Hardy completed 8 of his 15 throws for 97 yards and Troy's first three tallies. It was a brilliant comeback for a game youngster who lost something in the late games of the season and found the honor of starting yesterday's game allotted to his substitute, Ainslie Bell of U.C.L.A.

Bell did a splendid job of steering Troy during the first quarter and then came back in the final heat to take over the passing role and get S.C.'s closing tally.

**Fine Punt**

A fine punt by Jamison paved the way for the blocked Washington kick which gave the Trojans 2 points in the last quarter. This went out of bounds on the Husky 3 and a few plays later big Harry Planck banged through and planted his huge frame in front of Gerry Austin's effort to gain the safety.

Troy's superior reserve strength was telling on the Huskies, who found Milford Dreblow, third-string halfback, more than they could handle in the stretch. The guy with the storybook name reeled off two long runs and then Bell faded back from the 21 and shot a perfect pass to Gordon Gray in the end zone.

**Smashing Win**

Jamison's placement made the final count 29 to 0 in a smashing win over a team which, as recently as five days ago, was favored to triumph by 13 points.

When touchdowns were needed Messrs. Callanan and Gray were as prompt as a pair of bill collectors and their crafty catching helped to make Jim Hardy look so good.

Washington was dangerous on several occasions, but only when running the ball. The Huskies had no passer who could pitch with accuracy. At times the Huskies threw so poorly that it was a good thing they did, because if the throws had been good they would have been picked off by alert Trojans. As it was, Cravath's lads plucked off three shots, the first by George Callanan in the opening period halting a Washington drive on the Trojan 29. George got it on the 10 and raced back to the 36.

**Troy in Open**

This was late in the first stanza and Callanan's timely interception got Troy out in the open for the first time and seven plays later the second heat opened and Hardy came in to begin his brilliant pitching performance.

The Huskies didn't get close enough again to be really dangerous until S.C. was so far ahead it made no difference. Troy's terrific line play, with Capt. Norm. Verry, Bill Gray, Ferraro and Jamison as standouts, stymied every running threat.

**Verry, Gray Tops**

Seldom have two linemen played better ball in the Rose Bowl than Verry and Gray did yesterday. Norm's presence not only gave the Trojans great confidence, but in the early stages he was generally the man who nailed Washington's ball carriers when things didn't look too bright for his team. Backing up the line, Bill Gray was tremendous.

Robinson played a great game for the Huskies, shading Akins and Gordon Berlin slightly. The other Huskies were good, steady players but they just couldn't match Troy's superior speed.

**Robinson Dangerous**

Robinson was always dangerous running and had the Huskies elected to send him around the ends oftener they might have bagged a tally. For some reason Pest Welch's team didn't concentrate on the wings to the extent most of us had anticipated.

As a matter of fact I thought Washington's signal calling was not too hot. But you seldom

Turn to Page 14, Column 6

## HERE ARE BOYS WHO PLAYED LEADING ROLES IN TROY'S ROSE BOWL WIN

Jim Hardy

George Callanan

Eddie Saenz

Norm Verry

Bill Gray

Dick Jamison

Gordon Gray

Ainslie Bell

# DETROIT BEATS CUBS, 9-3; COPS SERIES

Los Angeles Times Sports

THURSDAY MORNING, OCTOBER 11, 1945

## The Sports Parade

By BRAVEN DYER

Deke Houlgate, one of the nation's top football dopesters, thinks both Bruins and Trojans will win their games Saturday. He figures that Bert LaBrucherie has started to get results through the air and says the Bruins will be vastly improved over their opener against S.C.

This series, which began with a scoreless tie in 1933, finds California holding a 9-to-4 edge, with one tie, in 14 games. They split last season, the Bears winning the first, 6 to 0, and the Bruins the second, 7 to 0. Deke says U.C.L.A. has a 6-point edge which, of course, will put an immediate end to LaBrucherie's blues.

Houlgate gives the Trojans an 18-point edge over San Diego Navy, which this department will bet him is too much. Deke says it depends on just how much Jeff Cravath decides to employ Verl Lillywhite, his ace quarterback and passer. This is rubber game, Sailors winning 10-7 in '43 and S.C., 28-21, last season.

For you gridball bugs, Deke sizes up other important games as follows:

**Oregon over Oregon State by 7**—With Jake Leicht in the line-up, Oregon can win by more than the touchdown margin given. While Oregon State captured the first game, 18-0, in 1894, and the last contest, 39-2, in 1942, Oregon is safely in front with 25 wins, 15 losses and 7 ties in 47 games. A standout battle of this series was Oregon's 13-6 win in 1918 when its team of "Iron Men" played the entire 60 minutes without substitution.

**W.S.C. Over Washington by 1**—Cougars have looked great in games with Idaho and Oregon State, but the balance of the season will show the importance of these wins. Huskies can be expected to bounce back from that upset by California and have tradition on their side since the game will be played in Seattle. Series which began with a 5-5 tie in 1900 gives Washington a big edge of 21 wins to 9 and 6 ties in 36 games. Last contest was 1942's 0-0 stalemate.

**Army over Michigan by 14**—Army's impressive win over a good Wake Forest eleven, 54-0, last Saturday merely confirmed the Cadets as the scoring powerhouse of the nation this fall. The way the deacons completed passes against the West Pointers, however, shows that Michigan has a chance, for the Wolverines unleashed a sensational passing attack to topple Northwestern, 20-7, the same day. Army still rates a two-touchdown edge and will make it more if any one of its many great backs has a good day. This is the first meeting between these teams.

**Navy over Penn State by 20**—The Middies' win over Duke was expected, but the margin of 3 T.D.'s provided a small surprise since the Blue Devils were known to be strong defensively. This week Navy should spoil another perfect record when it entertains undefeated, untied Penn State. Hoernschemeyer and company can win by more than three T.D.'s but that's the safe way to call it. The first game between these two was a 6-6 tie in 1894. Navy won last year, 55-14, and holds the series lead with 12 wins to 7, and two ties in 21 games.

**Ohio State over Wisconsin by 19**—Wisconsin looms as a much tougher hurdle for the Buckeyes than were the Hawkeyes last Saturday. The fact remains, however, that Coach Carroll Widdoes used his regulars sparingly against Iowa. If he shoots the works against the Badgers, it can be another lopsided win for the title-bound Ohio Staters. Wisconsin won the first game, 12-0, in 1913, and Ohio State the last, 20-7, in 1944.

**Indiana over Nebraska by 20**—A hapless Husker team hardly figures to defeat Indiana when Michigan, Northwestern and Illinois have failed. Last week's 61-7 beating by Minnesota has not done Nebraska much good either. Nebraska won the first of these annual games, 13-0, in 1936, but Indiana has triumphed the past two seasons, 54-13 in 1943 and 54-0 last fall.

**Notre Dame over Dartmouth by 28**—Pitching by Dancewicz is enough to give Notre Dame a four-touchdown edge over Dartmouth. Only the great stand shown by the Indians against Penn last week (0-12) makes for a closer game. Last year the Irish beat Dartmouth 64-0 in the only previous contest between the two.

**Oklahoma A. & M. over S.M.U. by 6**—The Cowboys, with two straight wins over Arkansas and Denver, must be favored over a Mustang team that has dropped its last two games—7-10 to Missouri last Saturday. In five previous games, S.M.U. has won three, with the other two tied.

**Texas Aggies over L.S.U. by 7**—Although running true to form against Oklahoma last week (19-14) the Aggies are no cinch against L.S.U., beaten under the lights on the same date 7-26 by Alabama. A. & M. won the first game, 52-0 in 1899, and took last year's contest, 7-0, to boost their series lead to nine wins against five and two ties in 16 games. One of the five Tiger wins was a 19-14 victory in the Orange Bowl at the end of the '43 season, after A. & M. had won 28-13 that same year.

**Texas over Oklahoma by 9**—Texas, looking more and more like the top team in the Southwest, should duplicate Texas Aggies' victory over a good Oklahoma eleven. The Sooners could provide a mild upset and for this reason, the Longhorns are picked by less than two touchdowns. Texas, which won the first game, 28-2 in 1900, and the last start, 20-0 in 1944, dominates the series with 26 wins to 11 losses and 2 ties in 39 games, including victories for the past five years.

**HAIL HAL!**—In the Detroit clubhouse after Tigers take series, teammate grabs cap of Hal Newhouser, winning hurler, third from left, as players crowd around and cheer. At Newhouser's left is Catcher Paul Richards.

## World Series Figures

Seventh game (at Chicago:)
Paid attendance—41,590.
Gross receipts—$204,177.
Commissioner's share—$30,626.55.
Each club's share—$43,387.61.
Each league's share—$43,387.61.

Total seven games:
a—Paid attendance—333,457.
b—Gross receipts—$1,492,454.
c—Players' share—$445,714.50.
Commissioner's share—$223,868.10.
Each club's share—$205,717.84.
Each league's share—$205,717.84.

a—Establishes all-time record for World Series paid attendance.
b—Coupled with $100,000 received for broadcasting rights, $1,592,454 establishes all-time revenue for World Series receipts.
c—Players participate in receipts of first four games only. They also participate in the $100,000 radio rights.

**RUN FOR MAYO**—Eddie Mayo is shown sliding home at Chicago yesterday. Ball bounces away from Livingston (11,) Cubs' catcher, toward Cullenbine, right, next batter for Detroit Tigers for whom Mayo, former local star, proved batting star in World Series.



## Composite Box Score

BY THE ASSOCIATED PRESS

DETROIT (A.L.)

| Player | G | AB | R | H | 2B | 3B | HR | RBI | BB | SO | Bat. Pct. | PO | A | E | Fldg. Avg. |
|---|---|---|---|---|---|---|---|---|---|---|---|---|---|---|---|
| Webb, ss | 7 | 27 | 4 | 5 | 0 | 0 | 0 | 1 | 2 | 1 | .185 | 9 | 24 | 1 | .971 |
| Hoover, ss | 1 | 3 | 1 | 1 | 0 | 0 | 0 | 1 | 0 | 0 | .333 | 1 | 1 | 0 | 1.000 |
| Mayo, 2b | 7 | 28 | 4 | 7 | 1 | 0 | 0 | 2 | 3 | 2 | .250 | 18 | 13 | 1 | .969 |
| Cramer, cf | 7 | 29 | 7 | 11 | 0 | 0 | 0 | 4 | 1 | 0 | .379 | 21 | 0 | 0 | 1.000 |
| Greenberg, lf | 7 | 23 | 7 | 7 | 3 | 0 | 2 | 7 | 6 | 5 | .304 | 8 | 1 | 0 | 1.000 |
| Mierk'wicz, lf | 1 | 0 | 0 | 0 | 0 | 0 | 0 | 0 | 0 | 0 | .000 | 0 | 0 | 0 | .000 |
| Cullenbine, rf | 7 | 22 | 5 | 5 | 2 | 0 | 0 | 4 | 8 | 2 | .227 | 8 | 0 | 0 | 1.000 |
| York, 1b | 7 | 28 | 1 | 5 | 1 | 0 | 0 | 3 | 3 | 4 | .179 | 67 | 8 | 1 | .987 |
| Outlaw, 3b | 7 | 28 | 1 | 5 | 0 | 0 | 0 | 3 | 2 | 1 | .179 | 5 | 15 | 0 | 1.000 |
| Richards, c | 7 | 19 | 0 | 4 | 2 | 0 | 0 | 6 | 4 | 3 | .211 | 46 | 5 | 1 | .981 |
| Swift, c | 3 | 4 | 1 | 1 | 0 | 0 | 0 | 0 | 2 | 0 | .250 | 9 | 1 | 0 | 1.000 |
| Newhouser, p | 3 | 8 | 0 | 0 | 0 | 0 | 0 | 1 | 1 | 1 | .000 | 2 | 6 | 1 | .857 |
| Benton, p | 3 | 0 | 0 | 0 | 0 | 0 | 0 | 0 | 0 | 0 | .000 | 0 | 3 | 0 | 1.000 |
| Tobin, p | 1 | 1 | 0 | 0 | 0 | 0 | 0 | 0 | 0 | 0 | .000 | 0 | 1 | 0 | 1.000 |
| Mueller, p | 1 | 0 | 0 | 0 | 0 | 0 | 0 | 0 | 0 | 0 | .000 | 0 | 0 | 0 | .000 |
| Trucks, p | 2 | 4 | 0 | 0 | 0 | 0 | 0 | 0 | 1 | 1 | .000 | 1 | 1 | 0 | 1.000 |
| Overmire, p | 1 | 1 | 0 | 0 | 0 | 0 | 0 | 0 | 0 | 0 | .000 | 0 | 1 | 0 | 1.000 |
| Bridges, p | 1 | 0 | 0 | 0 | 0 | 0 | 0 | 0 | 0 | 0 | .000 | 0 | 0 | 0 | .000 |
| Trout, p | 2 | 6 | 0 | 1 | 0 | 0 | 0 | 0 | 0 | 0 | .167 | 2 | 5 | 0 | 1.000 |
| Caster, p | 1 | 0 | 0 | 0 | 0 | 0 | 0 | 0 | 0 | 0 | .000 | 0 | 0 | 0 | .000 |
| Eaton, a | 1 | 1 | 0 | 0 | 0 | 0 | 0 | 0 | 0 | 1 | .000 | 0 | 0 | 0 | .000 |
| Hostetler, b | 3 | 3 | 0 | 0 | 0 | 0 | 0 | 0 | 0 | 0 | .000 | 0 | 0 | 0 | .000 |
| Borom, c | 2 | 1 | 0 | 0 | 0 | 0 | 0 | 0 | 0 | 0 | .000 | 0 | 0 | 0 | .000 |
| McHale, d | 3 | 3 | 0 | 0 | 0 | 0 | 0 | 0 | 0 | 1 | .000 | 0 | 0 | 0 | .000 |
| Walker, e | 2 | 2 | 1 | 1 | 1 | 0 | 0 | 0 | 0 | 0 | .500 | 0 | 0 | 0 | .000 |
| Maier, f | 1 | 1 | 0 | 1 | 0 | 0 | 0 | 0 | 0 | 0 | 1.000 | 0 | 0 | 0 | .000 |
| Totals | | 242 | 32 | 54 | 10 | 0 | 2 | 32 | 33 | 22 | .223 | 197 | 85 | 5 | .983 |

a—Batted for Benton in 4th inning of first game.
b—Batted for Richards in 9th inning of first game; for Benton in 9th inning of third game and for Webb in 7th inning of sixth game.
c—Batted for Mueller in 9th inning of first game and ran for Swift in 6th inning of third game.
d—Batted for Webb in 9th inning of first game; for Webb in 9th inning of third game, and for Caster in 6th inning of sixth game.
e—Batted for Overmire in 6th inning of third game and for Benton in 8th inning of sixth game.
f—Batted for Richards in 6th inning of sixth game

CHICAGO (N.L.)

| Player | G | AB | R | H | 2B | 3B | HR | RBI | BB | SO | Pct. | PO | A | E | Avg. |
|---|---|---|---|---|---|---|---|---|---|---|---|---|---|---|---|
| Hack, 3b | 7 | 30 | 1 | 11 | 3 | 0 | 0 | 4 | 4 | 2 | .367 | 12 | 13 | 3 | .875 |
| Johnson, 2b | 7 | 29 | 4 | 5 | 2 | 1 | 0 | 0 | 0 | 8 | .172 | 11 | 24 | 1 | .972 |
| Lowrey, lf | 7 | 29 | 4 | 9 | 1 | 0 | 0 | 0 | 1 | 2 | .310 | 21 | 1 | 0 | 1.000 |
| C'varretta, 1b | 7 | 26 | 7 | 11 | 2 | 0 | 1 | 5 | 4 | 3 | .423 | 71 | 3 | 0 | 1.000 |
| Pafko, cf | 7 | 28 | 5 | 6 | 2 | 1 | 0 | 2 | 2 | 5 | .214 | 24 | 2 | 1 | .963 |
| Nicholson, rf | 7 | 28 | 1 | 6 | 1 | 1 | 0 | 8 | 2 | 5 | .214 | 9 | 0 | 1 | .900 |
| Livingston, c | 6 | 22 | 3 | 8 | 3 | 0 | 0 | 4 | 1 | 1 | .364 | 22 | 4 | 0 | 1.000 |
| Gillespie, c, j | 3 | 6 | 0 | 0 | 0 | 0 | 0 | 0 | 0 | 0 | .000 | 3 | 0 | 0 | 1.000 |
| Hughes, ss | 6 | 17 | 1 | 5 | 1 | 0 | 0 | 3 | 4 | 5 | .294 | 13 | 17 | 0 | 1.000 |
| Merullo, ss | 3 | 2 | 0 | 0 | 0 | 0 | 0 | 0 | 0 | 1 | .000 | 4 | 2 | 0 | 1.000 |
| Schuster, ss, l | 2 | 1 | 1 | 0 | 0 | 0 | 0 | 0 | 0 | 0 | .000 | 1 | 2 | 0 | 1.000 |
| Borowy, p | 4 | 6 | 1 | 1 | 1 | 0 | 0 | 0 | 0 | 3 | .167 | 1 | 2 | 0 | 1.000 |
| Wyse, p | 3 | 3 | 0 | 0 | 0 | 0 | 0 | 0 | 0 | 2 | .000 | 0 | 0 | 0 | .000 |
| Vand'berg, p | 3 | 1 | 0 | 0 | 0 | 0 | 0 | 0 | 0 | 0 | .000 | 1 | 2 | 0 | 1.000 |
| Erickson, p | 4 | 0 | 0 | 0 | 0 | 0 | 0 | 0 | 0 | 0 | .000 | 0 | 1 | 0 | 1.000 |
| Derringer, p | 3 | 0 | 0 | 0 | 0 | 0 | 0 | 0 | 0 | 0 | .000 | 0 | 0 | 0 | .000 |
| Passeau, p | 3 | 7 | 1 | 0 | 0 | 0 | 0 | 1 | 0 | 4 | .000 | 1 | 3 | 0 | 1.000 |
| Prim, p | 2 | 0 | 0 | 0 | 0 | 0 | 0 | 0 | 0 | 0 | .000 | 0 | 1 | 0 | 1.000 |
| Chipman, p | 1 | 0 | 0 | 0 | 0 | 0 | 0 | 0 | 0 | 0 | .000 | 0 | 0 | 0 | .000 |
| Secory, g | 5 | 5 | 0 | 2 | 0 | 0 | 0 | 0 | 0 | 2 | .400 | 0 | 0 | 0 | .000 |
| Sauer, h | 2 | 2 | 0 | 0 | 0 | 0 | 0 | 0 | 0 | 2 | .000 | 0 | 0 | 0 | .000 |
| Becker, i | 3 | 2 | 0 | 1 | 0 | 0 | 0 | 0 | 1 | 1 | .500 | 0 | 0 | 0 | .000 |
| Williams, c, k | 2 | 2 | 0 | 0 | 0 | 0 | 0 | 0 | 0 | 1 | .000 | 1 | 1 | 0 | 1.000 |
| Block, m | 1 | 0 | 0 | 0 | 0 | 0 | 0 | 0 | 0 | 0 | .000 | 0 | 0 | 0 | .000 |
| M'C'lough, n | 1 | 1 | 0 | 0 | 0 | 0 | 0 | 0 | 0 | 1 | .000 | 0 | 0 | 0 | .000 |
| Totals | | 247 | 29 | 65 | 16 | 3 | 1 | 27 | 19 | 48 | .263 | 195 | 78 | 6 | .978 |

g—Batted for Wyse in 7th inning of second game; for Derringer in 5th inning of fourth game; for Derringer in 8th inning of fifth game; for Merullo in 12th inning of sixth game and for Erickson in 7th inning of seventh game.
h—Batted for Chipman in 6th inning of fifth game and for Vandenberg in 5th inning of seventh game.
i—Batted for Erickson in 9th inning of second game; for Hughes in seventh inning of fourth game and for Hughes in 9th inning of sixth game.
j—Batted for Vandenberg in 7th inning of fourth game and for Livingston in 9th inning of sixth game.
k—Batted for Merullo in 7th inning of fifth game.
l—Ran for Secory in 12th inning of sixth game.
m—Ran for Becker in 9th inning of sixth game.
n—Batted for Wyse in 9th inning of seventh game.

PITCHING SUMMARY

DETROIT

| Pitcher | G | CG | IP | H | R | ER | BB | SO | WP | HB | W | L | Pct. | ERA |
|---|---|---|---|---|---|---|---|---|---|---|---|---|---|---|
| Trucks | 2 | 1 | 13 1/3 | 14 | 5 | 5 | 5 | 7 | 0 | 0 | 1 | 0 | 1.000 | 3.38 |
| Newhouser | 3 | 2 | 20 2/3 | 25 | 14 | 14 | 4 | 22 | 1 | 0 | 2 | 1 | .667 | 6.10 |
| Trout | 2 | 1 | 13 2/3 | 9 | 2 | 1 | 3 | 9 | 0 | 0 | 1 | 1 | .500 | 0.66 |
| Overmire | 1 | 0 | 6 | 4 | 2 | 2 | 2 | 2 | 0 | 0 | 0 | 1 | .000 | 3.00 |
| Benton | 3 | 0 | 4 2/3 | 6 | 1 | 1 | 0 | 5 | 0 | 0 | 0 | 0 | .000 | 1.93 |
| Tobin | 1 | 0 | 3 | 4 | 2 | 2 | 1 | 0 | 0 | 0 | 0 | 0 | .000 | 6.00 |
| Bridges | 1 | 0 | 1 2/3 | 3 | 3 | 3 | 3 | 1 | 0 | 0 | 0 | 0 | .000 | 16.20 |
| Mueller | 1 | 0 | 2 | 0 | 0 | 0 | 1 | 1 | 0 | 0 | 0 | 0 | .000 | 0.00 |
| Caster | 1 | 0 | 2/3 | 0 | 0 | 0 | 0 | 1 | 0 | 0 | 0 | 0 | .000 | 0.00 |

CHICAGO

| Pitcher | G | CG | IP | H | R | ER | BB | SO | WP | HB | W | L | Pct. | ERA |
|---|---|---|---|---|---|---|---|---|---|---|---|---|---|---|
| Passeau | 3 | 1 | 16 2/3 | 7 | 5 | 5 | 8 | 3 | 0 | 0 | 1 | 0 | 1.000 | 2.70 |
| Borowy | 4 | 1 | 18 | 21 | 8 | 8 | 6 | 8 | 0 | 1 | 2 | 2 | .500 | 4.00 |
| Wyse | 3 | 0 | 7 2/3 | 8 | 7 | 6 | 4 | 1 | 0 | 0 | 0 | 1 | .000 | 7.04 |
| Prim | 2 | 0 | 4 | 4 | 5 | 4 | 1 | 1 | 0 | 0 | 0 | 1 | .000 | 9.00 |
| Erickson | 4 | 0 | 7 | 8 | 3 | 3 | 3 | 5 | 0 | 1 | 0 | 0 | .000 | 3.86 |
| Derringer | 3 | 0 | 5 1/3 | 5 | 4 | 4 | 7 | 1 | 0 | 0 | 0 | 0 | .000 | 6.75 |
| Vandenberg | 3 | 0 | 6 | 1 | 0 | 0 | 3 | 3 | 0 | 0 | 0 | 0 | .000 | 0.00 |
| Chipman | 1 | 0 | 1/3 | 0 | 0 | 0 | 1 | 0 | 0 | 0 | 0 | 0 | .000 | 0.00 |

COMPOSITE SCORE BY INNINGS

| | | | | | | | | | | | | |
|---|---|---|---|---|---|---|---|---|---|---|---|---|
| Chicago (N.L.) | 5 | 0 | 4 | 4 | 2 | 2 | 7 | 1 | 1 | 0 | 0 | 1—29 |
| Detroit (A.L.) | 5 | 2 | 1 | 4 | 4 | 4 | 4 | 6 | 2 | 0 | 0 | 0—32 |

SUMMARY

Earned runs—Chicago, 28; Detroit, 30. Sacrifices — Lowrey, Borowy, Johnson, 4; Cavarretta, Hughes, Pafko, Prim, Outlaw, Cullenbine, Greenberg. Double plays—Chicago (5,) Hughes to Johnson to Cavarretta; Johnson to Hughes to Savarretta; Johnson to Cavarretta; Johnson to Merullo to Cavarretta; Merullo to Johnson to Cavarretta. Detroit (4,) Mayo to York to Webb to Mayo; Mayo to Webb to Richards to Webb; Mayo to Hoover to York; Webb to Mayo to York. Stolen bases—Johnson, Pafko, Cullenbine, Outlaw, Cramer. Hit by pitcher — By Borowy (Greenberg;) Erickson (Cramer.) Left on bases—Chicago, 50; Detroit, 53. Passed balls—Richards, 2; Livingston, 1. Time of games—2h. 10m.; 1h. 47m.; 1h. 55m.; 2h.; 2h. 18m.; 3h. 28m.; 2h. 31m. Umpires—Summers (A.L.) Jorda (N.L.) Passarella (A.L.,) Conlan (N.L.) Attendances—First game, 54,637; second game, 53,636; third game, 55,500; fourth game, 42,923; fifth game, 43,463; sixth game, 41,708; seventh game, 41,590. Receipts—first game, $221,883; second game, $220,394; third game, $223,497; fourth game, $208,176; fifth game, $209,796; sixth game, $204,531; seventh game, $204,177.

## O'NEILL, HAPPY, LAUDS MAYO, HUGHES, PAFKO

BY CHARLES DUNKLEY

WRIGLEY FIELD, CHICAGO, Oct. 10. (AP)—The greatest thrill in the life of Stephen Francis O'Neill of Minooka, Pa., proud and happy manager of the conquering Detroit Tigers, came to him at 4:01 today at the age of 54.

At that moment, his victorious Tigers had presented O'Neill, up and down in the major and minor leagues for 36 years, with his first World Series championship while a manager.

Battered-nosed O'Neill, whose black hair is streaked with gray, was the happiest man in baseball as he walked among his yipping and yelling players in their steaming hot dressing room.

After the last ball was thrown, O'Neill first trotted over to the box occupied by Walter Briggs, owner of the Tigers, and his family near the Detroit dugout to congratulate him. Then he clattered up the concrete steps to the Tiger dressing room.

He found the tall, blond Newhouser quiet, as usual, but happy—particularly over the five runs his mates scored for him in the first inning.

**Correct Time**

"That was a great time to get them for me, wasn't it?" the lanky left-hander grinned.

Ford Frick, president of the National League, shouldered his way in to extend his hand in congratulation. Frick was followed by U.S. Sen. A. B. (Happy) Chandler, baseball's commissioner, and Will Harridge, president of the American League.

O'Neill singled out Newhouser, Richards, Skeeter Webb, Hank Greenberg and Eddie Mayo as standout players for the Tigers in the series.

O'Neill named Phil Cavarretta, Cubs' first baseman; Roy Hughes, veteran Chicago shortstop; Andy Pafko, fleet center fielder, and Pitcher Claude Passeau as the top performers for the National League champions.

## Records, Ties Chalked Up in World Series

Here are some of the records and ties just dug out of the baseball statistics.

Cavarretta tied other players who have batted more than .400 in two series.

Most chances by outfielder—Pafko, 27.

Most earned runs off pitcher who has won two or more games in a series—Newhouser, 14. Old record 12 in eight-game series.

Greenberg became 13th player to bat more than .300 in three series.

Most runs by losing team in a series—29 by Cubs. Record, 28 in 1909 and equaled in 1940.

Most bases on balls, one club, 33, by the Cubs. Old record 31 in 1926.

Most strikeouts by one club, 48 by the Cubs, old record 46 by the A's, 1931. All-time record in five-game series, Cubs.

Most strikeouts by a pitcher in modern series, 22 by Newhouser. Old record, 20 by three pitchers. Old-time record, 29, Bill Dineen, 1903.

Putouts by a third baseman in seven-game series, Hack, 12.

## Stephens Hits Pair of Homers in One Inning

Vern Stephens of the St. Louis Browns poked out two homers in the first inning of a game at Wrigley Field last night to spark the Vince DiMaggio Major League All-Stars to a 22-to-13 victory over the Kansas City Royals.

| | | R. | H. | E. |
|---|---|---|---|---|
| All-Stars | 13 23 300 001—22 | 22 | 2 |
| Royals | 1 00 310 200— 7 | 13 | 2 |

Barrett, Trichel and Salkeld. Mullican: Smith, Renfro, Hubbard and Marcell.

## Rowland to Put Ban on 'Beefs'

By a Times Correspondent

CHICAGO, Oct. 10.—President Clarence Rowland of the Pacific Coast League said here today that he will put into effect next season the rule that governed player-and-umpire relations in the World Series.

Nobody except managers and field captains were permitted to "beef" and even these were not allowed to argue on strike-and-ball calls.

Rowland plans to use a 13-man umpiring staff in 1946, with three arbiters working every game. One of the newcomers, incidentally, may be Lon Warneke, the Cubs' veteran pitcher.

Rowland also is going to slap fines on the clubs as well as the players for glaring transgressions, the idea being that then the individual offenders may have to pony up their own dough instead of having the clubs pay off.

The P.C.L. campaign will commence on March 26 and continue 28 weeks. Whether the play-offs will be abolished is to be decided at a meeting scheduled for Los Angeles Oct. 26.

Portland probably will train in Southern California next spring instead of at San Jose, Business Manager Bill Klepper said here today. Oakland will condition at Boyes Springs, San Francisco in Hawaii and all the others in the Southland, along with four major league outfits.

## Colonels Wallop Newark Bears, 8-3

NEWARK (N.J.) Oct. 10. (AP) Nemo Leibold's Louisville Colonels left the Newark Bears hanging on the ropes tonight, losers of three straight Little World Series tilts and faced with an early elimination, by rapping Frank Hiller and Jack Farmer for 13 hits and an 8-3 decision.

| | | R. | H. | E. |
|---|---|---|---|---|
| Louisville (A.A.) | 001 200 311—8 | 13 | 1 |
| Newark (I.L.) | 001 100 100—3 | 5 | 3 |

Terry and Walters: Hiller, Farmer and Van Grofski.
(Louisville leads, three games to none.)

## Figera's 68 Low Gross in Stakes

W. F. Figera, with 68, had low gross yesterday in the Monrovia sweepstakes, played as part of Santa Anita Open Week. Art Wild had low net with 83-15—68.

Each player received a $25 Victory Bond. About 50 players took part. Another sweepstakes event will be staged today.

## Tourney Revived

KANSAS CITY (Mo.) Oct. 10. (U.P.)—The women's international bowling congress announced tonight that its annual tournament would be resumed in 1946 after a lapse of five years.

## Hal Newhouser Pitches Brilliantly to Capture Record-Breaking Classic

BY AL WOLF, Times Staff Representative

CHICAGO, Oct. 10.—The 41,590 citizens who paid up to 50 bucks a ticket with the expectations of seeing 1945's zany World Series end in a frenzy of fireworks got a very flat finish for their dough today as the Detroit Tigers whammed the Chicago Cubs, 9 to 3.

The seventh and deciding game was decided almost before the echo of the announcer's "Play ball" had died away. The Bengals got five runs in the first inning and then merely went through the mechanics of playing 'er out.

With the grand climax coming at the start instead of the finish, the crowd (which boosted the series attendance to an all-time high of 333,457 and upped the "take" to another record of $1,592,454) started drifting out long before the curtain fell.

**Celebrate First Victory**

The Tigers' second series triumph came, appropriately enough, on the 10th anniversary of their first—which also was gleaned at the expense of the Cubs.

Ardent Cub fans, few of whom remember the glorious teams of 1907 and 1908, are beginning to wonder if they'll ever have another world's champion. Today's debacle made it seven straight series whippings for the burg's National League entry.

The story today was that overworked Hank Borowy wasn't ready, that overworked Hal Newhouser was.

Borowy, making his fourth appearance of the series after having won two games and lost one, gave hits to the first three Tigers to face him and then left the scene for good.

Before Paul Derringer could get the side out, the aforementioned five runs were in—and Newhouser frittered scarcely any of it away.

**Had Plenty on Ball**

The Detroit southpaw, although yielding 10 hits to 9 permitted by the half-a-dozen hurlers the Cubs used, had it when he needed it. He nipped a couple of early Chicago rallies in the bud and then went on to fan 10 men, a feat which made him the greatest strike-out artist in the series. Hal whiffed a total of 22 in his 20⅔ innings of work; the old mark for a seven-game series was 20.

Sharing honors with Prince Hal today was his battery mate, ancient Paul Richards.

Richards, crowning 20 years in organized ball by playing in his first World's Series, doubled to bash in three runs with the bases full and two away in the first frame—the blow that broke the Bruins' backs—and belted in another entirely unneeded tally in the seventh.

He was not around to be acclaimed at the finish, through having to quit in the eighth inning when he broke the little finger on his meat hand.

How could the Cubs get trounced so thoroughly and still outhit their adversaries?

**Control Is Answer**

The answer is control: Eight Bengals drew passes and four of them eventually scored. One of the toddlers even drove in a run. Let us go into the gory details—Skeeter Webb, Eddie Mayo and Doc Cramer began the ball game with solid singles and it was 1-0, nobody out, as Manager Cholly Grimm rushed afield to get his trumped ace out of there.

Paul Derringer, who pitched Cincinnati to victory over Detroit in the deciding game of the 1934 series, came in, but with a chance to duplicate that heroic stint a decade later, fizzled miserably.

Hank Greenberg put down a sacrifice bunt to advance the runners, whereupon Roy Cullenbine was purposely passed to fill the bases. Rudy York ran out the string, added several fouls and finally popped up.

With this dangerous gent out of the way and the bottom of the batting order coming up, Cub rooters breathed easier—for about two seconds.

Then lo and behold! Derringer walked Jimmy Outlaw on four pitches to force a run across the plate. Richards followed with a two-ply swat to the left cornor and it was 5-0. Newhouser ended the carnage by grounding out.

**Cubs Threaten**

The Cubs immediately started a counter-rally which threatened for a time to boost them right back into the ball game.

With one away in the Chicago half, Don Johnson doubled. Peanuts Lowrey was safe on Newhouser's error, whereupon Phil Cavarretta shot a single to right that scored Johnson and put Lowrey on third. Andy Pafko, a Dangerous Dan with the stick, was next up, but he grounded into a double play that not only retired the side but put Newhouser right back on the beam.

The Cubs had only two other "moments."

Cavarretta's single and Pafko's horseshoe triple, which Cramer misjudged horribly, gave Chicago a run in the fourth with but one away. Newhouser stopped that one personally by throwing out both Bill Nicholson and Mickey Livingston.

In the eighth, Lowrey and Cavarretta singled after one was out. Pafko fanned, but Nicholson doubled to bring in Peanuts, and put Phil on third. Again Hal was equal to the occasion. He fanned Livingston with a knuckler.

The Tigers tallied from time to time, but all these doings were utterly superfluous so we'll bore you no longer.

### THAT'S THAT!

DETROIT (A.L.)

| | AB | R | H | O | A |
|---|---|---|---|---|---|
| Webb, ss | 4 | 2 | 1 | 0 | 5 |
| Mayo, 2b | 5 | 2 | 2 | 2 | 1 |
| Cramer, cf | 5 | 2 | 3 | 2 | 0 |
| Greenberg, lf | 2 | 0 | 0 | 0 | 0 |
| Mierkowicz, lf | 0 | 0 | 0 | 0 | 0 |
| Cullenbine, rf | 2 | 2 | 0 | 2 | 0 |
| York, 1b | 4 | 0 | 0 | 8 | 1 |
| Outlaw, 3b | 4 | 1 | 1 | 1 | 2 |
| Richards, c | 4 | 0 | 2 | 9 | 0 |
| Swift, c | 1 | 0 | 0 | 2 | 0 |
| Newhouser, p | 4 | 0 | 0 | 1 | 2 |
| Totals | 35 | 9 | 9 | 27 | 11 |

CHICAGO (N.L.)

| | AB | R | H | O | A |
|---|---|---|---|---|---|
| Hack, 3b | 5 | 0 | 0 | 1 | 3 |
| Johnson, 2b | 5 | 1 | 1 | 1 | 3 |
| Lowrey, lf | 4 | 1 | 2 | 3 | 0 |
| Cavarretta, 1b | 4 | 1 | 3 | 10 | 0 |
| Pafko, cf | 4 | 0 | 1 | 6 | 0 |
| Nicholson, rf | 4 | 0 | 1 | 1 | 0 |
| Livingston, c | 4 | 0 | 1 | 4 | 1 |
| Hughes, ss | 3 | 0 | 1 | 1 | 1 |
| Borowy, p | 0 | 0 | 0 | 0 | 0 |
| Derringer, p | 0 | 0 | 0 | 0 | 0 |
| Vandenberg, p | 1 | 0 | 0 | 0 | 1 |
| Sauer, z | 1 | 0 | 0 | 0 | 0 |
| Erickson, p | 0 | 0 | 0 | 0 | 0 |
| Secory, zz | 1 | 0 | 0 | 0 | 0 |
| Passeau, p | 0 | 0 | 0 | 0 | 0 |
| Wyse, p | 0 | 0 | 0 | 0 | 0 |
| McCullough, zzz | 1 | 0 | 0 | 0 | 0 |
| Totals | 37 | 3 | 10 | 27 | 9 |

z—Batted for Vandenberg in 5th inning.
zz—Batted for Erickson in 7th inning.
zzz—Batted for Wyse in 9th inning.

SCORE BY INNINGS

Detroit ... 5 1 0 0 0 0 1 2 0—9
Chicago .. 1 0 0 1 0 0 0 1 0—3

SUMMARY

Error—Newhouser. Runs batted in—Cramer, Outlaw, Richards, 4; Cavarretta, York, Pafko, Mayo, Greenberg, Nicholson. Two-base hits—Richards, 2; Johnson, Mayo, Nicholson. Three-base hit—Pafko. Stolen bases—Outlaw, Cramer. Sacrifice—Greenberg. Double play—Webb to Mayo to York. Earned runs—Detroit, 9; Chicago, 3. Left on bases—Detroit, 8; Chicago, 8. Bases on balls—Off Derringer, 5 (Cullenbine, 2; Outlaw, Greenberg, York;) Vandenberg, 1 (Greenberg;) Erickson, 1 (Cullenbine;) Passeau, 1 (Webb;) Newhouser, 1 (Hughes.) Stuck out—By Newhouser, 10 (Hack, Hughes, 2; Sauer, Johnson, Pafko, 2; Secory, Livingston, McCullough.) By Vandenberg, 3 (Richards, Mayo, Cullenbine;) by Erickson, 2 (Greenberg, York.)

PITCHING SUMMARY

Borowy, 3 hits, 3 runs in 0 innings (none out in the first;) Derringer, 2 hits, 3 runs in 1⅔ innings; Vandenberg, 1 hit, 0 runs in 3⅓ innings; Erickson, 2 hits, 1 run in 2 innings; Passeau, 1 hit, 2 runs in 1 inning; Wyse, 0 hits, 0 runs in 1 inning. Wild pitch—Newhouser. Losing pitcher—Borowy. Umpires—Passarella (A.L.) p; Conlan (N.L.) 1b; Summers (A.L.) 2b; Jorda (N.L.) 3b. Time—2h. 31m.

## World Series at a Glance

BY THE ASSOCIATED PRESS

FINAL STANDING

| | W. | T. | Pct. |
|---|---|---|---|
| DETROIT (A.L.) | 4 | 3 | .571 |
| CHICAGO (N.L.) | 3 | 4 | .429 |

First game (at Detroit:)

| | | R. | H. | E. |
|---|---|---|---|---|
| CHICAGO (N.L.) | 403 000 200—9 | 13 | 0 |
| DETROIT (A.L.) | 000 000 000—0 | 6 | 0 |

Borowy and Livingston: Newhouser, Benton (3,) Tobin (5,) Mueller (8) and Richards.

Second game (at Detroit:)

| | | R. | H. | E. |
|---|---|---|---|---|
| CHICAGO (N.L.) | 000 100 000—1 | 7 | 0 |
| DETROIT (A.L.) | 000 040 00x—4 | 7 | 0 |

Wyse, Erickson (7) and Gillespie: Trucks and Richards.

Third game (at Detroit:)

| | | R. | H. | E. |
|---|---|---|---|---|
| CHICAGO (N.L.) | 000 200 100—3 | 8 | 0 |
| DETROIT (A.L.) | 000 000 000—0 | 1 | 2 |

Passeau and Livingston: Overmire, Benton (7) and Swift, Richards (7.)

Fourth game (at Chicago:)

| | | R. | H. | E. |
|---|---|---|---|---|
| DETROIT (A.L.) | 000 400 000—4 | 7 | 1 |
| CHICAGO (N.L.) | 000 001 000—1 | 5 | 1 |

Trout and Richards: Prim, Derringer (4,) Vandenberg (6,) Erickson (8) and Livingston.

Fifth game (at Chicago:)

| | | R. | H. | E. |
|---|---|---|---|---|
| DETROIT (A.L.) | 001 004 102—8 | 11 | 0 |
| CHICAGO (N.L.) | 001 000 201—4 | 7 | 1 |

Newhouser and Richards: Borowy, Vandenberg (6,) Chipman (6,) Derringer (7,) Erickson (9) and Livingston.

Sixth game (at Chicago:)

| | | R. | H. | E. |
|---|---|---|---|---|
| DETROIT (A.L.) | 010 000 240 000—7 | 13 | 2 |
| CHICAGO (N.L.) | 000 041 200 001—8 | 15 | 3 |

Trucks, Caster (5,) Bridges (6,) Benton (7,) Trout (8) and Richards, Swift (6:) Passeau, Wyse (7,) Prim (8,) Borowy (9) and Livingston, Williams (10.)

Seventh game (at Chicago:)

| | | R. | H. | E. |
|---|---|---|---|---|
| DETROIT (A.L.) | 510 000 120—9 | 9 | 1 |
| CHICAGO (N.L.) | 100 100 010—3 | 10 | 0 |

Newhouser and Richards, Swift (8:) Borowy, Derringer (8,) Vandenberg (2,) Erickson (6,) Passeau (8,) Wyse (9) and Livingston.

# ARMY ELEVEN WILL ACCEPT ROSE BOWL BID

## Sportscripts

by PAUL ZIMMERMAN
SPORTS EDITOR

Has the defense caught up with the T offense in college football?

The way Army and Notre Dame battled each other to a standstill Saturday furnishes some food for thought on this subject. Here we had two great, unbeaten teams who, by dint of thorough scouting held each other scoreless and for the most part kept the play within the 20-yard lines

Although these teams boasted of at least three backs who will make the first All-America eleven this year—Glenn Davis and Doc Blanchard for the Cadets and Johnny Lujack for the Irish—the average yardage gained all afternoon was 2.6. There were 160 plays run off in the 60 minutes.

**STRONG DISCIPLE**

A strong disciple of this belief is Paul Schissler, former college, professional and Army Air Forces coach, who is no babe in the woods on subjects football.

Schissler never has been completely sold on the T. An exponent of the box and single wing formations for the most part, the former Oregon State, National League and 4th Air Force mentor has become progressively more vehement in his arguments.

"It just doesn't make sense to me," says Paul, "to send backs into the line consistently without blockers or without the same number you could use on the old power plays. Once the quarterback feeds that ball he's of no earthly use. You just denude your ball carrier of that much protection.

**IS TROY SWITCHING?**

"I'm getting tired of seeing college teams send backs into the line naked of interference for two or three yards. Give me some blockers up ahead of a ball carrier and I'll get him loose oftener for longer gains than can be done with this fancy stuff."

In this vein, can it be that Coach Jeff Cravath is getting away from the T? Or did you overlook the fact that Troy's best passes yesterday were completed from the short punt formation and that Mickey McCardle scored on a spread formation?

And, while we are in the question asking mood, would you presume that the use of these formations against California presaged some of the stuff that Troy will have in store for the Bruins a week from next Saturday?

**GIVES HIM ROOM**

The T formation quarterback rarely runs. When he does he either has to depend on the quarterback sneak or else go with the ball after faking a pass, which never has been dependable. Of course, if he is a perfectionist like Bob Waterfield, he occasionally can hide the ball and go.

McCardle always was a fine ball carrier. But he needs room in which to maneuver. These new Trojan formations give him that room and the proof of the pudding was the fact that he was Troy's best ground gainer Saturday, averaging 5 yards a try, even if he did collect only 40 yards.

There is nothing startling about such yardage, but it gives you an idea of what might be forthcoming. As it was, the Trojans did not exploit their spread plays. The quarterback set them up with short jabs into the line but never got around to calling anything out to the flat.

**STAYS PUT**

But we have digressed.

The T formation can work better in pro football because you not only have the personnel adapted to it, but you have the time to spend on perfecting it.

Not all pro coaches who use the T are happy about the thing. Because of the shifting defenses used, the blockers find themselves with different players to block and different blocking angles than had been anticipated when the quarterback called the play. It gets to be a guessing contest and if the signal caller guesses right he's terrific. If he's wrong, he's a bum.

As one pro coach put it, "I could get more sleep coaching the single wing. The defense would have to sit tight to my right or I'd run all over him. It wouldn't dare shift around like it can with the T."

**HEAR AND THEIR**

Not a few college coaches are beginning to worry about their jobs . . . Frank Kimbrough of Baylor has been more or less on the hot seat all season . . . And there are rumblings in the Deep South about the future of Frank Thomas at Alabama . . . Some have named Paul Bryant of Kentucky as his successor already . . . Thomas was only the guy who was the toast of the land a year ago after walloping Troy in the Rose Bowl . . . He's been in poor health this fall, which may have something to do with 'Bama's three defeats.

P.S.: What became of the folks who picked them for the national championship?

## Luckman's Passes Tame Rams, 27-21

### Crowd of 68,381 Smashes Local Record for Pro Football Game

BY PAUL LOWRY

Sid Luckman, football's "T-That-Grew-in-Brooklyn," led the Chicago Bears to a thrilling 27-to-21 victory over the Los Angeles Rams in a game that drew the largest crowd in local professional football history to the Coliseum yesterday.

The turnout was 68,381, topping the record held by the Times charity game of 68,188 between the Rams and Washington Redskins last September.

Sparked by Luckman, who tossed three touchdown passes to Ken Kavanaugh in the end zone, the Bears put on a superdiller show that was all but matched by Bob Waterfield and company, but was nearly marred by what appeared to be extremely technical officiating.

**Touchdown Annulled**

The Rams had one clean touchdown taken away from them on the completion of a pass from Waterfield to Jim Benton because of alleged backs in motion (that was the ball game right there) and penalties ran the gamut of holding, clipping, running into kicker, offside, interference with pass receivers and one on Owner-Coach George Halas of the Bears for arguing with the referee.

In all a total of 31 penalties were called, which must be some kind of a record in a football game.

The Bears' win virtually assured them of the National League title (Western Division) and gave them their fifth victory in seven starts with one defeat and one tie. It was the third setback as against three wins for the Rams, who won the world's title last year.

**Gallarneau Sprints**

The Bears led, 20 to 7, at half time, thanks to a 52-yard sprint to a touchdown by Hugh Gallarneau, former Stanford star, five plays after the game opened and 38 and 34-yard tosses by Luckman for two other scores.

Waterfield hit Benton from 13 yards out for a Ram touchdown in the third period, but the irrepressible Luckman matched this with a 28-yard shot to Kavanaugh in the same quarter to lead, 27 to 14, while the Rams came back with their third score as the result of a short shot from Waterfield to Steve Pritko, 4 yards out, in the fourth quarter.

With the score 27 to 21 the Rams tried desperately to score again. A touchdown and a converted goal, after Matznicki had had his third attempt blocked, would give the Rams a victory.

**Intercepts Aerial**

But it was Luckman, spearhead of the Bear offense, who turned defensive hero when the Rams were riding dangerously close to the Bear goal line in the waning minutes of the game. With one hand he plucked a Waterfield pass off his shoe tops near the 5-yard line and ran the ball back to the Bear 29.

From that point Luckman, the Mister Quarterback of football, called nothing but line bucks, stalling for time until the game ended with the ball in Bear possession on the Ram 39.

It was a sensational conquest for Luckman and his mates, but on the other hand it was a tough game for Waterfield and company to lose, for the former Bruin virtually equaled his rival in pass completions. Luckman hit his men for 12 out of 22 and yardage of 245, while Waterfield completed 16 out of 30 and yardage of 180.

**Long Passes Click**

It was with the long passes that Luckman excelled, and with the pace-changing Kavanaugh to help him he made suckers of the Ram right halfbacks on the secondary line of defense. Although Luckman was rushed and it almost seemed impossible for him to get the ball away at times, somehow he did and there was Kavanaugh behind the Ram secondary to catch it, once over his head as he raced forward to the goal line.

Neither Bears nor the Rams could do much with the other

Turn to Page 9, Column 3

## Yankees' Rally Hands L.A. Dons 17-12 Trimming

BY DICK HYLAND

Times Staff Representative

NEW YORK, Nov. 10. — The New York Yankees, sparked by a wild, hard-running ex-Texan, Spec Sanders, put on a third-quarter rally to come from behind and defeat the Los Angeles Dons, 17-12, here today before 30,765 people.

The Dons took a 5-0 lead on a safety and a field goal in the second period, went behind, 7-5, then went ahead, 12-7, at the half, and saw the game grabbed from them in the third quarter when the surging Yanks tallied 10 points to win.

Typical of their last several games, the Dons outplayed their rivals except for the brief moments when fast scores were made against them. They bottled the powerhouse running attack of the Yanks today, giving up only 43 yards, and permitted but 87 yards from passes to be racked up against them. The Dons made 210 yards from rushing and passing.

**Radovich Breaks Through**

The Dons went ahead less than two minutes after the start of the second quarter via an automatic safety when ex-Trojan Bill Radovich broke through and blocked Ace Parker's kick on the Yank 10-yard line. The ball bounced behind the goal with Joe Aguirre going out of the end zone, chasing it, just as he got the ball. Three minutes later, stymied on the Yank 24 after a march from their own 48-yard line, the Dons took three more points when Aguirre kicked a field goal from the 32.

Five minutes later, Sanders, one of the greatest runners in football today, cut through two-thirds of the Don team after receiving a flat pass from Ace Parker on the Los Angeles 45-yard line to put the local team into a 7-5 lead when Harvey Johnson kicked his 23rd straight extra point.

**Dons Come Back**

Taking the ball on the ensuing kickoff the Dons marched to a touchdown in six plays. Just 36 seconds before the end of the half, Bob Seymour returned the kickoff 25 yards, Elsey and O'Rourke drove for 7 yards, Angelo Bertelli passed to Bob Seymour for 7 more and, with the ball on the Yanks' 47-yard line, Bertelli dropped a beautiful pass into Seymour's hands. He took the ball right away from Pug Manders on the Yank 15-yard line and scooted for the score.

Aguirre kicked the extra point.

In the third quarter the Yanks were given a penalty first down on the Don 26-yard line and Harvey Johnson kicked a field goal from the 17 when the Yanks became bogged down on the 12.

With the score 12-10 in their favor, outplaying the Yanks at all times, the Dons seemed safe enough when they kicked to Yank Halfback Ed Prokop on his own 33-yard line. The ex-

Turn to Page 9, Column 5

## Magyars Triumph at Soccer, 5-2

Bouncing back in the second half and breaking half-time deadlock of 1-1, Magyar A.C.'s soccermen thumped the Vikings, 5 to 2, yesterday in the feature tilt at Rancho La Cienega. A crowd of 1500 witnessed.

In the preliminary match Joe Edesa and Ray Brough hit pay territory to give the Hollywoods a 2-1 upset win over Victoria.

## BEAR HALFBACK ROMPS 52 YARDS FOR SCORE

Times photo by Art Rogers

GALLARNEAU GALLOPS—Hustling Hugh Gallarneau gallops 52 yards for first Bear touchdown early in first period. Ram players are Tom Harmon (98) and Mike Holovak (45.) Chicago pros whipped locals, 27-21.

## Cadets Play Bruin-Troy Game Victor

Continued from Page 1, Part I

Point also were willing to send their team west. But a possibility that there might be some slip-up in the War Department along with the attendant delay of getting approval forced the Coast Conference to make a quick decision in favor of Alabama.

Alabama was the only other logical Bowl contender and was being hard pressed by the Sugar Bowl for an answer to its offer.

Not only were authorities at West Point known to be interested in the game, but the team also was anxious to make the trip and it is known that the players were keenly dissapointed in not receiving the invitation.

There is no reason to believe that any of these circumstances have changed this year.

**Campaign Booster**

In addition to these, the Army is busy in a campaign of selling young men on the merits of serving their country and a Rose Bowl game presenting the Cadets to the West Coast for the first time since 1929 when they played Stanford at Palo Alto would do much toward this program.

Precedent for such a game was set back in 1924 when Navy met Washington in the annual Tournament of Roses game, playing to a 14-to-14 tie.

There is no reason why the Coast Conference should rush into an agreement with the Big Nine to compete in the Rose Bowl.

The West made repeated overtures to the then Big Ten in years gone by, always to be turned down, and there should be no great haste in closing a contract with that group now.

**Bruins Willing**

Especially is this true this year with every team in the Western Conference defeated and no great standout champion in prospect. Illinois, the current leader, voted against playing in the Rose Bowl.

The Bruins have indicated they would like to play Army, if they are invited and the Trojans gave the same indication a year ago.

As for the paying public, the majority has hankered for three years to see the great Cadet team with California's own Glenn Davis in the starring role.

Los Angeles Times Sports

MONDAY MORNING, NOVEMBER 11, 1946

## Redskins Swat Boston, 17-14

WASHINGTON, Nov. 10. (AP)—Dick Todd, hampered previously this season by a broken hand, led the Washington Redskins today to a hard-fought 17-14 National League football victory over the Boston Yanks.

Todd scored both touchdowns and his final thrust was the prettiest play of the day. This came in the last quarter with Boston ahead 14-10, before 33,691.

Todd hit the right side of the Yank line full steam ahead and never slowed down until he crossed the goal line, 30 yards away.

Although Todd, who previously has been limited to defense work because of his injured hand, was the hero, Dick Poillon's field goal from the 30-yard line in the second period proved to be the winning margin.

| Washington | | Boston |
|---|---|---|
| Peebles | L.E. | Goldman |
| Udams | L.T. | Deeks |
| Ward | L.G. | Badaczewski |
| Aldrich | C. | Domnanovich |
| Steber | R.G. | Canale |
| Young | R.T. | Pedersen |
| Cikers | R.E. | Crisler |
| Poillon | Q. | Scollard |
| Todd | L.H. | Dimancheff |
| Gaffney | R.H. | Micka |
| Jenkins | F. | Grigas |

SCORE BY QUARTERS

| | | | | |
|---|---|---|---|---|
| Washington | 0 | 3 | 7 | 7—17 |
| Boston | 0 | 7 | 7 | 0—14 |

Washington scoring: Touchdowns—Todd, 2. Points after touchdowns—Poillon, 2. Field goal—Poillon.

Boston scoring: Touchdowns — Famiglietti, 2. Points after touchdowns — Scollard, 2.

## Bombers Surprise Seagulls, 17 to 0

SAN DIEGO, Nov. 10. (AP)—San Diego's Pacific Coast League professional football Bombers defeated Salt Lake's Seagulls, 17 to 0, here today for their first victory of the season in six games. About 4000 fans saw the contest.

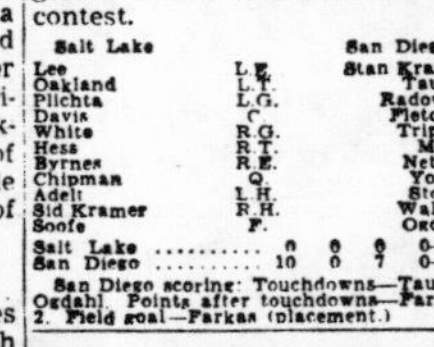

| Salt Lake | | San Diego |
|---|---|---|
| Lee | L.E. | Stan Kramer |
| Oakland | L.T. | Tauber |
| Plichta | L.G. | Radovich |
| Davis | C. | Fletcher |
| White | R.G. | Tripani |
| Hess | R.T. | Mena |
| Byrnes | R.E. | Nettles |
| Chipman | Q. | Young |
| Adelt | L.H. | Stoves |
| Sid Kramer | R.H. | Walden |
| Soofe | F. | Ogdahl |

| | | | | |
|---|---|---|---|---|
| Salt Lake | 0 | 0 | 0 | 0— 0 |
| San Diego | 10 | 0 | 7 | 0—17 |

San Diego scoring: Touchdowns—Tauber, Ogdahl. Points after touchdowns—Parkas, 2. Field goal—Farkas (placement.)

## Woodward, Chambers Triumph in Golf Duel

Jimmy Woodward and Mrs. T. E. Chambers defeated Mr. and Mrs. Marshall Springer, 1 up on the 19th green, to lead the way into the semifinal round of the Women's Southern California Golf Association mixed foursome tournament yesterday at Annandale Country Club. Results:

Jimmy Woodward-Mrs. T. E. Chambers def. Mr. and Mrs. Marshall Springer, 1 up on 19th; Mr. and Mrs. Jack Holmes won by default; Mr. and Mrs. Jim Ferrel def. Johnny Weissmuller-Allene Gates, 1 up; Boyer-Mrs. Montgomery def. Herb Hussey-Mrs. Denio, 3 and 2.

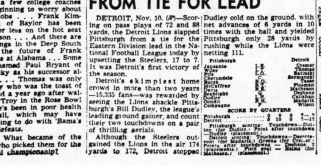

## Pro Grid Standings

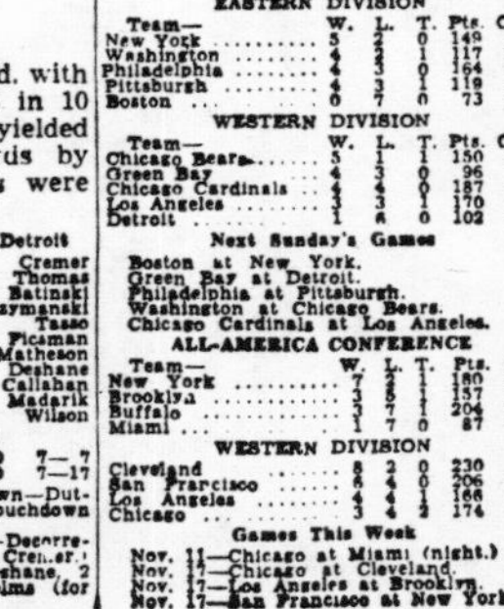

NATIONAL LEAGUE

EASTERN DIVISION

| Team— | W. | L. | T. | Pts. | O.P. |
|---|---|---|---|---|---|
| New York | 5 | 2 | 0 | 149 | 103 |
| Washington | 4 | 2 | 1 | 117 | 106 |
| Philadelphia | 4 | 3 | 0 | 164 | 162 |
| Pittsburgh | 4 | 3 | 1 | 119 | 93 |
| Boston | 0 | 7 | 0 | 73 | 174 |

WESTERN DIVISION

| Team— | W. | L. | T. | Pts. | O.P. |
|---|---|---|---|---|---|
| Chicago Bears | 5 | 1 | 1 | 150 | 108 |
| Green Bay | 4 | 3 | 0 | 96 | 89 |
| Chicago Cardinals | 4 | 4 | 0 | 187 | 147 |
| Los Angeles | 3 | 3 | 1 | 170 | 165 |
| Detroit | 1 | 6 | 0 | 102 | 180 |

Next Sunday's Games

Boston at New York.
Green Bay at Detroit.
Philadelphia at Pittsburgh.
Washington at Chicago Bears.
Chicago Cardinals at Los Angeles.

ALL-AMERICA CONFERENCE

| Team— | W. | L. | T. | Pts. | OP |
|---|---|---|---|---|---|
| New York | 7 | 2 | 1 | 180 | 138 |
| Brooklyn | 3 | 5 | 1 | 157 | 172 |
| Buffalo | 3 | 7 | 1 | 204 | 245 |
| Miami | 1 | 7 | 0 | 87 | 225 |

WESTERN DIVISION

| | | | | | |
|---|---|---|---|---|---|
| Cleveland | 8 | 2 | 0 | 230 | 92 |
| San Francisco | 6 | 4 | 0 | 206 | 158 |
| Los Angeles | 4 | 4 | 1 | 166 | 176 |
| Chicago | 3 | 4 | 2 | 174 | 198 |

Games This Week

Nov. 11—Chicago at Miami (night.)
Nov. 17—Chicago at Cleveland.
Nov. 17—Los Angeles at Brooklyn.
Nov. 17—San Francisco at New York.

## Giants Wreck Eagles, 45-17, to Lead East

NEW YORK, Nov. 10. (AP)—The New York Giants got more than even for a beating they absorbed a week ago by flailing the fumbling Philadelphia Eagles, 45 to 17, today to take over sole possession of the top spot in the National Professional Football League's eastern championship race.

For the entertainment of a sell-out crowd of 60,784 in the Polo Grounds, the Giants galloped to their biggest score in 13 years. And on that occasion, too, it was the Phillies who rolled over and played dead, 56-0, for Steve Owen's warriors.

**Eagles Slow Up**

The Eagles started out this time as if they were going to pick up where they left off last Sunday when they jolted the Giants, 24-14. But after they grabbed a quick 10-0 lead in the first five minutes on Augie Lio's 36-yard field goal and a 54-yard touchdown run with an intercepted pass by Gil Steinke, one-time Texas A.&I. ball carrier, the Giants found the combination and it was no contest the rest of the way.

Only in the fading minutes, when Al Sherman pitched 14 yards to Dick Humbert, were the Phillies able to hit the jackpot again.

Four times the Giants grabbed Eagle fumbles. Three of these fumbles were converted into New York touchdowns.

| Philadelphia | | New York |
|---|---|---|
| Ferrante | L.E. | Poole |
| Sears | L.T. | Cope |
| Lio | L.G. | Dobelstein |
| Lindskog | C. | Gladchuk |
| Maronic | R.G. | Younce |
| Wistert | R.T. | White |
| Cabrelli | R.E. | Howell |
| Thompson | Q. | Filipowicz |
| Vanburen | L.H. | Filchock |
| Pritchard | R.H. | Livingston |
| Muha | F. | Strong |

SCORE BY QUARTERS

| | | | | |
|---|---|---|---|---|
| Philadelphia | 10 | 0 | 0 | 7—17 |
| New York | 7 | 17 | 7 | 14—45 |

Philadelphia scoring: Touchdowns—Steinke (sub for Pritchard.) Humbert (sub for Cabrilli.) Points after touchdowns—Lio 2 (place kicks.) Field goal—Lio (place kick.)

New York scoring: Touchdowns—Poole, 2; Paschal (sub for Strong.) Mapes (sub for Strong.) Reagan (sub for Filchock.) Weiss (sub for Poole.) Points after touchdowns—Strong (place kicks.) Field goal—Strong (place kick.)

## Browns Drub '49'ers, 14-7

SAN FRANCISCO, Nov. 10. (AP) — Cleveland's Browns, putting together two great scoring drives in the first half, defeated the San Francisco '49'ers, 14 to 7, today in an All-America Conference professional football game witnessed by a crowd estimated at 48,000 fans. The victory gave the Browns a two-game lead over the local eleven, their closest rivals for Western Division honors of the league.

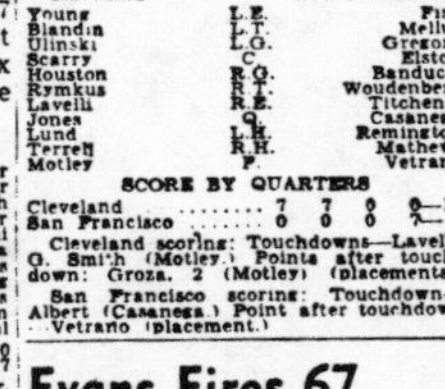

| Cleveland | | San Francisco |
|---|---|---|
| Young | L.E. | Fisk |
| Blandin | L.T. | Mellus |
| Ulinski | L.G. | Gregory |
| Scarry | C. | Elston |
| Houston | R.G. | Banducci |
| Rymkus | R.T. | Woudenberg |
| Lavelli | R.E. | Titchenal |
| Jones | Q. | Casanega |
| Lund | L.H. | Remington |
| Terrell | R.H. | Mathews |
| Motley | F. | Vetrano |

SCORE BY QUARTERS

| | | | | |
|---|---|---|---|---|
| Cleveland | 7 | 7 | 0 | 0—14 |
| San Francisco | 0 | 0 | 0 | 7— 7 |

Cleveland scoring: Touchdowns—Lavelli, G. Smith (Motley.) Points after touchdown: Groza, 2 (Motley) (placements.)

San Francisco scoring: Touchdown—Albert (Casanega.) Point after touchdown—Vetrano (placement.)

## Evans Fires 67 to Lead Golfers

Ralph Evans of Inglewood continued to pace the field yesterday in the first annual Long Beach medal play tournament at Meadow Lark golf course, adding a 5 under par 67 to a first-round 68 of yesterday.

Elmer Clements, stylist from Palos Verdes, put a 71 with his 69 of the first round to hold second spot in the title class with Smiley Quick, national public links champion, getting a 70 with a first round of 72 for third spot.

Fields in all classes will be cut today to the low 20 and ties with the first foursomes scheduled to tee off in the final round of the 54-hole tournament at 9:30 a.m.

Leaders in championship class: Ralph Evans (Inglewood,) 68-67—135. Elmer Clements (Palos Verdes,) 69-71—140. Smiley Quick (Inglewood,) 72-70—142. Jack Nounnan (Sunset Fields,) 71-72—143. Don Kennedy (Santa Ana,) 72-73—145.

## Ice Hockey Results

PACIFIC COAST LEAGUE

San Diego, 4; Fresno, 0.
Portland, 2; New Westminster, 1.
Seattle, 8; Vancouver, 2.

WESTERN INTERNATIONAL LEAGUE

L.A. Ramblers, 5; Kimberly Dynamiters, 4.
Trail, 5; Spokane, 4.

NATIONAL LEAGUE

Boston, 4; New York, 0.
Toronto, 4; Chicago, 2.
Detroit, 6; Montreal, 3.

AMERICAN LEAGUE

St. Louis, 4; Pittsburgh, 4 (tie.)
Springfield, 1; New Haven, 1 (tie.)
Providence, 7; Philadelphia, 3.
Buffalo, 1; Hershey, 0.
Cleveland, 3; Indianapolis, 2.

UNITED STATES LEAGUE

St. Paul, 4; Kansas City, 0.
Houston, 3; Ft. Worth, 2.

## Football Scores

NATIONAL LEAGUE PROS

Chicago Bears, 27; Los Angeles Rams, 21.
Washington Redskins, 17; Boston Yanks, 14.
Detroit Lions, 17; Pittsburgh Steelers, 7.
New York Giants, 45; Philadelphia Eagles, 17.
Green Bay Packers, 19; Chicago Cardinals, 7.

ALL-AMERICA PROS

New York Yankees, 17; Los Angeles Dons, 12.
Cleveland Browns, 14; San Francisco '49'ers, 7.
Buffalo Bisons, 17; Brooklyn Dodgers, 14.

COAST LEAGUE PROS

San Diego Bombers, 17; Salt Lake Seagulls, 0.

AMERICAN PRO LEAGUE

Jersey City Giants, 32; Wilmington Clippers, 0.
Long Island Indians, 14; Paterson Panthers, 3.

COLLEGE

Scranton, 13; Canisius, 13.
St. Norberts, 19; St. Ambrose, 7.

SERVICE

Ft. Benning, 38; Cherry Point Marines, 0.

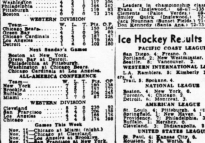

## Bruins to Get Two-Day Respite

Coach Bert LaBrucherie will make a very well-received speech to his undefeated U.C.L.A. footballers upon their arrival in Glendale this morning—"No practice today or tomorrow, fellows." With Montana this Saturday's Coliseum opponent — and with midterm examinations coming up later in the week—LaBrucherie decided to give his varsity hands a respite from their gridiron duties.

Playing in the mud against Oregon Saturday also left most of the boys hobbled by sore legs and scratched up from the sand that was strewn on the field to aid footing.

**Regulars to Start**

Although the Bruins will be favored to win as they please from the Grizzlies, LaBrucherie said he's planning to start his regular No. 1 combine. But reserves no doubt will play most of the time.

Nobody was seriously hurt in the 14-0 conquest of the Webfoots, but Tom Fears, Bill Clements, Moose Myers, Bob Mike and Skip Rowland picked up minor hurts and will take it easy this week.

## Raisin Bowl Game Pledges Received

SAN LUIS OBISPO, Nov. 10. (AP)—Representatives of the California Collegiate Athletic Association—strong little colleges in the West—today accepted the invitation of the Fresno Junior Chamber of Commerce to pledge the conference champion to meet the champion of a similar conference in the East or Midwest in Fresno's Raisin Bowl on Jan. 1.

Representatives of California Poly, College of the Pacific, Fresno State, San Jose State, Santa Barbara State and San Diego State participated in the meeting.

## St. Norbert's Eleven Keeps Record Spotless

DAVENPORT (Ia.) Nov. 10. (AP)—St. Norbert's College of West Depere, Wis., today handed St. Ambrose its first homecoming defeat in 12 years by a 19-to-7 count, and remained among the nation's undefeated football elevens.

## Fight Arenas Dark

Ocean Park Arena and Hollywood Legion Stadium will be dark tonight because of an Athletic Commission ruling barring boxing and wrestling on Armistice Day. Both arenas will resume their regular shows next Monday night.

## Ramblers Edge Dynamiters, 5-4

Staving off a desperate third-period rally, the Los Angeles Ramblers defeated the Kimberly Dynamiters, 5-4, in last night's Western International Ice Hockey League match at Westwood Ice Palace.

For the Ramblers it was their second win in as many nights, having edged the Canadian sextet, 4-3, Saturday night on the same rink.

A flare-up of fisticuffs in the second stanza featuring Hasse Young of the Ramblers and Sammy Calles of the Dynamiters supplied some extra excitement for the 3000 fans who witnessed the fray. Both bouters were ushered into the penalty box for five-minute stays.

Leading the Rambler attack was Max Labovich, right wing, who hit the netting twice.

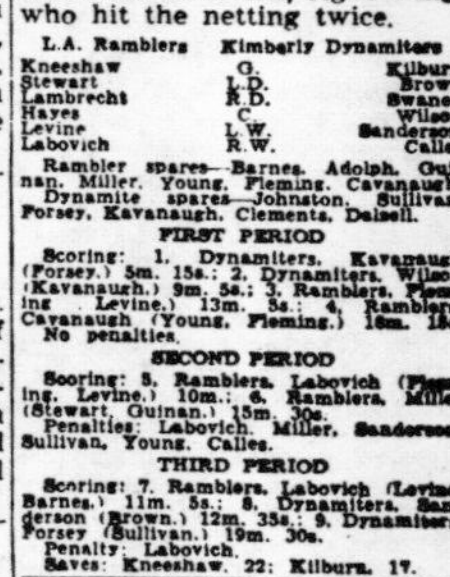

| L.A. Ramblers | | Kimberly Dynamiters |
|---|---|---|
| Kneeshaw | G. | Kilburn |
| Stewart | L.D. | Brown |
| Lambrecht | R.D. | Swaney |
| Hayes | C. | Wilson |
| Levine | L.W. | Sanderson |
| Labovich | R.W. | Calles |

Rambler spares—Barnes, Adolph, Guinan, Miller, Young, Fleming, Cavanaugh. Dynamite spares—Johnston, Sullivan, Forsey, Kavanaugh, Clements, Dalsell.

FIRST PERIOD

Scoring: 1, Dynamiters, Kavanaugh (Forsey,) 5m. 15s.; 2, Dynamiters, Wilson (Kavanaugh,) 9m. 5s.; 3, Ramblers, Fleming (Levine,) 13m. 5s.; 4, Ramblers, Cavanaugh (Young, Fleming,) 16m. 15s. No penalties.

SECOND PERIOD

Scoring: 5, Ramblers, Labovich (Fleming, Levine,) 10m.; 6, Ramblers, Miller (Stewart, Guinan,) 15m. 30s.
Penalties: Labovich, Miller, Sanderson, Sullivan, Young, Calles.

THIRD PERIOD

Scoring: 7, Ramblers, Labovich (Levine, Barnes,) 11m. 5s.; 8, Dynamiters, Sanderson (Brown,) 12m. 35s.; 9, Dynamiters, Forsey (Sullivan,) 19m. 30s.
Penalty: Labovich.
Saves: Kneeshaw, 22; Kilburn, 17.

## Indians Top Panthers

PATERSON (N.J.) Nov. 10. (AP)—The Long Island Indians beat the Paterson Panthers today, 14 to 3, in an American Professional Football League game before 4400.

## LIONS DROP STEELERS FROM TIE FOR LEAD

DETROIT, Nov. 10. (AP)—Scoring on pass plays of 72 and 88 yards, the Detroit Lions slapped Pittsburgh from a tie for the Eastern Division lead in the National Football League today by upsetting the Steelers, 17 to 7. It was Detroit's first victory of the season.

Detroit's skimpiest home crowd in more than two years—15,335 fans—was rewarded by seeing the Lions shackle Pittsburgh's Bill Dudley, the league's leading ground gainer, and count their two touchdowns on a pair of thrilling aerials.

Although the Steelers outgained the Lions in the air 174 yards to 172, Detroit stopped Dudley cold on the ground, with net advances of 6 yards in 10 times with the ball and yielded Pittsburgh only 28 yards by rushing while the Lions were netting 111.

| Pittsburgh | | Detroit |
|---|---|---|
| Jansante | L.E. | Cremer |
| Wiley | L.T. | Thomas |
| Fife | L.G. | Batinski |
| Cherundolo | C. | Szymanski |
| Bucek | R.G. | Tasso |
| McCaffray | R.T. | Piccman |
| Davis | R.E. | Matheson |
| Seabright | Q. | Deshane |
| Dudley | L.H. | Callahan |
| Condit | R.H. | Madarik |
| Compagno | F. | Wilson |

SCORE BY QUARTERS

| | | | | |
|---|---|---|---|---|
| Pittsburgh | 0 | 0 | 0 | 7— 7 |
| Detroit | 0 | 10 | 0 | 7—17 |

Pittsburgh scoring: Touchdown—Dutton (for Dudley.) Point after touchdown—Dudley (placement.)

Detroit scoring: Touchdowns—Decorrevont (for Madarik.) Greene (for Cremer.) Points after touchdowns — Deshane, 2 (placements.) Field goal — Helms (for Matheson.) (placement.)

## GLENN DOBBS' PASS BACKFIRES, BISONS WIN

BROOKLYN (N.Y.) Nov. 10. (AP)—Glenn Dobbs, Brooklyn's "one-man team," pitched both of his team's touchdowns but another one of his passes backfired into an interception which led to a Buffalo score and a Bison 17-14 victory over the Dodgers today in an All-America Professional Football Conference game at Ebbets Field.

Dobbs dazzled the crowd of 12,820 with 12 completions in 25 attempts, good for 258 yards, but his first heave, in the opening minutes of the game, was intercepted by Felto Prewitt on the Bisons' 10-yard line and the Buffalo center ran it back 42 yards to the Dodgers' 48.

| Buffalo | | Brooklyn Dodgers |
|---|---|---|
| Ebli | L.E. | McCarthy |
| Stanley | L.T. | Ruby |
| Perko | L.G. | Bernhardt |
| Prewitt | C. | Gibson |
| Pirro | R.G. | Buffington |
| Doherty | R.T. | Mieszkowski |
| Nelson | R.E. | Davis |
| Dekdebrun | Q. | McDonald |
| Johnston | L.H. | Dobbs |
| Juzwik | R.H. | Vantone |
| Zontini | F. | Mayne |

| | | | | |
|---|---|---|---|---|
| Buffalo | 10 | 0 | 7 | 0—17 |
| Brooklyn | 0 | 7 | 0 | 7—14 |

Buffalo scoring: Touchdowns—Johnston, Ebli. Points after touchdowns—Zontini, 2. Field goal—Zontini.

Brooklyn scoring: Touchdowns—Vantone, Tackett (sub for McDonald.) Points after touchdowns—Martinovich, 2 (sub for Buffington.)

# LEO DUROCHER SUSPENDED FOR 1947 SEASON

## The Sports Parade

By BRAVEN DYER

Bernie Kearney tells me the harness races which open at Hollywood Park tomorrow will be the best ever staged anywhere. Having known Bernie since his football days at Loyola, I am perfectly willing to accept his judgment. He learned long ago to play square with the press and public.

"We have the best horses, the best drivers and the best equipment," said the general manager of the Western Harness Racing Association yesterday. "In addition we have a new starting gate which has the unqualified approval of everybody connected with the sport."

**CONFIDENCE RESTORED**

I've seen this new gate operating and it's the cat's meow. Those who were reluctant to unlatch their wallets at Santa Anita last spring because of uncertain starts can now march up to the betting wickets with confidence.

Also the bar system (whatever that was) has been discarded and horses now are graded according to the amount of money they have won. This makes sense and gives the public an opportunity to find out what's going on. I suspect there was considerable chiseling among owners under the old bar rating.

Last year I never got overly enthused about harness racing, but with the improvements which have been made, plus Mr. Kearney's guarantee of several winners every day (oh, yeah) I confess my blood pressure is beginning to mount.

**NAMES TO REMEMBER**

To doubly insure my interest they have given me the probable winners of the two big races, the $50,000 Golden West Pace May 3 and the $50,000 Golden West Trot May 10, so that I can start saving up in my piggy bank for a few mutuel tickets on those big days. The favorites, they opine, will be Ensign Hanover in the pace and Victory Song in the trot, and both horses are from the Castleton Farm at Lexington, Ky., of Mr. and Mrs. James B. Johnson Jr.

They seek to entice me further with a look to the records, pointing out that Victory Song not only was the fastest 3-year-old trotter of 1946 but also the leading money winner among all trotters in the country, regardless of age. Victory Song opened his 1946 campaign at Santa Anita last spring where he won two races, the first in 2:10 and the second in 2:07¼. After being shipped east he won a couple more while prepping for the Hambletonian, the Kentucky Derby of harness racing, and he came to the big race co-favored with Chestertown.

**REVENGE AT LAST**

After winning the first heat of this traditional harness classic he came a cropper in the second and third heats in which he finished ninth and second, respectively, and lost the race to Chestertown. He won five straight heats after that, and in the Kentucky Futurity, second richest of the 3-year-old trotting races, he avenged his defeat in the Hambletonian by humbling Chestertown in two straight heats.

Victory Song started 27 times in 1946 and came up the winner on 19 of the occasions for a winning percentage of .704. That seems like much better than a fair country winning percentage, but wait until you hear what they tell me about Ensign Hanover.

**CONSISTENT WINNER**

The Ensign is a pacer, according to my informers, and they tell me he is the greatest money-winning pacer of all times, regardless of age or length of racing career, with earnings of $65,695. As a 2-year-old he won 22 out of 23 starts before hanging up his tack for the year. Last year he went to the post 26 times and visited the winner's circle after 19 of these outings. He thus goes into his third year of campaigning with a really great record of consistency and as a source of great comfort to the chalk players who insist that at last they've found that horse of Tin-Pan Alley fame "who couldn't go wrong."

Both Victory Song and Ensign Hanover are trained and driven by Sep Palin, one of the top trainers and drivers around the Grand Circuit for many years and who is often referred to as the "Johnny Longden of the Sulky."

The Johnsons are among the better known owners in the harness whirl, and always have taken keen and active interest in affairs of their horses.

Mrs. Johnson, herself an equestrienne of note, rode Greyhound, the now retired king of the sulky-steeds, to his record under saddle of 2:01¾ for one mile, established in 1940.

## Oaks Shade Seraphs in 10th, 4 to 3

BY AL WOLF

Oakland's Oaks played (and lost) four extra-inning ball games at San Diego last week.

So when the Stengelites found themselves working overtime again yesterday afternoon at Wrigley Field, they felt right at home—and proceeded to edge Los Angeles, 4-3, in 10 spasms.

Oren Baker, hero of the Angels' 12-inning victory over Portland a week ago, this time was the goat.

Taking over, at the start of the 10th after Red Adams had been lifted for a hitter, "Big Bake" was nicked for a single by Les Scarsella (who then stole second) and a double by Bill Hart.

It was a tight squeeze for fair.

**Scarsella Clinches Tie**

The Oaks put over a tying tally after two were dead in the ninth, Brooks Holder bashing it in with his fourth hit of the day. And when Scarsella romped home with the clincher, two also were out.

Jim Arnold started for the visitors and was victimized for two runs in the fourth. The Oaks came right back to knot the count in the top of the fifth. Arnold departed in favor of a batter during the rally and Damon Hayes took over in the bottom half of the frame, only to be rudely treated, indeed, by Cece Garriott, who belted the Angels' 12th homer of the fledgling campaign.

That made her 3-2, of course, and that's the way she stayed until the 1900 fans started streaking for the exits in the ninth. They soon streaked back.

Floyd Speer, who entered the fray in the ninth, was credited with the victory.

**Foul Tips**

Red Lynn (0-1) will chuck for the Cherubs at 2:30 today . . . It'll be Tom Reis (0-0) for the Acorns . . . Reis notched a 7-and-5 record with Kansas City last year . . . Yesterday's wind made life rugged for the outfielders.

Adams was called out in the fifth inning for straying off the line as he ran for first and getting hit by Catcher Ed Kearse's throw . . . Roy Paton has refused to report to Nashville, so the Angels are trying to option him elsewhere.

Glenn Crawford, signed t'other day by Oakland after getting the thumb from Portland, scored yesterday's tying run in the ninth after slapping a pinch single . . . Shortstop Billy Schuster of Los Angeles not only made a sensational backward catch of Ray Hamrick's short fly in the fifth, but turned it into a double play.

| Oakland | AB | H | O | A | Los Angeles | AB | H | O | A |
|---|---|---|---|---|---|---|---|---|---|
| Holder,lf | 5 | 4 | 3 | 0 | Garriott,cf | 5 | 1 | 2 | 0 |
| Smith,cf | 3 | 0 | 4 | 0 | Schuster,ss | 4 | 3 | 4 | 6 |
| Hamrick,ss | 5 | 0 | 2 | 4 | Bauer,rf | 4 | 1 | 1 | 0 |
| Scarsella,1b | 5 | 2 | 10 | 1 | Maddern,lf | 5 | 0 | 2 | 0 |
| Marshall,rf | 5 | 1 | 2 | 0 | Ostrowski,3b | 3 | 0 | 1 | 1 |
| Hart,3b | 5 | 2 | 3 | 4 | Stringer,2b | 3 | 1 | 3 | 3 |
| Burnett,2b | 2 | 0 | 1 | 4 | Richards,1b | 3 | 1 | 8 | 0 |
| Sabol,2b | 0 | 0 | 0 | 0 | Pawelek,a | 1 | 0 | 0 | 0 |
| Crawford,xx-2b | 1 | 1 | 0 | 0 | Otero,1b | 1 | 0 | 3 | 0 |
| Kearse,c | 2 | 0 | 4 | 2 | Malone,c | 3 | 1 | 6 | 1 |
| Gillespie,s | 1 | 0 | 0 | 0 | Treadway,b | 1 | 0 | 0 | 0 |
| Raimondi,c | 1 | 0 | 0 | 0 | Adams,p | 3 | 0 | 0 | 1 |
| Arnold,p | 1 | 1 | 0 | 0 | Glossop,aa | 1 | 0 | 0 | 0 |
| Barton,x | 1 | 0 | 0 | 0 | Baker,p | 0 | 0 | 0 | 0 |
| Hayes,p | 1 | 0 | 0 | 0 | | | | | |
| V. Bohays,zz | 1 | 0 | 0 | 0 | | | | | |
| Speer,p | 0 | 0 | 1 | 0 | | | | | |
| Totals | 39 | 11 | 30 | 15 | Totals | 37 | 8 | 30 | 12 |

x—Batted for Arnold in 5th.
xx—Batted for Sabol in 9th.
z—Batted for Hayes in 9th.
zz—Batted for Kearse in 9th.
a—Batted for Richards in 8th.
aa—Batted for Adams in 9th.
b—Batted for Malone in 10th.

Oakland ............0 0 0 0 2 0 0 0 1 1—4
Los Angeles ........0 0 0 2 1 0 0 0 0 0—3

PITCHERS' RECORDS

| | IP | AB | R | H | ER | BB | SO |
|---|---|---|---|---|---|---|---|
| Arnold | 4 | 16 | 2 | 4 | 2 | 1 | 0 |
| Hayes | 4 | 14 | 1 | 4 | 1 | 3 | 3 |
| Speer | 2 | 7 | 0 | 0 | 0 | 2 | 0 |
| Adams | 9 | 34 | 3 | 9 | 3 | 4 | 6 |
| Baker | 1 | 5 | 1 | 3 | 1 | 0 | 0 |

Summary: E—Hamrick, 2; Richards. HB—Crawford by Baker. LOB—Oakland, 10; Los Angeles, 11. PB—Kearse. 2B—Holder, Scarsella, Hart, Stringer, Bauer. 3B—Schuster. HR—Garriott. SH—Stringer. SB—Bauer, Holder, Smith, Scarsella. RBI—Holder, 2; Smith, Hart, Garriott, Maddern, Stringer. DP—Malone to Schuster; Schuster to Stringer; Stringer to Richards. Winner—Speer—Loser—Baker. Official attendance, 1900.

## Baseball Standings

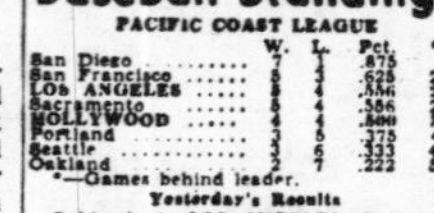

PACIFIC COAST LEAGUE

| | W. | L. | Pct. | * |
|---|---|---|---|---|
| San Diego | 7 | 1 | .875 | |
| San Francisco | 5 | 3 | .625 | 2 |
| LOS ANGELES | 5 | 4 | .556 | 2½ |
| Sacramento | 5 | 4 | .556 | 2½ |
| HOLLYWOOD | 4 | 4 | .500 | 3 |
| Portland | 3 | 5 | .375 | 4 |
| Seattle | 3 | 6 | .333 | 4½ |
| Oakland | 2 | 7 | .222 | 5½ |

*—Games behind leader.

**Yesterday's Results**

Oakland, 4; LOS ANGELES, 3 (10 innings.)
HOLLYWOOD, 7; San Francisco, 4 (10 innings.)
Sacramento, 7; Seattle, 4.
Portland, 4; San Diego, 4 (15-inning tie, called for curfew.)

**New Series Stand**

LOS ANGELES, 1; Oakland, 1.
HOLLYWOOD, 1; San Francisco, 0.
Sacramento, 1; Seattle, 1.
San Diego, 1; Portland, 0.

**Games Today**

Oakland at LOS ANGELES, Wrigley Field, 2:30 p.m.
HOLLYWOOD at San Francisco.
Seattle at Sacramento.
Portland at San Diego.

## Exhibition Baseball

Montreal (I.L.) vs. Brooklyn (N.) canceled, rain.

At Shreveport, La.: R. H. E.
Chicago (N.) ....... 000 230 200—7 9 0
Shreveport (T.) .... 000 000 000—0 5 0
Kush, Lade and Sheffing, Livingston; Dothager, Davis, Hill and Crompton, Rossi.

At Birmingham, Ala.: R. H. E.
Pittsburgh (N.) .... 200 000 002—4 15 1
St. Louis (A.) ...... 210 100 20x—6 9 0
Sewell, Singleton and Jarvis; Potter, Kramer and Moss.

At Hickory, N.C.: R. H. E.
New York (N.) ...... 000 001 420—7 11 1
Cleveland (A.) ..... 100 000 111—4 12 2
Kennedy, Carpenter and Lombardi; Black, Gettel, Lemon and Hegan, Lopez.

At Chattanooga, Tenn.: R. H. E.
Philadelphia (N.) .. 121 002 101—8 14 1
Washington (A.) .... 000 001 010—2 10 2
Judd, Hughes and Seminick, Hemsley; Wynn, Haefner and Evans.

At Savannah, Ga.: R. H. E.
Philadelphia (A.) .. 300 470 150—20 20 1
Savannah (S.A.) .... 000 010 010— 2 13 3
Flores, McCahan and Guerra; Clyde, Bernardini and Pobiak, Parks and Tanner.

At Kingsport, Tenn.: R. H. E.
Boston (A.) ........ 201 083 300—17 20 0
Cincinnati (N.) .... 021 000 030— 6 14 0
Ferriss, Johnson and Wagner; Riddle, Shound, Peterson and Lamanno, Lakeman.

At Richmond, Ind.: R. H. E.
Boston (N.) ........ 200 100 101— 5 8 3
Milwaukee (A.A.) ... 030 000 001— 4 12 4
Spahn, Macon and Masi; Karas, Nolan and Linden.

At Atlanta, Ga.: R. H. E.
Detroit (A.) ....... 000 100 002— 3 9 1
Atlanta (S.A.) ..... 020 000 000— 2 3 1
Newhouser and Tebbetts; Kinney, Bush and Ulisney.

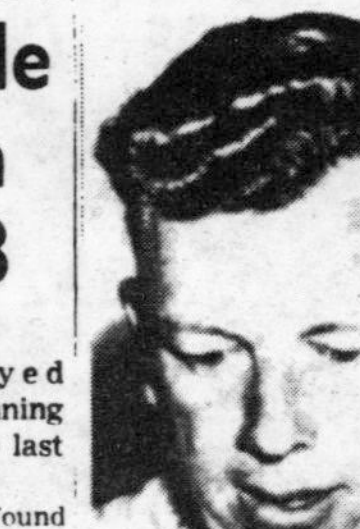

**PENALIZED**—Harold Parrott, left, traveling secretary of the Dodgers, drew $500 fine. Charles Dressen, right, former Dodger and now a Yankee coach, was suspended 30 days from April 15 by Commissioner Chandler.

## Gledhill, Shidler Now Third in A.B.C. Doubles

BY CAL WHORTON

A pair of 19-year-old youngsters, Don Gledhill and Jerry Shidler of Van Nuys, rolled into third place in the American Bowling Congress doubles yesterday afternoon at the Armory in Exposition Park.

Posting the highest two-man score of all local bowlers, Gledhill and Shidler turned in a series of 1262 to supplant another juvenile pair, Allen Shecter and Ken Hunt, from third spot in the doubles standings. This latter duo had rolled 1260 earlier in the tournament.

Gledhill, who carries a 165-average in the Van Nuys 875 Monday night classic loop, yesterday put together games of 226-176-232. Shidler, a 171 Van Nuys roller, manufactured games of 191-236-201.

**Good Singles Score**

Gledhill also turned in a commendable singles series of 203-208-225—636, but this, along with his fine doubles tally, failed to put him up among the all-events leaders. Gledhill, it seems, failed to do any better than 446 in his team kegling Tuesday night with the Van Nuys Eagles.

Two Southland teams moved into the "big 10" in last night's five-man competition. The 20th Century-Fox club, with a 2832, took over seventh spot, and four sticks behind was Hollywood Wholesale Electric Co. with 2828. Jesse Wolf sparked the Fox quintet with a 594 series and 232 high game. Elmer Davis set the pace for the Electricians with a 622 series and 237 high game.

An individual bowler moved into fifth place in the all-events when Dale Heysen of Santa Monica in team play added a 571 to his previous 686 doubles and 593 singles scores for a nine-game series of 1850.

**Brandt in Limelight**

Today's activities will start this morning at 10 o'clock and will run past midnight.

Five doubles and singles squads will tackle the maples during the daylight hours, to be followed by a Luxor booster outfit at 8:15 p.m. and a team of regulars at 10:15 p.m.

Particular interest this afternoon will settle around Allie Brandt, the mighty mite of bowlingdom who, with his partner, Herbert Richardson, will attempt to grab the lead in the two-man event on the 1:20 p.m. squad. Later Brandt will set his sights on the singles lead.

Brandt, who hails from Lockport, N.Y., is widely known in national kegling circles. He once rolled an 866 in league play. He's never copped an A.B.C. title, but year in and year out he's among the leaders and as such always a constant threat.

Another individual ball spinner who'll take to the lanes at 11:40 this morning is Murray Fowler, one-armed sensation out of Steubenville, O. Fowler, a middle-aged gent who rolls sans his left arm, was co-winner of the 1939 doubles championship in Cleveland.

## A.B.C. Leaders

REGULAR TEAMS

| Team | Score |
|---|---|
| Hermann Undertakers, St. Louis | 2992 |
| Old Pueblo Interceptors, Tucson, Ariz. | 2895 |
| El Charro Cafe, Lodi, Cal. | 2885 |
| Buddies Men's Shop, Luzerne, Pa. | 2859 |
| Ishley's Service Station, Luzerne, Pa. | 2853 |
| Hammond's Steak House, Los Angeles | 2844 |
| 20th Century-Fox Studio Club, Hollywood | 2832 |
| Hollywood Wholesale Electric Co., Holl'd | 2828 |
| Roy's Tavern, Cambridge, Wis. | 2821 |
| Reutbers Royal Bar, Wheeling, W.Va. | 2806 |

DOUBLES

|  |  |
|---|---|
| F. Matava-R. Lauman, St. Louis | 664 658—1322 |
| G. Palubiak-B. Janus, Chicago | 746-554—1300 |
| D. Gledhill-J. Shidler, Van Nuys | 634-628—1262 |
| A. Spector-K. Hunt, L.A. | 624-636—1260 |
| J. Pallardy-L. Badaracco, St. Louis | 656 592—1248 |
| W. Strubee-A. Lee, Prescott, Ariz. | 633-607—1240 |
| J. Palmieri-F. Rossi, Santa Rosa | 620-620—1240 |
| D. Heveren-F. Riccilli, Sta. Mon. | 686-553—1239 |
| N. Milanovich-J. Reuther, Wheeling, W.Va. | 567-668—1235 |
| C. Stafford-R. Leach, L.A. | 607-615—1222 |

SINGLES

|  |  |
|---|---|
| Ernest Del Dotto, Merced | 219-256-215—690 |
| Charles Yeager, Compton | 180-257-244—681 |
| Nolan Burton, L.A. | 233-216-224—673 |
| Angelo Reia, L.A. | 247-259-156—662 |
| P. Dusablon, Chicago | 235-248-179—662 |
| Les Gibson, Winnipeg, Can. | 234-215-212—661 |
| R. Nelson, L.A. | 166 248 246—660 |
| Gerald Funk, Beverly Hills | 216-233 211—660 |
| P. Gattanini, Seattle | 233-200-222—655 |

ALL EVENTS

|  |  |
|---|---|
| R. Lauman, St. Louis | 610 658 616—1884 |
| J. Pallardy, St. Louis | 605-656 645—1906 |
| G. Palubiak, Chicago | 561-746-585—1892 |
| J. Snyder, Wheeling, W.Va. | 610-612 635—1857 |
| Dale Heysen, Santa Monica | 686 593-571—1850 |
| P. Dusablon, Chicago | 599-569-662—1830 |
| A. Schwass, Luzerne, Pa. | 607-579-642—1828 |
| C. Yeager, Compton | 491 654-681—1826 |
| J. Schwab, Luzerne, Pa. | 598 550 642—1820 |
| G. Kosmos, Seattle | 579-557-643—1809 |

**THE VICTOR** — Larry MacPhail, president of the New York Yankees, was the winner in baseball's bitter row.

## Quick Leaves for Golf War

BY CHARLES CURTIS

With his heart strongly set on winning the British Amateur crown, Smiley Quick shoves off Saturday on the first leg of his golfing invasion of the British Isles.

The doughty little Irishman is going to England primarily as a member of American Walker Cup team on its first renewal of the international amateur golf series since 1938. The squad sails from New York on the Queen Elizabeth the 24th of this month.

**Aims at Crown**

But California's outstanding amateur golfing product since Lawson Little has his goal set very squarely—the British Amateur, May 26-31, at Scotland's famed Carnoustie course.

"I've been working with Olin Dutra and Willie Hunter on low wind shots. I've got the shot down now so I can hit short approaches or long irons and keep them low. And I've been practicing running long chip shots to big greens, because they tell me some of those greens over there are awfully big," says Smiley.

**Barely Misses**

Last year, after cleaning up the national public links crown, Quick came within a whisker of adding the national amateur when he bowed to Ted Bishop in an extra-hole final. He's held most of the sectional titles at one time or another and was tied for low amateur in the last U.S. Open.

Quick will play with Bud Ward against Frank Stranahan and Bishop at Garden City, L.I., shortly before leaving New York. Walker Cup matches, at St. Andrews, will be May 16-17 preceding the British Amateur. Quick's wife Hazel will accompany him on the trip which marks the first time a California amateur linksman has invaded Scotland since 1931.

## Golf News of Southland in Short Order Style

Two golf exhibitions are on tap today. This morning at 10 o'clock Herb Parsons, an exhibition shooter, will give a demonstration of "shotgun golf." Parsons' publicist says he can drive a golf ball 300 yards and make it hook or slice at will. The other exhibition takes place tonight when Keith Jacobs and his associates open their new Montebello driving range on Garfield Ave. near E. Third St. Johnny Dawson, Olin Dutra, Barney Clark, Jerry Barber and Clayton Aleridge will take part in the exhibition, starting at 7:30.

Official announcement of the dates for the 1948 United States Open, to be played at Riviera, was made yesterday by the U.S.G.A. It will be played June 10-12. The national public links, first slated for the Southland in 1948, has now been awarded to Atlanta, Ga.

Los Angeles Times Sports
THURS., APRIL 10, 1947

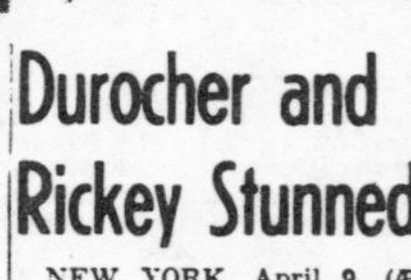

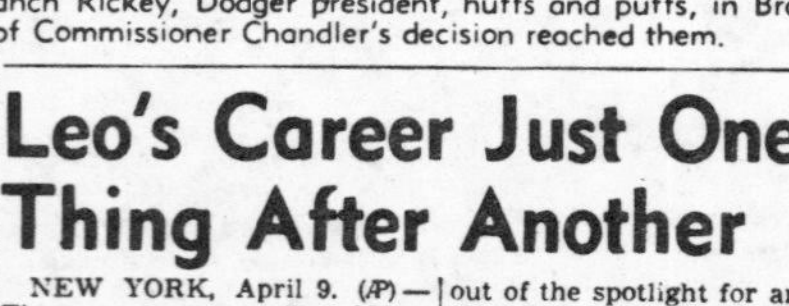

All (AP) Wirephotos

**SITTING THIS ONE OUT**—Leo Durocher, left, suspended yesterday for 1947 season, sits with arms folded as Branch Rickey, Dodger president, huffs and puffs, in Brooklyn club's office after news of Commissioner Chandler's decision reached them.

## Durocher and Rickey Stunned

NEW YORK, April 9. (AP)—President Branch Rickey of the Brooklyn Dodgers, recovering from the first shock of his manager's banishment from baseball for the 1947 season, told a press conference today that Commissioner Chandler's decision came as "quite a surprise" and that he was not yet ready to name a pilot to succeed Leo Durocher.

"All I can say for sure is that we will have a manager on the field when the season opens Tuesday," he said. "That's a certainty. I have an idea who it will be, but I can't tell you now."

Asked if Durocher's salary, reported to soar close to $70,000 a year, with bonuses, would be paid in the face of his suspension, Rickey dodged the issue with the reply that "his salary is not in the picture at this time at all—not until after I've seen Mr. Chandler's decision."

**Chandler Phones**

The Dodger president disclosed that Chandler called him by phone to advise him of his decision about 45 minutes after he had learned of it from newsmen. Asked if he would appeal, he said:

"I hadn't thought about it, but if I did there would be no one to take it to except the commissioner."

Durocher, who had been attending a full-dress conference of Dodger officials when the Chandler bombshell exploded, looked extremely crestfallen and would only repeat, "I have nothing to say. I don't know what I'll do."

## Lippy's Wife Postpones Air Trip to Coast

NEW YORK, April 9. (U.P.)—Film Actress Laraine Day, recent bride of Dodger Manager Leo Durocher, today postponed her departure for Hollywood 24 hours upon learning that her husband has been suspended from baseball for a year.

Durocher, she said, would not go with her, but would remain in New York.

## Padres, Beavers in 15-Inning Tie

SAN DIEGO, April 9. (AP)—The Portland Beavers and San Diego Padres battled to a 4-to-4 tie tonight in a game called at the end of the 15th inning by a Pacific Coast League curfew law. Score:

| Portland | AB | H | O | A | San Diego | AB | H | O | A |
|---|---|---|---|---|---|---|---|---|---|
| Smith,rf | 8 | 1 | 3 | 0 | Tran,ss | 6 | 0 | 3 | 5 |
| Radlovich,2b | 7 | 2 | 4 | 10 | Clay,cf | 6 | 2 | 4 | 0 |
| Escobar,lf | 6 | 3 | 3 | 0 | Barrett,rf | 5 | 2 | 3 | 0 |
| Storey,3b | 8 | 0 | 2 | 3 | Shupe,1b | 4 | 0 | 17 | 0 |
| Reich,rf | 6 | 1 | 2 | 0 | Gyselman,3b | 7 | 0 | 2 | 6 |
| Dobbins,ss | 5 | 0 | 2 | 4 | Cosgarait,2b | 4 | 2 | 2 | 3 |
| Crawford,1b | 6 | 1 | 21 | 2 | Hamilton,lf | 6 | 1 | 5 | 0 |
| Muratore,c | 6 | 2 | 8 | 0 | McDonnell,c | 1 | 0 | 5 | 1 |
| Bianco,p | 4 | 1 | 0 | 3 | Vitalich,c | 1 | 0 | 0 | 1 |
| Liska,p | 2 | 1 | 0 | 2 | Trinen,p | 5 | 0 | 1 | 1 |
| Lazor,x | 1 | 0 | 0 | 0 | West,a | 1 | 0 | 0 | 0 |
| Spaeter,z | 0 | 0 | 0 | 0 | Kerr,c | 2 | 0 | 3 | 0 |
| Holm,c | 0 | 0 | 0 | 0 | | | | | |
| Totals | 55 | 12 | 45 | 24 | Totals | 48 | 7 | 45 | 17 |

x—Batted for Muratore in 15th.
z—Ran for Lazor in 15th.
a—Batted for McDonnell in 9th.

Portland ............011 020 000 000 000—4
San Diego ...........110 020 000 000 000—4

PITCHERS' RECORDS

| | IP | AB | R | H | ER | BB | HB | SO |
|---|---|---|---|---|---|---|---|---|
| Vitalich | 1⅔ | 22 | 4 | 9 | 4 | 2 | 0 | 1 |
| Trinen | 10⅓ | 33 | 0 | 3 | 0 | 3 | 1 | 7 |
| Bianco | 9⅔ | 32 | 4 | 6 | 4 | 7 | 0 | 1 |
| Liska | 5⅓ | 16 | 0 | 1 | 0 | 2 | 0 | 2 |

Summary: Runs—Radlovich 2, Escobar, Dobbins, Tran, Clay, Cosgarait, McDonnell. Errors—Bianco. LOB—Portland 10, San Diego 11. 2B—Reich, Muratore, Clay. 3B—Radlovich. HR—Cosgarait. SH—Storey, Smith, Barrett, Shupe. SB—Clay, Barrett. RBI—Barrett 2, Muratore, Cosgarait, Reich, Escobar, Crawford, Clay. DP—Crawford to Robbins to Crawford; Dobbins to Radlovich, Crawford to Muratore. Attendance—4 575.

## Leo's Career Just One Thing After Another

NEW YORK, April 9. (AP)—The one-year suspension of Manager Leo Durocher of the Brooklyn Dodgers brings to a temporary check one of the most hectic careers in baseball, a career highlighted by great triumphs and bitter disappointments, by brawls and arguments and fines and court actions.

From the moment he stepped foot on a diamond as a pro back in 1925, to receive a brief tryout with the Yankees that same year, the garrulous, aggressive, fiery Lippy never has remained out of the spotlight for any prolonged period, and since his appointment as manager of the Brooklyn club by Larry MacPhail in January, 1939, his name has been almost constantly in the headlines.

A remarkable shortstop but known as the "all-America out" at the plate, Durocher's career carried him from Hartford to the Yankees to Atlanta to St. Paul, back to the Yankees, then to Cincinnati and the Cardinals, and finally to the Dodgers where his success reached its peak.

Always cocky, assertive, loud and truculent, Durocher found Brooklyn a natural setting for his style of play and he blossomed into something of a symbol of baseball as the Dodger fans seemed to love it.

**Umpire Baiter**

His association with MacPhail was unique. Both are outspoken, with temperaments that were bound to clash, but, although MacPhail is reported to have fired him and rehired him repeatedly after verbal clashes, when it came to a showdown they stuck together and, incidentally, brought to Brooklyn a National League pennant in 1941—the first in 21 years.

Lippy—the nickname was pinned on Durocher during his first training trip with the Yankees—as Dodger pilot became Exhibit A in the art of umpire baiting, and his run-ins with the men in blue resulted in fines and brief suspensions almost too numerous to enumerate.

## Faithful Fans of Flatbush Start Howling

NEW YORK, April 9. (AP)—The Flatbush baseball faithful who lost their Leo the Lip today reacted to the loss with an uproar of protest such as not even the most brazen umpire ever has had to face.

"I don't believe it . . ."
"You're kidding me . . ."
"They can't do that to Leo . . ."

This was the initial, incredulous reaction of Brooklyn's man in the street to the news that Baseball Commissioner A. B. Chandler had suspended Leo Durocher, manager of the Dodgers, for 1947.

George Pfeifer, a clerk, said: "They'd better have their extra cops out when Chandler comes to Ebbets Field."

In the familiar Brooklyn patois some call English, Dodger adherents blasted Chandler's decision as unfair and woefully concurred that it probably would cost the team this year's pennant.

## Solons Turn Back Rainiers, 7 to 4

SACRAMENTO, April 9. (AP) Hugh Orphan outlasted three Seattle pitchers and hurled the Sacramento Solons to a 7-4 victory over the Seattle Rainiers here tonight. Sacramento chased Ike Pearson with a six-run rally in the first inning.

| Seattle | AB | H | O | A | Sacramento | AB | H | O | A |
|---|---|---|---|---|---|---|---|---|---|
| Rucker,cf | 5 | 1 | 3 | 0 | Ramsey,cf | 4 | 0 | 1 | 0 |
| Vanni,cf | 5 | 1 | 0 | 0 | Schemer,1b | 3 | 1 | 10 | 1 |
| Sturm,1b | 4 | 1 | 12 | 0 | Mesner,3b | 5 | 1 | 1 | 0 |
| Novikoff,lf | 5 | 3 | 2 | 0 | Marty,lf | 3 | 3 | 1 | 0 |
| Layne,3b | 4 | 2 | 0 | 1 | Rizzo,rf | 3 | 1 | 4 | 0 |
| O'Neil,ss | 4 | 1 | 3 | 4 | T. Nelson,ss | 3 | 1 | 2 | 5 |
| Buzas,2b | 3 | 0 | 1 | 2 | Fitzgerald,c | 3 | 1 | 5 | 1 |
| Hill,c | 3 | 0 | 2 | [illegible] | Kampouris,2b | 3 | 1 | 3 | 5 |
| Pearson,p | 0 | 0 | 0 | 0 | Orphan,p | 4 | 1 | 0 | 1 |
| Orphal,p | 3 | 1 | 0 | 2 | | | | | |
| Mohr,a 2b | 0 | 0 | 0 | 0 | | | | | |
| White,xx | 1 | 0 | 0 | 0 | | | | | |
| Johnson,xxx | 1 | 1 | 0 | 0 | | | | | |
| Publicki,a | 0 | 0 | 0 | 0 | | | | | |
| Stagg,x | 0 | 0 | 1 | 0 | | | | | |
| Yelovic,p | 0 | 0 | 0 | 0 | | | | | |
| Carpenter,zz | 0 | 0 | 0 | 0 | | | | | |
| Totals | 38 | 11 | 24 | 9 | Totals | 31 | 10 | 27 | 13 |

Seattle .............0 0 3 1 0 0 0 0 0—4
Sacramento ..........6 0 0 0 0 1 0 0 x—7

PITCHERS' RECORD

| | IP | AB | R | H | ER | BB | SO |
|---|---|---|---|---|---|---|---|
| Pearson | ⅔ | 6 | 5 | 4 | 6 | 2 | 0 |
| Orphal | 6⅓ | 22 | 2 | 6 | 1 | 4 | 2 |
| Yelovic | 1 | 3 | 0 | 0 | 0 | 0 | 1 |
| Orphan | 9 | 38 | 4 | 11 | 3 | 2 | 4 |

Summary: E—Schemer 2, Mesner. HB—By Pearson (Fitzgerald), by Orphan (Mohr). LOB—Seattle 9, Sacramento 8. 2B—Marty 2. T. Nelson, Fitzgerald, Rizzo. 3B—Novikoff. SH—T. Nelson. SB—Vanni. RBI—Marty, T. Nelson 2, Orphan 2, Schemer, Novikoff 2, Layne, Rucker, Rizzo. DP—O'Neil (unassisted); Orphal to O'Neil to Sturm; Nelson to Kampouris to Schemer; Kampouris to Nelson to Schemer. Loser—Pearson. Attendance—3983.

## Gauchos Thump Bruins

College baseball at Santa Barbara.
U C L A ........... 000 110 300— 5 11 2
Santa Barbara ..... 103 001 06x—13 9 3
Frerks, Gilmore, Fairman and Handley; Nikcevich, Hicks, Scott, Mathew and Day, Mullaney.

## Twinks Wallop Seals in 10th

SAN FRANCISCO, April 9. (AP) Hollywood put on a furious finish tonight to beat San Francisco, 7 to 4, in their series opener with a three-run blast off Larry Powell in the 10th inning.

| Hollywood | AB | H | O | A | San Fran. | AB | H | O | A |
|---|---|---|---|---|---|---|---|---|---|
| Williams,2b | 6 | 2 | 1 | 4 | Uhalt,cf | 4 | 1 | 1 | 0 |
| Delsing,cf | 6 | 1 | 8 | 0 | Luby,2b | 4 | 0 | 1 | 2 |
| Lupien,1b | 4 | 0 | 9 | 1 | Jennings,3b | 5 | 0 | 1 | 2 |
| Kelleher,rf | 3 | 2 | 2 | 0 | Brovia,lf | 3 | 2 | 0 | 0 |
| Davis,ss | 5 | 2 | 2 | 0 | Henson,1b | 5 | 0 | 11 | 0 |
| Vaughn,3b | 5 | 1 | 5 | 2 | Sheridan,rf | 4 | 3 | 5 | 0 |
| Skurski,lf | 5 | 2 | 0 | 0 | Nicely,ss | 3 | 2 | 2 | 7 |
| Unser,c | 3 | 2 | 3 | 2 | Ogrodowski,c | 3 | 1 | 4 | 1 |
| Smith,p | 2 | 0 | 0 | 2 | Melton,p | 3 | 1 | 0 | 4 |
| Cox,x | 1 | 1 | 0 | 0 | White,z lf | 2 | 0 | 0 | 0 |
| Hufford,p | 2 | 1 | 1 | 0 | Rosso,p | 0 | 0 | 0 | 0 |
| Sheely,xx | 0 | 0 | 0 | 0 | Sanders,xx | 1 | 0 | 0 | 0 |
| Vezilich,aa | 0 | 0 | 0 | 0 | Taormina,xxx | 1 | 1 | 0 | 0 |
| Ross,aa | 0 | 0 | 0 | 0 | Chesnes,a | 1 | 0 | 0 | 0 |
| Cameron,aaa | 0 | 0 | 1 | 0 | Trower,x | 1 | 0 | 0 | 1 |
| | | | | | Leonard,c | 1 | 0 | 2 | 0 |
| | | | | | Powell,p | 0 | 0 | 0 | 0 |
| | | | | | Jensen,p | 0 | 0 | 0 | 0 |
| Totals | 42 | 14 | 30 | 11 | Totals | 41 | 11 | 30 | 17 |

x—Batted for Smith in 7th.
xx—Ran for Unser in 9th.
aa—Batted for Sheely in 10th.
aaa—Batted for Ross in 10th.
z—Ran for Brovia in 5th.
a—Batted for Rosso in 8th.
x—Batted for Nicely in 8th.
xxx—Batted for Ogrodowski in 8th.

Hollywood ..............000 100 300 3—7
San Francisco ..........100 110 010 0—4

PITCHERS' RECORD

| | IP | AB | H | R | ER | BB | SO |
|---|---|---|---|---|---|---|---|
| Smith | 6 | 26 | 8 | 3 | 2 | 1 | 2 |
| Melton | 6⅔ | 29 | 10 | 3 | 1 | 2 | 1 |
| Hufford | 4 | 15 | 3 | 1 | 1 | 2 | 1 |
| Rosso | 1⅓ | 4 | 0 | 1 | 0 | 1 | 0 |
| Powell | 1⅓ | 7 | 3 | 2 | 3 | 2 | 2 |
| Jensen | ⅔ | 2 | 1 | 1 | 1 | 0 | 1 |

Summary: Runs—Williams, Kelleher 2, Vaughn, Skurski 2, Cox, Uhalt, Luby, Sheridan 2. Errors—Davis, Unser, Nicely 2. 3B—Skurski 2, Taormina. 2B—Brovia, Kelleher, Davis, Sheridan, Hufford. RBI—Brovia 2, Davis, Ogrodowski, Cox, Lupien, Taormina, Skurski 2, Hufford. DP—Melton, Luby, Stern, Henson. Winner—Hufford. Loser—Powell. Attendance—5000.

## Today in Sports

BASEBALL—Oakland vs. Los Angeles, Wrigley Field, 2:30 p.m.; SC vs. Riverside (Sunset League) at Riverside, 8 p.m.
BOWLING—ABC, Exposition Park Armory. Doubles, 10 a.m.; teams, 8:15 p.m.
AMATEUR BOXING—CYO tourney opening, Olympic, 7 p.m.; Jeffries Barn, 8:30. Pasadena Junior College vs. Compton College, at PJC, 8 p.m.
WRESTLING—El Monte Legion Stadium, 8:30.

## Chandler's Crackdown Hits Bums

CINCINNATI, April 9. (AP) Leo (the Lip) Durocher, one of baseball's most explosive characters since he became manager of the Brooklyn Dodgers eight years ago, today was suspended for the 1947 season by Commissioner A. B. Chandler.

"Durocher has not measured up to the standards expected or required of managers of our baseball teams," Chandler said.

The suspension of the belligerent Leo, who left a shortstop's job to become baseball's highest paid manager—an estimated $70,000 a year—was the "result of the accumulation of unpleasant incidents in which he has been involved," Chandler said.

It was Chandler in new character today—a determined, punch-throwing commissioner who said in the same report that the people in baseball will not be permitted to associate "with known and notorious gamblers" and that "swift disciplinary action will be taken against any person violating the order."

**Warning Issued**

He said they "have been hitherto warned" against such association.

Chandler exonerated Larry MacPhail, president of the New York Yankees, from any association with known gamblers, and also said he was convinced that Branch Rickey, head of the Brooklyn club, had not made any statements which might be construed as detrimental to MacPhail's character and integrity.

But, "because their officials engaged in a public controversy damaging to baseball, the New York American League club and the Brooklyn club are hereby fined $2000 each," he added.

The commissioner also suspended Chuck Dressen, former Dodger coach, for 30 days beginning April 15, because he allegedly broke a verbal contract with Brooklyn to join the Yankees this year.

Harold Parrott, traveling secretary for the Brooklyn team, was fined $500 for "writing a deliberately derogatory" newspaper article about people in baseball. Parrott was "ghost" writer for Durocher in the Brooklyn Daily Eagle.

**All Parties Silenced**

"All parties to this controversy are silenced from the time this order is issued," read the closing line in Chandler's statement.

Chandler said both Rickey and Durocher had admitted making some statements regarding MacPhail's guests at the Havana game.

It was those statements, along with others made in a newspaper column under Durocher's name, that led to hearings in Florida recently and to Chandler's decision today. MacPhail brought the case to a head by filing charges of defamation against Durocher and Rickey.

Durocher in the newspaper column criticized MacPhail as trying "to knock me" after, he said, he declined to become manager of the Yankees.

Chandler said today he was convinced MacPhail never had offered the job to Durocher.

The three main characters in today's stunning action are one-time associates.

**Walker Not Considered**

Durocher starred at shortstop for the St. Louis Cards years ago. MacPhail and Rickey were with the same organization. Then MacPhail took a down-at-the-heels Brooklyn club, installed Durocher as manager and between them they whipped together one team that went into the World's Series.

Then Rickey took over the Brooklyn leadership when MacPhail left to join the Army, and last year the club tied St. Louis for the National League pennant. The Cards won in a play-off.

In New York Rickey said he had a new manager in mind but could not give his name at this time. Answering a question, he said it would not be Dixie Walker, veteran right-field star and slugger.

There was some talk that either Ray Blades or Pepper Martin might be chosen.

**Sukeforth Takes Reins**

Clyde Sukeforth, Brooklyn coach, tonight was named to manage the Dodgers in their exhibition game with the Montreal Royals at Ebbets Field tomorrow. For this game only, Sukeforth, a former big league catcher, scout and minor league pilot, will fill in the spot left open by the suspension of Leo Durocher for the 1947 season.

The now managerless Dodgers also are confronted with another problem, whether to install Jackie Robinson, Negro star, at first base. Robinson has been slugging the ball and fielding sensationally, although first is new to him.

# CITATION VICTOR OVER COALTOWN IN DERBY

## The Sports Parade

By BRAVEN DYER

When the history of sports for 1948 is written the author must devote considerable space to Jack Kramer when he swings into the chapter entitled "Surprises."

Most people have been surprised several times by what has happened since Jack and Bobby Riggs began their pro junket around the country. The list of "surprises" includes those who figured Riggs would kill Kramer, those who figured Kramer would kill Riggs, those who figured the entire shebang was as square as an apple pie and those who figured the whole thing was on the up and up.

Even as one who predicted that Kramer would prove Riggs' master, I've been surprised more than once; i.e. by (1) Kramer's sorry showing to begin with, (2) his complete flop in the first Pan-Pacific match and (3) his newfound ability to blast Bobby to smithereens.

**SURPRISING TURN**

Most surprising, I suppose, is the last, because, after all, this is a professional show and as such retains its popular appeal only as long as it continues to be a contest, or some semblance thereof.

All right, then, what happened?

Some say it all goes back to Friday the 13th—Friday the 13th of March in Tucson. The count stood 14 to 13 matches in Kramer's favor then. He had just begun to really feel his oats.

The first set in Tucson that night went 26 games, with Big Jake winning, 14 to 12. Riggs took the second, 6-4, but back came Kramer to bag the third, 18 to 16.

**ALL DOUBT REMOVED**

Riggs must have left something on that Tucson floor, because Kramer reeled off 20 wins in the next 22 matches to remove all doubt as to who was the master. The count is 52 to 19 now.

Bobby isn't mystified over what's happened to him—but he's mighty upset.

"I've got Kramer's style all figured out," said the cocky Angeleno the other day. "But I still can't do anything with the guy. You don't return what you can't reach or see. Why, the way Jack's playing today he's better than Don Budge or any of them."

Coming from Bombastic Bobby that's quite a tribute. Riggs speaks admiringly of Kramer's dogged determination and hails his "one-two punch" as the greatest in tennis.

**DESIRE TO WIN**

"You know, I usually figured I could beat a guy because I felt I wanted to win a little more than he did," continued Riggs. "But now it seems that Jack is the one who wants to win most. Lead or no lead, he just pours it on."

Kramer poured it on pretty good in Texas recently, blasting Bobby 6-0, 6-0. Promoter Jack Harris immediately began getting phone calls from anxious guys who had booked the tour.

Riding to their next stop, Harris mentioned this to Kramer. Jack wasted no time replying—"I'd like to beat Riggs six-love, six-love every night, and I would, too, if I could."

There is one other explanation, slightly technical, which may explain everything. It has to do with the way Kramer plays Riggs now.

When Riggs was leading in the early weeks of their tour Kramer was most unhappy. One night Kramer ran into his friend, Alrick Man, captain of the 1947 Davis Cup team.

**LOBS THE THING**

"You're playing Riggs wrong," said Man. "You keep trying to drive the ball past him when he comes to the net. Sure, you pass him some of the time; but he's been intercepting more than half those attempts and volleying 'em off for placements."

Man had the answer, too.

"Give Riggs a dose of his own lobbing medicine," advised Alrick. "Throw in a few lobs with your passing game. That way Bobby won't be able to get on top of the net. Right now he thinks you never lob. So he sits on the net. It's right down your alley—he's short and easy to lob over. Get in there."

Kramer got in there, all right, and he's been in there ever since.

Now that he's wrecked the tour, Big Jake might as well keep blasting Bobby all over the place. He'll be the big drawing card then when the new amateur king comes along—a much bigger drawing card than Riggs ever was—or will be.

## Today in Sports

BASEBALL—Portland vs Hollywood double-header 1:30 p.m. at Gilmore Field.

SOCCER—Three games at Rancho Cienega Stadium; first game at 11 a.m.

AUTO RACING—Stock-car racing at Carrell Speedway Gardena, time trials at 12 noon, first race at 2:30 p.m.; roadster racing at Bonelli Stadium, first race at 2:30 p.m.

QUARTER HORSE RACING—Vessels Ranch at Los Alamitos. Nine-race card, first race at 1 p.m.

## Tigers End Indians' Win Streak

CLEVELAND, May 1 (AP) The Cleveland Indians' unbeaten string came to an end today as the Detroit Tigers routed Bob Feller and handed the Tribesmen their first loss in seven games, 10 to 3, before a ladies' day crowd of 52,249.

The Indians' first six victories had brought them within two wins of the modern record for triumphs at the start of the season.

The Tigers, who had lost six of their last seven games, unleashed a 14-hit attack and enjoyed two big innings.

**Trout Pitches**

Paul (Dizzy) Trout set the Indians down with one run and five hits in the first eight innings but weakened in the ninth, when the Redskins tallied twice, and had to be replaced by Art Houtteman.

Feller, who wound up with his first loss instead of his third straight win, blanked the Tigers with two hits until the fifth when Detroit shelled him from the mound with a five-run uprising.

A walk to John Lipon, a pair of errors by Larry Doby, and singles by Eddie Mayo, George Kell, Pat Mullin, Hoot Evers, George Vico and Hal Wagner produced the five markers.

**Four-Run Attack**

Rookie Lyman Linde was the victim of a four-run assault by the Bengals in the eighth. Three Cleveland errors, a pair of walks, a double by Trout and singles by Mullin and Evers put the clincher on the game. The Tigers added another tally in the ninth on doubles by Lipon and Kell.

| Detroit | AB | H | O | A | Cleveland | AB | H | O | A |
|---|---|---|---|---|---|---|---|---|---|
| Lipon,ss | 4 | 3 | 2 | 3 | Tucker,cf | 5 | 2 | 3 | 0 |
| Mayo,2b | 4 | 1 | 2 | 5 | Doby,rf | 4 | 1 | 2 | 0 |
| Kell,3b | 4 | 2 | 2 | 2 | Boudreau,ss | 2 | 1 | 1 | 5 |
| Mullin,rf | 5 | 2 | 2 | 0 | Gordon,2b | 4 | 1 | 1 | 2 |
| Evers,cf | 5 | 2 | 2 | 0 | Robinson,1b | 4 | 0 | 10 | 0 |
| Outlaw,lf | 5 | 0 | 3 | 0 | Clark,lf | 4 | 0 | 2 | 1 |
| Vico,1b | 5 | 2 | 10 | 0 | Keltner,3b | 4 | 1 | 1 | 1 |
| Wagner,c | 5 | 1 | 4 | 1 | Hegan,c | 4 | 2 | 7 | 0 |
| Trout,p | 5 | 1 | 0 | 1 | Feller,p | 1 | 0 | 0 | 0 |
| Houtteman,p | 0 | 0 | 0 | 0 | Kennedy,p | 0 | 0 | 0 | 0 |
| | | | | | x-Peck | 1 | 0 | 0 | 0 |
| | | | | | Linde,p | 0 | 0 | 0 | 0 |
| | | | | | y-Mitchell | 1 | 1 | 0 | 0 |
| | | | | | Gromek,p | 0 | 0 | 0 | 0 |
| | | | | | z-Edwards | 0 | 0 | 0 | 0 |
| Totals | 42 | 14 | 27 | 12 | Totals | 34 | 9 | 27 | 9 |

x—Popped out for Kennedy in 6th.
y—Singled for Linde in 8th.
z—Walked for Gromek in 9th.

SCORE BY INNINGS

| | | | | | | | | | | |
|---|---|---|---|---|---|---|---|---|---|---|
| Detroit | 0 | 0 | 0 | 0 | 5 | 0 | 0 | 4 | 1 | —10 |
| Cleveland | 0 | 0 | 0 | 0 | 0 | 1 | 0 | 0 | 2 | — 3 |

E—Doby, 3; Keltner, Kell, Hegan, Gordon. RBI—Kell, 2; Mullin, 3; Evers, 2; Vico, Wagner, Doby, Outlaw, Clark, Keltner. 2B—Vico, Tucker, Trout, Kell, Gordon. DP—Kell to Mayo to Vico; Mayo to Lipon to Vico. LOB—Detroit, 12; Cleveland, 7. BB—Trout, 3; Feller, 2; Kennedy, 1; Linde, 2. SO—Trout, 4; Feller, 2; Kennedy, 2; Gromek, 1. Hits—Off Feller, 7 in 4⅔ innings; Kennedy, 2 in 1⅓; Linde, 3 in 2; Gromek, 2 in 1; Trout, 9 in 8⅔; Houtteman, none in ⅓. HB—Kell by Feller; Mayo by Gromek. Winner—Trout. Loser—Feller. Attendance, 34,624.

## Baseball Standings

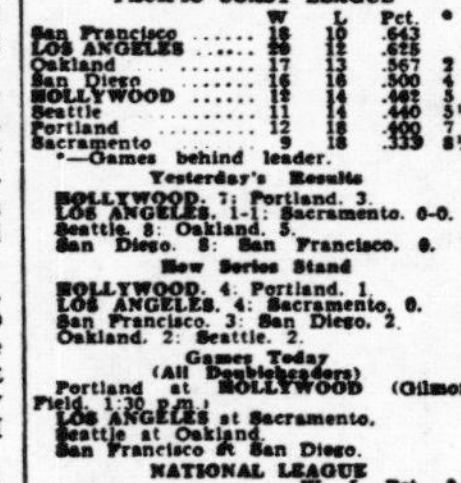

PACIFIC COAST LEAGUE

| | W | L | Pct. | * |
|---|---|---|---|---|
| San Francisco | 18 | 10 | .643 | |
| LOS ANGELES | 20 | 12 | .625 | |
| Oakland | 17 | 13 | .567 | 2 |
| San Diego | 16 | 16 | .500 | 4 |
| HOLLYWOOD | 12 | 14 | .462 | 5 |
| Seattle | 11 | 14 | .440 | 5½ |
| Portland | 12 | 18 | .400 | 7 |
| Sacramento | 9 | 18 | .333 | 8½ |

*—Games behind leader.

Yesterday's Results

HOLLYWOOD, 7; Portland, 3.
LOS ANGELES, 1-1; Sacramento, 0-0.
Seattle, 8; Oakland, 5.
San Diego, 8; San Francisco, 0.

How Series Stand

HOLLYWOOD, 4; Portland, 1.
LOS ANGELES, 4; Sacramento, 0.
San Francisco, 3; San Diego, 2.
Oakland, 2; Seattle, 2.

Games Today
(All Doubleheaders)

Portland at HOLLYWOOD (Gilmore Field, 1:30 p.m.)
LOS ANGELES at Sacramento.
Seattle at Oakland.
San Francisco at San Diego.

NATIONAL LEAGUE

| | W | L | Pct. | * |
|---|---|---|---|---|
| Pittsburgh | 7 | 4 | .636 | |
| New York | 7 | 5 | .583 | ½ |
| St. Louis | 5 | 4 | .556 | 1 |
| Brooklyn | 6 | 5 | .545 | 1 |
| Cincinnati | 6 | 7 | .462 | 2 |
| Boston | 6 | 7 | .462 | 2 |
| Philadelphia | 5 | 7 | .417 | 2½ |
| Chicago | 4 | 7 | .364 | 3 |

*—Games behind leader.

Yesterday's Results

Boston, 6; New York, 3.
Brooklyn, 2; Philadelphia, 1.
Pittsburgh, 7; Cincinnati, 2.
St. Louis, 4; Chicago, 0.

Games Today

Boston (Barrett, 1-0) at New York (Jansen, 1-1).
Brooklyn (Barney, 1-1, and Roe, 0-0) at Philadelphia (Heintzelman, 0-0, and Simmons, 0-2).
Chicago (Meyer, 1-1) at St Louis (Dickson, 1-1).
Cincinnati (Blackwell, 2-1, and Walters, 0-0) at Pittsburgh (Singleton, 1-0, and Queen, 0-0).

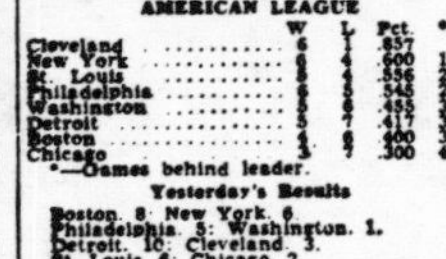

AMERICAN LEAGUE

| | W | L | Pct. | * |
|---|---|---|---|---|
| Cleveland | 6 | 1 | .857 | |
| New York | 6 | 4 | .600 | 1½ |
| St. Louis | 5 | 4 | .556 | 2 |
| Philadelphia | 6 | 5 | .545 | 2 |
| Washington | 5 | 6 | .455 | 3 |
| Detroit | 5 | 7 | .417 | 3½ |
| Boston | 4 | 6 | .400 | 3½ |
| Chicago | 3 | 7 | .300 | 4½ |

*—Games behind leader.

Yesterday's Results

Boston, 8; New York, 6.
Philadelphia, 5; Washington, 1.
Detroit, 10; Cleveland, 3.
St. Louis, 6; Chicago, 2.

Games Today

New York (Drews, 1-0) at Boston (Dobson, 0-2).
Detroit (Hutchinson, 0-1) at Cleveland (Lemon, 2-0).
St. Louis (Potter, 1-0, and Stephens, 0-0) at Chicago (Moulder, 0-0, and Pearson, 0-0).
Philadelphia (Brissie, 1-2, and Coleman, 0-1) at Washington (Haefner, 1-1, and Scarborough, 1-0).

AMERICAN ASSOCIATION

Minneapolis, 8; Columbus, 6.
Indianapolis, 10; Milwaukee, 1.
Toledo, 2; Kansas City, 1.
St. Paul, 5; Louisville, 4 (12 innings.)

INTERNATIONAL LEAGUE

Baltimore, 6; Rochester, 2.
Montreal, 7; Jersey City, 5.
Buffalo, 10; Newark, 6 (10 innings.)
Syracuse, 3; Toronto, 2 (10 innings.)

TEXAS LEAGUE

Ft. Worth, 10; Shreveport, 6.
Tulsa, 4; San Antonio, 1.
Houston, 4; Oklahoma City, 0.
Beaumont, 5; Dallas, 4.

SOUTHERN ASSOCIATION

No games scheduled.

CALIFORNIA LEAGUE

Bakersfield, 6; Fresno, 4.
San Jose, 13; Modesto, 7.

## College Track

SC, 73; California, 58.
UCLA, 80½; Stanford, 50½.
Washington, 89; Oregon State, 42.
University of Washington, 73; University of Oregon, 58.
Illinois, 72; Minnesota, 60.
Missouri, 87⅔; Nebraska, 43⅓.
Ursinus, 91; Pennsylvania Military College, 35.
Ohio State, 76; Penn State, 46.
Pennsylvania, 86; Cornell, 56.
Wisconsin, 90⅔; Iowa, 41⅓.
Hamline, 68; Augsburg (Minneapolis), 54.
Michigan, 68½; Indiana, 48½; Purdue, 44½.
Kansas, 70; Kansas State, 61.

CITATION WINS—Citation drives to finish line three and one-half lengths ahead of his stablemate, Coaltown, to win 74th running of Kentucky Derby. My Request runs third, followed by Billings. Estimated crowd of more than 100,000 saw Calumet Farm entry finish one-two.

## Indian Land Captures Pace After False Start Mars Race

Los Angeles Times Sports

SUNDAY MORNING, MAY 2, 1948

### Dr. Stanton Goes Half Mile Before Hearing Recall

BY JACK CURNOW

After a false start in which Dr. Stanton, the Cinderella horse owned and trained by Lindy Fraser burned himself out by running the first quarter in :27 and the half turn in 1:00 1-5, Indian Land went on to win the $50,000 Golden West Pace the second time it was started yesterday at Santa Anita.

But the crowd of 17,770 had nothing but boos for Little Joe O'Brien and Indian Land as they came into the winner's circle.

They gave Fraser and Dr. Stanton all the cheers, the first time when he came back because of the false start, the second time as Fraser dejectedly jogged his great pacer back in front of the stands on the way to the barns.

**Quick Pace**

"It's the lousiest deal I ever got," Fraser said. "My mistake was in not finishing out the first time."

Dr. Stanton for the second and real start, again cut out a quick pace. Coming from third tier in the field of 20 starters, Fraser again threaded his horse through traffic into the lead at the quarter in :28 3-5. He was still leading at the half in :59 1-5. But after going nearly three-quarters of a mile in horse-killing time, the great pacer just didn't have anything left.

He'd already paced a mile and a quarter (in two sections) in 2:30 1-5, which is one and four-fifths under the world record of 2:32 flat. He finished the big race in 18th place.

**Forbes Chief Second**

Second to Indian Land was Forbes Chief with Goose Bay third. The time was 2:33, a second off the mark held jointly by April Star and Jimmy Creed.

Indian Land was among several horses which pulled up before the first quarter in the false start; so was Forbes Chief and Goose Bay.

Fraser said that at a morning meeting with officials, there was mention made of a possible recall because of the large field. "But no one told us how they

Turn to Page 21, Column 1

## Bruins Impressive in 80-50 Romp Over Tribe

BY JOHN DE LA VEGA

Coach Ducky Drake's steadily improving UCLA tracksters, aided by a brisk breeze, registered a string of impressive marks yesterday as they dealt the Stanford Indians an 80¼ to 50¼ drubbing at Westwood.

Thus the Bruins earned the right to be at least even bets against SC next Saturday at the Coliseum in their Coast Conference dual meet title decider. The Troys defeated the Tribe, 71-60, two weeks ago.

While the Stanford athletes had plenty of excuses—bad weather prevented them from working out outdoors all week—the Bruins were mighty impressive. Five meet records were set and another tied.

**Dixon Rambles**

Lanky Craig Dixon of the Westwooders reeled off the flashiest 220-yard low hurdles race in the country this year when he was clocked in 22.7s. He had previously copped the high hurdles in 14.2s. Both marks were accepted as new meet records despite a wind estimated at between five and eight miles per hour. The low-stick mark was also a new school record.

Bruin Frank Fletcher bested George Grimes of Stanford and Teammate Frank Beck in a torrid 880 race that saw the trio hit the wire only five yards apart. The time, 1m. 54.7s., equaled the meet standard.

Stanford's terrific field event trio of Otis Chandler, Bill Larson and Gaylord Bryan accounted for the other three records. Chandler easily bested Jerry Shipkey of UCLA in the shot-put with a heave of 53ft. 2in. Shipkey did only 52ft. 4½in. Chandler's effort broke the old meet mark by almost a foot, the previous best being 52ft. 4¾in.

Turn to Page 18, Column 4

## Trojan Spikers Defeat Bears

BY JACK GEYER
Times Staff Representative

BERKELEY, May 1—One meet record was broken (as were the hearts of 7000 Golden Bear fans) when Coach Dean Cromwell's University of Southern California tracksters came with a rush to top California's game spikesters, 73 to 58, on Edwards Field here today.

Little Roland Sink opened the meet with a blazing 4m. 13.2s. mile, the fastest of his career. His time for the four laps smashed Louis Zamperini's 10-year-old standard of 4m. 13.7s., set by the SC speedster in 1938.

Sink trailed California's Kaare Vefling for the first three and one-quarter laps but as they rounded the first turn of the final go-around Sink poured it on and won by 20 yards. His teammate, Carmen Bova, caught Vefling in the stretch to grab a surprise second place.

Pell-Mell Patton, his eyes

Turn to Page 20, Column 7

OLD STORY FOR EDDIE—Jockey Eddie Arcaro holds up four fingers, signifying his number of Derby winners.

## Stars Clinch Series by Rapping Ducks, 7-3

BY AL WOLF

Hollywood sewed up its series with Portland last night by posting a 7-3 victory before 3717 Gilmore Field fans. It was the Stars' fourth decision in five starts this week.

Eddie Smith went the route to his second win, although yielding nine hits to the eight given up by Jake Mooty and Vince Di Biasi. Smith had a shutout until the eighth inning.

**Three Cheap Runs**

The Stars scored three cheap runs in the first inning.

After Mooty walked the bases full, Zernial brought in one marker with an infield hit and another followed immediately when Silvera threw the ball away. Libke's long fly accounted for the other moments later.

Portland finally drew blood in the top of the eighth—thanks to an error by Zernial. With one away, Lazor walked. Silvera doubled and Lazor scored when the ball went through Zernial. Silvera, however, was tagged trying for an extra base.

The Stars got to Di Biasi, who had replaced Mooty in the seventh, for four runs on five hits in the eighth.

**Foul Tips**

Rugger Ardizoia (3-2) and Vernon Kennedy (2-1) will work for Hollywood in today's twin bill . . . Tommy Bridges (2-2) and Duane Pillette (2-1) are next up for Portland . . . Bridges threw the Pacific Coast League's only no-hitter last season.

Babe Ruth, here to supervise the filming of his life story, will warm a box seat this afternoon . . . Outfielder Mayo Smith of the Beavers, who was hit in the head by a thrown ball Friday night, remained in the hospital yesterday, but will be back in uniform today.

| | | R | H | E |
|---|---|---|---|---|
| Portland | 000 000 012—3 | | 9 | 3 |
| Hollywood | 300 000 04x—7 | | 8 | 1 |

Mooty, DiBiasi (7) and Silvera; Smith and Kahn.

### Torrance Victor, 3-1

National Nightball League at Torrance:

| | | R | H | E |
|---|---|---|---|---|
| Riverside | 000 000 001— | 1 | [illegible] | 1 |
| Torrance | 010 000 20x— | 3 | 4 | 4 |

Trujillo, Kelly and Asdown; Hargis, Knight and Boden.

## Arcaro Sets Mark With 4th Triumph

BY PAUL LOWRY
Times Staff Representative

LOUISVILLE, Ky., May 1. Citation won America's most publicized horse race today and helped Eddie Arcaro to the all-time riding record of four Kentucky Derby victories.

The crowd was estimated at more than 100,000. Officials of rambling Churchill Downs declared that it was larger than last year because of added facilities.

Citation won by 3½ lengths from his stablemate, Coaltown, and as had been predicted by nearly everybody, the 74th Kentucky Derby was just a two-horse parade for Calumet Farm. My Request was third.

**Coaltown Leads**

Coaltown led at every stage of the mile-and-one-quarter journey except the homestretch, and there Eddie Arcaro sent Citation into command.

The only surprise about the race was the $2.80 return which the backers of Citation and Coaltown obtained on their money at 2-to-5 odds. The sloppy track was probably responsible for this situation.

After a week of sunshine and fast tracks the weatherman kicked up a fuss last night, and the clash of thunder and lightning brought a terrific rainstorm in its wake.

**Rain Dies Down**

The rain died down about the time the Derby gates were opened at 8 o'clock today, and spectators who had come from far and wide were spared a drenching. But the change in the racing strip generated new enthusiasm.

Frightened at the prospect of a minus pool the Churchill Downs management had ruled out anything but win betting. This sent the tourists shopping for something in the six-horse field to beat the Calumet entry.

Consequently, the early betting—wagering on the Derby itself starts at 9 a.m.—established Citation and Coaltown at 8-to-5, My Request 3 to 2, Escadru 7 to 2, Billings 8 to 1 and Grandpere 9 to 1.

Of the $670,833 wagered on the Derby, about half last year's total, so much went on horses with little or no chance that the Calumet backers benefited.

**Breaks Deadlock**

Arcaro's win with Citation broke a three-way deadlock in which he was involved with Isaac Murphy, colored rider of bygone days, and Earl (Handy Guy) Sande. The trio had three Derby winners apiece until sharp-nosed Eddie hit the wire in front under gloomy skies.

Plain Ben Jones also broke into the record column. He saddled both Citation and Coaltown for his fourth conquest to tie Derby Dick Thompson for Derby training honors.

The result of the race rather definitely established the fact that Coaltown cannot carry his blazing speed a mile and one-quarter, at least not in the mud. Maybe he can on a fast track. Many horsemen think so.

However, he beat My Request, a pretty fair mudder, by three lengths.

My Request bagged the third spot by one and one-half lengths over Billings, and 20 lengths behind came Grandpere, the only California-bred in the race.

**Escadru Last**

Grandpere got there by a nose in front of Escadru.

Coaltown failed to break as alertly as Citation and My Request at the start of the Derby, but by the time he had reached the clubhouse he was in front all by himself.

He added to his lead around the far turn as Citation, My Request and Grandpere were battling for second.

At the half-mile pole Coaltown was six lengths on top and Arcaro had Citation safely esconced in the second hole. Grandpere was third and My Request fourth.

As the field approached the far turn Arcaro began to move on the rapid Coaltown, and by

Turn to Page 20, Column 7

PROMISED LAND—It's Indian Land out in front by a length and a quarter crossing finish line to win $50,000 Golden West Pace at Santa Anita yesterday. Second was Forbes Chief (left) and Goose Bay (on rail) was third.

## CITATION TAKES DERBY



SEVENTH RACE—The Kentucky Derby, $100,000 added, for 3-year-olds; net value to winner, $83,400; second, $10,000; third, $5000; fourth, $2500. Winning breeder, $2000; second, $1000; third, $500. Winning trainer, $3000; second, $2000; third, $1000. Gold Cup to winner.

| Horse— | Wt. | PP. | St. | ½ | ¾ | 1 | Str. | Fin. | Jockey. | Odds $1 |
|---|---|---|---|---|---|---|---|---|---|---|
| a-CITATION | 126 | 1 | 2 | 2h | 2¹ | 2¹ | 1h | 1³½ | Arcaro | .40 |
| a-COALTOWN | 126 | 2 | 1 | 1⁴ | 1⁴½ | 1½ | 2⁴ | 2³ | Pierson | .40 |
| MY REQUEST | 126 | 6 | 3 | 4h | 4² | 3¹½ | 3¹ | 3¹½ | Dodson | 3.80 |
| BILLINGS | 126 | 5 | 6 | 5½ | 3h | 4⁸ | 4¹⁵ | 4²⁰ | Peterson | 14.70 |
| GRANDPERE | 126 | 4 | 4 | 3¹ | 6 | 6 | 5½ | 5nk | Gilbert | 17.80 |
| ESCADRU | 126 | 3 | 5 | 6 | 5⁶ | 5¹½ | 6 | 6 | Kirkland | 7.10 |

a—Calumet Farm entry.

Went to post at 4:32, off at 4:32½. Time, :12 1-5, :23 2-5, :34 3-5, :46 3-5, :59 1-5, 1:11 2-5, 1:24 3-5, 1:38, 1:51 2-5, 2:05 2-5. Winner, b.c. 3, by Bull Lea—Hydroplane II. Owner, Calumet Farm (Warren Wright). Trained by B. A. Jones. Start good from gate, won handily, place driving.

CITATION, away forwardly and losing ground while racing back of COALTOWN to stretch, responded readily to steady hand ride and, after disposing of latter, drew clear. COALTOWN began fast, established clear lead before going quarter and, making pace until inside stretch, continued willingly but was not good enough for CITATION although easily best of others. MY REQUEST, bothered slightly after start, was in hand while improving his position to stretch, then failed to rally when set down for drive. BILLINGS suffered interference after break when GRANDPERE bore to outside, was in close quarters at first turn when caught between ESCADRU and CITATION, then could not better his position when clear. GRANDPERE broke into BILLINGS after start, displayed speed for half mile, then gave way. ESCADRU, forced to take up when in close quarters entering the backstretch, could not reach serious contention thereafter and tired badly after going three-quarters of a mile.

# HOGAN'S RECORD 276 WINS OPEN GOLF TITLE

## The Sports Parade

By BRAVEN DYER

As the first to point out, locally at least, that Dink Templeton doubted Mel Patton's 9.3s. hundred at Fresno, and also that two or three northern scribes were quick to side with the onetime Stanford mastermind, I recently was quite intrigued by a letter from Harvey J. Quittner of Glendale.

Written several days before the Compton meet where Lloyd LaBeach tied one world's record and ruined another, the letter lends weight to the theory that Patton had to run 9.3s. to whip the pounding Panamanian. That's what this department contended from the start and subsequent events such as the Metric Merkle at the Coliseum only served to vindicate those of us who were naive enough to think that there was nothing fluky about Mel's mark in the first place.

**SAYS MR. QUITTNER**

But let Mr. Quittner mount the rostrum——

"Just what kind of egg do these guys want with their suds?

"I mean fellows like Bill Leiser of the Chronicle and Mr. Gregory of the Portland Oregonian.

"I've always been an admirer of the 'Sporting Green' and one of the reasons was the fine coverage of track and field and the fact that for quite a spell this was the only sports section that gave distances between the places. But this 'idea' of Leiser's that Mel Patton should do it again, please, or he doesn't get the big lollipop, leaves me not only cold, but irked.

"The thought comes to me that if Herman Wedemeyer ever ran a 9.3s. hundred (just for example) you'd never hear a peep like that out of Brother Leiser. Of course, in the Bay area, Herman is rated far above human mortals, and eulogized accordingly. And they talk about provincialism.

**SIMILAR BATCH**

"If you didn't catch Gregory's column on May 22, you missed a similar batch of baloney. This gentleman devotes a fair amount of space to the Fresno race; quotes Dink Templeton's 'fast 9.5s.'; quotes Patton saying he didn't think he was running that fast; raises the question of a guy running 9.3s. not being miles in front of the second-place man, and then launches into a discourse as to how human timers have never been able to judge the start anyhow, so how could they be right.

"Then, sez he, with so much doubt about the race, it certainly should never be certified as a world's record.

"Well—I wasn't aware there was any doubt about the race, and I don't see where Gregory proved any doubt by anything he said. For one thing, Templeton doesn't represent a 'doubt' by the fact he says he clocked a 9.5—I had 'em in 9.2. Secondly, almost anyone would discount Patton's statement, whether true or not. After all, what did that have to do with the timing of the race? Thirdly, those of us who have seen Lloyd LaBeach run this year are pretty sure that there's very little difference between his speed and Patton's. After all, LaBeach was clocked in 10.2 for the meters that same night, and without competition. And what about his races at Long Beach (9.4) and on that Coliseum track, 10.3?

**PARTICULAR PHOBIA**

"But this business about the timers.

"Granted that electric timing of some sort would be best method, but why make this race the scapegoat for one's own particular phobia. How about throwing all the records out of the books, and starting all over again, Mr. Gregory?

"You see, Braven, it all boils down to this one thing.

"A lot of the boys just won't let themselves believe that anyone can run 9.3. It used to be that 9.4 was all-too-sacred. George Anderson found that out at the Fresno Relays some years ago when he ran what might have been a 9.3, but turned out to be a 9.5. And that's the way it's been. 'They' just don't want to let themselves believe in a 9.3. So, it's going to really take something to make believers out of the lads.

**POP THEIR EYES**

"Unfortunately, Patton won't be running any more yardage races this year. That is, if the NCAA goes in meters as it did in '36. But I think that a whistling 100 meters, say about 10 flat (maybe even 10.1) will convince the lads. And that's what I hope Mel does, but good. And throws in a furlong that'll really pop their eyes. Maybe that would be good for what ails 'em.

"Anyway, Braven, don't cut down on your track and field writing. It always griped me that the sport which is conducted for the purpose of 'improving the breed' has to occupy so much space on the sports pages. I think we'd be better off to improve the breed of humans."

## Citation Captures 'Triple'

NEW YORK, June 12 (AP) Citation won the triple crown of America's racing today, wrapping up the Belmont Stakes easily as he carried the silks of Warren Wright's Calumet Farm to a six-length victory in record-equaling time.

The great 3-year-old champion, stumbling slightly as he broke from the gate, recovered quickly under Jockey Eddie Arcaro, then went on to pick up a $77,700 purse with only one brief challenge during the entire mile and one-half route.

It was just another romp for the Kentucky Derby and Preakness champion as he led King Ranch's Better Self to the wire by six lengths with the tiring Escadru from William L. Brann's stable third.

**Best Ever**

"He's the greatest horse I've ever seen, let alone ridden," Arcaro said as the infield board showed the brilliant bay son of Bull Lea-Hydroplane II had matched the stake record of 2:28 1/5 made by Mrs. John Hertz's Count Fleet in 1943.

"I shouldn't have let him win by so much but I couldn't take any chances for that kind of money," Arcaro added.

The crowd of 43,046 established Citation the 1-to-5 favorite, playing him so heavily for third that he caused a $3041.80 minus show pool. He paid $2.40, $2.30 and $2.10 across the board.

Citation boosted his 1948 money winnings to $389,020. With a two-season total of $544,700, the Calumet flyer now is just $16,461 behind Whirlaway, another Wright horse which holds fourth place in the world's cash-collecting list.

## Yanks Crush British in Wightman Cup

LONDON, June 12 (AP)—The U.S. Wightman Cup tennis team swept all four of today's matches with the British court queens and retained the international trophy, six matches to one.

The lone British tally was scored yesterday and is the only point the British have taken since the competition was resumed in 1946 after a seven-year lapse because of the war.

The Americans now have held the cup without interruption since 1931. Today's matches lured 5000 spectators to the Wimbledon Stadium.

In today's concluding match Mrs. Margaret Osborne DuPont of Wilmington, Del., and Louise Brough of Beverly Hills, Cal., made quick work of Mrs. Kay Stammers Menzies and Mrs. Betty Hilton, 6-2, 6-2.

Today's singles triumphs were registered by Mrs. DuPont, who mastered Mrs. Hilton, 6-3, 6-4; by Miss Brough, currently the U.S. champion, who conquered Mrs. Jean Bostock, 6-2, 4-6, 7-5, and by Doris Hart of Miami, who won 6-1, 6-4, from Joy Gannon.

## Matulich Signs With Rams

Wallace (Eagle) Matulich, 195-pound tailback from Mississippi State and one of the Southeastern Conference's outstanding stars last fall, today signed a professional grid contract with the Los Angeles Rams.

Rated by many as the South's top running back in 1946 and 1947, Matulich is a veteran of one freshman and three varsity campaigns at Mississippi State and was invited to participate in the annual North-South game at Montgomery, Ala.

Matulich, who stands 6 feet and is 25 years old, becomes the fifth rookie halfback to sign with the Rams this year.

## IT TOOK GREAT GOLF TO ANNEX OPEN CROWN

BY BRAVEN DYER

Dapper Jim Demaret, golf's riot of color from old Ojai, shot the last 36 holes of the National Open Golf Championship in 5 under par and all he got was second-place money.

His 278 over the entire tournament shattered a record which Ralph Guldahl hung up 10 years ago and which many golf critics began to suspect might stand like the Rock of Ages.

Unfortunately for popular Jim there was another hot shot kid out on the Riviera course yesterday. His name, of course, is Ben Hogan and quite likely there isn't another golfer in the whole wide world who could have beaten Demaret yesterday.

For you see, Ben was 5 under, too, for that last 36 holes, and, inasmuch as he started the day's links struggle two shots in front of Demaret, the Ojai fashion plate's magnificent try still got him nothing but second money.

As Willie Hunter, the host pro, said after it was all over, "and by next week nobody will even remember who was second."

Not that it really was needed, but yesterday's triumph by Hogan was the clincher. He goes into the record books indisputably now as the greatest golfer of all time.

Because, you see, not since 1922 when Gene Sarazen did it, has any man won both the Na-

Turn to Page 18, Column 6

TITLE BOUND—Bantam Ben Hogan belts one long and true off 15th tee during yesterday morning round of U.S. Open Golf Tournament at Riviera Country Club. Hogan shot a 68, tacked on an afternoon card of 69 to win title with 72-hole total of 276. It was his first Open crown.

SUNDAY MORNING, JUNE 13, 1948

## Ticket Sale Opens for Ram-Redskin Classic

BY PAUL ZIMMERMAN

Mail order ticket sales to the fourth annual Times Charities, Inc., pro football game between the Los Angeles Rams and Washington Redskins opens tomorrow, it was announced yesterday by Paul J. Schissler, general manager of the East-West pro classic.

More than 80,000 spectators poured into Memorial Coliseum a year ago to witness this contest—which officially opens the local grid season each fall—and Schissler says advance requests for ticket information already has been heavy.

**First Come, First Served**

Price for reserved seats is $3.60, including tax. Choice seats will be sold on the basis of first come, first served. Reservation requests should be mailed to Times Football Game, Room 200, Los Angeles Times, 202 W 1st St.

Box office sale will not start for several weeks and no telephone orders can be accepted at this time.

This year's classic will be held on the night of Sept. 2.

Coach Bob Snyder's Rams won the 1947 game, 20 to 7, and the Rams captured the 1946 game of this series by a 16-to-14 score. Both were wild, wide-open tussles featuring sharp passing and spectacular runs.

Since that game the Redskins have been vastly revamped. President George Preston Marshall untied his purse strings and bought some of the best players in the nation, headed by Harry Gilmer, Alabama's great passing and running star who was a standout in the Rose, Orange and Sugar bowls in successive years.

**Sammy the Great**

Gilmer will be called upon to spell the great Sammy Baugh, who holds virtually every passing record in the National League and set the circuit afire last year with his finest performance in a long series of terrific years as the top aerial artist of all time.

The Rams, who started out like a wild prairie fire on scoring last year and then ran into the most devastating series of injuries any pro team ever suffered in one season, will gamble largely on the sturdy squad that upset the National League championship Chicago Cardinals in convincing fashion.

Steve Bagarus and Bob Shaw, two of the finest pass catchers in the league, headed this list of injuries. Both were out for the season, but Coach Snyder says both are back in perfect health.

Back to do the passing, of course, is Bob Waterfield, the former Bruin star, who will find splendid support from Jim Hardy, Trojan Rose Bowl star of yesteryears.

And don't overlook Kenny

Turn to Page 18, Column 3

## Dillard Ties Own Record

DAYTON, O., June 12 (AP)—Harrison Dillard of Baldwin-Wallace College tied his own unofficial world record for the 220-yard low hurdles today in the district Amateur Athletic Union track and field meet.

The Baldwin-Wallace Negro speedster swept over the barriers in 22.3s., two-tenths of a second faster than the accepted world mark. He turned in the same time in 1947, but the mark has not been accepted for world recognition.

A 16-mile breeze at Dillard's back, officials said, probably would keep today's time from being recognized.

Dillard also tied the National Collegiate Athletic Association mark for the 120-yard high hurdles in 13.9s., bringing his string of race victories to 75.

Times photos by John Malmin

ALL SMILES—Ken Rogers, low amateur, and Hogan, at right, congratulate each other at cup presentation. Rogers was awarded medal. Hogan won trophy and $2000.

## How They Finished in U.S. Open Golf

Final 72-hole scores plus money winners of National Open Golf Tournament:

|  |  |
|---|---|
| **—276 ($2000)—** | |
| Ben Hogan, Hershey, Pa. | 67-72-68-69 |
| **—278 ($1500)—** | |
| Jimmy Demaret, Houston | 71-70-68-69 |
| **—280 ($1000)—** | |
| Jim Turnesa, Elmsford, N.Y. | 71-69-70-70 |
| **—282 ($800)—** | |
| Bobby Locke, Johannesburg, South Africa | 70-69-73-70 |
| **—283 ($600)—** | |
| Sam Snead, White Sulphur Springs, W.Va. | 69-69-73-72 |
| **—285 ($500)—** | |
| Lew Worsham, Oakmont, Pa. | 67-74-71-73 |
| **—286 ($400)—** | |
| Herman Barron, White Plains, N.Y. | 73-70-71-72 |
| **—287 ($300)—** | |
| Toney Penna, Cincinnati | 70-72-73-72 |
| Smiley Quick, Culver City, Cal. | 73-71-71-69 |
| John Bulla, Phoenix, Ariz. | 73-72-75-67 |
| **—288 ($200)—** | |
| Skip Alexander, Lexington, N.C. | 71-73-71-73 |
| George Schoux, Mamaroneck, N.Y. | 74-72-76-76 |
| x-Richard Mayer, Mamaroneck, N.Y. | 75-73-78-72 |
| John Dawson, Hollywood | 71-72-79-76 |
| **—289 ($150)—** | |
| Harold McSpaden, N.Y. | 74-69-69-77 |
| Charles Congdon, Tacoma, Wash. | 71-70-71-77 |
| **—290 ($114.28)—** | |
| Vic Ghezzi, Englewood, N.J. | 72-74-74-70 |
| Leland Gibson, Kansas City, Mo. | 71-76-69-74 |
| George Schneiter, Ogden, Utah | 73-68-75-74 |
| Ellsworth Vines, Iowa City, Ia. | 75-72-69-74 |
| Otto Greiner, Baltimore | 76-78-71-73 |
| Herman Keiser, Akron, O. | 71-71-73-75 |
| Herschel Spears, Birmingham, Ala. | 72-71-76-71 |
| **—291 ($100)—** | |
| Joe Kirkwood Jr., Pacific Palisades, Cal. | 72-70-72-77 |
| Lloyd Mangrum, Niles, Ill. | 71-72-74-74 |
| Alfred Smith, Winston-Salem | 73-72-77-69 |
| Cary Middlecoff, Memphis | 74-71-73-73 |
| **—292 ($100)—** | |
| Art Bell, Colma, Cal. | 72-75-71-74 |
| Pete Cooper, Ponteverde Beach, Fla. | 76-72-72-72 |
| George Fazio, Los Angeles | 72-72-76-72 |
| **—293 ($75)—** | |
| Chick Harbert, Northville, Mich. | 72-72-77-72 |
| Joe Kirkwood Jr., Abington, Pa. | 73-75-73-72 |
| Marty Furgol, Los Angeles | 72-74-73-74 |
| Frank Moore, Overland, Mo. | 73-75-73-72 |
| **—294—** | |
| Ralph Guldahl, Medina, Ill. | 73-75-75-71 |
| Zell Eaton, Montebello | 72-74-75-73 |
| **—295—** | |
| x-Ken Rogers, Oklahoma City | 69-76-72-78 |
| **—296—** | |
| Jack Harden, El Paso, Tex. | 72-73-73-78 |
| Bill Nary, Albuquerque | 73-75-75-73 |
| Jack Ryan, Louisville, Ky. | 74-69-76-77 |
| E. J. Harrison, Chicago | 75-72-72-77 |
| Jimmy Hines, Glenview, Ill. | 75-71-76-74 |
| John Palmer, Badin, N.C. | 74-74-76-72 |
| **—298—** | |
| x-Frank Stranahan, Toledo | 72-69-78-79 |
| **—299—** | |
| Jim Johnston, Farmington, Mich. | 76-71-77-75 |
| Ed Furgol, Royal Oak, Mich. | 75-73-77-74 |
| Dave Douglas, Wilmington, Del. | 74-73-78-84 |
| Jimmy Thomson, N.Y. | 77-71-76-76 |
| **—300—** | |
| Al Zimmerman, Portland, Or. | 71-74-77-78 |
| **—301—** | |
| Buck White, Battle Creek, Mich. | 75-73-80-73 |
| **—302—** | |
| Iverson Martin, Graham, Tex. | 73-73-80-76 |
| Ted Rhodes, Los Angeles | 70-76-77-79 |
| **—308—** | |
| Paul Runyan, Pasadena | 74-73-80-76 |
| **—313—** | |
| Andrew Mills, Kansas City | 71-75-83-84 |
| **WITHDREW** | |
| Tommy Armour, Boca Raton, Fla. | 74-74-81-xx |
| Ray Mangrum, Los Angeles | 75-71-84-xx |
| Chandler Harper, Portsmouth, Va. | 78-74-77-xx |

## Ross Surprises Gerry Karver

HARRISBURG, Pa., June 12 (AP)—Villanova College's Browning Ross scored a stunning upset today over Olympic hopeful Gerry Karver and set a new meet record in the Middle Atlantic AAU 1500-meter event.

His time of 3m. 57.8s. eclipsed the previous Middle Atlantic mark of 4m. 23s. set in 1934 by Ernie Federoff of Temple University.

## Today in Sports

**BASEBALL**—Hollywood vs. Los Angeles, Wrigley Field, double-header, starting at 1:30 p.m.

**SPEEDBOAT RACING**—Long Beach Marine Stadium, 11 events, 1:30 p.m.

**STOCK CAR RACING**—Carrell Speedway, qualifying at 12 noon; 250-lap race, 2:30 p.m.

**SOCCER**—Rancho Cienega Stadium, two games at 1 and 3 p.m.

## Demaret 2nd With 278; Turnesa 3rd

BY CHARLES CURTIS

Ben Hogan, a positive cinch on this course, romped away with golf's Hundred-Grander—the United States Open championship—yesterday over Riviera Country Club's 7020-yard distance.

Bantam Ben shattered all records for the 72-hole tournament scoring, firing an 8-under-par 276 on closing rounds of 68 and 69. And his brilliant triumph, coming on the heels of his second National Professional Golfers' Association match play triumph, is expected to net the Texas-born Irishman about $100,000 in the coming year.

Second was Jimmy Demaret at 278, next Jimmy Turnesa at 280. (Both of them cracked Ralph Guldahl's tournament record of 281.) Fourth was Bobby Locke at 282 and next Sam Snead with 283.

**Snead's Putter Cools**

Snead's fine putting of the first two days was just a myth—he returned to form yesterday, became the Sad Sam of the greens, and couldn't putt.

Yesterday's crowd was estimated by L.A. Junior Chamber of Commerce officials at 15,000, but the U.S. Golf Association guess for the entire three days was only 25,000, far below the record.

It was all Hogan's show and these are some of his accomplishments:

Became the first man since Gene Sarazen in 1922 to take both the PGA and Open crowns in the same season. This was Hogan's first Open triumph.

In addition to shattering the 72-hole scoring record by five strokes, his 54-hole total at the midway point yesterday clipped four shots off the mark for that distance.

Scored his third straight tournament win at Riviera. He took the Los Angeles Open of 1947 with 280 and the same event this year with 275. They'll make him Mayor of Pacific Palisades some day now and hand him the keys to the club house.

**Longest Course**

Posted rounds of 67-72-68-69 over the longest course ever the site of a National Open. He took a chunk of the first day lead with Defending Champion Lew Worsham, dropped a stroke back of Snead's pace at the midway point, and closed with a determined methodical drive yesterday.

If there is any explanation of all this rewriting to golf's record book it is certainly Ben Hogan's putter.

Only once in the 72 holes did Hogan take more than two putts on a green, and that lapse came at the 69th hole of play—the 15th of yesterday's final round—where he was on the extreme front of the huge carpet, some 75 feet from the pin, and took three shots to get down.

This ability to putt the Riviera greens was credited by Hogan after yesterday's triumph with a good share of credit for the victory.

**Read Greens Well**

"I guess ability to read the greens has been about my best asset at Riviera," Ben told press men. "But that stuff about golfers being a cinch on any particular course is nonsense." Which some local links followers must certainly question after Hogan's tour of duty at Riviera.

Hogan has no plans to try for the British Open next month. He acknowledged, to a leading question, that he feels he's a better golfer than he was before the war, which nobody present can deny.

Yesterday's punishing 36-hole test started as Sam Snead's show when he holed a 14-footer for an eagle at the very first green. But Sam took an extra shot to get down from the deep grass fringing the 3rd, missed a 7-foot putt there and then three-putted the 4th. After that he was never a serious threat.

But Demaret was of more solid substance.

Likeable Jimmy, brilliantly

Turn to Page 18, Column 3

## Herb M'Kenley Misses Mark

NEW YORK, June 12 (AP)—Herb McKenley missed his bid for a new world record at 400 meters today.

McKenley, fell 4/10ths of a second short of his announced assault on the world 400-meter record when he turned the distance in 46.4s.

But it was the fastest 400 meters ever run in New York and 1/10th of a second faster than the time which won for Archie Williams in the 1936 Olympics.

Charley Fonville, the Olympic shot-put favorite from Michigan, tossed the iron ball 56ft. 11in.—a heave he has bettered only with the 58ft. ¼in. with which he shattered the world record at the Kansas Relays.

SATURDAY MORNING, JUNE 26, 1948

# Louis Winner; Says He's Through

AND STILL CHAMPION—Joe Louis calmly looks down on Jersey Joe Walcott after knocking him out in 11th round. Referee Frank Fullam moves in to start count.

BUT NOT OUT—Champion Joe Louis takes a one-count after Jersey Joe caught him with a hard right hand in the third round of their heavyweight championship bout.

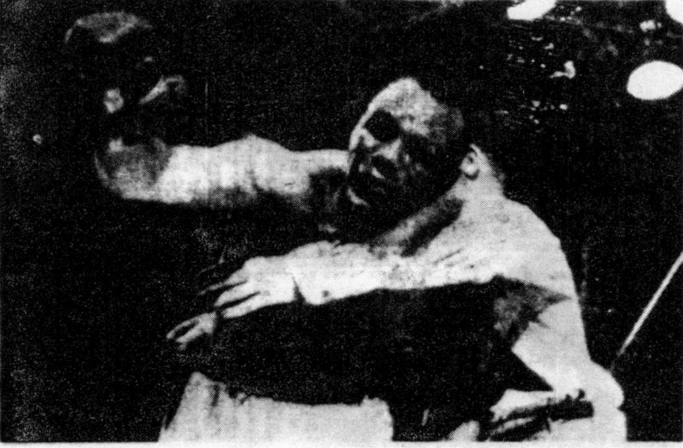

WHAT HIT ME?—Jersey Joe Walcott, still dazed by the smashing fists of the champion, is helped up by Referee Frank Fullam after being kayoed in 11th round. (AP Wirephotos)

## Jersey Joe Kayoed in 11th Round

BY JACK CUDDY

NEW YORK, June 25 (U.P.) Joe Louis ended one of the most glorious careers in boxing history tonight when he knocked out Jersey Joe Walcott in the 11th round to retain his world's heavyweight championship and then announced his retirement from the ring.

"That was it. That was my last fight," Louis said, a big smile on his face as he walked from the ring, after the 25th successful defense of his title.

"I'm a tired man," he said.

He looked it, too, for it took all the cunning and power which he had left to put away the challenger from Camden, N.J., at 2:56 of the 11th round.

**Dull and Listless**

Up to that point, it was an even fight, although a dull and listless one. Walcott had Louis on the floor once, for a count of one in the third round, but until Louis' flurry of rights and lefts ended the bout, there was very little fighting.

Louis became the second heavyweight champion in history to retire undefeated. Only Gene Tunney before him had done the same.

Louis had announced repeatedly before the fight that this bout would be his last. But had he lost tonight there was a chance of his changing his mind.

But his victory made the retirement definite and brought to an end the reign of one of the greatest champions in ring history. He won the title 11 years and three days ago from Jim Braddock in Chicago, and from that time on took on all comers.

**Longest Reign**

It was the longest reign in heavyweight history and the second longest in the history of any division. Only Johnny Kilbane, a featherweight, held a boxing championship longer. He held that crown from Feb. 22, 1912, until June 2, 1923, a period of 11 years and three months.

Twenty-five times Louis put his title at stake and each time he retained it, although he came close to losing it several times, including his first bout with Walcott last December at Madison Square Garden. He won that on a split decision, but he made it definite tonight that he was a better man than Walcott. That was the one thing Louis wanted to prove before he hung up his gloves for good.

The crowd of 42,667 gave Louis a tremendous ovation as he left the ring. Few knew then, how-

Turn to Page 13, Column 7

## Score Cards Tell Tale of Fight Before Kayo

YANKEE STADIUM, New York, June 25 (AP)—The score cards of the three officials of the Joe Louis-Jersey Joe Walcott fight. Referee Frank Fullam and Judges Harold Barnes and Jack O'Sullivan officiated.

(L — Designates Louis; W — Walcott; E—even round; the figures next to the initial designate points for the round.)

| | Fullam (Ref.) | O'Sullivan (Judge) | Barnes (Judge) |
|---|---|---|---|
| 1 | E | E | L-1 |
| 2 | L-1 | W-1 | W-1 |
| 3 | W-2 | W-3 | W-3 |
| 4 | L-1 | L-1 | W-1 |
| 5 | W-1 | L-1 | E |
| 6 | E | W-1 | W-2 |
| 7 | L-1 | L-1 | W-2 |
| 8 | L-1 | L-1 | L-1 |
| 9 | L-1 | W-1 | L-3 |
| 10 | E | W-1 | W-2 |
| 11 | Knockout by Louis | | |

## The Sports Parade

By BRAVEN DYER

Now that the Republicans have scratched all of their early eligibles and settled upon Governors Tom Dewey and Earl Warren as the entry they will send to the post next fall for the great Presidential Handicap, leave us turn to Hollywood Park where things have suddenly become very unsettled for the $25,000 Hollywood Lassie Stakes to be run this afternoon.

Mentioning Gov. Warren and a horse race in the same breath reminds me that the Governor is a solid racing fan as well as a boxing, football, baseball and grunion-grabbing enthusiast. Mrs. Warren has crowned the winner of the $100,000 Hollywood Gold Cup for the last two runnings and probably will do so again this season come the big day on July 17. The Governor is currently making a strong drive against bookmakers as he believes they may destroy the sport he loves if he does not chase them out of the State.

**VERSATILE NOMINEE**

Gov. Dewey is also a sportsman, so his backers tell us, and the cow-milking pictures that have been sent around to encourage the agricultural vote indicate that he might be a tough man to beat in the rope climb.

But to get back to today's Hollywood Park Lassie Stakes, which is for 2-year-old young lady hosses, the field is suddenly thrown wide open with two of the three favorites deciding they have the miseries. Jade's Jade, who might have been the public choice off her winning of the Maytime Stakes at Bay Meadows recently, went out on the track Thursday for a final work only to take a few steps and holler, "Ouch my corns," which immediately removed her from the contest.

Then yesterday, Tiger Inn, upon whom I was about to put the curse by selecting as the probable winner because of her three firsts and two seconds in six starts, knocked her shins against her stall, and Trainer Paul Lycan had to pacify her by telling her she could sunbathe this afternoon while the other girls were running. With Tiger Inn becoming Tiger Out, this leaves Cosmopolite, winner of one for one to date at Hollypark, as the one remaining member of the pre-race favorited trio, and I can't go for her simply because our Al Wolf has already selected her and no nag can carry that much weight.

**THREE-IN-ONE CHOICE**

Now young ladies are very unpredictable, so my young sons keep explaining earnestly to me these days (as if they were telling the old guy something he hadn't learned years ago the hard way) and so I won't try to predict the winner of today's feature race. No sir, I won't give you the winner—I'll give you three, all of them guaranteed to pay a big price—providing they get there first, of course.

No. 1 long-shot selection is Bomber Night. This little gal can't beat a gopher in her morning works, but when she runs in the p.m.—swish!! She made her first and only start at Hollypark just 10 days ago, got off badly, then circled the field, won—and paid $164.60 for two bucks.

Another longy to watch out for is Competing Lady, who has won two of her last three starts and beaten most of the hosses in today's field, but she is so lightly regarded when she goes to the post that last time she paid $40.80 for two.

For the third super special there is Sleeper's Jinx, a sleeper who won at Santa Anita but hasn't got home first yet at Hollywood Park and is about due at boxcar prices.

Leave Mr. Wolf spend his dough on the favored Cosmopolite. I'm going to take my threesome in a package deal and confidently expect one of them to cause a call to be made for the money trucks to help me home with my do-re-mi.

## Triple Play Helps Trojans Topple Yale

HYAMES FIELD, Kalamazoo, Mich., June 25—A ninth-inning triple play saved the game for Southern California here today as the Trojans beat Yale, 3-1, to take a one-up lead in the NCAA College World Series.

With the bases loaded and no outs, Yale's pinch-hitter, Jerry Breen, slapped a bouncer to Wally Hood, Trojan pitcher. Hood rifled the ball to Bob Zuber, catcher, for the first out, and Bob threw to Henry Cedillos at first to get Breen for out No. 2. Cedillos then zipped the ball to Bill Lillie at third who tagged the runner, Dick Mathews, who had rounded the bag, to end the game.

**Unearned Three**

The Trojans, trailing from the third inning when Yale scored its unearned run without benefit of a hit, rallied for three runs in the top of the ninth, apparently to clinch the triumph. Two dropped balls at the plate by Paul Russ, Yale catcher, helped the Trojans plenty as all three runs were unearned.

Then Hood, who had held the New Haven team to two hits, let down and two singles and a walk loaded the bases and set the stage for Breen's ill-fated appearances.

**Kipp To Hurl**

Tomorrow Lefty Tom Kipp throws for Troy and will oppose Frank Quinn, Yale ace righthander. If Yale wins, a third and deciding game will be played forthwith.

| SC | AB | H | O | A | Yale | AB | H | O | A |
|---|---|---|---|---|---|---|---|---|---|
| Jones,rf | 5 | 1 | 2 | 0 | Moher,ss | 4 | 0 | 1 | 1 |
| Mass'ian,2b | 4 | 1 | 0 | 2 | Goodyear,rf | 4 | 0 | 1 | 1 |
| Bridgew'er,ss | 3 | 0 | 6 | 4 | Bedden,cf | 3 | 0 | 0 | 0 |
| Workman,lf | 4 | 0 | 1 | 0 | Rosenweig,cf | 1 | 1 | 1 | 0 |
| McKelvey,c | 4 | 2 | 6 | 0 | Mathews,3b | 3 | 0 | 2 | 4 |
| a-Freeman | 0 | 0 | 0 | 0 | Fitzgerald,lf | 4 | 2 | 1 | 0 |
| Zuber,c | 0 | 0 | 1 | 1 | Frinke,c | 3 | 1 | 5 | 1 |
| Henley,rf | 4 | 1 | 6 | 0 | Russ,c | 0 | 0 | 0 | 0 |
| Lillie,3b | 4 | 1 | 2 | 2 | b-Breen | 1 | 0 | 0 | 0 |
| Cedillos,1b | 4 | 2 | 9 | 1 | Bush,1b | 3 | 0 | 10 | 1 |
| Hood,p | 3 | 1 | 0 | 2 | Smith,2b | 3 | 0 | 6 | 6 |
| | | | | | Duffus,p | 2 | 0 | 0 | 2 |
| Totals | 35 | 9 | 27 | 12 | Totals | 30 | 4 | 27 | 20 |

a—Freeman ran for McKelvey in 9th.
b—Breen hit into triple play for Russ in 9th.

SCORE BY INNINGS

Southern California ... 0 0 0 0 0 0 0 0 3—3
Yale .............. 0 0 1 0 0 0 0 0 0—1

E—Smith, 2; Bridgewater, Russ, 2. RBI—Goodyear, Jones. 2B—Fitzgerald. SH—Maxmanian. SB—Henley, Bridgewater. LOB—Southern California, 5; Yale, 5. DP—Moher to Smith to Cedillos to Lillie. TP—Hood to Zuber to Cedillos to Lillie. SO—Hood, 6; Duffus, 2. BB—Duffus, 3. Attendance—2500.

## Today in Sports

BASEBALL—San Diego vs. Hollywood, Gilmore Field, 8:15 p.m.

HORSE RACING—Hollywood Park, first post 1:30 p.m.

TENNIS—NCAA, Westwood, all day.

GOLF—Southern California amateur, Wilshire CC; city golf championship, Griffith Park. Play continues all day.

HORSE SHOW—Palomino Horse Show, 3200 Riverside Drive, 8 p.m.

HOT ROD RACES—Carrell Speedway (CRA), Gardena; time trials, 7; first race, 8:15.

## 'Referee Hounded Me,' Jersey Joe's Alibi

### Beaten Challenger Blames Official for Kayo Defeat

YANKEE STADIUM, New York, June 25 (AP) — "The referee beat me, that's what happened out there." Joe Walcott complained after being knocked out by Joe Louis in their heavyweight championship fight.

"It got so I was fighting the referee instead of Joe Louis," Jersey Joe moaned. "The ref kept hounding me, telling me to fight. 'Come on, make a fight of it,' he kept repeating. 'Let's have some action.' The ref kept yelling, 'Come on, Walcott, fight.' He never said, 'Come on, Louis, fight.'

**Changed Style**

"His hounding bothered me. It caused me to change my plans, my style of fighting."

Walcott thought he was ahead until he made "that fatal mistake."

"I know I made a mistake, but I don't know what it was," he said. "They tell me he hit me with everything in the book, but I only remember the first one. After that I don't know what happened, except that I was on the floor. I tried terribly hard to get up, but just couldn't."

Walcott, still dazed by the terrific battering he took in the final seconds of the 11th round, said he believed Louis was a much better fighter in their first meeting last December.

**Champ Slipped**

"Louis has slipped," he asserted. "There's no doubt about it. I had him licked, referee and all, until I made that mistake."

When informed about Louis' retirement announcement, Walcott shook his head and muttered, "I hope it's not true. I'd like to meet him again. I hope Joe changes his mind about retiring and gives me another chance. I know I can beat him."

Walcott said he planned to continue fighting.

"I feel fine," he said. "Joe never hurt me before that round. I'm awfully sorry that I let down all of my friends. I'm going to make it up to them, though. I'm going to fight until I win the heavyweight championship of the world. That's always been my life-long ambition."

### Joe Louis Admits He Has Slipped in Last Five Years

YANKEE STADIUM, New York, June 25 (AP)—Weary, and with his left eye slightly puffed, Joe Louis pushed his way through a milling crowd to his dressing room for the last time tonight.

Winner by a knockout over Jersey Joe Walcott in the 11th round of their heavyweight championship fight, the retiring champion—according to his own statement—said he was satisfied with his fight, and also intimated he still thought very little of Jersey Joe as a fighter.

**"Hokey-Pokey Stuff"**

"Five years ago I would have come out in the first round and got it over with in a hurry," Louis said, then added sadly, "but I'm not the fighter I was five years ago.

"I was determined to fight Walcott's fight and not be tricked into any moves by his hokey-pokey stuff. I would have been satisfied with a decision if I hadn't caught him, as I thought I could outpoint him. I thought I lost only two rounds—the third and the sixth."

The Champion's Trainer Manny Seamon, wasn't so sure, however.

"I told Joe at the end of the 10th round that it was an even fight and he'd better get in there or he'd blow his title, as anything could happen. Joe said at the end of nearly every round that he'd catch him, and Joe said about the 10th round he was beginning to catch on, that he was getting Walcott with his jab."

Louis, perspiring profusely as the mob of reporters and photographers hemmed him in, managed to blurt that he planned to enter politics.

**Speechmaking**

"Going to make any speeches, Joe?" someone asked.

"Sure, you can't be in politics without making speeches," he answered. Pressed as to what party he could side with, he sidestepped as neatly as Walcott did for 10 rounds. "I'll announce that next week," he said coyly.

## Stars Fall on Padres for Lopsided 12-0 Nod

BY AL WOLF

Hollywood's unfathomable Stars, who usually win 'em big or lose 'em close (with emphasis on the latter), ended a three-game losing streak by smashing San Diego, 12-0, last evening before 4379 Gilmore Field fans.

Four-hit pitching by Vernon Kennedy saddled the erstwhile sizzling Padres with their first shutout in a month. It was Kennedy's first whitewash job of the season, his fourth win and the stopper for a six-game personal losing streak that had extended 'way back to May 16.

Tom Seats cranked up against him and for three innings the two veterans tossed no-hit stuff. But Lee Handley doubled to spoil Kennedy's dreams, if any, with one away in the fourth.

And in the home half, singles by Gus Zernial and Don Ross and doubles by Frankie Kelleher and Lou Stringer not only soured Seats' impending perfecto but started him toward his fifth defeat.

Seats got the hook an inning later and Gordon Walden and Bob Kerrigan staggered the rest of the way. The trio coughed up 16 safeties, including Kelleher's 19th homer.

Kennedy managed to put the handcuffs on Jack Graham. For the first time this week, the Padre slugger went hitless, though drawing a pair of harmless passes.

**Foul Tips**

Pete Gebrian (7-4) will chuck for Hollywood tonight . . . Manager Rip Collins, apparently a whodunit fan, is making a great

Turn to Page 13, Column 1

## Seixas, Likas Tennis Finalists

BY BION ABBOTT

Top-seeded Vic Seixas of North Carolina and fifth-seeded Harry Likas of the University of San Francisco banged their way into the finals of the 64th annual National Intercollegiate tennis championships yesterday on the UCLA courts in Westwood.

Seixas simply slammed the ball too hard for fourth-seeded Herbie Flam of the Bruins, while Likas surprised second-seeded Jim Brink of Washington, outsteadying the towering Huskie star.

In the gathering dusk SC's Bobby Perez and Arnold Saul toppled the tourney's top-seeded doubles team, Flam and Gene Garrett of UCLA, in five sets, 6-2, 5-7, 1-6, 7-5, 6-3. The Bruin

Turn to Page 13, Column 7

## BERGELIN OUSTS PARKER IN LONDON NET UPSET

LONDON, June 25 (AP)—Lennart Bergelin, a long-legged Swede with a boarding house reach, pulled one of the classic upsets of Wimbledon tennis history today when he defeated Frankie Parker of Los Angeles in a gripping five-set struggle on the center court.

The 32-year-old American star, seeded first and a heavy favorite to win the singles title, went down by scores of 5-7, 7-5, 9-7, 0-6, 10-8, after more than three hours of play before 15,000 exhausted fans.

The unseeded Bergelin, only 23 and a favorite doubles partner of King Gustav of Sweden, played probably the greatest tennis of his career in battling his way to the quarter-finals.

Fighting his heart out to add a Wimbledon title to his long list of tennis honors, Parker led, at 5-3 in the deciding set, only to let Bergelin get away.

The Swede, only a game from defeat, swarmed to the net to pull the vital ninth game out of the fire after four deuces and then went on to victory.

Only one disturbing note marred the epic duel. That came in the same ninth game, when Bergelin developed a cramp in his right leg and began limping.

Parker, a thorough sportsman, asked his rival to rest a moment, and then obviously desisted from hitting sharply angled shots until the Swede had gotten over the worst of it.

From there to the end Bergelin did considerable limping. Yet on the final point he dashed to the net to smash away Parker's weak return and then vaulted

Turn to Page 12, Column 6

## Minyard Speeds to Midget Win

Hal Minyard won the main event, trophy dash and placed second in the semimain to steal the show in the midget races last night at 5-H Speedway, Roscoe. Bob Standcliff's automobile overturned in the semi-windup but he escaped unhurt.

Trophy dash (3 laps)—Hal Minyard, Speed Boardman, 46.22s.
Semimain (10 laps)—Jack Jordon, Hal Minyard, Bob Brown (no time, restart).
Main event (25 laps)—Minyard, Boardman, Jerry Curry, 8m. 34.[illegible]s.

## BABE RUTH IN HOSPITAL AGAIN

NEW YORK, June 25 (AP) Babe Ruth has gone back to the hospital, it was disclosed tonight.

A Memorial Hospital official said Ruth was admitted yesterday but gave no details of his condition.

He had been hospitalized several times since last November, when he entered French Hospital with a sinus infection. Later he underwent a throat operation.

## Riegel, Kraft Gain Finals

KANSAS CITY, June 25 (AP)—Skee Riegel of Glendale, Cal., the National Amateur champion, and the veteran John Kraft, Denver, won their way into the finals of the Trans-Mississippi Golf Tournament today without burning too much energy.

Riegel, the 1946 Trans-Mississippi champion, defeated Young Lawrence Glosser, Oklahoma City, 8 and 6, and Kraft, the 1942 titlist, breezed past Iri Olliver of Kansas City, 7 and 6.

Riegel and Kraft will meet for the championship in a 36-hole match.

## Baseball's Big Six

BY THE ASSOCIATED PRESS

(Three leaders in each league)

| Player and club | G | AB | R | H | Pct. |
|---|---|---|---|---|---|
| Williams, Red Sox | 57 | 211 | [illegible] | 87 | .412 |
| Musial, Cardinals | [illegible] | 233 | 52 | 85 | .365 |
| Boudreau, Indians | 57 | 214 | [illegible] | 78 | .364 |
| Ashburn, Phillies | 56 | 239 | [illegible] | 83 | .347 |
| Holmes, Braves | 51 | 206 | 37 | 71 | .345 |
| Zarilla, Browns | 55 | 197 | [illegible] | 66 | .335 |

RUNS BATTED IN

| American League | | National League | |
|---|---|---|---|
| Williams, Red Sox | 66 | Sauer, Reds | 56 |
| DiMaggio, Yanks | 63 | Kiner, Pirates | 51 |
| Stephens, Red Sox | 53 | Mize, Giants | 46 |

HOME RUNS

| American League | | National League | |
|---|---|---|---|
| DiMaggio, Yanks | 18 | Sauer, Reds | [illegible] |
| Keltner, Indians | 17 | Kiner, Pirates | [illegible] |
| Williams, Red Sox | 15 | Musial, Cards | [illegible] |
| | | Mize, Giants | [illegible] |

## Here's Blow-by-Blow Account of Louis Victory

BY THE ASSOCIATED PRESS

Here's blow-by-blow account of title clash:

**ROUND ONE**

They circled cautiously in midring. Walcott flicked out a left to the head with the first blow of the fight. Walcott tapped another left to head and another left to the body. Walcott was side-stepping as he did in the previous fight. Walcott tapped another light left to the head and took a left hook to the head for Louis' first blow to the head. Walcott flicked another left and took a left to the body in exchange. Louis was moving in steadily as Walcott stepped away. Walcott poked a left to the head of the champion and came back with another left to the body. Louis missed two lefts and received a light left to the head for his efforts. Louis ripped after Walcott with a left and right to the body. Walcott slapped a left to Louis' face and then danced away again from the pursuing champion as the bell sounded.

**ROUND TWO**

They circled around each other carefully waiting for an opening. Each missed light leading lefts. Walcott got in a light left to the body and then they exchanged lefts to the head. The crowd started to act up at the inactivity and then let out a roar as Walcott almost turned his back on Louis and moved away. Walcott was trying to feint but Louis wouldn't be caught open. They each got in lefts to the head. Walcott poked a left to the head and started dancing again. The crowd was now clapping hands as if they wanted the boys to get in there and start punching. Louis plodded forward and Walcott just side-stepped and danced away and the fans let go with a resounding chorus of boos at the bell.

**ROUND THREE**

Walcott flicked a light to the head, took one himself and took another soft in return. The champion poked a straight left to Walcott's body. Walcott was feinting and sidestepping and he made Louis miss a straight left. Louis nailed Walcott with a right to the jaw. The champion kept after the challenger. Louis dug another left to the body as Walcott moved away. Walcott flicked a left to Louis' head and then crossed a right to Louis' jaw for a count of one. Walcott drove a hard right to Louis' head and they exchanged punches. The crowd yelled as they both waited for an opening to get in a decisive blow.

**ROUND FOUR**

Walcott flicked a left and started moving forward. Walcott drove another left as Louis moved to counter punch. Walcott flicked two lefts to the head and then moved away again. The challenger connected with two more lefts to the head without taking any blows in return. Walcott jabbed over three more lefts. Walcott crossed a neat right to the head and then Louis came in with his first blow and pinned Walcott to the ropes. The champion got in a left and right to the body as the crowd roared. Walcott escaped another of Louis' rights and grinned as he back-pedalled away. Walcott crossed a right to Louis' head just before the bell. Louis' left eye was beginning to swell.

**ROUND FIVE**

Walcott tapped three lefts to Louis' face and then retreated before the incoming champion. Louis got in a beautiful left to the head and a right to the head. Walcott got in a left and Louis returned with a left to the body. The champion smashed a hard right to Walcott's jaw at the ropes. Walcott flicked a left and crossed two hard rights to Louis' head. Louis got in a stiff left to the head. Louis dug a right to the body and took a left and right in exchange. The champion got Walcott in a corner and stung him with a right to the head and got a right in exchange from Walcott.

**ROUND SIX**

Walcott flicked out three times but the champion caught all the blows with his gloves. Louis moved in on Walcott who moved away. Walcott jabbed two lefts to the head. The champion kept a careful eye on Walcott as the challenger poked out with his lefts. Walcott flicked over two more lefts without getting anything in return. The action slowed and the crowd began to yell for a little more business in the ring. Walcott grinned and swung a left to the body and took a left hook in return.

**ROUND SEVEN**

Louis' handlers worked on the champion's left eye during the interval. Walcott got in three lefts to the head and Louis caught as many on his gloves. Louis drove a left to Walcott's body. Walcott hooked a left to the head and then crossed a right to Louis' jaw. Louis moved in again but couldn't get anything in.

Walcott jabbed a left and crossed a right to the champion's head. The crowd laughed as Walcott stretched his hand upward. Walcott poked three lefts to Louis' head and Louis got in two lefts to the body. Louis moved forward and threw a left to Walcott's body.

**ROUND EIGHT**

Walcott danced, side stepped and back pedalled. In between he jabbed three times with his left to the champion's head. The champion poked a straight left to Walcott's body. Walcott crossed a long right to the champion's jaw. Walcott missed a right and Louis got in a right to Walcott's body. Louis stabbed a hard left to Walcott's head. Walcott got in a short left and right to Louis' head. The champion shot over a long left to the head and a short right to the body. Louis stabbed out with two stiff lefts to the head. Louis jabbed a left to the head and then the fighters circled away.

**ROUND NINE**

Louis drove a beautiful left to Walcott's head. Louis shot over another nice left to the head. Louis got in a nice right high on Walcott's head. Louis peppered Walcott with two lefts and followed it up with a left and right to the body. Walcott pinned Louis on the ropes and got in a left and right to the body. Louis stabbed another stiff left to the head. Louis ripped over two more straight lefts to the head. They exchanged hard lefts. Louis flicked two lefts to the head and Walcott gave him one back. They traded hard rights in mid-ring and they each got in one blow to the body at the bell.

**ROUND TEN**

Walcott pecked a left to the face and then moved away again. Walcott got in a light left and right to the head. The champion moved in as the challenger kept up his fancy dancing. The customers were rewarded by a light left by each. Louis poked in two lefts to the head. Walcott tapped two lefts to Louis' head and then moved away. Walcott peppered Louis' swollen eye with three lefts. Walcott got in two short rights to Louis' head. Louis' left eye was about half shut now. They circled carefully at the bell.

**ROUND ELEVEN**

Walcott flicked at the champion's swollen left eye. Louis sent over a straight left to the head. Walcott hooked a left to the body and missed a right to the head. Walcott danced and Louis moved forward and the crowd booed once more. Louis jabbed a left to the head. They exchanged lefts. Walcott got in a hard right to the head and followed up with a left to the head. Louis crossed a beautiful right to Walcott's head followed him up, pinning him against the ropes. Walcott then went down and was counted out.

Walcott was counted out after 2m. 56s. of the round.

PART 4

# Los Angeles Times

SPORTS

VOL. LXVII  CC  WEDNESDAY MORNING, AUGUST 4, 1948  Read Times Green for Latest Sports

## SPORTS PARADE

By BRAVEN DYER

From the Valhalla of Olympic champions the late Charles William Paddock, first world's fastest human, must have been truly proud of all the American sprinters who dominated the 100 and 200 meters in the current Olympic Games at London.

For the record book will now show that every American dash star finished in the money — a magnificent achievement when pitted against the world's greatest.

As the only previous Trojan ever to win an individual Olympic sprint title, Sir Charles (he was knighted in his heyday) must have been particularly proud of Melvin Emery Patton. For yesterday Pell-Mel finally hit the jackpot as he won the 200 meters after that heartbreaking disappointment in the 100 when everybody and his brother beat Dean Cromwell's pride and joy to the tape.

**ONLY OTHER ONE**

Cromwell, of course, has had many great sprinters and many champions. But until yesterday no Trojan student or grad had been able to match Paddock's sprint triumph 28 years ago at Antwerp.

Howard Drew made the Olympic team in 1912 as a Springfield (Mass.) schoolboy. Charles Borah was in the 200-meter dash in the 1928 Games. Frank Wykoff ran the 100 as a Glendale prep in 1928 and also made the teams of 1932 and 1936.

The late Foy Draper gained the '36 squad, but only as a relay man.

**DOUBLE WIN**

Sir Charles, fresh from winning both the 100 and 200 in the Inter-Allied Games in 1919, won the century crown at Antwerp in '20 in 10.8s. But when he attempted the longer sprint he was nipped by an American teammate, Allen Woodring, in 22s. flat.

Drew went unplaced in 1912. Paddock once more was second to Jackson Scholz of the United States in the 200 and fifth in the 100 in 1924, and in 1928 was a nonfinalist in the 200 after gallantly making the team for the third straight time.

Borah also failed to reach the finals in the 200 of 1928. Wykoff was fourth in the 100 that year, ran only on the winning sprint relay team of 1932 and repeated as fourth in the century of 1936.

**MERE TECHNICALITY**

Paddock's best time as a Trojan undergraduate in the yardage sprints were 9.6s. and 20.8s.—both world records. Later Paddock ran 9.5s. in the oft-discussed and disputed finish against Borah. Paddock's greatest race of all was 110 yards—slightly longer than 100 meters—in 10.2s., which now stands as the world record for the metric distance, although Paddock's name isn't included because of a technicality.

Patton has run the 100 in 9.3s., for a pending world record and was timed in 20.4s. for 220 yards and in 20.7s. around a turn for 200 meters, slightly less than a full furlong. Mel's time of 21.1s. in the 200 final was the second fastest time for that race in all Olympic history. Jesse Owens won in 20.7s. in 1936. Eddie Tolan did 21.2s. when he won in the Coliseum in the '32 Olympics.

**REVERSED STRATEGY**

The question immediately asked after Patton's 200-meter triumph yesterday was: "Well, what happened to him in the 100?"

It could be that Pell-Mel reversed his strategy. In gaining the finals of the 100 meters Patton was unbeaten and twice ran 10.4s., probably faster than he eventually ran the finals.

Yesterday he lost the 200-meter semifinal to Herb McKenley, the time being 21.4s., with both McKenley and Patton eased up. But when the blue chips were down, Pell-Mel was ready this time and it was McKenley, world record holder for both the 400 meters and 440 yards, who wound up fourth.

It's lucky for us Southern Californians that Patton reversed his strategy. Had he lost his second sprint, we might have had to move out! Him, too.

**HELP FROM PADDOCK**

It could be that the late Maj. Paddock, killed in a plane crash during the war, vicariously inspired Patton's victory yesterday.

How else can you explain Pell-Mel's unorthodox finish? Patton probably won't realize it himself until he sees a picture of his triumph, but that's Paddock's famed "Flying Leap" all over again!

I'm not much for the supernatural, but this time it looks for sure as if Paddock must have reached down from up there and patted Patton on the shoulder when Mel most needed it.

PATTON SHOWS HEELS TO FIELD IN 200 METERS

(AP) Wirephoto

Mel Patton of Southern California, third from left, is pictured winning the Olympic 200-meter finals in close finish with Teammate Barney Ewell, left. Finishers, left to right: Ewell, Cliff Bourland of LAAC, fifth; Patton, Lloyd LaBeach of Panama, third, and Herb McKenley of Jamaica, fourth. Both Patton and Ewell were timed at 21.1s.

RECORD-SETTER—With a record heave of 56ft. 2in., Wilbur Thompson of SC captures Olympic shot-put crown.

## YESTERDAY'S TRACK AND FIELD RESULTS

Results of yesterday's Olympic Games track and field results:

**Shot-put—Qualifying**

Qualifying distance 47ft. 10¾in.; three additional entries qualified on basis of best throws to make field of 12 for finals later today).

**James Fuchs, U.S.A.,** 52ft. 1in.; **Wilbur Thompson, U.S.A.,** 49ft. 6in.; **James Delaney, U.S.A.,** 49ft. 1½in.; Y. I. Lehtina, Finland, 48ft. 8½in.; J. A. Giles, Great Britain, 48ft. 7in.; P. J. Jouppila, Finland, 48ft. 3½in.; M. Lomowski, Poland, 48ft. 3in.; G. Arvidsson, Sweden, 48ft. 3in.; C. Yataganas, Greece, 48ft.; Kalina, Czechoslovakia, 47ft. 8½in.; Sigfus Sigurosson, Iceland, 47ft. 6in.; W. Gierutto, Poland, 47ft. 5in.

**Shot-put—Final**

**Thompson, U.S.A.,** 56ft. 2in. (new Olympic record, old record 53ft. 1¾in., set in Berlin in 1936 by Hans Woellke, Germany;) **2—Delaney, U.S.A.,** 54ft. 8½in. (also breaks former record); **3—Fuchs, U.S.A.,** 53ft. 10½in. (also breaks former record); 4—Lomoski, Poland, 50ft. 7½in.; 5—G. Arvidsson, Sweden, 50ft. 5in.; 6—Lehtina, Finland, 49ft. 4½in.

**Hop, Step and Jump—Qualifying**

(Qualifying distance 47ft. 6¾in.)

Gordon George Avery, Australia, 50ft. 3¾in.; K. J. V. Rautio, Finland, 48ft. 9in.; A. Hallgreen, Sweden, 48ft. 5¾in.; A. Pereira Da Silva, Brazil, 48ft. 2½in.; Wun Kwun Kim, Korea, 48ft. 1½in.; H. M. R. Rebello, India, 48ft. ¾in.; H. Coutinho Da Silva, Brazil, 48ft. ½in.; A. Ahman, Sweden, 47ft. 11in.; G. Oliveria, Brazil, 47ft. 10¼in.; L. Moberg, Sweden, 47ft. 9¾in.; Leslie A. H. McKeand, Australia, 47ft. 9in.; **W. E. Albans, U.S.A.,** 47ft. 9in.; K. Sarfalp, Turkey, 47ft. 9in.; Preben Kaj Larsen, Denmark, 47ft. 7½in.

**Hop, Step and Jump—Finals**

1—Ahman, Sweden, 50ft. 6¼in.; 2—Avery, Australia, 50ft. 4¾in.; 3—Sarfalp, Turkey, 49ft. 3½in.; 4—Larsen, Denmark, 48ft. 7¾in.; 5—Oliveria, Brazil, 48ft. 7½in.; 6—Rautio, Finland, 48ft. 2¾ in.

**200 Meters—Semifinals (218.72 Yards)**

(First three in each of two heats qualify for finals later today):

First heat: 1—Herb McKenley, Jamaica; **2—Mel Patton, U.S.A.; 3—Barney Ewell, U.S.A.** Time, 21.4s.

Second heat: **1—Cliff Bourland, U.S.A.;** 2—Lloyd LaBeach, Panama; 3—L. Laing, Jamaica. Time, 21.5s.

**200-Meter—Finals**

**1—Patton, U.S.A.,** (21.1s.); **2—Ewell, U.S.A.** (21.1s.); 3—LaBeach, Panama (21.2s.); 4—McKenley, Jamaica; **5—Bourland, U.S.A.;** 6—Laing, Jamaica. (Times of last three places not announced).

**110-Meter Hurdles—Qualifying (120.3 Yards)**

(First two in each of six heats qualify for semifinals tomorrow):

First heat: **1—Bill Porter, U.S.A.;** 2—P. Braekman, Belgium; 3—B. Recordon, Chile. Time, 14.3s.

Second heat: **1—Clyde Scott, U.S.A.;** 2—H. Frayer, France; 3—B. Rendin, Sweden. Time, 14.8s.

Third heat: 1—A. U. Triulzi, Argentina; 2—Peter John Gardner, Australia; 3—M. Molezun Suarez, Spain. Time, 14.6s.

Fourth heat: 1—J. H. Vickers, India; 2—H. Lidman, Sweden; 3—J. E. Sabater, Puerto Rico. Time, 14.7s.

Fifth heat: 1—Andre J. Marie, France; 2—O. H. Bernard, Switzerland; 3—S. F. Fosters, Jamaica. Time, 14.9s.

Sixth heat: **1—Craig Dixon, U.S.A.;** 2—R. H. Weinberg, Australia; 3—G. R. Omnes, France. Time, 14.2s.

**Women's 80-Meter Hurdles Qualifying (87.5 Yards)**

(First round: first three in each of four heats qualify for semifinals later today).

First heat: 1—F. E. Blankers-Koen, Holland; 2—J. M. Upton, Great Britain; 3—J. L. Toulouse, France; 4—M. L. James, Finland. Time, 11.3s. (equals world record set by C. Testoni of Italy in Dresden, Germany, in 1936, and later equaled by Mrs. Blankers-Koen in Amsterdam in 1942; also establishes new Olympic record; former mark 11.6s. set in Berlin in 1936 by T. Valla of Italy).

Second heat: 1—M. A. J. Gardner, Great Britain; 2—L. Lomska, Czechoslovakia; 3—N. Simonetto de Portela, Argentina; fourth place not announced. Time, 11.6s. (equals old Olympic record).

Third heat: 1—Y. Monginou, France; 2—Shirley B. Strickland, Australia; 3—Maria Oberbreyer, Austria. Time, 11.7s.

**Women's 80-Meter Hurdles Semifinals**

(First three in each of two heats qualify for finals Aug. 4).

First heat: 1—Blankers-Koen, Holland; 2—Oberbreyer, Austria; 3—Lomska, Czechoslovakia. Time, 11.4s.

Second heat: 1—Strickland, Australia; 2—Monginou, France; 3—Gardner, Great Britain. Time, 11.7s.

**3000-Meter Steeplechase Qualifying (3280.8 Yards)**

(Qualifying heats; first four in each of three heats qualify in finals Aug. 5).

First heat: 1—Erik Elmsaeter, Sweden; 2—A. Cuyodo, France; 3—Pentti Siltaloppi, Finland; 4—C. Mirando Justo, Spain. Time, 9m. 15s.

Second heat: 1—Raphael Pujazon, France; 2—G. Hagstroem, Sweden; 3—P. Segedin, Yugoslavia; **4—Browning Ross, U.S.A.** Time, 9m. 20.8s.

Third heat: 1—Tuhre S. Joestrand, Sweden, 2—A. Kainlauri, Finland; 3—E. Everaert, Belgium; 4—M. Chesneau, France. Time, 9m. 21s.

## Vicki Draves Scores Surprise Diving Win

WEMBLEY, Eng., Aug. 3 (AP)—A trio of California girls opened today's swimming session of the Olympic Games in the same manner that a quartet of American male swimmers closed it—with a rousing triumph for the Red, White and Blue.

Mrs. Victoria Manalo Draves of Pasadena, Cal.; Zoe Ann Olsen of Oakland, Cal., and Patricia Ann Elsener of San Francisco are the three girls. They finished in that order atop the contestants in the springboard diving.

The men swimmers swirled through the waters of the Empire Exhibition Poolhouse to slash 5½ seconds off the world and Olympic record in the 800-meter relay. The record now is 8m. 46s.

**Wolf on Team**

The foursome of Wally Ris, University of Iowa; Jimmy McLane of Akron, O.; Wallace Wolf of Los Angeles and Bill Smith of Honolulu traveled so fast that even the second-place Hungarian team cracked the old mark of 8m. 51.5s. That mark was set by Japan at Berlin in 1936.

The men swimmers now have three championships and two Olympic records to their credit. Additionally, the relay mark is the first at the current Games to be a world record.

The Americans had the race to themselves most of the way and Hungary had little dispute in its drive for second. Sweden was in third place through three legs, but when Alex Jany took over for France on the anchor, the Swedes soon dropped back to fourth.

The result of the women's dive was a minor surprise. Miss Olsen never had lost to Mrs. Draves prior to today and had beaten her for the national title three times.

**May Score Double**

Vicki was—and is—considered unbeatable in the tower diving and thus may be a double-crowned queen of the Olympics by Friday evening, when the high dive is completed.

The contest between the new champion and Zoe Ann was decided by the margin of 51/100 of a point—108.7 for Vicki and 108.23 for Zoe Ann after their eight dives.

Third place went to 18-year-old Patricia Ann Elsener of San Francisco, with 101.30 points.

Vicky remained poised throughout the two-day springboard program that began yesterday and wound up today as a chilly Lon-

Turn to Page 3, Column 2

## TICKETS ON SALE FOR TIMES GAME

Public sale of tickets for the Rams-Redskins game Sept. 2 at the Coliseum is now under way. They may be purchased at the following locations:

**Southern California Music Co., 737 S Hill St.**

**Desmond's, 616 S Broadway, and 3500 Wilshire Blvd.**

**Denels Music Shop, 6634 Hollywood Blvd.**

**Los Angeles Rams, 273 S Beverly Drive, Beverly Hills.**

**Los Angeles Times Information Desk, 202 W 1st St.**

**All Mutual Ticket Agencies.**

**All tickets $3.60 and $2.50, including tax.**

**Remember, please, no more mail orders!**

## OLYMPIC SCOREBOARD

BY WARD NASH

August 3, 1948

**TRACK AND FIELD ATHLETICS**

**200 METERS—MEN**

| First | Second | Third | Fourth | Fifth | Sixth |
|---|---|---|---|---|---|
| Patton U.S.A. | Ewell U.S.A. | LaBeach Panama | McKenley Jamaica | Bourland U.S.A. | Laing Jamaica |

**SHOT-PUT—MEN**

| First | Second | Third | Fourth | Fifth | Sixth |
|---|---|---|---|---|---|
| Thompson U.S.A. | Delaney U.S.A. | Fuchs U.S.A. | Lomoski Poland | Arvidson Sweden | Lehtina Finland |

**HOP, STEP AND JUMP—MEN**

| First | Second | Third | Fourth | Fifth | Sixth |
|---|---|---|---|---|---|
| Ahman Sweden | Avery Australia | Sarfalp Turkey | Larsen Denmark | Oliviera Brazil | Rautio Finland |

**SCORE BY COUNTRIES**

| Country— | 1 | 2 | 3 | 4 | 5 | 6 | * | † |
|---|---|---|---|---|---|---|---|---|
| United States | 7 | 3 | 6 | 5 | 2 | 3 | 36 | 174 |
| Sweden | 2 | 0 | 2 | 2 | 4 | 2 | 12 | 44 |
| France | 1 | 1 | 2 | 0 | 2 | 1 | 0 | 26 |
| Australia | 1 | 2 | 1 | 0 | 0 | 0 | 5 | 24 |
| Italy | 1 | 2 | 0 | 0 | 0 | 1 | 0 | 21 |
| Holland | 1 | 0 | 1 | 0 | 1 | 2 | 0 | 18 |
| Great Britain | 0 | 1 | 1 | 1 | 2 | 1 | 0 | 17 |
| Norway | 0 | 1 | 0 | 3 | 1 | 0 | 0 | 16 |
| Finland | 0 | 2 | 0 | 0 | 1 | 3 | 2 | 18 |
| Czechoslovakia | 1 | 1 | 0 | 0 | 0 | 0 | 0 | 15 |
| Hungary | 1 | 0 | 0 | 0 | 1 | 0 | 0 | 12 |
| Austria | 1 | 0 | 0 | 0 | 1 | 0 | 0 | 12 |
| Belgium | 1 | 0 | 0 | 0 | 0 | 1 | 0 | 11 |
| Jamaica | 0 | 1 | 0 | 1 | 0 | 2 | 4 | 10 |
| Panama | 0 | 0 | 2 | 0 | 0 | 0 | 4 | 8 |
| Denmark | 0 | 0 | 1 | 1 | 0 | 0 | 3 | 7 |
| Poland | 0 | 0 | 0 | 2 | 0 | 0 | 3 | 6 |
| Canada | 0 | 0 | 0 | 1 | 1 | 1 | 0 | 6 |
| Ceylon | 0 | 1 | 0 | 0 | 0 | 0 | 0 | 5 |
| Switzerland | 0 | 1 | 0 | 0 | 0 | 0 | 0 | 5 |
| Turkey | 0 | 0 | 1 | 0 | 0 | 0 | 4 | 4 |
| Yugoslavia | 0 | 1 | 0 | 0 | 0 | 0 | 0 | 5 |
| Brazil | 0 | 0 | 0 | 0 | 1 | 0 | 2 | 2 |

*Today's points. †Points to date.

Scoring system—First, 10 points; second, 5 points; third, 4 points; fourth, 3 points; fifth, 2 points; sixth, 1 point.

## TODAY IN SPORTS

**BASEBALL**—Seattle vs. Hollywood, Gilmore Field, double-header, 6:30; Sacramento vs. Los Angeles, Wrigley Field, single game, 8:15 p.m.

**HORSE RACING**—Del Mar, first post 2 p.m.

**MIDGET AUTO RACING**—Rose Bowl, qualifying heats 7 p.m.; first race 8:30 p.m.

**MEN'S SOFTBALL**—Sawtelle, one game, 7:30 p.m.

**ROADSTER RACING** — Carrell Speedway, trials 7 p.m.; races, 8:30 p.m.

**AMATEUR BOXING**—Pico Palace, 8:30 p.m.

**WRESTLING**—Olympic Auditorium, 8:30 p.m.

## Here's Slate for Today's Olympic Events

**MEN'S TRACK AND FIELD**

**Javelin Throw**

(Qualifying and finals)

Americans competing—**DR. STEVE SEYMOUR, LAAC;** Martin Biles, San Francisco Olympic Club; Bob Likins, San Jose State.

**110-Meter Hurdles**

(Semifinals and finals)

Americans competing—**CRAIG DIXON, UCLA;** Bill Porter, Northwestern; Clyde Scott, Arkansas.

**400-Meter Dash**

(Qualifying heats)

Americans competing—Mal Whitfield, Ohio State; George Guida, Villanova; Dave Bolen, Colorado.

**1500-Meter Run**

(Qualifying)

Americans competing—**ROLAND SINK, SC;** Clem Eischen, Washington State; Don Gehrmann, Wisconsin.

**SWIMMING**

**Men's Tower Diving**

(Qualifying)

Americans competing—**DR. SAMMY LEE, PASADENA;** Bruce Harlan, Ohio State.

**Men's 100-Meter Backstroke**

(Qualifying)

Americans competing — Allen Stack, Yale; Ensign Robert Cowell, U.S. Navy; Howard Patterson, Michigan State.

**Men's 400-Meter Free Style**

(Finals)

Americans competing—Jimmy McLane, Andover Academy; Bill Smith, Ohio State.

**Women's 100-Meter Backstroke**

(Semifinals)

Americans competing—Suzanne Zimmerman, Portland, Or.; **MURIEL MELLON, LOS ANGELES;** Barbara Jensen, Oakland.

Qualifying round starts also for Women's 400-Meter Relay.

**OTHER EVENTS**

**BASKETBALL**—United States vs. Egypt, Philippines vs. China, Canada vs. Brazil, Hungary vs. Uruguay, Korea vs. Iraq, Chile vs. Belgium, Britain vs. Italy and Eire vs. Iran.

**WATER POLO** — Second-round contests.

**WOMEN'S TRACK AND FIELD**—80-meter hurdle final, broad jump finals, shot-put finals.

**FENCING** — Men's individual foils, semifinals and finals.

**FIELD HOCKEY**—Preliminary round games.

**MODERN PENTATHLON** — 4000-meter cross-country run.

**SHOOTING**—Rapid-fire pistol at 25 meters.

**WRESTLING** — Greco-Roman elimination rounds.

**YACHTING**—Qualifying.

## Nice Goin', Moe

Moe Moffatt sank his tee shot on the 175-yard 17th hole yesterday at Lakewood. The ace helped give the Long Beach golfer a 38 for the side.

# PATTON, THOMPSON WIN OLYMPIC GAMES TITLES

## Mel Cops 200-Meters in 21.1s; Moose Shatters Shot Record

BY PAUL ZIMMERMAN, Times Sports Editor

WEMBLEY STADIUM, Aug. 3—The United States won four major Olympic titles today—including a world record in the 800-meter free-style swim relay—and three of them went to athletes from Southern California.

Wilbur (Moose) Thompson of Redondo Beach, the former Trojan who now competes for the Los Angeles Athletic Club, shattered the Olympic record in the shot put with every throw, winding up with a winning distance of 56ft. 2in. and heading America's first clean sweep in track and field.

**Patton Wins**

Mel Patton of SC picked the 200-meter sprint title out of the wreckage of his defeat in the 100 meters four days ago, beating Barney Ewell and Lloyd LaBeach in that order in 21.1s. over a slow, soggy track.

The third individual title came in the women's springboard diving when Vicki Draves, Pasadena matron, staged an upset by defeating Zoe Ann Olson of Oakland on her very last dive.

The world champion relay swim team, which defeated Hungary tonight in a brilliant final, included young Wally Wolf of Los Angeles, Trojan freshman. Wally Ris, Jimmy McLane and Bill Smith were also on the team, timed in 8m. 46s., compared to the former world and Olympic record of 8m. 51.5s., set by Japan at Berlin in 1936.

**Californians Shine**

The United States has now won seven men's track and field crowns, setting three Olympic records, and athletes from California have won six of them, chalking up all the new marks.

These Games of the XIV Olympiad never saw a record so completely shattered as the Americans did in the shot put. Thompson and his teammates, Francis (Jim) Delaney of the San Francisco Olympic Club and Jim Fuchs of Yale, all bettered the old record of 53ft. 1¾in., held by H. Wolke of Germany, on their very first tosses.

Thompson was best with 55ft. 8in. and then got off a prodigious push on his second effort to set the record. Moose, determined to set a mark as a lasting monument, got the ball out 56ft. 9 in. on his last trial, only to foul.

**Best of Career**

His mark is the best of his competitive career by more than 14 inches, and now places him among four in world track history ever to better 56 feet. The others are Jack Torrance, Louisiana State; the late Al Blozis, Georgetown, and Charles Fonville, Michigan.

Delaney was second in the iron ball event with a heave of 54ft. 8½in., while Fuchs got third with a 53ft. 10½in. toss.

"I'm sorry I didn't better 57 feet," said the 197-pound Thompson. "I've done it in practice and I should have done it here."

By comparison to his despondency after finishing fifth in the century, Patton was all smiles following his 200-meter victory.

"I guess I didn't let the home

Turn to Page 3, Column 1

### DEAN ALL SMILES

## Patton's Coach 'Happiest Man in the World'

LONDON, Aug. 3 (U.P.)—Californian Mel Patton was the second happiest man in the world today after his sparkling 21.1s. win in the 200-meter dash.

The world's happiest man was Patton's coach, Dean Cromwell.

"It justifies so many things," Cromwell said after the race. "It justifies Mel's world record 9.3s. for the 100-yard dash. It justifies his title of 'the fastest man on earth'—and a whole raft of other things."

**Takes Hot Shower**

Smiling Mel, lean and streamlined as a greyhound as he stood in a hot shower in the dressing room, said, "I felt in good shape today for the first time since reaching England. But I don't say I knew the race was in the bag. It's never in the bag till you break the tape and those other boys are fine runners."

Mel blamed his poor showing in the 100-meters event, where he finished fifth, on the fact that he has competed in only three meets since May 21 when he strained his right leg muscle in the Pacific Coast Conference championships at the Coliseum. After that, Mel said, he ran only in the national collegiate trials and in the Olympic trials before coming to London.

## Yank Hockey Team Blanked, 2-0

LONDON, Aug. 3 (AP)—Afghanistan's field hockey team defeated the United States, 2-0, in a group "B" match tonight. This was the Americans first game in the tourney. Neither they nor the Afghans reached a high standard of play.

Thirteen nations comprising three groups are in the hockey event and leaders of groups "A" and "B" and the first two teams in group "C" qualify for the semifinals after each team in each group has played a round robin.

## Belgium Cage Protest Denied

LONDON, Aug. 3 (AP)—W. R. Jones, British head of the Olympic basketball technical committee, announced that an Olympic jury had overruled Belgium's protest against its 36-34 overtime beating by China last night.

## KING GEORGE GETS LESSON IN GEOGRAPHY

LONDON, Aug. 3 (AP)—Two young American athletes found themselves standing in front of King George VI today without much to say. So they talked about the weather—and geography.

The two were Ann Curtis, swimming star from San Francisco, and Jack Robinson, the basketball playing pastor from Bayler University. They were among 10 members of the U.S. Olympic team who were invited, along with representatives of all other competing nations, to a royal reception at Buckingham Palace.

"There was an embarrassing pause after we were introduced," Miss Curtis explained afterwards.

"Apparently we were supposed to take our leave, but I guess Jack and I didn't grasp it immediately."

The King saved the situation with "a polite question about where we were from," Miss Curtis added.

When King George heard "California," he asked with a smile: "That's where they have the biggest and best of everything, isn't it?"

That was a bit too much for Robinson. As stiffly as one can to a King he said:

"Sir, I'm from Texas."

King George laughed. The ice was broken and the conversation continued.

GLORY—Vicki Draves, petite Pasadena housewife, won the women's springboard diving championship at Olympic Games yesterday—one of three Californians to sparkle.

PART 3 — Los Angeles Times — SPORTS

VOL. LXVII — CC — SATURDAY MORNING, AUGUST 7, 1948 — Read Times Green for Latest Sports

**HEROES**—Mrs. Vicki Draves of Pasadena, maker of Olympic history in women's diving events, clasps hands with a fellow-Pasadenan, Dr. Sammy Lee, Army medic, who captured the high platform diving championship in the Wembley pool. (AP) Wirephoto via Radio From London

# Mathias Wins Olympic Decathlon in Rain After 12-Hour Struggle

**WORLD'S GREATEST**—That's 17-year-old Bob Mathias of Tulare High School, who won the grueling Olympic Games decathlon after 12 hours of competition yesterday. Here he is throwing the discus 144ft. 4in. His winning point total was 7139. (AP) Wirephoto

## Youthful Tulare Schoolboy World's Greatest Athlete

BY PAUL ZIMMERMAN, Times Sports Editor

WEMBLEY STADIUM, Aug. 6—One of the greatest chapters in Olympic decathlon history was written here tonight by a sturdy 17-year-old native son of California when Bob Mathias, Tulare High School lad, defeated the world's finest all-around athletes after 12 gruelling hours of competition in rain and slush.

Finishing in virtual darkness with only the dim lights of the Wembley Stadium dog track to aid him in the pole vault and javelin, the gritty youth stood out like a giant Sequoia of his home State.

He rolled up 7139 points to best Ignace Heinrich of France by 165 digits. Except for adverse weather, untold delays and an almost total lack of light after twilight, Mathias may have shattered the world's record of Glenn Morris of the United States who posted a mark of 7900 in Berlin in 1936 under the best of conditions.

Mathias stopped at 11ft. 5¾in. in the pole vault without attempting the next height. To have gone ahead might have resulted in an injury that would have eliminated him from the remaining events.

**Took it Easy**

At the time it seemed certain he would win, he threw the javelin with caution and sauntered through the 1500 meters.

Never before in all the history of the Olympic Games did decathlon competitors perform under more adverse conditions and never before in the history of the event has anyone less than five years Bob's senior won this most exacting and fatiguing of all international track and field events.

The closest of these was Jim Thorpe, the Carlisle Indian star who won at Stockholm in 1912 and then had his medals shorn from his breast because of a charge of professionalism. He was 24.

In spite of Mathias' youth and despite his inexperience (this was only the third time in his life that he had gone through the 10 decathlon events) and regardless of the many adversities that shook the confidence of more veteran competitors, Mathias maintained his poise throughout.

**Fans Marvel**

A thousand-odd diehards who had stayed through since 10:30 a.m. today marveled at the 6-foot 1-inch, 191-pound lad who knew before he ever started to pole vault that the burden of taking the title back to America rested entirely on his shoulders. The javelin throw and the 1500 meters likewise were still to come.

Heinrich had finished hours before, shading Floyd Simmons of the Los Angeles Athletic Club. The 24-year-old Frenchman had chalked up an impressive 6974 points against 6950 for Simmons. Moon Mondschein, America's other entrant from New York University, had eliminated himself at the end of yesterday's competition when he failed to do well in his favorite events and finished out of the first six. His point total was 6715, which gave him eighth place.

**Bob Makes Move**

Fourth in the final reckoning was Enrique Kistenmacher, Argentine army lieutenant, with 6929 points. Eric Andersson of Sweden was fifth with 6877 and Peter Mullins of Australia was sixth with 6739 points.

Third behind Kistenmacher and Heinrich at the end of five events yesterday, Bob moved up into first spot on his second test today in the discus throw in which he led the field with a toss of

Turn to Page 4, Column 3

## Pair of U.S. Crews Bow in Prelims

HENLEY-ON-THAMES, Eng., Aug. 6 (AP)—Two United States crews were eliminated today from the Olympic regatta on the Thames River. One defeat led to a short-lived fuss over a twice-started race but tempers cooled quickly in a steady August rain.

Bow-man Ralph Stephan of Shaker Heights, O., and Stroke Festus Wade of St. Louis, represented the United States in the pairs without coxswain, finished six seconds behind Italy in one of the repechage—second chance—heats that give the first round losers another try for the semifinals.

**Hungary Wins**

The all-Philadelphia trio of Bow Jim Poland, Stroke Vincent Deency and Coxswain John McIntyre bowed to Hungary in their heat of the pairs with coxswain. Greece was third.

That was the first break in the United States representation at this marathon regatta. Neither of the eliminated teams, however, was rated as extremely strong—and the United States has won only one doubles title in all its Olympic trying. That was done at Los Angeles 16 years ago.

The defeat of Stephan and Wade looked for a time like it might produce a protest but Coach Allan Walz checked himself after letting off steam to Gason Mullegg, secretary of the International Rowing Federation, which runs the regatta. Walz didn't like the second start.

His boys got the jump on Italy and France and were three-fourths of a length up when their rivals collided. The umpire stopped the heat and ordered a rerun. The second time the Yanks never were in front. But they were content to let the result stand.

**Other Americans**

Five other United States teams won in the first round yesterday and there are good prospects of copping at least three titles. The University of Washington's four with coxswain is a favorite to win in tomorrow's quarterfinals in that event.

The other American survivors are the University of California eight, one to three betting favorite; Jack Kelly of Philadelphia in single sculls; Yale University's fours without coxswain and the double scullers, Art Gallagher of Bryn Mawr, Pa., and Joe Angyal of New York City.

How Americans made out today in repechage (second chance) heats of Olympic Games rowing:

Pairs with coxswain (winner of each heat qualifies for semifinals, losers eliminated).

First heat: 1—Hungary, 7m. 54.4s.; 2—U.S.A., 8m. 9.2s.; 3—Greece, 8m. 17.3s.

Pair without coxswain (winner in each heat qualifies for semifinals, losers eliminated).

First heat: 1—Italy, 7m. 24.8s.; 2—U.S.A., 7m. 30.5s.; 3—France, 7m. 42.3s.

## SPORTSCRIPTS

By PAUL ZIMMERMAN TIMES SPORTS EDITOR

LONDON, Aug. 6—Success of the United States diving forces has the swim experts of the world in a dither here at the Empire plunge just as it has in the last two Olympiads.

They can't quite comprehend why this regular sweep of the top places should be and, in fact, a number of coaches sharply criticize the American plan of training. The British insist that we don't know how to dive, yet our men and women continue to dominate the sport.

**TOP CREDIT**

Top credit must go, naturally, to a man whose vocation isn't coaching swimmers at all, but rather is that of an artist who dabbles in oils.

The gentleman is, of course, Fred Cady, the man with the waxed mustache. Fred is a graduate of the University of Pennsylvania and the Philadelphia school of fine arts. He's also recognized in Southern California as one of the top men in equestrian portraits, which are his specialty.

He's been dabbling in water as long as he has in oil, as a matter of fact, and while he once pursued coaching as something of a vocation his work has been part time in this field in recent years.

Cady started out with swimmers and gymnasts at Asher's Auditorium in Philadelphia more than a few years ago and also was a physical instructor at the Philadelphia YMCA.

**ART WORK HELPS**

"My art work helped me to learn of body muscles," says Fred, "but I also worked a lot with tumblers under the big top with the circus. All this fits in with divers."

How well it has fitted can be seen by the records. On top of the success of our divers here at Empire pool, he has had an impressive record for the last two Olympiads.

Cady first gained a place on the Olympic swimming team as a diving coach in 1928. His stars were just developing then and had to be content with a string of second places for such future greats as Mickey Riley, Georgia Coleman and Dutch Smith.

But in 1932 the California group really blossomed out under his careful coaching. Dutch and Dorothy Poynton won the high-diving championships in the Xth Olympiad at Los Angeles and Riley and Miss Coleman took the springboard events.

Georgia also got second in the high platform test and Frank Kurtz of World War II fame got a third.

Came the Berlin Games and things were no different with Marjorie Gestring, Poynton, Katherine Rawls, Velma Dunn, Marshall Wayne, Al Green and Elbert Root taking the top honors in a sweep.

**GETTING MONOTONOUS**

This thing is getting to be monotonous with the other nations, but so far they haven't found a solution. It's an understandable fact that many of the Olympic judges who are not American are inclined to score the Americans a little more closely and critically on their dives than they do the other competitors.

There is an equally natural leniency in giving a point extra here and there to athletes of other countries who are vainly trying to score. The Americans don't mind too much, since their superiority generally is pretty complete.

Cady says the problem of other nations is basic. We have more swimming facilities in America where divers can train the year around; and a system for training and coaching plus keen competition.

This may be true but we suspect Fred is being a little backward about tooting his own horn.

**P.S.:** Don't we have the same advantages in aquatic racing where our monopoly of championships is not so great?

## Vicki Draves Wins Second Diving Title

OLYMPIC POOL, Wembley, Eng., Aug. 6 (AP)—An American sweep of all men's Olympic swimming and diving events loomed tonight after six straight victories as the United States women celebrated Mrs. Vicki Manalo Draves' double diving win and a record-breaking performance by their Olympic championship 400-meter relay team.

This might well, in fact, be set down in Olympic annals as All-America day at the big poolhouse.

Mrs. Draves, petite, brunette beauty from Pasadena, Cal., won the women's platform diving, becoming the first woman to take both the Olympic's high and springboard diving championships. She won the springboard event Tuesday.

**Shatter Record**

The American girl swimmers, after failing to win a title in their first three final races, saved themselves from a shutout by taking the women's 400-meter free-style relay in Olympic record time of 4m. 29.2s.—almost seven seconds under the well-battered 1936 mark.

Ann Curtis, the tall 22-year-old blonde from San Francisco and the University of California, kicked the U.S. girl relayers home ahead of the favored Danish and Dutch women with an anchor leg win over Danish Fritze Nathansen Carstensen in sensational fashion.

**Stack Scores**

The Americans who won gold medals for the relay, beside Miss Curtis, were Marie Corridon of Norwalk, Ct., Thelma Kalama, an Hawaiian from Honolulu, and Brenda Helser of Los Angeles.

Denmark second, Holland third and Britain fourth, all beat the old Olympic relay record of 4m.

Turn to Page 4, Column 5

RIFLES ECHO IN HUNTS TODAY

## Nimrods Open First Half of Deer Season

BY FRED YOUNG

Strongly reminiscent of war days, the ear-tingling whine of high-powered rifles are echoing across the hills and valleys of our central and southern coastal mountain ranges today as hunters usher in the 1948 deer season.

The nimrods opened the first half of the '48 split season which runs until Sept. 16, in the central part of the State and Sept. 6, here in the Southland. Shooting time in both areas is one-half hour before sunrise to one-half hour after the setting of the sun.

**Outlook Bright**

Despite drouths of last winter that many feared would prove disastrous for the hunting clan, the outlook as the season breaks, is better than in many past years.

Plenty of feed is in evidence and the lack of water holes, where the "King of the Forest" is usually to be found, is reacting in the gunner's favor.

With the source of water supply far less this year than is the case in a normal season the highly prized buck will have to range far to quench his thirst and this will provide the hunters with fewer areas in which to make his shoot.

San Diego County, always a heavy producer of the fleet-footed buck, is hosting a large number of sportsmen as they make their opening week-end play.

Mt. Pinos and Pine Mountain, in Ventura County and the Ridge Route also had a representative body of nimrods. Cottonwood Flats, Sawmill Mountain and the district around Lake Elizabeth and Lake Hughes are also being heavily played.

Locally the Mt. Pacifico, Pinyon Flats, Horse Flats and Sulphur Springs area as well as the Mt. Waterman and Buckhorn sector will draw many.

Under the '48 ruling that the State F. and G. Department has made it legal for only one deer to be taken in the southern range many Southlanders have trekked north to the central coastal region where a two-buck limit is in force.

The new ruling states that in a one-buck district the "b" tags must be used and thus, any sportsman taking his deer in the southern sector, would automatically disqualify himself from the later high Sierra shoot which is also listed as a one-deer area.

## Decathlon Summaries

Scores at end of Thursday's five events:

| | |
|---|---|
| Enrique Kistenmacher, Argentina | 3897 |
| Ignace Heinrich, France | 3880 |
| Bob Mathias, U.S.A. | 3848 |
| Floyd Simmons, U.S.A. | 3841 |
| Irving Mondschein, U.S.A. | 3811 |
| Peter Mullins, Australia | 3713 |

110-METER HURDLES

| | Mark | Pts. |
|---|---|---|
| Simmons | 15.2s. | 896 |
| Mullins | 15.2s. | 896 |
| Heinrich | 15.6s. | 833 |
| Mathias | 15.7s. | 818 |
| Adamczyk, Poland | 15.8s. | 804 |
| Andersson, Sweden | 15.9s. | 770 |
| Ericksson, Sweden | 16.2s. | 749 |
| Kistenmacher | 16.3s. | 736 |

DISCUS THROW

| | | |
|---|---|---|
| Mathias | 144ft. 4in. | 834 |
| Dayer, Belgium | 136ft. 3½in. | 757 |
| Kistenmacher | 134ft. 10½in. | 746 |
| Heinrich | 134ft. 3½in. | 739 |
| Mondschein | 127ft. 1½in. | 674 |
| Andersson | 118ft. 6in. | 599 |
| Ericksson | 114ft. 6½in. | 567 |
| Mullins | 111ft. 4in. | 541 |
| Simmons | 107ft. 7½in. | 509 |

POLE VAULT

| | | |
|---|---|---|
| Andersson | 11ft. 5¾in. | 733 |
| Mathias | 11ft. 5¾in. | 733 |
| Mondschein | 11ft. 5¾in. | 692 |
| Simmons | 11ft. 2in. | 692 |
| Mullins | 11ft. 2in. | 692 |
| Ericksson | 10ft. 10in. | 613 |
| Heinrich | 10ft. 6in. | 575 |
| Kistenmacher | 10ft. 6in. | 575 |

JAVELIN THROW

| | | |
|---|---|---|
| Ericksson | 186ft. ½in. | 715 |
| Simmons | 170ft. 7in. | 624 |
| Mullins | 168ft. 4½in. | 612 |
| Andersson | 167ft. 5½in. | 607 |
| Mathias | 165ft. 1in. | 593 |
| Kistenmacher | 147ft. 10in. | 499 |
| Heinrich | 134ft. 5in. | 453 |
| Mondschein | 120ft. 9in. | 430 |

1500 METERS

| | | |
|---|---|---|
| Andersson | 4m. 34s. | 589 |
| Sprecher, France | 4m. 34s. | 589 |
| Ericksson | 4m. 35.8s. | 575 |
| Heinrich | 4m. 43.8s. | 517 |
| Kistenmacher | 4m. 49.6s. | 478 |
| Mondschein | 4m. 49.8s. | 477 |
| Simmons | 4m. 58s. | 436 |
| Mathias | 5m. 11s. | 354 |
| Mullins | 5m. 17.8s. | 321 |

FINAL SCORES

| | |
|---|---|
| 1—Bob Mathias, U.S.A. | 7139 |
| 2—Ignace Heinrich, France | 6974 |
| 3—Floyd Simmons, U.S.A. | 6950 |
| 4—Enrique Kistenmacher, Argentina | 6929 |
| 5—Eric Andersson, Sweden | 6877 |
| 6—Peter Mullins, Australia | 6739 |
| 7—Ericksson, Sweden | 6731 |
| 8—Irving Mondschein, U.S.A. | 6715 |

## OLYMPIC SCOREBOARD

BY WARD NASH

August 6, 1948

TRACK AND FIELD ATHLETICS

1500 METERS—MEN

| First | Second | Third | Fourth | Fifth | Sixth |
|---|---|---|---|---|---|
| Eriksson Sweden | Strand Sweden | Sliskuis Holland | Cevona Czechoslo. | Bergkvist Sweden | Nankeville Gt. Britain |

DECATHLON—MEN

| First | Second | Third | Fourth | Fifth | Sixth |
|---|---|---|---|---|---|
| Mathias U.S.A. | Henrich France | Simmons U.S.A. | Kisten-macher Argentina | Andersson Sweden | Mullins Australia |

200 METERS—WOMEN

| First | Second | Third | Fourth | Fifth | Sixth |
|---|---|---|---|---|---|
| Blankers-Koen Holland | Williamson Gt. Britain | Patterson U.S.A. | Strickland Australia | Walker Gt. Britain | Robb So. Africa |

SCORE BY COUNTRIES

| Country— | 1 | 2 | 3 | 4 | 5 | 6 | * | † |
|---|---|---|---|---|---|---|---|---|
| United States | 9 | 5 | 10 | 7 | 2 | 5 | 18 | 185 |
| Sweden | 4 | 2 | 4 | 1 | 7 | 3 | 19 | 86 |
| France | 2 | 2 | 2 | 3 | 2 | 1 | 5 | 52 |
| Holland | 3 | 0 | 2 | 1 | 2 | 2 | 14 | 47 |
| Australia | 1 | 2 | 2 | 1 | 2 | 1 | 4 | 36 |
| Finland | 1 | 2 | 0 | 1 | 2 | 3 | 0 | 30 |
| Great Britain | 0 | 3 | 1 | 1 | 3 | 2 | 8 | 30 |
| Italy | 1 | 3 | 0 | 0 | 0 | 1 | 0 | 26 |
| Hungary | 2 | 0 | 1 | 0 | 1 | 0 | 0 | 26 |
| Jamaica | 1 | 2 | 0 | 1 | 0 | 3 | 0 | 26 |
| Czechoslovakia | 1 | 1 | 0 | 1 | 1 | 1 | 3 | 21 |
| Austria | 1 | 0 | 1 | 0 | 2 | 1 | 0 | 19 |
| Norway | 0 | 1 | 0 | 4 | 1 | 0 | 0 | 19 |

| Country— | 1 | 2 | 3 | 4 | 5 | 6 | * | † |
|---|---|---|---|---|---|---|---|---|
| Belgium | 1 | 0 | 0 | 0 | 0 | 1 | 0 | 11 |
| Argentina | 0 | 1 | 0 | 2 | 0 | 0 | 3 | 11 |
| Panama | 0 | 0 | 2 | 0 | 0 | 0 | 0 | 8 |
| Denmark | 0 | 0 | 1 | 1 | 0 | 0 | 0 | 7 |
| Poland | 0 | 0 | 0 | 2 | 0 | 0 | 0 | 6 |
| Canada | 0 | 0 | 0 | 1 | 1 | 1 | 0 | 6 |
| Yugoslavia | 0 | 1 | 0 | 0 | 0 | 1 | 0 | 6 |
| Ceylon | 0 | 1 | 0 | 0 | 0 | 0 | 0 | 5 |
| Switzerland | 0 | 1 | 0 | 0 | 0 | 0 | 0 | 5 |
| Turkey | 0 | 0 | 1 | 0 | 0 | 0 | 0 | 4 |
| Brazil | 0 | 0 | 0 | 0 | 1 | 0 | 0 | 2 |
| South Africa | 0 | 0 | 0 | 0 | 0 | 1 | 0 | 1 |

*Today's points. †Points to date.

Scoring system—First, 10 points; second, 5 points; third, 4 points; fourth, 3 points; fifth, 2 points; sixth, 1 point.

## Cyril Walker Found Dead in Jail Cell

HACKENSACK, N.J., Aug. 6 (AP) Cyril Walker, 57, one of the nation's leading golfers in the 1920s, was found dead today in a cell at police headquarters where he had been given a night's lodging.

Walker, a native of England, won the U.S. Open Golf championship in 1924, defeating Bobby Jones by three strokes at Oakland Hills, Detroit.

Police Sgt. Daniel Bebus said Walker applied last night for lodging and was permitted to stay in a cell.

Bebus said he went to awaken Walker this morning and found him sitting in a chair. Death was due to natural causes, the police sergeant said.

## TICKETS ON SALE FOR TIMES GAME

Public sale of tickets for the Rams-Redskins game Sept. 2 at the Coliseum is now under way. They may be purchased at the following locations:

**Southern California Music Co., 737 S Hill St.**

**Desmond's, 616 S Broadway, and 5500 Wilshire Blvd.**

**Denels Music Shop, 6634 Hollywood Blvd.**

**Los Angeles Rams, 273 S Beverly Drive, Beverly Hills.**

**Los Angeles Times Information Desk, 202 W 1st St.**

**All Mutual Ticket Agencies.**

**All tickets $3.60 and $2.50, including tax.**

**Remember, please, no more mail orders!**

## TODAY IN SPORTS

**BASEBALL**—San Francisco at Hollywood, Gilmore Field, 8:15 p.m. L.A. Police vs. Ex-Major Leaguers, Wrigley Field, 2:15 p.m.

**HORSE RACING**—Del Mar, first post, 2 p.m.

**MIDGET AUTO RACING**—Carrell Speedway, Gardena, 8:30 p.m.

**INDOOR POLO**—Riverside Horse Palace, 8 p.m.

**PASSING TEST**—The University of California crew (left foreground) glides to victory in fourth heat of first round Olympic eight-oared crew race Thursday on Thames River. Yugoslavia, second; France, right, third. (AP) Wirephoto

PART 4 **Los Angeles Times** SPORTS

VOL. LXVII CC ★ TUESDAY MORNING, AUGUST 17, 1948 Read Times Green for Latest Sports

**THERE IT GOES**—A familiar cry when the Babe was at bat. In 1927 the Babe smacked 60 home runs, a record that has stood 21 years and might well stand 20 more.

# SPORTS-LOVING NATION MOURNS DEATH OF HOMER KING BABE RUTH

## Dread Malady Takes Life of Beloved Baseball Player

NEW YORK, Aug. 16 (U.P.)—Babe Ruth, 53, baseball's beloved home-run king, died in his sleep at 8:01 tonight, ending a career that had been devoted to baseball for more than a quarter of a century.

The famed Sultan of Swat, for 22 years a major leaguer, the man who hit 714 home runs in his lusty lifetime and who hit a record 60 in the 1927 season alone, died quietly after a two-year fight against cancer of the throat.

The Babe fought to the end, and in his last weeks only his stout heart kept him alive. His booming voice was all but gone, and his strength was sapped.

Ruth's family and close friends were by his side when he died. They had been on the alert for nearly a week, ever since Ruth was placed on the critical list last Wednesday after a pulmonary congestion set in.

Concern over Ruth's condition, expressed during the last few days in messages from all parts of the country and from distant points throughout the world, also was felt in the White House.

President Truman had telephoned the hospital last week from the capital to find out how the Babe was getting along. Tonight, advised of Ruth's death, the Chief Executive arranged to send a message of condolence to Ruth's widow.

In Albany, Gov. Thomas E. Dewey and his Vice-Presidential running mate, Gov. Earl Warren, expressed regret at the death of Babe Ruth.

"A spectacular baseball player whose equal may never be reached, Babe Ruth was above all a great American . . . In his passing I have lost a good friend," Dewey said.

Warren said, "Few men in American history have been a greater inspiration to the youth of our land . . . Throughout his life he played the game fair and hard and never gave up to the very end."

At his suite in the Waldorf-Astoria, former President Herbert Hoover described Ruth as "one of the great sportsmen of the United States."

**Hoover Hails**

Mr. Hoover then recalled a public gathering in Los Angeles when he was approached by a small boy who asked for his autograph.

"Would you mind giving me three?" the boy asked.

Mr. Hoover complied but asked the boy why he wanted three.

"Because it takes two of yours to trade for one of Babe Ruth's," he replied.

**The One and Only**

Two employees at the hospital where Ruth had lingered out his last illness were affected visibly when word of the Bambino's death spread throughout the institution.

Said 50-year-old William Stevenson:

"Gee, it's tough. I seen him when he opened up in the Yankee Stadium in 1923. I have not seen

Turn to Page 2, Column 5

**LAST PICTURE**—This picture, taken at New York Memorial Hospital July 29, is believed to be last picture taken of Babe Ruth. With him is Steve Broidy of movie studio, who is presenting him with check for Ruth Foundation for underprivileged children. (UP) photo

## SPORTSCRIPTS

By PAUL ZIMMERMAN TIMES SPORTS EDITOR

LONDON, Aug. 16—Avery Brundage, Hollywood hotel owner and part-time Southern California resident as he likes to point out, isn't a man to duck a controversial issue as was shown in the winter Games in Switzerland when he got himself right in the middle of the ice hockey team controversy.

For that reason, it is remarkable that the London Olympic Games failed to project Brundage, member of the International Olympic Federation and president of the American Olympic Committee, into anything more exciting than the usual discussion of "broken time" and the true meaning of amateurism.

Broken time involves the question of whether Olympic athletes should be paid by Olympic associations for money lost by being taken away from their normal professional or labor pursuits while competing in the world championships.

**NEVER CHANGE**

Brundage goes back to the dictionary and points out that amateurism means competition for the love of the game only and he adds that he feels professional sports belong on the entertainment pages of the newspapers since they are staged purely and simply for the enjoyment of the public and not the pleasure of the competitor.

Anyway, he insists you never can change the amateur rule because it is elemental.

The fact that Brundage was not in the middle here may be taken as a compliment to the athletes competing. There was no real untoward incident and the American team, especially, conducted itself as a group of ambassadors should.

**WELL-BEHAVED**

There were no champagne parties; no cases of athletes getting out of line; nothing of an exciting nature to report although the usual sensational element of the press tried to make incidents such as the absurd inference that one of our champions was a little tipsy at the reception staged by King George VI.

Brundage says this is by far the best-behaved American team we have taken to the Games. It may be for that reason that he was quick to push the protest of Coach Dean Cromwell when the American 400-meter team was disqualified — a disqualification that was overridden as soon as the motion pictures were seen.

Even if the pictures had shown that Barney Ewell and Lorenzo Wright had completed their baton pass outside the restraining zone, it is probable that Brundage, a member of the reviewing jury, would have argued for our team.

**IMPORTANT THING**

"I have always contended," said Brundage before he went in to view the films, "that the important thing in athletic competition is consideration of the competitor. Technicalities that prevent the best athletes from gaining a championship, so long as the violations are not of a serious nature and do not aid in that victory, do not merit consideration."

It is quite likely that Brundage would have projected himself into a controversy here, had the pictures failed to substantiate the American contention that the 400-meter relays were honestly run and victory well earned.

**POINT OF VIEW**

A long-time athletic competitor himself, Brundage is an official who certainly can see the contestant's point of view. The fact that he is a self-made man of considerable wealth while continuing amateur competition in his early years undoubtedly is one of the strong reasons why he is so set in his ways on the subject of absolute amateurism.

Although he has said that he is ready to resign as head of the American Olympic Committee, most of those who know Brundage well do not believe that it will be possible for him to turn his back completely on amateur athletics.

**P.S.:** Regardless of your personal feelings concerning the man, you have to admit that he has given freely of his time and money to further the cause of amateurism.

## Ruth Had One Name for All

The Babe always had trouble remembering names of teammates and rival players. So he called everybody "Kid." In '29, when Mickey Cochrane was at his peak as star catcher of the Athletics, he passed Babe on the street and said, "Hello, Babe." The Babe nodded and said, "Hello, kid," and strode on. Mickey ran after him, grabbed his arm and spun him around. "Listen, you," growled Mickey, "my name is Mickey Cochrane—and don't call me 'kid'." But the very next day the Babe saw Mickey again and said, "Hello, kid." And Mickey just shrugged his shoulders and let it go at that.

## 'YOUTH' VS. 'AGE'

"Youth" vs. "age," a question that has cropped up countless times in athletic history, will get still another airing when the Los Angeles Rams face the Washington Redskins for Los Angeles Times Charities, Inc., in the Los Angeles Coliseum on the night of Sept. 2.

The "age" will be supplied by Washington's Sammy Baugh, who, like Old Man River, keeps right on rolling along. Sammy's only 34 years old—young for a U.S. Senator but practically Social Security age for a professional football player.

His foe, representing "youth" and the Rams, will be Glenn Davis, 23-year-old Army lieutenant, who left frustrated tacklers sprawled on gridirons all over the East and Midwest during his four years as a West Point performer.

Baugh, who won't tell where he keeps his private fountain of youth, holds virtually every passing record in the National League. And this year railbirds say he's better than ever before.

Davis, a Southern California product, has never had a chance to show his wares here since his high school days. Until now, that is.

Although they're two entirely different types of players, they both have one thing in common—greatness. Who is greater? Come out and see for yourselves.

Tickets for the game may be obtained at any of the following locations:

Southern California Music Co., 737 S Hill St.; Desmond's, 616 S Broadway and 5500 Wilshire Blvd.; Denels Music Shop, 6634 Hollywood Blvd.; Los Angeles Rams, 273 S Beverly Drive, Beverly Hills; Los Angeles Times Information Desk, 202 W 1st St.; all Mutual ticket agencies.

All tickets $3.60 and $2.50, including tax.

## Colorful Babe's Life Ran Gamut

By the Associated Press

Baseball will never see another character quite like Babe Ruth. He was the game's mightiest slugger and most glamorous figure. He was the highest paid performer and greatest gate attraction. He was also its heaviest-fined "bad boy" and, as time marched on, its "forgotten man."

A street urchin from the dock district of Baltimore, the Bambino captured the fancy of the American public.

His tremendous slugging revolutionized baseball in the turbulent twenties, yet records still stand on the books that he made as a young southpaw pitcher. For glamour, color, thrills and achievement Ruth's career was unparalleled. During the "Golden Era" of sport after the first World War, Ruth shared with Jack Dempsey, Bobby Jones and Big Bill Tilden.

**Got $80,000 Salary**

In 1930 and 1931 he drew a salary of $80,000 per season, $5000 more than the President of the United States. And the $2,000,000 Yankee Stadium, largest and most modern baseball plant in the land, is still known as "The House that Ruth Built."

His early life is shrouded in mystery. Little is known of his parents and the date of his birth is uncertain. Old records say he was born at Baltimore, Feb. 7, 1894, but baseball records and his 1934 passport give Feb. 6, 1895, as the date.

Both his poverty-stricken parents were still living when 6-year-old George was taken off the streets and placed in St. Mary's Industrial School of Baltimore. School didn't interest the lad and he was soon back with his parents. But not for long, because they had neither the time nor means of preventing him from running wild with street gangs. So Father Matthias of St. Mary's took the young rebel back to school again to teach him the trade of shirtmaker.

**Coached by Cleric**

It wasn't long before Ruth found a real friend in Brother Gilbert, the school's baseball coach. He discovered that young George had more natural baseball ability than any lad in school. When Ruth became 18, Brother Gilbert recommended him to Jack Dunn, owner and manager of the Baltimore Orioles.

Dunn took out guardian papers and agreed to give Ruth $600 for the 1914 season. Ruth always claimed that his biggest thrill came when he went back to St. Mary's and told his schoolmates that he had signed a contract with the Orioles and was a real professional baseball player.

Ruth was a natural from the start. In his first season he won 22 games and lost nine for Baltimore and Providence. Before the season ended he was sold to the Boston Red Sox along with Pitcher Ernie Shore for $30,000. The Red Sox farmed him out to Providence but recalled him before the end of the season and he won two games and lost one.

**First Homer**

The next season Ruth, who had picked up the nickname of Babe while with Baltimore, hit his first major league homer against the New York Yankees May 6, 1915. Before he called it a day in 1935 Ruth hit 714 home runs, a mark that seems to stand.

Many say that if he had remained on the mound he would have gone down as one of the great left-handers. In 1915, his first full season with the Red Sox, he won 18 games and lost 6. The next season he copped 23 and lost 12 and achieved an earned run average of 1.75.

It wasn't until 1920 that he ter-

Turn to Page 2, Column 5

**THE BABE**—The famous grin, the lovable face, the big homely nose—the one and only, the great Babe Ruth. Today the whole sports world mourned his passing.

LIFELONG HERO PASSES

## Ruth Most Colorful of All Sports Greats

BY AL WOLF

Th' Babe is dead.

Th' Babe was our hero.

So it's not going to be a pleasant task writing this piece.

Babe Ruth was our hero when we were playing ball with the other neighborhood kids on weed-strewn vacant lots, with paving slabs for bases and a "nickel brick" for a ball. He was our hero long before we ever saw a professional game and he was still our hero when he died, long removed from the game.

No other sports figure ever challenged him closely for our affection and adoration. No one probably ever will.

**Babe Ruth** was much more than a great athlete—and he was a sensational fielder and a superb pitcher as well as the mightiest slugger of all time. He was more than the greatest personality in America's greatest game. Babe Ruth was the ultimate personification of an era in which sports "grew up"—from the Police Gazette to the front pages, from barns and bleachers to massive stadiums, from boozy, suspendered masculinity to socialite festoonings, from shoestring operations to big business.

The impetus that brought about this change in sports' status came in the postwar plenitude of the 20s.

And interest did not recede again with the stunning crash that ended that decade. There was a slight pause, until money again became something other than a museum piece, then a new forward surge that made fans of everybody, poured millions through the turnstiles and put athletes into the upper brackets, both socially and financially.

**Color did it.**

Sports in the "Roaring Twenties" were blessed with a tremendous concentration of athletic artists whose muscular talents were embellished by that tangible something that

Turn to Page 2, Column 3

## RUTH CALLED SHOT IN '32 WORLD SERIES

Of all Babe Ruth's homers, the most incredible was the one he blasted in the third game of the '32 World Series between the Yankees and Cubs in Chicago. Wrathful over the dugout taunts of the NL'ers, Babe warned Pitcher Charley Root he was going to hammer the first good pitch into the center field stands. Every fan in the crowd of 49,986 saw Babe dramatically wag his bat in the direction of the stands—and then belt the ball precisely into them!

## Flags to Fly at Half-Mast Tonight

President Clarence Rowland said last night that all flags in Pacific Coast League baseball parks will be at half mast tonight, honoring the memory of Babe Ruth. There will be one minute of silent tribute to the Babe before tonight's games.

"He was just the greatest of all baseball players," said Rowland. "He was America's sports hero—a hero to young and old. There will never be another like him."

## TODAY IN SPORTS

BASEBALL—Oakland vs. Los Angeles, Wrigley Field, 8:15.

HORSE RACING—Del Mar, first post 2.

MIDGET AUTO RACING—Culver City Speedway, time trials 7, first race 8:15.

WRESTLING—South Gate Arena, 8:30.

GIRLS' SOFTBALL—Monrovia vs. Ramblers, Montebello Park, 8:30.

PRO BOXING — Olympic Auditorium, 8:30 p.m.

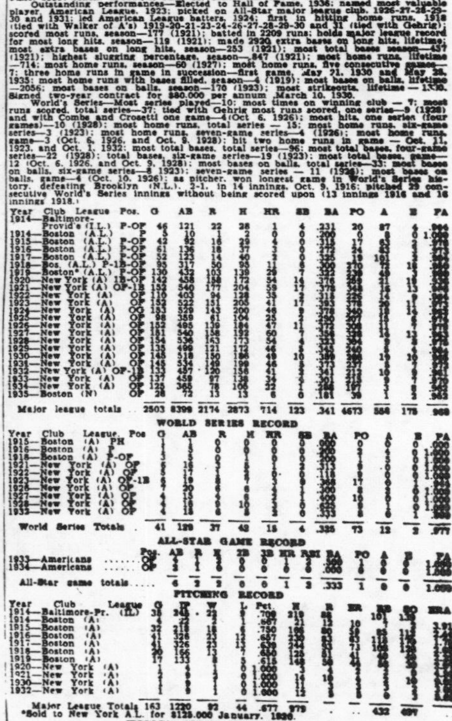



**TOGETHER AGAIN**—The Babe (right) shown in his heyday, with Yankee teammate, Lou Gehrig. Lou died in 1941. Babe was seventh member of 1927 Yankee team to die. (UP) photo

## BABE RUTH'S CAREER

Game's greatest home run hitter.
Born, Feb. 6, 1895, at Baltimore, Md.
Height, 6ft 2in. Weight, 215. Threw and batted lefthanded.
Married.

Vice-president and assistant manager, Boston, N.L., April, 1935; released, June, 1935; coach, Brooklyn, June 18, 1938 until end of campaign.

Outstanding performances—Elected to Hall of Fame, 1936; named most valuable player, American League, 1923; picked on All-Star major league club, 1926-27-28-29-30 and 1931; led American League batters, 1924; first in hitting home runs, 1918 (tied with Walker of A's) 1919-20-21-23-24-26-27-28-29-30 and 31 (tied with Gehrig); scored most runs, season—177 (1921); batted in 2209 runs; holds major league record for most long hits, season—119 (1921); made 2920 extra bases on long hits, lifetime; most extra bases on long hits, season—253 (1921); most total bases season—457 (1921); highest slugging percentage, season—.847 (1921); most home runs, lifetime—714; most home runs, season—60 (1927); most home runs, five consecutive games—7; three home runs in game in succession—first game, May 21, 1930 and May 25, 1935; most home runs with bases filled, season—4 (1919); most bases on balls, lifetime—2056; most bases on balls, season—170 (1923); most strikeouts, lifetime — 1330. Signed two-year contract for $80,000 per annum March 10, 1930.

World's Series—Most series played—10; most times on winning club — 7; most runs scored, total series—37; tied with Gehrig most runs scored, one series—9 (1928) and with Combs and Crosetti one game—4 (Oct. 6, 1926); most hits, one series (four games)—10 (1928); most home runs, total series — 15; most home runs, six-game series—3 (1923); most home runs, seven-game series—4 (1926); most home runs, game—3 (Oct. 6, 1926, and Oct. 9, 1928); hit two home runs in game — Oct. 11, 1923, and Oct. 1, 1932; most total bases, total series—96; most total bases, four-game series—22 (1928); total bases, six-game series—19 (1923); most total bases, game—12 (Oct. 6, 1926, and Oct. 9, 1928); most bases on balls, total series—33; most bases on balls, six-game series—8 1923); seven-game series — 11 (1926); most bases on balls, game—4 (Oct. 10, 1926); as pitcher, won longest game in World's Series history, defeating Brooklyn (N.L.), 2-1, in 14 innings, Oct. 9, 1916; pitched 29 consecutive World's Series innings without being scored upon (13 innings 1916 and 16 innings 1918.)

| Year | Club | League | Pos. | G | AB | R | H | HR | SB | BA | PO | A | E | FA |
|---|---|---|---|---|---|---|---|---|---|---|---|---|---|---|
| 1914 | Baltimore-Provid'e | (I.L.) | P-OF | 46 | 121 | 22 | 28 | 1 | 4 | .231 | 20 | 87 | 4 | .964 |
| 1914 | Boston | (A.L.) | P | 5 | 10 | 1 | 2 | 0 | 0 | .200 | 0 | 8 | 0 | 1.000 |
| 1915 | Boston | (A.L.) | P-OF | 42 | 92 | 16 | 29 | 4 | 0 | .315 | 17 | 63 | 2 | [illegible] |
| 1916 | Boston | (A.L.) | P-OF | 61 | 136 | 18 | 37 | 3 | 0 | .272 | 24 | 83 | [illegible] | [illegible] |
| 1917 | Boston | (A.L.) | P-OF | 52 | 123 | 14 | 40 | 2 | 0 | .325 | 19 | 101 | [illegible] | [illegible] |
| 1918 | Bos. | (A.L.) | P-1B-OF | 95 | 317 | 50 | 95 | 11 | 6 | .300 | 270 | [illegible] | 18 | [illegible] |
| 1919 | Boston* | (A.L.) | P-OF | 130 | 432 | 103 | 139 | 29 | 7 | .322 | [illegible] | 48 | [illegible] | [illegible] |
| 1920 | New York | (A) | 1B-OF | 142 | 458 | 158 | 172 | 54 | 14 | .376 | [illegible] | 21 | 19 | [illegible] |
| 1921 | New York | (A) | OF-1B | 152 | 540 | 177 | 204 | 59 | 17 | .378 | 348 | 16 | 13 | [illegible] |
| 1922 | New York | (A) | OF | 110 | 403 | 94 | 128 | 35 | 2 | .315 | 226 | 14 | [illegible] | [illegible] |
| 1923 | New York | (A) | OF | 152 | 522 | 151 | 205 | 41 | 17 | .393 | 378 | 20 | 11 | [illegible] |
| 1924 | New York | (A) | OG | 153 | 529 | 143 | 200 | 46 | 9 | .378 | 340 | 18 | 14 | [illegible] |
| 1925 | New York | (A) | OF | 98 | 359 | 61 | 104 | 25 | 2 | .290 | 207 | 15 | 6 | [illegible] |
| 1926 | New York | (A) | OF | 152 | 495 | 139 | 184 | 47 | 11 | .372 | 308 | 11 | 7 | [illegible] |
| 1927 | New York | (A) | OF | 151 | 540 | 158 | 192 | 60 | 7 | .356 | 328 | 14 | 13 | [illegible] |
| 1928 | New York | (A) | OF | 154 | 536 | 163 | 173 | 54 | 4 | .323 | 304 | 9 | 8 | [illegible] |
| 1929 | New York | (A) | OF | 135 | 499 | 121 | 172 | 46 | 5 | .345 | 240 | 5 | 4 | [illegible] |
| 1930 | New York | (A) | OF | 145 | 518 | 150 | 186 | 49 | 10 | .359 | [illegible] | 19 | 10 | [illegible] |
| 1931 | New York | (A) | OF | 145 | 534 | 149 | 199 | 46 | 5 | .373 | 237 | 5 | 7 | [illegible] |
| 1932 | New York | (A) | OF-1B | 133 | 457 | 120 | 156 | 41 | 2 | .341 | 212 | 10 | 9 | .961 |
| 1933 | New York | (A) | OF | 137 | 459 | 97 | 138 | 34 | 4 | .301 | 215 | 9 | 7 | .970 |
| 1934 | New York | (A) | OF | 125 | 365 | 78 | 105 | 22 | 1 | .288 | 197 | 3 | 8 | .962 |
| 1935 | Boston | (N) | OF | 28 | 72 | 13 | 13 | 6 | 0 | .181 | 39 | 1 | 3 | .963 |
| Major league totals | | | | 2503 | 8399 | 2174 | 2873 | 714 | 123 | .341 | 4673 | 586 | 175 | .968 |

WORLD SERIES RECORD

| Year | Club | League | Pos | G | AB | R | H | HR | SB | BA | PO | A | E | FA |
|---|---|---|---|---|---|---|---|---|---|---|---|---|---|---|
| 1915 | Boston | (A) | PH | 1 | 1 | 0 | 0 | 0 | 0 | .000 | 0 | 0 | 0 | .000 |
| 1916 | Boston | (A) | P | 1 | 5 | 0 | 0 | 0 | 0 | .000 | 2 | 4 | 0 | 1.000 |
| 1918 | Boston | (A) | P-OF | 3 | 5 | 0 | 1 | 0 | 0 | .200 | [illegible] | [illegible] | 0 | 1.000 |
| 1921 | New York | (A) | OF | 6 | 16 | 3 | 5 | 1 | 2 | .313 | [illegible] | 0 | 0 | 1.000 |
| 1922 | New York | (A) | OF | 5 | 17 | 1 | 2 | 0 | 0 | .118 | [illegible] | 0 | 0 | 1.000 |
| 1923 | New York | (A) | OF-1B | 6 | 19 | 8 | 7 | 3 | 0 | .368 | 17 | 0 | 0 | [illegible] |
| 1926 | New York | (A) | OF | 7 | 20 | 6 | 6 | 4 | 1 | .300 | [illegible] | [illegible] | 0 | 1.000 |
| 1927 | New York | (A) | OF | 4 | 15 | 4 | 6 | 2 | 1 | .400 | 10 | 0 | 0 | 1.000 |
| 1928 | New York | (A) | OF | 4 | 16 | 9 | 10 | 3 | 0 | .625 | [illegible] | [illegible] | 0 | 1.000 |
| 1932 | New York | (A) | OF | 4 | 15 | 6 | 5 | 2 | 0 | .333 | 8 | [illegible] | 1 | [illegible] |
| World Series Totals | | | | 41 | 129 | 37 | 42 | 15 | 4 | .325 | 73 | 12 | 2 | .977 |

ALL-STAR GAME RECORD

| Year | Club | Pos. | AB | R | H | 2B | 3B | HR | RBI | BA | PO | A | E | FA |
|---|---|---|---|---|---|---|---|---|---|---|---|---|---|---|
| 1933 | Americans | OF | 4 | 1 | 2 | 0 | 0 | 1 | 2 | .500 | 1 | 0 | 0 | 1.000 |
| 1934 | Americans | OF | 2 | 1 | 0 | 0 | 0 | 0 | 0 | .000 | 0 | 0 | 0 | 1.000 |
| All-Star game totals | | | 6 | 2 | 2 | 0 | 0 | 1 | 2 | .333 | 1 | 0 | 0 | 1.000 |

PITCHING RECORD

| Year | Club | League | G | IP | W | L | Pct. | H | R | ER | BB | SO | ERA |
|---|---|---|---|---|---|---|---|---|---|---|---|---|---|
| 1914 | Baltimore-Pr. | (IL) | 35 | 245 | 22 | 9 | .709 | 219 | 88 | | 101 | 139 | |
| 1914 | Boston | (A) | 4 | 23 | 2 | 1 | .667 | 21 | 12 | 10 | 7 | 3 | 3.91 |
| 1915 | Boston | (A) | 32 | 218 | 18 | 6 | .750 | 166 | 80 | 59 | 85 | 112 | 2.44 |
| 1916 | Boston | (A) | 41 | 326 | 23 | 12 | .657 | 230 | 83 | 63 | 118 | 170 | [illegible] |
| 1917 | Boston | (A) | 41 | 326 | 23 | 13 | .639 | 244 | 93 | 73 | 108 | 128 | [illegible] |
| 1918 | Boston | (A) | 20 | 166 | 13 | 7 | .650 | 125 | 51 | 41 | 49 | 40 | [illegible] |
| 1919 | Boston | (A) | 17 | 133 | 8 | 5 | .615 | 148 | 59 | 44 | [illegible] | [illegible] | [illegible] |
| 1920 | New York | (A) | 1 | 4 | 1 | 0 | 1.000 | 3 | [illegible] | [illegible] | [illegible] | [illegible] | [illegible] |
| 1921 | New York | (A) | 2 | 9 | 2 | 0 | 1.000 | 14 | 10 | [illegible] | [illegible] | [illegible] | [illegible] |
| 1930 | New York | (A) | 1 | 9 | 1 | 0 | 1.000 | 11 | [illegible] | [illegible] | [illegible] | [illegible] | [illegible] |
| 1932 | New York | (A) | 1 | 9 | 1 | 0 | 1.000 | 12 | [illegible] | [illegible] | [illegible] | [illegible] | [illegible] |
| Major League Totals | | | 163 | 1220 | 92 | 44 | .677 | 979 | . | .. | 432 | 497 | .. |

*Sold to New York A.L. for $125,000 January, 1920.

WORLD'S SERIES PITCHING RECORD

| Year | Club | League | G | IP | W | L | Pct. | H | R | ER | BB | SO | ERA |
|---|---|---|---|---|---|---|---|---|---|---|---|---|---|
| 1916 | Boston | (A) | 1 | 14 | 1 | 0 | 1.000 | [illegible] | [illegible] | [illegible] | [illegible] | [illegible] | [illegible] |
| 1918 | Boston | (A) | 2 | 17 | 2 | 0 | 1.000 | 13 | [illegible] | [illegible] | [illegible] | [illegible] | [illegible] |
| World's Series Totals | | | 3 | 31 | 3 | 0 | 1.000 | 19 | 3 | [illegible] | [illegible] | 8 | [illegible] |

Paul Zimmerman
Sports Editor

# Los Angeles Times

SPORTS

VOL. LXVIII — C C ★ — SUNDAY MORNING, DECEMBER 5, 1948 — PART I 25

**END OF LINE**—Bill Gay, Irish back, is finally downed by Don Doll's tackle following his spectacular 86-yard run which set up Notre Dame's last-minute touchdown. Gay was downed 13 yards short of goal. Times photo by Howard Maxwell

## SPORTSCRIPTS

By PAUL ZIMMERMAN TIMES SPORTS EDITOR

At last count there were more than 30 postseason bowl football games listed across the nation and it's entirely possible that several others have escaped our attention.

Except for the four major New Year's Day attractions at the Rose, Sugar, Orange and Cotton bowls, it would be difficult for even the best versed sports fan to name more than two or three of the others.

**UP FOR STUDY**

It is small wonder, then, that the National Collegiate Athletic Association has been giving this growing phase of intercollegiate football very serious study.

There is a strong sentiment forming in many high places in educational circles against this far-flung postseason grid business especially since the majority of the games are staged by promoters far outside the ken of collegiate circles.

President John C. Cavanaugh, CSC of the University of Notre Dame, was discussing this the other day after he arrived here with the Irish grid team.

**NO BOWLS FOR IRISH**

Asked if Notre Dame might consider a Rose Bowl bid if it ever were offered, Father Cavanaugh said:

"It has been our policy for a number of years now to reject bowl bids. It is remarkable the number of invitations and feelers we receive every year.

"Some of them are accompanied by strong appeals for fine charity causes for which the games are staged. These people seem to forget that universities are eleemosynary institutions themselves.

"We have several reasons for this policy. The football season is distracting enough for the players and where it is prolonged until January 1 the athlete does not have sufficient time in which to prepare for the examinations that come soon thereafter.

**SUGGESTS LIMIT**

"We also feel that to prolong the playing of football is to make improper inroads on our other sports, especially basketball.

"On top of that, with a few exceptions, these games are prompted by people or groups outside collegiate circles and this adds an aspect for which we do not care."

Ike Armstrong, Utah athletic director who will help Jeff Cravath coach the western team in the San Francisco Shrine All-Star game, comes up with a suggestion along this line.

"It is too much to keep football teams away from classes and in training for the long period from the end of the regular season until New Year's Day. A lot of my boys voted against playing in a bowl this year.

"Why not limit the four big games, the Rose, Cotton, Sugar and Orange bowls to Jan. 1 and play the others within two weeks after the season ends?"

**HURTS THE WEST**

Incidentally, Ike points out that the western team in the Shrine game is in a peculiarly tough spot for players this fall.

"We have been deprived of stars from at least eight major teams from west of the Mississippi who are in bowl games, so we have our work cut out for us when we face the East."

The list includes California and Oregon on the Coast; Texas, Southern Methodist, Baylor, Oklahoma and Oklahoma A&M in the Southwest and Missouri in the Midwest.

One glance at All-American selections will be enough to give you a fair idea how many senior stars from these clubs will be lost to the West as a result.

**WHITHER TO?**

This, of course, is a small item in the large general picture of bowl games.

What will happen to bowl games is anyone's guess. But it seems logical that these games will survive as long as the public shows enough interest in them to make them pay out.

It's hardly likely that public interest in the four major bowls ever will diminish to the point where these games will be abandoned.

California officials who have been trying to solve the problem of how to spread the Rose Bowl's 90,000 tickets over 900,000 potential purchasers probably would welcome the day when only 90,000 or even 80,000 were interested in this daddy of all these games.

P.S.: Maybe television will help 'em out.

# Fighting Trojans Battle Favored Notre Dame to 14-14 Stalemate

EVERYBODY'S SAD

## Troy Gloomy Despite Moral Victory Tie

BY AL WOLF

**You'd have thought SC had just lost to UCLA—or Vassar even.**

**The gloom was so thick in Troy's dressing quarters after yesterday's magnificent 14-14 "victory" over Notre Dame that the earthquake actually failed to penetrate it.**

From Head Coach Jeff Cravath down to the water boy—yes, and George Tirebiter, too—the Trojans were heart-broken over their failure to upset the Irish after leading 35 seconds from the finish.

They had stunned the nation by achieving a tie with the vaunted South Benders and by rights should have been reducing the Coliseum to rubble as the first step in wild celebration. But after being so close to going all the way, the "moral victory" soured into "moral defeat."

"Blame it all on to me," Cravath mumbled after emerging from a sweaty trance.

**Slow Getting Down**

"I suppose we should have kicked a 'squeegy' to them after we scored, figuring they might have trouble catching it and maybe even fumble. But if you can't cover kickoffs you don't deserve to win.

"Chuck Peterson kicked a beauty, high and clear to the goal. But we were slow getting down under it—maybe too cautious—and that fellow Gay got away."

(A "squeegy" is a kickoff in which the ball is simply placed flat on the ground. It generally curves erratically downfield when booted).

"We were hot and they were cold at that stage of the game," Jeff added after reflecting for a moment, "and so my whole thought was to get that ball way down there."

**Line Play Best**

Cravath said he was sorry his kids couldn't have won after putting up such a tremendous battle. He thought the Trojans' defensive line play was the best since he's been on the job, but he emphatically wouldn't pick out any individuals for special pats.

It was generally agreed, however, that George Schutte deserved top credit for opening the holes for Bill Martin's two touchdowns and that Jim Bird and Volney Peters hit the heights defensively.

Martin, who had tallied only once before this season, grinned wryly through a face that was an almost solid mass of bruises, welts and cuts.

"Sure was fun, but the line did all the work," he said. "I could have gone through both times

Turn to Page 26, Column 3

BAND WENT WILD

## Coach Leahy Honored by Troy Students

Southern California's rooting section and band went wild yesterday after the 14-to-14 tie between the Trojans and Notre Dame but showed utter impartiality (well, almost) as they serenaded the dressing rooms after the game.

They quite naturally concentrated on Coach Jeff Cravath and his boys, giving virtually every player a great cheer and a shoulder ride out of the enclosure.

But when Coach Frank Leahy emerged, they called on their tired vocal cords for one last big effort, hoisted the Irish mentor on the shoulders of three cheer leaders and demanded a speech.

**Astute Mr. Leahy**

The astute Mr. Leahy was up to the occasion.

"Without a doubt," said Leahy, "this is one of the best teams we met all year. Sterling coaching by Mr. Cravath and fine team play made possible your impressive showing today but the spirit of all of you also contributed to this fine performance this afternoon."

And then he added:

"This is the first time in my coaching career that I have been so highly honored by the student body of an opposing school."

## FOOTBALL RESULTS

**SC, 14; Notre Dame, 14!**

San Francisco City College, 24; Menlo JC, 9.

San Diego State, 28; Utah State, 19.

Santa Barbara, 46; Willamette, 7.

San Jose State, 71; Natural U of Mexico, 10.

March Field, 13; 8th Air Force, 7.

Alabama, 55; Auburn, 0.

Clemson, 20; Citadel, 0.

Arizona State (Tempe), 20; New Mexico U., 15.

Evansville, 13; Missouri Valley, 7 (Refrigerator Bowl).

San Jose, 71; National U of Mexico, 19.

Toledo, 27; Oklahoma City, 14 (Glass Bowl).

Kansas St. Tchrs. (Emporia), 34; Southwest Missouri State, 20. (Mo-Kan Bowl).

Hampton Institute, 20; Wilberforce State, 19 (Fish Bowl).

Everett JC, 39; Lassen (Cal.) JC, 20 (Evergreen Bowl).

Florida State, 33; Tampa, 18.

(Additional scores on Page 30.)

## TRIPUCKA MARVELS IN DRESSING ROOM

BY PAUL LOWRY

Huddled under blankets in the cold recesses of the Notre Dame dressing room, Frank Tripucka yesterday called signals for the winning touchdown that never materialized against the battling Trojans.

"Give 'em the 27 play, Bob," he implored as time was running out.

Tripucka had left the game at the end of the first half as the Irish froze the ball in the shadows of their own goal posts. Three times the Notre Dame first-string quarterback called a sneak into the line. The fourth time he took the ball on a spread play. Trojans swarmed all over him. The gun sounded the end of the half.

Tripucka's strategy had worked. The Irish left the field leading, 7 to 0, after staving off a Trojan touchdown drive. But Tripucka lay quite still. They had to carry him off the field on a stretcher. He is a senior, and it was his last game. Team physicians reported last night that Tripucka had suffered fractured processes of the spine, a fractured rib and a possible fracture of the vertebrae.

But Tripucka still lived up to the creed of the "fighting Irish."

A portable radio was at his side in the dressing room. He had heard the Trojans come from behind to tie the game at 7-7 in the fourth period and forge ahead, 14 to 7, with only two and one-half minutes left to play.

He was suffering the tortures of the damned along with his physical hurts.

But he still had faith.

Between clenched teeth he rooted for Bill Gay to go all the way on his long runback of the ensuing Trojan kickoff.

"God, what fighters," he said as Emil Sitko scored and Steve Oracko kicked the tying goal. "They've been that way all year."

"What men to play football with!"

"Did you take the Trojans too

Turn to Page 26, Column 4

## Grid Broadcast

Dons vs. San Francisco '49ers, KFWB, 2 p.m.

Rams vs. Washington Redskins, KMPC, 11:45 a.m.

## 'TWAS A GREAT DAY FOR COAST FOOTBALL

BY DICK HYLAND

It was a great day for the Irish. It was a great for the Trojans.

It was a great day for Coaches Frank Leahy and Jeff Cravath.

It was a great day for West Coast football. It was a great day for all football.

And it was a great day for 100,571 fans who left the Coliseum owing two great groups of boys more than ticket money could pay after seeing Notre Dame come from behind with less than a minute to play to tie Southern California 14-14 in one of the greatest games ever played in the West.

Such was the opinion of football experts who thrilled, tingled, giggled, groaned and guffawed as they watched what Frank Leahy says is the greatest "spirit" team he has ever coached get matched grunt for grunt for 60 minutes by the greatest Trojan team in a decade.

Southern Methodist's Matty Bell, Stanford's Marchie Schwartz, California's Lynn Waldorf, Washington's Howie Odell and Pepperdine's Ray Richards were among the coaches in the press box and they each bubbled with enthusiasm not only during the spectacle but afterward.

Marchie Schwartz, whose teams are noted for spirit, said, "The Trojans were up, up high, for this game. They were inspired and the

Turn to Page 26, Column 7

## TODAY IN SPORTS

**PRO FOOTBALL**—San Francisco '49ers vs. Los Angeles Dons, Coliseum, 2 p.m.

**AUTO RACING**—Hot-rod racing at Carrell Speedway, Gardena. 50-lap main event, first race at 2:30 p.m., time trials at 1 p.m.

**SOCCER**—Three games at Rancho Cienega Stadium, games to start at 11 a.m., 1 p.m. and 3 p.m.

**MUNICIPAL FOOTBALL**—[illegible] vs. Venice Athletic Club at Culver City Stadium, 2:15 p.m.

## 100,571 See Irish Rally to Save Unbeaten String

BY BRAVEN DYER

**The obvious lead, of course, is to say that two earthquakes hit Los Angeles almost simultaneously yesterday, the major one man-made by Jeff Cravath's fighting Trojans, who halted Notre Dame's 21-game win streak with a 14-14 tie.**

The obvious lead usually is best, so there it is.

But packed into that spectacular tie was more than two hours of heart-stabbing excitement which both players and 100,571 hysterical fans will be relating to their children's children for years to come.

The Trojans will say, and they could be right, that only a penalty against them in the last minute of play saved mighty Notre Dame from defeat, 14-7.

**Lucky to Break Even**

As it was, the proteges of Frank Leahy were lucky to finish on even terms with a traditional foe they had been doped to whip by three touchdowns.

And the Trojans, although terribly disappointed to have victory snatched away with but 34 seconds to play, gained the honor, for the third time in Notre Dame history, of halting long Irish winning streaks.

The current one ended at 21 straight as Cravath's gallant warriors fought their hearts out from whistle to whistle to score one of the most stunning upsets of the 1948 gridiron campaign.

While they escaped defeat the Irish made it 28 straight without a loss, the last team to hang one on them being Great Lakes in 1945. Army tied them in '46 and since then they're unbeaten.

Twenty-year-old Bill Gay, 170-pound halfback from Chicago, saved Notre Dame from what seemed to be certain defeat.

There was just 2m. 30s. to play after plunging Bill Martin, Trojan fullback, put the locals ahead, 14 to 7, with the second of his touchdown smashes.

SC rooters were hysterically happy . . . their underdog Trojans had whipped the mighty Irish . . . or so they thought while preparing for a long night of celebration.

Strong men grew weak slapping each other on the back and some even headed for the exits, certain that they'd seen a gridiron miracle.

Then it happened, as it does so often on the field of battle after a particularly strong emotional effort such as the Trojans gave to gain their second touchdown.

Gay grabbed the high kickoff on the 1-yard line and the clock showed less than 2m. 30s. to play as he set sail down the right sidelines.

Gaining speed and blockers as he pounded the bright turf, Gay sped past the Trojan bench and set sail for the promised land.

Jay Roundy, I believe it was, closed in, and forced him closer to the side lines. But Gay got away and then, as he cut back for more running room, Don Doll hit him from behind. And Gay hit the turf on the 13-yard line.

**With Great Restraint**

It is only with great restraint that I refrain from saying, at this point, that the Irish were having a Gay old time.

Quickly the Irish lined up and quickly Bob Williams, sophomore

Turn to Page 28, Column 2

## JEFF LAUGHS AT TALE HE'LL REPLACE LEAHY

Coach Jeff Cravath of SC was surrounded by the press following yesterday's 14-14 tie with Notre Dame. Questions poured at him. Grim, sweating, distracted, he tried to keep up. Jeff was plainly uncomfortable and unhappy.

Finally somebody cracked. "Is it true that you are going to replace Frank Leahy as Notre Dame's head coach next season?"

Jeff chuckled.

(Certain writers—not Times writers—had Leahy replacing him at the Trojan helm in 1949).

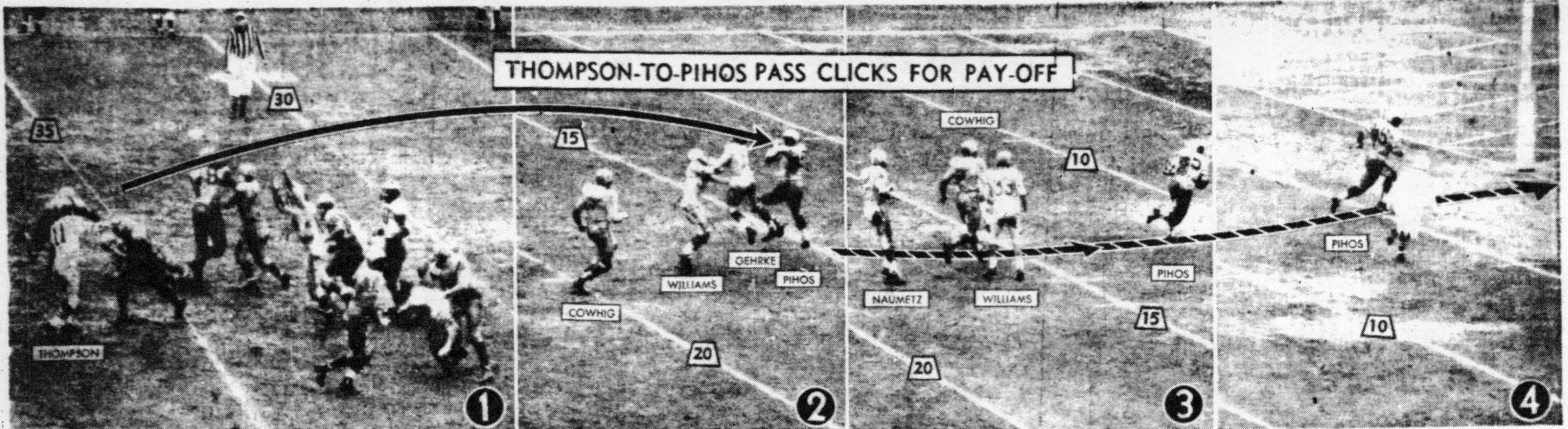


**EAGLE TOUCHDOWN**—Quarterback Tommy Thompson passes 16 yards to End Pete Pihos, who makes nifty catch on Ram 15 and runs for first Philadelphia touchdown in second period. Eagles whipped L.A. pros, 14-0, to keep NFL title. Times Miracle Eye Photos by Phil Bath

PART 4 **Los Angeles Times** SPORTS

VOL. LXIX CC MONDAY MORNING, DECEMBER 19, 1949 Read The Times for Latest Sports

**KICK BLOCKED**—Leo Skladany, Philadelphia lineman, blocks Bob Waterfield's punt on Rams' 2-yard line in third quarter. The former Pittsburgh star scooped up soggy ball, went over for Eagle's second touchdown. Note white towel used by Waterfield to dry his hands. Times photo by Art Rogers

# Eagles Blank Rams, 14-0, Before 22,245

## Philadelphians Keep Crown in Muddy Battle

BY FRANK FINCH

**A magnificent piece of precision pigskin machinery, the Philadelphia Eagle steamroller retained its National Football League championship yesterday by shutting out the Los Angeles Rams, 14 to 0.**

A disappointing crowd of 22,245 rain-drenched fans saw Greasy Neale's Eagles, paced by Steve Van Buren's record-breaking exhibition, completely dominate the Rams on the flooded Coliseum turf.

Van Buren lugged the leather 196 yards in 31 attempts to write three new NFL play-off records. His total broke the mark of 159 yards for one game, set two years ago by Elmer Angsman of the Chicago Cards in defeating the Eagles. Angsman carried the ball only 10 times. Van Buren also erased a record held by Bronko Nagurski of the Chicago Bears, who amassed 214 yards in 57 carries in four title games. Van Buren, on 75 attempts in three games, now has 320 yards rushing. His 31 carries broke his own mark of 27, set in 1947.

**Pihos Scores**

Ironically, the Bull of the Bayous, while right at home in the swamplike going, didn't score on the Rams.

Pete Pihos, Philly's All-Pro end, caught a 31-yard pass from Tommy Thompson in the second quarter for the initial tally and Left End Leo Skladany scored the clincher in the third period by blocking Bob Waterfield's attempted punt from the 2-yard line. Cliff Patton added both extra points.

The Rams couldn't raise a gallop against the monstrous Eagles. In fact, by gaining only 21 yards rushing, the Rams had the dubious distinction of setting another play-off record. Their rushing total was a yard less than the Washington Redskins gained when they were obliterated by the Chicago Bears in the 1940 play-off, 73 to 0.

The only L.A. "threat" came in the first quarter when Waterfield attempted a field goal from the Eagle 45. It was low and wide to the right.

"We never would be able to beat the Eagles under today's conditions," said Ram Coach Clark Shaughnessy. "Make no mistake, they're a truly great football team. Maybe we couldn't beat 'em on a dry field, either, but I think our chances went down the drain when it began to rain."

**Lights Turned On**

Rain fell steadily until midway through the third quarter, at just about the time the Coliseum lights were turned on.

Old-time Coliseum observers couldn't remember, positively, when it last rained there during a game, but everybody agreed it must have been sometime during the Pliocene Age.

While only 22,245 paying patrons braved the elements, a total of 27,980 seats were sold for the game. Gross receipts were $127,034.04. After Federal taxes and stadium rental were deducted, the net receipts amounted to approximately $107,978.94.

Seventy per cent of this amount, or approximately $75,585.25, went into the players' pool. Each Eagle's share was

Turn to Page 2, Column 3

### It's the Climate

The weatherman must have it in for the Rams and Eagles when they appear in NFL play-off games.

In 1945 the Rams, then playing under the Cleveland banner, defeated the Washington Redskins on a frozen field in sub-zero weather.

In 1948 the Eagles defeated the Chicago Cards in a blinding snowstorm at Shibe Park.

In 1949—man the lifeboats, men!

## Rams Lost Title Two Weeks Ago

BY DICK HYLAND

**The Philadelphia Eagles won the football championship of the world night before last. Yet the Los Angeles Rams lost it two weeks ago.**

Such were the considered opinions of, respectively, Eagle Coach Earle Neale and the Rams' Clark Shaughnessy. It was obvious to all concerned that the weather had considerable to do with the Eagles' 14-0 win in the Coliseum yesterday.

**Great Club**

The night before the game, in their Bel-Air hotel, the Eagles, who were to defend the championship they had won during 1948, met for a meeting called by Coach Neale. They took that one in stride. When Neale finished yakking at them, the Eagles yawned and prepared to exit from the room. Captain Al Wistert then popped to his feet and told the team a few homely truths. They were not ready for this game. . . . They were up against a great team on its home field. . . . They could not win with that attitude. . . . They had better get the lead out and begin the whoop and holler stuff, and right now, or bye-bye precious championship.

"That did it," said Coach Neale in the dressing room following the game. "We won the game right there. This is a great club. It is a family. It is close together on and off the field. It has great spirit. And when Captain Wistert called on them, they snapped out of it and produced."

**High Strung**

Shaughnessy said, "We were prepared for the Eagles today. They did not surprise us with one thing. They did just as we expected them to do—so soon as it came up mud. We could play them under the same conditions again tomorrow and the result would probably be the same.

"We really lost the title two weeks ago when the Cardinals beat us. That meant we had to

Turn to Page 2, Column 2

### OFFICIAL PAY-OFF ON PRO PLAY-OFF

Here are financial figures on yesterday's Philadelphia-Los Angeles game:

Paid attendance—27,980.
Gross receipts—$127,034.04.
Taxes and rental—Approximately $19,055.
Net receipts—Approximately $107,978.94.
Total players' pool—Approximately $75,585.25.
Winning players' pool—Approximately $40,816.03.
Losing players' pool—Approximately $27,210.68.
Each winning player's share—Approximately $1090.
Each losing player's share—Approximately [illegible].
Pool for sectional second-place clubs—Approximately $7558.

# EVERYONE BUT COMMISSIONER WANTED TITLE TILT POSTPONED

The fans wanted it postponed. So did the players, the coaches and the owners.

But back in Philadelphia the imperious commissioner of the National Football League, Bert Bell, flatly refused to postpone yesterday's Ram-Eagle game, so they went ahead and played it under miserable conditions.

In refusing to give everybody concerned a break, Bell said that it was impossible to defer the play-off game "because of radio network commitments and other factors."

Dan Reeves and Jim Clark, respective presidents of the Rams and Eagles, agreed yesterday morning that there should be a postponement.

The players, who lost heavily in play-off shares when the box-office sale dropped to zero with the first show of rain, were more than anxious to put it off.

Coaches Clark Shaughnessy and Earle (Greasy) Neale felt the same way.

More than 5000 fans who had purchased tickets refused to take a soaking to see the game.

Pleading ill-health, Commissioner Bell remained in Philadelphia.

After a long conversation with the mogul, Reeves issued this statement:

"Jim Clark, president of the Philadelphia Eagles, and I agreed early this morning to postpone this championship game because of inclement weather. We proposed to play the game Christmas Day and requested approval of the postponement from National Football League Commissioner Bert Bell.

"Hope of financial gain to the management of the two clubs did not affect our decision, since the game is played for the benefit of the players. We believe this will be a great football game and we feel it is a shame it cannot be presented to Southern California football fans under ideal weather conditions.

"Commissioner Bell, when we talked to him from 3000 miles away, informed us that postponement of the game was impossible because of radio network commitments and other factors."

## SPORTSCRIPTS

By PAUL ZIMMERMAN, TIMES SPORTS EDITOR

Monday morning's mullings:

Doak Walker, the Southern Methodist All-America back, will not be on hand to help his coach, Matty Bell, with the Western All-Stars in the Shrine game at San Francisco . . . Walker has a bruised muscle that needs rest from here on in, if he's to make the professional grade.

Matty and Jeff Cravath, the Southern California coach, could use him since they are going to ignore the T formation in the Crippled Children's classic . . . They will use the double wing, the short punt and, of course, some single wing, against their eastern opponents.

**WATCH WYATT**

If they can get him, Washington State authorities want Bowden Wyatt of Wyoming for their new grid mentor . . . He would replace Phil Sarboe, a swell guy who resigned recently . . . Wyatt turned in a great season for Wyoming this year . . . But his opportunities at Laramie may be too fine to make the change . . .

Washington State probably would make Ted Shipkey its first choice if it wasn't for the fact that he's coaching Montana which is in the Pacific Coast Conference . . . It's rather an unwritten rule that no conference school will take a top coach from another.

**RULE IS SILLY**

The Grizzlies probably would let Ted go if Washington State asked . . . After all the rule is silly . . . Shipkey was an All-America end at Stanford . . . He also did a fine job in the Los Angeles public school system before going to New Mexico before the war . . . When he came back he helped coach the Los Angeles Dons.

Wyatt is another one of the fine gridsters trained at Tennessee by Gen. Bob Neyland . . . A lot of Neyland's stars are in top coaching jobs around the nation . . . Coach Henry Sanders, who played many a game against him, says Neyland still is one of the best in the business.

Sarboe's name has been mentioned in connection with Fresno State . . . But Phil is a bit reluctant to take another head coaching job . . . The former Washington State mentor would like to play second fiddle . . . He figures he's qualified to assist and wants no more of the grief of the head coach.

**CREDIT TO JEFF**

Jeff Cravath's strong friends are excited about his getting a new contract at Southern California . . . They point to his impressive record with the Trojans in conference play as proof of his coaching ability . . . Cravath is a great coaches' coach . . . He's rugged and outspoken, but opposing mentors know he teaches the game according to the rules.

Films of the Rose Bowl game between California and Ohio State will be televised in the Bay area . . . A copy of KTTV's video display of the game here will be sent to San Francisco's KPIX for retelecast . . . It is safe to assume that Wisconsin has supplied Ohio State with game movies of its tilt with California during the regular season . . . By the same token California probably can have access to the films of the Trojan game vs. the Buckeyes if Coach Waldorf desires.

**IN FOR SURPRISE**

Not a few of the folks who attended the Coast Conference meeting at Carmel made it a point to tell the San Francisco scribes that they didn't see real major league football competi-

Turn to Page 2, Column 7

### TODAY IN SPORTS

**BOXING**—Ocean Park Arena, 8:30 p.m.

**WRESTLING**—Hollywood Legion Stadium, Pico Palace, Pasadena Arena, 8:30 p.m.

**AMATEUR BOXING**—South Gate Arena, 8:30 p.m.

**AMATEUR HOCKEY**—Pan-Pacific, 7:30 p.m.

## Rain Greets Bucks Here

BY AL WOLF

Ohio State's Buckeyes, the first footballers ever to fly out for a Rose Bowl game, arrived at International Airport in Inglewood at 5:45 p.m. yesterday after a 12-hour trip aboard a TWA charter plane.

Raindrops rather than roses provide the arrival motif. A chagrined Tournament of Roses welcoming committee escorted the visitors off the plane with umbrellas rather than sunbeams. In short, it was raining like heck, just as it had been all day.

However, a second reception was staged later at the Huntington Hotel in Pasadena and went off much better.

The weather even forced a change of plans. Burbank Airport was the original destination, but became "socked in."

Head Coach Wes Fesler said

Turn to Page 3, Column 3

WON'T POSTPONE GAME

## Rams, Eagles Miffed at Commissioner Bell

BY BRAVEN DYER

As Greasy Neale niftied after the game, "There are times when a coach's best friend is his mudder—meaning Steve Van Buren" . . . Whenever Frank Bull barked into the loud speaker, it seemed, this is what came out—"Van Buren carried the ball, and made five yards."

The players really were miffed over Bert Bell's refusal to postpone the game . . . It cost them beaucoup beans . . . One suggested that Czardine Bert leave his Philadelphia fireside and take a dive off the 75-foot tower which went unused yesterday because the scheduled aerialist wasn't related to Donald Duck.

**Time for Bath**

Sure wish I had the towel concession . . . Officials and players used 'em once over lightly and then discarded their dirty linen as if they were only Kleenex . . . This was one game where no official needed time out to wet his whistle . . . Things were damp enough as they were.

Bing Crosby and Bob Hope bought stock in the Rams just in time to take a bath . . . There is no truth to the report their next film will be entitled, "The Road to Bankruptcy" . . . Van Buren obviously was more at home than any other player . . . he was raised in the swamp lands of Louisiana.

**Waterfield Whapped**

If I were the Ram owners I'd ask Czar Bell for permission to play the '49ers here any time within the next two weeks . . . It would be a popular gesture with public and players . . . The worst Bertie could do would be to nix that, too . . . Think of the drama . . . Frankie Albert vs. Clark Shaughnessy 10 years after they cleaned up at Stanford.

Zilly's smashing tackle of Smackover Scott after Waterfield's punt was the first standout play of the game . . . The fans hooed something fierce when the Rams' tackle eligible pass to Dick Huffman gained 15 yards but went for naught because of a penalty . . . They roared with laughter when Vitamin Smith was almost drowned as he skidded into a deep lagoon out of bounds near the Eagle bench.

Bednarik bashed Waterfield after Bob's second punt and the penalty gave the Rams an auto-

Turn to Page 2, Column 5

## Longden Suffers Defeat at Hands of Girl Jockey

BY PAUL LOWRY

TIJUANA, Mex., Dec. 18—"She had the best horse, and she really gave me the business."

So said Johnny Longden, three-time national riding champion of America, after he lost the only mixed-match race in the records today.

Wantha Davis, piloting Northeast, beat Longden and Grey Spook by a length and three-quarters after a wild West rodeo race that was not settled in the stewards' stand because there was no betting.

The sum and substance of the race was that gal beat boy today because Wantha had the superior horse and Longden tried to play gentleman.

That is, he was playing nice until he decided that Wantha was giving him the works and then it was too late.

The girl queen of the jockeys (as far as quarter horses are concerned) carried Longden and Grey Spook almost to the outside fence after they came off the turn in the six-furlong match sprint.

"If I hadn't pulled up a bit, no telling where I would have wound up" said Longden.

When Longden finished he had cut to the inside of his rival, after Wantha had put his horse away and the race was practically over.

The time was 1:12 flat. Northeast carried 118, Grey Spook 123.

Wantha was all smiles as she rode into the winner's circle. Longden bagged some boos. He quickly jumped off his horse and beat it to the jockeys' room as the hecklers squawked at him, "What happened, Johnny?"

Johnny knows what happened.

"I'll never be a gentleman again in any kind of a match race," he said.

## Open Tourney Washed Out

Rain forced postponement to Saturday of the final round of the Montebello Open golf tournament yesterday. The same starting times will be in effect Saturday.

Jerry Barber held a one-stroke lead over Bob Gajda at the end of 36 holes in the $2500 event.

PART 4 **Los Angeles Times** SPORTS

VOL. LXIX CC★ THURSDAY MORNING, SEPTEMBER 28, 1950 Read The Times for Latest Sports

# Charles Takes Unanimous Verdict From Aging Louis

## SPORTS PARADE

By BRAVEN DYER

Tomorrow Wrigley Field, home of the Angels, will be 25 years old.

Many great athletes have appeared there, in addition to those who wore Angel uniforms.

Babe Ruth did an exhibition stint. Jimmy McLarnin scored one of his quickest knockouts, flattening Young Corbett in the first round of their 1933 bout for the title. Ace Hudkins twice thrilled big crowds with gutty fights against Sgt. Sammy Baker and Mickey Walker.

**FOOTBALLERS, TOO**

Tiny Roebuck, the greatest tackle I ever saw, played there. And so did John Levi, who threw passes farther than any man I ever saw. Johnny Drake of Purdue, I believe it was, played some of the finest football I ever saw, in a pro bowl game.

What would an all-star Angel team, limited to Wrigley Field performers, look like? I asked George Goodale, Seraph tub thumper, to buzz a few local experts, and this is what he offers:

**ALL-TIME ANGELS**

1B—James Oglesby, 1932-33-34-35.

2B—James Reese, 1933-34-35-36-40.

3B—Gene Lillard, 1932-33-34-35-38-40.

SS—Carl Dittmar, 1928-29-30-31-32-33-34-35-36-37-38.

UIF—Edward Mayo, 1938-39-40-41-42.

RF—Frank Demaree, 1934.

CF—Arnold (Jigger) Statz, 1925-26-29-30-31-32-33-34-35-36-37-38-39-40-41-42.

LF—Frank Baumholtz, 1950.

UOF—John Moore, 1930-31-38-39-40-41-42-43-44-45.

Catchers—Harry (Truck) Hannah, 1926-27-28-29-30-31-34-35 (coached and did not play in 1932-33-36). William (Gilly) Campbell, 1931-32-34-41-42.

Pitchers—Fay Thomas, 1933-34-36-37-38-39-40-41. Louis (Bobo) Newsom, 1933. Otis (Doc) Crandall, 1925-26-29. Ray Prim, 1936-37-38-39-40-41-42-44-47. Cliff Chambers, 1946-47.

Relief Pitcher—Jess Dobernic, 1941-42-46-47.

**MANY MARKS**

Take a closer look at these players.

Oglesby holds the Angel record for hitting safely in consecutive games, 44 in 1933. Batted .350 in 1935 and lifetime Angel swat mark is .324.

Reese has an Angel lifetime batting average of .300 and also holds fielding records. Oddly enough, he was the Angel bat boy in 1916. Dittmar's lifetime Angel batting figure is .285, led the club and league several seasons in sacrifice hits and holds several fielding records.

Lillard is the all-time Angel home run king, slugging 56 in 1935. In the same season hit eight homers in six consecutive games. Also led league in homers in 1933 with 43. Angel lifetime batting average is .317. Mayo played second, third and short in his five seasons with the club. Holds fielding marks at third and second and went 34 consecutive games without an error at second base in 1938. Lifetime Angel batting average is .303.

Statz needs no plaudits. He was an Angel for 18 years, 16 of them in Wrigley Field, and managed three years, in 1940-41-42. Holds Angel and league lifetime records in excess of a dozen in batting and fielding. Acknowledged the greatest of all Angels and his uniform number, No. 8, was retired to rest permanently in Angel historical archives when Statz quit the game.

Demaree holds the highest batting average of any Angel, .383, plus the season's highest mark in runs scored with 190 and most runs batted in with 173, both marks being set in 1934. Led league that year in batting, runs scored, home runs, runs batted in and total bases. Hit 45 homers.

Baumholtz bids fair currently to top Demaree's average. Now batting nearly .400 and leading the league in two-base hits. Had a consecutive game hitting streak of 33 and another one of 18. His total of 241 hits is the most any Angel has made since 1940. His total of two-base hits, now 53, is the most since Steve Mesner hit 55 in 1936.

Quite a ball club, isn't it?

Fans will see some of them again on Oct. 7 when two teams of former Angels play a three-inning game as part of the 25th birthday festivities of Wrigley Field. It will be held as a preliminary to the Angel-Seattle game.

## HAWKEYES ARRIVE FOR TROJAN TILT

BY BRAVEN DYER

Confident that they can continue the Big Ten's Rose Bowl mastery of our Pacific Coast Conference football teams, Iowa's experienced gridders hit the Southland yesterday for tomorrow night's game against SC at the Coliseum.

Coach Leonard Raffensperger and 39 athletes dropped in via United Air Lines after a quick flight from Cedar Rapids.

It is Iowa's first visit here since the Bruins of UCLA dumped them, 22 to 7, in 1947, and the Hawkeyes' initial start against SC since 1925 when they dropped an 18-0 tilt.

**Takes Top Job**

The game tomorrow night opens the season for both teams and it also marks the debut of Raffensperger as head coach of the invaders.

He was elevated from the freshman job to Iowa's top command last winter when Dr. Eddie Anderson decided to move on.

"We're happy to be here to play the Trojans," said Raffensperger yesterday afternoon as he prepared to take his athletes to the Coliseum for a night drill.

"We respect Jeff Cravath's team and the type of football you play. Last year we lost to UCLA and defeated Oregon. We hope to continue where we left off with Oregon, but realize that we are up against a real job."

**21 Lettermen**

Iowa players proved to be a husky lot with plenty of beef. They laughed at the 13-point rating in favor of the Trojans, who, as Cravath has often said, probably would be favored (in Los Angeles) to beat everybody but Notre Dame, the Chicago Bears and the Cleveland Browns.

Raffensperger brought a veteran squad to Los Angeles. There are 21 lettermen on his first two strings. The lone exception is Dudley Noble, 210-pound sophomore, at left tackle.

Midwest grid critics think Iowa has an excellent chance to finish in the first division.

That classy Hawk backfield impressed them last year and should be even better this time.

The all-veteran quartet of Glenn Drahn, Bill Reichardt, Jerry Faske and Mike Riley packs a powerful punch. Drahn and Reichardt are supposed to be the standouts, but nobody speaks disparagingly of the other pair.

Drahn is the senior quarterback, who pitches a football or a baseball with equal dexterity. Reichardt, as a sophomore last season, was named second all-Big Ten fullback, with a 5-yard average and 44 points, 28 in league games.

**Down on the Farm**

These Hawkeyes are competitors. They love their football. Drahn is the most experienced quarterback in the Big Ten, with poise and calmness. He hit for 735 yards and nine touchdowns last fall, and holds the Iowa record for most passes completed in a single game, 12 against UCLA in the opener.

Reichardt probably will play

Turn to Page 2, Column 3

## Oregon's Fell Breaks Ankle

EUGENE, Or., Sept. 27 (AP)—Halfback Bill Fell broke an ankle in scrimmage today, complicating the University of Oregon's backfield strategy against California.

The former Compton J.C. star who plays left half and is the Pacific Coast Conference's 100-yard dash champion, was tackled on an end run and fractured a small ankle bone and chipped the tibia, the large bone, in falling. Dr. George Guldager, team physician, said it was "a perfect break," but would idle the player for the season.

## PENNANT RACE AT A GLANCE

BY THE ASSOCIATED PRESS

| | W | L | Pct. | * | ** |
|---|---|---|---|---|---|
| New York | 96 | 55 | .636 | . | 3 |
| Detroit | 93 | 57 | .620 | 2½ | 4 |

*Games behind. **Games to play.

**Remaining Games**

New York—At home (0); away (3). Philadelphia, 1. Boston, 2.

Detroit—At home (4). St. Louis, 1: Cleveland, 3.

OUCH!—Challenger Joe Louis, left, grimaces with pain as Champion Ezzard Charles slashes a stinging right hand past the bruised and swollen face of the 36-year-old former titleholder. This punch occurred in the next to last round. Charles took a unanimous nod. (AP) Wirephoto

## Detroit Wins, Keeps Flag Hopes Alive

DETROIT, Sept. 27 (AP)—The Detroit Tigers found their claws again today as they outfought the St. Louis Browns, 5-4, to pick up a full game in the American League race and keep their slender pennant hopes alive.

The win moved the Tigers to within 2½ games of the pace-setting New York Yankees who bowed to Philadelphia. Ironically it was played before only 3335 fans—smallest turnout of the year at Briggs Stadium.

| St. Louis | AB | H | O | A | Detroit | AB | H | O | A |
|---|---|---|---|---|---|---|---|---|---|
| Wood,rf-lf | 5 | 1 | 4 | 0 | Priddy,2b | 4 | 1 | 3 | 1 |
| Coleman,cf | 4 | 1 | 3 | 0 | Kell,3b | 4 | 2 | 3 | 1 |
| Moss,c | 4 | 1 | 3 | 1 | Mullin,lf | 4 | 2 | 5 | 0 |
| Pillette | 0 | 0 | 0 | 0 | Keller,rf | 4 | 0 | 1 | 0 |
| Overm'e,p(L) | 0 | 0 | 0 | 0 | Groth,cf | 4 | 1 | 1 | 0 |
| Kokos,lf-rf | 4 | 1 | 1 | 0 | Kolloway,1b | 3 | 1 | 9 | 2 |
| Lenhardt,3b | 2 | 0 | 1 | 1 | Lipon,ss | 2 | 0 | 1 | 2 |
| Arft,1b | 4 | 0 | 9 | 0 | Ginsberg,c | 3 | 1 | 1 | 1 |
| Sommers,2b | 3 | 2 | 2 | 2 | Evers | 1 | 0 | 0 | 0 |
| Upton,ss | 3 | 1 | 2 | 3 | Houttem'n,p | 2 | 0 | 3 | 3 |
| Sievers | 1 | 1 | 0 | 0 | White,p(W) | 0 | 0 | 0 | 0 |
| DeMars,ss | 0 | 0 | 0 | 0 | | | | | |
| Starr,p | 2 | 1 | 0 | 0 | | | | | |
| Delsing | 1 | 1 | 0 | 0 | | | | | |
| Garver,p | 0 | 0 | 0 | 1 | | | | | |
| Lollar,c | 1 | 0 | 0 | 0 | | | | | |
| Totals | 34 | 10 | 25 | 8 | Totals | 31 | 8 | 27 | 10 |

One out when winning run scored.
Delsing singled for Starr in 7th.
Sievers doubled for Upton in 9th.
Pillette ran for Moss in 9th.
Evers flied out for Ginsberg in 9th.

| | |
|---|---|
| St. Louis | 000 010 102—4 |
| Detroit | 000 004 001—5 |

RBI—Wood, 2; Coleman, Moss, Kell, Mullin, 3; Evers, 2B—Wood, Sommers, Sievers, Coleman. 3B—Groth. HR—Mullin. SH—Lenhardt, Houtteman. LOB—St. Louis, 9; Detroit, 5. BB—Off Garver, 1; Overmire, 2; Houtteman, 5. SO—By Starr, 1; Garver, 1; Houtteman, 1. Hits—Off Starr, 5 in 6 innings; Garver, 2 in 2; Overmire, 1 in ⅓; Houtteman, 10 in 8⅔; White, 0 in ⅓. Winner—White (8-6). Loser—Overmire (8-12). Umpires—Summers, Stevens and Grieve. Time—2h. 1m. Attendance—3335.

## Chapman's Two-Run Homer in 9th Wrecks Yankees, 8-7

PHILADELPHIA, Sept. 27 (AP)—Sam Chapman of the Philadelphia Athletics snapped out of a paralyzing slump with a dramatic ninth-inning home run with Ferris Fain on base to beat the New York Yankees, 8 to 7, and extend the American League pennant race at least one more day.

And adding insult to injury, Chapman's blast into the left-field seats on a three-ball two-strike count pitch, lowered the boom on the Yankees' sensational rookie pitcher, Ed Ford. The 21-year-old left-hander had won nine straight games before today. Ford came in to pitch in the seventh after Johnny Hopp batted for Starter Ed Lopat.

**Still in Doubt**

As a result of the suddenlike Chapman poke, the Yankees still need two victories or two Detroit defeats, or a combination of the two, to win their 17th junior circuit flag.

Chapman, the likable Californian, had gone 10 times at bat before he connected on Ford. The big outfielder hadn't driven a run home in 19 games. Even today, against Lopat and Ford, his previous best was an infield-out hopper.

**Last-Ditch Homer**

The one-out, last-ditch homer spoiled a great Yankee rally which produced six runs in the seventh inning off Starting Pitcher Joe Coleman, the A's sore-armed right-hander.

As promised, Philadelphia Manager Connie Mack started Coleman, who hadn't won a game in 1950. Mack used Coleman against Detroit last week and the hurler was blasted for six runs in the first inning. The 87-year-old Mack said then he would start his onetime ace against New York.

| New York | AB | H | O | A | Phila'phia | AB | H | O | A |
|---|---|---|---|---|---|---|---|---|---|
| Woodling,lf | 5 | 2 | 4 | 0 | Lehner,lf | 5 | 1 | 5 | 0 |
| Rizzuto,ss | 5 | 0 | 2 | 2 | Valo,rf | 5 | 3 | 1 | 0 |
| Berra,c | 5 | 2 | 2 | 0 | Fain,1b | 3 | 2 | 10 | 1 |
| DiMaggio,cf | 3 | 0 | 2 | 0 | Chapman,cf | 5 | 1 | 2 | 0 |
| Mize,1b | 4 | 1 | 6 | 1 | Hitchc'k,2b | 4 | 0 | 3 | 5 |
| Ford,p(L) | 1 | 1 | 1 | 0 | Suder,3b | 4 | 2 | 0 | 1 |
| Brown,3b | 3 | 1 | 1 | 2 | Joost,ss | 4 | 1 | 3 | 5 |
| Johnson,3b | 1 | 0 | 0 | 0 | Tipton,c | 3 | 1 | 3 | 1 |
| Bauer,rf | 4 | 0 | 2 | 0 | J.Coleman,p | 3 | 0 | 0 | 0 |
| G.Cole'n,2b | 4 | 1 | 1 | 3 | Astroth | 0 | 0 | 0 | 0 |
| Lopat,p | 0 | 0 | 0 | 0 | Hoop'r,p(W) | 0 | 0 | 0 | 0 |
| Hopp,1b | 1 | 1 | 4 | 0 | | | | | |
| Totals | 36 | 9 | 25 | 8 | Totals | 36 | 11 | 27 | 13 |

One out when winning run scored.
Astroth walked for J. Coleman in 8th.

**SCORE BY INNINGS**

| | |
|---|---|
| New York | 000 100 600—7 |
| Philadelphia | 401 000 102—8 |

E—Rizzuto, Suder, Johnson. RBI—Hitchcock, Suder, 3; Joost, Chapman, 2; Berra, 4; Woodling, 2; Mize. 2B—Hopp. HR—Suder, Berra, 2; Mize, Chapman. DP—Mize to Rizzuto to Mize; Joost to Hitchcock to Fain; Joost to Hitchcock to Fain to Tipton. LOB—New York, 8; Philadelphia, 7. BB—Lopat, 2; Ford, 2; Coleman, 6. SO—By Lopat, 1; Coleman, 2. Hits—Off Lopat, 8 in 6 innings; Coleman, 8 in 8; Ford, 3 in 2⅓; Hooper, 1 in 1. Winner—Hooper (15-10). Loser—Ford (9-1). Umpires—McKinley, McGowan and Passarella. Time—2h. 23m. Attendance—2418.

## They Never Come Back--- Dempsey Knows

BY FRANK FINCH

Take it from the man who tried—and came within a whisker of doing it—they never come back.

Contentedly puffing on a perfecto in the quiet of his Santa Monica home, far from the madding throng at Yankee Stadium, Jack Dempsey listened on the radio last night while another former heavyweight champion tried to come back . . . tried and failed.

What vivid memories must have flashed through the old Manassa Mauler's mind . . . memories of how he had Gene Tunney down, and almost out, in the seventh round of their memorable "long-count" rematch in Chicago in 1927, a year after

Turn to Page 3, Column 3

## Ike Williams May Fight Davis Here

There was considerable long distance telephone buzzing yesterday between here and the East following John L. Davis' thrilling 12-round victory over Art Aragon Tuesday night at the Olympic.

Matchmaker Babe McCoy, more than satisfied with the Oakland Negro's terrific showing against the game Golden Boy, opened negotiations to match the State lightweight champion against World Titleholder Ike Williams.

If the match can be made, McCoy said he would stage the 15-round affair at the Olympic. Davis has already agreed to fight "for peanuts" just to get a chance at the crown.

## Gonzales Gains London Finals

LONDON, Sept. 27 (AP)—Pancho Gonzales, former American champion, reached the finals of the World Indoor Tennis Championships at Wembley today by beating Don Budge, 4-6, 6-1, 6-2, 6-2.

Gonzales will meet Welby Van Horn in the all-American final. Van Horn upset Bobby Riggs, 6-4, 2-6, 6-2, 6-3, in the other semi-final.

WHAMMO—Ezzard Charles, left, displays pain after Challenger Joe Louis cuffed him during 10th round of last night's title fight. Both Charles and Louis sported puffed left eyes which were closed at bout's end. (AP) Wirephoto

## Ex-Champion Badly Beaten in Title Go

**Cincinnati Boxer, 5-8½ Underdog, Wins Before 22,357**

YANKEE STADIUM, New York, Sept. 27 (AP)—Ezzard Charles, a much greater fighter than the world had thought he was, battered Joe Louis, the old champion, into bloody, helpless defeat tonight to prove once again that they never come back.

At the close of 15 savage rounds before 22,357 fans in Yankee Stadium the once peerless dark destroyer was so badly beaten that it appeared doubtful he could have answered more than another bell or two.

The unanimous decision of the two judges and Referee Mark Conn was only a formality after the two weary warriors had embraced at the finish. The Associated Press score card credited Charles with 12 rounds, gave Louis only two and called one even.

Louis, trying to regain at 36 the crown he wore for nearly 12 years before he retired in March of 1949, was completely unable to cope with the slender, relentless slasher from Cincinnati who was an 8¼-to-5 underdog in betting.

Toward the end, Charles, who conceded 33¾ pounds to the old Bomber, was trying for a knockout and Louis at times looked as though he might not weather the storm, though he never ceased to try to fight back.

**Sad Finish**

It was a sad finish for the once great champion in the eyes of the thousands who had seen him at the height of his ring glory. His left eye was pounded shut and blood poured from his nose as, in the 14th round, he held momentarily to the top rope and appeared uncertain whether he could continue.

Charles' left orb was sealed for the last five rounds, too, but he never ceased to bore in and batter the veteran who had sought to win back his title where such greats of the past as Bob Fitzsimmons, Jim Corbett, Jim Jeffries, Jack Dempsey and Max Schmeling had failed.

**Proves World Rating**

Charles, holder of the National Boxing Association version of world championship since he defeated Jersey Joe Walcott last summer, proved his claim to universal recognition. The confidence he gained tonight will make him a tough man to deprive of the bauble at any near future date.

Although scaling only 184¼ to Louis' 218, he met the issue squarely from the first bell, carried the fight to Joe most of the way and never flinched even when, on two occasions, Louis clipped him solidly and obviously hurt him.

Twice Ezzard was in trouble, in the fourth and 10th rounds. In the fourth Joe caught him flush with a left-right to the head and buckled his knees in the first 30 seconds but Charles survived the ensuing onslaught and was fighting back fiercely before the bell.

**Slow Reflexes**

Joe had his second and last chance in the 10th, which he won by a wide margin. He staggered the champion with a short right to the face at the outset of the round and dealt him a brutal beating from there until the bell as the crowd yelled madly for a knockout. But Joe could never corner his man and set him up for the one big, finish punch and the opportunity never came his way again.

There was no denying that

Turn to Page 3, Column 4

### Joe Says He's Through

NEW YORK, Sept. 27 (UP)—Joe Louis announced tonight that he would never fight again.

"I definitely am through," Louis said. "No more for me."

## TODAY IN SPORTS

**BASEBALL** — Sacramento vs. Hollywood, Gilmore Field, 8:15 p.m.

**HORSE RACING**—Pomona, 12:30 p.m.

**AMATEUR BOXING**—Wilmington Bowl, 8:30 p.m.

PART 4 **Los Angeles Times** SPORTS

VOL. LXX CC MONDAY MORNING, DECEMBER 25, 1950 Read Times Green for Latest Sports

# BROWNS EDGE RAMS, 30-28, TO WIN TITLE

**THAT DID IT**—Players from both teams stare with mixed emotions as ball (not shown) sails high between uprights to give Cleveland 30-28 victory over Los Angeles yesterday and National League crown. Browns' Lou Groza kicked the field goal from 16-yard line in final 20 seconds. (AP) Wirephoto

## Browns Offer Thanks After Thrilling Win

### Players Wouldn't Admit They Were Licked, Says Coach

**CLEVELAND, Dec. 24 (AP) The Cleveland Browns trooped into the dressing room after today's 30-28 victory over the Los Angeles Rams, and Capt. Tony Adamle called for silence.**

"Fellows," he said, "this is Christmas Eve. We have plenty to be thankful for. I don't believe we won this ball game all by ourselves.

"Let's pause for a minute of silence, during which I'd like to have each of you offer thanks, and a little prayer, each in his own way."

The squad, with bowed heads, responded.

**Buzz Starts**

As the boys lifted their heads and started stripping off their soiled uniforms, the hubbub started.

Tackle Coach Wilbur (Weeb) Ewbank roared:

"These kids just wouldn't admit they were licked."

And that remark just about wrapped up the sentiment of everyone who saw the four-time All-America Conference champs come back with a field goal in the last 20 seconds to subdue the magnificently equipped Rams for the national pro championship.

"This one will be remembered a long time," an emotionally exhausted Paul Brown declared. The champions' coach added:

**Luck Helped**

"We're very proud. They're as good and game a team as we ever played. It took a little bit of luck to win one like that and we had it."

In the quiet, downhearted atmosphere of the Rams' dressing room, their star quarterback, Bob Waterfield, didn't want to talk about the game much. "Just one of those things," he said.

Out in the Rams' chartered bus, Coach Joe Stydahar shooed visitors away from his boys with "please let 'em alone." And Stydahar echoed Waterfield's comment: "It was just one of those things."

The Rams mentor said he did not consider the weather an important factor. It was 29 deg. and very windy.

"It was a helluva good ball club that beat us," Stydahar concluded.

Bert Bell, the NFL commissioner, called the contest "the greatest football game I ever saw."

In the packed press box veteran football writers watched the pigskin twirl from Groza's

Turn to Page 4, Column 8

## Groza's Field Goal in Last 20s. Decides Exciting Grid Battle

BY FRANK FINCH, Times Staff Representative

**CLEVELAND, Dec. 24—Lou (the Toe) Groza, a hulking 238-pound tackle who has pulled the Cleveland Browns out of many a tight spot in the past five seasons, kicked the most important field goal of his career today.**

With 29,751 frozen fans roaring encouragement, the Toe stood on the 16-yard line directly in front of the Los Angeles Rams' goal posts and booted the ball through the uprights to defeat the Rams, 30 to 28.

The clock showed only 20 seconds to play.

Thus, the Browns proved what they have been saying all along since the All-America Conference was organized in 1946 . . . that they are the best football team in the world.

For four years they dominated the AAC, winning four consecutive championships. By whipping the Rams today they gave conclusive proof of their greatness.

**Two-Time Hero**

Joe Stydahar, the losing coach, hit the nail on the head in the morgue-like silence of the Rams' dressing room after the game, when he said:

"The Browns simply refused to quit. You've got to hand it to a ball club like that."

Until Groza performed his heroics—last week he beat the New York Giants in the American Conference play-off with two field goals — the Rams looked like the better ball club.

Performing in 27-deg. weather accentuated by snow flurries, Bob Waterfield played his heart out to give Los Angeles the league championship which he once gave the Rams when they represented Cleveland in 1945.

But the Browns' pass master, Otto Graham, was even greater today. He threw four touchdown passes and was the game's leading runner with 99 yards in 12 tries.

While the Rams held Fullback Marion Motley to 9 yards in six attempts, they couldn't stop Graham and his great gang of receivers.

Dante Lavelli caught two of Otto's pitches for touchdowns, while Rex Bumgardner and Dub Jones snagged one apiece.

Waterfield actually outpassed his opponent on a yardage basis, but four of Bob's passes were intercepted. These proved extremely costly in the final analysis.

The Rams had no excuses. In the second quarter alone they blew three golden opportunities when deep in Brownie territory. Once they reached the 7, only to lose the ball on an interception. Again they drove to the 9, but Waterfield missed an attempted 16-yard field goal. Back they bounced once more but the plucky Browns took the ball away from them.

**Fast Lead**

The Rams raced to a 7-0 lead on the very first play of the game when Waterfield passed to Glenn Davis for 82 yards. And at other stages of the exciting game they held leads of 14-7, 14-13, 21-20, 28-20 and 28-27. But the Browns just wouldn't give up and their guttiness paid off.

Despite the condition of the field, all players but a few of Cleveland lineman wore cleats. The exceptions played in basketball shoes.

Before the game Referee Ronald Gibbs ordered the Rams to put new cleats on their shoes, charging that they had filed them down too sharply. Even with the blunted edges, they seemed to have little trouble with their footing.

Davis demonstrated that right off the bat. With the ball on the Ram 18 after the opening kick-

Turn to Page 4, Column 5

### Van's Injury Revealed

CLEVELAND, Dec. 24 — Everyone was wondering today why Norm Van Brocklin, the NFL's passing champion, didn't get into the game until the last play. It seems that the Ram quarterback suffered a broken rib on the third play of last Sunday's Bear-Ram play-off and Coach Joe Stydahar kept it a closely guarded secret until after today's game.

## Here's How Pros Divided Game Money

CLEVELAND, Dec. 24 (AP)—The financial breakdown on today's National Professional League championship game in which the Cleveland Browns defeated the Los Angeles Rams, 30 to 28:

Paid attendance—29,751.

Gross receipts (including about $45,000 for radio and television)—$157,078.

Taxes and rental—$27,074.37.

Game operating expenses—$21,043.38.

Net receipts—$108,960.25.

Total players' pool (70% of net)—$76,272.18.

Winning players' pool—$41,186.98.

Losing players' pool—$27,457.98.

Each winning player's share (approximate)—$1113.16.

Each losing player's share (approximate)—$686.42.

Pool for sectional second-place clubs (Chicago Bears and New York Giants)—$7627.22.

## THE SEASON'S GREETINGS

BY BRAVEN DYER

This is the day when 'round the world, the Yuletide spirit reigns,
So to our friends we herewith send the following refrains:
Bring happiness to all, our boys in far-off lands away,
And hope that peace is soon to come, we all devoutly pray.
Be sure your sleigh goes Bob Hope's way, and don't pass up Steve Royce;
A heavy sack for Dempsey, Jack, and gifts for Hollis Moyse.

**Make Christmas bright** and extra cheery for Edna and Sir Walt McCreery,
Grant peace and rest with all the best for those who may be weary.
Don't turn your back on Stanley Hack nor overlook Jim Boyle,
And if it's what they really need, bring Fran and Wesson oil.
Leave something green for Red McQueen and F. McGee and Molly,
With Stydahar the coaching star, leave mistletoe and holly.
Let no snow fall on Helmsman Paul, nor rain on Allan Lane,
And make the day complete and gay for Rose Queen Elly Payne.

**A TV set please** don't forget for the H. L. Hoffman man,
And anything he thinks he needs for little Goodman, Dan.
Smile on Frank and Mary Roche and Oosterbaan the football coach,
And Sanders, too, and Sailie, Lew, along with Supervisor Roach.
Bring nuts and bolts and gags and poodles to Comic Showman Weaver, Doodles;
To Chasen, Dave, and Wayne B. Cave, be sure to give them oodles.
Let anthems ring for Crooner Bing and Dixie and the boys
And Tyrus Cobb and Bob the Cobb and all the Jason Joys.

**Back up your sled** for Hal and Ed, two Pauleys you must know,
And if you have a little left, leave Doctor Strub some dough.
Load high your bag for Lonnie Stagg, keep Grable's stocking full,
A Christmas grand for Harry Brand and records for Frank Bull.
To Schroeder, Ted, and Clampett, Fred, send anything that's nice,
Just double that and tip your hat to Kate and Grantland Rice.
May Longden, J., have quite a day, and wifey Hazel, too,
While youthful lovebirds everywhere buzz-buzz and bill and coo.

**For Weinberg, Bernie,** and Pinckert, Erny, leave off some snazzy gift,
And please for Peg and Jeff Cravath provide some special lift.
Hang no halter on Sam Balter, nor throttle Groucho Marx,
Make all the carol singers sound like Grade A meadowlarks.
For Kelly, Mark, and Cromwell, Dean, a hearty Christmas hail,
And lighten just a little bit Mike Fanning's Christmas mail.
The turkey fatten for Mel Patton and bring Tex Maule a toddy;
Drop gifts galore on Earl Gilmore, don't overlook a body.

**Jump up and down** with Joe E. Brown and dance with Nancy Chaffee,
And when his gin looks mighty grim, let Sid Ziff throw a "safey."
The Donald Ayres and Golden Bears and Metro-Goldwyn's L. B. Mayers,
We wish a joyous day; for Noor and all the thoroughbreds an extra load of hay.
The Delmer Daves and Doyle Naves deserve to have you stop,
And so do Jane and Freddie Funk, along with Warner, Pop.
A Christmas spray send on its way to Giesler, Lawman Jerry;
Just stop and say hello to Jones, the guy's first name is Perry,
Don't be late to have a date with Kukla, Fran and Ollie;
Plant a kiss on Russell, Miss, and make her Robert jolly.

**For Haney, Fred,** Narleski, Ted, make things just peachy keen,
A Christmas sprig take from your rig for Biscailuz the Gene.
What Smiths I know deserve no woe, instead give them first prize;
Heap high their plates with nuts and dates, but please forget the ties.
Make Waldorf, Pappy, victory happy, we hope he halts Koceski,
While Berkeley fans tear down the stands with cheers for J. Olszewski.
For Stengel, Casey, and Spencer Tracy cook up some special deal,
And give to every hungry lad the very bestest meal.

**To Myers, Bob, and** the Redwood mob, some bottles tall uncork;
And for the girls who want it thus, a call from old Doc Stork.
Drop in and sit with Victor Schmidt and call on Gorgeous Gussy,
I know from past experience that she "ain't" the least bit fussy.
For Eaton, Cal, and pert Aileen whip up a light libation,
And at the track, to win some jack, the inside information.
If you have time along the line, be kind to Frankie King.
And if there's one who wants it bad, be sure to leave "The Thing."

**Let your reindeer** look and listen for Arcaro, Neves and Glisson,
While we bettors pray to Allah that their winners won't be missin'.
Leave some loot for Charley Root and also Crisler, Fritz,
We fans who saw that Rose Bowl game won't soon forget the blitz.
More trophies bright and shiny for Bill and Wifey Schroeder,
And to that duckman, H. Burrell, a sure-fire musket loader,
I've missed a lot of friends on whom I'd like St. Nick to call,
But space runs out, so I'll just shout—

"A MERRY CHRISTMAS ALL."

## Top Athletes Yet to Get Their Gifts

Some of the world's greatest athletes haven't received their Christmas presents as yet, but they'll get them Wednesday night at the Cocoanut Grove when the eighth annual Los Angeles Times National Sports Award dinner unfolds.

Top performers in every field of athletic endeavor will be honored and, true to tradition, their names will be withheld until the actual moment of the presentation.

The honored sportsmen were selected after a thorough and painstaking search by the Times board of selection—Dean Cromwell, Bill Schroeder, Ellsworth Vines, Casey Stengel, Braven Dyer and Paul Zimmerman.

**Hope in Charge**

As eagerly awaited as the announcement of the award winners is the entertainment portion of the program which features Bob Hope as master of ceremonies.

Hope's task will be a pleasant one. He'll introduce such great performers as Dinah Shore, the lovely vocalist from the deep South; Dennis Day, whose comic

Turn to Page 2, Column 8

## North and South Teams Mix Tonight

MIAMI, Fla., Dec. 24 (AP)—An estimated 45,000 football fans, 60 young grid stars and some 500 unpaid Shriners will converge on the Orange Bowl tomorrow night to contribute talent and dollars for a giant Christmas gift to crippled children.

A crowd of 40,000 or more is expected to see the contest, with proceeds going to the Shrine's crippled children fund.

Each 30-man squad will be seeking the edge in games. Miami Coach Andy Gustafson's eleven won the opener, 24-14, and Yale Coach Herman Hickman's North squad won last year, 20-14. This game is rated a tossup.

Each side boasts a glittering array of stars from more than a score of colleges in the South, East and Middle West.

The South will count on the passing of John (Model T) Ford of Hardin-Simmons, the running of John Dottley of Ole Miss and the receiving of C. P. Youmans of Duke.

Georgia Tech's Bobby Dodd, who has handled the South squad while Gustafson was busy preparing his University of Miami team for its Orange Bowl game with Clemson, also has a wealth of other material, in the backfield and on the line.

Hickman's starting backfield is expected to be made up of John Miller of Northwestern, Reds Bagnall of Pennsylvania, Stu Tisdale of Yale and Jeff Fleischmann of Cornell.

Others in the North's backfield squad include Frank Miller of Cornell, Jack Martin of Army, Dick Gabriel of Lehigh, James Cain of Army, Carl Taseff of John Carroll, Bill Dechard of Holy Cross, Bill Roberts of Dartmouth, Gil Stephenson of Army, Bob Radcliffe of Wisconsin and Dick Doheny of Fordham.

Hickman said he expected to substitute freely but would not use the two-platoon system.

| SOUTH | | NORTH |
|---|---|---|
| Youmans (Duke) | LE | Pfeifer (Ford.) |
| Hannah (Ala.) | LG | Monahan (Dart.) |
| Molberg (Tex. AM) | LT | Strasheim (Neb.) |
| Bradshaw (Geo.) | C | Root (Rutgers) |
| Greiner (Tex. AM) | RG | Janosek (Purdue) |
| Rakestaw (Tulsa) | RT | Huxhold (Wis.) |
| Stribling (Miss.) | RE | Minarik (Mich. St.) |
| Ford (Hard.-Sim.) | Q | Tisdale (Yale) |
| Lucia (Louis.) | LH | Bagnell (Penn.) |
| Stinson (Kansas) | RH | Miller (N.W.) |
| Dottley (Miss.) | F | Fleischmann (Cor.) |

### Prep Hurler Pitches No-Hitter for Paramount

Bill Sperling, a right-hander from Bell High School, pitched a no-hit, no-run game for the Paramount Pirates over Long Beach yesterday at the Sawtelle diamond. The score was 7-0.

In mastering the beach nine, Sperling chalked up 17 strikeouts.

| | | R | H | E |
|---|---|---|---|---|
| Long Beach ....... | 000 000 000- | 0 | 0 | 0 |
| Paramount | 311 001 10x— | 7 | 12 | 2 |

Johnson; Sperling and Truitt

**RAMMING IT OVER**—Dick Hoerner (31), Los Angeles fullback, drives 3 yards for second touchdown against Cleveland yesterday. Rams' Tom Fears (55) is at left. Browns' No. 50 is Jim Martin. Cleveland won, 30-28.

STYDAHAR PRAISED

## Greatest Game I've Ever Seen, Says Bell

CLEVELAND, Dec. 24 (AP)—Commissioner Bert Bell of the National Pro Football League—a player, coach and commissioner for two score years—pulled no punches today as he termed the Cleveland Browns' 30-28 victory over the Los Angeles Rams "the greatest football game I've ever seen."

"In Los Angeles," the commissioner said, "we probably have the finest personnel any professional club ever boasted. But in the Cleveland Browns we probably have the most intensively coached club in history.

**'Extra Something'**

"This was an instance in which a magnificently coached club, which just wouldn't give up, overcame great opposition. The Browns overlook no detail in coaching or preparation for a game—they are ready for anything and they have that extra something of which champions are made.

"I would like to pay tribute to Joe Stydahar, the Los Angeles coach, who did a great job in his first year as head of the Rams. He did an outstanding job and we'll be hearing from him in the future. It was unfortunate that one of these two truly great teams had to lose."

Coach Paul Brown of the victors, answering scribes who wondered why the Browns didn't go for a touchdown in the waning 20 seconds, said:

"We had the ball, with a first down, on the Rams' 12, but the clock was running out. We have the greatest place-kicker in the world in Lou Groza. So we sent in word to run one play to the right, with Quarterback Otto Graham handling the ball, to get it right in front of the goal posts. Otto did a good job of it, and Lou booted the ball for the three points we needed, and that was the ball game. We felt we could hold the Rams after the kickoff—but our big need was those three points.

**Praises Coach**

"And speaking of those three points, I'd like to pay tribute to Ernie Godfrey of Ohio State, the finest teacher of place kicking I've ever known. Ernie taught Lou the art of place-kicking when Groza was a freshman at Ohio State, and I'll be eternally grateful to him for it.

"I would say, in the face of Lou's two place kicks which beat the New York Giants last week, and his game-winning kick today, that Ernie had a lot to do with Cleveland winning the pro championship. Ernie is just the best there is at teaching a youngster the place-kicking art."

Groza, after learning to place kick under Godfrey's tutelage, entered the service and then joined the Browns on his return, passing up a collegiate career.

### TODAY IN SPORTS

**WRESTLING** — Pasadena Arena, 8:30 p.m.

Paul Zimmerman
Sports Editor

# Los Angeles Times

SPORTS

6 PART II CC SUNDAY MORNING, JULY 15, 1951 VOL. LXX

# CITATION WINS GOLD CUP TO PASS MILLION

THE WINNER—Citation crosses finish four lengths ahead in 10-horse field in $100,000 Gold Cup at Hollywood Park yesterday. Bewitch, Calumet Farm stablemate, finished fast on outside to edge out Be Fleet for second place.
Times photo by Larry Sharkey

## SPORTS PARADE

By BRAVEN DYER

Seldom have I known a more dramatic story than the rescue of Ted Sierks at sea after having been tossed overboard en route to Honolulu.

When more than 24 hours had elapsed without any sign of the missing yachtsman, the odds were 100 to 1 that he'd never be recovered alive.

Thanks to the vigilance of the United States Navy and a lifetime aquatic training at Catalina. Ted today is basking on the beach at Waikiki and all his friends are thanking a merciful Providence for his astounding rescue.

**LONGTIME FRIENDS**

We of The Times have been pretty close to Ted and other members of his family for many years. His mother, Alma Overholt, has handled publicity from Avalon for the Wrigley interests ever since I can remember.

Ted not only assisted her, but also gained world-wide attention as a photographer . . . his knowledge of the ocean enabling him to take many unusual pictures.

Ted's younger sister Bobbie married Jack Singer, who wrote sports for The Times for many years. The minister who performed the ceremony is my father, Dr. Frank Dyer.

My memory being what it is, I wasn't sure who was Singer's best man. I thought it was Ted, so I called Alma for verification.

**GAVE BRIDE AWAY**

"Why, let me see," said Mrs. Overholt, "the best man was . . . why, you were the best man yourself. Ted gave the bride away."

Yes, that was it. In December of 1936, young Jack Singer and cute Bobbie Sierks were married in a swank Beverly Hills ceremony.

Jack lost his life in World War II. He was a correspondent for the International News Service when his ship, the aircraft carrier Wasp, was blown up in South Pacific waters . . . perhaps not far from where Ted slipped overboard last week.

Nobody could be happier over Ted's rescue than Bobbie, because, you see, she was on the yacht with him for this Honolulu race. And the swirling waters of the blue Pacific already marked the grave of one member of her family. The loss of Ted would have added another tragic chapter to the story of Bobbie Sierks and her loved ones.

**SAD, SAD STORY**

Speaking of sad stories which might have been, I'm reminded of a little literary effort I saw the other day. There was no official title to it, but it could be called "Ode to the Tax Collector" or "What Truman Is Doing to My Pocketbook." Goes like this:

"Tax the farmer, tax his fowl;
"Tax the dog and tax his howl.
"Tax the pig and tax his squeal;
"Tax his boots run down at heel.
"Tax his home and tax his bed;
"Tax the bald spot on his head.
"Tax his cow and tax her calf;
"Tax him if he dares to laugh;
"He is but a common man,
"So tax the cuss just all you can.
"Tax the lab'rer, but be discreet;
"Tax him for walking in the street.
"Tax his bread and tax his meat;
"Tax the shoes clear off his feet.
"Tax his pipe and tax his smoke;
"Teach him government is no joke.
"Tax the living, tax the dead;
"Tax the unborn before they're fed.
"Tax the water, tax the air;
"Tax the sunlight if you dare.
"Tax them all and tax them well;
"Do your best to make life h . . . ."

—AND STILL CHAMPION—Citation, loaded with flowers and Jockey Steve Brooks, stands in winner's circle as 50,625 fans give him tremendous ovation. Assisting in ceremonies, from left, are Mrs. Brooks and daughter; Lt. Gov. Goodwin Knight, Mrs. Jimmy Jones and Jimmy Jones, who trained Big Cy for his historic triumph.
Times photo

## Calumet Champion Four-Length Victor

### Bewitch Catches Be Fleet at Wire to Take Second Before 50,625 Fans

BY PAUL LOWRY

Citation reached the end of the $1,000,000 trail the easy way before a wildly cheering throng of 50,625 at Hollywood Park yesterday.

He ran away and hid from a field of nine rivals, including two of his own stablemates, in the $100,000 Gold Cup and sent his earnings skyrocketing to $1,085,760. Citation took command before he reached the half-mile pole, and the race was over right there.

He wasn't the Citation of old, but he was good enough yesterday to win the mile and one-quarter classic by four lengths and become the first horse in turf history to pass the six-figure mark in money totals.

Closest to him at the finish was his own running mate Bewitch. The little brown butterball of a mare caught Be Fleet in the last jump Alderman was fourth.

**Run One-Two**

Citation and Bewitch ran one-two in the American Handicap on the Fourth of July, and their repeat performance in the Gold Cup brought both of them immortal turf fame and glory.

For while Citation was going over the top Bewitch was doing likewise. Her secondary award of $20,000 makes her the greatest money-winning mare in history. She displaced Gallorette, who had $445,535. Bewitch's total is $462,605, and she is now eighth on the list of the world's leaders.

With 120 pounds on his back and Steve Brooks in the saddle Citation raced the Gold Cup distance in 2:01 flat. Noor's track record is 1:59-4/5.

The Calumet entry of Citation, Bewitch and All Blue was the 1-to-3 favorite of the crowd and paid $2.70, $2.40 and $2.10 across the board.

**Full of Drama**

It was a day full of drama and thrills. The huge crowd cheered Citation when he was led into the paddock to be saddled. They cheered some more when the big bay horse, his ears pricked and his nerves atune to the spirit of the occasion, arched his neck as he walked on the track. And they roared a deafening salute when he hit the wire in front.

For Trainer Jimmy Jones, who twice has patiently forged comebacks for Citation, it was a moment he will never forget.

"I guess I can probably say in all truth that this day has provided the greatest thrill of my life," said Jones after the race.

"He reached the peak of his Hollywood Park campaign today, but I don't know that he will get any better. He's not the Citation of old. He's six years old, you know.

**Citation's Future**

"We don't plan to retire him immediately as it would seem very foolish when he's as good as he is right now. There is a chance he may run in the Sunset Handicap next Saturday and probably once in Chicago. We might also point him for the Jockey Club Gold Cup in New York. Then he will be retired for good to enter stud in 1952."

Lt. Gov. Goodwin Knight crowned Big Cy in the winner's circle.

Adding color to the occasion a big gold blanket was thrown over Citation as he was leaving the winner's circle. It read:

**Citation**
**First Thoroughbred Millionaire**
**Hollywood Gold Cup—1951**

If Citation had finished second it had been planned to present him with the blanket in a special ceremony following the honoring of the winner. Even the secondary award would have made the son of Bull Lea and Hydroplane II a millionaire. If Citation had failed to win first

Turn to Page 11, Column 6

## BOSOX CLIP CHISOX AGAIN ON VOLLMER'S HIT IN 9TH, 3-2

CHICAGO, July 14 (AP)—The Boston Red Sox's money player, Clyde Vollmer, paid off again today with a two-run ninth-inning single for a 3-2 win over the Chicago White Sox in the finale of a torrid four-game set. Their third victory in as many days moved the first-place Red Sox a full game in front of the White Sox.

The fourth straight one-run decision of the crucial series came as the White Sox failed to score against Lefty Charley Stobbs after filling the bases with two out in the ninth. Chicago scored its only runs in the second.

**Sizzling Race**

It was Stobbs' first win of the season over the White Sox. He scattered six hits for his seventh victory against three defeats—all notched against him by the Pale Hose.

The triumph gave the Red Sox a 50-30 record for a .625 percentage, while the White Sox nestled into a .610 second-place rating with 50-32 after starting today's game only three percentage points behind the Red Sox.

**Ted Socks One**

Vollmer's line single to left after Bobby Doerr had singled and Billy Goodman doubled in the ninth won the game. It was the sixth time the big flychaser produced the winning punch for Boston in the last seven games.

Boston's first run today was on Ted Williams' 17th homer in the fourth.

It was a heartbreaking defeat for the White Sox, who showed signs of repeating their great comeback for a 19-inning, 5-4 win last night. They filled the bases in the ninth. But Stobbs wasn't to be denied.

| Boston | AB | H | O | A | Chicago | AB | H | O | A |
|---|---|---|---|---|---|---|---|---|---|
| DiMaggio,cf | 5 | 0 | 4 | 0 | Dillinger,3b | 4 | 0 | 1 | 2 |
| Pesky,ss | 2 | 1 | 2 | 5 | Baker,3b | 1 | 0 | 0 | 0 |
| Williams,lf | 4 | 1 | 4 | 0 | Fox,2b | 2 | 1 | 3 | 6 |
| Stephens,3b | 3 | 0 | 3 | 1 | Minoso,rf-lf | 4 | 1 | 2 | 0 |
| Doerr,2b | 4 | 1 | 2 | 2 | Haas,1b | 4 | 0 | 10 | 2 |
| Goodman,1b | 4 | 2 | 7 | 1 | Lenhardt,lf | 3 | 0 | 1 | 0 |
| Vollmer,rf | 3 | 1 | 1 | 0 | Zarilla,rf | 1 | 0 | 0 | 0 |
| Moss,c | 4 | 1 | 4 | 0 | Busby,cf | 3 | 1 | 2 | 0 |
| Stobbs,p | 2 | 1 | 0 | 1 | Masi,c | 1 | 0 | 1 | 0 |
| | | | | | Niarhos,c | 3 | 1 | 2 | 1 |
| | | | | | Carrasq'l,ss | 3 | 2 | 5 | 2 |
| | | | | | Holcombe,p | 1 | 0 | 0 | 2 |
| | | | | | Robinson | 0 | 0 | 0 | 0 |
| Totals | 31 | 8 | 27 | 10 | Totals | 30 | 6 | 27 | 15 |

Robinson walked for Holcombe in 9th.

SCORE BY INNINGS

Boston ........................000 100 002—3
Chicago .......................002 000 000—2

RBI—Minoso, 2; Williams, Vollmer, 2. 2B—Fox, Minoso, Goodman. HR—Williams. SB—Stephens, Carrasquel. SH—Holcombe, 2; Stobbs. DP—Carrasquel to Haas; Haas to Carrasquel to Haas, Doerr to Pesky to Goodman; Dillinger to Fox to Haas. LOB—Boston, 7; Chicago, 8. BB—Off Stobbs, 4; Holcombe, 5. SO—By Stobbs, 3; Holcombe, 2. HB—By Stobbs (Fox). WP—Stobbs. Winner—Stobbs (7-3). Loser—Holcombe (7-5). Umpires—Soar, Hubbard, Rommel and Paparella. Time—2h. 23m. Attendance—27,092.

## Big Cy Heaves Sigh of Relief, Counts Dough

BY JACK GEYER

Citation, the first horse in history who can stamp his footprint on a check for $1,000,000 without having it bounce, relaxed with a few old friends over a bowl of oats following his 4-length victory in the $100,000 Added Gold Cup yesterday.

There are people who say they never come back and there are others who say you can't take it with you. Citation, the 6-year-old Calumet charger, did both yesterday.

Old Cy didn't stand on ceremony.

**Gracious Host**

"Come in, come in," he said when your reporter knocked on the stable door.

Pushing aside some bags probably filled with gold, Citation gestured with his forefoot.

"Sit down. Don't sit on those five dollar bills. Too hard. Try that pile of twenties. Be comfortable."

"How does it feel, Citation," your reporter asked, brushing aside an impulse to call him Mr. Citation, "How does it feel to be the world's first equine millionaire?"

**Races Left**

"I suppose I could be corny and say it ain't hay," said Cy, "but I won't. It feels great. It looked like a million miles to that million until Steve Brooks moved me ahead at the half mile

Turn to Page 11, Column 5

## Stanley Loses 5-Up Lead, Wins Title on 38th Hole

MILWAUKEE, July 14 (AP)—Twenty-year-old Dave Stanley, the Los Angeles collegian, won the National Public Links Golf title today on his first try, but he had to go 38 holes to do it—the longest trek a fee course champ has ever made.

The youngster had a 5-hole bulge on Ralph Vranesic, Denver government worker, when they started out on what should have been the final 9 holes over Brown Deer Park's tree-bordered fairways.

But Vranesic, who had scrambled and scurried through most of the previous 27 holes, suddenly brought out a red hot putter. He 1-putted 5 greens—and the match was square for one of the greatest comebacks in history. Stanley, tiring badly and starting to tighten, didn't win a hole as they came in.

**Misses Easy Putt**

The kid, No. 1 man on the UCLA golf team as a sophomore last spring, apparently had the championship on the first extra hole. He was lying 3 with an 18-inch putt, but blew it and they started for No. 38 still even.

Both were in the rough on their second shots at the 425-yard hole. Vranesic's chip scooted 30 feet past the cup, but Stanley's settled down 18 inches away, the same as on the hole before. This time, though, he didn't miss, and won the cham-

Turn to Page 10, Column 8

## BROWNS SIGN SATCH PAIGE

ST. LOUIS, July 14 (U.P.)—Leroy (Satchel) Paige, the ancient Negro pitcher who has played exhibition and organized baseball longer than most fans care to remember, came to terms with the St. Louis Browns today.

Paige and Bill Veeck, new Browns' owner, agreed on terms of a contract late today. A Browns' spokesman said the contract would be signed Monday and Paige would join the club then.

## HOW THEY STAND IN PCL, MAJORS

**PACIFIC COAST LEAGUE**

| | W | L | Pct. | * |
|---|---|---|---|---|
| Seattle | 67 | 42 | .615 | |
| HOLLYWOOD | 63 | 47 | .573 | 4½ |
| LOS ANGELES | 54 | 54 | .500 | 12½ |
| Sacramento | 55 | 56 | .495 | 13 |
| Oakland | 54 | 58 | .482 | 14½ |
| Portland | 53 | 58 | .477 | 15 |
| San Diego | 47 | 62 | .431 | 20 |
| San Francisco | 46 | 62 | .426 | 20½ |

Yesterday's Results

LOS ANGELES, 8; Sacramento, 2.
HOLLYWOOD, 4; Portland, 2.
San Diego, 8; Oakland, 3.
San Francisco at Seattle, incomplete.

Games Today
(All double-headers)

Sacramento (Clough, 8-5, and Gillespie, 6-7) vs. LOS ANGELES (Lade, 2-3, and Moisan, 5-7), Wrigley Field, 1:30 p.m.

HOLLYWOOD (Lindell, 8-5, and Hood, 7-5) at Portland (Pieretti, 10-11, and Helser, 6-7).

San Francisco at Seattle.

San Diego at Oakland.

**NATIONAL LEAGUE**

| | W | L | Pct. | * |
|---|---|---|---|---|
| Brooklyn | 52 | 28 | .650 | |
| St. Louis | 42 | 36 | .538 | 9 |
| New York | 44 | 38 | .537 | 9 |
| Cincinnati | 38 | 38 | .500 | 12 |
| Philadelphia | 38 | 41 | .481 | 13½ |
| Boston | 34 | 42 | .447 | 16 |
| Chicago | 32 | 41 | .431 | 16½ |
| Pittsburgh | 31 | 47 | .397 | 20 |

*Games behind leader.

Yesterday's Results

Chicago, 5-11; Brooklyn, 4-7.
St. Louis, 4; New York, 3.
Cincinnati, 5; Boston, 0.
Philadelphia, 2; Pittsburgh, 0.

Games Today

Chicago (Rush, 5-4, and Klippstein, 4-4) at Boston (Spahn, 8-8, and Nichols, 4-3).

Cincinnati (Ramsdell, 6-9, and Blackwell, 8-7) at Brooklyn (Roe, 12-1, and Schmitz, 1-3).

Pittsburgh (Friend, 3-5, and Werle, 5-1) at New York (Maglie, 12-4, and Hearn, 7-5).

St. Louis (Poholsky, 4-6, and Brecheen, 5-1) at Philadelphia (Heintzelman, 3-8, and Johnson, 0-0).

**AMERICAN LEAGUE**

| | W | L | Pct. | * |
|---|---|---|---|---|
| Boston | 50 | 30 | .625 | |
| Chicago | 50 | 32 | .610 | 1 |
| New York | 46 | 31 | .597 | 2½ |
| Cleveland | 46 | 33 | .582 | 3½ |
| Detroit | 35 | 40 | .467 | 12½ |
| Washington | 33 | 45 | .423 | 16 |
| Philadelphia | 32 | 49 | .395 | 18½ |
| St. Louis | 23 | 55 | .295 | 26 |

*Games behind leader.

Yesterday's Results

Boston, 3; Chicago, 2.
Washington, 8; Detroit, 0.
Cleveland, 8; New York, 0.
Philadelphia, 10; St. Louis, 6.

Games Today

Philadelphia (Hooper, 3-7, and Zoldak, 2-3) at Chicago (Judson, 3-1, and Gumpert, 7-2).

Boston (Scarborough, 5-4, and Nixon, 6-1) at St. Louis (Kennedy, 1-4, and Garver, 11-4).

New York (Kuzava, 5-4, and Morgan, 3-1) at Detroit (Bearden, 2-1, and Hutchinson, 7-3).

Washington (Hudson, 3-5, and Marrero, 8-5) at Cleveland (Chakales, 3-2, and Garcia, 10-6).

## HIS FIRST MILLION

9759—SEVENTH RACE—MILE AND ONE-QUARTER. For 3-year-olds up. Hollywood Gold Cup. Purse $100,000 added. Net to winner (guaranteed), $100,000; second, $20,000; third, $10,000; fourth, $5000.

| Index | Horse. | Owner. | Wt. | PP. | St. | ¼ | ¾ | M | Str. | Fin. | Jockey. | Odds $1 |
|---|---|---|---|---|---|---|---|---|---|---|---|---|
| (9695) | a-Citation | (Calumet Farm) | 120 | 10 | 6 | 3 1½ | 7 h | 1 2 | 1 3 | 1 4 | Brooks | .35 |
| (9719) | a-Bewitch | (Calumet Farm) | 108 | 4 | 7 | 7 1½ | 7 4 | 5 1 | 4 h | 2no | Lasswell | .35 |
| 9695 | Be Fleet | (A. J. Crevolin) | 122 | 8 | 2 | 2 1 | 3 2 | 2 h | 2 h | 3 1 | Shoemaker | 12.45 |
| 9695 | Alderman | (Brel Stable) | 104 | 3 | 9 | 8 h | 8 2 | 8 h | 8 2 | 4nk | [illegible] | 18.15 |
| 9695 | Sturdy One | (Mr.-Mrs. F. Phelps) | 109 | 1 | 5 | 5 4 | 5 1 | 4 1 | 5 1½ | 5no | Neves | 12.15 |
| 9695 | Sudan | (C. Mooers) | 107 | 7 | 8 | 9 h | 9 2 | 9 1 | 7 h | 6 1½ | Glisson | 52.95 |
| 9695 | a-All Blue | (Calumet Farm) | 112 | 6 | 1 | 1 2 | 2 1 | 3 1 | 3 1 | 7nk | Balaski | .35 |
| 8799 | Lotowhite | (T. G. Benson) | 117 | 9 | 10 | 10 | 10 | 10 | 9 1 | 8nk | Longden | 16.35 |
| 9663 | Akimbo | (Brazan Stable) | 104 | 5 | 4 | 6 1 | 6 h | 7 2 | 6 h | 9 1½ | [illegible] | 31.95 |
| (9727) | Tantamount | (Silver Creek Ranch) | 103 | 2 | 3 | 4 h | 4 2 | 6 h | 10 | 10 | P. Moreno | 10.50 |

a—Calumet Farm entry.

Time, :23 2-5, :46 4-5, 1:10 3-5, 1:35 3-5, 2:01. Went to post at 5:22½, off at 5:23. Start good, from gate, won ridden out, second and third driving. Winner, b.h., 6, by Bull Lea—Hydroplane II. Trained by H. A. Jones. Overweight—All Blue, 1 pound, Tantamount, 2; Alderman, 1; Akimbo, 1. Mutuel pool, $852,963.

Two-dollar mutuels paid: a-CITATION, 2.70, 2.40, 2.10; a-BEWITCH, 2.40, 2.10; BE FLEET, 4.10.

CITATION, racing as if best, broke from outside, was allowed to drift toward rail in run to first turn while under light restraint, moved into contention on the clubhouse turn, moved up boldly to take command nearing half-mile pole and drawing clear was never in danger thereafter and won as rider pleased, although Brooks elected to hustle him along to wire. BEWITCH lacked early speed, was steadied early, began to move from far turn while losing some ground and although unable to threaten winner outfinished BE FLEET. Latter had early speed, was under pressure throughout and under hard riding through stretch held on stubbornly. ALDERMAN had no mishaps and was not too far away in a good effort. STURDY ONE was on inside much of the way, was shaken up at far turn and under the whip through the stretch also finished with courage. LOTOWHITE was never serious contender. ALL BLUE was used up setting early pace and had little left for the final drive. TANTAMOUNT was through early. AKIMBO could not keep up. No scratches.

PART 4 **Los Angeles Times** SPORTS

VOL. LXX CC THURSDAY MORNING, OCTOBER 4, 1951 Read The Times for Latest Sports

# YANKS FAVORED TO WIN WORLD SERIES

## SPORT SCRIPTS

By PAUL ZIMMERMAN
TIMES SPORTS EDITOR

Thursday's sport thoughts.

Those newspaper lads on the Helms Board who picked Bill Mais on the All-CIF team four years when he was at St. Anthony's, Long Beach, are happy that Coach Pappy Waldorf of California now has discovered him, too.

Mais was fourth-string quarterback at Berkeley last year . . . He was John Olszewski's signal caller and close friend at Long Beach . . . Olszewski refused to go to California unless Mais likewise was invited . . . Six or seven other St. Anthony lads followed . . . Including John Peterson and Dean O'Hare, halfbacks . . . Where are the rest?

Santa Clara has not lost a football game in Los Angeles since 1946 . . . That was the year the Broncos returned to football under Len Casanova . . . And dropped a 33-to-7 game to the Bruins . . . They upset an unbeaten Uclan eleven here in 1949, 14 to 0 . . . And went on to an Orange Bowl victory.

**TAKE ANOTHER PEEP**

If you're still high on the chances of Southern California over Washington Saturday, take another look at the national and Pacific Coast Conference statistics . . . Huskies set the PCC pace in passing and total offense . . . And are second in rushing and punt returns . . . Nationally they're second in passing and sixth in total offense . . .

Florida's quarterback, Haywood Sullivan, is 12th in the nation in pass completions with 46.7% . . . His Saturday night opponent, Don Klosterman of Loyola, is eight steps higher with a 50.7 average.

Frank Gifford of Troy is 12th in the nation on rushing, with 217 yards in 36 trips . . . UCLA's sophomore, Paul Cameron, stands 15th with 308 yards in 49 gallops . . .

**LARGE LIST**

A large list of Coast gridsters made the grade in the National Football League this fall . . . Eighteen in all . . . Start with Bob Moser, 245-pound College of Pacific center with the Chicago Bears . . . The Yanks have Al Pollard of Loyola and Army . . . Breck Stroschein, former UCLA tackle, now an end . . . And Jim Cullom, California tackle.

Two Westerners are with Detroit . . . They are LaVern Torgeson, Washington State center, and Dick Stanfel, USF guard . . . Dick has been on the injured list since the All-Star game . . . Add three with the Rams . . . Leon McLaughlin, UCLA center, Tom Dahms, San Diego State tackle, and Dick Daugherty, Oregon guard, make up this trio.

**SHAW GOT FIVE**

Those very much alive San Francisco Forty Niners grabbed off five . . . Bill Jessup, end, is the lone Trojan . . . Halfbacks Pete Schabarum and Jim Monachino of California Rose Bowl fame are on hand . . . Jim also has been hurt since the Chicago game in mid-August . . . Stanford's Halfback Bob White and Bill Wilson, San Jose State end, likewise grace Coach Buck Shaw's squad.

Loyola apparently has performed the hat trick by landing three with the Redskins . . . Gene Brito, end, and a pair of halfbacks, Neil Ferris and Jack Dwyer, are holding forth with Washington . . . Last, but not least, is that big Bruin end, Bob Wilkinson, with the Giants.

**HEAR AND THEIR**

Ed Powell, UCLA assistant to Johnny Wooden, and Sax Elliott, former Trojan captain now with Los Angeles State, are reported to be top candidates for the Oregon basketball coaching assignment . . . A real star with San Jose State this fall is Lynn Aplanalp, former Pasadena City College star . . . He completed 8 of 13 passes against Stanford for 82 yards.

James Lynah, former chairman of the NCAA sanity code panel, is urging that recruiting and subsidization of athletes be taken away from the coaches . . . He would put this privilege in the hands of conference commissioners . . . And the schools would requisition players from him by positions . . . Without regard to where the prep star might want to go.

**P.S.** So a chap desiring to take law could, instead, wind up taking animal husbandry at some agricultural college.

### TODAY IN SPORTS

**WRESTLING** — Long Beach Auditorium 8:30 p.m.

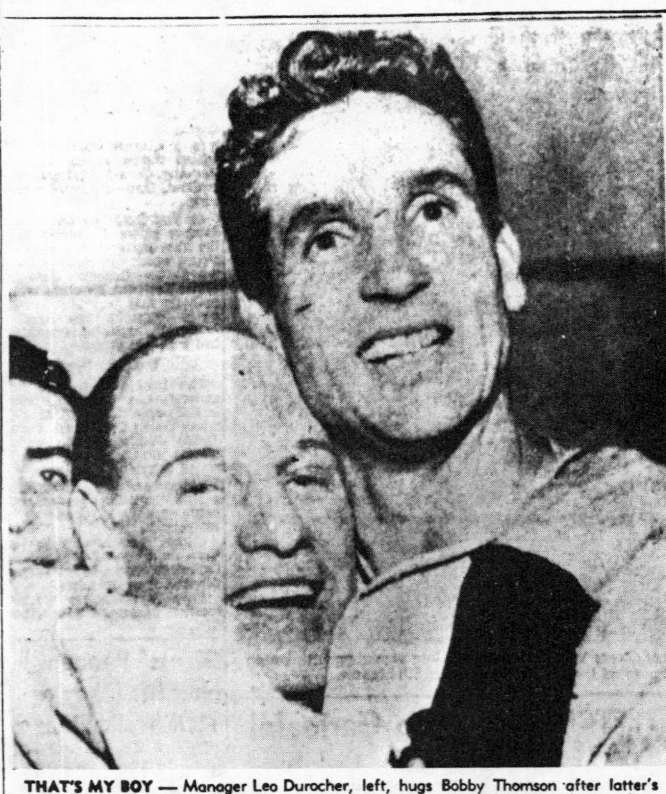

THAT'S MY BOY — Manager Leo Durocher, left, hugs Bobby Thomson after latter's three-run homer gave Giants 5-4 win over Brooklyn yesterday and National League flag.

CRAZY WITH JOY—Durocher gives Second Baseman Eddie Stanky a piggy-back ride as Hero Thomson streaks for home with the run that gave Giants thrilling victory.
(AP) Wirephotos

'A LITTLE INSIDE'

## Thomson Picked Out High, Fast Offering

NEW YORK, Oct. 3 (AP)—Bobby Thomson, Scottish-born resident of metropolitan New York, wrote a storybook finish to the spine-tingling National League pennant race late today and then pandemonium broke loose in the Polo Grounds.

Never in history has Coogan's Bluff, under which rests the home of the New York Giants, reverberated with such sound, as followers of the new National League champions cut loose with all their vocal cords.

They had been quiet most of the afternoon, especially after the Brooklyn Dodgers took a 4-1 lead in the eighth inning, but with a mighty roar that continued long afterward they opened all their pent-up emotions as Thomson's 32nd and most important home run of the year settled in the lower left-field stands with two mates aboard.

**'All Set'**

"It was a high, fast one and a little inside," Thomson shouted above the din of the dressing-room noise. "I saw Branca (Ralph) let loose with his fast pitch and I was all set."

The Giants' dressing room was such confusion that hardly anyone could get in a word.

But out of the backslapping, noise and general hullabaloo came:

"Never saw a greater finish," declared Ford Frick, newly elected baseball commissioner. "And I have been watching games for more than 30 years."

"It'll be Dave Koslo tomorrow," shouted Leo Durocher as he tried to catch his breath.

There was only one note of sadness to the Giants' first pennant since 1937. Don Mueller, whose single to right field kept the New Yorkers' ninth-inning rally going, will not be able to play the first and probably the second game of the World Series opening against the Yankees tomorrow.

Mueller sprained his left ankle going into third on Whitey Lockman's double to the left-field corner.

"Don will be out for two or three days," said Dr. Anthony Palermo, team physician.

Mueller lay on a table while Dr. Palermo looked at the ankle and joined with the Giants in shouting meaningless words.

Into the jam-packed, hot dressing room came Warren Giles, new president of the National League; Manager Charley Dressen of the Dodgers, Jackie Robinson, the Dodgers' great second baseman; Walter O'Malley, president of the Brooks, and scores of others.

"I told you we'd finish one, two," Dressen said as he congratulated Durocher. "I was right only we were second."

**Robbie on Hand**

Then in came Robinson to join with his manager in wishing Durocher and the Giants well in their coming Series.

"I don't feel sorry for myself," said Robinson, "but I do feel bad that we let the Brooklyn fans down."

Somebody grabbed Durocher around the shoulder and yelled that he did a great job of masterminding in the ninth inning.

"I sure did," said Durocher jokingly. "It didn't take much master-minding to get those hits that set it up for Bobby."

"We were lucky to win it," Leo said as he sat down at his desk, wiped the sweat from his brow and collected his thoughts.

"That's the toughest ball club in America next door," he said, nodding toward the Dodgers' dressing room. "When you beat them you know you're beating a great team."

"I knew I hit the ball hard but it started sinking very fast," said Thomson of his 32nd homer.

"But when I saw it go into the stands I don't think I touched the ground a single time the remainder of the way. I just floated around. It was that kind of feeling."

### It Figured!

From Braven Dyer's Sports Parade of April 17, 1951:

"This department picks the Yankees and Giants to meet in the 1951 World Series. Leo Durocher will get all the mileage possible out of the Giants. He and Casey Stengel are just about the best managers in baseball today."

## 'Wasn't a Bad Pitch,' Moans Beaten Branca

NEW YORK, Oct. 3 (AP)—Ralph Branca sat on the steps, eyes wet, his head buried in his arms. Manager Charley Dressen paced the floor like a nervous lion. Big Don Newcombe moved around, silently and aimlessly as if trying to figure out a reason for it all.

The others sat on the short, three-legged stools in their dressing room, eyes boring holes through the floor. None spoke. The room had a funereal quiet about it.

**And Then—Boom!**

These were the men of Brooklyn, wondering what they had done against destiny to make destiny treat them so.

"We are three runs ahead going into the ninth inning," said Jackie Robinson, the Dodgers' brilliant second baseman. "We see ourselves in the World Series. And then—boom—five minutes later we are sitting in the clubhouse."

Once before these Dodgers had started counting World Series money—amounting to $5000, maybe $6500. That was when they were 13½ games ahead on Aug. 11. Then the great Giants' surge collared them and they fought back twice from the brink of elimination to today's final game.

**Branca Loses Two**

Then it was all wiped out with one tremendous blow in the ninth inning by New York's Bobby Thomson, giving the

Turn to Page 2, Column 4

### SERIES ON TV, RADIO TODAY

Telecasts of today's first game of the World Series from New York between the Giants and the Yankees will be carried over both KHJ-TV (Channel 9) and KNBH (Channel 4) via the national network. The telecasts will start at 9:45 a.m.

Pregame shows are scheduled for both video stations with KNBH featuring Dizzy Dean at 9:30 and KHJ-TV showing a baseball movie at 8:35 and Bert Dunne's Series preview at 9:15. Dunne's guest will be Jack Salveson, Hollywood pitcher.

On radio, a play-by-play broadcast of the game will be aired by KHJ, local Mutual outlet.

BYE-BYE PENNANT—Dodger Andy Pafko looks up helplessly as Bobby Thomson's well-tagged blow sails into bleachers, giving Giants 5-4 play-off win and pennant.
(AP) Wirephoto

## Reynolds, Koslo Hurl in Opener

BY AL WOLF
Times Staff Representative

NEW YORK, Oct. 3—It's out of the frying pan into the fire for the New York Giants, who have accomplished the impossible and now must do it all over again.

Despite the Giants' pulsating performance in flagging down the Brooklyn Dodgers, an almost anticlimactical World Series will see the New York Yankees go off 8-5 favorites.

**Koslo Starts**

The big show starts tomorrow in Yankee Stadium. The perennial American League champions are well rested since clinching the pennant last Friday, and Manager Casey Stengel will open with Allie Reynolds (17-8) as his slinging selection. For the Giants, Manager Leo Durocher figures on Dave Koslo (10-9).

First two games are slated for the stadium, which seats 70,000, then play will move to the Polo Grounds (55,000) for two—or, if need be, three—games. If the title still is undecided, the Series then goes back to the Bronx.

**Series Slate**

Unless weather intervenes, play in the Series will be on these consecutive days:

Tomorrow and Friday, Oct. 5, Yankee Stadium; Saturday, Oct. 6, Sunday, Oct. 7 and Monday, Oct. 8, Polo Grounds; Tuesday, Oct. 9 and Wednesday, Oct. 10, Yankee Stadium.

All World Series seats have been sold and scalpers are asking two and even three times face value which is $6 for each reserved seat and $8 for each box seat.

**Dressen on Spot**

Yesterday, after New York dropped its play-off game to Brooklyn, Durocher was put on the grease for looking ahead to the World Series.

Today, after Brooklyn dropped the play-off series to New York, Manager Chuck Dressen of the Dodgers was fried in the fat by many critics.

Durocher was blasted for pitching Sheldon Jones yesterday instead of using Sal Maglie. Durocher protested that Maglie's tight arm needed more rest, but there was a widespread suspicion that Maglie was being saved for the Series opener against the Yankees—before the Giants were in the Series.

As events turned out, what with young Clem Labine throwing shutout ball, Maglie couldn't have won yesterday, anyhow. You can't beat a shutout, only

Turn to Page 2, Column 1

### UN-DRESSEN!

| BROOKLYN | AB | R | H | O | A |
|---|---|---|---|---|---|
| Furillo, rf | 5 | 0 | 0 | 0 | 0 |
| Reese, ss | 4 | 2 | 1 | 2 | 5 |
| Snider, cf | 3 | 1 | 2 | 1 | 0 |
| Robinson, 2b | 2 | 1 | 1 | 3 | 2 |
| Pafko, lf | 4 | 0 | 1 | 4 | 1 |
| Hodges, 1b | 4 | 0 | 0 | 11 | 1 |
| Cox, 3b | 4 | 0 | 2 | 1 | 3 |
| Walker, c | 4 | 0 | 1 | 2 | 0 |
| Newcombe, p | 4 | 0 | 0 | 1 | 1 |
| Branca, p | 0 | 0 | 0 | 0 | 0 |
| Totals | 34 | 4 | 8 | 25 | 13 |

| NEW YORK | AB | R | H | O | A |
|---|---|---|---|---|---|
| Stanky, 2b | 4 | 0 | 0 | 0 | 4 |
| Dark, ss | 4 | 1 | 1 | 2 | 2 |
| Mueller, rf | 4 | 0 | 1 | 0 | 0 |
| Hartung | 0 | 1 | 0 | 0 | 0 |
| Irvin, lf | 4 | 1 | 1 | 1 | 0 |
| Lockman, 1b | 3 | 1 | 2 | 11 | 1 |
| Thomson, 3b | 4 | 1 | 3 | 4 | 1 |
| Mays, cf | 3 | 0 | 0 | 1 | 0 |
| Westrum, c | 0 | 0 | 0 | 7 | 1 |
| Rigney | 1 | 0 | 0 | 0 | 0 |
| Noble, c | 0 | 0 | 0 | 0 | 0 |
| Maglie, p | 2 | 0 | 0 | 1 | 2 |
| Thompson | 1 | 0 | 0 | 0 | 0 |
| Jansen, p | 0 | 0 | 0 | 0 | 0 |
| Totals | 30 | 5 | 8 | 27 | 11 |

One out when winning run scored.

Rigney struck out for Westrum in 8th.

Thompson grounded out for Maglie in 8th.

Hartung ran for Mueller in 9th.

| | | |
|---|---|---|
| Brooklyn | 100 000 030—4 | |
| New York | 000 000 104—5 | |

E—None. RBI—Robinson, Thomson, 4; Pafko, Cox, Lockman. 2B—Thomson, Irvin, Lockman. HR—Thomson. SH—Lockman. DP—Cox, Robinson and Hodges; Reese, Robinson and Hodges. LOB—Brooklyn, 7; New York, 3. BB—Maglie, 4 (Reese, Snider, Robinson, 2); Newcombe, 2 (Westrum, 2). SO—Maglie, 6 (Furillo, Walker, 2; Snider, Pafko, Reese); Newcombe, 2 (Mays, Rigney). HO—Maglie, 8 in 8 innings; Jansen, 0 in 1; Newcombe, 7 in 8⅓; Branca, 1 in 0 (pitched to one batter in ninth). Winner—Jansen (23-11); Loser—Branca (13-12). Umpires—Jorda (plate); Conlan (1b); Stewart (2b); Goetz (3b). Time—2h. 28m. Attendance—34,320 (paid).

## GIANTS NOSE OUT DODGERS, 5-4!

Continued from Page 1, Part I

made that 4-1 deficit seem insurmountable in the short time left.

But the Giants long since had stricken the word "impossible" from their vocabularies.

**Giant Rally**

Alvin Dark opened this modern-day version of Custer's Last Stand with a sharp single off diving Gil Hodges' mitt. Don Mueller singled to right, sending the New York captain to third. Monte Irvin, top run producer in the league this season, popped out foul and a vast groan rumbled from the dry throats of die-hard Giant rooters.

Whitey Lockman drove one into left field and got credit for a cheap double when Andy Pafko juggled the ball. Dark scored, of course, and Mueller slid into third base (spraining his ankle and being carried off the field). Clint Hartung became the runner.

**Fans With Bases Full**

Branca replaced Newcombe in the box and up to bat came Thomson, the Great Scot from Glasgow. Only he was more goat than hero at the moment.

For he had fanned with bases full and two out in the third inning yesterday, the turning point as Brooklyn matched New York's first-game victory. Today, he had wrecked an incipient rally in the second inning by trying for second with that bag already occupied to convert his single into a foolish out, and then in the eighth had clumsily played two balls that went for run-producing hits.

He took a called first strike from the fellow he'd homered into defeat in game No. 1, then swung viciously on the next offering. Like an arrow, the ball sped toward the seats just inside the left-field foul line. With only about a three-foot clearance, it disappeared into the mass of humanity.

**Wrong Fluid**

And so the Giants became National League champions for the first time since 1937. But if they win every year hereafter until Gabriel toots that trumpet, they'll never again unfurl a pennant so richly deserved, so dramatically achieved—so utterly satisfying.

Technically, the defeat was Branca's. But most folks were inclined to charge it squarely to Manager Chuck Dressen's account for picking the wrong fireman in relieving with Branca, who came with a pail of gasoline instead of water.

**Lead Grows**

With victory but two outs away, the more logical choice seemed to be Clem Labine, who'd handcuffed Thomson while whitewashing the Giants yesterday—and who was also warmed up.

Larry Jansen got credit for the all-important win, though he worked but one inning. The one-time San Francisco ace merely retired the Brooks in 1-2-3 fashion in the top of the ninth, after Sal Maglie had been lifted for a batsman in the eighth.

Each tandem yielded eight hits.

The Dodgers got only three balls out of the infield against Maglie during their first seven turns, yet owned a 1-0 lead that was beginning to look big as the national debt.

With one away in the first round, Maglie briefly went out of control—and the Dodgers took control. Peewee Reese and Duke

Turn to Page 2, Column 3

### FINAL NATIONAL LEAGUE STANDINGS

(Play-off games included)

| | W. | L. | Pct. | |
|---|---|---|---|---|
| New York | 98 | 59 | .624 | |
| Brooklyn | 97 | 60 | .618 | 1 |
| St. Louis | 81 | 73 | .526 | 15½ |
| Boston | 76 | 78 | .494 | 20½ |
| Philadelphia | 73 | 81 | .474 | 23½ |
| Cincinnati | 68 | 86 | .442 | 28½ |
| Pittsburgh | 64 | 90 | .416 | 32½ |
| Chicago | [illegible] | [illegible] | [illegible] | [illegible] |

*Games behind winner.

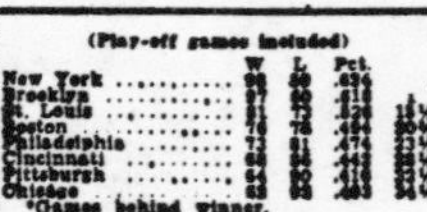

**Read 'Em and Weep**
SC, 21; California, 14.
Arkansas, 16; Texas, 14.
TCU, 20; Texas A&M, 14.
Indiana, 32; Ohio State, 10.
Rice, 28; SMU, 7.

Los Angeles Times — SPORTS

8 PART II — CC — SUNDAY MORNING, OCTOBER 21, 1951 — VOL. LXX

# SC'S SECOND-HALF BURST RUINS CAL, 21-14

OVER THE TOP—Leon Sellers, SC sophomore fullback, releases smile as he scores Trojans' third touchdown against California at Berkeley yesterday in fourth quarter. At left Bob Buckley, Troy halfback, gives victory sign while standing at right is dejected Ed Bartlett, Bear wingman (84). Sellers scored through right guard from 2-yard line. (AP) Wirephoto

## Troy Tumbles Bears From Unbeaten Ranks Before 81,490 Throng

BY BRAVEN DYER, Times Staff Representative

BERKELEY, Oct. 20 — An autumn-ic bomb exploded here today as mighty California fell before the might and courage of Jess Hill's never-say-die Trojans, 21-14, before 81,490 fans.

The victory goes into the record books as one of the greatest of all time for Southern California. Cal had been riding high on the crest of a 38-game regular season unbeaten streak and as late as this morning was ranked as the nation's No. 1 football team.

If the experts who make these ratings really know their onions, which I doubt, they'll just have the Trojans and Bears switch places when they go to the polls again.

Trailing by two touchdowns at the half, Hill's hard-hitting squad just simply knocked the daylights out of the Bears while scoring once in the third period and twice in the fourth.

**Two More Hurdles**

It was Cal's first regular season defeat since Jeff Cravath's 1947 club clobbered the Bears, 39-14. The win gives SC the inside track to the Rose Bowl, with Stanford and UCLA the only remaining Pacific Coast Conference foes to be met.

Troy's touchdowns were tallied by Frank Gifford, Co-Capt. Dean Schmeider and Leon Sellers, with gifted Gifford nudging all the extra points. But this trio, individually or collectively, would be the first to admit that it was a team triumph, scored by the combined efforts of both the offensive and defensive platoons.

It was Bakersfield's pride and joy, the Gifford boy, who stole all the offensive thunder today.

His 69-yard run midway in the third quarter was one of the most sensational touchdown gallops in Trojan history. He passed to Schneider for the second tally, 6 yards on a quickie which required alertness and accuracy; he twice punted out of bounds around Cal's 5-yard line and he completed five out of seven pitches for 59 yards while emerging as the game's greatest ground gainer with 115 yards to his credit.

**Cannamela Patted**

I know the other Trojans will understand if I pause just a moment to say that Pat Cannamela must be accorded equal ranking with the great Gifford.

Murderous Pat knocked Johnny Olszewski, Cal's famed back, clear out of the game the first time Johnny-O carried the ball. The blond bombshell returned periodically, but early in the third stanza Charley (Tugboat) Ane hit Cal's ace again and that was all for the great runner—his injured leg just couldn't stand any more.

One scout in the press box said: "If Les Richter is an All-American, then Cannamela is an All-Everything." And Richter played a whale of a game, too, but Gifford's 69-yard touchdown dash was over his side of the line.

Cal can point to Dick LemMon, defensive back, as her brightest star. Twice he recovered fumbles and once he was the only man between Gifford and another touchdown run. Dick didn't miss.

**Troy Turns Tide**

Hill probably won't ever tell us scribes what he told the officials at halftime, but it was plenty, after the horn blowers tagged SC for a flock of penalties in the first half. And what he said to his team in the dressing room could have been nothing more than routine instructions, with the promise that the same hard football, minus Troy's bobbles, could still overcome the 14-point deficit and bring glorious victory.

That's just the way the Trojans acted —as if they knew they could do it.

Hot as the Trojans were in the second half, it could be that Cal lost because of a strategical error soon after the third quarter began.

The Bears had marched with the kickoff to SC's 38. It was fourth and a skimpy yard to go for a first down. Pappy Waldorf sent in his punter, Tom Keough, who, with two exceptions, did a fine job of punting. This one sliced out of bounds for a mere 7 yards and there were the Trojans with the ball they wanted on their 31.

**Gifford Shakes Loose**

On the first play, the Trojans showed the shape of things to come, as Gifford broke around right end and behind devastating blocking, cut this way and that, to race across the goal line as the Trojan rooters loosed a mighty roar.

It was their first real chance to answer, in a semicivilized way, Cal's earlier bleats of "dirty Trojans, dirty Trojans," and "get No. 42, get No. 42." No. 42 is Cannamela. Gifford then put Cal in a hole shortly after the next kickoff by punting out of bounds on the 5.

Fleet Johnny Williams brought the Cal punt back 17 yards to the Bear 35 but Rudy Bukich missed a first down by inches on the 25 and Waldorf's warriors took over.

**SC Pulls Even**

Jim Sears returned the next punt to SC's 40 and this time Troy didn't miss, going 60 yards for the touchdown which knotted the score.

Gifford's pass to Schneider ate up 15 yards and then Cal, for the first time, drew a penalty for roughness and that moved the ball to the 18.

Gifford ripped right tackle to the 9 and Bob Buckley

Turn to Page 11, Column 4

## STANFORD EDGES SANTA CLARA, 21-14

### Mathias Scores Winning Touchdown With Two Minutes Remaining; Broncs' Burget Rolls

**PALO ALTO, Oct. 20 (AP)—A touchdown in the final two minutes by Olympic Decathlon Champion Bob Mathias gave the unbeaten Stanford Indians a 21-14 victory over the unheralded Santa Clara Broncos today.**

Through three periods, Stanford and Santa Clara fought on even terms before 21,000 spectators. Then, with only 2 minutes of play remaining, Stanford marched 67 yards for the winning margin.

Mathias raced 18 yards for the 6 points.

**Burget Rolls**

Twice the underdog Broncos came from behind to knot the count, moving mainly through the center of the Indian line. Fullback Hank Burget hammered out consistent gains.

Stanford scored first, taking the opening kickoff and moving the ball to the end zone on 18 plays. Mathias punched over from the 4.

Burget led the Santa Clara comeback that evened the score at halftime. He dived over the goal line from the 1 to cap the 54-yard march.

Stanford quickly regained the lead in the third quarter. Halfback Harry Hugasian did most of the heavy work in a ground offensive that carried to the Santa Clara 6. All-American End Bill McColl faked his way clear to the end zone and took a pass from Quarterback Bob Garrett.

**Broncs Bounce**

The Broncos bounced back once again. Quarterback John Pasco mixed up passes and running plays, flipping a 21-yarder to End Larry Williams that took the ball to the Stanford 14. Then he sent Fullback Melvin Lewis off tackle for the touchdown. John Daly booted his second conversion to make it 14-14.

The Indians, flat for most of the game, caught fire late in the fourth period, and moved 67 yards for their clincher in eight plays.

**SCORE BY QUARTERS**

| | | | | |
|---|---|---|---|---|
| Santa Clara | 0 | 7 | 7 | 0—14 |
| Stanford | 7 | 0 | 7 | 7—21 |

Santa Clara scoring: Touchdowns—Burget, Lewis. PAT—Daly 2.
Stanford scoring: Touchdowns—Mathias, 2; McColl. PAT—Kerkorian, 3.

**STATISTICS**

| | Santa Clara | St'ford |
|---|---|---|
| First downs | 14 | 23 |
| Rushing yardage | 134 | 264 |
| Passing yardage | 107 | 101 |
| Passes attempted | 18 | 21 |
| Passes completed | 9 | 10 |
| Passes intercepted | 1 | 2 |
| Punts | 5 | 2 |
| Punting average | 37.8 | 36 |
| Fumbles lost | 1 | 1 |
| Yards penalized | 60 | 25 |

## Late Illini Air Attack Beats Washington, 27-20

SEATTLE, Oct. 20 (AP)—Sophomore Tommy O'Connell, cool as a fall frost when the going was toughest, pitched Illinois to a fourth-quarter, tie-cracking touchdown and a 27-20 football victory today over the ever-challenging Huskies of the University of Washington.

The invading Illini, ranked eighth in the nation, had freed two flying phantoms—Johnny Karras and Pete Bachouros—in the first half to run up a 20-7 margin before a stunned crowd of 54,000.

Washington came pounding back for touchdowns in the third and fourth quarters to knot the count at 20-all and wreck the Illinois running attack.

With seven minutes left, O'Connell launched an 81-yard drive to the victory. Plunges took the Illini to midfield and when Washington threatened to halt the parade there, O'Connell went upstairs and pitched five strikes to reach the goal, throwing every one out of deep punt formation.

**SCORE BY QUARTERS**

| | | | | |
|---|---|---|---|---|
| Illinois | 7 | 13 | 0 | 7—27 |
| Washington | 7 | 0 | 7 | 6—20 |

Illinois scoring: Touchdowns—W. Tate, 2; Bachouros, Stevens. PAT—Rebecca, 3.
Washington scoring: Touchdowns—McElhenny, 2; Earley. PAT—Rockey, McElhenny.

**STATISTICS**

| | Ill. | Wash. |
|---|---|---|
| First downs | 12 | 7 |
| Rushing yardage | 171 | 96 |
| Passing yardage | 94 | 159 |
| Passes attempted | 14 | 28 |
| Passes completed | 9 | 10 |
| Passes intercepted | 1 | 3 |
| Punts | 6 | 5 |
| Punting average | 41 | 32 |
| Fumbles lost | 1 | 3 |
| Yards penalized | 127 | 40 |

## Bay City Writer Hails Gifford, Cannamela, SC

BY BILL LEISER
San Francisco Chronicle Sports Editor

MEMORIAL STADIUM, Oct. 20—Ouch, but this is it: Southern California Trojans, 21; California Bears, 14. Lest there be any misunderstanding, this is not the first-quarter or third-quarter count.

It is the final score as marked up on Fullback Leon Sellers' 2-yard touchdown smash over with a whirling dive atop left guard 2m. 44s. ahead of the timer's game-ending gun.

**Shocking Upset**

With Sellers' plunge the last emerged first once more. Four years and 38 Coast Conference and college games ago these same SC Trojans won the last game California lost in regular season competition. Today they drove doggedly and brilliantly from behind a 14-point first half deficit to overtrump America's up-to-now No. 1 gridiron power of the year—the same California Bears.

This achievement which will shock football centers from coast to coast tonight was accomplished by:

1—A comparatively short, chunky 205-pound linebacker from New London, Ct., Pat Cannamela, who personally shifted the vaunted Golden Bear attack into reverse gear toward the end of the second period, and carefully devoted himself to the business of seeing to it no points whatever were made available to Blue and Gold forces from there on out.

**Troy Hailed**

2—A one-man football machine capable of any type of advance or attack, 194-pound Frank Gifford of Bakersfield, who rode his blockers through 69 yards of territory in a single dash to the first Trojan score in the third period; who forward-passed to Dean Schneider after being twice trapped for the second t.d., and whose terrific presence motored the southerners through their final drive to the six-pointer which sealed up the whole deal.

(3) One swell team of football battlers who formed a supporting cast reminiscent of the

Turn to Page 14 Column 1

## TROJANS CONFIDENT THROUGHOUT GAME

### Frank Gifford's Fight Talk Sparks Triumph; Heart, Spirit, Morale Did It, Says Coach

BY PAUL ZIMMERMAN, Times Sports Editor

**BERKELEY, Oct. 20—With five minutes of the California-Southern California game to go, the score tied, 14 to 14, and the Golden Bears in possession of the ball, Frank Gifford called the offensive team together and said: "We've got 'em whipped now, fellows. Let's go."**

That Troy went on from there to whip California, 21 to 14, now is history, but the triumph set off no really spontaneous and riotous dressing room scene.

The Trojan players believed they were going to win all the time, which probably accounts for their comparatively subdued reaction and trust of the coaches and well-wishers who walked in through the unguarded door.

Everyone was welcome.

**Hill Happy**

"Heart, spirit, morale, that's what did it," said Coach Jess Hill. "Determination won for us. Nothing takes the place of fortitude." He sounded like a professor—not a coach.

"Fourteen points behind is a big deficit. When you're playing against California, it's no breeze. Don't forget that. But the boys overcame it.

"Frank Gifford was the outstanding back on the field today and Pat Cannamela was the outstanding linebacker.

"Johnny Olszewski is great and hard to stop. And Les Richter is fine backing up the line. But I'll still pick Frank and Pat over them.

"Pat is an All-American. Gifford isn't far behind and might be one too." What did these two stars have to say in their greatest hour of triumph?

**Pat Happy**

"I don't know what to say, I'm so happy."

That was all the stumpy, unbeautiful, 205-pound guard Cannamela from New London, Ct., via Ventura, could answer.

Gifford, who was running a high fever two days ago and was a doubtful starter until Dr. Willis Jacobus gave his approval this

Turn to Page 11, Column 2

## Scouts Unanimous in Hailing Pat and Frank

BY PAUL ZIMMERMAN, Times Sports Editor

BERKELEY, Oct. 20—Greater determination on the part of Southern California and the terrific play of Troy's Frank Gifford and Pat Cannamela brought California's triumph string to an end, 21-14, here this afternoon.

This was the unanimous opinion of the scouts who witnessed the bruising Trojan upset win over a rugged Golden Bear team many had said was Coach Lynn Waldorf's greatest.

"California got outhit and outtackled. That's all there is to it," said Billy Barnes, UCLA assistant.

"When Southern California went into the single wingback it really hurt the Bears, especially on those off-tackle plays with Gifford carrying the ball. The Trojans also hurt California with their passing.

"But don't let this game's outcome change your opinion. California still has a great football team."

Said Buster Brannon, Texas Christian spy who will be in Memorial Coliseum Saturday with the Horned Frogs of TCU:

"Southern California simply went after it harder. Those Trojans came here to play football.

"That No. 42 (Cannamela) is the finest linebacker I've ever seen. And No. 16 (Gifford) played a great game."

Capt. Bob St. Onge, here to report for Army, was greatly impressed with the play of Bob Van Doren.

"He was wonderful on rushing

Turn to Page 14, Column 1

## Waldorf Says Troy Played It 'Hard, Clean'

BY JIM SCOTT
Times Correspondent

BERKELEY, Oct. 20—A football dynasty crashed here this afternoon and there were tears in Strawberry Canyon tonight.

SC's decisive 21-14 conquest of California was the Bears' first loss in 39 games over a five-year span, exclusive of the Rose Bowl contests.

In the dressing room, old Blues charged that several of the Californians had been intentionally injured, but Coach Lynn O. (Pappy) Waldorf wouldn't hold still for this.

**No Alibi**

Asserted Waldorf, as he looked disdainfully down at his good-luck gold and maroon Trojan tie, plucked three years ago off the neck of Sam Barry, the late SC scout:

"I have no alibi and no complaint. I feel that SC played it hard but clean. Oh, there were one or two incidents which came up but the Trojans were promptly penalized.

"But I would remind you that these men were lost to our offensive platoon: Johnny Olzsewski (knee injury); Harry West (back); Ralph Krueger (knee); John Peterson (kept out by a pregame injury); Sam Williams (ankle); Paul Andrew (elbow), and Dwight Ely (knee injury on first kickoff).

"Don Robison (victim of pulled rib ligaments last week) wasn't able to kick but he was able to go in there and catch some passes at the end of the game. Bob Beal saw only a little action at end near the end of the game."

**To See Movies**

Here Waldorf paused again to caution that he was not trying to foment an alibi.

"But," a reporter asked, "have you ever lost so many men before in one game through injuries?"

"I guess not," replied the wise Walrus. "I actually couldn't tell what happened when Olszewski was injured," he went on, "but I'd like to see the movies of that play."

Olszewski's right knee was damaged early in the first period

Turn to Page 11, Column 8

| | | | | | |
|---|---|---|---|---|---|
| UCLA . . . . 41 | Stanford . . . 21 | Indiana . . . 32 | WSC . . . . . 26 | Illinois . . . . 27 | SC . . . . . . . 21 |
| Oregon . . . . 0 | Santa Clara . 14 | Ohio St. . . . 10 | OSC . . . . . 13 | Wash. . . . . 20 | Cal . . . . . . . 14 |

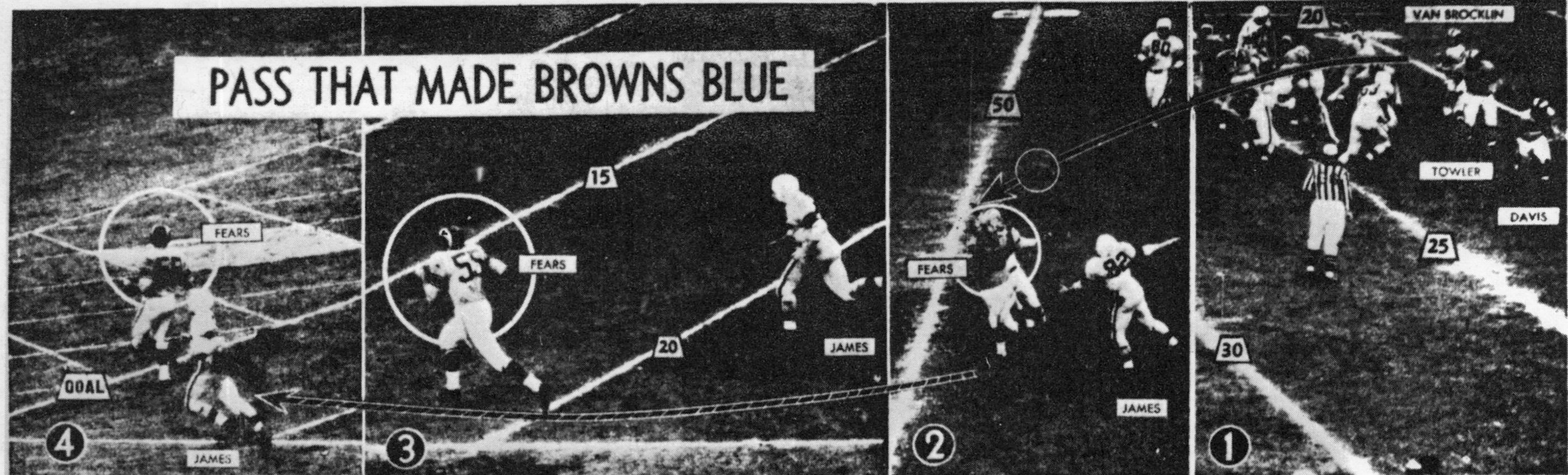


HERE'S THE PITCH—Norm Van Brocklin, Ram quarterback, unleashes a sensational pass late in the fourth quarter to End Tom Fears that was good for 73 yards and the winning touchdown as Rams whipped Cleveland Browns, 24-17.
Times Miracle Eye photos by John Malmin


PART 4 **Los Angeles Times** SPORTS

VOL. LXXI CC MONDAY MORNING, DECEMBER 24, 1951 Read Times Green for Latest Sports


# RAMS WHIP BROWNS, 24-17; WIN PRO TITLE

## SPORT SCRIPTS

By PAUL ZIMMERMAN
TIMES SPORTS EDITOR

If you can put your finger on one specific reason for the success of the Illinois football teams in the last decade you would have to say spirit probably has been its greatest asset.

Having said that, you naturally have to turn your eyes on the head coach, Ray Eliot, a gentleman with a wide grin, a pair of horn-rimmed spectacles and a pate slightly more denuded than is ours. Ray is the spirit stimulater.

**CAUTIOUS MAN**

What manner of man is the mentor of the Fightin' Illini?

Well, in the first place, he's a cautious sort of a chap who doesn't leave anything to chance. Some might call him "suspicious" but that's hardly the word.

Certainly, Ray treated the newspapermen cautiously on his first Rose Bowl visit out here. On this he is more relaxed.

If you corner him, he's apt to admit he was scared to death on that first junket. Everyone wanted Army out here instead of Illinois and Ray felt like something of an interloper.

**THINGS DIFFERENT**

Ray took advantage of that situation to get his boys steamed up for a terrific effort, defeating a well-manned UCLA team 45 to 14.

Things are different this time. Eliot knows he has no psychological advantage and is more cautious than ever in his preparatory plans. He brought the team here earlier than on the first trip because of miserable weather conditions that made satisfactory training at Champaign impossible.

He fretfully hopes this will not work against his lads with distracting influences in this "land of make believe" as Ray jokingly refers to Southern California.

**UP THE HARD WAY**

Eliot came up the hard way. A native of Massachusetts, he went to Illinois as a student because he had happened upon one of the school's brochures that stressed its fine physical education and coaching school.

"I always wanted to be a football coach," says Ray, "and Illinois offered the sort of training I wanted."

While playing tackle for Bob Zuppke he worked his way through school washing windows, waiting tables, shoveling snow and any other odd job he could pick up.

In his last year he came upon a steady job of managing a dance hall where the university students liked to gather for their social events.

**ONLY TWO JOBS**

He's held only two jobs since being graduated in 1932. After getting out of school he went to Illinois College and served as head coach there until Zuppke took him back to Champaign as his line mentor.

When Zup resigned Ray took over in 1942 and the Illini, who had been having trouble winning in Zuppke's declining years, promptly started a climb back up the Big Ten ladder.

In four years they won the

Turn to Page 4, Column 5

HOORAY!—Jumbo Joe Stydahar and players on Ram bench cut loose with roar as gun ended title-winning game at Coliseum yesterday.
Times photo by Art Rogers

## Van Brocklin's Pass to Fears Provides Late Victory Spark

BY FRANK FINCH

They beat the Browns!

In their finest hour the Los Angeles Rams abruptly ended football's longest reign of terror by conquering mighty Cleveland, 24 to 17, to capture the National Football League championship yesterday.

And it took a perfect play to do it—Norm Van Brocklin's 73-yard scoring shot to tall Tom Fears. Coming midway in the final quarter, the pay-off pitch shattered a 17-17 deadlock which had threatened to send this tremendous battle of the giants into a "sudden-death" overtime period.

Thus, finis was written to a proud dynasty built up over the past five years by Paul Brown.

For four seasons Brown's hand-picked team dominated the All America Conference and when the two leagues merged last year the Browns never broke stride.

**Run Rampant**

They whipped the Rams in the 1950 championship game, 30 to 28, and then ran rampant through their division this year on the crest of an 11-game winning streak.

The king is dead. Long live the king! For it was a great team that the Rams beat yesterday. Make no mistake of that.

They were 7-point favorites at kickoff time and certainly looked the part at the half when they left the field with a 10-7 lead.

But the inspired Rams, spurred on by the highly partisan crowd of 59,475 Coliseum fans, simply would not admit defeat to the team which had beaten them three times in as many previous meetings.

Twice the Rams were hurled back by the powerful Browns after having first downs on the 1-yard line during that dramatic second half. No less than eight times did the stubborn enemy dig in and repulse football's most potent offense inside the 5-yard line during those two scoring threats.

Most teams would have folded after blowing such golden opportunities, but not this ball club.

They fought their hearts out for Coach Joe Stydahar . . . Jumbo Joe, who faced the impossible task last July of building a championship contender without a single, solitary veteran tackle on the roster.

"This team will be 50% stronger than last year's team." Stydahar insisted despite jibes of the scoffers. Didn't the Rams have 13 rookies, they asked?

**Yearlings Perform**

They certainly did, and how those yearlings performed against the poised, proud champions from the shores of Lake Erie! Big Jim Winkler jamming up the ground plays . . . Andy Robustelli repeatedly creaming Otto Graham . . . Marv Johnson coming up with a clutch interception . . . Norb Hecker nailing Dub Jones with a shoestring tackle that stopped their last drive.

Much of the credit for Los Angeles' first championship team must be shared with the defensive ends, Robustelli and Larry Brink. They hopped, battered and blasted Graham so often that he finally wound up throwing passes directly into the arms of two very appreciative Rams, Don Paul and Johnson.

But although he was exhausted at the finish, Herr Otto played a superb game. He pinpointed 19 passes to such fine receivers as Mac Speedie, Dante Levelli, Jones and Ken Carpenter for 280 yards and wound up as the game's leading ground gainer with a 43-yard total.

**Provides Spark**

Capt. Bob Waterfield outkicked Horace Gillom, the league champion, by a wide margin and contributed a vital field goal and three extra points, but he did not provide the spark of victory.

It was his understudy, the Dutchman, who fired the fatal shots. Entering the fray for the first time with only two minutes left in the third quarter, Van Brocklin connected on four of half a dozen throws for 128 yards and the winning touchdown. Waterfield completed nine of 24 for 12[illegible] yards and had two intercepted.

And Fears, who made a great late-season comeback after an injury had laid him low for six games, came through in the clutch with four receptions which produced 146 yards, not to mention a Christmas bonus of $2108.44 for each of 34 Rams; Coaches Stydahar, Hamp Pool, Red Hickey and Ray Richards;

Turn to Page 2, Column 1

VIGOROUS RAMS

## Old Age, Angelenos Finally Catch Browns

BY BRAVEN DYER

Old age finally caught up with the Cleveland Browns.

The youthful vigor of the Rams gave Otto Graham the worst day of his pro career.

Line Coach Ray Richards had his speedy forwards following Otto like a bunch of hungry bloodhounds.

The great Graham was rushed so relentlessly that he actually "discovered" two new receivers—Marvin Johnson and Don Paul. This was rather embarrassing for good-looking Otto because Messrs. Johnson and Paul were playing against the Browns.

And if Graham lives to be 100 he'll probably see Larry Brink in his dreams at least every other night. Brink could become an author if he wishes, writing a treatise on "Inside Otto Graham" or "How I Pierced Paul Brown's Iron Curtain."

**Toughest Job**

The sports editors of this town knew what they were doing when the first man they named for the pro bowl game Jan. 12 was brother Brink. Ram forwards just gave Brown's line a tasty pasting.

The toughest job the Rams had all season was trying to carry Jumbo Joe Stydahar off the field when the final gun boomed. They never did make it. I often wonder how such a big guy can be so nice. Joe will wear his new laurels modestly even if all the Ram millionaire owners double his salary, which they should.

Bob Boyd and Norbert Hecker turned in two tremendous, timely tackles which saved the day at crucial moments.

**Right Dope**

There were four minutes to go, Browns in possession in midfield, when Graham, finding an opening, smartly decided to run. Rams had six halfbacks on defense then and Boyd, making up his mind in a split second, came tearing in from "way back" and nailed Otto for a two-yard loss.

A few minutes later Hecker did virtually the same thing on the other side of the field when the Browns needed only 2 yards for a first down—only this time Dub Jones was the victim.

Joe Muha and Mel Hein gave you the right dope in last

Turn to Page 2, Column 7

## Rams Pocket Biggest Pay-off --$2108 Each!

The victorious Los Angeles Rams collected $2108.44 each for winning the National League championship from the Cleveland Browns yesterday. Each losing Cleveland player got $1483.12.

The players' pool totaled $156,551.42 from a paid attendance of 57,540, the league announced last night. It is based on 70% of the net receipts.

The gross receipts, including $75,000 for the television and radio rights, was $325,970.

The gross and the players' share topped the previous high for the title game, set in 1946 between the Chicago Bears and the New York Giants at the Polo Grounds. The gross that year, which had no TV rights, was $282,955.25. The winning Bears collected $1975.82 apiece and the Giants, $1295.57.

Here are the figures:

Paid attendance—57,540.

Gross receipts, including television and radio—$325,970.

Taxes and rental—$62,624.98.

Game operating expenses—$34,078.13.

Net receipts—$223,644.89.

Total players' pool (70% of the net)—$156,551.42.

Winning players' pool—$84,537.77.

Losing players' pool—$[illegible].51.

Each winning players' share—$2108.44.

Each losing players' share—$1483.12.

Pool for sectional second-place clubs—$1[illegible].12.

HAILS THE DUTCHMAN

## Fears Calls Van Brocklin's Toss 'Best Thrown Pass I Ever Caught'

BY PAUL ZIMMERMAN

"That was the best thrown pass I ever caught in my life."

This was the high praise Tom Fears gave Norm Van Brocklin for the throw the Los Angeles Rams' big end took for the touchdown that beat the Cleveland Browns, 24 to 17, for the world's grid championship at Memorial Coliseum yesterday.

"He laid it right in there when I was going full stride," added Tom, who had faked himself into the clear on the 50-yard line to make the 73-yard scoring play possible.

While Fears' catch and run won the game, the consensus was that Los Angeles' great defensive play was the difference in the long run.

**Earns Contract**

Coach Joe Stydahar, who undoubtedly has earned himself a long-term contract with this victory, started out naming Ram stars and wound up mentioning almost everyone but Jack Zilly, who was in the press box letting his broken arm mend.

But when he got down to real cases, he bowed deepest to his defensive men. And Capt. Bob Waterfield, who was presented with the championship ball, seconded the motion.

"We kept the pressure on Otto Graham all the time," said genial Joe. "We gave him a bad time 'red dogging;' that is, rushing our linebackers as well as our line when he threw. In that last quarter, especially, we had the Browns upset the way we mixed up our defenses."

Curley Lambeau, for many years a great coach in the National League, likewise gave the Ram defense credit for the win.

**Short Conference**

Coach Paul Brown of the losers, with a smile on his face that belied defeat, walked through the Ram dressing room, congratulating the players who had just defeated Cleveland.

"Here's the guy who did it, right here!" said Brown as he put his hand on Fears' shoulder.

"We lost a football game, that's all," he said in the briefest press conference on record. "We played as hard as we could.

"It was Joseph's turn."

Brown was referring to the opposing coach in the formal fashion. Then he changed his tune.

"A little flick of the eyelash here or there could have changed things. As a matter of fact, we lost by an eyelash."

Then he dismissed the press with:

"That's all, gentlemen."

**More Mistakes**

Graham later visited the Ram dressing room to shake hands with friendly foes.

"We just made more mistakes than they did," said the great Otto.

"Great passing in there," said Don Paul, Ram linebacker.

"I sure threw a nice one to you," said Otto.

"I'm too slow," said Paul. "I should have scored on that interception."

Stydahar took the blame for the Ram play from place-kick formation at the start of the fourth quarter when Glenn Davis was thrown for a loss on fourth down.

"We went into a huddle at

Turn to Page 2, Column 6

### TODAY IN SPORTS

**WRESTLING**—Hollywood Legion Stadium, Pasadena Arena, 8:30 p.m.

PART 3 **Los Angeles Times** SPORTS

VOL LXXI CC ★ SATURDAY MORNING, MAY 31, 1952 Read The Times for Latest Sports

# RUTTMAN ROARS TO RECORD '500' VICTORY

**HI, CHAMP**—Troy Ruttman, left, 22-year-old Lynwood resident who drove the winning car in yesterday's 500-mile speed classic, shares his joy with Owner J. C. Agajanian, who built the winning racer. Ruttman averaged 128.922 in recording victory.

**TURNING POINT**—Fresno's Bill Vukovich bounces off wall at the northeast turn at Indianapolis Speedway yesterday. Accident occurred on 191st lap of 500-miler and knocked Vukovich out of the lead. Troy Ruttman went on to win. In foreground is George Fonder of Lansdale, Pa. Vukovich, unhurt, walked away from crack-up. (AP) Wirephotos

## Vukovich Cracks Up on 191st

BY JACK CURNOW
Times Staff Representative

INDIANAPOLIS, May 30. One of our Southern California "hot dog kids," 22-year-old Troy Ruttman from Lynwood, hit the jackpot here today in the fastest 500-miler ever raced. And a Northern Californian, Billy Vukovich, hit the fence while leading in a record-shattering speed duel.

Never worse than a brief third in the J. C. Agajanian Special from San Pedro, Cal., the 250-pound Ruttman sped home to the checkered flag at an average speed of 128.922. He had three laps on Jim Rathmann of Glendale, Cal., who wheeled the Granco-Wynn's Oil Special to second place.

**Records Fall**

Every record in the speed book fell here today as the kids up from the hot rod and midget ranks went full bore.

Between Ruttman and Vukovich, the "mad Russian" from Fresno, speed marks fell lap after lap. Vukie, doing a terrific job of chauffeuring Howard Keck's fuel injection Engineering Special from San Gabriel, Cal., cut a terrific pace most of the way, with Ruttman pressing him. It looked like the couple of midget kids going around Gilmore Stadium as Southland fans were used to seeing them on that tiny oval.

Ruttman got one of those assists that sometimes come along in professional racing, Lady Luck playing quite a part in this game of speed. Vukie spun on the 191st lap in the northeast turn while leading and with Ruttman getting closer to him all the time.

**Luck Steps In**

Here is the picture: Vukie and Rutt both have made their last pit stops, Ruttman losing the lead on his stop at the 147th lap to Vukie. Then the heat is really turned on, Vukie having 55 seconds to the good and Ruttman having 3 seconds on Rathmann. By 191 laps, Ruttman had cut down Vukie's lead to 19 seconds and is still gaining. Vukie has hopped his speed back up to 132, but is still losing precious ground to Ruttman who's strictly got his foot through the floorboard.

Then on lap 191 luck steps in,

Turn to Page 2, Column 5

## SPORTS PARADE

By BRAVEN DYER

Some of us with long memories who are going to the Olympic Games in Helsinki this summer will be watching Wednesday night's Compton track show with particular interest.

We'll be watching a young man named Ollie Matson, who has won considerable fame as a sprinter and footballer while carrying the colors of the University of San Francisco.

It could be, you see, that the amazing Mr. Matson will be the fifth consensus All-American football player to make the United States Olympic Games squad.

That should stamp the "Matson Liner" as one of the greatest athletes in all American history.

**EXCLUSIVE COMPANY**

Of course, you want to know right quick who are the four All-Americans who have performed for Uncle Sam in previous Olympic Games. Thanks to my efficient research department, I'm the guy to tell you.

The first was Jim Thorpe, who won the all-round title at at Stockholm in 1912 and likewise carried the mail for the Carlisle Indians.

The second was Harold P. (Brick) Muller, California's famed end of the early 20s, who was second in the high jump at Antwerp in 1920.

The third was Morton Kaer, great Trojan halfback of the mid 20s, who was sixth in the 1924 pentathlon at Paris.

And the fourth and last was Sam Francis, Nebraska's rugged fullback of 1936, who was fourth in the 1936 shot-put at Berlin.

**DANGEROUS GROUND**

I'm treading on dangerous ground by mentioning gridiron greats who carried Uncle Sam's shield into the Olympics, because I'm sure to miss some. But a partial list . . .

On the 1920 squad, for instance, there were Pesky Sprott of California, Dink Templeton and Reg Caughey of Stanford, Swede Evans of the Trojans, Bill Yount of Redlands, Charles Daggs of Pomona and Otto Anderson of Pomona High, later a corking halfback at SC.

The 1924 team included Chet Bowman of Syracuse, Tom Lieb of Notre Dame, Bill Neufeldt of California, Norm Anderson of SC and Cliff Argue of Occidental.

In 1928 there were Harlow Rothert of Stanford, Herman Brix (Bruce Bennett) of Washington and Ray Barbuti of Syracuse.

Jim Bausch of Kansas was the 1932 decathlon champion.

Jack Torrance of LSU played an all-star game at tackle, won the Olympic trials in the 1936 shot-put but was beaten at Berlin.

Glenn Morris of Colorado State captured the decathlon at Berlin after a fine gridiron career for the Aggies.

There was no All-American footballer on the 1948 Olympic squad, although Bob Mathias, with a break or two next fall, could attain such distinction. Clyde (Smackover) Scott of Arkansas was a top gridder and so was Willie Steele of San Diego State. Vic Frank and Jim Fuchs, both Yale, played football well and made the '48 Olympics.

In addition to Matson there are three footballers who might make it this time.

The best bet probably is Don Laz of Illinois. Others are Darrow Hooper of Texas and Bob Carey of Michigan State, who'll be playing for the Rams next fall.

Matson, 6-foot 2-inch, 202-pound 21-year-old, has compiled a fabulous record. He was a consensus All-American for USF last year, first player from that school to be accorded such an honor.

**TOPS IN NATION**

What the big San Francisco product accomplished on the gridiron still has Bay City writers talking. Big Ollie led the nation in yardage gained rushing and scoring last season. Pacing the Hilltop school to its only unbeaten, untied season, he outgained the opposition on the ground all by himself. In fact, it wasn't even close. Ollie rolled up 1092 more yards rushing than all USF's foes.

When Matson enrolled at USF, Dink Templeton, the veteran sage, said, "The U.S. loses the 1952 Olympic 400-meter champ and USF gains a boy that will develop into the greatest running back since Red Grange. With concentration on track, Matson could have run the quarter in 45 flat."

**ALL-OUT PITCH**

With football out of the way, Matson determined to make an all-out pitch this spring to show the promise he had displayed in '48, his senior year in high school. Then he was clocked in 47.1 in chasing Herb McKenley to the world's 440 record of 46.0

The big boy has had an amazing year. He ran two 9.6 100s in the Fresno Relays. Then he startled the track world with a sensational 46.9 quarter in the California Relays. No American has run faster since Dave Bolen's 46.7 in 1948.

Things are looking so good for Matson right now that he's concerned with the problem of which events to run. It looks as if he could win a spot in the 100, 220 or 440, which is why he's trying for the furlong and one-lap double in Herschel Smith's big Compton Invitational.

# 59,445 See Admiral Drake Triumph

## Oakland Hands Hollywood First Double Defeat

BY AL WOLF

Hollywood's Stars didn't have enough power yesterday to wind a watch, let alone drive home runs. The consequences, as might be anticipated, were horrendous.

They dropped their first double-header of the season, 6-1 and 3-0, to the Oakland Oaks, which was bad. They skidded from second to third in the Coast League standings, six lengths off the pace, which was worse. And it all happened right in front of 8495 Gilmore Field customers, which was worser.

Their only tally of the afternoon came on Carlos Bernier's theft of home.

That daring feat, beautifully executed, gave the Stars a 1-0 lead in the first fifth frame of the curtain raiser. And it still was the only score of the game as the Oaks took their bats in the eighth.

Then the lightning which scorched the locals Thursday night again hit in the same place.

The Hollywoodians went into the ninth inning of that scuffle owning a 1-0 advantage, only to

Turn to Page 2, Column 3

## Turf Wagering Records Fall

NEW YORK, May 30 (AP)—All Memorial Day race betting records were shattered today as 357,528 fans in attendance at 13 tracks shoved a total of $19,052,849 through the pari-mutuel windows.

Attendance at major-league baseball games, however, declined for the third straight year.

The breakdown:

BASEBALL

| National League | |
|---|---|
| New York at Philadelphia | 31.273 |
| St. Louis at Pittsburgh | 19.846 |
| Boston at Brooklyn | 30.703 |
| Cincinnati at Chicago | 35.999 |
| Total | 117.821 |
| **American League** | |
| Chicago at Cleveland | 36.064 |
| Philadelphia at New York | 30.005 |
| Washington at Boston | 28.767 |
| Detroit at St. Louis | 13.162 |
| Total | 107.998 |
| Grand total | 225.819 |

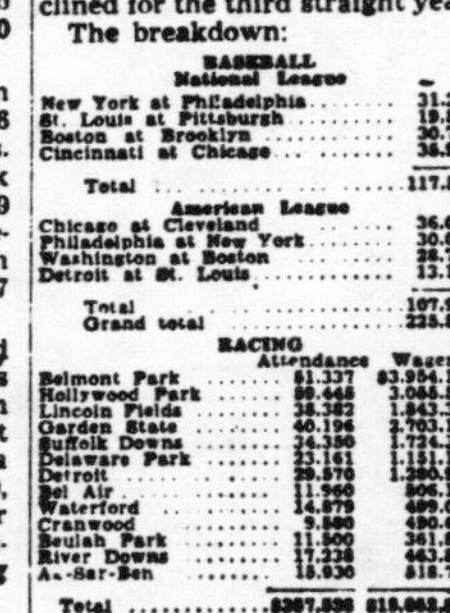

RACING

| | Attendance | Wagered |
|---|---|---|
| Belmont Park | 51.337 | $3.954.144 |
| Hollywood Park | 59.445 | 3.085.538 |
| Lincoln Fields | 38.382 | 1.843.344 |
| Garden State | 40.196 | 2.703.123 |
| Suffolk Downs | 34.350 | 1.724.398 |
| Delaware Park | 23.161 | 1.151.170 |
| Detroit | 29.570 | 1.280.951 |
| Bel Air | 11.960 | 806.127 |
| Waterford | 14.879 | 699.076 |
| Cranwood | 9.880 | 490.614 |
| Beulah Park | 11.500 | 361.887 |
| River Downs | 17.238 | 463.807 |
| Ak-Sar-Ben | 15.930 | 818.762 |
| Total | $357.528 | $19.052.849 |

**WELCOME ABOARD**—Admiral Drake whips home the winner by three lengths over Miche, the gray horse, in the $50,000-added Argonaut Handicap at Hollywood Park yesterday before 59,445 fans. Third went to Moonrush. The surprise victor paid $21.10. Times photo

## Miche Runs Second at Hollypark

BY PAUL LOWRY

Admiral Drake saved the best race of his life for the Memorial Day throng of 59,445 at Hollywood Park yesterday, and as a result Owner Abe Hirschberg is $33,550 richer this morning.

One of the lightweights in the field and not an intended starter in the Argonaut Handicap until Intent and Lights Up withdrew, Admiral Drake made a wire-to-wire victory of it, repelling Miche's stretch challenge by three lengths.

Moonrush was third and Sturdy One fourth in the nine-horse field.

**Simple Strategy**

The winner's strategy was simple and workable. He broke on top and stayed there. When Miche, the 3-to-4 favorite, who was taken back to dead last at the start, made one of his customary charges around the far turn and almost drew abreast at the three-sixteenths pole Admiral Drake merely let out another notch. He rolled away from the popular gray horse and left him stranded.

Apprentice Willie Marsh was aboard for the first stakes victory of his young life. "It was the biggest thrill of my life," said Willie. "I figured we had all the speed in the race, and it sure worked out that way over the added distance."

**Stable's Decision**

Admiral Drake has generally been restricted to sprints, but when he won an overnight mile easily Wednesday the stable figured he had a good chance with only 106 pounds on his back as against Miche's 123 in the mile and one-sixteenth feature that grossed $56,750.

The winner was a 9-to-1 shot on the tote board and paid $21.10, $7.40 and $4.70 across the

Turn to Page 5, Col. 4, Pt. 1

## Gil Hodges Slaps Two Homers, Bats in Eight Runs as Brooklyn Bags Pair

BROOKLYN, May 30 (AP)—Gil Hodges broke out of his dismal .198 batting slump to drive home eight runs today as Brooklyn knocked off Boston twice, 5-4 and 11-2, to slice New York's National League lead to a half game. The Braves now have lost all eight 1952 starts to the Dodgers.

Humiliated by the pitchers in early season, Hodges won the first game with his fifth home run, a three-run blast in the eighth inning that knocked out Jim Wilson. He nailed down the second game with another three-run poke in the fifth inning that finished Starter Dick Donovan.

With two hits in the opener and a perfect score of a homer, two singles and two walks in the second, Hodges picked up some 29 batting points during the holiday double.

In the second game, Carl Erskine allowed only one hit—Paul Burris' first major league homer—in a seven-inning relief job after replacing Johnny Schmitz. The Braves had only one other hit—a single by Burris—off Schmitz.

Although the second game was a rout, the opener was tight all the way. A pair of homers by Sid Gordon, his fifth and sixth,

Turn to Page 3, Column 8

## TODAY IN SPORTS

**HORSE RACING**—Hollywood Park, 1:30 p.m.

**BASEBALL**—Hollywood Stars vs. Oakland Oaks, 2:15 p.m.

**BOXING** — Hollywood Legion Stadium, 8:30 p.m.

**AUTO RACING**—Culver City Stadium, 8:30 p.m.

**WRESTLING**—Valley Garden Arena, 8:30 p.m., Pomona Stadium, 8:30 p.m.

**STOCK CAR RACING**—Huntington Beach Speedway, 8:30 p.m.

## STANDINGS

PACIFIC COAST LEAGUE

| | W | L | Pct. | * |
|---|---|---|---|---|
| San Diego | 39 | 21 | .650 | |
| Oakland | 32 | 25 | .561 | 5½ |
| HOLLYWOOD | 32 | 26 | .552 | 6 |
| LOS ANGELES | 29 | 29 | .500 | 9 |
| San Francisco | 28 | 31 | .475 | 10½ |
| Portland | 24 | 32 | .429 | 13 |
| Sacramento | 24 | 34 | .414 | 14 |
| Seattle | 23 | 33 | .411 | 14 |

*Games behind leader.

Yesterday's Results

Oakland, 6-3; Hollywood, 1-0.
San Francisco, 5-4; LOS ANGELES, 0-3.
San Diego, 5-1; Portland, 2-0.
Sacramento, 3-2; Seattle, 2-3 (second game, 13 innings).

How Series Stand

Oakland, 3; HOLLYWOOD, 1.
LOS ANGELES, 2; San Francisco, 2.
Sacramento, 3; Seattle, 2.
San Diego, 4; Portland, 1.

Games Today

Oakland (Gettel, 4-4) at HOLLYWOOD (Woods, 3-3), Gilmore Field, 2:15 p.m.
LOS ANGELES (Bacszewski, 0-2) at San Francisco (Roeder, 3-6).
Seattle (Davis, 3-3) at Sacramento (Elliott, 4-5).
Portland (Lint, 1-3) at San Diego (Olsen, 5-4).

NATIONAL LEAGUE

| | W | L | Pct. | * |
|---|---|---|---|---|
| New York | 27 | 10 | .730 | |
| Brooklyn | 26 | 10 | .722 | ½ |
| Chicago | 23 | 16 | .590 | 5 |
| Cincinnati | 19 | 20 | .487 | 9 |
| Philadelphia | 17 | 19 | .472 | 9½ |
| St. Louis | 18 | 22 | .450 | 10½ |
| Boston | 13 | 22 | .371 | 13 |
| Pittsburgh | 9 | 33 | .214 | 20½ |

*Games behind leader.

Yesterday's Results

Philadelphia, 3-2; New York, 0-4.
Brooklyn, 5-11; Boston, 4-2.
St. Louis, 3-3; Pittsburgh, 3-4.
Chicago, 7-11; Cincinnati, 6-6.

Games Today

Philadelphia (Possehl, 0-0) at Pittsburgh (Rickert, 0-0).
Cincinnati (Miller, 4-3) at Chicago (Minner, 4-1).
Only games scheduled.

AMERICAN LEAGUE

| | W | L | Pct. | * |
|---|---|---|---|---|
| Cleveland | 26 | 17 | .605 | |
| Boston | 22 | 16 | .579 | [illegible] |
| Washington | 21 | 17 | .553 | [illegible] |
| Chicago | 21 | 19 | .525 | [illegible] |
| New York | 18 | 17 | .514 | 3½ |
| St. Louis | 20 | 24 | .455 | 6 |
| Philadelphia | 15 | 19 | .441 | 6 |
| Detroit | 12 | 25 | .324 | 10½ |

*Games behind leader.

Yesterday's Results

Chicago, 7-2; Cleveland, 3-1.
Washington, 8-2; Boston, 2-8.
Philadelphia, 2-4; New York, 3-8 (first game 14 innings).
St. Louis, 3-8; Detroit, 3-6 (second game 12 innings).

Games Today

Cleveland (Lemon, 4-4) at New York (Lopat, 1-3).
Chicago (Grissom, 1-3) at Boston (Scarborough, 1-2).
St. Louis (Madison, 1-0) at Philadelphia (Harris, 0-4), night.
Detroit (Stuart, 1-2) at Washington (Sima, 3-0), night.

PART 4 **Los Angeles Times** SPORTS

VOL. LXXI CC ★ TUESDAY MORNING, JULY 22, 1952 Read Times Green for Latest Sports

# AMERICANS WIN FOUR OLYMPIC MEDALS

## SPORTS PARADE

BY BRAVEN DYER

HELSINKI, July 21—One of the never-to-be-forgotten features of this European safari was the pilgrimage which several of us made the other day to the world's most famous golf course—St. Andrews.

We were billeted in Edinburgh at the time and when Art Kivari found out that we were only a couple hours away from the shrine of all devout linksmen we made arrangements for the trip. Brother Kivari is a member in good standing at the Lakeside Golf Club and said as how he wouldn't dare go back to the Toluca Lake layout and face Marty Zahn, Maurie Luxford, Peter DePaolo and all the gang if they ever learned he had passed up St. Andrews.

**FERRY VOYAGE**

So the five of us — we included Ham Hamilton, Bill Hubbard and Col. Tommy Atkinson — hired an auto and away we went. By ferryboat we crossed the Firth of Forth, fabled in ancient and modern history, and landed after a 30-minute voyage. Our ferry had been a landing craft during the war and had been converted by the thrifty Scots.

An hour's drive up the rugged coast of Scotland brought us to the city of St. Andrews and in a few minutes we were standing on the first tee. On the first tee of what is called "the old course," that is.

There are four courses, the others being the new, the Eden and a mammoth putting layout which, once each week, is reserved for novelty putting. This means that all the children are allowed to take part and on the day of our visit they were scurrying all over the place by the hundreds, each with a putter in his or her hand, laughing, shouting and chasing the ball from one hole to the next. This is a regular Friday feature during the months of June, July and August, apparently when the kids are out of school.

**LISTEN TO IT WHISTLE**

There are three striking features about St. Andrews which are immediately apparent, even to those who do not play golf. In the order of their importance they are the whistling wind, the hundreds of bunkers and the complete absence of trees.

The wind should be called a gale. It blows all the time and may completely reverse itself at any moment. On some holes a slice or hook can land in the North Sea. There are bunkers all over the place and instead of trees there is an occasional bush. I don't know why there aren't any trees, except that they probably haven't discovered any type sufficiently strong to withstand the offsea gales.

The charge to play "the old course," which is the course, is 3 shillings and sixpence, roughly 48 cents. The other courses may be played for 2 shillings. Strangely, a caddie costs more . . . He gets 85 cents per 18 holes.

**SNEAD WON IN '46**

There is no Sunday golf, except on the Eden course. And there probably wouldn't be any there except that during the recent war the general in charge of allied servicemen billeted near St. Andrews requested that the boys be accommodated, and this concession was never reversed when hostilities ceased.

There have been many British Opens played at St. Andrews, of course, and the last, in 1946, was won by Sam Snead with a total of 290, beating Bobby Locke, the current champion, by 4 strokes. For this title event the course was extended from 6572 yards to 6883. Par is 73, so Slammin' Sam was the only man to break it in '46. Contrast that with some of our big money tournaments where the winner often is 14 under par with the first 10 bunched closely behind.

The wind and the rain keep the courses in wonderful shape, except that the greens are apt to be very hard most of the time. It is almost impossible to make a ball stick, hence the pitch-and-run shot is favored for approaches.

**A FAIR QUESTION**

I asked the official starter when the course was built. He gave me a withering look and replied in a rich brogue, "Nobody knows."

He could be right at that. The university which is located in the town was founded in 1411 and is the oldest in Scotland. It attracts 2000 students.

The Royal and Ancient Golf Club of St. Andrews was founded in 1754, so it must be that the course was built prior to this.

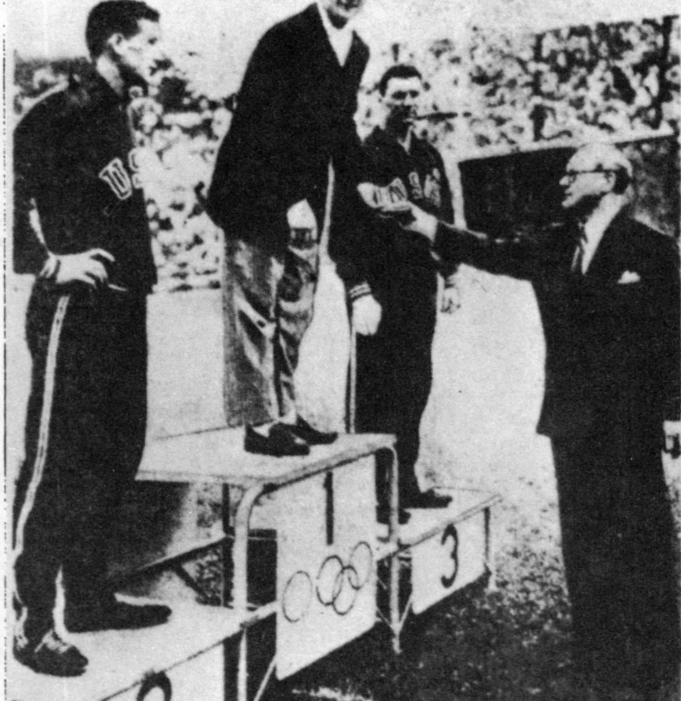

TO THE VICTOR — Parry O'Brien, SC shot-put star, receives gold medal for winning event in Olympics from Avery Brundage. Others are Hooper (left), second, Fuchs, third. (AP) Wirephoto

## Record Set by O'Brien in Shot-Put

BY PAUL ZIMMERMAN
Times Sports Editor

HELSINKI, July 21—Five times the world's greatest athletes paraded to the victory stand here today and on four of those occasions it was "The Star-Spangled Banner" that resounded through the stands in token of United States' triumphs.

For the first time in history of the Olympic Games an American and a Russian stood on the tribunal together. And Yankee Charles Moore, 400-meter hurdles champion, stood the higher.

One world record and two Olympic marks were posted this second day of the track and field competition, staged before a scattered crowd of 20,000 who braved a chill wind and occasional showers.

**O'Brien Wins Shot**

Witnessing the sharp competition, Italian Giuseppe Dordoni posted a world and Olympic mark of 4h. 28m. 7.8s. in the 50,000-meter walk.

A stalwart son of California, Parry O'Brien of Santa Monica and the University of Southern California, chalked up the other Olympic record when he won the shot-put as America swept the event.

The handsome, bronzed giant uncoiled himself with a terrific record-shattering toss of the first time he stepped in the ring for a 57ft. 1.43in. effort. Other red-white-and-blue shield wearers besides Moore and O'Brien who won gold medals this dreary day were Jerome Biffle, broad jump, and Lindy Remigino, 100 meters victor.

**Brown, Bagnes Miss**

It was an unhappy day for two of California's contingent. George Brown fouled all three efforts in the second qualifying round of the broad jump and failed to get into the final six. John Barnes, Occidental's NCAA champion, ran fourth in his semifinal heat of the 800 meters and will not be there for tomorrow's finals.

O'Brien had two throws over the 1948 record performance of Wilbur Thompson, also of SC, 56ft. 2in., and Darrow Hooper, finished second, likewise surpassed the mark with a toss of 57ft. 0.63in. Jim Fuchs was third but he never approached the two collegians.

**Close 100 Final**

Remigino's victory in the short sprint was scant inches over the amazing veteran Herb McKenley. Less than a foot separated the first four finishers, with McDonald Bailey of Britain third and Uncle Sam's Dean Smith of Texas U. fourth. Identical times of 10.4 were given all four.

The victor, a Manhattan College star, was off fast and led all the way, just barely chesting the tape ahead of the fast flying Jamaican who was still protesting at a late hour tonight that he won although the photo timer said no.

Arthur Bragg, the other United States sprinter, pulled up

Turn to Page 3, Column 4

### Gold Medal Winners

Yesterday's first-place finishers in Olympic track and field:

Shot-put — Parry O'Brien, U.S.A. (Southern California), 57ft. 1.43in.

Broad jump—Jerome Biffle, U.S.A. (Denver), 24ft. 10in.

400-meter hurdles — Charley Moore, U.S.A. (Cornell), 50.8.

100 meters — Lindy Remigino, U.S.A. (Manhattan), 10.4.

50,000-meter walk—Giuseppi Dordoni, Italy, 4h. 28m. 7.8s.

YOU CALL IT—Here's official photo finish that decided places in 100 meters. From top (with placings): Vladimir Soukharev, Russia; Herb McKenley, Jamaica; Lindy Remigino, U.S.; Dean Smith, U.S.; McDonald Bailey, Britain; John Treloar, Australia. (AP) Wirephoto

## Twinks Open Series With Sacs Tonight

BY AL WOLF

Is the Coast League pennant race all over—except for triumphant snake-dancing along Hollywood Blvd. by the Stars and their followers?

With two months of campaigning left, the answer obviously is no.

But after what happened last week, even the most conservative of railbirds agree that the Stars will be hard to stop—and that only the Oakland Oaks remain in serious contention.

In capturing seven out of eight from San Diego, Fred Haney's men vaulted from third place to first and pretty plainly knocked the Padres out of the running.

**Pair Fade**

Meanwhile, Seattle and Los Angeles likewise faded from the pennant picture.

San Diego now is five games back, Seattle 10½ and Los Angeles 12½.

Only a 1½-length spread separates the Stars and Oaks, though, and a driving finish between these two teams seems likely to ensue. Oakland, already boasting an 11-5 edge over Hollywood for the season, gets eight more cracks at the new leaders. The clubs clash in four games at Emeryville, Sept. 1-3, and in four more at Gilmore Field, Sept. 12-14.

Both contenders figure to make more hay this week.

**Walsh on Crag**

Hollywood meets last-place Sacramento in a seven-game series here, starting tonight. Oakland entertains seventh-place San Francisco in a nine-gamer.

The Stars, with 13 victories over the Sacs in 21 meetings, will pitch Jim Walsh (6-7) this evening. Manager Joe Gordon, faced with a make-up doubleheader against Portland last night, declined to look ahead, so the identity of the Sacto starting slinger tonight remains a puzzle—probably even to Gordon.

Walsh accounted for two victories, both via four-hitters, as Hollywood streaked to 10 straight wins before bowing to San Diego in Sunday's nightcap here, 1-0.

**Two New Faces**

There'll be two new faces in the Sacramento line-up tonight, belonging to First Baseman Ben Taylor and Outfielder Dino Restelli. They were forthcoming last week in the deal which sent First Sacker Bill Glynn to Cleveland. Taylor had been at Indianapolis and Restelli, a former Coaster, with Tulsa.

The week's fourth series sends Los Angeles to Seattle.

FONDEST AMBITION

## O'Brien Continues Long SC Win Tradition

BY BRAVEN DYER
Times Staff Representative

HELSINKI, July 21—"I was very fortunate to realize my fondest ambition by winning the Olympic shot-put," said modest Parry O'Brien, 218-pound University of Southern California junior after starting a sweep of male events in today's Olympic track program during alternate sun, showers and terrific applause by the fans.

"I was very happy to see my teammates, Hooper and Fuchs, come in second and third so the United States could finish one-two-three for the first time in the 1952 Olympics," continued the broad-shouldered husky from Santa Monica, the son of former star athlete Parry O'Brien Sr., who now has an important post at the MGM studio.

"If weather conditions had been better I feel that all of us Americans and other finalists could have exceeded marks we made from the heavy and muddy ring this afternoon.

"Yes, I heard the fans cheering for me," said O'Brien, answering whether he heard hundreds of Americans giving him the old college yell, 'Let's go, O'Brien.'"

American rooters gave this yell virtually every time O'Brien entered the circle even though he was leading the field after his very first put, on which he set new Olympic record of 57ft. 1.43in.

"It was the greatest thrill of my life when I stood on the victory stand and saw the American Flags go up for first three places and hear the band play 'The Star-Spangled Banner,'" said Parry.

As the first Californian to win a 1952 Olympic championship, O'Brien naturally was very popular with American rooters, at least half of whom hail from Southern California. They showed their appreciation for his record-breaking peformance

Turn to Page 3, Column 4

### TODAY IN SPORTS

**HORSE RACING**—Del Mar, 2 p.m.

**BASEBALL**—Sacramento vs. Hollywood, Gilmore Field, 8:15 p.m.

**BOXING** — Olympic Auditorium, 8:30 p.m.

**WRESTLING** — South Gate Arena, 8:30 p.m.; Wilmington Bowl, 8:30 p.m.

ARMY FLIER—Jerome Biffle of U.S. Army gets off leap of 24ft. 10.03in. to win broad jump in Olympic Games. (AP) Wirephoto

## Yankees Batter Bums, 5 to 3

NEW YORK, July 21 (AP) — In what 48,263 fans flocked to see as a "World Series preview" tonight, the New York Yankees retained their jinx over the Brooklyn Dodgers, soaring to a 5-3 victory on the wings of Mickey Mantle's homer with one aboard in the eighth and last inning.

Because of an agreement to enable the Yanks to catch their train west, the Dodgers never had a chance to bat in the ninth.

This marked the seventh straight year the Yanks have won the Mayor's Trophy from their N.L. rivals.

| | | | |
|---|---|---|---|
| Brooklyn (NL) | 000 100 02—3 | 6 | 0 |
| New York (AL) | 000 010 22—5 | 8 | 1 |

Game called after 8th inning to allow New York to catch train.

Schmitz, King (8) and Walker; Miller, Ostrowski (8) and Berra, Silvera (5).

Winner—Ostrowski. Loser—King. Home runs: Brooklyn—Robinson; New York—Mantle.

## DEL MAR INAUGURAL TODAY LURES ELEVEN

BY PAUL LOWRY
Times Staff Representative

DEL MAR, July 21—Earthquakes below or flying saucers above, Del Mar opens its 13th horse-racing season tomorrow to the old familiar tune oft warbled by Bing Crosby, "Where the Turf Meets the Surf." An opening-day crowd of 10,000 is anticipated.

It is distressing to this observer to report that there was a bit of a haze over the nearby ocean this morning instead of a bright and glowing sun but the natives insist things will be different in a day or two. They say summer weather is just around the corner and we hope they're right. They have been wrong for two or three years running.

The earthquake did no damage down this way and if anything it shook some pretty snappy drills out of a number of horses, including Big Noise, winner of the last Del Mar Futurity in the colors of Betty Grable and Harry James. He stepped five-eighths in 59 3-5 while such horses as Venerable and Red Bachelor were clocked in 34 2-5 and 34 4-5 for three-eighths, respectively, indicating the track is not exactly on the slow side.

The opening-day's feature will be the six-furlong Inaugural, a $5000 allowance race for fillies and mares 3 years old and up.

It drew 11 entries, with Mrs. Thelma Sneed's Fair Regards and Mr. and Mrs. R. H McDaniels' Great Dream likely to vie for the role of post-time favorite.

**Wins First Test**

Fair Regards won her first and only start at Hollywood Park during the latter part of the meeting after having been sidelined for nearly a year, while Great Dream was only beaten a nose by Ky. Lea in her last race.

The remainder of the field includes Miss Terri, Blue Lea, No Buts, Family Pride, Blue Cloth.

Turn to Page 4, Column 6

## BASEBALL STANDINGS

### PACIFIC COAST LEAGUE

| | Hollywood | Oakland | San Diego | Seattle | Los Angeles | Portland | San Francisco | Sacramento | Won | Lost | Percentage | Games Behind Leader |
|---|---|---|---|---|---|---|---|---|---|---|---|---|
| Hol. | | 5 | 17 | 8 | 6 | 10 | 8 | 13 | 67 | 45 | .598 | |
| Oak. | 11 | | 5 | 11 | 7 | 14 | 8 | 9 | 65 | 46 | .586 | 1½ |
| S.D. | 4 | 9 | | 9 | 7 | 9 | 16 | 8 | 62 | 50 | .554 | 5 |
| Sea. | 5 | 10 | 2 | | 12 | 5 | 9 | 10 | 54 | 53 | .505 | 10½ |
| L.A. | 7 | 7 | 7 | 9 | | 6 | 10 | 9 | 55 | 58 | .487 | 12½ |
| Port. | 4 | 7 | 7 | 5 | 15 | | 7 | 7 | 52 | 58 | .473 | 14 |
| S.F. | 6 | 3 | 5 | 5 | 6 | 7 | | 13 | 45 | 66 | .405 | 21½ |
| Sac. | 8 | 5 | 6 | 6 | 5 | 7 | 8 | | 45 | 69 | .395 | 23 |
| Lost | 45 | 46 | 50 | 53 | 58 | 58 | 66 | 69 | | | | |

Coast League standings appear in this style each Tuesday.

**Yesterday's Results**

Portland, 3-1; Sacramento, 1-2 (first game 11 innings, second game 13 innings). Only games scheduled.

**Games Today**

Sacramento (Johnson, 6-10) at HOLLYWOOD (Walsh, 6-7) Gilmore Field, 8:15 p.m.

LOS ANGELES (Moisan, 11-4) at Seattle (Davis, 6-5).

San Francisco (Lien, 6-11, and Bradford, 9-10) at Oakland (Hittle, 8-10, and Evans, 1-2).

Portland (Lint, 2-5) at San Diego (Fletcher, 10-10).

### AMERICAN LEAGUE

| | W | L | Pct. | * |
|---|---|---|---|---|
| New York | 54 | 34 | .614 | |
| Boston | 49 | 38 | .563 | 4½ |
| Washington | 49 | 39 | .557 | 5 |
| Cleveland | 49 | 40 | .551 | 5½ |
| Chicago | 48 | 43 | .527 | 7½ |
| Philadelphia | 39 | 42 | .481 | 11½ |
| St. Louis | 35 | 56 | .385 | 20½ |
| Detroit | 28 | 59 | .322 | 25½ |

*Games behind leader.

**Yesterday's Results**

No games scheduled.

**Games Today**

Boston (Parnell, 7-5) at Chicago (Grissom, 7-5), night.

Philadelphia (Shantz, 16-3) at St. Louis (Garver, 5-9), night.

Washington (Shea, 9-2) at Detroit (Trucks, 3-11), night.

New York (Raschi, 10-2, and Reynolds, 11-5) at Cleveland (Feller, 7-8, and Gromek, 5-3), twi-night double-header.

### NATIONAL LEAGUE

| | W | L | Pct. | * |
|---|---|---|---|---|
| Brooklyn | 59 | 22 | .728 | |
| New York | 53 | 31 | .631 | 7½ |
| St. Louis | 51 | 39 | .567 | 12½ |
| Chicago | 45 | 42 | .517 | 17 |
| Philadelphia | 43 | 45 | .489 | 19½ |
| Boston | 37 | 50 | .425 | 25 |
| Cincinnati | 36 | 53 | .404 | 27 |
| Pittsburgh | 25 | 67 | .272 | 39½ |

*Games behind leader.

**Yesterday's Results**

No games scheduled.

**Games Today**

Chicago (Rush, 9-7, or Klippstein, 6-7) at Boston (Bickford, 5-8), night.

Cincinnati (Wehmeier, 4-7) at Brooklyn (Roe, 7-0), night.

St. Louis (Staley, 12-8) at New York (Koslo, 6-3), night.

Pittsburgh (Main, 2-7, and Friend, 4-14, or Hogue, 1-0) at Philadelphia (Meyer, 6-12, and Drews, 6-10), twi-night double-header.

### Fights Last Night

BROOKLYN—Pat Manzi, 146, Syracuse, outpointed Ted Murray, 148, New York (8).

DARTMOUTH, Nova Scotia—Orlando Zulueta, 135, Havana, outpointed Noel Paquette, 140, Montreal (10).

NEW ORLEANS—Bernard Docusen, 146, New Orleans, T.k.o. (4) over Joe Hardegen, 142, New Orleans.

## U.S. Vaults Over Russ to Lead in Standings

HELSINKI, July 21 (AP)—The United States vaulted over Russia into first place in the team standings of the Olympic Games today with probably the biggest day of scoring by any nation in Olympic history.

American athletes scored 57 points to raise their country's total to 72. The Russians, meanwhile, added only 17 points for a two-day total of 40 points, good for second place.

Czechoslovakia ranked third with 15, Great Britain fourth with 14 and Italy fifth with 11.

The United States ran up its amazing 57-point total today with: First, second and third in the shot-put, first and second in the broad jump, first in the 400-meter hurdles, first and fourth in the 100 meters.

In two days of competition, the United States had won five track and field events. Russia, Czechoslovakia and Italy have won one each.

On the scoring basis of 10-5-4-3-2-1, the unofficial team standings after the second day were:

United States, 72; Russia, 40; Czechoslovakia, 15; Great Britain, 14; Italy, 11; Hungary, 8; Brazil, 7; Sweden, 6; Finland, 5; Jamaica, 5; France, 5; New Zealand, 4; Japan, 3; Austria, 2; Rumania, 2; Australia, 1.

# BOB MATHIAS SMASHES DECATHLON RECORD

## McMillen Step Behind Winner in 1500-Meter Classic

### SPORT SCRIPTS

By PAUL ZIMMERMAN
TIMES SPORTS EDITOR

HELSINKI, July 26—Urho E. Saari, coach of the El Segundo water polo team that is representing the United States in the Olympic Games here, is a chap with a problem.

Although American born, he is of Finnish parentage and had dreamed for years of visiting the land of his kin. Now he is here but so far Saari, who learned to speak the language from his folks, has seen only Helsinki.

**TOO BUSY**

Under the schedule of chartered Olympic planes the water polo team will leave Finland and fly directly back to the United States immediately after the conclusion of the competition. Up to the first official water polo competition tomorrow Coach Saari has been busy with workouts and practice games.

So, unless things work out differently, his visit to the native land is going to begin and end with Helsinki, period.

Roy, as Urho is known around the plunges and beaches at El Segundo, was born in Buffalo but his folks came to California about 10 years ago. He attended UCLA where he earned his teaching credentials and he's now in the El Segundo schools system.

**ROY GIGGLES**

When we asked Roy how he got started in water polo coaching he laughed and said: "You should know. I was stationed in Calcutta in the Army during the war when you were over there."

A staff sergeant with a fine knowledge of swimming, Saari landed in the replacement depot in Kanjaperi, near Calcutta. He went to the Red Cross canteen in Calcutta one night and ran into Fuzz Merritt, the Pomona College coach.

**GOT NEW JOB**

Fuzz immediately took him to Maj. John Trutter, special service officer for the area.

"Here," said Fuzz to the major, "is the man you've been looking for to run your GI swimming program." Gen. Bob Neyland, now recognized as one of the greatest football coaches in the land, was commanding the base there and had ordered a heavy athletic program for his troops.

So it was no trouble for the major to get Sgt. Saari transferred.

"I started developing a water polo team there," recalls Roy, "and we had a good one. We played the British army, navy and Indian teams and did exceptionally well. I've been at it ever since."

**BETTER TEAMS**

United States water polo teams haven't won a title since 1904 and this year probably will be no exception. However, this squad, composed of eight Southern Californians, should be better than the one we had at London in 1948.

The average age of the boys is 21 years and it probably is the youngest team in the competitions here. Bill Lake of El Camino JC is 19. Bob Hughes, Coast Guard; Harry Bisbey, Coast Guard and ex-Trojan; Jim Norris, SC; John Spargo and Pete Stange, UCLA, are all 21.

The "baby" of the squad is Bill Dornblaser of El Camino, who is 18. Marvin Burns, Whittier and SC, is the "old man" of the Southern California contingent at 23. However, he's overshadowed by two alternates, Bill Kooisten of the Illinois AC, who is 25, and Ed Jaworski of the New York AC, age 26.

**TOUGHEST TEAMS**

Coach Saari considers the Holland, Sweden, Hungary, Argentina and Italy teams to be the toughest in the competitions here.

"Most of the members of these teams are veterans who have been working together for several years," says Roy, "and they have the advantage of experience on us. However, we have youth and none of them will outgame us."

Saari would like nothing better than to spring an upset here with this El Segundo team in the land of his parents.

P.S.—His next choice still is to see something more of Finland.

HUSKY HEAVE—Bob Mathias of Tulare, who successfully defended his Olympic decathlon championship yesterday in Helsinki, tosses discus 153ft. 10.06in., good for 838 points. The 21-year-old Mathias totaled 7887 points, a new world record.
(AP) Wirephoto via radio from Helsinki

ANOTHER RECORD—Joseph Barthel (406) of Luxembourg noses out Bob McMillen, left, of Occidental, in new Olympic record time of 3:45.2. Third is Werner Lueg (739) of Germany. R. G. Bannister (177) of England finished fourth. The surprising McMillen was given the same time as Barthel. Old record was 3:47.8.
(AP) Wirephoto via radio from Helsinki

HAPPY TRIO—Congratulating each other after making one-two-three sweep in Olympic decathlon are: Bob Mathias, center; Milt Campbell, left, and Floyd Simmons.
(AP) Wirephoto

### OXY STAR JUST MISSES

## McMillen Says He Started Closing Sprint Just a Little Bit Too Late

BY BRAVEN DYER
Times Staff Representative

HELSINKI, July 26—"If I had started sprinting just a little sooner I think I may have won the race. But Barthel is a great runner and entitled to full credit for beating the world's best 1500-meter stars."

This was the comment of Occidental's Bob McMillen immediately after he ascended the Olympic Games victory stand to accept the second-place medal behind the stout-hearted ace from little-known Luxembourg, Joseph Barthel.

The slender Oxy runner lost by a foot after forcing the fading Barthel to break the Olympic record by more than two seconds. The finish was so close the officials gave McMillen the same time as the victor—3:45.2.

In fact it was so swift a race that all of the first six finishers cracked the record of 3:47.8 set 14 years ago by New Zealand's Jack Lovelock at Berlin.

"I felt fine before and during the race and I'm happy to be able to help bring additional points to the United States' team. Naturally, I would have liked to win. But I did my best and it wasn't good enough," the black-haired runner, a member of the 1948 team as a steeplechaser, said.

Dink Templeton, former Stanford track coach, was of the opinion that McMillen lost his winning chance on the next to last turn where there was much jostling and McMillen was forced wide. As reported here before, taking the turns in the Olympics is an art and the guy with the sharpest elbows and most European experience gets through the pack easiest.

Most of us American rooters were convinced McMillen would have won had the race been two yards longer. He clearly was the strongest at the finish and as he himself said, it could have been different had he begun to sprint a wee bit earlier. But the final lap in the Olympic 1500 meters looked much like a quarter-mile dash plus bargain day at Bullock's basement as all 12 run-

Turn to Page 9, Column 3

## TULARE GOES WILD OVER WIN BY FAVORITE SON, MATHIAS

TULARE, July 26 (AP)—Tulare went wild today when news of favorite son Bob Mathias' record win in the Olympic decathlon championship reached here.

An estimated 1000 persons staged demonstrations that almost got out of hand at times. Fire engines, ambulances and numerous cars formed an impromptu parade past the home of Dr. and Mrs. Charles Mathias, Bob's parents, and back through the downtown streets.

A special Associated Press teletype had been set up in a downtown hotel by the Tulare Advance-Register to bring bulletins from Helsinki to the fans crowding the hotel lobby and point scores were tabulated on a large bulletin board.

## Tulare's Titan Leads American Sweep in Event

BY PAUL ZIMMERMAN
Times Sports Editor

HELSINKI, July 26—The incomparable Bob Mathias, already the greatest athlete the world has ever known, outdid himself again tonight under the most trying conditions as he won the XVth Olympiad decathlon championship with 7887 points.

This grand total shattered his own global mark of 7825, posted at Tulare less than a month ago, and placed on the Olympic record books a mark that this universe's athletes will be shooting at for years to come.

Mathias' victory gave Uncle Sam's greatest array of color-bearers their 13th gold medal for the largest track and field total of all time.

**Sweep for Uncle Sam**

Second in the grueling two-day event, supreme test of a man's all-around ability, was a New Jersey high school lad, 18-year-old Milton Campbell, and third was Floyd Simmons of the Los Angeles Athletic Club who won the bronze medal for this same event in 1948. Campbell scored 6975 points while Simmons had a 6788 total.

By finishing one-two-three the decathlon heroes presented America with its fourth sweep of the Games.

The competition, which started at 10 a.m. today, lasted 12 hours under laden skies that occasionally spattered rain on the contestants.

In fourth place was Russian Vladimir Volkov with 6674 points. Sepp Hipp of Germany was fifth with 6559 and Goran Widenfelt of Sweden sixth with 6388.

**Frenchman Scratched**

Ignace Heinrich of France, hailed as Europe's best, withdrew in the morning with an injured ankle. Four events remained at the time but the Frenchman was already out of the placing and would have finished behind the American trio.

Twenty-one of the world's sturdiest athletes were in the event, but there were none in the same class with the strapping pride of Tulare, the 6-foot 3-inch, 198-pound giant who won this same event at London when he was only 17 years old.

Big Bob, a fullback on Stanford University's football team, suffered a slight muscle pull yesterday and wore a bandage wrapped around his left thigh today. But Bob said the injury didn't bother him.

More than 10,000 fans stayed in this huge stadium until after 10 p.m. to see the finish of the final event, the 1500 meters, and their cheers rent the air when it was announced Mathias had broken the record.

As Bob rested in the dressing

Turn to Page 9, Column 1

## Luxembourg's Barthel Nips Oxy Ace in Record-breaker

BY PAUL ZIMMERMAN
Times Sports Editor

HELSINKI, July 26—Lion-hearted Bob McMillen, a lean, lithe Southern Californian, came within a step of Olympic immortality here today.

From dead last as the field entered the final lap, the gallant runner from Occidental College unleashed a sensational, heart-pulling sprint that carried him to within a foot of Joseph Barthel of Luxembourg, the victor in one of the most thrilling 1500-meter races ever staged.

Barthel was clocked in the remarkable Olympic record time of 3:45.2 and the skinny Southlander, a product of Cathedral High and Glendale Junior College, was credited with the same time. It was the fastest race ever recorded by an American, the best previous clocking being 3:47.9 set by Walter Mehl at Fresno 12 years ago.

The first lap was a sizzling 57.2 and the last was an even more unbelievable 57. McMillen's time, obviously, was even swifter as he roared from far back and the clockings are taken off the lap leaders.

**Driving Finish**

Had the runners been able to continue at a similar pace for a mile—roughly 120 yards farther—they would have raced a 4:03 mile.

McMillen's driving finish in the 1500 meters was an upset which almost matched the victory of Horace Ashenfelter in the steeplechase yesterday as 50,000 roared full-voiced approval.

Third and fourth in the 1500 today were the favorites, Werner Lueg of Germany and Roger Bannister of Great Britain, respectively.

McMillen had not been given even an outside chance to finish in the first six by any of the experts prior to the race. In fact Warren Druetzler of the Army, who finished 12th today, had been rated ahead of McMillen who finished last in his steeplechase qualifying heat in the 1948 games.

**McMillen Surprised**

Even McMillen was pessimistic prior to the event.

"I didn't think I could do it," Bob gasped after the race. "Yes, I just prayed and hoped. If I had only started four yards sooner I could have caught Barthel. No, I shouldn't have said that. He's a fine runner and a very humble fellow. I never prayed so hard in my life. God's been awfully good to me."

Everyone agreed that McMillen should have started his kick a bit sooner. He was last going into the final lap. He spurted to fourth down the backstretch and held this spot around the final turn.

Suddenly, weaving his way between the weary runners like a halfback in a broken field, came the slender McMillen. He passed the faltering Lueg 10 yards from the tape and in one or two more strides he would have won as Barthel was fading rapidly.

Two Germans, Rolf Lamers and Lueg, were the early pace-setters with Druetzler at their heels. Bannister, a heavy choice, was far off the pace. McMillen stayed in last place until the final lap as Druetzler hung on and Barthel, the chemist from Luxembourg, moved up to press the German, Lueg. Barthel went to the front on the final turn and held a 3-yard advantage on Lueg as McMillen, flying like the wind, surged up.

"I got into trouble and almost didn't qualify yesterday trying to stay on the pace. Today I stayed out of trouble all the way. Oh, how I wish I had started my kick sooner," McMillen said.

The Americans won both their heats in the 400 and 1600-meter relays.

In the longer race the U.S. team of Ollie Matson, Gene Cole, Charlie Moore and Mal Whitfield was clocked in 3:11.5 but they'll have trouble with the powerful Jamaican team of Herb McKenley, Les Laing, Arthur Wint and George Rhoden which won its heat in 3:12.1.

In the sprint relay the team of Dean Smith, Harrison Dillard, Lindy Remigino and Andy Stanfield breezed to an easy victory in 40.3 despite some poor baton passing.

Marjorie Jackson of Australia won her second gold medal of the games when she took the 200-meter dash in 23.7 and Galina Zybina of Russia won the shot in 50ft. 2.58in., a new world and Olympic record.

## KILLER KIM STOPS MADRID IN 7TH ROUND AT HOLLYWOOD

BY CAL WHORTON

Phil Kim, the Honolulu assassin, is still socking 1.000 in his Stateside knockout league. The dour looking Korean kept his string intact last night at Hollywood Legion Stadium where he hammered out a seventh round t.k.o. over ever willing Manny Madrid in the scheduled 10-round main event before an excited, shirt-sleeved gathering of 4300 customers.

Kim won all the way but there were times along the route when he had to step to keep ahead of his game foe. Madrid, although staggered once in the first and again in the second, might have weathered Kim's brutal attack to the end had he not suffered a nasty, bloody cut on his lip in round seven.

Manny's handlers tried furiously to stem the flow of blood between rounds but the wound was too deep. Manager George Latka, just before the gong was to send the two gladiators into action for the eighth round, asked that the fight be called. Referee Frankie Van obliged and the fight went into the record books as another technical knockout for Kim in the seventh.

**Going Strong**

When he stopped the fracas Referee Van had the transplanted islander in front by four points. Kim was six ahead on the Times card. He was unmarked and going strong.

Kim had three really big innings — the first, second and sixth. Madrid rated a shade in the fourth, a round that found both working at close range. Manny rated no worse than an even shake in the fifth when he fought back like he was clawing for his very existance, taking powerful leather slugs to the head all the way.

In the sixth Madrid, evidently inspired by his ability to stand up to his power slugging foe the two previous rounds, actually tried to drive Kim back with a power attack. The plan worked only briefly and nearly proved disastrous for the Los Angeles Mexican. It served only to arouse Kim into high gear and, so aroused, Kim went to work like a man possessed. He bombed Madrid's head and body with cruel, hot belts. He never let up as Manny retreated, his left eye showing signs of tear from the merciless attack.

Kim, Hollywood's greatest crowd attraction since the build-up days of Aragon, weighed 140, Madrid 140½.

**First Loss**

Pete Janke, 154½, suffered his first professional defeat in 10 fights when he lost a unanimous six-round decision to Tony Renteria, 160, in the semi-windup.

Richie Lopez, 157½, nabbed a split decision over Everett Vasquez, 156, in a companion six-rounder.

Results of the four-rounders: [illegible] 160, dec. [illegible] 153, and Vincent Canto, 143½, dec. Al Cassanova, 143.

Paul Zimmerman
Sports Editor

# Los Angeles Times

SPORTS

VOL. LXXI — CC ★ — SUNDAY MORNING, AUGUST 3, 1952 — PART II 9

# UNITED STATES CLINCHES OLYMPIC TITLE

## SPORTS PARADE

BY BRAVEN DYER

STOCKHOLM, Aug. 2—One of the most intriguing angles to an excursion through Europe is the problem of currency exchange.

Traveler's checks are accepted at all banks, of course, and also at most hotels but there are times when you run short of the proper money and the safest way out is to open up the old wallet and extract an American bill. I have yet to find a place where one of our $1 bills isn't taken.

**RATE GOES UP**

In Finland the markka is the basic monetary exchange and you ordinarily get around 230 for $1. But to encourage buying during the Olympic Games the rate was jumped to 350 per dollar, which is quite a difference when you get to dealing in big money as sometimes happened at night clubs, etc.

The only difficulty with this was that you got the 350 rate only at banks and at a special exchange for us newspapermen at press headquarters. One evening at a night club when all of us men couldn't pool enough Finnish money to pay the bill we cashed traveler's checks and received only 228 markkas for each buck.

**ERRONEOUS REPORTS**

Reports that the Finnish people intended to hike all their prices for the Olympics were grossly unfair and erroneous. In the first place Finland has had price control since 1939 so the merchants couldn't put the bite on tourists even if they wanted to.

In the main, prices were cheaper than at home. A haircut, for instance, cost only 40 cents. Taxis were much cheaper than in Los Angeles and there were plenty of them. Hair dressing for the women at beauty parlors wasn't nearly as expensive as at home. Except at the more expensive restaurants, food prices were low by comparison with ours.

In other words, there was absolutely no gouging of visitors. Mostly the good Finns went out of their way to be sure that we Americans were getting a square deal and that we felt satisfied.

**MODEST FLAT**

Accommodations in private homes varied, of course. There were six members of our party quartered at the residence of Aino Keto, widow of the former City Manager of Helsinki. Her place was a modest four-room flat not unlike some of the dwellings erected in Chicago 50 years ago.

The six of us—Millie and Harold Hamilton, Helen and Bill Hubbard and the Dyers—thoroughly enjoyed Mrs. Keto's warm hospitality. Fortunately for us she understood and talked some English, so we got along famously.

She prepared breakfast for us every morning consisting of coffee, oranges or canned pineapple, eggs, bread and butter, tomatoes, cheese and generally some kind of canned meat. There was plenty of everything, such as cream and butter, and the coffee was excellent—and it isn't always easy to get good coffee in Europe by any means.

**FOUR BITS, ROUGHLY**

We paid Mrs. Keto 1000 markkas each morning for breakfast, roughly less than 50 cents each.

Lunch served at a special restaurant for the press cost 300 markkas, less than $1 and the food was excellent and you could eat all you desired and have as many cups of coffee or glasses of milk as you wished.

At the Olympic Stadium coffee and all manner of soft drinks were available within 50 feet of your seat and there were cakes, sandwiches, wieners, raw fish, candies and ice cream. Our seats were the best—$12 each per day and right on the finish line for all the races.

**NO PRIVACY**

The press section could have been improved, but I guess most of you Times readers know by now that we Los Angeles writers are spoiled by those wonderful accommodations Bill Nicholas arranged at the Coliseum. We were jammed in too much and there was no privacy nor protection from the wind.

But by and large things weren't too bad. I've worked in much worse press boxes in America — at Berkeley and Portland, for instance.

The grass field at the stadium was bright green—no need for green paint such as Nicholas has to employ at the Coliseum now and then. And the Olympic officials did a perfect job of covering the field of all but those absolutely necessary. They really put us to shame in this respect.

PEDEN PRODUCES—Les Peden crosses home plate after hitting game-winning ninth-inning homer yesterday. Peden is greeted by Willie Ramsdell, L.A.'s winning hurler. Times photo

## L.A. AGAIN KEEPS TWINKS IN LEAD

### Angel Catcher Les Peden Smacks Home Run With Two Out in Ninth for 4-to-3 Victory

BY AL WOLF

Hollywood lost its fifth straight game at San Francisco yesterday afternoon, but still leads the Coast League parade thanks again to Los Angeles, and particularly Les Peden.

For the hefty Angel catcher smacked a homer with two out in the ninth inning at Wrigley Field to transform a tie ball game into a 4-3 victory over Oakland.

And that defeat, the Oaks' fourth in five starts during the series, left 'em one percentage point behind the suddenly helpless Stars—helpless, that is, except for the Angels' inadvertent aid.

**Peden Wins**

Peden's belt, which came off Bill Evans on a no-balls-two-strikes count, made Willie Ramsdell's PCL return a triumphant thing, even though slightly squeaky.

Ramsdell, making his first Coastal appearance since 1949, when he helped Hollywood capture the pennant by achieving an 18-12 record, gave the Oaks only four hits and looked mighty good out there. Evans, who also went the route, was nicked for seven — of which three were homers.

Bobby Usher rode one out of the park in the fourth frame and Bobby Talbot duplicated in the sixth.

**Gilbert Homers**

But Tookie Gilbert squared matters in the seventh by homering with Spider Jorgenson on base. It was the 22nd round-tripper and the 85th and 86th runs batted in for the Oakland first baseman, who tops the league in both departments.

Successive doubles by Gene Baker and Talbot briefly put the Angels ahead again in the eighth, but Jorgenson produced a tying tally in the top of the ninth by

Turn to Page 14, Column 6

### Haney's Heroes

| Oakland | AB | H | O | A | Los Angeles | AB | H | O | A |
|---|---|---|---|---|---|---|---|---|---|
| [illegible],lf-rf | 4 | 0 | 4 | 0 | Baker,ss | 4 | 1 | 4 | 3 |
| N.Lenz,2b | 4 | 0 | 2 | 0 | Talbot,cf | 4 | 3 | 3 | 0 |
| Jorgensen,3b | 3 | 0 | 1 | 2 | Usher,lf-rf | 4 | 1 | 4 | 0 |
| Gilbert,1b | 4 | 1 | 7 | 0 | Northey,rf | 3 | 1 | 0 | 0 |
| Chapman,cf | 4 | 1 | 5 | 0 | Brinkopf,3b | 4 | 0 | 3 | 0 |
| [illegible],c | 4 | 0 | [illegible] | 1 | West,1b | 4 | 0 | 7 | 0 |
| [illegible],rf-lf | 4 | 1 | 1 | 0 | Peden,c | 4 | 1 | 4 | 2 |
| Bero,ss | 3 | 0 | 3 | 2 | [illegible],2b | 3 | 1 | 1 | 2 |
| Evans,p | 3 | 1 | 0 | 2 | Ramsdell,p | 3 | 0 | 0 | 1 |
| | | | | | Layton,lf | 0 | 0 | 1 | 0 |
| Totals | 3[illegible] | 4 | 26 | 7 | Totals | 33 | 7 | 27 | 8 |

SCORE BY INNINGS

| | | | | |
|---|---|---|---|---|
| Oakland | 000 | 000 | 201 | —3 |
| Los Angeles | 000 | 101 | 011 | —4 |

| Pitcher | IP | AB | R | H | ER | BB | SO |
|---|---|---|---|---|---|---|---|
| Evans | 8⅔ | 33 | 4 | 7 | 4 | 1 | 3 |
| Ramsdell | 9 | 30 | 3 | 4 | 3 | 3 | 4 |

[illegible] LOB—Oakland, 4; Los Angeles, 4. 2B—Baker, Talbot. [illegible] HR—[illegible], Talbot, Gilbert, Peden. [illegible] RBI—Gilbert 2, Chapman, Usher, Talbot, 2, Peden. Umpires—[illegible], Carlucci and Anske. Time—1h. 57m. Attendance—6515.

## STANDINGS

**PACIFIC COAST LEAGUE**

| | W | L | Pct. | * |
|---|---|---|---|---|
| HOLLYWOOD | 71 | 52 | .577 | |
| Oakland | 72 | 53 | .576 | |
| San Diego | 68 | 56 | .548 | 3½ |
| Portland | 62 | 61 | .504 | 9 |
| LOS ANGELES | 62 | 63 | .496 | 10 |
| Seattle | 59 | 61 | .492 | 10½ |
| San Francisco | 53 | 72 | .424 | 19 |
| Sacramento | 48 | 77 | .384 | 24 |

*Games behind leader.

**Yesterday's Results**

LOS ANGELES, 4; Oakland, 3.
San Francisco, 9; HOLLYWOOD, 4.
Portland, 3; Seattle, 2.
Sacramento, 6; San Diego, 5.

**How Series Stand**

LOS ANGELES, 4; Oakland, 1
San Francisco, 5; HOLLYWOOD, 0.
San Diego, 4; Sacramento, 1.
Portland, 5; Seattle, 1.

**Games Today**

Oakland (Ayers, 8-10, and Bamberger, 7-2) at LOS ANGELES (McLish, 8-11, and Hatten, 2-2), Wrigley Field, 1:30 p.m.

HOLLYWOOD (Walsh, 8-7, and Pettit, 10-5) at San Francisco (Singleton, 11-11, and Lien, 7-12).

San Diego (Flowers, 6-4, and Salveson, 11-10) at Sacramento (Flores, 6-15, and Gables, 5-7).

Seattle (Kindsfather, 13-8, and Nagy, 10-9) at Portland (Sanford, 13-4, and Ward, 9-6).

**AMERICAN LEAGUE**

| | W | L | Pct. | * |
|---|---|---|---|---|
| New York | 59 | 43 | .578 | |
| Cleveland | 57 | 45 | .559 | 2 |
| Boston | 55 | 44 | .556 | 2½ |
| Washington | 54 | 47 | .535 | 4½ |
| Philadelphia | 49 | 47 | .510 | 7 |
| Chicago | 53 | 51 | .510 | 7 |
| St. Louis | 43 | 61 | .413 | 17 |
| Detroit | 35 | 67 | .343 | 24 |

*Games behind leader.

**Yesterday's Results**

St. Louis, 11; New York, 6.
Philadelphia, 6; Cleveland, 4.
Chicago, 6; Washington, 1.
Boston, 10; Detroit, 5.

**Games Today**

New York (McDonald, 2-2, and Sain, 8-3, or Kuzava, 5-7), at St. Louis (Byrne, 6-10, and Garver, 7-9).

Boston (Brodowski, 5-3) at Detroit (Houtteman, 5-14).

Philadelphia (Scheib, 5-3, and Kellner, 8-9, or Newsom, 2-3), at Cleveland (Feller, 7-11, and Gromek, 6-4).

Washington (Shea, 9-3, and Marrero, 8-5) at Chicago (Pierce, 11-7, and Dorish, 5-3).

**NATIONAL LEAGUE**

| | W | L | Pct. | * |
|---|---|---|---|---|
| Brooklyn | 64 | 30 | .681 | |
| New York | 60 | 35 | .632 | 4½ |
| St. Louis | 58 | 43 | .574 | 9½ |
| Philadelphia | 53 | 47 | .530 | 14 |
| Chicago | 51 | 48 | .515 | 15½ |
| Boston | 41 | 57 | .418 | 25 |
| Cincinnati | 41 | 60 | .406 | 26½ |
| Pittsburgh | 28 | 76 | .269 | 41 |

*Games behind leader.

**Yesterday's Results**

New York, 4; Pittsburgh, 3 (game called end 6th, rain).
Cincinnati, 8; Boston, 3.
Chicago at Brooklyn (called in 5th, rain).
Philadelphia, 6; St. Louis, 2.

**Games Today**

Chicago (Klippstein, 7-8, and Kelly, 2-5, or Lown, 3-7) at Brooklyn (Erskine, 10-3, and Rutherford, 2-2).

Pittsburgh (Friend, 4-16, and Pollet, 4-11) at New York (Gregg, 0-1, and Lanier, 5-6).

St. Louis (Chambers, 4-2) at Philadelphia (Simmons, 9-4).

Cincinnati (Blackwell, 2-11, and Church, 2-6) at Boston (Spahn, 9-11, and Jester, 1-2).

## McCormick, Sanders Score Wins

### Five U.S. Fighters Triumph

BY PAUL ZIMMERMAN
Times Sports Editor

HELSINKI, Aug. 2—Led by Times Golden Gloves Champion Ed Sanders of Compton, the United States scored its greatest Olympic Games boxing triumph ever tonight, by winning five of 10 individual titles and a walkaway team victory.

Not since 1932 has an American won even one championship. But tonight before a packed house of 5000 spectators the Yankees were the whole show.

Sanders' heavyweight victory came as anticlimax and on disqualification after Americans had taken the flyweight, lightwelterweight, light-middleweight and light-heavyweight titles in a monotonous succession of victories.

**Refuses to Fight**

Referee Vaisberg of France threw Sanders' opponent out of the ring at the end of the second round for refusing to fight. He was Ingemar Johansson of Sweden, a 19-year-old lad who never tossed a punch and turned in the greatest retreat since the allies swept through Germany in World War II.

"Mr. Zimmerman, I had power tonight," said Sanders, the San Diego Navy giant, "but I never got a chance to use it. I never had a chance to hit him even once."

Big Ed, who read the Bible and prayed in his dressing room before the fight, had flattened three previous rivals in rapid succession.

**Wasn't So Dumb**

So the big Swede was not so dumb at that! Johansson had seen Sanders win his way to the finals with those terrific knockouts. And he refused to join battle in the championship fight. Johansson wanted no part of it. Sanders managed to corner him two or three times in the first round for short right chops to the head as Referee Vaisberg warned the Swedish scrapper against running away.

Midway through the second stanza, the referee stopped the fight and motioned the judges that he was taking points away for refusal to fight. Then just at the bell, he walked over and disqualified Johansson.

**Sanders Cheered**

The crowd, which had whistled and stomped feet in disdain, gave a great cheer for Sanders as Johansson was ordered from the ring.

Fans wildly applauded the victory ceremony. Second place on the stand was vacant and no flag raised on the pole. Officials later said Johansson completely disqualified himself so no silver medal was awarded in an unprecedented move.

"I never had any idea when I first fought in the Times Golden Gloves that I ever would have this greatest moment in my life," said Sanders. "And I'm only sorry that I didn't have a chance to demonstrate that I was ready to fight," said the happy former Compton College star who has been the sensation of the tournament and top crowd favorite.

**Boxing Lesson**

Another Californian NCAA champion from San Jose State, Charles Adkins, light welter-

Turn to Page 10, Column 5

RING KING — Ed Sanders, Los Angeles heavyweight, won Olympic Games title yesterday in Helsinki.

PAT PULLS THROUGH—Patricia McCormick, Los Angeles Athletic Club, executes dive in final of Olympic platform event, which she won yesterday for second gold medal.

SOUTHLAND SWEEP—Paula Jean Myers of Covina, left, second; Pat McCormick, winner, and Mrs. Juno Stover Irvin of Pasadena AC, third, after Olympics dive event. AP Wirephotos by radio from Helsinki

### Southland Girls Sweep High Dive

BY PAUL ZIMMERMAN
Times Sports Editor

HELSINKI, Aug. 2—Three sweet Southern California lassies swept the high diving and five United States boxers scored smashing victories here today in the 15th Olympiad to bring the United States storming from behind to lead the Russians, 610 to 553½, clinching the team title.

With barely 24 hours to go before the closing of the Olympic Games, victory by our swimmers and boxers, plus a win by the basketball team pulled the American team ahead.

Even under the Russian system of scoring, which gives seven instead of 10 points for first place, the United States is in front, 493 to 484½. The Yanks have taken 39 gold medals—three more than any other time in history.

**Record High**

Ever since Russia piled up a flock of points in men's and women's gymnastics, the U.S. team had trailed despite its virtual sweep of men's track and field. Here 14 first places were won for a record high.

Our Southland girls turned the tide with their 19 points in aquatics which put the U.S. in front of Russia for the first time since the Games began.

As expected, Pat McCormick of Los Angeles Athletic Club walked away with the high diving event to become the only U.S. double gold winner, with a 79.37 total in points.

**Miss Meyers Second**

Paula Jean Myers, sweet little 17-year-old Covina High School graduate and LAAC member, was second with 71.63. Juno Stover Irwin of the Pasadena AC was a close third at 70.49.

The American boxers who won five championships included Ed Sanders, Los Angeles Times Golden Gloves heavyweight champ, and Charley Adkins of Gary, Ind. who is a student at San Jose State.

Starting today, the next to last of competition here, the Soviets led in team standings by 24½ points, 523½ to 499. Now, at 610 to 553½, no matter what the Russians do in tomorrow's final equestrian events they cannot dislodge the Red, White and Blue.

**Win All the Way**

Mrs. McCormick, who previously won a gold medal in springboard competition, led from the very start in the high diving. Just to convince the 10,000 fans who packed the stands in this afternoon's warm sunshine, Pat topped off her marvelous performance with the day's best dive, a handstand cut through with one half gainer and layout good for 15.96 points.

Juno was second going into the final dive. But little Paula Jean, looking cute in pigtails, forged ahead with her last dive. Both girls were at their very best this afternoon but not good enough to outclass peerless Pat. Juno and Paula Jean were just a fraction of a point ahead of Nicole Pellissard of France going into the finals. After the first dives this afternoon, however, they left her far behind.

It was a big day for America in swimming and a tough one on records as three more Olympic marks were washed away.

Ford Konno of Hawaii and Ohio State trimmed 40 seconds

Turn to Page 11, Column 4

### Seals Tee Off on Stars Again

SAN FRANCISCO, Aug. 2 (AP) The resurgent San Francisco Seals took their fifth game in a row from the Hollywood Stars, 9-4, this afternoon, working over four Hollywood pitchers for 13 hits. It was the Seals' seventh straight win.

The Seals, who scored two runs in the first inning on a walk, a double by Frank Kalin and a single by Bill McCawley, added six more in the third, driving Hollywood Hurler Johnny Lindell from the mound. San Francisco scored another run in the fifth on a double by McCawley and a single by Lennie Ratto.

Then the Stars bounced back for four runs in the sixth, sending San Francisco Starter Bill Bradford to the showers.

| Hollywood | AB | H | O | A | San Fra'co | AB | H | O | A |
|---|---|---|---|---|---|---|---|---|---|
| [illegible],cf | 5 | 1 | 4 | 0 | Moran,2b | 5 | 2 | 2 | 4 |
| [illegible],2b | 4 | 2 | 3 | 2 | [illegible],cf | 4 | 1 | 1 | 0 |
| Stevens,1b | 4 | 2 | 9 | 0 | Grace,1b | 3 | 1 | 10 | 0 |
| [illegible] | 4 | 1 | [illegible] | 0 | Kalin,lf | 4 | 1 | 3 | 0 |
| [illegible] | [illegible] | 1 | 1 | 0 | McCawley,rf | 4 | 2 | 0 | 0 |
| Handley,3b | 3 | 0 | 0 | 4 | Orteig,c | 4 | 1 | 8 | 1 |
| Sandlock,c | 4 | 2 | 2 | 0 | [illegible],3b | 4 | 1 | 3 | 0 |
| [illegible],ss | 3 | 1 | 2 | 5 | Ratto,ss | 4 | 3 | 0 | [illegible] |
| Lindell,p-lf | 1 | 0 | 0 | 1 | Bradford,p-W | 3 | 1 | 0 | 1 |
| Lynn,p | 1 | 0 | 0 | 0 | [illegible],p | 0 | 0 | 0 | 0 |
| Phillips | 1 | 0 | 0 | 0 | | | | | |
| Muir,p | 0 | 0 | 0 | 0 | | | | | |
| Malone | 1 | 0 | 0 | 0 | | | | | |
| Shepard,p | 0 | 0 | 0 | 0 | | | | | |
| Totals | 34 | 10 | 24 | 13 | Totals | 35 | 13 | 27 | 8 |

Phillips struck out for Lynn in 6th.
Malone struck out for Muir in 8th.

SCORE BY INNINGS

| | | | | |
|---|---|---|---|---|
| Hollywood | 000 | 004 | 000 | —4 |
| San Francisco | 206 | 010 | 00x | —9 |

| Pitcher | IP | AB | R | H | ER | BB | SO |
|---|---|---|---|---|---|---|---|
| [illegible] | 2⅓ | 14 | [illegible] | 8 | [illegible] | 2 | 0 |
| [illegible] | 5⅔ | 21 | 4 | 5 | 4 | 3 | 2 |
| Lynn | 2⅓ | [illegible] | 1 | 2 | 1 | 0 | 0 |
| Muir | 2 | 9 | 0 | 3 | 0 | 1 | 1 |
| Shepard | 1 | 3 | 0 | 0 | 0 | 0 | 0 |
| [illegible] | 3⅓ | 15 | 0 | 5 | 0 | 2 | 5 |

LOB—Hollywood, 10; San Francisco, 7. 2B—Kalin, [illegible], McCawley. SB—Grace. RBI—Kalin, McCawley 2, Orteig, [illegible], Bradford 3, Ratto, [illegible], Sandlock 2. DP—[illegible] to Baczewski to Stevens, Ratto to Moran to Grace. Umpires—[illegible] and [illegible]. Time—2h. 10m. Attendance—[illegible].

### U.S. DEFEATS RUSSIA IN SLOW CAGE TILT

HELSINKI, Aug. 2 (AP)—America whipped Russia, 36-25, today to win the Olympic basketball championship for the third time in a game dominated almost to the very end by Soviet stalling tactics.

It was the eighth straight victory for the United States team in the Helsinki Games and its second over Russia.

No other country ever has won the Olympic title since basketball was introduced to the competition in the 1936 Games at Berlin.

The Americans started the game full of confidence but tightened up when the Russians threw an iron curtain around the hole beneath the American basket and settled down to play possession ball.

Both University of Kansas and AAU players who made up Uncle Sam's team got the jitters as Russia led, 7-4, after the first 11 minutes of this type of play.

The Americans were missing from outside and close up in the few scoring chances the Russians allowed them.

At half time the score had crept to 17-15 in America's favor but it was still anybody's ball game.

After three minutes of the second half Russia led, 20-21, but from then on the United States slowly forged in front and was pulling away at the game's end.

Phog Allen, the University of Kansas coach, said later "Russia played the best type of game for her purposes because she had tried a fast game in the previ-

Turn to Page 10, Column 3

### Polly Riley Wins Women's Western Golf Crown, 2-1, Over Miss Downey

BY JEANNE HOFFMAN

Polly Riley, the chunky 26-year-old bookkeeper from Ft. Worth, Tex., came out on the right side of the ledger yesterday with a brilliant 2-and-1 victory to defeat Mary Ann Downey of Baltimore, Md., for the women's western championship at the Los Angeles CC. It was her second western amateur title in three years.

The thrilling hard-fought match saw Mary Ann outputt Polly and score 7 birdies to Polly's four, but lose the silverware for the second consecutive year.

Polly had an 81 in the morning and Mary Ann's 80. In the 17 holes of the afternoon round Miss Riley was 3 over women's par and Miss Downey 4 over. Each was 9 over women's par for the distance of the match.

Polly led, 1 up, after the morning 18 and, except for Mary Ann's brief 1-up advantage at the 22nd, led the rest of the way. It was Mary Ann's Jonah hole which finally sent her crashing to defeat after dogging the Curtis Cupper all the way.

One down, the Baltimore lass had landed in the trap at the left of the 35th hole on her second shot. While Polly lay 3 on the green, Mary Ann blasted out, hitting the ball clean and sending it sailing clear over the green and over the heads of most of the gallery of 800.

The ball landed some 35 yards down in the barranca, almost buried in 5 inches of deep grass and there, actually, was the game. The determined Miss

Turn to Page 13, Column 1

PART 4 **Los Angeles Times** SPORTS

VOL. LXXI CC WEDNESDAY MORNING, SEPTEMBER 24, 1952 Read The Times for Latest Sports

# MARCIANO KO'S WALCOTT TO WIN TITLE

BY FRANK FINCH, Times Staff Representative

MUNICIPAL STADIUM, Philadelphia, Sept. 23—Exactly 26 years from the night that Jack Dempsey lost his title to Gene Tunney in this vast arena another heavyweight champion fell tonight.

Jersey Joe Walcott, holder of the crown for only 14 months, was knocked out in 43 seconds of the 13th round by a man 10 years his junior, Rocky Marciano.

A terrifying right cross to the point of the champion's chin felled him like a pole-axed steer and made the 28-year-old Brockton block buster the first white heavyweight champion since James J. Braddock ruled 15 years ago.

Referee Charley Daggert tolled the fatal "10" over Jersey Joe, but he could have counted in the hundreds.

Walcott was unconscious for nearly a minute after taking that thunderbolt on the button.

The crowd of 40,379 fans who had seen the balding champion build up a seemingly safe lead over the crude but dangerous Marciano was quite unprepared for the "sudden death" finish.

In the opening minute of the first round Walcott sent Marciano to the canvas with a savage left hook to the jaw. Rocky fought his way out of this jam but he never could overcome Jersey Joe's early lead.

In the 11th and 12th rounds Walcott seemed to have Rocky on his way out. He was boxing easily and cautiously, ripping over jolting counterblows as the challenger's wild swings whistled past him harmlessly.

Rocky, who never had traveled more than 10 rounds before—and very rarely then, what with a record of 37 knockouts in 42 fights—obviously was tiring from the furious pace.

Only a tremendous closing rush would bring the world's championship to the rugged son of an Italian shoe cobbler.

But Marciano likes to kill 'em off suddenlike, as he did when he met Joe Louis, Rex Layne and Harry Kid Matthews, to mention a few.

The 13th round had just begun when Marciano backed Walcott against the ropes.

Rocky wound up his right arm like a baseball pitcher. You could see it coming. Walcott saw it and he swung his right hand, too.

Jersey Joe missed but Rocky was right on target.

Even from my fourth-row seat across the ring I could

Turn to Page 2, Column 7

STRICKEN WARRIOR—Jersey Joe Walcott sags towards the canvas after receiving knockout right-hand punch from the new champion, Rocky Marciano, in the 13th round of heavyweight title bout. (AP) Wirephoto

## SPORTS PARADE

BY BRAVEN DYER

Last year a young man named Ray McKown came to town and scorched the Coliseum grass.

Against the Trojans he ran and passed for the staggering total of 340 yards. This constituted a new all-time record for mayhem against ol' SC.

His passing total of 270 yards likewise was a new mark.

McKown comes back this week end to engage the Bruins of UCLA as his alma mater, Texas Christian, strives to recover from the opening-game setback administered by Kansas.

**PERSONAL DUEL**

One of the greatest personal duels ever waged locally is apt to develop Saturday when McKown matches his talents with UCLA's phenomenal Paul Cameron.

It is doubtful if there were two more sensational sophomore tailbacks in the entire nation last fall.

Cameron set so many Bruin records they haven't finished compiling them yet.

His total of 1182 yards running and passing made him UCLA's greatest sophomore back in 33 years of football. He scored five touchdowns by running and 10 by passing. And only in the 41-0 rout of Oregon did he gain less than 100 yards . . . Red Sanders kept him bench-tied most of that afternoon.

Paul's outstanding scoring spree last fall was against Santa Clara when he passed for four touchdowns, thus breaking Bob Waterfield's game record of three. Cameron tied another Waterfield mark with his total of 306 yards for one contest.

**BIGGEST GUN**

If you consider some of UCLA's other foes a bit tougher than Santa Clara, here's what Cameron did against recognized major competition . . .

Nicked California for 266 yards, Illinois for 181 and SC for 128.

And without him last Saturday the struggling Bruins came within a whisker of being upset by the 1951 PCC doormat, Oregon. Even cagey Sanders admits the UCLA offense is weakened 30% when Cameron is idle.

McKown came so close to beating SC (26-28) last year that he was running up and down Hill's bed for weeks after.

For some inexplicable reason Coach Dutch Meyer started a sophomore, Roy Clinkscale, against Kansas last week, even though McKown had skippered Texas Christian to the Southwest championship less than 12 months ago.

The jittery sophomore got the Horned Frogs in a hole by fumbling the opening kick-off.

**REINSTATED QUICKLY**

McKown was reinstated as first string tailback almost instanter, and that's where he'll be playing Saturday. Against Kansas he completed 11 of 23 passes for 119 yards and ran four times for an additional 17. His punting average was just under 40 yards per kick.

When the 1951 season dawned young McKown was no better than Meyer's fourth string tailback. But a succession of injuries to other players moved Ray up notch by notch until he reached the top rung the week of the Trojan game.

During that afternoon he completed four perfect long passes of 20, 32, 43 and 74 yards, the latter (with run) for a touchdown.

One other shot went for a teedee and Ray himself scored a third.

**UNLUCKY HAPPENSTANCE**

He fumbled once in the end zone for what would have been his second tally and was unlucky enough to have one of his buddies drop a perfect shot while standing unmolested behind the goal line.

McKown and Cameron were so closely matched in yardage gained last season that it seems almost unbelievable. As I said, Paul ran and passed for 1482. McKown lugged the ball for 559, passed for 911, so wound up with a total of 1470.

Sanders and all Bruinville are convinced after the Oregon game that "as Cameron goes, so go the Bruins." Quite likely, after the Kansas game, Meyer and his associates feel the same way about McKown. Which makes Saturday's duel all the more intriguing.

**It is rather significant that the Trojans put Cameron and McKown on their all-opponent team of 1951 along with McElhenny of Washington and Lattner of Notre Dame. Pretty fast company, but in my book both boys deserved such recognition. Here's hoping Cameron is ready Saturday. If not, the Horned Frogs may be more than the Bruins can swallow.**

## Shantz Suffers Broken Wrist as A's Win 4-3

PHILADELPHIA, Sept. 23 (AP) Tiny Bobby Shantz suffered a broken bone in his pitching wrist today ending prematurely the southpaw's greatest major league season.

Shantz, smallest pitcher in the major leagues at 5 feet, 6 inches tall, was injured while batting in the second inning against Walter Masterson of the Washington Senators. A Masterson pitch caught Shantz flush on the wrist before he could jump back from the plate.

**Shantz Warned**

Masterson knew the pitch was bad and shouted, "Look out" as the ball headed for the plate. But Shantz couldn't get away and stood white faced, wringing his left hand as teammates rushed from the dugout to check the damage to their brilliant hurler.

Trainer Jim Tadley worked feverishly for about 10 minutes on the little left-hander as the game was delayed. Shantz finally trotted to first base and apparently everything was okay. He ran to second a moment later as Eddie Joost singled off Masterson.

**Ordered to Hospital**

But after the A's were retired it was evident that Shantz couldn't continue. He was unable to bend his fingers and Manager Jimmy Dykes immedi-

Turn to Page 4, Column 1

## AGGRESSIVE ROCKY SUBDUED CHAMPION

PHILADELPHIA, Sept. 23 (AP) Rocky Marciano, the cut, bruised and bleeding new heavyweight champion of the world, tonight proudly proclaimed his willingness to defend his title and termed Jersey Joe Walcott a "good, tough guy — a heluva fighter."

His dressing room after the bruising, dramatic fight was a scene of utter confusion. Men shouted, glaring lights brought sweat to everyone's face and in the midst of it all, the new titleholder looked small and subdued.

**Right, Left**

Finally Marciano was hoisted up on a bench and said in a low voice:

"I hit him with a right up against the ropes. His head was at one side and I hooked with a left and he went down."

"For four rounds he couldn't even see," said Al Weill, his chubby manager. "We thought it was because of some stuff on Walcott's shoulder but we're not accusing anybody and we aren't saying that's what it was."

After the fourth round Rocky seemed to peer uncertainly and blinked frequently but finally his eyesight cleared up.

Ordinarily a new champion would be talking freely from the moment he entered his dressing room, but not so with Marciano. Police cleared the way as he was brought to the far end of a narrow row of lockers and doctors went to work on him. There was a bad cut on his scalp, a big mouse under his left eye and a jagged gash on his right eyebrow. He managed to grin and rub his fist over his stomach to indicate he was both sick and tired.

Even after ice and restoratives brought him to his feet, Rocky was far from exuberant.

**Scalp Wound**

The scalp wound and the cut on the right eye, said Rocky, "were because we bumped heads, I guess."

The punch that floored Rocky in the first round he termed "the hardest I ever took."

Weill, not knowing that Walcott had decided to quit the ring and go into business, said that Rocky would fight Walcott "inside 90 days but he will fight where I want him to fight, not where he wants. Rocky is the champ now."

Walcott's retirement releases Marciano to make his own plans for future ring battles.

Off in a corner Rocky's father, Peter Marciano, sat on a bench and wept.

"I'm proud, I'm proud," he said over and over again.

## TODAY IN SPORTS

**HORSE RACING** — Los Angeles County Fair, Pomona, 12:30 p.m.

**AMATEUR BOXING** — South Gate Arena, 8:30 p.m.

**WRESTLING**—Olympic Auditorium, 8:30 p.m.; Ocean Park Arena, 8:30 p.m.

**AUTO RACING**—Long Beach Veteran Memorial Stadium, 8:30 p.m.

## Chisox Shatter Tribe Pennant Dreams, 10-1

CLEVELAND, Sept. 23 (AP) — Chicago's White Sox swatted the pennant-dreaming Cleveland Indians with a staggering 10-1 defeat today, making first place for Cleveland a longshot indeed.

Only 5377 fans showed up in cavernous Municipal Stadium to watch the high-flying Indians take their first defeat in seven games.

**Indians Fooled**

Pitcher Joe Dobson had them almost completely fooled, allowing only six hits, three singles in the third producing the only Indian run. The White Sox got 14 hits off four Indian pitchers, including Sherman Lollar's 13th homer.

The pennant picture now sizes up this way:

Even if Cleveland wins its three remaining games, the New York Yankees now would need to win only three of their remaining six games for a tie and four for the pennant.

**Rest of Schedule**

The Indians have one more game with Chicago here tomorrow, rest two days and wind up with two at Detroit Saturday and Sunday. The Yankees, rained out today, have three in Boston — a double-header tomorrow and a single game Thursday — and a final three-game series in Philadelphia Fri-

Turn to Page 4, Column 1

## DODGERS DIVIDE WITH PHILS, CLINCH NATIONAL LOOP FLAG

Illustrated on Page 2, Part IV

BROOKLYN, Sept. 23 (AP)—The Brooklyn Dodgers won their first National League pennant since 1949 tonight as they came from behind to edge the Philadelphia Phillies, 5-4, in the first game of a twi-night double-header. The Phils captured the anticlimatic game, 1-0 in 12 innings before 24,408 fans.

Little Johnny Rutherford, who wasn't on the Dodgers' spring roster, pitched the pennant clincher, Brooklyn's ninth since 1890. The victory gave the Dodgers 95 victories and made it impossible for the runner-up New York Giants to overhaul the flock. The Giants have 88 victories and only six games left to play.

**Dodgers Celebrate**

Manager Chuck Dressen started his regular line-up in the second game but most of them along with Chuck left before the game was over to celebrate the clinching of the pennant in the Dodgers' clubhouse.

Rutherford, a 26-year-old right-hander, was cuffed around in the early innings but steadied after the third and blanked the Phils on three hits the rest of the way to square his record at 7-7.

Karl Drews, a Dodger nemesis, started for Philadelphia and fielded a run in the first on a walk to Duke Snider and double by Jackie Robinson.

**Slender Lead**

Rutherford guarded his slender advantage until the third inning when Gran Hamner accounted for all of Philadelphia's runs with a grand-slam homer. A single, walk and error set the stage for Hamner's 17th homer of the season.

Drews, gunning for his fifth victory over Brooklyn, came to grief in the fifth. Gil Hodges singled to launch the pennant clinching rally. Rutherford sacrificed and the pitcher also was safe when First Baseman Ed Waitkus of the Phils erred on the play. Pee Wee Reese singled to drive in Hodges and Snider followed with a two-run double to insure the pennant.

Bedlam reigned in the Dodger clubhouse after the game. Dressen was lifted on their shoulders by a group of players.

When some semblance of order was restored, Jackie Robinson reached Dressen's side and said:

**Great Skipper**

"Skipper, you were great. If anybody has to be singled out for the most credit, it is you. I think you've done a tremendous job with the pitching staff. I don't think anybody could have done better. For that matter, I think you've handled the team excellently. And I think everybody should be made aware of it."

Dressen singled out reserve Outfielder George Shuba and Relief Ace Joe Black for praise.

"There's the difference between last year's club and this—Black and Shuba," Dressen said. "We'd have never won the pennant without them."

Dressen indicated that Black, who won 15 games and saved at least another 15, might start the first World Series game.

**Black May Start**

"Black may pitch the opening game of the World Series for us," Dressen said. "I'm trying to maneuver him into that spot. I'll have him pitch six innings

Turn to Page 2, Column 5

## PENNANT RACES AT A GLANCE

**AMERICAN LEAGUE**

| | W | L | Pct. | * | ** |
|---|---|---|---|---|---|
| New York | 90 | 58 | .608 | ... | 6 |
| Cleveland | 90 | 61 | .596 | 1½ | 3 |

Remaining games:

New York—Away (6). Boston, 3, Sept. 24 (2), 25. Philadelphia, 3; Sept. 26, 27, 28. At home (0).

Cleveland—At home (1). Chicago, 1, Sept. 24. Away (2). Detroit, 2, Sept. 27, 28.

**NATIONAL LEAGUE**

| | W | L | Pct. | * | ** |
|---|---|---|---|---|---|
| Brooklyn | 95 | 55 | .633 | ... | 4 |
| New York | 88 | 60 | .595 | 6 | 6 |

Remaining games:

Brooklyn—At home (4). Philadelphia, 1, Sept. 24. Boston, 3, Sept. 26, 27, 28. Away (0).

New York—At home (6). Boston, 3, Sept. 24 (2), 25. Philadelphia, 3, Sept. 26, 27, 28. Away (0).

*Games behind; **games left.

Read 'Em and Weep
Ohio State, 27; Michigan, 7.
Kentucky, 14; Tennessee, 14.
Penn State, 17; Pittsburgh, 0.
Northwestern, 28; Illinois, 26.
Alabama, 27; Maryland, 7.

Los Angeles Times SPORTS

6 PART II CC ★ SUNDAY MORNING, NOVEMBER 23, 1952 VOL. LXXI

# SC EARNS BOWL BID WITH RUGGED 14-12 WIN

## Bruins Lost Only on Score---Hyland

### Uclans Retain Fans' Respect Despite Narrow Two-Point Defeat

BY DICK HYLAND

The big golden bell, prize of the game, was there ready for either Bruin or Trojan to toll. With it went the glory of the Rose Bowl, the thrill of an undefeated season.

At the game's end, how, the short distance across a football field changed the tone of the prize bell. For the Trojans it was a paean of victory, a joyous song that at long last the war was over and triumph the reward. That is what 14 points did.

For the Bruins, it was a death knell of hope for athletic immortality, the end of a trail. It was defeat. That is what 12 points did.

**Both Teams Won**

There was no question of winner or loser on that Coliseum field yesterday, however. Both teams won. The Trojans took the conference championship but the Bruins took the respect of every individual who saw them in action.

Outmanned, outplayed, stymied at every turn, they yet battled on and not until the Trojans' final pass interception with just over two minutes to play remaining did any of the 96,869 fans present think for one moment that the game was over.

The "breaks" were pretty even, yet they decided the game.

**Breaks Decide It**

The Bruins gained one when Sears fumbled deep in his own territory when hit by Jack Ellena, and Myron Berliner recovered. Pete Dailey kicked a 22-yard field goal.

They gained another when Harold Han fumbled and was tossed to a safety by Berliner. That was two first-half breaks, two mistakes—and five points for the Bruins.

The Trojans got a break when Al Carmichael was grabbed and turned loose on the line of scrimmage, grabbed and his forward progress stopped 6 yards later — and lateraled to Jim Sears running free for a touchdown. The rules say that the ball is dead when the forward progress of the ball is stopped with the runner in the grasp of an opponent. The motion pictures may show that THAT play was illegal.

The Trojans got a break when Elmer Willhoite popped up in front of a Cameron pass. That pass never should have been thrown where it was. In seconds, from driving to a touchdown on the Trojan 18-yard line, the Bruins were defending on their 8. That led to seven Trojan points, the winning points.

A third possible break was when Willhoite was offside to move the ball from the Trojan 6 to the 1. That helped the Bruins score but they had been rolling and might have anyway.

Call Willhoite's goal line mistake a break and it comes out three for the Bruins, two for the Trojans. The three meant 12 points, the two breaks meant 14 points. How close can you get?

**Wasn't Close**

Actually the game was not that close. The Trojans were so superior on defense that little except sporadic offensive bursts could be expected from the Bruins almost from the opening kickoff. One march only, from their own 29 to the Trojan 18, where Willhoite intercepted Cameron's pass at the start of the second half, saw the Bruin offense puzzling the Trojan defense.

That was not because the Bruin offensive line was being handled. It wasn't. Trojan speed, however, enabled men who were not supposed to be able to, get in on the play to catch Cameron or Don Stalwick from behind or cut them down as they turned the corner. Trojans from the "other" side of the line followed, caught and stopped the Bruin play.

**In on Plays**

It was that desire to get in on every play taken onto the field by every Trojan yesterday that won them the ball game. Call it, if you wish, following up the play—but recognize that conditioning, mental and physical, prompted it and permitted it.

The Bruin passing game, if it

Turn to Page 10, Column 7

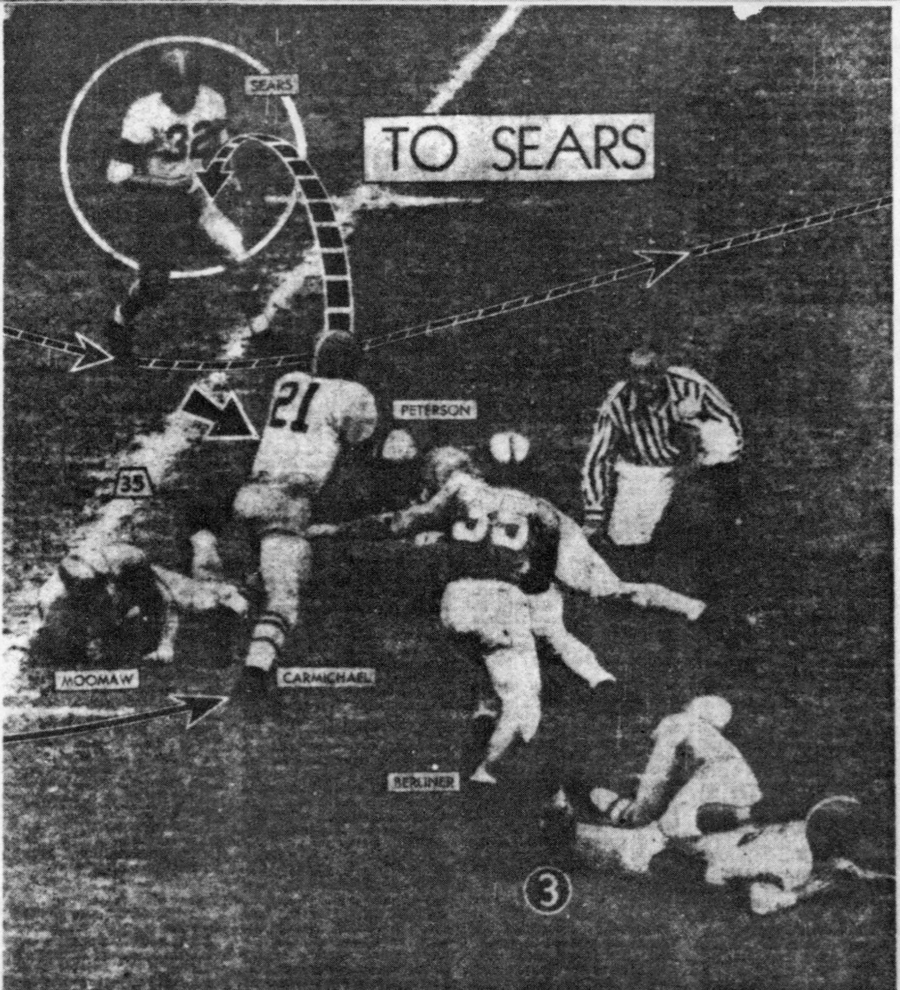


## 96,869 Fans See Sears Spark Troy

### SC's Wrecking Crew Paves Way; Two Long Gainers Ruin Bruins

BY BRAVEN DYER

Led by their brilliant all-purpose tailback, Jim Sears, and backed up by injured Bob Van Doren's rugged wrecking crew, the Trojans of Southern California smashed their way into the Rose Bowl yesterday by beating the gutty Bruins, 14 to 12, before 96,869 customers at the Coliseum.

The win made it nine straight victories for Jess Hill's great team this season and also made them Pacific Coast Conference champions.

They close their 1952 campaign next week end at South Bend against Notre Dame.

The Bruins finished second in the PCC derby, their lone loss administered by the Trojans.

**Bid Awaited**

Although official notification of their Pasadena invitation will not reach the Trojans until after next Saturday's game between Washington and Washington State, it is a foregone conclusion that they'll get the bid.

Southern California has been to the Crown City classic 10 times and off their showing this year they have a chance to make their 11th appearance a lucky one against either Wisconsin or Purdue, one of which will be selected by the Big Ten tomorrow.

**Storm Back**

Yesterday's thrill-packed battle had a little bit of everything. The teams were so evenly matched it was a shame one had to lose. Too bad they can't both go to the Rose Bowl and each play a half.

The Bruins led, 3 to 0, in the first quarter on Pete Dailey's 22-yard field goal.

SC came storming back with a two-man touchdown run, covering 70 yards, by Al Carmichael and the ever-dangerous Sears, to make it 7 to 3 early in the second quarter.

It became 7 to 5 a few minutes later when Harold Han, Trojan fullback, was nailed in the end zone for a safety.

Less than two minutes before the half ended it was 12 to 7 for the Bruins, Bill Stits climaxing a 30-yard drive by plunging through left guard for the only Westwood touchdown of the day.

Sears and Carmichael teamed up again six minutes into the third stanza to bag the clinching touchdown on a 4-yard pitch after Elmer Willhoite had run 72 yards to the Bruin 8 with a stolen pass.

**Tremendous Punting**

Tremendous punting by Paul Cameron and Bob Heydenfeldt gave the victors all manner of trouble in the first half and actually led up to all the UCLA points.

Both defensive platoons played magnificently and it took two "emergency" plays, as some of the football Wisenheimers call them, to put points on the scoreboard for Troy.

And after the Bruins lost the great Paul Cameron near the end of the third quarter SC's wrecking crew rushed Ted Narleski and Primo Villanueva so relentlessly that UCLA never quite got close enough to try a field goal which could have won the game.

Hill was mobbed by his jubi

Turn to Page 10, Column 1

## ROSE BOWL HANDICAP

(Final Standings)

| PACIFIC COAST | W | L | T | Pct. | Pts. | Op. |
|---|---|---|---|---|---|---|
| SC | 6 | 0 | 0 | 1.000 | 174 | 32 |
| UCLA | 5 | 1 | 0 | .833 | 166 | 48 |
| Wash. | 5 | 2 | 0 | .714 | 182 | 118 |
| California | 3 | 3 | 0 | .500 | 109 | 80 |
| Wash. State | 3 | 3 | 0 | .500 | 121 | 109 |
| Stanford | 2 | 5 | 0 | .286 | 110 | 198 |
| Oregon | 2 | 5 | 0 | .286 | 79 | 178 |
| Idaho | 1 | 3 | 0 | .250 | 61 | 101 |
| Oregon State | 1 | 6 | 0 | .143 | 95 | 243 |

| BIG TEN | W | L | T | Pct. | Pts. | Op. |
|---|---|---|---|---|---|---|
| Wisconsin | 4 | 1 | 1 | .750 | 158 | 97 |
| Purdue | 4 | 1 | 1 | .750 | 147 | 91 |
| Ohio State | 5 | 2 | 0 | .714 | 148 | 94 |
| Minnesota | 3 | 1 | 2 | .667 | 92 | 96 |
| Michigan | 4 | 2 | 0 | .667 | 128 | 86 |
| Illinois | 2 | 5 | 0 | .286 | 113 | 154 |
| N'rthwest'rn | 2 | 5 | 0 | .286 | 146 | 201 |
| Iowa | 2 | 5 | 0 | .286 | 107 | 167 |
| Indiana | 1 | 5 | 0 | .167 | 89 | 115 |

ALL THE WAY—Trojan Halfbacks Al Carmichael and Jim Sears combined talents on this 70-yard touchdown play. Al ran 6 yards, then lateraled to wide-open teammate.

Times Miracle Eye photos by Phil Bath

## Purdue, Wisconsin Tie for Crown

(Stories on Page 12)

## California Smothers Stanford, 26-0

(Story on Page 13)

# 1953
# 1962

ROGER BANNISTER, ARNOLD PALMER, ROCKY MARCIANO, SUGAR RAY ROBINSON, SANDY KOUFAX, BILL Shoemaker, Johnny Unitas, A. J. Foyt.

These are a few of the stars who arrived on stage during this decade while athletes such as Ben Hogan, Ted Williams, Maureen Connolly, and Eddie Arcaro were leaving it.

Every decade seems to have had more drama than a Broadway hit, but it would be hard to beat this one for exciting events. A few examples:

> Roger Bannister ran a mile in less than four minutes. Don Larsen of the Yankees pitched a perfect game. Major league baseball came to Los Angeles and San Francisco. A little-known golfer named Jack Fleck upset Ben Hogan in the U.S. Open. Ted Williams hit a home run in his last time at bat. Roger Maris hit sixty-one home runs to break Babe Ruth's record. Sandy Koufax pitched the first of his four no-hit games. The U.S. hockey team won the gold medal in the 1960 Olympics. Rocky Marciano retired as heavyweight champion, undefeated in all his forty-nine fights. Pittsburgh's Harvey Haddix pitched a perfect game for twelve innings but lost the decision to Milwaukee, 1–0, in the thirteenth. The Baltimore Colts, led by quarterback Johnny Unitas, beat the New York Giants, 23–17, in overtime, in one of professional football's most memorable games.

None of these events had as much worldwide impact as the result of the mile run in an obscure dual track meet between Oxford University and the British Amateur Association on May 6, 1954, in Oxford, England. Roger Bannister, a 6′ 1″, 150-pound British medical student, won the mile run that day in 3 minutes, 59.4 seconds. The 4-minute barrier, the target of the world's best runners for years, had finally been broken. Strangely, once Bannister did it, numerous runners broke it.

Don Larsen's perfect game had the perfect setting: the World Series. The world probably paid less attention to his feat than it did to Bannister's, but most of the United States watched on television as Larsen beat the Brooklyn Dodgers, 2–0, on October 8, 1956. The first perfect game in World Series history was achieved by a fellow whose career before and after was otherwise undistinguished.

Johnny Unitas also performed brilliantly in an important event—the National Football League's championship game. No NFL title had ever been decided in overtime, and when Alan Ameche scored the winning touchdown after 8 minutes, 15 seconds of the extra quarter, millions watching on television became captivated by the sport that would soon become America's number one game.

From 1953 to 1957 the Oklahoma Sooners under Coach Bud Wilkinson won more football games without a loss than any college in modern times. But on November 16, 1957, Notre Dame defeated the Sooners, 7–0, to stop their remarkable streak at forty-seven games.

The Dodgers, who had won their first World Series in Brooklyn by beating the Yankees in 1955, won their first championship in Los Angeles in 1959, defeating the Chicago White Sox after winning the pennant in a playoff with Milwaukee.

Ben Hogan, who had won four U.S. Open golf championships in six years, starting in 1948, was about to win his fifth when he was tied by Jack Fleck at San Francisco's Olympic Club in 1955. Fleck won an eighteen-hole playoff the next day. But golf in this decade belonged to the flamboyant Arnold Palmer, who stirred golf fans with his daring charges and gambling shots. Palmer met his match, too, losing the 1962 Open to a fat young rookie named Jack Nicklaus.

Floyd Patterson won the heavyweight boxing championship vacated by Marciano in 1956. Sweden's Ingemar Johansson took the title away from Patterson in 1959, but Patterson became the first fighter to regain it when he knocked out Johansson the following year. In 1962, however, Patterson was knocked out by Sonny Liston in a fight that lasted about two minutes.

The 1956 Olympic Games were held in Melbourne, Australia, only a few weeks after the Soviet Union had invaded Hungary. During a water polo match between the two nations, several fights broke out and the water became bloody. Hungary won, 4–0, and went on to win the gold medal.

In 1960 at Squaw Valley, California, the U.S. hockey team went undefeated in five matches and upset both Canada and the Soviet Union to win its first gold medal in the sport. It would have been no bigger upset if Canada and Russia had beaten the United States in baseball.

Records fell in bundles at the Summer Olympics at Rome that year. In four track and field events—the 110- and 400-meter hurdles, shot put, and discus—the United States swept all three medals in each event, but for the first time since 1928, Americans did not win either the 100- or 200-meter sprints. The gold medal in light-heavyweight boxing was won by a young fellow from Louisville, Kentucky, named Cassius Clay. As Muhammad Ali, he would be heard from later.

VOL. LXXII CC FRIDAY MORNING, JANUARY 2, 1953 Read The Times for Latest Sports

# TROJAN HORSE IN WINNER'S CIRCLE, 7-0

**HERE'S THE BALL GAME**—Rudy Bukich, subbing for injured Jim Sears, pitches to Al Carmichael in end zone for only touchdown of 1953 Rose Bowl game. Line of scrimmage was 22-yard line when Trojans broke deadlock.

Times Miracle Eye photos by Julian Robinson

HYLAND REPORTS

## Timberlake, Ane and Goux Hailed

BY DICK HYLAND

Your reporter has not, for the past few years, been one of those who thought the Big Ten (Midwest) could teach us anything about football.

They did, however, show us what could be done with a band. The Wisconsin band lived up to that tradition—and this time the Trojans went right along with them.

And thank you, Jess Hill.

**Awkward Game**

That "back in" to a report of a football game is awkward.

It was an awkward game to report.

For a long time it appeared that the pregame thought, "How can either one of them win?" would stand up. The Wisconsin defense was holding the ineffective Trojan offense. More important, from a western point of view, the Trojan defense was handcuffing the vaunted Badger offense, the best in the Midwest.

As a result, not much was happening so far as anyone could see unless the viewer happened to be a football technician. If he came under the latter group, by halftime he was delirious. Here was one of the finest defensive games ever played in the Rose Bowl.

In the second half "attrition" took over and the physical condition that Jess Hill had given his Trojans won the ball game. For once a western team did not fold in the second half. For once a western team beat a better ball club. For half a dozen years it has been the other way around.

**Bukich Wins**

In the press box just as the game was ending Bill Schroeder was polling sports writers to name the game's outstanding player. Rudy Bukich was finally named. It was a difficult decision. There was no outstanding player on that field, on either team.

Coming away from the game an observer had the impression that Wisconsin was almost always "up there" knocking on the door. Actually, the Badgers were in what could be called scoring territory five times. Only once, when Harland Carl dropped a touchdown pass from Jim Haluska with a minute and a half to go did the

Turn to Page 4, Column 2

## TD Pass Was a Beauty, Says Al Carmichael

BY FRANK FINCH

Al (Hoagy) Carmichael was talking about the touchdown pass that finally ended the Big Ten's reign of terror.

"It was a beautiful pass," said the tall, dark and handsome Trojan halfback. "But it came at me so slowly that I was afraid that some Wisconsin guy would pick it off."

Carmichael said that the winning play first was employed by the Trojans in the UCLA game.

"It didn't work that time," he said.

**Touchdown Play**

The maneuver calls for the ends to cross and for the right halfback (Carmichael) to delay two counts before taking off. Then he swings out wide and cuts back to the middle. Hoagy was flanked by two Badgers when he caught Rudy Bukich's pass, but neither one was in a position to interfere with the reception. Hoagy might have been worried about an interception, but in reality he had all day to catch it.

It was a "picture" pass.

**Bukich Protected**

"Except for one pass I had all the time I needed to throw," said Bukich, who filled the aching void left when Jimmy Sears was injured early in the first quarter.

"Man, oh man, did you see the protection I got from Lou Welsh, Ed Pucci, Don Stillwell and Bob Cox?" beamed Bukich.

Somebody asked Jess Hill if this was Troy's best game.

"When you beat the Big Ten in the Rose Bowl it has to be," he cracked. "That Wisconsin is the biggest 190-pound team I ever saw and Alan Ameche is

Turn to Page 2, Column 6

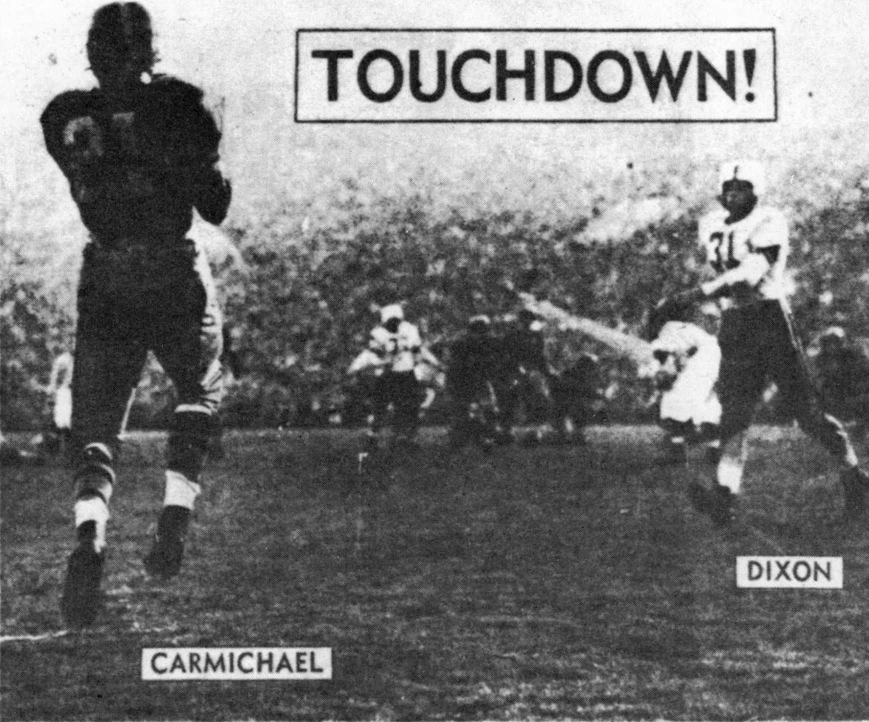


**END OF THE DROUGHT**—Al Carmichael (21) clutches ball for vital six points and Trojan victory. Wisconsin Defender John Dixon (31) was caught far from crucial spot as SC tallied to end long western loss string.

Times photo by Jack Gaunt

## AGING MOONRUSH WINS SAN PASQUAL

BY PAUL LOWRY

Moonrush, a veteran gelding that defies the advance of Father Time, added another jewel to his crown by winning the $25,000 San Pasqual Handicap before a New Year's Day crowd of 40,000 at Santa Anita yesterday.

Wresting command at the clubhouse turn in the mile and one-sixteenth feature Moonrush gamely held his slight but sufficient lead right down to the wire in a photo finish with Trusting and Horsetrader-Ed. A nose and a neck separated the trio.

Don Rebelde, the Mexican champion, came from far back in the early running to take fourth, two lengths behind the leaders. Eight started, with Deluge, Stormy Cloud, Simonsez and Danger Ahead trailing in the order named. Calbreds finished one-two-three in the race.

**Won It Also in 1951**

For Moonrush, 7-year-old son of Hunter's Moon IV and Bustle owned by Anita King and Gus Luellwitz, the San Pasqual victory was his second and the third for Jockey Ralph Neves in the same event. Moonrush previously captured the San Pasqual in 1951, the year he also triumphed in the Santa Anita Handicap. The ill-fated Your Host fell in the running of the '51 San Pasqual.

A bargain buy for $10,500 at the Louis B. Mayer sales of 1948 Moonrush, with his yesterday's cut of $15,550, advanced his lifetime earnings to $429,-530, and swept into 11th place in the world standings. He is now ahead of Hill Prince and just behind Seabiscuit.

Moonrush's previous start was in the Bay Meadows Handicap, where he scored his third win and set a new track record for a mile and one-quarter in beating the great mare Two Lea, winner of the last Hollywood Gold Cup.

**Sun Shines, Track Off**

The sun shone for the New Year's program at the Arcadia tureen, but the track was still off as the result of Tuesday's rain, and it was labeled "good" by the chart caller.

Moonrush's time, carrying top weight of 122 pounds, was 1:43 2-5, and all the fractions belonged to him—half in :46 2-5, six furlongs in 1:11 and mile in 1:37. He was the 3 to 2 favorite—one of five that clicked during the afternoon — and paid $5.10 on the front end.

Trusting lost ground at the

Turn to Page 7, Column 6

### LOS ANGELES OPEN GOLF PLAY STARTS

The 27th annual Los Angeles Open Golf Tournament for $20,000 purse begins today at Riviera Country Club. It will be played over 72 holes for four days. Details on Page 6, Col. 1.

### TODAY IN SPORTS

**HORSE RACING** — Santa Anita, 1 p.m.

**GOLF**—27th annual Los Angeles Open, Riviera Country Club, all day.

**BASKETBALL** — UCLA vs. California, UCLA gym, 8:30 p.m.

**WRESTLING** — Ocean Park Arena, 8:30 p.m.

## SC Finally Halts Big 10 Win Streak

### Jubilant Troy Rooters Tear Down Goal Posts After Rugged Victory

BY BRAVEN DYER

The Pacific Coast Conference had the horses yesterday—the Trojan horses—and the long string of victories by the Big Ten ended as Jess Hill stepped into the winner's circle to the tune of 7-0.

At precisely 4:43 p.m. the final gun barked in Pasadena's famed Rose Bowl and delirious Southern California rooters among the 101,500 fans poured on the field to tear the goal posts to toothpick size and cart them off to home and mother.

**Last PCC Victor**

Thus, just as the man said the other morning, after going to the New Testament for help, the last shall be first.

The Trojans, you see, were the last PCC team to win a Rose Bowl game 'way back there in 1945

Yesterday was their 11th visit to the Arroyo Seco saucer and the triumph over Wisconsin made their record nine wins and two defeats.

The lone score came as Rudy Bukich fired a Bob Feller strike to Al Carmichael in the end zone with 8:45 to play in the third quarter.

The line of scrimmage was on the Wisconsin 22 but Bukich threw from near the 30.

Little Sam Tsagalakis came in and, with Harry Welch holding, kicked the extra point.

**Flops on Fumble**

The pass by Bukich climaxed a 73-yard drive which began when Troy's wrecking crew, as had happened in many games this season, took the ball away from the Badgers as Bob Hooks flopped on a fumble deep in SC territory.

Hill's hard-hitting outfit won the game the hard way—without All-American Jim Sears, who was injured in the first five minutes and wound up in civilian clothes on the bench.

Bukich and Aramis Dandoy, a gutty sophomore, came along to bat for the unlucky Sears and thanks to the customary rock-ribbed defense by the wrecking crew these two standbys were able to put over the most important victory the PCC has ever scored in the Rose Bowl.

Wisconsin played magnificently and it is doubtful if the Badgers could have been held scoreless by any other team in the country yesterday.

The great Alan Ameche was just that . . . great. He rumbled along for the staggering total of 133 yards in 28 carries, thereby coming close to Bobby Grayson's Rose Bowl record of 151 made for Stanford against Columbia in 1934.

Jim Haluska, Wisconsin's terrific quarterback, did a brilliant passing job, connecting on 11 of 26 for 142 yards.

And Ivy Williamson's aggressive line did a lot of damage advancing the ball, but the Trojan defensive unit clapped shut like a bear trap every time it looked as if the Madison men were about to penetrate the promised land.

**First-Down Edge**

Wisconsin had an edge in first downs, 19 to 16, and a yardage superiority of 353 to 233.

Bukich completed 12 of 20 pitches for 137 yards and all told the Trojans hit 18 of 27, which broke the old record of 16 completions set by Navy against Washington in 1924. Navy that day hit on a lot of shorties . . . the Trojans were gaining an average of 10 yards per pitch.

In the second half the Trojans introduced their new short-punt formation which proved a considerable aid in

Turn to Page 2, Column 1

### Bowl Scores

**SALAD BOWL** — San Diego Naval Training Center, 81; Camp Breckinridge, 20.

**RICE BOWL**—Camp Drake, 25; Yokosuka Navy Base, 6.

**PRAIRIE VIEW BOWL**—Texas Southern, 13; Prairie View, 12.

**SPAGHETTI BOWL** — Salzburg Army Base, 12; Wiesbaden Air Force Command, 7.

**TANGERINE BOWL** — East Texas State, 33; Tennessee Tech, 0.

| ROSE | | SUGAR | | COTTON | | ORANGE | | GATOR | | SUN | |
|---|---|---|---|---|---|---|---|---|---|---|---|
| SC | 7 | Ga. Tech | 24 | Texas | 16 | Alabama | 61 | Florida | 14 | COP | 26 |
| Wisconsin | 0 | Mississippi | 7 | Tennessee | 0 | Syracuse | 6 | Tulsa | 13 | Miss. So. | 7 |
| | | Story on Page 5 | | Story on Page 5 | | Story on Page 6 | | Story on Page 6 | | Story on Page 8 | |

VOL. LXXIII CC ★ FRIDAY MORNING, MAY 7, 1954 Read The Times for Latest Sports

# BANNISTER RUNS RECORD MILE IN 3:59.4

## SPORTS PARADE

By BRAVEN DYER

It's a pretty safe bet that there were no mirrors broken in the home of Andrew J. Crevolin seven years ago. Because the phenomenal Crevolin racing luck began exactly seven years ago this spring and reached its spectacular climax last week with the winning of two $100,000 races on the same afternoon.

The true story of Andy's racing debut is tied in with a cocktail party, an auction of oat eaters and a young man named Irving Cummings Jr. The date is Feb. 27, 1947. The opening scene is the San Gabriel home of Jane and Andy Crevolin, where the cocktail party is just breaking up.

"I've got four tickets to the Louis B. Mayer dispersal sale at Santa Anita," offered Cummings to the Crevolins, "let's go out and see how they run one of these things."

**LONG-TIME FRIENDS**

Jane Ann Dohrman and Fran Greenlin had been close friends at Stanford in the middle 30s when Irving was a star end on Tiny Thornhill's football teams. Jane later married Crevolin and Miss Greenlin became Mrs. Cummings.

"The Crevolins accepted the invitation," recalled Irving, "and I joshingly said something about starting the C and C Stable, Crevolin and Cummings. And, believe it or not, I thought nothing more about it until I heard Andy bidding for a 2-year-old at the auction."

Before the evening ended the Crevolins had purchased Rising Prices for $18,500 and Flying Rhythm for $11,000. This was a real gamble for the auto dealer, inasmuch as Flying Rhythm never had been to the post and Rising Prices had started but once. And what's more, Andy didn't even have an owner's license at the time.

**RISING PRICES STILL RUNNING**

But he got one three weeks later, just in time for the meeting at Tanforan. After that it wasn't long before Crevolin's charges began hitting the jackpot. Rising Prices paid $90 for a $2 ticket and now, at the age of 9, still is running, but for another owner, after substantially enriching the Crevolin coffers. Hollywood Park bettors will remember Flying Rhythm without much difficulty. Andy's filly not only won the third running of the Hollywood Oaks in 1948 but set a stakes record high of $167.80 for $2. The purse of $19,050 alone returned more than the purchase price.

The Crevolin colors have hit the winner's circle many, many times since then. His Valquest won the Hollywood Westerner in 1950 and Be Fleet copped the Argonaut a year later. Imbros came along last year and cleaned up by taking the El Dorado, Debonair and Will Rogers at the Goose Girl track last summer. And then Determine bobbed up to capture the Santa Anita Derby, after which Imbros had the Hundred Grander won until Rejected came flying through the stretch.

**GIVES IT HIS ALL**

"Sure, Andy is lucky," said Cummings of his pal. "Everybody who makes a real success in life has to be lucky some of the time. But there's one thing about Andy . . . when he goes into something he's in it with all he has. I know that since he bought his first horse seven years ago he has displayed sound judgment and business acumen."

Oh, yes, at the Mayer sale in 1947 a man named Harry M. Warner bought a 2-year-old named Wedding Plans for $54,000. His wife paid $36,000 for another 2-year-old named Make-Up Man. All told, the Warners spent almost $500,000 for horseflesh that night seven years ago, and they're still looking for their first Kentucky Derby winner!

## QUEEN REGISTERS SIXTH WIN IN ROW

SAN DIEGO, May 6 (AP)—Mel Queen, big right-hander, registered his sixth straight victory tonight in pitching the Hollywood Stars to a 2-1 win over San Diego.

San Diego had the tying run on second in the ninth with two outs but Queen got Bob Elliott to fly out to end the game.

Queen and Padre Hurler Bob Kerrigan hooked up in a pitcher's duel for the first five innings, with Queen allowing only two hits during that time.

But in the sixth the Padres bunched three singles to break the scoreless duel. Dick Aylward led off with a single to left, advanced to second on a sacrifice and remained there as Lee Walls barely missed catching Al Federoff's bloop single to short right-center. Then Dick Sisler singled to load the bases.

Harry Elliott walked to force in Aylward and when Hollywood Manager Bobby Bragan protested Plate Umpire Al Mutart's call on the last pitch he was ejected from the game. Earl Rapp grounded out to end the inning.

Totals 36 10 27 9. Totals 31 7 27 11.

SCORE BY INNINGS

Hollywood 000 000 200—2
San Diego 000 001 000—1

## Tribe Edges Athletics, 3-2

PHILADELPHIA, May 6 (AP) A lead-off eighth-inning homer by Al Smith was enough margin to give the Cleveland Indians and Early Wynn a 3-2 win over the Philadelphia Athletics.

## Allie Shuts Door, 9-0, on Orioles

### Reynolds Pitches One-Hit Ball for Nearly Eight Frames

NEW YORK, May 6 (AP)—Allie Reynolds pitched one-hit ball until he was forced to retire in the eighth inning with a leg cramp as the New York Yankees today blanked Baltimore 9-0. The only hit off Reynolds was a lead-off single by Bobby Young in the first inning.

Bob Kuzava, who replaced Reynolds in the eighth, allowed singles by Dick Kryhoski and Young. Vic Wertz singled off Bob Grim in the ninth for the fourth Baltimore hit.

**Berra Homers**

The Yanks rapped Joe Coleman and his successors for 11 hits, including Yogi Berra's third homer of the year with Joe Collins on base in the first.

The one hit off Reynolds was a scratch infield single to McDougald that Young beat out. He walked three and struck out five before he had to retire.

Reynolds was pitching to Clint Courtney, first man up in the eighth, and had a 3-2 count on him when he had to leave. At first it was thought he pulled a tendon in his right leg but later word from the dugout was that he had suffered a cramp.

E—Hunter. RBI—Berra, 2; Collins, 3; Carey, Slaughter, McDougald, Noren, 2. 2B—Carey, Noren, Rizzuto, Collins. 3B—Collins. HR—Berra. DP—Young to Waltkus; Wertz to Kryhoski; Berry to Young to Kryhoski; McDougald to Rizzuto to Collins. LOB—Baltimore, 6; New York, 11. BB—Off Coleman, 4; Koslo, 1; Littlefield, 4; Stuart, 1; Reynolds, 3. SO—By Coleman, 1; Reynolds, 5; Grim, 1. Hits—Coleman, 3 in ⅔; Koslo, 3 in 6⅓; Littlefield, 5 in 2; Stuart, 0 in 1; Reynolds, 1 in 7; Kuzava, 2 in 1; Grim, 1 in 1. R and ER—Coleman, 4-4; Littlefield, 5-5. HB—By Littlefield (Berra). Winner—Reynolds (2-1). Loser — Coleman (1-1). Umpires — Chylak, Honochick, McGowan, Paparella. Time—2h. 28m. Attendance—4610.

## BASEBALL STANDINGS

**PACIFIC COAST LEAGUE**

| | W | L | Pct. | * |
|---|---|---|---|---|
| Oakland | 18 | 13 | .581 | |
| Sacramento | 18 | 13 | .581 | |
| San Diego | 17 | 13 | .567 | ½ |
| LOS ANGELES | 17 | 15 | .531 | 1½ |
| HOLLYWOOD | 15 | 15 | .500 | 2½ |
| Seattle | 15 | 16 | .484 | 3 |
| Portland | 14 | 15 | .483 | 3 |
| San Francisco | 8 | 22 | .267 | 9½ |

*Games behind leader.

**Last Night's Results**

LOS ANGELES, 4; Portland, 2.
HOLLYWOOD, 2; San Diego, 1.
Sacramento, 6; San Francisco, 1.
Seattle, 7; Oakland, 6.

**How Series Stand**

LOS ANGELES, 2; Portland, 1.
HOLLYWOOD, 3; San Diego, 0.
Seattle, 2; Oakland, 1.
Sacramento, 2; San Francisco, 1.

**Games Tonight**

Portland (Boemler 1-1) at LOS ANGELES (Jones 2-3), Wrigley Field, 8:15 p.m.
HOLLYWOOD (Hall 3-3) at San Diego (Erautt 3-3).
Seattle (Byrne 2-2) at Oakland (Nicholas 3-0).
San Francisco (Singleton 2-3) at Sacramento (Johnson 3-0).

**AMERICAN LEAGUE**

| | W | L | Pct. | * |
|---|---|---|---|---|
| Chicago | 14 | 7 | .667 | |
| Detroit | 9 | 5 | .643 | 1½ |
| Cleveland | 11 | 7 | .611 | 1½ |
| Philadelphia | 9 | 9 | .500 | 3½ |
| New York | 9 | 9 | .500 | 3½ |
| Washington | 7 | 11 | .389 | 5½ |
| Baltimore | 5 | 11 | .313 | 6½ |
| Boston | 4 | 9 | .308 | 6 |

*Games behind leader.

**Yesterday's Results**

New York, 9; Baltimore, 0.
Chicago, 5; Washington, 4.
Cleveland, 3; Philadelphia, 2.
Detroit at Boston, postponed, rain.

**Games Today**

Philadelphia (Martin, 1-1, or Portocarrero, 0-0) at New York (Morgan, 1-0).
Washington (Stobbs, 1-2) at Boston (Nixon, 1-1, or Kiely, 0-2), night.

**NATIONAL LEAGUE**

| | W | L | Pct. | * |
|---|---|---|---|---|
| Philadelphia | 11 | 6 | .647 | |
| Cincinnati | 12 | 8 | .600 | ½ |
| Brooklyn | 10 | 8 | .556 | 1½ |
| St. Louis | 10 | 9 | .526 | 2 |
| Milwaukee | 8 | 9 | .471 | 3 |
| Chicago | 7 | 8 | .467 | 3 |
| New York | 9 | 11 | .450 | 3½ |
| Pittsburgh | 7 | 15 | .318 | 6½ |

*Games behind leader.

**Yesterday's Results**

Milwaukee, 3; Pittsburgh, 0.
Chicago, 8; Brooklyn, 7; (11 innings).
Cincinnati, 5; New York, 4.
Philadelphia at St. Louis, postponed, rain.

**Games Tonight**

Brooklyn (Newcombe, 2-1) at Philadelphia (Simmons, 3-1).
New York (Antonelli, 2-1) at Pittsburgh (Law, 2-2).
St. Louis (Staley, 2-1) at Cincinnati (Valentine, 2-2).
Chicago (Hacker, 0-1) at Milwaukee (Buhl, 0-1).

MIRACLE MILER—This radio photo from London shows Roger Bannister, former Oxford star, breasting the tape in his historic race yesterday when he became the first man ever to beat four minutes flat in the mile. He was clocked in 3:59.4.
(AP) Wirephoto via radio from London

## Angels Triumph, 4 to 2, but Portland Protests

BY AL WOLF

Los Angeles trimmed Portland—temporarily at least—by a 4-2 score at Wrigley Field last evening.

Whether the victory becomes official is in the ample lap of Clarence Rowland, the Coast League president. For Manager Clay Hopper of the Ports entered a protest in the seventh inning.

Hawk-eyed Mr. Hopper detected John Pramesa, who Wednesday was placed on the Angels' disabled list, warming up Catcher Al Evans in the bull pen between halves of that round. Evans had been called into action cold when Hal Meek split his finger moments earlier.

Technically, players put on the disabled list must remain out of play at least 10 days. It remains to be seen if Rowland will construe bull-pen activity in the same light.

"It won't do Hopper any good, and you can bet on it!" Skipper Will Sweeney of the Angels predicted following the game, if any.

Los Angeles manufactured all its runs in the sixth round while Portland went scoreless until the ninth.

**Hardly Power Stuff**

The bilious-batting Angels didn't exactly overpower the opposition. Their scores resulted from two bunted singles, two walks and a pinch hit down the first base line which a more agile defender than Dino Restelli probably would have captured.

But it's not how you get 'em that counts.

Bob Spicer and Bob Alexander were locked in a lulu when the roof suddenly caved in on the latter.

**Close Play**

Dave Cunningham led off for Los Angeles in the decisive sixth and pushed a bunt that he beat out on a play so close that the Portlanders beefed at length on Umpire Emmett

Turn to Page 2, Column 4

## BRAVES BEAT BUCS ON 95 PITCHES

MILWAUKEE, May 6 (AP)—Lew Burdette scarcely wasted a pitch today, throwing only 95 as he shut out the Pittsburgh Pirate, 3-0, on five hits to move the Milwaukee Braves into fifth place in the National League on their third straight victory.

| Pittsburgh | AB | H | O | A | Milwaukee | AB | H | O | A |
|---|---|---|---|---|---|---|---|---|---|
| Abrams,lf | 4 | 0 | 2 | 0 | Bruton,cf | 4 | 2 | 1 | 0 |
| Cole,ss | 4 | 2 | 0 | 2 | O'Connell 2b | 4 | 2 | 2 | 7 |
| Skinner,1b | 3 | 1 | 13 | 2 | Mathews,3b | 2 | 2 | 0 | 1 |
| Thomas,cf | 3 | 0 | 6 | 2 | Pafko,rf | 3 | 1 | 1 | 0 |
| Lynch,rf | 2 | 0 | 4 | 0 | Adcock,1b | 4 | 1 | 10 | 0 |
| Ward,3b | 3 | 1 | 0 | 3 | Aaron,lf | 4 | 1 | 3 | 0 |
| Atwell,c | 3 | 0 | 1 | 0 | Logan,ss | 4 | 1 | 6 | 5 |
| Roberts,2b | 3 | 1 | 1 | 5 | Crandall,c | 3 | 1 | 3 | 0 |
| O'Donnell,p | 1 | 0 | 0 | 1 | Burdette,p | 3 | 0 | 1 | 2 |
| Henley | 1 | 0 | 0 | 0 | | | | | |
| LaPalme,p | 0 | 0 | 0 | 1 | | | | | |
| Hall | 1 | 0 | 0 | 0 | | | | | |
| Totals | 28 | 5 | 24 | 16 | Totals | 31 | 11 | 27 | 15 |

Henley grounded out for O'Donnell in 6th. Hall lined out for LaPalme in 9th.

Pittsburgh 000 000 000—0
Milwaukee 100 110 00x—3

RBI—Mathews, Burdette, Pafko. 2B—Aaron. 3B—Roberts. SB—Bruton, Mathews. SH—Burdette. SF—Pafko. DP—Thomas to Skinner; Roberts to Skinner; O'Connell to Logan to Adcock 2; Burdette to Logan to Adcock; Logan to O'Connell to Adcock. LOB—Pittsburgh, 3; Milwaukee, 9. BB—Off O'Donnell, 2; LaPalme, 1; Burdette, 2. SO—By LaPalme, 1; Burdette, 2. Hits—Off O'Donnell, 7 in 5; LaPalme, 4 in 3. R and ER—O'Donnell, 3-3. Winner—Burdette (2-2). Loser—O'Donnell (1-2). Umpires—Ballanfant, Barlick, Warneke, Donatelli. Time—1h. 52m. Attendance—11,886.

## TODAY IN SPORTS

**TENNIS**—Southern California Tournament, L.A. Tennis Club, 12 noon.

**QUARTER-HORSE RACING**—Los Alamitos, 1 p.m.

**BASEBALL**—Portland Beavers vs. Los Angeles Angels, Wrigley Field, 8:15 p.m.

**BOXING**—Wilmington Bowl, 8:30 p.m.

**WRESTLING**—Ocean Park Arena, 8:30 p.m.

## HOW BANNISTER WAS TIMED AT CHECKING POSTS

OXFORD, Eng., May 6 (AP) Here are Roger Bannister's times at every 220-yard check post en route to his fantastic 3:59.4 mile today:

220 yards: 28.7 seconds
440 yards: 57.5
660 yards: 1:27.5
880 yards: 1:58.2
1110 yards: 2:29.6
1320 yards: 3:00.5
1540 yards: 3:30.5
1760 yards: 3:59.4

## Evolution of Mile Record

NEW YORK, May 6 (AP)—Here is the evolution of world records in the mile run as listed in Frank G Menke's Encyclopedia of Sport:

| | | |
|---|---|---|
| 4:56.0 | Charles Lawes, Britain | 1864 |
| 4:36.5 | Richard Webster, Britain | 1865 |
| 4:29.0 | William Chinery, Britain | 1868 |
| 4:28.8 | W. C. Gibbs, Britain | 1868 |
| 4:26.0 | Walter Slade, Britain | 1874 |
| 4:24.5 | Walter Slade, Britain | 1875 |
| 4:23.2 | Walter George, Britain | 1880 |
| 4:21.4 | Walter George, Britain | 1882 |
| 4:19.4 | Walter George, Britain | 1882 |
| 4:18.4 | Walter George, Britain | 1884 |
| 4:18.2 | Fred Bacon, Scotland | 1894 |
| 4:17.0 | Fred Bacon, Scotland | 1895 |
| 4:15.6 | Thomas Conneff, U.S. | 1895 |
| 4:15.4 | John Paul Jones, U.S. | 1911 |
| 4:14.4 | John Paul Jones, U.S. | 1913 |
| 4:12.6 | Norman Taber, U.S. | 1915 |
| 4:10.4 | Paavo Nurmi, Finland | 1923 |
| 4:09.2 | J. Ladoumegue, France | 1931 |
| 4:07.6 | Jack Lovelock, N. Zeal'd | 1933 |
| 4:06.8 | Glenn Cunningham, U.S. | 1934 |
| 4:06.4 | S. Wooderson, Britain | 1937 |
| 4:06.2 | Gunder Haegg, Sweden | 1942 |
| 4:06.2 | Arne Andersson, Sweden | 1942 |
| 4:04.6 | Gunder Haegg, Sweden | 1942 |
| 4:02.6 | Arne Andersson, Sweden | 1943 |
| 4:01.6 | Arne Andersson, Sweden | 1944 |
| 4:01.4 | Gunder Haegg, Sweden | 1945 |
| 3:59.4 | Roger Bannister, Britain | 1954 |

## Bannister's Mile and Other Speed Marks Compared

NEW YORK, May 6 (AP)—Here is how Roger Bannister's mile compares with other speed records:

| | |
|---|---|
| Human swimming (John Marshall, 1950) | 19:49.4 |
| Human running (Roger Bannister, 1954) | 3:59.4 |
| Human skating (Del Lamb, 1948) | 2:29.7 |
| Horse trotting (Greyhound, 1938) | 1:55.25 |
| Horse pacing (Billy Direct, 1938) | 1:55.0 |
| Bicycle (Alf Goullet, 1912) | 1:51.0 |
| Horse running (Citation, 1950) | 1:33.6 |
| Speedboat (Slo-Mo-Shun IV, 1952) | 20.2 |
| Automobile (John Cobb, 1947) | :09.1 |
| Jet airplane (Scott Crossfield, 1953) | :07.7 |

## Four-Minute 'Dream' Bettered as Haegg's 4:01.4 Mark Topples

BY MILT MARMOR

OXFORD, Eng., May 6 (AP)—Roger Bannister tonight ended the athletic world's quest for the four-minute mile with a monumental effort in which he was timed at 3:59.4.

Competing in his first race of the year, and on his own track at Iffley Road, the shy former Oxonian burst through the legendary four-minute barrier as a meager crowd of 1000, mostly Oxford students, watched the memorable performance during which he drove himself mercilessly through a 58.9 final lap.

### Full Measure

OXFORD, Eng., May 6 (AP) — Surveyors measured the Oxford University track today immediately after Roger Bannister was timed in 3:59.4.

They found that the four-lap track exceeded the mile distance by one-half inch.

PIONEER—Here's a close-up of Roger Bannister, who ran 3:59.4 mile yesterday.
(AP) Wirephoto

Thus he thrust into the dust bin of sports history the world record mark of 4:01.4 established July 18, 1945, at Malmo, Sweden, by the great Gunder Haegg of Sweden. Bannister also unofficially equaled the 1500-meter world mark of 3:43 en route to his mile mark.

Bannister was pulled along through the first three laps by a fellow Oxonian, Chris Chataway, and a former Cambridge steeplechaser, Chris Brasher.

**1:58.2 for Half-Mile**

He kept on Brasher's heels for the first two laps, and when Chataway dashed into the lead Bannister stayed with him through the third lap.

He was clocked at 57.5 for the quarter and 1:58.2 for the half. When he passed the three-quarter mark in 3:00.5 the handful of spectators seated in the small pavilion and scattered about the field gave a lusty cheer.

The great runner bided his time until about 300 yards from the tape, when he urged himself to a supreme effort. With a machinelike, seemingly effortless stride he drew steadily away from Chataway, and, head thrown back slightly, he breasted the cool, stiff wind on the last turn to come driving down the home stretch to climax his spectacular performance.

**Half-Inch Over Mile**

Before Bannister's tremendous record can become official it must be approved by the International Amateur Athletic Federation, but chances appeared good as the meet was an official one and the race was run under standard conditions.

The track was immediately resurveyed, and the measurement showed it was half-inch longer than one mile.

Spectators and athletes surged around the exhausted Bannister after he finished. Two officials held him erect as he regained his breath. Then came the announcement of the great time.

Bannister quickly rushed over to Chataway and Brasher and embraced them. Then the three jogged across the infield, Bannister towering over his friends. The Oxford medical student stands 6 feet 1 inch.

**Good Luck Omen**

Bannister told reporters he had not decided to go all out for a world record until 15 minutes before the start of the race. It had rained rather heavily during the day and a strong wind had whipped the field. But less than a half-hour before race time the sun came out and a rainbow showed in the sky. It was a good luck omen for Bannister.

Brasher said he thought he had taken the first lap too quickly. Bannister said he had been shouting at Brasher to go faster.

**Best Time**

"Naturally I wanted to have a try at it," Bannister said. "I could not have done it without Chataway and Brasher."

Chataway, who finished second about 60 yards behind Bannister, was timed in 4:07.2, the best he has ever done for the mile.

Bannister said he had been training recently with an Austrian coach, Franz Stampl, who helped him strengthen his shoulders and legs with push-ups. Bannister is an effortless runner, with longer strides than usual, and many consider his style to be among the best.

"I have been doing a great deal of jumping and sprinting of late," he said. "During the

Turn to Page 3, Column 1

## Challenge for Americans Remains, Says Santee

Wes Santee, America's No. 1 miler, said yesterday he was "not exceptionally disappointed" when told of the 3:59.4 world record breaking mile of Roger Bannister.

Santee, who has made no secret of the fact that he expected to be the first to run the four-minute mile, said, "Of the milers capable of doing it, Bannister is the one I'd just as soon have break it. It has always been a fact that Europeans have been ahead of us in the mile.

"There is still the challenge," he added, "to see who will be the first American to do it . . . I haven't been permitted to concentrate."

Santee's coach, Bill Easton of Kansas, said he thought Santee could run better now that the pressure was off. "Not so much will be expected of him and he will be better able to concentrate." Santee's best time in the mile, 4:02.4, is the American record.

Bannister's performance was no surprise to the official world record holder, Gunder Haegg of Sweden.

Haegg predicted last month the four-minute mile would be run this season. Haegg said, "Bannister has brains. He doesn't overtrain the way many runners do." It was Haegg's mark of 4:01.4, set in 1945, that Bannister bettered.

Australia's John Landy was surprised at Bannister's performance and said he thought "Santee will be next—but not I."

Mal Whitfield, contacted in New York, said he was still determined to run the mile under four minutes.

## FASTEST MILES OF PAST

NEW YORK, May 6 (AP)—The fastest miles run before Roger Bannister broke the four-minute barrier today:

| | | | |
|---|---|---|---|
| Gunder Haegg | Sweden | 1945 | 4:01.4 |
| Arne Andersson | Sweden | 1944 | 4:01.6 |
| John Landy | Australia | 1953 | 4:02 |
| John Landy | Australia | 1952 | 4:02.1 |
| Wes Santee | United States | 1953 | 4:02.4 |
| John Landy | Australia | 1954 | 4:02.4 |
| Arne Andersson | Sweden | 1943 | 4:02.6 |
| John Landy | Australia | 1954 | 4:02.6 |
| John Landy | Australia | 1954 | 4:02.6 |
| Gaston Reiff | Belgium | 1952 | 4:02.8 |
| John Landy | Australia | 1953 | 4:02.8 |

Paul Zimmerman
Sports Editor

# Los Angeles Times

SPORTS

6 PART II | CC | SUNDAY MORNING, FEBRUARY 20, 1955 | VOL. LXXIV

# LONGDEN BOOTS SWAPS TO DERBY VICTORY

**LONGDEN IN FRONT**—Swaps, with the veteran Johnny Longden aboard, crosses finish line with half-length margin over Jean's Joe, ridden by Eddie Arcaro, in $137,500 Santa Anita Derby before 49,000 fans. Swaps led after leaving backstretch. The California-bred colt paid $9.20 for $2 and won $90,400 prize money.
Times photo by R. L. Oliver

## Cal-Bred Conquers Jean's Joe in Rich Race Before 49,000

BY PAUL LOWRY

Swaps, a chestnut colt bred on the Ontario farm of Owner Rex Ellsworth, raced to the most impressive conquest of his career before a roaring crowd of 49,000 at Santa Anita yesterday.

With Johnny Longden in the saddle for his seventh stakes win of the meeting, Swaps took the $137,500 Santa Anita Derby by half a length from Murcain Stable's Jean's Joe. It was Longden's fourth winning Derby at the Arcadia track.

Strung out down the track and really not figuring in the race were such highly regarded 3-year-olds as Murcain Stable's Blue Ruler, Calumet Farm's Trentonian, Sunnyside Stable's Beau Busher and others.

Blue Ruler, the best-liked half of the Murcain entry, was third in the mile and one-eighth special, four lengths back of the winner. Honey's Alibi, a 63-to-1 longshot, was fourth by another three lengths.

**Track 'Dead'**

Then came Bequeath, Nabesna, Trentonian, Fabulous Vegas, Blue Pencil, Treadgold, Trackmaster, Beau Busher, Right Down and Cover Me Up.

It was a bright sunny day for the 18th running of the Derby, but while the track was labeled fast it was still a bit dead from the midweek rains as indicated by the time of 1:50 flat. Your Host (1950) and Determine (1954) both won their Derbies in 1:48.4.

The winner of the 18th Derby is strictly a Southern California product. He broke his maiden at Hollywood Park last year and has never raced anywhere but at Hollypark and Santa Anita. He had previously won the San Vicente Stakes at the meeting but missed the San Felipe, which went to Jean's Joe.

**Assist for Bequeath**

An assist in the Derby goes to Swaps' stablemate, Bequeath, which ran down Right Down on the early pace while Swaps raced evenly in third place.

Right Down died on the far turn and Swaps passed Bequeath to take the lead by a length at the head of the stretch. Meanwhile Jean's Joe, making a fast move along the rail, mowed down horses with ease and was second when the field turned for home. Blue Ruler was challenging on the outside, but he lacked the zip of his stablemate and never got close enough to be dangerous.

Jean's Joe had come off the turn with such a rush that it looked as if he might catch Swaps, but cagey Longden, the 45-year-old Valentine ba-

Turn to Page 11, Column 6

### THE WINNERS

1—Competing Beau, $3.90.
2—Noir, $8.40.
3—Red Ran, $15.20.
4—Se Voya, $33.20.
5—Allied, $20.70.
6—First Baby, $13.80.
7—Swaps, $9.20.
8—Sun Deck, $7.90.

NICE JOB

## Training of Swaps Called Masterpiece

BY PETE PEDERSEN

Meshach Tenney, a sober-faced, twinkling-eyed individual with a Biblical name and a green thumb for horses, engineered a training masterpiece when he saddled Swaps for victory in the $137,500 Santa Anita Derby yesterday.

Swaps, which had not been postward for a month to the day, carried the California-bred banner against some beautifully bred runners from enemy territory. The chestnut son of the magnificent stallion Khaled turned in an effort which is a tribute to the training tactics of Tenney.

**Infection in Foot**

"He developed an infection in his right fore foot after his last race," explained the modest Tenney. "It came from a piece of dirt working up in a crack. I put a pad on, and then set a pattern that I hoped would get him up to the Derby. I spaced his works five days apart. That's why I scratched him in the Derby Prep (Feb. 11). I'd have loved to run him, knowing he should have a race, but it came right between his work program. I decided it was best to train him for the race."

Tenney personally shoes all of his horses. He and Owner Rex Ellsworth trim the feet of their young horses on the ranch and Tenney continues the practice at the track.

"I put a new set on Swaps Friday morning," said Tenney. He has a very thin shell on his right fore foot, and believe me, my heart was in my mouth when I set the nails."

**Named for Derby**

Swaps is named for the Kentucky Derby, but not the Preakness or Belmont Stakes. Ellsworth, a soft-spoken gent who has parlayed experience as an Arizona cowboy into a pretty fair turf empire, was not overly enthusiastic about the prospects of sending Swaps to Kentucky, nor was Tenney.

"We haven't talked about it," said Ellsworth. "It depends on a lot of things, and particularly how Tenney feels about it."

"We'll look at the pictures and decide if he was entirely used up," said Tenney. "Going into the race, I felt he was thoroughly inexperienced. He should improve considerably. If we do decide to send him, I imagine the best way is to get him up to top shape here, then fly to Kentucky. But I'll listen to Mr. Ellsworth. There's no better judge of horses any place, and I don't bar the world."

**'Full of Run'**

Johnny Longden, who had never ridden the colt before, said, "He was pretty rank early—full of run and I couldn't hold him. I went to the lead with his neck bowed. Then he saw the starting gate and ducked out with me, but once I got him straight I turned his head loose and went to knocking."

Eddie Arcaro, who rode the second horse, Jean's Joe, was 39 years old yesterday. "And that's an honest 39," he laughed, "not a Longden 39."

Arcaro, who could under-

Turn to Page 11, Column 7

## SPORTSCRIPTS

By PAUL ZIMMERMAN TIMES SPORTS EDITOR

There's nothing like getting a new head football coach started off on the right (or wrong) foot by quoting a few of his offhand observations on what the 1955 grid season holds forth.

Tommy Prothro was in the throes of moving the other day when we tackled him with a few questions. Nonplused by the problem of getting more things in trunk and bag than he had trunks and bags, he was an easy target.

**TROJANS AND BRUINS LOOK BEST**

After all, he was packing his worldly goods for the long northern trek and his new job at Oregon State.

"Now that you have severed your ties with Coach Red Sanders and UCLA," we stated, "perhaps you would feel free to take an impartial view of the Pacific Coast Conference grid situation as it revolves around the teams that have held the sway of power."

"I wouldn't want to come out and say this team or that one would win the championship," hedged Prothro. Then he plunged in.

"Southern California should be as good as it was last year," said Tommy, "and could be better. The Trojans have more good personnel than any team that did well in 1954.

"If UCLA is lucky it might be as good as last year but the Bruins play a much tougher schedule.

**STANFORD AND WASHINGTON IMPROVE**

"Stanford and Washington are the two teams with the best chances against Southern California and UCLA. California lost two great players that will be hard to replace (Paul Larson and Matt Hazeltine). The Bears may not be better this fall."

Before Prothro knew it his appraisal of the situation had taken him right up there in his new bailiwick.

"Oregon lost a lot of good football players and as for Oregon State I can only say I hope we can improve the situation."

Tommy saw where his words were leading him, so he quickly dropped back down south.

"The Bruins have some fine backs. Ronnie Knox could make a lot of difference. He's truly great. However, they lost a lot of fine linemen. You don't figure to replace men like Jack Ellena and Jim Salsbury."

**BEAVERS POINT FOR IDAHO**

Prothro suddenly remembered his Oregon Staters tangle with the Bruins down here next fall.

"I kinda hate to be quoted on the Bruins," he said, and turned the conversation upstate a bit.

"Stanford," he said thoughtfully, "had a young ball club last fall and a great freshman team. Washington also has some fine new boys coming on. I guess no team in the conference had as much bad luck as the Huskies did last year. If they'd have a turn of good luck this fall they will cause trouble."

Tommy said he was so busy on his two trips up to

Turn to Page 12, Column 4

## Hasty Road Wins $132,800 Widener

MIAMI, Fla., Feb. 19 (AP)—Hasty Road, last year's winner of the Preakness, proved his fitness today when he led all the way to win the $132,800 Widener Handicap at a mile and a quarter before 30,472 fans at Hialeah Park.

Alfred G. Vanderbilt's Social Outcast, 6-5 favorite in the field of 10, could do no better than third behind Brookmeade Stable's Capeador. Bruce S. Campbell's Ram o' War was fourth.

Hasty Road, owned by Hasty House Farms of Toledo, O., and carrying 122 pounds including the veteran jockey, Johnny Adams, forged ahead just after the start and stayed in front all the way, beating off the challenge of Cerise Reine, only mare in the race, and then Capeador.

Social Outcast, top-weighted at 126 pounds with Eric Guerin in riding, closed ground but couldn't reach the front runners and was two and three-quarters lengths back at the end.

Hasty Road's margin was only a neck, but it brought his owners, Mr. and Mrs. Allie Reuben, the winner's purse of $95,600.

Robert S. Lytle's Correlation, who was flown here from California for the race, finished last under 122 pounds, with Henry Moreno riding.

Hasty Road ran the mile and a quarter in 2:02 2-5 over a fast track and paid $7.90, $3.60 and $2.50 in the $2 mutuels. Capeador returned $7.80 and $4.10 with the show price on Social Outcast $2.50.

Jockey Hedley Woodhouse, on Capeador, claimed foul against Hasty Road, but the stewards did not allow it. Woodhouse claimed Hasty Road drifted out entering the stretch and bothered his mount.

**Early Lead**

Hasty Road held a clear early lead as the rounded the clubhouse turn with Cerise Reine and Capeador in close pursuit. Capeador replaced Cerise after the first mile and was only a head back of the leader as they turned for home.

Social Outcast improved his position after the first mile, but couldn't get at the top pair as they sped down the long stretch. Ram o' War was within hailing distance of the leaders most of the way, but failed to respond in the long stretch.

Cerise Reine faded to sixth, behind the 1954 grass champion, Stan, an entry with Hasty Road. Mister Black, another Hasty House horse, came from last to finish seventh, ahead of James Cox Brady's Artismo, Greentree Stable's Maharajah and Correlation.

Fractional times for the mile and a quarter were :24, :48, 1:12 and 1:36 3-5.

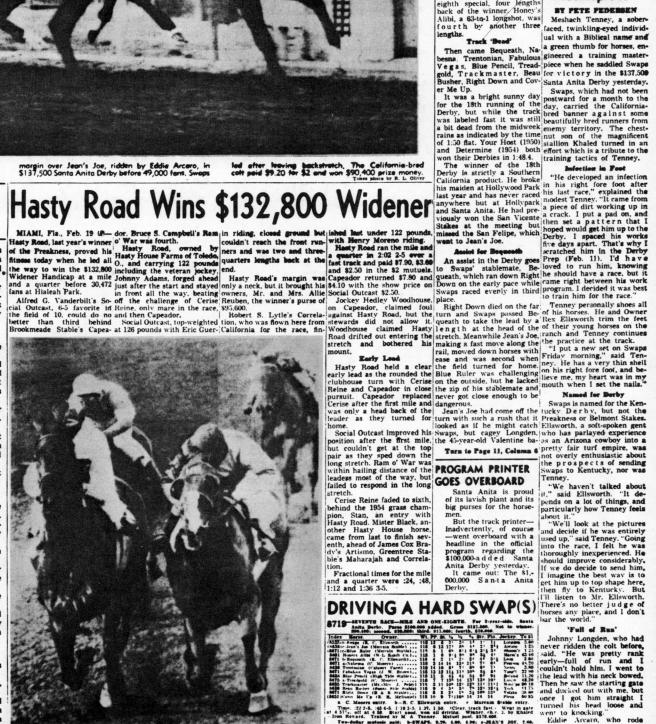

**MAKING HASTE**—Hasty House Farms' Hasty Road, right, ridden by Johnny Adams, comes down stretch to conquer Capeador in $100,000 Widener Handicap at Hialeah. Social Outcast, partially obscured by Capeador, finished third in race.

### PROGRAM PRINTER GOES OVERBOARD

Santa Anita is proud of its lavish plant and its big purses for the horsemen.

But the track printer—inadvertently, of course—went overboard with a headline in the official program regarding the $100,000-added Santa Anita Derby yesterday.

It came out: The $1,000,000 Santa Anita Derby.

## DRIVING A HARD SWAP(S)

**8719**—SEVENTH RACE—MILE AND ONE-EIGHTH. For 3-year-olds. Santa Anita Derby. Purse $100,000 added. Gross $137,500. Net to winner, $90,400; second, $20,000; third, $15,000; fourth, $10,000.

| Index | Horse. Owner. | Wt. | PP. | St. | ¼ | ½ | ¾ | Str. | Fin. | Jockey. | To $1 |
|---|---|---|---|---|---|---|---|---|---|---|---|
| (8535) | b-Swaps (R. C. Ellsworth) | 118 | 12 | 6 | $3^{1}$ | $3^{2}$ | $1^{2}$ | $1^{1}$ | 1½ | Longden | 3.60 |
| (8638) | c-Jean's Joe (Murcain Stable) | 118 | 6 | 13 | $12^{2}$ | $8^{h}$ | $4^{2}$ | $2^{2}$ | $2^{1½}$ | Arcaro | 1.25 |
| (8671) | c-Blue Ruler (Murcain Stable) | 118 | 5 | 1 | $6^{h}$ | $6^{1½}$ | $6^{1½}$ | $3^{1½}$ | $3^{2}$ | Shoem'r | 1.25 |
| 8691 | Honeys Alibi (W. L. Basch Co.) | 118 | 1 | 8 | $9^{1½}$ | $9^{h}$ | $9^{h}$ | 5½ | $4^{1}$ | Harm's | 63.40 |
| 8671 | b-Bequeath (R. C. Ellsworth) | 118 | 4 | 2 | $1^{1}$ | $2^{1}$ | $2^{2}$ | $4^{1}$ | $5^{1½}$ | Leon | 3.60 |
| 8671 | a-Nabesna (C. Mooers) | 118 | 2 | 14 | 14 | $13^{2}$ | $11^{5}$ | $7^{1}$ | $6^{2}$ | Pearson | 48.20 |
| 8638 | Trentonian (Calumet Farm) | 118 | 14 | 10 | $8^{2}$ | $7^{2}$ | $8^{h}$ | $6^{2}$ | $7^{1}$ | Neves | 3.80 |
| 8671 | Fabulous Vegas (J. W. Brown) | 118 | 13 | 12 | 11½ | $11^{1}$ | $10^{h}$ | 8½ | $8^{2}$ | Tang'l | 22.90 |
| 8638 | Blue Pencil (High Tide Stable) | 118 | 11 | 5 | 4½ | 4½ | 5½ | $9^{1}$ | 9½ | Boland | 11.20 |
| 8675 | a-Treadgold (C. Mooers) | 118 | 7 | 7 | $13^{h}$ | 14 | $13^{1}$ | $13^{2}$ | $10^{2}$ | [illegible] | 48.20 |
| 8635 | Trackmaster (Mr.-Mrs. J. Seley) | 118 | 3 | 11 | $10^{h}$ | $12^{1}$ | $12^{h}$ | $11^{2}$ | $11^{1½}$ | West'pe | 90.10 |
| 8638 | Beau Busher (Sunny Side Stable) | 118 | 9 | 4 | $5^{2}$ | $5^{2}$ | $7^{h}$ | $12^{1}$ | $12^{1½}$ | York | 11.75 |
| 8671 | Right Down (B & R Stable) | 118 | 8 | 3 | $2^{2}$ | $1^{h}$ | 3½ | $10^{h}$ | $13^{2}$ | Volzke | 38.60 |
| (8651) | Cover Me Up (R. H. McDaniel) | 118 | 10 | 9 | $7^{1}$ | $10^{h}$ | 14 | 14 | 14 | Plesa | 80.95 |

a—C. Mooers entry. b—R. C. Ellsworth entry. c—Murcain Stable entry.

Time, :22 2-5, :45 4-5, 1:10 3-5, 1:37, 1:50. (Clear, track fast.) Went in gate at 4:57½, off at 4:58. Start good, won all driving. Winner, ch.c. 3, by Khaled—Iron Reward. Trained by M. A. Tenney. Mutuel pool, $576,406.

Two-dollar mutuels paid: b-SWAPS, 9.20, 4.00, 4.90; c-JEAN'S JOE, 2.60, 2.00; c-BLUE RULER, 2.60.

SWAPS was prominent from the start, came around the leaders leaving the backstretch, bore out approaching the last eighth and then drifted in while stalling off JEAN'S JOE. Latter saved ground leaving the half-mile pole, came between horses entering the stretch and finished gamely. BLUE RULER was never a great distance back, moved up boldly entering the stretch and then hung in the drive. HONEYS ALIBI made up ground but could not get to the leaders. BEQUEATH had speed, held on to the stretch and weakened. NABESNA was slow to begin and made up ground. TRENTONIAN could not improve his position. RIGHT DOWN gave way badly after showing speed for seven-eighths.

PART 4 **Los Angeles Times** SPORTS

VOL. LXXIV CC MONDAY MORNING, JUNE 20, 1955 Read The Times for Latest Sports

# FLECK NABS OPEN TITLE BY THREE STROKES

## SPORTSCRIPTS

By PAUL ZIMMERMAN TIMES SPORTS EDITOR

Russia, for all we know, may walk off with Olympic Games honors at Melbourne in the gymnastics, weightlifting, fencing, etc., but you can wager the family jewels now that the boys from behind the Iron Curtain are not going to cut much of a swath with that U.S.S.R. scythe in track and field.

This was convincingly demonstrated by the collegians in the NCAA track and field championships at Memorial Coliseum Saturday. Even without the additional year of experience these rah-rah youths will have by 1956, they could come close to the United States' dominance of track and field at Helsinki in 1952.

**LOOK AT RECORDS**

Just take a look at the Coliseum performances in comparable events and match them with what Russia did in 1952 and you get the idea. Sure, the Soviets will be improved in 1956, but these marks give you as good a basis as any possible.

The first six shot-putters Saturday had better records than any Russian at Helsinki and Bill Nieder of Kansas eclipsed Parry O'Brien's Olympic record.

Des Koch was a little over 4 feet short of Sim Iness' Olympic record but 10 feet farther than the top U.S.S.R. performer.

In the high jump the first ten NCAA athletes did 6ft. 5in. or better and Russia's best was 6ft. 2¾in. Ernie Shelton's 6ft. 11¼in. bested Walt Davis' Olympic mark.

**BEST VAULTERS OF ALL TIME**

The NCAA pole-vault field was the best of all time. Don Bragg, a mere sophomore, would have beaten Bob Richards, and five of our callow collegians would have finished ahead of the 14ft. 5¼in, which was Russia's best.

The first two NCAA javelin stars had throws beyond Cy Young's Olympic record and 10 feet better than the top accomplishment of the U.S.S.R.'s best spearman.

Weakest of the NCAA field events was the broad jump, and yet the undergraduates would have placed four ahead of the very finest Russia had to offer at Helsinki.

**TRACK COMPARISON HARD**

Comparisons in the running events are difficult to make because of the different distances in yards and meters.

The one that closely matches is the half-mile with the 800-meter race. Even without Arnie Sowell, our best at this distance, the NCAA athletes would field six faster than the first Soviet of 1952.

Russia will concentrate on the events which normally do not grace our collegiate calendar such as the hammer, 400-meter hurdles, hop, step and jump, and distance races.

Even if we give them these—and we obviously will not—the athletes from behind the Iron Curtain couldn't hope to catch up with the United States.

You can depend upon it that no matter how successful we will be at Melbourne, the Russian controlled press will figure some method of scoring that will put the U.S.S.R. out in front as it did last time.

P.S. That's the Soviet system and thank goodness the Russians are the only ones who are stuck with it.

## L.A. WINS SERIES WITH SOLON SPLIT

SACRAMENTO, June 19 (AP)—The Sacramento Solons salvaged the final game of a Pacific Coast League doubleheader today by beating Los Angeles 4-2 after the Angels cinched the series with a 9-5 win in the opener.

The Angels took command in the opener with a run in the second on Steve Bilko's walk, Piper Davis' single and an infield out. Then they rallied for five in the second, chasing Ed Cereghino. Gale Wade and Gene Mauch launched the uprising with infield hits. Bilko lashed safely to left, Harry Bright kicked in an error and Jim Fanning singled. Marino Pieretti relieved, walked Bud Hardin and gave a single to Joe Hatten.

**Brazle Belted**

The Angels added three more in the ninth off Al Brazle when Mauch singled, Bilko was purposely passed and Piper Davis hit his fourth homer via left.

The Solons scored two off Hatten in the fourth on Al Heist's double. Bubba Church relieved in the fifth and was twice bumped for homers in the late innings. Danny Baich's first four-master scored two in the eighth and Tom Glaviano hit for the circuit in the ninth with the bags empty.

The Angels took a 1-0 lead in the nightcap in the first on Bob Usher's double and two wild pitches by Earl Harrist. But Bud Daley replaced Harrist and kept the Seraphs tied down until the seventh.

Harry Bright doubled home Sacramento's first run in the first inning. In the second, Turk Lown, essaying an Angel starting role, walked Jerry Streeter with the bags loaded and gave up a two-run single to Glaviano.

First game:

| Los Angeles | AB | H | O | A | Sacramento | AB | H | O | A |
|---|---|---|---|---|---|---|---|---|---|
| Wade,cf | 5 | 2 | 2 | 0 | Heist,cf | 4 | 2 | 2 | 2 |
| Usher,rf | 5 | 2 | 2 | 0 | Streeter,2b | 5 | 3 | 5 | 3 |
| Mauch,2b | 5 | 5 | 3 | 4 | Glaviano,ss | 2 | 2 | 4 | 5 |
| Rice,lf | 3 | 0 | 1 | 1 | Bright,3b | 4 | 0 | 0 | 2 |
| Bilko,1b | 3 | 1 | 12 | 1 | V. Jones,1b | 4 | 0 | 7 | 1 |
| Davis,3b | 5 | 2 | 2 | 3 | Crawford,rf | 4 | 2 | 2 | 0 |
| Fanning,c | 5 | 1 | 2 | 1 | Milne,lf | 4 | 0 | 2 | 0 |
| Hardin,ss | 4 | 1 | 2 | 7 | Baich,c | 3 | 2 | 5 | 0 |
| Hatten,p | 2 | 1 | 0 | 1 | Cereghino,p | 1 | 0 | 0 | 1 |
| Church,p | 3 | 0 | 1 | 0 | Pieretti,p | 2 | 0 | 0 | 1 |
| | | | | | Tobin | 1 | 0 | 0 | 0 |
| | | | | | Brazle,p | 0 | 0 | 0 | 0 |
| Totals | 40 | 15 | 27 | 15 | Totals | 34 | 11 | 27 | 15 |

Tobin flied out for Pieretti in 8th.

| | |
|---|---|
| Los Angeles | 015 000 003—9 |
| Sacramento | 000 200 021—5 |

E—Hardin, Glaviano, Bright, Baich. RBI—Hardin, Bilko, 2; Hatten, 2; Fanning, Davis, 3; Heist, 2; Baich, 2; Glaviano. 2B—Heist, 2; Hardin. HR—Baich, Glaviano, Davis. SB—Wade, 2; Davis, Fanning. SH—Glaviano, Rice. DP—Davis to Mauch to Bilko; Mauch to Hardin to Bilko. LOB—Los Angeles, 9; Sacramento, 8. BB—Hatten, 4; Church, 1; Cereghino, 1; Pieretti, 2; Brazle, 1. SO—Hatten, 2; Cereghino, 1; Pieretti, 3. Hits—Off Hatten, 7 in 4 innings plus; Church, 4 in 5; Cereghino, 7 in 2⅔; Pieretti, 6 in 5⅓; Brazle, 2 in 1. R and ER—Hatten, 2-2; Church, 3-3; Cereghino, 4-3; Pieretti, 2-0; Brazle, 3-3. WP—Pieretti. Winner—Church (1-2). Loser—Cereghino (1-5). Umpires—Pelekoudas, V. Smith and Carlucci. Time—2h. 8m.

Second game:

| Los Angeles | AB | H | O | A | Sacramento | AB | H | O | A |
|---|---|---|---|---|---|---|---|---|---|
| Wade,cf | 4 | 2 | 2 | 0 | Heist,cf | 3 | 1 | 0 | 0 |
| Usher,rf | 4 | 2 | 0 | 0 | Streeter,2b | 3 | 1 | 2 | 5 |
| Mauch,2b | 3 | 2 | 2 | 2 | Glaviano,ss | 3 | 1 | 4 | 2 |
| Rice,lf | 3 | 0 | 2 | 0 | Bright,3b | 3 | 1 | 2 | 2 |
| Bilko,1b | 3 | 0 | 7 | 1 | V. Jones,1b | 3 | 1 | 9 | 0 |
| Davis,3b | 2 | 0 | 0 | 3 | Crawford,rf | 3 | 2 | 2 | 1 |
| Pramesa,c | 2 | 1 | 5 | 0 | Milne,lf | 2 | 0 | 1 | 0 |
| Winceniak,ss | 3 | 1 | 0 | 1 | Baich,c | 1 | 0 | 1 | 1 |
| Lown,p | 1 | 0 | 0 | 2 | Harrist,p | 1 | 0 | 0 | 0 |
| Hardin | 1 | 1 | 0 | 0 | Daley,p | 1 | 0 | 0 | 0 |
| Elston,p | 0 | 0 | 0 | 1 | Candini,p | 0 | 0 | 0 | 0 |
| Clarkson | 1 | 1 | 0 | 0 | | | | | |
| Lary | 0 | 0 | 0 | 0 | | | | | |
| Totals | 27 | 10 | 18 | 10 | Totals | 23 | 7 | 21 | 11 |

Hardin singled for Lown in 5th.
Clarkson singled for Elston in 7th.
Lary ran for Clarkson in 7th.

| | |
|---|---|
| Los Angeles | 100 000 1—2 |
| Sacramento | 130 000 x—4 |

E—Lown, 2. RBI—Bright, Streeter, Glaviano, 2; Clarkson. 2B—Usher, Winceniak, Bright. SB—Heist. SH—Baich, Daley. DP—Streeter to Glaviano to V. Jones; Crawford to V. Jones; Glaviano to Streeter to V. Jones; Lown to Mauch to Bilko. LOB—Los Angeles, 7; Sacramento, 7. BB—Lown, 2; Harrist, 1. SO—Lown, 4; Elston, 1; Harrist, 1. Hits—Off Lown, 5 in 4 innings; Elston, 2 in 2; Harrist, 4 in 2⅓; Daley, 6 in 3⅔; Candini, 0 in 1. R and ER—Lown, 4-4; Elston, 0-0; Harrist, 1-1; Daley, 0-1; Candini, 0-0. HB—Davis, Pramesa by Harrist, Baich by Lown. WP—Harrist, 2. Winner—Daley (10-7). Loser—Lown (7-4). Umpires—V. Smith, Carlucci and Pelekoudas. Time—1h. 36m. Attendance—3011

### Daugherty to Coach

MIAMI, Fla., June 19 (AP)—Hugh Daugherty, head football coach at Michigan State, has been named one of the North coaches in the Mahi Shrine's 1955 Christmas night All-Star football game.

## Yanks Regain Lead With Double Win

**White Sox Fall Back After 7-1 and 5-2 Losses Before 40,060**

NEW YORK, June 19 (AP)—The New York Yankees moved back into first place in the American League today by taking a double-header from the Chicago White Sox, 7-1 and 5-2, before a crowd of 40,060 at the stadium.

Seventh inning home runs by Gil McDougald and Mickey Mantle broke a 2-2 tie in the second game after Veteran Pitcher Eddie Lopat won the opener, aided by homers by Elston Howard and Bill Skowron.

**McDougald Homers**

The double victory dropped the White Sox into second place, two games behind the Yankees, who were out of the league lead for just one day after Chicago took the first two of the 4-game series.

With two away in the seventh inning of the second game, McDougald slapped his seventh homer into the lower right-field stands. When Hank Bauer tripled to left center, Jack Harshman went to the showers and Sandy Consuegra came in to pitch for the Sox.

Mantle then walloped his 16th homer into the same section as McDougald, scoring Bauer ahead.

McDougald had a part in the first two Yankee runs, too. He led off the fourth inning with a triple to the right-field corner. Bauer walked, and after Mantle struck out, Yogi Berra doubled to left, with Bauer reaching third. Skowron was purposely passed to load the bases.

**Yogi Out at Plate**

When Howard lined a single to right, Bauer came home, but Jim Rivera's throw to Sherm Lollar caught Yogi at the plate.

Lopat scattered seven hits and struck out four men as he evened his season record at 4-4. The only Chicago run was unearned, set up by a passed ball by Berra in the sixth inning.

After hitting his fourth

Turn to Page 2, Column 1

## STANDINGS

**PACIFIC COAST LEAGUE**

| | W | L | Pct. | * |
|---|---|---|---|---|
| San Diego | 48 | 31 | .608 | |
| Seattle | 47 | 32 | .595 | 1 |
| Portland | 37 | 36 | .507 | 8 |
| HOLLYWOOD | 36 | 40 | .474 | 10½ |
| Oakland | 36 | 41 | .468 | 11 |
| LOS ANGELES | 36 | 42 | .462 | 11½ |
| San Francisco | 34 | 43 | .442 | 13 |
| Sacramento | 34 | 43 | .442 | 13 |

*—Games behind leader

**Yesterday's Results**

Portland, 9-5; HOLLYWOOD, 2-1.
LOS ANGELES, 9-2; Sacramento, 5-4.
San Diego, 7-3; Oakland, 2-1.
Seattle, 7-6; San Francisco, 3-1.

**How Series Ended**

Portland, 6; HOLLYWOOD, 1.
LOS ANGELES, 4; Sacramento, 3.
San Diego, 5; Oakland, 2.
Seattle, 7 San Francisco, 0.

**Games Today**

No games scheduled.

**Games Tomorrow**

San Francisco at LOS ANGELES, Wrigley Field, 8:15 p.m.
HOLLYWOOD at Oakland.
Seattle at Portland.
Sacramento at San Diego.

**AMERICAN LEAGUE**

| | W | L | Pct. | * |
|---|---|---|---|---|
| New York | 42 | 23 | .646 | |
| Chicago | 37 | 22 | .627 | 2 |
| Cleveland | 37 | 26 | .587 | 4 |
| Detroit | 32 | 27 | .542 | 7 |
| Boston | 31 | 32 | .492 | 10 |
| Kansas City | 24 | 37 | .393 | 16 |
| Washington | 23 | 37 | .383 | 16½ |
| Baltimore | 20 | 42 | .323 | 20½ |

*Games behind leader.

**Yesterday's Results**

Boston, 11; Cleveland, 7.
New York, 7-5; Chicago, 1-2.
Kansas City at Washington, postponed, rain.
Detroit at Baltimore, postponed, rain.

**Games Today**

No games scheduled.

**NATIONAL LEAGUE**

| | W | L | Pct. | * |
|---|---|---|---|---|
| Brooklyn | 46 | 16 | .742 | |
| Chicago | 36 | 28 | .563 | 11 |
| Milwaukee | 32 | 30 | .516 | 14 |
| New York | 31 | 31 | .500 | 15 |
| Philadelphia | 27 | 33 | .450 | 18 |
| Cincinnati | 26 | 32 | .448 | 18 |
| St. Louis | 25 | 33 | .431 | 19 |
| Pittsburgh | 21 | 41 | .339 | 25 |

*Games behind leader.

**Yesterday's Results**

Brooklyn, 7; St. Louis, 4.
Philadelphia, 1-7; Chicago, 0-8 (first game 13 innings, second game called end of 6th, darkness).
Milwaukee, 8; New York, 7.
Pittsburgh, 5-0; Cincinnati, 2-4.

**Games Today**

New York (Hearn, 7-6) at Cincinnati (Fowler, 1-4). Night.
Pittsburgh (Law, 2-2) at Milwaukee (Conley, 8-4). Night.
Philadelphia (Kuzava, 1-0) at St. Louis (Dickson, 4-4). Night.
Only games scheduled.

TO THE VICTOR—Ben Hogan; right, congratulates Jack Fleck after latter's three-stroke victory in 18-hole play-off to decide National Open Golf title. (AP) Wirephoto

## Punchless Twinks Drop Sixth Game to Beavers, 9-2, 5-1

BY AL WOLF

One string stretched and one string snapped at Gilmore Field yesterday afternoon—but both went the wrong way for Hollywood.

Portland swept the day's double-header, 9-2 and 5-1, before 6113 kibitzers to make it six straight following defeat in the series opener. And Red Munger, who had won six in a row, was the nightcap victim.

The Stars remained in fourth place, but with San Diego bagging a pair at Oakland and slipped 10½ lengths off the pace.

Earlier in the season, Hollywood likewise lost six times in succession.

Bob Alexander pitched a six-hitter before intermission and Bob Hall followed with a two-hitter.

Despite a 12-hit harvest Saturday, the hapless Hollywoodians aggregated but 33 blows during their six setbacks and scored only six runs.

Hoping to inject some punch into his club, Manager Bobby Bragan radically altered his line-up and batting order. In the first game yesterday he benched First Baseman R. C. Stevens and Outfielder Bobby Del Greco, replacing them with George Vico and Al Zarilla. In the nightcap he reinstated Del Greco but had Left Fielder Bobby Prescott and Third Baseman Carlos Bernier switch positions.

But nothing happened.

The Ports hammered Bob Garber, Georgie O'Donnell and Cholly Naranjo for 15 hits in the opener, including Joe Taylor's third homer of the series.

It came in the first inning with Artie Wilson aboard to give the visitors a wire-to-wire win. Prescott homered for the locals in the ninth.

Munger coasted a 1-0 edge after five rounds of the final, but six hits and two errors netted Portland three scores in the sixth and two more in the seventh. Three of those tallies were unearned.

Hollywood's lone run was not exactly the result of awesome power. Dick Smith walking with bases full in the third.

Carl Powis homered in the seventh for his fourth of the series. All told, the Ports put nine pitches over the fence during their visit. The Stars did it but twice.

**Foul Tips**

Los Angeles and San Francisco open a seven-game engagement at Wrigley Field tomorrow night, while Hollywood

Turn to Page 2, Column 7

### TODAY IN SPORTS

WRESTLING — Hollywood Legion Stadium, 8:30 p.m.

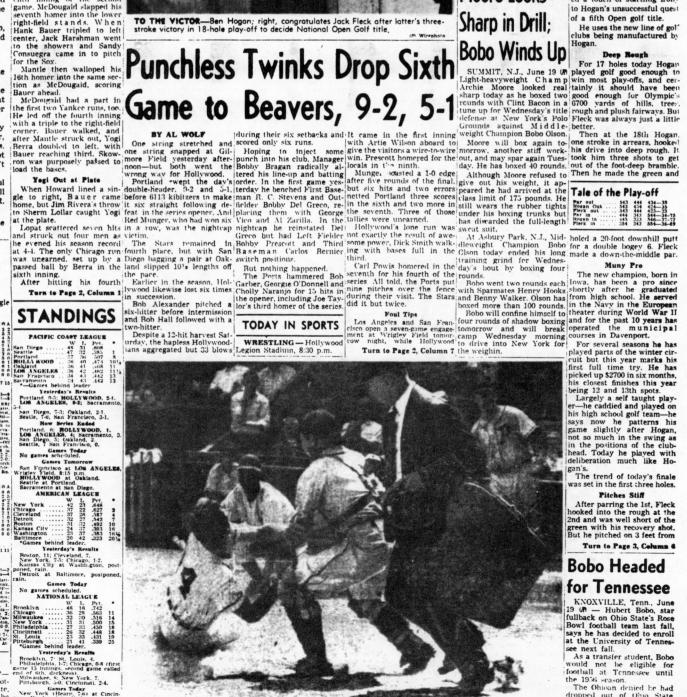

SHORT STRETCH—Lee Walls of Hollywood was tagged out by Portland Catcher Jim Robertson when he tried to stretch hit to left field, which got away from fielder, into home run. Stars lost double-header yesterday. Times photo by Larry Sharkey

## Iowa Dark Horse in Stunning Win Over Hogan, 69 Against 72

BY CHARLES CURTIS, Times Staff Representative

SAN FRANCISCO, June 19—Lightning, or a reasonable facsimile of same, struck the same spot two days running as Jack Fleck, 32-year-old municipal course pro from Davenport, Ia., won the 55th Open Golf Championship of the United States this afternoon.

Fleck, whose closest previous finish in any Open golf competition was an eighth place at Washington, D.C., last year, defeated Ben Hogan by three strokes in their 18-hole play-off at Olympic Country Club with a 69 to Hogan's 72.

Yesterday Fleck, one of the longest shots in the field, birdied the final hole for a 67 to tie Hogan with a 72-hole total of 287.

**Longshot List**

Today Fleck joined the list of U.S. Open golf champions which dates from 1895. And his triumph puts him in a longshot class with Cyril Walker, Sam Parks Jr. and Tony Manero, hitherto rated as the most surprising winners of golf's biggest title.

The amazing Mr. Fleck added a touch of startling irony to Hogan's unsuccessful quest of a fifth Open golf title.

He uses the new line of golf clubs being manufactured by Hogan.

**Deep Rough**

For 17 holes today Hogan played golf good enough to win most play-offs, and certainly it should have been good enough for Olympic's 6700 yards of hills, trees, rough and plush fairways. But Fleck was always just a little better.

Then at the 18th Hogan, one stroke in arrears, hooked his drive into deep rough. It took him three shots to get out of the foot-deep bramble. Then he made the green and

### Tale of the Play-off

| | | | |
|---|---|---|---|
| Par out | 543 | 444 | 434—35 |
| Hogan Out | 543 | 434 | 424—35 |
| Fleck out | 543 | 444 | 423—33 |
| Par in | 444 | 343 | 544—34-75 |
| Hogan in | 445 | 333 | 546—37-72 |
| Fleck in | 354 | 343 | 554—36-69 |

holed a 20-foot downhill putt for a double bogey 6. Fleck made a down-the-middle par.

**Muny Pro**

The new champion, born in Iowa, has been a pro since shortly after he graduated from high school. He served in the Navy in the European theater during World War II and for the past 10 years has operated the municipal courses in Davenport.

For several seasons he has played parts of the winter circuit but this year marks his first full time try. He has picked up $2700 in six months, his closest finishes this year being 12 and 13th spots.

Largely a self taught player—he caddied and played on his high school golf team—he says now he patterns his game slightly after Hogan, not so much in the swing as in the positions of the club-head. Today he played with deliberation much like Hogan's.

The trend of today's finale was set in the first three holes.

**Pitches Stiff**

After parring the 1st, Fleck hooked into the rough at the 2nd and was well short of the green with his recovery shot. But he pitched on 3 feet from

Turn to Page 3, Column 6

### RABBIT JUMPS BANTAM BEN

SAN FRANCISCO, June 19 (AP)—The little forest creatures really go for Ben Hogan, or maybe it's vice versa.

Yesterday a squirrel interrupted Ben's putt on one hole in the National Open Golf Tournament.

Today, on the 3rd, a rabbit jumped out of a bush, hopped onto the tee, slithered through Ben's legs and then raced away.

The squirrel yesterday brought Hogan good luck and a birdie 3. Not so the cottontail. Ben missed a short putt for a sure birdie and took a par three.

## Moore Looks Sharp in Drill; Bobo Winds Up

SUMMIT, N.J., June 19 (AP)—Light-heavyweight Champ Archie Moore looked real sharp today as he boxed two rounds with Clint Bacon in a tune up for Wednesday's title defense at New York's Polo Grounds against Middleweight Champion Bobo Olson.

Moore will box again tomorrow, another stiff workout, and may spar again Tuesday. He has boxed 40 rounds.

Although Moore refused to give out his weight, it appeared he had arrived at the class limit of 175 pounds. He still wears the rubber tights under his boxing trunks but has discarded the full-length sweat suit.

At Asbury Park, N.J., Middleweight Champion Bobo Olson today ended his long training grind for Wednesday's bout by boxing four rounds.

Bobo went two rounds each with Sparmates Henry Hooks and Benny Walker. Olson has boxed more than 100 rounds.

Bobo will confine himself to four rounds of shadow boxing tomorrow and will break camp Wednesday morning to drive into New York for the weighin.

### Bobo Headed for Tennessee

KNOXVILLE, Tenn., June 19 (AP)—Hubert Bobo, star fullback on Ohio State's Rose Bowl football team last fall, says he has decided to enroll at the University of Tennessee next fall.

As a transfer student, Bobo would not be eligible for football at Tennessee until the 1956 season.

The Ohioan denied he had dropped out of Ohio State because of scholastic deficiencies. He said he quit for personal reasons which he declined to disclose.

**PART 4** # Los Angeles Times **SPORTS**

VOL. LXXIV — CC ★★ — THURSDAY MORNING, SEPTEMBER 22, 1955 — Read The Times for Latest Sports

# ROCKY KNOCKS OUT MOORE IN 9TH ROUND

## SPORTS PARADE

By BRAVEN DYER

Eyes of the nation's football fans turn to Maryland this week end as UCLA's championship Bruins invade the effete East for the first time.

The game means more to the Bruins than any they've ever played.

There is a good chance that the American League pennant race will be decided by then, which means that every competent gridiron observer in the East will be on hand to see the Bruins and Jim Tatum's powerhouse.

Red Sanders and his staff have done a tremendous job of rebuilding the line which was shattered by graduation and barring injury to key men in Saturday's game I expect the Bruins to score the most important win in all their history.

**LT. DYER'S SCOUTING REPORT**

Lt. David Payne Dyer, public information officer at Ft. Leonard Wood, sends an interesting scouting report on the Maryland-Missouri game. Lt. Dyer grew up with the Bruins, has followed football all his life and might even become a writer someday unless I can steer him into some other means of making an honest living. His analysis follows:

Maryland is big and aggressive—Maryland seemed jittery to begin with, being off-side twice in the same series of plays. Their defense is sound, but has loopholes . . . lots of offensive punch . . . Pass defense seems somewhat weak—Knox, off his performance Friday night, should prove sensational against the Terps . . . Maryland's offense is quite diversified—keeps the opponent guessing all the time.

The split-T optional play didn't work too well today for the Terps. Harry Smith had his linemen ready and waiting . . . However, the Georgia Tech "inside belly series" hurt Missouri the most . . . Missouri was weak on defense at times, making Maryland function better than they probably will against UCLA . . . Looks like the Terps and Bruins will play a similar game Saturday as they did last year, except for Qnox's passing, which will probably break the game wide open.

**MIZZOU SHARP WITH SPREAD**

Missouri worked the spread formation to good advantage, giving Maryland cause for alarm . . . In the first half Maryland seemed to be toying with Missouri, although the Tigers were fighting all the way. Even so, the first half seemed somewhat dull, with Maryland leading 13-0 . . . But the second half was quite different. Missouri was fired up and Maryland seemed to wilt—possibly because of the 92 deg. temperature. The Terps were not in real danger until three-quarters through the third quarter—and then Missouri really caught fire. The Tigers scored 6 and then 6 more in the fourth. Maryland never threatened during that time.

It's hard to judge Maryland off this game because Missouri had the psychological advantage. All in all, the Tigers played the Terps to a standstill—and even had an edge in statistics (slight) . . . Maryland is tough inside its own 10 on the ground, but Missouri found its way through the air, scoring both TD's on passes . . . UCLA should definitely pass on Maryland—it's hard to run over them, although end sweeps worked pretty well for Missouri . . .

Quote from Don Faurot: "We had easier psychological preparation. Maryland is a fine ball club. The heat probably bothered them, but we were happy to have played them on even terms. They're a tough ball club—fine defensively. Ronnie Knox could have a good day against them."

**MARYLAND CAN BE HAD**

Maryland can be had off what I saw today. Pass defense seems weak and the Terps are vulnerable over right tackle . . . Linebacker Pellegrini of Maryland was in on many plays and was a key man in his team's defense.

On several occasions Missouri receivers were out in the open—really clear and at other times Tiger men caught the ball when surrounded . . . When the score was 13-12 late in the game, Missouri held Maryland brilliantly—pushing them to a fourth down and 29 to go . . . Maryland attempted a field goal while leading 13-0 from about 40 yards out—No good, of course . . . UCLA should rush Maryland's passer good—Missouri did on several occasions.

Of course, it's hard to tell about how UCLA will do—not having seen them Friday night. But from what I've heard and seen today, I'd pick the Bruins about 21-7. (Maryland might score twice, however.) But one way or other, I'd pick the Bruins definitely. Hope I'm right.

## AL Pennant Race at a Glance

| | W | L | Pct. | * | ** |
|---|---|---|---|---|---|
| New York | 94 | 56 | .627 | | 4 |
| Cleveland | 91 | 60 | .603 | 3½ | 3 |
| Chicago | 88 | 63 | .583 | 6½ | 3 |
| Boston | 82 | 68 | .542 | 12 | 4 |
| Detroit | 78 | 73 | .517 | 16½ | 3 |
| Kansas City | 63 | 89 | .414 | 31½ | 3 |
| Baltimore | 54 | 95 | .362 | 39½ | 2 |
| Washington | 51 | 98 | .342 | 42½ | 3 |

*Games behind leader. **Games left.

**Yesterday's Results**

New York, 7; Washington, 3.
Chicago, 7; Cleveland, 2.
Detroit, 10; Kansas City, 1.
Baltimore, 8; Boston, 7 (13innings).

**Games Today**

No games scheduled.

**Remaining Schedule**

NEW YORK (4): Away—(4) Boston, Sept. 23, 23, 24, 25.
CLEVELAND (3): Away (3)—Detroit, Sept. 23, 24, 25.

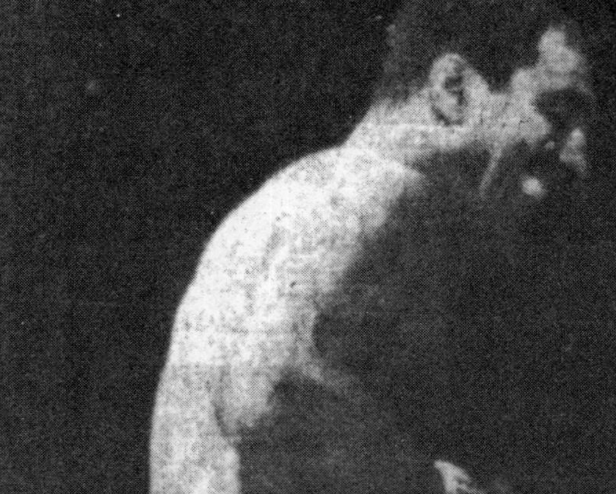

**BEGINNING OF THE END**—The mighty champ, Rocky Marciano, towers menacingly over Archie Moore after putting the challenger on the deck for the first time in the sixth round. Rallying from a second-round knockdown, Rocky went on to score a knockout in the 9th. (AP) Wirephoto

## Champion Floored in Second

**BY PAUL ZIMMERMAN**
**Times Sports Editor**

YANKEE STADIUM, N.Y., Sept. 21—If you run into a rock you get hurt.

Like 48 fighters before him, Archie Moore of San Diego ran into the rock that is Rocky Marciano here tonight and got himself knocked out after 1 minute and 19 seconds of the ninth round before a crowd of 61,574 rabid, riotous fans.

It was a vicious right in which the undefeated and untied world's heavyweight champion knocked the challenging light-heavyweight champion down three times

**Full page of Marciano-Moore fight pictures on Page 4, Part IV.**

before he could win on the fourth decking and the Rock himself was down for the count of four in the second round.

**Sizzling Hooks**

Moore hit the canvas twice in the sixth, once in the eighth and then was felled with two sizzling left hooks in his own corner in the disastrous ninth.

Thus ended the Cinderella effort of Archie to wrest the world's heavyweight title after a 19-year boxing campaign that took him through 144 bouts.

The challenger never was in it after the second round but he fought back gamely, tired as an old man would be fighting gamely to the bitter end. After the second stanza the champion took everything Moore threw and returned more of the same.

**Behind in Scoring**

Archie put up a valiant stand but was behind on all scorecards when the end came. Judge Harold Barnes gave Rocky five rounds to three in the first eight. Judge Artie Aidala had it seven to

**Turn to Page 3, Column 3**

### TODAY IN SPORTS

**TENNIS** — Pacific Southwest Championships, L.A. Tennis Club, all day.

**GOLF** — Women's Open, Clock CC, all day; Times Putting Championship; L.A. County Fair, 10 a.m.

**HORSE RACING** — L.A. County Fair, Pomona, 12:30 p.m.

**ICE SHOW** — Ice Follies, Pan-Pacific Auditorium, 8:30 p.m.

**BOXING** — Olympic Auditorium, 8:30 p.m.

**WRESTLING** — Long Beach Auditorium, 8:30 p.m.

**Today's sports section appears on Pages 1, 2, 3, 4, Part 4 and Pages 39, 40, 41, Part 1.**

## YANKEES CLINCH PENNANT TIE, HANG 7-3 LOSS ON SENATORS

WASHINGTON, Sept. 21 (UP)—The New York Yankees clinched at least a tie for the American League pennant tonight, belting the Washington Senators, 7-3, while the second-place Cleveland Indians lost a 7-2 decision at Chicago.

One more Yankee victory or Cleveland defeat will give New York its sixth championship in seven years.

**Four to Play**

The Yanks have four games to play, starting with a double-header at Boston Friday. Cleveland, four games behind on the "lost" side, has three remaining.

Billy Martin's three-run inside-the-park homer was the big blow for the Yanks tonight as they breezed to their eighth straight victory—their longest winning streak of the season.

Tonight's game was a dull, drab affair enlivened a bit by five Yankee double plays. Starter and Winner Bob Turley generously doled out seven walks, allowing Washington runners just about permanent entry on the base paths.

**Score Early**

The Yankees wrapped it up early, shelling Chuck Stobbs, who lost his 14th against four victories, from the game in the third inning as they built up a 4-0 lead on a six-hit barrage of extra-base blows.

Martin's wallop, his first home run since rejoining the Yankees Sept. 1, was hit off Relief Pitcher Ted Abernathy in the fifth with two out after Abernathy had walked Joe Collins and Elston Howard.

| New York | AB | H | O | A | Washington | AB | H | O | A |
|---|---|---|---|---|---|---|---|---|---|
| Cerv,cf | 5 | 2 | 0 | 0 | Yost,3b | 4 | 1 | 0 | 3 |
| Noren,cf | 0 | 0 | 0 | 0 | Oravetz,rf | 3 | 1 | 2 | 0 |
| McDougald,3b | 5 | 1 | 0 | 0 | Runnels 2b | 3 | 0 | 1 | 3 |
| Bauer,rf | 3 | 0 | 1 | 0 | Vernon,1b | 2 | 0 | 11 | 0 |
| Berra,c | 5 | 1 | 5 | 1 | Sievers,lf | 4 | 2 | 2 | 0 |
| Skowron,1b | 2 | 1 | 5 | 0 | Umphlett,cf | 4 | 0 | 2 | 0 |
| Collins,1b | 1 | 0 | 5 | 0 | Korcheck,c | 4 | 2 | 7 | 0 |
| Howard,lf | 3 | 0 | 3 | 0 | Valdivielso,ss | 2 | 0 | 2 | 2 |
| Martin,2b | 4 | 2 | 3 | 5 | Becquer | 1 | 0 | 0 | 0 |
| J Coleman,ss | 4 | 0 | 5 | 7 | Stewart,p | 0 | 0 | 0 | 1 |
| Turley,p W | 2 | 1 | 0 | 0 | Wright | 1 | 0 | 0 | 0 |
| G Coleman,p | 0 | 0 | 0 | 0 | Stobbs,p L | 0 | 0 | 0 | 0 |
| Grim,p | 0 | 0 | 0 | 0 | Abernathy,p | 1 | 0 | 0 | 1 |
| | | | | | Lemon | 0 | 0 | 0 | 0 |
| | | | | | Chakales,p | 0 | 0 | 0 | 0 |
| | | | | | McDermott | 1 | 1 | 0 | 0 |
| | | | | | Kline,ss | 0 | 0 | 0 | 0 |
| | | | | | Paula | 0 | 0 | 0 | 0 |
| Totals | 34 | 8 | 27 | 13 | Totals | 30 | 7 | 2 | 710 |

Collins walked for Skowron in 5th.
Lemon walked for Abernathy in 6th.
Becquer flied out for Valdivielso in 7th.
McDermott singled for Chakales in 7th.
Wright struck out for Stewart in 9th.
Paula walked for Kline in 9th.

| | |
|---|---|
| New York | 121 030 000—7 |
| Washington | 000 000 300—3 |

RBI—Berra, Turley, Cerv, Skowron, Martin, 3; McDermott, Oravetz, 2. 2B—Berra, Turley, Korcheck, Oravetz. 3B—Cerv, Skowron. HR—Martin. DP—Coleman to Skowron; Martin to Coleman to Skowron, 2; Coleman to Martin to Skowron, 2; Runnels to Valdivielso to Vernon. LOB—New York, 6; Washington, 8. BB—Turley, 7; Stobbs, 1; Abernathy, 4; Stewart, 1; G Coleman, 1. SO—Stobbs, 1; Turley, 4; Abernathy, 2; Stewart, 3; Grim, 1. Hits off Turley, 6 in 6⅔; G Coleman, 0 in ⅓; Grim, 1 in 2; Stobbs, 6 in 2⅓; Abernathy, 2 in 3⅔; Chakales, 0 in 1; Stewart, 0 in 2. R and ER—Turley, 3-3; G Coleman, 0-0; Grim, 0-0; Stobbs, 4-4; Abernathy, 3-3; Chakales, 0-0; Stewart, 0-0. WP—Turley. Winner—Turley (17-13). Loser—Stobbs (4-14). Umpires—Hurley, Hon[illegible], Chylak, Grieve. Time—2h. 41m. Atten[illegible]—5770.

### National League

| | W | L | Pct. | * |
|---|---|---|---|---|
| Brooklyn | 97 | 53 | .647 | |
| Milwaukee | 84 | 67 | .556 | 13½ |
| New York | 79 | 72 | .523 | 18½ |
| Philadelphia | 75 | 76 | .497 | 22½ |
| Cincinnati | 74 | 78 | .487 | 24 |
| Chicago | 70 | 80 | .467 | 27 |
| Chicago | 71 | 80 | .470 | 26½ |
| St. Louis | 66 | 85 | .437 | 31½ |

*Games behind leader.

**Yesterday's Results**

New York, 7-7; Pittsburgh, 2-3.
Cincinnati, 14; Milwaukee, 5.
Chicago, 7; St. Louis, 5 (13 innings).
Only games scheduled.

**Games Today**

No games scheduled.

### PAUL ZIMMERMAN TABBED ROCKY BY KNOCKOUT

Paul Zimmerman, Times Sports Editor, tabbed it right when he predicted a knockout triumph by Rocky Marciano over Archie Moore in last night's title fight.

In last Tuesday's editions, Zimmerman wrote: ". . . we pick Marciano to win in 10 rounds. It could be less if the Rock solves his opponent's defense earlier and gets to the aging Moore before he slows down to a walk."

### Major Leaders

(Based on 375 at bats)

**AMERICAN LEAGUE**

| | G | AB | R | H | Pct. |
|---|---|---|---|---|---|
| Kaline, Detroit | 148 | 575 | 119 | 196 | .341 |
| Power, K.C. | 142 | 578 | 89 | 184 | .318 |
| Kell, Chicago | 126 | 421 | 43 | 132 | .314 |
| *Williams, Boston | 93 | 311 | 77 | 110 | .354 |

*Fewer than 375 at bats.

**NATIONAL LEAGUE**

| | G | AB | R | H | Pct. |
|---|---|---|---|---|---|
| Ashburn, Phila | 137 | 522 | 90 | 180 | .345 |
| Campanella, Bkln. | 120 | 438 | 81 | 140 | .320 |
| Mays, New York | 147 | 5[illegible]4 | 120 | 178 | .316 |

**HOME RUNS**

| American League | | National League | |
|---|---|---|---|
| Mantle, N.Y. | 37 | Mays, New York | 50 |
| Zernial, K.C. | 29 | Kluszewski, Cinc. | 46 |
| Williams, Bstn | 28 | Banks, Chicago | 44 |

**RUNS BATTED IN**

| American League | | National League | |
|---|---|---|---|
| Jensen, Bostbn | 113 | Snider, Brklyn. | 134 |
| Boone, Detroit | 111 | Mays, New York | 122 |
| Berra, N.Y. | 108 | Ennis, Phila. | 119 |

## TRIBE FLAG HOPES FADE AFTER LOSS

CHICAGO, Sept. 21 (UP)—The Cleveland Indians all but lost their hopes of winning the American League Pennant tonight as they bowed to the Chicago White Sox, 7-2.

The loss put the Indians three and one-half games behind the New York Yankees, who defeated the Washington Senators, 7-3.

One more Cleveland defeat or New York win will mean the pennant for the Yankees. The Indians have three games to play, at Detroit Friday, Saturday and Sunday. The Yankees have four games to play, at Boston Friday, Saturday and Sunday.

Lefty Jack Harshman held the Indians in check before 16,856 at Comiskey Park tonight as the Sox scored two runs in the sixth and five in the eighth, knocking out Cleveland Pitcher Bob Lemon, who was seeking his 19th victory.

Lemon, seeking his fourth consecutive 20-victory season, blanked the Sox with four hits until Rookie Shortstop Carl Peterson opened the sixth inning with a double.

An error by Rookie Bill Harrell on Peterson's grounder paved the way for a five-run rally by the Sox in the eighth that finished Lemon.

| Cleveland | AB | H | O | A | Chicago | AB | H | O | A |
|---|---|---|---|---|---|---|---|---|---|
| Smith,rf | 2 | 0 | 1 | 0 | Peterson,ss | 3 | 1 | 2 | 2 |
| Fain,1b | 4 | 0 | 8 | 1 | Fox,2b | 5 | 1 | 4 | 3 |
| Avila,2b | 3 | 0 | 1 | 3 | Minoso,lf | 2 | 1 | 0 | 0 |
| Rosen,3b | 2 | 0 | 1 | 3 | Kell 3b-1b | 4 | 3 | 2 | 4 |
| Evers,lf | 3 | 0 | 2 | 0 | Nieman,rf | 3 | 2 | 2 | 0 |
| Doby,cf | 4 | 2 | 3 | 0 | Rivera | 0 | 0 | 0 | 0 |
| Harrell,ss | 2 | 1 | 1 | 2 | Dropo,1b | 3 | 0 | 7 | 0 |
| Hegan,c | 4 | 2 | 6 | 0 | Northey | 1 | 1 | 0 | 0 |
| Lemon,p L | 2 | 0 | 1 | 3 | Adams | 0 | 0 | 0 | 0 |
| Santiago,p | 0 | 0 | 0 | 0 | Kennedy,3b | 0 | 0 | 0 | 1 |
| Colavito | 1 | 0 | 0 | 0 | Lollar,c | 3 | 0 | 7 | 1 |
| | | | | | Busby,cf | 4 | 2 | 3 | 0 |
| | | | | | Harshman,p-W | 4 | 0 | 0 | 1 |
| Totals | 27 | 5 | 24 | 12 | Totals | 32 | 11 | 27 | 13 |

Northey singled for Dropo in 8th.
Adams ran for Northey in 8th.
Rivera ran for Nieman in 8th.
Colavito struck out for Santiago in 9th.

**SCORE BY INNINGS**

| | |
|---|---|
| Cleveland | 100 000 001—2 |
| Chicago | 000 002 05x—7 |

E—Harrell. RBI—Evers, Kell, 2; Nieman, 2; N[illegible], Lollar, [illegible] Hegan. 2B—Minoso, N[illegible], Peterson. 3B—Doby. SH—Lemon, Minoso, Evers, [illegible] Nieman [illegible], Lollar [illegible]. DP—Lemon to Harrell to Fain; Fox to Peterson to Dropo; Rosen to Avila to Fain; Kennedy to Fox to Kell. LOB—Cleveland, 7; Chicago, 7. BB—Lemon, 2; Harshman, 7. SO—Lemon, 5; Harshman, 7; Santiago, 1. Hits Off Lemon, 10 in 7 innings (faced 6 men in 8th); Santiago, 1 in 1. R and ER—Lemon, 7-5; Harshman, 2-2; Santiago, 0-0. HB—Peterson by Santiago. Winner—Harshman (11-7). Loser—Lemon (18-10). Umpires—Soar, Stevens, Runge, Summers. Time—2h. 33m. Attendance—14,956.

# LARSEN FEARED HE MIGHT FAINT IN NINTH

Los Angeles Times Sports

CC TUESDAY MORNING, OCTOBER 9, 1956 Part IV

## SPORTS PARADE

By BRAVEN DYER

## Don Larsen Hurls Perfect Series Game

### Only 27 Dodgers Face Yank Star in Record Performance

BY FRANK FINCH
Times Staff Representative

YANKEE STADIUM, New York, Oct. 8—The Yankees won today, 2 to 0, because the Dodgers weren't hitting. Don Larsen wouldn't let 'em.

When Larsen whizzed a third strike past Pinch Hitter Dale Mitchell of Brooklyn with two outs in the ninth he became the first pitcher in World Series history to hurl a no-hit game.

**Only No-Hitter**

The 27-year-old right-hander from San Diego couldn't have been better because this was a perfect game. Nary a Dodger reached first base as Larsen threw only 97 pitches in the full nine innings to beat the great Sal Maglie.

Besides being the only no-hitter in the 306 World Series games that have been contested since the big show first began back in 1903, Larsen's masterpiece was the first perfecto pitched by a major leaguer since 1922.

Charley Robertson of the Chicago White Sox performed the rare feat on April 30 of that year by blanking the Detroit Tigers, 2 to 0.

Larsen's victory, made possible by Mickey Mantle's home run in the fourth and another tally in the sixth, gave the Yankees a 3-2 lead after they'd blown the first two games at Brooklyn.

**Play at Ebbets**

The combatants return to Ebbets Field tomorrow to complete the Series. Clem Labine will pitch for the Dodgers while either Johnny Kucks or Bob Turley will go for the Yanks. Casey Stengel said he won't decide this all-important question until Kucks and Turley warm up tomorrow.

Alston announced that Don Newcombe will work the seventh game Wednesday, if it's necessary: Stengel ain't even thinking about it, or so he says.

The series has followed the identical pattern of the 1955 classic, when the Dodgers lost their first two games on a foreign field and came back to sweep three straight in their own park.

**Podres' Triumph**

Brooklyn finally won the series at Yankee Stadium, four games to three, on Johnny Podres' dazzling 2-0 triumph—the first time in series annals that a team won after losing the first two games.

Larsen, a 225-pounder who stands 6 feet 4 inches, was kayoed in the second inning of the second game at Ebbets Field last Thursday. Wildness cost him that one, yet he allowed only one hit during his stint.

But Larsen had pitched and won four low-hit games

Turn to Pg. 1, Pt. 4, Col. 4

## Yankees Now 3-1 Favorites

NEW YORK, Oct. 8 (AP)—With a 3-2 edge in games, the New York Yankees tonight were made 3-1 favorites to win the World Series from Brooklyn. Tomorrow's sixth game was rated even in the betting—11 to 10 and take your pick.

## TODAY IN SPORTS

**HARNESS RACING**—Hollywood Park, 1 p.m.

**WRESTLING** — Eastside Arena, 8:30 p.m.

# Labine Faces Kucks or Turley

## Stengel Undecided on Choice

BY FRANK FINCH
Times Staff Representative

NEW YORK, Oct. 8 — With the Yankees once again the top dog after their miraculous recovery at home, the World Series returns to Ebbets Field tomorrow for the sixth game.

The Yankees went one up on Brooklyn this afternoon on the strength of Don Larsen's matchless no-hitter, the seventh perfecto ever pitched in the big leagues, and they can close out the Series with another victory tomorrow. Whitey Ford, Tom Sturdivant and Larsen presented Casey Stengel with three completed games in a row, and ol' Case would like to come up with another good guess tomorrow.

Tonight he's mulling it over—Johnny Kucks or Bob Turley?

**One Or Other**

"It's gonna be one or the other, which both of them fellas are very good pitchers, but I don't think I'll decide on Kucks or Turley until I see 'em warm up tomorrow," said the great man. "I can't afford to be wrong now."

Walt Alston settled on Clem Labine without quibbling, passing up his 27-game winner, Don Newcombe, who never has beaten the Bronx Bombers.

Labine, a 30-year-old right-hander, suffered two defeats in relief against New York in the '53 Series and won as a fireman over New York last year in the game in which Larsen was the loser.

**Excellent Control**

He's not a "messy" hurler, boasting excellent control, good stuff that sinks and an explosive curve. Yankee home-run hitters, who've outslugged the Dodgers by an 8-3 margin so far, may have trouble lofting Labine's stuff out of the Brooklyn Bandbox.

The fences are so close that the Yankee outfielders, used to the wide, open spaces of their own stadium, suffer from claustrophobia when they play in Ebbets Field.

Clem mopped up Saturday's game in which Ford trimmed the Flatbushers, allowing one run and one hit in two frames while walking one and fanning a pair. He was 10-6 for the regular season.

Like Labine, Kucks features low, breaking stuff around the knees. He worked

Turn to Page 5, Column 3

### Good Weather Today

NEW YORK, Oct. 8 (AP)—The weatherman tonight promised another good day for baseball for the sixth game of the World Series at Ebbets Field tomorrow.

"Mostly fair and windy with highest temperatures in the 60s," was the forecast.

## Bruins Rate 13-Pt. Choice Over Cougars

UCLA was rated a 13-point favorite over Washington State, Washington a 7-point choice over Oregon and the California-Oregon State game was tabbed a tossup, according to the odds received from Canada yesterday. No quote was available on the Stanford-San Jose game.

The opening line:

Miami 9 over Maryland.
Syracuse 5½ over West Virginia.
Penn State 8½ over Holy Cross.
Princeton 7½ over Pennsylvania.
Brown 1½ over Dartmouth.
Cornell 11 over Harvard.
Michigan 7½ over Army.
Ohio State 7½ over Illinois.
Michigan State 24 over Indiana.
SMU 3 over Duke.
Georgia Tech 14 over LSU.
Notre Dame 7 over Purdue.
Clemson 7 over Wake Forest.
Iowa 4 over Wisconsin.
Minnesota 15 over Northwestern.
Oklahoma A&M 1 over Tulsa.
TCU 12½ over Alabama.
Kansas and Iowa State, even.
Georgia and North Carolina, even.
Oklahoma 21 over Texas.
Navy 5½ over Tulane.
Mississippi 10½ over Vanderbilt.
Baylor 7½ over Arkansas.
Washington 7 over Oregon.
Kentucky 2 over Auburn.
Texas A&M 7½ over Houston.

YOGI AND FRIEND—Yankee Catcher Yogi Berra executes flying scissors leap into arms of Pitcher Don Larsen after latter struck out last Dodger to complete a no-hit, no-run perfect game, first such effort in the history of the World Series. (AP) Wirephoto

## Larsen Hurls Perfect Game

**Continued from Page 1, Pt. 1**

during the month of September and Stengel reasoned that the big fellow couldn't go sour all at once.

**Pinpoints Control**

As usual the squire of Glendale was right. Larsen had pinpoint control today. Only one batter, Pee Wee Reese in the first inning, secured a count of "ball three" on the towering twirler. Reese then fanned, as did six other frustrated hitters.

Larsen said he threw sliders and fast balls, tossing in an occasional "nickel curve," as he put it. Consistently he was getting that first strike in there. Seventy-one of his 97 pitches were strikes.

The Dodgers hit very few pitches solidly.

Jackie Robinson bounced a shot off Andy Carey's glove in the second inning, but Gil McDougald retrieved the ball and threw out Robbie on a close play.

In the fourth, Duke Snider rode a ball high into the right-field stands but it was foul.

Mantle had to step on the gas to glove Gil Hodges' 450-foot smash backhanded in the fifth, and in the same inning Sandy Amoros pumped a liner into the right-field seats that was foul by the scantest of margins.

Gil McDougald made a nice play on Junior Gilliam's hard bouncer in the seventh inning and Andy Carey speared Hodges' low liner off his shoetops in the eighth.

**Growing Tension**

But mostly the Brooks were popping up or batting routine grounders and flies as Larsen cast a magic spell that mowed 'em down methodically.

By the time the seventh inning rolled around, you could fell the great tension in the crowd of 64,519 marveling fans. As each Dodger was retired, the fans would applaud enthusiastically.

The big Californian (by way of his native Indiana)

Turn to Page 7, Column 3

## ONLY SEVEN PERFECT NO-HIT, NO-RUN GAMES EVER PITCHED

NEW YORK, Oct. 8 (UP)—Here is a list of the seven perfect no-hit, no-run games in baseball history:

| Pitcher and Club | Opponent | Date | Score |
|---|---|---|---|
| Richmond, Worcester (NL) | vs. Cleveland | June 12, 1880 | 1-0 |
| Ward, Providence (NL) | vs. Buffalo | June 17, 1880 | 5-0 |
| D. T. (Cy) Young, Boston (AL) | vs. Phila. | May 5, 1904 | 3-0 |
| A. C. Joss, Cleveland (AL) | vs. Chicago | Oct. 2, 1908 | 1-0 |
| x-E. G. Shore, Boston (AL) | vs. Wash. | June 23, 1917 | 4-0 |
| C. C Robertson, Chicago (AL) | vs Detroit | April 30, 1922 | 2-0 |
| Larsen, New York (AL) | vs. Brooklyn (NL) | Oct. 8, 1956 | 2-0 |

x—Shore's performance in this game now is classified with "perfect games." Babe Ruth started as the Boston pitcher and was removed by Umpire Owens after giving up a base on balls to Morgan, the first Washington batter. Shore took Ruth's place and after Morgan was retired trying to steal, Shore retired the next 26 batters without allowing a man to reach base.

## Three Hurlers Had 1-Hitters in Series Play

NEW YORK, Oct. 8 — World Series records disclose that only three other pitchers ever approached a no-hit game and none came close to Don Larsen's "perfect game" performance.

The last of the near no-hitters was, of course, the game in 1947 when Floyd (Bill) Bevens of the Yankees saw his hopes go with Pinch Hitter Cookie Lavagetto's double which presented Brooklyn with a 3 to 2 victory. Bevens allowed 10 passes in that one and the Dodgers scored a run in the fifth on his wildness before Lavagetto's ninth inning double that drove in the deciding runs.

In the 1945 series between Chicago's Cubs and Detroit, Claude Passeau pitched a one-hitter. Rudy York got the single but was erased by a double play as the Cubs won 3 to 0.

It was away back in 1906 that the other near perfect game occured. Ed Reulbach of the Cubs pitched it against the White Sox. Big Ed gave up six bases on balls, allowed one hit, put another man aboard by hitting him with a pitch.

## LARSEN JUNKED WINDUP BEFORE WORLD SERIES

NEW YORK, Oct. 8 (AP)—Don Larsen, who pitched the first perfect World Series game in history today in beating the Brooklyn Dodgers 2-0, said he abandoned his windup in the final weeks of the season because he feared a rival coach was stealing his signs.

The Yankee right-hander didn't use the routine windup once in setting down 27 Dodgers in order at Yankee Stadium.

"It was after we clinched the pennant. I got a feeling Del Baker, first base coach of the Boston Red Sox, was stealing our signals," Larsen said. "So I thought I'd fool him by just not using a windup."

## Sad Dodgers Pay Homage to Larsen

NEW YORK, Oct. 8 (AP)—Sal Maglie, a sad and dejected athlete who had pitched a superb game himself, led the Brooklyn Dodgers today in paying homage to Don Larsen's great perfect performance in the World Series.

"I'm glad he got it, as long as we had to lose," said Maglie, and all the other Dodgers chimed in.

"That's the way it goes."

**Alston Agrees**

As Catcher Roy Campanella said:

"He had good control. Whenever we could hit it, it was either foul or right at someone. He deserves a lot of credit."

That was the sentiment of Manager Walt Alston.

"He pitched a helluva ball game," said the scholarly Alston, who rarely uses profanity even on the light side. "And don't forget that Maglie pitched a good game, too."

**No Bunt Called**

Alston said afterward in a second-guessing session that he did not call for any bunts because his ace hitters are allowed to bunt on their own.

"Not much was said about bunting on the bench, either," he said. "We kept thinking we'd get some hits."

In Alston's opinion, Maglie's five-hit, two-run performance was even better than the game he pitched in the opener which he won, 6-3.

"His stuff was a little better today," he said.

"When I walked out to the mound in the sixth, with two on and one out, I just wanted to find out how he felt, and as soon as he told me he was all right I didn't hesitate to leave him in. I wanted to talk to Pee Wee Reese and Junior Gilliam to set up a double play situation, too."

**Double Play**

Actually, Mickey Mantle hit into a double play, but not exactly by plan. He grounded sharply to Gil Hodges, who stepped on first and then threw to Campanel-

Turn to Page 7, Column 1

## No-Hit Ace Prays for Strength

NEW YORK, Oct. 8 (AP)—"I was so weak in the knees out there in the ninth inning I thought I was going to faint."

Big Don Larsen, admittedly "in a daze," said he also mumbled a little prayer for help before he finally completed his perfect, no-hit, no-run, no-man-to-first game against the Dodgers in the fifth World Series game.

**Realized in Seventh**

It was the first no-hit game in World Series history and the first perfect game—no man reaching first—since another obscure pitcher, Charley Robertson of the Chicago White Sox, did it in 1922 against the Detroit Tigers.

Larsen said he realized in the seventh inning that he had a no-hitter going, but added: "I didn't get nervous—my main object was to win the game."

Then, he said, came the ninth, and he felt the full impact of his performance.

"The thing I wanted to do was get out of the ninth inning," he said. "Once I mumbled a little prayer to myself. I said, 'Please help me through this.'"

**Get First One**

The towering right-hander from San Diego, Cal., said nobody on the Yankee bench mentioned that he had a perfect game going.

"The only word said to me was by Yogi Berra," Larsen said. "Yogi hit me in the seat of the pants and said, 'Go out there and let's get the first batter.'"

The Yankee dressing room—the dressing room of the "old pros"—was bedlam for the first time during the Series.

Yogi grabbed Larsen around the neck. Mickey Mantle, normally quiet and retiring, let out a resounding war whoop. Andy Carey jumped around the room, yelling loudly.

**'Beautiful,' Says Case**

"Beautiful, beautiful," said Casey Stengel, the Yankee manager, his creased face breaking into a broad smile. "This kid is a good pitcher."

Walter O'Malley, the president of the Brooklyn Dodgers, came in.

"You beat us and I'm not happy about that," he said, elbowing his way through the crowd around the beaming pitcher. "I have to congratulate you—do me a favor will you? Sign this ball."

Larsen, who came to the Yankees in December, 1954, as an insignificant part of the 19-player deal with Baltimore which brought the Yankees Bob Turley, said Berra's crafty signal-calling and the Yankees' fine defensive play deserve equal credit for his feat.

**Yogi's Calls**

"I was pitching fast balls and sliders mostly," he said, "but mainly I had pretty good control. I only shook off a couple of Yogi's signals, but

Turn to Page 5, Column 7

## WORLD SERIES ON TV, RADIO

Today's sixth World Series game will be carried on local television by both KRCA (4) and KHJ-TV (9), starting at 8:45 a.m.

Radio Station KHJ will broadcast the game starting at 8:35 a.m.

## NO-HIT 'LARSENY'

| Brooklyn | AB | R | H | O | A |
|---|---|---|---|---|---|
| Gilliam, 2b | 3 | 0 | 0 | 2 | 0 |
| Reese, ss | 3 | 0 | 0 | 4 | 2 |
| Snider, cf | 3 | 0 | 0 | 1 | 0 |
| Robinson, 3b | 3 | 0 | 0 | 2 | 4 |
| Hodges, 1b | 3 | 0 | 0 | 5 | 1 |
| Amoros, lf | 3 | 0 | 0 | 3 | 0 |
| Furillo, rf | 3 | 0 | 0 | 0 | 0 |
| Campanella, c | 3 | 0 | 0 | 7 | 2 |
| Maglie, p | 2 | 0 | 0 | 0 | 1 |
| Mitchell | 1 | 0 | 0 | 0 | 0 |
| Totals | 27 | 0 | 0 | 24 | 10 |

| New York (A) | AB | R | H | O | A |
|---|---|---|---|---|---|
| Bauer, rf | 4 | 0 | 1 | 4 | 0 |
| Collins, 1b | 4 | 0 | 1 | 7 | 0 |
| Mantle, cf | 3 | 1 | 1 | 4 | 0 |
| Berra, c | 3 | 0 | 0 | 7 | 0 |
| Slaughter, lf | 2 | 0 | 0 | 1 | 0 |
| Martin, 2b | 3 | 0 | 1 | 3 | 4 |
| McDougald, ss | 2 | 0 | 0 | 0 | 2 |
| Carey, 3b | 3 | 1 | 1 | 1 | 1 |
| Larsen, p | 2 | 0 | 0 | 0 | 1 |
| Totals | 26 | 2 | 5 | 27 | 8 |

Mitchell struck out for Maglie in 9th.

**Brooklyn (N)** ........ 000 000 000—0
**New York (A)** ........ 000 101 00x—2

RBI—Mantle, Bauer. HR—Mantle. S—Larsen. DP—Reese to Hodges; Hodges to Campanella to Robinson to Campanella to Robinson. LOB—Brooklyn, 0; New York, 3. BB—Maglie, 2. SO—Maglie, 5; Larsen, 7. HO—Larsen 0-9, Maglie 5-8. R&ER—Maglie 2-2. Winner—Larsen. Loser—Maglie. Umpires—Pinelli (N), plate; Soar (A), first base; Boggess (N), second base; Napp (A), third base; Gorman (N) Runge (A), foul lines. Time—2h. 6m. **Attendance—64,519.**

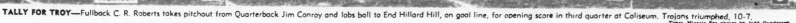

**TALLY FOR TROY**—Fullback C. R. Roberts takes pitchout from Quarterback Jim Conroy and lobs ball to End Hillard Hill, on goal line, for opening score in third quarter at Coliseum. Trojans triumphed, 10-7.
Times Miracle Eye photos by Judd Gunderson

# OUTCLASSED BRUINS BOW TO TROY, 10-7

## Aroused California Surprises Stanford in 20 to 18 Upset

Los Angeles Times Sports
CC★ SUNDAY MORNING, NOVEMBER 25, 1956 Part III

### ROSE BOWL HANDICAP

| PACIFIC COAST (Final) | W | L | T | Pct. | TP | OP |
|---|---|---|---|---|---|---|
| Oregon St. | 6 | 1 | 1 | .813 | 152 | 104 |
| *SC | 5 | 2 | 0 | .714 | 133 | 90 |
| *UCLA | 5 | 2 | 0 | .714 | 109 | 73 |
| *Washington | 4 | 4 | 0 | .500 | 190 | 139 |
| Oregon | 3 | 3 | 2 | .500 | 91 | 88 |
| Stanford | 3 | 4 | 0 | .429 | 151 | 130 |
| Wash. St. | 2 | 5 | 1 | .312 | 118 | 196 |
| California | 2 | 5 | 0 | .286 | 95 | 142 |
| Idaho | 0 | 4 | 0 | .000 | 64 | 121 |

| BIG TEN (Final) | W | L | T | Pct. | TP | OP |
|---|---|---|---|---|---|---|
| Iowa | 5 | 1 | 0 | .833 | 88 | 44 |
| Michigan | 5 | 2 | 0 | .714 | 143 | 96 |
| Minnesota | 4 | 1 | 2 | .714 | 84 | 67 |
| *Ohio State | 4 | 2 | 0 | .667 | 88 | 47 |
| *Mich. State | 4 | 2 | 0 | .667 | 133 | 49 |
| Northwest'n | 3 | 3 | 1 | .500 | 80 | 69 |
| Illinois | 1 | 4 | 2 | .286 | 69 | 106 |
| Purdue | 1 | 4 | 2 | .286 | 95 | 101 |
| Wisconsin | 0 | 4 | 3 | .214 | 46 | 116 |
| Indiana | 1 | 5 | 0 | .167 | 85 | 216 |

*Ineligible for Rose Bowl.

## Hawkeyes Batter Irish by 48 to 8

IOWA CITY, Ia., Nov. 24 (AP) — Iowa's Rose Bowl-bound Big Ten football champions put a golden touch to the best Hawkeye season in 35 years with a spectacular 48-8 rout of Notre Dame today.

Shortly after the game, Big Ten athletic directors officially designated the Hawkeyes as the Big Ten representative in the Rose Bowl at Pasadena, Jan. 1.

Iowa, stabbing Notre Dame with dazzling long runs, kept its partisans in the crowd of 56,632, huddled in slightly below freezing weather, wild and warm throughout the afternoon with by far its best offensive show of the season.

**Undisputed Champs**

The Hawks, headed for a New Year's Day Rose Bowl duel with Oregon State, ended their regular season with an 8-1 record and they picked up their first undisputed Big Ten championship since 1921 as a result of Michigan's 19-0 victory over Ohio State.

Iowa had a 5-1 conference record, landing the Hawks in first place for the first time since a share with Michigan in 1922.

Iowa, whose fans had feared there might be a letdown after last week's Bowl clinching 6-0 victory over Ohio State, dispelled all those thoughts in the first half by racing to a 28-0 lead under the expert direction and individual play of Quarterback Kenny Ploen.

**Ploen Stars**

Ploen went 10 yards for the first Iowa touchdown and set up the second with a 32-yard spurt to the Notre Dame 1-yard line. He got himself

Turn to Page 2, Column 4

## Joe Kapp Sparks Cal to Victory

BERKELEY, Nov. 24 (U.P.) California's aroused Bears kept faith with Coach Lynn (Pappy) Waldorf today by striking for two quick touchdowns and battling the rest of the way to earn a 20-18 upset victory over Stanford in the massive mentor's last game for the school.

Past performances went out the window as they usually do in the "Big Game" between these schools as a capacity crowd of 81,400 watched the Bears, who finished with a season record of three wins and seven losses, stun the Indians by taking a 14-0 lead before the game was 12 minutes old and then capitalizing on breaks in the second half to insure Waldorf's virtual mastery over the Tribe.

In his 10 seasons as coach of the Bears, Pappy's elevens beat Stanford seven times, lost to them once and played two ties. The upset triumph also gave Cal a one-game margin in the 59-year-old rivalry.

**Kapp Sparkles**

The keys to California's victory were carried in the strong hands of sophomore Quarterback Joe Kapp, who set up California's second and third touchdowns with runs of 28 and 11 yards to the Indian one from where Halfbacks Darrell Roberts and Jack Hart smashed over for touchdowns.

Once again Stanford was betrayed in the conversion department as the Indians went down to their fourth straight defeat and third in which the outcome rode on points after touchdown.

Two attempted placements by Mike Raftery were wide while a third was blocked by Substitute Guard Don Piestrup.

Waldorf announced last Tuesday he was stepping out as the Bears headed into their second straight bad sea-

Turn to Page 9, Column 2

## Kick by Kissinger Decides It

BY DICK HYLAND

For the first time in the 27-year-old series between the two teams, the Trojans kicked a field goal against the Bruins and Southern California gained victory over UCLA by just that margin in the Coliseum yesterday, 10-7.

A total of 63,709 fans saw the Trojans stalled on the Bruin 10-yard line with a second over 2 minutes gone in the final period, fourth down and 3 yards to go. They saw the Trojans take a 5-yard penalty to enable Ells Kissinger to get into the field with his kicking tee. And they saw the 21-year-old senior from York, Pa., swing his foot forward on the Bruin 22-yard line.

The ball barely lifted over the line of scrimmage, hung and moved slowly forward end over end to pass between the goal posts for the first field goal he has ever kicked. It was a game winner.

**3-Point Margin**

Kissinger had made the score 10-0, and the Trojan rooting section relaxed. As things turned out, it was well that Southern California had that 3-point margin.

The men of Troy, playing a power game that saw them throw but two passes the en-

Turn to Page 4, Column 1

### How They Scored

| SC | UCLA | | Time |
|---|---|---|---|
| | | THIRD QUARTER | |
| 6 | 0 | Hill. 14-yd. pass (Roberts) | 5:39 |
| 7 | 0 | Kissinger. conversion. | |
| | | FOURTH QUARTER | |
| 10 | 0 | Kissinger. 32-yd. field goal | 2:01 |
| 10 | 6 | Farber. 1-yd. smash | 14:08 |
| 10 | 7 | Duncan. conversion. | |

**FIELD GOAL**—This 32-yard field goal kick by Ells Kissinger (inset) early in final period provided margin of victory for SC over UCLA. Cameraman catches ball in flight coming toward the Bruin goal posts.
(AP) photo

### SPORTS TODAY ON RADIO, TV

**FOOTBALL**

Rams vs. Colts, KNXT (2), 11 a.m.; KHJ Radio, 10:50 a.m.

**AUTO RACING**

Jalopy races, KTTV (11), 2 p.m.; NASCAR stock-car races, KTLA (5), 2 p.m.

**OLYMPIC GAMES**

Opening Day Ceremonies, KTLA (5), 5 p.m.

## MAJOR GRID SCORES

**LOCAL**

SC, 10; UCLA, 7.

**SOUTHLAND**

Pepperdine, 23; Whittier, 13.

**PACIFIC COAST**

California, 20; Stanford, 18.
Washington, 40; Washington St., 26.

**EAST**

Boston College, 52; Brandeis, 0.
Villanova, 26; Iowa St., 0.
Yale, 42; Harvard, 14.
Penn St., 7; Pitt, 7.
Dartmouth, 19; Princeton, 0.
Columbia, 18; Rutgers, 12.

**MIDWEST**

Iowa, 48; Notre Dame, 8.
Michigan St., 38; Kansas St., 17.
Northwestern, 14; Illinois, 13.
Michigan, 19; Ohio St., 0.
Purdue, 39; Indiana, 20.
Tulsa, 14; Wichita, 6.
Wisconsin, 13; Minnesota, 13.
Oklahoma, 54; Nebraska, 6.

**SOUTH**

Clemson, 7; Virginia, 0.
Georgia Tech, 28; Florida, 0.
Duke, 21; N. Carolina, 6.
Tennessee, 20; Kentucky, 7.
Alabama, 13; Miss. Southern, 13.
Auburn, 13; Florida St., 7.
LSU, 21; Arkansas, 7.
Texas Western, 54; Trinity (Tex.), 0.

**SOUTHWEST**

TCU, 20; Rice, 17.
Baylor, 26; SMU, 0.
Houston, 20; Texas Tech, 7.
Hardin-Simmons, 38; New Mexico, 19.
New Mexico, 34; San Diego St., 6.
Arizona St. (Tempe), 19; COP, 6.
Colorado, 38; Arizona, 7.

**ROCKY MOUNTAIN**

Brigham Young, 34; Air Force Academy, 21.

Additional scores on page 8

### READ 'EM AN' WEEP

**California, 20; Stanford, 18.**
**Dartmouth, 19; Princeton, 0.**
**Penn State, 7; Pittsburgh, 7.**
**LSU, 21; Arkansas, 7.**
**Wisconsin, 13; Minnesota, 13.**

## Yank Stars Setting Torrid Olympic Pace

BY PAUL ZIMMERMAN
Times Sports Editor

MELBOURNE, Nov. 25 (Sunday)—Seven events and five gold medals for the United States!

That was the way the score stood in track and field events in the 16th Olympiad today as athletes caught their breath for a fresh start tomorrow.

Americans came crashing through even better than expected with four victories, including the first sweep ever as our lads ran 1-2-3 in the 400-meter hurdles.

Australians at Melbourne Cricket Grounds, 100,000 strong, heard the Star Spangled Banner played so often they were humming it on the way out, as might be expected.

Yankees accomplished two new Olympic records, one of them in the hammer throw where Boston's strongman, Hal Connolly, became the first U.S. victor since 1924. Hal beat his archrival from Russia with a record shattering toss of 207ft. 3½in. on his second to last throw.

And mighty Mikhail Krivonosov of the U.S.S.R., who had led up to that point, felt pressure so much that he fouled out on his last effort, obviously a beaten man.

After that Glenn Davis in the hurdles, Bobby Morrow in the 100 and Greg Bell in the broad jump each took their turn on the topmost step of the victory stand. And in each case one or more of their fellow stars stood there with them to receive vociferous plaudits from the multitude.

As if this were not enough, the United States qualified all three men in the 800 semifinals yesterday and appear certain to add this gold medal to the collection tomorrow (Monday).

Davis said he missed one hurdle, the second, on his great run clocked in record time of 50.1. This clipped .7 off the 400-meter hurdles record set by Charlie Moore in Helsinki. Eddie Southern, Texas freshman, also ran the same time in the semifinals and finished .6 back in the finals. Josh Culbreath of the Marines completed the sweep as Potgieter of South Africa

Turn to Page 7, Column 1

| | | | | | |
|---|---|---|---|---|---|
| Wash. ..... 40 | Michigan .. 19 | Wisconsin .. 13 | Oklahoma . 54 | Tennessee . 20 | TCU ...... 20 |
| Wash. St.... 26 | Ohio St. ... 0 | Minnesota .. 13 | Nebraska .. 6 | Kentucky .. 7 | Rice ....... 17 |
| (Story on Page 10) | (Story on Page 2) | (Story on Page 2) | (Story on Page 3) | (Story on Page 9) | (Story on Page 10) |

# AMERICANS SWEEP 200 METERS, DISCUS

CC★★ TUESDAY MORNING, NOVEMBER 27, 1956 Part IV

## SPORTS PARADE

By BRAVEN DYER

MELBOURNE, Nov. 26—At 10 minutes to 6 tonight over a slow runway and into a biting wind, the Rev. Bob Richards of La Verne became the first two-time pole vault king in all Olympic Games history. In the final rundown, with all other rivals eliminated, the vaulting vicar was locked in a three-way fight with Occidental's Bob Gutowski and Greece's George Roubanis, the lad who recently transferred to UCLA from Occidental.

Forty minutes after breaking his own Olympic record with a vault of 14 feet 11½ inches, the popular parson entered the interview room under the stands of Melbourne's historic Cricket Grounds. It's become something of a ritual with those of us who subject Olympic winners to the third degree. A ritual where we put a chair on top of a table and sit the champion down to be quizzed. Reporters of all nations crowd around and pop the questions. "What's this," laughed Richards as he was hoisted on high, "the block?"

**BOB BOTHERED BY STRAINED TENDON**

Bob was a little late in joining us and word had come through after some delay that his leg was bothering him, so the first questions were along this line.

"Yes, I strained a tendon in my lower left leg," he admitted, "but you don't notice those things too much while you're keyed up as we all were today. But you sure find out about it when you unwind. No, I don't think it will keep me out of the decathlon. At least, I hope not. That wind out there today was something.

"I feel, that under the circumstances, this was some of the greatest vaulting that I ever did. And I say the same thing for the other two boys, too.

**RUNWAY IN VERY BAD SHAPE**

"I don't want to appear to be knocking anything but the runway was bad. It was very slow and so soft. That's why I say the vaulting was great.

"But those Australian people . . . they are the greatest. I have been to three Olympic Games now and the Australian people are the most enthusiastic sports fans. It is wonderful to hear them cheer.

"This is it, men. I'm going to quit now. You see, I'm an old man of 30 and it's time for me to devote more time to my life work."

Bob does not have a pastorate now. But no one I have ever heard can deliver such a stirring plea for good citizenship and clean living as the La Verne preacher. Of course, Bob always is asked about prayer.

"Yes, I prayed today," he admitted, "but I think all the boys prayed, too. I know that the Lord helps all the boys and I was praying for all of them." And here again Richards emphasized the great vaulting in the face of serious obstacles.

**GUTOWSKI HANDICAPPTD THROUGHOUT**

Gutowski, who was bothered through the entire afternoon by a strained side muscle incurred a week ago, went out after clearing 14ft. 10¼in. When the bar was raised to the champion's winning height, Gutowski missed his first try and so did Richards. On his second attempt Gutowski didn't get off the ground. Richards hit the bar coming down on his second and winning try and it bounced up and down for several seconds.

"I lay there in the sawdust watching it jiggle," said Richards, "and I am sure it wasn't held on by more than a quarter of an inch. It could be that the chilly wind which was blowing against us all day actually held the bar on for me."

Asked if he wished to send any message to his mother, Bob replied: "Yes, I thank her for giving me a chance to compete here and for her steadfast interest in me. I also want to thank my wife for being so understanding. It is high time that I get home to them and our three children."

You could call the Rev. Bob Richards an old pro. He is the only American thus far to win medals in the last three Olympic Games and the typographical error in today's official program must have given him a real chuckle. It listed the record he established at Helsinki as having been made in 1852 or 100 years before he actually was crowned the champion in the Finnish stadium.

VAULTING VICAR—Rev. Robert E. (Bob) Richards, La Verne, Cal., clears bar on way to win Olympic pole vault event at stadium in Melbourne yesterday. Bob cleared the bar at 14ft. 11½in., thereby breaking his own Olympic record of 14ft. 11¼in. set in 1952.
(AP) Wirephoto via radio from Melbourne

# Rams Take Arnett as No. 1 Choice

## JOE KUHARICH INTERESTED IN CAL JOB

WASHINGTON, Nov. 26 (AP)—Joe Kuharich, coach of the Washington Redskins, indicated tonight he is willing to talk with the University of California about the job as head coach at the school.

Kuharich made the comment in an interview when asked about a story in the Stockton Record that he would succeed retiring Coach Lynn (Pappy) Waldorf at California.

Kuharich said he had "absolutely not" heard from the university, but added:

"I don't deny that I would be receptive to a discussion with them." He said he "spent five years out there and am very fond of it."

## SC Favored by 13 Over Notre Dame

SC opened as a 13-point favorite yesterday over Notre Dame when the traditional rivals play here Saturday afternoon in the Coliseum.

In another traditional game, Army and Navy are rated even for their colorful clash Saturday in Philadelphia.

Texas A&M plays Texas Thursday. In this one the Aggies have been installed a 7-point choice.

Other games:

Holy Cross ½ over Boston College.
Miami (Fla.) 6 over Florida.
Georgia Tech 7 over Georgia.
Missouri 6½ over Kansas.
Tennessee 8 over Vanderbilt.
Auburn 7 over Alabama.
Mississippi 7 over Mississippi St.
Tulane 7 over LSU.
Baylor 7 over Rice.
TCU 8 over SMU.

**Sunday's Pro Games**

Rams 2½ over Steelers.
Bears 3 over Lions.
Cardinals 4½ over Packers.
Browns 7 over Eagles.
Colts 6 over 49ers.
Giants 6 over Redskins.

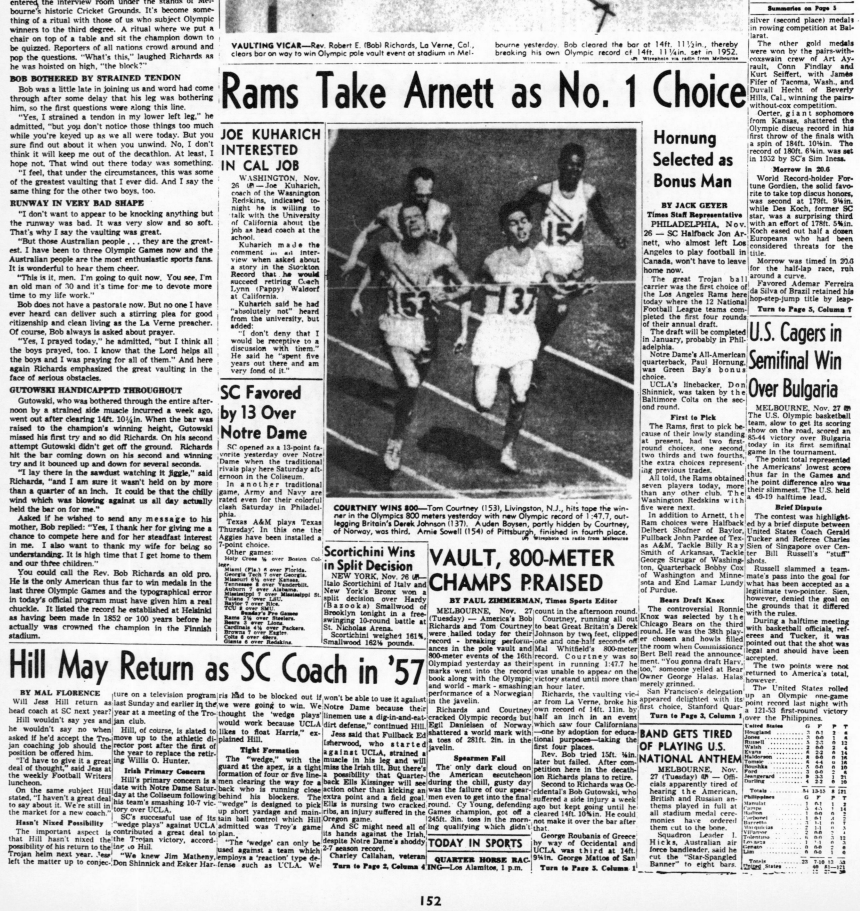

COURTNEY WINS 800—Tom Courtney (153), Livingston, N.J., hits tape the winner in the Olympics 800 meters yesterday with new Olympic record of 1:47.7, outlegging Britain's Derek Johnson (137). Auden Boysen, partly hidden by Courtney, of Norway, was third. Arnie Sowell (154) of Pittsburgh, finished in fourth place.
(AP) Wirephoto via radio from Melbourne

## Hornung Selected as Bonus Man

BY JACK GEYER
Times Staff Representative

PHILADELPHIA, Nov. 26 — SC Halfback Jon Arnett, who almost left Los Angeles to play football in Canada, won't have to leave home now.

The great Trojan ball carrier was the first choice of the Los Angeles Rams here today where the 12 National Football League teams completed the first four rounds of their annual draft.

The draft will be completed in January, probably in Philadelphia.

Notre Dame's All-American quarterback, Paul Hornung, was Green Bay's bonus choice.

UCLA's linebacker, Don Shinnick, was taken by the Baltimore Colts on the second round.

**First to Pick**

The Rams, first to pick because of their lowly standing at present, had two first-round choices, one second, two thirds and two fourths, the extra choices representing previous trades.

All told, the Rams obtained seven players today, more than any other club. The Washington Redskins with five were next.

In addition to Arnett, the Ram choices were Halfback Delbert Shofner of Baylor, Fullback John Pardee of Texas A&M, Tackle Billy Ray Smith of Arkansas, Tackle George Strugar of Washington, Quarterback Bobby Cox of Washington and Minnesota and End Lamar Lundy of Purdue.

**Bears Draft Knox**

The controversial Ronnie Knox was selected by the Chicago Bears on the third round. He was the 38th player chosen and howls filled the room when Commissioner Bert Bell read the announcement. "You gonna draft Harv, too," someone yelled at Bear Owner George Halas. Halas merely grinned.

San Francisco's delegation appeared delighted with its first choice, Stanford Quar-

Turn to Page 3, Column 1

## Scortichini Wins in Split Decision

NEW YORK, Nov. 26 (AP)—Italo Scortichini of Italy and New York's Bronx won a split decision over Hardy (Bazooka) Smallwood of Brooklyn tonight in a free-swinging 10-round battle at St. Nicholas Arena.

Scortichini weighed 161¾, Smallwood 162¼ pounds.

## VAULT, 800-METER CHAMPS PRAISED

BY PAUL ZIMMERMAN, Times Sports Editor

MELBOURNE, Nov. 27 (Tuesday) — America's Bob Richards and Tom Courtney were hailed today for their record-breaking performances in the pole vault and 800-meter events of the 16th Olympiad yesterday as their marks went into the record book along with the Olympic and world-mark-smashing performance of a Norwegian in the javelin.

Richards and Courtney cracked Olympic records but Egil Danielsen of Norway shattered a world mark with a toss of 281ft. 2in. in the javelin.

**Spearmen Fail**

The only dark cloud on the American escutcheon during the chill, gusty day was the failure of our spearmen even to get into the final round. Cy Young, defending Games champion, got off a 245ft. 3in. toss in the morning qualifying which didn't count in the afternoon round.

Courtney, running all out to beat Great Britain's Derek Johnson by two feet, clipped one and one-half seconds off Mal Whitfield's 800-meter record. Courtney was so spent in running 1:47.7 he was unable to appear on the victory stand until more than an hour later.

Richards, the vaulting vicar from La Verne, broke his own record of 14ft. 11in. by half an inch in an event which saw four Californians—one by adoption for educational purposes—taking the first four places.

Rev. Bob tried 15ft. ½in. later but failed. After competition here in the decathlon Richards plans to retire.

Second to Richards was Occidental's Bob Gutowski, who suffered a side injury a week ago but kept going until he cleared 14ft. 10¾in. He could not make it over the bar after that.

George Roubanis of Greece by way of Occidental and UCLA was third at 14ft. 9¼in. George Mattos of San

Turn to Page 5, Column 1

## BAND GETS TIRED OF PLAYING U.S. NATIONAL ANTHEM

MELBOURNE, Nov. 27 (Tuesday) (AP) — Officials apparently tired of hearing the American, British and Russian anthems played in full at all stadium medal ceremonies have ordered them cut to the bone.

Squadron Leader I. Hicks, Australian air force bandleader, said he cut the "Star-Spangled Banner" to eight bars.

## Morrow, Oerter Triumph

BY PAUL ZIMMERMAN
Times Sports Editor

MELBOURNE, Nov. 27 (Tuesday) — Americans scored their second and third sweeps of the Olympic track competition here today when Al Oerter took the discus and Bobby Morrow won his second sprint crown by flashing to the 200-meter championship. Both were new Olympic records.

A howling throng of 110,000, largest of the Games, saw Uncle Sam pocket his eighth and ninth gold medals on this, the fourth day of the Games.

Yale University's crew won the eight-oared championship to pace the United States to three gold medals and two

Summaries on Page 5

silver (second place) medals in rowing competition at Ballarat.

The other gold medals were won by the pairs-with-coxswain crew of Art Ayrault, Conn Findlay and Kurt Seiffert, with James Fifer of Tacoma, Wash., and Duvall Hecht of Beverly Hills, Cal., winning the pairs-without-cox competition.

Oerter, giant sophomore from Kansas, shattered the Olympic discus record in his first throw of the finals with a spin of 184ft. 10½in. The record of 180ft. 6½in. was set in 1952 by SC's Sim Iness.

**Morrow in 20.6**

World Record-holder Fortune Gordien, the solid favorite to take top discus honors, was second at 179ft. 9½in. while Des Koch, former SC star, was a surprising third with an effort of 178ft. 5½in. Koch eased out half a dozen Europeans who had been considered threats for the title.

Morrow was timed in 20.6 for the half-lap race, run around a curve.

Favored Ademar Ferreira da Silva of Brazil retained his hop-step-jump title by leap-

Turn to Page 5, Column 7

## U.S. Cagers in Semifinal Win Over Bulgaria

MELBOURNE, Nov. 27 (AP) The U.S. Olympic basketball team, slow to get its scoring show on the road, scored an 85-44 victory over Bulgaria today in its first semifinal game in the tournament.

The point total represented the Americans' lowest score thus far in the Games and the point difference also was their slimmest. The U.S. held a 49-19 halftime lead.

**Brief Dispute**

The contest was highlighted by a brief dispute between United States Coach Gerald Tucker and Referee Charles Sien of Singapore over Center Bill Russell's "stuff" shots.

Russell slammed a teammate's pass into the goal for what has been accepted as a legitimate two-pointer. Sien, however, denied the goal on the grounds that it differed with the rules.

During a halftime meeting with basketball officials, referees and Tucker, it was pointed out that the shot was legal and should have been accepted.

The two points were not returned to America's total, however.

The United States rolled up an Olympic one-game point record last night with a 121-53 first-round victory over the Philippines.

| United States | G | F | P | T |
|---|---|---|---|---|
| Hougland | 3 | 0-1 | 2 | 6 |
| Jones | 3 | 0-0 | 1 | 6 |
| Russell | 5 | 2-3 | 0 | 12 |
| Walsh | 2 | 0-0 | 2 | 4 |
| Evans | 6 | 2-2 | 0 | 14 |
| Haldorson | 8 | 0-0 | 0 | 16 |
| Tomsic | 6 | 4-4 | 0 | 16 |
| Boushka | 5 | 0-0 | 0 | 10 |
| Ford | 3 | 0-0 | 2 | 6 |
| Jeangerard | 9 | 3-3 | 1 | 21 |
| Darling | 4 | 2-2 | 0 | 10 |
| Totals | 54 | 13-15 | 8 | 121 |
| **Philippines** | **G** | **F** | **P** | **T** |
| Manulat | 1 | 0-1 | 1 | 2 |
| Camps | 5 | 4-5 | 1 | 14 |
| Badion | 1 | 0-0 | 0 | 2 |
| Carbonel | 1 | 0-1 | 3 | 2 |
| Barretto | 3 | 1-1 | 0 | 7 |
| Marquicias | 2 | 1-1 | 0 | 5 |
| Villamor | 2 | 0-0 | 2 | 4 |
| Tolentino | 6 | 0-0 | 3 | 12 |
| Lovzaga | 1 | 1-1 | 0 | 3 |
| Genato | 0 | 0-0 | 2 | 0 |
| Lim | 0 | 0-0 | 1 | 0 |
| Totals | 23 | 7-10 | 13 | 53 |

United States .... 40 81—121
[illegible]

# Hill May Return as SC Coach in '57

BY MAL FLORENCE

Will Jess Hill return as head coach at SC next year?

Hill wouldn't say yes and he wouldn't say no when asked if he'd accept the Trojan coaching job should the position be offered him.

"I'd have to give it a great deal of thought," said Jess at the weekly Football Writers luncheon.

On the same subject Hill stated, "I haven't a great deal to say about it. We're still in the market for a new coach."

**Hasn't Nixed Possibility**

The important aspect is that Hill hasn't nixed the possibility of his return to the Trojan helm next year. Jess left the matter up to conjecture on a television program last Sunday and earlier in the year at a meeting of the Trojan club.

Hill, of course, is slated to move up to the athletic director post after the first of the year to replace the retiring Willis O. Hunter.

**Irish Primary Concern**

Hill's primary concern is a date with Notre Dame Saturday at the Coliseum following his team's smashing 10-7 victory over UCLA.

SC's successful use of its "wedge plays" against UCLA contributed a great deal to the Trojan victory, according to Hill.

"We knew Jim Matheny, Don Shinnick and Esker Harris had to be blocked out if we were going to win. We thought the 'wedge plays' would work because UCLA likes to float Harris," explained Hill.

**Tight Formation**

The "wedge," with the guard at the apex, is a tight formation of four or five linemen clearing the way for a back who is running close behind his blockers. The "wedge" is designed to pick up short yardage and maintain ball control which Hill admitted was Troy's game plan.

"The 'wedge' can only be used against a team which employs a 'reaction' type defense such as UCLA. We won't be able to use it against Notre Dame because their linemen use a dig-in-and-eat-dirt defense," continued Hill.

Jess said that Fullback Ed Isherwood, who started against UCLA, strained a muscle in his leg and will miss the Irish tilt. But there's a possibility that Quarterback Ells Kissinger will see action other than kicking an extra point and a field goal. Ells is nursing two cracked ribs, an injury suffered in the Oregon game.

And SC might need all of its hands against the Irish, despite Notre Dame's shoddy 2-7 season record.

Charley Callahan, veteran

Turn to Page 2, Column 4

## TODAY IN SPORTS

**QUARTER HORSE RACING**—Los Alamitos, 1 p.m.

# BRUIN FACULTY VOTES FOR QUITTING PCC

## Calhoun Upsets Davis---13.5; O'Brien Breaks Shot Record

CC★ WEDNESDAY MORNING, NOVEMBER 28, 1956 Part IV

## SPORTSCRIPTS

By PAUL ZIMMERMAN Times Sports Editor

MELBOURNE, Nov. 28 (Wednesday)—Bill Russell, star center of the United States basketball team, has made it his purpose to come out of the Olympic Games the most-talked-about cagester in all the world.

A fun-loving chap at heart, he has been in dead earnest about his play here and will feel his time has been wasted if he isn't considered the top player of the globe.

Russell has lots of comedy in his make-up, but none of it shows on the court. Even the day the official team pictures were taken by Los Angeles' Lee Hansen, Bill refused to even smile when the squad was asked to laugh it up.

**BASKETBALL NOT CLOWNING GAME TO HIM**

Bill hasn't decided, he says, what his future plans may be but it is doubtful if he will join the Harlem Globetrotters, as has been intimated. He doesn't consider basketball a clowning game. To him it is a serious contest, and if he should turn professional he probably will join one of the big league teams after this is over.

Russell undoubtedly could have made the Olympic team as a high jumper but decided he couldn't do that and be in his best playing form on the courts. He probably could have won one of the top places here in that event because he cleared 6 feet 9¾ inches at Fresno last spring.

Bill was a one-man track team in high school at Oakland where he did just about everything including a 49s. 440 yards.

**BIG TEST WILL COME AGAINST RUSSIA**

"That's for the younger fellows," said Russell when we asked him why he gave up the running business for which he obviously was also well qualified. The fact that Bill is only 22 is the only evidence you have that he was kidding, because he didn't crack a smile as he said this.

Russell's big test will come against Russia if the U.S.S.R. team and the Americans come down to the wire in the finals on Saturday, as anticipated.

Coach Gerald Tucker considers that two elements have helped the United States team this time. In 1952 at Helsinki the offense got more advantage than the defense from officials compared to the game as it is played in America.

Tucker explains that the officiating in the United States last year more nearly approximated this international interpretation of the rules so our players have adjusted better.

**ITALIAN BALL DIDN'T HAVE TRUE BOUNCE**

The other advantage has been a change in the type of ball used. In 1952 an Italian ball, stitched in the fashion of a soccer ball, was the one in vogue. It didn't have the true bounce of the American ball and didn't hold its shape as well.

Little has been seen of the fabulous Russian, Vasily Akhtayer, who stands 7 feet 6½ inches. He can shoot well enough, but he doesn't have the ability to move around on the court as effectively as the average 6-foot 6-inch type player. Russia has a number of stars who are much better.

It will be interesting if and when he gets in against Russell.

**P.S.:** Bill Russell at 6 feet 9⅝ inches is a little guy by comparison but his muscles are like coiled springs.

## Toss of 60-11 Wins for Parry

BY PAUL ZIMMERMAN
Times Sports Editor

MELBOURNE, Nov. 28 (Wednesday) — Lanky Lee Calhoun edged out world record holder Jack Davis to lead a United States sweep in the 110-meter hurdles and Parry O'Brien came through with his expected shot-put win for the Yanks' 10th and 11th gold medals of the Olympic Games today.

Another turnaway crowd of 110,000 fans saw the American domination continue into the fifth day of track competition.

O'Brien of Santa Monica, who has a world record application of 63ft. 2in. up for approval, successfully defended his Olympic title with a winning record effort of 60ft. 11in. His listed Olympic mark was only 57ft. 1⅜in. He bettered that on all six tries today.

**Shankle Third**

Calhoun, who tied with Davis in the final Olympic trials, was awarded the gold medal after officials took a good look at the photo finish. Both were clocked in 13.5, well under the Olympic record of 13.7, set by the U.S.'s Harrison Dillard at Helsinki in 1952.

Joel Shankle of Duke completed the Yankee domination, well back at 14.1.

It was the fourth clean sweep by the Americans. Previously they had taken the gold, silver and bronze medals in the 400-meter hurdles, 200 meter and discus throw.

Calhoun, a 23-year-old Negro from North Carolina Col-

Turn to Page 5, Column 4

DAVIS SHADED—Jack Davis, former SC hurdler from Glendale, shown winning his heat in the 110-meter highs in Olympic Games at Melbourne, was second in a photo finish to Lee Calhoun of Gary, Ind., in the finals today. Both Calhoun and Davis were timed in 13.5, a new Olympic record. Joel Shankle, U.S., third.
(AP) Wirephoto via radio from Melbourne

## Allen and Sproul in Meeting

BY DICK HYLAND

UCLA yesterday officially conferred with University of California's President Robert G. Sproul at Berkeley upon the subject of the Bruins leaving the Pacific Coast Conference.

In the persons of Chancellor Raymond B. Allen, Dr. Bradford A. Booth, faculty representative to the PCC, and Director of Athletics Wilbur Johns, the Bruins conveyed to their superior the polled wishes of their division of the university, including faculty and other organic units.

A brief summation of their polite palaver would be this: UCLA desires to resign from the Pacific Coast Conference.

**Faculty Meeting**

The Bruin trio's sudden flight to Berkeley, five days before the regular PCC meeting scheduled for the Beverly Hilton Hotel here next Sunday, was sparked by a meeting of the UCLA faculty Monday evening.

At this meeting, attended by some 500 members of the potent Academic Senate, the faculty gave complete endorsement of the actions past and future of Chancellor Allen, Athletic Director Johns and Football Coach Red Sanders.

That the faculty members knew exactly what they were doing when they so voted, was indicated immediately after the regular meeting was adjourned.

**Favor Withdrawal**

A straw vote was taken unofficially and 80% of the Westwood faculty voted yes on the question: Should UCLA withdraw from the PCC? Ten per cent refrained from voting with the plea that they did not know enough of the subject and 10% voted to remain in the conference.

The effect of the Bruin withdrawal from the conference would be nil so far as the National Collegiate Athletic Association is concerned. The Bruins are already under a 3-year ban from the Rose Bowl and NCAA championship meetings. There is no precedent for other action, such as telling its members not to schedule or play the Bruins in football or any other sport.

**Code Cited**

The effect upon the members of the PCC is something else again. There is a specific part in the PCC code which states that no member shall play any other member that withdraws from the PCC.

The present contracts for

Turn to Page 2, Column 3

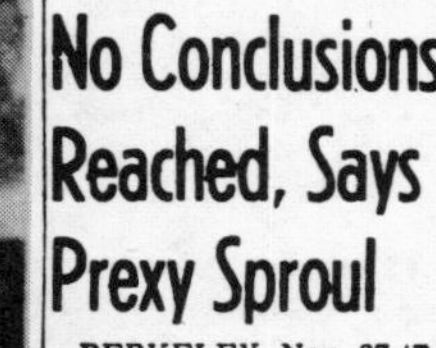

## No Conclusions Reached, Says Prexy Sproul

BERKELEY, Nov. 27 (AP)—Leaders of UCLA and the University of California today discussed possible withdrawal from the Pacific Coast Conference, but President Robert Gordon Sproul said "no conclusions were reached."

Sproul, whose authority extends to both the UCLA and Berkeley campuses, said the meeting was the type of caucus always held prior to meetings of the PCC presidents' council and the conference itself.

The council meets in San Francisco on Sunday while the conference faculty representatives hold their winter meeting in Beverly Hills, Sunday through Thursday.

**Discounts Reports**

Dr. Sproul discounted reports that Chancellor Raymond B. Allen and Athletic Director Wilbur Johns had come to this meeting to seek approval for withdrawal by UCLA, one of the schools hardest hit by conference penalties for illegal aid to football players.

"It was the regular type of session for clearing of views before meeting with the others in the conference," he said.

**Would Be Surprised**

He said it was stated that certain people in Southern California sought withdrawal but no conclusions were reached and no ultimatums issued.

"Because the presidents' council is going on with possible changes in the athletic setup and code, the group

Turn to Page 2, Column 1

## Russia Wins Pentathlon, U.S. Second

MELBOURNE, Nov. 28 (Wednesday) (AP)—Russia won the team championship in the Olympic modern pentathlon competition today, beating out the United States team which led through the first four events.

The Russian three-man team scored a total of 13,690.5 points in the five events. The U.S. finished second with 13,482 points.

Lars Hall of Sweden won the individual gold medal, retaining the title he won at Helsinki in 1952.

Hall scored 4833 points. Olavi Mannonen of Finland finished second with 4774 and Vaino Korhonen of Finland third with 4750.

## Yank Spikemen Score Sweeps in Discus, 200

BY PAUL ZIMMERMAN
Times Sports Editor

MELBOURNE, Nov. 28 (Wednesday)—United States track and field athletes rolled relentlessly on toward a smashing triumph in the XVI Olympiad here at the Melbourne Cricket Ground today with nine victories earned and seven Olympic records set.

As usual, a throng of 100,000 packed Melbourne Cricket Ground despite chilly, gusty weather. It was Bobby Morrow of Abilene Christian, as expected, in the 200 meters and Al Oerter of Kansas in the discus, which hadn't been expected. This was the golden anniversary of his university and Bobby now presented it with two gold medals, the first man to do this since Berlin.

**Never Any Doubt**

Again Russia was thwarted in quest of its second victory in track and field when Adhemar Da Silva of Brazil retained his Olympic title in the hop, step and jump with a leap of 53ft. 7⅝in. That made it three records broken for the day.

Morrow's time of 20.6 erased the mark which had been on the books since Jesse Owens put it there 20 years ago in Berlin. Jesse was in the stands yesterday to see it erased. Andy Stanfield, who tied it in victory at Helsinki four years ago, was a stride-

Turn to Page 6, Column 5

SCORES UPSET—Al Oerter, New Hyde Park, N.Y., whirls as he sets to throw discus yesterday at Melbourne. Oerter tossed discus 184ft. 10½in. to score upset over the favored Fortune Gordien, holder of world record from Brightwood, Or.
(AP) Wirephoto via radio from Melbourne

## SWAPS TOP HORSE OF YEAR IN POLL

NEW YORK, Nov. 27 (AP)—Swaps, the record-breaking thoroughbred currently recovered from a fractured leg, today was named Horse of the Year by staff members of the Morning Telegraph and Daily Racing Form.

The 1955 Kentucky Derby winner was an overwhelming choice, receiving 20 of the 33 votes cast for top honors in the 21st annual poll while Nashua, his chief rival got only 12 with one going to the D. & H. Stable's Needles, winner of the Kentucky Derby this season.

**Best Handicap Horse**

Swaps also was named the best handicap horse of the season, receiving 129 points against 101 for Nashua, owned by the Leslie B. Combs Syndicate, and 121 for Calumet Farm's Bardstown. Points were awarded on the basis of five for first place, two for second and one for third.

Swaps was third to Nashua and High Gun in Horse-of-the-Year voting a year ago but the brilliant son of Khaled changed that this season by setting four new world records and equaling a fifth.

Other divisional champions selected were Calumet Farm's Barbizon as the best two-year-old colt and best juvenile; Charlton Clay's Leallah as the best two-year-old filly; Needles as the best three-year-old colt and best sophomore; Claiborne's Doubledogdare as the best three-year-old filly; Woodlawn Farm's Blue Sparkler as the best handicap mare; River Divide Farm's Decathlon as the best sprinter; C. V. Whitney's Career Boy as the best grass runner; and Montpelier's Shipboard as the leader of the steeplechasers.

## Swaps Walks First Time Since Accident

CAMDEN, N.J., Nov. 27 (AP)—Swaps, California thoroughbred who ranks as one of the top race horses of all time, walked today for the first time since X rays disclosed he had fractured a tiny bone in his left hind leg during an Oct. 9 workout at Garden State race track.

Swaps, still wearing a small cast to protect the injured canon bone which veterinarians say has healed completely, walked from one stall to another one bedded with straw.

## TODAY IN SPORTS

**QUARTER HORSE RACING**—Los Alamitos, 1 p.m.

**WRESTLING** — Olympic Auditorium, 8:30 p.m.

## Paul Hornung Among All-Time Irish Greats

BY MAL FLORENCE

The Notre Dame team which faces SC Saturday at the Coliseum may be the worst club ever to come out of South Bend, but curiously Quarterback Paul Hornung is considered to be the greatest all-around back in Irish history.

Is this statement too bold? One must tread lightly when speaking of Irish grid lore.

How about George Gipp, the Four Horsemen, Frank Carideo, Marchy Schwartz, Angelo Bertelli, Johnny Lujack and Ralph Guglielmi? Where do they rate?

We deplore the "greatest" tag because the term becomes meaningless by misuse. But, Hornung can't be ignored even as to be compared with those backs whose feats have become part of the Notre Dame legend.

Hornung's a quarterback who plunges like a fullback and has the open-field instinct of a halfback. In fact, he's played briefly at fullback this season and it's reported he's been drilling at left half this week.

Southland fans who watched SC's spine-tingling 42-20 upset of Notre Dame here last year remember Hornung's incredible one-man performance. All Hornung did was set an all-time opponents individual record against the Trojans by passing and running for 354 yards.

Before the Trojans broke the game open in the fourth quarter on Jim Contratto's 64-yard touchdown pass to Jon Arnett, Hornung had shown his versatility.

Paul, a 6-foot 1-inch, 195-pound specimen from Pennsylvania, carried two tacklers into the end zone with him as he scored ND's first touchdown on a fourth-down-and-7 situation from SC's 8-yard line. He looked like a fullback.

Hornung teamed with Jim Morse for a 78-yard pass-and-run play for ND's second TD and set up the final Irish score when he and Morse clicked on a 60-yard gainer to the SC 6. Quarterback qualities.

In the third quarter Hornung turned left end and sprinted 59 yards to the SC 28. But, this drive died on

Turn to Page 3, Column 4

# SC, UCLA WITHDRAWAL THREATS DIE OUT

**CAMERA DAY**—Out for a morning workout is this string of thoroughbreds belonging to Rex Ellsworth stable now at Santa Anita. Trainer Mish Tenney, fourth from left, directs conditioning of valuable horseflesh. The Ellsworth Stable, which raced the famous Swaps, is awaiting Santa Anita opening Dec. 26.
Times photo by Larry Sharkey

Story on Page 4, Part IV

## SPORTSCRIPTS

By PAUL ZIMMERMAN TIMES SPORTS EDITOR

MELBOURNE, Dec. 4 (Tuesday)—Without question, the largest Olympic Games guest representation from any of the United States again has been Californian.

Just as the Sunshine State has been dominant in total competitors in all events, and total medal winners, it also has a terrific edge among the spectators in the stands.

No. 1 representative at all Olympiads always is John J. Garland of Pasadena, the best liked of all the United States members of the International Olympic Committee.

Second-place honors here went to Mayor Norris Poulson of Los Angeles, who came at the invitation of the Lord Mayor of Melbourne along with the Mayors of all the cities of the world that have held the Olympics.

**HALE HEADS SQUAW VALLEY CONTINGENT**

Strong, also, is the contingent of Squaw Valley 1960 Winter Olympics representatives, headed by Prentis C. Hale, San Francisco and Los Angeles department store owner, who is president of the Winter Games organizing committee.

With Hale are such luminaries in charge of the Winter Games spectacle as Alan E. Bartholemy, general secretary; Joseph A. Moore, vice-president of the organizing committee; H. D. Thoreau, executive secretary of the California committee for Squaw Valley; Dick Ham, committee member, and Ken Macker and Pete Rozelle.

In addition to Mayor Poulson from Los Angeles, the Memorial Coliseum Commission is represented by Dick Yeamans, president, and Bill Nicholas, general manager.

**LEE AND MATHIAS REPRESENT PRESIDENT**

Two of President Eisenhower's special representatives at the Games here are famous Californians, Dr. Sammy Lee of Santa Ana and Bob Mathias of Los Angeles, both two-time Olympic champions.

Add to these the coaches who have spent so much time in training many of the California stars who are being so successful here.

There also is a long list of coaches who are not connected with the team.

Perhaps we should top this with Payton Jordan of Stanford. He was the coach of both Bob Gutowski, who finished second, and George Roubanis, Greece, who was third in the pole vault. Then there are Herschel Smith, coach of victorious Charles Dumas of Compton in the high jump; Bud Winter, San Jose State, who had several competitors, and Bob Strehle, retired track coach from Pomona.

**EVEN CALIFORNIA PRESS LEADS NATION**

Add to this list Bud Lyndon of the Pasadena AC, who trained Juno Stover Irwin and other diving stars.

This only starts the list of California sportsmen present, including Carl Hansen, Oakland, president of the National AAU; Lee Hansen, Los Angeles photographer and former Trojan star; Cliff Henderson, Palm Desert, who used to run Pan-Pacific; Herm Albers, the great Trojan from General Petroleum; Don George, former Olympic and world's wrestling champion, etc.

You also might count Oympic officials like Bill Schroeder, Briggs Hunt, UCLA; Larry Houston, track and field manager; Jess Mortensen, assistant track coach; Ducky Drake, trainer, etc. Even the California press leads the nation.

**P.S.**: There are nine writers here from our State.

## 'The Stilt' Scores 52 in Debut

LAWRENCE, Kan., Dec. 3 (AP) — Seven-foot Wilt (The Stilt) Chamberlain made a sensational varsity debut tonight, scoring 52 points in sparking Kansas to an 87-69 basketball victory over Northwestern.

A season-opening crowd of 15,000 watched the heralded Negro star from Philadelphia play his first game under the Kansas varsity colors.

Chamberlain's point total shattered the school record of 44 points, held jointly by Clyde Lovellette and B. H. Born, former centers.

## Sugar Bout Postponed; Beef Erupts

NEW YORK, Dec. 3 (AP)—The middleweight championship fight between Sugar Ray Robinson and Gene Fullmer, scheduled for Dec. 12 at Madison Square Garden, was postponed until Jan. 2 today and Fullmer, through Manager Marv Jensen, promptly claimed the title by default.

The three-week delay was ordered after Robinson came down with a severe cold and brought a prompt reaction from Jensen, who said he would go before Chairman Julius Helfand of the New York State Athletic Commission tomorrow to claim the title from Sugar Ray.

**New Purse Split**

Jensen, who negotiated and waited for nearly six months to get the bout for his challenger, suggested that "Sugar Ray probably got sick watching old man Archie Moore on television Friday night."

Jensen said either the Dec. 12 contract will be honored by a fight or it ought to be voided and a new split of the purse drawn up.

Under current terms, Robinson would receive 47½% plus a big slice of the TV and radio receipts to 12½% and no TV or radio swag for Fullmer, whose home is in West Jordan, Utah.

Pending new arrangements, Jensen said Fullmer would stay in training at Grossinger, N.Y.

**Examined By Doctor**

The decision to order a postponement was made after Robinson, who has a notable case history of title bout delays, was examined by Dr. Alexander Schiff of the commission.

Dr. Schiff said he told the commission that, in his opinion, Robinson is not in condition to fight on Dec. 12 but should be sufficiently recovered by Jan. 2.

Fullmer was a 7-5 choice in the latest odds.

## Folley in Close Win Over Bethea

NEW YORK, Dec. 3 (UP)—Heavyweight Zora Folley of Chandler, Ariz., made a successful New York debut tonight by winning a split 10-round decision by the eyelash margin of one point over Wayne Bethea of New York in their 10-rounder at St. Nicholas Arena.

Folley, 25, piled up enough of a lead in the early rounds to barely salvage the verdict after he had run out of gas in the second half of the contest.

Folley, scaling 187 pounds to Bethea's 201¼, registered his sixth straight victory and may have earned a ranking among the top 10 by snapping Bethea's winning streak at seven straight.

## U.S. Water Poloists Need Two Wins for Third Place

CC TUESDAY MORNING, DECEMBER 4, 1956 Part IV

### Hughes Star of 4-3 Win Over Germany

BY PAUL ZIMMERMAN
Times Sports Editor

MELBOURNE, Dec. 4 (Tuesday) — The United States water polo team needs only two more victories to clinch third place, which would be its finest Olympic Games performance in many years.

The American team, composed of five Southern Californians and two Chicago competitors, defeated Germany, 4-3, yesterday in a crucial game and now meets Italy and Russia in round-robin competition.

Dr. Neill Kohlhase of Los Angeles, team coach, considers Russia toughest of the two upcoming opponents.

**Hughes Leads Attack**

Robert Hughes, star member of the U.S. team that finished fourth in Helsinki in 1952, scored three goals yesterday to lead the United States attack and Robert Horn of Fullerton at goal made numerous saves that

Turn to Page 6, Column 3

## Aragon Favored to Beat Poirier

BY CAL WHORTON

Idle since scoring a controversial knockout over Cisco Andrade last Aug. 29, Art (Golden Boy) Aragon goes out after a little Christmas spending money tonight when he faces Gene Poirier of Niagara Falls, N.Y., in the nontelevised 10-round headliner at Hollywood Legion Stadium.

Ranked fourth among contenders for Carmen Basilio's welterweight championship, the 29-year-old Aragon has been established a 3-1 favorite over his rugged eastern foe, who'll be making his initial start locally.

There have been some reports that Aragon is taking the unranked Poirier too lightly, that he has been neglecting serious training.

Weight for the match originally was set at 147 pounds, but was changed to 152 at Aragon's request.

Aragon is unbeaten in five starts this year. In addition to the knockout scored over Andrade, he also stopped Ramon Tiscareno, Danny Giovanelli and Raul Perez. He decisioned Jimmy Carter.

The 25-year-old Poirier is

Turn to Page 5, Column 3

## HUNGARY'S TABORI MAY SEEK ASYLUM

MELBOURNE, Dec. 4 (Tuesday) (AP) — Five members of Hungary's large Olympic delegation will seek asylum in Australia and famed runner Laszlo Tabori is among others seriously considering not returning home, a source close to the team told the Associated Press today.

Tabori, a quiet little man who is one of the world's 10 four-minute milers, said:

"I cannot say definitely now what I will do, but I am seriously considering staying in Australia. The trouble is none of us here knows what conditions are in Hungary. It is a great problem and a worry for all of us."

The five who are said definitely committed to remain here were not identified for security reasons. One of them is a famous champion runner like Tabori.

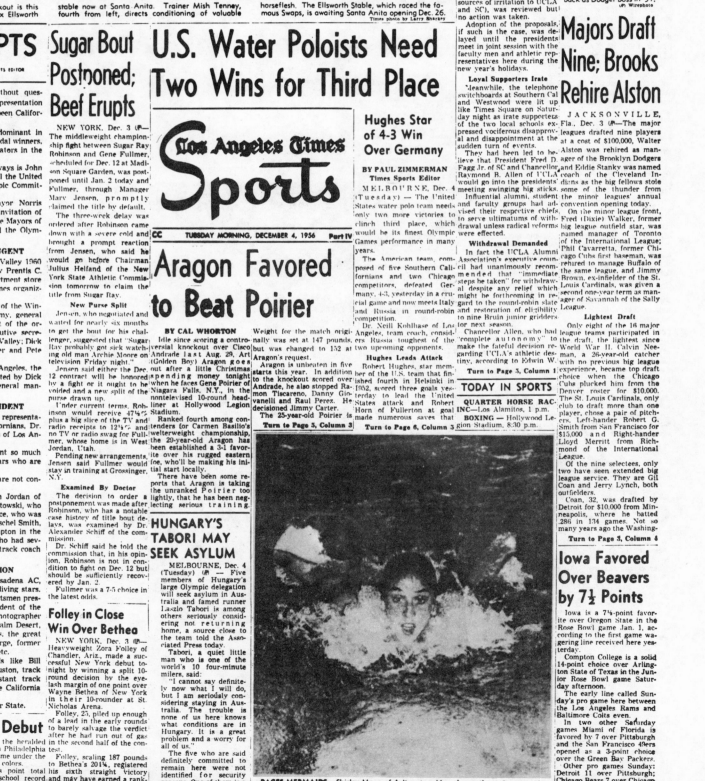

**PACES MERMAIDS**—Shirley Mann of Arlinugton, Va., churns the water en route to setting fastest time among qualifiers in the 100-meter butterfly swim in Olympic Games. Shirley was timed in 1:11.2. All three U.S. entries qualified in event.
Wide World photo

## Two Local Teams Remain Members of Coast Conference

BY FRANK FINCH

The fireworks expected to explode at the winter meeting of the Pacific Coast Conference which opened yesterday at the Beverly Hilton Hotel turned out to be complete duds.

UCLA and Southern California still are members of the PCC. Their threatened withdrawal from the conference turned out to be wishful thinking. It was obvious that alumni and undergrads felt they were shortchanged at the Sunday meeting of the PCC president's council.

**Reserved Comment**

Faculty representatives and athletic directors of the nine-member schools in joint session yesterday heard the report of the presidents' powwow, but reserved comment.

A 10-point proposal recommended to the meeting here by the presidents, which includes abolishing the present round-robin football schedule (one of the main sources of irritation to UCLA and SC), was reviewed but no action was taken.

Adoption of the proposals, if such is the case, was delayed until the presidents meet in joint session with the faculty men and athletic representatives here during the new year's holidays.

**Loyal Supporters Irate**

Meanwhile, the telephone switchboards at Southern Cal and Westwood were lit up like Times Square on Saturday night as irate supporters of the two local schools expressed vociferous disapproval and disappointment at the sudden turn of events.

They had been led to believe that President Fred D. Fagg Jr. of SC and Chancellor Raymond B. Allen of UCLA would go into the presidents' meeting swinging big sticks.

Influential alumni, student and faculty groups had advised their respective chiefs to serve ultimatums of withdrawal unless radical reforms were effected.

**Withdrawal Demanded**

In fact the UCLA Alumni Association's executive council had unanimously recommended that "immediate steps be taken" for withdrawal despite any relief which might be forthcoming in regard to the round-robin slate and restoration of eligibility to nine Bruin junior gridders for next season.

Chancellor Allen, who had "complete autonomy" to make the fateful decision regarding UCLA's athletic destiny, according to Edwin W.

Turn to Page 5, Column 1

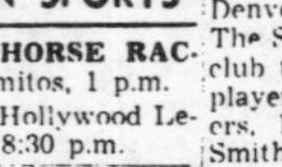

### TODAY IN SPORTS

QUARTER HORSE RACING—Los Alamitos, 1 p.m.

BOXING — Hollywood Legion Stadium, 8:30 p.m.

**REHIRED** — Walt Alston, Brooklyn manager, will be back as Dodger boss in '57.
(AP) Wirephoto

## Majors Draft Nine; Brooks Rehire Alston

JACKSONVILLE, Fla., Dec. 3 (AP)—The major leagues drafted nine players at a cost of $100,000, Walter Alston was rehired as manager of the Brooklyn Dodgers and Eddie Stanky was named coach of the Cleveland Indians as the big fellows stole some of the thunder from the minor leagues' annual convention opening today.

On the minor league front, Fred (Dixie) Walker, former big league outfield star, was named manager of Toronto of the International League; Phil Cavarretta, former Chicago Cubs first baseman, was rehired to manage Buffalo of the same league, and Jimmy Brown, ex-infielder of the St. Louis Cardinals, was given a second one-year term as manager of Savannah of the Sally League.

**Lightest Draft**

Only eight of the 16 major league teams participated in the draft, the lightest since World War II. Calvin Neeman, a 26-year-old catcher with no previous big league experience, became top draft choice when the Chicago Cubs plucked him from the Denver roster for $10,000. The St. Louis Cardinals, only club to draft more than one player, chose a pair of pitchers, Left-hander Robert G. Smith from San Francisco for $15,000 and Right-hander Lloyd Merritt from Richmond of the International League.

Of the nine selectees, only two have seen extended big league service. They are Gil Coan and Jerry Lynch, both outfielders.

Coan, 32, was drafted by Detroit for $10,000 from Minneapolis, where he batted .286 in 134 games. Not so many years ago the Washing-

Turn to Page 3, Column 4

## Iowa Favored Over Beavers by 7½ Points

Iowa is a 7½-point favorite over Oregon State in the Rose Bowl game Jan. 1, according to the first game wagering line received here yesterday.

Compton College is a solid 14-point choice over Arlington State of Texas in the Junior Rose Bowl game Saturday afternoon.

The early line called Sunday's pro game here between the Los Angeles Rams and Baltimore Colts even.

In two other Saturday games Miami of Florida is favored by 7 over Pittsburgh and the San Francisco 49ers opened as a 3-point choice over the Green Bay Packers.

Other pro games Sunday: Detroit 11 over Pittsburgh; Chicago Bears 7 over Chicago Cards; New York 8 over Cleveland and Washington 7 over Philadelphia.

# PCC Supports SC in NCAA Appeal

CHAMPION—Shelley Mann, right, of Arlington, Va., rests in the Olympic pool after winning 100-meter butterfly event in record time of 1:11. Teammates Mary Sears, left, and Nancy Jane Ramey finished third and second, respectively, as American girls swept event.
(AP) Wirephoto via radio from Melbourne

Los Angeles Times Sports

CC★ THURSDAY MORNING, DECEMBER 6, 1956 Part IV

## SPORTSCRIPTS

By PAUL ZIMMERMAN TIMES SPORTS EDITOR

MELBOURNE, Dec. 5—Australian sports fans differ from those in the United States in that they are more patient. Like us, they have an insatiable desire for athletic spectacles as exemplified in the Olympic Games.

They are willing to queue up in long lines for hours to pay their money for standing room only at Melbourne Cricket Ground.

Once they are in, most of them stay until the very last event has been concluded. Then, only, do they seem to get excited. There is a mad scramble to get out and a wild dash for taxis or trams.

A classic example of the Australian's determination to stay and see it all was the evening of the first track and field event when Charlie Dumas, the Compton jumper, and their own Charles Porter were still going until nearly 8 p.m. to resolve the championship.

**AND THE CROWD STAYS ON**

It was difficult, in the gloom, to see how many were still on hand, but well over half of a crowd of 100,000 had stayed on to the end. Naturally, the presence of one of their own performers had something to do with this but events since have indicated that is only a part of the reason.

Group attendance at the events here is done on a picnic basis. Families or parties come armed with baskets of food, thermos jugs of tea, beer, Cokes, etc. Some sit in the stands long after the events are concluded, have supper there, and then go home when the traffic has cleared out.

The festive atmosphere is much greater even than at our Rose Bowl game where our spectators park their cars and set up a picnic lunch.

At the Cricket Ground, parking facilities are almost negligible and these are taken up by official cars. The average citizen brave enough to drive must park far away. Most of the more than 100,000 spectators come by taxi or tram.

**AUSTRALIAN FANS COME EARLY**

Some spread a blanket on the spacious park grass and eat there, but the bulk of the spectators carry their luncheon into the stands so they can enjoy the electric atmosphere of the excited crowd while they eat.

At London and Helsinki only a few scattered thousands bothered to go to the stadium in the morning for qualifying trials in such events as the women's discus, "long jump," high jump, etc. Here the Cricket Ground was better than half filled and these folks stayed on all day—from 10 a.m. until the late end.

The Cricket Ground, for the most part, makes for a comfortable stay. The expensive seats have backs that contour to the body.

**BEER SERVED AT CRICKET GROUND**

In addition there are food bars where you can eat, drink coffee, tea and beer. Being a private corporation, the M.C.G. can serve beer just as we do at our baseball parks but can't at our local football stadia.

No hamburgers are included in the spectator's diet but they give you the hot dog giant size. It is twice as long as the American version, extending three inches each end of the bun, dripping with tomato sauce instead of mustard.

P.S.: The Australian sports spectator needs this to replenish the energy he burns up cheering the contestants.

SHELLEY MANN WINS

## All-Southland Sweep Looms in Men's Diving

BY PAUL ZIMMERMAN
Times Sports Editor

MELBOURNE, Dec. 6 (Thursday)—An all-Southern California victory in the men's platform diving competition appeared probable last night when the world's stars went through their polished, breath-taking acrobatics.

The last four tests of Olympic Games competition in this 10-meter platform event are expected to bring the United States its fifth gold medal in the aquatics events as the Americans began making inroads on Australia's dominance in the swimming events.

Dick Connor, of the Pasadena Athletic Club, was a surprise leader at the end of the six qualifying performances with a point total of 80.24.

**Tobian Fourth**

Gary Tobian, the favorite from Los Angeles, stood fourth at this juncture, but he was expected to advance because of his ability in the difficult optional dives in the competition tonight. The third Californian, Willie Farrell of Los Angeles, stood in the sixth place slot as he moved into the final rounds, but he, too, figured to improve over Joaquin Capilla of Mexico, who is second at the moment, and Joszef Garlach of Hungary, who was running third. These were the two closest competitors to the Southern California combination.

Connor had the highest score posted for one dive when he chalked up 19.68 on the difficult backward one-half with a half twist. This was as close to perfect as a diver can get without going into a string of decimal points.

**Mann Triumphs**

Shelley Mann brought the United States its fourth victory in the aquatic competition last night when she swam the 100-meter butterfly stroke in 1:11 flat for a new world's and Olympic record. This was America's first sweep in the tank department when Shirley's teammates, Nancy Romey and Mary Jane Sears, made

Turn to Page 5, Column 5

## Russ Close Gap on U.S. Games Lead

MELBOURNE, Dec. 6 (Thursday) (AP) — Russian athletes have surged to within 20 points of the United States in the ding dong battle for the unofficial team honors at the 1956 Olympic Games, and American hopes of pulling out victory virtually disappeared today.

After Russian successes in gymnastics yesterday the score stood at 538½ points for the United States and 518½ for Russia. This was under the system of 10 points for each first place, and five, four, three, two, one for the other five placings.

In gold medals the United States leads with 31, to 23 for Russia. The Soviets lead in second place, or silver medals, with 25, as against 22 for the United States. Bronze medals show 24 for Russia and 12 for the Americans.

**U.S. Hopes Fading**

Only a handful of swimming finals remain for the United States to pick up additional points, while Russia still has plenty to pick up in gymnastics, Greco - Roman wrestling and fencing.

Thus domination of the United States in the Olympics that began with the first modern Games in Athens in 1896 almost certainly is coming to an end.

The U.S.A. had an aggregate 538½ to 518½ with three days to go. Points are awarded on the basis of 10 for first place, five for second, etc.

|  |  |
|---|---|
| United States | 538½ |
| Russia | 518½ |
| Australia | 200½ |
| Germany | 190 |
| Hungary | 163 |
| Britain | 162½ |
| Italy | 140 |
| Sweden | 131 |
| Rumania | 94 |
| France | 85½ |
| Finland | 67 |
| Poland | 61 |
| Japan | 57½ |
| Czechoslovakia | 52 |
| Iran | 48 |
| Canada | 45 |
| Turkey | 36 |
| Ireland | 28½ |
| Denmark | 28 |
| Korea | 22 |
| New Zealand | 22 |
| Bulgaria | 21 |
| Norway | 21 |
| Argentina | 18½ |
| Chile | 17 |
| South Africa | 16 |
| Brazil | 12 |
| Yugoslavia | 11 |
| Belgium | 11 |
| Austria | 9 |
| Trinidad | 7 |
| Mexico | 7 |
| Switzerland | 5 |
| Iceland | 5 |
| Greece | 4 |
| Uruguay | 4 |
| Bahamas | 4 |
| Portugal | 3 |
| Nigeria | 2 |
| Malaya | 1 |
| Spain | 1 |
| Cuba | 1 |

## Troy Given Backing Should School Seek to Have Bans Eased

BY FRANK FINCH

Moral support for the University of Southern California, should it press an appeal for modification of athletic sanctions imposed on it by the NCAA, was assured yesterday by the Pacific Coast Conference.

A resolution pledging support was unanimously adopted during the afternoon session of PCC faculty representatives and athletic directors at the Beverly Hilton Hotel.

In another major development, it was disclosed that four more cases of illegal aid to University of Washington athletes by the so-called "downtown fund" of Seattle had been uncovered by Washington officials.

**Ban Lifted**

After the PCC placed Southern Cal, UCLA and Washington on probation and imposed blanket athletic sanctions, the conference later lifted the ban on sports other than football at SC.

But the NCAA not only affirmed the PCC's original action, but extended the ban on SC to include all sports until July 1, 1957. This meant that Trojan athletes and teams are prohibited from competing in all NCAA-sponsored events until that time.

SC has not decided whether to file an appeal, according to Athletic Director Willis O. Hunter, but in light of the PCC's support it seems certain that such action will be taken.

**Resolution Text**

Text of the PCC resolution, which was presented at a press conference by California's faculty man, Prof. Glenn T. Seaborg, follows:

"Moved that the NCAA council be informed that in connection with any appeal which may be taken by SC from the imposition of sanctions upon that institution by the NCAA, it is the present judgment of the conference that the sanctions and penalties imposed were and continue to be entirely adequate under all of the facts and circumstances involved in the SC case, and that of this date these penalties and sanctions are in full force and effect, and SC is in full compliance with respect to any obligations owed under those sanctions and penalties."

Prof. Seaborg said that "... quite a lot of progress is being made on uncovering illegal aid to athletes."

He announced that an investigation conducted by Washington's faculty man, Prof. Don Wollett, and Athletic Director George Briggs disclosed four new cases of illegal aid from the so-called slush fund that has since been dissolved.

**Other Cases**

In addition, "five or six" other cases were discovered by the Husky investigators, but the athletes involved already have graduated.

Three football players and a baseball player received varying amounts.

One football player received $25, purportedly to buy books. His case has not been adjudicated.

Another gridder received a $20 loan. He was declared ineligible for one year, but will regain his eligibility if he repays the loan by Feb. 1, 1957.

**Schmidt Support Pledged**

Yet another gridder lost a year's eligibility for receiving money from the fund. In his case the penalty will stick. The baseball player also was "benched" for a year. In neither of the latter two cases was the amount of money involved made public.

Assurance that full co-operation will be given to PCC Commissioner Victor O.

Turn to Page 3, Column 1

## Machen Scores Unanimous Win in TV Battle

SYRACUSE, N.Y., Dec. 5 (AP)—Eddie Machen, classy undefeated West Coast heavyweight, made his first eastern appearance a successful one as he won a unanimous 10-round decision tonight over Detroit's Johnny Summerlin. Machen weighed 190¼, Summerlin, 196.

Machen, clearly the boss throughout the bout, was nevertheless, unable to send the plodding Summerlin to the canvas.

Again and again it seemed as though Summerlin's legs would finally collapse as the sixth - ranked Detroiter seemed to counterpunch out of sheer instinct.

**Fancy Footwork**

Machen used a flicking left jab throughout to force Summerlin, who attempted to carry the fight to his opponent, to punch from long range. The Californian, showing fancy footwork, won the fight with his counterpunching ability.

Judges Richie Fazio and Dick Albino both scored it 7-3 for Machen. Referee Joe Paler had it 6-4. The Associated Press called it for Machen, 7-2-1.

**Machen's 19th Win**

The victory was Machen's 19th. Summerlin now has a 31-7-1 mark.

On the basis of his performance against Summerlin, Machen, fourth ranked in the National Boxing Association listings, was expected to get a shot at Tommy (Hurricane) Jackson.

## PAULA IN DIVING LEAD, PAT FOURTH

MELBOURNE, Dec. 6 (Thursday) (AP)—Pretty Paula Jean Myers of Glendora, Cal., surprised by leading qualifiers in the women's platform diving in the Olympics today while Defending Champion Pat McCormick ranked only fourth.

Mrs. McCormick, 26-year-old Lakewood (Cal.) housewife shooting to become the first two-time double champion in Olympic diving history, had been expected to lead qualifying as she tried to add the platform title to the springboard championship she already has won.

**Russia 2nd and 3rd**

Shapely Pat had been leading after the third of today's four dives but then Miss Myers, a University of Southern California junior, took command with a four-dive total of 52.96 points.

Russians ranked second and third as Raissa Vocokhovskaia tallied 52.64 points and Tatiana Kacackachiants scored 52.19. Then came Mrs. McCormick with 51.28 in fourth place and Juno Stover Irwin of Glendale, Cal., in fifth with 50.81.

Point totals from today's four dives carry over into Friday's final, where two more dives of each contestant's choosing will be held. However, today's field of 17 was cut to the top 12 for the final.

**Trail by 20 Points**

The United States was banking heavily on a gold medal in this event tomorrow, supposedly from Mrs. McCormick, in its touch-and-go effort to hold off a Russian surge in the over-all team competition in the Games.

The Soviets trailed by only 20 points at the start of to-

Turn to Page 5, Column 2

WATER POLO FRACAS

## Fists Fly, Blood Flows in Hungary-Russ Tilt

MELBOURNE, Dec. 6 (AP) Fists flew and blood flowed in the tension-packed Olympic pool today as a crowd of 5500 cheered undefeated Hungary to a 4-0 win over the lustily-booed Russian team in the final round of water polo.

Fighting occurred all the way through the match. Near the end of the game, Hungary's Ervin Zador left the pool with blood streaming down his face from a cut over the right eye where Russia's Valentine Prokopov had butted him.

"The final whistle has blown in this match," concerned officials announced as Zador was helped from the pool and furious Hungarians lined the pool's edge shaking their fists at the Russians gathered in a protective knot at one end.

Only the Olympic officials applauded the Russians as they climbed from the pool and marched to the dressing room through a torrent of booing from the spectators.

It was a pro-Hungarian crowd from the moment the two teams were introduced. The Russians drew a light spatter of applause but the crowd, heavily sprinkled with tight - lipped Hungarians, roared its acclaim as each member of the Hungarian team was introduced.

The game was only one minute old when Russia's Peter Mchvenieradze put a hammerlock on a Hungarian and was sent to the penalty box as the crowd showered him with catcalls.

**Thunderous Cheers**

The boos turned to thunderous cheers when Dezso Gymati of Hungary flailed his way in front of the Russian goal, caught a Russian's chin with his windup, and hurled Hungary into a 1-0 lead.

Hungary's heroes didn't get away with everything, either. Viapcheslav Kourennoi was sent off for slugging a Russian and again the crowd went wild as the short-handed Hungarians held off the Russian attack.

Russia's Boris Markarov delivered a haymaker to the right eye of Hungary's Antol Bolvari as the second half started and a free-for-all was developing until the referee's shrill whistle broke it off. Markarov was penalized and a minute later Zador scored for a 3-0 Hungarian lead.

Bolvari put it away with a fourth Hungarian goal—and they forgot all about playing water polo and went at it hammer and tongs, both above and below the water line.

## TODAY IN SPORTS

**QUARTER HORSE RACING**—Los Alamitos, 1 p.m.

**BOXING** — Olympic Auditorium, 8:30 p.m.

**WRESTLING**—South Gate Arena, 8:30 p.m.

CLOSE FINISH — Nine horses rush to wire in photo fnish at Los Alamitos with Little Raffles Joe winning.
Story on Page 4, Part IV
Official photos by Photochart

# PAT M'CORMICK SCORES DIVING DOUBLE

Los Angeles Times
Sports

CC★ SATURDAY MORNING, DECEMBER 8, 1956 Part II

## Tartars Favored in Jr. Rose Bowl

RIVAL QUARTERBACKS—Bob Hivner, above, will be at Compton helm and Bob Manning at Arlington QB today when teams collide in the Junior Rose Bowl game.

Times photos

## FINAL DIVES 'MY BEST AND MY LAST,' SAYS PAT

MELBOURNE, (Saturday) Dec. 8 (UP)—"They were my best—and my last."

With those words Mrs. Pat McCormick of Lakewood, Cal., summed up her unprecedented Olympic "diving double" and revealed today that she has decided to retire at the ripe old age of 26.

"I knew I had to do those last two dives (the two-and-a-half somersault and the one-and-a-half somersault with full twist) better than I ever did before," Mrs. McCormick said. "And, I guess I did."

"They were good ones," said the 5-foot 4-inch 128-pound mermaid. "And they also were my last competitive dives—forever."

## LAAC Star Wins 4th Gold Medal

BY PAUL ZIMMERMAN
Times Sports Editor

MELBOURNE, Australia, Dec. 8 (Saturday) — Patricia McCormick was being hailed today as the first woman ever to win four gold medals in Olympic Games swimming competition.

The Long Beach mother of a nine-months-old baby boy, pretty Patricia won it the hard way. She was fourth in qualifying and with only two dives left the Los Angeles Athletic Club star came through with amazing performances under the stress of bad international judging.

Her accomplishment today was the winning of the platform championship, which she added to her springboard title here and two victories in Helsinki four years ago. It was a clean sweep for Southern California as Juno Irwin, a Glendale mother of three, finished second and Paula Jean Myers of Glendora won the third-place medal.

**Final Competition**

This tremendous achievement marked the final competition for both Pat and Juno, but Miss Myers plans to continue her drive for a gold medal at Rome when the Olympics are held there in 1960.

The victory gave the Americans their fifth triumph in aquatic events, which were dominated by the Australian entrants.

The big Russian point total in gymnastics gave the Soviet Union the unofficial team championship by every means of computation. America won 32 gold medals to 37 for Russia, including the cheap victories in the gymnastics.

The Russians won in spite of serious International Olympic Committee consideration. However, the total will remain unchanged. No question about that. Nevertheless, the protest that Karl Michaels, coach of the men's diving team, over prejudiced decisions Thursday night in the men's competition, when Californians Gary Tobian and Dick Connors were jobbed out of first and second places, resulted in a changed situation that gave Pat McCormick the points to which she was entitled.

**Remarkable Windup**

Both of Pat's last dives were remarkable and earned her 18.17, which gave her a winning total of 84.85. Asked what her coach and husband said to her prior to last night's victorious performance, Pat said, "He told me I'd have to hit the last two better than ever before."

That's exactly what she did and then hurriedly asked if there was any place where she could make a call to her mother with the charges reversed, of course.

Juno turned in her greatest performance in winning second and proving that this is one event where mothers excel. She referred all questions of her proficiency to Coach Bud Lyndon of the Pasadena Athletic Club.

Paula Jean was leading going into the finals, but typical Russian and Hungarian downgrading clipped her.

Turn to Page 2, Column 4

SEEING DOUBLE—Pat McCormick of Los Angeles Athletic Club holds two gold medals won in springboard and platform diving in Olympic Games. Pat won some two championships four years ago in Helsinki.

AP Wirephoto via radio from Melbourne

## SPORTSCRIPTS

By PAUL ZIMMERMAN TIMES SPORTS EDITOR

MELBOURNE, Dec. 7 — Australians are a proud people and they can't help but exude enthusiasm over the successful manner in which they staged the XVI Olympiad and in their record outpouring of crowds. There can be little question that more people witnessed the events here than ever attended the Games before. before.

What the Melbourne folks are most proud of in their Games building program is the swim stadium that cost close to a million dollars. It probably is more than a coincidence that Australia came up with its finest set of men and women swimmers in years as a compliment to the structure.

**LARGER SEATING CAPACITY NEEDED**

The only real drawback to this spectacular concrete, steel and plate-glass natatorium seems to be that it doesn't hold enough. It seats 5500 and even with the swimming program televised, seats were selling for as much as £12 a night. The prices ranged from $2 to $6 a seat, so the expensive seats were being scalped for an $18 profit.

The building is the most modern of its kind in the world. It has no obscuring pillars. Both ends are glassed from the roof to the ground. The steel suspended roof beams are anchored outside by steel cables that hold up the top.

Sound-absorbent material has been placed in the ceiling and it is needed when an Australian star steps to the starting position for a race. The lighting is most modern and effective. An air-conditioning unit keeps the crowd and pool air temperatures even, but our divers report it is chilly upon the high platform.

The water temperature is maintained at close to 74 deg.

**PROVEN BY WIND-TUNNEL TESTS**

Basically, the structure consists of two main components—the stands and the roof. Wind-tunnel tests were carried out on a scale model to insure that the building was structurally sound against the stiff winds and suctions common to the area along the Yarra River where it is located.

Choice of the plan was made after a nationwide competition. The selected design was drawn up by four young Melbourne architects in co-operation with a construction engineer.

The walls outside the stadium are covered with multi-colored impressionistic ceramic murals 30 feet high in glazed terra cotta. Various figures of men and women have been worked into the pattern to symbolize the aquatic-sports theme as well as that of the Olympics.

**ONE ERROR IN STRUCTURAL PLAN**

There was only one error in the structural plan. After the place was erected it was discovered that not enough room was allowed above the high platform so that the performers could safely make their leaps without bumping against the roof.

What they had to do was dig the diving pool deeper and lower the water level three feet. The result of this was that many of those in the lower range of seats in the stadium cannot see the divers at their point of entry into the water.

**P.S.:** As experts know, the water entry is one of the most important judging points in the diving contests.

## Compton JC, Arlington St. Clash Today

BY DON SNYDER

Compton, the Oklahoma of JC football, reaches out for a second successive perfect season today when the nigh invincible Tartars play the Texas Rebels of Arlington State in the 11th Junior Rose Bowl game.

The crowd will be 50,000 and upward, the weather crisp and clear, the kickoff 1:30 p.m.

Now on a streak of 35 games without a loss, Compton is a popular 14-point pick to roust the Rebels, make it No. 36 and move a notch closer to the all-time JC undefeated string of 38 straight which the Broncs of Boise, Ida., put together some seasons ago.

**Quiet Coaches**

The opposing coaches have been unusually mum this time around.

Neither Tay Brown of the Tartar horde nor Claude Gilstrap of Arlington has offered a predicted score. But L. B. Chapman of the All-American Gridiron Index forecasts a Compton triumph by 26-13. This press rower sees a 26-20 Tartar victory.

Brown and his "best-balanced Compton team in history" mopped up on nine opponents and squeaked by another to collect the marbles 10 times this year.

Arlington's record has a couple of smudges. A tie and a defeat appeared along the way as the Pioneer Conference cochampions survived a

Turn to Page 5, Column 5

## HOW THEY LINE UP

KICKOFF AT 1:30 P.M.

| ARLINGTON STATE | | | | | COMPTON | |
|---|---|---|---|---|---|---|
| No. | Name | Wt. | Pos. | Wt. | Name | No. |
| 91 | Beasley | 190 | LER | 190 | Peasley | 88 |
| 79 | Butler | 215 | LTR | 220 | Burnett | 70 |
| 60 | Denney | 200 | LGR | 175 | E. McNeil | 68 |
| 55 | Nichols | 190 | C | 215 | D. Ane | 64 |
| 69 | Griffin | 205 | RGL | 230 | G. Ane | 65 |
| 93 | Lawler | 240 | RTL | 245 | Parrish | 79 |
| 84 | Rowland | 168 | REL | 210 | Thomas | 85 |
| 9 | Manning | 185 | Q | 170 | Hivner | 11 |
| 15 | Lee | 147 | LHR | 175 | C. McNeil | 21 |
| 34 | Yates | 147 | RHL | 165 | Cato | 41 |
| 33 | Foltyn | 168 | F | 180 | Beardman | 33 |

201—Average Weight Line—212
162—Average Weight Backs—172
187—Average Weight Team—192

**ARLINGTON STATE ROSTER**

| | | |
|---|---|---|
| 5 Darland, q | 51 Hill, c | 76 Baker, t |
| 6 Rose, q | 53 Uland, e | 78 Bielss, t |
| 7 Veach, e | 55 Nichols, c | 79 Butler, t |
| 8 Schnable, q-f | 60 Denney, g | 82 Hicks, e |
| 9 Manning, q | 65 Ingle, g | 84 Rowland, e |
| 13 Hanson, h | 66 Hays, g | 86 Bassett, e |
| 15 Lee, h | 67 McKinney, g | 87 Webster, e |
| 18 Edwards, f | 68 Welch, g-c | 89 Smith, e |
| 32 Hyden, h | 69 Griffin, g | 91 Beasley, e |
| 33 Foltyn, f | 70 Barron, c-t | 93 Lawler, t |
| 34 Yates, h | 74 Looper, t | |
| 46 Spencer, h | 75 Pevey, t | |

**COMPTON ROSTER**

| | | |
|---|---|---|
| 10 Galitz, q | 43 Silva, h | 75 Marks, t |
| 11 Hivner, q | 51 Whitby, e | 76 Verrecchia, t |
| 12 Davidson, q | 53 Cano, c | 77 Paine, t |
| 20 Hall, h | 54 Crawford, c | 78 Lasiter, t |
| 21 C. McNeil, h | 61 L. Baird, g | 79 Parrish, t |
| 22 Williams, h | 62 C. Baird | 80 Sullivan, e |
| 23 George, h | 64 D. Ane, c | 81 Bridgewater, e |
| 24 Saratore, f | 65 G. Ane, g | 82 Kunze, e |
| 30 Black, f | 66 Chavez, g | 83 Reed, e |
| 33 Beardman, f | 67 Albinger, g | 84 Butt, e |
| 34 Samera, h | 68 E. McNeil | 85 Thomas, e |
| 40 Wagerle, h | 70 Burnett, t | 86 Keawe, e |
| 41 Cato, h | 72 Harper, t | 87 Jennings, e |
| 42 Vinson, f | 73 Nesbitt, t | 88 Peasley, e |

## SPORTS TODAY ON RADIO, TV

**FOOTBALL** — Miami vs. Pittsburgh, KRCA (4), 11:15 a.m. Junior Rose Bowl Game, Radio KNX, 1:15 p.m. Packers vs. 49ers, KNXT (2), 1:30 p.m.

**HORSE RACING**— Quarter horse feature race from Los Alamitos, KTLA (5), 4 p.m.

**BOXING** — Hollywood Legion Stadium, 8:30 p.m.

**BASKETBALL** — SC vs. Wyoming, Radio KNX, 8:30 p.m.

## TODAY IN SPORTS

**QUARTER-HORSE RACING** — Los Alamitos, 12:30 p.m.

**JR. ROSE BOWL**—Compton vs. Arlington State, Rose Bowl, 1:30 p.m.

**BOXING** — Hollywood Legion Stadium, 8:30 p.m.

**BASKETBALL** — SC vs. Wyoming, Pan-Pacific Auditorium, 8:30 p.m. Regis College at Loyola U. gym, 8:30 p.m.

## 45 Hungarians Stay Behind

MELBOURNE, Australia, Dec. 8 (Saturday) (P)—Forty-five Hungarians who came to Australia for the Olympic Games chose freedom and stayed here today when their teammates headed for home. More may defect en route to Budapest.

Of the 175 athletes, coaches and managers from Hungary, only 130 are going back. The others elected to seek political asylum rather than return to their revolt-torn homeland under armed Soviet domination.

Among those staying here are some of Hungary's most noted athletes and the assistant chief of the Hungarian Olympic committee.

One who stayed behind said the two chartered French planes taking the Hungarian team back to Europe will stop at Milan, Italy, before they fly to Budapest, and it is likely that 20 more would drop off there.

Most going back to Hungary, he said, are doing so because they have wives and children at home—not be-

Turn to Page 2, Column 2

## Witte Selected on AP All-America

NEW YORK, Dec. 7 (AP)—A massive, mobile line which averages 226 pounds per man and backfield repeater Tommy McDonald of Oklahoma are features of the 1956 Associated Press All-America football team.

McDonald is joined on the squad by another representative from the National Championship Sooners—Center Jerry Tubbs.

The remainder of the backfield is composed of brilliant Tailback Johnny Majors, who led Tennessee to a perfect season; versatile Jimmy Brown of Syracuse and Fullback Don Bosseler of Miami, rated on a par with Doc Blanchard by Coach Andy Gustafson who worked with both.

The ends are Ron Kramer of Michigan (216 pounds) and Joe Walton of Pitt (201). Alex Karras of Iowa (235) and John Witte of Oregon State (232) are at tackles with Bill Glass of Baylor (230) and Jim Parker of Ohio State (262) filling the guard slots.

Tubbs weighs in at a trim 206.

The team was selected on the basis of recommendations from regional boards complete through all games of Dec. 1.

Because it was considered unfair to players who gave a full measure in every game, some fine talent was excluded from the first three teams.

**Hornung on Second Team**

Southern California Halfback Jon Arnett was limited to five games as part of the Pacific Coast Conference crackdown while Michigan State's Clarence Peaks was cut down by a midseason knee injury.

Paul Hornung, bonus pick in the National Football League, is in the second backfield with Iowa's Kenny Ploen, John Crow of the Texas Aggies and Bill Barnes of Wake Forest.

## AP ALL-AMERICA

NEW YORK, Dec. 7 (AP)—The 1956 All-America football teams selected by the Associated Press:

**FIRST TEAM**

| Pos. | Player | School | Class | Age | Wgt. | Hgt. |
|---|---|---|---|---|---|---|
| End | Joseph Walton | Pittsburgh | Sr. | 20 | 201 | 5'11" |
| End | Ronald Kramer | Michigan | Sr. | 21 | 216 | 6'3" |
| Tackle | Alex Karras | Iowa | Jr. | 21 | 235 | 6'2" |
| **Tackle** | **John Witte** | **Oregon State** | **Sr.** | **23** | **232** | **6'2"** |
| Guard | William Glass | Baylor | Sr. | 21 | 230 | 6'5" |
| Guard | James Parker | Ohio St. | Sr. | 21 | 262 | 6'3" |
| Center | Jerry Tubbs | Oklahoma | Sr. | 21 | 206 | 6'2" |
| Back | Tommy McDonald | Okla. | Sr. | 22 | 170 | 5'9" |
| Back | John Majors | Tennessee | Sr. | 21 | 162 | 5'10" |
| Back | James Brown | Syracuse | Sr. | 20 | 212 | 6'2" |
| Back | Donald Bosseler | Miami | Sr. | 21 | 205 | 6'1" |

| SECOND TEAM | THIRD TEAM |
|---|---|
| E—Walter Brodie, W'm & Mary | E—Kyle (Buddy) Kruze, Tenn. |
| **E—William Steiger, Wash. State** | E—Paul Lopata, Yale |
| **T—Paul Wiggin, Stanford** | T—Robert Hobert, Minnesota |
| T—Lou Michaels, Kentucky | T—Charles Krueger, Tex. A&M |
| **G—Esker Harris, UCLA** | G—John Barrow, Florida |
| G—Sam Valentine, Penn State | **G—Dick Day, Washington** |
| C—Donald Stephenson, Ga. Tech | C—John Matsko, Michigan St. |
| B—Kenneth Ploen, Iowa | **B—John Brodie, Stanford** |
| B—Paul Hornung, Notre Dame | B—James Swink, Tex. Christian |
| B—John Crow, Texas A&M | B—James Crawford, Wyoming |
| B—William Barnes, Wake For'st | B—Mel Dillard, Purdue |

**HONORABLE MENTION**
**(Pacific Coast Players)**

ENDS—Phil McHugh, Oregon; Ron Wheatcroft, California; Hal Smith, UCLA; Carl Isaacs, Stanford.

TACKLES—George Stugar, Washington; Dan Jesmer, Oregon State; John Nisby, College of Pacific.

GUARDS—Whitey Core, Washington; Don Gilkey, California; John Sniffen and Jim Brackins, Oregon State; Galen Laack, College of Pacific; Donn Carswell, Stanford.

CENTERS—Jim Matheny, UCLA; Karl Rubke, SC.

BACKS—Jon Arnett and C. R. Roberts, SC; Earnel Durden, Joe Francis and Tom Berry, Oregon State; Dean Derby, Washington; Bob Newman, Washington State; Jim Shanley, Oregon; Paul Camera and Lou Valli, Stanford; Art Powell, San Jose State; Barry Billington, UCLA.

# BASILIO WINS TITLE ON SPLIT DECISION

Los Angeles Times Sports

CC ** TUESDAY MORNING, SEPTEMBER 24, 1957 Part IV

## SPORTS PARADE

By BRAVEN DYER

The trials and tribulations of being a varsity football coach were brought home rather forcibly to three young men over the week end when Don Clark, Pete Elliott and Jim Owens failed to come up with a winner.

These gentlemen were lately installed as ringmasters at SC, California and Washington. Owens escaped with a tie while indulging in what was supposed to be a warmup with Colorado. But Clark and Elliott got the business from Oregon State and SMU.

One chap who came out unscathed, as usual, was Bud Wilkinson. George Dickson, chief Hawkshaw for the Trojans, sat in as Bud's Oklahoma Terrors trampled the Pitt Panthers. Says George:

"As you know, I've seen a few pretty good football teams. (The man has spied for ND and other teams over a period of years.) But I never saw a club on opening day with as much poise and in such condition as Oklahoma. (Ala Oregon State, Mr. Dickson, I'd say.)

"Oklahoma was in complete command all the way. Bud uses his first unit for seven minutes and then the second for eight minutes, and you don't see any difference. He has at least 22 very fine football players and in some respects they are more outstanding defensively than offensively.

**KRISHER TABBED TERRIFIC GUARD**

"A boy named Bill Krisher is a terrific guard. You'll hear a lot about him. Oklahoma's race-horse football electrified the Pitt crowd even though their team was taking a beating. The Sooners didn't pass much and they completed just four . . . but three were for touchdowns. I can't see how they'll lose a game this year.

"Pitt? Well, it's difficult to get enthused about a team which never was in the ball game, but I know one thing . . . Pitt will get better. They are very strong physically and they're bigger than we are. They lacked Oklahoma's experience and cohesion, so it wasn't easy for them to look good. I doubt if many clubs will look good against Bud's gang."

Pitt, as you may know, comes here next week to play SC.

**LEAVES NOTHING TO CHANCE**

Young Don Clark is leaving nothing to chance as he tries to build a winning football team at ol' SC.

The Trojan coach sprang quite a surprise on his players when they boarded the plane for their flight to Portland last week.

Each boy was handed a mimeographed document, 13 pages of single-spaced copy, dealing entirely with the Oregon State football team.

Included in the document were diagrams for 62 Oregon State plays! Of course, the Beavers don't actually have that many separate plays, but the analysis featured that many diagrams because of the variations which result from a right or left formation preceding the actual running of the play.

**PLAYERS LIKE IDEA**

The players had no idea the communique was coming up. They think it's the greatest. Never in my long association with football have I seen such a complete presentation of the problem confronting an athletic army on the eve of battle.

There were all manner of tips on the Beavers, both as a team and relating to the personal gridiron habits of individual players.

"The Beavers," said the prospectus, "will force you to go the hard way offensively and almost defy you to do so. They allow you short yardage with the belief that you will make a mistake. We have to be able to go the hard way without any mistakes. This Oregon State team can be beaten but only with your most aggressive physical efforts and complete mental concentration on your own responsibilities."

**INFORMATION BROKEN DOWN**

Information was broken down into special categories, such as "Offensive habits of Oregon State players," and "Types of blocks to watch for" and "Goal-line offense."

It took hours merely to put all the diagrams on paper, and the over-all information was the result of years of intensive study of the single-wing formation as employed by Red Sanders and those who came under his coaching spell, notably, of course, Tommy Prothro.

Well, you say, this wrinkle didn't help much, inasmuch as SC lost, 20-0. There were 14 Trojans playing their first minute of varsity ball against the experienced Beavers and the SC coaching staff had no cause to be ashamed of the way the boys conducted themselves. The prospectus helped to wise them up. So did the Beavers.

## Pirates Rehire Murtaugh

PITTSBURGH, Sept. 23 (UP)—Danny Murtaugh, a wise-cracking Irishman with a lot of baseball know-how, today was named manager of the Pittsburgh Pirates for 1958.

Murtaugh, who moved into the managerial job with the sudden dismissal of Bobby Bragan on Aug. 3 in Chicago, has fused the Pirates to a respectable .500 class, winnnig 24 and losing a like number since he replaced Bragan.

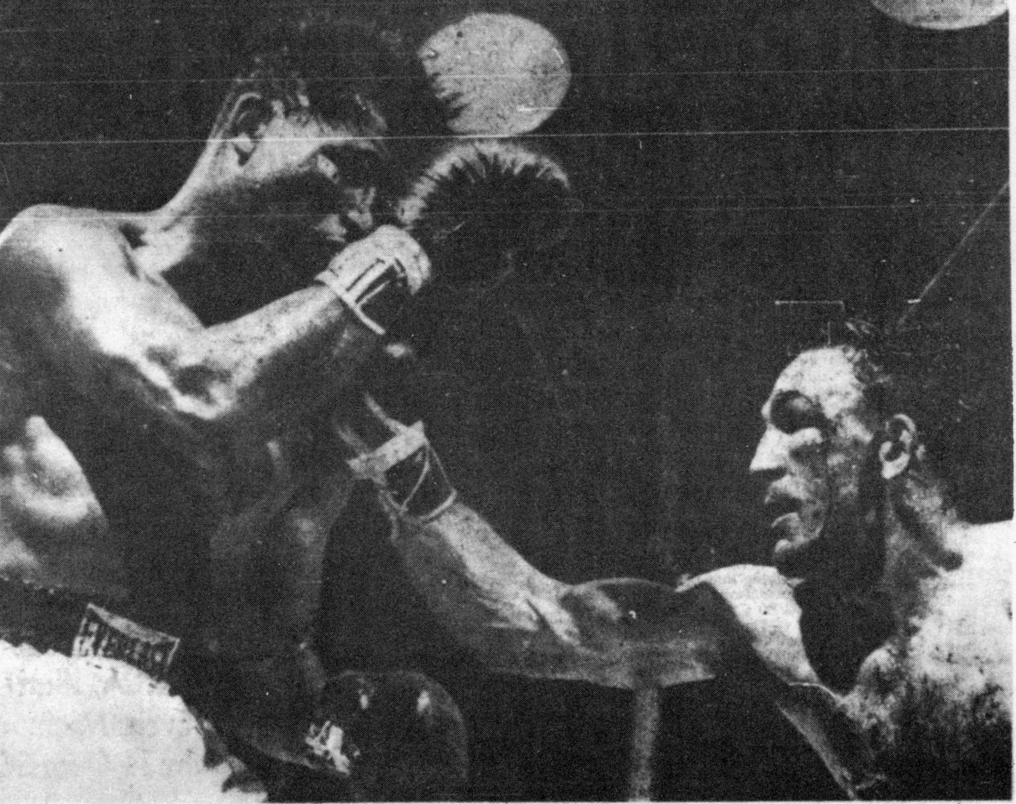

SUGAR DRAWS FIRST BLOOD—Challenger Carmen Basilio, bleeding from a cut over his right eye, tags Sugar Ray Robinson with a right to the jaw in the fourth round en route to winning a split decision and, with it, the middleweight championship of the world. AP Wirephoto

## Referee Votes for Sugar Ray

BY FRANK FINCH
Times Staff Representative

YANKEE STADIUM, Sept. 23—A grotesque, gory gargoyle at the finish, courageous Carmen Basilio had his hand raised over Ray Robinson tonight to become the world's middleweight champion.

The welterweight king, spotting aging Sugar Ray 6½ pounds and a long pull in height and reach, won a split 15-round decision that stunned many ringsiders but left plenty of experts satisfied with the verdict.

The crowd of approximately 38,000 paid an estimated $560,000 to see the fight.

The only ring official who thought Robinson had retained his 160-pound crown was Referee Al Berl. He gave Sugar Ray nine rounds, the challenger six.

But judges Artie Aidala and Bill Recht voted for the gutty Basilio by counts of 9-5 and 8-6-1, respectively.

**Vote for Sugar**

Your correspondent didn't think it was even close. He gave Robinson a 9-4-2 edge in rounds, and under the California 10-point must scoring system we had him by a decisive 145-127 margin.

A former heavyweight champion who once defended his title in this very arena against Billy Conn at $100 top for ringside seats, Joe Louis, saw the fight like we did. He called it 9-5-1 for Robinson.

But it was the kind of a scrap that is tough to judge, a hammer-and-tongs affair in which fists flew so furiously at times that it was impossible to record them on paper or brain tissue.

**Second in History**

Basilio became the second welterweight champion in history to also win the 160-pound belt. The only other one to achieve that feat was a fellow named Ray Robinson, who kayoed Jake LaMotta in 13 rounds in 1951.

The contract for this fight calls for a return match in 90 days. If it is made, and Robinson wins, it will mark the fifth time that he has been ruler of the middleweight division.

But the sleek Harlem

Turn to Page 3, Column 3

# Braves Win Flag, Edge Cards, 4-2

## NEW PROTEST OF BUMS HITS SNAG

### Holland Says Grading of Chavez Ravine Would Be Detrimental to Police Academy

BY PAUL ZIMMERMAN

The studied effort of Councilman John Holland to throw a monkey wrench into the moving of the Brooklyn Dodgers to Los Angeles failed again at the City Hall yesterday.

Holland called a special meeting of the Council as a member of the Police and Fire Committee to protest that the grading of Chavez Ravine, proposed Dodger Stadium site, would be a detriment to the Police Academy now located in the general area.

In the absence of a Council quorum because of a meeting of City Councilmen in Northern California, the matter was discussed by two other members of the Police and Fire Committee, Rosalind Wyman and James Corman.

In the end the vote was 2 to 1 that "no evidence presented at the hearing indicated that any of the facilities of the Police Academy would be injured."

This came after Negotiator Harold C. McClellan, whom the city appointed to deal with Dodger President Walter O'Malley, and Samuel Leask Jr., chief city administrative officer, stated that Holland was mistaken.

**No Trouble Seen**

Whereas Holland said there would be a 50-foot fill near the academy site, they said the facts are that there would be a 50-foot cut and that it could not possibly affect the facilities.

Nevertheless, Councilman Holland said he would again seek to get a quorum today for further discussion. This seemed unlikely.

Holland, who has opposed the sale of Chavez Ravine to the Dodgers all the way, sought unsuccessfully last week to get the Council to renege on its early action favoring the negotiations with Brooklyn.

In this connection, Councilwoman Wyman, who is chairman of the City Parks and Recreation Committee,

Turn to Page 2, Column 3

## Idle Yankees Win Flag as White Sox Bow

KANSAS CITY, Mo., Sept. 23 (UP) — The Chicago White Sox were beaten, 6-5, by the Kansas City Athletics tonight to give the New York Yankees the American League pennant.

The Yankees were idle; with five games remaining they lead the Sox by six and one-half games.

Arnold Portocarrero took

Turn to Page 5, Column 3

## STANDINGS

**NATIONAL LEAGUE**

| | W | L | Pct. | * |
|---|---|---|---|---|
| **Milwaukee | 92 | 57 | .617 | |
| St. Louis | 86 | 63 | .577 | 6 |
| Brooklyn | 82 | 68 | .547 | 10½ |
| Cincinnati | 77 | 71 | .520 | 14½ |
| Philadelphia | 74 | 76 | .493 | 18½ |
| New York | 69 | 82 | .457 | 24 |
| Pittsburgh | 60 | 91 | .397 | 33 |
| Chicago | 58 | 90 | .392 | 33½ |

*Games behind leader.
**Clinches pennant.

**Last Night's Results**

Milwaukee, 4; St. Louis, 2 (11 innings).
Only game scheduled.

**Games Today**

St. Louis (Jones, 12-8) at Milwaukee (Spahn, 20-10), night.
New York (Antonelli, 12-17) at Philadelphia (Simmons, 11-11), night.
Chicago (Mayer, 0-0, and Kaiser, 2-5, or Hillman, 5-11) at Cincinnati (Podbielan, 0-1, or Jeffcoat, 11-13), twi-night double-header.
Pittsburgh (R. Smith, 2-4) at Brooklyn (McDevitt, 6-4), night.

**AMERICAN LEAGUE**

| | W | L | Pct. | * |
|---|---|---|---|---|
| **New York | 93 | 54 | .638 | |
| Chicago | 88 | 60 | .595 | 6½ |
| Boston | 79 | 70 | .530 | 16 |
| Detroit | 75 | 74 | .503 | 20 |
| Baltimore | 72 | 75 | .490 | 22 |
| Cleveland | 72 | 76 | .486 | 22½ |
| Kansas City | 57 | 90 | .388 | 37 |
| Washington | 55 | 94 | .369 | 40 |

*Games behind leader.
**Clinches pennant.

**Last Night's Results**

Cleveland, 5; Detroit, 4 (11 innings).
Kansas City, 6; Chicago, 5.
Boston, 9; Washington, 4.
Only games scheduled.

**Games Today**

Chicago (Fischer, 7-7) at Kansas City (Brunet, 0-1).
Boston (Sullivan, 13-11) at Washington (Ramos, 12-16), night.
Only games scheduled.

## Aaron Belts Home Run in 11th Inning

MILWAUKEE, Wis., Sept. 23 (UP) — The Milwaukee Braves wiped out five years of frustration tonight by bringing the National League pennant to this city for the first time in history when Hank Aaron hammered a two-run homer in the 11th inning to defeat the St. Louis Cardinals, 4-2.

Milwaukee now will meet the New York Yankees in Yankee Stadium Wednesday, Oct. 2, in the World Series.

Aaron's game-winning wallop, his 43rd home run of the season, traveled 405 feet over the center field fence and drove in Johnny Logan, who had singled. The blow was struck off Billy Muffett who relieved Larry Jackson in the ninth inning.

**Seventh in Row**

The victory was the Braves' seventh straight and it gave them a six-game lead over the Cardinals with only five more games remaining to play.

Oddly, for a city which has seen the Braves finish second three times and third once since they transferred their franchise from Boston in March, 1953, Milwaukee accepted the victory in fairly solemn fashion, although part of the 40,926 fans hurdled the gates after Aaron's

Turn to Page 3, Column 1

## TODAY IN SPORTS

**HORSE RACING** — Los Angeles County Fair, Pomona, 12:30 p.m.

**RODEO** — L.A. County Fair, Pomona, 8 p.m.

## PARI-MUTUEL GUILD STRIKES TODAY; TANFORAN CLOSES

SAN BRUNO, Sept. 23 (UP)—The Pari-Mutuel Employees Guild definitely will go on strike at Tanforan race track tomorrow, it was announced today, when eleventh-hour negotiations between the union and track owners collapsed.

No new date for resumption of negotiations was set and Nicholas Daddario, guild president, said he would not be available for further parley until Friday "because of a court appointment."

The track did not take any entries for tomorrow which means that racing at the historic oval is off until there is a settlement.

The union is seeking a 7% wage increase.

The guild leader said he would go to Los Angeles tomorrow to ask the Los Angeles Central Labor Council for strike sanction against Hollywood Park and Santa Anita. The western harness meeting is scheduled to begin at Hollywood Park Oct. 3.

Other stories on Page 5, Part IV

## Robinson Says He Has No Squawks, Doesn't Know if He'll Fight Again

NEW YORK, Sept. 23 (AP)—A bitter and battered Sugar Ray Robinson, stripped of his middleweight championship he had won on four different occasions, said tonight he had no squawks about the split decision in favor of Carmen Basilio.

But he added dejectedly:

"I don't know whether I'll ever fight again. There are things about boxing I don't like. There is too much intrigue.

"I had to battle for everything I got in this fight. I'll decide in a few days whether I'll fight Basilio again."

**Barking Handlers**

As Robinson, his skin shining like polished copper under the glistening lights, talked in a quiet, smooth voice, his handlers barked above the crowd of newsmen.

"It was a steal," yelled Harold (Killer) Johnson, handler and onetime manager of the dethroned middleweight champion. "Those judges and the referee must have been watching another fight. Sugar Ray won easily."

Sugar Ray was asked if he thought he won.

"There were two judges and a referee," he said calmly. "I abide by their decision. I have no squawks."

**'Not Toughest'**

Robinson refused to say that Basilio, the plucky little welterweight champion, was the toughest man he ever fought.

"With all due credit to Carmen, who is a great champion, I don't think he is," Robinson said. "They don't come any tougher than Jake LaMotta and I think Randy Turpin had me in much worse shape before I knocked him out in our second fight."

The ex-middleweight champion, swathed in towels and suffering apparently only from exhaustion, said he thought he had Basilio in trouble several times but couldn't put over the decider.

"He's a real pro, that little guy," Robinson said. "Every time I set him up for what I thought might be a knockout he was smart enough to get out of it.

**'Didn't Hurt Me'**

"He never really hurt me. I always knew what I was doing. He hit me a couple of real good licks, but I never thought he had me in bad shape."

Robinson said he went into the 15th round thinking he was well ahead on points.

"I was sure I had it at that time," he added, "but that shows you can't ever tell."

## CARDS OF OFFICIALS

| | | | | | | | | | | | | | | | | B | R | E |
|---|---|---|---|---|---|---|---|---|---|---|---|---|---|---|---|---|---|---|
| Referee Berle | R | R | B | R | R | R | R | B | B | B | B | R | R | R | B | 6 | 9 | 0 |
| Judge Recht | R | E | B | R | B | R | R | R | B | B | B | R | R | R | B | 8 | 6 | 1 |
| Judge Aidala | R | E | B | R | B | R | R | B | B | B | B | R | B | R | B | 9 | 5 | 1 |
| Associated Press | R | R | B | R | B | R | B | E | B | B | B | R | E | R | E | 6 | 6 | 3 |

# Sanders Hurls Blackmail Charge at Hearing

BY AL WOLF

UCLA Football Coach Red Sanders hurled a charge of blackmail yesterday while testifying here before an Assembly committee that began a three-day hearing on intercollegiate athletics.

Under questioning by Francis Ruggieri, committee attorney, Sanders said:

"We went to the last (Pacific Coast) conference meeting hopeful of being allowed to play our seniors this season, at least in half the games as was the case in 1956. But another coach told me before the sessions ever started that his school would have to vote against the seniors or have support of the round-robin schedule withdrawn.

"I regard that as plain blackmail."

Sanders did not identify the coach or the school assertedly applying behind-the-scenes pressure.

Asked by Chairman Frank Bonelli if UCLA could continue in intercollegiate athletics without PCC membership, Sanders heatedly replied:

"I don't see how the conference itself can continue as things are now. We have existed the past couple of years in a climate of jealousy, intrigue and venom. The PCC must abolish its archaic code or abandon football."

Other highlights of Sanders' testimony:

Bonelli: "Did you hear it said that the fines and sanctions against UCLA would have been lifted if you had been removed?"

Sanders: "Yes, but just as hearsay."

Ruggieri: "Do you have doubts that there were infractions of the rules at UCLA?"

Sanders: "I have never authorized or approved violations of the rules at UCLA."

Harold Levering: "I represent the UCLA area and know my people are very indignant. They feel that it's a case where, if you can't beat the team on the field, you take away the players."

Sanders: "I know of no more effective way to get at a coach."

Ruggiari: "How do you feel about the system of fines and the suspension of seniors?"

Sanders: "The system of fines is not workable or helpful. I can't summon up the words to say how displeased I am over the matter of the seniors."

Charles Wilson: "Was that 72-0 beating UCLA gave Stanford in 1954 the real

Turn to Page 3, Column 1

# IRISH STUN OKLA., 7-0, END STRING AT 47

NORMAN, Okla., Nov. 16 (UP) — Oklahoma's all-time record of 47 straight football victories was shattered today by an underdog Notre Dame that marched 80 yards on the ground in the closing minutes for the all-important touchdown and a 7-0 triumph.

Oklahoma, No. 2 ranked in the nation and an 18-point favorite, couldn't move against the rock-wall Notre Dame line and the Sooners saw another of its national records broken — scoring in 123 consecutive games.

The defeat was only the ninth for Oklahoma Coach Bud Wilkinson since he became head coach at Oklahoma in 1947 and virtually ended any chance for the Sooners getting a third straight national championship.

Although the partisan, sell-out crowd of 62,000 came out for a Roman holiday, they were stunned into silence as the Sooners were unable to pull their usual last-quarter winning touchdowns—a Wilkinson team trade-mark.

As the game ended when Oklahoma's desperation passing drive was cut off by an intercepted aerial, the crowd rose as one and suddenly gave the Notre Dame team a rousing cheer.

It was a far cry from last year when the Sooners ran over Notre Dame, 40-0. The victory gave the Irish a 3-1 edge in the five-year-old series dating back to 1952.

The smashing, rocking Notre Dame line didn't permit the Sooners to get started either on the ground or in the air.

The Sooners were able to make only 98 yards on the ground and in the air just 47. Notre Dame, paced by its brilliant, 210-pound fullback, Nick Pietrosante, rolled up 169. In the air, the Irish gained 79 yards, hitting 9 of 20 passes, with Bob Williams doing most of the passing.

Notre Dame's lone touchdown drive, biting off short but consistent yardage against the Sooners' alternate team, carried from the 20 after an Oklahoma punt went into the end zone.

Time after time, Pietrosante picked up the necessary yardage when needed as the Irish smashed through the Oklahoma line. Notre Dame moved to the 8 and the Sooner first team came in to try to make the third Sooner goal-line stand of the day.

Pietrosante smashed 4 yards through center and Dick Lynch was stopped for no gain. On the third down, Williams went a yard through center.

Then Lynch crossed up the Sooners and rolled around his right end to score standing up. Monty Stickles converted to give Notre Dame the upset and end collegiate football's longest winning streak.

The closest Oklahoma could get to Notre Dame's goal was in the first quarter when the Sooners' alternate team moved to the 13 before being held on downs.

In the third period brilliant punting by first string Halfback Clendon Thomas and alternate Quarterback David Baker kept the Irish back on its

Turn to Page 7, Column 3

# Buckeyes Whip Iowa to Earn Trip West

BY PAUL ZIMMERMAN
Sports Editor

OHIO STADIUM, Columbus, Nov. 17—Man the Pacific Coast Conference football dikes!

Ohio State's devastating running attack rolled over fumbling Iowa here today to assure itself of the Big Ten championship and the Rose Bowl bid. The score was 17 to 13.

Robert White, a 212-pound sophomore third-string fullback and sometimes center from Covington, Ky., was the hero here before a record crowd of 82,935 delirious spectators who tore down the steel-pipe goal posts at the end.

Don Clark, who has been the driving force of the Buckeye attack this fall, sat the game out with a pulled leg tendon. If he is any more effective than White, Michigan's record Rose Bowl score of 49 to 0 will be in jeopardy come January 1.

White carried the ball on seven of the eight plays in that fourth-period winning touchdown drive of 67 yards and scored from the 5 to put Coach Woody Hayes' red-shirted Ohioans in front with less than four minutes to play.

As a matter of fact, he gained all but two of those yards, including a 28-yard run to the 26. White entered the game as a center and it took some arguing with the official statistician to get him to also put the man's name in the line-ups as fullback.

### Gains 157 Yards

This remarkable giant collected 157 yards in 22 runs for an average of better than 7 yards per carry, and then finished out the game as a linebacker and offensive center. No wonder his teammates carried him off the field on their shoulders after

Turn to Page 4, Column 2

## ROSE BOWL RACE

### PACIFIC COAST

| | W. | L. | T. | Pct. | P.F. | Op. |
|---|---|---|---|---|---|---|
| Oregon | 6 | 1 | 0 | .857 | 117 | 71 |
| *Oregon State | 5 | 2 | 0 | .714 | 137 | 103 |
| *UCLA | 4 | 2 | 0 | .667 | 116 | 75 |
| Wash. State | 4 | 3 | 0 | .571 | 119 | 122 |
| *Washington | 3 | 3 | 0 | .500 | 93 | 98 |
| Stanford | 3 | 3 | 0 | .500 | 134 | 99 |
| *SC | 1 | 5 | 0 | .167 | 45 | 108 |
| California | 1 | 5 | 0 | .167 | 85 | 109 |
| *Idaho | 0 | 3 | 0 | .000 | 19 | 50 |

### BIG TEN

| | W. | L | T. | Pct. | P.F. | Op. |
|---|---|---|---|---|---|---|
| Ohio State | 6 | 0 | 0 | 1.000 | 177 | 46 |
| Mich. State | 5 | 1 | 0 | .833 | 184 | 60 |
| *Iowa | 4 | 1 | 1 | .750 | 152 | 72 |
| Michigan | 3 | 2 | 1 | .583 | 131 | 110 |
| Wisconsin | 3 | 3 | 0 | .500 | 115 | 97 |
| Purdue | 3 | 3 | 0 | .500 | 106 | 83 |
| Minnesota | 3 | 4 | 0 | .429 | 149 | 167 |
| Illinois | 2 | 4 | 0 | .333 | 94 | 117 |
| Indiana | 0 | 5 | 0 | .000 | 20 | 218 |
| Northwestern | 0 | 6 | 0 | .000 | 38 | 196 |

*Ineligible for Rose Bowl

# Ducks Clinch Bowl, Beat Trojans, 16-7

## 30,975 See Morris Roll 212 Yards

BY BRAVEN DYER

Oregon's allegiance to the "Jack" Morris plan paid off yesterday as Len Casanova's club won the Rose Bowl bid by defeating Southern California, 16 to 7.

The 25-year-old former Air Force speedster broke all manner of records and Trojan hearts, too, as he rambled for 212 yards to clinch no less than a tie for the PCC crown and the dubious honor of facing Ohio State on New Year's Day.

The balding service veteran who has run the 100 well under 10 flat performed

### HOW THEY SCORED

| Oregon | SC | | Time |
|---|---|---|---|
| | | FIRST QUARTER | |
| 3 | 0 | Morris, 31-yd. field goal. | 3:50 |
| 9 | 0 | Morris, 63-yd. run. | 5:51 |
| 10 | 0 | Morris, conversion. | |
| | | SECOND QUARTER | |
| 16 | 0 | Shanley, 2-yd. run. | 9:02 |
| | | FOURTH QUARTER | |
| 16 | 6 | Buford, 7-yd. run. | 4:28 |
| 16 | 7 | Buford, conversion. | |

as if seeking a fat bonus check from the Los Angeles Rams, who drafted him two years ago. Morris was eligible then because he originally entered Oregon in 1951 before going into the Air Force.

It will be Oregon's first Pasadena game since 1920 when Harvard won, 7-6.

### Strike Quickly

A crowd of 30,975 fans saw the Ducks strike quickly yesterday to build up a 10 point lead in the first six minutes of play and then hold on grimly as the hot and cold Trojans gave 'em fits while scoring the lone touchdown of the second half.

No one man can put a team in the Rose Bowl, but if ever a player deserves such designation it is Oregon's 188-pound senior fullback.

He scored those first 10 points yesterday after previously having won the Idaho, Washington State and Stanford games with his educated toe, 9-6, 14-13 and 27-26.

Morris did everything yesterday but lead one of the 22 high school bands which tootled musically both before and during the game to highlight an otherwise drab and chilly afternoon for loyal SC followers who saw their team defeated for the seventh time in eight starts.

### SC Starts Slow

Many of the fans left the game with mingled feelings because Don Clark's greenies, after a horrible start, came back to outdown their rivals and came within 3 feet of matching Oregon's total yardage for the day.

A fumble on SC's second play set up the opening field goal by Morris and sloppy

Turn to Page 2, Column 4

Los Angeles Times
Sports
CC ★ SUNDAY MORNING, NOVEMBER 17, 1957 Part III

# UCLA Rolls Over Errant COP, 21-0

## Tailbacks Wilson and Kendall Suffer Leg Injuries in Game

BY AL WOLF, Time Staff Representative

STOCKTON, Nov. 16 — UCLA's little football magicians won their seventh game in nine starts here tonight by blanking College of Pacific, 21-0, before 23,000 fans.

But it wasn't easy, despite the decisive appearance of the score. And it may have proved costly, for Tailbacks Kirk Wilson and Chuck Kendall both came off the field with leg injuries. Whether they'll be in shape for SC remains to be seen.

Red Sanders' other tailback, Don Long, didn't play because of a sore shoulder, so Don Duncan wound up in the position.

### Clubs Run Wild

The big, bruising Tigers actually outgained and outdowned the Bruins as both clubs ran wild, but four fumbles and four interceptions helped keep 'em at bay. It was COP's first zero in 20 games—since another UCLA

### HOW THEY SCORED

| UCLA | COP | | Time |
|---|---|---|---|
| | | SECOND QUARTER | |
| 6 | 0 | Mason, 34-yd. run | 0:32 |
| 7 | 0 | Ger'sman, conversion. | |
| 13 | 0 | Wallen, 19-yd. pass from Kendall | 2:35 |
| 14 | 0 | Gertsman, conversion. | |
| | | FOURTH QUARTER | |
| 20 | 0 | Smith, 1-yd. dive | 7:21 |
| 21 | 0 | Duncan, conversion. | |

team turned the trick in 1955.

Pacific netted 200 yards rushing and 174 passing for an aggregate of 374. UCLA ran for 331 yards and passed for 34, thus totaling 365. The Tigers, mind you, rolled up 22 first downs without being able to score. The Bruins made 15.

UCLA, playing alertly, as usual, scored twice within two minutes early in the second quarter and finally buttoned it up with another touchdown midway through the final period.

### Mason Hero

Bill Mason was the Bruins' first hero of the evening, starting and finishing a swift 95-yard advance that produced the first TD. With the ball on the UCLA 5-yard line, he broke through for 47 yards from a fake punt formation. Kendall threw an incomplete pass and then rounded end for 13 to the

Turn to Page 5, Column 1

## READ 'EM AN' WEEP

**Notre Dame, 7; Oklahoma, 0.**
**Rice, 7; Texas A&M, 6.**
**Mississippi, 14; Tennessee, 7.**
**Yale, 20; Princeton, 13.**
**Washington, 35; California, 27.**
**Kansas St. 23; Missouri, 21.**
**Kansas, 13; Okla. St., 7.**

WEBFOOT NO TANGLEFOOT—Jack Morris, hero of Oregon's 16-7 victory over SC yesterday, eludes grasp of Rex Johnston (27) and gets away for 58-yard scamper in first quarter. Troy's Ed Isherwood, left, couldn't nail Morris, who gained 212 yards in game.
Times photo by Art Rogers

# TEXAS A&M UPSET BY RICE, 7 TO 6

HOUSTON, Tex., Nov. 16 (UP)—Rice's Owls combined a mighty defense with the fancy work of two senior quarterbacks, Frank Ryan and King Hill, to upset Texas A&M, the nation's No. 1 team, 7-6, today before a crowd of over 72,000.

The Owls, 7-point underdogs, drove 79 yards in the second period for a touchdown and then stopped three A&M threats inside the 20-yard line before yielding the Aggies a score on the second play of the final period.

The difference in the score was the extra point kicked by Hill. The conversion attempt by Lloyd Taylor, Aggie halfback, was wide.

It was the first defeat for Texas A&M in 15 games and the loss deprived the Aggies of at least immediate claim to the Southwest Conference championship. Rice and Texas now join the Aggies in a showdown race in the final two weeks of the title campaign. The defeat also knocked A&M out of an immediate invitation to be host team at the Cotton Bowl.

Hill scored the Rice touch-

Turn to Page 6, Column 7

# Francis Runs and Passes Beavers to 24-14 Victory Over Stanford

CORVALLIS, Or., Nov. 16 (UP)—Senior Halfback Joe Francis, a running and passing demon, turned in his most brilliant performance today to lead defending Pacific Coast Conference champion Oregon State to a 24-14 football victory over Stanford.

Francis, playing his final home game and cheered on by a crowd of 20,000, ran for two touchdowns and passed for another. The Honolulu Hurricane, who sat out last week because of the flu, also racked up a total of 289 yards rushing and passing, overcoming his mark of 203 yards in last season's Rose Bowl game against Iowa.

Operating behind Oregon State's bruising line, Francis ran for 138 yards and completed nine out of his 10 pass attempts for 136 yards.

Stanford was never in the ball game after Francis led the Beavers on two long scoring drives in the first half, one of 90 yards and the other for 74 yards. The first march was climaxed by his 10-yard scoring pass to End Bob DeGrant and the second by a 1-yard plunge by Fullback Nub Beamer.

Francis climaxed another 69-yard drive at the start of the second half with a 5-yard touchdown run and with just one minute and two seconds left in the game he went 5 yards for his other score to end an 88-yard march.

Stanford's Jack Douglas completed eight out of 14 passes and one of them went for 19 yards to Rick McMillen for the Indians' first score. Stanford scored again with only 13 seconds left on a 12-yard pass from Sub

Turn to Page 6, Column 6

## SPORTS ON RADIO, TELEVISION TODAY

### FOOTBALL

Rams vs. Packers, KNXT (2), 11 a.m.; Radio KMPC, 10:55 a.m.

Rhinos vs. Longshoremen, KTLA (5), 2 p.m.

Game of the Week, KHJ (9), 7 p.m.

PCC Highlights, KHJ (9), 7:30 p.m.

Big Ten Highlights, KHJ (9), 8:30 p.m.

## MAJOR GRID SCORES

### LOCAL

Oregon, 16; SC, 7.

### PACIFIC COAST

UCLA, 21; COP, 0.
Oregon St., 24; Stanford, 14.
Wash. St., 21; Idaho, 13.
Wash., 35; California, 27.

### EAST

Penn, 28; Columbia, 6.
Dartmouth, 20; Cornell, 19.
Boston College, 19; Marquette, 14.
Brown, 33; Harvard, 6.
Penn St., 14; Holy Cross, 10.
Navy, 52; G. Wash., 0.
Yale, 20; Princeton, 13.
Syracuse, 34; Colgate, 6.

### MIDWEST

Wisconsin, 24; Illinois, 13.
Notre Dame, 7; Okla., 0.
Colorado, 27; Nebraska, 0.
Kansas St., 23; Missouri, 21.
Michigan St., 42; Minnesota, 13.
Michigan, 27; Indiana, 13.
Kansas, 13; Okla. St., 7.
Purdue, 27; Northwestern, 0.
Ohio State, 17; Iowa, 13.

### SOUTH

Ga. Tech, 10; Alabama, 7.
Miss., 14; Tennessee, 7.
Auburn, 6; Georgia, 0.
Duke, 7; Clemson, 6.
Florida, 14; Vanderbilt, 7
Army, 20; Tulane, 14.
N. Carolina St., 12; Va Tech., 0.
S. Carolina, 13; Virginia, 0
W. Virginia, 27; Wake Forest, 14.
Miss St., 14; LSU, 6.

### SOUTHWEST

Rice, 7; Texas A&M, 6.
Texas, 14; TCU, 2.
SMU, 27; Arkansas, 22.

### ROCKY MOUNTAIN

Denver, 21; Utah St., 19.
Utah, 34; Air Force, 0.

Other Scores on Page 8

**Wash. .... 35**
**Cal....... 27**
(Story on Page 7)

**Mich. St. .. 42**
**Minnesota 13**
(Story on Page 4)

**Auburn .... 6**
**Georgia ... 0**
(Story on Page 4)

**Mississippi 14**
**Tennessee . 7**
(Story on Page 4)

**Army .... 20**
**Tulane ... 14**
(Story on Page 7)

**Wisconsin 24**
**Illinois ... 13**
(Story on Page 4)

# SILKY'S BIG STRETCH KICK WINS DERBY

**HERE COMES SILKY** — Silky Sullivan, somewhat closer to pack than in many races, starts to pick up speed as Santa Anita Derby field comes off backstretch. Aliwar and Old Pueblo pace the field at this point. Silky, with Jockey Willie Shoemaker astride him, staged powerful run from this point to massacre field of 3-year-old rivals in classic event.

Times photo by Art Rogers

## 'Pueblo' Falters to Fourth

BY PAUL LOWRY

Kentucky, here we come! The Golden State has another California bred to emulate the mighty Swaps.

Silky Sullivan made the $130,500 Santa Anita Derby an easy steppingstone to the Kentucky Derby by running away with the local classic yesterday before a crowd of 61,123, largest of the winter season.

But in victory Silky, darling of the hero-worshipers who groan at his trailing tactics and thrill to his pulverizing stretch charges, fooled even the most ardent.

Instead of spotting the leaders 30 to 40 lengths on the back stretch he was only 19 behind at the five-eighths pole.

He began to go after his 3-year-old rivals in the 10-horse field at that point, went into high gear around the far turn and through the stretch to win by three and one-half lengths from Harcall. The crowd roared as he went over the line.

Aliwar was third and Old Pueblo, which forced Aliwar's early pace, was fourth. Then came Martins Rullah, The Shoe, Furyvan, Carrier X. McTavish and Sabredale.

### Family Affair

Ridden by Chilly Willie Shoemaker and carrying 118 pounds with everybody else in the field, Silky Sullivan raced the mile and one eighth of the Derby in 1:49 2-5 over a track that changed from "good" to "fast."

He ran his last half in :48 2-5, the final quarter in :24 2-5. The early fractions of :22 4-5, :46 1-5, 1:10 3-5 and 1:36 4-5 all belonged to Aliwar.

Coupled with Harcall as an entry, Silky Sullivan as the 6 to 5 favorite paid $4.30, $5.10 and $3.30 across the board. Aliwar returned $5.80 for show.

The 1-2 finish of the favored entry made the race something of a family affair. Tom Ross and Phil Klipstein own Silky Sullivan while Harcall is the property of the El See Stable, nom de course of Mrs. Tom Ross.

### Largest Dividend

Mrs. Ross has her own trainer in Wayne Stucki, who saddled Harcall while Reggie Cornell put the girth on Silky Sullivan.

Harcall staged a game finish after Silky Sullivan

Turn to Page 8, Column 6

## SILKY SAILS

Here's clocking by furlongs showing how Silky Sullivan catches field and wins Santa Anita Derby by 3½ lengths. Listed in order are distance, leader's time, Silky Sullivan's time and lengths behind.

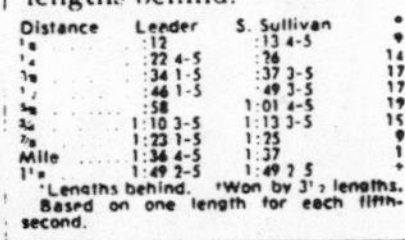

| Distance | Leader | S. Sullivan | * |
|---|---|---|---|
| 1/8 | :12 | :13 4-5 | 9 |
| 1/4 | :22 4-5 | :26 | 14 |
| 3/8 | :34 1-5 | :37 3-5 | 17 |
| 1/2 | :46 1-5 | :49 3-5 | 17 |
| 5/8 | :58 | 1:01 4-5 | 19 |
| 3/4 | 1:10 3-5 | 1:13 3-5 | 15 |
| 7/8 | 1:23 1-5 | 1:25 | 9 |
| Mile | 1:36 4-5 | 1:37 | 1 |
| 1 1/8 | 1:49 2-5 | 1:49 2 5 | † |

*Lengths behind. †Won by 3½ lengths. Based on one length for each fifth-second.

## THE WINNERS

1—Ali Von Dom, $10.10.
2—Ken's Chicle, $35.70.
3—Yard Bird, $6.60.
4—Lucky Bar, $15.80.
5—Gaelic Gold, $42.90.
6—Swirling Abbey, $8.80.
7—Silky Sullivan, $4.30.
8—Summer Story, $11.90.


# Los Angeles Times Sports

CC ★ SUNDAY MORNING, MARCH 9, 1958 Part III

**ALL HIS OWN** — Silky is flying away from rivals at the finish, boasting three-and-a-half-length margin over Harcall and Aliwar.

Times photo by John Malmin

## SPORTSCRIPTS

By PAUL ZIMMERMAN Times Sports Editor

MIAMI, March 8—If you could sit with the Dodger brain trust behind the screen during a practice game you would better appreciate the meticulous care with which they judge the performance of their prize players.

The experienced as well as the new performers get the eagle-eyed appraisal of Manager Walt Alston, Andy High, Fresco Thompson, etc.

"Watch and see if you see his finger give away that curve ball," Alston will say. Or, "I thought it was going to be a knuckler the way he was working with it in his glove but maybe the batter couldn't have seen it."

**ALSTON TALKS** as much to himself as to those next to him.

"I want to see how this boy hits the change of pace." Or, "I thought he took too big a stride on that pitch."

You learn what instructions have gone before. Take the example of Bill Harris, a Canadian hurler up from Montreal. "He's apt to throw before the catcher is set. I should have warned Joe (Pignatano)," said High.

"He probably won't throw as fast today," said Alston. "I suggested yesterday that he count to five before he goes into his windup."

To show you how all experienced eyes are watching everything, Alston commented on the fact that Jim Gentile at first base was stepping off the bag too soon after taking the long throw. "If he isn't careful he will get called on that," said Walt.

**IT DEVELOPED** that others were just as critical. Pee Wee Reese walked by Jim as they were leaving the field and confided:

"You were cheating a little too much out there, Jim, taking your foot off the bag, don't you think?"

Out on the coaching lines the same keen observance prevails. Chuck Dressen is an expert out there. In fact, many think he's the best coach in baseball today. His comments are sharp and precise.

"You can't read the signs if you don't look," he will chide one batter. "Protect that plate," he will shout at another. And so it goes.

**HALF A DOZEN** pairs of experienced eyes watch every pitch, every swing of the bat, every move of runner or fielder.

The psychological aspects are as keenly observed.

"Listen to Charley Neal (second baseman) chattering out there," says High. "He hardly spoke to anyone a year ago. Guess he feels he belongs on the club now. He's a southern boy and naturally would be more reluctant to pop off. Guess he's had what Mr. Rickey used to call 'indoctrination.' "

**P.S.:** What the Dodgers do in September will be the result of the careful observations here in March.

## Black Hawks Win Over Detroit, 4-3

CHICAGO, March 8 (AP)—Eddie Litzenberger scored his second goal of the game with a minute and two seconds left to play to give the Chicago Black Hawks a 4-3 victory over Detroit in a National Hockey League game this afternoon.

# Phillies Set Down Dodgers, 7 to 4

BY FRANK FINCH, Times Staff Representative

MIAMI, Fla., March 8—The Grapefruit League season opened on a note as sour as its name for the Los Angeles Dodgers tonight.

They got off to a sloppy start in the very first inning and never recovered as the Philadelphia Phillies waltzed to a 7-4 victory.

A rather disappointing crowd of 5966 turned out in muggy weather at Miami Stadium to see a major league team representing Los Angeles play its first game ever, unimportant as it was.

### Home Runs

Home runs with men aboard by Harry Anderson and Granny Hamner took all the fun out of the game for the handful of Los Angeles rooters in the park.

Anderson staked the Phillies to a lead they never relinquished with a poke off of loser Ron Negray in the opening round. Hamner hit one off of Southpaw Danny McDevitt in the sixth that traveled 380 feet and made it strictly "no contest."

Half of the Phillies' eight hits went for extra bases, while Los Angeles was restricted to six hits by Winner Don Cardwell and his successors, Bob Conley and Jim Hearn.

### No Test

Center Fielder Felipe Montemayor accounted for three of them, but two of the big Mexican's bingles were cheapies.

The game was no test of the rival teams' strength, of course, for Skippers Walter Alston and Mayo Smith elected to use second - line players and raw rookies for the most part.

Wallflowers included Duke Snider, Pee Wee Reese and Gil Hodges of the Dodgers and Wally Post and Richie Ashburn of the Phils.

However, Alston will start Don Newcombe in tomorrow's matinee against Ray Semproch, a 13-4 winner for

Turn to Page 5, Column 1

## SPORTS ON RADIO, TELEVISION TODAY

**EXHIBITION BASEBALL**

Dodgers vs. Phillies, Radio KMPC, 11:05 a.m.

**AUTO RACING**

Jalopies, KTLA (5), 2:30 p.m.

## Idaho Upsets Oregon State to Knot PCC

MOSCOW, Ida., March 8 (AP)—A magnificent second-half team effort gave Idaho a 62-55 upset victory over Oregon State and tied up the Pacific Coast Conference Basketball Championship tonight.

The loss left Oregon State and California with identical 12-4 records. A playoff between the two teams will come Monday night in a single game at Eugene.

| Oregon St. | G | F | P | T |
|---|---|---|---|---|
| Gambee | 10 | 5 | 3 | 25 |
| Nanson | 3 | 2 | 3 | 8 |
| Goble | 1 | 0 | 4 | 2 |
| Harman | 0 | 3 | 4 | 3 |
| Anderson | 5 | 0 | 3 | 10 |
| Copple | 3 | 1 | 0 | 7 |
| Moss | 0 | 0 | 1 | 0 |
| Totals— | 22 | 11 | 18 | 55 |

| Idaho | G | F | P | T |
|---|---|---|---|---|
| Liveious | 4 | 0 | 4 | 8 |
| Branom | 5 | 4 | 3 | 14 |
| McEwen | 3 | 1 | 3 | 7 |
| Coleman | 4 | 2 | 5 | 10 |
| Simmons | 5 | 7 | 0 | 17 |
| Jorgenson | 2 | 2 | 1 | 6 |
| Schaffer | 0 | 0 | 1 | 0 |
| Totals— | 23 | 16 | 17 | 62 |

SCORE BY HALVES

| | | | |
|---|---|---|---|
| Oregon State | 27 | 28 | 55 |
| Idaho | 19 | 43 | 62 |

# Silky Gets Job Done His Way

BY PETE PEDERSEN

An improbable sleep walker named Silky Sullivan came to life long enough yesterday to smother his field in the $130,500 Santa Anita Derby.

It was a triumph for free thinkers among the equine set. Silky is determined to get the job done his way. Today he could be elected President. On the independent ticket.

"I swear that Silky himself decided on the inside route," said Willie Shoemaker after he climbed off the antisocial runner. There was a wall of horses on the far turn and Silky went inside instead of resorting to the overland route.

### Had Lot Left

"He laid up a lot closer today and I never asked him to," continued Shoe. "He was just that much better. And all those other jocks expected me to go around. When you ask this horse, he's there. I think he won with a lot left."

Silky was a deep last in the early going but he was closer than in his heart-failure efforts before. Reginald Cornell, Canadian-born conditioner who deserves full credit for developing this colt, explained it:

"Shoe is getting to know this horse better. And we warmed him up slow and easy today. Also, I've trained him steady, with plenty of gallops and longer, slower works. That can put more speed in a horse than you might imagine. The track today (labeled fast, but definitely on the dull side) was probably a good cushion for a horse that hits as hard as he does."

Cornell revealed that he gave no prerace instructions to Shoemaker. "The horse laid up closer on his own accord," said Reggie.

There is no surcingle made large enough to encircle the tremendous girth of Silky Sullivan. Cornell has to have one made special. Also, he hits so hard that he runs in steel shoes (rather than aluminum) which are flat on all fours. Most horses run with a "sticker" on their hind shoes.

### Another Key

Another key to this horse is his prerace preparation. Cornell does not believe in "drawing" his horses, that is, muzzling them from eating hay and roughage. But Silky was muzzled the last three nights before the derby. He also has been outfitted in a hood which fits around his throat. Silky has had a wind affliction, does whistle while he works, and

Turn to Page 8, Column 8

# Bruins Rout Wash., 89-68

BY MAL FLORENCE

There's no place like home and UCLA knows it only too well as it sped to an impressive 89-68 victory over helpless Washington before a select gathering of 1000 fans last night in the Westwood gym.

The crowd was limited because of fire regulations.

By its victory, UCLA clinched third place in the conference with a 10-6 record. The Huskies wound up their season in seventh spot with a 5-11 mark.

It's been three long years since UCLA has had the privilege of playing in the cozy gym out west. But the Bruins didn't forget the pattern as they built up a 46-30 halftime lead and then added to that margin after intermission.

Center Ben Rogers, playing his last game for UCLA, topped all Bruin scorers with 23 points. Washington's Doug Smart was high for the game with 24 points, but most of his points came when the issue was already settled.

UCLA, which has been reluctant to run this season,

Turn to Page 4, Column 1

## PCC STANDINGS

PACIFIC COAST CONFERENCE

| | W | L | Pct. | PF | PA |
|---|---|---|---|---|---|
| Oregon State | 12 | 4 | .750 | 1031 | 864 |
| California | 12 | 4 | .750 | 952 | 873 |
| UCLA | 10 | 6 | .625 | 1018 | 977 |
| Idaho | 9 | 7 | .593 | 1115 | 1078 |
| SC | 8 | 8 | .500 | 1004 | 1026 |
| Stanford | 7 | 9 | .406 | 933 | 942 |
| Oregon | 6 | 10 | .375 | 997 | 1075 |
| Washington | 5 | 11 | .313 | 932 | 1031 |
| Washington State | 3 | 13 | .188 | 867 | 980 |

## SILKY'S BIG ROMP

**7823**—SEVENTH RACE—MILE AND ONE-EIGHTH. For 3-year-olds. The Santa Anita Derby. Purse $100,000 added. Gross $130,500. Net to winner, $83,400; second, $20,000; third, $15,000; fourth, $10,000.

| Index | Horse. Owner. | Wt. | PP | St. | 1/4 | 1/2 | 3/4 | Str. | Fin. | Jockey. | To $1 |
|---|---|---|---|---|---|---|---|---|---|---|---|
| (7749) | c-Silky Sullivan (Ross-Klipstein) | 118 | 7 | 10 | 10 | 10 | 97 | 3h | 13½ | Shoemaker | 1.15 |
| (7756) | c-Harcall (El See Stable) | 118 | 8 | 8 | 75 | 74 | 4h | 51½ | 2h | Boland | 1.15 |
| 7767 | Aliwar (Warner Ranch) | 118 | 6 | 1 | 1½ | 12 | 12 | 13 | 31½ | Neves | 12.05 |
| 7767 | a-Old Pueblo (Jelks-McBean) | 118 | 2 | 3 | 21½ | 25 | 24 | 22 | 4h | Arcaro | 1.75 |
| (7780) | d-Martins Rullah (Mrs G. Lewis) | 118 | 10 | 9 | 912 | 8½ | 81 | 76 | 5½ | Longden | 6.20 |
| 7767 | b-The Shoe (R. C. Ellsworth) | 118 | 5 | 2 | 53 | 52 | 3h | 41 | 62 | Burton | 10.85 |
| 7767 | Furyvan (M. Traub) | 118 | 4 | 7 | 61 | 61½ | 72 | 64 | 76 | Maese | 34.80 |
| 7780 | a-Carrier X. (Mrs. J. McMahen) | 118 | 1 | 6 | 8h | 912 | 10 | 93 | 8½ | Taniguchi | 1.75 |
| 7540 | b-McTavish (R. C. Ellsworth) | 118 | 3 | 4 | 41 | 41½ | 5½ | 8h | 93 | H.Moreno | 10.85 |
| 7767 | d-Sabredale (Kerr Stables) | 118 | 9 | 5 | 31 | 3h | 61 | 10 | 10 | I Val'z'la | 6.20 |

a—Mrs. J. L. McMahen-Jelks & McBean entry.
b—R. C. Ellsworth entry.
c—Ross & Klipstein-El See Stable entry.
d—Kerr Stables-Mr. & Mrs. G. Lewis Stable entry.

Time, :22 4-5, :46 1-5, 1:10 3-5, 1:36 4-5, 1:49 2-5. In gate 5:08, off at once. Start good, won easily, second and third driving. Winner, ch.c. 3, by Sullivan—Lady 'N Silk. Trained by R. Cornell. Mutuel pool, $512,802.

Two-dollar mutuels paid: c-SILKY SULLIVAN, 4.30, 5.10, 3.30; c-HARCALL, 5.10, 3.30; ALIWAR, 5.80.

SILKY SULLIVAN, not as far back as in some of his races, was in hand while outrun, saved ground to the stretch turn, was lucky to find room between horses entering the final quarter, closed boldly, drew out fast after taking command and won with something in reserve. HARCALL lacked early foot, began to advance after a half mile and finished gamely. ALIWAR made the pace in hand, saved ground, was put to a drive after three-quarters and held on fairly well. OLD PUEBLO followed the pace in hand, saved ground, was called upon entering the stretch and weakened in the final eighth. THE SHOE moved up menacingly on the stretch turn and hung in the drive. MARTIN'S RULLAH made up some ground. McTAVISH tired. SABREDALE stopped badly after five-eighths. No scratches.

# 78,672 SEE DODGERS BEAT GIANTS, 6-5

EFFECTIVE FOOTWORK—Dodger Charlie Neal slides into Bob Schmidt and separates Giant catcher from ball to score. Dick Gray (background at left) also tallied on miscue. Gino Cimoli's single to right touched off play.

Los Angeles Times
# Sports
CC SATURDAY MORNING, APRIL 19, 1958 Part II

## SPORTS PARADE

By BRAVEN DYER

There's something about the roar of the crowd at a sports event that brings out people's goose pimples.

Ernest Lawrence Thayer must have been thinking of this when he penned his "Casey at the Bat" and wrote, "From the benches dark with people went up a muffled roar."

Only yesterday at the mammoth Coliseum the deep-throated roar which dinned the ears of more than 78,000 spectators came from shirt-sleeved fans who welcomed major league baseball to Los Angeles under a warm summer sun.

**WE'VE ALL HEARD** followers of the Rams, Bruins and Trojans unload a rolling roar either in anticipation of or exultation over some magnificent, timely performance.

The fans gave the transplanted Dodgers the same full-throated reception yesterday. Time and again they roared for their favorites as Carl Erskine, Duke Snider, Gil Hodges, Dick Gray, Gino Cimoli and all the rest of Walter O'Malley's team made it a perfect day by outlasting the pesky Giants.

They cut loose with their first rumbling roar in the last of the third inning when Snider strode to the plate with Junior Gilliam on second, one out and the Dodgers behind, 1-0.

The onetime Compton football and baseball star could not have missed the rousing reception . . . and responded like the champion he is by slashing a single to center to tie the score.

**THE ROAR ROSE** again a few minutes later when the Duke slid into home plate in the most approved style, bum knee and all, to send his team ahead, 2-1.

Duke was greeted with another booming ovation

Turn to Page 2, Column 1

## DODGER BOX SCORE

| San Francisco | AB | R | H | * | E |
|---|---|---|---|---|---|
| Davenport, 3b | 5 | 1 | 3 | 0 | 0 |
| Kirkland, rf | 5 | 1 | 3 | 0 | 0 |
| Mays, cf | 4 | 0 | 2 | 0 | 1 |
| Spencer, ss-2b | 4 | 0 | 0 | 1 | 0 |
| Cepeda, 1b | 5 | 0 | 0 | 0 | 0 |
| Sauer, lf | 4 | 2 | 2 | 2 | 0 |
| Rodgers, ss | 0 | 0 | 0 | 0 | 0 |
| Schmidt, c | 3 | 1 | 2 | 0 | 1 |
| O'Connell, 2b | 2 | 0 | 0 | 0 | 0 |
| King | 0 | 0 | 0 | 0 | 0 |
| Gomez | 0 | 0 | 0 | 0 | 0 |
| Bressoud, 2b | 0 | 0 | 0 | 0 | 0 |
| Lockman | 0 | 0 | 0 | 0 | 0 |
| Worthington, p | 2 | 0 | 0 | 0 | 0 |
| McCormick, p | 0 | 0 | 0 | 0 | 0 |
| Speake | 1 | 0 | 0 | 0 | 0 |
| Antonelli, p | 0 | 0 | 0 | 0 | 0 |
| Jablonski | 1 | 0 | 0 | 0 | 0 |
| Grissom, p | 0 | 0 | 0 | 0 | 0 |
| Totals | 36 | 5 | 12 | 3 | 2 |

*Runs batted in.

| Los Angeles | AB | R | H | * | E |
|---|---|---|---|---|---|
| Gilliam, lf | 3 | 1 | 0 | 0 | 0 |
| Reese, ss | 4 | 0 | 1 | 0 | 0 |
| Snider, rf | 5 | 1 | 2 | 1 | 0 |
| Furillo, rf | 0 | 0 | 0 | 0 | 0 |
| Hodges, 1b | 4 | 0 | 0 | 0 | 0 |
| Neal, 2b | 3 | 1 | 2 | 1 | 0 |
| Gray, 3b | 3 | 2 | 2 | 1 | 1 |
| Cimoli, cf | 3 | 1 | 1 | 1 | 0 |
| Roseboro, c | 1 | 0 | 0 | 0 | 0 |
| Jackson | 1 | 0 | 0 | 0 | 0 |
| Pignatano, c | 1 | 0 | 0 | 0 | 0 |
| Erskine, p | 4 | 0 | 0 | 0 | 0 |
| Labine, p | 0 | 0 | 0 | 0 | 0 |
| Totals | 32 | 6 | 8 | 4 | 1 |

*Runs batted in.

Jackson grounded out for Roseboro in 5th.
King walked for O'Connell in 6th.
Speake struck out for McCormick in 6th.
Gomez ran for King in 6th.
Lockman sacrificed for Bressoud in 8th.
Jablonski struck out for Antonelli in 8th.

| | | | | | |
|---|---|---|---|---|---|
| SAN FRANCISCO | 001 | 101 | 011—5 | 12 | 2 |
| LOS ANGELES | 002 | 030 | 10x—6 | 8 | 2 |

PO-A—San Francisco, 24-7; Los Angeles, 27-11. DP—Erskine to Neal; Gray to Neal to Hodges. LOB—San Francisco, 9; Los Angeles, 9. 2B—Davenport, Kirkland. 3B—Schmidt, Kirkland. HR—Sauer, 2; Gray. SB—Neal. S—Lockman.

| Pitcher | IP | H | R | ER | BB | SO |
|---|---|---|---|---|---|---|
| Worthington-L (0-1) | 4⅓ | 7 | 5 | 3 | 5 | 4 |
| McCormick | ⅔ | 0 | 0 | 0 | 0 | 0 |
| Antonelli | 2 | 1 | 1 | 1 | 2 | 0 |
| Grissom | 1 | 0 | 0 | 0 | 0 | 1 |
| Erskine-W (1-0) | 8+ | 10 | 4 | 3 | 4 | 7 |
| Labine | 1 | 2 | 1 | 1 | 0 | 0 |

WP—McCormick, Erskine. Umpires—Venzon, Conlan, Secory and Dixon. Time—3h. Attendance—78,672.

NO ALIBI

## Davenport Admits Skull at 3rd Base

There was no cry of "we wuz robbed" in the Giant dressing room anent the fateful ninth-inning play which erased a big run.

Jim Davenport, San Francisco's sensational rookie third baseman, readily admitted he failed to touch third base. Dick Gray, Los Angeles' equally sensational rookie third baseman, spotted the miscue, called for the ball and Davenport was out.

**Feet Tangled**

"My feet tangled, causing me to get off stride," Davenport said. "I knew I missed the bag and started back. But there was Willie Kirkland coming in, so there was nothing to do but go ahead and hope nobody noticed it."

Davenport had doubled off the screen to open the ninth inning with the Giants trailing, 6-4. Kirkland followed with a triple off Gino Cimoli's glove in deep center. Davenport stopped short after rounding third, then sped across the plate, only to become an automatic out on what is called an appeal play.

**Scored on Mays' Single**

Kirkland subsequently scored on Willie Mays' single — and thus the score would have been tied had Davenport touched the base and legitimately scored.

Herman Franks, who ran the Giants yesterday in the absence of ailing Billy Rigney, was stationed in the third-base coaching box but didn't see the lapse.

"I have to be watching the ball on a play like that. I had cautioned Davenport to be careful, because his run didn't mean anything at the time. I didn't want him doubled or something like that.

"When he hesitated after rounding third, I figured he was making sure he had plenty of time to score."

Gray said Davenport cut

Turn to Page 2, Column 5

## TODAY IN SPORTS

**QUARTER-HORSE RACING**—Los Alamitos, 1:15 p.m.

**BASEBALL**—Los Angeles Dodgers vs. San Francisco Giants, Coliseum, 1:30.

**SPORTSMEN'S SHOW**—Pan-Pacific Auditorium, 1 p.m.

**COLLEGE BASEBALL**—SC vs. California, doubleheader, Bovard Field, 11 a.m.; UCLA vs. Santa Clara, Joe E. Brown Field, 2 p.m.

**TRACK**—UCLA vs. Fresno State, Trotter Track, 2 p.m.; Stanford at Occidental, 1:30 p.m.

**RUGBY**—GPC vs. Eagle Rock No. 2, 1:30 p.m.; Ontario vs. Eagle Rock AC, 3 p.m., Rancho Cienega Stadium.

**AUTO RACING**—100-lap midget race, Gardena Stadium, 8:30 p.m.

**BOXING**—Hollywood Legion Stadium, 8:15 p.m.

**TENNIS** — SC vs. UCLA, Westwood, 1 p.m.

LONG WAIT—Schmidt waits for ball which Pitcher Al Worthington retrieved after it rolled to backstop as Gray (partially hidden) slides into home plate.

TOO LATE—Gray comes home safely for second run as Schmidt gets ball too late. Ump is Tony Venzon.

Times photos by Larry Sharkey

## Daffy Running Costly to Giants

### L.A. Snares Coliseum Opener as Rookie Misses Base to Blow Run

BY FRANK FINCH

But for the size of the crowd—78,672, largest in National League history—you'd of thunk the Dodgers and Giants were back in Brooklyn yesterday instead of playing an opening date in the Coliseum.

Only this time it was the Giants, not the Dodgers, who were guilty of some daffy base running that cost them no less than a ninth-inning tie which could have sent the match into overtime.

The net result was a satisfying 6-to-5 triumph for the Dodgers, avenging San Francisco's inaugural triumph Tuesday in Bridgetown.

**Rivals Meet Two More Times**

The California sparring partners are all square at 2-2, with matinees in the current engagement remaining today and tomorrow.

The failure of Jim Davenport, the Giants' slugging rookie, to touch third base while "scoring" on Willie Kirkland's triple in the top of the ninth was the blow that killed father and, no doubt, brought on a relapse for the club's ailing skipper, Bill Rigney.

Kirkland came on in when Willie Mays beat out an infield single, but the Jints perished, a run shy, when Fireman Clem Labine took care of the next two guys.

In the first inning the Giants revived one of Mack Sennett's Keystone cop comedy scripts.

With one out and Davenport on second base and Kirkland on first, Daryl Spencer raised a weak little pop fly in front of Carl Erskine.

**Rule Invoked**

The Dodger pitcher lost the ball in the sun and it plopped on the emerald turf.

Erskine first thought to throw to first base, but he changed his mind and fired to Charlie Neal at second, who soon was surrounded by gray uniforms.

It so happened that the in-

Turn to Page 4, Column 4

## STANDINGS

**NATIONAL LEAGUE**

| | W | L | Pct. | * |
|---|---|---|---|---|
| Chicago | 3 | 0 | 1.000 | |
| Milwaukee | 2 | 1 | .667 | 1 |
| LOS ANGELES | 2 | 2 | .500 | 1½ |
| San Francisco | 2 | 2 | .500 | 1½ |
| Philadelphia | 1 | 1 | .500 | 1½ |
| Cincinnati | 1 | 1 | .500 | 1½ |
| Pittsburgh | 1 | 2 | .333 | 2 |
| St. Louis | 0 | 3 | .000 | 3 |

*Games behind leader.

**Yesterday's Results**

LOS ANGELES, 6; San Francisco, 5.
Cincinnati, 4; Pittsburgh, 1.
Chicago, 11; St. Louis, 6.
Milwaukee, 4; Philadelphia, 2.

**Games Today**

San Francisco (Gomez, 15-13) vs. LOS ANGELES (McDevitt, 7-4), Coliseum, 1:30 p.m.

St. Louis (Mizell, 8-10) at Chicago (Phillips, 3-2).

Milwaukee (Spahn, 21-11) at Philadelphia (Simmons, 12-11).

Cincinnati (Haddix, 10-13) at Pittsburgh (R. G. Smith, 2-4).

**AMERICAN LEAGUE**

| | W | L | Pct. | * |
|---|---|---|---|---|
| New York | 3 | 1 | .750 | |
| Baltimore | 2 | 1 | .667 | ½ |
| Chicago | 2 | 2 | .500 | 1 |
| Cleveland | 2 | 2 | .500 | 1 |
| Detroit | 2 | 2 | .500 | 1 |
| Kansas City | 2 | 2 | .500 | 1 |
| Washington | 1 | 2 | .333 | 1½ |
| Boston | 1 | 3 | .250 | 2 |

*Games behind leader.

**Yesterday's Results**

New York, 3; Baltimore, 1.
Cleveland, 7; Detroit, 5.
Chicago, 11; Kansas City, 7.
Only games scheduled.

**Games Today**

Chicago (Pierce, 20-12) at Kansas City (Urban, 7-4), night.

Boston (Fornieles, 10-13) at Washington (Ramos, 12-16).

Baltimore (O'Dell, 4-10) at New York (Shantz, 11-5).

Cleveland (Mossi, 11-10) at Detroit (Foytack, 14-11).

## Players Complain but Fans Happy

BY AL WOLF

The great experiment—big-league baseball in the Coliseum — was a great success. Except for the Giants.

For the Dodgers, yesterday's inaugural was doubly gratifying. They won the ball game. And that crowd of 78,672 not only broke the National League record (60,747) but also the major mark (78,382) for a regular season single game.

For the fans, it was a terrific show. Few left before the bitter end, even though it took three hours to determine the victor.

And though the Giants lost, their take-home check for yesterday's game alone should prove sweet balm. Especially after some of the "crowds" at the Polo Grounds the past few years.

The players of both clubs complained that the backgrounds made both batting and outfielding difficult. But the customers in the far reaches of the vast arena, who could scarcely see the ball at all, seemingly had a swell time.

From that distance, the game resembled a pantomime. You couldn't follow the ball, but the actions of the players told you what was happening. Nobody complained. In fact, the farther the plate the greater the enthusiasm.

Actually, the view from most seats was very good, all things considered. Fans located behind the left-field screen said what little visibility was lost by the wire was more than made up by the nearness to the infield.

That nearness failed to make the park a laughing-stock of baseball, at least for the nonce.

Only three homers materialized — and two of

Turn to Page 3, Column 2

# FIGURES PROVE: L.A. SPORTS CAPITAL OF WORLD

BY PAUL ZIMMERMAN, Sports Editor

The next time you get into an argument with someone over the question of the location of the sports capital of the world, throw this series of facts at him:

To start off, tell your doubting friend that 9,691,370 spectators attended major events in Southern

## SPORTSCRIPTS

California during the year approaching its conclusion.

As you might suspect, considering that 263 days are involved, horse racing sets the pace with a mark of 4,608,919 for all thoroughbred, harness and quarter-horse meetings this year.

Next comes baseball. In 77 home games the Los Angeles Dodgers attracted 1,845,556 paid customers and an estimated 816,000 more free fans and spectators who bought cut-rate tickets. That makes a total of 2,661,556 for baseball.

Football stands third. The pigskin sport attracted 1,426,694 to Memorial Coliseum and the Rose Bowl.

This one will surprise you. Motor racing in all of its phases drew 655,000 spectators. This includes sports cars, sprint cars, stock cars, midgets, jalopies and motorcycles.

Next in line is boxing. One hundred two shows at the Olympic and Hollywood Legion Stadium and three events at Wrigley Field attracted 237,442.

Unfortunately, we have no accurate estimate of college and AAU basketball, plus the several sellout games staged here by the Harlem Globetrotters. It is safe to say that over 100,000 more persons watched the roundball sport. This we have not included in the grand total.

The Los Angeles Open drew 55,000 spectators and other golf events in these parts quite probably would take the total for the links sport to another 100,000. Then there was the well-attended Pacific Southwest Tennis Tournament plus the appearance of the pro troupe here before capacity crowds for at least 50,000 more.

Here are a few individual crowd figures to startle you:

The Los Angeles Rams vs. Chicago Bears game brought out 100,470—the top football crowd in the National League. The second biggest grid gathering was the 100,202 total amassed for the Ram-Colt game.

Our biggest collegiate event was, of course, the Oregon-Ohio State game which brought a near-capacity total of 98,202 fans to the Rose Bowl.

The top racing crowd was the 61,123 who swarmed over Santa Anita on Derby Day to see Silky Sullivan run. On Memorial Day at Hollywood 60,659 were in attendance.

In track and field, the Coliseum Relays drew 34,722. Boxing's biggest gathering was the 21,988 who collected for the Carmen Basilio-Art Aragon fight last September. The world's heavyweight championship between Floyd Patterson and Roy Harris had an attendance of 21,951.

The Dodgers, of course, set all sorts of records. Their opening crowd of 78,672 was a National League

Please Turn to Pg. 4, Col. 2

# Colts Beat Giants in Sudden Death, 23-17

CC ★ MONDAY MORNING, DECEMBER 29, 1958

## Olmedo Wins as MacKay Beaten

BRISBANE, Australia, Dec. 29 (Monday) (AP)—Alex Olmedo, the first foreigner ever to play for the United States Davis Cup team, pushed the underdog Americans into a 1-0 lead in the challenge round today when he stunned Australian Ace Mal Anderson, 8-6, 2-6, 9-7, 8-6, in the first singles match.

But Ashley Cooper, after dropping the first set, rallied to give Australia the second match by topping Yankee Barry MacKay, 4-6, 6-3, 6-2, 6-4.

Play resumes tomorrow for the famed cup with a doubles match.

Olmedo, who is a citizen of Peru, although he has resided in the United States for some five years, proved to be a better "mudder" than Anderson.

**Slugging Match**

The center court in Milton Stadium was virtually a quagmire as a result of a night-long tropical rainstorm. It was covered with canvas, but the rain slipped under.

Once he got into action, though, the youngster who won the National Collegiate championship for Southern California last year, stood toe-to-toe with Anderson and slugged out every point.

**Uphill Struggle**

Actually, the tennis wasn't as good as the capacity crowd of more than 18,500 would have liked Both Anderson and Olmedo had trouble holding their footing and after two games in the first set both donned spikes.

Still, Anderson took a couple of headers.

Despite the victory, it was an uphill struggle for Ol-

Please Turn to Pg. 5, Col. 1

## Iowa Equal of Any Big 10 Team--Crisler

BY FRANK FINCH

"This Iowa team is as good as any that the Big 10 has sent to the Rose Bowl."

The authority for this statement is Athletic Director Fritz Crisler of Michigan, who arrived here Saturday to attend the Iowa-California game on New Year's Day.

Crisler was reminded that he was the coach of a Wolverine team which walloped Southern Cal's Trojans, 49-0, when Bob Chappius passed and ran for 279 yards, an all-time Rose Bowl record, in the '48 fracas.

**Fleming Praised**

"Do you mean to say that Iowa is as good as that Michigan team?" a reporter inquired incredulously.

"Yes, I do," said Crisler. "Michigan was a fine team, but it got all the breaks against SC. Don't underestimate Iowa.

"This Willie Fleming is simply tremendous. But for him, I think maybe the result (Iowa, 37-14) might have been different.

"Michigan gave Randy Duncan a bad time in that game, but we couldn't stop Fleming. He returned a punt 72 yards for a touchdown and broke loose for a 61-yard touchdown run from scrimmage."

Fritz shook his head, recalling Fleming's fireworks.

"If we had it to do over

Please Turn to Pg. 5, Col. 3

## TODAY IN SPORTS

**SPORTS AWARDS DINNER** — 16th annual Times Dinner, Ambassador's Cocoanut Grove, 6:30 p.m.

**WRESTLING** — Pasadena Arena, 8:30 p.m.

## DODGERS' DIGIOVANNA DIES OF HEART ATTACK

Charles Joseph DiGiovanna, 28, who became the Los Angeles Dodgers' bat boy when he was 13 and was presently clubhouse custodian for the team, died of a heart attack early yesterday at his home in Long Beach.

DiGiovanna collapsed at home and was taken to Seaside Hospital, but was pronounced dead on arrival there. Since childhood he had suffered from a heart ailment.

He leaves his widow, Shirley, of 3752 Hackett St., Long Beach; two sons, Gregory, 9, and Charles Jr., 5; a daughter, Rita, 7; his father Charles, and several brothers and sisters in his native Brooklyn, N.Y.

DiGiovanna was given his first job with the Dodgers

Please Turn to Pg. 2, Col. 6

Charles DiGiovanna

HORSE (AND WAGON) TRAIL—Alan (The Horse) Ameche of Colts lowers head and booms through gaping hole in Giants line to score decisive touchdown that gave Baltimore pro title in unprecedented sudden death overtime in New York yesterday. At left, Lenny Moore blocks out Giant Emlen Tunnell (45). Right, Giant Jim Patton (20) comes up to make tackle—too late. Score was 23-17. (AP) Wirephoto

TIMES DINNER

## Sports Champions to Be Feted Tonight

Who is the greatest baseball player of the past year?

Which football players, professional and collegiate, so distinguished themselves during 1958 that experts have decreed that they're best in their divisions?

And how about basketball players, swimmers, track athletes and all the others who have helped make headlines during the past year?

There's a champion among champions in each sport and these worthy lads and lassies will be individually honored tonight at the 16th annual Times Sports Award dinner in the Cocoanut Grove of the Ambassador Hotel.

Times Sports Editor Paul Zimmerman and the committee that works with him in choosing the outstanding sports talent of the nation call this year's line-up of athletes the greatest in history.

**Captains Attend**

In addition to the contemporary athletes, the Grove will be populated with many former champs plus present-day sports leaders.

Rival Rose Bowl coaches, Forest Evashevski of Iowa and Pete Elliott of California, will be at the head table, as will Fred Haney, manager of the Milwaukee Braves, and Casey Stengel, manager of the New York Yankees and also a member of the Times Sports Awards Committee.

The Big 10 will be represented by Tug Wilson, the Pacific Coast Conference by Bernie Hammerbeck. Backing up the coaches will be Paul Brechler, director of athletics at Iowa, and Greg Englehard, director of athletics at California.

Jack Hart and Joe Kapp, cocaptains of the Golden Bears, will be present, as will John Nocera, captain of the Hawkeyes.

And for entertainment — there'll be Connie Haines, pert southern miss who can send you with a snappy number or lull you with the blues, plus Tennessee Ernie Ford, nationally known song stylist who brings along his own brand of back-home philosophy.

## Kapp, Parque Rejoin Bears

Quarterback Joe Kapp and Larry Parque, both of whom missed one of Saturday's practice sessions because of colds, were completely recovered yesterday and participated fully in a one-hour sweat-suit workout held by the California Bears.

With their return, the entire squad is in good shape as the Pacific Coast Conference champions await their final pre-Rose Bowl drills. They'll work in the afternoons today, tomorrow and Wednesday, again at Beverly Hills High.

## MARCHETTI'S LEG BROKEN IN 2 PLACES

BALTIMORE, Dec. 28 (AP)—Gino Marchetti, defensive end for the professional champion Baltimore Colts, broke both bones in his right ankle in today's 23-17 victory over the New York Giants.

But Dr. Erwin Mayer, team physician, said Marchetti will be okay.

"Of course, he won't play in the Pro Bowl Game," Dr. Mayer said, "but we're not worried about him. He's resting comfortably and he'll be fine by next season."

Dr. Mayer said both the tibia and fibula in Gino's right ankle were broken when he made a tackle on Giant Halfback Frank Gifford in the closing minutes of the fourth quarter.

MODZELEWSKI 'MOUSED'

## Trap Play by Ameche Beat Giants--Unitas

NEW YORK, Dec. 28 (UPI) Quarterback Johnny Unitas jubilantly singled out Alan Ameche's 23-yard "trap" play as the wedge which broke the New York Giants' resistance and set up the Baltimore Colts' "sudden-death" touchdown worth $4700 per man.

On that particular play, New York Defensive Tackle Dick Modzelewski was the "mouse" who was trapped. He barged through the line fiercely to tackle Unitas as he had done several times before.

But this time Unitas handed the ball off to Ameche, who plowed through the hole left behind by Modzelewski's rush and ran all the way to the Giants' 20.

Two short passes by Unitas and Ameche's subsequent one-yard touchdown plunge earned Baltimore the National Football League championship.

"We were looking for the opportunity," Unitas related in the Colts' dressing room after the game. "Those Giant linemen were 'blowing' in on me pretty good. They even made me 'eat' the ball a few times.

"When we noticed that Sam Huff (Giants' middle linebacker) was laying back just a bit for pass protection, we figured that Modzelewski would come flying through there. He did and everything worked out as it was supposed to. Ameche went clean up the middle."

Coach Weeb Ewbank con-

Please Turn to Pg. 3, Col. 6

CHAMPIONS—Alan Ameche gives Johnny Unitas a victory kiss with Steve Myhra smiling happily on the left. This threesome starred for Baltimore in 23-17 sudden death triumph over New York in the NFL championship game at Yankee Stadium. Ameche scored two TD's including the game winner. (AP) Wirephoto

## Ameche's Late TD Ends Tilt

NEW YORK, Dec. 28 (AP) The Baltimore Colts, directed by the golden arm of Johnny Unitas and driven by the flying feet of Alan Ameche, roared back from almost certain defeat to defeat the New York Giants, 23-17, in a sudden death overtime period for the National Football League championship today.

It was Ameche who climaxed the winning 80-yard march by plunging over the goal line from the 1 for the pay-off touchdown after 8 minutes and 15 seconds of the extra period. And it was Unitas who spearheaded the drive by completing four passes for 46 yards, putting the Colts in the position to score.

**Kicks Field Goal**

The Giants appeared to have their fifth championship in the bag after coming from behind with a pair of electrifying second-half touchdowns to take a 17-14 lead.

But with 10 seconds remaining, Steve Myhra kicked a 20-yard field goal to tie the score and cast a pall over the highly partisan crowd of 64,185 Yankee Stadium spectators.

The emotion-spent crowd sensed a break for the Giants when they won the toss of the coin and elected to receive the extra-period kickoff. However, they couldn't move the ball and were forced to punt. It took the Colts 13 plays to score the winning touchdown.

The key play was Unitas' 21-yard pass to Ray Berry on third down and 15, which moved the Colts to the Giants' 43.

**Unitas' Key Play**

Ameche, a devastating runner for the Colts all afternoon, romped 23 yards down the middle to the 20. After L. G. Dupre failed to gain, Unitas connected with a 12-yard toss to Berry and hit Jim Mutscheller with a 6-yarder after Ameche had gotten a yard.

Now the Colts had third down on the 1. With the Giant line practically breathing down the necks of the Colts, Ameche hurtled over right guard for the score.

It was Ameche's second touchdown. He had scored the first touchdown of the game, plunging over from the 2 as the Colts overcame an early 3-0 Giant lead on Pat Summerall's 36-yard first-period field goal.

A 15-yard touchdown pass from Unitas to Berry in the second period, followed by Myhra's second point after touchdown gave the Colts a 14-3 half-time lead.

Baltimore appeared well on the way to its first championship in its seven years

Please Turn to Pg. 3, Col. 1

## Facts, Figures on NFL Title Game

NEW YORK, Dec. 28 (AP)—Financial facts and figures of today's championship play-off game in the National Football League at Yankee Stadium.

PAID ATTENDANCE 64,1[illegible]

GROSS RECEIPTS (including radio and television) $[illegible]

TAXES AND RENTAL $[illegible]

GAME OPERATING EXPENSES $[illegible]

NET RECEIPTS $[illegible]

TOTAL PLAYER POOL (70% of the net)—$372,310.[illegible]

EACH WINNING SHARE $4718.77 (42½ shares)

EACH LOSING SHARE—$3111.33 (42½ shares).

POOL FOR SECTIONAL SECOND-PLACE CLUBS—$37,231.06.

# HADDIX LOSES 'PERFECT GAME' IN 13, 2-0

Los Angeles Times

Sports

PART IV

CC WEDNESDAY MORNING, MAY 27, 1959 3 †

SPORTS PARADE

## New Giant Park Not on Schedule

BY BRAVEN DYER

SAN FRANCISCO, May 26—Although nobody in authority is willing to be quoted, it begins to look as if the Giants won't play any games in their spanking new ball park this season.

The contract specifies that Candlestick Park be ready by the end of August. But three different people who should know what they are talking about, even if I can't divulge their names, told me today that it'll take a major miracle to get the place ready for any of the 18 home games the Giants have scheduled in September.

I visited Candlestick Park today. It is a beautiful baseball stadium with a capacity for about 40,000 fans. From the Sheraton-Palace Hotel it is exactly seven miles to home plate. When completed the layout will have cost about $12,000,000. The grass is ready right now, so baseball could be played if the rabid fans didn't mind standing for a couple of hours.

Braven Dyer

Up here they are saying that the Dodgers can't possibly have their Chavez Ravine park ready for 1960. Actual construction on Candlestick Park began last November, so the job, when done, will have taken virtually a full year. But preliminary grading, much of which was started before all legal formalities had been completed, was going on many months before construction commenced. The Chavez Ravine terrain presents quite a problem.

### O'Malley May Switch to Wrigley Field

They're also saying in the best-informed 'Frisco baseball circles that the Dodgers won't play in the Coliseum next season. They claim that Walter O'Malley has just about decided to switch to Wrigley Field for 1960. Why? Mainly because he wants the concession money . . . and knows the Coliseum rental will be hiked.

You may have noticed some very interesting figures on major league baseball in today's paper. Los Angeles, of course, led all 16 clubs in home attendance. We shrug that off nonchalantly as something that is only normal for Southern California.

The most enlightening figure, to me, was 348,130 for San Francisco's home games. Only one other city (except Los Angeles) attracted anything close to this . . . Pittsburgh with 338,348. And in the National League all the rest were below 270,000.

### Seals Stadium Seats Only 22,000

This is most significant because the Giants seat only 22,000 fans. I understand their average attendance last year was just under 17,000 per game.

Wrigley Field, as it stands today, seats about the same as Seals Stadium. But at very little extra cost O'Malley can enlarge Wrigley Field by 10,000 and except for series with Milwaukee and the Giants this would be adequate . . . or almost so. And Walter then could stow away that concession money.

The Giants released no official figures relative to how much they profited from hamburgers, beer and hot dogs last year but I understand $250,000 showed up in Horace Stoneham's bank account when his money-changers finished balancing the concession books.

Gosh, if Walter O'Malley really has decided to move to Wrigley Field maybe he'll use some of the concession money in advance to buy a new pitcher. Maybe, I say.

## Tokyo, Innsbruck Get 1964 Olympic Games

MUNICH, Germany, May 26 (UPI)—Tokyo and Innsbruck, Austria, were selected today as the sites for the 1964 summer and winter Olympic Games by an overwhelming vote of the International Olympic Committee delegates.

Both were elected on the first ballot. Tokyo, which lost a chance to host the 1940 Olympics because of World War II, received 34 of 58 votes for the summer classic. Vienna received 10 votes, Detroit nine and Brussels five, according to authoritative sources.

If the games go through on schedule five years hence, it will mark the first time they are held in Asia. The Olympics have been held outside of Europe and the United States only in 1956, when they were staged at Melbourne, Australia.

In the voting for the winter games, Innsbruck received 49 votes, compared to nine for Calgary, Alberta. No votes were cast for Lahti, Finland, a third site under consideration.

This is the first time the winter games are to be held in Austria.

A two-man Detroit delegation, bearing a letter from President Eisenhower, failed in a bid to bring the Olympics to the United States.

PUTTERING AROUND—Mrs. Betty Loveys putts on 7th green in Southern California women's golf against Mrs. Lester Boyle. She missed putt, won match.
Story on Page 4, Part IV
Times photo by John Malmin

## Round Table Awarded 134 for Gold Cup

BY PAUL LOWRY

Round Table, the 1958 horse of the year, has been awarded top weight of 134 lb. for the renewal of the $100,000-added Hollywood Gold Cup on July 11.

Hillsdale, victorious in two successive stakes at the Inglewood track this summer, is next at 124 lb. He is the leading money-winning horse of the year with a total of $270,250 for '59.

Round Table is the money-winning king of all time with lifetime earnings of $1,363,189.

Amerigo, which was beaten a nose by Hillsdale in the California last Saturday when the weights were 123 and 107, respectively, gets into the mile-and-one-quarter Gold Cup with 112.

Racing secretary John Maluvius released the Gold Cup weights yesterday after long hours of study.

Currently Round Table is in Chicago, and has not raced since grabbing a quarter and finishing last to Hakuchikara in a field of 16 horses in the Washington's Birthday Handicap at Santa Anita.

Declared from the Santa Anita Handicap, for which he had been allotted 132 lb., Round Table was shipped to Chicago and it was an-

Please Turn to Pg. 7, Col. 6

### THE WINNERS

1—Vegas Jewell, $9.40.
2—Pez Vela, $3.90.
3—Rubidoux, $9.30.
4—Jaybil, $58.50.
5—Marianne, $17.10.
6—Shah Jehan II, $13.20.
7—Nascania, $7.30.
8—Ardent Love, $15.50.

### TODAY IN SPORTS

HORSE RACING—Hollywood Park, 1:45 p.m.

BASEBALL—Dodgers vs. Cubs, Coliseum, 8 p.m.

WRESTLING — Olympic Auditorium, 8:30 p.m.

K.C. TO RESCUE

## Yankees Trade Four to Get Terry, Lopez

NEW YORK, May 26.—The slumping New York Yankees again turned to Kansas City for help today, completing the 14th deal between the two clubs. The Yanks got infielder Hector Lopez and pitcher Ralph Terry for pitchers Tom Sturdivant and Johnny Kucks, infielder Jerry Lumpe and a fourth player to be named before the start of next season.

The Kansas City-New York shuffles, starting shortly after the A's moved west in 1955 into former Yankee farm territory, have involved 52 players. Several have made the trip both ways or to a minor-league outlet.

Terry, a 6-2 right-hander from Chelsea, Okla., toiled in the Yankee chain until 1957. Then he was tossed into the deal that also sent Billy Martin and Woody Held to the A's for Harry Simpson, Ryne Duren and two minor leaguers. Terry certainly will get into the starting rotation on the thin Yankee staff. In seven starts for the A's, the 23-year-old picther has managed a 2-4 won-lost record.

Lopez, in the midst of a sizzling batting streak with six hits, including two doubles, two triples

Please Turn to Pg. 3, Col. 2

## BASEBALL STANDINGS

NATIONAL LEAGUE

| | W | L | Pct. | * |
|---|---|---|---|---|
| Milwaukee | 24 | 14 | .632 | |
| San Francisco | 22 | 18 | .550 | 3 |
| Pittsburgh | 20 | 19 | .513 | 4½ |
| LOS ANGELES | 22 | 21 | .512 | 4½ |
| Chicago | 21 | 21 | .500 | 5 |
| Cincinnati | 19 | 21 | .475 | 6 |
| St. Louis | 17 | 22 | .436 | 7½ |
| Philadelphia | 15 | 24 | .385 | 9½ |

*Games behind leader.

**Yesterday's Results**

San Francisco, 6; LOS ANGELES, 4.

Milwaukee, 2; Pittsburgh, 0. (13 innings.)

Cincinnati, 2; Philadelphia, 1.

Only games scheduled.

**Games Today**

Chicago (Hobbie, 5-3) vs. LOS ANGELES (Drysdale, 4-4), Coliseum, KMPC Radio, 7:55 p.m.

St. Louis (Blaylock, 2-1) at San Francisco (Antonelli, 5-2).

Pittsburgh (Law, 4-1) at Milwaukee (Spahn, 5-5), night.

Philadelphia (Roberts, 2-3) at Cincinnati (Nuxhall, 2-2), night.

AMERICAN LEAGUE

| | W | L | Pct. | * |
|---|---|---|---|---|
| Cleveland | 24 | 13 | .649 | |
| Chicago | 23 | 16 | .590 | 2 |
| Baltimore | 23 | 17 | .575 | 2½ |
| Washington | 19 | 22 | .463 | 7 |
| Kansas City | 17 | 20 | .459 | 7 |
| Detroit | 17 | 22 | .436 | 8 |
| Boston | 16 | 21 | .432 | 8 |
| New York | 14 | 22 | .389 | 9½ |

*Games behind leader.

**Yesterday's Results**

Baltimore, 6; Washington, 5.
Boston, 12; New York, 2.
Cleveland, 3; Chicago, 0.
Detroit, 9; Kansas City, 5.

**Games Today**

Boston (Delock, 5-1) at New York (Maas, 2-2).

Cleveland (Bell, 4-2, or Grant, 3-0) at Chicago (Wynn, 6-3).

Detroit (Bunning, 5-3) at Kansas City (Daley, 2-3), night.

Washington (Griggs, 2-2) at Baltimore (Portocarrero, 0-3), night.

## Braves Win on 'Homer'

MILWAUKEE, May 26 (AP)—Pittsburgh left-hander Harvey Haddix pitched 12 perfect innings tonight, then lost 2-0 in the 13th to Milwaukee on an error, an intentional walk and a rule-book double by Joe Adcock—the Braves' only hit.

Haddix, credited with a 12-inning no-hitter, retired the first 36 men in order before Don Hoak's throwing error permitted Felix Mantilla to reach base leading off the 13th inning.

After Ed Mathews sacrificed, Haddix issued the intentional pass to Hank Aaron, but the strategy backfired when Adcock sent a long drive into the stands.

### Homer Erased

Adcock at first was credited with a home run. But he was declared out, and given only a double, when he passed Aaron between second and third.

A jubilant Aaron had cut across the diamond without touching third. His run was permitted to count, however, after he was sent back by his mates to touch third and then home. Adcock's run was nullified.

It was a heart-breaking climax for Haddix, who became the first pitcher in history to carry a perfect performance past nine innings. He did salvage, however, the longest no-hitter in major league history.

Seven other pitchers, including the New York Yankees' Don Larsen in the 1956 World Series, have registered perfect games. Two were National Leaguers, both before the turn of the century.

### Last One In 1922

The last pitcher to do it in a regular-season game was Charley Robertson of the Chicago White Sox against Detroit on April 30, 1922. He won 2-0.

Lew Burdette was the winning pitcher, pitching brilliantly while giving up a dozen hits. It was his eighth victory—tops in the majors — against two defeats.

A crowd of 19,194 sat in on the historic game as Haddix once again gave in to the Braves. This was his

Please Turn to Pg. 6, Col. 4

### Almost Haddix

| Pittsburgh | ab | r | h | * | Milwaukee | ab | r | h | * |
|---|---|---|---|---|---|---|---|---|---|
| Schofield,ss | 6 | 0 | 3 | 0 | O'Brien,2b | 3 | 0 | 0 | 0 |
| Virdon,cf | 6 | 0 | 1 | 0 | Rice | 1 | 0 | 0 | 0 |
| Burgess,c | 5 | 0 | 0 | 0 | Mantilla,2b | 1 | 1 | 0 | 0 |
| Nelson,1b | 5 | 0 | 2 | 0 | Mathews,3b | 4 | 0 | 0 | 0 |
| Skinner,lf | 5 | 0 | 1 | 0 | Aaron,rf | 4 | 1 | 0 | 0 |
| Mazeroski,2b | 5 | 0 | 1 | 0 | Adcock,1b | 5 | 0 | 1 | 2 |
| Hoak,3b | 5 | 0 | 2 | 0 | Covington,lf | 4 | 0 | 0 | 0 |
| Mejias,rf | 3 | 0 | 1 | 0 | Crandall,c | 4 | 0 | 0 | 0 |
| Stuart | 1 | 0 | 0 | 0 | Pafko,cf | 4 | 0 | 0 | 0 |
| Ch'topher,rf | 1 | 0 | 0 | 0 | Logan,ss | 4 | 0 | 0 | 0 |
| Haddix,p | 5 | 0 | 1 | 0 | Burdette,p | 4 | 0 | 0 | 0 |
| Totals | 47 | 0 | 12 | 0 | Totals | 38 | 2 | 1 | 2 |

*Runs by innings.
Stuart filed out for Mejias in 10th.
Rice flied out for O'Brien in 10th.

SCORE BY INNINGS

| | |
|---|---|
| Pittsburgh | 000 000 000 000 0—0 |
| Milwaukee | 000 000 000 000 2—2 |

E—Hoak. PO-A—Pittsburgh, 38-13 (two out when winning runs scored); Milwaukee, 39-21. DP—Logan to Adcock; Mathews, O'Brien to Adcock; Adcock to Logan. LOB—Pittsburgh, 8; Milwaukee, 0. 2B—Adcock. SH—Mathews.

| Pitcher— | IP | H | R | ER | BB | SO |
|---|---|---|---|---|---|---|
| Haddix-L (3-3) | 12⅔ | 1 | 2 | 1 | 1 | 8 |
| Burdette-W (8-2) | 13 | 12 | 0 | 0 | 0 | 2 |

Umpires—Smith, Dascoli, Secory, Dixon. Time—2h. 54m. Attendance—19,194.

## Grand Slam Nips Dodgers

### Wagner's Blow in Ninth Gives S.F. 6-4 Victory

BY FRANK FINCH, Times Staff Representative

SAN FRANCISCO, May 26—It shouldn't happen to a hound dog, but it happened to Sandy Koufax tonight.

On the verge of pitching his best game in several seasons, Sandy faltered in the ninth inning, Art Fowler relieved him with the bases loaded, and then Leon Wagner walloped a grand-slam pinch homer to dump the Dodgers, 6-4.

It was a blow that will go down in San Francisco Giant lore, for the Giants were practically as extinct as the dodo bird until Koufax finally faded when his first victory of the season was within his grasp.

### Whiffs Eleven

With 10 strikeouts to his credit, Sandy sailed into the last of the ninth by whiffing his 11th victim, Orlando Cepeda.

Then Koufax issued his third base on balls to Jackie Brandt.

The next hitter, Felipe Alou, got a lucky break when catcher Joe Pignatano failed to glove his foul ball behind the plate. Given new life, Alou blooped a single, and when Koufax walked Daryl Spencer on a 3-and-2 offering, Fowler relieved him.

Manager Bill Rigney made himself look like a genius by selecting Wagner, a wicked-swinging left-hander, to bat for Bob Schmidt.

Strike one, called.

Fowler's next serve never got across the plate. Wagner tied into it and parked it into

Please Turn to Pg. 2, Col. 3

### BOX SCORE

| Los Angeles | AB | R | H | RBI | E |
|---|---|---|---|---|---|
| Fairly, rf | 4 | 0 | 1 | 0 | 0 |
| Neal, 2b | 4 | 1 | 1 | 1 | 1 |
| Moon, lf | 4 | 1 | 1 | 1 | 0 |
| Demeter, cf | 3 | 1 | 1 | 0 | 0 |
| Hodges, 1b | 4 | 0 | 1 | 2 | 0 |
| Gray, 3b | 4 | 0 | 0 | 0 | 0 |
| Pignatano, c | 3 | 0 | 0 | 0 | 0 |
| Lillis, ss | 3 | 0 | 0 | 0 | 0 |
| Koufax, p | 3 | 1 | 2 | 0 | 0 |
| Fowler, p | 0 | 0 | 0 | 0 | 0 |
| Totals | 32 | 4 | 7 | 4 | 1 |

| San Francisco | AB | R | H | RBI | E |
|---|---|---|---|---|---|
| O'Connell, 3b | 4 | 0 | 0 | 0 | 0 |
| Rodgers, ss | 4 | 1 | 1 | 1 | 0 |
| Mays, cf | 2 | 1 | 1 | 0 | 0 |
| Cepeda, 1b | 4 | 0 | 1 | 0 | 0 |
| Brandt, lf | 3 | 1 | 0 | 0 | 0 |
| Alou, rf | 4 | 1 | 2 | 0 | 0 |
| Spencer, 2b | 3 | 1 | 0 | 0 | 0 |
| Schmidt, c | 3 | 0 | 0 | 0 | 0 |
| Wagner | 1 | 1 | 1 | 4 | 0 |
| Miller, p | 2 | 0 | 0 | 0 | 0 |
| Bressoud | 1 | 0 | 0 | 0 | 0 |
| G. Jones, p | 0 | 0 | 0 | 0 | 0 |
| Totals | 31 | 6 | 6 | 5 | 0 |

Bressoud struck out for Miller in 7th.
Wagner homered for Schmidt in 9th.

SCORE BY INNINGS

| | |
|---|---|
| Los Angeles | 010 003 000—4 |
| San Francisco | 100 001 004—6 |

PO-A—Los Angeles, 25-8 (one out when winning run scored); San Francisco, 27-15. DP—Pignatano to Neal, Spencer to Cepeda. LOB—Los Angeles, 2; San Francisco, 4. 2B—Mays, Koufax, 2; Neal. 3B—Demeter. HR—Rodgers, Wagner. SB—Moon.

| Pitcher— | IP | H | R | ER | BB | SO |
|---|---|---|---|---|---|---|
| Koufax-L (0-1) | 8⅓ | 5 | 5 | 4 | 4 | 11 |
| Fowler | 0+ | 1 | 1 | 1 | 0 | 0 |
| Miller | 6 | 5 | 4 | 4 | 1 | 3 |
| G. Jones-W (2-2) | 3 | 2 | 0 | 0 | 0 | 1 |

WP—Koufax. Umpires—Crawford, Delmore, Barlick and Jackowski. Time—2h. 22m. Attendance—18,471.

BAD PITCH

## Haddix Tells How Adcock Ruined Gem

MILWAUKEE, May 26 (AP)—"He hit a high slider but I tried to keep it down and away."

That was Pittsburgh southpaw Harvey Haddix's explanation of the key pitch of the only hit off him in a heart-breaking 2-0 loss tonight to the Milwaukee Braves.

Haddix retired 36 men in order. He was discouraged but not downhearted following his brilliant performance in becoming the longest perfect game pitcher in major league history.

### One Purpose

"All I kept thinking of was trying to keep them from scoring," the 33-year-old ace said. "I knew I had a no-hitter—knew it all the time. I didn't know I had a perfect game. I thought I might have walked a man somewhere along the line."

Harvey Haddix

Haddix retired the heavy hitting Braves in order for 12 innings until Felix Mantilla reached first on a throwing error by third baseman Don Hoak. The Pirates protested vigorously that Mantilla had rounded first and had been tagged out but the umpires disagreed.

After Eddie Mathews sacrificed Hank Aaron was intentionally walked. But Joe Adcock crossed up the strat-

Please Turn to Pg. 6, Col. 4

BRITISH LINE—Here's forward line that starts for England against United States All-Stars in soccer game at Wrigley Field tomorrow night. From the left, Warren Bradley, outside right; Jimmy Greaves, inside right; Kevan Derek, center; Johnny Haynes, inside left and Bobby Charlton, outside left.
Story on Page 4, Part IV
Times photo

# RAGS TO RICHES FOR CINDERELLA TEAM

## L.A. Beats Braves With Story Book Finish in 12th, 6-5

Los Angeles Times
Sports
PART IV
CC WEDNESDAY MORNING, SEPTEMBER 30, 1959 2†

### SPORTSCRIPTS

## Sox Have Edge in World Series

BY PAUL ZIMMERMAN, Sports Editor

You have to assume that the White Sox have a definite edge in physical condition going into the start of the World Series tomorrow at Chicago. Also, in their pitching assignments.

Not only has this been a rugged, dog-eat-dog last month in the pennant race for the Dodgers, but their two play-off games with Milwaukee have taken something out of the National League champions.

All you need to do is travel with a baseball team to realize how much this transcontinental hopping wears on players. After the Dodgers beat down the leading Giants, they had to fly to St. Louis. Then it was another leap to Chicago.

Paul Zimmerman

They got a day of rest after playing the Cubs, but had a bus trip to Milwaukee the morning of the first play-off game. Then it was "be packed in the bus an hour after the game" for the Monday night trip here.

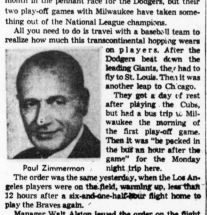

The order was the same yesterday, when the Los Angeles players were on the field, warming up, less than 12 hours after a six-and-one-half-hour flight home to play the Braves again.

Manager Walt Alston issued the order on the flight home Monday night that—same old story—have "your bags packed and at the locker room. We're leaving for Chicago immediately after the game."

#### Alston Admits Club Needs Rest

"It isn't so much that we need the practice," said the genial manager. "Sure, the surroundings at Comiskey Park are new, and the wind currents are treacherous. What we need more right now is the rest."

In the meantime the White Sox have been pretty much sitting on their hands, having the American League pennant in the bag. Certainly theirs has been no fatiguing problem of two cross-country flights and sundry short trips.

Manager Al Lopez has another distinct edge. His pitching rotation is in order. Alston is fortunate that the play-off didn't go to a third game where he would have called upon Roger Craig. Now Rog will be ready to start, but the rest of the hurlers are pretty well used up at the moment.

#### Giants Beaten After Similar Whirl

To give you some idea, the Giants were beaten by the Yankees in 1951 after they had knocked off Brooklyn in a similar play-off. And manager Durocher's team didn't have an energy-taxing six-hour plane ride on top of its climaxing game that won the pennant.

To refresh your memory, the Giants stood their ground for three games.

Then the wear and tear on them took its toll, even though they had the advantage of a day's postponement because of rain. Beaten to a frazzle by fatigue and pressure, they lost the next three and the championship.

#### Mental Strain Adds to Pinch

In addition to the general worn-down condition of the team, there is a matter of the mental wear and tear. Here are a couple of examples:

Warren Spahn, who pitched the Braves to an all-important 3 to 2 victory over Robin Roberts of the Phils Saturday, was suffering from an upset stomach all during the contest and before.

Monday, at Milwaukee, Jim Gilliam was affected by a similar ailment and was ill on the plane coming home.

Now here are a pair of case-hardened, vastly experienced campaigners. Both have been through the World Series mill. It may not have been nerves, but neither Spahn or Gilliam discounted the fact.

P.S.: Certainly, a much rested White Sox team has an edge when the World Series shooting starts.

### HOW THEY FINISHED

| | W. | L. | Pct. |
|---|---|---|---|
| Los Angeles | 88 | 68 | .564 |
| Milwaukee | 86 | 70 | .551 |

## Carl Furillo Center of Celebration

### Oldest Dodger Erases Memories of Past Play-offs

BY BOB THOMAS

The story just had to be Carl Furillo with postscripts by Gil Hodges.

The oldest pro of 'em all, Carl had gone down with the ship as a Brooklyn Dodger in 1946 and again in 1951 in the National League's only other play-offs.

As the only active Los Angeles Dodger who played on those teams, Carl carried some unhappy memories onto the field when he entered yesterday's all-important game with the Braves as a ninth-inning pinch hitter. In five previous post-season tilts—four of them losses to the Cardinals and Giants—Furillo had squeaked out only one hit in 22 times at bat.

**Center of Celebration**

But yesterday he was an immediate hero. And when the league's third such play-off series was over it was Furillo who was the center of a wild dressing room celebration, a dressing room clogged beyond belief with newsmen, cameramen, radio and TV equipment and well wishers.

Carl smacked Warren Spahn's second pitch in the ninth deep to right field to bring home Hodges from third base with the game-tying run, sending the battle into overtime.

Hodges, incidentally, was a bench warmer on that 1946 team which lost to the Cards, coming up at the end of the season as a rookie catcher from Newport News. He didn't get into a game, however.

**Crazy Victory**

And so it had to be Furillo and Hodges again in the 12th to sew up the craziest pennant victory in Dodger history.

Did Carl think he had the play at first beat out when Felix Mantilla made a bad throw allowing Hodges to score the winning run?

"I thought so," he said later amid the mob scene in the dressing room. Somehow

Please Turn to Pg. 7, Col. 3

THE BIGGEST MOMENT — Gil Hodges, arrow, crosses home plate with a pennant-winning grin after scoring from second on Carl Furillo's hit in 12th inning. Downcast catcher Del Crandall of Braves at upper right. Maury Wills is behind Hodges while manager Walt Alston (24), coach Charlie Dressen (7), Norm Larker (5) and catcher John Roseboro, jacket, rush out to swarm over triumphant mates. Air is filled with pieces of paper as the elated fans throw torn-up programs into air in jubilation.

Times photo by Larry Sharkey

## Seventh to First for Zany Club

BY BRAVEN DYER

The crazy, zany Cinderella story of the Dodgers was complete yesterday.

They beat last year's National League champion Milwaukee, 6-5, in 12 thrill-packed innings before 36,528 Coliseum cardiac cases to get their World Series shot against the Chicago White Sox.

Walter O'Malley had right Sunday night. After his club had tied the Braves for the pennant he said:

"You can win 'em the easy way and you can win 'em the hard way. But that doesn't satisfy the Dodgers. They've got to win 'em the Dodger way."

I understand Mr. O'Malley, before leaving for Chicago with the team last night signed his script writer to a new long term contract.

**Dodgers Defy Tradition**

Not even a panel of Hollywood's brightest authors could turn out anything to match the Dodgers rise from seventh place a year ago to the World Series of 1959.

No other National League club ever did it, but the Dodgers have been defying tradition ever since the '59 campaign began.

President Eisenhower has announced he's coming out this week to get rid of a cold. Actually, he's coming to pitch the first ball when the Series switches from Chicago to the Coliseum next Sunday. At least that's the way I get it now.

**Full of Tension**

I've seen major sports events of every description all over the world and many will stick with me forever.

For sustained tension though, nothing comes even close to matching the hour of diamond dramatics which the Dodgers and Braves furnished from the home half of the ninth inning through the history-making 12th.

Carl Furillo, at 37 the elder statesman of the Dodgers, was the last player to come to bat and his bounder behind second base with two out in the 12th started the play which sent Gil Hodges across with the winning run.

**Throw Goes Wild**

It was ruled a hit, but what actually cooked the Braves was Felix Mantilla's wild throw to first. The ball bounded in front of Frank Torre and then skidded by the Milwaukee first sacker, hit Dodger coach Greg Mulleavy on the shoulder and wound up in the stands while Hodges crossed the plate and ran into the wildest reception party in Coliseum history as all the Dodgers poured from the dugout and pounded him purple.

It was Furillo, too, who had knocked in the tying run during that mad ninth inning when Milwaukee seemed a cinch winner with a 5-2 lead.

Pinch hitting for John Roseboro, the old pro belted one a mile deep in right field. Hank Aaron caught it almost against the fence and Hodges, who had been

Please Turn to Pg. 2, Col. 1

Stan Williams

### OF PEBBLES AND BRAVES

## Torre Says Furillo Would Have Been Out but for Crazy Bounce

BY MAL FLORENCE

But for a freak carom of a ball the Dodgers and the Braves might still be battling for the National League pennant.

Milwaukee first baseman Frank Torre might be alone in his opinion but he staunchly believed that if Felix Mantilla's throw in the 12th inning yesterday hadn't eluded him Dodger Carl Furillo would have been out.

"If the ball had taken a normal bounce, sort of a skid, I could have dug it out," stated the articulate Torre in the Braves' dressing quarters.

**Didn't Touch Ball**

"But, as it was, the ball hit a ridge or stone and bounced over my head. It hit Mulleavy on the fly, so you can see it was a crazy bounce," continued Torre.

Torre was referring to Greg Mulleavy, the Dodger first base coach. The ball actually bounced off his shoulder.

There was no doubt in Torre's mind that Furillo was a dead Dodger at first, IF he could have gloved the ball.

"The ball had Furillo beat," said Torre emphatically. "No, my foot wasn't off the bag."

Torre went on to say that he never touched the ball. And he defended shortstop Mantilla, stating that the throw "wasn't that bad." Thus, some innocent pebble is the culprit.

Some people felt that Mantilla shouldn't have thrown to first at all what with Hodges on second, Pignatano on first and two outs. But Torre disagreed:

"His (Mantilla) only play was to first. There was no one at second as Avila was going for the ball, too. It's a shame it had to work out this way because Mantilla has been carrying the infield all season."

**Was Only Play**

A dejected Mantilla kept muttering, "it was my only play, it was my only play, I had to throw to first."

Mantilla, who had replaced the injured Johnny Logan at shortstop in the seventh inning, was near tears in his dressing cubicle.

"I was off balance when I grabbed the ball, "sobbed Felix. I thought I might have had a force play at second when the ball was hit. But it took a crazy bounce and pulled me across the bag before I got it."

One scribe asked Mantilla if he thought the Dodgers could beat the White Sox in the World Series.

"If they could beat us, they could beat the White Sox," snapped Felix.

**Haney Disgruntled**

Manager Fred Haney was disgruntled about the loss but also philosophical.

"If you can't hold a three-run lead in the ninth, you don't deserve to win," observed Haney.

As for the Mantilla play, Haney stated:

"He made a helluva good play just getting to the ball. It was just one of those things—he wasn't

Please Turn to Pg. 4, Col. 2

### TODAY IN SPORTS

**PRO BASKETBALL**—St. Louis Hawks vs. Philadelphia Warriors, L.A. Sports Arena, 8:15 p.m.

**HORSE RACING** — L.A. County Fair, Pomona, 12 noon.

**WRESTLING** — Olympic Auditorium, 8:30 p.m.

### FINAL STANDINGS

| | W | L | Pct. | * |
|---|---|---|---|---|
| LOS ANGELES | 88 | 68 | .564 | |
| Milwaukee | 86 | 70 | .551 | 2 |
| San Francisco | 83 | 71 | .539 | 4 |
| Pittsburgh | 78 | 76 | .506 | 9 |
| Chicago | 74 | 80 | .481 | 13 |
| Cincinnati | 74 | 80 | .481 | 13 |
| St. Louis | 71 | 83 | .461 | 16 |
| Philadelphia | 64 | 90 | .416 | 23 |

*Games behind winner.

**Yesterday's Results**

LOS ANGELES, 6; Milwaukee, 5 (play-off, 12 innings).

### FROM 7TH TO HEAVEN

| Milwaukee | AB | R | H | RBI | E |
|---|---|---|---|---|---|
| Bruton, cf | 6 | 0 | 0 | 0 | 0 |
| Mathews, 3b | 4 | 2 | 2 | 1 | 0 |
| Aaron, rf | 4 | 1 | 2 | 0 | 0 |
| Torre, 1b | 3 | 0 | 1 | 2 | 0 |
| Maye, lf | 2 | 0 | 0 | 0 | 0 |
| Pafko, lf | 1 | 0 | 0 | 0 | 0 |
| Slaughter | 1 | 0 | 0 | 0 | 0 |
| Demerit, lf | 0 | 0 | 0 | 0 | 0 |
| Spangler, lf | 0 | 0 | 0 | 0 | 0 |
| Logan, ss | 3 | 1 | 2 | 0 | 0 |
| Schoendienst, 2b | 1 | 0 | 0 | 0 | 0 |
| Vernon | 1 | 0 | 0 | 0 | 0 |
| Cottier, 2b | 0 | 0 | 0 | 0 | 0 |
| Adcock | 1 | 0 | 0 | 0 | 0 |
| Avila, 2b | 0 | 0 | 0 | 0 | 0 |
| Crandall, c | 6 | 1 | 1 | 0 | 0 |
| Mantilla, 2b-ss | 5 | 0 | 1 | 1 | 2 |
| Burdette, p | 4 | 0 | 1 | 0 | 0 |
| McMahon, p | 0 | 0 | 0 | 0 | 0 |
| Spahn, p | 0 | 0 | 0 | 0 | 0 |
| Jay, p | 1 | 0 | 0 | 0 | 0 |
| Rush, p | 1 | 0 | 0 | 0 | 0 |
| Totals | 44 | 5 | 10 | 4 | 2 |

| Los Angeles | AB | R | H | RBI | E |
|---|---|---|---|---|---|
| Gilliam, 3b | 5 | 0 | 1 | 0 | 0 |
| Neal, 2b | 6 | 2 | 2 | 1 | 1 |
| Moon, rf-lf | 6 | 1 | 3 | 1 | 0 |
| Snider, cf | 4 | 0 | 1 | 0 | 1 |
| Lillis | 0 | 1 | 0 | 0 | 0 |
| Williams, p | 2 | 0 | 0 | 0 | 0 |
| Hodges, 1b | 5 | 2 | 2 | 0 | 0 |
| Larker, lf | 4 | 0 | 2 | 2 | 0 |
| Pignatano, c | 1 | 0 | 1 | 0 | 0 |
| Roseboro, c | 3 | 0 | 0 | 0 | 0 |
| Furillo, rf | 2 | 0 | 2 | 1 | 0 |
| Wills, ss | 5 | 0 | 1 | 0 | 0 |
| Drysdale, p | 1 | 0 | 0 | 0 | 0 |
| Podres, p | 1 | 0 | 0 | 0 | 0 |
| Churn, p | 0 | 0 | 0 | 0 | 0 |
| Demeter | 1 | 0 | 0 | 0 | 0 |
| Koufax, p | 0 | 0 | 0 | 0 | 0 |
| Labine, p | 0 | 0 | 0 | 0 | 0 |
| Essegian | 0 | 0 | 0 | 0 | 0 |
| Fairly, cf | 2 | 0 | 0 | 0 | 0 |
| Totals | 48 | 6 | 15 | 5 | 2 |

Pafko flied out for Maye in 5th. Slaughter popped out for Pafko in 7th. Demeter lined out for Churn in 8th. Vernon called out on strikes for Schoendienst in 9th. Lillis ran for Snider in 9th. Pignatano ran for Larker in 9th. Furillo hit sacrifice fly for Roseboro in 9th. Essegian announced as batter for Labine in 9th. Fairly hit into force play for Essegian in 9th. Spangler walked for Demerit in 11th. Adcock hit into force play for Cottier in 11th. Two out when winning run scored.

| | | | | | |
|---|---|---|---|---|---|
| Milwaukee | 210 | 010 | 010 | 000 | — 5 |
| Los Angeles | 100 | 100 | 003 | 001 | — 6 |

PO-A—Milwaukee, 35-12 (two out when winning run scored). Los Angeles, 36-15.

E—Snider, Neal, Mantilla 2. DP—Wills, Neal and Hodges; Torre, Logan and Torre. LOB—Milwaukee 13, Los Angeles 11. 2B—Aaron. 3B—Neal, Crandall. HR—Neal, Mathews. SF—Mantilla, Furillo.

| | IP | H | R | ER | BB | SO |
|---|---|---|---|---|---|---|
| Drysdale | 4 1/3 | 6 | 4 | 3 | 2 | 3 |
| Podres | 2 1/3 | 3 | 0 | 0 | 1 | 1 |
| Churn | 1 1/3 | 1 | 1 | 1 | 0 | 0 |
| Koufax | 2/3 | 0 | 0 | 0 | 3 | 1 |
| Labine | 1/3 | 0 | 0 | 0 | 0 | 1 |
| Williams (W, 5-5) | 3 | 0 | 0 | 0 | 3 | 3 |
| *Burdette | 8 | 10 | 5 | 5 | 0 | 4 |
| 'McMahon | 0 | 1 | 0 | 0 | 0 | 0 |
| Spahn | 1/3 | 1 | 0 | 0 | 0 | 0 |
| Jay | 2 2/3 | 1 | 0 | 0 | 1 | 1 |
| Rush (L, 5-6) | 1 | 2 | 1 | 0 | 1 | 0 |

*Faced 3 batters in 9th.

'Faced 1 batter in 9th.

BB—Drysdale 2 (Mathews, Aaron), Podres 1 (Torre), Koufax 3 (Aaron, Torre, Demerit), Williams 3 (Mathews, Torre, Spangler), Jay 1 (Gilliam), Rush 1 (Hodges). SO—Drysdale 3 (Crandall 2, Mantilla), Podres 1 (Burdette), Koufax 1 (Bruton), Labine 1 (Vernon), Williams 3 (Mantilla, Jay, Rush), Burdette 4 (Snider 2, Hodges, Wills), Jay 1 (Williams). HBP—By Jay (Pignatano). WP—Podres. PB—Pignatano.

Umpires — Barlick, Boggess, Donatelli, Conlan, Jackowski, Gorman. Time—4:06. Attendance: 36,528.

# CINDERELLA DODGERS WORLD CHAMPS

CLIMAX ON THE HILL—Dodger Larry Sherry hurls final pitch, turns to watch fly hit to outfield, grabs John Roseboro's hand for a victory shake, then embraces battery mate after triumph.

(UP) Wirephoto

Los Angeles Times
Sports
PART IV
CC FRIDAY MORNING, OCTOBER 9, 1959 †

## SPORTSCRIPTS

## Great Field Set for Grand Prix

BY PAUL ZIMMERMAN—Sports Editor

Like a baseball player poised on second for the hit that will send him to the plate, the second annual U.S. Grand Prix of sports car racing awaits the starter's flag at Riverside this week end, ready to give the red-hot sports fans of Southern California something new to cheer about.

This Times-Mirror-sponsored 200-mile road race has attracted the finest array of drivers and cars ever assembled in the West for such an event.

Stirling Moss

Where else could you hope to see such name drivers in one race as Stirling Moss, classed as the greatest in the world; Phil Hill, the Santa Monican who went continental; Chuck Daigh, who won the inaugural a year ago; Dan Gurney, a Riverside resident who has become one of the top drivers; the Rodriguez brothers from Mexico, Ricardo and Pedro, and Roger Ward, Indianapolis winner, to name a few?

This, of course, is Moss' first appearance. He's a Britisher with a keen sense of humor. You'd hardly know he was a race driver until he climbs into his Aston Martin.

Moss should go into this classic as the favorite. Oddly enough, his greatest competition, say the experts in the pits, comes from three Southern Californians.

Hill, 32-year-old Ferrari factory driver, is the top American in European Grand Prix racing. He got his road racing start right here.

Riverside's Gurney came here from Long Island but also earned his speed honors in Southern California first. He's the son of a former opera singer and was a surprise second-place finisher 23 seconds back of Daigh a year ago.

### *Ginther Third Southland Entry*

The third Southlander is Richie Ginther of Granada Hills. By coincidence, he's a long-time friend of Hill. Like Phil and Dan, he will pilot a Ferrari.

Needless to say, there's a pronounced Southern California flavor in the race with such week-in and week-out local favorites as Ken Miles, Jack McAfee, Max Balchowsky, Billy Krause, Skip Hudson and Eric Hauser among them.

The Rodriguez youths add a distinct Pan-American touch. Ricardo, 18, and Pedro, 20, are the sons of a wealthy Mexican industrialist and they've raced all over the world with considerable success despite their tender age.

Ricardo is the better known here because of his Riverside victory in 1956 when he was only 15 years old.

With 65 drivers seeking to qualify for the field of 30 in the big race, it is self-evident that this is going to be another in the parade of major sports events for us this year.

**P.S.:** Where but in Southern California could the fan jump from the World Series in the Coliseum to the Grand Prix of sports car racing at Riverside in one week?

DUKE STARTS IT—With a mighty swing, Duke Snider whacks the ball out of the park for two-run homer in third inning to start Dodgers on road to their second World Series triumph in finale at Chicago yesterday. Dodgers won, 9-3.

(UP) Wirephoto

## 'MADE ME WORK HARD'

## Sherry Lauds Brother for Fame

BY LARRY SHERRY
As told to the United Press International

CHICAGO, Oct. 8 (UPI)—My older brother Norm didn't even get his name in the box score, but if it wasn't for him, my name wouldn't have been in it either during this World Series.

Norm is a catcher. He came up to the Dodgers this year from Spokane and wasn't eligible to play in the series even though he was with us and suited up each day before the game.

No one worked harder with me than he did. Even when we were kids, we'd spend hours working together. Sometimes I'd feel like

Please Turn to Pg. 4, Col. 1

### TODAY IN SPORTS

**HARNESS RACING** — Hollywood Park, 1 p.m.

**MOTORCYCLE RACING** —Ascot Stadium, 8:30 p.m.

## 'Greatest Team, It Never Quit,' Says Walt Alston

BY AL WOLF
Times Staff Representative

CHICAGO, Oct. 8—Picture six cans of sardines squeezed into one Add pandemonium, hysteria, screams, shoving and joyous back-slaps.

That was the Dodger dressing room scene following today's World Series triumph.

The players had no more than reached their already cramped quarters from the field when they were engulfed by a crush of sports writers, photographers, newsreel men and assorted visitors numbering in the hundreds.

So tight was the jam that the players could scarcely move, let alone congratulate each other, get their hands on bottles of beer, undress or make for the showers.

The Dodgers were wildly exultant as they scampered through the door. By the time they finally got breathing room, they were too spent to whoop or indulge in the usual horseplay. They just sat.

"This is the greatest team I ever was connected with," shouted manager Walt Alston, "or any manager ever was connected with. This team never quit; it came from behind all the way; it won against big odds.

"This team would make any manager look good, because whatever you did, they came through. So you couldn't guess wrong.

"I hate to single out any one player because it was teamwork every step of the way from spring training. But how about that kid, Larry Sherry? He gave us tremendous pitching the last part of the season and he carried us through this series. I just have to say something special about him."

**Hero of the Series**

Sherry, called up at mid-season, pitched his first Dodger game on July 4, lost it and another, then won seven straight — and topped that performance by winning two games and saving two others in the World Series.

Unquestionably, the 24-year-old Fairfax High grad is the hero of the 1959 show.

"Sure, this has to be the greatest thrill of my life," Sherry said as he leaned wearily against his locker. "No, I didn't get tired today, but I'm glad there's no game tomorrow that I might have to work in. I don't think I'd be much good.

"All I want now is to rest a little while. Then I'm go-

Please Turn to Pg. 2, Col. 1

## ARRIVAL OF CHAMPS ON TV

The Dodgers will arrive at International Airport at 4:10 this afternoon, deplaning from their chartered United Air Lines DC-7 directly east of United's east concourse.

The arrival will be telecast by KTTV and there will be interviews. Dodger executives and players' wives will arrive aboard a second chartered flight at 5:25 p.m.

## 4 GAMES TO 2

## Dodgers Rout Chisox, 9-3, to Take Series

Continued from Pg. 1, Pt. I

the Dodgers in the classic 1-0 fifth game in L.A.

Maury Wills singled in the first tally of the inning, Podres doubled Maury home to finish Wynn, Charlie Neal drove in two runs after Donovan walked Jim Gilliam, and Moon followed with a two-run homer as Donovan expired.

After Klu clouted his third homer in the last of the fourth, there was no more scoring until Essegian became the first player in World Series history to wallop a second pinch homer.

The former Stanford fullback, who also hails from Fairfax High, hit for Snider in the ninth and slugged Ray Moore's first pitch into the left-field seats. Chuck hit his other one in the second game here.

Their reward for a job well done? The lion's share of a record series melon of $892,-365.04 and the pride that goes with knowing they're the best damned baseball team in the world.

The comeback of Sherry parallels the rags-to-riches story of the Dodgers.

During the Dodgers' drive to the pennant Sherry posted seven consecutive victories and saved three other games. In relief his earned-run average was a microscopic 0.74.

**Sherry 'Chary'**

And in tying a series record with two wins in relief against Chicago, Sherry lowered his ERA to an even more minute 0.71.

In four appearances the kid with the blazing fast ball, big curve and sinker gave up

Please Turn to Pg. 2, Col. 4

## SHERRY TO CHAMPAGNE

| LOS ANGELES (N) | AB | R | H | RBI | PO | A |
|---|---|---|---|---|---|---|
| Gilliam, 3b | 4 | 1 | 0 | 0 | 0 | 2 |
| Neal, 2b | 5 | 1 | 3 | 2 | 4 | 4 |
| Moon, lf | 4 | 2 | 1 | 2 | 3 | 0 |
| Snider, cf-rf | 3 | 1 | 1 | 2 | 2 | 0 |
| Essegian | 1 | 1 | 1 | 1 | 0 | 0 |
| Fairly, rf | 0 | 0 | 0 | 0 | 0 | 0 |
| Hodges, 1b | 5 | 0 | 1 | 0 | 10 | 0 |
| Larker, rf | 1 | 0 | 1 | 0 | 0 | 0 |
| Demeter, cf | 3 | 1 | 1 | 0 | 4 | 0 |
| Roseboro, c | 4 | 0 | 0 | 0 | 2 | 0 |
| Wills, ss | 4 | 1 | 1 | 1 | 2 | 3 |
| Podres, p | 2 | 1 | 1 | 1 | 0 | 1 |
| Sherry, p | 2 | 0 | 2 | 0 | 0 | 2 |
| Totals ... | 38 | 9 | 13 | 9 | 27 | 12 |

| CHICAGO (A) | AB | R | H | RBI | PO | A |
|---|---|---|---|---|---|---|
| Aparicio, ss | 5 | 0 | 1 | 0 | 1 | 2 |
| Fox, 2b | 4 | 0 | 1 | 0 | 2 | 2 |
| Landis, cf | 3 | 1 | 1 | 0 | 2 | 0 |
| Lollar, c | 3 | 1 | 0 | 0 | 5 | 2 |
| Klus'wski, 1b | 4 | 1 | 2 | 3 | 10 | 0 |
| Smith, lf | 2 | 0 | 0 | 0 | 2 | 0 |
| Phillips, 3b-rf | 4 | 0 | 1 | 0 | 3 | 1 |
| McAnany, rf | 1 | 0 | 0 | 0 | 1 | 0 |
| Goodman, 3b | 3 | 0 | 0 | 0 | 0 | 1 |
| Wynn, p | 1 | 0 | 0 | 0 | 0 | 1 |
| Donovan, p | 0 | 0 | 0 | 0 | 0 | 0 |
| Lown, p | 0 | 0 | 0 | 0 | 0 | 0 |
| Torgeson | 0 | 0 | 0 | 0 | 0 | 0 |
| Staley, p | 0 | 0 | 0 | 0 | 1 | 0 |
| Romano | 1 | 0 | 0 | 0 | 0 | 0 |
| Pierce, p | 0 | 0 | 0 | 0 | 0 | 0 |
| Moore, p | 0 | 0 | 0 | 0 | 0 | 0 |
| Cash | 1 | 0 | 0 | 0 | 0 | 0 |
| Totals ... | 32 | 3 | 6 | 3 | 27 | 9 |

Demeter ran for Larker in 4th; Goodman struck out for McAnany in 4th; Torgeson walked for Lown in 4th; Romano grounded out for Staley in 7th; Essegian homered for Snider in 9th; Cash flied out for Moore in 9th.

SCORE BY INNINGS

| | | | | |
|---|---|---|---|---|
| **Los Angeles (N)** | 002 | 600 | 001 | —9 |
| **Chicago (A)** | 000 | 300 | 000 | —3 |

E—Aparicio. DP—Podres to Neal to Hodges. LOB—Los Angeles (N), 7; Chicago (A), 7. 2B—Podres, Neal, Fox, Kluszewski. HR—Snider, Moon, Kluszewski, Essegian. SH—Roseboro.

PITCHERS RECORDS

| | IP | H | R | ER |
|---|---|---|---|---|
| Wynn (L) | 3⅓ | 5 | 5 | 5 |
| Donovan | 0 — | 2 | 3 | 3 |
| Lown | ⅔ | 1 | 0 | 0 |
| Staley | 3 | 2 | 0 | 0 |
| Pierce | 1 | 2 | 0 | 0 |
| Moore | 1 | 1 | 1 | 1 |
| Podres | 3⅓ | 2 | 3 | 3 |
| Sherry (W) | 5⅔ | 4 | 0 | 0 |

Donovan faced 3 batters in 4th.

BB—Wynn, 3 (Snider, Larker, Moon); Donovan, 1 (Gilliam); Podres, 3 (Smith, 2, Lollar), Sherry, 1 (Torgeson). SO—Wynn, 2 (Gilliam, Neal); Pierce, 1 (Moon); Moore, 1 (Demeter); Podres, 1 (Wynn), Sherry, 1 (Goodman). HBP—By Podres (Landis). Umpires—Dascoli (N), plate; Hurley (A), first base; Secory (N), second base; Summers (A), third base; Rice (A), left field; Dixon (N), right field. Time—2h. 33m. Attendance—17,653.

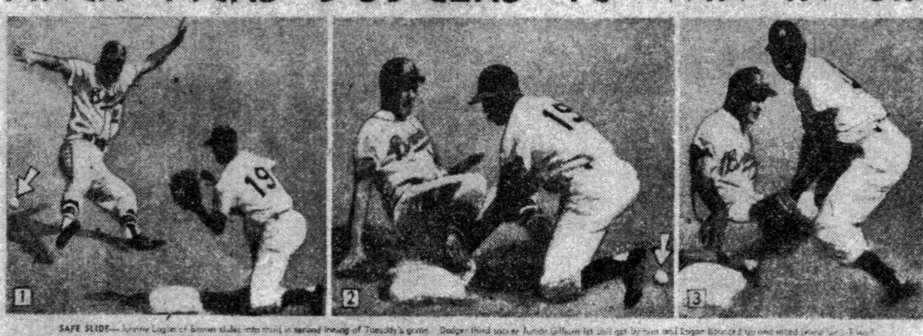

# FINCH PICKS DODGERS TO WIN IN SIX

SPORTS PARADE

Mantilla Threw Before Thinking

White Sox Interesting Ball Club

Speed, Hurling and Defense Wins for AL Champions

Los Angeles Times Sports PART IV

THURSDAY MORNING, OCTOBER 1, 1959

THE BULL PEN

WORLD SERIES ON RADIO, TV TODAY

Wynn, Craig Mound Rivals

Crowd of 50,000 Due for Chicago Opener

ON THE BUTTON—Times baseball reporter Frank Finch tabbed outcome of 1959 World Series right on the button when he forecast in October 1st editions that Dodgers would tip the Sox in six games.

Times photo

# 15,000 BRAVE STORM AS GAMES OPEN

**BEAUTIFUL SQUAW VALLEY**—Scene of the VIII Olympic Winter Games, this panoramic view shows the snow-covered valley and outdoor ice arena during yesterday's opening ceremonies.
Times photo by Ben Olender via UPI Wirephoto

## Snowfall Abates for Ceremony

**BY PAUL ZIMMERMAN**
**Times Sports Editor**

SQUAW VALLEY, Feb. 18—For one perfect hour the storm stood still today and in that interval, as if it were preordained, the picturesque opening ceremonies of the VIII Olympic Winter Games were held here.

Vice President Richard Nixon, always on a tight schedule, arrived on time despite the previous heavy snowfall, to pronounce the games open.

Ten inches of the flakey stuff had filtered down into Olympic Valley before the ceremony took place, stalling traffic and limiting the attendance to 15,000 hardy spectators.

Then, as if on prearranged schedule, just as the 800 colorfully clad athletes filed out of Blyth Memorial Arena, the storm swoomed in again with increased fury.

**Gorgeous Spectacle**

It was a gorgeous spectacle, made more remarkable by the hand of providence. The sun was shining bright when Andrea Mead Lawrence, twice a U.S. gold medal winner at Oslo, came skiing down Papoose Peak with the Olympic Torch held high.

The colorful throng of spectators on the hillside, augmented by the chorus of more than 2,500 students from California and Nevada high schools and their combined bands of 1,200 instruments, made a path for her as she swooped gracefully into the skating arena.

There she handed the torch to Kenneth Henry, U.S. speed skater, who made a precision-smooth circuit of the 400-meter racing course, climbed the steps and lighted the huge Olympic Torch amid resounding applause.

**Highways Clogged**

Several thousand hardy souls, intent on visiting this compact valley for the event, were still on the clogged highways when the flame flared forth.

Bill Henry of The Times, the voice of the 1932 Olympic Games in Los Angeles, had hardly made his initial announcement on the loudspeaker, when the storm stopped and the sun came out from behind the clouds over Papoose Peak.

Prentis C. Hale Jr., president of the Organizing Committee, bareheaded and furcoated, stepped up to the rostrum and made his welcoming speech, after the colorfully clad athletes had taken orderly position—30 nations of them—on the ice of the arena.

He called the athletes the "world's best equipped ambassadors of goodwill." He urged them to set a goal second to winning. "Make this Olympic Village a meeting place for competitors of all nations for the purpose of better international understanding.

"Before we master outer space," Mr. Hale cautioned, "let us conquer inner space

Please Turn to Pg. 2, Col. 3

### Partly Cloudy Today

SQUAW VALLEY, Feb. 18 (UPI)—The second day of the Winter Olympics should, weather-wise, be "considerably different" than today, the Weather Bureau promised tonight in forecasting a "good day." The official prediction was only partly cloudy conditions tomorrow in contrast to today's snowstorm.

## SPORTSCRIPTS

# Pigeons Almost Didn't Make It

**BY PAUL ZIMMERMAN—Sports Editor**

SQUAW VALLEY, Feb. 18—Olympic notes translated from hieroglyphics scratched in a snowbank:

An overzealous guard almost kept a load of caged homing pigeons from getting to the arena in time for the opening ceremonies . . . The driver of the station wagon didn't have necessary credentials . . . Someone suggested that not all of the birds had passes, either.

The California racing pigeon organization supplied the birds for the traditional "dove of peace" flight that always is a part of an Olympic opening ceremony . . . Why homing pigeons? . . . So they won't stay in the valley and eventually die of starvation.

### Skaters Are Often Cyclists

For some reason or other, speed skating and cycling go hand in hand . . . Coach Eddie Schroeder was on the U.S. ice teams in the 1932 and 1936 Winter Games . . . and also competed in bicycle events.

Seven members of the skate squad here also are cyclists . . . Several have a chance to make the team that goes to Rome . . . Jack Disney of Monrovia, a bike man at Melbourne for Uncle Sam in 1956, barely missed making the ice team here.

By the same token, many of the top European hockey players are soccer stars . . . There are only two ice rinks in all of South Africa, so the members of that team have competed with each other for years.

### Youngster Makes U.S. Team

Great Britain's Alpine squad has gone western . . . Its members wear broad-brimmed cowboy hats . . . The youngest jumper of the U.S. team is Ragnar Ulland of Seattle . . . He's 17 . . . Born in Norway, Ragnar is of a ski-jumping family . . . He came to America eight years ago.

Lattmar Ottsen, chairman of the U.S. Olympic Skating Committee, thinks the rarefied air here will make for high speeds . . . That is, if the skaters become properly acclimated.

The food dished up by Pete Rasmussen, chief chef at the Olympic Village, is so good coaches are fearful their stars will eat themselves out of contention . . . Some make their athletes weigh in each day . . . Sigvar Nordlund of Sweden says, "Let 'em stuff. I'll work it off of them."

### Many Birthday Cake Requests

Rasmussen says the daily intake of fruit for in-between snacks is astounding . . . One day's check showed 3,339 oranges, 2,100 apples and 1,200 bananas were devoured.

In addition to the regular meals, Rasmussen and his staff have been swamped with requests for special birthday cakes . . . He denies he is suspicious, but it

CC 2†

Please Turn to Pg. 2, Col. 3

# Yankee Puck Hopes Rise as Players Mend

**BY CHARLES CURTIS**
**Times Staff Representative**

SQUAW VALLEY, Feb. 18 — The snow-bound ice hockey teams of the United States and Czechoslovakia, which open the Olympic puck program tomorrow at 4 p.m., were idle today as only three squads were permitted to use the indoor rink for practice.

The ailing American team needed the day off and there was some good news amid the snowflakes.

**Ice Too Bumpy**

Wing Weldon Olson was discharged from the hospital after treatment for an infected throat. Goalie Laurence Palmer, who had been written off by coach Jack Riley yesterday because of his severely wrenched knee, is now considered to have a chance to get into later competition.

Center Paul Johnson and wing Roger Christian, both hurt in the Los Angeles games with the Czechs, are on the mend.

When John F. (Bunny) Aherne, the Irish-born president of the International Hockey Federation, which conducts the Olympics hockey program, ruled out the outside rinks because of bumpy ice, the hockey program was thrown all awry and into a night schedule at least for the first few days.

**U.S. Team Idle**

The big Swedish team, rated as a darkhorse prospect, faces Canada at 6:30 p.m. tomorrow, while Russia and Germany meet at 9.

Our forces are idle Saturday, then face Australia, not considered a top contender, Sunday at 5.

The Olympic rope trick, suspending strands from the open end of the arena to break up the sun's rays on the ice rink, was completed

Please Turn to Pg. 2, Col. 1

## OLYMPIC ACTION ON TV TONIGHT

Highlight's of today's Winter Olympic Games program at Squaw Valley will be televised over KNXT (2) from 11:15-11:30 p.m.

## WISHES RUSSIANS LUCK

# Nixon Big Hit in Village Tour

**BY GLEN BINFORD**
**Times Staff Representative**

SQUAW VALLEY, Feb. 18—Vice President Nixon, who himself skied and skated until deterred by the press of other activities, talked skiing and skating with the athletes of several countries here this afternoon.

And among the first Winter Olympic competitors with whom he spoke were two Russians—speed skater Lydia Skoblikova and hockey player Yrij Tsitsinov.

They shook hands all around and exchanged Soviet and American lapel pins, then the Vice President wished them luck.

He exchanged pins also with Miss Kyung Hoi Jim, Korean speed skater, and because of her excellent English, conversed with her for several minutes.

Nixon was constantly surrounded by crowds of young athletes after he went from the opening ceremonies in Blyth Memorial Arena to Olympic Village, the compact area reserved only for the competitors.

He trudged several hundred yards through the new, soft snow to the recreation hall, a large quonset hut full of malted milk machines, ping-pong tables and a juke box.

There he talked with California's own hope in the women's Alpine events, Linda Meyers of Mammouth Mountain. As he did with all of the athletes, he wished her good luck.

There was a brief interruption when a ping-pong table collapsed under Canadian figure skater Wendy Griner and she crashed to the floor. She escaped injury and made her way through the crowd to obtain the Vice President's autograph.

Others with whom he discussed winter sports were Cooky Matthews of South Africa, the 11-year-old figure skating whiz; American figure skater Carol Heiss, and Boris Kolchin, trainer of the USSR skating team.

Nixon said he and his wife skied in the big pines area near Wrightwood in

Please Turn to Pg. 3, Col. 1

# COMEBACK PAIR SCORE ANITA WINS

**BY BION ABBOTT**

Venerable St. Vincent and the comparative youngster, Restless Wind, each crowned a comeback with success yesterday at Santa Anita before 19,398 fans.

For St. Vincent his triumph in the Camino Real Distance Handicap was his first in slightly more than a year. The gallant 9-year-old gelding came from dead last to overtake Castlestone in the stretch and pull away by more than three lengths in the mile and one-half trek over the turf course.

**Top Sub**

Carefully rated by Bill Shoemaker, who filled in for injured pilot Johnny Longden, St. Vincent completed the trip in 2:28 2-5. This was only three seconds off the track record for the route he set in 1955 and still holds.

There to greet them in the winner's circle were Longden and his son Vance, the trainer, and Sir Gordon Richards. Sir Gordon was the world's winningest rider until Johnny passed his mark of 4,870 triumphs in 1956.

Llangollen Farm's Restless Wind, idle since his juvenile year when he ranked right behind First Landing and Tomy Lee, returned to the races with a flash of speed and ran off with the featured Palm Springs purse by a length and one-half.

**Plenty Left**

Now a 4-year-old, Restless Wind took command a few strides out of the gate and Eddie Arcaro merely let out another notch as Sir Salonga made a menacing motion along the rail near the eighth pole. Prize Host was third, three-quarters of a length behind Sir Salonga.

Restless Wind paced off

Please Turn to Pg. 6, Col. 7

## THE WINNERS

1—Hustle Bubble, $3.80.
2—Zero Night, $90.60.
3—Stepped Up, $11.40.
4—Gray Shark, $4.40.
5—Act Now, $6.00.
6—St. Vincent, $5.60.
7—Restless Wind, $10.40.
8—Blue Wind Boy, $16.00.

# Three Events Billed Today in Olympics

SQUAW VALLEY, Feb. 18 (AP)—Europeans and Canadians are favored to capture the gold medals tomorrow when the Winter Olympics switch from ceremony to competition.

The schedule includes championships in the men's 30-kilometer (18.64 miles) cross-country ski race and pairs in figure skating. The hockey tournament also gets under way.

Four medal winners in previous Olympics are the choices to battle it out for the cross-country prize.

They include defending champion Veikko Hakulinen of Finland; Sixten Jernberg, Sweden's "King of the skis"; Russia's Pavel Kolchin, and Norway's Hallgeir Brenden.

## TODAY'S SCHEDULE AT SQUAW VALLEY

8 a.m.—Men's 30-kilometer cross-country skiing, McKinney Creek.

10:30 a.m. — Pairs figure skating, Blyth Arena.

3 p.m.—Victory ceremonies, Blyth Arena.

4 p.m.—Hockey, United States vs. Czechoslovakia, Blyth Arena.

6:30 p.m. — Hockey, Canada vs. Sweden, Blyth Arena.

9 p.m.—Hockey, Russia vs. Germany, Blyth Arena.

## TODAY IN SPORTS

**HORSE RACING**—Santa Anita, 1:10 p.m.

**BASKETBALL** — UCLA vs. Stanford, 9 p.m., Sports Arena.

**BASEBALL**—SC vs. Negro Major All-Stars, Bovard Field, 2:30 p.m.

# DODGERS OFF FOR FLORIDA TOMORROW

**BY FRANK FINCH**

Tomorrow is Departure Day for the local Dodger colony, and when a planeload of players, club officials and writers takes off for Florida only a handful of players on the 40-man roster still will be unsigned.

Autographed contracts were received yesterday from Stan Williams, Tommy Davis, Norm Sherry and Tim Harkness, raising the list of signed athletes to 34.

Those who have yet to enter the fold are outfielder Chuck Essegian, pitchers Danny McDevitt, Fred Kipp and Bill Harris, and infielders Bob Lillis and Bobby Aspromonte.

Essegian, the pinch-hitting home-run hero of the World Series, is expected to come to terms momentarily.

Off his showing this winter for the champion Escogido Reds in the Dominican Republic, Williams seems to be on the verge of realizing his great potential. The oversized right-hander led the loop with 15 victories.

Williams was a big disappointment to Smokey Alston last year when he finished only two of 15 starts and split 10 decisions. In '58 he won 9 and lost 7.

Only 20, Davis captured the PCL batting title with a .345 average last year and led with 211 base hits. His bag included 18 homers, nine triples and 32 doubles. The husky outfielder is given a good chance to stick with the Dodgers.

Sherry, who had a brief stay with Los Angeles last year before being shipped to Spokane, will fight it out with Joe Pignatano as catcher Johnny Roseboro's understudy.

Harkness is a budding first-sacker who batted .316 for Green Bay last season. He was placed on the L.A. roster merely for protective purposes.

Pitchers and catchers, along with a few vets like Duke Snider, Wally Moon and Carl Furillo, will begin their vernal exercises Monday morning at Vero Beach. The balance of the squad, augmented by 48 farm hands, will report a week later.

PHOTO FINISH

# Linmold Captures Big 'Cap in Upset

Los Angeles Times
Sports
PART III
CC SUNDAY MORNING, FEBRUARY 28, 1960 2†

OLYMPIC GAMES

# U.S. Beats Russia in Ice Hockey, 3-2

**DRIVING FINISH**—Down the stretch, at left, Fleet Nasrullah leads by nose over Linmold with Amerigo coming up fast. At the finish, right photo, Linmold nudges ahead to win Santa Anita Handicap.
Times photo by Larry Sharkey

## HERE'S THE PITCH

## Braves Contending With Same Cast

BY FRANK FINCH

VERO BEACH, Fla., Feb. 27—Like the Dodgers, the Milwaukee Braves will offer virtually the same cast of characters this season as they did during the harrowing campaign of 1959. Neither club did any business in the winter trading marts.

Even with a dire second-base problem and a gimpy Wes Covington, Milwaukee missed bagging its third consecutive pennant by only a whisker last year, and already the Braves have been established as 7-to-5 favorites on the Las Vegas line.

Del Crandall

Chuck Dressen has said that ". . . If the Dodgers are the only club we have to worry about, then we've got no worries."

We don't agree with the gabby Milwaukee manager that the Dodgers won't provide any headaches for the Braves, but when you study the 1959 performance charts of the Sudsville nine you can't help but wonder how the Dodgers ever licked 'em.

Warren Spahn and Lew Burdette each won 21 games and Bob Buhl chipped in with 15 wins, including five over Los Angeles. Don McMahon and Bob Rush did sterling service in the bull pen.

Eddie Mathews won the major league home-run crown and Hank Aaron led the parade in batting average, slugging percentage, total hits and total bases. Mathews was right up there in most of these departments.

Los Angeles didn't possess a pitcher or a hitter who compared with these brilliant Braves on a basis of individual performances.

### Dressen Has Inside Dope on Dodgers

As a team, the Braves outhit, outscored and outslugged the Dodgers besides yielding fewer runs to the enemy. Only in fielding and baserunning did the Dodgers outdo them. Oh, yes, the Dodgers outgamed them, too, and that's what paid off.

When the Braves hired Chuck Dressen after Fred Haney called it quits to return to sportscasting, they scored a 10-strike. The canny little gamecock knows the National League inside out and, more important in this particular instance, he has the whole "book" on the L.A. ball club in his noggin.

The fact that L.A. took 14 of 22 games from Milwaukee in 1958, and 14 of 24 last season was no mere coincidence, and Dressen can share in the credit.

### Chuck Sincere in His Convictions

With his customary confidence, Chuck already is on record as predicting another pennant for Milwaukee. The man hardly could be expected to say otherwise, but he actually believes what he says.

Dressen is faced with some very tough problems. He has no assurances that Red Schoendienst can come back, or that Chuck Cottier can play second base in the majors. Spahn will be 40 years old soon after the season opens, and Burdette is nearing 34. Baseball's No. 1 receiver, Del Crandall, is the only experienced receiver on the staff. Del caught 150 games last year, an amazing feat, but he's not a superman and needs some help.

However, there's still a lot of run in the Braves, and Dressen is the guy who can get 'em to galloping.

## Stretch Run by Linmold Wins 'Cap

### Fleet Nasrullah, Amerigo, Bagdad in Blanket Finish

BY BION ABBOTT

Longshot Linmold fought his way forward inch by inch in the final strides of a spectacular stretch struggle to win the $145,000 Santa Anita Handicap before a roaring crowd of 49,448 who braved yesterday's dark and threatening clouds.

With a heart that must have been forged in the foundry for which he was named, Linmold lunged forward in the last jump to shade front-running Fleet Nasrullah by a head.

**Blanket Finish**

A blanket could have covered the first four at the end of this silver jubilee edition of the mile and one-quarter classic.

Only a nose behind Fleet Nasrullah came the fast-closing invader from Florida, Amerigo, and but a neck farther back was the 8-5 favorite, Bagdad.

A week ago winning trainer H. C. (Mac) McBride declared, "I don't see how my colt can catch Bagdad and First Landing."

Calm in a still stunned sort of way after the tremendous race, the friendly, curly-haired McBride looked thoughtfully through his horn-rimmed glasses and modestly attributed his success to luck.

**Credits Luck**

"You've got to have luck to win a race like that," he added.

But the fact remains, McBride took over Linmold, a colt which had a history of disabilities, at the start of the Santa Anita meeting and progressively improved him to the point where he won the toughest race of them all.

And Linmold's 2:00 3-5 for the golden gallop, only four-fifths off the track record, also minimizes the element of luck.

**Biggest Win for Pierce**

Jockey Don Pierce, recording the biggest triumph of his career, charged out of the starting gate and immediately placed Linmold in contending position. He

Please Turn to Pg. 3, Col. 1

### THE WINNERS

1—Slats, $18.00.
2—Queen's Choice, $34.80.
3—Kamasutra, $18.60.
4—Pirnie, $4.80.
5—Titanium, $6.80.
6—Gawain, $10.40.
7—Linmold, $26.00.
8—Lord Fauntleroy. $14.20.

# U.S. HOCKEY TEAM SURPRISES SOVIETS

BY PAUL ZIMMERMAN
Times Sports Editor

SQUAW VALLEY, Feb. 27—They said it couldn't be done, but the U.S. ice hockey team—driven by unquenchable determination—defeated Russia for the first time ever at Blyth Arena in the VIII Olympic Winter Games here today.

The final score was 3 to 2 with the winning goal scored by Bill Christian with only 5:01 remaining in the heart-stopping contest.

With Canada defeating Sweden, 6 to 5, the championship goes right down to the wire tomorrow. The U.S.A. meets Czechoslovakia, whom it has previously beaten here, and the Canadians face the USSR.

If Canada wins and the Americans lose, then the title will be decided on points scored in the championship round and our northern neighbors hold an edge of 3 goals here.

Nine thousand vociferous spectators, who jammed the rink, frantically called on the Yankees to hold the smart-passing Soviet sextet. When they did, the riotous fans stood and cheered for 10 minutes.

It was a come-from-behind performance of the first water. Russia led 2-1, after the first period and the shuddering thought ran through the throng that the game might turn into a Russian rout.

"We were too tight," said coach Jack Riley after the contest. "We left our first-period game in the dormitory, but for the first time, America outconditioned the Russians."

In five previous meetings, at Cortina four years ago and in world competition, the United States never had beaten the USSR. The triumph came on top of a remarkable 2-1 win over Canada two days ago, and kept the Yankee

Please Turn to Pg. 4, Col. 2

**BROTHER ACT WINS**—Crowd goes wild as U.S. scored decisive goal in 3-2 triumph over Russia in Olympics ice hockey game. Bill Christian, right, scored on assist from brother Roger, left. Yank No. 5 is Robert Owen. Russ goalie Nikolaj Puchkov is down while Genrikh Sidorenkov (No. 5) looks at crowd.
Times Photo by Ben Olender via (P) Wirephoto

KISSES

## Russ Rough on Ice, but Tender Later

BY CHARLES CURTIS
Times Staff Representative

SQUAW VALLEY, Feb. 27—"They're the kissin'est gang."

That was Bill Cleary, leading scorer of the U.S. hockey team, referring to the Russians after today's 3-2 victory for the United States.

Russian coach Anatoli Tarsov, who had bussed U.S. coach Jack Riley soundly Thursday after we beat Canada, repeated the treatment on Riley today. Then he grabbed Bill Cleary, who scored our first goal today, and gave him the full treatment.

**Great Guys**

One of the Russian players also gave Bill a similar type greeting.

"They're great guys," Cleary said of the Russians. "Only a couple of them speak a little English, but we've got to know them pretty well. They're wonderful sports."

The losers, who had been beaten by the United States for the first time in ice hockey, had stood on the ice after the game in a lonesome blue line, prepared to salute their conquerors as is the custom in these Olympic contests.

**Ceremony Delayed**

But the pileup of U.S. players and well-wishers delayed the ceremony for several minutes. Then the Russians filed into their dressing

Please Turn to Pg. 2, Col. 7

## Norwegian Carpenter Sets New World Distance Skating Record

BY BRAVEN DYER
Times Staff Representative

SQUAW VALLEY, Feb. 27—Knut Johannesen, gutty 26-year-old carpenter from Oslo, Norway, smashed all records for long distance skating here this morning as he won the killing 10,000-meter race with one of the most sensational performances of the eighth Winter Olympics.

Illustrated on Page 2, Part III

Closing with a terrific sprint after setting a spine-tingling pace over the 400-meter oval, the doughty European champion was clocked in 15:46.6 for the 25-lap grind of approximately six and one-third miles.

The old world's record of 16:32.6 belonged to a fellow Norwegian, Hjalmar Andersen. The pace was so swift this morning that the next four skaters behind Johannesen also fractured the old record.

Norway's champion had to be at his best to win because the great Russian army lieutenant, Viktor Koshichkin, was out gunning for his second gold medal, and against anybody but Johannesen he'd have made it.

Winner of the 5,000-meter race Thursday, Koshichkin matched the Norwegian's

Please Turn to Pg. 5, Col. 3

### SPORTS ON RADIO, TELEVISION TODAY

**PRO BASKETBALL**

Philadelphia vs. Detroit, KRCA (4), 11:15 a.m.

**WINTER OLYMPICS**

80 meter ski jump, closing ceremonies, KNXT (2), 2 p.m.

**AUTO RACING**

Hot rods, Gardena Stadium, KTLA (5), 2:30 p.m.

# FURILLO FIGHTS TO KEEP DODGER JOB

BY FRANK FINCH
Times Staff Representative

VERO BEACH, Fla., Feb. 27—The day of reckoning is at hand for Carl Furillo, one of the noblest Dodgers of them all.

"Furillo is the biggest question mark in camp," says general manager Buzzie Bavasi. "I know it's a hard thing to say of a man who has done so much for the club, but Carl will have to produce to stay with the Dodgers.

"We've got some fine young outfielders coming up, and we can't afford to carry Furillo — or anybody else, for that matter—out of sentiment and loyalty."

Furillo, who will be 38 on March 8, realizes he is on the spot as he prepares for his 15th season with the Dodgers.

"I've gotta bear down and battle these kids," he grinned as he mopped his sweaty brow after a long session in the batting cage this morning.

Furillo has been in Florida for the better part of a month, and has worked out every day since camp opened although he isn't officially slated to report until Monday.

A pulled hamstring muscle limited Skoonj's activities to only 50 games last year, including numerous pinch-hit appearances. 'He came through with some clutch blows, including a couple of

Please Turn to Pg. 4, Col. 1

# PALMER WINS OPEN WITH BLAZING FINISH

## Rigney Fired as Giants' Manager

SAN FRANCISCO, June 18 (UPI)—Bill Rigney was fired as manager of the second-place San Francisco Giants today and big Tom Sheehan, 66-year-old former minor league pilot, was named to succeed him.

Horace Stoneham, president of the Giants, said that Sheehan would be manager "two or three weeks, or possibly for the rest of the year."

Rigney, 41-year-old manager, was in his fifth year at the helm of the Giants. And Stoneham had expected his pilot to bring him home a winner this year.

"But we had to make the change now before it was too late," said Stoneham. "I was afraid that if I waited until next week, the way the team is going, we would drop back to the place where he couldn't regain first place."

Lack of hustle, rumors of dissension, front-office interference with players and other reasons were given for the firing of Rigney — but not by Stoneham.

"The decision was a hard one to make," said the Giant owner. "On the surface it looks like a criticism of Rigney, which it isn't. It's a combination of either the club's not as good as we thought it was, which we don't think is true, or it was a good club that couldn't get inspired. I'm sure all the players liked Rigney."

The Giants started the campaign in good shape and were only one game

Please Turn to Pg. 4, Col. 4

Los Angeles Times
Sports
SECTION H
CC SUNDAY, JUNE 19, 1960

## Hogan Bic Collapses Near End

DENVER, June 18 (UPI)—Arnold Palmer came fro 7 strokes off the pa with a 6-under-par-6 fourth round today ar won the National Open go title as Ben Hogan falterc on the final two holes i quest of his coveted and ur precedented fifth champior ship.

Never before in the 6 year history of the open ha a man made up more tha 5 strokes in the fina round. But today Palme flamed his way around th seared 7,004 yd. of the Che

### Fast Fairway Finish

| | | | |
|---|---|---|---|
| Par out | 444 | 453 | 434—35 |
| Par in | 453 | 443 | 454—36—71 |
| Palmer out | 333 | 352 | 344—30 |
| Palmer in | 443 | 443 | 454—35—6 |

ry Hills Country Club for total of 280 that brought hir the title to go with the Ma ters crown he won in Apri

Palmer, who meets a cha lenge as an old friend, start ed the 36-hold windup strokes behind Mike Sou chak and in a tie for 15t place. A 1-over-par 72 i the morning's third roun gave no indication of the fireworks ahead.

**Hogan Determined**

After lunch he torr through the first nine of the final round in 30 strokes tying the open record. He tallied six birdies, two pars and a bogey. Coming home he stayed closer to par as the hardened fairways and greens of the 35-36—71 layout alternately lifted and dropped the chances of the others.

Hogan, grim and determ mined, was even with Palme er until the final two holes. There the Hawk became the victim of the two water hazards. On the 17th he put his second into the mud near the moat. After knocking the ball on the green with still a chance for a par, he missed a 10-footer.

On the 18th, Hogan collapsed to a 3-over-par 7 when he drove into the lake and also encountered the rough and a trap before reaching the green.

**Souchak Skids**

Palmer is the first man to win the open with a subpar total since Hogan did the trick in 1953.

Souchak, the leader through the first three rounds after setting a 36-hole championship record, skidded to 73 and a total of 283.

Jack Nicklaus, the amateur champion, from Columbus, O., grabbed second place with a final round 71 for a 282 total. He knocked in an eagle 3 on the 538-yd. 5th, which he reached with two irons and took over the temporary lead at the 63rd hole.

Then he began 3-putting. His runner-up position is the

Please Turn to Pg. 2, Col. 3

# BUCS' RALLY BEATS DODGERS IN 10TH, 4-3

### HERE'S THE PITCH

## Sisler Simplifies Art of Batting

BY FRANK FINCH

Batters, from the majors down through the minors to the little-shaver leagues, would do well to hearken to the theory of hitting expounded by the great George Sisler, American League two-time batting champion with .407 in 1920 and .420 in 1922.

The way Sisler explains it, it sounds as easy as finding Kate Smith in a phone booth, but there's no gainsaying Sisler knows whereof he speaks.

George Sisler

"Hitting, to put it simply, is the act of putting the bat against the ball," explained the batting coach of the Pittsburgh Pirates. "You can correct flagrant faults in a hitter, but you can't teach him that.

"Once, in the minors, I saw a kid whose stance and swing were exactly like Stan Musial's. In fact, he even looked like Musial. But he couldn't hit the ball and he never made it in baseball.

"Stance has nothing to do with hitting. Al Simmons stood at the plate with his foot in the bucket, but his body was in the correct position to swing when the ball came over.

*Good Hitters Battle the Pitcher*

"Rocky Nelson of our club has a unique stance. His right foot points directly at the pitcher, but his left (back) foot points toward the third baseman. Still, he knows how to put the bat on the ball.

"Just looking at Smokey Burgess standing there you wouldn't dream he was the fine hitter he is. Some of those 'picture' hitters aren't so hot.

"And another thing; all good hitters are aggressive. They fight the pitcher on every pitch."

Like several other pretty fair batsmen, namely Musial, Babe Ruth and Lefty O'Doul, Sisler broke into professional baseball as a pitcher. He gained renown as a twirler for the University of Michigan and it may be news to you, gentle reader, that as a pitcher for the St. Louis Browns Sisler once scored a 1-0 victory over Washington's immortal Big Train, Walter Johnson.

*Hunch: Patterson in 7th by Kayo*

The sight of Ingemar Johansson bouncing his fists off Floyd Patterson's skull a year ago reminded us of a West Indies champion bongo thumper giving a spirited solo on the skins. The Swede threw more leather than the winner of the bulldogging contest at Sheriff's Rodeo.

Still and all, we're picking Patterson to regain the crown jools tomorrow night. And by a knockout, yet, in the seventh heat.

Like Patterson, we have the utmost respect for Ingemar's toonderbolts. Before flagellating Floyd, he cooled Eddie Machen in one round, which leaves little doubt concerning his destructive powers.

Johansson is a superb specimen, intelligent, and supremely self-confident. He yet has to prove that he is a great champion, and the same could have been said of Patterson before he was disconnected from his senses and his crown by Ingemar.

The dope points to Johansson, but we're riding with a hunch that Patterson will win, even though he looked like an umbay in every fight since he knocked out Archie Moore nearly four years ago.

## 63,699 Put Attendance Over Million

BY FRANK FINCH

The Dodgers and Pirates battled into extra innings last night before a huge ladies' night crowd of 63,699 which sent Coliseum attendance for the season over the million mark.

Pittsburgh won with a run in the 10th inning, 4-3.

Paid attendance was 50,062 to put the Dodgers' home total at 1,022,485 for 36 games.

Young Danny McDevitt appeared to have a 3-0 shutout victory "locked up" in the ninth inning when the Pirates erupted with the bases

### Counting the House

| | |
|---|---|
| Last night's attendance (paid) | 50,062 |
| 1960 attendance, 36 games | 1,002,485 |
| 1959 attendance, 36 games | 903,454 |

empty and two outs. A two-run homer by Buc catcher Hal Smith and a run-scoring pinch single by Smoky Burgess sent the game into overtime.

**Skinner Singles**

Skinner singled and Clemente walked in the top of the first, but McDevitt slipped the visitors a goose egg.

Friend did likewise despite Gilliam's lead-off bunt.

Both Hoak and Mazeroski walked in the second with one away, the latter being rubbed out when Friend grounded into a double play.

Howard struck out and Sherry and Neal were retired on grounders in the bottom half of the frame.

**Three Hits Fail**

After Skinner opened the third with his second safety, Groat forced him and Gilliam took Clemente's grounder to start another DP.

Three L.A. batters in the third — McDevitt, Gilliam and Larker—slapped singles, yet the home team failed to score. McDevitt was thrown out by Skinner when he attempted to stretch his hit, making it two away, and Moon was thrown out by Mazeroski.

L.A. executed its third double play in as many innings after Stuart and Smith walked in the fourth. L.A. also failed to score although Howard dropped a single over Groat's noggin.

**Two for Dodgers**

The Dodgers assumed a 2-0 lead in their share of the fifth. Wills opened with a single and took second on Friend's wild pitch that struck out McDevitt. Maury went to third when Gilliam lined an infield hit off Friend's glove, scoring on Larker's sacrifice fly.

Back-to-back singles by Moon and Snider plated Gilliam with the second run before Howard popped up. Moon's safety extended his

Please Turn to Pg. 3, Col. 2

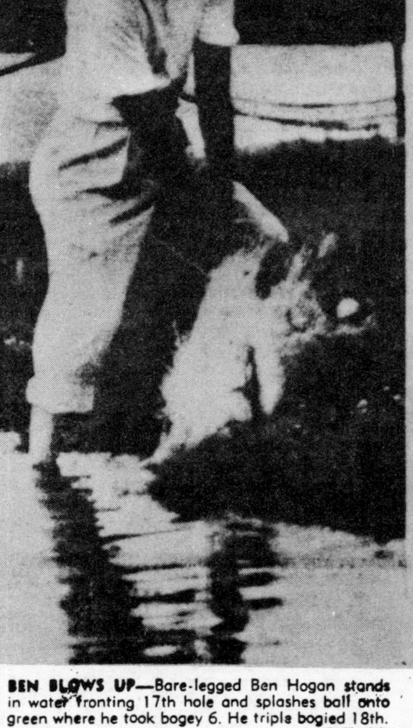

BEN BLOWS UP—Bare-legged Ben Hogan stands in water fronting 17th hole and splashes ball onto green where he took bogey 6. He triple bogied 18th. (P) Wirephoto

'I DID IT!'—Arnold Palmer jumps for joy after final putt drops for a 65 which gave him come-from-behind victory in National Open. He scored 280. (P) Wirephoto

## Bagdad Wins; Fleet Nasrullah Fades to 4th

BY BION ABBOTT

Bagdad bounced back to winning form to capture the $54,350 Inglewood Handicap as favored Fleet Nasrullah faded out of the money for the second straight time to surprise a crowd of 45,661 yesterday at Hollywood Park.

"He had run on his mind today," was the way jockey Bill Shoemaker explained the sudden resurgence of the winner.

Bagdad started to move on the far turn and simply mowed down the opposition through the stretch, finishing three-quarters of a length ahead of Sea Orbit in 1:40 4-5 for the mile and one-sixteenth.

Prize Host, longest shot on the board, at 22-1, gave one final lunge to nose Fleet Nasrullah out of third money, a little more than a length behind Sea Orbit. More than

Please Turn to Pg. 8, Col. 3

## Kansas Wins NCAA; SC 2nd as 10 Marks Fall

BY AL WOLF, Times Staff Representative

BERKELEY, June 18—Kansas retained its NCAA track and field championship here this afternoon by scoring 50 points.

The star-studded Jayhawkers racked up four firsts — Charlie Tidwell in the 100-meter and 200-meter dashes, Bill Alley in the javelin and Cliff Cushman in the 400-meter hurdles.

SC, left for dead after yesterday's preliminaries, rallied today and captured runner-up honors with 37 points. West Coast teams also finished third, fourth and fifth as UCLA bagged 31 points, Oregon and Oregon State 22 each.

**Records Tumble**

Nine meet records fell today and another was equaled twice—and one of those performances also shattered a national intercollegiate standard. In addition, a new shot-put mark was set yesterday by Troy's big Dallas Long.

SC's Luther Hayes, who couldn't even qualify in the broad jump yesterday, about-faced today and got his name in the record book with a hop-step-jump of 50ft. 11¼in.

Jim Johnson of UCLA came through with a winning performance in the 110-meter hurdles. Rafer's little brother traveled the course in 14s. flat, which was no record but helped mightily as the Bruins made a surprisingly strong showing.

**Cunliffe Upset**

The big race of the day, as anticipated, was the 800-meters.

Stanford's Ernie Cunliffe

Please Turn to Pg. 4, Col. 1

### Wolf on Beam

Al Wolf, Times track and field writer, picked 13 winners in the 17-event NCAA championships at Berkeley yesterday.

## BASEBALL STANDINGS

**NATIONAL LEAGUE**

| | W | L | Pct. | * |
|---|---|---|---|---|
| Pittsburgh | 37 | 20 | .649 | |
| San Francisco | 34 | 25 | .576 | 4 |
| Milwaukee | 29 | 22 | .569 | 4½ |
| St. Louis | 28 | 29 | .491 | 8½ |
| Cincinnati | 27 | 31 | .466 | 10 |
| **LOS ANGELES** | **26** | **31** | **.456** | **11** |
| Chicago | 23 | 29 | .442 | 11½ |
| Philadelphia | 20 | 37 | .351 | 17 |

*Games behind leader.

**Yesterday's Results**

Pittsburgh, 4; **LOS ANGELES, 3** (10 innings).
San Francisco, 7; Philadelphia, 4.
Milwaukee, 5; St. Louis, 0.
Cincinnati, 7; Chicago, 1.

**Games Today**

Pittsburgh (Haddix, 4-3) at LOS ANGELES (Koufax, 2-8), Radio KFI, 2 p.m.

Philadelphia (Roberts, 2-7) at San Francisco (Antonelli, 3-4, or O'Dell, 2-6).

St. Louis (Sadecki, 1-2, and Simmons, 0-0) at Milwaukee (Spahn, 4-3, and Willey, 3-3).

Chicago (Hobbie, 6-7, and Cardwell, 3-5, or Ellsworth, 3-3) at Cincinnati (O'Toole, 4-6, and McLish, 2-4).

**AMERICAN LEAGUE**

| | W | L | Pct. | * |
|---|---|---|---|---|
| New York | 31 | 22 | .585 | |
| Baltimore | 35 | 25 | .583 | |
| Cleveland | 30 | 23 | .566 | 1 |
| Detroit | 29 | 25 | .537 | 2½ |
| Chicago | 30 | 27 | .526 | 3 |
| Washington | 24 | 30 | .444 | 7½ |
| Kansas City | 23 | 34 | .404 | 10 |
| Boston | 19 | 35 | .352 | 12½ |

*Games behind leader.

**Yesterday's Results**

New York, 12; Chicago, 5.
Detroit, 5; Baltimore, 3.
Cleveland, 2; Boston, 1.
Washington, 7; Kansas City, 2.

**Games Today**

New York (Coates, 7-0, and Terry, 3-2) at Chicago (Shaw, 5-6, and Baumann, 3-3).

Baltimore (Wilhelm, 3-4, and Pappas, 4-5) at Detroit (Bunning, 4-3, and Mossi, 3-4).

Boston (Brewer, 4-6, and Monbouquette, 5-6) at Cleveland (Perry, 7-2, and Bell, 6-5).

Washington (Lee, 2-1) at Kansas City (Kucks, 1-1, or Trowbridge, 1-2).

## SPORTS ON RADIO, TELEVISION TODAY

**BASEBALL**

Dodgers vs. Pirates, Coliseum, Radio KFI, 2 p.m.

**TENNIS**

Jack Kramer's professional tennis troupe, San Francisco, KTLA (5), 2:30 p.m.

**AUTO RACING**

CJA hot rods, Gardena Stadium, KTLA (5), 4:30 p.m.

## ZIMMERMAN TO REPORT TITLE FIGHT

Times sports editor Paul Zimmerman is in New York to report tomorrow night's heavyweight championship fight between champion Ingemar Johansson and the man he dethroned a year ago, Floyd Patterson.

The excitement and drama of the title bout will be brought to Times readers Tuesday by Zimmerman and the staff of Associated Press and United Press-International writers who will report on the big night.

## Rams, Redskins to Play Aug. 19

BY MAL FLORENCE

George Preston Marshall, ebullient football figure, has already started talking on his favorite subject—the Washington Redskins.

Marshall might be excused if his enthusiasm gets out of bounds, because among other things, he owns the Redskins and he's not at all bashful in predicting that they're headed for a red-hot season.

"Mike Nixon and I are certain that we'll have the finest offensive and defensive lines we've had in years," Marshall declared recently. "And in Ralph Guglielmi we're well heeled at quarterback.

Marshall and his Redskins head west next month to start prepping for their annual skirmish against the Rams on Friday night, Aug. 19 in the Coliseum.

The game is being sponsored by Times Charities, Inc.

This will mark the 15th meeting between these two NFL powers. The series score favors the Rams, 8-6. Last year the Rams were heavy favorites, but were ambushed by Chief Marshall's scalp hunters, 23-21.

It could have been this shocking defeat, coming as it did in full view of 85,888 spectators, that triggered the Rams' dismal season. For a club that was the consensus pick to win the title, the Rams fell completely apart.

Collapse of the Rams naturally prompted a shake-up in coaching ranks. It was exit for Sid Gillman and entrance for Bob Waterfield.

Los Angeles fans will watch the Rams with par-

Please Turn to Pg. 4, Col. 4

## THE WINNERS AT HOLLYPARK

1—Mr. America, $4.60.
2—Taboo, $23.20.
3—Hechizo, $37.60.
4—Barbarian, $9.40.
5—Blank Check, $6.00.
6—Whiz Bam, $5.80.
7—Bagdad, $3.00.
8—Fair Dawn, $8.60.

## Patterson Picking Up Backers as Match With Johansson Draws Near

BY PAUL ZIMMERMAN
Times Sports Editor

NEW YORK, June 18—It was hardly earth-shaking, like the quake in Chile, but there was a definite strengthening of feeling here today that Floyd Patterson has a chance to become the first heavyweight in history to regain the world championship.

The fistic seismograph reading was 8 to 5 that the superb Swede, Ingemar Johansson, would still retain his crown after the festivities at the Polo Grounds Monday night, but more than a few of those who have been favoring him were wavering.

If you will recall, in the previous bout Patterson was a proud 4 to 1 favorite before Johansson unloosed his "toonderbolt" right that shook Floyd loose from his title.

"Maybe it is my patriotism and the hope that an American owns the title," said George Jessel, "but I like Patterson."

The toastmaster general of the United States doesn't qualify as an expert, as such, but who does?

"I'm no expert either,"

Please Turn to Pg. 3, Col. 3

## DARKEST DAY IN U.S TRACK HISTORY

# Russians Upset Thomas in High Jump; Hary Shades Sime in 100, Norton Last

PART IV

CC FRIDAY MORNING, SEPTEMBER 2, 1960 4†

**BLANKET FINISH?**—Olympic 100-meter finalists hit finish line in Rome. From left, Germany's Armin Hary (winner), Great Britain's Peter Radford (third), Cuba's E. Figueroa and the U.S.A.'s Ray Norton, Francis Budd and Dave Sime (second). Hary's 10.2 time tied Games' record. Sime also clocked 10.2.

## SPORTSCRIPTS

## India Has Threat in 400-Meters

**BY PAUL ZIMMERMAN—Sports Editor**

ROME, Sept. 1—From the rear the man looked like a pukka sahib from India with the typical ramrod bearing of the Hindu, a yellow turban smartly wound on his head, but he looked a little pale for a man from Hindustani.

The minute he turned around the cat was out of the bag. We recognized him immediately as Vincent Reel, the former Occidental star now coach of Claremont-Mudd College. He left last April to help coach the India track team.

Vincent Reel

Vincent has one of the top 400-meter sprinters in the Olympics here. He is a 25-year-old Sikh from the Punjab plains, named Milkha Singh.

"The race is wide open," said Reel, "with Carl Kaufmann of Germany, America's three stars and George Kerr of the West Indies perhaps the best.

"Kaufmann twice has beaten Singh but we're counting on the heat factor to work in our favor."

Any GI who served in India during World War II can tell you that it really gets hot on the arid plains of the Punjab. As Noel Coward pointed out in song, this is the place where only mad dogs and Englishmen venture out in the midday sun.

India never has had a great track athlete. Field hockey is its forte, but Reel believes it might have one in Singh.

"I suspect that Kaufmann, who is used to cool weather, is not going to like conditions here. The last time he and Singh met was at Cologne a few weeks ago and he beat my man by a very narrow margin. Singh was not running all out."

### *Spence's Chances Discounted*

Kaufmann's best mark this year is 45.4s. Mal Spence of South Africa, who has a fine 45.6s., is handicapped with a bad foot and many discount his chances.

Singh's best performance is 45.8s., turned in at the British Commonwealth games in London a month back.

Earl Young of the United States has run faster and Kerr has an identical best with Singh at 45.8s., along with Otis Davis, the Los Angeles star.

The Sikh first competed in the games at Melbourne but there it was too cold and he was eliminated in the trial heats.

In the All-India championships he won three events. He took the 100 in 10.4s.; the 220 in 20.7s., and the 400 in 46.1s.

Singh is a jemadar in the artillery. That is like being a sergeant in our Army.

"Since they have little or no college competition in India, most of the country's athletes come from the armed forces, the police or the government-run railroad," said Sahib Reel.

"Our problem is lack of competition so we corrected that by bringing Singh to Europe for more than a month of running against the top stars.

"This heat is almost as bad as India," said Reel as he unwound his turban to mop his brow. He put it back on as we walked out.

**P.S.:** Vincent Reel will be a pukka, pukka sahib if Singh wins here and you can bet that Milkha will wind up with a lieutenant's pips on his tunic.

## Snider's Hit Beats Phils in 11th, 3-2

**BY FRANK FINCH**

A bases-loaded pinch single by Duke Snider scored Tommy Davis with the deciding run in the last of the 11th inning as the Dodgers downed the Phillies again last night, 3-2, before a charity crowd of 28,946.

Duke's drive, coming off Dick Farrell (9-5), concluded a crackling contest that saw the fortunes of war swing from one side to the other like a pendulum.

**Sixth in Row**

Going the distance and striking out 13 Phillies, Don Drysdale (12-13) captured his sixth straight Coliseum decision. He allowed only seven hits.

Farrell, who relieved Gene Conley when the Dodgers came to bat in the ninth, retired eight batters in a row before Davis drilled a double off the top of the screen with one out in the 11th. The ball

**Please Turn to Pg. 2, Col. 1**

## BOX SCORE

| Philadelphia | AB | R | H | RBI | E |
|---|---|---|---|---|---|
| Malkmus, 2b | 3 | 0 | 0 | 0 | 0 |
| Dalrymple | 1 | 0 | 0 | 0 | 0 |
| Koppe, 3b, ss | 1 | 0 | 0 | 0 | 0 |
| Taylor, 3b, 2b | 5 | 1 | 3 | 0 | 0 |
| Callison, lf | 5 | 0 | 1 | 0 | 0 |
| Gonzalez, cf | 4 | 0 | 1 | 0 | 0 |
| Walters, rf | 5 | 0 | 0 | 0 | 0 |
| Herrera, 1b | 3 | 0 | 0 | 0 | 0 |
| Del Greco | 0 | 0 | 0 | 0 | 0 |
| Lepcio, 3b | 1 | 0 | 0 | 0 | 0 |
| Coker, c | 4 | 1 | 2 | 1 | 0 |
| Amaro, ss | 3 | 0 | 0 | 0 | 0 |
| Curry | 0 | 0 | 0 | 0 | 0 |
| Farrell, p | 0 | 0 | 0 | 0 | 0 |
| Conley, p | 3 | 0 | 0 | 0 | 0 |
| Walls, 1b | 1 | 0 | 0 | 0 | 0 |
| Totals | 39 | 2 | 7 | 1 | 0 |
| **Los Angeles** | | | | | |
| Wills, ss | 5 | 0 | 0 | 0 | 1 |
| Gilliam, 3b | 5 | 0 | 1 | 0 | 0 |
| Moon, lf | 4 | 1 | 1 | 0 | 0 |
| Larker, 1b | 5 | 1 | 2 | 0 | 0 |
| Davis, cf | 5 | 1 | 1 | 0 | 0 |
| Howard, rf | 3 | 0 | 0 | 0 | 0 |
| Roseboro, c | 4 | 0 | 2 | 2 | 0 |
| Neal, 2b | 4 | 0 | 1 | 0 | 0 |
| Snider | 1 | 0 | 1 | 1 | 0 |
| Drysdale, p | 3 | 0 | 1 | 0 | 0 |
| Totals | 39 | 3 | 10 | 3 | 1 |

Dalrymple struck out for Malkmus in 8th.

Del Greco ran for Herrera in 9th.

Curry intentionally walked for Amaro in 9th.

Walls hit into double play for Conley in 9th.

Snider singled for Neal in 11th.

SCORE BY INNINGS

| | |
|---|---|
| **Philadelphia** | 000 010 010 00—2 |
| **Los Angeles** | 000 200 000 01—3 |

PO-A—Philadelphia, 31-11 (one out when winning run scored in 11th); Los Angeles, 33-10. DP—Neal to Wills to Larker. LOB—Philadelphia, 8; Los Angeles, 10. 2B—Larker, Roseboro, Callison, Drysdale, Davis. 3B—Taylor. HR—Coker. SB—Gilliam. S—Drysdale, Coker.

| Pitcher— | IP | H | R | ER | BB | SO |
|---|---|---|---|---|---|---|
| Conley | 8 | 8 | 2 | 2 | 2 | 5 |
| Farrell-L (9-5) | 2⅓ | 2 | 1 | 1 | 2 | 2 |
| Drysdale-W (12-13) | 11 | 7 | 2 | 1 | 3 | 13 |

WP—Drysdale, 2. Balk—Farrell. PB—Roseboro. Umpires—Jackowski, Landes, Pelekoudas, Barlick. Time—2h. 55m. Attendance—28,946.

## Thomas Upset by Russian Jumpers

**BY PAUL ZIMMERMAN, Times Sports Editor**

ROME, Sept. 1—Germany and Russia combined here to make this the darkest day in United States Olympic track and field history.

First, Armin Hary, the brash sprinter from Frankfurt, won the 100-meter dash. Then, in the dusk of late evening, Robert Shavlakadze of the USSR, captured the high jump, beating heavily favored John Thomas of the United States.

These had been counted as almost sure gold medals for the highly vaunted American team. Instead Uncle Sam's stalwarts were lucky to get one silver and one bronze award.

**No Flash in Pan**

It was adding insult to injury because our 800-meter men were washed out in the semifinals and only Deacon Jones qualified for the steeplechase finals. Fortunately, all three of our 400-meter hurdlers got to the payoff race.

Hary, whose world record of 10.0 had been pooh-poohed by a lot of experts, proved he was no flash in the pan by winning the century sprint in Olympic record time of 10.2.

It was Dave Sime and not Ray Norton who chased him to the tape as the 80,000 spectators roared, but there was no question that the 23-year-old, 158-lb. blond had won.

Sime made a great dive at the tape and also was clocked in 10.2. Peter Radford of England was third and Norton, who has been struggling in every race he has run the last two days, finished sixth and last. Francis Budd of the U.S.A. was a tight fourth.

**Greater Upset**

As big an upset as this was, the defeat of Thomas in the high jump was greater. Three Russians, with rubber in their legs battled him all the way and the pressure told. Few in the huge crowd had gone when Shavlakadze, a 27-year-old mustached Georgian, cleared 7ft. 1in. on the first leap. By this time the lights were on. His teammate, little heard of Valeriy Brumel cleared it on the second leap and Thomas, who had the last turn, failed three times.

Shavlakadze never had cleared 7 ft. before but Brumel jumped 7-1½ two weeks ago. Both tried 7-1⅞ after

**Please Turn to Pg. 3, Col. 4**

### Games on TV, Radio

**TV** — KNXT (2), 8:30 p.m. (men's and women's track and field, women's fencing, boxing and basketball); 11:15 p.m. (men's swimming, basketball, boxing and women's swimming).

**RADIO**—KFI, 2:10, 3:50 and 6:25 p.m.; KABC, 4:50 p.m.

**OFFICIAL PHOTO**—Sprinters rocketing into tape in 100-meter dash are, from bottom to top, Hary, Radford, Figueroa, Norton, Budd, Sime. Hary won in 10.2. (AP) Wirephoto via radio from Rome

### TODAY IN SPORTS

**HORSE RACING** — Del Mar, 2:15 p.m.

**PRO FOOTBALL**—Chargers vs. Denver Broncos, 8 p.m.

**AUTO RACING**—CJA hot rods, Grand Prix, Gardena Stadium, 8:30 p.m.

**MOTORCYCLE RACING**—Ascot Stadium, 8:15 p.m.

## 'BEATEN FAIR AND SQUARE'—THOMAS

ROME, Sept. 1 (UPI) —John Thomas, obviously shaken by his surprise defeat in the Olympic high jump today but taking it calmly, said, "I don't have any alibis — I was beaten fair and square."

The Boston University star, whose victory had been predicted by almost everyone since long before the games began here, was questioned by newsmen as he sat eating his dinner in the Olympic Village.

As usual, the Cambridge (Mass.) Negro was quiet and spoke only in answer to questions.

How did he feel in today's competition?

"I felt good."

Was he disappointed?

"I was not disappointed. I won a bronze medal."

Did he think there was anything wrong with his training?

"I [illegible] no complaints ab[illegible] the training schedule."

Thomas, who has been pursued by fans and athletes ever since his arrival 'as people sought his picture, his autograph, and his opinion, was asked if all of this

**Please Turn to Pg. 4, Col. 6**

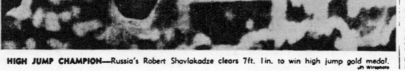

**HIGH JUMP CHAMPION**—Russia's Robert Shavlakadze clears 7ft. 1in. to win high jump gold medal. (AP) Wirephoto

## U.S. Just a Big Cry-baby at Rome

**BY OSCAR FRALEY**

ROME, Sept. 1 (UPI)—The giant of the athletic world has become a puling cry-baby today.

That's us. The United States.

For years we had it swinging tall, fat and pretty. We were the muscular marvels of the ages.

But now, thank goodness, we find we're just ordinary guys and it's a disturbing fact that we can't take it.

This fact has become glaringly and uncomfortably obvious during the early course of the current Olympic Games.

**Better to Grin**

Protest has become our middle name and it's a bad sign that we can't accept the defeat with a grin—even if it is rigged a bit on occasion.

U.S. protests have been coming from all quarters during this Olympiad. It must be admitted that some of them have a sound, legitimate basis.

Yet in making even the semi-valid ones we are hinting to the world that we put a tiny gold medal above sportsmanship. The carping complaints we have been making, and the amazing number of them, hints in a few places that we are trying to talk our way to victory.

**Swim Dispute**

One case involved a decision which Australia's John Devitt was awarded over Lance Larson of the U.S.A. in the men's 100-meter freestyle swimming. The judges considered all the facts and, whether they were right or not, gave the duke to the Aussie.

We screamed. We lost an appeal. So we produced some television film and we screamed some more. The case may go before swimming's supreme court a second time.

Personally, I'd like to see our kid win it. But not at the price.

Our girl swimmers complained vigorously about the caliber of the judging which cost them two diving championships.

But Sammy Lee, the straight-shooting diving coach, put his stubby mitt squarely on the cause and effect when he said:

"Our girls went into the competition as if they had the gold medals all wrapped up. Maybe what we needed was more effort."

The U.S. has showered down a regular torrent of protests and appeals. They have come in boxing and wrestling. There have been 12 from us in yachting alone.

Pete Newell, the basketball coach, grumped that "we have to make every basket a clean one or it's no good and we get a foul called on us."

But we haven't lost a game yet and, having all the talent in the world with us on the court, we shouldn't. So copping such a plea makes us sound small even though most of our guys are 7-ft. tall.

If we can't win 'em outright and beyond the slightest shadow of a doubt, we ought to forget 'em. Respect is the biggest victory we can carry home and this one, too, we're losing daily.

## BASEBALL STANDINGS

**NATIONAL LEAGUE**

| | W | L | Pct. | * |
|---|---|---|---|---|
| Pittsburgh | 79 | 49 | .617 | |
| Milwaukee | 71 | 55 | .563 | 7 |
| St Louis | 71 | 56 | .559 | 7½ |
| **LOS ANGELES** | 68 | 57 | .544 | 9½ |
| San Francisco | 62 | 63 | .496 | 15½ |
| Cincinnati | 57 | 72 | .442 | 22½ |
| Chicago | 51 | 75 | .405 | 27 |
| Philadelphia | 48 | 80 | .375 | 31 |

* Games behind leader

**Yesterday's Results**

**LOS ANGELES, 3**; Philadelphia, 2 (11 innings)

Milwaukee, 10, Chicago, 1.

Cincinnati, 7, St Louis, 4.

Pittsburgh, 6, San Francisco, 1.

**Games Today**

**LOS ANGELES** (Podres 11-10) at San Francisco (Sanford, 11-11). KTTV, radio KFI, 8:15 p.m.

Chicago (Cardwell, 8-12) at St. Louis (Simmons, 5-3), night.

Milwaukee (Jay, 5-7) at Cincinnati (McLish, 4-8), night.

Only games scheduled.

**AMERICAN LEAGUE**

| | W | L | Pct. | * |
|---|---|---|---|---|
| New York | 75 | 50 | .600 | |
| Baltimore | 76 | 53 | .589 | 1 |
| Chicago | 72 | 55 | .567 | 4 |
| Washington | 64 | 63 | .504 | 12 |
| Cleveland | 61 | 65 | .484 | 14½ |
| Detroit | 59 | 67 | .468 | 16½ |
| Boston | 55 | 71 | .437 | 20½ |
| Kansas City | 45 | 83 | .352 | 31½ |

* Games behind leader.

**Yesterday's Results**

Cleveland, 7, Kansas City, 3.

Only game scheduled.

**Games Today**

Washington (Lee, 6-4, and Woodeshick, 4-4) at Boston (Sullivan, 5-14, and Muffett, 4-2), twi-night.

New York (Ford, 9-7) at Baltimore (Pappas, 12-8), night.

Detroit (Regan, 0-3) at Chicago (Score, 4-8), night.

Cleveland (Locke, 1-4) at Kansas City (Hall, 7-10), night.

# RAFER JOHNSON WINS DECATHLON TITLE

Los Angeles Times
Sports
PART IV
CC WEDNESDAY MORNING, SEPTEMBER 7, 1960 2†

## HERE'S THE PITCH

## Parseghian Tabs Illinois to Win

BY FRANK FINCH

Ara Parseghian, the brilliant young coach who revived Northwestern's football fortunes, has joined the growing list of competent observers that tab Illinois to capture the Big Ten title this fall.

"I don't think it'll be decided until the last Saturday of the season," the Wildcat mentor was telling Dick Forbes of the Cincinnati Enquirer.

Ara Parseghian

"My favorite is Illinois. Off the finish Illinois had last year, and with what I think is the best line in the Big Ten with experience and depth, I like 'em.

"Michigan State is my second choice. The Spartans were young and they came along real strong at the end of the season. Duffy Daugherty had a great frosh team and a fine spring practice.

"Ohio State will be tough. They have good freshmen coming and with more platooning and use of more boys it'll help. But we don't play the Buckeyes, so they don't worry me.

"Michigan is a team about which I know nothing.

"Iowa has some extremely fast boys and all-around good team speed.

"Wisconsin had a good frosh team and I think the Badgers will fool a few people.

"Indiana, Minnesota and Purdue will cause a lot of trouble too."

### Wildcats Need Linemen

His own team's chances will ride on the development of linemen, said Parseghian, who used to play for Sid Gillman at Miami (O.) University.

"It all depends on our line," he said. "We'll have to build all over again from tackle to tackle. And replacing Ron Burton is going to be a real problem. We have a soph, Dutch Purdin, who has the best chance of taking Burton's job."

To refresh your memory, we'll print last season's Big Ten standings. It is shocking to note that those tuffies—Iowa, Michigan and Ohio State—were relegated to the second division:

| | W | L | T | | W | L | T |
|---|---|---|---|---|---|---|---|
| Wisconsin | 5 | 2 | 0 | Iowa | 3 | 3 | 0 |
| Michigan State | 4 | 2 | 0 | Michigan | 3 | 4 | 0 |
| Illinois | 4 | 2 | 1 | Ohio State | 2 | 4 | 1 |
| Purdue | 4 | 2 | 1 | Indiana | 2 | 4 | 1 |
| Northwestern | 4 | 3 | 0 | Minnesota | 1 | 6 | 0 |

ROUNDY COUGHLIN, the sage of Madison, Wis., who recently tipped us that the Wisconsin athletic director, Ivy Williamson, is heir-apparent to Tug Wilson's toga as Big Ten commissioner, has unearthed another candidate.

### Eliot Pushed for Commissioner Job

"I was in Chicago recently," Roundy writes, "and the talk there was that the strong Illinois alumni on La Salle St. and in the Loop are really pushing Ray Eliot, former Illinois football coach, as commissioner. Tell all my Big Ten friends in L.A. thanks for all the letters I got after you put my name in your paper."

We fervently hope that Johnny McKay's noble experiment in shifting his All-American end, Mike McKeever, to fullback will pay off better than a similar experiment conducted with another All-American end, Leon Hart. The huge Notre Dame star, who probably was as fast as McKeever, still was too slow hitting the line to be effective.

California's Bears will play three intersectional contests before taking on seven Coast opponents in a row. The Bears open at home Sept. 17 with Tulane, play the Irish in South Bend the next weekend, and then host Army at Berkeley Oct. 1.

## Groat's Wrist Broken by Pitch; Bucs Win, 5-3

PITTSBURGH, Sept. 6 (AP)—The league-leading Pittsburgh Pirates whipped the Milwaukee Braves, 5-3, tonight on a come-from-behind, eighth inning rally, but the Pirates lost the services of their shortstop, Dick Groat, for about four weeks.

Groat suffered a fractured left wrist in the first inning when hit by a Lew Burdette pitch.

Groat, unaware his wrist was broken, continued playing until the third when the swelling wrist forced him into the dugout. After the game, hospital X-rays showed the wrist was fractured.

Pirates' Gen. Mgr. Joe L. Brown said the injury would

Please Turn to Pg. 3, Col. 1

### TODAY IN SPORTS

**HORSE RACING** — Del Mar, 2:15 p.m.

**WRESTLING** — Olympic Auditorium, 8:30 p.m.

## Rafer's Win---Teacher Over Pupil

BY BRAVEN DYER
Times Staff Representative

ROME, Sept. 6 — The student almost caught up with the teacher in the longest Olympic decathlon test ever tonight.

Rafer Johnson, who has worked out with C. K. Yang at UCLA for two years, barely beat him out with a record-breaking total of 8,392 points.

Anyway you look at it, this was a 1-2 win for the Bruin school and Ducky Drake, the track coach they are talking of replacing. Vasily Kuznetsov of Russia was a distant third.

Johnson was only 58 points ahead of the 26-year-old representative of the Republic of China, pardon, Formosa which the International Olympic Commitee prefers.

### Work Cut Out

Rafer, who was the United States flag bearer in the opening ceremonies, had his work cut out for him as he led by only 67 points going into the final event, the 1,500 meters.

It appeared that Yang, always superior in this race, had the championship made. Johnson knew he had to stay with his Chinese opponent in the devastating final test and he did it.

Yang couldn't pull away . . . and, while he won over Johnson by six meters, the time differential was not enough to close the narrow point gap.

"I didn't care what the clock said. I made up my mind I was going to stay with him," said Rafer.

"I wasn't going to let him get away."

Johnson had to run his fastest race ever—4:49.7, 1.2 slower than the Chinese star, to accomplish victory.

Rafer had led at the halfway mark this morning but lost the advantage to Yang in the first event, the hurdles, when he hit an early barrier, lost his stride and turned in a mis-

Please Turn to Pg. 4, Col. 8

'MR. DURABLE'—Rafer Johnson, Kingsburg, Cal., hurls the discus while en route to winning grueling 10-event Olympic Games decathlon title with a record 8,392 points to beat C. K. Yang by 58.
(AP) Wirephoto via radio from Rome

## DRYSDALE BLANKS GIANTS IN FINALE

### L.A. Wins Series Before 9,753 Coliseum Fans; Larker Hits Homer in 7-0 Victory

BY FRANK FINCH

It was Melvin Miller Day at the Coliseum yesterday, but Don Drysdale stole the show.

Hurling his fourth shutout of the season and his seventh consecutive triumph in the local arena, Drysdale didn't allow a single pedestrian to advance past second base as he stifled the San Francisco Giants, 7-0.

The series finale, which saw Los Angeles nabbing the rubber match, drew only

### Counting the House

| | |
|---|---|
| Yesterday's attendance | 9,753 |
| 1960 attendance, 69 games | 2,124,457 |
| 1959 attendance, 69 games | 1,822,167 |

9,753 well-toasted fans, the smallest baseball gathering here since the Dodgers and Reds played before 8,001 on Aug. 27, 1958.

### Big Victory

In a way, it was a big victory for the Dodgers, since it put a little more daylight between them and the fifth-place Giants. The latter club now is four games back of their intrastate sparring partners.

The triumph also squared the seasonal skirmishing at 10 wins apiece, with two games remaining here after the Dodgers return from their last junket east of the Rockies.

Dumbo Larker's fourth homer with Maury Wills on base in the first inning slipped Georges Maranda the loss, but Drysdale (13-13) was given five more runs to toy with in the third round.

Wills, by the way, swiped his 41st base of the season and the 23rd in his last 26 attempts.

One of baseball's rarities — a muffed fly by Willie

Please Turn to Pg. 3, Col. 1

## BOX SCORE

| San Francisco | AB | R | H | RBI | E |
|---|---|---|---|---|---|
| Blasingame, 2b | 4 | 0 | 0 | 0 | 0 |
| Davenport, 3b | 4 | 0 | 1 | 0 | 0 |
| Mays, cf | 4 | 0 | 2 | 0 | 1 |
| Marshall, lf | 4 | 0 | 0 | 0 | 0 |
| Cepeda, 1b | 3 | 0 | 1 | 0 | 0 |
| Kirkland, rf | 3 | 0 | 1 | 0 | 0 |
| Landrith, c | 3 | 0 | 0 | 0 | 0 |
| Bressoud, ss | 2 | 0 | 0 | 0 | 1 |
| Amalfitano, ss | 1 | 0 | 1 | 0 | 0 |
| Maranda, p | 1 | 0 | 0 | 0 | 0 |
| Sh. Jones, p | 2 | 0 | 0 | 0 | 0 |
| Totals | 31 | 0 | 6 | 0 | 2 |

| Los Angeles | AB | R | H | RBI | E |
|---|---|---|---|---|---|
| Wills, ss | 5 | 1 | 1 | 0 | 0 |
| Gilliam, 2b | 4 | 1 | 1 | 0 | 0 |
| Moon, lf | 4 | 1 | 1 | 0 | 0 |
| Larker, 1b | 4 | 1 | 1 | 2 | 0 |
| Davis, cf | 3 | 1 | 0 | 0 | 1 |
| Hodges, 3b | 3 | 1 | 1 | 3 | 0 |
| Howard, rf | 4 | 0 | 0 | 0 | 0 |
| Roseboro, c | 2 | 1 | 0 | 0 | 0 |
| Drysdale, p | 2 | 0 | 1 | 2 | 0 |
| Totals | 31 | 7 | 6 | 7 | 1 |

SCORE BY INNINGS

| | |
|---|---|
| San Francisco | 000 000 000—0 |
| Los Angeles | 205 000 00x—7 |

PO-A—San Francisco, 24-10; Los Angeles, 27-10. DP—Larker to Wills to Larker; Hodges to Larker. LOB—San Francisco, 4; Los Angeles, 7. 2B—Hodges. 3B—Drysdale. HR—Larker. SB—Wills, Davis. SH—Drysdale.

| Pitcher— | IP | H | R | ER | BB | SO |
|---|---|---|---|---|---|---|
| Maranda-L (1-4) | 2⅔ | 5 | 7 | 4 | 3 | 1 |
| Sh. Jones | 5⅓ | 1 | 0 | 0 | 3 | 0 |
| Drysdale-W (13-13) | 9 | 6 | 0 | 0 | 0 | 8 |

WP—Drysdale. Umpires—Smith, Sudol, Boggess and Gorman. Time—2h. 18m. Attendance—9,753.

## STANDINGS

NATIONAL LEAGUE

| | W | L | Pct. | * |
|---|---|---|---|---|
| Pittsburgh | 82 | 51 | .617 | |
| St. Louis | 74 | 57 | .565 | 7 |
| Milwaukee | 74 | 58 | .561 | 7½ |
| LOS ANGELES | 70 | 61 | .534 | 11 |
| San Francisco | 66 | 65 | .504 | 15 |
| Cincinnati | 60 | 74 | .448 | 22½ |
| Chicago | 52 | 78 | .400 | 28½ |
| Philadelphia | 49 | 83 | .371 | 32½ |

* Games behind leader.

**Yesterday's Results**

LOS ANGELES, 7; San Francisco, 0.
Cincinnati, 6; Philadelphia, 1.
Pittsburgh, 5; Milwaukee, 3.
Only games scheduled.

**Games Today**

LOS ANGELES (Podres, 11-11) at Cincinnati (McLish, 4-11), radio KFI, 6 p.m.
Chicago (Cardwell, 7-12) at Philadelphia (Conley, 7-12), night.
St. Louis (Broglio, 17-7) at Pittsburgh (Law, 19-6), night.
San Francisco (Sanford, 12-11) at Milwaukee (Jay, 6-7), night.

AMERICAN LEAGUE

| | W | L | Pct. | * |
|---|---|---|---|---|
| Baltimore | 80 | 54 | .597 | |
| New York | 77 | 54 | .588 | 1½ |
| Chicago | 75 | 58 | .564 | 4½ |
| Washington | 67 | 66 | .504 | 12½ |
| Cleveland | 66 | 66 | .500 | 13 |
| Detroit | 61 | 72 | .459 | 18½ |
| Boston | 58 | 75 | .436 | 21½ |
| Kansas City | 47 | 86 | .353 | 32½ |

* Games behind leader.

**Yesterday's Results**

Boston, 7; New York, 1.
Cleveland, 10; Detroit, 8.
Kansas City, 3; Chicago, 2.
Only games scheduled.

**Games Today**

Baltimore (Pappas, 13-8) at Cleveland (Perry, 15-7), night.
New York (Ford, 9-8) at Chicago (Wynn, 11-9), night.
Boston (Sullivan, 5-15) at Detroit (Lary, 11-14), night.
Washington (Lee, 7-4) at Kansas City (Kucks, 4-8), night.

THANKFUL CHAMP

## Davis Offers Prayer After 400 Victory

ROME, Sept. 6 (AP)—Otis Davis of Los Angeles, today set an almost unbelievably fast world record for 400 meters — and then dropped his head in a long prayer of thanks.

"Something was pushing me out there," he told a teammate, "and it wasn't the wind. It must have been the Good Lord."

His superbly run race electrified the large audience in the huge Olympic Stadium.

### Victory Leap

When he saw he'd won, Davis leaped high in the air.

"Do it again," asked a photographer.

"Man, you don't have to ask me," replied Davis, "I'm doing it naturally. I'm jumping for joy, man."

And again he jumped.

He was the only person in the stadium who couldn't believe he'd won.

He kept shaking and shaking his head.

When he wasn't doing this, he was almost deliriously kicking his sweat pants around.

Then, when a voice over

Please Turn to Pg. 4, Col. 5

HUSTLIN' HERB—Australia's Herb Elliott breezes across the finish line of 1,500 meters in the record time of 3:35.6, the equivalent to a 3:52.5 mile.

## Otis Davis and Elliott Set Marks

BY PAUL ZIMMERMAN
Times Sports Editor

ROME, Sept. 6—UCLA's big Rafer Johnson ran his heart out tonight in the punishing 1,500-meter finale to win the Olympic decathlon championship by a scant 58 points over slender C. K. Yang, a fellow Bruin.

Herb Elliott earlier smashed the world record in the 1,500-meter run with a 3:35.6 clocking and Otis Davis of Los Angeles broke the world 400-meter mark with 44.9.

### Games on Radio, TV

Radio—KFI, 2:10, 3:50, 6:25 p.m.; KABC, 4:50 p.m.
TV—KNXT (2), 7:30, 11:15 p.m.

For good measure, Josef Schmidt of Poland also posted a new world hop, step and jump mark. It was the greatest day of record-breaking of this or any other Olympiad.

### Slim Lead

But to the crowd of 40,000 that stayed well into the cool Roman night, the emotional highlight came as Johnson, the world record holder, headed into the final 1,500-meter event of the decathlon with only a 67-point lead over Yang.

They were drawn in the same heat of the 1,500. And there Johnson hung grimly to the heels of Yang, finishing just a few yards behind him, to protect most of his point lead and win the championship.

His total of 8,392 points set an Olympic record. Yang had 8,334 for second and Russia's Vassily Kuznetsov 7,809 for a distant third.

### Best Time Ever

Johnson was timed in 4:49.7 for the metric mile, his fastest ever in decathlon competition, and Yang gained only nine points with his 4:48.5.

Davis, a 28-year-old former Manual Arts High School basketball star who didn't take up track until two years ago when he went to Oregon, broke the 45-second barrier in the 400 for the first time.

The crowd of 70,000 went into a frenzy when his time of 44.9 seconds was announced and hardly had any pent-up enthusiasm left when Elliott made a rout of the metric mile in 3:35.6.

### Lead of 3 Yd.

Davis, who barely qualified for this race in the trials, stood off Carl Kaufmann in the stretch to win by a foot. The clockers gave the German the same time.

You wouldn't have given the Oregon physical education student a nickel for his chances after the first 100 meters as Mal Spence of Africa and Milkha Singh of

Please Turn to Pg. 4, Col. 6

RECORD WIN—Otis Davis of Los Angeles hits tape first to nab Olympic Games 400-meter gold medal in record time of 44.9, as he noses out Germany's lunging Carl Kaufman, right. M. Spence, left, South Africa, was third; Earl Young, San Fernando, sixth.
AP Wirephotos via radio from Rome

# BATTEY'S HOMER RUINS ANGELS' OPENER

SLIDE, ALBIE, SLIDE!—Angel outfielder Albie Pearson hits infield and skids toward second while Minnesota's Billy Gardner prepares to tag in first inning. Gardner dropped ball and Albie was safe. The Twins won, 4-2.
Times photos by Larry Sharkey

Los Angeles Times
**Sports**
PART IV
CC FRIDAY MORNING, APRIL 28, 1961 †

## JIM MURRAY

### Boos and Bravos

Opening your mail each morning is like lining up a 10-ft. putt. You never know till you're through with it whether you're going to enjoy it or regret it. For instance:

"I read your column and noted your comments about the hunting of coyotes. I am sending this along to a friend of mine on the east coast who hunted coyotes. I am wondering if you have been given the proper information as to the activities of a coyote on a coyote hunt. Will pass correct information along to you after I receive it."

**Virg Davidson, Davidson-Chudacoff Meats**

(You do that, Virg. And wrap the answer in a steak, will you? I have to tell you though, if your friend hunts coyotes in the east, he MUST be an expert. Tell me, does he catch any?)

"You write a helluva fine column and I enjoy it and I'm sort of ashamed to think maybe you and your family will be tuned in to 'Gunsmoke' when Jim Arness takes me out with one sneak right hand."

**George Kennedy, Actor**

(I saw the punch, George. It wasn't sneak. In fact, I thought he telegraphed it. You're dropping your left, George, and letting him set you up. You'll never beat him till you overcome this.)

"We Dodger fans—and there are many of us—certainly take exceptions to your column. If you distort the facts and resort to sarcasm, we'd all consider you would be better off back in the east. So, Mr. Murray, simply consider that you've lost a big contingent of readers and so far as we are concerned you might as well go back where you came from."

**Robert G. Fitch, Dodger Fan**

(OK, Robert, but why pick on me? I was here 15 years before the Dodgers got here and would have come sooner if the mayor promised me a piece of Chavez Ravine. Seriously, I love the Dodgers, the finest bunch of fellows in the game. What I like most is THEY have a sense of humor.)

"Leo Durocher appears to be suffering from the hoof and mouth disease. Find out where Sonny Liston got $75,000—and let me know."

**William A. Sherwin, Attorney**

(Leo Durocher is suffering from a lot of things. If Sonny Liston's got $75,000, that'll set the Boy Scout program back 100 years.)

"From me, my wife and my grown kids, an Oscar . . ." **Frank Capra, Producer-Director**

(From me, heartfelt thanks, Frank. Forgive me for printing it but I've framed it. You see, I saw "It Happened One Night" 14 times, "Lost Horizon," almost as many, and you and I go back to "The Bitter Tea of General Yen" only you never knew it. I should send YOU telegrams.)

"You must read the junk you dish up every morning, then get awfully sick. What you don't know about sports could fill in the Grand Canyon with enough for Chavez ball park and a few city dumps. You are a paid mouth man for both Cus D'Amato and Floyd Patterson. You phony stiffs are all the same."

**Johnny Sullivan, Angry Man**

(I'll say one thing for you, Johnny: you sure get your point across.)

"I haven't cut out columns since Ring Lardner. I am

Please Turn to Pg. 4, Col. 5

## Ten More Cagers From 6 Schools Named in Scandal

NEW YORK (AP) — The spreading basketball scandal Thursday dragged in 10 more players from six colleges as a fantastic attempt to fix 29 games, mainly in the east and south, was disclosed by Dist. Atty. Frank S. Hogan.

Many of the fix attempts covering the past two seasons were successful, Hogan said, as Aaron Wagman, 29, a convicted football fixer from New York, was indicted on 37 counts of corruption and charge of conspiracy by the New York County Grand Jury.

Hogan said the investigation, which was first broken open last March 27 with the arrest of Wagman and Joseph Hacken of New York, is continuing.

The present probe threatens to rival the 1951 scandals which involved 33 players from seven colleges.

Named in the indictment Thursday were three players from St. Joseph's College of Philadelphia, two from the University of Connecticut, two from the University of Tennessee, and one each from LaSalle College of Philadelphia, Mississippi State and University of North Carolina.

In addition, William Minnerly, the co-captain of the University of Connecticut football team; two former Alabama basketball players, Jerry Vogel and Daniel Quindazzi, and Joseph Green, a New Yorker and close associate of Wagman, were named in the indictment as co-conspirators but not defendants. All four allegedly contacted basketball players, said Hogan.

Hogan said the players mentioned in the indictment allegedly accepted or agreed to accept sums ranging from $750 to $1,500 each for shaving points.

He named them as:

John Egan, senior, captain and outstanding star of St. Joseph's.

Frank Majewski, senior, St. Joseph's.

Vincent Kempton, senior, St. Joseph's.

Peter Kelly, senior, captain of the University of Connecticut team.

Glenn Cross, senior, University of Connecticut.

Richard Fisher, senior, University of Tennessee.

Edward Test, senior, Uni-

Please Turn to Pg. 5, Col. 1

## Sherluck Rolls in Blue Grass; Flutterby 2nd

**BY BION ABBOTT**
**Times Staff Representative**

LEXINGTON, Ky. — Flutterby turned the tables on his most recent tormentor, Mr. Consistency, but once again he was a runner-up this time failing by six spectacular lengths of catching speedball Sherluck Thursday in the $34,300 Blue Grass Stakes, at Keeneland.

Sherluck simply shot to the front from the extreme outside of the 10-horse field at the start and never stopped running, finishing the mile and one-eighth Derby test in a sparkling 1:48 3-5 and drawing away from his rivals through the final quarter.

Flutterby, rated in fourth place by Johnny Longden for most of the trip, overhauled California Derby winner, Mr. Consistency, by three-quarters of a length. The other half of the Kerr

Please Turn to Pg. 6, Col. 6

## STANDINGS

**AMERICAN LEAGUE**

| | W | L | Pct. | • |
|---|---|---|---|---|
| Minnesota | 9 | 3 | .750 | |
| Detroit | 8 | 3 | .727 | ½ |
| New York | 7 | 4 | .636 | 1½ |
| Boston | 6 | 5 | .545 | 2½ |
| Cleveland | 7 | 6 | .538 | 2½ |
| Chicago | 5 | 5 | .500 | 3 |
| Baltimore | 5 | 7 | .417 | 4 |
| Kansas City | 3 | 6 | .333 | 4½ |
| Washington | 4 | 8 | .333 | 5 |
| LOS ANGELES | 1 | 8 | .111 | 6½ |

**Thursday's Results**

Minnesota, 4; LOS ANGELES, 2.
Boston, 5; Detroit, 2.
New York, 4; Cleveland, 3.
Baltimore, 5; Washington, 0.
Chicago, 9; Kansas City, 1.

**Today's Games**

Minnesota, (Ramos, 2-0) at LOS ANGELES (Kline, 0-0), radio, KMPC, 8 p.m.

Chicago (McLish, 1-1) at Kansas City (Herbert, 1-0), night.

Boston (Brewer, 2-0) at Detroit (Bruce, 1-0), night.

Baltimore (Hall, 0-0) at Washington (Daniels, 0-1), night.

Cleveland (Perry, 2-0) at New York (Terry, 0-0), night.

**NATIONAL LEAGUE**

| | W | L | Pct. | • |
|---|---|---|---|---|
| San Francisco | 8 | 5 | .615 | |
| Pittsburgh | 7 | 5 | .583 | ½ |
| Milwaukee | 5 | 4 | .556 | 1 |
| Chicago | 7 | 6 | .538 | 1 |
| LOS ANGELES | 8 | 7 | .533 | 1 |
| St. Louis | 6 | 7 | .462 | 2 |
| Cincinnati | 5 | 8 | .385 | 3 |
| Philadelphia | 4 | 8 | .333 | 3½ |

**Thursday's Results**

Chicago, 5; Cincinnati, 2.
Only game scheduled.

**Today's Games**

LOS ANGELES (Koufax, 1-1) at Chicago (Ellsworth, 0-1), radio, KFI, 11:30 a.m.

Pittsburgh (Law, 0-3) at Cincinnati (Jay, 0-2), night.

San Francisco (Jones, 2-0) at Milwaukee (Spahn, 1-1), night.

Philadelphia (Roberts, 0-3) at St. Louis (Broglio, 1-2), night.

## REDS TRADE BAILEY FOR THREE GIANTS

CINCINNATI (AP) — The Cincinnati Reds Thursday traded catcher Ed Bailey to the San Francisco Giants for second baseman Don Blasingame, catcher Bob Schmidt and a third player to be announced later.

Bailey, 30, has a .260 lifetime batting average accumulated in five full seasons with the Reds and part of two others. He was starting catcher in the 1956 and 1957 All-Star games and played in the second 1960 game.

Blasingame, 29, has a .268 average for five seasons in the majors. He broke into the big leagues with the St. Louis Cardinals and last year moved to San Francisco.

Schmidt, 28, has a .253 batting record in three seasons with the majors.

Bill DeWitt, Reds' general manager, said the club had been negotiating with the Giants about the deal for about three weeks.

"We hated to part with Bailey," DeWitt said. "He's a fine catcher—but we needed a second baseman very badly. When you figure that we were going to get a second baseman who's a front line major leaguer and a catcher who's a front line major leaguer for Bailey—plus a third player—we felt we just had to deal."

TOO LATE

## Wind Shift 'Robs' Hunt of Home Run

**BY AL WOLF**

"An hour earlier and it would have been a home run," said Angel manager Bill Rigney of Ken Hunt's ninth-inning blast which drove Bob Allison back to the right-field screen for a one-handed catch that ended Thursday's Wrigley Field game.

"That's right," Rig said. "An hour earlier and the wind takes it out and we win. By then, though, the wind had shifted."

The Angels trailed, 4-2, at the finish, but had two runners on base.

**The Angel Story**

"That's been our story all the way though," Billy continued. "We can't get the hits when we need them. Six lead-off men got on. Only one of them got home. We have something going, then a double play or something and we're out of it."

At that point in his post-game press conference Rigney's phone rang.

"Hello, hello!" he

Please Turn to Pg. 2, Col. 1

## TODAY IN SPORTS

**QUARTER HORSE RACING**—Los Alamitos, 1:15 p.m.

**MOTORCYCLE RACING** — Ascot Stadium, 8:30 p.m.

**COLLEGE BASEBALL**—SC vs. Stanford, Bovard Field, 2:30 p.m.; UCLA vs. California, Joe E. Brown Field, 3 p.m.

**TRACK** — Mt. San Antonio Relays (High School, College, Junior College Division), 11:30 a.m., 6 p.m.

**BASEBALL** — Angels vs. Twins, Wrigley Field, 8 p.m.

## Only 11,931 See Twins Win, 4-2

### Seraphs Fail to Hit in Clutch, Drop 8th Straight at Wrigley

**BY BRAVEN DYER**

**The fallen Angels couldn't beat the opening-day jinx. Falling in line with all other American League teams, Bill Rigney's Seraphs lost their home inaugural, 4-2, to the Minnesota Twins on catcher Earl Battey's three-run homer in the sixth.**

Thus the cycle was completed with every home team dropping its opener.

It was the first American League game ever played on the West Coast and came only four months after Gene Autry, Bob Reynolds and Leonard Firestone received their franchise.

**Hunt Comes Close**

But the unlucky Cherubs went down swinging. With two on and two out in the ninth, Ken Hunt backed right fielder Bob Allison against the screen to snag his long smash with a leaping, one-handed catch that was only slightly less than sensational.

A disappointing and disappointed crowd of 11,931 fans saw the Angels leave 10 men stranded as the Twins came up with three fast double plays to help Camilo Pascual, the Cuban chucker, register his second win of the season without defeat.

**Battey Local Boy**

The Twins' ace flinger needed aid from 34-year-old Roy Moore, however, as the Seraphs got two on with one out in the eighth. Moore responded by getting Averill and Gene Leek in rather routine fashion.

## ANGEL BOX

| TWINS— | AB | R | H | RBI | E |
|---|---|---|---|---|---|
| Versalles, ss | 5 | 0 | 1 | 0 | 0 |
| Green, cf | 4 | 1 | 1 | 0 | 0 |
| Mincher, 1b | 4 | 1 | 2 | 0 | 0 |
| Allison, rf | 4 | 0 | 0 | 1 | 1 |
| Lemon, lf | 2 | 1 | 1 | 0 | 0 |
| Whisenant, lf | 0 | 0 | 0 | 0 | 0 |
| Battey, c | 4 | 1 | 2 | 3 | 0 |
| Bertoia, 3b | 4 | 0 | 0 | 0 | 0 |
| Gardner, 2b | 3 | 0 | 0 | 0 | 1 |
| Valo | 1 | 0 | 0 | 0 | 0 |
| Valdivielso, 2b | 0 | 0 | 0 | 0 | 0 |
| Pascual, p | 2 | 0 | 1 | 0 | 0 |
| Moore, p | 1 | 0 | 0 | 0 | 0 |
| Totals | 34 | 4 | 8 | 4 | 2 |

| ANGELS— | AB | R | H | RBI | E |
|---|---|---|---|---|---|
| Pearson, cf-rf | 4 | 0 | 1 | 0 | 0 |
| Aspromonte, 2b | 3 | 0 | 0 | 0 | 0 |
| Kluszewski, 1b | 3 | 0 | 1 | 0 | 0 |
| McBride | 0 | 0 | 0 | 0 | 0 |
| Hunt, cf | 1 | 0 | 0 | 0 | 0 |
| Cerv, lf | 4 | 0 | 0 | 0 | 0 |
| Bilko, rf-1b | 2 | 1 | 1 | 0 | 0 |
| Averill, c | 4 | 1 | 1 | 2 | 0 |
| Leek, 3b | 4 | 0 | 1 | 0 | 0 |
| Hamlin, ss | 2 | 0 | 0 | 0 | 0 |
| Becquer | 1 | 0 | 0 | 0 | 0 |
| Clevenger, p | 0 | 0 | 0 | 0 | 0 |
| Throneberry | 1 | 0 | 0 | 0 | 0 |
| Grba, p | 2 | 0 | 0 | 0 | 0 |
| Bowsfield, p | 0 | 0 | 0 | 0 | 0 |
| Wagner | 1 | 0 | 1 | 0 | 0 |
| Brickell, ss | 1 | 0 | 1 | 0 | 0 |
| Totals | 33 | 2 | 7 | 2 | 0 |

Becquer grounded out for Hamlin in 7th.
Wagner singled for Bowsfield in 7th.
Whisenant ran for Lemon in 8th.
Valo grounded out for Gardner in 8th.
McBride ran for Kluszewski in 8th.
Throneberry flied out for Clevenger in 9th.

**SCORE BY INNINGS**

| | |
|---|---|
| Minnesota | 000 103 000—4 |
| Los Angeles | 020 000 000—2 |

PO-A—Minnesota, 27-13 Los Angeles, 27-11. DP—Versalles to Gardner to Mincher; Gardner to Mincher to Versalles; Mincher to Versalles. LOB—Minnesota, 9; Los Angeles, 10. 2B—Mincher, Leek. HR—Averill, Battey. S—Allison(f) Versalles.

| Pitcher— | IP | H | R | ER | BB | SO |
|---|---|---|---|---|---|---|
| Pascual (W, 2-0) | 7⅓ | 6 | 2 | 2 | 5 | 4 |
| Moore | 1⅔ | 1 | 0 | 0 | 1 | 0 |
| Grba (L, 1-2) | 6⅓ | 6 | 4 | 4 | 3 | 4 |
| Bowsfield | ⅔ | 0 | 0 | 0 | 0 | 0 |
| Clevenger | 2 | 2 | 0 | 0 | 2 | 1 |

Umpires — Berry, Linsalata, Umont, Stewart. Time 3h. 13m. Attendance—11,931.

A former Jordan High School star, Battey rang up his first round tripper of the

Please Turn to Pg. 2, Col. 3

FIRST PITCH—Eli Grba of Angels fires ball to Zorro Versalles of Twins in Wrigley Field opener on Thursday before crowd of 11,931.
Times photo

# MARIS COMES OUT SWINGING, HITS 61ST

Los Angeles Times
# Sports
PART IV BUSINESS & FINANCE
CC MONDAY MORNING, OCTOBER 2, 1961 2†

BY FRANK FINCH, Times Staff Representative

NEW YORK—With one swish of his bat, Roger Maris Sunday earned himself an extra $100,000, broke the major league record for home runs, captured the American League runs batted in title and brought the Yankees a 1-0 victory over Boston.

There was a two-ball, no-strike count on the muscular Maris in the fourth inning when he pickled one of Tracy Stallard's fast balls and rocketed it into the right-field stands at Yankee Stadium for his 61st home run of the season.

At the crash of bat against ball there was no doubt about it.

It was a goner.

Even before the ball landed about 15 rows back in the lower right-field stands a crowd of 23,154 frenzied fans sent up a deafening roar.

And as the sturdy slugger trotted around the bases, made sure he touched home plate, and then disappeared amidst a welter of back-slapping teammates in the Yankee dugout, the ecstatic fans continued to give Roger a standing ovation.

Fellow players pushed him to the top of the dugout steps, where he waved his cap in gratitude, a mile-wide smile on his sharply chiseled face.

But the fans hadn't seen enough of their hero. Again he was obliged to step out and wave to the crowd while the game went on with nobody paying any attention to the next hitter, Yogi Berra.

Maris, a 27-year-old native of Hibbing, Minn., had accomplished something that even the fabled Babe Ruth never achieved.

On Sept. 30, 1927, in this very ball park, the Babe

Please Turn to Pg. 2, Col. 4

## JIM MURRAY
### Life in a Sports Car

The only thing I know about sports cars is that when I bought one four years ago, people in other ones started to wave at me.

As a veteran of a dozen conventional automobiles over the years, the experience was unnerving. The first time it happened, I jammed on the brakes and pulled over, shaking, to the side of the road to get out and see where it was afire. No one had ever acknowledged my presence on the same highway before except with a curse or a finger pointing to a tire that was going flat.

All of a sudden, I realized with a thrill what I had done: I had not just bought a car. I had initiated myself into a select fraternity.

My car was a little apple-green English job with black-leather bucket seats, a joy stick (at least that was what the salesman led me to believe) and a dashboard that was right out of a 1927 Essex. I was overjoyed at the waving caper. I could hardly wait to get out and buy myself a Madras cap, a tartan scarf to wear instead of a tie (and maybe a shirt) and, perhaps, a monocle.

#### Chance to Wave at Pretty Girls

I didn't smoke but I put a pack of English Ovals in the side pocket (glove compartments are for the colonies only) and it wasn't long before I was honking furiously and waving gaily to every other similar car that passed me. I waved at so many pretty girls—and vice versa—that one of us would have got arrested for mashing on the highway if we weren't driving the same cars.

I found the practice a little more of a bore when the waver was some middle-aged adolescent in a baseball cap and goggles and a middle so big around it looked as if the car had been strapped onto him. At night, it was treacherous. You found yourself waving at cars that were not quite the same make as yours. A couple of times some other upper-class hot-rodders waved at me too soon and then when they got on top of me and saw they had made a ghastly social error they staggered past looking stonily ahead with a look of strangled distress on their faces. I mean, two mistakes like that and you had to turn in your tachometer.

In a way, I was an impostor. But I never told anybody. I bought the car to save gas, not to win trophies. I never went near Agoura for fear somebody would put me in the entry box. I didn't mind waving at sports cars but I didn't want to race them.

#### Gaudy International Fraternity

Which brings me to a group of characters who drive sports cars not to save gas but to be able to buy it—an oil well at a time. This is the gaudy international fraternity of race drivers, a reckless, romantic bunch of fellows whose lives are like the final reels of those B-pictures starring Chester Morris, Richard Arlen and a cast of charred stunt men.

I am speaking of the likes of Stirling Moss, Jack Brabham, Olivier Gendebien, Briggs Cunningham, Chuck Daigh who will be on hand for the fourth annual Grand Prix for sports cars at Riverside the weekend of Oct. 14-15. The elite of the driving world will take to the track in sports cars that resemble mine only in that they have windshields, two seats and headlights but will be doing 170 m.p.h. at times in the 62-lap 200-mile oil-strewn rodeo.

Race drivers have as distinctive techniques as jockeys, ballplayers or golfers. Stirling Moss, for instance, is the acknowledged Sam Snead of the track. His form is impeccable, his reflexes razor-edged. But he not only out-drives his opposition, he out-drives his car — so

Please Turn to Pg. 8, Col. 1

## TIMES READERS TO GET TOP COVERAGE OF WORLD SERIES

When the New York Yankees and Cincinnati Reds open fire Wednesday in New York for the start of the 1961 World Series of baseball, Times sports page readers will be on the scene.

Columnist Jim Murray's enlightening and witty comments will be published on these pages daily. And baseball writer Frank Finch will cover the games and bring interesting sidelights.

In addition to these two fine writers, all the facilities of the Associated Press and United Press International, plus exciting pictorial coverage from both of these services, will enable Times readers to enjoy a box seat view of all the World Series games.

HISTORIC SWAT—Roger Maris of New York Yanks follows through swing after connecting for 61st home run of year against Boston Sunday in Yankee Stadium to top Babe Ruth's record 60 set in '27. AP Wirephoto

'MAN ENOUGH'

## Roger Salutes Bosox Hurler

NEW YORK (AP)—"Babe Ruth was a big man in baseball and I don't say I'm in his caliber but naturally I'm happy to go past Ruth's mark. I would have liked to have done it in 154 games but being as I didn't I'm glad now I didn't and got it when I did."

Roger Maris still wore a dazed expression as he met reporters in the New York Yankee clubhouse Sunday after hitting his 61st home run. He nervously squeezed an empty beer can with both hands as he talked.

**'Good Feeling'**

"It gives me a pretty good feeling to know I'm the only man in the history of baseball to hit 61 home runs."

Maris hit his 61st in the Yanks' 162nd decision (163rd game counting one tie) on the last day of the season. Commissioner Ford Frick had ruled Ruth's record of 60 could only be broken in 154 decisions. Maris had 59 at that stage of the season, so Ruth's record stands and Maris' mark goes into the books as a brand new high for a 162-game schedule.

The 27-year-old outfielder complimented the Boston pitcher, rookie Tracy Stallard, for giving him a chance to swing.

**'Man Enough'**

"I appreciate the fact that Stallard was man enough to pitch to me," said Maris. "He was trying to get me out and he did three times. (Actually he retired Maris twice and relief man Chet Nichols got him in the eighth).

"When he got behind he had to come over. I don't think he meant to get the ball over where he did. I hit a fast ball over the plate a little bit high.

"I knew this was the sink or swim day. I promised myself I'd go out swinging even if I went 0 for 4."

Somebody asked Maris what he thought when a fan raced out to shake his hand as he rounded third.

**'Mind a Blank'**

"I didn't even know he did it," said Maris. "I was so happy I wasn't paying attention to anything. My mind was a blank.

"This was the biggest home run I ever hit. When I hit the 60th I never thought I'd have a bigger thrill. This is absolutely the greatest."

# Rams Win on 96-yd. TD Thriller, 24-14

## Catch by Matson Snaps 14-14 Tie With Steelers

BY MAL FLORENCE

Old pro Ollie Matson renewed a career as a game saver when he sprinted 65 yd. with a Frank Ryan pass on a gloomy Sunday afternoon at the Coliseum.

The entire play spanned 96 yd., breaking a fourth-quarter 14-14 tie as the Rams went on to defeat the Steelers, 24-14, before a disappointing crowd of 40,707.

Until Matson cut loose, it was a grubby, dull, tug-of-war—a throw back to the days when the pros performed on vacant lots for the price of a meal.

**Unusual Game**

It was an unusual contest, a Keystone Cop-type fight near the end capping a day replete with intercepted passes, fumbles, personal fouls and injured personnel.

In the latter case, this means Ram quarterback Zeke Bratkowski, who suffered a sprained right ankle in the second quarter, surrendering control to Ryan for the remainder of the game.

**A Fight, Too**

The bizarre fight followed a 34-yd. pass interception (one of five by the Rams) by Ed Meador that set up Danny Villanueva's game-clinching 16-yd. field goal with 12 seconds remaining.

Meador was hit on the 8-yd. line by Steeler fullback John Henry Johnson. Meador objected to Johnson's knees-first tactics and retaliated by kicking the Steeler.

Ram linebacker Bill Jobko, assisting Meador, rammed into Johnson. Cornered, Johnson picked up a ply-

Please Turn to Pg. 4, Col. 1

### HOW THEY SCORED

| Steelers | Rams | | Time |
|---|---|---|---|
| | | **FIRST QUARTER** | |
| 0 | 6 | Bratowski, 2-yd. run | 4:59 |
| 0 | 7 | Villanueva, conversion. | |
| | | **SECOND QUARTER** | |
| 6 | 7 | Dial, 20-yd. pass (Bukich) | 4:58 |
| 7 | 7 | Layne, conversion. | |
| 13 | 7 | John Henry Johnson, 5-yd. run | 13:47 |
| 14 | 7 | Layne, conversion. | |
| 14 | 13 | Phillips, 15-yd. pass (Ryan) | 14:27 |
| 14 | 14 | Villanueva, conversion. | |
| | | **FOURTH QUARTER** | |
| 14 | 20 | Matson, 96-yd. pass (Ryan) | 12:19 |
| 14 | 21 | Villanueva, conversion. | |
| 14 | 24 | Villanueva, 16-yd. field goal | 14:48 |

### HOW THEY FINISHED

**AMERICAN LEAGUE**

| | W | L | Pct. | * |
|---|---|---|---|---|
| x-New York | 109 | 53 | .673 | |
| Detroit | 101 | 61 | .623 | 8 |
| Baltimore | 95 | 67 | .586 | 14 |
| Chicago | 86 | 76 | .531 | 23 |
| Cleveland | 78 | 83 | .484 | 30½ |
| Boston | 76 | 86 | .469 | 33 |
| Minnesota | 70 | 90 | .438 | 38 |
| **LOS ANGELES** | 70 | 91 | .435 | 38½ |
| Washington | 61 | 100 | .379 | 47½ |
| Kansas City | 61 | 100 | .379 | 47½ |

*Games behind leader.
x—Clinched pennant.

**Sunday's Results**
Cleveland, 8; LOS ANGELES, 5.
New York, 1; Boston, 0.
Detroit, 8; Minnesota, 3.
Kansas City, 3; Washington, 2.
Only games scheduled.

**NATIONAL LEAGUE**

| | W | L | Pct. | * |
|---|---|---|---|---|
| x-Cincinnati | 93 | 61 | .604 | |
| **LOS ANGELES** | 89 | 65 | .578 | 4 |
| San Francisco | 85 | 69 | .552 | 8 |
| Milwaukee | 83 | 71 | .539 | 10 |
| St. Louis | 80 | 74 | .519 | 13 |
| Pittsburgh | 75 | 79 | .487 | 18 |
| Chicago | 64 | 90 | .416 | 29 |
| Philadelphia | 47 | 107 | .305 | 46 |

*Games behind leader.
x—Clinched pennant.

**Sunday's Results**
LOS ANGELES, 8; Chicago, 2.
Pittsburgh, 3; Cincinnati, 1.
St. Louis, 2; Philadelphia, 0.
San Francisco, 8-2; Milwaukee, 2-3 (second game 10 innings).

### TODAY IN SPORTS

WRESTLING — Pasadena Arena, 8 p.m.

TUMBLER—Rams' Frank Ryan survived this rough landing to throw 96-yd. TD pass two plays later. Times photo by Art Rogers

| | | | | | |
|---|---|---|---|---|---|
| 49ers . . . . . . 49 | Colts . . . . . . 34 | Giants . . . . . 24 | Packers . . . . 24 | Browns . . . . 25 | Cards . . . . . . 30 |
| Lions . . . . . . 0 | Vikings . . . . 33 | Redskins . . . 21 | Bears . . . . . . 0 | Cowboys . . . 7 | Eagles . . . . . 27 |
| Story on Page 6 | Story on Page 6 | Story on Page 6 | Story on Page 6 | Story on Page 5 | Story on Page 6 |

# ANGELS' BELINSKY PITCHES NO-HITTER!

# Decidedly Wins Kentucky Derby in Record Time

CC SUNDAY, MAY 6, 1962 2†

## JIM MURRAY

## Decidedly Decidedly

LOUISVILLE—There are 8,000 race horses foaled every year someplace in the U.S. and it is the fond hope of the owner of every one of them that he will someday run in and win the Kentucky Derby.

It's a goofy kind of race. It's been won by a George Smith and a Paul Jones which is all right since nobody gives his right name in Louisville on Derby week.

Only 15 out of the 8,000 made it to the starting gate in this year's Derby after such a public display of inhospitality on the part of the track that the management was lucky it didn't have to send to Caliente for a field. A race horse's legs are as perishable as an egg and during Derby week, Churchill Downs is an omelet. The favorite and several lead ponies broke down on this rockpile before they even dropped the flag. The betting was even money three of them would bow in the post parade. It's the only race course in the world where the horses that harrow the track wear bandages.

The horse race is the least interesting part of Derby Day in Louisville. In fact, I wouldn't even go to it except there's no way out of it. If you walk out the front door to empty the garbage on Derby Day you get swept along in the traffic jam to Churchill Downs. Every year they announce the crowd at 100,000 and 10,000 of them are textile salesmen who were on their way to Toledo and got in the wrong cab.

### Cabs Take Roundabout Route

They bring cabs in from three states around for the Derby which may account for the fact you pass through so many of them on the way to the track. They take you on a route so roundabout you get the feeling the direct one is mined.

There's hardly a dry eye in the house when the strains of "My Old Kentucky Home" are struck up. There's hardly a dry throat, either. They begin hawking mint juleps at daybreak and even then there's a queue. This is the kind of drink that can give you the giggles and a throat rash at the same time. Mint is like mushrooms in that it might not be. It's kind of like a bourbon frappe, not so much a drink as an invitation to a basal fracture. Kentuckians have a saying that one is too many but three not nearly enough. The predominant decor around the track, other than fire hydrants, is tulips and the surest bet in Louisville is that sooner or later the juleps will be in the tulips. If you're smart, you'll pour them there before drinking.

The 15 horses that survived the week of workouts on Churchill Downs may not have been the best horses in America but they're the best bets to take to a fire sale. Fourteen of them were nice kids who mind their mother and sleep with their shoes off but one of them, Sunrise County, came to the race with a reputation for being a four-footed rat pack. But he didn't knock down a single horse because where he was running there weren't any.

### Decidedly's Daddy Won '54 Derby

The winner is a nice little prematurely-gray fellow whose daddy won this race as easily in 1954. He was ridden by a jockey who was everybody's best bet to lose the next popularity contest he's entered in. Bill Hartack has been on such a losing streak lately even Eddie Arcaro, who hasn't spoken to him for years, asked the writers to say something nice about him. But none of them could think of anything.

It's a little early in the year for flag-waving but if anybody was it would have the California bear on it. Decidedly is the third California-bred horse in history to win this race and the second in the last 7 years. He doesn't look like a Californian. In fact, he doesn't look much like a horse. He's grayer than Archie Moore.

His trainer is Horatio Luro, a South American of such aplomb he looks as if he should be either the male half of a tango team or in charge of an Andean firing squad.

Luro's training methods are of the Bear Bryant school. He makes the scrimmages so tough the game is a relief. For one thing, Luro puts a 150-lb. exercise boy on Decidedly in the morning. Then he sits back to see which one of them comes home on foot. When it was the horse, Luro knew his biggest problem was to fight through the crowd to the winner's circle on Saturday.

The owner, George Pope, runs ships on the side. He had an easy job on race day. The only other graybeard in it was Johnny Longden who came over the mountains to ride a horse that was still in the backstretch when last seen.

It probably makes very little difference to a horse where he's from. Either way there's always some rat

Please Turn to Pg. 9, Col. 2

**LIKE FATHER, LIKE SON**—Decidedly, a California-bred son of Determine, which won 1954 Derby, emulates his father with thrilling 2¼-length victory in 88th Run for the Roses Saturday at Churchill Downs. Ridden by Bill Hartack, Decidedly broke record. (AP) Wirephoto

**NEXT STOP: WINNER'S CIRCLE**—Turning for home, Decidedly is caught behind Ridan but on the move in Kentucky Derby. Fortunately for jockey Bill Hartack, Ridan bore over, giving Decidedly room. (AP) Wirephoto

## California Colt Pulls Derby Upset

BY BION ABBOTT
Times Staff Representative

LOUISVILLE—Decidedly, a galloping gray ghost which made running away a habit, ran off with the roses in record time this summery Saturday afternoon at historic Churchill Downs.

The 3-year-old California-bred son of another Kentucky Derby winner, Determine, erased Whirlaway's 21-year-old track mark as he roared under the wire in 2:00 2-5, a full second under the old standard for a mile and one-quarter.

It was a grinding, gruelling finish as jockey Bill Hartack sent Decidedly driving to the front for good just inside the final eighth.

**Pulling Away**

Decidedly opened up daylight in the last sixteenth and finished two and one-quarter lengths in front of the surprising 25-1 speed horse, Roman Line, whose mamma was another California star, Lurline B.

Ridan, the even-money favorite, was a close and challenging contender the whole torrid trip. While he couldn't hold off the first two, he

Please Turn to Pg. 8, Col. 2

## PALMER SHOOTS 69 TO LEAD CASPER, STEWART BY STROKE

BY PAUL ZIMMERMAN
Sports Editor

LAS VEGAS — Arnold Palmer Saturday finally broke the deadlock that has marked the 10th annual Tournament of Champions, but not by much.

The favorite and leading money winner of the tournament trail, fired a 69, three under par, for a 54-hole total of 208 and a one-stroke lead after a head-and-head match with one of his toughest adversaries, Bill Casper Jr.

Casper and Earl Stewart Jr., also shot 69s to put them into a second place tie of 209. The ever-present Doug Sanders likewise clipped three strokes off par to stay close to the pace with 210.

None of the 28 players set the course on fire Saturday as the tension mounted on the 7,073-yd., par 72 Desert Inn course, despite the fact that no more than a zephyr — hardly enough to cool the 97 degree temperature — blew across the course.

Saturday's best rounds were only a stroke better than those of the four leaders. Jay Hebert and Tommy Jacobs got 68s, but all this did for them was close the gap to seven strokes off the pace.

The casualties in the third round of the tournament that ends today for the na-

Please Turn to Pg. 6, Col. 2

**FARM YARD**—While a pair of geese waddle in the foreground, Earl Stewart Jr. putts for his par 3 on 17th hole at Desert Inn Course. Geese waddled out of lake at 17th green for closer look at Tournament of Champions. Stewart shot a 69 Saturday for 54-hole total of 209, one stroke off the pace. Times photo by Ben Olender via AP wirephoto.

## Big D, Camilli Lead Dodgers Past Pirates

BY FRANK FINCH
Times Staff Representative

PITTSBURGH — Don Drysdale came within one out of hurling a shutout against the Pirates Saturday, but he still was happy to settle for his fourth triumph of the season.

With Doug Camilli and Tommy Davis kicking up a storm as the Dodgers broke out of their batting slump by unloading a 15-hit bombardment, the Pirates were drubbed, 10-1, before a paid crowd of 13,366.

Drysdale's brilliant five-hitter squared the series, and if Los Angeles wins today's matinee it will keep intact its record of not losing a series this season.

Drysdale (4-1) had spaced three hits through the first eight rounds and only one Pirate had reached third base when Dick Groat doubled over Tommy Davis'

Please Turn to Pg. 3, Col. 3

## Southpaw Fans Nine in 2-0 Win

BY BRAVEN DYER

Bob (Bo) Belinsky, rookie southpaw drafted from a Baltimore farm club last winter, pitched a no-hit, no-run ball game at Dodger Stadium Saturday night as the Angels won their second straight from the Orioles, 2-0, before 15,886 wildly-cheering spectators.

It was the first no-hitter in the American League since Sept. 20, 1958, when Hoyt Wilhelm, ace Baltimore relief hurler, who watched Bo do his stuff Saturday

### 'O' BY BO

| ORIOLES— | AB | R | H | RBI | E |
|---|---|---|---|---|---|
| Temple, 2b | 4 | 0 | 0 | 0 | 0 |
| Williams, lf | 4 | 0 | 0 | 0 | 0 |
| B. Robinson, 3b | 4 | 0 | 0 | 0 | 0 |
| Gentile, 1b | 2 | 0 | 0 | 0 | 0 |
| Brandt, cf | 3 | 0 | 0 | 0 | 0 |
| Triandos, c | 2 | 0 | 0 | 0 | 0 |
| Nicholson, rf | 4 | 0 | 0 | 0 | 0 |
| Hansen, ss | 3 | 0 | 0 | 0 | 0 |
| Barber, p | 1 | 0 | 0 | 0 | 0 |
| Stock, p | 0 | 0 | 0 | 0 | 0 |
| Totals— | 28 | 0 | 0 | 0 | 0 |

| ANGELS | AB | R | H | RBI | E |
|---|---|---|---|---|---|
| Pearson, cf | 4 | 0 | 0 | 0 | 0 |
| Moran, 2b | 4 | 1 | 2 | 0 | 0 |
| Wagner, rf | 4 | 0 | 2 | 0 | 0 |
| Bilko, 1b | 4 | 0 | 0 | 0 | 0 |
| Torres, 3b | 3 | 0 | 0 | 0 | 1 |
| Averill, lf | 2 | 1 | 1 | 0 | 0 |
| L. Thomas, lf | 0 | 0 | 0 | 0 | 0 |
| Rodgers, c | 3 | 0 | 1 | 0 | 0 |
| Koppe, ss | 3 | 0 | 0 | 1 | 0 |
| Belinsky, p | 2 | 0 | 0 | 0 | 0 |
| Totals— | 29 | 2 | 6 | 1 | 1 |

L. Thomas ran for Averill in 6th.
Breeding struck out for Barber in 7th.

| | |
|---|---|
| Baltimore | 000 000 000—0 |
| Los Angeles | 110 000 00x—2 |

PO-A—Baltimore, 24-13; Los Angeles, 27-10. LOB—Baltimore, 7; Los Angeles, 5. 2B—Wagner, Rodgers. S—Belinsky.

| Pitcher— | IP | H | R | ER | BB | SO |
|---|---|---|---|---|---|---|
| Barber (L, 3-1) | 6 | 6 | 2 | 2 | 1 | 6 |
| Stock | 2 | 0 | 0 | 0 | 0 | 1 |
| Belinsky (W, 4-0) | 9 | 0 | 0 | 0 | 4 | 9 |

HB—Gentile and Barber, by Belinsky. WP—Barber. Umpires—Schwarts, Berry, Honochick, Smith. Time—2h. Attendance—15,886.

night, blanked the Yankees, 1-0.

Belinsky broke his own strikeout mark, a season's club high of eight, by striking out nine batters.

**[illegible] Great**

He walked four and hit two.

Bo set the last nine Orioles down in order.

"Yes, the tension was getting to me in the ninth," the happy Bo said, after it was all over. "But I honestly think I was exceptionally quick in that ninth inning.

"I want to thank manager Bill Rigney and coach Marvin Grissom for going along with me when I didn't look too good in spring training. If they hadn't stuck with me I wouldn't have had this wonderful night."

It was Bo's fourth win without defeat.

As official scorer for Belinsky's masterful performance, I can report that the Birds didn't even come close to getting a hit.

He began by fanning

Please Turn to Pg. 4, Col. 4

**PERFECTO**—Bo Belinsky, Angel southpaw, who pitched 2-0 no-hitter over Baltimore Saturday.

## BASEBALL STANDINGS

**NATIONAL LEAGUE**

| | W | L | Pct. | * |
|---|---|---|---|---|
| San Francisco | 19 | 6 | .760 | |
| St. Louis | 14 | 6 | .700 | 2½ |
| Pittsburgh | 14 | 9 | .609 | 4 |
| DODGERS | 15 | 10 | .600 | 4 |
| Philadelphia | 11 | 9 | .550 | 5½ |
| Cincinnati | 11 | 11 | .500 | 6½ |
| Milwaukee | 9 | 13 | .409 | 8½ |
| Houston | 8 | 12 | .400 | 8½ |
| Chicago | 6 | 18 | .250 | 12½ |
| New York | 3 | 16 | .158 | 13 |

*—Games behind leader.

**Saturday's Results**

DODGERS, 10; Pittsburgh, 1.
Philadelphia, 2; New York, 1.
Cincinnati, 8; St. Louis, 7.
Chicago, 12; San Francisco, 8.
Milwaukee, 6; Houston, 5 (12 innings).

**Games Today**

DODGERS (Williams, 1-1) at Pittsburgh (Mizell, 1-1), radio KFI, KWKW, 10.30 a.m.

San Francisco (O'Dell, 3-0) at Chicago (Buhl, 1-1).

New York (Hook, 1-1 and Moorhead, 0-0) at Philadelphia (Hamilton, 2-2 and Brown, 0-0), doubleheader.

St. Louis (Broglio, 1-0 and Washburn, 2-0) at Cincinnati (Jay, 3-3 and Ellis, 1-2 or Drabowsky, 0-2), doubleheader.

Houston (Farrell, 1-2 and Golden, 1-0) at Milwaukee (Spahn, 2-3, and Willey, 0-1), doubleheader.

**AMERICAN LEAGUE**

| | W | L | Pct. | * |
|---|---|---|---|---|
| New York | 13 | 6 | .684 | |
| Cleveland | 11 | 8 | .579 | 2 |
| Minnesota | 13 | 10 | .565 | 2 |
| ANGELS | 10 | 9 | .526 | 3 |
| Chicago | 12 | 11 | .522 | 3 |
| Boston | 10 | 10 | .500 | 3½ |
| Kansas City | 12 | 13 | .480 | 4 |
| Baltimore | 10 | 11 | .476 | 4 |
| Detroit | 9 | 10 | .474 | 4 |
| Washington | 3 | 15 | .167 | 9½ |

*Games behind leader.

**Saturday's Results**

ANGELS, 2; Baltimore, 0.
Boston, 8; Chicago, 3.
Minnesota, 7; Detroit, 2.
New York, 7; Washington, 6.
Kansas City, 18-2; Cleveland, 6-3.

**Games Today**

Baltimore (Estrada, 1-3) vs. ANGELS (McBride, 2-1), radio KMPC, 1:30 p.m.

Cleveland (Bell, 2-1) at Kansas City (Bass, 0-3).

Detroit (Mossi, 2-3) at Minnesota (Pascual, 4-1).

Washington (Stenhouse, 0-0 and Burnside, 2-1) at New York (Terry, 4-1 and Bouton, 0-0), doubleheader.

Chicago (Pizarro, 2-2 and Herbert, 1-2) at Boston (Conley, 2-2 and Fornieles, 1-1), doubleheader.

# HEAVEN CAN WAIT! ANGELS IN 1ST ON 4TH

## It's True! AND Dodgers, Too

AMERICAN LEAGUE

| | W | L | Pct. | * |
|---|---|---|---|---|
| ANGELS | 45 | 34 | .570 | |
| New York | 43 | 33 | .566 | ½ |
| Cleveland | 44 | 34 | .564 | ½ |
| Minnesota | 45 | 38 | .542 | 2 |

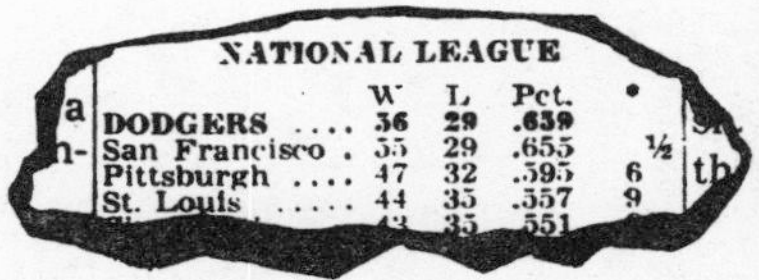

NATIONAL LEAGUE

| | W | L | Pct. | * |
|---|---|---|---|---|
| DODGERS | 56 | 29 | .659 | |
| San Francisco | 55 | 29 | .655 | ½ |
| Pittsburgh | 47 | 32 | .595 | 6 |
| St. Louis | 44 | 35 | .557 | 9 |

**CRAZY, MAN**—Tradition says that the team leading the pennant race on July 4 wins the flag. If that's true, it looks like a Freeway World Series.

## JIM MURRAY

### State of Mind City

San Francisco is not so much a city as a state of mind. It's a place which has given the rest of the world new marks to shoot at in alcohol and suicide. It has probably the only citizen in the world who would go right on eating crab and talking about art if the news came The Bomb was on its way. San Francisco, you have to say, has savoir-faire. Too much of it, in fact.

It is colder in the summer than it is in winter, consequently, you can recognize baseball fans by their chattering teeth, and football fans by their Bermuda shorts. It is a city which cannot make up its mind at night whether to go to the opera or the hungry i. No one wears shirt sleeves in San Francisco. In the first place, you'd shiver, in the second place, people would stare.

To give you an idea, San Francisco in the late 1800's used to have a character abroad in the streets who called himself "Emperor Norton I." He went around (and you could set your clock by him) in a uniform the Kaiser would have considered outlandish. He believed he was king and San Francisco let him. Anywhere else, they would have got a net over him but San Francisco permitted him to "levy" taxes, dine free in the best restaurants, and go his harmless way. It was hard to tell who was the biggest lunatic, he or San Francisco. He was terribly disappointed not to be assassinated.

#### *City Slumped When He Died*

The city hit a slump when he died. It might have been abandoned out of boredom if it weren't for the earthquake, which San Francisco characteristically ignored and grandly titled "The Fire," for the conflagration which followed, in the neatest bit of substituting effect for cause since the guy who killed both his parents pleaded for mercy on the ground he was an orphan.

But in 1958, things began to look up for San Francisco again and everybody sat up, alert for the fun. The New York Giants came to town. The city was overjoyed. Twenty-five Emperor Nortons in baseball suits!

The Giants were just perfect for San Francisco, a faintly-dotty band of athletes who had the good taste not to play the game too well. Of course, they had one super-player in the lineup, that fellow in centerfield, but San Francisco rejected Willy Mays' virtuosity as a bit vulgar. He seemed somehow to be missing the point.

#### *Giants Always Predictable*

But the rest of the Giants didn't. San Francisco was rocked for awhile as the Giants soared into contention for the league lead each year. But the Giants always caught themselves in time. So did the rest of the league. You couldn't set your watch by them, but you could set your calendar. In the hungry i, they would play the bit as follows: a business executive is standing in his office looking down over the city and dictating to his secretary. Suddenly, a falling figure shoots past the window. "Oh, oh," the man says, glancing at his chronometer. "It must be June. There go the Giants."

They built a new ballpark and the comedy got funnier. They went unerringly to the worst place in the city, if not the world, for it. Only the sides of Mt. Everest could have been more unsuitable. The Giants became the only team in the game who played all their home contests in the teeth of a gale. A batter hit a ball, then ducked so it wouldn't bean him on the way back. The slopes of Candlestick claimed so many climbers whose hearts gave out that they were thinking of having St. Bernards roaming the moraines of the parking lot.

The Giants hired a house detective as manager and the city's applause was deafening. The evidence was the Giants needed a house dick all right. But not on the field. This was what is known in the trade as a "fire escape team."

Clancy Sheehan gave up, rumor has it because the Giants switched fingerprints on him. The management hired a tithing church-goer. The city feared the worst. San Francisco wanted a pixie not a preacher. Alvin Dark was a man who didn't drink or smoke and was as out of place in San Francisco as a bikini. Plainly, he could be expected to put an improper emphasis on victory.

The town needn't have worried. Alvin may not have had any bad habits but the team took up the slack. Almost his first official act was to bail out a consider-

Please Turn to Pg. 6, Col. 5

## Rigneymen Take Two From Nats

BY BRAVEN DYER
Times Staff Representative

WASHINGTON — Those unbelievable Angels celebrated a safe — if not sane—Fourth of July by soaring into first place.

The Angels called on their brilliant bullpen to preserve 4-2 and 4-1 victories over the Washington Senators and enable them to climb over the New York Yankees in the torrid American League race.

**Yankees Split**

The Yankees, held to a split by the Kansas City Athletics, now trail the amazing Angels by half a game.

With the Dodgers leading the "other" league and tradition saying the leader on July 4 usually wins the pennant, it's not too far-fetched to start dreaming of a Freeway Series.

So, late Wednesday night, Manager Bill Rigney and his all-conquering Cherubs flew home after completing by far the most successful road trip in their brief history.

The count is 14 wins and eight defeats.

**Hectic Race**

They come home riding on Cloud Nine, leading the American League with their 45-34 record at the half-way mark of the most hectic race Joe Cronin's circuit has seen in many moons.

On the morning of July 5, 1961, they stood 33-48 and were 18½ games behind the league leaders.

This year they were in first place just once (April 15) and then for only one day. But for the past six weeks they've been the hottest club in their league and ever since they split with the Yankees over the weekend the rest of the loop finally has quit laughing at them.

**McBride Winner**

Great pitching, timely hitting and shrewd managing won the twin bill.

Ken McBride became the first Angel hurler to cop eight games and the owner of L.A.'s longest win streak (seven straight) by a pitcher to make his record 8-3 after the opener.

Dean Chance, 21-year-old all-purpose flinger, got his fourth save on the 22-game road trip by rescuing the classy Ken with two and one-third rounds of two-hit chucking.

Doughty Ted Bowsfield, gradually returning to his best form, went seven and two-thirds innings to win the nightcap, but needed relief by Art (The Hummer) Fowler with the tying run at bat in the eighth. It was Bowsfield's longest stint of the

Please Turn to Pg. 4, Col. 2

Los Angeles Times
Sports
PART III BUSINESS & FINANCE
CC THURSDAY MORNING, JULY 5, 1962 2†

## Dodgers Smash Phillies Twice

### All-L.A. World Series Possible; T. Davis, Howard Wield Hot Bats

BY FRANK FINCH

With the Dodgers and the Angels co-starring as Top Bananas of the big leagues after the last bean ball was fired Wednesday, the likelihood of an historic World Series between the local clubs no longer belongs in the realm of wishful thinking.

The way both clubs are flying high, it could happen next October.

When the bell rang in early April, a Dodgers Angels series to decide baseball supremacy was a fantastic million-to-one shot,

**Counting the House**

| | |
|---|---|
| Wednesday's attendance | 39,322 |
| 1962 attendance, 43 dates | 1,382,631 |
| 1961 attendance, 43 dates | 1,048,746 |

but both swept doubleheaders Wednesday to lead their respective races as they passed the traditional July 4 milestone.

**Often Enough**

Although being in first place on the Glorious Fourth doesn't necessarily guarantee a pennant, it has happened often enough to give one pause.

After cleaning up in Washington, the Angels already were winging homeward as the Dodgers destroyed the Phillies, 16-1, and 7-3, before 39,322 sun bathers at Dodger Stadium.

On the eve of their departure for a vital series in San Francisco, the Dodgers closed out a 12-8 home stand with a six-game winning streak, but during the stand L.A. saw its lead over the Giants shaved from two full games to a mere half-game.

**Fanned 10**

Sandy Koufax (12-4) didn't pitch another no-hitter, allowing five safeties that included Ted Savage's homer in the seventh inning, yet the opener was his easiest game of the year.

While Koufax was fanning 10 batters for the 40th time in his career and ninth time this season, the Dodgers pounded Chris Short (4-5), Cal McLish and Paul Brown for 18 resounding hits.

After only four innings

Please Turn to Pg. 2, Col. 3

## BASEBALL STANDINGS

AMERICAN LEAGUE

| | W | L | Pct. | * |
|---|---|---|---|---|
| ANGELS | 45 | 34 | .570 | |
| New York | 43 | 33 | .566 | ½ |
| Cleveland | 44 | 34 | .564 | ½ |
| Minnesota | 45 | 38 | .542 | 2 |
| Detroit | 40 | 38 | .513 | 4½ |
| Baltimore | 40 | 40 | .500 | 5½ |
| Chicago | 41 | 42 | .494 | 6 |
| Boston | 37 | 43 | .463 | 8½ |
| Kansas City | 37 | 45 | .431 | 9½ |
| Washington | 26 | 51 | .338 | 18 |

*Games behind leader.

**ANGELS**

Home 18 17 .514 Away 27 17 .614

**Wednesday's Results**

ANGELS, 4-4; Washington, 2-1.
Kansas City, 11-3; New York, 1-7.
Cleveland, 1-6; Detroit, 0-2 (first game 10 innings, second game 13 innings).
Baltimore, 7-2; Chicago, 3-5.
Minnesota, 8-5; Boston, 4-9.

**Games Today**

Detroit (Lary, 2-5) at Cleveland (Ramos, 4-5), night.
Baltimore (Fisher, 2-3) at Chicago (Zanni, 5-3), night.
Only games scheduled.

NATIONAL LEAGUE

| | W | L | Pct. | * |
|---|---|---|---|---|
| DODGERS | 56 | 29 | .659 | |
| San Francisco | 55 | 29 | .655 | ½ |
| Pittsburgh | 49 | 32 | .605 | 5 |
| St. Louis | 45 | 36 | .556 | 9 |
| Cincinnati | 43 | 35 | .551 | 9½ |
| Milwaukee | 40 | 41 | .494 | 14 |
| Philadelphia | 34 | 46 | .425 | 19½ |
| Houston | 32 | 46 | .410 | 20½ |
| Chicago | 30 | 54 | .357 | 25½ |
| New York | 21 | 57 | .269 | 31½ |

**DODGERS**

Home 31 16 .660 Away 25 13 .658

**Wednesday's Results**

DODGERS, 16-7; Philadelphia, 1-3.
San Francisco, 11-10; New York, 4-3.
Cincinnati, 8; Chicago, 6.
Pittsburgh, 7-4; Houston, 0-3.
Milwaukee, 7-0; St. Louis, 5-2 (first game completion of suspended July 3 game).

**Games Today**

DODGERS (Drysdale, 14-4) at San Francisco (McCormick, 4-2), KTTV (11), radio KFI, KWKW, 1 p.m.
Philadelphia (Owens, 2-2) at Pittsburgh (McBean, 7-5), night.

THERE ARE SMILES . . .—Angel manager Bill Rigney lights up big smile after his team moved into first in the American League by whipping Senators twice. (P) Wirephoto

## Prove It Wins as Gamble Pays Off in American 'Cap

BY BION ABBOTT

A big gamble on a split-second decision by jockey Henry Moreno paid off for Prove It Wednesday in the $55,350 American Handicap before a heavy-spending holiday crowd of 55,215 at Hollywood Park.

Moreno changed his course in midstretch, a pause that allowed Prove It to grab a big gulp of air, and then sent him flying in a final surge that whipped Windy Sands by a neck.

"If it works, I'm a champ," Moreno said afterward, with a big breath of relief. "If it doesn't, I look like a bum.

"The gamble wouldn't have worked with an ordinary horse. I felt a prolonged drive with his high weight of 124 lb. would have been too much for Prove It. He had to have a breather."

**Victory Streak**

This was the second straight success for Prove It and he handled the rugged mile and one-eighth in a sparkling 1:47 3-5.

Some of the cheers were

**THE WINNERS**

1—Stonager, $11.80.
2—Circumnavigator, $12.
**Daily Double—$61.20.**
3—Vetirok, $38.20.
4—Ronnie's Brother, $6.60.
5—Regally Yours, $25.40.
6—Sirri II, $6.60.
7—King Kameha, $14.80.
8—Prove It, $6.40.
9—Rapid Flight, $9.40.

reserved for Harpie, however. The horse that nobody wanted at one time dueled for the lead with Olden Times all the way to the final eighth. And it was Olden Times which gave way first, with Harpie collecting third money a length and one-quarter behind Windy Sands.

Olden Times faded to fourth, three lengths farther back but still a nose in front of heavily-supported T. V. Lark, a big disappointment for the second straight time.

They were followed, in order, by Rablero, Sea Orbit, which never reached contention; Cadiz and Typhoon II, which trailed the field by 17 lengths after stepping along a threatening third to the final turn.

Olden Times managed to

Please Turn to Pg. 9, Col. 1

## McCovey, Mays Homer Twice; Giants Win 2

SAN FRANCISCO (P) — Willie McCovey smashed two home runs in the opener and Willie Mays did the same in the nightcap Wednesday as San Francisco slugged the New York Mets twice, 11-4 and 10-3.

The sweep gave the Giants 11 wins in their last 13 games to set up a crucial series opening today with the Dodgers.

McCovey drove home seven runs in the first game with two-run and three-run homers plus a pair of sacrifice flies. He singled his other time up before a Candlestick Park holiday crowd of 33,253.

**GAME ON KTTV**

KTTV (11) will televise today's Los Angeles Dodger-San Francisco Giant game in Candlestick Park starting at 12:55 p.m.

The slugging performance gave McCovey 11 round-trippers in only 99 at-bats this season.

Ed Bailey and Jim Davenport added solo homers to help Bob Bolin win his third game against no losses.

Mays blasted a three-run shot with none out in the first inning of the second game and the Giants never were headed.

In the third inning, Mays switched his target from right field to left with a two-run homer, his 24th of the year. Both were off loser Bill Hunter (1-4).

Billy O'Dell won his 10th

Please Turn to Pg. 5, Col. 4

**PROOF POSITIVE**—Rex Ellsworth's Prove It, right foreground, with Henry Moreno in the irons, outgames Windy Sands, Milo Valenzuela aboard, to win $50,000-added American Handicap Wednesday at Hollywood Park. Harpie, right, was third in 1⅛ mile race. Times photo by Ken Dare

**TODAY IN SPORTS**

HORSE RACING — Hollywood Park, 1:45 p.m.

BOWLING—$5,000 Pro-Amateur, Ocean Lanes, Long Beach, 7 p.m.

# LISTON KO'S PATTERSON IN TWO MINUTES!

## Savage Left Hooks Dethrone Champion in First Round

THE MESSAGE—Sonny Liston lands pulverizing right on Floyd Patterson's jaw during punishing infighting that precedes first round knockout. Patterson winces as blow scores. End came seconds later at 2m. 6s.

AP Wirephoto

Los Angeles Times
Sports
PART III BUSINESS & FINANCE

CC WEDNESDAY MORNING, SEPTEMBER 26, 1962 3†

## JIM MURRAY

## The Thing Is Loose

CHICAGO — The Thing surfaced on the shores of Lake Michigan here Tuesday, blinked its eyes, strode through the ring on size-14 shoes and swatted the heavyweight champion of the world off him as though it had been a small gnat.

A creature so awesome, that if a ship saw it swimming in the North Atlantic it would radio for help, made a shambles of the heavyweight division with a couple of hooks that would capsize a destroyer.

The plot would never pass the censors. St. George has to get a rematch. The Dragon is one up and knighthood's flower is being pressed in the pages of a comic book.

Sonny Liston, who used to knock over people on the streets of St. Louis for nickels and dimes, knocked over a million dollars in the ring at Comiskey Park in a bigger score than a Boston bank robbery. You may have heard of rehabilitation but this is ridiculous. The heavyweight champion of the Missouri State Penitentiary became the heavyweight champion of the whole world in the biggest step-up in class since Stalin stopped throwing bombs from the street and did it from the Kremlin.

### *Not Confident, but Counterfeit*

The champion wasn't confident, he was counterfeit. Patterson might have had a chance if he could have come in the ring without his chin. He tried to hide behind his hands but he should have hidden in a phone booth. It wasn't a fight, it was an execution.

Patterson fought a fight as hysterical as a cry for help—which, by the way, would have been more use to

Please Turn to Pg. 4, Col. 1

COLTS WIN, 3-2, IN 10TH

## Dodgers, Wills (99) Still Sliding

**BY FRANK FINCH**

If the Dodgers intend to back into the pennant, they're certainly headed in the right direction.

Al Spangler's 10th-inning home run slipped Ed Roebuck his first defeat since 1960 as the Houston Colts bagged a 3-2 decision over the skidding Dodgers Tuesday night before 25,036 fans at Dodger Stadium.

Maury Wills stole his 98th and 99th bases, including home, but he made one of two errors that cost Don Drysdale an unearned run in the first inning and kept Los Angeles from winning the game in regulation time.

As a result, the rallying San Francisco Giants trimmed L.A.'s league lead to two games by defeating St. Louis.

With five games remaining for both the Dodgers and Giants, the magic number for the local varsity still is 4.

Although they've been no great shakes either, the Giants pruned two big, fat games from L.A.'s lead in a week as the listless, punchless Dodgers went through the motions of losing five of their last seven starts.

**Farrell Sharp**

Should they blow the Duke, they'll be the laughing stock of baseball, and the Giants will have avenged the humiliation poured on them by the Dodgers in '59.

Dick Farrell (10-19), who seems to pitch better against the Dodgers than when he was with them last year, scored his 10th career victory over them as he went the route and fanned seven.

Spangler packed most of the Colts' kick.

Errors by Wills and Larry Burright enabled Spangler to convert a potential double-play ball into a cheap run in the first inning.

Al's triple scored J. C.

Please Turn to Pg. 5, Col. 4

### Counting the House

| | |
|---|---|
| Tuesday's attendance | 25,036 |
| 1962 attendance 71 dates | 2,486,101 |
| 1961 attendance 71 dates | 1,749,919 |

## STANDINGS

**NATIONAL LEAGUE**

| | W | L | Pct. | * |
|---|---|---|---|---|
| DODGERS | 100 | 57 | .637 | |
| San Francisco | 98 | 59 | .624 | 2 |
| Cincinnati | 96 | 63 | .604 | 5 |
| Pittsburgh | 90 | 67 | .573 | 10 |
| Milwaukee | 84 | 74 | .532 | 16½ |
| St. Louis | 80 | 77 | .510 | 20 |
| Philadelphia | 79 | 78 | .503 | 21 |
| Houston | 62 | 93 | .400 | 37 |
| Chicago | 57 | 100 | .363 | 43 |
| New York | 39 | 117 | .250 | 60½ |

*Games behind leader.

**DODGERS**

**Home 52 24 .684 Away 48 33 .593**

**Tuesday's Results**

Houston, 3; **DODGERS, 2** (10 innings).
San Francisco, 4; St. Louis, 2.
Milwaukee, 7, New York, 3.
Cincinnati, 2; Pittsburgh, 1.
Only games scheduled.

**Games Today**

Houston (Brunet, 2-3) vs. **DODGERS (Podres, 14-12)**, Dodger Stadium, radio KFI, KWKW, 8 p.m.
Philadelphia (Short, 11-8) at Chicago (Buhl, 11-13).
St. Louis (Simmons, 9-9) at San Francisco (Marichal, 18-10).
New York (Craig, 10-23) at Milwaukee (Lemaster, 2-4), night.
Pittsburgh (Francis, 8-8) at Cincinnati (Maloney, 9-7), night.

**AMERICAN LEAGUE**

| | W | L | Pct. | * |
|---|---|---|---|---|
| New York | 93 | 65 | .589 | |
| Minnesota | 88 | 71 | .553 | 5½ |
| ANGELS | 84 | 73 | .535 | 8½ |
| Chicago | 83 | 75 | .525 | 10 |
| Detroit | 82 | 75 | .522 | 10½ |
| Cleveland | 77 | 81 | .487 | 16 |
| Baltimore | 76 | 81 | .484 | 16½ |
| Boston | 75 | 82 | .478 | 17½ |
| Kansas City | 71 | 86 | .452 | 21½ |
| Washington | 59 | 99 | .373 | 34 |

*Games behind leader.

**ANGELS**

**Home 40 41 .494 Away 44 32 .579**

**Tuesday's Results**

Detroit, 3; **ANGELS, 2.**
Boston, 4; Chicago, 0.
New York, 8; Washington, 3.
Cleveland, 5; Minnesota, 1.
Kansas City at Baltimore, postponed, rain

**Games Today**

**ANGELS** (Grba, 8-9) at Detroit (Bunning, 18-9), radio KMPC, 11:30 a.m.
Washington (Rudolph, 8-9) at New York (Terry, 22-12)
Chicago (Herbert, 18-9) at Boston (Wilson, 12-7)
Kansas City (Fischer, 4-10 and Pena, 5-4) at Baltimore (McNally, 0-0 and Roberts, 10-9), twi-night double-header
Only games scheduled.

ZIFF VIEWS FIGHT

## Patterson Proves Poor Excuse for Champion

**BY SID ZIFF, Times Staff Representative**

COMISKEY PARK, Chicago—Floyd Patterson gave up his title here Tuesday night in the poorest showing a heavyweight champion ever made. He was knocked out by Sonny Liston in 2:06 of the first round and ringsiders are still wondering why.

Joe Louis knocked out Max Schmeling in 2.04 but Schmeling at least wound up in the hospital.

Patterson didn't even have a mark.

The press was held out of his dressing room for over 30 minutes before Patterson would speak to reporters.

You'd have thought he got murdered but one indignant guy said he hasn't seen him get hit yet.

**Press Wait While Floyd Showers**

After a prolonged wait a character came out of Patterson's dressing room and said he was all right. He was just taking a shower.

"Anything wrong with that?" he demanded hotly. "Yeah," replied another angry scribe. "What's he showering for? He didn't even get up a sweat."

Liston obviously hit Patterson a couple of left hooks and fainting Floyd swooned in a daze.

I don't think he could take a punch any more if his wife hit him with a powder puff.

**Patterson Appears Scared to Death**

Now it is obvious why he boxed in secret. He was afraid people might catch on.

It appeared that Patterson was scared to death, like almost all the rest of Liston's opponents, before he stepped into the ring.

He lunged in a couple of times with punches to the body but people were expecting him to show an aggressive offense.

When Liston smashed a couple of left hooks to his

Please Turn to Pg. 4, Col. 4

## Kaline Triple Edges Angels in Ninth, 3-2

**BY BRAVEN DYER**
**Times Staff Representative**

DETROIT — Al Kaline's triple over the head of George Thomas with two out in the ninth drove home two of Detroit's three unearned runs on a chilly, autumn afternoon here Tuesday to beat the unlucky Angels, 3-2, before 51,267 empty seats.

Rookie Tom Satriano, batting for pitcher Don Lee, had clouted a pinch homer in the final round to spark an L.A. rally which produced two runs. It was the first round-tripper of the year for Rod Dedeaux's one-time USC star, who came up from Hawaii three weeks ago.

A walk to Rocky Colavito in the second inning, followed by Norm Cash's single to right, Leo Burke's error on the bingle and Dick McAuliffe's infield out produced Detroit's first tainted tally.

The smallest Tiger turnout of the year (1583) sat back

Please Turn to Pg. 6, Col. 4

## SONNY WINS TITLE WITH KO IN 2:06

### Champion Dethroned by Liston's Left Hook in One of Fastest Knockouts in Ring Annals

**BY PAUL ZIMMERMAN, Sports Editor**

CHICAGO — In one of the briefest heavyweight championship bouts ever fought, Charles (Sonny) Liston dethroned Floyd Patterson in 2m. 6s. of the first round Tuesday night at Comiskey Park.

The grim-visaged giant turned the trick as he had predicted, only much sooner. He set the stage with a rugged left hook to the body in mid-ring; fired another as Patterson leaned against the ropes, and then connected with a left and right to the head as the champion slumped to the canvas.

It was a bewildered champion who crouched there while referee Frank Sikora counted.

**Patterson Gets Up Too Late**

He was getting up as Sikora tolled 10, but not in time. Patterson looked questioningly, his out-of-focus eyes asking what happened, as Sikora took him by the hand and led him to his nearby corner.

"I asked him what his name was," said the referee after the bout, "and he couldn't answer me."

The crowd of 25,000 scattered through the White Sox ball park hardly had settled into its seats after the introductions when the end came.

**Third Shortest Heavyweight Bout**

It was the third shortest bout in the history of the heavyweight championship.

Tommy Burns knocked out Jim Roche in 1m. 28s. back in 1908. Joe Louis put Max Schmeling away in 2m. 4s. in their second meeting in 1938.

Liston had gone into the ring a 10 to 7 favorite but even his most optimistic partisans dared not expect that the end would come with such suddenness. Patterson, who was spotting his rugged challenger 25 lb.—214 to 189—and 13 in. in reach, got in only one punch worthy of the name before the somber, glowering Liston got to him.

**Fight Follows Expected Pattern**

The bout had started much as expected, with Sonny snaking his huge left fist at the title holder and Patterson bobbing and weaving; trying desperately to get inside for the combination punches he likes to throw.

Floyd's one solid contact was a desperation punch. He lunged at Liston, firing his right to the body.

Everything else landed lightly around the challenger's head as Patterson sought in vain to find the target inside Liston's massive fists.

It is safe to say that the new champion suffered greater punishment after the bout was over.

His handlers catapulted into the ring, followed by a host of admirers whom the ushers and police could not stop.

All of a sudden the ring was swarming with fans mingling with photographers trying desperately to get

Please Turn to Pg. 2, Col. 4

## YANKEES CLINCH FLAG

STORY ON PAGE 5

# CARDS SLAM BACK DOOR ON DODGERS

# Giants Win on Mays' Homer to Force Play-off Today

Los Angeles Times
Sports
PART III BUSINESS & FINANCE
CC MONDAY MORNING, OCTOBER 1, 1962 2†

## JIM MURRAY

## Wanted: 1 Pennant

WANTED: ONE NEARLY-NEW 1962 NATIONAL LEAGUE PENNANT, SLIGHTLY SOILED WITH TEAR STAIN IN THE CENTER.

LAST SEEN BLOWING TOWARD SAN FRANCISCO IN WINDS OF GALE VELOCITY. SCRAP OF CLOTH IS BELIEVED TO BE PROPERTY OF LOS ANGELES DODGERS AND FINDER PROMISED LIBERAL REWARD

ANY INFORMATION LEADING TO THE ARREST AND CONVICTION OF ANYONE ATTEMPTING TO TRANSMIT THIS STOLEN MATERIAL TO HORACE STONEHAM AND THE SAN FRANCISCO GIANTS, PLEASE COMMUNICATE IMMEDIATELY WITH WALTER O'MALLEY, CHAVEZ RAVINE, R.F.D. IN CASE OF A PHONE CALL, PLEASE REVERSE THE CHARGES.

WARNING: IF YOU RETURN PENNANT TO DODGERS DIRECT, PLEASE BE SURE TO TAPE IT TO THEIR HANDS.

This notice, as this is written, is being tacked up in all the better post-offices. Panic is in the freeways of Los Angeles. After 162 games, the National League pennant race is right back where it started. All that dust raised didn't mean a thing.

They're throwing down martinis by the tub-full in Candlestick Park. But the champagne is still on ice in Chavez Ravine. Two more losses and they will trade it in for a gross of aspirin.

### Small Order Hard to Deliver

The Dodgers have scored exactly no runs in 21 innings when 1 run at any time in most of those innings would have brought a pennant.

Western Union, the nation's press, the Sheraton-West hotel, the All-Year Club of Southern California, Yellow Cab and the Upland Oddfellows were all ready. Only the Dodgers said "Not yet." They dropped 10 of their last 13 games as easily as they had won 100 of the first 150. Just when they seemed to have the flag in their hands, they shoved it over to the Giants and said "Here, you take it." The Giants are eyeing it suspiciously themselves at the moment. They suspect a trick. There is one: the New York Yankees come with the pennant.

The Dodgers dropped three straight to a sixth-place ball club, the St. Louis Cardinals, despite two of the best pitching jobs in the major leagues this season.

There were over 40,000 people in the ball-park for each of the last 3 games setting a new all-time attendance record for the grand old game of 2,684,170, but Commissioner Ford Frick has not yet signified whether they are asterisks or real people.

But the Dodgers could have done better batting with pillows. They have been the victim of dirty tricks by St. Louis pitchers. Ernie Broglio threw curves. Curt Simmons just fluttered his sleeves and only let go of the ball after each Dodger had already swung. The Dodgers had come down with cancer of the pennant.

### Mays More Important Than Momentum

The momentum was all with the Giants. But sometimes momentum just carries you over the cliff. It depends on whether you have control of the wheel. Willie Mays is all with the Giants and that may be more important than momentum.

The Dodgers have had first place since July 8 but Manager Walt Alston has been trying to protect it with mirrors ever since. Sandy Koufax came down with a finger ailment in the one quarter-inch of his body that would make any difference and Alston has been trying to camouflage the defect by playing left-fielders on third base, right-fielders on first base and pitchers in the bullpen whose arms are held in place by chicken-wire and chewing gum.

He had the most active corpse in the National League for a month and a half until the Giants began to smell something and reached up and took the pulse.

The manager took each defeat in stride—as if none of them really surprised him. On Saturday night when 49,012 turned out in their party hats, ready for the snake dance downtown, with pie plates and noisemakers, the defeat found Manager Alston thoughtful as he peeled off his clothes in the locker room. "We have a

Please Turn to Pg. 6, Col. 1

## S.F. Nips Colts, 2-1, Gain Tie

SAN FRANCISCO (AP) — Willie Mays crashed his way out of a brief hitting slump with an eighth inning home run Sunday, clipping Houston, 2-1, and sending the San Francisco Giants into a playoff with Los Angeles for the National League pennant.

Mays' dramatic blast, the most important of the year for the most valuable Giant of them all — who won the home run title — combined with the St. Louis 1 to 0 triumph over Los Angeles to deadlock the Dodgers and Giants.

When the score of the St. Louis-Los Angeles game was announced, the capacity throng waiting here went wild, pitching cushions in the air, roaring with approval.

Dick Farrell had kept the Giants checked except for Ed Bailey's solo fourth inning homer.

**O'Dell Effective**

Lefty Billy O'Dell had been just as effective as his right handed pitching opponent but came out for a pinch hitter in the seventh. So Mays' mighty blast gave the triumph to reliever Stu Miller, putting his record at 5-8.

Mays hadn't hit in his previous ten times at bat when he faced Farrell as leadoff man in the eighth. With the count no balls and one strike, Willie whacked a ball over the left field fence—his 47th homer of the campaign, giving Farrell his 20th loss against 10 triumphs.

Bailey bombed San Francisco into a 1-0 fourth inning lead with his 17th homer of the year, a 400-ft. shot over the right field fence.

| Houston | ab | r | h | bi | San. Fran. | ab | r | h | bi |
|---|---|---|---|---|---|---|---|---|---|
| Warwick,cf | 4 | 0 | 0 | 0 | Kuenn,lf | 3 | 0 | 1 | 0 |
| Temple,2b | 4 | 0 | 0 | 0 | F.Alou,rf | 0 | 0 | 0 | 0 |
| Mejias,rf | 4 | 1 | 2 | 0 | M.Alou,rf-lf | 4 | 0 | 2 | 0 |
| Larker,1b | 3 | 0 | 0 | 0 | Mays,cf | 3 | 1 | 1 | 1 |
| Aspr'm'nte,3b | 4 | 0 | 2 | 0 | McCovey,1b | 4 | 0 | 0 | 0 |
| Pendleton,lf | 2 | 0 | 1 | 1 | Cepeda,1b | 0 | 0 | 0 | 0 |
| Roberts,lf | 1 | 0 | 0 | 0 | Bailey,c | 4 | 1 | 1 | 1 |
| Smith,c | 3 | 0 | 0 | 0 | Dav'nport,3b | 4 | 0 | 1 | 0 |
| Hartman,ss | 3 | 0 | 1 | 0 | Hiller,2b | 3 | 0 | 2 | 0 |
| Ranew | 1 | 0 | 0 | 0 | Pagan,ss | 3 | 0 | 1 | 0 |
| Farrell,p | 3 | 0 | 1 | 0 | O'Dell,p | 2 | 0 | 0 | 0 |
| Goodman | 1 | 0 | 0 | 0 | Haller | 1 | 0 | 0 | 0 |
| | | | | | Miller,p | 0 | 0 | 0 | 0 |
| Totals | 33 | 1 | 7 | 1 | Totals | 31 | 2 | 9 | 2 |

Haller filed out for O'Dell in 7th.
Roberts grounded out for Pendleton in 8th.
Ranew popped out for Hartman in 9th.
Goodman struck out for Farrell in 9th.

SCORE BY INNINGS

| | |
|---|---|
| Houston | 000 001 000—1 |
| San Francisco | 000 100 01x—2 |

E—None. PO-A — Houston, 24-6; San Francisco, 27-8. DP—Hartman to Larker; Farrell to Hartman to Larker. LOB—Houston, 8; San Francisco, 7. 2B—M. Alou, Hiller, Farrell. HR—Bailey, Mays. SB—Hartman. S—Pendleton.

| Pitcher— | IP | H | R | ER | BB | SO |
|---|---|---|---|---|---|---|
| Farrell-L (10-20) | 8 | 9 | 2 | 2 | 1 | 4 |
| O'Dell | 7 | 7 | 1 | 1 | 2 | 4 |
| Miller-W (5-8) | 2 | 0 | 0 | 0 | 0 | 1 |

HBP—By Farrell (Kuenn). Umpires — Smith, Steiner, Boggess, Landes. Time—2h. 28m. Attendance—41,327.

**DODGER DOLDRUMS**—Duke Snider and row of Dodgers have that glum look that means defeat as they sit in dugout in ninth inning of Sunday's game with St. Louis. The 1-0 loss forced the Dodgers into a best-of-three playoff for the pennant against the Giants starting this afternoon in San Francisco.
Times photo by Ken Dare

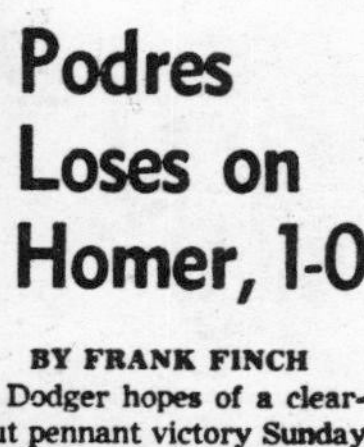

## Podres Loses on Homer, 1-0

BY FRANK FINCH

Dodger hopes of a clear-cut pennant victory Sunday rode out of the ball park with Gene Oliver's eighth-inning home run which gave St. Louis its second straight shutout victory, 1-0, and forced a play-off between Los Angeles and San Francisco.

Walt Alston will herd his crestfallen club aboard the Dodger Electra II at 9 o'clock this morning for the hop to Candlestick Park and the first game of the best-of-three playoff with the Giants.

**Swift Descent**

The second game and third, if necessary, will be played at Dodger Stadium. All games will commence at 1 p.m. and will be telecast locally over KTTV (11) and to the rest of the nation over the NBC network.

It would require a Herculean effort for the Dodgers to bounce back now and battle their way into a lucrative World Series with the Yankees.

**Reverse Gear**

The plucky Giants have the momentum and the bedraggled Dodgers apparently are stuck in reverse gear as they square off against their mortal enemies, who've won six of their last seven meetings with L.A.

Southpaw Billy Pierce (15-6), virtually invincible at

Please Turn to Pg. 4, Col. 4

## GIANTS CHEER AS CARDS PUT THEM INTO FLAG PLAY-OFF

BY PAUL ZIMMERMAN
Times Sports Editor

SAN FRANCISCO — "Come on. Let's get 'em."

This was the shout of Harvey Kuenn in the Giants clubhouse Sunday afternoon when the last Dodger out was reported from Chavez Ravine. Then the place shook with prolonged cheers.

The San Francisco players, who had left the field with a 2-1 victory over the Colts, had to wait a half hour before they knew Los Angeles lost and that they were in a playoff today.

In the absence of a direct radio report from down south, Russ Hodges, on the Giant network, stood by after the game and gave a reconstructed report from Western Union.

**Just Arrived**

The Giants had just arrived from the field when Gene Oliver hit his home run off Johnny Podres, and this started the back-slapping and cheering that spasmodically broke out after each telling play at Chavez Ravine.

Manager Alvin Dark wandered around the place as nervous as a hen hovering over its chicks. His chicks crowed like roosters when Jim Gilliam popped out to Julian Javier to end the game.

Then he held court in his office, answering questions between phone calls of congratulations.

"It will be Billy Pierce tomorrow and Jack Sanford Tuesday. After that I don't know," as he announced his pitchers.

**Tickled to Death**

Asked if he dislikes having to play the first game here with the next two in Los Angeles, Dark smiled thinly:

"I'm just tickled to death to play 'em anywhere."

Please Turn to Pg. 2, Col. 4

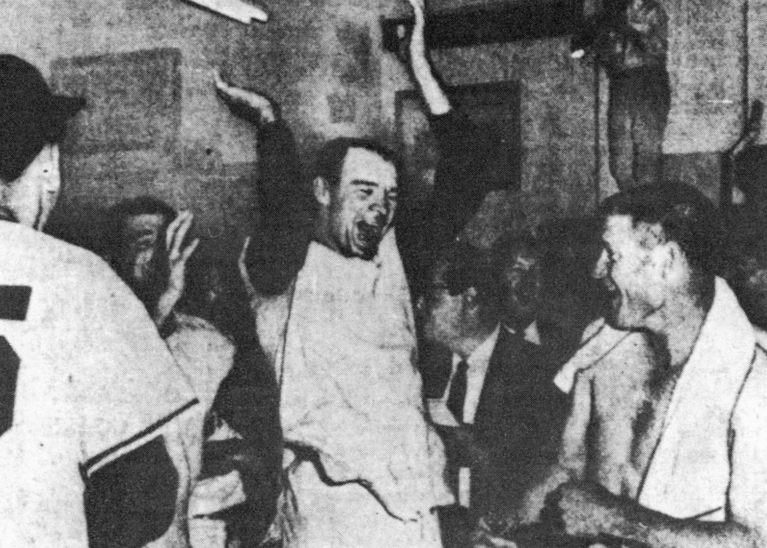

**WHOOPING IT UP**—While the Dodgers were blue, the Giants whooped it up in clubhouse after learning that L.A. had lost. In center Harvey Kuenn jumps for joy, while pitcher Billy O'Dell, right, laughs.
UPI Telephoto

## Rams Cut in on Dodger Act, Lose Again, 27-17

### Only 26,907 Fans See Dallas Pros Score Upset on LeBaron's 'Home Run' Aerials

BY MAL FLORENCE

In the city of futility, no one is more futile than the Rams.

While the baseball Dodgers were blowing to St. Louis in neighboring Chavez Ravine Sunday, the football Rams out did them at the Coliseum, stumbling before Dallas, an 11 point underdog, 27-17.

In one of their more listless performances of recent listless seasons, the Rams can be thankful of one thing: only 26,907 fans were present to witness their failure — the smallest crowd to watch an NFL game here in nine years.

And, the "crowd" seemed more interested in the proceedings at Dodger Stadium, the transistor throng departing midway through the fourth quarter when the Dodger score became final.

### HOW THEY SCORED

| Cowboys | Rams | | Time |
|---|---|---|---|
| FIRST QUARTER | | | |
| 6 | 0 | D. Perkins, 5-yd. run | 4:48 |
| 7 | 0 | Baker, conversion | |
| SECOND QUARTER | | | |
| 7 | 3 | Villanueva, 51-yd. field goal | 4:30 |
| 10 | 3 | Baker, 34-yd. field goal | 7:33 |
| THIRD QUARTER | | | |
| 16 | 3 | Marsh, 85-yd. pass from Le Baron | 3.35 |
| 17 | 3 | Baker, conversion | |
| FOURTH QUARTER | | | |
| 17 | 9 | Phillips, 16-yd. pass from Bratkowski | 5:23 |
| 17 | 10 | Villanueva, conversion | |
| 23 | 10 | Clarke, 66-yd. pass from Le Baron | 6:43 |
| 24 | 10 | Baker, conversion | |
| 27 | 10 | Baker, 48-yd. field goal | 9:54 |
| 27 | 16 | Atkins, 48-yd. pass (Gabriel) | 14.23 |
| 27 | 17 | Villanueva, conversion | |

**Half-Hearted Boos**

Even the booing was half-hearted, thus matching the Ram effort afield.

As for the game itself, daring Dallas quarterback Eddie LeBaron, who threw a pair of home run touchdown passes, and a stout Cowboy defense, frustrated the Rams.

The Eastern Conference Cowboys, who never trailed, earned their first victory of the season against a loss and a tie, while the Rams lost their sixth straight contest—three in league play.

This game was supposed to be a "laugher," one that would put the Rams back on the right road after narrow losses to Baltimore and Chicago. But the laugh was on Los Angeles.

**Led All the Way**

Dallas led at half, 10-3, expanded this margin to 17-3 after three quarters and never let the Rams come

Please Turn to Pg. 6, Col. 7

## PLAY-OFF AT A GLANCE

Here's the picture for the National League pennant play-off between the Giants and Dodgers and the World Series to follow:

The Giants and Dodgers meet in a best-of-three series which opens today at Candlestick Park at 1 p.m. The second and third if necessary, will be played at Dodger Stadium Tuesday and Wednesday. The games will be telecast by KTTV (11) and broadcast by KFI.

The World Series starts on Thursday even if the play-off goes three games. Games will be played in the National League park Thursday and Friday, at Yankee Stadium Sunday, Monday and Tuesday, and if necessary, the last two in the west on the following Thursday and Friday.

| | | | | | |
|---|---|---|---|---|---|
| Redskins...24 | Eagles.....35 | 49ers.......21 | Packers....49 | Giants......31 | Lions......29 |
| Cards.......14 | Browns.... 7 | Vikings.... 7 | Bears....... 0 | Steelers....27 | Colts.......20 |
| Story on Page 3 | Story on Page 3 | Story on Page 3 | Story on Page 3 | Story on Page 3 | Story on Page 3 |

# DODGERS THROW AWAY FLAG TO GIANTS

## Charity Begins at Home: Errors, Walks Beat L.A., 6-4

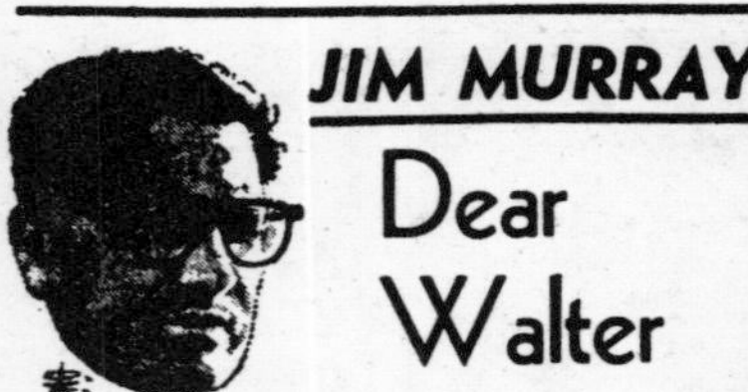

### JIM MURRAY

## Dear Walter

All right, Mrs. Higginbotham, dry your eyes, don't put your gum under the desk, do your nails on your own time and take a memo to Mr. Walter O'Malley. I want to tell him how it happened.

Dear Walter:

First off, never mind about those tickets. I won't be here for the Series. Neither will my bartender or that waitress at the Pig 'n Whistle. I'll be in San Francisco.

Next, you better come down and get your ball club. The last time I saw them they were all sitting in the clubhouse staring at their feet. A funny thing happened to them on the way to the World Series. The Giants.

I would make a few suggestions about your ball club, Walter. First of all, if I were you, I would start insisting they wear those batting helmets in the field.

Next, I would suggest at the next winter meeting, you recommend a few simple rule changes—like, make it legal to steal first base. That way, you might get to use the next batch of World Series tickets you print.

#### They Came From Behind

I suppose you prefer not to hear about the game. Well, your guys had it all the way. They came from behind—which, I don't have to tell you, is not the best thing they do. Tommy Davis and Maury Wills hit home runs. Tommy's went out of the park. Maury's went out of the infield. Maury, of course, stole second, third and then came home on a wild throw. But everybody in the league knows it's a home run if he gets on first base.

I went down in the locker room in the eighth inning. So did all the radio and TV guys. Buzzie Bavasi was pacing up and down. He not only had his fingers crossed, he had his eyes crossed. You had a 4-2 lead and the guttiest pitcher in the league going for you—Eddie Roebuck. But I was there to see Eddie come walking in the locker room, carrying his right arm as if it were overweight on an airline. He had pitched so much you could stick a pin in it and he wouldn't notice.

Willie Mays beat you. That doesn't put you in a very exclusive society in baseball. I have to say Willie has done it before. If Mays struck out in the ninth, this memo would now be addressed to Horace Stoneham, care of the Giants. But Willie Mays doesn't strike out. Not when it counts. Besides, when you lured Stoneham west with you, you told him he'd find fame and fortune, didn't you?

#### Alston Explained Strategy

A word about your manager, Walter Alston. This guy shows a lot of class. I think Fred Hutchinson is the best manager in the league, if you care. But your guy is right there. And, while his team was locked in the dressing room, Walter came out. He patiently explained every move he had made to a sometimes-hostile press. He acted as if he owed the world an explanation of his strategy. I know so many guys who wouldn't explain to their wives under those circumstances.

I know only one thing I would have done in Walter's situation that he didn't do. I would have gone out and gotten drunk.

The Dodgers are a young team and will win many pennants. Perhaps, too many. I would take Tommy Davis off third-base, if you care. Tommy is happy in left-field and I think the infield is happy to see him there. The demise of the Dodgers dates to the day Davis took third.

I know Mays threw that last ball he caught into the stands. But before you bill him, remember he cost Los Angeles more than he cost you. The Sheraton-West Hotel will be wide open for reservations and if you can use a ballroom full of teletype machines, I know where you can get a rate.

Willie and Alvin Dark didn't touch any of that champagne in the locker room. Willie went and got a strawberry pop. Alvin went on the air to tell people he didn't think he should be prevented from watering down his infield "considering O'Malley needs a one-ton roller to harden his enough to let his runners run."

#### Willie Isn't Starving

Mays was philosophical. "I don't need the World Series, money-wise, as much as the rest of these guys," he told me. "But it's an honor and a privilege to be in it."

I wish your team had been as big about it. Barring the locker room to the press I hope was due to their youth and inmmaturity and not, as some visiting writers felt, due to your public relations which sometimes seems to combine age and immaturity.

"It is the greatest thing that ever happened to me," Orlando Cepeda told me in fractured Spanish. "There is nossing like being champion."

All right, Mrs. Higginbotham, type that in triplicate. And cheer up. There's always next year.

## BUCKEYES ARRIVE FOR UCLA GAME

STORY ON PAGE 7

CC †

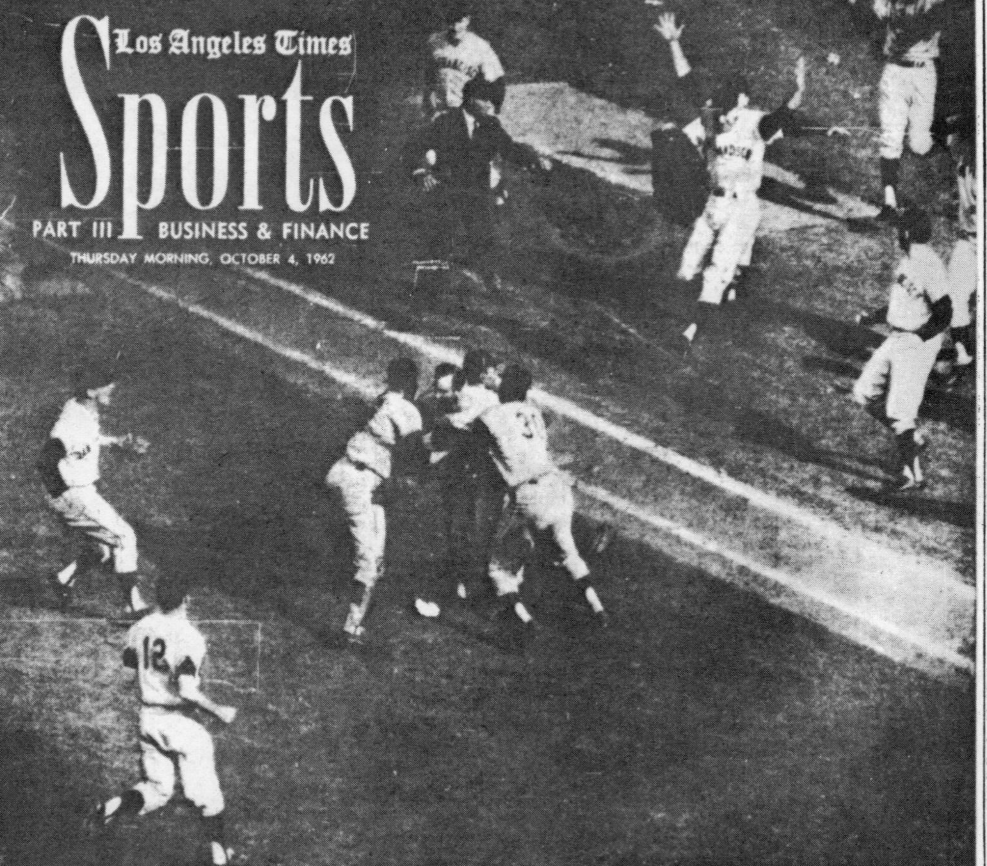


JOY IN GIANTVILLE—The San Francisco Giants have just won the National League pennant and pitcher Billy Pierce (hatless) is mobbed by teammates, catcher Ed Bailey and Orlando Cepeda (30), while other Giants rush up. Manager Al Dark is at the far right.

Times photo by Art Rogers

## S.F. Gets Crack at Yankees

BY FRANK FINCH

History caught up with the Dodgers again Wednesday when they blew a two-run lead over the Giants in the ninth inning of the third and deciding game of the National League play-offs, just as they'd done in '51 when Bobby Thomson did you-know-what.

Just when it looked like Los Angeles had its second pennant wrapped up, its pitching and defense capsized (does that sound familiar?) and San Francisco scored four times in the last act to capture a 6-4 victory before 45,693 Dodger Stadium spectators.

Thus, Al Dark's resourceful Giants qualified to challenge the world - champion New York Yankees in the 1962 World Series, which begins at noon today in Candlestick Park.

**Dodgers Go Ahead**

In the sixth inning, Tommy Davis sent the Dodgers ahead, 3-2, with a homer following Duke Snider's second hit.

And in the seventh, Maury Wills slapped his fourth straight single, stole second and third bases for a grand total of 104, and romped home on a poor peg to give L.A. a 4-2 lead.

At this juncture, with Ed Roebuck pitching smoothly in relief, lots of baseball authors canceled airplane reservations for San Francisco.

**Runs Out of Gas**

But the veteran relief hurler, making his seventh appearance in the last nine games, ran out of gas in the ninth, and the game was as good as lost before manager Walt Alston called in Stan Williams, relief winner of Tuesday's thriller.

Ten Giants traipsed to the plate as the Dodgers, once again performing like semipros, let a possible record cut of the series melon be swiped by the hard-knocking visitors from the north.

**Shades of 1951**

It was reminiscent, in a way, of the Dodger-Giant play-off decider at the Polo Grounds in '51.

Brooklyn led, 4-1, as Leo Durocher's Giants came to bat in the ninth. Before it was concluded, the Giants pushed over four runs, capped by Thomson's three-run homer.

The transplanted Giants used a different formula this time, however. They capitalized on four walks and L.A.'s fourth error, their offensive contributions being two singles and a sacrifice fly.

Batting for the winning pitcher, Don Larsen, Matty Alou rapped Roebuck's first serve for a single. Shortstop Wills made a fine play on Harvey Kuenn's smash to force Matty, but Kuenn beat

Please Turn to Pg. 6, Col. 1

## DODGERS SUFFER IN SILENCE AFTER BLOWING $12,000 GAME

BY JOHN HALL

Look ma, no pennant.

Three outs to go . . . the champagne was ready . . . the glasses iced . . . but the corks never popped.

In the depths of despair, the crushed Dodgers still couldn't believe it Wednesday as they crawled off the field after blowing a two-run lead and the National League championship in the ninth inning at the torture chamber known as Dodger Stadium.

The players were so stunned they refused to allow the press into their dressing room for 56 minutes, locking the doors to suffer in silence.

**No Exceptions**

"How the hell would you feel if you all just blew $12,000?" asked Wally Moon, who finally came outside the tomb-silent quarters to try to explain to the gang of locked-out reporters.

Moon, Dodger player representative, politely but firmly said there would be no visitors and no exceptions.

"The players just don't want to talk," said Wally. "They want to be alone. They've got to cool off. This wasn't easy.

"We had several chances to win it, but it's over. There's nothing to say. You can't lose like this without feeling bad."

"What's going on in there?" a reporter asked.

"Nothing," said Moon. "Just nothing. They're sitting around not saying a word."

A couple of players earlier emerged briefly from the gloom to run down the hall and grab a beer or ice.

None of them spoke.

Don Drysdale broke through the door, swearing loudly to himself. Jim Gilliam, Maury Wills and Duke Snider were grimly silent.

**Alston Talks**

Manager Walt Alston, as courteous as always, met the press in another room next to the clubhouse.

"We just came close, that's all," said Alston quietly.

"Our pitchers finally ran

Please Turn to Pg. 5, Col. 1

!★%?!!★$●

| Giants | ab | r | h | bi | Dodgers | ab | r | h | bi |
|---|---|---|---|---|---|---|---|---|---|
| Kuenn,lf | 5 | 1 | 2 | 1 | Wills,ss | 5 | 1 | 4 | 0 |
| Hiller,2b | 3 | 0 | 1 | 0 | Gill'm,2b-3b | 5 | 0 | 0 | 0 |
| McCovey | 0 | 0 | 0 | 0 | Snider,lf | 3 | 2 | 2 | 0 |
| Bowman,2b | 0 | 1 | 0 | 0 | Burright,2b | 1 | 0 | 0 | 0 |
| F.Alou,rf | 4 | 1 | 1 | 0 | Walls | 1 | 0 | 0 | 0 |
| Mays,cf | 3 | 1 | 1 | 1 | T.Davis,3b-lf | 3 | 1 | 2 | 2 |
| Cepeda,1b | 4 | 0 | 1 | 1 | Moon,1b | 3 | 0 | 0 | 0 |
| Bailey,c | 4 | 0 | 2 | 0 | Fairly,1b-rf | 0 | 0 | 0 | 0 |
| Davenport,3b | 4 | 0 | 1 | 1 | Howard,rf | 4 | 0 | 0 | 1 |
| Pagan,ss | 5 | 1 | 2 | 0 | Harkness,1b | 0 | 0 | 0 | 0 |
| Marichal,p | 2 | 1 | 1 | 0 | Roseboro,c | 3 | 0 | 0 | 0 |
| Larsen,p | 0 | 0 | 0 | 0 | W.Davis,cf | 3 | 0 | 0 | 0 |
| M.Alou | 1 | 0 | 1 | 0 | Podres,p | 2 | 0 | 0 | 0 |
| Nieman | 1 | 0 | 0 | 0 | Roebuck,p | 2 | 0 | 0 | 0 |
| Pierce,p | 0 | 0 | 0 | 0 | Williams,p | 0 | 0 | 0 | 0 |
| | | | | | Perranoski,p | 0 | 0 | 0 | 0 |
| Totals | 36 | 6 | 13 | 4 | Totals | 35 | 4 | 8 | 3 |

M. Alou singled for Larsen in 9th.
McCovey walked for Hiller in 9th.
Bowman ran for McCovey in 9th.
Nieman struck out for M. Alou in 9th.
Walls flied out for Burright in 9th.

SCORE BY INNINGS

| | |
|---|---|
| San Francisco | 002 000 004—6 |
| Los Angeles | 000 102 100—4 |

E—Marichal, Podres, Roseboro, Gilliam, Pagan, Bailey, Burright. PO-A—San Francisco, 27-7; Los Angeles, 27-13. DP—Gilliam to Wills to Moon; Wills to Gilliam to Moon; Wills to Burright to Fairly. LOB—San Francisco, 12; Los Angeles, 8. 2B—Snider, Hiller. HR—T. Davis. SB—Wills, 3; T. Davis. S—Hiller, Marichal, Fairly, Cepeda (f).

| | IP | H | R | ER | BB | SO |
|---|---|---|---|---|---|---|
| Marichal | 7 | 8 | 4 | 3 | 1 | 2 |
| Larsen-W (5-4) | 1 | 0 | 0 | 0 | 2 | 0 |
| Pierce | 1 | 0 | 0 | 0 | 0 | 0 |
| Podres | 5 | 9 | 2 | 2 | 1 | 0 |
| Roebuck-L (10-2) | 3⅓ | 4 | 4 | 3 | 3 | 0 |
| Williams | ⅓ | 0 | 0 | 0 | 2 | 0 |
| Perranoski | ⅓ | 0 | 0 | 0 | 0 | 1 |

(Podres pitched to three batters in 6th; Marichal pitched to one batters in 8th.)

WP—Williams. Umpire—Boggess, plate; Donatelli, 1b; Conlan, 2b; Barlick, 3b. Time—3h. Attendance—45,693.

## How to Lose a Pennant

THIRD INNING

Pagan singled to left. Marichal sacrificed and Pagan continued to third when Podres threw past second base into center field. Marichal reached first on the error. Kuenn singled sharply to left, scoring Pagan, Marichal stopping at second. Hiller missed a sacrifice attempt, and Marichal was hung up between second and third. Marichal reached third, however, when Roseboro's throw to second sailed into center field, Kuenn holding first. Hiller flied to Snider whose quick return to the infield kept Marichal at third. Kuenn, however, was hung up between first and second but returned to first safely when Gilliam's throw struck him in the back. Marichal scored on Gilliam's error. F. Alou singled to center and Kuenn reached third when W. Davis' throw hit him on the back. F. Alou took second on the throw. (No error.) Mays was purposely passed. Cepeda hit into a double play, Gilliam to Wills to Moon.

**Two runs, three hits, three errors, two left. (One run earned.)**

NINTH INNING

Matty Alou batted for Larsen and singled to right center. Kuenn forced M. Alou, Wills to Burright.

Willie McCovey batted for Hiller and walked on four pitches. Ernie Bowman ran for McCovey. F. Alou walked on a full count, filling the bases.

Mays cracked a line single off Roebuck's glove scoring Kuenn and leaving the bases filled. That was all for Roebuck. Stan Williams, right hander, came in to pitch for the Dodgers. Cepeda hit a low liner to Fairly in medium right, Bowman scoring on the sacrifice, to tie the score at 4-4, with F. Alou taking third after the catch.

Mays took second on a wild pitch. The ball glanced off Roseboro's outstretched mitt and did not roll away sufficiently for F. Alou to make a try for the plate. Bailey drew an intentional pass, filling the bases. Davenport walked on five pitches forcing F. Alou over the plate and putting the Giants ahead, 5-4.

Left hander Ron Perranoski replaced Williams on the mound. Burright fumbled Pagan's grounder to the right of second base and all hands were safe as Mays scored on the error, leaving the bases still filled. Bob Nieman batted for M. Alou and struck out.

**Four runs, two hits, one error, three left. (Three runs earned.)**

TOSSING THE BALL (GAME) AWAY—In crucial plays involving Dodger throwing errors in third inning, Jose Pagan is safe at second when Johnny Podres fielded Juan Marichal's bunt and threw wildly to Maury Wills and, at right, Harvey Kuenn is hit on back by Jim Gilliam's throw to Wally Moon.

Times photos

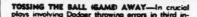

1963
1972

THE NATION WAS FAST BECOMING HOOKED. MORE PEOPLE THAN EVER WATCHED SPORTS AS NETWORK television brought major events from around the globe into their living rooms. Leagues expanded faster than fastfood franchises.

Headlines featured Sandy Koufax, Don Drysdale, Muhammad Ali, the UCLA basketball team, the Boston Celtics, Billy Casper, Jack Nicklaus, the Notre Dame and USC football teams, Denny McLain, George Allen, Lee Trevino, Joe Frazier, the Tokyo, Mexico City, and Munich Olympic Games, the Los Angeles Lakers, and a football game known as the Super Bowl.

Tokyo staged an impressive Olympics in 1964, featured by some splendid personal achievements in track and field. Peter Snell, the great New Zealand runner, won both the 800 and 1,500 meters. Al Oerter of the United States won his third straight gold medal in the discus, and another American, Bob Schul, was a surprise winner in the 5,000 meters. But it was Billy Mills, a twenty-six-year-old, part-Sioux Indian from South Dakota and the U.S. Marine Corps who stunned the world. He upset a strong field to win the 10,000 meters in 28 minutes, 24.4 seconds, an Olympic record.

The 1968 Olympics in Mexico City featured one of the most remarkable athletic feats ever achieved. The world record for the long jump was 27 feet, 4¾ inches, and Bob Beamon of the United States had not jumped farther than 27 feet, 4 inches. But on October 18, he exploded off the takeoff board in Estadio Olimpico and soared almost beyond the landing pit. He cleared the 28-foot barrier and sailed 29 feet, 2½ inches, a distance regarded then as unreachable. No doubt the 7,573-foot altitude aided Beamon in his jump—as it also helped other athletes in their events. Fifteen world records were set and two equaled. Furthermore Oerter won his fourth gold medal in the discus.

Tommie Smith and John Carlos, two black members of the U.S. team who had threatened to boycott the Games because of a racial dispute, stirred a controversy by raising clenched fists in a "black power" salute on the victory stand after Smith had won the 200-meter dash and Carlos had finished third. They were kicked off the team and sent home.

The worst moments in Olympic history came at Munich, Germany, in 1972. In the early morning hours of September 5, terrorists invaded the Olympic Village, killed two Israeli athletes, and took eleven hostage. After long hours of negotiation the terrorists and hostages were transferred to an air base to be flown out of the country, but in a gunfight with police, five terrorists, one policeman, and all the hostages were killed.

All events were suspended for a day of mourning, a memorial service was held, and competition resumed the next day amid protests by many who thought the Games should be canceled.

The competition itself featured a U.S. swimmer, Mark Spitz, who won seven gold medals; Valery Borzov of the USSR, who won the 100- and 200-meter dashes; Frank Shorter, who became the first American to win the marathon in sixty-four years; and seventeen-year-old Olga Korbut from the Soviet Union, who introduced Americans to the skill, grace, and athletic ability of gymnasts as she won two gold medals and one silver. The biggest upset: after sixty-three consecutive victories, the U.S. basketball team lost to the Soviet Union, 51–50.

Sandy Koufax was the talk of baseball in the early 1960s. In 1963 he pitched his second no-hit game, and in the World Series, which the Dodgers swept from the Yankees in four games, he set a record by striking out fifteen batters. He pitched his third no-hit game in 1964 and a perfect game against Chicago in 1965. He and Don Drysdale gave an old custom, holding out, a new twist the following year when they bargained with the Dodgers as a tandem. Koufax retired with arm trouble after the 1966 season and was elected to the Hall of Fame in 1972. Drysdale, meanwhile, set records in 1968 by pitching six consecutive shutouts and fifty-eight straight scoreless innings.

Muhammad Ali won the heavyweight boxing championship in 1964 when Sonny Liston did not answer the bell for the seventh round. Ali held the title until 1967 when it was taken away from him because he refused to accept induction into the army. It was not until 1970 that Joe Frazier won the vacated title, which he retained in 1971 with a fifteen-round decision over Ali.

UCLA's basketball dynasty began in 1964 when the Bruins won the first of ten national college championships. They won again in 1965 and starting in 1967 won seven in a row. The team, coached by John Wooden, won its last title in 1975, and Wooden retired. Led by center Bill Russell, the Boston Celtics won their eighth consecutive professional basketball championship in 1965. In 1972 the Los Angeles Lakers won a record thirty-three straight games and their first NBA championship.

In one of sports biggest comebacks—or collapses—Billy Casper made up seven strokes on Arnold Palmer in nine holes to tie him in the last round of the 1966 U.S. Open at San Francisco, and in a playoff the next day Casper won the championship.

On June 8, 1966, peace came to professional football as the American and National Leagues merged. And on January 15, 1967, at Los Angeles' Coliseum, Green Bay defeated Kansas City, 35–10, in the first Super Bowl.

# HORNUNG, KARRAS BANNED FOR BETTING

## NFL Stars Out Indefinitely; 5 Lions Fined

Paul Hornung

NEW YORK (UPI)—Paul Hornung of the Green Bay Packers and Alex Karras of the Detroit Lions, two of the National Football League's brightest stars, were suspended indefinitely Wednesday for betting on games in the league's biggest scandal since 1946.

Pete Rozelle, the 36-year-old NFL commissioner, meted out the harsh penalties with expressed regret following an intensive investigation that took more than 10 months and included 52 interviews related to players and officials connected with eight clubs.

"It was the most difficult decision I've ever had to make in my life," said Rozelle, in explaining that Hornung and Karras' cases could not possibly be reviewed before 1964 and that they are now "legally free" to play in any other league if they like.

However, both the American Football League and the Canadian League said the players would not be permitted to play.

In other simultaneous decisions by Rozelle:

Five of Karras' Detroit teammates—guard John Gordy, defensive back Gary Lowe, linebackers Joe Schmidt and Wayne Walker, and end Sam Williams—were fined $2,000 each for making a $50 bet on one game.

The Detroit team was fined $4,000 because head coach George Wilson didn't report certain findings to the league and because unauthorized persons were permitted to have sideline passes and sit on the Lions' bench during games.

The commissioner added that many players technically violated league rules by betting on $1 football cards and making token bets of little value with friends. He said these players, not mentioned by name, had been reprimanded and no further action on them was expected.

Rick Casares, veteran fullback for the Chicago Bears and Bob St. Clair, San Francisco 49ers tackle, were given a clean bill of health from rumors that they had associated with gambling elements.

An investigation is being continued regarding allegations that president Carroll Rosenbloom of the Baltimore Colts bet on league games during a period eight to 10 years ago.

Rozelle, chain-smoking at Wednesday's conference

Please Turn to Pg. 3, Col. 4

Alex Karras

Los Angeles Times
Sports
PART III BUSINESS & FINANCE
CC THURSDAY MORNING, APRIL 18, 1963 2†

### JIM MURRAY

## Baseball Faculty



I never thought I'd live to see the day I'd watch a major league baseball game with the athletic director of one of the teams—but I guess as long as Phil K. Wrigley is aboard in baseball, anything is possible.

The associated students of the University of Phil Wrigley, formerly the Chicago Cubs, spoiled the home debut of the Dodgers, a backward group of athletes who still believe in the divine right of manager's theory, the other night, in a triumph that was clearly mind over matter.

The Cubs are a bunch of downy-cheeked scholars whom managment has been systematically trying to extricate from the fabric of old fashioned baseball for several years now. The best guess is they're trying to get their affairs in order so they can get into the Big Ten—or possibly the intra-murals at the University of Chicago.

Like Notre Dame and Stanford, they deny that deemphasis was deliberate. It just worked out that way. It did so because they got rid of the manager, whom they deemed an unwholesome relic of the age of dictators, and spread the responsibility through a squad of touring coaches, some coming, some going, and some not knowing what the hell they were supposed to be doing. The team fielded nine men at a time only through force of habit because there was no one to tell them. The manager's office had more strangers in it than a highway motel.

### Only Headlines Are Complicated

The only thing really complicated about baseball are the headlines in the Sporting News ("Wingfoot Cline Chases Tepee Garden Gloom," or "Tribe's Tyro Trio Torrid Topic Along Cactus Trail"). But owner Wrigley even brought a computer machine to bear on his hapless team. And they easily ran that down to the point where it only made the same strangling noises as any other manager who looks out and sees three of his base-runners on the same base.

Wrigley's latest caper is the athletic director, Robert V. Whitlow, an old friend, with whom I sat the other night. Like all athletic directors, Whit didn't have much to do—so he charted the pitches and counted the runs. There are so few of these in Goose Egg Ravine, where the fences are so far a base on balls is a rally, that it was not much of a strain. His is a strange kind of athletic directorship. He doesn't need a tutor for the second baseman, a transcript of the grades of his starting pitchers and doesn't have to offer the father of his star first baseman a convertible to get him enrolled.

### Wrigley's First Consecutive Game

The game was honored by the presence—in addition to the Compton Elks, the Covina Lions, the gang from Casey's Club in Bell and Miss Winnie Willardson attending her 84th consecutive game—by P. K. Wrigley himself, attending his first consecutive game since Tinker stopped speaking to Chance.

Bob Whitlow is an ex-West Point and UCLA left tackle and pitcher who spent 20 years in the Air Force, some of them trying to explain De Gaulle to the State Department. That was when the French premier wanted out of France the American planes that his predecessors had been pleading for with tears in their eyes 23 years before. Bob also served democracy by recruiting the first successful Air Force Academy football teams when he was the first athletic director at that new installation. He also logged several years in the Pentagon, which I have the feeling prepared him better for the Chicago Cubs than any other.

The team by now is used to anything. Hardly an eyebrow would be raised if Wrigley put Betty Crock-

Please Turn to Pg. 7, Col. 1

# LAKERS' ONE-TWO PUNCH KO'S CELTS

UP IN ARMS—It's anybody's ball as Bill Russell (6) and Tom Sanders (16) of Celtics spring for a rebound with Lakers' Elgin Baylor during the third playoff game Wednesday night at Sports Arena. Times photo by Ken Dare

## West (42) and Baylor (38) Pace Win Before 15,493

BY DAN HAFNER

The Lakers shot back into the National Basketball Assn. final playoffs with a mighty bounce Wednesday night.

With their great one-two punch of Jerry West and Elgin Baylor banging in baskets from all over the place and the other Lakers hustling throughout, the club gave the Boston Celtics a 119-99 lacing before an all-time Sports Arena basketball record throng of 15,493.

The Lakers' finest performance in 10 play-off battles this year cut the Celtics' lead in the best-of-seven series to 2-1 and gave themselves a crack at tying the count Friday night before heading back to Boston.

While Baylor and West were magnificent, every Laker played a prominent role in the victory, decided when West and Baylor went wild in the last period.

**Lakers Fast Break**

Between them the superstars had 80 points — 42 for West — and 28 of them in the final quarter when the Lakers simply brushed aside the tired world champions with a blistering fast break that had the partisan crowd roaring.

But such other Lakers as Rudy LaRusso, Dick Barnett, Frank Selvy, Gene Wiley, Leroy Ellis and Jim Krebs hustled, fought and battled throughout.

Krebs, in a slump for quite awhile, played his best, blocking shots, and even driving in for a layup against Bill Russell.

Big Bill was brilliant in the first half, but he tired in the third period and Baylor, Wiley and others took the boards away from him — no mean feat.

Baylor wound up with 23 rebounds as the Lakers, after being beaten on rebounds for two games, came out with a big edge in this department, 65-42.

**Celtics Start Fast**

Only at the start of the game did the Celtics look as if they were en route to a four-game sweep. They started out with a 10-3 bulge, but it was already obvious the Lakers were ready for a top effort.

In the space of 94 seconds, they banged in nine straight points to grab a lead. They never trailed again, but they opened the last period by blowing a three point lead.

The Lakers, especially Baylor and West, were just getting their second wind. Baylor tossed in nine straight points, Krebs tallied on a layup, then West scored eight straight for L.A. All of

Please Turn to Pg. 2, Col. 3

## Professor Don Lee Teaches Twins Lesson, Blanks 'Em on 3 Hits, 4-0

BY BRAVEN DYER
Times Staff Representative

MINNEAPOLIS — Prof. Don Lee made his first 1963 major league start Wednesday since getting his degree from the University of Arizona and taught his old buddies a lesson by blanking the Minnesota Twins, 4-0, on three scattered hits before 4,850 chilled spectators.

The victory evened the series and upped Bill Rigney's Angels to .500 in the tight American League race with three wins and as many defeats.

**Only One Walk**

The son of a pitcher (Thornton Lee) retired the Twins in order in all but two innings as only two runners got as far as second base.

What's more, the 28-year-old right-hander did not issue a walk until the ninth round when Lennie Green also collected Minnesota's third safety. Don fanned three.

The Angels won the game with three runs off losing southpaw Jack Kralick (0-2) in the fifth and got their fourth tally on Bob Rodgers' second homer of the year off Bill Dailey in the eighth.

Lee's mates gave him perfect support and Don chimed in with an unusual game-ending double play from Lee

### ANGEL BOX

| LOS ANGELES | ab | r | h | bi | MINNESOTA | ab | r | h | bi |
|---|---|---|---|---|---|---|---|---|---|
| Pearson cf | 5 | 1 | 2 | 1 | Green cf | 4 | 0 | 1 | 0 |
| Moran 2b | 4 | 1 | 1 | 0 | Power 1b | 4 | 0 | 1 | 0 |
| L.Thom's 1b | 4 | 0 | 2 | 1 | Lemon lf | 3 | 0 | 0 | 0 |
| Torres 3b | 4 | 0 | 1 | 0 | Allison rf | 3 | 0 | 0 | 0 |
| Rodgers c | 4 | 1 | 2 | 1 | Ratliff c | 3 | 0 | 0 | 0 |
| G.Thom's rf | 4 | 0 | 0 | 0 | Banks 3b | 3 | 0 | 0 | 0 |
| Hunt lf | 4 | 0 | 1 | 0 | Allen 2b | 3 | 0 | 1 | 0 |
| Fregosi ss | 3 | 0 | 2 | 0 | Versalles ss | 3 | 0 | 0 | 0 |
| Lee p | 3 | 0 | 0 | 0 | Kralick p | 1 | 0 | 0 | 0 |
| | | | | | Stange p | 0 | 0 | 0 | 0 |
| | | | | | aHall | 1 | 0 | 0 | 0 |
| | | | | | Dailey p | 0 | 0 | 0 | 0 |
| | | | | | Pleis p | 0 | 0 | 0 | 0 |
| | | | | | bMincher | 0 | 0 | 0 | 0 |
| Totals | 35 | 4 | 11 | 3 | Totals | 28 | 0 | 3 | 0 |

a—Struck out for Stange in 6th; b—Walked for Pleis in 9th.

| | |
|---|---|
| Los Angeles | 000 030 010—4 |
| Minnesota | 000 000 000—0 |

E—Lemon. PO-A—Los Angeles 27-13, Minnesota 27-12. DP—Allen, Versalles and Power, Ratliff and Versalles; L. Thomas, Fregosi and Lee. LOB—Los Angeles 8, Minnesota 2.

2B—Hunt. HR—Rodgers. S—Lee.

| | IP | H | R | ER | BB | SO |
|---|---|---|---|---|---|---|
| Lee W. 1-0 | 9 | 3 | 0 | 0 | 1 | 3 |
| xKralick L. 0-2 | 5 | 7 | 3 | 3 | 2 | 2 |
| Stange | 1 | 0 | 0 | 0 | 1 | 2 |
| Dailey | 2 | 3 | 1 | 1 | 0 | 0 |
| Pleis | 1 | 1 | 0 | 0 | 0 | 0 |

x—Faced 1 man in 6th.

WP—Lee, Stange. U—Stewart, Salerno, Honochick, [illegible]. T—2:13. A—4,850.

Thomas to Jim Fregosi to the Seraph slabman.

"Marvin Grissom didn't try to change my style," said Lee last year when he came to the Angels in a trade for Jim Donohue. "Grissom told me I shouldn't take my eye off the catcher after getting the sign. Nobody ever told me that before and I was wild. It gave me a lot of confidence."

**Slow Start**

And where is Donohue? Out to lunch, for a long time . . . in the minors. Jim never did win a game for the Twins, while two of Lee's eight Angel wins in '62 were zeroes. He also helped record three others to give the Angels the best American League mark (15) in this department.

The one-time U of Arizona All-American started slowly in exhibitions, but posted a skimpy 1.71 ERA.

"I naturally wanted to pitch well here," said Don after dealing his zero. "Of course I'm not sorry the

Please Turn to Pg. 7, Col. 1

## 'Best of West' Paced Lakers

BY CAL WHORTON

Jerry West played his greatest game as a professional and mainly on the strength of this effort the Lakers managed to beat the Boston Celtics in the third game of the National Basketball Assn. playoffs Wednesday night at the Sports Arena.

"He's never been better," said Laker coach Fred Schaus of his former West Virginia pupil who moved into the pro ranks along with his coach.

**Celtics Blow Cold**

West, who totaled 42 points, shyly declared, "I thought I played pretty good, but I didn't think it was my best game."

While the weary Lakers grinned over their first play-off victory in three starts, the Celtics appeared to be a sullen group in their dressing quarters.

"We just ran out of gas when they (the Lakers) were getting hot," Boston coach

Please Turn to Pg. 2, Col. 1

## DODGERS WIN, 1-0, IN 10TH OVER CUBS

### Walls, Howard, Skowron Hit Singles to Break Deadlock Against Ellsworth

BY AL WOLF

It was frigid in Dodger Stadium Wednesday night, but Moose Skowron, who had been in deep freeze since the season began, somehow thawed out.

And the melt couldn't have come at a better time.

His 10th-inning single, following other one-basers by Lee Walls and Frank Howard, gave Walter Alston & Co. a 1-0 decision over the Cubs.

You might call it a case of double retribution.

**Ellsworth Loses**

For the victim was southpaw Dick Ellsworth, who had blanked the Dodgers on three hits in Chicago. And only Tuesday, the Cubs had made off with a 2-1 decision in 12 rounds here.

Wednesday's overtime show was viewed by only 15,617 Eskimos, making it the smallest turnout for a Dodger game since Walter O'Malley proudly opened the doors a year ago.

The previous turnstile low was 16,075 last May 16 for a Houston game.

Two were out when Ellsworth, who'd gone all the way and permitted only four hits, suddenly was solved like a mystery story when you peek at the last page first.

Walls banged one into center, Howard came through with his third successive hit of the evening into left and then Skowron belted a liner into right. The ball went through outfielder Lou

Please Turn to Pg. 5, Col. 1

### TODAY IN SPORTS

QUARTER HORSE RACING—Los Alamitos, 1:15 p.m.

BASEBALL — Dodgers vs. Chicago Cubs, Dodger Stadium, 8 p.m.

SOCCER—Germania vs. Costa Rica, State Cup replay, Rancho Cienega Stadium, 7:30 p.m.

## BASEBALL STANDINGS

**NATIONAL LEAGUE**

| | W | L | Pct. | * |
|---|---|---|---|---|
| Milwaukee | 6 | 2 | .750 | |
| San Francisco | 5 | 2 | .714 | ½ |
| St. Louis | 5 | 2 | .714 | ½ |
| Pittsburgh | 4 | 3 | .571 | 1½ |
| Philadelphia | 4 | 3 | .571 | 1½ |
| DODGERS | 4 | 4 | .500 | 2 |
| Chicago | 3 | 4 | .429 | 2½ |
| Cincinnati | 3 | 4 | .429 | 2½ |
| Houston | 3 | 5 | .375 | 3 |
| New York | 0 | 8 | .000 | 6 |

*Games behind leader.

**Wednesday's Results**

DODGERS, 1; Chicago, 0 (10 innings).

St. Louis, 7, Pittsburgh, 3

Cincinnati, 5; New York, 0

Milwaukee, 6; Philadelphia, 5

Houston, 2, San Francisco, 1 (13 innings).

**Games Today**

Chicago (Hobbie, 0-0) at DODGERS (Drysdale, 2-0), radio KFI, KWKW, 8 p.m.

Philadelphia (Mahaffey, 1-1) at Milwaukee (Hendley, 1-1).

Houston (Farrell, 1-1) at San Francisco (Sanford, 2-0).

Pittsburgh (Schwall, 0-0) at St. Louis (Broglio, 1-0), night.

**AMERICAN LEAGUE**

| | W | L | Pct. | * |
|---|---|---|---|---|
| Detroit | 5 | 2 | .714 | |
| Kansas City | 4 | 2 | .667 | ½ |
| New York | 4 | 3 | .571 | 1 |
| Baltimore | 4 | 3 | .571 | 1 |
| Cleveland | 3 | 3 | .500 | 1½ |
| ANGELS | 3 | 3 | .500 | 1½ |
| Boston | 3 | 4 | .429 | 2 |
| Chicago | 2 | 3 | .400 | 2 |
| Washington | 2 | 4 | .333 | 2½ |
| Minnesota | 2 | 5 | .286 | 3 |

*Games behind leader.

**Wednesday's Results**

ANGELS, 4; Minnesota, 0.

Detroit, 4; New York, 2.

Baltimore, 5; Boston, 4.

Washington at Cleveland, postponed, rain

Only games scheduled.

**Games Today**

ANGELS (McBride, 1-0) at Minnesota (Stigman, 0-1), radio KMPC, 11:30 a.m.

Kansas City (Rakow, 1-0) at Chicago (Herbert, 0-0).

Only games scheduled.

# Those Daffy Dodgers Sweep It in Four as Yankees Fall Flat on Pin Stripes, 2-1

Los Angeles Times
Sports
PART III BUSINESS & FINANCE
CC MONDAY MORNING, OCTOBER 7, 1963 †

BY FRANK FINCH

The Yankees must've known something Sunday when they packed their bags before they left for the ball park to play the Dodgers.

Locking the luggage was a wise idea, for the Yankees flew home to New York within several hours after Sandy Koufax pitched Los Angeles to an unbelievable four-game World Series sweep over the defending champions.

The score was 2-1 as Koufax set a new Series total strikeout record of 23 while besting Whitey Ford for the second time in the brief and stunning Series.

And the Dodgers did it the hard way, being held to two hits while capturing their second world championship since moving to Los Angeles and their third under Walter (Smokey) Alston's gifted guidance.

They say the Yankees never beat themselves, but they did Sunday before another capacity crowd of 55,912, the same as attended the third game Saturday at Dodger Stadium.

The score was 1-1 as a result of home runs by Frank Howard and Mickey Mantle, who tied Babe Ruth's all-time Series record with his 15th roundtripper, when the Dodgers came to bat in the last of the seventh.

Clete Boyer, a fabulous third baseman, left his feet to glove Jim Gilliam's high bouncer and made a routine peg to first baseman Joe Pepitone.

To the astonishment of all concerned, the ball struck the Fancy Dan on the inside of the right forearm, glanced off and rolled to the right-field stands as Gilliam sped all the way to third base. Later, Pepitone said he lost sight of the ball in the multi-colored background.

It was a monumental stroke of luck for the Dodgers, and they didn't pass up the opportunity to cash in.

Willie Davis lofted a well-kissed sacrifice fly to Mantle, and Gilliam scored standing up to give Koufax the go-ahead run that will enable the Dodgers to cut up the

Please Turn to Pg. 4, Col. 3

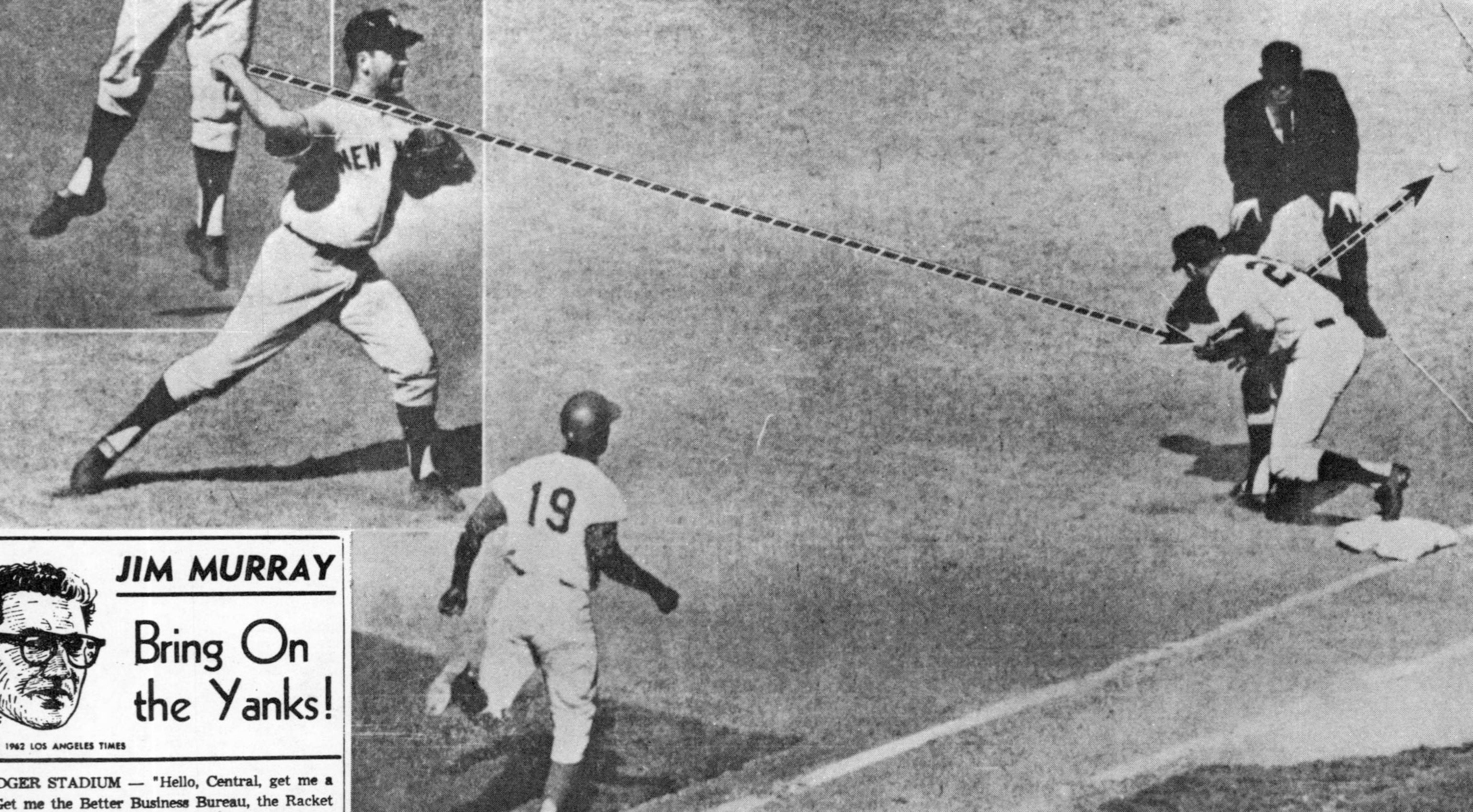

**BEGINNING OF THE END**—Yanks' Clete Boyer goes airborne to stab Jim Gilliam's bouncer, but Joe Pepitone's error on throw sets stage for the winning tally.

Times photos by Larry Sharkey

## JIM MURRAY

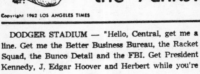

## Bring On the Yanks!



DODGER STADIUM — "Hello, Central, get me a line. Get me the Better Business Bureau, the Racket Squad, the Bunco Detail and the FBI. Get President Kennedy, J. Edgar Hoover and Herbert while you're at it.

"There's been a bunch of guys out here masquerading as the New York Yankees. It's the clumsiest impersonation I've ever seen. If these guys are the New York Yankees, I'm the Queen of England.

"I first began to suspect when they began to brag about beating you with a glove. I mean, since when do the New York Yankees beat you with a glove? The REAL New York Yankees, I mean. And they talked about beating you with their feet. You know, going and getting those ground balls. Why, the old Yankees wouldn't bother to stoop down for a ground ball. They just gave you a run and then went out and got 11 themselves.

"Beat you with a glove and footwork? I thought Fresco Thompson would die laughing! That's like the German Army launching a pillow fight or a guy in a duel getting a choice of weapons against a blind man and choosing tea-bags at 20 paces. The old Yankees chose cannons.

### *They Just Can't Be Legit*

"The reason I know they can't be legit is they chose the Dodger weapons. That's as stupid as getting in a fight with your wife with words. I don't know where they got those suits, but I have to think it was Western Costume.

"They were fighting fire with gasoline. The result was about what might have been expected, but it has to rank as an upset. I expect lightning might strike those statues of Ruth and Gehrig. If they beat guys with their feet it meant they stomped you to death. The old Yankees didn't even have to run. Where they hit the ball, you could get around the bases on crutches.

"Listen, Roger Maris hit 61 home runs, right? The REAL Roger Maris stood right in the dressing room last year and told us he wasn't going to crash into a fence for anybody. Right? I mean, the Yankees send other people crashing into fences. That's the way they play it. Well, THIS Roger Maris took one look at Sandy Koufax's fast-ball and he was glad to crash into a fence. I'm surprised he didn't just butt his head in the dugout wall.

"You know Mickey Mantle? I swear this guy out

Please Turn to Pg. 8, Col. 1

**IT ONLY TAKES ONE**—Hand, that is, when Frank Howard is the batter. Here the big Dodger outfielder connects for his fifth-inning home run into the second deck in left field off Whitey Ford Sunday.

**MOST HAPPY FELLOW**—Bursting with jubilation, Sandy Koufax gallops off field after halting Yanks.

Times photos by Ben Olender

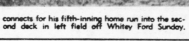

| | | | | | |
|---|---|---|---|---|---|
| Packers . . . 42 | Giants . . . . . 24 | Lions . . . . . . 26 | Bears . . . . . . 10 | Eagles . . . . . 24 | Cards . . . . . 56 |
| Rams . . . . . 10 | Redskins . . . 14 | 49ers . . . . . 3 | Colts . . . . . . 3 | Cowboys . . . 21 | Vikings . . . . 14 |
| STORY ON PAGE 7 | STORY ON PAGE 6 | STORY ON PAGE 6 | STORY ON PAGE 7 | STORY ON PAGE 6 | STORY ON PAGE 6 |

# 'I'VE UPSET THE WORLD!' CRIES CASSIUS

## Clay Wins TKO in 7th---Liston Takes it Sitting Down

CC WEDNESDAY MORNING, FEBRUARY 26, 1964 2†

### JIM MURRAY

## Upset-- or Set-Up



MIAMI BEACH—You will pardon me if the keys slip as I try to write this story. You see, I am trying to type with one hand and hold my nose with the other.

I am a little unclear at this point whether I have just seen the upset of the century or the set-up.

Cassius Clay, who looked like a hot prospect for a straight-jacket instead of a crown as late as an hour before fight time, is the heavyweight champion of the world. And Sonny Liston is just another ex-con with his arm in a sling.

The old champ was as clumsy as a guy groping for a light switch in the dark with a hangover. I have seen guys look more graceful falling down cellar stairs. They say Liston threw his shoulder in this fight. I only hope that's all he threw.

But if he did, I know how he did it — missing punches.

### *Sonny Unmasked at Last*

But we now know one thing: you can throw away that silver bullet. The "King Kong" of the ring has been unmasked as just a big stiff in a fur coat. If the real Sonny Liston stood up tonight, he couldn't scare a kid in a graveyard at midnight. You won't have to match him with Russia after all. Guys will be picking on him in barrooms now.

Cassius Clay was supposed to be exposed as a counterfeit in this fight. He was the three-dollar bill of boxing. Liston was something that ran you up a tree.

The first shock came when a mysterious red substance began to trickle down Liston's eye. It was unthinkable it was blood. But that's exactly what it was. Clay, who was not supposed to be able to stun a mosquito with a combination of one-two's, had the champion's face looking like a melon that had fallen off the back of a truck. He not only bleeds, he lumps. It was possible to feel pity for this mastodon.

Cassius appeared to believe it least of anybody. He fought as hysterically as a guy brushing off a swarm of bees. He was popularly believed to be the first fighter in the history of the ring who would need smelling salts BEFORE the fight. He would have to be revived to be introduced, was the word to the unwise.

### *The Lip Becomes the Limp*

This was the night the "Louisville Lip" was to become the "Louisville Limp." He came to the weigh-in like Donald Duck on a bender. To a man, the 400 onlookers were convinced they were looking at a man who had just seen his own ghost. The classic defense against fear, Charlie McCabe pointed out, is noise. Judging by the decibels Cassius raised, he was scared silly. His pulse rate beat the clock around the minute hand by double. It lapped it, in fact. It registered 120. Usually, a fight "physical" consists of holding a mirror up in front of a fighter's mouth. If it clouds, he's ready. Most fighters are so low pressure, you have to hold it there for a quarter-hour. They had to stick pins in Joe Louis. But Cassius' mirror would drop from across the room.

He showed up in a tuxedo and the crowd thought this was provident of him. That way, all the undertaker would have to do is take off the shoes.

But instead of Cassius in the morgue, the fight wound up with Liston in the hospital. Six days ago, you wouldn't have believed he'd have to go there for anything more serious than a tonsillectomy—or to visit Cassius Clay.

Cassius did not exactly rule the fight from the opening bell. In fact, Sonny came out as if he had nothing more trying to do than take the boy to the woodshed. But he kept looking around to see where Cassius went. A couple of times I expected him to tap the referee on the shoulder and ask him if he had seen anything of Cassius.

### *When the Stalk 'Stalled'*

You might say Liston "stalked" him. But the way he went at it, if he went for a polar bear, he'd wind up with a camel. He was so sure Cassius' heart beat would drown out the sound of his feet thumping on the canvas. he didn't telegraph his punches, he sent them by straight mail—fourth class. But it looked as if nothing short of a flood could stop him.

Cassius flurried wildly from time to time and, unaccountably, Liston looked like a man trying to crawl away from mortar. The crowd cheered wildly each

Please Turn to Pg. 2, Col. 6

**TYPICAL OF THE LIP** — Exultant in victory, Cassius Clay is caught in a characteristic pose—with his mouth open—as he and his handlers whoop it up moments after the Louisville Lip posted a TKO triumph over Sonny Liston Tuesday night for the title.

### NUMB SHOULDER

## Liston Pilot Says He Made Sonny Quit

MIAMI BEACH (AP)—Sonny Liston, his normally stolid face creased with pain, and complaining his left arm was numb from shoulder to wrist, was rushed directly from ringside to a hospital Tuesday night.

His handlers feared a possible shoulder fracture.

Liston didn't even bother to shower following his stunning seventh round technical knockout defeat at the hands of the brash young challenger, Cassius Clay, for the heavyweight championship of the world.

Jack Nilson, advisor of Liston, said at the hospital, that the hulking fighter had hurt the shoulder during training. He said Liston did not spar on Feb. 3, 4, 5 and 14th because of it.

Asked why he didn't postpone the fight, Nilon replied, "We thought we could get away with it."

But only last Sunday, before a packed house at his training camp and in

Please Turn to Pg. 3, Col. 3

**CASSIUS SWINGS . . .** A grimacing Cassius Clay sends a whistling right to the head of a ducking Sonny Liston during the first round of their heavyweight bout. Five rounds later, it was all over.

### MAYBE HE REALLY IS

## Clay Tells Everyone: 'I AM the Greatest'

MIAMI BEACH (UPI). The boy who went on a man's errand acted like a boy Tuesday night after proving himself a man.

Cassius Clay — almost unbelievably, the new heavyweight champion of the world —sat on a dressing room table and shouted jubilantly:

"I'm the greatest. I told the world I'd do it."

He said it over and over as he had so many times in the past weeks while he trained to fight Sonny Liston.

This time they had to believe him.

And, in a double-barrelled mouthful even for Clay, he whooped:

"Give some credit to Sugar Ray Robinson, all of you hypocrites," Cassius yelled. "You are hypocrites because none of you believed me."

It was a wild and tumultous scene as, for more than 10 minutes, Clay shouted his admiration for himself.

"Whatcha gonna say now," he demanded. "He's gonna go in one? He's gonna go in two? Well, I whipped him so bad I put him in the hospital and look at Cassius—I'm still pretty.

"Oh, I'm so great," he announced throwing his eyes toward the ceiling. "And don't," he said, "call it a fix."

Cassius frowned "I just played with him" but said,

Please Turn to Pg. 2, Col. 1

**. . . AND SONNY MISSES**—As Sonny Liston tries a long left, Cassius Clay exhibits one of his specialties, bobbing and weaving away from the punches. Clay's elusiveness paid off in a shocking upset.

## Sonny's Paycheck Held Up

**BY SID ZIFF**
Times Staff Writer

MIAMI BEACH — The ending was so weird people may always think it smelled, but throw out the suspicions.

Cassius Clay whipped Sonny Liston here Tuesday night and won the heavyweight championship of the world, fair and square.

When the bell sounded for Round Seven, Liston didn't come out. It goes in the record book as a TKO in the seventh.

"I've upset the world," yelled Cassius when the bout was halted.

**Surprise Finish**

Liston lost it officially in the only way that no one had figured. They say he threw his left shoulder out in the first round.

But the Miami Beach Boxing Commission has ordered Liston's purse held up pending an examination today by two orthopedic specialists, Dr. Lester Russin and Dr. Stan Weinkle.

The kid with the big mouth lived up to it and was winning the fight. He did a tremendous job of outboxing the ponderous champ.

No one guessed it during the fight but there was an indication that something might have gone wrong with Liston. He hit Clay some pretty good licks and nothing happened. The power was gone.

**Slumped on Stool**

The bout ended in total confusion. Everyone was left in the dark as to what happened.

Liston remained dejectedly in his corner, slumped wearily on the stool when the bell rang. He had a mouse under both eyes. He had been cut up badly.

The first impression was that he had quit. No doctor had been called up to look him over.

His handlers, Jack Nilon and Willie Reddish supposedly made the decision, not Liston.

**Ache in Arm**

They say Liston told them at the end of the first round that he had hurt his shoulder. He felt a dull ache in his arm which kept growing worse.

Liston was rushed to the St. Francis Hospital.

The dislocated shoulder would explain Liston's loss of punching power but he had already been exposed as

Please Turn to Pg. 2, Col. 3

### THE WINNERS

1—Eyebright, $20.20
2—Flying Dutchman, $6
**Daily double $69.40**
3—Taint Cricket, $6.20
4—My Boudoir, $8.40
5—King's Pie, $55.80
6—Natcherly, $7.60
7—Dr. Kacy, $14.80
8—Don Juan, $30.60
9—Lady Erin, $33.40

# BRUINS PUT '30' TO A PERFECT ENDING!

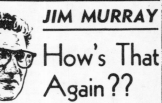

Los Angeles Times
Sports
SECTION C
CC SUNDAY, MARCH 22, 1964 3¢

# UCLA Spurts Past Duke for NCAA Title

**OUT OF REACH**—Jack Marin of Duke leans back in effort to get rebound, but UCLA's Keith Erickson comes down with ball during final round of national collegiate basketball championships at Kansas City. The Bruins defeated Duke, 98-83, for their 30th victory in a row and first NCAA crown. *Wirephoto*

## JIM MURRAY

### How's That Again??



Springtime again. A time when lions escape from the circus, ballplayers get away from their wives, managers adjust their syntax and the lively art of not saying what you mean is with us again.

It is the custom of this department to cut through the dense gorse of double-speak from time to time to give our readers the inner meaning of what a baseball manager says during the course of spring training which is usually a run of rhetoric divisible by three or more to arrive at a correct translation.

For instance, a manager who has just spent a sleepless night bailing his starting infield out of an Arizona drunk tank cannot be expected to admit as much in so many words. What he must say is, "I have every confidence in my boys and when the full facts in this case are brought out, I am sure in my heart they will be cleared."

What this translates out to, is "The club lawyer is right now over at the house of the guy whose glasses they broke with a pocket full of money to square the beef and the judge is being given a gold lifetime badge to the ball-park."

When a pitcher gets shot in the leg, the standard form calls for the explanation, "He was just trying to break up a fight." What you don't add is that the fight he was trying to break up was one he started in the first place.

#### *Diplomacy Watchword for Successful Pilot*

Diplomacy is the watchword for the successful manager. It's O.K. to offer to punch a sportswriter in the nose for calling you a bum manager but when the boss' wife sends down the suggestion that you let that cute Sandy Koufax play second base so he can play every day, the thing to say is, "It might not be a bad idea, some times, we in the front office or the dugout get too close to things to see them clearly. I would let Sandy play second-base but first we have to find out if he's subject to hemophilia."

A more sensible suggestion, coming from the traveling secretary draws an instant, "Who's running this club—you or me? Get back to your train schedules and see if we can't get a bus instead of a 4-wheeled gas chamber for a change!"

It goes on like that all spring. Here are some other alternative meanings to common locker room declamations:

"That kid we brought up from Kokomo is a major leaguer right now—he can do it all."—("Sure. He can drink, smoke, chew, swear, cheat at cards and break curfew and chase waitresses. He's ready.")

"If we don't start hitting, I'm going to shake up this team."—("I'll replace our centerfielder who's batting .270 and has been in a slump for two weeks with a guy who's batting .212 and has been in a slump all his life. THAT ought to show I'm awake.")

#### *Charge Accounts Threatened*

"Nobody's job is safe on this club." ("Particularly, mine. If the Old Man gives me one more vote of confidence, my wife's charge accounts will be closed up in every department store in town.")

"We can win without the Big Fellow."—("Against the Mets. If we have to play the Giants without him, I'm not even going to look.")

"We don't know what The Jolter is doing wrong in this slump but we're going to study films to find out." ("And the films will be taken by a private detective. That actress he's going with isn't America's Sweetheart but she's the American League's.")

"This kid pitcher can't miss."—("I'll say he can't. He's already hit everything in camp but home plate. He's made more ears bleed than Sonny Liston. The only reason he doesn't walk everybody who comes up is because he hits half of 'em. He couldn't put more guys in the hospital if he was throwing hand grenades.")

#### *Nice if Infielders Spoke to Each Other*

"There are no cliques on this team—we all pull together." —("Still, it would be nice if the infield spoke to each other. On the other hand, I can't think why. The last time they did, all the people in the box seats had to hold their ears.")

"We'll make a trade only if it will help the club."—("That's a laugh. The only trade that could help this club would be a 25-man swap. The only thing we could get for this pile of bush leaguers is unemployment pay. It would help the club if we could just get two ash trays apiece.")

"I'm happy to hear I'm getting a vote of confidence from the front office.—("You bet I am! It means I'll be leaving in a month. Start packing, honey, and tell your brother to stop playing the cash register in the

Please Turn to Pg. 7, Col. 1

## Yanks Finally Solve Koufax (Too Late) 5-3

**BY FRANK FINCH**
Times Staff Writer

FT. LAUDERDALE — The Yankees' paramount goal this year is not to avenge their crushing defeat by the Dodgers in the 1963 World Series, but to win the American League pennant.

"First things come first, and we're concentratin' on the pennant," said the Bronx Bombers' eloquent field boss, Lawrence Peter Berra, before Saturday's Yankee-Dodger exhibition.

However, the Yankees concentrated on Sandy Koufax long enough to score five times in the first two frames and post a 5-3 triumph before 5,638 fans. Roger Maris slammed a two-run homer in the first inning to insure Al Downing's victory.

**Relishes Rematch**

Lawrence Peter, who also answers to Yogi, conceded that his club would relish a big-money rematch with Los Angeles, but insists the Dodgers' stunning four game sweep is not a festering sore in the Yankees' hides.

"Why look back?" reasoned Berra as he puffed on a Perfecto, "We'll be plenty busy just tryin' to defend our league champeenship. There ain't no point in worryin' about the series now because maybe we won't get in it and maybe the Dodgers won't, either."

Yogi already shows signs of managerial astuteness by

Please Turn to Pg. 3, Col. 3

## LAKER 1-2 PUNCH HOT, 'TEAM' COLD

### Baylor, West Combine for 65 Points, but Scrappy Hawks Score 115-104 Playoff Win

**BY DAN HAFNER**
Times Staff Writer

ST. LOUIS — The Laker one-two punch clicked brilliantly, but little Lennie Wilkens stole the ball game for the St. Louis Hawks Saturday night.

A highly-partisan crowd of 7,214 roared with delight as Wilkens and his mates broke open a thriller in the last 90 seconds to score a 115-104 victory and take a 1-0 lead in the best-of-five Western Division play-off series.

**Bitter Rivals**

It was a bruising fight as usual when the two bitter rivals get together and more of the same can be expected tonight in the second affair, which will be televised in Los Angeles over KHJ-TV (9) at 6 p.m.

The Lakers, who were fighting from behind most of the night after a horrible start, trailed by a single point with 1:30 to play when Wilkens came up with the big play.

He took the ball right out of the hands of Rudy LaRusso and hurled a long pass to Cliff Hagan for the cripple and a three-point lead.

**Safe Lead**

It was all over but the shouting seconds later when the 6-1 former Providence star grabbed the next rebound and helped Richie Guerin make it five and safe.

Elgin Baylor and Jerry West did their part, combining for 65 points, the latter getting 35 of them, but their help was mediocre much of the time.

While coach Fred Schaus pointed out that Wilkens' play was the key one, he also felt LaRusso and Jim

Please Turn to Pg. 8, Col. 6

## Bombs Away! Giants Pound Angels, 10-1

**BY BRAVEN DYER**
Times Staff Writer

PALM SPRINGS — San Francisco's power-packed Giants invaded this swank desert spa Saturday for the first time this spring and bombed the anemic Angels, 10-1, before 4,105 shocked citizens.

Former President Eisenhower made his annual visit to Angels' Stadium, accompanied by Leonard Firestone and Freeman Gosden.

"I asked Ike if he had any advice about stopping these guys," said Skipper Bill Rigney, "but even he admitted it might be wise just to surrender."

This was San Francisco's eighth straight win Saturday while compiling a 12-1 record.

The Giants even left two of their big guns, Willie McCovey and Orlando Cepeda,

Please Turn to Pg. 2, Col. 6

## BRUINS WIN 30TH, BEAT DUKE, 98-83

### Unbeaten UCLA Breaks Game Open With 16-Point Blitz, Sets Tournament Record

**BY MAL FLORENCE**
Times Staff Writer

KANSAS CITY—There is no more room at the top. All of the space belongs to UCLA.

The superb Bruins joined the select ranks of college basketball's greatest teams Saturday night by smothering Duke, 98-83, to win the national championship.

Thus, the Bruins became the first team since North Carolina (1957) to go through a complete season undefeated, winning No. 30 in much the same manner they fashioned 29 previous victories.

UCLA turned the taller, proud Blue Devils into a jittery, frantic club late in the first half when it scored 16 straight points without retaliation.

The splendid spurt, which consumed 2min. 33s, left the Bruins with a 43-30 advantage and they easily held off the disenchanted Devils the rest of the way.

There were many heroes for the Bruins, but no one stood out more than substitute forward Kenny Washington and guard Gail Goodrich.

**Another Unselfish Team Effort**

Washington, who entered the game early in the first half, remained to score 26 points—his all-time Bruin high—and take rebounding honors with 12.

Goodrich, the clever, southpaw guard, recovered from his tournament "slump" to top all scorers with 27—17 in the first half when the game was decided.

But, we won't quibble if you want to say that Jack Hirsch, the driving force in the 16-point Bruin surge, or sub center Doug McIntosh or All-America guard Walt Hazzard were equally as proficient.

It's been that type of a year—the total, unselfish team effort.

In winning the school's initial national basketball championship and becoming the first California team since the Golden Bears to capture the NCAA title (1959), John Wooden's wonders wrapped themselves in positive statistics.

It marked the first time since 1957 that the nation's

Please Turn to Pg. 6, Col. 1

**Clay Title in Danger**
STORY ON PAGE 2

**Blades Win, Take Third**
STORY ON PAGE 5

**U.S. Horse, 18-1, Wins**
STORY ON PAGE 10

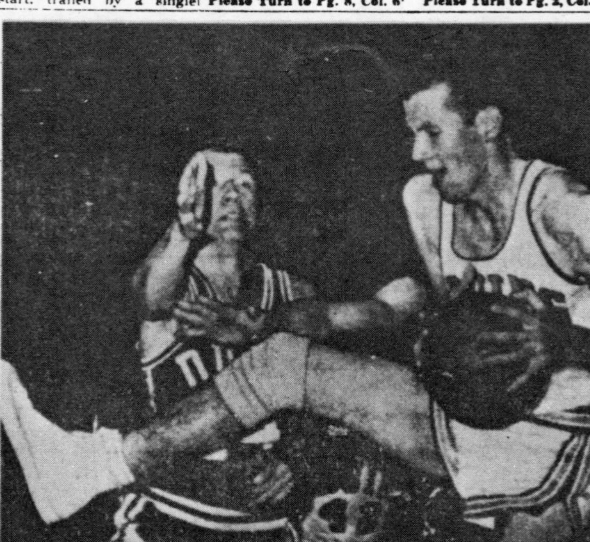

**ON THE REBOUND**—UCLA sophomore Doug McIntosh kicks high in the air as he blocks out Duke's Jack Marin going for rebound in the final NCAA game. *Times Photo*

## 'We're No. 1,' Rooters Chant; Bruins Prove It

**BY JEFF PRUGH**
Times Staff Writer

KANSAS CITY—Repetitously, a swarm of Bruin rooters chanted "We're No. 1," confirming, of course, what UCLA's whizbang basketball team had just finished proving to the live audience of 10,864 fans and millions more on television Saturday night.

And, almost intuitively, it made one recall the night of Dec. 27 last year in Los Angeles—the night when a No. 4-ranked UCLA quintet trounced No. 2-ranked Michigan, 98-80, to trigger local sentiments that the Bruins WERE the nation's No. 1 college team.

But, the stakes were

Please Turn to Pg. 6, Col. 1

# GRIM DOUBLE DEATH TRAGEDY STUNS INDY

## MacDonald, Sachs Die in Flaming Seven-Car Crash

FIERY DEATH—Blinded by smoke from burning cars in tragic Indianapolis 500 mile race, these drivers managed to ease past the burning wreckage unscathed. However, Eddie Sachs of Detroit and Dave MacDonald of El Monte, whose cars were aflame after colliding, died in holocaust Saturday. AP Wirephoto

### Pit Fire Sidelines Jones; Foyt Wins in 'Old-Time' Roadster

BY BOB THOMAS
Times Auto Editor

INDIANAPOLIS—The most tragic page in Indianapolis racing history was written Saturday when rookie Dave MacDonald from Southern California and veteran Eddie Sachs were killed in a fiery crash during the 48th running of the 500-mile auto race.

National champion A. J. Foyt's eventual victory seemed only incidental as the spectacle was dulled by the second-lap accident that snuffed out the lives of the two drivers before a record crowd of 300,000 at the Speedway and the first closed circuit TV audience ever to see the race.

Seven cars were involved in the flaming crash that occurred in full view of thousands of main grandstand spectators. None of the other drivers was hurt seriously.

**Fire Halts Race Over an Hour**

There was a one hour and forty-minute delay before the race could be restarted as fire-fighting crews battled the horrendous blaze that covered the track at a spot leading into the main straight and shot flames 30 or 40 ft. into the air.

Foyt's elapsed time on the track, however, established a new track record as he covered the 200-lap distance in 3 hrs. 23 min. 35.8 sec. for an average speed of 147.350 m.p.h. The old record was 143.137 m.p.h., set last year by Parnelli Jones of Torrance.

Jones was hospitalized after a hectic episode in which he received slight burns from a pit stop fire that erupted when his car's gas tank exploded.

Foyt, driving a conventional front-engine Offenhauser roadster, finished more than a lap in front of another two-time winner, Rodger Ward who drove a rear-engine Ford-powered racer. Foyt also won the classic in 1961.

The crash was triggered when MacDonald's car, a rear-engine Ford built in Long Beach by Mickey Thompson, went out of control as he came out of the fourth turn and into the straight. The car hit the inside wall, exploded into flames and bounced back across the track into the path of at least half of the field of cars. Flames engulfed their route. Sachs, who started in the sixth row directly behind MacDonald, was unable to avoid the rookie's car, striking it broadside.

**Sachs Dies in Roaring Blaze**

The 37-year-old driver from Detroit apparently died instantly as his car was consumed in the blaze. MacDonald, youngest driver in the race at 26, died two hours later in Methodist Hospital, according to the track's medical department.

A soft-spoken ex-dragster from El Monte, MacDonald was making his first appearance at the Speedway after rocketing to national racing prominence in last fall's Times Grand Prix for Sports Cars which he won.

Three other drivers were burned. Ronnie Duman of Dearborn, Mich., was taken to the hospital with first and second degree burns of the legs, face and neck. Johnny Rutherford of Ft. Worth and Bobby Unser of Albuquerque received burns on the neck. Also involved but not injured were Norm Hall of Los Angeles and Chuck Stevenson of Costa Mesa, Cal.

Rutherford explained the accident this way:

"I was running behind Sachs. I saw a commotion up ahead and saw MacDonald go sideways into the wall and explode into flames at least 30 ft. high. Sachs veered to the inside. When he did, he hit MacDonald dead broadside. Both cars came to a stop in a ball of fire. I went to the outside and was hit by Duman's car. I went over

Please Turn to Pg. 4, Col. 3

### Ziff: Death on TV

SEE COLUMN ON PAGE 3

Los Angeles Times
Sports
SECTION D
CC SUNDAY, MAY 31, 1964 †

### MacDonald, Sachs Exact Opposites

BY BOB THOMAS
Times Auto Editor

INDIANAPOLIS — A promising auto racing career was nipped in the bud and a familiar, jocular voice of the sport silenced in a single terrible stroke Saturday at the Indianapolis motor speedway.

Southern California's own Dave MacDonald, a newcomer, and the veteran, Eddie Sachs of Detroit, were two of the most popular figures involved in this year's speedway activity.

And there were no more contrasting personalities on the track than the two drivers who died in a second-lap crash.

MacDonald, a slight (5-ft. 10-in., 140-lb.) ex-dragster from El Monte, was quiet, almost withdrawn, but extremely friendly.

His spot in the racing sun came quickly. He started on the drag strips in 1956, moved into production sports cars in 1960 at Willow Springs and national recognition last fall. That was when he won The Times Grand Prix for sports cars in a Ford-powered Cooper.

Dave MacDonald Eddie Sachs

The victory sent the 27-year-old speedster into a position of national recognition, a rating soon expanded as a member of the Mercury factory racing team.

His all - round talents also earned him the eye of speed king Mickey Thompson, who signed MacDonald to drive for his Indianapolis racing team, although Dave had never seen the Indianapolis 500 or even the speedway.

MacDonald seemed to adapt himself well to the challenging oval, easily passing his driver's test. Just as convincingly, he put himself into the race by qualifying one of

Please Turn to Pg. 6, Col. 4

### JIM MURRAY

### I'm Glad You Ask



It's election year. The candidates have had their say about every burning issue from Outer Mongolia to Inner Sanctum. The oratory is so thick you could grow grass with it.

But I notice one important category the popoffs have ducked—sports. Not one word about what they're going to do about the infield fly rule and unlimited substitution. They're going to clean up the mess in Washington, they say, but that doesn't necessarily mean the Senators and the Redskins. All they promise to do for baseball is throw out the first ball.

With this in mind, I have decided to detach our crack interviewing team of Gruntly and Groanly to brace the top candidates to see what they propose to do about the really pressing questions of our time—like, how to pitch to Mickey Mantle.

Our first candidate is that square-jawed, square shooting, square guy, Sen. Wary Dishwater. He is carrying a sign with the chemical formula for dishwater, a tub with lettuce floating in it. Gruntly speaks.

**Gruntly:** "Senator, if elected, what is your platform for the grand old sports of America, if any?"

*No More Forward Passes*

**Senator:** "I'm glad you asked that, Mr. Gruntly. If elected, the first thing I will do for baseball is require players to go back to the handlebar moustaches. In football, I'll reinstate the flying wedge and outlaw the forward pass. In basketball, I will cut costs by going back to the peach baskets and wooden backboards. Boxing returns to bare knuckles. The Indianapolis 500 is with bicycles. Skeet-shooting is with bow-and-arrow."

**Gruntly:** "Senator, it has been reported you are against night baseball."

**Senator:** "You see the distortions my opponents have raised in this campaign! I am NOT against night baseball. Actually, I am against the electric light. You can play night baseball by kerosene. It was good enough for grandpappy and it should be good enough for Walter O'Malley. Why, sir, remember Lincoln learned to read by firelight. But when you have the government building dams to make electricity, just so Willie

Please Turn to Pg. 5, Col. 1

THE BEGINNING OF TRAGEDY—El Monte's Dave MacDonald looks out helplessly as his car goes into a spin that touched off the fatal crash in the opening minutes of the Indianapolis 500. Seconds later he was hit by car driven by Eddie Sachs. Both MacDonald and Sachs died as a result of the collison. UPI Telephoto

# U.S. TRACK JUGGERNAUT CRUSHES RUSS

**UP AND OVER**—Valeriy Brumel, Russia's world record holder in high jump, sails over bar at 7 feet, 3½ inches for victory in meet with U.S. Sunday. He tried for new mark of 7-6 but missed
Times photos by Joe Kennedy

Los Angeles Times
Sports
PART III BUSINESS & FINANCE
CC MONDAY MORNING, JULY 27, 1964 2†

## SID ZIFF
## Cheers For All

In sports you learn to win with a smile and lose the same way. The United States handed Russia its worst defeat in international track and field competition in their two-day meet at the Coliseum but it ended Sunday in a magnificent gesture of friendship.

The athletes formed a column of twos, pairing an American with a Russian, and holding hands, they marched in a moving ceremonial parade around the track while a crowd of 55,924 gave them a standing ovation.

It was Russia's darkest hour in international competition but the Soviet athletes swallowed their disappointment and responded to the cheers with smiles and waving hands.

The U.S. men's team won by a record score of 139 to 97. Our girls lost 59 to 48 but made their most remarkable showing. Last year in Moscow they scored only 28 points.

### *Strongest-Ever Squad for U.S.*

Analyzing our overwhelming men's victory you reach several conclusions. We have the strongest team we've ever had. Our athletes were in terrific condition and the Russians were not. In fact, several of them were astonishingly out of shape.

We won every race except the walk. We won four events that we have never been able to crack before in the history of the meet, the 5,000 meters, the 10,000 meters, the steeplechase and the triple jump.

We finally joined the world's elite in the distance races.

The rout was completely unexpected although the Russians had said bluntly that they were two months behind us in training. But even if they had been in shape, the result would not have been materially changed.

The overwhelming victory should end all fears that our athletes cannot hope to compete on even terms unless we subsidize them.

There's obviously nothing wrong with our system when our athletes are willing to make the effort to get in condition.

### *New Friends for Track and Field*

The meet with its color and pageantry made thousands of fans for track and field. Long after the closing ceremonies, perhaps 10,000 people remained in the stands to watch the finish of the decathlon.

George Young's dramatic victory in the steeplechase stole the second day spotlight. The meet also produced a second Wilma Rudolph. Leggy, lithe Edith McGuire, from the same school that gave us Wilma, ran just like her to win both sprints. She is also getting near Wilma's record time. They even look alike although Edith is 5 ft. 8 and Wilma was 6 ft. tall.

Despite competition from the Dodgers and Giants, who played in the afternoon, the second day crowd was larger than the 50,519 of Saturday. The Saturday program also had to buck Hollywood Park.

The track meet, however, drew a tremendous reserve seat crowd and in that respect was a substantial success.

The announcing by Dick Nash and Dick Bank, two

Please Turn to Pg. 4, Col. 4

**POURING IT ON**—Bob Schul grins as he uncorks sprint on last lap to lead American teammate Bill Dellinger to tape in 5,000-meter race against Russians Sunday for first American win in that event.
Times photo by Ben Olender

## Men's 139 to 97 Win Series High

### Combined Score Favors U.S. as Women's Total Best Ever

**BY PAUL ZIMMERMAN**
Times Sports Editor

The United States piled up its greatest point total, a smashing victory, over the Soviet Union in the sixth meeting of these two world track and field powers before 55,924 wildly partisan fans at Memorial Coliseum Sunday.

The men's team, in defeating the USSR 139 to 97, amassed 11 points more than ever before to warn the world it must be seriously reckoned with in the Tokyo Olympics come October.

And a vastly improved women's team scored its highest total ever as the Russians won by a score of 59 to 48. That was four more points than our gals made in 1958, the first year of this meet.

Even by the Soviet standard of counting, it was a United States victory, since the combined totals of the men's and women's teams was 187 to 156.

**U.S. Records**

No world records were added Sunday after the two posted Saturday by Dallas Long in the shot put and Fred Hansen in the pole vault, but the day was packed with applause-making thrills as three American records fell.

Valeriy Brumel, the great high jumper who has personally accounted for world records on three occasions in this classic, was the only one who came close. He tried 7 feet 6 inches after winning at 7-3½ but really didn't come close.

So fantastic was the Yankee performance that our male athletes won every running event over the two days.

Most impressive Sunday were our first-time triumphs in this series for the 3,000-meter steeplechase, where George Young and Jeff Fishback shut out the Russians, and again in the 5,000 when Bob Schul and Bill Dellinger ran away from the Soviets on the last lap. The great Pyotr Bolotnikov, 1960 Olympic 10,000 - meter champion, finished a distant last.

These victories, coming on top of Gerry Lindgren's 10,000 triumph on Saturday, established the fact that America no longer is a patsy in the distance events.

Another first for the USA since this meet started in 1958 came in the triple jump when Ira Davis leaped 53 feet, 11 inches to set an American record in victory.

Willye White, with an upset second in the women's long jump with a leap of 21 feet, 7¾ inches, joined Davis in the assault on American marks.

So did Leah Ferris, who ran the women's 800 meters in 2.08.8 while finishing third.

While the invaders obviously were not at their best, this should not detract from the performance of the Americans because five meet marks were erased.

Coliseum records took a terrific beating, with 18 going by the boards.

Schul's time of 14.12.4 for the 5,000 was not startling but, as he pointed out later, "Dellinger and I were just running to win."

"I could tell Bolotnikov didn't have much left with two laps to go and I was confident of victory then."

The two Americans made

Please Turn to Pg. 2, Col. 3

### TODAY IN SPORTS

**HORSE RACING** — Hollywood Park, 1:45 p.m.

**WATER POLO** — National AAU tournament, L.A. Swim Stadium, 9:30 a.m.

**BASEBALL** — Angels vs. Yankees, Dodger Stadium, 8 p.m.

**WRESTLING** — Pasadena Arena, 8:30 p.m.

## VENTURI NABS TITLE

STORY ON PAGE 8

## McArdle Wins Marathon

STORY ON PAGE 2

## Baseball Standings

**NATIONAL LEAGUE**

| | W | L | Pct. | * |
|---|---|---|---|---|
| Philadelphia | 56 | 40 | .583 | |
| San Francisco | 57 | 42 | .576 | ½ |
| Cincinnati | 54 | 45 | .545 | 3½ |
| Pittsburgh | 50 | 44 | .532 | 5 |
| Milwaukee | 50 | 47 | .515 | 6½ |
| St. Louis | 50 | 48 | .510 | 7 |
| Chicago | 48 | 48 | .500 | 8 |
| DODGERS | 48 | 49 | .495 | 8½ |
| Houston | 45 | 55 | .450 | 13 |
| New York | 30 | 70 | .300 | 28 |

*Games behind leader.

**Sunday's Results**

San Francisco, 5; DODGERS, 2.
St. Louis, 6-4, Philadelphia, 1-1.
Cincinnati, 7-1; Pittsburgh, 2-5.
Milwaukee, 11-15; New York, 7-10.
Chicago, 3; Houston, 0.

**Game Today**

Cincinnati (Maloney, 9-9) at Milwaukee (Lemaster, 10-6), night.
Only game scheduled.

**AMERICAN LEAGUE**

| | W | L | Pct. | * |
|---|---|---|---|---|
| New York | 59 | 36 | .621 | |
| Baltimore | 60 | 38 | .612 | ½ |
| Chicago | 59 | 38 | .608 | 1 |
| ANGELS | 53 | 50 | .515 | 10 |
| Boston | 50 | 51 | .495 | 12 |
| Minnesota | 48 | 51 | .485 | 13 |
| Detroit | 48 | 52 | .480 | 13½ |
| Cleveland | 43 | 54 | .443 | 17 |
| Kansas City | 38 | 61 | .384 | 23 |
| Washington | 38 | 65 | .369 | 25 |

*Games behind leader.

**Sunday's Results**

ANGELS, 3-4; Kansas City, 0-3 (second game, 10 innings).
New York, 11-5; Detroit, 6-4.
Washington, 4; Baltimore, 1.
Boston, 6-3; Cleveland, 1-1.
Chicago, 5-3; Minnesota, 4-0 (first game, 12 innings).

**Game Today**

New York (Terry, 2-8) vs. ANGELS (Newman, 8-3), Dodger Stadium, radio KMPC, 8 p.m.
Only game scheduled.

## Sandy Had It Locked Up, but ... Two Errors Let Giants Win, 5-2

**BY FRANK FINCH**
Times Staff Writer

Sandy Koufax had his 16th victory of the season all but locked up Sunday when errors by Jim Gilliam and Maury Wills opened the gates and let four unearned runs cross home plate that gave the hated Giants a 5-2 victory and the odd game of the series before 49,429 fans.

Before the defensive lapses cost him the decision, Koufax had won 11 games in a row, 10 straight at Dodger Stadium, and seven straight from San Francisco here.

**Counting the House**

| | |
|---|---|
| Sunday's attendance | 49,429 |
| 1964 attendance, 48 dates | 1,561,[illegible] |
| 1963 attendance, 48 dates | 1,312,[illegible] |

The gift win boosted the Giants to within one half game of the sagging Phillies, and they'll start a showdown series Tuesday in the Quaker City.

Meanwhile, Los Angeles fell below the .500 level again as the Giants beefed up their season edge to 10-3, clinching honors for 1964.

Of the Dodgers' last 10 defeats, four of them came on four-run rallies in the last inning. The hoodoo streak started in Houston July 9, and continued in Chicago July 12 and again in St. Louis July 14.

Willie Mays drove in the go-ahead tally with a double

Please Turn to Pg. 7, Col. 1

## Angels Fly to Fifth Straight Double Victory

**BY BRAVEN DYER**
Times Staff Writer

KANSAS CITY — The high-flying Angels climaxed their winningest road trip Sunday by sweeping a doubleheader from the Athletics, 3-0 and 4-3, the finale in 10 innings.

For 13 games Bill Rigney's rampaging red-hots posted a 10-3 record.

They are 16-6 since the All-Star game on July 7 and 18-9 for the month.

By drubbing the A's twice the Angels tied a major league record which has stood since 1906 — five straight sweeps.

The New York American League club owned the mark exclusively.

In consecutive twin bills the Cherubs beat the Minnesota Twins twice, Detroit and the White Sox prior to Sunday's sweep.

The nightcap was L.A.'s seventh extra-inning victory of the year against five defeats.

Making his first start of the season, Aubrey Gatewood (2-0) teamed with General Bob Lee to cop the opener.

Dean Chance (9-5), coming out of the bullpen for the first time since May 17, got credit for the nightcap victory.

Chance retired for pinch hitter Ed (Spanky) Kirkpatrick, who had as much to do with winning the game as anybody.

Spanky did his stuff in the 10th. Bobby Knoop, three-for-four in the finale, opened with a double off loser John Wyatt (7-7).

Kirkpatrick ripped a single to right, scoring Knoop to put L.A. ahead, 3-2.

When Rocky Colavito fumbled the ball, Spanky raced to second and moved to third on Bob Perry's ground out.

Third baseman Ed Charles tried to stop Vic Power's bounder with his chest and the Angels got their big insurance run as

Please Turn to Pg. 7, Col. 3

YANKEE BOMBERS — Home run hitters Roger Maris, Mickey Mantle and Joe Pepitone celebrate in New York locker room after their blasts helped Yanks rip Cards, 8-3, to even World Series at 3-3. UPI Telephoto

# Three Yankee Bombs Crush Cards--Sudden Death Today

BY FRANK FINCH
Times Staff Writer

ST. LOUIS—The Bronx Bombers wheeled up their heavy artillery Wednesday and bombarded the Cardinals into rubble, 8-3, with a barrage of home runs.

Back-to-back blasts by Roger Maris and Mickey Mantle in the sixth inning broke a 1-1 tie, and Joe Pepitone's grand slam in the eighth climaxed a five-run detonation to send the1964 World Series right down to the wire.

**Hunch Clues**

In today's seventh and final game, Mel Stottlemyre of New York and Bob Gibson of St. Louis will meet on the mound for the third time.

For the benefit of hunch players, it should be mentioned that Cardinal teams never have lost a seven-game Series while winning four of them, and the Yankees haven't lost two Series in a row since bowing to the New York Giants in 1921-22.

A capacity turnout of 30,805 pro-Redbird rooters was bitterly disappointed as the Yankees racked up their 99th victory in 29 World Series.

**Bouton's Steam**

The Cardinals had battled back to take the fourth and fifth games in New York and assume a 3-2 Series lead, and their partisans had high hopes of the club wrapping up its first world championship since 1946.

They reckoned without the crushing power in Yankee bats and the steam in Jim Bouton's right arm.

In the clubhouse, Bouton likes to jam a battered felt hat on his head, cross his eyes and screw up his mouth in a startling impersonation of Crazy Guggenheim. But he's crazy like a fox on the mound.

Although tiring in the ninth, Bouton posted his second victory of the Series with Steve Hamilton's help.

**Simmons Loser**

Jim's victim was the aging southpaw, Curt Simmons, who faced Bouton in the third game, but was not charged with the defeat. That was the game in which Barney Schultz fed Mantle a home-run pitch leading off the last of the ninth.

Home runs have figured very prominently in every game of this set.

Mike Shannon's shot sparked St. Louis' winning rally in the first game, and Phil Linz's rap gave New York a much-needed cushion in the ninth inning of the second.

Mantle decided the third with his 16th Series swat. Ken Boyer's slam clinched the fourth. Tim McCarver topped Tom Tresh's score-tying homer in the ninth round of Monday's thriller by hitting one with two aboard in the 10th.

**Record Shattered**

A Series record was broken, one was set, and several were tied during the festivities.

While improving his own record with his 17th homer, Mantle now has amassed 119 total bases, two more than his boss, Yogi Berra, achieved during his playing career.

The consecutive homers by Maris and Mantle matched a mark first set by Goose Goslin and Joe

Please Turn to Pg. 2, Col. 3

Los Angeles Times
Sports
PART III BUSINESS & FINANCE
CC THURSDAY MORNING, OCT. 15, 1964 2†

## JIM MURRAY

## War Party of One



TOKYO—The storms moved in overnight from the northwest. The rains fell steadily on Hokkaido, Honshu, Kyushu. They fell on the Emperor's moat and in the Bay of Tokyo, on the Imperial Gardens and the tourists struggling out of overcrowded hotel lobbies, on the Son of Heaven and some sons of a lower celestial order. They fell on barefoot runners from Kenya, on beribboned field hockey players from the ramparts of India, on Soviet "masters of sport," on spear throwers from Scandinavia and young lady high-jumpers whose hair is now a mess, on Robert Hayes and 5,000 guys with stop watches.

The symbol of this Olympics is not five rings but five sinuses, all dripping. Instead of gold medals they should give out mustard plasters. The motto is no longer "Citius, Altius, Fortius" but "Gesundheit."

The Olympic shield should be on a bottle of cough syrup. You get your choice of a bronze medal or a hundred aspirins. The only thing you can say in Japanese is "achoo." At night, you sit there and listen to the sizzle of your socks drying on the radiator. You don't need a masseuse running up and down your back because she might drown. The stadium is a sea of paper umbrellas. The Tokyo taxi drivers, who are conducting an Olympic of their own cheerfully, add wet brakes to the pleasure of the competition. The regular athletes add wet feet.

### No Decimals for Difficulty

It is a conceit of Americans that an Olympics is, after all, a contest of running, jumping and throwing. The rest is, at best, a diversion.

Track and field brings the magic of exactitude. There are no decimals for "degree of difficulty," no occult measurement of scratches on ice. You are at the mercy of the clock and the tape measure and God help you. It is the moment American tourists, American journalists and American hearts have been waiting for. You don't depend on a horse, a boat, a gun. You depend on you. The last stand of individualism. No committees, board of directors, table of organization. You don't go through channels. You go through a finish line tape. These gold medals are a little golder to Americans. The others turn green, a track and fielder is half convinced.

The 10,000 meters is a race Americans left to Finns, who had to chase mail trains and whose pulse you could clock with a calendar, and to Iron Curtain Captives who got used to running long distances to stay ahead of bayonets. It was not that we never won the 10,000 meters. That was bad enough. It was just that we keep the finish judges up way past their bedtime. We've been whistled off the track, pelted with laughter. We blushed when we entered it. We are too impatient to wait a half-hour for the result of a race.

### Mills Real Live Indian

Usually these races are half chess, half charge. This one was run like a prison break. The field started out like a raided crap game and kept going like prodded cattle. The winner is the kind of guy they would write songs about in a less sophisticated age.

Billy Mills is that most thrilling of American folk heroes, a real live Indian. Seven-sixteenths of all the blood that flows in his veins, by actual corpuscular count, is Sioux. Half of his grandparents were Indians

Please Turn to Pg. 4, Col. 4

# Mills Wins First U.S. Gold Medal in 10,000

## Oerter and Hayes Win Gold Medals

Exclusive to The Times from a Staff Writer

TOKYO — The United States continued to harvest gold medals in track and field today when burly Bob Hayes won the 100 meters in 10 seconds flat and big Al Oerter won his third discus gold medal with a throw of 200 feet 1½ inches.

Second in the discus was the world record holder, Ludvik Danek of Czechoslovakia, with 198-6½, with Dave Weill of Walnut Creek, Calif., third at 195-6.

Hayes, the big Florida A&M football star from Jacksonville, Fla., had clocked a world record shattering 9.9 seconds for the 100 meters in the semifinals, but it was disallowed because of a 12 mile per hour trailing wind.

Cuba's Enrique Figuerola was second and Canada's Harry Jerome third in the 100. Mel Pender of the U.S. pulled a muscle in a semifinal heat, while the other Yankee, Trenton Jackson, failed to qualify.

**More Wind**

The winds also wiped out a world record equaling 11.2 seconds in the women's 100 meters by Wyomia Tyus of Griffin, Ga., made in the semifinals. That clocking equaled the world mark held by Wilma Rudolph, America's gold medalist in the Rome Olympics in 1960.

Two of the three U.S. entrants in the men's 400-meter hurdles gained the final. Rex Cawley of Los Angeles made it by winning his semi-final in 49.8 seconds. Jay Luck of Watertown, Mass., qualified by finishing second in the semi-final won by John Cooper of Britain in 50.4 seconds. Luck also clocked 50.4.

**Hardin Misses**

But Billy Hardin of Baton Rouge, La., was eliminated when he trailed home in Cooper's heat.

Jerry Siebert of Willits, Calif., and Tom Farrell of Forest Hills, N.Y., both qualified for the finals in the 800 meters with second places in semi-finals. Siebert, in 1:47 flat, was second to Peter Snell of New Zealand, 1:46.9.

Armin Hary, 1960 Olympic champion and co-holder of the world record of 10 flat, and former Olympic gold medal winner Jesse Owens both were in the stands at capacity - packed National Stadium to see Hayes win the 100.

Janell Smith of Fredonia, Kan., was one of the 16 qualifiers for the semifinals in the women's 400 meter run. She was the only U.S. entry.

Because of the large field

Please Turn to Pg. 6, Col. 3

**TODAY IN SPORTS**

HARNESS RACING—Hollywood Park, 1 p.m.

RADIO-TELEVISION

OLYMPICS—Summer Games, Channel 4, 10 p.m. and 11:15 p.m. (tape).

BASEBALL—World Series, Channel 4, KFI, 11 a.m.

HARD-PRESSED YANK—Despite slight shove by Mohamed Gamoudi of Tunisia, Lt. Billy Mills, a U.S. marine, keeps lead in Tokyo to become first American to win Olympic 10,000-meter run. He set a record: 28 minutes, 24.4 sec. UPI Wirephoto

## Yank Splashers Win Four 'Golds,' Set Three Marks

Exclusive to The Times from a Staff Writer

TOKYO — The United States' mastery of the aquatic sports in the Olympic Games continued with a brilliant display Wednesday as Americans added four gold medals and three world records.

The U.S. men divers took a 1-2-3 finish in the springboard competition led by a come-from-behind rush by Ken Sitzberger of River Forest, Ill.

Californians dominated the record-breaking.

Cathy Ferguson, a 16-year-old high school student from Burbank, captured the backstroke in 1:07.7.

**Roth Beats Saari**

Dick Roth, a 17-year-old from Atherton, took the individual medley in 4:45.4, beating Roy Saari of El Segundo for the gold medal. Saari was timed in 4:47.1.

Don Schollander of Santa Clara teamed with Steve Clark of Los Altos, Gary Ilman of San Jose and Mike Austin of Rochester, N.Y., for a record-smashing relay victory in 3:33.2.

Wednesday's events fulfilled all of the promises of the American swimmers for a rich harvest of gold medals in this year's Games.

Miss Ferguson's victory was the most spectacular. She nipped the favored Christine Caron of France by two-tenths of a second and the crowd in Yoyogi Pool cheered wildly.

Miss Ferguson was naturally exuberant — and in tears.

"This is the greatest thrill of my life," she said. "I'm so nervous I can hardly stand it. This is a moment in my life I will never forget. My parents were here and I'm thankful for that."

**Ten Medals Won**

The United States enjoyed a field day Wednesday in the Olympics. Ten medals were won by the U.S.A. forces to raise their total to 20 for four days of competition, eight more than the Russians. Americans took four gold medals in the day's program.

Roth had been wrapped in ice packs Sunday after an appendicitis attack so he could compete in the heats Monday. But he said he was not bothered in the final.

"I decided to put the thought of my appendicitis attack out of my mind," he said. "I just didn't think about it. I was determined to go for a gold medal and a world record."

Sitzberger, who overtook Frank Gorman of New Yorok on the last three dives, said:

"It seems like I always do better on my last dives [illegible] the competition is toughest."

Sitzberger led a sweep in springboard diving, with Gorman second at 157:63 and Larry Andreason of Los Alamitos, Calif., third at 143:77.

The women's 400-meter freestyle relay team entered the finals with a 4:12.2 clocking. The team is composed of Jeane Hallock, Arcadia; Erika Bricker, Visalia; Lynne Allsup, Bloomington; and Patience Sherman of Upper Montclair, N.J.

**New Records**

Three U.S. girls cracked the Olympic record en route to the 100-meter butterfly semifinals, Kathy Ellis of Indianapolis starting off with a 1:07.8, Donna de Varona of Santa Clara, lowering it to 1:07.5 and Sharon Stouder of Glendora, finishing the heats with a 1:07.0.

Miss De Varona was also credited with an Olympic record today as she led three American girls into Saturday's finals of the women's 400 meter individual medley swim.

Miss De Varona covered the distance in 5:24.2, breaking the mark of 5:26.8 set in the preceding heat by Germany's Veronika Holletz.

Qualifying also with her were Martha Randall of Wayne, Pa., at 5:27.8 and Sharon [illegible], 18, of San [illegible], Calif., with a time of

## Pendleton Marine Scores Upset, Lindgren Ninth

BY PAUL ZIMMERMAN
Times Sports Editor

TOKYO—Unheralded and unsung before the XVIII Olympiad, William M. Mills is the toast of the track and field world today. The Camp Pendleton Marine lieutenant, with Sioux Indian blood pumping from his gallant heart, beat all the "name" distance runners of the world Wednesday at 10,000 meters and set a new Olympic record in the doing.

His time was 28:24.4 for the approximate 6.2 miles. A great sprint finish down a straightaway cluttered with runners who were a lap behind took him to victory by two strides over Mohamed Gamoudi of Tunisia.

Ron Clarke, the favorite from Australia, was 10 yards back in third place.

Eighteen - year - old Gerry Lindgren of America, who entered the race with a sprained ankle, finished ninth.

**Strong Finish**

Mills, who never was a resounding success, even as a collegian at Kansas, won by the simple expedient of staying with the leaders all the way and outspeeding them at the end.

"I knew I was in with five laps to go," enthused the 155-pound motor pool officer who never had run faster than 29:10.4 before.

"I guess I was the only one who thought I had a chance. I figured if I stayed up there with the leaders my speed would carry me in," he said.

**First for U.S.**

Mills' confidence in his sprint was bolstered Monday when he ran a 220 in 23.4 seconds.

"I knew if I stayed with Clarke I could beat him at the end. Gamoudi was the queston mark. He ran away from me the only time we ever met," Mills continued.

No American ever had won the 10,000 in the Olympics. The best we've ever done was the sixth by Max Truex at Rome and Mills washed out the American record Max posted there.

The USA triumph was only one of a series of upsets on the opening day of track that spelled disappointment for the Russians, who got only two bronze medals.

Terje Pedersen of Norway, who set a world record of over 300 feet in the javelin this summer, had to settle for a 236-6½ and failed to get past the preliminaries. Pauli Nevala of Finland won with a best of 271 feet 2½ inches.

Russia's Jan Lusis had to be content with third and Ed Red of the USA finished 11th.

**Four-man Race**

In the women's long jump, Mary Rand of Great Britain set a world's record of 22 feet 2 1/4 inches with Irna Kirszenstei of Poland second and former world record holder Tatyana Shchelkanova of the Soviet Union third.

But the big story of the opening day of track and field was the 10,000. Mills went right out with the leaders and stayed there, even though a big blister developed on his left foot along the way.

The race quickly developed into a four-man affair between Mills, Clarke, Gamoudi and Mamo Wolde of Ethopia.

Ptyor Bolotnikov, defend-

Please Turn to Pg. 6, Col. 7

**NINTH IN 10,000**

## 'I Felt Lousy,' Says Lindgren After Loss

TOKYO (UPI) — Little Gerry Lindgren could still muster a smile. But just barely.

The 18-year-old high school boy from Spokane, a 120-pounder running in a six-mile race against the big men, finished ninth in the field of 38 competitors in the 10,000-meter run.

An unhappier boy you never saw, but the smile came when he was asked about Billy Mills, 26-year-old Marine from Coffeyville, Kans., who won the race in a spine-tingling finish.

"Great," said Gerry. "Boy, he really took off and moved out."

Gerry has had the limelight here as much as any American athlete because of his victory over the Russians in the 10,000 in a dual meet in Los Angeles last summer. It never [illegible] to his head, but he knew that much was expected of him.

After the race Wednesday, he walked out of the great stadium all alone and entered a snack stand. He ordered a cup of chocolate drink and drank it down in one gulp. He was perspiring heavily, his hair was awry and he was anxious to get away by himself.

How did he feel during the race?

"I sure didn't feel good," he said. "In fact, I really felt lousy.

"I was never in a race like this before. There was a real mob coming out of the start and a lot of jolting and that took a lot out of me.

"At the 5,000-meter point I felt real bad and I didn't know if I was going to be able to finish. I came up behind Halberg (Murray Halberg of New Zealand) and he helped me to finish.

"I sure learned a lot."

WINNING HEAVE—Former USC great Dallas Long starts the toss that earned the Olympic Games gold medal in shot put. Long's best put was record 66-8½. UPI Radiotelephoto

# U.S. Spikers Still Good as Gold: Hansen, Long Set Olympic Marks

BY PAUL ZIMMERMAN
Times Sports Editor

TOKYO — The XVIII Olympiad had its own cold war here Saturday.

It came in the pole vault and Fred Hansen of Texas won it after 9 hours and 9 minutes of competition as first a Russian, then a Czechoslovakian and finally three Germans succumbed in the most gruelling single event competition in the history of the Olympic Games.

In that trying span of time—from 1 p.m. to 10:09—the tall athlete from the Lone Star state took only seven vaults. He eventually won at 16 feet 8¾ inches.

**German Misses**

To heighten the suspense, Hansen gambled by passing 16 feet 6¾ inches, which Wolfgang Reinhardt made, and then Hansen missed twice at the winning height before clearing it on the final try.

The German, who had taken 13 vaults on this long day, missed.

Twelve thousand of an original crowd of 72,000 who had thrilled to the day's competition stayed on to the bitter end. Even the moon had set before the vault, first event on the program, had run its course.

It had been a day of great excitement, and the Rice University pre-dental student's victory made it three gold medals for the United States to increase its total to seven in men's track and field.

Earlier in the day Uncle Sam's men had finished one-two in the shot put and 200 meter dash, making it three Olympic records in the bargain.

**O'Brien Fourth**

Dallas Long, competing for the last time in his illustrious career, won the shot put with a best toss of 66 feet 8½ inches as Randy Matson finished second. Four-time Olympian Parry O'Brien finished fourth, 7½ inches behind the third place Hungarian, Vilmos Varju.

Then Henry Carr came along and sped to a 20.3 victory in the dash with Paul Drayton of the U.S.A. his closest opponent.

Saturday's competition had one other noteworthy performance.

Russia finally collected a gold medal in track and

Please Turn to Pg. 6, Col. 6

SURVIVOR—That's Fred Hansen of U.S.A., who won Olympic pole vault.

Los Angeles Times
Sports
SECTION D
CC SUNDAY, OCTOBER 18, 1964 2†

## JIM MURRAY

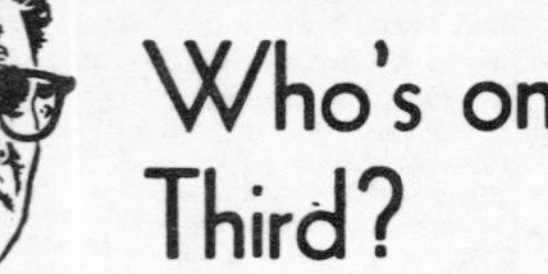

### Who's on Third?



TOKYO—John Curtis Thomas, a fairly proper Bostonian, can beat every highjumper in the world except one.

This is like saying Caruso could sing every high note except C, Sam Snead could win every golf tournament except the Open, a general could win every battle except the last. It's more of a tragedy than being last.

They pay off only on first place in this life. Second place is like being a butler. Nobody notices you. "Nobody remembers second place in the Olympics," Rex Cawley, the USC hurdler, observed as he pocketed his gold medal in his event last week. To paraphrase Bugs Baer, after first place, everything is Bridgeport.

John Thomas actually took third place in the last Olympics. But, if you don't finish first, third is like being given a seat by the kitchen. You show the medal at a dinner party 30 years hence and your guest coughs politely behind his hand and murmurs politely, "very nice. Tell me, who won?" You have put yourself inexorably in a shadow. You might be better off pulling a muscle or getting kicked off the team.

This is not meant to denigrate ALL third place finishers, but, in general, a man who finishes third may be one heartbeat away from the spotlight. The heartbeat may change his whole life. There are third place finishers who should be eighth. But there are also third place finishers who should be first.

#### *It's Not the Win That Counts*

A medal of gold is just seven dollars worth of cast metal with a gaudy ribbon on it. "The important thing is not the winning but the taking part," the Baron de Coubertin said. Let him ask John Thomas.

John Thomas was history's greatest high jumper in 1960. The event was a formality anyway. The U.S. had only lost it three times in the history of the Olympic Games and the band only brought the sheets for "The Star-Spangled Banner" with them for the high jump. Like the hot dog, apple pie and the Mississippi River, it could only happen in America.

John Thomas hit Rome like a state visit. It seemed a shame he had to come so far and go to all that trouble when they might just as well have mailed the gold medal to him. When he worked out, he put the bar at seven feet and as he went over he sneaked a look at the Russians who were standing with their jaws open. They had a highjumper who had a name that could only be pronounced with a noseful of pepper, Shavlakadze, who had a moustache and a trailing left leg and another, Valeriy Brumel, whom, most people thought, Thomas should have charged for lessons.

Thomas, one journalist noted, was a 1-10 shot going to the post. He jumped easily, confidently. The Russians trained in secret. The guess was, most of them couldn't jump over a privet hedge in less than three tries.

John Thomas passed the height at 6-11. It was be-

Please Turn to Pg. 12, Col. 1

# Bowl-Bound Bucks Trample Trojans, 17-0

## Ohio State Puts Clamp on Garrett

BY CHARLIE PARK
Times Staff Writer

COLUMBUS, Ohio—USC brought along its own weather (76 degrees) here Saturday afternoon and got blistered — badly — by a powerful, versatile Ohio State football team, 17-0.

The third largest crowd in the history of Ohio Stadium, 84,315, plus millions of TV viewers saw Woody Hayes' scarlet-clad bruisers pound and pass the Trojans into submission and become the prime favorite to go to the Rose Bowl.

It was the first time Troy had been slipped a blank job since playing a 0-0 tie with Washington in 1961, the span covering 28 games.

**Garrett Stopped**

Unless Mike Garrett makes a miraculous comeback, his bid for All-America honors probably came to an end here, too, as the burly Buck line contained the little speedster most of the afternoon.

His longest run from scrimmage was 18 yards and often he was blasted down before he could even get to the line. In 17 carries, he netted just 41 yards.

The Trojans made some goofs, but actually they didn't play badly at all. They were simply over-matched. Unbeaten Ohio State outgained them, 294 yards to 197, and monopolized the ball, pulling off a total of 84 plays to 55 for USC.

**Sander Big Noise**

The losers did have an edge in the air, Craig Fertig accounting for 133 yards on 8 completions in 26 tries, while State picked up 79 on 8 for 17—and a touchdown.

Willard Sander, 220-pound junior fullback, was the big noise in the Buckeye assault, crashing for 120 yards and one TD in 29 thrusts.

Hayes, who called every play, mixed up his traditional into-the-middle attack with devastating reverses featuring sophomore Bo Rein, pitchouts to Tom Bar-

Please Turn to Pg. 9, Col. 1

BELTING BUCKEYES—Trojan Mike Garrett finds things a little rough as he is tackled by Ohio State's Bill Spahr (82) and Dwight Kelley (53), with Tom Bugel (66) moving in for the kill. Garrett was held to only 41 yards in 17 carries by the rugged Buckeyes. AP Wirephoto

### HOW BUCKEYES . . .

| USC | Ohio State | | Time |
|---|---|---|---|
| | | FIRST QUARTER | |
| 0 | 6 | Sander, 2-yd. run | 6:40 |
| 0 | 7 | Funk, conversion | |
| | | SECOND QUARTER | |
| 0 | 13 | Lashutka, 16-yd. pass (Unverferth) | 13:57 |
| 0 | 14 | Funk, conversion | |
| | | FOURTH QUARTER | |
| 0 | 17 | Funk, 24-yd. field goal | 0:20 |

### . . . IRISH SCORED

| ND | UCLA | | Time |
|---|---|---|---|
| | | FIRST QUARTER | |
| 6 | 0 | Wolski, 1 yd. run | 8:20 |
| | | SECOND QUARTER | |
| 12 | 0 | Sheridan, 27-yd. pass from Huarte | 10:40 |
| | | THIRD QUARTER | |
| 18 | 0 | Snow, 16-yd. pass from Huarte | 1:24 |
| 24 | 0 | Farrell, 1-yd. run | 8:42 |

# Irish Give Bruins Huarte-to-Snow Job, 24-0

WHEN BRUINS MOVED — This untypical action shows UCLA fullback Paul Horgan powering for 15 yards against Notre Dame in third period of South Bend game. Unbeaten Irish drubbed Bruins, 24-0. AP Wirephoto

## Southland Kids Click for Two Aerial Scores

BY JOHN HALL
Times Staff Writer

SOUTH BEND—It wasn't exactly another Syracuse, but UCLA got its pocket picked again here Saturday as the unbeaten Fighting Irish of Notre Dame punched out its fourth straight victory, 24-0.

A cheer-cheer-cheering near capacity crowd of 58,385 saw the alert, recharged Irish force Larry Zeno into four fumbles, march all the way the first time they touched the ball and completely dominate the entire 60 minutes as the battered Bruins never moved closer than the Notre Dame 20 yard line.

**Californians Do It**

And it could have been worse.

The California kids had a ball, but these particular Californians happened to be wearing the wrong uniforms.

Every time it was necessary, Notre Dame's slick senior quarterback John Huarte of Anaheim would locate end Jack Snow of Long Beach for long yardage, and that was

Please Turn to Pg. 10, Col. 7

| | | | | | |
|---|---|---|---|---|---|
| California . 27 | Wash. . . . . . . 6 | Purdue . . . . . 21 | Kansas . . . . . 15 | Indiana . . . . 27 | Arkansas . . . 14 |
| Navy . . . . . . . 13 | Stanford . . . . 0 | Michigan . . 20 | Oklahoma . . 14 | Mich. St. . . . 20 | Texas . . . . . . 13 |
| STORY ON PAGE 2 | STORY ON PAGE 3 | STORY ON PAGE 11 | STORY ON PAGE 11 | STORY ON PAGE 11 | STORY ON PAGE 4 |

# RAMS STAGE 'TRACK MEET,' SCORE 42!

TOUCHDOWN TWINS — Ram Roman Gabriel tosses third touchdown pass of game to Bucky Pope, who catches ball on 3, runs between 49ers Ben Scotti (left), Elbert Kimbrough (45) to score.
Times photos by Larry Sharkey

## Gabriel Hits Pope for 3 TDs

BY MAL FLORENCE
Times Staff Writer

Once every four years, during the Olympic Games period, the Rams get in the spirit of things and stage a track meet at the Coliseum.

Sunday was the designated day as the Rams, relying on Roman Gabriel's arm and a record-breaking performance by the secondary, sped to a 42-14 victory over the San Francisco 49ers.

The Rams haven't scored over 40 points since 1960, another Olympic year, when they rolled up 48 points here on the Detroit Lions.

A crowd of 54,350, unaccustomed to such brash offensive displays, watched Gabriel and rookie star Bucky Pope take charge in the first half before surrendering the day to the defensive platoon.

**Three to Pope**

Gabriel, unruffled and accurate, hurled four touchdown passes—three to Pope—before intermission as the Rams mounted a 28-7 lead.

The big bomber lost his control in the final half (1 for 9), but, in true cavalry fashion, the secondary galloped to the rescue.

For the game, the Rams' deep backs picked off seven 49er passes, returning same 314 yards to shatter the former National Football League record (213) established by the Browns against the Bears in 1960.

Two of the thefts resulted in dazzling touchdowns, Bobby Smith bringing back one

Please Turn to Pg. 2, Col. 4

### HOW THEY SCORED

| Rams | 49ers | | Time |
|---|---|---|---|
| | | FIRST QUARTER | |
| 0 | 6 | Parks, 83-yd. pass (Brodie) | 7 40 |
| 0 | 7 | Davis kick | |
| 6 | 7 | McKeever 6-yd. pass (Gabriel) | 12 19 |
| 7 | 7 | Gossett kick | |
| | | SECOND QUARTER | |
| 13 | 7 | Pope, 48-yd. pass (Gabriel) | 1 54 |
| 14 | 7 | Gossett kick | |
| 20 | 7 | Pope, 68-yd. pass (Gabriel) | 11 46 |
| 21 | 7 | Gossett kick | |
| 27 | 7 | Pope, 18-yd. pass (Gabriel) | 14 17 |
| 28 | 7 | Gossett kick | |
| | | FOURTH QUARTER | |
| 28 | 13 | Kopay, 4-yd. pass (Mira) | 10 12 |
| 28 | 14 | Davis kick. | |
| 34 | 14 | Smith, 97-yd. interception return | 12 00 |
| 35 | 14 | Gossett kick | |
| 41 | 14 | Martin, 71-yd. interception return | 14 28 |
| 42 | 14 | Gossett kick. | |

## SID ZIFF

### Just as Expected

It looks wonderful, it is wonderful, but let's not get carried away by what's happening in the Olympic Games in Tokyo. We knew in advance we would dominate the swimming events. But the U.S. is doing just about what was expected, and no more, in track and field, according to Dick Nash, a leading Southern California expert on the subject.

We've gained victories in the 5,000 and 10,000 meters for the first time. But if you check back to the 1956 Olympics in Melbourne, we're just about where we were then. We're not any stronger.

The significant thing is that Russia has lost ground. The U.S.S.R. is being cut back by the rise of other countries, among them Hungary and Rumania. The African countries also are beginning to show strength.

America's improvement in the distance races, according to Nash, is the result of an acceptance by our athletes of the European training program, real, heavy, hard, day-after-day work. It is something they were unwilling to tackle in other years.

#### Keys to Cars Haven't Softened Kids

Indirectly, of course, our collection of gold medals proves that we have one less thing to worry about. Our youth is not going to pot. Our boys and girls aren't getting soft. They haven't forgotten how to run just because every kid has the key to a car by the time he is 16.

Nor will it be necessary for the United States to subsidize its athletes on a full-time basis to meet the competition of the Iron Curtain countries.

We can go along just as we have been doing. It's pretty difficult on the kids, they have to make a lot of sacrifices, but I don't think we'd want our athletics any other way.

We do have a certain amount of subsidization ourselves. Through the co-operation of the armed forces, certain athletes have actually benefited by detached service. Lt. Mills, for example, the winner of the 10,000 meters, has been a full-time athletic soldier for the last six months.

But in Russia, the athletes are on permanent detached service. There still exists a vast difference in our Olympic programs.

#### Off-Beat Color Fascinates Viewers

NBC regained some of its lost prestige with a well-rounded two-hour Olympic program on Saturday. I particularly enjoyed some of the off-beat shots. It was a poignant moment when the Argentine soccer team lost to lightly regarded Japan. The losers wrung their hands in despair. You had a feeling they may never get over the disgrace. To them, the world had come to an end.

Then there was the Yugoslavian fencer, who emoted all over the place during his losing match to a Russian. John Barrymore would have envied him. He was forever taking off his helmet and making an impassioned address to the judges, or perhaps he was just baring his soul for the spectators. In the end he would shrug his shoulders, apologize with an audible, "Pardon! Pardon!" and return to the fray. You had the impression that although the whole world was against him, he would go down, if he must, with flying colors.

One thing we noticed about the women's track events, the girls of today run like men. They don't duck waddle. You've got to be a real athlete to place

Please Turn to Pg. 8, Col. 4

## Larrabee Zips to 400-Meter Win

### Ex-Trojan Clocked in 45.1 Seconds

Exclusive to The Times from a Staff Writer

TOKYO — Veteran Mike Larrabee, a 30-year-old former University of Southern California runner from Fillmore, Calif., won the Olympic 400 meters today in a snappy 45.1 seconds as the United States added to its growing horde of gold medals in track and field.

At the same time, however, the United States track forces suffered perhaps their greatest disappointment when Tom O'Hara and young Jim Ryun failed to qualify for the 1,500 meter run, which will be staged Wednesday.

Meanwhile, Edith McGuire of Atlanta won the women's 200 meter dash in the Olympic record time of 23 seconds flat—a clocking which was just one-tenth of a second off the world mark.

**Gold and Glory**

The victories by Larrabee and Miss McGuire were the 11th and 12th in track and field for the United States and raised its total medal collection to 70, 31 of which are gold. Russia, which has yet to compete in some of her strongest events, has 41 medals, 13 of them gold.

Larrabee, a mathematics teacher at Monroe High School in Sepulveda, Calif., and captain of the Southern California Striders, gave the United States its third successive triumph in the 400 meters. His teammate, Ulis Williams of Compton, Calif., and a student at Arizona State University, finished fifth in 46 seconds flat.

**Closing Rush**

With a tremendous finishing kick, Larrabee won by an eyelash over Wendell Mottley, a Yale graduate running for Trinidad, who was timed in 45.2.

O'Hara and Ryun, the No. 2 and 3 men on a 1,500-meter squad that was considered the United States' best in four decades, failed to make the finals of the prestigious event, leaving Dyrol Burleson of Oregon the only U.S. qualifier.

Miss McGuire, a 20-year-old co-ed at Tennessee State who already owns a silver medal in the 100-meter dash, got off to a lightning start in the 200, quickly took the lead and never was headed. She

Please Turn to Pg. 4, Col. 1

### TODAY IN SPORTS

WRESTLING—Pasadena Arena, 8 p.m.
PRO-BOXING—Santa Monica Civic Auditorium, 8:30 p.m.
RADIO-TELEVISION
OLYMPICS—Summer Games, Channel 4, 11:15 p.m. (tape).

BOSTON LOSES TO BRITON

## Gold Rushes In: Schul, Jones Win

BY PAUL ZIMMERMAN
Times Sports Editor

TOKYO — Robert Keyser Schul further established the United States' new-found dominance in distance running Sunday when he added the 5,000 meters to a growing string of Yankee gold medals in the XVIII Olympiad.

He accomplished the remarkable feat on a cold, rainy day that sent Ralph Boston into a surprising defeat in the long jump. This upset, staged by Lynn Davies of Great Britain, came on the heels of an American double in the high hurdles and the Soviet Union's first men's gold medal of the track and field competition in the hammer throw.

The United States' victory total in this phase of the competition now stands at nine—the same number of gold medals garnered in Rome with six events to go. The USA can win three more.

"My next goal is to set a world's record in the event," said Schul, who ran past France's Michel Jazy on the final turn and went on to defeat Harald Norpoth of Germany by six strides in the time of 13:48.8. Under the conditions it was not a bad performance, but far from an Olympic record.

Bill Dellinger also ran by the faltering Jazy, a prime favorite with Schul, to take third. His time was 13:49.8.

Davies came through with a leap of 26 feet 5 3/4 inches in the final round and Boston, 1960 winner and world record holder, had to come back with a 26-4½ leap on his final effort to salvage the silver medal over Igor Ter-Ovanesyan of Russia. Ralph fouled on his best leap that would have taken it all.

"I'm sorry, boys," he said with a wan smile. "There's an awful lot of difference between a gold and silver medal."

The double came when Hayes Jones captured the hurdles in 13.6 seconds with Blaine Lindgren inches back

Please Turn to Pg. 5, Col. 2

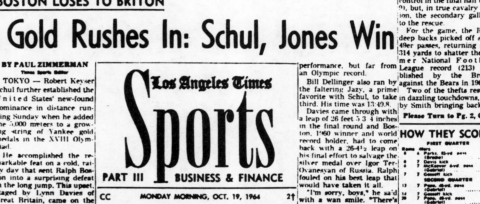

Los Angeles Times
Sports
PART III BUSINESS & FINANCE
CC MONDAY MORNING, OCT. 19, 1964 2†

IT'S CATCHING—Ram rookie Aaron Martin (left) comes up with one of seven interceptions which L.A. team pulled on San Francisco 49ers Sunday. Center, flankerback Bucky Pope, another first-year player with Rams, hauls in first of three touchdown passes he caught from Roman Gabriel—a 48-yard gainer. At right, Marlin McKeever latches onto a six-yard toss by Gabriel in end zone.
Times photos by Ben Olender and Art Rogers

| | | | | | |
|---|---|---|---|---|---|
| Colts . . . . . . 24 | Cardinals . . 38 | Browns . . . . 20 | Vikings . . . . 30 | Lions . . . . . . 10 | Eagles . . . . . 23 |
| Packers . . . . 21 | Redskins . . 24 | Cowboys . . . 16 | Steelers . . . . 10 | Bears . . . . . . 0 | Giants . . . . . 17 |
| STORY ON PAGE 6 | STORY ON PAGE 6 | STORY ON PAGE 7 | STORY ON PAGE 7 | STORY ON PAGE 6 | STORY ON PAGE 6 |

# USC SHOCKS NO. 1 IRISH, 20-17, BUT...

## ... Oregon State Comes Up Smelling Like a 'Rose'

Los Angeles Times
Sports
SECTION C
CC SUNDAY, NOVEMBER 29, 1964 3¢

### JIM MURRAY

## Irish Eyes Are Cryin'



Anybody want a good deal in used shamrocks? How about a fleet rate on green balloons?

If any Irish eyes are smiling today, bring a shillelagh down over his ears. You can hear the Angels sing, but who's listening? Anyone who'd smile and listen to music this day would water whiskey.

A little bit of heaven didn't fall from out of the skies, a little bit of football did. When it nestled in the arms of Rod Sherman once again the Irish jig was up.

They came into this town No. 1 on all the better polls. They got about as much chance of winning the next election as Slippery Rock. They'll fall so fast they'll think they hit a cake of soap.

The game had all the rock-ribbed defense of a saloon fight in the dark. USC can move the ball on the German army but they can't resist a pass any better than Mamie Stover. The only reason Notre Dame didn't score as many completions in the second half as in the first was because they didn't have the ball enough. On some of their more stunning gains, their halfbacks forgot to bring the ball along.

The first half of the game looked as if it were going to be less a game than a recital for four hands and three downs by their quarterback John Huarte. John played the Trojan defense like a giant organ he had the sheet music for. But in the second half someone threw a cat in the bellows. USC let the air out of them.

*Lost Game in Committee*

Notre Dame lost the game on a piece of legislation. They lost it in committee, so to speak. They had the ball in the fourth quarter on the one-foot line, give or take a few inches. The only Catholic Kantor you'll find anywhere in the world (in a gold helmet anyway) took the ball in for an apparent touchdown. Some official with a suspicious mind kept his eyes on the line and swore he caught a Notre Dame man holding. Notre Dame lost the touchdown, the ball and, ultimately, the game. This is known in story and song as the "Luck of the Irish." With luck like that, you don't need black cats.

After Huarte turned from Toscanini to Buster Keaton, Notre Dame's defense turned to mush. Craig Fertig, who could only complete 3 passes in the first half, completed 10 in the second. The Irish looked like a guy trying to hold onto a top hat in a snowball fight. For one thing, they were so afraid of USC's Mike Garrett, that five of them dove at him if he changed his seat on the bench.

*Guys From Western Costume*

They must have thought the rest of Troy's varsity was just a bunch of guys from Western Costume. Sherman went through them like Georgia. They looked like the Mets chasing fly balls. Of course, all USC won was the right to go to the Rose Bowl game—if they can buy tickets.

This was "Band Day" in the Coliseum, ten thousand tuba-tooters and enough cymbals to give you a headache for the whole second half. The joint was full of Swiss bell ringers and Roman collars. If you hollered "Hey, Pat," half the place would turn around. If you hollered "Hey, Pat," at the end of the game, your answer would be "Why don't you just shut the hell up? Have you no respect for the dead?"

I think I know what happened. It wasn't the stunting or the looping, the slant defenses. It wasn't the rapscallions who went to sleep during the sermons or

Please Turn to Pg. 8, Col. 2

IT'S A-OK FOR USC—A leaping Rod Sherman hauls in Craig Fertig's history-making pass that beat the Irish with 1:33 left.

USC'S WINNING PLAY

## Sherman Called It . . . and McKay Said 'OK'

BY JOHN HALL
Times Staff Writer

84-Z delay.

Remember the formula. It's not the number of a secret operator from another planet, but it's the name of the play that made Trojan football history.

It's the one that beat unbeaten, unbeatable Notre Dame Saturday to climax another dramatic, unbelievable USC finish and touch off a mass nervous breakdown at the Coliseum.

Or was it merely an earthquake?

**Greatest Ever**

It's also the play that one day will have the 83,840 stunned spectators telling their grandchildren about the time they saw Craig Fertig pass to Rod Sherman.

Forget Johnny Baker's field goal at South Bend in 1931, Doyle Nave to Al Krueger in the Rose Bowl and that frantic little preview performance against California just a couple of weeks ago.

Remember 84-Z delay. It was something.

"This was the greatest moment in USC's football history," said Trojan athletic director Jess Hill. "There's never been a comeback like this."

**Final Chance**

And it was all wrapped up into one neat package by a red-haired senior quarterback and a red-haired sophomore flanker, Fertig to Sherman, and WOW!

With less than two minutes to play—1:33 to be exact — it was fourth and eight on the Irish 15 and Troy was trailing 17-13.

It was the final chance as Sherman came trotting back from the sidelines to

Please Turn to Pg. 6, Col. 1

## Vote Puts Beavers in Bowl

BY CHARLIE PARK
Times Staff Writer

Notre Dame was supposed to be the miracle team, but USC had the magic touch Saturday and tumbled the previously unbeaten and No. 1 ranked Irish, 20-17, before 83,840 nailbiters in the Coliseum.

But in the end, it was the Trojans themselves who were "bowled over" as the faculty representatives of the eight AAWU schools selected Oregon State to challenge Michigan in the Rose Bowl game.

It was a shocking decision after the way John McKay's revved-up warriors stormed back in one of football's greatest and guttiest comebacks to prove that they were capable of playing a "representative" game against the Big Ten champion.

**Identical Records**

USC and Oregon State had finished the conference race with identical 3-1 records, but did not play each other. USC's stunning upset gave the Cardinal and Gold an overall season mark of 7-3 to Oregon State's 8-2.

When they wound up as co-champs a week ago, the AAWU voted to wait until after Troy's tussle with Notre Dame before choosing between them.

It took only one vote then to delay the decision, and now it would appear that perhaps USC was the only

Please Turn to Pg. 5, Col. 1

### HOW THEY SCORED

| USC | Irish | | Time |
|---|---|---|---|
| FIRST QUARTER | | | |
| 0 | 3 | Ivan 25-yd. field goal .. | 9.20 |
| SECOND QUARTER | | | |
| 0 | 9 | Snow 21-yd. pass (Huarte) ........ | 1.05 |
| 0 | 10 | Ivan kick. | |
| 0 | 16 | Wolski 5-yd. run ...... | 13.40 |
| 0 | 17 | Ivan kick. | |
| THIRD QUARTER | | | |
| 6 | 17 | Garrett 1-yd. run ...... | 6.04 |
| 7 | 17 | Brownell kick. | |
| FOURTH QUARTER | | | |
| 13 | 17 | Hill 23-yd. pass (Fertig) | [illegible] |
| 19 | 17 | Sherman 15-yd. pass (Fertig) .......... | 13.27 |
| 20 | 17 | Brownell kick. | |

## Army Plays It by Foot, Sinks Navy

PHILADELPHIA (AP) — Quarterback Carl Stichweh marshaled five years of Army frustration into a last quarter drive which produced a 20-yard field goal by Barry Nickerson and an 11-8 football upset over Navy Saturday.

The favored Middies, getting new life from a roughing the kicker penalty against John Carber, got to the Army 28 near the finish but a mauling Cadet defensive rush shoved the Sailors' Roger Staubach back to his own 47.

Stichweh, outdueling the more celebrated Staubach in a battle of senior field generals, was mindful of 1963 when the clock left him and his mates two yards shy of a stunning reversal.

Army saw an 8-0 lead erased on the second period efforts of Staubach and Pat Donnelly plus a two-point conversion pass to Phil Norton with 25 seconds left before intermission.

But when Navy's Tom Williams was far short and wide of a 49-yard field goal try moments before the end of the third quarter, Stichweh took firm command of the game.

Starting from his 20, Stichweh, the Williston Park, N.Y., Cadet, called on his talents for a key 17-yard fake pass and left end sweep to his 48.

On the next play, he lofted a long aerial to end Sam Champi, who hauled his reception to the 19, good for a 33-yard advance.

From the 13, Stichweh personally ushered the ball to the three where, on fourth down, Nickerson had his moment of retribution. His field goal kick was high and true, more than making up for the fact he was wide on

Please Turn to Pg. 6, Col. 3

. . . AND THAT'S ALL FOR IRISH — As Sherman spins into the end zone, Notre Dame's defender, Tony Carey, reflects the feeling of a team that was unbeaten and "unbeatable." But it all came to this.

Times photos by Cal Montney

Lakers Lose to Warriors
STORY ON PAGE 3

'RANKEST INJUSTICE,' SAYS USC'S HILL
STORY ON PAGE 4

Rams Draft Cougar Back
STORY ON PAGE 10

# BRUINS REPEAT AS NCAA CHAMPS, 91-80

Los Angeles Times
Sports
SECTION D
CC SUNDAY, MARCH 21, 1965 2†

## Worst of '64



I see where E. P. Dutton & Co. will shortly bring out its "Best Sports Stories of 1964." I can wait. I think I know what they'll be anyway. "My Greatest Day in Baseball—the Story of a Stout-Hearted Pitcher and His Greatest Challenge." "The Agony of Roger Maris." (The agony of Roger Maris is he only gets $72,000 a year for being booed which makes everyone cry except his banker.)

There'll be a soapy valentine or two to "The Fabulous Bill Russell" or "The Fabulous Willie Mays" or maybe "The Fabulous Larry Burright." There will be an "I Remember the Four Horsemen," a story that will recall for the 15th million time that Leo Durocher said, "Nice guys finish last" and a story on how television is taking over sports.

I didn't get to send in my own nominees partly because I don't remember the Four Horsemen, I think Leo has served his time for that one slip of the Lip, and I would gladly undertake the agony of Roger Maris if it comes out, as it does, to $500 a boo.

### *'A Slop's Fables'*

I would, however, like now to submit my own choices for the "Sports Stories of 1964." Don't try to remember where you read them because you didn't. These are exclusives and since they all have morals to point out Dutton may want to bring them out under "Worst Stories of 1964" or, simply, "A Slop's Fables." Here they are:

In darkest Africa, a famous old white hunter who was known to his customers as "Whitey" Hunter but to the native bearers simply as "Ofay," took a near-sighted young greenhorn from the Peace Corps out on a lion hunt one day. They found one in the dense jungle at the foot of Kilimanjaro where they had tea with Joan Bennett and Gregory Peck but by then, the Peace Corpsman had lost his glasses, torn his shirt and fouled up the firing mechanism of his gun. As they cornered mighty Simba, the white hunter cautioned his young friend, "Whatever you do, don't show fear." So the young Peace Corpsman stuck his tongue out at the lion. And the lion leaped and bit it off. The white hunter shot the lion but they had a long and tiresome journey back to the settlement. For one thing, the white hunter had no one to talk to. They marched all night and in the morning came to the government house where they had to register. The official was brusque as he told them to state their business. "Hunters—out of Nairobi," the white hunter told him, holding out their passports. "Here's both our papers." "What's the matter with your friend?" the official snapped. "Cat got his tongue?" "Why, yes," said the old hunter. "How'd you know?"

The moral of this story, of course, is never stick your tongue out at a lion. They get their feline's hurt.

### *Famous Duel at Old Heidelberg*

There were two students duelling at Old Heidelberg when one of them suddenly got a fly on his cheek. "Hold still! I'll get it!" the other one yelled. And he smote the insect with his sword. The fly was only slightly wounded in the wing but the other duellist fell dead. There were two repercussions to this: now there's a fly somewhere in Germany with a dented wing and

Please Turn to Pg. 5, Col. 1

GO-GO-GOODRICH—Gail Goodrich drives around Michigan's George Pomey for two of his 42 points in leading the Bruins to a 91-80 victory over the top-ranked Wolverines Saturday night in the NCAA basketball final. It was the second title in row for UCLA. UPI Telephoto

## Goodrich Scores 42 in Finale

BY MAL FLORENCE
Times Staff Writer

PORTLAND — The race and the national basketball championship belongs to the swift.

UCLA, courageous and collected, defended its NCAA title in convincing fashion here Saturday night, darting to a 91-80 victory over Michigan, which was judged to be the nation's best team at the conclusion of the regular season.

The fleet Bruins, urged on by All-America guard Gail Goodrich and "sixth man" Kenny Washington, proved conclusively before a record Memorial Coliseum crowd of 13,204 that wire-service rankings are specious.

UCLA, rated No. 2 for the bulk of the season, flew to a 47-34 halftime lead, stayed on top in the opening minutes of the second half and then resorted to a calculated 10-minute control game to seal the victory.

Goodrich was a will o' the wisp, scurrying among the burly Wolverines for deft layups and quick-handed jump shots. He wound up with 42 points to break his own school scoring record of 40 set against Brigham Young in the recent western regionals.

**Definite Factor**

As for Washington, you could pull out the old bromide that when the going gets tough, the tough get going.

The soft-spoken Bruin guard from South Carolina came on in relief of the injured Keith Erickson with 6:26 gone in the game and was a definite factor in the win.

He hit some key buckets as UCLA erased an early 20-13 Michigan lead and tightened up the Bruin zone press, a strategy which eventually upset the bewildered Wolverines.

Erickson started but his jumping was impaired as the result of a pulled left leg muscle incurred in practice here Thursday.

**Fifth In History**

Keith did come back in the final 10 minutes—replacing guard Freddie Goss as Washington moved to the backcourt — for ball control purposes.

Thus, UCLA becomes the fifth team in tournament history to win back to back titles. The feat was last accomplished in 1961-1962 by Cincinnati.

The Bruins also joined the University of San Francisco as a West Coast team that has won the NCAA title more than once.

UCLA coach John Wooden is building a dynasty on the West Coast as his Bruins have now won 58 of 60 games over a two-year span. They concluded the tournament and regular season with a splendid 28-2 mark.

As usual, it was a team victory in every sense of the word.

Centers Doug McIntosh

Please Turn to Pg. 4, Col. 4

FLEES BULLPEN

## Don Lee Makes Bid for Starting Role

BY JOHN HALL
Times Staff Writer

PALM SPRINGS — Streamlined Don Lee, the "other Lee" in the Angel bullpen, became one of the top candidates for a spot in the front four this year with a sparkling mound performance here Saturday as the well known "Roof" fell in on the Chicago Cubs.

Striking out five of the first six men he faced, Lee wound up with a total of eight whiffs in five frames, and rookie catcher Phil Roof made it a perfect ending with a game-winning two-run homer in the bottom of the ninth for a 3-2 Angel victory.

**Crowd of 3,419**

A crowd of 3,419 in ideal desert weather was treated to a mid-season display of major league baseball for a change. And it came to its feet with a roar when Roof lined his homer some 370 feet over the left field fence off Chicago's Dick Burwell.

They take these spring things rather seriously here, and it must have been catching as both clubs put on their best shows of the Cactus League campaign with sharp defense, spirited base running and strong pitching.

Don Lee's performance was particularly gratifying to pitching professor Marv Grissom, who has maintained all along that the 31-year-old veteran is his best bet as long man in the bullpen and also for a steady job as a spot starter this season.

**Happy With Results**

"Actually I'm tickled to death with the way things are coming along," said Don, who underwent surgery on his arm last November.

"I feel as good this spring as I've ever felt before. I sort of like the idea of working both as long man in relief and as a starter."

So do the Angels.

The 6-4 right-hander came into camp 20 pounds under his listed 215, and has been

Please Turn to Pg. 3, Col. 3

## SPORTS ON RADIO, TELEVISION TODAY

**BASKETBALL**

Dodgers vs. Baltimore Orioles, KFI, 11 a.m.; Angels vs. Chicago Cubs, Channel 5, radio KMPC, 1 p.m.

**PRO BASKETBALL**

Cincinnati at Boston, Channel 7, 2 p.m.

**ICE HOCKEY**

BLADES vs. San Francisco, KNX, 7 p.m.

## Yanks Fall, 9-6, as Roseboro, T. Davis Homer

BY FRANK FINCH
Times Staff Writer

FORT LAUDERDALE, Fla. — Tommy Davis and John Roseboro ripped three-run homers and Dick Smith slugged a solo job Saturday as the Dodgers slipped New York's Yankees their fourth straight loss, 9-6, before 5,553 sunkissed customers.

In becoming the first Los Angeles hurler to work five frames this spring, lefty Jim Brewer posted his second win. Off Brewer, Howie Reed and Bob Miller the Bombers scored only two earned runs.

**Ford Loser**

Loser Whitey Ford hadn't given up a run in eight previous frames before singles by Jim Lefebvre and Al Ferrara, plus Roseboro's sacrifice fly, produced a tally in the second inning.

Davis drove his second spring homer 420 feet to center after Maury Wills and Wes Parker singled in the third. Jim Bouton was the victim of Roseboro's three-run smash in the fifth and Smith's 400-footer in the sixth.

Elston Howard hit for the

Please Turn to Pg. 3, Col. 3

MICHIGAN TOO SLOW

## Speed, Quickness Pay Off for Bruins

BY JEFF PRUGH
Times Staff Writer

PORTLAND — From the standpoint of each team's qualitative merits, the match was attractive. UCLA's finesse and cunning, on the one hand, against Michigan's muscle and power, on the other.

The finesse and cunning won out, of course. But so did stamina, and UCLA had inexhaustible quantities of it.

**Michigan Tires**

The assessment of UCLA's impressive 91-80 conquest of top-ranked Michigan for a return trip to the throne room of college basketball here Saturday night was just about unanimous.

Coaches and players agreed: The Bruins are a monument to conditioning.

"I knew before the game," said the UCLA coach, John Wooden, with his customary composure, "that our speed and quickness would cause them (Michigan) to tire. And when you're tired, you don't shoot as well.

"My feeling was—and it's a natural thing—that players of that size (Michigan had three starters who weighed more than 218) cannot run with boys of the size that we had."

Dave Strack, coach of virtually the same Michigan team that had absorbed a 98-80 drubbing from the Bruins in the L.A. Classic of 1963, also was of the opinion his team tended to tire.

**Game of Emotions**

"But we didn't necessarily wear out in the second half," he said. "It was the first half (when UCLA erased a 20-13 lead and outscored the Wolverines, 34-14, to seal the Big Ten champs' doom) that did it. This is a game of emotions and momentum. Things went bad for us, and we couldn't come back.

One of UCLA's most glaring attributes in this championship game, which was reminiscent somewhat of the Bruins' 98-83 victory over Duke in the finals last year,

Please Turn to Pg. 4, Col. 3

## On Inside . . .

BAYLOR HITS MILESTONE
STORY ON PAGE 4

Bob Day Sets 2-Mile Mark
STORY ON PAGE 8

A CATCH IN THE RYE—Cub rightfielder Steve Fox of Covina makes sensational catch of fly ball hit by Les Kuhnz of the Angels Saturday. In next inning, Fox injured his ankle chasing another ball.

# DODGERS ON MARICHAL: 'KICK HIM OUT'

Los Angeles Times
Sports
PART III BUSINESS & FINANCE
CC MONDAY MORNING, AUGUST 23, 1965 2†

BY SID ZIFF
Times Staff Writer

SAN FRANCISCO—When the Dodgers play the Giants on their next trip at the Dodger Stadium, there won't be any trouble if Juan Marichal isn't in the ball park.

But if he gets off with a light suspension after using his baseball bat on Dodger catcher John Roseboro's head, it may take the National Guard to keep the peace.

Many of the Dodger players are calling for Marichal to be kicked out of baseball. If such a thing should happen, the Giants would be out of the baseball race entirely. But they say he could have killed Roseboro as he swung at him repeatedly with his bat.

Roseboro managed to throw up his left arm and back was turned to Marichal the first time he was hit with the bat.

In the wild melee that followed, several other Dodgers were slightly hurt. Pitcher Howie Reed was spiked on the ribs as he tried to get at Marichal.

Marichal went berserk his first time at bat after Sandy Koufax had thrown him a routine low inside pitch. The pitch was perfectly harmless, but we are told that Roseboro, when he returned the ball to Koufax, lessen the force of the blows while he tried to get at Marichal with his other hand. The Dodgers say his whizzed it so close to Marichal's head that it ticked his ear.

Marichal was hustled out of the park before he could make any statements. And Roseboro was sent to a hospital for observation after getting first aid treatment in the Dodger dressing room.

According to trainer Bill Buhler, Roseboro had a two-inch gash sustained above the forehead which was closed with butterfly stitches. "He had a knot in the middle of his skull that it would take your whole hand to cover," Buhler said.

It was because of the knot he was sent to the hospi-

Please Turn to Pg. 4, Col. 5

THE SWING THAT CONNECTED—Bat wielded by an infuriated Juan Marichal is about to strike the head of the Dodgers' John Roseboro as Sandy Koufax tries to defend his catcher—and himself. The Giant pitcher said Roseboro's throw ticked him on the ear. UPI Wirephoto

HEAT'S ON . . . FULL BLAST—His fist doubled and blood trickling down his chest protector, John Roseboro charges after Juan Marichal, who is restrained by umpire Shag Crawford. Moving in on Roseboro is the Giants' Willie McCovey. UPI Wirephoto

## M'KEEVER'S HEAD INJURY 'SEVERE'

### Ram's Career Threatened by Concussion Suffered During 21-19 Loss to Browns

BY MAL FLORENCE
Times Staff Writer

The Rams fought the good fight and lost a 21-19 preseason encounter to the Cleveland Browns Sunday afternoon at the Coliseum. But the game was of little significance as the football career of Ram tight end Marlin McKeever could be in jeopardy.

He suffered a severe concussion during the second quarter, was removed and later admitted to Hollywood Presbyterian Hospital, where he'll be kept under observation for the next three days.

McKeever, who was out on his feet for the better part of the quarter, will undergo an electro-encephalogram test today to determine "some reason for the injury," according to Dr. John Perry, the team physician.

**Brother's Injury**

Although Ram officials are hopeful that McKeever will have a normal recovery from the concussion and be back in the lineup in a few weeks, they are mindful of the head injury that ended the football career of Mike McKeever, Marlin's twin brother.

Mike, who was a star lineman along with Marlin at USC, suffered a head injury in his senior year (1960) which ruled out his further participation in football.

The Rams owned the draft rights to Mike, as well as Marlin, but would not sign him to a contract when he announced his intention of playing pro football a few years ago. This decision was made after Mike underwent additional physical examinations at the behest of the Rams.

Marlin, a five-year veteran who was shifted from linebacker to tight end last season, has been the rage of training camp this summer. His blocking and pass catching have been superb and Ram coaches have candidly admitted that he could be the best tight end in the league.

He was replaced by Bill Truax Sunday after it was ruled he had dropped—many observers felt he had retained possession—a crucial third-down pass from quarterback Bill Munson.

"We had a hard time keeping him on the sidelines in the second half," said a Ram spokesman. "He was determined to get back in the game."

After the game, Marlin could not remember the date or his coming to the Coliseum Sunday. It was then that Dr. Perry ordered his hospitalization.

As for the game itself, the Rams constructed a 9-0 lead and then frittered it away before a crowd of 29,580.

Chronologically, it was 9-0, 9-7 at halftime, 12-14 after three quarters and, finally, 19-21.

The Rams were still very much in the game in the final period when they trailed

Please Turn to Pg. 2, Col. 3

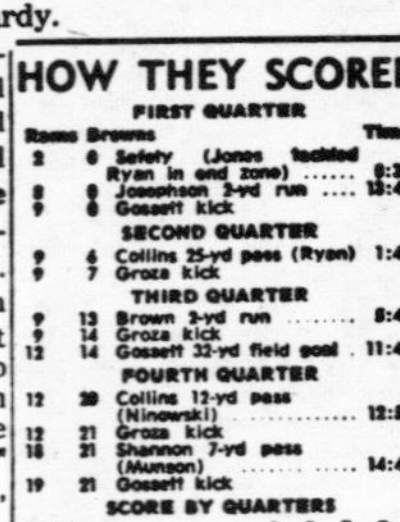

### HOW THEY SCORED

| Rams | Browns | | Time |
|---|---|---|---|
| FIRST QUARTER | | | |
| 2 | 0 | Safety (Jones tackled Ryan in end zone) | 8:36 |
| 8 | 6 | Josephson 2-yd run | 13:42 |
| 9 | 6 | Gossett kick | |
| SECOND QUARTER | | | |
| 9 | 6 | Collins 25-yd pass (Ryan) | 1:48 |
| 9 | 7 | Groza kick | |
| THIRD QUARTER | | | |
| 9 | 13 | Brown 2-yd run | 8:46 |
| 9 | 14 | Groza kick | |
| 12 | 14 | Gossett 32-yd field goal | 11:44 |
| FOURTH QUARTER | | | |
| 12 | 20 | Collins 12-yd pass (Ninowski) | 12:54 |
| 12 | 21 | Groza kick | |
| 18 | 21 | Shannon 7-yd pass (Munson) | 14:48 |
| 19 | 21 | Gossett kick | |

SCORE BY QUARTERS

| | | | | |
|---|---|---|---|---|
| Cleveland | 0 | 7 | 7 | 7—21 |
| Los Angeles | 9 | 0 | 3 | 7—19 |

### TODAY IN SPORTS

HORSE RACING—Del Mar, first post 2 p.m.

WRESTLING—Pasadena Arena, 8 p.m.

RADIO-TELEVISION

BASEBALL — Cleveland vs. Angels, KMPC, 8 p.m.; Dodgers at New York, KFI, KWKW, 5 p.m.

GOLF — Carling World Golf, Sutton, Mass., Channel 2, 4-6 p.m.

UMP CLOSES IN . . . As umpire Shag Crawford rushes in, Roseboro stumbles out of the way, leaving a visibly distressed Koufax a rather helpless target.

. . . TO GRAB MARICHAL—Wrestling with Marichal, Crawford tries to protect Koufax and Jim Gilliam from the fury of violence that injured Roseboro. UPI Telephotos

## Mays Breaks Up the Fight ---and the Ball Game, 4-3

BY FRANK FINCH
Times Staff Writer

SAN FRANCISCO — When Willie Mays wasn't breaking up a fight on the field Sunday, he was busy breaking up the Dodgers with his booming home-run bat.

Willie's fourth home run of the series, coming with two on in the third inning, resulted in a 4-3 loss for Sandy Koufax, whose heralded mound duel with Juan Marichal ended in confusion and disorder in the third when Marichal struck Dodger catcher John Roseboro with his bat.

Marichal's rash act, which brought about his ejection from the game, precipitated a mob scene that held up the game for 14 minutes and had a capacity crowd of 42,807 on edge as a general brawl threatened to break out.

In a role of peacemaker, Capt. Mays twice helped restrain the enraged Roseboro from getting back at Marichal, and in a touching tableau Willie tenderly wiped blood from Roseboro's forehead, which was cut when Juan swung his bat at him after they got into a dispute at the plate.

Lou Johnson, Howie Reed and coach Danny Ozark also had to be restrained by cooler heads during the melee. Big Willie McCovey once had Johnson in a bear hug, but Lou kept coming back for more, although he didn't harm anyone.

Earlier in the game, Marichal had decked Maury Wills and Ron Fairly the second time they came to bat after getting hits the first trip.

Koufax "retaliated" with a token fast ball that sailed far over Mays' head in the second inning, but there's no bad blood between these great players.

"I admire Marichal as a pitcher, but I'm more afraid of Mays," said Koufax (21-5), who had a four-game winning streak snapped.

In the excitement, the

Please Turn to Pg. 4, Col. 3

## BASEBALL STANDINGS

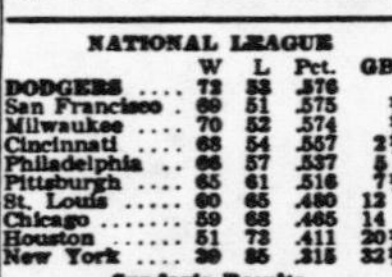

NATIONAL LEAGUE

| | W | L | Pct. | GBL |
|---|---|---|---|---|
| DODGERS | 72 | 53 | .576 | |
| San Francisco | 69 | 51 | .575 | ½ |
| Milwaukee | 70 | 52 | .574 | ½ |
| Cincinnati | 68 | 54 | .557 | 2½ |
| Philadelphia | 66 | 57 | .537 | 5 |
| Pittsburgh | 65 | 61 | .516 | 7½ |
| St. Louis | 60 | 65 | .480 | 12 |
| Chicago | 59 | 68 | .465 | 14 |
| Houston | 51 | 73 | .411 | 20½ |
| New York | 39 | 85 | .315 | 32½ |

**Sunday's Results**

San Francisco 4, DODGERS 3
Pittsburgh 5, Milwaukee 4 (11 innings)
Chicago 3, Houston 1
Philadelphia 6, Cincinnati 5
New York 7-4, St. Louis 5-2

**Today's Schedule**

DODGERS (Drysdale, 16-11) at New York (Miller, 1-2), KFI, KWKW, 5 p.m.

San Francisco (Perry, 8-10 or Spahn, 5-14) at Pittsburgh (Law, 14-8), night.

Cincinnati (Maloney, 14-6) at Milwaukee (Johnson, 13-8), night.

Chicago (Jackson, 11-15) at St. Louis (Simmons, 8-11), night.

Only games scheduled.

AMERICAN LEAGUE

| | W | L | Pct. | GBL |
|---|---|---|---|---|
| Minnesota | 79 | 46 | .632 | |
| Chicago | 71 | 51 | .582 | 6½ |
| Detroit | 70 | 53 | .569 | 8 |
| Baltimore | 67 | 53 | .558 | 9½ |
| Cleveland | 68 | 54 | .557 | 9½ |
| New York | 63 | 61 | .508 | 15½ |
| ANGELS | 56 | 68 | .452 | 22½ |
| Washington | 54 | 70 | .435 | 24½ |
| Boston | 45 | 78 | .366 | 33 |
| Kansas City | 41 | 80 | .339 | 36 |

**Sunday's Results**

ANGELS 4, Minnesota 3
Cleveland 3, Washington 0 (10 innings)
Detroit 2, Boston 1 (5⅔ innings, rain).
Chicago 8-2, Kansas City 2-1.
New York at Baltimore, doubleheader, postponed, rain.

**Today's Schedule**

Cleveland (Kralick, 5-9) vs. ANGELS (Lopez, 13-10), Dodger Stadium, KMPC, 8 p.m.

Detroit (Lolich, 11-6) at Kansas City (Krausse 1-0), night.

New York (Downing, 10-11) at Minnesota (Grant, 16-4), night.

Baltimore (Barber, 11-9) at Chicago (Buzhardt, 9-4), night.

Only games scheduled.

## JUAN MAY FACE ASSAULT CHARGES

Exclusive to The Times from the San Francisco Chronicle

SAN FRANCISCO — Dodger catcher John Roseboro indicated Sunday he may press criminal assault charges against San Francisco pitcher Juan Marichal for hitting him on the head with a baseball bat.

However, Roseboro added, "I just haven't decided what to do about it yet.

"I have no love for that man, and I don't believe in turning the other cheek; it's just not right to use a weapon on a man."

Herman Franks, manager of the Giants, said of the incident that flared into a free-for-all in the third inning of Sunday's game at Candlestick Park:

"Juan told me that when Roseboro threw the ball back to (Sandy) Koufax, it flicked his ear and that he turned to Roseboro and said, 'Why did you do that?' "

Two of Marichal's teammates, shotstop Tito Fuentes, who was only a few feet away in the on-deck circle, and Orlando Cepeda, on the bench, confirmed they heard Marichal ask the question. So did Willie Crawford, the Dodger outfielder.

Things obviously got tight on the Dodger bench after Maury Wills and Ron Fairly both hit the dirt on Marichal - thrown pitches in the third inning.

There was no doubt that Juan was trying to knock down Wills, who had beat out a bunt to open the game and scored the first

Please Turn to Pg. 4, Col. 6

## 'PUT HIM IN A ROOM WITH ME'---ROSEBORO

SAN FRANCISCO—John Roseboro, who was struck on his head by a bat wielded by San Francisco pitcher Juan Marichal Sunday, was asked what kind of penalty would be just for his assailant.

His reply: "He and I in a room together for about 10 minutes."

Here is Roseboro's version of the attack:

"When I threw the ball back to Koufax, Marichal told me I'd better not hit him with the ball. I certainly was close enough to hit him had I wanted to, but the ball didn't touch him.

"I took a step toward Marichal and that's when he began swinging his bat against my head. I don't know how many times he hit me because I don't remember much of what happened after his first swing. I was just trying to grab that bat.

"I do remember Willie Mays telling me my left eye was bleeding, and wiping my face. My eye was full of blood but it wasn't cut. Later on in the game, Mays came into our clubhouse to find out how I was.

"I'm not a great fan of Marichal. In fact, we're unfriendly."

To prevent untoward incidences, Roseboro and traveling secretary Lee Scott were escorted by two police officers from the dressing room to a taxi cab stand before the game ended and went directly to the airport.

# IT'S A PERFECT NIGHT AT DODGER STADIUM

## Koufax Becomes First Player to Pitch Four No-Hitters

### JIM MURRAY

## The Law Breaker

If the Pittsburgh Pirates win the 1965 National League pennant—and shop for a price if you think—don't bother to send champagne for the victory party. There won't be any.

And, if the Pittsburgh Pirates don't win the 1965 National League pennant, it will be because they won the 1960 N.L. pennant—and had a victory party.

It was on the bus back from the pennant-clinching win in Milwaukee. A few of the boys were whooping it up; the champagne was flowing, laced with beer. Elroy Face took his teeth out and put his hat on sideways, a quartet got going, off-key, in the back of the bus and everybody was happy.

Or, almost everybody. In a front seat, the team's most valuable member, the pitcher who was to win the Cy Young Award and beat the Yankees twice in the upcoming World Series, looked more like a guy who had just heard Paris fell.

When anyone sits this sombre in the midst of a gay party, you all know what the next scene is: some guy with a lampshade on his head and wearing a grass skirt, with his glasses fogged up, comes along and shouts, "Shay! You don't look like you're havin' fun!" And he empties a bottle of champagne over your new suit, or pushes you in the pool or dumps a giggling girl in your lap just as your wife enters the room.

#### *A Playful Yank Proved Expensive*

They didn't exactly do this to Vernon Sanders Law that September afternoon in 1960. But a utility player whose contribution to the victory that season could not be found without a microscope, came playfully up to Law and grabbed him by the foot. He gave it a yank—the most expensive leg pull in history. He not only sprained Law's ankle, he fractured Pittsburgh's pennant chances for four years.

Vernon Law pitched in the World Series, favoring an ankle that made him wince on every follow-through. What happened next is what always happens next when a pitcher favors an injured leg—the unnatural motion tore a rotator muscle in his shoulder. He beat the Yanks twice, but each pitch shortened his career. The next spring he showed up in camp with an arm so stiff and sore, it looked as if it were tacked on his side. The 20-game winner in 1960 became a 3-game winner in 1961. He pitched only 59 innings, but he had to clench his teeth to keep from screaming during most of them.

Vern Law occupies the same unique position on the Pittsburgh Pirates that Albie Pearson does on the Angels, Don Demeter on the Tigers, Bobby Richardson on the Yankees and a handful of other players around the leagues. He is a tither, a teetotaler. The Pirates call him "Deacon," because ballplayers call anybody "Deacon" who goes to church on Sundays and to bed before midnight.

#### *Profanity Cut to a Minimum*

Actually, Vern Law is an ordained Elder in the Mormon Church. The Pirates respect him for his beliefs even though they know if he wandered into Frankie's Band-Box saloon in Pittsburgh, it would be to use the phone or to get out of an earthquake. The profanity is cut to a minimum in his corner of the locker room where the scholarly Bob Veale and the abstemious Del Crandall also suit up. It is a section of the dressing room one of the players refers to affectionately as "The Monastery" and where he has recommended stained-glass windows for their shower.

Although Vern Law is the most expensive casualty of the post-pennant victory party, he is not the only one. In 1941, Leo Durocher's Brooklyn Dodgers were rolling south from Boston on the New York-New Haven-and-Hartford Railroad and the grape was flowing and the hats were on sideways. When the victory train rolled into 125th St. owner Larry MacPhail, never a man to pass up a drink, wanted to get aboard. "Drive on!" Leo instructed the trainmen. And they did—leaving MacPhail sputtering on the platform. Leo Durocher was the first manager ever to get fired while he was being carried off on the shoulders of his countrymen.

In 1960, when the Yankees celebrated winning their pennant, the pitcher, Ryne Duren, elected to push a lighted cigar into the mouth of a bullpen coach. The bullpen coach turned out to be Ralph Houk, and, the next season, Ralph Houk turned out to be the Yankee manager, and it turned out if he wanted to chew tobacco he didn't want it to be lighted, and Ryne Duren turned out to be on the Los Angeles roster by late spring.

Houk didn't get much for him, but rumor had it, he didn't want much for him—just a lot of geography. The feeling was Houk just traded him as far away as he could without a passport.

If the Pirates win this year, (and if they do, the biggest part of the reason will be the 16 games Law won this year between arm twinges) the victory party won't be bobbing for apples at the YMCA, or fruit punch and sarsparilla, but you can bet me that the Pirates' general manager, Joe Brown, will make sure anything his athletes do is not against the Law.

**Ralston Suffers Upset**

STORY ON PAGE 3

**HAPPY SANDY** — Dodgers' Sandy Koufax is congratulated by teammates Willie Davis and Ron Fairly moments after Sandy had completed hurling a perfect game agains tthe Chicago Cubs. It was Sandy's fourth major league no-hitter, an all-time baseball record. (AP) photo

## Hendley Loses, 1-0, on 1-Hitter

BY FRANK FINCH
Times Staff Writer

A Michelangelo among pitchers, Sandy Koufax produced his masterpiece Thursday night when he pitched a perfect no-hit, no-run game against the Chicago Cubs.

The score was a nervous 1-0, as Koufax's opponent, Bob Hendley, allowed Los Angeles only one hit in eight innings.

The game's sole tally was unearned.

Lou Johnson drew Hendley's only walk to begin the fifth inning. Sacrificed to second by Ron Fairly, the speedy outfielder then stole third base and kept on coming when catcher Chris Krug's hurried throw sailed into left field.

**Counting the House**

| | |
|---|---|
| Thursday's attendance | 29,139 |
| 1965 attendance, 65 dates | 2,077,238 |
| 1964 attendance, 65 dates | 2,021,112 |

Johnson also blooped a double in the seventh for the thriller's only hit.

**Huge Roar**

A crowd of 29,139 fans rocked Dodger Stadium with their roaring as Koufax struck out the last six batters for a total of 14—the 79th time in his career and the 18th time this season Sandy has fanned 10 or more batters in a game.

Koufax finally attained his 22nd victory after failing in five previous attempts and now leads both majors in wins and strikeouts. Juan Marichal of the Giants notched his 21st victory Thursday afternoon as the Giants remained a half-game ahead of Los Angeles and Cincinnati.

Tension in the last two innings was almost unbearable as the Cubs attacked Koufax in a vain effort to break his magic spell.

**Banks Fans**

In the eighth inning, he threw a called third strike past Ron Santo and sent Ernie Banks and rookie Byron Browne down swinging.

Now he needed just three more outs to become the first pitcher in history to record four no-hit games.

The first batter in the ninth was Krug, and he struck out swinging.

A tough pinch hitter, Joe Amalfitano, fanned on three serves.

**..... And It's Over**

Another crafty batsman, Harvey Kuenn, batted for Hendley. With a count of two balls and two strikes Kuenn swung viciously at a fast ball—and missed it by a mile.

Sandy danced off the

Please Turn to Pg. 2, Col. 4

## WOW!

| CHICAGO | ab | r | h | bi | LOS ANGELES | ab | r | h | bi |
|---|---|---|---|---|---|---|---|---|---|
| Young cf | 3 | 0 | 0 | 0 | Wills ss | 3 | 0 | 0 | 0 |
| Beckert 2b | 3 | 0 | 0 | 0 | Gilliam 3b | 3 | 0 | 0 | 0 |
| Williams rf | 3 | 0 | 0 | 0 | Kennedy 3b | 0 | 0 | 0 | 0 |
| Santo 3b | 3 | 0 | 0 | 0 | Davis cf | 3 | 0 | 0 | 0 |
| Banks 1b | 3 | 0 | 0 | 0 | Johnson lf | 2 | 1 | 1 | 0 |
| Browne lf | 3 | 0 | 0 | 0 | Fairly rf | 2 | 0 | 0 | 0 |
| Krug c | 3 | 0 | 0 | 0 | Lefebvre 2b | 3 | 0 | 0 | 0 |
| Kess'ger ss | 2 | 0 | 0 | 0 | T'cewski 2b | 0 | 0 | 0 | 0 |
| Am'f'ano ph | 1 | 0 | 0 | 0 | Parker 1b | 3 | 0 | 0 | 0 |
| Hendley p | 2 | 0 | 0 | 0 | Torborg c | 3 | 0 | 0 | 0 |
| Kuenn ph | 1 | 0 | 0 | 0 | Koufax p | 2 | 0 | 0 | 0 |
| Totals | 27 | 0 | 0 | 0 | Totals | 24 | 1 | 1 | 0 |

Chicago ........ 000 000 000—0
Los Angeles ........ 000 010 00x—1

E—Krug. LOB—Chicago 0, Los Angeles 1.
2B—Johnson. SB—Johnson. S—Fairly.

| | IP | H | R | ER | BB | SO |
|---|---|---|---|---|---|---|
| Hendley L, 2-3 ... | 8 | 1 | 1 | 0 | 1 | 3 |
| Koufax W, 22-7 .. | 9 | 0 | 0 | 0 | 0 | 14 |

T—1:43. A—29,139.

**Los Angeles Times**
**Sports**
PART III BUSINESS & FINANCE
CC FRIDAY MORNING, SEPTEMBER 10, 1965 2†

## Alston Would Prefer Twins to White Sox

BY CHARLES MAHER
Times Staff Writer

Walter Alston inspected the remaining National League schedule and conceded at once that Pittsburgh, among the five contenders, has the best of it on paper.

But Wlter Alston doesn't believe everything he reads on paper.

The Pirates have 19 games left. Except for three with Cincinnati this week, they're all against second-division teams.

"I don't think that means a helluva lot," the Dodger manager said. "For one thing, there's not that much difference between the top clubs and the rest of them, with maybe one or two exceptions.

"Like I've said before, I'd rather have my own club going good and playing the best of them than have it going not so good and playing the weaker ones. If you're not going good, about any of them can beat you."

Alston was asked which of the other four contenders concerns him most.

"Milwaukee has been the toughest for us to beat," he said. "But I think I'd agree with what Tom Haller (the San Francisco catcher) said the other day—that Cincinnati has the best balance."

The Dodgers, of course, are not without arresting attributes themselves. They have pitching and speed. Moreover, they have successfully inverted the formula of their gasoline sponsors and are eminently entitled to acclaim as the team that took the Pow! out of Power.

If their attack should develop enough thrust to put them in the World Series, Aston would rather have them play the Minnesota Twins than the Chicago White Sox. Minnesota's power worries him less than Chicago's lack of it.

"With our pitching," he said, "I'd just as soon play the hard-hitting club. Turning it around the oth-

Please Turn to Pg. 3, Col. 3

## Juan Cheered, Whips Astros for No. 21, 4-0

SAN FRANCISCO (AP) — Right-hander Juan Marichal made his first start in San Francisco's Candlestick Park since his Aug. 22 battle with John Roseboro and hurled the National League-leading Giants to a 4-0 triumph over Houston.

The crowd of 20,076 cheered Marichal when he went out for his pre-game warm-up and when he faced the first Houston batter.

Marichal notched his 21st victory of the campaign and his 10th shutout, limiting the Astros to four hits.

The Giants won their sixth straight, jumping into a two-run lead in the second inning on a walk to Willie McCovey, a triple by Len Gabrielson and Tom Haller's sacrifice fly.

| HOUSTON | ab | r | h | bi | SAN FRANCISCO | ab | r | h | bi |
|---|---|---|---|---|---|---|---|---|---|
| Maye lf | 4 | 0 | 0 | 0 | Schofield ss | 4 | 1 | 1 | 0 |
| Morgan 2b | 4 | 0 | 0 | 0 | J.Alou rf | 4 | 0 | 1 | 1 |
| Wynn cf | 3 | 0 | 1 | 0 | Mays cf | 3 | 0 | 0 | 0 |
| Bond 1b | 4 | 0 | 1 | 0 | Hend'son cf | 1 | 0 | 0 | 0 |
| Aspro'te 3b | 3 | 0 | 0 | 0 | McCovey 1b | 2 | 1 | 1 | 0 |
| Staub rf | 3 | 0 | 1 | 0 | Hart 3b | 3 | 0 | 0 | 0 |
| Brand c | 1 | 0 | 0 | 0 | G'br'ls'n lf | 3 | 1 | 1 | 1 |
| Adlesh c | 2 | 0 | 1 | 0 | Haller c | 2 | 1 | 1 | 2 |
| Kasko ss | 3 | 0 | 0 | 0 | Lanier 2b | 3 | 0 | 0 | 0 |
| Bruce p | 2 | 0 | 0 | 0 | Marichal p | 3 | 0 | 0 | 0 |
| Gentile ph | 1 | 0 | 0 | 0 | | | | | |
| Totals | 30 | 0 | 4 | 0 | Totals | 28 | 4 | 5 | 4 |

Houston ........ 000 000 000—0
San Francisco ........ 020 020 00x—4

Errors—None. DP—San Francisco 1. LOB—Houston 4, San Francisco 2.
2B—Schofield, Wynn. 3B—Gabrielson. HR—Haller (12). SB—Wynn. SF—Haller.

| | IP | H | R | ER | BB | SO |
|---|---|---|---|---|---|---|
| Bruce L, 9-18 .... | 7 | 5 | 4 | 4 | 1 | 4 |
| Raymond ........ | 1 | 0 | 0 | 0 | 0 | 2 |
| Marichal W, 21-10 | 9 | 4 | 0 | 0 | 1 | 5 |

WP—Bruce 2. T—1:55. A—20,076.

## TODAY IN SPORTS

**HORSE RACING**—Del Mar, first post 2 p.m.

**BASEBALL**—Houston vs. Dodgers, Dodger Stadium, 8 p.m.

**MOTORCYCLE RACING** — Ascot Park, National AMA 8-mile qualifying, novice program, 7 p.m.

**AUTO RACING** — Southgate Raceway, NMRA midgets, 8 p.m.

**RADIO-TELEVISION**

**BASEBALL** — Angels at Washington, KMPC, 5 p.m.; Houston vs. Dodgers, KFI, KWKW, 8 p.m.

ALL AGREED

## Even Koufax Admits Game 'Nearly Perfect'

BY CHARLES MAHER
Times Staff Writer

Sandy Koufax is normally as modest and unassuming as Clark Kent, but even he had to agree with the scorebook, which said the game he pitched against the Chicago Cubs Thursday night was nearly perfect.

"You mean," someone asked, "that there wasn't a pitch you didn't want back right after you threw it?"

"No," Koufax said, "I don't think so. Well, there was one I threw to Byron Browne in the second inning that I didn't want back as soon as I let it go. But I wanted it back after he hit it."

**Four No-Hitters**

Browne hit it on a line to center fielder Willie Davis, coming as close as the Cubs got to a hit all night.

Koufax has pitched a no-hitter a year for four seasons and he said this one gave him more satisfaction than the first two (against the Mets and the Giants) and as much as the third (against Philadelphia).

He conceded the fourth one should be most gratifying because no one else has ever pitched more than three. "But the third," he said, "was equally thrilling."

**Good Fastball**

"I think the stuff I had tonight was the best I've had all season," he said. "I had a real good fastball, and that sort of helps your curve. I thought the fastball was really working best the last three innings.

"You always know when you've got a no-hitter going, but you don't particularly pay attention to it early in the game. In the seventh, I really started to feel as though I had a shot at it.

"But I still had only one run to work on. I still had to win the game."

Koufax offered his sympathy to Bob Hendley, who followed the Dodgers only one hit, the bloop double in the seventh by Lou Johnson.

**Unearned Run**

The hit would have been meaningless if it hadn't broken up Hendley's no-hitter because the Dodgers scored their only run two innings before on a walk, a sacrifice, a stolen base by Johnson and a throwing error by catcher Chris Krug on Johnson's steal.

"It's a shame Hendley had to get beaten that way," Koufax said. "But I'm glad we got the run or we might have been here all night."

**Wanted Hit**

Koufax came closest to losing his perfect game in the seventh, when he went three balls and no strikes to Billy Williams.

"I threw him two curves low," Sandy said, "and then I was high with a fastball."

Williams was asked if he was looking for a walk at this point.

"I was looking for a base

Please Turn to Pg. 4, Col. 1

## BASEBALL STANDINGS

**NATIONAL LEAGUE**

| | W | L | Pct. | GBL |
|---|---|---|---|---|
| San Francisco . | 79 | 59 | .572 | |
| **DODGERS** .... | **80** | **61** | **.567** | **½** |
| Cincinnati .... | 80 | 61 | .567 | ½ |
| Milwaukee .... | 77 | 62 | .554 | 2½ |
| Pittsburgh .... | 77 | 66 | .538 | 4½ |
| Philadelphia .. | 71 | 68 | .511 | 8½ |
| St. Louis ..... | 70 | 71 | .496 | 10½ |
| Chicago ....... | 65 | 77 | .458 | 16 |
| Houston ...... | 60 | 81 | .426 | 20½ |
| New York .... | 45 | 98 | .315 | 36½ |

**Thursday's Results**

**DODGERS 1,** Chicago 0
Cincinnati 3, New York 2
Philadelphia at Milwaukee, postponed, rain
San Francisco 4, Houston 0
Only games scheduled

**Today's Schedule**

Houston (Roberts, 9-8) vs. **DODGERS** (Drysdale, 18-12), Dodger Stadium, KFI, KWKW, 8 p.m.

Milwaukee (Blasingame, 16-9) at New York (Fisher, 8-19), night.

St. Louis (Gibson, 17-10) at Philadelphia (Short, 16-9), night.

Cincinnati (Jay, 9-6) at Pittsburgh (Veale, 15-10), night.

Chicago (Ellsworth, 13-13) at San Francisco (Herbel, 9-7), night.

**AMERICAN LEAGUE**

| | W | L | Pct. | GBL |
|---|---|---|---|---|
| Minnesota .... | 89 | 54 | .622 | |
| Chicago ...... | 82 | 61 | .573 | 7 |
| Baltimore ..... | 80 | 60 | .571 | 7½ |
| Cleveland .... | 77 | 63 | .550 | 10½ |
| Detroit ....... | 78 | 64 | .549 | 10½ |
| New York .... | 69 | 75 | .479 | 21½ |
| **ANGELS** ..... | **66** | **77** | **.462** | **23** |
| Washington .. | 62 | 80 | .437 | 26½ |
| Boston ....... | 56 | 87 | .392 | 28 |
| Kansas City ... | 51 | 89 | .364 | 36½ |

**Thursday's Results**

**ANGELS 7,** Kansas City 2
Minnesota 10, Chicago 4
Only games scheduled

**Today's Schedule**

**ANGELS** (Brunet, 8-10) at Washington (Richert, 12-10), KMPC, 5 p.m.

Kansas City (Sheldon, 7-7 and Hunter, 6-6) at Baltimore (Pappas, 12-7 and J. Miller, 6-3), twi-night doubleheader.

Minnesota (Perry, 9-6) at Boston (Lonborg, 9-15), night.

Detroit (Lolich, 11-8) at Cleveland (Siebert, 14-6), night.

New York (Stottlemyre, 16-8) at Chicago (Peters, 9-11), night.

## Versalles, Desire Make Twins Tick

BY JOHN HALL
Times Staff Writer

CHICAGO — What puts the tick-tick in the American League time bomb known as the Minnesota Twins?

Al Campanis, L.A. Operator 007 whom the Dodgers dispatched here to investigate the lonely leaders in their latest moment of truth with the White Sox, opened his case full of charts and diagrams Thursday and delivered a preliminary diagnosis.

"Zoilo Versalles, underrated pitching, timely hitting and big desire," capsuled the chief of the Dodger scouts.

"But without Harmon Killebrew their power isn't overwhelming, their defense is average and they have real speed in only a couple of spots," he said.

"If the Dodgers can make it home in the National, it's going to be interesting to see what our pitching can do to their hitting. Dodger Stadium isn't going to help the Twins."

Without saying directly, Campanis gave the impression he agreed with the general suspicion that winning the World Series will be a much better bet for the Dodgers than surviving in the National League.

Nonetheless, the Twins continue to demonstrate they are tough to master.

Making it a two-in-a-row sweep over the suddenly flat and fractured Sox with a 10-4 death rattle Thursday, Minnesota moved a safe seven jumps ahead of Chicago and 7½ in front of the idle Baltimore and impressively erased all remaining doubts.

Sam Mele's lineup was the same for both battles at Comiskey Park, and it will probably be the same for the World Series opener Oct. 6 in Metropolitan Sta-

Please Turn to Pg. 4, Col. 3

# SANDY'S THE GREATEST--DODGERS WIN IT!

## Alston Leans to Left and Koufax Proves He's Right, 2-0

PART III BUSINESS & FINANCE

CC FRIDAY MORNING, OCTOBER 15, 1965 †

### JIM MURRAY

### Worker of Art

MINNEAPOLIS-ST. PAUL—If you want someone to play piano for you, get Horowitz.

Need a doctor? Get Jonas Salk's exchange on the phone. You want to win a golf bet, get Sam Snead for a partner.

If you want a conductor, try Leonard Bernstein. Heifetz will do on the violin. If you want to dance, see if Fred Astaire is busy. Want someone to sing nice, just hand the music to Andy Williams.

But if you want to win a pennant or a World Series, just hand the ball to Sanford Koufax. He gave a performance here Thursday afternoon that should go to Carnegie Hall. Or Westminster Abbey.

A Koufax-pitched game is a work of art, a tribute to the craftsmanship of Man—like the Kohinoor diamond or a Greek statue.

There have been lots of good pitchers. Even a few great ones. There are lots of diamonds, too. Quite a few people paint pictures for calendars. Just owning a curve ball doesn't make you a great pitcher. Just like an easel doesn't get you in the Louvre.

#### 'Genius' of Pitching

If such a word is possible in what is, after all, just a game, I would have to say Sandy Koufax is a "genius" at pitching. I think he rolled out of bed one morning with his fast ball, just the way Sam Snead did with his golf swing. You can't teach a guy a fast ball. If he's not born with it, he has to learn a knuckle-ball or a spitter —or take up parcheesi.

Sandy Koufax has long fingers, tremendous pride and back muscles that enable him to propel a baseball 60 feet 6 inches as fast or faster than anyone in history. The same physical attributes enable him to break off a curve that drops over the plate like an Indian falling off a horse.

He has now won 142 baseball games in his career. He has pitched four no-hitters. You can't hit his curve ball. You can't even hear his fast ball. He has now struck out 2,138 batters in his career. He struck out 29 of them in the past seven days.

What makes Sandy Koufax great is the same thing that made Walter Johnson great. The team behind him is the ghostliest-scoring team in history. They pile up runs at the rate of one every nine innings. This is a little like making Rembrandt paint on the back of cigar boxes, giving Paderewski a piano with only two octaves, Caruso singing with a high school chorus. With the Babe Ruth Yankees, Sandy Koufax would probably have been the first undefeated pitcher in history.

#### Walter's Wonderful Problem

The manager of the Dodgers, Walter Alston, woke up Thursday morning with a terrible problem: he didn't know whether to go with Drysdale or Koufax. This is the kind of terrible problem every manager in major leagues would like to have. It's like trying to decide whether to date Elizabeth Taylor or Jane Fonda, whether to buy a Cadillac or a Continental or Imperial, whether to take a million dollars in cash or stocks.

You are not exactly handing the world championship

Please Turn to Pg. 4, Col. 2

### Johnson's Home Run Decisive

BY FRANK FINCH
Times Staff Writer

MINNEAPOLIS-ST. PAUL—The man with the million-dollar arm, Sandy Koufax, pitched like a million dollars again Thursday as the Los Angeles Dodgers won their third world championship.

With another of his incredible performances, the southpaw nonpareil defeated the Minnesota Twins, 2-0, allowing three hits after only two days' rest. Sandy also blitzed the Twins last Monday in Los Angeles, 7-0, and in each game he struck out 10 batters.

The Dodgers wrapped it up with a fourth-inning flurry against Jim Kaat when the Cinderella Man, Lou Johnson, jolted his second home run of the series, followed by Ron Fairly's two-bagger and Wes Parker's single.

It was the 101st victory of a long and rugged season for the team that overcame a staggering string of injuries that would have made a lesser team roll over and be counted out.

As late as Sept. 16 L.A. trailed the Giants by 4½. Then Smokey Alston's troops stormed through a 13-game winning streak to pass the Giants and win the pennant by two lengths.

#### Historic Rally

Another rally was necessary, however, when the Twins stunned the Dodgers by taking the first two games of the Series.

In 61 previous Series, only three teams had survived losses in the first two contests and come back to win a seven-game series.

The first was Alston's Brooklyn Dodgers in 1955, and the New York Yankees accomplished the feat in 1956 and 1958.

Although beaten in the second game by Kaat, Koufax won a Chevrolet Corvette, courtesy of Sports Magazine, which annually honors the outstanding player in the Series. Sandy also won the award in 1963 by beating the Yankees twice.

When the announcement was made, a press-box inmate quipped, "Sandy can use the Chevvy to stand on when he's washing his Rolls-Royce."

#### Shaky Start

While posting his 28th victory and 10th shutout of the year, Koufax was so good that the heavy-hitting Twins, who use Metropolitan Stadium for target practice, managed to get only three runners as far as second base.

In a shaky first inning Koufax walked Tony Oliva and Harmon Killebrew with two out, and by then Don Drysdale, whose turn it was to start, hurriedly heated up in the bull pen.

Don sat down when Koufax struck out Earl Battey, but began throwing again in the third after Zoilo Versalles got his eighth hit with one out.

Zoilo stole second base, but umpire Ed Hurley ruled that the batter, Joe Nossek, inter-

Please Turn to Pg. 2, Col. 3

THE LOOK THAT CHILLS—This is the way dazzling Sandy Koufax looked to Minnesota batters Thursday as he finished off Twins with 2-0 three-hitter. It was his 2nd Series shutout in four days.
(AP) Wirephoto

### All the Way on One Pitch

BY PAUL ZIMMERMAN
Times Staff Writer

MINNEAPOLIS-ST. PAUL—It isn't often a man can win the World Series deciding game with only a fast ball, but that's exactly what Sandy Koufax did at the expense of the power-laden Twins here Thursday.

"It can't be done unless you are exceptional," praised John Roseboro who was catching him, "and Sandy is the most exceptional pitcher in the game today."

"I didn't have a curve ball at all," explained the great southpaw after he had held Minnesota to three hits and shut them out, 2-0.

"When I threw it I couldn't get it over. And those first few innings I really didn't know how long I was going to last.

#### Second Wind

"Then I seemed to get my second wind. In the last three the fastball seemed to move better and I felt I got stronger."

He was strong enough to strike out Earl Battey and Bob Allison—two of the big guns on the Twins—to close out the game in the ninth.

Asked if he had had other days when his curve ball was missing and he had depended on the fastball Koufax said:

"Yes, but if I had a choice I'd rather not have it happen in a World Series, like it did to me today."

"I was worried in the fifth and again in the sixth when I seemed to lose my rhythm. When Walt (Alston) came out to talk to me he told me not to try and get anything extra on the ball, just pitch to the spots."

"I didn't ever come close to taking him out of there," said the Dodger manager

Please Turn to Pg. 4, Col. 5

### THE KOufax PUNCH

| Minnesota | AB | R | H | BI | PO | A |
|---|---|---|---|---|---|---|
| Versalles, ss | 4 | 0 | 1 | 0 | 0 | 2 |
| Nossek, cf | 4 | 0 | 0 | 0 | 0 | 0 |
| Oliva, rf | 3 | 0 | 0 | 0 | 4 | 0 |
| Killebrew, 3b | 3 | 0 | 1 | 0 | 2 | 2 |
| Battey, c | 4 | 0 | 0 | 0 | 8 | 1 |
| Allison, lf | 4 | 0 | 0 | 0 | 1 | 0 |
| Mincher, 1b | 3 | 0 | 0 | 0 | 10 | 0 |
| Quilici, 2b | 3 | 0 | 1 | 0 | 1 | 3 |
| Kaat, p | 1 | 0 | 0 | 0 | 0 | 1 |
| Worth'gton, p | 0 | 0 | 0 | 0 | 1 | 1 |
| Rollins | 0 | 0 | 0 | 0 | 0 | 0 |
| Klippstein, p | 0 | 0 | 0 | 0 | 0 | 0 |
| Merritt, p | 0 | 0 | 0 | 0 | 0 | 0 |
| Valdespino | 1 | 0 | 0 | 0 | 0 | 0 |
| Perry, p | 0 | 0 | 0 | 0 | 0 | 0 |
| TOTALS | 30 | 0 | 3 | 0 | 27 | 10 |

| Los Angeles | AB | R | H | BI | PO | A |
|---|---|---|---|---|---|---|
| Wills, ss | 4 | 0 | 0 | 0 | 2 | 4 |
| Gilliam, 3b | 5 | 0 | 2 | 0 | 2 | 1 |
| Kennedy, 3b | 0 | 0 | 0 | 0 | 0 | 1 |
| W. Davis, cf | 2 | 0 | 0 | 0 | 1 | 0 |
| Johnson, lf | 4 | 1 | 1 | 1 | 3 | 0 |
| Fairly, rf | 4 | 1 | 1 | 0 | 0 | 0 |
| Parker, 1b | 4 | 0 | 2 | 1 | 6 | 0 |
| Tracewski, 2b | 4 | 0 | 0 | 0 | 1 | 0 |
| Roseboro, c | 2 | 0 | 1 | 0 | 12 | 0 |
| Koufax, p | 3 | 0 | 0 | 0 | 0 | 1 |
| TOTALS | 32 | 2 | 7 | 2 | 27 | 7 |

Rollins walked for Worthington in 5th.
Valdespino fouled out for Merritt in 8th.

**SCORE BY INNINGS**

| | | | | |
|---|---|---|---|---|
| Los Angeles (N) | 000 | 200 | 000 | —2 |
| Minnesota (A) | 000 | 000 | 000 | —0 |

E—Oliva. LOB—Los Angeles 9, Minnesota 6. 2B—Roseboro, Fairly, Quilici. 3B—Parker. HR—Johnson. S—W. Davis.

| | IP | H | R | ER | BB | SO |
|---|---|---|---|---|---|---|
| Koufax (W) | 9 | 3 | 0 | 0 | 3 | 10 |
| Kaat (L) | 3 | 5 | 2 | 2 | 1 | 2 |
| Worthington | 2 | 0 | 0 | 0 | 1 | 0 |
| Klippstein | 1 2/3 | 2 | 0 | 0 | 1 | 2 |
| Merritt | 1 1/3 | 0 | 0 | 0 | 0 | 1 |
| Perry | 1 | 0 | 0 | 0 | 1 | 1 |

Kaat faced 3 men in 4th.

### Lakers Trade Barnett

STORY ON PAGE 4.

LAMENT OF A LOSER

### 'Koufax Good, but Dodgers Kind of Lucky', Says Zoilo Versalles

BY CHARLES MAHER
Times Staff Writer

MINNEAPOLIS - ST. PAUL — Zoilo Versalles, Minnesota's most valuable player, took the outcome of the World Series the way he plays the game. Hard.

The skinny little shortstop from Cuba talked with reporters awhile, then walked idly around the clubhouse, wearing nothing but a look of despair.

"Koufax was good today," he said, "but the Dodgers were kind of lucky."

#### Sad Story

Versalles offered several examples of Dodger luck:

With one away in the third, Versalles singled. Then, with Joe Nossek at bat, Zoilo took out for second base. He appeared to have it stolen easily, but Nossek was declared out for interfering with catcher John Roseboro's throw to second.

So, instead of having a runner on second with one away, the Twins had a runner on first with two out. The next man, Tony Oliva, struck out.

"How could you get more lucky than that?" Versalles asked.

With one away in the Minnesota fifth, Frank Quilici doubled and pinch hitter Rich Rollins walked. Versalles then ripped a ball down the third base line. Jim Gilliam made an extraordinary stop and stepped on third for a forceout. Nossek hit into another force play and the Twins were out.

"On the ball I hit," Versalles said, "the third baseman doesn't even know he has it in his glove. If it goes through, that's the end for Koufax. Their manager has talked to him and is about ready to take him out."

A writer suggested Versalles might have had a two-run double if Gilliam hadn't stopped the ball.

"Two runs easy," Zoilo said, "and then we win the game. But the guy made a helluva play. And there goes the ball game, right there."

The Dodgers had scored both their runs in the fourth. Lou Johnson led off with a home run. The ball hit the left-field foul pole.

"It was fair by that much," Versalles said, holding two fingers an inch apart.

Zoilo said there was also

Please Turn to Pg. 3, Col. 3

### TODAY IN SPORTS

HORSE RACING—Hollywood Park, first post 1 p.m.

MOTORCYCLE RACING — Ascot Park, AMA flat track program, 8:15 p.m.

GOLF SHOW—Dodger Stadium, noon to 11 p.m.

RADIO-TELEVISION

FOOTBALL — Mt. San Antonio vs. Orange Coast, Channel 13, 8 p.m.

HOCKEY—Blades vs. San Francisco, Channel 5, 8:30 p.m.

BASKETBALL—Lakers vs. San Francisco, Channel 11, 8:30 p.m.

THE HOT CORNER—Jim Gilliam, Dodger third baseman, makes diving stop of Zoilo Versalles' grounder in 5th inning of Thursday's game and scrambles back to force Frank Quilici, snuffing out Twin rally.

# H-A-P-P-Y NEW YEAR! BRUINS WIN, 14-12

**CATCH AS CATCH CAN**—Kurt Altenberg makes an incredible catch of a Gary Beban pass to set up UCLA's second touchdown. The play covered 27 yards to the 1-yard line. Another view is shown in box below.
Times photos by Larry Sharkey and Ben Olender

SECTION D

CC SUNDAY, JANUARY 2, 1966 2†

## JIM MURRAY

© 1966 LOS ANGELES TIMES

## Mice Turn on the Cat

There were over 100,000 people who came to the Rose Bowl New Year's Day to see UCLA get thrown to the lions. Instead, they saw Michigan State get thrown to the mice.

If you check the neck of Michigan State fullback, Bob Apisa — if you can find a neck on that torso — you will find the fingerprints of a UCLA tackler named Jim Colletto on it. Another tackler named Bob Stiles got a slight concussion on the play and Michigan State isn't feeling too good either.

Bob Apisa, who came all the way from Samoa to play at Michigan State, will have a lot of explaining to do at the next luau. He sat down abruptly about two yards from the Hall of Fame.

It was a finish right out of a 1929 Richard Arlen movie. All it needed was Toby Wing fainting on the sidelines.

UCLA crushed Michigan State by two whole points. That made them 16 points better than the gamblers made them. I say "crushed" because when you beat the Big 10 in the Rose Bowl, you can be said to crush them if you tie. There are certain things not meant to occur in nature. The sun shows up at the same place every day, the horizon is fixed, the Pope goes to the Catholic church, husbands and wives fight—and the Big 10 wins in the Rose Bowl.

### *Touted as Greatest Thing Since '40 Bears*

They came here touted as the greatest thing in cleats since the 1940 Chicago Bears but they were like a cat watching the wrong mouse hole all day. UCLA decided early the only thing it could get trying to look them in the eye was a crick in the neck. Michigan State had altitude, latitude—the only thing they didn't have most of the day was the ball. Their quarterback was like a guy who kept trying to make a pair of treys stand up through three raises in a no-limit poker game. He kept throwing the ball when the only receivers still upright were in blue uniforms. He was either color blind or nervous.

Their safety man also tried for a 95-yard touchdown run with a punt once. He missed by 95½ yards but he couldn't have made it anyway because he forgot the ball. By the time he located it, there were two UCLA players lying on it.

UCLA, which had never won a Rose Bowl game, was held scoreless by Michigan State, which had never lost one, for all but the first 3 minutes and 10 seconds of the second quarter. UCLA held Michigan State scoreless for 50 minutes but they were beginning to turn blue from holding their finger in the dike as the shadows lengthened. The clock was the biggest star on the field most of the fourth quarter.

The game was a real mismatch as predicted for three quarters. The only switch was, Michigan State was the miss and UCLA was the match. The canaries were

Please Turn to Pg. 8, Col. 1

## UCLA's Inspired Defense Stuns Top-Rated Spartans

BY PAUL ZIMMERMAN
Times Sports Editor

Someone forgot to tell UCLA that Michigan State was the No. 1 football team in the nation.

Coach Tommy Prothro's Bruins out-fought, out-scrambled and out-scored the highly-vaunted Spartans, 14-12, before 100,087 startled spectators in the Rose Bowl on a beautiful New Year's Day.

UCLA got its two touchdowns in the second quarter and then staved off a typical Michigan State fourth-quarter comeback to win its first game in this classic after five unsuccessful efforts.

For coach Duffy Daugherty's previously undefeated Spartans, favored by two touchdowns, it was their first loss in three trips to Pasadena.

The torrid contest—which was won up front, as the coaches say — went right down to the last 30 seconds for a decision as desperate Michigan State gambled for two points after each of its belated touchdowns and failed both times.

Certainly it was one of the greatest games in the series of 52 in this daddy of all post-season gridiron classics.

The gracious Bruin coach said after the game that "Michigan State is still the No. 1 team in the nation," but he would have trouble getting a second to the motion from the throng which saw it go down in defeat Saturday.

Sure, the Spartans gained

Please Turn to Pg. 4, Col. 3

**LSU ENDS ARKANSAS WIN STREAK, 14-7**

STORY ON PAGE 7

**Alabama Passes Gun Down Nebraska, 39-28**

STORY ON PAGE 6

**MISSOURI HOLDS ON TO WIN SUGAR BOWL**

STORY ON PAGE 8

**Packers, Browns Battle for NFL Crown Today**

STORY ON PAGE 9

**BRUINS ON THE BALL**—UCLA's Dallas Grider is ready to pounce upon an on-side kick perfectly executed by Kurt Zimmerman in second quarter. The ball was recovered on the Michigan State 42-yard line and UCLA scored five plays later. No. 82 is Wade Pearson. At left is MSU's Joe Przybycki.
Times photo by Art Rogers

# WHAT AN ENDING! LONGDEN BY A NOSE

BY BION ABBOTT
Times Staff Writer

Somebody up there must have written the script.

It couldn't happen this side of a movie studio, but it did. And there are 60,792 witnesses who can testify—if they have recovered their voices—that the old master, John Longden, captured the climactic closing race of his riding career with George Royal in the $125,000 San Juan Capistrano Handicap Saturday at Santa Anita.

This turned out to be as thrilling a finale for both man and beast as any fiction writer could produce—only it was real.

George Royal nipped Plaque by a narrow nose at the end of the marathon mile and three-quarters in 2:48 4-5. Probably the Old Pumper's 40 years of riding experience made the winning difference during a spine-tingling seesaw struggle through the length of the stretch.

During those dramatic 25 seconds of the final quarter, George Royal headed Plaque at the top of the stretch, lost his lead halfway home and then came on again for Grandpa John in the final few steps to win with only a whisker to spare.

It did, indeed, Longden admitted afterward, top the thrill of his nose victory with Noor over Citation in the 1950 Capistrano, a spectacular struggle that until now ranked as the greatest spine tingler in Santa Anita history.

This was a statistical splurge as well as an emotional experience.

For the 59-year-old Longden, this increased his world record total of triumphs to 6,032. It was Sir John's 452nd stakes victory, his 67th stakes success at Santa Anita and his 25th triumph in a hundred grander.

And, really, it was anti-climactic.

The elder statesman of the saddle got his winner on the final day of his riding career in the fourth race, scoring by a head with favored Chiclero after an unexpectedly rugged stretch duel with Valiant Man. That was supposed to be the last visit to the winner's circle with a horse for the Pumper.

Please Turn to Page 10, Col. 7

BY A NOSE . . . AND HOW!—Carrying Johnny Longden on his last ride, George Royal, outside, overtakes Plaque down the stretch.
Times photo by Larry Sharkey

# Utah Turns Speed on Beavers, 70-64

## Oregon St. Falls Behind Early and Can't Stop Chambers (33)

BY MAL FLORENCE
Times Staff Writer

Oregon State, a team which got a lot of mileage out of a Model T basketball offense, broke down Saturday night. But, it wasn't entirely the Beavers' own doing.

Los Angeles Times
Sports
CC SECTION D 3¢
SUNDAY, MARCH 13, 1966 •

Slender Jerry Chambers simply bewildered the ball-control Beavers in leading Utah to a 70-64 victory in the finals of the NCAA Western Regional basketball tournament at Pauley Pavilion.

Chambers, the 6-4 Redskin forward-center with the soft touch and quick release, poured in 33 points as Utah earned the right to represent the West in the NCAA semifinals next Friday evening in College Park, Md.

The runnin' Redskins, champions of the Western Athletic Conference, will confront Texas Western, which prevailed over Kansas, 81-80, in a double-overtime session in the Midwest Regional.

**Semi-Control by Utah**

Although the final six-point spread at Pauley would suggest that the game was a closely contested affair, such was not the case.

Utah led at halftime, 41-24, and then resorted to a semi-control type offense in the final 5½ minutes to protect its advantage.

The Redskins, who overwhelmed the Beavers on the boards, 61-42, were never seriously threatened by OSU in the final half.

In a preliminary consolation game for third place, run-and-gun Houston shot down the University of Pacific, 102-91.

**Chambers Changes Attack**

Chambers, who banged in 40 points as Utah whipped UOP, 83-74, in Friday's semifinals, "owned" the tournament.

Not only did he soar high in the air to score with a floating outside jumper, but showed off a new wrinkle Saturday night.

He drove on the Beavers, capitalizing on quick passes from Utah's underrated guards, 6-2 Mervin Jackson and 5-11 Richard Tate.

It was evident over the weekend that you can't relax your vigil on Chambers for a moment. Once you do, it's a two-point mistake.

Ostensibly, Oregon State's fine floor leader, Charlie White, was assigned to Chambers. But, he got "help" of sorts from guard Scott Eaton and forward Loy Petersen.

**Fisher Injured**

Utah coach Jack Gardner, a USC alum who has won more than his share of titles in his 30-year coachnig career, stunned everyone when he said, "I actually debated bringing my team here."

"For one thing," explained Gardner, "we lost George Fisher, our best scorer and a defensive standout two games before the season ended. I thought we had had it.

Please Turn to Page 6, Col. 3

## JIM MURRAY

# What? No Longden? It's Sad, but It's True

Feel a little older this morning, do you?

Notice a few gray hairs that weren't there yesterday?

That pretty young thing at the office call you "Sir," did she?

Find yourself wondering irritably why they never play "Moonlight and Roses" any more? Do Boy Scouts try to help you cross streets?

Join the group. Now you know how a lot of us feel this gloomy Sunday. John Longden has hung up his tack.

A California race meeting without John Longden in the irons? Unthinkable! Insupportable! France without love. Paris without spring. Italy without music. Germany without bands. Baseball without beer. Weddings without tears.

A part of your youth gets off horseback with John.

Suddenly you notice the bifocals in the mirror. The ticking of the clock seems louder. The calendar is a mock.

Not see The Pumper in a backstretch?! Not watch a little silken gnome of a man giving the horse 1,100 pounds in the weights and 60 years in age and winning the wrestling match?! What do we do now—root for some young whipper-snapper?

Was it really 16 years ago that you watched him come down the homestretch, your heart pounding, in what may have been the greatest horse race ever? The great, wilful, black Noor, holding the mighty Citation on the rail where his rider couldn't whip and he could run on courage alone. Did Noor win that race? Or did Longden? Do birds sing? Trees grow? Does the sun shine?

Was it clear back in 1955 when he brought a great red-gold colt flashing home in front in the Santa Anita Derby and the magic racing word "Swaps" went out over the A-wire for the first time? Did they take Swaps away from John because they said he was "too old?"

Did he ever forgive the owners? Was he only 50 at the time?

Were we Keeping Cool With Coolidge when John first threw a leg over a no-chance mare in one of his first starts? Weren't we watching Cagney walk the Last Mile, singing "Brother, Can You Spare a Dime?" Wasn't it only yesterday?

Wasn't he an experienced rider about the time talking pictures came in? America's richest horse race paid a princely $25,000. Wasn't a goof named Hitler making an ass of himself in Europe about the time of his first thousand winners?

### Border to Belmont

Was there a trick he didn't learn from the bull ring tracks at the border, the leaky roof traps in the Appalachians, the neat hedge rows of Belmont, the half-mile ovals of Dixie?

Did he become the greatest of them all? Did he outlast Arcaro, Silvio Coucci, Neves, Sonny Workman, Sande, Laverne Fator? Did anybody write poems about him? Did any rider they wrote poems about ever let Longden out of his sight even in an overnight?

Did he ride in 32,500 races, win 6,032? Did any other rider?

Did he see two of his best friends killed on the track in front of him and yet did he get right back aboard himself in the next race? Did they pick him up in pieces a few times and yet he showed up in the paddock as soon as the cast was off?

Did they give him glue pots to ride in recent years? Did he complain or did he just ride them? Will we see his like again? Don't stand on tiptoe waiting.

Old age should creep up on a man. A gray hair here, a uniform that won't button any more there. A doctor saying "The old ticker's not getting any younger, you know."

You shouldn't find it out picking up a newspaper and seeing "Longden Retires — 'Too Old to Win,' Says."

Professor! Play "Melancholy Baby" just one more time. The hour grows late.

# Tommy D's Ankle Passes Test, but Dodgers Lose, 3-2

BY FRANK FINCH
Times Staff Writer

WEST PALM BEACH — The Dodgers blew the duke to the Atlanta Braves in typical fashion Saturday, on a two-strike pitch down the pipe and some heads-down base running, but Smokey Alston preferred to look at the bright side of the picture.

While Rico Carty singled with two on and two out in the ninth to give Atlanta a 3-2 victory in the Grapefruit League opener for both clubs, L.A.'s plusses outnumbered its minuses.

Tommy Davis doubled in the fourth inning and then gave his right ankle its sternest test of the spring by scoring from second on Jeff Torborg's single to left.

**'Ran All Out'**

Davis was going all out as he rounded third, and when Felipe Alou bobbled the ball he was able to score standing up.

"I had to find out if I could do it in that situation, so I ran all out. Let's hope it continues that way," said Tommy. "Yes. I had made up my mind to slide home because I've got to take that first slide sometime, but I didn't have to when Alou dropped the ball."

John Kennedy drew praise from Alston for his play at shortstop, where he appears to be the heir apparent to Maury Wills—unless Maury accepts the club's $75,000 take-it-or-leave-it offer which he finds unattractive.

**Lefebvre at Third**

"John made some pretty good plays out there, although he's got a sore arm. I also liked the way he swung the bat," Alston commented.

The slick glove man had two singles and a walk, and went one up on Wills by stealing a base.

Jim Lefebvre's debut at third base under fire was a revelation.

"I felt a little strange there, and the Braves were razzing me pretty good, but I think I'll get the hang of it," he grinned. Jim made two exceptional plays on a smash and a bunt by Frank Thomas, and clicked at bat

Please Turn to Page 2, Col. 6

## SPORTS ON RADIO, TV

**BASKETBALL**

Philadelphia vs. New York, channel 7, 11 a. m.

**BASEBALL**

Dodgers vs. Braves, KFI, 10:30 a.m.; Angels vs. Cubs, channel 5 and radio KMPC, 1 p.m.

**GOLF**

Doral Open, Channel 9, 1 p.m.

# WILLS PLANS MORE TALKS

Maury Wills expects to continue salary negotiations sometime this week with Dodger vice president Buzzie Bavasi, he told The Times Saturday night.

The Dodger captain said he would not believe reports that Bavasi said the $75,000 offer turned down by Wills was the club's "final offer," until Bavasi himself told him this was true.

"I think there has been too much written in the papers," said Wills. "I think, however, that we can still settle this thing. I expect to talk to Mr. Bavasi within a week."

BEAVER TRAP — Utah's Mervin Jackson (10) and Jerry Chambers put pressure on Oregon State's Charlie White in NCAA Western Regional final at Pauley Pavilion. The Utes defeated Beavers, 70-64.
Times photo by Joe Kennedy

# PEACE AT LAST! K&D RETURN TO FOLD

MOST HAPPY FELLAS—Happiness is a general manager signing two pitchers, especially if they happen to be the Dodgers' Don Drysdale, left, and Sandy Koufax, right. The third man in the "triangle" is jubilant GM, Buzzie Bavasi. Pitchers ended holdouts Wednesday, begin workouts today and will probably join team Friday night in Phoenix.

Times photo by Ben Olender

## Sandy Signs for $120,000, Don $105,000

BY CHARLES MAHER
Times Staff Writer

The Dodgers announced Wednesday that they have signed Chauncey Haines, "distinguished organist of the motion picture industry," to play the Dodger Stadium Wurlitzer this season.

Apparently as an afterthought, the Dodgers also announced they have signed a couple of out-of-work pitchers, Sandy Koufax and Don Drysdale.

Koufax and Drysdale are virtually unknown outside the solar system, but general manager Buzzie Bavasi said he would not be surprised if they work their way into the regular pitching rotation. Of course, it will take time. Say, 10 days.

As evidence of their faith in the potential of the two pitchers, the Dodgers will pay Koufax about $120,000 this season and Drysdale about $105,000. No salary figures were announced, but these are known to be authoritative estimates.

**Form a Two-Man Union**

Some time before spring training, Koufax and Drysdale formed a two-man union and asked the Dodgers for three-year contracts that would bring each about $166,666 a year. The club offered $100,000 to Koufax, $85,000 to Drysdale.

They rejected the offers and the club went to Florida without them.

This week, the Dodgers made what they described as a final offer of $210,000—$112,500 to Koufax and $97,500 to Drysdale. This also was rejected and club officials said they no longer had any hope of signing the two pitchers.

Then, Wednesday morning, Bavasi made another offer—whichever one comes after the final one—and it was accepted.

Koufax and Drysdale made about $75,000 apiece last season. So Koufax's salary goes up about $45,000, Drysdale's $30,000.

"I'm just happy to be back in the fold," Drysdale said at a news conference. "This is the most trying

Please Turn to Page 4, Col. 2

Los Angeles Times
Sports
BUSINESS & FINANCE
CC PART III 2†
THURSDAY, MARCH 31, 1966

*JIM MURRAY*

## Don't Let 'Em Fool You; Koufax Wanted to Pitch

VERO BEACH—There are a few things to settle at the outset of this column.

The first is that the next lie Sandy Koufax tells me will be the first. Oh, I've gotten "No comment" out of him or no answer or the busy signal. But when he tells you something, you can take it and put it in the bank. It's so solid, it will draw interest.

This is not the only thing that distinguishes Sandy in Baseball, but it's one of the things.

The second is that this is not the column I intended to bring you at this regularly scheduled time. It has been relinquished to bring you this news special.

The original column dealt with the unoriginal notion that Sandy Koufax did not want to play baseball this year. Or any other. It was a notion planted in my mind by, among others, E. J. (Buzzie) Bavasi. Sandy wasn't rejecting money, went the refrain; he was rejecting the game. He didn't want to bend that curve ball over on a 3-and-2 pitch with the world championship at stake any more. He wanted a job with a carpet on the floor, two phones in the Cadillac, and a hot line to the stock market.

He was turning his back on apple pie, Motherhood, the Fourth of July and the Boy Scout movement—the whole American concept. He wanted more money than Willie Mays. The club was bending every effort, but his price was put deliberately out of reason because he was sick of the monkey suit, the thunder-and-lightning flights, the distasteful publicity including the leering little stories in detestable penny-dreadful publications. Sandy was not trying to hold up Baseball; he was trying to escape it. So they said.

The notion depressed me. But I bought it. I went down to the minor league dressing room here where the crew-cut kids of all hues and nationalities are bucking for too-few jobs with too-little skills. I stared up at the signs. "Be proud your a Dodger." The misspelling was sadly amusing. You don't need grammar to make Spokane; you need a hop on your fast one, a hook on your deuce ball. "Learn the signs!" "Think Baseball!" ran other exhortations.

Why?

If the guy who made it beyond the wildest dreams of these kids says, "Baseball? who needs it?" who needs to bother with signs that say "Back up all bases!" "Hit the cutoff man!" and related tips from the top? Who needs Room At the Top if the guy who made it bailed out, who acted as if he were quitting the narcotic trade, the Mafia? Maybe it really wasn't Show Business, maybe it was just cleaning the elephant after all.

### *What Can You Do?*

I felt uneasy about it. So I started to phone Koufax—3,000 miles away.

"Do I want to leave Baseball?! Of course, I don't!" an angry young man answered me. "But what are you to do when you don't hear from the employer for over a month? What? Maybe my phone doesn't answer. But I get my mail."

What about movie offers, TV, business?

"Jim," said Sandy Koufax, "I like to eat. But Baseball has always treated us as if we had no choice but to sign, as if it were just a dumb charade. They just made us an offer and waited for us to crawl up to it like a desert water hole."

It was true. I had forcibly told the general manager only a few days before that I, as a 20th Century American, 700 years after the Magna Carta, would resent being told to get on a jet, eat 3,000 miles of crow and meekly get back in the cottonfield. A man who is as sure to get in the Hall of Fame as

Please Turn to Page 3, Col. 1

## Hawks Sweep, Play Lakers on Friday

### Bridges, Wilkens Pace 3rd Straight Win Over Bullets

ST. LOUIS (UPI)—The St. Louis Hawks made it three in a row over the Baltimore Bullets 121-112 Wednesday night and advanced to the finals of the Western Division playoffs against the Lakers, which open in Los Angeles Friday.

Retiring Baltimore coach Paul Seymour came close to keeping Baltimore's hopes alive in the playoffs when his team rallied from a 17-point deficit in the fourth period to within three points of the Hawks.

Don Ohl, who finished with a total 32 points, sank 15 points in the final period rally.

**Bridges' Career High**

Bill Bridges, also with 32 points, his career high, and 30 points by Len Wilkens pushed the Hawks to the victory.

Player-coach Richie Guerin, his team trailing 60-59 at the half, used reserve Paul Silas for Zelmo Beaty in the third period.

Silas dominated the boards and contributed four points while Bridges sank 12 points to move the Hawks to a 93-80 third period lead.

Coach Seymour used the injured Gus Johnson for the first time in the three-game playoff series. But he was of little help.

The Hawks built a 7-0 lead in less

Please Turn to Page 2, Col. 3

## TODAY IN SPORTS

**HARNESS RACING**—Santa Anita, 1 p.m.

**BOXING**—Joe Orbillo vs. Irish Tony Doyle. Olympic Auditorium, 8 p.m.

**SPORTSMEN'S SHOW**—Pan-Pacific Auditorium, 2 p.m. to 11 p.m.

**RADIO-TELEVISION**

**BASEBALL**—Dodgers vs. All-Stars, KFI, 10:30 a.m.; Angels vs. San Francisco, KMPC, 12 noon.

## Club Jubilant, Alston Expects Aces To Pitch During Season's First Week

BY FRANK FINCH
Times Staff Writer

VERO BEACH—Walter Alston, beneficiary of a stunning 11th hour windfall of the best 1-2 pitching punch in baseball, is confident Sandy Koufax and Don Drysdale will be pitching in games 10 days from now.

That means the ex-reluctant dragons could be doing their stuff, on a limited basis, in the final exhibition series with the Cleveland Indians April 9-10 at Dodger Stadium.

Jubilant at the change of heart in ending the most controversial hold-out siege in the game's history, the Dodger manager went on to say it is entirely possible that Sandy and Don could start with only two weeks of tuneups.

In that case, the Cy Young Award winners would be available during the Dodgers' first home stand against Houston and Chicago, beginning April 12 and ending April 17.

"I don't know how much they've thrown on their own this spring, but I don't think either has a weight problem. They looked pretty trim when I saw them in Los Angeles at the baseball writers' dinner," Alston added during a press conference Wednesday.

**Won't Rush Them**

"In spring training Drysdale and Koufax have taken three inning turns in intrasquad games after only 10 days in camp, and I know no reason why they shouldn't get ready just as quickly this season.

"Of course, I'm not going to rush them and risk hurting their arms. I won't pitch them until they tell me they're ready."

Alston, who suddenly inherited 49 victories from last year, Wednesday said the twin twirling titans will join the club in Phoenix either Friday night or Saturday. The Dodgers break camp this afternoon.

As boss of the team which now will be the favorite to repeat as National League champion, the usually unflappable Alston admitted Tuesday after Walter O'Malley announced that "the incident is closed" that he had given up hope of the K-D combo reporting this year.

On that premise, Alston prepared a pitching staff which included Claude Osteen ("He's my new ace') Johnny Podres, Phil Regan, Don

Please Turn to Page 2, Col. 4

HE'S A SWINGER—Jim Fregosi, at 24 a veteran of five seasons at the Angels' shortstop, batted .277 for the second year in a row in 1965. He will be in the lineup against the Giants in Phoenix today.

Times photo

Story on Page 2, Part III

Los Angeles Times

# Sports

BUSINESS & FINANCE

CC PART III 3†

FRIDAY, APRIL 29, 1966

# Boston Cage Capital, Crows Auerbach

BY CHARLES MAHER
Times Staff Writer

BOSTON — Los Angeles has been advertised by some of its more effusive promoters as "The sports capital of the world."

Red Auerbach, the retiring coach of the Boston Celtics, paused a moment Thursday night to protest that this is false advertising.

"I don't think that L.A. is the capital of the world in basketball," he said. "Not yet. This is the capital. Boston."

Auerbach's point was quite well taken. It was, in fact, unassailable, for his team had just won another NBA title by defeating the Lakers, 95-93, in the final game of the playoffs.

Having made his point, Auerbach suggested that reporters forget about him and talk to his players. "What the hell did I do tonight?" he said. "I didn't score many points."

By NBA standards, neither did his players. The thing they beat the Lakers with, everyone agreed, was defense. In the first half, for example, they held L.A. to 38 points. In the second quarter, the Lakers went more than 8½ minutes in one stretch without making a field goal.

"There is no question about it," said L.A. coach Fred Schaus. "Their defense was great in the first half. But there is no reason we should have let it bother us that much. They've been playing defense like that for years.

"Their press didn't bother us like that the last four games. But tonight they forced us into a lot of bad shots.

"We played like scared rabbits there in the first period.

"There was one thing I knew we couldn't let happen to us, and it did. They got on top of us with their defense.

"I don't think we got a loose ball the whole first half. We weren't going after the ball. We were just watching it."

Schaus talked with newsmen outside the Laker dressing room. More than a half hour after the game, he was still there, leaning against a wall, utterly depressed.

"I still can't believe it," he said.

It was a little chilly in Boston Garden when the game started. A reporter wondered if this had bothered the Lakers in the early going.

"It took me until the second half to get loose," said Elgin Baylor. "I don't know if it was the temperature or what."

"I just felt cold when I was shoot-

Please Turn to Page 5, Col. 1

## JIM MURRAY

### Fasten Your Belt

Frankly, the fastest I want to go across water is by the Australian crawl. I get dizzy in a canoe, seasick in a shower. I take Dramamine to cross a bridge. If you can't ring for the steward in a boat, it's too small. Any body of water you can't unplug with a finger is too big.

But if you will go down to the sixth annual Custom Car and Motorcycle Show at the Sports Arena this week and can tear yourself away from the candy paint and chrome-creased kiddie cars and take a look at the 3,000 h.p. rowboat called the "Miss Bardahl" and tell yourself this skims across riverbeds and spring lakes at 12,000 r.p.m., that makes that freeway-hopper of yours look like the family mare—something you could ride side-saddle and read a book on.

Ron Musson, who has driven the "Miss Bardahl" to three Gold Cup titles and the national high-point championship, is probably the best hydroplane pilot in the world today. Of course, there are only 18 of them. To get to be a hydroplane pilot in the first place is like getting into the Cuban social registry. Not many qualify.

You need to pass an airline pilot's physical, you have to prove you can steer a boat through a roostertail five stories high and you have to have as much mechanical knowledge as the first mate on the Queen Mary. You have to get your insurance at Lloyd's of London at the same premiums paid by a guy running a blockade. You don't strap yourself in the boat, but you strap your liver, kidneys, stomach and spleen in. You wear a life jacket because if you hit the water, you won't be conscious enough to swim.

The great names in powerboat racing (your grandfather used to call them "naphtha launches") were Gar Wood, Kaye Don, Stan Sayres, and, believe it or not, Guy Lombardo.

An English lord once donated a trophy called the "Harmsworth" which came to be known as the "Harm-self" when the Hudson and Detroit rivers became so littered with powerboat jockeys it looked like a scene from "Victory at Sea."

#### One-Way Record

Sir Malcolm Campbell and his son, Donald, used to hold the solo run championships in these things, usually running on Loch Ness where all he had to watch out for was the monster. John Cobb set the one-way speed record once—posthumously. Neither he nor the boat made it back.

As a spectator sport it makes the World Series look private. Over a half-million people have lined the banks to watch it. The only spectators it kills are salmon, but they have to drag the lake frequently for a driver. The things run at 110 deg. centigrade, and if you touch a pipe you won't have any fingerprints. In fact, you may not have any fingers.

The "Miss Bardahl" is barely able to make 170 m.p.h. So Musson is afraid he may get arrested for loitering in the next race. He has a new machine which has the engine in the rear and will go over the water at 200.2 m.p.h. As soon as he can make it do that in a straight line, he may make Gar Wood look like Grant Wood. His only problem is the Gold Cup is on the Detroit River this year which has a turn basin so narrow he may go through the corners by way of the Fisher Building lobby. And he keeps 100 pounds of fire extinguisher aboard so that, even if the outer shell glows at those speeds, he won't.

OLD HOME WEEK—Boston's Don Nelson (center), an ex-Laker, is surrounded by his old pals as he loses ball in final NBA playoff game. Lakers' Darrall Imhoff (right) tries to retrieve it as Gail Goodrich (11) and Elgin Baylor look on. Celtics won unprecedented eighth straight championship by beating L.A., 95-93.
UPI Wirephoto

# Celtics Totter, but Lakers Fall, 95-93

BY DAN HAFNER
Times Staff Writer

BOSTON—The bells are ringing and the champagne is flowing. The Boston Celtics, sports' greatest empire, tottered, but did not fall.

Bill Russell, taking advantage of the coldest-shooting night the Lakers have had in a long time, rallied his weary club to a tough defensive game Thursday night that gave it a 95-93 victory and presented retiring coach Red Auerbach with an unprecedented eighth straight NBA championship.

A screaming mob of 13,909 fans nearly tore down Boston's dirty old Garden with their celebrating, but they had to hold off their party until the final gun.

For the Lakers, a game group throughout this seven-game series, found their shooting eyes with 40 seconds to play, scored four-straight baskets and were still battling for a chance to tie it in the last two seconds.

**Red Lights Up**

Instead, it was the same old story, Auerbach lighted the victory cigar and the Lakers were the runners-up for the fourth time in five years.

The Lakers let Boston run up the first 10 points and they never could catch up against a rugged defense that harassed them all over the court. Coach Fred Schaus tried all sorts of combinations but nobody could hit with any consistency.

Russell spearheaded the defense, pulling down 32 rebounds and he made the key points every time the Lakers threatened to climb back into the battle. The Bearded Wonder also led his team in scoring with 25 points.

The Laker trouble was that they couldn't get more than one guy hot at any time. Elgin Baylor couldn't buy a basket in the first half and Jerry West, who wound up the leading scorer with 36, had only a few.

Then Baylor got hot in the third, and it was West in the final period, but except for a first quarter spurt by LeRoy Ellis and one by Walt Hazzard, the one-two punch didn't get much help.

The low point of the Laker season was reached in the second quarter when they went almost 10 minutes without a field goal. The amazing thing is that they didn't fall more than the 15 points they were behind at intermission.

The Lakers were back in the battle—eight points behind midway through the third—and then they went three more minutes without a field goal, and that was too much!

Boston was shooting its normal game, which is just about the worst in the league. However, when the Lakers hit a lull someone, almost always Russell, but once in a while Sam Jones or John Havlicek and at

Please Turn to Page 5, Col. 4

## LAKER BOX SCORE

| LOS ANGELES | FG-A | FT-A | R | A | P | T |
|---|---|---|---|---|---|---|
| Baylor | 6-22 | 6-6 | 14 | 1 | 1 | 18 |
| West | 12-27 | 12-16 | 10 | 3 | 3 | 36 |
| Ellis | 5-11 | 2-3 | 11 | 0 | 2 | 12 |
| Goodrich | 2-9 | 2-3 | 4 | 1 | 4 | 6 |
| King | 1-4 | 0-1 | 2 | 0 | 1 | 2 |
| Boozer | 0-0 | 0-0 | 2 | 1 | 1 | 0 |
| Hazzard | 5-7 | 2-5 | 2 | 3 | 2 | 12 |
| Imhoff | 0-1 | 0-0 | 3 | 0 | 3 | 0 |
| LaRusso | 2-7 | 3-4 | 6 | 0 | 5 | 7 |
| Team rebounds | | | 6 | | | |
| Totals | 33-88 | 27-38 | 60 | 9 | 22 | 93 |

Shooting: Field goals, 37.5%; free throws, 71.1%.

| BOSTON | FG-A | FT-A | R | A | P | T |
|---|---|---|---|---|---|---|
| Sanders | 3-9 | 1-1 | 4 | 3 | 5 | 7 |
| Havlicek | 6-21 | 4-6 | 16 | 2 | 3 | 16 |
| Russell | 10-22 | 5-5 | 32 | 1 | 5 | 25 |
| K. C. Jones | 2-9 | 1-1 | 2 | 3 | 5 | 5 |
| Sam Jones | 10-21 | 2-2 | 5 | 0 | 5 | 22 |
| Naulls | 0-1 | 0-0 | 1 | 0 | 3 | 0 |
| Nelson | 2-9 | 4-4 | 8 | 2 | 3 | 8 |
| Siegfried | 4-13 | 2-5 | 2 | 2 | 4 | 12 |
| Team rebounds | | | 7 | | | |
| Totals | 37-105 | 21-24 | 77 | 13 | 33 | 95 |

Shooting: Field goals, 35.2%; free throws, 87.5%.

SCORE BY QUARTERS

| | | | | |
|---|---|---|---|---|
| Los Angeles | 20 | 18 | 22 | 33—93 |
| Boston | 27 | 26 | 23 | 19—95 |

Officials—Earl Strom and Mendy Rudolph.
Attendance—13,909.

# All's Well; Dodgers' Big D Notches 1st Win

BY FRANK FINCH
Times Staff Writer

For the third straight game the Dodgers put it all together Thursday night — stout pitching, clutch hitting and a near-perfect defense.

The net result was Don Drysdale's first win of the season, an 8-2 cakewalk that gave the Dodgers a series sweep over the Atlanta Braves and enabled them to stay in a second-place tie with the Giants, only one length behind Pittsburgh.

Jim Lefebvre's fifth homer, and his first batting right handed, touched off a five-run rally in the second inning and the Dodgers batted around to drive Wade Blasingame to cover.

The world champs, definitely out of the slump that saw them lose three 2-0 games in succession, came back with a three-run spurt in the fourth inning against rookie Arnold Umbach.

Three other of Bobby Bragan's second-line hurlers held L.A. to one hit the balance of the way but by then the Braves were hopelessly behind.

The great Hank Aaron, who spoiled Don Sutton's shutout with a ninth-inning homer Wednesday, kept the Braves from suffering an utter rout again. Aaron doubled Gary Geiger home in the first inning and slugged his sixth homer in the sixth inning to tie Willie Mays for

Please Turn to Page 3, Col. 3

## Baseball Standings

NATIONAL LEAGUE

| | W | L | Pct. | GBL |
|---|---|---|---|---|
| Pittsburgh | 10 | 4 | .717 | |
| **DODGERS** | **10** | **6** | **.625** | **1** |
| San Francisco | 10 | 6 | .625 | 1 |
| Atlanta | 9 | 7 | .563 | 2 |
| Philadelphia | 6 | 5 | .545 | 2½ |
| Houston | 8 | 8 | .500 | 3 |
| St. Louis | 6 | 8 | .429 | 4 |
| New York | 4 | 6 | .400 | 4 |
| Cincinnati | 3 | 9 | .250 | 6 |
| Chicago | 3 | 10 | .231 | 6½ |

THURSDAY'S RESULTS

DODGERS 8, Atlanta 2
Houston 4, St. Louis 2
San Francisco 3, Cincinnati 0
Pittsburgh 9, Chicago 6 (10 innings).
Only games scheduled.

TODAY'S SCHEDULE

Cincinnati (O'Toole, 0-0) vs. DODGERS (Osteen, 3-1), Dodger Stadium, KFI, KWKW, 8 p.m.
New York (Gardner, 0-0) at Pittsburgh (Blass, 1-0), night.
Philadelphia (Bunning, 1-1) at Chicago (Ellsworth, 0-1).
Houston (Latman, 1-1) at Atlanta (Lemaster, 1-1), night
St. Louis (Sadecki, 1-0) at San Francisco (Shaw, 1-2), night

AMERICAN LEAGUE

| | W | L | Pct. | GBL |
|---|---|---|---|---|
| Cleveland | 10 | 0 | 1.000 | |
| Baltimore | 9 | 1 | .900 | ½ |
| Chicago | 9 | 3 | .750 | 2 |
| Detroit | 10 | 4 | .717 | 2 |
| **ANGELS** | **6** | **6** | **.500** | **5** |
| Minnesota | 4 | 6 | .400 | 6 |
| Boston | 3 | 9 | .250 | 8 |
| Washington | 3 | 9 | .250 | 8 |
| Kansas City | 2 | 9 | .189 | 8½ |
| New York | 2 | 11 | .154 | 9½ |

THURSDAY'S RESULTS

Cleveland 2, ANGELS 1
Detroit 13, Kansas City 5
Chicago at Boston, postponed, cold.
Washington at New York, postponed, rain.
Minnesota at Baltimore, doubleheader, postponed, cold.

TODAY'S SCHEDULE

Baltimore (Bunker, 1-1) at Detroit (Monbouquette, 2-1), night.
Chicago (Lamabe, 0-0) at Cleveland (Bell, 1-0), night.
Minnesota (Kaat, 1-1) at Washington (Richert, 0-3), night.
Only games scheduled.

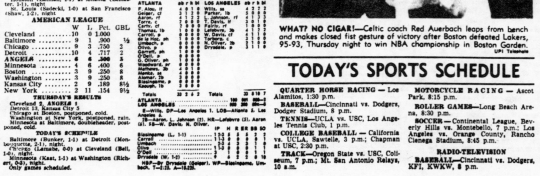

## DODGER BOX SCORE

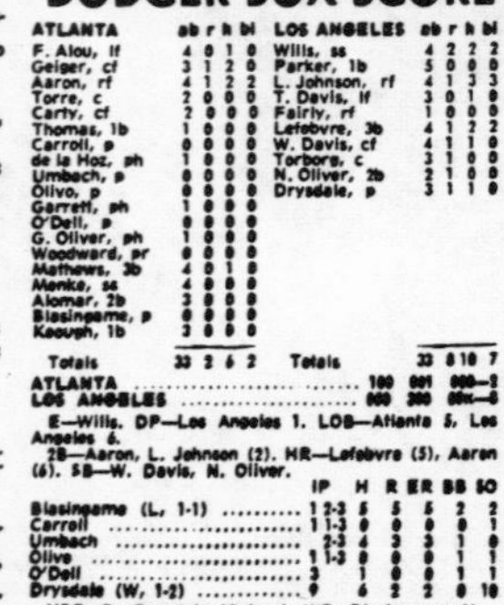

| ATLANTA | ab | r | h | bi |
|---|---|---|---|---|
| F. Alou, lf | 4 | 0 | 1 | 0 |
| Geiger, cf | 3 | 1 | 2 | 0 |
| Aaron, rf | 4 | 1 | 2 | 2 |
| Torre, c | 2 | 0 | 0 | 0 |
| Carty, cf | 2 | 0 | 0 | 0 |
| Thomas, 1b | 1 | 0 | 0 | 0 |
| Carroll, p | 0 | 0 | 0 | 0 |
| de la Hoz, ph | 1 | 0 | 0 | 0 |
| Umbach, p | 0 | 0 | 0 | 0 |
| Olivo, p | 0 | 0 | 0 | 0 |
| Garrett, ph | 1 | 0 | 0 | 0 |
| O'Dell, p | 0 | 0 | 0 | 0 |
| G. Oliver, ph | 1 | 0 | 0 | 0 |
| Woodward, pr | 0 | 0 | 0 | 0 |
| Mathews, 3b | 4 | 0 | 1 | 0 |
| Menke, ss | 4 | 0 | 0 | 0 |
| Alomar, 2b | 3 | 0 | 0 | 0 |
| Blasingame, p | 0 | 0 | 0 | 0 |
| Keough, 1b | 3 | 0 | 0 | 0 |
| Totals | 33 | 2 | 6 | 2 |

| LOS ANGELES | ab | r | h | bi |
|---|---|---|---|---|
| Wills, ss | 4 | 2 | 2 | 2 |
| Parker, 1b | 5 | 0 | 0 | 0 |
| L. Johnson, rf | 4 | 1 | 3 | 3 |
| T. Davis, lf | 3 | 0 | 1 | 0 |
| Fairly, rf | 1 | 0 | 0 | 0 |
| Lefebvre, 3b | 4 | 1 | 2 | 2 |
| W. Davis, cf | 4 | 1 | 1 | 0 |
| Torborg, c | 3 | 1 | 0 | 0 |
| N. Oliver, 2b | 2 | 1 | 0 | 0 |
| Drysdale, p | 3 | 1 | 1 | 0 |
| Totals | 33 | 8 | 10 | 7 |

| | | | |
|---|---|---|---|
| ATLANTA | 100 | 001 | 000—2 |
| LOS ANGELES | [illegible] | 300 | [illegible]—8 |

E—Wills. DP—Los Angeles 1. LOB—Atlanta 5, Los Angeles 6.
2B—Aaron, L. Johnson (2). HR—Lefebvre (5), Aaron (6). SB—W. Davis, N. Oliver.

| | IP | H | R | ER | BB | SO |
|---|---|---|---|---|---|---|
| Blasingame (L, 1-1) | 1 2-3 | 5 | 5 | 5 | 2 | 2 |
| Carroll | 1 1-3 | 0 | 0 | 0 | 0 | 1 |
| Umbach | 2-3 | 4 | 3 | 3 | 1 | 0 |
| Olivo | 1 1-3 | 0 | 0 | 0 | 1 | 1 |
| O'Dell | 3 | 1 | 0 | 0 | 1 | 1 |
| Drysdale (W, 1-2) | 9 | 6 | 2 | 2 | 0 | 10 |

HBP—By Drysdale (Geiger). WP—Blasingame, Umbach. T—2:25. A—18,223.

WHAT? NO CIGAR!—Celtic coach Red Auerbach leaps from bench and makes closed fist gesture of victory after Boston defeated Lakers, 95-93, Thursday night to win NBA championship in Boston Garden.
UPI Telephoto

## TODAY'S SPORTS SCHEDULE

**QUARTER HORSE RACING** — Los Alamitos, 1:30 p.m.

**BASEBALL**—Cincinnati vs. Dodgers, Dodger Stadium, 8 p.m.

**TENNIS**—UCLA vs. USC, Los Angeles Tennis Club, 1 p.m.

**COLLEGE BASEBALL** — California vs. UCLA, Sawtelle, 3 p.m.; Chapman at USC, 2:30 p.m.

**TRACK**—Oregon State vs. USC, Coliseum, 7 p.m.; Mt. San Antonio Relays, 10 a.m.

**MOTORCYCLE RACING** — Ascot Park, 8:15 p.m.

**ROLLER GAMES**—Long Beach Arena, 8:30 p.m.

**SOCCER** — Continental League, Beverly Hills vs. Montebello, 7 p.m.; Los Angeles vs. Orange County, Rancho Cienega Stadium, 8:45 p.m.

RADIO-TELEVISION

**BASEBALL**—Cincinnati vs. Dodgers, KFI, KWKW, 8 p.m.

# Tribe Nips Angels on Wagner's Fly to Tie Win Mark

BY JOHN HALL
Times Staff Writer

CLEVELAND—They are no longer the Cleveland Indians. Put them down as the Cleveland Vow Boys of 1966.

The Vow Boys nipped the Angels, 2-1, Thursday night to boom their record to 10-0, establish a new league record for wins at the start of the season and equal the major league mark shared by Brooklyn (1955) and Pittsburgh (1962).

Leon Wagner, whose heart has finally left Los Angeles, claimed here Thursday night that Cleveland's stunning early season success is due to a private meeting held the day before the American League season began.

"All the players got together and we vowed to go all out and win them all against the second-rate teams," said the Tribe outfielder.

"If we keep beating up the humpties consistently and break even with the top clubs, we'll win the pennant," said hero Wagner.

**Formula Not New**

Leon's formula is not exactly new, but the fact the athletes have taken it upon themselves to endorse the policy has added new zest to the frequently confused club that finished fifth in '65.

And, of course, "Daddy Wags" drove in the victory tally with a pinch-sacrifice fly in the eighth.

Wagner quickly made it clear he doesn't consider California to be one of the also rans.

"The Angels are going to be rough and right up there all the way," he said. "With pitchers like Marcelino Lopez, Dean Chance and Fred Newman, nobody is going to

Please Turn to Page 4, Col. 2

## Graustark Beaten

Story on Page 13

**JIM MURRAY**

# The Playoff: a Nice Guy (Billy Casper) Gets the Girl

SAN FRANCISCO — Look! There are certain things not meant to happen. You don't beat Man O' War. You don't strike out Babe Ruth with the bases loaded. You don't knock Joe Louis' head down onto the ring apron. The guys in the black hats don't win on television. John Wayne doesn't get shot in the back. You don't say, "What was so great about Bernard Baruch?" You don't throw eggs at the Queen.

And you don't beat Arnold Palmer or Ben Hogan in a playoff for the National Open.

But, we're living in an age of impudence. And the center of it, I'm afraid, is this sovereign city of San Francisco. This citadel of topless society, hallucinogenic headquarters of the universe, has no patience with idols.

Twice they'd held the National Golf Open here. The first time, Ben Hogan was beaten in a playoff by a club-cleaner from Davenport, Iowa, who rose to obscurity on the strength of the feat.

Monday, they put a banana peel under Arnold Palmer. I tell you, this place would scratch matches on the Mona Lisa.

Billy Casper, the player who beat Arnold Palmer, is a nice-enough young man. You'll never find him throwing stools in a bar, or eating stew with his fingers. You'd like your daughter to marry him—if your daughter was the kind who liked to stay home nights and watch television. And go fishing on the weekends.

Billy is exciting only when he's got a putter in his hands. Arnold Palmer is exciting just buttering toast.

Billy, however, is an impeccable golfer. His game is neat, dull, full of common sense. A bore, to be honest with you.

Arnold is as reckless as a salesman on convention. A round of golf for him is like a husband-and-wife fight—messy, noisy, usually unnecessary, and hard on the family. He goes after a golf course like a man chasing chickens. He plays the game like a guy playing blackjack who gets 19 and says, "Hit me again!"

The most interesting things about Billy Casper are his diet and his former waistline. He eats the same things that Sitting Bull used to eat. To give you an idea, his wife overdid the bear meat the night before the playoff, so Billy resigned himself to a breakfast of swordfish. In between he addressed the Mormon Church group at Petaluma. Billy is allergic to everything the normal man eats except soup. He doesn't even put ketchup on his rhinoceros chops.

Arnold Palmer plays golf like the Perils of Pauline. He ends up hanging on a cliff all day. Billy plays it like a guy going over the books of U.S. Steel.

This golf course has now performed the same service to golfing history as John Wilkes Booth did to America. If they fought World War II here, the Japanese would have won.

Arnold Palmer has every right to win a U.S. Open. He's won one and he's been in a playoff in three others. He's won almost every tournament worthy of being mentioned in Bobby Jones' presence. But he played a highly peccable two rounds of golf here at Olym-

Please Turn to Page 3, Col. 7

Los Angeles Times
Sports
PART III
TUESDAY, JUNE 21, 1966


HEADS UP—Billy Casper sends a shower of sand and the ball toward the cup on second hole of U.S. Open playoff match with Arnold Palmer. Casper got his par on hole and went on to a four-stroke victory.

# Casper Has Rich ($25,000) Diet That Includes Palmer

BY BILL SHIRLEY
Times Staff Writer

SAN FRANCISCO—Bill Casper won his second United States Open golf championship Monday with the help of a new "inner" strength, a "fantastic putting stroke" and a strategical blunder by Gen. Arnold Palmer himself.

The serious San Diego player shot a 1-under-par 69 over the Olympic Country Club's Lake course to win the 66th renewal of this historic tournament in an 18-hole playoff with Palmer. He also won $25,000 in loot and all the fringe benefits that accompany the sport's most important championship.

Palmer, meanwhile, in a repetition of Sunday's disaster on the second nine holes, shot a 3-over-par 73, blowing the match after leading by two strokes as late as the 10th hole. He won $12,500.

Each player also collected $1,500 from the gate receipts contributed by a crowd of 11,560 that witnessed the fourth Open playoff in the past five years. The weather was perfect—for San Francisco.

Make no mistake about it, Casper won this one, Palmer's retreat notwithstanding. Bill's 3-under-par 32 on the back side Sunday was a most uncommon performance. He was almost as good when he shot it in 34

**HOW CASPER WON IT**

| | | | | | |
|---|---|---|---|---|---|
| Par | Out | 543 | 444 | 434—35 | |
| Palmer | Out | 543 | 344 | 334—33 | |
| Casper | Out | 543 | 454 | 325—35 | |
| Par | In | 444 | 343 | 544—35—70 | |
| Palmer | In | 454 | 354 | 744—40—73 | |
| Casper | In | 434 | 243 | 663—34—69 | |

strokes Monday. Palmer was even worse, taking a five-over 40!

The second nine was Palmer's undoing all weekend and it will be a shock to his "army" to learn that its general clearly flunked a course in strategy. Arnold based his attack on the Lake course to survive the first five holes, the ones he thought would be the most difficult. In fairness to Palmer, most of the other professionals did too.

Arnie figured that if he came through "the chute," as the holes are labeled, in par or less, he would be in a good position to win. This he did every day but one, and then he was only one over.

However, he forgot about the rest of the course, and he did not reckon with Bill Casper. Bill shot him down there both days.

What happened? "I'd like to know that myself," answered a disgusted Palmer.

The new champion, who also won this tournament at Winged Foot, N.Y., in 1959, will be 35 Friday. He is noted for his putting, which was brilliant again Monday, and an allergy that has forced him on a diet that includes such exotic foods as buffalo and bear steaks. Someone suggested that his diet Monday included Arnold Palmer.

Bill is about as glamorous as a 3-putt green. He does not smoke or drink, use profanity or even own a jet airplane. Neither does he constantly hitch up his pants. The Mor-

Please Turn to Page 5, Col. 1

# Angels Weather Home Run Attack, Topple Twins, 5-3

BY JOHN HALL
Times Staff Writer

The Angels have come up with a sure fire formula in solving the Minnesota Twins.

It's simple enough. Walk Harmon Killebrew and dance all night.

Three times last week, Bill Rigney ordered the Killer walked intentionally in tense situations in Minneapolis.

Three times it paid off, all of which called for a fourth Monday night at Anaheim Stadium where the Angels opened a nine-game home stand with a 5-3 victory over their favorite opponent in the American League.

**Killebrew Given Walk**

With a 4-3 lead at stake in the eighth, the Twins started making unfriendly noises, putting men on second and third with two out.

Bob Lee, third Angel hurler of the evening, stared first at Killebrew strolling toward the plate and then at Rigney strolling up and down the Angel dugout.

The manager finally flashed his customary sign.

Lee promptly passed Harmon to load the bases, and then finished off the frustrated Twins by getting pinchhitter Sandy Valdespino to tap into a routine force.

Presto, it was the eighth Angel triumph in nine starts this season against the club that pressed the Dodgers to the final game last year in the World Series.

However, a welcome home turnout of 17,075 would perhaps insist there was a little more to it than chess.

Home runs by Killebrew and Don Mincher helped stake Jim Grant (5-9) to a 3-1 lead that stood up until the seventh when the Halos

Please Turn to Page 4, Col. 1

# Big D Gets Another F on Report Card, 4-2

BY FRANK FINCH
Times Staff Writer

HOUSTON — Venerable Robin Roberts battled to prolong his active baseball career Monday night while Don Drysdale fought desperately to escape the doldrums.

Roberts won his battle but Drysdale lost his.

The 39-year-old Roberts wasn't around to prance into the winner's circle at the finish as the Astros beat Los Angeles for the third straight time, 4-2, but he showed enough in seven innings to remain on Houston's pitching staff.

Meanwhile, Drysdale was knocked out in the eighth round when the upstart spacemen broke a 2-2 tie, to the immense delight of 33,347 Astrodome patrons.

Drysdale (4-9) sustained his fifth-straight defeat, matching his similar slump last season between June 15 and July 2.

And his career record over the expansionist Houston club is a very mediocre 8-7, including two defeats this season.

The L.A. management even flew Drysdale down here Sunday night ahead of the rest of the bunch so that he would be well-rested, but it didn't pan out as Rusty Staub led the charge by driving in two runs, including the deciding one.

Drysdale has preceded the team into other towns this season, but it didn't pay off then—except for the airlines.

Big D, a real bulldog even in adversity, continues to maintain that there is nothing wrong with him physically. "You tell me what's wrong, I certainly don't know," he said dejectedly rather than with rancor.

**Own Error Costs Run**

There is no gainsaying that breaks in his favor have been few and far between to date, but his own error in the first inning, when he dropped the ball after tagging Sonny Jackson, led to an unearned run, and he has nobody but himself to blame for that.

Before the series opener it was touch-and-go for whether Roberts, now in his 19th major league campaign, would remain on the active roster or be reassigned as a coach.

In 11 previous starts Robbie had gone the route only once, and failed to last more than six innings in his last six starts.

He was seeking his 285th career triumph but the laurels went to southpaw Mike Cuellar (5-0), who worked a fashionable eight round after Roberts retired for a pinch hitter in the home seventh.

During his stint the veteran right-hander limited L.A. to four singles, a walk and two runs, one of which was unearned as the Astros matched the Dodgers' three errors.

Had his brains been knocked out in the early going, Houston pilot Grady Hatton was ready to remove Roberts from the roster, but now

Please Turn to Page 4, Col. 4

**TODAY IN SPORTS**

**HORSE RACING**—Hollywood Park 1:45 p.m.

**BASEBALL** — Minnesota vs. Angels, Anaheim Stadium, 8 p.m.

**TENNIS** — Southern California junior boys and girls championships, L.A. Tennis Club, 8 p.m.

**ROLLER GAMES**—Olympic Auditorium, 7:30 p.m.

**BOXING** — Jose Medel vs. Rudy Corona; Dwight Hawkins vs. Jose Jiminez, Sports Arena, 8:30 p.m.

**RADIO-TELEVISION**

**BASEBALL** — Dodgers at Houston, KFI, KWKW, 6:30 p.m.; Minnesota vs. Angels, KMPC, 8 p.m.

**ROLLER GAMES**—Channel 5, 8 p.m.

PICTURE TELLS TALE — Billy Casper waves to crowd after sinking birdie putt while Arnold Palmer grimaces in background after missing his bird during their playoff for U.S. Open title. For second straight day, Palmer lost an early lead and finally bowed by four strokes. UPI Telephotos

# Baseball Standings

**AMERICAN LEAGUE**

| | W | L | Pct. | GBL |
|---|---|---|---|---|
| Baltimore | 42 | 22 | .656 | |
| Detroit | 38 | 23 | .623 | 2½ |
| Cleveland | 37 | 23 | .617 | 3 |
| **ANGELS** | **35** | **31** | **.530** | **8** |
| Minnesota | 30 | 32 | .484 | 11 |
| Chicago | 30 | 32 | .484 | 11 |
| New York | 26 | 33 | .441 | 13½ |
| Washington | 28 | 38 | .424 | 15 |
| Kansas City | 25 | 38 | .397 | 16½ |
| Boston | 22 | 41 | .349 | 19½ |

**MONDAY'S RESULTS**

ANGELS 5, Minnesota 3
Washington 4, Cleveland 2
Chicago 3, Kansas City 1
Only games scheduled.

**TODAY'S SCHEDULE**

Minnesota (Perry, 2-1) vs. ANGELS (Lopez, 3-6), Anaheim Stadium, KMPC, 8 p.m.
Chicago (John, 5-4) at Kansas City (Terry, 1-4), night
Detroit (McLain, 10-3) at Washington (Segui, 2-5), night
Baltimore (Bunker, 6-4 and Bertaina, 1-2) at New York (Stottlemyre, 6-6 and Peterson, 5-5), twi-night doubleheader
Cleveland (Bell, 6-2) at Boston (Sheldon, 4-8), night

**NATIONAL LEAGUE**

| | W | L | Pct. | GBL |
|---|---|---|---|---|
| San Francisco | 40 | 25 | .615 | |
| Pittsburgh | 37 | 25 | .597 | 1½ |
| **DODGERS** | **37** | **27** | **.578** | **2½** |
| Houston | 35 | 30 | .538 | 5 |
| Philadelphia | 35 | 31 | .530 | 5½ |
| St. Louis | 32 | 31 | .508 | 7 |
| Cincinnati | 29 | 34 | .460 | 10 |
| Atlanta | 30 | 38 | .441 | 11½ |
| New York | 24 | 37 | .393 | 14 |
| Chicago | 20 | 41 | .328 | 18 |

**MONDAY'S RESULTS**

Houston 4, DODGERS 2
St. Louis 4, New York 2
Atlanta 7, Philadelphia 5
Only games scheduled

**TODAY'S SCHEDULE**

DODGERS (Sutton, 7-5) at Houston (Farrell, 1-5), KFI, KWKW, 6:30 p.m.
New York (Shaw, 3-4) at St. Louis (Stallard, 1-2), night
San Francisco (Marichal, 12-2) at Chicago (Hands, 5-4)
Philadelphia (Jackson, 4-6) at Atlanta (Lemaster, 4-4), night
Pittsburgh (Blass, 5-1) at Cincinnati (Fischer, 2-4), night

CC 3†

# Bear Bryant Collapses at Grid Clinic

BY CHARLES MAHER
Times Staff Writer

Alabama football coach Paul (Bear) Bryant collapsed Monday while delivering a lecture at the sixth annual Pepperdine College coaching clinic.

"It's exhaustion; he fainted," said Bryant's physician, Dr. William Allen. "He is now being observed and studied. No serious problem has evidenced itself as yet."

Bryant, 53, was taken to Viewpark Community Hospital. His wife, Mary, joined him there.

"He doesn't look or talk like it's something real serious," Mrs. Bryant said. "They are giving him glucose and making electrocardiograms. He talks clearly and his color is good."

Dr. Harold Bailey, who treated Bryant until Dr. Allen reached the hospital, said the coach told him the had no history of heart trouble.

Dr. Bailey was quoted in one report as saying Bryant told him he had felt chest pains. Bailey said Bryant told him no such thing.

Pepperdine athletic director Duck Dowell said about 500 coaches from many parts of the nation turned out for Bryant's talk at Pepperdine's Friendship Hall.

"Bear had talked maybe two or three minutes," Dowell said, "when he stopped and said 'Something's wrong up here . . . Is there a doctor in the house?'

"Then he just fell over sideways on the platform . . . He didn't look good when he first stood up. He was wan. But he started his talk off rath-

Please Turn to Page 6, Col. 6

# SANDY ENDS THE AGONY---DODGERS DO IT!

Los Angeles Times
Sports
BUSINESS & FINANCE
CC PART III 2¢
MONDAY, OCTOBER 3, 1966

## Victory Bath: Champagne and Shaving Cream

PHILADELPHIA (AP) — Tommy Davis poured a full bottle of champagne over Sandy Koufax, and the Los Angeles Dodgers' pitching ace sputtered through the bubbles, "Thank God it's over."

The second-game victory behind Koufax that clinched the National League pennant for the Dodgers touched off a wild spree in the clubhouse.

Wes Covington ran from man to man, squirting shaving cream in their faces. Al Ferrara, a sub outfielder, stalked the range in a wide-brimmed sombrero while puffing on a cigar.

The Dodgers gave their radio announcer, Vince Scully, the shaving cream treatment.

Manager Walter Alston survived a champagne bath and retreated to his calm corner of the noisy room.

"Will you compare this pennant with the five others you won?" Alston was asked.

"Well, they are kind of similar," said the calmest man in the room who never loses his cool in the heat of battle.

Koufax revealed he had "popped" his back in the fifth inning and had undergone treatment and an application of "hot stuff" from trainers Bill Buhler and Wayne Anderson before he came out to bat in the sixth.

"It will probably be a little stiff tomorrow," said the 27-game winner. "I'll be ready for game No. 2 in the Series."

Alston said he would decide between Don Drysdale, who was knocked out by the Phillies in the first game Sunday, and lefthander Claude Osteen, the loser Friday night, for Wednesday's starting assignment against Baltimore at Dodger Stadium.

"Sandy probably will go in the second game," said Alston.

THAT CLASSIC FORM — Sandy Koufax, the Dodgers' masterful southpaw, displays the form that subdued the Phillies and won pennant for Los Angeles on last day of the National League season.

## Koufax Lifts L.A. to Flag Again, 6-3

BY FRANK FINCH
Times Staff Writer

PHILADELPHIA—Sandy Koufax, who pitches in pain, ended the Dodgers' agony after sundown Sunday by whizzing a third strike past Jackie Brandt to give the jittery Dodgers their second straight National League pennant.

When Brandt became Koufax's 10th strikeout victim, the Dodgers had a 6-3 victory over the Phillies which ended the gallant charge by the San Francisco Giants.

Earlier on the pressure-packed Sabbath, the Giants backed the Dodgers against the wall by rallying to defeat Pittsburgh after Los Angeles blew a 4-3 game to the Phillies in the first game of the doubleheader.

The Dodgers were not mathematically dead when they kicked the opener away as the Phillies rallied for two runs in the eighth, but they were in dire peril of missing a World Series date with the champion Baltimore Orioles Wednesday in Dodger Stadium.

**Giants Go Home**

A loss in the nightcap would have given San Francisco a chance to tie for first place by beating Cincinnati in a postponed game today, but instead the Giants headed for the Golden Gate after the Golden Arm staved off a last-round rally by the stubborn Phillies.

And the Dodgers flew home to prepare for the Series, which Don Drysdale will draw the honor of starting although he did not last long Sunday. "I'll be ready Wednesday," was Don's ominous promise.

After drinking the bitter dregs of defeat behind locked clubhouse doors following the opener, the Dodgers quaffed the exhilarating wine of victory in the frenzied madhouse of their quarters.

**Champagne Corks Pop**

Champagne corks popped like machine-gun fire and not all of the cold bubbly disappeared down throats. Gallons of it splashed and sprayed virtually everybody in the jam-packed clubhouse.

As the first National League champions to repeat since Fred Haney led the Milwaukee Braves into the winner's circle in 1957-58, the doughty Dodgers presented their loyal Los Angeles following with their fourth pennant in nine years. Three of them have come in the last four years.

They won in 1959, 1963 and 1965, and for the sake of hunch bettors it should be mentioned that they went on to bag World Series crowns from the White Sox, Yankees and Twins.

It was a year ago to the day that

Please Turn to Page 6, Col. 4

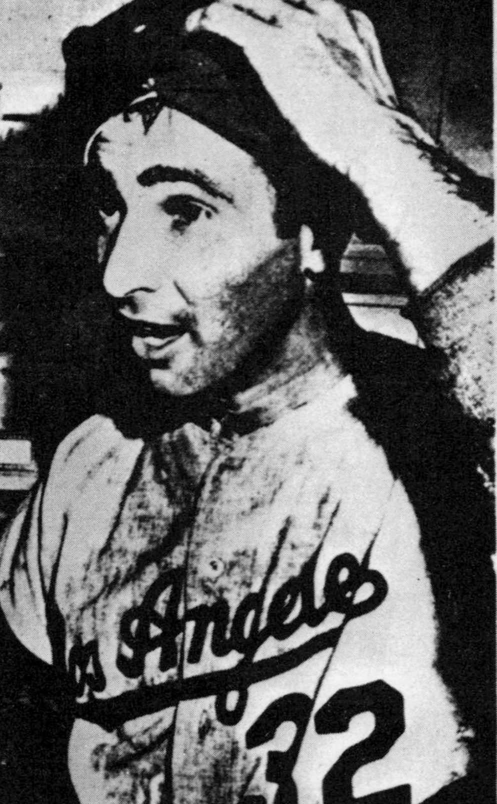

'GEE, —WE FINALLY WON'—Showing the pixie in him, Koufax cuts up with his mates in jubilant clubhouse celebration after the Dodgers clinched the pennant with a 6-3 victory over Philadelphia Phils. AP Wirephotos

## SID ZIFF

### Amazing Bruins Make Mistakes, Still Win

After that frantic finish in the National League race, I'm about ready to go along with the Chicago palmist who read Wes Parker's hand and said the Baltimore Orioles would win the World Series. It could be the year the big bat finally stops the league with the best pitching.

There are no easy outs in the Baltimore lineup. When you face Russ Snyder, Luis Aparicio, Boog Powell, Frank Robinson and Brooks Robinson in a row, it's too much.

Alvin Dark, Kansas City manager, told newsmen recently that Frank Robinson had as fine a season as a man can have.

"His 49 home runs and 121 runs batted in are two men's job," Dark said. "Split 'em in half and it is still a good day's work."

Many a high salaried major league star would settle for 24 homers and 60 RBI for the season.

Those UCLA Bruins continue to be amazing. They had their hands full beating Missouri, 24 to 15, Saturday, making a raft of mistakes, and yet it was all very impressive. It is never easy to beat a class outfit and they can't come much better than Mizzou. It's like playing Michigan State or Alabama.

The Bruins could be better this year than their Rose Bowl champs of '66. They had some defensive weaknesses in their opening game. They've been overcome. They have a whole new set of receivers and all of them are sharp. They have more good receivers than last year. And, if anything, the overall team is quicker.

"If we can keep our poise when we're behind and turn it on a little better offensively we could be better than last year," conceded UCLA's coach Tommy Prothro.

Dan Devine, Missouri's coach, said the Bruins aren't good — "they're great." He was overwhelmed by their quickness. "When you have great personnel, give them great coaching, and have a dedicated attitude, you've got a tough competitor," said Devine.

Of course, you still have to get the breaks to wind up in the Rose Bowl, so we're not declaring them in yet.

Gary Beban wasn't satisfied with his performance. He was disappointed because he didn't cash in on more opportunities. "We made enough mistakes to throw away two games," he said. "I'll have to improve my passing. I had three interceptions, although my arm was hit on one before I threw the ball. I shouldn't have thrown it. It was too dangerous."

Beban also lost a touchdown when he overran the line of scrimmage before he threw to Cornell Champion in the end zone.

"I could have cut the inside corner and run it over," he said. "I knew I'd run too far but I'd already made up my mind. I was hoping the officials hadn't spotted it."

*Farr's Problem*

Mel Farr's fumble on the goal line in the first quarter was another error that kept Mizzou in the game. But that's all the more reason why you're impressed with the Bruins. They don't let misfortune ruffle them. When they found themselves in danger in the fourth quarter, they moved 50 yards in a sensational manner to lock it up.

Farr's overall effort was superb but he is worried about his tendency to fumble. "That's the third one for me this season," he said. "I've had a fumble in all three games. I guess I'm jinxed when I get down there. All I can think of is crossing the goal line when I should be remembering that when you're down there they'll be grabbing for the ball."

It's a flaw in Farr's game but the only one.

The Bruins handled a team that was much heavier and also very well coached. It's the mark of a champion.

## Wilt Does Little, but Philly Still Tops Lakers, 116-109

BY DAN HAFNER
Times Staff Writer

The Philadelphia 76ers, with little help from the big man, Wilt Chamberlain, extended the Laker losing streak to six Sunday night by scoring a 116-109 victory. In the first part of a doubleheader that lured 10,196 fans to the Sports Arena, San Francisco whipped Cincinnati, 134-118.

Chamberlain, obviously well below top condition, played a little over half the game and scored only six points. But new 76er coach Alex Hannum used veterans almost exclusively and they came from far behind to score the victory.

Fred Schaus isn't about to panic. He proved this by using a rookie-dominated lineup throughout the final quarter after his regulars led most of the way.

Chamberlain wasn't the only fel-

Please Turn to Page 5, Col. 1

## PRO FOOTBALL

NATIONAL LEAGUE

Eastern Conference

| | W | L | T | Pct. | PF | PA |
|---|---|---|---|---|---|---|
| St. Louis | 4 | 0 | 0 | 1.000 | 114 | 58 |
| Dallas | 3 | 0 | 0 | 1.000 | 127 | 38 |
| Philadelphia | 2 | 2 | 0 | .500 | 81 | 84 |
| Cleveland | 2 | 2 | 0 | .500 | 114 | 76 |
| Washington | 2 | 2 | 0 | .500 | 78 | 98 |
| Pittsburgh | 1 | 2 | 1 | .333 | 88 | 94 |
| New York | 0 | 3 | 1 | .000 | 65 | 149 |
| Atlanta | 0 | 4 | 0 | .000 | 48 | 117 |

Western Conference

| | W | L | T | Pct. | PF | PA |
|---|---|---|---|---|---|---|
| Green Bay | 4 | 0 | 0 | 1.000 | 92 | 50 |
| RAMS | 3 | 1 | 0 | .750 | 97 | 58 |
| Baltimore | 2 | 1 | 0 | .667 | 77 | 61 |
| Detroit | 2 | 2 | 0 | .500 | 59 | 53 |
| Chicago | 1 | 2 | 0 | .333 | 33 | 55 |
| San Francisco | 0 | 2 | 1 | .000 | 37 | 90 |
| Minnesota | 0 | 3 | 1 | .000 | 70 | 99 |

Sunday's Results

Chicago 13, Minnesota 10
Cleveland 28, New York 7
Dallas 47, Atlanta 14
Green Bay 23, Detroit 14
Washington 24, Pittsburgh 10
St. Louis 41, Philadelphia 10

AMERICAN LEAGUE

Eastern Division

| | W | L | T | Pct. | PF | PA |
|---|---|---|---|---|---|---|
| New York | 3 | 0 | 1 | 1.000 | 111 | 58 |
| Buffalo | 3 | 2 | 0 | .600 | 141 | 127 |
| Houston | 2 | 3 | 0 | .400 | 147 | 126 |
| Boston | 1 | 2 | 1 | .333 | 72 | 101 |
| Miami | 0 | 4 | 0 | .000 | 62 | 144 |

Western Division

| | W | L | T | Pct. | PF | PA |
|---|---|---|---|---|---|---|
| San Diego | 4 | 0 | 0 | 1.000 | 124 | 37 |
| Kansas City | 3 | 1 | 0 | .750 | 133 | 83 |
| Oakland | 1 | 3 | 0 | .250 | 53 | 106 |
| Denver | 1 | 3 | 0 | .250 | 64 | 124 |

Sunday's Results

San Diego 44, Miami 10
Denver 40, Houston 38
Buffalo 20, Kansas City 14
New York 24, Boston 24

## GIANTS PLAY WAITING GAME AT THE AIRPORT

BY CHARLES MAHER
Times Staff Writer

PITTSBURGH—The San Francisco Giants won the game they had to win at Forbes Field Sunday, but they didn't make out so well at the Greater Pittsburgh Airport.

They were sitting in a passenger lounge there at 7:12 p.m. when Chub Feeney, the club vice president, walked in and said:

"It's all over at Philadelphia. The Dodgers won it, 6-3 . . . you guys did all you could. We're proud of you."

A little more than two hours earlier, the Giants had completed a sweep of their 3-game Pittsburgh series, breaking an 11th-inning tie on a 2-run homer by Willie McCovey and beating the Pirates, 7-3.

The Dodgers had lost the first game of their doubleheader in Philadelphia. If the Phillies beat Sandy Koufax in the second game, the Giants would go to Cincinnati to make up a rained-out game with the Reds. And if they won that, they'd be tied with the Dodgers and there would be a playoff.

But if the Dodgers won their second game, San Francisco would be eliminated. So, instead of going to Cincinnati, the Giants would go home.

By the time the Giants got to the airport, the Dodgers were leading, 4-0. Feeney was getting periodic reports on the game by phone and relaying them to the players in the lounge. After 8½ innings it was 6-0 Dodgers.

Giant pitcher Ron Herbel was standing outside the lounge. An airline employe said to him, "You guys don't even know where you're going, huh?"

"We know where we're going," Herbel said. "Superman is not going to give them seven runs in the ninth inning."

A few minutes later, however, the Giants got the word that the Phils had scored three in the ninth and had a man on second with one out. Bobby Wine was hitting for pitcher Darold Knowles.

The Giants were not greatly en-

Please Turn to Page 6, Col. 1

## FINAL STANDINGS

NATIONAL LEAGUE

| | W | L | Pct. | GBL |
|---|---|---|---|---|
| DODGERS | 95 | 67 | .586 | |
| San Francisco | 93 | 68 | .578 | 1½ |
| Pittsburgh | 92 | 70 | .568 | 3 |
| Philadelphia | 87 | 75 | .537 | 8 |
| Atlanta | 85 | 77 | .525 | 10 |
| St. Louis | 83 | 79 | .512 | 12 |
| Cincinnati | 76 | 84 | .475 | 18 |
| Houston | 72 | 90 | .444 | 23 |
| New York | 66 | 95 | .410 | 28½ |
| Chicago | 59 | 103 | .364 | 36 |

SUNDAY'S RESULTS

Philadelphia 4-3, DODGERS 3-6
San Francisco 7, Pittsburgh 3 (11 innings)
St. Louis 2, Chicago 0
Houston 6-8, New York 1-2
Atlanta 4, Cincinnati 2

AMERICAN LEAGUE

| | W | L | Pct. | GBL |
|---|---|---|---|---|
| Baltimore | 97 | 63 | .606 | |
| Minnesota | 89 | 73 | .549 | 9 |
| Detroit | 88 | 74 | .543 | 10 |
| Chicago | 83 | 79 | .512 | 15 |
| Cleveland | 81 | 81 | .500 | 17 |
| ANGELS | 80 | 82 | .494 | 18 |
| Kansas City | 74 | 86 | .463 | 23 |
| Washington | 71 | 88 | .447 | 25½ |
| Boston | 72 | 90 | .444 | 26 |
| New York | 70 | 89 | .440 | 26½ |

SUNDAY'S RESULTS

ANGELS 2, Cleveland 0
New York 2, Chicago 0
Baltimore 6-0, Minnesota 2-1
Kansas City 7, Detroit 5
Only games scheduled

## Bukich-to-Ditka Pass Sinks Vikes

MINNEAPOLIS-ST. PAUL (UPI) —The Chicago Bears, their offense tied up for most of the game, edged the Minnesota Vikings, 13-10, Sunday on a 19-yard touchdown pass from Rudy Bukich to Mike Ditka with less than three minutes to play.

The Bears, who got their first win of the season over the winless Vikings, had to settle for a pair of field goals before Ditka bulled his way over in the closing minutes.

Bukich hit Ditka on the 15 yard line. The rugged tight end bounced away from two Minnesota defenders and fell into the end zone for the winning score.

Fumbles proved costly to the Vikings who saw the bobbles lead to 10 points.

Bill Brown dropped Fran Tarkenton's lateral pass on the Viking 44 and Chicago linebacker Joe Fortunato recovered when none of the Vikings pursued the ball. The Minnesotans apparently thought the ball was an incomplete forward pass.

Carl Kassulke intercepted a Bukich pass on the Minnesota 4 on the next play but the Vikings were forced to punt and Chicago took over on the Viking 45 and scored three plays later.

On the game's opening play from scrimmage, Brown fumbled and Fortunato pounced on the ball on the Minnesota 17. The Bears could not move and Roger Leclerc kicked a 25-yard field goal.

Minnesota took a 7-3 lead with less than five mintues gone in the third period. Tarkenton hit Paul Flatley over the middle on the Chicago 15 and the swift spread-end sprinted in. Fred Cox kicked the extra point.

Cox kicked a 26-yard field goal with only 38 seconds gone in the fourth quarter to increase the Minnesota lead to 10-3. Chicago took the kickoff and marched from its own 35 to the rival 12 where the Viking defense held and forced Leclerc to settle for a 12-yard field goal.

Cox tried a 34-yard field goal on the last play of the game. But Chicago's Dick Evey broke through and blocked the kick. Bukich, who had a slow start, finished with 13 completions in 25 throws for 179 yards. Ronnie Bull and Gale Sayers were

Please Turn to Page 4, Col. 3

# BRUINS DO IT AGAIN! AWAIT BOWL BID

CC SECTION D †
SUNDAY, NOVEMBER 20, 1966

### *JIM MURRAY*

## Coliseum--- 3000 A.D.

The year will perhaps be 3000 A.D. when archaeologists, sifting through the radioactive dust of our civilization, will come upon a sensational discovery which will rival the unearthing of the Dead Land Scrolls of 2096 (which turned out to be back issues of the Sporting News) and the hypothesis published by Professor A. Conclusion Jumper Sr. that a significant majority of 20th century (a period of history identified chronologically to go along with the Ice Age and the Dark Ages as The Ash Age) lawmakers were thespians by profession — a contention hotly disputed by his colleagues, who will claim they were fry cooks and housewives.

The new discovery will center about an ancient ruin known as the "Los Angeles Coliseum" where diggers will uncover in sequence: 1) rotting series of multi-colored cards; 2) rolls of unraveled toilet paper which have obviously been heaved in the air; 3) shreds of decorative devices labeled by historic researchers as "pompons"; 4) banners translated as "Tromp the Trojans" which will momentarily baffle researchists who had tentatively tabled the Trojan era as 25 centuries earlier; 5) a bear costume; and 6) two glockenspiels with red and gold and blue and gold ribbons attached.

### *Tribal Outpouring*

At first, the discovery will be believed to be a fertility rite practiced by the savages who inhabited the area in that dawn of history but, eventually, a scholar will emerge who will conclusively label it a tribal rite known as "The Big Game."

"'The Big Game' was an enormous tribal outpouring some time just before the winter solstice where admission was limited to an elite and by ticket only with the pecking order arranged in seating precisely according to social standing.

"The proceedings were enlivened by cards manipulated to simulate animals performing human functions while on the field a factional dispute was settled between armed and helmeted ruffians recruited for the purpose from the back of tractors, the front of trucks, pool rooms, and class room, with the limiting factor that no one wearing a neck size under 18 was eligible.

"They appeared to have fought over an inflated pig bladder and the contest may have been lethal in some aspects in that, amid the debris surrounding the camps of the rival factions, called 'benches' from the crude wooden divans ón which they awaited the call to battle, were found stethoscopes, oxygen machines, towels with bloodstains on them, teeth and here and there, a stretcher.

### *U for Uncouth*

"Archaeologists are of the opinion each 'bench' held at least one doctor, presumably a surgeon, a first-aid man known as a 'trainer' and at least one priest and two interns who sat in a machine with red-lights and siren, presumably for rapid transit of the more seriously injured to base hospitals.

"The contending forces were identified alphabetically as 'USC' and 'UCLA' and the science of archaeology is temporarily baffled except that all members of the cipher division are agreed the first letter stood for 'Uncouth' until a similar set of findings were uncovered in New Haven, Conn., where a similar 'Big Game' rite

Please Turn to Page 15, Col. 1

TOUCHDOWN!—Norm Dow had quite a day filling in for UCLA's injured star, Gary Beban, against USC Saturday. Here, he scores first Bruin touchdown on 5-yard run around right end in third quarter as Trojan Bill Jaroncyk gives chase. The busy Dow gained 82 yards in 19 carries.

Times photo by Ben Olender

## Dow's Heroics Spill Trojans in 14-7 Upset

BY JOHN HALL
Times Staff Writer

Who's Gary Beban?

It's not only Bruin Town again, it's Dow Town.

Norman Dow, the shadow who had never started a game, began one and finished one Saturday as he burned up the Coliseum, burned down USC and directed the battling UCLA Bruins to another unbelievable 14-7 victory over the Trojans —a win that quite likely will also direct Tommy Prothro's machine right back into the Rose Bowl.

Not quite understanding what it was witnessing, a gathering of 81,980 saw Dow calmly turn an otherwise cloudless, perfect November afternoon into an early sunset for Troy.

The 21-year-old senior from Sunnyvale scored the first Bruin touchdown himself, set up the second with the biggest clutch run of the big day and happily turned the 37th renewal of the crosstown dogfight into his personal masterpiece.

**Clincher by Champion**

As it happened a year ago when the underdog Bruins bumped USC out of the Rose Bowl, the clincher came in the final quarter—Cornell Champion taking a reverse from Dow and dashing 21 yards around the left side for the tie-breaking touchdown.

There was 6:20 still on the clock, plenty of time for USC to retaliate, but it might as well have been six months.

This was UCLA's game.

After a scoreless first half, the Bruins took command impressively in the final 30 minutes, tallying first, recovering from a temporary Trojan comeback score and then opening distance as they won it going away.

As a result, USC's perfect AAWU mark was reduced to 4-1, UCLA climbed to 3-1, and it'll take a conference vote to determine which club—the blue or red—represents the West against Purdue Jan. 2 at

Please Turn to Page 10, Col. 3

## No. 1 Ranking Still Undecided as Irish, Spartans Tie, 10-10

### Battered Notre Dame Overcomes 10-0 Deficit, Then Plays Ball Control; Hanratty Hurt, Lost for USC Game

BY PAUL ZIMMERMAN
Times Sports Editor

EAST LANSING, Mich.—Notre Dame's great comeback led to a 10-10 tie with Michigan State here on a chilly Saturday afternoon, but the ball-control tactics of the Irish in the last minute of play led to boos from many of the 80,011 frigid fans.

The question of which team is No. 1 in the nation was left unanswered.

While the Spartans were stopping the clock in a forlorn hope of getting the ball back in the dying moments, Notre Dame stuck to the ground to save the tie. It was an expensive tie at that, because quarterback Terry Hanratty suffered a shoulder separation and cannot play against USC next Saturday at Los Angeles.

**Too Hard a Fight**

"I simply wasn't going to give away cheaply the tie our crippled team had fought so hard to obtain," said coach Ara Parseghian in defense of the ball-control game at the end. Notre Dame had trailed, 10-0, late into the second quarter.

"If we'd been in the middle of the field it might have been different. But with the ball on our 35, I wasn't going to risk a pass interception because of the great field goal-kicking ability of Michigan State's (Dick) Kenney.

"After all, the Spartans almost lost the game that way a few plays earlier when we intercepted and were in field goal position."

On that occasion, with five minutes left to go, Joe Azzaro's 41-yard attempt had enough carry but sailed wide by a couple of feet.

Although there was no question of Michigan State's intentions as it took time out after each Irish play in that closing minute, hoping for one chance to break the tie, coach Duffy Daugherty refused to condemn Notre Dame's strategy.

"That's not my area," said Duffy. "Anything I would say could be construed as a criticism."

Then he changed the subject.

"We think we are the best. I don't think anyone can say Notre Dame is better than us. We both deserve the national championship."

Getting back to Notre Dame's last-minute decision to protect the tie, coach Parseghian said:

"After we got that field goal on the first play of the final quarter, I certainly gave no consideration to a tie. I felt we had a good chance but it just didn't work out that way.

"At the end I had to feel that any team that could come back after being 10-0 behind, after losing its quarterback, its best runner, and its No. 1 center, deserved not to lose. I am

Please Turn to Page 6, Col. 5

### Rose Bowl Handicap

AAWU
Final

| | W | L | T | Pct. | PF | PA |
|---|---|---|---|---|---|---|
| USC | 4 | 1 | 0 | .800 | 101 | 44 |
| UCLA | 3 | 1 | 0 | .750 | 53 | 38 |
| Oregon State | 3 | 1 | 0 | .750 | 85 | 62 |
| Washington | 4 | 3 | 0 | .571 | 114 | 102 |
| California | 2 | 3 | 0 | .400 | 78 | 102 |
| Oregon | 1 | 3 | 0 | .250 | 42 | 47 |
| Washington St. | 1 | 3 | 0 | .250 | 40 | 94 |
| Stanford | 1 | 4 | 0 | .200 | 43 | 67 |

BIG TEN
Final

| | W | L | T | Pct. | PF | PA |
|---|---|---|---|---|---|---|
| *Michigan St. | 7 | 0 | 0 | 1.000 | 213 | 71 |
| Purdue | 6 | 1 | 0 | .857 | 192 | 88 |
| Illinois | 4 | 3 | 0 | .571 | 149 | 140 |
| Michigan | 4 | 3 | 0 | .571 | 171 | 110 |
| Minnesota | 3 | 3 | 1 | .500 | 75 | 89 |
| Ohio State | 3 | 4 | 0 | .429 | 72 | 76 |
| Wisconsin | 2 | 4 | 1 | .358 | 61 | 133 |
| Northwestern | 2 | 4 | 1 | .358 | 109 | 139 |
| Indiana | 1 | 5 | 1 | .215 | 87 | 160 |
| Iowa | 1 | 6 | 0 | .143 | 52 | 172 |

*Not eligible for 1967 Rose Bowl.

A CHAMPION AT WORK — Cornell Champion carried the ball only one time for UCLA Saturday and he made the most of it. He outruns USC defenders (top) and goes 21 yards for winning score.

Times photos

## Rose Bowl Story: It's Up to Vote

Some of the biggest upsets in Athletic Assn. of Western Universities football history have occurred when the conference representatives vote to select the team which will represent them in the Rose Bowl.

Monday at noon they will vote again in San Francisco to select someone to play Purdue at Pasadena Jan. 2. UCLA expects to get the bid after beating USC, 14-7, Saturday. However, the Trojans (4-1) are still conference champions so don't count them out.

Would you believe Oregon State, which finished with a 3-1 record to tie UCLA?

"Off hand," says UCLA coach Tommy Prothro, "I'd say a team with a 9-1 record (UCLA) deserves it over a 7-2 team (USC)."

Says USC coach John McKay, "I said before that I thought the conference champion should be invited."

## Stanford Beats Cal in the Mud

STORY ON PAGE 5

# IRISH HAND TROY WORST BEATING, 51-0

**TOUCHDOWN, THE HARD WAY**—Despite tight defense by USC's Nate Shaw (89) and Mike Battle, Notre Dame's Jim Seymour (85) snares 39-yard touchdown pass from Coley O'Brien.
Times photos by Larry Sharkey

## 88,520 See Notre Dame Gun for No. 1

**BY PAUL ZIMMERMAN**
Times Sports Editor

Either Notre Dame is No. 1 in the nation or USC is far from being the West's most representative team for the Rose Bowl — or both.

Before an astounded crowd of 88,520 at the Coliseum Saturday, the Irish amassed 51 points while holding the Trojans scoreless. It was the largest total ever chalked up against USC.

Either coach Ara Parseghian's Irish have improved vastly since their 26-14 opening game triumph against Purdue or the Trojans are in for another pasting when they tackle the Boilermakers in Pasadena come Jan. 2.

The whopping score was an eloquent answer to the critics who chided coach Parseghian for playing for the tie in that 10-10 game with Michigan State a week ago.

Now, the charge may be that Notre Dame poured it on Saturday, considering that the halftime score was 31-0, but the huge crowd was entitled to see the best each team had to offer. Besides, USC in its anxiety to stop the onslaught, contributed to the massacre.

**Irish The Greatest**

As limp and exhausted as his players after the game, coach John McKay agreed with the Notre Dame mentor, who said:

"This is the best balanced offensive and defensive team I've ever coached or seen."

"I guess I've never seen a better team than Notre Dame was today," was McKay's appraisal. "This will be a tremendous psychological handicap for us in the Rose Bowl."

There could be no doubt about it. Coley O'Brien and Jim Seymour spearheaded the Notre Dame attack to become the automatic selection as leading back and lineman of the game.

Playing his first full game for the Irish, O'Brien completed 21 of 31 passes for 255 of the 461 yards amassed by Notre Dame. Three of the passes went for touchdowns.

Seymour, the great sophomore end, caught 11 passes for 150 yards and two of the three touchdowns through the air.

**Troy Bewildered**

The bewildered USC defense, which had not allowed more than two touchdowns in any one game, saw Notre Dame accomplish this with ease in the first quarter.

When O'Brien was not throwing the ball, he was handing it off to All-American Nick Eddy, Larry Conjar and Dan Harshman for devastating yardage on the ground.

The closest the Trojans came to scoring was in the third period. With the score 38-0 against it, USC moved the ball to the Irish 9 on a series of passes after Adrian Young had returned an interception 43 yards to the Notre Dame 47. The vanquished were back on the 28 when they finally gave up the ball,

Please Turn to Page 8, Col. 3

***JIM MURRAY***

## It Just Goes to Show: You Can't Tie 'em All

Well, USC will show up in the Rose Bowl Jan. 2, all right. But first, we'll have to put 'em in a sack for you.

It may take a while to find all the pieces. When Notre Dame got through with them, they looked like a watch that had been dropped from the Empire State Building.

The last time I saw anything that one-sided, one of the parties was blindfolded.

This Notre Dame team can't play in states that ban capital punishment.

USC made lots of mistakes, not the least of which was showing up. To show you how bad things were, its mascot quit in the third quarter.

The trouble with this USC team is that only about 11 of them are ineligible for the Rose Bowl game. About 44 were ineligible for the Notre Dame game.

Notre Dame, which used to win one for the old Gipper, is now winning one for the old United Press.

Of course, this Notre Dame team showed you can't tie 'em all. The team that was looking under the bed and pulling the sheets over its head against Michigan State last week was hollering, "Let me at 'em!" against USC. They reminded me of a guy who had a bad day at the office, losing a sale and getting passed over for a promotion, going home and kicking the dog. They're good, game winners.

### *Irish Go Airborne*

Ara Parseghian, who wouldn't pass with the score tied and a minute to play last week, was passing with the score 44-0 Saturday.

USC scored a moral victory in holding the Irish scoreless during halftime, but I would say Notre Dame scored an immoral victory in not holding USC scoreless in the last three minutes. Parseghian put his scrubs in the minute he saw the timekeeper reaching for his gun.

Of course, the Trojans — who won the Rose Bowl bid even though they had to be revived to be told—had spent all week being told how bad they were till they vowed to do something about it. They did. They confirmed it.

On the basis of a 14-7 defeat last week, they were voted to go to the Rose Bowl. On the basis of this defeat, the conference will probably order them directly to the Hall of Fame.

Of course, this wasn't the most lopsided contest I've ever seen. Russia vs. Finland was. This one is no worse than seventh, though.

It didn't look as if they were playing the same game. Trojan halfbacks looked like four guys learning to ice skate. They went after Notre Dame ball-carriers like a guy applying for a loan—without collateral.

It was announced before the game that USC had just contracted to play Notre Dame for 10 more years—which will be bad news to the Coliseum scoreboard. The only thing USC outscored Notre Dame in was penalties. It got four to Notre Dame's one. Penalizing USC in this game for little things like pulling face masks is a little like hauling Poland before the World Court for putting out rat poison in advance of the invading Nazis.

Word has it that Rose Bowl rival Purdue sent a post-game wire to USC: "Are you still there?" Ten more minutes and all you would see would be a mushroom cloud.

### *Will USC Show Up?*

There are some who now fear USC will show up in the Rose Bowl swell-headed. And that's not the only place they will have swelling. Some are afraid they won't show up in the Rose Bowl now. Even more are afraid they will. Purdue is said to be checking the Humane Society to see whether the game is even allowable.

The legend of Notre Dame was started by a bald-headed, broken-nosed old codger—a high school dropout—who wouldn't beat you, 51-0, if he caught you robbing the poor box. And he wouldn't let you get away with a 10-10 tie while he still had the football if the end zone was mined.

Knute Rockne and George Gipp, a high-school dropout and a high-school kickout, set the "tone" for this institution which, essentially, only called for kicking a man when he was up. And for kicking back as long as you were up. You invoked the dead, you didn't kick them.

This team is a fine broth of bully-boys who may be first in the

Please Turn to Page 4, Col. 1

### HANDS UP!

Seymour's catch of O'Brien's touchdown pass is all the more remarkable when Shaw's defensive effort can be seen close-up. Shaw appears ← to have his hand on the ball as Battle helps pinch in the 6-foot-4 Irish soph. Seymour still manages to pull the ball away from Shaw to make it 31-0 at halftime.
Times photo by Joe Kennedy

## Irish Out to Show World and Troy Got in Way

**BY JOHN HALL**
Times Staff Writer

Notre Dame had a hunch there might be an earthquake.

The first thing the Fighting-mad Irish did Saturday when they took the field at the Coliseum was drape a banner over the back of their bench.

"To hell with UPI," it read, "we're No. 1."

Sixty minutes, seven touchdowns, six conversions and a field goal later, they hadn't changed their minds.

It wasn't USC the Irish were smashing, 51-0, in the worst-ever whipping suffered by the Trojans. It was the world.

"We're No. 1," they chanted as they raced up the parade tunnel and back to their street clothes.

"Michigan Who?"

"Break out the champagne."

"Who's No. 1?"

"We're No. 1!"

It was the end of the war. Name a war. Any war. Notre Dame won it. Notre Dame demanded unconditional surrender.

**'Best Ever'**

"This is by far the best football team I've ever coached," said Ara Parseghian surrounded by pencils, pens, paper, mikes and camera lights.

He knew where he was.

"Not only that," said the intense, black-haired, sparkling-eyed man who has been a head coach for 16 years, "it is the best-balanced college football team, offensively and defensively, I've ever seen in my life."

Parseghian stood in the middle of a mob, the game ball clutched under his left arm and his navy blue Notre Dame sweat shirt dripping from

Please Turn to Page 8, Col. 1

**TROJAN FRUSTRATION**—USC's Ron Drake (83) typifies the Trojans' frustration as he catches two Toby Page passes, only to have Notre Dame linebacker Dave Martin tackle him almost immediately.
Times photos by Ben Olender

# PACKERS PROVE NFL'S BRAND BEST, 35-10

**BY PAUL ZIMMERMAN**
Times Sports Editor

Like a stern parent chastizing a mischievous child, the Green Bay Packers soundly thrashed the upstart Kansas City Chiefs, 35-10, Sunday in Memorial Coliseum in the first Super Bowl game.

The outstanding master of the whip-lash on a gorgeous summer-like afternoon was Bryan Bartlett Starr, who had been playing in the NFL four years before the junior circuit was born.

The great Packer quarterback completed key third down passes with abandon to the amazement of 63,036 shirt-sleeved spectators, connecting on 16 of 23 throws for 250 yards and two touchdowns as he riddled the Kansas City defense. He was named player of the game.

Kansas City, the recalcitrant child, bitterly opposed the lessons its elders sought to teach in the first half, and left the field before the spectacular half-time show trailing only 14-10.

That was the end of the line for coach Hank Stram's Chiefs, who never got deep into Green Bay territory during the second half as the always rugged Packer defense turned back the AFL champions at the 40-yard line twice—the deepest penetrations.

"We mangled 'em a little bit," was the understatement of Packer fullback Jim Taylor after the game.

Victorious coach Vince Lombardi kindly called the vanquished a good team but honesty got the better of him when he added:

"The Chiefs are not as good as the Cowboys (who lost to Green Bay in the NFL playoff game). They are not as good as the good NFL teams."

The first championship game provided the answer to the question the football world had been asking ever since the AFL was formed.

Naturally, Stram didn't quite agree.

"After the first half I thought we could win. But once the Packers got their third touchdown we had to play to catch up," he pointed out.

That was when the Packer defense really asserted itself, early in the third quarter, blitzing quarterback Len Dawson and turning back the Kansas City ground game.

Stram felt Willie Wood's interception and 50-yard return with a Dawson pass turned the tide in Green Bay's favor. It set the stage for Elijah Pitts' 5-yard touchdown run.

"The interception changed the personality of the game," Stram said.

There was no question about that, but the Packers were going to accomplish the change sooner or later, anyway.

By a quirk of fate, 34-year-old Max McGee emerged from the contest as Starr's key receiver. The 11-year veteran end, who had caught only four passes for 90 yards all season, plus another in the playoff game, replaced the injured Boyd Dowler and snagged seven for 138 yards and a pair of touchdowns.

He made some fantastic catches as Starr riddled the Kansas City deep defenses behind a wall of superb protection.

It was McGee who started the scoring with as spectacular a catch as anyone would want

Please Turn to Page 3, Col. 1

## JIM MURRAY

## Fee, Fi, Fo ---Fumble!

No, Virginia, there is no Santa Claus. They pulled his whiskers off at the Coliseum Sunday and it turned out to be Vince Lombardi saying "Ho, ho, ho!"

Sorry, kids, fairy tales don't come true, after all. Sleeping Beauty was really dead. Hansel and Gretel never did get out of the oven. The giant ate Jack AND the beanstalk.

St. George got eaten by the dragon. The guys in the black hats got clean away with the cattle rustle.

Little Red Riding Hood didn't notice Grandma's ears 'til too late and she found out her teeth were too big the hard way. Goldilocks is just a big lie. The Easter Bunny doesn't really bring all those jelly beans. They get them at Thrifty Drug.

All of which is my way of telling you the clock struck midnight for the American Football League Sunday. Brute strength conquered in the end again. They played for money and them as has, got.

Goliath must have had an off-day. The little guys don't win these things.

What the Super Bowl needed was a rewrite by Walt Disney or Hans Christian Andersen. So it would come out like this:

The little, shy, frightened, big-eyed AFL, wandering through the forests cringing at shadows and shuddering at the roars emanating from the Ogre of the Woods, the NFL Colossus.

"Please, sir, won't you play with me?" asked the shy little league in the red cape and boots. "Fee, fi, fo, fum!" roared the NFL. "Go way and get yourself a football first."

So the little AFL huffed and puffed and he sued the court. And the NFL ate their lawyer. So the AFL said, "Well, I know a shortcut to Grandma's house, otherwise known as the Super Bowl" and sprinkled money around and bought lots of players. Only the giant bought even more.

### Sucker Will Pay

Then, the fairy godmother—the commissioner of football — came along and said, "Wait a minute. Put on this glass slipper and all of a sudden you'll be fairer than all the football leagues in the land." Out of the side of his hand he whispered to his own giant, "Don't worry. This way we'll make the sucker pay and then we'll eat Riding Hood's cape and all right in front of 63,036 people who will pay 12 bucks a head for the privilege of watching. Wouldn't you like to dispose of Little Red Riding Hood on national TV for 2½ million dollars?" And the big giant said, "Fee, fi, fo, fum! Pete has stuck in his thumb and pulled out a plum."

Well, you all know what happens next in fairy tales. Little Red Riding Hood outwits the wicked old wolf, or Jack slays the giant. Cinderella gets the prince.

Well, the Kansas City Chiefs just turned back into pumpkins. As a fairy tale, the Super Bowl wouldn't sell a copy. The Brothers Grimm would sit right down and cry. Peter Pan would crash. It'll never make a movie. Who wants to star the wicked old witch?

Of course, there's another way to look at the Super Bowl game (and you realize here I'm just looking at the thing in its broad literary aspects, not from a prosaic

Please Turn to Page 7, Col. 2

**HOT SHOT** — Packers' Max McGee gathers in 13-yard pass from Bart Starr for his second Super Bowl TD but it wasn't quite as easy as it looks. McGee gave Green Bay fans jitters as he juggled the ball.
Times photo by Ben Olender

PACKERS UNIMPRESSED

## KC Not in Class With NFL's Best--Lombardi

**BY MAL FLORENCE**
Times Staff Writer

For seven years—since the inception of the American Football League — most National Football League coaches have carefully avoided discussing or making any comparisons between teams in the rival professional organizations.

The silence was broken Sunday and Vince Lombardi, of all people, was the man to break it.

"I don't think that Kansas City compares with the top teams of the NFL," said the Green Bay coach whose team had swamped the Chiefs, 35-10, Sunday in the first Super Bowl game.

"That's what you wanted me to say, and I said it," shouted Lombardi from a podium in the cramped Packer dressing room. "It (the statement) has been a long time coming out."

Green Bay's quarters in the Coliseum resembled a snake pit. Hundreds of reporters surrounded Lombardi. Television cameras were hanging from every conceivable angle. Cables were wrapped around the coach, the players and the sports writers. There were as many microphones as there were people.

Lombardi quickly dropped the comparison issue. "I don't like to compare teams," he said. "Kansas City is a good team—let's leave it at that."

He was even loath to declare his team's decisive victory as a great achievement for the NFL as a whole.

"I don't have any ax to grind," he grinned. "I have no reason to hate anybody."

Vince Lombardi
Times photo

Lombardi did say that he thought Kansas City's defensive alignment worked to its disadvantage.

He explained that the Chiefs employed a "stack defense" which, in general layman terms, means that the linebackers were playing directly behind the defensive linemen.

"It's very difficult to run against such a defense, but it makes it easier to throw," continued Lombardi.

The statistics supported Lombardi, as quarterback Bart Starr completed 16 of 23 passes for 250 yards and two touchdowns. The Packers, despite the "stack defense," also managed to move for 130 yards on the ground.

Some football theorists have credited Kansas City coach Hank Stram with inventing the "stack defense," calling it appropriately, the "Stram stack."

"Not many NFL teams use it," said Lombardi dryly. "But Detroit has had it for years."

Lombardi also thought that the Kansas City secondary played his receivers rather "loose."

"They were daring us to pass," he said.

Although the Packers had a fight on their hands in the opening half and led only, 14-10, at halftime, Lombardi said he didn't make any

Please Turn to Page 2, Col. 4

## Goalby Captures San Diego Open

Story on Page 6

## WEST SCORES 39, LAKERS WIN ONE

Story on Page 7

**STARR STARTS IT OFF** — Green Bay's Bart Starr fires a pass toward end Max McGee, who made one hand grab and then evaded Chiefs' Willie Mitchell (22) for first Packer score.
Times photos by Larry Sharkey

# A PERFECT ENDING! UCLA ROUTS DAYTON

BY JEFF PRUGH
Times Staff Writer

LOUISVILLE—It was a symphony with a fast-tempo beat, the kind of performance that was typical of UCLA's "Firehouse Four Plus Lew" all season long.

And in the game that counted most of all, the Bruins made beautiful music together here Saturday night, proving once again that they indeed are unbeatable—so unbeatable, in fact, that they are likely to rule the college basketball world for a long time.

Lew Alcindor, the towering young man who did the most to make this Bruin team unbeatable, again was the most significant factor in his team's victory, a rather blase 79-64 conquest of Dayton's Cinderella team in the national championship game.

It was victory No. 30—a perfect ending to a perfect season. And like so many other Bruin victories, it was one that belonged to the whole team (everybody got into the act) and one that was pretty well assured before the game was even eight minutes old.

In fact, UCLA was so comfortably in front (28 points) with 4½ minutes to go) that the Bruins easily could have broken the NCAA title game record for the winning margin (Ohio State's 75-55 win over Cal in 1960), had coach John Wooden not removed his starting five.

In sweeping to its third NCAA crown in the last four years, UCLA got balanced scoring from Big Lew (20 points), and its dazzling pair of guards, Lucius Allen and Mike Warren, who threw in 19 and 17 points, respectively, many of them after Dayton went into a zone about three minutes before intermission.

Now, with another perfect season, the second in four years for UCLA and for Wooden, this Bruin team accomplished exactly what most everyone had anticipated it would do. It etched its name into college basketball immortality by becoming the youngest ever to win the grand prize.

With four sophomores and a junior on the starting five (and not a senior on the squad), the Bruins are younger than the Ohio State team that started three sophomores—Jerry Lucas, John Havlicek and Mel Nowell—and won the title in 1960, and are younger than Indiana's title-winning team of 1953, which had no senior, either, and was composed mostly of juniors.

For Wooden, who acquired Big Lew, Allen, Lynn Shackelford and Kenny Heitz off the high school All-America team only two years ago, it was perhaps his proudest hour as a coach.

He became the first coach to guide a team to perfect title-winning seasons twice, having done so in 1964 with a diminutive team that also went 30-0 and again this season with a giant of a player—Lew Alcindor, who made his presence known like no other sophomore has in college basketball annals.

The other coaches who led teams to perfect seasons were Phil Woolpert of USF (29-0) in 1956 and Frank McGuire of North Carolina (32-0) in 1957.

There were still other proud accomplishments by this Bruin team:

1. It made UCLA the second school to win at least three national basketball titles. Only Kentucky,

Please Turn to Page 3, Col. 1

## JIM MURRAY

## A Story for Easter

Fables for a modern Easter:

"The heavyweight champion of the world was a great, boastful giant who was widely considered unbeatable. The earth trembled when he walked and the ear shattered when he spoke, which was all the time. People laughed at all his jokes and bowed when he went by. He was so out of opponents that when the promoters led in this skinny, quiet little guy, the press was scandalized, legislators threatened to ban the match, arenas boycotted it. It was denounced in the pulpit and the world covered its eyes.

"The 'contender' was a foot shorter, a hundred pounds lighter and much quieter. Only the bloodthirsty showed up at ringside and the odds were 10-1 as the giant champion swaggered out and roared, 'OK. Sonny, WHAT'S MY NAME?' And the little guy said, 'How should I know—all I care about is where is your temple?' And the big guy said 'Oh, a wise guy, eh? Well, before I pinch your head off, what's yours?' And the little guy said 'David.' "

*Moral: Keep taking the 10-1. Even a heel has an Achilles.*

"Every sports writer in the country knows this story needed a rewrite. There was this kid, see? Born on the wrong side of the tracks and prejudiced against even in the womb. The night before he was born, there wasn't a hotel in town that would let his mother in; they were all restricted. Before he was a week old, the family had to run for the border one jump ahead of a lynch mob. The kids used to laugh at him over the stories he used to tell about his real father.

"He lived all his life in places where you'd be afraid to drink the water. If ever a guy was 20-1 to hate society, he was it. Now, the editors of Sport Magazine know what he SHOULD have done: Beat up old ladies, robbed poor-boxes, slugged his commanding officer, strangled cab drivers or stole from the government. Then he could have gone to prison where he could have learned fighting or football and when he came out they could make him heavyweight champion or give him a scholarship or put him in Congress so they could all sleep nights.

### Worked With Sick

"He was such a great natural athlete some people even said he could walk on water. But he passed all this up to work with the sick and comfort the aged. He should have hated everybody but he didn't hate anybody.

"Naturally, they couldn't leave a man like this at large. I mean, whose SIDE was he on, anyway? So they decided to put him to death. Only the judge didn't want to. 'Wait!' he said. 'Either I kill him

Please Turn to Page 6, Col. 1

**BRUINS' BOUNTY**—UCLA's Kenny Heitz, left, and Lucius Allen, right, lift Mike Warren up to cut off basketball net in traditional victory ceremony after Bruins had defeated Dayton to win NCAA championship. Jim Nielsen of UCLA joins teammates in post-game rites. UCLA built early lead and then coasted.

**IS IT A BIRD?** — No, it's UCLA guard Lucius Allen, who overruns ball retained by Dayton's Rudy Waterman in NCAA title game in Louisville. Bruins capped a perfect season by defeating Flyers, 79-64.

(AP Wirephotos)

## MET EVERY CHALLENGE

## Wooden Rates New Champs on Par With His '64 Team

BY CHARLES MAHER
Times Staff Writer

LOUISVILLE—When it was all over Saturday night, the Dayton cheering section began chanting, "We're No. 2!"

Like Avis, the Dayton fans seemed to relish their subordinate station. And, as a matter of fact, their delight was quite justified. Because a little earlier in the evening their team was so far behind it looked as though it might not even be able to finish as high as second in the final game of the NCAA basketball championship.

The Flyers from Dayton were shot down, 79-64, which is a fairly respectable score. But it was UCLA coach John Wooden who made it so—by putting his reserves in the game with more than five minutes to play. UCLA probably could have won it by 30.

Wooden said after the game that he ranks this UCLA team with his unbeaten national championship squad of three years ago. "They're equal," John said. "They both met every challenge. . .

"We'll have all our players back next year and we should have a better team. But we certainly can't accomplish any more than we did this year."

Someone wondered whether a team that dominates the game as UCLA is likely to do for the next

Please Turn to Page 3, Col. 3

## TROJANS CAPTURE 11 OF 17 EVENTS IN EASTER RELAYS

BY SHAV GLICK
Times Staff Writer

SANTA BARBARA—The 29th Easter Relays were turned into a showcase for USC's powerful track and field team Saturday as 7,000 fans watched the Trojans capture 11 of 17 open events. They set one collegiate, two school and four meet records in the process.

Sophomore Bob Seagren vaulted 17 feet 3 1/4 inches to wipe out ex-Bruin Marc Savage's year old national collegiate record of 16-9, but even this was overshadowed by Earl McCullouch, who earned athlete of the meet honors by winning the high hurdles in a record 13.7, running on the 440 and 880 record relay teams and placing third in the long jump.

McCullouch's 13.7 broke the oldest mark in the Easter Relays book, a 13.8 by Trojan Olympian Jack Davis clear back in 1956.

Eighteen records were set in four divisions as the relays were held in perfect weather conditions at La Playa Stadium overlooking Santa Barbara bay.

The only open record not set by a Trojan went to Arizona's Ed Caruthers with a 7-2½ high jump, second highest ever outdoors by an American. Only John Thomas' 7-3 3/4, made in 1960, has topped Caruthers' leap.

In the 880 relay, USC's Fred

Please Turn to Page 4, Col. 2

## Ryun Easy Winner: 4:05.1, 1:48.1

BY CHUCK GARRITY
Times Staff Writer

Jim Ryun proved one thing Saturday to the disappointment of 4,390 fans at the Coliseum during UCLA's 88-55 track conquest of Kansas: sub-four-minute miles are not every day occurrences, even for him.

The 19-year-old Kansas sophomore glided to an easy 4:05.1 victory in the mile, then came back 50 minutes later to run away with the half in 1:48.1.

And though the mile fans were disappointed at his time, Ryun was happy enough with his day's work.

"I'm running a little tired, but I'm pleased with both times," the personable young world record holder in the mile said. "We put in about 85 miles, mostly sprinting, the past week all between Sunday and Thursday. Then we got in here awfully early Friday (4:45 a.m.)

"So I just wanted to run an easy mile, then come back with a good half. I felt I accomplished both. I really thought the mile would go faster though."

### Identical Bursts

Ryun won both races with nearly identical bursts about 250 yards from the finish. He disposed of the Bruins' Rick Romero in the mile and won by 20 yards. He opened up again in the 880 to turn a close duel with Bruin Arnd Kruger into an 8-yard victory.

While Ryun commanded most of the attention, Kansas teammate Ben Olison came up with the day's best track performance. The former Bakersfield Junior College speedster dealt the heralded Bruin sprinters some embarrassment with a 9.6 victory in the 100 and a 21.2 win in the 220. He came back later with a 46.6 anchor leg for the victorious Jayhawker mile relay team.

Olison edged UCLA's Harold Busby in the 100, then posted the 220 triumph when the fast-starting

Please Turn to Page 4, Col. 7

**LOOKING FOR TROUBLE**—World mile record holder Jim Ryun of Kansas, right, looks around for running room during Saturday's mile against UCLA at the Coliseum. Rick Romero of UCLA, center, holds the lead on the first lap. But Ryun charged away for an easy 4:05.1 victory.

Times photo by Steve Fontanini

**BUD WILKINSON'S ANALYSIS**

# Three Super Plays Did It All for Explosive Trojans

BY BUD WILKINSON

It took three super plays to put USC in business Saturday.

If you took the film of the game and clipped out those three plays—along with the UCLA scoring plays—and then showed the film to any unbiased observer, he'd tell you UCLA had all the better of it.

You'd take out the interception by Pat Cashman that got the Trojans their first touchdown, the flanker reverse by Earl McCullouch that went for 52 yards and set up the second Trojan touchdown, and the 64-yard touchdown run by O. J. Simpson.

Clip out those plays and Southern Cal doesn't get close to the goal. But that's what football is all about. A team with the ability to explode is going to win a lot of games. And the Trojans certainly have that ability.

UCLA had much better field position. In fact, USC took over the ball only once in UCLA territory. The Bruins, on the other hand, got the ball twice in USC territory (once on the 47 and once on the 15) in the first half alone.

The punting of Zenon Andrusyshyn had a lot to do with UCLA's field position. The way I figure it, punting yardage is net yardage. That is, how far you kick the ball, less the return. In the first half, UCLA averaged 39.7 yards punting to 23.3 for USC, and in the second half it was 41 yards for UCLA to 24 for USC.

*Bud Wilkinson, the former University of Oklahoma coach whose teams won 12 consecutive Big Eight titles, prepared this analysis of the USC-UCLA game exclusively for The Times.*

But the fact that Andrusyshyn had two field goals blocked took a little of the edge off his performance. You figure he can kick a field goal just about any time he gets inside the 35. But the Bruins got him in there and he missed one and had two blocked.

The blocking of those two field goals was certainly a key to the game. The two blocks saved the Trojans.

USC overloaded the right side of its line on those two plays. It had five men rushing from the right side and only three from the left.

Bill Hayhoe, who stands 6-feet-8, was one of the men on the right side. I think he was responsible for the second block.

As great a kicker as Andrusyshyn is, he kicks a ball that takes off on a low trajectory. Naturally, this makes it easier to block.

Another big play, of course, was the blocked conversion attempt by Andrusyshyn. On this one, I thought there was a poor center snap.

This game more than lived up to expectations. Sometimes, in a game with a buildup like this, one of two things will happen. One side will get a hot hand and the score won't even be close. Or both teams will be so tight they won't execute and the game will get dull.

But you see a game like this and you wish football wasn't over in 60 minutes. You wish you could see these two teams play again next week.

I know how fierce this rivalry is and how much the game meant to both squads and both coaches. From the standpoint of tactics and strategy, effort and execution, it was apparent both teams deserved the rankings

Please Turn to Page 4, Col. 6

CC SECTION D 3†
SUNDAY, NOVEMBER 19, 1967

# A Change in Plans...An O. J. Run...And Roses!

A RUN FOR THE ROSES—USC's magnificent halfback, O. J. Simpson, heads down field behind teammate Bob Klein during his 64-yard touchdown dash in fourth quarter against UCLA Saturday at the Coliseum. O. J. gained 177 yards. For another view of the winning run see Page 5.

Times photo by Joe Kennedy

## Trojans Win It All, 21-20, From Bruins, Head for No. 1

BY PAUL ZIMMERMAN
Times Sports Editor

**An audible signal called at the line of scrimmage by quarterback Toby Page in the fourth quarter turned O. J. Simpson loose on a 64-yard touchdown run at Memorial Coliseum Saturday to put USC in the Rose Bowl.**

It was to have been a pass play to Ron Drake, hardly calculated to go the distance.

When Page saw the UCLA defense go into double coverage on his split end, he changed to a weak-side smash by his work-horse halfback. O. J. put on a spectacular burst of speed once he broke into the clear, reversed his field and went all the way for the score.

Sophomore Rikki Aldridge kicked the extra point, to give the Trojans a 21-20 victory after a rugged contest that had attracted a wild-cheering crowd of 90,772 and held the attention of an estimated 10 million television viewers.

**One of Greatest Games**

Whether that run earns Simpson the Heisman Trophy and moves coach John McKay's Trojans back as the No. 1 team in the nation remains for the voters to decide later. But the witnesses will remember this game as one of the greatest.

UCLA's brilliant quarterback, Gary Beban, completed 16 of 24 passes for 301 yards, although obviously hurting from a rib injury, to also keep alive his hopes for the coveted Heisman Trophy.

Perhaps because it was a USC victory, the writers named Simpson the back of the game.

No one could fault the choice because the big halfback with a sprinter's speed raced for 177 yards and scored two of the three Trojan touchdowns.

**Full Page of Pictures on Page 5**

"A lot of people in this town are going to say I'm a lot smarter than I was last year when we lost," quipped McKay, who then revealed the play he had sent in was countermanded by his quarterback for the winning touchdown.

The play Page called was identical to the one that broke Simpson loose for an 86-yard dash against Washington a few weeks ago.

**O. J. Takes Off**

O.J., after taking the handoff, faked to the strong side then swerved to the left as tackle Mike Taylor and guard Steve Lehmer opened the hole.

Center Dick Allmon knocked down the linebacker and Simpson did the rest, breaking two or three tackles as he went into high gear.

Safety Sandy Green seemed to get his hands on O.J., just as the swift Trojan reversed his field but there wasn't anyone fast enough to catch the 9.4 sprinter after that as he angled for the corner and fled into the end zone.

"It was a great call by Page when he saw the Bruins go into double cover on Drake," praised McKay.

What about Simpson?

"I haven't changed my mind. He's the greatest college runner I"ve ever

Please Turn to Page 6, Col. 5

**JIM MURRAY**

## Bruins Learn a Lesson in Higher Mathematics

Whew!

I'm glad I didn't go to the opera Saturday afternoon, after all. This was the first time in a long time where the advance ballyhoo didn't live up to the game.

The last time these many cosmic events were settled by one day of battle, they struck off a commemorative stamp and elected the winner President.

I'm talking about the USC-UCLA game. It had so much pre-game build-up that, if I'm betting, it had to be the biggest stinker since the last Anna Sten movie. A 0-0 tie, I told myself. A game they could play at night with the lights out.

It was a four heart-attack feature. More fun than watching Sophia Loren getting ready for bed with the shades up. A total of 41 points were scored. One more and UCLA is in the Rose Bowl.

Everything was at stake but French Equatorial Africa in this one. The Heisman Trophy, the Rose Bowl, the conference championship, the national championship and probably the Republican nomination.

On that commemorative stamp, they can put a double image—one of UCLA's Gary Beban and one of USC's Orenthal James Simpson. They can send that Heisman Trophy out with two straws, please.

O. J. Simpson plays the game like a pool hall hustler. He runs a few losing tables at the start and, just when you're sending home for fresh money or orders to hock the car and bring the check, he starts looking like Willie Hoppe. O. J. played the first half more like Wallis Simpson. He ran like a guy whose feet were killing him. You were beginning to think if they gave him the Heisman Trophy, he'd drop it. You were hoping it wasn't breakable.

The second half, as far as the Bruins were concerned, he just simply disappeared. You pictured them returning to the dressing room and asking each other, "whatever happened to that No. 32 they were playing in the first half—that real slow fellow who kept dropping things?"

He made 30 yards in the first half. He made 64 yards in one run in the second and 177 overall. If he had a light hanging on it, UCLA couldn't get his number.

Give that man one-half a Heisman Trophy.

If Gary Beban gets the Heisman Trophy, I hope they fill it with aspirin first. To give you an idea, Beban was disappearing under two tons of beef all afternoon when it hurt him even to turn over in bed. The cartilage is torn away from his ribs but it only hurts when he breathes. Gary was getting his breath by mail most of the game. It took him two minutes to inhale sometimes. Between screams.

If he had two yards more of tape, they would have had to turn him over to the County Museum. He

Please Turn to Page 9, Col. 1

**OTHER BIG ONES**

## Gophers Shatter Hoosiers' Hopes

**MINNESOTA 33, INDIANA 7**

Minnesota shattered Indiana's dream of a perfect season and took the inside track to the Rose Bowl classic. Both have 5-1 conference records, but Indiana must face Purdue (6-0) while Minnesota plays winless (0-5-1) Wisconsin (Story on Page 3).

**PURDUE 21, MICHIGAN ST. 7**

National scoring leader Leroy Keyes caught a pass for his 19th touchdown of the season, passed for another and picked up 193 yards in 24 carries to help keep Purdue unbeaten in the Big Ten (Story on Page 3).

**CALIFORNIA 26, STANFORD 3**

Sophomore quarterback Randy Humphries threw two touchdown passes in the last quarter and sneaked over for another as California scored its first "Big Game" victory over Stanford since 1960 (Story on Page 12).

## THE ROSE PARADE

**PACIFIC EIGHT**

| | W | L | T | Pct. | PF | PA |
|---|---|---|---|---|---|---|
| USC | 6 | 1 | 0 | .857 | 182 | 47 |
| UCLA | 4 | 1 | 1 | .750 | 193 | 90 |
| Oregon St. | 4 | 1 | 1 | .750 | 87 | 53 |
| Wash'gton | 3 | 3 | 0 | .500 | 75 | 97 |
| Stanford | 3 | 4 | 0 | .429 | 88 | 121 |
| California | 2 | 3 | 0 | .400 | 79 | 107 |
| Oregon | 1 | 5 | 0 | .167 | 60 | 119 |
| Wash. St. | 0 | 5 | 0 | .000 | 53 | 183 |

**BIG TEN**

| | W | L | T | Pct. | PF | PA |
|---|---|---|---|---|---|---|
| *Purdue | 6 | 0 | 0 | 1.000 | 211 | 72 |
| Minnesota | 5 | 1 | 0 | .833 | 106 | 70 |
| Indiana | 5 | 1 | 0 | .833 | 130 | 89 |
| Ohio State | 4 | 2 | 0 | .667 | 84 | 92 |
| Michigan | 3 | 3 | 0 | .500 | 90 | 112 |
| Mich. State | 2 | 4 | 0 | .333 | 98 | 84 |
| N'rthwestern | 2 | 4 | 0 | .333 | 98 | 102 |
| Illinois | 2 | 4 | 0 | .333 | 81 | 127 |
| Iowa | 0 | 5 | 1 | .083 | 94 | 133 |
| Wisconsin | 0 | 5 | 1 | .083 | 79 | 131 |

*Not eligible for Rose Bowl.

A CRIME THAT PAID—Trojan defensive back Pat Cashman steals ball from UCLA's Greg Jones and sprints 55 yards for USC's first touchdown Saturday Trojans' Jim Gunn and Jim Snow move in on play.

Times photo by Larry Sharkey

# BIG E STANDS FOR END OF BRUIN STREAK

**BY JEFF PRUGH**
Times Staff Writer

HOUSTON—It happened!

Some people said it would never be done. Never! Others muttered maybe—just maybe it would.

So, just as sure as death and Texas it happened here Saturday night. And the king is dead.

High and mighty UCLA, ruler of the college basketball world, finally went down to defeat, 71-69, to the muscular Houston Cougars and Elvin (Big E) Hayes, who pulled it off before the largest crowd ever to see a basketball game in the United States.

It was No. 2 conquering No. 1, the Big E upstaging a below-par Lew Alcindor. And it all happened before 52,693 in the Houston Astrodome and a television audience of millions more.

Hayes, a 6-8 All-American forward with massive shoulders and a feather touch, swished 39 points—including the two free throws that won the game with 28 seconds left—as the Cougars (17-0) turned back a team that many had labeled the greatest college team ever.

Not only was it the first defeat for UCLA, 13-1 this season, but it was the Bruins' first setback in 48 games. Their 47-game winning streak dated back to Feb. 19, 1966.

What's more, it was the first time Alcindor had played on a losing side in 72 games—since his senior year (1965) at New York's Power Memorial Academy, and it was the first time UCLA guard Lucius Allen had played for a loser since December, 1963 — his junior year at Wyandotte High School in Kansas City, Kan.

UCLA still may be No. 1—that may have to be decided in the national championship game in March—but coach John Wooden's Bruins certainly did not look the part here Saturday night.

They were not the crisp team with the thunder-clap offense that had been running the enemy into the floor. They were neither quick nor clever; their fast break looked like somebody sleepwalking — and they could not weather their coldest shooting night of the season, only 33.6%.

"The big difference," said Wooden afterward, "was the fact that we had too many turnovers. And we missed too many easy shots."

Probably UCLA's most costly mistake of all was that of being lulled into Houston's type of game. The Cougars threw a sticky 1-3-1 zone defense at the Bruins — with Hayes clinging to Big Lew and blocking three of his shots and also a layup by Edgar Lacey. The Cougars also picked off the crucial rebounds, got the "second shot" the Big E said they'd have to get, shut off UCLA's fast break and slowed the tempo to a walk.

Amazingly enough, in spite of perhaps its poorest game of the year, UCLA was able to make a game of it, thanks to Allen's 25 points and the board work of Jim Nielsen.

The Bruins kept jabbing and throwing uppercuts —catching the Cougars at 65-65 and 69-69 in the final three minutes — but couldn't connect with a knockout punch.

The second half was full of turning points, but the play that nailed UCLA came on a foul beneath the

Please Turn to Page 6, Col. 3

## JIM MURRAY

# The Man Who...

I hate to step into Walter Lippmann's line but there are times when good citizens cannot remain quiet. I would like to blow the whistle on a political scandal today.

You would think the Dallas Cowboys would be above that sort of thing but they have been guilty of bribing a state official.

They didn't offer him color TV sets, deep freezes, mink coats or free trips to New York or the Bahamas in the company plane, but cold, hard cash.

They didn't want highways, pipelines, oil leases or zoning variances but just a few feet of real estate in downtown Dallas—the Cotton Bowl, to be exact.

They lured him away from his responsibilities and duties as the duly-appointed state of New Mexico Director of Courtesy and Information.

I will leave the rest up to the attorney general but if this isn't the biggest miscarriage of public trust in New Mexico since the Teapot Dome, I'm Albert B. Fall.

The official's name is Donald Anthony Perkins and heretofore he has been a man of probity, albeit he has been known to fall on a fumble and sock a man over the helmet to protect the quarterback.

Don, you will recall, had decided to forego the crass commercialism of professional football and go into public service—to dedicate his life to serving his fellow man. There were those who thought that the last thing the State House in New Mexico needed was a fullback—but that's cavilling.

The last thing the Cowboys needed was a Director of Courtesy and Information. "They'll get plenty of courtesy and darn little information out of Don," predicted Dandy Don Meredith, the Drew Pearson of the Cowboy clubhouse. "Perk is going to be the 'Deputy Collector Of Internal Touchdowns,'" freely predicted another corner of the locker room. The rest of the team contented itself with calling him "The Governor" and "Your Excellency" and "E. Pluribus Perkins," and inquiring innocently whether he could fix parking tickets.

### Boss Schramm Acts

When they found out his political affiliation, they began to call him "Mr. Republican" and to inquire whether he wore spats in summer, too. "If you run for President, Perk, I know one bloc of votes you'll get—every defensive lineman and back in the league would rather see you in the White House than in the Cotton Bowl."

Alas! That's when the corrupt Tex Schramm Machine went to work. Wily old Tex, general manager of the Cowboys, veteran of thousands of smoke-filled rooms, a man who has bribed a generation of halfbacks into abandoning a career in the Boy Scouts or at the pinball machines and taking up one in football, began dangling the Murchison millions before the once-and-future politician. Perkins went back to fullback and New Mexico presumably went back to discourtesy and misinformation. Unlike Calvin Coolidge who, when he said, "I do not choose to run," stuck by his gums, Perk went back to his running.

Mr. Lippmann may want to speculate on the larger national issues involved. Like, if the Rt. Hon. Mr. Perkins once again turns his back on the commonweal in favor of football, will he be known as the

Please Turn to Page 12, Col. 3

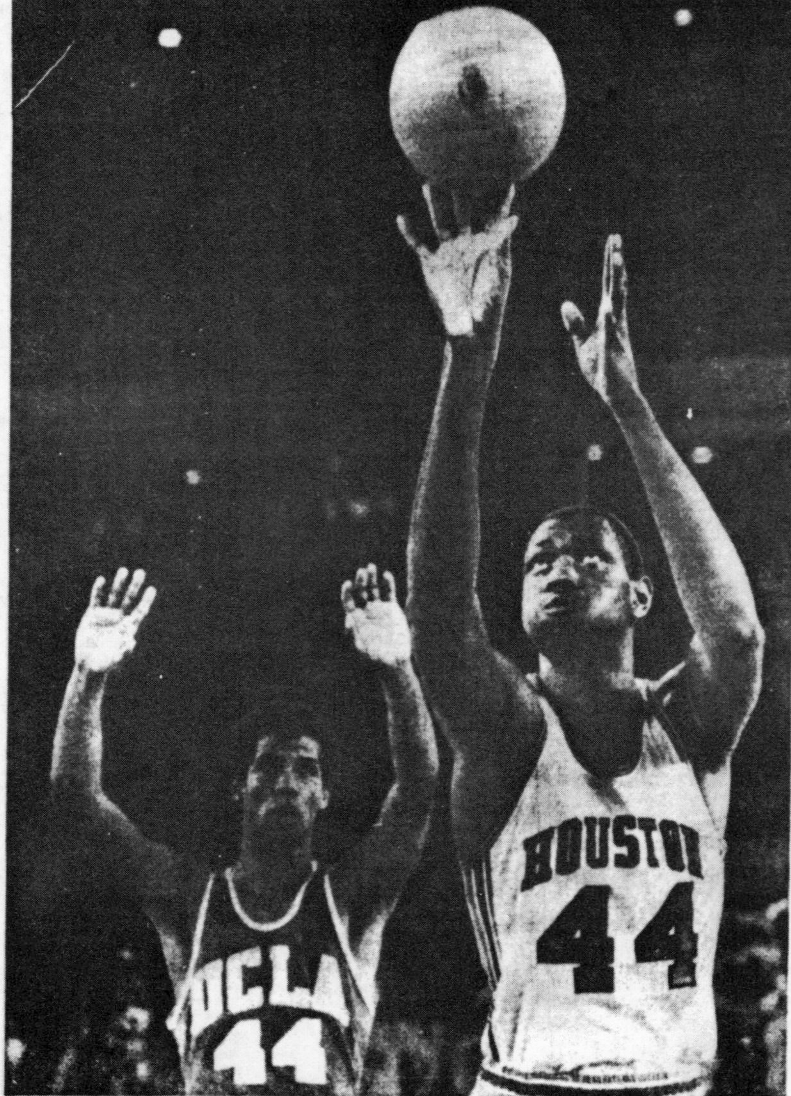


**HANDS TELL THE STORY**—UCLA's Mike Warren (left) seems to be signaling that free throw by Houston's Elvin Hayes is right on target. Hayes' two foul shots with 28 seconds to play gave Houston a 71-69 victory over UCLA, ending Bruins' win streak at 47 games. Hayes finished the game with 39 points.
UPI Wirephoto

# West Favored in Pro Bowl Today

**BY PAUL ZIMMERMAN**
Times Sports Editor

Contrary to the belief once expressed by Rudyard Kipling about the east and west, that "never the twain shall meet," they are on a collision course in Memorial Coliseum today.

The occasion is the 18th annual Pro Bowl game and it has attracted the finest football players of the Eastern and Western divisions of the National Football League.

This is the closing game of the NFL's long, fierce, successful season and more than 50,000 fans are expected to be on hand for the excitement as the curtain comes down on a campaign that started with early July practice sessions for these athletes. The kickoff comes at 1:05 p.m.

Coach Don Shula's Western All-Stars go into the game as nine-point favorites over the Eastern Conference team piloted by Otto Graham.

This seems to be based on the assumption that the Ram "front three," aided by All-Pro Willie Davis from the Packers, will harass East quarterbacks Don Meredith and Fran Tarkenton more effectively than the Eastern defenders will be able to trouble John Unitas and Roman Gabriel.

In the last two years, however, the West went into the game favored but the East scored convincing victories.

The West has collected wins in 10 of the 17 previous games, with Unitas taking command with such success in three of them that he was named on each occasion as winner of the George Halas Trophy, awarded to the game's outstanding performer.

Shula's Western squad is fortified with nine players off the world champion Packers. However, the Eastern group includes as many from the Dallas Cowboy aggregation that came within seconds of victory over Green Bay in the NFL title game.

The incentive in the game, in addition to the continuing controversy over whether the Eastern or Western Conference is superior, is money. Each of the 35 players on the winning team will receive $1,500,

Please Turn to Page 2, Col. 3

# Damascus Easy Victor; Payoff 'Anita's Lowest

## Shoe Boots Horse of Year to Two-Length Win Over Most Host; Backers 'Reap' $2.20

**BY BION ABBOTT**
Times Staff Writer

Financially speaking, dazzling Damascus trounced an all-star field of Round Table, Citation and Busher and for good measure he left T.V. Lark behind Saturday before 51,915 admirers at Santa Anita.

Actually, the 1967 Horse of the Year humbled Most Host by two lengths during his statistical splurge in the $56,950 San Fernando Stakes that caused a $7,177.92 minus pool to show.

Held under a stout hold all the way to the stretch by Bill Shoemaker, Damascus polished off his mile and one-eighth in a sparkling 1:48 4/5 after extremely slow early fractions. He was timed in a torrid :23 2/5 for his final quarter.

**Lowest Ever**

"Yes, on his best day, I do think he might be the best horse I've ever ridden." Shoemaker admitted after due consideration.

The financial figures bear out Shoemaker's belief.

The $2.20 that Damascus paid to win was the lowest in Santa Anita history. The former record of $2.30 was held jointly by Round Table (another Shoemaker favorite), Citation and Busher. A total of $155,773 was wagered to win on Damascus out of the $210,082 bet on all six starters.

The $34,450 that the 4-year-old son of Sword Dancer collected for his victory increased his career earnings to $906,106 and elevated him to 11th among the all-time money winners. His latest exhibition of excellence enabled Damascus to edge ahead of T. V. Lark and his $902,194.

**First Minus Pool**

The minus pool to show was the first of the Santa Anita season and it might have been monumental but for last year's ruling of the California Horse Racing Board that lowered the minimum payoff to $2.10. The bridge jumpers bet $110,217 to show on Damascus out of a total pool of $150,228.

The plungers hardly had a worried moment.

Damascus broke smoothly and Shoemaker dropped him over to the rail almost immediately. There he stayed until Shoe brought him out on the clubhouse turn to range alongside the pacesetter, Field Master, down the backstretch and around the far turn.

It appeared the only danger to Damascus might be death by strangulation as Shoemaker attempted to keep him from going to the front too soon.

"Sometimes he loafs in front," Shoe explained.

As a matter of fact, no one wanted to lead and Ismael Valenzuela sort of backed his way to the front with Field Master, at the start.

**Went to Front**

"There was nothing I could do about it," Valenzuela said, "so I tried to slow it up as much as I could."

This was responsible for the "walking time" of :24 2/5 for the first quarter, :49 flat for the half-mile and 1:13 flat for six furlongs.

Damascus finally poked a nose in front at the top of the far turn and once he straightened out in the

Please Turn to Page 12, Col. 3

AUTOMOTIVE

CC SECTION D 2¢

SUNDAY, JANUARY 21, 1968

# Aussie, Russian Stars to Compete in Times Games

A pair of crack Australian distance runners and a host of the Soviet Union's Olympic hopefuls head the list of international stars who will compete in The Times Indoor Games Feb. 10, at the Forum, meet director Glenn Davis announced Saturday.

Ron Clarke, who holds six world records, including the indoor two mile, and Kerry O'Brien, the Aussie steeplechaser who had a fantastic indoor season last year, form the contingent from Down Under.

Although this will be the ninth renewal of The Times Indoor Games, it will be the first meet held at the Forum, a site described by Davis as "perfect" for indoor track.

"Spectators will find that they are much closer to the action," he said, "and there will be more of the better seats."

**New Track Constructed**

A new track with Borden's "Fastrac" surfacing has been especially constructed for the Forum. It will be a standard 11 laps to a mile, high-banked track.

Clarke set the world record for the indoor two-mile at 8:28.8 in 1966 at San Francisco. At one time he held 11 world records. He still owns five outdoor world marks: two miles, three miles, six miles, 5,000 meters and 10,000 meters. O'Brien may give Clarke his stiffest challenge in the two-mile. The husky young Aussie ran in three indoor meets last year and captured all three two-mile races, setting a meet record in each one.

Among the Soviet stars competing will be Eduard Gushchin, fifth-ranked shot putter in the world last season (64-5 1/4); Valentin Gavrilov, young high jumper with a best of 7-1; Gennadiy Bliznyetsov, 17-foot pole vaulter, and Olyeg Raiko, sub-4-minute miler.

**DAMASCUS GETS RUN FOR THE MONEY** — The great Damascus outfinishes tenacious Most Host (7) and Ruken to score a two-length victory in the $56,950 San Fernando Stakes Saturday at Santa Anita. Jockey Bill Shoemaker guided 1967 Horse of the Year to his second straight 'Anita stakes win. Payoff of $2.20 was track record low.
Times photo by Art Rogers

# THE WINNER AND STILL CHAMPION---UCLA!

Los Angeles Times
Sports
CC SECTION D 2†
SUNDAY, MARCH 24, 1968

## JIM MURRAY

## A Fizzle at Arena

To give you an idea how the "great" game went, midway in the first period, UCLA put in a kid with glasses to guard Elvin Hayes.

The bravest thing I've seen in sports in a long time was Houston coming out for the second half.

Houston better get the guy who writes the military communiques to describe this one to the old folks at home. In a case like this, you say "despite heavy losses, the enemy is now answering the phone in the embassy."

The score was 101-69, but it wasn't that close.

It was supposed to be Dempsey-Firpo, St. George and the Dragon, the 1926 World Series. It was more like Dempsey-Fulton. The Dragon turned out to be a lizard photographed through a telescope.

UCLA wore out two baskets. UCLA coach John Wooden reached clean down in the student body for his last five players. He could have sent in a crew in handcuffs and still not kept the score under three figures.

The game proved what everybody already knew: Ferdinand Lewis Alcindor is the best college basketball team in history. The second most majestic peak in the state of California kept sweeping Houston players off the slopes like a monsoon raking down Everest.

Coach Adolph Rupp of Kentucky had described the UCLA team as complacent. It's a good thing they were or we might have been there till dawn adding the score. If this team ever gets aroused, we may have a shutout.

### Next a Blindfold?

Alcindor came on the court looking bored and, as soon as Houston got the ball, we found out why. If they ever play again, Lew will bring a good book. The last time he played Houston, he only had one eye. The next time, he may bring a blindfold.

The game was full of suspense right up until the time they left the dressing room. They put a fellow named Spain on Alcindor but you have to say the reign of Spain was mainly plain. I hope he never has to describe Alcindor in court because they may hang the wrong guy. As far as Spain is concerned, Alcindor is just another hit-and-run driver. He didn't even catch the number.

I'm sure Elvin Hayes is a very fine basketball player but Friday night Houston might as well have had Gabby. They kept him out on Figueroa Street all night. The Bruin press was so aggressive that, a couple of times, the ushers were looking suspiciously at Hayes as if they were about to say, "You got a ticket, bub?"

The Houston coach, Guy Lewis, sat there with a towel to his head all night long. The wonder is, he didn't throw it in. Someone asked him if he missed his regular guard. It was like asking Custer if he could have used one more trooper. Anybody who was ineligible for this last stand should thank the profs.

If they take the Houston team to see Mt. Whitney, they're not going to be at all impressed—they may even say, "It's nice—but until we see it jump we'll hold our judgement."

In the final game, it was North Carolina's turn to get a look at Mount Westwood. They couldn't plant a flag on it either.

There were about a thousand less people and forty less points at the

Please Turn to Page 12, Col. 1

LONG ARM OF LEW—Typical of North Carolina's frustration Saturday night was this play in which Charlie Scott tried to score over Lew Alcindor. Lew slapped ball away in one of many defensive gems.

## Alcindor Hits 34 in 78-55 Romp Over North Carolina

BY JEFF PRUGH
Times Staff Writer

That shiny gold numeral one that UCLA coach John Wooden has been sporting on his handkerchief pocket for the past couple of months did have a very special meaning, after all.

The Bruins are, indeed, the No. 1 collegiate basketball team in the land—and you probably won't find anybody from North Carolina to Houston who will ever deny that.

With Lew Alcindor at his devastating best, the mighty Bruins conquered North Carolina's Tar Heels, 78-55, Saturday night and came away with the NCAA championship for the second year in a row.

What's more, it was UCLA's fourth national crown in the last five years—and who's to say the Bruins won't be fast-breaking their way to the winner's circle again in 1969?

### Sixteenth Straight Win

Alcindor, the magnificent 7-footer who will be back to lead the charge to the finals in Louisville next year, poured in 34 points—and blocked five shots—as the Bruins finished with a 29-1 record and a 16-game victory streak, the nation's longest among major college teams.

In the process, the Bruins treated the crowd of 14,438 at the Sports Arena to another record-wrecking performance.

It was the widest margin of victory (23 points) ever achieved in the NCAA title game. The previous high: 20 points in Ohio State's 75-55 win over California in 1960.

It also made UCLA the only school ever to win back-to-back NCAA championships on two separate occasions. The Bruins also won in 1964 and 1965.

Moreover, Wooden became only the second coach to guide four NCAA championship teams. The other is Kentucky's Adolph Rupp in 1948, 1949, 1951 and 1958.

Against North Carolina, the Bruins were not nearly so sharp as they were the previous night in their 101-69 massacre of the Houston Cougars.

### UCLA BOX SCORE

| UCLA | FG-A | FT-A | R | A | P | T |
|---|---|---|---|---|---|---|
| Shackelford | 3-5 | 0-1 | 2 | 4 | 0 | 6 |
| Lynn | 1-7 | 5-7 | 6 | 4 | 3 | 7 |
| Alcindor | 15-21 | 4-4 | 16 | 1 | 3 | 34 |
| Warren | 3-7 | 1-1 | 3 | 1 | 2 | 7 |
| Allen | 3-7 | 5-7 | 5 | 5 | 0 | 11 |
| Nielsen | 1-1 | 0-0 | 1 | 0 | 1 | 2 |
| Heitz | 3-6 | 1-1 | 2 | 2 | 3 | 7 |
| Sutherland | 1-2 | 0-0 | 2 | 1 | 1 | 2 |
| Sweek | 0-1 | 0-0 | 0 | 0 | 1 | 0 |
| Saner | 1-3 | 0-0 | 2 | 1 | 2 | 2 |
| Team rebounds | | | 9 | | | |
| Totals | 31-60 | 16-21 | 48 | 19 | 16 | 78 |

Shooting: Field goals, 51.7%; free throws, 76.2%.

| NORTH CAROLINA | FG-A | FT-A | R | A | P | T |
|---|---|---|---|---|---|---|
| Miller | 5-13 | 4-6 | 6 | 3 | 3 | 14 |
| Bunting | 1-3 | 1-2 | 2 | 1 | 5 | 3 |
| Clark | 4-12 | 1-3 | 8 | 1 | 3 | 9 |
| Scott | 6-17 | 0-1 | 3 | 2 | 3 | 12 |
| Grubar | 2-5 | 1-2 | 0 | 1 | 2 | 5 |
| Fogler | 1-4 | 2-2 | 0 | 2 | 0 | 4 |
| Brown | 2-5 | 2-2 | 5 | 0 | 1 | 6 |
| Tuttle | 0-0 | 0-0 | 0 | 1 | 0 | 0 |
| Frye | 1-2 | 0-1 | 1 | 0 | 0 | 2 |
| Whitehead | 0-0 | 0-0 | 0 | 0 | 0 | 0 |
| Delany | 0-1 | 0-0 | 0 | 0 | 0 | 0 |
| Fletcher | 0-1 | 0-0 | 0 | 0 | 0 | 0 |
| Team rebounds | | | 10 | | | |
| Totals | 22-63 | 11-19 | 35 | 11 | 17 | 55 |

Shooting: Field goals, 34.9%; free throws, 57.9%.

SCORE BY HALVES

| | | |
|---|---|---|
| UCLA | 32 | 46—78 |
| North Carolina | 22 | 33—55 |

Officials—Steve Honzo & Charles Fouty.
Attendance—14,438.

But they were good enough to pick holes in Carolina's vaunted man-to-man defense—and only four teams had been able to do that to the Tar Heels in 32 games this season.

Alcindor tossed in 15 of his 21 field-goal attempts, and most of them came from close range against Carolina's 6-10 center, Rusty Clark.

It was a bit of a struggle in the first half. The Bruins led only 32-22, but not until after Carolina tried to slow down the tempo by leisurely playing catch with the ball.

Hoping to pull Alcindor away from the basket, Carolina planted Clark in the corner. The Tar Heels played their delay game even when they trailed by as many as 10 points in the first half.

But coach Dean Smith had his reasons.

"We wanted to keep them from

Please Turn to Page 12, Col. 6

## Kings Triumph 4-2 Over Flyers, Gain Tie for Top Spot

BY CHUCK GARRITY
Times Staff Writer

Two guys who hadn't scored in so long you'd think they'd have forgotten how swept the Kings into first place in the Western Division of the National Hockey League Saturday night with a 4-2 conquest of Philadelphia before a cheering throng of 14,003 at the Forum.

Dale Rolfe, who hadn't scored a goal in 52 games, and Gordon Labossiere, who hadn't connected in 17, came through in the clutch game of the season that allowed the Kings to climb into a tie for first with the Flyers going into the final week of the season.

### Hard-Hitting Thriller

This hard-hitting thriller was just what a game between the two best teams in a division should be. It had the crowd roaring and on its feet time after time as the Kings rammed in two final-period goals to break a 2-2 tie in their second successive wild windup. They cracked 18 shots at beleaguered Flyer goalie Bernie Parent in the last 20 minutes.

They demolished Minnesota with a four-goal burst in the final period Friday night to put them in position to make their move for the top Saturday.

And move they did. The Kings came out swinging for a knockout at the outset of the final period.

"I didn't have to tell 'em a thing before they went back on the ice," said coach Red Kelly, his face split with a wide smile. "They knew they

Please Turn to Page 4, Col. 3

LEAPING LUCIUS—Bruins' Lucius Allen sails through the air to pick off a loose ball and go in for an easy layup in NCAA final against North Carolina Saturday night at Sports Arena. No. 53 is UCLA's Lynn Shackelford. Bruins won, 78-55, for second national title in row.
Times photos by Ben Olender

## Sports: A World Where Blacks Are Just a Little More Equal

BY CHARLES MAHER
Times Staff Writer

*"Sports today provide for American Negroes the closest approach to the great goal they dream about, talk about, sing about, pray and work for, every moment of every living day . . . Only in sports, to such a high degree, has the wondering lament—'How long, oh Lord, how long?'—become passe. Total all that sports mean today to all other Americans and you'll find that sports mean still more to Negroes."*

—A. S. (Doc) Young, Negro author in "Negro First in Sports"

In his struggle for social equality in the United States, the Negro has won some major engagements, but not the war.

But, as Doc Young says, the world of sports is a different world. In fact, if the Negro's objective in sports was simply to achieve equality, he may have overshot his target. Of his performance to date, it is possible to argue that he has not become equal, but superior.

And he has done it in a remarkably short time. The 20th century was nearly half over before baseball decided to join it. Finally, on Oct. 23, 1945, the Brooklyn Dodgers signed a Negro player. He didn't play in the majors right away but it wasn't long. On April 10, 1947, Branch Rickey announced:

"The Brooklyn Dodgers today purchased the contract of Jackie Roosevelt Robinson from the Montreal Royals. He will report immediately."

From within baseball, as from without, there were mixed responses. A catcher then playing in the majors said of Negro ballplayers: "They'll never make it." On the other hand, an ex-Cleveland outfielder named Pat McNulty predicted: "They'll own the game."

Neither man was right. But McNulty's judgement, it developed, was eminently more astute than the catcher's.

At the last census, in 1960, the United States had a population of 179,323,175. Of this number, 18,871,831 were Negroes. So Negroes constituted less than 11% of the population. As we shall see, they are not nearly so badly outnumbered in the athletic population.

In baseball, each team has eight positions that may be filled by regulars—i.e., players who are on the field day after day. The pitcher, of course, is not a regular. With 10 teams, the National League has room for 80 regulars.

Of the 80 who might have been described as regulars last season, 27 were American Negroes. That works out to 33.75%. So the ratio of Negroes to whites was more than three times as great among regulars

Please Turn to Page 8, Col. 3

OFFICIAL SCORE CARD SUNDAY APR 14 1968

| 2 | 3 | 4 | 5 | 6 | 7 | 8 | 9 | Out |
|---|---|---|---|---|---|---|---|---|
| 555 | 355 | 220 | 450 | 190 | 365 | 530 | 420 | 3485 |
| 5 | 4 | 3 | 4 | 3 | 4 | 5 | 4 | 36 |
| 4 | 3 | 3 | 4 | 3 | 4 | 4 | 4 | 31 |

| 10 | 11 | 12 | 13 | 14 | 15 | 16 | 17 | 18 | In | Totals |
|---|---|---|---|---|---|---|---|---|---|---|
| 470 | 445 | 155 | 475 | 420 | 520 | 190 | 400 | 420 | 3495 | 6980 |
| 4 | 4 | 3 | 5 | 4 | 5 | 3 | 4 | 4 | 36 | 72 |
| 4 | 4 | 2 | 5 | 4 | 4 | 3 | 4 | 5 | 35 | 66 |

ED MY SCORE HOLE BY HOLE.

TURE [signature]

ROBERTO DE VICENZO

ATTEST [signature] 212 278

**MASTER MISTAKE**—Roberto de Vicenzo (left) sits stunned after learning he had signed scorecard (center) with wrong score on 17th hole (circle). It cost him a tie and gave top prize to a sympathetic Bob Goalby (right). AP Wirephotos

# DE VICENZO LOSES BY STROKE (OF PEN)


Los Angeles Times

Sports

BUSINESS & FINANCE

CC PART III 2†

MONDAY, APRIL 15, 1968


## Goalby Wins on Scorecard Error

BY BILL SHIRLEY
Times Staff Writer

AUGUSTA—A mathematical goof gave Bob Goalby the Masters Golf Championship and spoiled Roberto de Vicenzo's birthday party Sunday.

Roberto, the happy, popular professional from Argentina, seemingly had shot his way into a playoff with Goalby for the title, but then was suddenly banished to second place by the slip of Tommy Aaron's pencil—and his own "stupid mistake."

In the confusion of the most dramatic finish in the 32-year history of Bobby Jones' prestigious party, Roberto signed a scorecard that added up to a 66 instead of the 7-under-par 65 he shot because Aaron had given him a 4 on No. 17 instead of a 3.

Under the Rules of Golf, Roberto, who had not caught the error, had blown a stroke. His 72-hole total of 278 fell one shy of Goalby, who shot a 66 to win his first major championship with a 277, 11-under-par.

Roberto, a professional for 30 years, was 45 Sunday. And it was one of the saddest days of his life.

Who is to blame for the monumental goof? Roberto? The Rules of Golf? Aaron?

Roberto said: "We are professionals and we should know the rules. It is my fault."

The rules ARE hard, but, as Roberto said, "They have to be very hard so you can't make unfair advantage. The rule have to be fair."

Roberto's scorecard was clearly marked: "I have checked my score hole by hole."

**Player Responsible**

The total was not important. The Scoring Committee adds the figures, but each player is responsible for the hole-by-hole scores. If the score is higher, he is stuck with it. If it is lower, he is disqualified.

But Roberto is not alone in thinking that a player under pressure in a major tournament, where one shot can cost you $5,000 (which Roberto's mistake did), should not have to be a bookkeeper on the course.

And Aaron also was at fault because he, as Roberto's playing companion, kept the Argentine's score. When Roberto made the birdie 3 on No. 17 to go 12-under par, Aaron did not mark the figure on the card. Instead, he waited until they had finished the round and completed the card, which is common practice among the professionals. The bogey 5 Roberto made at No. 18 made Aaron's scores total 66. Aaron, a mathematics major at the University of Florida, discovered the error about 10 minutes too late.

But Roberto already had signed the card and under the rules he is to blame.

"Maybe it's Goalby's fault because he give such pressure to me I lose my brain," Roberto kidded later.

It was, in fact, a blow to Goalby, who shot spectacular Sunday, and who, because of the confusion and controversy, probably never will receive proper credit for his achievement. He had rounds of 70, 70, 71 and 66 over an Augusta National course that is never a soft touch, although it played shorter than usual Sunday because most of the pins were at the front of the

Please Turn to Page 4, Col. 1

## Bunning Zeroes In on Dodgers, Hurls Pirates' 3-0 Win

BY DAN HAFNER
Times Staff Writer

Major league baseball bats come in various shapes, weights and lengths. Each one costs about $4 and the average player will use about three dozen in the course of a season.

As you can see, it is an expensive item. It is even more so for Dodger management, because, for the most part, its players don't seem to be able to put them to use.

The Dodgers played their fourth game of the season Sunday at Dodger Stadium and most of the 27,136 partisans on hand were there to see if the club could score a run.

Jim Bunning, with help from Roberto Clemente, made sure that for the third time in four games the Dodgers did not score as he hurled the Pittsburgh Pirates to a 3-0 victory.

**One Homer**

When the Dodgers were shut out in the first two games of the season by lefthanders, it was felt that the big problem was that the team could not hit lefthanders. The truth is, they cannot hit any pitching.

Ron Fairly's home run, which gave Don Drysdale a 1-0 victory over the Mets Saturday, is still the only run the Dodgers have scored in 35 innings. They have made few threats and only 19 hits.

They made only five hits off Bunning, who is expected to make the Pirates a pennant contender, but Fairly came within inches of hitting another home run.

After Donn Clendenon hit a high

Please Turn to Page 2, Col. 5

**HISTORIC MOMENT**—Pirate hurler Jim Bunning delivers to Dodgers' Claude Osteen, who strikes out on pitch, giving Bunning his 1,000th strikeout in National League. The whiff made him only man other than Cy Young to reach the milestone in both major leagues.

## HARDLUCK BRUNET WINS WITHOUT HIS BEST STUFF

### Angel Hurler Wild With Curve Ball but Still Manages to Post First Victory as California Whips Orioles, 6-2

BY PAUL ZIMMERMAN
Times Sports Editor

BALTIMORE—After what happened at Memorial Stadium here Sunday, George Stuart Brunet is prepared to believe the adage that all things even out in baseball.

The Angel lefthander lost seven games last year by a run, and this season started off in the same pattern at New York, where he limited the Yankees to three hits but lost, 1-0.

"I had my good stuff that day. This afternoon all I had was a fast ball and these Orioles are good fast-ball hitters," said Brunet as he described the ordeal on the mound as California beat Baltimore, 6-2, before a crowd of 12,810.

Now the Angels move to Washington today with a .500 record.

"Oh, I had a curve ball, but I couldn't get it over," Brunet said. "After the first inning I knew it was going to be tough, but I had to challenge them.

"I don't recall when I couldn't get my curve over like today—even in the minors. All last year when I lost nine in a row I kept thinking things would even out. Maybe they will this year."

Brunet asked to be taken out after the seventh.

"My shoulder started tightening up a little bit," he said. "If it had been close I'd have stayed, because it wasn't that bad."

**Nervous Moment**

George admitted he had some uneasy moments, sitting in the clubhouse in the eighth listening to the radio as Jack Hamilton loaded the bases on three walks and Boog Powell came up to the plate.

"If the big guy hits it out, and he can, I'd probably have moved the clubhouse furniture around a bit," Brunet said.

The way things went, Clyde Wright got Powell on a fly ball to right and then, with the help of the Angels' third double play of the afternoon, polished off the bottom of the Oriole batting order in the ninth.

After being held to two singles on Saturday, California was back hit-

Please Turn to Page 2, Col. 4

## De Vicenzo's Error Cost Him---About One Million Dollars

BY BILL SHIRLEY
Times Staff Writer

AUGUSTA—"I make 3 on the 17th and my partner he put 4."

That was Roberto de Vicenzo's simple explanation of the mathematical mistake that Sunday cost him a chance to win the Masters championship.

It is what you would expect from the gregarious Gaucho from Buenos Aires. He is a simple, uncomplicated man. He would rather win friends than money.

"Thirty or 35,000 dollars a year is enough," he said recently. "I don't want to kill myself or lose friends for money."

**Very Costly Mistake**

When Tommy Aaron shanked with his pencil Sunday, giving Roberto a 4 on No. 17 instead of a 3, the error may have immediately cost the Argentine $5,000, the difference in first and second place money here. In a lifetime, however, the price may have hit $1 million. That is the tag the business agents have put on a Masters championship.

Of course, Roberto still might have lost to Bob Goalby in the playoff, but at least he would have had a chance at it.

Viewing it from Goalby's — or most any other professional's position — Roberto just goofed. The rule always has been in the book. Roberto knew it, and, in fact, said it was his fault.

But there are circumstances in Roberto's case that are not covered

Please Turn to Page 4, Col. 6

## 76ers Defeat Celts, Near Eastern Title

BOSTON (AP)—The Philadelphia 76ers withstood repeated Boston challenges and foul trouble Sunday in defeating the Celtics, 110-105, and taking a commanding 3-1 lead in the Eastern Division playoff finals.

Sharp-shooting Hal Greer led the 76ers with 28 points, but he had plenty of help from Philadelphia's fearsome trio of Wilt Chamberlain, Lucious Jackson and Chet Walker, who contributed 22 apiece.

The 76ers, defeating the Celtics for the second time in Boston in the playoffs, can wrap up the Eastern Division title with a victory in Philadelphia tonight.

The 76ers blew a 15-point lead in the second period, but bounced back to score eight straight points for a 68-62 halftime advantage.

The Celtics fell 14 points behind, 79-65, early in the third period, but fought back to within three points, 86-83, at the three-quarter mark.

Plagued by turnovers, the Celtics slumped badly at the outset of the final period. The 76ers, leading, 92-88, reeled off 11 straight points, including three straight field goals by Jackson, before the Celtics could get untracked.

Please Turn to Page 3, Col. 3

**NEVER LETS UP** — Following through so hard he falls off the mound, Jim Bunning of Pittsburgh breezed past the Dodgers Sunday, giving up only five hits as Pirates topped Los Angeles, 3-0. Times photos by Art Rogers

## BASEBALL STANDINGS

**NATIONAL LEAGUE**

| | W | L | Pct. | GBL |
|---|---|---|---|---|
| Houston | 4 | 1 | .800 | |
| St. Louis | 3 | 1 | .750 | ½ |
| Pittsburgh | 3 | 1 | .750 | ½ |
| San Francisco | 3 | 2 | .600 | 1 |
| Atlanta | 2 | 2 | .500 | 1½ |
| Chicago | 2 | 2 | .500 | 1½ |
| New York | 2 | 2 | .500 | 1½ |
| Los Angeles | 1 | 3 | .250 | 2½ |
| Cincinnati | 1 | 3 | .250 | 2½ |
| Philadelphia | 1 | 5 | .167 | 3½ |

**Sunday's Results**

Pittsburgh 3, Los Angeles 0
Cincinnati at Atlanta, postponed, rain
San Francisco 13-3, Philadelphia 2-1
New York 4, Houston 0
Chicago 7, St. Louis 6

**Today's Schedule**

Pittsburgh (Veale, 0-0) vs. Los Angeles (Singer, 0-1), Dodger Stadium, KFI, KWKW, 8 p.m.
St. Louis (Gibson, 0-0) at Atlanta (Jarvis, 0-1), night
New York (Seaver, 0-0) at Houston (Wilson, 1-0), night
Only games scheduled

**AMERICAN LEAGUE**

| | W | L | Pct. | GBL |
|---|---|---|---|---|
| Minnesota | 4 | 0 | 1.000 | |
| Detroit | 3 | 1 | .750 | 1 |
| Baltimore | 2 | 1 | .667 | 1½ |
| California | 2 | 2 | .500 | 2 |
| Boston | 2 | 2 | .500 | 2 |
| Cleveland | 2 | 2 | .500 | 2 |
| New York | 1 | 2 | .333 | 2½ |
| Oakland | 1 | 2 | .333 | 2½ |
| Washington | 1 | 3 | .250 | 3 |
| Chicago | 0 | 3 | .000 | 3½ |

**Sunday's Results**

California 6, Baltimore 2
Cleveland 7, Boston 4
Detroit 5, Chicago 4 (10 innings)
Minnesota 4, New York 3
Washington 8, Oakland 1

**Today's Schedule**

California (Ellis, 0-0) at Washington (Pascual, 0-1), KMPC, 10:30 a.m.
Minnesota (Boswell, 0-0 or Merritt, 1-0) at Baltimore (Phoebus, 1-0), night
Oakland (Odom, 0-0) at New York (Stottlemyre, 1-0)
Detroit (Wilson, 0-1) at Boston (Culp, 0-0)

# Drysdale Sets Record (58⅔), Then Gets KOd

Los Angeles Times
Sports
CC SECTION D 3†
SUNDAY, JUNE 9, 1968

## JIM MURRAY

## Real Fun of Open

Every time I am asked what my favorite sport is, I always answer, "Golf." "I love Golf," I say.

It's a big lie. I hate Golf. It's not a game, it's an aggravation, the most exquisite form of self-torture this side of a guy who lies down on a bed of nails or walks on coals.

"It's good for you," say the doctors. What good?! It gives you high blood pressure, acid indigestion. It ruins your disposition, hurts your feet, peels your nose, makes your hands bleed and takes a big chunk out of your day when you could be doing something useful. It can cause a divorce, poison ivy. You can lose a job shooting 69.

Name me one good it does.

You're out in the air, you say? Do you have ANY idea what the pollen count is out there? Or the stroke count? Did it ever occur to you that blackish water could be a breeding ground for yellow fever? Also golf balls?

But, look at the trees, the fresh air, the greenery, you shout.

Listen! To Joyce Kilmer, that's a tree. To a bird, it's a tree. To a golfer, it's an unprintable unmentionable put there by some unprin table unmentionable to catch the best tee shot you've hit all day.

### Leaves You Babbling

That "babbling brook," you say? Phooey! That's no "babbling brook." That's a "lateral wate. hazard" or a parallel one. That's a babbling 2-stroke penalty.

Smell the flowers, Walter Hagen said? YOU smell the flowers. I'll stay well clear of them. Ever try to hit a 2-iron off a geranium? Believe me, you'll HATE geraniums.

Part of the trouble is, I always see myself as a conqueror with a 1-iron on a course. Tamerlane the Magnificent bloodying 18 holes in his triumphant march to the winner's stand. I want to slash the ball out there 380 yards like Arnold Palmer. And I bang it out there 40 feet like Arnold Stang. I want to be Jack Nicklaus and I'm more like St. Nicholas.

I want to stride up to a green, hitching up my pants like Palmer, surveying a birdie putt. Instead, I am squinting through the under brush on the wrong fairway, murmuring "Anyone see a ball come over here—a No. 4 Dot with this little cut in it?"

This is why I duck tournaments like that recent one at Memphis where the scores soared clear up in the high 60s when the wind came up, where the pros could break 70 without dirtying 12 of the 14 clubs in the bag, where I saw a guy PUTT out of a sand trap.

### It Fights Back

But this week, I'm going to be like a kid locked in a candy store, a dog in a butcher shop.

I'm going to Rochester for the Open. That's the one tournament a year where the pros set out with a pocketful of balls and an adding machine. That's where you will find me, helpless with laughter, holding my sides while tears streak down my cheeks as I hide behind a tree laughing at a guy trying to hit a backward iron out of a tree basin.

This is not a fight between Joe Louis and a Bum-Of-The-Month. This course fights back. Oak Hill has been seriously weakened by the Dutch Elm blight which is defoliating the East, but Joe Dey of

RECORD-BREAKING PITCH—Don Drysdale forces Roberto Pena of the Phillies to ground out on this pitch, enabling Dodger righthander to break major league record of 56 shutout innings set by Walter Johnson in 1913. Drysdale went on to establish a new record of 58⅔ innings before giving up a run.

## Big D Leaves in 7th Inning of 5-3 Triumph Over Phils

BY DAN HAFNER
Times Staff Writer

As Don Drysdale walked slowly to the mound to the accompaniment of the roar of a turnaway crowd of 55,017 (50,060 paid) Saturday night at Dodger Stadium, he had only one goal left in his triumphant march through major league pitching records.

Drysdale accomplished his purpose with a flourish, breaking Walter Johnson's 55-year-old scoreless inning streak, extending the record to 58⅔ innings, then turned into a human being again shortly thereafter.

The 31-year-old righthanded ace of the Dodgers was knocked out of the box in the seventh inning and it took a brilliant relief chore by seldom-used Hank Aguirre to preserve a 5-3 victory over the Philadelphia Phillies.

Drysdale, who had pitched a record six consecutive shutouts, hurled the Dodgers into second place and kept their winning streak alive at six games, but the pressure that has mounted steadily for two weeks finally caught up with him.

As Tony Taylor crossed the plate with two out in the fifth inning after 32-year-old pinch-hitter Howie Bedell, just purchased from Reading, Pa., hit a fly to left, Drysdale gave the appearance of a man who had just had the weight of the world removed from his shoulders.

"I wanted the record so bad," admitted Drysdale, "but I'm relieved that it's over. I could feel myself go 'blah' when the run scored. I just let down completely. I'm sure it was the mental strain."

Drysdale denied that a hassle (which Philadelphia manager Gene Mauch sportingly waited until Johnson's record was broken to launch) had anything to do with his failure to finish.

#### Warned by Umpire

Mauch accused Drysdale of using a foreign substance on the ball and umpire Augie Donatelli concurred after closely examining Drysdale's left wrist and hair at the end of the Phils' half of the third inning.

Donatelli warned Drysdale not to touch the back of his head the rest of the game.

"I told him," said Donatelli, "that if he went to the back of his head with his pitching hand again, it would be automatic ejection from the game."

According to the rules, if Donatelli discovered that Drysdale was using an illegal substance on the ball, Drysdale should have been thrown out without a warning.

Following his amazing feat of pitching six consecutive shutouts, Drysdale needed 2⅓ scoreless innings to break Johnson's mark.

#### Don Starts Shakily

When he started out, it did not appear as though he would make it. Seven of his first eight pitches were balls. The one strike resulted in a line drive to Willie Davis in center.

After Johnny Briggs walked, Zoilo Versalles made a brilliant play. He hustled into the hole, backhanded Tony Gonzales' hot smash and made a fine throw to get Briggs at second. Then Johnny Callison lined to Davis.

Drysdale buckled down and retired the next four batters to earn the record.

"I didn't think Drysdale threw very well in the first inning," said manager Walt Alston. "Then he straightened out. Although his phenomenal streak had to end sometime, I think all that hassle hastened the end of it.

"I think you have to give Hank Aguirre a lot of credit. He hasn't pitched much, but he did a tremendous job. Jim Brewer has had the flu and I wanted a left-hander pitching to all those Philly left-handed hitters."

Aguirre, who had pitched only one inning since May 27, came to the rescue with the Dodgers leading, 4-3, runners on second and third and only one out in the seventh.

He disposed of pinch-hitter Gary Sutherland and Gonzalez, on popups, then breezed through the eighth and ninth.

Please Turn to Page 6, Col. 3

## BIG D'S RECORD

## Boyer Carefully Handles Slow Hopper for Record

BY DWIGHT CHAPIN
Times Staff Writer

He stood there on the mound, tall and straight, and he accepted the sign from catcher Tom Haller.

His arms went up over his head, the black mourning band on his left arm clearly revealed, he wheeled and went into the familiar sidearm motion.

The Phillies' shortstop Roberto Pena, had an 0-2 count and was protecting the plate. He hit the ball and it bounced on a high, slow hop toward Dodger third baseman Ken Boyer.

Boyer moved in ever so slowly, looking at his feet so he wouldn't get them crossed up, checking—it seemed—to see if he might have dropped his glove.

But he hadn't. He played the ball cleanly and carefully threw it over to first baseman Wes Parker.

That's how Don Drysdale became the greatest shutout pitcher in the 96-year history of major league baseball.

The crowd, which jammed nearly every seat of Dodger Stadium, rose almost in unison, yelling, screaming, letting the emotion go. It was 8:45 on a Saturday, and the big guy had done it.

Only he still wasn't shown the respect due a man who had accomplished what will probably rank as the foremost pitching achievement ever.

Please Turn to Page 6, Col. 4

## Gamely Noses Out Rising Market for Win in Inglewood

BY BION ABBOTT
Times Staff Writer

It took a great sense of timing for jockey Wayne Harris to get the great mare, Gamely, into the winner's circle at Hollywood Park Saturday.

First, he had to finish serving a five-day suspension and he got that out of the way by Friday while vacationing in his native Canada

Next, he had to get out of Canada He cut that a little fine, too. Harris won his case with the immigration department barely in time to catch a plane that got him to Hollypark Friday night.

Finally, and tightest of all, was the timing it took for Harris to help Gamely to the finish line a long nose in front of favored Rising Market in the $57,050 Inglewood Handicap.

"They sure named this baby right, didn't they?" Harris praised once he had a chance to draw a deep breath again.

#### Betting Favorite

The 40,193 spectators couldn't help but agree with Harris. They made Rising Market their 8-5 betting favorite but there was no doubt about the favorite in their hearts following one of Hollypark's great stretch duels.

From the time Gamely nosed to the front at the top of the stretch until she fought her way across the finish line, she and Rising Market were never more than a head apart.

The brilliant, bristling battle carried them under the wire in 1:47 1/5 for the season's fastest clocking for a mile and one-eighth.

THE END — Don Drysdale, right, watches his record Phils' Tony Taylor slides across home plate with the righthander. Catcher Tom Haller leaps high to string of scoreless innings come to an end as the first run in 58⅔ innings against the big Dodger get throw from rightfielder Len Gabrielson in fifth.

## Baseball Standings

**NATIONAL LEAGUE**

| | W | L | Pct. | GBL |
|---|---|---|---|---|
| St. Louis | 32 | 22 | .593 | |
| Los Angeles | 31 | 26 | .544 | 2½ |
| Atlanta | 28 | 24 | .538 | 3 |
| San Francisco | 28 | 26 | .519 | 4 |
| Philadelphia | 25 | 24 | .510 | 4½ |
| Cincinnati | 26 | 25 | .510 | 4½ |
| Chicago | 25 | 27 | .481 | 6 |
| New York | 24 | 27 | .471 | 6½ |
| Houston | 22 | 31 | .415 | 9½ |
| Pittsburgh | 20 | 29 | .408 | 9½ |

**Saturday's Results**

Los Angeles 5, Philadelphia 3
St. Louis 7, Cincinnati 2
Houston 3, Pittsburgh 2
New York at San Francisco, postponed
Atlanta at Chicago, postponed

**Today's Schedule**

Philadelphia (Fryman, 8-4) vs. Los Angeles (Singer, 5-5), Dodger Stadium, KFI, KWKW, 1 p.m.

New York (Koosman, 9-2 and Cardwell, 1-6) at San Francisco (McCormick, 4-7 and Perry, 6-3), doubleheader.

Atlanta (Johnson, 3-3 and Reed, 6-2) at Chicago (Jenkins, 5-6 and Hands, 6-2), doubleheader.

St. Louis (Carlton, 7-1 and Washburn, 3-2) at Cincinnati (Arrigo, 4-3 and Pappas, 2-5), doubleheader.

Pittsburgh (McBean, 8-5) at Houston (Dierker, 5-8).

**AMERICAN LEAGUE**

| | W | L | Pct. | GBL |
|---|---|---|---|---|
| Detroit | 35 | 19 | .648 | |
| Cleveland | 31 | 24 | .564 | 4½ |
| Baltimore | 30 | 24 | .556 | 5 |
| Minnesota | 28 | 26 | .519 | 7 |
| Boston | 26 | 28 | .481 | 9 |
| Oakland | 25 | 28 | .472 | 9½ |
| California | 25 | 30 | .455 | 10½ |
| New York | 24 | 30 | .444 | 11 |
| Washington | 23 | 30 | .434 | 11½ |
| Chicago | 22 | 30 | .423 | 12 |

**Saturday's Results**

California at New York, postponed
Detroit 3, Cleveland 1
Baltimore 8, Oakland 1
Chicago 4, Boston 0
Minnesota at Washington, postponed

**Today's Schedule**

California (Clark, 0-3 and Ellis, 3-5) at New York (Barber, 0-1 and Bahnsen, 5-3), doubleheader, Channel 5, KMPC, 10 a.m.

Cleveland (Tiant, 8-4) at Detroit (Dobson, 1-0).

Minnesota (Merritt, 4-4) at Washington (Coleman, 3-8).

Chicago at Boston, postponed

Oakland at Baltimore, doubleheader, post-

**JIM MURRAY**

# Ole for Trevino! He Carved Up Golf's Biggest Bull

ROCHESTER—Okay, break out the tequila! See if Herb Alpert and the Tijuana Brass got a gig.

Wake up that guy sleeping under the sombrero. Refry the beans. Order tacos for all hands. Tune up the Tipica band.

Cut the ears off this golf course here and ship them to El Paso. Tell the gang at La Golondrina it's margaritas all around. Salt the glasses, bartender. Cube the limes. See if the tamales are done.

Lee Buck Trevino picked a great spot to win his first professional tournament ever. He started at the top. He killed the biggest bull in all golf. A grade-school dropout, he joins history in the company of Yale's Bobby Jones, Ft. Worth's Ben Hogan, Nicklaus, Palmer. The biggest tournament he won before this one was the Texas State Open.

No one who ever watched him swing ever confused him with Sam Snead. The only place he ever wins money is in U.S. Opens. Or on the first tee at Horizon Country Club, where he sometimes makes bets he can break par with a broomstick, a Coke bottle and a pool cue—and he does.

He gets more excited at dog races than he does in National Opens. He plays a hustler's game. He can spot anybody in the game 100 yards from tee to green and still, when he gets to the green, smile sweetly and say, "You're away, pards."

Don't look around any pro shops for any Lee Trevino gloves, Lee Trevino shirts. He pays for his clubs just like everybody else. You'd expect to see him getting strokes on the first tee at Western Avenue, not accepting the greatest trophy in all golf. Smiley Quick would reach for his wallet if he saw him coming.

I think he's the first winner in the history of this tournament to have a tattoo. It wasn't too many years ago they had monocles. He drinks beer out of a bottle, makes noise eating soup and blows on his coffee. He's a happy-go-lucky Mexican or Mexican-American who goes around his home town leaking money.

He served two hitches in the Marine Corps because the parts of Texas he used to live in made a barracks seem like the Waldorf. He's a throwback to the day when this game was played by caddies, not collegians. The closest you can come to describing his swing is that it's a kind of upright chop. But he hasn't had a 3-putt green since the Alamo. He didn't have a single one here all week. He could two-putt an airport.

When he arrived at his first U.S. Open last year, some of the top pros weren't sure whether they should hand him their shoes in the clubhouse. But when he finished fifth, they weren't sure whether they should hand him their clubs.

He's only been married twice—but he's only 28. "I get rid of them when they get to be 21," he told the press cheerily after he had won the Open, a bit of marriage counseling that will never make the Readers' Digest.

The Oak Hill golf course he brought to its knees was not really a very brave bull. Its horns seemed to be shaved. The only water on it fell from the heavens. You didn't have to be long, just straight. Since Trevino just scrapes the ball down the fairway to where he can push it in the hole, he found the course as perfectly suited to his game as a fast backswing. The last four shots he hit on this golf course would have sent most of us back to the practice tee. But he parred the last

Please Turn to Page 3, Col. 2

WATCHING THE BIRDIE—Clenching his fist in triumph, Lee Trevino excitedly watches his putt drop into the 11th hole for a birdie 2 in Sunday's final round of the U.S. Open. Trevino fired a 69 and finished with a record-tying 275—four strokes ahead of Jack Nicklaus.

AP Wirephoto

# Trevino's Record 275 Wins Open by 4 Shots

## Wise-Cracking Mexican Scores First Pro Tournament Victory; Nicklaus 2nd at 279

BY BILL SHIRLEY
Times Staff Writer

ROCHESTER — Lee Buck Trevino talks a good game of golf. He plays it even better. The uninhibited little, wise-cracking Mexican from El Paso won the world's most important championship Sunday, the U.S. Open by four shots, breaking one record and equalling another.

While the flower of professional golf was being embarrassed over the narrow, impeccable fairways and deceitful greens of Oak Hill Country Club, the 28-year-old Trevino shot a 1-under-par 69 and tied Jack Nicklaus' 72-hole record of 275.

Lee, a grade school dropout in Dallas, also became the first player in the 68-year history of the United States Golf Assn. championship to shoot four consecutive subpar rounds, an incredible achievement that sets him apart from such players as Bobby Jones, Ben Hogan, Arnold Palmer and Nicklaus.

**First Professional Win**

The victory, Lee's first as a professional, was worth $30,000.

And his rounds of 69, 68, 69 and 69, five under par for 72 holes, were not shot on a rinky-dink course. Nicklaus, who came in on an alternately rainy, cloudy, sunny day in 67 strokes, was the only other player who could crack Oak Hill's par of 280 for the tournament. Jack, shooting what he said was the finest round he ever played in a U.S. Open, made it in 279.

Bert Yancey, who led the first three rounds, setting a 54-hole record of 205, faded fast under the intense pressure and shot a 76, six over par, for a total of 281 and third place. Bobby Nichols (69 Sunday) was fourth at 282.

Bill Casper, rated by many as the player to beat here, had another so-so round, shooting a 72 for a total of 286. Tied with him were Al Geiberger and Dave Stockton, who both had 72s Sunday.

**Embarrassing Moment**

Palmer, in what must have been one of his most embarrassing moments, played in the last threesome with two obscure amateurs and had another bad day. His 75, five over par, produced an unprofessional total of 301. He also shot rounds of 73, 74 and 79.

But Arnold still was a major attraction. Hundreds of spectators remained after Trevino and Yancey had passed to see him strike the ball.

Steve Spray of Indianaola, Iowa, enjoyed a fleeting moment of glory, too. He shot a 65 to equal the lowest fourth-round score ever shot in the Open, and his 30 on the back nine also tied a record. He made EIGHT birdies.

What looked like a two-man race at the start, Trevino vs. Yancey, soon developed into a three-man fight as Nicklaus gained five shots on Yancey, the leader, in five holes. Yancey, off to a shaky start with a

Please Turn to Page 2, Col. 3

Los Angeles Times
Sports
BUSINESS & FINANCE
CC PART III 2†
MONDAY, JUNE 17, 1968

# Angels Fail With Saturday's Script, Lose to Yanks, 4-3

BY JOHN WIEBUSCH
Times Staff Writer

The theatrics of the previous day fell one perfect throw short of repetition Sunday and the Angels lost to the New York Yankees, 4-3, at Anaheim Stadium.

The Angels were behind, 4-1, with one out in the ninth inning because Horace Clarke, who isn't supposed to hit home runs, and Mickey Mantle, who is, lashed two-run homers in the eighth inning.

Jim Fregosi, the man who tied Saturday's game against Washington with a two-run triple in the ninth, singled to left-field to ignite the comeback.

Rick Reichardt, the man who won Saturday's game with a 10th inning home run, followed with a single.

**Houk Makes Switch**

With Don Mincher due to bat, manager Ralph Houk switched from a right-handed pitcher, Dooley Womack, to a lefthander, Steve Hamilton.

Enter Bubba Morton. The man who started the ninth-inning rally 24 hours earlier with a single did the same again. He bounced a hit into left field to drive in a run and the Angels trailed by two.

Bobby Trevino fouled out, but the Angels had one more chance.

It appeared to be a forlorn opportunity when Bobby Knoop lofted a soft fly ball to short right field. Andy Kosco came in five steps to make the catch, but the ball dropped in front of him.

Reichardt scored easily from second base and it was 4-3. But Kosco recovered the ball and threw a strike to Jake Gibbs, the catcher. Gibbs tagged Morton and the game—and the Angels' three-game winning streak—was over.

"I lost the ball in the sun," said

Please Turn to Page 3, Col. 7

# BASEBALL STANDINGS

**AMERICAN LEAGUE**

| | W | L | Pct. | GBL |
|---|---|---|---|---|
| Detroit | 41 | 22 | .651 | |
| Baltimore | 32 | 28 | .533 | 7½ |
| Cleveland | 33 | 30 | .524 | 8 |
| Minnesota | 31 | 31 | .500 | 9½ |
| Boston | 29 | 29 | .500 | 9½ |
| Oakland | 30 | 31 | .492 | 10 |
| New York | 29 | 32 | .475 | 11 |
| California | 28 | 33 | .459 | 12 |
| Chicago | 26 | 32 | .448 | 12½ |
| Washington | 24 | 35 | .407 | 15 |

**Sunday's Results**

New York 4, California 3
Minnesota 4, Washington 2
Chicago 3-1, Detroit 2-6
Boston 5, Cleveland 3
Oakland 4-6, Baltimore 2-4

**Today's Schedule**

New York (Bahnsen, 6-2) at California (McGlothlin, 5-4), Anaheim Stadium, KMPC, 8 p.m.

Cleveland (Hargan, 4-6) vs. Chicago (Fisher, 1-3), at Milwaukee, night

Washington (Moore, 1-3) at Minnesota (Kaat, 3-3), night

Baltimore (Brabender, 4-2) at Oakland (Odom, 6-4), night

Only games scheduled

**NATIONAL LEAGUE**

| | W | L | Pct. | GBL |
|---|---|---|---|---|
| St. Louis | 38 | 25 | .603 | |
| San Francisco | 34 | 30 | .531 | 4½ |
| Atlanta | 32 | 29 | .525 | 5 |
| Los Angeles | 34 | 31 | .523 | 5 |
| Philadelphia | 28 | 28 | .500 | 6½ |
| Chicago | 30 | 31 | .492 | 7 |
| Cincinnati | 29 | 31 | .483 | 7½ |
| New York | 29 | 31 | .483 | 7½ |
| Pittsburgh | 27 | 31 | .466 | 8½ |
| Houston | 23 | 37 | .383 | 13½ |

**Sunday's Results**

Los Angeles 2, Philadelphia 1
St. Louis 4, Cincinnati 2
San Francisco 4-1, New York 1-3
Pittsburgh 3-11, Houston 1-2
Atlanta 1, Chicago 0 (11 innings)

**Today's Schedule**

Los Angeles (Drysdale, 8-4) at Philadelphia (Short, 4-6), KFI, KWKW, 4:30 p.m.

Cincinnati (Maloney, 6-4) at Atlanta (Jarvis, 6-4), night

Houston (Cuellar, 4-7) at Pittsburgh (McBean, 5-5), night

Only games scheduled

**L.A. SHADES PHILLIES, 2-1**

# Brewer Saves Day for Dodgers

BY DAN HAFNER
Times Staff Writer

PHILADELPHIA—Just when it appeared that the Dodger bullpen had sprung a leak, Jim Brewer sauntered out to the mound Sunday and saved a 2-1 victory for Claude Osteen over the Philadelphia Phillies.

Brewer had lost the second game Friday night and Hank Aguirre and Jack Billingham had also been roughed up in recent games, but Brewer was brilliant Sunday.

The left-handed reliever who has an Oklahoma drawl and just about the best screwball in the game, entered the scene before a Bat Day crowd of 20,084, with the bases loaded and one out in the seventh inning.

The first man he faced was Johnny Callison, and Brewer made him pop a foul to Bob Bailey. But he was far from out of trouble, because up stepped Richie Allen.

The usual mixture of cheers and boos greeted the powerful swinger. Brewer threw him two sliders and the count was even. Then he threw a screwball in the dirt and the eager Allen missed it. Another in the same place and again Allen went for it and missed to strike out.

In the last two innings, Brewer gave up only an infield hit as the Dodgers evened the marathon series at two games apiece.

"I'd rather not face Allen with the bases loaded," drawled Brewer. "In fact, I never enjoy seeing him with the bat in his hand. He may not be the most dangerous hitter in the game, but he sure looks mean to me."

Controversy follows Allen everywhere.

He seems to be the key figure in every game. Even when he contributes to the victory, which is often, the fans are not completely happy with him.

But when he strikes out in a key situation they delight in pouring it on.

Brewer's performance ruined the debut of Bob Skinner as Philadelphia

Please Turn to Page 3, Col. 3

## TODAY IN SPORTS

**BASEBALL**—New York vs. California, Anaheim Stadium, 8 p.m.

**TENNIS**—Southern California junior championships, L.A. Tennis Club, 9 a.m.

**AMATEUR BOXING**—Victoria Hall, 8 p.m.

**RADIO-TELEVISION**

**BASEBALL**—New York at California, KMPC, 8 p.m.; Los Angeles at Philadelphia, KFI, KWKW, 4:30 p.m.

# Wahoo Sam Crawford, Former Detroit Great, Dies at 88

Samuel E. (Wahoo Sam) Crawford, one of baseball's immortals who was elected to the Hall of Fame in 1957, is dead at 88.

The oldest living member of the Hall of Fame died Saturday at Hollywood Community Hospital, where he had been treated since May 26 when he suffered a stroke.

A teammate of the great Ty Cobb with the Detroit Tigers for 15 years, Crawford spent 19 years as a major league baseball player, four years with the Cincinnati Reds and the rest with Detroit.

Although basically an outfielder, Crawford also played first base and during his lengthy stay with the Detroit club he became one of the best known and best-liked players ever to perform for the Tigers.

Crawford got his nickname of "Wahoo Sam" because he came from the little town of Wahoo, Neb., where he started out playing semiprofessional baseball and quickly came to the attention of the major league scouts.

At the age of 19 he started playing professional baseball with Chatham of the Canadian League and in one season he went from that club to Grand Rapids of the Western League and then to the Cincinnati club.

The smooth-swinging Crawford quickly made his mark in the majors. In 1901, his second full season in the majors, he led the National League in home runs with 16 and batted .335.

The next year he led the National League in triples with 23 and batted .333.

It was in 1903 that Crawford was traded to the Detroit club of the American League where he was to spend the rest of his major league career until 1917.

During his lengthy span in the majors Crawford compiled a .309 batting average and set the major league record of 312 triples. He hit more than 20 triples in five seasons.

By leading the American League in home runs in 1908 with seven, Crawford became the only man ever to lead both leagues in that department.

Durability was another of his assets.

He played in 2,505 games and three World Series, and collected 2,961 hits.

Please Turn to Page 4, Col. 1

# DENNY DOES IT! RALLY HELPS HIM TO 30TH

DETROIT (AP)—Denny McLain was blinking at exploding flash bulbs and trying to contend with rapid-fire questions in the Detroit dressing room Saturday after winning his 30th game when Sandy Koufax grabbed his attention.

The former left-handed great of the Dodgers, now an announcer, yelled to McLain:

"No one's left the ball park. They're screaming out there for you."

"I'll go," said McLain. "I want to go."

"Wait until we get some protection," cautioned a Detroit official, and McLain complied.

Then he made his way through the mob scene in the dressing room and back through the dugout to step on the field and acknowledge the wildly cheering fans who still were massed in the stands awaiting one more look at baseball's latest hero.

Detroit rallied for two runs in the last of the ninth inning for a 5-4 victory over the Oakland Athletics to help McLain become the first pitcher in 34 years to win 30.

The victory also cut Detroit's magic number for clinching the American League pennant to four.

Two home runs by Reggie Jackson left McLain on the short end of a 4-3 score as the Tigers came to bat in the ninth. Al Kaline batted for McLain, who allowed six hits, and walked one. Klaine walked.

After Dick McAuliffe fouled out, Mickey Stanley singled to center and Kaline raced to third.

Then, with the infield drawn in, Jim Northrup bounced to first baseman Danny Cater. Kaline broke for the plate and Cater's high throw sailed over catcher Dave Duncan's head, allowing the tying run to score.

With the outfield drawn in, Willie Horton lifted a long drive that soared over the head of left fielder Jim Gosger and Stanley scored the winning run.

McLain raced from the dugout with the rest of the Tigers to embrace Horton.

McLain was rocked early by the A's but allowed only two hits over the five innings and struck out 10.

After McLain's walk back onto the field, more police had to be called to hold back a large group of strong-voiced youths who pounded on the Detroit dressing room and yelled over and over again, "We want Denny, we want Denny."

While that noise echoed through the dressing room, McLain finally admitted that he had been under pressure in the three days before his bid to become the first 30-game winner in the majors since Dizzy Dean in 1934.

"It's been on my mind the last couple of days," he said, although previously he had denied he had been giving it too much thought. "With all the business I was handling I really didn't have too much time to think—but then it just would pop into my head.

"It really built up right from the beginning of the game," he continued. "There was a great amount of pressure on us just trying to keep up close after we fell behind.

"But you probably could feel it too. The people out there went crazy

Please Turn to Page 6, Col. 6

Los Angeles Times
Sports
CC SECTION D 3†
SUNDAY, SEPTEMBER 15, 1968

## JIM MURRAY

# Autocratic Mr. Tennis

To Perry Thomas Jones, 80, the world is a tennis court—bounded on the east by Cahuenga Boulevard, on the west by a military academy and on the south by Clinton Street. On a clear day you can see the national singles winner.

It has been called the Vatican of Tennis. Which gives you an idea of the stature of Perry T. Jones. In some corners of the world they think he arrives each day by sedan chair.

The cramped 4½ acres there is the font of American tennis. Every great player of the last 40 years has either come through or out of the L.A. Tennis Club. The best players in the world habitually are found there. Also, the worst: the movie crowd, the oil rich, the land sellers are abroad on its courts.

There are probably only two really towering athletic mentors who ever came out of Los Angeles—and they were both named Jones. Howard taught football and Perry managed tennis.

Fussy, cantankerous, patrician, autocratic, Perry has ruled tennis the way Torquemada ruled the Inquisition. One word from him and you were banished to the public parks forever—Siberia, the dungeons of Tennis.

It was said he not only wanted to keep the costume of tennis white but the epidermis. It would help if even your hair was white. That for the first 20 years even brown eyes were unacceptable. If you had freckles, you played out back.

It wasn't true. Perry Jones didn't care what color you were. But you did have to know how to curtsy. You had to know which one was the salad fork. You had to have MANNERS. If you were under 21 you had to have a shave and a haircut. And be passing English.

They said Perry Jones didn't like poor people but the truth was, he threw more sons of riches off his courts because they threw racquets or tantrums. He told them they could take their Roman numerals and $50 sweaters and try Plummer Park—or badminton.

### A Case of Schooling

When he barred Pancho Gonzales, the fine old fraternity of do-gooders thought they detected the overripe odor of Anglo prejudice. With characteristic deportment (and no proof) they descended on Perry in a mob. All that was lacking was a rope. Perry faced them with the disdain of a dowager for a servant she has caught stealing—or kissing the butler: "All Richard (read, Pancho) has to do is go back to school," he scolded. "We're not running a teen club for dropouts here."

When a band of Peruvian patrons sent Alejandro Olmedo here with a restrung racquet and a note pinned to his coat, the Norteamericano branch knew right where to send him—P. T. Jones. Any postoffice in the country would know where to direct a letter marked "Mr. Tennis USA."

Controversial, contentious, tendentious, Perry Jones began his love affair with tennis back in the days when you had to chase the Indians off the court to play. Papa, who had migrated to Etiwanda from Cincinnati, went broke sinking millions into a dam to supply water to Los Angeles and San Bernardino only to have a judge rule that only the government could move water from one watershed to another.

Perry was a so-so player but he

Please Turn to Page 12, Col. 7

THE AGONY . . . Detroit's Denny McLain shows strain as he delivers fastball Saturday against A's in quest of his 30th victory of the season.

. . . AND THE ECSTASY—McLain embraces Willie Horton after latter hit single in ninth-inning rally to give Tigers and McLain 5-4 victory. AP Wirephotos

# Evans Speeds to World 400 Record But Is Disappointed

## San Jose Star Runs 44.0, Was Hoping for 43

BY PAUL ZIMMERMAN
Times Sports Editor

SOUTH LAKE TAHOE — Lee Evans took a half second off the world record and Larry James trimmed four-tenths from it, but neither was satisfied Saturday as they led the parade in the 400-meter Olympic trials at Echo Summit.

"I was hoping to run 43 today," said Evans, 21-year-old San Jose State junior, who was clocked in the fantastic time of 44 seconds flat.

"Forty-three what?" he was asked.

"Just 43," said the 6-foot, 172-pound collegian who wants to be a football player when the Olympics are over.

James, 20-year-old Villanova speedster, was more conservative.

"I planned to run 43.9," said the junior, who was leading with five meters to go, but his legs went rubbery at the end and Evans sped by him. James was clocked in 44.1.

### Matthews Fourth

Ron Freeman of Arizona State ran 44.6 for the third spot on the team, a split second back of Tommie Smith's record. The pace was so sizzling that Vince Matthews, who ran a 44.4 here only two weeks ago, had to settle for fourth. He still made the team as a member of the 1,600-meter relay quartet.

It was the fourth world mark shattered during the trials here, and a fifth might have been forthcoming in the long jump Saturday except for an aiding wind.

Bob Beamon, who has usurped the throne from Ralph Boston, got off a leap of 27-6½ on his first attempt, but the wind reading was 7.15 m.p.h. at the time and this deprived him of the record currently held by Boston and Igor Ter-Ovanesyan at 27-4¾.

Boston did 27-1 1/4 on his first effort with an aiding wind of 11 m.p.h. and the third spot went to veteran Charlie Mays, who missed the 1964 team by a quarter of an inch. His best of 26-9¼ also was wind aided.

The only other competition during the day was the first round of the 1,500 meters in which Jim Ryun, after his abortive attempt to make the

Please Turn to Page 7, Col. 1

# It's Okker vs. Smith Today in Net Play; Gonzales Triumphs

BY JEFF PRUGH
Times Staff Writer

The moment had arrived when everybody was to learn who Tom Okker's first opponent would be.

Jack Kramer, the official referee, reached into the large silver bowl, pulled out a piece of paper and told a small gathering at the L.A. Tennis Club the other night:

"Ladies and gentlemen, I hate to say it, but it's Stan Smith."

To the fans who hope to get their first look at Okker next Thursday when the Pacific Southwest Open moves to the Sports Arena, and to the promoters who want Okker as a box-office attraction, Stan Smith is a potential villain.

And those pulling for a local-boy-makes-good upset by Smith, the former USC Trojan, could not care less whether Okker lives up to his No. 3 seeding.

So, the Tom Okker-vs.-Stan Smith match at 2 p.m. today shapes up as the most attractive pairing of the tournament's second day of action.

It will offer a contrast in styles—Okker, the astonishingly quick groundstroke artist, against Smith, the serve-and-smash specialist.

Okker, the most exciting newcomer in tennis this year, has won more than $20,000 this season as a registered player—one who is permitted by his country to play for prize money, instead of expenses.

But Smith, the No. 7-ranking U.S. amateur, will be very much at home on the center court. The L.A. Tennis Club is where Smith has spent most of the past years practicing as a member of the USC varsity.

One thing, though, is certain. Not one of the seeded players has a tougher opening match than Tom Okker.

★

Pancho Gonzales is a man on a mission.

Some people might call it "Mission: Impossible," but don't tell it to Gonzales.

Even at 40, he is bent on winning

Please Turn to Page 12, Col. 4

# Ellis Scores Unpopular Decision

STOCKHOLM (UPI)—Jimmy Ellis, gamely fighting back after suffering a broken nose in the first round, retained his World Boxing Assn. heavyweight championship Saturday with an unpopular 15-round decision over former champ Floyd Patterson.

Referee Harry Valan of New York, the sole judge, gave Ellis a 9-6 edge and reaped such violent fan reaction he had to have police protection when he left the ring.

Most of the 25,000 fans thought Patterson was winning. He had scored the most obviously telling blows, including a right—the first real punch of the fight—in the first round which appeared to have broken Ellis' nose.

And, he connected in the 14th with two hooks that sent Ellis down, dragging Patterson with him. Valan began counting, but changed his mind and decided not to score it as a knockdown.

The referee, appearing in his fourth title fight, told newsmen later he did not score a knockdown because Ellis "just slipped."

Defending his controversial decision, Valan said in reference to Patterson: "You cannot win a fight backing away."

Patterson said he believed he won when he heard the final bell.

"I believed I had won—but, of course, it's the referee's decision," said the sad-eyed ex-champion. "I felt I was on top for most of the time. I don't count the punches in a fight but I suppose the referee does.

"But I must admit that I had high hopes when I stood there and waited for the decision. It was sort of a shock that it went against me."

Patterson, 33, said he had talked of quitting if he lost Saturday's fight. "But I'm not so sure now," he said. "After all it makes a difference how you lose. I think I had a very good fight tonight."

Patterson had only praise for his opponent.

He agreed with Valan and Ellis that there was no knockdown in the 14th round.

"Ellis slipped after he took a punch from me. I helped him up," Patterson said.

Patterson's handlers were not as diplomatic as their employer.

Please Turn to Page 6, Col. 1

ROCKET SHOT—Australia's Rod Laver, top seeded in men's singles, makes backhand return against John Norgauer in second round of Pacific Southwest Open tournament Saturday. Laver won, 6-0, 6-3. Times photo by Ben Olender

# STANDINGS

**NATIONAL LEAGUE**

| | W | L | Pct. | GBL |
|---|---|---|---|---|
| St. Louis | 92 | 58 | .613 | |
| San Francisco | 80 | 69 | .537 | 11½ |
| Cincinnati | 77 | 70 | .524 | 13½ |
| Chicago | 77 | 74 | .510 | 15½ |
| Atlanta | 75 | 74 | .503 | 16½ |
| Pittsburgh | 72 | 76 | .486 | 19 |
| Philadelphia | 71 | 78 | .477 | 20½ |
| Los Angeles | 68 | 81 | .457 | 23½ |
| New York | 67 | 83 | .447 | 25 |
| Houston | 67 | 83 | .447 | 25 |

**Saturday's Results**

Los Angeles 3, Atlanta 0
St. Louis 8, Houston 0
Philadelphia 4, Chicago 1
Pittsburgh 6, New York 0
San Francisco 9, Cincinnati 1

**Today's Schedule**

Atlanta (Stone, 6-3) at Los Angeles (Moeller, 1-0), Dodger Stadium, KFI, KWKW, 1 p.m.

Chicago (Jenkins, 17-14) at Philadelphia (G. Jackson, 1-3)

Pittsburgh (Ellis, 4-4) at New York (Cardwell, 7-12)

St. Louis (Carlton, 12-11) at Houston (Wilson, 13-14)

Cincinnati (Queen, 0-1 or Nolan, 9-2) at San Francisco (Marichal, 25-8)

**AMERICAN LEAGUE**

| | W | L | Pct. | GBL |
|---|---|---|---|---|
| Detroit | 95 | 54 | .638 | |
| Baltimore | 86 | 64 | .573 | 9½ |
| New York | 79 | 70 | .530 | 16 |
| Boston | 79 | 70 | .530 | 16 |
| Cleveland | 80 | 72 | .526 | 16½ |
| Oakland | 76 | 74 | .507 | 19½ |
| Minnesota | 70 | 79 | .470 | 25 |
| California | 64 | 86 | .427 | 31½ |
| Chicago | 62 | 88 | .413 | 33½ |
| Washington | 58 | 92 | .387 | 36½ |

**Saturday Results**

California 5, Chicago 4 (10 innings)
Detroit 5, Oakland 4
New York 4, Washington 1
Baltimore 5, Cleveland 3
Minnesota 7, Boston 3

**Today's Schedule**

California (Messersmith, 3-1) at Chicago (Nyman, 3-0), KMPC, Channel 5, 11:15 a.m.

Oakland (Krausse, 10-10) at Detroit (Lolich, 14-9)

New York (Peterson, 11-9) at Washington (Moore, 3-4 or Pascual, 13-11)

Minnesota (Kaat, 13-12) at Boston (Bell, 11-11)

Baltimore (Hardin, 18-10) at Cleveland (Williams, 11-10)

# Gambling Seagren Takes Pole Vault at 17-8½

CC PART III 2†
BUSINESS & FINANCE
THURSDAY, OCTOBER 17, 1968

BY PAUL ZIMMERMAN
Times Sports Editor

MEXICO CITY — Bob Seagren, taking chances that would put a Mississippi riverboat gambler to shame, preserved the United States' unbroken string of Olympic victories in the pole vault here Wednesday night, but just barely.

The USC senior, passing at such unbelievable heights as 17-2 3/4, and 17-6 3/4, finally won on fewer misses at 17-8½ from Claus Schiprowski of West Germany, and Wolfgang Nordwig of East Germany, who finished third.

This was a quarter of an inch short of Bob's pending world record of 17-8 3/4, but it bettered teammate Paul Wilson's existing mark of 17-7 3/4.

It was a day in which three recognized world records and five Olympic marks fell. Tommie Smith of Lemoore won the 200-meter dash by three yards in 19.8 seconds, after almost failing to make it to the finals because of a groin injury.

The other world record was posted in the triple jump qualifying by Giuseppe Gentile of Italy, at 56 feet 1 1/4 inches, to better the eight-year-old mark (55-10½) set by Josef Schmidt of Poland at Rome.

Two additional Olympic records were broken and one tied during the afternoon. Giula Zsivotzki of Hungary hurled the hammer 238 feet 2½ inches and Janis Lusis of the Soviet Union bettered a 12-year-old javelin mark, flinging the spear 295 feet 7 1/4 inches on his final throw to win the event. All three medalists broke the 281-2½ feet record set by Egil Danielsen of Norway at Melbourne.

Colette Besson of France tied an Olympic standard when she won the 400-meter finals for women in 52 seconds flat. America's lone representative, Jarvis Scott, faded to sixth in the stretch run.

For pure suspense, Seagren's performance in the marathon pole vault, which finished 7½ hours after it started, was the heartstopper on another day of terrific competition, in which George Young of the USA finished third in the steeplechase behind two Kenyans, Amos Biwott and Benjamin Kogo. The winning time of 8:51 flat, was understandably slow because of the high altitude.

Seagren was trailing Nordwig and Schiprowski with four misses, when he passed 17-2 3/4. He caught them there by clearing 17-4 3/4 on his first try as each had missed their first efforts but made it the second time around.

Then came the greatest gamble of them all, as he passed at 17-6 3/4—an unheard of thing. If he had missed at 17-8½ later, he wouldn't even have finished in the first three.

All three failed in their first effort at the winning height. Then, first Seagren and after him, Schiprowski, got over the bar. Nordwig did, too, but not until his third and final try.

In the final analysis, since none of these could make 17-10½, the great Trojan competitor emerged victorious, with Nordwig third. Chris Papanikolau, the San Jose State student from Greece, who stayed with them through 17-6 3/4 finished fourth ahead of John Pennell of the USA, who was fifth, again on the basis of fewer misses.

Young made a gallant bid for victory in the steeplechase. The 31-year-old Arizona high school teacher moved past Kogo into first place on the backstretch of the final lap, after

Please Turn to Page 4, Col. 3

THE WINNER!—Jubilant in victory, Tommie Smith of San Jose State speeds across the Olympic 200-meter finish line in world record time—19.8. Earlier, he suffered a muscle pull, winning a 20.2 heat, but came back strongly in the finals. Smith had held the former world record of 20 flat, set in 1965.

OLYMPIANS PROTEST — U.S. sprinters Tommie Smith (center) and John Carlos raise black-gloved hands in racial protest and stare at ground during playing of Star Spangled Banner after getting medals for finishing first, third in Olympic 200 meters Wednesday. Peter Norman, Australia, was second.
AP Wirephotos

## JIM MURRAY

# U.S. Gold Drain? Not When Oerter Competes

MEXICO CITY—The number of athletes who have four Olympic gold medals would not fill a German car.

The number of athletes who have won four in the same event comes to exactly one.

Before Alfred Adolph Oerter is through, he may fill a small German car with his medals alone. There would be no room for him. He weighs 275 pounds and stands 6 feet 4 inches.

You wouldn't think a four-pound discus would require that much heft. At first glance, it would seem like hiring a cannon to shoot a bird. Hundred-pound housewives have been known to get distance and accuracy with plates no heavier.

Al Oerter won his first Olympic discus in the administration of Dwight D. Eisenhower. His secret is the same as Sam Snead's or Ben Hogan's—a repeating, controlled swing in which his muscles have been trained to respond to a series of checkpoints. He's not so much an athlete as a computer. He has the ability to awaken from a sound sleep and four-month layoff and step out and dispatch a 200-foot toss as effortlessly as emptying a bucket of water.

His competition errs in striving for distance at the expense of accuracy. They are like golfers who can drive the ball 350 yards but in any direction except straight out.

The discus is not one of the glamour events of an Olympics—or any other track meet. The 100-meter dash winner becomes the "world's fastest human." But "the world's farthest plate-thrower" does not exactly set off ticker-tape parades. The medal, of course, is just as gold. But even a shot put champion is a celebrity by comparison.

"Oerter Wins Shot—Again" read the headline in the English language local newspapers Wednesday morning as Oerter, his wife, Corinne, and two small daughters, Christiana and Gabriela, sat down to breakfast in the married athletes' compound. Al shook his head. "Next edition they'll have me winning the javelin," he prophesied.

When I arrived at the compound gate, amid the babel of accents and threaded my way past the turbanned Asiatics, the fezzed Africans and the pink-cheeked Nordics milling about the information counter, I asked, "Which apartment is Al Oerter in?" "Is he an athlete?" the young lady asked politely. An overbearer, an African in the correct Oxonian accent of his people, corrected her. "Of course," he said. "He won the shot put. He is the world's champion in the shot put."

A pity, because, probably no athlete in Olympic history, to say nothing of any history, dominated his event as thoroughly as Al Oerter has. Only two ever won back-to-back discus events, let alone back-to-back-to-back-to-back.

Oerter was the first discus champion to break the 200-foot barrier. He set four world's records in 10 years but had been thought this year to be as extinct as silent movies. He came to the Olympics in the shadow of his teammate, Jay Silvester, the Utah strongboy who has a world record pending which broke the old one by over a foot. They were thinking of clearing the seats behind the landing area when Silvester threw this year. It would go so far, so they thought, it would have to be measured by bringing the curvature of the earth into the computation.

Poor Jay was as wild off the tee as a 20-handicapper with a built-in slice. If it was golf, he would have been laying 11 on the first hole. He was in the fairway only three out of his six tries. Three times, he flew it in the deep rough, and the other three he might as well have. He barely broke 200 feet, which was 24 full feet off his world mark. It was like Jimmy Hines running a 15-second 100, Bob Seagren missing out at 12 feet, the Harvard shell sinking. His discus wavered through the air like a burning airplane. He could have thrown a saucer farther with a cup in it.

Please Turn to Page 4, Col. 1

# Taxi-Squad Grads Sparkle as Stand-ins for Crippled Rams

BY BOB OATES
Times Staff Writer

On the 40-man Los Angeles football club today you can find only two players who, in George Allen's three seasons, have moved directly from college football to the Ram varsity.

"If anything," says George, "two rookies in three years are too many."

As a policy, this is unprecedented in professional football, but it works for Allen because he does not throw rookies away. He confines them instead to the reserve squad, which he calls the taxi squad, and they practice each day with the varsity.

And that is how the Rams beat Green Bay. On the turning-point plays in the crisis of the fourth quarter last week, Roman Gabriel's backfield consisted of two graduates of Allen's taxi squad—Henry Dyer and Mike Dennis.

Dyer and Dennis, what's more, will join young Willie Ellison as probably the only Ram running backs again this week. In the Atlanta game here Sunday, Tommy Mason and Dick Bass probably will not play and Lester Josephson is out.

When an NFL contender loses its entire backfield—both starters and the No. 1 replacement—it can expect to fall out of contention.

Usually in such a predicament, the coach must rely on rookies who have been filling places on the 40-man roster but who lack the experience to make a contribution on the field. Instead, the Rams are replacing experience with experience.

"The main thing is confidence," says Allen. "When a boy gets a year or two of experience on the taxi squad, he acquires the confidence that can only come from long

Please Turn to Page 14, Col. 3

## TODAY IN SPORTS

**HOCKEY**—Boston vs. Los Angeles, Forum, 8 p.m.

**HORSE RACING**—Quarter horses, Los Alamitos, first post 7 p.m.; Harness horses, Hollywood Park, first post 1 p.m.

**BOXING**—Andy Heilman vs. Andy Kendall, Olympic Auditorium, 8 p.m.

**POLO**—Will Rogers State Park, 2 p.m.

**RADIO-TELEVISION**

**HOCKEY**—Boston at Los Angeles, KNX, 8 p.m.

**OLYMPICS** — From Mexico City, Channel 7, 1 p.m., 4:30 p.m., 9.30 p.m.

**BOXING** — Olympic Auditorium, Channel 5, 8:30 p.m.

## SMITH, CARLOS CLENCH FISTS

# 'Black Power' on Victory Stand

BY SHIRLEY POVICH
Exclusive to The Times from the Washington Post

MEXICO CITY—The protest of American Negro athletes flared from the winner's stand at the Olympic Games late Wednesday with medal-winning sprinters Tommie Smith and John Carlos flaunting symbols of black power.

After running first and third in the 200-meter finals, they strode to the stand for the medal-bestowing ritual, shoeless but wearing long black stockings. Each held high one hand encased in a black glove. Smith wore a black scarf around his neck.

While the second-place medalist, Peter Norman of Australia, stood in respectful attention at the playing of the "Star Spangled Banner," both Smith and Carlos raised a black-gloved hand in a closed-fist gesture.

Avery Brundange, president of the International Olympic Committee (IOC), who had been quoted as saying any Negro athlete would be sent home if they wore black armbands or other symbols of protest in conflict with the U.S. Olympic uniform, did not make the medal presentations. Lord David Burghley, British Olympic official, did.

Some U.S. Negro athletes made it clear Tuesday they did not want to receive any medals from Brundage Wednesday. Brundage went to Acapulco, where the Olympic sailing races are in progress. Other Olympic officials said Brundage's Acapulco trip was not one of "convenience" on this day.

Smith and Carlos, both known as Negro militants, advised the U.S. track coaches before the ceremony that they would appear with black scarfs as a protest gesture. Head coach Payton Jordan and track assistant Stan Wright made no objection, but told the press they would have no comment.

In a post-race press conference Smith and Carlos emphasized their protest of the Negroes' position in America. Carlos said the closed-fist gesture was to show that black people are united.

"We both want you to print what I say the way I say it or not at all," said Carlos. "When we arrived, there were boos. We want to make it clear that white people seem to think black people are animals doing a job.

"We want people to understand that we are not animals or rats. We want you to tell Americans and all the world that if they do not care what black people do, they should not go to see black people perform.

"If you think we are bad, the 1972

Please Turn to Page 4, Col. 1

## BACKS 'BIGGER, FASTER' NOW

# In Drury's Day, You Played Entire Game—Without Rest

BY DWIGHT CHAPIN
Times Staff Writer

It was all so different then.

"The plays and systems weren't as complicated," said Morley Drury. "We never had more than 30 men on our squad. The tackles never went much over 190 pounds. And you played a whole game of football or you didn't play at all."

The man they named "The Noblest Trojan of Them All" was looking back, with pride but no sorrow.

"It's been a long time since you carried the ball 45 times in a game for USC," he was reminded.

"Yes," he answered, "41 years.

"We were playing California in the Coliseum and we beat 'em, 13-0. I played quarterback but under Howard Jones that was sort of like tailback is at USC today. But I remember when the fullback, Harry Edelson, got hurt, I moved over and took his spot."

It didn't matter. Drury still ran for 205 yards and destroyed the Bears.

**Record Falls to O. J.**

"No," he said, "I can't recall that I was particularly tired running that much. I always carried a lot. But I did know that I'd had a good day."

The 45 carries stood as a record through a depression, two wars and nearly half a century.

Saturday the record fell under the cleats of O. J. Simpson. The new mark is 47.

Morley Drury is happy.

"He's a terrific runner," Drury said. "He has a great change of pace. The thing I always like about a runner is the way he can reverse his field, and O. J. can.

"He's strong but he surprises you, too. He looks like he isn't going to do anything and then all of a sudden he goes. I liked Mike Garrett, too, but he seemed to get tired after he carried a lot of times. Simpson stays right in there, and he even gets stronger."

Drury, at 185 pounds, was a big back in his day. Simpson, at 204, is not overly large in his.

**They're Bigger Now**

"That's probably the main difference between my day and his," said Drury. "They're all so much bigger now, and faster, too."

Simpson, however, even though he carries 40 times or more a game, gets a chance to rest when his team is on defense. Drury never did.

"If we went out of a game," Drury said, "that was it."

The Noblest Trojan's role in USC history is assured. There is plenty of room for another man. Drury was asked just how Simpson would do if he were ushered into a time machine and whisked back to 1927.

"He would," said Dury without

Please Turn to Page 14, Col. 1

NOBLEST TROJAN—One of O. J. Simpson's admirers is Morley Drury, who carried the ball 45 times in the USC-California game 41 years ago.
Times photo

# U.S. Expels Smith, Carlos From Olympic Team

BY CHARLES MAHER
Times Staff Writer

MEXICO CITY—The U.S. Olympic Committee, under pressure from higher-ups, expelled Tommie Smith and John Carlos from the American team Friday for turning a victory ceremony into a black power demonstration.

There was talk early in the day that some other U.S. athletes might pull out of the Games, to indicate their displeasure with the committee action, but no such walkouts occurred.

Smith and Carlos were expelled for their conduct after the 200-meter race Wednesday. Smith, who won the gold medal, and Carlos, the bronze medalist, turned up for the victory ceremony wearing black socks. Also, each wore a black glove, and black scarves. While the Star-Spangled Banner was being played, they held their gloved hands aloft, with the fingers clenched. They fixed their eyes on the ground.

Smith said later that the clenched hands were symbols of black power and black unity, that the scarves symbolized their blackness and the socks were symbols of black poverty.

Early Thursday, the International Olympic Committee issued a statement saying Smith and Carlos deliberately violated a universally-accepted Olympic principle "by using the occasion to advertise domestic political views." The IOC said the U.S. Olympic Committee "carries the responsibility for its competitors."

Douglas F. Roby, president of the U.S. committee, said he called a committee meeting for 10 a.m. Thursday .But at 9 a.m., he said, he was called before the IOC.

"They were incensed at what occurred," he said. "They accused me and our committee of not having control of our teams."

Roby said nine members of the IOC executive committee were present and one asked him what the U.S. committee proposed to do.

"I asked the board a question," Roby said. "I asked, 'What if we do nothing?'

"Then that brought forth a statement from one member—and several others concurred — that they would have to take some drastic action so far as our team was concerned if we did not take action."

Roby told newsmen that the IOC did not imply, as one report said, that it might expel the entire U.S. team from the Games "I really don't think they would have disqualified the entire team," he said. "But there was concern that this might lead to a takeover, that there might be a broad demonstration."

Roby's committee met and issued this statement:

"The United States Olympic Committee expresses its profound regrets to the International Olympic Committee, to the Mexican Organizing Committee and to the people of Mexico for the discourtesy displayed by two members of its team in the parting from tradition during the victory ceremony . . .

"The untypical exhibitionism of these athletes also violates the basic standards of sportsmanship and good manners which are highly regarded in the United States, and therefore the two men involved are suspended forthwith from the team and ordered to remove themselves from the Olympic Village . . .

"A repetition of such incidents by other members of the USA team can only be considered a willful disregard of Olympic principles that would warrant the imposition of the severest penalties at the disposal of the U.S. Olympic Committee."

Smith and Carlos turned up for Friday afternoon's program at the Olympic Stadium. There they were interviewed by Brad Pye, a Negro member of the Los Angeles Park and Recreation Commission and a sports commentator on station KGFJ in Los Angeles.

Please Turn to Page 3, Col. 4

SWEET SUE—Sue Gossick of Tarzana is shown en route to a gold medal Friday in three-meter springboard event of Olympic Games.

# Bob Beamon in Long, Long Jump, Sets Record at 29-2½

Los Angeles Times
Sports
CC PART II 2†
BUSINESS & FINANCE
SATURDAY, OCTOBER 19, 1968

## Evans Breaks World Mark (43.8) as U.S. Sweeps 400 at Olympics

BY PAUL ZIMMERMAN
Times Sports Editor

MEXICO CITY—Bob Beamon got off an unbelievable leap of 29 feet 2½ inches in the long jump Friday to lead another world record-breaking parade in the Olympic Games. This was almost two feet beyond the recognized mark held by Ralph Boston and Igor Ter-Ovanesyan of 27 feet 4¾ inches.

Three global marks were washed away during the rainy afternoon, another tied, and five Olympic figures were rewritten.

One of the more spectacular of these was the 43.8 clocking turned in by Lee Evans, also of the USA, when he just did nip teammate Larry James at the tape. Ron Freeman made it a sweep, the first here by the United States. Not since the 1904 games at St. Louis have the Americans accomplished this feat in the 400.

Irina Kirszenstein of Poland won the women's 200-meter dash in 22.5, two tenths faster than her world mark, as the United States trio of Barbara Farrell, Wyomia Tyus, and Margaret Bailes ran fourth, sixth and seventh.

**Aussie Teenager Wins**

Seventeen-year-old Maureen Caird of Australia equaled the world mark of 10.3 in the women's 80-meter hurdles, a stride ahead of 29-year-old Pam Kilborn, also of Australia. blonde Pat Van Wolvelaere from the United States was fourth, just a step back of third-place finishing Chi Cheng of Taiwan.

After the dismissal of Tommie Smith and John Carlos for their victory podium Wednesday, there was a tense moment of suspense when Evans, James and Freeman took the stand.

They jauntily wore black berets, but doffed them at the playing of the National Anthem, after John Jewett Garland of Los Angeles presented the medals.

Douglas Roby, president of the United States Olympic Committee, said there was nothing objectionable about their dress or conduct.

Beamon took only two jumps Friday. When the rain came he quit.

**Boston's Advice**

"Ralph (Boston) talked to me before the start and told me to put everything into my first jumps, so I did," said the Texas (El Paso) star who wants to eventually play pro basketball.

"I have been having trouble with my step all week (he didn't qualify until his last leap Thursday) and I was surprised when I hit the board so perfectly.

"I knew it was a good jump but I didn't have any idea it was over 29 feet.

Please Turn to Page 2, Col. 1

## Confusion, Shock Grip U.S. Squad After Pair Ousted

MEXICO CITY (AP) — Confusion erupted around the United States headquarters at the Olympic Village Friday after the early morning shock announcement that Tommie Smith and John Carlos had been expelled from the team.

Athletes wandered around the Village, expressing shock and varying opinions on the action.

"It is unfair; it is ridiculous," said Art Walker, a Negro triple jumper from Los Angeles who has already competed.

"They say they are doing it because of a protest. This is silly. Since the early 1900s the United States team has been protesting similarly by failing to dip its flag when it passes the reviewing stand. All other countries do it. This is strictly political."

**Follow U.S. Protocol**

Most countries dip their flags when passing in review but it is against government regulations to dip the American flag under any circumstances. Flag bearers in the Olympic parade have always followed Army and Navy protocol in this respect.

Members of the Harvard rowing team, who had pledged support of the black athletes' civil rights movement, expressed regret but said that they would row in today's finals as scheduled.

"It is unfair and very tragic," said Scott Steketee of Toledo, No. 5 on the Harvard eight.

"Rowing is a team sport and those of us who disagree with this decision have an obligation to the boat and to the crew."

Two of Steketee's crew mates. Cleve and Mike Livingston, brothers from Carmichael, Calif., also said they were very dissapointed in the American action. Both insisted they would row as usual.

"I was with Hal Connolly, the hammer thrower, last night" said Cleve Livingston. "He was talking

Please Turn to Page 3, Col. 1

IT LOOKS EASY—Jim Ryun of the United States easily wins his elimination heat in 1,500 meters at Olympic Games Friday. He laid off pace, then sprinted to beat Hamadi Ben Haddou of Morocco in 3:45.7.
(AP) Wirephotos

## Dream Comes True; Sue Gossick Wins Diving Gold Medal

Exclusive to The Times from a Staff Writer

MEXICO CITY—There is a plaque in the den of the Tarzana home of Dr. Gustav Gossick which reads: "Future Olympic Champion Diver, 1957, Sue Gossick, United States Olympic Committee."

Sue Gossick was nine then and she represented a club known as the Puddle Jumpers.

It was the year after Pat McCormick had won the gold medal in three-meter springboard diving at the Melbourne Olympic Games and it would be 12 years before an American did it again.

Sue Gossick, 20, ended the wait and brought the inscription on that plaque to fruition Friday night when she won the three meter title of the XIX Olympiad.

Miss Gossick, The Times Woman of the Year in 1967, took the lead on her second dive Friday night and maintained it while scoring a total of 150.77 points, becoming the youngest ever to win this event.

Tamara Pogozheva of Russia, with an impressive final dive, finished second (145.30 points) and Keala O'Sullivan, a 17-year-old school girl from Honolulu, finished third (145.23 points).

The defending champion, Ingrid Kramer Gulbin of East Germany, who was a double gold medal winner eight years ago, finished fifth behind Micki King of the United States.

Miss Gossick, who attends Valley State and is expected to pursue a career in dentistry like her father, was fourth in the Olympic Games at Tokyo four years ago, won the Pan-American Games' springboard title a year ago and qualified for the Mexico City Games despite a sprained back.

Please Turn to Page 8, Col. 6

## M'KAY EXPECTS TROUBLE FROM 'PAL' AND HUSKIES

BY DWIGHT CHAPIN
Times Staff Writer

Jim Owens of the Washington Huskies and John McKay of the USC Trojans are close friends off the field.

And that just could be the reason why Owens' teams are almost always ready for McKay's on the field, too.

The oddsmakers say that the Trojans, newly installed as the No. 1 college team in the nation, are going to breeze past the Huskies by 20 points when they meet today at 1:30 at the Coliseum, before a crowd expected to reach 65,000.

But McKay would just as soon his team were not No. 1 in the country in the wire service polls, and he certainly cringes at the 20-point spread.

"The only way that 20 would help us would be if we could put it up on the scoreboard before the game starts," McKay said. "Washington is always very tough against us and I don't expect it to be any different this time."

Two things should help Washington. One, of course, is that it simply has nothing to lose, since its record is only 1-2-1, including two conference losses. The other is that two of the Huskies' best backs figure to be ready to play after persistent injuries.

Halfback Jim Cope, an extremely dangerous halfback both catching the ball and running with it, has played only sparingly but may start today.

And fullback Gary James, a speedy junior from St. Francis High, may be ready to play for the first time this season.

Coupled with the likes of Harvard Blanks, the breakaway wingback, Carl Wojciechowski, Buddy Kennamer and Bo Cornell, they give the Huskies a considerably talented ground attack.

Nowhere else, however, is Washington as fearsome.

Quarterback Jerry Kaloper has been ordinary and the defense, where Washington usually rules, has been somewhat soft all season, except in a rain-soaked, 3-0 win over punchless Oregon last weekend.

The assignment the Husky defense faces—containing O. J. Simpson—is something none of the other four Trojan foes this season has been able to complete.

Washington has given up an average of 131.5 yards per game on the ground. But Simpson has averaged 202 all by himself. Last season, on a slippery field in Seattle, Simpson had his most productive day of 1967, gaining 235 yards, including an

Please Turn to Page 5, Col. 1

## Greer, Clark Pace 76ers Over Lakers

PHILADELPHIA (AP)—Led by Hal Greer's 35 points, the Philadelphia 76ers built a 30-point lead and then held on to defeat the Los Angeles Lakers, 114-96, Friday night at the Spectrum.

The 76ers also got 20 points from Archie Clark, obtained in the big July trade that sent Wilt Chamberlain to the Lakers.

Chamberlain scored 15 points and grabbed 17 rebounds. He spent more time on the bench, however, than he usually did in any game during his 3½ years with the 76ers.

The 76ers showed a sell-out crowd of 15,244 their new style running game under first-year coach Jack Ramsay as the defending Eastern Division champions raced to a 31-14 first period lead.

Greer scored 16 of Philadelphia's last 17 points in the opening period. He had 12 field goals and 11 free throws for the night.

Clark, with 8 points, and Bill Cunningham, with 6 points in the second period, kept the pressure on the Lakers and their trio of superstars—Chamberlain, Elgin Baylor and Jerry West—increasing the 76ers lead to 61-38 at halftime.

It was 68-38 when Chamberlain was lifted for the first time. Led by Baylor and West, the Lakers cut the margin to 70-58, but Johnny Green

Please Turn to Page 6, Col. 6

PIT STOP—Bob Beamon sends sand flying with perfect landing, culminating unbelievable leap of 29-2½, which won the Olympic Games gold medal and established a world record for the long jump.

# Rams Lose a Down---and Shot at Title, 17-16

**BY MAL FLORENCE**
Times Staff Writer

The season ended prematurely for the Rams Sunday as they ran out of miracles in the gathering dusk of the Coliseum.

Too many mistakes—their own and possibly an official's error—rendered the final regular season game here next Sunday against the Baltimore Colts as meaningless.

It's all over. The Colts (12-1) are champions of the Coastal Division by default. The Rams (10-2-1), who have pulled out many a close game in the fading seconds during the George Allen administration, are dead—for this season, at least.

They almost survived their own miscues again Sunday but, in the end, the Chicago Bears were dancing in the dressing room after hanging on for a 17-16 upset victory.

A Tommy Mason fumble, a missed 35-yard field goal, a holding penalty—all in the final quarter—caught up and tripped the Rams.

And, let's not forget a wrong-down dispute that won't change the score of the game but will be a conversation piece at hot-stove Ram sessions during the winter.

Here's the situation:

The Rams, hemmed in by a pinching Bear defense for most of the game, were still fighting for survival with 29 seconds remaining.

Roman Gabriel, who had been knocked out in the second quarter but had returned early in the third, was on the prowl for a game-winning field goal.

His 32-yard pass to Jack Snow had produced a first down at the Chicago 32-yard line. Gabe wanted to incl. a little closer in order to put Bruce Gossett within comfortable range of a kick.

Gabriel fired a pass to Snow again that fell incomplete. Not disastrous. Now, an official signified holding against the Rams (Charlie Cowan)—a 21-yard penalty, since the infraction took place behind the line of scrimmage.

Seemingly the Rams had a first down on their own 47, but the yard marker unaccountably read second down. You don't lose a down on such an infraction after the defense accepts the penalty.

A long toss intended for Wendell Tucker, a short throw aimed at Mason and a bomb directed at Harold Jackson didn't make connections. Chicago took over with 5 seconds left; quarterback Jack Concannon fell on the ball and the Bears, Central Division co-leaders, were still in the running for the Western, NFL and Super Bowl championships. They could qualify for a Dec. 22 meeting with Baltimore by beating Green Bay at home next Sunday.

The official play-by-play concurred with reporters' tabulations: The Rams had only three downs after the penalty.

Norm Schachter, the referee, was unavailable for comment. However, Art McNally, the NFL supervisor of officials, was in attendance and did issue a statement:

"As far as the play-by-play is concerned, it appears that the Rams still had another down coming. However, the officiating crew did not think it made an error and the films will have to be reviewed for verification."

What if it turns out that the officials goofed, then what, someone asked McNally.

"Any further comment will have to come out of the commissioner's (Pete Rozelle's) office," he said. "The entire situation will be investigated thoroughly."

One down could mean nothing, or it could mean a season.

Allen and Gabriel were unaware at the time that the Rams may have been deprived of a down. "I was just concerned with the clock," said the Rams' coach.

George's eyes were red. He was emotionally exhausted. The small dressing cubicles that housed the Ram players were closed. You could hear the sounds of sobbing and no one wanted to go in.

"We have no excuses, no alibis," said Allen in a husky voice. "We've drained ourselves dry—three years of working and everything is down the drain. We have an axiom here that nobody can beat the Rams; the Rams lose because they beat themselves. The headline of this game is, 'Too Many Mistakes.'"

Allen, who had privately confided to friends that he was sure the Rams could beat the Colts in a showdown

Please Turn to Page 4, Col. 2

TWO BIG PLAYS DID IT

## Bears Earn Upset Victory

**BY BOB OATES**
Times Staff Writer

Los Angeles Times
Sports
BUSINESS & FINANCE
CC PART III 2†
MONDAY, DECEMBER 9, 1968

It will be remembered as the "lost down game." But this was not the first time a football team ever lost a down when the officials lost their heads.

This was not the first time a quarterback was knocked unconscious and recovered five minutes too late to save the season.

This was not the first time a team has blocked a punt out of bounds, for a 2-point safety, instead of into the end zone for a probable touchdown.

Nor was it the first time that a pro club has lost three separate field goal chances in the fourth quarter on a fumble, a holding penalty and a blown placekick from the 35-yard line.

But just possibly, it was the first time that all this ever happened on one day to one team. And because it happened to the Rams, they were beaten by one point Sunday in the Coliseum.

They lost everything when they lost to the Chicago Bears, 17-16, before a frustrated crowd of 66,368. Defeated only twice in 13 weeks, they are now just another second-place team. With one of the best records in pro football (10-2-1) they have forfeited the NFL's Coastal Division championship to Baltimore.

The crushing end to the season, which includes the last superfluous game next week, came on an afternoon when the Bears earned their upset with two big plays—an 88-yard kickoff run by Clarence Childs and a driving interception by Dick Butkus—setting up their only two touchdowns.

So the Bears earned it. They have the final score to prove that they were the better team on the day a dream ended in Los Angeles.

The interest of the game nonetheless lies in the series of events that took the Rams out of 1968—as follows:

1. The "lost down." Chicago and Los Angeles reporters all agreed that the officials allotted the Rams only three downs on their critical last series.

2. Roman Gabriel's injury. In the second quarter, the Ram quarterback was blind-sided by a blitzing Bear linebacker, Jim Purnell, and knocked unconscious. He returned at 5:00 of the third quarter, after the first Ram series. The interception thrown in that series was cashed by the Bears for their winning touchdown. After the game, strictly as a precautionary measure, Gabriel was taken to St. Joseph's Hospital in Orange for observation.

3. The safety play. Los Angeles blocked three Bear kicks (two punts and a field goal) but in the third quarter, Ram Dave Pivec blocked Jon Kilgore's punt too successfully. The ball scooted out of bounds—in the end zone—with three Rams close enough to cover it for a touchdown if it had stopped.

4. The fumble. After Clancy Williams intercepted for Los Angeles on the second play of the fourth quarter, Gabriel, on fourth and one at midfield, gambled the franchise on a pass to Tommy Mason—which sure-handed Tommy caught and carried 31 yards. But with a 2nd-and-2 on the Bear 9-yard line, Tommy never got control of the handoff. It bounced up to Butkus, who made a mid-air fumble recovery.

5. The blown field goal. One of the game's 22 penalties—on an afternoon when the officials seemed more nervous than the contestants—went against the Bears within

Please Turn to Page 4, Col. 1

**THE FALL OF ROMAN**—Ram quarterback Roman Gabriel is rendered temporarily unconscious from this blitz by the outside linebackers of the Chicago Bears late in the second quarter Sunday. Fullback Tommy Mason, top, blocks Doug Buffone, but Jim Purnell (53) has a clear course to Gabriel and his blindside tackle rocks Roman as he releases ball, leaving Mason with nothing to do but comfort fallen mate.

Times photos by Art Rogers

## Chiefs (7 Interceptions) Steal Chargers Blind in 40-3 Victory

**BY CHARLES MAHER**
Times Staff Writer

SAN DIEGO—Two Southern California teams were excused Sunday from further contention for a place in the Super Bowl. Only there were a lot of people here who were not ready to excuse the Chargers for the wretched performance they gave against the Kansas City Chiefs.

About four minutes into the first period, the Chargers recovered a fumble on the Kansas City 19. A minute later, a 28-yard field goal by Dennis Partee put San Diego ahead, 2-0.

The lead did not quite hold up. San Diego still had three points at the end. Kansas City had 40.

As the Ram loss to the Bears Sunday dropped L.A. from contention in the Coastal Division of the NFL, this one eliminated San Diego in the Western Division of the AFL. With one game to play the Chargers (9-4) are two games behind Oakland and Kansas City (11-2).

The Raiders meet the Chargers here next Sunday, while K.C. gets a softer touch playing at Denver. If the Raiders and Chiefs both win, or both lose, there will be a playoff at Oakland Dec. 22.

Before a standing-room-only crowd of 51,174 at San Diego Stadium, the Chiefs became the first team in more than four years to keep the Chargers from scoring a touchdown for 60 minutes.

The story here Sunday was interceptions. John Hadl of the Chargers threw six of them and his replacement, Jon Brittenum, threw one.

Hadl had a bad day, but he was not quite as bad as his interception total suggests. Four of the six balls he had picked off were deflected into the hands of Kansas City defenders.

Four of the seven K.C. interceptions led to touchdowns and one led to a field goal. That explains 31 of K.C.'s 40 points.

Please Turn to Page 2, Col. 1

## Lakers' Comeback Downs San Diego

**BY DAN HAFNER**
Times Staff Writer

Take three of the four greatest scorers in professional basketball history and put them on the same team. What do you get?

In the case of the Lakers, who acquired the No. 1 pointmaker, Wilt Chamberlain, when they already had No. 3 and 4, Elgin Baylor and Jerry West, it means a club that has trouble scoring points.

It seems rather weird, doesn't it? But going into Sunday's game at the Forum with the improved San Diego Rockets the Lakers had averaged only 100 points in their previous 10 games and 24 hours earlier managed only 81 in a 48-minute game.

Things did not look any better when the hungry young Rockets roared out to a 46-33 lead after 17 minutes of action that found the Lakers always at least one step behind.

Bill van Breda Kolff is a smart

Please Turn to Page 6, Col. 4

## Bears Remember, Win It for Halas

**BY DWIGHT CHAPIN**
Times Staff Writer

It was like the old days, the glory days. The "Monsters of the Midway" were shouting and snarling.

"Tell the Rams," said one of them, pounding his chest with his hands, "to keep pointing for that Baltimore game."

These are tough men, with scars on their bodies and destruction in their hearts and souls. They had won by one point and they had not been artistic. But they knew that the one was as big as a hundred on this smoggy Sunday.

They reminded you of a pack that used to play for George Halas, the old Papa Bear. And they didn't forget him, in victory.

The honorary game ball went to the old man.

Earlier in the week, the Bears had sent a cablegram to Manchester, England, where father Bear now is in hibernation, after hip surgery in late November.

"Our thoughts and prayers have been with you," the message read. "We're going to try to win it for you Sunday."

You could almost see Halas' grizzled smile shining through the debris in the locker room.

Halas has been replaced by Jim Dooley, whose face is smooth and whose clothes are "in." But he is of the usual Bear mold.

"Our main object," he said, "was to score 17 points. We thought if we could do that offensively and get a great game from our defensive unit, we could win it. But we didn't expect those two blocked kicks. We'd worked on preventing that all week."

He loosened his tie.

"We were very lucky on that first blocked kick that they could only get two points out of it."

Chicago, however, had done what it had to do.

"We knew we had to contain the ball on the Rams," Dooley said.

He had the NFL's leading ground gaining attack, statistically, to do it but the big man, Gale Sayers, was out of that attack because of knee surgery.

The scrambler from Boston College, Jack Concannon, was the man who kept the ball away from the Rams for great chunks of times. Often he kept the ball himself on rollouts that left the Rams standing in disarray.

He did it on a leg that wasn't sound after the first quarter. On one of his scrambles he had pulled a hamstring muscle.

Please Turn to Page 5, Col. 1

### Pro Grid Scores

**NATIONAL LEAGUE**

Chicago 17, Los Angeles 16
Cleveland 2[illegible], Washington 21
Philadelphia 29, New Orleans 17
Detroit 24, Atlanta 7
St. Louis 28, New York 21
Dallas 28, Pittsburgh 7
Minnesota 30, San Francisco 20

**AMERICAN LEAGUE**

New York 27, Cincinnati 14
Miami 38, Boston 7
Kansas City 40, San Diego 3
Oakland 33, Denver 27

# ALLEN FIRED; PLAYERS THREATEN REVOLT

A HAPPIER TIME—All was sweetness and light between Ram coach George Allen, left, and president Dan Reeves when this photo was made, but a "personality conflict" led to Allen's dismissal Thursday. During three seasons as the Rams' head man, Allen amassed 29-10-3 record plus division championship.

## We Don't Want a Loser---Cowan

BY MAL FLORENCE, Times Staff Writer

At approximately 8 a.m. Thursday George Allen received a telephone call from Ram owner Dan Reeves. When the conversation terminated Allen had been fired as head coach of the Rams.

Later, in a shocking post-Christmas announcement, Reeves said that the eminently successful coach had been relieved of his duties because of a "personality conflict."

Reeves gave no hint as to Allen's successor.

It was learned, however, that Ray Prochaska and Tom Catlin, the Rams' offensive line and defensive backfield coaches, are strong candidates to succeed Allen. Another candidate is New Orleans Saints' coach, Tom Fears, who is reportedly unhappy with his present employer. Fears is a former Ram end and assistant coach.

The Rams must find a replacement for Allen in the next month. The annual NFL-AFL player draft is scheduled Jan. 28 and it is important to the Ram organization for a coach to be named prior to the collegiate selection meeting.

Through Allen's trades, the Rams have three first-draft choices, including their own.

**Buffalo Owner Interested**

It was recently reported by The Times that Allen had unofficially been offered the head coaching job at Buffalo with the incentive of owning 10% of the franchise.

Allen denied he had been contacted by Buffalo, while owner Ralph Wilson was unavailable for comment at the time.

However, Thursday Wilson said he wants to talk to Allen about coaching his club.

Wilson said he would not have talked to Allen about the posts before. "However, now if he's relieved of his duties, why, certainly. I would be interested in talking to him. Dan Reeves is a good friend of mine. I would never talk to his head coach while he was working for Dan."

**News Shocks Allen**

Asked about his future plans, Allen said: "I'm not interested in anything right now."

There is a coaching vacancy at Pittsburgh where Bill Austin was recently fired. It has also been rumored that Otto Graham and Joe Kuharich may be relieved at Washington and Philadelphia, respectively.

It is customary to expect the unexpected from the Ram organization, but Reeves' decision caught everyone by surprise, especially Allen.

"This was probably the biggest Christmas shock of my life," said Allen, the 1967 NFL Coach of the Year and the man who restored the Rams to a position of prominence after seven losing seasons.

Allen had two more years left on a five-year contract estimated at close to $50,000 annually. A Ram spokes-

Please Turn to Page 6, Col. 1

Los Angeles Times
Sports
BUSINESS & FINANCE
CC PART III 3†
FRIDAY, DECEMBER 27, 1968

Charlie Cowan, the Rams' veteran offensive tackle, predicted late Thursday night that there would be at least "28 empty spots" on the Ram roster next year as the result of the firing of head coach George Allen.

"We don't want to come back and play for a loser and Dan Reeves told some of the players that he would just as soon settle for a 7-7 season," said Cowan, a member of the West Pro Bowl team.

Cowan was only one of many Ram players to publicly vent their discontent over the sudden, unexpected firing of Allen by Reeves.

Eddie Meador, the 10-year veteran All-Pro free safety, said he plans to retire while quarterback Roman Gabriel announced that he wants to be reunited with Allen at some other pro football franchise.

**'Want to Leave'**

"Reeves will have a young team next year," said Cowan. "I think that all the players with five or more years experience will want to leave Los Angeles."

Cowan, who plans to attend an Allen-ordered press conference today along with other veterans, said that telegrams supporting the coach and denouncing management will be in evidence at the gathering.

The tackle stated unequivocally that he would not return to the Rams next season. He also said that other players feel the same way, including Maxie Baughan, Jack Pardee, Deacon Jones, Tommy Mason, Meador and Gabriel, to name a few.

"Time is running out on us older players and we don't want to play here unless we have a chance to compete," he said.

Cowan, an eight-year veteran, said that he wants to continue playing football for a few more years—not in Los Angeles—but other veterans may just want to retire in the wake of Allen's ouster.

**Wants a Chance**

"I don't want to play if we can't possibly win a championship," he continued. "I want at least a chance to compete. But Reeves apparently doesn't want a winner."

Cowan intimated that the older Rams—its a veteran team—are in a state of revolt and will stand up and be counted at today's press conference.

"It's a little unbelievable," said Meador. "I had planned to play another year or so. Now, I'm sitting in my office and trying to figure out what I'm going to do. It doesn't look like I'll be back."

As for Gabriel, he wants to follow Allen out of Los Angeles.

"It's hard to understand," said the quarterback. "Allen is the third coach to be fired since I've been here (seven years) but we weren't winning the other times. Now, we have a winning team and have good relationships between the players and coaching staff.

"But I don't know if a picture can ever change here. I don't know if it's

Please Turn to Page 6, Col. 1

## McKay Switches Cowlings to End on USC Defense

BY DWIGHT CHAPIN
Times Staff Writer

The move probably figured.

Very early in the 1968 football season, USC coach John McKay called Alan Cowlings, the transfer from City College of San Francisco, "the fastest tackle I've ever coached."

The speed is now at work at a position—right defensive end—that has troubled the Trojans most of the season.

When Jim Grissum, who had taken over there hurt a knee in the UCLA game, USC was left without a truly reliable operator in that critical spot.

In the Rose Bowl press book, 6-8, 238-pound senior Bill Hayhoe is listed as the starter. But while his size is more than sufficient for the spot, his speed is not.

McKay's comment on the switch of Cowlings was terse.

"We just cannot continue to let people run around that end," he said.

The people he is immediately concerned about, of course, are Woody Hayes' Ohio State Buckeyes, who meet the Trojans in the Rose Bowl next Wednesday.

Cowlings, who made the Notre Dame all-opponent team as a tackle,

Please Turn to Page 8, Col. 3

*JIM MURRAY*

## Football's Easy, Woody, but Bands Need Talent

Well, it's time to make our guests welcome again. Take a letter to coach Woody Hayes, Miss Higginbotham:

"Dear Coach:

"I know you're going to persist in thinking of the Rose Bowl New Year's Day as an athletic exercise but, please, Woody, TRY to understand. We HAVE to play the National Anthem! And, no, we can't just pipe in the recording.

"I KNOW you got upset that time when it rained and they let the band march on the field at halftime, but, out here, Woody, we had an emergency meeting to see whether they would let the football team scuff up the field so it was unmarchable between the halves. We thought of cancelling the first half of the football game. I mean, ANYBODY can play football. But how many outfits can simulate a Mississippi River steamboat going up and down the field with REAL smoke coming out of the tubas? Let your clumsy athletes match THAT!

"Another thing, Woody, old boy. You think all those folks in the Thom McAn shoes jumping up and yelling 'Yea, Ohio!' are cheering a touchdown? Ha! Woody, what really happened was that somebody in the middle of that American Gothic section got up and yelled 'There's Bob Hope!,' and 18,000 people who came on the economy tour out of Chillicothe and Marion leaped to their feet with their autograph books and spilled all that fried chicken and potato salad over their calico dresses as they yelled, 'Where?'

"And those banners they wave? If you look closely you'll see they're protesting that 'Queen For a Day' isn't on the air anymore.

"Most of these folks will have a big time New Year's Eve—sitting up listening to frost warnings. But we're always glad to have them here, Woody, but you got to let the bands play. How else are these folks ever gonna catch up on the latest tunes like 'Painting The Clouds With Sunshine' or 'Sweet Leilani'? And, by the way, tell them to put away those autograph books. Mae West won't be here.

"Now to get to the sideshow of the day—the football game. Woody, O. J. Simpson is just a nice kid about 6 feet 1. He has two hands, two feet, 10 fingers, and all his teeth. He won't be hard to pick out on the SC offense: he'll be the one with the football.

"If he's got that ball more than 40 times, Woody, don't expect to be carried to the dressing room. If he's got that football 50 times, you'll be buying your own dinners all winter. You can spot him the first 25 times, because he just uses them to get the other team overconfident.

"I know you stopped Leroy Keyes and Ron Johnson, Woody, but, believe me, O.J. can run across quicksand and not get his soles wet. He doesn't run, he SKATES.

### *Miners and Milkers*

"I know you still think you don't get football players out of swimming pools or off surf boards, Woody. You get them down coal mines or in milk sheds. Right? All the same, I would instruct my boys to hit and then step back so they won't get squirted with the orange juice leaking out of the California kids. When your guys hit Jimmy Gunn, Jimmy Snow, Al Cowlings or Tony Terry, THEY might leak coal dust. Your milkers might curdle.

"Steve Sogge doesn't impress you with his arm — till you suddenly notice he's not passing for distance but for accuracy. He doesn't throw The Bomb, he throws the hand grenade. He's one of those 'Which eye do you want me to hit, coach?' passers. He's a catcher in baseball where you don't pick up any bad habits, like overthrowing.

"Mike Battle is going to surprise you. You're going to think they recruited him out of a chimney. He couldn't clog a water pipe. His helmet falls clear down to his numbers. All the same, just don't kick the ball to him, Woody. You'll find his last name is more of a description than a name.

"Well, that's all, Woody. And, just remember, if worse comes to worst, you can always enjoy the band!"

## Smith-Lutz Clinch Davis Cup for U.S. With Doubles Win

ADELAIDE, Australia (AP)—California collegians Stan Smith and Bob Lutz crushed Australia's Ray Ruffels and Jack Alexander in 67 minutes of devastating tennis today 6-4, 6-4, 6-2 for a doubles victory that returned the Davis Cup to the United States for the first time in five years.

On Thursday Clark Graebner and Arthur Ashe had given the U.S. a 2-0 lead by winning their opening singles matches. Graebner defeated Bill Bowrey, 8-10, 6-4, 8-6, 3-6, 6-1, while Ashe conquered Ruffels, 6-8, 7-5, 6-3, 6-3.

Smith and Lutz tossed their rackets in the air and leaped across the court when Ruffels failed to return a sizzling Smith service for the final point.

It was a great day for American tennis, which went into virtual eclipse after the Yanks won the Cup on these same Memorial Drive courts in 1963 and lost the following year in Cleveland, Ohio.

The smashing triumph by the USC students, who hold every American doubles record, was a blow to the veteran Australian captain, Harry Hopman, whose big gamble failed.

Hopman, who built up a reputation of miracle man in leading the Australians to 16 Challenge Round victories in 20 matches, made a bold move in naming 17-year-old Alexander, Wimbledon junior champion, as partner of Ruffels, hard-serving, left-hander. They had never played as a team before.

The Americans concentrated their attack on the slender six-footer, who was highly tense and nervous. They cracked Alexander's service for vital

Please Turn to Page 4, Col. 3

## Kings Cry Robbery as Stars Gain Tie

BY CHUCK GARRITY
Times Staff Writer

No one was really happy with the Kings' 4-4 tie with Minnesota's North Stars Thursday night. But coach John Muckler of the North Stars was more than willing to steal the point after being three goals behind in the second period.

Muckler didn't think his team played all that well. Coach Red Kelly hardly wanted to talk about the third period in which his Kings gave up two goals. And everybody was gouging away at the officials, including the 7,772 fans at the Forum who felt the last Minnesota goal was robbery.

The tying score came with just 1:58 left to play when Danny Grant banged in his 16th goal of the season from 15 feet out on the left side.

Just prior to the goal, Kings' winger Bob Wall was dropped flat on his face on what appeared to be tripping by the North Stars' Bill Collins.

Please Turn to Page 8, Col. 5

## Rising Market Rallies for Win

BY BION ABBOTT
Times Staff Writer

Frankly, the 33,552 enthusiasts on hand for the annual opening-day exercises at Santa Anita Thursday had a little difficulty handicapping the horses.

But the several thousand fans who failed to show apparently couldn't even handicap the weather.

It turned out to be a bright, brisk, beautiful afternoon.

A dark, drizzling dawn did the damage, discouraging the hesitant.

Santa Anita, however, seems to have a way with the weather and this day was no exception.

Sunshine streamed down upon the first spectators to arrive and after that it got better. Disappearing clouds traced artistic patterns over the purple mountain backdrop.

And the performances matched the panorama for sheer brilliance.

Of all the champions, Rising Market was the most.

In a tremendous effort, Rising Market ran down favored Tumiga to capture the $28,900 Palos Verdes Handicap and to maintain a peculiar winning tradition despite track conditions that were, for him, extremely adverse.

This was the third Santa Anita opening day in a row on which Rising Market has been a visitor to the winner's circle.

Apparently that tradition meant more to him than his renowned distaste for damp footing. The racing

Please Turn to Page 8, Col. 6

STRETCHING OUT --- Pounding hooves send dirt flying as jockeys urge their mounts on as field turns into the stretch at Santa Anita. A crowd of 33,552 turned out Thursday to launch the 75-day race meet.
Times photo by Joe Kennedy

### TODAY'S SPORTS SCHEDULE

HORSE RACING—Santa Anita, first post 12:30 p.m.

COLLEGE BASKETBALL — Trojan Invitational at Sports Arena: Tulsa vs. Texas (El Paso), 7 p.m., Montana State vs. USC 9 p.m.

RADIO-TELEVISION

COLLEGE BASKETBALL—Tulsa vs. Texas (El Paso), Channel 11, 7 p.m.; Montana State vs. USC, KNX, 9 p.m.; UCLA vs. Providence at New York, KMPC, 1 p.m., Channel 5, 11 p.m.

# Allen: 'I'm Back Because My Players Stood Up for Me'

# Reeves: 'Allen's Intense Loyalty, Devotion Sole Reason'

**SHOE STILL FITS**—It was only a stable pony named Baldy, but there was Bill Shoemaker back in the saddle again Monday morning at Santa Anita, returning for the first time since he fractured his left leg in a spill at the Arcadia track Jan. 23 of last year.

**POST TIME FOR MEMORIES**—It was like old times at Santa Anita Monday morning as Bill Shoemaker, right, returned to saddle for first time since fracturing a leg. He is accompanied to the track by trainer Johnny Longden. Only Longden has more career victories than Shoemaker, 6,032 to 5,758.

Story on Page 4

Times photos by Art Rogers

Los Angeles Times
Sports
BUSINESS & FINANCE
CC PART III 2†
TUESDAY, JANUARY 7, 1969

## Rams' Coach Is Rehired on Same Terms

BY BOB OATES
Times Staff Writer

The most dramatic chapter in the history of a football team that has been in ferment for more than 20 years was written Monday by George Allen when he succeeded himself as head coach of the Rams.

He had been out of a job since he was fired on the day after Christmas. He came back on his own terms—which he outlined as follows in an interview:

"They are the exact terms of my old contract as to salary and duration. And there is no indemnity clause. It would not have been fair play to hold up the Rams at a time like this. I came back for one reason—because my players stood up for me."

**Broader Authority?**

Allen resumes where he left off, at $40,000 a year, with only two years remaining on his original contract, plus a bonus plan which added about $20,000 to his Ram income in 1968.

One source said the only significant difference in Allen's arrangement with the Ram president, Daniel F. Reeves, is that Allen will now have broader authority in all areas bearing on the football team. However, Reeves said at a news conference Monday that Allen's authority will neither be broadened nor decreased.

Allen turned down two "incredible offers," one in each league, according to a spokesman for the Ram squad. The playe.., a veteran with extensive and close NFL contacts, said:

"We have reliable information from the city concerned that one club offered him two jobs, coach and general manager, at $85,000 a year. He would have had full control, which is what he wants, of course, and what you need to run a pro club today. And when they read that he owns a $150,000 home, they called back and offered him a rent-free $150,000 house. I couldn't have blamed him if he'd gone. It takes quite a man to come back to us just on a principle."

**Quiet Pressure**

Another source said it was pressure from Allen's players, who were united almost unanimously, which influenced the Rams to bring him back. A secondary factor, this source said, was the club's inability to land Vince Lombardi, the only other coach who, in the collective opinion of the Ram playing squad, "would have had a chance to maintain our winning momentum."

Reeves said at Monday's news conference that he was not influenced by player pressure and that Allen's job had not been offered to anyone else.

A Ram players' committee—Eddie Meador, Lamar Lundy, Merlin Olsen and Roman Gabriel—never actually met with owner Reeves. "But," said Gabriel, "we were so nearly unanimous that we were able to exert pressure quietly and in a dignified way."

It was learned that of the 40 Rams on the active squad, 38 supported

Please Turn to Page 4, Col. 5

## REEVES: ALLEN'S LOYALTY PROMPTED HIS REHIRING

### Owner Says Decision Was Not Affected by Public, Players; Two Other Coaches Had Been Considered

BY MAL FLORENCE
Times Staff Writer

George Allen's intense loyalty and devotion to the Rams was the sole reason he was rehired, according to owner Dan Reeves, who formally acknowledged the reconciliation at a press conference Monday.

Thus, the 12-day holiday war of nerves came to an end. And, in an almost unprecedented development, Allen succeeds himself as head coach.

Reeves carefully made it clear, though, that his decision was not influenced by pressure from the Ram players or the public.

He further stipulated that Allen is being retained under the same terms of his original contract. George had two more years to serve on a five-year contract when he was dismissed the day after Christmas.

**No Conditions**

The owner added that he imposed no conditions on Allen as a prerequisite for his reinstatement or that the coach has any "greater or less" voice in Ram management than he did before.

Reeves also revealed that "two other nameless coaches"—believed to be USC's John McKay and Green Bay general manager Vince Lombardi—were still under consideration for the Ram job when he decided to rehire Allen.

The Ram coach attended the news gathering at the Century Plaza but it was the owner's show. Allen read from a brief, prepared statement, shook hands with Reeves and then left.

Reeves then detailed the events leading up to the rehiring of Allen prior to answering questions from the floor. He declined, however, to elucidate on his original reasons for releasing Allen.

He dispensed with the subject by saying:

"There were valid and sufficient reasons in my mind at the time. But I'm not going to rehash it now. Perhaps the term 'personality clash' is a misnomer. It was a question of philosophy of operation."

Reeves and Allen arrived together and the coach went immediately to the podium and addressed the press:

"From the meetings which Dan and I have had in the last few days, it is clear that we have each, unintentionally, hurt the other. These discussions have, however, been greatly beneficial in establishing communication between us and thereby enabling us to view our problems with clarity and to resolve them with dignity.

"I am, therefore, very happy to be

Please Turn to Page 4, Col. 1

## TODAY IN SPORTS

**HORSE RACING**—Santa Anita, first post 12:30 p.m.

**CURLING**—Norwalk Ice Rink, 7 p.m.

**PRO BOWLING**—Pro-Am, West Valley Bowl, 5 p.m.

**RADIO-TELEVISION**

**PRO BASKETBALL**—Los Angeles Lakers at Baltimore, Channel 5, KNX, 6 p.m.

**HOCKEY**—Los Angeles at St. Louis, KNX, following Los Angeles-Baltimore basketball game.

### JIM MURRAY

## Rams Exciting to Watch During Off-Season, Too

For those of you banging the side of your heads today trying to understand the Ram situation, the answer is to be found on Page 110 of Alice's Adventures in Wonderland: "No, no!" said the Queen. "Sentence first — verdict afterwards."

The cavalry galloped in just in time to cut George Allen down but that figure still swaying from a lamppost is me. You'll find my predicament outlined on Page 24 of Alice: "I'll be the judge, I'll be the jury," said the cunning old Fury. "I'll try the whole cause and condemn you to death."

**Okay, readers, you're away!**

"Dear Lackey:

"Now for Reeves, huh? Why don't you paint the rest of your face to match your nose? To you, only money is sacred. Words sure aren't, not the way you use them . . . You have had a bad year and I devoutly hope 1969 will be worse. For you.

(signed) Gault, Santa Barbara"

—What's the matter, Gault, cat got your tongue?

"Dear Mr. Murray:

"On occasion I've found your sports feature . . . colorful and clever. On other occasions it seems to be 'huffing and puffing' in its effort . . . and ended up an insult to the intelligence of anybody with an IQ much above that of a moron. Speaking charitably, your column today would hardly qualify . . .
(signed) Rodney A. Stetson, M.D., Torrance"

—What should I do for it, Doc, take four aspirin and try to stay off my feet for awhile?

"Dear Mr. Murray:

"Well, after picking out and tossing away the usual descriptive and superfluous garbage so indicative of (your) column I was able to gather enough meaning from your remarks to ascertain that you and the rest of the subordinators of human privacy didn't like poor old Allan (sic) . . . Anyway, when you and reeves (sic) and the front office get over congratulating yourselves for being so strong and right, could you tell me what the citizens of Los Angeles are going to do for a PROFESSIONAL football team? Or is that important compared to the finer things in life?

(signed) Jack Christie"

—Well, Jack, after picking out and tossing away the superfluous garbage, I would say it's unimportant compared to penicillin, cancer research, schools and colleges and the San Andreas Fault. The citizens have bigger urban problems than their professional football team.

"Re George Allen Matter:

"Mr. Reeves is in name and in fact the owner of the Los Angeles Rams. The Mona Lisa has a legal owner also, but what happens to either is not the province only of the owner but all interested parties . . .

(signed) Thomas E. Cochran, Toluca"

—I get it. We turn the Mona Lisa over to the guy who wipes the glass off every morning.

"Dear Messrs. Murray and Reeves:

"Lynch won't be back. Up Stairway 7, down a little and turn to the left. Say hello to all the guys and sit down. No laughs, just his peculiar kind of fun. He won't be back, Dan. Some of the boys said Ed is acting too hasty. He thought he hadn't acted hastily enough.
(signed) Edward M. Lynch, Walker, Wright, Tyler & Ward"

—O.K., Ed. Try to help around the house on Sundays, y'hear?

I'll say one thing for the Rams: They're an exciting team to watch. Particularly during the off-season.

### PERFECT TRADEMARK

## Golfer Murphy Has New Name— Watermelon Man

BY ROSS NEWHAN
Times Staff Writer

He was professional golf's rookie of the year. His slice of the 1968 tour was $105,000. In 1969 you will call call him Watermelon Murphy.

Bob Murphy insists that it has nothing to do with his waist line, but the watermelon is now his trademark.

Murphy says that a watermelon will appear on his golf bag and, probably, on his shirts, replacing the penguin and alligator.

This could stir a revolution in the sport.

"It is merely an attempt to keep my name in front of the public," said Murphy, who blossomed in August by winning the Philadelphia and Thunderbird Classics on consecutive weekends.

**His Relaxation**

The Philadelphia was worth $25,000 to the 25-year-old Murphy. The Thunderbird added $30,000. Murphy won another $50,000 and that is why he is now in watermelons.

"I find relaxation," he said, "in securing business off the course. The only thing that bothers me is answering the phones."

The phones have been connected to the offices of Sports Investors in New York. "The company is small in golfers," said Murphy, "but big in business."

Sports Investors has affiliated Murphy with Shamrock watermelons.

"Watermelons," said Murphy, who lives in Bartow, Fla., "are a big business where I live. I figure that this affiliation will take root locally and then spread nationally."

Watermelon Murphy is in town to play in the Los Angeles Open. He tuned up erratically, firing a 75 and failing to qualify for the second and final round of last weekend's Southern California Open.

Murphy says that he is playing poorly because he is on a diet. His strength has ebbed as he's reduced from 220 to 215.

Murphy weighed 218 during torrid August. This is a young man who is only 5-10 in height. In the lexicon of the game, Murphy literally, hits all his shots "fat."

"I've got to get down to 200

Please Turn to Page 4, Col. 3

**BACK TOGETHER**—Dan Reeves (left) shakes hands with George Allen just before start of press conference at Century Plaza Monday when Reeves announced that Allen had been rehired as Rams' coach.

Times photo by Joe Kennedy

## JIM MURRAY

# Don't Look Now...but the Funny Little League Is No. 1

MIAMI—First of all, are you sitting down?

Be sure who you tell this to or they'll think you've been drinking.

On Sunday afternoon, the canary ate the cat. The mailman bit the police dog. The minnow chased the shark out of its waters. The missionaries swallowed the cannibals. The rowboat rammed the battleship. The mouse roared, and the lion jumped up on a chair and began to scream for help.

The first thing that's going to surprise you about the Super Bowl game is the closeness of the score. But, hang onto your hat. If you think THAT'S a shocker, wait till I get to the punchline.

The—come closer and let me whisper this—the NEW YORK JETS are the Super Champions of football! Cross my heart! That funny little team from that funny little league they left on pro football's doorstep a few years back. You know the one—the team whose checks bounced and so did their quarterbacks.

And you know that smart-alecky quarterback they got for $400,000 and the NFL sat down and like to have busted laughing? Well, turns out he was a bargain. You know, they called him "Broadway Joe" and he went around wearing women's fur coats and he closed up more bars than Carrie Nation? A sleep-to-noon guy who had been a model youth. He didn't smoke till he started kindergarten and he never drank in high school till the sun went down. And when someone said the Jets had a "Boozer" in the backfield, someone thought it was a description instead of a name.

They said (Norman Van Brocklin did) that Broadway Joe would be pl:'ng in his first professional game in the Super Bowl. Well, he likes it better than that game they play over in that other league. He got beat three times over in that league.

They said the Jets were the third-best team in their own league. If so, it's a good thing they didn't send the best. Everybody would have switched over to Heidi.

I would say, on the basis of what we saw Super Sunday, the NFL is a couple of years away. I mean they have INDIVIDUAL performers, but the AFL appears to be better in teams.

Namath said that the Colts' Earl Morrall would be third string on the Jets, but he may have overestimated him. Of the nine passes Morrall completed before his coach invited him to spend the rest of the game resting up for next year, only six went to his own team. He has a good arm, but they might check his color perception.

It could be said to be a contest only if you consider a public hanging a contest. As usual, if you want the executioner, you have to give points. But the funny thing in this game was, the books put their expert eyes on this match and said you could have the Jets and 17½ points and there was no limit to what you could bet. If you wanted Baltimore, you had to come up with 18 points. And they wouldn't take a check. Bookmakers are perched on ledges all over America today. For them, the score of the game at the payoff window was Jets 33½, Colts, 7.

I would say the Colts were terrible, but that would be an overstatement. They weren't that good. It's hard to believe this team went through 30 NFL games and only lost two in the past two years.

The Colts started the game as if the other guys hadn't showed up

Please Turn to Page 2, Col. 7

LOOKING 'EM OVER—Joe Namath surveys field as he drops back to pass, protected by Jet teammate Bill Mathis (left) during the AFL's most glorious hour—a 16-7 victory over the vaunted Colts Sunday. Namath, who predicted stunning upset, completed 17 of 28 passes against Baltimore to set game mark.

UPI Wirephoto

## JETS SHOCK COLTS, 16-7

# Broadway Joe Puts AFL in Lights

BY BOB OATES
Times Staff Writer

MIAMI—Think of the biggest surprise you've ever had. Then forget it.

Joe Namath beat the National Football League here Sunday. His ability to throw a football with more accuracy than perhaps any other passer — living or gone — destroyed Baltimore's famous defensive team in a 16-7 upset.

In the third Super Bowl, as Broadway Joe finished his fourth season at quarterback for the New York Jets, the champions of the 9-year-old American Football League finished off the champions of a 49-year-old league.

The AFL caught up in one hour in Miami. And there will be those who say it went ahead—when Joe went ahead, 16-0, in the fourth quarte

Before a capacity 75,377 on a warm, overcast day in the multi-colored Orange Bowl, Baltimore became the first NFL team to lose a world championship game, and it happened because the Colts had no defense for Namath's passes.

It also happened because the Colt quarterbacks, Earl Morrall and John Unitas, couldn't throw the ball straight on this of all days after the NFL flagbearers had sailed through a 15-1 season against NFL teams.

They were intercepted four times for the same two reasons—their inaccuracy primarily, and alert defense secondly—as Baltimore, an 18-point favorite, knocked itself out on the last play of the first half.

If Morrall had seen his receiver that time, he would have gone off the field 7-7 instead of 0-7, and the Colts would have come back, possibly, with the psychological advantage in the second half.

### A Good Play

It was a good play, too, that one. At midfield, with 25 seconds left, Morrall handed off to Tom Matte, who lateraled the ball back to Morrall, who threw it toward Jerry Hill as Jim Hudson intercepted for the Jets.

It failed because Morrall couldn't find his primary receiver, Jimmy Orr, who was wide open on the 5-yard line. There were two reasons for the oversight. First, Morrall was facing toward the center of the field when he got Matte's lateral. Second, by the time he turned to throw, Orr had stopped running.

A passer on this kind of play locates the target normally by the movement of the target. But Orr had stopped moving. His execution had been too successful—and it was this, ironically, that stopped the Colts in Miami.

They didn't make a first down with Morrall in the third quarter, astonishingly, and Unitas' sore-armed pitches could guide Baltimore to but one touchdown in the last quarter. By then it was all over.

Namath had won it. He had achieved an improbable upset with an 80-yard touchdown drive and three marches ending in field goals by Jim Turner.

"Congratulations," said Broadway Joe afterward, "to the American Football League."

Thinking next of his newspaper

Please Turn to Page 2, Col. 2

RARE OCCASION—New York fullback Matt Snell failed to gain when he tripped over Colts' Dennis Gaubatz on this play, but Snell paced the Jets by gaining a record 121 yards in 30 carries in Super Bowl.

UPI Wirephoto

# Sifford Gives Final Round Pressure a $20,000 Kick

BY BILL SHIRLEY
Times Staff Writer

Los Angeles Times
Sports
BUSINESS & FINANCE
CC PART III 2†
MONDAY, JANUARY 13, 1969

There was once a time when the pressure of the last round of a golf tournament weighed heavily upon Charlie Sifford. Life was a series of 74s and 75s and nothing but frustration on the last 18 holes at the PGA whistlestops.

But not anymore. Old Charlie has kicked the habit.

His metamorphosis began in 1967 at Hartford, when he became the first Negro to win a tournament on the tour by shooting a 64 in the last round.

Charlie held up magnificently again Sunday as he won the most important tournament of his life, the Los Angeles Open. He even played an extra hole to win it, shooting a birdie 3 at No. 15 to beat Harold Henning, a 34-year-old professional from South Africa. Henning made up three strokes on the 46-year-old Los Angeles resident by firing a 3-under-par 68 to tie him at the end of 72 holes with a score of 276, 8 under par.

### Tense, Exciting Windup

The tournament, which almost went to Sifford by default after he shot an 8-under-par 63 the first day, finally developed into a tense, exciting competition on another cold afternoon at Rancho Park.

Sifford continued to play steady, conservative golf, shooting his third consecutive even-par 71. So, for 63 holes, he was 1 under par after being 7 under on the back nine Thursday.

But the other players weren't going to let Charlie off that easy.

Henning, who had started his run Saturday with a 66, finally caught Sifford at 7 under par when Charlie bogeyed the 12th hole. In fact, there was a three-way tie at that point among Dave Hill, who finished with a 70-278, Henning and Sifford.

The South African took the lead by sinking a 20-foot birdie putt at No. 13 but Charlie tied him again by making one from the same distance at No. 16. That's the way it finished, but in the meantime, Bruce Devlin of Austrialia and Bill Casper had moved within one stroke of them.

Devlin, playing what he labeled "super golf," shot a 4-under-par 67 and Casper, firing four birdies and avoiding bogeys, made the same score to tie him with a total of 277. Devlin, in fact, left a 20-foot putt one inch from the dead center of the cup on the 18th green.

Whow! It was that close. The gallery, however, was smaller than usual, probably because of the telecast of the Super Bowl game. The sponsor, the Junior Chamber of Commerce, estimated that the football game probably cost it about $15,000.

Sifford, meanwhile, was making $20,000 and Henning $11,400 from the $100,000 tournament.

The victory, aside from all the loot, was especially satisfying to Charlie, not only because he withstood the pressure, but because it was achieved in his hometown.

"This is the most important tournament to me," he said, "because I'm gonna live in L.A. the rest of my life."

The former caddy (he started when he was 10) from North Carolina was overwhelmed by the response of the fans. "I didn't know I had so many fans in L.A." he said. "But I had as many as Arnold Palmer."

There is less pressure on Charlie Sifford these days. "You only get pressure in the last round when you don't have any money in your pocket," he says. But Charlie has lots of money in his pocket now. He won about $50,000 in 1967 and $33,000 more last year, some of which he has invested in real estate.

He couldn't have timed Sunday's victory better. Starting Feb. 15, the first Charlie Sifford autographed clubs will go on sale.

### Other Negroes on Tour

The pressure on Sifford also has been eased because he no longer is carrying all the load for his race on the tour. There were five other Negro players in the L.A. Open, for example; Pete Brown, Ray Botts, Jimmy Walker, Lee Elder and Charlie's nephew, Curtis Sifford.

Charlie became the first PGA card-carrying Negro on the tour in 1959. He won several non-tour events such as the Long Beach Open and the Gardena Open, which were 54-hole tournaments. He also won the U.S. Negro Open five times, but it was not until Hartford that he was able to achieve a measure of fame.

Charlie is popular with the other professionals but he can be cold with strangers. With his friends, however, he loosens up and flashes a sharp sense of humor.

Please Turn to Page 6, Col. 4

## L.A. Open Leaders

| | |
|---|---|
| 276 ($20,000) | |
| *Charlie Sifford | 63-71-71-71 |
| 276 ($11,400) | |
| *Harold Henning | 7^ 72-66-6. |
| 277 ($5,900) | |
| Bill Casper | 69-69-72-67 |
| Bruce Devlin | 69-72-69-67 |
| 278 ($4,100) | |
| Dave Hill | 66-73 69-70 |
| 280 ($3,600) | |
| Bert Yancey | 75-67-71 67 |
| 281 ($3,200) | |
| Howell Fraser | 72-73-70-66 |
| 282 ($2,716) | |
| Mac McLendon | 69-68-77-68 |
| Roy Pace | 71-69-72-70 |
| Tommy Shaw | 69-68-73-72 |

*Sifford won playoff on first extra hole

Complete Scores on Page 6

A $20,000 SMILE—Charlie Sifford is all smiles after sinking birdie putt on first hole of sudden-death playoff with Harold Henning to win the L.A. Open. The victory, second tour triumph for 46-year-old Los Angeles professional, was worth $20,000. Pair had tied at end of regulation 72 holes with 276s.

Times photo by Ben Olender

# A DAY TO REMEMBER FOR LEW, BRUINS

Los Angeles Times
Sports
CC SECTION D 2†
SUNDAY, MARCH 23, 1969

BY JEFF PRUGH
Times Staff Writer

LOUISVILLE—Across his face burst a smile that surely must have stretched 7 feet, 1 3-8 inches wide.

Around his neck hung the tangled strings of the basket and he was proudly waving his left index finger. And from his right hand sprouted three more long, delicate fingers.

He was standing there, waving at the UCLA rooters who had cheered him from the beginning—and who had waited so long for the inevitable to happen.

Soon he was arm-in-arm with his father, who had spent the afternoon playing first trombone in the Bruin band. And then he was holding both hands aloft again—three fingers raised on one, the index finger on the other.

Those were the fingers that had just etched his name into basketball immortality. They were the fingers of Ferdinand Lewis Alcindor Jr., and they had just finished molding the UCLA Bruins into the legend that everybody expected them to be four winters ago.

The Lew Alcindor Era, after 88 victories in 90 games, was over. A record three NCAA championships in a row—that's what the three fingers stood for. The No. 1 team in the land—that's what the index finger was all about.

And the ending came here Saturday afternoon with a smashing 92-72 victory over Purdue—a triumph that hoisted UCLA to an unprecedented fifth national crown in six years.

It was Big Lew's last recital—and perhaps his finest.

He treated 18,663 Freedom Hall witnesses and millions of television viewers to a virtuoso performance. He was the epitome of strength, speed and touch—37 points, 20 rebounds and all those intimidating things he does to the enemy.

It was a day to remember for Lew and for his father, Ferdinand L. Alcindor, 6-foot-2, a New York transit policeman and onetime jazz trombonist who had volunteered to play in the band.

They made beautiful music together on a day when UCLA (29-1) broke quickly from the gate and was never in trouble—and also on a day when John Wooden became the first coach ever to win five national titles, surpassing the Kentucky Baron, Adolph Rupp.

"I had no doubt that we were capable of winning it," said Wooden, who made it three in a row by beating his alma mater. "We were flat recently. We didn't play well against Drake, but when I saw them again today (in a 104-84 win over North Carolina for third place), I began to think that maybe we did."

And could he tell whether Lew Alcindor was going to play an inspired game?

"Yes, I could," he said, grinning. "And when I saw that he was really to play, I felt a lot more ready, too."

When it was over, Alcindor was decorated with more honors — the first player ever to win the tournament's Most Outstanding Player award for the third year in succession, bettering such back-to-back winners as Oklahoma A&M's Bob Kurland (1945-46), Kentucky's Alex Groza (1948-49) and Ohio State's Jerry Lucas (1960-61).

He also vaulted past Lucas and Jerry West into third place on the NCAA tournament's all-time scoring ladder, finishing with 304 points behind Elvin Hayes (358) and Oscar Robertson (324).

Typically, however, the afternoon

Please Turn to Page 4, Col. 1

## IM MURRAY

## New Angel 'Tantalizer'

PALM SPRINGS—Bob Feller uld throw a baseball 98.8 miles r hour. Pancho Gonzales could t a tennis ball 114 miles per hour.

Hoyt Wilhelm's ball goes just ster than a letter addressed to Occupant." Or a note dropped in a ttle. It would get arrested for tering. It would get waved over to the slow lane of a freeway. It ugs its way to its destination like farmer with a truckload of chickens and an overheated engine. It should be listed as a shot put. On bunt situations the first baseman could beat it to the plate. In fact, the right fielder could.

Frank Howard should get six rikes when he comes to bat gainst Hoyt Wilhelm. "Swing gain, there's still time, it won't be ere for several minutes yet," the atcher urges. It's like waiting for trolley.

Part of the trouble is, the ball omes to the plate like a kid on his ay to a bath. It takes more etours than a dog with a block full f hydrants.

Hoyt Wilhelm has been throwing since the days when most of the untry was still getting water om a backyard pump and light om kerosene.

It's commonly called a "knuckle" all but it's really a "finger" ball. ou grip it with the tips of your ngers. You get a strike and a anicure at the same time.

### Difficult to Describe

It's such an unimpressive pitch om the seats that, when someone ked Bill Rigney how to throw it scratched his head and said: Vell, first you put some soap a clay pipe . . ." Another anager, asked to describe it, dn't hesitate: "Well, did you ever e a drunk get thrown out of a r, then get up and dust his hat d then fall down again? Well, ilhelm's knuckler does all of ose things."

If it was human, you'd treat it for . Vitus Dance. You can't hit it d you can't catch it. Don rysdale and Walter Johnson lead e major leagues in hit batsmen. oyt Wilhelm leads in hit catchers. he ball disappears about three-arters of the way to the plate. 's not hard to catch, it's hard to nd. It's no threat to the batter. 's as easy to get out of the way of a glacier. If it came any slower, ey'd have to go out and look for . It's got so much backspin on it, ometimes the catcher doesn't ave to throw it back.

### Anybody's Guess

It's as easy on the arm as cutting ravy. Hoyt Wilhelm will be 46 ears old the Saturday after the ll-Star break this summer. Still, e pitched in 72 ball games last eason. He has pitched in 937 in his fe, more than any pitcher who ver lived. That kind of record was ought to have gone out with andlebar moustaches and free nches. He's in better shape than hunting dog.

He throws 85% "knuckle" balls ut that doesn't matter. Not only oesn't the batter know where it's oing, neither does Hoyt. "It never oes the same thing twice, even arming up," he admitted the ther day as he sat on a bench at e Angels' training camp here. He rves it up and says "Here, surise me."

Yogi Berra once hid in the clubuse in an All-Star game (at San

Please Turn to Page 13, Col. 1

LEW'S TERRITORY — UCLA's Lew Alcindor leaps high and stretches his 7-1⅜ frame to take a rebound against Purdue in the NCAA finals Saturday at Louisville. Jerry Johnson (31) of Purdue isn't in this battle as Lew has things under control. Bruins won an unprecedented third straight title, 92-72.

## Cordero Rides Taneb to Win in San Luis Rey

### Upset Lightning Strikes Three Other Times for Riding Champ Making Santa Anita Debut

BY BION ABBOTT
Times Staff Writer

So who's perfect? Angel Cordero, descending upon Santa Anita as if he really had a halo, finally made the mortal mistake of losing a race in Saturday's nightcap.

But the 1968 national riding champion already had convinced a crowd of 42,465 that he was really real by scoring spectacular upsets during the first four starts of his West Coast saddle debut.

The big win, of course, was Cordero's $17.40 shocker with the Florida invader, Taneb, in the $57,700 San Luis Rey Handicap. That really made believers of the bettors.

And that's about the only logical reason Cordero finally went to the post a favorite for the first time in the nightcap, a 5-2 choice on a 6-1 animal named Ben Ben. He figured fifth and finished fourth.

So a $9,300 win parlay on Cordero collapsed but it only cost $2, remember.

"I felt lucky today," explained the laughing, fun-loving Angel, nattily attired after the races in a lavender suit with lavender shirt and tie to match.

"That's all it takes in this business—luck," he repeated.

But anyone who watched him would have argued that it required a little more than luck to score this season's third saddle quadruple the first time he ever set eyes on Santa Anita outside of a movie projection room.

The audience applauded with appreciation when the champion brought longshot Conroy Kid back to the winner's circle following the second race. This $22.40 upset punctuated Cordero's first appearance on the West Coast.

The ovation commenced to grow when he did it again, turning in another riding gem to score a $21 surprise with Cabin Boy in the fourth race.

A spontaneous roar erupted after Angel's next superlative performance, a $9.80 victory with longshot Mayoworth in the sixth race.

Could longshot lightning strike a fourth time?

Please Turn to Page 10, Col. 3

## Kings Draw Blank From Seals; Hopes for Second Dashed

BY CHUCK GARRITY
Times Staff Writer

Second place has proved too much of a challenge for the Kings. But perhaps their next problem will be easier. For this one, they have to drop down, rather than climb up.

If they can manage to drop from third place into fourth in the final week of the season, they won't have to face the Western Division champion St. Louis Blues in the first round of the Stanley Cup playoffs.

And after their 4-0 shutout at the hands of the second-place Oakland Seals and goalie Gary Smith Saturday night at the Forum, the Kings appear ready to make a determined bid for fourth.

**Road Trip Ahead**

Philadelphia trails them by only a point and the Kings face a three-game road trip starting tonight in Oakland. Their 5-25-5 road record this season weighs heavily in their favor when trying to avoid the Blues.

Coach Red Kelly won't buy any of the talk that the Blues are tougher than anyone else, however, even in the light of St. Louis' runaway to the Western title.

"We still want to finish as high as we can," Kelly said. "St. Louis doesn't scare me. And look at Oakland. They were plenty tough tonight. Who's to say St. Louis will be any tougher?"

He has a point.

The Seals had lost four and tied two previous games against the Kings. But they were trying to put second place out of reach Saturday night and played like it after the first period.

**Fourth Shutout**

It was all Oakland could do to hold on in the first 20 minutes as the Kings produced much better shots. The difference was Smith, the 6-foot 4-inch goaltender, who picked up his fourth shutout of the season and frustrated the 10,835 fans.

Eddie Joyal, the Kings' leading goal scorer (30) had four excellent cracks at Smith in the opening 20 minutes. He was thwarted on two 1-on-1 breakaways and hit the goal post on two other occasions. Lowell MacDonald also had a point-blank shot bounce off of Smith.

Even with the Kings enjoying the best shots, the Seals skated off with a 1-0 lead on Mike Laughton's power play goal midway through the period. Then when the Kings' defense crumbled in the second period, the Seals' Gerry Ehman, Earl Ingarfield and Norm Ferguson put the game away. It was rookie Ferguson's 31st goal of the season and stamped him as a favorite for rookie of the year honors.

Please Turn to Page 11, Col. 3

## DAD SHARES SPOTLIGHT

## Relaxed, Poised Alcindor Opens Up to Interviewers

BY MITCH CHORTKOFF
Times Staff Writer

LOUISVILLE—John Wooden, the only man ever to coach three consecutive NCAA basketball championship teams, stepped to the microphone in the interview room at Freedom Hall Saturday.

"Gentlemen," he said. "I'd like one more privilege.

"I'd like to introduce the man responsible—or at least 50 per cent responsible—for giving us the greatest college basketball player of all time. Here is Ferdinand Lewis Alcindor."

There was applause and Lew Alcindor's father, a sign reading "UCLA, 1" stapled to the lapel of his suit, stepped forward.

**Yields to His Son**

He was on center-stage for a moment, and then he yielded it to his son, who was no longer in a basketball uniform. Lew had changed into slacks, a maroon turtleneck sweater and a blue sports coat.

The youngster was relaxed. Three years of mounting pressure had been lifted from his shoulders. He had led his team to an unprecedented third consecutive national championship. He had become the first three-time winner of the NCAA tournament's Most Outstanding Player award. Now he was ready to answer questions, joke with his interrogators, share his supreme moment with father and coach.

Lew Alcindor stayed there for nearly 30 minutes. He displayed skill and poise, just as he had on the basketball court, where he had scored 37 points and taken 20 rebounds in the 92-72 disposal of Purdue.

He discussed the tournament, the season, the Alcindor Era at UCLA, his present feelings, his future plans. His broadest grin resulted from a question about whether or not he was ready to get married.

"Nope," he replied in a most definite manner.

He spoke about the game in which he had just played.

"It was a question of attitude," he said. "We were ready. We were up. I was, and the whole team was. We weren't Thursday for Drake (a narrow, 85-82 victory).

"I felt our defense was a big factor," he said. "Purdue didn't shoot well, and I don't think it just happened to have a bad game. I think we had a lot to do with it."

**Choice Not Revealed**

The discussion turned to his future in professional basketball. Which league? That's what everyone wanted to know.

"Well, that's the next thing on the agenda," he admitted. But he wasn't about to reveal his choice.

"There are a whole lot of variables involved," he said.

He was willing to name a couple of them.

Please Turn to Page 4, Col. 5

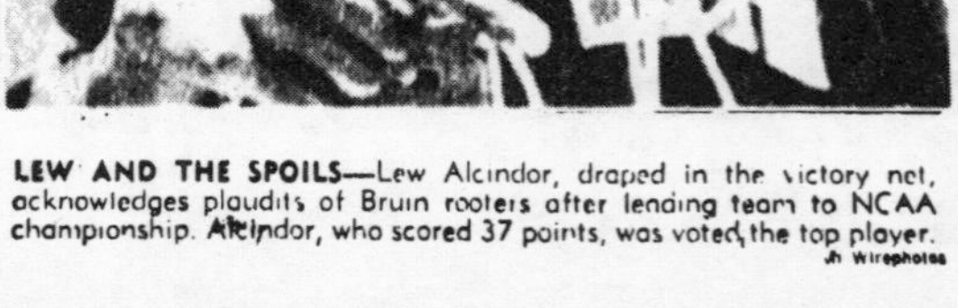

LEW AND THE SPOILS—Lew Alcindor, draped in the victory net, acknowledges plaudits of Bruin rooters after leading team to NCAA championship. Alcindor, who scored 37 points, was voted the top player.
AP Wirephotos

## TRAINS WRECKED BY SOCCER FANS

LONDON (AP)—British soccer fans went on the rampage again Saturday leaving a trail of wrecked trains and broken bones in their wake.

At least 20 persons were hurt when Glasgow fans rushed the gates at Hampden Park, where the Celtic team was playing Morton.

In London, gangs of rival teen-age fans smashed everything in sight at several subway stations. Fist fights started as the mob broke windows. Police were called in to break up one mob of about 200 at West London's Notting Hill station after frightened passengers abandoned a train.

# HO-HUM, ANOTHER USC MIRACLE, 14-12

## Jones' Bomb to Dickerson Beats UCLA in Last Seconds

CC SECTION D 2†

SUNDAY, NOV. 23, 1969


BY BOB OATES
Times Staff Writer

The miracle came with a minute and a half to play.

Quarterback Jimmy Jones threw the ball into a deep corner of the end zone, Sam Dickerson ran over and caught it, and USC won again.

The Trojans won by two points, 14-12, coming from behind as usual Saturday to fight their way into the Rose Bowl for an unprecedented fourth consecutive time.

With only 3:07 left, UCLA led. Dennis Dummit had parlayed a bomb and a short pass to steal ahead, 12-7.

It was the sixth time this year that USC had been tied or losing in the fourth quarter.

But the Trojan fans in the Coliseum crowd of 90,814 winked knowingly and sat back to await the miracle.

It developed on schedule. Jones, who had completed only one pass in the first 57 minutes, completed three out of four to get the decisive 68-yard drive under way — then pitched the winning pass 32 yards to Dickerson. Jones previously had missed on four straight passes but a fourth - down interference penalty against UCLA had presented him with another chance.

Of the 20 regular-season games the Trojans have played for coach John McKay in the last two years, they have won or tied 12 this way, with fourth-quarter rallies that broke the hearts of their opponents.

The last time these teams came together unbeaten, in 1952, the Trojans won by the same 14-12. That season they defeated Wisconsin, 7-0, to score the first decision for the West in the modern Rose Bowl era.

This time in Pasadena, USC will meet Michigan, the upset conqueror Saturday of mighty Ohio State.

A draw with UCLA would have been enough to send the Trojans against Michigan—but for the second time in the last three USC-UCLA games coach Tommy Prothro lost a tie to McKay when the Bruin special teams misfired.

In 1967, a missed conversion kick left USC in charge, 21-20.

In this 39th renewal of the Trojan series, the Bruins blew both conversion chances.

On each occasion they went for two points—after scoring the first touchdown in the 6-0 first quarter and after pulling ahead in the last few minutes—but the Trojans beat them out of both conversions with strong defensive plays.

The first was a fast charge by Charlie Weaver, who deflected Dummit's pass, and the second was a faster charge by Jimmy Gunn and

Please Turn to Page 6, Col. 1

**TROJAN TOUCHDOWN!**—Clarence Davis of USC, the nation's leading ground gainer, follows Charlie Evans into UCLA line and blasts 13 yards for the first Trojan score, leaving Bruin bodies strewn behind him.
Times photos by Larry Sharkey

***JIM MURRAY***

## Graham's Big Mistake: Larceny Before 90,000

There is a military proposition that holds that a small, elite strike force of well-drilled troops can overwhelm and take the sword away from a big mass of soldiery whose very size makes them clumsy, vulnerable and difficult to direct.

I don't know whether it was Clausewitz, Napoleon or Sergeant York who put it out but it seldom works. The British couldn't handle the American colonials, the Confederacy ran out of places to hide, even the Indians had to go back to the reservation. Napoleon got swallowed up in Russia.

And the Bruins can no longer hold off the Trojans.

To win with a thin line of forces, you have to have the element of surprise. You have to hit and smoke out of there. A fly can bring down an elephant with perseverance. You have to shrug off adversity.

And, you can never, never make mistakes.

Mistakes are your stock in trade. You force 'em, you don't commit 'em.

### *Under People*

UCLA probably made hundreds of mistakes out on the field in the football game for the Rose Bowl at the Coliseum Saturday. USC made more than the cast of a high school operetta.

But they were made under piles of people, down in corners, under cover of oblivion. There were 180,000 eyes on Danny Graham when he made his mistake Saturday.

Danny Graham is a cornerback for the UCLA Bruins. It's his job to tackle people. There is only one qualification. They should have the football. There isn't always time to frisk them.

Danny Graham made three clean tackles Saturday. Two of them show up in the defensive stats. The third one showed up on the scoreboard.

There was 1 minute and 45 seconds to go in the ball game. USC had the ball on the UCLA 43 and it was fourth down, 10 to go.

The USC quarterback, Jimmy Jones, wound up to throw the ball. Now, on the basis of earlier form, this was like pointing a water pistol at a tank. There was nothing in Jimmy Jones' previous performance that day to indicate he was a bigger aerial threat than Shirley.

The odds that this one would be any closer to the receiver than the same time zone weren't good. And it wasn't. Sam Dickerson, the receiver, was looking up at it and squinting when Danny Graham hit him.

Poor Danny had tackled the Rose Bowl.

### *The Ball Game*

Tackling a ballplayer who is licensed to catch a pass while a ball is still in the air is football larceny. The fine in this case was the ball game.

UCLA would have had the ball, first down, on the 43 and they could have calmly fallen into the Rose Bowl.

Jimmy Jones knows what to do with hot dice. The next play, he hit a friend in the end zone. Nobody tackled Sam Dickerson this time.

The Trojans habitually show up with more football players than Texas has cows. They don't look like a team, they look like a coalition. The pre-game exhortation on their blackboard was simply "Hustle — Cover Punts." That's like the general saying "Keep marching till you notice there's nobody underfoot any more." They don't have to crawl on their bellies like a guy in Indian country with a knife and a pack of matches. The Trojans have so many football players, some of 'em haven't met yet. Sometimes, they play like it.

The guys they got on defense—the ones they call "The Wild Bunch," after a slaughterhouse movie, Al Cowlings, Tody Smith, Jimmy Gunn, Charlie Weaver and Bubba Scott — would be even money against an avalanche.

Still the Bruins had them 12-7 with 2 minutes to go. The Bruins don't lose football games with 2 minutes to go.

Please Turn to Page 16, Col. 2

## Michigan Upsets Buckeyes, 24-12, Wins Bowl Bid

ANN ARBOR, Mich. (AP)—The Michigan Wolverines pulled one of the upsets of the decade, stunning No. 1-ranked Ohio State, 24-12, Saturday to clinch a Rose Bowl trip.

All the scoring came in the first half as the Wolverines snapped the Buckeyes' 22-game winning streak and gained a tie for the Big Ten Conference championship with the Bucks, who are ineligible to return to Pasadena.

"They outplayed us, outhustled us, and outcoached us," said disappointed Ohio State coach Woody Hayes. "Like every good thing, the winning streak had to come to an end."

Michigan was formally awarded the Rose Bowl bid by a telephone vote of conference athletic directors.

"We're No. 1. We're No. 1," chanted many of the 103,588 spectators who filled Michigan Stadium—largest crowd ever for a football game in Michigan.

Hundreds of fans surged onto the artificially surfaced field and tore down the goalposts before police cordoned it off. About 25,000 fans from Ohio State had journeyed from Columbus for the game—they were about the only ones to leave immediately after the stunning upset.

**Quick Touchdown**

The Wolverines took a surprising 7-6 first quarter lead on a three-yard touchdown run by fullback Garvie Craw and an extra point kick by Frank Titas. It was the first time this season the Buckeyes had trailed.

Ohio State scored first on a one-yard plunge by fullback Jim Otis at 7:22 of the first quarter.

The Buckeyes came back after Craw's first TD, with quarterback Rex Kern firing a 22-yard touchdown pass to Jan White. Stan White's extra point kick was good but the Bucks elected to take a Michigan penalty and try for a two-point conversion. But the hard-rushing Michigan defense tackled Kern before he could get off a pass.

Moorhead mixed his plays well, utilizing the running of sophomore tailback Billy Taylor and the pass catching of tight end Jim Mandich to full advantage.

Taylor set up Michigan's second touchdown with a 28-yard burst to the OSU five. Two plays later Craw

Please Turn to Page 10, Col. 1

## THE BIG GAME

**Stanford . . . . . . . 29**
**California . . . . . . 28**

Story on Page 4

**THE BRUIN LOCKER ROOM:**

## You Could Hear Rose Petal Fall...

BY DWIGHT CHAPIN
Times Staff Writer

It was so quiet you could hear a rose petal fall.

The only sound in the UCLA locker room was the occasional slam of a door as the players slowly made their way out of their cubicles and to the showers. The sound of the doors swinging shut would crack and then it would be quiet—very quiet—again.

Some of them sobbed behind those locker-room doors, unbelieving, waiting in the solitude for the reprieve that wasn't to come.

It was Danny Graham, the young man of misfortune, the young man guilty of pass interference that gave USC life—and later the ball game—who was able to articulate the sorrow best.

"It seems," he said, "like my whole life just went down the drain."

Wes Grant, the magnificent defensive end who led UCLA with eight unassisted tackles, was smiling bravely one minute, saying that "I really don't feel too badly about losing. I usually do, but our defense was awfully good today."

And then, moments later, he was greeting his coach, Tommy Prothro, and the emotion was too much. He put his head on Prothro's shoulder, the tears came and everyone looked away.

Ron Carver, the Mighty Mouse, the tiny sophomore who had played his heart out, as the rest of them had, dabbed at his eyes and his nose, too, as he talked about the final touchdown strike from Jimmy Jones to Sam Dickerson.

"We knew they'd have to pass," he said, "and we felt we could contain Jones' passing because he had been so erratic.

"We knew, too, that when they are in trouble they always go to Dickerson. On that play, they put (Bob) Chandler in motion to one side of the field—switching us back to man-to-man coverage on Dickerson.

"We still should have stopped them but SC always ends up with a great play. They always seem to come up with the ball, somehow."

Please Turn to Page 4, Col. 3

**THE MIRACLE**—Sam Dickerson falls to his knees and slides out of the corner of the end zone after catching a 32-yard touchdown pass from Jimmy Jones that enabled USC to defeat UCLA, 14-12, at Coliseum Saturday. Dickerson beat Doug Huff on the play and caught ball just inside the flag.

# Wicks Slays the Giant; Bruins Champs Again

BY DWIGHT CHAPIN
Times Staff Writer

COLLEGE PARK, Md.—Get the Bat Car ready for a return trip to Florida.

Artis Gilmore and Rex Morgan, the "Batman" and "Robin" of Jacksonville University, are in reality only wealthy socialite Bruce Wayne and his ward, Dick Grayson.

The UCLA Bruins, again, are the champions of the college basketball world, 80-69 victors over the Dolphins for a record fourth straight NCAA title and sixth in seven seasons.

For many nervous minutes here at the University of Maryland's Cole Fieldhouse Saturday afternoon, however, the Dynamic Duo and their friends were clipping along on the path of a stunning upset. Jacksonville led UCLA by nine points. The dynasty was wavering.

But then along came Superman, a guy who also goes by the name of Sidney Wicks.

UCLA's nine-point deficit was suddenly a 41-36 halftime lead. Superman had removed Batman's mask and exposed him to the country as an uncertain giant who wasn't quite up to what had become the first real challenge he'd faced in a long, long time.

When Gilmore, the Batman, was forced to pack up his cape and get ready to go back to the land of sunshine and palms, the rest of the Jacksonville team, the nation's tallest, had to follow suit.

It might be a little unfair to give all the credit to Sidney.

He had help . . . loads of it.

While Wicks was blocking five—that's right, five—of the 7-foot, 2-inch Gilmore's shots, scoring 17 points and taking down 18 rebounds, John Vallely, the Bruins' only senior starter, was rising again to the excellence he has shown in UCLA's last two tournament years. He held Gilmore's sidekick, Reckless Rex, to only 8 points, wheeled and dealed for five assists and scored 15 points.

In UCLA's time of trial, in the first half, Curtis Rowe was more or less conceded the medium-range jump shot by the Dolphins, and he took advantage of it for 14 points. His 19 for the game led UCLA.

Center Steve Patterson scored 17 points in a strong offensive performance and pulled down 11 rebounds.

And Henry Bibby, the fifth UCLA starter who played 38 minutes of the game, helped out with 8 points and four rebounds from his guard position.

But you almost have to concede that Wicks was the key in this title triumph—the big man in UCLA's fourth straight championship and most significant in that string, since it came without Lew Alcindor.

Jacksonville went into the game unawed and ready.

Spurred on by a bunch of uninhibited fans raising a green felt dolphin aloft and yelling, "We beat No. 1 (Kentucky) and we can beat No. 2" and "Go to hell, Bruins," Jacksonville burst into a fast early lead.

The spread was four points, then six, then eight, then nine, at 24-15 with 9:35 to play in the first half.

What was worse for the Bruins, Gilmore was tearing them apart.

Wicks was playing to the side or in front of Artis, and that wasn't working.

"So we had Sidney get behind Gilmore," said coach John Wooden, "and dropped Patterson off the high post to front him . . . and we made a couple of other moves that helped."

Then it happened.

Gilmore received the ball on the low post and went up in the air like an arrow. But Wicks, six inches shorter, was suddenly above him, jamming the ball right back at him.

From that point, Artis was never the same.

In the last portion of the first half and the first part of

Please Turn to Page 9, Col. 2

## JIM MURRAY

## Talk Cheap in Spring

Opening Day is almost upon us and, for some few teams, that may augur a season of bright promise. For most, it will be a Judgment Day, an Eye-Opening Day, the day a fraud was uncovered.

The nice thing about spring training is that it doesn't count. Does your cleanup hitter strike out? Pshaw! He's just trying to get his timing down. Your pitcher get racked? Pish-tush. He's just trying to perfect a new pitch. Your entire outfield overweight? Wait till the bell rings.

But the old managers aren't fooled. They know the percentages. Santa Claus is just a department store employe. If they pray at night, they know better than to ask for another Cobb, Ruth, Koufax. Just a journeyman ballplayer would do. A guy they can platoon. A guy who can hit a fair ball with a man on third. An outfield that can see at night. After all, the opposition isn't the 1927 Yankees. A handful of good players can take the pennant. Look at the Mets.

In the spring, though, the wise old manager also knows better than to kill the gate. He goes along with the gag. He's got a miracle up his sleeve, he implies to the press. "Don't sell us short," he warns. English translation: "We won't lose 'em all." Here are a few other stout promises — together with their slim prospects.

### Spring Talk

"He's matured as a hitter."—(He can hit a pitcher's mistakes.)

"He's going where the ball is pitched, he's not trying to pull everything."—(No power.)

"He's quit overswinging, he's going to wait for his pitch."—(He knows his best chance is a base-on-balls.)

"That's the best-looking infield I ever saw."—(Too bad it's not a dance.)

"He's not trying to overpower the hitters."—(You could sell advertising on his fastball.)

"He's got a real fine arm."—(He's got real fine teeth, too, and he can't throw the baseball much farther with one than the other. Also, his hair is curly but what's any of them got to do with the pennant?)

"He's going to try to out-guess the hitters."—(Since all he's got is a fastball, what is there for them to guess in the first place? What time it is?)

### Strong Bench

"We're going to do more hitting behind the runner."—(Yeah, we're going to pop it up on the infield grass. We're more apt to do more hitting behind the catcher.)

"He has a good chance to break into our rotation."—(Zsa Zsa Gabor has a good chance to break into our rotation. Our rotation calls for volunteers by Thursday.)

"Our bench is much stronger this year."—(Our showers have hotter water, too. It's the guys sitting on the bench I'm worried about. Most of them won't need a shower all season.)

"This kid has all the tools."—(Yeah! He could make a bat. But he couldn't hit anything with it. Carpentry goofed letting him get into baseball. So did baseball.)

"We're gonna be a gambling club."—(Gonna be! These guys wouldn't take a chance on a sinking line drive or take second on a wild pitch but they'll bet on a

Please Turn to Page 14, Col. 1

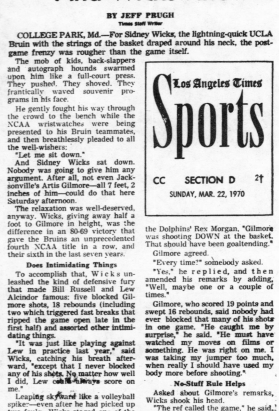

TWO-POINTER FOR UCLA—Despite aggressive guarding of Jacksonville's Rod McIntyre, Curtis Rowe (30) manages to get ball up for a basket as UCLA won its fourth consecutive NCAA basketball championship Saturday. Off to a shaky start, UCLA took lead just before half and won, 80-69.

LAST YEAR'S PRACTICE HELPS

## Gilmore's No Alcindor ---And Wicks Knew It

BY JEFF PRUGH
Times Staff Writer

COLLEGE PARK, Md.—For Sidney Wicks, the lightning-quick UCLA Bruin with the strings of the basket draped around his neck, the post-game frenzy was rougher than the game itself.

The mob of kids, back-slappers and autograph hounds swarmed upon him like a full-court press. They pushed. They shoved. They frantically waved souvenir programs in his face.

He gently fought his way through the crowd to the bench while the NCAA wristwatches were being presented to his Bruin teammates, and then breathlessly pleaded to all the well-wishers:

"Let me sit down."

And Sidney Wicks sat down. Nobody was going to give him any argument. After all, not even Jacksonville's Artis Gilmore—all 7 feet, 2 inches of him—could do that here Saturday afternoon.

The relaxation was well-deserved, anyway. Wicks, giving away half a foot to Gilmore in height, was the difference in an 80-69 victory that gave the Bruins an unprecedented fourth NCAA title in a row, and their sixth in the last seven years.

Los Angeles Times
Sports
CC SECTION D 2†
SUNDAY, MAR. 22, 1970

#### Does Intimidating Things

To accomplish that, Wicks unleashed the kind of defensive fury that made Bill Russell and Lew Alcindor famous: five blocked Gilmore shots, 18 rebounds (including two which triggered fast breaks that ripped the game open late in the first half) and assorted other intimidating things.

"It was just like playing against Lew in practice last year," said Wicks, catching his breath afterward, "except that I never blocked any of his shots. No matter how well I did, Lew could always score on me."

Leaping skyward like a volleyball spiker—even after he had picked up two fouls—Wicks staged one of the most memorable defensive shows ever seen in the NCAA finals, considering his height disadvantage.

The Jacksonville players in general, and Gilmore in particular, weren't altogether complimentary of Wicks' effort, however.

They insisted that Wicks should have been cited for goaltending.

"On a couple of those shots," said the Dolphins' Rex Morgan, "Gilmore was shooting DOWN at the basket. That should have been goaltending."

Gilmore agreed.

"Every time?" somebody asked.

"Yes," he replied, and then amended his remarks by adding, "Well, maybe one or a couple of times."

Gilmore, who scored 19 points and swept 16 rebounds, said nobody had ever blocked that many of his shots in one game. "He caught me by surprise," he said. "He must have watched my moves on films or something. He was right on me. I was taking my jumper too much, when really I should have used my body more before shooting."

#### No-Stuff Rule Helps

Asked about Gilmore's remarks, Wicks shook his head.

"The ref called the game," he said. "A couple of my shots should have been allowed, too, but that's neither here nor there."

Wicks added, however, that the rule against "stuffing" the ball gave him some help on defense.

"If he could have stuffed those shots," he said, "there's no way I could have stopped him. That's why

Please Turn to Page 8, Col. 2

## FIDDLE ISLE BREAKS U.S. RECORD IN SAN LUIS REY

### Runs 1½ Miles in 2:23 for One of Shoe's Four Winners; Quilche Wins Second Half of Handicap in $8.20 Upset

BY BION ABBOTT
Times Staff Writer

A fabulous final half-mile enabled high-weighted and heavily-favored Fiddle Isle to record the fastest 1½ miles ever run Saturday in the spectacular first half of the split San Luis Rey Handicap before 44,725 spectators at Santa Anita.

Anything less would not have been enough because Fiddle Isle barely nosed out Hitchcock in a bristling battle through the stretch that carried them to the wire in a world-beating 2:23 flat.

It will count only as an American record, however, because of varying conditions among the world's grass courses. The old mark of 2:23 2/5 was established just last November by Czar Alexander over the Santa Anita course that slopes gently downward for the first quarter of a mile.

Fiddle Isle, carrying 124 pounds, just fiddled around for the first mile, then charged from last to first during his final half-mile that had to be down around :46 flat.

The victory was one of four during the sunny afternoon for Bill Shoemaker, who also participated in the season's first win dead heat while fashioning his first quadruple of this campaign.

In the anticlimactic second division of the San Luis Rey Handicap Quilche's $8.20 upset over the Santa Anita Handicap winner, Quicken Tree, was the result of a strategic chess game and just about as slow.

Jockey Jerry Lambert made the key moves that enabled Quilche to outrush Quicken Tree by a half-length in a :23 4/5 final quarter that completed their leisurely journey in 2:25 2/5. Lambert simply shut off the pace when none would challenge front-running Quilche and they merely breezed the mile in 1:37 3/5 and 1 1/4 miles in 2:01 3/5.

Although Quilche traveled more than two seconds slower, he made just as much money as Fiddle Isle. There were eight starters in each division after Tampa Trouble was

Please Turn to Page 14, Col. 5

## WINGS BEAT KINGS AS CROZIER STARS

BY DAN HAFNER
Times Staff Writer

A couple of seasons ago the Kings whipped the Detroit Red Wings, 8-6. It was such a shattering experience for the losing goalie, Roger Crozier, that he announced his retirement at the age of 25.

The retirement was only temporary and it was a different Roger Crozier tending the nets for the Red Wings Saturday night at the Forum.

Crozier, making one spectacular save after another, blanked the Kings for 50 minutes as the Red Wings, moving to within two points of first place in the torrid Eastern Division race, skated to a 4-1 victory before 10,209 fans who were treated

Please Turn to Page 7, Col. 1

AMONG HIS SOUVENIRS—Riding the shoulders of Bruin teammate Steve Patterson, senior guard John Vallely cuts down the net as a memento of Bruins' impressive win over Jacksonville Dolphins.

**JIM MURRAY**

# An Ontario First: A Texas Dropout in the 'Ugly One'

ONTARIO—Move over Indianapolis, LeMans, Monza, Daytona. And move over Ray Harroun.

Make room for the Ontario 500 and, er, ah—well, I think, Jim McElreath.

In a race too fast to be clocked by anything human, a computer singled him out of a contest that was mostly full of mangled iron and, greatly to the surprise of 180,223 spectators, this high school dropout from Texas who had never won anything but a few miles of races in places like Langhorne and Trenton won $146,850 and a permanent place in auto racing history. He is the first winner of what is sure to become an American Classic sports fixture, the Big O's California 500.

McElreath thought so little of his chances, he sent his clothes on to Texas before the race. He thought he would be flying to Texas for a 600-mile overnight trip to DuQuoin, Ill., to drive a dirt race on a horse race track today, Labor Day.

He was driving a "backup" car. English translation: The leavings. If cars were sisters, the "backup" car in a team would be the ugly one. In a family, it would be the poor relation. They put fuel in it but not much faith. They then try not to wreck it. But they expect it'll be back in the garage, not the winner's circle, by the end of the afternoon. In every car race, just as in a horse race, there's always a bunch of things just to fill up the field.

McElreath qualified it in the caboose of the race, the outside of the sixth row. Cars that start there, in 18th position, can usually win only if there's a 17-car collision up in front of them that they're too slow to catch up to.

But, when this 500-mile race was finished, the only car McElreath had to beat was one which started in 32nd place. Even it passed him with two laps to go. He beat it by two whole seconds.

He led the race for only five laps. Fortunately they were the crucial five, the final five. To give you an idea, Al Unser led the race for 166 laps. With only 35 miles to go, Unser was 3 1/2 miles in front of his nearest competition which was Peter Revson, who had made the mistake a lot of car owners do. He turned his car into a mechanic for a checkup. By the time his pit crew got through with it, the sun was beginning to set, and it seemed the Ontario 500 could be won by Unser in second gear.

But all of a sudden, cars began to drop off like swatted flies. The racetrack looked like a parking lot. It looked as if the last laps would be run by tow trucks.

That's when two drivers, whose total age was 85 and whose positions in the starting grid totaled 50, suddenly found that every other car had died and willed them the race. There were so many smoking vehicles about, it looked like Rommel's retreat.

A. J. Foyt spent most of the day parked in the pits, and was about 80 laps behind the leaders when he unaccountably put the thing in gear again and started out. He had

Please Turn to Page 4, Col. 1

**END OF THE LINE**—Dan Gurney of Santa Ana pulls to a stop as wheel on his car flies down the track during running of California 500 Sunday at Ontario Motor Speedway. Dick Simon in car No. 44 is about to pass Gurney. The smudge on the wall is where Gurney's car hit in Turn 3.

# 180,223 See McElreath Win 500 by 2 Seconds

## Dramatic Finish Marks Inaugural Race; Pollard Second

**BY SHAV GLICK**
Times Staff Writer

ONTARIO—The first California 500 produced a storybook finish and a picture postcard setting as 180,223 spectators helped inaugurate Ontario Motor Speedway Sunday.

In one of the most dramatic 500-mile finishes in history, 42-year-old Jim McElreath survived a race of attrition which saw the lead change hands five times in the last 20 miles—twice on the next to last lap—to win $146,850 out of a $727,500 purse.

McElreath was driving a "backup car" for owner-driver A. J. Foyt, a Coyote powered by a turbocharged Ford, but it took some hustle by his boss before Jim could grab the lead on the 196th lap, 12½ miles from the finish. Foyt had crashed his Coyote while the leaders were on the 191st lap and it appeared the race might finish under the yellow caution light, with no passing allowed.

**Foyt Gives a Push**

Art Pollard, at 43, the oldest driver in the race, was the leader at the time.

Foyt, however, jumped out of his battered car in Turn 4 and helped the wrecking crew push it off the track.

"I knew they were running 1-2 at the time and in a wreck like that I would just hate to see it end under a yellow and that's why I was down there trying to drag my car off the track," said Foyt. "I knew it would be a fantastic finish and I thought that one thing Ontario deserved was a good finish in its first 500. And it proved to be a fantastic one."

The cleanup took five laps and as the green light flashed on, McElreath swept past Pollard in front of the packed grandstands and took the lead. But Pollard, who had started in the back row in 32nd place, wasn't finished yet.

**Pollard in Too Deep**

On the 198th of the 200-lap race, when McElreath bobbled slightly in Turn 3, Pollard shot past him and into the short shoot toward Turn 4. This time it was Pollard who went in too deep and McElreath dropped down and took him on the inside as the crowd came cheering to its feet for the final laps.

"I was surprised when he passed me," admitted McElreath, "as I had blown by him without much trouble earlier. Then, when I saw him going so far into the turn I was sure he was going to be in trouble and I ducked down under him fast before he could recover."

McElreath's margin at the end was two seconds — out of a 3-hour 7-minute 22-second race.

Please Turn to Page 6, Col. 1

Jim McElreath

# Mechanical Failures Eliminate Al Unser, Ruby, Other Stars

**BY PAT RAY**
Times Staff Writer

ONTARIO—"It was running perfectly and all at once it began missing and then finally just stopped," said Al Unser.

—"When the yellow light came on for (Joe) Leonard's wreck it looked like the perfect time to make a pit stop for the final 10 gallons of fuel we needed to finish," said crew chief Tyler Alexander of Team McLaren.

—"That was the longest 10 minutes of my life," said Peter Revson.

—"I was just more or less sitting there waiting out the laps when it happened," said LeeRoy Yarbrough.

The words were different but they all meant the same thing Sunday at Ontario Motor Speedway as fame and fortune went down the drain in the closing 20 laps of the California 500.

The events of the final 20 laps turned what had been a rather dull, runaway performance by Unser into one of the most thrilling of all 500-mile races.

Things had gone pretty much as expected with Unser headed for a repeat win of his Indy victory of last May and Revson and Yarbrough, his only challengers, both a lap back.

All Al had to do was make a decent final pit stop and victory was his — but it wasn't to be.

On the 174th lap the yellow light came on when Joe Leonard, Unser's Johnny Lightning teammate, spun into the infield. Unser, Revson and Yarbrough all headed to the pits for their final stop.

Unser and Yarbrough both got in and out but Revson's engine died and wouldn't restart.

Please Turn to Page 4, Col. 1

# RIGNEY BOOED BUT GETS LAST LAUGH WITH SWEEP

## Former Angel Manager Gives Victory Sign After Twins Boost Lead to 6 with 3-1 Win; It's Not Over, Phillips Says

**BY ROSS NEWHAN**
Times Staff Writer

He was booed vigorously by fans of the team he managed for eight years. But, the last hurrah belonged to Bill Rigney.

He stood in front of the visitors' dugout at Anaheim Stadium late Sunday afternoon, raised both arms exultantly and, with the index and middle fingers of each hand, formed the victory sign.

Rig's Twins had just completed a crushing sweep of the Angels before 19,641, a crowd that put the Angels over the million mark (1,013,878) for the fourth time in their five years in Anaheim.

Later, Rig sat in the clubhouse, his face flushed, his eyes sparkling.

"Damn, what a lift," he said. "They can have the boos; I'll take the three wins."

The score Sunday was 3-1 and now the Angels and Athletics are tied for second, six games behind Minnesota.

Rigney was asked if the race in the West is over.

"Hell, no," he said smiling. "According to the schedule, it won't be over until Oct. 2."

The doors to the Angels' clubhouse were locked for the first time this season. When they were opened, there was silence. Then, manager Lefty Phillips spoke.

**Phillips Won't Surrender**

"First of all," he said, "we'll just have to forget what happened this weekend. We're six out, but it's not over. We've been a team that's battled, that's had the odds against us and I don't think we'll quit now.

"However, today I had some players who didn't use their heads, who forgot fundamentals, who tried to do things they have no right doing."

The game was lost by the weak response to the pitching of Tom Hall and Ron Perranoski. The latter saved the series opener and came on in the ninth inning Sunday to rescue Hall, the slender southpaw from Riverside.

The Angels scored only four runs in the series, eight in the six games of the homestand and collected only four hits off Hall and Perranoski.

Phillips' anger was aroused in the fourth. Trailing 2-0 and with one out, Jim Fregosi singled and Alex Johnson doubled, putting the tying runs in scoring position.

Hall then struck out Ken McMullen and got Tommy Reynolds on a tap-back to the mound.

"With the type team that has to take every run it can get and with

Please Turn to Page 2, Col. 5

# Mota's Single in 9th Beats Houston, 4-3

HOUSTON—A ninth-inning single by Manny Mota drove in the winning run Sunday as the Dodgers defeated Houston, 4-3, after the Astros had tied the game by scoring three runs in the last of the eighth.

Mota's hit scored Bill Grabarkewitz, who led off the ninth with a single and moved to third on a single by pinchhitter Tom Haller.

Houston, blanked on four hits and trailing 3-0 going into the eighth, tied it on a solo homer by Cesar Cedeno, a single by John Edwards, and a pinch-hit homer by Norm Miller. Miller hit the first pitch by reliever Pete Mikkelsen, who had taken over for Joe Moeller.

The Dodgers scored their first two runs on one hit in the second inning. Ted Sizemore beat out an infield hit down the third-base line, Bill Russell walked and Grabarkewitz was hit by a pitch to load the bases.

Sizemore scored the first run on a wild pitch and Russell moved to third, where he scored as Moeller grounded out to second. The third

Please Turn to Page 2, Col. 2

**QUICK KNOCKOUT**—Jim Hurtubise didn't complete the first lap of the California 500 at the Ontario Motor Speedway Sunday. His front-engine car hit the wall on the third turn, losing a wheel. Hurtubise, the last of the 33 qualifiers, was uninjured.
Times photos by Larry Sharkey

**THE WINNING MOVE**—Jim McElreath's Coyote racer (14) shoots inside of Art Pollard in car No. 64 to take over lead on the 198th lap of the California 500. McElreath, who had finished in the top six at the Indianapolis 500 five times in the past nine years, went on to win.

# Stanford Finds It's Faster, Easier by Air, 27-17

CC PART III †

SATURDAY, JAN. 2, 1971

### JIM MURRAY

## 'Yes, Pater, We Won!'

Well, bust my monocle! Lay out my white tie and tails, I believe we'll be dressing for dinner tonight. Break out the '09 Dom Perignon, phone up the class of ought-eight, see if you can wake up the crowd in the lobby of the Union League Club. Ring up Aunt Mame out on Long Island. Get pater on the ship-to-shore radio to his cruise in the Caribbean.

STANFORD WON THE ROSE BOWL!

I mean, dear, how will we EVER explain this at the Yale Club. I mean, really! It's just too gauche, now, really, but there it is!

They have struck a blow for silk sheets, governesses, silver spoons, dining off tablecloths, teeth braces, baby pictures, prep school, upstairs maids. I mean, one couldn't be more surprised if Marie Antoinette won the French Revolution.

Kids from San Marino, Altadena, South Pasadena, San Mateo, Burlingame, Beverly Hills and Phillips Exeter aren't even supposed to BE in the Rose Bowl—except with a hamper of champagne and turkey sandwiches and damask napkins on the 40-yard-line.

Tell Grandmere to tune up her ear trumpet. This will take a bit of explaining. She thought they were going to be a FLOAT in the Rose Parade. She may need smelling salts when she finds out they were playing tackle with some ruffians from Ohio. I mean, really, we don't KNOW anybody from Ohio, do we?

As a matter of fact, Stanford usually does play in the Rose Bowl as if it was covered with rose petals or made out of cymbidium orchids. They act as if they were competing for the sweepstakes in the noncommercial division. They usually can keep the kids from the other side of the tracks off for the first few minutes but they always get their nose bloodied and their eyes blacked at the end.

### *It Was Embarrassing*

New Year's Day, it was Stanford passing out nosebleeds. The score was downright embarrassing—27-17. I don't expect we'll EVER get Harvard back on the schedule now. Stanford has always adhered to the principle no gentleman ever plays a game too well but I'm afraid we've really sullied our image.

It may have been the greatest victory in the history of the Rose Bowl. Ohio State came out here with a coach who can make a lion with a sore paw seem lovable. Stanford all but drove Woody Hayes into an underground bunker Friday.

The problem was, his team made touchdowns like a guy laying bricks. Stanford got theirs almost by inheritance by comparison. They had the ball for 6½ minutes at the end of the third quarter and the beginning of the fourth—and on fourth down and inches to go, their best runner was abruptly seated well short of it by a political science major from Glendora named Ron Kadziel.

It didn't seem serious at the time for Ohio. They had a 4-point lead. The only thing was, they just didn't have the ball. This appeared to confuse them. It wasn't in the game plan. Ohio State ALWAYS

Please Turn to Page 8, Col. 5

THE BIG PLAY — Stanford was trailing Ohio State, 17-13, in the fourth quarter of the Rose Bowl game Friday when Jim Plunkett, the Indians' quarterback scrambled to his right and hit tight end Bob Moore with a 35-yard pass to the Ohio State 2-yard line. Moore leaps high to make spectacular catch between Tim Anderson, left, and Mike Sensibaugh. Three plays later the Indians scored to take lead.
Times photo by Rick Browne

## 103,839 See Ohio State Finally Lose

BY BOB OATES
Times Staff Writer

The Stanford air force brought down the Ohio State infantry Friday afternoon in one of the most dramatic Rose Bowl games of the first 57.

A classic matchup of passes against runs was won in the fourth quarter by Big Jim Plunkett and the Indians, who came from behind to score two touchdowns in the last 10 minutes, 27-17.

Two crafty receivers named Bob Moore and Randy Vataha helped Plunkett bail out the Stanford team and overturn the nation's last undefeated and untied football power save one, Arizona State.

It was Moore's leaping catch for 35 yards gained to the 2-yard line that doomed Ohio State on Plunkett's decisive 80-yard drive in the final period.

A record Rose Bowl crowd of 103,-839 came out on a lazy, hazy day to see the downfall of a 10-point favorite. Coach Woody Hayes' Buckeyes, who outgained Stanford in ground yardage, 364-143, had lost only once before in the last three seasons.

**Stanford Resembles Pro Team**

At Stanford, John Ralston coaches a different kind of football. The Indians, who outgained Ohio State in air yardage, 265-75, closely resemble a good pro club.

Thus two of the most celebrated running teams of college football, undefeated Texas and Ohio State, both failed the climactic test of the season on New Year's Day.

The main event at Pasadena was a strange game of peaks and valleys and long drives by both sides, starting with Stanford's early thrust to a 10-0 lead followed by an Ohio State rally that earned the Big 10 champions a 14-10 halftime lead.

Throughout the third quarter, Ohio State seemingly held the momentum as Rex Kern controlled the ball from one minute to the next and from one series to the next as Plunkett chafed on the sideline.

**Only 3 Points in Third**

But Kern earned only three points in that third quarter of Buckeye domination. Seldom before has a college game offered a more poignant example of the insufficiency of ground-play, ball-control football when unaccompanied by touchdowns.

The Buckeyes were ahead by only four points, 17-13, when the game turned against them on the first play of the fourth quarter. They had marched out from their 6-yard line on 14 consecutive running plays, and now, on the Stanford 19, it was fourth and one. More exactly, it was fourth and one foot.

Five times on fourth down, Hayes, the Ohio signal-caller, asked the Bucks to run the ball with inconclusive results. Sometimes they made it and sometimes they missed. On this occasion, against the surprisingly

Please Turn to Page 6, Col. 1

## TEXAS CHOKES ON IRISH DEFENSIVE 'WISHBONE'

### Notre Dame Ends Longhorns' Win Streak at 30 Games, 24-11; Theismann Scores Twice, Passes for Touchdown

BY MAL FLORENCE
Times Staff Writer

DALLAS—Texas, which rode a Wishbone-T offense to 30 straight victories, choked on a defensive version of it Friday in the 35th Cotton Bowl game.

Notre Dame, employing a new Wishbone defense, contained every runner in the Longhorns' famed backfield except slick quarterback Eddie Phillips, in defeating the nation's No. 1 team, 24-11, before 72,-000 fans on a clear, mild afternoon.

It has to rate as one of the most satisfying victories for Notre Dame—a school that is rich in football tradition.

The Fighting Irish had their own perfect season spoiled last month by USC and many felt that, perhaps, Notre Dame was overrated.

Texans won't buy it and neither will anyone else now.

In a game in which the scoring was confined to the first half, clever Joe Theismann guided the Irish to an early 21-3 lead. Then the defense took over.

"What we did was to mirror their Wishbone-T in our secondary," said Ara Parseghian, the Notre Dame coach. "We were lining up in our own Wishbone."

In avenging last year's 21-17 defeat to Texas in the Cotton Bowl game, Notre Dame's brutish linemen and quick defensive backs made life miserable for All-American Steve Worster.

**Irish Shadow Worster**

The strong Worster had company wherever he went—even when he was blocking. As a result, he gained only 42 yards in 16 carries (2.6 average) and fumbled four times. He lost possession twice, depriving Texas of advantageous field position when it was trying to get back into the game in the second half.

In fact, turnovers ruined the Longhorns. One fumble at the Texas 13 set up an Irish touchdown and another at the Notre Dame 12 was the Longhorns' last offensive gasp in the final quarter.

Still, this was Notre Dame's game all the way. Theismann, blending passes and the runs of chunky John Cieszkowski, ripped the Texas defense like no other team has in the past two years.

Theismann, the runnerup to Jim Plunkett in the Heisman Trophy balloting, scored two touchdowns himself on keepers and threw 26 yards to wide receiver Tom Gatewood for another.

He probably would have had one

Please Turn to Page 8, Col. 1

## ORANGE BOWL

**Nebraska . . . . . . . 17**
**LSU . . . . . . . . . . . 12**

Story on Page 7

## SUGAR BOWL

**Tennessee . . . . . . 34**
**Air Force . . . . . . . 13**

Story on Page 9

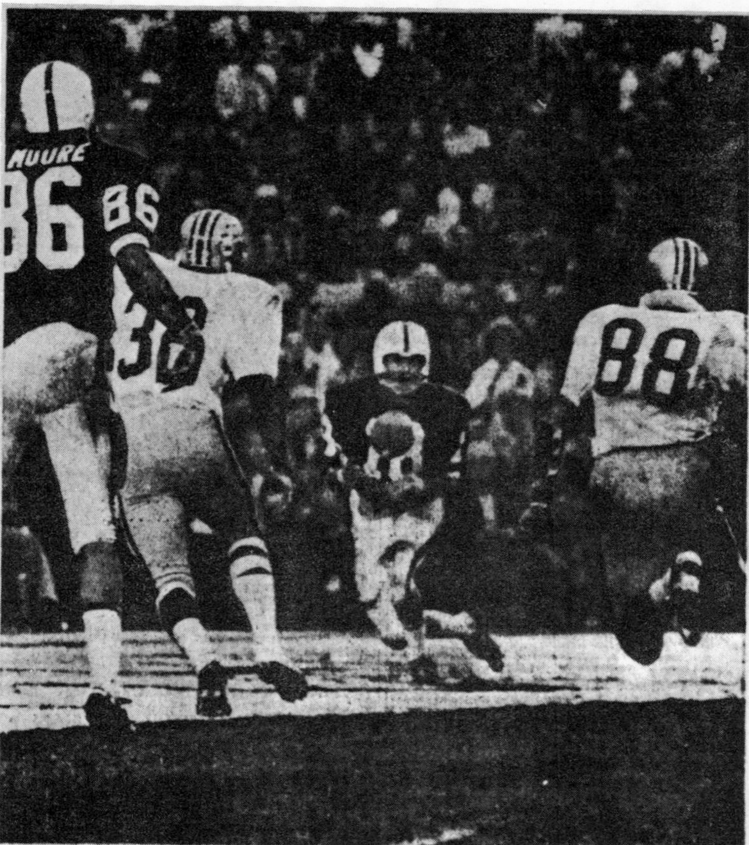

THE NEEDLE IS THREADED — Randy Vataha, Stanford's little flanker, catches a 10-yard pass from Jim Plunkett for the Indians' last TD. Plunkett threw between Stan White (88), Jack Tatum.
Times photo by Art Rogers

# FRAZIER WINS, DECKS ALI IN 15TH ROUND

## Joe Retains Heavyweight Title on Unanimous Decision

Los Angeles Times
Sports
BUSINESS & FINANCE
CC PART III 3†
TUESDAY, MAR. 9, 1971

BY CHARLES MAHER
Times Staff Writer

NEW YORK—Nine hours before the fight, Muhammad Ali said:

"I'll tell you: if Joe Frazier whips me, I'm going to get on my knees and crawl across the ring, look up a' d say, 'You are the greatest. You are the champion of the whole world.'"

Ali didn't get down on his knees at Madison Square Garden Monday night, but he got knocked on his pants in the 15th round and, whether he believes it or not, Joe Frazier really is the champion of the whole world.

Joe took a lot of good shots, and looked more battered than the man he beat at the end, but he won a clear decision. One official called it 8-6 and 1 even, another 9-6, the third 11-4.

Frazier didn't score the knockout that many expected of him, but he fought the fight the way everyone knew he would. He kept after his man like a bill collector.

Joe got his nose opened up, and his face was as red as it was brown after a few rounds. But he kept coming forward in his characteristic re'ntless manner.

Finally, in the 11th round, Frazier got off one of the two really big punches of the fight. He nailed Ali with a withering left hook and Muhammad's knees buckled.

There was about a minute left in the round. For about half that minute, Ali was stumbling around drunkenly. He did not figure to last the round.

But he not only made it through that one. He came back and gave a fair account of himself in the 12th.

Then, about 20 seconds intothe final round, Frazier landed his second big punch. It was another left hook and it put Ali down. It was the only knockdown of the fight.

The way Ali hit, you didn't know if he could get up. But he was on his feet at the count of 3 and managed to stumble through the rest of the round.

When it was over, Ali had a badly swollen right cheek. Ringside gossip was that he might have suffered a broken jaw. He was taken to a hospital for examination.

Ali didn't win a lot of the early rounds but he was boxing beautifully much of the time. When he did get hit, he would shak his head trying to tell the crowd not to get excited; there was nothing really wrong with him.

In fact, there didn't really seem to be anything seriously wrong with him until the 11th. Except that he was tiring. Maybe his 3½-year layoff was having the anticipated effect. Or maybe—the way Frazier was hammering at the body with both hands and occasionally landing a good hook—it wouldnt' have mat-

Please Turn to Page 4, Col. 2

***JIM MURRAY***

## Feet of Clay

NEW YORK—You were expecting maybe Armageddon? The Apocalypse?

It was a schoolyard fight. It was the most unprofessional fight I have ever seen for 150 bucks top.

But, Lord, it was exciting!

As this is written, at midnight in the catacombs under Madison Square Garden, the word is, Muhammad Ali's jaw was broken. It's for sure his heart was.

I never thought I would live to hear Ali described as a "fighter who can take it." His whole life style is based on dealing out punishment and then disappearing like some poltergeist with 8-ounce gloves. The state, the government, the press, the establishment could never lay a glove on him.

Joe Frazier laid about 50 on him. The one that counted was a left hook that Joe Frazier started just south of Weehawken. Ali had started a right. He was still holding it, cocked, when he thudded to the canvas. The butterfly had turned into a cocoon. The old magic was taking an 8-count.

★

**I suppose** it will be taken in some quarters as a victory for hot dogs and apple pie, the Fourth of July and moonlight along the Wabash. And it's safe to belong to the American Legion again and "pick up your troubles in your old kit bag"—but actually it was just a fist fight.

Ali, the wunderkind, the beautiful icon of the ghettoes, had such implicit faith in his destiny that he released a handwritten, boastful ode to his own success practically on his way down the aisle. Defeat was as incomprehensible to him as Einstein's Theory.

He was like a guy going to the electric chair buying a new car.

He thought he was going right to the kingdom of all boxing. Instead, he was going to the hospital. He thought Joe Frazier was just another doll to stick pins in, make faces at, and then, in the dark of the moon, turn it into a zombie. He made up poems, pulled all the old shticks, humiliated his opponent publicly, privately, in rhyme and in simple declarative sentences.

★

**He sneered** at his opponent's punches, jeered and shook his head "No, No!" at the most violent shots.

Even when his jaw looked like the world's biggest hunk of bubblegum, he pretended it wasn't happening. Reality has never been Ali's bag. He lives in a kind of Arabian Nights fantasy world.

But Joe Frazier was not a confused, fearful, spooked pug. Joe Frazier comes to work, like a guy who brings his lunch in a pail, turns on the machine and doesn't stop till the whistle blows.

Ali tried to punch him out of his one-track mind, then, to talk him out of it.

It was like trying to con and oncoming train. Frazier felt the mighty Ali crumpling under his punches as early as the sixth round. Then, for awhile, it was Frazier's turn to underestimate his opponent.

Make no mistake about it, Muhammad Ali is no pug. But he is a fighter. Leaden-legged, taking punches he never knew existed in his previous 150 fights, absorbing blows to the stomach that will come out as blood clots for a week, he had turned into the immoveable object.

His only offensive weapon was

Please Turn to Page 4, Col. 7

**ON THE DECK**—Legs kicking, Muhammad Ali is sent sprawling to the canvas after Joe Frazier connected with a left hook in 15th round Monday night. Frazier went on to retain his world heavyweight championship, winning a 15-round unanimous decision.

## ...And Still Champion

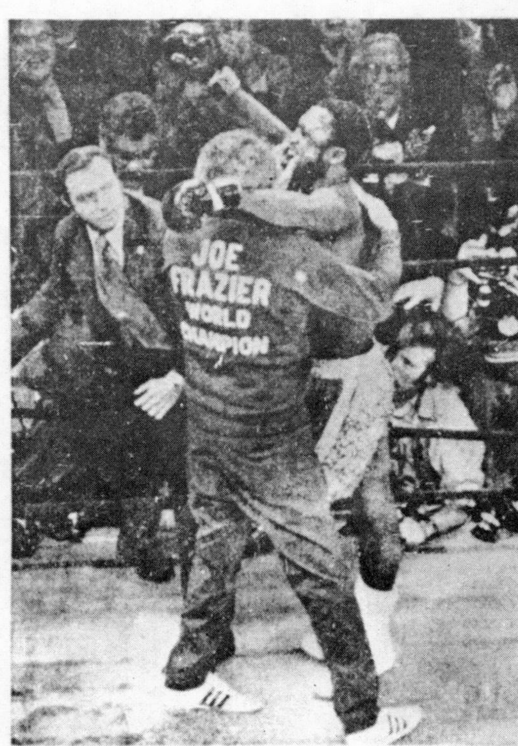



**MOST HAPPY FELLA**—Joe Frazier is embraced by his manager, Yank Durham, after retaining his world heavyweight title Monday.

**ON THE BUTTON**—Joe Frazier lands a hard left to the jaw and sends Muhammad Ali against the ropes during their 15-round world heavyweight title bout at Madison Square Garden Monday night

# NCAA BASKETBALL STILL 'BRUIN WORLD'

## UCLA Booed for Stall as Villanova Falls, 68-62

BY DWIGHT CHAPIN
Times Staff Writer

HOUSTON—The crown tipped and wavered but did not fall. The dynasty lives.

It was tough—tougher than any of their other championship games have been.

But the UCLA Bruins, thanks primarily to a pair of players—Steve Patterson and Henry Bibby— who were in the doghouse only a couple of weeks ago because of their shooting, fought off the determined Villanova Wildcats, 68-62, at the Astrodome here Saturday afternoon for their fifth straight national basketball title.

Some in the record crowd of 31,765 —largest ever to see an NCAA tournament game—sneered at this one. Some in the audience, which seemed almost unanimously allied to bring on the Bruins' demise, said that UCLA could have blown it.

They were right, but that didn't take away the fact. The king is still up there on his perch, looking down at everybody. And it's now 28 straight tournament victories and seven national championships in the last eight years—a string many consider the most amazing in sports history—for a team that had no worlds left to take this season but refused to believe it.

Ironically, if UCLA had fallen, the man who has coached the team through all of the big years, John Wooden, would have been blamed.

After blistering Villanova's 2-3 zone with 51.4% shooting (much of it from far outside) for a 45-37 halftime lead, the Bruins came out in a stall at the start of the second half.

It was designed to draw the Wildcats out of their zone.

After a bit of tugging and hauling and some shouts from the Villanova players of "You're the national champions, play ball," it achieved its purpose.

But Wooden knew something else could happen if the Bruins went to a delay. He knew they could lose their momentum . . . and that's exactly what happened.

It wasn't an all-at-once type of thing. UCLA even had extended its lead to 12 points with 11:35 to go.

But then the Wildcats—who had been shocked by Patterson's 20 points in the first half—inexorably began to cut it down. And, to UCLA's surprise, they did it uncharacteristically, with a man-to-man defense that got them the ball.

At 5:09, a sweeping hook shot by leaping Howard Porter brought Villanova to within four points, 58-54. At 2:38, the Wildcats moved to within three, 61-58, on another Porter specialty — a baseline, turn-around jump shot.

UCLA's momentum and poise both were drooping badly now.

But then came what probably was the play of the game.

Bibby worked free underneath on a pick by Patterson, took a Sidney Wicks pass from the corner and put in a lay-in for a 63-58 Bruin lead.

Porter answered with a 15-footer but 63-60 was as close as the Wildcats got.

The Bruins handled the pressure from that point as they have all season—calmly and adeptly. Bibby hit three free throws and Patterson a lay-in on which Porter was called for goaltending and it was over.

The margin was six. UCLA's closest calls previously in final games were a pair of 11-pointers over Jacksonville (1970) and Michigan (1965).

"We know it wasn't easy this time," said Bibby, the junior guard. "But we've played so many games the same way this year we knew how to handle it. We knew we could just hold out, be patient and play good basketball."

For a half, UCLA didn't resort to

Please Turn to Page 6, Col. 1

FLYING HIGH—The NCAA tourney standout, Villanova's Howard Porter, towers over Bruins and teammates during finale at Astrodome, won by UCLA for fifth straight time. In last year's tournament Sidney Wicks (right) of the Bruins was hailed as the best player.

### JIM MURRAY

## Stylish Miscast

VERO BEACH—When Maurice Wesley Parker IV was going to Bel-Air Town and Country School and just beginning to master the Greek alphabet, Plutarch's Lives, and the minor British poets, it was considered a foregone conclusion he would be earning $75,000 a year at age 31.

He would have two telephones, a rug on the floor, a cable address, an ulcer, an office in New York, a seat on the Exchange, a box at the opera, and be complaining about how hard good help was to get and keep these days. He would belong to the L.A. Country Club, the Republican Party, play dominoes at the California Club, and sail at the Newport Yacht Club. He was to be "Mr. Plastic — Maurice Wesley Plastic."

He went to Harvard Military Academy where he carried a saber. His roommates were the sons of Gregory Peck, Doris Day and Jack Carson. He was a star athlete, but most of the other kids' sports activities had been confined to riding their ponies. If Wes Parker got his picture in Sports Illustrated, it would be in a polo helmet.

★

**Well, now he's 31,** and making $75,000 a year and Wes never did make the Junior Chamber of Commerce, the Harvard Business School or the executive suite. He wears a gray flannel suit, but it's got a number on the back.

But business is fine, thank you. While the rest of the country was going through a recession, M. W. Parker, Inc., had its best year ever last year. The industrial average was up 41 points over the year before and the lifetime average was up around 70 points.

Production doubled in two-base hits, which is the firm's bread-and-butter product, and runs-batted-in were four times what they were two years ago. Gains were up, you might say, on all issues traded.

Wes Parker had a tougher time getting into baseball than Mickey Mantle would have getting into Harvard. "Look, sonny, they don't play this game on horseback," they told him. Or, "A shutout isn't called 'love' here, boy." They couldn't believe the game could be played by anyone who would go to military school without being drafted.

★

**No one overcame** more handicaps to play baseball than Wes Parker. He came up the hard way. Baseball players come from orphan asylums, not military academies. A game which scattered hundreds of thousands of dollars to guys who had never graduated from Spokane wouldn't give a dime to a guy who graduated from Harvard.

No one believed Wes Parker loved baseball. They thought he was just collecting material for a book, that he would turn out to be a Paper Dodger.

Wes Parker was collecting material for a career. He was as deadly serious as Ty Cobb. "I felt like a guy who's in love with a girl, only she thinks he's only after her money." Baseball's reasoning was, "Parker doesn't need the money, therefore, he doesn't need baseball." Or, "As soon as they start curving him, he'll want to take his ball and go home."

Wes persevered. He was easily the most stylish first baseman the league has seen since Hal Chase. In 1965, he led the league in fielding, but they gave the Golden Glove to Bill White.

In 1968, Wes Parker made only one error—and that was question-

Please Turn to Page 10, Col. 2

### BRUINS IN A 'WALK'

## It's Routine as UCLA Wins 5th Straight Title

BY JEFF PRUGH
Times Staff Writer

HOUSTON—All the post-game whoopla was as old as the late, late show. The chants of "We're No. 1" and "Five in a Row." The beaming faces and fond embraces. The hoisting of Sidney Wicks up to the baskets, where he ceremoniously snipped the strings off the rims and draped them around his neck.

Los Angeles Times
Sports
CC SECTION C 2†
SUNDAY, MAR. 28, 1971

UCLA, which didn't exactly save its best for the last, was the monarch again here Saturday afternoon—king of the college basketball world for the seventh time in eight years.

But the mood was starkly different this time.

For coach John Wooden, the architect of possibly the greatest dynasty in all of sport, it was the feeling of a man on trial.

"I'm not a betting man," he said in the subdued UCLA dressing room after his team's scary 68-62 win over Villanova. "But I would have bet my life that they weren't going to beat us."

He was stoutly defending his strategic ploy, an unusual stall-tempo game that admittedly "backfired" and nearly knocked the Bruins right on their NCAA crowns.

Here was UCLA, of all teams, actually WALKING the ball up the court, passing and waiting and rarely shooting, hoping to force Villanova out of its zone defense.

**Create Another Problem**

Well, the Bruins did exactly that. But they found themselves entangled in a scrappy Villanova man-for-man defense that pestered UCLA much more than the zone ever did.

And here was John Wooden, rehashing the game that almost slipped away from him before a record NCAA crowd of 31,765 in the Houston Astrodome.

"I didn't feel, in any way, that we would lose it," he said, "If we made 'em play us man-to-man. I felt we could beat Villanova's man-for-man.

"If we had let them stay in their zone, I was afraid we might have hit a cold spot and started missing our shots for three or four minutes. Actually, I didn't think they would come within three points of us, either. Yet they did (61-58 and 63-60). But even if they caught us, I knew we'd get it right back."

Wooden admitted, too, that his slowdown was motivated partly by one of his old peeves—the lack of a clock to prevent stalling in the college game.

"I've always wanted a 30-second clock" he said. "Maybe now the Rules Committee will think a little bit more about putting one in."

Even though the Bruin coach nearly lost a game by proving a point, his strategy paid off at the outset of the second half.

"We were able to kill five minutes," he said, "and pick up four points."

It was true. UCLA, to the accompaniment of "Bruins are Bush" chants from the Villanova rooting section, froze the ball and got two baskets, widening its eight-point halftime lead to 49-37.

Then, with 15 minutes to go, Villanova finally scrapped its 2-3 zone and began chasing the Bruins all over the court.

The Wildcats may have chased them into the Gulf of Mexico had it not been for those ingredients that carried UCLA to the finals—poise and patience—as well as a weapon the Bruins didn't find most of the year, the outside shooting of Steve Patterson (29 points) and Henry Bibby (17 points).

Please Turn to Page 7, Col. 1

## TRY SHEEP SURPRISES HIS OWNERS, TOO, PAYS $110.40

BY BION ABBOTT
Times Staff Writer

Try Sheep, a horse with a habit of running into trouble, ran into the Santa Anita winner's circle instead Saturday for a stunning $110.40 surprise in the $82,000 San Luis Rey Handicap.

A perfect, rail-skimming ride by Fernando Alvarez enabled Try Sheep to overtake the 6-1 outsider, Tampa Trouble, by a head in a sparkling 2:25 flat for the marathon of 1½ miles over the turf course.

They outfinished third-place Bacuco by four lengths and the Laffit Pincay-powered even-money favorite, Drumtop, was a distant fourth, beaten nearly seven lengths by the winner.

But Pincay still made his first $1 million of the meeting, increasing the earnings of his 491 mounts to $1,017,390 with one Saturday winner, one second, three thirds, one fourth and two fifths.

If Try Sheep took the 38,114 spectators by surprise, they had company—the owners, Mrs. Cecilia DeMille Harper and Mr. and Mrs. Clinton La Tourette, and trainer Noble Threewitt.

"We had him nominated for next Tuesday's $40,000 San Bernardino Handicap, too," disclosed Mrs. Harper, breeder of the 5-year-old son of Determine and Can't Sleep. "We finally decided the longer distance today would suit him better."

**Biggest Thrill**

Threewitt confessed in the winner's circle, "It's a bigger thrill when you don't think you have much of a chance."

This was the ninth $100 winner of the season, the second in a major stakes. War Heim, who paid an even $100 for winning the $132,100 Strub Stakes, was fifth this trip, less than a length behind Drumtop.

Only Alvarez was confident—and that was after Try Sheep swung off the rail at the top of the stretch.

"Once we got in the clear, I was sure we were going to get there because my horse was really running," Alvarez said. "But Tampa Trouble wasn't giving up, either.

"We were lucky to run on the best part of the track most of the way."

That part of the track was right next to the rail, and Alvarez was hugging it all the way around. Re-

Please Turn to Page 12, Col. 4

## HADL THROWN OFF HORSE, SUFFERS SKULL FRACTURE

SAN DIEGO—Quarterback John Hadl of the San Diego Chargers suffered a skull fracture, facial fractures and a concussion Saturday when he was thrown from a horse. He was taken to Grossmont Hospital where Dr. E. Paul Woodward, team physician, said Hadl's head injuries did not appear to be critical.

However, he was scheduled to undergo surgery for one of the facial fractures near a vital optic nerve.

Hadl was riding with his wife, Charneil, and Charger defensive end Steve DeLong and his wife, Jackie, at Rancho Monte Vista. Hadl's horse stumbled over a log entering a ravine at high speed and threw him.

The former Kansas All-America, 31, who will start his 10th season with the Chargers this year, has never missed a game because of injuries in his career.

HAWKING THE BALL—Two players with but a single thought—retrieve the ball—are Villanova's Chris Ford (42) and UCLA's Terry Schofield as they pursue the loose ball during the championship game at the Astrodome. UCLA's stalling tactics drew some boos, but led to a 68-62 triumph.

# It's Over...Jabbar, Bucks Stop Lakers at 33

Los Angeles Times
Sports
BUSINESS & FINANCE
CC PART III 2†
MONDAY, JAN. 10, 1972

BY MAL FLORENCE
Times Staff Writer

MILWAUKEE—The win streak is dead at 33.

Kareem Abdul Jabbar and the Milwaukee Bucks accomplished something that no other NBA team could in more than two months—defeat the Lakers.

And, they did it with a flourish Sunday afternoon, running away from the careless Lakers in the fourth quarter for a 120-104 victory before a capacity crowd of 10,746 at Milwaukee Arena and a national television audience.

The streak—the longest in American major league professional team sports—had to end sometime, but the Lakers were disappointed that it expired against NBA champion Milwaukee and the manner in which it did.

"We lost it. Milwaukee didn't win it," said forward Jim McMillian.

There's justification for his attitude because the Lakers slumped as a team. There wasn't any third or fourth quarter spurt that has occurred almost automatically since the streak began Nov. 5—only turnovers (24), inaccurate shooting (39.3%) and porous defense.

The Bucks, of course, contributed to the Lakers' defeat. Jabbar, maintaining advantageous floor position, couldn't be contained by Wilt Chamberlain and the other Lakers.

The graceful 7-footer battered the Lakers' defense with sweeping hooks, short jumpers and intimidating stuff shots.

He finished with 39 points, 20 rebounds and a technical "knockout" over Happy Hairston.

Early in the second quarter Jabbar became incensed when fouled by Hairston and threw a right-hand chop—without the ball—that landed flush on Happy's jaw. Hairston remained motionless on the floor for several seconds as Chamberlain gently led Jabbar away from the fallen Laker.

"I simply lost my temper," said Jabbar, who could have been ejected from the game. However, he only drew a personal foul.

"Sure, I fouled him," said Happy. "Fouls are part of basketball but slugging isn't."

Then, Hairston turned his head so reporters could view the lump that was prominent on the right side of his face.

When asked what kind of foul he committed, Happy snorted: "That's the silliest question I've ever heard. A foul is a foul."

Hairston became entangled with Jabbar's legs under the Milwaukee basket when the Bucks' center unloaded on the Laker forward.

The Bucks were unloading the entire day, namely Jabbar, and reserves John Block and Lucius Allen, who divided 35 points. Block, the former USC star, also grabbed some timely rebounds (10). It was one of the 6-9 cornerman's most effective performances as a pro.

There weren't many positive aspects to attribute to the Lakers, however. Jerry West, whose personal win streak ended at 41 games, threw the ball away several times and was only 5-of-16 from the field (20 points). Oscar Robertson forced Jerry to work hard at both ends of the floor.

The other Laker shooters were misfiring, too. Gail Goodrich was 5-for-20 (18 points) while McMillian was 7-for-19 (18). Many of the shots were high percentage attempts.

The Lakers warmed up a bit in the second half after shooting only 29.5% in the first 24 minutes in which they experienced a miserable, 17-point second quarter.

It was in this period that the Bucks probably should have put the Lakers away but they were missing easy shots themselves.

Please Turn to Page 4, Col. 5

IT LOOKS GOOD — Dave Hill strokes his final 20-foot putt in the 46th Glen Campbell Los Angeles Open and he and his caddie, Junior Moore, begin to get the idea the ball is going to roll in for a birdie and allow Hill to tie for the lead and join a three-man playoff.

# Three for Money in Open Playoff

## Archer, Hill Catch Aaron, Force 18-Hole Round at Rancho Today

BY BILL SHIRLEY
Times Sports Editor

Tommy Aaron kept telling himself he didn't have it made.

The 34-year-old Georgian was playing some of the best golf of his life at Rancho Park Sunday and led the Glen Campbell Los Angeles Open by two strokes as late as the 13th hole. He just had made a birdie 4 on the hole, the 67th of the tournament, and was sailing along 14 under par.

But Tommy has been on the tour for 11 years and he knew the two professionals trailing him by two shots, George Archer and Dave Hill, were too close for comfort.

He told himself, "I've got to make some more birdies." Saturday night he had said, "You can't stand still with these guys; you can count on them making birdies."

He was right. Archer and Hill each made two birdies on the last five holes and finished in a deadheat with Aaron at 270, 14 under par. Starting the day three strokes behind Aaron, the 54-hole leader, Archer and Hill each shot 66, 5 under par on the 6,827-yard municipal course. Aaron didn't do badly himself, shooting a 69, and again playing without a bogey on a gorgeous Sunday afternoon. He made only two in 72 holes.

So, for the fourth straight year, a playoff will determine the winner of the $125,000 tournament. Only this time, Aaron, Archer and Hill will play 18 holes today to settle the championship. Usually the players tee off in a sudden-death fight the same afternoon. In the past three years, Charlie Sifford defeated Harold Henning; Billy Casper beat Hale Irwin and last year Casper lost to Bob Lunn.

The format was changed this year to accommodate CBS, which didn't like to cut into prime time in the East to telecast sudden-death com-

Please Turn to Page 6, Col. 1

### L.A. OPEN SCORES

| | |
|---|---|
| x-Tommy Aaron | 69-65-67-69—270 |
| x-Dave Hill .... | 70-67-67-66—270 |
| x-G. Archer ... | 66-69-69-66—270 |
| Chris Blocker .. | 69-71-65-70—275 |
| Hale Irwin .... | 66-74-68-68—276 |
| Bob Rosburg .. | 71-68-71-66—276 |
| Tom Weiskopf.. | 68-68-71-70—277 |
| Forrest Fezler . | 69-72-72-65—278 |
| Curtis Sifford .. | 66-68-71-73—278 |
| Bob E. Smith .. | 66-73-67-72—278 |
| Johnny Miller .. | 69-68-70-71—278 |

x—18-hole playoff today for first place.

Complete scores on Page 7

# Attlesey's the Name

## Teen-aged Kim follows dad, ex-USC star Dick, in bid for track records

BY EARL GUSTKEY, Times Staff Writer

NEWPORT BEACH—After an absence of 20 years, the name Attlesey is back in the sports headlines.

Two decades ago it was Dick Attlesey, USC world record-setting hurdler.

Now it's his 18-year-old daughter, Kim, one of the nation's brightest prospects in the women's long jump.

"I get the same excitement out of going to her meets as I did when I competed," says Attlesey, 42, an insurance executive. "My heart still thumps the same way."

Kim Attlesey

Kim is training hard for the Sunkist Invitational at the Los Angeles Sports Arena Jan. 22, first Southland meet of the Olympics year.

"Kim really wants to go to the Munich games," her father says. "I sure hope she makes it. But I want her to do it on her own. I don't meddle in her training program. She's the type who gets bugged by someone hovering over her. My wife and I keep our noses out of it."

A knee injury in 1948 and a muscle pull in 1952 kept Attlesey out of the Olympics. In between, in the seasons of 1950 and 1951, he lost only one race. He broke world records in the 120-yard and 110-meter high hurdles.

Miss Attlesey's L.A. Track Club coach, Dave Rodda, forecasts a brilliant future for his still-inexperienced pupil.

"The amazing thing about this girl is that she's only been jumping competitively for a year," says Rodda, 31.

"I've never seen a girl with such great natural ability for the event. She can go as far as sh ewant to. Potentianlly, she's the greatest woman long jumper this country's ever had. She has an excellent shot at the Olympic team and she's a potential world record holder."

The women's world long jump record is 22-5¾, set by Heidi Rosendahl of West Germany. Miss Attlesey's best is 20-8, which

Please Turn to Page 5, Col. 1

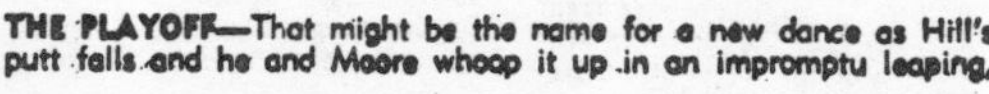

THE PLAYOFF—That might be the name for a new dance as Hill's putt falls and he and Moore whoop it up in an impromptu leaping, laughing celebration. Hill shot 270 to tie Tommy Aaron and George Archer. The trio play off today at 11:10 a.m. at Rancho Park.
Times photos by Ben Olender

# ANOTHER PERFECT ENDING FOR BRUINS

Los Angeles Times
Sports
CC SECTION C 2†
SUNDAY, MAR. 26, 1972

## UCLA Upset Because Florida State Makes It Close, 81-76

**BY JEFF PRUGH**
Times Staff Writer

The script would have been just as believable as all the others were—even if Clifford Irving had written it.

It was UCLA all the way. A perfect ending to a perfect season. Six national titles in a row and eight in the last nine years. So what else is new?

Plenty.

The Walton Gang had to withstand its toughest challenge of the season Saturday afternoon at the Sports Arena to conquer tall and quick Florida State, 81-76, in the NCAA basketball finals.

But to see all the pouting faces among the Bruin players, you would have thought they'd been arrested for stealing the championship.

While fans and alumni were whooping it up over UCLA's third 30-0 season, Bill Walton was upset that the victory wasn't typically one-sided. Henry Bibby said, "It gets to be old after awhile." And Larry Hollyfield and Greg Lee sat disconsolately on the bench during the trophy presentations.

Maybe it wasn't UCLA's most artistic triumph. Maybe it wasn't typical of a team which many observers were saying was the greatest of all Bruin teams.

But it was good enough to beat Florida State's Seminoles, who had withstood a barrage of criticism over recruiting on the eve of the game to play the Bruins better than anybody had all season.

They raced away to the biggest lead against UCLA this season, 21-14 (the previous high: 4-0 by Oregon), and rode the deadly corner shooting of Ron King and inside scoring of 6-11 Lawrence McCray after Walton got into foul trouble to make it close at the finish.

Things got so close, in fact, that Bruin coach John Wooden had to summon Lee off the bench to run a keepaway-tempo game and protect a 79-72 lead in the last 5 minutes.

But the Seminoles blew several chances to make it closer, if not topple a dynasty, by committing costly turnovers.

And while they were losing the ball, the Bruins were not losing their poise.

"The most pleasing thing to me," said Wooden afterward, "was that when we got behind early, we showed patience. But later I thought we became cautious when we lost Walton. We seemed to lose our movement. We weren't cutting and passing and we were dribbling too much."

But most of the mistakes—19 in all—were committed by Florida State.

"I thought we had a chance near the end," said coach Hugh Durham, who added that his team was not affected "one way or the other" by critical remarks the previous day by outgoing president Bill Wall of the National

Please Turn to Page 12, Col. 2

BRUIN STEAL—UCLA's Henry Bibby goes high to intercept a pass intended for Florida State's Greg Samuel in NCAA finals.

CRASH DRIVE—Tommy Curtis of Bruins falls to floor after fouling while trying to drive on Reggie Royals Saturday at Sports Arena.

PRESS PAYS OFF—Florida State's Otis Cole, double-teamed by Larry Farmer (left) and Bibby, loses the ball. Bruins won sixth straight title, 81-76.
Times photos by Art Rogers

***JIM MURRAY***

## Sermon On the Mound

VERO BEACH—They say you can't learn pitching from a book. But Don Sutton did.

It's more than a thousand pages long and its lessons are indivisible. You won't find how to pitch a screwball in it, or how to hold a curve. It's not that specialized. It doesn't tell you how to pitch Aaron with a 3-and-2 count but it can fit you with a philosophy for that, as well as larger contests.

It can tell you how to get out of a bases-loaded jam in life as well as in the World Series. It can tell you how to live and how to love. No, it's not a sex manual, any more than it's a manual of off-speed pitches.

The pitching coaches Don Sutton turns to whenever the fat part of the batting order comes up in life are Matthew, Mark, Luke and John. Sutton would rather learn how to hold the Devil on first than Lou Brock.

★

**Pitchers,** as a class, do not tend to be ecclesiastical. Occasionally, they would call a guy "Deacon Danny" but this would be apt to be in honor of the fact he wore eyeglasses, not a turned collar. Pitchers' nicknames, historically, ran more to "Dizzy," "Daffy," "Goofy," "Rube," "Bugs," or even "Lefty." Pitchers ran off to join fire departments, chased chorus girls, broke barroom mirrors. One of them jumped the club bus to catch a plane for Israel a couple of years ago. Another jumped the club once and returned, bleary-eyed, several days (and fifths) later to report he had been kidnaped while his captors poured whiskey down his throat. Some others, as the press noted, "staggered through the late innings," and they meant it all too literally.

The pitchers' mound, in short, is not always a pulpit. You do not expect a sermon on the mound.

There have been outstanding young men of exemplary conduct who have thrown the high, hard ones at batters in the past—a Christy Mathewson, Tom Seaver, Walter Johnson, to name a few.

But the very nature of the job is believed to bar excessive piety, to (in some cases) fatally limit trust in the Lord. The banjo hitter, for instance, getting a good pitch on the fists but somehow managing to bloop it into left field for a game-winning hit, is not conducive to praising the Lord.

★

**Pitchers have** broken up more clubhouse furniture than any other eight positions put together. A pitcher who loses a one-hitter, or even a no-hitter, as has happened, usually is well able to restrain himself from psalm-singing. He may pray, of course—that he gets traded to a club that can hit.

"Christianity or being a Christian doesn't guarantee winning," admits Don Sutton. Neither, to be sure, does it insist on losing. The Scriptures do not rule out a winning rally in the home half of the ninth.

What Christianity does guarantee, Sutton feels, is a perspective which prevents winning or losing from interfering with the product of faith, which is the good life regardless of the hits, runs or errors.

How did Don Sutton, a major league right-hander with a curveball the hitters feel is right out of Hell, become an Evangelical Christian? "Well, I didn't fall off a donkey on the road to Damascus," grins Sutton. "No hole opened up on the highway.

"I think it started very early in my life, because my parents were true Christians who lived their faith. Our home was a happy place, even when they were raising their family on $25-a-month on share crops as tenant farmers."

Please Turn to Page 14, Col. 1

## BASEBALL'S 'QUIET MAN'

### The Calm and Consistent Mr. Alston: He's Not Too Tough and Not Too Soft

**BY RON RAPOPORT**
Times Staff Writer

VERO BEACH—"Good managing is like holding a dove in your hand," says Dodgers vice president Al Campanis. "Squeeze it too tight and it dies; not tight enough and it flies away."

Walter Alston, in Campanis' view, has a nice touch with the dove . . . not too tough, not too soft.

That, perhaps, goes a long way toward explaining why Alston is now in his 19th year with the Dodgers. Average tenure is 2½ years.

This year, as always, he has only a one-year contract. But no one doubts that baseball's "quiet man" is as secure as it's possible to be in his line of work.

But it wasn't always thus.

There were many doubters when the club hired a man whose major league career consisted entire-

*'He's same when he wins a pennant as when he finishes fourth or fifth'*

ly of one at bat—a strikeout—and who had managed only in the minors, among them a sizable number of Dodger players.

"A lot of people thought he'd be a failure," recalls Carl Erskine, a star pitcher of that era. "I predicted he wasn't forceful enough to be a manager and a lot of the players were skeptical.

"He didn't bring any ready-made credentials and at that time—and still in some places today—the image of a manager was some kind of dynamo, like Leo Durocher. Walt was such a departure from that.

"Before spring training was over the writers were coming to us and saying, 'What's with this guy? He doesn't tell us much.' With Charlie Dressen (previous manager) you'd just open the door and get a flood of words on yesterday, today and tomorrow.

"Another handicap was he came to the Dodgers to manage a group of men who were successful—remember, there were Hodges, Reese, Robinson, Furillo, Snider, Campanella, Newcombe, Loes, myself—most of whom were making more money than he was.

"He's very gracious in his recollections of those years—he says we all helped him become a mana-

ger—but I remember we thought he'd have problems because of his personality."

The supreme irony, in looking back, is that it generally is agreed the one quality which accounts for Alston's lasting nearly two decades, is this very equanimity, this lack of outward forcefulness many thought would cause his early downfall.

Now it's hard to find a baseball man with anything but kind words for Walt.

As Erskine puts it, "The things that in the beginning seemed weaknesses because they didn't fit

*'A lot of people thought he'd fail . . . a lot of players were skeptical'*

the managerial pattern of the day turned out to be strengths."

Now these qualities are recognized and admired almost universally.

"All of us tend to make big things out of little things," says Sparky Anderson, manager of the Cincinnati Reds. "But he doesn't. That's what I'm trying to learn from him. I can't do it yet. He's the same when he wins the pennant as when he finishes fourth or fifth."

"There's a saying," says Campanis, "that if you can't play for Alston, you can't play for anybody. He's patient and understanding and he doesn't

Please Turn to Page 10, Col. 3

BRUIN ACE TESTY

## Walton and Bibby Unimpressed, but Wooden Satisfied

**BY DWIGHT CHAPIN**
Times Staff Writer

It was UCLA's sixth straight national basketball championship—and Bill Walton's first.

But the college Player of the Year took the 81-76 victory over Florida State like a defeat.

When he arrived in the interview room after the win, with teammate Henry Bibby and coach John Wooden, the Bruin sophomore center obviously was far from joyous. In fact, he was a trifle testy.

Asked by writers in the back of the room to raise the microphone and speak louder, he snapped: "I can hear myself. It (his voice) is bouncing off the back wall."

He first informed Bibby to "get off my shoestrings". That remark sounded facetious. The rest of what he said did not.

Asked again to talk louder, he said:

"There are a lot of empty seats up front."

**'Not That Elated'**

When the questions finally came, Walton said, "I'm not that elated because we didn't play that well. Florida State is an excellent team but we didn't dominate the game like we know we can. If we had played our game the way we can it would have been different. No excuses but I don't like to back into things. I like to win convincingly."

Then he added:

"I felt like we lost it."

Bibby agreed that "we didn't play that well. But I'm happy we won. We made mistakes we shouldn't have made, but any team would like to be in our position now."

This was Bibby's third straight national championship team.

"It gets to be old after a while," he said, but he smiled when he said it.

He was asked to compare this year's team with the Sidney Wicks-Curtis Rowe-Steve Patterson units he played with the last two seasons.

"Neither of those teams went undefeated," he said. "This one did."

It appeared, for a brief time in the

Please Turn to Page 13, Col. 1

# L.A. GOES WILD! LAKERS WORLD CHAMPS

Los Angeles Times
Sports
BUSINESS & FINANCE
CC PART III 2¢
MONDAY, MAY 8, 1972

## Wilt Shrugs Off Injury, Leads 114-100 Win Over Knicks

BY MAL FLORENCE
Times Staff Writer

The deliriously happy crowd poured onto the court and hoisted Wilt Chamberlain to its shoulders, while Jerry West, laughing and, perhaps, crying a little, barely beat the mob to the dressing room.

The Forum organist played "Happy Days Are Here Again" and why not?

Finally, after 12 years of frustration, the Los Angeles Lakers attained the goal that has eluded them so many times in the past—champions of the National Basketball Assn.

They accomplished it with a withering, fourth-quarter assault Sunday night at the Forum, defeating the determined New York Knicks, 114-100, to win the playoff in five games.

Chamberlain, not expected to play because of a severely sprained right wrist, shrugged off the injury and was a dominating factor in the victory—the Lakers' first in eight appearances in the final series.

The 7-2 center was also voted the Most Valuable Player in the championship round and will get an automobile to add to his fleet.

Wilt got the green light to play after the swelling in his wrist subsided—an injury he suffered during Friday night's game in New York.

He performed with a football-type pad wrapped around his huge right hand.

"It's an unbelievable feeling . . . something I've always wanted to experience," said an elated West. "Now, I know what it feels like to be a champion."

The 33-year-old All-Pro all-time guard has received almost every honor imaginable in his career. But a championship was the thing he coveted the most.

Jerry is the only Laker who has been with the team since its inception in Los Angeles and he has been in seven previous championship series, only to taste defeat, sometimes in the fleeting seconds of the seventh game.

At a time like this, one has to wonder how Elgin Baylor feels. The great Laker forward retired at the outset of the season but as he said earlier, "I still am part of the team in spirit. If they win, I win."

The win capped an incredible season in which the club won a record 69 games while compiling a 33-game win streak—the longest in major league sports history.

And, the man who brought it all about is coach Bill Sharman, who has now won championships in three pro leagues—ABL, ABA and now NBA.

When Sharman accepted the job this year, he was advised by critics that the Lakers were too old and set in their ways to win a title. But Bill molded them together as a team

Please Turn to Page 8, Col. 4

THE BIG MAN—Wilt Chamberlain of Lakers, playing despite a sprained right wrist, and a bruised left hand, goes up to grab rebound Sunday night in title-clinching win over New York Knicks. Chamberlain scored 24 points and led in rebounds with 29.

FRUSTRATING SEASONS PAST

## West Finally Plays on an NBA Winner

BY DWIGHT CHAPIN
Times Staff Writer

*"I guess it just wasn't meant for me to be a member of a championship team. Maybe there'll be another year, another chance. I don't think so right now."—Jerry West, 1969, in his autobiography, "Mr. Clutch: The Jerry West Story."*

Jerry West was wrong. There was another chance.

It was a quiet moment amid the bedlam of a championship locker room.

Jerry West stood surrounded by reporters and dripping sweat, a man in a happy trance. A long arm reached over the crowd and grabbed his shoulder.

West turned and his eyes met those of Bill Russell. For an instant, there were no words. Between two old adversaries, a silent look was enough.

Six times West and the Lakers went against Russell and the Boston Celtics in the NBA finals. Six times, West and the Lakers lost.

"Congratulations," Bill Russell said, as West shared at last the triumph Russell had known so often.

West and Russell shook hands . . . once, twice.

"I know now how you felt all those times," West said.

Russell then prepared to return to his job as a TV commentator, but first he was asked how he felt for a longtime rival—a man who came so close so many times but never beat him.

"I'm just glad," Russell said, "to see this finally happen to him."

The microphones were in West's face now. Radio, television. The reporters surged around him. Notebooks, pens. His sons, David and Mike, joined him, standing shyly at his sides. He held a full bottle of champagne, open but as yet untouched.

### Trials of Defeat

And you couldn't help—in a time of victory—thinking back to all the trials of defeat.

The first three losses—1962, 1963 and 1965—were to the Celtics. He was a young player then, a skinny kid out of West Virginia—and defeat didn't hurt as much.

Then it began to tell.

1966—The Lakers lose to Boston in the seventh game, 95-93. Jerry West says: "I just felt cold when I was shooting. I really thought we were going to win this game. They were taking us much too lightly. But when you score 93 points you're not going to beat anybody. I said before the series that we'd have to shoot well to beat them. We did shoot well—every game but tonight."

1968—The Lakers lose to Boston in the sixth game, 124-109. Jerry West says: "I thought we gave them two games in this series but tonight they won easily. They were just really ready. Bill Russell back there doesn't allow you to get any layups. That hurt us and it's awfully hard to play catchup against them."

1969—The Lakers lose to Boston in the seventh game, 108-106. Jerry West says: "I just hate to sit here in this locker room and listen to all that noise over there in the other room. It's very difficult to try to appear happy because I'm not. We lost

Please Turn to Page 9, Col. 1

## THE CHAMPIONS!

NEW YORK

| | Min. | FG-A | FT-A | R | A | P | T |
|---|---|---|---|---|---|---|---|
| DeBusschere | 35 | 6-15 | 1-3 | 14 | 2 | 6 | 13 |
| Bradley | 35 | 4-16 | 4-4 | 1 | 2 | 3 | 12 |
| Lucas | 47 | 5-14 | 4-4 | 9 | 5 | 4 | 14 |
| Frazier | 47 | 14-24 | 3-6 | 7 | 10 | 3 | 31 |
| Meminger | 18 | 2-3 | 0-0 | 2 | 1 | 3 | 4 |
| Jackson | 24 | 4-6 | 2-2 | 3 | 1 | 3 | 10 |
| Monroe | 29 | 4-15 | 8-8 | 2 | 3 | 1 | 16 |
| Mast | 1 | 0-0 | 0-0 | 0 | 0 | 0 | 0 |
| Miles | 1 | 0-0 | 0-0 | 0 | 0 | 0 | 0 |
| Paulk | 1 | 0-0 | 0-0 | 0 | 0 | 1 | 0 |
| Rackley | 1 | 0-1 | 0-0 | 0 | 0 | 0 | 0 |
| Barnett | 1 | 0-0 | 0-0 | 1 | 1 | 0 | 0 |
| Team rebounds | | | | 8 | | | |
| Totals | 240 | 39-94 | 22-27 | 47 | 25 | 24 | 100 |

Shooting: Field goals, 41.5%; free throws, 81.5%

LOS ANGELES

| | Min. | FG-A | FT-A | R | A | P | T |
|---|---|---|---|---|---|---|---|
| Hairston | 42 | 4-8 | 5-5 | 14 | 3 | 2 | 13 |
| McMillian | 45 | 8-15 | 4-5 | 3 | 0 | 4 | 20 |
| Chamberlain | 47 | 10-14 | 4-9 | 29 | 4 | 2 | 24 |
| Goodrich | 38 | 6-18 | 13-14 | 4 | 3 | 4 | 25 |
| West | 42 | 10-28 | 3-5 | 5 | 9 | 3 | 23 |
| Ellis | 8 | 0-0 | 0-0 | 8 | 1 | 1 | 0 |
| Riley | 15 | 2-8 | 3-4 | 3 | 0 | 3 | 7 |
| Robinson | 1 | 0-1 | 0-0 | 0 | 0 | 0 | 0 |
| Trapp | 1 | 0-0 | 0-0 | 0 | 1 | 0 | 0 |
| Cleamons | 1 | 1-2 | 0-0 | 1 | 0 | 0 | 2 |
| Team rebounds | | | | 9 | | | |
| Totals | 240 | 41-94 | 32-42 | 76 | 21 | 19 | 114 |

Shooting: Field goals, 43.6%; free throws, 76.2%

SCORE BY QUARTERS

| | | | | |
|---|---|---|---|---|
| New York | 24 | 29 | 25 | 22—100 |
| Los Angeles | 26 | 27 | 30 | 31—114 |

Technical fouls—Holzman, Goodrich
Officials—Richie Powers & Jack Madden
Attendance—17,505

## Sutton's One-Hitter Wasted; Dodgers Lose in 13th, 1-0

BY RON RAPOPORT
Times Staff Writer

MONTREAL—Teetering on the edge of a sudden-death defeat for four tense innings Sunday, the Dodgers were finally pushed over the brink by an unearned run in the 13th as Montreal dealt them a 1-0 loss, their third straight.

A brilliant one-hit pitching performance over 10 innings by Don Sutton—"He can't pitch any better than that," said manager Walt Alston—went for naught when, with one out in the 13th, reliever Pete Richert couldn't handle a bases-loaded grounder to the right of the mound and the winning run scored on the error.

The Dodgers had escaped tight situations several times in the game—most notably in the 11th when Montreal loaded the bases but couldn't score—before they found themselves in one they couldn't get out of.

After they stranded two runners of their own in the top of the 13th to run their left-on-base total for the game to 13, Richert came in to pitch to the Expos and gave up a leadoff single to John Boccabella. It was Montreal's second hit of the game as Sutton had allowed only a seventh-inning single to Bob Bailey.

Ron Woods then bunted foul to Bill Buckner at first, but Ron Hunt singled up the middle, Boccabella taking second. A passed ball got by catcher Duke Sims and pinch-hitter Clyde Mashore was walked intentionally to load the bases.

Please Turn to Page 4, Col. 3

SLEIGHT OF HAND — Bill Bradley of Knicks looks one way and throws another as he slips pass to Walt Frazier (right) Sunday night at Forum.

Jim McMillian (5) of Lakers pressures Bradley as Pat Riley (12) looks on. Los Angeles won game, 114-100, to win National Basketball Assn. crown.
Times photos by Art Rogers

## Brewers' Sunday Punch KOs Angels

### Milwaukee Finds Winning Formula on Weekends, 5-2

BY DAVE DISTEL
Times Staff Writer

Dave Bristol smiled impishly as writers filed into his office in the basement of Anaheim Stadium and circled his desk.

"I figured I'd see you guys today," he dead-panned. "We always win on Sunday."

Milwaukee's fourth win of the season was a 5-2 decision over the Angels Sunday afternoon before 7,940 fans. Of those four, three have come on Sundays, the other on a Saturday.

The Brewers seemingly have come up with the ideal week, working on weekends and taking the other five days off.

But, the game is played daily, hence, the Brewers are tied for last in the American League East.

### Hitting Woes

Milwaukee's problem has been hitting. The Brewers' earned run average of 2.95 was not enough to compensate for a batting average of .159. Giving up less than three runs a game does not suffice if the hitters are scoring only 19 in their first 13 games.

Bristol, whose previous managerial assignment was in Cincinnati, is not accustomed to such mass offensive futility.

"I've tried to keep my cool," he said, "if I possibly could. I look at the records and I know they're better hitters than they've shown."

Sunday's key punches were thrown by Billy Conigliaro, the outfielder obtained in the 10-man, off-season trade with Boston. He hit a 2-run homer in the sixth inning, doubled and scored in the ninth.

Please Turn to Page 6, Col. 3

## Now Maybe My Fans Can Walk in Peace---Chamberlain

BY CHARLES MAHER
Times Staff Writer

Pat Riley started the celebration by popping open a bottle of champagne. He looked around for a head to pour it over and found one—his own.

Happy Hairston, apparently unaware of the kind of drinking the occasion called for, sat down and opened a can of Pepsi.

John Q. Trapp got out his Polaroid to take some pictures.

Coach Bill Sharman, who has been suffering from strained vocal chords for months, said: "I can holler, all right, but I still can't talk."

Dean Meminger of the Knicks came in and took a turn around the room, congratulating the Lakers.

That's how it was in the Los Angeles dressing room a minute or two after the Lakers had won their first NBA championship.

The place was crawling with people. Players, writers, radio and TV men, club officials. They were milling around, shaking hands, bumping into each other. A few availed themselves of the champagne being poured into long-stemmed glasses.

Then the big man came in. Wilt Chamberlain, named player of the series by Sport magazine, stood behind a counter in a corner normally occupied by trainer Frank O'Neill. Chamberlain had writers in front of him, beside him, behind him.

"For a long time," he said, "fans of mine had put up with people saying Wilt couldn't win the big ones. Now maybe they'll have a chance to walk in peace like I do.

"They've been with me a long, long while. These are people from all over the country. From Philadelphia (where Wilt played on a championship team five years ago) and San Francisco and L.A. All over."

The sweat was oozing out of Chamberlain. Also the satisfaction. He had sprained his right wrist Friday night in the fourth game of the series and there was doubt he'd even be able to play Sunday.

He played, all right. Twenty-four points. Twenty-nine rebounds. It was his game. He controlled it.

"There wasn't really enough pain in the hand to make that much difference," he said. "As of yesterday they didn't want me to play. But the swelling went down quite a bit in 24 hours.

"I really felt last night if I played I wouldn't be any particular help. I wanted to see Leroy Ellis in there.

"I used ice and the whirlpool at my house. I treated myself 30 hours or so—right up to game time. They left it up to me somewhat whether I'd play. I guess it was some time this afternoon I decided I could do it."

Dave DeBusschere of the Knicks came by to congratulate Chamberlain. "Thanks," Wilt said, extending his hand.

A writer asked if this was Wilt's most satisfying achievement.

"Right now . . can't think of any greater," Wilt said.

"Not even when you were with Philly and you beat the Celtics?"

"That Philadelphia team was picked to beat anybody," Wilt said. "At the start of this season, we weren't."

As the series MVP, Chamberlain will get a car from Sport magazine. He'll also get a winner's share, about $17,000.

"The money doesn't mean anything," he said. "I don't think it's that much money. (If you're making $200,000 or so a year, maybe it isn't.)

"I'd say it's more the personal price," Wilt added.

Please Turn to Page 9, Col. 4

**JIM MURRAY**

# Angry U.S. Sprinters Blame Coach for Disqualification

MUNICH—I have seen lots of guys lose gold medals—but never sitting in front of a TV set watching themselves do it.

I had just wandered over to the ABC bungalow hard by the gate of the Olympic Village. I was in search of another story when one of the saddest stories since they took Jim Thorpe's medals away erupted before these astonished eyes.

Eddie Hart, Reynaud Robinson and Robert Taylor are three 9.9 100-meter sprinters, but the Olympic Stadium was thousands of meters away as one of them pointed to a TV monitor on the wall showing the lineup of the first quarter-final heat in the 100 meters at the stadium. "Is that on tape or somethin'?" Reynaud Robinson asked in sudden panic.

It was live and in color. The missing spots in the lineups should have been filled by Reynaud Robinson and Eddie Hart.

They piled in a car for a breakneck dash to the stadium, past startled cops and scattering spectators.

They arrived only in time for Robert Taylor to pull off his sweat suit and dash to the starting blocks for his heat. He finished second. Reynaud Robinson and Eddie Hart finished last. They had been beaten by, probably, the only two sprinters who could have done it—Eddie Hart and Reynaud Robinson.

They were also eliminated by an overage, overweight non-competitor—their coach, Stan Wright. The boys had been given an incorrect time to appear for the quarter-finals.

They were driven back to the ABC hut where Wright, near tears,

### U.S. Officials' Excuse: 'We Followed Wrong Schedule'

Story on Page 6

fled to the Olympic Village with Hart, who was weeping. With announcer Howard Cosell in awkward pursuit, Wright flung only heartbroken answers over his shoulder as he disappeared into the Village—"It was my fault, my fault. I'll talk to you later."

Howard, whose best track years are well behind him, turned to the stunned Robinson. "Get my jacket. We're going on television to tell it like it is," he barked.

Robinson stood with his pals, the Olympic quarter-milers, John Smith and Wayne Collett of UCLA, and sprinter Chuck Smith of Occidental.

The stunned young man was handed a telephone. Someone had phoned his wife at home in Florida. "I can't believe it. I don't believe it. Can you believe this?" he murmured. Seconds later, he was on TV tape. His words were controlled. Yes, he was sure coach Wright felt badly. But, well, he was a veteran coach, wasn't he? "I thought he had himself together."

I caught up with him outside as he walked, head slumped, back to his quarters. There were no tears in his eyes now. This was not national TV, this was a reporter and two friends. This was the rich, private language of the ghetto. This was anger, cold and raging.

"I don't care, the man is a coach, he can say he's sorry. What about three years, what about torn ligaments, pulled muscles, a broken leg? What about all those bleep meets, all that bullsmoke in Tuskegee and Alabama State? Shee! This is the big one. This is what it's all about! And we sit there looking at pictures! We thought we had three hours. He told us 7 o'clock. We were going over to warm up. The man's a coach. He supposed to get his sprinters on the blocks. What else he got more important to do? A man who lives by the stopwatch. Two 9.9 sprinters out of the Olympics! Do you dig that? Do you, man? Dig on that for a minute!"

Behind him, on tape delay, Cosell was telling America of America's costliest elimination. "An American tragedy!" pronounced Howard in his best doomsday English. He turned to the athletes. "This young man will be scarred by this all his

Please Turn to Page 8, Col. 2

LOOKING AT A WINNER—Mark Spitz of Carmichael, Calif., won his fourth and fifth Olympic gold medals in swimming Thursday. After one race he gives 'V' for victory sign, left. Later, on victory stand, Spitz acknowledges cheers from the crowd and then covers face with hands.

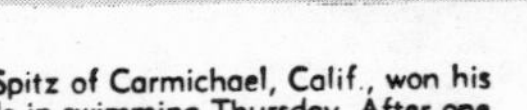

Wirephotos

# Spitz Makes It 5-for-5 With Two Races to Go

Los Angeles Times
Sports
BUSINESS & FINANCE
CC PART III 2†
FRIDAY, SEPTEMBER 1, 1972

### Swimmer Victorious in 100 Butterfly, Anchors Relay Rout

MUNICH (AP)—Mark Spitz, becoming the greatest swimmer in Olympic Games history, thrashed to his fourth and fifth gold medals Thursday night and has two more events still on his schedule.

The 22-year-old swimmer from Carmichael, Calif., churned to glory with a world record clocking of 54.27 seconds in the 100-meter butterfly and swam the anchor leg on the United States' victorious 800 meter freestyle relay team.

Spitz' log at the Munich Games has been incredible—five events, five gold medals, five world records.

"I swam with the three greatest Americans I have ever worked with in a relay," Spitz said.

**Spitz Starts 15 Meters Ahead**

His teammates in the 800 freestyle relay—John Kinsella of Oak Park, Ill., Fred Tyler of Winter Park, Fla. and Steve Genter of Lakewood, Calif.—gave Spitz a 15-meter lead and he completed the race in 7:35.78, bettering the world record of 7.43.3 held by the U.S.

Spitz' double-medal sweep highlighted a good day for the Americans. The U.S. freestyle wrestlers won 3 gold medals, 2 silvers and a bronze, and the California-based water polo team gained the final round with a 5-0 record after upsetting defending champion Yugoslavia, 5-3. No U.S. water polo team ever gained the finals without a defeat before.

In the two championship events of this opening day of track and field competition, Heide Rosendahl, a bespectacled, 25-year-old teacher, gave West Germany its first gold medal with a victory in the women's long jump to the chants of "Heidi, Heidi," and Peter Frenkel, 33, a decorator and designer from East Germany, won the 20-kilometer walk in an Eastern European sweep.

Dave Wottle kept America's gold medal hopes bright when his ailing knee held up under the pressure of the final 100 meters of his 800-meter trial.

Wottle qualified easily, using his blistering kick and showing that tendinitis in his left knee had eased. His second-place time was 1:47.6.

Dick Wohlhuter of the U.S. fell in the first 100 yards of his 800-meter heat, but got up and caught up with the field. He moved into what appeared to be a comfortable third-place position with 100 meters to go, but lost his chance to qualify when Tunisia's Mansour Guettaya came with a blistering finishing kick to finish second. Wohlhuter fell back to fourth.

**Russians Take Medal Lead**

Gail Neall of Australia won the women's 400-meter individual medley swimming race in the world record time of 5:02.91, with the U.S., failing to place.

With 56 championships decided—25 of them Thursday—the Soviet Union took over the medals lead with 34, including 14 golds. The United States, with 12 golds, 11 silvers and 8 bronzes for a total of 31, was second. East Germany remained third with 23 medals, 8 of them gold.

Bruce Robertson of Canada, (55.56) was second to Spitz in the 100-meter butterfly and Jerry Heidenreich, 22, of Dallas, (55.74) won the bronze for the U.S.

Please Turn to Page 5, Col. 1

# Osteen Beats Cubs for No. 15; Chisox Bid for Crawford

**BY ROSS NEWHAN**
Times Staff Writer

CHICAGO—Bidding to win 20 games for the second time in his career, Claude Osteen gained his 15th Thursday as the Dodgers beat the Cubs, 5-3.

The season's final month may mean more to Osteen than his team, which remains well behind Cincinnati in the National League West.

Nevertheless, the Dodgers might be the determining factor in two other circuits.

—In the American League West, the surprising White Sox are attempting to strengthen their outfield for the September showdown with Oakland through the acquisition of the Dodgers' Willie Crawford.

—In the Pacific Coast League, the Dodgers have recalled pitcher Doug Rau, depriving Albuquerque, which has already won the pennant, of its ace during the championship playoffs.

"The parent club comes first," said Dodger manager Walter Alston. "Our situation necessitated another arm."

The Dodgers play a doubleheader in St. Louis tonight and a doubleheader against Cincinnati in Los Angeles Monday night.

Besides the demanding schedule, two Dodger pitchers, Osteen and Tommy John, are nursing leg injuries that could eliminate them from the rotation if aggravated.

Please Turn to Page 8, Col. 6

**ONTARIO BREAKDOWN**

# 'Wait—and Win' Strategy May Pay Off in 500 Again

**BY SHAV GLICK**
Times Staff Writer

ONTARIO—The route to victory in the last two California 500s has been that taken by the tortoise. The hares have failed to finish.

This year is not likely to be different.

All 33 cars in Sunday's race are equipped with huge rear wings called air foils, that exert tremendous pressure on the rear wheels, keeping them glued to the track as they roar through corners at close to 200 m.p.h.

The foils add as much as 1,000 pounds of pressure to the normal weight of the car, making for speed and stability, but the stress is murder on engines and rear ends. Most drivers, particularly those in the Eagles and McLarens, don't let up on the throttle except for a brief flash as they enter Turns 1 and 3 at the end of long straightaways.

Thus the engines receive no "breathing" time, no rest from revolutions per minute that reach as high as 9,200.

Jim McElreath won the inaugural California 500 from 18th position, taking the checkered flag after Al Unser, Peter Revson and LeeRoy Yarbrough broke down while leading. McElreath didn't lead until the final turn when he passed Art Pollard.

"He was the only driver I passed all day," said McElreath in Victory Lane.

Last year Joe Leonard followed a similar route, coming from 11th to win after Mark Donohue ran out of fuel and Al Unser and A. J. Foyt broke down and Bobby Unser crashed. Leonard did not lead until the 161st lap of the 200-lap race. Pollard, another tortoise, was second again.

This year's 500 mile race at Indianapolis followed a similar pattern.

Although Donohue, the Indy winner, started third he used a smaller

Please Turn to Page 11, Col. 2

# MRS. COURT OPENS FOREST HILLS BID BY ROUTING FOE

FOREST HILLS, N.Y. (AP)—Margaret Court, on a comeback after a year's absence, displayed the devastating game that once made her the world's ranking women's player as she swept past Pat Pretorius, 6-0, 6-1, Thursday in the U.S. Open Tennis Championships.

"My service is better and my ground strokes are better," Mrs. Court, a lanky Australian, said, "I think I'm all the way back now."

She left little doubt among the crowd that swarmed into the sun-splashed West Side Tennis Club Stadium to watch her lightning triumph over South Africa's top-ranked woman.

The match was in the preliminary round, necessitated when the wom-

Please Turn to Page 11, Col. 1

# Olympic Pressure So Severe It Even Blots Out Memory

**BY DWIGHT CHAPIN**
Times Staff Writer

MUNICH—Pressure.

It's an ever-present factor at an Olympic Games, particularly for track and field athletes who have waited and waited and waited for the start of their competition this week.

"I've got to get out of here for a few days," said Steve Prefontaine, the distance runner from Oregon. "I'm really getting bugged. Got to get up in the mountains and relax."

Female distance runner Doris Brown of Seattle has been sick to her stomach most of the time in Munich. She doesn't know why.

**Foggy Memory**

Hurdler Patty Johnson of San Clemente, Calif., ran in the Olympic Stadium the other day—and admitted she had the shakes worse than Don Knotts. And this isn't her first Olympics. She was fourth at Mexico City in 1968.

"All I can remember of that race," Patty says, "is when I was in the 'set' position. Everything after that was a blur. But I guess that's good. If you actually said to yourself, 'Here I am in the Olympic Games,' you'd probably swoon on the spot."

Bill Toomey is a television commentator now but he was the Olympic gold medalist in the decathlon four years ago.

"The pressure was on from the moment I stepped off the plane in

Please Turn to Page 6, Col. 4

# PATTERSON: A SOLITARY MAN

**Floyd's still a 'hermit,' even training in chicken coop for upcoming fight with Ali**

**BY CHARLES MAHER**
Times Staff Writer

Floyd Patterson, a coming young heavyweight of 37, is training in a chicken coop back of his home in New Paultz, N.Y., a hundred miles north of New York City.

A chicken coop? Swell. Just what boxing needed. Another stink.

Actually, it's not as bad as it sounds. The chickens have moved out. Patterson's handlers were afraid one of them would walk across the ring during a sparring session and they'd have to stop it or account of a fowl.

What Floyd is training for is a Sept. 20 fight that could lead to smaller things. His opponent is Muhammad Ali.

The folks at Madison Square Garden would prefer that Patterson train at some less-secluded spot, so he'd be more accessible to the media. Floyd prefers privacy. Solitaire is his game It involves the ideal number of people.

"This has always been my way of training," he was saying on the phone the other day. "I tried the other way and it didn't work. In my own secluded gymnasium here, I can try different things and it doesn't matter if they're successful or not. If I'm out in the public, I won't try these things. If they don't work, it's embarrassing. And I can concentrate better with no one around. I'm more relaxed and all."

Patterson, a two-time heavyweight champion who last held the title a generation or so ago, has won nine straight fights. So they offered him a shot at Joe Frazier and he said no thanks. He'd rather have Ali, who, he says, is still Cassius Clay to him. ("His mother calls him Cassius Clay. When she starts calling him Muhammad Ali, I'll call him Muhammad Ali.")

"Why would you want Ali," Patterson was asked, "when you could fight the champion?"

"I've always wanted a return match with Clay," Floyd said. "It's not revenge or anything. I'd just like to fight him with a good back."

The first time they fought, in 1965, Floyd spent much of the evening in what looked like an arthritic crouch.

"I'd had back trouble since 1956," he said. "A guy who'd been a construction worker read a book on how to be a chiropractor and somebody in my camp hired him. He'd put me on a table and crack my back. One day he did it and I got a sharp pain. It bothered me several times when I was in training, including before

Please Turn to Page 10, Col. 6

NICE TRY—Some golfers will try anything to avoid taking penalty strokes. Cathy Yamamato of Los Angeles tries a chip shot out of a pond during Junior World golf tournament at San Diego. But after several swings she gave up, leaving the ball in the water.

Wirephoto

**SPRINT WINNER**—Valeriy Borzov of Russia raises his arms as he crosses finish line to win Olympic 100 meters in 10.14. Robert Taylor of Houston is second in 10.24 and Lennox Miller of Jamaica, a former Trojan, is third in 10.33. It was Russia's first Olympic sprint win. (AP Wirephoto)

# Borzov Wins 100, Says He's Fastest

## Russian Clocks 10.1; Taylor of U.S. 2nd in 10.2

Los Angeles Times
Sports
BUSINESS & FINANCE
CC PART III 2¢
SATURDAY, SEPTEMBER 2, 1972

BY DWIGHT CHAPIN
Times Staff Writer

MUNICH—Is Valeriy Borzov of the Soviet Union really the world's fastest human?

He thinks so—and so do a lot of people who saw him win an easy victory in the 100 meters at the 20th Olympic Games on a dark, chilly day Friday.

But because of an incredible tragicomedy of errors that removed the two top U.S. sprinters from the competition, there is no way to tell.

In the interview room after his win, Borzov, a blond, 22-year-old student from Kiev, said (and had his words translated into about a hundred languages) he was sorry the Americans weren't present in full force but that he'd beaten U.S. runners the six times he's met them, anyway.

Then the man known in Russia as "The White Flash" added:

"At present, the American sprinters seem to have reached a point of stagnation, while the European sprinters are making good progress."

**Taylor Second**

Robert Taylor of Houston finished second in 10.2 to Borzov's 10.1. But the only American finalist didn't come to the interview room to discuss his performance or defend the potential of his countrymen. He sent word he was starving for lack of food all day and had to dine.

He paused in the dressing room tunnel, however, and said he got the best start of his career. "But the Russian got out there and I couldn't catch him."

Bronze medalist Lennox Miller of Jamaica might have had something to say on the subject of U.S. sprinters, but Miller, who went to USC and has competed with and against Americans for years, wasn't in the interview room, either. He was in the training room, being treated for a leg injury suffered at the end of the race.

So the only version offered was Borzov's. He is a strong, smooth sprinter and there was no doubt that when he tossed up his hands as he crossed the finish line he was clearly the best in the eight-man field.

But his top 100 time is 10 flat. Both Eddie Hart and Rey Robinson—the Vanishing Americans—have run 9.9, the world record. Robinson had been nursing a leg injury but it's possible Hart, a University of California star, could have beaten the Russian.

As it was, Borzov became the first Soviet runner to win an Olympic sprint gold medal and the first white man to win one since Armin Hary in 1960.

But the glamor just wasn't there.

It departed Thursday when Hart and Robinson failed to show for their quarter-finals and were disqualified.

The track world still was stunned

Please Turn to Page 5, Col. 3

**MEDAL WINNERS** — Robert Taylor and Kathy Schmidt won medals for the United States Friday. Taylor, shown giving black power salute, was second in 100-meter final, while Kathy, of Long Beach, won the bronze medal in the javelin throw. She is shown here during competition at Valencia, Calif. (AP Wirephotos)

IN BED 3 DAYS

## Long Beach Girl Sick, but Takes Third in Javelin

Exclusive to The Times from a Staff Writer

MUNICH—Kathy Schmidt should have been in bed Friday.

That's where she had spent three of the last five days, trying to shake a sore throat and cold.

But the Olympic Games transcend things like that.

So Kathy, a tall, 19-year-old brunette from Long Beach, got up, went to the Olympic Track Stadium and threw the javelin 196 feet, 8 inches to win a bronze medal behind two husky East Germans, Ruth Fuchs and Jacquelin Todten.

Almost everyone was surprised. But not Kathy. Nor was she impressed.

"I didn't expect to win," she said, "but I could have thrown farther.

**First Throw Best**

"I was pulling out on my throws and I wasn't coming back on the javelin enough. I probably did everything wrong you can do as far as technique goes".

Her best throw was her first. She held second place for a long time but things got tough toward the end of the competition. She sat down after one weak throw and put her head in her hands.

"I just did that for the television cameras," she said, smiling.

It was cold and windy but Kathy, who had a red, polka-dot bandana around her long hair in the interview room; said the weather did not bother her.

"Just my technique," she said.

The gold medalist, Mrs. Fuchs, was asked how training methods in East Germany—supposedly highly concentrated and regimented—compare with those in the United States.

"I have no way to compare," she answered, "unless I saw those in the United States."

But a BBC television commentator, after watching Kathy Schmidt throw, didn't hesitate to make the comparison.

"I'd really like to see her over in those East German training camps," he said. "What a tremendous prospect she is."

## DEMONT WINS ONLY GOLD IN SO-SO DAY FOR YANKS

### San Rafael Swimmer Sets 400-Meter Freestyle Mark; American Water Poloists Blow Big Lead, Get 4-4 Tie

MUNICH (UPI)—Rich DeMont of San Rafael, Calif., splashed to a Games record in the men's 400-meter swimming freestyle Friday brightening an otherwise so-so day for Americans at the Olympics.

DeMont's victory, in 4:00.26, came after:

—Russia's Valeriy Borzov ran off with the gold medal in the 100-meter dash—only the sixth time in Olympic history the United States has not won the race.

—Shane Gould, Australia's teenage swimming star, got her third victory and third world record—2:03.56—in the women's 200-meter freestyle.

—Japan's Mayumi Aoki won the women's 100-meter butterfly in the world-record time of 1:03.34 as three American girls finished fourth, fifth and sixth.

—Eastern European nations, led by Russia, won all the medals in two shooting finals.

—The United States water polo team blew a 4-1 lead and settled for a 4-4 tie with West Germany.

All the news wasn't bad, though. There were a few pluses for the American team, but not enough to keep Russia from increasing its lead in the race for medals. After six days of competition, Russia led with 19 golds and a total of 43 medals, with the United States second with 13 golds and a total of 38. East Germany was third with 10 and 27.

DeMont's victory gave the U.S. men their sixth gold medal in nine events, but it was the first by a male other than Mark Spitz.

Please Turn to Page 6, Col. 7

## 'When You're Hot . . . and I Am Hot,' Says Joe Leonard of 500

BY SHAV GLICK
Times Staff Writer

ONTARIO—The more times you walk through the garage area or along the pit wall at Ontario Motor Speedway, the more you hear the same talk.

Can Mario Andretti keep his car together and win the California 500? Can Jerry Grant go wire-to-wire for his first championship win? Can Bobby Unser get from 23rd to first without breaking his engine?

The questions swirl around every car as drivers prepare for Sunday's $670,000 California 500 on Ontario's 2½-mile course. But the name of Joe Leonard is seldom heard.

Leonard will be sitting quietly in the third row, behind the front row of Grant, Peter Revson and Gordon Johncock and the all-Indy 500 winner second row of Al Unser, Andretti and A. J. Foyt.

Leonard's credentials are overwhelming, yet he never seems to fit the favorite's role. He is:

1. Defending U.S. Auto Club national driving champion.

2. Defending California 500 winner.

3. Current leader for the 1972 driving championship with 3,040 points, nearly double that of his Viceroy Pack teammate, Al Unser, who has 1,620.

4. Winner of the last three USAC championship car races, the Michigan 200, Schaefer 500 at Pocono and the Milwaukee 200.

Still, most race followers think of

Please Turn to Page 6, Col. 3

## DODGERS, CARDS DIVIDE; ALSTON RAPS WILLIE D.

BY ROSS NEWHAN
Times Staff Writer

ST. LOUIS—After losing the opener of Friday night's doubleheader to the Cardinals, 5-1, the Dodgers won the second game, 2-1, behind Al Downing's 4-hitter.

Downing drove in the winning run and retired the last 16 Cardinals in order. It was his victory, his alone, and his manager, Walter Alston, refused to take even partial credit.

A man who generally locks only the doors to his house and hotel room, Alston locked the doors to the clubhouse between games and lectured with such ferocity that one veteran Dodger said, "I've never seen him as angry."

Indeed, uncharacteristically, Al

Please Turn to Page 7, Col. 6

## BALTIMORE ENDS ANGEL STREAK, 3-2

BY RON RAPOPORT
Times Staff Writer

Until the seventh inning of Baltimore's 3-2 victory over the Angels at Anaheim Stadium Friday night, Oriole pitcher Dave McNally had allowed one hit and two baserunners but was nevertheless trailing by a run.

It came as no surprise to McNally.

"Maybe I've seen it so much it doesn't bother me any more," said McNally after the game,

What he's seen is loss after loss in which he pitched well but simply didn't get enough runs. For the first time in 5 seasons, in fact, he will not win 20 games even though his earned-run average is presently better than it's been the last 4 seasons.

McNally (13-13) had lost his last 3 starts before breaking the Angels' 5-

Please Turn to Page 6, Col. 6

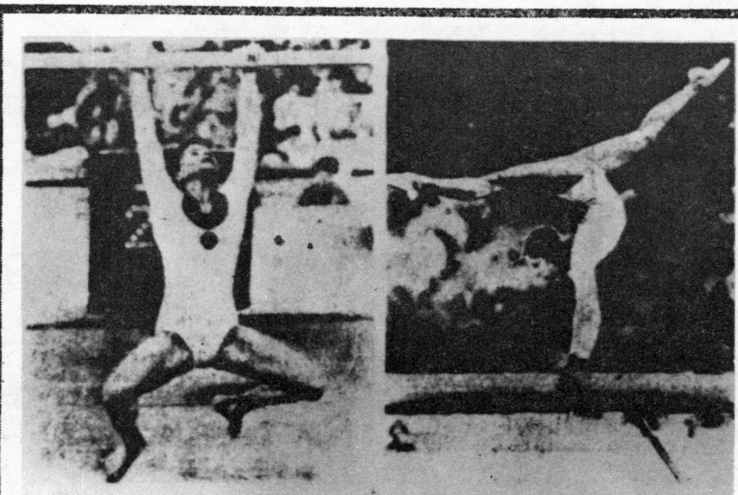

**UPS AND DOWNS**—Olga Korbut, 17, of Russia is the darling of Olympic gymnastics. But she had a bad moment, left, when she slipped. At right, she shows form which won her a gold medal. (AP Wirephotos)

## Gymnastics Set Flips Over the Olga Show

### *'Unknown' Russian girl flabbergasts experts with her daring, verve in winning three medals*

A tiny Russian doll with an impish smile, saucy style and astonishing daring is the new darling of the international gymnastics set.

Olga Korbut, 17, 4-11 and a wispy 84 pounds, won two gold medals and a silver at the Munich Olympic Games, stealing the spotlight from a bevy of taller and more conventionally graceful performers.

The Olga Korbut Show began early in the week when, in the uneven parallel bars event, she whirled to the top of the high bar, stood erect, then did a soaring back flip. She caught the bar on the way down then, after another blur of stunts, made a stunning dismount leap.

Some experts said they'd never seen anything like it. The act brought down the house.

Those were the heights. Before long, Olga knew the depths. In the all-around competition, same event, she scuffed her feet as she mounted the low bar, missed again while performing on the high bar, and her act came to a dangling, pathetic halt. She missed a simple "kip" that was needed to get started anew. Finally, she finished almost mechanically and went sobbing to her seat.

But by Thursday night she had rallied her confidence—with stunning effect. In the uneven bars she was a marvel again, moving in a distinctive fast, gee - I'm - having - fun style. And when she was judged to have enough points only to tie for a silver medal, the crowd howled and whistled for minutes, so loudly that the competition came to a halt.

Miss Korbut sat solemnly as the pretty, perfectly poised, picture-book-graceful Karin Janz of East Germany took the gold.

But the judges as well as the crowd were with her as she won the

Please Turn to Page 5, Col. 1

**GOLDEN GIRL**—Olga Korbut proudly displays gold medal she won in the Olympics. (AP Wirephoto)

Los Angeles Times
Sports
BUSINESS & FINANCE
CC PART III 3†
TUESDAY, SEPTEMBER 5, 1972

WORLD'S NO. 1 SPORTS HERO

# Spitz Wins 7th Gold Medal, Quits

MUNICH (AP) — Mark Spitz, the swimming dentist-to-be, may jump out of the Olympic tank to the richest job since Johnny Weissmuller pulled on a loincloth as Tarzan of the movies.

The bicuspids may have to wait.

Spitz sped to a record seventh gold medal Monday with a dazzling butterfly leg as the United States cracked a world record in the 400-meter medley relay. It was a great day all-around for the U.S. team.

Karen Moe of Santa Clara, Calif., led a United States sweep of the women's 200-meter butterfly in world record time. Melissa Belote of Washington, D.C., won her second Olympic individual gold medal with a world record in the women's 200-meter backstroke. And Mike Burton of Sacramento, cracked the world mark of Rick DeMont of San Rafael, Calif., in winning a gold in the 1,500 freestyle after DeMont, the favorite, was barred on medical grounds.

But it was Spitz' day. No competitor in any event has won more than five golds at an Olympics. Spitz' feat was enhanced by virtue of the world records that fell with each of his wins.

The 22-year-old from Carmichael, Calif., a dental student at Indiana University, said after his last race that he was through competitively.

"All the way down that last lap I kept saying, 'just a few more strokes and it will be over,'" he said. "I couldn't wait to get out of the pool."

The future? "I may postpone the completion of my education a little bit. I got an awful lot of letters and telegrams during the competition and there were some suggestions of things. I just may want to find out whether there are things I can do as well as swimming."

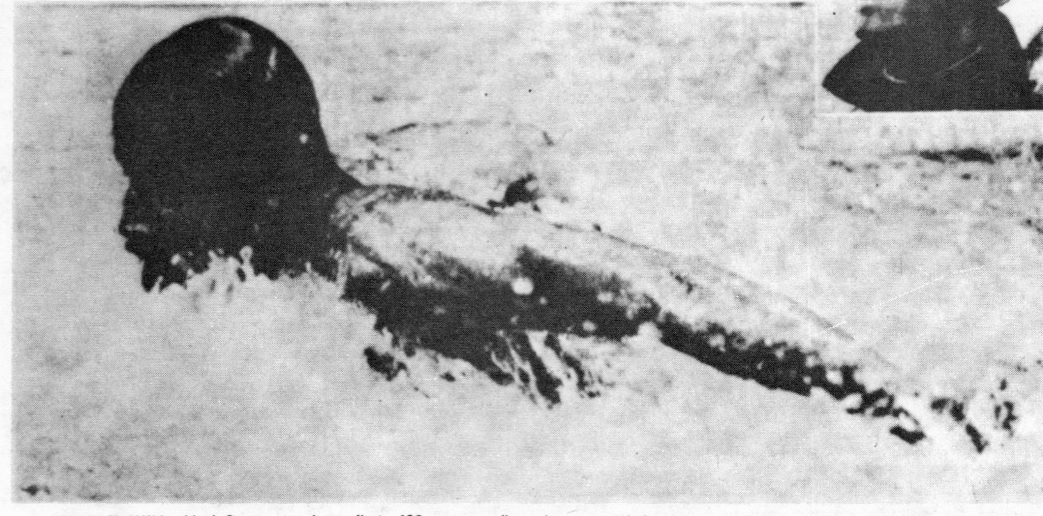

AN EASY WIN—Mark Spitz swims butterfly in 400-meter medley relay victory, helping set record and winning his seventh gold medal.
AP Wirephoto

Two West German sporting goods manufacturers reportedly have their vault doors open and an invitation for the California manfish to come in and shop around.

"God loves a winner," says Arnold Spitz, his father.

A week ago, millions of words flowed from Munich regarding Spitz's medal hopes, centering mainly on his individual failure at the Mexico City Olympics of 1968. Mark had predicted he would win five, maybe six gold medals. He managed only two golds as a member of the winning U.S. teams in the 400-meter freestyle relay and the 800-meter freestyle relay.

Mark now wants to change places with nobody in the world. If such a switch were possible, he'd like to be "a man that looks like Mark Spitz and can swim as well as Mark Spitz."

A triumph in his final event was important to the kid who looks like a watery Omar Sharif. He said before the event:

"I have a feeling I can beat all the others, but, on the other hand, I feel I have enough medals already. Naturally, when I can do it, I will take the other medals, too. My competitive sports life ended Monday night and I want to stop at the high point."

With such striking looks, does Hollywood enter his mind for the fu-

Please Turn to Page 5, Col. 1

## JIM MURRAY

# High-Rise Robbery

MUNICH—It wasn't a victory, it was a heist.

The gold medal the East Germans won in pole vaulting should at least be wearing a mask and a black hat.

My hustling Uncle Ed, who used to boil dice for a living, always told me, "Never play the other man's game."

Bob Seagren should have been listening. Ed also said, "Never get in a card game with a guy on a train and be sure you shower with your wallet in your hand in a strange rooming house."

Seagren now knows what it's like to be standing on a corner with a bill of sale for the Brooklyn Bridge you just bought from a guy whose suit made your eyes hurt.

He knows what it's like to sit in on a hand, lay down four 5s, reach for the pot and have the dealer say, "I'm sorry I forgot to tell you 5s are no good in this game," and you ask, "What is good?" and he starts to turn his cards over and says, "Just a minute, I'll tell you."

★

He knows what it is to get in a game where the other guy pulls out a deck from his breast pocket and says, "Let's play with these," and you suddenly know for the next hour you're going to be looking at handfuls of treys and busted straights.

He knows what it is to get in a fight and suddenly realize the guy holding your coat is the brother of the guy you're fighting. You know you're going to have this ringing in your ears before the cops break it up.

He knows what it's like to fade the shooter and suddenly notice what long sleeves he has and realize you're going to be looking at a tableful of boxcars all night long because you're going to get the pair he shakes out of his cuffs.

The Olympic pole vault, it says here, was won by the East Germans and a guy named Wolfgang Nordwig. Well, that's half-right. It was won by the East Germans, all right. They slipped Seagren a pinochle deck at the last minute.

First, you have to understand that East Germany is a nation of 17 million stiff-necked socialists. Which is OK. A man's religion is his own business. Personally, I'd rather be a king — but who's going to argue with a bayonet?

★

Anyway, the East Germans pour almost a billion marks a year into their sports program. They comb the country for world class athletes and they even prowl the cribs and perambulators. They have 20 special schools where they stash promising young athletes.

Wolfgang Nordwig is a product of this intense training program. Kind of too bad because maybe he could have been Wolfgang Mozart if left to his own.

Anyway, the East Germans had high hopes for Wolfgang in this year's pole vault until, suddenly, they heard the shocking news that three American pole vaulters went over 18 feet and Seagren went over at 18 feet, 5 3/4 inches. Every Hans and Fritz in Leipzig knew something would have to be done or all that loot would have been wasted.

The East Germans went to the International Amateur Athletic Federation, a collection of septuagenarians who promptly outlawed the new pole Seagren had been using. They didn't specify the sport go back to wrapped bamboo or fresh-cut saplings but they just said, "Whatever you were using at Eugene, don't." And then went back to nodding over their domino boards.

Now, you have to understand the Olympic and international athletic rules say you can pole vault with anything that isn't ticking or trailing smoke. The pole is the only

Please Turn to Page 8, Col. 4

# DODGERS MAKE 7 ERRORS TO GIVE REDS NIGHTCAP

## Mota's Double in Ninth Inning Decides Opener, 6-5; Defensive Lapses Allow Cincinnati to Gain Split, 8-4

BY ROSS NEWHAN
Times Staff Writer

The Dodgers demonstrated Monday night that they cannot catch Cincinnati when they cannot catch the ball.

And in the second game of the holiday doubleheader, after defeating the Reds, 6-5, in the opener, the Dodgers caught only a continuous chorus of boos from many of the 40,366 fans at Dodger Stadium.

The home team made 7 errors, more than in any game since the move from Brooklyn, and was routed by the Reds, 8-4.

Tht return of the midsummer fielding lapses erased the momentum of a 4-game winning streak and the modest hope generated by the win in the first game.

Cincinnati emerged with the 11-game lead over the Dodgers that it had taken into the doubleheader, but now Los Angeles has only 26 games left.

And the Dodgers are burdened with a record that characterizes the summer of defensive misfortune.

The previous mark was 5 errors, accomplished several times, including once this year in a game against Cincinnati.

In establishing the new record, Bobby Valentine and Russell each made 2 errors while Bill Grabarkewitz, Chris Cannizzaro and Steve Garvey each erred once.

Only 2 of Cincinnati's runs were unearned, but the rhythm of starter Claude Osteen was disrupted.

Osteen had won 4 of his last 5 decisions, but he was chased in the fifth and the Reds went on to collect 12 hits in support of Don Gullett and Pedro Borbon.

A 2-run homer by Frank Robinson in the eighth was too little too late.

Of the errors, 4 were made by third basemen, although Grabby made his at second after opening the game at third, an honor he was accorded following a pinch-hit homer in the opener.

An injury suffered by Lee Lacy sent Grabarkewitz to second in the second inning and brought on Garvey, who promptly tripled, errored and left the game with a migraine headache.

That brought back Valentine, who had gone hitless in the opener, making it easier for manager Walter Alston to start Grabarkewitz.

Grabby responded with 3 singles, enjoying his biggest night of a season in which he has been seen infrequently since being removed from the lineup in mid-April because of a slow start.

His first-game homer, in fact, was

Please Turn to Page 7, Col. 3

# CANADIANS EVEN RUSSIAN SERIES WITH 4-1 VICTORY

TORONTO (AP) — Team Canada scored three goals in the third period, including one by Peter Mahovlich with the team playing shorthanded, to defeat Russia, 4-1, Monday night and even their eight-game hockey series at one triumph apiece.

Phil Esposito, Yvan Cournoyer and Frank Mahovlich scored the other Canadian goals, while Russia's Alexandre Yakushev broke goalie Tony Esposito's shutout bid in the third period.

Unlike their first meeting Saturday, when the Russians won, 7-3, the Canadians controlled the tempo of the game and closely checked their opponents.

Canadian coach Harry Sinden said prior to the contest that his players

Please Turn to Page 2, Col. 1

# U.S. TRACK TEAM STILL UPSET BY TIME SNAFU

## Wright Apparently Misread Clock When Two Sprinters Failed to Show for Race

BY DWIGHT CHAPIN
Times Staff Writer

MUNICH — The 20th Olympic Games are 10 days old, track has been going on for 5 and the United States still has just one gold medal in that sport.

Maybe that's not too surprising, since many of the Americans' best events come in the final four days of competition starting Wednesday.

But Larry Black, who finished second to Valeriy Borzov of Russia Monday in the 200 meters, said "The whole U.S. team has been greatly affected because our sprinters didn't make it in the 100 meters."

**U.S. Mail Sympathetic**

Two American co-holders of the 100-meter record of 9.9 seconds, Eddie Hart and Rey Robinson, were to compete in the second round of the event last Thursday.

But Stan Wright, the U.S. assistant coach in charge of sprinters, apparently misread the time, they showed up at the stadium too late and were scratched.

"It's hard to look either Rey or Eddie straight in the face now," Black said Monday.

The mailman has been stopping a lot at Wright's door the last few days.

By Monday morning he had received 55 telegrams and 30 letters from the U.S.—and nearly all the writers said they were sorry—for him.

**Scheduled for 4:15 P.M.**

Wright's monumental blunder guaranteed him a place in history alongside such people as Roy Riegels, who ran the wrong way in the Rose Bowl, and Fred Merkle, who failed to touch second base and lost his team a pennant.

The 100-meter second round was to begin at 4:15 p.m., Munich time, last Thursday. Wright's year-old schedule showed the event at 16:15, and on the 24-hour clocks used in Europe that is 4:15 p.m. But Wright apparently took the figures to mean 6:15.

So, while he and his sprinters watched on television what they thought were earlier heats, they

Please Turn to Page 5, Col. 4

Valeriy Borzov

# Borzov No Fluke! Speeds to 200 Win

## Kip Keino Breaks Record in 3,000-Meter Steeplechase

Exclusive to The Times from a Staff Writer

MUNICH—Valeriy Borzov of the Soviet Union didn't show up at the interview room after winning his second gold medal in the sprints at the Olympics Monday.

The interpreters explained that Borzov hadn't liked a question a reporter asked him after he won the 100 meters Friday.

So, after he sped to a 20 flat win in the 200 meters, he fled to his room in the Olympic village.

But Larry Black, 21, of Miami, who finished second to Borzov in 20.2, talked enough for both men. He was a surly loser.

"When I first heard of Borzov," said Black, "he said all Americans have big mouths. Well, I'm not coming down on him; I respect him. But he's like a clown to me."

Black made reference to Borzov looking over his shoulder, almost haughtily, in a couple of heat races, to see how far the pack was behind him.

"The day will come when he'll look

Please Turn to Page 2, Col. 4

# Ryan Streak Ends, but Angels Divide

## California Edges A's, 2-1, After Wright 10-5 Loser

BY RON RAPOPORT
Times Staff Writer

OAKLAND — Reggie Jackson swung and sent a fly ball medium deep to left field in the first inning. It was far from the most glorious moment of the Athletic slugger's career, but it served to put out of their misery Don Drysdale, Jim McGlothlin and the ghost of Walter Johnson.

For after the catch, Bert Campaneris dashed in from third base to score the run that broke Nolan Ryan's consecutive scoreless inning streak at 34 and ended his bid for a fourth straight shutout.

Thus, Drysdale's major league record is safe at 58 2/3 innings and so is Johnson's American League mark of 56. And on a smaller plane, Ryan will have to start all over again to get to McGlothlin's Angel record of 36, or to break his three straight shutout mark.

What Ryan did achieve, however, was his 16th victory of the season as he held Oakland scoreless the rest of the way for a 2-1 triumph and a split of the Labor Day doubleheader. The A's routed Clyde Wright in the opener and won, 10-5.

Please Turn to Page 6, Col. 4

# Goolagong Bows to Teeguarden in Upset Wave at Forest Hills

FOREST HILLS, N.Y. (AP)—Slender Pam Teeguarden, a Los Angeles longshot, defeated Australia's Evonne Goolagong, 7-5, 6-1, in the most stunning of a wave of upsets Monday in the third round of the U.S. Open Tennis Championships.

"I've dreamed of this day for a long, long time. I'm glad it finally came," the 21-year-old Miss Teeguarden said after the biggest victory of her career. She'd never before gone beyond the round of 16 at the West Side Tennis Club and was unseeded in this tournament.

The early-round defeat for Miss Goolagong, in her first visit to Forest Hills, ended an amazing string of international successes for the 21-year-old daughter of a shepherd in New South Wales.

Miss Goolagong emerged from the Australian outback two years ago and vaulted into world fame with her 1971 Wimbledon victory. She was a beaten finalist in this year's Australian, French and Wimbledon championships.

"I guess I just got a bit careless," said the bitterly disappointed Evonne, who was the No. 2 seed in the women's ranks.

"Pam played very well," she said. "She didn't let me do anything that I wanted to do. When I got behind I thought I could come back, but she wouldn't let me do it."

(Miss Teeguarden is the daughter of tennis professional Jerry Teeguarden of Cheviot Hills Tennis Center in Los Angeles. In addition to having coached his daughter, he also coached Margaret Court of Australia.)

Three of the men's seeds, No. 5 John Newcombe of Australia, No. 7 Tom Okker of the Netherlands and No. 10 Manuel Orantes of Spain, also were upset victims in the bright, warm sunshine. All were beaten by unseeded players.

Newcombe, the 1971 Wimbledon King, lost to fellow Australian Fred Stolle, 7-6, 6-4, 5-7, 7-6, with the rangy Stolle taking the tie-breakers, 5-1 and 5-3.

Roscoe Tanner, a 20-year-old Stanford senior from Lookout Mountain, Tenn., scored 21 aces on a devastating service in his 6-4, 3-6, 7-5, 6-3 victory over Okker, a veteran international player.

"Easily the biggest win of my life,"

Please Turn to Page 3, Col. 1

# Football's Fun at Bears' Mod Training 'Camp'

BY JEFF PRUGH
Times Staff Writer

SANTA BARBARA—Everything about the California football team is new. The head coach. The uniforms. The training rules. The team morale. And the pre-season camp.

Actually, it's not a camp, it's a resort. The Golden Bears have been headquartered at a UC Santa Barbara coed dormitory (sans coeds) called the Tropicana Gardens, complete with swimming pool, sub-tropical foliage, billiards lounge featuring piped-in rock music and handmade signs that read "OUT-HIT COLORADO" (that's the Bears' first opponent Saturday at Boulder) . . . "POISE" . . . "CONCENTRATION" . . . "FULL SPEED."

There is no curfew, thanks to a curfew committee of players who decided that bed-checks were passe. Grooming regulations are recommended by a "dress and appearance committee," also composed of players, who favor long hair and leather jackets and ties.

The architect of Cal's renaissance is the new head coach, Mike White, 36, an intense, dynamic tactician who last January found himself with an attractive vocational choice. He was simultaneously offered the head coaching jobs at Stanford, where he assisted John Ralston for seven years, and at Cal, where he competed in four sports and later coached the frosh and served as varsity end coach.

He chose his alma mater, he said, because of athletic director Dave Maggard, 32, whose fresh, imaginative approach toward relating to athletes coincides with White's.

"I'm a goal-oriented guy," said White, explaining his training camp rules. "I believe in achievement through personal analysis, encouraging each player to know himself and reach his potential. I saw things at Stanford that worked and, frankly, things that did not work. I saw coaches mishandle players and not allow them to reach their potential. I saw players come under all sorts of coaches. I merely evaluated how a coach could—and could not—communicate to his players."

White's philosophy differs from the iron-fisted rule of a Woody Hayes or a Bear Bryant. He says it is a byproduct of a changing society.

"I believe in team involvement—I saw it work, to a great degree, at Stanford," says White, who was offensive coordinator of the Don Bunce-led Rose Bowl champs. "You start off by communicating with as many players as possible to break down barriers. Kids nowadays need reasons for everything. We feel we're creating a receptive atmos-

Please Turn to Page 8, Col. 6

Los Angeles Times
**Sports**
BUSINESS & FINANCE
CC PART III 2†
THURSDAY, SEPTEMBER 7, 1972

*'I'll run but I don't feel like running . . . I thought Olympics were . . . something important . . . What's important after this?'*

**Ken Moore, U.S. marathon runner**

*When the early morning knock on the door came 'I knew what was happening . . . I have lived with that sort of thing. I ran.'*

**Shaul Ladany, Israeli distance walker**

# Olympic Reaction: Life Must Go On---but Fun Is Gone

*BY DWIGHT CHAPIN, Times Staff Writer*

MUNICH—"The Olympic Village is no longer a city of refuge," said U.S. marathon man Ken Moore. "I don't know that there are any left.

"It wasn't fun here even before the killings. People everywhere, swarms of them. I'm used to running 30 miles and seeing only two deer and a bobcat. Right now, all I want to do is see them again.

"I'll run but I don't feel like running. Until now, I think almost everyone felt the Olympics were a symbol of something so important.

"Now this insanity. What's important after this?"

★

Wednesday morning, after a memorial service at the track stadium for the Israelis killed by Arab guerrillas, things were almost back to normal in the village.

There was still tight security around the athletes quarters, particularly Building 31, where the Israelis had been.

Germans stood guard with guns on their hips, clubs in their hands and armored trucks near by . . . and alongside them were flowers, scores of flowers, put there by the people of the world.

Israel had never won an Olympic medal. The chances they would have this year were long, but it was enough to be here, to compete, to enjoy.

And then came the guns of morning.

Now there's a sign written on the cobblestone path from the Israeli quarters to the track stadium. It is a circle, with an "X" drawn inside. And there's one word written across the "X": MURDER.

★

"It's my opinion," said George Frenn, the American hammer thrower, "that what happened yesterday will mean the dissolu-

Please Turn to Page 9, Col. 1

MUNICH—When the knock on the door came, Shaul Ladany didn't have to be told who was there.

There had been another morning knock on the door of his home in Hungary when he was a boy of 8. That was 28 years ago and he and his family were taken to a Nazi prison camp, Bergen-Belsen.

This time, when the knock came Ladany, an Israeli walker, reacted instinctively.

"I have lived with that sort of thing," he said. "I knew what was happening. I ran."

Eleven Israeli coaches and athletes died Tuesday in the Arab attack on the Olympic Village and in the hours that followed it.

Ladany, because he had experienced terror, is now cloistered somewhere in the village.

He said he had seemed to sense that something might happen several days before it did. He read of Arab guerrilla activity in downtown Munich and he told Steve Hayden, an American race walker, how upset he was that German officials weren't dealing with the situation more firmly.

At the same time, he talked about his youth and about why he didn't visit Dachau, just 10 miles from Munich, with other members of the Israeli team.

"I didn't want to go," he said. "I didn't want to raise memories."

There were 100,000 people in Bergen-Belsen. Ladany is one of 2,000 who got out, ransomed through money deposited by American Jews in a Swiss bank.

Ladany, world record holder in the 50-mile walk, is often asked how he can speak German so well.

"I answer arrogantly — arrogantly and proudly," he said, "that I learned it in Bergen-Belsen. Arrogantly because of what

Please Turn to Page 9, Col. 1

## JIM MURRAY

# Blood on Olympus

MUNICH — "Seventeen dead, three wounded" is hardly an Olympics statistic. This was supposed to be a track meet, not a war.

Incredibly, they're going on with it. It's almost like having a dance at Dachau.

How can they have a decathlon around the bloodstains, run the 1,500 over graves?

There is a wreath at Building 31 in the Olympic Village right under the bullet hole. But there will be ribbons on the playing field and the bands are playing.

How do you put a funeral service on the sports page? Is an autopsy a field event? Is Beethoven a fight song?

Hardboiled? No. Bitter, perhaps. Incredulous. Cynical. Shouldn't the Olympics have a wreath placed on its chest? Why does the high jump have to go on? Do we need a guy riding a horse in a high hat? Can't we just let poppies grow on this Olympics? Shouldn't things be All Quiet On The Western Front?

The Games should not be covered from the press box but from the war room. By communique, not communication.

★

**The most important** memento of this Olympiad, joining the succession of Jim Thorpe's shoes, Cornelius Warmerdam's pole, or Rafer Johnson's javelin is an Arab guerrilla's machine gun.

The Olympic Stadium at Munich with its soaring center-poles reaching for the sky like railroad cannon, or its central tower jutting heavenward like a launch pad for heaven, will never match a bullet-scarred billet or airfield for Olympic symbolism. An automatic should go to Helms Hall before Mark Spitz's trunks. Seven gold medals pale before 17 corpses.

The German communique from the airfield at Furstenfeldbruck should have read: "Heavy casualties were inflicted on the enemy. One of our Olympic teams is missing."

It remains to be seen whether the Olympics have been turned into rubble, whether the closing ceremonies were really at 4:50 in the morning on the 5th of September or whether indeed, the memorial ceremony in the Olympic Stadium on September 6 was really for the Games themselves.

★

**The Germans never seem** to be able to run the country efficiently without the generals, and the firing at Furstenfeldbruck could scarcely have been more disastrous. A group of us managed to break into the Village Tuesday morning after a lively game of "Hogan's Heroes" at three gates. We saw a tableau where armed Germans managed to walk around the sealed-off compound in the sweatsuits of a hundred track athletes and were impressed at the restraint, discipline and even bravery of the secret police. It is not a German tradition to hold fire, but if a fire fight had broken out in the village, they might be burying the dead in 20 languages.

No one thought, as this Olympics opened, that Terror would be in Lane 1. It is evident that, as the United States and other nations convened for their qualification meets, so did the Arabs' Black September squad. Not even the East Germans were better prepared.

We stood outside Building 31, a shrine of Olympian brotherhood, Wednesday. It was heavily guarded by blue-suited security police. There was nothing to guard but bloodstains and bullet holes, but orders are orders.

Outside, a lively little man from Hong Kong, a small bore (prone) rifle shooter from that Chinese outpost, whose team was quartered on the second and third floors of Building 31, above the first-floor Israelis,

Please Turn to Page 10, Col. 1

OVER THE TOP — Billie Jean King, returning a volley, moved into the semifinals of the U.S. Open tennis tournament at Forest Hills, N.Y., Wednesday, beating Virginia Wade of Britain, 6-2, 7-5. UPI Wirephoto

# Evert Pulls Out Match After Near-Defeat by Russian Girl

**BY JEFF PRUGH**
Times Staff Writer

FOREST HILLS, N.Y.—All afternoon long it was the pony-tailed American against the pig-tailed Russian.

And when it was over Chris Evert, the Princess Charming of tennis, breathed a deep sigh of relief and said: "I didn't think I could win."

In a stirring quarter-final match Wednesday against Russia's net-attacking Olga Morozova, the teenager from Ft. Lauderdale, Fla., came breathtakingly close to becoming another victim in the U.S. Open's wave of upsets that has felled such stars as Rod Laver, Ken Rosewall, John Newcombe and Evonne Goolagong.

Miss Evert stormed back from a 6-5 deficit in the final set by brilliantly breaking service at love, then won a tense tie-breaker to pull it out, 3-6, 6-3, 7-6.

"I don't think I've ever won after coming this close to losing," she said. "When she had me at 6-5 on her serve, that really scared me! But that's when you've gotta take chances, to start putting shots away."

That's exactly what she did by ripping off two doublefisted backhands—a passing shot and a service return. Then she got Miss Morozova to err on a forehand, and finally she came back with a marvelously placed lob into the corner to send the match into overtime.

The crowd of 8,972 roared louder than it had during any of the other matches on a day when Billie Jean King and Margaret Court also battled into the semifinals (they will meet Friday), as did Australia's Kerry Melville, who foiled the Cinderella dream of Los Angeles' Pam Teeguarden, 6-0, 6-2. Miss Teeguarden upset Miss Goolagong three days ago.

In men's singles, the remaining quarter-final berths were filled

Pleae Turn to Page 2, Col. 4

## TEXAS HANDYMAN

# Rams' Bertelsen Complete Player

**BY MAL FLORENCE**
Times Staff Writer

It was a routine power play designed for a maximum 4 or 5 yards. Nothing fancy. Hardly exciting.

But the runner, Jim Bertelsen, made something of it. He cut back quickly after clearing the hole, faked two Charger defenders with a stutter step and gained 27 yards.

"That's the most yardage we've ever gotten out of that play," said veteran guard Joe Scibelli, one of the blockers who created the opening Saturday night in San Diego.

For those who attach significance to exhibition games this hasn't been a memorable summer for the Rams. They've won but once in five outings and have been beset by nagging injuries.

Yet, at some future point, 1972 may be recalled as the year Jim Bertelsen came aboard.

The rookie from Texas demonstrated a touch of class on his first pro touchdown last month when he smashed through two Dallas linebackers on a 5-yard sweep.

Since then, he's been the primary running threat in the absence of injured veterans Willie Ellison, Les Josephson and Larry Smith. He's the leading rusher with 35 attempts for 159 yards and a 4.1 average. He also performs on all but one special team.

Bertelsen is a compact 5-11 and 200

Please Turn to Page 6, Col. 4

# Grabarkewitz Hits Homer, but Dodgers Bow to Cincy, 6-3

**BY ROSS NEWHAN**
Times Staff Writer

It was in 1970 that Bill Grabarkewitz, emerging from anonymity, was nicknamed Billy Who?

That sobriquet may still apply, for only in the last few days has Grabarkewitz escaped from the bench to conduct a refresher course in the spelling of his name.

Grabby hit a 3-run homer Wednesday night at Dodger Stadium, but it was his team's first and last hurrah as Cincinnati defeated Los Angeles, 6-3, before 16,965.

Wayne Simpson scattered 7 hits before Clay Carroll came out of the bullpen to gain his 26th save, retiring Steve Yeager and Jim Lefebvre with 2 on in the ninth.

**Wants Regular Job**

A persistent, 10-hit Cincinnati attack, led by Pete Rose, who had 3 singles, driving in one run and scoring 2, produced Al Downing's 7th loss in 15 decisions.

Grabarkewitz made it close, but only temporarily, and that is what may be said about the opportunity he is currently receiving.

"I hope this winter," said Grabby, "that the Dodgers make a trade so that I can play regularly or that they trade me.

"I have the feeling now that I'll only be a utility man here and I know I can play regularly for a lot of clubs."

He played regularly for the Dodgers in 1970, earning selection to the National League All-Star team through a write-in vote.

He went on to lead the Dodgers with 17 home runs, but his bright future took a turn last spring when he suffered a shoulder injury.

Grabby spent most of 1971 on the disabled list, returned to open the current season as the starting third

Please Turn to Page 5, Col. 4

# RUSSIANS RALLY, TIE CANADA, 4-4

WINNIPEG, Man. (UPI)—The Russian ice hockey team rallied with two goals late in the second period Wednesday night and tied Team Canada 4-4 in the third game of an international exhibition series.

Each team has a victory plus the tie thus far in the 8-game series. The next game will be played in Vancouver Friday, and the final 4 matches will be held in the Soviet Union.

Russia's Alexander Bodunov slapped in his first goal of the series with an assist from Vyacheslav Anisin at 18:48 of the second period to tie the score 4-4.

The Canadians took 38 shots on goal, 13 more than the Russians.

Please Turn to Page 4, Col. 4

DROPPED SOMETHING—Vasily Alexeyev of Russia drops the weight and somersaults backwards during heavyweight event in the Olympic Games. Alexeyev recovered and won gold medal anyway.
Story on Page 8 UPI Wirephoto

# CALIFORNIAN STRIPPED OF SWIMMING VICTORY

## IOC Takes 400 Freestyle Gold Medal From Rick DeMont for Using Drug He's Needed Since Childhood for Asthma

MUNICH (UPI)—American swimmer Rick DeMont, winner of the 400-meter freestyle in the Olympic Games, was stripped of his gold medal Wednesday because a drug the 16-year-old Californian takes for asthma is on the banned list.

The action came as Games competition resumed. Events were suspended Tuesday afternoon due to a raid by Arab guerrillas on Israeli quarters that culminated in the slayings of 11 Israeli team members. Tuesday's schedule was completed Wednesday and competition will continue as planned, a day late.

The executive board of the International Olympic Committee made the decision to take DeMont's medal away.

No gold medal will be awarded in the event. Brad Cooper of Australia won the silver medal and Steve Genter of Lakewood, Calif., took the bronze.

Traces of the drug, Ephedrine, which DeMont has taken for an asthma condition since he was a small boy, were found in his urine after the 400 freestyle victory Friday.

As a result, DeMont was scratched Sunday from the 1,500-meter freestyle, an event in which he held the world record. Mike Burton of Sacramento won that race.

DeMont was not available for comment.

The young swimmer's mother said, "Rick takes the medicine in order to breathe."

However, Ephedrine is specifically listed among the drugs banned for use by Olympic contestants.

DeMont said, when the routine doping test given all Olympic winners revealed the drug, that he had listed the fact that he took it on all his pre-Olympic forms.

American team officials said they had failed to notify Olympic officials that DeMont took the drug.

Prince Alexandrew De Merode of the medical commission of the IOC said that some other Olympic teams had approached his group to discuss the use of medications containing Ephedrine, and were advised to switch to other preparations.

Please Turn to Page 8, Col. 1

# HOCKEY: IT'S SOVIET GAME

## Canadian Manpower Supply Can't Keep Pace With Russians

*A Commentary*

*BY CHARLES MAHER*

There is probably no longer such a thing as major league hockey in North America.

Maybe the Canadians have enough good players to handle the Russians in the so-called World Series of Hockey, in which each team has won once and played one tie.

But they don't have enough to supply all the teams that will be playing in the United States and Canada between October and May.

The National Hockey League has been spread thin, practically to the point of emaciation, by expansion and loss of players to the new World Hockey Assn. The WHA, even with dozens of NHL defectors signed up, will be weaker than its emaciated rival.

The predicament of North American hockey occurs to you as you watch Russia play Team Canada. The Soviet team is astonishingly good. And Russia has the human resources to make it better.

That's where North American hockey is in trouble. Virtually all our players come from Canada. Now, with 16 teams in the NHL and 12 in the WHA, there aren't enough good players to go around. Canada lacks the human resources. Its population is only a tenth of Russia's.

Between periods of the first Russian-Canadian game, an Air Canada official who spent five years in Russia tells you hockey has become the second most popular spectator sport (after soccer) in the Soviet Union. Three million Russians play hockey. Three million! If the Soviets keep at it, there's no way the Canadians can stay abreast.

Say a hockey superstar comes along once every thousand players. Russia, over the years, figures to produce more superstars than Canada simply because Russia will produce more thousands of players.

In most sports, all a populous nation needs to excel is the will to excel. There are exceptions. It is unlikely, for example, that Japan will ever become a basketball power. For this sport, the Japanese are built too close to the floor.

But hockey doesn't demand exceptional size.

Please Turn to Page 10, Col. 1

'OH, SAY CAN YOU SEE . . .'—While two Olympic officials stand at attention, Olympic 400-meter winner Vince Matthews (far right) and silver medalist Wayne Collett slouch on the podium during the playing of U.S. National Anthem during victory ceremony. Crowd of 80,000 booed their actions.

# Matthews and Collett Booed on Victory Stand by Fans

Los Angeles Times
Sports
BUSINESS & FINANCE
CC PART III 3†
FRIDAY, SEPTEMBER 8, 1972

## Fidgeting During U.S. Anthem Angers Crowd; Disrespect Denied

BY DWIGHT CHAPIN
Times Staff Writer

MUNICH—Vince Matthews said Thursday no disrespect was meant when he and Wayne Collett fidgeted and chatted on the victory stand during the U.S. National Anthem after they ran one-two in the 400 meters at the Olympics Thursday.

He said he couldn't understand the boos from the crowd of 80,000 at Olympic Stadium. Collett's Black Power salute, he said, was just a way of saying "Hi, ya."

Matthews, of Brooklyn, third in the U.S. track trials, won by a stride in 44.7 seconds over Collett, of Santa Monica, timed in 44.8. Julius Sang of Kenya was third in 44.9. John Smith of Los Angeles, the third United States finalist, pulled up lame.

On the victory stand, as Sang stood at attention during the anthem, Collett stepped up to the top, or winner's, level and stood alongside Matthews. They stood sideways to the flag. Matthews had his arms folded. Collett had his hands on his hips. Neither was at attention.

The boos and whistling began when they stepped down. As Matthews left he twirled his gold medal around a finger. When Collett came back to pick up a sweat suit, and got more boos and whistles, he raised his right fist in salute to the crowd.

The gesture was not as flagrant as the black-gloved salute at Mexico City four years ago by sprinters John Carlos and Tommie Smith, which resulted in the expulsion of the two athletes from the Olympic Village, but there was speculation it might draw censure from the U.S. Olympic authorities.

### Matthews Seldom Still

Matthews, 24, a social worker who dropped out of track four years ago, then made a comeback, told a press conference: "The reason Collett came on the stand with me was not a protest. We consider ourselves the best quarter-milers in the world—Wayne Collett, John Smith, Lee Evans and myself. On the right day in the right lane, any of us can win. Collett stepped up to show we are a team. If we wanted to protest we could do a better job than that. People are trying to make something out of nothing."

The fidgeting? "Those who know me know I'm hardly ever still, and after running 400 meters I was tired."

The salute? "If you were in the Village at all, you would see us giving the sign to each other, the same as other people say, 'Hi, ya.'"

Collett said the black power salute was directed not at the crowd, but

Please Turn to Page 11, Col. 1

A 'FRIENDLY' HELLO?—Dour expressions greet Wayne Collett after he raised his right fist in Olympic Stadium Thursday. The clenched fist was explained later as a way of saying, "Hi, ya."
AP Wirephotos

**JIM MURRAY**

## A Charger From Kenya

MUNICH—One of the romances of sport is the triumph of the natural man over the forces of training, organization, breeding and money.

The legend of an old Indian leading a buffalo pony up to the starting line at the Kentucky Derby and, with a 150-pound naked brave riding bareback, winning by 100 lengths, dies hard with the sportswriter tired of seeing Oldmoney Acres Farms or Rich House Stud win.

We thrill to stories of Jim Thorpe arriving at a tryout and saying, "Which end do you want me to hold on this spear?" Or, "You mean I can jump over those little fences any way I want to?" Or, "All I have to do is push that little ball?" Then, he dashes his competition into the ground as easily as Sitting Bull at Little Big Horn.

We like the story of the big farmer boy who puts on the gloves with the champ in the carnival and knocks him out with one punch. The weightlifter who picks up the floor and all with the barbells on it. The swordfighter with no technique who flips his opponent's epee up in the rafters with one lightning unorthodox thrust. The Eskimo who shows up in a fur suit and a sealskin kayak—and wins the repechages with a hand-hewn whalebone paddle.

★

**The nearest thing to that** I have seen in the Olympics is a lean, bony half-man, half-hartebeest with the unlikely name of Kipchoge Keino.

You reconstruct how they must have found him. They came into a clearing one day and here was this pride of lions with their tongues hanging out and a rich lather of sweat on their flanks—and the tracks show they had been on the spoor of this man who is calmly staying safely ahead of the lions relay team while munching a sandwich.

Or they gave him a message to take from Nairobi to Johannesburg on the train, only he missed the train. So he beat it to Johannesburg on bare feet.

Perhaps he beats a leopard to a zebra carcass or, as a policeman in Nairobi, he saw the bullet coming and beat it to the wall. He didn't climb Mt. Kilimanjaro, he ran up it and down the other side. Before dinner.

They say they found Paavo Nurmi running across the frozen fjords so fast he wasn't out in the air long enough over 20 miles in 50-below weather to have his teeth chatter. An ordinary man would have had plenty of time to turn blue halfway or to ice before the finish line.

Mark Spitz? Rats! Mark Spitz learned his craft after millions of man hours in chlorine and heated pools with soft water. Duke Kahanamoku, the original Mahi-Mahi, was the one who had to learn to swim fast because sharks could. Beating a man was no trick to a man who could beat a dolphin.

★

**Kipchoge Keino** came off the slopes of Mt. Kenya about a decade ago with no more idea of how to run formfully than a rhinoceros. He knew nothing of the nuances of the sport, the strategy, the way to conserve oneself in heats, the interval training or the rest of the bullsmoke they run on about when track and field nuts gather at dual meets. He simply ran all the time as if he had just heard a loud roar from the tree on the right or there was a thrashing sound in the bushes or just noticed that tree limb had eyes and a forked tongue.

A man who runs the mile might possibly double in the half-mile. Anything over that, they need wheels.

In Mexico, Kipchoge won the mile with ludicrous ease—after a week in which he (1) fell off the track after setting a blistering pace in the 10,000, (2) jumped back up as they came for him with a stretcher and ran back on the track and finished the race, (3) finished a closing second in the 5,000 after winning his heat; (4) got the gold medal in the metric mile. With heats and all, he had probably run the equivalent of the coastline of Chile in seven days. He took a victory lap around the track all the same.

He did not, however, enter the marathon. Since American blacks (and American whites) seem to consider anything over 800 meters as a cross-country, the astonishment was world-wide. It was finally reasoned the altitude was responsible, not the African.

The finals came up in such a way in Munich this year that Keino had to rearrange his appearances. The finals of the 5,000 and the 1,500 come up the same day and not even an antelope could survive heats and finals under those circumstances.

Please Turn to Page 11, Col. 4

## Ashe Surprises Smith by Winning in Straight Sets

BY JEFF PRUGH
Times Staff Writer

FOREST HILLS, N.Y.—Arthur Ashe said he felt the "pressure was too much" for Stan Smith and that he had an excellent chance of upsetting him Thursday.

But the former UCLA star had no idea he would do it so convincingly.

"If I thought it would be three sets, I would have bet 15-1 odds," he said after crushing the king of Wimbledon and Forest Hills, 7-6, 6-4, 7-5, to reach the semifinals of the $160,000 U.S. Open tennis tournament.

Ashe wasn't even breathing heavily after his lightning backhand propelled him to perhaps his biggest victory since he won the inaugural Open here four years ago as an amateur.

"Midway through the second set," he said, "I could see Stan was mentally tired. He needs a rest. He was just rolling his arm over on his serve and barely getting to the net. Since January, he's played an awful lot of tennis, including Davis Cup matches. That's tough—it's a lot of pressure. The pressure was too much."

Smith, the former USC star from Pasadena, took the loss hard. He refused to talk to newsmen immediately afterward, and stood disconsolately at his locker, alone with his thoughts, until he was consoled by his college coach, George Toley.

Then he spoke softly to a reporter. "I was sluggish," he said. "I just didn't hang in there. I wasn't even nervous. Maybe that was the trouble."

He indicated, too, his displeasure with the USLTA for its schedul-

Please Turn to Page 7, Col. 2

## Aaron Checked, but 2 Braves Homer and Dodgers Fall, 4-2

BY ROSS NEWHAN
Times Staff Writer

Over the course of 11 years, Hank Aaron has hit 15 home runs in Dodger Stadium.

Some hitters contend that only Yellowstone is a tougher park to hit the ball out of.

The night air is heavy in Chavez Ravine and the distance to the fences increases sharply from the 330 at the corners.

There were three home runs Thursday night as Atlanta defeated the Dodgers, 4-2.

Aaron didn't homer, but he did hit one drive that was caught on the warning track in center and another that was caught on the warning track in left.

"Both," said Bad Henry later, "would have been home runs in Atlanta."

Aaron is 38 and in his 19th major league season. He has had other drives caught at the fence. He does not throw his helmet or pace the clubhouse in anger.

Aaron sat at his locker and said that he has met with good fortune in Dodger Stadium.

"I'd say that my luck has been very good here," he said. "I think 15

Please Turn to Page 6, Col. 3

## Yank, Soviet Cage Teams Reach Finals

### IOC Will Review Order That Cost DeMont Medal

MUNICH (AP)—The United States sent its never-beaten basketball team into the finals against Russia and picked up two victories in track Thursday but could not catch the Soviet Union in the gold medal race of the Olympic Games.

Hank Iba's youthful cagers, led by the scoring of Jim Forbes of Texas-El Paso with 14 points and Tom Henderson of Hawaii with 10 and the great defensive work of Mike Bantom of St. Joseph's crushed Italy, 68-38, and qualified to meet America's traditional court rival, Russia, for the championship Saturday night. The older and more experienced Russians came from behind for a 67-61 triumph over Cuba.

At the end of the day's events, the Soviet Union—with two victories in track and field, one in equestrian and another in women's volleyball—still led the United States in gold medals, 31-26. But the United States maintained its edge in total medals, 75-69. East Germany is third in both categories with 53 medals, 18 of them gold.

U.S. runners won the men's 400-meter race and 110-meter hurdles Thursday.

In basketball the Soviet team weathered an 18-5 first-half explosion by Cuba to take a 6-point triumph in the semifinal game.

The United States and Russia have

Please Turn to Page 10, Col. 5

## Hofbrauhaus: Symbol of All That Is German

Exclusive to The Times from a Staff Writer

MUNICH—The Hofbrauhaus is a beer garden where beer not only flows down throats but onto tables, onto floors, onto everything and everyone sooner or later.

Huge, smoky, noisy, it is somehow a symbol of all that is German, all that is Bavarian. It opens at 9 in the morning and closes, well, you can stay up and see if you wish—but those one-liter steins of beer are potent mixes.

At 5 p.m. on the day Arab terrorists were killing Israeli athletes and coaches the Hofbrauhaus was filled with drunks, happy drunks, perhaps unaware of the tragedy a few miles away, perhaps uncaring.

Later, national groups formed at tables and pounded their steins on them and got up and sang and danced on them, as a Bavarian band oomph-paa-paahed in the background.

A barmaid about 4-feet-10 inches tall, and wide, lugged 14 full liter steins, without a tray, to a serving area and plopped them down. As she began sliding them down a long table to thirsty customers a man about 6-3 and 220 sneaked up behind and tried to swipe one.

The barmaid saw him, turned, planted her right hand on his chest and shoved him backwards 50 feet, blistering him with German swear words. Cowed, he sat down and waited his turn.

Downtown Munich, a melange of old and the new. Gray, ugly, American-style apartment buildings and department stores rising alongside baroque and Gothic museums and churches and opera houses.

Some say 45% of the city was destroyed during World War II, others say 75%.

Every major building but one has been fully restored. The one? A munitions museum.

Munich, where Hitler began building the Reich that was to last forever, is trying hard to forget the bloodshed and the shame Adolf Hitler brought Germany. Dachau is a 15-minute drive from Munich. That, alone, is enough.

There is great beauty in Munich . . . The opera house, built in 1753 for a king, made solely of wood, seating 480, looking like a mu-

Please Turn to Page 9, Col. 1

# Ryun Takes Fall; Matthews, Collett Kicked Out

## Kansan Fails to Qualify in 1,500 Meters

MUNICH — All the heartbreaks, frustration and failures of the 20th Olympic Games — star-crossed almost from the start—seemed to be symbolized for a moment Friday when Jim Ryun lay sprawled on the runway at the track stadium.

He stumbled and fell, tangling his legs with those of another runner, and he was knocked senseless briefly. He was spiked on both ankles.

He got up and ran in pursuit of an elusive dream, an Olympic gold medal in the 1,500 meters. But in this, his third Games, in what had seemed an ordinary qualifying heat, he finished 9th in a field of 10 and was out of competition.

So ended four years of effort to atone for the 1968 Olympics at Mexico City where he lost in the high altitude to Kenya's Kipchoge Keino. Oddly, Keino was in the same heat Friday as Ryun, winning it in 3:40.0, fastest of seven such heats.

Elsewhere in the Games, American swimmer Rick DeMont finally lost his gold medal beyond further appeal.

Russians were one-two in the decathlon and the East Germans picked up another gold medal in the women's 100-meter hurdles. The United States picked up a yachting gold, and Americans moved only one man into the boxing finals.

Ryun, for years the king of the distance runners and the most glamorous figure in track and field, was in the fourth of seven Friday heats. The top four from each went into the semifinals. There appeared no way the world record holder at 3:33.1 could miss—unless he fell down.

And that's what he did.

The stoic Kansan was a lap and a half from the finish, running last. Keino had just gone outside and begun to move up into the pack. Ryun decided to move, too.

Instead of going outside, he tried inside. But the gap he'd spotted was closed suddenly by Ugandan Vitus Ashaba. Ryun stumbled and went down, tangling with Billy Fordjour of Ghana, who fell over him.

Ryun, who besides his spike wounds suffered an abrasion on his right knee, a contusion of the throat and a strained ankle, lay there for

Please Turn to Page 5, Col. 1

## IOC Bans Pair for 'Insulting' Behavior

*BY DWIGHT CHAPIN, Times Staff Writer*

MUNICH—Mark Spitz waved a pair of shoes over his head on the Olympic victory stand. He won seven gold medals.

Dave Wottle wore his billed cap on the stand during the National Anthem, but he held his hand over his heart. He got to keep his gold medal for a win in the 800 meters.

Gold and silver medalists Vince Matthews and Wayne Collett, the U.S. 400 meter men, talked and slouched during the Anthem after their victory Thursday, and Matthews twirled his gold medal as he left the stadium.

Friday, the executive board of the International Olympic Committee, tossed Matthews and Collett out of the Games . . . depriving the U.S. of two of its 4 x 400-meter relay men.

"The whole world saw the disgusting display of your two athletes when they received their gold and silver medals for the 400-meter event yesterday," IOC president Avery Brundage wrote Clifford Buck, president of the U.S. Olympic Committee.

"This is the second time the USOC has permitted such occurrences on the athletic field. It is the executive board's opinion that these two athletes have broken rule 26, paragraph 1, in respect of the traditional Olympic spirit and ethics and are, therefore, eliminated from taking part in any future Olympic competition.

"If such a performance should happen in the future, please be advised that the medals will be withheld from the athletes in question."

Brundage was making obvious reference to Mexico City, 1968, when U.S. sprinters John Carlos and Tommie Smith raised gloved fists in a "black power" salute at the Games.

Did Matthews of Brooklyn and Collett of UCLA have the same thing in mind as Smith and Carlos?

"No," said Matthews. "This wasn't really a protest or a planned demonstration. It was a spontaneous thing, a feeling Wayne and I had."

Neither faced the Flag during the Anthem and at one point Collett stepped up to the winner's level with Matthews. They conceded Friday they had a purpose, if not a plan.

Please Turn to Page 5, Col. 3

**QUEST FOR GOLD MEDAL ENDS**—Jim Ryun, right, world record holder in the mile, ends his bid for an Olympic gold medal Friday sprawled on the track in Munich with Ghana's Billy Fordjour. Ryun collided with Uganda's Vitus Ashaba and fell, failing to qualify in 1,500-meter heat.

AP Wirephoto

Los Angeles Times
Sports
BUSINESS & FINANCE
CC PART III 2†
SATURDAY, SEPTEMBER 9, 1972

# AUSTRALIAN BEATS EVERT; BILLIE JEAN GAINS FINAL

### Florida Teen-ager's Defeat by Kerry Melville in U.S. Open Delays 'Dream Match'; Mrs. King Eliminates Mrs. Court

**BY JEFF PRUGH**
Times Staff Writer

FOREST HILLS, N.Y. — The "Princess" fell. The "Old Lady" survived. And the dream tennis match between them may have to wait until next season.

For the second year in a row, teenage Chris Evert was defeated in the U.S. Open Women's single semifinals here Friday when 25-year-old Kerry Melville of Australia scored a 6-4, 6-2 upset that was surprisingly one-sided.

The victory sends Miss Melville into today's finals against defending champion Billie Jean King for the $10,000 first prize.

Mrs. King, nicknamed the "Old Lady" by rival players on the tour, turned back Australia's Margaret Court, 6-4, 6-4, avenging a stunning defeat to her last week in a tournament at Newport, R.I.

It was a day off in men's single competition. The men will play semifinals today for the right to battle for the $25,000 winner's prize. Ilie Nastase, the clowning Romanian who is playing perhaps the best tennis of the tournament, is expected to beat Seattle's Tom Gorman, while Arthur Ashe is favored over his ex-David Cup teammate, Cliff Richey.

It took what seeded Miss Melville called "the best tennis of my life" to finish off the third-seeded Miss Evert, who was never really in the match and will now return to Ft. Lauderdale, Fla., for her senior year of high school.

"Usually I make a lot of errors," said Miss Melville, the fourth-leading money winner on the Virginia Slims tour, "but I hardly made any today."

Miss Evert, attractive as usual in ribbons and ruffles, was again the heart-throb of a near-capacity gallery of more than 9,000 who groaned in anguish when Miss Melville hit winner after winner.

The ninth-seeded Australian chased Chris all over the court, keeping her off-balance with deftly placed drop shots, then passing her at the net before she could recover.

She broke Miss Evert's service twice to open the final set for a 2-1 lead, then got the crucial break she needed by sweeping four points to widen her lead, 5-2, and all but sew up the match.

"Kerry played too tough," said Miss Evert, who lost to Mrs. King in the semifinals here last year. "Even after I lost the first set, I thought I could win. But I didn't slow the pace down enough. Eventually, she got

Please Turn to Page 6, Col. 6

# WOOO PIG SOOOIIEE!

### *Eerie cry of Arkansas football fans is one way of showing state's pride in Razorback teams*

**BY BILL SHIRLEY**
Times Sports Editor

LITTLE ROCK, Ark.—WOOoooo PIG SOOOiieeee!

The startled visitor from California almost dropped a forkful of black-eyed peas as the eerie yell interrupted the quiet talk and soft music in the elegant rooftop restaurant. WOOOoooo PIG SOO-Oiieeee!

The yell was louder this time as other diners and dancers joined the fun.

Then, one more time—the yell always comes in threes, the visitor was told—the cry erupted before the University of Arkansas football fans went back to eating and dancing.

The visitor's host laughed and said: "That's nothing. Wait until you hear it tomorrow night."

Hearing it tonight will be the USC Trojans, who open the season against Arkansas in War Memorial Stadium before what is expected to be a record crowd of more than 54,000. It will be an experience the Trojans probably will want to forget because when that many people yell, even a pig with good sense would run and hide.

Arkansas, once known as the Cardinals, adopted Razorbacks as a nickname when someone suggested that the championship team of 1909 "played like a bunch of razorback hogs." A razorback is a mean, skinny wild hog with a ridged back and long legs which once roamed Arkansas' swamps. However, nobody has seen one around here for 40 or 50 years. Big Red, the Razorback mascot, is nothing but a fat pig.

The yell starts low and drawn out and builds to a crescendo. "It's eerie," says sports editor Orville Henry of the Arkansas Gazette, who has heard it hundreds of times.

"It makes cold chills in ya," says one Texas coach.

Not that the Arkansas football team needs any help. The Razorbacks are rated one of the strongest teams in the nation and are favored tonight by 2 to 6 points.

In fact, they're saying here coach Frank Broyles' experienced team is so strong it probably will go 12-0—if it beats USC.

Please Turn to Page 7, Col. 4

# Larry Jaster Back, Tops Dodgers Again

### Former Shutout Star Wins, 4-3, for Braves

**BY RON RAPOPORT**
Times Staff Writer

For six years, Larry Jaster's name has been in the record book alongside that of Grover Cleveland Alexander.

But for the last year and a half, Jaster has been in the minor leagues trying to recover the promise of 1966 when he was 21 years old and seemed to be on his way.

And it was only fitting that it should be against the Dodgers that Jaster should gain his first victory since joining Atlanta from the minors recently, a 4-3 triumph in relief in Dodger Stadium Friday night.

It was the Dodgers, of course, whom Jaster blanked five times in 1966. Only Alexander in the National League ever shut out the same team (Cincinnati) five times in a season before Jaster, and it hasn't been done since Larry's super season.

"I think I am more nervous now than I was then," the left-hander said after the game. "There's more

Please Turn to Page 4, Col. 1

# JENKINS REACHES 20 VICTORIES FOR 6TH YEAR IN ROW

PHILADELPHIA (AP)—Ferguson Jenkins moved into select company Friday night as he hurled the Chicago Cubs to a 4-3 victory over the Philadelphia Phillies.

The win was the 20th of the season for Jenkins, making it six consecutive 20-victory seasons for the big right hander. Only three pitchers since 1920—Lefty Grove, Robin Roberts and Warren Spahn — ever had that many in a row.

And only two others—Christy Mathewson with 12 consecutive seasons and Walter Johnson with 10—did it in the dead-ball era.

"It's something no pitcher could ever dream of doing," said Jenkins, who admits he'd like to make it seven in a row. "Nobody in the National League ever did that in modern times. I'd like that record.

"Just being in the same class with

Please Turn to Page 2, Col. 5

# 49ers Nip Rams, 17-14; Fans Boo

**BY BOB OATES**
Times Staff Writer

Gene Washington's extraordinary ability to find open ground when circling out for passes decided a close game in favor of the 49ers here Friday night.

It all came down to third and 16 at the 49er 44 with 2 minutes to play, at which time split end Washington bolted down the middle to take Steve Spurrier's 21-yard pass.

Four plays later Bruce Gossett kicked a 38-yard field goal and the 49ers had won for only the second time in their last 13 Ram games, 17-14.

This extended the Los Angeles losing streak to five, making it a 1-5 summer for the Rams—their worst preseason of all time—and there was booing in the stands as the 60,807 walked out.

**Gabriel Gets 7-0 Lead**

The spectators, forming the Coliseum's fourth straight plus-60,000 crowd for NFL exhibitions this summer, had dreamed through a dull first half in which Los Angeles quarterback Roman Gabriel outscored San Francisco's John Brodie, 7-0.

Pete Beathard, playing in relief of Gabriel, and Spurrier, San Francisco's second-stringer, livened it up in the second half. But the scoring flurry made no difference to the fans when the Rams finally blew it.

Except for Washington, the teams looked dead even. His catch that set up the field goal came at what seemed a most unpromising time for him, inasmuch as Spurrier, on the preceding play, had been sacked for minus 9 by a rookie Ram lineman, Larry Brooks.

Larry's big play had the appearance of knocking the 49ers out of field goal position, and so it would have been, had Washington been defended on the next play. Two Ram safetymen, Dave Elmendorf and Eddie Phillips, tried. And when the ball came in, Dave was close enough to wrestle Gene for it. But with the game on the line, Gene wasn't giving it up.

With their next three plays, all runs, the 49ers gained only a yard, but that was close enough for Gossett. In the second quarter, it hadn't been close enough for David Ray of the Rams, who missed what proved to be the tying field goal from 38 yards away.

Earlier he had succeeded on what would have been the tying field goal from 47 yards out. But on this one, the Rams were offside. That's the kind of summer they've had, which is to say, not good.

But they're better than their record. Although their coach, Tommy Prothro, was a loser for the first time in his four 49er starts, he has a

Please Turn to Page 7, Col. 1

# Bruins' Wishbone T, McAlister Face No. 1 Nebraska Tonight

**BY MAL FLORENCE**
Times Staff Writer

UCLA, with a prayer and a wishbone, opens its season tonight at the Coliseum against the nation's most renowned college football team.

The young Bruins draw No. 1 ranked Nebraska, riding a 32-game unbeaten streak and after an unprecedented third straight national championship.

Nebraska is a three-touchdown favorite in the 8:05 p.m. game. The crowd is expected to be 70,000.

"Our team feels like you would expect a young team to feel," said UCLA coach Pepper Rodgers. "Nervous. Apprehensive. But we've got some cards ourselves . . . we're not without a few aces."

This is the hand Pepper will be playing:

—A new formation for UCLA, the wishbone T, which spreads the defense for long runs or passes if executed properly.

—The debut of halfback James McAlister, considered the best collegiate running prospect since USC's O.J. Simpson. James wears the same No. 32.

—A poised but untested quarterback in Mark Harmon, son of Tom Harmon, Michigan's famed runner of yesteryear.

—The element of surprise ("We know more about them than they do about us").

On the negative side, the Bruins, trying to redeem themselves after a 2-7-1 season, are woefully inexperienced—especially on defense.

Rodgers starts one senior, left cornerback Allan Ellis, and 10 underclassmen. Of the first defensive 11,

Please Turn to Page 6, Col. 7

**NO ROOM**—Larry Schreiber, 49er fullback, gets just two yards on pass from John Brodie as Rams' Coy Bacon, on ground, trips him up. Jack Reynolds (64) and Merlin Olsen, right, come up to help.

Times photo by Art Rogers

**JIM MURRAY**

# The 20th Olympiad: A Showcase for Ugly Americans

CC SECTION D 2†

SUNDAY, SEPTEMBER 10, 1972

MUNICH—On the far turn on the Olympic track, two races away from the goal of his life, a gold medal, the greatest miler America ever produced ran up on the heels of a Ugandan plodder, 17 seconds slower than he, and tumbled heavily to the track and lay there—then rose forlornly to trot after the rest of his company like a puppy whose bone has been stolen by a bigger dog.

In a way, Jim Ryun symbolized the American track effort in these Olympics. It ranged from the purblind to the ridiculous.

This is not a team, it's an impractical joke. It doesn't need a coach, it needs a couch. It doesn't need a trainer, it needs a headshrinker.

The evidence is, this is the biggest collection of spoiled brats, foul-ups, crybabies and human beings ill-suited to their purpose who have ever been gathered in one team photo.

The Germans must be sorry they surrendered.

This is a team which has fallen on its prat in a shower of gold medals which other countries are running around eagerly picking up.

It's not a team, it's a series of one-liners. "What if they gave a race and no one showed up? Why, in that case, the A m e r i c a n s would." "What has 400 arms, 400 legs, and no medals?" "The Americans are sure making their absence felt in these Olympics." "How do you make the American team? Either have no speed, no form—or no manners."

The things that have happened to the American team the past week would make a great plot for a Chaplin movie. Ringling Bros. should sign up the whole act intact and put it on a train. The rubes would love it. It's "Laugh Out"—"Laugh In" outdoors and with heats.

I'd like to tell you everything that went wrong but my visa is only good till Sept. 15.

At the weightlifting the other night, the German announcer, perfectly oblivious of the connotation, announced importantly that some wheelhoister "can now set a new Olympic jerk record."

That record was retired by a bunch of guys who couldn't lift anything heavier than a cocktail. The International Olympic Committee which, if fingerprinted, would show the prints of Avery Brundage, banned two Olympic sprinters because, on the victory stand, they behaved like Americans—spoiled and arrogant. Like, why should these tourists be any different?

In a sense, they had an excuse. They were in unfamiliar surroundings, the victory platform, and, it was clear, they didn't know what to wear for the occasion. They also didn't know what to do with their gold and silver medals—which is also not surprising. We hadn't had many. So, they were kind of like the South Seas natives who put eyeglasses on their feet. They twirled the medals. They also talked during the "Star Spangled Banner"—which ain't easy.

The Germans acted as if they caught them using somebody else's toothbrush.

You see, the 20th Olympiad, which probably should not even have been going on since it already had cost 17 lives, had had its fill of

Please Turn to Page 16, Col. 4

HUSKER WALL CRACKS—UCLA's Mark Harmon (7) squirms through wall of Nebraska linemen to pick up first down Saturday night at the Coliseum. The 2-yard gain set up Bruin field goal. Among Nebraska players are Dave Mason (25), John Dutton (90) and Jim Branch (51).
Times photo by Art Rogers

# Russia Ends U.S. Basketball Reign

## USC's Williams Leaps 27-0½ to Win Long Jump

BY DWIGHT CHAPIN, Times Staff Writer

MUNICH—"All I could think of up there was that it was good to be from the U.S.A. and watch that Flag go up."

The words—explaining his emotions on the Olympic Games victory stand—came from a black teen-ager from Compton, Calif., who provided a refreshing high point Saturday in a generally miserable performance by the U.S. track team.

Randy Williams and his magic bear salvaged one of U.S. track's worst days Saturday with a long jump of 27 feet ½-inch on his first try for a gold medal—only one of the day for the American squad. And he did it after hurting his leg.

Williams, who smiles a lot, was the first American to mount the stand since 400-meter runners Vince Matthews and Wayne Collett were banished for "insulting" fidgeting and facing away from the Flag Thursday.

Williams, 19, 5-10 and 152 pounds, stood at attention, bit his lip and gulped a couple of times during the Anthem. Then he said:

"I don't think there's been too much emphasis on flags at the Olympics. They've a l w a y s been there. And the Flag is an essential part of our country."

The USC freshman was the fourth American to win a track event at the Games. The United States' lowest track gold total was eight in 1920 and 1928. It seems unlikely this

Please Turn to Page 13, Col. 3

## Yanks Protest 51-50 Loss, Say Time Ran Out

MUNICH—You're not going to believe this, but . . .

The United States, which had not lost one of its 63 previous Olympic basketball games, lost one early today. Or did it?

The victor—maybe—was Russia. The score—possibly—was 51-50.

The hero—perhaps—was a tall, blond Russian, Alexsander Belov, who had blood streaming down his face when he made the final basket. Or was the hero the referee, or the timekeeper, or whoever it was who gave the ball to the Russians out of bounds after the scoreboard clock showed the American had won?

The final score on the board gave the game to the Soviets, 51-50. United States officials filed an immediate protest.

The International Amateur Basketball Federation delayed awarding the medals, met secretly for three hours, then said it would announce its decision on the protest later today.

The scene during the final minute of play was incredibly confused and after the action was over there was no unanimous agreement on what happened.

This is what appeared to happen.

The U.S., playing without movement on offense and sloppily on defense, fell behind an experienced Russian team by as much as 10

Please Turn to Page 11, Col. 1

# Bruins Defeat Nebraska; USC Wins

## No. 1 Team Upset on Late Goal by Herrera

BY MAL FLORENCE
Times Staff Writer

Who is No. 1 now? Would you believe UCLA's astonishing Bruins?

That's what the ecstatic Bruin rooters were shouting late Saturday night after their 3-touchdown underdog team upset No. 1 ranked Nebraska, 20-17, shattering a 32-game unbeaten streak that began early in 1969.

It was accomplished in dramatic fashion. Efren Herrera kicked a 30-yard field goal with only 22 seconds remaining as UCLA launched its wishbone T era with a flourish.

This wasn't any ordinary team the Bruins knocked off before a Coliseum crowd of 67,702, including 15,000 red-clad Nebraska fans.

The Cornhuskers were bidding for an unprecedented third straight national title and, although they had lost some starters from last year's team, many experts figured they would accomplish their goal.

### UCLA Never Trailed

It was not to be. The opportunistic Bruins, a team depending heavily on sophomores a n d junior c o l l e g e transfers, never trailed.

They opened up a 10-0 lead, were tied at halftime, 10-10, and pulled away to 17-10 before Nebraska caught up again. Then Herrera finished off the Huskers, acclaimed as the greatest college team of all time in 1971.

The win has to rank as one of the most noteworthy accomplishments in UCLA football history—even surpassing the 14-12 Rose Bowl victory over Michigan State in 1966.

As for the hulking Huskers, boasting two bona fide Heisman Trophy candidates in slotback Jimmy Rodgers and middle guard Rich Glover, they were a stumbling, bumbling giant.

Nebraska committed 5 turnovers on interceptions and fumbles and UCLA turned these errors into 17 of its 20 points.

But, on the winning field goal drive, a 57-yard push, the Bruins did it on their own without any assis-

Please Turn to Page 14, Col. 1

**THE BIG ONES**

## Colorado Beats Cal, 20-10

Ed Shoen returned a third-period interception 48 yards to score and Fred Lima kicked two long field goals in an otherwise sluggish Buffalo offense that had difficulty with Bears.

Story on Page 3

**WASH. ST. 18, KANSAS 17**
Thoroughly beaten for three quarters, Cougars scored all their points in last period, winning on a 2-point conversion by quarterback Ty Paine.

Story on Page 3

**TENNESSEE 34, GA. TECH 3**
Volunteers used a head-hunting defense to smother the Yellowjackets, recovering 5 fumbles and intercepting 3 passes.

Story on Page 9

**MISSOURI 24, OREGON 22**
Oregon appeared to have won when the Tigers recovered a fumble on Missouri 11. Then Greg Hill kicked 31-yard field goal with six seconds left.

Story on Page 3

## Osteen Takes Joy Out of Lip's New Life as Dodgers Win, 4-0

BY ROSS NEWHAN
Times Staff Writer

The Lip was shaving, preparing for his Los Angeles debut as manager of the Houston Astros.

"A great group," said Leo Durocher, thrusting a razor toward his players, suiting up Saturday in the visitor's clubhouse at Dodger Stadium.

"Not like the Cubs," he continued, the words coming in the manner of a machine gun. "I'd take a Chicago player out of the lineup and he'd beef, moan and sit there sulking.

"With this group, a guy comes out of the lineup and he's on the bench rooting for the other guy. I'm really not used to it."

Another thing Durocher is not used to is losing, but it was fortunate he put the razor to his throat before, rather than after, Claude Osteen hurled the Dodgers to a 4-0 victory.

The loss prevented Houston from gaining a game on the Reds, who lost to San Francisco.

The Astros are 7-5 under Durocher and 8 behind Cincinnati. The only race in the National League West appears to be for second place.

Houston leads the Dodgers by 2 games. More than pride is at stake. Each Dodger received $1,140 for finishing second last year. Each Astro received only $350 for finishing third.

Please Turn to Page 4, Col. 6

## TIMES GRAND PRIX TO DECIDE TITLE

BY SHAV GLICK
Times Staff Writer

Is this the final year of the Team McLaren dynasty in the Can-Am?

For six years the orange-colored machines designed by the late Bruce McLaren have dominated the Canadian-American Challenge Cup series as no team ever has dominated a racing series.

The deciding event in this year's $1 million, 9-race series will be the 15th annual Times Grand Prix, Sunday, Oct. 29, at Riverside International Raceway.

Between 1966 and 1972 the low-slung McLarens won 39 of 43 races.

Please Turn to Page 17, Col. 1

## Arkansas Bows to Troy, 31-10; Rae 18-24-269

BY BILL SHIRLEY
Times Sports Editor

LITTLE ROCK, Ark.—Mike Rae started his first game as quarterback for USC Saturday night and it looks as if he finally has earned the job.

The senior from Lakewood, who played second string to Jimmy Jones for two years, directed a strong USC team to a 31-10 victory over Arkansas in the opening game of the s e a s o n and, surprisingly, looked sharper than the Razorbacks' Heisman Trophy prospect, Joe Ferguson.

Rae, firing to flankers Lynn Swann and Dave Boulware, split ends Edesel Garrison and J. K. McKay and tight end Charles Young, completed 18 of 24 passes for 269 yards. He did not have any intercepted.

Ferguson, the much-publicized senior who completed 59% of his passes last season, hit 10 of 36 for 223 yards but had 2 intercepted. He's not bad, either, although he improved his statistics by connecting several times in the final minutes when the Trojans were giving him short yardage.

### 117 Yards for McNeill

Thus, it looks as if USC coach John McKay has a sharper passing attack to go with his usual strong ball-control game, which was awesome at times Saturday night. The USC runners netted 208 yards, led by tailback Rod McNeill, who looked as if he has recovered from the hip injury that prevented him from playing last season. He was a workhorse, getting 117 yards in 28 carries.

Presumably, the USC win can be listed as an upset because Arkansas, which started as a 6-point favorite, was still a 2-point choice at kickoff.

The record crowd of 54,461 Arkansas fans in War Memorial Stadium on a warm, humid evening probably wondered why. Once the well-conditioned Trojans began rolling in the second half they wore down coach F r a n k Broyles' highly-regarded forces, which were not as strong physically and did not appear sharp for a team rated so high.

Please Turn to Page 6, Col. 1

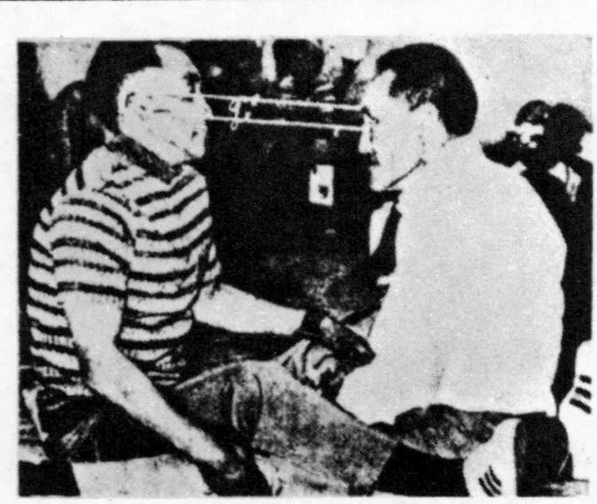

EAR-PULLING—One of the events in the Eskimo Olympics is the ear-pulling contest. The winner is decided when one contestant submits, or in some instances, suffers loss of his ear.

**TEST OF PAIN, ENDURANCE**

## Eskimos Hold Olympics

FAIRBANKS, Alaska—A crowd of 1,500 watches silently. The air is hot and tacky, heavy with the strain of concentration. Reggie Joule, a young Alaskan Eskimo from Kotzebue, studies the high kick target which dangles almost two feet above his head. Twice he has failed to kick it in a style acceptable to the judges.

*This article is reprinted by permission of the Tundra Times and the Alicia Patterson Fund.*

If he fails again he is sure the Eskimo Olympic title will go to a Canadian.

Watching quietly nearby is Mickey Gordon, a 27-year-old athlete from the raw tundra of Inuvik on the MacKenzie River Delta. Back in Canada he holds the high kick record. He has jumped against Joule before and won. But something has happened to the Alaskan in the five months since he competed at the Canadian Winter Games. His style is better. He has knocked off some awkward edges.

Please Turn to Page 15, Col. 1

# DAVIS! DAVIS! DAVIS! DAVIS! DAVIS! DAVIS!

**THE BEGINNING**—USC sophomore Anthony Davis shocks Notre Dame and 75,243 Coliseum fans with this 97-yard touchdown run with opening kickoff Saturday. He scored five more TDs in USC's 45-23 rout of the Irish.

**AGAIN**—Davis drives into the end zone from one yard away for his second touchdown, climaxing a 63-yard drive in the first quarter. Victory made it a perfect, 11-0, regular season for USC.

## Anthony Scores Six TDs; Trojans Rout Irish, 45-23

**BY BOB OATES**
Times Staff Writer

To overcome the Irish, John McKay's big maroon machine needed a 6-touchdown performance from Anthony Davis and got it Saturday as the undefeated Trojans won their 11th straight, 45-23.

Notre Dame outgained the nation's No. 1 team but couldn't defense Davis, USC's sophomore sensation, who broke the backs of the Irish with touchdown runs of 97, 1, 5, 4, 96 and 8 yards.

A 185-pound blur standing 5-9, Davis won it with two long kickoff returns to put McKay on the doorstep of his third national championship. UPI votes Monday. The final AP poll will be taken after USC's last game against Ohio State in the Rose Bowl.

It was in the first 13 seconds that Davis brought 75,243 to their feet in the Coliseum with his explosive 97-yard trip with the opening kickoff to key a 19-3 first quarter lead that was cut to 19-10 at the half.

But Notre Dame's sophomore quarterback, Tom Clements, was outplaying the Trojans during almost every series in the first 45 minutes and at 13:41 of the second half

Clements hit his third touchdown pass to pare USC's lead to 25-23.

That was a moment of uncomfortable tension for the Trojans and their fans and the nervousness was hardly reduced when Notre Dame's coach Ara Parseghian gambled and lost on a 2-point shot at 25-25.

The Irish, as of that moment, had survived damaging fumbles and interceptions to seize the momentum, on the accurate arm of a 19-year-old quarterback.

Then Davis killed them.

He put the Notre Dame kickoff in the end zone, 96 yards distant, and the Irish at long last were done, 32-23.

The sag was immediately noticeable. The famous Irish spirit which had sustained them for three quarters had been beaten out of them by Davis' second big run. And in the confusion, the Trojans made it a rout with two touchdowns in the fourth quarter, pouring it on with a 15-yard pass in the last 3 minutes to set up their last six points.

McKay's best team—and quite possibly USC's best of all time—spent a hard afternoon turning back one of the most spirited challenges ever made by an underdog in this long series.

Notre Dame led in yards, 360-320; first downs, 19-18, and by a significant margin in total plays, 75-61.

Another upset was clearly in the making in the third quarter. The measure of the Trojans at this high point in McKay's career is that they

**Please Turn to Page 4, Col. 1**

### JIM MURRAY

## 'Ouch!'--Ara the Coach

"Well," says I to Kinsella, "what's so grand about football? 'Tis only a game, after all."

"Ye may be right," says Kinsella. "Let's go have a pint."

—From the Collected Post-Game Sayings of Gonigle the Poet.

"Heathen!"

—Culligan the Theologian as Richard Wood ran down an ND halfback.

"Do ye think the man has any idea in the world what the game is all about?"

—Fogarty the Undertaker of Parseghian the Coach, third period.

"Well, let's put it this way, he's no Rockne, now, is he?"

—Clancy the Scholar in the third period.

"Ryan downed the punt for the Trojans?! Why, the man's little better than an infarmer to turn on his own that way! He'd be afraid to leave his bed in the old days after a trick like that!"

—Casey the Used-Car Salesman on Mike Ryan, the punt-downer.

"D'ye think prayers help a'tall when officials are crooked?"

—Halloran, the Unemployed Carpenter as a penalty was called against ND.

"Well, I wish they would stop calling them 'Irish.' I shouldn't be surprised there's an Ulsterman among them. A pity some people can't tell an Irishman from an Orangeman."

—Costello the Streetcar Conductor as the score mounted.

"Well, it's a good thing they teach them something, now, isn't it? You could scarcely call that algebra now, could you?"

—Kelly the Laundromat Operator of the USC halftime card stunts.

"What'd ye expect when they stopped saying the Mass in Latin and you could eat on your way to Communion and they let guitars in church and not bingo?"

—Hannigan the Unpublished Author and Part-Time Bartender.

"Is he as good as George Gipp?"

—Fagan the Pants-Presser as Anthony Davis scored 6th touchdown.

"The ball was heavier in Gipp's day."

—Kerrigan the Expert on Everything.

"The saddest thing is, there's no part for Paddy O'Brien, the fillum actor, in the whole lot. He can't play that Parsahoogan, he's some kind of an atheist, now, isn't he?"

—Duffy the Movie-Goer.

"We've got them now!"

—Cassidy the Optimist as Notre Dame drove to 1-yard line.

"Well, the Lord does work in mysterious ways. They say everything always works for the Best."

—Cassidy the Optimist a minute later as the Irish's Art Best fumbled.

"God must be sitting on a rock some place today and weeping."

—Boyle the Altar Boy as the score went to 45-23.

"It's a cinch he can't feel too good about it."

—Kinsella the Judge.

"How would a man write about a terrible thing like this?"

—Hennessy the Dry Cleaner in the fourth quarter.

"'Outlined against a blue-gray December sky, the One Horseman rode again.' His name in dramatic lore is 'Anthony Pestilence.' "

—Gogarty the Publican.

"D'ye think if we all said a good Act of Contrition before the Orange Bowl?"

—Conway the Cop.

"Well, we can sure put away the beads today."

**Please Turn to Page 15, Col. 1**

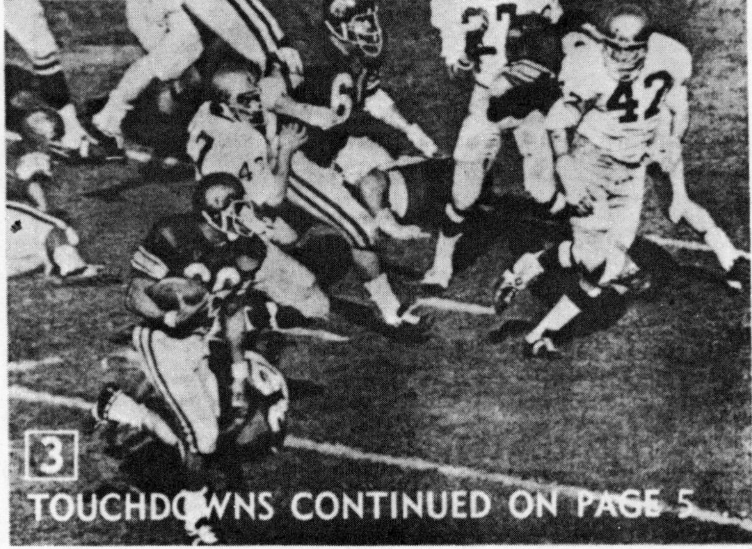


**. . . AND AGAIN**—As Trojan blockers clear his path to the goal line, Davis streaks around right end for his third TD on 5-yard sweep. Fumble recovery set up USC score that made it 19-3.

**Times photos by Larry Sharkey and Rick Browne**

### RECORDS TUMBLE

## Davis Predicted Breakaway Plays Two Weeks Ago

**BY JEFF PRUGH**
Times Staff Writer

The toughest run Anthony Davis had to make all afternoon was from the USC dressing room to the showers.

Newsmen swarmed around him like mosquitoes. The crush was as heavy as a New York subway ride at 6 p.m.—certainly more suffocating than anything the Notre Dame defense threw at him while getting trampled Saturday by the Trojans, 45-23.

As Davis fielded questions again and again like a courtroom witness, teammate Glenn Byrd shouted a battle cry for this season—or maybe 1973 and 1974:

"Anthony Davis for the Heisman Trophy!"

Characteristically, Davis stood there poker-faced and gave answers more predictable than his moves with the football.

**Huskies Hit Harder**

No, he doesn't "worry about records." Yes, he thinks this is the best college football team ever assembled, to which a teammate yelled, "You tell 'em, A.D.!" No, Notre Dame wasn't the hardest-hitting team he'd faced—the Washington Huskies were. And, no, he had never scored 6 touchdowns in one game. "I scored 5 in one game in high school," said the sophomore from San Fernando. "It was a Valley record."

If just about everybody was left spellbound by Davis' performance, Anthony himself seemed nonchalant about it. Two weeks ago, he had sat quietly with a writer in the USC dining room and pondered the game with the Fighting Irish.

"They're big and strong," he had said, "but if I can get outside—get into the open—I think I can go all the way a few times."

As it was, Davis probably could have run forever.

When it was over, Davis took a deep breath and expressed a sentiment that typified the "team unity"

**Please Turn to Page 6, Col. 2**

## NO. 2 'RAMA BOWS AS AUBURN BLOCKS TWO PUNTS, 17-16

BIRMINGHAM, Ala. (AP) — Bill Newton blocked two punts in the final quarter and David Langner ran the ball for touchdowns both times as ninth-ranked Auburn upset second-ranked Alabama, 17-16, Saturday.

Langner sealed Alabama's doom in the incredible upset shortly after his second touchdown by intercepting a pass at the Auburn 41.

It was the first regular season loss for Alabama in 22 games, and virtually ruined the Tide's chances for a national title.

Alabama will take its 10-1 record into the Cotton Bowl against Texas,

**Please Turn to Page 8, Col. 5**

## Bruins Win 48th Straight With 81-48 Romp Over Pacific

**BY RON RAPOPORT**
Times Staff Writer

University of the Pacific, helpful to a fault, has outfitted its basketball players this season in uniforms bearing their names on the back. Considering what happened to the Tigers at Pauley Pavilion Saturday night, however, they might have preferred anonymity.

Belted about virtually at will in an 81-48 defeat by UCLA, Pacific found itself helping to establish several milestones. Had it not been for the honor, the visitors probably would have wished it had happened to someone else.

The victory was not only UCLA's 48th in a row—its longest streak ever and the second most extensive in the history of college basketball—but also was the 804th win in 1,000 games for coach John Wooden, including his 11 years as a high school coach and 2 at Indiana State.

Although Pacific didn't try to stall as Bradley had on Friday night, it took the Tigers even longer than the 6 minutes the Braves needed to get on the scoreboard. The game was 8 minutes and 14 seconds old before forward Jim McCargo scored Pacific's first points on its 10th shot of

**Please Turn to Page 10, Col. 2**

**MIRACLE PLAY**—With only 5 seconds left in the game, Pittsburgh scored on this freak play to beat Oakland, 13-7, Saturday in AFC playoff. At left, John Fuqua of Steelers falls to turf after he and Oakland's Jack Tatum (31) collided going for pass from the Steelers' Terry Bradshaw. The ball (circled) rebounds into hands of Pittsburgh's Franco Harris who clutches it (right) and takes off on 60-yard TD. AP Wirephotos

# A Day in NFL: One Miracle Deserves Another


Los Angeles Times

Sports

CC SECTION D 2†

SUNDAY, DECEMBER 24, 1972


## Steelers Beat Raiders on Freak Pass

BY BOB OATES, Times Staff Writer

PITTSBURGH—For the first time in the history of football—a sport that has been around in professional form for 53 years—television's instant replay camera was used to uphold the referee on the big call here Saturday.

NFL officials seated in the press box served as a court of last resort, ruling in Pittsburgh's favor on one of the freakiest and most controversial plays of the century.

The play was a pass thrown by Steeler quarterback Terry Bradshaw. It hit one or two players on the Oakland 35-yard line and bounced back to Pittsburgh's Franco Harris, who made a shoestring catch and ran it 42 yards for the winning touchdown with only 5 seconds left.

Officially it was a 60-yard pattern, Bradshaw to Harris, deciding a 13-7 thriller Pittsburgh's way as pro football opened its third annual three-week Super Bowl tournament in Three Rivers Stadium.

Two minutes earlier Oakland had seemingly won it, 7-6, on a 30-yard touchdown scramble by lefty quarterback Kenny Stabler against a Pittsburgh blitz.

Although the Steelers were probably the better team and may have deserved to win, only a miracle could have saved them in the last minute.

The miracle came on 4th-and-10 at the Pittsburgh 40 when Bradshaw unloaded his disputed pass.

Please Turn to Page 4, Col. 1

## Staubach Strikes Down 49ers, 30-28

BY MAL FLORENCE, Times Staff Writer

SAN FRANCISCO—It was a day when Northern California professional football teams slid into the Pacific Ocean.

In Pittsburgh, the Steelers stole a game from Oakland in the last 5 seconds and the same drama was repeated late Saturday afternoon at Candlestick Park.

The Dallas Cowboys, apparently beaten 28-16, scored 2 touchdowns in 38 seconds in the final minute and a half to knock the 49ers out of the NFL playoffs, 30-28.

So, the Super Bowl champions, who made the post-season tournament as the wild card entry, are one victory away from defending their title Jan. 14 in Los Angeles. The Cowboys meet the Green Bay-Washington winner next weekend and they'll be a road team again.

A good portion of a crowd of 61,214 was already on the Bayshore Freeway when Roger Staubach, disabled most of the season, worked his magic.

When the scrambling quarterback reached Billy Parks with a 20-yard scoring pass with only 1½ minutes left, it was generally considered a token touchdown — something that would make the final score seem respectable.

Dallas' next move was obvious—an onside kick—and San Francisco was prepared for it. Toni Fritsch dribbled the ball the required 10 yards and it nestled in Preston Riley's midsection.

Please Turn to Page 4, Col. 5

*JIM MURRAY*

## And Don't Forget...

**All right, Santa Claus,** put away those electric trains and toy guns. Never mind the peppermint candy and the stockings hung with care. We got a bigger list for you.

Give O. J. Simpson a block now and then.

Give Roman Gabriel back Bernie Casey.

Give the Dodgers back Richie Allen.

Give Bill Singer back his fastball.

Give Casey Stengel another 20 years.

Give Henry Aaron plenty of good pitches to hit.

Give Jerry Quarry a guy he can hit.

Give Willie Mays back five years.

Give Johnny Bench 20 more years.

Give Philadelphia a winner.

Give the Olympics back to the athletes not the politicians.

★

**Give Joe Louis** peace of mind and a tableful of 7s every night.

Give football a Bart Starr, baseball a Sandy Koufax, basketball a Bob Cousy and take back all those loudmouths and bright-lighters.

Give Arnold Palmer back those 30-foot putts.

Give Bob Hope our love.

Give Bo Schembechler the ball back on the one-yard line so he can kick his way into the Rose Bowl.

Give Notre Dame another Gipp.

Give the Army and the Navy a football team so the kids won't get the idea we're going to be a breather on Russia's schedule some day.

Give me a tee shot I can depend on.

Give every ghetto kid a ball and a bat to hit it with or a net to throw it through or a line to run it around, and give the rich kids a night in the tenements so they'll know what they missed.

Give Andretti a car he can race and not park.

Give A. J. Foyt the pole one more time.

Give Joe Leonard a straight track.

Give Shoemaker another Swaps.

Give the fight game another Dempsey.

★

**Give Sugar Ray Robinson** another unanimous decision—over narcotics use among the kids he works with.

Give the bantamweights a division where everybody isn't named Rafael Herrera.

Give Danny (Little Red) Lopez a title shot.

Give Vida Blue an owner he can work with.

Give Pete Rose a base to hit with his head.

Give Gale Sayers back his knees and hand him a football.

Give the guys who go to church equal time with the guys who go to Mr. Laffs.

Give the Dodger infield whatever you want but hand it to them, don't roll it or throw it.

Give Duane Thomas an answering service.

Give Jack Nicklaus golf.

Give Jerry West the ball; he'll take care of the rest.

Give Roberto Clemente a guy who takes a wide turn at first or tries to stretch a double.

★

**Give Gene Tenace** a wake-up call.

Give Sinatra one more session with Gordon Jenkins.

Give Rod Laver one more match-point at Wimbledon.

Give the Cubs a pennant and explain to them what it is.

Give Norm Van Brocklin a chance to put Bud Grant in the Super Bowl—and have him try to do it.

Give all the hackers wide fairways and two-a-side.

Give all the guys waiting in the Western Union office for a money order from home a page that their money has come.

Fix the game so that any pair gets you into heaven.

Give Art Rooney a championship and fix it so each and every guy out there who goes to work with a lunch pail or a briefcase or a shovel or a set of mops to scrabble for a living gets no worse than a tie in life.

**THE GRAND SLAM**—Cowboys' Ron Sellers slams ball to turf after catching winning pass as official signals touchdown. Score came in closing minutes of NFC playoff game as 49ers bowed, 30-28. AP Wirephoto

## Notre Dame Makes It 'Tough;' UCLA Wins 51st, 82-56

BY RON RAPOPORT
Times Staff Writer

There was nothing in UCLA's 82-56 victory over Notre Dame at Pauley Pavilion Saturday night that remotely compared with the drama of the day's events in Pittsburgh or San Francisco. But there might have been some storm warnings raised over a game the Bruins will play a month from now.

In winning its 51st straight game, John Wooden's team got what was clearly its sternest opposition of the season from a fighting Notre Dame team that has perhaps as much determination as talent.

Even though the margin of victory was wider than Friday night's 89-73 win over Pitt, this one was closer for longer. More importantly, the Irish, whose 1-5 record belies their ability, may be expected to put to good use the experience they got playing the Bruins when next they meet.

That will be on Jan. 27 when the situation will be considerably different. For one thing, UCLA will in all likelihood be going for its 61st consecutive victory, the one that would break the major-college record set by the University of San Francisco during Bill Russell's time there.

And for another, the game will be played in South Bend, Ind., where

Please Turn to Page 2, Col. 3

## HOME ICE STILL PLUS FOR KINGS—SABRES LOSE, 2-0

BY DAN HAFNER
Times Staff Writer

The Kings and the Buffalo Sabres go along with the theory that the home ice is a definite advantage in the National Hockey League.

The Kings, giving goaltender Rogatien Vachon more help than they do on the road, ended a four-game losing streak Saturday night by whipping the Sabres, 2-0, before 8,752 enthusiastic supporters at the Forum.

Los Angeles now is 12-3-3 at home, but only 2-13-1 on the road. The Sabres, who had won eight in a row before losing to California Friday night, are 3-10-4 away and 15-0-3 in Buffalo.

Please Turn to Page 2, Col. 7

## George Allen: Early Bird Who Gets the Win

### Redskin coach will 'pay any price' to achieve victory ... Is he fanatic or phony?

BY SANDY PADWE
Exclusive to The Times from Newsday

WASHINGTON — Jack Pardee groped through the darkness and reached for the ringing telephone. He snapped on the light then looked at the clock. It was 2 in the morning.

The caller was George Allen, Pardee's coach with Los Angeles and now with Washington. "He was watching films," Pardee said. "He found something and he wanted to tell me about it. That's his way of communicating. When you get a call at that hour, you tend to remember what he was calling about."

Pardee calls the defensive signals for the Redskins. It's a job Maxie Baughan used to have for the Rams. "Sure," Baughan said, chuckling, "I got calls. That's George Allen. I don't remember exactly what time they were but I know I was asleep. See, he studies the films and breaks them down so thoroughly that if he spots something he wants you to know right away, not the next morning."

Bill Kilmer, one of the Redskins' quarterbacks, said he has escaped the early-morning calls so far. "Maybe that's because he's primarily a defensive coach," Kilmer said. "But Sonny Jurgensen has gotten calls. Maybe not early in the morning. Not long ago Sonny was telling me that he was having dinner in Washington and about 10 o'clock he gets a call in the restaurant from George.

"George is watching films and getting ready for a game against the Giants and he notices something about Norm Snead. So he knows that Sonny knows Norm pretty well. The question in his mind had something to do with Snead's personality—you know; how he reacts to certain situations. So he called Sonny because he wanted the answer right then. Not the next day.

"There's no detail too small for Allen," Kilmer continued. "I've never played for a coach who wants to win so badly. It's an obsession. That goes from everything that happens on the field to this office. If he felt those doorknobs over there weren't helping us win, he'd have the doorknobs changed. To him every game is a new life. He feels like he's reborn."

George Burman played for Chicago when Allen was a Bear assistant. Later he played on the offensive line for Allen at Los Angeles. Now he, too, is with Washington. Burman is working for his doctorate in labor economics

**MOVIE BUFF** — By the hour, Washington coach George Allen watches the game films of his Redskins and their NFL opponents. AP Wirephoto

at the University of Chicago. His dissertation, "The Economics of Discrimination: the Impact of Public Policy," is nearly complete.

Burman is a George Allen watcher and enthusiast. "It's not just football that he's

Please Turn to Page 7, Col. 4

# 1973
# 1983

SPORTS IN THIS DECADE BECAME ALMOST AS MUCH A BUSINESS AS FUN AND GAMES. SALARIES ESCALATED quicker than a Nolan Ryan fastball and made millionaires of many baseball, basketball, and tennis players. Athletes hired agents and signed multiyear contracts that guaranteed and deferred their income. Teams raised ticket prices to pay their affluent employees.

Athletes also got more freedom to move from one team to another and went on strike if their demands were not met. Unions had become fixtures in all sports.

The networks paid millions to televise events, subsidizing leagues and teams and even the Olympic Games with their largess. Commercialism was rampant. Hardly a tennis or golf tournament was played that wasn't supported by corporate money. Companies paid millions to use the Olympic Games logo.

But probably the biggest story of the era, for Americans at least, was a victory by a bunch of amateur hockey players at the Lake Placid Winter Olympic Games in 1980. On February 22, the little-known U.S. players upset the Soviet Union, 4–3, and an entire nation cheered. The Americans then won the gold medal by beating Finland, 4–2. The hockey victory overshadowed a remarkable performance by a U.S. speed skater, Eric Heiden, who won five gold medals.

Protesting the Soviets' invasion of Afghanistan, President Carter ordered the U.S. Olympic team to boycott the Moscow Games in 1980. Several other Western nations also pulled out, leaving the Communist powers, Russia and East Germany, to dominate the competition. Chances are they would have dominated it anyway, because starting at Munich in 1972, they had been winning medals in bundles.

At Innsbruck, Austria, in 1976, the U.S. stars of the Winter Olympics were figure skater Dorothy Hamill, who won the gold medal, and cross-country skier Bill Koch, who won a silver medal in the 30-kilometer race, a competition which is about as American as borsch. Cuban runner Alberto Juantorena and Romanian gymnast Nadia Comaneci stole the show in the Summer Games at Montreal that year. Leading U.S. stars were decathalete Bruce Jenner, hurdler Edwin Moses, and the entire men's swimming team.

Tennis became a popular sport as millions of Americans took up the game. Jimmy Connors, Bjorn Borg, Billie Jean King, Chris Evert-Lloyd, Martina Navratilova, and John McEnroe became household names for their skill, income, and, on occasion, their behavior on court. Borg, in 1980, won his fifth consecutive men's singles championship at Wimbledon. But few tennis matches attracted as much attention as an exhibition in 1973 between a professional hustler, Bobby Riggs, and Billie Jean King. The women's lib movement got a big lift when King beat Riggs.

It was the decade of Secretariat, Seattle Slew, and Affirmed. All three horses won the Triple Crown —Secretariat in 1973, Seattle Slew in 1977, and Affirmed in 1978. A filly, Genuine Risk, won the 1980 Kentucky Derby, the first to do so since Regret won in 1915.

O. J. Simpson of the Buffalo Bills and the University of Southern California gained more than two thousand yards in one season, a National Football League record, and made more money than any football player in history. The Super Bowl became the nation's biggest sports event and television attraction. The Pittsburgh Steelers dominated the championship game, winning it four times.

Pitcher Nolan Ryan set a major league record in 1974 by striking out nineteen batters, and in 1981 he pitched his fifth no-hit game, surpassing Sandy Koufax's record of four. Fernando Valenzuela, a fat young Mexican pitcher, became baseball's biggest gate attraction in 1981 and led the Dodgers to a World Series victory over the Yankees.

One of baseball's most glamorous records, Babe Ruth's career total of 714 home runs, was broken in 1974 by Atlanta's Henry Aaron, who hit number 715 in Atlanta on April 8. Another slugger, Reggie Jackson of the Yankees, hit three home runs in one game to beat the Dodgers in the 1977 World Series.

An Englishman, Sebastian Coe, had lowered the record for the mile run to 3 minutes, 47.33 seconds by 1981. Another runner became famous by not running as far as she was supposed to. Rosie Ruiz was the first woman to finish the 1980 Boston Marathon, but officials disqualified her when they learned she had slipped into the race near the finish line.

Muhammad Ali defended his heavyweight title in some strange places, fighting in Zaire and the Philippines. He lost his championship to Leon Spinks in 1978 at Las Vegas and won it back from him at New Orleans the same year. After retiring in 1979 he tried once more to regain his title in 1980 but lost to Larry Holmes.

A more famous punch in those days was thrown by a football coach, Woody Hayes of Ohio State. He struck an opposing player on national television in 1978 and was fired.

The Los Angeles Rams started 1983 as they had a lot of other years. They fired their coach, Ray Malavasi, and hired John Robinson, who had quit the University of Southern California, he said, because he was tired of coaching and wanted to do something else with his life.

The nation lost a folk hero when Paul (Bear) Bryant, the winningest college football coach in history, died on January 26. In Alabama, and other Southern precincts, Bryant was a historical monument.

A noted Los Angeles public figure, Steve Garvey of the Dodgers, caused a flap among the city's baseball fans, especially women, when he refused his team's best offer and fled to San Diego for more money. Raising taxes would have caused less of a fuss.

It took seventy-one years but Jim Thorpe was finally recognized as the winner of the decathlon and pentathlon in the 1912 Olympic Games. On January 18, 1983, the International Olympic Committee gave to Thorpe's children the medals that had been taken away from him because he had violated the IOC's sacred rules of amateurism.

# THE ROSE PARADE: USC 42, OHIO STATE 17

Los Angeles Times
Sports
CC PART III 2†
TUESDAY, JANUARY 2, 1973

## JIM MURRAY

### Stone Age Football

**Well, I can see why** Woody Hayes kept his Ohio State team hidden. He should have locked them in a closet on game day, too. He should chain them to a bed when company is coming, or keep them in a sealed wing of the mansion.

It wasn't so much a game as a target practice. SC has a tougher time with tackling dummies.

Woody Hayes, who's a great student of military history, must have gotten his game plan from Mussolini. You don't really need an alphabet to describe his "attacks." It was so Cro-Magnon, you should do it in cave drawings. I don't know how Ohio came to the game, but I bet it was on stone wheels.

Woody Hayes' team made touchdowns like a guy laying carpet. They had all the razzle-dazzle of Princeton-Rutgers in 1869. Woody's team was so slow pigeons kept trying to light on them. I have seen guys move faster on canes.

★

**I felt sorry** for all those Ohio people who had to sell all that hay and save up for the trip out here and get the buttons on their shoes polished and then have to be embarrassed like this. They always sit in this one corner of the field near the end zone, eating sauerkraut and looking around for Bessie Love or the Gish Sisters. They all have their hair parted in the middle.

Woody's attack was exciting if you like to see the quarterback fall on the snap from center all day. He gave the impression he was running out the clock. On the opening kickoff. Might not have been a bad idea, because every time SC got the ball, Ohio looked like a housewife chasing a mouse with a broom.

Imagine blowing the egg money to come out here and get beat by a bunch of Hollywood wise guys who probably sit around their swimming pools and look at Paris postcards.

Ohio was undone by an identified flying object, a guided muscle from Santa Barbara named Sam Cunningham. All Ohio got to see of him was a blip.

★

**Sam Cunningham** gets touchdowns the same way we get to the moon. He lifts off, orbits the line of scrimmage, and then does a flaming reentry and splashdown in the end zone. The only way to stop that is, if they get him on the pad. Once he blasts off, you have to stand around and wait for him to come down. Sam set a Rose Bowl record for happy landings. His four touchdowns wiped out the Rose Bowl records of Elmer Layden, Jack Weisenburger and Mel Anthony. Laid end to end, his four touchdowns probably wouldn't make more than a birdie putt. But, vertically, they probably set altitude records.

Woody Hayes' team had some trouble with some unidentified flying objects, too. These turned out to be footballs. Woody's team had no idea they could be thrown. They appeared to be as shocked by the appearance of a ball not in the stomach of a fullback, but flying through the air, as if an elephant suddenly went overhead.

Woody Hayes kept sending in plays. He mixed his attack well. He sent the fullback right, he sent the fullback left, and he sent the fullback center. I don't know why they bothered to blow up the football. Behind 42-10, with only a few minutes left to play, Woody sent in a series of line bucks. This is like helping your kidnapper tie you in your trunk.

Please Turn to Page 8, Col. 1

STORY OF THE DAY—Fullback Sam Cunningham of USC scored four touchdowns Monday and all four looked just like this. Here he dives over Ohio State's Doug Plank (28). His TD flights covered 2, 1, 1 and 1 yards as No. 1 Trojans routed Buckeyes, 42-17, in the Rose Bowl.
Times photo by Larry Sharkey

## Cunningham Scores 4 TDs in Runaway

BY BOB OATES
Times Staff Writer

There were two parades in Pasadena Monday, including the one USC led in the second half at the Rose Bowl with Ohio State following far behind.

It was a 42-17 rout in which the unbeaten Trojans scored the first five times they had the ball in the last two quarters after a 7-7 struggle in the first two.

The 50-year-old bowl may never before have seen such a parade. The record 106,869 there may never have seen such a backfield:

—Quarterback Mike Rae's passes (18 of 25 for 229 yards) broke the game open.

—Flanker Lynn Swann's six catches and tailback Anthony Davis' 157-yard explosion on 23 runs moved the ball.

—Fullback Sam (Bam) Cunningham moved it over. Scoring a Rose Bowl-record four touchdowns with high dives from the 1- and 2-yard lines, Cunningham ruined one of coach Woody Hayes' proudest possessions, his goal-line defense.

**Trojans Finish Undefeated**

And so the Trojans finished the season 12-0 as the country's only major undefeated team, bringing coach John McKay his third national championship in 13 years.

Beyond doubt this is McKay's best team and one of the finest yet organized in college football. The 42 points were the most ever scored against Hayes at Ohio State.

Because of the demands of television, the Trojans had played only twice since Nov. 4—with two-week layoffs before the UCLA and Notre Dame games—and they were plainly out of practice in the first half.

This was most noticeable when they tried to tackle the Buckeyes. Often they didn't.

But in the 30-minute scrimmage before the break, their timing came back, and in the third quarter the Trojans broke Hayes' heart.

Asked if this is the greatest team he's played against, Woody replied: "Yes, I'd say so."

**Fourth Pac 8 Win in Row**

As a West Coast entry beat the Big 10 for the fourth straight time in the Rose Bowl, USC marched 57, 56 and 67 yards to 3 touchdowns and scored 3 others after turnovers at the Ohio State 38, 32 and 41-yard lines.

It was Hayes' fear of Anthony Davis, who had overwhelmed Notre Dame in November with two touchdowns on kickoff returns, that got the Trojans going in the third quarter. The Bucks kicked off short to avoid Davis, giving the Trojans field position at their 43 and 44-yard lines.

The massive crowd sat back expecting the Bucks to hold the line again, as they had in the first half, but the Trojans flattened Ohio's defense both times with an ease reminiscent of their other big wins this golden season.

It was all over, 28-10, before the end of the third quarter.

Please Turn to Page 8, Col. 1

## BOWL INCIDENT

### Hayes Shoves, Injures Times Photographer

BY MAL FLORENCE
Times Staff Writer

As Times photographer Art Rogers was taking a picture at the Rose Bowl Monday, Ohio State football coach Woody Hayes shoved Rogers' camera into his face. He later required medical treatment.

Rogers said he was one of a half dozen persons photographing the coach huddling with his team during warmup drills five minutes before the Rose Bowl game.

Rogers was crouched low, using a long lens, when the huddle broke up and Hayes charged out and jammed the camera into his forehead, Rogers said.

"That ought to take care of you, you son of a bitch," Rogers quoted Hayes as saying.

Rogers said there was no provocation. He is 55 and has been a Times photographer 33 years.

Rogers received medical aid before the game then remained at the Rose Bowl and photographed the first half.

The photographer left the Rose Bowl in the second half and checked into The Times medical department. He complained of double vision, inability to focus and extreme brightness in his sight.

He was sent to a specialist who said there was swelling in both eyes and damage to the right eye. But the specialist did not think the damage would be permanent.

Rogers was not hospitalized.

Hayes kept reporters waiting for 20 minutes—as he said he would—before submitting to a post-game interview in a special meeting room near the Ohio State dressing room.

For almost five minutes he was genial and courteous while he discussed his team's 42-17 loss to the Trojans.

However, when Hayes was asked to give his version of the Rogers incident, he exploded.

"Oh, for Jesus Christ's sake, forget it," he snapped and threw a microphone he was holding onto the floor. "That's the end of this interview. Those are really big stories."

Hayes stormed brusquely past writers to the Ohio State dressing room.

Before parting, Woody snapped: "He (Rogers) wasn't hurt."

When informed that Rogers received medical aid, Hayes muttered something inaudible, then secluded himself behind the Buckeye dressing room doors.

ANTHONY GETS HIS KICKS—High-stepping Anthony Davis of USC kicks out of grasp of Ohio State's Neal Colzie in end zone after twisting 20-yard run for third Trojan touchdown Monday. Davis gained 157 yards in 23 carries before giving way to reserves in the latter stages.
Times photo by Steve Fontanini

## Bowl Results

**ORANGE**

| | |
|---|---|
| Nebraska | 40 |
| Notre Dame | 6 |

Story on page 2

**COTTON**

| | |
|---|---|
| Texas | 17 |
| Alabama | 13 |

Story on Page 3

## NOBODY PLAYED THE GAME HARDER

### Clemente: Complex Person Known to Few

PITTSBURGH (AP) — Nobody played the game of baseball any harder than Roberto Clemente, a complex man who legged out every infield grounder as if the World Series were at stake.

Those close to him during his 18 seasons as a Pittsburgh Pirate knew him for much more than his public image as a supposed hypochrondriac who could hop out of a hospital bed and line a double to right.

"Maybe we as teammates didn't know him as well as we could have," said Pirate pitcher Steve Blass. "But I think we knew him better than some of the fans. He was more than a great baseball player."

Thousands of stories have been written about Roberto Clemente, No. 21 for the Pirates. But there were other sides to Clemente that were unpublicized. He seemed to want it that way.

A frequent visitor to hospital patients, he had planned some day to open a boys' camp in his native Puerto Rico.

When he was lost in a plane crash Sunday off the coast of Puerto Rico, he was on a mission of mercy to deliver supplies to survivors of an earthquake in Nicaragua.

"Clemente's work with the relief effort was typical," said Pirate home-run hitter Wilver Stargell. "Roberto was always trying to help someone."

The record books will show that Clemente collected his 3,000th hit Sept. 30 against the Mets at Pitts-

Please Turn to Page 13, Col. 1

Roberto Clemente

# Who Said Nobody's Perfect? Dolphins Go 17-0

Los Angeles Times
Sports
BUSINESS & FINANCE
CC PART III 2†
MONDAY, JANUARY 15, 1973

## Miami Makes It All the Way by Beating Redskins, 14-7, in Super Bowl

BY BOB OATES
Times Staff Writer

It was Don Shula's finest hour. The football team he has coached for three years, the Miami Dolphins, won the world championship Sunday with a performance that stopped just short of perfection when Garo Yepremian turned out to be a lousy passer.

Yepremian, the little Miami tie-maker who doubles as a place-kicker, tried to stretch his talents too far in the fourth quarter. Attempting a pass after a blocked kick, the 170-pound Cypriot fumbled to Mike Bass for a 49-yard Washington touchdown.

This was the main thing the Redskins did right in Super Bowl VII, which Miami won, 14-7, after a 14-0 first half that looked like 28-0. The Dolphins, masterfully prepared by Shula, were much the better team, scoring once with their offense (a 28-yard Bob Griese pass after a 63-yard drive) and once with their defense (Nick Buoniconti's 32-yard interception return setting up Jim Klick's 1-yard touchdown).

And so the National Football League has a new champion. More than that, it has a champion with a perfect record for the first time.

After a 14-0 season, the Dolphins won all three in the Super Bowl tournament for a 17-0 mark that has never been approached and may never be duplicated. The NFL's only other undefeated teams in 53 years (the Chicago Bears in 1934 and 1942) both lost in the championship game.

The odds against Shula were enormous. But on an 80-degrees-plus, smoggy afternoon in the Coliseum, before a Super Bowl record crowd of 90,182, he had one thing going for him. He and his players had been there before. They were humiliated in last ;ear's Super Bowl by Dallas, 24-3.

This was the first championship appearance for coach George Allen's Redskins — and this is an event that has never been won by the club with the least Super Bowl experience.

Title game experience, in fact, has been decisive in the NFL finals most of the time since 1960, when Vince Lombardi was a loser in his first championship bid against a Philadelphia team quarterbacked by Norm Van Brocklin, a playoff veteran.

There is something about pro football championships, including Super Bowl matches particularly, that makes most athletes freeze in the first-time pressure.

On the Coliseum stage this time the Redskins were plainly tense and tight. They at no time resembled the loose, poised team that beat up on Dallas two weeks ago.

In January, 1972, it was the Dolphins who were tense and tight as they lost to Dallas. But they have spent the last 12 months campaigning to make somebody pay for it, and Washington, a one-point favorite, did.

Strategically, the difference was that Miami opened up with first-down passes before Washington got around to it. The turning point was Griese's first-down pass to Paul Warfield for 18 yards in the last minute of the first quarter,

Please Turn to Page 8, Col 1

SETUP—Jim Mandich, Miami Dolphins' tight end, makes a diving catch of this 19-yard pass from quarterback Bob Griese on Washington's 2-yard line to set up second TD in the Super Bowl Sunday at the Coliseum. Jim Kiick scored moments later to make the score 14-0. Miami won game, 14-7.
UPI photo

TWILLEY SCORES FIRST — Miami receiver Howard Twilley clutches the ball after taking a pass from Griese for a 28-yard touchdown that started Dolphins toward their 17th straight win.
Times photo by Ben Olender

'SO SCARED . . .'

## Garo's Goof: Cypriot Kicker Is No Passer

BY JEFF PRUGH
Times Staff Writer

"My mind went blank," said tiny Garo Yepremian, describing the zany moment when he picked up the ball in the Super Bowl and handled it like a hot potato.

The man who grew up in Cyprus kicking soccer balls, not throwing footballs, stood in th. Miami dressing room Sunday and repeatedly described the blocked field-goal try which boomeranged into Washington's only touchdown.

"I just picked up the ball and thought I could throw to somebody," he said in the wake of his team's 14-7 victory. "I saw two teammates who were open, two white jerseys. But the ball—when I tried to throw—just slipped out of my hand."

Result: the Redskins' Mike Bass caught the ball and ran it back 49 yards for a touchdown with only 2:07 to play. And for several anxious moments, Yepremian thought he had kicked away the whole game.

"I was so scared," said the 5-foot-8 specialist. "Scared maybe I could've lost the game. I should have just fallen on the ball. I shoulda ate it, but I made a mistake. Coach (Don) Shula told me the same thing when I got to the sidelines. He told me, 'Next time, just fall on it.'"

Yepremian reflected on the possible consequences.

"Wouldn't it have been terrible?"

Please Turn to Page 4, Col. 4

JIM MURRAY

## It Was Super Bore VII

**You're not going to believe this** but you know that funny little team with the sardines on its helmets—ones no one would recognize unless they were wearing numbers?

Well, they won the Super Bowl Sunday. The pauper made prince. The little old lady with the egg money broke the bank at Monte Carlo. The claimer won the Derby. The charlady got asked to the ball. The help is sleeping in the master bedroom.

I know next you'll be telling yourself this guy is going to tell us Truman beat Dewey or Russia bought a seat on the Stock Exchange.

You got me pegged for the kind of guy who leaves cookies out for Santa Claus. You're saying, get a net over this guy or next he'll be telling us there is an Easter bunny. You'll figure me for a guy who writes to the Tooth Fairy or who thinks Cinderella was a documentary.

Well, Miami Kiicked hell out of those Establishment types from Washington. Griese wasn't kid stuff. Little wasn't chicken. Mercury Morris is not a guy who repairs thermometers. He got his name from taking footballs, not temperatures. Miami got a Great Scott.

★

**I have seen better games** at New Britain State Teachers College when Hoover was President. In fact, I have seen better games where the mothers made the uniforms. The football was right out of Walter Camp. So was the score.

When two of the greatest teams in the universe compete in front of 80 million people for $15,000 per man you might expect something that was better than what was, essentially, a 2-1 game. Most of the game looked like 22 guys stuck in a revolving door.

The only excitement of the game came when Garo Yepremian, who weighs 168 pounds and never touched a football with anything but his toe, decided to throw a forward pass with a blocked field goal. I don't know whether it was supposed to be a down-and-out, a post pattern or who the primary receiver was or whether Garo was bucking to be backup quarterback next year, but this was the poorest forward pass ever seen in a Super Bowl. Even for an Armenian tie salesman from Cyprus, it was poor.

Two passes won it for the Dolphins. The funny thing is, they were both thrown by Billy Kilmer, who is supposed to work for the other guys. The only significant completions Billy had all day were (1) to Nick Buoniconti, an aging middle linebacker who returned it 32 yards despite the fact he can run just faster than he can crawl, and (2) to Jake Scott, who caught the pass in the end zone and brought it out to midfield. It was the only pass Kilmer got in the end zone all day.

★

**The Buoniconti interception** was turned into a touchdown in five plays, Jim Kiick going over from the 1 and the Scott interception came with only 5 minutes to play. So Kilmer's two most spectacular passes gained 83 yards — for Miami.

Not if you had Mt. Palomar's telescope could you find anything Super about this Bowl. They could have played the game in a tar pit for all the offense it generated. It had all the thrills of a poker game in Orange County.

The two teams were so similar it looked like two sisters dancing. They could have swapped uniforms at the half and no one would have been the wiser. They could have played it by phone.

In addition to three interceptions, Kilmer hit the goal posts with another pass. Kilmer threw at anything that didn't move. The teams were so similar even he couldn't tell them apart.

Miami is now the only team in the long history of the NFL to go undefeated. The suspicion that their record was like Young Stribling's — padded with fights with his chauffeur—now must be laid aside. I don't think Washington could be 17-0 against their second team. If they have one.

Please Turn to Page 8, Col. 2

## Kilmer Shoulders Blame for Defeat: 'Didn't Throw Well'

BY MAL FLORENCE
Times Staff Writer

George Allen has often said that his Washington Redskins win and lose as a 40-man team, but quarterback Bill Kilmer departed from his coach's policy and blamed himself for the 14-7 Super Bowl loss to Miami.

"I just didn't throw very well," said Kilmer, "and two of my three interceptions had a lot to do with the outcome. One set up a Dolphin touchdown and the other took one away from us."

An interception by Miami middle linebacker Nick Buoniconti led to the Dolphins' second touchdown and a 14-0 halftime lead.

Then, when the Redskins were on the Dolphin 10-yard line in the fourth quarter, Kilmer was intercepted in the end zone by free safety Jake Scott, who returned it 55 yards.

"Both times I tried to force the ball," said Kilmer, a onetime UCLA tailback. "On the pass Buoniconti intercepted, they were blitzing their strong side backer and I had no one to pick him up because both of the backs were in pass patterns. It was either throw it or get sacked and I probably shouldn't have thrown it.

"On the Scott interception, Charley Taylor was open for a moment but Jake just jumped in front of him."

The previous down Kilmer aimed a pass at tight end Jerry Smith but

Please Turn to Page 6, Col. 1

## WEST'S DEFT THEFT LEADS LAKERS TO 102-100 VICTORY

With 1½ minutes left in Sunday's game against Atlanta, the Lakers held a 95-94 lead and Jerry West had already scored 33 points.

But the best was yet to happen as West came up with a quick-handed steal of the ball from Pete Maravich and scored two baskets on layups to lead the Lakers to a 102-100 victory over the Hawks in Atlanta.

The victory enabled the Lakers to finish their 7-game road trip with a 4-3 record—the last three wins in a row—and gave Los Angeles a 4-game lead over Golden State in the NBA's Pacific Division.

Please Turn to Page 10, Col. 4

TOUCHDOWN . . . BARELY—Twilley barely gets the ball into the end zone as the rest of his body twists out of bounds after he was hit by Redskin Pat Fischer. Official starts to signal touchdown.
Times photo

MANNY IN ON 10 TACKLES

## Unsung Fernandez Foils Redskin Rushers

BY CHARLES MAHER
Times Staff Writer

A few days before the Super Bowl, Manny Fernandez was approached by a writer. "Got a minute?" the writer asked.

"Hell, I got all day," Fernandez said.

As one of the no-names in the Miami defense, Fernandez had probably been pestered for interviews about as often as the cymbals player in the Keokuk firemen's band.

It all changed for Manny Fernandez Sunday. An hour and 15 minutes after the Super Bowl, Manny still hadn't made it to the showers.

Reporters, he finally discovered, can be harder to fight off than offensive linemen.

The reason they were after him was that he was probably the player of the game. The honor actually went to Miami safetyman Jake Scott, who made two interceptions, but Fernandez was probably the biggest single problem the Washington Redskins had Sunday.

"Stopped by Fernandez," the public-address announcer kept saying. They should have put it on one of those tapes where at the end you hear, "This is a recording."

Fernandez was in on 10 tackles, one a sack. Washington would give Larry Brown the ball and Brown would start one way, then cut back. And there would be Fernandez, waiting to embrace him.

"We knew they were going to cut back," Manny said later in the dressing room," and we wanted 'em to. We were waiting for 'em."

Manny has a hoarse voice, a Fu Manchu moustache and long, stringy hair. He put on his silver-rimmed glasses as soon as he got to the locker room. He's nearsighted.

"That's why I can't let the runners get away from me," he said. "I'll lose them."

"Was this your best game?" he was asked.

"Oh, hell no. I made 12 tackles against Buffalo and stole a handoff. But for a Super Bowl, this was probably my best game."

Please Turn to Page 4, Col. 4

# Wonderful World of Walton---It's UCLA, 87-66

BY DWIGHT CHAPIN
Times Staff Writer

ST. LOUIS—Bill Walton may not be playing for the UCLA Bruins, the Philadelphia 76ers or any other earthly team next season. He's already in another world.

The redhead scored an NCAA final-game record 44 points Monday night as UCLA remained where it's been for seven straight years—at the top of college basketball—by wearing down and then slaying the Memphis State Tigers, 87-66, at St. Louis Arena before a crowd of 19,301.

The point total was 2 more than the record set by ex-Bruin Gail Goodrich in 1965. The way Walton did it was amazing.

He made 21 of the 22 shots he tried, missing only in the first half on a high lob pass. Many of the points came on those same, soaring lob passes from the Bruins' forgotten guard, Greg Lee, who had 14 assists.

It was the night the lights went out in Missouri for Memphis State—champions of the Missouri Valley Conference—but the Tigers didn't go early, or easily.

Using a 1-2-2 zone defense, they deadlocked UCLA, 39-39, at halftime and stayed close for the first 10 minutes of the second half.

But they had no defense for the Red Baron, even though he played the last 9 minutes 27 seconds with 4 fouls, and left the game with 2:51 remaining after twisting an ankle.

Clean John Wooden, whose Bruins won their seventh straight NCAA title, ninth in the last 10 years, 75th straight game, 36th in a row in tournament play of 30 this season, clearly outcoached Clean Gene Bartow of Memphis State, making his first appearance in the na-

Please Turn to Page 7, Col. 2

BY JEFF PRUGH
Times Staff Writer

ST. LOUIS—He sat there at courtside as newsmen and cameras and microphones converged on him tighter than Memphis State's zone defense.

Bill Walton of UCLA was on center stage again Monday night, even though he didn't seem to want to be.

Again and again, when they tried to quiz him about perhaps his finest hour in basketball, his eyes gazed sullenly at the floor—at no one—and he answered, tersely:

"I don't want to talk about it, man."

The UCLA Bruins had written another perfect ending to a perfect season—their fourth in nine winters of NCAA championships. They laughed and hand-slapped and embraced after beating a good Memphis State team, 87-66. They happily accepted congratulatory handshakes from UCLA chancellor Charles Young, who gleefully said, "Unbelievable! . . . Great game, Greg! . . ."

In a moment, coach John Wooden moved down the bench to whisper into Walton's ear. Then he smiled and affectionately rumpled the thick, red hair of the young man who had thrown in 44 points to break ex-Bruin Gail Goodrich's NCAA title-game record 42, set in 1965 against Michigan.

And when somebody queried Walton about the extent of his ankle injury, which he got in a spill late in the game, he shot back:

"I don't know. It just hurts."

Moments later, he limped slowly through the swarm of well-wishers on the St. Louis Arena court, toward the Memphis bench.

Please Turn to Page 7, Col. 5

**UP FOR GRABS**—Bill Walton of UCLA (left) and Ronnie Robinson of Memphis State reach for ball during NCAA finals Monday night at St. Louis. Walton had 44 points to lead Bruins to 87-66 win.

*JIM MURRAY*

## Pitfalls Passed By

VERO BEACH—When Donald Howard Sutton came up to the big leagues in 1966, packing a Bible and a curveball and announcing he owed it all to God, no one got too excited.

Baseball had seen this immorality play once too often. The downy-cheeked kid with the grace of God purring in his heart hadn't seen Broadway yet. The girls back home weren't 38-22-36 and hanging around the clubhouse door in mink and limousines. The flesh pots weren't open till 4 a.m. in the morning for starting pitchers or star quarterbacks back home.

The usual thing is to check this kid out 10 years later and he's sitting in the clubhouse with a paunch on his belly, red eyes, and the veins in his nose broken, and there's a paternity suit, a divorce, a car wreck or two, and an advance on his salary to pay off the bad investments he made with cocktail acquaintances. And, when someone asks him about his relationship with God, he says "Who?"

★

**He thinks St. Paul is a city,** the "Bible" is The Sporting News, "Genesis" is a rock group. He wonders how he could have been so naive as to trust in anyone but himself.

All of this, one was sure, was in store for Donald Sutton. "Just wait till they start hitting his curveball," was the dire prediction. God would get knocked down. Religion would get it in the ear.

Well, now it's eight years later and Donald Sutton's curveball has been whacked pretty well, particularly in 1969 when 38 home runs and a league-leading 127 runs were scored off it.

Sutton threw a fastball through a locker in St. Louis, kicked a bucket up into the electric lights in Chicago. But he didn't grab a bottle, a dame, or prowl the Sunset Strip looking for one or the other or both. Nor did he typically blame the manager. Not even when they sent him down to the minor leagues (where he struck out 19 guys in 16 innings and the managers there complained, "If you got someone better than him on the major league roster why don't you just send him to Cooperstown?").

The players called him "Elmer" (for Gantry) or "Oral" (for Roberts) and the journalists periodically waited around the hotel lobbies hoping to find him coming home hiccuping or with lipstick on his collar or in his room.

★

**They never even caught him** in an "R" movie. Piety is no guarantee you can get your fastball by Henry Aaron, otherwise the sawdust trail would be crowded with right-handed pitchers but, wherever his strength comes from, Don Sutton was just about the most effective right-hander in the National League last year. He led the league with nine shutouts, gave up only 13 home runs and 63 walks. He won 19. The manager would put up with those kinds of statistics even from a guy who had to be given coffee and cold showers between innings.

Sutton did this with a defense which can be mercifully described as "porous" in that porosity was only one of its problems. Sutton greeted his support—or lack of it—with a shrug. "They don't get mad at me when I throw a home run," he explained.

Sutton is the last to suggest the secrets of getting the side out can be found in Deuteronomy. But he doesn't think it can be found in a

Please Turn to Page 6, Col. 7

**HELPING HAND**—UCLA's Bill Walton, a virtual one-man show in NCAA title game Monday night, finally needed some help late in game after spraining his ankle and Memphis State's Larry Finch provides his shoulder to lean on as Walton hobbles off the court.
(AP) Wirephotos

## George Sisler, 80, Hall-of-Famer and .400 Hitter, Dies

ST. LOUIS (UPI)—George Sisler, a baseball Hall of Fame first baseman who twice batted over .400 despite serious eye problems, died Monday following a brief illness.

Sisler, who was 80 Saturday, had been a patient for the last eight days at St. Mary's Health Center.

Hospital officials never specified Sisler's illness but said only he had been in a "generally run-down condition." He was taken off the critical list on his birthday Saturday when a hospital spokesman said he appeared "chipper."

**Keen Interest**

The spokesman said Sisler had maintained a keen interest in baseball since his hospitalization.

Sisler, born March 24, 1893, at Manchester, Ohio, was nicknamed "Gorgeous George" because of his all-round abilities as a hitter and fielder. A two-time .400 hitter, with a top of .420 for the St. Louis Browns in 1922, Sisler helped perfect the first-short-first double play.

Sisler, left-handed all the way, was elected to the Hall of Fame in 1939 after compiling a .340 batting average for the Browns, Washington Senators and Boston Braves from

Please Turn to Page 5, Col. 1

ANGELS' ATTITUDE 'LOUSY'

## 'Nice Guy' Winkles Explodes After Club Trounced Again

BY RON RAPOPORT
Times Staff Writer

PHOENIX—Angel manager Bobby Winkles, angry over his team's play and attitude during spring training, blasted his players Monday.

"If my Arizona State team had played this badly," the former college coach said, "I'd take them out collectively and run them till they vomit. With professionals, that's senseless, but you can be sure that if we have to put up with this during the season there will be some heavy donations to a lot of charities."

Winkles' comments were made after the Angels dropped their fourth straight exhibition game, 7-1, to the Cubs in Scottsdale.

"I've sent my razor and my belt home," he said sardonically. "And I've had a guy come up here and put bars on the windows. But I wouldn't expect Harry Dalton (general manager) to put up with what he sees on the field, or with the manager."

Winkles said he is not upset as much over the Angels' losses—the club is 5-9—as he is at the margin of defeat and the players' attitude. The last four losses were 6-1, 14-4, 8-3 and 7-1.

"When you get beat by seven and eight runs a game," he said, "you're lousy. One thing about defeat — it doesn't bother our ball club. They'd lay right down beside it and go to sleep. They know I'm upset about it but, they don't play any better and they can't play any worse. Baseball is a game of peaks and valleys, but we've seen nothing but valleys.

"All spring, I've been a nice guy, but I haven't been able to communicate. They don't seem to listen. They didn't listen last year. What's the answer? The answer hasn't been found over 11 years of losing. It's presumptuous of me to think I can change it in one spring."

Winkles said he is particularly concerned about the Angels' pitching which is considered perhaps the team's strongest point, but which has given up 35 runs in the last four games.

"That's 25 too many," Winkles said. "The one thing I expected to carry us while I experimented was our pitching and it hasn't even come close. Nobody's making an effort to see what the situation is."

Of the rest of the team he said, "We don't have a great deal of ability. We have to use scrap and hustle. We have to win by intellect."

The manager named no players as targets of his unhappiness and made it clear he was upset with the club as a whole. In 14 games this spring, the Angels have committed 26 errors.

# Lakers Counting on Counts to Help Defend Championship

BY MAL FLORENCE
Times Staff Writer

Mel Counts has been flopping around the National Basketball Assn. for nine years. All arms and legs. A 7-footer without a home. His problem: he doesn't have the strength to be a center and is seemingly out of position at forward.

From Boston to Baltimore to Los Angeles to Phoenix to Philadelphia and back to Los Angeles has been the nomadic life of the gentle, blond giant as a pro.

His second stop in Los Angeles may be his last, however, because Counts is giving the Lakers a lift at a time when many people say the world champions are hard-pressed to defend their title.

He'll come off the bench tonight at the Forum in a final regular-season showdown with Milwaukee and even though he may resemble Ichabod Crane the opposition isn't laughing.

Since Mel moved up in the rotation as the Lakers' seventh man early this month, he has frustrated rival forwards with his shooting (52%) and rebounding (7 a game) while averaging 17½ minutes playing time.

"Sure, a smaller forward may get around Mel when he's on defense," says Dave DeBusschere, the New York Knicks' All-Star cornerman, "but Counts creates a lot of problems at the other end of the court."

There's no way a 6-5 forward can prevent the 7-0 Counts from releasing his jump shot. But Counts might still be on the bench if Wilt Chamberlain hadn't suggested to coach Bill Sharman that he could help the Lakers.

Chamberlain remembered Counts' contributions during his first tour of duty with the Lakers from 1968 through 1970.

Counts concedes he's comfortable at forward—only because he is playing with Chamberlain. "Maybe I couldn't play forward with some other team," said Mel, "but knowing that Wilt is behind me makes me feel more at ease. I've never been known for my defensive ability but if my man gets around me, he has to run into Wilt—and nobody gets by him.

"But knowing that Wilt is there hasn't made me slack off on defense. In fact, I try harder."

Sharman stresses defense and the gangling Counts said he has benefited from the example set by Chamberlain, Jerry West, Jim McMillian, Keith Erickson and Bill Bridges.

"It's a contagious thing," said the native of Coos Bay, Ore. "When you see other people stealing the ball and hustling you want to do it, too. It's fun and it's also a matter of pride. You don't want to let anyone down."

Counts is hardly the picture defensive player. There's not much meat on his bones—only 225 pounds. He thrashes around the court like a windmill. But no Laker tries harder than Mel. However, his hustle often results in fouls. At one time he led the league in technicals for berating officials.

Please Turn to Page 7, Col. 1

# It's a Ms.-Match---Riggs (Oink) Slaughtered

Los Angeles Times
Sports
BUSINESS & FINANCE
CC PART III 4¢
FRIDAY, SEPTEMBER 21, 1973

Bobby Riggs' summer-long ego trip ended in a humiliating 6-4, 6-3, 6-3 defeat by Billie Jean King in the Houston Astrodome Thursday night but Riggs seemed to be the only one who didn't realize it.

"I want a rematch," Riggs announced after Mrs. King had reduced him to a tired old man playing pitty-pat tennis on 55-year-old legs that not even 400 vitamin pills a day could rejuvenate.

If anyone else wanted a repeat, they didn't speak up.

The largest crowd in the history of tennis, 30,472, saw the the rout from $100 courtside seats and more distant places in the Astrodome and a television rating service in New York somehow came up with an instant estimate that 50 million more saw it on television. There is no doubt that the battle of the libber and the lobber, the feminist and the admitted male chauvinist pig, the 29-year-old star of the present and the middle-aged star of the past had caught the fancy of the country, including people who are titillated by wrestling and the Roller Derby. But, it seemed to be agreed, enough is too much.

In the era of the put-on (Alice Cooper, Andy Warhol, Miss America, platform shoes) Riggs engineered the most marvelous put-on of all but in the end he was exposed. His mixture of junk deceived Mrs. King not at all; she returned everything he put across the net and, presumably, sent him back where he belongs, playing in over-50 tournaments.

The bandy-legged little veteran was a crestfallen figure after the 2 hour-4-minute match in the air-conditioned arena.

Asked what happened, Riggs replied, "She was just too quick. I couldn't get the ball past her. She didn't get a break but still won."

Billie Jean was ecstatic.

"This is a culmination of 19 years of tennis for me," she said. "I've wanted to change the sport and tonight a lot of non-tennis people saw the sport for the first time."

She said she was inspired by the boisterous, cheering crowd, the blaring bands and circus-like atmosphere surrounding the match.

"This was a dream come true," she said. "I've always wanted people to scream at matches."

Asked about Bobby's request for a rematch, Billie Jean said, "Give me 24 hours and a beer — and I'll think about it."

She gave Mrs. Margaret Court, who was beaten by Riggs, 6-2, 6-1, on Mother's Day, credit for advice on how to beat Bobby. "She told me to play his backhand," she said.

Please Turn to Page 10, Col. 4

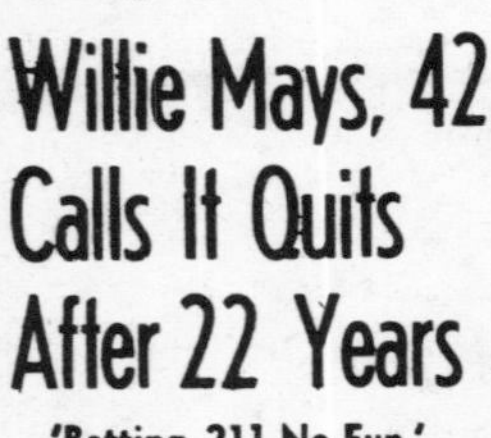

## Willie Mays, 42, Calls It Quits After 22 Years

### 'Batting .211 No Fun,' Says Mets' Superstar; Will Finish Out Season

NEW YORK (AP)—Willie Mays announced his retirement from baseball Thursday the same way he's always played—with grace and style.

"Maybe I'll cry tomorrow or the next day," the 42-year-old superstar said, "but not today. I've got too many friends in this room to feel sad."

With pride, Mays recalled the highlights of a fabulous 22-season career that has reached its climax in the shadows of the New York Mets dugout, where he nursed a series of nagging injuries that an athlete his age must expect.

"I have to face facts," said Mays, who has been limping along with a .211 batting average this season. "The body catches up with you in the long run. It's time to get out when the game stops being fun, and batting .211 is no fun. I've been in slumps before and I've always come out of them. But not at 42."

Mays hit six homers this season, pushing his career total to 660, third on the all-time list behind Babe Ruth and Hank Aaron. Even with his struggling 1973 season, Mays still has a .302 career batting average. His 3,283 hits are seventh on the all-time list.

"I've had a love affair with baseball," said Mays. "Now we will part, but only as a player."

Willie made it clear that he intends to remain active in the game that carried him from the sandlots of Westfield, Ala., through Negro league baseball in Birmingham and eventually to major league stardom with the Giants, first in New York and then in San Francisco.

When Mays came to the Mets last season, the deal included a guaranteed $50,000 per year contract for his post-playing days. His duties have not been spelled out, but he feels he can help the club and the game in several areas.

"There are a number of things I would like to do," he said. "Work with youngsters in the organization. Teaching them."

That sounds like a coaching job, but Mays frowned on the traditional one. "I don't want to be standing on first base, not doing anything," he said. "I think I can do more than coach."

It's entirely likely that in the dwindling days of the 1973 season, Mays will play one or two more games as the Mets make a run for the National League's East Division title. It was the quest for the division championship that caused Mays to announce his retirement now.

"I didn't want to interfere with them," he said. "Look at the last two or three weeks, coming from 12 games behind to one. Somebody is doing something, and I don't want to interfere by telling them I want to play."

Mays' last appearance came in Montreal 11 days ago when he bruised his ribs when he ran into into a metal railing trying to catch a foul pop fly. "They still hurt," he

Please Turn to Page 7, Col. 1

**TIRED OLD MAN**—Bobby Riggs, 55, slumps in his chair and tries to regain his composure during a break in his match at the Astrodome with Billie Jean King. Riggs lost in three straight sets. AP Wirephoto

## Lopes' Homer in 12th Wins for Dodgers, 5-3

### Aaron Homer-less as Crawford Hits 2; L.A. Only 4½ Back

BY RON RAPOPORT
Times Staff Writer

Dave Lopes, 708 home runs shy of Babe Ruth's record, hit a two-run homer in the bottom of the 12th inning Thursday night to give the Dodgers a 5-3 victory over the Braves and move them within 4½ games of the Reds in the National League West.

Hank Aaron was kept in the ballpark, though not off the bases, as he failed in six at-bats to hit his 712th homer, the one that would bring him within two of Ruth.

The homer was the sixth of the year for the rookie Lopes and came off Atlanta reliever Roric Harrison after Von Joshua had led off the inning with a single and taken second on Dusty Baker's error in center.

The win gave the Dodgers some slim hope that they may yet catch the Reds who open a three-game series in Dodger Stadium tonight. The Dodgers all but certainly need a sweep if they are to stay alive.

In winning their fourth straight game, the Dodgers got two home runs from Willie Crawford and a tense three-inning relief job from Charlie Hough who, if he keeps it up, may soon be known as the Cardiac Kid.

In each of the three extra innings Hough worked, the Braves got two men on base as he gave up four hits and walked two. But each time the 25-year-old knuckleballing right-hander managed to extract the final out before a run was able to score.

Aaron doubled twice in the game, drove in two runs and scored one himself. He also had a single in the eighth that was his 3,500th career hit.

The Dodgers took a 2-0 lead after four on Crawford's first homer in the second inning and Tom Paciorek's double-play grounder in the fourth that drove in Crawford, who had doubled.

Aaron doubled in two unearned runs and scored a third off Al Downing in the sixth. The runs were set up by Downing's inability to field a Ralph Garr grounder near the first-base line.

But in the bottom of the inning, Crawford hit his 14th homer of the year off the top of the bullpen screen to tie the score. An inch or two lower and it would have bounced back on the field.

In all, the Dodgers had 12 hits, four of them doubles, to go with the three home runs. But they left eight runners on base and hit into three double plays.

Thus frustrated, the Dodgers went into extra innings hanging on behind Hough.

In the 10th, Darrell Evans singled with one out and Aaron walked, to the boos of the crowd in the left-field pavilion that was hoping to do battle for the 712th homer. But Baker hit into a double play.

Please Turn to Page 4, Col. 5

## M'CLUSKEY ADDED TO FIELD FOR CHAMPIONS' RACE

BY SHAV GLICK
Times Staff Writer

Newly crowned U.S. Auto Club driving champion Roger McCluskey is the final addition to the International Race of Champions, Oct. 27-28, at Riverside International Raceway.

McCluskey, 43, completes the finest 12-driver field in auto racing history, comprising world and national champions in sports cars, stock cars and Indy-type championship cars.

The International Race of Champions highlights a weekend of action that features the 16th annual Times Grand Prix, final race in the Canadian American Challenge Cup series.

McCluskey is one of racing's most versatile drivers. Although this is his first championship car title, he won USAC driving crowns in stock cars in 1969 and 1970 and sprint cars in 1963 and 1964.

The Tucson veteran had a remarkable record in the three 500-mile races this year. He was third at Indianapolis, second at Pocono and fourth at Ontario.

Please Turn to Page 10, Col. 1

## British Surprise Leaders, 5½-2½, in Ryder Cup Golf

EDINBURGH, Scotland (UPI)—With Jack Nicklaus and Arnold Palmer managing no better than a split for a long day's work and Tom Weiskopf losing twice, the United States Ryder Cup team trailed Britain, 5½-2½ Thursday on the opening day of the Ryder Cup competition.

Losers only three times in the previous 19 editions of this biennial tournament, the U.S. could win only two of the eight matches.

Today's program calls for four four-ball matches in the morning and four singles in the afternoon, with the competition ending Saturday with eight singles matches.

Palmer and Nicklaus got the Americans their first point in the morning foursomes by trouncing Maurice Bembridge and Eddie Polland, 6 and 5. Then, in the afternoon fourball competition, Lee Trevino and Homero Blancas beat Neil Coles and Christy O'Connor, 2 and 1.

But that was it for the visitors, who managed only another half-point when Chi Chi Rodriguez and Lou Graham halved their foursomes with Tony Jacklin and Peter Oosterhuis.

Weiskopf, who won the British Open and the World Series of Golf this year, was a surprise double loser. He and J.C. Snead fell to Coles and O'Connor, 3 and 2, in the foursomes and then, along with new partner Billy Casper, was victimized in the fourball by Jacklin and Oosterhuis, 2 and 1.

"We just don't get enough experience in this kind of play," said Jack Burke, the non-playing U.S. captain. "I'm not happy with our position."

Trailing 2½ to 1½ after the foursomes, the Americans were unable to rally in the fourball over the par-71, 6,917-yard Muirfield course.

Even Nicklaus and Palmer, impressive winners in the morning, fell to Bembridge and his new partner, Brian Huggett, 3 and 1.

The American pair, four down at one time, rallied to trail by one hole at the 14th, but Bembridge chipped in from 25 yards for a birdie three to take Britain two points ahead again.

Scotsmen Brian Barnes and Bernard Gallacher were double winners for the British, defeating Trevino and Casper by one hole in the foursomes and then crushing Tommy Aaron and Gay Brewer, 5 and 4, in the four-ball.

Burke, who captained the American team when it last lost to Britain 16 years ago, said he was surprised how easily the course played.

Please Turn to Page 6, Col. 4

Jim Murray is on vacation.

MADE RIGHT DECISION

## Ramirez Upsets Ashe in Pacific Southwest

BY JEFF PRUGH
Times Staff Writer

It hasn't taken Raul Ramirez very long to convince himself—and the tennis world—he made the right move by turning professional last June.

Since quitting the USC tennis team, he has won $20,000 on the world tour—and Thursday he defeated Arthur Ashe, 6-4, 4-6, 6-3, in the Pacific Southwest Open, staying on the road to more riches.

"It was my best win, that's for sure," said Ramirez, who grew up in Mexico, a protege of the late Rafael Osuna. "But I really can't say whether it's the best I've played."

Actually, Ramirez has sparkled throughout the $75,000 tournament. He is unseeded and unsung, but certainly not unnoticed by the L.A. Tennis Club galleries.

Two days ago, he upset ex-Stanford star Roscoe Tanner, 6-3, 7-6, although the win wasn't all that startling to Ramirez because he had beaten Tanner in college.

Then came Ashe, who was seeded No. 3 behind Stan Smith and Ilie Nastase and who had never played Ramirez.

It figured that Ashe and Tanner, armed with two of the fastest services in tennis, would prevail—particularly on fast cement.

But Ramirez, who played summers at the L.A. Tennis Club as a teen-ager, knew how to exploit his marvelous counter-punching game, to say nothing of his service returns.

"My style of play," he said, "can give guys with big serves a few problems."

It gave Ashe problems in the second game of the third set. That's when Ramirez got a crucial service break at love to make it 2-0. And when Ramirez held service in the next game by unleashing three spectacular shots for winners, it was all over.

At 1 p.m. today, Ramirez will meet

Please Turn to Page 10, Col. 2

## The Game Is FOOTball

### And, Van Brocklin Says, the Way to Get to the Super Bowl Is on Foot

BY BOB OATES
Times Staff Writer

Norman Van Brocklin, the former Ram quarterback who coaches the Atlanta Falcons, says he had two thrills in his first 24 years in the National Football League.

"The first," he says, "was in 1951 when we won the championship in Los Angeles. Then in 1960 we won it in Philadelphia. Those were big years. I don't remember the other 22 years."

However, a third thrill is imminent, Van Brocklin believes. He is rounding out his first quarter century in pro football with his best team. Indeed, the Ram-Falcon winner in the Coliseum Sunday will be co-favored with the 49ers for the NFC's Western Division title.

It has been Van Brocklin's lot to coach nothing but expansion clubs, first in Minnesota for six seasons and next in Atlanta for six. He is now a serious contender for the first time since, 13 years ago, he became the only quarterback to beat Vince Lombardi in a world championship game.

Van Brocklin's 1960 achievement in Philadelphia—whose team was second-rate before he arrived and third-rate when he left—may have been the most brilliant in the NFL's first 53 years, considering (a) it was basically a one-man achievement and (b) he had to beat Lombardi, who in the next seven years was to win five world titles, including two Super Bowls.

But Ram fans still opt for 1951, when a Van Brocklin bomb brought them their only world championship. The receiver was Tom Fears, whose touchdown upset Cleveland, 24-17, on a 73-yard play.

In today's pro games when good teams get together such a play is almost impossible. What's happened to the forward pass?

"The human race has always learned from those who succeed," says Van Brocklin, the South Dakota-born son of a watchmaker who moved to California in the 1930s. "And in pro football success means the Super Bowl. Miami and Washington got there on foot last year. The name of the game is football. Check the stats."

*The 1972 statistics show Miami with an average of 10 completions a game in 17 pass attempts. Miami and Washington ran the ball three times out of four. What's happened to passes?*

"NFL teams pass some," says Van Brocklin. "We've always passed some but this has never been a passing league. It's been a running league all the time I've been in it."

*Didn't you play on a Ram team that set 20 passing records or so in one season?*

"Yes, but that team also ran well. For 25 years pro clubs have always run more than they passed."

*It hasn't always seemed as lopsided as it's been lately.*

"Well, the NFL got its reputation as a passing league in the years when the colleges hardly threw at all. By comparison with college teams, the pros threw a lot of passes 10 or 15 years ago. Colleges only threw when necessary. The pros had the pass in their game plan. That was the difference—but even then, pro teams were running more than passing. Check the stats."

*So what's happened is that the colleges have changed, not the pros.*

"They've both changed but the colleges are throwing more than they used to — which

Please Turn to Page 8, Col. 2

# THE STREAK ENDS ON FEAT OF CLAY

**Irish 71**
**UCLA 70**

Los Angeles Times
Sports
CC PART III 2†
SUNDAY, JANUARY 20, 1974

NO. 1, NO. 1, NO. 1, NO. 1—It's unanimous as far as Notre Dame fans are concerned. That's Irish freshman Adrian Dantley above the crowd and chances are the Irish basketball team, after ending UCLA's 88-game streak Saturday, 71-70, will be above the crowd in this week's polls.

## Bruins Shoot 70% in First Half, 0% in the Last 3:30

**BY JEFF PRUGH, Times Staff Writer**

SOUTH BEND, Ind.—If God made Notre Dame No. 1, as Irish fans shouted in the bedlam Saturday after The Streak had ended, He got considerable help from UCLA in a basketball game with a wildly improbable finish.

The score was Notre Dame 71, UCLA 70—a shocking ending to the longest winning streak in the history of college basketball, 88 games, and to a 139-game string for Bill Walton, who hadn't lost a game since his junior year in high school.

Even 'he winning couch, Digger Phelps, and his players sat dazed, spellbound, in their dressing room.

"Did we win?" asked Phelps, half-grinning, sweating profusely, tieless, after he finally fought his way through the mob of roaring fans to a tiny room jammed with newsmen.

"Yes," somebody said.

"Well, then," said Phelps, catching his breath, "I believe it."

It ended in, of all places, the same arena where UCLA had last been beaten three years ago—and it happened in a way that nobody would have predicted in his wildest dreams.

Notre Dame's Fighting Irish, seemingly knocked over the cliff and without even a prayer for victory, miraculously regained their poise in the last 3½ minutes while UCLA and coach John Wooden seemed to lose theirs.

In those frantic final minutes, Notre Dame ran off 12 points without retaliation—including the game-winning basket by guard Dwight Clay, a fall-away jumper from the right-hand corner with 29 seconds left.

At the same time, the Bruins were blowing a 70-59 lead with more rapid-fire mistakes than they'd made in years.

They missed easy shots. They lost the ball against Notre Dame's full-court, man-to-man press. And those who say college basketball is perfectly all right without a 30-second clock are probably saying, "I told you so," because the Bruins threw the ball away even while trying to stall and protect their lead.

And the winning streak—one of sport's most celebrated accomplishments—crumbled, piece by piece, before the eyes of the man who had

Please Turn to Page 10, Col. 1

### A MOST UNUSUAL DAY

## Digger Told His Players: It Will Be Unbelievable

*"This is not just an ordinary day. The chances are good that years from now you will look back on this day as one of the memorable ones in your life. Is this melodramatic? I don't think so . . ."*

THE REV. EDMUND P. JOYCE.
Executive Vice President of Notre Dame
at Saturday morning's team Mass

**BY FRANK DOLSON**
Knight News Service

SOUTH BEND, Ind.—This was such an extraordinary day that Pete Crotty's older brother, Mike, a New York school teacher, drove all night to be a part of it.

It was so important to Dwight Clay's mother that she rode the bus all the way from Pittsburgh.

It was so meaningful to freshman Adrian Dantley's mother that when her plane was fogbound in Cleveland, she, too, came by bus.

It was so out of the ordinary to Dick Harter that the Oregon basketball coach stayed up all night to get here. "I'd walk all the way to see you beat them," Harter told his former Penn assistant, Digger Phelps, the Notre Dame coach.

It was so big, so important, so exciting in the life of John Shumate that his parents phoned him from Elizabeth, N.J., at 6:30 a.m. to make sure he was ready to face it.

"They were praying with me on the phone," said the 6-9 minister's son who had to face Bill Walton on this day. "Not for victory, but that I would have faith in myself, my coach and my team; confidence that we could accomplish anything."

Even the near impossible.

Even a victory over UCLA.

"No matter what happens," John Shumate's mother had warned her son, "don't lose faith and confidence in yourself."

He didn't. None of them did, although the temptation must have been great on more than one occasion.

Not many teams can hope to spot UCLA 17 points and make a game of it, no less win.

Not many teams can spot anybody 11 points with just over three minutes to go and win.

Please Turn to Page 14, Col. 1

### JIM MURRAY

## Mantle of Greatness

**Mickey Charles Mantle** was born with one foot in the Hall of Fame. Unfortunately, the other one was in a brace.

If Mickey Mantle had had TWO Hall of Fame legs, he probably wouldn't have had to go through the formality of 18 big league seasons and 12 World Series. He's the first guy who limped his way to the Hall of Fame.

Mantle probably should be in the Smithsonian, too. He may be the last of a breed, as extinct as the brontosaur—the last of the great New York Yankee myths. Mickey played most of his career on one leg—and in dead silence. I don't think I ever heard him speak above a whisper. He behaved as if a ballpark were a library. He was as shy as a schoolgirl, the only superstar I ever saw blush. He was as private as the Pope.

He was, in the words of one reporter, The Man Who Wasn't Babe Ruth. And it infuriated the fans, the press, the league, the world, the front office, the backroom. He was as aloof as a German spy. He couldn't stand to be laughed at. When he missed a fly ball or a curveball, he went into a raging, silent sulk. But he punched things, not people.

"Mickey's got a hitting streak of 56 straight water-coolers," Whitey Ford once observed.

★

**Mantle gave the impression** on the field he didn't give a damn, that he was just waiting for the 5 o'clock whistle. But Mantle was as competitive as a shark.

"He hated pitchers that wouldn't give him nothin' sound to hit," ruminated Casey Stengel, who managed Mantle on a more or less friendly basis, mostly less, for 10 years.

Mantle went from a zinc mine to Broadway, from Oklahoma to Times Square, at the age of 19. "He never seen concrete before," Stengel explained as Mantle stood in frightened silence in right field at Yankee Stadium.

The Yankee press, used to the gregarious, bellowing Babe Ruth, for whom the big city held no more terror than a base on balls, resented Mantle's taciturnity and it showed in their copy. I doubt any player that great got that booed. I doubt any player that disabled got that great.

When Mantle showed up in Arizona as a raw recruit signed for a miserly $1,100 bonus and bus fare, sportswriters retired his number before he had been issued one. "He could have embarrassed my writers if it turned out he could not hit the curveball. They had him in Cooperstown in knickers," grunted Stengel.

Mantle's career could have been traced in X-rays. He had more cartilage and bone taken out of him than most people have. He was built like something that should have horns. He had to be careful on hunts. Even the moose thought he was one of them.

He was a haunted figure. The men in the Mantle family, including his dad, Elvin (Mutt) Mantle, died of cancer as young men. A well-bruited story about Mickey concerns the time a TV newsman asked him what his goal was. "Forty," he responded. "Home runs?" asked the telecaster. "Years," said Mantle grimly.

★

**He played in a World Series** once with a hole where the back of his hip should be. He tore his leg apart settling under a Willie Mays fly ball in his first World Series. "He tripped over one of them faucets out there," recalls Stengel.

He started out his career with a history of osteomyelitis, a bone disease which kept him out of the Army. He was lucky it didn't keep him out of shoes. Playing a game where you run into things with osteomyelitis is like digging tunnels under rivers with tuberculosis.

"You'd see him, he'd go down the dugout steps and his knees would shake. But he was the greatest hitter for distance I ever managed," recalls Stengel. "The distance of those balls were outstanding. He hit one in Washington one day and they had to send a cab after it as Red Patterson—he was the club publicity man—stepped it off and he says, 'My goodness, what if it was a thousand feet?' And I says, 'What if you have to send a boat after it?' And Griffith—he was the owner of the Washingtons in those days—he put a mark up where the ball went out of the park. But he had them take it down as it was commencing to scare his pitchers."

Please Turn to Page 2, Col. 1

DIGGER'S DEE-LIGHTED—Digger Phelps (right), the Notre Dame coach, savors his greatest victory, realizing it is only seven days until his team has to play UCLA again, this time on the UCLA home court. "I'm hoping for President Nixon to call and cancel our flight," Phelps said. "I hope we run out of gas before we have to go out there." Rematch is Saturday night at Pauley Pavilion.
AP Wirephotos

## Nolan Ryan

### Angels' pitching star is just ordinary citizen in hometown of Alvin, Texas

**BY BOB OATES, Times Staff Writer**

ALVIN, Tex.—This is the place that gave the world Nolan Ryan, the Angel who pitched two no-hitters and two one-hitters last year and struck out 383 American League hitters, breaking Sandy Koufax' major league record.

A bare 15 miles from the Gulf of Mexico, Alvin is a synonym for hot and humid—very hot and insufferably humid.

> *'My goals are to be consistent and keep respect of my fellow players'*

Probably nobody would live the life of a small-town citizen in this part of Texas who could live as a celebrity in New York or California; nobody, that is, except Nolan Ryan.

For the last six years, after getting the last man out at his places of employment, east or west—in two of the most populous and popular centers of civilization on the North American continent—Ryan has dropped thankfully into the driver's seat of his station wagon and tooled home to Alvin, pop. 11,702.

In Alvin he owns six cows, who bless him with six calves a year. In Alvin he has friends who will hunt with him two or three times a week. He squires his beautiful wife, Ruth, to the modest homes of their best friends: the young men and women they knew at Alvin Grammar School, Alvin High and Alvin Junior College. In Alvin he patches the shingles on his mother's house, and here he is raising Robert Reid Ryan, 2, to be an honest, happy Texan like Lynn Nolan Ryan, 27. In Alvin he lives.

In California this winter, conceivably, he would be brooding on the fate that denied him the Cy Young Award as the best pitcher in the American League last year, which he probably was. In California he would be reminded of the slight night and day.

In Alvin, when asked about it, he smiles. The eyes light up and he stands a little straighter, smoothing out the wrinkles in his sport shirt and work pants.

"Fellow down to Galveston mentioned it the other day," he says. The voice combines Irish music

Please Turn to Page 8, Col. 1

## Van Zijl Surprises in a 4:04.4 Mile; Liquori Finishes 2nd

### Mary Decker Sets Only World Record in 1,000 in Sunkist Before 13,601

**BY HARLEY TINKHAM**
Times Staff Writer

They wouldn't let him run at Mexico City and they wouldn't let him run at Munich, but South Africa's Fanie Van Zijl keeps right on running and continues to beat everything the United States has to offer.

Van Zijl, 25-year-old campaigner from Randfontein, capped a night of surprises and disappointments by holding off Marty Liquori to win the featured mile run in the 15th annual Sunkist Invitational before a sellout crowd of 13,601 at the Sports Arena Saturday night.

Coming off a dreadfully slow pace which saw the runners pass the three-quarters mark in 3:06.0, Van Zijl surged into the lead and gamely repulsed repeated bids by Liquori to win by two yards in 4:04.4.

Liquori was clocked in 4:04.7 and Dave Wottle, admittedly not in shape, was a badly beaten third in 4:09.5.

It remained for little Mary Decker to establish the night's only world record and for Dwight Stones to send the fans home happy by clearing 7-4¼ for a new American indoor record in the high jump.

Miss Decker, a 15-year-old 90-pounder from Garden Grove who upset the Soviet girls last summer in the USA-USSR meet in Minsk, set an indoor record of 2:26.7 in the women's 1,000-yard run.

Steve Prefontaine was a runaway winner in the two-mile, running 8:33.0, and George Woods scored the first surprise of the night, inching out world outdoor record holder Al Feuerbach in the shot put.

Woods, two-time Olympic silver medalist and world indoor record holder at 69-6½, threw 68-2 3/4 to Feuerbach's 68-2 1/4. Feuerbach's outdoor record is 71-7.

Although Prefontaine's time failed to approach his American record of 8:24.6, he indicated he's ready for bigger things by covering the final mile in a swift 4:12.7.

He'll be back for the Times Indoor Games, Feb. 8 at the Forum. Heading the two-mile in that one will be Belgium's Emiel Puttemans, world indoor record holder at 8:13.2.

The ballyhooed 880 showdown between Rick Wohlhuter and Italy's Marcello Fiasconaro failed to materialize. They met, but not at 880 yards. Fiasconaro's coach, after his arri-

Please Turn to Page 6, Col. 2

# UCLA LOSES POISE, LEAD, STREAK, TITLE

THEIR BIG MOMENT—North Carolina State's reserves are jubilant as Wolfpack scores an 80-77 win over UCLA in NCAA semifinals at Greensboro, N.C., Saturday. The double overtime victory ended a string of 38 NCAA playoff wins by the Bruins. Second from right is winning coach, Norm Sloan.

## N.C. State Wins, 80-77, After Trailing by 7 in 2nd Overtime

BY DWIGHT CHAPIN, Times Staff Writer

GREENSBORO, N.C.—It's over. The winning streak that may well be the greatest in sports history ended here Saturday as North Carolina State defeated UCLA, 80-77, in double overtime in the NCAA semifinals at Greensboro Coliseum.

It was a case of David (Thompson) slaying Goliath.

But Goliath—mighty UCLA, which had won a record 38 straight NCAA tournament games—was something of a setup, too.

Thompson made the short bank shot that gave North Carolina State the lead in the second overtime and two free throws that insured the victory.

But that was after UCLA blew the lead, something it had been doing much of this season. The Bruins did it twice this time, throwing away an 11-point lead in the second half, a seven-point lead in the final overtime period.

UCLA had gotten away with it numerous times, the last in a triple overtime victory over Dayton in the Western Regionals last week. But against the nation's No. 1-ranked team, and playing before a roaring, partisan Carolina crowd of 15,829, the Bruins simply couldn't escape again.

So the Wolfpack (29-1) advances into the Monday night's final, against Marquette (25-4), which beat Kansas, 64-51, in the other semifinal. And UCLA (25-4) gets to play the Jayhawks (23-5) for third place, an ignominious way to end a season after seven straight national championships, nine in the last 10 years.

North Carolina State did what few teams have been able to do effectively against the Walton Gang. It played UCLA straight up, man-on-man. Coach John Wooden of UCLA responded in kind, refusing to tinker with his offense as he had in recent weeks . . . and going to the bench sparingly.

Despite the Wolfpack's excellence, UCLA should have won it—and Wooden knew it.

"We had the game in hand twice and then made critical mistakes," he said. "We took three shots we shouldn't have with the 11-point lead and then made a couple of crucial mistakes in the second overtime."

The battle of the superstars was even. Bill Walton of UCLA had 29 points and 18 rebounds, Thompson 28 points and 10 rebounds. The battle of stars was almost even. Keith Wilkes of UCLA had 15 points and 7 rebounds, Tom Burleson of N.C. State 20 points and 14 rebounds.

But the following things happened

Please Turn to Page 8, Col. 4

Los Angeles Times
Sports
CC PART III 2¢
SUNDAY, MARCH 24, 1974

## Walton, Other Bruins May Sit Out Last Game

BY ROSS NEWHAN
Times Staff Writer

GREENSBORO, N.C.—Greg Lee, the UCLA guard, said, "You should always win when you have the kinds of leads we had."

Keith Wilkes, the UCLA forward, said, "Give them credit. They came back, but they couldn't have come back if we hadn't made the number of mistakes and turnovers that we did."

Bill Walton, the UCLA center, said very little, and, yet, may have said everything, as he was besieged by reporters following his team's 80-77 double overtime loss to North Carolina State Saturday.

It was more than the end of the UCLA streaks—the seven straight NCAA titles, the 38 straight playoff victories.

It may have been Walton's final game as a Bruin. When asked if he would play in Monday's meaningless consolation game with Kansas, he said, "I'm due for a rest."

And if he and some of the other Bruin starters don't play, they'll have the blessing of coach John Wooden.

"I think consolation games are for the birds," Wooden said. "Several of my players probably won't play and it will be all right with me."

"I don't know who's going to play and who isn't," Lee said. "There has been some discussion about it. As the coach said, our season is over. I imagine it will be left up to the guys who have eligibility left."

The UCLA dressing room, normally closed to reporters, appeared to be off limits again. The initial word to a small group of journalists huddled outside the locked door was that they would not be admitted.

Then information director Vic Kelley whispered into the ear of Wooden, who had left the dressing room on his way to an interview area.

Wooden stopped and reentered the dressing room. He emerged again, told Kelley that the players had said they would talk with the press, but to allow them another few minutes by themselves.

It was 20 minutes before the door opened, before athletic director J. D. Morgan waved approximately two dozen writers into the small room in the catacombs of the Greensboro Coliseum.

Dave Meyers was still in uniform, slumped on a bench, his back against the wall, staring into space.

Please Turn to Page 8, Col. 1

### JIM MURRAY

## Sun Sets on Bruin Empire

GREENSBORO, N.C.—Well, the sun did set on the British Empire, didn't it?

The Ark did hit Mt. Ararat finally.

Rome did decline and fall. The glaciers went back. The dinosaur vanished.

The Titanic went down. The waters of Johnstown receded. The Pharaohs departed. Even Methuselah died.

Napoleon was conquered, Caesar slain.

Nobody's perfect.

But they didn't have a 7-point lead with 3 minutes to play. They succumbed like great trees sawn in half. Their throats rattled. They had time for deathbed scenes like Camille. They went out, coughing, like the final act of a Verdi opera. People had their obits ready. There was a death watch.

UCLA died Saturday in the blush of health. Their cheeks were pink, their color good. They didn't even look as if they needed a doctor.

Anyone would have written their insurance as late as 2 o'clock Saturday. No one knows what time the end came. Because no one was expecting it. One minute they were waving their arms in the air signifying, "We're No. 1!" And the next minute, they had the pennies over their eyes. They drew the sheet over a dynasty.

They didn't even have a twilight of the gods. They just mysteriously disappeared like Judge Crater or the sardine off the coast.

The archaeologists of the future will be puzzled. Because they went down at their battle stations. They will be found frozen in inaction, as if felled by some mysterious force they didn't see coming. The autopsy will puzzle sports pathologists for centuries.

One minute, the UCLA Bruins' dynasty was in full flower. The barbarians were at the gates but the barbarians had a 7-point deficit. And they didn't even have the ball.

Napoleon got felled by the flower of the Russian, German, Austrian and British armies. The Bruins, so to speak, got beaten by people they were chasing up trees.

For 11 years, the Bruins have been the monarchs of basketball. The only championship they lost in that time was one they weren't in.

• ★

Great kings are felled by great adversaries. Caesar had Brutus; Napoleon, Wellington. Lee had Grant. But this was more like the dinosaur succumbing to the tsetse fly.

They threw some great challenges at the Bruins in the past. Elvin Hayes of the Houston Cougars comes to mind. The "Big E," they called him. There have been Big "E's" and Big "A's," "E's," "I's," "O's," and "U' s." And the Bruins always come walking out of the locker room alive, dusting their hands and saying, "You'll find the Big What's-His-Name in there. Bring a stretcher."

The 1974 Bruins were supposed to have been the greatest kings of all the reign. I mean, they won 88 straight games. Without breathing hard. They were as unbeatable as Alexander, as unsinkable as Molly Brown. Bill Walton played a game that was right out of Lourdes. This was George Gipp, Babe Ruth and Superman in sneakers.

North Carolina State, on the other hand, looked as if it played the game for laughs. The first time

Please Turn to Page 6, Col. 4

## FRED BROWN GETS 58 TO KO WARRIORS

OAKLAND (AP) — Fred Brown scored 58 points, including a 20-foot basket at the final buzzer, to give the Seattle SuperSonics a 139-137 victory over Golden State Saturday night.

Brown's total was the highest in an NBA game since Feb. 9, 1969, when Wilt Chamberlain scored 66 for the Lakers.

Brown made 24 of 37 shots.

The defeat virtually eliminated the Warriors from play-off contention, dropping them 2½ games behind the first-place Lakers in the Pacific Division. The Lakers have two games remaining, the Warriors three.

Please Turn to Page 3, Col. 1

MIXED EMOTIONS—Bruin center Bill Walton, left, mops his chin and listens intently to coach John Wooden during a time-out in Saturday's double overtime game. North Carolina State's coach Norm Sloan, right, yells at his players when the game appears to be getting away.

AP Wirephotos

## Wolfpack Will Hear Footsteps, Predicts Marquette Coach

From a Times Staff Writer

GREENSBORO, N.C.—Those who had said it would be merely a junior varsity preliminary to the UCLA-North Carolina State game were wrong.

It wasn't that exciting.

Marquette defeated Kansas, 64-51, Saturday in the opening game of the NCAA semifinals at the Greensboro Coliseum and will meet North Carolina State for the championship Monday night.

Prior to Saturday's second game and after his own team had qualified for the finals, Marquette coach Al McGuire said he didn't care who his opponent would be.

"On paper," he said, "we're not as good as either UCLA or North Carolina State, but we'll make sure that whoever we play hears some footsteps."

McGuire said previously his team was not as good as other Marquette teams which had failed to reach the semifinals and was "not good enough" to be ranked among the nation's top four.

Please Turn to Page 8, Col. 3

## Kings Win, 5-0, Run Streak to 10 Games

BY DAN HAFNER
Times Staff Writer

It has not been a good year for Gary Edwards, but in the closing weeks it's improving. He started in goal for only the third time in three months Saturday night at the Forum and nobody could have been any better.

He fashioned his fourth shutout of his young National Hockey League career as the Kings whipped the Vancouver Canucks, 5-0, to extend their unbeaten string to a club record-tying 10 games.

He did it before 12,946 fans. When it was over and he was named the top player, there was a loud ovation.

Edwards missed nearly three months because of a broken finger and because when he was ready to return Rogie Vachon was on a hot streak. In his three appearances, he has two victories and a 4-4 tie with Boston when the Bruins scored

Please Turn to Page 4, Col. 4

## LEO THE LIP

### Durocher Turns Author and Claims Astros' Cedeno Can Be as Great as Willie Mays, but There Are 'Ifs'

BY BOB OATES, Times Staff Writer

After 48 years in baseball, Leo Durocher, 67, is taking a few days off in Palm Springs to write a book in which he will say that Willie Mays, Pete Reiser and Cesar Cedeno were the greatest young ballplayers of his life and times.

Because only Mays has fulfilled his potential, the thought doesn't make Durocher entirley happy.

Reiser, a Dodger outfielder of the 1940s, chipped the edge off his great talent running into fences and walls. The accidents drove him out of the lineup prematurely.

Cedeno, 23, the Houston outfielder, has seemed to be the best young player in the majors since he became an Astro regular five years ago. But in Santo Domingo this winter Cedeno was convicted of involuntary homicide, fined $100 and eventually released from jail after a 19-year-old girl was found shot to death in his motel room.

"As a ballplayer," Durocher says, "Cedeno can be as great as Mays. It only depends on two things. He's got to want to be a super superstar, really want it, and he will have to take care of himself physically."

Durocher, who is calling his book "Nice Guys Finish Last," divides the galaxy of baseball into stars, superstars and super superstars. The highest classification includes those who can run, field, throw, hit and hit with power, who desperately want to do all that well, and who are athletes with plenty of charisma.

Few players, in Durocher's opinion, have the all-round talent. Fewer still have the desire to succeed. And only twice has he managed young players who had it all: Reiser in the 1940s and Mays in the 50s and 60s.

In the 70s, Cedeno would be the third.

A gifted producer, Cedeno is certain to be a marked man from now on. The tragedy of last December in a Santo Domingo motel room guarantees this.

The world is Cedeno's in the 1970s, Durocher firmly believes, if the young man can handle it.

Durocher is an expert on charisma. One of the most colorful performers in his sport for nearly half a century, he was among the most charismatic baseball people.

But not the first.

That could have been Babe Ruth, whom Durocher knew in the 1920s when they were teammates on the New York Yankees.

Please Turn to Page 5, Col. 1

# No. 715...It Belongs to Aaron and Nobody Else

## DOWNING AND THE BABE ARE THE VICTIMS

**NO. 44 LEADS ALL THE REST**—Henry Aaron, shown here hitting the most celebrated home run in the history of baseball, the 715th of his major league career, now stands alone, ahead of Babe Ruth (714), Willie Mays (660), Frank Robinson (552), Harmon Killebrew (546) and all the other home run hitters in the game.

**BY ROSS NEWHAN**
Times Staff Writer

ATLANTA—The home run was hit at 9:07 Monday night. Approximately five minutes later, on the scoreboard at Atlanta Stadium, the following message appeared:

"George Herman Ruth also shares this great moment with all of us tonight—by setting the standard of 714 which made the great chase possible.

"Hail To The Babe."

The legend may never die, but the record, the most hallowed of all baseball records, the record that belonged to Babe Ruth for 39 years, now belongs to Henry Louis Aaron.

Aaron drove a fastball thrown by Dodger left-hander Al Downing through the mist and wind in the fourth inning, and when it landed 400 feet away in left-center, home run No. 715 was a part of baseball history.

A record baseball crowd in a city that had displayed a measure of apathy toward Aaron's pursuit last year, 53,775, saw the dramatic home run.

It lifted the heavy burden from Aaron's back and brought the fans out of their seats and may have been the most appropriate of all Henry's homers because it came in Atlanta's controversial home opener and it came on a night dedicated to Aaron.

"Atlanta Salutes Henry Aaron" is what they called it. And when it was over, the 40-year-old Aaron, a man whose grace and composure have held up so remarkably, said:

"It is a happy moment and I'm glad it's over with. I feel I can relax now and that my teammates can relax and that I can go on to have a great year, a year comparable to my last one.

*'I'd rather not talk about the commissioner but I . . . was happy Irvin was booed'--Aaron*

"It probably won't be until tomorrow morning that I'll wake up and realize the significance of everything that has happened.

Right now I'm just happy that this home run contributed to a win. The win is the most important thing that happened tonight."

The Braves won, 7-4, as the Dodgers provided a slapstick accompaniment to Aaron's artistic achievement by committing six errors.

In the privacy of the Atlanta clubhouse, owner Bill Bartholomay, National League president Chub Feeney and Braves manager Eddie Mathews each offered a champagne toast to Aaron.

Aaron, his wife Billye, and Bartholomay then walked into an interview room where 200 writers greeted his appearance with applause.

It was a night of constant applause, of standing ovations, but Aaron couldn't help but be aware of the one man who wasn't there—commissioner Bowie Kuhn.

It was Kuhn who had ordered Aaron to play Sunday in Cincinnati and it was Kuhn who had promised Aaron he would be the first to shake his hand when he hit No. 715.

He made that promise when Aaron complained about the commissioner's failure to send him a congratulatory telegram following his 700th home run last July.

But the first man to shake Aaron's hand Monday night was Dodger second baseman Davey Lopes. The two clasped hands as Aaron rounded the bag. Shortstop Bill Russell patted him on the back.

Two youths who jumped out of the stands caught up to Aaron between second and third. Aaron gently brushed them aside and finished his unemotional tour of the bases.

Teammate Ralph Garr was the first to shake his hand at the plate and then Aaron was mobbed by players coming out of the dugout

BUSINESS & FINANCE
CC PART III 2†
TUESDAY, APRIL 9, 1974

and others racing from the left field bullpen.

Mr. and Mrs. Herbert Aaron, Henry's parents, came out of a special box near the Braves dugout and embraced their son.

"I never knew Mom could hug so hard," Henry said later.

Then Aaron went to that box and kissed his wife. The crowd was on its feet in a thunderous ovation. Downing walked to the dugout, where he waited out much of the 11-minute delay, during which Aaron, Batholomay and Monte Irvin, representing the commissioner, addressed the crowd.

Irvin was booed as he gave Aaron a $3,000 watch featuring a diamond-studded 715 engraved on the face.

Irvin later said he did not know where the commisioner was, that he

Please Turn to Page 4, Col. 2

### JIM MURRAY

## An Oscar Overlooked

**Quick now**, the most overlooked super athlete in his sport is (choose one): (a) Walter Johnson, (b) Hack Wilson, (c) Sam Snead, (d) Bart Starr, (e) Oscar Robertson.

A good case could be worked up for all of the above. Walter Johnson didn't get into a World Series till he was in his dotage and often pitched for crowds that totaled well up in the hundreds. Hack Wilson set the major league record for runs-batted-in and the National League record for home runs—but he's not in the Hall of Fame. Sam Snead never won the U.S. Open and so tends not to be thought of on the same plane as Ben Hogan or Bobby Jones though he belongs there. Bart Starr was usually considered as something Vince Lombardi put away in a trunk every night.

Oscar Robertson is "the Big O," and "The Big Ah" and the "Oh, yes, of course, there's Oscar." But how many people know he's the second-most-effective basketball player of all time? By any yardstick?

★

**Only Wilt Chamberlain** scored more points in the history of the game. No one's even close in free throws made, assists, or rebounds by a backcourt man. Only Chamberlain played more minutes, made more field goals. No active player has as high a free-throw percentage.

Yet, you will look in the bookstalls in vain for tomes on the life and times of this wizard of the dribble. The "O" stands for zero in the publishing field. There's no Academy Award for this Oscar. The books are all about "Clyde: The Walt Frazier Story," "View From the Rim—the Willis Reed Story," "Red Holtzman's Winning Tactics and Strategy," "The Open Man—Dave DeBusschere," "Miracle on Thirty-Fourth St., the New York Knicks Come Through."

Oscar, like most of the overlooked stars listed above, never played Broadway. Or even the Midway. Doris Day never came to the Cincinnati Royals games. Oscar was always a long-distance call from the Ed Sullivan Show, Madison Ave., or Publishers' Row. President Nixon never called.

The proof of Oscar's virtuosity is that, in his waning years, overweight and overage, and plagued with the slow-healing infirmities these conditions produce, Oscar was able to steer a team to a world championship. In 1970-71, Oscar went from a team that had everything but a center to one which had nothing but a center.

★

**To understand basketball** you have to understand that the center is the pontiff of this religion. Without one, you have a team of caddies. It was Oscar's melancholy lot to be playing not only off-Broadway, but off-center most of his life. He came along in the days of the territorial rights, a double-infringement of one's constitutional rights, and, if it weren't for the statistics, and the late-life trade to a team which had Kareem Abdul-Jabbar in the pivot, Oscar might as well have stayed on the Crispus Attucks Playground in Indianapolis.

His 26,710 points is a record for people under 7 feet tall. His nearly 10,000 assists is a record for anyone with only two arms. It has been said Oscar could pass the ball through a keyhole or across Lake Michigan and hit the open man. There was a period, when he was playing on a team whose shooting percentage was just better than Mussolini's army, when critics complained Oscar "hogged" the ball too much. This was like complaining that Nick the Greek has the deal.

Oscar may finally get to play one more time in the Palace. The Milwaukee Bucks, a mixed bag of

Please Turn to Page 6, Col. 4

## Mom's Mop Handle Was First Bat for Young Henry Aaron

**BY BILL LIVINGSTON**
Knight News Service

He learned the game in the hard, spare way of blacks in the Deep South of three decades ago.

A skinny kid who played baseball far into the night in Mobile, the energy crisis of that day was solved by flares fashioned from kerosene-soaked rags. He used a mop handle for a bat and a soda bottle cap for a ball and even then he could hit with such ferocity that he often got in trouble for cutting up his mother's mops by the force of his swing.

From those beginnings, Hank Aaron stands today at the pinnacle of achievement that was once thought beyond reach. He has surpassed baseball's record of the ages —714 home runs hit in an almost mythic career by Babe Ruth.

Aaron is only the most recent in a line of black athletes who have assailed and overcome records set in another era by white men. But before Wilt Chamberlain ever dipper-dunked, O.J. Simpson followed a block, Maury Wills stole a base or Bob Hayes ran a footrace, there was Jackie Robinson. It was Robinson who really kindled Aaron's interest in baseball as a youth.

"He was always crazy about playing baseball but I'd never thought about him becoming a player until the Brooklyn Dodgers came to Mobile for an exhibition game when Henry was 11," recalls his father, Herbert, a retired dock worker who presided over the eight children Estellar Aaron bore him.

"I took him out to see the game and he told me that night at the ball park, 'I'm going to be in the big leagues myself, Daddy, before Jackie Robinson is through playing.'"

The name Robinson was the memorable catalyst for Aaron. Oddly, he does not even remember hearing of the man whose record he has pursued since 1954.

"I know I never remember hearing the name of Babe Ruth when I was a youngster," Aaron said. "What he accomplished was virtually meaningless to black kids. We paid little attention to the records of the white professional players. It wasn't until

Please Turn to Page 5, Col. 1

### THE TIE-BREAKER

**Date:** April 8, 1974.
**Site:** Atlanta Stadium.
**Weather:** Overcast, windy and cool, occasional drizzle, 62 degrees.
**Inning:** Fourth.
**Time:** 9:07 p.m., EDT.
**Opposing pitcher:** Al Downing, Dodgers.
**Men on base:** One.
**Score:** 3-1 Dodgers.
**Distance:** 400 feet.
**Direction:** Left-center field.
**Count:** 1-0.
**Outs:** 0.
**Type of pitch:** Fastball.

SEVEN-ONE-FIVE—The imposing number 715 appears on wall over head of beaming Henry Aaron as he appears at press conference following his dramatic record-setting home run Monday night. AP Wirephoto

## . . . OH, YES, THE DODGERS LOST FOR FIRST TIME, 7-4

From a Times Staff Writer

ATLANTA—Meanwhile, on the cold, rainy night when Henry Aaron made history, the Dodgers made six errors and lost their first game of the season, 7-4.

Manager Walt Alston had seen it coming. Boarding the bus at Dodger Stadium Sunday afternoon after his team had swept three games by outscoring San Diego, 25-2, Alston said, "I know they won't all be that easy. I wish we had saved some of those runs."

However, what the Dodgers needed most Monday night was defense. The six errors, two by Bill Russell and one each by Ron Cey, Bill Buckner, Dave Lopes and Joe Ferguson, were not a record for an L.A. Dodger team but they were close. They made seven once in 1972.

The sudden collapse by the young Dodger defenders spoiled pitching performances by Al Downing, Mike Marshall and Charlie Hough that ordinarily would have been good enough to win. They allowed only four hits. Downing and Marshall, who came on in the fourth inning, each allowed two hits and Hough pitched two hitless innings in a fine mop-up job.

Only three of Atlanta's runs were earned. Downing was responsible for two of them, including *the* home-run serve.

Marshall, who likes to work almost every night, made his first appearance (the first three Dodger starters went the distance against San Die-

Please Turn to Page 4, Col. 1

## MARTIN FIGURES RANGERS, AT 150-1, ARE 50% BETTER

**BY JEFF PRUGH**
Times Staff Writer

A year ago, the Texas Rangers were baseball's designated losers.

They finished far enough out of the pennant race to warrant a missing-persons report. They had the majors' worst record (57-105) and wound up 37 games out of first place in the American League West.

But their new manager, Billy Martin, believes nobody should feel sorry for the Rangers anymore.

Talking about his team, he uses words like "contender" and "potential" and "much improved."

Contender?

"You bet," said Martin. "We've improved 50 per cent. Last year Las Vegas listed us at 200-1 to win and this year we're down to 150-1."

When the Texans play the Angels tonight in the 1974 Anaheim Stadium opener, they'll have some faces

Please Turn to Page 6, Col. ●

# A.D. Turns Irish Around, Upside-Down, 55-24

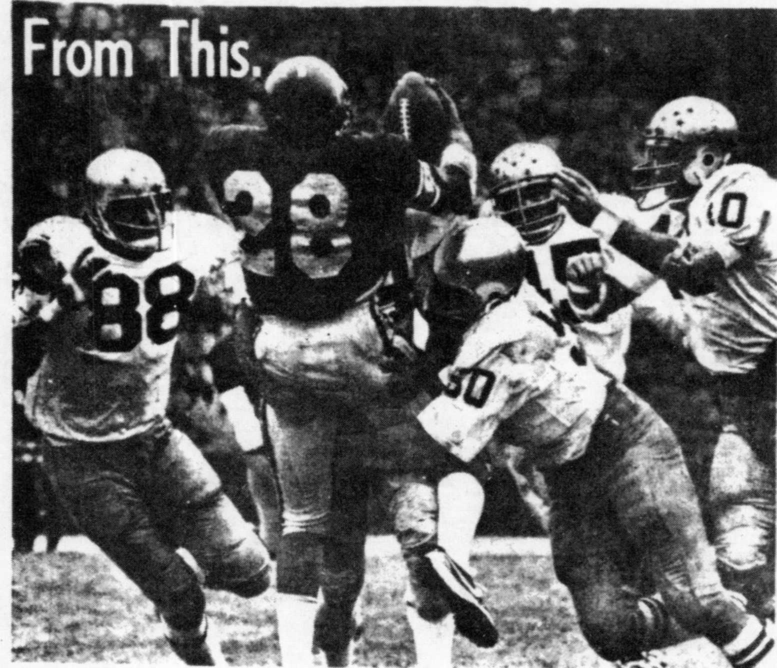


HELP!!!—Five Notre Dame defenders close in on USC's Anthony Davis in the first quarter at the Coliseum Saturday. Davis lost four yards and the Trojan offense was bottled up in the first half.
Times photo by Art Rogers

## Behind 24-0, USC Hurries Back

Los Angeles Times
Sports
CC PART III 2†
SUNDAY, DECEMBER 1, 1974

**BY MAL FLORENCE**
Times Staff Writer

Notre Dame 24, USC 6. That was the first-half score.

But are you ready for USC 49, Notre Dame 0 in the second half?

In what might be the most improbable comeback in college football history, the Trojans routed the Fighting Irish, 55-24, Saturday afternoon before an almost unbelieving Coliseum crowd of 83,552 and a national television audience.

As anyone might guess, the man who started the touchdown landslide was Anthony Davis, a Notre Dame nemesis.

Davis returned the second-half kickoff 102 yards to a touchdown and the Trojans, a badly beaten team in the first half, came alive.

So did the USC rooters in the crowd. They didn't stop yelling through a pulsating third quarter in which USC scored 35 points on Notre Dame.

This wasn't Occidental or Pomona the Trojans were battering but the No. 1 defensive team in college football.

Davis, who scored a first-half touchdown on a short pass from Pat Haden, had four for the game, three in the third quarter. He scored 11 touchdowns and 68 points against the Irish in his career—three on long-distance kickoff runs.

The 55 points scored on Notre Dame were four short of the record 59-0 blitz by the Glenn Davis-Doc Blanchard Army team in 1944.

The Trojans were scoring touchdowns so fast in the third quarter that the scoreboard couldn't handle it and went on the blink.

In a little less than 9½ minutes, USC had compiled 28 points. And in less than 17 minutes of the second half, the Trojans scored seven touchdowns.

The scoring binge ended early in the fourth quarter when Charles Phillips sprinted 58 yards to a touchdown after intercepting a Tom Clements pass. That gave USC eight touchdowns for the day, as many as 10 previous Irish opponents had scored.

Phillips' interception was his third and he totaled 101 yards on returns.

Davis made another strong bid for the Heisman Trophy with his performance—almost as remarkable as his six-touchdown show against Notre Dame in 1972 (including kickoff runs of 97 and 96 yards).

But there were other Trojans who asserted themselves on a gloomy, overcast day, such as:

—Quarterback Haden, who completed his first six passes in the final half for 139 yards and three touchdowns.

—Split end John McKay, the coach's son, who burned the young Irish secondary in the tension-packed third quarter, in which he caught four passes for 110 yards and two touchdowns.

—An aroused Trojan defense that mopped up on Clements, fullback Wayne Bullock and the other strong Notre Dame runners after being pushed around in the opening half.

Art Riley, Gary Jeter, Danny Reece, Kevin Bruce, Marvin Cobb, Richard Wood and Phillips did the most damage to an Irish offense that moved almost at will on the way to a 24-0 lead in the first half.

By winning, the Trojans improved their record to 9-1-1 and are bound to move up in the national rankings. They were ranked sixth by Associated Press and fourth by UPI before the game.

And John McKay's team gave Ohio State's Woody Hayes some food for thought. The Buckeye coach watched the game as a television commentator and fans, spotting him in the booth, raised their fists in challenging gestures.

Please Turn to Page 8, Col. 3

BYE, BYE—It took Davis only a little more than 13 seconds to get rolling in the second half, however, as he returned the Irish kickoff 102 yards for the touchdown that started USC on the way to its 55-24 victory.
Times photo by Ben Olender

***JIM MURRAY***

## The Divil, They Say

**OK, put away the beads.** Never mind lighting any more candles. It's OK to sleep through the sermon today. We have nothing more to lose.

Us again, huh, Lord?

Sat out the second half on us, huh?

Look! Don't anybody tell any Pat and Mike jokes for awhile. Put away the corned beef and cabbage. Nobody feels like eating. See if there's a drop in that bottle. It's going to be a long, chilly evening.

Never mind saying hello to your sister Kate down on the garden gate. Tell her to go home and feed the pigs. The hussy! If Hennessy-Tennessy tootles the flute, may he choke on it. Tell MacNamara nobody feels like singing, either. If McCarthy thumps the old bassoon, thump him. Does he have no respect for the dead?

Never mind the shamrocks. They're just weeds, after all. And what good did the Blarney Stone do if you can't even hold a 24-0 lead? Just a damn boulder after all.

★

**Don't bother** with Paddy O'Brien, the fillum star. Tell him we've got Earl Butz for the next speaker at the Friendly Sons of St. Patrick.

Check and see if Judas Iscariot went to USC. And wore No. 28.

There'll be no wearing of the green this weekend. If you see a leprechaun, step on him.

You knew it had to come to this what with the eating of meat on Friday and the terrible things they did to St. Christopher and Santa Claus.

You had to believe somebody up there didn't like us.

Would you believe anything that didn't have cannons could score 55 points in a row on Notre Dame—55 POINTS?! And I don't mean in a game, I mean in 30 minutes and 10 seconds!

Can you believe we're in the state of grace when someone runs a kickoff back 102 yards in under 13 seconds and not in a straight line?

Anthony Davis should now get permanent possession of Notre Dame. He's scored 11 touchdowns on the Irish. That's more than Army scored on them in 20 years.

Get an exorcist. That second half of football has to be the work of the devil. Surely we should have listened for the banshees this week instead of all the choruses of "Mother Machree" and "Danny Boy."

★

**Where was the Gipper?** Don't we always beat these heathens? We did when Rockne was alive.

But surely there were spirits out there, knocking the ball out of Irish hands, whispering into Anthony Davis' ear, "Just go up the left side and follow me. Nobody will see me but you." That's the THIRD time this man has run a kickoff back for a touchdown against Notre Dame. This positively cannot be done unless he turns invisible for parts of the run.

Irish eyes are not smiling. Irish hearts are unhappy. I suppose some people will blame it on the guitar Mass and the fact it isn't said in Latin anymore. But, pshaw, all Latin would do would be make the score LV-XXIV.

Please Turn to Page 15, Col. 2

## Trojans Ecstatic, Call Comeback Win Wild and Fantastic

**BY TED GREEN**
Times Staff Writer

"The greatest, most incredible game," Anthony Davis said. "We had some magic . . . We turned into madmen."

"I still don't know what happened," Johnny McKay said. "I can't understand it. I'm gonna sit down tonight and have a beer and think about it. Against Notre Dame? Maybe against Kent State . . . but *Notre Dame?*"

"Ten years from now," Charles Phillips said, "I'll probably be watchin' the USC-Notre Dame game and sayin', 'Do you remember 1974? I was in that crazy game.' "

"If someone with crystal ball had told me beforehand what was going to happen," Pat Haden said, "I would have said, 'Put that guy away.' It was pure fantasy."

Fantasy. Lunacy. Ecstasy.

Those were the kind of words the USC Trojans used to describe the indescribable: *eight* touchdowns in slightly more than a quarter of playing time against Notre Dame and a 55-24 victory.

In the excitement of what some described as the wildest, most emotional 16 some-odd minutes of football in the history of the Coliseum—maybe anywhere—the memory of Notre Dame's 24-0 lead in the second quarter Saturday was all but obliterated.

Yes, USC's players said afterward, we sort of knew we were behind. No, no one on the sidelines gave up. No, we never thought we were out of it. No, McKay didn't scream at us at halftime.

All the answers seemed perfunctory, almost predictable. All they could *really* think about, laugh

Please Turn to Page 10, Col. 1

## Ara Feared Second-Half Collapse

**BY JEFF PRUGH**
Times Staff Writer

They were more shocked than anguished, more philosophical than demoralized when it was over.

Ara Parseghian, the head coach, understandably had difficulty remembering—and rehashing—exactly how it all happened.

Linebacker Greg Collins, his eyes slightly moist, asked, "What *was* the final score, anyway?"

And they all sat for 5 minutes of stony silence behind closed doors before the press was permitted to enter.

These were Notre Dame's Fighting Irish late Saturday afternoon in the wake of one of their darkest hours.

The shock of their 55-24 defeat by USC's Trojans hadn't yet worn off as they dressed hastily—and quietly—before moving into the chill darkness outside.

"Well . . . c'mon!" snapped Parseghian, as reporters crowded around him in the coaches' dressing quarters. "Let's get it over with."

He then answered questions about "momentum" and "mistakes," but he also said, in retrospect, that USC's astonishing second-half explosion was something he had feared all week.

"We've never played a good second half out here," he said, "And there's more significance to that than meets the eye. You saw what happened to Minnesota (against the Rams) out here last weekend. They had a good first half but a poor second half."

The significance of the Irish collapse, he said, was traced to the cold, snowy conditions back home in South Bend which made it virtual-

Please Turn to Page 9, Col. 1

## UCLA Makes It Look Easy, 79-64

**BY DWIGHT CHAPIN**
Times Staff Writer

Those UCLA basketball babies grew up in a hurry against De Paul Saturday night at Pauley Pavilion.

The Bruins looked strong, healthy and potentially worthy of their all-star predecessors as they buried the Blue Demons, 79-64, before a crowd of 12,101.

On display were not only the usual Bruin faces but a bundle of youngsters that John Wooden gave long looks—including Brett Vroman, a freshman center who apparently has much talent, Ray Townsend, Gavin Smith, Casey Corliss and Marvin Thomas.

Everybody played and, in contrast to Friday night's game with Wichita State, nearly everybody played well as the Bruins easily dispatched a team that has been one of the Midwest's most ballyhooed independents.

By halftime the Bruins had a 39-22 lead and played just about as they pleased after that.

UCLA extended its lead to 74-51 with 4:52 left in the game before

Please Turn to Page 12, Col. 4

## KINGS' EDWARDS DEALS BOSTON ANOTHER BLANK

**BY DAN HAFNER**
Times Staff Writer

The tougher the assignment, the better the Kings' Gary Edwards likes it. He went out Saturday night before a sellout 16,005 at the Forum and shut out Boston, 2-0, ending the Bruins' six-game winning streak.

Rogatien Vachon has been the fans' favorite for several years, but Edwards quietly does an important job. He's called the backup goalie, but it's a misnomer. His second shutout of the season gave him a 5-1-2 record, not bad for the man who usually faces the Stanley Cup champion Philadelphia Flyers and the Bruising Bruins.

Don Kozak scored the only goal Edwards needed just before the five-minute mark of the second period when he took a Bob Berry pass while on his knees and backhanded the puck into the net. Berry clinched the victory halfway through the final period when he stole the puck and beat goaltender Gilles Gilbert from 25 feet.

Only an outstanding effort by Gilbert kept the game from getting out of hand, as after the first few minutes the Kings dominated. They outskated and outhustled the talented Bruins. Gilbert stopped 37 shots, many of them when Kings skated in unmolested.

There was one Bruin, though, who wasn't outplayed. Bobby Orr. The brilliant defenseman, who leads the league in scoring, played more than 40 minutes. Unfortunately for the Bruins, he had to have occasional rest. He was sitting on the bench when both goals were scored.

Phil Esposito, the other half of the best one-two punch in the sport, was not at his best. Maybe it was because Frank St. Marseille was hounding him all night, but Esposito, the NHL goal-scoring leader with 21, had only one weak shot on goal and it came in the final minute.

St. Marseille's performance was a further indication that bench strength is one reason the Kings are going so well. Coach Bob Pulford, seeking more scoring punch, had put Butch Goring at center for a couple of games with Bob Nevin and Dan Maloney. But St. Marseille, one of the team's best defensive centers,

Please Turn to Page 6, Col. 7

## JIM MURRAY

# What Odds? McKay Doubles Pot, Rolls a Natural

Los Angeles Times
Sports
BUSINESS & FINANCE
CC PART III
THURSDAY, JANUARY 2, 1975

If you're ever in a shipwreck, do yourself a favor and try to get in the same lifeboat as John McKay.

If you're in a crap game, back his play.

Follow him to the hundred-dollar window at the track.

Buy half of his ticket in a lottery. Stand next to him in a lightning storm. Follow him during a bombardment.

The man is a walking four-leaf clover. He would bet into an ace-high straight held by a guy wearing two guns even if he had seen only three cards himself.

He belongs on a riverboat with a checked vest and a $20 gold piece.

Find out what kind of stock he buys and call your broker.

I don't know whether you know it or not but coaching is a gloomy profession. A football coach can always see what could go wrong. They spend their life holding their cards close and praying a lot. Most of them would punt on first down if they could. They go for field goals on the one-yard line. If the country was settled by football coaches, the West still wouldn't be discovered. They wouldn't put the Indians on the schedule.

But John McKay is a football coach who always thinks the next card will be an ace, that there will be oil on the lot he bought by mail. If he bought a gold brick from a guy on a street corner—and he would—he would expect it to be real.

John McKay won a football game in the Rose Bowl on the first day of 1975 that puts him right up there with guys who sell the house to get down on 100-1 shots.

Listen! You don't give Nick the Greek an extra card. You wouldn't give Billy the Kid the first shot, would you? Would Custer spot the Indians another tribe?

Well, in the second quarter of a football game in the Rose Bowl Wednesday, John McKay gave Woody Hayes and the Ohio State Buckeyes 3 points.

There was a lot of time left at the time—easily 20 seconds. The Trojans had just kicked a field goal from the 22. I mean, it was GOOD! THR_E points—or twice as many as the Trojans had at the time.

It seemed a good note to go into the locker rooms for the half on. Only, it turned out Ohio State was offside. The Trojans could have a first down and a few ticks of the clock.

The odds looked great to McKay. He contemptuously threw back the 3 points. Personally, I would say he was taking a chance on a dry hole. And he was. USC went into the locker room without their 3 points.

But the thing about gamblers is they never learn. They blow the rent money on a 40-1 shot and the next race they're back

Please Turn to Page 4, Col. 5

# Trojans Gamble and Make 8 the Hard Way, 18-17

CATCH THIS ACT, PART I . . . — Johnny McKay (circle) has Pat Haden's 38-yard touchdown pass in his arms as he runs into and through end zone Wednesday in Rose Bowl. The catch, with 2:03 left in game, was next-to-last big play for USC in 18-17 win over Ohio State. Times photo by Ben Olender

## Haden Passes to McKay, Diggs to Top Buckeyes in Rose Bowl

BY MAL FLORENCE
Times Staff Writer

Pat Haden, John McKay and the wide receiver's gambling father, the USC coach, teamed in memorable fashion to provide USC with a stirring, 18-17 comeback win over Ohio State Wednesday in the 61st annual Rose Bowl game.

A crowd of 106,721 watched Haden drive the Trojans 83 yards in the closing minutes, covering the last 38 yards with a towering touchdown pass to McKay.

The score came with a little more than two minutes remaining and left USC trailing, 17-16. A conservative coach would have settled for a point-after-touchdown kick and an almost certain tie with the favored Buckeyes.

But coach John McKay, who has lost some big games by gambling on two-point conversions late in games, went for broke. And this time he was a winner as Haden passed to flanker Shelton Diggs deep in the end zone for the two-pointer.

Ohio State, behind its scrambling, clever quarterback, Cornelius Greene, made USC partisans in the crowd nervous as he marched his team to the USC 45.

But time ran out on him and Tom Skladany, normally a punter, was short on a 62-yard field-goal try as the game ended.

It was a strange, turnover-prone contest in which the Trojans lost their All-American tailback, Anthony Davis, with a bruised sternum and ribs for the second half.

But Allen Carter, an experienced reserve, performed commendably in Davis' absence, gaining 75 yards for a 4.2 average.

By winning, USC now has a chance to win the UPI version of the national championship. No. 1 ranked Alabama lost to Notre Dame in the Orange Bowl Wednesday night. So its possible that the No. 4 Trojans could advance to the top of the ratings with their victory over No. 2 Ohio State.

Most of the action on a matchless afternoon came in the fourth quarter when the lead changed hands three times after Ohio State carried a 7-3 advantage into the final 15 minutes.

The Buckeyes had apparently put the game out of reach on Greene's 3-yard touchdown run and Tom Klaban's 32-yard field goal following a Haden fumble.

But Haden didn't panic by throwing desperation passes with six minutes remaining. He sent Carter and fullbacks Dave Farmer and Ricky Bell through the line for sizeable gains.

Then, with a first down on the Ohio State 38, he retreated to pass. He waited until McKay, his high school buddy from Bishop Amat, got clear behind cornerback Steve Luke in the corner of the end zone.

The high, arching pass was per-

Please Turn to Page 6, Col. 1

## ARNIE JONES STRUCK

## Hayes Hits Own Player 'To Get Him Fired Up'

BY JEFF PRUGH
Times Staff Writer

As USC was driving toward its winning points, Ohio State coach Woody Hayes struck middle linebacker Arnie Jones and angrily shook him as they exchanged heated words late in Wednesday's Rose Bowl game.

Hayes, who said he did it to "get him fired up," was observed striking Jones in the chest and shaking him by the face mask while chewing him out along the sidelines.

Asked about the incident in the wake of USC's 18-17 win, Hayes explained why he did it, raising his voice as he was interviewed by newsmen.

"He was not playing particularly good football today," said the 61-year-old coach, "and he is a good player and capable of playing better than he was."

Jones, a 240-pound senior from Dayton, gave his version of the altercation calmly afterward and did not seem particularly outraged by Hayes' actions.

"He was just tryin' to get me fired up, I guess," he said with a half-shrug in the Buckeyes' locker room.

The incident reportedly occurred moments after USC had crossed midfield on a 6-yard run by fullback Ricky Bell during its game-winning drive.

Jones said Hayes was upset that the Trojans were moving the ball so easily. "He asked me, 'What are you doin'?'" said Jones. "And I told him, 'They're cutting back against us.' He just said, 'Stay with 'em.' "

The chunky linebacker stood on a bench in streetclothes as he talked. He wore a Fu Manchu and had a gash over his right eyebrow—not, he said, from the Hayes confrontation.

Jones said he was surprised by

Please Turn to Page 5, Col. 4

. . . AND PART II—Shelton Diggs, on his back in the end zone, has the ball on the play that followed, a two-point conversion pass from Haden, which he dove for and caught—just barely. The nearest Ohio State player is Neal Colzie (20) and that's McKay exulting at left. AP photo

## This Time USC Had What It Needed: the Big Plays

BY BOB OATES
Times Staff Writer

Like all gamblers, coach John McKay wins some and loses some. And like all passers, Pat Haden throws completes, incompletes and touchdowns.

So the Trojans could have lost Wednesday's game. Although they

### ANALYSIS

outplayed Ohio State most of the way, they were seven points down with two minutes left.

They won from the Buckeyes because, in the pressure of the fourth quarter, Haden completed two of three passes—both for touchdowns—and McKay won a dramatic gamble for a two-point conversion.

Only rarely before has McKay successfully rolled the dice. In the second quarter of this game, he took three points off the board, tried for seven and lost the roll.

And with 2:03 left there were still three possible results for USC: 16-17, 17-17 and 18-17. McKay made it 18-17 because he was ready with a formation that his opposite number, Woody Hayes of Ohio State, couldn't handle.

It was a formation with two wide receivers on the right flank: the coach's son, Johnny McKay, and Shelton Diggs. The Buckeyes, obliged to single-cover them, didn't. Both were open, McKay deep in the end zone and Diggs in front of him. McKay threw, Diggs dug it out for two points and Hayes was done.

Coming from behind twice in the fourth quarter, the Trojans had lined up in the same formation to get their first touchdown. That time, Haden had faked right and thrown left to tight end Jim Obradovich for 9 yards.

Please Turn to Page 10, Col. 1

## Bowl Games

### ORANGE

| | |
|---|---|
| Notre Dame | 13 |
| Alabama | 11 |

Story on Page 2

### COTTON

| | |
|---|---|
| Penn State | 41 |
| Baylor | 20 |

Story on Page 10

## JOHN HALL

## McKay Plays it Straight . . . Afterward

"Gentlemen, we didn't come in here to play for a tie," said the red-coated riverboat gambler known as John McKay, the Dangerous Dan McGrew of the Arroyo Seco.

McKay, always the sideline iceman, the portrait of Mr. Cool during the battle, was still shaking with emotion, throat tight and hands trembling, as he came off the field to meet the press following Wednesday's 18-17 royal flush finish in Rose Bowl No. 8 for the USC coach.

"Ohio State has a wonderful team. Make no mistake about that," he said. "We were very fortunate to win. It was their misfortune to lose. It was quite a game. I don't think anybody knew who was going to win until it was over."

The silver-haired McKay, 51, has now tied Howard Jones as a Rose Bowl winner. Obviously never happier, he sat in a folding chair on a platform in a little tent outside the USC dressing room, a battery of mikes under his nose and tried to catch his breath while explaining how it all happened.

"Are you proud of your son?" somebody shouted.

McKay, the sometimes hard-hitting wit with a quip for every occasion, was fresh out. He beamed and said yes.

"Yes, I'm very proud. I'm proud of both my daughters and both my sons."

John Kenneth McKay, the wide receiver, finished his final game for USC and the old man as the star of stars—clutching the 38-yard pass in the final two minutes from his old high school mate and roommate, Pat Haden (who lived in the McKay home during his senior prep year) that led to the winning two-point conversion gamble that led to old dad getting off the hook where some would most certainly have hung him.

So Johnny McKay goes out with stars on his helmet and the pot of gold at the end of the rainbow, and here comes Richie, the last of the McKays, the 10th grade

Please Turn to Page 3, Col. 1

# Bruins Give Wooden 10th One for the Road

BUSINESS & FINANCE

CC PART III 3†

TUESDAY, APRIL 1, 1975

## UCLA Wins NCAA Title, 92-85

**BY DWIGHT CHAPIN**
Times Staff Writer

SAN DIEGO—John Wooden isn't the sort of man to be carried off the basketball court on his team's shoulders—after any game.

So, in his final hour as a college coach here Monday night, his UCLA Bruins simply gave him his 10th national championship as a going-away present, and then walked off the floor after him—quietly, calmly, happily.

There was something special, however, in the Bruins' 92-85 victory over a rugged, stubborn Kentucky team, something that comes along perhaps once or twice in a lifetime.

UCLA has won so many championships that some of them seemed almost humdrum.

But this one was different, for the fans—most of whom seemed to be rooting for UCLA—and for the Bruin players.

Senior guard Pete Trgovich used just a few words to explain:

"We wanted to win it bad," he said. "For The Man."

All season, this was a team that had merged beautifully with The Man and his methods. Cool. Under control.

"We're not a team," Trgovich said, "that jumps and screams before games. But I could look at each of the guys tonight and just tell. We were all ready, in our own ways."

It had to be that way for the Bruins to win in John Wooden's farewell because Kentucky, too, was ready, particularly forward Kevin Grevey.

Grevey scored 34 points—many of them as Kentucky hung close to the Bruins late in the game.

But—in a sense—he might also have lost the game for coach Joe B. Hall's Wildcats, who were seeking their fifth national title, their first without the Baron, Adolph Rupp.

With eight minutes to play, Kentucky began to move and to muscle—the thing it does best—and cut UCLA's lead from 74-67 to 76-75.

Just 6:23 was left to play when UCLA's captain, David (The Spider) Meyers, went up for a jump shot. He and Grevey crashed to the floor. Official Hank Nichols called an offensive foul on Meyers.

The emotion spilled over. Meyers banged the floor and Nichols whistled him for a technical foul.

It could have been a five-point play for Kentucky.

Grevey had a one-and-one free throw, plus the technical foul to shoot. He missed the first of the one-and-one. He missed the technical. Kentucky got the ball out of bounds but James Lee was called for an offensive foul.

It remained tense the rest of the way. But the Bruins regained their poise after Grevey missed and Lee turned over the ball. And they kept that—and the lead—the rest of the way.

"There was no way," said guard Andre McCarter, "We were going to lose coach's last game."

Meyers didn't think UCLA would have lost—even if Grevey had connected and Kentucky had made its five-point play.

"I was upset on the call because I felt he went under me as I got off to the shot," Meyers said. "I was square onto the basket and he ducked under me. But I don't really blame Grevey or the officials. They have an awfully

Please Turn to Page 4, Col. 1

**THE INTIMIDATORS**—Neither team was given much breathing room in Monday night's NCAA championship game at the San Diego Arena, as depicted in these photos. At left, UCLA's Dave Meyers dives for the ball, which is picked off by Kentucky's Rick Robey and held high as the Bruin heads for the floor. Above, UCLA's Marques Johnson maintains control of the ball while closely guarded by Mike Phillips. The Bruins, playing their final game under retiring coach John Wooden, rolled to a 92-85 victory and the championship. The title was Wooden's 10th in 12 years.

AP Wirephotos

## JIM MURRAY

## He Dared Stand Alone

**Don't bang the drums** slowly. Don't muffle the caissons, or lead a riderless horse. Strike up the band. Let the trumpets roll. Never mind the 21-gun salute, just bring a plate of fudge. Raise your glasses in a toast if you must—but fill them with malted milk.

John Wooden is not going out as a great general or field leader. This is not Old Blood and Guts or Old Hickory, this is Mr. Chips saying goodby.

John Wooden never wanted to be thought of as a fiery leader. Life to him was a one-room school house with pictures of George Washington, Christ and a pair of crossed flags. Outside, the pumpkins ripening under a harvest moon. A pedagogue is all he ever wanted to be or remembered as. A simple country teacher.

His precepts were right off a wall motto. His idols were gentle Hoosier poets, not the purple-prose artists of the sports pages. A reserve guard stumbled out of a pre-game meeting once to mumble in some shock to a frat brother, "Our game plan is by Edgar A. Guest, and our front line seems to be made up of Faith, Hope and Charity."

★

**John Wooden,** someone once said, was "the only basketball coach from the Old Testament." Others preferred to think of him as New Testament—"St. John," who walked to work across Santa Monica Bay.

His lifestyle was embodied in a cornerstone of philosophy which he called the "Pyramid of Success," which looked like a collection of Horatio Alger titles. They were real easy to follow—if you lived in a convent.

His basketball was 20th Century, but his life lessons were B.C. "Dare to be a Daniel! Dare to stand alone!" He spouted more poems than Lord Byron. Most of his thoughts for the day had a strong odor of new-mown hay about them or sycamores in the candlelight, and sometimes the ghetto kids from New York, more used to subway graffiti than "The Old Oaken Bucket" or "Moonlight Along The Wabash," wished he'd stick to setting picks.

Critics contend that it was easy to put your faith in the Bible when your center was between 7 and 8 feet tall and as agile as an acrobat, but that you would have to turn to more recent works when your whole team could come to the games in a single Volkswagen. Wooden went out and won NCAA championships with nothing more than 6-foot-5 centers and the Book of Leviticus.

★

**In the world of modern** sport, piety in a coach is as suspect as piety in a faro dealer. The fabric of recruitment is as corrupt as a military junta, and it was hard to believe anyone in it could not sooner or later be found in possession of 30 pieces of silver he couldn't account for.

Every time John Wooden hinted at retirement in recent years, the scribes—to say nothing of the Pharisees—nodded sagely and said, "Aha! Now comes the NCAA investigation!" So, Wooden would get tight-lipped—and stay on for another two years.

An act like this might have been hard to maintain at a little church school in the middle of the Dakotas. At UCLA, a campus surrounded by Gomorrah by the Sea, it was believed impossible. No one believed the mysteries of the zone defense could be equated with Deuteronomy, but Wooden quietly went his winning way with the Bible in one hand and a basketball in the other.

When he came to UCLA, bas-

Please Turn to Page 4, Col. 6

## If He's a Coach, He's Rumored for Wooden's Job

From a Staff Writer

SAN DIEGO—Speculation over John Wooden's successor as UCLA basketball coach continued Monday at NCAA tournament headquarters.

USC's Bob Boyd and the Lakers' Bill Sharman were among those mentioned as possibles. "I've not been contacted. That's an absurd rumor," said Boyd. "All my thoughts are with the Lakers," said Sharman, who added that he has not been contacted.

For what it's worth, a Pacific 8 basketball coach who correctly tabbed Wooden's retirement ahead of time picks Boyd as his replacement. The coach asked anonymity.

Other names that came up were those of Gene Bartow of Illinois, Denny Crum of Louisville and Dave Gavitt of Providence.

Bartow, former Memphis State coach whose team lost to UCLA in the 1973 NCAA finals, said he'd thought about the job but hadn't been contacted.

Said Crum, a former Wooden assistant: "Because of speculation going on, I told my school I intend to honor my contract at Louisville. I have not been contacted by UCLA."

## INDIANA BETTER TEAM—GREVEY

From Times Wire Services

Kevin Grevey, whose Kentucky Wildcats were defeated by UCLA Monday night for the NCAA championship in San Diego, said he thought Indiana was a better team than the Bruins.

"It's a great effort we gave against Indiana that beat them," Grevey said. "But we didn't play that well against UCLA."

Grevey, whose 34 points led the Wildcats, said, "We played a little tight tonight."

He said that Kentucky's normal game plan, which includes physical domination of both backboards, usually intimidated opponents.

"But it didn't intimidate UCLA.

Please Turn to Page 3, Col. 1

## TITLE A RETIREMENT GIFT

## Wooden Goes Out a Champion

**BY TED GREEN**
Times Staff Writer

SAN DIEGO—It began as so many of his 766 other games as UCLA basketball coach had.

The small smile as he walked in for the warmups, the little wave of the folded program as the applause for him crescendoed, a handshake with a friend a few minutes before tipoff, a word in the ear of his assistant coach as the ball went up.

Yet so much of what went on afterward was different.

Oh, there was another victory, this one 92-85 over Kentucky, another national championship, this one the 10th, another team picture afterward, another long and by now familiar post-game interview, another hug from his wife.

But for John Wooden Monday night it was the last victory of 620 at UCLA, the last championship, the last picture, the last post-game interview, the last hug in a crowded, locker room corridor.

The players knew it. The fans at the Sports Arena here—responsive to his every move—knew it. And even though he preferred to talk about something else, anything else, Wooden showed that he knew it, too.

There was the raised fist he shook again and again when UCLA scored at a critical time. And shook again when a jump shot by Richard Washington danced around the rim and fell in late in the game. And shook a final time when the buzzer went off and the floor was flooded by TV cameras, photographers, reporters and fans.

And there was the uncharacteristically bitter words for an official who called a technical foul on Dave Meyers. No one could remember Wooden having to be restrained from moving toward a referee, as he was by Meyers and the other official.

And when it was over, there was the uncharacteristic emotion: an embrace with Marques Johnson, a long and warm handshake with Meyers, a hug from a female fan who was crying, a kiss on the cheek from an old friend who happened to be a man.

He walked into an interview room, and some of the 200 or so newsmen let their objectivity slip. They applauded.

Then, the same old questions and same old answers, about turning points, physical play, substitutions. John Wooden answered, dutifully as always. Praised the other team and praised his. Used the word "pleasing" to describe what No. 10 meant. Said he was "annoyed" at the official who called the technical foul, and that it wasn't good to show that kind of emotion.

The image he'd worked at for 27 years at UCLA was familiar again, and John Wooden wouldn't have it any other way.

"I guess to say that I thought we would go this far would be stretching the point," Wooden said. "But I did think we had a chance. I'm extremely happy; I'm just glad it's over."

Please Turn to Page 3, Col. 1

**FINAL TRIBUTE**—Amid cheers and adulation, UCLA John Wooden wears smile and basketball net after ending his career with NCAA title.

AP wirephoto

Los Angeles Times

# Sports

BUSINESS & FINANCE
PART III
MONDAY, SEPTEMBER 29, 1975

THE STREETS OF LONG BEACH—With the city's buildings and the bleachers near the course crammed with spectators, the Formula 5000 cars in the Long Beach Grand Prix race around the first lap Sunday. Brian Redman of England won the race in his Lola, averaging 86.325 m.p.h. and sewing up his second straight Formula 5000 championship before a crowd estimated at 75,000.

Times photo by Joe Kennedy

## 75,000 SEE REDMAN WIN AT LONG BEACH

### Grand Prix Race Through Streets a Roaring Success; British Driver Clinches Formula 5000 Championship

BY SHAV GLICK
Times Staff Writer

Billboards on the approaches to Long Beach proclaim it as the International City, not withstanding its public reputation as Iowa West.

Sunday it truly was an International City.

Drivers from around the world roared through its streets and along its harbor front in a racing panorama that turned the clock back 50 years to the delight of more than 75,000 spectators. More European writers were on hand than for any previous U.S. race.

And it was an international finish to the richest Formula 5000 race ever held as foreign drivers took the first six places.

Brian Redman, 38-year-old defending Formula 5000 champion from Yorkshire, Eng., drove a "tidy race" to win easily after watching early leaders Al Unser, Tony Brise and Mario Andretti succumb to the torturous demands the 2.02-mile Long Beach course made on their machinery in 50 laps.

Following Redman, who clinched the 1975 championship with his win, were Vern Schuppan of Australia, Eppie Wietzes of Canada, Chris Amon of New Zealand, David Hobbs of England and Warwick Brown of Australia.

The first American finisher was seventh place Evan Noyes of Indianapolis, two laps behind the winner.

Only Schuppan, driving a Dan Gurney-prepared Jorgensen Eagle, was on the same lap with Redman when he took the checkered flag in a dramatic race that was a dress rehearsal for a world championship Formula I race next March 28 on the same downtown Long Beach circuit.

Unser and Andretti, in identical Vel's-Parnelli Jones Viceroy-Lolas, and Brise, the 23-year-old Formula I star from England, put on a tremendous battle during the early stages as Redman lay back, saving his Jim Hall-prepared Lola.

But the back and forth antics of the leaders did precisely what Redman figured it would, it put such pressures on transmissions, brakes and drive trains that on the 35th lap Redman found himself in the lead, breezing along with nearly a minute

Please Turn to Page 8, Col. 3

FOLLOW THE LEADER—Al Unser leads the pack into Turn 2 at Long Beach Grand Prix Sunday. Good brakes were a must. Those tires are for drivers who took it too fast. Brian Redman won.

Times photo by Ben Olender

## 4 A's Pitchers No-Hit Angels and Set Record

From Times Wire Services

Four pitchers—Vida Blue, Glenn Abbott, Paul Lindblad and Rollie Fingers—made major-league history Sunday when they pitched the A's to a 5-0, no-hit victory over the Angels on the final day of the season. It was the first time more than two pitchers had combined on a no-hitter.

The only previous combined no-hitters were a losing effort by Baltimore's Steve Barber and Stu Miller in 1967, and a winning one in 1917 by Babe Ruth and Ernie Shore of the Boston Red Sox. In that game, Shore relieved after Ruth walked the first batter and was ejected from the game. The runner was immediately thrown out trying to steal and Shore then retired 26 straight batters. Shore subsequently was credited with a perfect game.

Starting pitcher Blue, who went the first five innings to pick up his 22nd victory and permitted the game's only baserunners on a pair of walks and a Bert Campaneris error said, "I knew I was coming out. It

Please Turn to Page 8, Col. 3

### *Crandall, Quilici Fired*

Story on Page 8

## Rams Get Their Kicks---23-14

### 49ers Lose 10th in Row to L.A.

BY BOB OATES
Times Staff Writer

SAN FRANCISCO—Tom Dempsey, the new placekicker, kept the Rams in the game until they could win it Sunday, 23-14, on a blocked punt and a couple of well-thrown passes by quarterback James Harris.

For awhile against the 49ers, there was nobody for Los Angeles fans to applaud except Dempsey, whose third field goal carried 51 yards with the wind in Candlestick Park to tie a club record.

But this was a game in which, ultimately, there was as much good footballs as bad—by both sides—as Chuck Knox' team (1-1) moved into undisputed possession of first place in the NFC West.

In the crisis of the fourth quarter, with the Rams barely ahead, 16-14, they forsook the conservative strategy for which they are justly well known and nailed down their first win of the two-week-old season with forward passes—including Harris' bomb to Harold Jackson for 52 yards and his touchdown throw to Lawrence McCutcheon on a 22-yard play.

Knox, in the fourth quarters of his two seasons as a big winner in pro ball, has often played it close to the chest in defense of a small lead. But this time, with 5 minutes left, second-and-9 on the Los Angeles 22, Knox, as the signal-caller, ordered Harris to hit away with a long pass down the middle.

Jackson was fighting across the 50-yard line against the challenge of 49er cornerback Bruce Taylor when Harris unloaded one that carried 40-plus yards.

As Jackson caught it, Taylor was there, but only close enough for Jackson to drag him another 10 yards to the San Francisco 26.

Four plays later, on third-and-7, McCutcheon drifted behind the San Francisco secondary to take the touchdown pass that preserved his team's jinx over the 49ers, who have now lost 10 straight regular-season games to the Rams.

Knox is 7-0 against the 49ers. San

Please Turn to Page 6, Col. 1

GUESS WHO KICKED IT—As Rams and 49ers watch, Ram field goal kicker Tom Dempsey (10) raises his arms in jubilation. He knew 51-yarder in Sunday's game was good. Rams won, 23-14.

AP Wirephoto

## O.J.'S DAY: 227 YARDS, 88-YARD TD; STEELERS BOW

PITTSBURGH (UPI)—O. J. Simpson rushed for 227 yards, including an 88-yard touchdown burst, to lead the Buffalo Bills to an upset 30-21 victory Sunday over the defending Super Bowl champion Pittsburgh Steelers.

Simpson's 227 yards fell 23 short of the NFL single game record of 250 yards he gained in a 1973 contest with the New England Patriots. The Juice carried the ball 28 times in rushing for 100 or more yards for the 26th time in his career.

Joe Ferguson added two touchdown passes and 270-pound defensive tackle Mike Kadish lumbered 26 yards for another TD as the Bills beat the Steelers for the first time in four meetings.

The Bills owned a 3-0 lead on John

Please Turn to Page 7, Col. 1

### 'BALL KEPT GOING . . .'

## Dempsey Put Foot in It, 49er Put Hand on It

BY DWIGHT CHAPIN
Times Staff Writer

SAN FRANCISCO—Somebody got a hand on the 51-yard field goal that Tom Dempsey kicked to beat the San Francisco 49ers here Sunday.

"I didn't see who it was," said Dempsey. "Had my head down. But I heard the ball get tipped and I thought, 'Oh, God, no; it's been blocked! Here we go again.' "

But no. The ball kept on going—and going—like a wounded goose, and fluttered over the crossbar.

"That took some kind of leg, to get it that far after it was tipped," someone suggested.

Somebody else asked Dempsey what it was like to kick a 51-yarder, which tied a Ram record shared by Danny Villanueva and Lou Michaels.

Bad question . . .

Dempsey not only holds the National Football League field goal record of 63 yards, but he's a team player now.

"Maybe personal goals meant more to me when I kicked that ball 63 yards (in 1970)," Dempsey said. "But, hell, I know now no kick means as much as a win—however you do it.

"I never played on a team that won more than seven games in a season before. It was sort of fun down in New Orleans with the Saints, but we were a Gashouse Gang more than a team. It's great to know I'm with somebody who can win now."

Apart from a special teams' unit that blocked a 49er punt into a Ram touchdown, it was pretty much Dempsey's game Sunday . . . 47-yard field goal in the first quarter, 37-yarder in the third, 51-yarder in the fourth, two extra points.

Please Turn to Page 6, Col. 5

† CC

## Pro Football

Los Angeles 23, San Francisco 14
Detroit 17, Atlanta 14
Minnesota 42, Cleveland 10
Miami 22, New England 14
Washington 49, N.Y. Giants 13
Oakland 31, Baltimore 20
Chicago 15, Philadelphia 13
Dallas 37, St. Louis 31 (OT)
Houston 33, San Diego 17
N.Y. Jets 30, Kansas City 24
Cincinnati 21, New Orleans 0
Buffalo 30, Pittsburgh 21

# UCLA MAKES HISTORY AGAIN, 23-10

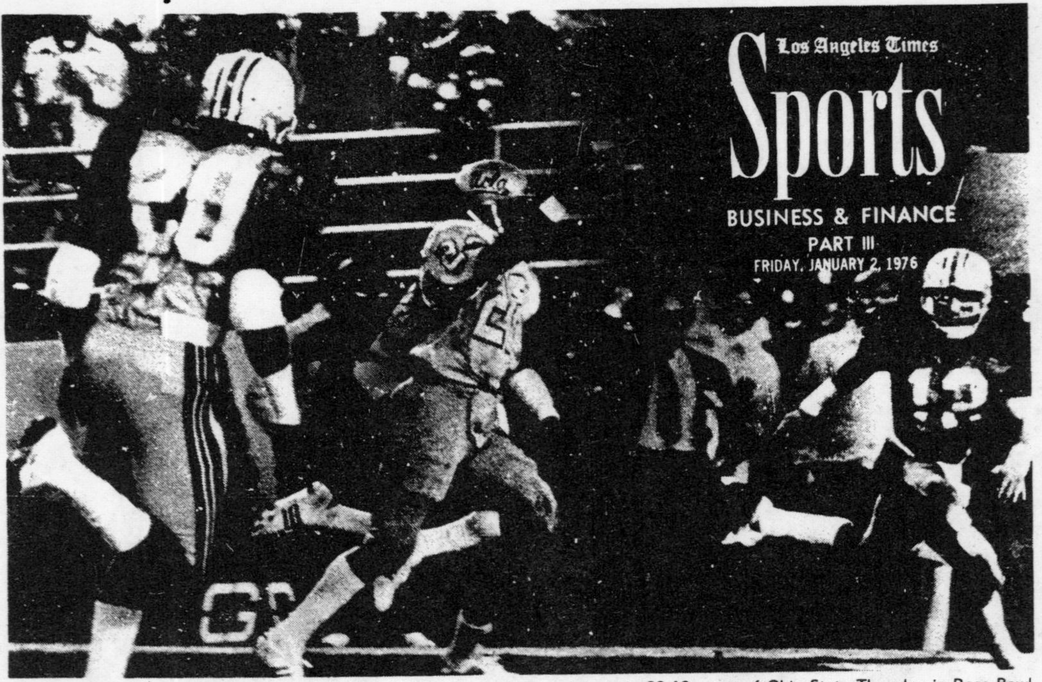


**THE CLINCHER**—Wendell Tyler holds ball aloft triumphantly as he crosses goal on 54-yard sprint in fourth quarter for UCLA's final touchdown in 23-10 upset of Ohio State Thursday in Rose Bowl. Buckeye defenders are Leonard Mills (20) and Tim Fox (12).

Times photo by Bill Varie

## Bruins Upset Another No. 1 Team in Rose Bowl

BY MAL FLORENCF
Times Staff Writer

Woody Hayes is a history buff and to the Ohio State coach's chagrin, he relearned an old truth: history *does* repeat itself.

UCLA's Bruins most likely knocked Ohio State out of the national championship New Year's Day with an upset 23-10 victory in the 62nd annual Rose Bowl game in Pasadena.

Another UCLA team performed the same number on Michigan State 10 years ago in the Rose Bowl—beating the previously unbeaten and top-ranked Spartans, 14-12.

In both instances UCLA had lost to the Big 10 teams during the regular season.

UCLA, a 14-point underdog Thursday, played like one in the first half when Ohio State mauled the Bruins but could net only a field goal for its efforts.

It was turnabout for Dick Vermeil's team in the last half. The Bruin veer, inoperative earlier, began functioning behind All-American quarterback John Sciarra, who threw two touchdown passes—plays covering 16 and 67 yards to Wally Henry, the little flanker.

The Bruins, trailing 3-0 at halftime, stretched out to a 16-3 lead in the third quarter on Sciarra's scoring tosses and 33-yard field goal by Brett White.

Then, after Ohio State marched 65 yards to cut the lead to 16-10 early in the fourth quarter, quarterback Cornelius Greene took his team out of the game with two badly thrown passes that were intercepted.

It remained for Wendell Tyler, UCLA's underrated halfback, to apply the clincher. With slightly more than four minutes left, Tyler shot through a large hole on the left side, ran by some Buckeye defenders and cut back at the perfect instant.

When Tyler was through running, he had covered 54 yards and provided the Bruins with the touchdown insurance they needed.

Tyler, labeled a fumbier this season, held the ball securely against the Buckeyes and had a big day—172 yards rushing, 8.2 average.

The UCLA halfback's total is something when you consider the Bruins gained only *nine* yards rushing in the first half to Ohio State's 155.

Moreover, the Bruins had the ball for only 9 minutes 8 seconds the first 30 minutes and didn't make a first down until more than 11 minutes had elapsed in the second quarter.

But UCLA maintained ball control most of the second half—18:09 minutes to 11:51—in spoiling Ohio State's previously perfect (11-0) season and atoning for a 41-20 loss to the Buckeyes last October at the Coliseum.

It was a bitter defeat for Hayes, who was knocked out of a share of the national title by losing to USC, 18-17, last year in the Rose Bowl.

For the 39-year-old Vermeil, this may be the start of something big. In only two seasons as UCLA coach he has got his team to the Rose Bowl—and won it—at the same age that former USC coach John McKay scored his first victory at Pasadena in 1963.

UCLA's stunning victory reaffirmed the Pacific 8's recent dominance over the Big 10 in what many regard as the most prestigious of all bowl games.

Please Turn to Page 5, Col. 1

## Bowl Results

### ORANGE

Oklahoma .......... 14
Michigan .......... 6

Story on page 7

### COTTON

Arkansas .......... 31
Georgia .......... 10

Story on page 8

## JIM MURRAY

## A Funny Thing Hap . . .

**It was supposed** to be a parade, not a game.

Ohio State wasn't sure whether to bring the first team or the whole squad.

Ohio State was supposed to be on the way to a national championship. UCLA was supposed to be on the way to a fumble. It was the thing they do best.

It was supposed to be the Miami Dolphins against Yale. You could always tell the UCLA team, the story went, because it had this big hole in the middle. It wasn't a team, it was a tunnel. And so on.

Ohio State had all these Heisman Trophies and the flower of the Pennyslvania coal mines in the line. The first team was the 1975 All-American.

They had this coach who wouldn't let them lose. He invented the game. He was always giving lectures to the world on how to live. After he won the Rose Bowl, he was going to straighten out the mess in Africa. His team had all these battle ribbons tacked on their helmets. He got mentioned in the same breath with Gen. Patton—and Gen. Ludendorf and Grant, for that matter.

★

**UCLA was** a fumbling team but it didn't matter. They wouldn't have the football that much.

Woody Hayes decided he would let the team go to Disneyland, stay up clear to 10 o'clock and even see some movies that had girls in them and John Wayne didn't necessarily win Iwo Jima.

He even let them pass the football—the rankest kind of indulgence for an Ohio State team. Clearly, Woody Hayes didn't think there would be too much suspense in the game.

I don't know how coach Hayes got so overconfident as to allow his team all those liberties. Except that he beat this very same UCLA team by 41-20 earlier in the year without taking the "A" game out.

But, a funny thing happened to Ohio State's national championship in the Rose Bowl. It got intercepted twice. You usually can't do that to coach Woody Hayes championships. Because he never puts them in the air in the first place. Woody's teams like the covered wagon approach.

Which is why a lot of people were shocked when Ohio State turned out to be "Woody Hayes' Aerial Circus." Ohio State played like a team that is outmanned. The team that is supposed to be 14 points better than some standing armies pulled a game plan that was right out of the way Swarthmore might try to play Notre Dame.

★

**He put the ball** in the air 18 times, a season high for an Ohio State team and maybe a career high. They seemed to play as if they were 14 behind at kickoff.

UCLA couldn't believe its good luck. Ohio State putting that ball up there where everyone could get a shot at it is like the Rockefellers throwing their money out of skyscraper windows. Usually, Ohio State just gets the ball, holds it for a day or two and you get to see the ball only on kickoffs. The guess was, the UCLA Bruins wouldn't get to see it much even then. After all, they fumbled ELEVEN times in the USC game. They fumbled SIX in the Oregon State game.

They started out the game like guys searching for a bomb in a dark cellar. They did everything but ask Ohio State for autographs. They had the ball a total

Please Turn to Page 4, Col. 4

**KING HENRY I**—Wally Henry catches 16-yard pass from John Sciarra for UCLA's first touchdown in third quarter. The defender is Craig Cassady. The score gave the Bruins a 9-3 lead.

Times photo by Joe Kennedy

**KING HENRY II**—Henry comes right back to make it 16-3 in third quarter on 67-yard pass play from Sciarra. On the ground is Cassady and in futile pursuit is Ray Griffin (44) who was taunted by Henry at the goal. Henry caught five passes for 113 yards.

Times photos by Rick Meyer

## Bruins Knew It at Halftime: Everything Would Be Fine

BY DWIGHT CHAPIN
Times Staff Writer

They floated into the locker room on clouds. Some of them laughed. Some of them cried. All of them smiled the incredulous smiles that come with upsetting the No. 1 team in college football.

They said things like "I still can't believe it" and "It's the most unreal feeling I've ever felt."

And they scribbled a chalk message on the blackboard that read: "Rose Bowl Champs. The Spirit of '76."

This was UCLA revisiting the Rose Bowl for the first time in 10 years, and UCLA in another incredible upset of a Big 10 behemoth.

As Bruin athletic director J. D. Morgan said, with his best cat-that-ate-the canary grin:

"We don't go to the Rose Bowl very often, but when we do we do it right."

There was Wendell Tyler, the former fumbler, grimacing and then crying out in pain as trainer Ducky Drake cut a thick bandage off his cracked left wrist, then just as quickly letting out a throaty laugh and saying he'd like to make All-American next year . . . and win the Heisman Trophy.

There was All-American quarterback John Sciarra being asked what adjustments UCLA's offense made after it was scoreless at the half and

Please Turn to Page 4, Col. 1

## BENGALS' BROWN QUITS AS COACH

CINCINNATI (UPI)—Paul Brown, who has coached more football victories than anyone else in history, resigned Thursday night as coach of the Cincinnati Bengals.

Brown, 67, bowed out with a 351-134-16 record after 41 seasons as a football coach from high school to the pros.

Brown said he would continue as general manager of the Bengals, an expansion team he formed eight years ago. He also is a major stockholder in the club.

Please Turn to Page 10, Col. 4

## JOHN HALL

## Woody: The Vanishing Buckeye

"Buckeye" is described in the reference books as a sort of bitter nut that grows on the state tree of Ohio.

Woody Hayes, the head Buckeye, regarded by many as the perfect definition, didn't disappoint his faithful critics Thursday afternoon and Thursday evening and even later Thursday night in the aftermath of Ohio State's shocking collapse against UCLA in the 62nd Rose Bowl.

In 61 previous chapters of this thing they call grandaddy, nobody came close to matching his matchless behavior—unless it was old Woody himself in one of his eight visits to what he regards as his private shrine—as he established a new record in rudeness and childishness.

With 8 seconds to go in the game and all the money in the Bruin bank, Hayes strolled across the field in a glorious solo flight in full view of the 105,464 to make a grandstand play in congratulating winning coach Dick Vermeil over UCLA's 23-10 shocker. It really wasn't quite that pretty.

"Congratulations," Hayes grunted to Vermeil. "But they (our guys) screwed up." These were his last words, the last sound heard from him as he then vanished like Claude Rains taking off the tape in "The Invisible Man."

With his chances for a fourth national championship and another unbeaten season going down in flames, it was too much for the 62-year-old Ohio State coach of 25 seasons, a man who often boasts he takes pride in being pre-

Please Turn to Page 3, Col. 1

CC †

Los Angeles Times
Sports
BUSINESS & FINANCE
CC PART III †
TUESDAY, JULY 20, 1976

# The Nadia & Olga Show

BY BILL SHIRLEY
Times Sports Editor

MONTREAL—Capacity crowds are not uncommon in the Forum, Montreal version. A team called the Canadiens fills it all the time.

But those haven't been hockey games packing them into the old arena lately. Monday night, for the fourth night this week, it was sold out—for some calisthenics known as team optional exercises in Olympic Games gymnastics.

Gymnastics, at the rate it's going, may soon replace track and field as the most popular sport in the Games. Two of the sellouts were for *rehearsals!*

Monday night the streets around the Forum were crowded with people trying to buy tickets at scalpers' prices. The 16,000 tickets had been sold long ago for the Nadia Comaneci & Olga Korbut Show.

It's easy to see why, judging from Monday night's performances. Little Nadia of Romania, who looks as if she ought to be in bed at 9 p.m.—or in kindergarten—was a knockout. The 14-year-old doll, who Sunday night became the first gymnast in Olympic Games history to make a perfect score of 10 (on the uneven parallel bars), got two more Monday night, one on the balance beam and another on the parallel bars.

Her stunning performance established her as the world's No. 1 women's gymnast and, for a while at least, little Olga Korbut has been knocked off the throne she ascended at the Munich Games in 1972.

Korbut, in fact, had an off night, although she had a near-perfect 9.9 on the parallel bars. In the other events, the beam, vault and floor exercises, she slipped and stumbled several times, almost as if she was losing her cool under the pressure applied by Comaneci.

But the judges were kind to the little Soviet star and she qualified for the all-around finals with a score of 39.15, only the third best total on her team. Comaneci's score was 39.70. Three gymnasts from each nation qualify.

At least three times during the night both Comaneci and Korbut were performing simultaneously and each time the

## All the World's a Stage for Gymnastics Dolls of Romania and USSR

crowd applauded Korbut but gave its strongest enthusiasm to Comaneci.

After her performance, Comaneci said through an interpreter, "I was very glad, but I've done it (achieved a perfect score) 19 times. "And my teammates are always helping me."

Nelli Kim at 39.45 and Ludmila Tourischeva at 39.40, who at 23 surely must feel like a grandmother out there with all those kids, led the Soviet Union to the team gold medal. Romania won the silver and East Germany got the bronze. The United States

Please Turn to Page 4, Col. 1

# Hey, Naber, Silence Isn't Golden at the Pool

THE GOLD RUSH—John Naber of U.S. and USC heads into pool and a gold medal Monday in 100-meter backstroke at Olympic Games in Montreal. Naber, 20, of Menlo Park set a world and Olympic record with time of 55.49—breaking own mark in prelims.
AP Wirephoto

## USC Swimmer Gets Win, Record; So Does Furniss

BY DWIGHT CHAPIN
Times Staff Writer

MONTREAL—A British writer called him "an American hotdog" Monday night. Teammate Jim Montgomery calls him "a fruitcake."

But John Naber isn't really a culinary delight. He's just a delight.

Naber broke his own world record—the one he set only Sunday night—in winning the men's 100-meter backstroke, then nearly edged his USC teammate and roommate Bruce Furniss (who also set a world record) in the 200 freestyle on the second day of swimming at the Olympic Games.

After that, Naber—who probably has shaken as many hands and acknowledged as many cheers here as Jimmy Carter did at the Democratic National Convention—talked about his style, which is gloriously uninhibited.

"I am what you see I am," Naber said. "I'm not being a hypocrite. I'm emotional, and sensitive, and I like to show it. If I offend anyone, I'm sorry. But I have to be myself.

"I like to see a lot of attention go to my sport because it's probably the only true amateur sport around. There's pure, genuine sacrifice in swimming and I'd like to see people realize it. I don't like to play the role of clown and I don't think I do. I just like to involve the crowd."

Naber did more than that Monday night as he led another record-breaking show.

In addition to his new 100-meter backstroke mark (55.49, which topped his previous 56.19); and Furniss' 1:50.29 in the 200 freestyle (which bettered his 1:50.32); records were set by East Germany's Kornelia Ender, 55.65 in the women's 100 freestyle (her former mark was 55.81) and American John (Rocket Man) Hencken of Stanford, who broke his world mark of 1:03.88 in the men's 100 breaststroke semifinals with a 1:03.62.

The only other final of the evening, the women's 200 butterfly, was swept by East Germans Andrea Pollack (2:11.41, an Olympic record), Ulrike Tauber and Rosemarie Gabriel.

The American women again followed in East Germany's wake. Karen Moe Thornton nearly touched out Gabriel for third in the 200 butterfly, and Kim Peyton was fourth in the 100 freestyle, but Shirley Babashoff—after a false start—got off badly in the 100 and finished fifth, a full second and a half behind the durable Ender.

Babashoff didn't congratulate Ender after her win, and U.S. women's coach Jack Nelson wouldn't let his

Please Turn to Page 6, Col. 1

## SOVIET STAR IS DISQUALIFIED FOR CHEATING

From Reuters

MONTREAL—A Soviet contestant, alleged to have cheated in the modern pentathlon, was expelled from the Olympic Games Monday after officials discovered his weapon was wired to score a hit without touching his opponent.

In an astonishing incident that destroyed the Soviet Union's chances of repeating its 1972 Munich gold medal win in the event, Boris Onischenko, 38, was found to have a piece of wire concealed on his epee to trigger the electronic scoring machine. Epees are wired to blink a light over the judges' desk when a hit is registered.

Please Turn to Page 3, Col. 4

## Kingman Hurt, Out for 6 Weeks

### Home Run Leader Has Surgery on His Thumb

From Times Wire Services

Dave Kingman of the New York Mets, the major league home run leader with 32, will be sidelined for about six weeks as the result of a thumb injury sustained in Monday night's game against Atlanta.

Kingman underwent surgery Monday night at Manhattan Roosevelt Hospital for torn ligaments in his left thumb.

Kingman was injured diving for a double down the left-field line in the third inning in the Mets' 4-2 loss to Atlanta. After being examined on the field, Kingman finished the inning but was removed in the fourth.

The initial prognosis by physicians indicated that Kingman's thumb would be placed in a cast for approximately four weeks. They also indicated that at least two additional weeks of therapy and exercise would be required before Kingman could return to active duty.

In addition to his 32 homers, King-

Please Turn to Page 7, Col. 1

## *JIM MURRAY*

## Olympic Hipsters

MONTREAL—For Olympian Ron Laird, it's the same old story. Work for years on your event, live for it, eat for it, sleep for it, sacrifice for it—and then, one day, you'll be able to turn pro and cash in on it. After all, basketball players do it, ice skaters, skiers, hockey players, even fighters.

Ron is ready right now. He could become a letter carrier tomorrow. Or a waiter. Night watchman. The post office is missing a good prospect. So is Luchow's. He'd make a great beat cop.

The Ice Capades gave Peggy Fleming millions. The NBA regularly signs Olympic centers to multiyear contracts. But nobody from the post office has even contacted Ron Laird. He doesn't even have an agent.

Ron Laird is a long-distance walker, an event that is an orphan of track and field. When they wanted to trim the bulk of events this year, the first thing they threw out was the 50-kilometer walk.

★

**For all of that,** Ronald Owen Laird is an historical track and field figure. This will be his fourth Olympics. But it's the only Olympic event that moves just faster than the opening-day ceremonies.

You have to be able to run the 100 in 10.2 to make the Olympic qualifying standard. You have to do the metric mile in 3:40 or better. Even the 10,000 meters allows you only 28 minutes. But in the 20,000 kilometer walk, just get in by dark.

The first look you get at a walking race, it looks like 50 guys doing Charlie Chaplin. You wonder what they did with their canes. They got the hip movement of a conga line. They are the comedy relief of every track meet. But they are as deadly serious about what they do as jewel thieves.

They really suffer for their sport. Dogs chase them. People hoot at them. Cops stop them. The press ignores them. They are constantly accusing each other of cheating. In Tokyo, after a grueling 20,000 kilometer walk, an official nastily ran up to Ron Laird and waved a red flag in his face and ordered him off the track as he entered the stadium with a lap to go. "Your form is awful!" he snarled.

Things keep happening to Ron Laird. When he was in the Army in Philadelphia, he paid a guy $12 to pull his KP for him once while he went to Franklin Field where he won the U.S. walking championship. The sergeant was unimpressed and ordered him arrested on his return, medal and all.

★

**He is 38 years old,** but for walkers, that is a youth movement. It's never really caught on in the playgrounds and there is one walker in here, Alex Oakley of Canada, who is 50—the oldest competitor ever in track and field. A West German walker is 45.

Ron Laird was in a low mood the day I caught up with him in the Olympic Village. He had the sniffles. "What a time to get a cold, eh?" he sniffled. He also had had trouble finding his girlfriend an apartment. He had been bunked in with the high jumpers, Dwight Stones and Bill Jankunis, whose life-styles call for late and noisy arrivals to the 12-to-a-room quarters. His name had been left out of the United States Olympic team book. Also he had just been bitten by a large German shepherd. He dropped his pants to show me the scar.

He doesn't have any real expectations of a medal. After all, the best he's ever done in the Olympic walk is 19th (Rome, 1960). He got red-flagged off the

Please Turn to Page 5, Col. 2

## Phils Knock Out Hooton and Beat Dodgers in Ninth

BY ROSS NEWHAN
Times Staff Writer

The Dodgers went down to an emotional 2-1 defeat Sunday, and Monday night there was another blow to the psyche and to the standings.

A Dodger Stadium crowd of 37,109 saw the Phillies rally for three runs in the ninth inning and a 5-3 victory that left the Dodgers seven back of Cincinnati in the National League West.

The only solace for Los Angeles seemed to be that Burt Hooton emerged in one piece.

It was significant solace for Hooton, although for eight innings it appeared that he would also emerge with his seventh victory of the season and his eighth in a row over the Phillies.

But after Philadelphia scored an unearned run in the eighth to close to 3-2, all of Hooton's rewards were wiped out in the ninth when Hooton himself was almost wiped out by a line drive off the bat of Greg Luzinski, the strong man they call The Bull.

Mike Schmidt opened the ninth with a single to center, the Phils' seventh hit off Hooton, who they had last defeated Sept. 6, 1974.

Luzinski was now the batter and he jumped on a fastball that was up and over the plate, nailing it squarely. The ball was on top of Hooton before he could come out of his follow through, which was fortunate.

The pitcher was still bent over, his right arm reaching toward the dirt of the mound, his momentum spinning him toward first base.

Luzinski's drive struck Hooton on the right hip and struck him on the belt, popping high into shallow left where it fell in front of the charging Bill Buckner as Schmidt raced to third and Luzinski lumbered into second with a double.

Hooton later said the ball came back at him so fast that he did not have time to think, but because it hit his belt it did not hurt.

Manager Walter Alston said, however, that since Hooton had given up the two shots to open the ninth and since there had been two other

Please Turn to Page 7, Col. 2

## RED SOX FIRE JOHNSON AND KEEP THE TEAM

BOSTON (AP)—Darrell Johnson, who led the Boston Red Sox to within one victory of a World Series championship in 1975, was fired Monday. A club statement said it was easier to fire him than the team.

Third base coach Don Zimmer was named manager for the rest of the season.

"The way the team's been going lately I don't blame (general manager) Dick O'Connell or the Red Sox one bit," said Johnson, who was reached by telephone in Arlington, Tex., where the Red Sox were playing the Texas Rangers.

"In my opinion it was time for a change. But I wouldn't change anything I did one bit."

Please Turn to Page 2, Col. 3

## THEY'RE OUT OF THE RUNNING

## Political Pawns Are Heard From

From a Times Staff Writer

MONTREAL—Mike Boit would rather not be a symbol of the 1976 Olympic Games.

He would rather leave the political machinations and the shouting to others. He would rather just run—as few men alive today can run.

But as it now stands, Mike Boit of Kenya will not run here, will not get a gold medal or any other kind in the 800 meters. Mike Boit, today or Wednesday, will be on a charter plane back to Africa.

He is one of the best of hundreds of African and Third-World athletes who, barring change, will not compete here because of complicated political issues—largely the fact that New Zealand, which played South Africa in a rugby game, is here. "I am very, very disappointed to be leaving," Boit said. "I am not going to enjoy watching. As of now we are out. I keep hoping for change, and I'm still around. But I don't truthfully see much chance."

Neither does Kenya marathoner Phillip Ndoo, a teammate of Boit's at Eastern New Mexico.

"All of this," he says, "is nothing new to me. I am personally disappointed but when politicians are at war with each other they will use any weapon—including people—to win their point of view.

"We athletes don't really understand much about this. I wish someone had the answers."

He said his understanding first was that Kenya and the other African nations would not compete only if a New Zealand competitor was entered in the same event. "Now it is not clear. It seems we are out of everything."

Boit was asked if he might defy his government's order and compete anyway.

"No," he said, "I would not be able to do that."

Ndoo is concerned about reaction in Kenya to his team's withdrawal.

"We have had no monetary help from our government to come to the Olympics," he said. "It has all come from our people. What will they think? Will they want to support us in 1980? But the decision of the government is final and it may be a tragedy for us. If we have wasted the people's money the government may be forced to take over the team and there will be much more control."

The pullout of nations will mostly affect four sports—track and field, boxing, soccer and field hockey.

Garry Hill, editor of Track and Field News, says, "If the Africans and others are out, track will be drastically affected in nearly every running event from the 200 up. It bodes well for the Americans, but you can throw your form charts out the window."

There are a bundle of big names and contenders among the missing, including:

James Gilkes, Guyana, sprints; Stephen Chepkwony and Charles Asati of Kenya and Dele Udo of Nigeria, 400 meters; Boit and Dan Omwanza of Kenya in the 800; Filbert Bayi of Tanzania (former co-favorite with New Zealand's John Walker); Boit and Wilson Waigwa of Kenya in the 1,500; James Munyala and Nathan Lagat of Kenya and Yo-

Please Turn to Page 4, Col. 4

**JIM MURRAY**

# Oh! Say, Can You See ... What's Going On?

ORANGE COUNTY

CC PART III †

SUNDAY, JULY 25, 1976


MONTREAL—Does anyone here remember how "The Star-Spangled Banner" goes?

Oh! Say, can you see, if our Flag is still there?

We haven't seen it around here in a long while.

When did Olympic Games stop being "Stars And Stripes Forever"? Who took Francis Scott Key out of the repertoire?

When was the last time you remember when the U.S. didn't win a medal in the Olympic 100? Shucks, we used to take *all* of them.

How long has it been since we got shut out in the shot put? Didn't guys named "O'Brien" used to win this thing? Or guys named "Bill," "Clarence"? Or "Dallas"? Or "Randy"?

When did guys named "Udo" and "Evgeni" start to take this event from us?

What do we lose next—the World Series?

Remember when the pole vault was an American parade? Well, we lost that the last time for the first time ever.

But when did the 100 stop being an All-American event and become a No-American event? How come guys named "Hasely" and "Valeriy" are winning this thing? Whatever happened to "Charley" and "Bobby" and "Jesse," for heaven's sake?

Why don't these foreigners keep the 10,000 meters and the 5,000 and the steeplechase and render to America the things that are American? OK, so they can have the gymnastics and those funny little sports. But we own the sprints, don't we? We win the shot put 14 out of every 16 times, don't we? We at least take second, don't we?!

What is going on here? It's all very well to get out of Southeast Asia or Angola, but do we have to get out of the hundred?

I can remember Olympics when they played "The Star-Spangled Banner" so often it was embarrassing. It sounded as if the Olympic stadiums were playing a medley of our National Anthem. They wore out 20 American Flags at Olympics hauling them up and down the flagpole.

Now all you hear is that East German hymn or the Internationale or a steel-band anthem from the Caribbean that sounds like a limbo dance.

Speed has always been an American asset. It was hard to imagine anyone from Kiev beating anyone from Alabama. Or anyone named "Jones."

The United States of America is being beaten by the United States of America. In 1972, we didn't get our best sprinters to the start line because our coaches didn't know what time it was. In Europe, anyway. This year, we didn't because our method of selection is just better than picking a team out of the phone book. Terry Albritton got to the Olympics only on the scoreboard. His listed world record—21.82 meters (71 feet 7 inches)—got to the Olympics but he didn't.

We are beginning to find new ways to lose. It isn't easy. On Saturday, our best half-miler (and the world's), Rick Wohlhuter, who sells insurance for a living, was breezing along in a heat of the 800.

It was only a heat, and all he had to do was finish fourth. Rick Wohlhuter could do that on a

**Please Turn to Page 8, Col. 2**

# The Darkest Day: U.S. Shut Out in 100, Shot

**NO YANKS IN SIGHT**—With the United States shut out, Trinidad's Hasely Crawford raises right arm in victory as he crosses finish line first in Olympic 100-meter dash Saturday in Montreal. Jamaica's Donald Quarrie (574) won the silver medal and Valeriy Borozov (877), the Soviet sprinter who won at Munich four years ago, finished third. Bulgaria's Petar Petrov (127) was seventh. AP Wirephoto

## Glance, Feuerbach Both Fourth; Crawford Surprises in Sprint

**BY DWIGHT CHAPIN**
Times Staff Writer

MONTREAL—So you thought Munich was bad for the U.S. track and field team . . .

The Americans had one of their blackest days in Olympic history here Saturday. For the first time since 1928, the U.S. failed to win a medal in the men's 100 meters. And for the first time since 1936, it was shut out in the shot put.

Rick Wohlhuter

Brenda Morehead, America's top woman sprinter, pulled up in a second round heat in the 100 meters and is doubtful with a hamstring injury. Madeline Manning Jackson, 1968 Olympic champion in the 800 meters, finished eighth and last in her semifinal heat.

But it could have been much worse.

Rick Wohlhuter, the top U.S. 800-meter man and one of the favorites for a gold medal here today, won his semifinal Saturday and then was disqualified for what a judge called a bumping infraction with about 250 meters to go in the race.

Dr. Leroy Walker, the U.S. men's coach, immediately filed an appeal, however, and less than 30 minutes later the race referee overturned the ruling—saying the videotape of the race showed no infraction.

So Wohlhuter officially is back, to try to restore some of that lost American pride today. But the way Alberto Juantorena of Cuba ran in winning his 800 semifinal (1:45.88) Wohlhuter, too, may have trouble winning a gold medal.

The only track medal the U.S. got Saturday was Kate Schmidt's bronze in the women's javelin. But Schmidt, who won the bronze in Munich, had been expected to do better than that here, too.

The 100 meters—in one of those upsets that comes along every couple of decades, went to Hasely Crawford of Trinidad-Tobago, who went to school at Eastern Michigan.

His 10.06 beat Don Quarrie of Jamaica (10.08) and Valeriy Borzov of the Soviet Union (10.14). Harvey Glance, the teen-ager from Auburn University, was fourth in 10.19.

In the shot put, the best the U.S. could do was Al Feuerbach's fourth. This one went to a surprise winner, too, young (20-year-old) Udo Beyer of East Germany, who threw 69-0¾ to 69-0 for Evgeni Mironov and 68-10¾ for Alexander Barisnikov, both of the Soviet Union. Geoff Capes of Great Britain and George Woods of the U.S., favored along with Feuerbach, were sixth and seventh.

And where would you be today if you'd made a parlay bet back in—say—January, on Hasely Crawford

**Please Turn to Page 6, Col. 1**

# Briton Snaps U.S. Men's Swim String at 9

## USC's Naber Wins 4th Gold Medal

**BY BILL SHIRLEY**
Times Sports Editor

MONTREAL—The U.S. men swimmers can't win 'em all.

Just when it appeared they would sweep the 13 Olympic Games events, they lost a race Saturday night when David Wilkie of Great Britain took the 200-meter breaststroke.

Of course, it took a world record to break the U.S. string at nine. But then it usually takes a record to win a race these days, especially in the Olympic Games, the most important races of a swimmer's life unless his opponent is a shark.

Wilkie swam the distance in 2:15.11 to beat John Hencken of Stanford University by about 2 yards. Hencken held the record of 2:18.21 and beat that himself with a 2:17.26. Rick Colella of the U.S. won the bronze medal and another U.S. swimmer, Charles Keating, finished fifth.

So the U.S. men enter tonight's final events with a 10-1 record, with two races to go. Every time they have won here in the gorgeous new Olympic Swim Stadium they have set a world record.

They broke two more Saturday night. John Naber of USC set one and won his fourth gold medal (he also has a silver) when he beat two teammates, Peter Rocca and Dan Harrigan, in the 200-meter backstroke. His time was 1:59.19. He already held the record at 2:00.64, which Rocca also beat with a 2:00.55.

Jim Montgomery broke the other

**Please Turn to Page 6, Col. 4**

**PLUNGING FOR MORE GOLD**—USC's John Naber casts off in 200-meter backstroke, and minutes later dips under water, raising four fingers to indicate his fourth gold medal Saturday. AP Wirephoto

# Dodgers Chase Jones but Fail to Get Relief

**BY ROSS NEWHAN**
Times Staff Writer

SAN DIEGO—For the first time in four confrontations this year, the Dodgers did not lose to Randy Jones Saturday night.

Neither did they beat him, although they had him down and out, 5-1, after seven innings. What happened after that is what has been happening consistently to the Dodgers during the second half.

Manager Walter Alston went looking for relief and found it only in trainer Bill Buhler's medicine chest. Alston's headache became acute as he watched the Padres score four times in the eighth and once in the ninth for a 6-5 victory that enabled Jones, a 17-game winner, to escape his fifth defeat.

The win that was San Diego's ninth in 12 games with the Dodgers also enabled Cincinnati to move seven games ahead of Los Angeles in the National League West and prompted Alston to say.

"The same relief pitchers who did a

**Please Turn to Page 4, Col. 3**

# Angels Toast Sherry With a Double, 8-0, 4-3

**BY RON RAPOPORT**
Times Staff Writer

When Norm Sherry entered the Angel dressing room at Anaheim Stadium Saturday afternoon, he got a standing ovation from the ballplayers.

The new Angel manager appreciated it, of course, but he was even happier about what came next.

That was the sweep of a doubleheader from the Texas Rangers, 8-0 and 4-3. Rookie Paul Hartzell pitched his first major league complete game and his first shutout in the opener, allowing only three hits, while the Angels supported him with a 13-hit attack. He threw only 79 pitches.

Don Kirkwood and John Verhoeven combined to hold Texas off in the second game as Bobby Bonds drove in what turned out to be the deciding run with a ground ball in the fifth. Bonds now has driven in runs in eight straight games and 12 of his last 13.

There were two reasons for the cheers Sherry received from the Angels as he began his managerial duties. The players were glad Dick Williams had gone and they were glad Norm Sherry was there.

Many of them had played for Sherry at one time or another in California's minor league systems and those questioned gave him high marks as a manager and a motivator. During the course of the season, many of the Angel players had complained about the way Williams, who was fired Friday, had tried to motivate them.

"He had 11 of us in the minors," said infielder Dave Chalk of Sherry, who moved from the third-base coaching box under Williams to the manager's office. "I think people know him a little better and can talk to him a little easier maybe than they talked to Dick.

"There's not a doubt in my mind we'll be more relaxed." I think the situation with Dick affected everybody to a certain extent. Everybody was unhappy with it."

"In my book," said third baseman Ron Jackson of Sherry, "he's a good

**Please Turn to Page 10, Col. 1**

# Pincay Wins 5, Passes Hawley

## Upset Win in Feature Finishes a Big Day

**BY BION ABBOTT**
Times Staff Writer

Laffit Pincay caught and then passed Sandy Hawley with five trips to the winner's circle and capped the season's first quintuple with an upset victory aboard Bastonera II in the $65,800 Beverly Hills Handicap before 48,369 fans Saturday at Hollywood Park.

Pincay, who trailed Hawley by 27 wins after the first three weeks of the season, now has a three-winner advantage, 122-119, going into the final two days.

His $9.40 victory with Bastonera II in the feature snapped a win streak of four straight by heavily-favored Miss Toshiba and compromised her chances of being named horse of the meeting.

Bastonera II beat Miss Toshiba by a head in 1:50 1/5 for 1⅛ miles on

**Please Turn to Page 12, Col. 2**

# GLITTER OF OLYMPIC GOLD

**BY STEVE JACOBSON**
Newsday

## *Former Champions Recall What Medal Meant to Them*

"The Olympics. I can feel all four of mine, but the one farthest away—20 years ago—I can feel the whole competitive thing," Al Oerter said, his voice full of wonder at the freshness of his own image. "I can feel exactly where I was and what I was thinking.

"There isn't very much time that goes by in any day in my life when something about the Olympics doesn't really sink home to me. I'll think about it and I sit there with a big smile on my face.

"It's a very real emotion. It stays with you."

"You stood on the victory stand," Bobby Joe Morrow said, "while they played the Stars and Stripes and you could hear a pin drop among 120,000 people.

"I can visualize where the victory stand was; where I walked to get there and what I did afterward. I'm really constantly thinking about that whole time. Really."

Bobby Joe Morrow raises cotton and grain near Rangerville, Texas, in the Rio Grande Valley. He won gold medals for the 100-meters, 200-meters and ran the anchor leg of the winning 400-meter relay at the Melbourne Olympics in 1956. Twenty years ago he was the world's fastest human.

Al Oerter is 39, lives on Long Island and is manager of data communications at Grumman. He won his first Olympic gold in the discus at Melbourne and won again at Rome, Tokyo and Mexico City. No other athlete ever won gold medals at four consecutive Olympic Games.

He retired after the 1968 Games but his competitive urge was merely banked. When he became involved in production of the films about the Olympic Games for public television, he felt the urge grow. It was too late for him to catch up to the world for Montreal, but he's working toward Moscow in 1980.

That's four years from now. He'll be 43 years old. He wants that sensation again. "And that's why I'm going back," Oerter said.

Olympic gold made Oerter and Morrow celebrities. It bathed their ego. It gave them satisfaction they say can be appreciated only by someone who's stood on the victory stand. They say it didn't put a dollar in their pockets. But then, they say, that wasn't what they were there for.

Olympic gold has been gold in the marketplace for a lot of athletes over the years. It made Cassius Clay, Floyd Patterson, Joe Frazier and George

**Please Turn to Page 10, Col. 1**

# Moses, Wilkins Put U.S. Back on Gold Standard

## Hurdler Shatters Akii-Bua's World Mark

BY DWIGHT CHAPIN
Times Staff Writer

MONTREAL—Silent Edwin Moses has been around track seven years, and never did much until he took up the hurdles fulltime in March.

Four months later, on a cool, sunny day at the Olympic Games, Ed Moses set a world record.

"Maybe it was about time," he said in that quiet way of his, "that something came around."

The "something" was a 47.64 time in the 400-meter hurdles which broke the world record of 47.82 John Akii-Bua of Uganda set in Munich in 1972. Akii-Bua wasn't in the field Sunday. Uganda has long since pulled out of the Games. But it's doubtful Akii-Bua, who's been hurting lately, could have done anything about Moses.

Moses was the big winner on a day when there were some of other kinds—including a patriotic winner, Alberto Juantorena of Cuba, who knocked off Rick Wohlhuter in world record time, 1:43.50, in the 800 meters and then said he did it for his country and for Castro; and a sore winner, American discus thrower Mac Wilkins, who rapped himself, the U.S. Olympic Committee and just about everyone else in sight.

And then there was the modest winner, Annegret Richter of West Germany, who set a world women's 100-meter dash record at 11.01 in the semifinals, and came back to beat defending gold medalist Renate Stecher of East Germany.

Taking them one at a time:

—"I got the slowest start I ever had," Moses said. "I had to really pick it up down the back straight (to catch the man who finished third—Evgeniy Gavrilenko of the Soviet Union)."

When Moses went into overdrive, however, everyone just watched in amazement, including Mike Shine of Penn State, who won the silver medal.

"The last 60 or 70 meters," Shine said, "I couldn't believe him. I didn't think anyone could pull away that fast."

"I'd planned to run a 47.5 today," Moses said. "I guess 47.6 isn't too bad."

He said he won because "I pushed hard on the last five hurdles. Anyone can run the first five, but what decides who wins a race is the last five."

When they finished, Moses and Shine embraced in a classic picture that was flashed on both electronic scoreboards in the stadium. Then, holding hands, they ran a victory lap, playfully knocking over a couple of hurdles as the crowd cheered.

"We were talking about what we had said before the race," said Shine who was timed in 48.69. "We wanted the U.S. to go one-two-three. We didn't care what order we were in."

(Quentin Wheeler was fourth in 49.86 to Gavrilenko's 49.45.)

For Moses, 27, it closed a chapter.

"I had to give up a lot in my engineering studies (at Morehouse College of Atlanta) to train," he said. "I'm glad I got a gold medal and I'm glad it's all over."

Wohlhuter, who had to survive a

Please Turn to Page 9, Col. 1

## JIM MURRAY

### A Man in Pain

MONTREAL—It was the night before the 800-meter final and the world's second-best half-miler and early favorite to win this event briefly weighed whether to have another beer or go for some more of the white wine. Service had been slow in the Cafe Martin, one of the plush Frenchtown restaurants, but it was still well before midnight—at least 40 minutes, in fact.

The onion soup was resting easy in his stomach, the rib steak was smothered in french fries, each of which he dipped in the gravy before eating. He eyed the dessert table with its mounds of whipped cream.

To be sure, there were still 15 hours before his event but any coach would have fainted dead away at the sight and, upon being revived, would have fired him off the team and out of the Olympics.

The trouble was, somebody already had. This was Mike Boit, one of those marvelous Kenyans who have stormed the Olympics these past eight years like a flight of wildebeest over the veldt. This was to have been Mike's gold-medal year. He won the bronze at Munich. He ran the second-fastest 800 meters (1:43.8) ever. He was no worse than even money in this year's Olympic 800.

★

**But an unfunny thing** happened to Mike on his way to the victory stand. He got caught in the political squeeze which removed the African ring from the five-continents Olympic flag. No one cared this night if Mike Boit drank champagne out of a slipper, ate oysters and got the gout.

If Mike Boit fully comprehends what has happened to his four years of hard work, sacrifice, pain and dedication, it shows only in his diet. His conversation eerily dwelt on strategy he would employ in the race, pique at the prerace quotes of his principal competitor, a grand overview of what the race would mean in history. Like Gloria Swanson, in "Sunset Boulevard," Mike thinks he is still a star and not yesterday's news.

"Why," he said in that clipped singsong Oxonian accent affected by Africans, "did Wohlhuter (he pronounced it "Well-hootah") say in Sports (pronounced "Spots") Illustrated that I am easy to beat because I do not have good strategy in a race? Do you think he really said that—or some journalist?" (The story was written by Kenny Moore, an ex-Olympic marathonist, so Boit's hearers were uncomfortable with the question.)

★

**"Tomorrow," said Boit,** flashing an amiable gold-toothed smile, "I would have taken the race out slowly with a slow 200, then I would have turned it on with the third 200. Wohlhuter will miss me. He will not know how to race as well with me not there. How can he say I am not a good tactician when I have beat him six times out of eight last year? If I do that, and I do not have any strategy, that does not make him such a good runner, does it? He will need me tomorrow."

The subject was changed. It is not good to see a man in pain. Mike Boit with his pathetic little relics of his Olympics—buttons he exchanged with other athletes before he left the Olympic Village—was man in torment.

For him, the 800 meters was like attending the wedding of your very best girl, watching somebody else raise your child, steal your birthright. Athletics took Mike Boit from a thatched hut and a hardpan floor life to a

Please Turn to Page 6, Col. 1

**RECORD RUN**—Cuba's Alberto Juantorena (right) outsprints Belgium's Ivo Van Damme (left) and Rick Wohlhuter of Chicago in winning 800 meters in world record time of 1:43.50 Sunday at Olympic Games in Montreal. Wohlhuter, 880 record-holder, was timed in 1:44.12.

**HAPPY HURDLER**—Edwin Moses of Dayton shows elation after winning 400-meter hurdles in world record time of 47.64 seconds Sunday at Montreal Olympics. Mike Shine of Youngsville, Pa., was second.

AP Wirephotos

# At the Very End, American Women Swim to Gold

**AT LAST, SOME GOLD**—U.S. women won their first swimming gold medal of Montreal Olympic Games Sunday night in 400-meter freestyle relay—setting world record of 3:44.82. Happy Americans are, from left: Kim Payton, Shirley Babashoff, Wendy Boglioli and Jill Sterkel.

AP Wirephoto

## Americans Beat East Germans in Relay; Montgomery Goes 49.99 in 100 Freestyle

BY BILL SHIRLEY
Times Sports Editor

MONTREAL—Until Sunday night, it had been an embarrassing Olympic Games for the United States' women swimmers. While their male teammates broke records so fast it appeared they were swimming downhill, the women collected only silver and bronze medals as the East Germans won almost all the gold in sight.

And with the defeats came a considerable amount of ridicule and questions such as "Why don't American women lift weights and grow muscles like the East Germans?"

Well, the U.S. women got a measure of revenge—without all those muscles. Down to the last of 13 races, they finally won a gold medal. And they won it convincingly.

The names were Kim Peyton, Wendy Boglioli, Jill Sterkel and Shirley Babashoff. The race was the 400-meter freestyle relay. The time was 3:44.82, a world record. They knocked almost four seconds off the old mark of 3:48.80.

To get the medals and record, they defeated the flower of East Germany and its sensational star, Kornelia Ender, who was shooting for her fifth gold medal. The East Germans also broke the old record with a time of 3:45.50.

The last night of the week-long competition produced four world records in five events. U.S. men accounted for two, Jim Montgomery of Indiana University becoming the first person in history to break 50 seconds in the 100-meter freestyle with an incredible 49.99 and Rod Strachan of USC swimming the 400-meter individual medley in 4:23.68.

The other record was set by East German's Petra Thumer, who swam the 800-meter freestyle in 8:37.14 to break Shirley Babashoff's old mark of 8:39.63 set in the Olympic trials at Long Beach last month.

It was another heart-breaking race for Babashoff, who finished a fraction of a second behind the 15-year-old East German in 8:37.59 and won

Please Turn to Page 9, Col. 1

## Dodgers at a Standstill but Sizemore's Moving

BY ROSS NEWHAN
Times Staff Writer

SAN DIEGO—A starter during each of his seven previous major league seasons, Ted Sizemore started Sunday only because Bill Buckner didn't. He said later he won't go through another season like this, that he will seek to go to another team next winter via an avenue provided in the new Basic Agreement.

Sizemore is the first Dodger to indicate he will take advantage of a provision in the reserve system that was restructured after Andy Messersmith played out his option and proved his right to do so in court.

The provision is this: If a player has five years in the majors, he can, between the dates of Oct. 15 and Oct. 30, request his club to trade him while listing six clubs in each league he will not go to. The club then must trade him. Sizemore could also play out his option next year but he said he is unwilling to sacrifice another year as a utility man.

Only time will tell if other Dodgers follow Sizemore's apparent lead. Time is becoming increasingly important to the Dodgers, who have 65 games left following Sunday's 1-0 win over San Diego in which Doug Rau (10-6) pitched a six-hitter for his fourth straight win, three of them complete games.

The loss went to Dave Freisleben (6-8), who has lost seven straight after once being 6-1. The win kept the Dodgers seven back of Cincinnati in the National League West and stemmed from a seventh-inning run that saw Bill Russell walk, steal second and score on a double by Lee Lacy, who later expressed some of the same frustration as Sizemore.

Sizemore opened at second base as Davey Lopes moved to the outfield after Buckner (bruised wrist) joined Dusty Baker (assorted bruises) on the bench. The 31-year-old Sizemore has been employed primarily as a replacement for the oft-injured Lopes and with his 1-for-4 Sunday is now batting .269, having hit in nine of his last 11 games while playing the field in a superior fashion. Sizemore is also 5 for 7 as a pinchhitter, having delivered the five hits in consecutive assignments.

"The Dodgers have a chance to win and I'll do anything to help them do so," Sizemore said. "I finished second four of my five years with St. Louis

Please Turn to Page 4, Col. 2

## AN ANXIOUS LADY IN WAITING

### *Standing in Rain for a Glimpse of the Princess Was the Queen*

BY SALLY QUINN
The Washington Post

MONTREAL—It was rather mucky out. Not the sort of day to go riding.

Bromont, the small green village in Quebec an hour's drive from Montreal, was soaked.

At 8 o'clock Saturday morning the clouds were nestled against the hills, barely revealing the jumps and hurdles which the equestrians would have to take during the endurance test that day.

The officials, glancing nervously upward as enormous drops of rain began to spatter on the ground were thinking seriously of postponing the whole thing. Not canceling, you understand. Just postponing. The ground was wet, muddy, slippery. Dangerous for the horses and the riders as well.

In the back of everyone's mind, however, was only one rider. No. 62. HRH Princess Anne. On Goodwill.

But no. They would jolly well stick it out. The endurance test, second in the three-day event, would go on.

The dressage Thursday had less than happy results for the princess, and dispatches from the stable at Bromont indicated that she was not at all pleased. Not at all.

Her mother, the queen, who is staying aboard the yacht Brittania in Montreal harbor, had been there to watch when Goodwill acted up badly and added points to her score. The queen remained unemotional while watching Anne's disappointing performance.

Anne, on the other hand, did not.

When she returned to the stable her younger brother, Prince Andrew, asked her how she had done, and she reportedly snapped back at him, "How do *you* think I did?"

So Saturday, with the hardest event of all ahead of her, everyone naturally expected her to be in a foul humor as well. Especially because, as 9 a.m. rolled around and her time to begin the roads and tracks approached, it was really starting to drizzle.

There is only a small group of 10 or so huddling around the fence of "Depart A," where she is meant to leave from as Goodwill is brought in by a groom.

One of the young women sucks in her breath and in a loud stage whisper announced, "That's her horse, that's her horse."

"Big deal," says someone else.

Then Capt. Mark Phillips arrives. He is Princess Anne's husband, and looking quite handsome in blue jeans, racing sneakers, a red sweatjacket and a white canvas hat. His father, Mr. Peter Phillips, is even nattier in a tweed golfing hat, tattered tattersal shirt, jeans and a windbreaker. They begin fussing with the horse as it continues to drizzle.

Just then a couple of blue Land Rovers pull up and out pops a small brown-haired woman in flat brown leather shoes, a green and white skirt just above her knees, a khaki rain cape and a print scarf over her head. Around her neck is a Leica camera. She approached the fence and looks around—obviously another tourist looking for a shot of HRH Princess Anne.

Please Turn to Page 9, Col. 1

# Jenner Wins Some Gold... and Waits for More

## San Jose Athlete Sets Decathlon World Record

**HAPPY WINNER**—Bruce Jenner proudly displays the gold medal he won in the decathlon. AP Wirephoto

Los Angeles Times
Sports
CC PART III †
SATURDAY, JULY 31, 1976

BY DWIGHT CHAPIN
Times Staff Writer

MONTREAL—There was Bruce Jenner, the new world record holder and Olympic champion in the decathlon, running around the track with an American Flag in hand—reminiscent of George Foreman when he won the heavyweight boxing title in 1968.

But Foreman's patriotic display was premeditated. When a man leaped out of the stands to hand the flag to Jenner, he was just plain surprised.

"I thought at first maybe he was going to shoot me," Jenner said.

He carried the Flag for awhile, then kept on running around the track with his arms raised over his head in a victory salute. And finally he stopped to hug his wife, Chrystie.

It was the end of a seven-year journey.

Jenner of San Jose had just run the 1,500 meters to finish two days of decathlon competition—which more or less judges who's the best amateur track athlete in the world—with 8,618 points. That was 164 more than the world electronically timed record Nikolay Avilov of the Soviet Union set in Munich in 1972, and 94 more than Jenner's own hand-timed record. Avilov finished third here with 8,367 points. West Germany's Guido Kratschmer took the silver medal with 8,411.

"There was a lot of pressure on me," Jenner said. "Dave Roberts is my roommate at the Games and I sat there earlier in the week and watched the rain come down and saw him lose the pole vault, when he was by far the best pole vaulter out there. That scared me a little bit."

He felt the pressure—and then he rose to it.

"The first day of competition (Thursday) I had five personal bests," he said. "I was shocked when I saw I was 30 points ahead of anything I'd ever done."

Then came a night to reflect.

"I just lay in bed," he said, "and convinced myself all I had to do was make good marks Friday in order to win."

The only event of the 10 in the decathlon he won was the discus. But points came nearly everywhere.

His second-day performance—a

Please Turn to Page 7, Col. 1

**VICTORY SALUTE**—Bruce Jenner's wife, Chrystie, cheers his world-record decathlon performance. AP Wirephoto

# McKay to Get Look at Most of Rams Tonight

### Knox Plans to Rotate His Players Against Bucs in Times Game

BY BOB OATES
Times Staff Writer

Chuck Knox and John McKay will be looking at each other across a football field for the first time competitively tonight in the 31st annual Times Charity Game at the Coliseum.

In his three years as coach of the Rams, Knox has won 34 and lost eight for an .810 regular season mark that tops the National Football League.

McKay won 127 games at USC, lost 40 and tied 8 in a 16-year career that encouraged the Tampa Bay Buccaneers to hire him as their first head coach.

Tonight is their first game and McKay's first in professional football. The kickoff is at 7, a crowd of 60,000 is expected, and the Rams are favored by 14 points in their exhibition season opener.

For those who think the Rams should be favored by more than 14, here's Jimmy (The Greek) Snyder's explanation:

"McKay's team will be gung-ho—going all out to win for the Silver Fox in his native habitat. And the Rams are looking at a lot of rookies, now. They have a big cast of characters."

There are, for example, three Ram quarterbacks and Knox is going to show them all to Tampa Bay in a precise rotation system: James Harris in the first half, Ron Jaworski in the third quarter, Pat Haden in the fourth quarter.

Knox says he'll begin rotating running backs in the first quarter and use eight in all. The four fullbacks will appear in this order: Lawrence McCutcheon, John Cappelletti, Rod Phillips, Jim Jodat. The four halfbacks: Jim Bertelsen, Cullen Bryant, Rob Scribner, Mack Herron.

The Rams, moreover, plan to unleash four new kick runners—two at a time, of course—of whom much is expected this season: Herron and three quick freshmen wide receivers, Dwight Scales, Freeman Johns and (if his sore thigh permits) Jerrald Taylor.

McKay, who also has a lot to learn about his team this summer, will begin the experiments with a backfield that includes two former University of Florida performers, quarterback Steve Spurrier and rookie fullback Jimmy DuBose, and halfback Manfred Moore, who played with Spurrier in San Francisco.

John McKay, the coach's son, is the

Please Turn to Page 4, Col. 1

**MORE GOLD**—Lasse Viren of Finland wins 5,000 meters Friday at Montreal Olympics for second gold medal. Earlier, he had won 10,000. Dick Quax (691) of New Zealand was second while Klaus Hildenbrand of West Germany dives across line in third place. Viren was timed in 13:24.76. AP Wirephoto

# Viren Wins 5,000, Runs Marathon Today

### Modern Flying Finn Could Duplicate Zatopek With Olympic Distance Triple

From a Times Staff Writer

MONTREAL—Lasse Viren, the Flying Finn of the modern age of track and field, will try to pull an Emil Zatopek here today.

Viren won the 5,000-meter run Friday in a thriller over Dick Quax of New Zealand and is entered in the marathon today. If he wins, he'll be the only man other than Zatopek, the Czech who did it in 1952, to win that triple at the Olympic Games.

And Viren might have a little more incentive than Zatopek.

Viren, who is quickly becoming as controversial as the Flying Finn of another age—Paavo Nurmi—reportedly will get $10,000 from a shoe company for every race he wins here.

After the 5,000 meters Friday, he didn't mention money. Asked what he hopes to do in the marathon, he said only (through an interpreter), "I hope I can finish the race honorably."

He finished more than honorably in the 10,000 and 5,000 here—and with his victory in the 5,000 he became the only man ever to win both races in back-to-back Olympics. (He'd taken the same double in Munich.)

There was another repeat performer Friday—Soviet triple jumper Viktor Saneyev. He won his third straight Olympic gold medal in that event, jumping 56-8¾ to beat James Butts of the United States and world record holder Joao De Oliveira of Brazil.

Saneyev then said he wants to do two things—travel to Mexico, where Oliviera set the world mark of 58-8¼, to try to break it, and then get ready for the 1980 Moscow Olympics, where he hopes to tie Al Oerter for most track and field gold medals in one event—four.

In Friday's other final, Tatyana Kazankina of the Soviet Union, who had won the women's 800 meters, took the 1,500 meters, too, in 4:05.48. American Jan Merrill finished eighth in a field of nine.

Most questions for Viren in a packed interview room were controversial. Most of his answers were evasive.

The most persistent rumor here is that the Finnish veteran has some new blood this time around. It's been widely reported Viren and other European athletes have been engaging in something called blood doping. Simply, it means a competitor has two units (1,000 c.c.) of blood taken out of his body within 4 to 6 weeks of competition. The body builds the blood supply back and the athlete then gets back the old blood as well.

This reportedly allows the blood to

Please Turn to Page 7, Col. 2

## CAMERON, TWO OTHERS BANNED FOR STEROID USE

MONTREAL (AP)—Olympic officials closed in on the anabolic steroids menace after years of research Friday and disqualified two men and a woman for using the notorious body-building drugs.

The athletes in disgrace—the first ever disqualified from the Olympic Games for using steroids—were Mark Cameron, a 23-year-old U.S. heavyweight weightlifter from Middletown, R.I.; Peter Pavlasek, Czechoslovakian super-heavyweight weightlifter; and Danuta Rosuni, Polish woman discus thrower.

Please Turn to Page 8, Col. 2

# Spoiler Giants Defeat Dodgers

### L.A.'s 5-3 Loss Boosts Reds' Margin to 8½

BY ROSS NEWHAN
Times Staff Writer

SAN FRANCISCO—The Giants were expected to be the sleeper in the National League West and until recently they seemed to be just that—a team asleep.

Thirteen games under .500 and last in the West, San Francisco has now shown signs of coming awake, a team that may yet have an impact on the division race.

Now a spoiler rather than sleeper, the Giants whipped the Reds both Tuesday and Wednesday nights and did the same to the Dodgere in Friday night's opener of a four-game series, 5-3.

"We're starting to act like a team and we don't intend to make it easy for either Los Angeles or Cincinnati," manager Bill Rigney said after the Giants improved their record to 10-6 since the All-Star break and sent the Dodgers reeling 8½ games back of the Reds, who rebounded from the

Please Turn to Page 4, Col. 1

# Hayes Admits Turning in MSU

CHICAGO (AP)—Woody Hayes, Ohio State football coach, admitted Friday that he exposed Michigan State for recruiting violations which resulted in the Spartans receiving severe penalties from the NCAA and the Big 10.

Hayes, speaking at the Big 10's kickoff football luncheon, warmed up to his admission by noting that baseball will draw its one billionth fan this weekend.

Hayes then referred back to the Black Sox scandal and baseball's strong commissioner, Kenesaw Mountain Landis, in reviving the integrity of the game.

"I sat up during the football season last fall to watch the greatest baseball World Series I've ever seen," said Hayes. "There was no question they were playing to win. It was in-

Please Turn to Page 8, Col. 1

THE WILKINS PLAN

# Help! It's a Familiar Cry From U.S. Athletes

BY BILL SHIRLEY
Times Sports Editor

MONTREAL—Wind up a U.S. athlete at the Olympic Games and he'll complain about his country's amateur sports program.

The frustrating thing is, they say, they don't know who's responsible for the mess they're in. But when they're interviewed, they usually flail away at the nearest target, the U.S. Olympic Committee.

The USOC has won no medals at these Olympic Games. This week alone it's been called everything from inept to absurd.

While East Germans are winning medals for the Socialist Unity Party and the Cubans are running and fighting for Fidel Castro and the revolution, a lot of U.S. athletes are going around saying they are winning their medals for themselves.

And they're doing it, they say, without the help of the U.S. government, the U.S. Olympic Committee and the Daughters of the American Revolution.

Arnie Robinson, who won a gold medal in the long jump, said his wife supported him for three years so he could make the Olympic team.

Mac Wilkins, world record holder in the discus who created a flap when he said he won his gold medal here for himself, not his country, said Friday that no one helped him train. "I'm on my own; I supported myself," he said.

Please Turn to Page 8, Col. 1

BOOS FOR THE CRITIC

## Olympic Crowd Jumps All Over Stones

From Times Wire Services

Because he had criticized everything from the Canadian Olympic Organizing Committee ("They've done a bum job") to the accommodations at Olympic Village—not to mention the condition of the stadium track and the food in Montreal—quite a few in a crowd of 68,000 were ready for American high jumper Dwight Stones during qualifying Friday.

qThey booed when he first appeared, cheered when he missed his first try at the qualifying height of 7-1, booed when he cleared it on his next try and booed again when he jumped up and derisively blew kisses to the crowd.

"They'll be sorry they gave me so much static," said Stones, the world record holder and gold medal favorite in today's final. "Those people don't know what they're doing for me. They're psyching me out of my mind."

Stones said he wouldn't have missed at 7-1 the first time had it not been for a judge who apparently didn't like his Mickey Mouse T-shirt.

"He was giving me a lot of static about the shirt," he said. "He said, 'This isn't a show, it's the Olympics.' And I said that the Olympics *are* a show . . ."

Stones, who was quoted in a Montreal newspaper as saying, "I hate French-Canadians" ("What I actually said was that the Olympic officials were rude not to have gotten the stadium ready in six years"), said the booing didn't bother him.

In fact, he apparently liked it. But, referring to the fact that some Americans in the crowd countered by booing Canadian jumpers as they made their runs, Stones said:

"I don't want Canada and the United States to get into a shouting match."

He also said he'd conform to Olympic rules to "keep from turning this into a U.S.-Canada confrontation" but . . ."I'll probably go berserk when I get off the victory stand."

**PLAYING TO THE CROWD**—Dwight Stones of Long Beach hams it up before crowd at stadium after clearing qualifying height of 7-1 in high jump. He'd been booed by fans before jumping. AP Wirephoto

# Stones Flops to 3rd; Spinks & Spinks Win

## High Jumper Settles for Bronze

BY DWIGHT CHAPIN, Times Staff Writer

MONTREAL—World record-holder Dwight Stones missed the high jump gold medal at the Olympic Games here Saturday but left with a couple of things he considered more important—his health and his life.

Stones was moving toward the gold when it began to rain late Saturday afternoon.

"With the kind of run and takeoff I have," said Stones, whose flop-style has lifted him to a world record of 7 feet 7 inches, "there's no way I could jump well in rain like that. If I had to plant hard, chances are I'd have broken my knee. And I like walking."

He also likes living—which is why he was quite upset when told of a threat on his life after he'd finished his competition and won the bronze medal.

"These four policemen came out and said please follow them," he said. "I knew I didn't have any dope in my (clothes) bag so it was something else. They said someone had called and said he was going to shoot me. They said I could stay in the tunnel or go back outside and they'd protect me."

Stones stayed in the tunnel but later he did go out to the victory stand. "I was scared to death as I walked out there, to put it mildly," he said.

Stones was widely criticized earlier in the week for making derogatory remarks about Canadians and their handling of the Games, and when he came out to warm up Saturday

Please Turn to Page 6, Col. 1

CC PART III †
SUNDAY, AUGUST 1, 1976

## Five U.S. Boxers Gain Victories

BY BILL SHIRLEY, Times Sports Editor

MONTREAL—"I was yelling for them so hard somebody asked me for my autograph," Kay Spinks of St. Louis said.

There she was Saturday night, sitting among a mob of cheering, flag-waving U.S. fans at the Forum, watching her two sons win Olympic boxing gold medals and throw kisses to her.

Quite a switch from earlier in the week, when Mrs. Spinks watched her boys in action on a borrowed television set in her small apartment in a housing project back home. She was staked to a trip here by a St. Louis man who read about her in a newspaper. He wants to be anonymous.

Michael and Leon Spinks were just two of five U.S. boxers who won championships in 11 final matches. Five out of six ain't bad. Only bantamweight Charles Mooney, a U.S. Army sergeant from Fayetteville, N.C., had to settle for a silver medal.

Winning gold medals along with the Spinks brothers were flyweight Leo Randolph of Tacoma, lightweight Howard Davis of Glen Cove, N.Y., and light-welterweight Ray Charles Leonard of Palmer Park, Md.

That's four more gold medals than the U.S. boxing team won in Munich in 1972. The Americans tried a little harder this time. They held 35 clinics around the country and engaged the Russians, Poles and Hungarians in a series of international matches. It was a young but

Please Turn to Page 9, Col. 1

WINGING IT HOME—John Walker spreads his arms and throws back head, thankful of victory in the 1,500 meters Saturday at Montreal. Ivo Van Damme (103) of Belgium is second and Paul Wellman (446) of West Germany third. Rick Wohlhuter (far right) of the U.S. finished sixth.

AP Wirephoto

# Rams Have No Trouble Holding Tampa at Bay

BY BOB OATES
Times Staff Writer

James Harris quarterbacked two touchdown drives in the first half Saturday night, completing 11 of 13 passes, and Pat Haden directed the other touchdown drive in the fourth quarter, completing 5 of 7, as the Rams turned back the Tampa Bay Buccaneers, 26-3, in the 1976 exhibition opener at the Coliseum.

A crowd of 54,787, attending the 31st annual Times Charity Game, saw Ron Jaworski complete 1 of 5 in the third quarter, when the Rams scored their last of three field goals.

Coach John McKay's Tampa Bay team played stronger football than the score suggests, moving twice against the Los Angeles defense.

The first time the clock beat the Buccaneers after they had reached the Los Angeles 3 just before the half, forcing a third down field goal by Pete Rajecki, whose 18-yard kick averted a shutout for the new Florida team.

Moving again in the fourth quarter, the Buccaneers marched to the Ram 1, where a fumble knocked them out of a seemingly sure touchdown.

John McKay, the coach's son, made an impressive National Football League debut, speeding into the open to catch three passes on plays measuring 27, 10 and 13 yards.

But otherwise, the Ram defense was usually in control, sacking Tampa Bay quarterbacks seven times.

Coach Chuck Knox, who seldom loses in the Coliseum, made sure of a win in the first half, leaving his first-stringers in until they had opened a 10-0 lead and leaving his first-string quarterback in until the score was 17-0, the halftime margin.

But thereafter, with rookies and reserves in most of the Los Angeles positions, the performance was distressingly ragged. Many of the reserves are individually promising—as they have proved in training camp this summer—but as a team they were without smoothness most of the way.

The Buccaneers actually seemed the more disciplined team in the second half until Haden finally produced the only touchdown of those 30 minutes at 12:47 of the fourth quarter.

On play after play in the second half the Rams were jumping offside or missing assignments or fumbling or dropping passes.

Jaworski only had possession twice in the third quarter and drops stopped him once. The clock stopped him next, time running out with the Rams on the Tampa Bay 24.

Haden went in there, on third-and-5, and was sacked, ending the threat.

It was when middle linebacker Jim Youngblood gave him a second good chance, intercepting at midfield, that Haden came through with a 45-yard touchdown drive.

Jim Jodat, the rookie fullback, scored that time on an alert 5-yard slant at Tampa Bay's outside linebacker. The earlier Los Angeles touchdowns also came on short plays, a one-yard run by Lawrence McCutcheon ending a 73-yard drive and a short sneak by Harris at the end of an 80-yard series.

The two Los Angeles field goals were kicked by candidates for Tom Dempsey's job, George Jawenko, formerly of the Oakland Raiders, who

Please Turn to Page 12, Col. 1

## Shorter Comes Up Short in Rain; E. German Wins

### Cierpinski Goes 26 Miles 385 Yards in 2:09:55; Finland's Viren Finishes Fifth in Try for Triple

From a Times Staff Writer

MONTREAL—Dwight Stones wasn't the only American who had a little rain fall on his parade here Saturday.

Defending marathon champion Frank Shorter was all wet before he started his 26-mile 385-yard run on the last day of track competition at the Olympic Games.

"I don't like rain," Shorter said. "It makes me stiff. When the gun went off today, I looked up at the sky and just said, 'Oh, hell.'"

For a long time Shorter didn't run as if the rain was affecting him. He was on the pace—or leading—until the 32-kilometer mark, about three-quarters of the way through.

That's when Waldemar Cierpinski of East Germany made his move.

"He got everything on me in the space of about half a mile," Shorter said.

Cierpinski, who finished in Olympic record time of 2:09:55 but behind Derek Clayton's world record of 2:08:34, agreed.

"I started going faster at about 30 kilometers," he said, "and at about 32 I was able to break away a little from Shorter. It was a small distance at first but I was able to increase it at about 35 kilometers, then add from there."

Shorter had no idea who that guy up in front of him was.

"I thought it was Lopez (Hipolito Lopez of Honduras)," he said. "Then I heard him speaking German."

Lasse Viren of Finland, who was trying to become the second man to win the 5,000 and 10,000 meters and the marathon (Emil Zatopek did it in 1952), started off well. The look in his eyes was that of a man possessed.

Viren seemed interested in staying with Shorter.

"I think his tactics were to just watch me and stick with me wherever I went," Shorter said.

Fine, but they were both watching Cierpinski when matters got serious.

"About three miles from the stadi-

Please Turn to Page 6, Col. 5

***JIM MURRAY***

## The Umlaut Olympics

MONTREAL—These were supposed to be the "white" Olympics—they lost a whole continent before a gun was fired or a bell rung.

But, as the flags flutter down and the handkerchiefs wave and auld acquaintance is forgot, these will be known as the "Umlaut" Olympics. You can put two little dots over the "O."

The Olympics belong to the flying frauleins from East Germany, who routed the flower of world womanhood on land and on sea. They made it possible for East Germany, a satellite of only 17 million people, to outmedal the United States (and nearly Russia) in such a dazzling display of virtuosity as to give rise in the Olympic Village to the conundrum:

Q. What do you get if you mate an East German girl swimmer with an American boy swimmer?

A. German-speaking dolphins.

The medals have been won, the anthems sung, the Swiss timers have been turned off but we should like to pause today to salute the Olympians who performed over and beyond the call of duty and to give them our own special awards. If you will strike up the Olympique protocolaire fanfare, Professor, please, we will get to them.

★

ALBERTO JUANTORENA—The Cuban Comet gets the memorial Hitler Youth Award as the most-perfectly programmed devotee to leader and Fatherland since Helmut Dantine movies. Alberto accompanied his every gold medal with a stern lecture to the assembled journalists on the superiority of the socialist system as a breeding ground for athletes and the decadence of the West who were paying for their sins in the 400 and the 800 as well as in Custer's Last Stand. Juantorena's commendation is in the form of an Iron Cross with "Ein Reich, Ein Volk, Ein Fuehrer" on it and an oak leaf cluster titled "Forget the Maine!"

MAC WILKINS—Gets the Whose Side Are You On, Anyway? Award for hugging an East German who has just beaten out his teammate for a silver medal. Wilkins also qualifies because he suggested that he won his discus medal in spite of, rather than because of, the United States. Mac's award is either the collected works of Benedict Arnold—or two years in Leipzig.

★

LASSE VIREN—Lasse wins the Great Equivocator Award. Lasse, after he won his second gold medal in the 5,000, was asked about the recurrent rumors he had undergone "blood doping," a method in which a quantity of blood is removed from the athlete a month or so prior to the race to be stored and frozen, then thawed just before the race and reinjected into the system. This supposedly raises the red-blood count and enables the runner to retain or convert oxygen more easily. The colloquy with Viren went as follows:

Q. Stories have been circulating that you have been involved in blood doping, can you confirm or deny that?

A. Can you confirm it?

Q. But can you deny it?

A. Can I deny what?

Q Can you deny that you engaged in blood doping?

A. What is blood doping?

Please Turn to Page 10, Col. 1

## The Count Beats Club He Hates the Most, 6-3

BY ROSS NEWHAN
Times Staff Writer

SAN FRANCISCO—The manager of the Giants said Saturday that it will take an "absolute miracle" for the Dodgers to catch Cincinnati.

Bill Rigney said it after the Giants had defeated the Dodgers, 6-3, and what he said could not really compare to what was said by the man who is recognized here as Speaker of the House.

John Montefusco wasn't at his best against the team he hates most, scattering 11 hits in improving his season record to 10-9 and his career record against the Dodgers to 6-3, but the irrepressible nature of his clubhouse responses showed him to be in familiar form.

"I'm glad to win but I'm not overwhelmed," he said. "I wanted to shut 'em out so I could shut up (coach Tommy) Lasorda. He's been all over my case. He's been saying I'll never beat 'em again.

"Man, it's good to beat 'em, it's good to beat 'em by any score.

"Can the Dodgers catch Cincinnati? No way. They don't have the ballclub Cincinnati does. It's not even close. The Dodgers aren't even as good as we are. We've proved it in our season's series (the Giants are 8-3) with them.

"We can handle the Dodgers and Reds (5-3) and hold our own with Philadelphia (4-5) but we can't beat the weaker teams. I don't know what it is. We don't seem to get up. I know I don't. It's like when you're playing in Montreal and Houston you're playing nowhere. Maybe I shouldn't say that about Montreal. That's where the Olympics are and I'd have liked to have been there to see it. I wonder if Bruce Jenner can pitch. He can do everything else."

A smile played at the corners of Montefusco's mouth as he talked. He is a man who puts out on the field

Please Turn to Page 14, Col. 1

A DIFFERENT TWIST—Jim Bertelsen of Rams has his helmet twisted while being tackled by Ted Jornov (on ground) and Council Rudolph of Tampa Bay. The Rams won the exhibition opener.

Times photo by Steve Fontanini Jr.

# JACKSON KO'S DODGERS ON 3 SWINGS

## And the Yankees Win the World Championship in Six Games, 8-4

**BY CHARLES MAHER**
Times Staff Writer

NEW YORK—There's no today. It's been canceled on account of Reggie Jackson, who had a game few if any have matched in the 74-year history of the World Series.

But it's not all that bad for the Dodgers. While they lost another one to the Yankees Tuesday night, they can take comfort in the knowledge it doesn't even count in the regular-season standings. So they lost no ground to the Cincinnati Reds, who were idle.

New York's 8-4 victory does count, however, in the World Series standings, which show the Yankees won four of the first six games. That means that Game 7, if necessary, isn't.

So the Yankees have won the Series for the first time in 15 years and the American League has won it five times in the last eight years.

But about Jackson:

He hit three home runs in consecutive at-bats, drove in five runs and scored four. But his home run string is even more improbable than that makes it appear.

He homered his last time up in Game 5 and walked on four pitches his first time up Tuesday. In each of his next three at-bats, he homered on the first pitch. So, at game's end, he had four homers in his last four swings.

When they added it all up, it turned out Jackson had:

—Set an individual record for most home runs in one Series (5), even though this Series went only six games.

—Become the first man ever to hit three homers in a Series game in consecutive at-bats.

—Set a record by scoring 10 runs in one Series, again even though this one didn't go the distance.

—Set a record for most total bases in one Series (25).

—Tied a record with 12 total bases in one game.

—Tied a record by scoring four runs in one game.

Jackson also finished with the highest batting average of the Series (.450), going 9 for 20. At the conclusion, then, it was foregone that Sport Magazine would give him its most Valuable Player award.

Among other Yankee stars Tuesday night, Mike Torrez was probably foremost. The big right-hander allowed nine hits (one more than the Yankees got) but gave up only two earned runs. He got his second victory of the Series, having picked up the first with a seven-hitter in Game 3.

It was a cool but not unpleasant evening at Yankee Stadium and 56,407 turned out. When it was over, there was the customary display of idiocy. Hundreds, maybe thousands, jumped over the rails and raced onto the field. Jackson, who put on a helmet in the ninth inning to protect himself from possible bombardment, took off like a sprinter after the last out.

First, he tried to cut across center field, perhaps aiming for the third-base dugout, but a mob cut him off. So he reversed his field and, swinging to scare off fans who tried to grab him, finally threw himself into the Yankee dugout behind first base.

Before the field was finally cleared, fans had ripped up patches of grass in maybe two dozen places, leaving at lease several bare areas the size of shotput circles.

For a few minutes there early in the game, it looked as if the New York celebration might have to be postponed at least a day. The Dodgers seemed intent on coming from near dead (which is where they were after losing three of the first four games) to dead even.

They got two unearned runs in the first inning. Bucky Dent, a usually reliable shortstop, was their benefactor. With two out, he went to his right and stopped, then dropped, a sharp bouncer by Reggie Smith.

Please Turn to Page 4, Col. 1

Los Angeles Times
Sports
BUSINESS & FINANCE
CC PART III †
WEDNESDAY, OCTOBER 19, 1977

TAKING A BOW—Reggie Jackson doffs his cap to acknowledge cheers from crowd upon return to outfield after hitting second homer Tuesday night. Jackson later hit third homer.
AP Wirephoto

***JIM MURRAY***

## Reggie Renames House Ruth Built

NEW YORK—Excuse me while I wipe up the bloodstains and carry off the wounded. The Dodgers forgot to circle the wagons.

Listen! You don't go into the woods with a bear. You don't go into a fog with Jack the Ripper. You don't get in a car with Al Capone. You don't get on a ship with Morgan the Pirate. You don't go into shark waters with a nosebleed. You don't wander into Little Big Horn with General Custer.

And you don't come into Yankee Stadium needing a win to stay alive in a World Series. Not unless you have a note pinned to you telling them where to send the remains. If any.

They told us these weren't the *real* Yankees. I mean, not like the genuine article of years gone past, the Murderers' Row Yankees, the Bronx Bombers. These were just a bunch of pussycats dressed up in gorilla costumes.

These were Yankees who had "take" signs in the playbook. These were Yankees who talked of "beating you with the glove." These were "hit-and-run Yankees," not the old kind who just stood there and hit balls into the stratosphere and played "hit and walk" baseball.

★

**That's what they** told us. That's what the scouting report said.

They said these Yankees weren't even speaking to each other. You wondered why they dared show up.

Years ago, oldtimers remembered, on the 1927 Yankees the right fielder in World Series used to stand there and hit back-to-back home runs out of the park. Why, he hit three in one game in World Series *twice*!

Well, the 1977 Yankees' right fielder has just hit home runs on his last four consecutive official at-bats. And he became only the second player in history to hit three home runs in a game.

He became the first player in history to hit five home runs in a single Series.

You have the feeling the Dodger pitchers are longing to see Babe Ruth step in there. He might be a welcome relief.

"If I played in New York, they'd name a candy bar after me," boasted Reggie Jackson before the season started. They may name an entire chocolate factory after him now.

Once again these were the Yanks who had your back to the wall when you were ahead only 2-0. Once again they were headhunters. If they were fighters they'd never go to the body. Once again, they're a bunch of guys who go for the railroad yards in bombing runs or shell Paris with railroad guns.

These are the Yankees who let you store up runs like a squirrel putting nuts in his cheek. When you get them all neatly piled up, the Yankees come along and pile up more with two swings of a bat.

★

**These Yanks are** store-bought. They're not homemade like a proper ballclub should be, stitched at home with tender, loving care. George Steinbrenner just went out and ordered them like a new car. Expense was no object. It didn't matter. With George, it was either a question of buying a ball club—or buying Rhode Island.

There's an old familiar smell in the Yankee locker room—fermenting grapes. The wine of victory spreads across the floor, the water fall of success. Where Ruth or Gehrig once dribbled champagne across their chins, Reggie Jackson does now.

The reporters are 10-deep around Jackson's locker in this the House That Ruth Built. It is Jackson's Yankees now. "Mr. October." The most dangerous World Series hitter since Ruth used to call his shots.

No one has ever seen more devastating homeruns than Reggie Jackson ripped out of Yankee Stadium Tuesday night. Two were on so-so fastballs but the third was a knuckler down and away. "He hit a helluva pitch," Da Manager Tom Lasorda confessed later, still in some shock.

The pitchers' union is not

Please Turn to Page 7, Col. 2

THE PRICE OF STARDOM—Reggie Jackson pays the price of being a superstar as he tries to get off the field after World Series Tuesday night. An unidentified fan is about to be sent head over heels.
AP Wirephoto

**'ROOM SERVICE'**

## Inside Pitches Provide Feast for Jackson

**BY ROSS NEWHAN**
Times Staff Writer

NEW YORK—Mike Torrez, the pivotal pitcher of a World Series that now belonged to his Yankees, stood under a champagne shower Tuesday night and said:

"Now I believe him. Now I know why he calls himself Mr. October."

Mr. October, of course, is Reggie Jackson, who had just reawakened the ghosts of former Yankee immortals with three home runs and five RBI in the 8-4 victory that made it possible for the best team money can buy to indeed be known as the best team money can buy.

Jackson was bought for $2.9 million over five years and he made the biggest return yet on that investment against a Los Angeles team that refused to meet those terms last winter and which, according to Jackson, refused to change its pitching pattern against him.

"You've got to pitch me in," he said, surrounded by reporters in a packed clubhouse, "but you can't just live there.

"The Dodgers tried to do it all Series and it was like ordering room service."

Jackson grew fat on the inside offerings. Five home runs. Eight RBI. A 9 for 20 that earned him recognition as the Series MVP and the keys to a sports car that he said he would give to his 29-year-old sister Tina.

"A great feeling, what a great feel-

Please Turn to Page 7, Col. 1

## Jabbar Scores KO Over Benson

### Laker Ace Ejected Early in 117-112 Loss

**BY TED GREEN**
Times Staff Writer

MILWAUKEE—The National Basketball Assn. season had barely gotten off the ground Tuesday night when Kent Benson, the Milwaukee Bucks' rookie center from Indiana and the first collegian drafted last June, was *on* the ground. Laker center Kareem Abdul-Jabbar put him there with one powerful punch.

It happened, swiftly and unexpectedly, only two minutes into the first quarter of the Lakers' first game of 1977-78, a game they lost, 117-112, without the league's Most Valuable Player. Abdul-Jabbar was ejected.

Just minutes after he lost his cool, a composed Abdul-Jabbar said the punch—which put Benson down for five minutes, blackened and cut his eye and sent him to the hospital with a mild concussion—was retaliatory.

Abdul-Jabbar said Benson, out of view of the referees, swung an elbow into his stomach and knocked the wind out of him.

"It was a sneak attack," Abdul-Jabbar said. "I was standing there trying to get position and he elbowed me in the gut. It was totally uncalled for. I'm not out there to take a beating. And when someone deliberately tries to hurt you, when it's not inadvertent, that's something you can't take."

And then Abdul-Jabbar walked the mile back to his hotel room, where he

Please Turn to Page 10, Col. 1

## DETENTE COMES TO THE BRONX: MARTIN STAYS

**BY ROSS NEWHAN**
Times Staff Writer

NEW YORK—The Yankees held a press conference Tuesday to announce they are not going to fire manager Billy Martin.

Denying it was a vote of confidence ("a vote of confidence is a kiss of death and I'm not about to kiss Billy"), club president Gabe Paul said that the final two years of Martin's contract will definitely be honored and in recognition of "the fine job he has done" Martin will receive "a substantial bonus."

Part of that bonus is a Lincoln Continental. "Blue," Martin said, "to match my eyes." He also will receive cash estimated at between $20,000 and $50,000.

"Billy has two years left on his

Please Turn to Page 5, Col. 1

## Dodgers Explain Defeat With One Word—Reggie

**By JOHN HALL**
Times Staff Writer

NEW YORK—Well, the Big Dodger In The Sky finally went out to lunch—blown right out of his heavens by a Reggie Jackson attack like never ever.

"What was it? I'll tell you what it was," said Lee Lacy, the Dodger utility ace, Tuesday night.

"Reggie Jackson . . . Reggie Jackson . . . Reggie Jackson."

Who could say anything otherwise? The controversial Yankee right fielder broke all the fences and all the Dodger hearts with his three home runs off Burt Hooton, Elias Sosa and Charlie Hough in the 8-4 sixth game burial of the Dodgers in the 1977 World Series.

"I think he was able to release all his emotional tension of the entire season in this one game," Steve Garvey said. "It was just a tremendous performance."

Although in a state of silent shock in the gloom room that is any losing clubhouse after a classic confrontation, all the Dodgers were quick to praise Reggie . . . Reggie . . . Reggie.

"He's the MVP, you bet, and his most impressive move all night was the broken field run he made to get back to the dugout and escape those crazies at the end of the game," innocent bystander Don Sutton said.

Hough was trying to explain what he threw Jackson. He was sitting on a trunk in the clubhouse, looking more like a broken prize fighter than a butterfly artist and trying to cheer himself up when Lacy, who ended it all

Please Turn to Page 8, Col. 1

## AFTER THE MUTINY: RED MILLER

### The Broncos Are Riding High With Their New Coach

**BY BOB OATES, Times Staff Writer**

DENVER—When the Denver Broncos offered Bob (Red) Miller a job last winter he turned them down. At that time he was a New England assistant coach who didn't want to make a lateral move to an assistant's job here.

Two weeks later the Broncos solved their problem, and Miller's by offering him another job—as head coach. His acceptance was the beginning of a new era in Denver, an era that reached an unexpected landmark the other day when the Broncos upset the Oakland Raiders.

It wasn't just an upset, it was a smashing. The seemingly invincible Raiders, whose 17-game winning streak had included a rout over Minnesota last January in Super Bowl XI, were overwhelmed, 30-7, as Denver intercepted Kenny Stabler seven times.

Was it a fluke?

Nobody in the Raider organization thinks so. And nobody thinks so here. The undefeated Broncos were winning their fifth straight game that day, and, although their schedule this year is one of the most difficult in the National Football League, they appeared to have the resources to contend indefinitely.

These resources include a powerful, veteran defensive team which has had the same coordinator (Joe Collier) under Denver's last three head coaches; a new quarterback, 34-year-old Craig Morton, and a bright new leader, Miller, whose approach to his work blends everything that's solid and time-tested in football with a bit of gimmickry.

The decisive play of the Oakland game was a fake field goal in which the gimmick was a forward pass to the placekicker. After pretending to kick the ball, Jim Turner sneaked out and caught a touchdown throw.

"That was the gas-blower," says Denver's defensive end Lyle Alzado. "It took all the gas out of Oakland."

"Every week," says Miller, "we toss two or three special plays of that kind into the game plan. I've

Please Turn to Page 12, Col. 1

# ALI FINALLY TAPS OUT IN LAS VEGAS

## Young Spinks Dethrones a Legend on a Split Decision

Los Angeles Times
Sports
BUSINESS & FINANCE
CC PART III †
THURSDAY, FEBRUARY 16, 1978

**BY JACK HAWN**
Times Staff Writer

LAS VEGAS—As the world was saying, Leon Spinks doesn't stand a chance.

"There's a new heavyweight champion," a ringsider remarked moments before the decision was announced.

"I'll bet anyone right now Muhammad Ali walks out of this ring as the heavyweight champion," another said. "I gave the fight to Spinks but

The roaring began to subside as a Hilton Pavilion crowd of 5,298—a flea speck among the millions watching on television—awaited Wednesday night's decision.

"It's a split decision," were the announcer's first words, and he then began to read the judges' point totals as fans filled the arena with booing.

After revealing Art Lurie's card (143-142 for Ali) and judge Lou Tabat's total (145-140 for Spinks), the announcer said, "Judge Harold Buck: 144-141. The new . . ."

And that was it. Justice finally prevailed, the crown has fallen off the head of a legend and a virtual amateur is king of the world of boxing—Leon Spinks, Olympic 1976 light-heavyweight champion, now 7-0-1 as a professional and a 24-year-old believer of miracles.

It was "Rocky" in full bloom in the 15th round as the 10-1 underdog battled toe-to-toe with the 36-year-old man and it was one of Ali's most electrifying finishes.

Still, all three officials gave the final round to the new champion, a former marine from St. Louis, now living in Philadelphia.

Ali, who first won the title in 1964 when he knocked out Sonny Liston Feb. 25 in Miami Beach in the seventh round, knew the end was at hand long before the official verdict was rendered.

After the 14th round, he sat wearily on his stool, his head heavy, his eyes on the floor. It was pathetic, actually, as he contemplated what he must do to retain the crown he had successfully defended 19 times. His only hope was to knock out this brash young man who had shown such unexpected endurance.

Ali, huffing and puffing as he lumbered into action, gave it one of his most honest efforts, ripping hooks and firing jabs and taking equally damaging blows in return. It was a slugfest in which both were close to going down. But they continued punching dramatically as the crowd roared.

"I didn't know he could fight that type of fight after 10 rounds," Ali said later in an interview room that was not void of laughter or even a bit of wisecracking.

Ali, who has no intentions of quitting, at least at the moment, told the roomful of reporters, "You didn't know it either."

Please Turn to Page 8, Col. 1

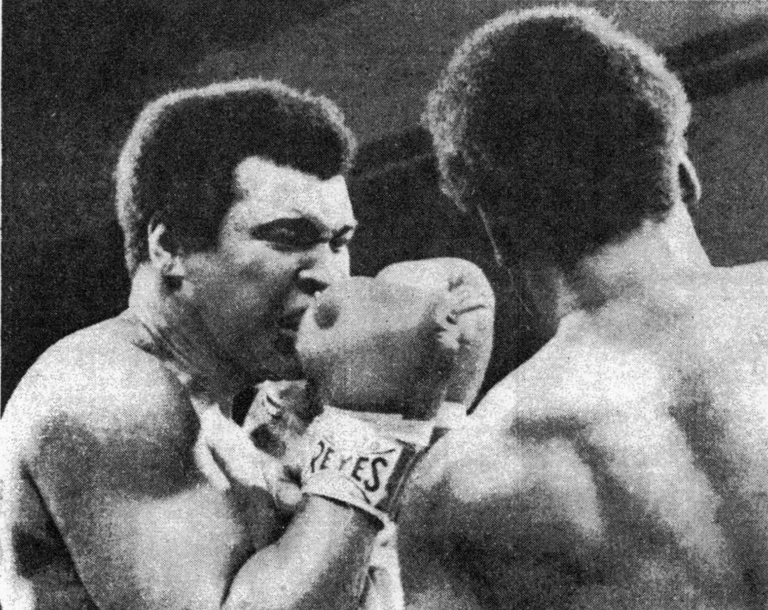

A MARKED MAN—Muhammad Ali, on the way to losing his world heavyweight championship for the second time (the first time in the ring), covers up (left) in the first round and stands back to reveal a fat lip in the fifth round. Upstart challenger Leon Spinks, an early aggressor while the champion waited for him to punch himself out, finished strong to win the title on a split decision.

AP Wirephotos

***JIM MURRAY***

## When Music Stopped

**There was no** such person as Johnny Miller. He was a product of Central Casting. He was the invention of the same wonderful people who brought you Bambi or Edward G. Robinson as Little Caesar, Cagney as a hood or Ingrid Bergman as a nun. Perfect typecasting. Somebody at MGM phoned up MCA and said "Send me over a golfer. Blond, blue eyes, all these curls hanging over his forehead. Be sure he looks good in slacks and an alpaca."

Sears Roebuck's clothing department drooled. Teen-age girls swooned. Madison Avenue went bonkers.

Now, if he could only play golf! One Laura Baugh was all the toothpaste ads could take.

★

**Johnny Miller could** play golf as if somebody reached in back and wound him up. His putter was Excalibur. They didn't make a hole he couldn't birdie. He could eagle Rhode Island. He didn't drink, smoke, chew or swear. Lochinvar. A character right out of King Arthur or Ivanhoe. All this and an Open winner, too. Man, he'd sell all the toothpaste they could make! There wouldn't be a pair of slacks on the rack.

It wasn't a career, it was a parade. He birdied life. The big home in Napa. Australia was on the phone. Would he come down and play for $45,000 or so a week? Sponsors took numbers and lined up.

Then, suddenly, the music stopped. The lights went out. The drives started landing in the rough. Excalibur turned into a wet noodle. Lochinvar missed the cut. Sir Lancelot was shooting 85s.

In January of 1974, Miller won the Crosby, the Phoenix and the Tucson Opens and made $4,000 in Hawaii. He shot one 62, one 66, one 67 and several 68s and 69s in that stretch. He made $91,804 for the month. He was running neck and neck with the Bank of England for the period.

In January, 1975, Miller won the Phoenix by 14 shots, the Tucson by nine shots and the Hope by a bunch. He shot *two* 61s, two 64s and a whole bunch of 66s and 67 and 68s. He made $107,318 for the period.

In January, 1976, Miller won the Tucson by three shots and the Hope by three more and he shot one 63 and the usual batch of 67s, 68s and 69s.

The months of January belonged to him. No one had ever seen such a brilliant run of golf as Johnny Miller in January. "Cactus John," they called him. In three Januarys, he piled up $243,482 on the golf course alone.

Would you care to guess how much Cactus John has made *this* January? $4,525. And no cents. A little more than Stan Lee and Phil Hancock but not nearly as much as Tim Simpson, Jim Chancey and the other greats.

Miller used to make that much in the first pro-am in January. The man who is 11th on the all-time money list with $1,148,590 earned—and he's only 30—suddenly was making less than streetcar conductors or auto workers.

The 61s, 62s and 63s gave way to 85s. Miller, who shot 64-69-72-66-68 in winning the Hope in 1975—and who shot 71-69-73-68-63 winning the Hope in 1976—shot 76-80-72-85 in missing the cut in 1978. At 85, he was suddenly 24 shots a round worse than his best desert scores.

You pictured somebody screaming into the phone to Central Casting. "Dammit! I said 'golf,' not 'goof.' If I sent for Elizabeth Taylor you'd send me Phyllis Diller." You couldn't save this act with a dog.

★

**Golf is not** a game, it's an adversity. It looks easy. It is like long-distance running. The first 10 miles are a breeze. Then, the field hits the "Wall of Pain," the threshold at which the lungs burst, the feet seize, the calves spasm and the runner wants to scream. Or quit.

It happens to the best of them. Hogan went through it. He threw his clubs in the back of the car one day and went home vowing to get rid of his duck hook or go into real estate. Fortunately for golf, he did the former.

Gene Littler went through it. He won a tournament before even turning pro, was hailed as the greatest Gene since Sarazen. Suddenly, he began to slap the ball around like a tennis ball. It hurt to watch. He played his way out of it. You have to. There are

Please Turn to Page 10, Col. 1

## Kotey Easier This Time, Says Lopez After KO

**BY JACK HAWN**
Times Staff Writer

LAS VEGAS—"It was easier than I thought it would be. I could do just about what I wanted."

Danny Lopez, beaming in his dressing room after retaining his World Boxing Council featherweight championship by knocking out David Kotey in the sixth round Wednesday night on the Ali-Spinks card, didn't worry even *before* the rematch. He had predicted a KO midway in the scheduled 15-rounder. It came a bit earlier—at 1:18 of the sixth.

A right-left combination to the head staggered the 27-year-old African and another right dropped him.

Kotey, who lost the 126-pound title to the Alhambra redhead Sept. 20, 1975, in Accra, Ghana, in a fierce battle that went the distance, had no opportunity to recover after the knockdown.

Kotey, 125, regained his feet at the count of seven, but was on rubbery legs and virtually defenseless.

Lopez, 25, making his second defense after stopping Jose Torres last September at the Olympic Auditorium in Los Angeles, charged in for the anticlimactic finish.

Firing a barrage of blows, Lopez had the challenger backed against the ropes, sagging and beaten.

"He would've gone down if he wasn't against the ropes," Lopez said. "I hit him one good right when the referee stopped the fight."

Lopez, a 2½-1 favorite, recalled "two good right hands in the third or fourth round on the side of the jaw

Please Turn to Page 9, Col. 1

PROMISES EX-CHAMP A REMATCH

## Ali's a Fallen Idol as Spinks Takes Over

From Times Wire Services

LAS VEGAS—The first thing the new world heavyweight champion did was visit the old one to pay his respects.

"You're a great fighter and a fine man," said Leon Spinks to Muhammad Ali, whom he had just beaten in a 15-round split decision Wednesday night.

"Thanks," mumbled Ali, holding a cold compress to his swollen features. "You ain't so bad yourself."

The next thing the 24-year-old Spinks did was go to his own dressing room where he kneeled down and said his thanks to God for helping him win the championship.

"Ali was my idol since I was a kid," said Spinks, a St. Louis native, who first gained national prominence by winning a Gold Medal during the 1976 Olympics in Montreal. "He's still my idol. I can't honestly say I feel sorry for him, in my heart I mean, because this is something I always wanted so I could become somebody. But I can't say anything bad about the man. He gave me a great fight."

Spinks' victory over the 36-year-old Ali represented the biggest upset in world heavyweight title history since Ali, an 8-1 underdog himself at the time, dethroned the late Sonny Liston in Miami Beach in 1964. It ranked right alongside Jim Braddock's upset over Max Baer in 1935, Jersey Joe Walcott's title victory over Ezzard Charles in 1951 and Ingemar Johansson's title win over Floyd Patterson in 1959.

In this magical mecca of gambling, there was next to none on Spinks who was quoted as an 8-1 underdog. That meant if you wanted to bet on Ali to keep his title, there was no one at the Vegas gambling parlors that would accept your bet.

"Odds don't make a fight," said Spinks, who showed remarkable poise considering he had only seven previous pro fights. "I knew about the odds but I didn't worry about them. If I were a betting man, I would have had to bet on myself."

Please Turn to Page 8, Col. 2

## ARIZONA STATE GETS GITTENS, 3 TEAMMATES

**BY SCOTT OSTLER**
Times Staff Writer

Frank Kush, head coach at Arizona State, is sometimes referred to as the meanest man in college football because of his boot-camp training techniques. But Kush can also be a persuasive salesman, as he demonstrated Wednesday by signing at least six top Southland preps, including four from one school.

Willie Gittens of Fountain Valley, the most sought-after prep running back in the Southern California and one of the top prospects in the nation, was Kush's big prize. But Arizona State's traveling four-man contingent of coaches also signed three of Gittens' teammates, and two other

Please Turn to Page 11, Col. 1

## Canadiens Defeat Blues, 6-2, to Set NHL Record

Coach Bob Pulford of the Chicago Black Hawks, who may once again be the National Hockey League Coach of the Year, is convinced that Scotty Bowman of the Montreal Canadiens is doing the best job of coaching.

"The hardest thing is to have great talent like the Canadiens, win with it, and keep winning with it," said Pulford, Coach of the Year three years ago with the Kings. "It's like making money and then keeping it. Not easy. Taking a mediocre team and making them respectable is not nearly as hard."

And Scotty Bowman keeps winning with his talent. Wednesday night, as skillful Guy Lafleur scored twice and assisted on two other goals, the Canadiens trounced the Blues, 6-2, in St. Louis to set an NHL record of 24 consecutive games without losing.

Over that stretch the Canadiens are 19-0-5. They broke the record they held jointly with the Boston Bruins of 1940-41 and the Philadelphia Flyers of 1975-76.

"The thing I like best about the record," said Bowman, "is that 15 games were on the road. We have pride. First we wanted to tie the record and then we wanted to break it. Both came on the road."

The Canadiens' surge began after they had lost successive games to Minnesota and Pittsburgh in mid-December, giving up eight goals in the two games. The loss to Pittsburgh was the seventh of the season for a team that lost only eight during the 1976-77 season.

Please Turn to Page 4, Col. 2

## NICKLAUS: HE'S STILL GOLF'S MAN TO BEAT

***Despite Exaggerated Reports of His Boredom With Game, Golden Bear Insists He's Still in His Prime***

**BY ROSS NEWHAN**
Times Staff Writer

On the practice tee at Riviera Country Club, Jack Nicklaus was giving a lesson to fellow pro Jerry Pate, working on his address, swing and stance.

Later, joining a reporter for a soft drink in the clubhouse lounge, Nicklaus was asked about his own stance—on competitive golf.

It has been suggested that at 38, after 63 tour victories and more than $3 million in career earnings, Nicklaus has become bored, that varied business interests have cut into his golf schedule, that time he once spent reading greens is now spent reading financial ledgers.

Nicklaus takes to the suggestions like he would take to a shank. He said that while he now has periods of diminishing intensity, he is not bored. He said he has curtailed his schedule to spend more time with his family and reduce these periods when his intensity lags.

"I am still somewhere in my prime," he said, "still as capable as ever of taking advantage of my ability.

"The records I have set will someday be broken but it would be a shame if I didn't push them out to a point where they will be more difficult to break. That is my goal and one reason I have cut back on my schedule.

"At the same time, in some ways, I'm playing more golf than ever. I went home (North Palm Beach) from the Crosby (his only tournament appearance of 1978) and played golf for nine or 10 days in a row. In the past I'd have gone fishing. I'd have gone flying. I'd have never picked up a club between tournaments. Why I did it, I don't know. It was just something I wanted to do."

He ran his fingers over the frost on his glass and said, "I like this feeling I now have, this feeling of *wanting* to play golf."

Nicklaus may like it but it is doubtful that those who must play against him this week do. He is still considered the man to beat in the $200,000 Glen Campbell Los Angeles Open which begins today at Riviera.

He is still probably the man to beat in any tournament.

"I would be surprised," he said, "if at this time of the year, not yet at tournament sharpness, I could put together four rounds of the type that will be necessary to win. On the other hand, I would not be surprised to win considering my background of tournament experience.

"This course is one of the best in the country and it is in better shape than I have ever seen it. I have said many times that the tougher the course, the better I seem to play."

This is one of only five tournaments Nicklaus will play in before the Masters in April. The four events that comprise the elusive Grand Slam—the Masters, PGA, U.S. Open and British Open—remain his objective, and he will probably play in fewer

Please Turn to Page 6, Col. 1

JIM MURRAY

# It's Affirmed: The Best in the West Is THE Best

LOUISVILLE—It was supposed to be the race of the mid-century. It was to make everybody forget whatever happened on a racetrack before. Compared to this, Noor-Citation was a schottische. Dempsey-Firpo was a debate. Man o' War and John P. Grier were underbred.

This was going to be a ride like Paul Revere's. It would go right into the history books, poems would be written about it. It would be a celebration of the horse. No Canonero II, Dust Commander, no quarter horse. This field had the look of eagles, all right. These were the kind that won the wars, settled the West, delivered the mail. These kind caught Geronimo, beat Montezuma, conquered Peru and almost saved Lee.

But, sometimes, great expectations sour. You expect Dempsey-Firpo and you get Dempsey-Gibbons. You want a Super Bowl and you get Harvard-Yale. You get two Hall of Fame pitchers and they're both chased by the third inning. "Carmen" is announced but "Naughty Marietta" is performed.

Well, you can pump up the trumpets for the 1978 Kentucky Derby. Pull the stops, wave the flags. A great, marvelous, well-mannered colt, as gold as bullion, as orange-red as a Canadian sunset, put away a blue chip field in the Derby as easily as Too Tall Jones might drop a quarterback or Musial pull a fastball off the fence.

He beat a blue-ribbon panel without really appearing to have to reach in to take out the capital of his talent.

Impeccably trained by a Cuban who appears to be able to talk to horses, skillfully ridden by an unexcitable 18-year-old who looks as if he should be sweeping chimneys in 19th century London, Affirmed won a picture-book Derby. One for the lithographs.

There was one undefeated colt, three bums, a mystery colt, a couple of so-whats? and four very real runners in the race.

You can never tell about colts. They make eggs look sturdy. But Affirmed looked every inch a colt for the lithographs. He went about his work with the bored efficiency of a Joe DiMaggio getting under a line drive, Sugar Ray working his man into a corner, Dempsey measuring a palooka. He looked like Bobby Layne picking a defense apart, Nick the Greek betting a pat hand.

He did what he had to do on the day he had to do it—as the great ones always do. This was the seventh game of the World Series, the fourth quarter, the main event and the 15th round. It doesn't matter in this game what you do at Pimlico next week or Arlington Park next summer. The Kentucky Derby is a grueling mile-and-a-quarter rockpile a chain gang should work on.

Lazaro Barrera, the trainer who has been acting all week as if the colt told him he would win

Please Turn to Page 13, Col. 1

TOO LATE—Alydar (left), with Jorge Velasquez aboard, moves up on the outside of Affirmed, with Steve Cauthen up, but it's too late.

Native son Cauthen and Affirmed gave the field a Kentucky fried lickin' in the 104th Kentucky Derby Saturday. Believe It (rear) was third.

# Cauthen Whips Affirmed; Affirmed Whips 'Em All

## Trainer Says They Were Toying With the Field in the Stretch

CC PART III †
SUNDAY, MAY 7, 1978

BY SKIP BAYLESS
Times Staff Writer

LOUISVILLE—All week long, Lazaro Soto Barrera's Cuban blood boiled as he heard the criticism from rival trainer John Veitch and an Eastern press that Barrera regarded as prejudiced toward Alydar, the early Kentucky Derby favorite.

Affirmed had no competition in California, Barrera heard. Affirmed hadn't improved as much over the winter as Alydar (whom Affirmed beat four of six times as a 2-year-old). Affirmed wasn't bred to go the Derby's mile and a quarter distance. Affirmed wouldn't get the ride he'd need from 18-year-old Steve Cauthen in his first Derby.

Barrera, 52, held his tongue until Friday, when he indirectly told the 32-year-old Veitch to keep his mouth shut until Alydar had won.

Late Saturday afternoon at Churchill Downs, Barrera was the one doing the talking after Affirmed put away Alydar and the rest of what was supposed to be one of the strongest Derby fields.

"Maybe now some people believe in my horse," Barrera said. "Now I don't want to hear any more excuses from them (the Alydar people)."

Affirmed, his little orange ball of fire, had, he said, just toyed with the field, playfully pricking his ears through the stretch, waiting for an Alydar charge that came too late.

Affirmed finished a length and a half in front of Alydar but Barrera and Cauthen said they could have named the margin. Affirmed won, they said, just like they thought he would, settling into the third position, moving up to second at the mile pole, taking the lead coming out of the far turn.

Affirmed's time of 2:01 2/5 was the fastest since Secretariat's record 1:59 2/5 in 1973 and the fifth fastest of all time.

The 9-5 second choice of the crowd of 131,004, Affirmed paid $5.60, $2.80 and $2.60. Alydar (6-5) returned $2.60 and $2.40. Wood Memorial winner Believe It (the 7-1 fourth choice), made a move at Affirmed in the far turn but finished third, a 1¼ lengths behind Alydar. Sensitive Prince, the third betting favorite, led for awhile and faded to sixth.

The excitement generated by the race seemingly prompted the crowd to bet record numbers: $4,425,828 on the Derby (the '77 record was $3,-655,225) and $10,336,443 on the card (last year's mark: $8,811,486.).

And afterward, Barrera was excited—and caustic.

"Just because we run in California no matter," Barrera said, rolling his r's. "If we run in China this is a good horse. He no run all out (through the stretch). We need better competition to see how fast he can really run."

The not-so-subtle needle obviously was aimed in Veitch's direction. The cocky young Calumet trainer was nowhere to be found—he said before the race that he'd jump off a bridge into the Ohio River if Alydar lost—but Jorge Velasquez, Alydar's jockey, was located.

"The track was very, very hard," the Panamanian said. "He couldn't handle it. He just did not respond. That is why he dropped back so far (he was eighth after three-fourths of a mile). I kept whipping him but he would not get going. He did not start running until the last eighth."

Cauthen whipped Affirmed sharply

Please Turn to Page 12, Col. 1

# Dodgers Lose Game, 3-2; Maybe Reggie Smith, Too

## Right Fielder Aggravates Old Groin Pull Running After Parker's Hit on a Cold Day in Pittsburgh

BY ROSS NEWHAN
Times Staff Writer

PITTSBURGH—The Dodgers lost to the Pirates, 3-2, Saturday and may also have lost their clutch-hitting right fielder, Reggie Smith, for an indefinite time.

Disregarding the recommendation of doctors and his manager that he give a groin pull incurred during the final week of spring training time to heal properly, Smith again remained in the lineup on a cold, gray afternoon and aggravated the injury while running after Dave Parker's triple in the fifth inning.

Smith came out two innings later and was back at the team's downtown hotel even before relief pitcher Grant Jackson struck out Teddy Martinez with runners at second and third and two out in the ninth.

"I'm concerned," manager Tom Lasorda said when asked about Smith. "We really need him. He's one of the people we could least afford to lose for any amount of time."

If Smith is unable to play in today's trip finale—and trainer Bill Buhler said it was doubtful—he will be replaced by Lee Lacy, who proved again Saturday that he can handle the difficult demands of irregular work while also proving to himself again that he should be playing regularly.

After collecting two singles as Ron Cey's replacement in Friday night's game, Lacy was called on to pinch hit for Glenn Burke, who had replaced Smith, as the leadoff hitter in the ninth.

Lacy promptly slugged his second pinch-hit homer in the 10 games of the trip (he's 3 for 5 with 5 RBI as a pinch hitter), cutting the Pittsburgh lead to 3-2 and sending John Candelaria to the clubhouse.

The homer by the 30-year-old Lacy brought on Kent Tekulve, who promptly retired Cey and Steve Garvey on infield grounders. Dusty Baker singled up the middle and Rick Monday delivered a drive to left center that bounced once on the hard Tartan turf and caromed over the fence for what Monday later called "a synthetic rule double."

It was a bad bounce for the Dodgers since it deprived them of the tying run. Baker was already around third and halfway home when third base umpire Ed Vargo waved him to a stop. The rule limits a runner to two bases on a hit of that nature.

Lasorda bemoaned the break later, forgetting that the Pirates had lost a run in a similar fashion in the fourth. Reminded of it, Lasorda said, "ours came at a more critical time."

"But," said a reporter, "the Pirates would still have been credited with a

Please Turn to Page 8, Col. 1

## LAFLEUR SCORES TWO; MONTREAL GOES THREE UP

TORONTO (AP)—Guy Lafleur scored two goals and an assist while Jacques Lemaire had a goal and two assists Saturday night as the Montreal Canadiens defeated the Toronto Maple Leafs, 6-1, and moved to within a victory of the National Hockey League playoff finals.

The defending champions got first-period goals from Steve Shutt, Rick Chartraw and Yvon Lambert for a 3-0 lead before George Ferguson scored Toronto's goal at 8:05 of the middle session.

Lefleur, who had assisted on the goal by Shutt, then scored his pair around one by Lemaire to complete the scoring against Toronto goalie Mike Palmateer and give the Canadiens a 3-0 lead in the best-of-seven

Please Turn to Page 7, Col. 1

# Angels Win, 7-3, on Rettenmund's Pinch-Hit Slam

BY SCOTT OSTLER
Times Staff Writer

The two oldest Angels, Merv Rettenmund (34) and Ron Fairly (39), pounded the Cleveland Indians into submission Saturday night at Anaheim Stadium, leading a 7-3 win that gave the Angels a two-game sweep and moved them a game closer to the first-place Oakland A's.

Rettenmund, a free agent picked up by the Angels this spring as an extra outfielder and pinch hitter, hit a grand slam homer with two out in the seventh. It thrilled the Angel fans in the Jacket Night crowd of 40,750 but looked otherwise insignificant until the Indians scored twice in the ninth and left two men on base.

Fairly homered in the first inning with a man aboard, which made Angel starter Chris Knapp feel a little better. Knapp gave up a homer to the game's leadoff hitter, ex-Angel Paul Dade, but settled down to strike out the side that inning and look good until the ninth, when Paul Hartzell was called on to get the last two outs.

Rettenmund was pinch-hitting for Ken Landreaux when he hit the grand slam off reliever Dennis Kinney, who came in at the start of the inning. It was Rettenmund's third career grand slam and the first pinch-hit grand slam in Angel history. For an encore, Rettenmund reached into the stands in left field to grab Andre Thornton's foul fly for the first out in the ninth, with two men on base.

Fairly's homer was his third of the homestand and all three have come in the first inning with a man on.

The Angels, who tied a season high with 12 hits Friday night against Cleveland, carried that momentum into the first inning of Saturday's game. After Rick Miller led off with a walk, Dave Chalk doubled him home.

Chalk, elevated to the No. 2 spot in the lineup and moved to shortstop Friday night, had two hits and a sacrifice fly in his first four times at bat.

Paxton, making only his second start of the season, didn't give up another run but gave way to Dennis Kinney to open the seventh.

With one out, Chalk and Lyman Bostock had chop hits, Chalk's over third baseman Buddy Bell and Bostock's over first baseman Andre Thornton. Bostock hustled his into a double.

After pinch hitter Ron Jackson flied to shallow right, the Indians

Please Turn to Page 8, Col. 3

THAT'S MY BOY—Derby winner Steve Cauthen gets a hug and a kiss from his mother, Myra, in winner's circle at Churchill Downs.
AP Wirephotos

# CURT FLOOD STILL MAKES WAVES AND PAINTS PICTURES

## Exiled Baseball Rebel Returns as Oakland A's Color Announcer

BY CHARLES MAHER, Times Staff Writer

OAKLAND—It's been a season of radio novelty for fans of the Oakland A's.

First, they were getting their play-by-play from two college students on a 10-watt station.

Now, they're hearing the voice of a baseball revolutionary. Curt Flood, the man who helped radically change baseball's reserve system, is the expert analyst in the Oakland radio booth.

A conclusion after the expert did his first game the other evening: Flood can really paint a picture for you.

That's if you give him a brush and canvas. He is a professional artist. A professional broadcaster he ain't. Not yet, anyway. In the first game, he excelled mainly at long pauses.

But it figured to be a difficult beginning. Flood had never worked in a broadcast booth and, indeed, had no on-the-air experience except in the comparatively undemanding role of interview subject.

He knew what was coming. Before the game he said, "I'm going to be a little tight in the beginning. I can tell you right now."

But how did this famous rebel wind up in a broadcast booth, working at least indirectly for management?

As the season approached, nobody knew for sure whether the A's would play here or in Denver. This uncertainty discouraged major stations from bidding for the radio package. So, club owner Charlie Finley sold the rights to a little FM station run by the University of California.

The deal was for the first 16 games only and the station didn't want to continue preempting its regular programs.

Enter the Bercovich Furniture Co., which for years has sponsored local sports programs, including several Flood had participated in as a youngster. The company bought the radio rights and made a deal with a 5,000-watt country-music station.

Please Turn to Page 6, Col. 1

REBEL RETURNS—Curt Flood teams with play-by-play announcer Bud Foster on Oakland A's broadcasts.
AP Wirephoto

# Hayes' 33-Year Career Ends on One Punch

**CAUGHT IN THE ACT**—This picture, shot from a monitor at ABC studio in Washington, shows Ohio State coach Woody Hayes throwing a punch at Clemson's Charlie Bauman. The incident, which occurred in Friday's Gator Bowl game, cost Hayes his job.
AP Wirephoto

## Ohio State Coach Is Fired for Hitting Clemson Player in Gator Bowl Defeat

Los Angeles Times
Sports
CC PART III †
SUNDAY, DECEMBER 31, 1978

From Times Wire Services

COLUMBUS, Ohio—Woody Hayes, the fiery head coach at Ohio State University for 28 years and the fourth winningest coach in college football history, was fired Saturday for punching a Clemson player in the Gator Bowl.

Sources close to the Ohio State football program say that Arkansas coach Lou Holtz, a one-time Hayes assistant, will be named to succeed his former 65-year-old mentor.

Ohio State athletic director Hugh Hindman said he fired Hayes after meeting most of the night with university president Harold Enarson in Jacksonville, Fla., following the Gator Bowl which the Buckeyes lost, 17-15.

When asked why he fired Hayes, Hindman said, "I think it's obvious."

"There is not a university or athletic conference in this country which would permit a coach to physically assault a college athlete," Enarson said.

Hayes returned to Columbus with the team and was quickly escorted into a police car and driven to his home in suburban Upper Arlington, where he remained in seclusion.

Freshman quarterback Art Schlichter said the team was not told of Hayes' firing until the plane was landing and then it was just "very, very quiet."

The players and assistant coaches were utterly shaken when they left the chartered jetliner and several had tears in their eyes.

National television caught the incident in the Gator Bowl. It was one of many that clouded an otherwise brilliant 33-year college coaching career in which Hayes compiled a record of 238-72-10.

Hayes struck Clemson middle guard Charlie Bauman after Bauman intercepted a pass by Schlichter in the waning minutes of the game. Hayes later grabbed an official.

Hindman announced Hayes' firing shortly before the team left Jacksonville.

"Coach Hayes has been relieved of his duties as head football coach at Ohio State University," the announcement said. "This decision has the full support of the president of the university."

However, Hayes telephoned the Columbus Dispatch early Saturday and said he had resigned.

Hindman said that "I told him (Hayes) this morning at the hotel about the decision."

"It was the toughest decision I will ever have to make," said Hindman, who played for Hayes at Miami of Ohio one season and coached under him at Ohio State for seven years.

Hindman said Hayes' actions

Please Turn to Page 6, Col. 3

### JIM MURRAY

## The Best of 1978

**OK, let's hear** it for 1979! As for 1978, throw the bum out!

As you know, it is the custom of the wire services, networks, Art Buchwald and the Missouri School of Journalism each new year to pick out the best news stories of the year. Naturally, they miss a few. Besides, Buchwald and the wire services only pick regular news stories. Among a few missed are my favorites in the sports field:

Moe Gull, the owner of the Pittsburgh Plutocrats, was negotiating a contract with free-agent Pete Petunia, whose nickname is "Charlie Costly." When told the openers were $3 million in tax-deferred income plus a lifetime position with the corporation as vice-sinecure, he replied: "Listen, Klutz! My father worked 50 years in the mines, chopping a ton of coal a day for $16 a week, and he died owing the company store $980 and the lung hospital $1,500, and you want me to pay you $3 million to get a hit off Lance Rautzhan six out of every 20 times up not counting walks and sacrifice flies, and standing in right field doing absolutely nothing for days on end?! No way! I'd rather give the money to a polo players' relief fund!"

★

**Coach Woody Head** of the Slippery State Rockeyes was sitting in his room near the Rose Bowl when his star quarterback, and 60% passer and Heisman Trophy winner, "Scatter" Armour, came in on New Year's Eve and said: "Coach, I hate to tell you this but I've got four makeup lab tests I have to finish in time for Jan. 2 and I don't see any way I can make the Rose Bowl game tomorrow. I know the guys will do all right without me, and they sure have my best wishes, but you know how the head of the chemistry department is counting on me." And Coach Head said: "Son, don't give it another thought. It's just a lousy game, after all. I'm sure NBC will understand, too, and send along its best wishes. As for the public, don't worry about it. I'm sure everybody in the state will realize it's more important for you to work on a cure for the gout than to beat Southern Cal. Besides, there's about seven other first-stringers who may not make it. They're going to a New Year's party down in Laguna, and they told me if they're not here by 2 to start without them."

★

**Lord Hawhawin** of the International Olympic Committee announced to the press the 1984 Olympic Games had been awarded to a small village in Thuringia, which promised only to sweep the sidewalks to get ready for the Games. The mayor of the village also promised to clear an area a quarter of a mile square for the track and field events, and the swimming and diving would be held in the local swimming hole, and the kayak pairs on the village pond. He invited the world to come along so long as everybody brought their sleeping bags, and promised there would be no commemorative coins unless, of course, you wanted change for a dollar when you got there. Admission would be free. "Since the athletes run for free, why should you pay to see them?" he asked.

Please Turn to Page 7, Col. 1

# A Breeze for Steelers, Squeeze for Cowboys

## Stallworth Star of Victory Over Broncos, 33-10

BY MIKE LITTWIN
Times Staff Writer

PITTSBURGH—Meet John Stallworth. He's the other guy. Lynn Swann catches the passes and the glory. Stallworth merely makes passes at glory and settles for leftovers.

But not in Saturday's American Football Conference playoff game between Pittsburgh and Denver. Swann was the decoy and Stallworth made sitting ducks of the Denver secondary. Terry Bradshaw hit Stallworth 10 times as the Steelers beat the Broncos, 33-10.

Stallworth can pick his spots. One he liked particularly was the middle of the field.

As the Broncos blitzed one linebacker and double-teamed Swann with another, they left Stallworth open to maneuver as he pleased.

"Our game plan was to go to John because of the way they cover Swann," said Bradshaw, who couldn't look up without seeing Stallworth in the clear. "And the last time we played them, John had beaten (Steve) Foley deep, so we figured he would have room."

Not just room, he had a clearing. The score could have been worse. "I thought we should have had 54 points," said Swann.

The 33 were plenty. Avenged was Pittsburgh's playoff loss last year to the Broncos, the Cinderella team of 1977. No one can recall Cinderella's second dance, however. And the solid Steelers, seven straight years in the playoffs, had two weeks to practice eating glass slippers for lunch.

"I don't think Denver knew what was going on initially," said Stallworth, five years out of Alabama A&M. "You have to double someone like Lynn. But this might make the team we play next week think a little."

Yes, it could. Stallworth's 10 receptions were an division playoff record in the National Football League. Franco Harris, meanwhile, gained 105 yards—the sixth time he has rushed for more than 100 yards in a playoff game. That, too, is a record. Records were broken like Denver's spirit.

This was devastation. The Broncos couldn't get to Bradshaw and they couldn't get away from Pittsburgh's defensive line, the Steel Curtain.

"They got themselves into a whirlwind," said Steeler defensive back Ray Oldham.

After Denver took a 3-0 lead in the first quarter, on Jim Turner's 37-yard field goal, the offense shut down. The

Please Turn to Page 8, Col. 3

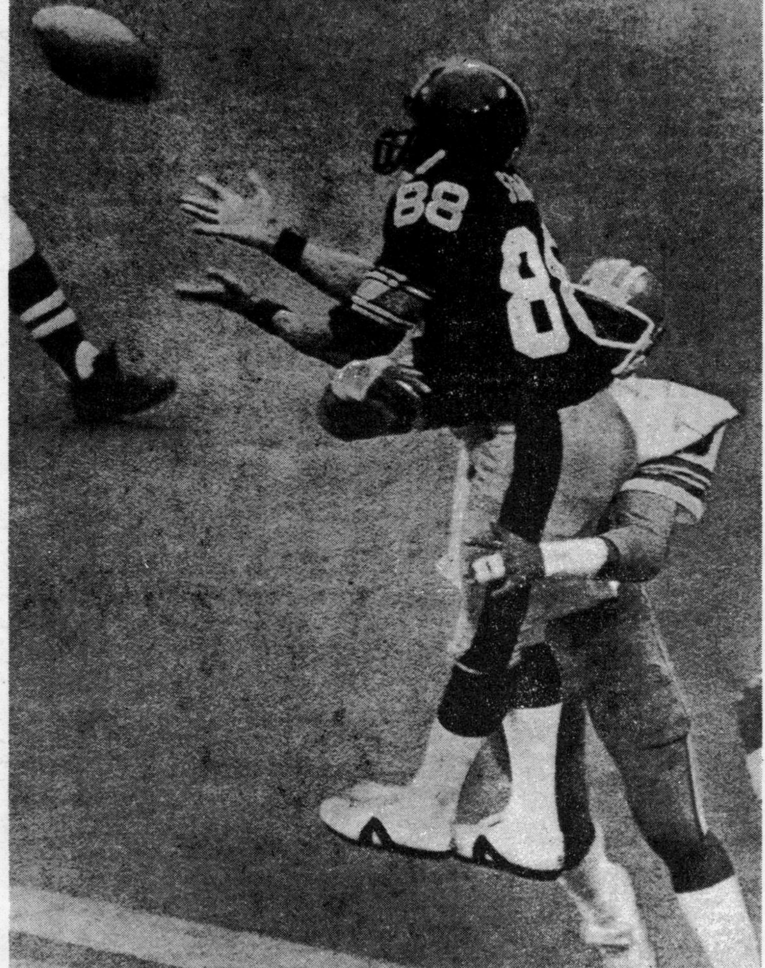

**BREAKING THE BRONCOS**—Steelers' Lynn Swann catches 38-yard touchdown pass despite defense of Broncos' Bill Thompson in fourth quarter. Broncos protested score in vain.
AP Wirephoto

## Staubach Hurt; White Rallies Dallas, 27-20

BY BOB OATES
Times Staff Writer

DALLAS—Atlanta's surprising Falcons, a 14-point underdog, outplayed Roger Staubach Saturday, outpointed him and knocked him out of the game in the first half with a blatantly foul hit.

But in the second half they couldn't handle Dallas backup quarterback Danny White, who in a cool and confident performance brought the Cowboys from behind to the 27-20 win that put them in the National Football Conference championship game next Sunday.

The turning point came in the last minute of the first half when, with Atlanta leading by the halftime margin, 20-13, linebacker Robert Pennywell sprinted up the middle on a typical Falcon blitzing play and knocked Staubach unconscious with a late hit after the Cowboy quarterback had thrown the ball.

This enraged Dallas' Doomsday Defense, which following its lethargic first half, kept Atlanta from scoring again.

The decisive play came in the fourth quarter, when after White's rollout passes had evened things for Dallas, 20-20, Cowboy safetyman Charlie Waters rushed Atlanta's John James into a 10-yard punt. In evading Waters, who would have blocked it if James had punted straightaway, the Falcon kicker let the ball slide off his foot.

This left the Cowboys only 30 yards from the go-ahead touchdown. And with an assist by Pennywell on another personal foul they won the game four plays later. All four were runs by backup fullback Scott Laidlaw, gaining the last 16 yards.

Afterward, Dallas coach Tom Landry, who in normal circumstances might have been relishing his close-shave win, raged at length against Pennywell, a 23-year-old third-year pro who on his legal plays typified Atlanta's rough-house defense.

"There's no place in football for that kind of shot," Landry said of the blow that felled Staubach. "And it should be dealt with by the commis-

Please Turn to Page 8, Col. 1

## MARYLAND BEATS USC FOR TITLE IN TOURNAMENT

COLLEGE PARK, Md. (UPI)—Sophomores Albert King and Ernest Graham scored 20 points each Saturday night to lead Maryland to an 83-79 victory over USC in the championship game of the Maryland Invitational tournament.

King earned Most Valuable Player honors as Maryland (9-2) won its tournament for the seventh time in eight years.

Graham hit three free throws in the final 31 seconds after the Trojans had twice cut an 11-point Maryland lead to three in the final minute.

Maurice Williams' 15-foot jump shot pulled the Trojans (7-2) to 77-73 with two minutes left.

Larry Gibson's three-point play boosted the Terrapins' margin to 80-73 with 1:46 left but Williams and Dean Jones scored for USC before Graham's final free throws iced the contest.

Please Turn to Page 4, Col. 1

## Rams Challenge Minnesota's Jinx

### L.A. Seeks 1st Playoff Win Over the Vikings

BY TED GREEN
Times Staff Writer

There will be matchups within the matchup—lots of them—when the Rams play the Minnesota Vikings at 2 o'clock this afternoon at the Coliseum in a National Football League quarter-final playoff game which is blacked out in Los Angeles. They include:

—The Rams vs. the So-Called Minnesota Jinx. The score so far stands Jinx 4 playoff victories, Rams 0.

—The Rams vs. the Choke-in-the-Playoffs Stigma. Los Angeles has made the postseason tournament annually since 1973 but can't seem to get past the NFC title game. Last season the Rams' frustrations became almost laughable when, heavily favored, they lost to Minnesota, 14-7, in the first round on a rainy Monday at the Coliseum.

—The Rams vs. the weatherman. The weatherman's ahead here, too, but the Rams figure to cut into his lead because the forecast calls for a cool, clear, *rainless* day.

—The Rams' Ray Malavasi, in his

Please Turn to Page 10, Col. 2

## USC'S ROBINSON SNIFFS ROSES

### *Coach Says Bowl Game Is Ideal Showcase for Talented Athletes*

BY BOB OATES
Times Staff Writer

Rounding out his third year as USC's football coach, John Robinson is back in Pasadena, where the Trojans have won a record 15 Rose Bowls in 21 New Year's Day appearances and where Monday's game will be watched by dozens—perhaps hundreds—of future Trojans.

It is the pomp and glory and tradition of the Rose Bowl, Robinson believes, that makes USC what it is in football, attracting the most gifted of each new generation.

"The Rose Bowl," he says, "appeals to youngsters who have an abundance of two things—talent and ambition. And that's what we want at USC. We're looking for the player who wants to be the best and dreams of being the best. You have a better shot at greatness if you dream about it. The Rose Bowl provides an ideal showcase for that kind of player. The kids know it and we know it and I think that's why we keep coming back."

Ambition can be measured as readily as ability, Robinson says, explaining:

"When I talk with them (prospects for USC) about the effort it takes to be great, they tend to react in different ways. Some are turned off completely—some of the better prep players. Other very talented youngsters are frightened by the challenge. And a few will tell themselves: 'Heck,

Please Turn to Page 9, Col. 2

# USC Wins Rose Bowl but the Replay's a Tie

## White Scores (or Did He?) as Trojans Beat Michigan, 17-10

BUSINESS

CC PART III †

TUESDAY, JANUARY 2, 1979


**BY MAL FLORENCE**
Times Staff Writer

Thirty years ago in the Rose Bowl, Northwestern's Art Murakowski scored a disputed touchdown—the margin of victory in a 20-14 victory over California.

He fumbled while surging towards the end zone, and Cal partisans maintain to this day that he didn't break the plane of the goal line before losing the ball.

History might have repeated itself to a degree in the 65th Rose Bowl New Year's Day as USC held off Michigan to win, 17-10, in a defensive war before a crowd of 105,629.

Charles White, USC's tailback, sky dived for the end zone in the second quarter. But the ball was stripped from his grasp by linebacker Ron Simpkins and Michigan apparently recovered near its 1-yard line.

White pounded the turf with his fist in frustration.

However, line judge Gilbert Marchman raised his hands over his head, signifying a touchdown. Then umpire Don Mason signaled that Michigan had possession.

After the officials huddled for a few seconds, head linesman Lee Joseph reaffirmed it was a touchdown.

Referee Paul Kamanski explained later what happened, saying, "The line judge says the ball broke the plane. He is in charge of forward progress of the ball. He instantaneously made the signal. The umpire, who doesn't rule on forward progress, saw a fumble. The line judge was emphatic about it and he was in perfect position and he gave the signal. So it should be no problem."

No problem? Most observers who watched the instant replay on television were convinced that White lost the ball before he crossed the goal line. Others weren't so sure.

It was Kamanski, coincidentally, who made a controversial ruling in USC's 27-25 victory over Notre Dame in November, calling quarterback Paul McDonald's apparent fumble an incomplete pass, thereby keeping alive the Trojans' winning field goal drive.

Anyway, White's 3-yard dive and the subsequent conversion gave the Trojans a 14-3 lead and enough points to deal Bo Schembechler, the Michigan coach, his sixth bowl defeat without a win—five setbacks in the Rose Bowl.

So the Wolverines contend they got no worse than a tie but it will go into the books as another win for the Pacific 10 over the Big 10 in this series—the ninth in the last 10 years.

This was a game in which defenses

**Please Turn to Page 10, Col. 1**

### NOW, WHO IS NO. 1 TEAM IN THE LAND?

| The Candidates | Record | Last Ranking | Comment |
|---|---|---|---|
| Alabama | 11-1 | No. 2 | Beat No. 1 team Monday |
| USC | 12-1 | No. 3 | Defeated Alabama, 24-14 |
| Oklahoma | 11-1 | No. 4 | Avenged only loss Monday |

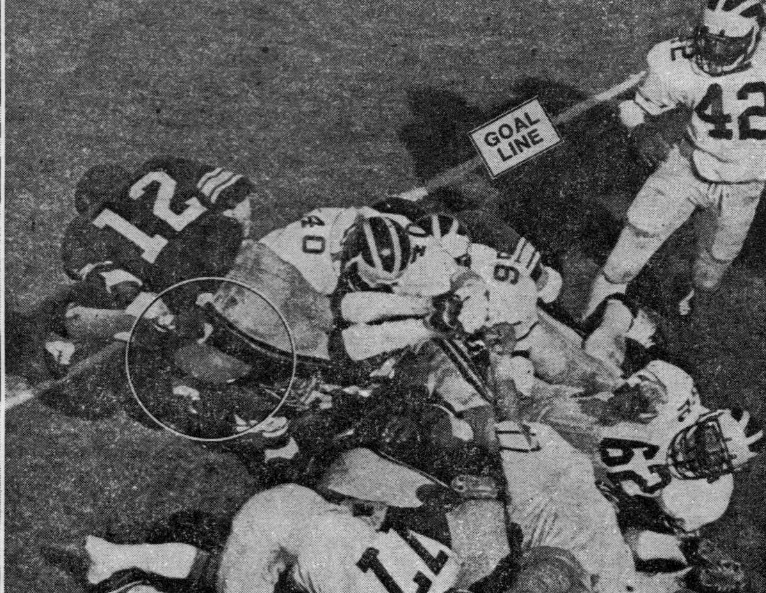


**DISPUTED PLAY**—USC tailback Charles White fumbles as he dives for end zone during the second quarter of Monday's Rose Bowl game. It appears (right) that White fumbled before crossing the goal line, but officials ruled White had scored. Michigan linebacker Ron Simpkins (40) caused the fumble and the Wolverines recovered. The Trojans went on to win by a touchdown, 17-10.

Times photos by George Rose and Larry Sharkey

***JIM MURRAY***

## The Phantom Touchdown

**Every so often** a Rose Bowl game is one for the ages. Roy Riegels runs the wrong way. The Four Horsemen run wild. A Doyle Nave comes off the bench to score on a team that had never been scored on. USC and Wisconsin throw up 79 points.

The 1979 game was distinguished because it managed to cram more inaction into 60 minutes of football than the old Pitt-Fordham scoreless ties. If it was a fight it would have been all clinches. It began with a whimper and ended with one.

It was a great game if you're crazy about 1-yard losses, passes behind the line of scrimmage, a whole lot of punts—681 yards of punts—and a game that ends with the quarterback falling on the ball. It was trench warfare, as boring as a day at the office or guarding a cannon in the park.

Still, it will probably go down in the books as the game of the Phantom Touchdown.

★

**I don't know** about you but where I grew up you were supposed to have the football with you when you went into the end zone for a touchdown. When Charles White "scored" for USC with 7:28 remaining in the second period, he seemed to have forgotten one small detail—the ball.

An official decided it was inconsequential. I guess he figured anybody could score carrying the ball. You have to admire a man who can put points on the board without it.

The situation was this: USC, with a 7-3 lead, had just driven 47 yards to the Michigan 3-yard line. It was second down and the quarterback handed the ball off to Charles White, who dove at the goal line in a soaring arc.

He had the football when he took off. But he didn't have it when he landed. A Michigan player had it by then.

One official, doubtless an old-fashioned type who thought the ball had to accompany the ball-carrier, signaled it was Michigan's ball somewhere on the one-inch or one-foot line. He was overruled.

And that, sports fans, was the old ball game. A field goal in the last two seconds of play at the half made the score 17-3. Michigan scored in the second half but spent most of the rest of it on its own 10-yard line looking like a fly trying to get out of a spider web.

Frankly, I wouldn't want to get into the same lifeboat with this Michigan team. In fact, I would not get into an elevator with them. I wouldn't want to back their play at a casino but I would bet the limit against them even if they had three aces showing. Because these guys would have to get luckier to be even considered snakebit. I'm surprised they didn't bring rain. These are the kind of guys who would be lucky enough to get a last-minute reservation on the Titanic.

Michigan had a quality team but they do some funny things. Like, with 2 minutes 50 seconds left in the game, and their ball on the USC 48-yard line, and fourth down, they—you're not going to believe this—PUNT!! You heard me. They gave up the football. It's like handing over your sword. They folded the three aces, said "I pass."

★

**They had enough** bad luck without getting that kind of advice or leadership from the bench. USC's running backs managed a couple of first downs and were in a position to do three fall-downs and end the game like a tilted pinball game.

It was typical of everything they did all day. The game was barely two minutes old when the Michigan quarterback tried a pass from his own 29-yard line and dropped it in the hands of the enemy, USC's Ron Lott. USC quickly scored. In three plays it was 7-0.

With only eight seconds remaining in the first half, quarterback Rick Leach threw another interception and, with two seconds remaining, USC turned it into a field goal and, as it happened, their final scoring for the day.

That was the kind of a day it was for Michigan. Wide open receivers twice dropped touchdown passes. With that kind of luck,

**Please Turn to Page 12, Col. 3**

## Bo Says, 'We Didn't Play Well Enough to Win'

**BY SCOTT OSTLER**
Times Staff Writer

Maybe Reggie Jackson's baseline rhumba didn't cost the Dodgers a World Series game, and eventually the entire Series, last October.

Maybe that official didn't enable USC to beat Notre Dame last month when he ruled incomplete pass on what many believed to be a fumble by quarterback Paul McDonald.

And maybe USC tailback Charles White didn't really carry the ball over the goal line in the second quarter of Monday's Rose Bowl game against Michigan on the play that gave the Trojans a 14-3 lead that proved insurmountable, as the Trojans won, 17-10.

But those are the types of plays that make for lively discussion down through the years.

White dove over the Michigan goal line from 3 yards out on the controversial play. The ball was knocked loose somewhere in flight and fell to the ground on the one-yard line, where it was pounced upon by two eager Michigan players.

Did White lose his precious cargo before or after crossing the goal line? Did the officials botch the play by giving conflicting signals (touchdown and recovered fumble) or hesitating before making the call? If the play had been ruled in Michigan's favor, would it have changed the outcome of the game or made any difference in the cosmic scheme of things?

To that last question the answer is probably not. Bo Schembechler's Michigan teams seem unable to win a bowl game (they're 0-6). However, the controversial play is worth further consideration.

Schembechler had his opinion of

**Please Turn to Page 8, Col. 1**

***Robinson: We're No. 1***

Story on Page 9

### ORANGE BOWL

| | |
|---|---|
| Oklahoma | 31 |
| Nebraska | 24 |

Story on Page 4

### COTTON BOWL

| | |
|---|---|
| Notre Dame | 35 |
| Houston | 34 |

Story on Page 6

**'YOU'VE GOT TO BE KIDDING'**—That seems to be the reaction of Michigan players as head linesman Lee Joseph, after a brief discussion, confirms that Charles White scored on controversial dive. One official had ruled that White had fumbled and Michigan had recovered.

Times photo by George Rose

## No. 1? The Tide Defense Rests

### Alabama Stops Penn State Twice at 1-Foot Line in 14-7 Win

**BY BOB OATES**
Times Staff Writer

NEW ORLEANS—Paul (Bear) Bryant, 65, won his 284th football game Monday in the Sugar Bowl as Alabama's Crimson Tide toppled error-prone, erratic, previously undefeated Penn State, 14-7.

"Alabama outcoached us," Joe Paterno, the leader of the Nittany Lions, said candidly, graciously, perceptively and truthfully after No. 2 Alabama did this to No. 1 Penn State:

—Broke up a brilliant first-half defensive fight in the last eight seconds and took a 7-0 lead when Tide split end Bruce Bolton dropped to his knees and elbows in the end zone to catch a 30-yard pass from quarterback Jeff Rutledge.

—Broke a 7-7 tie in the third quarter when halfback Lou Ikner cleverly ran a Penn State punt 62 yards to set up the 11-yard Alabama touchdown drive that was to prove decisive.

—Took advantage of an embarrassing penalty against the Lions for having 12 men on the field on a shanked Alabama punt which sailed out of bounds on the Crimson Tide 29 with less than six minutes left. The penalty enabled Alabama to retain possession for several valuable minutes, and when again forced to punt, Woody Umphrey boomed one from his 35 to the Penn State 21, a difference of 50 yards in potential field position.

—Made a spectacular goal-line stand at the Alabama 1-foot line in the fourth quarter when two diving Nittany Lions were tackled on third and fourth downs after an 18-yard march that began with a Tide fumble on its 19.

Paterno thus was halted 12 inches short of his first national championship in what had to be the most disappointing defeat of his fine career as Alabama opened the door to a national debate over who's No. 1.

The key fact in the debate, possibly, is that USC's offensive team wrecked a defense that Penn State could hardly budge in the 45th Sugar Bowl.

Last September, in the third week of the season, after Alabama had tuned up against Nebraska, 20-3, Trojan tailback Charles White ran through Alabama for 199 yards as USC breezed, 24-14.

By contrast, the entire Penn State backfield gained a net of 19 yards rushing against Alabama, proving that Bryant's defense is indeed a majestic weapon—except when contending with the Trojans.

**Please Turn to Page 13, Col. 1**

# White Runs for 246 Yards and Dives for 1

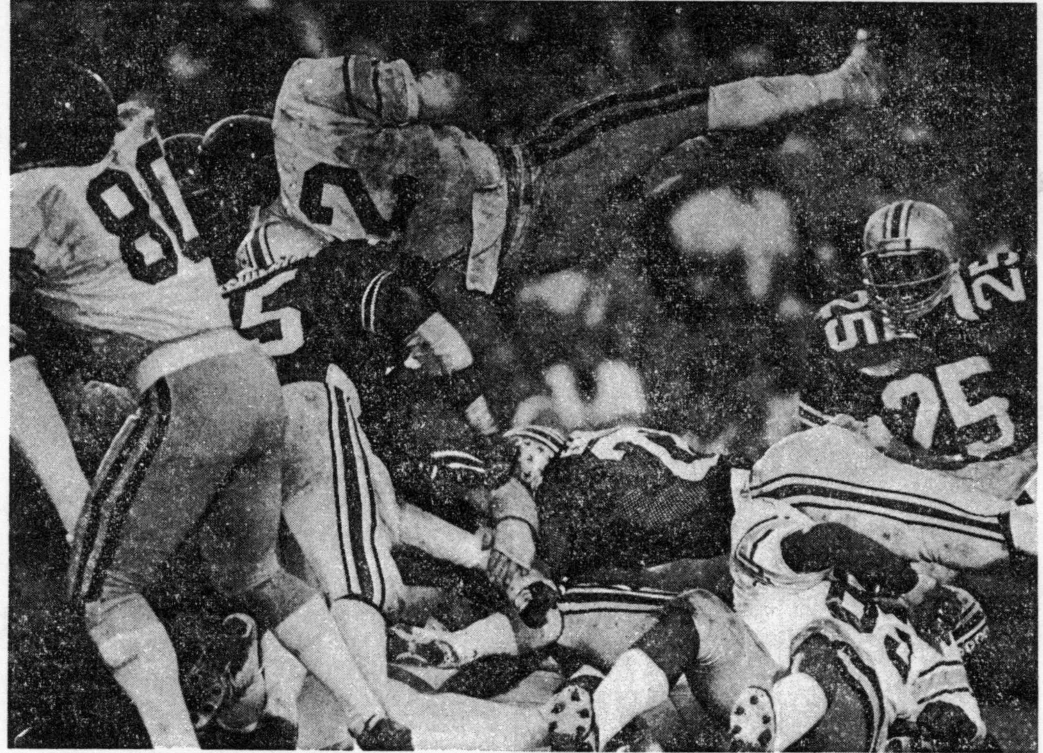


## Tailback Powers USC Past Buckeyes for Roses, 17-16

By MAL FLORENCE
Times Staff Writer

PASADENA—It will be remembered as the Charles White drive when historians talk about the 1980 Rose Bowl game.

It was White, USC's Heisman Trophy-winning tailback, who went on a running rampage late in the fourth quarter of the 66th Rose Bowl game with Ohio State New Year's Day.

He accounted for 71 yards of an 83-yard, stay-on-the-ground assault as the Trojans came from behind to beat the impressive Buckeyes, 17-16, before 105,-526 fans.

And it was White, who sky-dived over a pile inches away from the goal line for the winning touchdown with 1:32 remaining that preserved an unbeaten season for USC (11-0-1) and marred a previously perfect season for Ohio State (11-1).

Seldom has a back taken charge of a game as White did in the waning minutes of a slightly overcast Tuesday afternoon. The Trojans needed White at his best because Art Schlichter, the poised, Ohio State quarterback, had apparently beaten USC with his big-play passes.

White, playing his final game for USC, ran into the record books. He gained 247 yards on 39 carries to break the Rose Bowl record held by Iowa's Bob Jeter, 194 yards against California (1959), and the rushing attempts mark (34) shared by Stanford's Ernie Nevers (1925) and Cal's Vic Bottari (1938).


Los Angeles Times

Sports

CC PART III †

WEDNESDAY, JANUARY 2, 1980


USC, a 7½-point favorite, had stuttered repeatedly against an aroused Ohio State defense and the Trojans' passing game had betrayed them at critical junctures of the game.

So it was back to basics, a throwback to the Thundering Herd days of Howard Jones and the John McKay power-I formation of student body right, left or every way.

USC, trailing, 16-10, with 5:21 to play, was in an uncompromising position at its own 17-yard line. Surely, the Trojans must pass if they expected to win.

But USC Coach John Robinson probably crossed up Ohio State by electing to run from such poor field position. For sure, there was ample time.

On first down, White charged through a huge hole at right guard for 32 yards. Then, from USC's 49, he swept right end—student body right—for 28 yards and another first down at the Buckeye 23.

White, who was named the game's Most Valuable Player, then went out for a brief breather. Reserve tailback Michael Hayes reeled off seven yards and fullback Marcus Allen followed with five and a first down at the 11.

Then, waving to the cheering crowd, White returned to the game. White slammed for three, five and then two yards and a first down just short of the goal line.

Naturally, it was White, who jackknifed over the middle for the touchdown, juggling the ball a bit as he scored.

There was still time, of course, for Schlichter to make a counterattack—perhaps like he did last Sept. 29 when he completed six straight passes in the last 2:21 to beat UCLA, 17-13.

But Schlichter, setting up at his own 20 after a touchback, wasn't close on three throws and his fourth was almost picked off by cornerback Ron Lott.

So the Trojans took over at the Buckeye 20 and weren't about to rub it in as they let time run out after White gained 16 yards on three carries.

It remains to be seen whether USC will gain a share of the national championship by defeating Ohio State. The Buckeyes were ranked No. 1 in the Associated Press poll coming into the game with Alabama second and USC third.

'Bama beat Arkansas, 24-9, in the Sugar Bowl Tuesday and because the Crimson Tide was previously ranked No. 1 by UPI probably will retain that status.

Now it's a question of whether the

Please Turn to Page 12, Col. 1

### JIM MURRAY

## Back to the Trenches

PASADENA—Well, the lions et the Christians again. Don't hold the presses. The bride showed up. It's dog-bites-man stuff. USC wins Rose Bowl. And the sun rises in the East and water is two parts hydrogen and one part oxygen. Don't bother to wake anybody up with this scoop. It's Germany-Loses-War stuff. The Ohio State Buckeyes came up a nickel short.

It will come as no surprise to Woody Hayes. The defrocked Ohio State coach hated a lot of things in his life—long hair, people who didn't stand up when the Anthem was played and the pipsqueak who forced General Patton to slap him in the face. But Woody Hayes hated the forward pass more than any of them. Woody would lecture on the evils of the forward pass the way a temperance lecturer would take on the bottle. First, it's wine from a glass and then it's beer from the bottle and, next thing you know, it's a forward pass. A guy who would throw a forward pass would plow in a tractor with a radio in it, buy picture postcards from Paris and get his hair cut without a bowl on it. Sodom and Gomorrah was probably the direct result of the forward pass.

★

**"He who lives by the pass,** dies by the run," Woody used to warn direly.

He was so right on the lovely sunny day that was New Year's Day 1980 in Pasadena.

USC won the football game by going back to sound, fundamental Walter Camp football that was about as nifty as a steamroller rolling tar. It was standard give-the-football-to-the-big-guy and everybody-knock-somebody-down football. A guy in moleskins would have felt right at home.

USC won the game only 17-16 and they should be ashamed of themselves. It was like taking four aces and only winning a dollar and a quarter, using a battleship to gun down a canoe.

USC came into the game All-Everything. They were dripping with Heisman Trophies, they lost count of the All-Americans they had. Playboy magazine had already awarded them the national title before they picked up a football or put their helmets on. This was the school John Wayne came from. It seemed a shame they had to play these Midwestern hicks when they should really probably be taking on the Houston Oilers.

★

**They managed to fritter** away almost 57 minutes before they really regrouped and started to pay attention to business. Up to the fourth quarter, Charlie Heisman's (nee, White's) principal contribution to the holiday had been to fumble on a touchdown run on which he was open. Charlie White was so surprised to be caught from behind by anything that didn't have claws that he forgot he had the football.

Up to that time, USC's game plan seemed modelled more for Magic Johnson or Dr. J than Heisman winners. With an offensive line that blotted out the sun and resembled the Houston skyline, they felt they had to resort to deceit, trick plays, clever passes.

Ohio State, on the other hand, had no choice. Their only chance was 67-yard passes, devious routes by receivers and to hope USC wouldn't be able to figure out which was the one with the ball because him they would hold upside-down until he coughed it up.

But when they were down to their last nickel, the last five minutes of football, the USC Trojans suddenly remembered they were the ones with the muscle. They had the cards, the guns. The other guys were doing it with mirrors.

They launched an infantry attack. They dusted off the old reliable "Student Body Left, Student Body Right" which has been the bread-and-butter staple of USC teams since the football was round. It was as if someone said

Please Turn to Page 14, Col. 1

**GREAT WHITE WAY**—There was a hole cleared (bottom) for Charles White with 1:32 to play in Rose Bowl Tuesday; it was just that the USC running back had to go several feet off the ground (top) to find it. And find it he did as he scored the winning touchdown from one yard in USC's 17-16 victory. White rushed for 71 of the 83 yards in the Trojans' final scoring drive.

Times photos by Andy Hayt and Rick Meyer

**COTTON BOWL:**

| | |
|---|---|
| Houston | 17 |
| Nebraska | 14 |

Story on Page 4

**ORANGE BOWL:**

| | |
|---|---|
| Oklahoma | 24 |
| Florida St. | 7 |

Story on Page 5

### A WORK OF ART

## Schlichter Plays Up to His Billing

By MARK HEISLER
Times Staff Writer

PASADENA—He hit town billed as the quarterback prospect of the new decade, a big-play player and about a dozen other things that effusive. What Arthur Schlichter of Ohio State did was complete 11 of his 21 passes for 297 yards to hold his team in a fantastic Rose Bowl Game all afternoon. . .

. . . And leave town glum, his last four passes having fallen incomplete, the Buckeyes having lost that fantastic game, 17-16, to USC Tuesday afternoon.

"It's just a disappointment for me," Schlichter said a little later. "My long-time goal was to be a national champion, to play on a national champion. We didn't get it this year. For me, it's a disappointment, a great disappointment, probably one of the greatest disappointments of my life."

And Schlichter's accomplishments included:

—On third and four in the first period, he hit Gary Williams on a 53-yard pass play to the USC two, after which the Trojans threw the Buckeyes back on four cracks at the line.

"They were jamming the middle," Schlichter said. "Their guards were pinching and the linebackers were coming in behind them. We just didn't blow them off. We didn't go after 'em.

Please Turn to Page 13, Col. 1

## McDonald and White Take the Winning Drive in Stride

### 'That's Our Style, Our Game,' Says USC Tailback, Who Played Key Role Again Despite Having Flu

By RICHARD HOFFER
Times Staff Writer

PASADENA—As dusk gathered over the Rose Bowl Tuesday, so seemingly did USC's confidence.

As they have in other games this season, the Trojans rallied in the fourth quarter to beat both time and their opponent. The Trojans, who are now 11-0-1 because of this ability to come back in the final minutes, beat Ohio State this time, 17-16.

Down 16-10, USC marched 83 yards in the final five minutes, 17-16, scoring the winning points with less than two minutes left.

"I didn't think anything in particular had to be said," senior quarterback Paul McDonald explained, when asked to describe his motivational techniques. With 5:21 and 83 yards to go, McDonald simply called plays, variations, according to running back Charles White, of "power" and "sweep."

White, the Heisman Trophy winner who ran for 71 of the 83 yards in the drive, including the winning touchdown, likewise downplayed the winning charge. "That's our style, our game," he said, his palms upwards, as if it were simply too ordinary to talk about. "We wear people down. That's what USC does."

White, who finished with a Rose Bowl record 247 yards on a Rose Bowl record 39 carries (6.33 per carry), ripped off runs of 32 and 28 in that drive, hurtling the last one for the score. To White, the runs were scarcely worth discussing. "Paul called the plays and the rest blocked," he said. "They were audibles. Marcus Allen made some blocks and I was off to the races."

When asked what the plays were, White turned secretive, although as a senior, he no longer requires the USC playbook. "Let's just call them 'power' and 'sweep,'" he said.

White's understatement should be understood in light of past accomplishments—1,803 yards this season, coming into the game, and 5,598 regular-season yards, second best in college football history.

But his accomplishments were not overlooked elsewhere. USC quarterback coach Paul Hackett, who accords USC comebacks the respect most onlookers do (105,526 Tuesday), was astonished.

"The guy's got an incredible supporting cast, I know," Hackett said. "But holy smoke. The big man is incredible. He takes over. He's a wild man."

Hackett might have been even more astonished if he had realized White was playing sick. The 185-pound "big man" spent the pregame

Please Turn to Page 14, Col. 2

# Tide Sugarcoats Its Bid, 24-9

By BOB OATES
Times Staff Writer

NEW ORLEANS—Lou Holtz, Arkansas football coach, was saying the other day that the academic standing of his football players should have been questioned when they voted to play Alabama on New Year's Day.

"I really think the NCAA ought to investigate them," he said.

It turns out that Holtz knew something. Attacking Arkansas aggressively, Alabama made a powerful bid for the national football championship Tuesday with an easy 24-9 win in the Sugar Bowl.

"The point spread is enough to win the national championships," Alabama Coach Paul (Bear) Bryant said. "It tickled me to death. One point would have been enough for me. I really believe we have the best team in the country."

Alabama dominated the Razorbacks all three ways—offensively, defensively and kicking, as Holtz acknowledged.

"The thing that makes Alabama what they are is that they can run, pass, defend and kick," the Arkansas coach said. "I voted for them (in the polls) virtually all year and I'm going to do it again. The only thing I can't understand is why our team wanted to play them. Personally, I wanted New Hampshire."

Bryant used nine different running backs to open a 17-3 halftime lead with touchdown marches of 82 and (after a fumble) 22 yards. Then, when the Razorbacks briefly made it a game in the third quarter, 17-9, the Tide rolled 98 yards in the final period to knock them out with an awesome nine-play series.

"I thought we had them until they suddenly went 98," Arkansas' best running back, freshman Gary Anderson, said.

So, after playing a suspect schedule against mostly overmatched teams, Alabama, in its decisive test of the season, proved itself by clobbering a good team—the co-champion of the tough Southwest Conference—to put Bryant on the precipice of his fifth national championship.

Please Turn to Page 10, Col. 1

# Rams Shed the Hollywood Image but It's Not Enough

BUSINESS

CC PART III

MONDAY, JANUARY 21, 1980


**JIM MURRAY**

PASADENA—In a game which the NFL managed to sandwich in between rounds of cocktail parties, press conferences, ballroom dances, parades, card tricks, community sings, and round-the-clock TV hype, the (ho-hum!) Pittsburgh Steelers won another Super Bowl Sunday.

In case you missed it between the exploding palm trees, mirrored cards, silver streamers, snake dancing, and jitterbugging the score was 31-19. This was of only minor interest to the peasantry who came out with their bodies painted black and gold or their head shaved and replaced with paint bearing some football player's number. The parking lots were a sea of catered champagne parties.

It was a moral victory for the Rams. Moral victories you can take to the store and get your nickel back.

The game was quite good considering it was the most minor of the events on the Super Week calendar. The score belongs on the society pages. To preserve the spirit of the occasion, the teams should have played in tuxes or swallow-tail coats and corsages. It's not an athletic event any more, it's a carnival. Mardi Gras with first downs.

The outcome was as predictable as San Diego weather. Pittsburgh Steelers *always* win Super Bowl games. They're getting monotonous. But they must have thought somebody else showed up in Ram uniforms. These were no Hollywood sissies, no college of profiles, no rhinestone cowboys, no Sunset-and-Vine lilacs waiting for their big break in pictures, no guys bucking for a screen test. The Rams didn't show up with mirrors or makeup men, they were scratching, scrambling, stubborn, socking team of alley fighters, swarmers spoiling for a scrap.

They came into the game with a rookie at quarterback, their best player playing on a broken leg and a 9-7 record and a team that scored only 323 points and gave up 309. They shouldn't even have been able to get tickets. The first 50-0 game in Super Bowl history was freely predicted, indeed, expected.

Pittsburgh is such a tough town Bugs Baer once said even the canaries sing bass there. It's a harsh slag heap of a city with sausage and beer on its chin and our options are the coal mine or the steel mill, you wear a hard hat and a lunchpail and leave the change on the bar till you're through drinking and nobody raised on orange juice or under palm trees are supposed to be able to knock heads with you. They get guys out of Penn State who have had to shovel snow—or coal—to live to knock you down, they get even their quarterbacks out of little canebrake schools where the student body didn't start to wear shoes till a few years before they enrolled.

You didn't give the Rams much chance against these cavemen, guys who call the wife "the old lady" and have American flags and "Dora" tattooed on their arms. It's a town with hair on its chest and a team to match the Rams' best chance seemed to be a bus wreck on the Pasadena Freeway.

**TOWER OF POWER**—Pittsburgh's receiving corps—Lynn Swann, Bennie Cunningham and John Stallworth (from top to bottom)—is a key reason the Steelers have won four Super Bowl championships. Swann, signaling his team is No. 1, is hoisted in the air by Cunningham following 46-yard touchdown reception in the third quarter of the Steelers' 31-19 victory over the Rams Sunday.

Associated Press photo

# Year of the Ram Belongs to Steelers

## They Overtake L.A. in Fourth Quarter, 31-19

PASADENA (UPI)—The Pittsburgh Steelers, sparked by a 73-yard touchdown pass play, Terry Bradshaw to John Stallworth,and a game-saving interception by Jack Lambert, surged to their fourth NFL title in the last six years Sunday when they rallied for a 31-19 victory over the dogged Los Angeles Rams in Super Bowl XIV.

The unprecedented fourth Super Bowl victory did not come easily as the lead changed hands six times before Bradshaw finally put the heavily favored Steelers ahead to stay with 12:04 left on the spectacular bomb to Stallworth.

Trailing 19-17, the Steelers were bogged down with a third-and-eight at their 27. But Bradshaw, who had his difficulties with three interceptions, calmly stepped back and hit Stallworth in full stride at the Rams' 30. The All-Pro wide receiver easily outraced the opposition to the end zone.

The scoring pass was Bradshaw's second of the game and ninth in his Super Bowl career, breaking the record held by Dallas' Roger Staubach. Stallworth also set a record with his third lifetime Super Bowl scoring reception.

Bradshaw, who hit 14 of 21 passes for 309 yards, was named the game's Most Valuable Player. It was the second time he has won the award, tying the honor held by Green Bay's Bart Starr in the first two Super Bowls.

Los Angeles, an 11-point underdog, refused to give in and with young Vince Ferragamo guiding them, moved to a first-and-10 at the Steelers' 32. But Ferragamo tested the Pittsburgh secondary once too often and Lambert, the Steelers' All-Pro middle linebacker, ended the Rams' dream of winning a Super Bowl in their first appearance in the NFL title game by picking off Ferragamo's pass over the middle and returning it 16 yards to the Steelers' 30.

Bradshaw applied the crushing blow when he threw a 45-yard pass to Stallworth to the Los Angeles 22, setting up Franco Harris' second touchdown of the game—a one-yard burst off left tackle. Harris' touchdown dive came with 1:49 remaining after a pass interference penalty against Rams cornerback Pat Thomas.

The Steelers extended the AFC's domination over NFC rivals in the Super Bowl with the 10th victory for the conference in the 14 games since the AFL and the NFL merged. The Steelers won all three of their previous Super Bowls, beating Dallas twice and Minnesota once. A Super Bowl record crowd of 103,985 watched Pittsburgh clinch its fourth title.

Pittsburgh, which trailed 13-10 at halftime, roared into the lead on its first possession of the second half when Larry Anderson, who turned in a record kickoff-returning perfor-

Please Turn to Page 7, Col. 5

**HE'S UP FOR IT**—Pittsburgh's John Stallworth goes high into the air as he catches a Terry Bradshaw pass in the second quarter despite Rod Perry's defensive efforts. Rams' Nolan Cromwell offers a helping hand. The reception was good for three yards and gave the Steelers the ball on the one. From there. Franco Harris scored a touchdown. The Steelers won, 31-19

Times photo by Ben Olender

# 'THEY DIDN'T OUTPLAY US AT ALL'

## Malavasi Looks Ahead to Next Year, Says Lucky Plays Beat Rams

From Times Wire Services

PASADENA—The Rams, bitter and disappointed, spoke in hushed tones of "lucky plays" and of next season.

The Rams, 11-point underdogs who were knocked out of the NFC playoffs the past six years, made their Super Bowl debut Sunday and came away 31-19 losers to the Pittsburgh Steelers.

"They didn't outplay us at all," said Coach Ray Malavasi. "They got a couple of lucky plays on us and that pretty much did it. They made a couple of big plays and we didn't.

"We didn't get it this time, but by God we'll get another shot at it. Pittsburgh doesn't try to surprise anyone. They executed and they won."

Los Angeles defensive end Fred Dryer agreed with most of the players that Pittsburgh quarterback Terry Bradshaw's 73-yard touchdown pass to John Stallworth midway through the final quarter was the clincher. That score gave the Steelers a 24-19 lead.

"Their pass offense is very experienced and that helped them tremendously," Dryer said. "That's what makes them different from us and Dallas. They have the ability to go real long any time.

"We knew we'd be somewhat vulnerable on the ground, but we knew they couldn't beat us on the ground. I think Bradshaw knew that also. The game's over. I had a good time."

Offensive tackle Doug France, showing more disappointment than any other player on the Rams, said it was hard to think about next year.

"We played a damn good game," said France. "We gave them a long pass and we gave them an interception. But we proved we're one hell of a team.

"As Houston said earlier, we knocked on the door and next year we're gonna knock the damn thing down."

Quarterback Vince Ferragamo, who completed 15 of 25 passes for 212 yards, was intercepted late in the game by linebacker Jack Lambert, killing a drive that could have lifted the Rams back into the lead. But Ferragamo, at 25 the second-youngest quarterback to ever start a Super Bowl, said it wasn't a bad throw, just a good play on Lambert's part.

"The offense played well and the defense played well," Ferragamo said. "We played good enough football to win. We all played well. It's too bad we couldn't win.

"On the interception, (Billy) Waddy went deep and Lambert made a deep drop into the zone. He made a good interception. I probably should have gone deep into the end zone with it."

Malavasi said his team's defense

Please Turn to Page 7, Col. 1

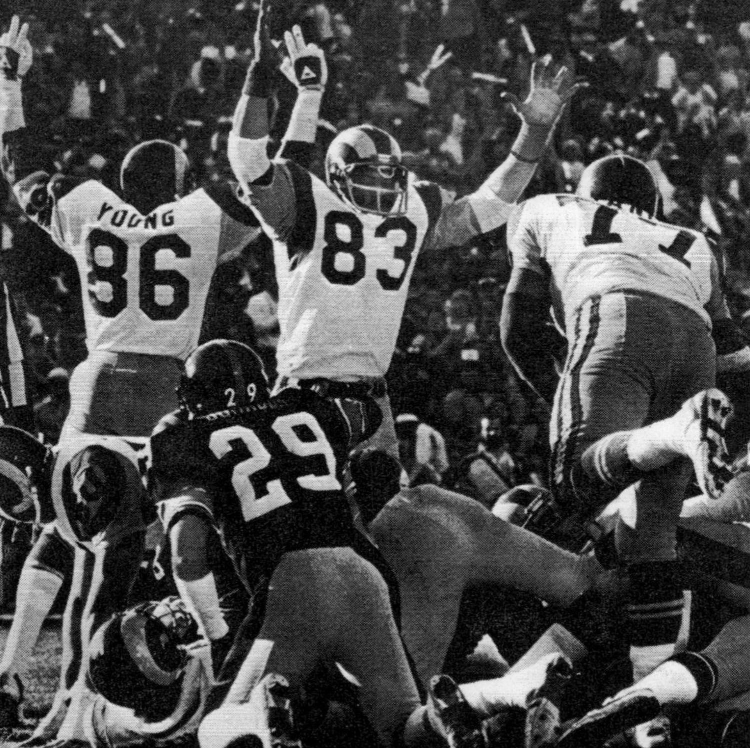


**NO DOUBT ABOUT IT**—Charle Young (86) and Terry Nelson (83) of the Rams signal touchdown after Cullen Bryant's one-yard scoring run in first quarter of Super Bowl in Pasadena.

Times photo by George Rose

# AMERICANS PUT SOVIETS ON ICE, 4-3

## U.S. Can Take the Gold by Beating Finland Sunday

Los Angeles Times
Sports
BUSINESS
CC PART III †
SATURDAY, FEBRUARY 23, 1980

By TED GREEN
Times Staff Writer

LAKE PLACID, N.Y.—There was cheering in the press box and dancing in the streets. This wasn't just a hockey game, it was a happening. And what happened had to be seen to be believed.

The United States hockey team's college kids and minor-league rejects played the game of their young lives and defeated the Soviet Union, 4-3, in the Winter Olympics' medal round late Friday afternoon.

Now these American kids, having beaten the very best hockey team in the world, a team that had not lost an Olympic game in 12 years, can win the gold medal by also beating Finland in their final match Sunday morning.

Finland tied Sweden, 3-3, in the other semifinal game, so a win Sunday guarantees the gold for the Americans. The Soviets and Swedes, who meet in Sunday's other game, also can win the gold, based on medal-round standings and, in case of ties in them, goal differential. The U.S. leads the standings with three points, to two each for the USSR and Sweden and one for Finland.

But this much is all but certain: The Americans will leave with more than their cowboy hats and Olympic pins. They're probably going to leave with a medal.

And none of those kids will soon forget the night they virtually clinched it, because they did it in a wildly emotional game that ended with the players hugging and throwing sticks in the air while the Soviets stood clustered at center ice, staring impassively at this incredible scene. Some of the same fans who had thrown flowers onto the ice, to salute figure skaters the night before, this time threw American flags.

This would have been *The Game* at the Games, regardless of politics, because the Soviets, who have hockey down to a science, have won every Olympic gold medal in the sport since 1960. And now an unlikely bunch of college kids—who lost to this same Soviet team, 10-3, in a tuneup game two weeks ago—was trying to take it away from them. The Americans were Rocky to Russia's Apollo Creed.

President Carter's call for a U.S. boycott of the 1980 Summer Olympics in Moscow because of Soviet military intervention in Afghanistan only added further political overtones, not that they are ever needed when East meets West in sports.

This combination of Cinderella

Please Turn to Page 7, Col. 1

FIRST, BUT NOT LAST—The first U.S. goal in the Americans' 4-3 upset victory against the Soviet Union in Olympic hockey brings cheers and flag waving from the crowd and a swarm of teammates around the scorer, Bill Schneider, at Lake Placid Friday.
Associated Press photo

# Phil Mahre Lights Up Silver Medal Screen

## Stenmark Changes Script to Win Gold but American Co-Stars, Takes Second

By BOB LOCHNER, Times Staff Writer

LAKE PLACID, N.Y.—"OK, places everyone. Now, Phil, you gotta make this look convincing, because it's basically a corny script.

"See, you've just skied the fastest time in the first run. An American man has never won a gold medal in an Alpine event at the Winter Olympics. Your three teammates have wiped out, and you're all the United States has left. But you're first—they gotta catch you in the second run.

"Forget those guys in second and third. The big stud is Stenmark, the Super Swede. He's only .58 of a second back, and that's where he likes to be. He won the giant slalom gold medal a couple of days ago just that way—coming from behind in the second run.

"No question, you're hearing footsteps, like Lynn Swann with George Atkinson bearing down from behind. But the crowd is cheering. You're on your home turf at Whiteface Mountain. It's the Olympic Games and this is America's moment. OK, roll it . . ."

Friday, the script was not "Downhill Racer," and the star wasn't Robert Redford. It was the real Olympic men's slalom, and the central character was Phil Mahre of White Pass, Wash. Unfortunately for the U.S., the ending of this real-life melodrama didn't turn out quite as well as "Downhill Racer," either.

But let's pick up the action as the second run began on the steep 60-gate course. It had begun to snow lightly, but visibility was not a problem.

Ingemar Stenmark, three-time winner of the World Cup, started second and twisted rhythmically down the course in a manner that he later said "was not perfect. I made no mistakes, but I could have been faster." His time was 50.37 seconds, for a total of 1:44.26.

Two racers later, Mahre moved into the starting shack, awaiting the countdown for the run that could make American Olympic skiing history. The noise began to build as the thousands of spectators alongside the course cheered. Four Alpine races had been held in these XIII Winter Games and the medal total for the U.S. was zero. The Europeans were beginning to whisper and point, then break into laughter.

Mahre later described what followed: "As I was waiting to start my second run, I heard a time being announced, but I really didn't know if it was Stenmark's, and it was too early

Please Turn to Page 8, Col. 1

# Decker Sets 880 Mark of 1:59.7; Bayi Wins Mile

By MAL FLORENCE
Times Staff Writer

SAN DIEGO—Mary Decker, Mary Decker. It isn't a soap opera spoof, but merely the crowd at Friday night's Jack-in-the-Box meet cheering the outstanding runner, who set her fourth world record this year.

Decker, setting her own pace, broke the women's record for the 880, timing 1:59.7 and came within four-tenths of a second of tying the world record at 800 meters.

The 21-year-old runner from Orange, now living in Eugene, Ore., wasn't the only record breaker at the San Diego Sports Arena.

Larry Myricks improved on his own long jump record by a quarter of an inch with a jump of 27-6 and Mike Boit of Kenya tied the world 880-yard record by timing 1:47.9.

Moreover, Filbert Bayi held off Eamonn Coghlan and John Walker in a strategic mile, clocking 3:55.5 as the winner. And Kenya's Henry Rono ran the second fastest indoor mile of all time—8:15.9.

It was probably the showcase meet of the indoor season and a crowd of 12,106 seemed to enjoy every minute of it.

Decker had to be her own rabbit

Please Turn to Page 5, Col. 1

***U.S. Jumps to 2-0 Lead in Davis Cup***

Story on Page 2

# Watson's Edge: 20 Years and 1 Stroke on January

By MIKE LITTWIN
Times Staff Writer

Tom Watson, who finally and reluctantly admits he is the best player in golf, mused Friday about the time he might not be. Not that he was in any hurry.

"The day will come," he said, half seriously. "Maybe in about 20 years."

Watson is 30, in his prime. In 20 years, he'll be middle-aged, occassionally short of breath, not quite as long off the tee, maybe a bit shaky on the green. He'll also be the same age Don January is now.

After 36 holes of the Glen Campbell Los Angeles Open, Watson is leading the tournament. If that surprises you, you haven't been paying attention. Maybe you were expecting Ben Hogan.

Watson shot a 66, five-under-par, for a two-round total of 135, one stroke better than a group of three.

Among that trio is January.

And January, who took 67 strokes Friday, had some good news for Watson, saying: "I shot about the same I did 20 years ago. No worse, no better."

January has stopped the clock. He's not sure how he does it, or why he seems to have been exempted from suffering the ravages of time. He plays 20 or 25 times a year, wins his share of money, and now and again contends for a title.

Tied with him for second are former U.S. Amateur champion Bill Sander (who wasn't born when January joined the PGA tour in 1956) and Bob Gilder (who was five). Sander shot a 65 and Gilder a 66.

January would have had a 66 of his own but he bogeyed his last hole of the day, three-putting from 35 feet. That did nothing to dampen his spir-

Please Turn to Page 9, Col. 1

# LAKERS WALLOP NETS, 132-110, CATCH SONICS

By SCOTT OSTLER
Times Staff Writer

INGLEWOOD—Laker owner Jerry Buss' next project should be to rent a bulldozer and gouge out a moat around the Forum, add a drawbridge and let the next storm fill up the moat. It would be the perfect touch for the Fabulous Fortress—or Forum—where the Lakers have become, for the last couple months at least, unbeatable.

Friday night the Lakers bludgeoned another opponent, this time the New Jersey Nets, by a score of 132-110. It was their 16th straight win at home, their fifth win overall and 10th win in the last 12 games.

The Lakers are now 28-3 at home and in their 16-game win streak they have outscored their opponents by an

Please Turn to Page 5, Col. 1

# Good Guys Win and Cheering's OK in Pressbox

By BILL SHIRLEY
Times Sports Editor

LAKE PLACID, N.Y.—It was just a game. Yes, and the Bolshoi is just a ballet and Horowitz is just a piano player.

It was the West vs. East, Capitalism vs. Communism, the good guys against the bad guys. The final score was USA 4, USSR 3. The good guys won.

What set this victory apart, however, was not politics but the sport. This was *hockey*. The Soviets usually play it like they invented it, when in fact they played their first international match in 1954. But they beat the National Hockey League, don't they? They all skate like Eric Heiden and move the puck around the way the Globetrotters pass a basketball.

To give you an idea how good the Soviets usually are, they won the Olympic hockey gold the first time they played, in 1956. In the next five Olympics, they won four more gold medals. And, of course, you remember who won the other one: The U.S. at Squaw Valley, Calif., in 1960. And the Americans set it up with that extraordinary win over the Soviets. It was like the Soviets beating the Yankees in baseball.

Once the USSR learned to play the game, they won 16 world champion-

Please Turn to Page 9, Col. 3

FABULOUS PHIL—Phil Mahre of White Pass, Wash., zips by a flag on the way to the silver medal in men's slalom at the Olympics. Sweden's Ingemar Stenmark won the gold medal.
Associated Press photo

# Heiden Corners the Olympic Gold Market With Fifth

## Speed Skater Carves Himself a Place Among All-Time Olympians With 10,000 Win

Los Angeles Times
Sports
CC PART III †
SUNDAY, FEBRUARY 24, 1980

By TED GREEN
Times Staff Writer

LAKE PLACID, N.Y.—With this town still abuzz over the United States hockey team, which goes for a gold medal today after upsetting the Soviet Union, Eric Heiden quietly and methodically went about the business of becoming an Olympian for all times.

Heiden won the 10,000-meter race Saturday morning to complete an unprecedented and heretofore unthinkable sweep of men's speed skating events at the 13th Winter Olympics.

Five Races, ranging in distance from an outright sprint (500 meters) to Saturday's mini-marathon of 6.25 miles, five Olympic records, and one world record, which he broke Saturday by more than six seconds. And five gold medals, the only five the United States has so far won as this quadrennial festival closes today.

The wonderskater from Wisconsin, skating in the second pair, clocked 14:28.13 at the Main Street oval, winning the toughest race with almost scandalous ease. The silver medalist, the Olympic champion at 10,000 meters in 1976, Piet Kleine of the Netherlands, finished nearly eight seconds behind (14:36.03). Tom Erik Oxholm of Norway won the bronze at 14:36.60. Dr. Mike Woods of the U.S. was fourth, almost three seconds away from a medal.

Heiden, far and away the individual star of these Games, surpassed the four speed skating gold medals won by the Soviet Union's Lydia Skoblikova, a Siberian schoolteacher who swept the women's races in 1964. Now Eric Heiden, 21, of the skating Heidens from Madison, Wis., stands alone as the winningest Winter Olympian since these Games began in 1924.

It is not lost on the people who report these things that Heiden won more gold medals than all but two—the Soviet Union and East Germany—of the 37 nations represented here. You've heard of the tiny country of Liechtenstein, which produces medal-winning skiers. Now there's Heidenstein, a country unto himself.

Nor does it seem any less remarkable that this living advertisement for Middle America won five golds in eight days after it took generations of American speed skaters 52 years to win 11.

Yet here's the rub: this son of an orthopedic surgeon, a kid who trained maniacally to stand out in his odd, obscure sport, apparently couldn't care less about his golden haul. Oh, he's happy to have won and happier still that he lived up to his own expectations. But that, he said, is as far as it goes.

"The medals may sit in my mom's drawer and collect dust," Heiden said. "After today, I may not see them for a long time.

"The gold medals just don't mean that much to me. Skating your best, that means something. What can you

Please Turn to Page 8, Col. 1

**JIM MURRAY**

## Making of a Man

*"Tom appeared on the sidewalk with a bucket of whitewash and a longhandled brush. He surveyed the fence and all the gladness left him and a deep melancholy settled on his spirit. Life to him seemed hollow and existence but a burden. Work consisted of what a body is obliged to do. Play is what a body is not obliged to do."*

—The Adventures of Tom Sawyer

*"I'm in the gunsights now. It's not a game, it's a responsibility. It means no more breakfasts alone. It means ringing phones and you're a louse if you have to say 'No.'"*

—The Adventures of Tom Watson

**Fortunately** for Mark Twain, Tom Sawyer is always going to be 15 years old and whitewashing that fence. Huck Finn is always going to be barefoot and fishing.

Imagine what a sad sight it would be to see Tom Sawyer working in a bank, wearing a tie and carrying a briefcase. Like to think of Huckleberry Finn in an office with shoes on?

Their fellow Missourian was not so lucky. Ten years ago, when young Tom Watson came on the golf tour with his freckled face and shock of red hair, he looked like something that stepped right out of the imagination of Samuel Clemens. Or, arrived by raft with a runaway slave. You kept looking around for Becky Thatcher. He looked as if he had just landed a string of catfish. If he had a wood in his hands it should have a string and a hook on it. You looked at him and you could hear the steamboat whistles.

★

**Alas, he is now** no longer young Tom Watson, he's Thomas Watson, Esq. He's not a country kid from the banks of the Mississippi, he's a corporation, earnings last year $462,636 from the golf division alone, probably double that from all sources.

He's the most improbable-looking captain of industry you'll ever see. He looks like he's playing hooky. Not too long ago, if you saw him on the street you would have bought him a balloon and told him not to cry, that you'd find his folks for him.

The Watsons go back as far in Missouri lore as Twain or the James boys. Horse traders, likely, maybe river men, they were a fearless lot. Great grandfather Isaac Newton Watson broke up the Prendergast machine in Kansas City in the '30s when that was about as easy—or as advisable—as breaking up a Mafia picnic.

"I. N.," as he preferred to be called, put FBI men on his payroll (at $50 a week) and brought so many truckloads of affidavits and depositions to court that old Tom Prendergast himself went to jail. If you think that wasn't brave, you don't know Kansas City. While the rest of law enforcement concentrated on Bonnie & Clyde, I. N. went after the real public enemies.

★

**That's probably why** Tom Watson never saw anything to be particularly afraid of in a 10-foot putt or a 3-wood over water. When you come from a long line of people who have to be careful starting their cars or standing in a lighted window at night, what's a double bogey?

Competitors say the thing which distinguishes a Watson round of golf is his inability to sulk over a bad shot, a bad hole or a bad round. He plays an attacking game and, like a fighter who comes on, he expects to take some punishment. I don't know whether you know it or not but golfers, as a class, tend to what

Please Turn to Page 17, Col. 1

**PROBLEMS WITH FORM**—Jan Holmlund of Sweden loses control midway through his jump in the 90-meter competition Saturday in Winter Olympics. Holmlund, 22, landed 75 meters below the ramp and hit going about 60 m.p.h. He was hospitalized with a broken left clavicle.

OLYMPIC ROUNDUP ON PAGE 9

Associated Press photo

# Poetzch Edges Linda but It Doesn't Figure

## East German 3rd in Free Skating, 4th in Short Program Yet Beats Fratianne

By TED GREEN
Times Staff Writer

LAKE PLACID, N.Y.—Anett Poetzch of East Germany won the gold medal, Linda Fratianne of the United States won the silver and the competition confirmed, for the umpteenth time, this much about their subjective, political sport! You just can't figure it.

Poetzch, Fratianne's longtime rival, finished third in Saturday night's free-skating program, the highlight of the women's singles in figure skating. The East German girl also finished fourth earlier in the week in the short program. But Poetzch built a big enough lead in the compulsory figures, which open the competition, that Fratianne couldn't quite catch her.

So Poetzch, even though she was outskated in two categories that count 70% in the scoring—free skating is 50% and short program 20%—won anyway because the judges liked her figures better. The compulsory (or school) figures count 30%.

If all this seems confusing, don't feel bad. Figure skating is a sport where the judges are just about the only people in the arena who allegedly know what they're seeing. Everyone else only *thinks* they know.

Case in point Saturday night: Poetzch (pronounced Putch) wasn't much. She seemed wooden and skated a conservative program with one double jump after another. She had more doubles than Rod Carew . . . or Dean Martin.

Fratianne, on the other hand, hit all four triple jumps she tried. And though she failed to project—that is, create the illusion of intimacy between skater and audience—her lone weakness, lack of a jazzy personality on the ice, did not detract too much from her performance.

Dagmar Lurz, meanwhile, may as well have been Dagwood Bumstead, the way she skated. But she got high enough marks to hold onto third place.

In the meantime, all three medal winners were upstaged by Denise Biellmann, a 17-year-old Swede. She skated such an exciting program as the last performer of the evening that she jumped from eighth to fourth place and won a prolonged standing ovation from the more than 10,000 fans who packed the new Olympic field house.

Please Turn to Page 8, Col. 3

# Hanni Wenzel Gives Tiny Liechtenstein Second Gold

By BOB LOCHNER
Times Staff Writer

LAKE PLACID, N.Y.—First, it should be reported that the Carter Administration has denied it is considering statehood for Liechtenstein. Too bad. As the 13th Olympic Winter Games draw to a close, it appears that might be the only way to make the U.S. ski team truly competitive with the Alpine powers of Europe.

The little principality gained its fourth Olympic medal Saturday, a gold in the slalom by Hanni Wenzel, who thereby equaled West German Rosi Mittermaier's two gold-one silver performance at Innsbruck in 1976.

And the best the United States could do in the final race on Whiteface Mountain was an eighth place by Christin Cooper of Sun Valley, Ida. The team's leader, Cindy Nelson, finished 11th—just two days after she'd chewed out a radio reporter who had dared ask, "Why, except for a few isolated exceptions, isn't the U.S. more competitive."

On that ocassion, Nelson, 24 and considering retirement, said, "I totally disagree with you. I've been competitve. I won the bronze medal in the downhill in '76. This is a young team; it's tough for them competing in Europe and living out of a suitcase six months a year. You've got to have faith. Give them a chance and some more experience and with a couple of more years of hard work, they should be there."

As she spoke, Nelson's voice rose and she became emotional. A few minutes later, she reopened the argument but after a few words said, "Forget it," and walked away, crying.

The "isolated exception" here was Phil Mahre's silver medal (behind Sweden's Ingemar Stenmark) in the men's slalom, and it was a stirring example of courage and skiing ability. But Mahre, too, is thinking about quitting at the advanced age of 22, and he mentioned one reason for U.S. ineffectiveness in ski racing when he said, "I've lost a lot of interest in skiing over the last two years . . . I guess what it boils down to is there are a lot of other things in life. That's how it is in America."

Nelson, who had cheered up Saturday as a result of acquiring the silver medal awarded by the International Ski Federation for the second-best combined finishes in three races, touched upon another reason when she said, "There are more opportuni-

Please Turn to Page 10, Col. 1

# Gilder Goes One-Up on Watson

By SHAV GLICK
Times Staff Writer

Maybe there's something to feeling lousy when you play golf. If you're sick enough, they say, it slows down your backswing.

Bob Gilder, a successful but not spectacular professional from Corvallis, Ore., could hardly have more things wrong with him this week. He spent most of his vaction between the 1979 and 1980 seasons arguing with the Internal Revenue Service. When he resumed the tour he said he didn't feel like playing, he felt like he never got refreshed.

When he stayed in Hawaii last week trying to get over a nagging cold he ended up taking a boat trip and getting violently seasick. He came to the Riviera Country Club this week feeling so sluggish and tired that he never hit a practice ball to get ready for the Glen Campbell Los Angeles Open.

So what's he doing now? He's leading the $250,000 tournament after 54 holes with three subpar rounds of 70-66-68 for a nine-under-par 204—one shot ahead of everyone's favorite, Tom Watson.

**L.A. Open Leaders**

| | |
|---|---|
| **204** | |
| Bob Gilder | 70-66-68 |
| **205** | |
| Tom Watson | 69-66-70 |
| **206** | |
| Bill Sander | 71-65-70 |
| Don January | 69-67-70 |
| **209** | |
| Hale Irwin | 73-68-68 |

Gilder shot his way around the 7,029-yard Riviera course Saturday without putting a 5 on his scorecard. He birdied all three par-5 holes and played the other 15 holes in par.

"I'm pretty proud of that," he said, referring to the absence of 5s. "I don't know if I ever did that before."

Watson, who started Saturday's third round one shot ahead of Gilder, 50-year-old Don January and young Bill Sander, led most of the day until he bogeyed the last hole for a 70 to leave Gilder alone at the top. January and Sander had matching 70s to share the 206 third position. After the top four it was a drop back to 209 and U.S. Open champion Hale Irwin.

Ironically, it was Watson who took Gilder and his wife, Peggy, on the deep sea fishing trip off the big island of Hawaii last week.

Please Turn to Page 12, Col. 1

# Tired Flyers Take It Easy in 5-1 Victory Over Kings

By ALAN GREENBERG
Times Staff Writer

INGLEWOOD—The Kings didn't have to contend with the Spectrum jinx Saturday night. They had only to contend with the Philadelphia Flyers. The tired Philadelphia Flyers.

It didn't matter. After a scoreless first period, the Flyers manhandled the Kings and bulled their way to an easy 5-1 win at the Forum. Winger Mike Murphy scored the Kings' only goal on a power play, averting a shutout at 13:54 of the final period.

The Kings have not beaten the Flyers since Oct. 10, 1975.

The Flyers broke the game open in the second period with three goals to take a 3-0 lead. Their attack, so quiet in the first period, accounted for 15 shots.

Philadelphia took a 1-0 lead on Ken Linseman's 15th goal of the season with 6:20 elapsed in the period. Linseman, breaking from the blue line and outskating defenseman Brad Selwood, shot the puck between goalie Mario Lessard's legs to make it 1-0.

The highlight of the period for the Kings came when the capacity crowd of 16,005 applauded them wildly for successfully killing four minutes with Randy Holt in the penalty box for slashing and tripping.

But the Flyers scored again with 11:48 elapsed when Linseman streaked down the right side and passed to Brian Propp, who ended up tangled in the goal with Lessard. In the confusion, the puck was pushed out to the left point, where Jimmy Watson slapped it in against Lessard, who hadn't had time to pick up his stick (it was at his feet) and whose only defensive move was a half-hearted hip shake as the shot zoomed by to make it 2-0.

Winger Al Hill scored at 17:43 of the period to make it 3-0. The Philadelphia second-period scoring ended a shutout streak by Kings goalies of 117:31. Until Linseman's goal, the last opponent goal had been Reed Larson's at 8:49 of the second period Monday night at Detroit.

Please Turn to Page 4, Col. 1

# SMILING WITH A STIFF UPPER LIP

## *'Well, It Happens and That's All There Is to It,' Is the Soviet Reaction to Their Hockey Team's Embarrassing 4-3 Loss to Young Americans*

By KEVIN KLOSE
The Washington Post

MOSCOW—"Our front line is more than a hundred years old, so what can we expect?" the Soviet said, a smile floating uncertainly on his unhappy face.

"Yours are so young, I congratulate you!" said another.

"Well, it happens and that's all there is to it."

Embarrassment, sportsmanlike stiff upper lips and fatalism—all were found here Saturday as the Soviets dealt with the surprising 4-3 loss of their powerful veteran Olympic hockey team to the Americans Friday.

This capital of a hockey-mad country virtually shut down at mid-morning Saturday as Moscovites retired to their small flats to watch the taped television broadcast of the crucial game. Many already knew the outcome from the official radio, but probably millions of others hadn't a clue that their "hockeyists" were about to be outhustled by the U.S.

Let it be said that many Soviets were drawn immediately to the young Americans when they first appeared on Soviet television screens more than a week ago as the Games began. "They look like children," one man said with unconcealed awe and possibly delight.

And they had some warning that their own team of veterans, drawn chiefly from officer-players of the Central Army Sports Club in Moscow, were not doing so well. The Soviets came close to losing to the Finns and the Canadians on their way to defeat by the Americans.

The military newspaper Red Star declared going into the match with the United States that "the performance of (our) defensemen is a source of some concern. They make blunders at times in absolutely harmless situations."

But the official Tass news agency in a dispatch Saturday from Lake Placid manfully called the defeat "perhaps the greatest surprise of the Olympics. It is difficult to explain how come the most experienced Soviet players conceded to the team they

Please Turn to Page 9, Col. 1

# THE AMERICAN DREAM TURNS TO GOLD

## U.S. Kids Beat Finland to Win Hockey Title

TO THE VICTORS—After the U.S. won the gold medal in hockey at Lake Placid Sunday, some friends of the players came onto ice to celebrate 4-2 win over Finland, giving goalie Jim Craig, who stopped 21 of 23 shots in game, the American flag he clutches. Associated Press photo

By TED GREEN
Times Staff Writer

LAKE PLACID, N.Y.—The United States hockey team made an American dream come true Sunday by beating Finland, 4-2, and winning the gold medal at the 13th Winter Olympics.

The dream was this: That a bunch of college hockey players in their teens and early 20s, as close to true amateurs as our times permit, could compete against the cream of international hockey and come out on top.

It was a silly, unattainable dream but somehow these confident kids from the East and Midwest gave it life. They never backed down against the older and more experienced players from Europe. They tied the Swedes. They clobbered the Czechs en route to the medals round. And there they beat the Russians, who had not lost an Olympic hockey game in 12 years.

The United States' 4-3 win Friday night over the *really* Big Red Machine, in a game that was more of a national catharsis than an athletic contest, put the Americans in position to win the gold medal outright in the first final-round game Sunday morning. And the kids won it by scoring three goals in the third period for their sixth come-from-behind victory of the seven-game tournament.

And so, on the 13th and last day of an Olympics filled with internal foul-ups, quite possibly the last Olympics of this quadrennial for the U.S. if it boycotts the Summer Games in Moscow, an improbable little hockey team captured a nation's fancy by completing the biggest team upset in Olympic history and one of sports' biggest upsets in years.

Games come, games go, memories fade. But we may remember this one awhile.

"You people watched a group of kids who startled the athletic world," U.S. Coach Herb Brooks said. For once, it wasn't a coach's hyperbole.

The Americans' victory turned this town upside down and gave the U.S. its first and only gold medal *not* won by speed skater Eric Heiden, who won five to emerge as the individual star of these Games. And it proved, among other things, that crazy dreams do come true every 20 years or so.

**'WE AREN'T AWED'**
**Please . . . Nobody Tell the U.S. Hockey Team It Has No Chance**

By TED GREEN, Times Staff Writer

When the United States hockey team opens play at the Wi[torn] Olympics against Sweden on Feb. 12 it will be almos[torn] day that a Nat[torn] Hockey Leag[torn] star team, [torn] be[torn] players [torn] merica, [torn] by [torn]

Prophetic feelings of hockey team appeared in Feb. 2 Times

It was 20 years ago, in 1960, that an older, amateur hockey team from the U.S. upset the Canadians, Russians and Czechs to win the hockey gold medal. That was in Squaw Valley, the last time the Winter Olympics were held in this country. It was also the last time the Soviets, just beginning to master hockey, lost the gold. They won in 1964, 1968, 1972 and 1976, and were odds-on favorites to win here. Then the newest version of the Comeback Kids came along and stunned everyone.

The Soviets, knowing they couldn't win the gold this time if they invaded Sweden, took it out on the Swedes, anyway. The USSR hammered them, 9-2, in Sunday's second game to win the silver medal. Sweden, which tied the U.S. for first place in challenge-round play with a 4-0-1 record, won the bronze. Finland, which tied Sweden, 3-3, in the other medals game Friday night, finished fourth.

Sunday's early game between the U.S. and Finland, a finesse team with superior skaters, was played before a standing-room-only crowd of more than 10,000 at the new Olympic Fieldhouse on Main Street. American flags of all sizes carried in by fans there nearly outnumbered stocking caps. As the clock wound down after the U.S. scored three goals in nine minutes to erase a 2-1 deficit, those flags were waved in all their glory.

But that was nothing compared to the celebration that was about to take place on the ice.

When the final horn sounded, the players who banded together six months ago to begin a tough, 60-game, worldwide schedule mobbed each other, deliriously happy. They tossed their sticks and gloves into the stands, souvenirs for a lucky few. Then about 25 fans, some friends and girlfriends of the players, climbed

Please Turn to Page 6, Col. 1

WINNING SMILES—U.S. hockey players receive congratulations from fans after receiving gold medals in the awards ceremony. Associated Press photo

## Abdul-Jabbar Gets in Late and Just in Time for Lakers

### Despite a Migraine, the Captain Leads L.A. Into First-Place Tie With 112-100 Win Over Rockets

By SCOTT OSTLER
Times Staff Writer

INGLEWOOD—About the time the Lakers were falling nine points behind the Houston Rockets in the first quarter of Sunday's game, Laker center Kareem Abdul-Jabbar was tooling along the freeway in his Mercedes, late for work.

Actually he had called in sick with a severe migraine headache and wasn't expected to show up at the game at all. When he walked into the Forum early in the third quarter, to a standing ovation from the 15,889 fans, the Lakers were ahead by two points.

Kareem proceeded to block five shots in the quarter, presumably telling the Rocket shooters, "Not this afternoon, I have a headache."

With their captain back in action, hitting six of seven shots, the Lakers won going away, 112-100. Jamaal Wilkes, who is on most Laker opponents' all-migraine team, scored 29 points and had seven rebounds.

It was the Lakers' sixth straight win, and 17th in a row at home. And it allowed them to move back into a tie for first place in the Pacific Division with Seattle. The SuperSonics will be at the Forum Tuesday night.

The only negative note for the Lakers was an injury to Magic Johnson, who somehow injured his left eye early in the second half and left the game. He was examined by an ophthalmologist, who diagnosed the injury as an abrasion of the cornea. Magic was wearing an eyepatch when he left the doctor, but is expected to play Tuesday.

Kareem's late entrance was dramatic, but he didn't intend it that way. He's not big on dramatic entrances. He just got to the game as soon as his headache would allow.

"It's a situation where I've worked with these guys, but they're also my friends," Abdul-Jabbar explained quietly. "I knew they needed my help."

Please Turn to Page 10, Col. 2

## Lake Placid Bids Olympics Adieu a Second Time

By BOB LOCHNER
Times Staff Writer

LAKE PLACID, N.Y.—Athletes from 37 nations marched without their flags and joyously embraced each other Sunday as the Olympic flame was extinguished and the Moscow boycott, at least for the moment, was lost in the crowd.

It was the second flameout for the Games in Lake Placid, which also hosted the Winter Olympics in 1932.

With stirring music and flashing skates, with pomp and simple humanity, the 13th Olympic Winter Games officially ended after 13 days of competition that saw East Germany and the Soviet Union virtually tie for the unofficial medals championship.

East German skaters and skiers won 23 medals to 22 for the Soviet athletes, but the latter had the edge on the gold market, 10 to 9. The United States was third with 12 medals, six of them gold.

But this kind of nationalism was not in evidence Sunday night as the

Please Turn to Page 2, Col. 3

## Watson Is Up to Par and Wins

### L.A. Open Is His When January and Gilder Both Bogey Final Hole

By MIKE LITTWIN
Times Staff Writer

Tom Watson, who can win often enough on his own, required assistance Sunday in the Glen Campbell Los Angeles Open. It wasn't Watson alone who vanquished his rivals. Pressure played at least an equal role.

Hubert Green probably summed it up best, once saying of himself: "When it came time to stand up and be counted, I sat down."

In which case, they should have placed chairs at Riviera's 18th hole for Don January and Bob Gilder. Each had only to par the final hole to force a playoff with Watson.

Instead, both settled for bogeys.

And Watson, whose credentials on a golf course assure him entry anywhere, took the back door Sunday and found a $45,000 winner's check awaiting him there.

Watson shot a 71 for a 72-hole total of 276, eight-under par. Gilder, who led after 54 holes, shot a 73 Sunday and January a 71 to finish a stroke back. They each won $22,000.

It was the second win in four starts this year for Watson, who is popularly accepted as the tour's preeminent performer. But it didn't come as easily as it might. He did some backing up himself Sunday, losing what was once a three-stroke lead, and fully expected to have to contend with playoff pressure.

"When I parred 18," said Watson, who was playing a hole ahead of his rivals, "I thought for sure there would be a playoff. Number 18 just wasn't playing that hard."

Not when you could draw back the club, it wasn't.

A golfer playing under pressure is most likely to hit short. Let it be noted that neither January, the wizened veteran, nor Gilder, a one-time winner, reached the par-4 18th in two. Then both chipped well short, January by 20 feet.

January missed his putt first and Gilder, who was eight feet away, also missed.

Watson couldn't hide his smile.

"It looked like everyone tried to play giveaway out there," Watson said. "I'm just glad I was on the right end this time."

In 1976, Watson, who had never won here before, led Hale Irwin by three strokes going into the final

Please Turn to Page 9, Col. 2

### L.A. Open Scores

| | |
|---|---|
| **276—$45,000** | |
| Tom Watson | 69-66-70-71 |
| **277—$22,000** | |
| Bob Gilder | 70-66-68-73 |
| Don January | 69-67-70-71 |
| **280—$12,000** | |
| Don Pooley | 70-69-72-69 |
| **281—$9,500** | |
| Scott Simpson | 72-67-71-71 |
| Mike Reid | 70-72-72-67 |
| **282—$6,292** | |
| George Archer | 74-68-68-72 |
| Hale Irwin | 73-68-68-73 |
| Tom Weiskopf | 67-71-72-72 |
| John Fought | 70-70-70-72 |
| Johnny Miller | 69-71-71-71 |
| Jay Haas | 70-68-72-68 |
| Gil Morgan | 70-70-71-71 |
| Fuzzy Zoeller | 72-69-71-70 |
| Lanny Wadkins | 70-75-68-69 |

SWEET SWINGER—Tom Watson lashes a wood shot during Sunday's final round of L.A. Open at Riviera Country Club. Watson took the $45,000 first prize by one stroke when both Don January and Bob Gilder made bogeys on the final hole of tournament. Times photo by Ben Olender

## THE ATHLETES WON AFTER ALL

### *Wenzel, Heiden, Stenmark and a Bunch of Unknown Kids Turned Discord and Disorder Into Memories, Tears and, Finally, Beauty*

By BILL SHIRLEY, Times Sports Editor

LAKE PLACID, N.Y.—First there was discord and near-ruinous disorder. But then, as is always the case in these Olympian affairs, when the politicians stopped meddling and the civic organizers stopped blundering, young athletes restored order and, yes, beauty to the 13th Olympic Winter Games.

They flew down mountains and skated around rinks at breathtaking speeds. And in the arenas they dazzled us with extraordinary virtuosity and vivacity. They shed tears of frustration and joy and beat their hands in the snow in anger and disgust. There were names we'll remember when Olympic history is recited. Ingemar Stenmark, Eric Heiden, Hanni Wenzel. And some we will not recall, but should, such as the young members of the U.S. hockey team, a bunch of rosy-cheeked kids (average age: 22) who beat the Soviets out of the gold medal and showed us what enthusiasm can do for a sport the National Hockey League still doesn't understand.

There were disappointments, but no tragedies. Canada's daredevil downhill racer, Ken Read, crashed at the top of Whiteface Mountain and a medal was lost when his ski binding opened. He showed no emotion and handled the inevitable interview with aplomb.

And long remembered will be Randy Gardner's exit from the Olympics, sliding embarrassingly across the ice on his burgundy pants after falling for the fourth time while warming up for the pairs free-skating competition he and his partner, Tai Babilonia, were co-favored to win. Gardner's groin-pull injury forced them to withdraw without even competing in the Games that had been their goal for years.

Many Alpine skiers never made it down the mountain. Daniela Zini of Italy didn't in the giant slalom and she fell over into the snow and cried.

Beth Heiden, Eric's sister, cried, too. But her tears came after she had finally won a medal, for third place, in her last speed skating race. She was fighting them back as she told reporters, "This year I felt I was skating for the press. I like to skate for myself, so to hell with you guys." But as she an-

Please Turn to Page 4, Col. 1

*Times Staff Writers Ted Green and Bob Lochner also contributed to this story.*

Los Angeles Times
Sports

CC PART III †

TUESDAY, APRIL 22, 1980

# Did Rosie Run a Fast One—or Pull One?

## Marathon Winner May Not Have Gone the Distance; Rodgers Leaves No Doubt

**By ALAN GREENBERG, Times Staff Writer**

BOSTON—When it was over, the nearly 6,000 runners looked like characters from "Night of The Living Dead." But the women's winner seemed awfully fresh for having just run 26 miles 385 yards in surprisingly fast time.

Was that because she hadn't? Did Rosie Ruiz, 30, who says she fled Castro's Cuba in 1961 for New York City, pull the greatest sting in these parts since the Brink's Robbery? Did she hide among the estimated one million people who lined the route for Monday's 84th Boston Marathon, then slip onto the course undetected somewhere past the 22-mile mark and cross the finish line 147th overall but first among the races's 449 women.

"Yes," some runners and track officials said. Quite possibly, said an infuriated Will Cloney, the Boston Marathon's meet director since 1946.

Definitely not, Ruiz said when questioned nearly an hour after Gov. Edward King presented her with a gold medal. Back in her hotel room, besieged by visits and calls from reporters, she broke into tears but continued to deny any impropriety.

LEGITIMATELY TIRED?—Rosie Ruiz is helped by a policeman after being first woman to finish Monday's Boston Marathon. But there is doubt as to whether the 30-year-old woman ran full distance.
Associated Press photo

The did-she-or-didn't-she fuss over Ruiz thrust her into the spotlight that had been focused on Bill Rodgers, 32, who easily won his third straight Boston Marathon—for a total of four—in 2 hours 12 minutes 11 seconds, a full 2:44 slower than his record time last year. One difference: Monday's relatively warm temperatures, in the 70s, compared to the 40s a year ago.

"She's a definite phony," Fred Lebow said of Ruiz. He is president of the New York Roadrunners Club and meet director of the New York City Marathon, the only one Ruiz had run in before Boston. "She had none of the signs of having run a marathon. There were no salt stains (from excessive sweating) on her face. Her hair wasn't frazzled in the back like the other women's. Her shirt on the sides was completely dry."

"I don't remember seeing her at any time during the race," said 27-year-old Jacqueline Gareau of Montreal, who placed second among the women with a time of 2:34:28.

"Yeah, I was surprised, I was second place going into the hills and they told me I was second when I crossed the finish line," said the third-place finisher, local favorite Patti Lyons, 25, of suburban Quincy.

Malcolm Robinson, the editor of the New York Running News, charted

**Please Turn to Page 6, Col. 1**

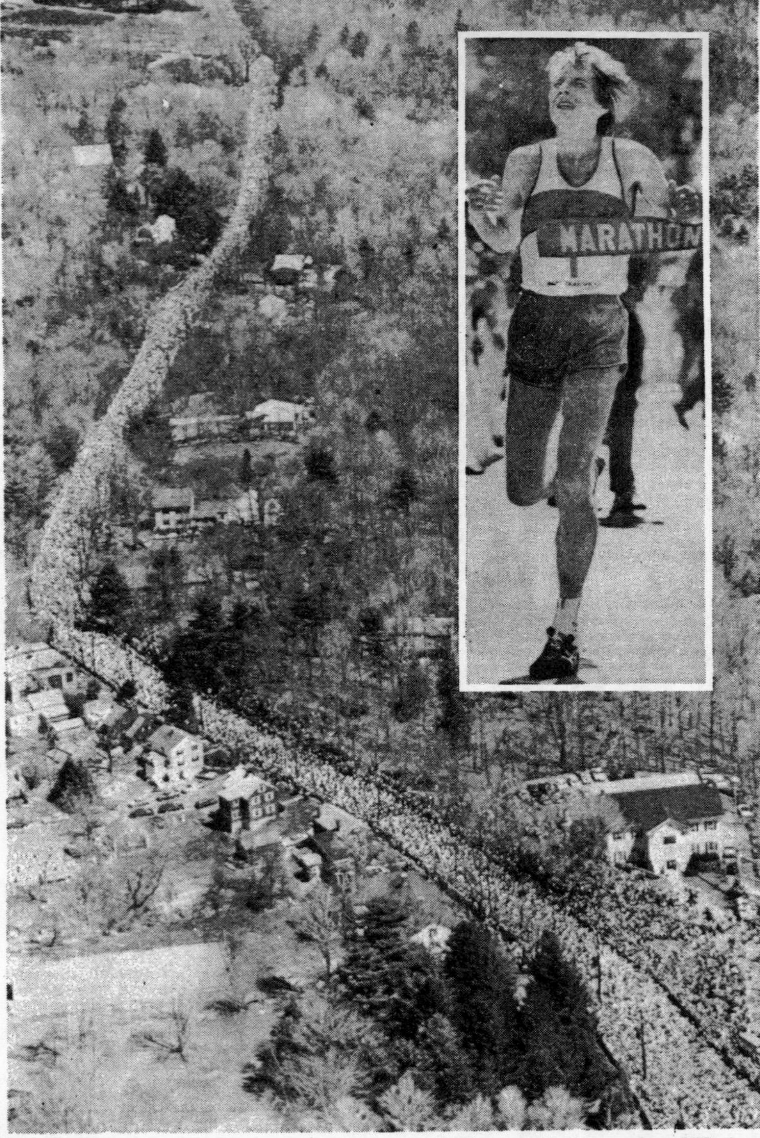


GROUP PHOTO—The nearly 6,000 runners in Monday's Boston Marathon look like ants as the race begins in Hopkinton, Mass. Bill Rodgers (inset) ran 2:12:11 to win for the fourth time.
Associated Press photo

***JIM MURRAY***

# A Car to Remember

**I guess the United States** of America has turned out more motor cars than anyone else on earth, most of them highly forgettable hunks of chrome and steel about as stylish as a housecoat on a fat lady, about as dashing as a plow. Detroit never could get the hang of class and fashion, and kept turning out things like the 1953 DeSoto and some models that seemed to be trying to duplicate the camel.

The most obscene efforts were those monsters of the 1950s with the huge fins on the back. They were positively hideous, and seemed often to be driven by little old ladies in blue hair who had about as much chance of parking them as they had of docking the Berengaria.

Detroit thought they were just swell, although connoisseurs of the automobile as an art form covered their eyes and acted as if someone had just brought home from an auction a statue with a clock in its belly.

★

**One trouble was,** Detroit changed the styling a little every year, not so much to make it better as to make it different. Sometimes, the effect was like ketchup on ice cream, but the American consumer wanted everybody to know his, by God, car was a 1937, not a 1934. This conspicuous consumption did in the Packard, a graceful, partly hand-tooled car which had hit upon a design uniquely its own. Trouble was, you couldn't tell a 1930 Packard from a 1935 except by the serial number. So, people bought lesser cars and Packard drifted out of the business.

Some car companies even thought things like safety and engineering and comfort sold cars—but they soon got disbused. Another trouble was, the carmakers hired European carriage builders in the early days, and these guys thought cars were just going to be automotive surreys with a fringe on top, or stagecoaches with horns. They seemed to think they should design them so horses could pull them when the oil ran out.

The auto show was the big social event of the year when you were a kid in those depression-locked years of the 30s, and I'll never forget the time the one and only truly classic American car made its appearance. I believe it was 1936 and the car was the Cord, the brainchild of a flamboyant huckster from the Middle West, Errett Lobban Cord, the head of the then-Auburn Motorcar Co.

★

**It was a gorgeous thing,** the Cord, the nearest thing to a yacht you would find in that roomful of barges. It had pipes coming out from the sides, and it made the throaty purring sound of a mighty cat when its instant ignition was turned on. The car was made with loving care, only a couple of thousand were ever turned out, and, out in Hollywood, every cowboy star or actress married to royalty promptly turned in their Duesenbergs (which Cord also made) for the new Cord cars. It was only fitting. They were not made to carry eggs to the market, they were sleek racing machines, and deserving of the finest ownership.

E. L. Cord didn't put his masterpiece in a showroom with a ribbon around it, he put it on a racetrack in Atlantic City where it drove a 24-hour endurance test at an average speed of 103 mph. Cord's Cord was not just another pretty grille, it was a top performer.

This weekend, at Riverside, another Cord will be on the track—not the car, the scion. Chris Cord is the grandson of the late

**Please Turn to Page 10, Col. 1**

# A Couple of Bolts Out of Blue

## Smith and Cey Hammer Giants' Ace Early; Dodgers Win, 4-3

**By MIKE LITTWIN**
Times Staff Writer

Reggie Smith, at age 35, has never made it to recognized superstar status, for too many reasons to list here. But Smith can do what so-called superstars are said to do—he can carry a team.

He carried one Monday night. He hit a two-run homer in the first to get the Dodgers going and then made the defensive play of the game in the eighth to keep them going.

And so the Dodgers, just as they did so often last year, beat the rival San Francisco Giants, this time 4-3 before 29,779 Dodger Stadium fans on a night so cool that you might have guessed the game was being played at Candlestick Park.

All the scoring was done early, but the Giants threatened once late. Darrell Evans led off the eighth with a single to center against relief pitcher Steve Howe, who had just replaced starter Burt Hooton. He was moved to second on a sacrifice, setting up the play of the game.

Larry Herndon singled to right and Evans was off and running, home plate in mind. But Smith, whose arm is among the best in baseball, fired straight and true to rookie catcher Mike Scoscia and Evans (who would have been out 20 feet) stopped midway down the line and headed back to third.

Herndon, seeing that the ball wasn't cut off, headed for second. Scoscia's throw to second baseman Davey Lopes beat him there. Willie McCovey grounded out and the inning and the would-be rally was over.

"There are only two or three right fielders in baseball who could have stopped Evans from scoring," Giants Manager Dave Bristol said. Smith, of course, among them.

He already has two assists this season and he's hit in 11 straight games (sitting out one). He and Ron Cey had first-inning homers and the Giants, who lost 14 of 18 to the Dodgers last year, never could catch up.

Smith has been playing that way against everyone. It hasn't always helped the Dodgers, who are 5-7, and 3-2 on this home stand, but he hasn't hurt them. In fact, he's one big reason the team has stayed afloat.

"That's what I expect of myself, to

**Please Turn to Page 4, Col. 2**

## ANGELS LOSE DOWNING WITH BROKEN ANKLE

**By ROSS NEWHAN**
Times Staff Writer

BLOOMINGTON, Minn.—It was disclosed Monday the Oakland A's four-game weekend sweep of the Angels was also a case of adding injury to insult.

Catcher Brian Downing, the American League's leading right-handed hitter (.326) last year, suffered a fractured left ankle in the first inning of Sunday's second game of a double-header and is expected to be sidelined for at least three weeks.

"There's not much I can say except that it's a very serious loss," Manager Jim Fregosi said Monday. "Brian is not only an aggressive hitter, he's an aggressive player, period. He's a leader and he'll be missed."

Downing suffered the injury on an

**Please Turn to Page 2, Col. 1**

### LAKERS AND SONICS START TONIGHT

# Western Matchup: 1979's Best vs. 1980's Favorite

**By SCOTT OSTLER**
Times Staff Writer

For the two teams who will begin tonight the battle for the National Basketball Assn.'s Western Conference title, it has been a strange and wonderful season—strange for the Seattle SuperSonics and wonderful for the Lakers.

The opener of the best-of-seven series at the Forum will be televised locally (Channel 9, 8 p.m.). Game 2 is Wednesday night, also at the Forum, then the action moves to Seattle for games Friday and Sunday.

The Lakers won 60 regular-season games and took the Pacific Division, then blew the Phoenix Suns out of the league tournament, four games to one. The Lakers are favored to win the NBA title. They couldn't be playing better if they had signed a working agreement with the Big Laker in the Sky.

The Sonics had trouble getting untracked early in the season, then had trouble getting retracked at the end. Even though they won 56 games, dozens of What's Wrong With the Sonics theories popped up in Seattle. It took the Sonics three games to beat lowly Portland in the first-round miniseries, and they had to come from behind to nudge the Cinderella Bucks in the seven-game semifinal series which ended Sunday.

During that series, Laker scouting reports noted that the Bucks were much the better team. Surprise! The Sonics, not the Bucks, flew into LAX Monday evening. What happened?

"The Sonics," Laker forward Jamaal Wilkes said, "have people who believe that when they have to make a play, they will make it."

In other words, the Sonics are a tough, experienced, clutch group which seems to have recaptured the confidence that helped win the league championship last season.

The Lakers? They have a little confidence, too.

"We're going to beat them (the Sonics) basically because we're a better team than they are," said Laker forward Jim Chones, never one to soften his opinions for fear of offending the opposition. "It's just a matter of us getting on the floor and doing

**Please Turn to Page 5, Col. 1**

# SPURS OFFER GERVIN $8.775 MILLION FOR 40 YEARS...

## ... But He's Worried About What Inflation Will Do to the Package and His Agent Says It's 'Not Even Close' to What Gervin Wants; ONLY $5.1 Million Is Guaranteed

SAN ANTONIO (UPI)—The San Antonio Spurs Monday offered George Gervin $8.775 million over the next 40 years, but the offer is "not even close" to what he wants, his agent said.

"It looks like five million dollars over a million years," Gervin said. "At this point, until I find out more about it, I have nothing to say. The way inflation in the economy is going, there's no telling what this works out to be."

The guaranteed portion of the contract totals $5.1 million for five years of service, including a $100,000 signing bonus, $400,000 a year for five years, plus $100,000 a year for 30 years beginning in 1990 when Gervin likely will be retired.

He could earn the other $3.675 million during the second five years on optional one-year "make-good" contracts starting at $625,000 in 1985-86 and increasing to $900,000 by 1989-90.

Pat Healy, the Tacoma, Wash., attorney who represents the 6-7 guard, said in a telephone interview he was shocked that Spurs President Angelo Drossos called reporters together and spelled out the terms of the offer. Drossos said he did so to show the rest of the nation the Spurs were not "some kind of poor-boy operation."

"My first impression was total shock that a private negotiation, which is of a sensitive nature, would be thrust into the media," Healy said. "At no time have I ever disclosed terms of any negotiation."

But Healy contends Gervin is the best and most consistent basketball player in the NBA—on the basis of being the runner-up MVP the past three years and winning the scoring championship the past three years.

Healy contended the Spurs' offer would still leave Gervin about fifth in the league in salary and that the total—with the 30-year pension payments worked in—breaks down to $452,000 a year during the first five years of the contract.

"I can't even talk money. It's not fair," Healy said. "The cash money is not even

**Please Turn to Page 4, Col. 1**

### The Gervin Package

*Terms of the "lifetime" contract that could pay San Antonio Spurs guard George Gervin $8.775 million over the next 40 years:*

—$100,000 signing bonus
—1980-81 $400,000 cash guaranteed
—1981-82 $400,000 cash guaranteed
—1982-83 $400,000 cash guaranteed
—1983-84 $400,000 cash guaranteed
—1984-85 $400,000 cash guaranteed
—1985-86 $625,000 cash option
—1986-87 $650,000 cash option
—1987-88 $700,000 cash option
—1988-89 $800,000 cash option
—1989-90 $900,000 cash option
—1990-91 $100,000 a year for next 30 years.

GAME OF BREAKS—Here's one way to stop Philadelphia's Mike Schmidt. The slugger's bat snaps in half as he grounds out Saturday against the Dodgers. Otherwise, he homered for second straight day as Phils beat L.A. again in Philadelphia, 7-3. Catcher is Mike Scioscia.
Associated Press photo

# The Risk Was Genuine... but the Filly Was More So

## Derby Has First Female Winner in 65 Years; Rumbo Is Second

Los Angeles Times
Sports
CC PART III †
SUNDAY, MAY 4, 1980

By ROSS NEWHAN, Times Staff Writer

LOUISVILLE—Proving that this lady definitely is no tramp, Genuine Risk Saturday became the first filly in 65 years and only the second ever to win the Kentucky Derby.

Diana Firestone's chestnut daughter of Exclusive Native—the sire of 1978 Triple Crown winner Affirmed—wrested the lead from 2-1 favorite Rockhill Native at the top of the Churchill Downs stretch, shook off Jaklin Klugman, who momentarily pulled even with her, and then withstood the anticipated charge of the eccentric Rumbo.

Rumbo, second to Codex in both the Santa Anita and Hollywood derbies, finished one length back of the winner and one length ahead of Jaklin Klugman, who was four lengths ahead of yet a third Californian, Super Moment.

Rockhill Native, setting the type of slow pace that seemed to be all to his advantage, faded to fifth while Plugged Nickle, the 5-2 second choice, shadowed Rockhill Native for a mile before finishing seventh in the 13-horse field.

Genuine Risk, whose trainer, the veteran Leroy Jolley, had initially opposed running her against the colts and geldings but was apparently overruled by the owners, went off at 13 to 1 and returned an across the board payoff of $28.60, $10.60 and $4.80 to her supporters in a crowd of 131,859, many of whom were jammed into the infield in what is Kentucky's annual answer to Woodstock.

Among those who went to the parimutuel windows to illustrate their approval of the feminist movement (Genuine Risk was only the 31st filly ever and first since Silver Spoon in 1959 to start a Derby) were Mrs. Gerald Ford and Phyllis George Brown, wife of Kentucky Gov. John Y. Brown. This was ladies' day in more ways than one since a filly named Excitable Lady, co-owned by the governor's wife, won the $25,000 Debutante Stakes, run two races before the 106th Derby.

Genuine Risk became the only filly other than Regret in 1915 to win what is known as the Run for the Roses by covering the 1¼ miles on a fast track in 2:02, two-fifths faster than Spectacular Bid's time of last year but 13 lengths (each fifth representing a length) behind Secretariat's 1973 race record.

This was something of a dartboard derby, a shut-your-eyes-and-take-a-pick-type race. None of the 1980 3-year-olds had demonstrated the obvious ability and superiority of Affirmed, Seattle Slew or Spectacular Bid, one reason Diana and Bert Firestone insisted on starting their valuable filly.

Jockey Jacinto Vasquez, scoring his second Derby victory and his second for Jolley (who won previously with Foolish Pleasure in 1975), touched on the caliber of this year's crop when he was asked if he was surprised at Genuine Risk's ability to go 1¼ miles.

"No," Vasquez said, "She could run *two* miles with this kind of competition."

Asked if he considered Genuine Risk superior to Ruffian, the great filly who was destroyed after breaking down under Vasquez in the 1975 match race with Foolish Pleasure, Vasquez said, "I refuse to answer on the grounds it may incriminate me."

The questionable quality of this year's Triple Crown cast was also cited by Darrel McHargue, who was up

Please Turn to Page 14, Col. 1

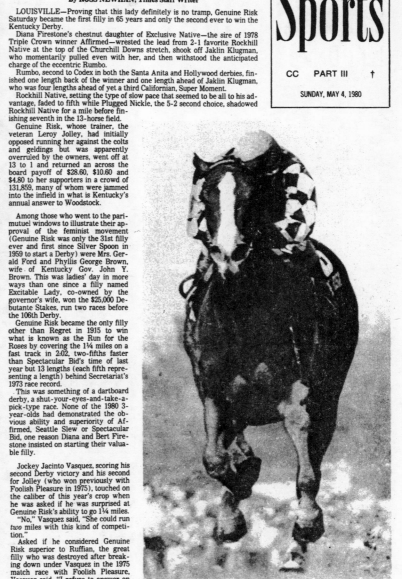

GENUINE ARTICLE—Genuine Risk, with Jacinto Vasquez up, comes flying home at Churchill Downs Saturday, the first filly to win the Kentucky Derby since Regret did it in 1915.
Associated Press photo

***JIM MURRAY***

## He's Smooth, That Silk

**Whenever you run** into a guy whose nickname is Silk, one thing you don't do is play cards with him. You don't let him deal. You don't try to pick the shell with the pea under it. If he's got the dice, you don't fade him. You back his play. You play the "come."

Don't bother calling for a new deck. If he's betting, fold. Never hand him your watch. Never put your money in a bag with him because, sure as sunset, you're going to wind up with a bagful of torn paper and his phone's going to be disconnected.

If the croupier winks at him, pull in your chips. If a jockey nods at him in the post parade, skip the race. If he says he'll take a quarter out of your ear, get ready for an earache. If he offers you shots on the golf course, pretend you didn't hear him. If he bumps into you, count your fingers.

On the Lakers, they call Jamaal Wilkes, "Silk." Right there, if I were an opposing forward, I wouldn't play him till I found out precisely why. Because usually when you do, it's too late. By then your money and your watch are gone, you can't remember what he looked like.

★

**Jamaal even looks** like a guy called "Silk." One-iron thin, he has these cool green eyes and he looks like he's trying not to laugh at you as he deals. He has the look on his face of a guy who's going to say "Pick a card—any card—and remember what it is," and you know damn well he's going to pick it out of a floorful of cards in a minute.

In another era, Silk Wilkes might be wearing a pinchback suit and a checkered vest with a goldpiece on his watch chain and a beaver hat and be working the upper deck on the old Mississippi river boats. He looks like four aces just standing there. He'd be looking for a guy with the egg money.

They said he was too small and too slight to play forward in this league. Hah! They said that, in this game, forward had turned into a thug position and, to play it, you had to practice nights in Central Park. There was no place for a guy with touch. The only way Jamaal could play these guys is with a club.

★

**That was before Silk** rolled up his sleeves to show the marks there was nothing under them. That was before he started to take the basketball out of ears of the registered goons of the game and innocently inquire "Is this it?"

Silk would have made a great spy. He's so thin he looks like a registered letter. When he stands sideways, he disappears. He seems to be standing there just minding his own business but the next thing you know, he has the ball and is running down-court ahead of hot pursuit like a puppy that just stole a roast and is dashing out to bury it.

His statistics are not awesome—until you realize you're dealing with a forward only 6-6 and (it says on the program) 190 pounds. Wilkes is the only guy on the court who makes the basketball look heavy. Actually, you could poke a fire with him. Nevertheless, he is the second-leading scorer on the Lakers with 1,644 points for an average of 20 a night.

Please Turn to Page 12, Col. 1

## Phils' 7-3 Win Over the Dodgers a Murder Mystery

By RICHARD HOFFER
Times Staff Writer

PHILADELPHIA—As far as the Dodgers are concerned, Veterans Stadium is a kind of major league Bermuda Triangle. Season after season they enter Philadelphia air space, flying high, only to be wiped from National League radar screens. Sometimes the wreckage is discovered, sometimes not. It gets pretty mysterious.

"I sure don't know what it is," Dodger Manager Tom Lasorda said Saturday after the Phillies had beaten his club, 7-3, "Seems like we've had problems here ever since the (1978) playoffs. What are we here 0-8? And four of those by one run. We came in here last year three different times leading in the eighth inning. And lost."

The Dodgers were 0-6 here last year but the statistic wasn't all that significant. The Dodgers, struggling most of the season, lost in other parks, too. More important, they are now 0-2 this season, going into today's series-ending game. All it took was a trip to Veterans Stadium to turn a 10-game Dodger winning streak into a two-game losing streak—less than 24 hours.

As bad and as unexplained as the Dodgers' luck has been here over the last two seasons (they were 3-3 here in the 1978 season), there was absolutely no mystery to Saturday afternoon's game, played before 35,011 fans.

Here's what it came down to: Dodger pitcher Burt Hooton couldn't keep his pitches down and Philly sluggers Greg Luzinski and Mike Schmidt couldn't help get them up.

Hooton, normally tough on the

Please Turn to Page 20, Col. 1

***Honeycutt Stops Angels for Fifth Victory, 2-0***

Story on Page 2

# SANFORD RUNS RACE OF CENTURY

## Blazes 100 Meters in Wind-Aided 9.88; USC Bows to UCLA

By MAL FLORENCE
Times Staff Writer

USC's James Sanford ran the second fastest 100 meters of all time, a wind-aided 9.88, and the Trojans had speed to burn Saturday, but, in the long run, UCLA won the annual dual track meet, 83-71, at Drake Stadium.

Sanford said he got only a fair start, but he was accelerating at the finish and barely missed getting credit for breaking Jimmy Hines' world record of 9.95.

The wind reading was 5.1 miles per hour, barely over the legal limit of 4.47 m.p.h. Only William Snoddy of Oklahoma has run faster, 9.87, at the Dallas Invitational in 1978. But Snoddy was pushed along by a gale—a wind estimated at 25 m.p.h. And, considering that Hines' 9.95 record was set in the 7,000-feet altitude of Mexico City in the 1968 Olympic Games, track purists contend Sanford's 9.88 was, indeed, the fastest 100 meters in history.

But Sanford's speed and that of Billy Mullins, Bill Green and Bill Wang (an upset winner in the 800) couldn't offset UCLA's strength in the distance races.

The score was tied 70-70 on a warm afternoon with only two events remaining—the 5,000 meters and mile relay. The Trojans had to get a second in the 5,000 to stay in contention.

But, as expected, UCLA's Ron Cornell and Steve Ortiz ran away and hid in the 5,000, finishing 1-2 and providing the Bruins with eight points to clinch the meet before the mile relay (which UCLA won).

USC is short-handed in the distance races and this was a determining factor in a typically, competitive Bruin-Trojan dual watched by 11,973.

"We wanted to win it before the mile relay, so I could relax," said UCLA Coach Jim Bush, whose team concluded an undefeated dual meet season (7-0) and probably will be named the U.S. dual meet champion by Track & Field News.

Bush's dope sheet that he had kept secret until after the meet had the Bruins ahead, 78-71, prior to the mile relay. That race, the UCLA coach, said was a tossup.

Please Turn to Page 8, Col. 2

# Finally, an NBA Final With Some Glamour: Lakers vs. 76ers

## For a Change, the Best and the Brightest (Not the Most Muscular) Have Survived

Billy Cunningham

By SCOTT OSTLER
Times Staff Writer

OK, cue the footage of Dr. J's flying jacknife reverse dunk. Looks good.

Now cut to the shot of Magic's double-take, double-fake, double-bounce pass on the break. Nice rhyme, eh?

Fade to Kareem's 18-foot skyhook in the lane with those three defensive guys hanging on his jersey like San Francisco cable car riders.

Good. Now we'll finish with the clip of Dawkins doing his Chocolate Thunder dunk. As the backboard shatters, freeze the frame and cue the voice-over . . .

". . . Live! From the Forum in Los Angeles! It's the 1980 National Basketball Assn. championship playoffs, featuring the Los Angeles Lakers and the Philadelphia 76ers!"

The NBA has come up with a great gimmick to kick off the decade. They've arranged for the best championship series matchup in years, starting this afternoon at 12:30. The game will be carried live on local TV (Channel 2). No tape delay. These are the Ready For Prime Time Players, baby.

No offense to Seattle, Washington, Golden State and all you other dockworker-style teams who have been slugging your way into the finals the last few years, but what this league has been needing is some hardcore *glamour*.

**Profiles of the Lakers and 76ers, back at the NBA's summit again, begin on page 3. The Lakers are profiled by Times Staff Writer Ted Green and the 76ers by Times Staff Writer Mark Heisler.**

And this best-of-seven series is probably the most appealing matchup since the Lakers vs. Knicks in '73.

The Lakers lost that one, and haven't been back in the finals since. The 76ers were in the finals in '77, when they won the first two games from Portland, then folded the circus tent and lost four straight.

This series is one that fans can sink their teeth into. For the casual observer, there is the glitter of big names. Nobody in basketball has a more electric court presence and big play potential than 76er Julius (Dr. J) Erving, unless it's Laker Earvin (Magic) Johnson. No player in the game is more intimidating than Kareem Abdul-Jabbar, unless it's Darryl Dawkins.

For dedicated and sophisticated NBA followers, there is guts beneath the glamour. These are two very solid teams—teams that play defense, execute a textbook fast break and move the ball around the floor like people who are on a first-name basis with one another.

The credentials have been established. The 76ers battled Boston to the wire in the regular season in the Eastern Division, winning 59 games. They

Please Turn to Page 10, Col. 2

Paul Westhead

*'How else can I explain those rainbows when there is no rain?*

# It's MAGIC!' The New Starting Center Puts Lakers Over the Top, 123-107

—From the Doris Day hit song, "It's Magic," 1948, by Sammy Cahn and Jules Styne

Los Angeles Times
**Sports**
BUSINESS
CC PART III †
SATURDAY, MAY 17, 1980

By SCOTT OSTLER
Times Staff Writer

PHILADELPHIA—When they erect the statue of Magic Johnson in some prominent location in L.A., as they surely will soon, chiseled on the pedestal will be Magic's favorite saying:

"It's winnin' time."

That's what time it was Friday night in the Spectrum when Magic, a 20-year-old rookie, led the Lakers to one of the true upsets in National Basketball Assn. playoff history, a 123-107 win over the 76ers.

With center Kareem Abdul-Jabbar watching the game from the comfort of his living room, 3,000 miles away, his sprained left ankle propped up on a coffee table, the Lakers won the championship of the NBA four games to two.

Magic, who literally laughed at the added pressure when Abdul-Jabbar was scratched, started at center and scored 42 points, grabbed 15 rebounds and handed out seven assists. He made 14 of 23 field-goal attempts and 14 of 14 free-throw attempts.

The Lakers outplayed the 76ers from the start but with five minutes left, Philadelphia pulled within two points, 103-101.

As 18,276 Spectrum fans sat back and waited for reality to take over from fantasy, the Lakers outscored the 76ers, 20-6. Magic had 11 of those 20 points.

When Jamaal Wilkes threw down a dunk to give the Lakers an unsurmountable 12-point lead with 50 seconds left, Abdul-Jabbar must have spiked his TV to his living room carpet in jubilation.

It is the Lakers' first NBA championship since 1972, a perfect anniversary present for the team's 20th season. In those 20 years, the team has been in the finals 10 times, and won twice.

Johnson was voted the Most Valuable Player in the series, Abdul-Jabbar's monumental contributions in the first five games notwithstanding.

Magic had help.

Who can believe . t. t.

—Quiet Jamaal Wilkes, a non-All-Star, outplaying Julius (Dr. J) Erving? Wilkes scored 37 points, the most he's had since high school. Erving had 27 points.

—Brad Holland, laker rookie, outscoring teammate Norm Nixon, 8 to 4? Until Friday night, Holland was the Human Victory Cigar, entering games only when the outcome was decided. He scored six straight points near the end of the first half.

—The Lakers—without Abdul-Jabbar, remembered—outrebounding the 76ers, 52-36 (17-7 on the offensive boards)? It's called desire. Wilkes, Jim Chones and Mark (the Shark) Landsberger had 10 rebounds each. No 76er had 10.

—Jim Chones, the reluctant standin for Abdul-Jabbar, outplaying Darryl (Chocolate Thunder) Dawkins? Chones had 11 points and 10 re-

Please Turn to Page 6, Col. 1

PARTY TIME

## Magic Tells the Captain: Let's Dance

By TED GREEN
Times Staff Writer

PHILADELPHIA—The season started with Magic Johnson gleefully hugging Kareem Abdul-Jabbar after the captain tossed in a skyhook at the final buzzer to win the opener in San Diego.

Six months later, the season ended with Magic Johnson gleefully hugging the National Basketball Assn.'s championship trophy.

"I know your ankle hurts, Kareem," Johnson said, "but why don't you get up and dance, anyway?"

All the Lakers were dancing late Friday night, and pouring champagne on each other, and praising Abdul-Jabbar, after they won the 1979-80 championship with a 123-107 victory over the Philadelphia 76ers in Game 6 of the final series.

This was an improbable win, and an improbable end to a season that had an almost dreamlike quality, for it was accomplished without the game's most dominate player. Abdul-Jabbar watched the clincher on TV, having sprained his left ankle the previous game.

So for a few minutes, dreamlike minutes, the Lakers' locker room seemed strangely subdued. Maybe because reality hadn't set in. Maybe because Captain Kareem had not been there to share it. Maybe just because.

As he did the first of many TV interviews, you could see those were tears, not just sweat, under Magic Johnson's eyes.

But then Butch Lee popped open a bottle of champagne, someone started spraying another and it wasn't a dream, anymore. Before long, Coach Paul Westhead's three-piece, pinstriped suit and perfectly styled hair were drenched in the bubbly, too.

Johnson eventually joined in, but first he said he had something important to say.

"Big fella," he said. "We did it for you."

And: "Kareem is the one who got us this far. And he was with us (in spirit) tonight."

It was a nice gesture from the man of the hour, from the series' Most Valuable Player, from the rookie who scored 42 points and proved that he is not only a man for all positions but for all leagues.

From an NCAA title a year ago last March to an NBA title in May, it could only be Magic.

"Magic Johnson is the Mr. Opportu-

Please Turn to Page 7, Col. 1

### THE MAGIC NUMBERS

LOS ANGELES

| | Min | FG | FT | R | A | P | T |
|---|---|---|---|---|---|---|---|
| Chones | 43 | 5-9 | 1-1 | 10 | 3 | 2 | 11 |
| Wilkes | 42 | 16-30 | 5-5 | 10 | 2 | 4 | 37 |
| Johnson | 47 | 14-23 | 14-14 | 15 | 7 | 3 | 42 |
| Nixon | 40 | 1-10 | 2-2 | 3 | 9 | 3 | 4 |
| Cooper | 39 | 4-9 | 8-9 | 4 | 6 | 4 | 16 |
| Lndsbrgr | 19 | 2-7 | 1-2 | 10 | 0 | 4 | 5 |
| Holland | 9 | 3-4 | 2-2 | 0 | 0 | 2 | 8 |
| Byrnes | 1 | 0-0 | 0-0 | 0 | 0 | 0 | 0 |
| Totals | 240 | 45-92 | 33-35 | 52 | 27 | 22 | 123 |

Shooting: Field goals, 48.9%; free throws, 91.4%.

PHILADELPHIA

| | Min | FG | FT | R | A | P | T |
|---|---|---|---|---|---|---|---|
| Erving | 39 | 13-23 | 1-4 | 7 | 3 | 4 | 27 |
| CJones | 26 | 2-3 | 2-2 | 6 | 2 | 4 | 6 |
| Dawkins | 31 | 6-9 | 2-5 | 4 | 1 | 5 | 14 |
| Hollins | 26 | 5-13 | 3-4 | 1 | 6 | 4 | 13 |
| Cheeks | 40 | 5-11 | 3-3 | 2 | 8 | 2 | 13 |
| BJones | 29 | 4-8 | 0-0 | 9 | 1 | 4 | 8 |
| Bibby | 21 | 4-10 | 0-2 | 3 | 3 | 2 | 8 |
| Mix | 25 | 8-11 | 2-2 | 4 | 2 | 1 | 18 |
| Spanrkl | 1 | 0-0 | 0-0 | 0 | 1 | 0 | 0 |
| Toone | 1 | 0-0 | 0-0 | 0 | 0 | 1 | 0 |
| Richrdsn | 1 | 0-1 | 0-0 | 0 | 0 | 0 | 0 |
| Totals | 240 | 47-89 | 13-22 | 36 | 27 | 27 | 107 |

Shooting: Field goals, 52.8%; free throws, 59.1%.

SCORE BY QUARTERS

| | | | | |
|---|---|---|---|---|
| Los Angeles | 32 | 28 | 33 | 30—123 |
| Philadelphia | 29 | 31 | 23 | 24—107 |

Three-point goals—Johnson 0-1; Landsberger 0-1; Erving 0-2; Hollins 0-1; Bibby 0-2; Richardson 0-1
Attendance—18,276

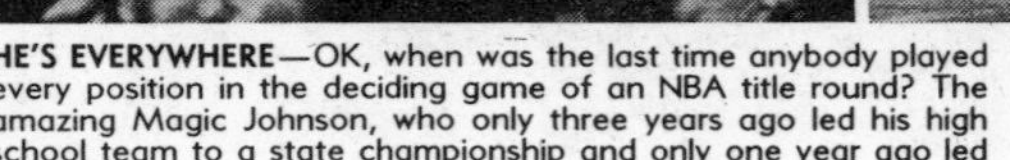

HE'S EVERYWHERE—OK, when was the last time anybody played every position in the deciding game of an NBA title round? The amazing Magic Johnson, who only three years ago led his high school team to a state championship and only one year ago led his college team to the NCAA championship, put on a showstopper Friday night and did it at center (above left, he scores over Darryl Dawkins), at forward (above right, he goes head-to-head with Julius Erving) and at guard (below, he hits open man).

Times photos by Joe Kennedy

PAINFUL LESSON

## 76ers' Fondest Dream Winds Up a Nightmare

By ALAN GREENBERG
Times Staff Writer

PHILADELPHIA—The 76ers learned a painful lesson Friday night: That sometimes the worst thing that can happen is for your fondest wish to come true. You may live to regret it.

Throughout his career, many teams have suggested that the best way to defense Kareem Abdul-Jabbar is to keep him from showing up. Well, he didn't Friday night because of a sprained left ankle suffered in game five, and watched game six on TV from his home.

Over the long run, nobody would dare argue that the Lakers without Abdul-Jabbar are as good as they are with him.

But this was not the long run. Just 48 minutes. Forty-eight minutes of Magic Johnson and Jamaal Wilkes playing the games of their lives, and an inspired Lakers team reminding anyone who might have forgotten that no man-even basketball's ultimate weapon-is indispensable.

He didn't beat us. It was the Lakers that beat us," Caldwell Jones said. "He wasn't here in person but I'm sure he was here in spirit, and the Lakers played like they could feel him in spirit. They won it for their captain. They played with the intensity you need to be a champion"

The 76ers certainly didn't and they knew it. All series long, they talked about how they had to get tough and keep the Lakers from dominating the backboards.

"It's something we never really solved," Julius Erving admitted. "And we certainly didn't solve it tonight."

Please Turn to Page 6, Col. 3

## Reuss Gives the Dodgers a Start and an 8-6 Win

By RICHARD HOFFER
Times Staff Writer

Don Stanhouse, whose relief has mostly been comic since he's been removed from the bullpen and installed in the trainer's room, adopted a posture of outrage, instead of his usual outrageous posture.

"Damn it," he said to Jerry Reuss, who was trying to gather some concentration before Friday night's game in a dark corner of the trainer's room, "you found yourself a niche and now you go screwing it up. You're a *reliever*, for goodness sakes."

Reuss had been a reliever and, with Stanhouse on the disabled list, was one of the Dodgers' most effective. He had three wins, three saves and an ERA of 1.42.

But Friday night, with scheduled pitcher Dave Goltz down with the flu, Reuss was a starter, much to his colleague's mock chagrin. And a very effective one at that, much to the world champion Pirates' chagrin.

The once-reluctant reliever weathered two shaky innings—pitching five scoreless innings in his innings of work—to register a win (his first as a starter tihis year) in the Dodgers' come-from-behind, 8-6 defeat of the Pirates, the hottest team in baseball these days.

Reuss, a starter most of last year, figured again to be in the rotation this year. But he was unhappily surprised to find himself very much out of it, even though he performed more than adequately in spring training.

Yet he adapted well enough to bullpen duty. He never pretended he liked it, but he didn't ask to be traded either.

He never really asked for anything, as far as that goes. Friday night's

Please Turn to Page 4, Col. 2

*Angels Make a Big Hit in K.C. and Win, 11-1*

Story on Page 2

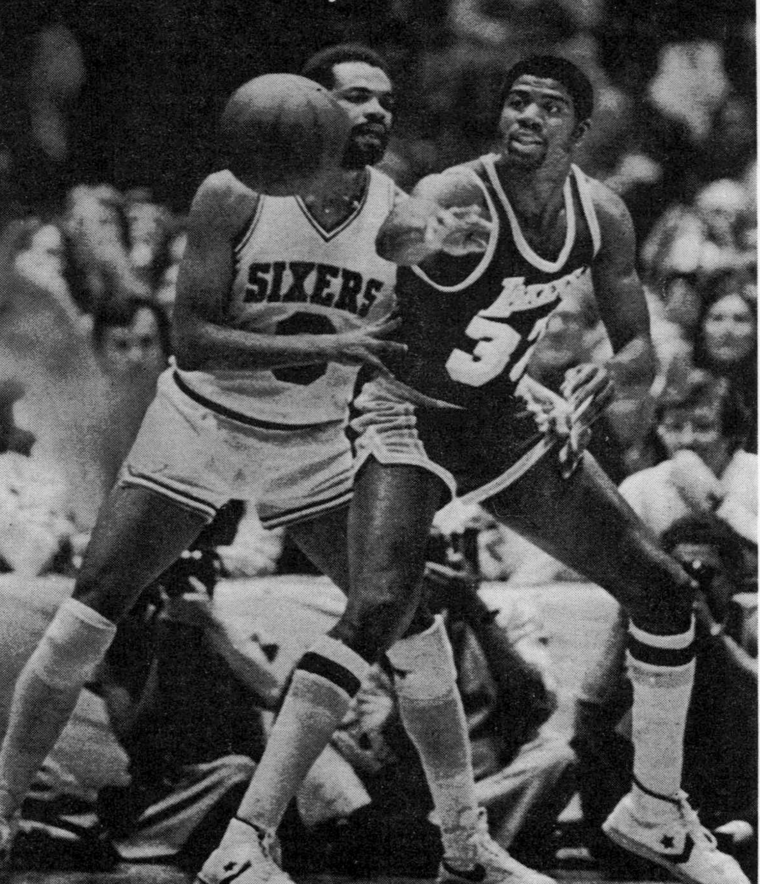

## FILLY VS. NEW FACES IN PREAKNESS

By ROSS NEWHAN
Times Staff Writer

BALTIMORE—Genuine Risk, only the second filly to win a Kentucky Derby, tries today to become only the fifth to win a Preakness, last won by a filly (Nellie Morse) in 1924.

Pimlico's 105th renewal, having drawn Santa Anita and Hollywood Derby winner Codex from California and the front-running Colonel Moran from New York, has generated some of the anticipatory excitement that seemed absent in Louisville until the lady had her day.

If she never has another, the roses will always be hers.

"It doesn't really matter what she does now," co-owner Bertram Firestone said Friday, "because she's already won the greatest race in the world. We've received calls and letters from people who wouldn't know the Arc de Triomphe from a claiming race. All they know is the Kentucky Derby. What I'm saying is that it's recognized as the greatest race anywhere and so whatever happens now we've still had a very good year."

It could get better today, though Firestone said even disregarding the improved competition he has believed for some time that this would be the toughest of Genuine Risk's Triple Crown tests. At 1 3/16 miles, it is shorter than both the Derby (1¼ miles) and Belmont Stakes (1½), and Genuine Risk is bred for distance.

The filly's father was Exclusive Native, who also sired Triple Crown winner Affirmed, a winner at just about *every* distance en route to becoming the sport's all-time leading money winner. Affirmed did it with cool detachment and now Genuine Risk has been displaying some of the same traits.

"Nothing seems to be bothering her," trainer Leroy Jolley said Friday. "She has the greatest temperament of any horse I've ever been around. She's very kind and very quiet and very much like Affirmed in that way."

As a winner of seven of eight career starts, she's much like Affirmed in other ways, too.

"The more I think about her performance in the Kentucky Derby," Jolley said, "the more I think it was a super effort. She came off a soft slow pace to finish with the ninth-fastest time in the 106 years of the Derby. It was faster than I thought she was capable of. She's smaller and lighter than most of the colts, but she has the same rugged determination as Foolish

Please Turn to Page 8, Col. 3

Los Angeles Times
Sports
CC PART III †
SUNDAY, JULY 6, 1980

# McEnroe Breaks the Tie, but He Can't Break Borg

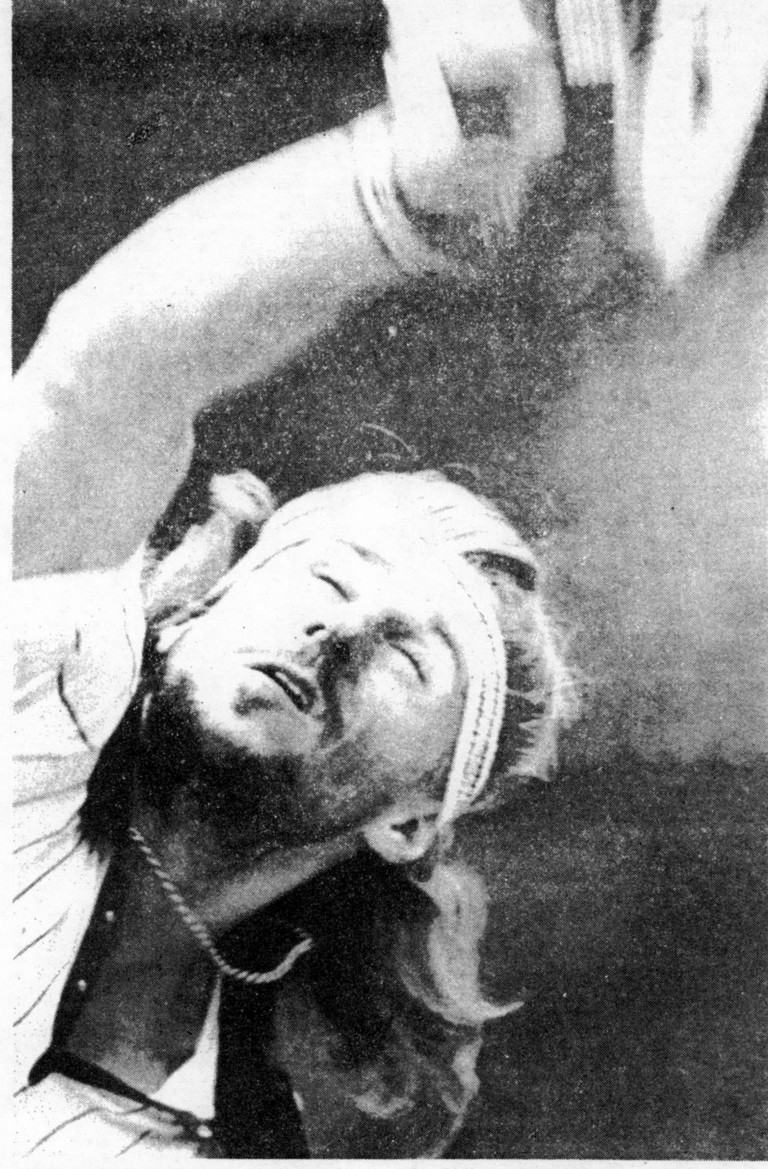

**WITH HIS EYES CLOSED**—By now, Bjorn Borg ought to be able to win at Wimbledon blindfolded. Well, almost. Here the camera catches him blinking while he serves in Saturday's nearly four-hour final with John McEnroe. Borg withstood a big challenge to win his fifth title.
Associated Press photo

## The Swede Wins the Fifth Set ... and His Fifth Title in a Row

By TED GREEN
Times Staff Writer

WIMBLEDON, England—For sheer drama and sustained suspense; for a clash of two indomitable wills, each refusing to give an inch; for slam bang action between the best players in the business; for a struggle that made superlatives seem, well, senseless, Bjorn Borg and John McEnroe may have played the tennis match to end all tennis matches Saturday.

And when Borg blasted one last crosscourt backhand just past a lunging McEnroe at the net, finally ending the match after nearly four hours and five sets, even old stuffed shirts at the All-England Club, men who tend to cling to the past, said they had never seen a better Wimbledon final.

Borg beat McEnroe, the United States Open champion, 1-6, 7-5, 6-3, 6-7, 8-6, to win his fifth successive men's singles title at Wimbledon, a streak unprecedented in modern tennis.

Willie Renshaw won seven straight titles in the late 1800s and Laurie Doherty won five consecutively at the turn of the century, but those streaks can't be mentioned in the same breath with Borg's.

They played a challenge round then, meaning defending champions were seeded directly into the final and had to win only one match for a title.

Borg had to win seven matches each of the last five summers, so his Wimbledon match streak now stands at 35. That is also a record. Rod Laver held the old record of 31 before Borg broke it earlier this week in the fourth round.

Additionally, Borg's fifth singles title moved him past Laver, who won four here (1961-62, 1968-69). So the shy, stoic Swede, who dreamed of being a hockey player as a child, has now won Wimbledon more than any man who picked up a tennis racket from Bill Tilden on.

Borg's records—which include five victories in another major tournament, the French Open—invite historical comparisons. The fact is, he has won the most Wimbledons on grass, even though he is, at heart, a baseline player who is far more at home on clay.

Thus you can argue that, at 24, Bjorn Rune Borg may already be the best tennis player ever, which just happens to be his career ambition.

McEnroe did everything possible with a tennis racket and still couldn't beat him.

For instance, McEnroe saved *seven* match points in the fourth set with at least that many great shots, every one hit without a trace of nerves.

And he won perhaps the most dramatic 7-6 tiebreaker since tournament tennis installed the system in 1971. The tiebreaker score was 18 points to 16 and both players hit more screaming winners on the dead run, from improbable angles, during that tense time than you're likely to see in some five-set matches.

From 5-5 in the fourth set, after McEnroe saved the first two match points with Borg serving at 40-15 and then broke serve to tie the set, the emotionless Swede and emotional New Yorker for the next half hour played at a level other players only dream about.

What happened after McEnroe finally won that outrageous tiebreaker told you everything you need to know about Bjorn Borg's character and temperament, about his self-control, will to win and belief in himself.

Instead of being dispirited or at least losing a little confidence, Borg got 25 of 31 first serves in during the final set. As a result, he lost a measly three points on his serve the entire set, despite the fact that McEnroe returns serve almost as well as anyone in tennis.

Borg appropriately ended this 3-hour 53-minute struggle by breaking McEnroe's serve in the 14th game of the set and 55th game of one of the longest Wimbledon finals.

Please Turn to Page 8, Col. 1

***JIM MURRAY***

## Baseball's Nobodies

**Do you know** who Ernie Koob is? Bob Groom?

Well, they pitched back-to-back no-hit games for the St. Louis Browns in 1917 over the Chicago White Sox. On May 5 and 6. Koob won only five other games that year. Groom lost 19 that year. But, that's nothing. He lost 26 in 1909.

No-hit games are the strangest of baseball artifacts. There's no form on them. They're as unpredictable as earthquakes, as full of surprises as boarding house stew.

They have a fascinating lure. For instance, did you know that, when Johnny Vander Meer was pitching his second consecutive no-hitter, the manager sneaked a relief pitcher down to the bullpen to warm up to be ready to go in in the seventh inning? Think about that for a while. A manager who would do that would set fire to a Rembrandt.

★

**When Jerry Reuss** pitched his no-hitter for the Dodgers the other night, the sporting press noted that it was a bid "to join the immortals of the game."

Actually, Jerry was joining some of the great nobodies of the profession. In addition to Koob and Groom, such luminaries, non-bubble gummers, loom as Bill Dietrich, Bob Keegan, Dick Bosman, Ed Head. There is also Weldon Henley, James S. Lavender, John Lush, Earl Moore and Malcolm Eason. George Culver completed only seven games in his major league career and one was a no-hitter.

And, let us not forget Bobo Holloman. Bobo pitched a no-hitter in the first game he ever started in the major leagues, and the only game he ever finished. He won only two other games and was down in the bush leagues before the season ended. Bobo wasn't a hungry pitcher, he was a thirsty one.

Speaking of thirsty pitchers, Grover Cleveland Alexander never pitched a no-hitter—even though one year he threw four one-hitters. Lefty Grove never pitched a no-hitter. Neither did Dizzy Dean or Whitey Ford. The Hall of Fame is full of guys who never pitched a no-hitter.

★

**Yet, Bill Stoneman** pitched *two*. And his lifetime record was 54-85. Grove's was 300-141. Alexander's was 373-208. Walter Johnson won 415 other games, but only one no-hitter. This put him behind such all-time greats as Steve Busby, Frank Smith and Ken Holtzman.

To be sure, Carl Hubbell, Bob Gibson, Tom Seaver, Chief Bender, Rube Marquard, Nap Rucker and Ted Lyons had no-hitters. Sandy Koufax got four. So has Nolan Ryan. Bob Feller got three. So did Cy Young. Christy Mathewson, Addie Joss, Allie Reynolds, Dutch Leonard and Warren Spahn got two. So, a no-hitter isn't always pitched by a nobody. Hoyt Wilhelm pitched in more games than any pitcher who ever lived, 1,070 of them, but only one was a no-hitter. It was one of only 20 games that he completed.

Did you know that the first no-hit game was lost? There have been 192 no-hit games, and 11 were lost. Harvey Haddix pitched 12 innings of *perfect* ball (no walks, no errors, nobody reached first base) in 1959. He lost in the 13th as Milwaukee beat Pittsburgh on Joe Adcock's home run. Haddix had pitched the greatest game ever pitched—and lost.

Jim Maloney pitched a 10-inning no-hitter for the Reds

Please Turn to Page 14, Col. 1

# DODGERS GO BACK IN FRONT, 3-2

## Victory Over Giants Puts Them a Game Ahead of the Astros

By RICHARD HOFFER
Times Staff Writer

A crowd of 41,587 at Dodger Stadium watched a couple of All-Star pitchers work Saturday night, Dodger Bob Welch and Giant Ed Whitson. It was a nice preliminary to Tuesday's All-Star game.

Welch pitched a routine—for him—game, allowing just a pair of runs and four hits before he left in the seventh, victim of his own wildness. And Whitson, who replaced injured teammate Vida Blue on the National League staff, likewise pitched according to form, yielding just six hits and three runs in his seven innings.

But the Dodgers' 3-2 win over the Giants proved to be more than just a crowd-builder for Tuesday's game. With the victory, the Dodgers shot into first place for the first time since June 9, a full game ahead of the Houston Astros, who lost twice to the Cincinnati Reds. It's been a long time —25 games—since the Dodgers occupied so lofty a position.

That the Dodgers are in first is not entirely a result of Saturday night's All-Star pitching. Welch got the win —he's 9-3—but, really, it was up to the Dodgers' much-maligned bullpen —Bob Castillo, specifically—to accomplish victory.

Welch, who had yielded nothing more damaging than Milt May's solo homer in the fifth, began to get into trouble in the seventh. He gave up a single to Max Venable, then loaded the bases by hitting May with a pitch and walking pinch-hitter Willie McCovey. You can't be too careful with McCovey, even if he is out of baseball after today's game. Welch then gave up a run-scoring walk to Rich Murray.

And then Welch went back to the clubhouse, presumably to concentrate on his next workout. That would be Tuesday when he pitches—probably —part of the All-Star game.

Castillo came in and got pinch-hitter Jim Wohlford on a nubber back to the mound to end the inning.

Castillo, who got his third save by enduring that inning and two more scoreless innings, says there was no lack of motivation when he came out to replace Welch.

"We heard in the bullpen that Houston had lost two and that we could get back into first," he said. "So it was a big one for me in that situation. Anyway, I wanted to save one for Bobby."

Welch got some offensive help early when Reggie Smith cracked his 15th homer—and second in two nights off the Giants—off Whitson (7-8). Welch got a little more help in the sixth when Rudy Law and Smith scored, Law on Steve Garvey's single and Smith on Dusty Baker's sacrifice fly. But they were both advanced by Whitson's throwing error. It was one of the few bad pitches Whitson has made in the last month.

Whitson had thought to pick Law off at second but threw wildly into center instead. Law and Smith both advanced a base, making it a lot easier on Baker and Garvey.

Please Turn to Page 6, Col. 4

## 'Do You Know Me?'

Baseball's Old-Timers games provide fans a chance to see some of the sport's top stars. Some are well known because they have remained in baseball or otherwise are in the public eye. But many, once familiar names in box scores, are today only memories. Some could qualify for that well-known credit card commercial. One of the largest collections of famous names will appear today in the Dodgers' annual Old-Timers game. How are the players faring today after notable careers in the sport? A Times reporter provides an update on some famous names starting on Page 7.

## Brewers Hold On to Beat Angels

By MIKE LITTWIN
Times Staff Writer

MILWAUKEE—Scoreboard watching is at least as old as, well, scoreboards. Everyone does it. Some won't admit to it, but you know better.

George Bamberger, who manages the Milwaukee Brewers, is a veteran scoreboard watcher. He admits it. But that doesn't mean he's proud of it. In fact, he thinks it might be a significant mistake.

"Damn the Yankees," Bamberger said (or words similar thereto) after his Brewers had beaten the Angels, 4-3, Saturday night. "I've got enough to worry about just managing this team."

The Brewers are in second place, but a distant second, 7½ back. The Yankees, as you might expect, are in first, 7½ ahead. You knew that if you

Please Turn to Page 4, Col. 1

# Today Is Forever

## After 22 Years, Willie McCovey Becomes Reluctant Early Retiree

By RICHARD HOFFER, Times Staff Writer

Willie McCovey suits up for his last baseball game today, playing the Dodgers in Los Angeles to conclude a remarkable career in the major leagues.

He has hit 521 home runs, the most ever for a left-handed hitter in the National League. He has been named Rookie of the Year, National League Most Valuable Player and Comeback Player of the Year. He has played in six All-Star games and a World Series.

And he has had the additional satisfaction of playing most of his career in San Francisco, where he has been much beloved, a kind of landmark on the civic landscape—but a landmark whose impermanence is taking a lot of people by surprise these days.

It has taken McCovey by surprise. By any accounting he has had a full and satisfying career and should be able to drift noiselessly into a front office job with the Giants on the way to the Hall of Fame. Yet McCovey is testy about the prospect of his midseason retirement, not at all as gracious in the face of this city-to-city well-wishing as you'd hope. He is kind of burned up, actually. It has been just—what?—22 years. It looked like forever.

Some folks close to the ballclub say the Giants were highly persuasive in organizing McCovey's retirement—McCovey really did think it was forever. They had this kid Mike Ivie, who could hit home runs and drive a lot of other guys home. He was getting anxious in McCovey's long shadow, required to play at some position other than first, if he wanted to play at all. Ivie didn't like it, right up to when *he* retired.

Also, the Giants had a "phenomenon," young Rich Murray, just called up from Phoenix. The last phenomenon the Giants had, well, that would have been Willie McCovey. They made Hank Sauer retire when McCovey came up. That's just something they do when such players come up. They do it everywhere, not just in San Francisco. There are better places for landmarks than in a musty dugout.

So the Giants, the reports have it, explained to McCovey that his day had come, after all. He wouldn't be playing a lot. He wouldn't be swinging a bat much. And he could get out of baseball the best way he could.

McCovey, after 22 years in the National League, has been getting out as well as he knows how. It's just not something he's prepared for. The sudden attention grates on him, for one thing. A couple of networks wanted to interview him—not some local affiliate, but the networks. "That's hard to figure," he said, a little edge in his voice, his brown eyes unusually cold. "I've been playing 22 years, no network ever wanted to talk to me. You'd think with my stats, I'd have had national attention during my career. Too low profile, I guess."

Every day, ever since he announced his retirement, he has been besieged by newspaper, radio and TV reporters. And he doesn't like it that much. "I'm talked out," he said, turning his back when he can, sitting down for a grilling when he can't. At least, he didn't do a tour of the National League cities—"where they could all have 'days' for me, like they did for Lou Brock," he snorted. What do they want, anyway, but to remind him he's through?

And the questions bother him, too. They're all pegged to the same angle. After he went to the plate last week and destroyed the Dodgers with a pinch double in the ninth—just sort of flicking that bat out, effortlessly (later, his teammates were walking around the clubhouse imitating that swing, in unconscious homage)—the crowd demanded his return, standing, almost begging for an encore. McCovey came back out of the clubhouse to tip his hat. "Did

Please Turn to Page 6, Col. 1

# Were the Soviet Track Judges Caught Red-Handed?

## Allegations of Cheating Bring Outside Officials on the Field at Lenin Stadium

Los Angeles Times
Sports
CC PART III †
THURSDAY, JULY 31, 1980

By BILL SHIRLEY
Times Sports Editor

MOSCOW—A dispute over Soviet judging in Olympic track and field erupted Wednesday, and International Olympic Committee officials said IOC President Lord Killanin had asked for an investigation into allegations of cheating.

But Adrian Paulen of Holland, president of the International Amateur Athletic Federation and the man Killanin reportedly asked to do the investigating, said: "That is absolutely a lie. He has never talked to me."

Killanin could not be reached for comment.

Allegations of judging irregularities centered on the discus, javelin, pole vault and triple jump events where it appeared to some that Soviet judges may have given their own athletes an edge.

The IAAF supervises international track and field competition and is in charge of the Olympic events at Lenin Stadium until Wednesday. However, IAAF members had observed from the stands rather than from points nearer the action on the field as they have at past Olympics.

The reason for this, IOC officials said, was that the Soviets protested that their judges would be offended by close IAAF supervision, saying it would suggest they were unreliable.

*Dan Fisher and Kenneth Reich, Times Staff Writers, assisted on this story.*

Paulen, 78, who is up for reelection in his IAAF post next year, at first denied that the Soviets had objected to having federation officials on the field. But upon further questioning, he later admitted that the Soviet request was made in May when federation delegates came to Moscow for a technical meeting.

In other Olympic sports, the judging is by a panel of international officials but in track and field officials are from the host country. Paulen said this system has been in existence since 1912. "We train these people for six months and then they have to take an examination," he said. "Besides, it's a hell of a job to get 600 judges from international sources."

Among the IAAF officials making their first appearance "in the ring" (on the field) Wednesday was Paulen, who personally observed the pole vault and said, "Everything was quite correct."

Why, suddenly, did they decide to go onto the field?

"To protect the (Soviet) judges from unfair and even scandalous rumors that have appeared in the Western press," Paulen said.

Paulen confirmed that the IAAF executive committee had discussed the judging situation Tuesday at a meeting aboard a boat on the Moscow River and agreed that its members should go onto the field. The

Please Turn to Page 10, Col. 4

### JIM MURRAY

## Overt Disdain

MOSCOW—Journalists, like kids at Saturday matinees, wrestling promoters and comic strips, need good guys and bad guys.

In an Olympics full of communists, Third World bombast, visiting Arab terrorists and reports host-country judges are helping the home team by calling fouls on visitors and using two sets of measuring sticks, one for them and one for us, Western journalists have found their villain.

He's English-speaking. He's a capitalist. To the best of anyone's knowledge he has never hijacked a plane or even eaten peas with a knife or his hat on. He's never stuck up a bank, pushed women and children out of a lifeboat or even stolen a horse.

But you would think Steve Ovett had shot Santa Claus, burned the flag or even said a kind word about the Russian judges. All he does is win races. That's his big trouble right there.

★

**You see,** these races are supposed to be won by his countryman, a slim, elegant, smiling young man with the poetic looks of a young Lord Byron, the engaging manner of a British public school athlete with well-scrubbed cheeks and curly locks, a young British dandy who stares brazenly out at you from a dozen Georgian portraits. Sebastian Coe is Little Lord Fauntleroy in this morality drama.

Enter now (hiss!) the evil Dr. Ovett himself. Paint him in a cape and top hat sneering. He's up to no good.

As proof, he's won 44 straight footraces, the most recent over (Zounds! What a scoundrel!) young Master Coe himself. He's snatched away Coe's record in the mile. It seemed as soon as young Master Coe set a record, this dastard broke it or tied it.

It was all wrong. I mean, what would this blackguard be doing next, insulting the queen?

Well, in a sense, he did. He turned down an invite to Buckingham Palace, no less. Egad! Is there no limit to the cheek of the man?

Steve Ovett does not look like Little Lord Fauntleroy. He looks more like Little Lord Fauntleroy's family coachman. He looks a little like actor John Ireland when John was playing a stagecoach robber.

★

**Worst of all,** he disdains press conferences. Consider the plight of several planeloads of Western journalists adrift in Moscow, awash with victorious athletes who have to have their post-game remarks translated into as many as three languages before they make sense, finding their great hero cutting them off at the tape recorders.

When Sebastian Coe arrived, he graciously consented to a mass press conference with instant translation in six tongues via headsets. And he manfully answered questions, loaded and innocent, not to say inane, from the assembled reporters of the world. Coe now wears the white hat.

Unfortunately, he doesn't wear the gold medal. Some elements of the British press dubbed Ovett "Mr. Arrogance." Seb Coe was "Mr. Nice," but this was a case of nice guys finishing second.

You would think Westerners, minus their cleanup hitters, the Americans and the West Germans, would be starved for a winner—any winner. You would think Steve Ovett would have them throwing their hats in the air. You would think they would want him to stand for prime minister.

All they want him to do is

Please Turn to Page 10, Col. 1

HAPPY LANDING—Wladyslaw Kozakiewicz of Poland heads for a pit stop after winning the gold medal and setting a world record of 18 feet 11½ inches in pole vault at Olympics.
Associated Press photo

# An Upper-Case Pole Pole Vaults 18-11½

## Kozakiewicz Breaks the World Record; Alexeyev's Career Ends With a Whimper

From Times Wire Services

MOSCOW—Wladyslaw Kozakiewicz, a 26-year-old Pole from the shores of the Baltic Sea, set a world pole vault record; Steve Ovett and Sebastian Coe advanced toward Showdown II; the Yugoslavian men and the Soviet women won gold medals in basketball, and Vasily Alexeyev bombed out of his last Olympics and then said he is retiring.

These were among the dramatic highlights Wednesday on the 11th day of competition in the Olympic Games, but there was some intrigue, too, as the integrity of Soviet officials was called into question. (See separate story.)

Kozakiewicz, ranked No. 1 in the world in 1975, 1977 and 1979, regained the world record and won the gold medal with a vault of 18 feet 11½ inches and then came close at 19 feet 1¼ inches. He had to survive a lot of jeering and hooting and whistling from groups of Soviet and French fans in jam-packed, 103,000-seat Lenin Stadium before claiming the world mark, the first set in men's track here. The pockets of Soviet, French and Polish fans took turns cheering their favorites and trying to unnerve the vaulters from the other countries.

**A Plea Goes Ignored**

At one time, the public address announcer even pleaded with the enthusiastic, flag-waving fans to be quiet while the vaulters were jumping. But the fans ignored the plea—until only Kozakiewicz was left in the competition.

"I think it hampered performances slightly," Kozakiewicz said. "I have trained myself to concentrate in such a way that I have no idea what the other athletes are doing, or what is happening in the stadium. But the whistling hampered us. We all wanted to win but not at any price."

The nerveless Kozakiewicz overcame all the early distractions and soared over the bar cleanly, breaking the world mark of 18-11¼ set by Philippe Houvion of France on July 17, only two days before the start of the Olympics.

After clearing the record height, the bushy-haired Pole smiled

Please Turn to Page 10, Col. 1

## Reuss Wins, 3-0, but Guerrero Gets the Rave Notices

By MIKE LITTWIN
Times Staff Writer

It had been a while between wins for Jerry Reuss. Three starts, 19 days. For Reuss, this year, that's a drought.

Which says something about what kind of year it has been for Reuss (11-4), the ex-Pirate, who shut out Pittsburgh on four hits Wednesday, 3-0, before a sellout crowd of 50,308 at Dodger Stadium.

"If you look at the past few games," he said, "you can see that with a break here or there, we might have won one or two of those."

**Outstanding Defense**

That's because Reuss, even when he hasn't pitched very well, still hasn't pitched badly. Let's say, he's been there, close. In his last start, some shabby defense hurt more than a little.

On Wednesday, he credited "outstanding defense" as a major factor in his victory.

A look at the defense: Pete Guerrero was playing centerfield. Mickey Hatcher was playing right. With Davey Lopes back in the lineup, the infield was its old self. Steve Yeager caught.

They all played well, it seemed.

Please Turn to Page 12, Col. 3

### RAMS' FANS IRATE

## What's All the Shouting About? Ticket Locations

By PETE DONOVAN and RICH ROBERTS
Times Staff Writers

ANAHEIM—Irate ticket buyers, complaining about their seat locations at Anaheim Stadium, have been calling the Ram ticket office, the Ram general office, the stadium switchboard and newspapers this week.

"I paid $15,000 for my 84 tickets on April 5," said Gordon Fields of Los Angeles, who has bought Ram tickets for 25 years. "They moved me about 10 yards further away (to the 30-yard line) and downstairs on the field level where I don't think you can see as well. They (the Rams) did a nice job on the people of Los Angeles. They don't care. I think they want to eliminate the L.A. people and get their own fans down there.

"I kind of expected it. I'll go this year and then just wait for the Raiders to move here (the Coliseum) from Oakland."

**Goal to Goal: 21,000 Seats**

Don Nims, the Rams' ticket manager, said his phones have been ringing "constantly" since Monday.

"I'm ready to hit the panic button and go to Mexico," he said, managing a joke. "Just as soon as you hang one up, it's ringing again.

"Not all of them are irate. Some are just curious. They don't really understand what they've got. I can't help but feel if they get down there and look, they're not going to be as unhappy."

The problems, the Rams said, have been created by fewer seats (21,000 compared to 26,000 at the Coliseum) between the goal lines; difficulties in attempting to make an equitable transition, and the allocation of tickets a month later than scheduled.

Jack Teele, vice president for administration for the Rams, said, "We knew it (the avalanche of complaints) would happen because any change upsets a season ticket buyer.

"There are a lot of plusses that people should consider. Anaheim is a triple-decked stadium, so the sight lines are much better than in a one-level stadium (such as the Col-

Please Turn to Page 9, Col. 1

## U.S. Swimmers Break 2 World Records at Irvine

By JOHN WEYLER
Times Staff Writer

IRVINE—America's swimmers may be boycotting, but they certainly aren't on strike and they proved it again Wednesday night at the U.S. swimming championships, leaving two world records and one American record in their wake.

Mary T. Meagher, tears of "pain, not happiness" flowing down her face, still had a smile for a swarm of reporters at the Heritage Park Aquatics Complex after she broke her world record in the 200-meter butterfly with a time of 2:06.37.

The Louisville 15-year-old had just escaped one mob scene in the pool, where the other swimmers hugged and kissed her.

"This time I was going for that world record," Meagher said, explaining that when she set the mark she was just trying to win.

"It was a very painful race. I just kept thinking about keeping my arms high out of the water. The crowd really helped."

About 4,000 fans and nearly 1,000 other swimmers screamed when they saw her split time of 1:00.83 (well ahead of worldrecord pace). And they screamed some more as Meagher came out of her final turn.

**Beardsley Sets Mark**

It started out as Craig Beardsley's day when he set a world record in the 200-meter butterfly and the 19-year-old from Harrington Park, N.J., ended up in the spotlight as well.

Beardsley broke Mike Bruner's world record in the preliminaries, shaving more than a second off the mark of 1:59.23 set by Bruner at Montreal in '76—with a 1:58.21.

He came back to win the final (in 1:58.46) as the American men showed their dominence of the butterfly. All eight swimmers in the final beat the silver medalist time from Moscow.

Beardsley, Bruner who was second with 1:59.13 (also bettering his world mark) and Bill Forrester (1:59.40) all were ahead of Sergey

Please Turn to Page 13, Col. 1

### *Angels on Win Streak: Three Straight*

Story on Page 3

### PIPINO CUEVAS

## All Fireworks but No Flair

By RICHARD HOFFER
Times Staff Writer

DETROIT—Pipino Cuevas defends his World Boxing Assn. welterweight title Saturday night when he fights top-ranked Tommy Hearns here. Cuevas, 22, of Mexico City, has successfully defended his 11 times, 10 by knockout and 5 of those by the third round. Hearns, 21, of Detroit, is undefeated in 28 bouts and has left just two opponents upright. Of Hearns' 26 KOs, 19 have come by the fourth round.

This is the fight ringsiders have voted least likely to go the distance. Advises veteran trainer Angelo Dundee: "Get your hot dogs *before* the fight."

Yet, the prospect of the collision does not have the country in a lather, even though it may be even more explosive than that other welterweight title fight, the Brawl in Montreal where Roberto Duran bulled his way past Sugar Ray Leonard to win the World Boxing Council's championship.

Not a lot of folks are buying tickets, for one thing. As of Monday,

Please Turn to Page 8, Col. 1

## J. R. RICHARD HAS SURGERY ON BLOCKED ARTERY

HOUSTON (AP)—J.R. Richard, the Houston Astros' million-dollar pitcher, was listed in good condition Wednesday night after he underwent emergency surgery to remove a blood clot in a neck artery, a hospital spokeswoman said.

"J.R. Richard was found to have a blocked artery in his neck. The surgery was successfully accomplished to remove the blockage and he was moved to the intensive care unit," she said.

Richard was rushed into surgery at Houston Methodist Hospital after he collapsed during a workout at the Astrodome earlier Wednesday, team officials announced in Philadelphia, where the Astros played the Phillies.

A hospital spokesman said the blood clot could have been "a life-or-death situation."

Please Turn to Page 13, Col. 4

# Coe Gets a Kick and Gold Medal This Time; Ovett 3rd

By BILL SHIRLEY
Times Sports Editor

MOSCOW—There is nothing satisfying about a tie in any sport. Just ask Notre Dame or Michigan State.

And now the world must wait again for who knows how long to determine whether Sebastian Coe is a better middle-distance runner than Steve Ovett. The Englishmen broke even in their heralded races at the Olympic Games, settling absolutely nothing.

Coe got even with his rival Friday night, winning a slow 1,500 meters in 3:38.4. Ovett finished third in 3:39, losing the silver medal to East Germany's Jurgen Straub.

So each Englishman won a gold medal, Ovett taking the 800 meters last Saturday, also in a rather slow time (1:45.4), at least for fellows at their level. After all, they hold all the middle-distance world records.

Coe finished second in the 800, running, in his words, a dreadful race.

Oddly, each runner won the race the other was supposed to win, so the argument over who is No. 1 was further compounded. They share the world 1,500-meter record at 3:32.1, but until Friday night they had not met over that distance. And until last Saturday they had not raced each other in two years. Ovett came into the 1,500 final unbeaten in 45 races at that distance or the mile.

After beating the stronger Ovett in a race to the finish line over the last 100 meters or so, Coe made it clear he would have preferred to win the 800.

"Saturday was a terrible disappointment," he said. "I would have preferred for it to have gone right on Saturday, in a way, rather than tonight. That's the one I came for.

"But I'm not complaining about tonight; I thought I was equally well prepared. There was just this thing in the back of my mind all the time that really it was impossible to run quite as badly again, certainly not within a few days."

Coe said he had a fairly uncluttered run for the tape and that's what he was hoping for. The surprise was his ability to outfoot Ovett over those last 100 meters because Ovett usually has a stronger kick to the tape.

Ovett had said he had a 90% chance of winning the longer race because, "Steve Ovett is a miler." Steve Ovett also had won 28 races in a row.

There was no immediate comment after the race from Ovett, who rarely talks to reporters.

The race, the feature event of the last night of track and field competition, was run on a warm evening under a bright sun. A capacity crowd of 103,000 watched in Lenin Stadium.

Straub raced into the lead almost immediately, but Coe stuck close to his heels. They went to the first 400 meters in 61.7 seconds. Ovett at first seemed content to run back in the eight-man field. Straub and Coe held the same positions through 800 meters at 2:04.9 and passed 1,200 in 2:59.5. With 200 meters to go, Ovett had moved into a close third place. The stage was set for the race to the wire.

"Soon after the halfway Straub took it up, and the pack broke up," Coe said. "I was able to do what I can do best—that is, to run freely."

Please Turn to Page 6, Col. 1

GOLD RUSH—Sebastian Coe (254) holds off British countryman Steve Ovett around the final turn (left) and wins the gold medal in the 1,500 meters Friday night at Moscow. Ovett, winner of the 800, finished third behind Jurgen Straub (338) of East Germany.

# East German Breaks Record in High Jump

## Wessig Leaps 7-9; Yifter Gets Second Gold Medal; Cierpinski Wins Marathon

From Times Wire Services

MOSCOW—Ethiopia's Miruts Yifter won the 5,000 meters Friday to become the only double gold medalist in Moscow Olympics track competition and East Germany's Gerd Wessig set a world high jump record of 7 feet 9 inches.

In other action before 103,000 at Lenin Stadium, Sebastian Coe beat British arch-rival Steve Ovett in their long-awaited 1,500-meter showdown (see separate story) and Waldemar Cierpinski of East Germany became the second man to win Olympic marathons back to back.

Los Angeles Times
Sports
ORANGE COUNTY
BUSINESS
CC PART III †
SATURDAY, AUGUST 2, 1980


The scrawny, balding Yifter, who won the 10,000-meter gold medal Monday, took the 5,000 with his usual devastating kick in 13 minutes, 21.0 seconds.

Wessig, 21, won the gold with a leap of 7-8¼ and then went on to break the world mark of 7-8½ shared by Poland's Jacek Wszola and Dietmar Mogenburg of West Germany. Wszola, the 1976 Olympic champion, took the silver by clearing 7-7.

### Two-Time Champion

Cierpinski's time was 2 hours 11 minutes 3 seconds. The only other two-time marathon champion was Abebe Bikila of Ethiopia, who took the 26-mile, 385-yard race for the first time in 1960 while running without shoes and repeated in 1964 while wearing shoes.

In other individual events, Tatyana Kazankina of the Soviet Union won the women's 1,500-meter gold medal for the second consecutive time with an Olympic record clocking of 3:56.6. And Evelin Jahl of East Germany repeated as a Games champion with an Olympic record 229-6 in the women's discus.

East Germany's women's 400-meter relay team of Romy Muller, Barbel Wockel, Ingrid Auerswald and Marlies Gohr cracked its world record with a time of 41.60 seconds. The Germans had run 41.85 on July 13 for the previous mark.

Soviets took the other three relays. They won the men's 400 in 38.26, a European record; the men's 1,600 in 3:01.1 and the women's 1,600 in 3:20.2.

### Monument in Gold

On the next-to-last full day of competition, the Soviets continued to build a monument in gold medals and total medals that seems unlikely to ever be torn down. In the first Games without an American team participating, the Soviets have won 77 golds and 179 total medals, far surpassing their marks of 50 golds at Munich in 1972 and 125 total medals in Montreal in 1976.

Boxing headlines the Olympic agenda today with 11 final bouts, including Cuban heavyweight Teofilo Stevenson's bid to win a third consecutive Olympic gold medal. He fights Pyotr Zaev of the Soviet Union. Besides this matchup, Cubans and Soviets will be paired in four other finals. In all, eight Cubans and seven Soviets reached the championship round.

In today's other major event, defending champion East Germany

Please Turn to Page 6, Col. 1

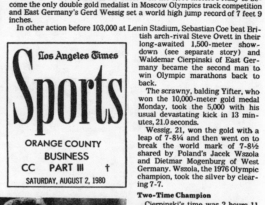

JOLLY GOOD SHOW—Coe takes a moment to catch his breath and reflect on his victory in the 1,500 meters at the Olympics (left), but he's on his feet seconds later and taking a victory lap around Lenin Stadium after making up for his disappointment in losing the 800 meters to Ovett earlier in Moscow Games.

Associated Press photos

# Dodgers Beat Cards on Ferguson Homer in 10th, 2-1

By MIKE LITTWIN
Times Staff Writer

Joe Ferguson began Friday's game on the bench. Probably unhappily.

But he ended it at home plate in the arms of his manager, Tom Lasorda, who's given to hugging a game-winner, especially if it's Ferguson.

All Ferguson did was homer to open the 10th inning against Bob Forsch to give the Dodgers a 2-1 victory over St. Louis.

The Dodgers did it the hard way. In the ninth, Jay Johnstone homered against Forsch, thus providing the game's equalizer. They loaded the bases that inning, but Forsch got a double play ball and new life.

Not, however, long life.

It was the third straight win for the Dodgers, and more important, it was the third straight night in which they picked up a game on faltering Houston.

A 3½-game lead by the Astros in the National League West has diminished to a half-game. There were at least a few Dodgers to thank for that.

One was Dave Goltz, who is soon to reappear in the starting rotation. On Friday, he took over in the ninth for Don Sutton and pitched two shutout innings to get the victory.

That figured, with Sutton pitching. In eight innings, he allowed all of two hits—one a George Hendrick homer. But the Dodgers haven't been scoring runs for Sutton, who is 5-0 at home and 7-3 overall.

But they do tend to score once he leaves. In the 10 games he's started at Dodger Stadium, the Dodgers are unbeaten.

They're also 5-2 so far this homestand, 36-14 at home overall.

And they got that way by winning more than occasionally the way they did Friday night. Johnstone, who hadn't expected to play, was in right field in place of injured Reggie Smith. Hitless that night and without a homer all season, Johnstone, who's just slightly flakey, turned back to Lasorda and said: "I'm going to hit one out."

But it was Ferguson's, on a 1-2 pitch, that was the crusher.

"He (Forsch) didn't make a good pitch and he knew it," said Ferguson, who entered the game in the ninth and was batting for the first time. "He tried to get a fastball in, but he missed. I knew it was gone as soon as I hit it and so did he. He started walking off the mound."

Forsch had pitched extremely well, just a little too long, it turned out.

Please Turn to Page 10, Col. 2

# Despite a World Record, Barrett Misses Moscow

By JOHN WEYLER
Times Staff Writer

IRVINE—A sign in the stands this week at the Heritage Park Aquatics Complex reads: "We couldn't bear to be in Moscow, but we love Irvine."

The consensus of most of the swimmers here at the U.S. swimming championships, however, is very much to the contrary.

Bill Barrett, a UCLA junior from Alpharretta, Ga., set a world record in the 200-meter individual medley (a non-Olympic event) Friday in preliminaries. After he won the final in just over his record time, he was asked if he would trade his world record for a chance to swim in Moscow.

"I wish I was there," he said. "In this sport that's the ultimate. I guess . . . well . . . I just can't answer that."

Barrett wasn't the only winner who was less than overjoyed.

"The people here have done everything they could to make this a big event," said Rowdy Gaines, America's premier freestyle swimmer, after winning the 200-meter freestyle.

"But it's just not the same. I know if I was there (Moscow), I would have won a couple of golds," said the Winter Haven, Fla., resident who won the 100 freestyle earlier this week.

"This is nice though. I guess I couldn't get any better of a feeling unless those medals were hanging around my neck."

Winner after winner has expressed the same empty feeling. There's just something missing.

But Barrett, if he can hang in there until 1984, could get a chance to swim the 200 individual medley in the Olympics. It's been added as an Olympic event for '84.

"That was the toughest race I've

Please Turn to Page 10, Col. 1

# It's Showdown Time in Motown

By RICHARD HOFFER
Times Staff Writer

DETROIT—It's a low-rent "Brawl in Montreal," a blue-collar counterpart to Roberto Duran's recent seizure of Sugar Ray Leonard's World Boxing Council welterweight title.

It's a World Boxing Assn. companion piece in which Tommy Hearns challenges Pipino Cuevas for the "other" welterweight title. In comparison to the Leonard-Duran fight, which was suffused with the personal style of the two boxers, tonight's match figures, on the basis of its promotion, to have all the panache of a gangland slaying.

Hearns, 21, the challenger who lives in Detroit, where he has scored many of his 26 knockouts (he's 28-0), is being promoted as the HitMan.

Cuevas, 22, a knockout specialist (he's flattened 10 of 11 challengers during his four-year reign) from Mexico City, where he owns four

Please Turn to Page 4, Col. 2

# HILL, PEACOCK IN THE RUNNING

## Starting Job With Rams Is Available, at Least Temporarily

By RICH ROBERTS
Times Staff Writer

FULLERTON—Only Eddie Hill and Elvis Peacock know what they felt deep in their hearts when they heard Wendell Tyler had dislocated a hip in a plunge down a West Virginia mountain.

Concern for a friend, certainly, but they couldn't be faulted for also allowing themselves a flutter of hope for their own professional football careers.

Hill and Peacock are the leading contenders to start at halfback for the Rams, at least until Tyler returns—and that's all either is counting on.

Peacock said, "There's a chance for me, and I have to try to take advantage of it. But when Wendell gets back he gets his job back and things will go from there. If I have been playing well up to that point, I feel that Ray (Malavasi) probably will use both of us in the backfield."

Malavasi's oft-stated policy is to return injured starters to the lineup when they're healthy. Hill agreed it's a good policy.

"I don't really see, regardless of how well I play, me winning the job from Wendell," Hill said.

### Deserves Starting Position

"He won the position last year. He has great natural running skills and he has a lot of heart. I admire Wendell a great deal. To go out and execute and take the punishment that Wendell had to take last season, I think he deserves the starting position."

When Tyler arrived at training camp on crutches, Hill asked him about his hip.

"He said it was doing OK and I said he was looking good," Hill said. "He said, 'No, you're looking good. You're the one that's carrying the mail now.' I said, 'Myself and Peacock.' "

Hill is not about to claim anything he hasn't earned.

"I don't believe a person should get anything for free," he said.

But he paid a large part of his dues as a rookie last season, rushing 29 times for 114 yards and returning 15 kickoffs.

"I think I contributed in various ways," he said, "just being ready whenever they needed me. Knowing Ram policy over the years, they just don't like to play young ballplayers much, especially if it's a situation where a mistake would hurt them. But by the end of the season last year I felt that Ray and the offensive coaches thought I could play if necessary."

When they drafted Hill and Peacock, the Rams thought they *both* could play. In fact, both were drafted higher than Tyler: Hill a No. 2 in '79 out of Memphis State, Peacock a

Please Turn to Page 11, Col. 2

***Formula One Driver Depailler Is Killed***

Story on Page 2

# The Ballad of Muhammad Ali: a Sad Song at the End

**JIM MURRAY**

LAS VEGAS—OK, stop the music. Take off the paper hats. Take down those streamers from the ceiling. Tell the piano player to cool it. Hold the confetti. Close the bar. Nobody feels like a drink at a time like this. Cancel the parade. Dim the lights, muffle the drums. Get out the black suit. The party's over.

Muhammad Ali is mortal. He turned back into a pumpkin well before midnight. The dazzling pretty boy who flashed out of the Louisville ghetto 20 years ago to beguile the world with the most improbable career in the annals of fistiana was finally caught up with by the Gray Stranger. His appointment in Samarra was kept, his rendezvous with fate met.

And Larry Holmes has shot Santa Claus. He has closed the circus. He couldn't do any worse if he burned Disneyland and poisoned Mickey Mouse.

We're not going to have Muhammad Ali to kick us around any more. He belongs with the Joe Louises, James J. Jeffrieses, the Jack Johnsons and Jack Dempseys now. He's yesterday's roses, he belongs to the scrapbooks.

But what a lovely light when he burned his brightest, if Edna St. Vincent Millay will pardon me. What a glow he lit in a sport grown moribund when he first burst on it.

They'll talk into the night around the old gyms of the flashing footwork, the blazing combinations, the fights he fought that were more ballet than brutal. He did things in a ring Nureyev couldn't do at the Bolshoi. It was when boxing became an art not a murder.

I'd like to spare you the details. I mean who cares what the train thinks when it rolls through a bus at a crossing? Who wants to interview a flood? Larry Holmes was just there, is all. He didn't beat Ali, he beat the ghost of Ali, a memory, is all. The real Ali, the Arabian Knight, the boy boxer from the bluegrass, would have beat Larry Holmes and knitted an Afghan in his days of glory. Holmes would have spent the night wondering where he kept disappearing to. He would have thought it was raining gloves.

This 38-year-old replica of the real thing would have had trouble getting out of the way of a glacier. He was like a general who keeps sending messages

**Please Turn to Page 12, Col. 2**

VICTOR AND VANQUISHED—Larry Holmes (left) raises arms in victory after 11th-round KO win over Muhammad Ali Thursday night in Las Vegas. At right, trainer Angelo Dundee gives the word to Ali (seated) that he is ordering the fight stopped.

Associated Press photo

# Ali's Last Hurrah Is Without Any Cheer

## He Reaches Back and Finds He Has Nothing as Holmes Scores KO in 11

**By RICHARD HOFFER**
Times Staff Writer

LAS VEGAS—It was a brief, yet surprisingly complete retrospective, a hurried, yet comprehensive, walk through the gallery of modern boxing. The mugging, the histrionics, the taunting and theatrics, the jabs, hooks and idiosyncratic defenses. They were all there Thursday on a hot desert night, there for everyone to see in the middle of a hotel parking lot.

In the end, as was anticipated before Muhammad Ali had worked his spell on his vast public, World Boxing Council champion Larry Holmes retained his title with an 11th-round knockout. He exposed Ali, his old master, for the relic he is, a three-time champion now blasted with antiquity, a product of his own golden age, and a far more distant age than anyone had believed.

It was after the 10th round, when Ali, slumped on his stool, was unable to answer the bell that the decision was officially rendered. Referee Richard Green, who had
een cautiously observed the former three-time champion the previous four rounds, stopped it, with the whole-hearted approval of Ali's cornerman, Angelo Dundee.

But the decision had been delivered long before that, a decision ordained by the orderly progression of age. Ali, 38, coming off a two-year retirement and crash diet, was little more than a shell of his former greatness, aged, slow and seemingly deprived of the reflexes that carried him through a marvelous era of boxing. He was no match, never a factor in the fight, even with all the old psychological tools still in evidence.

And Holmes, a former sparring partner for Ali who has long been denied the respect and awe that was accorded Ali so many years, finally exorcised the demon of boxing's memory. He did it reluctantly, holding off a number of times after Ali had become defenseless. He threw the shroud off Ali and revealed a museum-piece. Yet, even so, the respect was offered grudgingly. "Holmes, you're nothing," shouted one of the 25,000 fans who filled the makeshift arena in a Caesers Palace parking lot, "you're still nothing. All you beat is an old man."

**Crash Diet Was Successful**

That Ali is an old man, in terms of professional boxing, had been obscured by Ali's wonderfully public bombast, an increasingly persuasive argument that assured a purse of $8 million for himself, $4 million for Holmes and lots more for promoter Don King, who marketed the fight to closed circuit and subscription television.

Ali, who has fought 16 years, winning the heavyweight title three times, losing it once in the ring, once in the courts and once by actual retirement, had found retirement satisfying only in a gastronomic sense. Fat, but boared, he announced his comeback six-and-a-half months ago and trained beyond anyone's expectations, carving 50 pounds from a once-embarrassing body.

**Please Turn to Page 12, Col. 1**

SCREWBALL SEASON

# Teen-Age Beer-Drinker Is Now Dodger Stopper

**By MIKE LITTWIN**
Times Staff Writer

Fernando Valenzuela's midsection is as rounded as his favorite pitch, which curves down and away and nearly always out of the batter's reach.

But if the newest Dodger sensation has a body by Rubens, he also has a screwball by Brewer, or maybe Hubbell.

And nobody minds, even in the age of physical fitness, that this 19-year-old pitcher has come along bent on giving the beer gut a good name.

The Dodgers, who paid $120,000 for this overweight, left-handed Mexican pitcher a year ago while wondering if they had overspent, have themselves a bargain. Just figuring dollars per pound.

No matter that Valenzuela's nickname should be Pauncho, if the Dodgers somehow win the National League West, no one will have played a greater role down the stretch than Fernando Valenzuela.

Since coming to the club last month he has pitched 11⅔ innings without allowing an earned run while saving one game and winning another. And this from a kid who's never relieved in all of his 19 years.

But his philosophy on pitching is sound for either starter or reliever: Don't let the other team score, ever.

In his last 35 innings at San Antonio, the Dodgers' Double A farm club, he didn't allow a run. Somehow, they're not boring, all those consecutive zeroes.

His success is based on his screwball, taught him last year by Bobby Castillo, now his teammate. No one mastered that pitch in a year, until Valenzuela did it. Carl Hubbell, whose screwball took him to the

**Please Turn to Page 10, Col. 1**

CORNERED—Holmes maneuvers Ali into a corner, and the former three-time champion is almost helpless to defend himself from the onslaught near the end as Holmes hits Ali at will.

Associated Press photos


*The Anonymous Astros of Houston, Texas*

Story on Page 3

*The Last Grand Prix at Watkins Glen?*

Story on Page 7


ART SCHLICHTER

# The Guy UCLA Can't Forget

**By RICHARD HOFFER**
Times Staff Writer

UCLA, in some people's top 10 this week, visits Ohio State Saturday afternoon. Ohio State is in everybody's top 2. This is considered a significant differential in college football. But there are additional concerns for the Bruins as they prepare to wind up their Big 10 schedule.

First of all, there's Ohio Stadium, home to 88,000 loyal Buckeye fans every game day in Columbus; it takes UCLA two weeks at the Coliseum to see that many people. Second, there's the recently announced regional TV (ABC); the Bruins haven't been on the tube for a while and there's always stage fright to think about.

These things concern UCLA Coach Terry Donahue enough that he's included pictures of Ohio Stadium and a television in his weekly scouting report. Just to give the team a more graphic idea of what it's up against. One more thing in the Donahue photo album: A picture of Art Schlichter.

**Please Turn to Page 11, Col. 1**

# Dodgers Lose—Now Must Sweep Astros Just to Tie

## Houston Rolls On, Beats Braves, 3-2

From Times Wire Services

Joe Niekro pitched a six-hitter with last-out relief help and Joe Morgan hit a two-run single Thursday night at Houston as the Astros beat the Atlanta Braves, 3-2, and moved within one game of winning the National League West.

"I am confident we can win one of three games," Houston Manager Bill Virdon said of the season-closing series with the Dodgers. "But that victory won't be easy. The game will be tough."

Said Morgan: "I came here to help Houston win the championship and to find the Joe Morgan that had been lost the last couple of years. I have corrected my swing and I know I will be a good hitter the rest of the way."

"This team could not have won the championship in April but we can do it now," he said.

**THE NL RACES**

**WEST**

| | W | L | Pct. | GB | Left |
|---|---|---|---|---|---|
| Astros | 92 | 67 | .579 | | 3 |
| Dodgers | 89 | 70 | .560 | 3 | 3 |

**Tonight, Saturday and Sunday:** Astros at Dodgers.

**EAST**

| | W | L | Pct. | GB | Left |
|---|---|---|---|---|---|
| Expos | 89 | 70 | .560 | | 3 |
| Phillies | 89 | 70 | .560 | | 3 |

**Tonight, Saturday and Sunday:** Phillies at Expos.

Niekro struck out four and walked none in 8⅔ innings to run his record to 19-12 in his last scheduled start of the regular season. He left in the ninth after allow g a double to Gary Matthews. Joe Sambito relieved and surrendered an RBI single to Chris Chambliss before Frank LaCorte came on to record his 11th save by striking out Dale Murphy to end the game.

**Please Turn to Page 5, Col. 1**

## Giants Score Twice in 8th for a 3-2 Victory

**By MIKE LITTWIN**
Times Staff Writer

The Dodgers' chances of winning the National League West fell a giant notch Thursday, from slim to remote.

With a 3-2 come-from-ahead loss to San Francisco, they slipped to three games behind Houston, with three to play, on a two-run bloop single in the eighth by Darrell Evans.

And so begins the much-awaited showdown at Dodger Stadium tonight, three games between the two leaders. But this is a Wild West showdown with a twist.

The Astros come with all the guns.

They have only to win once to claim their first West Division championship. And because the Dodgers lost Thursday and Houston won, they get an extra game with which to win it.

Should the Dodgers sweep the three-game series, they still wouldn't win the West. There would be a one-game playoff for the title.

The Dodgers took a 2-1 lead into the eighth on the strength of a two-run homer by Steve Garvey and Dave Goltz' fine pitching.

But the Giants were determined not to be swept by the Dodgers. Manager Dave Bristol was quoted in a San Francisco paper saying, "I'd give 10 years off my life to beat the Dodgers."

After singles by Milt May and Max Venable and a flyout, Goltz left the game with a cramp in his right thigh. Bobby Castillo walked Jack Clark to load the bases. Steve Howe was brought in to face Darrell Evans, who blooped a single over second baseman Derrel Thomas' head in shallow right, two runs scoring.

The Dodgers lost by a run, for the 23rd time in 30 one-run decisions on the road.

"I think we can do it," Dusty Baker said. "I really do. But I'm sure the Astros think they can too."

There's no reason why the Astros shouldn't. They've won nine of their last 13, having just swept Atlanta, and they're close enough to a title to taste it.

One game.

They'll send Ken Forsch (12-12) against Don Sutton (13-5) to get it. But Sutton, who leads the league in earned run average, has been the Dodgers' most consistent starter.

And it will be an emotional game for the winningest pitcher in Dodger history. It could well be his last as a Dodger. In the last year of a four-year contract, Sutton appears headed for the free-agent market.

But all the negotiating he'll be doing will be on the mound, where he must try to buy time.

**Please Turn to Page 16, Col. 1**

# SPORTS

Sunday, November 23, 1980 — Los Angeles Times — CC†/Part III

# USC Gives UCLA a Winning Tip

JAYNE KAMIN / Los Angeles Times

On the play that finished Troy, UCLA's Freeman McNeil follows the bouncing ball (above left) that has been tipped by USC's Jeff Fisher (40) and brings it in as he goes by Dennis Smith (above right). In full flight (right), McNeil completes 58-yard play for winning score.

## McNeil Turns It Into a 20-17 Victory

By RICHARD HOFFER, *Times Staff Writer*

UCLA, which has long suffered in the deep shadows of USC, finally had its day in the sun Saturday, beating the Trojans, 20-17, before 83,491 pom pon-shaking, card-flashing fans in the Coliseum.

It was the Bruins' (8-2) first victory over crosstown rival USC (7-2-1) in five years and all it took was a tricked-up volleyball play that went for a 58-yard touchdown in the fourth quarter, a brand new defensive alignment that held the nation's top rusher to a 1.95 average on 37 carries, a 9-for-11 passing day from a second-string quarterback and three deflected passes by a free safety who, doctors said, should have spent the day in the hospital, not the secondary.

All it took was the game of their lives, on a day on which the Trojans, playing without their senior quarterback and much of a passing attack, were prepared to play the game of theirs.

All it took was a game that is entirely typical of this half-century-old series, one that's sometimes bitter, but always important to the two teams and their fans and always, it seems, decided in the last minute. A game, finally, typical of two teams which have been ranked as high as No. 2 in the nation this year and which, no matter what happens, will finish with fine records.

The victory, which wasn't accomplished until the last play of the game when USC, disdaining a try for a game-tying field goal, failed to complete a drive at the UCLA 29, was the first for almost everybody connected with UCLA football these days.

UCLA Coach Terry Donahue had failed to beat USC in any of the last four years. And that's how long Donahue has been head coach. Nobody, as a result, had become more aware than Donahue of how this particular game is able to confer the notion of success or failure of a team, its games beyond or behind notwithstanding.

Was the monkey, if that's what it was, finally off Donahue's back? "More like a gorilla," he said. "It wasn't a spider monkey, it was a gorilla." But did Saturday's victory make it all worthwhile? He shook his head. "All the blood, sweat and tears. . .it's been very expensive."

The payoff Saturday was not easily gained, not by any means. Although USC did not have its total offense at hand, quarterback Gordon Adams having been injured and operated on in the last week, the Trojans capitalized on Bruin mistakes and strange bounces to hold leads of 10-7 early in the second half and 17-14 early in the fourth quarter.

With sophomore Scott Tinsley at quarterback, untested except for some action in the Trojans'

Please see UCLA, Page 14

---

*Jim Murray*

## Rams' Kansas Legend

**They tell a story** in Kansas about the Rams scout who was combing the territory for football prospects and a coach asked him, "By the way, how is Nolan Cromwell doing with the Rams?" "He's holding for place-kicks," the scout told him. There was a pause. Then, the coach said, "If that's the best Nolan Cromwell can do, you're wasting your time down here. We don't have anybody who can even hold kicks for you."

The cliche about Nolan Neil Cromwell is, "He's the best athlete on the Rams, maybe in the league." It's the first thing anybody says about the Rams free safety. They don't say he's "blue-eyed" or "6-1" or "fast." They say "Nolan Cromwell, best athlete."

You get a picture of Nolan Cromwell intercepting a pass in a game, then going to the sidelines to match long drives with Jack Nicklaus or going to bat against Steve Carlton, going one-on-one with Magic Johnson, or racing a horse, doing pole vaults or, between halves, swimming to Catalina. Or maybe he just bench presses the back of freight cars. Or gives a prize to anyone who can stay three rounds with him in a ring.

★

**The legends** grow the farther you get from the Rams practice field. Nolan Cromwell used to outrun rabbits in his hometown on the prairies. He once jumped the Missouri River at Kansas City. From a standing start. He used to run home from school every day—a distance of 26 miles, 385 yards. He never bowled under 300 in his life. He birdied 18 straight holes in a state amateur once. He could eagle Rhode Island.

Nolan Cromwell was so fast as a pitcher they thought he was Nolan Ryan. He was so fast as a college quarterback he used to catch his own passes. He encountered a great white shark skin diving one time—and ate him. And so on.

The facts are heroic enough. In the first place, Cromwell is not 7-3 or 280 pounds. He does not look like something that was roped and broken. He looks like a guy who might be called "Fast Eddie" in a pool hall. He looks—well, ready, if you know what I mean. He doesn't look like a guy who would ever be taken by surprise. Or would even pick the wrong shell at a carnival. There is no hay sticking out of Cromwell's ears despite his humble rural beginnings.

★

**Nolan Cromwell is,** for sure, the best athlete ever to come out of Ransom, Kan. That's just a couple of hundred miles due west of Salina, and with a population of 387, unless it's exploded since Nolan was growing up there. If you ask folks there what position Nolan played on the football team they'll tell you, "Nolan *was* the football team."

Cut away the frontier myth and you find that Cromwell was a two-way high school football player, he was a pitcher and shortstop in baseball. But he never beat up the town bully or saved the banker's daughter from drowning or ran the Dalton Gang out of town. But every school in the Big 8 was after him, which tells you something. He chose Kansas because he would not have to concentrate solely on football but could run track.

He was a world-class inter-

Please see MURRAY, Page 18

---

## Leafs Shut Out Kings, but Then the Game Starts

By GORDON EDES
*Times Staff Writer*

TORONTO—When the Kings arrived at Maple Leaf Gardens for their pregame skate Saturday morning, they were told they could not take the ice.

The reason?

"Harold's flipped out," left winger Glenn Goldup said.

That's Harold as in Ballard, the 75-year-old curmudgeon who oversees the operations of the arena and its principal tenants, the Toronto Maple Leafs. Ballard, whose avocation it is to tweak the noses of foes and friends alike (last season he carried on a widely publicized fight with his star players), believed his team had been slighted on its last visit to L.A. Thus, the "No Trespassing" signs.

But Saturday night the matter was out of Ballard's hands. And the Kings, free to roam, celebrated the return of right wing Dave Taylor with a 5-2 win over the Leafs, their third win in a row and sixth against three losses and a tie on the road.

The one who did the most celebrating was Taylor. Idled for seven games with a shoulder injury, Taylor slipped right back into stride to score two goals and assist on two

Please see KINGS, Page 18

---

*3 Years of Frustration Turns to Joy*

## Last Dance Best for Bruin Seniors

By ALAN GREENBERG, *Times Staff Writer*

When it was over, safety Kenny Easley grabbed linebacker Avon Riley and they danced off the field, a pair of whirling human dervishes spinning arm-in-arm toward the joyous UCLA locker room, totally absorbed in the greatest moment of their college football lives.

With all due respect to the 0-10 Oregon State Beavers, whom UCLA plays in Tokyo next Saturday, this game-USC-was the last dance for Easley, Riley, Freeman McNeil and the rest of UCLA's 18 seniors.

In the recent past, UCLA seniors enjoyed this dance only if they liked getting their feet stepped on. Or worse. In 1976 (24-14), 1977 (29-27) and 1978 (17-10), USC did a cha-cha on UCLA.

Last year, USC did the mashed potato, 49-14.

So deep was last year's UCLA humiliation that Easley, who usually can't be silenced by anything less than a vacuum, stared into his locker afterward and refused to talk about the game.

This year, he and a couple teammates invaded the weight room the first day of spring practice and affixed a sign to the mirrors there:'49-14.'

"Nobody forgot last year's game when we needed to get things done out there today," Easley said. "We just wanted it more than they did. There was no way we were gonna lay down and die for USC."

Especially not Easley, a high school quarterback in Chesapeake, Va., who became a starter the second game of his freshmen year and went on to become the greatest defensive back in UCLA history. Easley entered the game with a badly bruised shoulder suffered two weeks ago in the loss to Oregon. He aggravated it tackling Hoby Brenner, USC's 6-6, 240-pound tight end, in the first quarter.

"From then on, I had ice on my shoulder (on the bench) so I couldn't feel any pain," Easley said. "SC's got so many big guys. I thought I'd hit the small guys and the big guys would leave me alone. I looked at

Please see BRUINS, Page 15

---

## USC's Fisher Says He Can't Believe One That Got Away

By MAL FLORENCE, *Times Staff Writer*

Jeff Fisher figured the odds were in his favor when he moved in to intercept a pass intended for Freeman McNeil late in the fourth quarter of Saturday's game between USC and UCLA at the Coliseum.

But it wasn't Fisher, a cornerback, who got the ball, rather McNeil, UCLA's tailback, who carried it to the end zone to complete a 58-yard scoring play.

So instead of Fisher preserving an apparent USC victory, it was McNeil who enabled UCLA to win, 20-17, after four frustrating years of losing to the Trojans.

"That ball would have been intercepted or fallen incomplete nine out of 10 times," Fisher said as he reconstructed the play in the USC dressing room.

Here's what happened:

UCLA quarterback Jay Schroeder threw a pass intended for McNeil near the sideline. But Fisher deflected ball into McNeil's hands at the USC 35-yard line and the Bruin tailback had a clear field ahead of him.

"We were in a zone coverage and I had the receiver in the flat—about 15 yards deep," Fisher said. "I found the receiver, looked back for the

Please see USC, Page 13

---

## Ohio St. Settles for 3 Points and a Cloud of Dust

By BOB OATES, *Times Staff Writer*

COLUMBUS, Ohio—When the Michigan and Ohio State teams meet on a football field in this era they seldom play to win. They play not to lose. And so Michigan's 9-3 decision over the Buckeyes here Saturday was neither spectacular nor very artistic.

The Wolverines made their way into the Rose Bowl by combining one perfect touchdown pass with some good defense and a heap of conservative signal-calling by their opponent, the coach of last year's Big 10 champions, Earle Bruce.

"We thought we could run on them," Bruce said afterward, "but we didn't get it done. Perhaps, looking back, we should've passed more."

Hardly waiting for a room full of reporters to nod collectively, the Ohio State coach continued:

"So often in a game like this, you're better off when you are able to jam it in there. There is a point where we have to test them."

Before a crowd of 88,827 on a brisk (50 degrees) and breezy afternoon in hazy sunshine, the Buckeyes failed that test and the Wolverines passed it—both defensively and offensively. Their good defense overpowered the Ohio State passer, Art Schlichter. And when the game was on the line in the third quarter after a 3-3 half, Michigan quarterback John Wangler won it with a 13-yard touchdown pass to his 161-pound flanker, Anthony Carter.

"The touchdown came on an automatic—yes, an audible call—by our quarterback," Michigan Coach Bo Schembechler said of the play that won the Big 10 title for the Wolverines and put them in the Rose Bowl Jan. 1 against Washington.

Said "Wangler: "I changed the call when I saw the (Ohio State)

Please see MICHIGAN, Page 9

# It's Coe's Turn: He Breaks Mile Mark by 1.07 Seconds

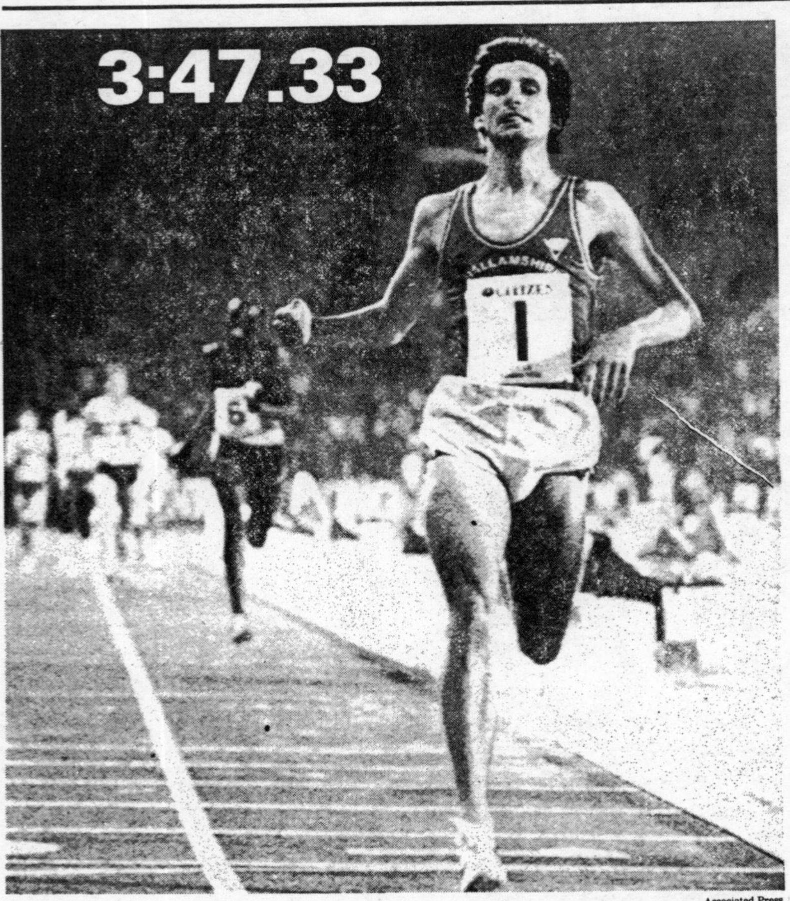


Associated Press

Sebastian Coe puts quite a bit of distance between him and the field in reclaiming world record in mile.

BRUSSELS, Belgium (AP)—Britain's remarkable Sebastian Coe regained the world mile record Friday, shaving more than one second off the previous mark with a time of 3 minutes, 47.33 seconds in the Ivo van Damme Memorial track and field meet before a wildly cheering crowd of nearly 50,000 at Heysel Stadium.

As soon as the 24-year-old Coe crossed the finish line in the "Golden Mile," the words "World Record" were flashed onto the stadium scoreboard.

It was the second time in three days the world record had been shattered, and the third time in 10 days—the most concentrated assault ever on the mile mark.

Steve Ovett, Coe's countryman and bitter rival, had lowered the record to 3:48.40 at Koblenz, West Germany Wednesday. That was exactly one week after Coe bettered Ovett's 1980 mark of 3:48.80 with a time of 3:48.53 at Zurich, Switzerland.

**Coe Predicted He Would Do It**

Following Ovett's achievement at Koblenz, Coe was unnerved. He went to sleep early that night without commenting on the record, then Thursday was quoted as saying he would break Ovett's mark by more than just a fraction of a second.

He kept his promise, clipping 1.07 seconds off Ovett's short-lived record.

Coe had said he needed the cooperation of the other runners in the race to help him break the record. And he got it.

Tom Byers of the United States, who had upset Ovett in the 1,500-meter race at the Bislett Games in Oslo, Norway, June 26, was Coe's early pacesetter.

He took the Briton through a first lap of 54.92 seconds, a time Coe had said he would need to set him up for the record. After 800 meters, the time was 1:52.67, also right on schedule.

**Says He Has More**

In comparison, Ovett was timed in 55.63 and 1:53.59 at Koblenz.

Coe appeared to stumble slightly during the third lap, but he did not lose his pace.

After his remarkable performance, Coe, a student at the University of Loughborough, said he could go even faster.

"It was fast," he said of his latest race. "But I still have a bit more to come out of it. I'm very, very pleased."

Coe, 24, also holds world records in the 800 meters and 1,000 meters, and won the gold medal in the 1,500 meters at the 1980 Olympic Games in Moscow.

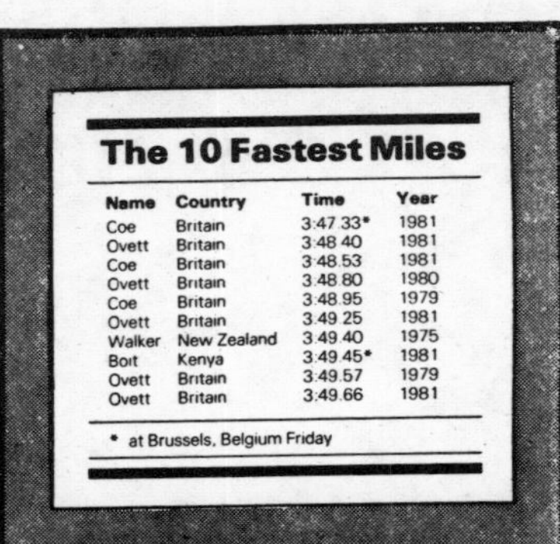

**The 10 Fastest Miles**

| Name | Country | Time | Year |
|---|---|---|---|
| Coe | Britain | 3:47.33* | 1981 |
| Ovett | Britain | 3:48.40 | 1981 |
| Coe | Britain | 3:48.53 | 1981 |
| Ovett | Britain | 3:48.80 | 1980 |
| Coe | Britain | 3:48.95 | 1979 |
| Ovett | Britain | 3:49.25 | 1981 |
| Walker | New Zealand | 3:49.40 | 1975 |
| Boit | Kenya | 3:49.45* | 1981 |
| Ovett | Britain | 3:49.57 | 1979 |
| Ovett | Britain | 3:49.66 | 1981 |

* at Brussels, Belgium Friday

"I've always run well here. And this crowd . . . it is well, the best in the world."

He and Ovett never have met over the mile distance. It was believed the temperamental Ovett would run in the Golden Mile, but he declined a couple of weeks ago, saying that when—and if—he met Coe over that distance, he wanted it to be in their home country.

Conditions were ideal for Coe's latest record race. The temperature was a comfortable 71 degrees and the crowd was enthusiastic, built to great expectations by Coe's pre-race prediction.

Mike Boit of Kenya was a distant second in 3:49.45 and Steve Scott of the U.S. came third in 3:51.48, followed by Sydney Maree of the U.S. (3:51.48), Thomas Wessinghage of West Germany (3:52.60) and John Walker of the New Zealand (3:52.97).

Two other outstanding marks were turned in by American women. Pam Spencer leaped 6-5 1/2 in the high jump to break her own American record by one-quarter of an inch and Evelyn Ashford won the 200 in 21.84, missing her U.S. record by .01. Both efforts are tops in the world this year.


**See Brussels track summaries on Page 8**


# Angels Get Lots of Help and Witt Gets a 9-2 Win

By MIKE LITTWIN, *Times Staff Writer*

BALTIMORE—If the state of the art looked a bit shaky here Friday night—and it did—youngster Mike Witt was unnaturally calm.

The 6-7 rookie, 21 years old and given to a more-than-occasional case of the shakes himself, rose above the confusion that was Memorial Stadium to pitch the Angels to a 9-2 victory over Baltimore.

The Orioles, who had won four straight, made five errors, three by third baseman Doug DeCinces, and treated the Angels to six unearned runs. They played the field as if it had been mined.

**Had Been Demoted**

And they hit . . . well, they didn't hit much, getting just seven against Witt and his wicked curveball. The Angels got 11 hits, 4 by Rick Burleson, playing despite a badly jammed ankle.

Witt, already notorious as a poor starter, allowed both runs by the time he had faced three batters. And if anyone was going to crack, he was the obvious candidate.

In his first two games against the Orioles, he didn't last past the second inning. A regular in the pre-strike starting rotation, he had been demoted to spot starter.

"Those two games were in the back of my mind," Witt said. "Maybe I was a little nervous. Once I got to the third inning, I figured I was OK. I'd never got that far before."

Once he got there, he never


**Please see ANGELS, Page 9**

RICK MEYER/Los Angeles Times

Dodgers' Steve Sax gets a force-out on Chicago's Leon Durham at second, but Durham's slide broke up a double play.

# Sax Plays a Part as Dodgers Hit High Notes, 6-1

By MARK HEISLER, *Times Staff Writer*

In the middle of a heat wave, the visiting Chicago Cubs succumbed Friday night to a Dodger attack that was led in part by a little breath of fresh air, which is what Tom Lasorda calls his rookie second baseman, 21-year-old Steve Sax.

The little breath of fresh air singled twice, scored twice and played his usual enthusiastic second base as the Dodgers won their fifth game in a row, 6-1 over the Cubs. Helping out were Bob Welch, Dave Stewart and many others, including Ron Cey (a homer, three other hits, two RBIs) and Steve Garvey (an RBI single, giving him eight RBIs in three games).

The victory put the Dodgers back into first place in the National League West, one game ahead of the Braves. It put Cey at .288, up from .264 three games ago after going 10 for 13, Garvey at 52 RBIs and Sax at .333.

**Cey Hits 10th Homer**

Even before he started hitting, Sax was running out routine grounders ferociously that people feared he was was going to wipe himself out on first base. He made an error Friday night and holed up in the trainer's room, unhappy about it until Stewart talked him out of it.

"The thing I like about you Saxy," Stewart said, "is when I'm out there, you excite the hell out of me."

Welch was coming off two straight losses, one at Chicago in which he pitched fairly well, and one in St. Louis in which he was bombed. Welch said after the Cardinal pounding that he'd had about the worst fastball of his career going, which made things tough for him since he is a fastball pitcher. But Friday night, he had a better one.

Welch pitched four scoreless innings, by which time Ron Cey had gotten him the lead with his 10th home run, a blast over the centerfield fence in the fourth inning.

The Cubs tied it moments later, on Bobby Bonds' double, a hard grounder that ricocheted off Cey's right forearm, and a single by Jody Davis.

In the bottom of the fifth, the Dodgers untied it. Bill


**Please see DODGERS, Page 9**


# Rams Get Needed Backup

## Jeff Rutledge Is Very Much Improved This Year but He Wants No Part of Quarterback Controversy

By TED GREEN, *Times Staff Writer*

A funny thing happened to the Rams on the way to finishing exhibition play.

Just when people were saying the club would be in big trouble if Pat Haden got hurt, what with Bob Lee gone and two young, inexperienced quarterbacks behind Haden, the Rams seemingly found a solid backup—Jeff Rutledge.

The third-year man from Alabama raised his standing in the organization, not to mention some eyebrows at Anaheim Stadium, by completing seven of nine passes for 156 yards and two touchdowns in 23 minutes against Minnesota Thursday night.

Rutledge replaced Haden (who had cramps in both calves) with 8:13 remaining in the third quarter. And the Rams scored three touchdowns in 10 minutes to go from a 17-7 deficit to a 27-17 lead.

The Rams ultimately won, 34-31, to finish the summer 2-2. Their next game, the season opener against Houston a week from Sunday in Anaheim, counts.

Rutledge, 24, was a wishbone quarterback under Bear Bryant at Alabama. The run-oriented wishbone does not exactly prepare quarterbacks for pro football, so when the Rams drafted him on the ninth round in 1979 they weren't sure about his arm, even though he had broken Joe Namath's school record by throwing 30 career touchdown passes.

Now, having played a little (four regular-season appearances and one start in two years) but practiced and observed a lot, Rutledge has shown that his arm is good enough. Maybe even better than that.


**Please see RUTLEDGE, Page 8**

Associated Press

Backup quarterback Jeff Rutledge takes snap during victory over Vikings.

# Fed-Up Michael Says He Told Steinbrenner, 'Fire Me If You Want'

CHICAGO (AP)—Manager Gene Michael said Friday night he's tired of George Steinbrenner's interference and has told the New York Yankees owner to fire him if that's what he wants.

"I told him to quit threatening me," Michael said before the Yankees' 6-1 victory over the Chicago White Sox. "If he wants me to go, make the move—don't wait.

"I can' take it any longer," said Michael, who said he knew what he was getting into when he took the job, "but I didn't think it would be so direct."

"Yest, I've talked with George," Michael said after emerging from a meeting with slumping star Reggie Jackson. "I told him to quit threatening me. If he wants me to go, make the move, don't wait.

"I can live with anything," the Yankee manager said. "My mother died in 1978, I went through a divorce, I had friends


**Please see MICHAEL, Page 6**

# Ryan Beats Dodgers (and Koufax, Too) With His Fifth No-Hit Game, 5-0

By MARK HEISLER, *Times Staff Writer*

HOUSTON—When it finally happened, ol' Nolan Ryan, 34 years old now and as emotional as ever, just ducked his head a little bit and threw his right fist into the air. Then he walked calmly toward the Astro dugout, until a human wave assault of his ecstatic teammates crushed him.

They picked him up and carried him off. He waved to the crowd and hugged his wife, who had run down to the field, and was interviewed on national TV and finally, after years of narrow misses, it was over.


✔ **Plate umpire Bruce Froemming took it all in stride. He didn't know it was Nolan Ryan's fifth no-hitter. Bill Dwyre's story on Page 3.**

✔ **Ryan's fifth no-hitter, as seen by some history writers. Story on Page 3.**

✔ **Buzzie Bavasi, Angels' executive vice president, won't say his team made a mistake letting Ryan become a free agent. Story on Page 3.**

✔ **The five days baseball was overmatched and the box scores of those games. Page 3.**


Someone somewhere once decided that pitchers who throw no-hitters become immortal, but now Nolan Ryan was an immortal above all the other immortals. He had pitched his fifth no-hitter, a dramatic, 129-pitch, 11-strikeout, 5-0 victory over the Dodgers Saturday afternoon, retiring the last 19 of them in a row, before 32,115 in the Astrodome, to break the career record for no-hitters he had shared with Sandy Koufax for six years.

It had been that long since Ryan, then 28, threw his fourth no-hitter as a member of the Angels, for whom he'd also thrown his first three. That one came late in another crummy Angels season, against the Orioles. "I always kind of favored that one," Ryan said late Saturday afternoon, smiling, "because I threw it with a bad arm. My arm was killing me. I had it operated on after the season."

In the six years that passed, there were so many near-misses that Ryan began to doubt his ability to go hard enough long enough to get No. 5. His peers, however, teammates and opponents alike, hadn't quite given up on him. Here's what some of them said Saturday:

Don Sutton, an ex-Dodger and an ex-teammate of Koufax: "That brings back memories of Sandy Koufax pitching, when a foul ball was a moral victory."

Davey Lopes: "Anytime he goes out there, you don't know, he might throw one. That's the kind of stuff he has.

"Look at where the ball was hit today. How many balls did we hit hard? I hit one (a first-inning ground out). (Mike) Scioscia (a long drive to right-center that Terry Puhl ran down in the seventh). Ron Roenicke (a liner right at Puhl in the fifth), Derrel Thomas (a ground out in the eighth)."

Scioscia, asked about Ryan's stuff: "Pshhh . . . Outstanding. Nice question."

Astros pitching coach Mel Wright: "I've seen him throw as well or better."

Sutton: "He blew away Montreal here one day this year when he had better stuff than he did today."

**Please see DODGERS, Page 22**

### *Koufax Says, 'It's Great'*

Sandy Koufax, apparently awakened at 10:45 Saturday night at his home near Paso Robles for his reaction to Nolan Ryan's fifth no-hitter, said, "I think it's great. Congratulations to Nolan. I knew he'd get it sooner or later."

Koufax, who had been out most of the day, said he heard of Ryan's no-hitter on the radio.

Did Koufax think pitching four no-hitters was his greatest accomplishment?

"I don't rate them," he told the caller. "I have nothing to say about anything I did."

# USC Gets Off the Deck to Stay No. 1, 28-24

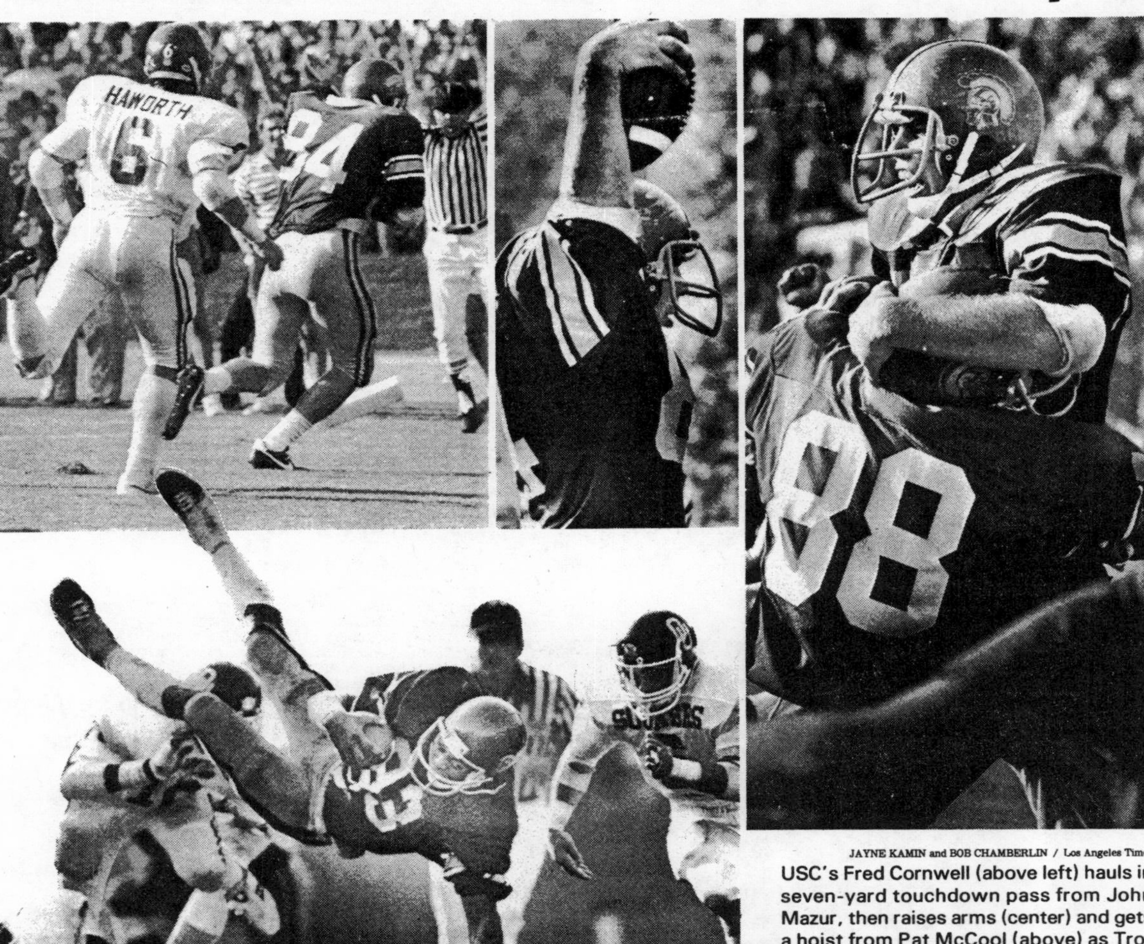

JAYNE KAMIN and BOB CHAMBERLIN / Los Angeles Times

USC's Fred Cornwell (above left) hauls in seven-yard touchdown pass from John Mazur, then raises arms (center) and gets a hoist from Pat McCool (above) as Trojans beat Oklahoma in final two seconds, 28-24, at the Coliseum. At left, Marcus Allen hurtles for yardage in final drive. Allen rushed for 208 yards, scoring twice.

## Oklahoma Falters in Last 2 Seconds

By MAL FLORENCE, *Times Staff Writer*

John Robinson compared his USC football team Saturday to Sugar Ray Leonard, a fighter who was trailing but came on at the end to stop Thomas Hearns in their recent fight.

It wasn't a bad analogy because the Trojans, seemingly whipped by Oklahoma's whiplash wishbone, got up from the Coliseum grass to win in the final two seconds.

John Mazur, the sophomore quarterback, threw a seven-yard touchdown pass to tight end Fred Cornwell to climax USC's surge in the fourth quarter with a 28-24 comeback victory.

By winning, USC most likely preserved its ranking as the No. 1 team in the country. Oklahoma came into the came as the nation's No. 2-rated team, and the Sooners were on the verge of becoming No. 1. They led, 24-14, in the fourth qaurter and seemed in control of the game.

The Trojans probably won't encounter another team as fast or quick-striking as Oklahoma—until they meet the Sooners at Norman in 1982.

But the Sooners, with all of their devastating ground power—307 yards rushing—and surprising passing attack, seemed to tire in the final quarter as the Trojans got stronger.

✔ **Once Fred Cornwell got his hands on the ball, he refused to let go. Mike Littwin's story on Page 15.**

It seemed for a while that the Sooners would run away with the game, but the wishbone is a mistake-prone offense with so many backs handling the ball. Oklahoma fumbled 10 times Saturday, losing five. The Trojans didn't have a turnover, and this had to be a factor in their victory.

It was another showcase game for Marcus Allen in the tailback's quest to win the Heisman Trophy. He rushed for 208 yards on 39 carries and scored two touchdowns. Allen has now rushed for 200 or more yards in three consecutive games, tying an NCAA record held by four other running backs.

"Marcus Allen is the best tailback I've seen play on this field," said Robinson, who has seen such great USC running backs as Charles White, Ricky Bell and Anthony Davis perform at the Coliseum.

What Allen is doing now is cutting back sharply, looking for openings, along with his power running. His 27-yard touchdown run in the first quarter was an example of the way he cuts across the grain now.

The game, watched by a Coliseum crowd of 85,651 and a national television audience, has to be ranked as one of the most entertaining in some time. It will also be remembered by Trojan fans as one of those classic late wins reminscent of stirring victories over UCLA and Notre Dame and in the Rose Bowl.

Robinson was disheveled in the locker room. He was sweating profusely and his voice was hoarse as he said: "Marcus said in a prayer after the game that if God stands by us, we won't blink the rest of the season. And I said, 'Amen, we're No. 1.'"

**Please see USC, Page 16**

# The Sooners Had It in Their Hands, the Worst Place Possible

***Jim Murray***

In the mid-30s, Princeton's Tigers, desirous of a Rose Bowl bid, played in a game against Yale in which their star quarterback, Kats Kadlec, fumbled several times. Finally, as they lined up for a last desperate play in a losing cause, Yale's great end, Larry Kelley, leaned across the line of scrimmage and drawled, "Hey, Kadlec, has that Rose Bowl got handles on it?"

In one of the great football games played in any bowl, the mythical national championship had to have handles on it for the Oklahoma Sooners Saturday afternoon.

At the start of the second half, the USC band piped up a stirring rendition of "Send In the Clowns." At that moment, the Oklahoma varsity showed up—and promptly committed their 7th, 8th 9th and 10th fumbles of the afternoon. They turned a rout into a cliffhanger and a victory into a defeat.

Oklahoma was the better football team except in one very important category. An awesome attack force, they roll up 450-500 yards every game. But they sometimes forget to bring the ball with them. They fumbled 10 times against USC and lost the ball five of them. Impressive as this was, this was hardly their greatest moment. They once fumbled 13 times in a single game and 58 times in a season. They lost the ball by fumble 36 times in 1979. That is bearing down, you'd have to say. This is a team which would be better off without the football. This team doesn't need a coach, it needs a gluepot.

They were driving for the touchdown which would have put them ahead by two touchdowns to none when they fumbled on the USC 23-yard line in the first quarter. USC took the ball and tied the score.

They were leading 17-14 in the second quarter and had stopped USC cold on its 23 when their punt-returner fumbled the USC kick and USC had the ball on the Oklahoma 40. USC drove in for a touchdown with only 42 seconds left in the half. They kept aborting their own drives in the third quarter. They seemed to have no trouble running through or around USC. They handled the ball like a guy feeling around the floor of the shower for a bar of soap with lather in his eyes. The team motto should be "Oops!"

They could be excused. The 85,651 was the largest number of people collected in one place they had ever seen before. And Oklahoma is a team that can fumble at Iowa State.

At that, they only came up two seconds short, as their coach, Barry Switzer was to point out afterward.

The USC Trojans are now No. 1 again, thanks to that devastat-

**Please see MURRAY, Page 16**

## INSIDE

## *UCLA Loses Its Offense and Game in Iowa, 20-7*

Story on Page 2

| | | | | |
|---|---|---|---|---|
| Purdue . . . . . . . 15 | Penn St. . . . . .30 | San Jose St. . 27 | Ohio St. . . . . . .24 | Scoreboard — See Page 5 |
| Notre Dame . . 14 | Nebraska . . . .24 | Cal . . . . . . . . . . .24 | Stanford . . . . .19 | Summaries — See Page 20 |
| Story on Page 6 | Story on Page 8 | Story on Page 4 | Story on Page 2 | |

# SPORTS



# It's Champagne With a Twist of Lemon

Associated Press

Manager Tom Lasorda throws his arms in the air as he rushes to the mound to join celebrants following the Dodgers' 9-2 victory in World Series clincher.

## Dodgers KO Yanks After the Manager Pulls Tommy John

By MARK HEISLER, *Times Staff Writer*

NEW YORK—Wednesday night in the South Bronx, where they'd been used for a punching bag for the last half-decade, the incredible, battling Dodgers got it all back.

Behind Burt Hooton, who won his fourth postseason game, and Pedro Guerrero, who drove in five runs, they simply flattened George Steinbrenner's pride of New York, the Yankees, 9-2, before 56,513 in Yankee Stadium and that gave them the 78th World Series, four games to two, after having trailed, two games to none. For the first time since the era of Sandy Koufax, the Dodgers are champions of the world.

"There'll really never be another moment like it," Steve Garvey said afterward.

Sixteen minutes after the game's end, copies of a statement by Steinbrenner, the Yankee owner, were passed out in the press box, meaning the statment must have been prepared while the game was still on. It read:

"I want to sincerely apologize to the people of New York and to fans of the New York Yankees everywhere for the performance of the Yankee team in this series. I also want to assure you that we will be at work immediately to prepare for 1982 . . ."

Before this one, the Dodgers had lost their last four World Series, in '66, '74, '77 and '78, falling in four, five, six and six games, respectively. In '77 and '78, they lost to these same Yankees, and in '78 the Series was the exact reverse of this one. The Dodgers, the favorites, won the first two games at home and then lost four straight. Their infield played badly, they spent a lot of time complaining about the New York fans, and they were remembered for all of that for a long time afterward. All the way up until this week.

After their three-game Dodger Stadium sweep, an off day Monday and Tuesday's rainout, they fell behind, 1-0, Wednesday night on Willie Randolph's third-inning homer, but tied it an inning later when Steve Yeager knocked in his fourth run of the Series with a ground single between short and third, out of the reach of the diving Graig Nettles.

And then, in the bottom of the fourth, in his most second-guessed move of a second-guessed Series, Yankee Manager Bob Lemon sent Bobby Murcer up to hit for his starting pitcher, Tommy John.

There were two runners on and two out, Tom Lasorda

Please see SERIES, Page 3

### *Jim Murray*

## One Man's Vote: Davey Lopes

NEW YORK—The World Series, the first one in history where the two teams were certifiably not the best in Baseball, came to a merciful end in Yankee Stadium Wednesday. The Dodgers, who would have been second in their division and third in the league had a full schedule been played, beat the Yankees, who would have been third in their division and fourth in the league.

The game may have been lost in the dugout.

It is the bottom of the fourth inning in this Series where the DH or designated hitters are not permitted on this alternate year. The score is tied, 1-1, and the Yankees have a runner on second with two outs. The pitcher is coming up next, Tommy John, no threat to Stan the Man at the plate. Tommy Lasorda, the Dodger manager, hits on a stratagem. He will walk batter Larry Milbourne. This will force Yankee Manager Bob Lemon to an agonizing decision. Tommy John is pitching a masterful game. But Lemon needs that run on second. Or thinks he does. He sighs, sends up a pinch hitter. Bobby Murcer pops out.

★

**The Dodgers feast** on the pitchers who succeed John. For only the second time in eight tries, they manage to win in New York.

It is an anticlimactic end to the most bewildering season in all baseball annals. Scholars will search the box score for a guy to give the gold watch and the scholarship.

I have my own candidate and it may be an exclusive. Bear with me while I make my case.

This Dodger team which finally broke through to a world championship was put together by the

Please see MURRAY, Page 6

*'I can't believe that'*

Associated Press

Tommy John stares out of the Yankee dugout in disbelief after being lifted for a pinch-hitter by Manager Bob Lemon, who said, "All I was doing was trying to get us a lead."

## Tommy John Is Sour on Lemon's Decision to Pull Him in Fourth

By ROSS NEWHAN, *Times Staff Writer*

NEW YORK—The television camera captured the normally passive Tommy John pacing the Yankee dugout Wednesday night, shaking his head, waving his arm and obviously saying, "I can't believe that."

It was the fourth inning of Game 6 of the World Series and John had just been lifted for a pinch hitter with two on, two out and the score tied, 1-1.

The pinch-hitter, Bobby Murcer, flied deep to right, after which John's successor, George Frazier, gave up three runs in the fifth inning, propelling the Dodgers to a 9-2 win that earned them their first world's championship in 16 years.

In the Yankee clubhouse, now wearing street clothes, John said he still found the decision of Manager Bob Lemon hard to believe.

**'I'm Paid to Pitch'**

"That was a pitcher reacting on the spur of the moment," he said of his dugout emotions, "but you can say I definitely didn't agree with the move.

"I didn't try to talk him out of it because I never argue with the manager. I'm only paid to pitch.

"It just seems highly unlikely that you'd take out your best pitcher—at least I assume that your starting pitcher of that night is your best pitcher—that early in a tie game.

"I mean I was throwing well. I wasn't getting cuffed around. I'd just completed 13 innings against a club of that caliber and held it to one run. I wanted to keep pitching and thought I would.

Please see JOHN, Page 8

## The Dodgers Win Before That Old Gang Is Broken Up

By MIKE LITTWIN, *Times Staff Writer*

NEW YORK—Start spreading the news.

The Dodgers are World Champions for the first time in 16 years, champions after losing four straight World Series, champions for the first time in the history of the Garvey-Lopes-Cey-Russell-Yeager-Lasorda Dodgers.

And they wanted the world to know it.

"We're the champs," Manager Tom Lasorda shouted. "Can't nobody in this room take that away from us."

He wasn't the only Dodger shouting after Wednesday's 9-2 victory over the New York Yankees allowed the Dodgers to win the Series in six games after losing the first

Please see DODGERS, Page 10

### *Scott Ostler*

## George Learns You Have to Earn It

This is the way it was out at the old ball park on the memorable night the Dodgers won the world:

**Around the batting cage:** Tommy John, the Yankees starting pitcher, talks about how he spent the day raking leaves on his 3½ acre farm in New Jersey, and how tomorrow (today) he'll pick up a load of sheep manure to spread on his vegetable garden. Unless Bob Lemon sends in a relief gardener.

Burt Hooton, who will start for the Dodgers, says he spent the day doing "Nothing." Good old Burt, always good for a colorful pregame anecdote.

**First Inning:** Fans boo Steve Garvey, the All-American guy. The fans are ready.

Ron Cey comes to bat, his first plate appearance since being skulled by a Goose Gossage fastball. Tommy John is the perfect pitcher for Cey to return against. John, no fireballer, beaned a guy once and the batter didn't know it until the umpire told him. Cey singles.

In the Yankees' half of the inning, Willie Randolph steals second base and the stadium organist plays "Somebody Stole My Gal." Later, as 60,000 sets of teeth chatter in the background, he plays "Sunny Side of the Street." Is there is gong in the house?

**Second inning:** It's a Baskin-Robbins inning for first baseman Steve Garvey—two large scoops. He digs out low throws from Cey (who made a leaping stab to get the ball) and then Bill Russell. When Garvey checks into a hotel, the clerk throws the key at his ankles. The Dodger infield, reliable most of the season, seems intent on removing the term "routine play" from the baseball dictionary.

**Third inning:** The stadium lights fade. Are the fans stealing bulbs? You've gotta keep everything locked up in this town. It's only a power failure. Bowie Kuhn, in his box near the Yankee dugout, springs to action. He makes a phone call. An inning later his pizza arrives.

The wind is getting very brisk. Up in the ABC-TV booth, it takes three production assistants to hold down Howard Cosell's toupee.

Graig Nettles makes his first steal of the night, robbing Davey Lopes of a hit. A minute later he robs Gar-

Please see OSTLER, Page 7

Associated Press

Yankees owner George Steinbrenner was tight-lipped after his club lost the World Series.

## Steinbrenner Makes an Apology to the Fans for How Yankees Played

*NEW YORK (AP)—Owner George Steinbrenner of the Yankees issued the following statement Wednesday night, immediately following his team's defeat by the Dodgers in the World Series:*

"I want to sincerely apologize to the people of New York and to fans of the New York Yankees everywhere for the performance of the Yankee team in the World Series.

"I also want to assure you we will be at work immediately to prepare for 1982.

"I also want to extend my congratulations to Peter O'Malley and the Dodger organization—a fine team that didn't give up—and to my friend Tom Lasorda, who managed a superb season, playoffs and a brilliant World Series."

# SPORTS



# Alabama Beats Auburn; Bryant Beats Stagg

## Late Rally Gets the Bear a 28-17 Victory ... and a Piece of College Football History

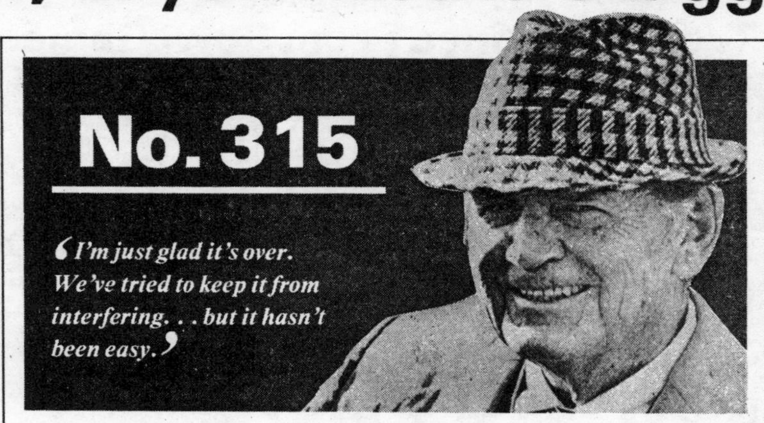

No. 315
‘I'm just glad it's over. We've tried to keep it from interfering. . . but it hasn't been easy.’


By BOB OATES, *Times Staff Writer*

BIRMINGHAM, Ala.—Although football has been played in America for more than a century, it was only 12 years ago that a young Kansas City sports researcher found out that a man named A. A. Stagg had coached his teams to a record 314 wins—with Paul (Bear) Bryant far down the list at 187.

Stagg, who died at 103, never knew he was the champion.

Nor did Pop Warner ever know he held the record at 313 until 1946 when Stagg broke it.

Sports longevity statistics are somewhat artificial, but Bear Bryant will take the record he set here Saturday when his Alabama team came from behind in the fourth quarter to beat both Auburn, 28-17, and Stagg, 315 to 314.

And even in his hour of triumph, the 68-year-old coach was thinking of his future.

"I liked coming from behind," he said. "Give me my druthers and we'll come from behind like that. It proved to our players that they have class and character, and it showed them what can be done in the future."

For Bryant, win No. 315 came on two dramatic, exciting, beautifully coached touchdown drives in the last 10 minutes after Auburn—which outplayed Alabama much of the way—had opened a 17-14 lead at the top of the final period.

"This was one of the greatest games ever played," Bryant said, standing bareheaded, for a change. Someone had pilfered his familiar houndstooth hat in the instant the game ended—but no matter. He owns several hundred others. In fact, he owns the factory that makes the hats.

"It hasn't set in yet," he said when asked how it feels to wear the record. "I feel like I ought to go back and check the scoreboard to make sure we won."

Staying in character, Bryant

Please see ALABAMA, Page 7

Associated Press

Matt Bradley of Penn State tosses the football in the air as he exults after a fourth quarter pass interception in 48-14 upset of No. 1 Pitt.

# Pitt Sees Dream Turn to Nightmare

## Penn State Comes From 14-Point Deficit to Beat No. 1 Team, 48-14

By JOHN FEINSTEIN, *Washington Post*

PITTSBURGH—As dusk fell on Pitt Stadium Saturday, the Penn State band struck up college football's theme song for 1981: "Another One Bites The Dust."

It was a jubilant rendition, one that few Pittsburgh fans were around to hear. Because Saturday, with 60,260 chilled spectators watching in amazement, Penn State crushed Pitt, 48-14, making the Panthers the sixth No. 1 team to fall this season.

Pitt's loss left Clemson as the only major unbeaten, untied team in college football and an almost sure bet to become the seventh No. 1-ranked team this season when the polls come out next week.

"We just got the momentum turned against us the wrong way," said Pitt Coach Jackie Sherrill, whose 10-1 team had a 17-game winning streak broken. "We had the locomotive going against us . . . and nothing to stop it with."

What made the lopsided outcome so astonishing was the way the game began. Pitt came out as if it intended to chase Penn State back into the Nittany Mountains, rolling to touchdowns on its first two possessions. First the Panthers drove 53 yards, scoring on Dan Marino's 28-yard pass to Dwight Collins, then went 64 yards to score on Marino's nine-yard pass to Collins.

"The first quarter Marino was just unbelievable," Penn State Coach Joe Paterno said. "We had to make some adjustments against him."

When that quarter ended, Pitt was leading, 14-0, had driven to the Lions' 31 and had held Penn State to minus-one yard in offense. Marino had completed 9 of 10 passes for 121 yards.

"It looked like we were going to blow them out," Collins said. "I think maybe we relaxed a little bit, let down and let them get back in it."

But from the first play of the second quarter, when Marino tried to find Collins with a pass lobbed into the corner of the end zone and was intercepted by Roger Jackson, until the end, the Panthers appeared helpless. That was the first of the Pitt quarterback's four interceptions; for the

Please see PITT, Page 10

### Jim Murray

# He's Playing in Handcuffs

**If I were an NFL quarterback,** whenever Rams defensive end Jack Youngblood begins thumping his right foot on the ground before the snap of the ball, I would call time and send out for a cape and a sword and light a candle in the dressing room or make a call to my priest.

"We know he's coming, he doesn't have to paw the ground," Roger Staubach once observed irritably.

If all this suggests Jack Youngblood is a lot of bull, well, it is the view of opposing quarterbacks and offensive linemen that he sure is. They think they should be allowed to stick banderillas in his neck before he charges. Or fight him from horseback. Unlike the fiesta brava bulls, though, Youngblood is frequently the one who gets the ears and tails.

Jack Youngblood has been strewing quarterbacks around gridirons like sacks of mail for 11 years. He has flattened more people than holiday traffic. Quarterbacks would rather see the rent bill coming. If he did have horns, they'd run out of penicillin.

★

**Jack Youngblood is one** of the four or five best defensive ends ever at the position. He may be even better than that. For the simple reason that he persisted into an era when the game, in a sense, shaved the horns of defensive ends, penned them up, straitjacketed them.

Defensive ends, when Youngblood came up, used to be able to slap the ears off would-be blockers. Deacon Jones used to get to the quarterback through a series of right crosses to the helmet that would have made an ox cross-eyed. Sometimes the helmet would keep ringing for a half an hour after the blocker took it off.

After punching-bag workouts, you used to be

Please see MURRAY, Page 7

# *For Sampson, Growing Was Easy, but Growing Up Wasn't*

By MIKE LITTWIN, *Times Staff Writer*

CHARLOTTESVILLE, Va.—Growing always came naturally to Ralph Sampson and his overactive pituitary gland. It was what they did best.

As a third grader, little Ralph was taller than his teacher. She made him sit in the back of the class so he wouldn't obscure the blackboard. As a seventh grader, Sampson was 6-3 and his recreation basketball league set a rule limiting him to 15 points a game. In the 10th grade, he was 6-10 and required special desks to accomodate his gangly body. Is bigger really better, he wondered.

Well, yes. He didn't get to be a 7-footer until the 11th grade, about the time he became a high school All-American. Now he's a certified, honest-to-gosh 7 feet 3¾ inches, and the certified best college basketball player in the land. The old pituitary has finally taken a well-deserved rest. Any taller, Sampson could swat down airplanes.

No wonder his teammates at the University of Virginia look up to him. Everyone looks up to Ralph Sampson.

But growing is one thing; growing up, another.

It took Ralph Sampson 21 years, just about on schedule actually, to grow up. But he had to fast-break to get there on time.

Two years ago, as a freshman at Virginia, Sampson was 7-3¾ worth of surly, lacking the social graces expected of a gentleman attending Mr. Jefferson's university. Today he's as pleasant as a fall day at the foot of the Blue Ridge Mountains. He's a speech major and, what's more, talks like one. Sampson has blossomed here. If not like a rose, like a cornstalk. Or an oak tree.

"It's been amazing," says his coach, Terry Holland.

"It's been more gratifying to see the progress Ralph has made," says Craig Littlepage, a Virginia assistant coach, "than to get to the (NCAA basketball) Final Four last year."

It was also a little unexpected.

Al McGuire has said Ralph Sampson will one day be the greatest basketball player ever. Jack McCloskey, general manager of the Detroit Pistons, once said Sampson should be declared illegal as a college player.

It's easy to understand all the fuss. Sampson is 7-4 (in not-so-round figures) and he dribbles the ball behind his back or through his legs, shoots a 20-foot jumper, blocks shots, rebounds, jams, hooks and amazes. He's the big-

Please see SAMPSON, Page 12

COLLEGE BASKETBALL

See Page 3

# UCLA Gets Farmer a Win, 76-69

## But Pepperdine Takes the Bruins Right Down to the Wire

By RICHARD HOFFER, *Times Staff Writer*

This much is clear, even after just two games: The UCLA basketball season will be an exciting one, though hardly in ways first imagined. Saturday night, the Bruins were involved in another last-minute decision, this one a 76-69 victory over Pepperdine.

The Bruins, who lost to Brigham Young by four points a night earlier when an alternating jump ball in the final minute alternated the other way, struggled again before getting rookie coach Larry Farmer his first win.

After running up leads as great as nine points in the second half, they allowed Pepperdine to come back within three points with 33 seconds left. An aborted fast break, some desperate fouls and Pepperdine was out of the game just seconds later. But it was a scare for many of the 11,257 in Pauley Pavilion nevertheless.

For Pepperdine, the outcome was an improvement on last year's game here. The Waves lost that one by 18. Pepperdine returned all five starters from a 16-12 team, and all of them evidently improved with age.

It was Pepperdine senior Boot Bond who created a lot of the excitement in the Waves' season opener, scoring a game-high 24 points, 16 in the first half. But it was teammate Dane Suttle, a junior guard, who made the finish close.

Suttle, who missed all three of the his first-half shots, got hot in the second half, scoring all 12 of his points then. He scored eight in a row midway through the half to help the Waves draw within a point.

Then in the final minute, while three fellow starters were fouling out, Suttle got hot again. With the Waves down, 72-65, Suttle drove unguarded for a layup. Then, the UCLA's Darren Daye inbounding the ball immediately afterward, Suttle grabbed an errant pass and left-handed it into the basket, making it a 72-69 game with 33 seconds left.

There was not enough time and UCLA was not going to blow that many more possessions. Even the memory of Pepperdine's Bill Sadler making a half-court shot at the first-half buzzer couldn't keep the Pauley Pavilion ticket buyers off the roads.

UCLA was doing its part to make it another exciting

Please see UCLA, Page 8

### Inside

*Steelers Have Regained Form; Will the Rams?*

See story on Page 6

*Chargers Plan on Making Race a Three-Way Tie*

See story on Page 6

# Keans, Kings Are Sharp; Canuck Goes After a Fan

By GORDON EDES, *Times Staff Writer*

Naturally, goalie Doug Keans wanted out of the minor leagues and a return to L.A.

But little did he know he'd have to drive a cab to get there.

Keans, summoned from the Kings' New Haven farm club to replace Jim Rutherford, was behind the wheel Friday night in upstate New York, when we had to transport himself to an airport in Syracuse. The cabbie assigned to take Keans from Binghamton, N.Y., to Syracuse, a $100 fare, showed up "a little inebriated," Keans said.

"So I ended up driving while he slept in the back seat."

Saturday, Keans was still in the driver's seat, so to speak, as he stopped 41 shots in the Kings' 3-2 win over the Vancouver Canucks.

The game was disrupted with 1:18 left to paly when Vancouver's Dave (Tiger) Williams, leaving the ice after his second fight of the night, went into the stands in pursuit of a fan who threw a handful of ice at him, striking the player in the forehead.

Three of Williams' teammates—Stan Smyl, Ron Delorme and Curt Fraser—followed Williams into a sparsely occupied area of the stands. Police accosted the alleged offender, a man described in his early 20's, and security men moved in to keep the players from advancing any further.

Vancouver Coach Harry Neale blamed the lack of Forum security measures. In similar incidents in the past, the most recent occurring last season in Detroit when a number of New York Rangers went into the stands, league officials have reacted

Please see KINGS, Page 4

# USC IS HIT HARD BY NCAA PENALTIES

## Trojans Banned From Bowl Games, TV for 2 Years

By MAL FLORENCE, *Times Staff Writer*

The NCAA came down hard on USC's football program Friday, prohibiting the school from appearing in bowl games during the 1982-83 and 1983-84 academic years, and from appearing on television in 1983 and 1984.

But USC got one concession in its appeal to the NCAA Council Thursday. It was learned that the NCAA Infractions Committee had requested the university to permanently disassociate assistant football coach Marv Goux from the athletic department for allegedly selling the players' tickets. This meant no coaching, fund-raising or recruiting.

Goux, instead, will have his salary frozen and not be allowed to recruit for two years. But friends of Goux told The Times that the long-time assistant coach could probably live with this arrangement.

Although USC got some relief from the NCAA on Goux's behalf, the university was hit with one of the most severe penalties in the history of the NCAA.

Charles Alan Wright, chairman of the Infractions Committee, used strong language in denouncing USC, saying Goux's activities were "the most flagrant example of willful circumvention of NCAA legislation" in the case.

The NCAA also chastied USC for "lack of administrative control of the conduct of its atheltic program." This would presumably mean President James H. Zumberge, Athletic Director Dick Perry and head football Coach John Robinson, as well as their predecessors.

The Times reported earlier that USC has been sanctioned by the NCAA with three years of probation and two years of direct penalties—banning bowl games and television appearances. USC appealed the findings of the Infractions Committee but didn't win on these counts.

USC will appear on television next season because NCAA rules permit this if a school has made commitments prior to sanctions.

There was no comment from USC officials on the penalties, but President Zumberge said USC would respond at a press conference Monday afternoon on campus.

Please see USC, Page 13

### THE USC PROBATION

**The Offense:** From 1971 through 1979, an assistant coach sold complimentary football tickets in excess of face value and gave the cash to participating players.

**NCAA's Comment:** "The most flagrant example of willful circumvention of NCAA legislation."

**Probation Term:** Three years.

**Bowls:** Banned from all bowls in 1982-83 and 1983-84 academic years.

**Television:** May appear this season, but not during 1983 or 1984 regular seasons.

*Commentary*

## NCAA Wording Spells It All Out: USC a Cheater

By BILL DWYRE, *Times Sports Editor*

The NCAA action against USC announced Friday night shouldn't come as a shock, but it does. Nor should it stir much emotion, but it does.

The basic revelations were reported by this newspaper about a month ago. USC did, indeed, get three years of probation and two years of hard-time penalties—no TV appearances and bowl games for that time, meaning a hefty dent in the school's athletic program cash flow.

But the basic revelations, when put in the context of an official, final, no-tomorrow decree—rather than a newspaper's reporting of what it had come to believe from some highly reliable sources—is sobering stuff. And when put in the-pull-no-punches words of NCAA officials, one has some real reason for wondering what in the world was going on at USC.

The NCAA language, as quoted in wire service reports, is stunning, to say the least. Remember, the NCAA, partly by necessity of the delicate nature of its dealings and partly by some inherit badge of dullness that it wears with pride, *never* makes statements that are anything but dry, middle-of-the-road and painfully void of any emotion.

So what do we get in the statements about USC? Examples:

"The most flagrant example of willfull circumvention of NCAA legislation in this case," said Charles Alan Wright, chairman of the NCAA Committee on Infractions, "involved an assistant football coach who, during the period 1971-'79, deliberately violated NCAA rules by selling complimentary tickets . . ."

Did you get that? "Flagrant example of willful circumvention?"

Another statement, from Wright:

(The violations) "represent a significant and extensive pattern of improper benefits made available to en-

Please see COMMENTARY, Page 13

MIKE MEADOWS / Los Angeles Times

**Hush before the storm**—No, these aren't poachers getting an early start on the Eastern Sierra trout season, which opens today. The two fishermen are enjoying some legal angling Friday along Lower Owens River, where they may fish the year around.

## Penguin at Home in Candlestick, Leads 9-0 Romp

By DAN HAFNER, *Times Staff Writer*

SAN FRANCISCO—It seems there is more criticism than ever for the wind tunnel that passes for a ballpark called Candlestick.

After spending last season here, Enos Cabell learned to hate the place. He said it was terrible and frustrating, especially for the Giants, who must play 81 games here every season.

Even Giants Manager Frank Robinson damns the place with faint praise, saying: "All parks have a different character." Few people are so kind. There is a move afoot to cover the place, but it may be too late to save it.

**Cey Loves the Place**

There is one Dodger who wouldn't want to change a thing about Candlestick Park. He is Ron Cey. The veteran third baseman loves it.

In his first appearance in this favorite park on the road, the Penguin had four hits, including a three-run home run as the Dodgers smashed the Giants, 9-0.

Cey figured in all four scoring innings, driving in four runs and scoring three as the Dodgers made it easy for Bob Welch to win his third game without a defeat.

Welch struggled in the early innings but finished with a seven-hitter. He was the third Dodger in a row to pitch a complete-game victory. In the last 30 innings, Dodger pitchers have yielded only one earned run.

The story, though, was Cey and Candlestick Park. His home run, an opposite field shot off Dan Schatzeder in the eighth was his 15th at Candlestick. It's the most he's hit anywhere except at home.

**Fowlker the Loser**

In the fourth Cey doubled and scored a run to start Alan Fowlkes, the rookie from Brawley, on the way to his first defeat after two victories.

In the fifth, he drove in a run with a single, and in the seventh, he singled and scored again.

"I can't knock the ark," he said. "It's been good to me and the club,"

"The Chicken", brought in by a radio station to entertain the fans, and the slowness of the pitchers were the highlights of the first three innings.

Not only did the pitchers take a long time between pitches, they used a lot of them. Fowlkes gave up a hit and a walk in the first inning and two walks in the second. He struck out Welch and Sax to end the second.

Welch gave up a hit in each of the

Please see DODGERS, Page 4

## *Americans Are Arming the Hammer*

By MAL FLORENCE, *Times Staff Writer*

The remote field at West Los Angeles College is pockmarked with small craters, each made by a metal ball attached to a steel wire and a hand grip.

The contraptions are known as 16-pound hammers and the people who throw them have been a back-lot act for years in this country.

Football coaches don't want their fields torn up by the hammers, and throwers are kept out of other open areas for fear that a wild throw—the hammers hurtle well over 200 feet—could hurt someone.

So hammer throwers, for the most part, practice and compete almost in anonymity, which hasn't helped to popularize the event in this country.

Ed Burke, a former American record-holder, observed wryly: "You don't get much reward by training alone and, when you're competing almost alone, that's worse yet."

Please see HAMMER, Page 8

Steve Rohovit, Cal State Long Beach hammer thrower, works out for Sunday's Mt. San Antonio Relays. He says he also needs more practice in the technique of keeping his tongue in his mouth.

KEN HIVELY
Los Angeles Times

## Keough Chased, but Not by Angels

### Pitcher's Ejection Brings On Dispute as California Wins, 7-2

By ROSS NEWHAN, *Times Staff Writer*

Umpire Rich Garcia chased Oakland starting pitcher Matt Keough Friday night, probably depriving the Angels of that distinction.

The Angels, who went on to beat the A's, 7-2, before an Anaheim Stadium crowd of 36,585, were already leading, 4-1, when Keough, described recently by California Manager Gene Mauch as Oakland's leading dispenser of spitballs, was ejected by Garcia for twice bringing his pitching hand in contact with his mouth while standing on the mound.

Third base umpire Garcia delivered the first warning before Keough had even delivered his first pitch to Bobby Grich, leading off the third inning. It automatically put Keough behind on the count by one ball. Keough delivered another ball, then was cited again by Garcia for going to his mouth, the umpire making a broad wave of his right arm to indicate the automatic ejection under rule 8.02 (b).

Keough and Manager Billy Martin stormed after Garcia, as they has an inning earlier when Martin came racing out of the dugout to engage Garcia in a finger-pointing, head-bobbing debate prompted obviously because Martin felt Garcia had been jawing at and disrupting his pitcher, who, when not at his mouth, was constantly fingering the bill of his cap, the nape of his neck, the

Please see ANGELS, Page 11

RANDY McBRIDE / Los Angeles Times

Jim Adams (lower right) smiles after he drove a Lola-Chevrolet (above) on a lap of 118.354 m.p.h Friday at Riverside to win the pole position for Sunday's Times/Toyota 6-hour Endurance race.

## Adams' Lola Takes Wing, Wins Pole for Times 6-Hour

By SHAV GLICK, *Times Staff Writer*

RIVERSIDE—When Jim Adams left the track after Thursday's practice for the Times/Toyota 6-Hour race, he felt like not coming back for Friday's qualifying.

"The car was so far off I didn't think it was worth coming out," said the 43-year-old former Ferrari driver from Hollywood.

Things weren't much better Friday morning during last-minute testing for Sunday's race at Riverside International Raceway. Then a crewman on the Lola T-600 owned by Chris Cord set the wing at a different angle and Adams went back out for one last lap during qualifications.

Adams found the 3.2-mile track free of traffic and responded with a lap at 118.354 m.p.h., good enough to take the pole away from Ted Field. Field, also in a Lola, had run 118.096 and appeared to have won his first pole since driving in the International Motor Sports Assn. series.

"Our problems started last week testing at Willow Springs with a broken spring that we didn't know about," Adams said. "We made all kinds of changes hoping to compensate for the problem the broken spring caused. Then, when we did discover the problem, all our other

Please see ADAMS, Page 9

Los Angeles Times

# SPORTS

Wednesday, June 9, 1982 CC†/Part III

# A Memorable, Magical Night for Lakers

## Beating 76ers May Not Mean a Dynasty, But It Is, in Riley's Words, Much to Savor

By RANDY HARVEY, *Times Staff Writer*

For the second time in the last three years, the Lakers are on top of the National Basketball Assn. While that hardly constitutes a dynasty, this is a team that won't soon be forgotten.

Few will be writing epics about Game 6 of their best-of-seven final series against the Philadelphia 76ers. The Lakers simply did what they had to do Tuesday night at the Forum, beating the 76ers, 114-104.

But when it was over, and the Lakers had clinched the championship, four games to two, the moment was no less satisfying. To use one of Coach Pat Riley's favorite words, there was much to savor.

For Riley, 37, it was a triumphant conclusion to his most bizarre experience in professional basketball. He took over the team 11 games into the season from Coach Paul Westhead, who was fired, and, admittedly often directing by instinct, emerged with a championship.

"I wouldn't have believed it if somebody had told me this eight months ago," he said. "But it's here now, and I believe it."

For Magic Johnson, it was his second championship in three years since he left Michigan State, where he also won a championship, and the second time he has taken home the trophy as the Most Valuable Player in the final series.

Two years ago, against the 76ers, he won the MVP award for his 42-point, 15-rebound magical performance in the decisive Game. This time, he won it for his blue-collar consistency.

Against the 76ers, Johnson, 23, led the Lakers in rebounds (10.8) and was second in assists (8.0). He also averaged 16.2 points. Tuesday night, he had 13 points,

**Please see LAKERS, Page 6**

JOE KENNEDY / Los Angeles Times

Magic Johnson (left) and Jamaal Wilkes embrace after the Lakers beat the Philadelphia 76ers, 114-104, to win the NBA title Tuesday night at the Forum. Wilkes led the Lakers with 27 points, while Johnson had 13 points, 13 rebounds and 13 assists and was voted the MVP of the series.

**Scott Ostler**

## Team Hollywood Comes Into Focus

JAYNE KAMIN / Los Angeles Times

Coach Pat Riley hugs wife Chris in locker room as Lakers celebrate their second title in three years.

**Team Hollywood finally** got its makeup on straight, made its cue and remembered its lines.

The Lakers, the slick guys from the coast who wouldn't win the NBA playoffs because they were too busy making movies and commercials, firing coaches and fighting over the ball, did.

How could you love the Lakers? Magic terminated his coach, a heck of a nice guy. Kareem was unpopular and frequently booed, and that was by his teammates. Nixon was always griping about Magic. Jamaal was about as visible as the vice president of the United States, whoever *he* is. McAdoo was just another NBA malcontent looking for another team to sabotage. Kurt Rambis was an NBA joke.

And so on. That was the popular view of the Lakers a few months ago, and that popular view wasn't completely wrong.

What happened? Here's how coach Pat Riley explained it before the playoff series with Philly started:

"After a while," he said, "there became a tacit agreement that each player had an identity and an image that they put out to the public with their style of play, and after a while, nobody ever really tried to trespass in their area. They accepted one another's image, because that was his business.

"It was OK for a certain guy, for instance, to be Magic. It was OK for Coop to be Coop-a-loop, for Norman to be

**Please see OSTLER, Page 7**

LARRY SHARKEY / Los Angeles Times

Kareem Abdul-Jabbar, sandwiched by Bobby Jones (left) and Darryl Dawkins (left photo) loses his balance as Dawkins backs into him (right).

***Lakers' Big Plus***

## For McAdoo, Proof Is All in the Winning

By MIKE LITTWIN, *Times Staff Writer*

Now it can be told. Bob McAdoo, who many said could never play for a winner, was apparently destined to make off with an NBA championship this season.

The only question was with which team he would do it.

For if McAdoo hadn't signed with the Lakers on the day before Christmas, soon after Mitch Kupchak was injured, he might have signed later with the 76ers when Darryl Dawkins went down.

And if he had, the 76ers, who had been negotiating with him, might have been slurping Dom Perignon.

"I would think so," said McAdoo.

You can be certain of one thing: McAdoo was the difference for the Lakers, who took Philadelphia in six games, winning Tuesday at the Forum, 114-104.

McAdoo contributed 16 points, 9 rebounds and 3 blocked shots. He took a charge, against Darryl Dawkins no less. He even got in a scuffle with Mike Bantom. Everything he did seemed to be inspirational, especially his third-quarter block of a Julius Erving layup that would have given the 76ers the lead.

And for the first time in years, nobody wanted to call McAdoo a loser.

"Thank God for Bob McAdoo," said Pat Riley, his coach. "Thank God we were geniuses and signed him."

The only thing Bob McAdoo didn't do Tuesday night was win the MVP award. A lot of people thought he should have. McAdoo, who has won MVP awards, was more concerned about winning an NBA championship.

**✓No championship ring again for Dr. J. Story on Page 5.**

And for the people who thought we never would, McAdoo had this to say:

"I proved that to people that I can play. People said I wasn't a winner. I think this proved that I am. People said I wouldn't fit in, that I'd disrupt things. Well, I fit in. A year ago, I was playing for the worst team in the league and this year I'm playing for the best. That has to prove something."

The Lakers took McAdoo off the unemployment lines. Once a superstar, the 6-9 center-forward had become known as a malcontent, dumped by three teams in less than a year. But the Lakers were desper-

**Please see McADOO, Page 6**

***L.A. Trails by 6½ Games***

## Dodgers Less Than Happy Amid Braves Madness, 4-3

By MARK HEISLER, *Times Staff Writer*

Happy returned to Dodger Stadium Tuesday night, but not quite happiness. Burt Hooton came off the disabled list and went five good innings, which would have been a well-received development, indeed, except that he worked another 1⅓ innings after that, gave up three more runs and took the loss.

The Braves beat him—the National League West front-running Braves—coming from a 3-1 deficit in the sixth inning to win their second game in this series, 4-3, ending it with one scoreless, dramatic inning of relief from their Mad Hungarian, Al Hrabosky, and two from Gene Garber.

Hrabosky came in to protect the Braves lead in the seventh, and got into a massive psych-out contest with the Dodgers and the 33,153-strong Dodger crowd. He stepped off the mound three times pitching to pinch-hitter Jose Morales, with the crowd booing louder each time, then retired Morales on a ground ball.

Then, with the trying run at second, he started to work on Steve Sax, who'd driven in all the Dodger runs. With the count 1-2, Sax hit a long smash into the left-field seats, but it hooked fouled by a couple of yards.

**Please see DODGERS, Page 12**

**Inside**

**ANGELS WIN, 11-4**

Reggie Jackson hit his eighth home run as the Angels rolled over Toronto, 11-4. (Story on Page 2.)

## San Diego May Get Lakers (on TV)

### A Cable Deal Could Soothe Buss in Move of Clippers to L.A.

By CHRIS COBBS, *Times Staff Writer*

San Diego is probably going to lose the Clippers to Los Angeles. But in return it may gain the Lakers on cable TV.

And as a direct result of a Clippers shift, the L.A. Coliseum and the Sports Arena would be a giant step closer to lining up sponsors for $7-million worth of scoreboards and message boards—equipment that would be used in the 1984 Olympics.

A move into a vacated San Diego market would help the Lakers heal any financial hurt they might suffer because of a shift to the Sports Arena by their closest National Basketball Assn. rivals, the Clippers. Lakers owner Jerry Buss has already suggested he would want a $5-million indemnity from the Clippers.

By sending the Lakers to San Diego over the airwaves, Buss would be tapping the largest cable system in the country. More than 325,000 homes receive cable-TV broadcasts in San Diego County.

"It would certainly be something we would look at," a spokesman for Buss said Tuesday. "It would not be an even tradeoff for the Clippers coming to L.A. But it is not impossible our games could be shown in San Diego this year."

The spokesman said Buss not long ago vetoed one cable-TV company's proposal to package Lakers games in the San Diego market. "But it had nothing to do with the principle (of cable in San Diego), it was more the specifics of the proposal that was turned down," the spokesman said.

Clippers owner Donald Sterling, for his part, never packaged his team on cable TV from San Diego. He said the San Diego Sports Arena would not allow him to have a cable-TV deal. And a losing team such as the Clippers probably would not have nearly the appeal for cable TV that a team such as the Lakers would have.

While it now appears Buss stands to gain more than had been previously supposed from a Clippers shift, the Coliseum Commission definitely will earn a handsome return on its offer to Sterling.

By securing a second major tenant in addition to the Oakland Raiders, the commission greatly strengthened

**Please see CLIPPERS, Page 10**

# A Chip-Shot Artist Wins Open

**NO. 17**

Tom Watson chips from off the 17th green (above) and makes the birdie (right) that virtually sealed his first U.S. Open win.

## Watson's Birdie From the Rough on No. 17 Decides It; Nicklaus Finishes 2 Shots Back

By SHAV GLICK, *Times Staff Writer*

PEBBLE BEACH—The U.S. Open, the tournament Tom Watson wanted more than any other in the world, came to him Sunday in the most improbable way.

With Jack Nicklaus sitting on the sidelines at Pebble Beach, believing he had already won his fifth Open, Watson made an unlikely shot—a cut-shot wedge out of deep grass, 16 feet downhill to the pin on a green sloping away from him—that went in the cup for a birdie on the 17th hole to snatch the victory away from Nicklaus.

The dramatic shot, followed by another birdie on No. 18, gave Watson a four-under-par 282 (72-72-68-70), two shots ahead of Nicklaus (74-70-71-69), and his first U.S. Open championship to go with two Masters and three British Opens.

"When I finished my round, I saw where Tom's ball landed on 17," said Nicklaus, "and I knew I had no worse than a tie. There was no way in the world he could save par there so I figured he'd have to birdie 18 just to get in a playoff. I couldn't see the ball after Tom hit it, but I saw him jumping around and I figured he'd lipped the cup. It never dawned on me it could go in the hole."

Ironically, it was at the same hole, the 209-yard 17th that juts out into Carmel Bay, that Nicklaus clinched his third Open title in 1972 by hitting the flagstick with his 1-iron tee shot for a cinch birdie.

British Open champion Bill Rogers, who was paired with Watson after they shared the 54-hole lead, said, "If you took 100 balls and pitched them by hand from there, you couldn't do any better. I was in absolute shock when I saw the ball go in the hole."

Nicklaus went Rogers one better. He said, "Make it a thousand balls," when told of Rogers' comment. "You couldn't drop a ball on the green and stop it."

**U.S. Open Leaders**

| | |
|---|---|
| Tom Watson .. | 72-72-68-70—282 |
| Jack Nicklaus .. | 74-70-71-69—284 |
| Bob Clampett .. | 71-73-72-70—286 |
| Bill Rogers .... | 70-73-69-74—286 |
| Dan Pohl ...... | 72-74-70-70—286 |
| Gary Koch .... | 78-73-69-67—287 |
| Jay Haas ..... | 75-74-70-68—287 |
| Lanny Wadkins . | 73-76-67-71—287 |
| David Graham .. | 73-72-69-73—287 |

Watson, who played Pebble Beach often while attending Stanford University, said before he hit the delicate chip shot that he firmly expected to make it.

"I told Bruce (caddy Bruce Edwards) that I wasn't going to try to come close, that I was going to make it," said Watson. "I had a good, clean lie and I knew all I had to do was open the blade, slice across the ball and pop it in the air. When it hit the fringe, I knew it was in the hole. It was still rolling when I said to Bruce, 'I told you so.'"

Watson said the shot, 16 feet in distance, had a foot and a half break.

"There was no question, though, it was dead center," he said, calling it "the best shot, the most important shot, I ever made in my life."

Estimates varied as to how far the ball might have rolled had it not hit the cup. Nicklaus said 20 feet, Rogers 10 feet and Watson 5

Please see U.S. OPEN, Page 10

**Jim Murray**

## Watson Wins the One He Needed

PEBBLE BEACH—Well, we're well out of that!

Laffit Pincay has never won a Kentucky Derby, Ernie Banks never played in a World Series, William Jennings Bryan never made President.

But Tom Watson has won a U.S. Open. Finally.

He leaves the forlorn company of guys-who-can't-win-the-big-one. He leaves Sam Snead standing alone as a tragic figure, a victim of historic injustice. Sam won 100 tournaments around the world, a record 84 on the U.S. tour and nobody ever swung a club any sweeter. But he never won the Open. He was runner-up four times.

But the pro from Mark Twain finally got the blue coat. And he beat the heavyweight champion of golf to do it. I never saw Dempsey at Toledo or the great Whirlaway charging down a stretch, but I saw Jack Nicklaus fight Pebble Beach out of a crouch in a relentless attack, the kind that left Willard bleeding and battered and the kind that left the other horses with Whirlaway wondering what just went by them.

Tom Watson did his best to toss this Open back on the table for the other players to pick up. He was looking more like Sam Snead on every hole up to 10. He couldn't put away Bill Rogers, the young British Open-winning pro he was outdriving by 30 to 50 yards. On hole No. 7, a piddling little piece of real estate surrounded on three sides by water and on the fourth by sand barely 100 yards long from tee to green, Tom Watson laid a nice little wedge up there two feet from the hole. His playing partner, Rogers, dumped it in the sand. Rogers came out with the kind of sand shot truck drivers make.

Please see JIM MURRAY, Page 6

**NO. 18**

If any doubt remained about who was going to win the 1982 U.S. Open, Watson ended it with another birdie at 18 and then threw his golf ball (above) into the crowd. At right, he hugs his caddy.

LARRY SHARKEY and JOE KENNEDY / Los Angeles Times

*An American Record*

## Olson, Ripley Clear 18-9¼ in Pole Vault

By MAL FLORENCE, *Times Staff Writer*

KNOXVILLE, Tenn.—In the late 30s, USC had a pair of pole vaulters, Bill Sefton and Earl Meadows, who were called the "Heavenly Twins" because they set a world record of 14-11 on the same day at the Coliseum.

The U.S. now has a modern counterpart to Sefton and Meadows.

Billy Olson and Dan Ripley each cleared 18-9¼ to set an American record Sunday night in the U.S. track and field championships at Tom Black Track.

The bar was then raised to a world record height of 19-1 but the two vaulters, exhausted by then, didn't really come close to making it.

Still, the competition was exhilarating between the two and, earlier, among most of the competitors as eight vaulters cleared 18-1½.

The pole vault used to be an American domain but, in recent years, the Europeans have dominated the event. Now U.S. vaulters, particularly Olson and Ripley, are resurging.

Olson, 23, formerly of Abilene Christian, held the previous U.S. outdoor record at 18-8¾ established March 20. He is the world indoor record holder at 18-10. Ripley, 28, is a veteran vaulter who serious-

Please see TRACK, Page 11

ROBERT LACHMAN / Los Angeles

Chicago's Carlton Fisk can't tag Reggie Jackson out if he can't see him, or the ball.

## Angels Win as Reggie Has Day to Make a Father Proud

By PETE DONOVAN, *Times Staff Writer*

He can be baseball's most dramatic performer, a role he has risen to repeatedly over his career. So with his father in the hospital after undergoing hip surgery Friday what did you expect from Reggie Jackson on Father's Day?

A big day, of course.

Jackson singled three times, scored two runs, stole a base and hit a towering solo home run in the sixth inning as the Angels defeated the White Sox, 3-1, before a crowd of 49,567 at Anaheim Stadium Sunday.

Jackson, of course, has a flair for this kind of thing. He has always been at his best in front of national television audiences, during the playoffs and in the World Series.

Sitting in the corner of the Angel clubhouse after the game, Jackson was surrounded by the customary throng of reporters.

He talked quietly and with some emotion about his father. "We had a good chapel service this morning and my father was a big part of it," he said. "He had the operation Friday (replacing a hip) and I talk to him every day.

"I told him I'd call him back if I had a good day. I guess my prayers were answered. I'll call him again. It was a nice Father's Day present."

Jackson's contributions helped give the Angels their fifth victory in seven games against one of their chief rivals in the American League West, Chicago.

Mike Witt, continuing to pitch with consistency and growing poise since his return to the starting rotation, went the distance to improve his record to 4-1. He gave up nine hits, but walked just one and benefited from some

Please see ANGELS, Page 8

## Dodgers Beat Seaver, but for Lasorda Something's Missing

By MARK HEISLER, *Times Staff Writer*

CINCINNATI—The rampaging Dodgers beat Tom Seaver Sunday, but that can't be said to be quite the coup that it once was. Seaver has 11 decisions this season, eight of them losses, and opponents have been critiquing his stuff with things like: "He's got nothing."

The Dodgers, longtime admirers, were more courtly. Besides, Seaver pitched well enough that the Reds were beaten only 4-2. Jerry Reuss went the first seven innings for the Dodgers before a blister forced him to ask out. Steve Howe went a hitless eighth and ninth and the Dodgers had won six in a row, all on this trip.

Joy in the Dodger clubhouse knew few bounds and only one man could find anything at all to complain about.

"WHO ATE MY DAMN CHICKEN?" yelled Tom Lasorda, bouncing out of his office and drowning out three postgame interviews. "THAT'S A BLEEPING CRIME!"

Assistant player representative Pedro Guerrero was summoned. Guerrero started asking around who ate the manager's chicken. It turned out to be Fernando Valenzuela, so no fine was announced.

There was another non-banner crowd of 25,968 in Riverfront Stadium Sunday to see another of their heroes, Johnny Bench, hit the bench. Bench has a bruised thumb on his right hand, not to mention a .215 batting average, and there was some speculation that he wanted no part of a left-hander like Reuss who throws all those fastballs on right-handed hitters' hands.

Anyway, one of the few remaining Cincinnati stars was pitching. That one managed to go two hitters before Ron Roenicke took him out of the park for his first big league home run.

"A fastball I was trying to drive away," Seaver said, with an expression that suggested a connoisseur's distaste. "I just threw it down the middle of the plate, the middle half in, with not much on it."

Reuss gave a first-inning run, himself, on a single, a sacrifice, and an RBI single by Dave Concepcion. But in the fourth, Ron Cey hit his seventh homer, over the left-field fence, and the Dodgers were ahead to stay.

"A hanging slider out over the plate," Seaver said, no happier at this memory, "nothing on it."

An inning later, Ken Landreaux scored from second base on Steve Garvey's infield hit, easily, because the Reds first base

Please see DODGERS, Page 9

GEORGE ROSE / Los Angeles Times

UCLA Coach Terry Donahue raises his arm in triumph as he's given a ride after Rose Bowl win.

GARY FRIEDMAN / Los Angeles Times

UCLA tailback Danny Andrews dives into the end zone to score a touchdown on a nine-yard run that put the Bruins ahead, 17-7, in the third quarter.

## A New Year . . . but an Old Story

### UCLA Repeats Itself Against Michigan, 24-14, With Ramsey Showing the Way

By TRACY DODDS, *Times Staff Writer*

The Rose Bowl game on New Year's Day, 1983, was Tom Ramsey's Rose Bowl game.

Not just because he was the quarterback who led UCLA to a 24-14 victory over Michigan. Not just because he is one of the many seniors topping off a 10-1-1 season with a dream victory before 104,991 on what, just this season, became the Bruins' home field.

It was Tom Ramsey's game because it was so much like Tom Ramsey. He made the game his game, played it his way, and it went his way.

It even adopted his personality—not much.

But, like Ramsey, the Bruin victory was solid and impressive. No flash, no drama, no nonsense, no doubt.

Even Michigan Coach Bo Schembechler, who lost to Ramsey and the Bruins for the second time this season, was impressed. He said, "To UCLA's credit, they never turned the ball over . . . To UCLA's credit, they ran the ball pretty well on us . . . To UCLA's credit, they drove the ball 80 yards on us and scored, just after we had closed to within three. Then we were down by 10 again. That drive took us out of the game."

That drive had the Ramsey touch all the way.

It was in the third quarter, and Michigan had just scored on a fourth down pass play from stand-in quarterback David Hall to another unlikely hero, fullback Eddie Garrett.

A routine touchback put the Bruins on the 20, and from there Ramsey launched what for him, this season, could be called a routine drive.

On third-and-10 from the UCLA 20, after two incomplete passes, Ramsey made a pinpoint perfect pass to flanker Jojo Townsell at the left sideline, good for 12 yards. On third-and-five from the UCLA 37, Ramsey made another pinpoint perfect pass to Townsell at the right sideline, good for 10 yards. On second-and-eight from the UCLA 49, Ramsey found all his receivers covered, considered for a moment, then scrambled for 15 yards.

On second-and-eight from the Michigan 34, Ramsey found wide receiver Cormac Carney for the first time, firing a bullet 11 yards to hit Carney between defensive back Jerry Burgei and linebacker Mike Boren.

Tailback Kevin Nelson gained nine yards on the next play, and tailback Frank Cephous gained five for the

Please see UCLA, Page 6

INSIDE

**The Rose Bowl**



**Jim Murray**

## If Bo Loses, It Must Be a Rose Bowl

**Not one of your** vintage Rose Bowl games . . .

I mean, once again, nobody ran the wrong way, nobody fumbled on the goal line only to have the referee signal a touchdown anyway.

It will not be remembered in the same breath with the year the Four Horsemen came to Pasadena. No one came off the bench a la Doyle Nave or Antelope Al Krueger to retrieve a lost cause in the final seconds.

It was just the football equivalent of a pretty good club fight, a $20,000 claiming race, not the Kentucky Derby, a card game in the firehouse, not Nick the Greek's bucking the house.

Hurry Up Yost would be bound to misunderstand. His Point-A-Minute teams used to win Rose Bowl games 49-0 in contests shortened to three periods in the interest of mercy.

★

**Michigan Coach** Bo Schembechler is now becoming a legend in his own time in Rose Bowl lore. He's now lost six Rose Bowl games in a little over a decade and has a chance to make the world forget the Minnesota Vikings.

Bo's team lost its best tackle on the third play of the game and its only quarterback in the second quarter of the game. Michigan wasn't a good enough team to write off those kinds of losses and the kid who came in to quarterback was, in the words of his coach, "a guy who has never had to win a game in his life and now he's asked to win the biggest." David Hall is a decathlete by athletic preference whose chief function on Bo's squad up to now has been to mop up in 52-14 games and warm up the receivers in spring practice drills.

The flower of American journalism was prepared to make the press box awash with "Cinderella" allusions if Hall came

Please see MURRAY, Page 21

Associated Press

Michigan's Steve Smith (left, on sidelines) goes down and out of game after a tackle by UCLA's Don Rogers (7).

## Mr. Rogers' Neighborhood

### It Wasn't a Friendly Place for Some Tourists From Michigan

By MAL FLORENCE, *Times Staff Writer*

Don Rogers says he hasn't patterned his style of play after Kenny Easley, but the UCLA free safety hits with the same devastating force as the former UCLA All-American.

Steve Smith, Michigan's starting quarterback, will remember Rogers—and may grimace with pain at the thought—for some time.

Smith was turning upfield on an option play in the second quarter of Saturday's Rose Bowl game when Rogers smashed him. It was a jolting, clean tackle and it knocked Smith out of the game with a separated right shoulder.

It was one of many big plays—and big hits—by Rogers. He made 11 tackles, intercepted a Smith pass when Michigan was threatening and broke up three other passes. As a result, Rogers, a junior, was named co-player of the game along with UCLA quarterback Tom Ramsey.

UCLA's offense has received considerably more recognition than its defense this season. But it was the Bruin defense that was, perhaps, the decisive factor in UCLA's 24-14 win over Michigan in the 69th Rose Bowl.

"I was reading the option play," said Rogers, talking about his hit on Smith. "I don't think he saw me and I caught him off guard. I didn't think he would be out of the game."

Someone asked Rogers if he said anything to the Michigan quarterback.

"I didn't say anyting to him and he didn't say anything either," Rogers said.

Although Rogers was the key player on UCLA's defensive unit, he said that his teammate, inside linebacker Blanchard Montgomery, made the turning-point play of the game.

UCLA led, 17-7, midway through the fourth quarter and Michigan was back-

Please see SMITH, Page 8

## Paterno Takes Sweet With Bitter, 27-23

By MIKE LITTWIN, *Times Staff Writer*

NEW ORLEANS—In case the point was lost on anyone, as his players carried him off the field Penn State Coach Joe Paterno raised a finger to the sky indicating that he, at last, was No. 1.

There can be little room for doubt this time, no further disappointments. Not when Penn State, second ranked in the country, has beaten top-rated Georgia, 27-23, in the Sugar Bowl.

"I hope nobody doubts it after today," Paterno said Saturday night in the Superdome. "We beat three or four of the top five football teams in the country. This is the best team I ever had."

He's had three unbeaten teams in 17 years at Penn State, but none of them was voted No. 1 by the pollsters, who decide such matters. Once, even a President lobbied against him.

But, this time, Penn State had a chance to win it on the field. It looked like it might be easy when the Nittany Lions built a 20-3 lead. Suffice it to say, it wasn't. There was question until the final minute in a game that, eventually, nearly lived up to its billing.

In the end, it was Penn State's offensive balance—running and passing—that made the difference. Penn State tailback Curt Warner ran for 117 yards and quarterback Todd Blackledge threw for 228, including a 47-yard strike to Gregg Garrity in the fourth quarter. The touchdown pass gave Penn State a 27-17 advantage, a lead it could not lose.

Warner, plagued by leg cramps for much of the night in hot indoor stadium, outrushed the more heralded Herschel Walker, who got 103 yards on 28 carries.

"It confirms what said, that they have one of the best best offensive teams I've seen since I've been coaching,"

Please see PENN STATE, Page 17

### McIlhenny and SMU Make a Pitch for No. 1 Ranking and Beat Pittsburgh, 7-3

By BOB OATES, *Times Staff Writer*

DALLAS—On their most important football afternoons this season, Southern Methodist's undefeated Mustangs played only as well as they had to play to win narrowly, or, on one occasion tie Arkansas.

And their final game was a struggle Saturday, as usual. But against Pittsburgh's passing team, it was SMU's running team that got off the big pass to knock out the Panthers in the Cotton Bowl, 7-3.

Quarterback Lance McIlhenny threw it 42 yards to reserve split end Bobby Leach—the sophomore known as the "Mustang Miracle Man"—to set up the only touchdown on a cold, rainy day. The touchdown came a moment later in the fourth quarter on McIlhenny's nine-yard keeper.

And on the first day of 1983, still bidding for the national championship, SMU had finished the 1982

Please see SMU, Page 16

JOSE GALVEZ / Los Angeles Times

In Los Angeles Tuesday, Jack Thorpe (above) accepts the decathlon medal his father earned at Stockholm in 1912 (right).

# Thorpe's Victory

## Olympic Medals Returned to His Family 70 Years After They Were Taken Away

By KENNETH REICH, *Times Staff Writer*

To the sound of Indian whoops from many of his 29 grandchildren and great-grandchildren, Jim Thorpe was posthumously awarded his Olympic gold medals Tuesday, 71 years after he won them.

In a ceremony at a downtown hotel, President Juan Antonio Samaranch of the International Olympic Committee and other IOC executive board members presented the medals the Sac-Fox Indian won in the pentathlon and decathlon at the 1912 Stockholm Olympics but later had taken away because he violated amateur rules.

On the victory stand after the decathlon competition, Sweden's King Gustav had told Thorpe, "Sir, you are the greatest athlete in the world." Thorpe reportedly replied, "Thanks, King."

Tuesday, Samaranch seemed startled and then visibly impressed as the Thorpe family whoops came from one side of the room while the medals were being returned to six out of seven Thorpe children who flew in for the occasion. As they whooped, many of the children and great-grandchildren wept.

Medals or replica medals were presented to each of the children and each made short remarks. One of Thorpe's sons, Chief John Thorpe of the Sac and Fox tribe of Oklahoma, the athlete's native state, called the event "one of the first times in the history of the United States that an Indian has his honors restored to him."

Grace Thorpe, one of the daughters said, "It's a very joyous occasion. You kind of want to laugh and cry at the same time."

The IOC's decision last October to

Please see MEDALS, Page 6

## Those Who Saw Him Say He Was Best Ever

By RAY DIDINGER, *Philadelphia Daily News*

Abel Kiviat is 90 and his memory isn't what it used to be, but, yeah, he remembers Jim Thorpe. You spend three weeks on the U.S. Olympic team ship with the world's most celebrated athlete, you train with him, room with him, drink beer with him, chase Swedish girls with him, you remember.

"If you're lucky, you might see real greatness once or twice in your lifetime," Kiviat said. "You don't forget it. And, believe me, Jim Thorpe *was* greatness."

Kiviat was the 1,500-meter runner on the 1912 U.S. Olympic team. He held the world record at the time and was favored to win the gold at the Stockholm games. Thorpe was the decathlon and pentathlon man, an All-American football player from the Carlisle Indian School. No one knew quite what to expect from him.

"The Indians were different," said Kiviat, a retired Penn Relays official who now lives in Tom's River, N.J. "They were hard to figure.

Please see THORPE, Page 10

*David Woodley*

## He Quietly, Efficiently Does a Job

By ROSS NEWHAN, *Times Staff Writer*

He has been described in print as having a "hermitlike lack of charisma."

Quiet. Modest. Intensely protective of his privacy. A loner to the extent that he secured only one autograph for his high school yearbook—that of his favorite wide receiver.

He was the 13th quarterback and 214th player selected in the 1980 National Football League draft, a Louisiana State product who started his pro career as a fourth stringer and, in the view of one writer, nothing more than a "sacrifical lamb," an extra arm during training camp.

David Woodley is now in his third season as the Miami Dolphins' *starting* quarterback. He is no longer considered a sacrificial lamb, though it is only in the last three games, perhaps, that he has buried speculation that Miami will attempt to acquire draft rights to Stanford's John Elway through a trade for the Baltimore Colts' No. 1 choice.

Only by his performance in the last three games, perhaps, has Woodley left Coach Don Shula less inclined to rush in reserve Don Strock and risk compounding a quarterback-rivalry situation of the type Rams fans are familiar with, a situation known in Florida as "Woodstrock."

Sunday, of course, Shula will do what he has to do because the AFC title is at stake when Miami plays host to the New York Jets.

Woodley is on his best-ever roll as he approaches it. Which is not to say his 24-10 record as the Miami starter and seven touchdown passes in the last three game have convinced every cynic that he is something more than a very mobile quarterback with an erratic arm.

Please see WOODLEY, Page 13

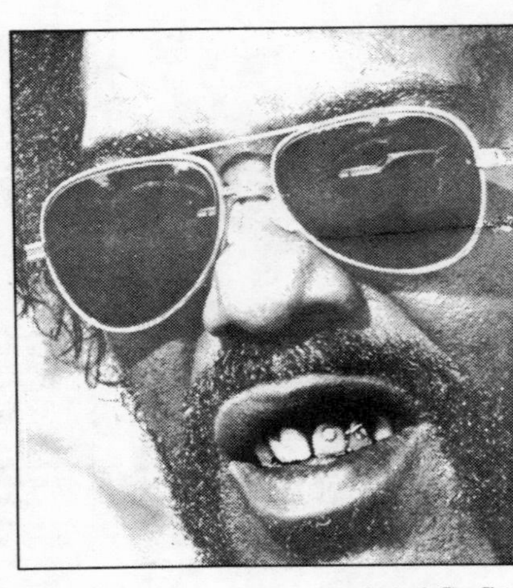

Los Angeles Times Photo

Calvin Peete used to sport diamonds in his teeth (above); now his appearance is more conservative.

## Now, Peete Flashes His Swing Instead of a Diamond Smile

By SHAV GLICK, *Times Staff Writer*

LA QUINTA—Calvin Peete, best known for the diamonds in his teeth when he started playing golf, now is known as one of the game's finest shotmakers.

He likes the new identification better.

"When I first came on the tour seven years ago, people called me Jim Dent or Lee Elder when they saw me," Peete said. "Now they know who Calvin Peete is. That gives me a lot of satisfaction."

This week Peete, the son of migrant farm workers, will walk the fairways of some of America's plushest country clubs in quest of $67,500 for five days work—first prize for a win in the Bob Hope Desert Classic.

Peete will be one of the tournament's most recognizable performers, not because he is black but because of the way he swings a club. As the 1982 PGA season closed, he was the

Please see PEETE, Page 12

## 3-3 Tie Is as Good as Win to the Kings

By SAM McMANIS, *Times Staff Writer*

For one night at least, Wayne Gretzky, center for the Edmonton Oilers and usually the center of attention, was overshadowed both on and off the ice.

Off the ice, former heavyweight boxing champion Muhammad Ali made an appearance around the press area between periods and received a lot of attention from the crowd. And on the ice, Gretzky was overshadowed by the team he usually dominates—the Kings.

Before 14,754 fans, the third largeest Forum crowd of the season, the Kings played one of their best games of the season. They outskated and outchecked the Oilers and held Gretzky pretty much in check—one goal, one assist. There was one problem, though: They didn't win. But they also didn't lose.

The Kings earned a 3-3 tie with the Oilers, but as far as Kings Coach Don Perry is concerned, it was a win. When you've won only twice in the last 19 games, you begin to appreciate ties more.

"It almost feels like a win when you come from behind and play like that," a smiling Perry said. "You won't see a game like that often, with that kind of determination."

Edmonton Coach Glen Sather, however, was less than pleased with his team. He blamed it on penalties —12 against the Oilers. "The referee was 15 steps behind everybody," Sather said.

The Kings were able to handle Edmonton with pretty much the same combination of things they did last season when they upset the Oilers in the first round of the playoffs—excellent goaltending,

Please see KINGS, Page 6

*Wesley Walker*

## Sure Hands, Quick Feet but Only One Good Eye

By EARL GUSTKEY, *Times Staff Writer*

In the aftermath of the Raiders' demise in the NFL playoffs Saturday, it's been pointed out they were victims of an unlucky matchup on the one-yard line with 11 minutes to play.

Cornerback Ted Watts found himself having to cover one of the NFL's best wide receivers with a thumb he'd broken earlier. Wesley Walker caught the ball, a 45-yard pass from Richard Todd. New York scored on the next play to achieve the final score, 17-14.

What *isn't* generally known is that Walker is virtually a one-eyed receiver. Throughout his remarkable football career, Wesley Darcel Walker has had more trouble with eye charts than defensive backs.

On the morning of the 1977 NFL player draft, the Jets' scouting staff had him rated the 10th best college player in the country, at any position. They were surprised to find him still available on the second round and selected him, despite not needing wide receivers.

When contract negotiation began the Jets sent their trainer, Bob Reese, to Berkeley to examine Walker's knee, which had been operated on midway through his

Please see WALKER, Page 13


■ **Oerter Gets Ready Again**

At the age of 46, Al Oerter is shoveling snow and preparing to throw the discus in another Olympic Games.

Please see Scott Ostler on Page 3.

■ **Share of Pirates Sold**

Warner Communications announced it will purchase 48% of the stock in the Pittsburgh Pirates for an estimated $10 million.

Please see Page 4.

■ **Right by Wright**

UCLA's Brad Wright says that it doesn't bother him to sit on the bench.

Please see Page 2.

# Bear Bryant Dies of Heart Attack

Los Angeles Times

Associated Press

After seeing his team struggle to a 7-4 record, Bear Bryant retired a winner (right) when his team beat Illinois in the Liberty Bowl on December 30. Two weeks ago, he was in Los Angeles (above) to receive an American Football Coaches Assn. award from Jerry Claiborne.

## Alabama Coach Had Retired a Month Ago After 323 Wins

By RICHARD HOFFER, *Times Staff Writer*

Paul (Bear) Bryant, who insisted his teams won in spite of him but who nevertheless managed to win more games than any other coach in college football history, died Wednesday of a massive heart attack in Tuscaloosa, Ala. He was 69.

Bryant had been retired less than a month after a 38-year career at Maryland, Kentucky, Texas A&M and Alabama, where he was as much reluctant caretaker to his own legend as he was coach of the Crimson Tide.

Bryant, as well recognized for his self-depreciation as his houndstooth hat, had been admitted to Druid City Hospital in Tuscaloosa on Tuesday after complaining of chest pains. Doctors detected no heart damage at that time and Bryant was reported in "good spirits" with his vital signs stable. Wednesday morning he joked with doctors and nurses, saying, according to Dr. William Hill, "the one thing he wanted to do was go back to Arkansas and do some duck hunting."

But at 12:24 p.m. (EST), while talking to nurses, Bryant went into "sudden cardiopulmonary arrest." Dr. Hill, the attending physician, put a pacemaker in Bryant's chest wall and was able to restore a weak heartbeat, which subsequently failed.

"We quit working with him and pronounced him dead at 1:30 p.m.," Dr. Hill said.

So ended a remarkable life, and with it a remarkable era, during which the craggy-faced Bryant, practically a caricature of a college football coach with his characteristic slump and rumpled suits, won a record 323 games, losing just 85.

Please see BRYANT, Page 10

*He Sent 45 Into Coaching*

## Bear Bryant Has Left His Legacy on Sidelines

*From Times Wire Services*

All the things that were said about Paul (Bear) Bryant Wednesday were the kinds of things he never would have said about himself. He spent a lifetime downplaying the kind of praise he received from President Reagan, who called him a hero who "made legends out of ordinary people."

But in death, the tributes stand unchallenged by the self-mocking coach who won more games than anyone in the history of college football and refused—publicly, anyway—to take credit for any of them.

"He always appeared to be indestructible," said Penn State Coach Joe Paterno, who won a national championship last season but lost to Bryant's Alabama team. In four tries, two of them in the Sugar Bowl, Paterno never beat the Bear.

"He was a monumental figure in intercollegiate athletics, a man who set standards not easily attainable by men," Paterno said. "He was a giant and we will miss him."

Bryant's reputation was unrivaled among his colleagues in the coaching fraternity. So many of those coaches either played for, or worked under, Bryant. The Alabama press guide lists 45 of "Bear's Boys" who went on to become head coaches at either the college or

Please see REACTION, Page 11

Jim Murray

## *He's Little Big Man of Redskins*

**There is, in Washington,** this personality known as "The Great Communicator."

He's got this crest of brown hair in tufts, rosy cheeks, a nice smile, an engaging manner, is kind of outdoorsy and extroverted and has a sort of love-hate relationship with the nation's capital.

He's kind of a public monument. He holds press conferences from time to time to answer his critics in the media. He stops traffic wherever he goes and everyone in town has an opinion on him one way or the other. He has this kind of identification with the legend of Notre Dame and he's theatrical in the extreme.

Ronald Reagan? Are you crazy? Who'd he ever hit with a 30-yard bomb with 30 seconds to play? Did he ever befuddle the Minnesota Vikings with a quarterback keeper? Did he ever take Washington to the Super Bowl?

No, the Washington monument in question is the Rt. Hon. Joe Theismann and, if he's not first in peace and first in war, he is at least in the NFC.

Joe Theismann goes through life as if he's running for office. He's gregarious, talkative, breezy. Hubert Humphrey in cleats. You couldn't send him to funerals because he would have a hard time looking sad.

He's always had a firm grasp of the dramatic. He's the only guy in history to change his name to rhyme with his profession's top award. I mean, would Barrymore change his name to "Oscar" to win the Academy? Well Joe's name is "Theesman" if you ask his father.

Please see MURRAY, Page 12

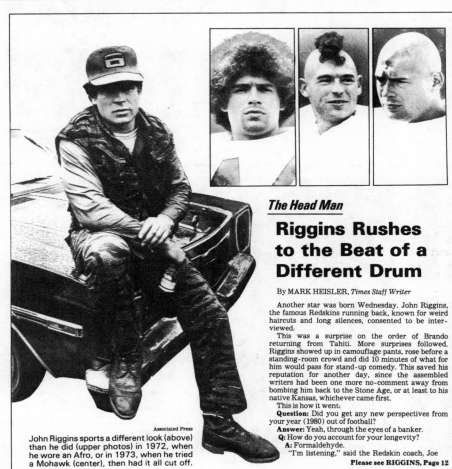

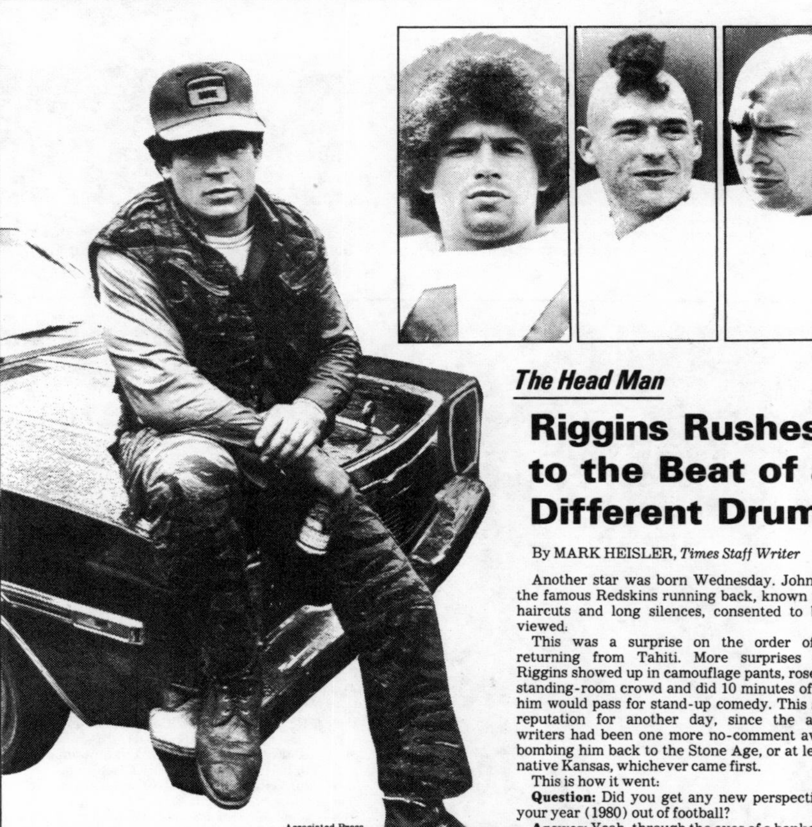

Associated Press

John Riggins sports a different look (above) than he did (upper photos) in 1972, when he wore an Afro, or in 1973, when he tried a Mohawk (center), then had it all cut off.

*The Head Man*

## Riggins Rushes to the Beat of a Different Drum

By MARK HEISLER, *Times Staff Writer*

Another star was born Wednesday. John Riggins, the famous Redskins running back, known for weird haircuts and long silences, consented to be interviewed.

This was a surprise on the order of Brando returning from Tahiti. More surprises followed. Riggins showed up in camouflage pants, rose before a standing-room crowd and did 10 minutes of what for him would pass for stand-up comedy. This saved his reputation for another day, since the assembled writers had been one more no-comment away from bombing him back to the Stone Age, or at least to his native Kansas, whichever came first.

This is how it went:

**Question:** Did you get any new perspectives from your year (1980) out of football?

**Answer:** Yeah, through the eyes of a banker.

**Q:** How do you account for your longevity?

**A:** Formaldehyde.

"I'm listening," said the Redskin coach, Joe

Please see RIGGINS, Page 12

## Lakers Show Bucks but Not a Lot, 115-113

By RANDY HARVEY, *Times Staff Writer*

Even though he didn't know it at the time, Milwaukee guard Sidney Moncrief issued a challenge to the Lakers after the Bucks beat Phladelphia Sunday. He said the 76ers are the National Basketball Assn.'s best team.

Although all the evidence this season supports Moncrief's claim, the Lakers, Coach Pat Riley in particular, took exception to it. They felt they had something to prove to the Bucks before a sellout crowd of 17,505 Wednesday night at the Forum.

The Lakers won the game, 115-113, but whether they proved anything to Milwaukee is questionable. That doesn't mean they weren't pleased with the victory, their sixth straight and their 15th in the last 17 games. This one gave them an eight-game Pacific Division lead over Portland and Phoenix.

But if the Bucks were impressed, they certainly didn't show it on the court. Playing on the road, and without All-Star Moncrief for the entire second half because of a strained calf, Milwaukee had a seven-point lead in the fourth quarter and didn't give in until the final second.

They lost it when Lakers guard Michael Cooper forced Junior Bridgeman's 20-foot jump shot off its mark, and Bucks center Dave Cowens' follow shot from underneath the basket as time ran out rolled off the rim. That would have sent the game into overtime.

"I missed the shot, that's all," Cowens said. "I didn't get fouled. I just missed it."

When it was over, and the Bucks had lost for only the sixth time in the last 23 games, Riley paid the Central Division leaders a supreme compliment.

"They're a great basketball team," he said. "They're equal to us as far as athletes go. It helped us when Moncrief couldn't come back, but they kept bringing guys off the bench."

Opposing coaches usually say the same thing about the Lakers, whose bench is one of the deepest in the NBA. But, Wednesday night, the Bucks' reserves outscored the Lakers' reserves, 63-32.

As he has been almost since the beginning of the season, Milwaukee forward Marques Johnson was outstanding. He had 30 points and 10 rebounds.

But it was guard Charlie Criss' performance off the bench, especially in the second half when he scored 16 of his 20 points, that brought the Bucks back after they

Please see LAKERS, Page 15

■ **Flashback**

Len Dawson had to beat more than Minnesota in 1970.
Please see Page 3.

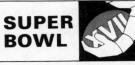

■ **Quarterbacks**

The Super Bowl quarterbacks are not the NFL's best.
Please see Page 3.

■ **Laskoski Is Back**

Goalie Gary Laskoski was recalled by the Kings from New Haven, where he failed to play.
Please see Page 5.

■ **Knox a Seahawk**

As expected, Chuck Knox was named coach at Seattle, one day after leaving Buffalo.
Please see Page 6.

Los Angeles Times

Monday, January 31, 1983 CC†/Part III

# SPORTS

# Super Bowl Really Hog Heaven

JOE KENNEDY / Los Angeles Times

Washington's John Riggins breaks away on 43-yard touchdown run that put Redskins ahead, 20-17, in fourth quarter. Miami's Glenn Blackwood (47) gives futile pursuit

## Redskins Leave No Doubt, Take No Prisoners

By ALAN GREENBERG, *Times Staff Writer*

In 1942, the last time the Redskins won the world championship, there was world war. Art imitated life. Everyone adopted he-man heroes.

Now, life imitates art. Our modern he-men, pro football players adopt cartoon characters as heroes. Smurfs scamper across football fields instead of TV screens. The Fun Bunch frolics in the end zone.

But don't be deceived. There was nothing odd or otherworldly about the Redskins' resounding 27-17 win over the Miami Dolphins in Super Bowl XVII Sunday at the Rose Bowl before 103,667.

Sure, the Redskins took the sting out of the Dolphins' defense with some new formations, particularly the tight end in motion. Sure, Dolphin quarterbacks David Woodley and Don Strock, who completed exactly *none* of their 11 second-half passes, moved as if they'd been knocked into the Twilight Zone by the Redskin defense.

But what made the difference Sunday was as blunt and basic, as simple and down-to-earth as a hog's life. The Smurfs and the Fun Bunch, wouldn't be much without the Redskin offensive line—affectionately known as The Hogs.

The Hogs root, root, rooted the Dolphin defenders off the line of scrimmage as if they were blocking their food trough. They made ample room for the Head Hog—fullback John Riggins—to pound the Dolphins 38 times for 166 yards, both Super Bowl records. That included his 43-yard touchdown on a fourth-and-one with 10:09 to go, when he slipped cornerback Don McNeal's tackle at the line of scrimmage and raced down the sideline to the longest touchdown run from scrimmage in Super Bowl history.

"That's our bread and butter," Redskins center Jeff Bostic said. "When you get caught in a squeeze, you go with your best play."

McNeal, who had lost his footing at the start of the play following the Redskin tight end in motion, had to dive at Riggins' side, instead of hitting him head-on.

"I wanted to make him bounce outside," McNeal said, "but I never got my arms all the way around him. He was like a train."

Capped by Mark Moseley's conversion, it gave the Redskins a 20-17 lead, their first lead of the game. The only lead they'd need.

"We pounded it all day," Bostic said. "They never really stopped us."

The Redskins, the NFC champions, were here because nobody else had either. They swept through the NFL's four-game playoff tournament, beating the Lions, Vikings, Cowboys and Dolphins with a run-oriented offense geared to the 235-pound Riggins. In the playoffs, 172 of the Redskins' 261 offensive plays were runs. Riggins carried 136 times for 610 yards.

"John Riggins is our consistency factor, our common denominator," quarterback Joe Theismann said. "If you can't run, you have to throw into all that coverage. We just turned all our Hogs loose."

Although the Dolphins led until Riggins' score, the Redskins dominated. They had the ball for 36:15 of the game's 60 minutes. They outgained the Dolphins, 400-176, and had 24 first downs to the Dolphins' 9. The Dolphins gained only 34 yards in the second half, with two first downs—both in the third quarter.

Third-year pro Woodley, who had been on a roll earlier in the playoffs, wasn't rushed hard; he was just inept, completing only 4 of 14 passes for 97 yards, a touchdown and an interception.

The Dolphin offense consisted of one big play—Woodley to Jimmy Cefalo on a 76-yard pass play with 8:11 left in the first quarter that gave Miami a 7-0 lead. The Dolphins scored their only other touchdown on a 98-yard Fulton Walker kickoff return 1:38 before halftime to lead at intermission, 17-10.

"At halftime, I told them we had been in tougher spots," Redskin

Please see SUPER BOWL, Page 15

Jim Murray

## *Super Bowl Magic: Dolphins Disappear*

**Anybody seen** the Miami Dolphins? The football team?

They disappeared during halftime of a football game Sunday, a game in which they were comfortably ahead, breathing easy and under the command of a man widely accepted as three times smarter than anyone else in his business and definitely not accustomed to losing things, not teams or games.

They were last seen in the vicinity of the Rose Bowl wearing those funny little blue-green uniforms with the fishes on the helmets.

If anyone knows of their whereabouts, contact Coach Don Shula, who thought they were right behind him leaving the locker room at around 5 o'clock Sunday. Some minutes later, he realized with a shock that the players on the field, whoever they were, were not the ones he brought with him in the first half. They were impostors. Not very clever ones at that.

Now we know the secret of an exciting Super Bowl game. Take two lousy teams who don't belong there, give them the football, wish them luck and close your eyes and pray. Sometimes you get lucky. The NFL did Sunday.

You see, neither of these teams beat anybody to get here. Not since Primo Carnera got a title shot fighting his chauffeur across the country and/or people who owed his managers money, has a championship featured two principals with more suspect credentials.

The Washington Redskins missed out playing the Dallas Cowboys (the first time), the Pittsburgh Steelers, San Francisco 49ers, Cincinnati Bengals. The Dolphins got to pass on playing the Packers, Chargers (the first time), the Raiders and Bengals. What was left was like playing with your sister.

Still, for XVI years, the NFL has been sending its registered titans to the game and they have been dispensing clinkers, grim defensive outfits so scared of each other they barely needed the air in the football.

Please see MURRAY, Page 16

Associated Press

Joe Theismann celebrates after throwing four-yard touchdown pass to Alvin Garrett for first Washington touchdown in second quarter of Super Bowl XVII. This tied the score at 10-10.

## Celtics Use Lakers and Television to Get a Point Across

By RANDY HARVEY, *Times Staff Writer*

BOSTON—On the flight here from Los Angeles Saturday morning, Lakers Coach Pat Riley said he wanted his team to make a statement to the rest of the National Basketball Assn.: Take a seven-game winning streak into the Boston Garden, beat the Celtics and don't lose again before the Feb. 13 All-Star break.

Let the league know who is really the best team. Period.

But upon arriving at the Boston Garden, the Lakers discovered that the Celtics had an announcement of their own. They shouted it over national television and ended it with an exclamation point, beating the Lakers, 110-95.

The Celtics did it the way they've been doing it for years, with hard work. Like the blue-collar laborers they are, they overwhelmed the Lakers in the effort departments—defense and rebounding.

That's not to say the Lakers didn't want it. They just didn't want it as much as the Celtics did.

But then the Celtics needed it more. Although their 34-10 record is the NBA's third best, a loss Sunday would have dropped them five games behind Philadelphia in the Atlantic Division.

Also, while they had won 12 of their last 14 games, the two losses were to Cleveland and Washington. Some of the victories weren't all that impressive. The critics were beginning to question the Celtics' hearts.

There were other problems. Point guard Tiny

Please see LAKERS, Page 25

Associated Press

Laker rookie James Worthy has shown he can go to the basket, but this time Celtics' Larry Bird blocks the way and the shot.

## Jackson and Fields Do Their Numbers on the Irish Again

By TRACY DODDS, *Times Staff Writer*

Once again it was Ralph Jackson who did in the unlucky Irish, coming through to give UCLA a last-second victory.

Jackson did a little bit of everything down the stretch as UCLA beat Notre Dame, 59-53, Sunday morning before a crowd of 11,425 and a national television audience.

UCLA, holding for the moment to its No. 1 ranking, ran its record to 14-2, while Notre Dame dropped to 11-6.

But the record Jackson was enjoying was his 6-0 against the Irish.

Jackson, who rolled in a layup with three seconds left to win the game at Notre Dame earlier this season, has never lost to Notre Dame. He—and another Bruin junior, Kenny Fields—have had a hand in beating the Irish in six straight. In this series, which UCLA leads, 20-11, neither team had ever won six straight before.

Giving his usual little smile, Jackson admitted, "I said to Kenny before the game, we've never lost to them. This is no time to start."

So, when time came to win the game, Fields and Jackson stepped forward.

The game had been close, and Notre Dame guard John Paxson had just brought the Irish within two points with a pair of free throws. Then with 1:19 to play, Fields backed in toward the basket, knocking Notre Dame forward Tim Kempton aside, to put up a shot that

Please see UCLA, Page 24

**■ Analysis**



SUPER BOWL

**■ More on the Victorious Redskins**



**■ TV, the Dolphins, and Statistics**

## Jim Murray

### Cruelty, Thy Name Is Golf

**Golf is the most unfair** of games. In most sports, you get what you deserve. But golf metes out what Aristotle called "undeserved misfortune." It takes great delight in punishing the guiltless. If it were human, it would be Ivan The Terrible. Himmler. Bobby Jones called the golfer "the dogged victim of inexorable fate." I.e., doomed.

Consider the case of Jack Renner, a golfer of mild repute from San Diego. If you were watching Sunday, you saw Jack win his third tournament on the PGA tour, the Hawaiian Open. I mean, Jack left the 17th green all tied with Japanese golfer Isao Aoki at 18 under par. Then, Jack proceeded to ice the tournament, for all intents and purposes.

He slammed a gorgeous drive off the par-5 18th. Long and solid, it came to rest so far down the fairway, Renner had no trouble going for the green with his second shot. He hit a textbook 3-wood to the front of the green and it bounced to within 15 feet of the cup. He was looking at a makeable eagle 3.

Meanwhile, back on the tee, the golfing samurai, Aoki, appeared to have fallen on his sword. He slammed a hacker's drive to the right into stubble so unnegotiable that his fairway wood shot out of it was hooked badly into the left rough, a ball so mired in the broccoli that it looked like his best club was a pair of tweezers.

Here was the picture then: Renner was on the green, 15 feet from the hole, in 2. Aoki was in the rough, 128 yards from the green, in two. The game's over, right? Renner makes 3, Aoki makes 6, right?

You don't know golf. It dreams of setups like this. It's like the practical joker who works all his life to get the pail of water in the right place, the cayenne in the sugar jar, the phony wallet just right to humiliate the unsuspecting.

□

**Renner missed that** little putt. Well, he didn't exactly miss it. Golf is not so kind. It hit the hole and lipped out. Never mind. Aoki is still out there in lion country. He's looking at 5—if he's lucky. Renner makes his tap-in 4. Even if the roof falls in, he now makes no worse than a playoff.

Aoki then chips in. Well, make that "pitches" in. One hundred and 28 yards is not exactly a chip. It's more like a hole in one, a 100,000-to-1 shot.

Isolated instance? Not at all. Golf is full of perversions like that. It's a sport for the Marquis de Sade.

It seldom rewards the just. It punishes the worthy. Who can forget a PGA played in Columbus, Ohio, in 1964? Tee to green that year, Arnold Palmer played an impeccable round of golf on the final day. Bobby Nichols, the ultimate winner, played by the way of Philadelphia. Hole after hole, Palmer would be found standing on a green in regulation with a short putt for birdie and Nichols would be out in the briars looking for his ball. All of a sudden, twigs would fly, stones rattle, cans scatter, branches and squirrels would run all over the place—and Nichols' ball would come screaming out of the garbage and stop one foot from the pin. Shaken, Palmer would miss the putt. Palmer would never win a PGA. Golf is relentless, too.

□

**You can recall** Lee Trevino winning a British Open with a skull shot out of a trap that hit the flag and dropped straight down into the cup. If it misses the stick, it's in the Firth of Forth or Scapa Flow or someplace nestled around the sunken subs.

Who can forget Tom Watson, hip deep in the weeds, chipping in from the edge of a ledge to win last year's U.S. Open? A colleague, Lyle Spencer, watching with me, leaned over to tap me on the shoulder as Watson studied his disaster lie. "He'll lose now. He'll make a 4 from that lie. Or a 5, maybe," he said. "What if he makes 2?" I challenged. You see, I know golf for the perverse dastard that it is.

You make a good pitch in baseball, you get the guy out. Chances

**Please see MURRAY, Page 4**

JAYNE KAMIN / Los Angeles Times

Georgia Frontiere, owner of the Rams, helps her newest employee, Coach John Robinson, try his new hat on for size. Presumably he'll be given another one that fits.

## New Ram Coach Starts Off With a Reverse

### John Robinson's 2½-Month Retirement Comes to a Rather Abrupt End

By MIKE LITTWIN, *Times Staff Writer*

Surprise, surprise. John Robinson, apparently not the retiring kind, landed Monday in the embrace of the Rams, ending the team's six-week hunt for a head coach. He then spent the afternoon trying to hurdle the credibility gap he'd created.

It was only 2½ months ago that Robinson, 47, quit as USC coach to accept a position as the school's senior vice president for university relations, saying, "I've committed myself to another type of life."

Almost as quickly as you can say John Robinson, that commitment has ended.

No one was happier about it than Rams owner Georgia Frontiere, who introduced Robinson at a Beverly Hills press conference by telling the assembled media, "Happy Valentine's Day. I brought you a gift because I love you all."

Landing Robinson is a coup for the Rams, who finally are taking steps in an attempt to shore up the team's sagging fortunes. In the wake of a 2-7 record, their second losing season in a row, the Rams have hired Ray Nagel to run the front office and Robinson to replace Ray Malavasi as coach.

Perhaps no other coach would have been as well received locally as the popular Robinson, whose record was 67-14-2 in seven years as head man at USC.

But it was Robinson's credibility, not the team's, that came under question Monday. As usual, he handled the press deftly, saying that his decision was nothing more or less than a change of heart.

"I missed it," he said of coaching. "Maybe I made a mistake on how I read myself . . . You make a decision (and) this is it. Deep down in your stomach you know."

But it wasn't so long ago that deep down in his stomach Robinson knew that giving up coaching was the right decision. He left it behind for the life of a university fund-raiser. As recently as last Friday, he was mapping plans for his department to reporters.

And, privately, he had been telling friends that he wouldn't be interested in the Ram job if for no other reason than the often chaotic state of the franchise.

But all that apparently changed in a hurry. According to Robinson, it was only a week ago Monday that he and the Rams first got together. Robinson met with Frontiere and other Rams officials Wednesday and then again on Saturday. Frontiere said he accepted the job only Sunday and that she had an interview with another candidate lined up for Monday had Robinson refused the offer.

"He's the perfect package, everything we want," she said.

Robinson last year turned down a five-year, $2.5-million contract from New England. Terms of his Rams deal were not announced, but it was believed to be for five years.

He accepted the Rams' offer knowing that people would wonder how he could change his mind so quickly or if a deal already had been struck when he left his USC coaching job.

"People can basically think what

**Please see ROBINSON, Page 6**

## Ed Hookstratten Sold Frontiere on Robinson

By RICH ROBERTS, *Times Staff Writer*

As the Rams' meet-the-coach press conference was breaking up, Georgia Frontiere called to Ed Hookstratten across the room.

"Thanks, Ed," the Rams' owner said. "I couldn't have done it without you." True, but *wouldn't* might be more accurate.

There have been eight head coaching changes in the National Football League since the end of last season. The Rams created one of the first vacancies by firing Ray Malavasi but were the last to fill theirs by hiring John Robinson. What took so long?

"We didn't want to rush," Frontiere said. "It's easy to say, 'OK, we've got to get someone,' and maybe make a mistake. In the backs of our minds, the latest date was Feb. 15—that's tomorrow, isn't it?"

But according to all principals, the first significant contact with Robinson wasn't made until only

**Please see HIRING, Page 5**

Ed Hookstratten

## Scott Ostler

### Rams Put One Over on Good Old Davis

**Sorry, Al Davis,** wherever you are. The day after Valentine's day is a lousy time to stick a knife in your heart, but I've got some bad news for you.

You have just been out-Al-Davised.

True, you are the recognized genius at bugging, intimidating, scheming and surprising your opponents. Moving the Raiders from Oakland to L.A. is still the classic sports prank. Were the Rams and Georgia Frontiere steamed at that one! Man, you stole their town!

But they just paid you back. You might say the ball is now in your court. Or in your throat.

What Georgia did was hire John Robinson to be her new head coach. Can you believe it? John Robinson, the former Raider assistant and more recently the head coach at USC?

Isn't that a stunner, Al? Here the Rams were the laughing stock of the league, making one bungle after another. Then your team came to town and made things even hotter for the Rams by being so impressively efficient. It was "Pride and Poise" vs. "Pies and Pratfalls."

Let's face it, the Rams were in big trouble.

And now, with one move, they have made themselves credible. You think you were crafty, stealing the fans' hearts by getting Marcus Allen and by moving into the Coliseum. Well, Marcus is a hero in L.A., but John Robinson is more than a hero here. He's sort of a guru, junior grade. Shoot, John Robinson *invented* Marcus Allen.

You're surprised, Al, because you thought John Robinson had retired from football coaching. That's what he swore 2½ months ago, when he walked away from the USC job. He said that he was no longer interested in coaching in general and no longer interested in coaching the Rams in particular.

So he surprised us.

In recent weeks, the three biggest lies have been: 1. The check is in the mail; 2. I promise I'll respect you in the morning; And 3. "I'm not interested in the Rams' coaching job."

As one prospective coach after another stepped forward to voice fib No. 3, we all winked. However, when John Robinson said it, we *believed*. Robinson has more credibility around L.A. than Santa Claus or Vidal Sassoon.

Maybe you think Robinson threw away his credibility Monday, but that doesn't seem to be the case. He's the only guy I know who could make this kind of philosophical turnaround in such a short time and have people believe him. Get this: At his press conference, Robinson even took a verbal shot at the sportswriters who, 2½ months ago,

**Please see OSTLER, Page 5**

## Sitton Sits—but USC Falls, 62-50

By MAL FLORENCE, *Times Staff Writer*

CORVALLIS, Ore.—Charlie Sitton, Oregon State's star center, was on the bench most of the game with foul trouble but the Beavers still beat USC, 62-50, Monday night at Gill Coliseum.

It was Oregon State's sixth straight victory and kept the Beavers' hopes alive for a second or third-place finish in the Pacific 10 race.

USC had a four-game winning string snapped and, after a brief stay in second place, fell to third with a 7-3 record. The Beavers are 7-4.

OSU outscored USC, 12-2, at the start of the second half, and that run was definitive. The Trojans came within four points of tying the score twice, but the Beavers pulled away on each occasion.

The game got out of hand in the last three minutes with OSU leading, 52-42, when an official gave USC a basket it didn't make (the field goal was eventually taken away). Many in a sellout crowd of 10,000 booed lustily and some paper objects were thrown on the floor.

Oregon State Coach Ralph Miller grabbed a microphone and berated the crowd. "Now damn it, you shape up," he said.

The crowd applauded the rebuke by Miller.

The Trojans had a chance for a five-point play at the time as guard Jacque Hill went to the line for two shots and wingman Cedric Bailey was ready to shoot a technical foul because of the crowd's behavior.

Hill made one free throw and Bailey made the technical foul. But after the Trojans inbounded the ball, they couldn't score.

Sitton, who is averaging 18 points a game, got just nine as he played only 10 minutes 15 seconds. He got his third and fourth fouls early in the second half and didn't return to the floor until 4:42 remained in the game.

But the Beavers got 17 points from forward A.C.

**Please see USC, Page 7**

**■ Off the Wall**

It was a very upsetting day at Daytona for Cale Yarborough—he crashed.

Please see Page 8.

**■ Death in New York**

Sonny Dove, the former basketball star at St. John's, was killed when the cab he was driving slid off a drawbridge and fell into an icy canal.

Please see Page 4.

**■ Second Thoughts**

Lakers writer Randy Harvey reconsiders picking Kareem Abdul-Jabbar on his team.

Please see Page 3.

# Fernando Hits Jackpot for Million

## Some Expert Witnesses Named Campanis and Lasorda Help Him Win Arbitration

By MARK HEISLER, *Times Staff Writer*

VERO BEACH, Fla.—In the time it took arbitrator Tom Roberts to place a call from his home in Rolling Hills Estates to the Major League Players Assn. in New York City, 22-year-old Fernando Valenzuela became the highest-paid Dodger, the highest-paid third-year player in baseball history and the first man ever to be awarded $1 million in arbitration.

Roberts decided Saturday for Valenzuela and against the Dodgers, who had submitted a $750,000 offer.

That ended the Dodgers' arbitration win streak at three and enabled Valenzuela's lawyer, Dick Moss, 3-1 in arbitrations, to tie Bob Walker, the heretofore undefeated Dodger counsel, who is now 3-1 himself.

"I would like to congratulate Tony DeMarco and Dick Moss for what must have been a very impressive case," said Dodger owner Peter O'Malley here Saturday night.

"We gave the arbitrators four tough cases (the team beat Pedro Guerrero, Steve Howe and Mike Scioscia). We thought they were very fair, very professional. We appreciate the job the arbitrators did."

This is how impressive Valenzuela's case was: It included endorsements from Al Campanis and Tom Lasorda, who are the Dodger executive vice president for personnel and the Dodger manager, respectively.

**The Biggest Winners**

Baseball's Top Five Arbitration Awards

| Player (Team) | Year | Award Per Year | Team Offer |
|---|---|---|---|
| 1. Fernando Valenzuela (Dodgers) | 1983 | $1,000,000 | $750,000 |
| 2. Bruce Sutter (Cubs)* | 1980 | $700,000 | $500,000 |
| 3. Mario Soto (Reds) | 1983 | $625,000 | $450,000 |
| 4. Steve Kemp (Tigers)* | 1981 | $600,000 | $350,000 |
| 5. Rickey Henderson (A's) | 1982 | $535,000 | $350,000 |

* no longer with team

This was done in a 3½-minute videotape, accepted by Roberts during the Friday hearing only after Walker objected and Moss counterobjected for close to half an hour.

The tape included Lasorda, being interviewed in 1981, Valenzuela's rookie year, at the height of Fernandomania. On the tape, Lasorda says things like:

"Everywhere we go the fans are clamoring for Fernando."

And:

"Fernando is a player who comes along once in a lifetime."

And:

"I'm the luckiest manager in the world."

Campanis was interviewed, also in 1981, standing on an empty baseball diamond. A friend of Valenzuela's, who saw the tape, insists Campanis even had tears in his eyes. Campanis says something like:

"Mr. Walter O'Malley must be looking down and smiling. When we moved to Los Angeles, he asked me, 'Al, do you think we can find a good Mexican player?' Fernando is the answer to all our dreams and prayers. We're so lucky."

Years later, the Dodgers have a good Mexican player,

Please see VALENZUELA, Page 9

Associated Press

Fernando Valenzuela scored a big victory Saturday, winning a $1-million contract at arbitration.

DON KELSEN / Los Angeles Times

Cal State Fullerton guard Leon Wood (above and right) is getting a lot of attention from NBA scouts.

## When Leon Wood Has the Ball, It's Cal State Wow

By ALAN GREENBERG, *Times Staff Writer*

Leon Wood keeps two basketballs in his closet, two more in his car trunk. Got to be ready for anything.

He plays 365 days a year. Last year. This year. Every year. In between, he goes to class and the coaches' office to watch game films. He watches every pro and college game on TV. Not most. Every. Starting lineups? He knows ESPN's, the NBA's and those of more than 100 NCAA teams by heart. Women's teams, too.

"When I'm watching games, I hate being interrupted," Wood says. "I don't like people coming in and talking about other things."

Sometimes, in school, he's had to do book reports on famous people. He's done Pete Maravich, Connie Hawkins, Wilt Chamberlain, Walt Frazier, Jerry West. He also makes collages—of basketball players.

George McQuarn is Wood's coach at Cal State Fullerton. McQuarn, 41, coached at Verbum Dei High in South Central Los Angeles and at Nevada Las Vegas before moving to Fullerton for the 1980-81 season. Like most coaches, he's a basketball junkie. But even he is impressed by Wood's single-mindedness.

Please see WOOD, Page 13

## UCLA Maintains Its Mastery of Cal With a 70-60 Victory

By TRACY DODDS, *Times Staff Writer*

UCLA chalked up another in a series of victories over California Saturday afternoon.

The Bruins' 70-60 win kept intact a streak against the Bears which is now at 48 games; kept the Bruins in first place in the Pac-10 with a record of 11-1; ran the Bruins' overall record to 19-3, and filled some regional-TV time for NBC.

It was a W, as the coaches say.

And the crowd of 9,244, which did not quite pack Pauley Pavilion, was mostly pleased with that.

But that was about all it was. Just a W. Not one that will stand out in this long-standing series.

Forward Kenny Fields, who hasn't seemed to lose any of his effectiveness since hurting his shoulder last Saturday at Oregon State, had a perfect shooting game, hitting nine of nine from the floor to lead the Bruins with 18 points. He also led UCLA with eight rebounds.

The other bright spot for UCLA was the defense on Cal center Michael Pitts. The Bears' 6-11 junior center averages 15.6 points and 6.3 rebounds. He ended up with 15 points Saturday, but he got most of them when it was too late. Pitts was held to three points in the first half, hitting 1 of 7 from the floor and 1 of 4 from the line.

"I thought the turning point of the ballgame was the fact that we only shot 37% in the first half," Cal Coach Dick Kuchen said. "That took us out of the game, we lost contact."

UCLA Coach Larry Farmer, who started 6-10 sophomore Brad Wright in place of injured 7-foot center Stuart Gray, liked the defensive play of both Wright and backup Gary Maloncon.

"I wanted both Brad and Gary to sacrifice offensively if they had to in order to give their best effort defensively," Farmer said. "They both really did that. . .

"This is definitely one of the better Cal teams in a while. There's no doubt in my mind tht Michael Pitts is one of the outstanding centers in our league."

But while Pitts was not scoring, guard Michael Chavez was. Chavez, a 5-9 guard, led Cal with 19 points, making some Rod Foster-like shots from outside.

The Bruins stayed with their man-to-man defense all the way.

Please see UCLA, Page 8

JAYNE KAMIN / Los Angeles Times

Rod Foster finds an opening in the fast lane to basket during UCLA's 70-60 win over Cal Saturday. Jeff Thilgen is the defender.

Jim Murray

## *New Thoughts on the Grand Old Game*

**The subject for today**, class, is "So You Think You Know Baseball?"

One answer and one answer only. Neatness counts. First prize is a picture of the Dodgers' front office refusing to sign free-agent Joe Morgan to a one-year contract. Second prize is the ball Joe Morgan hit over the fence to knock the Dodgers out of the 1982 pennant.

We will skip right over "How many years did Ty Cobb hit over .400?" and the trivia faithfuls like "Who played third base in the Tinker-to-Evers-to-Chance combination?" We are concerned here with the artistic aspects of the grand old game, not the mechanics. Ready? Places, everybody.

**Question.** What is meant in baseball by the term "arbitration"?

**Answer.** Arbitration is a device whereby a layman who has never seen a game of hardball, or at least not since the Philadelphia Athletics were in the league, is asked to decide whether a .211 hitter gets a half-million dollars a year or three-quarters of a million. He does not know the infield-fly rule intimately, he probably thinks the St. Louis Cardinals are an ecclesiastical group convened to elect a Pope, and he thinks Vida Blue is a disease, but he has the power at one stroke of the pen to dole out more money than Babe Ruth made in his lifetime. He allows players to bring in videotapes of one of their two sensational catches from the year before, but management cannot bring in a montage of the 811 infield pop outs or double-play balls he hit.

Q. What does the "designated hitter" rule do?

Please see MURRAY, Page 14

Herschel Walker

## Walker, at Banquet, Denies Reports of Signed Contract

ATLANTA (AP)—Heisman Trophy winner Herschel Walker, denying reports of new meetings with officials of the New Jersey Generals, said again Saturday night that he has not signed a contract with the United States Football League team.

CBS-TV, using an unidentified source in a report similar to the Boston Globe's a day earlier, said Walker had signed a contract with the USFL club and was meeting with Generals officials Saturday.

"No, I haven't met with anyone," Walker said as he arrived at an Atlanta hotel to attend the Georgia Sports Hall of Fame's annual banquet, where he was to be honored.

Asked if he had signed anything at all, Walker said, "No." He was quickly whisked into the banquet area by Hall of Fame officials and answered no further questions.

Georgia Coach Vince Dooley, also in Atlanta for the banquet, said he was convinced his star running back had not jeopardized his eligibility.

Dooley said that when he heard the reports of Walker signing, "the first thing I did was check back with Herschel. I don't have any doubt in

Please see WALKER, Page 15

**■ Keeping It All in the Family**

The best-known father-son combination in basketball was probably LSU Coach Press Maravich and his son, Pistol Pete, but it wasn't the only one.

Please see Page 3

**■ USC Scores a Basketball Sweep**

USC's men's team got even with Stanford for an earlier defeat, 90-76, and the Trojan women beat Cal State Long Beach, 90-75.

Please see Page 4.

Los Angeles Times

# SPORTS/BUSINESS

Saturday, March 26, 1983

CC†/Part III

# Former Bruin and Ram Bob Waterfield Dies

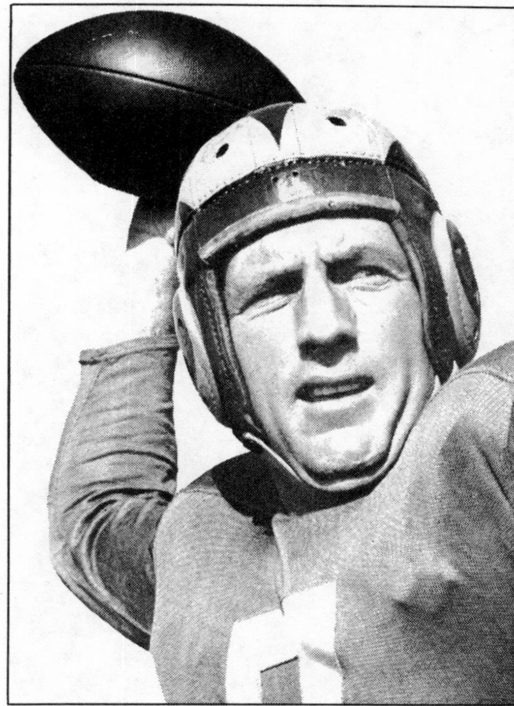

## Respiratory Failure Claims Legendary Quarterback at 62

Bob Waterfield, former star quarterback with the Rams and UCLA Bruins, who later coached the Rams, died Friday of respiratory failure following a lengthy illness. He was 62.

A spokesman for St. Joseph Medical Center in Burbank said Waterfield, who entered the hospital March 11, was pronounced dead about 1:30 p.m. His wife, Jan, and one of his three children, Robert John, were at his bedside.

Waterfield came out of UCLA to join the Cleveland Rams in 1945 and led them to the NFL championship in his rookie season.

After the 1945 season, Waterfield signed a three-year contract at $20,000 a year, making him the "highest-paid football player in the world," and he was Ram owner Dan Reeves' main selling point when he convinced other owners that his team would be successful in Los Angeles. The team moved in 1946, becoming the first major professional sports franchise to play on the West Coast.

Waterfield played with the Rams for eight years and was named professional football's Most Valuable Player in 1945 and 1950. He was runner-up to Pittsburgh's Bill Dudley in 1946.

Waterfield still holds the Rams' club record for the longest punt, 88 yards against Green Bay in 1948. He kicked 315 conversions, another Ram record, and his five field goals against Detroit in 1951 is still a team high. In his seventh year with the Rams, Waterfield was elected team captain.

During his later years with the Rams, he competed with Norm Van Brocklin for the starting quarterback position and, on Dec. 1, 1952, Waterfield, "Mr. Ram himself," announced his retirement at the age of 32.

In 1965, Waterfield was unanimously selected to pro football's Hall of Fame at Canton, Ohio.

Of Waterfield, former Ram teammate Don Paul once said: "I have always felt that the greatest all-around football player I have ever known is Bob Waterfield. He could do everything . . . offense, defense, punt, place-kick, run, pass, the whole bit. Norm Van Brocklin was a great quarterback and the purest passer I've ever seen. But for all-around ability, Waterfield was my guy."

In January, 1960, Waterfield succeeded Sid Gillman as coach of the Rams and signed a five-year contract. He resigned two years later in November, 1962 "for the good of the team." At the time, the Rams were 1-7. They had finished 4-7-1 under Waterfield in 1960 and 4-10 in 1961. Waterfield was replaced by Harland Svare.

Asked what kind of a coach he thought he was, Waterfield replied, "Losing."

Waterfield played for UCLA in 1941-42 and 1944. During the 1942 season, he led the Bruins to the Rose Bowl, where they lost, 9-0, to Georgia on Jan. 1, 1943. A 42-yard pass play from Waterfield to All-American end Burr Baldwin

Please see WATERFIELD, Page 12

Los Angeles Times photos

Bob Waterfield is shown toward the end of his playing career as Ram quarterback (above); after a game as Ram coach in 1961, shaking hands with former teammate Norm Van Brocklin, then coach of the Minnesota Vikings (right), and with actress Jane Russell, whom he married in 1943 (far right). Waterfield, who died Friday of respiratory failure following a lengthy illness, played for UCLA, then the Rams and later became Ram coach in 1960.

## Waterfield Remembered as an Outstanding Athlete and a Loyal Friend

By LARRY STEWART, *Times Staff Writer*

Bob Waterfield was, first and foremost, a great all-around athlete. He was also a private person who shunned publicity. And he was a person who was loyal to his friends.

That's what his friends and former teammates were saying about him Friday.

San Diego Chargers General Manager Johnny Sanders was a lifelong friend of Waterfield's. They went to Van Nuys High School together. Sanders was hired as a part-time scout for the Rams during the Waterfield era, and the friendship blossomed. When Sanders married his wife Peggy in 1946, Waterfield and Jane Russell drove them to Las Vegas.

"He wasn't easy to get to know, but once he liked you, his heart was full of gold," Sanders said. "He couldn't do enough for you.

"Bob was a great athlete, a great competitor at heart. A lot of people don't know he was an outstanding gymnast. He competed in gymnastics in high school and at UCLA. Bob was also a very brilliant person."

The first Ram quarterback controversy involved Waterfield and Norm Van Brocklin. "There was no controversy," said Van Brocklin from his home near Atlanta Friday. "The newspapers created it. There were five L.A. papers back then, and they were in competition with each other."

The impression was that Waterfield and Van Brocklin didn't get along. But Van Brocklin said, "We were always friends.

"He was a natural-born athlete. He was born ambidextrous. He was an outstanding golfer and was one of the best handball players you'll ever see.

"He was a real fine person. Very shy, a withdrawn type of guy."

Former Ram teammate Tom Fears said: "He was the best athlete I ever saw in my life. He shunned publicity, but nobody could pass any better or kick a ball any better. He was from the old school. He even ran beautiful (pass) patterns. Of course, he didn't have to because he was a quarterback. I learned a lot from him.

"He never said too much. He didn't get frustrated if you ran the wrong route. He never said anything derogatory. He was an easy-going guy. He liked his privacy to the point of being an introvert.

"But he was very congenial, though he never volunteered anything in a conversation. It was funny, because he was very intelligent.

"I'm sorry it (Waterfield's death) happened, but it wasn't a shock. We were kind of prepared for it. He was real sick a couple of years ago. I hate to see great contemporaries dying off like this. He was a wonderful man."

Former teammate Elroy Hirsch, Wisconsin athletic director, was reached in Grand Forks, N.D., site of the NCAA hockey championships.

"I've always said that Bob was the finest all-around athlete to ever play football," Hirsch said. "As a quarterback, he was a tremendous leader and passer. He also kicked off, punted, kicked field goals and extra points and could also run the bootleg. He called the signals, was a general in the huddle, and when he first started out in the pros he even played defense."

Sanders: "At one time he was one of the best defensive backs in the league."

Hirsch also mentioned Waterfield's prowess at gymnastics and handball. And Sanders said, "He spent a lot of time hunting and fishing. He loved to hunt and fish."

## For Lakers, Spurs Are a Real Pain

By RANDY HARVEY, *Times Staff Writer*

There are nights when the Lakers just don't have it and they lose, but everyone still goes home happy. They know it was just one of those nights.

But the 132-120 loss to San Antonio Friday night before a sell-out crowd of 17,505 at the Forum wasn't like that.

The Lakers had it this time. They led by 11 points in the second quarter and by 10 in the third. But the Spurs had more.

There were a lot of long faces in the Lakers' dressing room following the game. It hasn't been that quiet in there since a thief stole the money out of their wallets during a game last season.

Even Jamaal Wilkes was a little testy when a radio reporter asked a question the easy-going forward didn't like.

"Where's the perspective?" Wilkes asked. "We lost the season series (three games to two) to them last year and beat them four straight in the playoffs.

"It hurts. They outplayed us. They put some things in our minds to think about. They're a different team this year with Artis Gilmore. But let's see what happens in the playoffs."

The playoffs are a concern, because if there are no upsets in the early rounds, the Lakers and Spurs

Please see LAKERS, Page 13

Associated Press

Ohio State's Troy Taylor fends off Michael Jordan of North Carolina while dribbling ball.

## Georgia Knocks Beast Out of the East, 70-67

By ALAN GREENBERG, *Times Staff Writer*

SYRACUSE, N.Y.—Tradition enthralls fans. Tradition enthralls the media. They imbue it with mythical power.

But tradition doesn't mean a whole lot to a bunch of 20-year-old kids, especially the ones from Georgia who swept aside favored St. John's, 70-67, Friday night in the NCAA East Regional semifinals before a crowd of 23,268 at the Carrier Dome.

St. John's (28-5), its winningest season abruptly ended, has a basketball tradition, all right. This was St. John's 38th year in a postseason tournament, tops in the nation. It was Georgia's third, and only the Bulldogs' first NCAA. It's a football school, right? In Herschel Walker We Trust.

Well, Walker's gone, and it's a new dawn. And Sunday, the Southeastern Conference tournament winners (23-9) willmeet defending national champion North Carolina (28-7) for the right to represent the East at the Final Four in Albuquerque next weekend.

North Carolina, which beat Ohio State,

Please see NCAA EAST, Page 10

## Houston, Villanova Win With Games on the Line

By MAL FLORENCE, *Times Staff Writer*

KANSAS CITY, Mo.—It's difficult to find many weaknesses on No. 1 ranked Houston, but the Cougars' critics have contended that sub-par free throw shooting would eventually catch up with Guy Lewis' team.

But Memphis State Coach Dana Kirk said that the "weakness was their strength" Friday night after Houston beat his team, 70-63, in an NCAA Midwest Regional semifinal game before a crowd of 17,036 at Kemper Arena.

Houston, a 60.9% foul shooting team, made 16 of 20 from the line—some key ones in the closing seconds—to advance to the regional final Sunday afternoon against Villanova.

The Wildcats (24-7) also survived by sharp foul shooting. Center John Pinone made two key free throws with 12 seconds remaining as Villanova defeated Iowa, 55-54, in the other semifinal game.

The brothers of Phi Slamma Jama—that's Houston's new nickname this season—probably have had better games but they extended their winning streak to 24 in beating Memphis State, which was still in contention until the final seconds.

Please see NCAA MIDWEST, Page 10

**■ Bruce Jenner at 33**

Seven years after his gold medal at Montreal, Bruce Jenner is enjoying life more than ever.

Please see Page 5.

**■ Battle of the Ratings**

The U.S. Football League faces a variety of competition in its battle for television ratings and sports spectators' dollars.

Please see Page 8.

**■ The Other NCAA Regionals**

North Carolina State and Virginia are rematched in the West final, while Kentucky and Louisville finally meet in the Mideast.

Please see Pages 10 and 11.

# Garvey Gets Record, That's It

THE RETURN OF

**Steve Garvey**

**First Inning**—Popped out to first baseman Greg Brock with runner on first.

**Third Innning**—Grounded back to pitcher Fernando Valenzuela with runner on second.

**Fifth Inning**—With a runner on first, grounded into a double play.

**Seventh Inning**—With none on, flied out to Dusty Baker in left.

BATTING LINE

| | AB | R | H | HR | BI | Ave. |
|---|---|---|---|---|---|---|
| **Friday** | 4 | 0 | 0 | 0 | 0 | .000 |
| **Season** | 41 | 6 | 10 | 1 | 4 | .244 |

## He Goes 0 for 4, Brock Homers and Dodgers Win, 6-2

By MARK HEISLER, *Times Staff Writer*

Steve Garvey came home, saw old friends, got a two-minute standing ovation from a full house and played in his 1,117th straight game, tying Billy Williams' National League record. He did all that before Friday night's game was five minutes old, but then harder times set in.

He went 0 for 4. His teammates got stepped on and his manager was ejected. His replacement as Dodger first baseman, Greg Brock, hit his third home run in three days. As returns go, this was the equivalent of MacArthur catching a wave in the face.

Fernando Valenzuela struggled with everyone else in the Padre lineup, but the Dodgers got him an early lead and he wound up with a tidy 11-hitter for 8⅔ innings. Joe Beckwith got the last out and the Dodgers won, 6-2, before 52,392 in Dodger Stadium, their largest crowd in almost two years. They can thank Garv for more than some memories.

Garvey popped up in front of the plate in the first, tapped back to Valenzuela with a runner at second base in the third, grounded into a double play in the fifth and flied to left in the seventh. He said he hadn't been nervous, though.

"I was swinging freely," he said, "but not squarely."

Brock wound up 2 for 4. He now has four homers, which ties him for the league lead. Hitting a home run in Garvey's return might have appeared poetic, or dramatic, but not to Brock.

"I don't think I stole any show from Garv," Brock said. "This was his night. The fans were great. What he did for the Dodgers, this was their thank you. I don't think anybody could take anything away from him. . .

"I looked at it as another ball game. That's the way I had to. The home run felt good. Just like any other home run."

Valenzuela got the first hitter he faced, but after that he started struggling in earnest. The second hitter, Juan Bonilla, slammed a single up the middle. The third was Garvey, who popped up, but No. 4

**Please see DODGERS, Page 14**

JAYNE KAMIN / Los Angeles Times

Steve Garvey strikes a familiar pose as he stretches for a throw that puts out his former Dodger teammate Bill Russell at first base Friday night in Garv's return to Dodger Stadium.

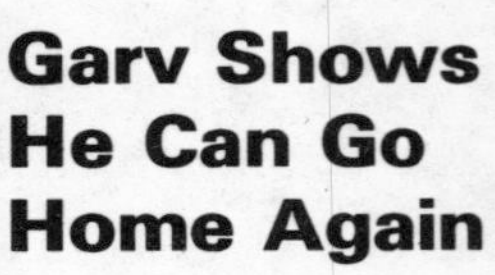

## Garv Shows He Can Go Home Again

By MIKE LITTWIN,
*Times Staff Writer*

As far as Steve Garvey was concerned, he could have danced all night. But what can you do when the music stops?

When the last note was played Friday, Garvey was kneeling in the on-deck circle, not wanting the night to end. He stayed there while everyone else ran off the field. For the first time all night, he was alone with his thoughts.

"I was giving thanks," he said.

Maybe so. But, if Garv really is human, he must have been thinking that with one more chance at bat he could have made this night to remember one never to forget.

It was Steve Garvey Night, after all, at Dodger Stadium, and 52,392

**Please see GARVEY, Page 14**

JAYNE KAMIN / Los Angeles Times

Steve Garvey lets Dodger fans know they're No. 1 as they give him a two-minute standing ovation before he bats in the first inning.

***One Out Short***

## Wilcox Is Just About Perfect

*From Times Wire Services*

CHICAGO—Milt Wilcox says any time he can pitch near his birthday, he's a candidate to throw a perfect game.

Wilcox, who will be 33 on Wednesday, came within one out of pitching the major league's 12th perfect game when he stopped the Chicago White Sox, 6-0, on a chilly Friday night before 19,483 at Comiskey Park.

Pinch-hitter Jerry Hairston spoiled Wilcox's bid for baseball immortality when he lined the first pitch from the right-hander up the middle for a clean base hit for Chicago's only baserunner of the game.

"I had a one-hitter on my birthday last year so I knew if I pitched around it this year I'd have a chance at a perfect game," said Wilcox, who struck out eight and didn't walk a batter in overcoming 43-degree temperatures.

"They fined me in the kangaroo court $1 for giving up that one hit."

Wilcox said Hairston's hit was an inside fastball.

"It was just a bad pitch, and he hit it," he said. "I was trying to keep it down to him. If I had to throw it over, the only thing different would be I would throw it lower."

Wilcox (1-1) who had surrendered six runs on eight hits in losing to Chicago, 6-3, one week ago, mixed a strong fastball with an effective curve in mystifying White Sox hitters until Hairston delivered the only hit.

"I was disappointed, yes. If you pitch a perfect game, you go into the Hall of Fame," said Wilcox, who has a career record of 91-85 over 13 major-league seasons. "That's the only way I'll get in there."

Hairston, considered the White Sox's best pinch-hitter, said he was looking to hit the first pitch when he stepped up to the plate with the fans standing and cheering Wilcox.

**Please see WILCOX, Page 5**

BOB CHAMBERLIN / Los Angeles Times

**A winner**—Jimmy Connors returns shot in 2-6, 6-3, 6-4 win over Sandy Mayer Friday in Pacific Southwest Open. (Story, Page 2.)

# Dome Fixed—Angels Bust Fences

## Jackson, Lynn and Grich Homer in 8-2 Victory Over Twins

By ROSS NEWHAN, *Times Staff Writer*

MINNEAPOLIS—They reinflated the Metrodome roof Friday, after which the Angels attempted to bring down the fences.

In a hitter's haven that yielded 191 home runs last year, the Angels routed the Twins, 8-2, with 15 hits, including:

—Reggie Jackson's first homer of the year, a sub-orbital blast in the second that caromed off the auxiliary seats behind the 408-foot sign in dead center and was calculated by the Metrodome computer to have traveled 472 feet at point of impact, the longest ever here. Informed of that, Jackson shrugged and said, "That's only because I haven't been coming here that long."

—Fred Lynn's second homer of the year, a three-run, fifth-inning drive that broke a 1-1 tie and a right-field seat or two, traveling a computerized 397 feet.

—Bobby Grich's second of the year, a two-run, sixth- inning drive that also caromed off the right-field seats after a flight of 378 feet.

It added up to a laugher for Ken Forsch, who wasn't laughing after capturing his second win in as many decisions, having scattered eight hits, including an RBI double by Gary Ward in the first and a solo homer by John Castino in the sixth.

Forsch, who came to the Angels from the Astrodome, where a howitzer is required to get the ball out, stood at his locker later, still experiencing claustrophobia after his first complete game in the Metrodome.

"I don't think about it (the number of home runs hit here)," he said, "until they hit a fly ball. Then I bite my lip until it's caught. I guess you could adjust, but I wouldn't want to have to pitch here regularly."

Forsch had 48 hours to think about it since he arrived Wednesday night, having been sent ahead to avoid the Angels' scheduled 6 a.m. Thursday arrival following the Wednesday night game in Anaheim.

A blizzard that deposited 13 1/2 inches of snow here forced the Angels to land in Chicago instead and postponed the Thursday night series opener. Forsch's teammates finally joined him at noon Friday, but the possibility of a game was still in doubt since an ice slide had opened a 20-foot tear in the Teflon coated, fan-supported roof late Thursday night.

The roof was deflated Friday morning, allowing for repairs estimated at $5,000. The fans were turned on, the roof raised and

**Please see ANGELS, Page 12**

## Knight Keeps Olympics Job, With Apology

By KENNETH REICH,
*Times Staff Writer*

COLORADO SPRINGS, Colo.—The United States Olympic Committee has decided to retain Indiana University's Bobby Knight as coach of the 1984 basketball team, USOC President William Simon said Friday.

The decision was made despite the fiery coach's recent off-color, anti-Puerto Rican comments.

Simon told a meeting of the USOC Executive Board that he had a "long talk" with Knight about his remarks at a hospital employees' banquet in Gary, Ind. "He recognizes he told a bad story," Simon said.

According to published reports, a reference was made at the dinner to Knight's conviction for aggravated assault for punching a Puerto Rican policeman at a practice session of the American basketball team during the 1979 Pan-American Games in San Juan. Knight then told the audience that he made an obscene gesture to the people of Puerto Rico the day he flew out of San Juan.

"I stood up, unzipped my pants,

**Please see KNIGHT, Page 13**

Bobby Knight

## Lakers Defeat Seattle, Take a Look at Mix

By RANDY HARVEY,
*Times Staff Writer*

With only two shopping days remaining before the National Basketball Assn. playoffs, the Lakers met with veteran power forward Steve Mix Friday and were expected to decide by today whether to sign him.

Mix, 6-7, 222, worked out by himself Friday afternoon at the Forum and watched the Lakers game against Seattle. Lakers owner Jerry Buss met with team President Bill Sharman and Coach Pat Riley following a 100-99 victory over the Seattle SuperSonics to decide whether to offer Mix a contract.

As Pacific Division champions, the Lakers have a bye through the first round of the playoffs but still must submit their final 12-man

**Please see LAKERS, Page 8**

**■ Astros Win**

The Houston Astros break their nine-game losing streak with a 7-6 win over Montreal.

Please see Page 4.

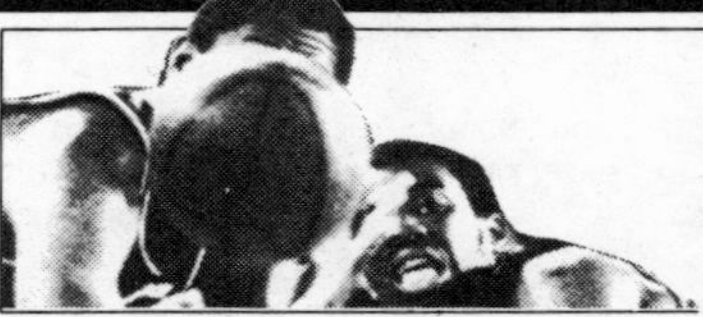

**■ Knicks Have Knack**

The New York Knicks gain a spot in the NBA playoffs with a 100-83 victory over Detroit.

Please see Page 8.

**■ Smog Lifts**

A dispute over what time of day to run the marathons in the Olympics ends.

Please see Page 13.

1984
1990

By Earl Gustkey

NO ONE WAS REALLY SURPRISED THAT THE LOS ANGELES RAIDERS WON THE 1984 SUPER BOWL. AFTER ALL, THE Raiders had won the 1981 game and were, three seasons later, still one of the National Football League's dominant teams. But on January 22, at Tampa Stadium, no one was prepared for the *way* the Raiders beat the Washington Redskins, 38–9.

The headline said it all. It really was a slaughter.

And for Marcus Allen, the brilliant running back from USC who was passed over by nine NFL teams in the 1982 draft, it was his greatest day in football. He set a Super Bowl rushing record, 191 yards, including a terrific broken field run of 74 yards on the last play of the third quarter. That run boosted the Raiders' lead to 35–9.

Los Angeles, in October, 1978, was awarded the 1984 Summer Olympic Games. The anticipation level of Southern Californians seemed to increase a tick almost daily, as sports sections contained Olympic news and features years before the Games.

Finally, on July 28, 1984, the hour had arrived. Capping an unforgettable Olympic Games opening ceremonies featuring 84 piano players who played Gershwin classics (OK, OK—the music was partially recorded, but this was L. A., right?), two figures appeared to kick-start the Olympics.

Gina Hemphill, granddaughter of America's hero of the 1936 Berlin Olympics, Jesse Owens, appeared first. She emerged from out of the Coliseum tunnel, carrying the Olympic torch. She ran one lap and handed the flame to Rafer Johnson, who had won the 1960 Olympic decathlon gold medal in Rome. Johnson's assignment, at the age of 48, was to carry the torch up 99 steep steps and ignite the Coliseum flame. While 92,655 people in the Coliseum and a billion more on worldwide television watched, he made it to the top, where he put the flame to the Games.

These Games would demonstrate that cities can stage Olympic Games without risking bankruptcy. And in fact, the Los Angeles Olympic Organizing Committee would clear a profit of $222,716,000, money that would fund Southern California youth sports facilities for generations to come.

Late in the Games, a white-hot controversy developed. Mary Decker Slaney, America's queen of track and field and the world champion in the event, was leading the women's 3,000-meter final near the end of the fourth lap. But as the runners were tightly grouped coming off a turn, Slaney was suddenly down, writhing in pain on the infield. She was also out of the race. Her hulk of a husband, discus thrower Richard Slaney, carried his 105-pound, weeping wife off the track.

Immediately, fingers were pointed at the barefooted wonder from South Africa (via England), 18-year-old Zola Budd. In what would be one of the most replayed sports incidents in video history, everyone, it seemed, had an opinion: Budd kicked Slaney and knocked her down...Slaney shouldn't have been running in dense traffic...Slaney tripped over her own feet...Slaney should have shoved Budd out of the way...Budd bumped Slaney with her hip....

So enduring was the controversy that the winner of the race, Maricica Puica of Rumania, was within a couple of years the answer to a trivia question: Who won the race in the '84 Olympics when Mary Decker Slaney and Zola Budd collided?

The fight of the eighties? Probably when Sugar Ray Leonard, who had fought once in the previous 62 months, challenged Marvelous Marvin Hagler in Las Vegas. Few gave the 1976 Olympic champion and former welterweight champion much chance. Hagler was ferocious, powerful, and seemingly indestructible. But only a handful accounted for one factor—Leonard's heart. He won a split decision that night, time and again fighting back bravely each time Hagler hurt him. It was an epic presentation of all the characteristics Americans treasure in their athletes: bravery, tenacity, and the will to win.

Said *Sports Illustrated* boxing writer Pat Putnam just hours after the fight: "If you could cut Ray Leonard's heart up into little pieces, you'd have enough to supply the entire First Marine Division."

It was beginning to look as if no National Basketball Association team would ever win consecutive championships again. Until the Los Angeles Lakers beat the Detroit Pistons in Game 7 of the 1988 NBA finals, no team since the 1969 Boston Celtics had won a pair, back-to-back. And for the Magic Johnson-led Lakers, it was their fifth NBA title of the eighties.

When Mike Tyson became the youngest fighter, at age 20, ever to win a heavyweight championship in 1986, he was a prodigy. But on the night of June 27, 1988, he became a boxing legend. After that match, many boxing fans were ready to compare him to such greats as Muhammad Ali, Joe Louis, and Jack Dempsey. In 91 seconds, he savagely demolished his last credible opponent, Michael Spinks. Tyson, two days short of 22, was now 34–0 and in hot pursuit of Rocky Marciano's all-time heavyweight unbeaten record of 49–0.

Sports editors love news. They get paid for putting it in the newspaper, right? Sure—but please, no more days like September 26, 1988. First, word comes from the Seoul Olympics that sprinter Ben Johnson has had his 100-meter gold medal yanked after he flunked his steroid test. Then, that afternoon in Denver, the Raiders put together a whirlwind finish to overcome a 24–0 halftime deficit and beat the Broncos, 30–27. Also that afternoon, Greg Louganis becomes the first diver to win back-to-back double gold medal events in the Olympics. Finally, that night, the Dodgers clinch the National League West championship in San Diego.

Said Paul Gelormino, a Times Sports Department slot man that night: "It was the greatest news night I've ever seen."

Oh, about the Dodgers. Orel Hershisher delivered a command performance in Game 5 of the 1988 World Series, a 4-hit, 5–2 victory over the favored Oakland A's, to give the Dodgers their first World Series victory since 1981.

Los Angeles Times

# SPORTS

Monday, January 23, 1984 CC††/Part III

# Raiders Send Hogs to Slaughter, 38-9

United Press International

Marcus Allen, the Super Bowl MVP, darts for a few of his record 191 rushing yards in the Raiders' 38-9 victory over Washington. Allen also scored two touchdowns.

## Allen Gains 191 Yards in Super Romp

By ALAN GREENBERG, *Times Staff Writer*

TAMPA, Fla.—It wasn't a game, it was an execution. Redskins-Raiders in the Super Bowl. Before the game, people called it a dream match. If this were boxing, today they'd be calling for an investigation.

It was Raiders 38, Redskins 9 the most lopsided game in the Super Bowl's 18-year history, eclipsing Vince Lombardi's Green Bay Packers' 35-10 win over the Kansas City Chiefs in the first Super Bowl.

Of course, that was January, 1967, even before the National and American Football Leagues had merged, and not many people believed the upstart Chiefs belonged on the same field with the Packers.

You got the same feeling watching the Washington Redskins—winners of 31 of their last 34 games—futilely flailing away at the Raiders Sunday at Tampa Stadium. They didn't look like they belonged. But then, the way the Raiders looked at it, nobody did.

"This," Raiders Pro Bowl free safety Vann McElroy said, "is the culmination of the way the Raiders can play. They tell you all season, 'Don't peak too soon.' We peaked just right."

And they drove the Redskins to their nadir. The Redskins' 90 net rushing yards were their fewest this season. And the Raiders' 231 rushing yards—of which game MVP Marcus Allen had 191—were the most rushing yards given up by the Redskins, who led the league in rushing defense, in 1983.

"The way they play football, they have to dominate the line of scrimmage (to win)," Raiders linebacker Matt Millen said. "And they didn't. We went down the matchups before the game of what they needed to d to beat us. We figured no way

Please see SUPER BOWL, Pa

## Scott Ostler

### To Win Super Bowl, the Raiders Put In Calls for Jensen, Squirek

TAMPA, Fla.—Going into Sunday's game, there were three obvious Super Bowl angles the nation's media had carelessly ignored:

(1) The possibility that the Hogs might be named to a presidential cabinet post, like Secretaries of Posterior.

(2) The potential damage to the earth's ozone layer from the millions of helium balloons released before the game and at halftime.

(3) The possibility that Derrick Jensen and Jack Squirek, who play football for the Raiders, might have a little to do with the outcome of the game.

The Tampa Stadium P.A. announcer wasn't ready for that angle Number 3, either. When Squirek intercepted a Joe Theismann pass and ran it back for a five-yard touchdown that wrapped up the game seven seconds before halftime, the P.A. man credited the heroic deed to, ah . . .

"I think he said 'Squirrel,' " Squirek said.

The only other play of the game worth mentioning was Derrick Jensen's block of the Redskins' first punt and subsequent recovery for the Raiders' first touchdown.

Asked to evaluate the impact of his deed, Jensen said: "Let's see—It was six points out of 38. So it was 3/19ths, I guess."

He guessed wrong. It was 50%. That play knocked the Redskins down. Squirek's play was the other 50%. It knocked the Redskins out. Everything else on the field Sunday was filler between commercials. No offense, Marcus.

Woodward and Bernstein caused less heartache in Washington, D.C. than Squirek

Please see OSTLER, Page 25

## Louisville Puts Pressure on UCLA —and It Pays Off in 86-78 Victory

By MIKE LITTWIN, *Times Staff Writer*

LOUISVILLE, Ky.—When Charles Jones left the floor Sunday to a standing ovation, a few UCLA players came over to shake the Louisville center's hand.

Not surprisingly, Stuart Gray didn't get there in time.

Jones, only 6-8, dominated play inside, scoring a career-high 27 points and grabbing 15 rebounds while erasing a few painful memories of Gray in the process. Not coincidentally, Louisville beat UCLA, 86-78, in a game that wasn't nearly that close.

Don't be fooled by the score. If you got up in time to watch this one, you know that Louisville jumped out to a 42-19 lead—making 18 of 24 shots—and then just sort of hung on.

UCLA came out as if it had no idea that the Cardinals, as they always do, would be pressuring the ball.

"We knew what we had to do against them," UCLA guard Ralph Jackson said. "We just didn't get it done."

The first thing any team has to do against Louisville is get the ball upcourt. On their first possession, the Bruins couldn't even get the ball inbounds.

The second thing most teams try to do is get

Please see UCLA, Page 6

United Press International

A somewhat startled Joe Theismann looks up at Raiders linebacker Jeff Barnes after being sacked Sunday. Barnes gets a congratulatory slap on the helmet from defensive end Greg Townsend. Theismann was sacked six times for 50 yards.

*Allen's Big Day*

## Move Over, Riggo—It's All Marco

By RICK REILLY, *Times Staff Writer*

TAMPA, Fla.—It had been a week for singing the praises of the one, the only John Riggins. It was Riggins with his own press conference. It was Riggins dressed in an Air National Guard jumpsuit, complete with hero's medals. It was Riggo's Rangers. It was Riggins, Boss Hog. It would be Riggo right, Riggo left, Riggo up the middle until all that was left was to guess what kind of funny hat that nutty Riggo would wear to his coronation as King of the Universe.

But somewhere in there they forgot about Marcus Allen, who didn't have his own press conference, wasn't marketing his own line of camouflage clothing, didn't even have his own car commercial. Marcus Allen went through the week getting plenty of sleep and never once having to meet with Brent Musburger for breakfast.

But this morning the nation remembers Marcus Allen again. This morning they will read how he went through the Redskins defense for 191 pretty yards, the most ever in XVIII of these Super Bowls. They will read how he surgically removed the spirit of the Washington team with two second-half touchdowns, one a remarkable 74-yard reverse-field job, the worst cutback to hit the city of Washington since the days of David Stockman.

And they will read how he won the Most Valuable Player trophy, which he will cart home in his new

Please see ALLEN, Page 24

SUPER BOWL XVIII / INSIDE

**■ Bob Oates' Analysis**
In talent, the Redskins just don't stack up to Raiders like Bruce Davis (left). Please see Page 2.

**■ Mark Heisler: Grin, Bear It**
Commissioner Pete Rozelle hands the Lombardi Trophy to Al Davis again. Please see Page 3.

**■ Rich Roberts: Hogs Update**
In just one game, the Redskins go from hog heaven to hogwash. Please see Page 3.

**■ Larry Stewart's TV View**
Even announcer Irv Cross gets sacked by the Raiders. Please see Page 3.

**■ The Cornerbacks**
Lester Hayes and Mike Haynes corner the market on Smurfs. Please see Page 10.

**■ The Game Summary**
Complete scoring summary plus team and individual statistics. Please see Page 29.

Los Angeles Times

SPORTS

Tuesday, April 7, 1987

CC†/Part III

# Marvelous One Is Really Leonard

## He Stuns Hagler With Split Decision

By RICHARD HOFFER,
*Times Staff Writer*

LAS VEGAS—Sugar Ray Leonard's enormous bravado, which was nearly offensive in the prefight buildup, became a promise fulfilled Monday night when, after what was essentially a five-year layoff, he returned and upset boxing's dominant champion, Marvelous Marvin Hagler. The sheer audacity of what he attempted was somehow matched by the strategic elegance with which he did it.

The comeback, culminated before the largest world audience to ever see a bout, had been judged foolhardy by most. The symmetry of their careers, their destinies so intertwined, somehow forgave the circumstances of the obvious mismatch. They deserved each other five years ago, but this was better than never.

Still, only those who believed in time travel gave Leonard any chance against Hagler. Leonard would have to return five years, to a time when hands were fast and legs tireless, to meet the foreboding Hagler on anything near equal terms.

Well, he wasn't the welterweight of 1982, when he first retired after eye surgery. But there was more about Leonard than his tasseled shoes that recalled his time of greatness. For 12 tactically brilliant rounds, he circled and countered, confusing and confounding the bewildered middleweight champion, until he had secured a split decision.

Though the judges did not entirely agree on what they saw—Lou Fillippo had it 115-113 for Hagler, Dave Moretti 115-113 for Leonard, and JoJo Guerra 118-110 for Leonard—the only person near the ring in the parking lot at Caesars Palace to voice any genuine surprise at the decision was Hagler himself. "I beat him and you know it," he said immediately afterward. "I stayed aggressive. C'mon. I won the fight."

But Leonard's game plan never let Hagler in the fight. He circled outside, daring Hagler to stalk him, occasionally entangling the champion in a brisk flurry. Hagler missed monumentally as he chased Leonard. Although neither was hurt or in any danger of going down, it was clear that Leonard was hitting more than Hagler was.

It was also clear that Leonard meant to clinch as often as possible, perhaps turning Hagler and gain-

Please see FIGHT, Page 4

Associated Press

His work done, Sugar Ray Leonard leaps with joy as he learns that he has won a split decision over Marvelous Marvin Hagler.

## Jim Murray

### Sugar Ray Shows What Boxing Is All About

LAS VEGAS—It wasn't even close . . .

Hey, maybe Jeffries couldn't do it. Maybe, Johnson, Dempsey, a half dozen other famous names from out of the past.

But, don't put Sugar Ray Leonard in there.

He did it. He came back. Did he ever.

Calling on skills you wouldn't think he could even remember, he put the hurt on Marvelous Marvin Hagler in the parking lot at Caesars Palace Monday night. But that was nothing to what he did to Father Time. He stopped that old impostor right in his tracks.

You imagine if Peter Pan were a fighter, this is how he would do it. It was pretty, dazzling, daring. He not only turned back the clock, he made the most fearsome pugilist in a ring today look like a clumsy old character in a gorilla suit.

He didn't just outpoint Hagler, he exposed him. He made him look like a guy chasing a bus. In snowshoes. Marvelous Marvin Hagler should have put stamps on his punches. He kept aiming them at places Sugar Ray had left much earlier in the evening. Sometimes, you expected Hagler to tap the referee on the shoulder and say, "Excuse me, did you see a little fellow, about 5 foot 10 with dark hair and a nice smile go by here tonight? I was supposed to fight him but I guess he couldn't make it."

The moral of the story?

Please see MURRAY, Page 4

United Press International

Sugar Ray Leonard shows some of the power of a middleweight as he pummels Marvelous Marvin Hagler in fight at Las Vegas.

Al Campanis

## Campanis Questions Ability of Blacks

By BILL DWYRE,
*Times Sports Editor*

Al Campanis, third-ranking executive in the Los Angeles Dodger organization, implied in a nationally televised interview Monday night that blacks had not advanced as far or as often in major league baseball's executive hierarchy because of some inherent shortcomings.

The interview took place on ABC's "Nightline," during a segment of the show in which Ted Koppel, the show's anchor, interviewed both Campanis and Roger Kahn, author of "The Boys of Summer," a best-selling book about the Dodgers. Both Koppel and Kahn took exception to Campanis' remarks during the interview, Koppel at one stage referring to statements Campanis made as "garbage."

When Koppel asked why there are no black managers in the major leagues, Campanis replied: "Mr. Koppel, you have to pay your dues. You generally have to go to the minor leagues. And the pay there is low."

To which Koppel asked "Is there still that much prejudice?"

And Campanis answered: "No. It's just that they may not have some of the neces-

See CAMPANIS, Page 6

ANGEL PREVIEW
1 9 8 7

## Mauch's New Element: Speed

By MIKE PENNER, Times Staff Writer

When Butch Wynegar looks back on the recent past of the Angels, he does so through eyes that once peered from behind the mask of an opposing catcher. And those eyes used to tell him that whenever the Angels were on the schedule, heaven couldn't be far behind.

"You'd come in here and, as a catcher, it'd almost be like three days off," says Wynegar, who spent 11 seasons with Minnesota and the New York Yankees. "Keep Gary [Pettis] off base and you'd have nothing to worry about. If your arm wasn't feeling too good, you could give it a little rest before going into that series with Kansas City."

The Angels were slow motion without the instant replay. They were baseball's oldest team and they looked it. Get on base and don't try anything rash. Conserve your energy and wait for a home run.

In 1983, the Angels stole 41 bases as a team. Rickey Henderson had them beaten by June. The club's stolen base leader was a 25-year-old

Please see ANGELS, Page 5

# Dodgers Start Out Short a Star and Short a Run

Associated Press

The hard-sliding Billy Hatcher sends Dodger shortstop Mariano Duncan leaping for safety while successfully breaking up a double play in first inning Monday.

By SAM McMANIS,
*Times Staff Writer*

HOUSTON—By their own doing, the Dodgers were denied an appearance by Fernando Valenzuela in their season opener here Monday night. What they didn't expect was also being deprived of slugger Pedro Guerrero, who had a bad reaction to a routine injection into his right knee.

That doesn't figure to be the recommended way to open the season, especially when you're facing Houston Astro pitcher Mike Scott. But it did seem quite familiar in several respects.

A 4-3 loss to the Astros before 44,585 in the Astrodome was frustratingly familiar to a team that specialized in one-run losses last season and also became quite accustomed to life without Guerrero.

If the Dodgers could derive anything positive from this one, it's that Guerrero is expected to be out only a few days, and that they managed to get eight hits and three runs off Scott, the split-fingered sorcerer.

It turned out to be one run too few, though, after veteran Astro outfielder Jose Cruz broke a 3-3 tie in the seventh inning with a solo home run to dead center field off Orel Hershiser, a loser in his first season-opening assignment of his Dodger career.

Hershiser, awarded the first-game honor that automatically went to Valenzuela the last four years, made few mistakes before the Astros' 39-year-old left fielder launched a Cruz missile that even Mike Ramsey, the Dodgers' fleet young center fielder, could not run down.

Actually, none of those involved called the low, outside fastball Cruz hit a mistake.

"I was lucky to hit it out," Cruz said. "I hit it hard, but it was a good pitch."

That was of little solace to Hershiser, who gave up eight hits and three earned runs in seven innings. He wanted to enable the Dodgers to be 1-0 going into Valenzuela's debut here tonight.

"I'd throw it again to him," Hershiser said. "You're going to make good pitches and they are

Please see DODGERS, Page 6

- **A Big Opener:** Rookie center fielder Mike Ramsey, known better for his good glove, is a pleasant surprise at the plate. Ross Newhan's story, Page 6.
- **Angel Cuts:** Veterans Rob Wilfong and Jerry Narron are released. Mike Penner's story, Page 5.

INSIDE

**Lakers Rout Clippers**

The Lakers clinch the home-court advantage throughout the NBA playoffs with a 135-112 rout of the Clippers.

Please see Page 2.

**Umpires Go to Work**

Major league umpires go to work on opening day after their union reaches a last-minute labor agreement with the leagues.

Please see Page 3.

INDEX

Los Angeles Times

Wednesday, June 22, 1988

CC††/Part III

# SPORTS

# Lakers Repeat Their Title Feat

## Mike Downey

### Lakers Are Worthy of Another One

And they'll win it next year, too.

Not just because they have Earvin (Magic) Johnson, America's Player, coming back for more, more, more.

Next year, too.

Not just because they have Kareem (Magic) Abdul-Jabbar, coming back for 1989's Farewell Tour.

Next year, too.

Not just because they have Michael (Magic) Cooper, who, when all was said and dunked, was a friend in need and a friend indeed.

Next year, too.

Not just because they have Byron (Magic) Scott, who was hot from the first shot, and good to the last drop.

Next year, too.

Not just because they have A.C. (Another Championship) Green, a perfect fit as the last piece of the Laker puzzle.

Next year, too.

Not just because they have Mychal (Magic) Thompson, who is coming back for thirds.

Next year, too.

Because the Los Angeles Lakers next year—and the year after that, and the year after that—will still have James (Sometimes Even More Magic Than Magic Himself) Worthy, the nobleman from North Carolina, the feet-off-the-ground Tar Heel, the classical Gastonian, who went out Tuesday night and wrapped up not one, not two, but three National Basketball Assn. titles:

Please see DOWNEY, Page 7

**LAKERS vs. PISTONS**

| NBA CHAMPIONSHIP SERIES | |
|---|---|
| Game 1 | Pistons 105, Lakers 93 |
| Game 2 | Lakers 108, Pistons 96 |
| Game 3 | Lakers 99, Pistons 86 |
| Game 4 | Pistons 111, Lakers 86 |
| Game 5 | Pistons 104, Lakers 94 |
| Game 6 | Lakers 103, Pistons 102 |
| Game 7 | Lakers 108, Pistons 105 |

**INSIDE**

- **Scott Ostler:** Those motivational speeches that Pat Riley gave the Lakers all season finally pay off in a big way. Column, Page 6.
- **He'll Be Back:** Kareem Abdul-Jabbar announces after the game that he plans to return for his 20th NBA season. Chris Baker's story, Page 6.
- **Detroit's Bad Boy:** Bill Laimbeer does what he has to do and doesn't worry about what the fans think. Tracy Dodds' story, Page 8.

STEVE DYKES / Los Angeles Times

James Worthy, the series' most valuable player, scores 2 of his 36 points as the Lakers win their second title in a row.

## L.A. Wins for Fifth Time in the '80s

By GORDON EDES, *Times Staff Writer*

It took both the suddenness of a sprinter and the heart of a marathoner, but the Lakers crossed the finish line of their two-year run Tuesday night at the Forum with history borne triumphantly on their shoulders and brazen guarantees safely tucked away in their memories.

With James Worthy carrying the baton in Game 7, the Lakers outdistanced the Detroit Pistons, 108-105, to become the first team since the Boston Celtics in 1969 to repeat as champions of the National Basketball Assn. Worthy, voted the most valuable player of the series, chose this night to have the first triple-double of his career—36 points, 16 rebounds and 10 assists—bringing the Lakers to what may be the end of their championship ring cycle—five rings in the '80s.

"I don't have any feelings left just now—I feel raw for them," said Laker Coach Pat Riley, who had pledged the Lakers to another title within a half-hour of the team's championship victory over the Boston Celtics in 1987.

"At the end of the game, what were we doing? We were watching a great basketball team hold on. We were holding on, and we had a big enough lead to do so."

But barely. The Lakers, who had burst ahead of the Pistons by making their first 10 shots of a third quarter that began with Detroit ahead by 5 and ended with the Lakers up by 10, nearly had a 15-point lead expire in the last 7:27.

Detroit, which limped into the game with Isiah Thomas playing on one good leg, pulled within one point, 106-105, on Bill Laimbeer's three-point basket

Please see LAKERS, Page 9

## For Thomas, It's Painful Way to Go

By MARK HEISLER, *Times Staff Writer*

You take your silver linings where you find them, so when Isiah Thomas' debut in the National Basketball Assn. Finals ended a little short of his dreams—say, by one wrenched back, one wrenched ankle and one title wrested away—he smiled his Isiah smile and counted his blessings.

He had his wealth, he had most of his health, he has a new baby, who could ask for anything more?

Don't answer that.

OK, he could.

"Do I hurt more than I let on?" he said late Tuesday night. "That's a good question.

"Yeah, I hurt. But I've come to realize, I've come to learn that basketball is only one segment of my life."

This hasn't been an easy lesson. Unhappy that the Pistons weren't going anywhere, or that he wasn't taking them anywhere, Thomas used to consider retirement on an annual basis. As anyone who saw his 25-point third quarter on one leg Sunday must have noted, this is not a man who considers himself bound by known limits. Isiah dreams things that never were, and asks, "Why not me?"

But after the show was over Sunday, he had only a sore right ankle and 48 hours for it to get well before the biggest game of his life.

He spent much of it at Raider headquarters at El Segundo, where they had rolled out the silver and black carpet. He got more treatment Tuesday and was entertained by Howie Long and Todd Christensen in the bargain.

"They were fun to be around," Thomas said of the Raider players. "They were fun, down-to-earth guys. They treated me like a king.

"My injury compared to one of theirs? It was nothing. They're, like: 'Hey, just shoot it up!' The difference in mentality between football players and basketball players is amazing."

Please see THOMAS, Page 8

WIMBLEDON TENNIS CHAMPIONSHIPS

## Victorious McEnroe Wins Them Over

By RICHARD HOFFER, *Times Staff Writer*

WIMBLEDON, England—John McEnroe, rehabilitated by age and absence, returned to Wimbledon and, if he didn't get a royal welcome—there was no royalty at Wimbledon Tuesday—he did get a nice hand.

This followed a gift, his No. 8 seeding, by a previously hostile management.

This, in turn, was followed by the equally generous opposition of somebody named Horst Skoff, whose clowning turned one-time Superbrat into a comparative model of maturity and decorum, much appreciated by the crowd at the All England Lawn Tennis Club.

Mac's back, as the tabloids are hysterically proclaiming. And he is heralded as he has never been before. This from the Daily Mirror: "Mac's a Good Guy." Subhead: "He's a new man now."

This could be premature, of course. Such statements always have been. But his lack of showmanship stole the show on a day that historically belongs to the women.

Chris Evert, in her 100th singles match here, beat Alexia Dechaume, 6-1, 6-2, in first-round play and nobody cared.

Martina Navratilova, who is gunning for a record ninth women's singles Wimbledon title, beat Sabrina Goles, 6-1, 6-2, and nobody noticed.

Steffi Graf, who is looking to complete the first Grand Slam since Margaret Smith Court did it in 1970, went through Hu Na, 6-0, 6-0, to little hurrah.

And Gabriela Sabatini, seeded fifth and tennis' new pinup, swept through former pinup Carling Bassett Seguso, 6-2, 6-2, and a throng of young males at court No. 2 *did* pay attention to that match.

Most of the attention, though, was on three-time champion McEnroe, back after a two-year absence, during which he had injuries, children and, he says, he grew up. In anticipation of this new maturity, a standing-room-only crowd on Court 1 gave him a rousing, perhaps thunderous, welcome as he strode forth. He raised his hand in acknowledgment, and the crowd went wild.

Please see TENNIS, Page 4

Associated Press

John McEnroe, who has the support of the crowd, defeats Horst Skoff, 6-1, 7-5, 6-1.

## Leary Beats Braves, 2-1, on 4-Hit Complete Game

By SAM McMANIS, *Times Staff Writer*

Adversity visited the Dodgers again Tuesday night, the unwelcome guest this time bringing the burdensome news that ace reliever Jay Howell had been put on the disabled list because of a fractured rib.

But, just as they have done after the loss of Alfredo Griffin, their best defensive player, and Pedro Guerrero, their best offensive player, the Dodgers vowed to continue winning despite the growing body count of casualties.

They absorbed Howell's loss, on Tuesday night at least, quite painlessly thanks to starter Tim Leary, who pitched a complete-game four-hitter in the Dodgers' 2-1 win over the Atlanta Braves before a Dodger Stadium crowd of 18,485.

Unfazed, seemingly, by the injury siege, the Dodgers equaled their season-high with five straight wins, coming against the Braves and San Diego Padres, the National League West's lower-echelon teams. Tuesday's win also kept the Dodgers 2½ games ahead of the Houston Astros in the West.

It isn't known yet whether the Dodgers will be able to survive—and, occasionally, thrive—without Howell as they have done without Griffin (broken hand) and Guerrero (neck stiffness). This night, Leary made that question moot with a dominating effort.

Please see DODGERS, Page 3

INSIDE

**Angels Win Again**

Chili Davis hits a two-out home run in the 10th inning as the Angels beat the Minnesota Twins, 5-4, for their sixth straight victory.

Please see Page 2.

**Tigers Rally to Beat Yankees**

Alan Trammell's two-out, ninth-inning grand slam climaxes a six-run rally as the Detroit Tigers beat the New York Yankees, 7-6.

Please see Page 3.

INDEX

# Tyson Does a Minute-and-a-Half Waltz

United Press International

Mike Tyson's first-round knockout of Michael Spinks was the 31st of his professional career and made his record 35-0. It was the first loss Spinks has suffered as a pro.

## It Takes 1:31 to Make Spinks a Lightweight

By EARL GUSTKEY, *Times Staff Writer*

ATLANTIC CITY, N.J.—With his last remaining credible opponent, Michael Spinks, having been assisted out of the Atlantic City Convention Hall Monday night—actually Tuesday morning—it now looks as if the only man in Mike Tyson's appointment book who can prevent him from a long, sensationally rich reign as the world's greatest fighter is Mike Tyson.

That's assuming he wants to do this any more. He left that small matter up in the air in a chaouc post-fight press conference when he said, almost off-handedly: "As far as I know, this might be my last fight."

What came down here Monday night was Michael Spinks, in 1 minute 31 seconds.

Tyson hit Spinks often, hard and so accurately that a $70-million mismatch was under way before the ring announcer had taken his seat.

This, obviously, was not the classic, boxer-puncher confrontation in which many had hoped. It was a demolition derby, a Boardwalk mugging. Ten days ago, Tyson told his close friend, Jose Torres, he wanted to kill someone.

And that's exactly what it looked like, to the 21,785 who paid up to $1,500 to watch. Tyson defeated Spinks coldly and savagely . . . breaking him with hooks to the body and then finishing him with a solid right hand to the chin.

And, remember, Spinks was supposed to be the master defensive boxer, harder to hit squarely than anyone around.

Spinks came out with the characteristic stutter-step, lurching defense. But Tyson simply shattered Spinks' defense.

Ten seconds into the bout, Spinks, who entered the ring a 4-1 underdog, looked like 400-1.

"When I looked at him when I got in the ring, I didn't think he looked ready," Tyson said. "The first punch I hit him with, he kind

Please see TYSON, Page 7

## This Fight Wasn't a Mismatch, It Was Really a Non-Match

### Jim Murray

ATLANTIC CITY, N.J.—Well, the train won the wreck. The tank won the war. The rope won the hanging. The river won the flood. The cannon beat the spear. The battleship sank the canoe. The mugger got the watch. The flood got Johnstown. The bank got the money.

Brute strength conquered in the end. It usually does.

A creature so awesome you wondered what they did with the tusks of what surfaced in the Convention Hall here Monday night and squashed a 212-pound fighter who thought he was the heavyweight champion of the world as if he were something he found crawling up his leg.

The last time anyone saw anything this ferocious it had a horn on its nose and it lived in a river and charged land rovers. It walked through Michael Spinks as if he wasn't there.

It wasn't a fight, it was a felony. It was a fight only if you consider the iceberg and the Titanic a tossup. They should have blindfolded Michael Spinks. Or, better yet, Mike Tyson.

They said Michael Spinks' very awkwardness would work for him. Well, he wasn't all that awkward. He fell straight down like everybody else. It was just as well gravity was working. He got hit so hard, if he went straight up, he wouldn't have come down yet. The ground broke his fall. Tyson almost broke his back.

At least Tyson didn't eat him.

Never have so many paid so much for so little. The "fight" lasted 1 minute 31 seconds. Tyson probably could have knocked him out on the way out of the locker room. Or on the way in.

The public paid in excess of $70 million for this insult to the intelligence. Barnum must be crying someplace today. The public has a taste for catastrophes. This one was as one-sided as an orphanage fire. If you missed it, get some films of the German Army going through Belgium or those baby seals getting clubbed on a rock in the St. Lawrence river.

Michael Spinks said he liked to put a little terror in his life. For an encore he should go find a castle

Please see MURRAY, Page 7

## COURTING THE GAME

### Bob Boyd Taking a Year Off From His Retirement

By MAL FLORENCE, *Times Staff Writer*

In Bob Boyd's first season as a Division I coach at Seattle University, his team qualified for the National Collegiate Athletic Assn. basketball tournament and came close to rewriting history.

It was a watershed year, 1964, since John Wooden was laying the foundation for his championship dynasty at UCLA. Yet . . .

Seattle was UCLA's opponent in an NCAA regional game at Corvallis, Ore., and, as Boyd recalls, his team had a seven-point lead with five minutes to play.

"Then our center, L.J. Wheeler, tore up his knee near the end of the game and we lost, 95-90," Boyd said. "I never got that close again. But at the time, I thought it could be done every year."

Boyd didn't know it then, but his coaching career would be largely overshadowed by Wooden's legendary accomplishments at UCLA.

"I have no ill feeling about it, but I was at the right place at the wrong time," Boyd said of his 13 years as USC's coach, 9 of which were in direct competition with Wooden.

Boyd has spent the last two seasons in retirement, but he recently decided to return to coaching and has taken a job similar to the one with which he launched his career. He will coach Riverside Community College next season, as a one-year replacement for Dave

Please see BOYD, Page 10

WIMBLEDON TENNIS CHAMPIONSHIPS

Associated Press

**It isn't as easy anymore**—Fourth-seeded Chris Evert (above) holds off 19-year-old Katrina Adams in 3 sets, but No. 5 Gabriela Sabatini is upset. (Wimbledon Roundup, Page 9.)

## Down a Match Point, Lendl Prevails

### He Has 21 Double Faults, 24 Aces in Win Over Woodforde

By RICHARD HOFFER, *Times Staff Writer*

WIMBLEDON, England—Afterward you heard the loser's happy refrain: "The guy's No. 1 and I had match point on him."

The happy losers—they're different all the time—never make match point. The guy's still No. 1.

Ivan Lendl, the No. 1 guy, always wins these five-set matches. He has won his last eight here, since 1981.

He never wins Wimbledon, which he regards as something more than a minor failure, but when battles with top-20 players—top 54 in this case—become a matter of nerve, he does tend to emerge from Wimbledon's growing dusk with his racket held high. He did so Monday, to begin Week 2 of this tournament, in a remarkable fourth-round match that stretched 4 hours 46 minutes and 68 games, not a dull one among them.

Still, Lendl will have to beat better than Mark Woodforde, which he did, 7-5, 6-7, 6-7, 7-5, 10-8, to

Please see LENDL, Page 9

## Dodger Pitchers and Wins Keep Adding Up

By SAM McMANIS, *Times Staff Writer*

■ **Dodgers to Sign Soto:** Former Cincinnati pitcher joins team today. Story, Page 6.

HOUSTON—Good thing that the Dodgers, impulse shoppers in the free-agent market, agreed to terms with Mario Soto Monday. Can't you just tell this team could use more pitching?

Hours after acquiring the recently released veteran pitcher, the Dodgers once again showed that they need another pitcher like their manager needs another plate of pasta. But then, some people collect coins; the Dodgers collect pitchers.

"You don't understand," catcher Mike Scioscia said. "You can have 15 good pitchers, and you're always looking for No. 16."

Monday night, the Dodgers used four more-than-adequate pitchers to turn back the Houston Astros, 4-0, before 27,185 fans at the Astrodome. The win, the Dodgers' 4th straight and 9th in their last 10 games, extended their lead in the National League West to a season-high 4½ games.

Please see DODGERS, Page 6

1988 NBA DRAFT

## Clippers Are Working Deal to Get No. 3

Michael Cage

By GORDON EDES, *Times Staff Writer*

The Clippers, who already have the luxury of making Danny Manning the No. 1 choice in today's National Basketball Assn. draft, have engineered a three-way deal with the Philadelphia 76ers and Seattle SuperSonics that, barring last-minute complications, will net them the third pick in the first round but will cost them Michael Cage, the league's leading re-

Please see NBA, Page 4

INSIDE

■ **Lewis Wins in France**

Carl Lewis overcomes his usual slow start and wins the 100-meter dash in a wind-aided 9.95 seconds at an international meet in France.

Please see Page 4.

■ **Wilson Gets an Offer**

The Green Bay Packers have reportedly offered former Raider quarterback Marc Wilson a contract worth $400,000.

Please see Page 4.

INDEX

| NATIONAL LEAGUE CHAMPIONSHIP SERIES | | |
|---|---|---|
| DODGERS vs. METS | | |
| BEST-OF-SEVEN SERIES | | |
| Date | Where | Time |
| Oct. 4 | Mets at Dodgers | 5 p.m. |
| Oct. 5 | Mets at Dodgers | Noon |
| Oct. 7 | Dodgers at Mets | 5 p.m. |
| Oct. 8 | Dodgers at Mets | 9 a.m. |
| *-Oct. 9 | Dodgers at Mets | 5 p.m. |
| *-Oct. 11 | Mets at Dodgers | 5 p.m. |
| *-Oct. 12 | Mets at Dodgers | 5 p.m. |

*—Games 5, 6 and 7 if necessary. All times Pacific.

# Dodgers Uncork NL West Title

By SAM McMANIS, *Times Staff Writer*

SAN DIEGO—The coronation of the Dodgers as National League West champions, expected days ago, finally is official. No more pondering the mathematical possibilities, slim as they were. No more deferring to superstition for Manager Tom Lasorda, who would not discuss the impending playoff series until the race really was over.

With a 3-2 victory over the San Diego Padres Monday night before 18,552 fans at Jack Murphy Stadium, the Dodgers proved many skeptics wrong and became the first National League team in the 1980s to win four divisional titles.

It was not an easy climb from being among the West's downtrodden to its elite for the Dodgers, so it was fitting that the Dodgers' title-clinching victory was not easy.

They needed Mickey Hatcher's run-scoring single in the eighth inning to break a 2-2 tie, three scoreless innings from Alejandro Pena and Jay Howell's 21st save to hold off the Padres for the win.

Amid the chaos that was the Dodger clubhouse—the beer and champagne flowed at high tide for more than 30 minutes afterward—Lasorda moved from player to player, administering spleen-jarring hugs.

"They really believed," Lasorda bellowed. "I really believed, right from when we left spring training. This team has been in first place almost the whole way [since May 26] because they believed they could do it.

Please see DODGERS, Page 10



THE SEOUL GAMES / DAY 11

## Louganis Dives Right Into History

### He Repeats His Double Gold-Medal Feat of 1984 on Final Chance of Games

By TRACY DODDS, *Times Staff Writer*

SEOUL—Even before the winning scores flashed on the board, Greg Louganis was in the arms of his coach, Ron O'Brien, crying tears of relief.

It was finally over. He had stood up to the pressure that had continued building right up until the moment that he left the 10-meter platform for the last time.

He had hit that last, most challenging, most dangerous dive—a reverse 3½ somersault tuck with a difficulty rating of 3.4—to win his second gold medal of the 1988 Olympic Games at the Chamshil Swimming Pool Tuesday morning.

In order to add the gold medal for platform competition to the gold medal he already had won here on the 3-meter springboard, he needed to score 8.5s on his final dive. He needed more than 85.56 points to beat 14-year-old Xiong Ni of China on the 10-meter platform in the closest international competition he has ever won.

And he did it.

Louganis averaged 8.5s to score 86.70 points on the dive, finishing with 638.61 points. Xiong took the silver with 637.47 points. A distant third, with 594.39 points, was bronze medalist Jesus Mena of Mexico.

With the dive, Louganis completed the sweep of Olympic gold for the second time. He also won gold medals on both the springboard and platform in Los Angeles in 1984.

Added to the silver medal he won on the platform in the 1976 Games, Louganis has five Olympic

Please see LOUGANIS, Page 3

**MORE COVERAGE**

- **Apology:** Two U.S. swimmers apologize to South Korean people for stealing a decorative plaster mask. Story, Page 3.
- **Men's Basketball:** The U.S. can't reset the clock, but at last it has a chance to even the score with the Soviet Union. Story, Page 4.
- **Facts and Figures:** Page 9.

PATRICK DOWNS / Los Angeles Times

Greg Louganis composes himself before making the dive off the 10-meter platform that earns him his second gold medal of the 1988 Olympics.

## Johnson Loses Gold to Drugs

By RANDY HARVEY, *Times Staff Writer*

SEOUL—Canadian Ben Johnson, whose explosive strength enabled him to become the world's fastest man, was stripped of his 100-meter gold medal Tuesday by the International Olympic Committee after testing positive for an anabolic steroid commonly used by bodybuilders.

Johnson, 26, faces a two-year suspension by the International Amateur Athletic Federation, which governs track and field, and likely will be prevented from competing at least through the 1992 Olympic Games by the Canadian Olympic Assn.

With the disqualification, an IAAF spokesman said Tuesday that the gold medal will be awarded to the United States' Carl Lewis, who finished second to Johnson in Saturday's 100-meter final at the Olympic Stadium.

Lewis thus became the only man ever to repeat as the Olympic 100-meter champion and, after finishing first in the long jump Monday, could win four gold medals for the second consecutive Olympics. He competes Wednesday in the 200

Please see JOHNSON, Page 7

**WHAT ELSE JOHNSON MAY LOSE**

- **Shoe contract** . . . . . . $2.5 million, 4 years.
- **Existing endorsements** . . . All in jeopardy.
- **Endorsements to be signed** . . . Unknown.
- **Oct. 5 Tokyo race** . . . Minimum $100,000.
- **Outdoor meets** . . . . . . . . $25,000 a meet.
- **Indoor meets** . . . . . . . . . . $15,000 a meet.
- **In addition:** (1) Johnson will likely be suspended for 2 years by the IAAF; (2) His 100-meter world-record time of 9.79 seconds will likely be invalidated, but he will retain the record at 9.83 seconds.

**MORE COVERAGE**

- **Seoul Reaction:** It's about time that a big-name athlete was made an example of in the fight against drugs. Story, Page 6.

## Mike Downey

### His Fall From the Top Is Equally Fast

SEOUL—How in the world did he ever believe he would get away with it?

How do you go to the Olympic Games on banned chemical substances and expect to get away with it?

A better question might be: How many others *are* getting away with it?

Is Ben Johnson just one of the very few who *won't* get away with it?

What was Johnson thinking?

What got into him—besides the fairly obvious?

Is there any chance that this guy is the most innocent dupe of all time?

We suppose several possibilities exist.

One is that the lab messed up the 100-meter champion's drug test, in which case these International Olympic Committee folks have a hell of a lot of apologizing to do.

That one's unlikely.

You do not take away a gold medal from a track man for the first time in 24 Olympic Games on a drug rap without checking and cross-checking and triple-checking first.

You do not take away a gold medal and a world record—9.79 seconds, the man ran—and pretend the person was never even here without being damned certain of your facts.

Another possibility is that somebody else slipped steroids into Ben Johnson's system. Johnson's agent already is howling that this is nothing short

Please see DOWNEY, Page 7

## Raiders Trail at Half, 24-0, and Win

### Bahr's 2 Field Goals Climax 30-27 Overtime Victory in Denver

By STEVE SPRINGER, *Times Staff Writer*

DENVER—For the Denver Broncos, it was sudden death.

But for the Raiders, it meant sudden life.

Sudden life for a team seemingly going nowhere because of a bad mix of new personnel, never-ending injuries and a last-minute quarterback trade.

Sudden life for a club embarrassed in the first half by one of the worst 30-minute demonstrations ever staged by players wearing the silver and black.

Sudden life for a quarterback who came 3,000 miles seeking redemption, only to find himself in the middle of another budding quarterback controversy.

Sudden life for a reserve defensive back who hadn't played a previous down all night.

Sudden life for a kicker who may have been on the verge of kicking himself out of a job.

They all came together Monday night at Mile High Stadium to equal the biggest comeback in Raider history with a 30-27 overtime victory, won with just 2:25 remaining in the extra period on a 35-yard field goal by Chris Bahr.

"I hit the ball good," Bahr said. "What the heck. It was nice to get some kicks. I needed a game like this."

That he did. The 13-year veteran had made just 2 of 6 attempts this season before Monday, but he came through on three occasions against the Broncos.

First, he hit a 28-yard field goal early in the fourth quarter. Then with his club trailing, 27-24, and time running out, the Raiders drove down to the Bronco 27. Just 8 seconds remained.

It would take a 44-yard kick to tie the game. Bahr's longest this year had been a 29-yard boot.

No problem.

He put the ball through with plenty of room and 4 seconds to spare, creating the overtime he would eventually win.

Great story?

Here's a better one.

Zeph Lee used to be a running back, who was switched to the secondary when it became obvious that he wasn't going to get into a

Please see RAIDERS, Page 14

- **Which Schroeder?:** Raiders come up with a new model. Bob Oates' column, Page 14.
- **Summary** . . . . . . . . . Page 13.

United Press International

Denver's Dennis Smith stops Marcus Allen during the Raider win.

**INSIDE**

**Rams Lose Gary Jeter**

The Rams learn that defensive tackle Gary Jeter will be out 3 weeks to a month with a knee injury suffered Sunday against the Giants.

Please see Page 2.

**Boston's Magic Number Still 3**

The Boston Red Sox lose to the Toronto Blue Jays, 11-1, and their magic number for winning the American League East remains at 3.

Please see Page 11.

INDEX

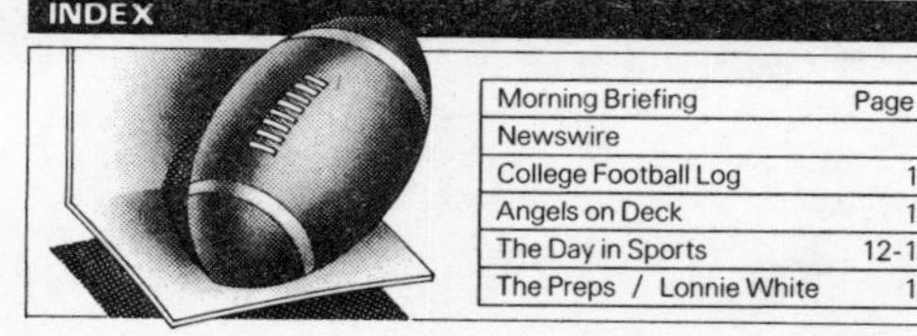

THE WORLD SERIES
OAKLAND ATHLETICS vs. LOS ANGELES DODGERS

# It's a Title Out of the Blue

## Jim Murray

### Another Mickey Is Series Hero

OAKLAND—The "weakest team in the history of the World Series" won it Thursday night.

The team from Lourdes did it. They came in on crutches, so to speak, and went out dancing and wearing halos at a rakish angle. It was a script right out of "The Song of Bernadette." As this is written, they're throwing champagne around the visiting team clubhouse. They should be throwing holy water.

World champions!? The Dodgers!? You got to be kidding!

I mean, look, gang, we're not talking the 1927 Yankees here. We're talking more banjos than a minstrel show.

This wasn't even the varsity. This was the Dodgers' No. 1 farm club. This was the Los Angeles Scrubs. The B team. The one you send off on long bus trips in spring training when the A team stays at the base to play the Yankees.

Everyone thought this was a club running on empty. With their best pitcher and their worst line-up going, they were spotting the most physical team in baseball a lot of muscle, to say nothing of homers, doubles, triples and runs batted in. On paper, it looked like the Bayonne Bleeder vs. Mike Tyson.

Orel Hershiser for President! Orel, who has had a season that's right out of Frank Merriwell, won it like Billy Graham. He stood out on the mound, thinking the good thought and humming hymns.

Ordinarily, when you face the Oakland lineup, the hymn that comes to mind is "Nearer My God to Thee."

The game was won by the Bash Brothers—Mickey Hatcher and Mike Davis.

When you get beat on home runs by Mickey Hatcher and Mike Davis, you begin to listen for voices or watch for tables to start lifting by themselves and lighted saucers to begin landing on the front lawn.

Mickey Hatcher may be E.T. He came into this Series with a record of having hit exactly one (1) home run this season. I think it went out in the air. But Mickey doesn't take any chances. He runs out home runs the way Carl Lewis

Please see MURRAY, Page 13

United Press International

Pitcher Orel Hershiser gets a bearhug from Rick Dempsey as the Dodgers start to celebrate their World Series victory after beating the Oakland A's, 5-2, Thursday night to win, 4 games to 1.

## Hershiser's 4-Hitter Lifts Never-Say-Die Dodgers to Clincher Over A's, 5-2

By SAM McMANIS,
*Times Staff Writer*

OAKLAND—Fact and fantasy had mingled for weeks, like a Hollywood creation slowly unfolding. But now they have somehow intertwined, and the Dodgers' improbable dream of winning the World Series is a reality.

Thursday night at the Oakland Coliseum, the final scene was played in a Dodger season of expectations not only fulfilled but surpassed.

The Dodgers used the tireless right arm of pitcher Orel Hershiser, the leading man, and the efforts of their corps of "Stuntmen" to beat the Oakland Athletics, 5-2, and win baseball's championship in a startling 5 games.

As Hershiser, the Series' most valuable player, struck out Tony Phillips in the dramatic climax of the Dodgers' championship season, he looked skyward to give thanks. But he also may have been asking, "Is it real?"

It certainly was. Reality may have hit the A's like a forearm bash to the midsection, but it cascaded over the Dodgers like champagne.

"It wasn't supposed to happen," relief pitcher Jay Howell said. "People weren't supposed to write this. I think we are as overwhelmed as anyone by this. We didn't think we'd beat the [New York] Mets in the playoffs, and we weren't sure about the A's."

There is no mistake: It is the Dodgers, not the seemingly more talented A's, who are officially crowned baseball's best. This is the Dodgers' sixth World Series title, the second in Manager Tom Lasorda's tenure.

Typical of the Dodgers' rise, contributions were made by many sources. Most notable on a night of stars was another dominating pitching effort by the indefatigable Hershiser, who pitched a 4-hitter, and another offensive windfall off the bat of Mickey Hatcher, who hit a 2-run home run as he became the offensive star of the Series.

Those are the facts. Now for the fantasy. Even as late as 2 weeks ago, hardly anyone not wearing blue gave the Dodgers a chance to beat the Mets in the National League championship series. And once the Mets were dismissed, the Dodgers were said to have no chance against the all-powerful A's, who won 104 regular-season games.

Yet, it was as if Lasorda knew the script in advance and used it to his team's advantage. Every time the Dodgers were counted out, Lasorda pointed it out to his club.

"I planned it," Lasorda said. "I

Please see DODGERS, Page 10

## DOGGONE GOOD

### Orel Hershiser Proves His Bark Can Be as Devastating as His Bite

By ROSS NEWHAN,
*Times Staff Writer*

OAKLAND—Bulldog?

Orel Hershiser proved the appropriateness of the nickname again Thursday night.

He did it with both bark and bite.

"I don't usually get emotional on the mound, but when I get upset it just makes me pitch better," the amazing Hershiser said after restricting the Oakland Athletics to 4 hits and pitching the Dodgers to a 5-2 victory and the championship of the 85th World Series.

Hershiser got upset at himself in a tense eighth inning after earlier getting upset at the A's attempt to disrupt his rhythm by repeatedly stepping in and out of the batter's box.

"They were trying anything," said Hershiser, who finally had enough of it while Tony Phillips was batting in the fifth inning.

"I walked in to talk to [catcher] Rick Dempsey, but I talked loud enough to let Phillips and the umpire hear me," he said. "I asked Rick at what time and how often can they do it [step out].

"I wanted to let them know I didn't like it and that anytime I get aggravated I become a better pitcher.

"I wanted to let them know it was inspiring me and not affecting me adversely. People would have better luck if they tried to lull me to sleep. The A's made sure I stayed awake."

Please see OREL, Page 11

**HOW THEY DID IT**

| | |
|---|---|
| Game 1 | Dodgers 5, Athletics 4 |
| Game 2 | Dodgers 6, Athletics 0 |
| Game 3 | Athletics 2, Dodgers 1 |
| Game 4 | Dodgers 4, Athletics 3 |
| Game 5 | Dodgers 5, Athletics 2 |

■ Dodgers win World Series, 4-1.

**MORE COVERAGE**



## Scott Ostler

### Hatcher Has the Name of His Life

*That guy hit a home run, Hatcher What's-his-name.*
—DAVE PARKER, reliving a nightmare.

OAKLAND—Exactly as predicted and advertised, one World Series team bashed the ball over the fences game after game and the other team went down meekly, its dejected fans leaving the ballpark early to beat the traffic.

The A's were beaten by the Jayvees, 4 games to 1, in the World Series shocker of at least the last 2 decades.

Naturally, the Dodgers did it unnaturally, completely outplaying the A's with a lineup only Tom Lasorda could love.

And Mickey Hatcher, the unknown soldier, supplied the inspiration Thursday night with a first-inning, 2-run homer.

That's the same Mickey Hatcher who hit a first-inning, 2-run homer in Game 1 of this Series.

"Luckily, they didn't check my bat," Hatcher said.

If they did, they would have found it filled with Tinkerbell's fairy dust. Or, knowing Mickey the prankster, a sign would have popped out that said, "BANG!"

Or "BASH!"

Who would've thought Mickey Hatcher would emerge as the offensive star of the World Series?

Who would've imagined any of this nonsense? The Amazin' A's, a team of already legendary power, beaten by a cartoon gang—Mickey, Bulldog, Moose, Gibby, Saxy, Tommy. . . .

With a lineup that looked and sounded more like a Mouseketeer roll call, the Dodgers cruelly mugged the A's.

The A's were an emerging

Please see OSTLER, Page 12

THOMAS KELSEY / Los Angeles Times

Dodger Mike Davis (right) gets a high-five from Mickey Hatcher after hitting a 2-run home run in the fourth inning of Game 5.

**INSIDE**

■ **3 Killed, Reggie Rogers Hurt**

Three teen-agers are killed and defensive end Reggie Rogers of the Detroit Lions suffers a broken neck in an automobile crash.

Please see Page 4.

■ **Gastineau Says He's Quitting**

Defensive end Mark Gastineau tells the New York Jets that he doesn't want to play football anymore, citing personal reasons.

Please see Page 4.

**INDEX**

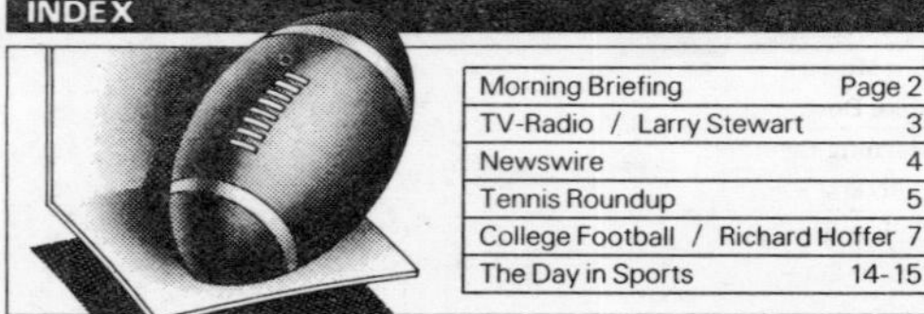

SECTION C
SUNDAY
FEBRUARY 11, 1990 CC†† 
Los Angeles Times

# SPORTS

## HIGHLIGHTS



**NHL SCORES**

- Pittsburgh 7, Kings 6 **C1**
- Detroit 7, Calgary 5
- N.Y. Islanders 4, Boston 3 OT
- Minnesota 6, Chicago 4
- Hartford 6, Toronto 2
- Montreal 7, Quebec 2
- St. Louis 7, New Jersey 0

Roundup **C14**

**TV's BEST BET**

**PRO BASKETBALL**

- NBA All-Star game, 12:15, Ch2

Complete listings **C16**

**ON THE RECORD**

'I'll probably think I'm playing with the Lakers.'

—**Akeem Olajuwon** of the Houston Rockets on starting with Magic Johnson, James Worthy and A.C. Green of the Lakers for the West team, coached by Pat Riley, in the NBA All-Star game today at Miami. **C6**

**INDEX**



# Tyson Era Goes Buster

United Press International

James (Buster) Douglas knocks out heavyweight champion Mike Tyson with left hook during 10th round at the Tokyo Dome.

■ **Boxing:** Douglas scores knockout in 10th round, but appears to have benefited from a long count in the eighth.

By EARL GUSTKEY
TIMES STAFF WRITER

TOKYO—For Iron Mike Tyson, unbeaten in 37 fights and thought to be on his way to Rocky Marciano's career heavyweight record of 49-0, the unthinkable happened in Tokyo Sunday afternoon.

Before about 30,000 in the Tokyo Dome, Douglas won nearly every round, closed Tyson's left eye and knocked him out in the 10th round.

Tyson had nearly pulled it out in the eighth round. He dropped Douglas with a hard right uppercut, and whether or not Douglas beat the count at the end of the round was the subject of heated debate afterward.

Tyson's manager, promoter Don King, filed a protest. Two hours after the fight, the heads of the WBA, WBC and the Japan Boxing Federation announced there would be a news conference several hours later.

The president of the Japan Boxing Federation said videotape showed Douglas was down for 12 seconds in the eighth round.

(Videotape replays by The Times showed that Douglas was down for 13 seconds.)

Said King: "Buster Douglas was knocked out. He was down for 12 seconds. All we want is a fair result."

The controversy brought to mind the Long Count that occurred during the heavyweight title fight between Jack Dempsey and Gene Tunney in Chicago Sept. 22, 1927. After being knocked down in the seventh round, Tunney had more than 10 seconds to recover because referee Dave Barry waited for Dempsey to go to a neutral corner before starting the count. Tunney, too, went on to win the fight.

The result seemed fair to Douglas, whose chances were thought to be so hopeless that most Las Vegas casinos posted no odds.

As Tyson lay on his back in Douglas' corner in the 10th round, Douglas raised both hands over his head and walked calmly, not even smiling, back to his corner.

The final scene played out here was almost impossible to believe. There was Tyson, who had his mouthpiece in backward, held upright in the embrace of referee Octavio Meyrom of Mexico.

Please see FIGHT, C15

James (Buster) Douglas stands over Mike Tyson after knocking him down. Tyson was counted out by referee Octavio Meyrom of Mexico at 1:23.

Associated Press

## MIKE DOWNEY

### Only One Boxer Was Inspired

Buster! The way Cassius shocked Sonny, the way Leon amazed Muhammad, that was the way Buster Douglas beat the belt right off of Iron Mike Tyson on a crazy February night in Tokyo, and if you were lucky enough to see it, in person or on TV, it must have made your hair stand straight up in the air, exactly like Don King's.

Buster! What a night, what a fight! This Mr. X of the boxing world, this mystery guest, this nobody from nowhere, just stepped right up and knocked the sass out of the undefeated, undisputed heavyweight champion of the world, turning him horizontal 1 minute 23 seconds into the 10th round of a fight he controlled from start to finish.

Buster! He did it. Believe it or not, he did it.

How?

"Because I wanted it," Douglas said.

But HOW, Buster? HOW?

"I did it for my mother," Buster said, crying. Here he was, a couple of minutes after beating up the meanest bully on Earth, and he was weeping like a baby.

"God bless her heart," he said.

Buster! He's the toughest thing on two legs Japan has seen since Godzilla. James Douglas took the fight to Mike Tyson for seven straight rounds—never mind

Please see DOWNEY, C15

## JIM MURRAY

### King of the Air Is Missing Crown

He's rich, famous, good looking. He's the best in the world at what he does. He soars above his sport—literally—the way only a gifted few in history have. His mere image sells shoes, soft drinks, cars and tickets. He's well-liked, well-rounded and as cheerful as a bluebird.

So why do I feel sorry for Michael Jordan? Why do I look at him and see a tragic figure of history like the prisoner of Shark Island or Joan of Arc or, closer to home, Sam Snead, Ernie Banks, Walter Johnson, O. J. Simpson?

It's probably because I have this foreboding of doom. Oh, it's not that I think he will get hit by a truck or drown in the bathtub. I'm beginning to wonder—so is he, I have to think—if he's ever going to win a championship.

Sam Snead never won the U. S. Open. Ernie Banks never won a pennant. O. J. Simpson never got to a Super Bowl. Walter Johnson never got in a World Series till he was well in his dotage. His famous fastball was gone and his arm creaking before he finally made it.

Will Michael Jordan join this melancholy company of super superstars who never got to put their act on Broadway? It's like Gable never getting to play Rhett Butler, John Wayne getting shot in the third reel, Caruso singing "Melancholy Baby" in supper clubs.

Oh, it may be too early to don sackcloth and ashes or muffle the drums for Michael. The cortege may be premature. Michael Jordan is only 26 and in the full flower of his youth and vigor.

That's what bothers you. Here you have Michael Jordan

Please see MURRAY, C7

LARRY WOODALL / Los Angeles Times

UCLA's Gerald Madkins launches a shot over Arizona's Casey Schmidt Saturday. Madkins missed all six of his attempts.

### Lemieux Gets His Point, Penguins Get a Victory

By STEVE SPRINGER
TIMES STAFF WRITER

PITTSBURGH—The pain begins the moment Mario Lemieux wakes up.

Just walking into the arena can be a chore.

Putting on his skates is almost unbearable.

But when he gets out on the ice, when he hears the cheers of the crowd as he skates in pursuit of a legend, the herniated disk in his back is temporarily forgotten.

Once again Saturday night, in a 7-6 victory over the Kings, the Pittsburgh Penguin center went through the whole ordeal. Once again, he struggled out onto the ice, and, once again, he got a point, extending his point-scoring streak to 45 consecutive games.

Please see KINGS, C14

### Frigid-Shooting UCLA Falters Up Front, 83-74

By JERRY CROWE
TIMES STAFF WRITER

TUCSON—UCLA's most glaring weakness is its lack of a powerful center. Usually, however, the Bruins are able to compensate.

But when they make only 39.2% of their shots, as they did Saturday in an 83-74 loss to Arizona in front of 13,627 in the McKale Center, their weaknesses magnify.

Arizona extended the nation's longest home winning streak to 44 games and handed UCLA its fourth loss in its last six road games.

The Bruins, who dropped into third place in the Pacific 10 Conference, hadn't shot so poorly since their opener Nov. 25, when

Please see UCLA, C10

SECTION C

MONDAY
MARCH 5, 1990 CC††

# SPORTS

Los Angeles Times

## HIGHLIGHTS

TAMMY LECHNER / Los Angeles Times

**ROUTINE WIN:** Martina Navratilova lost one set, but still defeated Helena Sukova in the final of the women's tennis tournament at Indian Wells. **C3**

**A.C. TURNS IT ON:** A.C. Green scored 27 points to lead the Lakers to a 115-96 win over the Minnesota Timberwolves. **C1**

**WILSON'S FINALE:** Senior Trevor Wilson, playing his final game at Pauley Pavilion, had 13 points and 15 rebounds in UCLA's 74-61 win over Washington. **C2**

**KING POWER SHORTAGE:** Thomas Steen scored twice and the Winnipeg Jets had four power-play goals to beat the Kings, 5-2. **C2**

**TREVINO WINS AGAIN:** Lee Trevino struggled with his putter, but still won his third Senior PGA Tour title in four weeks. **C5**

**NEWSWIRE:** North Carolina State officials met with the agent of Coach Jim Valvano to discuss a $500,000 contract buyout clause if he is dismissed. **C8**

Associated Press

**SENT AWAY:** Georgetown Coach John Thompson was charged with three technical fouls while being ejected. His outburst helped Syracuse turn a six-point deficit into a nine-point lead. The Orangemen won the game in overtime, 89-87. **C7**

### NBA SCORES

- Lakers 115, Minnesota 96 **C1**
- Chicago 118, Boston 114
- Phoenix 108, Cleveland 96
- Detroit 111, Indiana 105

Roundup **C15**

### NHL SCORES

- Winnipeg 5, Kings 2 **C2**
- Washington 4, New Jersey 3
- Boston 4, Chicago 1
- Buffalo 5, Quebec 3
- Pittsburgh 8, Minnesota 6
- Edmonton 6, Vancouver 3

Roundup **C15**

### TV's BEST BET

**PRO HOCKEY**

- Kings/Calgary, 6:30

Prime Ticket

Complete listings **C18**

### INDEX



# Gathers Collapses, Then Dies

GARY FRIEDMAN / Los Angeles Times

Loyola Marymount center Hank Gathers lies semiconscious on court after collapsing during game against Portland Sunday. Gathers, 23, died after being hospitalized.

**MIKE DOWNEY**

## He Didn't Receive a Fighting Chance

Six days after Hank Gathers buckled and fainted at the free-throw line of a December college basketball game, I waited for him to keep an appointment in a lonely corner of Loyola Marymount's basketball pavilion. He wandered in a little late, a little woozy, a little wobbly, I thought. He did not look good. He looked listless.

"How are you feeling?" I asked.

"Is *that* what we're going to talk about?" he asked.

Hank was longing to get back to shooting hoops. A doctor had tested and tested him, X-rayed and examined him, taken his blood pressure and pulse, aimed a penlight beam into his eyes, monitored his heartbeat. He seemed OK. He *felt* OK. Loyola had basketball dates the following week with Oregon State and Oklahoma, so naturally, Hank Gathers was dying to play.

Was dying to play.

Was dying to play.

He gave me a shrug that day and said: "The doc's got a job to do. If he clears me to play basketball, and then I go out there and collapse again, he'd better be able to show that he ran every test there was on me."

Go out there and collapse again.

Go out there and collapse again.

More than two months have passed. It is a bone-chilling Sunday in the California oceanside community of Marina del Rey, where yacht brokerages dot the main boulevard, where boat sails flap from the channel's evening breeze. A nearby hospital has just ushered into its emergency room a handsome young man, a young man who three weeks before had celebrated his 23rd birthday, a young man who

Please see DOWNEY, C13

GARY FRIEDMAN / Los Angeles Times

Lucille Gathers is consoled after her son Hank collapsed during West Coast Conference tournament.

## Loyola Star, 23, Is Taken Off Court During a Game

By ALAN DROOZ
TIMES STAFF WRITER

In a frightening scene played out before much of his family, Loyola Marymount University basketball star Hank Gathers collapsed in a game at Loyola Sunday and died shortly thereafter at Daniel Freeman Marina Hospital.

Gathers, 23, had brought the crowd to its feet with a powerful dunk moments before when he started upcourt, then fell unconscious near midcourt.

Almost immediately Gathers sat up, then fell back to the floor and appeared to suffer convulsions. He was taken from the court on a stretcher and team physician Benjamin Schaeffer began cardiopulmonary resuscitation. Schaeffer was joined moments later by a paramedic crew from the L.A. Fire Dept.

Please see GATHERS, C12

- **TOURNAMENT CANCELED:** Conference officials award Loyola Marymount the WCC's automatic bid to the NCAA tournament. **C12**
- **REACTION:** Gathers' death is mourned by coaches, friends and teammates. **C12**
- **THE SCENE:** The moment turned from spectacular to a horror as Gathers collapsed seconds after completing an alley-oop slam dunk. **C12**
- **SUDDEN DEATHS:** Doctors cannot pinpoint a recurring trend in sudden death of athletes. **C13**
- **POOH REMEMBERS:** Pooh Richardson, a childhood friend of Gathers, said the Loyola star gave no indication in a recent conversation that he was feeling ill. **C14**

## Ortiz Doesn't Repeat Error, Wins L.A. Race

By JULIE CART
TIMES STAFF WRITER

Canadian Peter Fonseca, running in his first marathon, found himself in a pack of three runners leading the race with only one mile to go in Sunday's Los Angeles Marathon.

Alongside Fonseca, 23, were two men who were a decade older and had run scores of world-class marathons. Suddenly, the men began to run with almost wild abandon, sprinting hard after running 25 miles.

It was a pivotal moment for Fonseca, and a telling moment, too. For in marathons, as in life, experience is the best teacher.

Fonseca lacked only an education Sunday, and was left to watch ruefully as Pedro Ortiz of Colombia and Toni Niemczak of Poland swiftly pulled away in what would be the race's turning point. Ortiz was the swifter, winning in 2 hours 11 minutes 54 seconds on a damp and cloudy day—ideal marathon conditions.

Please see RACE, C11

CON KEYES / Los Angeles Times

At the end, Pedro Ortiz of Colombia was lone leader of the pack in L.A. Marathon.

## Lakers Beat Pesky Timberwolves

By SAM McMANIS
TIMES STAFF WRITER

The outcome is not predetermined whenever the Lakers play an expansion team. Once every decade or so, they will shock the NBA world by losing to one of the league's new and underprivileged.

Since the Lakers already lost to the Orlando Magic this season, the prospect of another loss Sunday night, to the Minnesota Timberwolves at home in this case, seemed unfathomable.

It was. The Timberwolves offered only minimum resistance, losing, 115-96, to the Lakers before 17,505 at the Forum.

Give Minnesota this much: they have not made it as easy for the Lakers as other expansion teams. December in Minnesota, the Timberwolves took the Lakers to overtime before losing. In Sunday's rematch, they at least put up a fight before facing the inevitable.

In the end, however, it was another predictable easy Laker win. It was their

Please see LAKERS, C16

## Ruhlmann Wins Big 'Cap at 22-1

By BILL CHRISTINE
TIMES STAFF WRITER

Trainer Charlie Whittingham had won a record seven Santa Anita Handicaps before Sunday, but none was as improbable as No. 8—a wire-to-wire, 1¾-length victory by Ruhlmann, a 5-year-old who had never run 1¼ miles.

After Ruhlmann's victory at 22-1 in the $1-million race, Whittingham, 76, said the horse's front-running style reminded him of Ack Ack, who in 1971 had given him his third Big 'Cap victory.

"Ack Ack could steal 'em, too," Whittingham said.

But Ack Ack went off at 4-5, typical of Whittingham's previous Big 'Cap winners, none of whom paid more than $9.60. Ruhlmann paid $47.80, the fourth-highest price in the 53-year history of the race. On a topsy-turvy day for the tote board, he was the seventh choice in a field of 10.

Please see BIG 'CAP, C17